THE DIRECTORY OF
MAIL ORDER
CATALOGS

2018

32nd Edition

THE DIRECTORY OF
MAIL ORDER
CATALOGS

GREY HOUSE PUBLISHING

PUBLISHER: Leslie Mackenzie
EDITOR: Richard Gottlieb
EDITORIAL DIRECTOR: Laura Mars

PRODUCTION MANAGER & COMPOSITION: Kristen Hayes
MARKETING DIRECTOR: Jessica Moody

Grey House Publishing, Inc.
4919 Route 22
Amenia, NY 12501
518.789.8700
FAX 845.373.6390
www.greyhouse.com
e-mail: books@greyhouse.com

Thirty-second edition published 2018

The directory of mail order catalogs.

v. 27.5 cm.
Annual, 1991
Irregular, 1981-1989
Includes indexes.
ISSN: 0899-5710

1. Mail-order business—United States—Directories. 2. Commercial catalogs—United States—Directories. I. Grey House Publishing, Inc.
   HF5465.5.D58 016.381'14'0973—dc21

ISBN 13: 978-1-68217-386-2 softcover

Printed in Canada

Table of Contents

Consumer Catalogs

Table of Contents

Table of Contents

Table of Contents

Business to Business Catalogs

Table of Contents

Table of Contents

Introduction

This thirty-second edition of *Directory of Mail Order Catalogs* represents Grey House Publishing's longest-running annual reference directory. In this age of e-commerce, the American Catalog Mailers Association is so intent on proving that print catalogs are not dead, their website offers a running list of articles discussing compelling reasons why print catalogs live on, including:

- Catalogs are so effective in driving online sales that Internet-first companies have joined the ranks of lifestyle-inspired catalog producers;
- Catalogs support storytelling—the new gold marketing standard;
- Catalogs enable personalized messaging and targeted outreach;
- New catalogs are inventive, inexpensive and easy to produce;
- Millennials (84% of them) respond to a low-tech marketing approach—paper in a mailbox;
- Catalogs cut through the digital noise yet enable digital experiences.

With these reasons in mind, this edition of *Directory of Mail Order Catalogs* includes more than 100 new catalogs throughout the chapters. And we continue to remain true to our mission—no online-only catalogs.

Directory of Mail Order Catalogs is two distinct directories. Section One, Consumer Catalogs arranged in 43 major chapters, from Animals to Travel & Leisure. These 43 chapters are further defined into 220 subcategories. Section Two, Business Catalogs, is aimed at the business buyer, listing catalogs in 39 major chapters, from Agriculture to Work Apparel.

These sections are separated by a colorful divider card for easy reference, and the Table of Contents is a helpful guide to the directory's nearly 800 pages. Many catalogs are included in more than one chapter, and five indexes allow you to search by catalog name, company name, geographical location, and product.

Each listing includes dozens of important, updated data points, from basic contact information—13,264 key executive names, 5,710 fax numbers, 6,616 web sites and 4,809 e-mails—to more specific fields, including company size, sales and the catalog's physical features.

The Directory of Mail Order Catalogs has five indexes:

- Consumer Catalog & Company: Consumer catalogs and catalog companies.
- Business Catalog & Company: Business catalogs and catalog companies.
- Consumer Geographical Index: Consumer catalog companies by state.
- Business Geographical Index: Business catalog companies by state.
- Product Index: Catalogs in more than 5,000 product categories.

For even easier access to data, *Directory Mail Order Catalogs* is available on our online database platform, http://gold.greyhouse.com. Subscribers have access to all of this business-building detail, and can search by geographic area, printing information, key contacts, sales volumes, employee size, keyword and so much more. Plus, subscribers can download contact sheets to create their own mailing list of sales leads. Visit the site or call 800-562-2139 to set up a demo of the online database.

1 America's Finest Pet Doors
Patio Pacific, Inc.
202 Tank Farm Road
Bldg. F-1
San Luis Obispo, CA 93401-7168 800-826-2871
Fax: 805-781-9734
customerservice@petdoors.com
www.petdoors.com

Pet doors

President: Alan Lethers
Marketing Manager: Rachel
Customer Satisfaction Jedi: Kelsey
CEO: Nick
Shipping & Receiving: David
Credit Cards: AMEX; MasterCard
In Business: 39 years

2 Bass Equipment Company
Bass Equipment Company
PO Box 352
Monett, MO 65708
417-235-7557
800-798-0150
Fax: 417-235-4312
sales@bassequipment.com
www.bassequipment.com

Rabbit and kennel supplies

President: Gary Bass
Number of Employees: 20
Sales Volume: $1.4 Million

3 Birds Choice
Birds Choice, Inc.
477 Vogt Lane
Chilton, WI 53014
800-817-8833
Fax: 920-849-4415
www.birdschoice.com

Bird feeders, baths, houses and accessories

4 Brisky Pet Products
Brisky Pet Products
PO Box 186
Franklinville, NY 14737
716-557-2464
800-462-2464
Fax: 716-676-3908
sales@brisky.com
www.brisky.com

Exotic pet products

President: Jeffrey Brisky
Credit Cards: AMEX; MasterCard
Catalog Cost: Free

5 Cherrybrook Chris Christensen Catalog
Cherrybrook Premium Pet Supplies
181 Bronico Way
Phillipsburg, NJ 8865
908-689-7979
800-524-0820
Fax: 908-689-7988
www.cherrybrook.com

Pet products for dogs and cats such as supplements, foods, treats, grooming supplies, accessories and gifts; also an international supplier of dogshow products

President: Claudia and Roy Loomis
Co-Owner: Roy Loomis
Co-Owner: Claudia Loomis
Catalog Cost: Free
In Business: 45 years

6 Doctors Foster & Smith
Doctors Foster & Smith
2253 Air Park Road
PO Box 100
Rhinelander, WI 54501
715-369-0312
800-381-7179
customerservice@drsfostersmith.com
www.drsfostersmith.com

Wide range of products and supplies for pets

Co-Founder: Race Foster
Co-Founder: Marty Smith
Merchandising Manager: Brenda Reinhard
Credit Cards: AMEX; MasterCard
Catalog Cost: Free
Printing Information: 160 pages in 4 colors on Glossy Stock
Binding: Saddle Stitched
In Business: 32 years
Number of Employees: 617

7 EntirelyPets
EntirelyPets
34501 7th st.
Union City, CA 94587
800-889-8967
sales@entirelypets.com
www.entirelypets.com

Pet medications, supplies, toys, treats, food, and supplements for dogs and cats

Catalog Cost: $0.01
In Business: 15 years

8 Farriers' Greeting Cards
Farriers' Greeting Cards-Hoofprints
13849 N 200 E
Alexandria, IN 46001
765-724-7004
800-741-5054
Fax: 765-724-4632
gina@hoofprints.com
www.hoofprints.com

Unique products for the Equine and Canine enthusiast

President: Gina Keesling
Catalog Cost: Free
In Business: 25 years
Number of Employees: 2
Sales Volume: $97,000

9 Goober Pet Direct
Goober Pet Direct
220 S. Mulberry St.
Mesa, AZ 85202
480-668-4994
Fax: 480-668-5052
www.gooberpetdirect.com

Pet grooming supplies, food, supplements, treats, toys and accessories

10 Gr8 Dogs
Gr8 Dogs
414 West St.
PO Box 947
Berlin, MD 21811
877-478-3647
Fax: 410-641-1504
www.gr8-dogs.com

Apparel, gifts and accessories for dogs

11 Hoover's Hatchery
Hoover's Hatchery
PO Box 200
Rudd, IA 50471
641-395-2730
800-247-7014
Fax: 641-395-2208
hoovers@omnitelcom.com
www.hooovershatchery.com

Poultry equipment and medications

President: Mary Halstead
Credit Cards: MasterCard
Printing Information: in 4 colors
In Business: 71 years
Sales Volume: $500M to $1MM

12 Horse.com
Pets United LLC
PO Box 369
Louisiana, MO 63353
800-637-6721
Fax: 888-262-3655
www.horse.com

Horse equipment

Credit Cards: MasterCard
Catalog Cost: Free
In Business: 38 years

13 Howell Book House
Wiley, Inc.
10475 Crosspoint Boulevard
Indianapolis, IN 46256-3386
317-572-3000
877-762-2974
Fax: 317-572-4000
info@wiley.com

Dog and equestrian books

Chairman: Peter Booth Wiley
President: Stephen M. Smith
CFO: John Kritzmacher
EVP, Human Resources: MJ O'Leary
SVP and Corporate Controller: Edward J. Melando
EVP/General Counsel: Gary M. Rinck
Credit Cards: AMEX; MasterCard; Visa
In Business: 49 years

14 In the Company of Dogs
In The Company of Dogs
P.O. Box 6529
Chelmsford, MA 01824-929
877-757-3477
800-544-4595
Fax: 800-866-3235
help@inthecompanyofdogs.com
www.inthecompanyofdogs.com

Gifts for canines and their best friends including personalized collars, tags, and feeding bowls, doghouses, custom leashes, cages, crates, and covers, chew toys and treats, pet beds and furniture

Chairman: Jack Rosenfeld
President: John Fleischman
Credit Cards: AMEX; MasterCard
Catalog Cost: Free
Printing Information: 51 pages in 4 colors on Glossy Stock
Binding: Saddle Stitched
In Business: 52 years

15 Lafeber Pet Bird Food Catalog
Lafeber Company
24981 North 1400 E. Rd
Cornell, IL 61319
815-358-2301
800-842-6445
info1@lafebermail.com
www.lafeber.com

Bird food catalog, veterinary resources

16 Light Livestock Equipment
Light Livestock Equipment
697 Glen Road
Jay, NY 12941
866-999-2821
Fax: 518-946-2188
info@lightlivestockequipment.com
www.lightlivestockequipment.com

Livestock equipment and supplies.

17 Marine Depot
Marine Depot Aquarium Supplies
14271 Corporate Drive
Garden Grove, CA 92843
714-385-0080
800-566-3474
Fax: 714-385-0180
www.marinedepot.com

Aquarium equipment and accessories, nutrition and supplements for fish

18 Northwest Pack Goats & Supplies
Northwest Pack Goats & Supplies
147 Wilson Creek Road
Weippe, ID 83553
208-435-4614
888-ACK-OAT
Fax: 208-435-4374
sales@northwestpackgoats.com
www.northwestpackgoats.com

Pack goat equipment and supplies

President: Terri Summerfield
Co-Owner: Rex Summerfield
Credit Cards: AMEX; MasterCard
Catalog Cost: Free
Catalog Circulation: to 1500

Printing Information: 24 pages
In Business: 20 years
Number of Employees: 2
Sales Volume: $130,000

19 Pet Castle
Armeria LLC
890 W 23rd Street
San Pedro, CA 90731
323-522-4156
Fax: 310-832-2026
info@rotocast.com
www.rotocast.com

Pet shelters

CFO: Randy Morris
In Business: 48 years

20 Pet Doors USA
Pet Doors USA Inc
4523 30th Street W
#E502
Bradenton, FL 34207-1072
941-758-1951
800-749-9609
Fax: 941-758-0274
sales@dogdoors.co.uk
www.dogdoors.com

Pet doors, kennel doors and cat doors

President: Joe Ambrose
Marketing Manager: Deidre Ambrose
SVP Marketing
Credit Cards: MasterCard
Catalog Cost: Free
Mailing List Information: Names for rent
In Business: 31 years
Number of Employees: 9
Sales Volume: $1.2 Million

21 Pet Solutions
Pet Solutions
802 N Orchard Lane
Beavercreek, OH 45434
800-737-3868
Fax: 937-320-4310
petinfo@petsolutions.com
www.petsolutions.com

Aquarium supplies, live fish and reptiles, dog, cat and bird supplies

Credit Cards: AMEX; MasterCard
Catalog Cost: Free
In Business: 65 years
Number of Employees: 70

22 PetEdge
PetEdge Inc.
PO Box 1000
Beverly, MA 01915-701
800-738-3343
800-638-5754
Fax: 800-329-6372
support@petedge.com
www.petedge.com

Pet care products and equipment for petcare professionals

President: Andrew S Katz
Founder: Loeb Katz
Credit Cards: AMEX; MasterCard
Catalog Cost: Free
In Business: 59 years
Sales Volume: $10MM to $20MM

23 PetSolutions
802 N. Orchard Lane
Beavercreek, OH 45434
800-737-3868
Fax: 937-320-4310
petinfo@petsolutions.com
www.petsolutions.com

Pet products and supplies

Live Deliveries Manager: John Flynn

24 Powder River Ranch, Cattle & Livestock Equipment
Powder River
PO Box 50758
Provo, UT 84605
800-453-5318
Fax: 801-377-6927
www.powderriver.com

Ranch, cattle and livestock equipment.

25 Pure Country Pet Boutique
22796 SW Lincoln Street
Sherwood, OR 97140
Fax: 626-657-2910

Country pet supplies

Co-Owner: Dean
Co-Owner: Wendy

26 Rock N Pooches
Rock N Pooches
238 Austin Street
New Bedford, MA 02740
508-993-0341
Fax: 508-993-0341
rocknpooches@hotmail.com

Coats, blouses, hoodies, shirts, pants and dresses for your dog

Credit Cards: MasterCard
Catalog Cost: $1

27 Showing & Grooming
eNasco Arts & Crafts Store
901 Janesville Avenue
PO Box 901
Fort Atkinson, WI 53538-901
920-563-2446
800-558-9595
Fax: 920-563-6044
custserv@enasco.com
www.enasco.com

Products for showing and grooming livestock; halters, clippers and blades, grooming chutes, show boxes, hoof care products, barn fans, blowers, dryers, vaccums, shampoos and soaps, curry combs

President: Andrew Reinen
Marketing Manager: Phil Niemeyer
Manager, Data Processing: Mike Wagner
Catalog Cost: Free
Catalog Circulation: to 25000
In Business: 74 years
Number of Employees: 540

28 SkyMall
Skymall Holdings, LLC
2 Bergen Turnpike
Ridgefield Park, NJ 07660
800-759-6255
Fax: 602-254-6075
customerservice@skymall.com
www.skymall.com

Pet travel and pet care items, pet treats and comfy and stylish beds for both dogs and cats

President: Christine Aguilera
CFO: Scott Wiley
Marketing Manager: Theresa McMullan, VP
Credit Cards: AMEX; MasterCard
Catalog Cost: Free
In Business: 26 years
Number of Employees: 33

29 UPCO Wholesale Pet Supplies
UPCO
3705 Pear Street
PO Box 969
St Joseph, MO 64503-969
816-233-8800
800-254-8726
Fax: 816-233-9696
sales@upco.com
www.upco.com

Supplies for dogs, cats, horses, reptiles, small animals and birds

Chairman: Frank J Evans
President: Walter J Evans

General Manager: Kyle Evans
Founder: Charles Evans
Credit Cards: AMEX; MasterCard
Catalog Cost: Free
Printing Information: 200 pages
Binding: Perfect Bound
In Business: 63 years
Number of Employees: 28
Sales Volume: $2.9 Million

30 Valley Vet Supply
Valley Vet Supply
1118 Pony Express Hwy
Marysville, KS 66508
800-419-9524
Fax: 800-446-5597
service@valleyvet.com
www.valleyvet.com

Animal supply and care, nutritional health supplements and products for household pets as well as farm and ranch animals.

31 Wildlife Control Supplies
PO Box 538
East Granby, CT 06026
877-684-7262
Fax: 860-413-9831
sales@wildlifecontrolsupplies.com
www.wildlifecontrolsupplies.com

Bird and animal controls and traps.

Animal Health Care

32 All About Dog Grooming
All About Dog Grooming
4720 Salisbury Rd.
Jacksonville, FL 32256
904-710-8318
888-800-1027
learntogroom@comcast.net
www.learntogroom.com

Health care and grooming supplies

Chairman: Carol Doggett
President: Richard Doggett
Co-Founder: Richard Doggett
Co-Founder: Carol Doggett
Credit Cards: AMEX; MasterCard
Catalog Cost: Free
In Business: 40 years

33 American Pet Pro
23575 Cabot Blvd.
Suite 207
Hayward, CA 94545
510-732-2781
800-543-9480
Fax: 510-732-1261

Pet supplies

34 Animal Medic
Animal Medic
3910 North George Street
PO Box 575
Manchester, PA 17345
717-266-5611
800-767-5611
Fax: 717-266-2594
amedicor@animalmedic.com
www.animalmedic.com

Animal health, pet, farm and home supplies

President: Jay Miller
amedicjm@animalmedic.com
Vice President: Barry Noll
amedicbn@animalmedic.com
Vice Presidet: Tom Borders
borders_tom@yahoo.com
Business Manager: Sharon St. Hart
sharon@animalmedic.com
Catalog Circulation: Mailed 2 time(s) per year
Printing Information: 64 pages
In Business: 45 years
Number of Employees: 48
Sales Volume: $13.7 Million

35 Cherrybrook Chris Christensen Catalog
Cherrybrook Premium Pet Supplies
181 Bronico Way
Phillipsburg, NJ 8865 908-689-7979
.... 800-524-0820
Fax: 908-689-7988
www.cherrybrook.com

Pet products for dogs and cats such as supplements, foods, treats, grooming supplies, accessories and gifts; also an international supplier of dogshow products

President: Claudia and Roy Loomis
Co-Owner: Roy Loomis
Co-Owner: Claudia Loomis
Catalog Cost: Free
In Business: 45 years

36 EntirelyPets
EntirelyPets
34501 7th st.
Union City, CA 94587 800-889-8967
sales@entirelypets.com
www.entirelypets.com

Pet medications, supplies, toys, treats, food, and supplements for dogs and cats

Catalog Cost: $0.01
In Business: 15 years

37 Goober Pet Direct
Goober Pet Direct
220 S. Mulberry St.
Mesa, AZ 85202 480-668-4994
Fax: 480-668-5052
www.gooberpetdirect.com

Pet grooming supplies, food, supplements, treats, toys and accessories

38 Gr8 Dogs
Gr8 Dogs
414 West St.
PO Box 947
Berlin, MD 21811 877-478-3647
Fax: 410-641-1504
www.gr8-dogs.com

Apparel, gifts and accessories for dogs

39 Heartland Veterinary Supply & Pharmacy
Heartland Veterinary Supply & Pharmacy
401 W 33rd Street
Hastings, NE 68901 800-934-9398
Fax: 888-424-0484
info@heartlandvetsupply.com
www.heartlandvetsupply.com

Horse, dog and cat products, supplements

President: David Behl
Catalog Cost: Free
In Business: 34 years

40 KV Vet Supply
KV Vet Supply
3190 N Road
PO Box 245
David City, NE 68632 402-367-6047
.... 800-423-8211
Fax: 800-269-0093
www.kvvet.com

Vet, pet, and equine supplies and equipment at wholesale prices, livestock supplements, supplies and equipment at wholesale prices

President: Raymond Metzner
Credit Cards: AMEX; MasterCard
Catalog Cost: Free
Mailing List Information: Names for rent
In Business: 30 years
Number of Employees: 900
Sales Volume: $20.8 million

41 Lambert Vet Supply
Lambert Vet Supply
714 5th Street
Fairbury, NE 68352 800-344-6337
Fax: 866-787-1177
cservice@lambertvetsupply.com
www.lambertvetsupply.com

Pet pharmacy, pet medications, pet medical supplies and supplies for dogs, cats, small animals, cattle horse swine and sheep

President: Douglas Lambert
Marketing Manager: Nels Sorensen
Credit Cards: AMEX; MasterCard
Catalog Cost: Free
In Business: 21 years
Number of Employees: 92
Sales Volume: $14 Million

42 Omaha Vaccine Company/Pet Supplies Delivered
CSR Company Inc.
11701 Centennial Road
Suites 2 & 3
La Vista, NE 68128 800-367-4444
Fax: 800-242-9447
www.omahavaccine.com

Kennel and pet supplies for all animals

Chairman: Scott Remington
President: C. Remington
Credit Cards: MasterCard; Visa
Catalog Cost: Free
Catalog Circulation: Mailed 1 time(s) per year to 1.6MM
Printing Information: 150 pages in 4 colors
Mailing List Information: Names for rent
List Company: Total Media Concepts
222 Cedar Lane, Suite 201
Teaneck, NJ 07666
201-692-0018
In Business: 401 years
Number of Employees: 200

43 PBS Animal Health
PBS Animal Health
2780 Richville Drive SE
Massillon, OH 44646 330-834-9252
.... 800-321-0235
Fax: 330-830-2762
info@pbsanimalhealth.com
www.pbsanimalhealth.com

Distributor of animal health products & livestock pharmaceuticals

President: Robert Matthews
Credit Cards: AMEX; MasterCard
Catalog Cost: Free
Printing Information: 172 pages

44 Pet Edge
Pet Edge
PO Box 1000
Beverly, MA 01915-0701 800-738-3343
.... 800-698-9062
Fax: 800-329-6372
support@petedge.com
www.petedge.com

Pet care products and equipment for petcare professionals

President: Andrew S Katz
Credit Cards: MasterCard
Catalog Cost: Free
Printing Information: 124 pages in 4 colors on Glossy Stock
Binding: Saddle Stitched
In Business: 59 years

45 Pet Supplies Delivered
CSR Company Inc
11701 Centennial Rd La Vista
Omaha, NE 68128-2332 800-367-4444
Fax: 800-242-9447
customerservice@omahavaccine.com

Vaccines, pharmaceuticals, flea and tick control, dental & health care, grooming, training aids, bedding, toys and rawhide treats for dogs, cats, birds, ferrets and small animals

President: C S Remington
CFO: Tammy O'Donnell
Marketing Manager: Chris Mazza
Credit Cards: MasterCard
Catalog Circulation: to 7
Printing Information: 128 pages
In Business: 50 years
Number of Employees: 65
Sales Volume: $9 Million

46 PetEdge
PetEdge Inc.
PO Box 1000
Beverly, MA 01915-701 800-738-3343
.... 800-638-5754
Fax: 800-329-6372
support@petedge.com
www.petedge.com

Pet care products and equipment for petcare professionals

President: Andrew S Katz
Founder: Loeb Katz
Credit Cards: AMEX; MasterCard
Catalog Cost: Free
In Business: 59 years
Sales Volume: $10MM to $20MM

47 PetMeds
PetMeds
1441 SW 29th Ave
Pompano Beach, FL 33069 954-979-5995
.... 800-738-6337
Fax: 800-600-8285
customerservice@1800petmeds.com
www.1800petmeds.com

Licensed pharmacy that dispenses all major brand medications, supplements, and products for dogs, cats, and horses

President: Menderes Akdag
Catalog Cost: Free

48 Star Ridge
Star Ridge Company
1849 E Overcrest St
PO Box 10571
Fayetteville, AZ 72703-3030 479-582-1980
.... 800-447-8836
Fax: 479-575-9064
support@star-ridge.com
www.star-ridge.com

Hoof boots and natural hoof care products

Catalog Cost: Free
Catalog Circulation: Mailed 1 time(s) per year
In Business: 22 years
Number of Employees: 2
Sales Volume: $96,000

49 Tractor Supply Blue Book
Tractor Supply Company
5401 Virginia Way
Brentwood, TN 37027 615-440-4000
.... 877-718-6750
customerservice@tractorsupply.com
www.tractorsupply.com

Rural lifestyle products from generators and animal feed to men's and women's workwear.

Chairman: Cynthia T. Jamison
President: Gregory A. Sandfort
CFO: Anthony F. Crudele
Catalog Cost: Free
Catalog Circulation: Mailed 1 time(s) per year
Printing Information: 356 pages in 4 colors
In Business: 78 years
Number of Employees: 2300
Sales Volume: $6.2 Billion

50 United Vet Equine
14101 W. 62nd. St.
Eden Prairie, MN 55346   800-328-6652
                                        Fax: 952-937-1119
                                heather@lakevet.com
                                www.unitedvetequine.com
Equine health and nutritional products

51 Valley Vet Supply
Valley Vet Supply
1118 Pony Express Hwy
Marysville, KS 66508   800-419-9524
                                        Fax: 800-446-5597
                                service@valleyvet.com
                                www.valleyvet.com
Animal supply and care, nutritional health supplements and products for household pets as well as farm and ranch animals.

52 Valley Vet Supply Catalog
Valley Vet Supply
1118 Pony Express Highway
Marysville, KS 66508   800-419-9524
                                        Fax: 800-446-5597
                                service@valleyvet.com
                                www.valleyvet.com
Complete line of products and services for pets and livestock
President: Ray Schultz
Marketing Manager: Rebecca Pierce
Catalog Cost: Free
Mailing List Information: Names for rent
In Business: 31 years
Sales Volume: $50MM to $100MM

53 Vet-Vax, Inc.
Vet-Vax, Inc.
PO Box 400
Tonganoxie, KS 66086   913-845-3760
                                        800-369-8297
                                        Fax: 913-845-9472
Vaccines, medications, supplements and grooming equipment for pets and livestock; and a complete line of pet toys and training equipment including field and lap dog enthusiast's supplies
President: Bill Maritel
International Marketing Manager: Bud Moomau
Buyers: Scott Johnson
Credit Cards: AMEX; MasterCard; Visa
Catalog Cost: Free
Catalog Circulation: Mailed 2 time(s) per year to 50M
Average Order Size: $68
Printing Information: 191 pages in 1 color on Newsprint
Press: Web Press
Binding: Saddle Stitched
Mailing List Information: Names for rent
List Manager: Bud Moomau
In Business: 27 years
Number of Employees: 14

54 Zoo Med Product Catalog
Zoo Med Laboratories Inc.
3650 Sacramento Drive
San Luis Obispo, CA 93401   888-496-6633
                                        Fax: 805-542-9295
                                zoomed@zoomed.com
                                zoomed.com
Medicine and healthcare for animals

Birds

55 2015 Master Poultry Catalog
Meyer Hatchery
626 State Route 89
Polk, OH 44866   888-568-9755
                                Fax: 419-945-9841
                        info@meyerhatchery.com
                        www.meyerhatchery.com

Offers different breeds of poultry.
Printing Information: 103 pages
In Business: 30 years

56 ABA Sales
American Birding Association
P.O. Box 3070
Colorado Springs, CO 80904   302-838-3660
                                        800-850-2473
                                        Fax: 302-838-3651
                                info@aba.org
                                www.aba.org

Birding books and supplies.
Chairman: Louis M. Morrell
President: Jeffrey A. Gordon
jgordon@aba.org
Marketing Manager: Bill Stewart
bstewart@aba.org
Web Developer & Administrator: David Hartley
dhartley@aba.org
Events Coordinator: George Armistead
garmistead@aba.org
Birding Editor: Ted Floyd
tfloyd@aba.org
Credit Cards: MasterCard; Visa
Catalog Circulation: Mailed 2 time(s) per year
In Business: 43 years
Number of Employees: 17

57 BIRD-X
Bird-X, Inc.
300 N Oakley Blvd
Chicago, IL 60612   312-226-2473
                                        800-662-5021
                                        Fax: 312-226-2480
                                josh.p@bird-x.com
                                www.Bird-X.Com

Bird control products, goose repellers
President: Dennis Tillis
Owner: Glenn Steigbigel
Owner: Ronald Schwartz
Credit Cards: MasterCard; Visa
Catalog Cost: Free
Catalog Circulation: Mailed 2 time(s) per year to 200M
Printing Information: 6 pages in 4 colors on Glossy Stock
Binding: Folded
Mailing List Information: Names for rent
In Business: 51 years
Number of Employees: 35
Sales Volume: $13MM

58 Bird Cage Catalog
CagesByDesign.com
7260 Commerce plaza Dr.
Neenah, WI 54956   920-886-1220
                                        800-941-2243
                                www.cagesbydesign.com
Building cages for personal use.
Owner/Operator: Rustin Keller
Owner/Operator: Adam Keller
In Business: 17 years

59 Birds Choice
Birds Choice, Inc.
477 Vogt Lane
Chilton, WI 53014   800-817-8833
                                        Fax: 920-849-4415
                                www.birdschoice.com
Bird feeders, baths, houses and accessories

60 Brinsea Products
Brinsea Products
704 N Dixie Avenue
Titusville, FL 32796   321-267-7009
                                        888-667-7009
                                        Fax: 321-267-6090
                                sales@brinsea.com
                                www.brinsea.com

Egg incubators, hatchers and brooders for parrot, falcon, poultry, chicken, duck, quali, pheasant and other birds or reptiles
President: Frank Pearce
Printing Information: in 4 colors
In Business: 39 years
Number of Employees: 5
Sales Volume: Under $500M

61 Droll Yankees
Droll Yankees
55 Lathrop Road Ext
Plainfield, CT 06374   860-779-8980
                                        800-352-9164
                                        Fax: 860-564-8031
                                drollbird@drollyankees.com
                                www.drollyankees.com

Quality bird feeders and acessories with a lifetime warranty on squirrel damage
President: Betsy Puckett
CFO: Betsy Puckett
Marketing Manager: Jennifer Masiello
Credit Cards: AMEX; MasterCard
Catalog Cost: Free
Catalog Circulation: Mailed 1 time(s) per year to 15000
Average Order Size: $50
Printing Information: 36 pages in 4 colors on Glossy Stock
Binding: Saddle Stitched
Mailing List Information: Names for rent
In Business: 62 years
Number of Employees: 30

62 Duncraft-Wild Bird Superstore
Duncraft
102 Fisherville Road
Concord, NH 03303   888-879-5095
                                        Fax: 603-226-3735
                                info@duncraft.com
                                www.duncraft.com

Wild bird specialities, feeders, baths, quality seeds, houses, hardware accessories, garden decor, field guides and more
President: Michael M Dunn
Marketing Manager: Shelby Dunn-Kimball
Operations Manager: Scott Hoyt
Customer Service Manager: Heidi Babb
Credit Cards: AMEX; MasterCard
Catalog Cost: Free
Catalog Circulation: Mailed 12 time(s) per year to 30000
Average Order Size: $50
Printing Information: 64 pages in 4 colors on Matte Stock
Press: Web Press
Mailing List Information: Names for rent
List Company: The Millard Group
Peterborough, NH
In Business: 63 years
Number of Employees: 70
Sales Volume: $5MM to $10MM

63 EggCartons.Com
EggCartons.Com
9 Main Street, Suite 1F
PO Box 302
Manchaug, MA 01526-302   508-476-0084
                                        888-852-5340
                                        Fax: 508-476-7703
                                www.eggcartons.com

Discount supplier of egg cartons, poultry supplies, egg baskets, feeders, laying nests, incubator, gifs, and books
President: Paul Boutiette
Marketing Manager: Scott Stankus
Credit Cards: MasterCard
Catalog Circulation: Mailed 1 time(s) per year to 45000
Printing Information: 12 pages in 4 colors on Matte Stock
Press: Web Press
Binding: Saddle Stitched
Mailing List Information: Names for rent

In Business: 12 years
Number of Employees: 10
Sales Volume: $1MM to $3MM

64 Final Flight Outfitters
Final Flight Outfitters
5933 Martin Hwy
Union City, TN 38261   731-885-5056
Fax: 731-885-5337
sales@finalflight.net
www.finalflight.net

Archery accessories and duck hunting equipment

65 Global Pigeon Supplies
Global Pigeon Supplies
2301 Rowland Ave
Savannah, GA 31404-4447   912-356-1320
800-562-2295
Fax: 912-356-1691
gpswo@aol.com
www.globalpigeon.com

Supplies for racing pigeon hobby including lofts and medication

President: Bert Oostlander
Credit Cards: AMEX; MasterCard
Catalog Cost: Free
Catalog Circulation: Mailed 1 time(s) per year to 20M
Average Order Size: $100
Printing Information: 88 pages in 2 colors on Newsprint
Press: Web Press
Binding: Saddle Stitched
Mailing List Information: Names for rent
In Business: 25 years
Number of Employees: 7
Sales Volume: $5MM to $10MM

66 Great Companions Bird Catalog
Great Companions
PO Box 166
Orange City, IA 51041   800-829-2138
Fax: 800-734-4750
custserv@greatcompanions.com
www.greatcompanions.com

Bird supplies

Credit Cards: AMEX; MasterCard
Catalog Cost: Free
In Business: 25 years

67 H Potter
H Potter
PO Box 3502
Coeur d Alene, ID 83814   509-921-1640
Fax: 509-921-1644
www.hpotter.com

Bird feeders and baths.

In Business: 15+ years

68 Harrison's Bird Foods
Harrison's Bird Foods
7108 Crossroads Blvd.
Suite 325
Brentwood, TN 37027   800-346-0269
Fax: 615-221-9898
www.harrisonsbirdfoods.com

Provides proper nutrition for your bird's lifetime care.

Main Developer: Dr. Greg Harrison

69 Hoover's Hatchery
Hoover's Hatchery
PO Box 200
Rudd, IA 50471   641-395-2730
800-247-7014
Fax: 641-395-2208
hoovers@omnitelcom.com
www.hovershatchery.com

Poultry equipment and medications

President: Mary Halstead
Credit Cards: MasterCard
Printing Information: in 4 colors
In Business: 71 years
Sales Volume: $500M to $1MM

70 Jim's Supply Co., Inc.
Jim's Supply Co., Inc.
3530 Buck Owens Blvd.
Bakersfield, CA 93308   800-423-8016
Fax: 661-324-6566
info@jimssupply.com
www.jimssupply.com

Bird netting for vineyards

71 Lafeber Pet Bird Food Catalog
Lafeber Company
24981 North 1400 E. Rd
Cornell, IL 61319   815-358-2301
800-842-6445
info1@lafebermail.com
www.lafeber.com

Bird food catalog, veterinary resources

72 Nixalite of America
Nixalite of America
1025 16th Avenue
PO Box 727
East Moline, IL 61244   309-755-8771
888-624-1189
Fax: 309-755-0077
birdcontrol@nixalite.com
www.nixalite.com

Complete line of bird and wildlife control products

Chairman: Marie Gellerstedt
President: Cory Gellerstedt
Production Manager: Jon Gellerstedt
VP: Keith Gellerstedt
Catalog Cost: Free
Printing Information: 8 pages in 4 colors on Glossy Stock
Press: Web Press
Binding: Saddle Stitched
Mailing List Information: Names for rent
In Business: 61 years
Number of Employees: 15
Sales Volume: $1.8 Million

73 Poultry Solutions
Premier1Supplies
2031 300th Street
Washington, IO 52353   319-653-7622
800-282-6631
Fax: 800-346-7992
www.premier1supplies.com

Electric fencing and electric netting, sheep and goat supplies, clippers and shearers, ear tags, poultry products

Printing Information: 56 pages
In Business: 30+ years

74 QA Supplies
QA Supplies LLC
1185 Pineridge Road
Norfolk, VA 23502   757-855-3094
800-472-7205
Fax: 757-855-4155
info@qasupplies.com
www.qasupplies.com

Pest control, temperature measurement, scales, weather monitoring, humidifiers, alarm and security systems

75 Randall Burkey Company
Randall Burkey Company
PO Box 1090
Boerne, TX 78006   800-531-1097

In Business: 68 years

76 Revival Animal Health
Revival Animal Health, Inc
1700 Albany Place SE
PO Box 200
Orange City, IA 51041-200   800-786-4751
Fax: 800-734-4750
info@revivalanimal.com
www.revivalanimal.com

Assortment of pet supplies for dogs, cats, birds, fish, small animals and horses

President: Roy Nielsen III DVM
Marketing Manager: Deidra De Leeuw
Credit Cards: AMEX; MasterCard
Catalog Cost: Free
In Business: 26 years
Number of Employees: 65
Sales Volume: $3.3 Million

77 The Bird Barrier Product Catalog
Bird Barrier
20925 Chico Street
Carson, CA 90746   310-527-8000
800-503-5444
Fax: 310-527-8005
customercare@birdbarrier.com
www.birdbarrier.com

Manufacturer and supplier of pest bird control products

President: Cameron Riddell
Vice President: Steve Blyth
Vice President Operations: Ron Richter
Senior Accounts Manager: Tony Jetton
In Business: 22 years

78 Welp, Inc.
Welp, Inc.
PO BOX 77
Bancroft, IO 50517   800-458-4473
Fax: 515-885-2346
bkollasch@welphatchery.com
www.welphatchery.com

Offers a wide variety of chickens and other poultry

In Business: 86 years

79 Wild Bird Supplies
Wild Bird
4815 N Oak St
Crystal Lake, IL 60012-3300   815-455-4020

Wild bird feeders, supplies and accessories

President: Gerald W Thon
Credit Cards: AMEX; MasterCard; Visa
Catalog Cost: Free
Catalog Circulation: Mailed 2 time(s) per year
Printing Information: 32 pages in 2 colors on Matte Stock
Press: Web Press
Binding: Saddle Stitched
In Business: 27 years
Number of Employees: 2
Sales Volume: $500M to $1MM

Cats

80 Azure Standard Product Catalog
Azure Standard
79709 Dufur Valley Road
Dufur, OR 97021   971-200-8350
Fax: 971-645-4759
info@azurestandard.com
www.azurestandard.com

In Business: 44 years

81 **Cat Claws**
Cat Claws
900 West Church Street
PO Box 1001
Morrilton, AR 72110
501-354-5015
800-783-0977
Fax: 501-354-4843
meow@catclaws.com
www.catclaws.com

Unique cat products including scratching pads, toys, treats and accessories
President: Bill Seliskar
Credit Cards: AMEX; MasterCard
Catalog Cost: Free
Average Order Size: $38
In Business: 23 years

82 **Cat Fence-In**
Cat Fence-In
PO Box 880
Norco, CA 92860
888-738-9099
www.catfencein.com

Patented cat containment systems
President: Georgia Heath
Credit Cards: MasterCard
In Business: 14 years

83 **Custom Gifts & More**
Floria Designs
375 Lincoln Place
Suite 1J
Brooklyn, NY 11238-5700
718-636-0453
Fax: 718-493-0929
LNF151@aol.com
www.floriadesigns.com

T-shirts for cat lovers
President: Linda Nesbit-Floria
Marketing Manager: Donald Dobson
Catalog Cost: $1
Catalog Circulation: Mailed 2 time(s) per year
Printing Information: 5 pages in 4 colors on Matte Stock
Press: Web Press
Mailing List Information: Names for rent
In Business: 10 years
Number of Employees: 5
Sales Volume: $100,000

84 **Great Companions Dog/Cat Catalog**
Great Companions
PO Box 166
Orange City, IA 51041
800-829-2138
Fax: 800-734-4750
custserv@greatcompanions.com
www.greatcompanions.com

Dog and cat supplies
Credit Cards: AMEX; MasterCard
Catalog Cost: Free
In Business: 25 years

85 **KV Supply**
KV Supply
3190 N Rd
David City, NE 68632
402-367-6047
800-423-8211
Fax: 800-269-0093
www.kvsupply.com
Credit Cards: AMEX; MasterCard

86 **Only Natural Pet Store**
Only Natural Pet Store
5541 Central Ave
Suite 201
Boulder, CO 80301
720-406-7475
888-937-6677
Fax: 720-406-7522
www.onlynaturalpet.com

Natural dog and cat food, treats, vitamins, flea control, supplements, medicine, herbal remedy treatments, shampoo, raw and organic food and more

President: Marty Grosjean
Marketing Manager: Christine Sandoval
Catalog Cost: Free
Printing Information: 60 pages
In Business: 7 years
Number of Employees: 40
Sales Volume: $8 Million

87 **Pet King, Inc.**
Pet King, Inc.
112 West 34th Street
Suite #811
New York, NY 10001
800-424-229
www1.babyking.com/petking_index.php
Pet products.

88 **Solid Gold Northland Health Products for Pets**
Northland Natural Pet
3830 Dight Ave South
Minneapolis, MN 55406
612-729-7748
800-706-0807
Fax: 612-729-0822
office@northlandnaturalpet.com
www.northlandnaturalpet.com

Wholesale distributor of pet products.
In Business: 20 years

89 **The Pet Health and Nutrition Center**
The Pet Health and Nutrition Center
PO Box 334
Harwinton, CT 6791
860-482-8383
888-683-3339
www.pethealthandnutritioncenter.com

Provides products and advices that improve the health of their client's dogs and cats.

Dogs

90 **Border Collies in Action**
Border Collies in Action
375 E Pavillion Road
Pavillion, WY 82523
307-856-7601
Fax: 307-856-7601
hope@bordercollies.com
www.bordercollies.com

Products and equipment to teach your dog to herd sheep
President: Donald Duerr
Owner: Hope Dennis
Catalog Cost: $5
Number of Employees: 5
Sales Volume: $200,000

91 **Canine Training Systems**
Canine Training Systems
9325 East Saint Charles Road
Columbia, MO 65202
573-214-0900
Fax: 573-214-0909
info@caninetrainingsystems.com
www.caninetrainingsystems.com

Canine training videos, books and aids
President: Douglas Calhoun
Credit Cards: AMEX; MasterCard
Catalog Cost: Free
Printing Information: 141 pages
In Business: 28 years

92 **Care-A-Lot Pet Supply**
Care-A-Lot Pet Supply
1924 Diamond Springs Rd
Virginia Beach, VA 23455-2320
757-457-9431
800-343-7680
Fax: 757-460-7326
customerservice@carealotpets.com
www.carealotpets.com

Full line of pet supplies for dogs and cats, birds, fish, reptiles, and small animals
President: Robert Clarke
Store Manager: Bret Borsey

Credit Cards: AMEX; MasterCard
Catalog Cost: Free
Catalog Circulation: Mailed 4 time(s) per year
Average Order Size: $100
Printing Information: 124 pages in 4 colors on Glossy Stock
Press: Web Press
Binding: Saddle Stitched
Mailing List Information: Names for rent
In Business: 25 years
Number of Employees: 1
Sales Volume: $52,000

93 **Cat Claws**
Cat Claws
900 West Church Street
PO Box 1001
Morrilton, AR 72110
501-354-5015
800-783-0977
Fax: 501-354-4843
meow@catclaws.com
www.catclaws.com

Unique cat products including scratching pads, toys, treats and accessories
President: Bill Seliskar
Credit Cards: AMEX; MasterCard
Catalog Cost: Free
Average Order Size: $38
In Business: 23 years

94 **Central Metal Products: Dog Kennels**
Central Metal Products, LLC
234 N Independence St
Tipton, IN 46072-1745
765-945-7677
800-874-3647
Fax: 765-945-7084

Dog kennels and accessories
President: Thomas Roseberry
In Business: 47 years
Sales Volume: $3MM to $5MM

95 **Collar Clinic**
Collar Clinic
1517 Northern Star Drive
Traverse City, MI 49696-8837
231-947-2010
800-430-2010
Fax: 231-947-6566
comments@collarclinic.com
www.collarclinic.com

Electronic dog training equipment
President: Jeff Gonda
Secretary/Treasurer: Diane Gonda
Credit Cards: AMEX; MasterCard
Catalog Cost: Free
In Business: 25 years
Number of Employees: 10
Sales Volume: $890,000

96 **Dogs Unlimited**
Dogs Unlimited LLC
725 Cedar Street
P.O. Box 570
Hudson, CO 80642
303-536-4373
800-338-3647
Fax: 303-536-4033
customerservice@dogsunlimited.com
www.Dogsunlimited.Com

Specializes in hunting, dog training equipment and supplies, dog training collars, books and DVDs
President: Alan Davison
Credit Cards: AMEX; MasterCard
Catalog Cost: Free
Printing Information: 92 pages
In Business: 44 years
Sales Volume: Under $500M

97 FetchDog
In The Company Of Dogs
P.O. Box 6529
Chelmsford, MA 01824-929   800-595-0595
                                   877-757-3477
                              Fax: 800-866-3235
help@InTheCompanyOfDogs.com
www.inthecompanyofdogs.com

Dog supplies and accessories

President: Gretchen Kruysman
CEO: Claude Sheer
Catalog Cost: Free
In Business: 20 years
Number of Employees: 13
Sales Volume: $910,000

98 GW Little
GW Little
80 W Cochran Street
Suite A
Simi Valley, CA 93065   866-495-4885
                              Fax: 805-233-6644
cs@gwlittle.com
www.gwlittle.com

Accessories for small dogs

President: John Grieco
VP: Angela Grieco
Credit Cards: AMEX; MasterCard
Catalog Cost: Free
In Business: 6 years
Number of Employees: 8
Sales Volume: $400,000

99 Gr8 Dogs
Gr8 Dogs
414 West St.
PO Box 947
Berlin, MD 21811   877-478-3647
                              Fax: 410-641-1504
www.gr8-dogs.com

Apparel, gifts and accessories for dogs

100 Great Companions Dog/Cat Catalog
Great Companions
PO Box 166
Orange City, IA 51041   800-829-2138
                              Fax: 800-734-4750
custserv@greatcompanions.com
www.greatcompanions.com

Dog and cat supplies

Credit Cards: AMEX; MasterCard
Catalog Cost: Free
In Business: 25 years

101 Groomer's Choice
6283 S. Valley View Blvd
Suite H
Las Vegas, NV 89118   888-364-6242
help@groomerschoice.com
www.groomerschoice.com

Dog grooming

President: Dan Dressen
Executive Vice President: Katy Dressen

102 J and J Dog Supplies
J and J Dog Supplies
975 Ford St.
Colorado Springs, CO 80915   719-434-5980
                                   800-642-2050
                              Fax: 719-380-9730
sales@jjdog.com
www.jjdog.com

Dog training equipment and supplies

Chairman: Mark R Godsil
President: John Oakley
Credit Cards: AMEX; MasterCard
Catalog Cost: Free
In Business: 48 years
Number of Employees: 25
Sales Volume: $3.4 Million

103 Kennel-Aire
Petmate
2300 E Randol Mill Rd
PO Box 1246
Arlington, TX 76011-1246   888-367-5624
                                   800-346-0134
                              Fax: 785-242-8383
kennelaire@aol.com
www.petmate.com

Dog cages, kennels and supplies

CFO: Trygve Pederson
VP: Robert Tyley
Manager: Jeff Schaper
Catalog Cost: Free
In Business: 53 years
Number of Employees: 45

104 Mason Company
Mason Company
P.O. Box 365
260 Depot Street
Leesburg, OH 45135   937-780-2321
                                   800-543-5567
                              Fax: 937-780-6336
info@masonco.com
www.masonco.com

Modular dog cages and kennels

President: Greg Taylor
CEO: Greg Taylor
Founder: Henry Mason
Catalog Cost: Free
In Business: 122 years

105 Only Natural Pet Store
Only Natural Pet Store
5541 Central Ave
Suite 201
Boulder, CO 80301   720-406-7475
                                   888-937-6677
                              Fax: 720-406-7522
www.onlynaturalpet.com

Natural dog and cat food, treats, vitamins, flea control, supplements, medicine, herbal remedy treatments, shampoo, raw and organic food and more

President: Marty Grosjean
Marketing Manager: Christine Sandoval
Catalog Cost: Free
Printing Information: 60 pages
In Business: 7 years
Number of Employees: 40
Sales Volume: $8 Million

106 Orvis Dogs
The Orvis Company Inc.
178 Conservation Way
Sunderland, VT 05250-4465   802-362-1300
                                   888-235-9763
                              Fax: 802-362-0141
www.orvis.com

Dog supplies and accessories.

CEO: Leigh H. Perkins Jr.
Catalog Cost: Free
In Business: 160 years
Number of Employees: 1700
Sales Volume: $340 Million

107 Risdon Rigs
Risdon Rigs, Inc.
PO Box 127
Laingsburg, MI 48848   517-651-6960
                              Fax: 517-651-6970
risdon3p@risdonrigs.com
www.risdonrigs.com

Dog sleds, rigs, harnesses, show hooks and dog bags

President: Patricia Risdon
Catalog Circulation: Mailed 1 time(s) per year to 1m
Printing Information: 8 pages in 1 color
In Business: 43 years
Number of Employees: 1

108 Solid Gold Products
Solid Gold Pets, LLC.
148 River Street
Suite 120
Greenville, SC 29601   800-364-4863
                              Fax: 864-603-2000
dane@solidgoldhealth.com
www.solidgoldhealth.com

Natural, holistic nutrition for dogs and cats, dry and canned foods, nutritional supplements, treats and topical products

President: Sissy Harrington-McGill
CFO: Teresita Bacani
Credit Cards: AMEX; MasterCard
Catalog Cost: Free
In Business: 41 years
Number of Employees: 7

Horses & Domestic Livestock

109 Agri Supply Co.
Agri Supply Company
                                   800-345-0169
www.agrisupply.com

Farm machinery, trailers and tires, lawn and garden equipment.

110 Agricultural Sciences
Nasco Arts & Crafts Store
901 Janesville Avenue
PO Box 901
Fort Atkinson, WI 53538-901   920-563-2446
                                   800-558-9595
                              Fax: 920-563-6044
custserv@enasco.com
www.enasco.com

Instructional aids for all areas of agriculture; agriculture, horticulture, agronomy, and farm supplies

President: Andrew Reinen
Marketing Manager: Phil Niemeyer
Manager, Data Processing: Mike Wagner
Catalog Cost: Free
Catalog Circulation: to 25000
In Business: 74 years
Number of Employees: 540

111 Barnmaster
2501 E I20
Midland, TX 79701-1704   432-687-6800
                                   800-500-2276
www.barnmaster.com

Various barns, garages, haybarns, arenas, corrals, round pens, products are fire resistant, crib proof, chew proof and customizable

President: Jeff Nowell
In Business: 25 years
Number of Employees: 122
Sales Volume: $10MM to $20MM

112 Big Dee's Tack & Vet Supplies
Big Dee's Tack & Vet Supplies
9440 State Route 14
Streetsboro, OH 44241   330-626-5000
                                   800-321-2142
sales@bigdweb.com
www.bigdweb.com

Standardbred & Thoroughbred racing, English & Western riding, horse blankets, custom stable wear & nameplates, vaccines, dewormers, nutritional supplements and more.

Catalog Cost: Free
In Business: 40 years

113 Centaur Forge
Centaur Forge
117 N Spring Street
Burlington, WI 53105
262-763-9175
800-666-9175
Fax: 262-763-8350
info@centaurforge.com
www.centaurforge.com

Manufacturers and distributors of over 10,000 items of blacksmith's, farriers and horseshoers' supplies
President: Ernest Litynsky
Marketing Manager: Mary Nelson
Purchasing Director: Becky Baas
General Manager/VP Sales: Vicky Klawitter
General Manager: Thomas Riddle
Catalog Cost: Free
Printing Information: 50 pages
Mailing List Information: Names for rent
In Business: 55 years
Number of Employees: 9
Sales Volume: $1.7 Million

114 Cheval International
Cheval International
PO Box 706
Black Hawk, SD 57718
605-787-6486
Fax: 888-296-0022
horses@chevalinternational.com
www.chevalinternational.com

Animal coat enhancers, horse bit cleaners and other horse products

115 Classic Equine Equipment
100 Wulfert Drive
Fredericktown, MO 63645
573-783-2999
800-444-7430
Fax: 573-783-4747
sales@classic-equine.com
www.classic-equine.com

Equine products and supplies

116 Country Manufacturing
Country Manufacturing Inc
333 Salem Ave
PO Box 104
Fredericktown, OH 43019
740-694-9926
800-335-1880
Fax: 740-694-5088
info@countrymfg.com
www.countrymfg.com

Horse stalls and equipment
President: Joe Chattin
General Manager/VP: Chad Chattin
Credit Cards: AMEX; MasterCard
Catalog Cost: Free
Printing Information: on Glossy Stock
Mailing List Information: Names for rent
In Business: 33 years
Number of Employees: 15
Sales Volume: $1.7 Million

117 Dover Saddlery
Dover Saddlery
P.O. Box 1100
Littleton, MA 01460
800-406-8204
Fax: 978-952-6633
customerservice@doversaddlery.com
www.doversaddlery.com

Equipment for horse and rider
President: Stephen L Day
CFO: David R Pearce
Credit Cards: AMEX; MasterCard
Catalog Cost: Free
In Business: 38 years
Number of Employees: 497
Sales Volume: $78 Million

118 EggCartons.Com
EggCartons.Com
9 Main Street, Suite 1F
PO Box 302
Manchaug, MA 01526-302
508-476-0084
888-852-5340
Fax: 508-476-7703
www.eggcartons.com

Discount supplier of egg cartons, poultry supplies, egg baskets, feeders, laying nests, incubator, gifs, and books
President: Paul Boutiette
Marketing Manager: Scott Stankus
Credit Cards: MasterCard
Catalog Circulation: Mailed 1 time(s) per year to 45000
Printing Information: 12 pages in 4 colors on Matte Stock
Press: Web Press
Binding: Saddle Stitched
Mailing List Information: Names for rent
In Business: 12 years
Number of Employees: 10
Sales Volume: $1MM to $3MM

119 Equine Breeding Supply
400 South Main Street
Walworth, WI 53184   *Fax:* 888-242-1925
www.equinebreedingsupply.com

Horse breeding equipment and supplies
President: Suzan Dyer
Printing Information: 8 pages in 3 colors on Matte Stock
Binding: Saddle Stitched
In Business: 17 years

120 Equissage
Equissage
PO Box 447
Round Hill, VA 20142
540-338-1917
800-843-0224
Fax: 540-338-5569
info@equissage.com
www.equissage.com

Equine and companion animal books and videos
President: Mary A Schrieber
CFO: Nelson Schrieber
Catalog Cost: Free
In Business: 26 years
Number of Employees: 4
Sales Volume: $750,000

121 General Livestock
American Livestock and Pet Supply
4602 Domain Drive
Menomonie, WI 54751
800-356-0700
Fax: 800-309-8947
info@americanlivestock.com
www.americanlivestock.com

Beef, dairy, swine, sheep, goat and poultry supplies
VP: Punkaj Jain
Public Relations: Michelle McNamara
Credit Cards: AMEX; MasterCard
Catalog Cost: Free
Catalog Circulation: Mailed 3 time(s) per year
In Business: 43 years
Number of Employees: 4
Sales Volume: $310,000

122 Heartland Veterinary Supply & Pharmacy
Heartland Veterinary Supply & Pharmacy
401 W 33rd Street
Hastings, NE 68901
800-934-9398
Fax: 888-424-0484
info@heartlandvetsupply.com
www.heartlandvetsupply.com

Horse, dog and cat products, supplements
President: David Behl
Catalog Cost: Free
In Business: 34 years

123 Hoffman Hatchery
Hoffman Hatchery
PO Box 129
Gratz, PA 17030
717-365-3694
info@hoffmanhatchery.com
www.hoffmanhatchery.com

Chicks, turkeys, ducklings, goslings, guineas, gamebirds, bantams, swans, equipment and books
President: Anna Hoffman
In Business: 67 years

124 Hoover's Hatchery
Hoover's Hatchery
PO Box 200
Rudd, IA 50471
641-395-2730
800-247-7014
Fax: 641-395-2208
hoovers@omnitelcom.com
www.hovershatchery.com

Poultry equipment and medications
President: Mary Halstead
Credit Cards: MasterCard
Printing Information: in 4 colors
In Business: 71 years
Sales Volume: $500M to $1MM

125 Horse Catalog
American Livestock Supply
4602 Domain Drive
Menomonie, WI 54751
608-223-3232
800-356-0700
Fax: 608-223-3223
info@americanlivestock.com
www.americanlivestock.com

Horse and pet related products
President: Mary Bohne
mary.bohne@americanlivestock.com
Credit Cards: AMEX; MasterCard
Catalog Cost: Free
In Business: 43 years
Sales Volume: $1MM to $3MM

126 Horse Health USA
Horse Health USA
2780 Richville Drive SE
Massillon, OH 44646
330-834-3000
800-321-0235
Fax: 330-830-2762
info@horsehealthusa.com
www.horsehealthusa.com

Horse supplies and supplements
Chairman: J D Mathews
CFO: Edward Cutcher
Marketing Manager: Bridget Gillogly
VP Operations: Sandy Gatewood
VP: Robert Matthews
Credit Cards: AMEX; MasterCard
Catalog Cost: Free
Printing Information: 142 pages
In Business: 63 years
Number of Employees: 60
Sales Volume: $22 Million

127 Horse Supply Catalog
American Livestock and Pet Supply
4602 Domain Drive
Menomonie, WI 54751
608-223-3232
800-356-0700
Fax: 608-223-3223
www.americanlivestock.com

Horse related products
President: Michael J Ripp, VP
Credit Cards: MasterCard
Catalog Cost: Free
Catalog Circulation: Mailed 4 time(s) per year
Printing Information: 60 pages in 4 colors
Binding: Saddle Stitched
In Business: 43 years

128   Horses Prefer
Vets Plus, Inc.
302 Cedar Falls Road
Menomonie, WI 54751   715-231-1234
                             800-468-3877
                        Fax: 715-231-1235
                        www.vets-plus.com

Quality equine health and nutrition products

President: Raj Lall
In Business: 25 years

129   Jeffers Livestock
Jeffers
310 W. Saunders Road
Dothan, AL 36301   334-793-6257
                          800-533-3377
                     Fax: 334-793-5179
          customerservice@jefferspet.com
                     www.jefferspet.com

Livestock supplies

Chairman: Dorothy Jeffers
President: Jennifer Martin
CFO: Michael Hawke
Purchasing Director/VP Marketing: Ruth
Jeffers
Catalog Cost: Free
In Business: 42 years
Number of Employees: 215
Sales Volume: $55 Million

130   Laboratory Sampling Products Catalog
Nasco Arts & Crafts Store
901 Janesville Avenue
PO Box 901
Fort Atkinson, WI 53538-901   920-563-2446
                                 800-558-9595
                            Fax: 800-372-1236
                         custserv@enasco.com
                            www.enasco.com

**Wide range of products used for sampling in
the food, dairy, water, sewage, medical,
pharmaceutical, veterinary, environmental,
soil, forage, cosmetic and industrial markets**

President: Andrew Reinen
Marketing Manager: Phil Niemeyer
Manager, Data Processing: Mike Wagner
Catalog Cost: Free
Catalog Circulation: to 25000
In Business: 74 years
Number of Employees: 540
Sales Volume: Under $500M

131   Light Livestock Equipment
Light Livestock Equipment
697 Glen Road
Jay, NY 12941   866-999-2821
                      Fax: 518-946-2188
          info@lightlivestockequipment.com
             www.lightlivestockequipment.com

Livestock equipment and supplies.

132   Livestock Supply Catalog
American Livestock And Pet Supply, Inc.
1118 Pony Express Hwy.
Marysville, KN 66508-3104   800-419-9524
                          Fax: 800-446-5597
                          www.valleyvet.com

**Beef, dairy, swine, sheep, goat and poultry
supplies**

President: John Kuehl
Credit Cards: MasterCard
Catalog Cost: Free
Catalog Circulation: Mailed 4 time(s) per year
Printing Information: 8 pages in 4 colors
Binding: Saddle Stitched
In Business: 43 years

133   Murray McMurray Hatchery
Murray McMurray Hatchery
191 Closz Drive
PO Box 458
Webster City, IA 50595   515-832-3280
                               800-456-3280
                          Fax: 515-832-2213
                     www.mcmurrayhatchery.com

Chickens and poultry supplies

President: Mike Lubbers
Owner/President: Murray J McMurray
Catalog Cost: Free
Printing Information: 108 pages
In Business: 94 years
Number of Employees: 15
Sales Volume: $1.2 Million

134   Nanric
Nanric Inc
131 South Main Street
Lawrenceburg, KY 40342   502-839-6742
                               877-462-6742
                          Fax: 502-839-6766
                          redden@nanric.com
                          www.nanric.com

Equine podiatry products & knowledge

President: Nancy Redden
General Manager: Shannon Redden
Catalog Cost: Free
Printing Information: 48 pages
In Business: 14 years
Number of Employees: 3
Sales Volume: $190,000

135   National Bridle Shop
National Bridle Shop
815 E Commerce Street
Lewisburg, TN 37091   800-251-3474
                          Fax: 931-359-8551
                        nbs@nationalbridle.com
                      www.nationalbridleshop.com

**Horse saddles and horse health supplies,
stable supplies, clothing & apparel, books,
videos and gifts**

President: Robert M Beech
Credit Cards: AMEX; MasterCard
Catalog Cost: Free
In Business: 66 years
Number of Employees: 27
Sales Volume: $3.3 Million

136   National Ropers Supply
National Ropers Supply
1410 S FM 51
Decatur, TX 76234-2416   940-627-3131
                               800-467-6746
                          Fax: 940-627-0101
                        support@nrsworld.com
                          www.nrsworld.com

**Saddles, ropes, headstalls, bits, cowboy
boots and hats, wrangler jeans, western gifts
and home decor**

President: David Isham
Catalog Cost: Free
Number of Employees: 35

137   Poultry & Gamebreeders Catalog
GQF Manufacturing Company
2343 Louisville Road
Savannah, GA 31415-1619   912-236-0651
                          Fax: 912-234-9978
                        sales@gqfmfg.com
                          www.gqfmfg.com

**Incubators, feeders, waterers, medicine and
supplies**

President: Richard McGhee
Buyers: Steven McGhee
Credit Cards: AMEX; MasterCard
Catalog Cost: Free
Catalog Circulation: Mailed 2 time(s) per year
Printing Information: 24 pages in 1 color
In Business: 58 years

Number of Employees: 55
Sales Volume: $10,000,000 - $25,000,000

**138   Powder River Ranch, Cattle & Livestock
Equipment**
Powder River
PO Box 50758
Provo, UT 84605   800-453-5318
                          Fax: 801-377-6927
                          www.powderriver.com

Ranch, cattle and livestock equipment.

139   Ramm Fence
Ramm and Horse Stalls and Horse Fencing
13150 Airport Highway
Swanton, OH 43558   419-825-2422
                               800-434-8456
                          Fax: 419-825-2433
                        ramm@rammfence.com
                          www.rammfence.com

Horsefencing, stalls and equipment

President: Debbie Disbrow
debbie@rammfence.com
CFO: Glen Johnson
glen@rammfence.com
CEO: Mike Disbrow
mike@rammfence.com
Catalog Cost: Free
In Business: 23 years
Number of Employees: 20
Sales Volume: $15 Million

140   Reich Poultry Farm
Reichs Poultry Farm, Inc.
1625 River Rd
Marietta, PA 17547-9504   866-365-0367
                          www.reichspoultryfarm.com

**Chickens, ducks, geese, turkeys and guinea
hens**

President: Jay Reich
VP: George Reich
Manager: Shirl Reich
Catalog Cost: Free
Catalog Circulation: to 8000
Printing Information: 9 pages in 4 colors on
Glossy Stock
Press: Offset Press
Binding: Saddle Stitched
In Business: 50 years
Number of Employees: 3
Sales Volume: $160,000

141   Ridgeway Hatchery
Ridgway Hatcheries Inc
615 N High St
Box 306
LaRue, OH 43332-306   740-499-2163
                               800-323-3825
                          Fax: 740-499-2828
                        RidgwayEgg@aol.com
                          www.ridgwayhatchery.com

**Chicks, ducklings, turkeys, guineas,
gamebirds, goslings and quail eggs, books,
supplies and egg cartons**

President: Dean Ridgway
Credit Cards: MasterCard
Catalog Cost: Free
In Business: 91 years
Number of Employees: 15
Sales Volume: $820,000

142   Schneider Saddlery
8255 E. Washington St.
Chagrin Falls, OH 44023   440-543-2700
                               800-365-1311
                          Fax: 440-543-2710
                          www.sstack.com

Products for the equestrian industry

Customer Service Manager: Renee Miller
Retail Store Manager: Wendy Peterson
Sales Volume: $3MM to $5MM

143

SmartPak Equine
SmartPak Equine
40 Grissom Road
Suite 500
Plymouth, MA 02360

774-773-1000
888-752-5171
Fax: 774-773-1444
email@e.smartPak.com
www.smartpakequine.com

Horse supplement, equestrian clothing & tack

Chairman: Teddy Johnson
President: Paal Gisholt
CFO: Tom McCain
Marketing Manager: Colby Balazs
Production Manager: Kevin Wilson
SVP/Founder: Becky Minard
VP Purchasing: Melissa Hamlet
VP Operations: Dodd Corby
Credit Cards: AMEX; MasterCard
Catalog Cost: Free
In Business: 16 years
Number of Employees: 175
Sales Volume: $9 Million

144

Standardbred Catalog
Big Dee's Tack & Vet Supplies
9440 State Route 14
Streetsboro, OH 44241

330-626-5000
800-321-2142
Fax: 330-626-5011
sales@bigdweb.com
www.bigdweb.com

Supplies for Standardbred racing and training

President: Dennis Osterholt
Marketing Manager: Elaine Konesky
Purchasing Manager: Gail Linsley
Credit Cards: AMEX; MasterCard
Catalog Cost: Free
Printing Information: 52 pages
In Business: 38 years
Number of Employees: 17
Sales Volume: $2 Million

145

Stockyards Ranch Supply
6990 US Hwy. 85
Commerce City, CO 80022

303-287-8081
contact@stockyardsupply.com
stockyardsupply.com

Supplies for livestock and horses

146

Stromberg's Chicks
Stromberg's Chicks & Game Birds
100 York Street
PO Box 400
Pine River, MN 56474

218-587-2222
800-720-1134
Fax: 218-587-4230
info@strombergschickens.com
www.strombergschickens.com

Baby chicks, poultry supplies, incubators and brooders

President: Loy Stromberg
VP: Janet Stromberg
Credit Cards: AMEX; MasterCard
Catalog Cost: Free
In Business: 94 years
Number of Employees: 6
Sales Volume: $950,000

147

Tack Catalog
K&B Saddler
11003 192nd Street
Dept ITN
Council Bluffs, IA 51503-6903

712-366-1026
Fax: 712-366-1026
www.kbsaddlery.com

Saddles and tack equipment

President: Kinze M Williams
Credit Cards: AMEX; MasterCard
Catalog Cost: $1

In Business: 44 years
Number of Employees: 3
Sales Volume: $2,00,000

148

The Black Book
The Black Book
2310 Hanover Pike
P.O. Box 339
Hanover, PA 17331

717-637-8931
Fax: 717-637-6766
harrisburgsale@theblackbook.com
theblackbook.com

Horse breading and sale

Chairman: Russell C. Williams
rcwilliams@hanoverpa.com
President: Paul F. Spears
pfspears@hanoverpa.com
CFO: Shaun R. Eisenhauer
seisenha@mwn.com
Production Manager: Dale Welk
dwelk@hanoverpa.com
Catalogs & Registration: Vivian Jewitt
vjewitt@hanoverpa.com
Catalogs & Registration: Susan Sentz
ssentz@hanoverpa.com
Catalogs & Distribution: JenniferThompson
jthompson@hanoverpa.com
Catalog Cost: Free
Number of Employees: 10
Sales Volume: $70,700,000

149

Thoroughbred Catalog
Big Dee's Tack & Vet Supplies
9440 State Route 14
Streetsboro, OH 44241

330-626-5000
800-321-2142
Fax: 330-626-5011
sales@bigdweb.com
www.bigdweb.com

Supplies for Thoroughbred racing and training

President: Dennis Osterholt
Marketing Manager: Elaine Konesky
Purchasing Manager: Gail Linsley
Founder: Dennis Osterholt
Credit Cards: AMEX; MasterCard
Catalog Cost: Free
Printing Information: 152 pages
In Business: 39 years
Number of Employees: 17
Sales Volume: $2 Million

150

Tractor Supply Blue Book
Tractor Supply Company
5401 Virginia Way
Brentwood, TN 37027

615-440-4000
877-718-6750
customerservice@tractorsupply.com
www.tractorsupply.com

Rural lifestyle products from generators and animal feed to men's and women's workwear.

Chairman: Cynthia T. Jamison
President: Gregory A. Sandfort
CFO: Anthony F. Crudele
Catalog Cost: Free
Catalog Circulation: Mailed 1 time(s) per year
Printing Information: 356 pages in 4 colors
In Business: 78 years
Number of Employees: 2300
Sales Volume: $6.2 Billion

151

Valley Vet Supply
Valley Vet Supply
1118 Pony Express Hwy
Marysville, KS 66508

800-419-9524
Fax: 800-446-5597
service@valleyvet.com
www.valleyvet.com

Animal supply and care, nutritional health supplements and products for household pets as well as farm and ranch animals.

152

Valley Vet Supply Catalog
Valley Vet Supply
1118 Pony Express Highway
Marysville, KS 66508

800-419-9524
Fax: 800-446-5597
service@valleyvet.com
www.valleyvet.com

Complete line of products and services for pets and livestock

President: Ray Schultz
Marketing Manager: Rebecca Pierce
Catalog Cost: Free
Mailing List Information: Names for rent
In Business: 31 years
Sales Volume: $50MM to $100MM

Snakes & Exotic Breeds

153

Bean Farm
The Bean Farm
32514 NE 77th
Carnation, WA 98014-6701

425-861-7964
877-708-5882
Fax: 425-333-4205
beanfarm@beanfarm.com
www.beanfarm.com

Supply company specializing in reptile husbandry products

President: Giovanni Fagioli
Credit Cards: MasterCard

154

Exotic Nutrition Pet Company
737 Industrial Park Drive
Newport News, VA 23608

757-988-0301
Fax: 757-988-0321
exoticdiet@verizon.net
www.exoticnutrition.com

Pet supplies and nutition for exotic animals

President: Ken Korecky

Fish

155

Fish Place Catalog
That Fish Place-That Pet Place
237 Centerville Rd
Lancaster, PA 17603

717-299-5691
888-842-8738
Fax: 717-295-7210
www.thatpetplace.com

Aquarium, fish and pet supplies

President: Scott Lebowitz
Credit Cards: AMEX; MasterCard
Catalog Cost: Free
Catalog Circulation: Mailed 8 time(s) per year
Mailing List Information: Names for rent
In Business: 41 years

156

Ken's Fish Farm
Ken's Hatchery and Fish Farm, Inc.
24533 Highway 129 North
PO Box 449
Alapaha, GA 31622-449

229-532-6135
877-536-3474
Fax: 229-532-7220
kensfish@usa.com
www.kens-fishfarm.com/

Fish traps, wildlife feeders, worms, bait, books and DVDs

President: Jason Holyoak
Secretary: Judye Holyoak
Credit Cards: MasterCard; Visa; Discover
Catalog Cost: Free
Catalog Circulation: Mailed 1 time(s) per year to 10000
Printing Information: 65 pages in 4 colors on Glossy Stock
In Business: 45 years
Number of Employees: 15
Sales Volume: $670,000

157 **Marine Depot**
Marine Depot Aquarium Supplies
14271 Corporate Drive
Garden Grove, CA 92843   714-385-0080
                           800-566-3474
                       Fax: 714-385-0180
                       www.marinedepot.com

Aquarium equipment and accessories, nutrition and supplements for fish

158 **MarineDepot.com**
Marine Depot Aquarium Supplies
14271 Corporate Drive
Garden Grove, CA 92843   714-385-0080
                           800-566-3474
                       Fax: 714-385-0180
                       www.marinedepot.com

Fish supplies

Arts & Graphic Arts
Frames & Framing Equipment

159 **Art Display Essentials**
Art Display Essentials
2 W Crisman Road
Columbia, NJ 07832-2709   908-496-4951
                           800-862-9869
                       Fax: 908-496-4956
                       info@artdisplay.com
                       www.artdisplay.com

Display stands, bases, acrylic cases, risers, easels and display accessories for art, antiquities and collectibles

President: William Stender
Production Manager: Chris Midkiff
Credit Cards: AMEX; MasterCard
Catalog Cost: $2
Average Order Size: $50
Printing Information: 44 pages in 4 colors on Glossy Stock
Binding: Folded
Mailing List Information: Names for rent
Number of Employees: 20
Sales Volume: $500,000- 1 Million

160 **Delta Picture Frame Company**
8076 NW 74 Ave
Miami, FL 33166   305-592-6456
                           800-327-5482
                       Fax: 305-594-9085
                       www.deltapictureframe.com

Picture frames and framing services

President: Jeff Mandel

161 **Exposures**
Exposures
1 Memory Lane
PO Box 3690
Oshkosh, WI 54903-3690   855-202-7390
                       Fax: 800-699-6993
                       csr@exposuresonline.com
                       www.exposuresonline.com

Picture frames, photo albums, photo-related gifts, curio cabinets, and photograph storage systems.

Catalog Cost: Free
Printing Information: in 4 colors

162 **Frames & Insignia Products Catalog**
Church Hill Classics
594 Pepper Street
Monroe, CT 06468   203-268-1535
                           800-477-9005
                       Fax: 203-268-2468
                       info@diplomaframe.com
                       www.diplomaframe.com

Custom diploma frames, certificate frames, insignia desk accessories and photo frames.

163 **Gallery Leather**
Gallery Leather Company, Inc.
27 Industrial Way
Trenton, ME 00460   877-811-7901
                       service@galleryleather.com
                       www.galleryleather.com

Handcrafted leather goods, specially designed planners, journals, albums, and organizers

Catalog Cost: Free
In Business: 30 years

164 **LeWinter Moulding & Supply Company**
LeWinter Moulding & Supply Company
137 23rd Street
Pittsburgh, PA 15215   412-782-2220
                           800-633-8886
                       Fax: 800-643-9907
                       www.lewintermoulding.com

Frames

President: Marc LeWinter
marc@lewintermoulding.com
Catalog Cost: $15
Number of Employees: 25
Sales Volume: $10-20 Million

165 **Magnolia Frame & Moulding**
                           800-398-3512
                       magnoliaframe.com

Photo frames and custom mouldings

166 **Potdevin Machine Company**
Potdevin Machine Company
26 Fairfield Place
West Caldwell, NJ 07006-1409   201-288-1941
                       Fax: 201-288-3770
                       sales@potdevin.com
                       www.potdevin.com

Framing equipment

Chairman: Robert A. Potdevin
President: Robert S Potdevin
Marketing Manager: James Byrnes
Printing Information: 4 pages
In Business: 122 years
Number of Employees: 40
Sales Volume: $5-10 Million

167 **Stu-Art Supplies**
Stu-Art Supplies
2045 Grand Ave
Baldwin, NY 11510   516-546-5151
                           800-645-2855
                       Fax: 516-377-3512
                       supplies@stu-artsupplies.com
                       www.stu-artsupplies.com

Picture frames, pre-cut and custom-cut matting, plastic glazing and shrink wrap

President: Lisa Hubley
Credit Cards: MasterCard; Visa
Catalog Circulation: to 5M
Printing Information: 19 pages
In Business: 50 years
Number of Employees: 10
Sales Volume: $500,000 - $1,000,000

168 **Ten Plus**
Ten Plus, Inc.
13620 Excelsior Drive
Santa Fe Springs, CA 90670   562-404-0088
                           888-944-8899
                       Fax: 562-404-9700
                       tenplusframe@msn.com
                       www.tenplusframes.com

Picture & ready made frames and mouldings

Credit Cards: MasterCard
Catalog Cost: Free
Printing Information: 32 pages
In Business: 44 years
Number of Employees: 7
Sales Volume: $3-5 Million

169 **Vermont Hardwoods**
PO Box 769
Chester, VT 05143   802-875-2550
                           888-442-7396
                       Fax: 802-875-2101
                       sales@vfh.us
                       vermonthardwoods.com

Lumber & millwork, picture framing services

170 **XYLO Molding Catalog**
XYLO Molding
2606 Gregory Street
Savannah, GA 31404   912-236-1870
                           800-627-5040
                       Fax: 912-233-2441
                       info@xyloframes.com
                       www.xyloframes.com

Picture frames and restoration moldings

President: Ron Horton
Production Manager: Cheryl Horton
Credit Cards: MasterCard; Visa
Catalog Circulation: to 6M
Printing Information: 20 pages
In Business: 30 years
Number of Employees: 10
Sales Volume: Under $500,000

171 **Ziabicki Import Company Catalog**
Ziabicki Import Company
PO Box 081004
Racine, WI 53408-1004   262-633-7918
                       Fax: 262-633-8711
                       info@ziabicki.com
                       www.ziabicki.com

Picture-hanging supplies

President: Tom Wolff
Credit Cards: AMEX; MasterCard
Printing Information: in 2 colors
Mailing List Information: Names for rent
In Business: 60 years
Number of Employees: 6
Sales Volume: $300,000- 750,000

172 **pictureframes.com**
2103 Brentwood St.
High Point, NC 27263   800-332-8884
                       www.pictureframes.com

Picture frames and framing materials

President: Geo Krieg
CEO: Lauri Feinsod

Materials & Supplies

173 **1 Stop Square**
1 Stop Square
9105 Anthony Lane
Spring Grove, IL 60081   815-675-2751
                       Fax: 815-675-2751
                       www.1stopsquare.com

Crafting and scrapbooking supplies, eductional supplies, rubber stamps

174 **Archival Products**
Archival Products
P.O. Box 1413
Des Moines, IA 50306-1413   800-526-5640
                       Fax: 888-220-2397
                       info@archival.com
                       www.archival.com

Handcrafted products and the development of solutions for preserving items

Account Representative: Phet Louvan
phetl@archival.com
Division Manager: Janice Comer
janicec@archival.com
Catalog Cost: Free

175 Argus Steel Products
Argus Steel Products
PO Box 25133
Richmond, VA 23260-5133   804-359-4840
                            800-368-2082
                      Fax: 804-358-3415
                      sales@argussteel.com
                      www.argussteel.com

Perforated metals, wire cloth, expanded metals

President: JW Boltger
Marketing Manager: BP Eggleston
Production Manager: Tom Rich
Credit Cards: MasterCard; Visa
Printing Information: 8 pages
In Business: 20 years
Number of Employees: 12

176 Arnie's Arts & Crafts
Arnie's Arts & Crafts
3741 West Houghton Lake Drive
Houghton Lake, MI 48629   989-366-8794
                            800-563-2356
                      Fax: 989-366-5931
                      www.basketpatterns.com

Basket making kits and supplies, gourd patterns and tools, lamp and leather kits, weaving tools

Chairman: Roberta Goupil
President: Arnold Goupil
Catalog Cost: Free
In Business: 29 years
Number of Employees: 5
Sales Volume: $300,000

177 Art Supply Warehouse
Art Supply Wholesale Club
6104 Maddry Oaks Court
Raleigh, NC 27616   919-878-5077
                            800-995-6778
                      Fax: 919-878-5075
                      www.aswexpress.com

Art supplies and materials

President: David Goldstein
Credit Cards: AMEX; MasterCard
Catalog Cost: Free
Catalog Circulation: Mailed 2 time(s) per year
Printing Information: 67 pages in 1 color on Newsprint
Press: Web Press
Binding: Saddle Stitched
In Business: 35 years
Number of Employees: 70
Sales Volume: $1-3 Million

178 Art-In-A-Pinch
Art-In-A-Pinch
PO Box 416
Hackensack, MN 56452   218-675-5374
                            888-369-4500
                      www.artinapinch.net

Quilt and rug hangers

President: Heather Roensch
In Business: 24 years

179 Arts & Crafts
Nasco Arts & Crafts Store
901 Janesville Avenue
PO Box 901
Fort Atkinson, WI 53538-901 920-563-2446
                             800-558-9595
                       Fax: 920-563-6044
                       custserv@enasco.com
                       www.enasco.com

Supplies and teaching materials for art history, sculpture, drawing, painting, tile work, leather crafts, ceramics, metal enameling, jewelry making, weaving, woodcraft, and stained glass

President: Andrew Reinen
Marketing Manager: Phil Niemeyer
Manager, Data Processing: Mike Wagner

Catalog Cost: Free
Catalog Circulation: to 25000
In Business: 74 years
Number of Employees: 540

180 Azerty
Azerty
13 Centre Dr
Orchard Park, NY 14127-2291 716-662-0200
                             800-888-8080
                       Fax: 716-662-7616
                       azwebsales@essendant.com
                       www.Azerty.Com

Wholesale information processing supplies, peripherals and office products

President: Kevin Bowman
Printing Information: 174 pages
In Business: 32 years
Number of Employees: 100

181 Backdrop Outlet
Backdrop Outlet
3540 Seagate Way
Oceanside, CA 92056   760-547-2900
                             800-466-1755
                       Fax: 760-547-2899
                       cs@backdropoutlet.com
                       www.backdropoutlet.com

A full line of backgrounds, props, sets, studio stands and studio props

President: Jay Gupta
Credit Cards: AMEX; MasterCard
Catalog Cost: Free
Catalog Circulation: Mailed 1 time(s) per year to 75000
Printing Information: 60 pages in 4 colors on Glossy Stock
In Business: 24 years
Number of Employees: 25
Sales Volume: $1-3 Million

182 Becker's School Supplies
Becker's School Supplies
1500 Melrose Highway
Pennsauken, NJ 08110-1410   800-523-1490
                       Fax: 856-792-4500
                       customerservice@shopbecker.com
                       www.shopbecker.com

School supplies, including art supplies

President: George Becker
Credit Cards: MasterCard
Catalog Cost: Free
Catalog Circulation: Mailed 1 time(s) per year
Printing Information: 272 pages in 4 colors
In Business: 89 years
Sales Volume: $20-50 Million

183 Bermar Associates
Bermar Associates
433 Minnesota Drive
Troy, MI 48083-9430   248-589-2460
                             800-394-2460
                       Fax: 248-589-2461
                       inquiries@bermarassociates.com
                       www.bermarassociates.com/

Urethane machine tool wipers and injection molded plastic parts

President: Janet Roncelli
office@bermarassociates.com
VP/GM: D.Gorney
dgorney@bermarassociates.com
Number of Employees: 10
Sales Volume: $1,000,000 - $5,000,000

184 Blue Line Pro
168 Mt. Zion Rd.
Florence, KY 41042   859-282-0096
                       Fax: 859-282-9412
                       www.bluelinepro.com

Comic book supplies

185 Daniel Smith
Daniel Smith
4150 First Avenue South
PO Box 84268
Seattle, WA 98124-5568   206-223-9599
                             800-426-7923
                       Fax: 206-224-0404
                       customer.service@danielsmith.com
                       www.danielsmith.com

Watercolors, oil colors and acrylic paint

Chairman: Daniel Smith
President: John Cogley
CFO: John Bole
Marketing Manager: Scott Bhyre
Catalog Cost: Free
In Business: 45 years
Number of Employees: 100
Sales Volume: $31.4 Million

186 Dharma Trading Company
Dharma Trading Company
1604 Fourth St.
PO Box 150916
San Rafael, CA 94915   707-283-0390
                             800-542-5227
                       Fax: 707-283-0379
                       service@dharmatrading.com
                       www.dharmatrading.com

Textile craft supplies and clothing blanks, tools, fabric markers,transfer paper, dyes, kits, and how to books

President: Isaac Goff
Credit Cards: AMEX; MasterCard
Catalog Cost: Free
Catalog Circulation: Mailed 2 time(s) per year to 150k
Printing Information: 120 pages in 1 color on Glossy Stock
Press: Web Press
Binding: Saddle Stitched
Mailing List Information: Names for rent
In Business: 31 years
Number of Employees: 50
Sales Volume: $3-5 Million

187 Dick Blick Art Materials
Dick Blick Art Materials
PO Box 1769
Galesburg, IL 61402-1267   309-343-6181
                             800-828-4548
                       Fax: 800-621-8293
                       info@dickblick.com
                       www.dickblick.com

America's widest selection of fine artist and craft materials and a tradition of service since 1911

Chairman: Jack Wyatt
President: Robert Buchsbaum
Credit Cards: AMEX; MasterCard
Catalog Cost: Free
Number of Employees: 575

188 Discount School Supply
Discount School Supply
PO Box 6013
Carol Stream, IL 60197-6013   800-627-2829
                       Fax: 800-879-3753
                       customerservice@discountschoolsupply.com
                       www.discountschoolsupply.com

Thousands of arts and crafts materials, school supplies and educational toys

President: Ron Elliott
CFO: Kelly Crampton
Credit Cards: AMEX; MasterCard
Catalog Circulation: Mailed 6 time(s) per year to 2.6M
Printing Information: 500 pages
In Business: 25 years

189 Dixie Art Airbrush
Dixie Art Airbrush
P.O. Box 6433
Metairie, LA 70009-6433   504-733-6509
800-783-2612
Fax: 504-733-0668
artdixie@aol.com
www.dixieart.com

Discount fine art supplies, free shipping
President: Don Aunoy
Credit Cards: AMEX; MasterCard
Catalog Cost: Free
Catalog Circulation: Mailed 1 time(s) per year
Printing Information: 42 pages in 2 colors on Matte Stock
In Business: 80 years
Number of Employees: 5
Sales Volume: $1-3 Million

190 Dove Brushes
Dove Brushes
280 Terrace Rd.
Tarpon Springs, FL 34689-7553   727-415-6588
800-334-3683
Fax: 727-934-1142
mrdove23@aol.com
www.dovebrushes.com

A complete line of artist's brushes and tools that service tole, ceramic, porcelain and fabric painters as well as general craft equipment
President: George Dovellos
Credit Cards: MasterCard
Catalog Cost: $2.5
Printing Information: 12 pages
In Business: 35 years
Number of Employees: 5
Sales Volume: $3-5 Million

191 Ecstasy Crafts
Ecstasy Crafts
630 Shannonville Rd.
Shannonville, ON K0K 3   613-968-4271
888-288-7131
Fax: 613-968-7876
info@ecstasycrafts.com
www.ecstasycrafts.com

String art, embroidery on paper, card stock for paper crafts, and stencil art
President: Anthony Oskamp
CFO: Mary Oskamp
Vice President & Board Member: Dennis Oskamp
Catalog Cost: Free
In Business: 20 years

192 GS Direct Graphic Supplies
GS Direct Inc.
6490 Carlson Dr
Eden Prairie, MN 55346-1729   952-942-6115
800-234-3729
Fax: 952-942-0216
info@gs-direct.com
www.gsdirect.net

Graphic supplies and drawing equipment including plotters, workstations, plotting media
President: Chuck Ehlers
Credit Cards: AMEX; MasterCard
Catalog Cost: Free
Catalog Circulation: Mailed 8 time(s) per year to 750M
Printing Information: 60 pages in 4 colors on Glossy Stock
Press: Web Press
Binding: Saddle Stitched
Mailing List Information: Names for rent
List Manager: Rich Trewilgas
In Business: 13 years
Number of Employees: 8
Sales Volume: $1.5 Million

193 Hecht Rubber Corporation
Hecht Rubber Corporation
6161 Philips Highway
Jacksonville, FL 32216   904-731-3401
800-872-3401
Fax: 888-340-3401
sales@hechtrubber.com
www.hechtrubber.com

Industrial rubber products for business, industry, government and safety
President: Larry Hecht
Credit Cards: MasterCard; Visa
Catalog Cost: Free
Catalog Circulation: Mailed 4 time(s) per year to 175K
Average Order Size: $150
Printing Information: 96 pages in 1 color on Newsprint
Press: Web Press
Mailing List Information: Names for rent
In Business: 73 years
Number of Employees: 33
Sales Volume: $20MM to $50MM

194 Holum & Sons Company
Holum & Sons Company Inc
740 N. Burr Oak Drive
Westmont, IL 60559-1196   630-654-8222
800-447-4479
Fax: 630-654-2929
sales@holumandsons.com
www.holumandsons.com

Catalog, ring and looseleaf binders, presentation folders, books and easels
President: Richard Holum
In Business: 82 years
Number of Employees: 100
Sales Volume: $ 10-20 Million

195 Howard Decorative Packaging
Howard Decorative Packaging
3462 W Touhy Avenue
Skokie, IL 60076   800-323-1609
888-772-9821
info@howardpkg.com
www.howardpkg.com

Custom printed packaging, offers packaging programs to fit your need and budget
President: Ron Watson
rwatson@howardpkg.com
C.S. Manager: Debbie Brazier
csmanager@howardpkg.com
Credit and Receivables: Susan Malinowski
smalinowski@howardpkg.com
Shipping and Receiving: Dean Voss
dvoss@howardpkg.com
Catalog Cost: Free
Printing Information: 28 pages
In Business: 58 years
Sales Volume: $20MM to $50MM

196 Jerrys Artarama
Jerry's Artarama
PO Box 58638J
PO Box 58638J
Raleigh, NC 27658-8638   919-878-6782
800-827-8478
Fax: 919-876-0966
cs@jerrysartarama.com
www.jerrysartarama.com

Acrylic paints, brushes, canvas and boards, drawing tools
Partner: Ira Goldstein
Partner: David Goldstein
Credit Cards: AMEX; MasterCard; Visa
Catalog Cost:
Printing Information: 556 pages
In Business: 45 years
Number of Employees: 2
Sales Volume: $90,000

197 Johnson Bros Metal Forming Catalog
Johnson Bros Metal Forming Company
5744 McDermott Drive
Berkeley, IL 60163-1102   708-449-7050
Fax: 708-449-0042
www.johnsonrollforming.com

Custom roll formed: angles, channels, mouldings; special shapes in straight lenght and/or ring form; also lockseam and open buttseam tubing
President: Edwin O. Johnson
VP & General Manager: Brad Johnson
Catalog Cost: Free
Mailing List Information: Names for rent
In Business: 70 years

198 Kolo
Kolo Retail LLC
1224 Mill Street, Bldg B
East Berlin, CT 06023-1515   800-833-5979
Fax: 860-547-0598
www.kolo-usa.com

Albums, binders, accessories, storage boxes, archival quality storage/display, scrapbooking supplies, wedding; retail or wholesale
President: Keith Horner
Catalog Cost: Free
In Business: 12 years
Number of Employees: 15
Sales Volume: $20-50 Million

199 Light Impressions
Light Impressions
100 Carlson Raod
Rochester, NY 14610   800-975-6429
Fax: 866-592-8642
help@fdmbrands.com
www.lightimpressionsdirect.com

Archival storage, display & presentation materials for negatives, transparencies, CDs, photographs, artwork, & documents
President: Gabe Bristol
Credit Cards: AMEX; MasterCard
Catalog Cost: Free
Catalog Circulation: Mailed 52 time(s) per year
Printing Information: 116 pages in 4 colors on Glossy Stock
Press: Web Press
Binding: Saddle Stitched
Mailing List Information: Names for rent
List Manager: MSGi
In Business: 48 years
Number of Employees: 80
Sales Volume: $36 Million

200 Literary Calligraphy
Literary Calligraphy
5326 White House Road
Moneta, VA 24121   540-297-7938
800-261-6325
Fax: 540-297-1599
susanloy@literarycalligraphy.com
www.literarycalligraphy.com

Catalog of calligraphy text with illustrations, great wedding or special gifts
President: Ron Ayers
Catalog Cost: Free
Catalog Circulation: Mailed 1 time(s) per year
Average Order Size: $60
Printing Information: 16 pages in 4 colors on Glossy Stock
Press: Sheetfed Press
Binding: Saddle Stitched
In Business: 14 years
Number of Employees: 8
Sales Volume: Under $500M

201 McClain's Printmaking Supplies
15685 SW 116th Avenue PMB 202
King City, OR 97224-2695
503-641-3555
Fax: 503-641-3591
mail@imcclains.com
www.imcclains.com

Pressers, blocks and plates, brushes, books, bayers, carving tools, engraving tools, inks, papers and sharpeners

202 Neil Enterprises
Neil Enterprises
450 E Bunker Ct
Vernon Hills, IL 60061
847-549-7627
800-621-5584
Fax: 847-549-0349
info@neilenterprises.com
www.neilenterprises.com

Promotional product/photo novelty manufacturer and supplier/distributor of instant photographic equipment serving the photographic, printing/screenprint, craft, educational and ad specialty industries

President: Jerry Fine
Catalog Cost: Free
Catalog Circulation: Mailed 1 time(s) per year
Printing Information: 52 pages in 4 colors on Glossy Stock
Press: Web Press
Binding: Perfect Bound
Mailing List Information: Names for rent
In Business: 56 years
Number of Employees: 25
Sales Volume: $50-100 Million

203 Neil Holiday Catalog
Neil Enterprises
450 E Bunker Ct
Vernon Hills, IL 60061
847-549-7627
800-621-5584
Fax: 847-549-0349
info@neilenterprises.com
www.neilenterprises.com

Promotional product/photo novelty manufacturer and supplier/distributor of instant photographic equipment serving the photographic, printing/screenprint, craft, education and ad specialty industries

President: Jerry Fine
Catalog Cost: Free
Catalog Circulation: Mailed 1 time(s) per year
Printing Information: 12 pages in 4 colors on Glossy Stock
Press: Web Press
Binding: Perfect Bound
In Business: 56 years
Number of Employees: 25
Sales Volume: $50-100 Million

204 New York Central Art Supply
New York Central Art Supply
62 Third Avenue
New York, NY 10003
212-473-7705
800-950-6111
Fax: 212-475-2513
sales@nycentralart.com
www.nycentralart.com

Art and drafting materials

President: Steve Steinberg
Credit Cards: AMEX; MasterCard; Visa
Catalog Cost: $3
Catalog Circulation: to 10M
Printing Information: 111 pages
In Business: 109 years
Number of Employees: 30
Sales Volume: $5-10 Million

205 Oriental Art Supply
21522 Surveyor Circle
Huntington Beach, CA 92646   714-969-4470
info@orientalartsupply.com
www.orientalartsupply.com

Chinese brushes, shuen paper, ink stones and sticks, Chinese seals, Chinese painting books and instructional videos

206 Paper Wishes
Hot Off The Press, Inc.
1250 NW Third Avenue
Canby, OR 97013
888-300-3406
www.paperwishes.com

Craft projects, tools, storage containers, card making kits, jewelry making kits, stencils, books, CDs and DVDs

President: Paulette Jarvey
Marketing Manager: Melissa Farrier
Owner: Paulette Jarvey
VP Operations: Sandy Bundy
Credit Cards: AMEX; MasterCard; Visa
Catalog Cost: Free
Printing Information: 79 pages on Glossy Stock
Binding: Saddle Stitched
In Business: 35 years
Number of Employees: 59
Sales Volume: $7.80 Million

207 S&S Worldwide
S&S Worldwide
75 Mill Street
P.O. Box 513
Colchester, CT 06415
860-537-3451
800-288-9941
Fax: 800-566-6678
cservice@ssww.com
www.ssww.com

Hands-on learning products for children

Catalog Cost: Free
Catalog Circulation: Mailed 4 time(s) per year
Printing Information: in 4 colors
Mailing List Information: Names for rent
In Business: 109 years
Sales Volume: $20MM to $50MM

208 Sax Arts & Crafts
School Specialty, Inc
PO Box 1579
Appleton, WI 54912-1579
888-388-3224
800-558-6696
Fax: 888-388-6344
orders@schoolspecialty.com
www.schoolspecialty.com

Artist's supplies, full line of weaving looms and aids, basketry and batik supplies

Chairman: James R. Henderson
President: Joseph M. Yorio
CFO: Kevin Baehler
Principal: Justin Lu
Portfolio Manager: Madhu Satyanarayana
EVP, Distribution: Patrick T. Collins
Printing Information: 600 pages in 7 colors
Binding: Perfect Bound

209 Shillcraft
Shillcraft
P.O. Box 325
Bonsall, CA 92003
951-674-4307
Fax: 951-674-4325
support@shillcraft.com
www.shillcraft.com

Latch hook kits, materials, and accessories

Catalog Cost:
In Business: 64+ years

210 Solo Horton Brushes
Solo Horton Brushes, Inc.
151 Ella Grasso Avenue
Torrington, CT 06790
800-969-7656
Fax: 800-899-4765
solo@snet.com
www.solobrushes.com

Art, wire, paint, power, tube and foam brushes

President: L Skeie
Secretary: Nan Skeie
Credit Cards: AMEX; MasterCard; Visa
Catalog Cost: Free
Catalog Circulation: Mailed 2 time(s) per year
Printing Information: 41 pages in 2 colors on Matte Stock
Press: Web Press
Binding: Saddle Stitched
In Business: 95 years
Number of Employees: 5
Sales Volume: $500,000 - $1,000,000

211 Stampendous
Stampendous, Inc.
1122 N Kraemer Pl,
Anaheim, CA 92806
714-688-0288
877-412-7467
stamp@stampendous.com
www.stampendous.com

Rubber stamps, stickers, and other paper crafting accessories

Owner/CEO: Fran Seiford
Catalog Cost:
Printing Information: 104 pages
In Business: 30+ years

212 Testrite Visual Products
Testrite Visual
216 South Newman Street
Hackensack, NJ 07601
201-543-0240
888-873-2735
Fax: 201-543-2195
display@testrite.com
www.testrite.com

Easels, presentation products

Chairman: Harold Rubin
President: Larry Rubin
Vice President of Sales: Paula Goodelman
paula@testrite.com
VP, Retail Development: Ken Allen
ken@testrite.com
VP, Business Development: Mitchell Lewis
mitchell@testrite.com
Catalog Cost: Free
Catalog Circulation: Mailed 1 time(s) per year to 6.5M
Printing Information: 187 pages in 4 colors on Matte Stock
Binding: Saddle Stitched
In Business: 98 years
Number of Employees: 130
Sales Volume: $16 Million

213 Utrecht Art & Drafting Supply
Utrecht Manufacturing Corporation
6 Corporate Dr
Cranbury, NJ 08512-3616
309-341-5710
800-223-9132
Fax: 800-382-1979
customerservice@utrecht.com
www.utrecht.com

Art supplies, oil and acrylic colors, canvas, pads, etc

President: John Dowers
Credit Cards: AMEX; MasterCard
Catalog Cost: Free
Catalog Circulation: Mailed 2 time(s) per year
Printing Information: 48 pages in 4 colors
In Business: 66 years
Number of Employees: 85
Sales Volume: $23.3 Million

214 WEBS - America's Yarn Store
WEBS-America's Yarn Store
75 Service Center Road
Northampton, MA 01060
800-367-9327
Fax: 413-584-1603
customerservice@yarn.com
www.yarn.com

Yarns, weaving looms & equipment, spinning wheels, fibers and books

In Business: 41 years

215 Yankee Candle
The Yankee Candle Company, Inc.
16 Yankee Candle Way
PO Box 110
South Deerfield, MA 01373-110   413-665-8306
800-243-1776
Fax: 413-665-4815
info@yankeecandle.com
www.yankeecandle.com

Candles
Chairman: Craig W Rydin
President: Harlan Kent
CFO: Bruce Hartman
Marketing Manager: Richard R Ruffolo
Credit Cards: AMEX; MasterCard
Catalog Cost: Free
Catalog Circulation: Mailed 4 time(s) per year
Printing Information: in 4 colors
In Business: 36 years

Original Art

216 2015 Auction Catalog
Jackson Hole Art Auction
130 East Broadway
P.O. Box 1568
Jackson, WY 83001   866-549-9278
registrar@jacksonholeartauction.com
jacksonholeartauction.com

Art event, defined by the high standard of works offered in a variety of genres including wildlife, sporting, figurative, landscape and Western art by both renowned past masters and contemporary artis
Printing Information: 228 pages
In Business: 8 years

217 Heartland Music
Heartland Music
17822 Gillette Avenue
Suite A
Irvine, CA 92614   630-919-2287
888-339-0001
www.heartlandmusic.com

Vinyl records, CDs, DVDs and Blu-rays
Chief Executive Officer: Jeff Walker
Credit Cards: AMEX; MasterCard
Catalog Cost: Free

218 Joseph Sheppard
Joseph Sheppard
c/o Rita St. Clair Associates, Inc.
1009 North Charles Street
Baltimore, MD 21201   410-752-1313
Fax: 410-752-1335
josephssheppard@gmail.com
www.josephsheppard.com

Portraits
President: Joseph Sheppard
Catalog Cost: $45
Printing Information: 38 pages

219 Mt Nebo Gallery
Will Moses
PO Box 94
Eagle Bridge, NY 12057-94   518-686-4334
800-328-6326
www.willmoses.com

Fine art, prints and lithographs, cards and puzzles
President: Will Moses
Credit Cards: AMEX; MasterCard; Visa
Catalog Cost: Free
Catalog Circulation: Mailed 1 time(s) per year
Printing Information: 15 pages in 4 colors on Glossy Stock
Binding: Saddle Stitched
In Business: 31 years
Number of Employees: 6
Sales Volume: $1MM to $3MM

220 Rachel Davis Fine Arts
Rachel Davis Fine Arts
1301 West 79th St.
Cleveland, OH 44102   216-939-1190
Fax: 216-939-1191
info@racheldavisfinearts.com
www.racheldavisfinearts.com

Auctioneer and appraiser of fine and decorative arts
In Business: 28 years

221 Royal Athena Galleries
Royal Athena Galleries
153 E 57th Street
New York, NY 10022   212-355-2034
Fax: 212-688-0412
ancientart@aol.com
www.royalathena.com

Greek, Etruscan, Roman and Egyptian antiquities: coins, prints, drawings, photographs
President: Jerome Eisenberg, PhD
Comptroller: Betty W Eisenberg
Associate Director: F Williamson Price
Gallery Photographer: Ramon Perez
Credit Cards: AMEX; MasterCard; Visa
Catalog Cost: $5
Catalog Circulation: Mailed 1 time(s) per year
Printing Information: 96 pages in 4 colors on Glossy Stock
Press: Web Press
Binding: Saddle Stitched
Mailing List Information: Names for rent
In Business: 72 years
Number of Employees: 8
Sales Volume: $6.0 Million

222 Sarkis Studio
Sarkis Studio
306 Westfield St.
Greenville, SC 29601   864-232-8157
800-793-0337
Fax: 864-232-0888
www.sarkisstudio.com

Decorative Arts Studio specializing in manufacturing and finishing fine drapery hardware
Credit Cards: MasterCard

223 Wendell August Forge Catalog
Wendell August Forge
390 Lincoln Ave, Gate 15
PO Box 109
Grove City, PA 16127   724-450-8700
800-923-4438
Fax: 724-458-0906
info@wendell.com
www.wendellaugust.com

Framed metal art, platters, trays, tin, bowls and jewelry
President: Will Knecht
Credit Cards: AMEX; MasterCard; Visa
Catalog Cost: Free
In Business: 92 years
Number of Employees: 79
Sales Volume: $7.0 Million

224 Works on Paper: 20th Anniversary Catalog
Elrick-Manley Fine Art
Marianne Elrick-Manley
118 Riverside Drive
New York, NY 10024   212-873-7282
marianne@elrickmanley.com
www.elrick-manley.com

Private art dealer
In Business: 25 years

Prints & Reproductions

225 Audubon Prints and Books
Audubon Prints and Books
9720 Spring Ridge Ln
Vienna, VA 22182   703-759-5567
Fax: 703-759-5578
audubonprints@aol.com
www.audubonprints-books.com

Antique prints
President: Ed Kenney
Partner: Robert Kenney
Catalog Cost: $3
Catalog Circulation: Mailed 1 time(s) per year
Printing Information: 29 pages in 2 colors
Sales Volume: Under $500,000

226 Carruth Studio
Carruth Studio, Inc.
1178 Farnsworth Rd
Waterville, OH 43566-1074   419-878-3060
800-225-1178
Fax: 419-878-3261
info@carruthstudio.com
www.carruthstudio.com

Planters, plaques, all cast from original designs
Chairman: George Carruth
President: Deb Carruth
Marketing Manager: Sharon Larowe
Public Relations: Karen Michaelis
Credit Cards: MasterCard
Catalog Cost: $3
Printing Information: 34 pages in 4 colors
Press: Sheetfed Press
Binding: Folded
In Business: 30 years
Number of Employees: 13
Sales Volume: $2.30 Million

227 Circa Home Living
Circa Home Living
384 HL Dow Hwy
Suite 12
Eliot, ME 3903   888-887-1820
CircaHomeLiving@gmail.com
www.circa1820.com

228 Complete Catalog Fine Art Poster & Print-on-Demand
Editions Limited
4090 Halleck Street
Emeryville, CA 94608   510-923-9770
800-228-0928
Fax: 510-923-9777
customerservice@editionslimited.com
www.editionslimited.com

Wholesale publisher and distributor of fine art posters
Printing Information: 200 pages

229 Fine Art & Art Instruction
Dover Publications
31 E 2nd Street
Mineola, NY 11501-3852   516-294-7000
Fax: 516-742-6953
www.doverpublications.com

Art books, coffee table books, and educational books on art
President: Christopher J Kuppig
Marketing Manager: Kristine Anderson
Acquisitions Editor: Nora Rawn
Account Manager: Christopher Higgins
Catalog Cost: Free
In Business: 76 years
Number of Employees: 135
Sales Volume: 40MM

230 Fine Art Presses Etching & Lithography
Conrad Machine Company
1525 South Warner Street
Whitehall, MI 49461-1826 231-893-7455
Fax: 231-893-0889
tom@conradmachine.com
www.conradmachine.com
Manufacturer of fine art etching and lithography presses
President: Tom Conrad
Advertising: Shaun Conrad
shaun@conradmachine.com
Catalog Cost: Free
Printing Information: 11 pages
In Business: 59 years
Number of Employees: 10
Sales Volume: $1-3 Million

231 Lone Star Western Décor Fall 2015 Catalog
Lone Star Western Décor
P.O. Box 297
Jenks, OK 74037-297 877-493-3779
Fax: 580-237-5009
www.lonestarwesterndecor.com
Print catalog and internet business specializing in home decor and lighting products for cabins and lodges.

232 Modern Digital Canvas
Modern Digital Canvas
PO Box 1582
Sag Harbor, NY 11963 888-345-0870
service@md-canvas.com
www.md-canvas.com
Your own images or digitally photographed images.
In Business: 15 years

233 Red Baron Antiques
Red Baron Antiques
8655 Roswell Rd
Sandy Springs, GA 30350 770-640-4604
Fax: 770-640-7172
info@rbantiques.com
www.rbantiques.com
Architectural antiques
President: Linda Brown
Credit Cards: AMEX; MasterCard; Visa
Catalog Cost:
Printing Information: 48 pages in 4 colors
In Business: 25 years
Number of Employees: 4
Sales Volume: $260,000

234 Robert Duncan Studios
Robert Duncan Studios
260 E. Main Street
Midway, UT 84049 800-282-0954
www.robertduncanstudios.com
Limited Edition Prints, Posters, Art Cards, and Calendars.

235 Sacred Silks
Sacred Silks International
7668 El Camino Real
Suite 104-179
Carlsbad, CA 92009 760-431-2781
Fax: 760-431-0306
info@coppolacreations.com
www.sacredsilks.com
Reproductions on silk of stained glass windows and other designs from around the world
President: Angela Coppola
Credit Cards: AMEX; MasterCard; Visa
Printing Information: 32 pages
Mailing List Information: Names for rent
In Business: 7 years
Number of Employees: 3
Sales Volume: $260,000

236 Schiffer Antiques, Collectibles & Art
Schiffer Publishing Ltd.
4880 Lower Valley Rd
Atglen, PA 19310-1768 610-593-1777
Fax: 610-593-2002
info@schifferbooks.com
www.schifferbooks.com
Antiques and collectibles
President: Peter Schiffer
VP: Nancy Schiffer
Catalog Cost: Free
In Business: 42 years
Number of Employees: 36
Sales Volume: $4.20 Million

237 Special Ideas
Special Ideas
511 Diamond Rd
Heltonville, IN 47436 800-326-1197
info@special-ideas.com
www.special-ideas.com
CEO: Karen
In Business: 34 years

238 Spring at MoMA
The Museum of Modern Art Store/MoMA Stor
11 West 53 Street
New York NY 212-708-9888
800-793-3167
wholesale@moma.org
www.momastore.org
Finest collection of modern and contemporary art.
In Business: 83 years

239 Stefani Photography
Stefani Photography
1830 High ST SE
Salem, OR 97302-5242 503-378-0636
hello@stefaniphotography.com
stefanigallery.com
Printings, prints, canvases

240 The Studio EI 2015 Sourcebook
Editions Limited
4090 Halleck Street
Emeryville, CA 94608 510-923-9770
800-228-0928
Fax: 510-923-9777
customerservice@editionslimited.com
www.editionslimited.com
Wholesale publisher and distributor of fine art posters

241 Things Deco
Things Deco
130 E 18 Street
Suite 8F
New York, NY 10003-2441 212-362-8961
thingsdeco@hotmail.com
www.thingsdeco.com
Art Deco and early 20th Century design books, stationery, posters, calendars, holiday cards and ornaments, jewelry, ceramics and home accessories.
President: Harriet Seltzer
Production Manager: Robert Josen
Catalog Circulation: to 60000
Printing Information: 52 pages in 4 colors
Binding: Saddle Stitched
In Business: 23 years

242 Wesley Gallery
Wesley Gallery
27008 Ranch Road 12 South
Dripping Springs, TX 78620 512-858-9758
888-806-0678
art@wesleyprints.com
www.wesleygallery.com

Variety of fine art images: landscapes, civil war art, spiritual art, sports subjects, southern and southwestern themes
Printing Information: 12 pages

243 Winn Devon Fine Art Collection Catalog
CAP & Winn Devon
6311 Westminster Highway
Unit 110
Richmond, BC V7C-4V4 604-276-4551
800-663-1166
Fax: 604-276-4552
sales@encoreartgroup.com
www.winndevon.com
Limited edition prints and fine art posters
CEO: Lisa Krieger
Credit Cards: AMEX; MasterCard; Visa
Catalog Cost: $60
Catalog Circulation: Mailed 2 time(s) per year to 5000
Printing Information: 800 pages in 4 colors on Glossy Stock
Press: Sheetfed Press
Mailing List Information: Names for rent
In Business: 27 years
Number of Employees: 10
Sales Volume: $1.20 Million

244 World Art Group 2015 Product Catalog
World Art Group
8080 Villa Park Drive
Richmond, VA 23228 804-213-0600
Fax: 804-213-0700
orders@theworldartgroup.com
www.theworldartgroup.com
Leading art publisher.
In Business: 40+ years

245 American Surplus
American Surplus
1 Noyes Ave
Rumford, RI 02916-3370 401-434-4355
800-876-3736
Fax: 401-434-7414
asi@americansurplus.com
www.Americansurplus.Com
New and used warehouse and industrial equipment
President: Bill Di Maio Jr
bill@americansurplus.com
Production Manager: Joe Archambault
joea@americansurplus.com
Chief Executive Officer: Claire DiMaio
claired@americansurplus.com
General Manager: Bill DiMaio Sr
wdimaiosr@verizon.net
Traffic Manager: SusanTusino
stusino@americansurplus.com
Credit Cards: MasterCard
Printing Information: 27 pages
In Business: 24 years

246 American Tubing
American Tubing
2191 Ford Avenue
Springdale, AR 72764-4701 479-756-1291
800-447-0284
Fax: 479-756-1346
www.americantubing.com
Copper tubing components and assemblies for refrigeration and air conditioning
President: Chuck Lewis
clewis@americantubing.com
Sales Engineer: James Laughter
jlaughter@americantubing.com
Service Representative: Kathy Franklin
kfranklin@americantubing.com
Quality Assurance Manager: BradGreathouse

bgreathouse@americantubing.com
Number of Employees: 115
Sales Volume: $25,000,000 - $50,000,000

247 Ametek Equipment Gauges
Ametek Equipment Gauges
205 Keith Valley Road
Horsham, PA 19044-2628   215-293-4100
                                Fax: 215-323-9450
                                usg.sales@ametek.com
                                www.Usgauge.Com

General purpose gauges
President: Joe Karpov
Printing Information: 12 pages
In Business: 111 years
Number of Employees: 500

248 Ametek Special Purpose Equipment Gauges
Ametek Special Purpose Equipment Gauges
205 Keith Valley Road
Horsham, PA 19044-2628   215-293-4100
                                Fax: 215-323-9450
                                usg.sales@ametek.com
                                www.Usgauge.Com

Gauges for refrigeration, air conditioning, boilers and water systems
President: Joe Karpov
Printing Information: 12 pages
Number of Employees: 500

249 Atlas Copco Industrial Compressors
Atlas Copco Industrial Compressors
1800 Overview Drive
Rock Hill, SC 29730-1641   803-817-7200
                                Fax: 413-536-0091
                                www.Atlascopco.Us

Industrial air compressors
President: Ronnie Leten
VP: Stephen Kuhn
Printing Information: 8 pages
In Business: 141 years
Number of Employees: 340

250 Audio Advisor
Audio Advisor
3427 Kraft Ave SE
Grand Rapids, MI 49512   616-254-8870
                                800-942-0220
                                Fax: 616-254-8875
                                sales@audioadvisor.com
                                www.audioadvisor.com

Fine end audio products including hard to find accessories, loudspeakers, analog and digital audio, audio/video cables, equipment racks, and power conditioners
President: Mike Hawkins
Vice President Finance: Gene Thaler
It Staff; President: Wayne A Schuurman
Sales Representative: Joe Darmogray
jdarmogray@audioadvisor.com
Credit Cards: AMEX; MasterCard
Printing Information: 80 pages in 4 colors on Glossy Stock
Press: Web Press
Binding: Saddle Stitched
In Business: 33 years
Number of Employees: 17

251 Aufhauser Brothers Corporation
Aufhauser Corporation
39 West Mall
Plainview, NY 11803-4288   516-694-8696
                                800-645-9486
                                Fax: 516-694-8690
                                sales@aufhauser.net
                                www.Brazing.Com

Products for brazing and welding
President: Keith Aufauser
In Business: 78 years

252 Belleville Wire Cloth
Belleville Wire Cloth
18 Rutgers Ave
Cedar Grove, NJ 07009-1444   973-239-0074
                                800-631-0490
                                Fax: 973-239-3985
                                contactus@bwire.com
                                www.Bwire.Com

Wire cloth for acoustics, food and chemical processing
President: James Crowley
Credit Cards: MasterCard
Printing Information: 4 pages
In Business: 96 years
Number of Employees: 20

253 Bon Tool
Bon Tool Company
4430 Gibsonia Road
Gibsonia, PA 15044-7945   800-444-7060
                                sales@bontool.com
                                www.bontool.com

Construction supplies and tools
President: John Bongiovanni
Credit Cards: MasterCard
Catalog Circulation: Mailed 4 time(s) per year
In Business: 59 years
Number of Employees: 60
Sales Volume: $20MM to $50MM

254 CCI Solutions
CCI Solutions
1247 85th Ave. SE
Olympia, WA 98501   360-943-5378
                                800-562-6006
                                Fax: 360-754-1566
                                info@ccisolutions.com
                                www.ccisolutions.com

Offers audio-visual consulting, products, technical systems and expertise.
Catalog Cost: Free
Printing Information: 72 pages in 4 colors
In Business: 40 years

255 CSI\SPECO
Speco Technologies
200 New Highway
Amityville, NY 11701   631-957-8700
                                800-645-5516
                                Fax: 631-957-9142
                                www.csi-speco.com

Residential and commercial audio and video security products specializing in CCTV cameras, video monitors, in-wall speakers, PA amplifiers and megaphones
President: Todd Kellar
Marketing Manager: Peter Botelho
In Business: 52 years
Number of Employees: 40
Sales Volume: $ 8.5 Million

256 Catalog of Professional Audio/Video Services
WTS Media
2841 Hickory Valley Road
Chattanooga, TN 37421-6600   423-894-9427
                                888-987-6334
                                www.wtsmedia.com

Blank audio and video tape CD's, A/V equipment and duplication services
President: Tom Salley
Credit Cards: AMEX; MasterCard
Printing Information: 15 pages in 4 colors
Mailing List Information: Names for rent
In Business: 40 years
Number of Employees: 40
Sales Volume: $5MM to $10MM

257 Concept Catalog
AVI-SPL
6301 Benjamin Rd.
Suite 101
Tampa, FL 33634   866-708-5034
                                sales@avispl.com
                                www.avispl.com

AV system design and integration, consulting, creative show services, rental, event staging and production, sales, repair and extended warranty.
CEO: John Zettel
Printing Information: 58 pages in 4 colors
Mailing List Information: Names for rent
In Business: 37 years
Number of Employees: 1500
Sales Volume: $577 Million

258 Fingerhut Spring Big Book
Fingerhut
PO Box 166
Newark, NJ 7101-166   800-208-2500
                                www.fingerhut.com

In Business: 67 years

259 Griffin Manufacturing Company
Griffin Manufacturing Company
1656 Ridge Rd
Webster, NY 14580   585-265-1991
                                800-344-6445
                                Fax: 585-265-2621
                                www.grifhold.com

Artist's hand tools, specialty tools, hobby knives and knife sets
President: Theresa Papia
Production Manager: Gary Papia
Catalog Circulation: to 75M
Printing Information: 30 pages
In Business: 69 years
Number of Employees: 20
Sales Volume: $500,000-1 Million

260 HK Holbein
Holbein
175 Commerce St
PO Box 555
Williston, VT 05495   802-862-4573
                                800-682-6686
                                Fax: 802-658-5889
                                info@holbeinusa.com
                                www.holbeinhk.com

Artist quality oil color, watercolor and acrylics
Fulfillment: Timothy Hopper
tim@holbeinusa.com
Credit Cards: MasterCard
Catalog Cost: $7
Printing Information: 100 pages
In Business: 85 years
Sales Volume: $1-3 Million

261 Industrial Arts Supply Company
Industrial Arts Supply Company
5724 West 36th Street
Minneapolis, MN 55416-2594   952-920-2947
                                888-919-0899
                                sales@iasco-tesco.com
                                www.iasco-tesco.Com

Industrial art supplies; plastics, tools, molds, electronics and hobby items
Credit Cards: MasterCard; Visa
Catalog Cost: $3
Catalog Circulation: to 50M
Printing Information: 165 pages in 1 color
In Business: 39 years
Number of Employees: 20
Sales Volume: $1-3 Million

262 Lowel-Lighting Equipment
Lowel-Lighting Equipment
90 Oser Avenue
Hauppauge, NY 11788   631-273-2500
                             800-645-2522
                        Fax: 631-273-2557
                      techsupport@tiffen.com
                             www.lowel.com

Light systems, light controls, stands and mounts, cases and light kits

President: Ross Lowell
Manufacturing Engineer: Joseph Yu
Catalog Cost: Free
Catalog Circulation: Mailed 1 time(s) per year
Printing Information: 88 pages
In Business: 55 years
Number of Employees: 40
Sales Volume: $10,000,000 - $25,000,000

263 Luxury Made Easy
Luther Appliance & Furniture Sales
129 Oser Avenue
Suite A
Hauppauge, NY 11788   800-358-6466
                        Fax: 631-236-4434
            generalquestions@luthersales.com
                           luthersales.com

Furniture and appliance purchases, computers, TVs, jewellery and electronics purchases

In Business: 48 years

264 MFJ Enterprises, Inc.
MFJ Enterprises, Inc.
PO Box 494
Mississippi State, MS 39762   662-323-5869
                             800-647-1800
                        Fax: 662-323-6551
            mfjcustserv@mfjenterprises.com
                     www.mfjenterprises.com

Ham radios and accessories

President: Martin F Jue
Founder: Martin F. Jue
Credit Cards: AMEX; MasterCard; Visa
Catalog Cost: Free
Catalog Circulation: Mailed 1 time(s) per year
Printing Information: 136 pages
In Business: 42 years
Number of Employees: 150
Sales Volume: 12.6 M

265 Music Direct
Music Direct
1811 W Bryn Mawr Ave
Chicago, IL 60660   312-433-0200
                             800-449-8333
                        Fax: 312-433-0011
                       www.musicdirect.com

Audio equipment, record albums, and accessories

President: Jim Davis
Sales Volume: $3MM to $5MM

266 Outwater Plastics Industries
Outwater Plastics Industries,Inc
24 River Road
P.O. Box 500
Bogota, NJ 07603   800-631-8375
                        Fax: 800-888-3315
                           www.outwater.com

Extrusions, furniture and cabinet components, knobs and pulls, injection molded parts, casters, store fixture components, lighting, engineering plastics, hardware, and architectural moulding/millwork.

President: Peter Kessler
Marketing Manager: Joey Shimm
Credit Cards: AMEX; MasterCard; Visa
In Business: 45 years
Number of Employees: 200
Sales Volume: $10,000,000 - $25,000,000

267 S&S Worldwide
S&S Worldwide
75 Mill Street
P.O. Box 513
Colchester, CT 06415   860-537-3451
                             800-288-9941
                        Fax: 800-566-6678
                       cservice@ssww.com
                             www.ssww.com

Hands-on learning products for children

Catalog Cost: Free
Catalog Circulation: Mailed 4 time(s) per year
Printing Information: in 4 colors
Mailing List Information: Names for rent
In Business: 109 years
Sales Volume: $20MM to $50MM

268 Safina Office Products
9916 Brooklet Dr.
Houston, TX 77099   832-327-0316
                             800-247-2344
                        Fax: 832-327-0314
                       www.safinaoffice.com

Office products and supplies

269 Seventh Avenue
Seventh Avenue
1112 7th Ave.
Monroe, WI 53566-1364   800-218-3945
                       www.seventhavenue.com

Furniture and home décor, jewellery, electronics, cookware, apparel

Printing Information: 115 pages

270 Source
Wholesale Tape and Supply Co.,Inc
2841 Hickory Valley Road
Chattanooga, TN 37421   423-894-9427
                             888-987-6334
                        Fax: 423-894-7281
            customerservice@wtsmedia.com
                          www.wtsmedia.com

Blank audio cassettes, blank video tapes, blank CD's, audio and video duplication services and equipment, including duplicators, microphones, mixing boards, CD burners, and other presentation products

President: Michael Salley
Marketing Manager: Greg Giordano
Sales Manager: Marianne Mankin
Credit Cards: AMEX; MasterCard
Catalog Cost: Free
Catalog Circulation: Mailed 4 time(s) per year to 12000
Average Order Size: $150
Printing Information: 64 pages in 4 colors on Glossy Stock
Press: Web Press
Binding: Saddle Stitched
Mailing List Information: Names for rent
In Business: 40 years
Number of Employees: 40
Sales Volume: $5MM to $10MM

271 Tape Resources
Tape Resources
845 N Church Ct.
Elmhurst, IL 60126-1036   630-993-4673
                             800-827-3462
                        Fax: 888-827-3329
                       www.polylinecorp.com

Software, audio cassettes, batteries, hard drives, discs, inkjet cartridges and printers

President: David Durovy
SVP Administration: Jeanette Freeman
Credit Cards: AMEX; MasterCard; Visa
Catalog Cost: Free

272 Universal Art Images
Universal Art Gallery
PO Box 698
Bentonville, AR 72712   941-966-3632
                             800-326-1367
                        Fax: 941-966-4069
                        ucslide@aol.com

Slides, paintings, drawings and architecture

Credit Cards: MasterCard; Visa
Catalog Circulation: to 150M
Printing Information: 56 pages
In Business: 62 years
Number of Employees: 10
Sales Volume: $500,000- 1 Million

273 Valiant IMC
Valiant National AV Supply
80 Little Falls Road
Fairfield, NJ 07004-1709   201-229-9800
                             800-825-4268
                        Fax: 800-453-6338
                    sales@valiantnational.com
                    www.valiantaudiovisual.com

Audio-visual products and supplies at wholesale prices; video equipment, computer equipment and supplies

Chairman: Martin Siegel
President: Sheldon Goldstein
Managing Director: Scott Schaefer
Credit Cards: AMEX; MasterCard; Visa
Catalog Cost: Free
Catalog Circulation: Mailed 1 time(s) per year to 200M
Printing Information: 212 pages in 4 colors on Glossy Stock
Binding: Perfect Bound
Mailing List Information: Names for rent
In Business: 20 years
Number of Employees: 100
Sales Volume: $ 13 Million

274 White's Metal Detectors
White's Electronics Factory, U.S.A.
1011 Pleasant Valley Road
Sweet Home, OR 97386   541-367-6121
                             800-547-6911
                        Fax: 541-367-6629
                  sales@whiteselectronics.com
                    www.whiteselectronics.com

Manufactures metal detectors for recreation, security, and industry

President: Ken and Mary White
Catalog Cost: Free
In Business: 64 years

275 World Catalog of Oil Spill Response Products
World Catalog of Oil Spill Response Prod
200-1140 Morrison
Ottawa, ON K2H-8S9   613-232-1564
                        Fax: 613-232-6660
                       jake@slross.com
                    www.oilspillequipment.com

Oil spill response products from distributors and manufacturers worldwide

Catalog Cost: $275
Catalog Circulation: to 1500
Printing Information: 1000 pages
Binding: Perfect Bound
In Business: 37 years

Automotive Products
Accessories

276 4 Wheel Parts
4 Wheel Parts
400 W Artesia Boulevard
Compton, CA 90220   310-900-5500
                             800-421-1050
                        Fax: 310-900-5560
customerservice@4wheelparts.com
www.4wheelparts.com

4 wheel drive parts and accessories.

Credit Cards: AMEX; MasterCard
Catalog Cost: Free
In Business: 54 years

277 AGV Sport
AGV Sports Group, Inc.
PO Box 378
Buckeystown, MD 21717   619-401-4100
                        Fax: 301-663-8950
catalog@agvsport.com
www.agvsport.com

278 ATI Performance Products
ATI Performance Products, Inc.
6747 Whitestone Road
Gwynn Oak, MD 21207   410-298-4343
                             877-298-5039
                        Fax: 410-298-3579
tech@atiracing.com
www.atiracing.com

High performance race car parts that include Compu-Flow Valve Bodies, Flexplates, Treemaster Converters, Torsional Super Dampers, and adapter kits

President: James C Beattie
CFO: Rose Mudgett
Printing Information: 84 pages
Number of Employees: 50
Sales Volume: $7.5 Million

279 AW Direct
AW Direct
401 S. Wright Road
Janesville, WI 53546   608-373-2797
                             800-243-3194
                        Fax: 800-828-9678
contactus@awdirect.com
www.awdirect.com

Towing tools, straps & equipment, truck equipment & lightbars, long reach tools and kits, arrow/directional lights, safety/traffic cones, portable jump packs, air compressors & safety apparel

President: Richard Thibodeau
Catalog Cost: Free
Number of Employees: 70

280 Accessory Center
TRUCKNVANS
2207 E. 4th Street
Ontario, CA 91764-5723   909-944-0252
                             800-924-0647
                        Fax: 909-941-6625
info@trucknvans.com
www.trucknvans.com

Automobile and truck accessories

President: John Filice
Production Manager: Jason Filice
Credit Cards: AMEX; MasterCard
In Business: 10 years
Number of Employees: 2
Sales Volume: $1,000,000

281 Advanced Graphics
Advanced Graphics Inc.
342 Williams Point Blvd
Cocoa, FL 32927-4828   321-632-0115
                             800-927-8247
sales@advancedgraphicsinc.com
www.Advancedgraphicsinc.Com

Airbrushed license plates & frames, signs, magnets, stickers and clothing

President: Rick Dean
Credit Cards: AMEX; MasterCard; Visa
In Business: 37 years
Number of Employees: 25
Sales Volume: $5,000,000 - $10,000,000

282 American Bass
American Bass USA
31200 Solon Road suit 4
Solon, OH 44139   216-662-2522
                             800-798-9311
                        Fax: 440-248-5858
info@americanbassusa.com
www.americanbassusa.com/

Subwoofers, amplifiers, electronic crossovers, power/speaker cable, installation accessories, interconnect cables, and more for automobiles

President: Bob Ahuja
Printing Information: 15 pages in 8 colors
Binding: Folded
In Business: 24 years
Number of Employees: 10
Sales Volume: $1MM to $3MM

283 American Muscle
American Muscle
1 Lee Boulevard
Unit 2
Malvern, PA 19355   610-251-2397
                             866-727-1266
                        Fax: 610-981-4720
support@americanmuscle.com
www.americanmuscle.com

F-150 and Mustang custom parts

President: Steve Voudouris
In Business: 14 years

284 American Van Equipment
American Van Equipment, Inc.
149 Lehigh Avenue
Lakewood, NJ 08701   800-526-4743
                        Fax: 800-833-8266
salesservice@amvanequip.com
www.americanvan.com

Van and truck equipment

President: Charles Richter
CFO: Joseph Fallon
Credit Cards: AMEX; MasterCard
Catalog Cost: Free
In Business: 36 years
Sales Volume: $10MM to $20MM

285 Andy's Autosport
Andy's Auto Sport
15005 Concord Circle
Morgan Hill, CA 95037   800-419-1152
                        Fax: 408-762-4478
info@andysautosport.com
www.andysautosport.com

Racing seats, exhaust systems, headlight, body kits, exhaust systems and mufflers

General Manager: Andy Ferguson
Credit Cards: AMEX; MasterCard
Catalog Cost: Free
Number of Employees: 100
Sales Volume: $10 Million

286 Auto Custom Carpets
Auto Custom Carpets, Inc
1429 Noble Street
P.O. Box 1350
Anniston, AL 36202-1350   800-352-8216
                        Fax: 256-236-7375
www.Accmats.Com

Original replacement carpets for cars and trucks from the 1940's to current models

President: Ken Howell
Production Manager: Tim Gaskin
Credit Cards: AMEX; MasterCard; Visa
Catalog Circulation: Mailed 1 time(s) per year to 10M
Printing Information: 50 pages in 4 colors on Glossy Stock
Binding: Saddle Stitched
In Business: 38 years
Number of Employees: 180
Sales Volume: $10 million

287 Auto Sport
Auto Sport
1552 Insurance Lane
Unit 100
Charlottesville, VA 22911   800-788-4495
                        Fax: 434-227-5150
www.autosportcatalog.com

Line of automotive accessories

President: Paul Opiela
CFO: Bill Sauer
Credit Cards: AMEX; MasterCard
In Business: 38 years

288 BW Inc
B.W. Inc.
316 W. Broadway
Box 150
Browns Valley, MN 56219-150 320-695-2691
                             800-525-7710
                        Fax: 320-205-3095
JB@CareSecrets.com
www.caresecrets.com

Custom covers, seat covers, floor mats and storage covers for automobiles, motorcycles, RV's and boats

President: Jeff Backer Jr
Credit Cards: AMEX; MasterCard; Visa
Catalog Cost: Free
Number of Employees: 10
Sales Volume: $1MM

289 Baer Claw Brake Systems
Baer Brakes
2222 West Peoria Ave
Phoenix, AZ 85029   602-233-1411
                        Fax: 602-352-8445
baerbrake@gmail.com
www.Baer.Com

Brake systems

President: Hal Baer
Marketing Manager: Chan Martinez
Credit Cards: AMEX; MasterCard
Catalog Cost: $5
In Business: 19 years
Sales Volume: $3 million

290 Cable Organizer Office and Home
CableOrganizer.Com, Inc.
6250 NW 27th Way
Fort Lauderdale, FL 33309   954-861-2000
                             866-222-0030
                        Fax: 954-861-2001
sales@cableorganizer.com
www.cableorganizer.com

Cable covers, wire looms, cable tags and fire protection for auto and marine wiring

President: Valerie Holstein
Marketing Manager: Juan Ribero
Credit Cards: AMEX; MasterCard
Catalog Cost: Free
In Business: 13 years

291 Cerwin-Vega!
Cerwin-Vega! Inc
772 S Military Trail
Deerfield Beach, FL 33442
954-949-9600
800-444-2766
Fax: 954-949-9590
www.cerwinvega.com

Home and professional speakers

President: Mike Quandt
CFO: Tim Dorwart
Credit Cards: AMEX; MasterCard
In Business: 52 years
Number of Employees: 246

292 Chrome Trim Accessories Catalog
Jae Enterprise
209 Radio Road
Almo, KY 42020
270-753-5585
800-626-3367
Fax: 877-626-3367
sales@jaeeagle.com
www.jaeeagle.com

Home of quality Eagle Flight® brand automotive accessories.

Credit Cards: AMEX; MasterCard
Printing Information: 12 pages

293 Comfort Products
Comfort Products inc.
122 Gayoso Avenue
Memphis, TN 38104
800-971-4630
Fax: 901-248-7196
marketing@comfortproducts.net
www.comfortproducts.net

Seat cushion and mats, including Kool Kushion, Slumber Zone, Comfort Fit

President: Gary Land
In Business: 96 years
Number of Employees: 120

294 Corvette America
Corvette Parts And Accessories
100 Classic Car Drive
Reedsville, PA 17084-8851
717-667-3004
800-458-3475
Fax: 717-667-3174
www.corvetteamerica.com

Interiors, parts, wheels and accessories for Vintage 3rd generation (1953-1982) and 4th-6th generation (1984-2009) Corvettes

President: David Hall
Marketing Manager: Susie Cannon
Printing Information: 208 pages
In Business: 40 years
Number of Employees: 110
Sales Volume: $11.6 Million

295 Creative Consumers Products
Creative Consumers Products
5630 Lassiter Rd
Las Cruces, NM 88001-7806
575-527-0018
Fax: 575-527-0227
www.musictote.com

Auto accessories and parts

President: James Carter
Marketing Manager: Mary Carter
Credit Cards: AMEX; MasterCard; Visa
Catalog Cost: Free
In Business: 5 years
Number of Employees: 4
Sales Volume: Under $500M

296 Currie Enterprises
Currie Enterprise
382 North Smith
Corona, CA 92880-1605
714-528-6957
Fax: 951-549-0267
info@currieenterprises.com
www.Currieenterprises.Com

Rear end specialist; mfg high performance rear ends/parts, including forged alloy axles, drum/disc brake kits, heavy duty housings, gear cases and positractions

President: John Currie
Marketing Manager: Kent Anderson
Sales Rep: Tom Nissley
tom@currieenterprises.com
Sales Rep: Chris Nissley
chris@currieenterprises.com
Accounts Manager: Kent Anderson
kent@currieenterprises.com
Buyers: Nick Pathiakis
Credit Cards: MasterCard; Visa
Catalog Cost: Free
In Business: 45 years
Number of Employees: 49
Sales Volume: $5MM to $10MM

297 Custom Accessories
Custom Accessories
5900 Ami Drive
Richmond, IL 60071
815-678-1600
weborders@causa.com
www.causa.com

Auto accessories, car and wheel covers, mirrors, license frames

Catalog Cost: Free
Catalog Circulation: Mailed 1 time(s) per year
Printing Information: 124 pages in 4 colors
In Business: 43 years
Number of Employees: 100
Sales Volume: $1,000,000 - $5,000,000

298 Custom Autosound
Custom Autosound
1030 W. Williamson Ave
Fullerton, CA 92833-2746
714-773-1423
800-888-8637
www.casmfg.com

Custom accessories for classic cars, custom cars and streetrods

President: Carl Sprague
Credit Cards: AMEX; MasterCard
Catalog Cost: Free
Sales Volume: $20MM to $50MM

299 Dallas Mustang Parts
Dallas Mustang
10720 Sandhill Rd
Dallas, TX 75238-1216
214-349-0991
800-687-8264
Fax: 214-553-8538
sales@dallasmustang.com
www.dallasmustang.com

Mustang performance parts, restoration, gifts and accessories

President: Richard Meditz
Customer Service Manager: Carl Carson
Credit Cards: AMEX; MasterCard
Catalog Cost: Free
Printing Information: 130 pages in 4 colors on Glossy Stock
Press: Offset Press
Binding: Perfect Bound
Mailing List Information: Names for rent
Number of Employees: 25
Sales Volume: $1 Million

300 Davis Instruments Corp.
Davis
3465 Diablo Ave
Hayward, CA 94545-2746
510-732-9229
800-678-3669
Fax: 510-670-0589
sales@davisnet.com
www.davisnet.com

A vehicle monitor which tracks speed, acceleration, deceleration and distance for a comprehensive driving record

Chairman: James Acquistapace
President: Bob Selig
CFO: Susan Tatum

Marketing Manager: Susan Foxall
Production Manager: Winston Wyckoff
International Marketing Manager: Russ Heihg
Credit Cards: MasterCard; Visa
Catalog Cost: Free
Catalog Circulation: Mailed 1 time(s) per year to 150M
Average Order Size: $300
Printing Information: 16 pages in 4 colors on Glossy Stock
Press: Web Press
Binding: Saddle Stitched
In Business: 52 years
Number of Employees: 100
Sales Volume: $10,000,000 - $25,000,000

301 Dayton Wheel Products
Dayton Wire Wheels
115 Compark Rd
Dayton, OH 45459-4803
937-438-0100
888-559-2880
Fax: 937-438-1215
www.Daytonwheel.Com

Wire wheels for cars, trucks and motorcycles

President: Charlie Schroeder
Credit Cards: AMEX; MasterCard; Visa
Catalog Cost: $10
Printing Information: 24 pages
In Business: 99 years
Sales Volume: $5MM to $10MM

302 Delta Truck Storage Solutions
Delta Consolidated Industries
14600 York Rd.
Suite A
Sparks, MD 21152
800-643-0084
Fax: 877-356-4081
www.deltatruckstorage.com

Truck storage containers, tanks and chests.

Printing Information: 64 pages in 4 colors
Number of Employees: 300

303 Domestic Trucks Performance Products
4 Wheel Drive Hardware Inc
400 W Artesia Boulevard
Compton, CA 90220
800-578-8132
Fax: 310-900-5560
cs@performance4trucks.com
www.performanceproducts4trucks.com

Ford, Chevy, GMC and Dodge truck accessories and high performance parts

President: Barry Ryan
Credit Cards: AMEX; MasterCard
Catalog Cost: Free
Printing Information: in 4 colors

304 Eagle Wings Catalog
Jae Enterprise
209 Radio Road
Almo, KY 42020
270-753-5585
800-626-3367
Fax: 877-626-3367
sales@jaeeagle.com
www.jaeeagle.com

Home of quality Eagle Flight® brand automotive accessories.

Credit Cards: AMEX; MasterCard
Printing Information: 16 pages

305 Fremont Die Consumer Products
Fremont Die Consumer Products
1709A Endeavor Dr
Williamsburg, VA 23195-6239
757-872-6438
800-336-8847
Fax: 757-872-6958
cs@fremontdie.com
www.Fremontdie.Com

Automotive signs and novelties, NFL auto accessories

President: James Hotze
Credit Cards: AMEX; MasterCard; Visa

Catalog Cost: Free
In Business: 32 years
Number of Employees: 15
Sales Volume: $3MM to $5MM

306   International Autosport
Auto Sport
1552 Insurance Lane
Unit 100
Charlottesville, VA   2291   800-788-4495
                                   800-953-0814
                    Fax: 434-227-5150
customerservice@autosportcatalog.com
          www.autosportcatalog.com
Car care, auto and travel accessories for all cars
President: Paul Opiela
Buyers: Kim Painley
Credit Cards: AMEX; MasterCard; Visa
Catalog Cost: Free
Printing Information: 50 pages
Number of Employees: 50-1

307   JOBOX Premium Storage Solutions
Delta Consolidated Industries
14600 York Rd.
Suite A
Sparks, MD   21152   800-643-0084
                    Fax: 877-356-4081
      www.deltatruckstorage.com
Truck storage containers, tanks and chests.
Printing Information: 56 pages in 4 colors
Number of Employees: 300

308   Jeep Parts Catalog
4 Wheel Drive Hardware Inc
PO Box 57
Columbiana, OH   44408   330-482-4924
                                   800-555-3353
                    Fax: 330-482-5035
          custserv@4wd.com
                www.4wd.com

Parts and accessories
President: Barry Ryan
Credit Cards: AMEX; MasterCard
Catalog Cost: Free
In Business: 38 years

309   MacNeil Automotive Products
MacNeil Automotive Products
841 Remington Blvd
Bolingbrook, IL   60440   630-769-1500
                                   800-441-6287
                    Fax: 630-769-0300
      sales@weathertech.com
          www.weathertech.com
Automotive accessories including floor mats, cargo and floor liners, side window deflectors, and a variety of other functional automotive accessories
Credit Cards: AMEX; MasterCard
Catalog Cost: Free
Printing Information: 29 pages
Mailing List Information: Names for rent
In Business: 25 years

310   Mercedes Performance Products
Performance Products for Mercedes
5200 S. Washington Avenue
Titusville, FL   32780   818-779-2823
                                   888-843-2822
                    Fax: 800-243-8893
      www.ecklersmbzparts.com
Parts and accessories
Credit Cards: AMEX; MasterCard
Catalog Cost: Free
In Business: 53 years

311   Mid America Motorworks
Mid America Motorworks
17082 N. US Highway 45
PO Box 1368
Effingham, IL   62401-6764   217-540-4200
                                   866-350-4543
                    Fax: 217-540-4800
      mail@mamotorworks.com
          www.mamotorworks.com
Parts and accessories for corvettes, air cooled volkswagons and porsches
President: Mike Yager
Mike.Yager@mamotorworks.com
CFO: Eric Calhoun
Chief Cheerleader: Mike Yager
mike.yager@mamotorworks.com
Corporate Director: Laurie Yager
laurie.yager@mamotorworks.com
President Performance Choice: SteveOlson
Steve.Olson@performancechoice.com
Catalog Circulation: Mailed 8 time(s) per year
Average Order Size: $125
In Business: 41 years
Number of Employees: 150
Sales Volume: 5MM-10MM

312   Midland Radio Corporation
Midland
5900 Parretta Drive
Kansas City, MO   64120-2134   816-241-8500
                    Fax: 816-241-5713
      mail@midlandradio.com
          www.midlandradio.com
Consumer two-way communication products, including FRS and GMRS radios, CB radios, weather monitors, and accessories
President: Dan Devling
International Marketing Manager: Noe Tabaras
Credit Cards: AMEX; MasterCard
Catalog Cost: Free
Printing Information: 3 pages
Mailing List Information: Names for rent
In Business: 50 years
Number of Employees: 120
Sales Volume: $20MM to $50MM

313   Montgomery Ward
Montgomery Ward
3650 Milwaukee St.
Madison, WI   53714   877-784-2836
                                   888-557-3848
Mail order business
Printing Information: 115 pages
In Business: 143 years

314   Motorbooks Catalog
Quarto Knows
400 First Avenue North
Suite 400
Minneapolis, MN   55401   612-344-8100
                                   800-458-0454
                    Fax: 612-344-8691
      customerservice@quartous.com
          www.quartoknows.com
Transportation books covering classic motorcycles, cars and trucks
Chairman: Tim Chadwick
President: Ken Fund
kfund@quaysidepub.com
CFO: Michael Connole, FCA
Director, Quarto International Co-e: David Breuer
Group Director of Operations: Michael Clarke
Managing Director, Books & Gifts Di: Joe Craven
Credit Cards: AMEX; MasterCard; Visa
Catalog Cost: Free
In Business: 39 years

315   Music Direct
Music Direct
1811 W Bryn Mawr Ave
Chicago, IL   60660   312-433-0200
                                   800-449-8333
                    Fax: 312-433-0011
      www.musicdirect.com
Audio equipment, record albums, and accessories
President: Jim Davis
Sales Volume: $3MM to $5MM

316   Mustangs Unlimited
Mustangs Unlimited
440 Adams Street
Manchester, CT   06042-2767   770-446-1965
                                   800-243-7278
                    Fax: 860-649-1260
      info@mustangsunlimited.com
          www.mustangsunlimited.com
Classic parts and accessories for your Mustang, Cougar or Shelby
President: Melissa Letenere
Marketing Manager: Anthony Coles
Credit Cards: AMEX; MasterCard
Catalog Cost: Free
Catalog Circulation: Mailed 24 time(s) per year
Printing Information: 352 pages
In Business: 39 years
Number of Employees: 60
Sales Volume: $5MM to $10MM

317   National Automotive Lines, Inc.
National Automotive Lines, Inc.
38 West Franklin Street
Shelbyville, IN   46176   317-392-1713
                                   800-428-4300
                    Fax: 888-442-9222
      www.natauto.com
Credit Cards: AMEX; MasterCard

318   Parts & Accessories Catalog
LMC Truck
15450 W 108th Street
PO Box 14991
Lenexa, KS   66285   913-541-0684
                                   800-562-8782
                    Fax: 913-599-0323
      CustomerCare@LongMotor.net
          www.lmctruck.com
Truck parts and accessories for GMC, Chevy, Ford and Dodge trucks and SUV's
President: Rebecca Hanrahan
Credit Cards: AMEX; MasterCard; Visa
Catalog Cost: Free
Printing Information: 180 pages

319   Pierce Sales
Pierce Sales
549 U.S. Highway 287 S.
Henrietta, TX   76365   940-538-5643
                                   800-658-6301
                    Fax: 940-538-4382
      info@piercesales.com
          www.piercesales.com
Stainless Jeep parts, grill guards, towing accessories, vehicle lighting, winch cables & accessories, wiring & connectors, hydraulics and wrecker parts
President: Jeff Pierce
Credit Cards: AMEX; MasterCard
Catalog Cost: $3
Printing Information: 80 pages
In Business: 39 years
Number of Employees: 25

320 Pit Pal Products
Pit Pal Products
2009 Horizon Court
Zion, IL 60099
847-872-7257
888-748-7257
Fax: 847-872-7258
sales@pitpal.com
www.pitpal.com

Garage, shop and trailer organizers
Catalog Cost: Free
In Business: 32 years

321 Plastic View ATC
Plastic View ATC, Inc
4585 Runway
Suite B
Simi Valley, CA 93063
805-520-9390
800-468-6301
Fax: 805-520-0260
info@pvatc.com
www.pvatc.com

See thru windows shades for automotives and homes; air traffic control ower cabs
President: Sonny Voges
CFO: Sonny Voges
Marketing Manager: Ryan Voges
Production Manager: Hector Moreno
Fulfillment: Sandra Estrada
International Marketing Manager: Ryan Voges
Buyers: Ryan Voges
Catalog Cost: Free
Printing Information: 20 pages on Glossy Stock
Press: Letterpress
Mailing List Information: Names for rent
List Manager: Sandra Estrada
In Business: 68 years
Number of Employees: 9
Sales Volume: $500M to $1MM

322 Raceline Direct
Raceline Direct
85 Main Street
Suite 200
Johnson City, NY 13790
800-454-8929
Fax: 607-644-1551
info@racelinedirect.com
www.racelinedirect.com

Automotive accessories and racing fan apparel
Credit Cards: MasterCard; Visa
Catalog Cost: Free
In Business: 16 years

323 Rik's Corvette Parts Catalog 63-82 Parts
Rik's Corvette Parts
3783 NC 18 S
Morganton, NC 28655
828-433-6506
888-745-7838
Fax: 828-437-7166
riksvet@riksvet.com
www.riksvet.com

324 Security Chain Company
Peerless Chain Company
PO Box 949
Clackamas, OR 97015-949
503-656-5400
Fax: 503-656-4836
custserv@peerlesschain.com
www.peerlesschain.com

Cable, tire and hardware chains, load straps, tow straps and other winter traction products
Catalog Circulation: Mailed 1 time(s) per year to 40M
Average Order Size: $2000
Printing Information: 48 pages in 2 colors on Glossy Stock
Press: Web Press
In Business: 98 years
Number of Employees: 120
Sales Volume: $5,000,000 - $10,000,000

325 Show Your Pride Catalog
Comet Products
Box 8165
Cherry Hill, NJ 08002
856-795-4810
Fax: 856-354-6313
webmaster@infosheet.com
www.cometproducts.com

Car grille emblem badges made of brass, chrome plated, with brilliant baked-on enamel colors; over 500 kinds are available
President: Marvin Schwartz
Credit Cards: MasterCard; Visa
Catalog Cost: $3
Average Order Size: $40
Printing Information: 16 pages
Mailing List Information: Names for rent
In Business: 20 years
Number of Employees: 4

326 Skyjacker Suspensions
Skyjacker Suspensions
PO Box 1678
West Monroe, LA 71294-1678
318-388-0816
866-423-3253
Fax: 318-388-2608
info@skyjacker.com
www.skyjacker.com

Ford, Chevrolet, Dodge, Jeep and Toyota suspension parts
Chairman: Nell McCury
President: Lonnie McCurry Sr.
Marketing Manager: Lee McGuire
Executive Director: Cindy M. Acree
Credit Cards: MasterCard
Catalog Cost: $5
Printing Information: 200 pages in 4 colors
In Business: 45 years
Number of Employees: 10
Sales Volume: 3mm-5mm

327 Speedgear
Speedgear
30A Locust Ave
Berkeley Heights, NJ 07922
908-286-1886
800-777-4453
Fax: 908-286-0002
info@speedgear.com
www.speedgear.com

Licensed racing apparel
Credit Cards: AMEX; MasterCard
In Business: 25 years

328 Superior Auto Extras Catalog 2015
Superior Auto Extras
12601 Encinitas Ave.
Sylmar, CA 91342
818-362-5554
800-445-XTRA
Fax: 818-362-2775
info@superiorautoextras.com
www.superiorautoextras.com
Owner: Gene Student
Sales VP: Chris Wade
chris@superiorautoextras.com
Operationa VP: Patrick Almalem
patrick@superiorautoextras.com
Printing Information: 73 pages
In Business: 24 years

329 USA Promo Items
USA Promo Items
Inland Empire, CA 92336
888-407-9929
Fax: 909-371-0281
sales@usapromoitems.com
www.usapromoitems.com

330 Universal Vintage Tire Company
Universal Vintage Tire Company
2994 Elizabethtown Rd
Hershey, PA 17033-9322
717-534-0715
877-454-3954
Fax: 717-534-0719
sales@universaltire.com
www.universaltire.com

Vintage tires for vintage and classic autos, wheel hardware and accessories, brass running board molding
President: Eric Maxwell
Credit Cards: AMEX; MasterCard; Visa
Catalog Cost: Free
Printing Information: 23 pages
In Business: 47 years
Number of Employees: 3
Sales Volume: $1MM to $3MM

331 Wheel Simulator and Accessories Catalog
Jae Enterprise
209 Radio Road
Almo, KY 42020
270-753-5585
800-626-3367
Fax: 877-626-3367
sales@jaeeagle.com
www.jaeeagle.com

Home of quality Eagle Flight® brand automotive accessories.
Credit Cards: AMEX; MasterCard
Printing Information: 16 pages

332 Wheel Trim Catalog
Jae Enterprise
209 Radio Road
Almo, KY 42020
270-753-5585
800-626-3367
Fax: 877-626-3367
sales@jaeeagle.com
www.jaeeagle.com

Home of quality Eagle Flight® brand automotive accessories.
Credit Cards: AMEX; MasterCard
Printing Information: 8 pages

333 Yakima-Destination Hardware
Yakima Products, Inc.
15025 SW Koll Pkwy
Beaverton, OR 97006-6056
971-249-7500
888-925-4621
www.yakima.Com

Racks for cars
President: Jay Wilson
CFO: PJ Peacock, VP Finance
Marketing Manager: Dean Hart, VP Marketing
International Marketing Manager: Chris Chadwick, VP Sales
Printing Information: 40 pages in 4 colors on Matte Stock
Press: Sheetfed Press
Mailing List Information: Names for rent
In Business: 35 years
Number of Employees: 155
Sales Volume: $20MM to $50MM

Antique Cars & Parts

334 1909-1927 Model T & TT - 2014-2015 Issue
MAC's Antique Auto Parts
PO Box 238
Lockport, NY 14095
716-210-1340
800-828-1051
Fax: 716-210-1370
customerservice@macsauto.com
www.macsautoparts.com

335 1928-1931 Model A & AA - 2014-15 Issue
MAC's Antique Auto Parts
PO Box 238
Lockport, NY 14095
716-210-1340
800-828-1051
Fax: 716-210-1370
customerservice@macsauto.com
www.macsautoparts.com

336 **1932-1948 Early V8 - 2014-2015 Issue**
MAC's Antique Auto Parts
PO Box 238
Lockport, NY 14095
716-210-1340
800-828-1051
Fax: 716-210-1370
customerservice@macsauto.com
www.macsautoparts.com

337 **1948-1979 Pickup Truck - 2014-2015 Issue**
MAC's Antique Auto Parts
PO Box 238
Lockport, NY 14095
716-210-1340
800-828-1051
Fax: 716-210-1370
customerservice@macsauto.com
www.macsautoparts.com

338 **1949-1959 Full-Size Ford & Mercury - Includes 1958**
MAC's Antique Auto Parts
PO Box 238
Lockport, NY 14095
716-210-1340
800-828-1051
Fax: 716-210-1370
customerservice@macsauto.com
www.macsautoparts.com

339 **1955-1979 Thunderbird - 2014-2015 Issue**
MAC's Antique Auto Parts
PO Box 238
Lockport, NY 14095
716-210-1340
800-828-1051
Fax: 716-210-1370
customerservice@macsauto.com
www.macsautoparts.com

340 **1960-1970 Falcon & Comet - 2014-2015 Issue**
MAC's Antique Auto Parts
PO Box 238
Lockport, NY 14095
716-210-1340
800-828-1051
Fax: 716-210-1370
customerservice@macsauto.com
www.macsautoparts.com

341 **1960-1972 Full-Size Ford & Mercury - 2013-2014**
MAC's Antique Auto Parts
PO Box 238
Lockport, NY 14095
716-210-1340
800-828-1051
Fax: 716-210-1370
customerservice@macsauto.com
www.macsautoparts.com

342 **1962-1971 Fairlane & Torino - 2014-2015 Issue**
MAC's Antique Auto Parts
PO Box 238
Lockport, NY 14095
716-210-1340
800-828-1051
Fax: 716-210-1370
customerservice@macsauto.com
www.macsautoparts.com

343 **1964-1973 Mustang - 2014-2015 Issue**
MAC's Antique Auto Parts
PO Box 238
Lockport, NY 14095
716-210-1340
800-828-1051
Fax: 716-210-1370
customerservice@macsauto.com
www.macsautoparts.com

344 **1965-1973 Mustang Parts**
California Mustang Parts & Accessories
19400 San Jose Avenue
City of Industry, CA 91748
909-598-3383
800-775-0101
Fax: 909-598-5611
csmustang@cal-mustang.com
www.cal-mustang.com

Restoration and performance parts for 1965-1973 Ford Mustangs.

Catalog Cost: Free
In Business: 39 years

345 **1967-1969 Camaro Parts & Accessories**
Ricks Camaros
5200 S. Washington Ave.
Titusville, FL 32780
706-546-9217
844-447-7693
Fax: 877-548-8581
custsvc@rickscamaros.com
www.rickscamaros.com

Restoration and performance parts for 1967-1969 Chevrolet Camaros.

Credit Cards: AMEX; MasterCard
Catalog Cost: Free
Mailing List Information: Names for rent
In Business: 54 years
Sales Volume: $10MM to $20MM

346 **1979-1993 Mustang Parts**
California Mustang Parts & Accessories
19400 San Jose Avenue
City of Industry, CA 91748
909-598-3383
800-775-0101
Fax: 909-598-5611
csmustang@cal-mustang.com
www.cal-mustang.com

Restoration and performance parts for 1979-1993 Ford Mustangs.

Catalog Cost: Free
In Business: 39 years

347 **4WD Vintage Jeep Parts & Accessories**
4Wheel Drive Hardware
44488 State Route 14
Columbiana, OH 44408
330-482-4924
800-555-3353
Fax: 330-482-5035
custserv@4wd.com
www.4wd.com

Vintage Jeep replacement parts and accessories for models from 1941-1975.

President: Roy Lenjoski
Store Manager: Robert Plute
Retail@4wd.com
Customer Service Manager: Heidi Eisenbraun
Call Center Supervisor: Becky Warner
Credit Cards: AMEX; MasterCard
Catalog Cost: Free
In Business: 38 years

348 **American Autowire**
American Autowire, Inc.
150 Heller Pl #17W
Suite 17
Bellmawr, NJ 08031-2503
856-933-0805
800-482-9473
Fax: 856-933-0805
www.americanautowire.com

Wiring harnesses, accessories and parts for GM restoration, modified original and custom street rods

President: Michael Nanning
Marketing Manager: Dave McKelvey
Chief Operating Officer: Jim Cardona
Vice President: Frank Colonna
Vice President, I.T.: Jeff Moore
Credit Cards: AMEX; MasterCard
Catalog Cost: Free
In Business: 32 years
Sales Volume: $1MM to $3MM

349 **Antique Auto Parts & Accessories**
LeBaron Bonney Company
6 Chestnut Street
Amesbury, MA 01913
978-388-3811
800-221-5408
Fax: 978-388-1113
sales@lebaronbonney.com
www.lebaronbonney.com

Specialty items for Fords 1928-1954 with many other items suitable for other antique cars and trucks

Catalog Cost: Free
Mailing List Information: Names for rent
In Business: 77 years

350 **Auto Krafters**
Auto Krafter's Inc.
214 E Old Cross Road
PO Box 1100
New Market, VA 22844
540-740-8000
800-228-7346
Fax: 540-740-8011
www.autokrafters.com

60's - 70's classic Ford and Mercury parts and accessories

President: Ron Miller
Production Manager: Donna Clark
Credit Cards: AMEX; MasterCard; Visa
Catalog Cost: $5
Average Order Size: $200
Mailing List Information: Names for rent
In Business: 5 years
Number of Employees: 45
Sales Volume: $3MM to $5MM

351 **Bill Hirsch Automotive**
Bill Hirsch Auto
396 Littleton Avenue
Newark, NJ 07103
973-642-2404
800-828-2061
Fax: 973-642-6161
info@hirschauto.com
www.hirschauto.com

Antique, classic and exotic automotive restoration products

President: Bill Hirsch
Catalog Cost: Free
In Business: 40 years

352 **Buick Parts Catalog**
Bob's Automobilia
3352 S El Pomar
Templeton, CA 93465
805-434-2963
Fax: 805-434-2626
bob@bobsautomobilia.com
www.bobsautomobilia.com

New and used restoration parts for 1920-1958 era Buicks

President: Robert Carrubba Sr
CFO: Beverly Carrubba
Marketing Manager: Robert Carrubba Jr
Catalog Cost: $6
Catalog Circulation: to 3500
Average Order Size: $100
Printing Information: 112 pages on Matte Stock
Press: Letterpress
Binding: Perfect Bound
List Manager: Alvin Cable
In Business: 36 years
Number of Employees: 6
Sales Volume: $1,000,000

353 **C & P 55-57 Chevy Passenger Cars**
C & P Automotive
PO Box 348
Kulpsville, PA 19443
610-584-9105
800-235-2475
Fax: 610-584-9509
sales@cpchevy.com
www.cpchevy.com

Restoration supplies and customizing parts for 1955 thru 1957 Chevrolet passenger cars

Credit Cards: AMEX; MasterCard
Catalog Cost: $5
In Business: 25 years

354 C & P 55-59 Chevrolet Trucks
C & P Automotive
PO Box 348
Kulpsville, PA 19443 610-584-9105
800-235-2475
Fax: 610-584-9509
sales@cpchevy.com
www.cpchevy.com

Restoration supplies and customizing parts for 1955 2nd series thru 1959 Chevrolet trucks

Credit Cards: AMEX; MasterCard
Catalog Cost: $3
In Business: 25 years

355 Clark's Corvair Parts
Clark's Corvair Parts
400 Mohawk Trail
Shelburne Falls, MA 01370 413-625-9776
888-267-8247
Fax: 413-625-8498
clarks@corvair.com
www.corvair.com

Corvair engines and parts - high performance, new, reproduced and used, original interiors and trim, over 14,000 listed

President: Calvin Clark
Catalog Cost: $6
Catalog Circulation: to 15
Printing Information: 700 pages
Mailing List Information: Names for rent
In Business: 44 years
Number of Employees: 22
Sales Volume: $3MM to $5MM

356 Classic Thunderbird Illustrated
Classic Auto Supply Company, Inc.
795 High Street
Coshocton, OH 43812 740-622-8561
800-374-0914
Fax: 740-622-5151
casco@classictbird.com
www.classictbird.com

Parts and accessories for 1955-1957 Thunderbirds

Catalog Cost: Free
Printing Information: 89 pages
In Business: 45 years

357 Cliff's Classic Chevrolet
Cliff's Classic Chevrolet
619 S.E. 202nd Avenue
P.O. Box 1957
Portland, OR 97233 503-667-4329
Fax: 503-669-4268
clifchev@aol.com
www.cliffsclassicchevrolet.net

Quality used, new, and reproduction parts for your original, modified or hot rod, 1955-57 Chevrolet and 2nd series 55-59 truck parts

President: Cliff Waldron
Credit Cards: MasterCard
Catalog Cost: $5
In Business: 18 years
Sales Volume: Under $500M

358 Collector Car Restorations
Greg Donahue Collector Car Restorations
12900 South Betty Point
Floral City, FL 34436 352-344-4329
Fax: 352-344-0015
www.gregdonahue.com

1963 and 1934 Ford Galaxie parts: new, reproduction, NOS

President: Greg Donahue
Credit Cards: MasterCard; Visa
Catalog Cost: $8
Printing Information: 198 pages
Mailing List Information: Names for rent
In Business: 30 years

359 Danchuk Manufacturing
Danchuk Manufacturing
3201 South Standard Ave.
Santa Ana, CA 92705 714-751-1957
800-648-9554
Fax: 714-850-1957
custserv@danchuk.com
www.danchuk.com

Classic auto parts

President: Danny Danchuk
CFO: Steve Brown
Marketing Manager: Bill Roche
Production Manager: Sara Portillo
Credit Cards: AMEX; MasterCard
Catalog Cost: $5
Printing Information: 300 pages
In Business: 39 years
Number of Employees: 71
Sales Volume: $11.10 Million

360 Dutchman 1955-1957 Chevy Car Catalog
Dutchman Motorsports
1250 E. Piper Ct.
PO Box 20517
Meridian, ID 83642 503-257-6604
Fax: 503-253-6564
www.dutchmanaxles.com

1955-1957 Chevy front suspension systems

President: Todd A Ebeling
Credit Cards: MasterCard
Catalog Cost: Free
Mailing List Information: Names for rent
In Business: 13 years
Number of Employees: 11
Sales Volume: $1.1 Million

361 Dutchman Motorsports
Dutchman Motorsports, Inc.
1250 E. Piper Ct.
PO Box 20517
Meridian, ID 83642 503-257-6604
Fax: 503-253-6564
www.dutchmanaxles.com

Alloy axle shafts, rearends, and drivetrain components for any year car or truck

President: Todd A Ebeling
Credit Cards: MasterCard
Catalog Cost: Free
Mailing List Information: Names for rent
In Business: 13 years
Number of Employees: 11
Sales Volume: $1.1 Million

362 East Coast Chevy
East Coast Chevy
4154A Skyron Drive
Doylestown, PA 18902 215-348-5568
Fax: 215-348-0560
ted@eastcoastchevy.com
www.eastcoastchevy.com

1955-1957 Chevy parts

President: Ted Wieckowski
Credit Cards: AMEX; MasterCard
Catalog Cost: $6
Printing Information: 240 pages
Mailing List Information: Names for rent
In Business: 39 years
Number of Employees: 18
Sales Volume: $1,000,000

363 Eckler's 1953-2001 Corvette Parts and Accessories
Eckler's Corvette
5200 S. Washington Ave
Titusville, FL 32780-7318 877-748-4555
800-284-3906
Fax: 321-383-2059
sales@ecklers.net
www.ecklers.com

Suppliers of parts and accessories for Corvettes dating from 1953 to present

President: Gary Mills
Marketing Manager: Michael Wilson
Mailing List Information: Names for rent
In Business: 54 years
Number of Employees: 50
Sales Volume: $20MM to $50MM

364 Egge Machine Company
Egge Machine and Speed Shop
11707 Slauson Avenue
Santa Fe Springs, CA 90670-2217 562-945-3419
800-866-3443
Fax: 562-693-1635
info@egge.com
www.egge.com

Parts and services for nostalgic motors

President: Robert Egge
CFO: Ernie Silvers
Marketing Manager: Tony Colombini
Credit Cards: AMEX; MasterCard
Catalog Cost: Free
Printing Information: 190 pages
In Business: 100 years

365 El Camino Store
El Camino Store
5200 S. Washington Ave.
Titusville, FL 32780 888-685-5987
Fax: 877-548-8581
sales@elcaminostore.com
www.elcaminostore.com

Parts and accessories for 1959 thru 1987 El Caminos

President: Russell Woodward
Credit Cards: AMEX; MasterCard; Visa
Catalog Cost: Free
Printing Information: 65 pages
In Business: 54 years
Number of Employees: 5

366 Filling Station
Filling Station
990 S 2nd Street
Lebanon, OR 97355 541-258-2114
800-841-6622
Fax: 541-258-6968
fssales@fillingstation.com
www.fillingstation.com

1916-1964 Chevrolet cars and 1918-1987 Chevy and GMC trucks reproduction parts

President: Stephen Kassis
Catalog Cost: $7
Printing Information: 400 pages
Mailing List Information: Names for rent
In Business: 36 years

367 Italian Car Parts
5665 Hood Street
#515
West Linn, OR 97068 503-655-9811
ICP@ItalianCarParts.com
www.italiancarparts.com

Products for maintenance and restoration of Italian cars

368 **Jim Carter's Antique Truck Parts**
Jim Carter
1508 East 23rd Street
Independence, MO 64055-1657   800-336-1913
800-842-1913
Fax: 800-262-3749
info@oldchevytrucks.com
www.oldchevytrucks.com

New and used antique parts for Chevy and GM trucks from 1934-1972

President: J L Carter
Owner: Jim Carter
General Mnager: Lynn
Vice President: Dave
Credit Cards: MasterCard; Visa
Catalog Cost: $5
Printing Information: 144 pages
In Business: 76 years
Number of Employees: 25
Sales Volume: $3MM to $5MM

369 **John's Mustang**
John's Mustang
5234 Glenmont Dr
Houston, TX 77081-2108   713-668-5646
800-869-6894
Fax: 713-664-3327
info@johnsmustang.com
www.johnsmustang.com

Mustang parts and accessories for 1964-1973 and 1979-2001 cars

President: John Sasitorn
Secretary/Treasurer: Wanicha Sasitorn
Catalog Cost: $12
In Business: 26 years
Number of Employees: 5
Sales Volume: $750,000

370 **Long Island Corvette Supply**
Long Island Corvette Supply
1445 S Strong Ave
Copiague, NY 11726-3227   631-225-3000
800-466-6367
Fax: 631-225-5030
www.licorvette.com

Automotive parts and accessories, offering parts for specific makes and models, specializing in 1963 to 1967 Corvette parts

Credit Cards: AMEX; MasterCard; Visa
Catalog Cost: $3
Printing Information: 87 pages in 1 color
Mailing List Information: Names for rent
In Business: 14 years
Number of Employees: 6
Sales Volume: $1MM to $3MM

371 **Luttys Chevys - Warehouse Catalog**
Luttys Chevys
2385 Saxonburg Blvd
Cheswick, PA 15024   724-265-2988
Fax: 724-265-4773
sales@luttyschevy.com
www.luttyschevy.com

1955 to 1957 Chevelle Monte Carlo, Camaro, Nova, Impala and 1947-1972 Chevy truck restoration parts and accessories

President: Darlene Lutty
International Marketing Manager: Chad Bevan
Buyers: Greg Jones
Credit Cards: AMEX; MasterCard; Visa
Catalog Cost: Free
Catalog Circulation: Mailed 1 time(s) per year to 30000
Mailing List Information: Names for rent
In Business: 33 years
Number of Employees: 12
Sales Volume: $5MM to $10MM

372 **Max Merritt Auto-Parts Master Catalog**
Max Merritt
235 Terre Haute Street
Franklin, IN 46131   317-736-6233
800-472-2573
Fax: 317-736-6235
www.maxmerrittauto.com

New, used and reproduction Packard parts and accessories

President: Max Merritt
In Business: 54 years

373 **Mustang Plus**
Mustang Plus
2353 N Wilson Way
Stockton, CA 95205   209-944-9977
800-999-4289
Fax: 209-944-9980
mustangs@mustangsplus.com
www.mustangsplus.com

Complete parts and accessories for Mustangs, etc.

Credit Cards: MasterCard; Visa
Catalog Cost: $2
Printing Information: 404 pages
In Business: 34 years

374 **Obsolete & Classic Auto Parts**
Obsolete & Classic Auto Parts, Inc.
8701 South Interstate 35
Oklahoma City, OK 73149   405-631-3933
800-654-3247
Fax: 405-634-6815
info@classicautoparts.com
www.classicautoparts.com

Worldwide retailer and distributor of antique, classic, street rod, and Obsolete Chevrolet and Ford parts and accessories

General Manager: Mike Forehand
Assistant Manager: Kevin Billins
Accounting: Sara Moheit
Catalog Cost: Free
Catalog Circulation: to 1
In Business: 39 years

375 **Pete's Fabrications**
Petes Fab'S
2364 Blue Level Rd
Bowling Green, KY 42101-9007   270-842-6016
Fax: 270-781-6579
petesfab@aol.com
www.petesfab.com

Billet aluminum accessories for 55-57 Chevys, Impala SS, trucks, and 97-98 Covettes

President: Pete Ausbrooks
Director: Mark Parsons
Credit Cards: MasterCard
Catalog Cost: Free
Printing Information: 9 pages
In Business: 17 years
Number of Employees: 3
Sales Volume: $150,000

376 **Restoration Specialties & Supply**
Restoration Specialties & Supply, Inc
148 Minnow Creek Lane
Windber, PA 15963-328   814-467-9842
Fax: 814-467-5323
info@restorationspecialties.com
www.restorationspecialties.com

Restoration parts for cars manufactured prior to 1980

President: David A Mihalko
Credit Cards: MasterCard
Catalog Cost: $3.5
Printing Information: 232 pages
In Business: 41 years
Number of Employees: 16
Sales Volume: $1 Million

377 **Rubber Parts for Classic Cars**
Metro Moulded Parts, Inc.
P.O. Box 48130
11610 Jay Street NW
Minneapolis, MN 55448-130   877-399-2562
800-878-2237
MetroSales@metrommp.com
www.metrommp.com

Weatherstripping and rubber parts for classic cars and trucks dated 1929-1975

President: Douglas Hajicek
CFO: Chuck Falloon, COO
Marketing Manager: John Rohling
Buyers: Joe Frascella
Credit Cards: AMEX; MasterCard; Visa; Discover
Catalog Cost: Free
Catalog Circulation: to 20000
Average Order Size: $85
Printing Information: 200 pages in 1 color on Matte Stock
Press: Web Press
Binding: Perfect Bound
Mailing List Information: Names for rent
In Business: 72 years
Number of Employees: 50

378 **Sherman & Associates**
Sherman & Associates, Inc.
61166 Van Dyke Road
Washington, MI 48094   586-677-6800
800-345-9487
Fax: 586-677-6801
info57@shermanparts.com
www.shermanparts.com

Automotive body parts, panel and accessories from 1949 to 2010 models for vintage, domestic and import cars and trucks

Credit Cards: AMEX; MasterCard
Catalog Cost: $12
In Business: 28 years

379 **Snyder's Antique Parts**
Synder's Antique Auto Parts, Inc
12925 Woodworth Rd
New Springfield, OH 44443-9753   330-549-5313
888-262-5712
Fax: 330-549-2211
www.snydersantiqueauto.com

Parts for 1909-1931 Model T and Model A Fords

President: Don Snyder III
Credit Cards: AMEX; MasterCard
Catalog Cost: Free
In Business: 60 years
Number of Employees: 30
Sales Volume: $3.5 million

380 **Steele Rubber Products**
Steele Rubber Products
6180 E NC 150 HWY
Denver, NC 28037   704-483-9343
800-447-0849
Fax: 704-483-6650
magosta@steelerubber.com
www.steelerubber.com

Rubber parts for the restoration of classic and collector cars

President: Matt Agosta
CFO: Debra Lail
Marketing Manager: Eric Saltrick
Production Manager: Eddie Lial
Founder: Lynn Steele
Credit Cards: AMEX; MasterCard
Catalog Cost: Free
Printing Information: 576 pages
Mailing List Information: Names for rent
In Business: 57 years
Number of Employees: 50-1
Sales Volume: $5.4 Millions

381 Stoudt Auto Sales
Stoudt Auto Sales, Inc.
1350 Carbon St
Reading, PA 19601-1696   610-375-8595
                          800-482-3033
                          Fax: 610-372-7283
                          sales@stoudtautosales.com
                          www.stoudtautosales.com
1953-2007 Corvettes and Corvette parts
President: Jay Stoudt
Secretary: Steven Stoudt, Corvette Parts
Credit Cards: AMEX; MasterCard; Visa
Catalog Cost: Free
Catalog Circulation: Mailed 1 time(s) per year
to 15000
Printing Information: 42 pages in 4 colors
Binding: Saddle Stitched
In Business: 92 years
Number of Employees: 15
Sales Volume: $2.7 Million

382 Thunderbird Price and Accessory Catalog
Thunderbird Headquarters Inc
4020 Pike Lane
Concord, CA 94520-1227   925-825-9550
                          800-227-2174
                          Fax: 800-964-1957
                          parts@tbirdhq.com
                          www.tbirdhq.com
Ford licensed parts, including OEM and re-production parts for classic Ford Thunderbirds
President: Don Johnson
Marketing Manager: Scott LeBean
Founder: Don Johnson
Founder: Sandy Johnson
Credit Cards: AMEX; MasterCard; Visa
Catalog Cost: Free
Average Order Size: $200
Printing Information: 99 pages in 1 color on Newsprint
Press: Web Press
Binding: Saddle Stitched
Mailing List Information: Names for rent
In Business: 36 years
Number of Employees: 23
Sales Volume: $3MM to $5MM

383 Thunderbird and Lincoln Catalogs
Classique Cars Unlimited
4523 Highway 589
Sumrall, MS 39482   601-758-3357
                     800-543-8691
                     Fax: 601-758-3116
                     parts@classiquecars.com
                     www.classiquecars.com
Switches, mouldings, relays, suspension, front end parts, brakes, decals and shop manuals
President: Karen A Williams
parts@datasync.com
Catalog Cost: $15-25
Printing Information: in 1 color on Matte Stock
Press: Sheetfed Press
Mailing List Information: Names for rent
In Business: 40 years
Number of Employees: 2
Sales Volume: $4,99,000

384 Vintage
Corvette America
100 Classic Car Drive
Reedsville, PA 17084   717-667-3004
                        800-458-3475
                        Fax: 717-677-3174
                        www.corvetteamerica.com
Interiors, parts and accessories for 1st-3rd generation Corvettes (1953-1982)
President: Peggy H Lekander
Marketing Manager: Susie Cannon
Printing Information: 336 pages
In Business: 38 years

Number of Employees: 110
Sales Volume: $11.6 Million

385 Vintage Tire Hotline
Coker Tire Company
1317 Chestnut Street
Chattanooga, TN 37402   423-265-6368
                         866-516-3215
                         www.cokertire.com
Supplier of vintage and classic tires and wheels to the collector car hobbylist
Founder: Harold Coker
Credit Cards: AMEX; MasterCard; Visa
Catalog Cost: Free
Printing Information: 63 pages
In Business: 57 years

386 Virginia Classic Mustang
Virginia Classic Mustang
195 W Lee Street
PO Box 487
Broadway, VA 22815   540-896-2695
                      Fax: 540-896-9310
                      www.virginiaclassicmustang.com
Parts and accesories for 1964 1/2-1973 Mustangs
President: Robert Halterman
Catalog Cost: Free
In Business: 29 years
Number of Employees: 14
Sales Volume: $5.2 Million

387 YearOne Catalog
Year One
P.O. Box 521
Braselton, GA 30517   706-658-2140
                       800-932-7663
                       Fax: 706-654-5355
                       info@yearone.com
                       www.yearone.com
New and reproduction restoration parts for 64/72 Chevelle, 64/72 Skylark, auto accessories and apparel, 66-74 Dodge Plymouth, 64-72 Cutlass, 67-81 Firebird, 67-81 Camaro, 64-72 GTO and others
President: Kevin King
Credit Cards: AMEX; MasterCard; Visa
Catalog Cost: Free
Mailing List Information: Names for rent
In Business: 35 years
Number of Employees: 490
Sales Volume: Under $500M

Campers, Off Road & RVs

388 Advance Adapters Buyer's Guide
Advance Adapters, Inc.
4320 Aerotech Center Way
P.O. Box 247
Paso Robles, CA 93446   805-238-7000
                         800-350-2223
                         Fax: 805-238-4201
                         sales@advanceadapters.com
                         www.advanceadapters.com
Engine and transmission conversion adapters
President: Mike Partridge
mike@advanceadapters.com
Marketing Manager: Dustin Bellew
dustin@advanceadapters.com
Production Manager: Scott Corgiat
scott@advanceadapters.com
Office/Accounting Manager: Angela Partridge
angela@advanceadapters.com
Purchasing Manager: Randy Cronkright
randy@advanceadapters.com
Shipping Manager: Tom U.
tom@advanceadapters.com
Credit Cards: AMEX; MasterCard
Catalog Cost: Free
Printing Information: 88 pages
Mailing List Information: Names for rent
In Business: 44 years

Number of Employees: 44
Sales Volume: $7.3 Million

389 American Tailgater
American Tailgater
855 N Skokie Highway
Suite J
Lake Bluff, IL 60044   888-215-1490
                        888-844-4263
                        Fax: 847-235-2093
                        orders@americantailgater.com
                        www.americantailgater.com
Camping equipment, tailgating or outdoor picnicing equipment
President: Michael Lincoln
Credit Cards: AMEX; MasterCard; Visa
Catalog Cost: Free
Printing Information: 32 pages
In Business: 8 years

390 Cabela's Auto and ATV
Cabela's Inc.
One Cabela Dr.
Sidney, NE 69160   www.cabelas.com

Winches, add-ons and kits to outfit a vehicle for hunting and outdoor adventure.
CFO: Ralph Castner
CEO: Thomas Millner
COO: Michael Copeland
Catalog Cost: Free
Catalog Circulation: Mailed 4 time(s) per year
Printing Information: in 4 colors
List Company: Chilcutt Direct
In Business: 55 years
Sales Volume: $3 Billion

391 Camping World
Camping World Inc
650 Three Springs Road
Bowling Green, KY 42104   866-645-8579
                           888-626-7576
                           Fax: 800-334-3359
                           www.campingworld.com
RV appliances and supplies, furniture and equipment
Chairman: Marcus Lemonis
Marketing Manager: Tamara Ward
Credit Cards: AMEX; MasterCard
Catalog Cost: Free
In Business: 42 years

392 Dennis Kirk Off Road Catalog
Dennis Kirk
955 South Frandsen Avenue
Rush City, MN 55069   320-358-4791
                       800-969-7501
                       Fax: 320-358-4019
                       customerservice@denniskirk.com
                       www.denniskirk.com
Dirt bikes and ATVs riding apparel, performance parts and accessories
President: Bob Behan
Marketing Manager: Renita Twingstrom
VP of Finance: Heidi Scheffer
Credit Cards: AMEX; MasterCard
Catalog Cost: Free
In Business: 46 years

393 Desert Rat Off-Road
Desert Rat Off Road Centers
3705 S Palo Verde Rd
Tucson, AZ 85713-5401   520-790-9550
                         866-444-5337
                         Fax: 520-750-1918
                         info@desertrat.com
                         www.desertrat.com
Accessories, tires and wheels for pickups and 4WD
President: Mike Furrier
Credit Cards: AMEX; MasterCard
Catalog Cost: Free

Average Order Size: $159
Printing Information: 40 pages
Mailing List Information: Names for rent
Number of Employees: 30
Sales Volume: $3MM to $5MM

394 Early Bronco Catalog
James Duff Enterprises Inc
3231 NW Park Drive
Knoxville, TX 37921   865-938-6696
                        Fax: 865-938-6746
                     www.jamesduff.com

Parts and accessories for 1966-1977 Broncos

Credit Cards: AMEX; MasterCard
Catalog Cost: $5
Printing Information: on Newsprint
Mailing List Information: Names for rent

395 JBG 66-77 Ford Bronco
Jeff's Bronco Graveyard
7843 Lochlin Drive
Brighton, MI 48116   248-437-5060
                        Fax: 248-437-9354
              info@broncograveyard.com
              www.broncograveyard.com

Bronco parts 1966-1996

President: Jeff Trapp
Credit Cards: MasterCard; Visa
Catalog Cost: $2
Catalog Circulation: Mailed 4 time(s) per year
to 10000
Printing Information: 100 pages in 2 colors on
Matte Stock
Binding: Saddle Stitched
In Business: 49 years

396 JOES Racing
JOES Racing
1410 80th St SW
Everett, WA 98203   877-267-1525
                     www.joesracing.com
Credit Cards: AMEX; MasterCard

397 Lance Camper Manufacturing
Lance Camper Manufacturing
43120 Venture Street
Lancaster, CA 93535-4510   661-949-3322
                        Fax: 661-949-1262
                 info@lancecamper.com
                 www.lancecamper.com

Recreational vehicles

President: Jack Cole
Catalog Cost: Free
In Business: 51 years
Number of Employees: 250
Sales Volume: $50m

398 Motosport Off Road
Motosport Inc
15353 SW Sequoia Parkway
Portland, OR 97224   503-783-5776
                            888-676-8853
                        Fax: 503-783-5696
                     www.motosport.com

Parts and accessories for your dirt bikes, ATV and other off-road adventures

President: Jon White
Credit Cards: AMEX; MasterCard
Catalog Cost: Free
In Business: 16 years

399 RCV Performance Products
RCV Performance Products
611 Beacon Street
Loves Park, IL 61111   815-877-7473
                        Fax: 815-877-1218
              sales@rcvperformance.com
              www.rcvperformance.com

In Business: 60 years

400 Reid Racing
Reid Racing
1917 Oak Park Blvd.
Plesant Hill, CA 94523   925-935-3025
                        Fax: 925-935-2287
              race.mail@reidracing.biz
                     www.reidracing.biz

High quality transmission and off-road products.

In Business: 9 years

401 Rocky Mountain ATV/MC
Rocky Mountain ATV/MC
1551 American Way
Payson, UT 84651   801-465-3140
                            800-336-5437
                        Fax: 801-465-3457
              sales@rockymountainatv.com
              www.rockymountainatvmc.com

Street gear, protective gear and apparel, ATV parts, brakes, engines, exhausts, helmets, boots and handlebars

President: Malynda Lewis
CFO: McMohan Chantale
Marketing Manager: Everett Hoffman
Owner/President: Dan Thomas
General Manager/Sales Exec VP: Ray Butts
Credit Cards: AMEX; MasterCard
Catalog Cost: Free
In Business: 30 years
Number of Employees: 150
Sales Volume: $11.2 Million

402 Smittybilt Catalog
Smittybilt Inc.
400 W Artesia Boulevard
Compton, CA 90220   310-762-9944
                            888-717-5797
                        Fax: 310-762-2297
                 info@smittybilt.com
                 www.smittybilt.com

4WD trucks and accessories

President: Shawn Angues
Credit Cards: AMEX; MasterCard; Visa
Catalog Cost: Free
Printing Information: 51 pages
In Business: 59 years
Number of Employees: 200
Sales Volume: $10MM to $20MM

403 Toyota Power
LC Engineering
2031 Holly Avenue
Lake Havasu City, AZ 86403-2862 928-505-2501
                            877-505-2501
                        Fax: 928-505-2503
              sales@lcengineering.com
                 www.lcengineering.com

Toyota 4 Cylinder 20R-22R-22RE Performance: engines, top end, short block kits, headers, camshafts, carburetor kits for circle track, drag race, off road, street performer

Credit Cards: MasterCard; Visa
Catalog Cost: $6.95
Catalog Circulation: Mailed 52 time(s) per
year to 10000
Average Order Size: $250
Printing Information: 240 pages in 4 colors on
Glossy Stock
Press: Web Press
Binding: Perfect Bound
Mailing List Information: Names for rent
In Business: 17 years
Number of Employees: 14
Sales Volume: $20,00,000

404 Wild Horses Four Wheel Drive Catalog
Wild Horses Four Wheel Drive
1045 S Cherokee Lane
Lodi, CA 95240   209-400-7200
                        Fax: 209-943-7923
              sales@wildhorses4x4.com
              www.Wildhorses4x4.Com

1966-79 Bronco parts and off-road vehicle parts, accessories, apparel, gifts and books

President: Jim Creel
Credit Cards: MasterCard; Visa
Catalog Cost: $5
Printing Information: 116 pages
In Business: 26 years
Number of Employees: 11
Sales Volume: $1MM to $3MM

Car Care

405 AMSOIL
AMSOIL
925 Tower Avenue
Superior, WI 54880-1582   715-399-8324
                            800-956-5695
                        Fax: 715-392-5225
                     www.amsoil.com

Manufactures premium synthetic lubricants for automotive, RV, marine, sport and heavy equipment applications for increased performance

President: Albert J. Amatuzio
CFO: Dean Alexander
EVP, Chief Operating Officer: Alan Amatuzio
Credit Cards: AMEX; MasterCard; Visa
Catalog Cost: Free
Catalog Circulation: to 1M
Average Order Size: $82
Printing Information: 48 pages on Glossy
Stock
Press: Web Press
Binding: Saddle Stitched
Mailing List Information: Names for rent
In Business: 45 years
Number of Employees: 200
Sales Volume: $35 Million

406 AVW Equipment Company
AVW Equipment Company, Inc.
105 S 9th Ave
Maywood, IL 60153-1340   708-343-7738
                        Fax: 708-343-9065
              info@avwequipment.com
              www.avwequipment.com

Car washing equipment

President: Milovan Vidakovich
Credit Cards: AMEX; MasterCard; Visa
Catalog Cost: Free
Printing Information: 40 pages
In Business: 27 years
Number of Employees: 15
Sales Volume: $1,000,000 - $5,000,000

407 Berkebile Oil Company
Berkebile Oil Company
PO Box 715
Somerset, PA 15501-715   814-443-1656
                            800-732-9235
                        Fax: 814-443-2873
              info@berkebileoil.com
              www.berkebileoil.com

2x2 antifreeze, power steering, brake fluids, degreasers, rust penetrant, and cleaners

President: Catherine Poorbaugh
In Business: 61 years
Number of Employees: 40
Sales Volume: $10,000,000 - $25,000,000

408   Buffalo Industries
Buffalo Industries LLC
99 S Spokane Street
Seattle, WA 98134
206-682-9900
800-683-0052
Fax: 206-682-9907
office@buffaloindustries.com
www.buffaloindustries.com

Car wash towels, Chamois products, shop towels, sponges, detail towels, oil sorbents, spill kits & containment products
President: Mark Benezra
mark@buffaloindustries.com
Marketing Manager: Matt Benesch
International Marketing Manager: Larry Benezra
Catalog Cost: Free
Printing Information: 24 pages
In Business: 70 years
Number of Employees: 150
Sales Volume: $10,000,000 - $25,000,000

409   Car-Freshner Catalog
Car-Freshner Corporation
21205 Little Tree Drive
P.O. Box 719
Watertown, NY 13601-719
315-788-6250
800-545-5454
Fax: 315-788-7467
domestic@car-freshner.com
www.car-freshner.com

Air fresheners and car care products
President: Jody Lalone
CFO: Laura Tousant
Production Manager: Robert Swank
International Marketing Manager: Linda Frasher
Buyers: Dolly Bidwell
Catalog Circulation: Mailed 2 time(s) per year
Printing Information: 30 pages
Mailing List Information: Names for rent
Number of Employees: 130
Sales Volume: $10MM to $20MM

410   DQB Industries
DQB Industries
32165 Schoolcraft Rd
Livonia, MI 48150-1894
734-525-5660
800-722-3037
Fax: 734-525-0437
sales@dqb.com
www.Dqb.Com

Brushes for the automotive industry
President: Donald Weinbaum
Marketing Manager: John Avgoustis
Production Manager: Carl Lebamoff
In Business: 128 years
Number of Employees: 70
Sales Volume: $10,000,000 - $25,000,000

411   Good Vibrations Motorsports
Good Vibrations Motorsports
8858 Painter Avenue
Suite E
Whittier, CA 90602
562-945-7669
800-576-7661
sales@dragparts.com
www.goodvibesracing.com

Car parts for motor racing
General Manager: James Michael Maher
Catalog Cost: Free
Catalog Circulation: Mailed 1 time(s) per year
Printing Information: 64 pages in 4 colors
In Business: 29 years

412   ITW Automotive Products
ITW Consumer
10 Columbus Blvd
Hartford, CT 06106
561-845-2425
877-376-2839
Fax: 561-845-2504
info@itwconsumer.com
www.itwconsumer.com

Gasket sealants, chrome polish, rear view mirror adhesive
President: Walt Polcuyn
Credit Cards: AMEX; MasterCard; Visa
Catalog Cost: Free
Number of Employees: 200
Sales Volume: $10,000,000 - $25,000,000

413   Inlinetube
Inline Tube
15066 Technology Drive
Shelby Township, MI 48315-3950
586-532-1338
800-385-9452
Fax: 586-532-1339
Office01@inlinetube.com
www.inlinetube.com

Computer precision brake and fuel lines, flex hoses, brake cables, and clamps
President: James Kryta
CFO: John Kryta
Production Manager: James Kryta
Credit Cards: AMEX; MasterCard; Visa
Catalog Cost: $3
Catalog Circulation: Mailed 52 time(s) per year
Average Order Size: $170
Printing Information: 60 pages in 2 colors on Glossy Stock
Binding: Saddle Stitched
Mailing List Information: Names for rent
Number of Employees: 12
Sales Volume: $3MM to $5MM

414   International Auto Parts
International Auto Parts
1220 Commerce Court
Lafayette, CO 80026
303-447-0239
888-750-2532
Fax: 303-447-0257
www.centerlinealfa.com

Specializes in the sales and distribution of parts and accessories for Italian cars such as the Fiat, Lancia, and Alfa Romeo
Catalog Cost: Free
In Business: 35 years

415   Iroquois Products Catalog
Iroquois Industries Corporation
2220 W 56th Street
Chicago, IL 60636-1047
773-436-4900
800-453-3355
Fax: 800-453-3344
sales@iroquoisproducts.com
www.iroquoisproducts.com

Packaging & shipping supplies, car cleaning/care supplies and marine cleaning/care supplies
President: Alan Gordon
Credit Cards: AMEX; MasterCard; Visa
Catalog Cost: Free
Catalog Circulation: Mailed 1 time(s) per year
Printing Information: 204 pages in 4 colors
In Business: 58 years
Number of Employees: 20
Sales Volume: $10MM

416   Jegs.com
101 JEGS Place
Delaware, OH 43015
800-345-4545
Fax: 740-362-7017
www.jegs.com

Auto parts and accessories

417   Nation/Ruskin
Nation/Ruskin, Inc.
206 Progress Drive
Montgomeryville, PA 18936
267-654-4000
800-523-2489
Fax: 267-654-4010
www.nationruskin.com

Buckets, car washing brushes, cloths, latex gloves, paint accessories, scouring pads, scrubbers, sponges, squeegees, towels
President: Raymond Adolf
In Business: 37 years
Number of Employees: 35
Sales Volume: 5MM-10MM

418   Obsolete & Classic Auto Parts
Obsolete & Classic Auto Parts, Inc.
8701 South Interstate 35
Oklahoma City, OK 73149
405-631-3933
800-654-3247
Fax: 405-634-6815
info@classicautoparts.com
www.classicautoparts.com

Worldwide retailer and distributor of antique, classic, street rod, and Obsolete Chevrolet and Ford parts and accessories
General Manager: Mike Forehand
Assistant Manager: Kevin Billins
Accounting: Sara Moheit
Catalog Cost: Free
Catalog Circulation: to 1
In Business: 39 years

419   Pit Pal Products
Pit Pal Products
2009 Horizon Court
Zion, IL 60099
847-872-7257
888-748-7257
Fax: 847-872-7258
sales@pitpal.com
www.pitpal.com

Garage, shop and trailer organizers
Catalog Cost: Free
In Business: 32 years

420   Prothane Motion Control
Dee Engineering
3560 Cadillac Avenue
Costa Mesa, CA 92626-1490
888-776-8426
prothane.com

Urethane performance products, sports seats, performance parts for Volkswagens
President: Rick Sadler
Catalog Circulation: Mailed 1 time(s) per year
Printing Information: 72 pages in 4 colors
In Business: 25 years
Sales Volume: $20MM to $50MM

421   Ranger Design
Ranger Design
20600 Clark-Graham
Baie D'Urfe, QC H9X-4B6
800-565-5321
www.rangerdesign.com

Van shelving, van storage bins, ladder racks, bulkhead partitions, storage systems
Marketing Manager: Yves L,veill,
Managing Director: Ron Cowie
Owner: Derek Cowie
Credit Cards: AMEX; MasterCard
Catalog Cost: Free
In Business: 29 years
Number of Employees: 200

422   Rightlook.com
Rightlook.com, Inc.
8525 Arjons Drive, Suite C
San Diego, CA 92126
858-271-4271
800-883-3446
Fax: 858-271-4303
www.rightlook.com

Offers the highest quality training, equipment, supplies, business consulting and marketing services for auto reconditioning and auto appearance
Catalog Cost: Free
In Business: 17 years

423 **TP Tools & Equipment**
TP Tools & Equipment
7075 State Route 446
PO Box 649
Canfield, OH 44406-649   330-533-3384
    800-321-9260
Fax: 330-533-2876
www.tptools.com

Supplier of restoration and auto body repair tools

President: Robert Zwicker
Credit Cards: AMEX; MasterCard
Sales Volume: $1MM to $3MM

424 **USA Weld**
USA Weld
180 Joey Drive
Elk Grove Village, IL 60007-1304 847-357-0700
    800-872-9353
Fax: 847-357-0744
customerservice@usaweld.com
www.usaweld.com

Welding supplies for automotive and fabrication, farm, aviation and cycle repair

President: Jeff Noland
Catalog Cost: Free
Mailing List Information: Names for rent
In Business: 17 years

425 **West Coast Corvettes**
1210 N Kraemer Blvd.
Anaheim, CA 92806   714-630-6396
    888-737-8388
Fax: 714-630-1422
sales@westcoastcorvette.com
www.westcoastcorvette.com

Corvette parts and accessories

Foreign Cars & Parts

426 **Bavarian Autosport**
Bavarian Autosport
275 Constitution Avenue
Portsmouth, NH 03801   603-427-2002
    800-535-2002
Fax: 800-507-2002
info@bavauto.com
www.bavauto.com

BMW parts and accessories

President: Dave Wason
CFO: Mark Stevens
Catalog Cost: Free
Printing Information: 132 pages on Glossy Stock
Binding: Saddle Stitched
In Business: 43 years
Number of Employees: 61
Sales Volume: $23.7 Million

427 **CB Performance**
CB Performance Products, Inc.
1715 N Farmersville Boulevard
Farmersville, CA 93223-2302 559-733-8222
    800-274-8337
Fax: 559-733-7967
info@cbperformance.com
www.cbperformance.com

Racing parts for VW's

President: Rick Tomlinson
Marketing Manager: Susie Canvassar
Production Manager: Patrick Downs
Fulfillment: Kevin Lewis
Office Manager: Susie Canvasser
susie@cbperformance.com
CB Sales Team: Daniel Watson
daniel@cbperformance.com
CB Sales Team: Marieanne Martin
marieanne@cbperformance.com
Credit Cards: AMEX; MasterCard
Catalog Circulation: Mailed 1 time(s) per year
to 10000

Printing Information: 200 pages
Number of Employees: 260

428 **California Pacific/Jbugs**
1338 Rocky Point Dr.
Oceanside, CA 92056   760-722-2535
    800-231-1784
Fax: 760-477-8505
sales@jbugs.com
www.jbugs.com

Volkswagen parts

Owner: Gary Vogl

429 **Centerline Alfa Products**
Centerline Alfa Products
1220 Commerce Court
Lafayette, CO 80026-4376 303-447-0239
    888-750-2532
Fax: 303-447-0257
www.centerlinealfa.com

Parts for Alfa Romeo

Catalog Cost: Free
Printing Information: 40 pages
Mailing List Information: Names for rent
In Business: 30 years
Number of Employees: 10
Sales Volume: $500,000

430 **Corvette/Volkswagen**
Mid America Motorworks
17082 N. US Highway 45
P.O. Box 1368
Effingham, IL 62401-1368 217-540-4200
    866-350-4543
Fax: 217-540-4800
mail@mamotorworks.com
www.mamotorworks.com

Parts and accessories for Corvettes and air-cooled Volkswagens

President: Mike Yager
Corporate Director: Laurie Yager
laurie.yager@mamotorworks.com
Corporate Director: Michael Yager
michael.yager@mamotorworks.com
Corporate Director: Blake Yager
blake.yager@mamotorworks.com
International Marketing Manager: Jason
Vahling
Buyers: Saney Corrett
Gene Henderson
Credit Cards: AMEX; MasterCard; Visa
Catalog Cost: Free
Printing Information: 168 pages
Mailing List Information: Names for rent
List Manager: Karen Rueter
List Company: Jason Vahling, International
In Business: 36 years
Number of Employees: 100
Sales Volume: $20MM to $50MM

431 **International Auto Parts**
International Auto Parts
1220 Commerce Court
Lafayette, CO 80026   303-447-0239
    888-750-2532
Fax: 303-447-0257
www.centerlinealfa.com

Specializes in the sales and distribution of parts and accessories for Italian cars such as the Fiat, Lancia, and Alfa Romeo

Catalog Cost: Free
In Business: 35 years

432 **Jaguar Master Catalog**
XKs Unlimited
850 Fiero Lane
San Luis Obispo, CA 93401-8399 805-544-7864
    800-444-5247
Fax: 805-544-1664
customerservice@xks.com
www.xks.com

Antique car parts

President: Jason Len
Catalog Cost: $15
In Business: 42 years

433 **Karl Performance**
5927 NE Industry Dr.
Des Moines, IA 50313   515-963-8788
    888-771-5574
Fax: 515-963-3487
www.karlperformance.com

Performance parts for racing and street engines

434 **Korman Autoworks**
Korman Autoworks
2629 Randleman Rd
Greensboro, NC 27406-5107 336-275-1494
    Fax: 336-274-8003
service@kormanautoworks.com
www.KormanAutoworks.Com

High performance BMW auto parts

President: Ray Korman
Credit Cards: AMEX; MasterCard; Visa
Catalog Cost: Free
Average Order Size: $500
Printing Information: 15 pages
Mailing List Information: Names for rent
In Business: 37 years
Number of Employees: 10
Sales Volume: $1MM to $3MM

435 **Mid America Motorworks Air-Cooled VW**
Mid America Motorworks
17082 N US Highway 45
PO Box 1368
Effingham, IL 62401-6764 217-540-4200
    866-350-4543
Fax: 217-540-4425
mail@mamotorworks.com
www.mamotorworks.com

Parts and accessories for 1950-1979 air-cooled Volkswagons

President: Mike Yager
Mike.Yager@mamotorworks.com
Marketing Manager: Henk van Dongen
Production Manager: Scott Bohannon
Scott.Bohannon@mamotorworks.com
Fulfillment: Tim Curtis
Director of Information Technologie: Shannon
Klein
shannon.klein@mamotorworks.com
Corporate Director: Laurie Yager
laurie.yager@mamotorworks.com
President Performance Choice: Steve Olson
Steve.Olson@performancechoice.com
Catalog Circulation: Mailed 8 time(s) per year
Average Order Size: $125
In Business: 41 years
Number of Employees: 150
Sales Volume: $5MM to $10MM

436 **Motorsport Auto**
Motorsport Auto
1139 W Collins Avenue
Orange, CA 92867   714-639-2620
    800-633-6331
Fax: 714-639-7460
info@motorsportauto.com
www.zcarparts.com

Datsun Z/ZX and Nissan Z/ZX parts

President: Ken Smith
Marketing Manager: Joseph Carrubba
Administration: Sandra Smith
Sales Manager: Abraham DeGalicia
Marketing/Customer Service: Garrett Fleig
Credit Cards: AMEX; MasterCard
Catalog Cost: Free
Mailing List Information: Names for rent
In Business: 36 years

437 **Racing Beat**
Racing Beat, LLC
4789 E Wesley Dr
Anaheim, CA 92807-1941   714-779-8677
Fax: 714-779-2902
www.racingbeat.com

Mazda RX-7 technical manuals and catalogs

President: Ryusuke Oku
Credit Cards: AMEX; MasterCard; Visa
Catalog Cost: $5.55
Printing Information: 80 pages
Sales Volume: $3MM to $5MM

438 **Roadster Factory**
The Roadster Factory
328 Killen Road
PO Box 332
Armagh, PA 15920-332   814-446-4491
800-678-8764
Fax: 814-446-6729
trfmail@aol.com
www.the-roadster-factory.com

Reproduction parts for Triumph and MG sport cars

President: Charles A Runyan
CFO: Dabra Gawlas
Marketing Manager: John Swauger
Buyers: Marie Pella
Frank Stoddard
John Swauger
Credit Cards: AMEX; MasterCard; Visa
Catalog Cost: Free
Catalog Circulation: to 100
Average Order Size: $150
Printing Information: 150 pages in 5 colors on Glossy Stock
Press: Web Press
Binding: Saddle Stitched
Mailing List Information: Names for rent
In Business: 37 years
Number of Employees: 30
Sales Volume: $2.8 Million

439 **Stoddard Imported Car Parts**
Stoddard Imported Car Parts
190 Alpha Park
Highland Heights, OH 44143   440-869-9890
800-342-1414
Fax: 440-946-9410
www.stoddard.com

Porsche parts

President: Bruce Schwartz
bschwartz@stoddard.com
Credit Cards: AMEX; MasterCard
Catalog Cost: $5
Printing Information: 356 pages
Mailing List Information: Names for rent
In Business: 58 years
Number of Employees: 57
Sales Volume: $3MM to $5MM

440 **Terry's Jaguar Parts**
Terry's Jaguar Parts
5775 Venture Park Drive
Kalamazoo, MI 49009   269-375-1000
800-851-9438
Fax: 269-375-1026
jagsales@terrysjag.com
www.terrysjag.com

New, used and rebuilt parts for Jaguars

Catalog Cost: Free
In Business: 41 years
Number of Employees: 11
Sales Volume: $2.1 Million

441 **Z&ZX Parts & Accessories Catalog**
Z&ZX Parts & Accessories
1139 W Collins Avenue
Orange, CA 92876   714-639-2620
800-633-6331
Fax: 714-639-7460
info@motorsportauto.com
www.zcarparts.com

Parts and supplies for Datsuns

President: Ken Smith
Marketing Manager: Joseph Carrubba
Founder and Vice-President: Greg Smith
Sales Manager: Abraham DeGalicia
Administration: Pat Smith
Credit Cards: AMEX; MasterCard; Visa
Catalog Cost: Free
Printing Information: 165 pages
In Business: 36 years

Parts & Supplies

442 **4Wheel Drive Hardware**
4Wheel Drive Hardware
44488 State Route 14
Columbiana, OH 44408   800-555-3353
www.4wd.com

Jeep parts and accessories.

Catalog Cost: Free
Printing Information: 196 pages in 4 colors
In Business: 39 years

443 **A&A Manufacturing Parts**
A&A Manufacturing
19033 174th Ave
Spring Lake, MI 49456   616-846-1730
800-473-1730
Fax: 616-846-5999
sales@aa-mfg.com
www.aa-mfg.com

Stock car, drag and buggy car components

President: Larry Marcinak
Catalog Cost: Free

444 **Adcole Corporation**
ADCOLE
669 Forest Street
Marlborough, MA 01752-3067   508-485-9100
Fax: 508-481-6142
info@adcole.com
www.adcole.com

Electro-optical instrumentation used in crankshafts, camshafts and pistons

President: Michael Foley, PhD
CFO: Doug Vandenberg
Marketing Manager: Daniel P. Harkins
VP, Software Development: William Smith
Vice President of Engineering: Stephen Corrado
Vice President of Aerospace: Tom MacDonald
In Business: 58 years
Number of Employees: 165
Sales Volume: $10,000,000

445 **Air-Drive**
Air Drive, Inc.
4070 Ryan Rd
Gurnee, IL 60031-1253   847-625-0226
Fax: 847-625-7422
sales@airdrive.com
www.airdrive.com

Aluminum and steel fan blades

President: James H. Gilford
Printing Information: 40 pages in 4 colors
In Business: 53 years
Number of Employees: 20
Sales Volume: $5 million

446 **Aluminum Tank & Truck Accessories**
Aluminum Tank and Tank Accessories, Inc.
2702-B N. Nichols
Fort Worth, TX 76106   817-378-8455
800-773-3047
Fax: 817-378-9765
attatank@gmail.com
www.attatank.com

Designs and manufactures aluminum tanks and fuel tank systems

Credit Cards: AMEX; MasterCard
Catalog Cost: Free
Printing Information: 23 pages

447 **American Muscle**
American Muscle
1 Lee Boulevard
Unit 2
Malvern, PA 19355   610-251-2397
866-727-1266
Fax: 610-981-4720
support@americanmuscle.com
www.americanmuscle.com

F-150 and Mustang custom parts

President: Steve Voudouris
In Business: 14 years

448 **Ames Performance Engineering**
Ames Performance Engineering
10 Pontiac Drive
P.O. Box 572
Spofford, NH 03462   800-421-2637
Fax: 603-363-7007
customer.service@amesperf.com
www.amesperformance.com

Pontiac parts and accessories

President: Don Emory
Buyers: Lee Selby
Credit Cards: AMEX; MasterCard; Visa
Catalog Cost: Free
Average Order Size: $175
Printing Information: 219 pages
Mailing List Information: Names for rent
In Business: 32 years
Number of Employees: 25
Sales Volume: $5MM-$10MM

449 **Andy's Autosport**
Andy's Auto Sport
15005 Concord Circle
Morgan Hill, CA 95037   800-419-1152
Fax: 408-762-4478
info@andysautosport.com
www.andysautosport.com

Racing seats, exhaust systems, headlight, body kits, exhaust systems and mufflers

General Manager: Andy Ferguson
Credit Cards: AMEX; MasterCard
Catalog Cost: Free
Number of Employees: 100
Sales Volume: $10 Million

450 **Anti-Seize Technology**
Anti-Seize Technology
2345 17th Avenue
Franklin Park, IL 60131-3432   847-455-2300
800-991-1106
Fax: 847-455-2371
sales@antiseize.com
www.antiseize.com

Sealants lubricants, anti-seize compounds, thread sealers, instant gaskets penetrants, protectants, coatings greases, cleaners, degreasers, silicones

President: John Heydt
Marketing Manager: Kristy Rivera
VP, Research & Development: Allen Majeski
International Marketing Manager: Barbara Swanson
Buyers: Jim Michalewicz
Catalog Cost: Free
Catalog Circulation: Mailed 1 time(s) per year to 3M
Average Order Size: $4500
Printing Information: 32 pages
Mailing List Information: Names for rent
List Manager: Jeffery J Heydt
In Business: 46 years
Number of Employees: 15
Sales Volume: $20,000,000

451 Auto Body Toolmart
Auto Body Toolmart
2545 Millenium Drive
Unit B
Elgin, IL 60124　　　　847-462-9243
　　　　　　　　　　　800-382-1200
　　　　　　　　　　　Fax: 847-462-9247
　　　　　　　　　　　info@abtm.com
　　　　　　　www.autobodytoolmart.com
Complete line of auto body & automotive repair tools and machines
President: Matt Dorfman
Credit Cards: MasterCard
Catalog Cost: Free
In Business: 35 years

452 Auto Restoration Car Parts
Mill Supply, Inc
19801 Miles Road
P.O. Box 28400
Cleveland, OH 44128　　　216-518-5072
　　　　　　　　　　　800-888-5072
　　　　　　　　　　　Fax: 216-518-2700
　　　　　　　　　info@millsupply.com
　　　　　　　　　www.millsupply.com
Automotive restoration parts and supplies for American and foreign cars; over 3000 panels listed including rockers, fenders, quarter panels, door bottom, floor pans, gas tanks and dash tops
President: Dave Schuld
Marketing Manager: John Shega
Fulfillment: David Schuld
Credit Cards: AMEX; MasterCard
Catalog Cost: Free
Printing Information: 96 pages in 1 color on Newsprint
Press: Web Press
Binding: Saddle Stitched
Mailing List Information: Names for rent
In Business: 65 years
Number of Employees: 30
Sales Volume: $6,000,000

453 Automotive Airfilters
K&N Engineering, Inc.
1455 Citrus Street
Riverside, CA 92507-1329　　951-826-4000
　　　　　　　　　　　800-858-3333
　　　　　　　　　　　tech@knfilters.com
　　　　　　　　　　　www.knfilters.com
High performance air filters, exhaust (cat back systems)
President: Nate Shelton
CFO: Steve Rogers
Marketing Manager: Diane Camp
Credit Cards: Visa
Catalog Circulation: Mailed 1 time(s) per year to 150M
Printing Information: 100 pages in 6 colors on Glossy Stock
Press: Web Press
Binding: Perfect Bound
Mailing List Information: Names for rent
In Business: 28 years
Number of Employees: 400
Sales Volume: $50MM to $100MM

454 Backyard Buddy
Backyard Buddy
140 Dana St NE
Warren, OH 44483-3845　　330-395-9372
　　　　　　　　　　　800-837-9353
　　　　　　　　　　　Fax: 330-392-9311
　　　　　　　　sales@backyardbuddy.com
　　　　　　　　www.backyardbuddy.com
Free-standing, electric four-post lifts and accessories for automobiles
President: Larry Gross
In Business: 27 years

455 Bar's Leaks
Bar's Products, Inc.
Po Box 187
Holly, MI 48442　　　　800-345-6572
　　　　　　　　　　　800-521-7475
　　　　　　　　　　　Fax: 810-603-1335
　　　　　　　　　www.barsproducts.com
Power steering products, cooling system and engine products
President: Joseph Pasuit
CFO: William Christinsen
Marketing Manager: Welford Samuel
Production Manager: John Bovie
In Business: 67 years
Number of Employees: 10
Sales Volume: $ 3-5 Million

456 Belle Tire Distributors
Belle Tire Distributors
1000 Enterprise Drive
Allen Park, MI 48101-3530　　888-462-3553
　　　　　　　　　　　www.belletire.com
Tires, auto glass and automotive accessories
Chairman: Robert Barnes, II
President: Don Barnes, Jr.
Marketing Manager: Robert Barnes, III
In Business: 92 years
Number of Employees: 110
Sales Volume: $10-20 Million

457 Big Red Catalog
Taylor Wings, Inc.
3720 Omec Circle
Rancho Cordova, CA 95742-7303　916-851-9464
　　　　　　　　　　　800-634-7757
　　　　　　　　　　　Fax: 916-851-9466
　　　　　　　　　　　terryt@taylorwings.com
　　　　　　　　　　　www.taylorwings.com
Full range of wings with internal ram system available in all sizes
President: Terry Taylor
CFO: Terri Taylor
Marketing Manager: Linda Nieves
Production Manager: Chris Roberts
Fulfillment: Thomas Bridgham
Sales Contact: Terry Taylor
terryt@taylorwings.com
Production Contact: Chris Roberts
chrisr@taylorwings.com
Programming Contact: Scott Holden
srholden@taylorwings.com
Credit Cards: AMEX; MasterCard; Visa
Printing Information: 16 pages
In Business: 37 years

458 Billet Specialties
Billet Specialties
1112 E Nakoma Street
La Grange Park, IL 60526-2072　708-588-0505
　　　　　　　　　　　800-245-5382
　　　　　　　　　　　Fax: 708-588-7181
　　　　　　　　　www.billetspecialties.com
Large slection of rims for cars and trucks
President: Paula Kind
Catalog Cost: Free
Sales Volume: $ 5-10 Million

459 Bob's Classic Chevy Catalog
Bob's Classic Chevy
4735 East Falcon Drive
Mesa, AZ 85215　　　　480-981-1600
　　　　　　　　　　　866-572-4389
　　　　　　　　　　　Fax: 480-981-1675
　　　　　　　　　www.bobsclassicchevy.com
Accessories, restoration parts, upgrades, manuals and books for Classic 1949-1957 Chevy's
Credit Cards: AMEX; MasterCard; Visa
In Business: 24 years

460 Borgeson Universal Company
Borgeson Universal Company
91 Technology Park Drive
Torrington, CT 06790-3098　　860-482-8283
　　　　　　　　　　　Fax: 860-496-9320
　　　　　　　　　　　sales@borgeson.com
　　　　　　　　　　　www.borgeson.com
Steering universal joints and components for the automotive, military, and aerospace industries
President: Gerald Zordon
Catalog Cost: Free
In Business: 101 years

461 Bradish Tractor Parts
George Bradish Tractor Parts
3865 State Route 982
Latrobe, PA 15650-3914　　724-539-8386
　　　　　　　　　　　Fax: 724-539-3808
　　　　　info@georgebradishtractorparts.com
　　　　　www.georgebradishtractorparts.com
Ford tractors and Dearborn implements parts
President: George Bradish
Credit Cards: MasterCard; Visa
In Business: 68 years

462 Burden Sales
Surplus Center
1015 West O Street
P.O. Box 82209
Lincoln, NE 68528　　　800-488-3407
　　　　　　　　　　　Fax: 402-474-5198
　　　　customerservice@surpluscenter.com
　　　　　　　　　www.surpluscenter.com
Pneumatics, electrical, engines/automotive, hydraulics, power transmission, water pumps, wheels/casters, winches and more
President: David P Burden
Credit Cards: AMEX; MasterCard
Catalog Cost: Free
In Business: 81 years
Number of Employees: 40
Sales Volume: $13 Million

463 Cabela's Auto and ATV
Cabela's Inc.
One Cabela Dr.
Sidney, NE 69160　　　www.cabelas.com
Winches, add-ons and kits to outfit a vehicle for hunting and outdoor adventure.
CFO: Ralph Castner
CEO: Thomas Millner
COO: Michael Copeland
Catalog Cost: Free
Catalog Circulation: Mailed 4 time(s) per year
Printing Information: in 4 colors
List Company: Chilcutt Direct
In Business: 55 years
Sales Volume: $3 Billion

464 Cable Organizer Office and Home
CableOrganizer.Com, Inc.
6250 NW 27th Way
Fort Lauderdale, FL 33309　　954-861-2000
　　　　　　　　　　　866-222-0030
　　　　　　　　　　　Fax: 954-861-2001
　　　　　　　　　sales@cableorganizer.com
　　　　　　　　　www.cableorganizer.com
Cable covers, wire looms, cable tags and fire protection for auto and marine wiring
President: Valerie Holstein
Marketing Manager: Juan Ribero
Credit Cards: AMEX; MasterCard
Catalog Cost: Free
In Business: 13 years

465 California Car Cover
California Car Cover
9525 DeSoto Avenue
Chatsworth, CA 91311
818-998-2100
800-423-5525
Fax: 818-998-2442
info@calcarcover.com
www.calcarcover.com

Custom car & truck covers, accessories, canopies, apparel, performance enhancement parts, motorcycle accessories, cleaning products and garage items/tools
President: Jim DeFrank
Credit Cards: AMEX; MasterCard; Visa
Catalog Cost: Free

466 California Mustang
California Mustang
19400 San Jose Ave.
City of Industry, CA 91748
800-775-0101
Fax: 909-598-5611
csmustang@cal-mustang.com
www.cal-mustang.com

Parts for restoration of Mustangs
President: Gary Lovett
In Business: 39 years

467 Camaro Connection
Camaro Connection
250 Akron Street
Lindenhurst, NY 11757-3612
631-226-7982
Fax: 631-225-8824
shop@eastcoastrestorations.com
www.Camaroconnection.Com

Camaro parts, services and restorations
President: Tom Marcantonio
In Business: 28 years
Sales Volume: $500M to $1MM

468 Castrol USA Catalog
BP Lubricants USA
P.O. Box 485
Lewiston, NY 14092-8427
973-633-2200
800-462-0835
Fax: 973-633-9867
Contactus@bp.com
www.Castrolusa.Com

Power steering and brake fluids, oils, transmission fluids
President: Stanley Mussington
Marketing Manager: Paul Giblett
Regional VP: Naveen Kshatriya
Regional Manage: Brian Gregory
Marketing Operations Manager: Lee Eng Han
In Business: 114 years
Number of Employees: 1200

469 Cheyenne Pick Up Parts
Chevelle World, Inc.
PO Box 959
Noble, OK 73068-959
405-872-3399
Fax: 405-872-0385
sales@cheyennepickup.com
www.cheyennepickup.com

Parts for 1960-87 full size Chevy pickups and 1969-87 Chevy Blazers
President: Henry Nunn
Vice- President: Linda Nunn
Credit Cards: MasterCard; Visa
Catalog Cost: $4
Catalog Circulation: Mailed 1 time(s) per year
Printing Information: 120 pages

470 Chicago Corvette Supply
Chicago Corvette Supply
7322 S Archer Road
Justice, IL 60458
800-872-2446
Fax: 708-458-2662
contact@chicagocorvette.net
www.chicagocorvette.net

Automotive parts and accessories for specific make and model corvettes as well as a large selection of carburetors for all cars
Credit Cards: MasterCard

471 Classic Auto Air Manufacturing
Classic Auto Air Manufacturing
4901 Rio Vista Avenue
Tampa, FL 33634
813-251-2356
877-342-5526
Fax: 813-254-7419
sales@ClassicAutoAir.com
www.classicautoair.com

Air conditioning parts and systems for 1970's and older cars and trucks
President: Al Sedita
Catalog Cost: $5
Catalog Circulation: Mailed 2 time(s) per year
Printing Information: 56 pages in 1 color on Glossy Stock
Press: Sheetfed Press
Binding: Perfect Bound
Mailing List Information: Names for rent
In Business: 35 years
Number of Employees: 18
Sales Volume: $1MM to $3MM

472 Classic Chevrolet Parts
Classic Chevrolet Parts Inc.
8723 South Interstate 35
Oklahoma City, OK 73149
405-631-4400
800-354-4040
Fax: 405-631-5999
info@classicchevroletparts.com
www.classicchevroletparts.com

Parts for Chevys and GMCs
President: Dale Bliss
Catalog Cost: $15
Printing Information: 206 pages
In Business: 20 years

473 Classic Industries: Camaro
Classic Industries
18460 Gothard St
Huntington Beach, CA 92648-1229 714-848-9501
800-854-1280
Fax: 714-848-9501
info@classicindustries.com
www.classicindustries.com

Classic industry parts and accessories restoring Chevrolet Camaros
President: Jeffrey Leonard
In Business: 39 years

474 Classic Industries: Chevrolet
Classic Industries
18460 Gothard Street
Huntington Beach, CA 92648-1229 714-848-9501
800-854-1280
Fax: 714-848-9501
info@classicindustries.com
www.classicindustries.com

Classic industry parts and accessories for restoring classic Chevrolets
President: Jeffrey Leonard
In Business: 39 years

475 Classic Industries: Firebird
Classic Industries
18460 Gothard Street
Huntington Beach, CA 92648-1229 714-848-9501
800-854-1280
Fax: 714-848-9501
info@classicindustries.com

Classic industry parts and accessories for Firebirds
President: Jeffrey Leonard
Catalog Circulation: to 10000
Printing Information: 600 pages in 4 colors on Glossy Stock
Press: Offset Press

Binding: Perfect Bound
In Business: 39 years

476 Classic Mustang
24-A Robert Porter Road
Southington, CT 06489
860-276-9704
800-243-2742
Fax: 860-276-9986
mustangrestoration@yahoo.com
www.cmustang.com

Parts for restoring Mustangs
President: David Scranton
Catalog Cost: $3

477 Classic Parts of America
Classic Parts of America
1 Chevy Duty Drive
Riverside, MO 64150
816-741-8029
800-741-1678
Fax: 816-741-5255
customerservice@classicparts.com
www.classicparts.com

Parts and supplies for Chevy trucks
President: Mark S Jansen
Marketing Manager: Robert Mata
Credit Cards: AMEX; MasterCard
Catalog Cost: $3
Catalog Circulation: to 25M
Average Order Size: $150
Printing Information: 80 pages in 4 colors on Matte Stock
Press: Web Press
Binding: Saddle Stitched
Mailing List Information: Names for rent
In Business: 12 years
Number of Employees: 19
Sales Volume: $3MM to $5MM

478 Coast Distribution RV Catalog
The Coast Distribution System, Inc.
350 Woodview Ave
Suite 100
Morgan Hill, CA 95037-8105
408-782-6686
800-495-5858
Fax: 408-782-7790
customerservice@coastdist.com
www.coastdistribution.com

RV parts and accessories
Chairman: Thomas R. McGuire
President: James i Musbach
CFO: Sandra A. Knell
Executive VP - Operations: David A. Berger
Executive VP Manufacturing: Dennis A. Castagnola
Catalog Circulation: Mailed 1 time(s) per year
Printing Information: 220 pages
In Business: 52 years
Number of Employees: 300

479 Coker Tire
1317 Chestnut Street
Chattanooga, TN 37402-4418
866-516-3215
www.coker.com

Tires and accessories
President: Corky Coker
Catalog Circulation: Mailed 1 time(s) per year
Printing Information: 80 pages
Number of Employees: 35
Sales Volume: $1MM to $3MM

480 Cooper Industries
Eaton
600 Travis Street, Suite 5400
P. O. Box 4446
Houston, TX 77002-1001
713-209-8400
Fax: 636-527-1405
www.cooperindustries.com

Automotive fuseholders and fuses
Chairman: Alexander M. Cutler
President: John Monter
CFO: Richard H. Fearon
Marketing Manager: Scott Robinson

Production Manager: John Monter
Vice Chairman, COO: Craig Arnold
Vice Chairman, COO: Thomas S. Gross
SVP & Chief Information Officer: William W. Blausey Jr.
In Business: 114 years
Number of Employees: 850

481 Corvette Central
Corvette Central
13550 Three Oaks Road
PO Box 16
Sawyer, MI 49125-9328   269-426-3342
                               800-345-4122
                          Fax: 269-426-4108
mail@corvettecentral.com
www.corvettecentral.com
Corvette parts and accessories
President: Jerry Kohen
CFO: Dan Baber
Credit Cards: MasterCard
Catalog Cost: Free
Printing Information: 14 pages in 4 colors
Binding: Perfect Bound
In Business: 40 years

482 Corvette Pacifica Motoring Accessories
Italia Productions
8981 La Linia Unit 1
PO BOX 2360
Atascadero, CA 93423   805-466-6293
                         Fax: 805-466-4782
info@italiareproductions.com
www.italiareproductions.com
Corvette accessories
President: John Fortney
Printing Information: 40 pages
Sales Volume: $3MM to $5MM

483 Corvette World
Corvette World
12491 Route 30
Irwin, PA 15642-1315   724-863-0410
                              800-327-0185
                         Fax: 724-863-5968
www.Corvettedept.Com
1953-2006 Covette restoration parts and accessories
President: Jared George
Credit Cards: AMEX; MasterCard
Catalog Cost: Free
Catalog Circulation: Mailed 1 time(s) per year to 10M
Average Order Size: $250
Printing Information: 120 pages in 2 colors on Glossy Stock
Press: Web Press
Binding: Saddle Stitched
Mailing List Information: Names for rent
In Business: 20 years
Number of Employees: 4
Sales Volume: $500M to $1MM

484 Delta Lights
Delta Tech Industries
1901 S Vineyard Avenue
Ontario, CA 91761   909-673-1900
                      Fax: 909-673-1990
sales@deltalights.com
www.deltalights.com
Lighting products for Jeeps, Hummers, trucks, emergency, motorcycles and ATVs
President: Bogdan Durian
Marketing Manager: Joseph Glass
Production Manager: Joel Moran
Fulfillment: Andrew Pierce
Buyers: Andrew Pierce
Printing Information: 56 pages
In Business: 39 years

485 Dennis Carpenter Ford Restoration
Dennis Carpenter
4140 Concord Parkway South
Concord, NC 28027   704-786-8139
                          800-476-9653
                     Fax: 704-786-8180
info@dennis-carpenter.com
www.dennis-carpenter.com
Ford restoration parts
President: Daniel Carpenter
Marketing Manager: Terry Rodenhuis
Owner: Dennis Carpenter
Credit Cards: AMEX; MasterCard

486 Dennis K Burk
Dennis K. Burk Inc.
284 Eastern Avenue
Chelsea, MA 02150-917   617-884-7800
                               800-289-2875
                          Fax: 617-884-7638
support@burkeoil.com
www.burkeoil.com
Petroleum products, gasoline and motor oil
Chairman: Ed Burke
President: Ted Burke
CFO: Joe Cote
Marketing Manager: Kelly Anderson
Director of Operations: Dan Hill
Executive Administrator: Meaghan Burke
Safety Director: Matthew Manoli
In Business: 54 years
Number of Employees: 52
Sales Volume: $20MM to $50MM

487 Detroit Body Products
Detroit Body Products
49750 Martin Drive
Wixom, MI 48393-159   800-521-8383
www.detroitbodyproducts.com
Synthetic and natural fiber fabrics
President: JP Kraft Sr
Credit Cards: AMEX; MasterCard

488 Douglas Battery Manufacturing Company
Douglas Battery
500 Battery Drive
Winston Salem, NC 27107   336-650-7000
                                 800-368-4527
                            Fax: 336-650-7072
www.Douglasbattery.Com
Batteries
Chairman: Tom S Douglas III
President: Charles Douglas
Marketing Manager: Tom Douglas
Production Manager: Stanley Turbeville
Credit Cards: AMEX; MasterCard
Printing Information: 26 pages
In Business: 94 years
Number of Employees: 250
Sales Volume: $100MM-$500MM

489 EFDYN
Efdyn Incorporated
7734 East 11th Street
Tulsa, OK 74112-5718   918-838-1170
                              800-950-1172
                         Fax: 918-835-3334
sales@efdyn.com
www.efdyn.com
Shock absorbers, recoil dampers, buffers
President: Carrie Wilkinson
Marketing Manager: Robert Walkerby
Credit Cards: AMEX; MasterCard
Printing Information: 40 pages
In Business: 59 years
Number of Employees: 36
Sales Volume: $1,000,000 - $5,000,000

490 EGT Exhaust Gas Technologies
EGT Exhaust Gas Technologies
15642 DuPont Ave.
Suite B
Chino, CA 91710-1421   909-548-8100
                              800-348-4678
                         Fax: 909-680-3226
sales@exhaustgas.com
www.exhaustgas.com
Manufactures a wide range of thermocouple assemblies, sensors for ATV vehicles, diesel trucks, drag racing, go-karts, snowmobiles, PWC - personal watercraft and professional race teams
President: Dennis Lawler
Credit Cards: AMEX; MasterCard
In Business: 12 years

491 Eagle Equipment-Automotive Equipment
Eagle Equipment
4810 Clover Road
Greensboro, NC 27405   800-336-2776
                         Fax: 800-590-9814
info@eagleequip.com
www.eagleequip.com
Above ground lifts, many models and styles include two post lifts, four post lifts, alignment lifts, scissor lifts, low and mid rise
CFO: Lisa Carlson
Marketing Manager: Marc DelChercolo
Credit Cards: AMEX; MasterCard
Catalog Cost: Free
Printing Information: 40 pages in 4 colors on Glossy Stock
Press: Web Press
Binding: Saddle Stitched
Mailing List Information: Names for rent
In Business: 61 years
Number of Employees: 70

492 Eastwood Unique Automotive Tools & Supplies
The Eastwood Company
263 Shoemaker Road
Pottstown, PA 19464   866-759-2131
                             800-343-9353
www.eastwood.com
Unique automotive tools and supplies
Credit Cards: AMEX; MasterCard
Catalog Cost: Free
Catalog Circulation: Mailed 12 time(s) per year to 500T
Printing Information: 84 pages in 4 colors on Glossy Stock
Press: Offset Press
Binding: Saddle Stitched
In Business: 35 years

493 Eaton Corporation World Headquarters
Eaton Corporation
1111 Superior Ave E # 19
Cleveland, OH 44114-2584   440-523-4400
                                  800-386-1911
                             Fax: 216-523-4787
www.eaton.com
Automotive, appliance, energy, industrial controls and components
Chairman: Alexander M Cutler
CFO: J Carmont
Marketing Manager: Jeff Obrock
Vice Chairman and COO: Craig Arnold
Senior Vice President and CIO: William W. Blausey Jr.
Executive Vice President, Chief HR: Cynthia K. Brabander
Number of Employees: 7300
Sales Volume: $20 million

494 Eckler's Classic Chevy
Eckler's Classic Chevy
5200 S Washington Ave
Titusville, FL 32780
925-516-7267
800-284-4096
Fax: 321-383-2059
sales@classicchevy.com
www.classicchevy.com

Parts for classic Chevys
President: James A Bruce
In Business: 54 years

495 Eckler's Corvette Parts
Eckler's Industries Inc
5200 S Washington Avenue
Titusville, FL 32780
800-284-3906
Fax: 321-383-2059
sales@ecklers.net
www.ecklers.com

Parts and accessories for Corvettes; different catalogs for different years
Catalog Cost: Free
In Business: 54 years

496 Eckler's El Camino
El Camino Store
5200 S Washington Avenue
Titusville, FL 32780
706-546-9217
888-685-5987
Fax: 877-548-8581
custserv@elcaminostore.com
www.elcaminostore.com

1959-1987 restoration parts and accessories for Chevrolet El Camino and GMC variants
Credit Cards: AMEX; MasterCard
In Business: 54 years

497 Edelbrock Corporation
Edelbrock Corporation
2700 California Street
Torrance, CA 90503
310-781-2222
800-416-8628
Fax: 310-320-1187
www.edelbrock.com

A complete line of parts for Chevrolet, Ford, Pontiac, Oldsmobile and Harley-Davidson
Chairman: O Victor Edelbrock
President: O Victor Edelbrock
CFO: Norm Judd
Marketing Manager: Jason Snyder
Production Manager: Wayne P Murray
Director of Advertising: Eric Blakely
eblakely@edelbrock.com
Technical Sales Coordinator: Smitty Smith
smitty@edelbrock.com
Printing Information: 207 pages
In Business: 75 years

498 Empire Motor Sports
Empire Vehicle Accessories
9261 Bally Ct
Rancho Cucamonga, CA 91730 909-980-8922
Fax: 909-980-8926
info@empirevehicleaccessories.com
www.Empiremotorsports.Com

Parts for trucks
President: Brett Brinkman
In Business: 23 years
Sales Volume: $3MM to $5MM

499 Everett-Morrison Motorcars
Everett-Morrison Motorcars
2800 Nolan Rd.
Suite 100
Baytown, TX 77520
281-839-7921
Fax: 281-837-3181
cobras@ix.netcom.com
www.everett-morrison.com

Catalogs of automotive parts and accessories, offering replica and conversion kits, specializes in replica car kits

President: Buford R Everett
CFO: Bruce M Everett
Marketing Manager: Buford R Everett
Production Manager: Brett D Everett
International Marketing Manager: Buford R. Everett
Buyers: Gina L Schmidt
Credit Cards: MasterCard; Visa
Catalog Cost: $4
Catalog Circulation: to 5000
Printing Information: 50 pages in 4 colors on Glossy Stock
Press: Letterpress
Binding: Perfect Bound
Mailing List Information: Names for rent
In Business: 32 years
Number of Employees: 25

500 Fiberglass Trends
Fiberglass Trends Mitcom
986 N Elm Street
Orange, CA 92867-5439
714-532-6140
Fax: 714-532-6144
www.california-webbusiness.com

High performance fiberglass accessories
Credit Cards: MasterCard; Visa
Catalog Cost: Free
Number of Employees: 20
Sales Volume: Under $500M

501 Fine Lines
Fine Lines, Inc.
127 Hartman Rd
Wadsworth, OH 44281-9402
330-335-5000
800-778-8237
Fax: 330-335-5009
info@finelinesinc.com
www.sstubes.com

Reproduction brake and fuel lines
President: Bob Grosser
bob@finelinesinc.com
Information / Sales: Rick Armbrust
rarmbrust@finelinesinc.com
Research and Development / Mark: Josh Stamper
jstamper@finelinesinc.com
Research & Development: JeremySimms
Jeremy@finelinesinc.com
Credit Cards: AMEX; MasterCard
Sales Volume: $3MM to $5MM

502 Finish Line
Finish Line, Inc.
777 Arnold Drive
Suite 200
Martinez, CA 94553
954-436-9101
888-436-9113
Fax: 954-436-9102
info@finishlineaccessories.com
www.finishlineaccessories.com

Parts and accessories for a Cobra replica
Credit Cards: AMEX; MasterCard
Catalog Cost: $5
Printing Information: 45 pages
In Business: 22 years

503 Firewheel Classics
Firewheel Classics, Inc.
119 Regency Dr
Wylie, TX 75098-7017
972-941-6623
800-711-0125
Fax: 972-941-8644
camaro@firewheelclassics.com
www.firewheelclassics.com

67-69 Camaro parts and accessories
President: Patti Stinson
Credit Cards: AMEX; MasterCard
In Business: 18 years
Number of Employees: 4
Sales Volume: $500M to $1MM

504 Flaming River
800 Poertner Drive
Berea, OH 44017
440-826-4488
800-648-8022
Fax: 440-826-0780
bdomin@flamingriver.com
www.flamingriver.com

Car parts
President: Jeanette Ladina
Sales Manager: Brett Domin

505 Force Control Industries
Force Control
PO Box 18366
3660 Dixie Highway
Fairfield, OH 45014-366
513-868-0900
800-829-3244
Fax: 513-868-2105
info@forcecontrol.com
www.forcecontrol.com

Clutches, brakes, transmission equipment and various auto parts
President: Michael Besl
Marketing Manager: R Kelly
In Business: 46 years
Number of Employees: 60
Sales Volume: $5,000,000 - $10,000,000

506 Ford Parts Specialists
JobLot Automotive, Inc.
98-11 211th Street
P.O. Box 75
Queens Village, NY 11429-1005   718-468-8585
Fax: 718-468-8686
www.joblotauto.com

Automotive parts and supplies covering 1928-1970 Ford cars, and 1928-1970 Ford trucks
President: Robert Schaeffer
CFO: Harold Brensilber
Credit Cards: MasterCard
Catalog Cost: $2
Catalog Circulation: Mailed 1 time(s) per year to 60M
Printing Information: 120 pages on Newsprint
Press: Web Press
In Business: 50 years

507 G.H. Meiser & Company
G.H. Meiser & Co.
2407 W. 140th Place
P.O. Box 315
Posen, IL 60469-315
708-388-7867
Fax: 708-388-4053
info@ghmeiser.com
www.ghmeiser.com

Tire gauges and cleaners
President: Brian Parduhn
Marketing Manager: Bruce Parduhn
Production Manager: Herman Parduhn
In Business: 106 years
Number of Employees: 35
Sales Volume: $1,000,000 - $5,000,000

508 Gast Manufacturing Corporation
Gast Manufacturing, Inc.
2300 M-139 Highway
P.O. Box 97
Benton Harbor, MI 49023-0097   269-926-6171
Fax: 269-927-0808
www.gastmfg.com

Compressors, vacuum pumps
President: Warren E Gast
Marketing Manager: K Gast
In Business: 95 years
Number of Employees: 600
Sales Volume: $50MM to $100MM

509 Gates Product Corporation
Gates Product Corporation
1551 Wewatta Street
Denver, CO 80202   303-744-1911
www.gates.com

Belts, hoses, hydraulics and power transmission belting for automotives

Chairman: James Nicol
President: Ken Friedman
CFO: John Zimmerman
Chief Administrative Officer: Dave Carroll
SVP, Human Resources: Heather Duma
VP, Research & Development: Ken Parks
In Business: 29 years
Number of Employees: 1100

510 Giant Industrial Corporation
Giant Industrial Corp
1 Baiting Place Rd
Farmingdale, NY 11735-6200   631-293-8282
Fax: 631-293-8132
www.GicBrake.Com

Brake pads and shoes, filters, water pumps

President: Isaac Youssian
Marketing Manager: Eli Youssian
Catalog Cost: Free
Catalog Circulation: Mailed 2 time(s) per year to 5M
Printing Information: in 4 colors
Binding: Perfect Bound
In Business: 18 years
Number of Employees: 10
Sales Volume: $5MM to $10MM

511 Gold Effects
Gold Effects, LLC
13130 56th Court
Suite 609
Clearwater, FL 33760-4021   727-573-1990
800-603-4343
Fax: 727-573-1360
sales@goldeffects.com
www.goldeffects.com

Auto supplies

President: Dan Mc Laughlin
Production Manager: Bob French
Credit Cards: AMEX; MasterCard
In Business: 25 years
Sales Volume: $480,000

512 Good Vibrations Motorsports
Good Vibrations Motorsports
8858 Painter Avenue
Suite E
Whittier, CA 90602   562-945-7669
800-576-7661
sales@dragparts.com
www.goodvibesracing.com

Car parts for motor racing

General Manager: James Michael Maher
Catalog Cost: Free
Catalog Circulation: Mailed 1 time(s) per year
Printing Information: 64 pages in 4 colors
In Business: 29 years

513 Goodmark Retail Catalog
Goodmark
625 E. Old Norcross Road
Lawrenceville, GA 30045   770-339-8557
877-477-3577
Fax: 770-339-7562
www.goodmarkindustries.com

Restoration parts and accessories for classic cars and trucks

President: Anthony Frank
Credit Cards: AMEX; MasterCard
Catalog Cost: $5
In Business: 23 years
Sales Volume: $3MM to $5MM

514 Goodson Tools & Supplies for Engine Builders
Goodson Shop Supplies
156 Galewski Drive
P.O. Box 847
Winona, MN 55987-847   507-452-1830
800-533-8010
Fax: 507-452-2907
orderdesk@goodson.com
www.goodson.com

Tools and supplies for engine building and repair

Chairman: Scott Biesanz
President: Mike Pulk
Marketing Manager: Dave Monyhan
Production Manager: Juan Roque
Credit Cards: AMEX; MasterCard
Catalog Cost: $5
Catalog Circulation: Mailed 1 time(s) per year
Printing Information: 136 pages in 4 colors on Glossy Stock
Press: Sheetfed Press
Binding: Perfect Bound
In Business: 67 years
Number of Employees: 50
Sales Volume: $5,000,000

515 Granatelli Motor Sports
Granatelli Motor Sports, Inc.
1000 Yarnell Pl
Oxnard, CA 93033-2454   805-486-6644
Fax: 805-486-6684
gmssales@granatellimotorsports.com
www.granatellimotorsports.com

Air flow sensors, turbo systems, components, accessories, valve covers, electronics and ignitions

President: J.R. Granatelli
Executive Assistant: Eric Mass
Catalog Cost: Free
Printing Information: 32 pages in 4 colors
In Business: 25 years
Sales Volume: $17 Million

516 Graphite Metalizing Corporation
Graphite Metalizing Corporation
1050 Nepperhan Ave
Yonkers, NY 10703-1421   914-968-8400
Fax: 914-968-8468
sales@graphalloy.com
www.graphalloy.com

Oil free bearings and bushings

President: Eben T Walker
Marketing Manager: Robert C Stowell
Catalog Cost: Free
Printing Information: in 2 colors on Matte Stock
Press: Web Press
Binding: Folded
Mailing List Information: Names for rent
In Business: 100 years
Number of Employees: 65
Sales Volume: $5MM to $10MM

517 Grove Gear Industrial Gear Drives
Grove Gear
1524 15th Avenue
Union Grove, WI 53182   262-878-1221
www.grovegear.com

Speed reducers and gear motors

President: Larry Minnich
Catalog Cost: Free
Catalog Circulation: Mailed 1 time(s) per year
Printing Information: in 1 color
In Business: 70 years
Number of Employees: 200
Sales Volume: $25,000,000 - $50,000,000

518 Grumpy's Truck Parts
Grumpy's Truck Parts
17829 N Black Canyon Hwy
Phoenix, AZ 85023-1207   602-375-9200
800-457-8679
Fax: 602-942-8633
grumpysrus@aol.com

1947-87 Chevrolet & GMC full-size pickup parts, weather-strip, lenses, wire harnesses, bumpers, bed parts, grills, glove boxes, carpet kits

President: Evelyn Rogers
Marketing Manager: Evelyn Rogers
General Manager: Robert Rogers
Credit Cards: AMEX; MasterCard; Visa
Catalog Circulation: to 5000
Printing Information: 40 pages in 2 colors on Matte Stock
Binding: Saddle Stitched
In Business: 27 years
Number of Employees: 4
Sales Volume: $530,000

519 HRP World
Hoerr Racing Products
9804 W Primrose Lane
Edwards, IL 61528   309-691-8789
866-851-7223
Fax: 309-691-8796
info@hrpworld.com
www.hrpworld.com

Auto racing parts, supplies and apparel

President: Irv Hoerr
Credit Cards: MasterCard
Catalog Cost: Free
In Business: 55 years

520 Header Parts
Headers By Ed, Inc
2710 - 16th Avenue South
Dept. WS-M
Minneapolis, MN 55407-1291   612-729-2802
Fax: 612-729-5638
info@headersbyed.com
www.headersbyed.com

V8 automotive and vertical exit exhaust headers, header kits, header parts for over 100 4, 6, V6, V8, V12, US made engines

President: Ed Henneman
Credit Cards: MasterCard
Catalog Cost: $4.5
Catalog Circulation: Mailed 3 time(s) per year to 5M
Average Order Size: $170
Printing Information: 32 pages in 1 color on Matte Stock
Press: Letterpress
Binding: Saddle Stitched
Mailing List Information: Names for rent
In Business: 52 years
Number of Employees: 3
Sales Volume: $500,000 - $1,000,000

521 Heidts Suspension Systems
Heidts Automotive
800 Oakwood Road
Lake Zurich, IL 60047   800-841-8188
sales@heidts.com
www.heidts.com

Front and rear suspension systems

522 High Performance Catalog
Auto Meter
413 W Elm Street
Sycamore, IL 60178   815-895-8141
866-248-6356
www.autometer.com

Tachometers, auto gage instruments, battery testers, LTM performance and charging system analyzers

President: Jeff Kingberg
Marketing Manager: Jeep Worthan

Credit Cards: AMEX; MasterCard; Visa
Catalog Cost: $5.95
Printing Information: 120 pages in 4 colors
In Business: 60 years
Number of Employees: 195
Sales Volume: $20MM to $50MM

523   Hitran Corporation
Hitran Corporation
362 Highway 31
Flemington, NJ 08822-5799   908-782-5525
Fax: 908-782-9733
www.hitrancorp.com

Transformers, chokes and reactors
President: John C Hindle Iii
In Business: 95 years
Number of Employees: 150
Sales Volume: $25,000,000 - $50,000,000

524   Hydro-E-Lectric
Hydro-e-lectric
5530 Independence Court
Punta Gorda, FL 33982-1700   941-639-0437
800-343-4261
Fax: 941-639-0376
info@Hydro-E-Lectric.com
www.hydroe.com

Convertible tops and top cylinders, motor pumps, hose sets, top latches, weatherstripping, carpet sets and much more
President: Paul Wiesman
CFO: Virginia Wiesman
Secretary: Erika Woody
Credit Cards: AMEX; MasterCard; Visa
Catalog Cost: Free
Catalog Circulation: to 12000
Printing Information: 46 pages in 4 colors on Glossy Stock
Binding: Saddle Stitched
Mailing List Information: Names for rent
In Business: 34 years
Number of Employees: 8
Sales Volume: $250,000

525   J & W Nova Parts
J & W Nova Parts
8253 Mount Cross Road
Danville, VA 24540-6745   434-685-4310
www.novaparts.com

Nova products, accessories and detail items
Credit Cards: MasterCard; Visa
Catalog Cost: Free
Catalog Circulation: Mailed 2 time(s) per year
Printing Information: 56 pages
Number of Employees: 7

526   J-Mark
J-Mark
2790 Ranchview Lane
Plymouth, MN 55447-1996   763-559-3300
800-328-6274
Fax: 763-559-4806
oem@j-markproducts.com
www.j-markproducts.com

Tailgate protectors, running boards, splash guards, bedliners, side bed caps
President: Gary Henriksen
Marketing Manager: Jerry Moore
Production Manager: Matt Henriksen
Buyers: Todd Slawson
Credit Cards:
Catalog Cost: $2
In Business: 35 years
Number of Employees: 35
Sales Volume: $5,000,000 - $10,000,000

527   Jeep Parts Catalog
4 Wheel Drive Hardware Inc
PO Box 57
Columbiana, OH 44408   330-482-4924
800-555-3353
Fax: 330-482-5035
custserv@4wd.com
www.4wd.com

Parts and accessories
President: Barry Ryan
Credit Cards: AMEX; MasterCard
Catalog Cost: Free
In Business: 38 years

528   Jegs.com
101 JEGS Place
Delaware, OH 43015   800-345-4545
Fax: 740-362-7017
www.jegs.com

Auto parts and accessories

529   Joblot Automotive
JobLot Automotive, Inc.
98-11 211th Street
P.O. Box 75
Queens Village, NY 11429   718-468-8585
Fax: 718-468-8686
www.joblotauto.com

Automotive parts and supplies
President: Robert Schaefer
CFO: Harold Brensilber
Catalog Cost: $2
Catalog Circulation: Mailed 1 time(s) per year to 60M
Printing Information: 120 pages on Newsprint
Press: Web Press
In Business: 52 years
Sales Volume: $5MM to $10MM

530   Kanter Auto Products
Kanter Auto Products
76 Monroe St
Boonton, NJ 07005-2160   973-334-9575
800-526-1096
Fax: 973-334-5423
sales1@kanter.com
www.kanter.com

Auto restoration parts and supplies for American cars and trucks from 1930-1990
Chairman: Dan Kanter
President: Fred Kanter
Credit Cards: MasterCard
Printing Information: 72 pages
In Business: 50 years
Sales Volume: $5MM to $10MM

531   Kent-Moore Automotive
SPX
13320 Ballantyne Corporate Place
Charlotte, NC 28277-5509   810-574-2332
800-345-2233
Fax: 810-578-7375
www.spx.com

Special service tools for transportation industry
Chairman: Christopher J. Kearney
President: Christopher J. Kearney
Marketing Manager: N Robert Kindig
CEO: Christopher J. Kearney
EVP: Robert B. Foreman
SVP, Secretary and General Counsel: Kevin L. Lilly
Buyers: Patti Barone
Credit Cards: MasterCard
Catalog Cost: Free
Catalog Circulation: Mailed 1 time(s) per year to 50M
Printing Information: 200 pages
Press: Web Press
Binding: Perfect Bound
In Business: 113 years
Number of Employees: 150

532   King Motorsports
King Motorsports Unlimited, Inc.
2130 South Danny Road
New Berlin, WI 53146-1601   262-522-7558
Fax: 262-522-7559
info@kingmotorsports.com
www.Kingmotorsports.Com

Automotive parts and accessories for specific makes and models, specializes in Acura parts and accessories
President: Scott Zellner
CEO: Scott Zellner
Founder: Jim Dentici
In Business: 34 years
Sales Volume: $1MM to $3MM

533   LMC Truck
LMC Truck
15450 W. 108th Street
Lenexa, KS 66219   913-541-0684
800-562-8782
Fax: 800-541-8525
customercare@longmotor.net
www.lmctruck.com

Chevy, Ford, GMC truck parts and accessories
President: Becky Hanrahan
Credit Cards: AMEX; MasterCard; Visa
Catalog Cost: Free
Printing Information: 124 pages
Number of Employees: 100
Sales Volume: $50MM to $100MM

534   Lisle Corporation
Lisle Corporation
807 E. Main Street
PO Box 89
Clarinda, IA 51632-89   712-542-5101
Fax: 712-542-6591
info@lislecorp.com
www.lislecorp.com

Automotive specialty tools, lubrication & tire products and creepers
Chairman: John Lisle
President: William Lisle
Production Manager: Fred Lisle
EVP: Mary Landhuis
Advertising Mgr/Marketing Director: John Bielfeldt
Catalog Cost: Free
Printing Information: 64 pages
In Business: 112 years
Number of Employees: 248
Sales Volume: $22.8 Million

535   Lokar Performance Products
Lokar Performance Products
2545 Quality Lane
Knoxville, TN 37931   865-824-9767
877-469-7440
Fax: 865-824-9761
tech@lokar.com
www.lokar.com

Automotive and truck performance parts
President: Van Walls
CFO: Deborah Walls
COO: Amanda Leblanc
Manager: Lawanda McClure
Credit Cards: MasterCard; Visa
Catalog Cost: Free
Printing Information: 84 pages
In Business: 22 years
Number of Employees: 40
Sales Volume: $5.9 Million

536   M&R Products
M&R Products
2210 San Joaquin
Fresno, CA 93721   856-696-9450
800-524-2560
Fax: 559-243-1111
info@mrproducts.com
www.mrproducts.com

Race car and dragster tie-downs and hardware, window nets, lever latch and rotary cam locks

Credit Cards: AMEX; MasterCard; Visa

537 Mercedes Performance Products
Performance Products for Mercedes
5200 S. Washington Avenue
Titusville, FL 32780   818-779-2823
                           888-843-2822
                 Fax: 800-243-8893
                 www.ecklersmbzparts.com

Parts and accessories

Credit Cards: AMEX; MasterCard
Catalog Cost: Free
In Business: 53 years

538 Mike's A Ford-able Parts
Mike's A Ford-Able Parts
124 Model A Drive
Maysville, GA 30558   706-652-3866
                           888-879-6453
                 Fax: 706-652-2492
                 mike@mikes-afordable.com
                 www.mikes-afordable.com

Specializes in Model A Ford parts and accessories

Credit Cards: MasterCard
Catalog Cost: Free
Printing Information: 320 pages in 4 colors

539 Morrison
Art Morrison Ent.
5216 7th St E
Fife, WA 98424   866-321-4499
                         800-929-7188
                 Fax: 253-922-8847
                 info@artmorrison.com
                 www.artmorrison.com

Automotive parts and supplies for classic cars

Marketing Manager: Kevin Kosair
Sales Team: Scott Randle
scottr@artmorrison.com
Sales Team: Kevin Kosir
kevink@artmorrison.com
Sales Team: Brock Baker
brockb@artmorrison.com
Credit Cards: MasterCard; Visa
Catalog Cost: $5
Printing Information: 68 pages

540 Moss Motors
Moss Motors
440 Rutherford Street
Goleta, CA 93117   800-667-7872
                 Fax: 805-692-2525
                 www.mossmotors.com

Supplier of parts for restoration of British cars

Marketing Manager: Carolyn Grimes
In Business: 67 years

541 Mostly Mustangs
Mostly Mustangs Inc
55 Alling St
Hamden, CT 06517-3103   203-562-8804
                 Fax: 203-562-4891

Ford Mustang restoration parts

President: Bill Fioretti
Marketing Manager: Gus Fioretti
Credit Cards: MasterCard
Catalog Circulation: Mailed 1 time(s) per year to 1000
Printing Information: 20 pages on Matte Stock
Mailing List Information: Names for rent
In Business: 28 years
Number of Employees: 3
Sales Volume: $1 million

542 Munchkin Motors
P.O.Box 266
Eastford, CT 06242-266   860-974-2545

Automotive supplies and books

President: Jack Larson
Marketing Manager: Jack Larson
Mailing List Information: Names for rent
Sales Volume: Under $500M

543 National Parts Depot
National Parts Depot
900 SW 38th Avenue
Ocala, FL 34474   352-861-8700
                         800-874-7595
                 Fax: 352-861-8706
                 www.npdlink.com

Car parts: Mustang, T-Bird, Ford Bronco and trucks, Camaro, Chevelle, Malibu, El Camino, Firebird, Trans-AM

President: James A Schmidt
Printing Information: in 4 colors
In Business: 39 years

544 Noco Company
The Noco Company
30339 Diamond Parkway #102
Glenwillow, OH 44139-5400   216-464-8131
                            800-456-6626
                 Fax: 216-464-8172
                 info@noco-usa.com
                 www.noco-usa.com

Battery cables, testers, terminals and cleaners, booster cables and spark plug wire sets

Chairman: William Nook, Chairman/CEO
CFO: Fred Barr
Marketing Manager: Johnathan L Nook
In Business: 101 years
Number of Employees: 99
Sales Volume: $20 to 50 million

545 Northern Auto Parts
Northern Auto Parts
801 Lewis Boulevard
Sioux City, IA 51105   712-258-4131
                         800-831-0884
                 Fax: 712-258-0088
                 info@northernautoparts.com
                 www.northernautoparts.com

Wide line of auto parts for many cars

President: Clifford E Tufty
In Business: 25 years

546 Northern Hydraulics
Northern Tool & Equipment
2800 Southcross Drive West
Burnsville, MN 55306   952-894-9510
                         800-221-0516
                 Fax: 954-894-1020
                 intlenglishsales@northerntool.com
                 www.northerntool.com

Hydraulic parts

President: Donald L. Kotula
Founder, CEO: Donald L. Kotula
In Business: 32 years

547 Obsolete Chevrolet Parts Company
Obsolete Chevrolet Parts Company
524 Hazel Avenue
PO Box 68
Nashville, GA 31639-2582   229-686-5812
                           800-248-8785
                 Fax: 229-686-3056
                 chevy@obschevy.com
                 www.obschevy.com

Hard to find Chevorlet parts

President: Tim Tygart
CFO: Maryland Lancaster
Printing Information: 100 pages in 2 colors on

Glossy Stock
In Business: 36 years

548 Olympic Auto Accessories
Olympic 4*4 Products
2645 Yates Ave
Commerce, CA 90040-2621   323-726-6988
                 Fax: 323-727-2936
                 info@olympic4x4products.com
                 www.olympic4x4products.com

Truck parts

President: Eric Lichtbach
Credit Cards: AMEX; MasterCard
Catalog Cost: $1
Catalog Circulation: Mailed 1 time(s) per year
Printing Information: 6 pages in 1 color
In Business: 64 years
Number of Employees: 40
Sales Volume: $3MM to $5MM

549 Original Parts Group
Original Parts Group, Inc.
1770 Saturn Way
Seal Beach, CA 90740   562-594-1000
                         800-243-8355
                 info@opgi.com
                 www.opgi.com

18,000 different parts and accessories, GM body parts

Credit Cards: AMEX; MasterCard
Printing Information: 260 pages

550 PIC Design
PIC Design Inc.
86 Benson Road
PO Box 1004
Middlebury, CT 06762-1004   203-758-8272
                            800-243-6125
                 Fax: 203-758-8271
                 sales@pic-design.com
                 www.pic-design.com

Auto parts and supplies

Marketing Manager: Donna Schuld
Printing Information: 292 pages
Mailing List Information: Names for rent
In Business: 52 years
Number of Employees: 98

551 PRO-TOOLS
PRO-TOOLS, Inc.
7616 Industrial Ln
Tampa, FL 33637-6715   813-986-9000
                 Fax: 813-985-6588
                 info@pro-tools.com
                 www.pro-tools.com

Large selection of professional tools - mechanical bender, manual and electric bead rollers, notchers, brakes, shrinker, tube and pipe notchers and much more

President: Mike Mullen
Marketing Manager: Dean Gordon
VP: Cindy Mullen
International Marketing Manager: Dean Gordon
Credit Cards: AMEX; MasterCard; Visa
Catalog Cost: Free
Catalog Circulation: Mailed 1 time(s) per year
Average Order Size: $1000
Printing Information: 25 pages on Glossy Stock
Binding: Perfect Bound
In Business: 26 years
Number of Employees: 20
Sales Volume: $1.8 Million

552 Pacer Performance
Pacer Performance
3901 Medford St
Los Angeles, CA 90063-1608   323-881-4311
                             800-423-2442
                 Fax: 323-263-3948
                 info@pacerperformance.com
                 www.pacerperformance.com

Truck lights and accessories

President: Bill Longo
Marketing Manager: Cathy Cripps
Printing Information: 20 pages
In Business: 50 years
Number of Employees: 4
Sales Volume: $3MM to $5MM

553 Parts Place For All Volkswagons
Parts Place, Inc.
5510 E 10 Mile Rd
Warren, MI 48091   586-757-2300
                          Fax: 248-373-5950
                sales@partsplaceinc.com
                www.partsplaceinc.com

Volkswagon parts and recycled parts

Printing Information: 176 pages
In Business: 30 years

554 Pegasus Auto Racing Supplies
Pegasus Auto Racing Supplies
2475 S 179th Street
New Berlin, WI 53146   262-317-1234
                          800-688-6946
                      Fax: 262-317-1201
          CustSvc@PegasusAutoRacing.com
               www.pegasusautoracing.com

Auto racing books and supplies, items for the racer including many unique and hard to find products

Personnel Director: Carla Heitman
Warehouse Manager: Joel Webber
Treasurer: Christopher Heitman
Buyers: Michael Marmurowicz
Credit Cards: AMEX; MasterCard
Catalog Cost: Free
Catalog Circulation: Mailed 1 time(s) per year to 120M
Average Order Size: $170
Printing Information: 164 pages in 1 color on Matte Stock
Press: Web Press
Binding: Perfect Bound
Mailing List Information: Names for rent
In Business: 40 years
Number of Employees: 15
Sales Volume: $5.3 Million

555 Performance
Performance
7733 Hayvenhurst Ave
Titusville, FL 32780   818-787-7500
                          888-787-3626
                      Fax: 800-752-6196
                ppe_sales@ecklers.net
                www.automotion.com

Automotive parts and accessories

President: Mel Kay
Credit Cards: AMEX; MasterCard
Catalog Cost: $3
Catalog Circulation: Mailed 4 time(s) per year to 25000
Printing Information: 115 pages in 4 colors on Matte Stock
Press: Web Press
Binding: Saddle Stitched
Number of Employees: 25
Sales Volume: $3MM to $5MM

556 Performance Years
Ames Performance Engineering
10 Pontiac Drive
PO Box 572
Spofford, NH 03462   800-421-2637
                      Fax: 603-363-7007
          CUSTOMER.SERVICE@amesperf.com
               www.performanceyears.com

Pontiac restoration parts

President: Chris Casperson
Marketing Manager: John Buchta
Production Manager: Ed Walter
Catalog Cost: Free
Printing Information: in 1 color on Matte Stock

Binding: Perfect Bound
Mailing List Information: Names for rent
In Business: 29 years
Number of Employees: 14
Sales Volume: $1MM to $3MM

557 Perry Company
The Perry Company
500 South Valley Mills Dr
PO Box 7187
Waco, TX 76711-7187   254-756-2139
                          800-792-3246
                      Fax: 254-756-2166
                info@perry-co.com
                www.perry-co.com

Tractor canopies

President: Jeff Weaver
Catalog Circulation: Mailed 1 time(s) per year
In Business: 69 years
Number of Employees: 47
Sales Volume: $5,000,000 - $10,000,000

558 Philips Lighting Company
Philips Office solutions
501 Fulling Mill Road
Middletown, PA 8875-6800 732-667-4900
                      Fax: 732-563-3641
                www.phillips.com

Headlamps and bulbs

Chairman: Edward Dolman
President: Michael McGinnis
Marketing Manager: James Gonedes
Credit Cards:
In Business: 219 years
Number of Employees: 500

559 Phoenix Graphix
PhoenixGraphix, Inc.
400 S 79th St
Chandler, AZ 85226-4720   480-941-4550
                          800-941-4550
                      Fax: 480-345-8685
                www.phoenixgraphix.com

Offers decals, stencils and stripe kits f/Muscle cars, Trans AM, Z28, El Camino, Plymouth, Dodge, AMC and Ford licensed kits restore cars to original appearances

President: Brian Kotarksi
CFO: Anne Kotarksi
Fulfillment: Nathan Shipe
Credit Cards: AMEX; MasterCard
Catalog Cost: $5
Printing Information: 64 pages in 1 color on Glossy Stock
Press: Web Press
Binding: Saddle Stitched
Mailing List Information: Names for rent
List Manager: Bryan Kotarski
In Business: 30 years
Number of Employees: 10
Sales Volume: $910,000

560 Piper's Corvette Specialties
Piper's Auto Spec Inc
308 Water Street
PO Box 140
Vermilion, IL 61955   217-275-3743
                          800-637-6111
                      Fax: 217-275-3515
                parts@pipersauto.com
                www.pipersauto.com

Corvette parts

President: Jon T Piper
Credit Cards: AMEX; MasterCard
Catalog Cost: $3
Catalog Circulation: Mailed 1 time(s) per year to 20000
Printing Information: 24 pages in 1 color on Glossy Stock
Press: Web Press
Binding: Perfect Bound
In Business: 33 years

Number of Employees: 7
Sales Volume: $1 Million

561 Pirelli Armstrong Tire Corporation
Pirelli Tire NA LLC
100 Pirelli Drive Rome
Rome, GA 30161-7000   706-368-5800
                          800-747-3554
                      Fax: 706-368-5832
                www.us.pirelli.com

Farm tires

President: Hugh D Pace
Catalog Circulation: Mailed 1 time(s) per year
Number of Employees: 500

562 Pit Pal Products
Pit Pal Products
2009 Horizon Court
Zion, IL 60099   847-872-7257
                          888-748-7257
                      Fax: 847-872-7258
                sales@pitpal.com
                www.pitpal.com

Garage, shop and trailer organizers

Catalog Cost: Free
In Business: 32 years

563 Prestige Thunderbird
Reed Publication
10215 Greenleaf Avenue
Santa Fe Springs, CA 90670-3417 562-944-6237
                          800-423-4751
                      Fax: 562-941-8677
          tbirds@prestigethunderbird.com
               www.prestigethunderbird.com

Thunderbird parts

President: Richard Harbaugh
Catalog Cost: $2
Catalog Circulation: Mailed 1 time(s) per year to 4000
Printing Information: 96 pages in 2 colors on Glossy Stock
Press: Sheetfed Press
Binding: Perfect Bound
In Business: 40 years
Number of Employees: 9
Sales Volume: $1MM to $3MM

564 Quadratec Essentials Jeep Parts
Quadratec
1028 Saunders Lane
West Chester, PA 19380   610-701-3336
                          800-745-6037
                      Fax: 610-701-2402
                info@quadratec.com
                www.quadratec.com

Jeep parts and accessories

565 Racer Walsh Company
Racer Walsh Company
1849 Foster Drive
Jacksonville, FL 32216   904-721-2289
                          800-334-0151
               www.racerwalsh.zoovy.com

Ford auto parts and accessories

President: Eddie Miller
Credit Cards: AMEX; MasterCard; Visa
Catalog Cost: Free
Catalog Circulation: to 20000
Average Order Size: $245
Printing Information: 29 pages in 2 colors
Press: Sheetfed Press
Binding: Folded
In Business: 32 years
Number of Employees: 2
Sales Volume: $240,000

566   Racer Wholesale
Racer Parts Wholesale
411 Dorman
Indianapolis, IN 46202   317-639-0725
                                800-397-7815
                           Fax: 678-832-1100
info@racerpartswholesale.com
www.racerwholesale.com

Auto racing safety equipment

Credit Cards: MasterCard
In Business: 15 years
Number of Employees: 10
Sales Volume: $1MM to $3MM

567   Ranger Design
Ranger Design
20600 Clark-Graham
Baie D'Urfe, QC H9X-4B6   800-565-5321
www.rangerdesign.com

Van shelving, van storage bins, ladder racks, bulkhead partitions, storage systems

Marketing Manager: Yves L,veill,
Managing Director: Ron Cowie
Owner: Derek Cowie
Credit Cards: AMEX; MasterCard
Catalog Cost: Free
In Business: 29 years
Number of Employees: 200

568   Raybuck Autobody Parts
Raybuck Autobody Parts, LLC
1723 W. North Ave
Pittsburgh, PA 15233   814-938-5248
                                800-334-0230
                           Fax: 814-938-4250
service@raybuck.com
www.raybuck.com

Aftermarket autobody parts and accessories for pickups, vans, SUVs and Jeeps

President: Lisa Raybuck
Marketing Manager: Randy Raybuck
Credit Cards: MasterCard
Catalog Cost: $3
Catalog Circulation: Mailed 12 time(s) per year to 25M
Printing Information: 50 pages in 1 color on Matte Stock
Press: Web Press
Binding: Saddle Stitched
Mailing List Information: Names for rent
In Business: 29 years
Number of Employees: 6
Sales Volume: $1MM to $3MM

569   Regitar USA
Regitar USA, Inc.
2575 Container Dr
Montgomery, AL 36109-1004   334-244-1885
                           Fax: 334-244-1901
info@regitar.com
www.Regitar.Com

Power tools, auto parts, ignition moduler, ignition, voltage reulators, rectifiers, ignitions coils, pick-up coils, distributor caps, rotors, diode trio, solenoids, condensers and more

President: Yu-Tueng Tsai
CFO: Chau L Tsai
Marketing Manager: Leo Manni
Production Manager: Ken Jimmerson
Fulfillment: Andrea Naranjo
Buyers: Chau Lee Tsai, Power Tools
Catalog Cost: $5
Catalog Circulation: Mailed 12 time(s) per year to 5000
Average Order Size: $250
Printing Information: 80 pages in 2 colors on Matte Stock
Press: Web Press
Binding: Saddle Stitched
Mailing List Information: Names for rent
List Manager: Yu-Tueng Tsai
In Business: 16 years
Number of Employees: 25
Sales Volume: $1,000,000 - $5,000,000

570   Repco
Repco Inc.
6 Eves Drive
Marlton, NJ 08053   856-762-0172
                               800-822-9190
                          Fax: 800-424-9224
sales@repcoinc.com
www.repcoinc.com

A variety of automotive parts, supplies and accessories

President: John Lowlor
Credit Cards: AMEX; MasterCard; Visa
Catalog Cost: Free
Catalog Circulation: Mailed 2 time(s) per year
Printing Information: 25 pages in 2 colors on Newsprint
Press: Web Press
Binding: Saddle Stitched
In Business: 39 years
Number of Employees: 30
Sales Volume: $3MM to $5MM

571   Republic Auto Supply
Republic Auto Supply
PO Box 35069
Dallas, TX 75235-69   214-630-8571
                          Fax: 214-630-7940
www.republicautosupply.com

Automotive parts store

President: Jack M Cleaveland

572   Ron Francis Wiring
Wire Works
200 Keystone Road
Suite #1
Chester, PA 19013-1430   610-485-1981
                               800-292-1940
www.ronfrancis.com

Wiring harnesses, fuel injection harnesses, wiring aids, grounding lighting and accessories for race cars

Chairman: Ronald Francis
President: Scott Bowers
Marketing Manager: Connie Francis
Production Manager: Gary DuRoss
Catalog Cost: $2
Catalog Circulation: Mailed 1 time(s) per year
Printing Information: 60 pages
In Business: 34 years
Number of Employees: 12
Sales Volume: $1,000,000 - $5,000,000

573   SLP Performance Parts
SLP Performance Parts
39555 Schoolcraft Rd
Plymouth Township, MI 48170   732-349-2109
                               855-757-7373
                          Fax: 732-244-0867
www.slponline.com

Automotive supplies and parts

President: Edward Hamburger
Catalog Cost: $3
Printing Information: 52 pages in 4 colors on G
Mailing List Information: Names for rent
In Business: 28 years
Number of Employees: 75
Sales Volume: $10MM-$20MM

574   Scoggin Dickey Parts Center
5901 Spur 327
Lubbock, TX 79424   806-798-4108
                               800-456-0211
                          Fax: 806-798-4086
sdparts.com

Automotive performance parts

575   Simpson
Simpson
328 FM 306
New Braunfels, TX 78130   830-625-1774
                               800-654-7223
                          Fax: 830-625-3269
texassales@teamsimpson.com
www.simpsonraceproducts.com

Full range of automotive racing products

In Business: 45 years

576   Sinclair's
Sinclair's Impala Parts
508 Charming Road
Danville, VA 24541   434-685-2337
                          Fax: 434-685-3346
Info@impala-parts.com
www.impala-parts.com

Impala parts and accessories

Credit Cards: MasterCard
Catalog Cost: Free
Printing Information: 64 pages in 6 colors on Newsprint
Binding: Saddle Stitched
In Business: 20 years

577   Snap-On Tools
Snap-on Incorporated
2801 80th Street
Kenosha, WI 53141   877-762-7664
                               877-777-8455
store.snapon.com

Hand tools, auto tools

Chairman: Jack Michaels
President: Alan Biland
Marketing Manager: Andrew Ginger
Chief Information Officer: Jeanne Moreno
Vice President, Investor Relations: Leslie H. Kratcoski
leslie.h.kratcoski@snapon.com
Credit Cards: AMEX; MasterCard; Visa
Catalog Circulation: Mailed 1 time(s) per year
Printing Information: 800 pages in 4 colors
In Business: 96 years
Number of Employees: 295
Sales Volume: $51.90 MM

578   Speedway Motors Race and Street Rod Catalogs
Speedway Motors Inc
340 Victory Lane
Lincoln, NE 68528   402-323-3200
                               800-971-8411
                          Fax: 800-736-3733
sales@bluediamondclassics.com
www.speedwaymotors.com

Race car parts and accessories such as engine storage stands, radiators, carburetors and steering wheels

President: 'Speedy' Bill Smith
Credit Cards: AMEX; MasterCard
Catalog Cost: Free
Printing Information: 352 pages in 4 colors
In Business: 66 years
Number of Employees: 50
Sales Volume: $5.7 MM

579   Speedway Motors Street Catalog
Speedway Motors Inc
340 Victory Lane
Lincoln, NE 68528   402-323-3200
                               800-971-8411
                          Fax: 800-736-3733
sales@speedwaymotors.com
www.speedwaymotors.com

Street rod, classic and muscle car parts for cars from 1962 to 1985

President: Speedy Bill Smith
Credit Cards: AMEX; MasterCard
Printing Information: 336 pages in 4 colors
In Business: 66 years

580 Springfield Rod & Custom
Springfield Rod & Custom
219 Buxton Ave
Springfield, OH 45505-1339   937-323-1932
                                     800-752-9763
                                  Fax: 937-323-1973
                                  fredyerkey@att.net

Vintage auto parts and accessories
President: Larry Chaney
Sales Volume: Under $500M

581 Sprint & Midget Catalog
Speedway Motors Inc
340 Victory Lane
Lincoln, NE 68528   402-323-3200
                                     800-979-0122
                                  Fax: 800-736-3733
                                  sales@speedwaymotors.com
                                  www.speedwaymotors.com

Sprint and midget racing products
President: Speedy Bill Smith
Credit Cards: AMEX; MasterCard
Printing Information: 336 pages in 4 colors
In Business: 63 years

582 Stallard Chassis and Components
Stallard Chassis and Components
123 Sandy Drive
Sandy Brae Industrial Park
Newark, DE 19713   302-292-1800
                                  Fax: 302-292-1802
                                  markstalchas@aol.com
                                  www.stallardchassis.com

250cc micro and 600cc multi sprints, wings and wing sliders, fiberglass body parts, tires, wheels, splined rear assemblies, suspension components and more
President: Mark Stallard
Webmaster: Ben Shelton
Printing Information: 25 pages in 2 colors on Glossy Stock
Binding: Folded
In Business: 44 years

583 Steiner Tractor Parts
Steiner Tractor Parts
1660 S M-13
Lennon, MI 48449   810-621-3000
                                     800-234-3280
                                  Fax: 800-854-1373
                                  sales@steinertractor.com
                                  www.steinertractor.com

New replacement tractor parts: fenders, steering wheels, grills, emblems, maniforlds, battery boxes, magnetos
President: Daniel Steiner
VP: Jeniffer Steiner
Catalog Cost: $5
Printing Information: 482 pages
In Business: 38 years
Number of Employees: 28

584 Stencils & Stripes
Stencils & Stripes Unlimited, Inc.
1108 South Crescent
Park Ridge, IL 60068-4846   847-692-6893
                                  Fax: 847-692-6895
                                  info@stencilsandstripes.com
                                  www.stencilsandstripes.com

Factory decals and stripes
President: Ralph Greinke
Credit Cards: AMEX; MasterCard; Visa
Catalog Cost: $6
Catalog Circulation: to 5000
Printing Information: 60 pages in 1 color on Matte Stock
Press: Letterpress
Binding: Folded
Mailing List Information: Names for rent
In Business: 32 years
Number of Employees: 5
Sales Volume: $499,000

585 Stock Drive Products
Stock Drive Products / Sterling Instuume
2101 Jericho Turnpike
Box 5416
New Hyde Park, NY 11040-5416   516-328-3300
                                     800-819-8900
                                  Fax: 516-326-8827
                                  sdp-sisupport@sdp-si.com
                                  www.sdp-si.com

Engine and machine parts; small mechanical components
Marketing Manager: Herb Arum
Catalog Cost: Free
Catalog Circulation: Mailed 1 time(s) per year to 50m
Printing Information: 1200 pages in 2 colors on Glossy Stock
Press: Web Press
Binding: Perfect Bound
Mailing List Information: Names for rent
In Business: 50 years
Number of Employees: 350
Sales Volume: $5,000,000 - $10,000,000

586 Summit Racing Equipment
Summit Racing Equipment
PO Box 909
Akron, OH 44309-0909   330-630-3030
                                     800-230-3030
                                  Fax: 330-630-5333
                                  www.summitracingequipment.com

Performance gear, parts and accessories for street and off-road racing
President: Ray Tatko
Credit Cards: AMEX; MasterCard
Catalog Cost: Free
Printing Information: 364 pages
In Business: 28 years
Number of Employees: 175

587 Surplus Center
Surplus Center
1015 West O Street
Lincoln, NE 68528   800-488-3407
                                  Fax: 402-474-5198
                                  customerservice@surpluscenter.com
                                  www.surpluscenter.com

Automotive engines, hydraulics, power transmissions, and water pumps

588 TA Performance
16167 N. 81st Street
Scottsdale, AZ 85260   480-922-6807
                                  Fax: 480-922-6811
                                  taperf@aol.com
                                  www.taperformance.com

Performance parts, aluminum engine blocks

589 Tomco
Tomco, Inc.
7208A Weil Avenue
St Louis, MO 63119   314-646-5300
                                     800-325-9972
                                  www.tomco-inc.com

Fuel and emission control parts
Catalog Cost: Free
Catalog Circulation: Mailed 1 time(s) per year to 20M
Printing Information: 46 pages in 1 color
In Business: 45 years
Number of Employees: 70
Sales Volume: $10,000,000 - $25,000,000

590 Torque Tech
Torque Tech & Co., Inc.
2632 Marine Way
Mountain View, CA 94043   888-465-1454
                                  Fax: 229-242-5353
                                  www.torquetechexh.com

Header and manifold applications, performance exhaust systems

Credit Cards: MasterCard; Visa
In Business: 27 years

591 Troy Lee Designs
Troy Lee Designs
155 East Rincon Street
Corona, CA 92879-1328   951-371-5219
                                     800-239-6566
                                  Fax: 951-371-5272
                                  info@troyleedesigns.com
                                  www.troyleedesigns.com

Racing helmets for car races, motorcycle races, ATV races, etc.
President: Troy Lee
Marketing Manager: Greg Skibel, Sales Manager
Catalog Cost: $3
Catalog Circulation: to 30000
Printing Information: 124 pages in 4 colors on Glossy Stock
Press: Sheetfed Press
Binding: Perfect Bound
In Business: 30 years
Number of Employees: 35
Sales Volume: 10MM-20MM

592 True Choice
Truechoice Motorsports
352 W Olentangy St
Powell, OH 43065   614-799-9530
                                     800-388-8783
                                  Fax: 614-799-9532
                                  info@truechoice.com
                                  www.truechoice.com

Parts and accessories for auto racing
Credit Cards: AMEX; MasterCard; Visa
Catalog Cost: Free
Printing Information: 140 pages
In Business: 10 years
Number of Employees: 20

593 Tuff Country E-Z Ride Suspension
Tuff Country, Inc
4172 West 8370 South
West Jordan, UT 84088-5905   801-280-2777
                                     800-288-2190
                                  Fax: 801-280-2896
                                  customerservice@tuffcountry.com
                                  www.Tuffcountry.Com

Auto suspension lift kits, leveling kits, axle pivot brackets, leaf springs, shock absorbers, sharing and pitman arms
President: Troy Davis
Catalog Cost: $3
In Business: 27 years
Number of Employees: 18
Sales Volume: $10MM to $20MM

594 Two Brothers Racing
Two Brothers Racing
401 South Grand Ave.
Santa Ana, CA 92705-4102   714-550-6070
                                     800-211-2767
                                  Fax: 714-550-9661
                                  www.twobros.com

Full line of TBR exhaust systems, custom accessories, performance clothing and parts, Ferodo pads and rotors, Goodridge brake lines, D.I.D. chain
Chairman: Jeff Whitten
President: Craig Erion
Credit Cards: AMEX; MasterCard; Visa
Catalog Cost: Free
Printing Information: 215 pages
In Business: 29 years
Number of Employees: 5
Sales Volume: 5MM-10MM

595 Unlimited Products
Unlimited Products
8770 Caliente Road
Hesperia, CA 92344
760-948-0055
877-735-7772
Fax: 760-947-8333
NET55@aol.com
www.up22.com

Fiberglass hoods, scoops and body parts for race cars, trucks and street machines
Credit Cards: AMEX; MasterCard
Catalog Cost: Free
Printing Information: 24 pages
In Business: 34 years

596 VDO Automotive Instruments
United Speedometer Service
2179 Macbeth Place
PO Box 51957
Riverside, CA 92507-1314
951-742-7117
800-877-4798
Fax: 951-742-7113
info@speedometershop.com
www.speedometershop.com

Speedometers, temperature gauges, clocks, tachometers, etc., for automobiles
President: Richard Workman
Printing Information: 44 pages
Binding: Saddle Stitched
In Business: 49 years
Number of Employees: 20-5

597 VISTA
B&F System, Inc.
3920 S Walton Walker
Dallas, TX 75236-1510
214-333-2111
Fax: 214-333-1511
service@bnfusa.com
www.bnfusa.com

Apparel to auto supplies at wholesale prices.
President: John Meyer
CFO: Don Meyer
Marketing Manager: Steve Mallon
Production Manager: Donna Pirkle
Credit Cards: MasterCard; Visa; Discover
Catalog Cost: $1.8
Catalog Circulation: to 150M
Printing Information: 200 pages
In Business: 65 years
Number of Employees: 120

598 Vintage Model Catalog
IPD
11744 NE Ainsworth Circle
Portland, OR 97220
503-257-7500
800-444-6473
Fax: 503-257-7596
info@ipdusa.com
www.ipdusa.Com

Aftermarket Volvo and Subaru accessories
President: Scott Hart
scott@ipdusa.com
CFO: David Precechtil
david@ipdusa.com
Marketing Manager: Bryan Cotrell
bryan@ipdusa.com
Production Manager: Cameron Daline
cdaline@ipdusa.com
CEO: Sue Hart
Sue@ipdusa.com
General Manager: Chris Delano
chris@ipdusa.com
Purchasing Manager: Michael Bernardi
mbernardi@ipdusa.com
Credit Cards: AMEX; MasterCard; Visa
Catalog Cost: Free
Catalog Circulation: Mailed 4 time(s) per year
Average Order Size: $130
Printing Information: 84 pages in 4 colors on Glossy Stock
Press: Sheetfed Press
Binding: Saddle Stitched
Mailing List Information: Names for rent
In Business: 52 years

Number of Employees: 20-5
Sales Volume: $5,000,000 - $10,000,000

599 Warner Electric
Warner Electric
449 Gardner Street
South Beloit, IL 61080-1326
815-825-6544
800-825-6544
Fax: 815-389-2582
info@warnerelectric.com
www.warnerelectric.com

Electric brakes, clutches and various auto parts
President: Carl Christenson
Production Manager: Shelley Smith
In Business: 70 years
Number of Employees: 800

600 Whelen Engineering
Whelen
51 Winthrop Road
Chester, CT 06412-0684
860-526-9504
Fax: 860-526-4078
custserv@whelen.com
www.whelen.com

Visual and audible signaling products for vehicular applications
President: John Olson
Purchasing Manager: Norm Lowery
Catalog Cost: Free
Printing Information: 68 pages
In Business: 65 years
Number of Employees: 400
Sales Volume: $50,000,000 - $100,000,00

601 Willys & Jeep Parts Catalog
The Jeepsterman, Inc.
238 Ramtown Greenville Rd
Howell, NJ 07731-2788
732-458-3966
Fax: 732-458-9289
JeepstermanInc@AOL.com
www.thejeepsterman.com

Willys and Jeep parts 1942 to present - all hard to find parts, manuals, rubber parts, exhaust systems, sheet metal tops, side curtains, rugs, mats, etc
President: Morris Ratner
Marketing Manager: Shelley Ramhurst
Catalog Cost: Free
Catalog Circulation: Mailed 1 time(s) per year to 2000
Mailing List Information: Names for rent
In Business: 30 years
Number of Employees: 10-J
Sales Volume: Under $500M

602 Wilmar Corporation
Wilmar Corporation
PO Box 88259
Suite 115
Tukwila, WA 98138-2628
425-970-6970
800-426-1262
Fax: 206-394-2130
tools@wilmarcorp.com
www.wilmarcorp.com

Hand and air tools, car/truck covers, specialty and heavy duty equipment
President: William Bellando
International Marketing Manager: Mike Cantalini
Buyers: Dan Cantalini
Catalog Cost: Free
List Manager: Mike Cantalini
In Business: 43 years
Number of Employees: 25

603 Wire Works Catalog
Ron Francis Wiring
200 Keystone Road
Suite 1
Chester, PA 19013
610-485-1981
800-292-1940
Fax: 610-485-1933
www.ronfrancis.com

Wiring systems for automotives and boats
Chairman: Ronald Francis
Production Manager: Gary DuRoss

604 Wood & Parts for Classic Pickups
Bruce Horkey's Wood and Parts
46284 440th Street
Windom, MN 56101-3310
507-831-5625
Fax: 507-831-0280
sales@horkeyswoodandparts.com
www.horkeyswoodandparts.com

Wood & metal parts for customizing and restoring 1928-current pickup trucks, complete pickup boxes & boxsides, front panels, tailgates & covers, running boards, and hardwood
President: Bruce Horkey
Production Manager: Ted Horkey
Credit Cards: MasterCard; Visa
Catalog Cost: $4
Catalog Circulation: Mailed 1 time(s) per year to 4000
Average Order Size: $350
Printing Information: 41 pages in 4 colors on Glossy Stock
Press: Sheetfed Press
Binding: Saddle Stitched
Mailing List Information: Names for rent
In Business: 35 years
Number of Employees: 7
Sales Volume: $500M to $1MM

Aviation Products
Accessories

605 Aircraft Spruce & Specialty Company
Aircraft Spruce West
225 Airport Circle
Corona, CA 92880
951-372-9555
877-477-7823
Fax: 880-329-3020
www.aircraftspruce.com

Aircraft instruments and accessories, especially for ultralights, kitplane and homebuilts
President: Jim Irwin
CFO: Debbie Moss
Marketing Manager: Rob Irwin
Vice President: Nancy Irwin
Director of Operations - West: Tom Marracci
Director of Operations - East: Don Arrington
Credit Cards: AMEX; MasterCard
Catalog Cost: Free
Catalog Circulation: Mailed 1 time(s) per year
Printing Information: 1124 pages in 4 colors
Mailing List Information: Names for rent
In Business: 52 years
Number of Employees: 150
Sales Volume: 70M

606 Aircraft Tool Supply Company
Aircraft Tool Supply Company
1000 Old US 23
PO Box 370
Oscoda, MI 48750-370
989-739-1447
800-248-0638
Fax: 989-739-1448
info@aircraft-tool.com
www.aircraft-tool.com

Sheet metal tools, riveting equipment and aircraft engine repair and maintenance tools
President: Desmond Lynch
Production Manager: Bryan MacDonald
General Manager: Gaye Pappas

Catalog Cost: Free
Printing Information: 176 pages
In Business: 41 years
Number of Employees: 30
Sales Volume: $6 MM

607 All About Dance
All About Dance

800-775-0578
info@allaboutdance.com
www.allaboutdance.com

Name brand dance clothing, shoes, and accessories

Catalog Cost: Free
In Business: 18 years

608 Areoflash Signal
Areoflash Signal
1715 W Carroll Avenue
Chicago, IL 60612-2503
312-733-3513
800-322-2052
Fax: 312-733-0192
info@AeroFlash.com
www.aeroflash.com

Strobe lights, accessories for school buses, and warning systems

President: Cari Murray
CEO: Cari Murray
In Business: 120 years

609 Aviation Book Company
225 Airport Circle
Suite C
Corona, CA 92880
951-372-9555
877-477-7823
Fax: 951-372-0555
sales@aviationbook.com
www.aircraftspruce.com

Books and gifts for that aviation lover in your house

Owner: Nancy Griffith
General Manager: Kristin Potter
Credit Cards: AMEX; MasterCard
Catalog Cost: Free
Catalog Circulation: Mailed 3 time(s) per year to 12000
Printing Information: 32 pages in 4 colors on Matte Stock
Press: Web Press
Binding: Saddle Stitched
Mailing List Information: Names for rent
In Business: 29 years
Number of Employees: 7
Sales Volume: 1.6M

610 Aviator's Store
The Aviator's Store
225 Airport Circle
Suite C
Corona, CA 92880-3804
951-372-9555
877-477-7823
Fax: 951-372-0555
sales@aviationbook.com
www.aircraftspruce.com

Books, apparel, gifts and holiday items

Owner: Nancy Griffith
General Manager: Kristin Potter
In Business: 29 years
Number of Employees: 7
Sales Volume: 1.6M

611 Back In The Saddle
Back In The Saddle
P.O. Box 3336
Chelmsford, MA 00182-0936
877-756-5068
800-865-2478
Fax: 800-866-3235
help@BackInTheSaddle.com
www.backinthesaddle.com

Horseback riding gear, clothing, jewelry, and accessories for horse lovers

Catalog Cost: Free
In Business: 22 years

612 Bag Making Accessories
H.A. Kidd & Co
5 Northline Road
Toronto, ON M4B-3P2
416-364-6451
800-387-1753
Fax: 888-236-8204
info1@hakidd.com
www.hakidd.com

Supplies and tools for handmade bags and accessories

Marketing Manager: Lynda Macham
VP, Chief Operating Officer: Jim Thielen
Controller, Human Resources: Amir Mirza
Credit Cards: MasterCard
Catalog Cost: Free
Catalog Circulation: Mailed 1 time(s) per year
Printing Information: 32 pages in 4 colors on Matte Stock
In Business: 93 years
Sales Volume: $20MM to $50MM

613 Betty's Attic
Betty's Attic
PO Box 25600
Bradenton, FL 34206-5600
941-747-5566
800-311-0733
Fax: 800-551-4406
customerservice@bettysattic.com
www.bettysattic.com

Nostalgic items and collectibles from the 1920s to the 1970s

President: Ralph Hoenle
CFO: David Crofoot
Marketing Manager: Kim Boyd
Buyers: Tom Ronzi
Catalog Cost: Free
Catalog Circulation: Mailed 52 time(s) per year
Printing Information: 64 pages
Mailing List Information: Names for rent
List Manager: Carolyn Foley
In Business: 101 years
Number of Employees: 100
Sales Volume: $500M to $1MM

614 Brahmin
Brahmin USA
77 Alden Road
Fairhaven, MA 00271
508-994-4000
800-229-2428
www.brahmin.com

Handbags, wallets, bracelets, and other accessories

Catalog Cost: Free
In Business: 32 years

615 Buggies Unlimited
Buggies Unlimited
3510 Port Jacksonville Pkwy
Jacksonville, FL 32226
888-444-9994
Fax: 888-444-6364
support@buggiesunlimited.com
www.buggiesunlimited.com

Golf cart parts and accessories

Catalog Cost: Free

616 California Power Systems
California Power Systems
225 Airport Circle Drive
Corona, CA 92880-3213
510-357-2403
800-247-9653
Fax: 951-372-0555
info@800-airwolf.com
www.cps-parts.com/

Ultralight and sport aircraft parts and accessories

President: Jim Irwin
Credit Cards: AMEX; MasterCard
Catalog Cost: $6.95

Printing Information: 160 pages
In Business: 34 years

617 Chief Aircraft
Chief Aircraft Inc.
Grants Pass Airport
1301 Brookside Blvd.
Grants Pass, OR 97526-7209
541-476-6605
800-447-3408
Fax: 541-479-4431
info@chiefaircraft.com
www.chiefaircraft.com

Electronic aviation equipment and accessories, all aircraft parts for privately owned planes

President: Dana Blix
Finance Executive: Sandy Anderson
Vice President: Ventura Rigol
Credit Cards: AMEX; MasterCard
Catalog Cost: Free
Printing Information: on Glossy Stock
In Business: 28 years
Number of Employees: 23
Sales Volume: 2.8M

618 Gulf Coast Avionics Products
Gulf Coast Avionics Corporation
3650 Drane Field Road
Lakeland Linder Regional Airport
Lakeland, FL 33811
863-709-9714
800-474-9714
Fax: 863-709-9736

Catalog of aircraft and aero activities, offering avionics and communications equipment, specializes in ready-to-install custom instrument panels for kit planes

Marketing Manager: Craig Jaroski
VP: Rick Garcia
Credit Cards: AMEX; MasterCard; Visa
Catalog Cost: Free
In Business: 29 years
Number of Employees: 22
Sales Volume: 2.3M

619 Kipp
Kipp Toys
491 W. Muskegon Drive
Greenfield, IN 46140
800-428-1153
Fax: 800-832-5477
www.kipptoys.com

Toys, novelties, and party supplies

Catalog Cost: Free
In Business: 134 years

620 Lockwood Aviation Supply
Lockwood Aviation Supply
1 Lockwood Lane
Sebring, FL 33870
863-655-5100
800-527-6829
Fax: 863-655-6225
Tisha@lockwood.aero
www.lockwood-aviation.com

Parts and accessories for light sport aircraft

President: Phillip Lockwood
General Manager: Tisha Lockwood
Tisha@lockwood.aero
Credit Cards: AMEX; MasterCard; Visa
Catalog Cost: Free
Printing Information: 205 pages
In Business: 25 years
Number of Employees: 3
Sales Volume: 310K

621 Magic Cabin
Magic Cabin
7021 Wolftown-Hood Rd.
Madison, VA 22727
888-623-3655
www.magiccabin.com

Children's toys, games, craft kits, and other accessories

622 McFarlane Aviation Products
696 East 1700 Road
Baldwin City, KS 66006 785-594-2741
866-920-2741
Fax: 785-594-3922
www.mcfarlane-aviation.com

Aviation products

Marketing Manager: Autumn Eckman
Tech Support: Fred McClenahan

623 Mountain High Equipment & Supply Company
Mountain High E&S Co.
2244 SE Airport Way
Suite 100
Redmond, OR 97756-9606 541-923-4100
800-468-8185
Fax: 541-923-4141
sales@mhoxygen.com
www.Mhoxygen.Com

Custom carry on or built in aviation oxygen systems

President: Patrick McLaughlin
Catalog Cost: Free
Printing Information: 42 pages
Mailing List Information: Names for rent
In Business: 26 years
Sales Volume: $3MM to $5MM

624 PS Engineering
PS Engineering, Inc.
9800 Martel Road
Lenoir City, TN 37772 865-988-9800
800-427-2376
Fax: 865-988-6619
contact@ps-engineering.com
www.ps-engineering.com

Aircraft audio selector panels and components, intercoms, digital recorders, wire harnesses and modified headsets

President: Mark Scheuer
Credit Cards: AMEX; MasterCard; Visa
Catalog Cost: Free
Printing Information: 12 pages
In Business: 30 years

625 Pacific Coast Avionics
Pacific Coast Avionics
Aurora State Airport
22783 Airport Road
Aurora, OR 97002 503-678-6242
800-353-0370
Fax: 503-678-6292
info@pca.aero
www.pacificcoastavionics.com

Avionics instruments, communications equipment and accessories, kitpanels and GPS gear

VP/COO: Dewey Conroy
dewey@pca.aero
Sales Team Leader: Randy Wright
randay@pca.aero
Sales: Sergio Gemoets
sergio@pca.aero
Credit Cards: AMEX; MasterCard
Catalog Cost: Free
In Business: 24 years
Number of Employees: 19
Sales Volume: 2M

626 Poly Fiber Aircraft Coatings
Consolidated Aircraft Coatings
P.O. Box 3129
Riverside, CA 92519 951-684-4280
800-362-3490
Fax: 951-684-0518
www.polyfiber.com

Aircraft fabric covering and painting

Credit Cards: MasterCard; Visa
Catalog Cost: Free
Printing Information: 151 pages
In Business: 40 years

Number of Employees: 20
Sales Volume: $3MM to $5MM

627 Sahalie
Bluestem Brands, Inc.
7075 Flying Cloud Drive
Eden Prairie, MN 55344 877-718-7902
www.sahalie.blair.com

Casual clothing, shoes & accessories for men and women

President: Steve Nave
CFO: Pete Michielutti
EVP, COO, & Chief Digital Officer: Vince Jones
EVP & President of Credit Services: Jim Slavik
Credit Cards: AMEX; MasterCard
Catalog Cost: Free
In Business: 46 years
Sales Volume: $50MM to $100MM

628 Sarasota Avionics
120 Airport Avenue West
Venice, FL 34285 941-360-6877
866-539-4078
Fax: 941-360-6878
support@sarasotaavionics.com
sarasotaavionics.com

Avionics and other aviation products

President: Kirk Fryar
VP/ Sales Manager: Ryan Van Kirk

629 Selkirk Aviation
3377 W. Industrial Lp
Coeur d'Alene, ID 83815 208-664-9589
800-891-7687
Fax: 208-665-9597
selkirkav@selkirk-aviation.com
www.selkirk-aviation.com

Fiberglass interior parts, extended baggage kits, glareshields, nose bowls and composite cowling for Cessna airplanes

630 Shillcraft
Shillcraft
P.O. Box 325
Bonsall, CA 92003 951-674-4307
Fax: 951-674-4325
support@shillcraft.com
www.shillcraft.com

Latch hook kits, materials, and accessories

Catalog Cost:
In Business: 64+ years

631 Sigtronics Corporation
178 East Arrow Highway
San Dimas, CA 91773 909-305-9399
Fax: 909-305-9499
info@sigtronics.com
www.sigtronics.com

Aviation communication products

632 Stampendous
Stampendous, Inc.
1122 N Kraemer Pl,
Anaheim, CA 92806 714-688-0288
877-412-7467
stamp@stampendous.com
www.stampendous.com

Rubber stamps, stickers, and other paper crafting accessories

Owner/CEO: Fran Seiford
Catalog Cost:
Printing Information: 104 pages
In Business: 30+ years

633 Univair Aircraft Corporation
2500 Himalaya Road
Aurora, CO 80011 303-375-8882
888-433-5433
Fax: 303-375-8888
info@univair.com
www.univair.com

Parts and supplies for general aviation

634 Wick's Aircraft Supply Catalog
Wick's Aircraft Supply
410 Pine Street
Highland, IL 62249 618-654-7447
800-221-9425
Fax: 888-440-5727
info@wicksaircraft.com
www.wicksaircraft.com

Aircraft kits, parts and accessories

President: Scott Wick
General Manager: Eric Cleveland
Credit Cards: AMEX; MasterCard; Visa
Catalog Circulation: to 2000
Printing Information: 250 pages
In Business: 288 years
Number of Employees: 17
Sales Volume: 3.50M

635 Yankee Candle Catalog
The Yankee Candle, Company, Inc.
16 Yankee Candle Way
PO Box 110
South Deerfield, MA 00137-0110 413-665-8306
800-243-1776
info@yankeecandle.com
www.yankeecandle.com

Candles and accessories

Catalog Cost: Free

Aircraft

636 Aerospace Composite Products
ACP Composites
78 Lindbergh Ave
Livermore, CA 94551 925-443-5900
800-811-2009
Fax: 925-443-5901
info@acp-composites.com
www.acpsales.com

Composite tubes, panels and rods for the medical, automotive, aerospace and defense industries

President: George Sparr
CFO: Lori Herren
Sales: Justin Sparr
jsparr@acpsales.com
Customer Service: Jessica Sparr
jrsparr@acpsales.com
In Business: 30 years
Sales Volume: $5MM to $10MM

637 Avionics International Supply
Aerospace Products International
3778 Distriplex Dr. N.
Memphis, TN 38118 901-365-3470
888-274-2497
Fax: 901-375-2626
sales@apiworldwide.com
order.apiworldwide.com

Electronic installation accessories for aviation

President: Andy Trosper
CFO: Jim Howell
Vice President- Sales & Marketing: Denis Boucher
Vice President: Eric Waller
Printing Information: 4 pages

638 Barnett Rotor Craft
Barnett Rotor Craft
4307 Olivehurst Ave
Olivehurst, CA 95961-4706   530-742-7416
Fax: 530-743-6866

Helicopter and gyroplane kits
President: Jerrie Barnett
Credit Cards: MasterCard; Visa
Catalog Cost: Free
In Business: 51 years
Sales Volume: $1MM to $3MM

639 Brown Aviation Tool Supply
Brown Aviation Tool Supply
2536 S.E. 15th Street
Oklahoma, OK 73129   405-688-6888
800-587-3883
Fax: 405-688-6555
information@browntool.com
www.browntool.com

Browntool is aviation tool supply company. Product Line includes Abrasives / Wire Brushes, Air Tools, Borescopes Bucking Bars, Bushing Tools, Clamps, Clecos, Cherry/Huck Tools, Carbide Burrs, etc.,
Credit Cards: AMEX; MasterCard
Catalog Cost:
Printing Information: 180 pages
In Business: 24 years

640 CGS Aviation
CGS Aviation
8970 Hunter Road
Grand Bay, AL 36541-5210   251-454-0579
cgsaviation.danny@gmail.com
www.cgsaviation.com

Ultra light and light aircraft used for recreation and utility
President: Charles Slusarczyk
Credit Cards: MasterCard; Visa
Catalog Cost: $10
Mailing List Information: Names for rent
In Business: 41 years
Number of Employees: 5
Sales Volume: $5,000,000

641 Glass Goose Catalog
Quikkit Inc
9002 Summer Glen
Dallas, TX 75243-7445   214-349-0462
Fax: 214-349-0462
www.glassgoose.com

Catalog of aircraft and aero activities, offering aircraft kits-fixed wing powered, specializes in two-place amphibians
President: Tom Scott
Sec/Treasury: Toni Scott
Credit Cards: MasterCard; Visa
Catalog Cost: $25
In Business: 21 years
Number of Employees: 5
Sales Volume: 590K

642 Grove Aircraft Landing Gear Systems
Grove Aircraft Landing Gear Systems
1800 Joe Crosson Drive
El Cajon, CA 92020   619-562-1268
Fax: 619-562-3274
www.groveaircraft.com

Grove Aircraft can provide a complete custom landing gear, ready to bolt on, designed for individual airplane. Product line includes designs, wheels and brakes, landind gear and accessories

643 Leading Edge Air Foils
Leading Edge Air Foils
1216 North Road
PO Box 231
Lyons, WI 53148   262-763-4087
800-532-3462
Fax: 262-763-1920
info@leadingedge-airfoils.com
www.leadingedge-airfoils.com

Catalog of ultralight and aero activities, offering aircraft kits-fixed wing powered, specializes in one and two-place open-cockpit biplane
President: Bill Reed
CFO: Mary Myers
Catalog Cost: Free
Printing Information: 132 pages
Mailing List Information: Names for rent
In Business: 36 years
Number of Employees: 8
Sales Volume: 910K

644 Quad City Ultralight Aircraft
Quad City Ultralight Aircraft Corp.
PO Box 370
Moline, IL 61266-370   309-764-3515
Fax: 309-762-3920
qcukaren@aol.com
www.Quadcitychallenger.Com

Aircraft and aero activities, offering aircraft kits-fixed wing powered, specializing in one- and two-place high-wing aircraft
President: Dave Goulet
VP: William Ehlers
Credit Cards: AMEX; MasterCard
Catalog Cost: $12
In Business: 29 years
Number of Employees: 12
Sales Volume: $1.02 MM

645 Ram Aircraft Parts Catalog
RAM Aircraft
7505 Karl May Drive
P.O. Box 5219
Waco, TX 76708   254-752-8381
Fax: 254-752-3307
www.ramaircraft.com

Airplane products and services to professional maintenance facilities and owners of piston-engine aircraft.
In Business: 39 years

646 Robinson Helicopter
Robinson Helicopter company
2901 Airport Dr
Torrance, CA 90505-6115   310-539-0508
Fax: 310-539-5198
pr@robinsonheli.com
www.Robinsonheli.Com

Catalog of aircraft and aero activities, offering aircraft kits-helicopters and gyroplanes, specializing in one-place helicopters
President: Kurt Robinson
CFO: Tim Goetz
Production Manager: Wayne Walden
Director of Sales & Marketing: Terry Hane
Public Relations: Lorretta Conley
pr@robinsonheli.com
Catalog Cost: Free
In Business: 42 years
Number of Employees: 970
Sales Volume: 76.4M

647 Sporty's Pilot Shop
Sportsman's Market Inc.
Clermont County/Sporty's Airport
2001 Sporty's Drive
Batavia, OH 45103   513-735-9000
800-776-7897
Fax: 800-543-8633
csmgr@sportys.com
www.sportys.com

Headsets, intercoms, flight computers, aviation charts, logbooks, radio's and scanners, books and DVD's
Chairman: Hal Shevers
President: Michael Wolf
CFO: Daniel Robinson
Credit Cards: MasterCard; Visa
Catalog Cost: Free
In Business: 50 years
Number of Employees: 172
Sales Volume: 14.4M

648 Starduster Catalog
Air Craft Spruce & Specialty Company
PO Box 4000
225 Airport Circle
Corona, CA 92880-4000   800-861-3192
877-477-7823
Fax: 951-372-0555
info@aircraftspruce.com
www.aircraftspruce.com

Aircraft and aero activities, offering aircraft kits-fixed wing powered, specializes in one and two-place biplanes
President: Jim Irwin
CFO: Nanci Irwin
Credit Cards: AMEX; MasterCard; Visa
In Business: 58 years
Number of Employees: 150

649 US Industrial Tool
US Industrial Tool & Supply Company
14083 S. Normandie Ave
Gardena, CA 90249   310-464-8400
800-521-7394
Fax: 310-464-8880
info@ustool.com
www.ustool.com

Aircraft tools, hand tools and sheetmetal tools
President: Mark Marinovich
Founder: William Marinovich
Credit Cards: MasterCard
Catalog Cost: Free
Catalog Circulation: to 30m
Printing Information: 188 pages in 4 colors on Glossy Stock
Binding: Saddle Stitched
Mailing List Information: Names for rent
In Business: 59 years
Number of Employees: 47
Sales Volume: $5,000,000 - $10,000,000

650 Van's Aircraft Accessories
Van's Aircraft, Inc.
14401 Keil Road NE
Aurora, OR 97002-9467   503-678-6545
Fax: 503-678-6560
info@vansaircraft.com
www.Vansaircraft.Com

Catalog of aircraft and aero activities, offering aircraft kits-fixed wing powered, specializes in one- and two-place low-wing aircraft
Chairman: Richard VanGrunsven
President: Scott Risan
Credit Cards: MasterCard; Visa
Catalog Cost: Free
In Business: 43 years
Sales Volume: $20MM to $50MM

651 WAG Aero Group
Wag-Aero
1216 North Road
Lyons, WI 53148   262-763-9586
800-558-6868
Fax: 262-763-7595
wagaero-sales@wagaero.com
www.wagaero.com

Aircraft.
Chairman: William E Read
President: Mary M Meyers
Catalog Circulation: to 600M

Printing Information: 124 pages
In Business: 50 years
Number of Employees: 35
Sales Volume: 6.4M

652   Zenith Aircraft Catalog
Zenith Aircraft Company
1881 Airport Road
Mexico Memorial Airport
Mexico, MO 65265-650   573-581-9000
                      Fax: 573-581-0011
                      info@zenithair.com
                      www.zenithair.com

Catalog of aircraft and aero activities, offering aircraft kits-fixed wing powered, specializes in two-place low- and high-wing aircraft

President: Chris Heintz
Credit Cards: MasterCard; Visa
Catalog Cost: $35
In Business: 22 years
Number of Employees: 18
Sales Volume: 1M

Pilot Safety & Equipment

653   EV Roberts & Associates
E.V. Roberts
18027 Bishop Avenue
Carson, CA 90746-4019   310-204-6159
                      800-374-3872
                      Fax: 310-202-7247
                      info@evroberts.com
                      evroberts.com

Epoxies, silicones, urethanes and adhesive coatings

President: Ronald Cloud
Credit Cards: AMEX; MasterCard
Number of Employees: 62
Sales Volume: $10MM to $20MM

654   Gibson & Barnes Flight Suits
Gibson & Barnes
1900 Weld Blvd
#140
El Cajon, CA 92020   619-440-2700
                      800-748-6693
                      Fax: 619-440-4618
                      store@ombps.com
                      www.gibson-barnes.com

High-quality, made-to-order flightsuits, uniforms, leather jackets and flying helmets for aviation, emergency medicine, and law enforcement

President: James A Wegge
Marketing Manager: Dan Longbrake
Catalog Circulation: to Weekl
In Business: 37 years

655   King School
King School
3840 Calle Fortunada
San Diego, CA 92123-1825   858-541-2200
                      800-854-1001
                      Fax: 858-541-2201
                      www.kingschools.com

Aviation education related products

President: Dave Jackson
CFO: Jim MacKay
Vice President of Operations/ CFO

Baby Products
Accessories

656   ABaby
A Baby Inc.
1958-59th Street
Brooklyn, NY 11204   877-552-2229
                      Fax: 718-972-0397
                      info@ababy.com
                      www.ababy.com

Nursery furniture, bedding, accessories, cradles, bassinets, gifts toys, and decor.

President: Issac Greenfeld
Catalog Cost: Free
Printing Information: 46 pages
In Business: 13 years
Number of Employees: 16
Sales Volume: $1,000,000

657   Baby Bunz & Company
Baby Bunz & Company
PO Box 113
Lynden, WA 98264   360-354-1320
                      800-676-4559
                      Fax: 360-354-1203
                      info@babybunz.com
                      www.babybunz.com

Diapering, baby care, baby clothing, toys, books and mother care

President: Carynia Van Buren
Credit Cards: MasterCard
Catalog Cost: $1.00
Average Order Size: $75
Printing Information: 32 pages in 4 colors on Matte Stock
Press: Web Press
Binding: Saddle Stitched
Mailing List Information: Names for rent
In Business: 24 years
Number of Employees: 4

658   Baby Works
Oregon Litho Print
PO Box 91268
Portland, OR 97231   503-224-4696
                      800-422-2910
                      customerservice@babyworks.com
                      www.babyworks.com

Eco-friendly diapers, diaper systems and accessories, baby clothes, nursing items

President: Paula DeVore
Credit Cards: MasterCard; Visa
Catalog Circulation: to 10000
Printing Information: 40 pages
Binding: Saddle Stitched
In Business: 20 years

659   Babystyle
Right Start
2001 N Sepulveda Blvd
Manhattan Beach, CA 90266   310-939-1147
                      888-856-8004
                      www.rightstart.com

Specialty maternity and baby clothing, gifts and toys

President: Laurie McCartney
Credit Cards: AMEX; MasterCard
Catalog Cost: Free
Catalog Circulation: Mailed 4 time(s) per year to 300M
Average Order Size: $100
Printing Information: 48 pages in 4 colors
In Business: 29 years

660   Chasing Fireflies
Chasing Fireflies
5568 West Chester Rd
West Chester, OH 45069   206-574-4500
                      888-700-9474
                      Fax: 800-989-4510
                      customerservice@chasing-fireflies.com
                      www.chasing-fireflies.com

Children's, newborn and infant's clothes, toys and accessories

President: Dina Alhadeff
Co-Owner: Lori Liddle
Co-Owner: Amy Grealish
Credit Cards: AMEX; MasterCard
Catalog Cost: Free
Number of Employees: 100
Sales Volume: $10 Million

661   Company Kids
The Company Store
500 Company Store Road
La Crosse, WI 54601-4477   800-323-8000
                      Fax: 800-238-0271
                      custserv@thecompanystore.com
                      www.companykids.com

Great prices on quality baby bedding

President: John Schomer
Vice President/Treasurer: Edward O'Brien
Credit Cards: AMEX; MasterCard; Visa
In Business: 104 years

662   Fat Brain Toys
Fat Brain Toys, LLC
1405 N. 205th Street
Ste 120
Elkhorn, NE 68022   402-779-3181
                      800-590-5987
                      Fax: 402-779-3253
                      cs@fatbraintoys.com
                      www.fatbraintoys.com

Open-ended toys, gifts and games that educate and entertain

CFO: Dean Giesselmann
Co-Founder: Mark Carson
Co-Founder: Karen Carson
Credit Cards: AMEX; MasterCard
Catalog Cost: Free
Printing Information: 30 pages in 4 colors on Glossy Stock
Press: Sheetfed Press
Binding: Folded
In Business: 12 years
Number of Employees: 100-
Sales Volume: $ 5-10 Million

663   Fisher-Price
Fisher-Price
636 Girard Avenue
East Aurora, NY 14052   716-687-3000
                      Fax: 716-687-3636
                      customerservice@fisher-pricestore.com
                      www.fisher-price.com

Toys, layette items

Chairman: Christopher A. Sinclair
President: Margaret Georgiadis
CFO: Joseph J. Euteneuer
Chief Operating Officer: Richard Dickson
Chief Technology Officer: Sven Gerjets
Chief Supply Chain Officer: Peter D. Gubbons
Credit Cards: AMEX; MasterCard; Visa
Catalog Cost: Free
Catalog Circulation: Mailed 5 time(s) per year
Printing Information: 41 pages in 4 colors on Glossy Stock
Press: Web Press
Binding: Saddle Stitched
In Business: 87 years
Number of Employees: 830
Sales Volume: $47.8 MM

664   Garnet Hill
Garnet Hill Inc
231 Main Street
Franconia, NH 03580   603-823-5545
                      800-870-3513
                      Fax: 888-842-9696
                      www.garnethill.com

Quality natural fabric baby clothing and linens, maternity clothes

President: Russ Gaitskill
CFO: Brian Gowen
Buyers: Diane Brush
Credit Cards: AMEX; MasterCard
Catalog Cost: Free
Catalog Circulation: Mailed 7 time(s) per year
Average Order Size: $190
Printing Information: 120 pages in 4 colors on Glossy Stock
Press: Web Press
Binding: Saddle Stitched
Mailing List Information: Names for rent
In Business: 41 years

Number of Employees: 175
Sales Volume: $ 11 Million

665 JC Penney Baby Book
JC Penney
PO Box 8178
Manchester, CT 06040-1463   972-431-3400
                                         800-842-9470
jcpinvestorrelations@jcpenney.com
                                www.jcpenney.com

Baby clothes, furniture and accessories, including cribs, bedding, matresses, safety items, car seats, strollers and swings

CFO: Edward Record
Marketing Manager: Debra Berman
Chief Executive Officer: Mike Ullman
EVP, General Counsel and Secretary: Janet Dhillon
EVP, Chief Information Officer: Scott Laverty
Credit Cards: AMEX; MasterCard; Visa
Printing Information: 50 pages

666 Koo Koo Bear Kids
Koo Koo Bear Kids, Inc
12060 Etris Road
Roswell, GA 30075   770-771-5665
                                   800-475-6909
                           Fax: 770-998-3136
www.kookoobearkids.com

Children, nursery and baby furniture, room decor, bedding, lighting and accessories

President: Tara Mediate
In Business: 11 years

667 Land of Nod
8135 River Drive
Morton Grove, IL 60053   800-933-9904
                                   Fax: 847-656-4750
customerservice@landofnod.com
                                www.landofnod.com

Furniture, beding, gear, toys, books and holiday decorations

668 Little Tikes Catalog
Little Tikes
2180 Barlow Road
Hudson, OH 44236   330-656-1348
                                   800-321-0183
                           Fax: 330-287-2864
www.littletikes.com

Riding toys, play toys, funiture and outdoor playground furniture

Production Manager: Bill Singer
Executive Vice President: Tom Fish
Operations Director: William Holcomb
In Business: 40 years
Sales Volume: Under $500,000

669 Mother-Ease Cloth Diapers
Mother-Ease Inc
6391 Walmore Road
Niagara Falls, NY 14304-1613   905-988-5188
                                       800-416-1475
                               Fax: 905-988-1110
diapers@mother-ease.com
                                www.mother-ease.com

Offers soft, convienient, leak free cloth diaper systems

President: Ricky Froese
Founder/Owner: Erika Froese
Owner: Rick Froese
Credit Cards: AMEX; MasterCard; Visa
Catalog Cost: Free
Mailing List Information: Names for rent
In Business: 24 years

670 Right Start
LMC Right Start
4643 S Ulster Street
Suite 1200
Denver, CO 80237   720-974-8198
                                  888-856-8004
                          www.rightstart.com

Children's books, clothing, furniture, car seats and strollers

President: Chris Seahorn
chris.seahorn@rightstart.com
CFO: Scott Henry
VP Operations: Gigi Healy
Credit Cards: AMEX; MasterCard
Catalog Cost: Free
Number of Employees: 80
Sales Volume: $5 million

Clothing

671 Acacia
Acacia
PO Box 8310
West Chester, OH 45069-8310   800-944-0474
customerservice@acacialifestyle.com
                                www.acacialifestyle.com

Clothing, shoes, jewelry, accessories, home decor and garden sculptures

President: Mark Stevens
CEO: Miguel Penella
Rozanne Hakala
Catalog Cost: Free
Printing Information: 47 pages in 4 colors on Glossy Stock
Binding: Saddle Stitched

672 Arhaus Jewels
Arhaus Jewels
7700 Northfield Rd
Walton Hills, OH 44146   877-857-4158
                            www.arhausjewels.com

Jewelry, clothing, accessories, and footwear

Catalog Cost: Free
In Business: 25+ years

673 Baby News
Baby News
6909 Las Positas Rd
Suite A
Livermore, CA 94550   925-245-1370
                                   Fax: 925-245-1376
                           www.babynewsonline.com

A complete children's catalog including furniture, bedding, layette, car seats, strollers and much more

Executive Vice President: William Cartan

674 Back in the Saddle
Back In The Saddle
2 BITS TRAIL
PO Box 3336
Chelmsford, MA 00182-0936   800-865-2478
                                    877-756-5068
                            Fax: 800-866-3235
help@backinthesaddle.com
                            www.backinthesaddle.com

Clothes, accessories and items for people who love horses.

675 Bargain Catalog Outlet
Bargain Catalog Outlet (BCO)
2300 Southeastern Ave.
Indianapolis, IN 46283-8320   888-289-2261
                                      888-355-3099
                              Fax: 888-355-3098
                              www.bcoutlet.com

Clothing and accessories for plus sizes

Catalog Cost: Free

676 Blue Generation
WestPro, Inc.
2294 Mountain Vista Lane
Provo, UT 84606-6206   801-373-2525
                                   Fax: 801-373-8778
steve@westpro.net
                                www.westpro.net

Casual wear and custom sportswear, including direct embroidery and screen printing

President: Steven Clements
CFO: John M Edmunds
Credit Cards: MasterCard
Catalog Cost: Free
Catalog Circulation: Mailed 1 time(s) per year
Printing Information: 16 pages in 4 colors on Glossy Stock
Press: Web Press
Binding: Perfect Bound
In Business: 36 years
Number of Employees: 45
Sales Volume: $3-5 Million

677 Boston Proper
Boston Proper
1155 Broken Sound Parkway NW
Boca Raton, FL 33487-8294   561-241-1700
                                     800-243-4300
                             Fax: 561-241-1055
customerservice@bostonproper.com
                                www.bostonproper.com

Upscale apparel and accessories

Chairman: Michael Tiernan
President: Sheryl Clark
Production Manager: Mike Manerie
Credit Cards: AMEX; MasterCard
Catalog Circulation: to 2500
Printing Information: 76 pages
In Business: 25 years
Number of Employees: 155
Sales Volume: $5-10 Million

678 Boston Proper Travel Clothing
Boston Proper
1155 Broken Sound Parkway NW
Boca Raton, FL 33487-8294   561-241-1700
                                     800-243-4300
                             Fax: 561-241-1055
customerservice@bostonproper.com
                                www.bostonproper.com

Wrinkle-free twills, swimwear, golf and tennis coordinates and lighweight luggage and accessories

Chairman: Michael Tiernan
President: Sheryl Clark
CFO: Ken Fischer
Marketing Manager: Margaret Moraskie
Production Manager: Mike Manerie
Credit Cards: AMEX; MasterCard
Catalog Circulation: to 2.5M
Printing Information: 76 pages
In Business: 25 years
Number of Employees: 155
Sales Volume: $5-10 Million

679 Cardinal Jackets
Cardinal Activewear
P.O. Box 1029
Grundy, VA 24614   800-647-7745
                                   Fax: 276-935-4970
info@cardinalactivewear.com
                                www.cardinalactivewear.com

Nylon coach's windbreakers; Satin baseball jackets; Nylon baseball jackets; Nylon hooded pullover jacket; Mesh lined micro-twill windshirt

President: Mark Shortridge
CFO: Laura Barden
Marketing Manager: Mark Shortridge/Teresa Damron
Buyers: Teresa Damron
Credit Cards: AMEX; MasterCard; Visa
Catalog Cost: Free
Catalog Circulation: to 400m

Printing Information: 4 pages in 4 colors
Mailing List Information: Names for rent
In Business: 40 years
Number of Employees: 4
Sales Volume: $110 Thousand

680 Catherines, Inc.
Catherines, Inc.
777 S. State Road 7
Margate, FL 33068-2803   954-970-2205
                                866-886-4720
catherines.lanebryant.com

Career and casual clothing for plus sized women, sizes 16W - 34W and OX - 5X
Chairman: Alan Rosskamm
President: Lori Twomey
CFO: Eric Specter
Credit Cards: AMEX; MasterCard; Visa
Catalog Cost: Free
In Business: 55 years

681 Cattle Kate Catalog
Cowboy Outfitters
7303 Mesco Dr
Bryan, TX 77808   979-314-1700
                                800-791-7264
                           Fax: 800-878-3970
info@cowboyoutfitters.com
www.cowboyoutfitters.com

Contemporary clothing, western clothing, saddles, gear
President: Kathy Bressler
Catalog Cost: $3
Catalog Circulation: to 50000
Printing Information: 24 pages
In Business: 14 years
Sales Volume: $500,000- 1 Million

682 Chef Revival
Chef Revival
7240 Cross Park Drive
North Charleston, SC 29418   262-723-6133
                                800-858-8589
                           Fax: 843-767-0494
customercare@chefrevival.com
www.chefrevival.com

Chef jackets, tunics, pants, hats, aprons and accessories, footwear and specialty products
President: Bill Rosenblum
CFO: Sandi Piscitello
Credit Cards: AMEX; MasterCard; Visa
Catalog Circulation: to 100M
Printing Information: 19 pages
In Business: 29 years
Number of Employees: 20
Sales Volume: $5-10 Million

683 Esprit
Esprit International, LLP
1370 Broadway, 16th Floor
New York, NY 10018   212-401-1122
                           Fax: 212-401-1130
hotline@esprit.com
www.esprit.com

Clothing, such as sportswear, bodywear, and footwear, as well as accessories made from natural products and materials, and other bed, bath, and kitchen products for the home.
Founder: Susie Buell
Co-Founder: Doug Tompkins
Catalog Cost: Free
In Business: 47 years

684 FootSmart
FootSmart.com
4651 Hickory Hill Road Suite 101
Memphis, TN 38141   800-707-9928
                           Fax: 800-841-3843
info@footsmart.com
www.footsmart.com

Foot and lower body healthcare products—men's and women's shoes, slippers, socks, and hosiery
Catalog Cost: Free
In Business: 25 years

685 Fort Western Outfitters
Fort Brands
5601 S 56th Street
Alamo #4
Lincoln, NE 68516-1886   402-421-3678
                                866-843-3678
help@fortwestern.com
www.fortbrands.com

Western clothing, boots and accessories
President: Carl Wohlfarth
Credit Cards: AMEX; MasterCard
In Business: 43 years
Sales Volume: $ 5-10 Million

686 Fort Western Outpost
Fort Brands
903 Central Ave
Nebraska City, NE 68410-2334   402-873-7388
                                866-843-3678
help@fortwestern.com
www.fortbrands.com

Accessories and clothing for the horse and rider
President: Steve Wohlfarth
CFO: C.S. Wohlfarth
Production Manager: Jeanne Smothers
Credit Cards: AMEX; MasterCard
Catalog Cost: $4
Printing Information: 96 pages
In Business: 43 years
Number of Employees: 50
Sales Volume: $ 5-10 Million

687 Fullbeauty
Fullbeauty.com
P.O. Box 8360
Indianapolis, IN 46283-8360   915-225-4970
                                800-400-4481
                           Fax: 800-528-5152
www.fullbeauty.com

Bras, undergarments, sleepwear, and swimwear for plus size women
Catalog Cost: Free

688 GK Men's Team Competitive
Elite Sportswear LP
2136 N 13th Street
PO Box 16400
Reading, PA 19604-6400   610-921-1469
                                800-345-4087
                           Fax: 610-921-0208
info@gkelite.com
www.gkelite.com

Women's and men's warmup apparel
President: Dan Casciano
COO: Alan Robezzoli
CEO: Sallie Weaver
Credit Cards: AMEX; MasterCard
Catalog Cost: $1.85
In Business: 30 years
Number of Employees: 250
Sales Volume: $15 Million

689 Garnet Hill
Garnet Hill Inc
231 Main Street
Franconia, NH 03580   603-823-5545
                                800-870-3513
                           Fax: 888-842-9696
www.garnethill.com

Quality natural fabric baby clothing and linens, maternity clothes
President: Russ Gaitskill
CFO: Brian Gowen
Buyers: Diane Brush

Credit Cards: AMEX; MasterCard
Catalog Cost: Free
Catalog Circulation: Mailed 7 time(s) per year
Average Order Size: $190
Printing Information: 120 pages in 4 colors on Glossy Stock
Press: Web Press
Binding: Saddle Stitched
Mailing List Information: Names for rent
In Business: 41 years
Number of Employees: 175
Sales Volume: $ 11 Million

690 Gloria Kay Uniforms
Gloria Kay Uniforms
3720 N 124th St
Unit G
Wauwatosa, WI 53222-2100   414-464-1400
                                800-242-7454
                           Fax: 414-464-1402
info@gloriakay.com
www.Gloriakay.Com

Uniforms, aprons, embroidery screen printing, shirts, jackets, caps
President: Mike Weinfhel
Credit Cards: AMEX; MasterCard
Catalog Circulation: to 200M
Printing Information: 52 pages
In Business: 65 years
Number of Employees: 10
Sales Volume: $ 1-3 Million

691 J.L. Powell The Sporting Life
J.L. Powell
1015 Cindy Lane
PO Box 9109
Carpinteria, CO 93013   805-456-4242
service@jlpowell.com
www.jlpowell.com

Sportswear for men including shoes and jewelry
President: J.R. Rigley
CFO: Michelle Fehr
CEO: Mark E. Jacobs
Catalog Cost: Free
Catalog Circulation: Mailed 4 time(s) per year
Printing Information: 66 pages in 4 colors
In Business: 38 years
Sales Volume: 5000000

692 Jasco Uniform Catalog
Allheart
700 Corporate Woods Pkwy
Vernon Hills, IL 60061-3153   847-821-7755
                                800-222-4445
                           Fax: 847-821-8885
customerservice@allheart.com
www.jascouniform.com

Scrubs, uniforms and accessories for nursing and medical professionals
President: Bobbie Veil
Credit Cards: AMEX; MasterCard
Printing Information: 44 pages
In Business: 25 years
Sales Volume: $ 10-20 million

693 Jean Hardy Patterns
Jean Hardy Patterns
2151 La Cuesta Dr
Santa Ana, CA 92705-2522   714-544-1608
jeanharpat@cox.net

Men's and women's riding clothes patterns for English, Western, and Saddle Seat riding
President: Jean Hardy
Catalog Cost: $1
In Business: 41 years

694 Life Uniform
Life Uniform
2770 University Square Dr
Tampa, FL 33612   813-971-5736
888-238-8104
Fax: 813-971-5736
customerservice@lifeuniform.com
www.lifeuniform.com

Healthcare uniforms

President: Jim Rudd
jrudd@lifeuniform.com
CFO: Brian Graiff
bgraiff@lifeuniform.com
Marketing Manager: Dana Colasono
Credit Cards: MasterCard; Visa
Catalog Cost: Free
In Business: 48 years

695 Marisota
Marisota
777 South State Road 7
Margate, FL 33068   855-308-6282
inquiries@Marisota.com
www.marisota.com

Clothing, lingerie, footwear, apparel, and swimwear

Catalog Cost: Free
In Business: 7 years

696 Merrell
Merrell
1400 Industries Rd.
Richmond, IN 47374   800-288-3124
customerservice@merrell.com
www.merrell.com

hiking and outdoors footwear and active gear.

697 Naturalizer
Brown Shoe Company
8300 Maryland Avenue
St. Louis, MO 63105   866-746-3748
www.naturalizer.com

Women's shoes.

698 Newport News
Spiegel Brands Inc
110 William St, 11th Fl.
New York City, NY 10038   212-986-2585
800-759-3950
Fax: 212-916-8281
customerservice@spiegel.com
www.newportnews.com

Women's clothing and accessories

President: Geralynn Madonna
Credit Cards: AMEX; MasterCard
Printing Information: 84 pages
In Business: 49 years
Number of Employees: 700
Sales Volume: $ 50-100 Million

699 Norm Thompson
Bluestem Brands, Inc.
7075 Flying Cloud Drive
Eden Prairie, MN 55344   877-718-7899
800-547-1160
normthompson.blair.com

Men and womens' clothing, footwear, gifts, and gourmet food

President: Steve Nave
CFO: Pete Michielutti
EVP, COO, & Chief Digital Officer: Vince Jones
EVP & President of Credit Services: Jim Slavik
Credit Cards: AMEX; MasterCard
Catalog Cost: Free
In Business: 68 years
Sales Volume: $50MM to $100MM

700 Old Frontier Clothing Company
Old Frontier Clothing Company
4818 W Adams Blvd
Los Angeles, CA 90016-2821   323-643-0000
Fax: 323-643-0001
ofc1123@yahoo.com
www.oldfrontier.com

Line of old time frontier clothing and accessories

President: Larry Bitterman
Founder: Larry Bitterman
Credit Cards: MasterCard; Visa
Catalog Cost: $3
Printing Information: 16 pages
In Business: 26 years
Sales Volume: Under $500,000

701 Olive Juice
Olive Juice
125 Noble Street
Norristown, PA 19401   877-655-4375
800-595-8870
customerservice@olivejuice.com
www.olivejuice.com

Clothing, shoes, socks, swimwear and accessories for infants, children and teens

President: Maryellen Kane
Marketing Manager: Barbara Sawby
Sales Volume: Under $500,000

702 Plus Woman
FSA Plus Woman
85 Laurel Haven
Fairview, NC 28730-9117   828-628-3562
800-628-5525
Fax: 828-628-2610
info@pluswoman.com

Large and supersized clothing for women size 22 and up

Marketing Manager: Gregg Adams
Printing Information: 32 pages
In Business: 24 years
Sales Volume: $ 500,000- 1 Million

703 Queensboro Shirt Company
The Queensboro Shirt Company
1400 Marstellar St
Wilmington, NC 28401-6067   910-251-1251
800-847-4478
Fax: 910-251-7771
www.queensboro.com

Custom embroidery logos on polos, woven shirts, turtlenecks, sweatshirts, outerwear, caps, t-shirts and accessories

President: Fred Meyers
fredm@queensboro.com
Marketing Manager: Beverly Duke
Contact: Jane Eustace
Contact: Lorna Warner
Contact: Rachel Collins
Credit Cards: AMEX; MasterCard
Printing Information: 40 pages
In Business: 33 years
Number of Employees: 50
Sales Volume: $ 6 Million

704 Right Start
LMC Right Start
4643 S Ulster Street
Suite 1200
Denver, CO 80237   720-974-8198
888-856-8004
www.rightstart.com

Children's books, clothing, furniture, car seats and strollers

President: Chris Seahorn
chris.seahorn@rightstart.com
CFO: Scott Henry
VP Operations: Gigi Healy
Credit Cards: AMEX; MasterCard
Catalog Cost: Free

Number of Employees: 80
Sales Volume: $5 million

705 Romans
Romans
2300 Southeastern Ave
Indianapolis, IN 46283-8360   800-677-0229

Plus sized clothing, shoes, jewelry and fragrances for women

Credit Cards:
In Business: 100 years

706 Saks Fifth Avenue
Saks Fifth Avenue
12 E 49th St
New York, NY 10017   212-753-4000
877-551-7257
www.saksfifthavenue.com

Upscale women's and men's apparel, jewelery and accessories, shoes and handbags, and home decor catalog

Chairman: Stephen Sadove
President: Ronald Frasch
CFO: Kevin Wills
Credit Cards: AMEX; MasterCard; Visa
Printing Information: 84 pages
In Business: 114 years
Number of Employees: 900
Sales Volume: Over $1 Billion

707 Scottish Lion Import
The Scottish Lion
27 Cricket Lane
Concord, NH 03301   800-956-5458
Fax: 902-468-2178
info@scottishlion.com
www.scottishlion.com

Scottish imported clothing and gifts

President: Judith Hurley
CFO: Jack Hurley
Credit Cards: AMEX; MasterCard; Visa
Catalog Circulation: to 50000
Printing Information: 64 pages
Number of Employees: 45
Sales Volume: $ 3-5 Million

708 Scrubs Catalog
Tafford Uniforms, LLC
PO Box 481912
Charlotte, NC 28269   800-669-0094
800-697-3321
Fax: 888-588-8590
customerservice@tafford.com
www.tafford.com

Men's and women's solid and print scrub tops, jackets, shoes, stethoscopes and nursing books

President: Robert Shoenfeld
Marketing Manager: David Kaplan
Production Manager: Marc Kohn
Credit Cards: AMEX; MasterCard
In Business: 29 years
Number of Employees: 60
Sales Volume: $ 3-5 Million

709 Silhouettes Catalog
Hanover Direct Inc
1500 Harbor Boulevard
Weehawken, NJ 07086   608-791-6000
Fax: 608-791-5790
custserv@silhouettes.com

Fashion and accessories for women in sizes 12W to 34W

President: Wayne Garten
Credit Cards: AMEX; MasterCard; Visa
Printing Information: 80 pages
In Business: 102 years
Number of Employees: 200
Sales Volume: $500 Million to 1 Billion

710 Spiegel
Spiegel LLC
110 William St
11th Fl.
New York City, NY 10038-5367   800-222-5680
800-253-4742
customerservice@spiegel.com
www.spiegel.com
General merchandise, clothing and jewelry
President: Geralynn Madonna
CFO: Thomas C Pacelli, VP Finance
Credit Cards: AMEX; MasterCard; Visa
Catalog Cost: $5
Catalog Circulation: to 10000
Printing Information: 96 pages
In Business: 149 years
Number of Employees: 1000
Sales Volume: 769MM

711 Stafford's
Stafford's
715 Smith Ave
Thomasville, GA 31792   229-226-4306
800-826-0948
Fax: 229-226-1287
customerservice@staffordscatalog.com
www.stafford-catalog.com
Outdoor apparel, hunting clothes, gifts, luggage and accessories
President: Warren Stafford
Credit Cards: AMEX; MasterCard; Visa
Printing Information: 64 pages
In Business: 70 years
Number of Employees: 20
Sales Volume: $ 1-3 Million

712 Talbots Misses/Petites
The Talbots Inc
One Talbots Drive
Hingham, MA 02043   781-741-4028
800-825-2687
Fax: 781-741-4136
customer.service@talbots.com
www.talbots.com
Specialty retailer, cataloger and e-tailer of classic women's, missy, petites, kids, men's apparel, shoes and accessories
Chairman: Gary Pfeiffer
President: Trudy Sullivan
CFO: Michael Scarpa
Founder: Rudolph Talbot
Founder: Nancy Talbot
In Business: 67 years
Number of Employees: 9096
Sales Volume: Over $1 Billion

713 Talbots Woman
The Talbots Inc
One Talbots Drive
Hingham, MA 02043   781-741-4028
800-825-2687
Fax: 781-741-4136
customer.service@talbots.com
www.talbots.com
Specialty retailer, cataloger and e-tailer of classic women's, missy, petites, kids, men's apparel, shoes and accessories
Chairman: Gary Pfeiffer
President: Trudy Sullivan
CFO: Michael Scarpa
Founder: Rudolph Talbot
Founder: Nancy Talbot
In Business: 67 years
Number of Employees: 9096
Sales Volume: Over $1 Billion

714 Territory Ahead
Territory Ahead
500 Bic Drive
Building 4
Milford, CT 06461-2304   805-962-5558
800-882-4323
Fax: 800-232-9882
service@cs.ttahead.com
www.territoryahead.com
Outdoor clothing and accessories for men and women
President: George Ittner
Credit Cards: AMEX; MasterCard; Visa
Catalog Circulation: to 40000
Printing Information: 86 pages
In Business: 25 years
Number of Employees: 150
Sales Volume: $ 20-50 Million

715 Tri-Mountain
WestPro, Inc.
2294 Mountain Vista Lane
Provo, UT 84606-6206   801-373-2525
Fax: 801-373-8778
steve@westpro.net
www.westpro.net
Custom sportswear, including direct embroidery and screen printing
President: Steve Clement
CFO: John M Edmunds
Credit Cards: MasterCard
Catalog Cost: Free
Catalog Circulation: Mailed 1 time(s) per year to 2000
Average Order Size: $2000
Printing Information: 292 pages in 4 colors on Glossy Stock
Press: Web Press
Binding: Perfect Bound
In Business: 36 years
Number of Employees: 45
Sales Volume: $3-5 Million

716 Watercraft by Dennis Kirk Catalog
Dennis Kirk, Inc.
955 South Field Avenue
Rush City, MN 55069   320-358-1917
800-969-7501
Fax: 320-358-4019
info@denniskirk.com
www.denniskirk.com
Men and womens apparel for Harley Davidsons, snowmobiles and metric bikes, including parts and accessories
President: Dennis Kirk
Credit Cards: AMEX; MasterCard
In Business: 45 years

717 WearGuard Catalog
WearGuard Corp
1101 Market St.
Philadelphia, PA 19107-1609   781-871-4100
800-388-3300
Fax: 800-436-3132
www.shoparamark.com
Work clothes, uniforms and accessories
Chairman: Joseph Neubauer
President: Eric J. Foss
CFO: L Frederick Sutherland
Marketing Manager: Charles Seelig
Production Manager: Tom McDermott
EVP/General Counsel/Secretary: Stephen R. Reynolds
EVP, Human Resources: Lynn B. McKee
Chief Operating Officer: Marc Bruno
Credit Cards: AMEX; MasterCard
Catalog Circulation: to 35MM
Printing Information: 99 pages
In Business: 77 years
Number of Employees: 250,
Sales Volume: $100-500 Million

718 WestPro Catalog
WestPro, Inc.
2294 Mountain Vista Lane
Provo, UT 84606-6206   801-373-2525
Fax: 801-373-8778
steve@westpro.net
www.westpro.net
Custom sportswear, embroidered and screen printed clothing and blank hats
President: Steven Clement
CFO: John M Edmunds
Credit Cards: MasterCard; Visa
Catalog Circulation: to 1000
Printing Information: 6 pages
In Business: 36 years
Number of Employees: 45
Sales Volume: $ 3-5 Million

719 Western Promotion Sportswear
WestPro, Inc.
2294 Mountain Vista Lane
Provo, UT 84606-6206   801-373-2525
Fax: 801-373-8778
steve@westpro.net
www.westpro.net
Custom sportswear, including direct embroidery and screen printing
President: Steven Clement
CFO: John M Edmunds
Credit Cards: MasterCard
Catalog Cost: Free
Catalog Circulation: Mailed 1 time(s) per year to 2000
Average Order Size: $2000
Printing Information: 100 pages in 4 colors on Glossy Stock
Press: Web Press
Binding: Perfect Bound
Mailing List Information: Names for rent
In Business: 36 years
Number of Employees: 45
Sales Volume: $ 3-5 Million

720 Work n' Gear Catalog
Work n' Gear, LLC
2300 Crown Colony Drive
Quincy, MA 02169   800-987-0218
info@workngear.com
www.workngear.com
Uniforms for healthcare, hospitality and industrial workers
President: Anthony DiPaolo
Credit Cards: AMEX; MasterCard; Visa

Boating Products
Accessories

721 Archival Products
Archival Products
P.O. Box 1413
Des Moines, IA 50306-1413   800-526-5640
Fax: 888-220-2397
info@archival.com
www.archival.com
Handcrafted products and the development of solutions for preserving items
Account Representative: Phet Louvan
phetl@archival.com
Division Manager: Janice Comer
janicec@archival.com
Catalog Cost: Free

722 Arhaus Jewels
Arhaus Jewels
7700 Northfield Rd
Walton Hills, OH 44146   877-857-4158
www.arhausjewels.com
Jewelry, clothing, accessories, and footwear
Catalog Cost: Free
In Business: 25+ years

723 Atwood Mobile Products
Atwood Mobile
1120 N Main St
Elkhart, IN 46514-3203   800-825-4328
                                800-546-8759
                    www.atwoodmobile.com

Boat trailers and accessories
President: Timothy Stephens
Number of Employees: 400

724 Bargain Catalog Outlet
Bargain Catalog Outlet (BCO)
2300 Southeastern Ave.
Indianapolis, IN 46283-8320   888-289-2261
                                888-355-3099
                    Fax: 888-355-3098
                    www.bcoutlet.com

Clothing and accessories for plus sizes
Catalog Cost: Free

725 Bluewater Books & Charts
Bluewater Books & Charts
3233 SW 2nd Ave.
Fort Lauderdale, FL 33315   954-763-6533
                                800-942-2583
                    Fax: 954-522-2278
                    help@bluewaterweb.com
                    www.bluewaterweb.com

Marine books, charts, navigation software and accessories.
Chairman: Vivien Godfrey
President: John Mann III
Catalog Cost: Free
Printing Information: in 4 colors on Glossy Stock
In Business: 31 years
Number of Employees: 24

726 Boatlife
Life Industries Corporation
4060 Bridge View Dr
North Charleston, SC 29405-7471 843-566-1225
                                800-382-9706
                    Fax: 843-566-1275
                    info@boatlife.com
                    www.boatlife.com

Marine sealant compounds, finishes, waxes, cleaners
President: Grace Schmidt
Credit Cards: AMEX; MasterCard
Catalog Cost: Free
Catalog Circulation: Mailed 1 time(s) per year to 10000
Average Order Size: $20
Printing Information: 16 pages in 4 colors on Glossy Stock
Press: Sheetfed Press
Binding: Folded
Mailing List Information: Names for rent
In Business: 50 years
Number of Employees: 20
Sales Volume: $3-5 Million

727 Boston Proper
Boston Proper
1155 Broken Sound Parkway NW
Boca Raton, FL 33487-8294   561-241-1700
                                800-243-4300
                    Fax: 561-241-1055
                    customerservice@bostonproper.com
                    www.bostonproper.com

Upscale apparel and accessories
Chairman: Michael Tiernan
President: Sheryl Clark
Production Manager: Mike Manerie
Credit Cards: AMEX; MasterCard
Catalog Circulation: to 2500
Printing Information: 76 pages
In Business: 25 years
Number of Employees: 155
Sales Volume: $5-10 Million

728 Brahmin
Brahmin USA
77 Alden Road
Fairhaven, MA 00271   508-994-4000
                                800-229-2428
                    www.brahmin.com

Handbags, wallets, bracelets, and other accessories
Catalog Cost: Free
In Business: 32 years

729 Crown Galleries
Crown Galleries
1706 Morrissey Drive
Bloomington, IL 61704   800-544-8200
                    Fax: 309-663-6691
                    customercare@crowngalleries.com
                    www.crowngalleries.com

Fine and costume jewelry
President: Richard Owen
Credit Cards: MasterCard
Catalog Cost: Free
In Business: 42 years
Number of Employees: 11
Sales Volume: $1.5 Million

730 Edson Accessories Catalog
Edson Marine Accessory Store
146 Duchaine Boulevard
New Bedford, MA 02745-1292   508-995-9711
                    Fax: 508-995-5021
                    info@edsonintl.com
                    www.edsonmarine.com

Fish supplies
President: William N. Keene
General Manager: Henry R. Keene

731 Esprit
Esprit International, LLP
1370 Broadway, 16th Floor
New York, NY 10018   212-401-1122
                    Fax: 212-401-1130
                    hotline@esprit.com
                    www.esprit.com

Clothing, such as sportswear, bodywear, and footwear, as well as accessories made from natural products and materials, and other bed, bath, and kitchen products for the home.
Founder: Susie Buell
Co-Founder: Doug Tompkins
Catalog Cost: Free
In Business: 47 years

732 Femail Creations
Femail Creations
P.O. Box 8300
#100
Little Rock, AR 72222-5949   702-896-3770
                                800-575-9255
                    Fax: 877-213-3660
                    customerservice@femailcreations.com
                    www.femailcreations.com

Products, items and accessories for women including Bath and Body items, home furnishings, books, clothing and artwork
President: Lisa Hammond
Credit Cards: MasterCard
Catalog Circulation: to 500m
Printing Information: 87 pages
In Business: 15 years
Number of Employees: 10
Sales Volume: $7 Million

733 FootSmart
FootSmart.com
4651 Hickory Hill Road Suite 101
Memphis, TN 38141   800-707-9928
                    Fax: 800-841-3843
                    info@footsmart.com
                    www.footsmart.com

Foot and lower body healthcare products—men's and women's shoes, slippers, socks, and hosiery
Catalog Cost: Free
In Business: 25 years

734 Marine Performance Accessories
Land & Sea Inc
25 Henniker Street
Concord, NH 03301-8528   603-226-DYNO
                                866-396-6648
                    Fax: 603-226-4329
                    sales@land-and-sea.com
                    www.land-and-sea.com

Marine performance equipment
President: Robert Bergeron
Production Manager: Peter Bergeron
Catalog Cost: Free
Printing Information: on Glossy Stock
Mailing List Information: Names for rent
In Business: 36 years
Number of Employees: 55
Sales Volume: $ 6 Million

735 Panama Marine
PO Box 1879
202 W. 6th St.
Panama City, FL 32401   850-785-4661
                                800-262-8243
                    Fax: 850-763-4422

Fish and aquarium supplies

736 Pompanette
Pompanette
1515 SE 16th St
P.O. Box 1200
Charlestown, NH 03603-1782   603-826-5761
                    Fax: 603-826-4125
                    pompanette@pompanette.com
                    www.pompanette.com

Equipment for yachts, pleasure boats, sail boats, sport fishing boats and commercial vessels
President: Colin O'Neil
Credit Cards: AMEX; MasterCard
Catalog Cost: Free
Printing Information: 40 pages in 4 colors
Number of Employees: 4
Sales Volume: $ 1-3 Million

737 Prestons - Ships & Sea
S.T. Preston & Son, Inc.
102 Main Street
P.O. Box 2115
Greenport, NY 11944-967   800-836-1165
                    Fax: 631-477-8541
                    www.prestons.com

Decorative nautical items
President: Peter Rowsom
Credit Cards: AMEX; MasterCard
Printing Information: 55 pages in 4 colors
In Business: 125 years
Sales Volume: $ 3-5 Million

738 Shaw & Tenney
Shaw & Tenney
20 Water Street
PO Box 213
Orono, ME 04473-213   207-866-4867
                                800-240-4867
                    info@shawandtenney.com
                    www.shawandtenney.com

Oars, paddles, hardware and canoe accessories
President: Steven Holt
In Business: 157 years
Sales Volume: $ 3-5 Million

739 **West Marine Master Catalog**
West Marine
500 Westridge Dr.
Watsonville, CA 95076-4100   831-728-2700
                              800-262-8464
                              www.westmarine.com

Boat supplies and accessories.

CFO: Jeffrey Lasher
President & CEO: Matt Hyde
Printing Information: 1116 pages in 4 colors
Mailing List Information: Names for rent
Number of Employees: 5000
Sales Volume: $700 Million

Boat Kits

740 **Chesapeake Light Craft**
1805 George Avenue
Annapolis, MD 21401   410-267-0137
                       Fax: 410-267-5689
                       info@clcboats.com
                       www.clcboats.com

Boats and boating kits, plans, gear and supplies

Production Manager: David
VP Marketing: Matt

741 **G3 Boats**
G3 Boats
901 Cowan Drive
Lebanon, MO 65536   800-588-9787
                      www.g3boats.com

Pontoon boats, aluminum fishing boats, jon boats, deep v or hunting boats.

742 **Geodesic Airolite Boats**
Monfort Associates
50 Haskell Rd.
Westport Island, ME 04578   207-882-5504
                              bettemonfort@roadrunner.com
                              www.gaboats.com

Ultra lite geodesic airolite boat plans and kits.

President: Bette Monfort
Catalog Cost: $5
Catalog Circulation: to 500
Printing Information: 30 pages in 3 colors
Mailing List Information: Names for rent
Number of Employees: 1

743 **Sailrite Marine Catalog**
Sailrite Enterprises, Inc.
2390 E 100 S
Columba City, IN 46725   260-244-4647
                           800-348-2769
                           Fax: 260-818-2005
                           info@sailrite.com
                           www.sailrite.com

Sailing kits, fabric, and sewing machines

President: Matt Grant
Co-Owner: Hallie Grant
Credit Cards: AMEX; MasterCard
Catalog Cost: Free
Catalog Circulation: Mailed 1 time(s) per year
Printing Information: 260 pages in 4 colors
In Business: 48 years
Number of Employees: 12

744 **Spring Creek Canoe Accessories**
Spring Creek, Inc.
8873 Main Street
Mountain Iron, MN 55768-246   218-735-8719
                                800-937-8881
                                Fax: 218-735-8018
                                www.springcreek.com

Car tops, truck racks, sail kits, canoes and yokes, paddles, motor mounts, seats, backrest rowing, wheels and stabilizers for canoes and kayaks

Chairman: Charles Newberg
President: Ted Newberg

CFO: Vydetta Newberg
Marketing Manager: Chuck Newberg
Catalog Cost: Free
Catalog Circulation: Mailed 1 time(s) per year to 7000
Average Order Size: $100
Printing Information: 32 pages in 4 colors on Matte Stock
Press: Letterpress
Binding: Saddle Stitched
Mailing List Information: Names for rent
List Manager: Krista Newberg
In Business: 27 years
Sales Volume: $500,000

Boats

745 **2015 Formula Catalog**
Formula Boats
2200 W. Monroe St.
P.O. Box 1003
Decatur, IN 46733-5003   260-724-9111
                           800-736-7685
                           Fax: 260-724-1194
                           www.formulaboats.com

Formula Boats

In Business: 59 years

746 **2015 Veranda Marine Boats Catalog**
Veranda Marine
199 Extrusion Place
Hot Springs, AR 71901   501-262-3876
                          www.verandamarine.com

Boats and accessories

747 **2015 Xpress Boats Catalog**
Xpress Boats
199 Extrusion Pl.
Hot Springs, AR 71901   501-262-5300
                          Fax: 501-262-5053
                          custserv@xpressboats.com
                          xpressboats.com

Aluminium boats

In Business: 49 years

748 **Accon Marine**
Accon Marine
13665 Automobile Blvd.
Clearwater, FL 33762   727-572-9202
                         Fax: 727-572-7621
                         Info@acconmarine.com
                         www.acconmarine.com

Manufacturer of transistor bases, superior quality marine hardware and other precision metal stampings.

In Business: 27 years

749 **Aire Catalog**
AIRE, Inc.
PO Box 186
Meridian, ID 83680-186   208-888-1772
                           800-247-3432
                           Fax: 208-884-2089
                           info@aire.com
                           www.aire.com

Whitewater rafts, kayaks, paddles, and accessories.

President: Greg Ramp
Marketing Manager: Dan Allanbaugh
Catalog Cost: Free
Printing Information: 30 pages
In Business: 22 years
Number of Employees: 30
Sales Volume: $5 Million

750 **Boston Whaler**
Boston Whaler
100 Whaler Way
Edgewater, FL 32141   877-294-5645
                        www.bostonwhaler.com

Sport fishing boats, pleasure boats, yacht tenders and dingies

751 **Cabela's Boating & Marine**
Cabela's Inc.
One Cabela Dr.
Sidney, NE 69160   www.cabelas.com

CFO: Ralph Castner
CEO: Thomas Millner
COO: Michael Copeland
Catalog Cost: Free
Catalog Circulation: Mailed 4 time(s) per year
Printing Information: in 4 colors
List Company: Chilcutt Direct
In Business: 55 years
Sales Volume: $3 Billion

752 **Carolina Skiff**
Carolina Skiff LLC
3231 Fulford Rd.
Waycross, GA 31503   912-287-0547
                       800-422-7282
                       www.carolinaskiff.com

Skiff boats

753 **Cascade Outfitters**
Cascade Outfitters
604 E 45th Street
Boise, ID 83714   208-322-4411
                    800-223-7238
                    Fax: 208-322-5016
                    www.cascadeoutfitters.com

Rafts, kayaks and boating accessories, whitewater equipment, rivercamping and clothing, paddles, oars, repairs and pumps, rescue and saftey, camping and cooking, gift ideas

President: Doug Tims
Credit Cards: AMEX; MasterCard; Visa
Catalog Cost: Free
In Business: 27 years
Number of Employees: 8
Sales Volume: Under $500,000

754 **Chesapeake Light Craft**
1805 George Avenue
Annapolis, MD 21401   410-267-0137
                        Fax: 410-267-5689
                        info@clcboats.com
                        www.clcboats.com

Boats and boating kits, plans, gear and supplies

Production Manager: David
VP Marketing: Matt

755 **Classic Airboaters Catalog**
Classic Airboats
306 Shearer Blvd.
Cocoa, FL 32922-7293   321-633-4026
                         800-247-2628
                         Fax: 321-632-6043
                         classic@classicairboats.com
                         www.classicairboats.com

Airboats and accessories

President: Bishop Jordon
Marketing Manager: Jay Betzel
Credit Cards: MasterCard; Visa
Catalog Cost: $3
Catalog Circulation: Mailed 1 time(s) per year to 30000
Printing Information: 54 pages in 4 colors on Matte Stock
Press: Offset Press
Binding: Folded
Mailing List Information: Names for rent
In Business: 35 years
Number of Employees: 20
Sales Volume: $2 Million

756 Clipper Canoes
Paddling.net, Inc.
7500 Thornapple River Dr. SE
Caledonia, MI 49316-8464   616-233-3295
www.paddling.net

Canoes and kayaks

757 EdgeWater Power Boats
EdgeWater Power Boats
211 Dale Street
Edgewater, FL 32132   386-426-5457
info@ewboats.com
www.ewboats.com

Boats

Director, Sales and Marketing: Peter Orlando
info@ewboats.com
Customer Service Manager: Christine Washington
Christine@ewboats.com
In Business: 23 years

758 Folbot Corporation
Folbot Corporation
4209 Pace Street
Charleston, SC 29405   843-744-3483
800-533-5099
Fax: 843-744-7783
sales@folbot.com
www.folbot.com

Folding boats and kayaks

Chairman: Tony Mark
President: David Avrutick
Owner: Philip Cotton
Credit Cards: AMEX; MasterCard
Catalog Cost: Free
In Business: 82 years
Number of Employees: 16
Sales Volume: $ 3 Million

759 G3 Boats
G3 Boats
901 Cowan Drive
Lebanon, MO 65536   800-588-9787
www.g3boats.com

Pontoon boats, aluminum fishing boats, jon boats, deep v or hunting boats.

760 Grady-White Boats
Alumacraft
315 W. Saint Julien St.
St. Peter, MN 56082   507-931-1050
customerservice@alumacraft.com
www.alumacraft.com

Aluminium fishing boats

761 Hyde Drift Boats
Hyde Drift Boats
1520 Pancheri Drive
Idaho Falls, ID 83402   800-444-4933
Fax: 208-529-4397
www.hydeoutdoors.com

Boats

CEO: Jim Kunz
Owner: J. Ann Hyde
Owner: LaMoyne Hyde
Credit Cards: AMEX; MasterCard

762 Legend Boats
Legend Boats
117 Dillard Drive
Midway, AR 72651   870-481-6750
info@legendmarine.com
legendmarine.com

Bass boats

763 Lund Boats
Lund Boats
info@lundboats.com
www.lundboats.com

Manufactures aluminum boats for fishing, water skiing and cruising

764 Marine Catalog
Bass Pro Shops
2500 E Kearney
Springfield, MO 65898   417-873-5000
800-227-7776
Fax: 417-873-5060
www.basspro.com

Boats and boating accessories.

President & CEO: James Hagale
Catalog Cost: Free
Catalog Circulation: Mailed 1 time(s) per year
Printing Information: 124 pages in 4 colors
In Business: 45 years
Number of Employees: 2200
Sales Volume: $4.45 Billion

765 Melton Tackle
Melton International Tackle, Inc.
1375 S. State College Blvd.
Anaheim, CA 92806   714-507-4177
800-372-3474
Fax: 714-978-9299
www.meltontackle.com

Lures, reels, rods, gamefishing accessories, boat accessories, clothing and gifts

766 Mid Shore Boat Sales
Mid Shore Boat Sales
11430 Trussum Pond Road
Laurel, DE 19956   302-875-8099
Fax: 302-348-8100
sales@midshoreboatsales.com
www.midshoreboatsales.com

New and used boats.

Service Technican: Brian Kelly
Parts, Warranty: Chad Miller
Sales & Service: Jerry Banks

767 Northwest River Supplies
Northwest River Supplies
2009 S Main St
Moscow, ID 83843-8913   208-882-2749
877-677-4327
Fax: 208-882-1744
service@nrs.com
www.nrsweb.com

Kayaking gear, rafting supplies and boating equipment

President: Bill Parks
Catalog Cost: Free
In Business: 40 years
Sales Volume: $ 10-20 Million

768 NuCanoe Fishing Kayaks
NuCanoe, Inc.
2125 Humboldt St.
Bellingham, WA 98225   360-543-9019
888-226-6310
Fax: 360-483-5613
info@nucanoe.com
www.nucanoe.com

Fishing and hybrid kayaks

769 Osage Canoes
Osage Canoes, LLC
301 Carmeco Rd
PO Box 871
Lebanon, MO 65536-871   417-532-7288
866-532-7299
Fax: 417-532-3565
info@osagian.com
www.osagian.com

Boats, boating supplies, fishing and sport products

President: Jeff Carr
Marketing Manager: Lynn Myers
Production Manager: Larry Denny
Catalog Circulation: Mailed 1 time(s) per year to 20000
Printing Information: 3 pages in 4 colors on Glossy Stock

Press: Web Press
Binding: Folded
Number of Employees: 12
Sales Volume: $500,000- 1 Million

770 Perception Kayaks
Perception Kayaks
575 Mauldin Road
Suite 200
Greenville, SC 29607-2433   864-859-7518
888-525-2925
Fax: 864-855-5995
www.perceptionkayaks.com

Kayaks, canoes, paddles and accessories

President: Susanne Rechner
Production Manager: Keith Butdorf
Catalog Circulation: Mailed 1 time(s) per year
Printing Information: 20 pages in 1 color
In Business: 30 years
Number of Employees: 150
Sales Volume: $ 20 Million

771 Porta-Bote
Porta-Bote International
1074 Independence Avenue
Mountain View, CA 94043-1602   650-961-5334
800-227-8882
Fax: 650-961-3800
sk@portaboat.com
www.porta-bote.com

Boats, portable boats, folding boats, inflatable boats

President: Sandy Kaye
Marketing Manager: Paul Mintz
Production Manager: Chester Hudson
International Marketing Manager: Cindy Dixon
Credit Cards: MasterCard
Catalog Cost: Free
Catalog Circulation: Mailed 4 time(s) per year to 150
Average Order Size: $1800
Printing Information: 6 pages in 4 colors on Glossy Stock
Mailing List Information: Names for rent
In Business: 42 years
Number of Employees: 35
Sales Volume: $4,000,000

772 Professional River Outfitters
Professional River Outfitters
PO Box 635
Flagstaff, AZ 86002-635   928-779-1512
800-648-3236
Fax: 928-213-0936
info@proriver.com
www.proriver.com

Rafting equipment

President: Bruce Helin
Operations Manager: Beth Roeser
Logistics Cordinator: Doug Hall
Menu Coordinator: Eli Yard
Credit Cards: AMEX; MasterCard
Catalog Circulation: Mailed 52 time(s) per year
Printing Information: 4 pages in 1 color on Matte Stock
Press: Web Press
Binding: Saddle Stitched
Mailing List Information: Names for rent
Number of Employees: 4
Sales Volume: Under $500,000

773 Pygmy Boats
Pygmy Boats Inc
355 Hudson Street
PO Box 1529
Port Townsend, WA 98368   360-385-6143
Fax: 360-379-9326
info@pygmyboats.com
www.pygmyboats.com

Precision precut wood kayak kits, rowing and paddling gear, hull gear, boat building supplies, books and DVD's

President: John Lockwood
Credit Cards: MasterCard
Catalog Cost: $4
Number of Employees: 5
Sales Volume: Under $500,000

774   Ranger's Bass Series Catalogs
Ranger Boats
927 Highway 178 N
PO Box 179
Flippin, AR 72634   870-453-2222
                           800-373-2628
                      Fax: 870-704-2666
                  www.rangerboats.com

Freshwater fishing boats and saltwater fishing boats

President: Randy Hopper
CFO: Lendl Hewis
Co Founder: Nina M Wood
Co Founder: Forrest L Wood
Catalog Cost: Free
Number of Employees: 800

775   Rendezvous River Sports
Rendevouz River Sports
945 W. Broadway
Jackson, WY 83001   307-733-2471
                      Fax: 307-733-7171
            info@jacksonholekayak.com
               www.jacksonholekayak.com

Kayak tours, lessons and gear

President: Aaron Pruzan
In Business: 19 years
Number of Employees: 10
Sales Volume: $500,000- 1 Million

776   SOAR Inflatables, Inc.
Soars Inflatable
20 Healdsburg Avenue
Healdsburg, CA 95448   707-433-5599
                           800-280-7627
                      Fax: 707-433-4499
                     info@soar1.com
                     www.soar1.com

Line of canoes and boating supplies

President: Larry Laba
In Business: 19 years
Sales Volume: Under $500,000

777   Sailrite Home Catalog
Sailrite Enterprises, Inc.
2390 E 100 S
Columbia City, IN 46725   260-244-4647
                           800-348-2769
                      Fax: 260-818-2005
                     info@sailrite.com
                     www.sailrite.com

Home sewing machines, fabrics, and supplies

President: Matt Grant
Co-Owner: Hallie Grant
Catalog Cost: Free
Catalog Circulation: Mailed 1 time(s) per year
Printing Information: 260 pages in 4 colors
In Business: 48 years
Number of Employees: 12

778   Sailrite Marine Catalog
Sailrite Enterprises, Inc.
2390 E 100 S
Columba City, IN 46725   260-244-4647
                           800-348-2769
                      Fax: 260-818-2005
                     info@sailrite.com
                     www.sailrite.com

Sailing kits, fabric, and sewing machines

President: Matt Grant
Co-Owner: Hallie Grant
Credit Cards: AMEX; MasterCard
Catalog Cost: Free
Catalog Circulation: Mailed 1 time(s) per year
Printing Information: 260 pages in 4 colors

In Business: 48 years
Number of Employees: 12

779   Sea Eagle Inflatable Boats
Sea Eagle Boats, Inc
19 N Columbia Street
Suite 1
Port Jefferson, NY 11777-2165   631-473-7308
                           800-748-8066
                      Fax: 631-473-7398
                  staff@seaeagle.com
                  www.seaeagle.com

Inflatable boats and kayaks

Marketing Manager: Lori Michel
Vice President: John Hoge
International Marketing Manager: Navneet Syal
Buyers: John Hoge
Catalog Cost: Free
Printing Information: 64 pages
In Business: 55 years
Sales Volume: $ 8 Million

780   SeaArk Catalog
SeaArk Boats
728 W. Patton
P.O. Box 803
Monticello, AR 71655   870-367-5317
                       seaarkboats.com

Aluminium boat building

In Business: 57 years

781   Shearwater Boats
Shearwater Boats
83 Captain Perry Drive
Phippsburg, ME 04562   207-386-0129
                  eric@shearwater-boats.com
                  www.shearwater-boats.com

Kayak, canoes and small boats

President: Eric Stromme
In Business: 32 years

782   Shell Boats
561 Polly Hubbard Road
St Albans, VT 05478   802-524-9645
                      Fax: 802-524-9645
                  shellboats@gmail.com
                  www.shellboats.com

Sailboat and rowboat kits, boat plans and finished boats

783   Stratos Boats
Stratos Boats
PO Box 179
Flippin, AR 72634   870-453-2222
                           877-978-7286
                  www.stratosboats.com

784   Triton Boats
Triton Boats
13 Bluegrass Dr.
Ashland City, TN 37015   615-792-4600
                           888-887-4866
                      Fax: 615-792-4615
                  www.tritonboats.com

Boats

785   War Eagle Boats
War Eagle Boats
2039 Hwy 35 East
P.O. Box 430
Monticello, AR 71657   870-367-1554
                      Fax: 870-367-0260
                  info@wareagleboats.com
                  www.wareagleboats.com

Boats and boating accessories for sports from hunting to fishing

President: Michael Ward
Sales Representative: Nick Carter
Sales Representative: Bill Stephens
Sales Representative: Jay Draffkorn

Catalog Cost: Free
In Business: 23 years
Number of Employees: 106
Sales Volume: $ 11 Million

786   Water Master Rafts
Big Sky Inflatables LLC
476 Wines Way
Stevensville, MT 59870   406-777-5970
                           800-239-7238
            info@bigskyinflatables.com
            www.bigskyinflatables.com

Rafts and raft supplies

Chairman: Amy Stuber
President: Rich Stuber
Catalog Cost: Free
Catalog Circulation: to 2000
Printing Information: 6 pages in 4 colors on Glossy Stock
Binding: Folded
In Business: 9 years

787   Wenonah Canoe Catalog
Wenonah Canoe
1254 Bundy Blvd.
PO Box 247
Winona, MN 55987   507-454-5430
                      Fax: 507-454-5448
                     info@wenonah.com
                     www.wenonah.com

Canoes, kayaks and paddle sports accessories

President: Michael Cichanowski
CFO: Barb Marshall
Marketing Manager: Tom Watson
Production Manager: Dave Hall
International Marketing Manager: Rich Enochs
Buyers: Chris Sayre
Credit Cards: MasterCard; Visa
Catalog Cost: Free
Catalog Circulation: Mailed 1 time(s) per year to 12000
Average Order Size: $75
Printing Information: 42 pages in 4 colors on Glossy Stock
Press: Web Press
In Business: 45 years
Number of Employees: 120
Sales Volume: $ 12 Million

788   WildWasser Sport USA
WildWasser Sport
P.O.Box 4617
Boulder, CO 80306-4617   303-444-2336
                      Fax: 303-444-2375
                     info@wildnet.com
                     www.wildnet.com

Boats, kayaks and accessories

President: Landis Arnold
CFO: Ivana Arnold
Production Manager: Elizabeth Murphy
Number of Employees: 18
Sales Volume: $ 2 Million

789   WoodenBoat Store
Naskeag Road
84 Great Cove Drive
Brooklin, ME 04616   207-359-4647
                           800-273-7447
                      Fax: 207-359-7799
                  wbstore@woodenboat.com
                  www.woodenboatstore.com

Boats and boat kits

Equipment & Supplies

790 AMSOIL
AMSOIL
925 Tower Avenue
Superior, WI 54880-1582   715-399-8324
                               800-956-5695
                          Fax: 715-392-5225
                          www.amsoil.com

Manufactures premium synthetic lubricants for automotive, RV, marine, sport and heavy equipment applications for increased performance
President: Albert J. Amatuzio
CFO: Dean Alexander
EVP, Chief Operating Officer: Alan Amatuzio
Credit Cards: AMEX; MasterCard; Visa
Catalog Cost: Free
Catalog Circulation: to 1M
Average Order Size: $82
Printing Information: 48 pages on Glossy Stock
Press: Web Press
Binding: Saddle Stitched
Mailing List Information: Names for rent
In Business: 45 years
Number of Employees: 200
Sales Volume: $35 Million

791 Adolph Kiefer and Associates, Inc.
Adolph Kiefer & Associates Inc
1700 Kiefer Drive
Zion, IL 60099-4093   847-872-8866
                              800-323-4071
                         Fax: 800-654-7946
                         info@kiefer.com
                         www.kiefer.com

Complete line of life guard accessories, water rescue and safety devices, first aid kits, chairs, umbrellas, swimwear and apparel
Chairman: Adolph Kiefer
President: Greg Howard
VP: Dan Kiefer
CEO: Jack Kiefer
Credit Cards: MasterCard; Visa
Printing Information: in 4 colors
In Business: 68 years
Number of Employees: 60
Sales Volume: $15 Million

792 Barr Marine Products
Barr Marine by EDM
100 Douglas Way
Natural Bridge Station, VA 24579 540-291-4180
                                  866-255-9265
                           Fax: 540-291-4185
                           sales@barrmarine.net
                           www.barrmarine.net

Marine exhaust parts and accessories
Marketing Manager: Michael Gibbs
Production Manager: Robert Ellmann
Credit Cards: MasterCard; Visa
Catalog Cost: $5
Printing Information: 155 pages
In Business: 82 years
Number of Employees: 50

793 Cabela's Boating & Marine
Cabela's Inc.
One Cabela Dr.
Sidney, NE 69160   www.cabelas.com

CFO: Ralph Castner
CEO: Thomas Millner
COO: Michael Copeland
Catalog Cost: Free
Catalog Circulation: Mailed 4 time(s) per year
Printing Information: in 4 colors
List Company: Chilcutt Direct
In Business: 55 years
Sales Volume: $3 Billion

794 CatfishConnection
PO Box 476
Pana, IL 62557   800-929-5025
       customerservice@catfishconnection.com
                 www.catfishconnection.com

Rods, reels, products and accessories for catfishing

795 Defender Marine Buyer's Guide
Defender Industries, Inc.
42 Great Neck Rd
Waterford, CT 06385-3336   860-701-3420
                            800-628-8225
                       Fax: 800-654-1616
                       info@defender.com
                       www.defender.com

Boating, marine and watersports equipment, accessories and supplies; marine electronics; inflatable boats, outboard motors
President: Sheldon Lance
Marketing Manager: Andrew Lance
Credit Cards: AMEX; MasterCard; Visa
Catalog Cost: $4.95
Catalog Circulation: Mailed 1 time(s) per year
Printing Information: 324 pages in 1 color on Matte Stock
Press: Web Press
Binding: Perfect Bound
Mailing List Information: Names for rent
In Business: 77 years
Number of Employees: 120
Sales Volume: $ 12 Million

796 Discount Inboard Marine
2113 1/2 Wessinger Road
Chapin, SC 29036   803-345-0996
                      Fax: 803-345-0972
                      sales@skidim.com
                      www.skidim.com

Inboard ski boat engine parts and accessories

797 Dock Builders Supply
6202 Powell Road
Gibsonton, FL 33534   813-677-4000
                           800-677-4710
                      Fax: 800-734-0335
                      www.dockbuilders.com

Marine construction supplies and materials

798 Dock Doctors
19 Little Otter Lane
Route 7
Ferrisburgh, VT 05456   802-877-6756
                           800-870-6756
                      Fax: 802-877-3147
                      info@thedockdoctors.com
                      thedockdoctors.com

Residential and commercial waterfront products

799 Forespar
22322 Gilberto
Rancho Santa Margarita, CA 92688 949-858-8820
                                  800-266-8820
                           Fax: 949-858-0505
                           sales@forespar.com
                           www.forespar.com

Sailboat and powerboat equipment
Vice President: Bill Hanna
OEM and Int'l Sales Manager: Art Bandy

800 Freeport Marine Supply Company
Freeport Marine Supply
47 West Merrick Road
P.O. Box 840
Freeport, NY 11520-840   516-379-2610
                           800-645-2565
                      Fax: 516-379-2909
                      sales@freeportmarine.com
                      www.freeportmarine.com

Boating and marine supplies and equipment
President: Irwin Ross
Owner: Justin Ross
Credit Cards: AMEX; MasterCard; Visa
Catalog Circulation: Mailed 1 time(s) per year
Average Order Size: $100
Printing Information: 280 pages in 1 color on Newsprint
Press: Web Press
Binding: P
Mailing List Information: Names for rent
In Business: 76 years
Number of Employees: 10
Sales Volume: $ 2.5 Million

801 Hobie Kayak Collection
Hobie Company
4925 Oceanside Blvd
Oceanside, CA 92056-3099   760-758-9100
                       Fax: 760-758-1841
                       info@hobiecat.com
                       www.hobiecat.Com

Gear and equipment for Hobie Cats and sailors
Chairman: Richard Rogers
President: Doug Skidmore
CFO: Bill Baldwin
Buyers: Bill Tsutsui
Credit Cards: MasterCard
Catalog Cost: Free
Catalog Circulation: Mailed 1 time(s) per year to 100M
Printing Information: 24 pages in 4 colors on Glossy Stock
Press: Web Press
Binding: Saddle Stitched
Mailing List Information: Names for rent
In Business: 54 years
Number of Employees: 140
Sales Volume: $ 19.4 Million

802 Jamestown Distributors
Jamestown Distributors
17 Peckham Drive
Bristol, RI 02809   401-253-3840
                           800-497-0010
                      Fax: 401-254-5829
                      www.jamestowndistributors.com

Boatbuilding and woodworking supplies
President: Michael Mills
Manager of Accounting and HR: Barbara Smith
Manager: Melanie Curley
Warehouse Manager: Rui Fernandes
Catalog Cost: Free
In Business: 43 years
Number of Employees: 45
Sales Volume: $ 12 Million

803 Marine Catalog
Bass Pro Shops
2500 E Kearney
Springfield, MO 65898   417-873-5000
                           800-227-7776
                      Fax: 417-873-5060
                      www.basspro.com

Boats and boating accessories.
President & CEO: James Hagale
Catalog Cost: Free
Catalog Circulation: Mailed 1 time(s) per year
Printing Information: 124 pages in 4 colors
In Business: 45 years
Number of Employees: 2200
Sales Volume: $4.45 Billion

804 McDonnell Marine Service
63 Old Windsor Road
Bloomfield, CT 06002   860-243-9114
                      Fax: 860-286-0861
                      mcdonnellmarine@comcast.net
                      www.mcdonnellmarine.com

Volvo Penta marine parts
Founder/ Head: Brian McDonnell
Service Manager: Dan Gavioli

805 **Minn Kota**
Johnson Outdoors
121 Power Dr.
Mankato, MN 56001   800-227-6433
                    Fax: 800-527-4464
                    www.minnkotamotors.com

Electric trolling motors and accessories.

Chair & CEO: Helen Johnson-Leipold
Catalog Cost: Free
Printing Information: 42 pages in 4 colors
Mailing List Information: Names for rent
In Business: 84 years
Sales Volume: $262 Million

806 **North Sports**
Northwave
406 Oak Street
Hood River, OR 97031   509-493-4938
                    Fax: 509-493-4966
                    www.north-windsurf.com

Equipment and supplies for boats

President: Blake Richards

807 **Raritan**
Raritaneng Engineering Company
530 Orange Street
Millville, NJ 08332-4031   856-825-4900
                    sales@raritaneng.com
                    www.raritaneng.Com

Boat sanitation and water systems

Marketing Manager: Kim Shinn
Cheif Executive Officer: Vinod Mehta
Buyers: Terri Worrall
Catalog Cost: Free
Catalog Circulation: Mailed 1 time(s) per year
to 15000
Printing Information: 36 pages in 4 colors on
Glossy Stock
Mailing List Information: Names for rent
In Business: 59 years
Number of Employees: 50
Sales Volume: $ 5-10 Million

808 **Sailrite Marine Catalog**
Sailrite Enterprises, Inc.
2390 E 100 S
Columba City, IN 46725   260-244-4647
                    800-348-2769
                    Fax: 260-818-2005
                    info@sailrite.com
                    www.sailrite.com

Sailing kits, fabric, and sewing machines

President: Matt Grant
Co-Owner: Hallie Grant
Credit Cards: AMEX; MasterCard
Catalog Cost: Free
Catalog Circulation: Mailed 1 time(s) per year
Printing Information: 260 pages in 4 colors
In Business: 48 years
Number of Employees: 12

809 **TackleDirect**
6825 Tilton Road
Bldg C
Egg Harbor Twp, NJ 08234-4426 609-788-3819
                    888-354-7335
                    Fax: 877-803-6229
                    sales@tackledirect.com
                    www.tackledirect.com

**Fishing gear for saltwater, freshwater and fly
fishing**

810 **VETUS**
Vetus America
7251 National Drive
Hanover, MD 21076-1781   410-712-0740
                    Fax: 410-712-0985
                    sales-service@vetus.com
                    www.vetus.com

**Marine accessories, bowthrusters, flexible
tanks, exhaust systems, decorative lights,
engines, ventilators and barographs**

President: John Mardall
CFO: Laura Railberg
Marketing Manager: Babette van Waes
CEO, VETUS-Maxwell APAC Ltd.: Andy
Stephens
Director - Purchase & Supply Chain: Hessel
de Vries
Director Finance: Bram Buermans
Credit Cards: MasterCard; Visa
Catalog Cost: Free
Catalog Circulation: Mailed 2 time(s) per year
to 36000
Average Order Size: $400
Printing Information: 75 pages in 4 colors on
Glossy Stock
Binding: Perfect Bound
Mailing List Information: Names for rent
In Business: 48 years
Sales Volume: $ 10-20 Million

811 **West Marine Master Catalog**
West Marine
500 Westridge Dr.
Watsonville, CA 95076-4100   831-728-2700
                    800-262-8464
                    www.westmarine.com

Boat supplies and accessories.

CFO: Jeffrey Lasher
President & CEO: Matt Hyde
Printing Information: 1116 pages in 4 colors
Mailing List Information: Names for rent
Number of Employees: 5000
Sales Volume: $700 Million

812 **West Marine Spring Waterlife**
West Marine
500 Westridge Dr.
Watsonville, CA 95076-4100   831-728-2700
                    800-262-8464
                    www.westmarine.com

Waterlife footwear, apparel and accessories.

CFO: Jeffrey Lasher
President & CEO: Matt Hyde
Printing Information: 1116 pages in 4 colors
Mailing List Information: Names for rent
Number of Employees: 5000
Sales Volume: $700 Million

Radio & Navigation Equipment

813 **B&B Electronics Manufacturing Company**
B&B Electronics Manufacturing Company
707 Dayton Road
PO Box 1040
Ottawa, IL 61350   815-433-5100
                    800-346-3119
                    Fax: 815-433-5109
                    support@bb-elec.com
                    www.bb-elec.com

Data communication products

President: Don Wiencek
Credit Cards: AMEX; MasterCard; Visa
Catalog Cost: Free
Printing Information: 122 pages
In Business: 34 years
Number of Employees: 100

814 **Bluewater Books & Charts**
Bluewater Books & Charts
3233 SW 2nd Ave.
Fort Lauderdale, FL 33315   954-763-6533
                    800-942-2583
                    Fax: 954-522-2278
                    help@bluewaterweb.com
                    www.bluewaterweb.com

**Marine books, charts, navigation software
and accessories.**

Chairman: Vivien Godfrey
President: John Mann III
Catalog Cost: Free
Printing Information: in 4 colors on Glossy
Stock

In Business: 31 years
Number of Employees: 24

815 **Communications Electronics Journal**
Communications Electronics Inc.
PO Box 1045
Ann Arbor, MI 48106-1045   734-996-8888
                    800-297-1023
                    Fax: 734-663-8888

**Electronic shortwave radios, scanners, CB
radios phones**

President: Ken Ascher
Marketing Manager: Sam Ascher
Credit Cards: AMEX; MasterCard; Visa Dis-
cover Optima
Catalog Circulation: to 800M
Printing Information: 64 pages
In Business: 24 years
Number of Employees: 25
Sales Volume: $ 1-3 Million

816 **Davis Instruments**
Davis
3465 Diablo Ave
Hayward, CA 94545-2778   510-732-9229
                    800-678-3669
                    Fax: 510-670-0589
                    sales@davisnet.com
                    www.davisnet.com

**Weathering monitoring stations, vehicle
monitoring stations, marine products**

President: Bob Selig
CFO: Susan Tatum
Credit Cards: MasterCard; Visa
Catalog Cost: Free
Average Order Size: $700
Mailing List Information: Names for rent
In Business: 52 years
Number of Employees: 100
Sales Volume: $12.30

817 **McDonnell Marine Service**
63 Old Windsor Road
Bloomfield, CT 06002   860-243-9114
                    Fax: 860-286-0861
                    mcdonnellmarine@comcast.net
                    www.mcdonnellmarine.com

Volvo Penta marine parts

Founder/ Head: Brian McDonnell
Service Manager: Dan Gavioli

818 **Minn Kota**
Johnson Outdoors
121 Power Dr.
Mankato, MN 56001   800-227-6433
                    Fax: 800-527-4464
                    www.minnkotamotors.com

Electric trolling motors and accessories.

Chair & CEO: Helen Johnson-Leipold
Catalog Cost: Free
Printing Information: 42 pages in 4 colors
Mailing List Information: Names for rent
In Business: 84 years
Sales Volume: $262 Million

819 **Port Supply**
PO Box 50070
Watsonville, CA 95077-70   831-728-4417
                    800-621-6885
                    Fax: 800-825-7678
                    www.portsupply.com

Marine products and accessories

Vice President: Kevin Osborn
Marketing Director: Chris Pearson

820 **Stanley Supplies and Services**
Stanley Supply &Services, Inc.
335 Willow Street
North Andover, MA 01845-5995 978-682-9844
                    800-225-5370
                    Fax: 800-743-8141
                    www.stanleysupplyservices.com

Tool kits, cases, test instruments, tools and equipment for technicians and service personnel in electronics and communications

President: Ken Lyon
Marketing Manager: Jeff Richardson
Credit Cards: AMEX; MasterCard
Catalog Cost: Free
Catalog Circulation: Mailed 2 time(s) per year
Printing Information: 300 pages in 4 colors on Glossy Stock
Binding: Saddle Stitched
Mailing List Information: Names for rent
In Business: 48 years
Number of Employees: 75
Sales Volume: $ 3-5 Million

821 TackleDirect
6825 Tilton Road
Bldg C
Egg Harbor Twp, NJ 08234-4426   609-788-3819
888-354-7335
Fax: 877-803-6229
sales@tackledirect.com
www.tackledirect.com

Fishing gear for saltwater, freshwater and fly fishing

822 Universal Radio
Unifersal Radio, Inc.
6830 Americana Parkway
Reynoldsburg, OH 43068-4113   614-866-4267
800-431-3939
Fax: 614-866-2339
dx@universal-radio.com
www.universal-radio.com

Shortwave, amateur and CB communications equipment, antennas, books and accessories

President: Fred Osterman
Sales: Craig
Founder: F.R. Gibb W8IJ
Store Manager: Eric
Credit Cards: MasterCard
Catalog Cost: Free
Printing Information: 124 pages
In Business: 73 years
Number of Employees: 18
Sales Volume: $6.2 Million

823 West Marine Master Catalog
West Marine
500 Westridge Dr.
Watsonville, CA 95076-4100   831-728-2700
800-262-8464
www.westmarine.com

Boat supplies and accessories.

CFO: Jeffrey Lasher
President & CEO: Matt Hyde
Printing Information: 1116 pages in 4 colors
Mailing List Information: Names for rent
Number of Employees: 5000
Sales Volume: $700 Million

Books
Antique & Historical

824 Applewood Books
Applewood Books
1 River Road
Carlisle, MA 01741-1889   781-271-0055
800-277-5312
Fax: 781-271-0056
bookorder@awb.com
www.awb.com

Books from America's past

President: Phil Zuckerman
Credit Cards: AMEX; MasterCard; Visa
Catalog Cost: Free
Mailing List Information: Names for rent
In Business: 39 years
Number of Employees: 5
Sales Volume: $3MM to $5MM

825 Art Catalog
Ashgate Publishing Company
110 Cherry Street
Suite 3-1
Burlington, VT 05401-3818   802-865-7641
800-535-9544
Fax: 802-865-7847
ashgate.online@ashgate.com
www.ashgate.com

Books of illustrated scholarship and reference, including Classical, Byzantine and Medieval Art; Early Modern Art; Eighteenth/Nineteenth/Twentieth Century Art; Religion and History

Fulfillment: Suzanne Sprague
Catalog Circulation: Mailed 1 time(s) per year
Printing Information: 24 pages
Press: Web Press
In Business: 40 years

826 Astragal Press
Astragal Press
5995 149th Street West
Suite 105
Apple Valley, MN 55124   952-469-6699
800-858-8515
Fax: 800-330-6232
info@finneyco.com
www.astragalpress.com

Books on antique tools, trades, science and technology

President: Alan E. Krysan
Marketing Manager: Ann Prescott
Catalog Cost: Free
Catalog Circulation: Mailed 4 time(s) per year to 15000
Printing Information: 64 pages in 4 colors
In Business: 34 years
Number of Employees: 5
Sales Volume: Under $500M

827 Bas Bleu
Bas Bleu
5581 Hudson Industrial Pkwy
Hudson, OH 44236   800-433-1155
www.basbleu.com
In Business: 21 years

828 Betty's Attic
Betty's Attic
PO Box 25600
Bradenton, FL 34206-5600   941-747-5566
800-311-0733
Fax: 800-551-4406
customerservice@bettysattic.com
www.bettysattic.com

Nostalgic items and collectibles from the 1920s to the 1970s

President: Ralph Hoenle
CFO: David Crofoot
Marketing Manager: Kim Boyd
Buyers: Tom Ronzi
Catalog Cost: Free
Catalog Circulation: Mailed 52 time(s) per year
Printing Information: 64 pages
Mailing List Information: Names for rent
List Manager: Carolyn Foley
In Business: 101 years
Number of Employees: 100
Sales Volume: $500M to $1MM

829 China Books
China Books
360 Swift Avenue #48
South San Francisco, CA 94080   800-818-2017
Fax: 650-872-7808
info@chinabooks.com
www.chinabooks.com

Books on Chinese language, culture and society.

President: Wang Xin
Marketing Manager: Eva Lai
Fulfillment: Limin Yam
Senior Managing Editor: Chris Robyn
Sales Manager: Kelly Feng
Design Manager: Tiffany Cha
In Business: 55 years

830 Classical Academic Press 2015 - 2016 Catalog
Classical Academic Press
2151 Market Street
Camp Hill, PA 17011   717-730-0711
866-730-0711
Fax: 717-730-0721
classicalacademicpress.com

Educational publishing company

National leader, author, and speake: Dr. Chris Perrin
Printing Information: 60 pages

831 Clearfield Company
Genealogical Publishing Company
3600 Clipper Mill Road
Suite 260
Baltimore, MD 21211   410-837-8271
800-296-6687
Fax: 410-752-8492
info@genealogical.com
www.genealogical.com

Genealogy books and CD's

President: Barry Chodak
CFO: Curtis Diering
Marketing Manager: Joe Garonzik
Production Manager: Eileen Perkins
Credit Cards: MasterCard
Catalog Circulation: Mailed 1 time(s) per year
Printing Information: 34 pages in 1 color on Newsprint
Press: Letterpress
Binding: Saddle Stitched
Mailing List Information: Names for rent
In Business: 50 years
Number of Employees: 10
Sales Volume: $1MM to $3MM

832 Collector Books
Collector Books
PO Box 3009
Paducah, KY 42002-3009   270-898-6211
800-626-5420
Fax: 270-898-8890
info@collectorbooks.com
www.collectorbooks.com

Books for every kind of collector, price guides to collectibles and antiques

President: Bill Schroeder Jr
Marketing Manager: Rick Loyd
Buyers: Mike Hovekamp
Catalog Cost: Free
Average Order Size: $105
Printing Information: 32 pages in 4 colors on Glossy Stock
Press: Letterpress
Binding: Saddle Stitched
Mailing List Information: Names for rent
In Business: 39 years
Number of Employees: 65

833 Crane Hill
Crane Hill
3608 Clairmont Avenue S
Birmingham, AL 35222-3508   205-714-3007
Fax: 205-714-3008
www.cranehill.com

Books that reflect the history, perceptions, experience and customs of people in regional locales around the United States

834 DreamHaven Books
DreamHaven Books
2301 East 38th Street
Minneapolis, MN 55406
612-823-6161
Fax: 612-823-6062
dream@dreamhavenbooks.com
www.dreamhavenbooks.com

New, used, and rare and collectible books, comics, paperbacks and periodicals, science fiction, fantasy, horror
President: Greg Ketter
Fulfillment: Elizabeth LaVelle
Credit Cards: AMEX; MasterCard; Visa
Catalog Circulation: Mailed 12 time(s) per year to 1500
Printing Information: 20 pages in 2 colors on Matte Stock
Press: Sheetfed Press
Binding: Folded
Mailing List Information: Names for rent
In Business: 25 years
Number of Employees: 10
Sales Volume: $500M to $1MM

835 Easton Press Leather Bound Books
Easton Press
47 Richards Ave.
Norwalk, CT 06857
203-855-8717
800-243-5160
customerservice@eastonpress.com
www.eastonpress.com

Leather bound books
Printing Information: 41 pages in 4 colors
In Business: 30 years

836 Edward R Hamilton Bookseller
Edward R Hamilton Bookseller
PO Box 15
Falls Village, CT 06031-15
800-677-3483
comments@edwardrhamilton.com
www.edwardrhamilton.com

Books and audio cassettes on history, politics, religion, travel, sports, wildlife and pets, gardening, art and architecture, fiction, cookbooks, computer, children's books and more at bargain prices
President: Edward R Hamilton
Catalog Cost: Free
Catalog Circulation: Mailed 4 time(s) per year
Printing Information: 98 pages in 1 color on Newsprint
Press: Web Press
Binding: Perfect Bound

837 Embroidery Research Press
10800 Alpharetta Highway
Roswell, GA 30076-1490
770-223-8620
Fax: 770-512-7837

Rare and out of print titles
President: Dolly Norton Fehd
Catalog Cost: Free

838 Empire Books
PO Box 2634
Ormond Beach, FL 32175-2634
386-677-7314
Fax: 386-677-7324

Ancient Greek and Roman coins and history books
President: Dennis Kroh
Catalog Cost: $5
Catalog Circulation: Mailed 1 time(s) per year
Number of Employees: 5
Sales Volume: Under $500M

839 French Reflection
French Reflection
6110 W. Pico Blvd.
Suite B
Los Angeles, CA 90035
310-659-3800
800-421-4404
Fax: 310-659-3800
frenchreflection.com

Books relating to French culture
President: Alice Myers
Sales Volume: $1MM to $3MM

840 General Military History
Q M Dabney
PO Box 849
Princeton Junction, NJ 08550
609-298-1003
Fax: 609-298-0070
qmdabney@qmdabney.com
www.qmdabney.com

Out of print military books
Credit Cards: AMEX; MasterCard
Catalog Cost: Free
Catalog Circulation: Mailed 12 time(s) per year
Printing Information: 125 pages in 4 colors

841 Heritage Books
Heritage Books Inc.
5810 Ruatan St.
Berwyn Heights, MD 20740
410-876-6101
800-876-6103
Fax: 877-552-4884
www.Heritagebooks.Com

Titles in genealogy, history, military history, historical fiction, and memoirs
President: Craig Scott
Sales Volume: $1MM to $3MM

842 Huntington Library Press
The Huntington
1151 Oxford Road
San Marino, CA 91108-1299
626-405-2100
Fax: 626-585-0794
publicinformation@huntington.org
www.huntington.org

18th century British and American literature, American history, gardens
Chairman: Stewart R. Smith
President: Steven Koblik
CFO: Alison Sowden
Marketing Manager: Jean Patterson
Vice President for Operations: Laurie Sowd
Vice President for Communications: Susan Turner-Lowe
Exe Assistant to the President: Anne Gustus
Catalog Cost: Free
Catalog Circulation: to 5000
Printing Information: 6 pages in 1 color on Matte Stock
Binding: Folded
Mailing List Information: Names for rent
In Business: 96 years
Number of Employees: 60
Sales Volume: Under $500M

843 Liberty Fund Books
Liberty Fund, Inc.
8335 Allison Pointe Trail
Suite 300
Indianapolis, IN 46250-1684
800-955-8335
Fax: 708-534-7803
libertyfund@ware-pak.com
www.libertyfund.org
Chairman: T. Alan Russell
President: Chris L. Talley
Executive Vice President and COO: Emilio J. Pacheco
Vice President of Educational Progr: Douglas J. Den Uyl
Vice President of Publishing: Patricia A. Gallagher

844 Library of America
Library of America
P.O. Box 37910
Boone, IA 50037-0910
800-964-5578
info@loa.org
loa.org

Nonprofit publisher of classic American writing, including literature, poetry, nonfiction works, and historical documents
President: Cheryl Hurley
Catalog Cost: Free
In Business: 38 years

845 Medieval Catalog
Ashgate Publishing Company
110 Cherry Street
Suite 3-1
Burlington, VT 05401-3818
802-865-7641
800-535-9544
Fax: 802-865-7847
ashgate.online@ashgate.com
www.ashgate.com

Topics/titles include Roman and Byzantium eras; The Crusades; Middle East, Africa and Asia; Medieval West; Philosophy and Theology; Art; Architecture and Music
Marketing Manager: Martha McKenna
mmckenna@ashgate.com
Fulfillment: Suzanne Sprague
ssprague@ashgate.com
Number of Employees: 25

846 Messianic Jewish Resources International Catalog
Messianic Jewish Publishers & Resources
6120 Day Long Lane
Clarksville, MD 21029
410-531-6644
800-410-7367
Fax: 410-531-9440
customerservice@messianicjewish.com
messianicjewish.net

847 Military Book
Thesis of History
PO Box 4470
Cave Creek, AZ 85327-4470
480-488-1377
800-564-6164
Fax: 800-488-1316
www.pohind.com

Military books
President: Lowell Jackson
Catalog Cost: $2
Printing Information: 60 pages in 1 color on Glossy Stock
Press: Web Press
Binding: Saddle Stitched
In Business: 15 years

848 Minnesota Historical Society
Minnesota Historical Society
345 W. Kellogg Blvd.
St. Paul, MN 55102
651-259-3000
800-657-3773
webmaster@mnhs.org
www.mnhs.org
President: William R. Stoeri
CFO: Peggy Ingison
Marketing Manager: Lory Sutton
VP: Ruth Huss
1st Vice President: Phyllis Rawls Goff
Director & Chief Executive Officer: D. Stephen Elliott
In Business: 166 years

849 Mountain Press Publishing
Mountain Press Publishing
PO Box 2399
Missoula, MT 59806
406-728-1900
800-234-5308
Fax: 406-728-1635
info@mtnpress.com
www.mountain-press.com

Books on natural history and geology, western history and western Americana
President: John Rimel
CFO: Rob Williams
Catalog Cost: Free
Mailing List Information: Names for rent
In Business: 63 years
Number of Employees: 10
Sales Volume: $500M to $1MM

850 Native American Collection
Cherokee Publications
PO Box 430
Cherokee, NC 28719
828-488-8856
800-948-3161
Fax: 828-488-6934
www.cherokeepublications.net

Videos, tapes and books on Native Americana

Credit Cards: MasterCard; Visa
Catalog Cost: $1
In Business: 58 years
Number of Employees: 4
Sales Volume: Under $500M

851 Obsolete & Classic Auto Parts
Obsolete & Classic Auto Parts, Inc.
8701 South Interstate 35
Oklahoma City, OK 73149
405-631-3933
800-654-3247
Fax: 405-634-6815
info@classicautoparts.com
www.classicautoparts.com

Worldwide retailer and distributor of antique, classic, street rod, and Obsolete Chevrolet and Ford parts and accessories

General Manager: Mike Forehand
Assistant Manager: Kevin Billins
Accounting: Sara Moheit
Catalog Cost: Free
Catalog Circulation: to 1
In Business: 39 years

852 Purple Mountain Press
Purple Mountain Press LTD
1060 Main St
PO Box 309
Fleischmanns, NY 12430-309
845-254-4062
800-325-2665
Fax: 845-254-4476
purple@catskill.net
www.catskill.net/purple/reach.htm

Hard-to-find books about New York State and maritime books

President: Wray & Loni Rominger
Credit Cards: AMEX; MasterCard
Catalog Cost: Free
Sales Volume: Under $500M

853 Schiffer Antiques & Collectibles
Schiffer Publishing Ltd.
4880 Lower Valley Rd
Atglen, PA 19310-1768
610-593-1777
Fax: 610-593-2002
info@schifferbooks.com
www.Schifferbooks.Com

Reference books for collectors, dealers and designers

President: Peter Schiffer
Credit Cards: MasterCard; Visa
Catalog Cost: Free
Mailing List Information: Names for rent
In Business: 42 years
Number of Employees: 30
Sales Volume: $10MM to $20MM

854 Scholar's Bookshelf
The Scholar's Bookshelf
110 Melrich Rd # 5
Cranbury, NJ 08512-3524
609-395-6933
Fax: 609-395-0755
www.Scholarsbookshelf.Com

Books and videos: military, history, fine arts, literature, philosophy, religion, music

President: Abbot Friedland
Fulfillment: Ginny Goss
Buyers: John Breenberg
Loren Hoeuzen
Credit Cards: MasterCard; Visa
Catalog Cost: Free
Catalog Circulation: Mailed 18 time(s) per year to 2.5MM

Average Order Size: $55
Printing Information: 64 pages in 2 colors on Newsprint
Press: Web Press
Binding: Saddle Stitched
Mailing List Information: Names for rent
List Manager: Jeanne Mael
List Company: Conrad Direct
300 Knicker Bocker Road
Cresskill, NJ 07526
In Business: 30 years
Number of Employees: 25
Sales Volume: $1MM to $3MM

855 US Naval Institute Holiday
US Naval Institute Holiday
291 Wood Road
Annapolis, MD 21402-5034
410-268-6110
800-233-8764
Fax: 410-571-1703
customer@usni.org
www.usni.org

Historical art prints, miniature ship models, gift items, books and DVD's

President: Tom Wilkerson
CFO: Robert G Johnson
Marketing Manager: W. Scott Gureck
CEO: VADM Peter H. Daly
EVP, Development: Kirk McAlexander
VP, Planning & Operations: A. Denis Clift
Credit Cards: MasterCard; Visa
In Business: 41 years
Sales Volume: $10MM to $20MM

Audio Books

856 American Audio Prose Library
American Audio Prose Library
PO Box 842
Columbia, MO 65205
573-443-0361
Fax: 573-499-0579

Readings and illuminating conversations with authors on cassette

President: Kay Binett
Average Order Size: $75
Mailing List Information: Names for rent
Number of Employees: 1
Sales Volume: Under $500M

857 Audio Diversions Johnson
3428 Blair Road
Falls Church, VA 22041-1412
800-628-6145
Fax: 703-442-9344
www.audiodiversions.com

Audio books on cassettes and CD's

President: Frank Johnson Jr
Credit Cards: AMEX; MasterCard; Visa
Catalog Cost: Free
Printing Information: 48 pages on Matte Stock
Press: Web Press
Binding: Saddle Stitched
In Business: 10 years

858 Audio Editions
Audio Editions
131 E. Placer St.
PO Box 6930
Auburn, CA 95604-6930
530-888-7801
800-231-4261
Fax: 530-888-1840
info@audioeditions.com
www.audioeditions.com

Line of books on cassette and CD

President: Linda Olsen
CEO: Grady Hesters
In Business: 30 years

859 Audio Forum
Audio Forum
1 Orchard Park Road
Madison, CT 06443-2272
203-245-0195
800-243-1234
Fax: 888-453-4329
www.audioforum.com

Spiritual masterpieces read and sung by world-renowned authorities and performers

Chairman: Jeffrey Norton
President: Jeffrey Norton
Credit Cards: AMEX; MasterCard
Catalog Cost: Free

860 AudiobookStand.com
Brilliance Publishing, Inc.
1702 Eaton Drive
P.O. Box 481
Grand Haven, MI 49417
800-854-7859
800-854-7859
Fax: 616-846-0630
help@audiobookstand.com
www.audiobookstand.com

Catalog of books on tape, CD and MP3 at discounted prices

Owner, Director of Sales: Steve Woessner
Vice President: Susan M Volkers
Managing Director: Laura Bryant
Catalog Cost: Free
Catalog Circulation: Mailed 12 time(s) per year
Printing Information: 16 pages in 4 colors on Glossy Stock
Binding: Saddle Stitched
Mailing List Information: Names for rent
In Business: 29 years
Number of Employees: 150
Sales Volume: $17.5 MM

861 BBC Audiobooks America
AudioGo
42 Whitecap Drive
N Kingstown, RI 02852-7445
800-621-0182
Fax: 877-492-0873
www.audiogo-library.com/

Unabridged audiobooks and radio dramatizations for adults and children; direct to library sales; formats include CD, MP3, and Playaway

Marketing Manager: Michele Cobb
Principle: Jim Brannigan
Credit Cards: AMEX; MasterCard; Visa
Catalog Cost: Free
Catalog Circulation: Mailed 7 time(s) per year to 18000
Printing Information: 65 pages
Mailing List Information: Names for rent
In Business: 20 years
Number of Employees: 40

862 Balcony Publishing
Balcony Publishing
PO Box 2175
Georgetown, TX 78627-2175
512-868-2061
800-777-7949
Fax: 512-868-8803
mail@balconypublishing.com
www.balconypublishing.com

Paperback books, audio and video cassettes concerning religion and women's concerns

President: Francis Heatherley
Credit Cards: MasterCard; Visa
Catalog Cost: Free
Printing Information: on Matte Stock
In Business: 13 years
Number of Employees: 3
Sales Volume: Under $500M

863 Balticshop.com
Balticshop.com, LLC
2842 Main St #333
Glastonbury, CT 6033-1036   371-292- 643
                                   800-506-2312
                                   info@balticshop.com
                                   www.balticshop.com

Internet store offering original items from the three Baltic states of Estonia, Latvia, and Lithuania.

Credit Cards: AMEX; MasterCard
Printing Information: 35 pages
In Business: 17 years

864 Blackstone Audio Books
Blackstone Audio Books
1124 E Nakoma Street
Ashland, OR 97520   800-621-0182
                          Fax: 800-482-9294
                          sales@blackstoneaudio.com
                          www.blackstoneaudio.com

Unabridged recordings of great books - fiction, history, biography, mystery, humor, art, business, children's, politics, economics, philosphy and religion

President: Craig W Black
Marketing Manager: Paul Coughlin
Production Manager: Debbie Stanton
Buyers: Warren Schnibbe
Credit Cards: AMEX; MasterCard; Visa
Catalog Cost: Free
Catalog Circulation: Mailed 1 time(s) per year
Average Order Size: $40
Printing Information: 270 pages in 2 colors on Newsprint
Press: Web Press
Binding: Perfect Bound
Mailing List Information: Names for rent
Number of Employees: 18
Sales Volume: 1MM

865 Books on Tape
Books on Tape, A Division of Random Hous
400 Hahn Road
Attn: Customer Service
Westminster, MD 21157   800-733-7046
                              Fax: 800-940-7046
                              www.booksontape.com

Unabridged audio books for rent or sale

Chairman: Duval Y. Hecht
President: Ron Prowell
Marketing Manager: Katrin Bandhaver
Production Manager: Sigrid Hecht
Buyers: Judy Garber
Credit Cards: MasterCard; Visa
Catalog Cost: $5
Catalog Circulation: Mailed 1 time(s) per year to 150
Average Order Size: $25
Printing Information: 430 pages in 4 colors on Newsprint
Press: Web Press
Binding: Perfect Bound
Mailing List Information: Names for rent
In Business: 35 years
Number of Employees: 130

866 Capstone Library
Capstone Publishing
1710 Roe Crest Drive
North Mankato, MN 56003   800-747-4992
                                Fax: 888-262-0705
                                www.capstonepub.com

Fiction and non-fiction publications for children

Chairman: James P. Coughlan
President: Robert J. Coughlan
CFO: Steve Robinson
Marketing Manager: Matthew A. Keller
Chief Executive Officer: G. Thomas Ahern
Chief Operating Officer: William R. Rouse
Catalog Cost: Free
Catalog Circulation: Mailed 4 time(s) per year

Printing Information: 164 pages in 4 colors
In Business: 26 years

867 Conners Publications
Conners Publications
503 Tahoe Street
Natchitoches, LA 71457-5718   318-357-0924
                                    ALMEI@aol.com
                                    www.music-usa.org/conners/

868 ElderSong Fall 2015 Catalog
ElderSong Publications, Inc.
P.O. Box 74
Mount Airy, MD 21771   800-397-0533
                             info@eldersong.com
                             www.eldersong.com

Publisher and distributor of books, videos, and recordings for activity directors, recreation and creative arts therapists, occupational and rehab therapists

Printing Information: 16 pages
In Business: 30 years

869 Forecast International
Baker & Taylor
2550 W. Tyvola Road
Suite 300
Charlotte, NC 28217   800-775-1800
                            Fax: 704-998-3100
                            btinfo@baker-taylor.com
                            www.baker-taylor.com

Promotes new and forthcoming adult hardcover, paperback and spoken word audio titles

Chairman: Thomas Morgan
President: George F. Coe
CFO: Jeff Leonard
Marketing Manager: Whitney Grones
EVP of Merchandising / Digital Medi: David Cully
Executive Vice President, Baker & T: Sydney joined
Senior Vice President, Operations: Gary Dayton
Credit Cards: MasterCard
Printing Information: 50 pages
Number of Employees: 20-5
Sales Volume: $10,000,000 - $25,000,000

870 Grodner Comprehensive Catalog of Music, Books, Rec
Lemur Music
32240 Paseo Adelanto, Suite A
P.O. Box 1137
San Juan Capistrano, CA 92675   949-493-8323
                                       800-246-2277
                                       Fax: 949-493-8565
                                       lemur@lemurmusic.com
                                       www.lemurmusic.com

Instruments & Supplies for Upright Bass

871 Harper Audio/Caedmon
HarperCollins US
195 Broadway
New York, NY 10007-5299   212-207-7000
                                Fax: 212-207-6964
                                www.HarperCollins.Com

Adult and children's books on audio cassette

President: Brian Murray
CFO: Janet Gervasio
Chief Executive Officer: Mark Schoenwald
SVP, Human Resources: Diane Bailey
EVP, Operations: Larry Nevins
Credit Cards: MasterCard; Visa
Catalog Circulation: Mailed 1 time(s) per year
Number of Employees: 4500

872 Pelican Publishing
Pelican Publishing Company
1000 Burmaster St
Gretna, LA 70053-2246   504-368-1175
                              800-843-1724
                              Fax: 504-368-1195
                              sales@pelicanpub.com
                              www.pelicanpub.com

Books and audiocasettes, including the Maverick Guide Series, recent releases, and children's books including Christmas books from the past

President: Milburn Calhoun
Marketing Manager: Kathleen Calhoun
Credit Cards: MasterCard
Catalog Cost: Free
Catalog Circulation: Mailed 3 time(s) per year
Printing Information: 48 pages in 4 colors on Matte Stock
Press: Web Press
Binding: Saddle Stitched
Mailing List Information: Names for rent
In Business: 89 years
Number of Employees: 35
Sales Volume: $5MM to $10MM

873 Sing 'n Learn
Sing 'n Learn
5404 Lafayette Dr
Frisco, TX 75035   800-460-1973
                         www.singnlearn.com

Musical sets, auditory products such as story CDs, audio books, and radio theater.

In Business: 24 years

874 Unabridged Audiobooks
Blackstone Audio, Inc.
31 Mistletoe Rd.
Ashland, OR 97520   800-729-2665
                          800-621-0182
                          Fax: 877-492-0793
                          libraryservices@blackstoneaudio.com
                          www.blackstoneaudio.com

Unabridged recorded books

President: Josh Stanton
CFO: Heather Johnson
Marketing Manager: Anne Ashbey
ashbey@blackstoneaudio.com

875 West Music 2015 - 2016 School Year Catalog
West Music
P.O. Box 5521
Coralville, IA 52241   319-351-2000
                             800-397-9378
                             Fax: 888-470-3942
                             www.westmusic.com

Instruments and accessories

Printing Information: 200 pages

Business & Industry

876 AICPA Self-Study & On-Site Training Catalog
AICPA
1211 Avenue of the Americas
New York, NY 10036-8775   212-596-6200
                                888-777-7077
                                Fax: 212-596-6213
                                service@aicpa.org
                                www.aicpa.org

Books for CPAs; self-study for professional development

Chairman: Tommye E. Barie, CPA
tbarie@aicpa.org
President: Barry C. Melancon, CPA, CGMA
bmelancon@aicpa.org
CFO: Tim LaSpaluto, CPA, CGMA, CITP
tlaspaluto@aicpa.org
Marketing Manager: Matty Carr
SVP, Strategy, People & Innovation: Lawson

Carmichael
lcarmichael@aicpa.org
SVP, Public Practice & Global Allia: Susan Coffey, CPA, CGMA
scoffey@aicpa.org
Senior Vice President: JaniceMaiman, CAE
jmaiman@aicpa.org
In Business: 128 years

877 Association for Information & Image Management
AIIM
1100 Wayne Avenue
Suite 1100
Silver Spring, MD 20910-5642   301-587-8202
                                 800-477-2446
                            Fax: 301-587-8202
                              aiim@aiim.org
                              www.aiim.org

Books

Chairman: Paul Engel
President: John F Mancini
CFO: Felicia Dillard
Chief Evangelist: Atle Skjekkeland
Chief Information Officer: Laurence Hart
VP and CMO: Peggy Winton
Catalog Circulation: Mailed 1 time(s) per year
Printing Information: 62 pages in 4 colors
Binding: Perfect Bound
Number of Employees: 100

878 Atlantic Publishing Company
Atlantic Publishing Company
1405 SW 6th Avenue
Ocala, FL 34471   352-622-1825
                      Fax: 352-622-1875
                  sales@atlantic-pub.com
                    www.atlantic-pub.com

Books

Printing Information: 52 pages
In Business: 25+ years

879 Bailey's Master Catalog
Bailey's
1210 Commerce Ave.
Suite 8
Woodland, CA 95776   707-984-6133
                          800-322-4539
                      Fax: 530-406-0895
                  baileys@baileysonline.com

Books, DVDs, chainsaws, grinders, outdoor power equipment and tree care supplies

President: Judith Baileys
CFO: Janet Peper
Marketing Manager: John Conroy
Credit Cards: AMEX; MasterCard
Printing Information: 266 pages
In Business: 40 years
Number of Employees: 50
Sales Volume: $19,000,000

880 Book Publishing Resources
Para Publishing.com
530 Ellwood Ridge
Santa Barbara, CA 93117-1047   805-968-7277
                                800-727-2782
                            Fax: 805-968-1379
                        info@parapublishing.com
                        www.ParaPublishing.com

Books, manuals and other resources on book publishing

President: Dan Poynter
Fulfillment: Becky Carbone
Catalog Cost: Free
Catalog Circulation: Mailed 1 time(s) per year to 15000
Average Order Size: $68
Printing Information: 16 pages in 1 color on Matte Stock
Press: Sheetfed Press
Mailing List Information: Names for rent
List Manager: Becky Carbone

In Business: 42 years
Number of Employees: 2

881 Brody Professional Development
Brody Professional Development
115 West Avenue
Ste 114
Jenkintown, PA 19046   215-886-1688
                             800-726-7936
                         Fax: 215-886-1699
                           info@brodypro.com
                           www.brodypro.com

Releases one new title each year in the business/self help categories; business communication skills books, self-help and career titles

President: Marjorie Brody
Marketing Manager: Laura Kemp
Account Manager: Tina Altman
Tina@BrodyPro.com
Account Manager: Tom Gill
TGill@BrodyPro.com
Operations Support: Suzanne P. Harkinson
Suzanne@BrodyPro.com
Mailing List Information: Names for rent
In Business: 30 years
Sales Volume: Under $500M

882 Business Guidebooks
Quality Small Business Books
PO Box 1240
Willits, CA 95490   707-459-6372
                            800-515-8050
                        Fax: 707-459-6372
                  publisher@bellsprings.com
                    www.bellsprings.com

Publisher of business guides

President: Sam Leandro
Mailing List Information: Names for rent
In Business: 30 years
Number of Employees: 3
Sales Volume: $100,000

883 China Decorator Library
The China Decorator
PO Box 575
Shingle Springs, CA 95682-575   530-677-1455
                             Fax: 530-677-1408
                          support@chinadec.com
                            www.chinadec.com

200+ books, 1,000 studies for painters

Catalog Cost: $1
Printing Information: 64 pages
In Business: 56 years

884 Construction Book Express
Construction Book Express
990 Park Center Drive
Suite E
Vista, CA 92081-8352   888-264-2665
                              800-253-0541
                          Fax: 760-734-1540
                    www.constructionbook.com

Construction books, manuals, audio and video tapes

President: Scott Forde
Credit Cards: AMEX; MasterCard; Visa
Catalog Cost: Free
Catalog Circulation: Mailed 3 time(s) per year
Printing Information: 64 pages in 4 colors on Glossy Stock
Press: Web Press
Binding: Saddle Stitched
Mailing List Information: Names for rent
List Manager: Michelle Gray
In Business: 17 years
Number of Employees: 20

885 Contractor's Guide to QuickBooks Pro
Craftsman Book Co.
6058 Corte Del Cedro
Carlsbad, CA 92011   760-438-7828
                             800-829-8123
                         Fax: 760-438-0398
                     www.craftsman-book.com

Construction books and computer programs that cover cost guides, estimating, carpentry, construction contracting, electrical work, plumbing, concrete work, heavy construction, painting and remodeling

President: Gary Moselle
Marketing Manager: Bill Grote
Credit Cards: MasterCard
Catalog Cost: Free
Catalog Circulation: Mailed 1 time(s) per year to 250K
Printing Information: 40 pages on Glossy Stock
Press: Web Press
Binding: Saddle Stitched
Mailing List Information: Names for rent
In Business: 35 years
Number of Employees: 50
Sales Volume: $5MM to $10MM

886 Disability Bookshop Catalog
Twin Peaks Press
PO Box 8
Vancouver, WA 98666   360-694-2462
                    www.allaboutdisabledtravel.com

More than 400 titles relating to disability, medical, health, travel, home business and computers

President: Helen Hecker
Production Manager: Victoria Nova
Managing Director: Simon Pitts
Marketing Director: Anne Nolan
anolan@ashgatepublishing.com
Credit Cards: AMEX; MasterCard
Catalog Cost: $5
Catalog Circulation: Mailed 6 time(s) per year to 50000
Printing Information: 40 pages in 1 color on Matte Stock

887 Doolco
Doolco
11258 Goodnight Lane
Suite 105
Dallas, TX 75229-3395   972-241-2326
                              800-886-2653
                          Fax: 972-243-4381
                        jimdoolin@doolco.com
                          www.doolco.com

Books on refrigeration, air conditioning and heating

President: James P Doolin
Credit Cards: AMEX; MasterCard
Catalog Cost: Free
Catalog Circulation: Mailed 1 time(s) per year
Printing Information: 3 pages in 4 colors
Mailing List Information: Names for rent

888 Fairchild Books & Visuals
Fairchild Books
1385 Broadway
5th Floor
New York, NY 10018   202-419-5300
                              800-932-4724
                          Fax: 212-630-3868
                        www.fairchildbooks.com

Books for fashion industry and home sewers

CFO: William Sarr
william.sarr@bloomsbury.com
Marketing Manager: Sonia Dubin
sonia.dubin@bloomsbury.com
Production Manager: Ginger Hillman
ginger_hillman@condenast.com
Associate Director of Sales: Melanie Sankel
melanie.sankel@bloomsbury.com
Senior Account Manager: Allison Jones

allison.jones@bloomsbury.com
ExecutiveEditor: Olga Kontzias
olga.kontzias@bloomsbury.com
Catalog Cost: Free
Printing Information: 52 pages
In Business: 105 years

889   Fall 2015 Eerdmans Trade Catalog
Wm. B. Eerdmans Publishing Company
2140 Oak Industrial Dr. NE
Grand Rapids, MI 49505   616-459-4591
                             800-253-7521
                        Fax: 616-459-6540
                        info@eerdmans.com
                        www.eerdmans.com

Publisher of religious books, from academic works in theology, biblical studies
Printing Information: 32 pages
In Business: 104 years

890   Grey House Publishing
Grey House Publishing, Inc.
4919 Route 22
PO Box 56
Amenia, NY 12501   518-789-8700
                        800-562-2139
                   Fax: 518-789-0556
                   books@greyhouse.com
                   www.greyhouse.com

Reference directories in business, demographics, statistics, health and education as well as general reference encyclopedias
President: Richard Gottlieb
Marketing Manager: Jessica Moody
Production Manager: Kristen Hayes
Publisher: Leslie Mackenzie
Editorial Director: Laura Mars
Credit Cards: AMEX; MasterCard; Visa
Catalog Cost: Free
Catalog Circulation: Mailed 3 time(s) per year to 20M+
Average Order Size: $185
Printing Information: 12 pages in 4 colors on Glossy Stock
Press: Web Press
Binding: Saddle Stitched
In Business: 36 years
Number of Employees: 75

891   HW Wilson Company
Grey House Publishing, Inc.
4919 Route 22
PO Box 56
Amenia, NY 12501   518-789-8700
                        844-630-6369
                   Fax: 518-789-0556
                   www.hwwilsoninprint.com

Library reference books
Marketing Manager: Jessica Moody
Production Manager: Kristen Hayes
Editorial Director: Laura Mars
Credit Cards: AMEX; MasterCard; Visa
Catalog Cost: Free
Catalog Circulation: Mailed 2 time(s) per year
Printing Information: 40 pages in 4 colors on Glossy Stock
Press: Web Press
Binding: Saddle Stitched
Mailing List Information: Names for rent
In Business: 117 years

892   Human Kinetics Academic & Professional Resources
Human Kinetics
1607 N Market Street
PO Box 5076
Champaign, IL 61820-5076   800-747-4457
                        Fax: 217-351-1549
                        info@hkusa.com
                        www.humankinetics.com

Information on physical activity success in sports

Facility Manager: Bill Squires
Sport Club Management: Matthew Robinson
Credit Cards: AMEX; MasterCard; Visa
Catalog Cost: Free
Printing Information: 57 pages in 4 colors on Glossy Stock
Binding: Saddle Stitched
In Business: 40 years
Number of Employees: 80

893   IBM, Training Solutions
IBM
1133 Westchester Avenue
White Plains, NY 10604-3505   800-426-4968
                        Fax: 800-426-4329
                        www.ibm.com

Technology course catalogs - 4 books
Marketing Manager: Timothy F Hamill
Production Manager: Paul Humbles
Average Order Size: $1000

894   IFSTA
Fire Protection Publications (FPP)
930 N Willis Street
Stillwater, OK 74078-8045   405-744-5723
                        800-654-4055
                   Fax: 405-744-8204
                   customer.service@osufpp.org
                   www.ifsta.org

Curriculums, software, videos and books pertaining to fire training
Credit Cards: AMEX; MasterCard; Visa
Catalog Cost: Free
Catalog Circulation: Mailed 1 time(s) per year
Printing Information: 65 pages in 4 colors on Glossy Stock
In Business: 81 years

895   International Wealth Success
International Wealth Success
PO Box 186
Merrick, NY 11566-186   516-766-5850
                        800-323-0548
                   Fax: 516-766-5919
                   admin@iwsmoney.com
                   www.iwsmoney.com

Newsletters on small business covering topics including finance, loans, venture capital, IPOs, and grants in the areas of real estate, import-export, e-commerce, etc
President: Tyler Hicks
Credit Cards: AMEX; MasterCard
Catalog Cost: $3
Catalog Circulation: Mailed 12 time(s) per year to 5000
Printing Information: 52 pages in 1 color on Matte Stock
Press: Web Press
Binding: Saddle Stitched
In Business: 49 years

896   Jane's Catalog
IHS Jane's 360 Inc.
110 N. Royal Street
Alexandria, VA 22314-1693   703-683-3700
                        800-447-2273
                   Fax: 703-836-0297
                   customerservice.us@janes.com
                   www.janes.com

Directories, books and magazines on aerospace, aviation, and militaria
President: Alfred Rolington
CFO: Michael Staton
Marketing Manager: Greg Wallace
Production Manager: Lois Smith
Operations Manager: Peter Baxter
Executive Director: Charles Cunningham
International Marketing Manager: Lynne Samuel
Credit Cards: AMEX; MasterCard; Visa
Catalog Cost: Free
Catalog Circulation: Mailed 2 time(s) per year to 60M

Average Order Size: $500
Printing Information: 60 pages in 4 colors on Glossy Stock
Press: Web Press
Binding: Saddle Stitched
Mailing List Information: Names for rent
List Manager: Lynne Samuel
List Company: Merkle Computer Systems
In Business: 30 years
Number of Employees: 70

897   Lindsay's Technical Books
Lindsay's Technical Books
PO Box 538
Bradley, IL 60915   *Fax:* 815-935-5477
                   gluehead@lindsaybks.com
                   www.lindsaybks.com

Plans, lost secrets, forgotten how-to and strange books teach how to melt metal, be a machinist, blacksmith, mad scientist, homestead, build a working solar cell, shortwave radio
Credit Cards: MasterCard; Visa
Catalog Circulation: to 50000
Printing Information: on Glossy Stock
Binding: Folded

898   Literary Studies
Ashgate Publishing Company
110 Cherry Street
Suite 3-1
Burlington, VT 05401-3818   802-865-7641
                        800-535-9544
                   Fax: 802-865-7847
                   orders@ashgate.com
                   www.ashgate.com

Scholarly books, topics/titles include: Classical and Medieval Literature; Early Modern Literature; Early Modern Drama and Shakespeare Studies; Eighteenth, Nineteenth and Twentieth-Century Literature
Fulfillment: Suzanne Sprague
Number of Employees: 25

899   Motorbooks
Quarto Knows
400 First Avenue North
Suite 400
Minneapolis, MN 55401   800-458-0454
                        Fax: 612-344-8691
                   customerservice@quartous.com
                   www.quartoknows.com

Automotive books, shop manuals and restoration books
Chairman: Tim Chadwick
President: Ken Fund
CFO: Michael Connole, FCA
Director, Quarto International Co-e: David Breuer
Group Director of Operations: Michael Clarke
Managing Director, Books & Gifts Di: Joe Craven
Credit Cards: AMEX; MasterCard; Visa
Catalog Circulation: Mailed 4 time(s) per year
Printing Information: 40 pages in 4 colors
In Business: 39 years
Number of Employees: 110

900   Osborne/McGraw-Hill
McGraw-Hill Education
2600 10th Street
P.O. Box 182605
Columbus, OH 43218-2522   800-338-3987
                        Fax: 609-308-4480
                   customer.service@mheducation.com
                   www.osborne.com

Computer books
President: Larry Levitsky
Marketing Manager: Kendal Andersen
Buyers: Allen Wyatt, Computers/Printers
Bill Emrick, Office Supp./Furn.
Credit Cards: AMEX; MasterCard; Visa
Catalog Cost: Free

Catalog Circulation: Mailed 5 time(s) per year to 500K
Printing Information: 44 pages in 4 colors on Glossy Stock
Press: Web Press
Mailing List Information: Names for rent
List Manager: Kendall Andersen
In Business: 15 years
Number of Employees: 55
Sales Volume: $10,000,000 - $25,000,000

901 Page Computer
Page Computers
4665 Melrose Avenue
Los Angeles, CA 90029-3342   323-665-7777
                                     888-557-2557
                                Fax: 323-660-0444

Books on computers

President: Jay Dardashti
Catalog Circulation: to 100
In Business: 15 years

902 Parlay International
Parlay International
712 Bancroft Rd
505
Walnut Creek, CA 94598   800-457-2752
                            Fax: 925-939-1414
                            info@parlay.com
                            www.parlay.com

Collection of reproducible resources: one-page handouts on a variety of topics for insurance companies, hospitals, military personnel

President: Robert Lester
In Business: 28 years
Sales Volume: $500M to $1MM

903 Paul Gaudette Books
AbeBooks.com
PO Box 17389
Tucson, AZ 85731-7389   520-791-3868
                                800-874-3097
                           Fax: 520-751-4454
                           www.abebooks.com

Aviation, military and naval - 1900 to present

President: Sharon Pappas
Catalog Cost: $4
Catalog Circulation: Mailed 10 time(s) per year
Average Order Size: $35
Printing Information: 50 pages in 2 colors on Matte Stock
Press: Letterpress
Mailing List Information: Names for rent
In Business: 20 years
Number of Employees: 10-J
Sales Volume: Under $500M

904 Pegasus
Leverage Networks, Inc
PO Box 2786
Acton, MA 01720   978-206-1448
                          800-272-0945
                     Fax: 781-894-7175
                     rebecca@leveragenetworks.com
                     www.leveragenetworks.com

Books and publications for marketing and management

President: Kris Wile
kris@leveragenetworks.com
Director, Marketing & Operations: Kate Skaare
kate@leveragenetworks.com
Printing Information: 29 pages
In Business: 23 years

905 Publishing Pointers
Para Publishing.com
PO Box 8206-240
Santa Barbara, CA 93118-8206   805-968-7277
                             Fax: 805-968-1379
                             info@parapublishing.com
                             www.parapublishing.com

Book writing, publishing and promotion

President: Dan Poynter
Production Manager: Becky Carbone
Credit Cards: AMEX; MasterCard
Catalog Cost: Free
Catalog Circulation: Mailed 26 time(s) per year
Average Order Size: $66
Printing Information: 20 pages in 2 colors
Mailing List Information: Names for rent
List Manager: Becky Carbone
In Business: 34 years
Number of Employees: 3
Sales Volume: Under $500M

906 Rand McNally
Rand McNally & Company
9855 Woods Drive Skokie
Skokie, IL 60077-9915   847-329-8100
                                800-777-6277
                           Fax: 800-934-3479
                           ctsales@randmcnally.com
                           www.randmcnally.com

Business and marketing data books

President: Robert S Apatoff
Credit Cards: AMEX; MasterCard; Visa
Catalog Cost: Free
Catalog Circulation: Mailed 1 time(s) per year to 10M
Printing Information: 48 pages in 4 colors
In Business: 159 years
Number of Employees: 600

907 SAE International
SAE International
400 Commonwealth Drive
Warrendale, PA 15096-1   724-776-4841
                                 877-606-7323
                            Fax: 724-776-4970
                            publications@sae.org
                            www.sae.org

Annual listing of books and services by the Society of Automative Engineers listed by topic

President: Dr Richard W Greaves FREng
CFO: Dana Pless
Marketing Manager: Greg Muha
Chief Executive Officer: David L. Schutt, PhD
Chief Information Officer: Brian Kaleida
Director of Human Resources: Sandra L. Dillner
Catalog Cost: Free
Printing Information: 96 pages in 4 colors on Glossy Stock
Press: Letterpress
Binding: Perfect Bound
Mailing List Information: Names for rent
List Manager: Jodie Mohnkern
In Business: 100 years
Number of Employees: 200
Sales Volume: Under $500M

908 Salem Press
Grey House Publishing, Inc.
4919 Route 22
PO Box 56
Amenia, NY 12501   518-789-8700
                           800-221-1592
                      Fax: 518-433-4739
                      sales@salempress.com
                      www.salempress.com

Award-winning history, literature, science and health titles that serve as excellent research tools for high school and undergraduate level students. Most titles include complementary online access.

Marketing Manager: Jessica Moody
Production Manager: Kristen Hayes
Editorial Director: Laura Mars
Sales Manager: Jim Wright
jwright@salempress.com
Catalog Cost: Free
Printing Information: 92 pages in 4 colors on Glossy Stock
Press: Web Press
Binding: Saddle Stitched
In Business: 66 years

909 Scarecrow Press
Scarecrow Press
4501 Forbes Blvd
Suite 200
Lanham, MD 20706   301-459-3366
                           800-462-6420
                      Fax: 301-429-5748
                      customercare@rowman.com

Reference and scholarly books on numerous subjects including art and architecture, business and economics, children's and young adult services, music, film, religious studies and history

President: James E Lyons
Marketing Manager: Mary Jo Goodman
International Marketing Manager: Lita Orner
Credit Cards: MasterCard; Visa
Catalog Cost: Free
Catalog Circulation: Mailed 8 time(s) per year
Printing Information: 32 pages in 2 colors on Matte Stock
Press: Sheetfed Press
Binding: Saddle Stitched
Mailing List Information: Names for rent
In Business: 55 years
Number of Employees: 54
Sales Volume: $20MM to $50MM

910 Self Publishing Catalog
Safety Technology
1867 Caravan Trail
Suite 10
Jacksonville, FL 32216   904-720-2188
                                 800-477-1739
                            Fax: 904-720-0651

Non-fiction online marketing resource center

Catalog Cost: Free
Catalog Circulation: Mailed 12 time(s) per year
Printing Information: 8 pages in 3 colors on Glossy Stock
Press: Sheetfed Press
Binding: Saddle Stitched
Mailing List Information: Names for rent
In Business: 3 years
Number of Employees: 5
Sales Volume: Under $500M

911 Simmons-Boardman Publishing Corporation
Simmons-Boardman Publishing Corporation
55 Broad Street
26th Floor
New York, NY 10004   212-620-7200
                             800-257-5091
                        www.simmonsboardman.com

Magazines, books, directories, e-newsletters, conferences, educational materials, websites

912 Social Studies Catalog
Films Media Group
132 West 31st Street
17th Floor
New York, NY 10001-2053   800-322-8755
                                  800-257-5123
                             Fax: 800-678-3633
                             custserv@films.com
                             www.films.com

Social studies books

President: Steve Jones
Buyers: Vickie Meadows
Credit Cards: AMEX; MasterCard; Visa
Catalog Circulation: Mailed 12 time(s) per year to 30000
Printing Information: 48 pages in 2 colors on Glossy Stock
Press: Web Press
Binding: Saddle Stitched
Mailing List Information: Names for rent
List Company: Stevens-Knox
In Business: 13 years
Number of Employees: 5
Sales Volume: 1MM-3MM

913   Sociology and Social Policy
Ashgate Publishing Company
110 Cherry Street
Suite 3-1
Burlington, VT 05401-3818   802-865-7641
                                  800-535-9544
                            Fax: 802-865-7847
                      ashgate.online@ashgate.com
                                www.ashgate.com

Books on social issues, topics/titles include: Welfare Theory; Comparative Social Theory; Poverty and Social Exclusion; Race, Migration and Social Integration; Education Policy; Aging, and Gender

Fulfillment: Suzanne Sprague
Credit Cards: AMEX; MasterCard; Visa
Catalog Cost: Free
In Business: 40 years
Number of Employees: 15

914   The Met Store
The Metropolitan Museum of Art
1000 Fifth Avenue
New York, NY 10028   800-468-7386
               customer.service@metmuseum.org
                             store.metmuseum.org

Jewelry, apparel, home d,cor, prints & posters, books, stationery & calendars inspired by the Metropolitan Museum of Art

Catalog Cost: Free
In Business: 96 years

915   The Original Privacy Catalog
Eden Press
PO Box 8410
Fountain Valley, CA 92728   714-968-8472
                                  800-338-8484
                        edenpressinc@hotmail.com
                               www.edenpress.com

Books and videos that deal with privacy, money, home businesses, jobs, new identity, credit, degrees, cash business, foreign opportunities, residence and passports.

President: Barry Reid
Catalog Cost: Free
Printing Information: 16 pages on Newsprint
Press: Web Press
Binding: Saddle Stitched
Mailing List Information: Names for rent
In Business: 46 years
Sales Volume: $410K

916   UN Publications
United Nations Publications Customer Ser
15200 NBN Way
PO Box 190
Blue Ridge Summit, PA 17214   800-254-4286
                            Fax: 800-338-4550
                       unpublications@nbnbooks.com
                                    shop.un.org

Books published by the United Nations relating to international affairs, trade, business, development, disarmament, children's books and more

President: Susanna H Johnston
Marketing Manager: Fred Doulton
Credit Cards: MasterCard; Visa
Catalog Cost: Free

Catalog Circulation: Mailed 1 time(s) per year
Printing Information: 200 pages in 1 color on Matte Stock
Binding: Saddle Stitched
List Manager: Chris Woodthorpe
In Business: 68 years
Number of Employees: 1050

917   Working Library
Screen Web
PO Box 1060
Skokie, IL 60076-9785   847-763-4938
                              800-925-1110
                        Fax: 847-763-9030
                          SPTG@halldata.com
                             www.screenweb.com

Signmaking books

President: Ted Swormstedt
Marketing Manager: Jean Greenwell
Production Manager: Trish Hill
Credit Cards: AMEX; MasterCard; Visa
Catalog Cost: Free
Catalog Circulation: Mailed 4 time(s) per year to 50000
Printing Information: 6 pages
Number of Employees: 115
Sales Volume: $10MM to $20MM

918   Yestermorrow
Yestermorrow, Inc
7865 Main Street
Warren, VT 05673   802-496-5545
                         888-496-5541
                   Fax: 802-496-5540
                     www.yestermorrow.org

Design/Build school teaching courses for both design and construction

Executive Director: Kate Stephenson
Dev & Comm Director: Dave Thurlow
Facilities Manager: Dave Warren

919   Zenith Aviation
Zenith Aviation
1321 Lafayette Boulevard
Fredericksburg, VA 22401   540-361-7700
                                 800-458-0454
                           Fax: 540-361-7800
                        rfq@zenithaviation.com
                            www.zenithaviation.com

Aviation literature and videos

President: Robert F. Stanford
rstanford@zenithaviation.com
CFO: Martin Coster
General Manager/Executive Vice Pres:
Angela Shawaryn
ashawaryn@zenithaviation.com
VP, Operations / Quality: Donald A. Capwell
dcapwell@zenithaviation.com
Director, Business Development:
ScottNordstrom
snordstrom@zenithaviation.com
Credit Cards: AMEX; MasterCard; Visa
Catalog Circulation: Mailed 1 time(s) per year
Printing Information: 24 pages in 4 colors
Mailing List Information: Names for rent
In Business: 33 years
Number of Employees: 90
Sales Volume: $10,000,000 - $25,000,000

Children

920   Adventure Publications
Adventure Publications
820 Cleveland St S
Cambridge, MN 55008   800-678-7006
                        Fax: 877-374-9016
                  custservice@adventurepublications.net
                        www.adventurepublications.net

Publisher of regional, nature and outdoors books

In Business: 24+ years

921   B Shackman
B. Shackman Company, Inc
PO Box 247
Galesburg, MI 49053   844-505-3229
                            800-221-7656
                      Fax: 212-656-1903
                            www.shackman.com

Paper novelties, greeting cards, childrens picture books, stickers and toys

President: Dan Durett

922   Baby Bunz & Company
Baby Bunz & Company
PO Box 113
Lynden, WA 98264   360-354-1320
                         800-676-4559
                   Fax: 360-354-1203
                     info@babybunz.com
                        www.babybunz.com

Diapering, baby care, baby clothing, toys, books and mother care

President: Carynia Van Buren
Credit Cards: MasterCard
Catalog Cost: $1.00
Average Order Size: $75
Printing Information: 32 pages in 4 colors on Matte Stock
Press: Web Press
Binding: Saddle Stitched
Mailing List Information: Names for rent
In Business: 24 years
Number of Employees: 4

923   Baby-Go-To-Sleep Parenting Resources
Audio-Therapy Innovations, Inc
PO Box 550
Colorado Springs, CO 80901   719-473-0100
                               800-537-7748
                        terry@audiotherapy.com
                           www.babygotosleep.com

Music therapy recordings to help baby stop crying and sleep all night, soothes colic

President: Terry R Woodford
Credit Cards: AMEX; MasterCard
Catalog Cost: Free
Average Order Size: $28
Printing Information: 12 pages in 4 colors on Glossy Stock
Binding: Saddle Stitched
Mailing List Information: Names for rent
In Business: 30 years
Number of Employees: 9

924   Bahai Publishing Trust
Bahai Distribution Service
401 Greenleaf Ave
Wilmette, IL 60091-2886   847-425-7950
                                800-999-9019
                          Fax: 847-425-7951
                               bds@usbnc.org
                          www.bahaibookstore.com

History and religion books and multimedia materials

President: Tim Moore
Sales Volume: $3MM to $5MM

925   Bellerophon Books
Bellerophon Books
PO Box 21307
Santa Barbara, CA 93121-1307   805-965-7034
                                 800-253-9943
                           Fax: 805-965-8286
                     sales@bellerophonbooks.com
                         www.bellerophonbooks.com

Coloring books and art books for children of all ages

President: Harry Knill
Catalog Cost: Free
Printing Information: 20 pages in 2 colors on Matte Stock
Binding: Folded
Mailing List Information: Names for rent

In Business: 46 years
Number of Employees: 6

926 Boyds Mill Press
Boyds Mill Press
815 Church Street
Honesdale, PA 18431   570-253-1164
800-490-5111
www.boydsmillspress.com
High-quality fiction and nonfiction books
In Business: 25 years

927 Capstone Classroom
Capstone Publishing
1710 Roe Crest Drive
North Mankato, MN 56003   888-747-4992
Fax: 888-262-0705
www.capstonepub.com
Fiction and non-fiction publications for children
Chairman: James P. Coughlan
President: Robert J. Coughlan
CFO: Steve Robinson
Marketing Manager: Matthew A. Keller
Chief Executive Officer: G. Thomas Ahern
Chief Operating Officer: William R. Rouse
Catalog Cost: Free
Catalog Circulation: Mailed 1 time(s) per year
Printing Information: 164 pages in 4 colors
In Business: 26 years

928 Capstone Library
Capstone Publishing
1710 Roe Crest Drive
North Mankato, MN 56003   800-747-4992
Fax: 888-262-0705
www.capstonepub.com
Fiction and non-fiction publications for children
Chairman: James P. Coughlan
President: Robert J. Coughlan
CFO: Steve Robinson
Marketing Manager: Matthew A. Keller
Chief Executive Officer: G. Thomas Ahern
Chief Operating Officer: William R. Rouse
Catalog Cost: Free
Catalog Circulation: Mailed 4 time(s) per year
Printing Information: 164 pages in 4 colors
In Business: 26 years

929 Capstone Young Readers
Capstone Publishing
1710 Roe Crest Drive
North Mankato, MN 56003   800-747-4992
Fax: 888-262-0705
www.capstonpub.com
Fiction and non-fiction publications for children
Chairman: James P. Coughlan
President: Robert J. Coughlan
CFO: Steve Robinson
Marketing Manager: Matthew A. Keller
Chief Executive Officer: G. Thomas Ahern
Chief Operating Officer: William R. Rouse
Catalog Cost: Free
Catalog Circulation: Mailed 4 time(s) per year
Printing Information: 164 pages in 4 colors
In Business: 26 years

930 Children's Book of the Month
Children's Book of the Month Club Inc
PO Box 916400
Rantoul, IL 61866-6400   717-697-0311
www.cbomc.com
Children's books, board books, puzzles and games
President: Stuart Goldfarb
Fulfillment: Christine Miller
Credit Cards: AMEX; MasterCard
Catalog Cost: Free

931 Children's Books
Sterling Publishing
387 Park Avenue S
New York, NY 10016-8810   212-532-7160
800-367-9692
Fax: 212-213-2495
custservice@sterlingpublishing.com
www.sterlingpublishing.com
Children's books
President: Charles Nurnberg
CFO: Joe Guadango
Marketing Manager: Mary Ann Q Canapi
Production Manager: Rick Willett
Credit Cards: MasterCard; Visa
Catalog Cost: Free
Catalog Circulation: Mailed 2 time(s) per year to 30000
Printing Information: 100 pages in 4 colors on Glossy Stock
Press: Web Press
Binding: Perfect Bound
In Business: 50 years
Number of Employees: 70

932 Children's Books & Activities
Dover Publications
31 E 2nd Street
Mineola, NY 11501-3852   516-294-7000
Fax: 516-742-6953
www.doverpublications.com
Books and activity kits for children, including literary, paper dolls, coloring books, origami, stickers, mazes, puzzles, and more
President: Christopher J Kuppig
Marketing Manager: Kristine Anderson
Acquisitions Editor: Nora Rawn
Account Manager: Christopher Higgins
Catalog Cost: Free
In Business: 76 years
Number of Employees: 135
Sales Volume: 40MM

933 Chinaberry
Chinaberry
6655 Shelburne Road
Suite 100
Shelburne, VT 05482   802-860-1300
888-481-6744
service@chinaberry.com
www.chinaberry.com
Books, audio books, toys, games and crafts
Credit Cards: AMEX; MasterCard
Catalog Cost: Free
Printing Information: 120 pages in 3 colors on Glossy Stock
Binding: Folded
Mailing List Information: Names for rent
In Business: 36 years
Number of Employees: 45
Sales Volume: $11.5 Million

934 Cobblestone Publishing
Cobblestone & Cricket
30 Grove Street
Suite C
Peterborough, NH 03458   800-821-0115
Fax: 603-924-7380
customerservice@caruspub.com
www.cobblestonepub.com
Children's magazines and teacher resources, fiction and non-fiction children's magazines for grades K-10 middle grade and VA novels; teacher resources
Managing Art Director: Suzanne Beck
Editorial Director and Editor: Alice Letvin
Credit Cards: AMEX; MasterCard; Visa
Catalog Cost: Free
Printing Information: 36 pages
Mailing List Information: Names for rent
In Business: 41 years
Number of Employees: 13

935 Coloring Books
Dover Publications
31 E 2nd Street
Mineola, NY 11501-3852   516-294-7000
Fax: 516-742-6953
www.doverpublications.com
Adult coloring books
President: Christopher J Kuppig
Marketing Manager: Kristine Anderson
Acquisitions Editor: Nora Rawn
Account Manager: Christopher Higgins
Catalog Cost: Free
In Business: 76 years
Number of Employees: 135
Sales Volume: 40MM

936 Cricket
Cricket Media
30 Grove St
Ste C
Peterborough, NH 03458   603-924-7209
800-821-0115
customerservice@caruspub.com
www.cricketmag.com
Children's books and magazines for toddlers to teens
President: Andre Carus
CFO: Jason Patenaude
Marketing Manager: Mark Fagiano
Editorial Director: Alice Letvin
Managing Art Director: Suzanne Beck
Customer Service Manager: Cathy Sutton
Credit Cards: AMEX; MasterCard
Catalog Cost: Free
Printing Information: 48 pages
In Business: 40 years

937 Early Learning Essentials
Nasco Arts & Crafts Store
901 Janesville Avenue
PO Box 901
Fort Atkinson, WI 53538-901   920-563-2446
800-558-9595
Fax: 920-563-6044
custserv@enasco.com
www.enasco.com
Learning toys, games, manipulatives, puzzles, and books, plus supplies for art, music, movement, dramatic play
President: Andrew Reinen
Marketing Manager: Phil Niemeyer
Manager, Data Processing: Mike Wagner
Credit Cards: AMEX; MasterCard
Catalog Cost: Free
Catalog Circulation: to 25000
In Business: 74 years
Number of Employees: 540

938 Fall 2015 Eerdmans Books for Young Readers Catalog
Wm. B. Eerdmans Publishing Company
2140 Oak Industrial Dr. NE
Grand Rapids, MI 49505   616-459-4591
800-253-7521
Fax: 616-459-6540
info@eerdmans.com
www.eerdmans.com
Publisher of religious books, from academic works in theology, biblical studies
Printing Information: 32 pages
In Business: 104 years

939 Gallaudet University Press
Gallaudet University
800 Florida Ave NE # Emg
Washington, DC 20002-3695   202-651-5000
800-621-2736
Fax: 800-621-8476
www.Gallaudet.Edu

Books on deaf related subjects, including sign language, deaf studies and culture, general interest, parenting and children's bestsellers

President: Dr. T. Alan Hurwitz
Marketing Manager: Daniel Wallace
Production Manager: Jill Porco
Provost: Dr. Carol Erting
VP, Administration and Finance: Paul Kelly
VP, Development and Alumni Relation: Paul Julin
Sales Volume: $10MM to $20MM

940 Heyday
Heyday
P.O. Box 9145
Berkeley, CA 94709 510-549-3564
Fax: 510-549-1889
heydaybooks.com

Well-crafted books, public events, and innovative outreach programs

Chairman: Guy Lampard
President: Richard D. Baum
Marketing Manager: Mariko Conner
Publisher: Malcolm Margolin
Finance Director: David Isaacson
Sales Manager: Christopher Miya
Printing Information: 20 pages
In Business: 40+ years

941 Highlights
Highlights for Children
1800 Watermark Drive
P.O. Box 269
Columbus, OH 43216-0269 888-372-6433
Fax: 614-487-2700
www.highlights.com

Children's books and fun with a purpose, including toys, games, puzzles, and activity kits

Marketing Manager: Shelly Stotzer
Production Manager: Sarah Bergman
CEO: Kent Johnson
Editor in Chief: Christine French Cully
Buyers: Lisa Hess
Erin Fogarty
Credit Cards: MasterCard; Visa
Catalog Circulation: Mailed 6 time(s) per year
Average Order Size: $60
Printing Information: 52 pages in 4 colors on Glossy Stock
Press: Web Press
Binding: Saddle Stitched
In Business: 69 years
Sales Volume: $10MM to $20MM

942 Hundelrut Studio
Hundelrut Studio
584B Tenney Mountain Hwy.
Rte. 25
Plymouth, NH 3264 603-536-4396
info@hundelrutstudio.com
www.hundelrutstudio.com
In Business: 26 years

943 Klutz
Klutz
450 Lambert Ave
Palo Alto, CA 94306 650-687-2600
800-737-4123
Fax: 650-857-9110
thefolks@klutz.com
www.klutz.com

Children's activity books

President: Dewitt Durham
Credit Cards: MasterCard
Catalog Cost: Free
Catalog Circulation: Mailed 2 time(s) per year to 70000
Average Order Size: $35
Printing Information: 25 pages
Mailing List Information: Names for rent
In Business: 28 years
Number of Employees: 70

944 Leaflet Missal Annual Catalog
Leaflet Missal
976 W Minnehaha Ave
St Paul, MN 55104 800-328-9582
www.leafletonline.com

945 Lots and Lots of DVD Gifts for Kids
Marshall Publishing & Promotions Inc
123 S Hough Street
Barrington, IL 60010 224-238-3530
888-300-3455
Fax: 224-238-3531
info@marshallpublishinginc.com
www.marshallpublishinginc.com

Kid's videos, DVDs, CDs and books

Credit Cards: AMEX; MasterCard
Catalog Cost: Free
Catalog Circulation: Mailed 1 time(s) per year
Average Order Size: $50
Printing Information: 10 pages in 4 colors on Glossy Stock
Press: Web Press
Binding: Folded
Mailing List Information: Names for rent
List Manager: Glaser Direct
In Business: 8 years
Number of Employees: 1
Sales Volume: $500M to $1MM

946 Magic Cabin
Magic Cabin
7021 Wolftown-Hood Rd.
Madison, VA 22727 888-623-3655
www.magiccabin.com

Children's toys, games, craft kits, and other accessories

947 National Geographic Learning PreK-12 Catalog
Cengage Learning
20 Channel Center St.
Boston, MA 02210 617-289-7700
Fax: 617-289-7844
ngl.cengage.com

Books and learning materials.

CEO: Michael Hansen
Catalog Cost: Free
Printing Information: 604 pages
Mailing List Information: Names for rent
In Business: 9 years
Sales Volume: $1.7 Billion

948 One Step Ahead
One Step Ahead
1112 7th Ave.
Monroe, WI 53566-1364 888-557-3851
Fax: 847-615-7236
www.onestepahead.com

One stop shopping for moms and kids, from clothing to books and toys

President: Karen Scott
CFO: Susan O'Malley
Marketing Manager: Bob Patton
Credit Cards: AMEX; MasterCard
Catalog Cost: Free
Catalog Circulation: Mailed 12 time(s) per year to 10M
Average Order Size: $65
Printing Information: 48 pages in 4 colors on Glossy Stock
Press: Web Press
Binding: Saddle Stitched
Mailing List Information: Names for rent
List Manager: ALCNY
In Business: 23 years
Number of Employees: 150
Sales Volume: $ 9 Million

949 Redleaf Press 2015 Fall
Redleaf Press
10 Yorkton Court
St. Paul, MN 55117-1065 651-641-0508
800-423-8309
Fax: 800-641-0115
customerservice@redleafpress.org
www.redleafpress.org

Non-profit publisher of exceptional curriculum, management, and business resources

President: Barbara Yates
CFO: Kristen Harinen
Marketing Manager: Eric Johnson
SVP, COO: Ray Aboyan
SVP, Chief Advancement Officer: Todd Otis
Director of Development: Janet Bisbee
In Business: 42 years

950 Scholastic Reading Club
Scholastic Inc.
557 Broadway
New York, NY 10012 800-724-6527
www.scholastic.com

Educational materials and resources including learning games and activities, books and videos, pocket charts, storage centers and more.

Chair, President and CEO: Dick Robinson
Catalog Cost: Free
Catalog Circulation: Mailed 12 time(s) per year
Printing Information: in 4 colors
In Business: 96 years
Number of Employees: 8400
Sales Volume: $1.6 Billion

951 Soundprints
Palm Kids
50 Washington Street
Norwalk, CT 06854-1552 800-409-2457
800-228-7839
Fax: 203-846-1776
customercare@palmkids.com

Children storybooks, audio cassettes, dolls and stuffed animals

President: Ashley C Andersen
Number of Employees: 30

952 Spilsbury
Spilsbury
P.O. Box 10
Guilford, IN 47022-6408 800-772-1760
Fax: 513-354-1487
service@spilsbury.com
www.spilsbury.com

Puzzles, books, toys and games

Credit Cards: AMEX; MasterCard
Catalog Cost: Free
Printing Information: 70 pages in 4 colors on Glossy Stock
Binding: Saddle Stitched
In Business: 32 years

953 The Learning Connection
The Learning Connection
4100 Silver Star Road
Suite D
Orlando, FL 32808 800-218-8489
Fax: 407-292-2123
ryan@tlconnection.com
www.tlconnection.com

Educational books for children

General Manager: Ryan Handberg
Catalog Cost: Free
In Business: 23 years

954 Young Explorers
Young Explorers
2 BITS Trail
PO Box 3338
Chelmsford, MA 01824-0938   877-756-5058
                        Fax: 800-866-3235
                        help@youngexplorers.com
                        www.youngexplorers.com

Educational toys

President: John Fleischman
Credit Cards: AMEX; MasterCard; Visa
Catalog Cost: Free
In Business: 52 years

Education

955 2015 Professional & Academic Catalog
Concordia Publishing House
3558 South Jefferson St.
Louis, MO 63118   314-268-1000
                        800-325-3040
                        Fax: 800-490-9889
                        order@cph.org
                        www.cph.org

Sound materials for churches and individuals

President: Dr. Bruce G. Kintz
bruce.kintz@cph.org
CFO: Collin Bivens
collin.bivens@cph.org
Marketing Manager: Loren Pawlitz
loren.pawlitz@cph.org
Vice President & Corporate Counsel: Jonathan D. Schultz
jonathan.schultz@cph.org
Director of Graphic Design: Tim Agnew
tim.agnew@cph.org
Director of Sales: Paul Brunette
paul.brunette@cph.org
Printing Information: 36 pages
In Business: 146 years

956 AAVIM
Amn. Assoc. for Vocational Instructional
220 Smithonia Rd.
Winterville, GA 30683   706-742-5355
                        800-228-4689
                        Fax: 706-742-7005
                        sales@aavim.com
                        www.aavim.com

Instructional materials for vocational education.

President: Marion Fletcher
CFO: Jimmy McCully
Production Manager: Kim Butler
Fulfillment: Kim Butler
Vice President: Brad Bryant
Catalog Cost: Free
Catalog Circulation: to 10000
Mailing List Information: Names for rent
List Manager: Karen Seabaugh
List Company: Market Data Retrieval
In Business: 67 years
Number of Employees: 3
Sales Volume: $400K

957 AIAA Winter/Spring Publication Catalog
American Institute of Aeronautics and As
1801 Alexander Bell Drive
Suite 500
Reston, VA 20191-4344   703-264-7500
                        800-639-AIAA
                        Fax: 703-264-7551
                        custserv@aiaa.org
                        www.aiaa.org

Books - astronautical and aeronautical

President: James F. Albaugh
CFO: Laura McGill
Executive Director: Dr. Sandra Magnus
Vice President, Education: Dr. Steven E. Gorrell
Vice President, International Activ: Dr. John D. Evans

Printing Information: 50 pages in 7 colors
Binding: Folded
In Business: 85 years
Sales Volume: $380,000

958 Accelerated Development
Renaissance Learning
2911 Peach Street
Wisconsin Rapids, WI 54494   715-424-3636
                        800-338-4204
                        Fax: 715-424-4242
                        answers@renaissance.com
                        www.renaissance.com

Psychologically-based books for mental health practitioners and educators, including counselors, therapists, psychologists and other professionals in the human services, social work and education

Chairman: Derek Mapp
CFO: Mary T Minch
Marketing Manager: Julie Blystone
Chief Executive Officer: John J. Lynch Jr.
Executive Vice President of Sales: Samir Joglekar
Chief Marketing Officer: D. Andrew Myers
In Business: 31 years
Number of Employees: 950

959 American Press
American Press
60 State St # 700
Boston, MA 02109-5717   617-247-0022
                        Fax: 617-247-0022
                        americanpress@flash.net
                        www.Americanpressboston.Com

Handbooks, study guides, lab manuals, textbooks for college

President: Becky Fox
Sales Volume: $1MM to $3MM

960 Amsco School Publications
Amsco School Publications
1000 N Second Avenue
Logan, IA 51546-0500   800-831-4190
                        Fax: 800-543-2745
                        orders@perfectionlearning.com
                        www.amscopub.com

School publications on literature, language arts, science, math, social studies, and test preparations

President: Larry Beller
Marketing Manager: Irene Rubin
Production Manager: Richard Ausburn
Editorial Director,Science: Madalyn Stone
Mstone@amscopub
In Business: 91 years
Sales Volume: $20MM to $50MM

961 Astro Communication Services
Astro Communication Services, Inc.
PO Box 1646
El Cajon, CA 92022-1314   603-734-4300
                        866-953-8458
                        Fax: 619-631-0180
                        www.astrocom.com

Communication aids for educational purposes

President: David Reecher
Fulfillment: Judith Curran
Printing Information: 66 pages
Binding: Folded
In Business: 42 years

962 Books For Global Mindfulness
Booksource
1230 Macklind Ave.
St. Louis, MO 63110   314-647-0600
                        800-444-0435
                        Fax: 800-647-1923
                        SERVICE@booksource.com
                        www.booksource.com

Largest selection of new and classic titles and classroom collections.

Printing Information: 64 pages
In Business: 41 years

963 Boy's Town Press
Father Flanagan's Boy's Home
14100 Crawford Street
Floor 2
Boys Town, NE 68010-7520   402-498-1320
                        800-282-6657
                        Fax: 402-498-1310
                        btpress@boystown.org
                        www.boystownpress.org

Books, DVD's, CD's and poster for educators, parents and youth-serving professionals

General Manager: Barbara Lonnborg
Project Manager: Alex Grossman
IT Manager: Nick Cavallaro
Catalog Cost: Free
Catalog Circulation: Mailed 12 time(s) per year to 40000
Printing Information: 36 pages in 4 colors on Glossy Stock
Press: Web Press
Binding: Saddle Stitched
Mailing List Information: Names for rent
In Business: 20 years
Number of Employees: 7
Sales Volume: $1,000,000

964 Brookes Publishing
Brookes Publishing
PO Box 10624
Baltimore, MD 21285-624   800-638-3775
                        Fax: 410-337-8539
                        custserv@brookespublishing.com
                        www.brookespublishing.com

Books and videos on education, developmental disabilities, early childhood, early interaction, literacy, mental health, communication and language and related subjects

Chairman: Paul H. Brookes
President: Jeffrey D. Brookes
EVP: Melissa A Behm
Vice President & Publisher: George S. Stamathis
Credit Cards: AMEX; MasterCard; Visa
Catalog Cost: Free
Mailing List Information: Names for rent
In Business: 35 years
Number of Employees: 50

965 CABI North America
CABI Publishing
745 Atlantic Avenue
8th Floor
Boston, MA 02111   617-682-9015
                        800-552-3083
                        cabi-nao@cabi.org
                        www.cabi.org

Books, journals and electronic products on life sciences

President: Carol Mc Namara
Marketing Manager: Bob Nickerson
Regional Sales Manager, Latin Ameri: Claudio Plaza
Regional Sales Manager, USA and Can: Hope Jansen
Strategic Partnerships Manager: Patricia Neenan Kilmartin
p.neenan@cabi.org
In Business: 104 years
Sales Volume: $500M to $1MM

966 CQ Press
Sage Publications
2300 N Street
Suite 800
Washington, DC 20037 202-729-1900
customerservice@cqpress.com
www.cqpress.com

Books on American politics, federal and state government, American institutions, campaigns & elections, current events and world affairs

President: Blaise Simqu

967 Capstone Classroom
Capstone Publishing
1710 Roe Crest Drive
North Mankato, MN 56003 888-747-4992
Fax: 888-262-0705
www.capstonepub.com

Fiction and non-fiction publications for children

Chairman: James P. Coughlan
President: Robert J. Coughlan
CFO: Steve Robinson
Marketing Manager: Matthew A. Keller
Chief Executive Officer: G. Thomas Ahern
Chief Operating Officer: William R. Rouse
Catalog Cost: Free
Catalog Circulation: Mailed 1 time(s) per year
Printing Information: 164 pages in 4 colors
In Business: 26 years

968 Capstone Library
Capstone Publishing
1710 Roe Crest Drive
North Mankato, MN 56003 800-747-4992
Fax: 888-262-0705
www.capstonepub.com

Fiction and non-fiction publications for children

Chairman: James P. Coughlan
President: Robert J. Coughlan
CFO: Steve Robinson
Marketing Manager: Matthew A. Keller
Chief Executive Officer: G. Thomas Ahern
Chief Operating Officer: William R. Rouse
Catalog Cost: Free
Catalog Circulation: Mailed 4 time(s) per year
Printing Information: 164 pages in 4 colors
In Business: 26 years

969 Capstone Young Readers
Capstone Publishing
1710 Roe Crest Drive
North Mankato, MN 56003 800-747-4992
Fax: 888-262-0705
www.capstonpub.com

Fiction and non-fiction publications for children

Chairman: James P. Coughlan
President: Robert J. Coughlan
CFO: Steve Robinson
Marketing Manager: Matthew A. Keller
Chief Executive Officer: G. Thomas Ahern
Chief Operating Officer: William R. Rouse
Catalog Cost: Free
Catalog Circulation: Mailed 4 time(s) per year
Printing Information: 164 pages in 4 colors
In Business: 26 years

970 Channing Bete Company
Channing Bete Company
1 Community Place
South Deerfield, MA 01373-7328 800-477-4776
Fax: 800-499-6464
custsvcs@channing-bete.com
www.channing-bete.com

Educational resources and publications, human services, public health and community safety publications & resources and military resource programs

President: Michael Bete
Senior Vice President: Daniel E. Carmody
Credit Cards: MasterCard; Visa
Catalog Cost: Free
Catalog Circulation: to 30000
Printing Information: 64 pages in 4 colors on Matte Stock
Press: Offset Press
In Business: 81 years
Number of Employees: 250
Sales Volume: $20MM

971 Common Core State Standards
Booksource
1230 Macklind Ave.
St. Louis, MO 63110 314-647-0600
800-444-0435
Fax: 800-647-1923
SERVICE@booksource.com
www.booksource.com

Largest selection of new and classic titles and classroom collections.

Printing Information: 196 pages
In Business: 41 years

972 Development Studies
Ashgate Publishing Company
110 Cherry Street
Suite 3-1
Burlington, VT 05401-3818 802-865-7641
Fax: 802-865-7847
info@ashgate.com
www.ashgate.com

Publisher of educational materials

President: Richard Slappey
Marketing Manager: Sue White
swhite@gowerpublishing.com
International Sales Director: Richard Dowling
Credit Cards: AMEX; MasterCard

973 Early Childhood Collections
Booksource
1230 Macklind Ave.
St. Louis, MO 63110 314-647-0600
800-444-0435
Fax: 800-647-1923
SERVICE@booksource.com
www.booksource.com

Largest selection of new and classic titles and classroom collections.

Printing Information: 72 pages
In Business: 41 years

974 Edupress Catalog
Highsmith, LLC
PO Box 8610
4810 Forest Run Road
Madison, WI 53708-8610 608-241-1201
800-694-5827
Fax: 800-835-2329
www.highsmith.com/edupress

Standards-based language arts, math, science and social studies materials for PreK through eighth grade

Catalog Cost: Free

975 Elementary STEM Catalog
Pitsco Education
P.O. Box 1708
Pittsburg, KS 66762-1708 620-231-0010
888-835-0686
Fax: 800-533-8104
orders@pitsco.com
www.pitsco.com

Science, Technology, Engineering and Math teaching resources

President: Harvey R. Dean
Production Manager: Kyle Bailey
Chief Operating Officer: Lisa Paterni
Catalog Cost: Free
Catalog Circulation: Mailed 1 time(s) per year

Printing Information: 112 pages in 4 colors
In Business: 46 years
Number of Employees: 200
Sales Volume: $50MM to $100MM

976 Environmental Media Corporation
Environmental Media Corporation
PO Box 99
Beaufort, SC 29901 843-474-0147
800-368-3382
Fax: 843-986-9093
www.environmentalmedia.com

Books and other materials that support environmental education for the classroom and community

President: Bill Pendergraft
Credit Cards: AMEX; MasterCard; Visa
Catalog Cost: Free
Catalog Circulation: Mailed 4 time(s) per year
Printing Information: 40 pages in 4 colors
Binding: Saddle Stitched
Mailing List Information: Names for rent
In Business: 27 years
Number of Employees: 2

977 Fine Art & Art Instruction
Dover Publications
31 E 2nd Street
Mineola, NY 11501-3852 516-294-7000
Fax: 516-742-6953
www.doverpublications.com

Art books, coffee table books, and educational books on art

President: Christopher J Kuppig
Marketing Manager: Kristine Anderson
Acquisitions Editor: Nora Rawn
Account Manager: Christopher Higgins
Catalog Cost: Free
In Business: 76 years
Number of Employees: 135
Sales Volume: 40MM

978 Free Spirit Publishing
Free Spirit Publishing
6325 Sandburg Road
Suite 100
Minneapolis, MN 55427-3674 612-338-2068
Fax: 612-337-5050
help4kids@freespirit.com
www.freespirit.com

A catalog for children, parents and teachers about learning to cope with bullies, homework, and life in general

President: Judy Galbraith
CFO: Beth Kininkas
Marketing Manager: Angela Henchen
Executive Director: Linda Crawford
Purchasing Manager: Kimberly Kittleson-Hurley
Credit Cards: AMEX; MasterCard
Catalog Cost: Free
Catalog Circulation: Mailed 10 time(s) per year
Printing Information: in 4 colors
Press: Web Press
Binding: Saddle Stitched
Mailing List Information: Names for rent
In Business: 34 years
Number of Employees: 31
Sales Volume: $4.3 MM

979 Grades 6-12 Catalog
Booksource
1230 Macklind Ave.
St. Louis, MO 63110 314-647-0600
800-444-0435
Fax: 800-647-1923
SERVICE@booksource.com
www.booksource.com

Largest selection of new and classic titles and classroom collections.

Printing Information: 204 pages
In Business: 41 years

980 Grades K-6 Catalog
Booksource
1230 Macklind Ave.
St. Louis, MO 63110   314-647-0600
                            800-444-0435
                       Fax: 800-647-1923
SERVICE@booksource.com
www.booksource.com

Largest selection of new and classic titles and classroom collections.

Printing Information: 308 pages
In Business: 41 years

981 Health Care Educational Materials
Nasco Arts & Crafts Store
901 Janesville Avenue
PO Box 901
Fort Atkinson, WI 53538-901   920-563-2446
                                800-558-9595
                           Fax: 920-563-6044
custserv@enasco.com
www.enasco.com

DVDs, games, computer software and a variety of anatomical models, charts and replicas

President: Andrew Reinen
Marketing Manager: Phil Niemeyer
Manager, Data Processing: Mike Wagner
Contract Sales Manager: Dave Johnson
Director: Tim Taggart
ttaggart@eNasco.com
Catalog Cost: Free
Catalog Circulation: to 25000
In Business: 74 years
Number of Employees: 540

982 Heinemann Resources for Teachers K-8
Heinemann
P.O. Box 6926
Portsmouth, NH 03802-6926   603-431-7894
                              800-225-5800
                         Fax: 877-231-6980
custserv@heinemann.com
www.heinemann.com

Books for English teaching K-8

President: Lesa Scott
Sales Services Manager: Lori Lampert
Credit Cards: AMEX; MasterCard; Visa
Catalog Cost: Free
In Business: 37 years

983 High School Science Catalog
PASCO Scientific, Inc.
10101 Foothills Boulevard
Roseville, CA 95747-7100   916-786-3800
                             800-772-8700
                        Fax: 916-786-7565
www.pasco.com

Teaching supplies for high schol level science

President: Paul A. Stokstad
Catalog Cost: Free
Catalog Circulation: Mailed 1 time(s) per year
Printing Information: 192 pages in 4 colors
In Business: 53 years
Number of Employees: 160
Sales Volume: $50MM to $100MM

984 Homespun Music Instruction
Homespun Tapes
Woodstock NY
                             800-338-2737
                        Fax: 845-246-5282
www.homespun.com

Instructional books, CDs, DVDs, and supplies to learn how to play a variety of instruments

President: Happy Traum
Co-Founder/Vice President: Jane Traum
Office Manager: Susan Robinson
Customer Service/Production Assoc.: Joyce Rado

Catalog Cost: Free
In Business: 48 years

985 Human Kinetics Physical Education and Dance
Human Kinetics
1607 N Market Street
PO Box 5076
Champaign, IL 61825-5076   217-351-5076
                             800-747-4457
                        Fax: 217-351-1549
info@hkusa.com
www.humankinetics.com

Informational resources for K-12 teachers and recreation and dance professionals, and textbooks and references for educators and researchers

President: Rainer Martens
Marketing Manager: Bill Sunderland
Credit Cards: AMEX; MasterCard; Visa
Catalog Cost: Free
Printing Information: in 4 colors on Glossy Stock
Binding: Saddle Stitched
In Business: 30 years

986 IFSTA
Fire Protection Publications (FPP)
930 N Willis Street
Stillwater, OK 74078-8045   405-744-5723
                              800-654-4055
                         Fax: 405-744-8204
customer.service@osufpp.org
www.ifsta.org

Curriculums, software, videos and books pertaining to fire training

Credit Cards: AMEX; MasterCard; Visa
Catalog Cost: Free
Catalog Circulation: Mailed 1 time(s) per year
Printing Information: 65 pages in 4 colors on Glossy Stock
In Business: 81 years

987 IVP Academic Catalog
InterVarsity Press
430 Plaza Dr
PO Box 1400
Westmont, IL 60559   630-734-4000
                       800-843-9487
                  Fax: 630-734-4350
email@ivpress.com
www.ivpress.com

Christian books

Printing Information: 52 pages
In Business: 70+ years

988 K-9 Science Catalog
ETA/Cuisenaire
500 Greenview Court
Vernon Hills, IL 60061   847-816-5050
                           800-875-9643
www.hand2mind.com

Educational and supplemental materials for PreK and grades K-12

President: Bill Chiasson
Marketing Manager: Shannon Cerny
Production Manager: Dr. Barbara diSioudi
Vice President, Sales: Soren Sofhauser
CPA, Controller: Gregg Tonkery
In Business: 40 years

989 KidSafety of America
KidSafety of America
6288 Susana Street
Chino, CA 91710   909-627-8700
                    800-524-1156
               Fax: 909-627-8777
info@kidsafetystore.com
www.kidsafetystore.com

Educational books and videos to promote the health and safety of children and their families

President: Peter D Osilaja
Buyers: Virginia Anorade
Credit Cards: AMEX; MasterCard; Visa
Catalog Cost: Free
Mailing List Information: Names for rent
In Business: 23 years
Number of Employees: 10
Sales Volume: $930,000

990 Knowledge Unlimited
Knowledge Unlimited
2320 Pleasant View Rd
P.O. Box 52
Middleton, WI 53562   608-836-6660
                        800-356-2303
                   Fax: 608-836-6684
csis@newscurrents.com
www.thekustore.com

Instructional materials for the educator looking for value; Posters, books, videos, teching kits, and current events programs suitable for grades 3 and up

President: Judith Laitman
Buyers: Melanie Wearing
Credit Cards: AMEX; MasterCard; Visa
Mailing List Information: Names for rent
In Business: 32 years
Number of Employees: 26
Sales Volume: $1MM to $3MM

991 Leveled Reading Catalog
Booksource
1230 Macklind Ave.
St. Louis, MO 63110   314-647-0600
                        800-444-0435
                   Fax: 800-647-1923
SERVICE@booksource.com
www.booksource.com

Largest selection of new and classic titles and classroom collections.

Printing Information: 244 pages
In Business: 41 years

992 Library Books K-12
Enslow Publishers
101 West 23rd Street
Suite #240
New York, NY 10011-398   908-771-9400
                           800-398-2504
                      Fax: 877-980-4454
customerservice@enslow.com
www.enslow.com

Books on multicultural studies, American history and biographies

Chairman: Brian Enslow, VP
President: Mark Enslow
Founder: Ridley M. Enslow, Jr.
Author: Nathan Aaseng
Author: Brian Aberback
Catalog Cost: Free
Printing Information: 142 pages in 4 colors on Glossy Stock
In Business: 38 years

993 Literature & Humanities
Dover Publications
31 E 2nd Street
Mineola, NY 11501-3852   516-294-7000
                      Fax: 516-742-6953
www.doverpublications.com

Fiction and nonfiction publications

President: Christopher J Kuppig
Marketing Manager: Kristine Anderson
Acquisitions Editor: Nora Rawn
Account Manager: Christopher Higgins
Catalog Cost: Free
In Business: 76 years
Number of Employees: 135
Sales Volume: 40MM

994 Literature Resources
Booksource
1230 Macklind Ave.
St. Louis, MO 63110   314-647-0600
                          800-444-0435
                     Fax: 800-647-1923
               SERVICE@booksource.com
                   www.booksource.com

Largest selection of new and classic titles and classroom collections.

In Business: 41 years

995 Mathematics & Science
Dover Publications
31 E 2nd Street
Mineola, NY 11501-3852   516-294-7000
                     Fax: 516-742-6953
             www.doverpublications.com

Books on general science, mathematics, physics, chemistry, engineering, astronomy and more

President: Christopher J Kuppig
Marketing Manager: Kristine Anderson
Acquistions Editor: Nora Rawn
Account Manager: Christopher Higgins
Catalog Cost: Free
In Business: 76 years
Number of Employees: 135
Sales Volume: 40MM

996 Mayer-Johnson
Mayer-Johnson
2100 Wharton St.
Suite 400
Pittsburgh, PA 15203   412-381-4883
                          800-588-4548
                     Fax: 866-585-6260
               MJQ@tobiidynavox.com
                   www.mayer-johnson.com

Special educational software.

997 Middle School Science Catalog
PASCO Scientific, Inc.
10101 Foothills Boulevard
Roseville, CA 95747-7100   916-786-3800
                          800-772-8700
                     Fax: 916-786-7565
                   www.pasco.com

Teaching supplies for middle school grades

President: Paul A. Stokstad
Catalog Cost: Free
Catalog Circulation: Mailed 1 time(s) per year
Printing Information: 56 pages in 4 colors
In Business: 53 years
Number of Employees: 160
Sales Volume: $50MM to $100MM

998 Music is Elementary
Music is Elementary
5228 Mayfield Road
Lyndhurst, OH 44124   800-888-7502
                     Fax: 440-461-3631
               info@musiciselementary.com
                   www.musiciselementary.com

Items such as books, CDs, instruments, and accessories for elementary music education, music therapy, and anyone with an interest in music

Music Consultant: BethAnn Hepburn
Credit Cards: AMEX; MasterCard
Catalog Cost: Free

999 NYC Grades 6-12 Catalog
Booksource
1230 Macklind Ave.
St. Louis, MO 63110   314-647-0600
                          800-444-0435
                     Fax: 800-647-1923
               SERVICE@booksource.com
                   www.booksource.com

Largest selection of new and classic titles and classroom collections.

In Business: 41 years

1000 NYC Grades K-6 Catalog
Booksource
1230 Macklind Ave.
St. Louis, MO 63110   314-647-0600
                          800-444-0435
                     Fax: 800-647-1923
               SERVICE@booksource.com
                   www.booksource.com

Largest selection of new and classic titles and classroom collections.

In Business: 41 years

1001 NYC Leveled Reading Catalog
Booksource
1230 Macklind Ave.
St. Louis, MO 63110   314-647-0600
                          800-444-0435
                     Fax: 800-647-1923
               SERVICE@booksource.com
                   www.booksource.com

Largest selection of new and classic titles and classroom collections.

In Business: 41 years

1002 National Geographic Learning PreK-12 Catalog
Cengage Learning
20 Channel Center St.
Boston, MA 02210   617-289-7700
                     Fax: 617-289-7844
                   ngl.cengage.com

Books and learning materials.

CEO: Michael Hansen
Catalog Cost: Free
Printing Information: 604 pages
Mailing List Information: Names for rent
In Business: 9 years
Sales Volume: $1.7 Billion

1003 Nienhuis Educational Catalog
Nienhuis Montessori USA
150 South Whisman Road
Mountain View, CA 94041-1512 650-964-2735
                          800-942-8697
                     Fax: 650-964-8162
               info@nienhuis-usa.com
                   www.nienhuis.com

Books by and about Dr. Maria Montessori and her method, books for teachers and parents, and for reference

President: Dick K P Luijendijk
Founder: Albert Nienhuis
Credit Cards: AMEX; MasterCard; Visa
Catalog Cost: Free
In Business: 86 years

1004 Parlay International
Parlay International
712 Bancroft Rd
505
Walnut Creek, CA 94598   800-457-2752
                     Fax: 925-939-1414
               info@parlay.com
                   www.parlay.com

Collection of reproducible resources: one-page handouts on a variety of topics for insurance companies, hospitals, military personnel

President: Robert Lester
In Business: 28 years
Sales Volume: $500M to $1MM

1005 Peterson Publishing
Peterson
121 S 13 Street
Lincoln, NE 68508   877-433-8277
               support@petersons.com
                   www.petersons.com

Books, directories and college guides for parents and students

President: Tom McGee
In Business: 52 years
Number of Employees: 250
Sales Volume: $50MM to $100MM

1006 Peytral Publications
Peytral Publications
PO Box 1162
Minnetonka, MN 55345-162   952-949-8707
                          877-739-8725
                     Fax: 952-906-9777
                   www.peytral.com

Educational books for teachers

Credit Cards: MasterCard
Catalog Cost: Free
Printing Information: 16 pages in 4 colors on Glossy Stock
Press: Web Press
Binding: Saddle Stitched
Mailing List Information: Names for rent
Number of Employees: 3
Sales Volume: $500M to $1MM

1007 Pitsco Maker Space Catalog
Pitsco Education
P.O. Box 1708
Pittsburg, KS 66762-1708   620-231-0010
                          800-835-0686
                     Fax: 800-533-8104
               orders@pitsco.com
                   www.pitsco.com

Activities, project kits, supplies, furniture, and storage to create maker spaces for robobits and other science activities.

President: Harvey R. Dean
Production Manager: Kyle Bailey
Chief Operating Officer: Lisa Paterni
Catalog Cost: Free
Catalog Circulation: Mailed 1 time(s) per year
Printing Information: 64 pages in 4 colors
In Business: 46 years
Number of Employees: 200
Sales Volume: $50MM to $100MM

1008 Planetary Publications/HeartMath
Heartmatt LLC
14700 W Park Avenue
Boulder Creek, CA 95006-9318 831-338-8700
                          800-450-9111
                     Fax: 831-338-9861
               info@heartmath.com
                   www.heartmath.com

Books, audiobooks, music videos, learning programs based on the research of the Institute of Heartmath with resources based on heart/mind research, health, parenting, self-help, and child development

Chairman: Doc Childre
President: Bruce Cryer
CFO: Chris Jacob
Marketing Manager: Lisa Lehnnoff
Production Manager: J J McCraty
Credit Cards: AMEX; MasterCard
Catalog Cost: Free
Catalog Circulation: Mailed 2 time(s) per year to 50000
Average Order Size: $75
Printing Information: 4 pages in 2 colors
Press: Sheetfed Press
Binding: Folded
Mailing List Information: Names for rent
In Business: 21 years
Number of Employees: 10

1009 Pre K-12 Math & Science Catalog
ETA/Cuisenaire
500 Greenview Court
Vernon Hills, IL 60061   847-816-5050
     800-288-9920
Fax: 800-875-9643
info@etacuisenaire.com
www.etacuisenaire.com

Educational and supplemental materials for
PreK and grades K-12

President: Dennis K Goldman
In Business: 39 years

1010 Pre K-8 Literacy Solutions Catalog
ETA/Cuisenaire
500 Greenview Court
Vernon Hills, IL 60061   847-816-5050
     800-288-9920
Fax: 800-875-9643
info@etacuisenaire.com

Educational and supplemental materials for
PreK and grades K-12

President: Dennis K Goldman
In Business: 39 years

1011 Professional Resources for Teachers K-8
Heinemann
P.O. Box 6926
Portsmouth, NH 03802-6926   603-431-7894
     800-225-5800
Fax: 877-231-6980
custserv@heinemann.com
www.heinemann.com

Professional resources and educational services for teachers kindergarten through 8th grade

President: Lesa Scott
Credit Cards: AMEX; MasterCard
In Business: 39 years
Sales Volume: $20MM to $50MM

1012 Prufrock Press
Prufrock Press
PO Box 8813
Waco, TX 76714-8813   254-756-3337
     800-998-2208
Fax: 254-756-3339
info@prufrock.com
www.prufrock.com

Activity books, teaching resources, identification instruments, journals and magazines for teaching and educating gifted children

General Manager: Ginny Bates
Marketing Assistant: Elizabeth Harp
Credit Cards: AMEX; MasterCard
Catalog Cost: Free
In Business: 23 years
Number of Employees: 7
Sales Volume: $660,000

1013 Robotics
Pitsco Education
P.O. Box 1708
Pittsburg, KS 66762-1708   620-231-0010
     800-835-0686
Fax: 800-533-8104
orders@pitsco.com
www.pitsco.com

science, Technology, Engineering, Math, and Robotics teaching resources

President: Harvey R Dean
Production Manager: Kyle Bailey
Chief Operating Officer: Lisa Paterni
Catalog Cost: Free
Catalog Circulation: Mailed 1 time(s) per year
Printing Information: 68 pages in 4 colors
In Business: 46 years
Number of Employees: 200
Sales Volume: $50MM to $100MM

1014 Sage Publications
Sage Publications
2455 Teller Road
Thousand Oaks, CA 91320   805-499-9774
     800-818-7243
orders@sagepub.com
www.sagepub.com

Journals on adolescent studies, anthropology, criminology, economics, family studies, history, marketing, philosophy, regional studies, social work, sociology and urban studies

Chairman: Sara Miller McCune
President: Blaise R Simqu
CFO: Chris Hickok
Marketing Manager: David Walsh
EVP, Chief Operating Officer: Tracey A. Ozmina
Global Chief Information Officer: Phil Denvir
Director: Gretchen Bataille
Credit Cards: AMEX; MasterCard
In Business: 52 years
Number of Employees: 1500
Sales Volume: $50MM to $100MM

1015 Sargent Welch
Sargent Welch
PO Box 92912
Rochester, NY 14692-9012   800-727-4368
Fax: 800-676-2540
customerservice@sargentwelch.com
www.sargentwelch.com

Science education equipment, supplies and lab furniture

In Business: 150 years

1016 Slosson Educational Publications
Slosson Educational Publications, Inc.
PO Box 280
East Aurora, NY 14052-280   716-652-0930
     888-756-7766
Fax: 800-655-3840
slossonprep@gmail.com
www.slosson.com

Educational testing, school screening, achievement, speech language, special needs, intelligence, apitude, developmental abilities, assessment therapy, emotional/behavioral, test preperations

President: Steven Slosson
CFO: Janet Slosson
Marketing Manager: David Slosson
Production Manager: John Slosson
Credit Cards: AMEX; MasterCard
Catalog Cost: Free
Catalog Circulation: Mailed 1 time(s) per year to 500M
Printing Information: 82 pages in 4 colors on Glossy Stock
Press: Web Press
Binding: Saddle Stitched
In Business: 22 years
Number of Employees: 15

1017 Spanish and ELL Collections
Booksource
1230 Macklind Ave.
St. Louis, MO 63110   314-647-0600
     800-444-0435
Fax: 800-647-1923
SERVICE@booksource.com
www.booksource.com

Largest selection of new and classic titles and classroom collections.

Printing Information: 100 pages
In Business: 41 years

1018 Spring/Summer 2015 Eerdmans Academic Catalog
Wm. B. Eerdmans Publishing Company
2140 Oak Industrial Dr. NE
Grand Rapids, MI 49505   616-459-4591
     800-253-7521
Fax: 616-459-6540
info@eerdmans.com
www.eerdmans.com

Publisher of religious books, from academic works in theology, biblical studies

In Business: 104 years

1019 SteinerBooks
Anthroposophic Press
PO Box 960
Herndon, VA 20172-0960   703-661-1594
Fax: 703-661-1501
service@steinerbooks.org
www.steinerbooks.org

Education books of all kinds including works on and by Rudolf Steiner and Waldorf educations

President: Gene Gollogly
CFO: Christopher Bamford
Production Manager: Stephan O'Reilly
Director: Mary Giddens
Editor: Marsha Post
Credit Cards: AMEX; MasterCard
Catalog Cost: Free
Catalog Circulation: Mailed 4 time(s) per year
In Business: 72 years
Number of Employees: 7

1020 Texas Essential Knowledge and Skills 2013-2014
Booksource
1230 Macklind Ave.
St. Louis, MO 63110   314-647-0600
     800-444-0435
Fax: 800-647-1923
SERVICE@booksource.com
www.booksource.com

Largest selection of new and classic titles and classroom collections.

Printing Information: 102 pages
In Business: 41 years

1021 The Learning Connection
The Learning Connection
4100 Silver Star Road
Suite D
Orlando, FL 32808   800-218-8489
Fax: 407-292-2123
ryan@tlconnection.com
www.tlconnection.com

Educational books for children

General Manager: Ryan Handberg
Catalog Cost: Free
In Business: 23 years

1022 Timberdoodle Co
Timberdoodle Co
1510 E Spencer Lake Road
Shelton, WA 98584   360-426-0672
     800-478-0672
Fax: 360-427-5625
customerservice@timberdoodle.com
www.timberdoodle.com

Educational books, activities, kits, courses, and toys

Credit Cards: AMEX; MasterCard
Catalog Cost: Free
In Business: 32 years

1023 UCLA Bear Wear
University of Los Angeles California
308 Westwood Plz
Los Angeles, CA 90095-8355   310-825-4321
bookzone@asucla.ucla.edu
www.Asucla.Ucla.Edu

College books and accessories

President: Bob Williams
Marketing Manager: Lisa Perez
Mailing List Information: Names for rent
In Business: 96 years

1024 Units of Study for Reading & Writing - Lucy Calkin
Booksource
1230 Macklind Ave.
St. Louis, MO 63110   314-647-0600
800-444-0435
Fax: 314-647-1923
SERVICE@booksource.com
www.booksource.com

Largest selection of new and classic titles and classroom collections.

Printing Information: 126 pages
In Business: 41 years

1025 World Quest Learning Catalog
World Quest Learning
PO Box 654
Lewis Center, OH 43035   614-245-0647

Educational books and supplies

President: Freda Seabolt

New Age & Religion

1026 2015 - 2016 Christian Education Catalog
Concordia Publishing House
3558 South Jefferson St.
Louis, MO 63118   314-268-1000
800-325-3040
Fax: 800-490-9889
order@cph.org
www.cph.org

Sound materials for churches and individuals

President: Dr. Bruce G. Kintz
bruce.kintz@cph.org
CFO: Collin Bivens
collin.bivens@cph.org
Marketing Manager: Loren Pawlitz
loren.pawlitz@cph.org
Vice President & Corporate Counsel: Jonathan D. Schultz
jonathan.schultz@cph.org
Director of Graphic Design: Tim Agnew
tim.agnew@cph.org
Director of Sales: Paul Brunette
paul.brunette@cph.org
Printing Information: 16 pages
In Business: 146 years

1027 ACS Publications
ACS Publications
334 Calef Highway
Epping, NH 03042   603-734-4300
866-953-8458
Fax: 603-734-4311
www.acspublications.com

Titles on astrology, holistic health, metaphysics and related subjects.

President: Judith Curran
Marketing Manager: James D McLain
Production Manager: Daryl Fuller
Credit Cards: AMEX; MasterCard; Visa
Catalog Circulation: Mailed 4 time(s) per year to 25000
Printing Information: 30 pages in 1 color on Matte Stock
Binding: Saddle Stitched
In Business: 32 years
Number of Employees: 11
Sales Volume: $500,000

1028 Artscroll
Artscroll Publications
222 44th Street
Brooklyn, NY 11232   718-921-9000
800-637-6724
Fax: 718-680-1875
info@artscroll.com
www.artscroll.com

Books relating to Judiasm

President: Meir Zlotowitz
Credit Cards: MasterCard; Visa
Catalog Cost: Free
Catalog Circulation: Mailed 1 time(s) per year to 20000
Printing Information: 40 pages in 4 colors
Number of Employees: 40
Sales Volume: $5MM to $10MM

1029 Augsburg Fortress
Augsburg Fortress
PO Box 1209
Minneapolis, MN 55440-1209   612-330-3300
800-328-4648
Fax: 612-330-3455
customerservice@augsburgfortress.org
www.augsburgfortress.org

Religious gifts, plaques, crucifixes and church materials

President: Beth Lewis
Marketing Manager: Jim Donohue
International Marketing Manager: Brad Gray
Credit Cards: AMEX; MasterCard
Catalog Cost: Free
Catalog Circulation: Mailed 1 time(s) per year
Printing Information: in 4 colors on Glossy Stock
Binding: Saddle Stitched
Mailing List Information: Names for rent
In Business: 125 years
Number of Employees: 300

1030 Auromere Books
Auromere Ayurvedic Imports
2621 W Highway 12
Lodi, CA 95242-9200   209-339-3710
800-735-4691
Fax: 209-339-3715
www.auromere.com

Spiritual books from India, classical spiritual texts, such as the Vedas, Upanishads, Tantra, Vedanta, and Bhagavad Gita; children's books from India, Sanskrit and Hindi

President: Dakshina Vanzetti
Marketing Manager: Vishnu Eschner
Credit Cards: AMEX; MasterCard
Average Order Size: $50
Mailing List Information: Names for rent
In Business: 25 years
Number of Employees: 4
Sales Volume: $370,000

1031 Aurora Press
Aurora Press
PO Box 573
Santa Fe, NM 87504-573   505-989-9804
Fax: 505-982-8321
info@aurorapress.com
www.aurorapress.com

Alternative health products, titles on astrology and metaphysics

Chairman: John Guffey
Catalog Cost: Free
Printing Information: 48 pages
In Business: 48 years

1032 Autom Inspirational Gifts
Autom
5226 S 31st Place
Phoenix, AZ 85040   800-521-2914
Fax: 800-582-1166
www.autom.com

Catholic and Christian books and related items

President: Paul DiGiovanni
CFO: Thomas DiGiovanni
Credit Cards: AMEX; MasterCard
Catalog Cost: Free
Catalog Circulation: Mailed 1 time(s) per year
Printing Information: 56 pages
Binding: Perfect Bound
In Business: 65 years

1033 AzureGreen
AzureGreen
16 Bell Road
P.O. Box 48
Middlefield, MA 01243   413-623-2155
800-326-0804
Fax: 413-623-2156
azuregreen@azuregreen.com
www.azuregreen.net

Metaphysical, witchcraft, pagan, spell crafts and new age supplies including; books, CDs, videos, ritual & spell craft supplies, amulets, jewelry, herbs, incense, cauldrons, statuary and candles

President: Adair Cafarella
Credit Cards: MasterCard; Visa
Catalog Cost: $5
Average Order Size: $100
Printing Information: 200 pages
Mailing List Information: Names for rent
In Business: 31 years
Number of Employees: 25
Sales Volume: $3,500,000

1034 Bahai Publishing Trust
Bahai Distribution Service
401 Greenleaf Ave
Wilmette, IL 60091-2886   847-425-7950
800-999-9019
Fax: 847-425-7951
bds@usbnc.org
www.bahaibookstore.com

History and religion books and multimedia materials

President: Tim Moore
Sales Volume: $3MM to $5MM

1035 Baptist Spanish Publishing House
Baptist Spanish Publishing House
P.O. Box 1749
Conway, AR 72033   800-333-1442
info@discipleguide.org
www.discipleguide.org

Publications/product categories include: Sunday School; Christian Growth Ministry; Youth 1-to-1; Girl's Missionary Auxiliary; Galileans; Spanish Curriculum, and Children's Christian Growth Ministry

Publishing Staff: Ken Adams
Credit Cards: AMEX; MasterCard; Visa
Catalog Cost: Free
Catalog Circulation: Mailed 4 time(s) per year to 80000
Printing Information: 96 pages in 4 colors on Glossy Stock
Press: Sheetfed Press
Binding: Saddle Stitched
In Business: 99 years
Number of Employees: 65
Sales Volume: $3,000,000

1036 Beacon Hill Press
Nazarene Publishing House
PO Box 419527
Kansas City, MO 64141-6527   816-931-1900
800-877-0700
Fax: 816-753-4071
www.nph.com

Books for spiritual growth, ministry resources and textbooks for Christian colleges

President: Hardy Weathers
CFO: Mark Brown
Marketing Manager: Barry Russell
Production Manager: Kevin Brown
Director Of Human Resources: Mark A. Parker
Human Resources Manager: Bruce Lampley
Administrative Assistant: Stacey Stark
International Marketing Manager: Barry Russell
Credit Cards: AMEX; MasterCard; Visa
Catalog Cost: Free
Printing Information: 52 pages in 4 colors on Glossy Stock
Binding: Saddle Stitched
Mailing List Information: Names for rent
In Business: 90 years
Number of Employees: 250
Sales Volume: $3MM to $5MM

1037 Best Book Catalog in the World
Loompanics Unlimited
1099 E Nakoma Street
Port Townsend, WA 98368-997   360-385-2230
800-380-2230
Fax: 360-385-7785
www.loompanics.com

How tos, alternative lifestyles, underground information, privacy, political activism, Americana and much, much more

President: Mike Hoy
Credit Cards: MasterCard; Visa
Catalog Cost: $5
Catalog Circulation: Mailed 5 time(s) per year
Printing Information: 300 pages in 1 color on Newsprint
Press: Web Press
Binding: Perfect Bound
Mailing List Information: Names for rent
Number of Employees: 10

1038 Biblical Archaeology Society Collection
Biblical Archaeology Society
4710 41 Street NW
Washington, DC 20016-1706   202-364-3300
800-221-4644
Fax: 202-364-2636
info@biblicalarchaeology.org
www.biblicalarchaeology.org

Books, videos and hi-res images on CD

President: Susan Laden
Marketing Manager: Loren Weisman
Production Manager: Heather Metzger
International Marketing Manager: Anne Barasso
Credit Cards: MasterCard; Visa
Catalog Cost: Free
Catalog Circulation: Mailed 2 time(s) per year
Average Order Size: $25
Printing Information: 16 pages in 4 colors on Matte Stock
Press: Web Press
Binding: Saddle Stitched
Mailing List Information: Names for rent
In Business: 41 years
Number of Employees: 15

1039 Bridge Building Images
Bridge Building Images
PO Box 1048
Burlington, VT 05402-1048   802-864-8346
800-325-6263
Fax: 802-893-1687
bbi@bridgebuilding.com
www.bridgebuilding.com

Religious cards and gifts including advent calendars, Christmas carols, greeting cards, prayer cards, prints, plaques and magnets

President: William J Flynn
Catalog Cost: Free
Catalog Circulation: to 100M
Printing Information: 28 pages in 4 colors on Glossy Stock
Press: Web Press
Binding: Saddle Stitched
In Business: 20 years

1040 CBD Academic
Christian Book Distributors
140 Summit St.
Peabody, MA 01960   800-247-4784
customer.service@christianbook.com
www.christianbook.com

Scholarly resources for students, professors and pastors.

President: Ray Hendrickson
Catalog Cost: Free
Mailing List Information: Names for rent
In Business: 39 years
Number of Employees: 500

1041 CBD Bible
Christian Book Distributors
140 Summit St.
Peabody, MA 01960   800-247-4784
customer.service@christianbook.com
www.christianbook.com

Bibles in every translation, binding, size, etc.

President: Ray Hendrickson
Catalog Cost: Free
Mailing List Information: Names for rent
In Business: 39 years
Number of Employees: 500

1042 CBD Clearance
Christian Book Distributors
140 Summit St.
Peabody, MA 01960   800-247-4784
customer.service@christianbook.com
www.christianbook.com

Special offers on Christian products.

President: Ray Hendrickson
Catalog Cost: Free
Mailing List Information: Names for rent
In Business: 39 years
Number of Employees: 500

1043 CBD Gift
Christian Book Distributors
140 Summit St.
Peabody, MA 01960   800-247-4784
customer.service@christianbook.com
www.christianbook.com

Christian gifts and home decor

President: Ray Hendrickson
Catalog Cost: Free
Mailing List Information: Names for rent
In Business: 39 years
Number of Employees: 500

1044 CBD Pastor
Christian Book Distributors
140 Summit St.
Peabody, MA 01960   800-247-4784
customer.service@christianbook.com
www.christianbook.com

Ministry, preaching, administration and church supplies.

President: Ray Hendrickson
Catalog Cost: Free
Mailing List Information: Names for rent
In Business: 39 years
Number of Employees: 500

1045 CBD Supply
Christian Book Distributors
140 Summit St.
Peabody, MA 01960   800-247-4784
customer.service@christianbook.com
www.christianbook.com

Bibles, music, pastoral resources, outreach materials and more.

President: Ray Hendrickson
Catalog Cost: Free
Mailing List Information: Names for rent
In Business: 39 years
Number of Employees: 500

1046 CM Almy General
CM Almy
228 Sound Beach Avenue
Greenwich, CT 06870-2644   203-531-7600
800-225-2569
Fax: 203-531-9048
almyaccess@almy.com
www.almy.com

Supplier of decorative furnishings, apparel, worship related products and gifts to churches, religious institutions, their clergy and members

President: Stephen Sendler
CFO: Mike Mc Gown
Credit Cards: MasterCard
Catalog Cost: Free
Printing Information: 208 pages in 4 colors on Glossy Stock
In Business: 123 years
Sales Volume: $5MM to $10MM

1047 Catalog of Meditation Supplies
DharmaCrafts
60 Island Street
Lawrence, MA 01840-1835   866-339-4198
www.dharmacrafts.com

Buddhist meditation supplies, Asian furnishings, premier supplies of products related to mediation and spiritual enrichment

President: Dyan Eagles
Credit Cards: AMEX; MasterCard
Catalog Cost: Free
Catalog Circulation: Mailed 3 time(s) per year to 500m
Average Order Size: $106
Printing Information: 48 pages in 4 colors on Glossy Stock
Press: Web Press
Binding: Saddle Stitched
Mailing List Information: Names for rent
In Business: 27 years
Number of Employees: 8
Sales Volume: $1MM to $3MM

1048 Celebrate the Wonder
Amber Lotus Publishing
5018 Ne 22nd Ave Studio A
PO Box 11329
Portland, OR 97211-329   503-284-6400
800-326-2375
Fax: 503-284-6417
info@amberlotus.com
www.amberlotus.com

A collection of Christian books, Bibles, music and gifts

VP: Leslie Gignilliat-Day
VP: Tim Campbell
Credit Cards: AMEX; MasterCard; Visa
Printing Information: 24 pages
5018 NE 22nd Avenue Studio A
Portland, OR 97211
503.284.6400
In Business: 27 years
Number of Employees: 7
Sales Volume: 1.3M

1049 Christian Schools International
Christian Schools International
3350 East Paris Avenue SE
Grand Rapids, MI 49512-3054   616-957-1070
800-635-8288
Fax: 616-957-5022
info@csionline.org
www.Csionline.Org

Christian products and services

Chairman: David Dykhouse
President: Joel Westa
jwesta@CSIonline.org
CFO: John Wolters
JWolters@csionline.org
Marketing Manager: Jane Mulder
JMulder@csionline.org
VP, Member Services: Jeff Blamer

JBlamer@CSIonline.org
VP, Corporate Development: Darryl Shelton
DShelton@CSIonline.org
Benefits Assistant: Kathy Doezema
KDoezema@csionline.org
In Business: 95 years

1050 Christian Tools of Affirmation

Christian Tools of Affirmation
1625 Larkin Williams Rd
PO Box 1205
Fenton, MO 63026-1205 636-305-3100
800-999-1874
Fax: 800-315-8713
customerservice@ctainc.com
www.ctainc.com

Christian products and gifts such as bracelets, books, keychains, mugs, ornaments, stationery, videos, magnets and prayer journals

President: Terry Knoploh
CEO: Terry Knoploh
Credit Cards: MasterCard; Visa
Catalog Cost: Free
In Business: 15 years
Sales Volume: $5MM to $10MM

1051 Church Identification Products

Lake Shore Industries Inc
1817 Poplar Street
PO Box 3427
Erie, PA 16508-427 800-458-0463
Fax: 814-453-4293
info@lsisigns.com
www.lsisigns.com

Books, plaques, architectural letters and recognition walls, as well as cemetery signs and markers

President: Leo Bruno
Marketing Manager: Shirley Bruno
Production Manager: David Mays
Credit Cards: MasterCard
Mailing List Information: Names for rent
In Business: 106 years
Number of Employees: 19
Sales Volume: $1,400,000

1052 Classical Academic Press 2015/2016 Catalog

Classical Academic Press
2151 Market Street
Camp Hill, PA 17011 717-730-0711
866-730-0711
Fax: 717-730-0721
classicalacademicpress.com

Educational publishing company

National leader/Author/Speaker: Dr. Chris Perrin
Printing Information: 60 pages

1053 Deseret Book Company

Deseret Books
P.O.Box 30178
Salt Lake City, UT 84130-178 888-846-7302
800-453-4532
Fax: 801-517-3338
service@deseretbook.com
www.deseretbook.com

Religious scripture, books, music, movies, gifts, clothing and home furnishings

President: Sheri Dew
Marketing Manager: Jeanne Crippen
Production Manager: Anne Sheffield
Intellectual Property: Michelle Spiron
mspiron@deseretbook.com
Marketing Division: Jennifer Hortin
jhortin@deseretbook.com
Media Inquiries: Gail Halladay
gail.halladay@deseretbook.com
Credit Cards: AMEX; MasterCard
Catalog Cost: Free
Printing Information: 23 pages
In Business: 149 years

Number of Employees: 700
Sales Volume: $5MM to $10MM

1054 Deseret Books

Deseret Books
P.O.Box 30178
Salt Lake City, UT 84130-178 888-846-7302
800-453-4532
Fax: 801-517-3338
service@deseretbook.com
www.deseretbook.com

LDS books, scriptures, standard works, and Mormon gifts

President: Sheri Dew
Marketing Manager: Mark Standing
Production Manager: Anne Sheffield
Intellectual Property: Michelle Spiron
mspiron@deseretbook.com
Marketing Division: Jennifer Hortin
jhortin@deseretbook.com
Media Inquiries: Gail Halladay
gail.halladay@deseretbook.com
Credit Cards: AMEX; MasterCard
Catalog Cost: Free
Catalog Circulation: Mailed 4 time(s) per year
Printing Information: 23 pages in 4 colors on Glossy Stock
Binding: Folded
Mailing List Information: Names for rent
In Business: 149 years
Number of Employees: 700
Sales Volume: $20MM to $50MM

1055 Explorations

Gaiam
833 W South Boulder Rd
PO Box 3095
Boulder, CO 80307-3095 303-222-3600
877-989-6321
Fax: 303-222-3700
customerservice@gaiam.com
www.explorations.com

Films, documentaries, books and tools on spirituality, ancient wisdom, relationships, health and healing, and the frontiers of science and human potential

Chairman: Jirka Rysavy
President: Lynn Powers
CFO: Vilia Valentine
Credit Cards: AMEX; MasterCard; Visa
Catalog Cost: Free
Catalog Circulation: Mailed 4 time(s) per year
Printing Information: 60 pages in 4 colors on Glossy Stock
Binding: Folded

1056 Gateway Films Vision Video

Vision Video
PO Box 540
Worcester, PA 19490 610-584-3500
800-523-0226
support@visionvideo.com
www.Visionvideo.Com

Christian video and DVD selections

President: William Curtis
Credit Cards: AMEX; MasterCard
Catalog Cost: Free
Catalog Circulation: Mailed 1 time(s) per year
In Business: 33 years
Number of Employees: 20
Sales Volume: $3MM to $5MM

1057 General Association of Regular Baptist Churches

Regular Baptist Press
3715 N.Ventura Dr.
Arlington Heights, IL 60004-7678 847-843-1600
800-727-4440
Fax: 847-843-3757
rborders@garbc.org
www.garbc.org

Offers curriculum, books, teaching resources, and more

Catalog Circulation: to 80000
Printing Information: 108 pages in 4 colors on Matte Stock
Binding: Folded
In Business: 30 years

1058 Ghirelli Rosaries

Ghirelli USA, Inc.
990 Green Bay Road-Suite 2A
Winnetka, IL 60093 847-446-5121
usa@ghirelli.com
www.ghirellishop.com

Rosaries, religious bracelets, pendants, sculptures, etc.

Catalog Cost: Free
In Business: 27 years

1059 Gompa

Gompa
PO Box 1777
Arlington, TX 76004-1777 817-860-0129
Fax: 817-460-5125
thegompa@aol.com
www.thegompa.com

Books and videotapes relating to Oriental health philosophies

President: John P. Painter
Credit Cards: AMEX; MasterCard; Visa
Catalog Circulation: Mailed 1 time(s) per year
Printing Information: in 1 color on Newsprint
Press: Sheetfed Press
Binding: Saddle Stitched
In Business: 41 years
Sales Volume: Under $500M

1060 Gospel Advocate Bookstores

Gospel Advocate Bookstore
1006 Elm Hill Pike
Nashville, TN 37210 615-254-8781
800-251-8446
Fax: 615-254-7411
order@gospeladvocate.com
www.gospeladvocate.com

Religious books

President: Kerry G Anderson
Publisher: Neil W. Anderson
neil.anderson@gospeladvocate.com
GA Editor: Gregory Alan Tidwell
greg.tidwell@gospeladvocate.com
VP Finance: Keaton Bell
keaton.bell@gospeladvocate.com
Credit Cards: AMEX; MasterCard; Visa
Catalog Cost: Free
Catalog Circulation: Mailed 1 time(s) per year to 10000
Printing Information: 96 pages in 1 color
In Business: 160 years
Number of Employees: 30
Sales Volume: $3MM to $5MM

1061 Hamilton New Age Mystical Arts Supplies

Hamilton New Age Supplies
PO Box 1258
Moorpark, CA 93020-1258 805-529-5900
Fax: 805-529-2934
info@hamiltonnewage.com

Tarot cards, runes stones, books, talisman jewelry, candles, oils, incense, wands, crystal balls, ceremonial garments, scrying mirrors, pendulums, chalices, cauldrons, herbs

President: Carol Hamilton
Credit Cards: AMEX; MasterCard
Printing Information: in 4 colors on Glossy Stock
Press: Web Press
Binding: Saddle Stitched
Mailing List Information: Names for rent
In Business: 40 years

1062 Hampton Roads Publishing Company
Red Wheel/Weiser/Conari
65 Parker Street
Suite 7
Newburyport, MA 01950-8719   978-465-0504
400-423-7087
Fax: 978-465-0243
info@rwwbooks.com
www.hamptonroadspub.com/index.php

Shamanic journeys, health, past-life experience, UFOs and new science, out-of-body experiences, spirituality and metaphysics

President: Michael Kerber
Publisher: Jan Johnson
Catalog Cost: Free
Catalog Circulation: Mailed 4 time(s) per year
Printing Information: 32 pages in 4 colors on Glossy Stock
Press: Sheetfed Press
Binding: Saddle Stitched
Mailing List Information: Names for rent
In Business: 15 years
Number of Employees: 22
Sales Volume: Under $500M

1063 Himalayan Institute
Himalayan Institute
952 Bethany Turnpike
Honesdale, PA 18431   570-253-5551
800-822-4547
Fax: 570-253-9078
info@himalayaninstitute.org
www.himalayaninstitute.org

Yoga and meditation instructional books, DVDs, tapes and retreats, botanicals, gifts, health products, and jewelry

Chairman: Irene Pertyszak
President: Rolf Fovik
Marketing Manager: Alena Miles
Founder: Swami Rama
Catalog Cost: Free
In Business: 44 years
Number of Employees: 60

1064 Hohm Press
Hohm Press
PO Box 4410
China Valley, AZ 86323   800-381-2700
Fax: 928-636-7519
hppublisher@cableone.net
www.hohmpress.com

Books on natural health, women's issues, poetry, children, transpersonal psychology, religious studies

President: Dasya Zuccarello
Credit Cards: MasterCard
Catalog Cost: Free
Printing Information: in 4 colors on Glossy Stock
Press: Letterpress
Binding: Saddle Stitched
Mailing List Information: Names for rent
List Manager: Frank Delano
In Business: 25 years
Number of Employees: 10-J

1065 International Bible Society
Bible Gateway
P.O.Box 35700
Colorado Springs, CO 80935-3570719-488-9200
800-524-1588
Fax: 719-488-3840
www.gospelcom.net

Bibles, new testaments and scripture related materials

President: David Passman
CFO: Bob Dinolfo
Marketing Manager: Phil Wilcoxson
Production Manager: Dennis Metzger
Credit Cards: MasterCard; Visa
Catalog Cost: Free
Catalog Circulation: Mailed 1 time(s) per year to 150

Printing Information: 34 pages in 4 colors on Glossy Stock
Binding: Saddle Stitched
List Manager: Ron Besonen
In Business: 5 years
Number of Employees: 105
Sales Volume: $5MM to $10MM

1066 Jewish Lights Publishing
Jewish Lights Publishing
Route 4
PO Box 237
Woodstock, VT 05091   802-457-4000
800-962-4544
Fax: 802-457-4004
sales@jewishlights.com
www.jewishlights.com

Book subject categories include spirituality, philosophy, theology, life cycle, healing/recovery and children's issues

President: Stuart M Matlins
Publisher: Stuart M Matlins
Credit Cards: MasterCard; Visa
Catalog Cost: Free
Catalog Circulation: Mailed 2 time(s) per year
Average Order Size: $40
Printing Information: 55 pages in 4 colors on Glossy Stock
Binding: Saddle Stitched
Mailing List Information: Names for rent
In Business: 10 years
Number of Employees: 20

1067 Llewellyn Worldwide
Llewellyn Worldwide
2143 Wooddale Drive
Woodbury, MN 55125   651-291-1970
877-639-9753
Fax: 651-291-1908
CustomerService@llewellyn.com
www.llewellyn.com

Publisher of books

In Business: 114 years

1068 Lynch & Kelly
Lynch & Kelly
23 Devereux St
PO Box 342
Utica, NY 13503   315-724-8215
888-548-3890
Fax: 315-792-4624
www.lynchkelly.com

Knights of Columbus books and supplies

President: Brian G. Kelly
Printing Information: 32 pages

1069 Magus Books
Magus Books
1309 4th Street S.E.
Minneapolis, MN 55414   612-379-7669
Support@MagusBooks.com
www.magusbooks.com

Books

In Business: 23 years

1070 Ministry Resources
Saint Mary's Press
702 Terrence Heights
Winona, MN 55987-1320   507-457-7900
800-533-8095
Fax: 800-344-9225
smpress@smp.org
www.smp.org

Catholic books

President: John Vitek
CFO: Steve Skifton
Marketing Manager: Joan Gamoke
Founder: Alphonsus Pluth
Credit Cards: MasterCard
Catalog Circulation: Mailed 2 time(s) per year to 18000
Printing Information: 64 pages in 4 colors on

Matte Stock
Press: Web Press
Binding: Saddle Stitched
Mailing List Information: Names for rent
In Business: 72 years
Sales Volume: $5MM to $10MM

1071 Monastery Store
Dharma Communications
831 Plank Road
PO Box 156
Mount Tremper, NY 12457   845-688-7993
Fax: 845-688-7995
support@dharma.net

Meditation cushions, clothing, books, DVDs, CDs, MP3s and artwork

1072 Mystic Trader
Pacific Spirit Corporation
1334 Pacific Avenue
Forest Grove, OR 97116-2315   503-357-1566
800-634-9057
Fax: 503-357-1669
csrservice@mystictrader.com
www.mystictrader.com

Spiritual books, art, jewelry, and other items

Credit Cards: MasterCard
Catalog Cost: Free
Catalog Circulation: Mailed 12 time(s) per year to 5m
Printing Information: 48 pages in 4 colors on Glossy Stock
Press: Web Press
Binding: Saddle Stitched
Mailing List Information: Names for rent
List Manager: Nam Marling
In Business: 20 years

1073 New Book Catalog
Dover Publications
31 E 2nd Street
Mineola, NY 11501-3852   516-294-7000
Fax: 516-742-6953
www.doverpublications.com

A selection of recent Dover publications in literature, arts & culture, math & science, children titles, history, music, and more

President: Christopher J Kuppig
Marketing Manager: Kristine Anderson
Acquisitions Editor: Nora Rawn
Account Manager: Christopher Higgins
Catalog Cost: Free
In Business: 76 years
Number of Employees: 135
Sales Volume: 40MM

1074 Pacific Spirit
1334 Pacific Ave
Forest Grove, OR 97116-2315   503-357-1566
800-634-9057
Fax: 503-357-1669
csrservice@mystictrader.com
www.pacificspiritcatalogs.com

Spiritual books and items from around the world

President: Mark Kenzer
CFO: Tripti Kenzer
Marketing Manager: Joseph Myer
Credit Cards: AMEX; MasterCard
Catalog Circulation: Mailed 6 time(s) per year to 60000
Printing Information: 48 pages in 4 colors on Newsprint
Press: Offset Press
Binding: Saddle Stitched
In Business: 4 years
Sales Volume: $5MM to $10MM

1075   Red Wheel/Weiser LLC
Red Wheel
65 Parker Street
Suite 7
Newburyport, MA 01950   978-465-0504
800-423-7087
Fax: 877-337-3309
info@rwwbooks.com
www.redwheelweiser.com

Books: new age, astrology, oriental philosophy, tarot, self-development, western mystery and Kabbalahi

Chairman: Jan Johnson
President: Michael Kerber
Production Manager: Jen Brown
Credit Cards: AMEX; MasterCard; Visa
Printing Information: 100 pages in 4 colors on Matte Stock
Press: Sheetfed Press
Binding: Perfect Bound
Mailing List Information: Names for rent
In Business: 20 years
Number of Employees: 30
Sales Volume: $5MM to $10MM

1076   SISU Home Entertainment/Sifriyat Ami
Kol Ami, Inc.
22-19 41st Avenue
Suite 509
Long Island City, NY 11101   212-947-7888
800-223-7478
Fax: 212-947-8388
sisu@sisuent.com
www.sisuent.com

Jewish and Israeli music, videos, DVDs, books and CD-roms

President: Haim Scheininger
Credit Cards: AMEX; MasterCard
Catalog Circulation: Mailed 4 time(s) per year to 250M
Average Order Size: $60
Printing Information: 32 pages in 4 colors on Matte Stock
Press: Web Press
Binding: Saddle Stitched
Mailing List Information: Names for rent
In Business: 27 years
Number of Employees: 6
Sales Volume: $500,000

1077   Schiffer Body, Mind & Spirit
Schiffer Publishing Ltd.
4880 Lower Valley Rd
Atglen, PA 19310-1768   610-593-1777
Fax: 610-593-2002
info@schifferbooks.com
www.Schifferbooks.Com

Reference books on astrology, ghosts and paranormal, metaphysics, numerology, shamanism, regional books, history, biographies, and The Planet Series

President: Peter Schiffer
CFO: Pam Braceland
Marketing Manager: Tina Skinner
Fulfillment: Erine Barrett
Catalog Circulation: Mailed 2 time(s) per year
Printing Information: in 4 colors on Glossy Stock
Binding: Folded
Mailing List Information: Names for rent
In Business: 42 years
Number of Employees: 30
Sales Volume: $10MM to $20MM

1078   Shambhala Publications
Shambhala Publications
300 Massachusetts Ave
Boston, MA 02115   617-424-0030
Fax: 617-236-1563
www.shambhala.com

Buddhism inspired books and other spiritual resources

President: Richard Reoch
Credit Cards: AMEX; MasterCard
Catalog Cost: Free
In Business: 55 years

1079   St. Patrick's Guild Book Catalog
St. Patrick's Guild
1554 Randolph Ave.
St. Paul, MN 55105   651-690-1506
800-652-9767
Fax: 651-696-5130
info@stpatricksguild.com
www.stpatricksguild.com

Religious gifts, books, music, and church supplies

In Business: 66 years

1080   The Catholic Company
The Catholic Company
615 E Westinghouse Blvd.
Charlotte, NC 28273   866-522-8465
www.catholiccompany.com

Religious products.

Catalog Cost: Free
Printing Information: 36 pages in 4 colors
In Business: 19 years

1081   Wisdom's Gate Catalog
Wisdom's Gate Ministries
PO Box 374
Covert, MI 49043-374   269-764-1467
Fax: 269-764-1710
wisgate@wisgate.com
www.wisgate.com

Christian publishing company that provides materials for families, and books related to home education

President: Skeet Savage
Catalog Circulation: Mailed 4 time(s) per year to 11000
Average Order Size: $40
Printing Information: 96 pages in 2 colors on Newsprint
Press: Sheetfed Press
Binding: Perfect Bound
Mailing List Information: Names for rent
In Business: 15 years
Number of Employees: 8
Sales Volume: Under $500M

Parenting

1082   Active Parenting Publishers
Active Parenting Publishers
1220 Kennestone Circle
Suite 130
Marietta, GA 30066-6022   770-429-0565
800-825-0060
Fax: 770-429-0334
cservice@activeparenting.com
www.activeparenting.com

Parenting programs, stepparenting, divorce, school success, and character education.

President: Michael H. Popkin, Ph.D.
Marketing Manager: Virginia Murray
Manager of Christian Resources: Melody Popkin
Sales Manager: Cheryl Cromer
Art Director: Gabrielle Tingley
Printing Information: 46 pages
In Business: 35 years

1083   Adoption Book
Tapestry Books
131 John Muir Drive
Amherst, NY 14228   716-544-0204
Fax: 609-737-5951
info@tapestrybooks.com
www.tapestrybooks.com

Books, CD's, DVD's for adoptive parents

President: Shepard Morrow
Owner: Shepard Morrow
Credit Cards: MasterCard
In Business: 21 years

1084   Atlantic Publishing Group
Atlantic Publishing Group
1405 SW 6th Avenue
Ocala, FL 34471   352-622-1825
Fax: 352-622-1875
sales@atlantic-pub.com
www.atlantic-pub.com

Books

Printing Information: 52 pages
In Business: 25+ years

1085   Bureau for At-Risk Youth
The Bureau for At-Risk Youth
PO Box 170
Farmingville, NY 11738   800-999-6884
Fax: 800-262-1886
info@at-risk.com
www.at-risk.com

Health and educational books and videos on topics including drugs, self-esteem, safe schools, parenting and professional development

President: James Werz
Credit Cards: MasterCard; Visa
Catalog Cost: Free
Printing Information: 48 pages

1086   Child Management
CM Services Inc
800 Roosevelt Road
Building C, Suite 312
Glen Ellyn, IL 60137-5899   630-858-7337
800-613-6672
Fax: 630-790-3095
rickc@cmservices.com
www.Cmservices.Com

Books,audio videos on the subjects of parenting and Attention Deficit Disorder

CFO: Nancy Roe
Trade Show Director: Maria Prior
Head Coach: Rick Church
rickc@cmservices.com
Credit Cards: AMEX; MasterCard; Visa; Discover
Catalog Cost: Free
Catalog Circulation: Mailed 2 time(s) per year to 20000
Average Order Size: $60
Printing Information: 12 pages in 4 colors on Glossy Stock
Binding: Perfect Bound
Mailing List Information: Names for rent
In Business: 39 years
Number of Employees: 3
Sales Volume: $3MM to $5MM

1087   Childswork/Childsplay
Childswork/Childsplay
303 Crossways Park Drive
Woodbury, NY 11797   516-496-4863
800-962-1141
Fax: 800-262-1886
info@childswork.com
www.childswork.com

Books, games and playtime activities for childhood development

President: Lawrence Shapiro
Credit Cards: AMEX; MasterCard; Visa
Catalog Cost: $25
Printing Information: 57 pages
Mailing List Information: Names for rent
In Business: 10 years
Number of Employees: 25

1088 Feldheim Publishers

Feldheim Publishers
208 Airport Executive Park
Nanuet, NY 10954
845-356-2282
800-237-7149
Fax: 845-425-1908
sales@feldheim.com
www.feldheim.com

Publishing house
In Business: 76 years

1089 Free Spirit Publishing

Free Spirit Publishing
6325 Sandburg Road
Suite 100
Minneapolis, MN 55427-3674
612-338-2068
Fax: 612-337-5050
help4kids@freespirit.com
www.freespirit.com

A catalog for children, parents and teachers about learning to cope with bullies, homework, and life in general

President: Judy Galbraith
CFO: Beth Kininkas
Marketing Manager: Angela Henchen
Executive Director: Linda Crawford
Purchasing Manager: Kimberly Kittleson-Hurley
Credit Cards: AMEX; MasterCard
Catalog Cost: Free
Catalog Circulation: Mailed 10 time(s) per year
Printing Information: in 4 colors
Press: Web Press
Binding: Saddle Stitched
Mailing List Information: Names for rent
In Business: 34 years
Number of Employees: 31
Sales Volume: $4.3 MM

1090 Gallaudet University Press

Gallaudet University
800 Florida Ave NE # Emg
Washington, DC 20002-3695
202-651-5000
800-621-2736
Fax: 800-621-8476
www.Gallaudet.Edu

Books on deaf related subjects, including sign language, deaf studies and culture, general interest, parenting and children's bestsellers

President: Dr. T. Alan Hurwitz
Marketing Manager: Daniel Wallace
Production Manager: Jill Porco
Provost: Dr. Carol Erting
VP, Administration and Finance: Paul Kelly
VP, Development and Alumni Relation: Paul Julin
Sales Volume: $10MM to $20MM

1091 Goodheart-Willcox Publisher

Goodheart-Willcox Publisher
18604 West Creek Drive
Tinley Park, IL 60477-6243
708-687-5000
800-323-0440
Fax: 888-409-3900
custserv@g-w.com
www.g-w.com

Print and digital textbooks

1092 KidSafety of America

KidSafety of America
6288 Susana Street
Chino, CA 91710
909-627-8700
800-524-1156
Fax: 909-627-8777
info@kidsafetystore.com
www.kidsafetystore.com

Educational books and videos to promote the health and safety of children and their families

President: Peter D Osilaja
Buyers: Virginia Anorade
Credit Cards: AMEX; MasterCard; Visa
Catalog Cost: Free
Mailing List Information: Names for rent
In Business: 23 years
Number of Employees: 10
Sales Volume: $930,000

1093 Love and Logic

Love and Logic
2207 Jackson Street
Golden, CO 80401-2300
303-278-7552
800-338-4065
Fax: 800-455-7557
www.loveandlogic.com

Practical tools and techniques that help adults achieve respectful, healthy relationships with their children.

President: Charles Fay, Ph.D.
Founder: Jim Fay
Founder and psychiatrist: Foster W. Cline, M.D.
Printing Information: 36 pages
In Business: 38 years

1094 Meadowbrook Press

Meadowbrook Press
6110 Blue Circle Drive
Suite 237
Minnetonka, MN 55343
952-930-1100
800-338-2232
Fax: 952-930-1940
info@meadowbrookpress.com
www.Meadowbrookpress.Com

Books on parenting, kid's, baby names and humor

President: Bruce Lansky
Author: Ann Kepler
Author: April Bolding
Author: Bruce Lansky
Credit Cards: MasterCard; Visa
Catalog Cost: Free
Catalog Circulation: Mailed 1 time(s) per year
Printing Information: 8 pages
In Business: 39 years
Number of Employees: 18
Sales Volume: $5MM to $10MM

1095 New Harbinger

New Harbinger Publications
5674 Shattuck Avenue
Oakland, CA 94609-1662
800-748-6273
Fax: 800-652-1613
customerservice@newharbinger.com
www.newharbinger.com

Books on parenting and childrens activities

President: Matthew McKay
Founder: Matthew McKay
Founder: Patrick Fanning
In Business: 42 years
Sales Volume: $10MM to $20MM

1096 Parenting & Family Life

Films Media Group
132 West 31st Street
17th Floor
New York, NY 10001
800-322-8755
Fax: 800-678-3633
custserv@films.com
www.films.com

Newborn care, baby-sitting, pregnancy and drug free healthy livingbooks and videos

President: Steve Jones
CFO: Jason McClure
Marketing Manager: Melinda Ball
Production Manager: Kim Keiffer
Buyers: Vickie Meadows
Credit Cards: AMEX; MasterCard; Visa
Catalog Circulation: Mailed 12 time(s) per year to 30000
Average Order Size: $100
Printing Information: 48 pages in 4 colors on

Matte Stock
Press: Web Press
Binding: Saddle Stitched
Mailing List Information: Names for rent
List Company: Stevens-Knox
In Business: 17 years
Number of Employees: 40
Sales Volume: $5MM to $10MM

Self-Help

1097 ARE Press

Edgar Cayce's A.R.E.
Association for Research and Enligh
215 67th St
Virginia Beach, VA 23451-2061
757-428-3588
800-333-4499
are@edgarcayce.org
www.edgarcayce.org

Edgar Cayce and related books and tapes for personal transformation and spiritual development

Chairman: Arthur P. Strickland
President: Charles T Cayce
CFO: Brenda Butler
Marketing Manager: Jennie Taylor Martin
Production Manager: Cassie McQuagge
Vice-Chairperson: William Austin
Trustee Emeritus: Ruben Miller
Executive Director & CEO: Kevin J. Todeschi, MA
Credit Cards: MasterCard; Visa
Catalog Cost: Free
Catalog Circulation: Mailed 3 time(s) per year to 21000
Average Order Size: $30
Printing Information: 50 pages in 4 colors
Press: Web Press
Mailing List Information: Names for rent
In Business: 84 years
Number of Employees: 100
Sales Volume: $400,000

1098 ASCP Catalog

American Society for Clinical Pathology
33 W Monroe Street
Suite 1600
Chicago, IL 60603
312-541-4999
800-267-2727
Fax: 312-541-4998
info@ascp.org
www.ascp.org

Books and information about pathology and laboratory medicine

Chairman: Evelyn Bruner
President: William G. Finn, MD, FASCP
Treasurer: Gregory N. Sossaman, MD, FASCP
Vice President: William E. Schreiber, MD, FASCP
Secretary: Melissa Perry Upton, MD, FASCP
Credit Cards: MasterCard; Visa
Catalog Cost: Free
Average Order Size: $200
Mailing List Information: Names for rent
List Manager: Holly Monahan
In Business: 93 years
Number of Employees: 175
Sales Volume: $500,000

1099 Aging Resources

Attainment Company Inc
504 Commerce Parkway
PO Box 930160
Verona, WI 53593-160
608-845-7880
800-327-4269
Fax: 608-845-8040
customerservice@attainmentcompany.com
www.attainmentcompany.com

Senior education books and DVDs to improve mental health

President: Don Bastian
Director of Software Development: Scott Meister

scott@attainmentcompany.com
Administrative Supervisor: Theresa O'Connor
theresa@attainmentcompany.com
Graphic Designer: Sherry Pribbenow
sherry@attainmentcompany.com
Credit Cards: MasterCard; Visa
Catalog Cost: Free
In Business: 36 years
Number of Employees: 23

1100 American Health Information Management Catalog
The American Health Information Manageme
233 N Michigan Avenue 21st Floor
Chicago, IL 60601-5809　　312-233-1100
　　　　　　　　　　　　　　800-335-5535
　　　　　　　　　　Fax: 312-233-1090
　　　　　　　　　　info@ahima.org
　　　　　　　　　　www.ahima.org

Health related books and seminars

Chairman: Cassi Birnbaum, MS, RHIA, CPHQ, FAH
President: Melissa M. Martin, RHIA, CCS, CHTS-
CFO: Sandy Fuller
Marketing Manager: Lori Osbourne
Production Manager: Rebecca Gordan
Chief Operating Officer: Laura Pait, RHIA, CDIP, CCS
Chief Executive Officer: Lynne Thomas Gordon, MBA, RHIA, CAE
Secretary: Virginia (Ginna) Evans, MBA, RHIA,
Catalog Circulation: to 50000
In Business: 87 years

1101 Aunt Lute Books
Aunt Lute Books
PO Box 410687
San Francisco, CA 94141-687　　415-826-1300
　　　　　　　　　　Fax: 415-826-8300
　　　　　　　　　　books@auntlute.com
　　　　　　　　　　www.auntlute.com

Women issues

President: Joan Pickvoss
Marketing Manager: Marielle Gomez
Production Manager: Shay Brawn
Catalog Cost: Free
Printing Information: 16 pages
Binding: Folded
In Business: 33 years

1102 Avery Health Books
Penguin.com
375 Hudson Street
New York, NY 10014-3657　　212-366-2000
　　　　　　　　　　　　　　800-632-8571
　　　　　　　　　　Fax: 212-366-2933
　　　　　　　www.us.penguingroup.com/

Books on contemporary health and wellness

Chairman: John Makinson
President: Susan Petersen Kennedy
CFO: Coram Williams
Chief Executive Officer: David Shanks
President of Penguin Young Readers: Don Weisberg
EVP of Business Operations for Peng: Doug Whiteman
Credit Cards: MasterCard; Visa
Printing Information: 72 pages
In Business: 17 years

1103 Bayou Publishing
Bayou Publishing
2524 Nottingham
Nottingham, TX 77005-1412　　713-526-4558
　　　　　　　　　　　　　　800-340-2034
　　　　　　　　　　Fax: 713-526-4342
　　　　　　　www.bayoupublishing.com

Products for schools and families

Publisher: Victor Loos, PhD
Printing Information: 2 pages
In Business: 20+ years

1104 Compassion Books
Compassion Books, Inc.
7036 State Highway 80 South
Burnsville, NC 28714-9569　　828-675-5909
　　　　　　　　　　　　　　800-970-4220
　　　　　　　　　　Fax: 828-675-9687
　　　　　orders@compassionbooks.com
　　　　　www.compassionbooks.com

Books, DVDs, and audios on grief, bereavement, losses of all kind

President: Donna O'Toole
Vice President: Bruce Greene
Catalog Cost: $3
Catalog Circulation: Mailed 1 time(s) per year to 40000
Average Order Size: $100
Printing Information: 32 pages in 4 colors on Glossy Stock
Press: Web Press
Binding: Saddle Stitched
Mailing List Information: Names for rent
In Business: 34 years
Number of Employees: 5
Sales Volume: $499,000

1105 Davies Publishing
Davies
32 South Raymond Avenue
Suites 4 and 5
Pasadena, CA 91105-1961　　626-792-3046
　　　　　　　　　　　　　　877-792-0005
　　　　　　　　　　Fax: 626-792-5308
　　　　　　www.daviespublishing.com

Medical books, reviews for professionals taking AROMS exam, videotapes, audiocassettes and CD-ROMS

President: Michael Davies
Operations Manager: Janet Heard
Product Development Specialist: Christian Jones
Art Director: Bill Murawski
Credit Cards: AMEX; MasterCard
Catalog Cost: Free
Catalog Circulation: Mailed 6 time(s) per year
Average Order Size: $100
Printing Information: 28 pages in 4 colors on Matte Stock
Press: Sheetfed Press
Binding: Folded
Mailing List Information: Names for rent
In Business: 36 years
Number of Employees: 4
Sales Volume: $1MM to $3MM

1106 Guidance, Life Skills and Work, work, work!
Linx Educational
4311 Salisbury Rd
Jacksonville , FL 32216　　904-296-6707
　　　　　　　　　　　　　800-717-LINX
　　　　　　　　　　Fax: 888-546-9338
　　　　　　　　　sales@linxedu.com
　　　　　　　　　www.linxedu.com

Educational materials for career and life skills, videos, books, posters and games

Printing Information: 48 pages

1107 Guilford Psychology Catalog
Guilford
370 Seventh Avenue
Suite 1200
New York, NY 10001-1020　　212-431-9800
　　　　　　　　　　　　　　800-365-7006
　　　　　　　　　　Fax: 212-966-6708
　　　　　　　　　info@guilford.com
　　　　　　　　　www.Guilford.Com

Books and other resources in psychology and psychiatry, mental health, self help, and many other topics

President: Bob Matloff
CFO: Andrew Kraft
Marketing Manager: Andrea Lansing
Exhibits Manager: Dorothy Avery

Art Director: Paul Gordon
Publisher: Kitty Moore
kitty.moore@guilford.com
Credit Cards: AMEX; MasterCard
Catalog Cost: Free
Catalog Circulation: Mailed 4 time(s) per year to 25000
Printing Information: 32 pages in 4 colors on Glossy Stock
Press: Web Press
Binding: Saddle Stitched
Mailing List Information: Names for rent
List Manager: Names in the News
In Business: 41 years
Number of Employees: 75
Sales Volume: $6.9 MM

1108 Health Master
Stressmarket.Com
PO Box 127
Port Angeles, WA 98362　　360-457-9223
　　　　　　　　　　　　　　800-578-7377
　　　　　　　　　　Fax: 360-457-9466
　　　　　　　　　　info@cliving.org
　　　　　　　　　　www.cliving.org

Audio cassettes, books and stress cards for self help

President: Tim Lowenstein
Credit Cards: MasterCard; Visa
Catalog Cost: Free
Printing Information: in 4 colors on Glossy Stock
Press: Web Press
Number of Employees: 3
Sales Volume: Under $500M

1109 Jist Publishing
875 Montreal Way
St Paul, MN 55102　　800-535-6865
　　　　　　　　　Fax: 800-328-5464
　　　　　　　　　educate@emcp.com

Books on career development, job searching & educational training books, as well as healing guides

President: Mike Farr
Printing Information: 80 pages

1110 OPTP Tools for Fitness Catalog
OPTP
3800 Annapolis Lane
Suite 165 PO Box 47009
Minneapolis, MN 55447-9　　763-553-0452
　　　　　　　　　　　　　　888-819-0121
　　　　　　　　　　Fax: 763-553-9355
　　　　　　　customerservice@optp.com
　　　　　　　www.optp.com

Books on strengthening, stretching and rehabilitation

President: Shari Schroeder
Marketing Manager: Cathy Lindvall
Owner: Mark Bookhout
VP Administration: Gloria Woog
Business, Finance & Purchasing Dir.: Paul Youleau
Buyers: Michelle Braun
Credit Cards: AMEX; MasterCard
Catalog Cost: Free
Average Order Size: $50
Printing Information: 100 pages in 4 colors
Binding: Perfect Bound
Mailing List Information: Names for rent
In Business: 42 years
Number of Employees: 23
Sales Volume: $2.9 MM

1111 Reader's Digest Books, Videos & Music
Readers Digest
222 Rosewood Drive
Davers, MA 01923　　978-750-8400
　　　　　　　　　　800-234-9000
　　　　　　　Fax: 978-750-4470
　　　　　　　letters@rd.com
　　　　　　　www.rd.com

Select editions, reading series, books on do-it-yourself, home improvement, cooking, health, gardening and other topics, children's books, young families products, and recorded music collections

Chairman: Michael A Brennan
President: Thomas O Ryder
Credit Cards: AMEX; MasterCard; Visa; Discover
Catalog Cost: Free
Catalog Circulation: Mailed 4 time(s) per year
Printing Information: 50 pages in 4 colors on Glossy Stock
Press: Web Press
Binding: Saddle Stitched
Number of Employees: 5000
Sales Volume: $20MM to $50MM

1112 Research Press Publishers
Research Press Publishers
P.O. Box 7886
Champaign, IL 61822
217-352-3273
800-519-2707
Fax: 217-352-1221
orders@researchpress.com
www.researchpress.com

Books and videos on counseling, therapy, psychology, education, parent training and developmental disabilities

President: Gail Salyards
Credit Cards: AMEX; MasterCard; Visa; Discover
Catalog Cost: Free
Catalog Circulation: to 600M
Average Order Size: $200
Printing Information: 52 pages in 4 colors on Glossy Stock
Press: Web Press
Binding: Saddle Stitched
Mailing List Information: Names for rent
In Business: 47 years
Number of Employees: 14
Sales Volume: $1MM to $3MM

1113 Self Healing Through Mind Body Medicine
Emmett Miller MD
P.O. 803
Nevada City, CA 95959
530-478-1807
800-528-2737
Fax: 530-478-0160
www.drmiller.com

Self healing tapes, CDs, books and training materials

President: Emmett Miller, MD
Production Manager: Susan McGuire
productmanager@drmiller.com
Fulfillment: Dr. Miller
General Manager: Aeron Miller
Client/Patient Services: Lisa Gorbet
Social Media Manager: Cabrina Channing
Credit Cards: MasterCard
Catalog Cost: Free
Printing Information: 16 pages in 3 colors
Press: Web Press
Mailing List Information: Names for rent
In Business: 40 years
Sales Volume: Under $500M

1114 Simple Truths
Simple Truths
1935 Brookdale Road
Suite 139
Naperville, IL 60563
630-946-1460
800-900-3427
Fax: 630-961-2168
www.simpletruths.com

Books

Credit Cards: AMEX; MasterCard
In Business: 10 years

1115 Sunrise River Press
Sunrise River Press
838 Lake St S
Forest Lake MN
651-277-1400
800-895-4585
Fax: 651-277-1203
info@sunriseriverpress.com
www.sunriseriverpress.com

Publishes books

In Business: 24+ years

1116 The Original Privacy Catalog
Eden Press
PO Box 8410
Fountain Valley, CA 92728
714-968-8472
800-338-8484
edenpressinc@hotmail.com
www.edenpress.com

Books and videos that deal with privacy, money, home businesses, jobs, new identity, credit, degrees, cash business, foreign opportunities, residence and passports.

President: Barry Reid
Catalog Cost: Free
Printing Information: 16 pages on Newsprint
Press: Web Press
Binding: Saddle Stitched
Mailing List Information: Names for rent
In Business: 46 years
Sales Volume: $410K

Sports & Hobbies

1117 5 T'S Embroidery Supply
Blue Moon Embroidery Supply
5709 Barber Hill Rd
Geneseo, NY 14454
585-382-9600
800-466-7945
Fax: 585-243-1092
ask5ts@5ts.com
www.5ts.com

Embroidery materials and supplies.

President: Dan Johnson
Credit Cards: AMEX; MasterCard
Catalog Circulation: to 6000
Printing Information: 34 pages in 2 colors
Binding: Saddle Stitched
In Business: 11 years
Sales Volume: Under $500M

1118 ABA Sales
American Birding Association
P.O. Box 3070
Colorado Springs, CO 80904
302-838-3660
800-850-2473
Fax: 302-838-3651
info@aba.org
www.aba.org

Birding books and supplies.

Chairman: Louis M. Morrell
President: Jeffrey A. Gordon
jgordon@aba.org
Marketing Manager: Bill Stewart
bstewart@aba.org
Web Developer & Administrator: David Hartley
dhartley@aba.org
Events Coordinator: George Armistead
garmistead@aba.org
Birding Editor: Ted Floyd
tfloyd@aba.org
Credit Cards: MasterCard; Visa
Catalog Circulation: Mailed 2 time(s) per year
In Business: 43 years
Number of Employees: 17

1119 ASN Publishing
Annie's
1455 Linda Vista Drive
San Marcos, CA 92069
800-345-1752
800-345-1752
Fax: 760-591-0230
www.annies-publishing.com

Pattern books, crafts

Chairman: Roger Muselman
President: Tom Muselman
CEO: David McKee
Director: Jeanne Voigt
Number of Employees: 35

1120 America's Foremost Sporting Books
Wolfe Publishing Co
2180 Gulfstream
Suite A
Prescott, AZ 86301
928-445-7810
800-899-7810
Fax: 928-778-5124
wolfepub@riflemag.com
www.riflemagazine.com

Western, adventure, wildlife, firearms, hunting, military and reloading books

President: Mark Harris
CFO: Roberta Montgomery
Credit Cards: MasterCard; Visa
Catalog Circulation: Mailed 2 time(s) per year to 10000
Printing Information: 47 pages in 4 colors on Glossy Stock
Press: Web Press
Binding: Saddle Stitched
In Business: 40 years
Number of Employees: 10
Sales Volume: $1,000,000

1121 Appalachian Mountain Club Books & Maps
Appalachian Moutain Club
10 City Square
Boston, MA 02129
617-523-0636
800-262-4455
AMCinformation@outdoors.org
www.outdoors.org

Appalachian Mountain Club books

Chairman: Rol Fessenden
President: John D. Judge
CFO: Chuck Johnston
Senior Vice President: Walter Graff
VP of Outdoor Learning/Leadership: Stefanie Brochu
VP of Outdoor Operations: Paul Cunha
Credit Cards: MasterCard; Visa
Catalog Cost: Free
Catalog Circulation: Mailed 1 time(s) per year
Printing Information: 4 pages in 2 colors
Press: Web Press
Binding: Saddle Stitched
In Business: 141 years
Sales Volume: $10MM to $20MM

1122 Arts and Crafts
Sterling Publishing
1166 Avenue of the Americas
17th Floor
New York, NY 10036
212-532-7160
800-367-9692
Fax: 212-213-2495
custservice@sterlingpub.com
www.sterlingpub.com

Arts and crafts books

President: Lincoln Boehm
Marketing Manager: Charles Nvrnberg
Production Manager: Rick Willet
Credit Cards: MasterCard; Visa
Catalog Cost: Free
Catalog Circulation: Mailed 2 time(s) per year to 30000
Printing Information: 100 pages in 4 colors on Glossy Stock
Press: Web Press
Binding: Perfect Bound
List Manager: Rena Kornbluh
In Business: 40 years
Number of Employees: 145

1123 Autograph Collector
Autograph Collector
PO Box 25559
Santa Ana, CA 92799   951-734-9636
                              800-996-3977
                              Fax: 714-557-2105
www.autographcollector.com

Books on autograph collecting

President: Steve Cyrkins
Marketing Manager: Jeena Narula
Catalog Circulation: to 5000
Printing Information: 100 pages in 7 colors on
Glossy Stock
Press: Sheetfed Press
Binding: Perfect Bound
In Business: 15 years

1124 Baron/Barclay Bridge Supplies
Baron/Barclay Bridge Supplies
3600 Chamberlain Lane
#206
Louisville, KY 40241   502-426-0410
                              800-274-2221
                              Fax: 502-426-2044
baronbarclay@baronbarclay.com
www.baronbarclay.com

Bridge supplies and books

President: Randy Baron
VP: Mary Baron
Credit Cards: AMEX; MasterCard
Catalog Cost: Free
Catalog Circulation: Mailed 2 time(s) per year
to 20000
Printing Information: 64 pages in 6 colors on
Glossy Stock
Press: Web Press
Binding: Saddle Stitched
Mailing List Information: Names for rent
In Business: 25 years
Number of Employees: 13
Sales Volume: $500,000

1125 Baseball Direct
Baseball Direct
PO Box 7563
Charlottesville, VA 22906   800-558-6273
                              888-244-8837
                              Fax: 434-974-4986
baseball@cstone.net
www.baseballdirect.com

Baseball video tapes, books, CDs, DVDs, audio tapes, calendars and other nostalgic collectibles

President: Reuben Holden
Credit Cards: MasterCard; Visa
Catalog Cost: Free

1126 Baseball Overlay
Baseball Overlay
800 South Main St
Las Vegas, NV 89101   702-382-7555
                              800-522-1777
                              Fax: 702-382-7594
info@gamblersbookclub.com
www.gamblersbook.com

Baseball books, videotapes, and computer software

In Business: 51 years

1127 Books for Cooks
Books for Cooks
1147 E Nakoma Street
Elkridge, MD 21075-5505   410-799-0122
                              888-247-3779
                              Fax: 410-799-0517
www.books-for-cooks.com

Cookbooks, current and out-of-print

Catalog Cost: $4
Printing Information: 8 pages
Brarglen Drive
Elkridge, MD 21075
410.799.0122

1128 C&T Publishing
C&T Publishing
1651 Challenge Drive
Concord, CA 94520-5206   925-677-0377
                              Fax: 925-677-0373
sales@ctpub.com
www.ctpub.com

Books on quilting, ranging from traditional classics to contemporary art quilts and cover techniques such as hand applique and machine quilting

Chief Executive Officer: Todd Hensley
Credit Cards: MasterCard; Visa
Catalog Cost: Free
Catalog Circulation: Mailed 52 time(s) per
year to 80000
Printing Information: 60 pages in 4 colors on
Glossy Stock
Press: Web Press
Binding: Saddle Stitched
Mailing List Information: Names for rent
In Business: 34 years
Number of Employees: 50
Sales Volume: $10,000,000

1129 CQ VHF Ham Radio Magazine
CQ VHF
25 Newbridge Road
Hicksville, NY 11801-2887   516-681-2922
                              800-853-9797
                              Fax: 516-681-2926
cqcomm.com/cq_portal_corp_contact.html

A wide selection of radio books, videos, CDs and CQ calendars

President: Richard Ross
Marketing Manager: Don Allen, Advertising
Manager
Business Manager: Dorothy Kehrwieder
Editorial Director: Richard S. Moseson
Art Director: Elizabeth Ryan
Catalog Circulation: Mailed 4 time(s) per year
Printing Information: in 4 colors
In Business: 30 years
Sales Volume: $10MM to $20MM

1130 Cane Masters
Cane Masters Inc.
288 Village Blvd.
PO Box 5151
Incline Village, NV 89451   755-832-6560
                              800-422-2263
                              Fax: 775-831-8440
info@canemasters.com
www.canemasters.com

Custom-made canes for self-defense, sport and fitness, how-to video packages

President: Mark Shuey Sr.
Catalog Cost: Free
Catalog Circulation: to 5000
Average Order Size: $125
Printing Information: 10 pages in 4 colors on
Matte Stock
Press: Sheetfed Press
Binding: Folded
Mailing List Information: Names for rent
In Business: 10 years
Number of Employees: 5
Sales Volume: $275,000

1131 Championship Productions Baseball Catalog
Championship Productions
2730 Graham St.
Ames, IA 50010   515-232-3687
                              800-873-2730
                              Fax: 515-232-3739
info@ChampionshipProductions.com
www.championshipproductions.com

Instructional Sports Videos

Printing Information: 16 pages

1132 Championship Productions Basketball Catalog
Championship Productions
2730 Graham St.
Ames, IA 50010   515-232-3687
                              800-873-2730
                              Fax: 515-232-3739
info@ChampionshipProductions.com
www.championshipproductions.com

Instructional Sports Videos

Printing Information: 24 pages

1133 Championship Productions Field Hockey Catalog
Championship Productions
2730 Graham St.
Ames, IA 50010   515-232-3687
                              800-873-2730
                              Fax: 515-232-3739
info@ChampionshipProductions.com
www.championshipproductions.com

Instructional Sports Videos

Printing Information: 8 pages

1134 Championship Productions Football Catalog
Championship Productions
2730 Graham St.
Ames, IA 50010   515-232-3687
                              800-873-2730
                              Fax: 515-232-3739
info@ChampionshipProductions.com
www.championshipproductions.com

Instructional Sports Videos

Printing Information: 24 pages

1135 Championship Productions Golf Catalog
Championship Productions
2730 Graham St.
Ames, IA 50010   515-232-3687
                              800-873-2730
                              Fax: 515-232-3739
info@ChampionshipProductions.com
www.championshipproductions.com

Instructional Sports Videos

Printing Information: 8 pages

1136 Championship Productions Hockey Catalog
Championship Productions
2730 Graham St.
Ames, IA 50010   515-232-3687
                              800-873-2730
                              Fax: 515-232-3739
info@ChampionshipProductions.com
www.championshipproductions.com

Instructional Sports Videos

Printing Information: 8 pages

1137 Championship Productions Lacrosse Catalog
Championship Productions
2730 Graham St.
Ames, IA 50010   515-232-3687
                              800-873-2730
                              Fax: 515-232-3739
info@ChampionshipProductions.com
www.championshipproductions.com

Instructional Sports Videos

Printing Information: 12 pages

1138 Championship Productions Soccer Catalog
Championship Productions
2730 Graham St.
Ames, IA 50010   515-232-3687
800-873-2730
Fax: 515-232-3739
info@ChampionshipProductions.com
www.championshipproductions.com
Instructional Sports Videos
Printing Information: 12 pages

1139 Championship Productions Softball Catalog
Championship Productions
2730 Graham St.
Ames, IA 50010   515-232-3687
800-873-2730
Fax: 515-232-3739
info@ChampionshipProductions.com
www.championshipproductions.com
Instructional Sports Videos
Printing Information: 16 pages

1140 Championship Productions Swimming Catalog
Championship Productions
2730 Graham St.
Ames, IA 50010   515-232-3687
800-873-2730
Fax: 515-232-3739
info@ChampionshipProductions.com
www.championshipproductions.com
Instructional Sports Videos
Printing Information: 16 pages

1141 Championship Productions Tennis Catalog
Championship Productions
2730 Graham St.
Ames, IA 50010   515-232-3687
800-873-2730
Fax: 515-232-3739
info@ChampionshipProductions.com
www.championshipproductions.com
Instructional Sports Videos
Printing Information: 8 pages

1142 Championship Productions Track & Field Catalog
Championship Productions
2730 Graham St.
Ames, IA 50010   515-232-3687
800-873-2730
Fax: 515-232-3739
info@ChampionshipProductions.com
www.championshipproductions.com
Instructional Sports Videos
Printing Information: 16 pages

1143 Championship Productions Volleyball Catalog
Championship Productions
2730 Graham St.
Ames, IA 50010   515-232-3687
800-873-2730
Fax: 515-232-3739
info@ChampionshipProductions.com
www.championshipproductions.com
Instructional Sports Videos
Printing Information: 16 pages

1144 Championship Productions Wrestling Catalog
Championship Productions
2730 Graham St.
Ames, IA 50010   515-232-3687
800-873-2730
Fax: 515-232-3739
info@ChampionshipProductions.com
www.championshipproductions.com
Instructional Sports Videos
Printing Information: 20 pages

1145 Chessieshop
Cheasepeak and Ohio
312 E Ridgeway Street
Clifton Forge, VA 24422-1325   540-862-2210
800-453-COHS
Fax: 540-863-9159
cohs@cohs.org
www.cohs.org
Books on the history of certain sports and hobby items related to the C&O Railway
President: Thomas W Dixon Jr
Art Director: Mac Beard
Credit Cards: AMEX; MasterCard; Visa
Catalog Circulation: Mailed 1 time(s) per year to 5000
Printing Information: 12 pages in 4 colors on Glossy Stock
Binding: Saddle Stitched
Mailing List Information: Names for rent
In Business: 35 years
Number of Employees: 5
Sales Volume: Under $500M

1146 Cutter and Buck
Cutter and Buck
101 Eliott Avenue W
Suite 100
Seattle, WA 98119   800-713-7810
help@cutterbuck.com
www.cutterbuck.com
Men's and women's golf apparel, shoes and other sportswear
President: Joel Freet
CFO: David Hauge
Marketing Manager: Julie Snow
Credit Cards: MasterCard
Catalog Cost: Free
Catalog Circulation: Mailed 6 time(s) per year
Printing Information: 123 pages in 4 colors on Glossy Stock
Binding: Perfect Bound
In Business: 28 years
Number of Employees: 225
Sales Volume: $ 58 Million

1147 Dance Horizons
Princeton Book Company
614 Route 130
Hightstown, NJ 08520   609-426-0602
800-220-7149
Fax: 609-426-1344
pbc@dancehorizons.com
www.dancehorizons.com
Dance books and videos
President: Charles H Woodford
Production Manager: Elaine Cinque
Credit Cards: AMEX; MasterCard; Visa
Catalog Cost: Free
Catalog Circulation: Mailed 1 time(s) per year
Average Order Size: $120
Printing Information: 80 pages in 1 color on Matte Stock
Press: Sheetfed Press
Binding: Saddle Stitched
Mailing List Information: Names for rent
In Business: 35 years
Number of Employees: 4
Sales Volume: $500,000

1148 Deer & Hunting Books Catalog
Krause Publications Inc
700 E State Street
PO Box 50096
Iola, WI 54945   715-445-2214
800-258-0929
Fax: 715-445-4087
zielkec@krause.com
www.krausebooks.com
Gun and hunting books
President: Roger Case
Marketing Manager: Corinne Zielke
Tour Manager: Bob Boris
Credit Cards: AMEX; MasterCard; Visa
Catalog Cost: Free
Catalog Circulation: Mailed 2 time(s) per year to 40000
Average Order Size: $30
Printing Information: 800 pages in 4 colors on Glossy Stock
Press: Web Press
Binding: Saddle Stitched
In Business: 63 years
Number of Employees: 570

1149 Deja Vu Collector's Gallery
Deja Vu Collector's Gallery
2934 Beverly Glen Circle
Suite 309
Los Angeles, CA 90077-1724   818-996-6137
Fax: 818-996-6147
dejavugallery@socal.rr.com
www.dejavugallery.com
Large collection of autographed photos, movie posters, lobby cards, books and old magazines
President: Stephen Pierson
Production Manager: Jason Knopinski
Credit Cards: AMEX; MasterCard; Visa
Catalog Cost: Free
Printing Information: 28 pages in 4 colors
In Business: 34 years
Number of Employees: 4
Sales Volume: under$500m

1150 Delta Press
Delta Press LTD.
215 S Washington Ave
El Dorado, AR 71730-5927   870-862-3811
Fax: 870-862-9671
info@deltapress.com
www.deltapress.com
Gun and survival books and videos
Credit Cards: AMEX; MasterCard
Catalog Cost: Free
Catalog Circulation: Mailed 2 time(s) per year
Average Order Size: $80
Printing Information: 16 pages in 4 colors on Glossy Stock
Press: Web Press
Binding: Saddle Stitched
Mailing List Information: Names for rent
In Business: 15 years
Number of Employees: 18
Sales Volume: $5MM to $10MM

1151 Design Originals
Design Originals
1970 Broad Street
East Petersburg, PA 17520-1411   717-560-4703
800-457-9112
Fax: 717-560-4702
d-originals.com@foxchapelpublishing.com
www.D-Originals.Com
Craft project books
President: Suzanne Mc Neil
Marketing Manager: Barbara Barnett
Production Manager: Kathy McMillan
Fulfillment: Dean Rothing
Credit Cards: AMEX; MasterCard
Catalog Cost: $3
Catalog Circulation: Mailed 3 time(s) per year
Printing Information: 30 pages on Glossy Stock

Mailing List Information: Names for rent
In Business: 24 years
Number of Employees: 40
Sales Volume: $3MM to $5MM

1152 Family Album
4887 Newport Rd
Kinzers, PA 17535-9793 717-442-0220
Fax: 717-442-7904
rarebooks@pobox.com

Antique books and library supplies, appraisal and restoration services

President: Ron Lieberman
Credit Cards: MasterCard; Visa
Catalog Cost:
Catalog Circulation: to 2000
Average Order Size: $50
Printing Information: 100 pages in 1 color on Matte Stock
Press: Sheetfed Press
Binding: Perfect Bound
Mailing List Information: Names for rent
Number of Employees: 1
Sales Volume: Under $500M

1153 Feather Craft Fly Fishing
National Feather Craft Co., Inc.
8307 Manchester Rd
PO Box 440128
St. Louis, MO 63144 314-963-7876
800-659-1707
Fax: 314-963-0324
orders@feather-craft.com
www.feather-craft.com

Fly fishing rods, reels, waders, flies and fly tying materials

President: Ed Story
Executive Director: Brian Flinchpaugh
Vice President: Robert Story
Treasurer: Janel Story
Printing Information: 100 pages in 4 colors on Glossy Stock
Binding: Saddle Stitched
In Business: 33 years
Number of Employees: 31
Sales Volume: $3.3 MM

1154 Fishing Hot Spots, Inc.
Fishing Hot Spots, Inc.
1853 N Stevens Street
PO Box 1167
Rhinelander, WI 54501-2163 715-365-5555
800-ALL-MAPS
Fax: 715-365-5575
customerservice@fishinghotspots.com
www.fishinghotspots.com

Fishing publications and maps

President: George Swierczynski
CFO: Dawn Richter
Production Manager: Steve Swierczynski
Fulfillment: Nicole Stein
Credit Cards: AMEX; MasterCard; Visa
Catalog Cost: Free
Catalog Circulation: Mailed 2 time(s) per year to 2000
Printing Information: 10 pages in 4 colors on Matte Stock
Press: Offset Press
Binding: Saddle Stitched
In Business: 40 years
Number of Employees: 20
Sales Volume: $2 MM

1155 Flyfisher's Paradise
Flyfisher's Paradise
2603 E College Avenue
State College, PA 16801 814-234-4189
Fax: 814-238-3686
information@flyfishersparadise.com
www.flyfishersparadiseonline.com

Fly fishing books, equipment and lures

President: Steve Sywensky
Credit Cards: MasterCard; Visa
Catalog Cost: Free

Catalog Circulation: Mailed 1 time(s) per year to 40000
Printing Information: 64 pages in 2 colors on Glossy Stock
Press: Web Press
Binding: Saddle Stitched
In Business: 34 years
Number of Employees: 4
Sales Volume: $500M to $1MM

1156 From the Neck Up
Madhatter Press
PO Box 7480
Minneapolis, MN 55407 612-822-1102
info@hatbook.com
www.hatbook.com

Comprehensive books on hatmaking

President: Denise Dreher
Number of Employees: 5

1157 Gambler's Book Shop
GBC Press
800 South Main Street
Las Vegas, NV 89101 702-382-7555
800-522-1777
Fax: 702-382-7594
info@gamblersbook.com
www.gamblersbook.com

Books, computer software, videotapes on the subject of gambling in 30 different categories

President: Maryann Guberman
Marketing Manager: Howard Schwartz
Production Manager: Mike Figueroa
Credit Cards: MasterCard; Visa
Catalog Cost: Free
Catalog Circulation: Mailed 1 time(s) per year
Printing Information: 80 pages in 4 colors on Matte Stock
Press: Web Press
Binding: Saddle Stitched
Mailing List Information: Names for rent
In Business: 47 years
Number of Employees: 10
Sales Volume: $500M to $1MM

1158 Gardening Books
Sterling Publishing
387 Park Avenue S
New York, NY 10016-8810 212-532-7160
800-367-9692
Fax: 212-213-2495
custservice@sterlingpub.com

Gardening books

President: Charles Nurnberg
Marketing Manager: Ronny Stolvenberg
Production Manager: Eli Hausknetht
Credit Cards: AMEX; MasterCard; Visa
Catalog Cost: Free
Catalog Circulation: Mailed 2 time(s) per year to 30000
Printing Information: 100 pages in 4 colors on Glossy Stock
Press: Web Press
Binding: Perfect Bound
In Business: 50 years
Number of Employees: 70

1159 Genealogical Publishing Company
Genealogical Publishing Company
3600 Clipper Mill Rd
Suite 260
Baltimore, MD 21211 410-837-8271
800-296-6687
Fax: 410-752-8492
info@genealogical.com
www.genealogical.com

How-to, reference books, CD-ROMS on genealogy and local history

President: Barry N Chodak
CFO: Michael Tepper
Marketing Manager: Joe Garonzik
Production Manager: Eileen Perkins
Fulfillment: Roger Sherr

Credit Cards: MasterCard
Catalog Cost: Free
Catalog Circulation: Mailed 12 time(s) per year to 100M
Average Order Size: $40
Printing Information: 126 pages in 1 color on Matte Stock
Press: Web Press
Binding: Saddle Stitched
Mailing List Information: Names for rent
In Business: 52 years
Number of Employees: 9
Sales Volume: $3,000,000

1160 Hard-to-Find Needlework Books
Hard-to-Find Needlework Books
416 Fenlon Boulevard
Clifton, NJ 07014-1206 617-969-0942
Fax: 617-969-0942
hardtofind@needleworkbooks.com
www.needleworkbooks.com

Needlework books

President: Bette Feinstein, Needlework Books
Credit Cards: MasterCard
Catalog Cost: $1
Catalog Circulation: Mailed 12 time(s) per year
Printing Information: 20 pages in 1 color on Newsprint
Binding: Folded
Mailing List Information: Names for rent
In Business: 39 years
Number of Employees: 1
Sales Volume: Under $500M

1161 Heart Zones Company
Heart Zones
2636 Fulton Ave
Suite #100
Sacramento, CA 95821-5731 916-481-7283
Fax: 916-481-2213
www.heartzone.com

Books on a variety of fitness, sports and health topics such as running, triathalons, heart rate monitors and logs

President: Sally Edwards
Marketing Manager: Melissa McKenzie
Credit Cards: MasterCard; Visa
Catalog Cost: Free
Catalog Circulation: Mailed 4 time(s) per year to 25000
Printing Information: 4 pages in 2 colors on Glossy Stock
Press: Web Press
Binding: Saddle Stitched
Will Trade Names: Yes
In Business: 22 years
Number of Employees: 2
Sales Volume: Under $500M

1162 Hemming's Motor News
Hemming's
PO Box 100
Bennington, VT 05201 802-442-3101
800-227-4373
Fax: 802-447-9631
hmnmail@hemmings.com
www.hemmings.com

Automotive books, automobilia, calendars

Production Manager: Ed Heys
Manager: Perez Ehrich
Credit Cards: MasterCard; Visa
Catalog Cost: Free
Catalog Circulation: Mailed 2 time(s) per year to 400M
Printing Information: 12 pages in 4 colors on Matte Stock
Mailing List Information: Names for rent
List Manager: Marian Savage
In Business: 45 years
Number of Employees: 150
Sales Volume: Under $500M

1163 High-Lonesome Books
High-Lonesome Books
PO Box 878
Silver City, NM 88062-878   575-388-3763
    800-380-7323
Fax: 575-388-5705
orders@high-lonesomebooks.com
www.high-lonesomebooks.com

New, used, rare and out-of-print books on the Southwest, outdoor adventure, natural history, hunting, fishing and country living

President: M H Salman
Credit Cards: AMEX; MasterCard; Visa
Catalog Cost: Free
Catalog Circulation: Mailed 4 time(s) per year
Average Order Size: $100
Printing Information: 48 pages on Newsprint
Press: Web Press
Binding: Saddle Stitched
Mailing List Information: Names for rent
In Business: 29 years
Number of Employees: 10-J
Sales Volume: Under $500M

1164 Hitching Post Supply
Hitching Post Supply
10312 210th ST SE
Snohomish, WA 98296-1809   360-668-2349
    800-689-9971
Fax: 360-668-0721
vickie@hitchingpostsupply.com
www.hitchingpostsupply.com

Cowboy and western music, books and gear, horsehair by the pound

President: Vickie Mullen
In Business: 27 years

1165 Hobby House Press
Hobby House Press
1 Corporate Dr
Grantsville, MD 21536-1261   301-895-3792
    800-554-1447
Fax: 301-895-5029
www.hobbyhouse.com

Great books to help you organize your collections

President: Gary Riddel
CFO: Nick Brown
Marketing Manager: Mark Brown
Production Manager: Brenda Wiseman
Credit Cards: MasterCard; Visa
Catalog Cost: Free
Catalog Circulation: to 10000
Mailing List Information: Names for rent
Number of Employees: 45
Sales Volume: Under $500M

1166 Human Kinetics Sports and Fitness
Human Kinetics
1607 N Market Street
PO Box 5076
Champaign, IL 61825-5076   217-351-5076
    800-747-4457
Fax: 217-351-1549
info@hkusa.com
www.humankinetics.com

Features instructional titles on specific sports, coaching education, and sports administration as well as fitness/training topics for consumers

Fulfillment: Rin Martin
Buyers: Ernie Noa
Credit Cards: AMEX; MasterCard; Visa
Catalog Cost: Free
Catalog Circulation: to 20000
Printing Information: 45 pages in 4 colors on Glossy Stock
Press: Offset Press
Binding: Saddle Stitched
List Manager: Bryan Holbing
In Business: 30 years

1167 Insect Lore
Insect Lore
PO Box 1535
Shafter, CA 93263-1535   800-548-3284
Fax: 661-746-0334
livebug@insectlore.com
www.insectlore.com

Books and supplies for bug catching

President: Carlos White PhD
Marketing Manager: John White
Credit Cards: MasterCard; Visa
Catalog Cost: Free
In Business: 40 years
Number of Employees: 48
Sales Volume: $10 Million

1168 International Center of Photography
International Center Of Photography
1114 Avenue of the Americas at 43rd
New York, NY 10036   212-857-0001
    800-688-8171
Fax: 212-768-4688
store@icp.org
www.icp.org

Photography books and related gifts

President: Jeffrey A. Rosen
CFO: Victor Quinomes
Executive Director: Mark Lubell
Executive VP: Stephanie H. Shuman
VP: Renee Harbers Liddell
Catalog Cost: $1
Printing Information: 16 pages in 7 colors on Newsprint
Binding: Folded
In Business: 49 years
Number of Employees: 75

1169 International Marine Boating Books
International Marine-Ragged Mt. Press
90 Mechanic Street
Camden, ME 04843   207-230-7033
    800-262-4729
Fax: 609-308-4484
www.mhprofessional.com

Nautical books, videos and computer software

Credit Cards: AMEX; MasterCard; Visa
Catalog Cost: Free
Catalog Circulation: Mailed 1 time(s) per year to 80000
Average Order Size: $40
Printing Information: 48 pages in 2 colors on Newsprint
Press: Web Press
Binding: Saddle Stitched
List Company: Media Marketplace
PO Box 500
Newton, PA 18940
215-968-9410
In Business: 40 years
Number of Employees: 9

1170 John Neal Bookseller
John Neal, Bookseller
1833 Spring Garden St.
1st Floor
Greensboro, NC 27403   336-272-6139
    800-369-9598
Fax: 336-272-9015
info@johnnealbooks.com
www.johnnealbooks.com

Books, tool and materials for calligraphy and bookbinding

President: John Neal
Production Manager: John Neal
Buyers: John Neal
Credit Cards: MasterCard; Visa
Catalog Circulation: Mailed 1 time(s) per year to 20000
Printing Information: 64 pages in 1 color on Newsprint
Press: Web Press
Binding: Folded
In Business: 14 years

Number of Employees: 10
Sales Volume: $500M to $1MM

1171 Judith Bowman Books
CPI Printers
98 Pound Ridge Rd
Bedford, NY 10506-1241   914-234-7543
Fax: 914-234-0122

Sporting books including angling, hunting, sporting dogs, archery, canoeing, out of print books

President: Judith Bowman
Credit Cards: MasterCard; Visa
Catalog Cost: $5
Catalog Circulation: to 1000
Average Order Size: $250
Printing Information: 56 pages in 1 color on Matte Stock
Binding: Saddle Stitched
Mailing List Information: Names for rent
In Business: 25 years
Number of Employees: 1
Sales Volume: Under $500M

1172 Knollwood Books
W248s7040 Sugar Maple Drive
Waukesha, WI 53189-9329   608-835-8938
    books@tdsnet.com

Books on astronomy, meteorology and space

President: Peggy Price
Buyers: Lee Price
Credit Cards: MasterCard; Visa
Catalog Cost: Free
Catalog Circulation: Mailed 4 time(s) per year
Printing Information: 33 pages in 1 color on Matte Stock
Press: Web Press
Binding: Perfect Bound
Mailing List Information: Names for rent
Number of Employees: 10
Sales Volume: $500,000

1173 Lacis
Lacis
3163 Adeline St
Berkeley, CA 94703-2401   510-843-7178
Fax: 510-843-5018
www.lacis.com

Books, tools and materials for the textile arts with emphasis on the crafts of lace, embroidery, tatting, braiding, weaving, beadwork and costume

President: Jules Kliot
General Manager: Perrin Kliot
Manager: Erin Algeo
Buyers: Kaethe Kliot
Credit Cards: MasterCard; Visa
Catalog Circulation: Mailed 1 time(s) per year to 6000
Average Order Size: $60
Printing Information: 90 pages in 4 colors on Matte Stock
Press: Letterpress
Binding: Folded
Mailing List Information: Names for rent
In Business: 48 years
Number of Employees: 9
Sales Volume: $346,000

1174 MF Athletic Company
MF Athletic Company
1600 Division Road
West Warwick, RI 02893   401-942-9363
    888-556-7464
Fax: 800-682-6950
mfathletic@mfathletic.com
www.everythingtrackandfield.com

Track and field supplies, books, DVDs, timing and measuring equipment and ez up tents

President: Eric Falk
eric.falk@mfathletic.com
Founder: Bill Falk

bill.falk@mfathletic.com
General Manager: Mark Strawderman
marks@mfathletic.com

1175 Manny's Woodworkers Place
Manny's Woodworkers Place
881 Nandino Blvd
Unit 9
Lexington, KY 40511   800-243-0713
                    Fax: 859-255-5444
purchasing@mannyswoodworkersplace.com
www.mannyswoodworkersplace.com
Woodworking books and videos on a variety of topics including woodturning, carving, carpentry, and furniture making, toy making and others
President: Manny Shambu
Marketing Manager: James Shambhu
Production Manager: Steve Gibbs
Buyers: Manny Shambhu
Credit Cards: AMEX; MasterCard
Catalog Cost: Free
Printing Information: 64 pages in 1 color on Matte Stock
Press: Web Press
Binding: Saddle Stitched
Mailing List Information: Names for rent
In Business: 22 years
Number of Employees: 3
Sales Volume: under $500M

1176 Mary Jane's Cross 'N Stitch
Mary Jane's Cross N' Stitch
120 E. FM544 Suite 72, #294
Murphy, TX 75904   800-334-6819
email@maryjanes.com
www.maryjanes.com
Craft books
Credit Cards: MasterCard
In Business: 37 years

1177 Mountaineers Books
The Mountaineers Books
1001 SW Klickitat Way
Suite 201
Seattle, WA 98134-1161   206-223-6303
                    800-553-4453
                    Fax: 206-223-6306
mbooks@mountaineersbooks.org
www.Mountaineersbooks.Org
Outdoor books by experts; 450+ titles on hiking, paddling, cycling, climbing, packbacking, skiing, snowboarding, snowshoeing and more, plus outdoor how-to's and guidebooks
President: Helen Cherullo
CFO: Art Freeman
artf@mountaineersbooks.org
Marketing Manager: Doug Canfield
dougc@mountaineersbooks.org
Production Manager: Jen Grable
jeng@mountaineersbooks.org
Publisher: Helen Cherullo
helenc@mountaineersbooks.org
Accounting Manager and HR: Gayle Grything
gayleg@mountaineersbooks.org
*Accounting & Office Coordinator:*Connie Saxon
connies@mountaineersbooks.org
Credit Cards: MasterCard; Visa
Catalog Cost: Free
Catalog Circulation: Mailed 2 time(s) per year
Printing Information: 43 pages in 4 colors on Newsprint
Binding: Saddle Stitched
Mailing List Information: Names for rent
In Business: 46 years
Number of Employees: 35
Sales Volume: 10MM-20MM

1178 Paladin Press
Paladin Press
5540 Central Avenue
Boulder, CO 80301-2997   303-443-7250
                    Fax: 303-442-8741
service@paladin-press.com
www.paladin-press.com
Publishes books on exotic weapons, espionage and investigations, martial arts, military science and firearms
Buyers: Tom Laidlaw
Credit Cards: MasterCard; Visa; Discover
Catalog Cost: Free
Catalog Circulation: Mailed 6 time(s) per year
Average Order Size: $120
Printing Information: 100 pages in 4 colors on Glossy Stock
Press: Web Press
Binding: Saddle Stitched
Mailing List Information: Names for rent
List Company: StatListics
11 Lake Avenue Ext.
Danbury, CT 06811
203-778-8700
In Business: 42 years
Number of Employees: 25
Sales Volume: $3MM to $5MM

1179 RTS Unlimited
RT Sun Limited
PO Box 150412
Lakewood, CO 80215-412   303-403-1840
                    Fax: 303-403-1837
RTSUnlimited@earthlink.net
www.rtsunlimited.com
Comic book supplies, back issues and related items
President: Tim Collins

1180 Rip Off Press
Rip Off Press
PO Box 4686
Auburn, CA 95604-4686   530-885-8183
                    800-468-2669
                    Fax: 530-885-8219
mail@ripoffpress.com
www.ripoffpress.com
Adult and underground comics, books and related items
Credit Cards: AMEX; MasterCard; Visa; Discover
Catalog Cost: $1
Catalog Circulation: Mailed 1 time(s) per year to 20000
Average Order Size: $40
Printing Information: 28 pages in 2 colors on Matte Stock
Press: Sheetfed Press
Binding: Saddle Stitched
Mailing List Information: Names for rent
In Business: 46 years
Number of Employees: 2
Sales Volume: Under $500M

1181 Robert A Madle Sci-Fi/Fantasy Books
Rainbow Sandals
4406 Bestor Drive
Rockville, MD 20853-2137   301-460-4712
                    www.sfsite.com
Science fiction, fantasy books, horror, old pulp magazines
President: Robert A Madle
Publisher/Managing Editor: Rodger Turner
Site Engineer: Wayne MacLaurin
Forum Administrator: Rick Norwood
Catalog Circulation: Mailed 2 time(s) per year to 10000
Printing Information: 96 pages in 1 color on Glossy Stock
Press: Web Press
Binding: Saddle Stitched
In Business: 34 years
Number of Employees: 1
Sales Volume: Under $500M

1182 Schiffer Aviation History
Schiffer Publishing Ltd.
4880 Lower Valley Rd
Atglen, PA 19310-1768   610-593-1777
                    Fax: 610-593-2002
info@schifferbooks.com
www.Schifferbooks.Com
Reference books subjects of which include aviation history, Great Britain, Japan and Russia, Luftwaffe, post WWII, and the Jet Age
President: Peter Schiffer
CFO: Pam Braceland
Marketing Manager: Tina Skinner
Fulfillment: Ernie Barrett
Catalog Circulation: Mailed 2 time(s) per year
Printing Information: 48 pages in 4 colors on Glossy Stock
Binding: Folded
Mailing List Information: Names for rent
In Business: 42 years
Number of Employees: 30
Sales Volume: $10MM to $20MM

1183 Smoky Mountain Knife Works
Smoky Mountain Knife Works, Inc.
2320 Winfield Dunn Parkway
P.O. Box 4430
Sevierville, TN 37864   865-453-5871
                    800-251-9306
                    Fax: 865-428-5991
help@smkw.com
Knives and accessories for hunting, tactical-military, cutlery, martial arts, and camping
President: Kevin Pipes
Catalog Cost: Free
In Business: 45 years

1184 Sportime Catalog
School Specialty Inc
PO Box 1579
Appleton, WI 54912-1579   888-388-3224
                    800-283-5700
                    Fax: 888-388-6344
orders@schoolspecialty.com
www.schoolspecialty.com
Innovative audio/video products for physical education & recreation, sensory solutions, school supplies, early childhood and special needs products and equipment
Chairman: James R. Henderson
President: Joseph M. Yorio
CFO: Kevin Baehler
Principal: Justin Lu
Portfolio Manager: Madhu Satyanarayana
EVP, Distribution: Patrick T. Collins
Credit Cards: AMEX; MasterCard
Catalog Cost: Free
Catalog Circulation: Mailed 1 time(s) per year
Printing Information: 400 pages

1185 Storey Publishing
Storey Publishing
210 MASS MoCA Way
North Adams, MA 01247   413-346-2100
                    Fax: 413-346-2199
feedback@storey.com
www.storey.com
Books, calendars, gifts on gardening, cooking, crafts, building and animals
Credit Cards: AMEX; MasterCard; Visa
Catalog Cost: Free
Catalog Circulation: Mailed 2 time(s) per year to 250
Average Order Size: $40
Printing Information: 56 pages
Mailing List Information: Names for rent
List Company: AZ Marketing
PO Box 904
Cos Cob, CT 06807
203-629-8088
In Business: 31 years

Number of Employees: 100
Sales Volume: $20MM to $50MM

1186 Sysko's

Sysko's
PO Box 287
Warrensburg, MO 64093   *Fax:* 855-546-5784
www.syskos.com

Instructional Basketball and Football books and videos

1187 Things Deco

Things Deco
130 E 18 Street
Suite 8F
New York, NY 10003-2441   212-362-8961
thingsdeco@hotmail.com
www.thingsdeco.com

Art Deco and early 20th Century design books, stationery, posters, calendars, holiday cards and ornaments, jewelry, ceramics and home accessories.

President: Harriet Seltzer
Production Manager: Robert Josen
Catalog Circulation: to 60000
Printing Information: 52 pages in 4 colors
Binding: Saddle Stitched
In Business: 23 years

1188 Timber Press

Timber Press
133 SW 2nd Avenue
Suite 450
Portland, OR 97204   800-327-5680
800-827-5622
Fax: 503-227-3070
info@timberpress.com
www.timberpress.com

Books on gardening and horticulture

President: Peter Workman
Credit Cards: AMEX; MasterCard
Catalog Cost: Free
Catalog Circulation: Mailed 4 time(s) per year to 200K
Average Order Size: $100
Printing Information: 32 pages in 1 color on Glossy Stock
Press: Web Press
Binding: Saddle Stitched
Mailing List Information: Names for rent
List Manager: Michael O Campbell
In Business: 29 years
Number of Employees: 35
Sales Volume: $10MM to $20MM

1189 Turtle Press

Turtle Press
PO Box 34010
Santa Fe, NM 87594-4010   800-778-8785
www.turtlepress.com

Martial arts books and DVDs

President: Josh Rappaport
In Business: 26 years

1190 US Chess Federation

USCF Sales
295 A Cochran Road SW
Huntsville, AL 35824   931-787-1234
888-512-4377
Fax: 256-851-0560
customerservice@uscfsales.com
www.uscfsales.com

Chess sets, books, software and computer chess games

President: Bill Hall
Credit Cards: AMEX; MasterCard
Catalog Cost: Free
Catalog Circulation: Mailed 4 time(s) per year
Printing Information: 100 pages in 4 colors on Glossy Stock
In Business: 80 years

1191 Wood Violet Books

3814 Sunhill Drive
Madison, WI 53718-6283   608-837-7207
877-477-4977
Fax: 608-837-7207

Herb and gardening books

President: Debbie Cravens
Buyers: Debbie Cravens
Credit Cards: AMEX; MasterCard
Catalog Cost: $2
Catalog Circulation: Mailed 1 time(s) per year
Average Order Size: $40
Printing Information: 60 pages in 4 colors on Glossy Stock
Mailing List Information: Names for rent
In Business: 16 years
Number of Employees: 10-J
Sales Volume: $500M to $1MM

1192 Wrestling Superstore Catalog

Wrestling Superstore
12826 Commodity Place
Tampa, FL 33626   813-749-0800
Fax: 813-749-0804
info@wrestlingsuperstore.com
www.wrestlingsuperstore.com

Wrestling merchandise such as shirts, belts, DVDs, replica masks and pendants

CFO: Anthony Balasco
Credit Cards: MasterCard
Catalog Cost: $2
In Business: 26 years

1193 YMAA Products Catalog

Trans Continental Prints
PO Box 480
Wolfeboro, NH 03894   603-569-7988
800-669-8892
Fax: 603-569-1889
www.ymaa.com

Martial arts books and DVDs and Tai Chi uniforms

President: David Ripianzi
CFO: David Ripianzi
Marketing Manager: Phil Goldman
Production Manager: Tim Comrie
Credit Cards: AMEX; MasterCard
Catalog Circulation: Mailed 1 time(s) per year
Average Order Size: $84
Printing Information: 54 pages in 4 colors on Glossy Stock
Press: Web Press
Binding: Saddle Stitched
Mailing List Information: Names for rent
In Business: 27 years
Number of Employees: 9
Sales Volume: $1MM to $3MM

Travel

1194 Adventure Life

Adventure Life
712 W. Spruce St.
Suite 1
Missoula, MT 59802   406-541-2677
800-344-6118
Fax: 406-541-2676
www.adventure-life.com

Travel information, deals and events.

1195 Aims International Books

Aims International Books
7709 Hamilton Avenue
Cincinnati, OH 45231   513-521-5590
800-733-2067
Fax: 513-521-5592
www.aimsbooks.com

Books in spanish, children books

In Business: 22+ years

1196 Bess Press

Bess Press
3565 Harding Avenue
Honolulu, HI 96816   808-734-7159
800-734-7159
Fax: 808-732-3627
customerservice@besspress.com
www.besspress.com

All general interest and educational titles including Hawaiian and Pacific Island studies

President: Benjamin Bess
publisher@besspress.com
Catalog Cost: Free
Catalog Circulation: Mailed 2 time(s) per year to 3000
Printing Information: 20 pages in 4 colors on Glossy Stock
Press: Letterpress
Binding: Saddle Stitched
In Business: 35 years
Number of Employees: 6
Sales Volume: $1,000,000

1197 Daedalus Books & Music

Daedalus Books & Music
P.O. Box 6000
Columbia, MD 21046-6000   410-309-2706
800-944-8879
custserv@daedalusbooks.com
www.daedalusbooks.com

Books, CDs and DVDs

In Business: 35 years

1198 Ebags

eBags, Inc.
5500 Greenwood Plaza Blvd.
Suite 160
Greenwood Village, CO 80111   303-694-1933
800-820-6126
Fax: 303-694-9491
info@ebags.com
www.ebags.com

Handbags, luggage, backpacks, carry-ons, computer cases, wallets and purses and travel accessories

Chairman: Jon Nordmark
President: Mike Edwards
CFO: Mark DeOrio
Marketing Manager: Keith Bristol
CEO & Director: Vince Jones
Credit Cards: AMEX; MasterCard; Visa
Catalog Cost: Free
Printing Information: 32 pages in 4 colors
Binding: Perfect Bound
In Business: 16 years
Number of Employees: 72
Sales Volume: $4.6 Million

1199 ElderSong Publications

ElderSong Publications
P.O. Box 74
Mount Airy, MD 21771   800-397-0533
info@eldersong.com
www.eldersong.com

Publisher and distributor of books, videos, and recordings for activity directors, recreation and creative arts therapists, occupational and rehab therapists

Printing Information: 16 pages
In Business: 30 years

1200 Geological Highway Maps

1444 S Boulder Avenue
Tulsa, OK 74119-3604   918-584-2555
Fax: 918-560-2665
www.aapg.org

Highway maps for each section of the country

President: Pat Gratton
Marketing Manager: Ronald Hard
Catalog Circulation: to 30000
Printing Information: 48 pages in 4 colors on

Glossy Stock
Press: Web Press
Binding: Saddle Stitched
In Business: 87 years
Number of Employees: 60

1201 George F Cram Company
Herff Jones
301 S Lasalle Street
Indianapolis, IN 46201-4336   317-635-5564
                                800-227-4199
                           Fax: 317-635-2720
                    www.herffjones.com

World globe and map publisher

President: William Douthit
CFO: Bryan Hollingsworth
Marketing Manager: Jennifer Douthit
Buyers: Julie Desjean
Credit Cards: AMEX; MasterCard; Visa
Catalog Circulation: Mailed 1 time(s) per year
Printing Information: 19 pages
In Business: 94 years
Number of Employees: 100
Sales Volume: $19.3 Million

1202 Graphic Arts Center Publishing Company
3019 NW Yeon Avenue
Portland, OR 97210-1519   503-226-2402
                            800-453-3032
                       Fax: 800-355-9685
                    www.gacpc.com

Books on Alaska, Western Canada and the Northwest; topics include history, geography, culture, arts, sports and recreation

Marketing Manager: Mike Jones

1203 High-Lonesome Books
High-Lonesome Books
PO Box 878
Silver City, NM 88062-878   575-388-3763
                              800-380-7323
                         Fax: 575-388-5705
            orders@high-lonesomebooks.com
                www.high-lonesomebooks.com

New, used, rare and out-of-print books on the Southwest, outdoor adventure, natural history, hunting, fishing and country living

President: M H Salman
Credit Cards: AMEX; MasterCard; Visa
Catalog Cost: Free
Catalog Circulation: Mailed 4 time(s) per year
Average Order Size: $100
Printing Information: 48 pages on Newsprint
Press: Web Press
Binding: Saddle Stitched
Mailing List Information: Names for rent
In Business: 29 years
Number of Employees: 10-J
Sales Volume: Under $500M

1204 Holiday Expeditions
Holiday Expeditions
544 East 3900 South
Salt Lake City, UT 84107   801-266-2087
                             800-624-6323
                        Fax: 801-266-1448
                    www.bikeraft.com

Whitewater rafting, mountain biking, ranch vacations

President: D Holiday
Operations Manager: Tim Gaylord
Catalog Cost: Free
Sales Volume: $1MM to $3MM

1205 John F. Blair Publisher
John F. Blair Publisher
1406 Plaza Drive
Winston-Salem, NC 27103   336-768-1374
                            800-222-9796
                       Fax: 336-768-9194
              sakowski@blairpub.com
                    www.blairpub.com

Publisher

President: Carolyn Sakowski
Marketing Manager: Anna Sutton
Editor-in-Chief: Steve Kirk
kirk@blairpub.com
Director of Design & Production: Debra Long Hampton
hampton@blairpub.com
Publicist: Sally Johnson
dickerson@blairpub.com
Printing Information: 36 pages
In Business: 61 years

1206 Magellan's
Magellan's
PO Box 3390
Chelmsford, MA 01824   888-450-7714
                    Fax: 800-866-3235
              help@magellans.com
                    www.magellans.com

Travel accessories, luggage and clothing

President: John Mc Manus
CFO: Michael Szele
Credit Cards: AMEX; MasterCard; Visa; Discover Optima
Catalog Cost: Free
Catalog Circulation: Mailed 6 time(s) per year
Average Order Size: $72
Printing Information: 68 pages in 4 colors on Matte Stock
Binding: Saddle Stitched
Mailing List Information: Names for rent
List Company: Names & Addresses
160 E Marquerdt Drive
Wheeling, IL 60090
847-465-1500
In Business: 25 years
Number of Employees: 100
Sales Volume: $20MM to $50MM

1207 Mazda Publishers
Mazda Publishers
PO Box 2603
Costa Mesa, CA 92628   714-751-5252
                    Fax: 714-751-4805
              mazdapub@aol.com
                www.mazdapublishers.com

Middle East, North Africa, Persian and Central Asia books

President: A. K. Jabbari, Ph.D.
Marketing Manager: Maryam Bayat
Vice President: Fay Zamani
Editor-in-Chief: George A. Bournoutian
Editor-in-Chief: Richard G. Hovannisian
Catalog Cost: Free
Catalog Circulation: Mailed 1 time(s) per year to 12000
Printing Information: 32 pages in 4 colors on Newsprint
Press: Web Press
Binding: Saddle Stitched
In Business: 34 years
Number of Employees: 5
Sales Volume: Under $500M

1208 Rizzoli Lifestyles & Interior Design
Rizzoli Publications
300 Park Avenue S
New York, NY 10010   212-387-3400
                       800-733-3000
                  Fax: 212-387-3535
        submissions@rizzoliusa.com
                    www.rizzoliusa.com

Books on design and decor, travel, and tourism, living and lifestyles of certain locales

President: Gianfranco Monacelli
Marketing Manager: William Gworkin
Production Manager: Paul Williams
Credit Cards: AMEX; MasterCard
Catalog Cost: Free
Catalog Circulation: Mailed 1 time(s) per year
Printing Information: 125 pages in 4 colors on Glossy Stock
In Business: 83 years

1209 Slavica Catalog
Slavica Publishers
1430 N. Willis Drive
Bloomington, IN 47404-2146   812-856-4186
                               877-752-8422
                          Fax: 812-856-4187
                    www.slavica.com

Scholarly books and textbooks on the languages, peoples, literature, cultures, and history of the former USSR and Eastern Europe

Production Manager: Dan Florek
Director: George Fowler
gfowler@indiana.edu
Assistant Manager: Christian Flynn
Managing editor: Vicki Polansky
vpolansky@slavica.com
In Business: 49 years

1210 Stenhouse Publishers
Stenhouse Publishers
480 Congress Street
PO Box 11020
Portland, ME 4101-3400   207-253-1600
                           800-988-9812
                      Fax: 800-833-9164
        customerservice@stenhouse.com
                    www.stenhouse.com

Books

President: Dan Tobin
dtobin@stenhouse.com
Marketing Manager: Rebecca Eaton
reaton@stenhouse.com
Production Manager: Jay Kilburn
jkilburn@stenhouse.com
Editorial Director: Philippa Stratton
philippa@stenhouse.com
Video Editor: Nate Butler
nbutler@stenhouse.com
Online Content Editor: Zsofia McMullin
zmcmullin@stenhouse.com
In Business: 22 years

1211 The Travel Collection
Interlink Publishing
46 Crosby Street
Northampton, MA 1060-1804   413-582-7054
                              800-238-LINK
                 info@interlinkbooks.com
                    www.interlinkbooks.com

Publishing house

In Business: 28 years

1212 TravelSmith Outfitting Guide and Catalog
TravelSmith Outfitters
773 San Marin Drive
Suite 2300
Novato, CA 94945   800-770-3387
                Fax: 800-950-1656
          service@travelsmith.com
                www.travelsmith.com

Travel gear and accessories

Printing Information: 84 pages
In Business: 23 years

1213 Windjammer Barefoot Cruises
Sailing Ship Adventures
1759 Bay Road
PO Box 190120
Miami Beach, FL 33139-1413   877-882-4395
                               800-327-2601
                          Fax: 305-674-1219
                www.sailingshipadventures.com

Caribbean cruises

President: Susan Burke
In Business: 5 years

1214 eBags Catalog
eBags Inc
5500 Greenwood Plaza Blvd.
Suite 160
Greenwood Village, CO 80111-4803 303-694-1933
800-820-6126
Fax: 303-694-9491
info@ebags.com
www.Ebags.Com

Handbags, luggage, backpacks, carry-ons, computer cases, wallets and purses and travel accessories

President: Mike Edwards
CFO: Mark DeOrio
Marketing Manager: Peter Cobb
EVP Marketing: Peter Cobb
EVP Financial Planning: Steve Neptune
SVP, Technology: Mike Frazzini
Credit Cards: AMEX; MasterCard
Catalog Cost: Free
Printing Information: 32 pages in 4 colors
Binding: Perfect Bound
In Business: 15 years
Sales Volume: $500M to $1MM

Camping Products
Army & Navy

1215 Bear & Son Cutlery
Bear & Son Cutlery, Inc.
1111 Bear Blvd S.W.
Jacksonville, AL 36265-3396 256-435-2227
800-844-3034
Fax: 256-435-9348
info@bearandson.com
www.bearandsoncutlery.com

Knives and cutlery including lockbacks, hunting, traditional, military, plus axes and shears

President: Matt Griffey
Marketing Manager: Ken Griffey
Catalog Cost: Free
Number of Employees: 55
Sales Volume: $ 5.7 Million

1216 Benchmade Catalog
Benchmade
300 Beavercreek Road
Oregon City, OR 97045 503-496-1853
800-800-7427
www.benchmade.com

Knives, including custom orders and accessories

President: Les de Asis
Catalog Cost: Free
Catalog Circulation: Mailed 1 time(s) per year
Printing Information: 102 pages in 4 colors
In Business: 29 years
Number of Employees: 10

1217 Big Ray's
Big Ray's
507 2nd Ave
Fairbanks, AK 99701-4728 907-452-3458
800-478-3458
Fax: 907-456-2413
classicweb@classicalaska.com
www.bigrays.com

Army and navy surplus clothing

President: Monty Rostad
Marketing Manager: Cindy Clark
Credit Cards: MasterCard; Visa
Catalog Cost: Free
In Business: 65 years
Number of Employees: 18
Sales Volume: $ 8 Million

1218 Day One Camouflage
Dan's Comp
1 Competition Way
Mt Vernon, IN 47620-2111 812-838-2691
888-888-3267
Fax: 812-838-2693
customerservice@danscomp.com
www.danscomp.com

Parkas, vests, and shirts designed for the serious hunter

President: Gary Christoffersen
garydayonecamo@qwestoffice.net
Credit Cards: AMEX; MasterCard
Catalog Cost: Free
Mailing List Information: Names for rent
In Business: 25 years
Number of Employees: 10
Sales Volume: Under $500,000

1219 Galaxy Army Navy
PO Box 230515
Gravesend, NY 11223-515 718-345-2222
800-766-9691
Fax: 718-345-2222
info@gan.com
www.galaxyarmynavy.com

Military tactical gear

1220 Gold Nugget Army Surplus
215 Globe Street
Radcliff, KY 40160-9504 270-351-1450
800-942-8769
Fax: 270-351-1480
www.goldnuggetsurplus.com

New and used military issued clothing and accessories

1221 Perret's Army Surplus
2514 Williams Blvd
Kenner, LA 70062 504-466-2532
Fax: 504-466-2607
cs@perrets.com
perretsarmysurplus.com

Military products and gear

1222 Quartermaster
Quartermaster, LLC
17600 Fabrica Way
P.O. Box 4147
Cerritos, CA 90703 562-304-7300
866-673-7645
Fax: 562-304-7335
gsa@qmuniforms.com
www.qmuniforms.com

Public safety, security and military uniforms and equipment

Credit Cards: MasterCard
Catalog Cost: Free
Average Order Size: $75
Mailing List Information: Names for rent
List Company: Alan Drey Company
333 N Michigan Avenue
Chicago, IL 60601
312-236-8508
In Business: 37 years
Number of Employees: 90
Sales Volume: $ 5-10 Million

1223 Ranger Joe's
325 Farr Road
Columbus, GA 31907-6248 706-689-0082
800-247-4541
Fax: 706-682-8840
customerservice@rangerjoes.com
www.rangerjoes.com

Military and law enforcement gear

Sales Volume: $5MM to $10MM

1224 US Cavalry
U.S. Cavalry
1222 East 38th St
Chattanooga, TN 37407-9000 270-351-1164
800-777-7172
Fax: 270-352-0266
service@uscav.com
www.uscav.com

Army/navy surplus and military related equipment; outdoor adventure equipment

Chairman: Patrick Garvey
President: Wayne Weissler
Buyers: David Acton
Jeanine Mason
Credit Cards: AMEX; MasterCard; Visa
Catalog Cost: Free
Mailing List Information: Names for rent
List Manager: Carmen Shelton
In Business: 42 years
Number of Employees: 110
Sales Volume: $ 28 Million

1225 US Patriot Tactical
212 Candi Lane
Columbia, SC 29210 803-832-0096
800-805-5294
admin@uspatriottactical.com
uspatriottactical.com

Military and law enforcement products

Co-Owner: Phil Dee
Co-Owner: Paul Yod

Equipment & Supplies

1226 Best Made Company
Best Made Company
36 White Street
New York, NY 10013 646-478-7092
Fax: 888-708-7824
contact@bestmadeco.com
www.bestmadeco.com

Clothing, jackets, hats and accessories, footwear, bags, camping gear, tools, home and office supplies

President: Peter Buchanan-Smith
CFO: Steve Molineaux
Chief Merchandising Officer: Tom Girard
Chief Operations Officer: Ben Lavely
Customer Experience Manager: Ali Bradley
Credit Cards: AMEX; MasterCard
Catalog Cost: Free
In Business: 9 years

1227 Brunton
Brunton
1900 Taylor Avenue
Louisville, CO 80027 307-857-4700
800-443-4871
Fax: 303-996-3758
support@bruntongroup.com
www.brunton.com

Product line includes binoculars, camping and backpacking equipment, headlamps, portable power supplies, gps units, lighters and compasses

President: Mike Jones
Marketing Manager: Jason Kintzler
Credit Cards: AMEX; MasterCard; Visa
Catalog Cost: Free
Mailing List Information: Names for rent
In Business: 121 years
Number of Employees: 40
Sales Volume: $ 13 Million

1228 Cabela's Camping
Cabela's Inc.
One Cabela Dr.
Sidney, NE 69160 www.cabelas.com

Supplies and gear for outdoor recreation.

CFO: Ralph Castner
CEO: Thomas Millner

COO: Michael Copeland
Catalog Cost: Free
Catalog Circulation: Mailed 1 time(s) per year
Printing Information: in 4 colors
List Company: Chilcutt Direct
In Business: 55 years
Sales Volume: $3 Billion

1229 Campmor
Campmor
400 Corporate Drive
PO Box 680
Mahwah, NJ 07430   201-335-9064
                          800-525-4784
                          Fax: 201-445-3151
                          www.campmor.com

Camping gear and equipment, outerwear, sporting gear, etc.
Chairman: Morton Jarashow
President: Daniel Jarashow
Credit Cards: AMEX; MasterCard
In Business: 36 years
Number of Employees: 100
Sales Volume: $ 14 Million

1230 CatfishConnection
PO Box 476
Pana, IL 62557   800-929-5025
customerservice@catfishconnection.com
www.catfishconnection.com

Rods, reels, products and accessories for catfishing

1231 Cloudveil
Cloudveil
830 Broad Street
Suite 3
Shrewsbury, NJ 7702   781-631-6157
                             866-785-3343
                             Fax: 781-631-5371
                             www.cloudveil.com

Outdoor, technical clothing and accessories for men, women, and children
President: Jim Reilly
Production Manager: Camron Burker
Credit Cards: AMEX; MasterCard
Catalog Cost: Free
Catalog Circulation: Mailed 4 time(s) per year
Printing Information: in 4 colors
Number of Employees: 34

1232 Colorado Yurt
Colorado yurt company
28 W South 4th St
PO Box 1626
Montrose, CO 81401-3459   970-240-2146
                                 800-288-3190
                                 Fax: 970-240-2146
                                 info@coloradoyurt.com
                                 www.coloradoyurt.com

Fine wall tents
President: Dan Kigar
Marketing Manager: Jennie Redwine
Credit Cards: MasterCard; Visa
Catalog Cost: Free
Printing Information: 16 pages in 4 colors
In Business: 39 years
Number of Employees: 30
Sales Volume: $ 2.5 Million

1233 Crazy Creek
Crazy Creek Products, Inc.
1401 South Broadway Avenue
P.O. Box 1050
Red Lodge, MT 59068-1050   406-446-3446
                                   800-331-0304
                                   Fax: 406-446-1411
                                   chairs@crazycreek.com
                                   www.crazycreek.com

Outdoor portable chairs and ThermaLoungers, chair sleeping pad combo, wrist warmers and a full line of hammocks
President: Rob Hart
Credit Cards: MasterCard; Visa
Catalog Cost: Free
Average Order Size: $40
Mailing List Information: Names for rent
Number of Employees: 10
Sales Volume: $ 2 Million

1234 GCI Outdoor
66 Killingworth Road
Higganum, CT 06441   860-345-9595
                             800-956-7328
                             Fax: 860-345-2966
                             info@gcioutdoor.com
                             www.gcioutdoor.com

Camping and outdoor gear and supplies
Founder/ Co-owner: Dan Grace
Co-owner: Jeffrey Polk

1235 Hilleberg Tent Handbook
Hilleberg
14790 NE 95th St.
Redmond, WA 98052-2541   425-883-0101
                                 866-848-8368
                                 Fax: 425-869-6632
                                 tentmaker@hilleberg.com
                                 www.hilleberg.com

Backpacking and mountaineering tents
President: Bo Hilleberg
Marketing Manager: Petra Hilleberg
Catalog Cost: Free
In Business: 44 years
Number of Employees: 5
Sales Volume: $ 500,000- 1 Million

1236 JM Cremps
PO Box 439
850 1st ST N
Dassel, MN 55325   877-469-0673
                           info@jmcremps.com
                           www.jmcremps.com

Outdoor clothing, accessories and gear
Co-Owner: Maria Asplin
Co-Owner: Jay Asplin

1237 Major Surplus & Survival
Major Surplus & Survival
435 W Alondra
Gardena, CA 90248   310-324-8855
                            800-441-8855
                            Fax: 310-324-6909
                            CustomerCare@MajorSurplus.com
                            www.majorsurplus.com

Military surplus items, disaster preparedness and survival products, outdoor and camping supplies
President: Steve Adkisson
CFO: Latonya Woods
Credit Cards: AMEX; MasterCard; Visa
Catalog Cost: Free
Mailing List Information: Names for rent
In Business: 20 years
Number of Employees: 30
Sales Volume: $ 4 Million

1238 Music is Elementary
Music is Elementary
5228 Mayfield Road
Lyndhurst, OH 44124   800-888-7502
                              Fax: 440-461-3631
                              info@musiciselementary.com
                              www.musiciselementary.com

Items such as books, CDs, instruments, and accessories for elementary music education, music therapy, and anyone with an interest in music

Music Consultant: BethAnn Hepburn
Credit Cards: AMEX; MasterCard
Catalog Cost: Free

1239 New England Camp Discounter
New England Camp Discounter
PO Box 7087
Dallas, TX 75209   888-909-8809
                           Fax: 888-909-5899
                           feednec@sportsupplygroup.com
                           www.campexpress.com

Full line of camp and recreational equipment
President: Adam Blumfeld
CFO: John Pitts
Credit Cards: AMEX; MasterCard; Visa
Catalog Cost: Free
Mailing List Information: Names for rent
In Business: 22 years
Number of Employees: 400
Sales Volume: $ 1-3 Million

1240 Outfitters Supply
Outfitters Supply, Inc.
7373 US Highway 2 E
Columbia Falls, MT 59912-9107   406-892-3650
                                  888-467-2256
                                  Fax: 406-892-4234
                                  gopackn@outfitterssupply.com
                                  www.outfitterssupply.Com

Camping gear, horse saddlebags, books, videos, maps, wall tents and gifts
President: Russ Barnett
Credit Cards: AMEX; MasterCard
In Business: 29 years
Number of Employees: 5
Sales Volume: $500,000

1241 Overton's
Overton's
111 Red Banks Rd
Greenville, NC 27858   252-355-2923
                               800-334-6541
                               Fax: 252-355-2923
                               www.overtons.com

Camping, hunting equipment, dog and horse supplies
President: Larry Carroll
CFO: Mark Metcalfe
Marketing Manager: Marisa Dore
Credit Cards: AMEX; MasterCard; Visa
Catalog Cost: Free
Catalog Circulation: Mailed 2 time(s) per year to 16000
Printing Information: 284 pages in 4 colors on Matte Stock
Binding: Perfect Bound
Mailing List Information: Names for rent
In Business: 45 years
Sales Volume: $ 13 Million

1242 Panther Primitives
Panther Primitives
P.O. Box 32
Normantown, WV 25267   304-462-7718
                               800-487-2684
                               Fax: 304-462-7755
                               info@pantherprimitives.com
                               www.pantherprimitives.com

Historical camp gear, supplier of reproduction tents and supplies for re-enactors and collectors
Catalog Cost:
Printing Information: 135 pages

1243 Parts Express
Parts Express
725 Pleasant Valley Dr
Springboro, OH 45066   800-338-0531
                               Fax: 937-743-1677
                               sales@parts-express.com
                               www.parts-express.com

Home audio and video subwoofers, in-wall speakers, cables, adapters and connectors

President: Jeffrey Stahl
VP of Operations: Dale Ditmer
VP Finance/Controller: John Kirsch
VP Marketing: Karl Keyes
Credit Cards: AMEX; MasterCard; Visa
Printing Information: 260 pages
In Business: 29 years

1244 Pilot Rock Park, Street and Camp Site Products
R.J. Thomas Mfg. Co. Inc.
PO Box 946
Cherokee, IA 51012-946   712-225-5115
                               800-762-5002
                          www.pilotrock.com

Outdoor and camping furnishings

1245 RedHead Hunting Master
Bass Pro Shops
2500 E Kearney
Springfield, MO 65898   417-873-5000
                               800-227-7776
                          Fax: 417-873-5060
                          www.basspro.com

Top-quality gear for hunting, camping, boating, fishing and other outdoor activities.

President & CEO: James Hagale
Catalog Cost: Free
Catalog Circulation: Mailed 1 time(s) per year
Printing Information: 600 pages in 4 colors
In Business: 45 years
Number of Employees: 2200
Sales Volume: $4.45 Billion

1246 Reese Tipis
Reese Tipis
2291 J Waynoka Road
Colorado Springs, CO 80915   719-265-6519
                               866-890-8474
                          Fax: 719-265-1018

Tipis

President: Richard Reese
Credit Cards: AMEX; MasterCard; Visa
Catalog Cost: Free

1247 South Summit
South Summit Survival
1819 Firman Dr
Suite 101
Richardson, TX 75081-6710   972-690-1812
                               800-234-8654
                          Fax: 972-690-6903
                          www.southsummit.com

Blowguns, knives, camping equipment and preparedness products

President: Dana Ellington
Credit Cards: MasterCard
Catalog Cost: Free
In Business: 10 years
Sales Volume: 1-10 M

1248 Swordsswords.com
PMB369, 457 Nathan Dean Blvd,
Ste 105
Dallas, GA 30132   770-443-1405
                               877- 57- 673
                          Fax: 770-443- 140
                          sales@swordsswords.com
                          www.swordsswords.com

Swords, knives, daggers, self-defense weapons and outdoor gear.

Clothing
General

1249 Adventure Edge
Sierra Trading Post
5025 Campstool Road
Cheyenne, WY 82007-1898   307-775-8000
                               800-713-4534
                          Fax: 800-378-8946
                  customerservice@sierratradingpost.com
                          www.sierratradingpost.com

Gear and action apparel

President: Keith Richardson
CFO: Gary Imig
Production Manager: Shelia Russell
Fulfillment: Robin Jahnke
Credit Cards: AMEX; MasterCard; Visa
Catalog Cost: Free
Mailing List Information: Names for rent
In Business: 29 years
Number of Employees: 565

1250 Alloy
Alloy
PO Box 6145
Westerville, OH 43086-6145   888-452-5569
                          Fax: 888-312-5569
                  contactus@alloymerch.com
                          www.alloy.com

Jeans, outerwear, shoes, sweaters and dresses

Credit Cards: AMEX; MasterCard; Visa

1251 Alloy Apparel & Accessories
Alloy Apparel & Accessories
348 Poplar St
Hanover, PA 17331   888-502-5569
                          www.alloyapparel.com

Clothes for women

Printing Information: 80 pages
In Business: 19 years

1252 Amplestuff
Amplestuff
Department WS
PO Box 116
Bearsville, NY 12409-116   845-679-3316
                               866-486-1655
                          Fax: 845-679-1206
                  helpdesk@amplestuff.com
                          www.amplestuff.com

Plus size fanny packs, clothes hangers, high limit scales, XL blood pressure cuffs, airline seatbelt tenders, bra liners, XL portable folding chairs, etc.

President: William Fabrey
Owner: Bill Fabrey
Credit Cards: MasterCard
Catalog Cost: Free
Catalog Circulation: Mailed 1 time(s) per year to 5000
Average Order Size: $70
Printing Information: 32 pages in 1 color on Matte Stock
Press: Sheetfed Press
Binding: Saddle Stitched
Mailing List Information: Names for rent
List Manager: R Cooper
In Business: 27 years
Number of Employees: 3
Sales Volume: $170,000

1253 Artful Home
Artful Home
931 E Main Street
Suite 9
Madison, WI 53703   608-257-2590
                               877-223-4600
                          Fax: 608-257-2690
                  info@artfulhome.com
                          www.artfulhome.com

Apparel, jewelry, gifts, ceramics, art glass, wall art, ornaments, lighting and furniture

Chairman: Scott Potter
President: Toni Sikes
CFO: Bill Lathrop
Marketing Manager: Terry Nelson
CEO: Lisa Bayne
VP of Finance: Bill Lathrop
Credit Cards: AMEX; MasterCard
Catalog Cost: Free
Catalog Circulation: Mailed 4 time(s) per year
Printing Information: 60 pages
In Business: 30 years
Number of Employees: 35
Sales Volume: $3.1 Million

1254 Bedford Fair
Bedford Fair Lifestyles
108 Telegraph Road
Bedford, PA 15522-6558   800-964-9030
                  international@blair.com
                          www.bedfordfair.blair.com

Women's clothing apparel and shoes

President: Steve Nave
CFO: Pete Michielutti
EVP, COO, & Chief Digital Officer: Vince Jones
EVP & President of Credit Services: Jim Slavik
Credit Cards: AMEX; MasterCard
Catalog Cost: Free
In Business: 19 years
Sales Volume: $ 50-100 Million

1255 Belk New Directions
Belk
2801 W Tyvola Road
Charlotte NC   800-669-6550
                          care@belk.com
                          www.belk.com

Casualwear for women, men, and children, jewelry, footwear, home furnishings and appliances

President: Lisa Harper
CFO: Scott Hurd
Marketing Manager: Barb Pellegrino
Chief Operating Officer: Don Hendricks
Chief Stores Officer: Randy Whitaker
Product Sourcing & Technical Design: Tanya Cauren
Catalog Cost: Free
Printing Information: 12 pages in 4 colors
In Business: 129 years

1256 Beretta Seasonal Catalog
Beretta USA
17601 Beretta Dr.
Accokeek, MD 20607   www.berettausa.com

Outdoor apparel and footwear.

CFO: Steve Biondi
Catalog Cost: Free
Printing Information: in 4 colors
In Business: 44 years
Number of Employees: 400
Sales Volume: $100MM to $500MM

1257 Best Made Company
Best Made Company
36 White Street
New York, NY 10013   646-478-7092
                          Fax: 888-708-7824
                  contact@bestmadeco.com
                          www.bestmadeco.com

Clothing, jackets, hats and accessories, footwear, bags, camping gear, tools, home and office supplies

President: Peter Buchanan-Smith
CFO: Steve Molineaux
Chief Merchandising Officer: Tom Girard
Chief Operations Officer: Ben Lavely
Customer Experience Manager: Ali Bradley
Credit Cards: AMEX; MasterCard

Catalog Cost: Free
In Business: 9 years

1258 Blank Shirts

Blank Shirts
1780 Forrest Way
Carson City, NV 89706

775-885-1364
800-332-6576
Fax: 877-813-7626
sales@blankshirts.com
www.blankshirts.com

White and solid color tees, polos shirts, jackets and hats

CFO: Brian Tuttle
CEO: Pat Drudge
Credit Cards: AMEX; MasterCard
Catalog Cost: Free
Catalog Circulation: Mailed 1 time(s) per year
Printing Information: 500 pages
In Business: 12 years
Number of Employees: 6
Sales Volume: $600,000

1259 Block Division

Block Division, Inc
618 Front Street
PO Box 1297
Wichita Falls, TX 76307-1297

940-723-0214
800-433-0921
Fax: 940-723-0214
info@blockdivision.com
www.blockdivision.com/

Pulleys and tackle blocks for small wire rope

President: Paula White
Vice President of Operations: Matthew White
Senior Plant Manager: Bobby Day
Bobby@BlockDivision.com
Plant Floor Manager: Joe Garcia
Joe@BlockDivision.com
Printing Information: 8 pages
In Business: 55 years

1260 Boden

Boden
180 Armstrong Road
Pittston, PA 18640-9628

570-883-5000
866-206-9508
custserv@bodenusa.com
www.bodenusa.com

Quality and affordable clothing and accessories for men, women and children

President: Johnnie Boden
EVP: Tricia Lewis
Printing Information: in 4 colors
In Business: 23 years
Number of Employees: 140
Sales Volume: $ 4 Million

1261 Carhartt

Carhartt
5750 Mercury Drive
Dearborn, MI 48126

800-833-3118
just_ask_us@carhartt.com
www.carhartt.com

Men and womenswear and gear for outdoor activities such as camping, horseback riding, boating, ski/snowboarding, farming, home gardening, woodworking, offreading, fishing, and hunting

Chairman: Mark Valade
President: Linda Hubbard
Credit Cards: AMEX; MasterCard
Catalog Cost: Free
Catalog Circulation: Mailed 4 time(s) per year
Printing Information: 55 pages in 4 colors on Glossy Stock
In Business: 128 years

1262 Carol Wright Gifts

Carol Wright Gifts
PO Box 7823
Edison, NJ 08818-7821

732-225-0100
800-267-5750
Fax: 732-572-2118
www.carolwrightgifts.com

Gifts, personal care, apparel, household helps, kitchen items, and outdoor and garden

President: Gary Giesler
Credit Cards: AMEX; MasterCard
Catalog Cost: Free
Average Order Size: $32
Printing Information: 63 pages in 4 colors on Glossy Stock
Binding: Saddle Stitched
In Business: 43 years
Number of Employees: 650

1263 Casual Wear Catalog

Bob's Cycle Supply
65 Viking DR W
St Paul, MN 55117

651-482-8181
888-306-2627
Fax: 651-482-0974
bobs@bobscycle.com
www.bobscycle.com

Casual clothing

President: Scott Muellner
Marketing Manager: Leisha Olson
Purchasing: Josh Lane
Team Manager: David Pingree
Credit Cards: AMEX; MasterCard
Catalog Cost: Free
Catalog Circulation: Mailed 12 time(s) per year
In Business: 40 years
Number of Employees: 47
Sales Volume: $10 million

1264 Christmas

Bass Pro Shops
2500 E Kearney
Springfield, MO 65898

417-873-5000
800-227-7776
Fax: 417-873-5060
www.basspro.com

Toys, casual wear and gifts.

President & CEO: James Hagale
Catalog Cost: Free
Catalog Circulation: Mailed 1 time(s) per year
Printing Information: 220 pages in 4 colors
In Business: 45 years
Number of Employees: 2200
Sales Volume: $4.45 Billion

1265 Delia's

Delia's
50 W 23rd Street
New York, NY 10010

212-590-6200
866-293-3268
Fax: 212-590-6300
customerservice@deliasmerch.com
store.delias.com

Teen clothing, shoes, jewelry, and accessories

Chairman: Carter S Evans
President: Walter Killough
CFO: David J Dick
Marketing Manager: Douglas Sietsma
Credit Cards: AMEX; MasterCard; Visa
Catalog Cost: Free
Catalog Circulation: Mailed 1 time(s) per year to 65mm
Printing Information: 74 pages on Glossy Stock
Binding: Perfect Bound
In Business: 16 years
Number of Employees: 50
Sales Volume: $217MM

1266 Ebbets Field Flannels

Ebbets Field Flannels
119 South Jackson Street
Seattle, WA 98104

506-382-7249
888-896-2936
Fax: 206-382-4411
customerservice@ebbets.com
www.ebbets.com

Flannel baseball, hockey, and football clothing and accessories in authentic vintage styles; team uniforms and custom orders available

President: Jerry Cohen
Credit Cards: AMEX; MasterCard
Catalog Cost: Free
Catalog Circulation: Mailed 12 time(s) per year to 12500
Printing Information: 16 pages in 4 colors on Glossy Stock
Press: Web Press
Binding: Saddle Stitched
In Business: 25 years

1267 Especially Yours

Especially Yours
PO Box 105
South Easton, MA 02375

800-952-5926
Fax: 508-238-1965
customerservice@especiallyyours.com
www.especiallyyours.com

African American wigs, hairpieces, hair extensions, hair weaves and stylish clothing for the fashion-concious black woman.

Catalog Cost: Free
Printing Information: in 4 colors

1268 Essentials by Anthony Richards

AmeriMark Direct
6864 Engle Rd.
Cleveland, OH 44130

866-345-1388
www.amerimark.com

Loungewear, sleepwear and intimate apparel.

CFO: Joe Albanese
CEO & President: Gareth Giesler
Catalog Cost: Free
Printing Information: in 4 colors
In Business: 47 years
Number of Employees: 700
Sales Volume: $400 Million

1269 Feel Good Store

FeelGood Store
6864 Engle Road
Cleveland, OH 44130

866-439-4572
www.feelgoodstore.com

Selection of wellness, health, fitness, massage, relaxation, home, sleep, marital health, shoes, beauty, skin care, bath, and body support products that aid in comfort.

In Business: 46 years
Number of Employees: 600

1270 Gudrun Sjoden

Gudrun Sj"d,n
50 Greene Street
New York, NY 10013

212-219-2510
877-574-1486
customerservice@gundrunsjoden.com
www.durunsjoden.com

Clothing and home furnishings

President: Gudron Sj"d,n
Credit Cards: MasterCard
Catalog Cost: Free
In Business: 41 years

1271 Herrington
Herrington
3 Symmes Drive
Londonderry, NH 03053-2142   866-558-7467
800-903-2878
Fax: 603-437-3492
customerservice@herringtoncatalog.com
www.herringtoncatalog.com
Apparel, electronic gifts, tools and gadgets
President: Lee Herrington
Credit Cards: AMEX; MasterCard; Visa
Catalog Cost: Free
Catalog Circulation: Mailed 8 time(s) per year
Printing Information: 48 pages in 4 colors on
Glossy Stock
Binding: Saddle Stitched
In Business: 35 years
Number of Employees: 160
Sales Volume: $ 10 Million

1272 Ibex Outdoor Clothing
Ibex Outdoor Clothing, LLC
132 Ballardvale Drive
White River Junction, VT 05001   802-359-4239
800-773-9647
info@ibex.com
shop.ibex.com/CS/FAQ
Designer of outdoor clothing, outdoor apparel and gear
President: John Fernsell
Marketing Manager: Jinesse Reynolds
Catalog Circulation: Mailed 4 time(s) per year
Number of Employees: 40
Sales Volume: $1-3 Million

1273 J. Peterman Company
J Peterman Company
PO Box 637394
Blue Ash, OH 45263-7394   513-985-3400
888-647-2555
Fax: 513-985-0514
orders@jpeterman.com
www.jpeterman.com
Hard-to-find unique and nostalgic items from around the world; both clothing and houshold goods and furnishings, as well as fine art, and collectibles
President: John Peterman
Credit Cards: AMEX; MasterCard
Catalog Cost: Free
Catalog Circulation: Mailed 5 time(s) per year
Printing Information: 50 pages in 4 colors on
Glossy Stock
Press: Offset Press
Binding: Perfect Bound
List Manager: Audrey Peterman
List Company: Chilcutt Direct
Number of Employees: 35
Sales Volume: $ 5 Million

1274 J.Crew Style Guide
J.Crew
770 Broadway
New York, NY 10003   800-562-0258
www.jcrew.com
Casual clothes and accessories for men, women and children.
Chairman and CEO: Millard Drexler
President and Creative Director: Jenna Lyons
Catalog Cost: Free
Printing Information: in 4 colors
In Business: 33 years
Number of Employees: 1560
Sales Volume: $2.27 Billion

1275 L.L.Bean Christmas
L.L.Bean Inc.
15 Casco St.
Freeport, ME 04033   207-552-2000
www.llbean.com
Christmas decorations and men's and women's casual apparel.

Chairman: Shawn Gorman
President: Stephen Smith
Catalog Cost: Free
Printing Information: 204 pages in 4 colors
In Business: 105 years
Number of Employees: 5000
Sales Volume: $1.6 Billion

1276 L.L.Bean Outsider
L.L.Bean Inc.
15 Casco Street
Freeport, ME 04033   207-552-2000
www.llbean.com
Women and men's sportswear and outdoor clothing and accessories
Chairman: Shawn Gorman
President: Stephen Smith
Credit Cards: AMEX; MasterCard
Catalog Cost: Free
Printing Information: 68 pages in 4 colors
In Business: 105 years
Number of Employees: 5000
Sales Volume: $1.6 Billion

1277 LAT Apparel
LAT Apparel
1200 Airport Drive
Ball Ground, GA 30107   770-479-1877
800-414-5650
Fax: 770-479-9739
www.latapparel.com

Clothes
President: Gina Watson
gina@latapparel.com
CFO: Mickie Schneider
mickie@latapparel.com
Executive Vice President of Sales: Chuck
Phares
cphares@latapparel.com
Vice President of Production Planni: Mindy
Anastos
mindy@latapparel.com
National Sales Manager: RegDunston
rdunston@latapparel.com
In Business: 30+ years

1278 Lands' End
Lands' End, Inc.
1 Lands' End Lane
Dodgeville, WI 53595   800-963-4816
Fax: 800-332-0103
www.landsend.com
Casual clothing, luggage and home furnishings.
Co-interim CEO: James Gooch
Co-interim CEO: James Boitano
Catalog Cost: Free
Printing Information: in 4 colors
Mailing List Information: Names for rent
List Company: Millard Group
In Business: 53 years
Number of Employees: 5300
Sales Volume: $1.42 Billion

1279 Lillian Vernon
Lillian Vernon Corporation
P.O. Box 35022
Colorado Springs, CO 80935-3522 800-545-5426
www.lillianvernon.com
Clothing and accessories; housewares; holiday decor; toys
President: Tom Arland
Credit Cards: AMEX; MasterCard
Catalog Cost: Free
Catalog Circulation: Mailed 6 time(s) per year
Printing Information: 80 pages in 4 colors on
Glossy Stock
Press: Web Press
Binding: Folded
In Business: 66 years
Number of Employees: 175
Sales Volume: $ 10-20 Million

1280 Macy's
Macy's
7 W 7th Street
Cincinnati, OH 45202   800-289-6229
www.macys.com
Clothing and accessories for men, women and children
Production Manager: Dan Cook
Credit Cards: AMEX; MasterCard; Visa
Catalog Cost: Free
Catalog Circulation: Mailed 24 time(s) per
year
Printing Information: 44 pages in 4 colors on
Glossy Stock
Binding: Saddle Stitched
In Business: 158 years
Sales Volume: $ 10-20 Million

1281 MensHats
MensHats
2615 Boeing Way
Stockton, CA 95206   800-357-4287
Fax: 888-746-7558
www.menshats.com
Men's hats and accessories
President: Steve Singer
steve@menshats.com
Credit Cards: AMEX; MasterCard; Visa
Catalog Cost: Free
Catalog Circulation: Mailed 2 time(s) per year

1282 Offroad Catalog
Bob's Cycle Supply
65 W Viking Drive
St Paul, MN 55117   651-482-8181
888-306-2627
Fax: 651-482-0974
www.bobscycle.com
Off-road riding gear from apparel to helmets, boots and more
President: Scott Muellner
Marketing Manager: Leisha Olson
Purchasing: Josh Lane
Credit Cards: AMEX; MasterCard
Catalog Cost: Free
In Business: 42 years
Number of Employees: 47
Sales Volume: $10 million

1283 Old Pueblo Traders
Bluestem Brands, Inc.
7075 Flying Cloud Drive
Eden Prairie, MN 55344   800-362-8410
oldpueblotraders.blair.com
Men and Women's clothing, shoes, and accessories; and home decor
President: Steve Nave
CFO: Pete Michielutti
EVP, COO, & Chief Digital Officer: Vince
Jones
EVP & President of Credit Services: Jim
Slavik
Credit Cards: AMEX; MasterCard
Catalog Cost: Free
In Business: 71 years
Sales Volume: $50MM to $100MM

1284 Orvis Men
The Orvis Company Inc.
178 Conservation Way
Sunderland, VT 05250-4465   802-362-1300
888-235-9763
Fax: 802-362-0141
www.orvis.com
Men's casual clothing and accessories.
CEO: Leigh H. Perkins Jr.
Catalog Cost: Free
In Business: 160 years
Number of Employees: 1700
Sales Volume: $340 Million

1285 Orvis Women
The Orvis Company Inc.
178 Conservation Way
Sunderland, VT 05250-4465   802-362-1300
                               888-235-9763
                          Fax: 802-362-0141
                               www.orvis.com

Women's casual clothing and accessories.
CEO: Leigh H. Perkins Jr.
Catalog Cost: Free
In Business: 160 years
Number of Employees: 1700
Sales Volume: $340 Million

1286 Peggy Lutz Plus
Peggy Lutz Plus
1813 Empire Industrial Court
Suite A
Santa Rosa, CA 95403-1979   707-578-0108
                               www.plus-size.com

Fine clothing for plus and supersize women, sizes 14, 16, and up, petite, medium, and tall; Career wear, cruise wear, evening clothes
President: Margaret Lutz
Catalog Cost: $5
In Business: 26 years
Sales Volume: Under $500,000

1287 Peter Millar
Peter Millar LLC
4300 Emperor Blvd.
Suite 100
Durham, NC 27703   888-926-0255
                       communications@petermillar.com
                       www.petermillar.com

Fine clothing and accessories for men and women

1288 Rocky Mountain Connection
Rocky Mountain Connection
141 E. Elkhorn Avenue
Box 2800
Estes Park, CO 80517-2800   970-586-3361
                               800-679-3600
                          Fax: 800-814-4900
                          office@rmconnection.com
                          www.rmconnection.com

Outdoor rugged and technical clothing and equipment
Chairman: Pep Petrocine
President: E J Petrocine
epetrocine@gmail.com
Credit Cards: AMEX; MasterCard; Visa
Catalog Cost: Free
Catalog Circulation: Mailed 4 time(s) per year to 90000
Average Order Size: $80
Printing Information: 16 pages in 4 colors on Matte Stock
Press: Web Press
Binding: Saddle Stitched
In Business: 97 years
Number of Employees: 20
Sales Volume: $1-3 Million

1289 Sahalie
Bluestem Brands, Inc.
7075 Flying Cloud Drive
Eden Prairie, MN 55344   877-718-7902
                             www.sahalie.blair.com

Casual clothing, shoes & accessories for men and women
President: Steve Nave
CFO: Pete Michielutti
EVP, COO, & Chief Digital Officer: Vince Jones
EVP & President of Credit Services: Jim Slavik
Credit Cards: AMEX; MasterCard
Catalog Cost: Free
In Business: 46 years
Sales Volume: $50MM to $100MM

1290 Sgt Grit's Marine Specialties
Sgt Grit Inc
7100 SW 44th St
Oklahoma City, OK 73179   405-602-5490
                              888-668-1775
                         Fax: 405-602-5470
                         custserv@grunt.com
                         www.grunt.com

Marine Corps clothing, uniforms and USMC merchandise
President: Don Whitton
Production Manager: Crystal Butler
VP: Laurie
Purchasing: Karen
Customer Service: Teresa
Credit Cards: MasterCard
Catalog Cost: Free
Catalog Circulation: Mailed 52 time(s) per year
Printing Information: 135 pages
In Business: 27 years
Number of Employees: 40
Sales Volume: $ 5 Million

1291 Street Catalog
Bob's Cycle Supply
65 W Viking Drive
St Paul, MN 55117   651-482-8181
                        888-306-2627
                   Fax: 651-482-0974
                   www.bobscycle.com

Aftermarket parts, apparel and accessories for ATV, Snowmobile, Street or Off-Road Motorcycle
President: Scott Muellner
Marketing Manager: Leisha Olson
Purchasing: Josh Lane
Credit Cards: AMEX; MasterCard
Catalog Cost: Free
In Business: 42 years
Number of Employees: 47
Sales Volume: $10 million

1292 Swell
Swell
121 Waterworks Way
Suite 101
Irvine, CA 92618   949-234-4600
                       800-255-7873
                  Fax: 949-234-4672
                  customerservice@swell.com
                  www.swell.com

Surf clothing, gear and accessories
Credit Cards: AMEX; MasterCard
In Business: 16 years

1293 Tafford Uniforms
Tafford Uniforms
PO Box 481912
Charlotte, NC 28269   800-669-0094
                          888-823-3673
                     Fax: 888-588-8590
                     customerservice@tafford.com
                     www.tafford.com

Nursing scrubs, nursing uniforms and medical scrubs
CFO: Gene J Caputo Jr
Marketing Manager: David Kaplan
Credit Cards: AMEX; MasterCard
Catalog Cost: Free
In Business: 28 years
Number of Employees: 60
Sales Volume: $3.8 Million

1294 Team Leader Sports
Team Leader Sports
2901 Summit Ave
Suite 300
Plano, TX 75074   214-340-2288
                      877-365-7555
                 info@teamleader.com
                 www.teamleadersports.com

Uniforms and accessories for cheerleaders, dance teams, drill teams, team sports, color guard and band

1295 Uncommon Goods
Uncommon Goods
140 58th St.
Buidling B Suite 5A
Brooklyn, NY 11220   888-365-0056
                         www.uncommongoods.com

Modern and trendy accessories and gifts.
Editor-in-Chief: Cassie Tweten Delaney
Assistant Editor: Jen Coleman
Contributor: Emily Hodges
In Business: 16 years

1296 Urban Outfitters
UrbanOutfitters.com
30 Industrial Park Blvd
Trenton, SC 29847   800-282-2200
                        800-988-7726
                   Fax: 800-959-8795
                   www.urbanoutfitters.com

Men and women's clothing, shoes and accessories an home furnishing
Marketing Manager: Teresa Lee
Credit Cards: AMEX; MasterCard
Catalog Circulation: Mailed 12 time(s) per year
Number of Employees: 29

1297 Vermont Country Store
The Vermont Country Store
5650 Main Street
Manchester Center, VT 05255-9718 802-362-4667
                                  800-564-4623
                             Fax: 802-362-8288
                             www.vermontcountrystore.com

Apothecary products, women's clothing, men's apparel, vermont maple syrup and home furnishings
Chairman: Lyman Orton
President: William Shouldice
Credit Cards: AMEX; MasterCard
Catalog Cost: Free
Catalog Circulation: Mailed 5 time(s) per year
Printing Information: 104 pages in 4 colors on Newsprint
Binding: Saddle Stitched
In Business: 69 years
Number of Employees: 600

1298 Vineyard Vines
Vineyard Vines
181 Harbor Drive
Stamford, CT 06902-6349   203-862-0793
                              800-892-4982
                         Fax: 800-892-3606
                         tieguys@vineyardvines.com
                         www.vineyardvines.com

Clothes for men, women, boys and girls; also men's ties
President: Shep Murray
Credit Cards: AMEX; MasterCard
Catalog Cost: Free
Number of Employees: 85
Sales Volume: $ 3-5 Million

1299 Whitehorse Gear
Whitehorse Gear
107 East Conway Road
Center Conway, NH 03813-4012   603-356-6556
                               800-531-1133
                          Fax: 603-356-6590
                          www.whitehorsepress.com

Motorcycle gear, apparel, books, videos, accessories and tools
President: Daniel Kennedy
In Business: 14 years
Number of Employees: 8
Sales Volume: $ 1.7 Million

1300 Wholesale Buyers Guide
Buyers Guide
6433 Topanga Canyon Ave
Suite 544
Canoga Park, CA 91331   818-342-5357
Fax: 818-343-0319
sales@wholesalebuyersguide.com
www.wholesalebuyersguide.com

Business to business wholesale apparel, cell phones, toys, electronics, footwear, handbags, hats, health & beauty, jewelry, perfumes, tobacco & pipes, sporting goods, uniforms and dvd & video movies

President: Robin Zonte
Credit Cards: AMEX; MasterCard; Visa
Catalog Cost: Free
Catalog Circulation: Mailed 2 time(s) per year
Printing Information: 116 pages in 4 colors on Glossy Stock
Press: Web Press
Binding: Saddle Stitched
Mailing List Information: Names for rent
List Company: Direct Media
200 Pemberwick Road
Greenwich, CT 06830
203-532-3713
In Business: 117 years
Number of Employees: 120
Sales Volume: $ 10-20 Million

1301 Wintergreen Northern Wear Catalog
Wintergreen Northern Wear
205 East Sheridan Street
Ely, MN 55731   218-365-6602
                              800-584-9425
                       Fax: 218-365-6451
www.wintergreennorthernwear.com

Winter jackets, pants, shirts and accessories

President: Rebecta Stacey
SVP: Curt Stacey
Credit Cards: MasterCard; Visa
In Business: 25 years
Number of Employees: 22
Sales Volume: $ 2 Million

1302 Woolrich Catalog
Woolrich
2 Mill Street
P.O. Box 189
Woolrich, PA 17779   877-512-7305
                              800-966-5372
service@woolrich.com
www.woolrich.com

Sportswear for both men and women, blankets and home furnishings, slippers and shoes, gloves, hats, and socks

President: James Griggs
Production Manager: Bruce Heggenstaller
Credit Cards: AMEX; MasterCard; Visa
Catalog Cost: Free
Catalog Circulation: Mailed 12 time(s) per year
In Business: 187 years
Number of Employees: 618
Sales Volume: $95 Million

Accessories

1303 Alan Sloane & Company
Alan Sloane & Company, Inc.
80 Kean Street
West Babylon, NY 11704-1221   631-643-2260
                              800-252-6266
                       Fax: 631-643-1015
asloaneco@hotmail.com
www.alansloaneinc.com

Men's and women's clothing accessories

President: Alan Sloane
Credit Cards: AMEX; MasterCard; Visa
Catalog Circulation: Mailed 1 time(s) per year
Printing Information: 15 pages in 4 colors
In Business: 38 years

Number of Employees: 5
Sales Volume: $630,000

1304 Ames Walker Support Hosiery
Ames Walker International
300 Industrial Park Avenue
PO Box 1027
Asheboro, NC 27204   336-625-3979
                              877-525-7224
                       Fax: 336-629-0632
customerservice@ameswalker.com
www.ameswalker.com

Support hosiery, foot care products and accessories

President: Ken Walker
Production Manager: Ryan Zell
Credit Cards: AMEX; MasterCard
Catalog Cost: Free
Printing Information: 88 pages
In Business: 11 years
Number of Employees: 11

1305 Anthony Richards
AmeriMark Direct
6864 Engle Rd.
Cleveland, OH 44130   866-345-1388
www.amerimark.com

Affordable women's apparel, shoes, cosmetics, jewelry and accessories.

CFO: Joe Albanese
CEO & President: Gareth Giesler
Catalog Cost: Free
Printing Information: in 4 colors
In Business: 47 years
Number of Employees: 700
Sales Volume: $400 Million

1306 Anthropologie
Anthropologie
5000 South Broad St.
Philadelphia, PA 19112-1495   215-454-5500
www.anthropologie.com

Women's apparel and accessories, home furniture and decor.

CEO, Anthropologie Group: David McCreight
Catalog Cost: Free
Printing Information: in 4 colors
In Business: 46 years
Sales Volume: $311 Million

1307 Bella Taylor
Victorian Heart Company, Inc.
P.O. Box 17
Kirbyville, MO 65679   888-334-3099
                       Fax: 417-973-0423
info@vhcbrands.com
www.vhcbrands.com

Quilted handbags, purses, and backpacks

Chairman: Billy Kline
President: Kenneth Kline
Key Accont Manager: Josh Ellig
Mid-Atlantic Central Account: David Brown
dbrown@vhcbrands.com
Sales Manager: Joe Morimoto
jmorimoto@vhcbrands.com
Catalog Cost: Free
Catalog Circulation: Mailed 1 time(s) per year
Printing Information: 78 pages in 4 colors
In Business: 21 years
Number of Employees: 25
Sales Volume: $3.3 Million

1308 Bemidji Woolen Mills
Bemidji Woolen Mills Inc
301 Irvine Avenue NW
Bemidji, MN 56601-279   218-751-5166
                              888-751-5166
                       Fax: 218-751-4659
bjiwool@bemidjiwoolenmills.com
www.bemidjiwoolenmills.com

Hats, gloves and blankets, woolen garments

President: Bill Batchelder
Marketing Manager: Phil Johnson
Buyers: Ronald Betchelder
Credit Cards: AMEX; MasterCard; Visa
Catalog Cost: Free
Catalog Circulation: Mailed 1 time(s) per year
Printing Information: 40 pages in 4 colors
In Business: 93 years
Number of Employees: 16
Sales Volume: $5 million

1309 Ben Silver
Ben Silver
149 King St
Charleston, SC 29401-2227   843-577-4556
                              800-221-4671
                       Fax: 843-723-1543
contact@bensilver.com
www.bensilver.com

Authentic English silk neckties, tailored clothing, shirts, and jewelry

President: Bob Prenner
Marketing Manager: James Prenner
Credit Cards: AMEX; MasterCard; Visa
Catalog Cost: $5
Catalog Circulation: Mailed 10 time(s) per year to 40000
Printing Information: 88 pages in 4 colors on Glossy Stock
Press: Web Press
Binding: Saddle Stitched
Mailing List Information: Names for rent
In Business: 50 years
Number of Employees: 41
Sales Volume: $5-10 Million

1310 Best Made Company
Best Made Company
36 White Street
New York, NY 10013   646-478-7092
                       Fax: 888-708-7824
contact@bestmadeco.com
www.bestmadeco.com

Clothing, jackets, hats and accessories, footwear, bags, camping gear, tools, home and office supplies

President: Peter Buchanan-Smith
CFO: Steve Molineaux
Chief Merchandising Officer: Tom Girard
Chief Operations Officer: Ben Lavely
Customer Experience Manager: Ali Bradley
Credit Cards: AMEX; MasterCard
Catalog Cost: Free
In Business: 9 years

1311 Boden
Boden
180 Armstrong Road
Pittston, PA 18640-9628   570-883-5000
                              866-206-9508
custserv@bodenusa.com
www.bodenusa.com

Quality and affordable clothing and accessories for men, women and children

President: Johnnie Boden
EVP: Tricia Lewis
Printing Information: in 4 colors
In Business: 23 years
Number of Employees: 140
Sales Volume: $ 4 Million

1312 Bullock & Jones
Bullock & Jones
5121 Innovation Way
Dock B
Chambersburg, PA 17201   800-227-3050
                       Fax: 800-922-9920
service@bullockandjones.com
www.bullockandjones.com

Classic, stylish, tailored clothing for men

President: Sidney Goodwill
Marketing Manager: Eric Goodwill

Credit Cards: AMEX; MasterCard; Visa
In Business: 162 years

1313 Chadwicks of Boston

Chadwicks of Boston
500 Bic Drive
Building 4
Milford, CT 06461   877-330-3393
service@cs.chadwicks.com
www.chadwicks.com

Women's clothing, shoes and accessories.

CEO: Aldus Chapin II
Catalog Cost: Free
Printing Information: 64 pages in 4 colors
In Business: 33 years

1314 Dance Catalog

GTM Sportswear
520 McCall Road
Manhattan, KS 66502   877-597-8086
800-377-8527
Fax: 877-908-7033
info@igtm.com
www.gtmsportswear.com

Dance apparel, uniforms and accessories

President: John Strawn
Credit Cards: AMEX; MasterCard; Visa
Catalog Cost: Free
Catalog Circulation: Mailed 3 time(s) per year
Printing Information: 28 pages in 4 colors on
G
Press: S
Binding: S
In Business: 26 years
Number of Employees: 650

1315 Dennis Kirk Snowmobile Catalog

Dennis Kirk
955 South Frandsen Avenue
Rush City, MN 55069   320-358-4791
800-969-7501
Fax: 320-358-4019
customerservice@denniskirk.com
www.denniskirk.com

Snowmobile apparel, protective gear and performance parts

President: Bob Behan
Marketing Manager: Renita Twingstrom
VP of Finance: Heidi Scheffer
Credit Cards: AMEX; MasterCard
Catalog Cost: Free
In Business: 46 years
Number of Employees: 3
Sales Volume: $250,000

1316 Diamond Nexus

Diamond Nexus
5050 W. Ashland Way
Franklin, WI 53132   704-253-9444
info@diamondnexus.in
www.diamondnexus.com

Jewellery

In Business: 11 years

1317 Discount Dance Supply

Discount Dance Supply
180 Welles St
Suite 500
Forty Fort, PA 18704   714-999-0955
800-328-7107
Fax: 714-970-6075
www.discountdance.com

Dance apparel and accessories

President: Brian Hill
Marketing Manager: Ellie Booms
Credit Cards: AMEX; MasterCard
Catalog Cost: Free
Catalog Circulation: Mailed 1 time(s) per year
Printing Information: 120 pages
In Business: 16 years
Number of Employees: 5

1318 Donnelly/Colt Progressive Resources

Donnelly/Colt Progressive Resources
PO Box 188
Hampton, CT 06247-188   860-455-9621
Fax: 860-455-9597
clay@donnellycolt.com
www.donnellycolt.com

In-stock and custom printed buttons, decals, t-shirts, posters, mugs, pens and tote bags, magnets, t-shirts, postcards, banners, hats, temporary tattoos, etc.- all made in the USA

Credit Cards: AMEX; MasterCard
Catalog Cost: Free
Catalog Circulation: Mailed 5 time(s) per year
Printing Information: in 4 colors on Matte Stock
Press: Web Press
Binding: Perfect Bound
Mailing List Information: Names for rent
In Business: 38 years
Sales Volume: Onder $100,000

1319 Duluth Trading Catalog for Men

Duluth Trading Company
PO Box 409
Belleville, WI 53508-409   608-424-1544
866-300-9719
Fax: 888-950-3199
customerservice@duluthtrading.com
www.duluthtrading.com

Men's work clothes, footwear and accessories

President: Steve Schecht
Production Manager: Dan Moeller
VP, Product Development: Mike Hollenstein
VP, Marketing: Peggy Langenfeld
Credit Cards: AMEX; MasterCard
Catalog Cost: Free
Printing Information: 116 pages
In Business: 24 years
Number of Employees: 150
Sales Volume: $ 15.6 Million

1320 Duluth Trading Catalog for Women

Duluth Trading Company
PO Box 409
Belleville, WI 53508-409   608-424-1544
866-300-9719
Fax: 888-950-3199
customerservice@duluthtrading.com
www.duluthtrading.com

Women's work clothes, footwear and accessories

President: Steve Schecht
VP, Product Development: Mike Hollenstein
VP, Marketing: Peggy Langenfeld
Credit Cards: AMEX; MasterCard
Catalog Cost: Free
Printing Information: 72 pages
In Business: 24 years
Number of Employees: 150
Sales Volume: $ 15.6 Million

1321 Floriana

Floriana
5581 Hudson Industrial Parkway
PO Box 2599
Hudson, OH 44236-99   844-304-7878
866-846-1668
Fax: 800-950-9569
www.shopfloriana.com

Apparel, jewellery, accessories

1322 Foot Traffic

Foot Traffic
PO Box 412895
Kansas City, MO 64141-2895   816-444-4446
800-789-3668
www.foottraffic.us

Specialty socks, tights, hosiery and slippers

President: Charles Barnard
CFO: Victoria Barnard

Credit Cards: AMEX; MasterCard
In Business: 29 years
Number of Employees: 9
Sales Volume: $740,000

1323 GTM Sportswear Inc.

GTM Sportswear Inc.
520 McCall Road
Manhattan, KS 65502   877-597-8086
800-377-8527
Fax: 877-908-7033
info@gtm.com
www.gtmsportswear.com

Cheerleading apparel, uniforms and accessories

President: John Strawn
Credit Cards: AMEX; MasterCard; Visa
Catalog Cost: Free
Catalog Circulation: Mailed 3 time(s) per year
Printing Information: 68 pages in 4 colors on
G
Press: W
Binding: P
In Business: 25 years
Number of Employees: 650

1324 Gavilan's

Gavilan's
Gavilan Hills, CA 92599   800-713-0493
800-777-0327
Fax: 951-940-1388
customerservice@gavilans.com
www.gavilans.com

General merchandise, jewelry, books, handbags, servingware, etc.

Credit Cards: AMEX; MasterCard
Catalog Cost: Free
In Business: 3 years
Number of Employees: 1
Sales Volume: $70,000

1325 Gudrun Sjoden

Gudrun Sj"d,n
50 Greene Street
New York, NY 10013   212-219-2510
877-574-1486
customerservice@gundrunsjoden.com
www.durunsjoden.com

Clothing and home furnishings

President: Gudron Sj"d,n
Credit Cards: MasterCard
Catalog Cost: Free
In Business: 41 years

1326 Hangers.com

Hangers
3933 Spicewood Springs Road
Suite 304
Austin, TX 78759   305-477-6967
800-336-2802
Fax: 305-477-4254
sales@hangers.com
www.hangers.com

Wooden, satin, wavy, metal, and velvet hangers; garment racks and steamers

President: Devon Rifkin
Credit Cards: AMEX; MasterCard
Catalog Cost: Free
Printing Information: 40 pages on Glossy Stock
In Business: 25 years

1327 Hartford York Hats

Hartford York
PO Box 337
French Camp, CA 95231-337   800-936-5646
Fax: 800-564-6291
steve@hartfordyork.com
www.hartfordyork.com

Hats for men and women

President: Steve Singer
Catalog Cost: Free

Catalog Circulation: Mailed 2 time(s) per year
In Business: 7 years
Number of Employees: 10

1328 Honors Military Catalog
Hoovers Manufacturing Company
4133 Progress Boulevard
PO Box 547
Peru, IL 61354-0547   800-223-1159
                              815-223-1159
                      Fax: 888-333-1499
                  hoover@hmchonors.com
                  www.hmchonors.com

2500+ military designs army, navy, air force, and marines; hat pins, medals, ball caps, buckles, and patches
President: David Hoover
Credit Cards: AMEX; MasterCard; Visa
Catalog Cost: Free
Printing Information: on 0
Mailing List Information: Names for rent
In Business: 52 years
Number of Employees: 15
Sales Volume: $ 1-3 Million

1329 Hugger Mugger
Hugger-Mugger Yoga Products
1190 South Pioneer Road
Salt Lake City, UT 84104   801-268-9642
                                800-473-4888
                         Fax: 801-268-2629
              comments@huggermugger.com
              www.huggermugger.com

Products and gear for the mind, body and spirit
President: Thomas Chamberlain
Founder: Sarah Chambers
Credit Cards: MasterCard
Catalog Cost: Free
In Business: 28 years
Number of Employees: 30
Sales Volume: $ 3 Million

1330 J.Crew Style Guide
J.Crew
770 Broadway
New York, NY 10003   800-562-0258
                  www.jcrew.com

Casual clothes and accessories for men, women and children.
Chairman and CEO: Millard Drexler
President and Creative Director: Jenna Lyons
Catalog Cost: Free
Printing Information: in 4 colors
In Business: 33 years
Number of Employees: 1560
Sales Volume: $2.27 Billion

1331 JJ Hat Center
JJ Hat Center
310 5th Avenue
New York, NY 10001   212-239-4368
                             800-622-1911
                      Fax: 212-971-0406
                  info@jjhatcenter.com
                  www.jjhatcenter.Com

Hats and caps
President: Aida O'Toole
Buyers: Aida O'Toole
Credit Cards: AMEX; MasterCard; Visa; Discover Optima
Catalog Cost: Free
Catalog Circulation: Mailed 1 time(s) per year to 10000
Printing Information: 32 pages in 4 colors on Glossy Stock
Binding: Saddle Stitched
In Business: 102 years
Number of Employees: 6
Sales Volume: $500,000- 1 Million

1332 Jos. A. Bank Clothiers
Jos. A. Bank Clothiers
500 Hanover Pike
PO Box 1000
Hampstead, MD 21074-4000   800-999-7472
                       www.josbank.com

Tailored and casual clothing, footwear & accessories for men.
CFO: Jon W. Kimmins
CEO: Douglas S. Ewert
Catalog Cost: Free
Catalog Circulation: Mailed 4 time(s) per year
Printing Information: 52 pages in 4 colors
In Business: 111 years
Number of Employees: 6300
Sales Volume: $1 Billion

1333 Josh Bach Neckties
Josh Bach Ltd
133 Beekman Street
2nd Floor
New York, NY 10038-2022   212-964-5419
                       Fax: 212-964-5470
                  info@joshbach.com
                  www.joshbach.com

Men's silk ties, underwear and accessories
President: Josh Bach
Credit Cards: AMEX; MasterCard; Visa
Catalog Cost: Free
Sales Volume: $ 3-5 Million

1334 K. Jordan
K Jordan
913 First Avenue
Chippewa Falls, WI 54774   800-944-4803
                         Fax: 800-446-2329
                  service@kjordan.com
                  www.kjordan.com

Womens clothing, shoes and accessories
Credit Cards: AMEX; MasterCard; Visa
Catalog Cost: Free
Printing Information: 48 pages in 4 colors on Glossy Stock
Binding: Saddle Stitched

1335 L.L.Bean Outsider
L.L.Bean Inc.
15 Casco Street
Freeport, ME 04033   207-552-2000
                       www.llbean.com

Women and men's sportswear and outdoor clothing and accessories
Chairman: Shawn Gorman
President: Stephen Smith
Credit Cards: AMEX; MasterCard
Catalog Cost: Free
Printing Information: 68 pages in 4 colors
In Business: 105 years
Number of Employees: 5000
Sales Volume: $1.6 Billion

1336 Lands' End Kids
Lands' End, Inc.
1 Lands' End Lane
Dodgeville, WI 53595   800-963-4816
                       Fax: 800-332-0103
                  www.landsend.com

Clothing and accessories for children.
Co-interim CEO: James Gooch
Co-interim CEO: James Boitano
Catalog Cost: Free
Printing Information: in 4 colors
Mailing List Information: Names for rent
List Company: Millard Group
In Business: 53 years
Number of Employees: 5300
Sales Volume: $1.42 Billion

1337 Lands' End Men
Lands' End, Inc.
1 Lands' End Lane
Dodgeville, WI 53595   800-963-4816
                       Fax: 800-332-0103
                  www.landsend.com

Weekend wear, suits, and dress shirts for men.
Co-interim CEO: James Gooch
Co-interim CEO: James Boitano
Catalog Cost: Free
Printing Information: in 4 colors
Mailing List Information: Names for rent
List Company: Millard Group
In Business: 53 years
Number of Employees: 5300
Sales Volume: $1.42 Billion

1338 Lands' End Plus
Lands' End, Inc.
1 Lands' End Lane
Dodgeville, WI 53595   800-963-4816
                       Fax: 800-332-0103
                  www.landsend.com

Clothing proportioned to fit women 16W-26W as well as some styles in regular sizes 14-18.
Co-interim CEO: James Gooch
Co-interim CEO: James Boitano
Catalog Cost: Free
Printing Information: in 4 colors
Mailing List Information: Names for rent
List Company: Millard Group
In Business: 53 years
Number of Employees: 5300
Sales Volume: $1.42 Billion

1339 MensHats
MensHats
2615 Boeing Way
Stockton, CA 95206   800-357-4287
                       Fax: 888-746-7558
                  www.menshats.com

Men's hats and accessories
President: Steve Singer
steve@menshats.com
Credit Cards: AMEX; MasterCard; Visa
Catalog Cost: Free
Catalog Circulation: Mailed 2 time(s) per year

1340 Monticello Catalog
The Shop Monticello
PO Box 318
Charlottesville, VA 22902-318   800-243-0743
                                   800-243-1743
                  catalog@monticello.org
                  www.monticellocatalog.org

Wide selection of gift ideas selected to reflect Thomas Jefferson's taste for elegance and quality
Marketing Manager: Liesel Nowak
Founder: Thomas Jefferson
Credit Cards: AMEX; MasterCard
Catalog Cost: Free
Catalog Circulation: Mailed 2 time(s) per year
Printing Information: 48 pages in 4 colors on Glossy Stock
Binding: Saddle Stitched
In Business: 90 years

1341 Musk Ox Producers Cooperative
Oomingmak
604 H Street
Anchorage, AK 99501-3415   907-272-9225
                                888-360-9665
                         Fax: 907-258-4225
                  qiviut@gci.net
                  www.qiviut.com

Handmade qiviut hats and scarves
Chairman: Sigrun Robertson
President: Mesonga Atkinson
In Business: 46 years

Number of Employees: 7
Sales Volume: $ 1 Million

1342 One Hanes Place

One Hanes Place
PO Box 748
Rural Hall, NC 27098-748　800-671-1674
　800-671-5056
Fax: 800-545-5613
www.onehanesplace.com

Lingerie and hosiery for women

Chairman: Lee Chaden
President: Richard Noll
Credit Cards: AMEX; MasterCard; Visa
Catalog Cost: Free
Printing Information: 84 pages
In Business: 40 years

1343 PalmBeach Jewelry

PalmBeach Jewelry
6400 East Rogers Circle
Boca Raton, FL 33409 www.palmbeachjewelry.com

Beautiful jewellery, accessories and designer fragrances

Credit Cards: AMEX; MasterCard
In Business: 63 years

1344 Paragon Gift Catalog

The Paragon
P.O. Box 4068
Lawrenceville, IN 47025-4068　855-557-4658
Fax: 513-354-1294
customerservice@theparagon.com
www.theparagon.com

Handbags, belts, bath accessories, dishes, gifts and toys

President: Steve Rowley
CFO: Michael Wood
Marketing Manager: Peg Wave
Production Manager: Eileen Houlihan
Buyers: Mary Jane Spooner
Credit Cards: AMEX; MasterCard; Visa
Catalog Cost: Free
Catalog Circulation: Mailed 8 time(s) per year to 40000
Average Order Size: $50
Printing Information: 71 pages in 4 colors on Glossy Stock
Press: Web Press
Binding: Saddle Stitched
Mailing List Information: Names for rent
List Company: Fasano & Associates
In Business: 44 years
Number of Employees: 400
Sales Volume: $ 10-20 Million

1345 Rewards

Rewards
9722 Great Hills Trail
Suite 300
Austin, TX 78759-5687　512-502-9799
　800-292-0195
Fax: 512-502-5193
shprewards@aol.com
www.shoprewards.com

Belt buckles (sets), belt buckles (single), belts, cufflinks and studs, money clips and key rings, alligator wallets, jewelry, horseshoe necklaces, watches, golf accessories and knives

President: Claudia Stromberg
Owner: Russell Stromberg
Credit Cards: AMEX; MasterCard; Visa
Catalog Circulation: Mailed 1 time(s) per year
Printing Information: 40 pages in 4 colors on Matte Stock
Press: Sheetfed Press
Binding: Perfect Bound
Mailing List Information: Names for rent
In Business: 16 years
Number of Employees: 7
Sales Volume: $550,000

1346 Rods Western Palace

Rods Western Palace
3099 Silver Dr.
Columbus, OH 43224　614-268-8200
　866-326-1975
Fax: 614-268-8203
www.rods.com

Western apparel, tack, unique Western gifts and home decor

1347 Sahalie

Bluestem Brands, Inc.
7075 Flying Cloud Drive
Eden Prairie, MN 55344　877-718-7902
www.sahalie.blair.com

Casual clothing, shoes & accessories for men and women

President: Steve Nave
CFO: Pete Michielutti
EVP, COO, & Chief Digital Officer: Vince Jones
EVP & President of Credit Services: Jim Slavik
Credit Cards: AMEX; MasterCard
Catalog Cost: Free
In Business: 46 years
Sales Volume: $50MM to $100MM

1348 Samantha's Style Shoppe

Collections Etc., Inc.
PO Box 7985
Elk Grove Village, IL 60009-7985　620-584-8000
　888-468-1666
Fax: 847-350-5701
www.collectionsetc.com

Clothing for women including jewelry

President: Shelley Nandkeolyar
Marketing Manager: Karl Steigerwald
Fulfillment: Bruce Getowicz
CEO/Founder: Todd Lustbader
COO: Paul Klassman
Credit Cards: AMEX; MasterCard; Visa
Catalog Cost: Free
In Business: 50 years
Number of Employees: 200
Sales Volume: 12.7M

1349 Spartina 449

Spartina 449
10 Hunter Rd.
Hilton Head Island, SC 29926　843-681-8860
Fax: 843-681-8830
www.spartina449.com

Women's handbag and accessory

Company Founder, CEO: Kay Stanley

1350 Stauer

Stauer
14101 Southcross Drive West
Burnsville, MN 55337　888-201-7123
　888-333-2012
Fax: 651-393-9728
www.stauer.com

Fine watches, jewelry and sunglasses, apparel, handbags, luggage, home accessories, coins and collectibles

President: Michael Bisceglia
Average Order Size: $55

1351 SuspenderStore

SuspenderStore
407 Headquarters Drive, Unit #3
P.O. Box 273
Millersville, MD 21108　410-987-4212
　800-393-4508
Fax: 410-987-4214
info@suspenderstore.com
www.suspenderstore.com

High quality suspenders

Credit Cards: AMEX; MasterCard
In Business: 16 years

1352 The Vermont Country Store

The Vermont Country Store
5650 Main Street
Manchester Center, VT 05255-9718 802-362-4667
　800-547-7849
Fax: 802-362-8288
www.vermontcountrystore.com

Clothing, accessories and footwear

Chairman: Lyman Orton
President: William Shouldice
VP Operations: Lynn Jefferies
Buyers: Nancy McLenithan, Food
Susan Rawls, Womens
Credit Cards: AMEX; MasterCard; Visa
Catalog Cost: Free
Catalog Circulation: Mailed 5 time(s) per year
Printing Information: 104 pages in 4 colors on Newsprint
In Business: 69 years
Number of Employees: 600

1353 Tumi, Inc.

Tumi, Inc.
1001 Durham Ave
South Plainfield, NJ 07080-2300　908-756-4400
　800-299-8864
Fax: 908-756-5878
info@tumi.com
www.tumi.com

Luggage, backpacks, handbags, wallets, cosmetic cases, belts, key chains, laptop covers, umbrellas

President: Jerome Griffith
CFO: Michael Mardy
Credit Cards: AMEX; MasterCard; Visa
Mailing List Information: Names for rent
In Business: 40 years
Number of Employees: 100
Sales Volume: $ 20-50 Million

Casual Wear

1354 Appleseed's

Bluestem Brands, Inc.
35 Village Road
Middleton, MA 01949　800-546-4554
international@blair.com
appleseeds.blair.com

Women's clothing, footwear, and accessories

President: Steve Nave
CFO: Pete Michielutti, EVP
EVP, COO, & Chief Digital Officer: Vince Jones
EVP & President of Credit Services: Jim Slavik
Credit Cards: AMEX; MasterCard
Catalog Cost: Free
In Business: 71 years
Sales Volume: $50-100 Million

1355 Big Ray's

Big Ray's
507 2nd Ave
Fairbanks, AK 99701-4728　907-452-3458
　800-478-3458
Fax: 907-456-2413
classicweb@classicalaska.com
www.bigrays.com

Army and navy surplus clothing

President: Monty Rostad
Marketing Manager: Cindy Clark
Credit Cards: MasterCard; Visa
Catalog Cost: Free
In Business: 65 years
Number of Employees: 18
Sales Volume: $ 8 Million

1356 Blair Men's

Blair
220 Hickory St.
Warren, PA 16366　800-821-5744
www.blair.com

Full line of men's clothing and footwear.

President: Marisa Smith
Catalog Cost: Free
Printing Information: in 4 colors
In Business: 106 years
Number of Employees: 2000
Sales Volume: $1 Billion

1357 Blue Generation
WestPro, Inc.
2294 Mountain Vista Lane
Provo, UT 84606-6206
801-373-2525
Fax: 801-373-8778
steve@westpro.net
www.westpro.net

Casual wear and custom sportswear, including direct embroidery and screen printing

President: Steven Clements
CFO: John M Edmunds
Credit Cards: MasterCard
Catalog Cost: Free
Catalog Circulation: Mailed 1 time(s) per year
Printing Information: 16 pages in 4 colors on Glossy Stock
Press: Web Press
Binding: Perfect Bound
In Business: 36 years
Number of Employees: 45
Sales Volume: $3-5 Million

1358 Crazy Shirts
Crazy Shirts
99-969 Iwaena St.
Aiea, HI 96701
800-771-2720
www.crazyshirts.com

Men's and women's t-shirts and shorts.

In Business: 52 years

1359 Hot Deals
Sierra Trading Post
5025 Campstool Road
Cheyenne, WY 82007-1898
307-775-8090
800-713-4534
Fax: 800-378-8946
customerservice@sierratradingpost.com
www.sierratradingpost.com

Outdoor, casual clothes, footwear, home decor, outdoor sports gear and more

President: Keith Richardson
CFO: Gary Imig
Production Manager: Shelia Russell
Fulfillment: Robin Jahnke
Credit Cards: AMEX; MasterCard; Visa
Catalog Cost: Free
Printing Information: 60 pages
Mailing List Information: Names for rent
In Business: 26 years
Number of Employees: 565

1360 J.Crew Style Guide
J.Crew
770 Broadway
New York, NY 10003
800-562-0258
www.jcrew.com

Casual clothes and accessories for men, women and children.

Chairman and CEO: Millard Drexler
President and Creative Director: Jenna Lyons
Catalog Cost: Free
Printing Information: in 4 colors
In Business: 33 years
Number of Employees: 1560
Sales Volume: $2.27 Billion

1361 J.L. Powell The Sporting Life
J.L. Powell
1015 Cindy Lane
PO Box 9109
Carpinteria, CO 93013
805-456-4242
service@jlpowell.com
www.jlpowell.com

Sportswear for men including shoes and jewelry

President: J.R. Rigley
CFO: Michelle Fehr
CEO: Mark E. Jacobs
Catalog Cost: Free
Catalog Circulation: Mailed 4 time(s) per year
Printing Information: 66 pages in 4 colors
In Business: 38 years
Sales Volume: 5000000

1362 Jessica London
Jessica London
One New York Plaza
New York, NY 10004
jessicalondon.com

Plus-size apparel, lingerie and shoes.

CEO: Paul Tarvin
Catalog Cost: Free
In Business: 105 years
Number of Employees: 6400
Sales Volume: Over $1 Billion

1363 Jim Morris Environmental T-Shirt Company
Jim Morris Environmental T-Shirt Company
5660 Valmont Road
PO Box 18270
Boulder, CO 80308-1270
303-444-6430
800-788-5411
Fax: 303-786-9095
wolf@jimmorris.com
www.jimmorris.com

Designs printed on a wide variety of garments, including t-shirts, sweatshirts, organic cotton t-shirts, hats and totebags

President: Jim Morris
Credit Cards: MasterCard; Visa
Catalog Cost: Free
Catalog Circulation: Mailed 3 time(s) per year to 150
Printing Information: 32 pages in 4 colors
Press: Web Press
Mailing List Information: Names for rent
In Business: 38 years
Sales Volume: $620,000

1364 Jockey
Jockey International, Inc.
2300 60th Street
Kenosha, WI 53140
800-562-5391
jockey.com

Sleepwear and casualwear for men, women, and children

President: Debra S. Waller
Marketing Manager: Prateek Kumar
SVP, Chief Supply Chain Officer: Tim Taylor
Catalog Cost: Free
In Business: 141 years
Number of Employees: 1600
Sales Volume: Over $1 Billion

1365 KingSize
KingSize
One New York Plaza
New York, NY 10004
www.kingsizedirect.com

Men's big and tall clothing.

CEO: Paul Tarvin
Catalog Cost: Free
In Business: 105 years
Number of Employees: 6400
Sales Volume: Over $1 Billion

1366 Lands' End Men
Lands' End, Inc.
1 Lands' End Lane
Dodgeville, WI 53595
800-963-4816
Fax: 800-332-0103
www.landsend.com

Weekend wear, suits, and dress shirts for men.

Co-interim CEO: James Gooch
Co-interim CEO: James Boitano
Catalog Cost: Free
Printing Information: in 4 colors
Mailing List Information: Names for rent
List Company: Millard Group
In Business: 53 years
Number of Employees: 5300
Sales Volume: $1.42 Billion

1367 Lands' End Plus
Lands' End, Inc.
1 Lands' End Lane
Dodgeville, WI 53595
800-963-4816
Fax: 800-332-0103
www.landsend.com

Clothing proportioned to fit women 16W-26W as well as some styles in regular sizes 14-18.

Co-interim CEO: James Gooch
Co-interim CEO: James Boitano
Catalog Cost: Free
Printing Information: in 4 colors
Mailing List Information: Names for rent
List Company: Millard Group
In Business: 53 years
Number of Employees: 5300
Sales Volume: $1.42 Billion

1368 Liza & Rose
AmeriMark Direct
6864 Engle Rd.
Cleveland, OH 44130
866-345-1388
www.amerimark.com

Fashion jewelry, fragrances, cosmetics, casual wear and footwear.

CFO: Joe Albanese
CEO & President: Gareth Giesler
Catalog Cost: Free
Printing Information: in 4 colors
In Business: 47 years
Number of Employees: 700
Sales Volume: $400 Million

1369 Massage Warehouse & Spa Essentials
Massage Warehouse & Spa Essentials
360 Veterans Parkway
Suite 115
Bolingbrook, IL 60440-4607
630-771-7400
800-910-9955
Fax: 888-674-4380
support@massagewarehouse.com
www.massagewarehouse.com

Apparel and fitness, gifts, massage and spa, treatment supplies, books, videos, yoga and fitness

President: Robert Cooper
Marketing Manager: Heather Zdan
Credit Cards: AMEX; MasterCard; Visa
Printing Information: 12 pages
In Business: 52 years
Number of Employees: 126
Sales Volume: $ 13 Million

1370 Orvis Gifts for Men
The Orvis Company Inc.
178 Conservation Way
Sunderland, VT 05250-4465
802-362-1300
888-235-9763
Fax: 802-362-0141
www.orvis.com

Hunting and fishing equipment and clothing.

CEO: Leigh H. Perkins Jr.
Catalog Cost: Free
In Business: 160 years
Number of Employees: 1700
Sales Volume: $340 Million

1371 Orvis Women
The Orvis Company Inc.
178 Conservation Way
Sunderland, VT 05250-4465   802-362-1300
                              888-235-9763
                              Fax: 802-362-0141
                              www.orvis.com

Women's casual clothing and accessories.

CEO: Leigh H. Perkins Jr.
Catalog Cost: Free
In Business: 160 years
Number of Employees: 1700
Sales Volume: $340 Million

1372 Roaman's
Roaman's
One New York Plaza
New York, NY 10004   roamans.com

Plus-size business and casual clothing, shoes and intimate apparel.

CEO: Paul Tarvin
Catalog Cost: Free
In Business: 105 years
Number of Employees: 6400
Sales Volume: Over $1 Billion

1373 Samantha's Style Shoppe
Collections Etc., Inc.
PO Box 7985
Elk Grove Village, IL 60009-7985 620-584-8000
                                  888-468-1666
                                  Fax: 847-350-5701
                                  www.collectionsetc.com

Clothing for women including jewelry

President: Shelley Nandkeolyar
Marketing Manager: Karl Steigerwald
Fulfillment: Bruce Getowicz
CEO/Founder: Todd Lustbader
COO: Paul Klassman
Credit Cards: AMEX; MasterCard; Visa
Catalog Cost: Free
In Business: 50 years
Number of Employees: 200
Sales Volume: 12.7M

1374 Schweitzer Nightwear
Schweitzer Linen
1053 Lexington Avenue
New York, NY 10021   212-570-0236
                              800-554-6367
                              Fax: 212-737-6328
                              www.schweitzerlinen.Com

Cashmere robes, intimates, jackets, long gowns, nite shirts

President: Elena Schweitzer
Manager: Ileana Jovica
Credit Cards: AMEX; MasterCard
Catalog Cost: $2
Printing Information: 32 pages in 3 colors on Glossy Stock
Press: Web Press
Binding: Saddle Stitched
In Business: 40 years
Number of Employees: 8
Sales Volume: $ 1-3 Million

1375 Serengeti
Serengeti
PO Box 3349
Chelmsford, MA 01824-949   800-426-2852
                              Fax: 800-866-3235
                              help@serengeticatalog.com
                              www.serengeticatalog.com

Line of womens clothing and accessories

Chairman: Jack Rosenfeld
President: John Fleischman
CFO: Steven Steiner
Credit Cards: AMEX; MasterCard; Visa
Catalog Cost: Free
Printing Information: 63 pages in 4 colors on Glossy Stock

Binding: Saddle Stitched
In Business: 27 years

1376 Sierra Woman Catalog
Sierra Trading Post
5025 Campstool Rd
Cheyenne, WY 82007-1898   307-775-8000
                              800-713-4534
                              Fax: 800-378-8946
                              customerservice@sierratradingpost.com
                              www.sierratradingpost.com

Clothes for the active woman with a passion for fitness

President: Keith Richardson
CFO: Gary Imig
Production Manager: Shelia Russell
Fulfillment: Robin Jahnke
Credit Cards: AMEX; MasterCard
Catalog Cost: Free
Mailing List Information: Names for rent
In Business: 28 years
Number of Employees: 565
Sales Volume: $ 20-50 Million

1377 Soft Surroundings
Soft Surroundings
1100 N Lindbergh Blvd
St Louis, MO 63132-2914   800-240-7076
                              Fax: 314-569-8471
                              customerservice@softsurroundings.com
                              www.softsurroundings.com

At home clothing of soft, easy care fabrics

President: Robin Sheldon
Marketing Manager: Mandy Dorrance
Catalog Cost: Free
Catalog Circulation: Mailed 2 time(s) per year
Average Order Size: $170
Printing Information: 80 pages in 4 colors on Glossy Stock
Binding: Saddle Stitched
In Business: 15 years
Sales Volume: $500,000- 1 Million

1378 The Company Store
The Company Store
500 Company Store Road
La Crosse, WI 54601-4477   608-791-6000
                              800-323-8000
                              Fax: 800-238-0271
                              CustServ@TheCompanyStore.com
                              www.thecompanystore.com

Linens, home decor, apparel, bath

President: John DiFrancesco
Catalog Cost: Free
Printing Information: 103 pages in 4 colors on Glossy Stock
Binding: Saddle Stitched
In Business: 103 years
Number of Employees: 120
Sales Volume: $6 Million

1379 Tog Shop
Bluestem Brands, Inc.
7075 Flying Cloud Drive
Eden Prairie, MN 55344   800-262-8888
                              www.togshop.blair.com

Offers updated classic apparel for mature women

President: Steve Nave
CFO: Pete Michielutti
EVP, COO, & Chief Digital Officer: Vince Jones
EVP & President of Credit Services: Jim Slavik
Credit Cards: AMEX; MasterCard
Catalog Cost: Free
In Business: 77 years
Sales Volume: $50MM to $100MM

1380 What on Earth
What on Earth
5581 Hudson Industrial Parkway
PO Box 2599
Hudson, OH 44236   800-441-2242
                             800-945-2552
                             Fax: 800-950-9569
                             shop@whatonearthcatalog.com
                             www.whatonearthcatalog.com

Catalog full of great gifts, from t-shirts to home decor

President: Jared Florian
Buyers: Karyn Vajner
Credit Cards: AMEX; MasterCard; Visa
Catalog Cost: Free
Catalog Circulation: Mailed 12 time(s) per year
Printing Information: 63 pages in 4 colors on Glossy Stock
Press: Web Press
Binding: Saddle Stitched
Mailing List Information: Names for rent
List Company: Mokrynski & Associates
401 Hackensack Avenue
Hackensack, NJ 07601
In Business: 125 years
Number of Employees: 75
Sales Volume: $ 10-20 Million

1381 Woman Within
Woman Within
One New York Plaza
New York, NY 10004   www.womanwithin.com

Plus-size casual clothing.

CEO: Paul Tarvin
Catalog Cost: Free
In Business: 105 years
Number of Employees: 6400
Sales Volume: Over $1 Billion

1382 Woman Within Catalog
Redcats USA
PO Box 8320
Indianapolis, IN 46283-8320   800-228-3120
                              800-228-3120
                              Fax: 800-456-9838
                              www.womanwithin.com

Casual plus sized women's clothing

President: Eric Faintreny
CFO: Olivier Marzloff
Credit Cards: AMEX; MasterCard; Visa
Catalog Cost: Free

Children

1383 B Coole Designs
B Coole Designs
2631 Piner Rd
Santa Rosa, CA 95401-4036   707-575-8924
                             800-992-8924
                             www.bcoole.com

Period clothing, women's clothing, knits, kids, leggings, bike shorts, bras, leotards, babies and toddlers, nursing pads, cotton diapers, socks, bags, scarves, hats, and women's health products

President: Barbara Coole
Catalog Circulation: Mailed 1 time(s) per year
Number of Employees: 2
Sales Volume: Under $500M

1384 Belk New Directions
Belk
2801 W Tyvola Road
Charlotte NC   800-669-6550
                             care@belk.com
                             www.belk.com

Casualwear for women, men, and children, jewelry, footwear, home furnishings and appliances

President: Lisa Harper
CFO: Scott Hurd
Marketing Manager: Barb Pellegrino
Chief Operating Officer: Don Hendricks
Chief Stores Officer: Randy Whitaker
Product Sourcing & Technical Design: Tanya Cauren
Catalog Cost: Free
Printing Information: 12 pages in 4 colors
In Business: 129 years

1385 Brooks Brothers
Brooks Brothers
100 Phoenix Avenue
Enfield, CT 06082   800-274-1815
Fax: 800-274-1010
www.brooksbrothers.com

Complete line of mens, women and childrens shirts, polos & tees, sweaters, casual and dress pants, suits, formalwear, sport coats and blazers

President: Claudio Del Vecchio
CFO: Brian Baumann
SVP Operations: Debra Del Vecchio
Credit Cards: AMEX; MasterCard; Visa
Catalog Cost: Free
Catalog Circulation: Mailed 5 time(s) per year
Printing Information: 80 pages in 4 colors on Glossy Stock
Press: Web Press
Binding: Saddle Stitched
Mailing List Information: Names for rent
In Business: 198 years
Number of Employees: 3500
Sales Volume: $ 20-50 Million

1386 CWDkids
Cute Well-Dressed Kids
7021 Wolftown-Hood Road
Madison, VA 22727   800-551-9168
www.cwdkids.com

Brand name children's clothing, ages 0-12

Credit Cards: AMEX; MasterCard; Visa
Catalog Circulation: Mailed 17 time(s) per year to 15000
Average Order Size: $110
Printing Information: 31 pages in 4 colors on Glossy Stock
Press: Web Press
Binding: Saddle Stitched
Mailing List Information: Names for rent
List Company: Millard Group Peterborough, NH
In Business: 30 years
Number of Employees: 20
Sales Volume: $ 20 Million

1387 Hanna Andersson
Hanna Andersson
1010 NW Flanders St
Portland, OR 97209-3199   503-242-0920
800-222-0544
Fax: 503-321-5289
customerservice@hannaandersson.com
www.hannaandersson.com

Full line of baby clothes and toys, as well as clothing, shoes and sleepwear for the whole family

President: Adam Stone
CFO: Rod Rice
Marketing Manager: Alison Hiatt
VP, Stores: Jessica Polonsky
VP, Operations: Randy Rieder
VP, Design: Lisa Strubel
Printing Information: 65 pages
In Business: 28 years
Number of Employees: 115
Sales Volume: $ 22 Million

1388 Kelly's Kids
Kelly's Kids
391 Liberty Road
PO Box 1367
Natchez, MS 39120   601-443-6185
800-837-2066
customerservice@kellyskids.com
www.kellyskids.com

Classic, quality childrens clothing

President: Lynn James
CEO: Ashton James
CCO: Caroline James
In Business: 29 years
Sales Volume: $ 5-10 Million

1389 Kipp
Kipp Toys
491 W. Muskegon Drive
Greenfield, IN 46140   800-428-1153
Fax: 800-832-5477
www.kipptoys.com

Toys, novelties, and party supplies

Catalog Cost: Free
In Business: 134 years

1390 KooKoo Bear Kids
KooKoo Bear Kids
12060 Etris Road
Roswell, GA 30075   770-771-5665
800-475-6909
Fax: 770-998-313
www.kookoobearkids.com

Kid's furnitures

In Business: 12 years

1391 L.L.Bean Back to School
L.L.Bean Inc.
15 Casco Street
Freeport, ME 04033   207-552-2000
www.llbean.com

Children's clothing and back to school acessories

Chairman: Shawn Gorman
President: Stephen Smith
Credit Cards: AMEX; MasterCard
Catalog Cost: Free
Catalog Circulation: Mailed 1 time(s) per year
Printing Information: 72 pages in 4 colors
In Business: 105 years
Number of Employees: 5000
Sales Volume: $1.6 Billion

1392 Lands' End Kids
Lands' End, Inc.
1 Lands' End Lane
Dodgeville, WI 53595   800-963-4816
Fax: 800-332-0103
www.landsend.com

Clothing and accessories for children.

Co-interim CEO: James Gooch
Co-interim CEO: James Boitano
Catalog Cost: Free
Printing Information: in 4 colors
Mailing List Information: Names for rent
List Company: Millard Group
In Business: 53 years
Number of Employees: 5300
Sales Volume: $1.42 Billion

1393 Lands' End School Outfitters
Lands' End, Inc.
1 Lands' End Lane
Dodgeville, WI 53595   800-963-4816
Fax: 800-332-0103
www.landsend.com

Uniforms in sizes to fit grades K-12

Co-interim CEO: James Gooch
Co-interim CEO: James Boitano
Catalog Cost: Free
Printing Information: in 4 colors
Mailing List Information: Names for rent

List Company: Millard Group
In Business: 53 years
Number of Employees: 5300
Sales Volume: $1.42 Billion

1394 Lilly's Kids
Lillian Vernon Corporation
PO Box 35980
Colorado Springs, CO 80935-5980   800-545-5426
800-901-9291
custserv@lillianvernon.com
www.lillianvernon.com

Clothing, gifts and toys for kids of all ages

President: Tom Arland
CFO: Kirby Heck
Marketing Manager: John Buleza
Buyers: Norma Zambano
Credit Cards: AMEX; MasterCard
Catalog Cost: Free
Catalog Circulation: Mailed 10 time(s) per year to 10000
Average Order Size: $45
Printing Information: 79 pages in 4 colors on Glossy Stock
Press: Web Press
Binding: Saddle Stitched
Mailing List Information: Names for rent
Will Trade Names: Yes
In Business: 64 years
Number of Employees: 150

1395 LittleMissMatched
MissMatched Inc
307 7th Avenue
Suite 501
New York, NY 10001   201-902-0056
customerservice@littlemissmatched.com
www.littlemissmatched.com

Mismatched girls socks, bedding, pajamas, accessorise, clothing and more

Co-Founder/CEO: Jonah Staw
Catalog Cost: Free

1396 Mini Boden Girls
JP Boden & Co., Ltd.
180 Armstrong Road
Pittston, PA 18640-9628   570-883-5000
866-206-9508
custserv@bodenusa.com
www.bodenusa.com

Girl's clothing

EVP: Tricia Lewis
Catalog Circulation: Mailed 4 time(s) per year
In Business: 24 years
Number of Employees: 800
Sales Volume: $ 4 Million

1397 One Step Ahead
One Step Ahead
1112 7th Ave.
Monroe, WI 53566-1364   888-557-3851
Fax: 847-615-7236
www.onestepahead.com

One stop shopping for moms and kids, from clothing to books and toys

President: Karen Scott
CFO: Susan O'Malley
Marketing Manager: Bob Patton
Credit Cards: AMEX; MasterCard
Catalog Cost: Free
Catalog Circulation: Mailed 12 time(s) per year to 10M
Average Order Size: $65
Printing Information: 48 pages in 4 colors on Glossy Stock
Press: Web Press
Binding: Saddle Stitched
Mailing List Information: Names for rent
List Manager: ALCNY
In Business: 23 years
Number of Employees: 150
Sales Volume: $ 9 Million

1398 Palumba Natural Toys and Crafts
Palumba
221 Felch Street, #2C
Ann Arbor, MI 48103-3353   734-995-5414
866-725-7122
hello@palumba.com
www.palumba.com

Natural wood toys, organic kids clothing, organic toys and furniture

President: Judy Alexander
Marketing Manager: Mickey Dean
Credit Cards: AMEX; MasterCard
Catalog Cost: Free
Sales Volume: Under $500,000

1399 Posh Tots
Posh Tots
825 Greenbrier Circle
Suite G
Chesapeake, VA 23230   804-935-6188
800-927-5164
Fax: 804-935-0844
Sales@PoshTots.com
www.poshtots.com

Baby furniture, accessories, luxury baby bedding and children's clothing

President: Andrea Edmonds
Production Manager: Susan Lindeman
Credit Cards: AMEX; MasterCard
Catalog Cost: Free
Printing Information: 100 pages in 4 colors on Glossy Stock
Binding: Perfect Bound
In Business: 10 years
Number of Employees: 43
Sales Volume: $ 3-5 Million

1400 Serena & Lily Baby Catalog
Serena & Lily
10 Liberty Ship Way
Suite 350
Sausalito, CA 94965   415-331-4199
866-597-2742
Fax: 415-331-1435
hamptons@serenaandlily.com
www.serenaandlily.com

Home and lifestyle

Chief Creative Officer: Serena Dugan
CEO: Lily Kanter
In Business: 12 years

1401 SoulFlower
Soul Flower
801 Boone Ave N
Golden Valley, MN 55427-801   651-251-1028
866-294-8074
Fax: 651-251-1029
yourbuds@soul-flower.com
www.soul-flower.com

Natural cotton clothing for women's and children, hand bags, jewelry and accessories

President: Mike Shoafstall
Marketing Manager: Sarah
Director of Corporate Optimization: Chad
Designer: Jennifer
Agent: Joe
Credit Cards: AMEX; MasterCard; Visa
Catalog Cost: Free
Catalog Circulation: Mailed 2 time(s) per year
Printing Information: 39 pages on Glossy Stock
Binding: Saddle Stitched
In Business: 15 years

1402 Tea Collections
Tea Collections
1 Arkansas St
Studio B
San Francisco, CA 94107-2482   415-621-9400
866-374-8747
Fax: 415-321-2477
service@teacollection.com
www.teacollection.com

Children's clothing

President: Leigh Rawdon
CFO: Laura Joukovski
Chief Creative Officer & Co-Founder: Emily Meyer
CEO & Co-Founder: Leigh Rawdon
Credit Cards: MasterCard
Catalog Circulation: Mailed 4 time(s) per year
Sales Volume: $ 5-10 Million

1403 The Wooden Soldier Fall/Winter 2015 Catalog
The Wooden Soldier
24 Kearsarge St.
P.O. Box 800
North Conway, NH 3860   603-356-7041
800-375-6002
Fax: 603-356-6016
info@woodensoldier.com
www.woodensoldier.com

Children's clothing

Printing Information: 36 pages
In Business: 35+ years

1404 The Wooden Soldier Spring/Easter 2015 Catalog
The Wooden Soldier
24 Kearsarge St.
P.O. Box 800
North Conway, NH 3860   603-356-7041
800-375-6002
Fax: 603-356-6016
info@woodensoldier.com
www.woodensoldier.com

Children's clothing

In Business: 35+ years

1405 Wooden Soldier
Wooden Soldier
PO Box 800
North Conway, NH 03860   603-356-7041
800-375-6002
Fax: 603-356-3530
info@woodensoldier.com
www.woodensoldier.com

Infants and children's clothing

President: David Mennella
Marketing Manager: Yvonne Mennella
Credit Cards: AMEX; MasterCard; Visa
Catalog Cost: Free
Catalog Circulation: Mailed 2 time(s) per year
Printing Information: 60 pages in 4 colors on Glossy Stock
Press: Web Press
Binding: Saddle Stitched
Mailing List Information: Names for rent
List Company: Mokreynski & Associates
401 Hackensack Avenue
Hackensack, NJ 07601
201-488-5656
In Business: 35 years
Number of Employees: 36
Sales Volume: $10 Million

1406 bella bliss
bella bliss
209-211 North Limestone
Lexington, KY 40507   866-846-5295
order@bellabliss.com
www.bellabliss.com

Clothing

1407 5.11 Tactical
5.11 Inc.
4300 Spyres Way
Modesto, CA 95356-9259   209-527-4511
866-451-1726
Fax: 209-527-1511
www.511tactical.com

Tactical apparel for law enforcement, military, EMS and firefighters.

President: Francisco Morales
CFO: Jeff Hamilton
CEO: Dan Costa
Credit Cards: AMEX; MasterCard; Visa
Catalog Cost: Free
Printing Information: 180 pages
Number of Employees: 180
Sales Volume: $ 8.7 Million

1408 Alfred Angelo
Alfred Angelo
1625 S Congress Avenue
Delray Beach, FL 33445   888-218-0044
customercare@alfredangelo.com
www.alfredangelo.com

Wedding dresses, bridesmaid dresses, prom dresses, flower girl dresses and mother of the bride dresses

President: Vincent C Piccione
Chief Creative Officer: Michele Piccione
Catalog Cost: $12.5
In Business: 82 years

1409 Alphabet U
Anderson's Alphabet U
4875 White Bear Parkway
White Bear Lake, MN 55110   800-338-3346
Fax: 800-213-8166
service@andersons.com
www.andersons.com

Preschool and kindergarten personalized school supplies, graduation apparel, award and recognition and classroom accessories

President: Troy Ethan
Credit Cards: AMEX; MasterCard; Visa
Catalog Cost: Free
Printing Information: 31 pages in 4 colors
In Business: 45 years

1410 Amy Lee Bridal
Amy Lee Bridal
3905 Braxton Dr
Houston, TX 77063   361-765-3043
832-704-8205
Fax: 713-532-9486
amyleebridals@gmail.com
www.amyleebridal.com

Bridal apparel

President: Amy Lee
Mailing List Information: Names for rent
In Business: 35 years
Number of Employees: 20
Sales Volume: $500,000- 1 Million

1411 Anderson's School Spirit Catalog
Anderson's
4875 White Bear Pkwy
White Bear Lake, MN 55110-3325 651-426-1084
800-338-3346
Fax: 800-213-8166
service@andersons.com
www.andersons.com

Custom imprinted school spirit products and cheerleading apparel

President: Charles Anderson
Marketing Manager: Annette Munns
Credit Cards: AMEX; MasterCard; Visa
Catalog Cost: Free
Printing Information: 147 pages in 4 colors

In Business: 45 years
Sales Volume: Under $500,000

1412 Balance: Gymnastics & Cheerleading
Ares Sportswear
3704 Lacon Rd
Hilliard, OH 43026 614-767-1950
800-439-8614
Fax: 614-527-3794
info@areswear.com
www.areswear.com

Gymnastics and cheerleading apparel and uniforms

President: Mike Leibrand
Production Manager: Christopher Olsen
Owner: Michael Campbell
Credit Cards: AMEX; MasterCard; Visa
Catalog Cost: Free
Printing Information: 68 pages
In Business: 18 years
Number of Employees: 100
Sales Volume: $ 7.5 Million

1413 Baum's Dancewear
Baum's Dancewear
1805 East Passyunk Avenue
Philadelphia, PA 19148-2127 215-923-2244
800-832-6246
Fax: 215-592-4194
info@baumsdancewear.com
www.baumsdancewear.Com

Dance and theatrical products

President: Peter Cohen
Credit Cards: AMEX; MasterCard; Visa
Catalog Cost: Free
Catalog Circulation: Mailed 2 time(s) per year
Printing Information: 100 pages in 4 colors on Glossy Stock
Press: Sheetfed Press
Binding: Perfect Bound
Mailing List Information: Names for rent
In Business: 126 years
Number of Employees: 18
Sales Volume: $ 3 Million

1414 Boosters: Bands & Clubs
Ares Sportswear
3704 Lacon Rd
Hilliard, OH 43026 614-767-1950
800-439-8614
Fax: 614-527-3794
info@areswear.com
www.areswear.com

Booster club shirts and spirit wear

President: Mike Leibrand
Production Manager: Christopher Olsen
Michael Campbell:
Owner
Credit Cards: AMEX; MasterCard; Visa
Catalog Cost: Free
Printing Information: 64 pages
In Business: 20 years
Number of Employees: 100
Sales Volume: $ 7.5 Million

1415 Buckaroo Bobbins
Buckaroo Bobbins
PO Box 1168
Chino Valley, AZ 86323-1168 928-636-1885
Fax: 928-636-8134
buckaroobobbins@gmail.com
www.buckaroobobbins.com

Sewing patterns for vintage 1860-1900 Western clothing, as well as cowboy accessories

President: Roger Eads
Co-Owner: Geneva Eads
Catalog Cost: $2
Catalog Circulation: to 10000
Printing Information: 16 pages in 2 colors on Newsprint
Press: Web Press
Binding: Folded
Mailing List Information: Names for rent

In Business: 22 years
Sales Volume: $400,000

1416 Cashs of Ireland
Cashs of Ireland
6185-K Huntley Rd
Ste K
Columbus, OH 43229 614-430-8180
800-999-0655
Fax: 614-430-8728
info@crystalclassics.com
www.cashs.com

Irish and European clothing, crystal, china, gifts and tableware

President: Maxine Stotler
Marketing Manager: Bruno Bergman
Credit Cards: AMEX; MasterCard; Visa
Printing Information: 52 pages
In Business: 37 years
Number of Employees: 26
Sales Volume: $ 1.2 Million

1417 Celtic Croft
Celtic Croft
8451 Xerxes Ave N.
Brooklyn Park, MN 55444 763-569-4373
888-569-4373
Fax: 763-549-3583
sales@thecelticcroft.com
www.kilts-n-stuff.com

Scottish kilts, gifts and jewelry

President: Joseph Croft
Marketing Manager: Lorie Croft
Co-Owner: Joseph Croft
Co-Owner: Lorie Croft
Credit Cards: AMEX; MasterCard
Catalog Cost: Free
Catalog Circulation: Mailed 2 time(s) per year
Printing Information: in 4 colors
In Business: 8 years
Sales Volume: $500,000- 1 Million

1418 Choir Robes Online Choral Attire Catalog
Choir Robes Online
2203 West Oak Island Drive
Oak Island, NC 28465 910-619-7492
info@choirrobesonline.com
www.choirrobesonline.com

Robes

1419 Choir Robes Online Church Dresses Catalog
Choir Robes Online
2203 West Oak Island Drive
Oak Island, NC 28465 910-619-7492
info@choirrobesonline.com
www.choirrobesonline.com

Robes

1420 Choir Robes Online Church Wear Catalog
Choir Robes Online
2203 West Oak Island Drive
Oak Island, NC 28465 910-619-7492
info@choirrobesonline.com
www.choirrobesonline.com

Robes

1421 Choir Robes Online Qwick-Ship Catalog
Choir Robes Online
2203 West Oak Island Drive
Oak Island, NC 28465 910-619-7492
info@choirrobesonline.com
www.choirrobesonline.com

Robes

1422 Cloudveil
Cloudveil
830 Broad Street
Suite 3
Shrewsbury, NJ 7702 781-631-6157
866-785-3343
Fax: 781-631-5371
www.cloudveil.com

Outdoor, technical clothing and accessories for men, women, and children

President: Jim Reilly
Production Manager: Camron Burker
Credit Cards: AMEX; MasterCard
Catalog Cost: Free
Catalog Circulation: Mailed 4 time(s) per year
Printing Information: in 4 colors
Number of Employees: 34

1423 Coconut Telegraph
Margaritaville
424A Fleming Street
Key West, FL 33040-6529 305-296-9089
800-262-6835
Fax: 305-296-1084
info@margaritaville.com
www.margaritaville.com

Fun catalog of clothing and gifts for those who like Jimmy Buffet's Margaritaville

President: Jimmy Buffet
Executive Director: Diane Sutton
VP: Kevin Boucher
Buyers: Amy Jamison
Catalog Circulation: Mailed 5 time(s) per year
Printing Information: 20 pages on Glossy Stock
Binding: Folded
In Business: 26 years
Number of Employees: 28
Sales Volume: $1.5 Million

1424 Costumakers Zippers & Accessories
H.A. Kidd & Company Limited
5 Northline Road
Toronto, ON M4B-3P2 416-364-6451
800-387-1753
Fax: 888-236-8104
info1@hakidd.com
www.hakidd.com

Zippers and accessories

Marketing Manager: Lynda Macham
VP, Chief Operating Officer: Jim Thielen
Controller, Human Resources: Amir Mirza
Credit Cards: MasterCard
Catalog Cost: Free
Printing Information: 16 pages in 4 colors
In Business: 93 years
Sales Volume: $20MM to $50MM

1425 Costume Armour
Costume Armour, Inc.
2 Mill Street,Building 1
Suite 101
Cornwall, NY 12518-1265 845-534-9120
Fax: 845-534-8602
info@costumearmour.com
www.costumearmour.com

Custom made period armour, sculptures and props

President: Nino Novellino
nino@customearmour.com
Marketing Manager: Brian Wolfe
brian@customearmour.com
Production Manager: Michelle Truncale
michelle@customearmour.com
Printing Information: 8 pages in 2 colors on Glossy Stock
Press: Letterpress
Binding: Folded
In Business: 50 years
Number of Employees: 16
Sales Volume: $ 1-3 Million

1426 Cruisin USA/Bowlingshirt
Cruisin USA Inc
6262 Olive Blvd
St Louis, MO 63130-3300 314-426-4886
800-444-1685
Fax: 314-426-1713
sales@bowlingshirt.com
www.bowlingshirt.com

Old bowling shirts; embroidery, custom work, poodle skirts, saddle shoes, and custom screenprinting
President: Helene Spetner
Marketing Manager: Tim Coggeshall
Production Manager: Deb Roach
CEO: Alan Spetner
Credit Cards: AMEX; MasterCard
Catalog Cost: Free
Catalog Circulation: Mailed 1 time(s) per year to 2000
Printing Information: 12 pages
In Business: 30 years
Number of Employees: 22
Sales Volume: $ 2.4 Million

1427 Dancewear Solutions
Dancewear Solutions
6750 Manchester Avenue
St Louis, MO 63139 866-542-6500
Fax: 877-773-5175
info@dancewearsolutions.com
www.dancewearsolutions.com

Dancewear at a discount; Dance shoes, apparel and supplies
President: Selina Evans
Catalog Cost: Free
Printing Information: 131 pages in 4 colors on Glossy Stock
Binding: Perfect Bound

1428 Fright Catalog.com
Fright Catalog
45 Fernwood
Edison, NJ 08837 605-271-5062
888-925-0412
Fax: 732-862-1107

Halloween costumes, supplies and accessories
President: Mark Arvanigian
Marketing Manager: Kristine Malo
Production Manager: Nicole Apelian
Credit Cards: AMEX; MasterCard
In Business: 22 years
Sales Volume: Under $500,000

1429 GK Back to School Workout Essentials
Elite Sportswear LP
2136 N 13th Street
PO Box 16400
Reading, PA 19612-6400 610-921-1469
800-345-4087
Fax: 888-866-9884
info@gkelite.com
www.gkelite.com

Gymnastics and dance apparel
President: Dan Casciano
Production Manager: Alan Robezzoli
CEO: Sallie Weaver
Credit Cards: AMEX; MasterCard
Catalog Cost: Free
In Business: 30 years
Number of Employees: 250
Sales Volume: $15.4 Million

1430 GK Womens Competitive Catalog
Elite Sportswear LP
2136 N 13th Street
PO Box 16400
Reading, PA 19604-6400 610-921-1469
800-345-4087
Fax: 888-866-9884
info@gkelite.com
www.gkelite.com

Gymnastics leotards and dance clothes
President: Dan Casciano
Production Manager: Alan Robezzoli
CEO: Sallie Weaver
Credit Cards: AMEX; MasterCard
Catalog Cost: Free
In Business: 30 years
Number of Employees: 250
Sales Volume: $15 Million

1431 Galls
Galls
1340 Russell Cave Road
Lexington, KY 40505 866-673-7643
800-944-2557
Fax: 877-914-2557
international@galls.com
www.galls.com

Printing Information: 400 pages
In Business: 50+ years

1432 Holiday Collection
National Wildlife Federation
11100 Wildlife Center Drive
Reston, VA 20190 800-822-9919
Fax: 800-525-5562
www.nwf.org

Christmas cards, calendars and apparel with a wildlife theme
Chairman: Deborah Spalding
President: Collin O'Mara
CFO: Dulce Zormelo
CEO: Collin O'Mara
Credit Cards: AMEX; MasterCard; Visa
Catalog Cost: Free
Catalog Circulation: Mailed 6 time(s) per year to 20MM
Printing Information: 48 pages in 4 colors on Glossy Stock
Press: Web Press
Binding: Saddle Stitched
Mailing List Information: Names for rent
In Business: 63 years
Number of Employees: 350

1433 James Townsend & Son
James Townsend & Son
133 North First Street
PO Box 415
Pierceton, IN 46562 574-594-5852
800-338-1665
Fax: 574-594-5580
www.jas-townsend.Com

Speciality clothing
President: Jonathan Townsend
In Business: 35 years
Number of Employees: 26
Sales Volume: $ 3 Million

1434 Just For Kix
Just For Kix
7842 College Rd
Baxter, MN 56425 218-829-7107
800-762-3347
Fax: 218-829-7618
products@justforkix.com
www.Justforkix.Com

Dance wear supplies and apparel
President: Stephen Clough
Credit Cards: AMEX; MasterCard
Catalog Cost: Free
Printing Information: 14 pages
In Business: 30 years
Sales Volume: $ 3-5 Million

1435 Making It Big
Making It Big
525 Portal Street
Cotati, CA 94931-3023 707-795-1997
Fax: 707-795-4874
mib@makingitbig.com
www.makingitbig.com

Plus size clothing line

In Business: 31 years

1436 Marketplace: Handwork of India
Marketplace: Handwork of India
PO Box 365
New Windsor, MD 21776 847-328-4011
800-726-8905
Fax: 888-294-6376
customerservice@marketplaceindia.com
www.marketplaceindia.com

Women's fashions and accessories of India
President: Pushpika Freitas
Owner: Kimberly German
Credit Cards: MasterCard; Visa
Catalog Cost: Free
Catalog Circulation: Mailed 2 time(s) per year to 10000
Average Order Size: $90
Printing Information: 32 pages in 4 colors
Press: Web Press
Binding: Saddle Stitched
Mailing List Information: Names for rent
In Business: 26 years
Sales Volume: $ 1-3 Million

1437 Mon Cheri Bridals
David Tutera
1018 Whitehead Road Extension
Trenton, NJ 08638-2406 609-530-1900
Fax: 609-530-9500
custinfo@mcbridals.com
davidtuteraformoncheri.com

Wedding gowns and accessories
President: Stephen Lang
Owner: Yolanda Carita
Designer: David Tutera
Designer: Martin J. Thornburg
Credit Cards: AMEX; MasterCard; Visa
Catalog Cost: $20
Catalog Circulation: Mailed 2 time(s) per year to 25000
Printing Information: 60 pages in 4 colors
Binding: Folded
In Business: 24 years
Number of Employees: 65
Sales Volume: $ 9.3 Million

1438 Omni Cheer
Omni Cheer
12375 World Trade Drive
San Diego, CA 92128 800-299-7822
Fax: 858-613-1976
customerservice@omnicheer.com
www.omnicheer.com

Cheerleading apparel and accessories

1439 Online Dancewear
Online Dancewear
3904 Central Avenue
Suite A, PMB 118
Cheyenne, WY 82001-1327 800-410-1556
Fax: 800-411-4763
feedback@onlinedancewear.com

Dance apparel and accessories
Production Manager: Clarke Milner
Credit Cards: AMEX; MasterCard
Catalog Cost: Free

1440 Opening Night
Concert Dress
436 Godwin Drive
Monroeville, AL 36460 215-575-5197
Fax: 251-575-3463
angie@concertdress.com
www.concertdress.com

Concert dress clothes, organists shoes
President: Carol Carlson
Credit Cards: AMEX; MasterCard; Visa
Catalog Circulation: Mailed 1 time(s) per year
Average Order Size: $50
Printing Information: in 4 colors on Glossy Stock
Press: Sheetfed Press

Binding: Folded
Number of Employees: 4

1441 Our Designs

Our Designs, Inc.
314 E. McLoughlin Blvd.
Suite 200
Vancouver, WA 98663   360-567-2530
800-382-5252
Fax: 800-347-3367
sales@ourdesigns.com
www.ourdesigns.com

Great gifts for your favorite EMT's, firefighters, paramedics

President: Tony Johnson
Founder: Ralph Daugherty
Credit Cards: AMEX; MasterCard
Catalog Cost: Free
Printing Information: 56 pages in 4 colors on Glossy Stock
Press: Web Press
Binding: Saddle Stitched
Mailing List Information: Names for rent
List Manager: Tony Johnson
In Business: 38 years
Number of Employees: 25
Sales Volume: $ 3 Million

1442 Peace Frogs

Peace Frogs
7546 John Clayton Memorial Highway
Gloucester, VA 23061   804-695-1314
800-447-3223
info@peacefrogs.com
www.peacefrogs.com

Clothing, toys, computer accessories, more

President: Catesby Jones
Marketing Manager: Spotfwood Jones
Production Manager: Nicole Baker
Credit Cards: AMEX; MasterCard; Visa
Printing Information: 31 pages in 7 colors on Newsprint
Binding: Saddle Stitched
Mailing List Information: Names for rent
In Business: 21 years

1443 ShopIrish

Shop Irish
PO Box 8300
Little Rock, AR 72222   866-851-7918
866-851-7916
Fax: 877-213-3660
www.shopirish.com

Irish clothing, gifts, jewelry, accessories, home and garden, kitchen items and Irish books and records

Credit Cards: AMEX; MasterCard

1444 Sleeping Indian Designs

PO Box 8517
355 S. Millward
Jackson, WY 83002-8517   307-739-9802
800-334-5457
Fax: 307-739-9804

Camouflage clothing for hunting

President: Ted Ranck
Vice President: Steven Ranck
Credit Cards: AMEX; MasterCard; Visa
Catalog Cost: Free
Catalog Circulation: Mailed 1 time(s) per year
Printing Information: 16 pages in 4 colors
Binding: Saddle Stitched
Number of Employees: 5
Sales Volume: $500,000- 1 Million

1445 Spec-L

Spec-L, Inc.
849 Performance Drive
Stockton, CA 95206   209-465-1981
800-445-1981
Fax: 888-709-8709

Adaptive clothing and accessories

President: Roger Fortun
CFO: Betty Fortun
Manager: Jemmie Minor
Credit Cards: AMEX; MasterCard; Visa
Catalog Cost: Free
Printing Information: 50 pages in 4 colors on Glossy Stock
Binding: Saddle Stitched
In Business: 30+ years
Number of Employees: 7
Sales Volume: $680,000

1446 Stone River Outfitters

Stone Rivers Outfitters, LLC
132 Bedford Center Rd
Unit C
Bedford, NH 03110-5457   603-472-3191
800-331-8558
Fax: 603-472-3105
sales@stoneriveroutfitters.com
www.stoneriveroutfitters.com

Fly fishing, fly tying supplies and equipment

President: Dan Fitzgerald
dan@stoneriveroutfitters.com
Credit Cards: AMEX; MasterCard; Visa
Catalog Cost: Free
Catalog Circulation: Mailed 1 time(s) per year
Average Order Size: $15
Printing Information: in 4 colors on Glossy Stock
Binding: Folded
In Business: 10 years
Sales Volume: $ 1-3 Million

1447 Stumps Spirit & Homecoming

Stumps
One Party Place
PO Box 305
South Whitley, IN 46787   800-348-5084
Fax: 260-723-6976
csr@stumpsparty.com
www.stumpsparty.com

Cheer gear and homecoming gear and accessories

President: Shep Moyle
Co-owner: Wendy Moyle
Catalog Cost: Free
Printing Information: 500 pages in 4 colors
In Business: 89 years

1448 Team Cheer

Team Cheer
133 Main Street
Suite 1
Geneseo, NY 14454-1242   585-243-0841
800-350-1562
Fax: 877-243-5268
www.teamcheer.com

Cheerleading clothes and accessories

President: Randy Cofield
VP: Linda Cofield
Territory Manager: Tammy Klemanski
tammy.klemanski@athleticausa.com
Territory Manager: Sue Krieger
sue.krieger@athleticausa.com
Credit Cards: AMEX; MasterCard; Visa
Printing Information: 104 pages
In Business: 24 years
Number of Employees: 25
Sales Volume: $ 4.6 Million

1449 Tibet Collection

Tibet Collection
150 Pleasant St # 320
Easthampton, MA 01027-1547   413-527-4500
800-318-5857
Fax: 413-527-6300
info@tibetcollection.com
www.tibetcollection.Com

Designs from Tibet

President: Mac McOy
Marketing Manager: Tomeka Davis
Catalog Cost: Free

In Business: 64 years
Sales Volume: Under $500,000

1450 Tuxedos & Blazers

Chillbert & Company LLC
1001 Fourth Avenue
Coraopolis, PA 15108   412-264-3700
800-289-2889
Fax: 412-262-2622
info@chilbert.com
www.chilbert.com

Formalwear, blazers, tuxedos and suits

President: Ray Petronio
Owner: Guy Tucci
Credit Cards: AMEX; MasterCard; Visa
Catalog Cost: Free
Printing Information: 32 pages in 4 colors on Glossy Stock
Press: Web Press
Binding: Saddle Stitched
In Business: 35 years
Number of Employees: 3
Sales Volume: $5,00,000

Fitness & Swimwear

1451 Activa Sports

Road Runner Sports
5549 Copley Dr
San Diego, CA 92111-7904   858-636-7652
800-743-3206
Fax: 800-453-5443
listening@roadrunnersports.com
www.roadrunnersports.com

Women's fitness, sportswear, and gear

President: Debra Christal
Credit Cards: AMEX; MasterCard
In Business: 32 years
Number of Employees: 800

1452 Adolph Kiefer & Associates

Adolph Kiefer & Associates Inc
1700 Kiefer Dr
Zion, IL 60099-4093   847-872-8866
800-323-4071
Fax: 847-746-8888
info@kiefer.com
www.kiefer.com

Swimming supplies and training equipment

President: Adolph Kiefer
Catalog Cost: Free
Catalog Circulation: Mailed 2 time(s) per year
Printing Information: 40 pages in 4 colors on Glossy Stock
Press: Web Press
Binding: Saddle Stitched
In Business: 68 years
Number of Employees: 45
Sales Volume: $15 Million

1453 As We Change

As We Change
250 City Center
Oshkosh, WI 54901   855-202-7392
Fax: 888-534-8469
help@aswechange.com
www.aswechange.com

Nutrition, beauty, skin care, exercise, personal care and lifestyle products for women ages 40-50+ years.

Catalog Cost: Free
In Business: 20 years

1454 Athleta

Athleta
1450 Technology Lane
Suite 150
Petaluma, CA 94954   614-744-3913
877-328-4538
www.athleta.gap.com/?

Athletic clothing and accessories for women including jackets and outerwear, pants and bottoms, skirts and dresses and footwear

President: Joseph E Teno
Marketing Manager: John Monteleone
Human Resources Director: Mona Patel
Credit Cards: AMEX; MasterCard
Catalog Cost: Free
Catalog Circulation: Mailed 1 time(s) per year
Printing Information: 24 pages
In Business: 16 years
Number of Employees: 110
Sales Volume: $6.7 MM

1455 Blue Sky Swimwear

Blue Sky Swimwear
729 E International Speedway Blvd.
Daytona Beach, FL 32118-4555   386-255-2590
800-799-6445
Fax: 386-253-5938
sales@blueskyswimwear.com
www.blueskyswimwear.com

Line of womens swimwear

President: Linda Kaplan
Catalog Cost: Free
Printing Information: 47 pages
Sales Volume: $500,000- 1 Million

1456 California Crazee Wear

California Crazee Wear
37321 Ski Side Ave.
Prairieville, LA 70769   225-673-2957
800-888-4439
Fax: 225-313-4180
info@crazeewear.com
www.crazeewear.com

Clothes and accessories

1457 Carushka Bodywear

Carushka Bodywear
PO Box 4835
Valley Village, CA 91617   818-643-3708
844-238-6022
Fax: 818-574-6851
contactus@carushka.com
www.carushka.com

Women's exercise clothing and sportswear

VP: Kristine Kreska
kristine@carushka.com
Designer: Carushka Jarecka
carushka@carushka.com
Credit Cards: AMEX; MasterCard
Catalog Cost: $5
Catalog Circulation: Mailed 12 time(s) per year to 30000
Average Order Size: $130
Printing Information: 32 pages in 4 colors
In Business: 36 years
Sales Volume: $ 3-5 Million

1458 Coolibar

Coolibar, Inc.
2401 Edgewood Avenue South
Suite 400
Minneapolis, MN 55426-2860   952-922-1445
800-926-6509
Fax: 952-922-1455
service@coolibar.com
www.coolibar.com

Line of sun protective clothes, sun hats, sun protective, swimwear, sunglasses, umbrellas, sunscreens and sunblock

President: Ann Danaher
CFO: Dennis Thalhuber
Marketing Manager: Alan Higley
CEO: Donna Avery
Printing Information: 48 pages
In Business: 14 years
Number of Employees: 15
Sales Volume: $ 1-3 Million

1459 Cyberswim

Cyberswim, Inc.
519 George Street
Pen Argyl, PA 18072   800-291-2943
Fax: 610-863-5052
www.cyberswim.com

Direct supplier of Miraclesuit swimwear

Catalog Cost: Free
In Business: 16 years

1460 Gaiam Living

Gaiam
833 W. South Boulder Road
P.O. Box 3095
Louisville, CO 80027-2452   303-222-3719
877-989-6321
Fax: 303-222-3750
customerservice@gaiam.com
www.gaiam.com

Organic/natural fiber bedding, bath and clothing; energy-saving products; earth-friendly cleaners; air & water filters; eco-conscious furnishings; fair trade decor & jewelry; natural wellness tools

President: Lynn Powers
CFO: Janet Mathews
CEO: Jirka Rysavy
Manager: Kraig Corbin
Director of Customer Relations: Christopher Fisher
Credit Cards: AMEX; MasterCard; Visa
Catalog Cost: Free
Catalog Circulation: Mailed 4 time(s) per year
Printing Information: in 4 colors
In Business: 20 years

1461 Gopher Sports Equipment

Gopher Sports Equipment
2525 Lemond Street SW
P.O. Box 998
Owatonna, MN 55060-998   507-451-7470
800-533-0446
Fax: 800-451-4855
www.gophersport.com

Physical education, recreation and athletic products

President: Joel Jennings
Marketing Manager: Pam Haas
Production Manager: Rhonda Studer
Buyers: Bill Disher, Sports Equipment
Credit Cards: AMEX; MasterCard
Catalog Cost: Free
Catalog Circulation: Mailed 2 time(s) per year to 40000
Printing Information: 180 pages in 4 colors on Glossy Stock
Press: Web Press
Binding: Perfect Bound
In Business: 65 years
Number of Employees: 180
Sales Volume: $ 10 Million

1462 Gymnastic Solutions

Dancewear Solutions
6750 Manchester Avenue
St. Louis, MO 63139   866-542-6500
866-542-6500
Fax: 877-773-5175
info@dancewearsolutions.com
www.dancewearsolutions.com

Exercise and dancewear; tops, pants, shorts, dresses, skirts, unitards, tights, shoes and accessories

Catalog Cost: Free
Printing Information: in 4 colors
In Business: 50 years

1463 HYDRO-FIT Gear

Hydro-Fit, Inc
160 Madison St
Eugene, OR 97402-5031   541-484-4361
800-346-7295
Fax: 541-484-1443
info@hydrofit.com
www.hydrofit.com

Water fitness and therapy gear, shoes, equipment, accessories, clothing and teaching/training tools

Chairman: David Sarett
President: Craig Stuart
Director: Craig Stuart
Catalog Circulation: Mailed 1 time(s) per year
In Business: 25 years
Number of Employees: 12
Sales Volume: $ 1.7 Million

1464 Hugger Mugger

Hugger-Mugger Yoga Products
1190 South Pioneer Road
Salt Lake City, UT 84104   801-268-9642
800-473-4888
Fax: 801-268-2629
comments@huggermugger.com
www.huggermugger.com

Products and gear for the mind, body and spirit

President: Thomas Chamberlain
Founder: Sarah Chambers
Credit Cards: MasterCard
Catalog Cost: Free
In Business: 28 years
Number of Employees: 30
Sales Volume: $ 3 Million

1465 Jacques Moret Bodywear

The Moret Group
1411 Broadway
8th Floor
New York, NY 10018-7702   212-354-2400
800-441-1999
Fax: 212-354-5544
info@moret.com
www.moret.com

Bodywear for men, women and children

President: Joseph Harary
CFO: Irwin Luxembourg
Credit Cards: AMEX; MasterCard; Visa
Catalog Circulation: Mailed 4 time(s) per year
Printing Information: 36 pages in 4 colors on Glossy Stock
Press: Web Press
Binding: Saddle Stitched
In Business: 40 years
Number of Employees: 250
Sales Volume: $20MM to $50MM

1466 Jazzertogs

Jazzercise, Inc.
2460 Impala Drive
Carlsbad, CA 92010-7226   760-476-1750
800-348-4748
Fax: 760-602-7180
jazzertogs@jazzercise.com
www.Jazzercise.com

World-wide aerobic, dance-fitness apparel, accessories and fitness products

President: Shanna Missett Nelson
CFO: Sally Baldridge
CEO: Judi Sheppard Missett
Director of Merchandising: Joan Marie Wallace
Director of Training: Sarah Buehler
Buyers: Susan Hammer, Fitness
Credit Cards: AMEX; MasterCard; Visa
Catalog Cost: Free
Catalog Circulation: Mailed 10 time(s) per year
Average Order Size: $75
Printing Information: 16 pages in 4 colors on Glossy Stock

Press: Web Press
Binding: Saddle Stitched
Mailing List Information: Names for rent
3599 Cahuenga Blvd. W-4th Floor
Los Angeles, CA 90068
In Business: 45 years
Number of Employees: 100
Sales Volume: $6.4 Million

1467 Just for Kix
Just For Kix
7842 College Rd
Baxter, MN 56425
218-829-7107
800-762-3347
Fax: 218-829-7618
products@justforkix.com
www.justforkix.com

Dancewear, shoes and accessories

President: Stephen Clough
Marketing Manager: Robert Clough
Co-owner: Cindy Clough
Credit Cards: AMEX; MasterCard; Visa
Catalog Cost: Free
Printing Information: 14 pages
In Business: 30 years
Number of Employees: 12
Sales Volume: $ 3-5 Million

1468 Little G.I. Joe's Military Surplus
Little G.I. Joe's Miltary Surplus
83 Hunts Neck Rd.
Poquoson, VA 23662
757-852-9200
877-344-5637
GIJOESINC@AOL.COM
www.gijoesmilitarysurplus.com

Military surplus clothing

Credit Cards: AMEX; MasterCard; Visa
Catalog Cost: $3.95
Printing Information: 298 pages

1469 NiteLite
NiteLite
P.O. Box 8300
Little Rock, AR 72222
479-754-5540
800-332-6968
Fax: 479-754-5669
www.huntsmart.com

1470 Otomix
Otomix
7585 Commercial Way Suite E
Henderson, NV 89011
800-597-5425
800-444-6620
Fax: 310-215-6105
otomix3@aol.com

Printing Information: 26 pages

1471 Prevail Sport
Prevail Sport
PO Box 93099
Atlanta, GA 30377
404-892-6576
Fax: 404-815-3113
customercare@prevailsport.com
www.prevailsport.com

Clothing

1472 ProMotion Wetsuits
ProMotion Wetsuits
416 Cascade Ave
Hood River, OR 97031-2023
541-386-3278
800-798-1628
promo@wetsuit.com
www.wetsuit.com

Wetsuits for triathalons

President: Dana Love
Credit Cards: AMEX; MasterCard
In Business: 30 years
Number of Employees: 6
Sales Volume: $500,000- 1 Million

1473 Sunup/Sundown
Sunup Sowndown
PO Box 11899
Fort Lauderdale, FL 33339
954-801-2883
800-926-8081
Fax: 954-564-1515
customer@sunupsundown.com

Men's and women's exotic swimsuits and other beachwear including wrap skirts and dresses

President: Thomas Farley
Credit Cards: AMEX; MasterCard; Visa
Catalog Circulation: Mailed 4 time(s) per year to 50000
Printing Information: 16 pages in 4 colors on Glossy Stock
Press: Web Press
Binding: Saddle Stitched
Mailing List Information: Names for rent
List Company: TCI
North Hollywood, CA
In Business: 38 years
Number of Employees: 2
Sales Volume: $ 500,000- 1 Million

1474 UnderGear
Undergear
455 Park Plaza Drive
La Crosse, WI 54601
717-633-3413
800-853-8555
Fax: 717-633-3214
service@undergear.com
www.undergear.com

Men's fitnesswear and swimsuits

Chairman: Alan Quasha
President: Don Wilson
Credit Cards: AMEX; MasterCard; Visa
Catalog Cost: Free
Catalog Circulation: Mailed 4 time(s) per year
Printing Information: 45 pages in 4 colors on Glossy Stock
Binding: Saddle Stitched
Number of Employees: 200

1475 Venus
Venus
11711 Marco Beach Drive
Jacksonville, FL 32224-7615
904-997-4000
888-782-2224
Fax: 800-648-0411
email@venus.com
www.venus.com

Line of womens swimwear, clothing, shoes, jewelry and accessories

President: Daryle Scott
CEO: Roger Reifensnyder
Credit Cards: MasterCard; Visa
Catalog Cost: $5
Catalog Circulation: Mailed 3 time(s) per year
Printing Information: 100 pages in 4 colors on Glossy Stock
Press: Web Press
Binding: Saddle Stitched
Mailing List Information: Names for rent
In Business: 33 years
Sales Volume: $ 6.6 Million

1476 Y Catalog
The Y Catalog
8325 Linda Vista Av
Atascadero, CA 93422
805-460-6342
Fax: 310-460-1719
infotheYcatalog@gmail.com
www.theycatalog.com

Yoga, eco-minded clothing, accessories, apparel, equipment and health products

President: Keri Lassalle
Credit Cards: AMEX; MasterCard
Catalog Circulation: Mailed 4 time(s) per year to 200M
Average Order Size: $80
Printing Information: 44 pages

1477 Allett
Allett
302 Washington Street #152
San Diego, CA 92103
800-642-2226
sales@allett.com
www.all-ett.com

Wallets

In Business: 20 years

1478 Bates Leathers
Bates Leathers
3671 Industry Ave
Unit C5
Lakewood, CA 90712
562-426-8668
Fax: 562-426-4001
info@batesleathers.com
www.batesleathers.Com

Leather clothing accessories including hats and gloves

President: Dawn Grindle
Catalog Cost: $5
Catalog Circulation: Mailed 1 time(s) per year
Printing Information: 8 pages in 1 color on Glossy Stock
Binding: Saddle Stitched
Mailing List Information: Names for rent
In Business: 50 years
Number of Employees: 15
Sales Volume: $ 3-5 Million

1479 Budd Leather Company
Budd Leather Company
699 Callowhill Rd.
Perkasie, PA 18944
215-258-2833
800-332-BUDD
Fax: 215-258-2810
info@buddleather.com
www.buddleather.com

Leather accessories and gifts

President: Charles Brous
In Business: 71 years
Number of Employees: 3

1480 Col. Littleton
Col. Littleton
755 Abernathy Rd.
Lynnville, TN 38472
800-842-4075
www.colonellittleton.com

In Business: 27 years

1481 Fabulous-Furs
Donna Salyers Fabulous-Furs
25 West Robbins Street
Covington, KY 41011-3005
859-291-3300
800-848-4650
custserv@fabulousfurs.com
www.fabulousfurs.com

Faux fur coats, hats, gloves/muffs, handbags, luggage, throws, rugs, accessories, jewelry,

President: Earl Holliman
VP: Kevin Nickell
Credit Cards: AMEX; MasterCard
Catalog Cost: Free
Catalog Circulation: Mailed 3 time(s) per year to 300M
Average Order Size: $100
Printing Information: 64 pages in 4 colors on Glossy Stock
Press: Web Press
Binding: Saddle Stitched
In Business: 26 years
Number of Employees: 40
Sales Volume: $ 10 Million

1482 La Pelleterie
La Pelleterie
PO Box 127
Arrow Rock, MO 65320   660-837-3261
info@LaPelleterie.com
www.lapelleterie.com

Custom made 18th and 19th century clothing, leather coats, moccasins, gun cases and accessories

President: Karalee Tearney
Credit Cards: MasterCard; Visa
Catalog Cost: $5
Catalog Circulation: Mailed 1 time(s) per year
Printing Information: 30 pages in 1 color on Matte Stock
Binding: Saddle Stitched
In Business: 19 years
Number of Employees: 2
Sales Volume: $83,000

1483 Leather Coats Etc
Leather Coats Etc
1700 Burlington Ave
Kewanee, IL 61443-3278   800-466-6663
Fax: 309-852-0690
customerservice@leathercoatsetc.com
www.leathercoatsetc.com

Women's and men's leather coats and accessories

President: Sharyn Russell
Credit Cards: AMEX; MasterCard; Visa
Catalog Cost: Free
Printing Information: 55 pages in 4 colors on Glossy Stock
Binding: Saddle Stitched
In Business: 80 years
Number of Employees: 200

1484 Leather Factory
Tandy Leather Factory, Inc.
1900 SE Loop 820
Fort Worth, TX 76140-4388   877-532-8437
tlfhelp@tandyleather.com
www.tandyleatherfactory.com

Offers retail and wholesale pricing on quality leather, and leathercraft supplies to individuals, institutions and businesses

President: Jon Thompson
CFO: Shannon Greene
Marketing Manager: Worth Jackson
Credit Cards: MasterCard
Catalog Cost: Free
Catalog Circulation: Mailed 6 time(s) per year to 178M
Printing Information: 188 pages in 2 colors on Matte Stock
Press: Sheetfed Press
Binding: Saddle Stitched
Mailing List Information: Names for rent
In Business: 37 years
Number of Employees: 466
Sales Volume: $60 Million

1485 Leather Unlimited
Leather Unlimited
7155 Hwy B
PO Box L
Belgium, WI 53004-911   920-994-9464
800-993-2889
Fax: 920-994-4099
service@leatherunltd.Com
www.leatherunltd.Com

Leather hides, leather goods, cycle accessories, belts, buckles, hardware, kits, lace, feathers, black powder, Indianlore

President: Joseph M O'Conell
CFO: Bruce Comdohr
Buyers: Diane Keller
Credit Cards: AMEX; MasterCard; Visa
Catalog Cost: $5
Catalog Circulation: Mailed 4 time(s) per year to 250
Average Order Size: $75
Printing Information: 100 pages in 2 colors on

Matte Stock
Press: Web Press
Binding: Saddle Stitched
Mailing List Information: Names for rent
List Company: The Other List Company
In Business: 45 years
Number of Employees: 12
Sales Volume: $ 500,000- 1 Million

1486 Maida's Belts and Buckles
Maida's Belts and Buckles
5727 Westheimer Rd
Suite K
Houston, TX 77057   713-524-2800
800-785-6036
www.maidasbelts.com

Belts, buckles

Printing Information: 39 pages

1487 Moore & Giles
Moore & Giles
1081 Tannery Row
PO Box 670
Forest, VA 24551   434-846-5281
800-737-0169
Fax: 434-846-1404
www.mooreandgiles.com

Leather bags and accessories

In Business: 82 years

1488 Trask
Trask
1415 Murfreesboro Road
Suite 190
Nashville, TN 37217   800-298-8253
traskcustomerservice@trask.com
www.trask.com

1489 Uber
Century Leather Products
308 Adams Ave
Owatonna, MN 55060   507-451-0762
Fax: 507-444-0727
www.clpuber.com

Deerskin clothing and accessories

President: Harley A. Uber
Director: Jared Rinerson
Credit Cards: AMEX; MasterCard; Visa
Catalog Circulation: Mailed 4 time(s) per year
Printing Information: 22 pages in 1 color on Newsprint
Binding: Saddle Stitched
In Business: 150 years
Number of Employees: 12
Sales Volume: $ 1-3 Million

Lingerie & Undergarments

1490 Blair Women's
Blair
220 Hickory St.
Warren, PA 16366   800-821-5744
www.blair.com

Full line of women's clothing and footwear.

President: Marisa Smith
Catalog Cost: Free
Printing Information: in 4 colors
In Business: 106 years
Number of Employees: 2000
Sales Volume: $1 Billion

1491 Bra Smyth
Bra Smyth
10300 Sanden Dr
Suite 100
Dallas, TX 75238   800-272-9466
Fax: 214-553-0210
info@brasmyth.com
www.brasmyth.com

Fine designer lingerie, intimate and other apparel

President: Becky Simon
Credit Cards: AMEX; MasterCard
Catalog Circulation: Mailed 4 time(s) per year
In Business: 22 years

1492 Chock Catalog.com
Chock Catalog Corp
3011 Avenue J
Brooklyn, NY 11210-1315   718-252-4340
800-222-0020
Fax: 212-941-6787
questions@chockcatalog.com
www.chockcatalog.com

Line of underwear, hosiery and sleepwear for men women and children

President: Josh Frankel
CEO: Josh Frankel
In Business: 94 years

1493 Decent Exposures
Decent Exposures
12554 Lake City Way NE
Seattle, WA 98125   206-364-4540
800-524-4949
info@decentexposures.com
decentexposures.com

Everyday wear, bras, underwear, swimwear, activewear etc.

President: Pat Marcus
In Business: 15+ years

1494 Flirt
Flirt
2346 E Pacifica Pl
Rancho Dominguez, CA 90220   877-825-2860

Women's apparel and lingerie

President: Ronald Alan Abeles
VP: Dan Deyoung
Buyers: Ronald Alan Abales
Credit Cards: AMEX; MasterCard
Catalog Cost: $2
Catalog Circulation: Mailed 5 time(s) per year
Average Order Size: $10
Printing Information: 40 pages in 4 colors on Glossy Stock
Press: Web Press
Binding: Saddle Stitched
Mailing List Information: Names for rent
In Business: 23 years
Number of Employees: 6
Sales Volume: $4 million

1495 Four Corners Direct
Four Corners Direct
8520 S. Tamiami Trail
PO Box 4800
Sarasota, FL 34230-4800   800-560-6100
800-550-5700
www.fourcorners.com

Electronic products, health and beauty items, clothes and shoes

1496 Fullbeauty
Fullbeauty.com
P.O. Box 8360
Indianapolis, IN 46283-8360   915-225-4970
800-400-4481
Fax: 800-528-5152
www.fullbeauty.com

Bras, undergarments, sleepwear, and swimwear for plus size women

Catalog Cost: Free

1497 Jodee Post-Mastectomy Fashions Catalog
Jodee Inc.
3100 N 29th Avenue
Hollywood, FL 33020   800-932-4115
www.jcpenney-jodee.com

Post masectomy fashions

1498 Just My Size
Just My Size
PO Box 748
Rural Hall, NC 27098-748   800-522-9567
                                    Fax: 800-848-1237
                                 www.justmysize.com

Plus size fashions and intimates for women sizes 14W - 40W
President: William Nictakis
Credit Cards: AMEX; MasterCard; Visa
Catalog Cost: Free
Catalog Circulation: Mailed 4 time(s) per year
Printing Information: 65 pages in 4 colors on Glossy Stock
Press: Web Press
Binding: Saddle Stitched
In Business: 25 years

1499 Lady Grace
Lady Grace
5 Commonwealth Avenue
Unit 1
Woodburn, MA 01801-5523   877-381-4629
                                   800-922-0504
                                  Fax: 800-437-9123
                              info@ladygrace.com
                                 www.ladygrace.com

Camisoles, slips, loungewear, sleepwear and undergarments
President: Steven Barsen
Credit Cards: AMEX; MasterCard; Visa
Catalog Cost: Free
Catalog Circulation: Mailed 8 time(s) per year
Average Order Size: $65
Printing Information: 52 pages in 1 color
Press: Web Press
Binding: Saddle Stitched
Mailing List Information: Names for rent
In Business: 77 years
Number of Employees: 130

1500 Marisota
Marisota
777 South State Road 7
Margate, FL 33068   855-308-6282
                            inquiries@Marisota.com
                                 www.marisota.com

Clothing, lingerie, footwear, apparel, and swimwear
Catalog Cost: Free
In Business: 7 years

1501 National Wholesale Co., Inc.
National, Inc.
400 National Blvd.
Lexington, NC 27294   336-248-5904
                                  800-433-0580
                                 Fax: 336-249-9326
                     customerservice@shopnational.com
                               www.shopnational.Com

Ladies' hoisery, lingerie and apparel
President: Lynda Smith Swann
Marketing Manager: Betty Allred
Credit Cards: AMEX; MasterCard; Visa
Catalog Cost: Free
Catalog Circulation: Mailed 6 time(s) per year
Average Order Size: $55
Printing Information: 80 pages in 4 colors on Glossy Stock
Press: Web Press
Binding: Saddle Stitched
Mailing List Information: Names for rent
In Business: 63 years
Number of Employees: 140
Sales Volume: $ 34 Million

1502 Pajamagram
The PajamaGram Company
6655 Shelburne Road
Shelburne, VT 05482-6500   888-518-2327
                                  800-448-3757
                                 Fax: 802-985-1311
                               www.pajamagram.com

Luxurious pajamas for women, men and children
President: Elisabeth Robert
Catalog Cost: Free
Catalog Circulation: Mailed 4 time(s) per year to 57000
Average Order Size: $94
Printing Information: 63 pages in 4 colors on Glossy Stock
Binding: Saddle Stitched
In Business: 7 years
Sales Volume: $ 50-100 Million

1503 Schweitzer Nightwear
Schweitzer Linen
1053 Lexington Avenue
New York, NY 10021   212-570-0236
                                  800-554-6367
                                 Fax: 212-737-6328
                             www.schweitzerlinen.Com

Cashmere robes, intimates, jackets, long gowns, nite shirts
President: Elena Schweitzer
Manager: Ileana Jovica
Credit Cards: AMEX; MasterCard
Catalog Cost: $2
Printing Information: 32 pages in 3 colors on Glossy Stock
Press: Web Press
Binding: Saddle Stitched
In Business: 40 years
Number of Employees: 8
Sales Volume: $ 1-3 Million

1504 Soma
Soma
11215 Metro Parkway
Fort Myers, FL 33966   239-277-6200
                                  866-768-7662
                          customerservice@soma.com
                                   www.soma.com

Clothing for women
Printing Information: 24 pages

1505 Thai Silks
Thai Silks
1959 Leghorn St
Mountain View, CA 94043-2813   650-948-8611
                                  800-722-7455
                                 Fax: 650-948-3426
                              silks@thaisilks.com
                                 www.thaisilks.Com

Silk, fabric, lingerie and pre-hemmed scarves
President: Rosi Valqui
Owner: Deanne Shute
Buyers: Mary Carter
Credit Cards: AMEX; MasterCard
Catalog Circulation: to 60M
Average Order Size: $100
Printing Information: 5 pages in 2 colors on Matte Stock
Binding: Folded
In Business: 51 years
Number of Employees: 12
Sales Volume: $ 1-3 Million

1506 Wickers America Catalog
Wickers America
340 Veterans Memorial Hwy # 1
Commack, NY 11725-4368   631-543-1700
                                  800-648-7024
                                 Fax: 631-543-1378
                              inquiry@wickers.com
                                 www.Wickers.Com

All weather underwear for men and women
President: Anthony Mazzenga
Marketing Manager: Andrew Long
VP: Diane Basso
Catalog Cost: Free
Mailing List Information: Names for rent
In Business: 30 years

Number of Employees: 9
Sales Volume: $ 1.2 Million

1507 Winter Silks Catalog
Winter Silks
7075 Flying Cloud Drive
Eden Prairie, MN 55344   800-718-3687
                              www.wintersilks.blair.com

Silk ready-to-wear apparel, intimate wear
President: Steve Nave
CFO: Pete Michielutti
EVP, COO, & Chief Digital Officer: Vince Jones
EVP & President of Credit Services: Jim Slavik
Credit Cards: AMEX; MasterCard; Visa
Catalog Circulation: Mailed 12 time(s) per year to 18000
Printing Information: 52 pages in 4 colors on Glossy Stock
Binding: Folded
Mailing List Information: Names for rent
Will Trade Names: Yes
In Business: 38 years
Number of Employees: 150
Sales Volume: $ 3-5 Million

Maternity

1508 Babystyle
Right Start
2001 N Sepulveda Blvd
Manhattan Beach, CA 90266   310-939-1147
                                  888-856-8004
                                 www.rightstart.com

Specialty maternity and baby clothing, gifts and toys
President: Laurie McCartney
Credit Cards: AMEX; MasterCard
Catalog Cost: Free
Catalog Circulation: Mailed 4 time(s) per year to 300M
Average Order Size: $100
Printing Information: 48 pages in 4 colors
In Business: 29 years

1509 Eve Alexander
Eve Alexander
P.O. Box 906
Duluth, GA 30096   305-433-4550
                             evealexandernursing.com

Maternity/nursing lingerie

1510 Fit Maternity & Beyond
Fit Maternity & Beyond
5122 Lake Shastina Drive
Weed, CA 96094   530-313-5138
                                  888-961-9100
                                 Fax: 530-313-5138
                              info@fitmaternity.com
                                www.fitmaternity.com

Exercise clothing for expectant mothers; maternity unitards, jackets, maternity bras, sport bras and sport nursing bras, shorts, swimwear and skin care products
President: Laurie Bagley
LaurieBagley.com
Accountant: Mike Karseboom

1511 Garnet Hill
Garnet Hill Inc
231 Main Street
Franconia, NH 03580   603-823-5545
                                  800-870-3513
                                 Fax: 888-842-9696
                                 www.garnethill.com

Quality natural fabric baby clothing and linens, maternity clothes
President: Russ Gaitskill
CFO: Brian Gowen
Buyers: Diane Brush
Credit Cards: AMEX; MasterCard

Catalog Cost: Free
Catalog Circulation: Mailed 7 time(s) per year
Average Order Size: $190
Printing Information: 120 pages in 4 colors on Glossy Stock
Press: Web Press
Binding: Saddle Stitched
Mailing List Information: Names for rent
In Business: 41 years
Number of Employees: 175
Sales Volume: $ 11 Million

1512 Motherwear
Motherwear International, Inc.
110 Lyman Street
Suite L 109
Holyoke, MA 01040   413-536-3569
                         800-950-2500
                    Fax: 413-532-4058
customerservice@motherwear.com
www.motherwear.com

Line of products and clothing for nursing moms

President: Tom Poalsse
CEO: Jeanne Taylor
In Business: 30 years
Sales Volume: Under $500,000

1513 Support Hose Store
Support House Store
906 South Jefferson St
Suite 100
Amarillo, TX 79101-4632   800-515-4271
                             800-515-4271
                        Fax: 888-235-8257
customerservice@supporthosestore.com
www.supporthosestore.com

Support stockings by Jobst, Sigvaris and Mediven

President: Vanda Lancour
CFO: Rod Lancour
Credit Cards: AMEX; MasterCard
Catalog Cost: Free
In Business: 10 years
Number of Employees: 10
Sales Volume: $ 1-3 Million

Menswear

1514 Apparel World
Sweet Company
4407 N. Beltwood Parkway
Suite 104
Dallas, TX 75244   214-887-8999
                        800-397-3086
                   Fax: 972-980-8493
myjumpsuits@aol.com
www.myjumpsuit.com

Line of mens jumpsuits, warmups, shirts, jackets and pants

President: Harold Sweet
Marketing Manager: Alan Sweet
Production Manager: Betty Chow
Credit Cards: AMEX; MasterCard; Visa
Catalog Circulation: to 80000
Printing Information: 12 pages on Glossy Stock
Press: Letterpress
Mailing List Information: Names for rent
In Business: 91 years
Number of Employees: 15
Sales Volume: $1.5 Million

1515 Bachrach
Bachrach
323 W. 39th Street
11th Floor
New York, NY 10018-9340   877-522-2472
contact@bachrach.com
www.bachrach.com

Line of menswear, shoes, and accessories

President: Chris Arnold
Credit Cards: AMEX; MasterCard

In Business: 137 years
Sales Volume: $ 3-5 Million

1516 Ben Silver
Ben Silver
149 King St
Charleston, SC 29401-2227   843-577-4556
                               800-221-4671
                          Fax: 843-723-1543
contact@bensilver.com
www.bensilver.com

Authentic English silk neckties, tailored clothing, shirts, and jewelry

President: Bob Prenner
Marketing Manager: James Prenner
Credit Cards: AMEX; MasterCard; Visa
Catalog Cost: $5
Catalog Circulation: Mailed 10 time(s) per year to 40000
Printing Information: 88 pages in 4 colors on Glossy Stock
Press: Web Press
Binding: Saddle Stitched
Mailing List Information: Names for rent
In Business: 50 years
Number of Employees: 41
Sales Volume: $5-10 Million

1517 Blair Men's
Blair
220 Hickory St.
Warren, PA 16366   800-821-5744
www.blair.com

Full line of men's clothing and footwear.

President: Marisa Smith
Catalog Cost: Free
Printing Information: in 4 colors
In Business: 106 years
Number of Employees: 2000
Sales Volume: $1 Billion

1518 Brighton Tuxedo Shop
Brighton Tuxedo Shop
8692 W. Grand River Ave
Brighton, MI 48116   810-227-1677
                   Fax: 810-227-1868
brightontuxshop.net

Tuxedos

In Business: 40+ years

1519 Brooks Brothers
Brooks Brothers
100 Phoenix Avenue
Enfield, CT 06082   800-274-1815
                   Fax: 800-274-1010
www.brooksbrothers.com

Complete line of mens, women and childrens shirts, polos & tees, sweaters, casual and dress pants, suits, formalwear, sport coats and blazers

President: Claudio Del Vecchio
CFO: Brian Baumann
SVP Operations: Debra Del Vecchio
Credit Cards: AMEX; MasterCard; Visa
Catalog Cost: Free
Catalog Circulation: Mailed 5 time(s) per year
Printing Information: 80 pages in 4 colors on Glossy Stock
Press: Web Press
Binding: Saddle Stitched
Mailing List Information: Names for rent
In Business: 198 years
Number of Employees: 3500
Sales Volume: $ 20-50 Million

1520 Bullock & Jones
Bullock & Jones
5121 Innovation Way
Dock B
Chambersburg, PA 17201   800-227-3050
                       Fax: 800-922-9920
service@bullockandjones.com
www.bullockandjones.com

Classic, stylish, tailored clothing for men

President: Sidney Goodwill
Marketing Manager: Eric Goodwill
Credit Cards: AMEX; MasterCard; Visa
In Business: 162 years

1521 Cabela's Men's Clothing & Footwear
Cabela's Inc.
One Cabela Dr.
Sidney, NE 69160   www.cabelas.com

Casual clothing and footwear for active lifestyles.

CFO: Ralph Castner
CEO: Thomas Millner
COO: Michael Copeland
Catalog Cost: Free
Catalog Circulation: Mailed 4 time(s) per year
Printing Information: in 4 colors
Binding: 0
List Company: Chilcutt Direct
In Business: 55 years
Sales Volume: $3 Billion

1522 Carbon2Cobalt
Carbon2Cobalt
6385 Rose Ln.
Suite A
Carpinteria, CA 93013   805-687-7442
                           805-687-7400
service@carbon2cobalt.com
www.carbon2cobalt.com

Casual clothes like jackets, sweaters, shirts, pants, shorts, tees, polos, henleys, sweats, pullovers

1523 Carhartt
Carhartt
5750 Mercury Drive
Dearborn, MI 48126   800-833-3118
just_ask_us@carhartt.com
www.carhartt.com

Men and womenswear and gear for outdoor activities such as camping, horseback riding, boating, ski/snowboarding, farming, home gardening, woodworking, offreading, fishing, and hunting

Chairman: Mark Valade
President: Linda Hubbard
Credit Cards: AMEX; MasterCard
Catalog Cost: Free
Catalog Circulation: Mailed 4 time(s) per year
Printing Information: 55 pages in 4 colors on Glossy Stock
In Business: 128 years

1524 Charles Tyrwhitt
Charles Tyrwhitt
377 Madison Ave
New York, NY 10017-2543   212-286-8988
                             866-797-2701
                        Fax: 212-370-7302
madison@ctshirts.com
www.ctshirts.com

Mens & womens dress shirts, jackets, suits & separates, casual wear, shoes, accessories and cufflinks

President: Nick Wheeler
Marketing Manager: Valerie Sharrin
Partner: Peter Higgins
Credit Cards: AMEX; MasterCard
Catalog Cost: Free
In Business: 29 years
Number of Employees: 8
Sales Volume: $500,000- 1 Million

1525 Cooper Jones
Cooper Jones
1034 Windward Ridge Parkway
Alpharetta, GA 30005   888-706-6767
customercare@cooperjones.com
cooperjones.com

Men clothing, shirts, sweaters, jackets, pants, shorts

Printing Information: 56 pages

1526 DeSantis Collection

DeSantis Collection
4500 Oak Circle
Suite B-9
Boca Raton, FL 33431-4212   800-501-8437
Fax: 888-388-7321
service@desantiscollection.com
www.desantiscollection.com

Upscale men's ties

President: Carl DeSantis
Credit Cards: AMEX; MasterCard
Catalog Cost: Free
In Business: 17 years
Sales Volume: Under $500M

1527 J.L. Powell The Sporting Life

J.L. Powell
1015 Cindy Lane
PO Box 9109
Carpinteria, CO 93013   805-456-4242
service@jlpowell.com
www.jlpowell.com

Sportswear for men including shoes and jewelry

President: J.R. Rigley
CFO: Michelle Fehr
CEO: Mark E. Jacobs
Catalog Cost: Free
Catalog Circulation: Mailed 4 time(s) per year
Printing Information: 66 pages in 4 colors
In Business: 38 years
Sales Volume: 5000000

1528 Jos. A. Bank Clothiers

Jos. A. Bank Clothiers
500 Hanover Pike
PO Box 1000
Hampstead, MD 21074-4000   800-999-7472
www.josbank.com

Tailored and casual clothing, footwear & accessories for men.

CFO: Jon W. Kimmins
CEO: Douglas S. Ewert
Catalog Cost: Free
Catalog Circulation: Mailed 4 time(s) per year
Printing Information: 52 pages in 4 colors
In Business: 111 years
Number of Employees: 6300
Sales Volume: $1 Billion

1529 KingSize

KingSize
One New York Plaza
New York, NY 10004   www.kingsizedirect.com

Men's big and tall clothing.

CEO: Paul Tarvin
Catalog Cost: Free
In Business: 105 years
Number of Employees: 6400
Sales Volume: Over $1 Billion

1530 Lands' End Men

Lands' End, Inc.
1 Lands' End Lane
Dodgeville, WI 53595   800-963-4816
Fax: 800-332-0103
www.landsend.com

Weekend wear, suits, and dress shirts for men.

Co-interim CEO: James Gooch
Co-interim CEO: James Boitano
Catalog Cost: Free
Printing Information: in 4 colors
Mailing List Information: Names for rent
List Company: Millard Group
In Business: 53 years

Number of Employees: 5300
Sales Volume: $1.42 Billion

1531 Ledbury

Ledbury
117 South 14th Street
Richmond, VA 23219   804-441-8040
customer-service@ledbury.com
www.ledbury.com

Shirts, ties etc.

1532 Linksoul

Linksoul
1034 Windward Ridge Parkway
Alpharetta, GA 30005   760-231-7069
888-217-4911
info@linksoul.com
linksoul.com

Printing Information: 17 pages

1533 Norm Thompson

Bluestem Brands, Inc.
7075 Flying Cloud Drive
Eden Prairie, MN 55344   877-718-7899
800-547-1160
normthompson.blair.com

Men and womens' clothing, footwear, gifts, and gourmet food

President: Steve Nave
CFO: Pete Michielutti
EVP, COO, & Chief Digital Officer: Vince Jones
EVP & President of Credit Services: Jim Slavik
Credit Cards: AMEX; MasterCard
Catalog Cost: Free
In Business: 68 years
Sales Volume: $50MM to $100MM

1534 Orvis Men

The Orvis Company Inc.
178 Conservation Way
Sunderland, VT 05250-4465   802-362-1300
888-235-9763
Fax: 802-362-0141
www.orvis.com

Men's casual clothing and accessories.

CEO: Leigh H. Perkins Jr.
Catalog Cost: Free
In Business: 160 years
Number of Employees: 1700
Sales Volume: $340 Million

1535 Paul Fredrick MenStyle

Paul Fredrick
223 W Poplar St
Fleetwood, PA 19522-1507   610-944-0909
800-247-1417
Fax: 610-944-7600
www.paulfredrick.Com

Men's dress shirts, formal wear and accessories

President: Paul Sacher
CFO: Ross Alaimo
Marketing Manager: Scott Drayer
Allen Abbott:
EVP
Buyers: Alan Mayman
Credit Cards: AMEX; MasterCard; Visa
Catalog Cost: $1
Catalog Circulation: Mailed 6 time(s) per year
Printing Information: 45 pages in 4 colors on Glossy Stock
Press: Web Press
Binding: Saddle Stitched
Mailing List Information: Names for rent
List Company: Mokrynski & Associates
401 Hackensack Avenue
Hackensack, NJ 07601
201-488-5656
In Business: 27 years
Number of Employees: 85
Sales Volume: $ 38 Million

1536 Paul Stuart

Paul Stuart
Madison Avenue at 45th Street
New York, NY 10017-1601   212-682-0320
800-678-8278
info@paulstuart.com
www.paulstuart.com

Men's and women's clothing and accessories

President: Michael Ostrove
Buyers: Arthur Grodd, Men's Clothing
Paul Ostrova, Business Apparel
Brian Baker, Casual
Credit Cards: AMEX; MasterCard; Visa
Catalog Cost: $5
Catalog Circulation: Mailed 4 time(s) per year to 14000
Printing Information: 44 pages in 4 colors on Matte Stock
Press: Web Press
Binding: Saddle Stitched
Mailing List Information: Names for rent
In Business: 77 years
Number of Employees: 200

1537 Pendleton Woolen Mills

Pendleton Woolen Mills
PO Box 3030
Portland, OR 97208   503-226-4801
877-996-6599
Fax: 503-535-5777
pendletoncatalog@penwool.com
www.pendleton-usa.com

Woolen men and women clothing, home collection and blankets

Chairman: John Bishop
President: Clarence Bishop
Credit Cards: MasterCard
Catalog Cost: Free
Catalog Circulation: Mailed 8 time(s) per year
Printing Information: 85 pages in 4 colors
Binding: Perfect Bound
In Business: 104 years
Number of Employees: 1000

1538 Peruvian Connection

Peruvian Connection
Canaan Farm
Box 990
Tonganoxie, KS 66086   913-845-2450
800-221-8520
Fax: 800-573-7378
sales@peruvianconnection.com
www.peruvianconnection.com

Peruvian sweaters, skirts, pants, dresses, coats, jackets, jewelry and accessories

President: Annie Hurlbut
CFO: Lori Green
Credit Cards: AMEX; MasterCard
Catalog Cost: Free
Catalog Circulation: Mailed 5 time(s) per year
Printing Information: 48 pages in 4 colors
In Business: 39 years
Number of Employees: 100
Sales Volume: $10 Million

1539 Peter Millar

Peter Millar LLC
4300 Emperor Blvd.
Suite 100
Durham, NC 27703   888-926-0255
communications@petermillar.com
www.petermillar.com

Fine clothing and accessories for men and women

1540 Rochester Big and Tall Catalog

Casual Male Rbt, LLC
555 Turnpike St
Canton, MA 02021-2724   781-828-9300
855-746-7395
Fax: 781-575-9866
www.rochesterclothing.com

High-end apparel for big and tall men

President: Fillman Teklai
CFO: Dennis Hernreich
Marketing Manager: Brenda Murphy
VP: Steven Sockolov
VP: William Sockolov
Manager: Chris Fisher
Credit Cards: AMEX; MasterCard; Visa
Catalog Circulation: Mailed 3 time(s) per year
Printing Information: in 4 colors on Glossy Stock
Press: Web Press
Binding: Saddle Stitched
In Business: 106 years
Number of Employees: 200
Sales Volume: $ 5 Million

1541 Sierra Home and Gift
Sierra Trading Post
5025 Campstool Rd
Cheyenne, WY 82007-1898   037-775-8000
                                  800-713-4534
                          Fax: 800-378-8946
customerservice@sierratradingpost.com
www.sierratradingpost.com

Home furnishings, daily essentials for him and her, slippers, gifts, outdoor gear and camping equipment & supplies

President: Keith Richardson
CFO: Gary Imig
Production Manager: Sheila Russell
Fulfillment: Robin Jahnke
Credit Cards: AMEX; MasterCard
Catalog Cost: Free
Mailing List Information: Names for rent
In Business: 20 years
Number of Employees: 135
Sales Volume: $20-50 Million

1542 Sierra Traditions For Men
Sierra Trading Post
5025 Campstool Rd
Cheyenne, WY 82007-1898   307-775-8000
                                  800-713-4534
                          Fax: 800-378-8946
customerservice@sierratradingpost.com
www.sierratradingpost.com

Quality, classic style and value clothes for men

President: Keith Richardson
CFO: Gary Imig
Production Manager: Shelia Russell
Fulfillment: Robin Jahnke
Credit Cards: AMEX; MasterCard
Catalog Cost: Free
Mailing List Information: Names for rent
In Business: 28 years
Number of Employees: 135
Sales Volume: $20-50 Million

1543 Turtleson
Turtleson
                                  423-217-4950
                                  888-602-0652
customercare@turtleson.com
www.turtleson.com

Menswear for on and off the golf course

1544 Undergear
Undergear
455 Park Plaza Drive
La Crosse, WI 54601   717-633-3413
                                   800-853-8555
                           Fax: 717-633-3214
service@undergear.com
www.undergear.com

Classic clothing for men

Chairman: Alan Quasha
President: Don Wilson
Buyers: Valerie Nadalini-Howarth
Credit Cards: AMEX; MasterCard
Catalog Cost: Free

Catalog Circulation: Mailed 2 time(s) per year
Printing Information: on Glossy Stock

1545 Vivre
Voyager Spirit
11 E 26th St
15th Floor
New York, NY 10010-1421   212-739-6193
                                  800-411-6515
                          Fax: 212-739-1736

Women, men and kids footwear, outerwear and accessories; home furnishings and gifts

Chairman: James Robinson
President: Eva Jeanbart-Lorenzotti
Marketing Manager: Eileen Shulock
EVP: Meg Galea
mgalea@vivre.com
Credit Cards: AMEX; MasterCard
Catalog Cost: $10
Catalog Circulation: Mailed 2 time(s) per year to 1.5MM
Average Order Size: $600
Printing Information: 80 pages
In Business: 17 years
Number of Employees: 25
Sales Volume: $ 1-3 Million

1546 Westport Big & Tall Catalog
Westport Big & Tall
1034 Windward Ridge Pkwy
Alpharetta, GA 30005-3992   770-667-8833
                                  877-937-8767
                          Fax: 800-314-1137
customercare@westportbigandtall.com
www.Westportbigandtall.Com

Apparel, dress clothing and accessories for big and tall men

President: Loren Poley
Credit Cards: AMEX; MasterCard; Visa
Catalog Cost: Free
Catalog Circulation: Mailed 12 time(s) per year to 4M
In Business: 22 years
Sales Volume: $ 3-5 Million

1547 Williams & Kent
Williams & Kent
1034 Windward Ridge Pkwy
Alpharetta, GA 30005-3992   888-577-9898
customercare@williamsandkent.com
williamsandkent.com

Men clothing

Natural Fibers

1548 Amazon Drygoods
Amazon Drygoods
3788 Wilson Street (Napoleon)
Osgood, IN 47037-1510   812-852-1780
                                  800-798-7979
                          Fax: 812-689-1385
www.amazondrygoods.com

Victorian home accessories, including carpets and draperies

President: Janet Burgess
Founder: Janet Burgess
Credit Cards: AMEX; MasterCard
Catalog Cost: Free
Printing Information: 92 pages
In Business: 32 years
Sales Volume: $ 1-3 Million

1549 Kasper Organics
Kasper Organics
6500 Hazeltine Ave
Van Nuys, CA 91401-1551   818-988-3924
                                  866-913-5234
www.kasperorganics.com

1550 Peruvian Connection
Peruvian Connection
Canaan Farm
Box 990
Tonganoxie, KS 66086   913-845-2450
                                  800-221-8520
                          Fax: 800-573-7378
sales@peruvianconnection.com
www.peruvianconnection.com

Peruvian sweaters, skirts, pants, dresses, coats, jackets, jewelry and accessories

President: Annie Hurlbut
CFO: Lori Green
Credit Cards: AMEX; MasterCard
Catalog Cost: Free
Catalog Circulation: Mailed 5 time(s) per year
Printing Information: 48 pages in 4 colors
In Business: 39 years
Number of Employees: 100
Sales Volume: $10 Million

1551 Synergy Organic Clothing
Synergy Organic Clothing
1126 Soquel Ave
Santa Cruz, CA 95062   888-466-0411
websales@synergyclothing.com
synergyclothing.com

Clothing and yoga apparel for women

1552 Tomorrow's World Catalog
Organic Comfort Zone
201 W Ocean View Ave.
Norfolk, VA 23503-1504   757-480-8500
                                  800-229-7571
                          Fax: 757-480-3148
www.tomorrowsworld.Com

Natural fashions, men and women, organic cotton, hemp, wool and flax

Chairman: Richard Hahn
President: Cheryl Hahn
Credit Cards: AMEX; MasterCard; Visa
Catalog Cost: $2
Catalog Circulation: Mailed 12 time(s) per year to 1M
Average Order Size: $85
Printing Information: 64 pages in 4 colors on Matte Stock
Press: Web Press
Binding: Saddle Stitched
In Business: 24 years
Number of Employees: 6
Sales Volume: $500,000- 1 Million

1553 WinterSilks
WinterSilks
PO Box 196
Jessup, PA 18434-196   800-648-7455
                                  800-718-3687
                          Fax: 800-247-8477
wintersilks.blair.com

Men, women apparel, sleepwear, lingerie, accessories

In Business: 30+ years

Sportswear

1554 Activa Sports
Road Runner Sports
5549 Copley Dr
San Diego, CA 92111-7904   858-636-7652
                                  800-743-3206
                          Fax: 800-453-5443
listening@roadrunnersports.com
www.roadrunnersports.com

Women's fitness, sportswear, and gear

President: Debra Christal
Credit Cards: AMEX; MasterCard
In Business: 32 years
Number of Employees: 800

1555 Adventure Edge
Sierra Trading Post
5025 Campstool Road
Cheyenne, WY 82007-1898   307-775-8000
                                800-713-4534
                          Fax: 800-378-8946
customerservice@sierratradingpost.com
www.sierratradingpost.com

Gear and action apparel

President: Keith Richardson
CFO: Gary Imig
Production Manager: Shelia Russell
Fulfillment: Robin Jahnke
Credit Cards: AMEX; MasterCard; Visa
Catalog Cost: Free
Mailing List Information: Names for rent
In Business: 29 years
Number of Employees: 565

1556 Adventure Motorcycle Gear
Frank Cooper's Adventure Motorcycle Gear
P.O. Box 52
Gilbert, AZ 85299   800-217-3526
                          Fax: 480-507-0900
info@adventuremotogear.com
www.adventuremotogear.com

Motorcycle clothing

President: Frank Cooper
Credit Cards: AMEX; MasterCard

1557 All Pro Team Sports
All Pro Team Sports
11615 Crossraods Circle
Suite H
Baltimore, MD 21220   410-335-9804
contacts@allproteamsports.com
www.allproteamsports.com

Sportswear, sporting equipment, gear, and uniforms

President: Steve Bottcher
steve@allproteamsports.com
Credit Cards: AMEX; MasterCard
Catalog Cost: Free
In Business: 8 years

1558 American Rugby Outfitters
American Rugby Outfitters
1510 Midway Court
Unit E6
Elk Grove Vlg, IL 60007-6691   847-981-1242
                                800-467-8429
                          Fax: 847-981-1224
www.americanrugby.Com

Specialty sportswear, rugby apparel, jerseys and warm-up suits

President: Willie Johnson Sr
Marketing Manager: Curt Hacker
Credit Cards: MasterCard; Visa
Catalog Cost: Free
Catalog Circulation: Mailed 2 time(s) per year
Printing Information: 32 pages in 4 colors on Glossy Stock
Press: Web Press
Binding: Saddle Stitched
In Business: 30 years
Number of Employees: 10
Sales Volume: $ 1-3 Million

1559 Athleta
Athleta
1450 Technology Lane
Suite 150
Petaluma, CA 94954   614-744-3913
                            877-328-4538
www.athleta.gap.com/?

Athletic clothing and accessories for women including jackets and outerwear, pants and bottoms, skirts and dresses and footwear

President: Joseph E Teno
Marketing Manager: John Monteleone
Human Resources Director: Mona Patel
Credit Cards: AMEX; MasterCard

Catalog Cost: Free
Catalog Circulation: Mailed 1 time(s) per year
Printing Information: 24 pages
In Business: 16 years
Number of Employees: 110
Sales Volume: $6.7 MM

1560 Athletic Connection
Athletic Connection
1901 Diplomat Drive
Farmers Branch, TX 75234   800-527-0871
                          Fax: 885-858-8337
www.athleticconnection.com

Sportswear, sporting equipment, gear, and uniforms

Credit Cards: AMEX; MasterCard
Catalog Cost: Free
Catalog Circulation: Mailed 1 time(s) per year
Printing Information: 364 pages in 4 colors

1561 Augusta Sportswear
425 Park West Drive
Grovetown, GA 30813   800-237-6695
                          Fax: 888-432-9749
sales@augustasportswear.com
www.augustasportswear.com

Sportswear, bags, totes, aprons and accessories

President: Eric Runckel
Director, Manufacturing/Operations;: Chris Bailey
In Business: 39 years
Number of Employees: 6
Sales Volume: $610,000

1562 Barracuda USA
Skyline Northwest
117 Foothills Rd
Lake Oswego, OR 97034-3105   503-697-3225
                                800-547-8664
                          Fax: 800-238-4658
Skyline@SkylineNW.com
www.skylinenw.com

Swimwear, goggles and accessories

President: Eric Runckel
Director, Manufacturing/Operations;: Chris Bailey
In Business: 39 years
Number of Employees: 6
Sales Volume: $610,000

1563 Bit of Britain Saddlery
Bit of Britain Saddlery
141 Union School Road
Oxford, PA 19363   800-972-7985
sales@bitofbritain.com
www.bitofbritain.com

Women and men horse care supplies

Marketing Manager: Helena
CEO, Owner: John Nunn
Photographer/Videographer: Amy
Operations & Finance: Suzanne
In Business: 28 years

1564 Blank Shirts
Blank Shirts
1780 Forrest Way
Carson City, NV 89706   775-885-1364
                                800-332-6576
                          Fax: 877-813-7626
sales@blankshirts.com
www.blankshirts.com

White and solid color tees, polos shirts, jackets and hats

CFO: Brian Tuttle
CEO: Pat Drudge
Credit Cards: AMEX; MasterCard
Catalog Cost: Free
Catalog Circulation: Mailed 1 time(s) per year
Printing Information: 500 pages
In Business: 12 years
Number of Employees: 6
Sales Volume: $600,000

1565 Blue Generation
WestPro, Inc.
2294 Mountain Vista Lane
Provo, UT 84606-6206   801-373-2525
                          Fax: 801-373-8778
steve@westpro.net
www.westpro.net

Casual wear and custom sportswear, including direct embroidery and screen printing

President: Steven Clements
CFO: John M Edmunds
Credit Cards: MasterCard
Catalog Cost: Free
Catalog Circulation: Mailed 1 time(s) per year
Printing Information: 16 pages in 4 colors on Glossy Stock
Press: Web Press
Binding: Perfect Bound
In Business: 36 years
Number of Employees: 45
Sales Volume: $3-5 Million

1566 CC Filson Company
Filson
PO Box 34020
Seattle, WA 98124   866-860-8906
                                800-624-0201
www.filson.com

Rugged outdoor clothing and accessories

President: Stan Kohls
Marketing Manager: Amy Terai
Manager, Sales Department: Dan Drust
Credit Cards: AMEX; MasterCard; Visa
Catalog Cost: Free
Catalog Circulation: Mailed 2 time(s) per year
Printing Information: 103 pages in 4 colors
In Business: 115 years
Number of Employees: 150
Sales Volume: $10 Million

1567 Camo Trading
CamoTrading
PO Box 297
Jenks, OK 74037-0297   800-605-0915
                                877-208-6125
info@camotrading.com
www.camotrading.com

Clothing, bedding and decor featuring a camouflage pattern.

1568 Cutter and Buck
Cutter and Buck
101 Eliott Avenue W
Suite 100
Seattle, WA 98119   800-713-7810
help@cutterbuck.com
www.cutterbuck.com

Men's and women's golf apparel, shoes and other sportswear

President: Joel Freet
CFO: David Hauge
Marketing Manager: Julie Snow
Credit Cards: MasterCard
Catalog Cost: Free
Catalog Circulation: Mailed 6 time(s) per year
Printing Information: 123 pages in 4 colors on Glossy Stock
Binding: Perfect Bound
In Business: 28 years
Number of Employees: 225
Sales Volume: $ 58 Million

1569 David Morgan
David Morgan
11812 North Creek Parkway N.
Suite 103
Bothell, WA 98011   425-485-2132
                                800-324-4934
                          Fax: 425-486-0224
catalog@davidmorgan.com
www.davidmorgan.com

Akura hats, outdoor imported clothing and accessories

President: David Morgan
Credit Cards: AMEX; MasterCard; Visa
Catalog Cost: Free
Catalog Circulation: Mailed 2 time(s) per year
Printing Information: on Matte Stock
Press: Web Press
Binding: Saddle Stitched
Mailing List Information: Names for rent
In Business: 53 years
Number of Employees: 7
Sales Volume: $500,000 - 1 Million

1570   De Soto Sport Company
De Soto Sport Company
7584 Trade St
San Diego, CA 92121-2412   858-578-6672
                              800-453-6673
                         Fax: 858-578-6021
                    contact@desotosport.com
                       www.Desotosport.Com

Triathlon and running gear

President: Emilio De Soto
Credit Cards: AMEX; MasterCard; Visa
Catalog Cost: Free
Catalog Circulation: Mailed 2 time(s) per year
7584 Trade Street
San Diego, CA 92121
858.578.6672
In Business: 25 years
Number of Employees: 20
Sales Volume: $ 3-5 Million

1571   Dennis Kirk Watercraft Catalog
Dennis Kirk
955 South Frandsen Avenue
Rush City, MN 55069   800-969-7501
                    Fax: 320-358-4019
           customerservice@denniskirk.com
                  www.denniskirk.com

Outdoor apparel and sporting goods

President: Bob Behan
Marketing Manager: Renita Twingstrom
VP of Finance: Heidi Scheffer
Credit Cards: AMEX; MasterCard
Catalog Cost: Free
Catalog Circulation: Mailed 4 time(s) per year
Printing Information: 132 pages in 4 colors
In Business: 48 years
Sales Volume: $ 50-100 Million

1572   Eastbay
Eastbay
111 S First Ave.
Wausau, WI 54401   715-845-5538
           asktheexperts@eastbay.com
                 www.eastbay.com

Athletic footwear and apparel.

President & CEO: Dowe Tillema
Catalog Cost: Free
In Business: 36 years
Number of Employees: 1500
Sales Volume: $200 Million

1573   Filson
Filson
P.O.Box 34020
Seattle, WA 98124-1020   866-860-8906
                            800-624-0201
                        www.filson.Com

Durable outdoor clothing, hats for hunting, fishing, rugged outdoor applications

President: Stan Kohls
Catalog Cost: Free
Printing Information: 112 pages in 4 colors on Glossy Stock
Press: Web Press
Binding: Saddle Stitched
In Business: 118 years
Number of Employees: 150
Sales Volume: $ 10 Million

1574   Finals
The Finals
21 Minisink Ave
Port Jervis, NY 12771-2320   845-858-4141
                                800-345-3485
                         www.thefinals.com

Swim wear and accessories, competition and fitness swimwear and swim accessories, male and female

President: Nancy Piccolo
CFO: Joseph Olliver
In Business: 35 years
Number of Employees: 40
Sales Volume: $ 5-10 Million

1575   Fox Head
FoxActive
16752 Armstrong Ave.
Irvine, CA 92606-2819   408-776-8800
                          888-369-7223
                     Fax: 408-852-6913
              webmaster@FoxHead.com
                   www.foxhead.com

Complete line of motorcycle helmets and dirtbike apparel

President: Peter Fox
Credit Cards: AMEX; MasterCard; Visa
Catalog Cost: Free
Catalog Circulation: Mailed 4 time(s) per year to 17500
Printing Information: 64 pages in 4 colors on Glossy Stock
Press: Web Press
In Business: 40 years
Number of Employees: 40
Sales Volume: $ 5-10 Million

1576   GK Back to School Workout Essentials
Elite Sportswear LP
2136 N 13th Street
PO Box 16400
Reading, PA 19612-6400   610-921-1469
                            800-345-4087
                       Fax: 888-866-9884
                         info@gkelite.com
                        www.gkelite.com

Gymnastics and dance apparel

President: Dan Casciano
Production Manager: Alan Robezzoli
CEO: Sallie Weaver
Credit Cards: AMEX; MasterCard
Catalog Cost: Free
In Business: 30 years
Number of Employees: 250
Sales Volume: $15.4 Million

1577   GK Continue the Quest
Elite Sportswear LP
2136 N 13th Street
PO Box 16400
Reading, PA 19604-6400   610-921-1469
                            800-345-4087
                       Fax: 610-921-0208
                         info@gkelite.com
                        www.gkelite.com

Authentic US National team leotards

President: Sallie Weaver
Production Manager: Alan Robezzoli
Credit Cards: AMEX; MasterCard
Catalog Cost: Free
In Business: 30 years
Number of Employees: 250
Sales Volume: $15 Million

1578   GK Spring/Summer Skating Wear Catalog
Elite Sportswear LP
2136 N 13th Street
PO Box 16400
Reading, PA 19604-6400   610-921-1469
                            800-345-4087
                       Fax: 610-921-0208
                         info@gkelite.com
                        www.gkelite.com

Figure skating dresses

President: Dan Casciano
COO: Alan Robezzoli
CEO: Sallie Weaver
Credit Cards: AMEX; MasterCard
Catalog Cost: Free
In Business: 30 years
Number of Employees: 250
Sales Volume: $15 Million

1579   GK Team Workout Wear Catalog
Elite Sportswear LP
2136 N 13th Street
PO Box 16400
Reading, PA 19604-6400   610-921-1469
                            800-345-4087
                       Fax: 610-921-0208
                         info@gkelite.com
                        www.gkelite.com

Workout and gymnastics apparel and accessories

President: Dan Casciano
CEO: Sallie Weaver
COO: Alan Robezzoli
Credit Cards: AMEX; MasterCard
Catalog Cost: $5
In Business: 30 years
Number of Employees: 250
Sales Volume: $15 Million

1580   GK Womens Competitive Catalog
Elite Sportswear LP
2136 N 13th Street
PO Box 16400
Reading, PA 19604-6400   610-921-1469
                            800-345-4087
                       Fax: 888-866-9884
                         info@gkelite.com
                        www.gkelite.com

Gymnastics leotards and dance clothes

President: Dan Casciano
Production Manager: Alan Robezzoli
CEO: Sallie Weaver
Credit Cards: AMEX; MasterCard
Catalog Cost: Free
In Business: 30 years
Number of Employees: 250
Sales Volume: $15 Million

1581   Gear Pro-Tec
Athletic Connection
1901 Diplomat Drive
Farmers Branch, TX 75234   800-527-0871
                         Fax: 888-858-8337
                 www.athleticconnection.com

Football gear, equipment, and uniforms

Credit Cards: AMEX; MasterCard
Catalog Cost: Free
Catalog Circulation: Mailed 1 time(s) per year
Printing Information: 32 pages in 4 colors

1582   Gorsuch
Gorsuch
263 E Gore Creek Dr.
Vail, CO 81657-4512   970-476-2294
                         800-525-9808
             customercare@gorsuch.com
                   www.gorsuch.com

Ski apparel for men, women and children.

Catalog Cost: Free
In Business: 50 years
Number of Employees: 75

1583   Green Pepper
The Green Pepper, Inc
PO Box 42073
Eugene, OR 97404   541-689-3591
                      800-767-5684
                 Fax: 541-689-3591
             www.thegreenpepper.com

Active sportswear patterns, fabrics, hardware and zippers

President: Arlene Haislip
Owner: Susan Downs
Buyers: Susan Downs
Credit Cards: MasterCard
Catalog Cost: $2
Catalog Circulation: Mailed 2 time(s) per year to 35000
Printing Information: 43 pages in 1 color on Newsprint
Press: Web Press
Binding: Perfect Bound
In Business: 41 years
Number of Employees: 3
Sales Volume: Under $500,000

1584 Hank's Clothing

Hank's Clothing
3119 Pearl St
Endicott, NY 13760   607-754-0601
866-444-2657
www.hanksclothing.com

Men's clothing

President: Henry Calleo
In Business: 66 years

1585 Healy Awards

Healy Awards
N94 W14431 Garwin Mace Drive
Menomonee Falls, WI 53051   800-558-1696
Fax: 800-900-3773
sales@healyawards.com
www.healyawards.com

Sports gear

Printing Information: 48 pages
In Business: 55 years

1586 High Five Sportswear

High Five Sportswear
18300 Cascade Avenue
Suite 220
Seattle, WA 98188   800-222-4016
Fax: 206-574-0276
customercare@high5sportswear.com
www.high5sportswear.com

Jerseys, scrimmage vests, shorts, outerwear, socks and bags

1587 Jockey

Jockey International, Inc.
2300 60th Street
Kenosha, WI 53140   800-562-5391
jockey.com

Sleepwear and casualwear for men, women, and children

President: Debra S. Waller
Marketing Manager: Prateek Kumar
SVP, Chief Supply Chain Officer: Tim Taylor
Catalog Cost: Free
In Business: 141 years
Number of Employees: 1600
Sales Volume: Over $1 Billion

1588 Junonia

JunoActive
1355 Mendota Heights Rd
Suite 290
Mendota Heights, MN 55120-1285 651-365-1830
800-586-6642
Fax: 920-967-0404
customerservice@junonia.com
www.junonia.com

Line of womens activewear, swimwear, inti-mates and outerwear for sizes 14 and up

President: Anne Kelly
annekellyfounder@junonia.com
Catalog Circulation: to 60000
Printing Information: 52 pages in 4 colors on Glossy Stock
Press: Offset Press
Binding: Saddle Stitched
Mailing List Information: Names for rent
In Business: 19 years

Number of Employees: 25
Sales Volume: $ 3-5 Million

1589 Kast-A-Way Swimwear

Kast-A-Way Swimwear
9356 Cincinnati-Columbus Rd
Route 42
Cincinnati, OH 45241-1197   513-777-7967
800-543-2763
Fax: 513-777-1062
sales@kastawayswimwear.Com
www.Kastawayswimwear.Com

Line of competition swimwear and accesso-ries

President: Patty Kast
Credit Cards: AMEX; MasterCard; Visa
Catalog Circulation: Mailed 2 time(s) per year
Average Order Size: $75
Printing Information: 6 pages in 4 colors on Matte Stock
Press: Web Press
Binding: Saddle Stitched
Mailing List Information: Names for rent
Number of Employees: 30
Sales Volume: $ 3-5 Million

1590 Kevin's Fine Outdoor Gear & Apparel

122 Plantation Oaks Drive
Thomasville, GA 31792   800-953-8467
Fax: 229-228-4380
customerservice@kevinscatalog.com
www.kevinscatalog.com

Outdoor clothing, sunglasses, knifes and accessories

Catalog Circulation: Mailed 1 time(s) per year
Printing Information:
Binding: Perfect Bound
Sales Volume: $3MM to $5MM

1591 King Louie Sports

King Louie America
8788 Metcalf Ave
Overland Park, KS 66209-2039   913-648-2100
www.kinglouie.com

Bowling shirts, sweaters, activewear and hats

President: Brett Hackworth
Marketing Manager: Gary Ruhnke
CEO: Brett Hackworth
VP, Sales & Marketing: John McMillan
Catalog Cost: Free
Catalog Circulation: Mailed 1 time(s) per year to 200M
Printing Information: 64 pages in 4 colors on Glossy Stock
Press: Web Press
Binding: Saddle Stitched
In Business: 78 years
Number of Employees: 13
Sales Volume: $1MM to $3MM

1592 L.L.Bean Outsider

L.L.Bean Inc.
15 Casco Street
Freeport, ME 04033   207-552-2000
www.llbean.com

Women and men's sportswear and outdoor clothing and accessories

Chairman: Shawn Gorman
President: Stephen Smith
Credit Cards: AMEX; MasterCard
Catalog Cost: Free
Printing Information: 68 pages in 4 colors
In Business: 105 years
Number of Employees: 5000
Sales Volume: $1.6 Billion

1593 Lancaster Archery Supply 2015 - 16 Archer's Wishbo

Lancaster Archery Supply
2195-A Old Philadelphia Pike
Lancaster, PA 17602   717-394-7229
855-922-7769
Fax: 717-394-8635
www.lancasterarchery.com

Products related to archery

President: A. Robert Kaufhold
Printing Information: 420 pages
In Business: 29+ years

1594 Merrell

Merrell
1400 Industries Rd.
Richmond, IN 47374   800-288-3124
customerservice@merrell.com
www.merrell.com

hiking and outdoors footwear and active gear.

1595 Midwest Volleyball Warehouse Volleyball Catalog

Midwest Volleyball Warehouse
14050 Judicial Road
Burnsville, MN 55337   952-808-0100
800-876-8858
www.midwestvolleyball.com

Sportswear - men and women

Printing Information: 60 pages

1596 Moosejaw

Moosejaw
32200 North Avis
Suite 100
Madison Heights, MI 48071   248-246-4000
877-666-7352
Fax: 248-246-4001
eliteservice@moosejaw.com
www.moosejaw.com

Outerwear, skiwear, accessories and foot-wear

President: Harvey Kanter
CFO: Ken Carson
VP: Julie Wolfe
Catalog Cost: Free
In Business: 20 years
Number of Employees: 100
Sales Volume: $ 13 Million

1597 NASCAR Superstore

NASCAR
PO Box 2875
Daytona Beach, FL 32120-2875   386-681-5977
866-290-4569
Fax: 386-947-6816
www.nascar.com

Nascar officially logged sportswear and ac-cessories

President: John Saunders
Catalog Cost: Free
Catalog Circulation: Mailed 2 time(s) per year
Printing Information: 32 pages
In Business: 68 years
Sales Volume: $10MM to $20MM

1598 Nite-Lite Company

NLC Products, Inc.
3801 Woodland Hgts Road, Suite 100
PO Box 8300
Little Rock, AR 72222   501-227-9050
800-332-6968
Fax: 479-754-5669
www.huntsmart.com

Hunting and dog supplies

Chairman: Henry Mariani
President: Tim Mariani
Marketing Manager: J McCay
Finance: Gina Terry
Human Resources: Tricia Mariani

Business Manager: John Carlton
Credit Cards: MasterCard; Visa
Catalog Cost: Free
Catalog Circulation: Mailed 2 time(s) per year
Printing Information: 96 pages in 1 color
In Business: 5 years
Number of Employees: 70
Sales Volume: $13 MM

1599 Offroad Catalog
Bob's Cycle Supply
65 W Viking Drive
St Paul, MN 55117   651-482-8181
    888-306-2627
    Fax: 651-482-0974
    www.bobscycle.com

Off-road riding gear from apparel to helmets, boots and more

President: Scott Muellner
Marketing Manager: Leisha Olson
Purchasing: Josh Lane
Credit Cards: AMEX; MasterCard
Catalog Cost: Free
In Business: 42 years
Number of Employees: 47
Sales Volume: $10 million

1600 Patagonia
Patagonia
259 W Santa Clara St.
Ventura, CA 93001   805-643-8616
    www.patagonia.com

Outdoor apparel for men and women.

CEO: Rose Marcario
Catalog Cost: Free
Catalog Circulation: Mailed 12 time(s) per year
Printing Information: in 4 colors
In Business: 43 years
Number of Employees: 2000
Sales Volume: $600 Million

1601 Patagonia Fish
Patagonia
259 W Santa Clara St.
Ventura, CA 93001   805-643-8616
    www.patagonia.com

Outdoor apparel for men and women.

CEO: Rose Marcario
Catalog Cost: Free
Catalog Circulation: Mailed 1 time(s) per year
Printing Information: in 4 colors
In Business: 43 years
Number of Employees: 2000
Sales Volume: $600 Million

1602 Patagonia Kids
Patagonia
259 W Santa Clara St.
Ventura, CA 93001   805-643-8616
    www.patagonia.com

Outdoor clothing for children.

CEO: Rose Marcario
Catalog Cost: Free
Catalog Circulation: Mailed 1 time(s) per year
Printing Information: in 4 colors
In Business: 43 years
Number of Employees: 2000
Sales Volume: $600 Million

1603 Patagonia Surf
Patagonia
259 W Santa Clara St.
Ventura, CA 93001   805-643-8616
    www.patagonia.com

Outdoor apparel for men and women.

CEO: Rose Marcario
Catalog Cost: Free
Catalog Circulation: Mailed 1 time(s) per year
Printing Information: in 4 colors
In Business: 43 years
Number of Employees: 2000
Sales Volume: $600 Million

1604 Rocky Mountain ATV/MC
Rocky Mountain ATV/MC
1551 American Way
Payson, UT 84651   801-465-3140
    800-336-5437
    Fax: 801-465-3457
    sales@rockymountainatv.com
    www.rockymountainatvmc.com

Street gear, protective gear and apparel, ATV parts, brakes, engines, exhausts, helmets, boots and handlebars

President: Malynda Lewis
CFO: McMohan Chantale
Marketing Manager: Everett Hoffman
Owner/President: Dan Thomas
General Manager/Sales Exec VP: Ray Butts
Credit Cards: AMEX; MasterCard
Catalog Cost: Free
In Business: 30 years
Number of Employees: 150
Sales Volume: $11.2 Million

1605 Rocky Mountain Connection
Rocky Mountain Connection
141 E. Elkhorn Avenue
Box 2800
Estes Park, CO 80517-2800   970-586-3361
    800-679-3600
    Fax: 800-814-4900
    office@rmconnection.com
    www.rmconnection.com

Outdoor rugged and technical clothing and equipment

Chairman: Pep Petrocine
President: E J Petrocine
epetrocine@gmail.com
Credit Cards: AMEX; MasterCard; Visa
Catalog Cost: Free
Catalog Circulation: Mailed 4 time(s) per year to 90000
Average Order Size: $80
Printing Information: 16 pages in 4 colors on Matte Stock
Press: Web Press
Binding: Saddle Stitched
In Business: 97 years
Number of Employees: 20
Sales Volume: $1-3 Million

1606 Sierra Trading Post
Sierra Trading Post
5025 Campstool Rd.
Cheyenne, WY 82007 www.sierratradingpost.com

Outdoor gear and apparel for men, women and kids.

CEO: Keith Richardson
President: Gary Imig
Catalog Cost: Free
In Business: 30 years
Sales Volume: $200 Million

1607 Soccer.com
Soccer.com
431 US Highway 70A E
Hillsborough, NC 27278   919-644-6800
    800-950-1994
    custserv@sportsendeavors.com
    www.soccer.com

Footwear, apparel, equipment and uniforms.

In Business: 32 years

1608 Sporthill
Sporthill Direct Inc
725 McKinley St
Eugene, OR 97402-2756   541-345-9623
    800-622-8444
    info@sporthill.com
    www.sporthill.com

Running, skiing and adventure wear for men and women

President: Jim Hill
Catalog Cost: Free
Printing Information: 24 pages in 4 colors
Mailing List Information: Names for rent
In Business: 21 years
Sales Volume: $ 1-3 Million

1609 Sprint Aquatics Catalog
Rothhammer International Inc., D.B.A Spr
PO Box 3840
San Luis Obispo, CA 93403   805-541-5330
    800-235-2156
    Fax: 805-541-5339
    info@sprintaquatics.com
    www.sprintaquatics.com

Swimming goggles, water aerobics, toys, games, educational items, competitive swimming items

President: Laurel Maas
Marketing Manager: Alex Smith
Buyers: Laurel Maas
Credit Cards: AMEX; MasterCard; Visa
Catalog Cost: Free
Catalog Circulation: Mailed 1 time(s) per year to 50000
Average Order Size: $150
Printing Information: 63 pages in 4 colors on Newsprint
Press: Web Press
Binding: Folded
Mailing List Information: Names for rent
In Business: 43 years
Number of Employees: 6
Sales Volume: $ 500,000- 1 Million

1610 Stackhouse Athletic
Stackhouse Athletic
1450 McDonald St. NE
Salem, OR 97301   503-363-1840
    800-285-3604
    Fax: 503-363-0511
    www.stackhouseathletic.com

Team or individual athletic and sporting equipment and accessories

1611 Stafford's Catalog
Stafford's
715 Smith Ave
Thomasville, GA 31792   229-226-4306
    800-826-0948
    Fax: 229-226-1287
    customerservice@staffordscatalog.com
    www.stafford-catalog.com

Outdoor apparel, hunting clothes, gifts, luggage and accessories

President: Warren Stafford
Buyers: Beth Stafford
Credit Cards: AMEX; MasterCard; Visa
Catalog Cost: Free
Catalog Circulation: Mailed 1 time(s) per year
Average Order Size: $120
Printing Information: 64 pages in 4 colors on Glossy Stock
Press: Web Press
Binding: Saddle Stitched
Mailing List Information: Names for rent
In Business: 70 years
Number of Employees: 20

1612 Sun Precautions
Sun Precautions, Inc.
2815 Wetmore Ave
Everett, WA 98201-3517   425-303-8585
    800-882-7860
    Fax: 425-303-0836
    www.sunprecautions.com

30+ SPF sun protective clothing and other products for people who are hypersensitive to the sun

President: Shaun Hughes
Catalog Cost: Free
Printing Information: 40 pages in 4 colors
In Business: 30 years
Sales Volume: $ 500,000- 1 Million

1613 Tattoo Golf
Tattoo Golf
2764 N. Lincoln Street
Burbank, CA 91504
818-953-7173
800-996-6939
support@tattoogolf.com
www.tattoogolf.com

Golf shirts, hats, outerwear, shoes, golf bags, golf packs and sunglasses
Marketing Manager: Bill Anderson
Credit Cards: AMEX; MasterCard; Visa
Catalog Cost: Free
In Business: 12 years
Sales Volume: $5,00,000

1614 Team Leader Sports
Team Leader Sports
2901 Summit Ave
Suite 300
Plano, TX 75074
214-340-2288
877-365-7555
info@teamleader.com
www.teamleadersports.com

Uniforms and accessories for cheerleaders, dance teams, drill teams, team sports, color guard and band

1615 Terry Precision Cycling
Terry Precision Cycling, Inc.
47 Maple Street
Burlington, VT 05401
802-861-7610
800-289-8379
Fax: 802-861-2956
www.terrybicycles.com

Clothing for bicycling
President: Georgena Terry
CFO: Peter Mellen
Marketing Manager: Jackie Marchand
Founder: Georgena Terry
Catalog Cost: Free
Catalog Circulation: Mailed 10 time(s) per year
Average Order Size: $100
Printing Information: in 4 colors on Matte Stock
Press: Web Press
Binding: Saddle Stitched
In Business: 25 years
Number of Employees: 16
Sales Volume: $ 2.5 Million

1616 Tilley Endurables
Tilley Endurables Corp.
60 Gervais Drive
Building A
Toronto, CA M3C 1-1069
866-441-3166
800-363-8737
Fax: 416-444-6977
tilley@tilley.com
www.tilley.com

Travel and adventure clothing
Chairman: Alexander Tilley
President: Mary Shanahan
Production Manager: Zoe Zwolak
Credit Cards: AMEX; MasterCard; Visa
Catalog Cost: Free
Catalog Circulation: Mailed 2 time(s) per year to 20000
Average Order Size: $110
Printing Information: 90 pages in 4 colors on Glossy Stock
Press: Web Press
Binding: Saddle Stitched
Mailing List Information: Names for rent
In Business: 24 years
Number of Employees: 25
Sales Volume: $ 7 Million

1617 Tri-Mountain
WestPro, Inc.
2294 Mountain Vista Lane
Provo, UT 84606-6206
801-373-2525
Fax: 801-373-8778
steve@westpro.net
www.westpro.net

Custom sportswear, including direct embroidery and screen printing
President: Steve Clement
CFO: John M Edmunds
Credit Cards: MasterCard
Catalog Cost: Free
Catalog Circulation: Mailed 1 time(s) per year to 2000
Average Order Size: $2000
Printing Information: 292 pages in 4 colors on Glossy Stock
Press: Web Press
Binding: Perfect Bound
In Business: 36 years
Number of Employees: 45
Sales Volume: $3-5 Million

1618 Turtleson
Turtleson
423-217-4950
888-602-0652
customercare@turtleson.com
www.turtleson.com

Menswear for on and off the golf course

1619 Tuttle Distinctive Sportswear
Tuttle
1068 North Farms Rd
Bldg 2
Wallingford, CT 06492-888
203-949-4290
800-854-3437
Fax: 203-949-4288
www.tuttlecatalog.com

Distinctive sportswear for men and women
President: Adam Mosher
Marketing Manager: Tom Kothman
Production Manager: Tom Kothman
Credit Cards: AMEX; MasterCard; Visa
Catalog Cost: Free
Catalog Circulation: to 1MM
Average Order Size: $320
Printing Information: 48 pages in 4 colors on Glossy Stock
Press: Web Press
Binding: Saddle Stitched
Mailing List Information: Names for rent
In Business: 23 years
Number of Employees: 12
Sales Volume: $ 3-5 Million

1620 West Marine Spring Waterlife
West Marine
500 Westridge Dr.
Watsonville, CA 95076-4100
831-728-2700
800-262-8464
www.westmarine.com

Waterlife footwear, apparel and accessories.
CFO: Jeffrey Lasher
President & CEO: Matt Hyde
Printing Information: 1116 pages in 4 colors
Mailing List Information: Names for rent
Number of Employees: 5000
Sales Volume: $700 Million

1621 WestPro Catalog
WestPro, Inc.
2294 Mountain Vista Lane
Provo, UT 84606-6206
801-373-2525
Fax: 801-373-8778
steve@westpro.net
www.westpro.net

Custom sportswear, embroidered and screen printed clothing and blank hats
President: Steven Clement
CFO: John M Edmunds
Credit Cards: MasterCard; Visa

Catalog Circulation: to 1000
Printing Information: 6 pages
In Business: 36 years
Number of Employees: 45
Sales Volume: $ 3-5 Million

1622 Western Promotion Sportswear
WestPro, Inc.
2294 Mountain Vista Lane
Provo, UT 84606-6206
801-373-2525
Fax: 801-373-8778
steve@westpro.net
www.westpro.net

Custom sportswear, including direct embroidery and screen printing
President: Steven Clement
CFO: John M Edmunds
Credit Cards: MasterCard
Catalog Cost: Free
Catalog Circulation: Mailed 1 time(s) per year to 2000
Average Order Size: $2000
Printing Information: 100 pages in 4 colors on Glossy Stock
Press: Web Press
Binding: Perfect Bound
Mailing List Information: Names for rent
In Business: 36 years
Number of Employees: 45
Sales Volume: $ 3-5 Million

1623 Wilderness Dreams
Wilderness Dreams
615 Nokomis St.
Suite 400
Alexandria, MN 56308
320-762-2816
Fax: 320-763-9762
info@wildernessdreams.com
www.wildernessdreams.com

Lingerie, Loungewear and Swimwear
Printing Information: 44 pages

1624 Yale Sportswear Catalog
Yale Sportswear, Inc.
1500 Industrial Park Rd
Federalsburg, MD 21632-2656
410-754-5500
800-922-9253
Fax: 410-754-5555
info@yalesports.com
www.yalesports.com

Line of sportswear and accessories
President: Charlie Nemphos
CFO: Bob Krebs
Marketing Manager: George Curtis
Production Manager: Lee Parot
Catalog Cost: Free
Catalog Circulation: Mailed 1 time(s) per year
Printing Information: 12 pages in 4 colors on Glossy Stock
In Business: 30 years
Number of Employees: 100
Sales Volume: $ 50-100 Million

Uniforms & Workwear

1625 Algy Team Collection
Algy
440 NE First Avenue
Hallandale, FL 33009
954-457-8100
800-458-2549
Fax: 888-928-2282
customerservice@algyteam.com
www.algyteam.com

Costumes and marching band uniforms
Chairman: Herbert Lieberman
President: Susan Gordon
CFO: Laurie Godbout
Chief Executive Officer: Sue Gordon
Credit Cards: AMEX; MasterCard
Catalog Cost: Free
Catalog Circulation: Mailed 2 time(s) per year to 50000
Printing Information: 102 pages in 4 colors on

Glossy Stock
Press: Sheetfed Press
Binding: Perfect Bound
Mailing List Information: Names for rent
In Business: 75 years
Number of Employees: 55
Sales Volume: $10-20 Million

1626   Baseball Express
Baseball Express
5750 Northwest Parkway
Suite 100
San Antonio, TX 78249-3374   210-348-7000
                                  800-937-4824
                        Fax: 210-525-9339
customer.service@teamexpress.com
www.baseballexpress.com

Full line of baseball uniforms and accessories

President: Pat Cawles
CFO: Geoff Westmoreland
Credit Cards: AMEX; MasterCard
In Business: 25 years
Number of Employees: 7

1627   Carhartt
Carhartt
5750 Mercury Drive
Dearborn, MI 48126   800-833-3118
just_ask_us@carhartt.com
www.carhartt.com

Men and womenswear and gear for outdoor activities such as camping, horseback riding, boating, ski/snowboarding, farming, home gardening, woodworking, offreading, fishing, and hunting

Chairman: Mark Valade
President: Linda Hubbard
Credit Cards: AMEX; MasterCard
Catalog Cost: Free
Catalog Circulation: Mailed 4 time(s) per year
Printing Information: 55 pages in 4 colors on Glossy Stock
In Business: 128 years

1628   Chef Works
Chef Works
12325 Kerran Street
Poway, CA 92064-6801   858-643-5600
                             800-372-6621
                   Fax: 858-643-5624
orders@chefworks.com
www.chefwork.com

Designer chef clothing and accessories

President: Henry Singer
CFO: David Forster
Credit Cards: AMEX; MasterCard
Catalog Cost: Free
In Business: 51 years
Number of Employees: 75
Sales Volume: $ 14 Million

1629   Chefwear
Chefwear
2300 Windsor Ct
Suite C
Addison, IL 60101   630-396-8337
                          800-568-2433
                Fax: 630-396-8393
carol.mueller@chefwear.com
www.chefwear.com

Clothing and accesories for chefs and home gourmets

President: Rochelle Huppin
Marketing Manager: Carol Mueller
carol.mueller@chefwear.com
VP-Sales & Marketing: Carol Mueller
carol.mueller@chefwear.com
Customer Service/Sales Manager: Michelle Schmuhl
mschmuhl@chefwear.com
Credit Cards: AMEX; MasterCard
Catalog Cost: Free

Printing Information: 40 pages in 4 colors
Press: Web Press
Binding: Saddle Stitched
Mailing List Information: Names for rent
In Business: 25 years
Number of Employees: 45
Sales Volume: $ 3 Million

1630   Dance Catalog
GTM Sportswear
520 McCall Road
Manhattan, KS 66502   877-597-8086
                            800-377-8527
                  Fax: 877-908-7033
info@igtm.com
www.gtmsportswear.com

Dance apparel, uniforms and accessories

President: John Strawn
Credit Cards: AMEX; MasterCard; Visa
Catalog Cost: Free
Catalog Circulation: Mailed 3 time(s) per year
Printing Information: 28 pages in 4 colors on G
Press: S
Binding: S
In Business: 26 years
Number of Employees: 650

1631   Ebbets Field Flannels
Ebbets Field Flannels
119 South Jackson Street
Seattle, WA 98104   506-382-7249
                          888-896-2936
                Fax: 206-382-4411
customerservice@ebbets.com
www.ebbets.com

Flannel baseball, hockey, and football clothing and accessories in authentic vintage styles; team uniforms and custom orders available

President: Jerry Cohen
Credit Cards: AMEX; MasterCard
Catalog Cost: Free
Catalog Circulation: Mailed 12 time(s) per year to 12500
Printing Information: 16 pages in 4 colors on Glossy Stock
Press: Web Press
Binding: Saddle Stitched
In Business: 25 years

1632   GK Warmup Catalog
Elite Sportswear LP
2136 N 13th Street
PO Box 16400
Reading, PA 19604-6400   610-921-1469
                               800-345-4087
                     Fax: 610-921-0208
info@gkelite.com
www.gkelite.com

Women's and men's warmup apparel

President: Dan Casciano
CEO: Sallie Weaver
COO: Alan Robezzoli
Credit Cards: AMEX; MasterCard
Catalog Cost: $6
In Business: 30 years
Number of Employees: 250
Sales Volume: $15 Million

1633   GTM Sportswear Inc.
GTM Sportswear Inc.
520 McCall Road
Manhattan, KS 65502   877-597-8086
                            800-377-8527
                  Fax: 877-908-7033
info@gtm.com
www.gtmsportswear.com

Cheerleading apparel, uniforms and accessories

President: John Strawn
Credit Cards: AMEX; MasterCard; Visa
Catalog Cost: Free

Catalog Circulation: Mailed 3 time(s) per year
Printing Information: 68 pages in 4 colors on G
Press: W
Binding: P
In Business: 25 years
Number of Employees: 650

1634   Happy Chef
Happy Chef Inc
22 Park Place
Butler, NJ 07405   973-492-2525
                         800-347-0288
               Fax: 973-492-0303
www.happychefuniforms.com

Chef coats, pants and footwear, server pants and women's chefwear

Chairman: Joseph Nadler
President: Jim Nadler
CFO: Howard Curtain
Credit Cards: AMEX; MasterCard
Catalog Cost: Free
In Business: 47 years
Number of Employees: 45
Sales Volume: $8 million

1635   Head-To-Toe Catalog
Lion Apparel
7200 Poe Avenue
Suite 400
Dayton, OH 45414-2655   800-548-6614
www.lionprotects.com

Protective clothing

President: Stephen Schwartz
Sr. VP: Terry Smith
VP Military Programs: Dennis Dudek
VP Stratergic Business Development: Jay Pavlick
Catalog Cost: Free
Catalog Circulation: Mailed 1 time(s) per year
Printing Information: 4 pages in 4 colors
In Business: 120 years
Sales Volume: $50MM to $100MM

1636   Lands' End School Outfitters
Lands' End, Inc.
1 Lands' End Lane
Dodgeville, WI 53595   800-963-4816
                   Fax: 800-332-0103
www.landsend.com

Uniforms in sizes to fit grades K-12

Co-interim CEO: James Gooch
Co-interim CEO: James Boitano
Catalog Cost: Free
Printing Information: in 4 colors
Mailing List Information: Names for rent
List Company: Millard Group
In Business: 53 years
Number of Employees: 5300
Sales Volume: $1.42 Billion

1637   Lydia's Uniforms
Lydia's Uniforms
2547 Three Mile Rd NW
Suite F
Grand Rapids, MI 49534-1358   888-222-8919
                                    800-942-3378
                          Fax: 616-453-8629
customerservice@lydiasuniforms.com
www.lydiasuniforms.com

Professional uniforms and accessories

President: Martha Fotis
VP of Operations: Jim Fotis
Credit Cards: AMEX; MasterCard
Catalog Cost: Free
Printing Information: 68 pages in 4 colors on Glossy Stock
Binding: Folded
In Business: 40 years
Number of Employees: 140
Sales Volume: $ 6 Million

1638 Mad About Mouths Catalog
Lydia's Professional Uniforms
2547 Three Mile Road NW
Suite F
Grand Rapids, MI 49534-1358 888-222-8919
Fax: 616-453-8629
customerservice@lydiasuniforms.com
www.lydiasuniforms.com

Fun professional uniforms for the dental industry
President: Martha Fotis
Catalog Cost: Free
In Business: 40 years
Number of Employees: 100
Sales Volume: $ 6 Million

1639 Modren Process Company Barber Catalog
Modren Process Company
3533 South Derenzy Road
Suite A
Bellaire, MI 49615 231-533-6700
www.modernprocess.net

Casual workwear, accessories
In Business: 40+ years

1640 Modren Process Company Education Catalog
Modren Process Company
3533 South Derenzy Road
Suite A
Bellaire, MI 49615 231-533-6700
www.modernprocess.net

Casual workwear, accessories
In Business: 40+ years

1641 Modren Process Company Postal Casual Wear Catalog
Modren Process Company
3533 South Derenzy Road
Suite A
Bellaire, MI 49615 231-533-6700
www.modernprocess.net

Casual workwear, accessories
In Business: 40+ years

1642 Modren Process Company Rural Letter Carrier Catalo
Modren Process Company
3533 South Derenzy Road
Suite A
Bellaire, MI 49615 231-533-6700
www.modernprocess.net

Casual workwear, accessories
In Business: 40+ years

1643 Modren Process Company School Cafeteria Catalog
Modren Process Company
3533 South Derenzy Road
Suite A
Bellaire, MI 49615 231-533-6700
www.modernprocess.net

Casual workwear, accessories
In Business: 40+ years

1644 Plastex Protective Products
Plastex Protective Products
661 Pleasant Street
Suite 600
Norwood, MA 02062 781-769-8000
888-752-7839
www.ppprainwear.com

Manufacturer & importer of quality safety and protective rain gear and safety gear, boots and footwear
President: Bob Shankman
VP: Kathleen Shankman
In Business: 77 years

Number of Employees: 9
Sales Volume: $ 1 Million

1645 Pro-Am Safety
Pro-Am Safety,Inc
551 Keystone Drive
Warrendale, PA 15086-6585 724-776-1818
800-351-2477
Fax: 724-776-2263
www.pro-am.com

Line of safety equipment, uniforms and accessories
President: Jim Di Nardo
Marketing Manager: John Gieder
Credit Cards: AMEX; MasterCard
In Business: 33 years
Sales Volume: $ 20-50 Million

1646 Regency Cap & Gown
Regency Cap & Gown Company
7534 Atlantic Blvd
Jacksonville, FL 32211-8783 904-724-3500
800-826-8612
Fax: 904-721-1444
catalog@rcgown.com
www.rcgown.Com

Graduation, choir and pulpit robes and accessories
President: Bob Walker
Marketing Manager: Lisa Cork
Catalog Cost: Free
In Business: 31 years
Number of Employees: 130
Sales Volume: $ 6 Million

1647 Rehan's
Rehan's Uniforms
2018 South St. Aubin Street
Sioux City, IA 51106-2406 712-276-1432
800-798-1432
Fax: 712-276-1672
rehans@cableone.net
www.rehansuniforms.Com

Uniforms and accessories
President: George Rehan
Marketing Manager: Cindy Cook
Co-Owner: Sara Rehan
In Business: 51 years
Number of Employees: 5
Sales Volume: Under $500,000

1648 Restaurant Uniforms
Cheap Aprons
599 Canal Street
Lawrence, MA 01840 978-689-0694
844-275-2795
Fax: 603-294-1797
info@cheapaprons.com
www.cheapaprons.com

Uniforms and apparel for the restaurant and hospitality industry
President: Sheri Alorich
CFO: Rick Kurman
Marketing Manager: Rick Kurman
Production Manager: Rick Kurman
Catalog Cost: Free
Catalog Circulation: to 200M
Printing Information: 32 pages
In Business: 35 years
Number of Employees: 20
Sales Volume: $500,000- 1 Million

1649 S&H Uniforms
S&H Uniforms
1 Aqueduct Rd
White Plains, NY 10606-1003 914-937-6800
800-210-5295
Fax: 914-937-0741
customerservice@sandhuniforms.com
www.sandhuniforms.com

Line of work uniforms and apparel

President: Glen Ross
Sales Manager: Patricia Kraft
Credit Cards: AMEX; MasterCard; Visa
Catalog Cost: Free
Catalog Circulation: Mailed 5 time(s) per year to 90MM
Average Order Size: $50
Printing Information: 96 pages in 1 color on Matte Stock
Press: Web Press
Binding: Perfect Bound
Mailing List Information: Names for rent
In Business: 54 years
Number of Employees: 65
Sales Volume: $ 10 Million

1650 Scrubs & Beyond
Scrubs & Beyond
PO Box 313
Louisiana, MO 63353 800-310-1580
866-972-2849
Fax: 800-313-5579
guestservice@scrubsandbeyond.com
www.scrubsandbeyond.com

Medical scrubs and accessories
President: Karla Bakersmith
Credit Cards: AMEX; MasterCard
Catalog Cost: Free
Catalog Circulation: Mailed 2 time(s) per year
Printing Information: 36 pages in 4 colors on Glossy Stock
Binding: Perfect Bound
In Business: 15 years

1651 Scrubs Catalog
Tafford Uniforms, LLC
PO Box 481912
Charlotte, NC 28269 800-669-0094
800-697-3321
Fax: 888-588-8590
customerservice@tafford.com
www.tafford.com

Men's and women's solid and print scrub tops, jackets, shoes, stethoscopes and nursing books
President: Robert Shoenfeld
Marketing Manager: David Kaplan
Production Manager: Marc Kohn
Credit Cards: AMEX; MasterCard
In Business: 29 years
Number of Employees: 60
Sales Volume: $ 3-5 Million

1652 Sgt Grit's Marine Specialties
Sgt Grit Inc
7100 SW 44th St
Oklahoma City, OK 73179 405-602-5490
888-668-1775
Fax: 405-602-5470
custserv@grunt.com
www.grunt.com

Marine Corps clothing, uniforms and USMC merchandise
President: Don Whitton
Production Manager: Crystal Butler
VP: Laurie
Purchasing: Karen
Customer Service: Teresa
Credit Cards: MasterCard
Catalog Cost: Free
Catalog Circulation: Mailed 52 time(s) per year
Printing Information: 135 pages
In Business: 27 years
Number of Employees: 40
Sales Volume: $ 5 Million

1653 Some's Uniforms
Some's World-wide Uniforms
314 Main Street
Hackensack, NJ 07601 201-843-1199
Fax: 201-843-3014
someunif@somes.com
www.somes.com

Military uniforms, badges, insignia, medals, certificates, citation bars, footwear and defense equipment

President: Jerome S. Some
CFO: Heschel Some
Administrative Executive: Lily Rivera
Director of Sales: Jason Some
Chief Executive Officer: Andrea Some
Catalog Cost: Free
In Business: 59 years
Sales Volume: $ 3-5 Million

1654 Team Leader Sports
Team Leader Sports
2901 Summit Ave
Suite 300
Plano, TX 75074   214-340-2288
877-365-7555
info@teamleader.com
www.teamleadersports.com

Uniforms and accessories for cheerleaders, dance teams, drill teams, team sports, color guard and band

1655 The Cruise Uniform Book
Cintas Corporation
6800 Cintas Blvd.
Cincinnati, OH 45262   513-459-1200
www.cintas.com

Traditional and formal collections for day, evening and cold weather.

President: J. Phillip Holloman
CEO: Scott Farmer
Catalog Cost: Free
In Business: 87 years
Number of Employees: 3000
Sales Volume: $4.1 Billion

1656 The Security Uniform Book
Cintas Corporation
6800 Cintas Blvd.
Cincinnati, OH 45262   513-459-1200
www.cintas.com

Security apparel.

President: J. Phillip Holloman
CEO: Scott Farmer
Catalog Cost: Free
Printing Information: 12 pages in 4 colors
In Business: 87 years
Number of Employees: 3000
Sales Volume: $4.1 Billion

1657 The Sourcebook
Cintas Corporation
6800 Cintas Blvd.
Cincinnati, OH 45262   513-459-1200
www.cintas.com

Uniform apparel featuring popular brand names including: Carhartt, Nike, Timberland and Dickies.

President: J. Phillip Holloman
CEO: Scott Farmer
Catalog Cost: Free
Printing Information: 212 pages in 4 colors
In Business: 87 years
Number of Employees: 3000
Sales Volume: $4.1 Billion

1658 The Uniform Book
Cintas Corporation
6800 Cintas Blvd.
Cincinnati, OH 45262   513-459-1200
www.cintas.com

Specialized products and services from corporate identity uniform programs to tile and carpet cleaning.

Chairman: Robert J. Kohlhepp
President: J. Phillip Holloman
CEO: Scott Farmer
Catalog Cost: Free
Printing Information: 76 pages in 4 colors
In Business: 87 years

Number of Employees: 3000
Sales Volume: $4.1 Billion

1659 Uniform Advantage Medical Uniforms
Uniform Advantage
150 South Pine Island Road
Suite 300
Plantation, FL 33324   954-626-2100
800-283-8708
Fax: 954-626-2112
www.uniformadvantage.com

Medical uniforms

President: Susan Fields
Production Manager: Melba Smith
Credit Cards: MasterCard
Catalog Cost: Free
Catalog Circulation: Mailed 1 time(s) per year
Printing Information: 64 pages in 4 colors
Binding: Perfect Bound
In Business: 30 years
Number of Employees: 33
Sales Volume: $ 3 Million

1660 Uniform Wizard
Uniform Wizard
2219 Clay Street
Kissimmee, FL 34741   888-999-4660
wizard@uniformwizard.com
www.uniformwizard.com

Uniforms, career apparel, promotional apparel, safety products and floor mats

Credit Cards: AMEX; MasterCard

1661 Vantage Apparel
Vantage Apparel
100 Vantage Dr
Avenel, NJ 07001-1080   732-340-3000
800-221-0020
Fax: 732-340-3165
customerservice@vantageapparel.com
www.vantageapparel.com

Apparel of the names and logos of the country' leading corporations, resorts, golf courses, colleges and casinos

President: Ira Neaman
Catalog Cost: Free
In Business: 35 years
Sales Volume: $ 20-50 Million

1662 Veterinary Apparel Company
Veterinary Apparel Company
847 Main Street
Battle Creek, MI 49014   269-963-7810
800-922-1456
Fax: 269-963-0341
pvac@professionalapparel.com
www.veterinaryapparel.com

Clothing for veterinarians

President: Sharon Van Vrankan
Credit Cards: AMEX; MasterCard
Catalog Cost: Free
Printing Information: 43 pages in 4 colors on Glossy Stock
Binding: Saddle Stitched
In Business: 30 years
Sales Volume: $5MM to $10MM

1663 Wasserman Uniforms
Wasserman Uniforms
700 NW 57th Place
Fort Lauderdale, FL 33309   800-848-3576
Fax: 800-204-0416
custserv@wassermanuniform.com
www.wassermanuniform.com

Carries a large selection of uniforms and accessories for the postal industry.

Catalog Cost: Free
In Business: 46 years
Sales Volume: $5MM to $10MM

Number of Employees: 3000
Sales Volume: $4.1 Billion

1664 WearGuard Catalog
WearGuard Corp
1101Market St.
Philadelphia, PA 19107-1609   781-871-4100
800-388-3300
Fax: 800-436-3132
www.shoparamark.com

Work clothes, uniforms and accessories

Chairman: Joseph Neubauer
President: Eric J. Foss
CFO: L Frederick Sutherland
Marketing Manager: Charles Seelig
Production Manager: Tom McDermott
EVP/General Counsel/Secretary: Stephen R. Reynolds
EVP, Human Resources: Lynn B. McKee
Chief Operating Officer: Marc Bruno
Credit Cards: AMEX; MasterCard
Catalog Circulation: to 35MM
Printing Information: 99 pages
In Business: 77 years
Number of Employees: 250,
Sales Volume: $100-500 Million

1665 Work n' Gear Catalog
Work n' Gear, LLC
2300 Crown Colony Drive
Quincy, MA 02169   800-987-0218
info@workngear.com
www.workngear.com

Uniforms for healthcare, hospitality and industrial workers

President: Anthony DiPaolo
Credit Cards: AMEX; MasterCard; Visa

1666 Worker's Choice
Dickies
509 West Vickery Blvd.
Fort Worth, TX 76104   800-342-5437
customerservice@dickies.com
www.dickies.com

Workwear, casual wear and footwear for men, women and kids.

Chairman & CEO: Philip Williamson
Catalog Cost: Free
Catalog Circulation: Mailed 2 time(s) per year
Printing Information: 48 pages in 4 colors
In Business: 95 years
Sales Volume: $100MM to $500MM

1667 eMarinePX Catalog
eMarine PX
PO Box 2329
Grass Valley, CA 95945   877-915-6772
emarinepx@emarinepx.com
www.emarinepx.com

Marine patches, apparel and USMC gear

Credit Cards: AMEX; MasterCard
Catalog Cost: Free
Printing Information: in 3 colors
In Business: 13 years
Sales Volume: Under $500M

Western Gear

1668 Buckaroo Bobbins
Buckaroo Bobbins
PO Box 1168
Chino Valley, AZ 86323-1168   928-636-1885
Fax: 928-636-8134
buckaroobobbins@gmail.com
www.buckaroobobbins.com

Sewing patterns for vintage 1860-1900 Western clothing, as well as cowboy accessories

President: Roger Eads
Co-Owner: Geneva Eads
Catalog Cost: $2
Catalog Circulation: to 10000
Printing Information: 16 pages in 2 colors on Newsprint
Press: Web Press
Binding: Folded

Mailing List Information: Names for rent
In Business: 22 years
Sales Volume: $400,000

1669 Drysdales

Drysdales
3220 S Memorial Dr
Tulsa, OK 74145-1355   918-664-6481
                             800-444-6481
                        Fax: 918-832-8900
customerservice@drysdales.com
www.drysdales.com

Fashion and traditional western clothing, gifts and accessories

President: Jim Mc Clure
Credit Cards: AMEX; MasterCard
Catalog Cost: Free
Catalog Circulation: Mailed 8 time(s) per year
Average Order Size: $78
Printing Information: 56 pages in 4 colors on Glossy Stock
Press: Web Press
Binding: Perfect Bound
Mailing List Information: Names for rent
In Business: 34 years
Number of Employees: 200
Sales Volume: $10MM to $20MM

1670 Hobby Horse Clothing Company

Hobby Horse Clothing Company
13775 Stockton Avenue
Chino, CA 91710-7035   909-613-1686
                             800-569-5885
                        Fax: 800-462-2439
customerserv@hobbyhorseinc.com
www.hobbyhorseinc.com

Full line of accessories and western clothing

President: Suzi Vlietstra
Catalog Cost: Free

1671 King Ranch Saddle Shop

King Ranch Saddle Shop
201 E. Kleberg
PO Box 1090
Kingsville, TX 78363-1090   361-595-1524
                             800-282-5464
                        Fax: 361-595-1011
krsaddleshop@king-ranch.com
www.king-ranch.com

Saddles and entire line of fine leather purses, men's and women's apparel, luggage, and hunting gear

CFO: William Gardiner
Production Manager: Joann Samora
Wildlife Manager: Justin Field
jfeild@king-ranch.com
Credit Cards: MasterCard; Visa
Catalog Cost: Free
Mailing List Information: Names for rent
In Business: 21 years
Number of Employees: 35
Sales Volume: $1MM to $3MM

1672 NRS World

NRS World
1410 S. FM 51
Decatur, TX 76234   800-467-6746
                        Fax: 940-627-3131
support@nrsworld.com
www.nrsworld.com

1673 Overland Sheepskin Co.

Overland Sheepskin Co.
2096 Nutmeg Avenue
Fairfield, IA 52556   641-472-8434
                             800-683-7526
                        Fax: 641-472-6614
service@overland.com
www.overland.com

Coats, jackets, footwear, accessories, rugs, covers

1674 Rand's Custom Hats

Rand's Custom Hats
2205 1st Ave. North
Billings, MT 59101   406-259-4886
                             800-346-9815
                        Fax: 406-259-5634
hatmaker45@hotmail.com
www.randhats.com

Hats

In Business: 30+ years

1675 Rod's Western Palace

Rod's Western Palace
3099 Silver Drive
Columbus, OH 43224   614-268-8200
                        Fax: 614-268-8203
rods@rods.com
www.rods.com

Western apparel, western gifts and home decor

President: Scott Hartle
Production Manager: Terry Frakes
In Business: 39 years
Number of Employees: 100
Sales Volume: $ 4 Million

1676 Smith Brothers

Smith Brothers
PO Box 2700
Denton, TX 76202-2700   940-565-0886
                             800-784-5449
                        Fax: 940-565-8232
info@smithbrothers.com
www.smithbrothers.com

Show clothing and supplies for the Western horseman

President: Jim Smith
Credit Cards: AMEX; MasterCard
Catalog Cost: Free
Catalog Circulation: Mailed 1 time(s) per year
Printing Information: 184 pages
Binding: Perfect Bound
In Business: 37 years
Sales Volume: Under $500M

1677 The Hat Store

The Hat Store
5587 Richmond Ave
Houston, TX 77056   713-780-2480
Gary@thehatstore.com
www.thehatstore.com

Hats

In Business: 100 years

1678 The Working Person's Store

The Working Person's Store
1608 Commerce Drive
South Bend, IN 46628   866-720-6841
                             877-652-9675
workingperson.com

Apparel, footwear

In Business: 20 years

Womenswear

1679 Anthony Richards

AmeriMark Direct
6864 Engle Rd.
Cleveland, OH 44130   866-345-1388
www.amerimark.com

Affordable women's apparel, shoes, cosmetics, jewelry and accessories.

CFO: Joe Albanese
CEO & President: Gareth Giesler
Catalog Cost: Free
Printing Information: in 4 colors
In Business: 47 years
Number of Employees: 700
Sales Volume: $400 Million

1680 Anthropologie

Anthropologie
5000 South Broad St.
Philadelphia, PA 19112-1495   215-454-5500
www.anthropologie.com

Women's apparel and accessories, home furniture and decor.

CEO, Anthropologie Group: David McCreight
Catalog Cost: Free
Printing Information: in 4 colors
In Business: 46 years
Sales Volume: $311 Million

1681 Ashro Lifestyle

Ashro
999 Oakmont Plaza Drive
Suite 360
Westmont, IL 60559-8736   630-515-8811
                             800-810-8964
                        Fax: 630-852-3133

Women's ethnic clothing and accessories

President: Rajiv Khartau
Vice President: Sandra Ford
sandra@ashro.com
Printing Information: 45 pages

1682 Athleta

Athleta
1450 Technology Lane
Suite 150
Petaluma, CA 94954   614-744-3913
                             877-328-4538
www.athleta.gap.com/?

Athletic clothing and accessories for women including jackets and outerwear, pants and bottoms, skirts and dresses and footwear

President: Joseph E Teno
Marketing Manager: John Monteleone
Human Resources Director: Mona Patel
Credit Cards: AMEX; MasterCard
Catalog Cost: Free
Catalog Circulation: Mailed 1 time(s) per year
Printing Information: 24 pages
In Business: 16 years
Number of Employees: 110
Sales Volume: $6.7 MM

1683 Blair Women's

Blair
220 Hickory St.
Warren, PA 16366   800-821-5744
www.blair.com

Full line of women's clothing and footwear.

President: Marisa Smith
Catalog Cost: Free
Printing Information: in 4 colors
In Business: 106 years
Number of Employees: 2000
Sales Volume: $1 Billion

1684 Brahmin

Brahmin USA
77 Alden Road
Fairhaven, MA 00271   508-994-4000
                             800-229-2428
www.brahmin.com

Handbags, wallets, bracelets, and other accessories

Catalog Cost: Free
In Business: 32 years

1685 Brooks Brothers

Brooks Brothers
100 Phoenix Avenue
Enfield, CT 06082   800-274-1815
                        Fax: 800-274-1010
www.brooksbrothers.com

Complete line of mens, women and childrens shirts, polos & tees, sweaters, casual and dress pants, suits, formalwear, sport coats and blazers

President: Claudio Del Vecchio
CFO: Brian Baumann
SVP Operations: Debra Del Vecchio
Credit Cards: AMEX; MasterCard; Visa
Catalog Cost: Free
Catalog Circulation: Mailed 5 time(s) per year
Printing Information: 80 pages in 4 colors on Glossy Stock
Press: Web Press
Binding: Saddle Stitched
Mailing List Information: Names for rent
In Business: 198 years
Number of Employees: 3500
Sales Volume: $ 20-50 Million

1686 Cali and York

Cali and York
1034 Windward Ridge Pkwy
Alpharetta, GA 30005-3992   888-571-2774
Fax: 888-571-1822
customercare@caliandyork.com
www.caliandyork.com

Women clothing

Printing Information: 60 pages

1687 Chadwicks of Boston

Chadwicks of Boston
500 Bic Drive
Building 4
Milford, CT 06461   877-330-3393
service@cs.chadwicks.com
www.chadwicks.com

Women's clothing, shoes and accessories.

CEO: Aldus Chapin II
Catalog Cost: Free
Printing Information: 64 pages in 4 colors
In Business: 33 years

1688 Cheeks Cape May

Cheeks Cape May
101 Ocean Street
Cape May, NJ 08204   609-884-8484
866-524-3357
Fax: 609-884-2249
info@cheekscapemay.com
www.cheekscapemay.com

Flax clothing in regular and plus sizes

President: Chris Hey
Credit Cards: MasterCard
Catalog Cost: Free
In Business: 32 years
Sales Volume: Under $500M

1689 Chico's

Chico's
11215 Metro Pkwy.
Fort Myers, FL 33966   www.chicos.com

Line of women's apparel and accessories.

President: Shelley Broader
Catalog Cost: Free
Catalog Circulation: Mailed 12 time(s) per year
Printing Information: 48 pages in 4 colors
In Business: 33 years
Number of Employees: 2370
Sales Volume: $2.6 Billion

1690 Coward Shoes

Old Pueblo Traders
PO Box 188
Jessup, PA 18434-188   800-351-5203
800-351-5205
Fax: 800-964-1975
oldpueblotraders.blair.com

Womens shoes and accessories

President: Steve Lightman
Credit Cards: MasterCard; Visa
Catalog Cost: Free
Catalog Circulation: Mailed 12 time(s) per year
Average Order Size: $80

Printing Information: in 4 colors on Glossy Stock
Press: Web Press
Binding: Saddle Stitched
Mailing List Information: Names for rent
In Business: 60 years
Sales Volume: $ 50-100 Million

1691 Crow's Nest Trading Company

Crow's Nest Trading Company
3205 Airport Blvd
Wilson, NC 27896   800-900-8558
Fax: 800-900-3136
ldolliver@thecrowsnesttrading.com
www.thecrowsnesttrading.com

Rustic furniture, southwestern decor and women's western apparel

President: Doug Tennis
CFO: Gary Tennis
Catalog Cost: Free
Catalog Circulation: Mailed 4 time(s) per year
Printing Information: 84 pages in 4 colors on Glossy Stock
Press: Web Press
Binding: Saddle Stitched
In Business: 16 years
Number of Employees: 20
Sales Volume: $3MM to $5MM

1692 Cyberswim

Cyberswim, Inc.
519 George Street
Pen Argyl, PA 18072   800-291-2943
Fax: 610-863-5052
www.cyberswim.com

Direct supplier of Miraclesuit swimwear

Catalog Cost: Free
In Business: 16 years

1693 Delia's

Delia's
50 W 23rd Street
New York, NY 10010   212-590-6200
866-293-3268
Fax: 212-590-6300
customerservice@deliasmerch.com
store.delias.com

Teen clothing, shoes, jewelry, and accessories

Chairman: Carter S Evans
President: Walter Killough
CFO: David J Dick
Marketing Manager: Douglas Sietsma
Credit Cards: AMEX; MasterCard; Visa
Catalog Cost: Free
Catalog Circulation: Mailed 1 time(s) per year to 65mm
Printing Information: 74 pages on Glossy Stock
Binding: Perfect Bound
In Business: 16 years
Number of Employees: 50
Sales Volume: $217MM

1694 Draper's & Damon's

Bluestem Brands, Inc.
9 Pasteur
Suite 200
Irvine, CA 92618   866-654-2195
www.drapers.blair.com

Line of womens clothing and accessories

President: Steve Nave
CFO: Pete Michielutti
EVP, COO, & Chief Digital Officer: Vince Jones
EVP & President of Credit Services: Jim Slavik
Credit Cards: AMEX; MasterCard
Catalog Cost: Free
Catalog Circulation: Mailed 1 time(s) per year
In Business: 89 years
Sales Volume: $50MM to $100MM

1695 Duluth Trading Company

Duluth Trading Company
PO Box 200
Belleville, WI 53508-9739   608-424-1544
866-300-9719
Fax: 888-950-3199
customerservice@duluthtrading.com
www.duluthtrading.com

Women & men clothing & accessories

President: Steve Schlecht
Production Manager: Dan Moeller
Credit Cards: AMEX; MasterCard
Catalog Cost: Free
In Business: 24 years
Number of Employees: 150
Sales Volume: $ 15 Million

1696 First Frost

Coldwater Creek
1176 E Dayton Yellow Springs Rd.
Fairborn, OH 45324   888-678-5576
www.coldwatercreek.com

Women's apparel, jewelry, accessories and gifts.

CEO: Dave Walde
President: Brenda Koskinen
Catalog Cost: Free
Printing Information: 88 pages in 4 colors
In Business: 32 years
Number of Employees: 100
Sales Volume: $780 Million

1697 Flirt

Flirt
2346 E Pacifica Pl
Rancho Dominguez, CA 90220   877-825-2860

Women's apparel and lingerie

President: Ronald Alan Abeles
VP: Dan Deyoung
Buyers: Ronald Alan Abales
Credit Cards: AMEX; MasterCard
Catalog Cost: $2
Catalog Circulation: Mailed 5 time(s) per year
Average Order Size: $10
Printing Information: 40 pages in 4 colors on Glossy Stock
Press: Web Press
Binding: Saddle Stitched
Mailing List Information: Names for rent
In Business: 23 years
Number of Employees: 6
Sales Volume: $4 million

1698 GK Spring/Summer Skating Wear Catalog

Elite Sportswear LP
2136 N 13th Street
PO Box 16400
Reading, PA 19604-6400   610-921-1469
800-345-4087
Fax: 610-921-0208
info@gkelite.com
www.gkelite.com

Figure skating dresses

President: Dan Casciano
COO: Alan Robezzoli
CEO: Sallie Weaver
Credit Cards: AMEX; MasterCard
Catalog Cost: Free
In Business: 30 years
Number of Employees: 250
Sales Volume: $15 Million

1699 Isabella Bird Collection

The Territory Ahead
500 Bic Drive
Building 4
Milford, CT 06461-2304   805-962-5558
800-882-4323
Fax: 800-232-9882
service@cs.ttahead.com
www.territoryahead.com

Women's clothing and accessories including jackets, shirts and tops, sweaters, pants, skirts, dresses, shoes and jewelry

President: Bruce Willard
Catalog Cost: Free
Printing Information: 65 pages on Matte Stock
Binding: Saddle Stitched
In Business: 25 years
Sales Volume: $ 1-3 Million

1700 J. Jill
J. Jill
100 Birch Pond Dr.
P.O. Box 2006
Tilton, NH 03276-9900

603-266-2600
800-343-5700
Fax: 603-266-2802
www.jjill.com

Women's apparel and accessories

President & CEO: Paula Bennett
Catalog Cost: Free
Printing Information: in 4 colors
In Business: 55 years
Sales Volume: $545 Million

1701 Jessica London
Jessica London
One New York Plaza
New York, NY 10004

jessicalondon.com

Plus-size apparel, lingerie and shoes.

CEO: Paul Tarvin
Catalog Cost: Free
In Business: 105 years
Number of Employees: 6400
Sales Volume: Over $1 Billion

1702 Junonia
JunoActive
1355 Mendota Heights Rd
Suite 290
Mendota Heights, MN 55120-1285

651-365-1830
800-586-6642
Fax: 920-967-0404
customerservice@junonia.com
www.junonia.com

Line of womens activewear, swimwear, intimates and outerwear for sizes 14 and up

President: Anne Kelly
annekellyfounder@junonia.com
Catalog Circulation: to 60000
Printing Information: 52 pages in 4 colors on Glossy Stock
Press: Offset Press
Binding: Saddle Stitched
Mailing List Information: Names for rent
In Business: 19 years
Number of Employees: 25
Sales Volume: $ 3-5 Million

1703 Ladies Collection 2
Bass Pro Shops
2500 E Kearney
Springfield, MO 65898

417-873-5000
800-227-7776
Fax: 417-873-5060
www.basspro.com

Ladies' clothing for fall and winter.

President & CEO: James Hagale
Catalog Cost: Free
Catalog Circulation: Mailed 1 time(s) per year
Printing Information: 160 pages in 4 colors
In Business: 45 years
Number of Employees: 2200
Sales Volume: $4.45 Billion

1704 Lafayette 148 New York
Lafayette 148 New York
148 Lafayette St.
New York, NY 10013

212-965-9606
www.lafayette148ny.com

Women's fashion

CEO & Co-founder: Deirdre Quinn
Catalog Cost: Free
Printing Information: in 4 colors
In Business: 20 years

1705 Lands' End Plus
Lands' End, Inc.
1 Lands' End Lane
Dodgeville, WI 53595

800-963-4816
Fax: 800-332-0103
www.landsend.com

Clothing proportioned to fit women 16W-26W as well as some styles in regular sizes 14-18.

Co-interim CEO: James Gooch
Co-interim CEO: James Boitano
Catalog Cost: Free
Printing Information: in 4 colors
Mailing List Information: Names for rent
List Company: Millard Group
In Business: 53 years
Number of Employees: 5300
Sales Volume: $1.42 Billion

1706 Long Elegant Legs
Long Elegant Legs
2 Jill Court
Hillsborough, NJ 08844

800-344-2225
www.tallwomensclothes.com

Clothing made especially for tall women

President: Ron Kordalski
Founder: Tricia Kordalski
Credit Cards: AMEX; MasterCard; Visa
Catalog Cost: Free
In Business: 23 years
Number of Employees: 30
Sales Volume: $1MM to $3MM

1707 Marisota
Marisota
777 South State Road 7
Margate, FL 33068

855-308-6282
inquiries@Marisota.com
www.marisota.com

Clothing, lingerie, footwear, apparel, and swimwear

Catalog Cost: Free
In Business: 7 years

1708 Metrostyle
Metrostyle
500 Bic Drive
Building 4
Milford, CT 06461

877-327-1328
service@cs.metrostyle.com
www.metrostyle.com

Line of womens clothing and accessories

Credit Cards: AMEX; MasterCard
Catalog Cost: Free

1709 Norm Thompson
Bluestem Brands, Inc.
7075 Flying Cloud Drive
Eden Prairie, MN 55344

877-718-7899
800-547-1160
normthompson.blair.com

Men and womens' clothing, footwear, gifts, and gourmet food

President: Steve Nave
CFO: Pete Michielutti
EVP, COO, & Chief Digital Officer: Vince Jones
EVP & President of Credit Services: Jim Slavik
Credit Cards: AMEX; MasterCard
Catalog Cost: Free
In Business: 68 years
Sales Volume: $50MM to $100MM

1710 OneStopPlus.com
OneStopPlus.com
P.O. Box 8320
Indianapolis, IN 46283

800-400-4481
Fax: 800-456-9838
www.onestopplus.com

Clothing, apparel, shoes, and accessories for plus-size women

Catalog Cost: Free
In Business: 6 years

1711 Orvis Women
The Orvis Company Inc.
178 Conservation Way
Sunderland, VT 05250-4465

802-362-1300
888-235-9763
Fax: 802-362-0141
www.orvis.com

Women's casual clothing and accessories.

CEO: Leigh H. Perkins Jr.
Catalog Cost: Free
In Business: 160 years
Number of Employees: 1700
Sales Volume: $340 Million

1712 Peggy Lutz Plus
Peggy Lutz Plus
1813 Empire Industrial Court
Suite A
Santa Rosa, CA 95403-1979

707-578-0108
www.plus-size.com

Fine clothing for plus and supersize women, sizes 14, 16, and up, petite, medium, and tall; Career wear, cruise wear, evening clothes

President: Margaret Lutz
Catalog Cost: $5
In Business: 26 years
Sales Volume: Under $500,000

1713 Peruvian Connection
Peruvian Connection
Canaan Farm
Box 990
Tonganoxie, KS 66086

913-845-2450
800-221-8520
Fax: 800-573-7378
sales@peruvianconnection.com
www.peruvianconnection.com

Peruvian sweaters, skirts, pants, dresses, coats, jackets, jewelry and accessories

President: Annie Hurlbut
CFO: Lori Green
Credit Cards: AMEX; MasterCard
Catalog Cost: Free
Catalog Circulation: Mailed 5 time(s) per year
Printing Information: 48 pages in 4 colors
In Business: 39 years
Number of Employees: 100
Sales Volume: $10 Million

1714 Peter Millar
Peter Millar LLC
4300 Emperor Blvd.
Suite 100
Durham, NC 27703

888-926-0255
communications@petermillar.com
www.petermillar.com

Fine clothing and accessories for men and women

1715 Pure Collection
Pure Collection
Department Pure
6-10 Nassau Avenue
Inwwod, NY 11096

866-864-8199
usaservice@purecollection.com
www.us.purecollection.com

Clothing and accessories for women

Co-Founder & Managing Director: Nick Falkingham

Credit Cards: AMEX; MasterCard
Catalog Cost: Free

1716 Roaman's
Roaman's
One New York Plaza
New York, NY 10004   roamans.com

Plus-size business and casual clothing, shoes and intimate apparel.
CEO: Paul Tarvin
Catalog Cost: Free
In Business: 105 years
Number of Employees: 6400
Sales Volume: Over $1 Billion

1717 Samantha's Style Shoppe
Collections Etc., Inc.
PO Box 7985
Elk Grove Village, IL 60009-7985   620-584-8000
    888-468-1666
    Fax: 847-350-5701
    www.collectionsetc.com

Clothing for women including jewelry
President: Shelley Nandkeolyar
Marketing Manager: Karl Steigerwald
Fulfillment: Bruce Getowicz
CEO/Founder: Todd Lustbader
COO: Paul Klassman
Credit Cards: AMEX; MasterCard; Visa
Catalog Cost: Free
In Business: 50 years
Number of Employees: 200
Sales Volume: 12.7M

1718 Share the Spirit!
Coldwater Creek
1176 E Dayton Yellow Springs Rd.
Fairborn, OH 45324   888-678-5576
    www.coldwatercreek.com

Women's apparel, jewelry, accessories and gifts.
CEO: Dave Walde
President: Brenda Koskinen
Catalog Cost: Free
Printing Information: 96 pages in 4 colors
In Business: 32 years
Number of Employees: 100
Sales Volume: $780 Million

1719 SimplySoles
SimplySoles
12107 Nebel Street
Rockville, MD 20852   202-232-0072
    800-909-3679
    Fax: 301-656-6465
    customerservice@simplysoles.com
    www.simplysoles.com

Designer women's shoes, handbags and accessories
President: Kassie Rempel
Marketing Manager: Karen Hollingsworth
Production Manager: Megan Dickens
Credit Cards: AMEX; MasterCard
Catalog Cost: Free
Printing Information: in 4 colors on Matte Stock
Press: Sheetfed Press
Binding: Saddle Stitched
Mailing List Information: Names for rent
In Business: 10 years
Number of Employees: 9
Sales Volume: $500,000- 1 Million

1720 Soft Surroundings
Soft Surroundings
1100 N Lindbergh Blvd
St Louis, MO 63132-2914   800-240-7076
    Fax: 314-569-8471
    customerservice@softsurroundings.com
    www.softsurroundings.com
At home clothing of soft, easy care fabrics

President: Robin Sheldon
Marketing Manager: Mandy Dorrance
Catalog Cost: Free
Catalog Circulation: Mailed 2 time(s) per year
Average Order Size: $170
Printing Information: 80 pages in 4 colors on Glossy Stock
Binding: Saddle Stitched
In Business: 15 years
Sales Volume: $500,000- 1 Million

1721 SoulFlower
Soul Flower
801 Boone Ave N
Golden Valley, MN 55427-801   651-251-1028
    866-294-8074
    Fax: 651-251-1029
    yourbuds@soul-flower.com
    www.soul-flower.com

Natural cotton clothing for women's and children, hand bags, jewelry and accessories
President: Mike Shoafstall
Marketing Manager: Sarah
Director of Corporate Optimization: Chad
Designer: Jennifer
Agent: Joe
Credit Cards: AMEX; MasterCard; Visa
Catalog Cost: Free
Catalog Circulation: Mailed 2 time(s) per year
Printing Information: 39 pages on Glossy Stock
Binding: Saddle Stitched
In Business: 15 years

1722 Time for Me
Time for Me
6864 Engle Road
Cleveland, OH 44130-7910   866-345-1386
    www.timeformecatalog.com

Women's apparel and accessories, shoes, sleepwear, foot care products, beauty essentials, fitness, health and diet
President: Louis Giesler
Credit Cards: AMEX; MasterCard; Visa
Catalog Cost: Free
Catalog Circulation: Mailed 11 time(s) per year to 3mm
Printing Information: 48 pages in 4 colors on Glossy Stock
Press: Web Press
Binding: Saddle Stitched
In Business: 44 years
Number of Employees: 600
Sales Volume: $ 20-50 Million

1723 Title Nine Sports
Title Nine
6201 Doyle St.
Emeryville, CA 94608   858-454-4666
    800-609-0092
    Fax: 510-655-9191
    www.titlenine.com

Sportswear and accessories for women
President: Missy Park
Credit Cards: MasterCard; Visa
Catalog Circulation: Mailed 8 time(s) per year
Printing Information: 71 pages in 4 colors on Glossy Stock
Press: Web Press
Binding: Saddle Stitched
Mailing List Information: Names for rent
In Business: 23 years
Number of Employees: 170
Sales Volume: $ 1-3 Million

1724 Ulla Popken
Ulla Popken
12201 Long Green Pike
Glen Arm, MD 21057-9705   800-245-8552
    Support@ullapopken.com
    www.ullapopken.com

Women's apparel in sizes 12 - 30
President: Phyliss Mosca
Founder: Johann Popken

CEO: Diane Cantor
Credit Cards: AMEX; MasterCard; Visa
Catalog Cost: Free
Printing Information: 60 pages in 4 colors on Glossy Stock
In Business: 135 years
Number of Employees: 265
Sales Volume: $ 5-10 Million

1725 Woman Within
Woman Within
One New York Plaza
New York, NY 10004   www.womanwithin.com

Plus-size casual clothing.
CEO: Paul Tarvin
Catalog Cost: Free
In Business: 105 years
Number of Employees: 6400
Sales Volume: Over $1 Billion

1726 Women's Catalog
Duluth Trading Company
PO Box 200
Belleville, WI 53508-200   608-424-1544
    866-300-9719
    Fax: 888-950-3199
    customerservice@duluthtrading.com
    www.duluthtrading.com

Women's clothing, tools, accessories and more for hardworking women
Production Manager: Dan Mueller
COO: Carol Mueller
Catalog Cost: Free
Printing Information: 72 pages
In Business: 11 years
Number of Employees: 150
Sales Volume: $ 16 Million

1727 WomenSuits Catalog
WomenSuits
655 S Flower Street
Suite 333
Los Angeles, CA 90017   213-744-0754
    866-595-7848
    info@womensuits.com
    www.womensuits.com

Women's suits, dresses and hats
Credit Cards: AMEX; MasterCard
Catalog Cost: Free
Catalog Circulation: Mailed 2 time(s) per year
In Business: 17 years
Sales Volume: Under $500M

Collectibles
Specialty Gifts

1728 Alaska Wild Berry Products
Alaska Wild Berry Products, Inc.
5225 Juneau St
Anchorage, AK 99518-1483   907-562-8858
    800-280-2927
    Fax: 907-562-5467
    info@akwbp.com
    alaskawildberryproducts.com

Wild berry products including jams and jellies, chocolates, candies, caramels, corporate gifts and gift baskets
President: Peter G. Eden
CFO: Thomas Purcell
Marketing Manager: Drew Hamilton
Production Manager: William McDonald
Vice President: Mercedes Eden
Credit Cards: AMEX; MasterCard; Visa
Catalog Cost: Free
Printing Information: 16 pages in 4 colors
Binding: Saddle Stitched
Mailing List Information: Names for rent
In Business: 69 years
Number of Employees: 40
Sales Volume: 4M

1729 Barker Animation Art Galleries
Barker Animation Art Galleries
1188 Highland Ave
Cheshire, CT 06410-1624   203-272-2357
                                 800-995-2357
                          Fax: 203-699-1188
gallery@barkeranimation.com
www.barkeranimation.com

Production cels, limited edition cels, sericels, vintage or comic strip art, lithographs, production drawings, model sheets, lobby cards, movie and fine art poster, press books, etc from major studios
President: Herb Barker
Catalog Circulation: Mailed 1 time(s) per year
Printing Information: 50 pages in 4 colors
Number of Employees: 4

1730 Bell Company
Bell Company, Inc.
106 Morrow Ave
PO Box 92
Trussville, AL 35173-92   205-655-2135
                                 800-828-3564
                          Fax: 205-655-2138
sales@bellcoinc.com
www.bellcoinc.com

Personalized badges, signs and desk name plates, engraving machines, materials and supplies, ADA Signage, Photo-2-Canvas printing, put your photo on almost anything
President: Neil H Bell
Marketing Manager: Tina Kirk
VP/Accounting: Virginia Bell
President, A.D.A. Sales: Christopher Bell
General Manager / A.D.A. Sales: Tina Kirk
Credit Cards: AMEX; MasterCard
Catalog Cost: Free
Printing Information: 40 pages
In Business: 68 years
Number of Employees: 30
Sales Volume: $50,000,000 - $100,000,00

1731 Big-Bang Cannons
Conestoga Company Inc
323 Sumner Ave.
Allentown, PA 18102-1856   610-866-0777
                                 800-987-2264
                          Fax: 610-433-8406
customerservice@bigbangcannons.com
www.bigbangcannons.com

Cannons made of cast iron and sheet metal, for display when not in use, three sizes and ammo available, also a collectors series of past products
President: David Spinosa
Credit Cards: AMEX; MasterCard; Visa
Catalog Cost: Free
Average Order Size: $160
Mailing List Information: Names for rent
In Business: 57 years
Number of Employees: 8
Sales Volume: $680,000

1732 Biordi Art Imports
Biordi's Art Imports
412 Columbus Ave
San Francisco, CA 94133-3902   415-392-8096
                          Fax: 415-392-2608
info@biordi.com
www.biordi.com

Italian majolica ceramics such as dinnerware, countertop and serving pieces, decorative items, vases, planters, gift items and jewelry
President: Giovanni Savio
Catalog Cost: Free
Catalog Circulation: Mailed 1 time(s) per year
In Business: 69 years
Number of Employees: 8

1733 Bowling Delights
Bowling Delights
400 Morris Ave
Ste 118
Denville, NJ 07834   862-244-8111
                                 877-777-2646
                          Fax: 800-569-4250
customerservice@bowlingdelights.com
www.bowlingdelights.com

Bowling gifts and collectibles
President: Parker Bohn
Credit Cards: AMEX; MasterCard; Visa
Catalog Cost: Free
In Business: 10 years

1734 Celtic Treasures
Celtic Treasures Irish Gift Shop
456 Broadway
Saratogo Springs, NY 12866   518-583-9452
                                 800-583-9452
                          Fax: 518-583-3270
sales@celtictreasures.com
www.celtictreasures.com

Imported goods and largest selection of Irish gifts
President: Paul O'Donnell
Catalog Cost: Free
Printing Information: in 3 colors
In Business: 22 years
Number of Employees: 6
Sales Volume: $450,000

1735 Collector's Paperweights
L.H. Selman, Ltd.
410 S. Michigan Avenue
Suite 207
Chicago, IL 60605   312-583-1177
                                 800-538-0766
                          Fax: 312-583-0111
info@selman.com
www.theglassgallery.com

Antique and modern paperweights for collectors
President: Lawrence Selman
Credit Cards: AMEX; MasterCard; Visa
Catalog Cost: $25
Average Order Size: $200
In Business: 42 years
Number of Employees: 10
Sales Volume: $ 1-3 Million

1736 Cottage Shop
The Cottage Shop
PO Box 4836
Stamford, CT 06897   203-762-1777
                                 800-965-7467
                          Fax: 203-762-0888
thecottageshop@aol.com
www.thecottageshop.com

Fine collectibles, upscale gifts, Limoges
Catalog Cost: Free
In Business: 30 years

1737 Creations and Collections
Creations and Collections
Po Box 8300
Little Rock, AR 72222   800-575-9255
                          Fax: 877-213-3660
www.creationsandcollections.com

Gifts, collectibles, taxidermy, home decor, sculptures

1738 Creative Concepts Golf
Creative Concepts Golf
365 E. Avenida de los Arboles
Suite 1008
Thousand Oaks, CA 91360   805-491-2929
                          Fax: 805-491-2922
lj@creativeconceptsgolf.com
www.creativeconceptsgolf.com

Distinguished line of gifts and awards.

In Business: 20 years

1739 David Orgell
David Orgell
262 North Rodeo Drive
Beverly Hills, CA 90210-5196   310-273-6660
                                 800-367-4355
                          Fax: 310-273-0399
info@davidorgell.com
www.davidorgell.com

Jewelry, watches, specialty gifts, crystal, china, antiques
President: Rahim Soltani
Marketing Manager: Korosh Soltani
Credit Cards: AMEX; MasterCard; Visa
Catalog Cost: Free
Mailing List Information: Names for rent
In Business: 59 years
Number of Employees: 28
Sales Volume: $ 4 Million

1740 Diecast Direct
Diecast Direct
3005 Old Lawrenceburg Road
Frankfort, KY 40601-9351   502-227-8697
                                 800-718-1866
                          Fax: 502-227-9484
www.diecastdirect.com

Collectible die cast metal cars, trucks, buses, planes and other vehicles
President: Kevin Black
Controller: Beth McFarland
Credit Cards: MasterCard
Catalog Cost: Free
In Business: 30 years
Number of Employees: 15
Sales Volume: $ 1-3 Million

1741 Faganarms
Faganarms Inc.
33915 Harper Avenue
Clinton Twp, MI 48035   586-465-4637
                          Fax: 586-792-6996
info@faganarms.com
www.faganarms.com

All cultures and periods antique armor, daggers, swords, etc
President: William Fagan
Credit Cards: MasterCard; Visa
Catalog Cost: Free
Catalog Circulation: Mailed 6 time(s) per year
In Business: 50 years
Sales Volume: $ 1-3 Million

1742 Fest for Beatles Fans
Fest for Beatles Fans
15 Charles Street
Westwood, NJ 07675   201-666-5450
                                 866-843-3378
                          Fax: 201-666-8687
mark@thefest.com
www.thefest.com

Beatles shirts, CDs, DVDs, books, calendars, mugs, musicskins, puzzles, blankets, posters and memorabilia
President: Mark Lapidos
Credit Cards: AMEX; MasterCard; Visa
Catalog Cost: $1
Catalog Circulation: to 10000
In Business: 43 years
Number of Employees: 4

1743 Festal Creations Catalog
Festal Creations
522A Avenue C
Redding Beach, CA 90277   877-455-4223
                                 800-747-9245
                          Fax: 800-903-4266
www.festalcreations.com

Religious gifts for gift stores and churches
President: Philip Tamoush
CFO: Artie Tamoush

Marketing Manager: James Tamoush
Buyers: Phil Tamoush
Catalog Cost: Free
Catalog Circulation: to 6000
Printing Information: 27 pages in 4 colors
Press: Offset Press
Binding: Perfect Bound
Mailing List Information: Names for rent
In Business: 15 years
Number of Employees: 3
Sales Volume: Under $500,000

1744 For Counsel: Catalog for Lawyers
For Counsel: Products And Gifts for Lawy
8050 SW Nimbus Ave
Beaverton, OR 97008   503-430-8894
                              800-637-0098
                    Fax: 503-430-8903
          forcounsel@forcounsel.com
                www.forcounsel.com

Products and gifts for the legal profession; both traditional and irreverent

President: Art Kroos
Marketing Manager: Carol Emory
Production Manager: Jane Ruggles
VP of Operations: Jennifer Leveille
Credit Cards: AMEX; MasterCard; Visa
Catalog Circulation: to 2MM
Printing Information: 56 pages
In Business: 26 years
Number of Employees: 6
Sales Volume: $860K

1745 Franklin Mint
The Franklin Mint
801 Springdale Dr
Suite 200
Exton, PA 19341   800-843-6468
                    Fax: 610-459-6880
          info@franklinmint.com
                www.franklinmint.com

Die-cast cars and airplanes, precision modeling, collectibles, jewelry, seasonal giftware

Chairman: Moshe Malamud
President: Steven Sisskind
CFO: Noah Becker
Credit Cards: AMEX
Catalog Cost: Free
Catalog Circulation: Mailed 4 time(s) per year
Printing Information: 60 pages
In Business: 49 years
Number of Employees: 42
Sales Volume: $6.2MM

1746 Fun-Tronics
Fun-Tronics, LLC
1415W.Water Street
PO Box 582
Teutopolis, IL 62467   217-857-1759
                    Fax: 217-857-3959
          fun-tronics@hotmail.com
                www.fun-tronicsllc.com

Vintage Coca-Cola machine restoration parts

President: Rod Heuerman
Credit Cards: MasterCard; Visa
Catalog Cost: $6.5
In Business: 39 years

1747 Gerald Fried Display & Packaging
Gerald Fried Display & Packaging
2727 Broadway Street
Cheektowaga, NY 14227   800-828-7701
                    Fax: 716-692-5458
          sales@gfried.com
                www.gfried.com

Custom jewelry boxes, pouches and displays

President: Val Racine
Credit Cards: AMEX; MasterCard; Visa
Catalog Cost: Free
Printing Information: 115 pages

In Business: 60 years
Number of Employees: 30
Sales Volume: $2.5 Million

1748 GiftsForYouNow.com
GiftsForYouNow.com
109 Shore Drive
Burr Ridge, IL 60527   630-771-0095
                              866-443-8748
                    Fax: 630-771-0098
          service@giftsforyounow.com
                www.giftsforyounow.com

Personalized gifts, products, and accessories for all occasions

Catalog Cost: Free
In Business: 16 years

1749 Grafton Village Cheese Company
Grafton Village Cheese
400 Linden Street
Brattleboro, VT 05301   800-472-3866
                    Fax: 802-246-2210
          info@graftonvillagecheese.com
                www.graftonvillagecheese.com

Handmade, all natural Vermont cheddars and Vermont specialty products, bacon and ham

CFO: Peter Mohn
Marketing Manager: Meri Spicer
Plant Manager: Richard Woods
Credit Cards: MasterCard; Visa
Catalog Cost: Free
Catalog Circulation: to 10000
Printing Information: 8 pages
Number of Employees: 18

1750 Hampshire Pewter
Hampshire Pewter
350 Route 108
Unit 201
Somersworth, NH 03878-4328   603-569-4944
                              800-639-7704
                    Fax: 603-569-4524
          hpgifts@hampshirepewter.com
                www.hampshirepewter.com

Pewter gifts, collectibles and ornaments

President: Robert Steele
Credit Cards: MasterCard; Visa
Catalog Cost: Free
Catalog Circulation: Mailed 1 time(s) per year to 15 M
Average Order Size: $80
Printing Information: 32 pages in 4 colors on Matte Stock
Press: Web Press
Binding: Saddle Stitched
In Business: 28 years
Number of Employees: 20
Sales Volume: $ 1-3 Million

1751 John Rinaldi Nautical Antiques
John F. Rinaldi Nautical Antiques & Rela
Box 765
Dock Square
Kennebunkport, ME 04046-765   207-967-3218
                    Fax: 207-967-2918
          john@jfrinaldi.com
                www.johnrinaldinautical.com

Nautical antiques, antique scrimshaw, naval items, ship models, instruments, carvings, marine paintings

President: John Rinaldi
Credit Cards: MasterCard; Visa
Catalog Cost: $5
In Business: 40 years
Number of Employees: 2
Sales Volume: under $500,00

1752 Lenox Holiday Decor & Gifts
Lenox
P.O. Box 735
Bristol, PA 19007-0806   800-223-4311
                www.lenox.com

Kitchen collectibles, figurines and gifts, dishes and crystal.

CEO: Katrina Helmkamp
Catalog Cost: Free
Printing Information: in 4 colors
In Business: 127 years

1753 NorthStyle
NorthStyle
Northwoods Trail
PO Box 6529
Chelmsford, MA 01824-929   877-756-4075
                              800-336-5666
                    Fax: 800-866-3235
          help@northstyle.com
                www.northstyle.com

Jewelry, clothing,homegoods and gifts.

President: Jack Rosenfeld
Buyers: Dawn Beausoleil
Credit Cards: AMEX; MasterCard
Catalog Cost: Free
Printing Information: 70 pages in 7 colors on Matte Stock
Binding: Saddle Stitched
In Business: 23 years
Number of Employees: 200
Sales Volume: $20-$50 Million

1754 Polart: Poland by Mail
Polart Distribution USA Inc
5700 Sarah Ave
Sarasota, FL 34233-3446   941-927-8983
                              800-278-9393
                    Fax: 941-927-8239
                www.polandbymail.com

Polish gifts and collectibles

President: Jarek Zaremba
Credit Cards: AMEX; MasterCard
Catalog Cost: Free
Catalog Circulation: Mailed 12 time(s) per year
Printing Information: in 4 colors on Glossy Stock
Press: Web Press
Binding: Saddle Stitched
Mailing List Information: Names for rent
In Business: 10 years
Sales Volume: Under $500,000

1755 Potpourri and Stitches
Potpourri Gift
PO Box 3337
Chelmsford, MA 01824-0937   877-758-6929
                    Fax: 800-866-3235
          help@potpourrigift.com
                www.potpourrigift.com

Clothing, gifts, jewelry, collectibles

President: Jack Rosenfed
Marketing Manager: William Knowles Jr
Production Manager: Edward Knowles
Fulfillment: Jeff Porter
In Business: 42 years
Number of Employees: 150

1756 Precious Moments
Precious Moments
4105 Chapel Road
Carthage, MO 64836   800-445-2220
                www.preciousmoments.com

Precious Moments figurines available for almost every occasion including weddings and baby showers

Chairman: Jon Butcher
President: Samuel J Butcher
Catalog Cost: Free
In Business: 27 years
Number of Employees: 15
Sales Volume: $2.6 Million

1757 Rockabilia
Rockabilia
P.O. Box 39
Chanhassen, MN 55317 953-556-1121
Fax: 952-556-1131
www.rockabilia.com
Rock music themed gifts and memorabilia
Chief Information Officer: David Perry
Credit Cards: AMEX; MasterCard
Catalog Cost: Free
In Business: 30 years

1758 ShopIrish
Shop Irish
PO Box 8300
Little Rock, AR 72222 866-851-7918
866-851-7916
Fax: 877-213-3660
www.shopirish.com
Irish clothing, gifts, jewelry, accessories, home and garden, kitchen items and Irish books and records
Credit Cards: AMEX; MasterCard

1759 Source for Everything Jewish
Hamakor Judaica, Inc.
6333 Gross Point Rd
Niles, IL 60714 847-966-4040
800-426-2567
Fax: 847-966-4033
service@jewishsource.com
www.jewishsource.com
Catalog of Jewish items and gifts for home and friends
President: Herschel Strauss
Marketing Manager: Naomi Strauss
Production Manager: Chris MacPherson
Credit Cards: AMEX; MasterCard; Visa
Catalog Cost: Free
Mailing List Information: Names for rent
In Business: 39 years
Number of Employees: 10
Sales Volume: $ 1 Million

1760 Steinland Gifts & Collectibles
Steinland Gifts & Collectibles
1070 Dundee Avenue
Suite A
East Dundee, IL 60118 847-428-3150
800-498-3215
Fax: 847-428-3170
steinland@aol.com
www.steinland.com
Collectible steins - Budweiser, Miller, German steins, character steins, beer related collectibles
President: Tony Steffen
Buyers: Linda McArthur
Catalog Cost: $1
Mailing List Information: Names for rent
In Business: 20 years
Sales Volume: Under $500,000

1761 The Christmas Book
Neiman Marcus
1618 Main St.
Dallas, TX 75201 214-741-6911
www.neimanmarcus.com
Women's apparel, shoes and handbags; jewelry and accessories; men's apparel; electronics; beauty and fragrance; home and entertaining; and various gifts
President: Karen Katz
Printing Information: 300 pages in 4 colors
Mailing List Information: Names for rent
Sales Volume: Over $1 Billion

1762 The Parks Company
The Parks Company
PO Box 284
Marylhurst, OR 97036 503-699-0252
888-596-4004
Fax: 503-699-6457
mike@theparksco.com
www.theparksco.com
National Park art, jewelry, furniture, books, gifts, apparel and more.
Catalog Circulation: Mailed 1 time(s) per year

1763 United Way Store
United Way Store
85 S Bragg St Suite 600
Suite 600
Alexandria, VA 22312 703-813-2400
800-813-9564
Fax: 703-813-2419
UnitedWayStore@staples.com
www.unitedwaystore.com
Films, banners, buttons and awards
President: Lisa Carol
CFO: Mary Joyce Flinn
Marketing Manager: Bob Gradijan
VP Sales: Greg Magnani
Credit Cards: AMEX; MasterCard; Visa
Catalog Cost: Free
Printing Information: 100 pages
In Business: 20 years
Number of Employees: 16
Sales Volume: $ 6 Million

1764 Wild Horsefeathers Catalog
Wild Horsefeathers
113 School House Lane
Portsmouth, RI 02871 401-683-4998
800-298-4998
Fax: 401-682-1848
pony@wildhorsefeathers.com
www.wildhorsefeathers.com
Annual catalog for horse lovers
President: Carol Manchester
Owner: Kimberly Dunn
Credit Cards: AMEX; MasterCard; Visa
Catalog Cost: Free
Catalog Circulation: Mailed 1 time(s) per year
Mailing List Information: Names for rent
In Business: 19 years
Number of Employees: 16
Sales Volume: $ 1-3 Million

1765 Wind & Weather Catalog
Wind & Weather
7021 Wolftown Hood Road
Madison, VA 22727 540-948-2272
877-255-3700
Fax: 800-843-2509
www.windandweather.com
Weather instruments for the home, rain gauges, garden statuary and decor, collectibles, gifts, and outdoor furniture
President: Peter Rice
Fulfillment: Peggy Rice
Credit Cards: AMEX; MasterCard; Visa
Catalog Cost: Free
Printing Information: 76 pages in 4 colors on f
Binding: Saddle Stitched
In Business: 30 years

1766 Worldwide Collectibles & Gifts Catalog
Worldwide Collectibles & Gifts
P.O. Box 158
Berwyn, PA 19312-0158 800-266-1664
800-644-2442
Fax: 610-889-9549
customerservice@wwcag.com
www.worldwidecollectibles.com
Variety of collectibles and gifts from around the world
President: Frank Cusumano
Credit Cards: AMEX; MasterCard; Visa

Catalog Cost: Free
Catalog Circulation: Mailed 1 time(s) per year
Printing Information: 64 pages in 4 colors
In Business: 43 years
Sales Volume: $ 3-5 Million

Americana

1767 American Flag and Gift Catalog
American Flag and Gift
1101 Highland Way
Suite B
Grover Beach, CA 93433 805-473-0395
800-448-3524
Fax: 805-473-0126
flags@anyflag.com
www.anyflag.com
Flags and flag poles
Chairman: John Solley
President: Bridgett Solley
Catalog Cost: $5
Mailing List Information: Names for rent
In Business: 23 years
Number of Employees: 8

1768 Americana Catalog
Americiana
P.O. Box 322
Avondale Estates, GA 30002 404-377-0306
800-269-5697
Fax: 404-377-1120
staff@shutterblinds.com
www.shutterblinds.com
American collectibles, authentic wooden shutters and blinds for both interior and exterior
President: Earl Austin
CFO: Bayne Cathy
Marketing Manager: Wayne Austin
Vice President: John Austin
Average Order Size: $2000
Mailing List Information: Names for rent
In Business: 78 years
Number of Employees: 25
Sales Volume: $ 1-3 Million

1769 Big-Bang Cannons
Conestoga Company Inc
323 Sumner Ave.
Allentown, PA 18102-1856 610-866-0777
800-987-2264
Fax: 610-433-8406
customerservice@bigbangcannons.com
www.bigbangcannons.com
Cannons made of cast iron and sheet metal, for display when not in use, three sizes and ammo available, also a collectors series of past products
President: David Spinosa
Credit Cards: AMEX; MasterCard; Visa
Catalog Cost: Free
Average Order Size: $160
Mailing List Information: Names for rent
In Business: 57 years
Number of Employees: 8
Sales Volume: $680,000

1770 Bits and Pieces
Bits and Pieces
P.O. Box 4150
Lawrenceburg, IN 47025 855-489-2539
www.bitsandpieces.com
Jigsaw puzzles, brain teaser puzzles and gift ideas through our mail order catalog.
In Business: 32 years

1771 Cardsone
Cardsone
PO Box 3777
Cleveland, TN 37320-3777   423-472-3140
      888-472-3140
Fax: 423-472-3148
rsales@cardsone.com
store.cardsone.com
Credit Cards: AMEX; MasterCard
In Business: 25 years

1772 Cotswold Collectibles
Cotswold Collectibles
5550 Vanbarr Place
PO Box 716
Freeland, WA 98249   360-331-5331
      877-404-5637
Fax: 360-331-5344
cotswold@whidbey.net
www.gijoeelite.com

GI Joe, military collectible toys, one-sixth scale military and pop culture action figures full sets and parts plus vintage GI Joe collecting

President: Tina Windeler
Marketing Manager: Greg Brown
Credit Cards: MasterCard; Visa
Catalog Cost: Free
Catalog Circulation: to 50000
Average Order Size: $100
Printing Information: 32 pages in 4 colors on G
Press: W
Binding: S
Mailing List Information: Names for rent
In Business: 29 years
Number of Employees: 10
Sales Volume: $ 1-3 Million

1773 Desperate Enterprises
Desperate.com
PO Box 604
Sharon Center, OH 44274   330-239-0500
      800-732-4859
Fax: 330-239-0600
shane@desperate.com
www.desperate.com

Tin signs, thermometers and switch plates

President: Dan Hutchings
CFO: Jon Hutchings
Credit Cards: AMEX; MasterCard
Catalog Cost: Free
Average Order Size: $400
Mailing List Information: Names for rent
In Business: 28 years
Sales Volume: $ 5-10 Million

1774 George H. LaBarre Galleries
George H. LaBarre Galleries
P.O. Box 746
Hollis, NH 3049   603-882-2411
      800-717-9529
Fax: 603-882-4797
collect@glabarre.com
www.glabarre.com
Credit Cards: AMEX; MasterCard
Printing Information: 36 pages
In Business: 35 years

1775 History Hollywood Auction 65
Profiles in History
26662 Agoura Rd.
Calabasas, CA 91302   310-859-7701
Fax: 310-859-3842
info@profilesinhistory.com
www.profilesinhistory.com

Historical documents and autographs

President: Joseph M. Maddalena

1776 Huggins and Scott Auctions
Huggins and Scott Auctions
2301 Broadbirch Dr.
STE 150
Silver Spring, MD 20904   301-608-0355
auction@hugginsandscott.com
www.hugginsandscott.com

A Sports Memorabilia Auction House selling baseball cards, football cards, graded cards, signed autographed vintage sports, Boxing, ice hockey & Americana Memorabilia.

1777 Mountain Press Publishing
Mountain Press Publishing
PO Box 2399
Missoula, MT 59806   406-728-1900
      800-234-5308
Fax: 406-728-1635
info@mtnpress.com
www.mountain-press.com

Books on natural history and geology, western history and western Americana

President: John Rimel
CFO: Rob Williams
Catalog Cost: Free
Mailing List Information: Names for rent
In Business: 63 years
Number of Employees: 10
Sales Volume: $500M to $1MM

1778 PM Research
PM Research,Inc
4110 Niles Hill Rd
Wellsville, NY 14895-9608   585-593-3169
      800-724-3801
Fax: 585-593-5637
PMRgang@pmresearchinc.com
www.pmmodelengines.com

Model kits and finished models; steam and stirling engines, machine shop tools, boilers, accessories

President: Gary Bastian
Catalog Cost: $3
In Business: 39 years
Number of Employees: 18
Sales Volume: $ 3 Million

1779 Written Heritage Catalog
Written Heritage, Inc.
53196 Old Uneedus Rd.
PO Box 1390
Folsom, LA 70437   985-796-5433
      800-301-8009
Fax: 985-796-9236
info@writtenheritage.com
www.writtenheritage.com

American Indian books and educational DVDs.

President: Jack Heriard
jack@writtenheritage.com
Credit Cards: AMEX; MasterCard
Catalog Cost:
Catalog Circulation: Mailed 1 time(s) per year to 10000
Average Order Size: $65
Printing Information: 64 pages in 4 colors on Glossy Stock
Press: Web Press
Binding: Saddle Stitched
Mailing List Information: Names for rent
In Business: 48 years
Number of Employees: 2
Sales Volume: $190,000

1780 Yesteryear Toys & Books Catalog
Yesteryear Toys & Books
PO Box 537
Alexandria Bay, NY 13607   613-475-1771
      800-481-1353
Fax: 613-475-3748
info@yesteryeartoys.com
www.yesteryeartoys.com

Over 130 different models of steam engines and accessories

President: Frank VanMeeuwen
Catalog Cost: $6.95
Printing Information: 43 pages in 4 colors
In Business: 41 years
Number of Employees: 6

Coins

1781 Air-Tite Holders
Air-Tite Holders Inc
1560 Curran Highway
North Adams, MA 01247-3900   413-664-2730
      800-521-1248
Fax: 413-664-2733
sales@airtiteholders.com
www.airtiteholders.com

Protective holders for coins and medallions

Chairman: Norm Therriam
President: Scott Therrien
Co-owner: Glenn Therrien
Credit Cards: MasterCard; Visa
Catalog Cost: Free
In Business: 32 years
Number of Employees: 16
Sales Volume: $ 1.7 Million

1782 American Coin and Stamp Brokerage
American Coin and Stamp Brokerage Inc
30 Merrick Avenue
Merrick, NY 11566   516-546-2300
      800-682-2272
Fax: 516-546-2315
support@acsb.com
www.acsb.com

US and foreign coins, stamps and baseball cards

President: Richard Cincotta
Buyers: Mark Roth
Credit Cards: AMEX; MasterCard; Visa
Catalog Cost: Free
Average Order Size: $250
Mailing List Information: Names for rent
List Company: Media Management Group
In Business: 28 years
Number of Employees: 8
Sales Volume: $ 1.5 Million

1783 Coast to Coast Coins and Currency
9365 Gerwig Lane
Columbia, MD 21046   800-638-8869
Fax: 410-309-1626
info@coastcoin.com
www.coastcoin.com

Coins and currency

1784 Collectible America
Collar Clinic
1517 Northern Star Drive
Traverse City, MI 49696-8837   231-947-2010
      800-430-2010
Fax: 231-947-6566
www.collarclinic.com

Collectible US coins, currency and supplies

President: Jeff Gonda
Credit Cards: AMEX; MasterCard
Catalog Cost: Free
Catalog Circulation: Mailed 6 time(s) per year to 1.5 M
Average Order Size: $150
Printing Information: 52 pages in 4 colors on G
Press: W
Binding: S
Mailing List Information: Names for rent
In Business: 30 years
Sales Volume: $ 3-5 Million

1785 Danbury Mint
47 Richards Avenue
Norwalk, CT 06857   203-838-3800
800-243-4664
customerservice@danburymint.com
www.danburymint.com

Coins

1786 Ginny's
1112 7th Ave.
Monroe, WI 53566-1364   800-290-9514

Home products and furniture for bed and bath

1787 GovMint.com
14101 Southcross Drive
Burnsville, MN 55337   800-642-9160
customerservice@govmint.com
www.govmint.com

Coins and currency
President: Bill Gale

1788 Hard to Find US Coins & Bank Notes
Littleton Coin Company LLC
1309 Mount Eustis Road
Littleton, NH 03561-3734   603-444-5386
800-645-3122
Fax: 603-444-0121
info@littletoncoin.com
www.littletoncoin.com

Coins and paper money
President: David Sundman
CFO: Patricia Redzinski
Marketing Manager: Paul Charlton
Production Manager: Mike Morelli
Credit Cards: AMEX; MasterCard; Visa
Catalog Cost: Free
Catalog Circulation: Mailed 4 time(s) per year to 40000
Printing Information: 68 pages in 4 colors
In Business: 67 years
Number of Employees: 325
Sales Volume: $ 14.5 Million

1789 Hoffman Mint
Hoffman Mint
1400 N.W. 65th Place
Fort Lauderdale, FL 33309-1902   954-917-5451
800-227-5813
Fax: 954-917-3079
sales@hoffmanmint.com
www.hoffmanmint.com

Tokens, medals, coins and key tags
President: Abram Ackerman
In Business: 34 years
Sales Volume: Under $500,000

1790 International Coins and Currency
Iccoin
62 Ridge Street
Montpelier, VT 05602-6100   800-451-4463
Fax: 800-229-3239
info@iccoin.org
www.iccoin.com

Coins and collectibles
President: Michael Boardman
Marketing Manager: John Devitt
Credit Cards: AMEX; MasterCard; Visa
Catalog Cost: Free
Catalog Circulation: Mailed 12 time(s) per year
Printing Information: 23 pages in 2 colors
Mailing List Information: Names for rent
In Business: 40 years
Number of Employees: 20
Sales Volume: $ 3-5 Million

1791 National Collector's Mint
8 Slater Street
Port Chester, NY 10573   800-452-4381
Fax: 914-935-3321
www.ncmint.com

Coins
President: Avram Freedberg

1792 Rare Coin & Currency
Southern Coin Investments
PO Box 720714
Atlanta, GA 30358-2714   770-393-8000
Fax: 770-396-1734
sales@southerncoin.com
www.southerncoin.com

Coins and collectibles
President: William Hodges
Credit Cards: MasterCard; Visa
Catalog Cost: Free
Catalog Circulation: Mailed 2 time(s) per year
Mailing List Information: Names for rent
In Business: 39 years
Number of Employees: 8
Sales Volume: $ 10-20 Million

1793 Stauer
Stauer
14101 Southcross Drive West
Burnsville, MN 55337   888-201-7123
888-333-2012
Fax: 651-393-9728
www.stauer.com

Fine watches, jewelry and sunglasses, apparel, handbags, luggage, home accessories, coins and collectibles
President: Michael Bisceglia
Average Order Size: $55

1794 Village Coin Shop
Village Coin Shop
51c Route 125
PO Box 207
Plaistow, NH 03865   603-382-5492
800-782-9349
Fax: 603-382-5682
coins@villagecoin.com
www.villagecoin.com

Coins, currency and supplies for the numismatist
President: Domenic J Mangano
Vice President, Treasurer: Antonia A Mangano
Founder: Mary Emma Beasley
Credit Cards: AMEX; MasterCard
Catalog Cost: $3.95
Catalog Circulation: Mailed 3 time(s) per year to 20000
Average Order Size: $65
Printing Information: 14 pages in 1 color on Matte Stock
Press: Web Press
Binding: Folded
Mailing List Information: Names for rent
In Business: 56 years
Number of Employees: 6
Sales Volume: $2.3 MM

1795 Willabee & Ward
47 Richards Avenue
Norwalk, CT 06857   800-282-9412
customerservice@willabeeandward.com
www.willabeeandward.com

Coins, jewelry and collectibles

Comic Books

1796 Bud's Art Books
Bud's Art Books
PO Box 1689
Grass Valley, CA 95945-9305   530-273-2166
800-242-6642
Fax: 530-273-0915
info@budsartbooks.com
www.budsartbooks.com

Books, prints, graphic novels, comic books and comic strips, illustrations, animation, and art history
President: Bud Plant
Credit Cards: AMEX; MasterCard
Catalog Cost: $2
Average Order Size: $80
Mailing List Information: Names for rent
List Manager: Dave Cowie
In Business: 45 years
Number of Employees: 25
Sales Volume: $ 5-10 Million

1797 Comic Heaven Auction Catalog
PO Box 900
Big Sandy, TX 75755   comicheaven@earthlink.net
www.comicheaven.net

Comic books
Owner: John Verzyl

1798 Creative Therapy Store
625 Alaska Ave.
Torrance, CA 90503-5124   424-201-8800
800-648-8857
Fax: 424-201-6950
help@creativetherapystore.com
www.creativetherapystore.com

Therapeutic games, books and toys

1799 Golden Age Comics
2430 Ridgeway Avenue
Rochester, NY 14626   *Fax:* 585-227-0617
joe@goldenagecomics.com
www.goldenagecomics.com

Comic books

1800 Rainbow Resource Center
655 Township Rd. 500E
Toulon, IL 61483   888-841-3456
info@rainbowresource.com
www.rainbowresource.com

Educational products for homeschooling

Dolls & Accessories

1801 American Girl
American Girl
PO Box 620497
Middleton, WI 53562-0497   800-845-0005
www.americangirl.com

Children's dolls, gifts, books and clothing.
President: Katy Dickson
Catalog Cost: Free
Printing Information: 88 pages in 4 colors
In Business: 30 years
Number of Employees: 2300
Sales Volume: $572 Million

1802 Antina's Doll Supply
Antina's Doll Supply
PO BOX 2130
Estacada, OR 97023   503-630-1900
800-257-9450
Fax: 503-630-1905
customerservice@dollsupply.com
www.dollsupply.com

Doll supplies and accessories
President: Antina Berray
Credit Cards: MasterCard; Visa
Catalog Cost: $3

In Business: 35 years
Number of Employees: 12
Sales Volume: $ 5-10 Million

1803 Barbie Top 10 Holiday Picks

Mattel, Inc.
333 Continental Blvd.
El Segundo, CA 90245-5012   310-252-2000
800-491-7514
www.thebarbiecollection.com

Barbie dolls and accessories for the collector

Chairman & CEO: Christopher A. Sinclair
Catalog Cost: Free
Printing Information: 24 pages in 4 colors
In Business: 71 years
Sales Volume: $6 Billion

1804 CR's Bear & Doll Supply

CR's Crafts
PO Box 8
Leland, IA 50453-8   641-567-3652
877-277-2782
Fax: 641-567-3071
CRService@crscraft.com
www.crscraft.com

Everything needed to make dolls and teddy bears; over 7,000 items

President: Michael Brown
Owner: Clarice Brown
Credit Cards: MasterCard; Visa
Catalog Cost: $4
Catalog Circulation: Mailed 1 time(s) per year
Printing Information: 70 pages in 4 colors on Glossy Stock
Press: Web Press
Binding: Saddle Stitched
Mailing List Information: Names for rent
In Business: 29 years
Number of Employees: 12
Sales Volume: $ 1 Million

1805 Dee's Delights

Dee's Delight Inc
3150 State Line Road
North Bend, OH 45052-9731   513-353-3390
Fax: 513-353-3933
www.deesdelights.com

Model and doll making supplies and accessories

President: Jerry Hacker
Printing Information: 650 pages in 4 colors
Press: Offset Press
Binding: Perfect Bound
In Business: 43 years
Number of Employees: 25
Sales Volume: $ 3 Million

1806 Dollmasters

Dollmasters
2148 Renard Court
PO Box 2319
Annapolis, MD 21401-6756   410-224-4386
800-966-3655
Fax: 410-571-9605
www.dollmasters.com

Doll-related items including books, clothing

President: Florence Theriault
Production Manager: Sharon Moran
Credit Cards: MasterCard
Catalog Cost: Free
Catalog Circulation: Mailed 2 time(s) per year to 14000
Average Order Size: $150
Printing Information: 38 pages in 4 colors on Glossy Stock
Press: Web Press
Binding: Saddle Stitched
Mailing List Information: Names for rent
In Business: 40 years
Number of Employees: 16
Sales Volume: $500,000- 1 Million

1807 Edinburgh Imports

Edinburgh Imports
3551 Voyager Street
Unit B
Torrance, CA 90503   310-370-5800
800-334-6274
Fax: 310-370-5802
info@edinburghimports.com
www.edinburghimports.com

Teddy bear fabrics and craft supplies

President: Elke Block
CFO: Ronald Block
Credit Cards: AMEX; MasterCard
Catalog Circulation: Mailed 1 time(s) per year
Printing Information: 32 pages in 1 color on Matte Stock
Mailing List Information: Names for rent
In Business: 32 years
Number of Employees: 26

1808 Ginny's

1112 7th Ave.
Monroe, WI 53566-1364   800-290-9514

Home products and furniture for bed and bath

1809 Goldenwest Manufacturing

GOLDENWEST Mfg., Inc.
13100 Grass Valley Ave.
Ste. A
Grass Valley, CA 95945-1148   530-272-1133
Fax: 530-272-1070
sales@goldenwestmfg.com
www.goldenwestmfg.com

Dolls

In Business: 44 years

1810 House of Caron

House of Caron
10111 Larrylyn Drive
Whittier, CA 90603   562-947-6753
800-432-8992
Fax: 562-943-5103
houseofcaron@houseofcaron.com
www.houseofcaron.com

Molds and supplies to make miniature dolls; how-to books, patterns for 1/2 inch and 1 inch scale dolls, costume patterns, knit patterns, glass eyes, stands, mohair, miniature wigs

President: Jackie Caron
Credit Cards: AMEX; MasterCard; Visa
Catalog Cost: $5.95
Mailing List Information: Names for rent
In Business: 23 years
Number of Employees: 2
Sales Volume: $40,000

1811 Intercal Trading Group

Intercal Trading Group
1760 Monrovia Avenue
A-17
Costa Mesa, CA 92627   949-645-9396
877-910-5400
Fax: 949-645-5471
mohair@intercaltg.com
www.intercaltg.com

Mohair and teddy bear making supplies, English and German mohairs, glass eyes, wool felt and jointing systems as well as patterns and kits for teddy bear making

President: K Enevoldsen
Credit Cards: MasterCard
In Business: 28 years
Sales Volume: Under $500,000

1812 Molds & Dollmaking Supplies

Collectible Doll Company LLC
1401 American Way
Cedar Hill, TX 75104   469-272-7722
800-566-6646
Fax: 972-291-9601
www.jeannordquistdolls.com

Doll collection items, including: molds, miniatures, workbooks, patterns, leather shoes, human hair and mohair wigs, outfits, and jewelry

President: Jean Nordquist
Credit Cards: MasterCard; Visa
Catalog Cost: $3
Average Order Size: $50
Printing Information: 54 pages
In Business: 26 years
Number of Employees: 3
Sales Volume: Under $500,000

1813 Paradise Galleries

Paradise Galleries
PO Box 57086
Irvine, CA 92619   858-793-4050
800-673-6557
Fax: 949-743-8974
customerservice@paradisegalleries.com
www.paradisegalleries.com

Collectible dolls

President: David Brownlee
Credit Cards: MasterCard; Visa
Catalog Cost: Free
In Business: 24 years
Number of Employees: 60
Sales Volume: $8.6 MM

1814 Seaway China

Seaway China
485 South Federal Highway
Dania Beach, FL 33004   786-464-1818
800-968-2424
Fax: 786-464-1950
sales@seawaychina.com
www.Seawaychina.Com

China dolls/figurines

Chairman: Gregg Whittecar
President: Arron Rimpley
Credit Cards: AMEX; MasterCard
Catalog Cost: Free
Printing Information: in 3 colors
Mailing List Information: Names for rent
In Business: 20 years
Number of Employees: 20
Sales Volume: $ 1-3 Million

Fossils & Shells

1815 Eloxite Corporation

806 10th Street
PO Box 729, Dept. 8
Wheatland, WY 82201   307-322-3050
Fax: 307-322-3055
president@eloxite.com
www.eloxite.com

Jewelry making and crafting supplies

President: Pat Murphy

1816 Home Science Tools

665 Carbon Street
Billings, MT 59102   800-860-6272
Fax: 888-860-2344
service@homesciencetools.com

hands-on science supplies and resources

Co-Founder: Frank Schaner
Co-Founder: Debbie Schaner

1817 Nature's Expression
PO Box 2812
Blaine, WA 98231   604-278-6403
                                          800-723-6403
                                     Fax: 604-278-6414
                             www.naturesexpression.com

Natural gifts and souvenirs

CEO: Greg Stump
VP Sales & Marketing: Linda-Ann Bowling

1818 Nature-Watch
5312 Derry Avenue
Unit R
Agoura Hills, CA 91301   818-735-3555
                                          800-228-5816
                                     Fax: 800-228-5814
                             info@nature-watch.com
                             www.nature-watch.com

Educational nature products and crafting supplies

1819 Safari Ltd
5960 Miami Lakes Drive
Miami Lakes, FL 33014   800-554-5414
                                     Fax: 305-766-7840
                             sales@safariltd.com
                                          safariltd.com

Figurines

Co-Founder: Bernard Rubel
Co-Founder: Rosemarie Rubel

Gemology

1820 Ebersole Lapidary Supply
Ebersole Lapidary Supply
5830 W Hendryx Ave
Wichita, KS 67209-1298   316-945-4771
                                          877-323-7765
                                     Fax: 316-945-4773
                             ebersolerocks@sbcglobal.net
                             www.ebersolelapidary.com

Lapidary and jewelry making supplies and equipment

President: Delbert Ebersole
Vice President: Leonard Ebersole
Credit Cards: AMEX; MasterCard; Visa
Catalog Cost: $5
Mailing List Information: Names for rent
In Business: 72 years
Number of Employees: 4
Sales Volume: $500,000- 1 Million

1821 Graves Company
Graves Company
1800 N Andrews Ave
Pompano Beach, FL 33069   954-960-0300
                                          800-327-9103
                                     Fax: 954-960-0301
                             www.gravescompany.com

Gemology and lapidary equipment and supplies

President: Emanuel Vanzo
Credit Cards: MasterCard; Visa
Catalog Cost: Free
Printing Information: 54 pages
Mailing List Information: Names for rent
In Business: 69 years
Number of Employees: 10
Sales Volume: $700,000

1822 Sadigh Gallery Ancient Art
Sadigh Gallery Ancient Art Inc
303 5th Ave # 1603
Suite 1603
New York, NY 10016-6636   212-725-7537
                                          800-426-2007
                                     Fax: 212-545-7612
                             info@sadighgallery.com
                             www.sadighgallery.Com

Genuine Egyptian, Mid Eastern Classical and Pre-Columbian artifacts, jewelry and collectibles,and more
President: Mehrdad Sadigh
Credit Cards: AMEX; MasterCard; Visa
Catalog Cost: Free
Printing Information: in 3 colors
Mailing List Information: Names for rent
In Business: 37 years
Number of Employees: 5
Sales Volume: Under $500,000

1823 Silver Moon Jewelers
Silver Moon Jewelers
1832 Union Street
San Francisco, CA 94123   415-775-9968
                             info@silvermoonjewelers.com
                             www.silvermoonjewelers.com

Silver jewelry.

In Business: 10 years

1824 Smyth Jewelers
Smyth Jewelers
2020 York Road
Timonium, MD 21093   410-252-6666
                                          800-638-3333
                             www.smythjewelers.com

Jewelry Store.

1825 Stone Age Industries
Stone Age Industries
PO Box 383
Powell, WY 82435-0383   307-754-4681
                                          888-331-7625
                                     Fax: 307-754-4681
                             stoneage@tritel.net
                           ᵀ www.stoneageindustries.com

Gemology, insology supplies, gemstone gifts, lapidary equipment

President: William Beebe
Production Manager: Linna M Beebe
Buyers: Linna M Beebe
Credit Cards: MasterCard; Visa
Catalog Cost: $3
Printing Information: in 1 color
Mailing List Information: Names for rent
List Manager: Linna M Beebe
In Business: 30 years
Sales Volume: Under $500,000

Historical Documents

1826 75th Historical Document Catalog
The Raab Collection
PO Box 471
Ardmore, PA 19003   877-405-4085
                             questions@raabcollection.com
                             www.raabcollection.com

Autograph and manuscript collections

Founder: Steven Raab

1827 Cohasco
Cohasco, Inc.
PO Box 821
Yonkers, NY 10702   914-476-8500
                                     Fax: 914-476-8573
                             info@cohascodpc.com
                             www.cohascodpc.com

Historical documents and collectibles

President: Bob Snyder
Credit Cards: MasterCard
Catalog Cost: $10
Mailing List Information: Names for rent
In Business: 68 years
Number of Employees: 3
Sales Volume: Under $500,000

1828 Rainbow Resource Center
655 Township Rd. 500E
Toulon, IL 61483   888-841-3456
                             info@rainbowresource.com
                             www.rainbowresource.com

Educational products for homeschooling

Maps

1829 Hake's Americana & Collectibles
PO Box 12001
York, PA 17402   717-434-1600
                                          866-404-9800
                             hakes@hakes.com
                             www.hakes.com

Collectibles

1830 International Military Antiques
1000 Valley Road
Gillette, NJ 07933   908-903-1200
                             www.ima-usa.com

Military antiques

1831 Rainbow Resource Center
655 Township Rd. 500E
Toulon, IL 61483   888-841-3456
                             info@rainbowresource.com
                             www.rainbowresource.com

Educational products for homeschooling

1832 Raven Maps & Images
Raven Map
PO Box 850
Medford, OR 97501-850   541-773-1436
                                          800-237-0798
                                     Fax: 541-773-6834
                             info@ravenmaps.com
                             www.ravenmaps.com

Shaded-relief wall maps; world, North America and Mexico maps, and individual state maps, suitable for framing

President: Michael Beard
Credit Cards: AMEX; MasterCard; Visa
Catalog Cost: Free
Average Order Size: $75
Mailing List Information: Names for rent
In Business: 31 years
Sales Volume: $ 1-3 Million

1833 Tag-A-Long Expeditions
452 North Main Street
Moab, UT 84532   435-259-8946
                                          800-453-3292
                                     Fax: 435-259-8990
                             tagalong@tagalong.com
                             www.tagalong.com

Utah river and wildlife expeditions

1834 Universal Map
Kappa Map Group, LLC
6198 Butler Pike
Blue Bell, PA 19422   386-873-3010
                                          800-829-6277
                                     Fax: 386-873-3011
                             info@kappamapgroup.com
                             www.universalmap.com

Maps

President: Stuart Dolgins
CFO: Robert Bellone
Marketing Manager: Richard Strug
Production Manager: Sara Oscalon
Credit Cards: AMEX; MasterCard; Visa
Printing Information: 60 pages
In Business: 38 years
Number of Employees: 100

1835 VinMaps
Tacoma WA   253-329-2649
                             sales@vinmaps.com
                             www.vinmaps.com

Maps showing wineries and vinyards

1836 Wilderness Press Catalog
C/O Keen Communications
2204 First Avenue South
Suite 102
Birmingham, AL 35233
800-443-7227
Fax: 205-326-1012
www.wildernesspress.com
Outdoor books and maps
President: Roslyn Bullas
Credit Cards: AMEX; MasterCard; Visa
Catalog Cost: Free
Mailing List Information: Names for rent
In Business: 40 years
Number of Employees: 11
Sales Volume: $ 1-3 Million

Militaria

1837 Atlanta Cutlery
Altanta Cutlery
2147 Gees Mill Rd.
Conyers, GA 30013
770-922-7500
800-883-0300
Fax: 770-388-0246
www.atlantacutlery.com
Cutlery, hunting and pocket knives, miltary knives and swords, antique knives, early american bowie reproductions, blades and materials for custom knifemaking.
Catalog Cost: Free
Printing Information: 76 pages in 4 colors
In Business: 45 years

1838 Benchmade Catalog
Benchmade
300 Beavercreek Road
Oregon City, OR 97045
503-496-1853
800-800-7427
www.benchmade.com
Knives, including custom orders and accessories
President: Les de Asis
Catalog Cost: Free
Catalog Circulation: Mailed 1 time(s) per year
Printing Information: 102 pages in 4 colors
In Business: 29 years
Number of Employees: 10

1839 Catalog of Antique Replica Ordinance
South Bend Replicas Inc
61650 Oak Road
South Bend, IN 46614
574-289-4500
www.southbendreplicas.com
Antique artillery reproductions and muzzle loading cannon replicas
President: Paul Barnett
Credit Cards: MasterCard; Visa
Catalog Cost: $10
Catalog Circulation: Mailed 1 time(s) per year
Printing Information: 144 pages
In Business: 43 years
Sales Volume: Under $500,000

1840 Cheaper Than Dirt
PO Box 162087
Fort Worth, TX 76161www.cheaperthandirt.com

Ammunition, firearms

1841 Collector's Armoury
Collector's Armoury, Ltd.
442 Westridge Parkway, Building 100
PO Box 2948
McDonough, GA 30253
678-593-2660
877-276-6879
Fax: 678-593-2670
sales@collectorsarmoury.com
collectorsarmoury.com
Replica guns

President: Jim Kemp
In Business: 47 years

1842 Cotswold Collectibles
Cotswold Collectibles
5550 Vanbarr Place
PO Box 716
Freeland, WA 98249
360-331-5331
877-404-5637
Fax: 360-331-5344
cotswold@whidbey.net
www.gijoeelite.com
GI Joe, military collectible toys, one-sixth scale military and pop culture action figures full sets and parts plus vintage GI Joe collecting
President: Tina Windeler
Marketing Manager: Greg Brown
Credit Cards: MasterCard; Visa
Catalog Cost: Free
Catalog Circulation: to 50000
Average Order Size: $100
Printing Information: 32 pages in 4 colors on G
Press: W
Binding: S
Mailing List Information: Names for rent
In Business: 29 years
Number of Employees: 10
Sales Volume: $ 1-3 Million

1843 Galati International
PO Box 124
Villa Ridge, MO 63089
800-444-2550
Fax: 636-584-0580
support@galatiinternational.com
www.galatiinternational.com
Gun holsters and accessories

1844 HJ Saunders/US Military Insignia
Saunders US Military Insignia
PO Box 1831
Naples, FL 34106-1831
239-776-7524
800-442-3133
Fax: 239-431-5602
info@saundersinsignia.com
www.saundersinsignia.com
Offering over 15,000 different insignia from 1940 to present
President: Earl Keaton
CFO: Anna Labra
Buyers: Aracely Rangel
Credit Cards: AMEX; MasterCard
Catalog Cost: Free
Catalog Circulation: to 1000
Average Order Size: $50
Printing Information: 250 pages in 1 color on Matte Stock
Press: Offset Press
Binding: Saddle Stitched
Mailing List Information: Names for rent
List Company: George Mann & Associates
569 Abbington Drive
Hightstown, NJ 08520
609-443-1330
In Business: 47 years
Sales Volume: $500,000 - 1 Miliion

1845 Honors Military Catalog
Hoovers Manufacturing Company
4133 Progress Boulevard
PO Box 547
Peru, IL 61354-0547
800-223-1159
815-223-1159
Fax: 888-333-1499
hoover@hmchonors.com
www.hmchonors.com
2500+ military designs army, navy, air force, and marines; hat pins, medals, ball caps, buckles, and patches
President: David Hoover
Credit Cards: AMEX; MasterCard; Visa
Catalog Cost: Free
Printing Information: on 0

Mailing List Information: Names for rent
In Business: 52 years
Number of Employees: 15
Sales Volume: $ 1-3 Million

1846 International Military Antiques
1000 Valley Road
Gillette, NJ 07933
908-903-1200
www.ima-usa.com
Military antiques

1847 Knights Edge
Knights Edge
5696 N Northwest Hwy
Chicago, IL 60646-6136
773-775-3888
Fax: 773-775-3339
sales@knightsedge.com
www.knightsedge.com
Medieval swords, armor, jewelry, figurines and home decor
President: Marion Bastle
Credit Cards: MasterCard
Catalog Cost: Free
Printing Information: 64 pages in 4 colors on Glossy Stock
In Business: 21 years
Number of Employees: 4
Sales Volume: $ 1 Million

1848 Medals of America
Medals of America
114 Southchase Blvd
Fountain Inn, SC 29644-9019
864-862-0635
800-308-0849
Fax: 864-862-7495
customerservice@usmedals.com
www.medalsofamerica.com
Military medals and display cases for veterans and family
President: Linda Foster
Marketing Manager: Pamela Foster
Vice President: Lee Foster
Credit Cards: AMEX; MasterCard; Visa
Catalog Cost: Free
In Business: 36 years
Number of Employees: 48
Sales Volume: $10-20 Million

1849 Military & Law Enforcement Product Catalog
Smith & Wesson
2100 Roosevelt Avenue
Springfield, MA 01104
413-781-8300
800-331-0852
Fax: 413-747-3317
www.smith-wesson.com
Firearms and firearm safety/security products
President: P. James Debney
CFO: Jeffrey Buchanan
Credit Cards: AMEX; MasterCard
Catalog Cost: Free
Printing Information: 84 pages in 4 colors
In Business: 165 years

1850 Mossberg Catalog
O.F. Mossberg & Sons
7 Grasso Avenue
North Haven, CT 06473
203-230-5300
Fax: 203-230-5420
www.mossberg.com
Firearms, parts, accessories, hunting apparel and gear
Chief Executive Officer: Alan Iver Mossberg Jr
Director of Media Relations: Linda Powell
Credit Cards: AMEX; MasterCard
Catalog Cost: Free
Catalog Circulation: Mailed 1 time(s) per year
Printing Information: 92 pages in 4 colors
In Business: 98 years
Sales Volume: $24.6 Million

1851 Reddick Militaria
PO Box 847
Pottsboro, TX 75076   903-786-2287
Fax: 903-786-9059
www.reddickmilitaria.com
Military books, insignia

1852 Schiffer Military History
Schiffer Publishing, Ltd.
4880 Lower Valley Rd
Atglen, PA 19310-1768   610-593-1777
Fax: 610-593-2002
info@schifferbooks.com
www.schifferbooks.com
Reference books subjects of which include military history (United states, Germany, Russia and Great Britain), the Navy, uniforms, medals, and insignia
Chairman: John Cook
President: Peter Schiffer
Marketing Manager: Tina Skinner
Catalog Circulation: Mailed 2 time(s) per year
Printing Information: 96 pages in 3 colors on Glossy Stock
Binding: Folded
Mailing List Information: Names for rent
In Business: 42 years
Number of Employees: 36
Sales Volume: $ 3.8 Million

1853 US Military Insignia
Ira Green
177 Georgia Avenue
Providence, RI 02905   401-467-4770
800-663-7487
Fax: 401-467-5557
contact@iragreen.com
www.iragreen.com
Patches, badges, wings, ribbons and medals
President: Michael Allister
VP Sales: Bob Strenk
Vice President: Robert Gilmartin
In Business: 72 years
Number of Employees: 211
Sales Volume: $ 26 Million

Miniatures

1854 Florence & George
Florence & George
PO Box 2319
Annapolis, MD 21404   410-224-4386
800-966-3655
Fax: 410-224-4386
info@florenceandgeorge.com
www.florenceandgeorge.com

1855 Hobby Builder's Supply
HBS/Miniatures.com
2388 Pleasantdale Rd
Atlanta, GA 30340-3152   800-926-6464
800-223-7171
Fax: 770-242-1497
hbs@miniatures.com
www.miniatures.com
Dollhouses, collectible miniatures and doll house kits
CFO: Paul Benamy
Credit Cards: AMEX; MasterCard
Catalog Cost: Free
Sales Volume: $ 5-10 Million

1856 Micro-Mark, The Small Tool Specialists
Micro-Mark
340 Snyder Ave
Berkeley Heights, NJ 07922   908-464-2984
800-225-1066
Fax: 908-665-9383
info@micromark.com
www.micromark.com
Hard to find tools and supplies

President: Tom Piccirillo
Credit Cards: MasterCard
Catalog Cost: Free
Printing Information: 104 pages in 4 colors on Glossy Stock
In Business: 87 years

1857 Reaper Miniatures
PO Box 2107
Lake Dallas, TX 75065-2107   940-484-6464
Fax: 940-484-0096
business@reapermini.com
www.reapermini.com
Pewter miniature figurines
Reaper Game Store Manager: Gus Landt

1858 The Golden Egg of Idaho
The Golden Egg of Idaho
167 E. Main St.
P.O. Box 11
Rigby, ID 83442   208-745-8080
800-828-2823
Fax: 208-745-0081
contactus@thegoldeneggofidaho.com
www.thegoldeneggofidaho.com
Full line of egging products.

Movie & Sports Memorabilia

1859 Acorn
Acorn
P.O. Box 1670
West Chester, OH 45071-1670   800-870-8047
www.acornonline.com
British entertainment—mysteries, dramas, comedies, documentaries, and more—plus quality gifts from around the globe.

1860 George H. Labarre Galleries
George H. Labarre Galleries
P.O. Box 746
Hollis, NH 3049   603-882-2411
800-717-9529
Fax: 603-882-4797
collect@glabarre.com
www.glabarre.com
Credit Cards: AMEX; MasterCard
Printing Information: 36 pages
In Business: 35 years

1861 Grey Flannel Auctions
Grey Flannel Auctions
13 Buttercup Lane
Westhampton, NY 11977   631-288-7800
Fax: 631-288-7820
Info@GreyFlannelAuctions.com
catalog.greyflannelauctions.com/default.aspx

1862 Pro Sports Store
Sports Deli
1157 McKinney Lane
Pittsburgh, PA 15220-3417   412-919-5880
www.prosportsstore.com
Sports memorabilia
President: Michael Autierri
Credit Cards: AMEX; MasterCard
Catalog Cost: Free

1863 Script City
Script City
8033 Sunset Boulevard
#315
Hollywood, CA 90046   818-701-0012
800-676-2522
Fax: 818-701-0015
info@scriptcity.com
www.scriptcity.com
Movie scripts

Credit Cards: AMEX; MasterCard; Visa
Catalog Cost: Free
Printing Information: in 1 color

Music Boxes

1864 MadisonAveMall
MadisonAveMall
5014 16th Avenue
Suite 330
Brooklyn, NY 11204   917-450-4472
800-377-0535
www.madisonavemall.com
Credit Cards: AMEX; MasterCard

1865 West Music
West Music
P.O. Box 5521
Coralville, IA 52241   319-351-2000
800-397-9378
Fax: 888-470-3942
www.westmusic.com
West Music is also proud to provide a full array of services with our repair technicians, delivery crew, music therapists, lesson teachers, road representatives, classroom consultants, and customer se
Credit Cards: AMEX; MasterCard
In Business: 74 years

1866 Woodcraft Supply Catalog
Woodcraft Supply LLC
P.O. Box 1686
Parkersburg, WV 26102-1686   304-422-5412
800-535-4486
Fax: 304-422-5417
custserv@woodcraft.com
www.woodcraft.com
Woodworking supplies and books, clock parts, musical movements, glass domes, specialty tools and plans
Chairman: Samuel Ross
President: Jeffrey Forbes
International Marketing Manager: Tim Rinehart
Catalog Cost: Free
Catalog Circulation: Mailed 12 time(s) per year
Printing Information: 176 pages in 4 colors
In Business: 89 years
Number of Employees: 75
Sales Volume: $ 38 Million

Stamps & Accessories

1867 100 Proof Press
100 Proof Press Inc
PO Box 621
St Paris, OH 43072   937-663-4047
Fax: 800-511-2100
info@100proofpress.com
www.100proofpress.com
Art rubber stamps and accessories.
President: Sara Vukson
Credit Cards: MasterCard; Visa
Catalog Cost: $7
Printing Information: 168 pages
In Business: 35 years

1868 Ameri Stamp/Sign-A-Rama
AmeriStamp - Sign-A-Rama
1300 N Royal Avenue
Evansville, IN 47715   812-477-7763
800-223-3086
Fax: 812-477-7898
websales@signsoveramerica.com
www.signsoveramerica.com
Full service sign company selling banners, outdoor signs, vehicle graphics, golf signs and more

President: Walter Valiant
VP of Public Relations: Grant Valiant
grant@signsoveramerica.com
Client Account Specialist: Sherri Hill
sherri@signsoveramerica.com
Account Executive: Matt Effinger
mteffinger@signsoveramerica.com
In Business: 57 years
Number of Employees: 17
Sales Volume: $ 1 Million

1869   Ampersand Press

Ampersand Press
750 Lake St
Port Townsend, WA 98368-2216   360-379-5187
800-624-4263
Fax: 360-379-0324
info@ampersandpress.com
www.ampersandpress.Com

Stamps, accessories and educational games

President: Lou Haller
Credit Cards: AMEX; MasterCard
Catalog Cost: Free
Mailing List Information: Names for rent
In Business: 39 years
Number of Employees: 4
Sales Volume: Under $500,000

1870   Brandtjen & Kluge

Brandtjen & Kluge
539 Blanding Woods Road
St Croix Falls, WI 54024-9001   715-483-3265
800-826-7320
Fax: 715-483-1640
sales@kluge.biz
www.kluge.biz

Embossing, die cutting and foil stamping presses, folding and gluing equipment, blanking systems, UV coaters

Chairman: Michael Aumann, CEO
President: Hank Brandtjen
Marketing Manager: Scott Hansen
Production Manager: Don Kronschnable/Mutt Wilson
International Marketing Manager: Thomas Andersen
Buyers: Kevin Robbins
In Business: 96 years
Number of Employees: 30
Sales Volume: $10,000,000 - $25,000,000

1871   Clacritter Designs

Clacritter Designs
1406 Triple S Trail
Johnson City, TX 78636   512-426-6236
Fax: 830-868-4272
leslie@clacritter.com
www.clacritter.com

Animal rubber stamps

President: Leslie Falteisek
Mailing List Information: Names for rent
In Business: 40 years
Number of Employees: 1
Sales Volume: Under $500,000

1872   Delta Creative

Delta Creative, Inc.
2690 Pellassier Place
City of Industry, CA 90601   800-842-4197
800-423-4135
Fax: 562-695-4227
www.plaidonline.com

Stencil, paint, and stamp products for creative projects

Chairman: Andreas Keller
President: William George
CFO: Carl Chestelson
Marketing Manager: Peggy Smith
Printing Information: in 3 colors
In Business: 50 years
Number of Employees: 105

1873   Ducks, Ducks & More Ducks Catalog

Michael Jaffee Stamps, Inc.
PO Box 61484
Vancouver, WA 98666-1484   360-695-6161
800-782-6770
Fax: 360-695-1616
mjaffe@brookmanstamps.com
www.duckstamps.com

Federal and state duck stamps and prints

President: Michael Jaffe
Credit Cards: AMEX; MasterCard
Catalog Cost: $5
Average Order Size: $150
Mailing List Information: Names for rent
In Business: 41 years
Number of Employees: 4
Sales Volume: $1 Million

1874   Earl P L Apfelbaum

Apfelbaum News & Events
The Pavilion
261 Old York Road, Suite 831
Jenkintown, PA 19046   267-763-0216
800-523-4648
Fax: 215-763-0227
info@apfelbauminc.com
www.apfelbauminc.com

Stamps for collectors

Chairman: Diane Apfelbaum
President: Missy Apfelbaum
Executive VP: John Apfelbaum
Vice President: Ken Apfelbaum
Credit Cards: AMEX; MasterCard
Catalog Cost: Free
In Business: 105 years
Number of Employees: 30

1875   Family Labels

Family Labels
PO Box 207
Peru, IN 46970   954-969-9500
800-935-3864
Fax: 954-969-9833
www.familylabels.com

Return address labels customized with caricatures of your entire family

President: William Berg
Credit Cards: AMEX; MasterCard; Visa
Catalog Cost: Free
In Business: 19 years
Sales Volume: Under $500,000

1876   HE Harris & Company

Whitman Publishing, LLC
3103 Clairmont Rd NE
Suite B
Atlanta, GA 30329-1044   404-214-4304
800-546-2995
Fax: 256-246-1116
info@whitmanbooks.com
www.whitman.com

Stamps and coins for collectors

President: Mary Counts
Production Manager: David Crenshaw
Credit Cards: MasterCard
Printing Information: 64 pages
Binding: Saddle Stitched
In Business: 85 years
Sales Volume: $ 1-3 Million

1877   HG Forms/Tenenz

Tenenz, Inc
9655 Penn Avenue South
Minneapolis, MN 55431   952-277-1713
800-888-5803
Fax: 800-638-0015
mail@tenenz.com
www.tenenz.com

Accounting and tax supples, envelopes, labels, presentation materials, stationery, and software

President: Robert Tenner
In Business: 40 years
Number of Employees: 23

1878   Kenmore Stamp Company

Kenmore Stamp Company
119 West Street
Milford, NH 03055   603-673-1745
800-225-5059
Fax: 603-673-3222
www.kenmorestamp.com

US and foreign postage stamps

President: Henry Harris
Marketing Manager: Richard Basha
Sales Executive: Joe Perez
Credit Cards: MasterCard
Catalog Cost: Free
In Business: 83 years
Number of Employees: 40
Sales Volume: $ 4.5 Million

1879   Lady & the Stamp

Lady & the Stamp
209 Broadway
Chesterton, IN 46304-2421   219-926-9063
www.ladyandthestamp.com

Stamps and stamp accessories

President: Lynn Marble

1880   Mystic Stamp

Mystic Stamp
9700 Mill Street
Camden, NY 13316   315-245-2690
866-660-7147
Fax: 800-385-4919
info@mysticstamp.com
www.mysticstamp.com

Postage stamps for collectors

President: Donald Sundman
VP: David Sundman
Owner: Kim Frank
Credit Cards: AMEX; MasterCard
Catalog Cost: Free
Printing Information: 148 pages
Mailing List Information: Names for rent
In Business: 92 years
Number of Employees: 150
Sales Volume: $ 10 Million

1881   PCS Stamps & Coins

PCS Stamps & Coins
47 Richards Avenue
Norwalk, CT 6857   800-641-8026
service@pcscoins.com
www.pcscoins.com

PCS Stamps & Coins markets a wide range of numismatic, philatelic, and other collectible products.

1882   Roberts Company Inc.

Roberts Company Inc.
180 Franklin St.
Framingham, MA 01702   800-729-1482
Fax: 508-879-3735
www.firecatalog.com

Merchandise for Firefighters.

Catalog Cost: Free
In Business: 56 years

1883   SAFE Collecting Supplies

SAFE Publications
331 W. County Line Rd
Hatboro, PA 19040   215-674-8150
877-395-7233
Fax: 866-395-5372
sales@safepub.com
www.safepub.com

Albums and accessories for stamp, coin, banknotes, postcard, pin and button collectors and paper memorabilia

President: Alex Braun
Vice President: Kurt Braun
Credit Cards: AMEX; MasterCard; Visa
Catalog Cost: $6
Catalog Circulation: Mailed 1 time(s) per year
Average Order Size: $100
Printing Information: 56 pages in 4 colors on Glossy Stock
Press: Web Press
Binding: Saddle Stitched
Mailing List Information: Names for rent
In Business: 62 years
Sales Volume: $500,000- 1 Million

1884   Stamp & Collectibles
Jamestown Stamp Company
117 Cheney Street
Jamestown, NY 14701-19   716-488-0764
                              888-782-6776
                         Fax: 716-664-2211
info@stamp-co.com
www.stamp-co.com

US and Worldwide postage stamps, stamp collecting supplies, albums, special offers and deals, and valuable collector information

President: Sandra Kavanaugh
Principal: Daniel Kavanaugh
Credit Cards: MasterCard; Visa
Catalog Cost: Free
Mailing List Information: Names for rent
In Business: 76 years
Number of Employees: 30
Sales Volume: $ 2 Million

1885   Whitman Publishing Catalog
Whitman Publishing LLC
3103 Clairmont Road
Suite B
Atlanta, GA 30329   404-214-4304
                              800-546-2995
                         Fax: 256-246-1116
info@whitmanbooks.com
www.whitmanbooks.com

Stamps and coins for collectors

President: Mary Counts
Production Manager: David Crenshaw
Credit Cards: AMEX; MasterCard; Visa
Catalog Cost: Free
In Business: 80 years
Sales Volume: $ 1-3 Million

Computers
Computers & Accessories

1886   Action Party Rentals
620 Union Boulevard
Allentown, PA 18109   610-435-8900
                         Fax: 610-435-7316
sales1@actionpartyrentals.com
www.actionpartyrentals.com
President: Sue Horn
Convention Services Manager: Randy

1887   B&R Industrial Automation Corporation
B&R Industrial Automation Corp.
1250 Northmeadow Parkway
Suite 100
Roswell, GA 30076   770-772-0400
                         Fax: 770-772-0243
office.us@br-automation.com
www.br-automation.com

Programmable controllers, industrial computers, software and support

Marketing Manager: Andreas Enzenbach
Credit Cards: MasterCard; Visa
In Business: 25 years
Sales Volume: $ 3-5 Million

1888   BG Micro
BGMicro.com
3024 Lincoln Ct
Garland, TX 75041   972-205-9447
                              800-276-2206
                         Fax: 972-278-5105
bgmicro@bgmicro.com
www.bgmicro.com

IC's, crystals, eproms and RAMS for computers

President: John Gage
Owner: Jerry Gage
Credit Cards: MasterCard; Visa
Catalog Cost: Free
Catalog Circulation: Mailed 4 time(s) per year to 35M
Printing Information: 24 pages in 1 color on Matte Stock
Mailing List Information: Names for rent
In Business: 30 years
Number of Employees: 3
Sales Volume: $500,000- 1 Million

1889   Brodart
Brodart
500 Arch Street
Williamsport, PA 17701   570-326-2461
                              888-820-4377
                         Fax: 800-283-6087
www.shopbrodart.com

In Business: 70 years

1890   CNA 2015 Catalog
Computer Network Accessories
5520 Burkhardt Rd.
Dayton, OH 45431   937-258-2708
                              800-516-1262
                         Fax: 800-236-5672
sales@cnaweb.com
www.cnaweb.com

1891   Cablexpress Technologies
Cablexpress
5404 South Bay Road
P.O. Box 4799
Syracuse, NY 13212-4799   315-476-3000
                              800-913-9465
                         Fax: 315-455-1800
info@cablexpress.com
www.cablexpress.com/

Computer networking equipment

President: William Pomeroy
VP: Barbara Ashkin
Credit Cards: AMEX; MasterCard; Visa
Printing Information: 68 pages
In Business: 34 years
Number of Employees: 310
Sales Volume: $ 72 Million

1892   Champs Software
Champs Software
1255 N Vantage Point Dr
Crystal River, FL 34429-8717   352-795-2362
                         Fax: 352-795-9100
mmelfi@champsinc.com
www.champsinc.com

Computerized maintenance management systems

President: Kaushik Patel
Marketing Manager: Chris Skinnerr
CEO: Chandra Patel
Owner: John Patel
Credit Cards: MasterCard; Visa
Printing Information: 8 pages
In Business: 36 years
Number of Employees: 28
Sales Volume: $ 3 Million

1893   Conde Systems
Conde
5600 Commerce Boulevard East
Mobile, AL 36619   251-633-5704
                              800-826-6332
                         Fax: 215-633-3876
saleshelp@conde.com
www.conde.com

Sublimation and heat transfer imprinting supplies, inks, paper, imprintables, systems, heat press machines, training, videos, workshops and more

President: David Gross
Production Manager: Martin Porter
President/CEO: William Gross Jr
Credit Cards: AMEX; MasterCard
In Business: 20 years
Number of Employees: 70
Sales Volume: $ 4 Million

1894   Connection
Connection
Route 101A, 730 Milford Road
Merrimack, NH 03054-4631   603-355-6005
                              888-213-0260
customerservice@pcconnections.com
www.connection.com

Electronics, computers, cables, adaptors, accessories, virus protection software, printers, office equipment

President: Timothy McGrath
Credit Cards: AMEX; MasterCard
Catalog Cost: Free
In Business: 35 years
Number of Employees: 2500
Sales Volume: $2.7 billion

1895   Cyberguys.com
Cybers Guys
11321 White Rock Rd
Rancho Cordova, CA 95742-6505 916-631-9000
                              800-892-1010
                         Fax: 916-858-1009
info@cyberguys.com
www.cyberguys.com

Hard to find and innovative computer accessories, electronics and workplace accessories

President: Wes Sumida
CFO: Terry Iwashige
Marketing Manager: Kelly Carlson
Buyers: Terrie Wilson
Credit Cards: AMEX; MasterCard
Catalog Cost: Free
Catalog Circulation: Mailed 12 time(s) per year
Printing Information: 190 pages in 4 colors on Newsprint
Press: Web Press
Binding: Saddle Stitched
Mailing List Information: Names for rent
In Business: 20 years
Number of Employees: 50
Sales Volume: $ 6.2 Million

1896   HRO Catalog
Ham Radio Outlet
110 Tampico
Suite 110
Walnut Creek, CA 94598-3432   925-831-1771
                         Fax: 925-831-1892
www.hamradio.com

Ham radio equipment

President: Bob Ferrero
Credit Cards: AMEX; MasterCard
In Business: 44 years
Sales Volume: $20MM to $50MM

1897 Hewlett Packard
HP
11445 Compaq Center W Dr
Houston, TX 77070-2000   281-370-0670
     800-333-1917
Fax: 281-514-1740
www.hp.com

Computer equipment and accessories

Chairman: Raymond Lane
President: Margaret Whitman
Catalog Circulation: to 45000
Average Order Size: $2600
Printing Information: 120 pages in 4 colors on Glossy Stock
Press: Web Press
Binding: Saddle Stitched
Mailing List Information: Names for rent
In Business: 73 years
Number of Employees: 3000
Sales Volume: Over $1 Billion

1898 Homeschool Catalog
Alpha Omega Publications
804 N 2nd Avenue E
Rock Rapids, IA 51246   800-622-3070
Fax: 712-472-4856
www.aophomeschooling.com

Annual catalog filled with home school curriculum choices, resources, and support services

President: Beth Grotenhuis
Catalog Circulation: to 1000
In Business: 38 years

1899 Indus International
Indus
340 South Oak Street
West Salem, WI 54669-890   608-786-0300
     800-843-9377
Fax: 608-786-0786
support@ventyx.com
www.indususa.com

Optical disk systems, micrographic readers and printers

President: Ameen Ayoob
Marketing Manager: Don Seawall
Owner: Sanober Ayoob
Credit Cards: MasterCard; Visa
Catalog Circulation: Mailed 12 time(s) per year
Mailing List Information: Names for rent
In Business: 29 years
Number of Employees: 21
Sales Volume: $ 2 Million

1900 Infosource
Infosource Inc.
1300 City View Center
Oviedo, FL 32765   407-796-5200
     800-393-4636
Fax: 407-796-5190
isisale@howtomaster.com
www.infosourcelearning.com

Computer software

President: Thomas Warrner
Marketing Manager: Kacy Keller
Catalog Circulation: to 2MM
Number of Employees: 105

1901 JDSU Company
JDS Uniphase Corporation
430 N McCarthy Boulevard
Milpitas, CA 95035   408-546-5000
Fax: 408-546-4300
www.jdsu.com

Portable computer products and supplies

Chairman: Martin Kaplan
President: Thomas Waechter
CFO: Rex Jackson
Marketing Manager: Paul McNab
CEO: Thomas Waechter
Executive Operations: Judith Kay

Human Resources: Brett Hooper
Printing Information: 6 pages
In Business: 32 years
Number of Employees: 320
Sales Volume: Over $1 Billion

1902 Kolobags
Kolobags
2512 Artesia Blvd #305F
Redondo Beach, CA 90278   310-374-4453
     866-405-KOLO

Laptop bags and accessories

President: Elaine Goodman
In Business: 8 years
Sales Volume: Under $500,000

1903 Microbiz
Microbiz
655 Oak Grove Avenue
Suite 493
Menlo Park, CA 94026-493   702-749-5353
     800-937-2289
Fax: 650-440-4870
info@microbiz.com
www.microbizonline.com

Computer hardware, software and complete systems

President: Kevin Kogler
Chief Architect: Tim Robidoux
In Business: 30 years

1904 Mobility Electronics
IGO
17800 N Perimeter Drive
Suite 200
Scottsdale, AZ 85255-5449   480-596-0061
     800-311-3274
Fax: 480-368-2856
support@igo.com
www.igo.com

Accessories for computer notebooks

Chairman: Michael Larson
President: Michael Heil
CFO: Darryl Baker
Credit Cards: AMEX; MasterCard
Printing Information: 8 pages
In Business: 16 years
Number of Employees: 62
Sales Volume: $ 43 Million

1905 Network Access & Connectivity Product Line
Patton
7622 Rickenbacker Drive
Gaithersburg, MD 20879-4773   301-975-1000
Fax: 301-869-9293
support@patton.com
www.patton.com

Short range modems, converters, etc

President: Robert R Patton
Marketing Manager: Chris Christner
VP Finance/Administration: Bruce E Patton
VP Manufacturing: Steve Schrader
Sr. Director of Engineering: Joachim Wlotzka
Catalog Cost: Free
Printing Information: 150 pages
In Business: 33 years
Number of Employees: 175
Sales Volume: $ 5-10 Million

1906 New England Business Service
Deluxe Business Corporation
3680 Victoria Street North
Shoreview, MN 55126-2966   651-483-7111
     888-823-6327
Fax: 800-234-4324
customerservice@nebs.com
www.deluxe.com

Top quality business and computer forms, checks and promotional products

President: Richard Schulte
CFO: Terry Peterson

CEO: Lee J. Schram
VP, Chief Information Officer: Michael S. Mathews
Senior Vice President: John D. Filby
In Business: 100 years
Number of Employees: 3611

1907 Office City
Office City
604 Price Avenue
Redwood City, CA 94063   650-364-4311
     877-484-3633
Fax: 650-364-2677
www.theofficecity.com

Computers

President: Stacey Leandro
Marketing Manager: Bill Jones
CEO: Dick Dodge
Regional Sales Manager: Amy Nieva
Credit Cards: AMEX; MasterCard
Catalog Cost: Free
In Business: 54 years
Number of Employees: 20
Sales Volume: $ 9 Million

1908 PC America
PC America
One Blue Hill Plaza
Floor 16
Pearl River, NY 10965-1943   845-920-0800
     800-722-6374
Fax: 845-920-0880
sales@pcamerica.com
www.pcamerica.com

Computerized registers

President: Richard Rotbard
CEO: David Gosman
Credit Cards: AMEX; MasterCard
Catalog Circulation: to 1k
Printing Information: 20 pages
In Business: 27 years
Number of Employees: 21
Sales Volume: $ 5-10 Million

1909 PC Connection Express
PC Connection, Inc.
Route 101A, 730 Milford Road
Merrimack, NH 03054-4631   603-355-6005
     800-800-0013
Fax: 603-683-5766
customerservice@pcconnection.com
www.pcconnection.com

Computers and computer accessories as well as other electronics

Chairman: Patricia Gallup
President: William Cooper
Production Manager: Anne Coyne
Credit Cards: AMEX; MasterCard; Visa
Catalog Cost: Free
Catalog Circulation: Mailed 12 time(s) per year
Printing Information: 172 pages in 4 colors on Glossy Stock
Press: Web Press
Binding: Saddle Stitched
In Business: 33 years
Number of Employees: 1400
Sales Volume: $ 20-50 Million

1910 Pioneer Hi-Bred International
DuPont Pioneer
PO Box 1000
Johnston, IA 50131-184   515-535-3200
Fax: 515-535-4415
www.pioneer.com

Computer and farming software

President: Rick McConnell
Production Manager: Mike Gumina
VP, Finance: Gregory Friedman
Credit Cards: AMEX; MasterCard
Catalog Circulation: to 30M+
In Business: 89 years
Number of Employees: 450
Sales Volume: $ 5-10 Million

1911 Premise Wiring
Premise Wiring
565 Brea Canyon Road
Ste A
Walnut, CA 91789   626-964-7873
800-346-6668
Fax: 626-964-7880
info@unicomlink.com
www.unicomlink.com

Voice and data networking products

President: Jeffrey Lo
Marketing Manager: Brian Milliken
Production Manager: Chris Lin
Credit Cards: MasterCard
Catalog Cost: Free
Catalog Circulation: to 100M
Printing Information: 100 pages in 4 colors on Glossy Stock
Binding: Perfect Bound
Mailing List Information: Names for rent
In Business: 16 years
Number of Employees: 40
Sales Volume: $ 3-5 Million

1912 Pro-tect Computer Products
Pro-tect Computer Products
P.O.Box 1002
Centerville, UT 84014-5002   801-295-7739
800-669-7739
Fax: 801-295-7786
protectcov@aol.com
www.protectcovers.com

Computer products, keyboards and covers

President: Gil Workman
Production Manager: Ted Larkin
Credit Cards: AMEX; MasterCard
Printing Information: 4 pages
In Business: 27 years
Number of Employees: 18
Sales Volume: $ 1-3 Million

1913 ProVantage
ProVantage
7576 Freedom Avenue NW
North Canton, OH 44720-7143   330-494-8715
800-336-1166
Fax: 330-494-5260
sales@provantage.com
www.provantage.com

Computer hardware

Chairman: Arno Zirngibl
President: Mike Colarik
Owner: Renee Ebert
Credit Cards: AMEX; MasterCard
Catalog Cost: Free
Catalog Circulation: Mailed 4 time(s) per year
Printing Information: in 4 colors
In Business: 31 years
Number of Employees: 50
Sales Volume: $ 5-10 Million

1914 Production Basics
Production Basics
31 Dunham Road
Billerica, MA 1821   617-926-8100
800-318-2770
Fax: 617-926-8010
sales@pbasics.com
www.pbasics.com

1915 Provantage
Provantage LLC
7576 Freedom Ave NW
North Canton, OH 44720   330-494-8715
800-336-1166
Fax: 330-494-5260
Sales@provantage.com
www.provantage.com

Sources for computer software and hardware

Chairman: Arno Zirngibl
President: Mike Colarik
Credit Cards: AMEX; MasterCard

Printing Information: 84 pages
In Business: 30 years
Number of Employees: 50
Sales Volume: $ 5-10 Million

1916 Publishing Perfection
Publishing Perfection
21155 Watertown Rd
Waukesha, WI 53186-1898   262-717-0600
800-782-5974
Fax: 262-717-0745
marketing@pubperfect.com
www.publishingperfection.com

Desktop and other computer equipment and accessories; Computer software and software for the publishing and graphics markets

President: Rick Wintersberger
Purchasing Manager: Jessica Lau
Sales Manager: David Bates
Credit Cards: AMEX; MasterCard
Printing Information: 64 pages
In Business: 22 years
Number of Employees: 20
Sales Volume: $ 3 Million

1917 RMS Technology
RMS Technology, Inc.
195 Montague St
Brooklyn, NY 11201   567-223-4123
800-533-3211
Fax: 503-829-6568
info@rmstek.com
www.rmstek.com

Flight planning computer software and moving map software, electronic flight bags

President: Warren Christman
CFO: Christine Christman
Marketing Manager: Allyson Overton
Production Manager: Neisa Lockett
Assistant Professor: Gregory Babbitt
Assistant Professor: Amit Batabyal
Assistant Professor: Mario Gomes
Credit Cards: AMEX; MasterCard; Visa
Printing Information: 8 pages
In Business: 30 years
Number of Employees: 8

1918 Salescaster Displays Corporation
Salescasterr Displays Corporation
2095 Protland Avenue
Scotch Plains, NJ 07076   800-346-4474
Fax: 908-322-3049
sales@salescaster.com
www.salescaster.com

Electronic visual displays

President: Dennis Tort
VP: Mark Tort
Printing Information: in 3 colors
In Business: 65 years

1919 Sealevel Systems
Sealevel Systems
PO Box 830
Liberty, SC 29657-3300   864-843-4343
Fax: 864-843-3067
support@sealevel.com
www.sealevel.com

Ports and products including PCI, USB and ISA Bus adapters, Windows COM

President: Ben O'Hanlan
beno@sealevel.com
Marketing Manager: Earle Foster
earlef@sealevel.com
CEO: Tom O'Hanlan
tom.ohanlan@sealevel.com
Human Resource Director: Nancy Gilreath
nancy.gilreath@sealevel.com
VP of Sales: Bill Hanrahan
bill.hanrahan@sealevel.com
In Business: 30 years

1920 Stinson Stationers
Stinson's
1108 Baker St
Bakersfield, CA 93305-4322   661-323-7611
Fax: 661-327-5299
supplies@stinsons.com
www.stinsons.com

Computers

President: Ben Stinson
ben@stinsons.com
Marketing Manager: DebbieAdams
dadams@stinsons.com
Production Manager: John Cowan
VP: Russ Haley
rhaley@stinsons.com
Customer Service: Kitty Emerson
kemerson@stinsons.com
IT Manager: Tim Davis
tdavis@stinsons.com
In Business: 66 years
Number of Employees: 53
Sales Volume: $ 12 Million

1921 Technoland Systems
IBASE Techonology (USA), Inc.
1050 Stewart Drive
Sunnyvale, CA 94085-3916   408-992-0888
800-292-4500
Fax: 408-992-0808
sales@ibase-usa.com
www.technoland.com

Price list of PC computer parts, supplies and accessories

President: Jeff Hsu
Credit Cards: MasterCard
In Business: 14 years
Number of Employees: 30
Sales Volume: $ 4.5 Million

1922 Telstar Products
Telstar Products
77 Beaver Street
Brooklyn, NY 11206   718-455-4500
888-828-1680
Fax: 718-455-6790
daniel@telstarpro.com
www.telstarpro.com

In Business: 28 years

1923 Viziflex Seels Computer Protection Products
Viziflex Seels, Inc.
406 N Midland Ave.
Saddle Brook, NJ 07663-6831   800-307-3357
800-627-7752
Fax: 201-487-3266
info@viziflex.com
www.viziflex.com

Computer accessories and static control products

President: Mike Glicksman
Production Manager: Sergio Gonzalez
VP: Andrea Glicksman
Buyers: Mike Dominguez, Computer Supplies
Catalog Circulation: Mailed 6 time(s) per year to 60M
Average Order Size: $850
Printing Information: 20 pages in 4 colors on Matte Stock
Press: Web Press
Binding: Perfect Bound
Mailing List Information: Names for rent
List Manager: Loretta Afif
In Business: 33 years
Sales Volume: $ 3 Million

1924 Zahn Dental
Henry Schein
135 Duryea Rd
Melville, NY 11747-3834   631-843-5500
Fax: 631-843-5675
investor@henryschein.com
www.henryschein.com

Wholesale healthcare products and computers for doctors

Chairman: Stanley Bergman
President: James Breslawski
Executive Vice President, Chief Adm: Gerald A. Benjamin
Senior Vice President and Chief Tec: James A. Harding
Senior Vice President, Corporate &: Michael S. Ettinger
In Business: 83 years
Number of Employees: 700
Sales Volume: Over $1 Billion

Graphic Supplies, Printers & Equipment

1925 Printers Plus
Printers Plus
1181 Belanger Ave
Ottawa, ON 63040-499   866-242-1153
                         Fax: 888-521-1056
                      www.printersplus.net

Printers and related supplies

Credit Cards: AMEX; MasterCard

1926 Voltexx
Voltexx, LLC
2100 N 15th Ave, Unit C
Melrose Park, IL 60160-1226   708-223-3858
                              800-211-5554
                         Fax: 708-223-3859
                   cminervino@voltexx.com
                         www.voltexx.com

Ink, toner and laser supplies for fax machines, copier and printing

President: William Zaggle
Credit Cards: AMEX; MasterCard
In Business: 7 years

Peripherals & Systems

1927 CDW
CDW
75 Tri-State International
Lincolnshire, IL 60069   866-782-4239
                              800-800-4239
                            www.cdw.com

Macintosh computer items and supplies

Chairman: Thomas E. Richards
CFO: Collin B. Kebo
Marketing Manager: Christina M. Corley
SVP/Chief Coworker Services Officer: Dennis G. Berger
SVP of Operations & CIO: Jonathan J. Stevens
SVP of Strategic & Marketing: Mark Chong
Credit Cards: AMEX; MasterCard; Visa
Catalog Cost: Free
Catalog Circulation: Mailed 1 time(s) per year to 20000
Printing Information: 208 pages in 4 colors
Press: Web Press
Number of Employees: 80
Sales Volume: $50MM to $100MM

1928 GEI International
GEI International, Inc.
PO Box 6849
Syracuse, NY 13217-6849   315-463-9261
                         Fax: 315-463-9034
                       info@geionline.com
                        www.geionline.com

Optical, measuring and graphic tools

President: Peter Anderson
Credit Cards: AMEX; MasterCard
Printing Information: 48 pages
In Business: 54 years
Number of Employees: 20
Sales Volume: $1-3 Million

1929 Global Datacom
GlobalComputer.com
2319 Highway 35
Holmdel, NJ 07733   516-608-7000
                              800-446-9662
                         Fax: 732-888-8316
                    investinfo@systemax.com
                     www.globalcomputer.com

Computers and accessories

President: Robert Leeds
Credit Cards: MasterCard

1930 Jameco Electronics
Jameco Electronics
1355 Shoreway Road
Belmont, CA 94002   650-592-8097
                              800-831-4242
                         Fax: 650-592-2503
                        Sales@jameco.com
                          www.jameco.com

Electronic & computer parts and components

President: Phil Greeves
CFO: Ester Baldovino
Marketing Manager: Greg Harris
CEO: James Farrey
VP: Gil Orozco
Director of Information Technology: Matt Smith
Catalog Cost: Free
In Business: 35 years
Number of Employees: 100
Sales Volume: $5 million

1931 Maysteel
Maysteel LLC
6199 Highway W
PO Box 902
Allenton, WI 53002   262-251-1632
                              877-629-7833
                         Fax: 262-629-1612
                          www.maysteel.com

Computer and communication equipment and systems

President: Kevin Matkin
CFO: Randy Gromowski
Marketing Manager: Suzy Moody
Director of Program Management: Jeffrey Henn
Allenton Plant Manager: David Dembinski
VP, Business Development: Don Lawinger
In Business: 78 years
Number of Employees: 118
Sales Volume: $10MM to $20MM

1932 Option PC
GlobalComputer.com
11 Harbor Park Drive
Port Washington, NY 11050-4650 516-625-3663
                              800-8GL-OBAL
                         Fax: 516-625-0038
                     www.globalcomputer.com

Computer and accessories

President: Bruce Leeds
Credit Cards: MasterCard

1933 PC & MacConnection
PC Connection
730 Milford Rd
Route 101A
Merrimack, NH 03054-4631   603-355-6005
                              888-213-0607
                         Fax: 603-423-5748
                 customerservice@pcconnection.com
                      www.pcconnection.com

Macintosh computer hardware, software and accessories

Chairman: Pat Gallup
President: Patricia Gallup
CFO: Jack Ferguson
Marketing Manager: Robert Wilkins
Credit Cards: AMEX; MasterCard; Visa

Catalog Circulation: Mailed 12 time(s) per year to 12000
Printing Information: 172 pages in 4 colors on Glossy Stock
Press: Web Press
Binding: Saddle Stitched
Mailing List Information: Names for rent
In Business: 33 years
Number of Employees: 1400
Sales Volume: $1MM to $3MM

1934 PC Systems Handbook
CyberResearch, Inc.
25 Business Park Drive
Branford, CT 06405-2932   203-643-5000
                              800-341-2525
                         Fax: 203-643-5001
                   sales@cyberresearch.com
                     www.cyberresearch.com

Rugged industrial PC systems, data acquitions and motion control

President: Robert C. Molloy
Credit Cards: AMEX; MasterCard; Visa
Catalog Cost: Free
Catalog Circulation: Mailed 2 time(s) per year to 30M
Printing Information: 212 pages in 4 colors on Matte Stock
Press: Web Press
Mailing List Information: Names for rent
List Manager: Jerry Abramczyk
List Company: Edith Roman
In Business: 32 years
Number of Employees: 2225
Sales Volume: $1,000,000 - $5,000,000

1935 Polywell Computers
Polywell Computers,Inc
1461 San Mateo Ave
S San Francisco, CA 94080-6553 650-583-7222
                              800-999-1278
                         Fax: 650-583-1974
                       info@polywell.com
                        www.Polywell.Com

IBM personal computers compatible 386, 486

President: Sam Chu
Marketing Manager: James Thomas
Production Manager: VP Sam Chu
Buyers: Eva Chu
Sam Chu
Credit Cards: AMEX; MasterCard
Catalog Cost: Free
Catalog Circulation: Mailed 4 time(s) per year to 50M
Printing Information: 8 pages in 4 colors on Glossy Stock
Press: Letterpress
Mailing List Information: Names for rent
List Manager: David Peters
In Business: 28 years
Number of Employees: 30
Sales Volume: $10MM to $20MM

1936 Power Up!
Global Computer Supplies Inc.
2139 Highway 35 Holmdel
Port Washington, NY 07733-4656 516-625-3663
                              800-446-9662
                         Fax: 516-625-0038
                     www.globalcomputer.com

Computer peripherals and systems

President: Bruce Leeds
In Business: 50 years

1937 ProStar
Pro Star Inc.
4752 W California Ave
Salt Lake City, UT 84104-1348 626-839-6472
                              888-576-4742
                         Fax: 626-854-3438
                         www.prostar.com

Notebook computers and accessories

President: Matt Williams
Credit Cards: AMEX; MasterCard
Number of Employees: 100

1938 Rose Electronics

Rose
10707 Stancliff Rd
Houston, TX 77099-4344   281-933-7673
   800-333-9343
Fax: 281-933-0044
sales@rose.Com
www.Rose.Com

Computer peripherals, printers and data switches

President: Joe Galenski
Marketing Manager: Sam Sekhavaty
Vice President Operations: Sheila Pearson
Vice President Sales: Allen Vineberg
Managing Director: Paul Naish
Printing Information: in 1 color
In Business: 30 years
Sales Volume: $20 million

1939 Server Management Products

Rose Electronics
10707 Stancliff Road
Houston, TX 77099-4306   281-933-7673
   800-333-9343
Fax: 281-933-0044
sales@rose.com
www.rose.com

Data communication equipment and computer peripheral sharing equipment

President: David Rahvar
Marketing Manager: Dick Baker
Credit Cards: MasterCard; Visa
Catalog Cost: Free
Catalog Circulation: to 70K
Printing Information: 25 pages in 4 colors on Glossy Stock
Press: Web Press
Binding: Perfect Bound
Mailing List Information: Names for rent
In Business: 31 years
Number of Employees: 130
Sales Volume: $10,000,000 - $25,000,000

1940 Teacher Direct

Teacher Direct
P.O. Box 12063
Birmingham, AL 35202   888-322-4377
Fax: 888-628-5678
customerservice@teacherdirect.com
www.teacherdirect.com

Teacher Direct offers everything from classroom whiteboards to wholesale school supplies to curriculum products for the following subjects: Language Arts, Math, Science, and Social Studies.

1941 Twinhead Corporation

GammaTech Computer Corporation
48303 Fremont Blvd
Fremont, CA 94538-6510   510-492-0828
   800-995-8946
Fax: 510-492-0820
sales@gammatechusa.com
www.gammatechusa.com

Computer systems and laptops

President: Bill Liu
Credit Cards: AMEX; MasterCard; Visa
Catalog Cost: Free
Catalog Circulation: Mailed 4 time(s) per year to 10M
Printing Information: 10 pages in 4 colors on Glossy Stock
Press: Letterpress
Mailing List Information: Names for rent
In Business: 10 years
Number of Employees: 26
Sales Volume: $10MM to $20MM

1942 V-Infinity Power Quick Guide Catalog

CUI Inc
20050 SW 112th Avenue
Tualatin, OR 97062   503-612-2300
   800-275-4899
Fax: 503-612-2383
sales@cui.com
www.cui.com

An overview of the V-Infinity power supply and dc-dc converter lines

President: Matt McKenzie
CFO: Dan Ford
Senior VP: Mark Adams
VP Operations: John Hulden
Chief Technical Officer: Don Li
In Business: 25 years

1943 Z-World

Digi International Inc.
11001 Bren Road East
Minnetonka, MN 55343-6809   952-912-3444
   877-912-3444
Fax: 952-912-4952
www.digi.com

Remote control kits

President: Ron Konezny
CFO: Mike Goergen
Vice President, Chief Marketing Off: Jeff Liebl
Vice President of Manufacturing Ope: Jon Nyland
Vice President of Talent and Inform: Tracy Roberts
In Business: 30 years
Number of Employees: 100

Software

1944 Accu-Time Systems

Accu-Time Systems
420 Somers Road
Ellington, CT 06029-2629   860-870-5000
   800-355-4648
Fax: 860-872-1511
sales@accu-time.com
www.accu-time.com

Time clocks and data collection terminals

President: James Mchale
CFO: Lisa Gladysz
Marketing Manager: David Hopkins
Production Manager: Martin Seelig
Director of Human Resources: Karen Blovish
VP of Strategic Alliances: Jim Cox
VP of Strategic Alliance: Larry Dawson
International Marketing Manager: Karen Parrott
Buyers: John Cappuccilli
Credit Cards: AMEX; MasterCard; Visa
Mailing List Information: Names for rent
List Manager: Karen Parrott
In Business: 24 years
Number of Employees: 40
Sales Volume: $5.6 Million

1945 American Business Systems

American Business Systems
315 Littleton Road
Chelmsford, MA 01824-3392   800-356-4034
Fax: 978-250-8027
sales@abs-software.com
www.abs-software.com

Business software for accounting, retail point of sale, and wholesale distributors

President: Jim Hamilton
Marketing Manager: Jim Hanlon
Catalog Cost: Free
Mailing List Information: Names for rent
In Business: 39 years
Number of Employees: 16
Sales Volume: $3MM to $5MM

1946 Baron Barclay Bridge Supply

Baron Barclay Bridge Supply
3600 Chamberlain Lane
Suite 206
Louisville, KY 40241   502-426-0410
   800-274-2221
Fax: 502-426-2044
www.baronbarclay.com

Bridge book in print and anything needed for playing contract or duplicate bridge. They also have videos, computer programs, electronic bridge games, a wide selection of the world's finest playing car

1947 Complete Real Estate Software Catalog

Z-Law Software, Inc.
80 Upton Avenue
PO Box 40602
Providence, RI 02940-602   401-331-3002
   800-526-5588
Fax: 401-421-5334
Sales@z-law.com
www.z-law.com

PC and MAC software for realtors, investors, developers, property managers, and anyone involved in real estate

President: Gary L. Sherman, Esq.
Marketing Manager: William Sherman
Credit Cards: AMEX; MasterCard
Printing Information: 72 pages in 2 colors
Press: Sheetfed Press
Binding: Saddle Stitched
Mailing List Information: Names for rent
In Business: 22 years

1948 Connection

Connection
Route 101A, 730 Milford Road
Merrimack, NH 03054-4631   603-355-6005
   888-213-0260
customerservice@pcconnections.com
www.connection.com

Electronics, computers, cables, adaptors, accessories, virus protection software, printers, office equipment

President: Timothy McGrath
Credit Cards: AMEX; MasterCard
Catalog Cost: Free
In Business: 35 years
Number of Employees: 2500
Sales Volume: $2.7 billion

1949 Data Impressions Technology Catalog

Data Impressions
17418 Studebaker Rd.
Cerritos, CA 90703   562-207-9050
   800-777-6488
Fax: 562-207-9053
www.dataimpressions.com
In Business: 36 years

1950 EZAutomation

EZAutomation.net
4140 Utica Ridge Road
Bettendorf, IA 52722   877-774-EASY
Fax: 877-775-EASY
sales@ezautomation.net
ezautomation.net

Computer parts

President: Vikram Kumar
Credit Cards: AMEX; MasterCard
Catalog Cost: Free
In Business: 16 years

1951 Flatt Stationers

Flatt Stationers
206 West Commerce
Mexia, TX 76667   254-562-3843
   800-792-3281
Fax: 254-562-7331
info@flattstationers.com
flatts.ssiwebonline.com

In Business: 77 years

1952 GovConnection

GovConnection
7503 Standish Pl
Rockville, MD 20855-2731   301-340-1100
800-998-0009
Fax: 603-423-6192
customercare@govconnection.com
www.govconnection.com

IT solutions for government and education

President: Patricia Gallup
CFO: Jack Ferguson
Printing Information: in 4 colors
In Business: 32 years
Number of Employees: 180
Sales Volume: $ 9 Million

1953 HR Direct

HR Direct
PO Box 452049
Sunrise, FL 33345-2049   800-888-4040
Fax: 954-846-0777
questions@hrdirect.com
www.hrdirect.com

Office products, holiday greeting cards, calendars and software

Catalog Cost: Free
Mailing List Information: Names for rent
In Business: 31 years
Number of Employees: 300

1954 Health Education Services

Social Studies School Service
P.O.Box 802
10200 Jefferson Blvd.
Culver City, CA 90232-802   310-839-2436
800-421-4246
Fax: 310-839-2249
access@socialstudies.com
www.socialstudies.com

Software

President: Irwin Levin
Owner: Stan Weiner
CEO: David Weiner
Printing Information: 48 pages in 4 colors on Matte Stock
Press: Web Press
Binding: Saddle Stitched
In Business: 50 years
Number of Employees: 65
Sales Volume: $ 12 Million

1955 Infosource

Infosource Inc.
1300 City View Center
Oviedo, FL 32765   407-796-5200
800-393-4636
Fax: 407-796-5190
isisale@howtomaster.com
www.infosourcelearning.com

Computer software

President: Thomas Warrner
Marketing Manager: Kacy Keller
Catalog Circulation: to 2MM
Number of Employees: 105

1956 Medical Arts Press Medical Reference Catalog

Medical Arts Press Medical Reference Cat
PO Box 43200
Minneapolis, MN 55443-200   763-493-7300
800-328-2179
Fax: 800-328-0023
www.medicalartspress.com

Medical, dental, optometry, podiatry and veterinary office supplies including coding & billing, filing, furniture, labels, forms, software, stationery and breakroom supplies

President: Lindee Weed
Marketing Manager: Barb Boyer

Production Manager: Terry Schwarting
Credit Cards: AMEX; MasterCard; Visa
Catalog Cost: Free
Catalog Circulation: Mailed 2 time(s) per year
Printing Information: 792 pages in 4 colors
Mailing List Information: Names for rent
In Business: 64 years
Number of Employees: 460
Sales Volume: $ 32 Million

1957 Neopost

Neopost
2304 Tarpley Road
Suite 134
Carrollton, TX 75006   510-489-6800
800-636-7678
Fax: 510-489-4367
www.Neopostinc.com

Mailing machines, shipping systems and software solutons

Chairman: Denis Thiery
CFO: Bertrand Dumazy
Sales Manager: Carol Chaney
In Business: 90 years
Number of Employees: 300

1958 NewHaven Software

NewHaven Software
9840 Willows Rd Suite 102
P.O. Box 3456
Redmond, WA 98073-3456   425-861-7120
Fax: 425-861-7460
sales@newhavensoftware.com
www.newhavensoftware.com

Mail Order Wizard, Mail List Monarch and other software packages

President: Tom Danner
CEO: Tom Danner
Credit Cards: MasterCard
Printing Information: 4 pages in 2 colors
In Business: 14 years
Number of Employees: 12

1959 PC/Nametag

PC/Nametag
124 Horizon Drive
Verona, WI 53593   888-354-7868
Fax: 800-233-9787
sales@pcnametag.com
www.pcnametag.com

Software equipment and supplies

President: Nick Topitzes
ntopitzes@pcnametag.com
International Marketing Manager: Darren Walker
Credit Cards: AMEX; MasterCard
Catalog Circulation: Mailed 4 time(s) per year
Printing Information: 68 pages in 4 colors on Glossy Stock
Press: Web Press
Binding: Saddle Stitched
Mailing List Information: Names for rent
In Business: 29 years
Number of Employees: 25
Sales Volume: $ 3-5 Million

1960 Paper Access

Paper Access
23 W 18th St
New York, NY 10011-4601   212-463-7035
Fax: 212-463-7022
info@paperpresentation.com
www.paperpresentation.com

Stationery and matching envelopes and printing software

President: Chris Brown
VP: Arthur Rejay
Credit Cards: AMEX; MasterCard; Visa
Catalog Cost: Free
Catalog Circulation: Mailed 2 time(s) per year to 20M
Printing Information: 64 pages in 4 colors
Mailing List Information: Names for rent
List Manager: Venture Communications

List Company: Venture Communications
60 Madison Avenue, 3rd Floor
New York, NY 10010
212-684-4800
In Business: 20 years
Number of Employees: 25
Sales Volume: $ 3.6 Million

1961 Pioneer Hi-Bred International

DuPont Pioneer
PO Box 1000
Johnston, IA 50131-184   515-535-3200
Fax: 515-535-4415
www.pioneer.com

Computer and farming software

President: Rick McConnell
Production Manager: Mike Gumina
VP, Finance: Gregory Friedman
Credit Cards: AMEX; MasterCard
Catalog Circulation: to 30M+
In Business: 89 years
Number of Employees: 450
Sales Volume: $ 5-10 Million

1962 Product Pak

Dialogic Corporation
4 Gatehall Drive
Parsippany, NJ 07054   408-750-9400
800-755-4444
Fax: 973-967-6006
insidesales@dialogic.com
www.dialogic.com/default.htm

Voice processing hardware and software

President: Bill Crank
CFO: Bob Dennerlein
SVP Product Management & Marketing: Jim Machi
SVP Product Development and Operati: Kevin Gould
VP Human Resources: Guy F. Pedelini
Credit Cards: AMEX; MasterCard
Catalog Circulation: to 7.5M
Printing Information: 20 pages
In Business: 26 years
Number of Employees: 300
Sales Volume: $ 100-500 Million

1963 Rapid Forms

Rapid Forms
PO Box 1186
Lancaster, CA 93584-9961   800-257-8354
Fax: 800-451-8113
service@rapidforms.com
www.rapidforms.com

Checks and banking supplies, software, business cards and stationery

President: Lee Schram

1964 Rep Profit Management System

RPMS, LLC
PO Box 15298
Lenexa, KS 66210-2782   913-800-8750
800-776-7435
Fax: 913-800-8756
www.rpms.com

Profit management system software

Marketing Manager: Brent Charles
Production Manager: Steve Goold
Director of Research & Development: JimAdam
In Business: 53 years
Number of Employees: 10
Sales Volume: $ 1 Million

1965 RockWare

RockWare
2221 East St
Suite 1
Golden, CO 80401   303-278-3534
800-775-6745
Fax: 303-278-4099
info@rockware.com
www.rockware.Com

Software products for earth science

President: Jim Reed
Marketing Manager: Amy Lunt
Credit Cards: AMEX; MasterCard
Catalog Circulation: Mailed 1 time(s) per year to 200K
Average Order Size: $300
Printing Information: 44 pages in 3 colors on Matte Stock
Press: Web Press
Binding: Saddle Stitched
Mailing List Information: Names for rent
In Business: 29 years
Sales Volume: $5 million

1966 Software Express Educators Catalog

4128 South Blvd # A
Charlotte, NC 28209-2643   704-522-7638
                                   800-527-7638
                              Fax: 704-529-1010
                      nicepeople@swexpress.com
                           www.swexpress.com

Educational software

President: Ken Heptig
Marketing Manager: Jennifer Cochran
Director of Sales: Sally Shorb
Catalog Circulation: to 200K
Average Order Size: $1384
Printing Information: 52 pages in 4 colors on G
Press: W
Binding: S
Mailing List Information: Names for rent
In Business: 28 years
Number of Employees: 30
Sales Volume: $ 6 Million

1967 Tenenz

Tenenz, Inc.
9655 Penn Avenue South
Minneapolis, MN 55431   952-227-1713
                                800-888-5803
                           Fax: 800-638-0015
                           mail@tenenz.com
                           www.tenenz.com

Accounting supplies, presentation materials, tax forms, business checks, stationery and software

Credit Cards: AMEX; MasterCard; Visa
Catalog Cost: Free
Printing Information: on Glossy Stock
Press: Web Press
Binding: Saddle Stitched
Mailing List Information: Names for rent
List Manager: Lee Myers
In Business: 40 years
Sales Volume: Under $500,000

1968 Tiger Direct Bussiness

Tiger Direct Business
1940 E Mariposa Avenue
El Segundo, CA 90245   888-278-4437
                           www.tigerdirect.com

Computer software, peripherals and accessories

Credit Cards: AMEX; MasterCard; Visa
In Business: 33 years
Number of Employees: 260
Sales Volume: $ 50-100 Million

1969 VPC

Virginia Panel Corporation
1400 New Hope Road
Waynesboro, VA 22980   540-932-3300
                           Fax: 540-932-3369
                           info@vpc.com
                           www.vpc.com

Designs, manufactures and markets Interface Connector products for commercial, military, telecommunications, aerospace, medical, automotive, and consumer electronic applications.

President: Sandy Powers
Chief Operating Officer: Robert Coward
Catalog Cost: Free
Catalog Circulation: Mailed 1 time(s) per year
Printing Information: 295 pages in 4 colors
In Business: 58 years
Number of Employees: 100

1970 Valiant IMC

Valiant National AV Supply
80 Little Falls Road
Fairfield, NJ 07004-1709   201-229-9800
                                   800-825-4268
                              Fax: 800-453-6338
                       sales@valiantnational.com
                         www.valiantaudiovisual.com

Audio-visual products and supplies at wholesale prices; video equipment, computer equipment and supplies

Chairman: Martin Siegel
President: Sheldon Goldstein
Managing Director: Scott Schaefer
Credit Cards: AMEX; MasterCard; Visa
Catalog Cost: Free
Catalog Circulation: Mailed 1 time(s) per year to 200M
Printing Information: 212 pages in 4 colors on Glossy Stock
Binding: Perfect Bound
Mailing List Information: Names for rent
In Business: 20 years
Number of Employees: 100
Sales Volume: $ 13 Million

1971 Zones

Zones, Inc.
1102 15th St SW # 102
Suite 102
Auburn, WA 98001-6509   253-205-3000
                                800-248-9948
                           Fax: 253-205-2673
                     customerservice@zones.com
                           www.zones.com

PC and Mac components, software, hardware, accessories

Chairman: Firoz Lalji
President: Murray Wright
CFO: Ronald McFadden
Marketing Manager: Sean Hobday
SVP, Operations/CIO: Anwar Jiwani
SVP, Partner & Product Marketing: Derrek Hallock
Senior Vice President, SMB Sales: Robert McGowen
Credit Cards: AMEX; MasterCard; Visa
Catalog Cost: Free
Catalog Circulation: Mailed 12 time(s) per year
Printing Information: 140 pages
In Business: 24 years
Number of Employees: 705
Sales Volume: $ 39 Million

Consumer Electronics
Products

1972 Adorama

Adorama
42 W 18th St
New York, NY 10011   212-741-0063
                             800-223-2500
                        Fax: 212-463-7223
                        sales@adorama.com
                           www.adorama.com

Cameras and camera accessories, TV's, computers, home theater systems and more

President: Mendel Mendelowits
Credit Cards: AMEX; MasterCard
In Business: 35 years
Number of Employees: 110

1973 Atlanta Cable Sales

ACS Solutions Inc.
495 Horizon Dr NE
Suite 200
Suwanee, GA 30024-7745   678-775-0208
                                 800-241-9881
                            Fax: 678-775-0209
                         acs@acssolutions.com
                           acssolutions.com

Telecommunications and audio/video cables

Production Manager: Mark Keating
CEO: Bryan Glutting
Vice President: Dave Fox
Credit Cards: MasterCard; Visa
Catalog Cost: Free
In Business: 34 years
Sales Volume: $ 5-10 Million

1974 Audio Accessories

Audio Accessories, Inc.
25 Mill Street
PO Box 360
Marlow, NH 03456   603-446-3335
                      Fax: 603-446-7543
                      audioacc@patchbays.com
                           www.patchbays.com

Audio accessories including jacks and panels, pre-wired patchbays, cords, holders, and cleaning tools

President: Robert Stofan
Production Manager: Tim Symonds
Credit Cards: MasterCard; Visa
In Business: 66 years
Number of Employees: 40
Sales Volume: $ 5 Million

1975 BestBuy

BestBuy
Best Buy Corporate Customer Care
PO Box 9312
Minneapolis, MN 55440   888-237-8289
                        onlinestore@bestbuy.com
                           www.bestbuy.com

Best Buy carries computers, home and car audio systems, personal electronics, appliances and more

President: Hubert Joly
CFO: Sharon McCollam
President, U.S. Retail & Chief HRO: Shari Ballard
President, Services: Chris Askew
President, e-Commerce: Mary Lou Kelley
In Business: 48 years
Number of Employees: 1400

1976 Bretford

Bretford
11000 Seymour Ave
Franklin Park, IL 60131-1230   847-678-2545
                                       800-521-9614
                                  Fax: 847-678-0852
                                  www.bretford.com

AV computer carts, notebook carts, tables, workstations, seating, shelving and projection screens

Chairman: David Petrick
President: Mike Briggs
Marketing Manager: Trudy Brunot
CEO: Chris Petrick
Catalog Cost: Free
Catalog Circulation: Mailed 1 time(s) per year to 2MM
Printing Information: 76 pages in 4 colors on Matte Stock
Press: Web Press
Binding: Saddle Stitched
Mailing List Information: Names for rent
In Business: 46 years
Sales Volume: $2 Million

1977 Crutchfield
Crutchfield Corporation
1 Crutchfield Park
Charlottesville, VA 22911-9097   434-817-1000
844-347-7281
Fax: 434-817-1010
support@crutchfield.com
www.crutchfield.com

Audio and video components, home theater, car stereos, telephones, pagers and digital satellite systems

CEO: William G Crutchfield Jr
Founder and CEO: Bill Crutchfield
Credit Cards: AMEX; MasterCard
Catalog Cost: Free
Catalog Circulation: Mailed 6 time(s) per year
Average Order Size: $275
Printing Information: 52 pages in 4 colors
Mailing List Information: Names for rent
List Manager: The Specialists
In Business: 43 years
Number of Employees: 550
Sales Volume: $50MM to $100MM

1978 DHC
DHC USA Inc.
5021 Louise Drive
Mechanicsburg, PA 17055-6916   800-342-2273
Fax: 888-650-7118
www.dhccare.com

Provides beauty products including skincare, body care, and makeup items

Catalog Cost: Free
In Business: 20 years

1979 Da-Lite Screen Company
Da-Lite Screen Company
3100 North Detroit Street
P.O. Box 137
Warsaw, IN 46582   574-267-8101
800-622-3737
Fax: 877-325-4832
info@da-lite.com
www.da-lite.com

Designers and manufacturers of projection screens - rear, manual or electric for permanent or portable applications

President: Richard Lundin
CFO: Jerry Young
Marketing Manager: Wendy Long
EVP: Judith D Loughran
Coordinator Bids & Quotations: Alisa Leek
Domestic Sales Partner: David Huntoon
International Marketing Manager: Adam Teevan
Catalog Circulation: Mailed 1 time(s) per year
Printing Information: 150 pages in 4 colors on Matte Stock
Press: Sheetfed Press
Binding: Perfect Bound
In Business: 105 years
Number of Employees: 415
Sales Volume: $ 31 Million

1980 Gunther Gifts Wedding Catalog
Gunther Gifts Inc.
2717 Loker Ave. West
Carlsbad, CA 92010   760-476-9131
877-544-0814
Fax: 775-890-6571

Personalized gifts, products, accessories, and engravings

Catalog Cost: Free
In Business: 29+ years

1981 Headsets.com
Headsets
211 Austin Street
San Francisco, CA 94109-5473   415-474-1106
800-432-3738
Fax: 800-457-0467
info@headsets.com
www.headsets.com

Headsets for cell phones, telephones and computers

President: Mike Faith
Production Manager: Chris Hicken
CEO: Mike Faith
Shipping Manager: Jake Cohen
jake@headsets.com
Credit Cards: AMEX; MasterCard
Catalog Cost: Free
Catalog Circulation: to 12M
Printing Information: 48 pages in 4 colors on Glossy Stock
Binding: Saddle Stitched
In Business: 15 years
Sales Volume: $ 10-20 Million

1982 Home Controls
Home Controls
8525 Redwood Creek Lane
San Diego, CA 92126   858-693-8887
800-266-8765
Fax: 858-693-8892
Tracking@HomeControls.com
www.homecontrols.com

Z-Wave Lightning and Appliance control, motion - activated plug - in LED, Z-Wave Plus smoke detector, Indoor Chime, Security sensors, Home speakers, volume control, home theatre, audio and video distr

Credit Cards: AMEX; MasterCard
In Business: 26 years

1983 Kicker
Kicker
3100 N Husband St
Stillwater, OK 74075-1706   405-624-8510
800-256-5425
Fax: 405-377-3272
questions@kicker.com

Auto stereo accessories and equipment, including subwoofers

President: Steve Irby
CFO: Rebecca Irby
Marketing Manager: Charlie Schultz
Laurie Crook:
VP
VP, Sales & Marketing: Charlie Schultz
Printing Information: 20 pages in 4 colors on Glossy Stock
In Business: 42 years
Number of Employees: 197

1984 Mayer-Johnson
Mayer-Johnson
2100 Wharton St.
Suite 400
Pittsburgh, PA 15203   412-381-4883
800-588-4548
Fax: 866-585-6260
MJQ@tobiidynavox.com
www.mayer-johnson.com

Special educational software.

1985 Parts Express
Parts Express
725 Pleasant Valley Dr
Springboro, OH 45066   800-338-0531
Fax: 937-743-1677
sales@parts-express.com
www.parts-express.com

Home audio and video subwoofers, in-wall speakers, cables, adapters and connectors

President: Jeffrey Stahl
VP of Operations: Dale Ditmer
VP Finance/Controller: John Kirsch
VP Marketing: Karl Keyes
Credit Cards: AMEX; MasterCard; Visa
Printing Information: 260 pages
In Business: 29 years

1986 Perfumax
Perfumax
Blythourne Station
P.O. Box 191213
Brooklyn, NY 11219   718-854-6136
800-300-7800
Fax: 888-755-7373
www.perfumax.com

Name brand fragrances, skin, bath and body care products

Catalog Cost: Free

1987 Speco Audio Products
Speco Technologies
200 New Highway
Amityville, NY 11701   631-957-9142
800-645-5516
Fax: 631-957-3880
sales@specotech.com
www.specotech.com

Residential and commercial audio and video security products specializing in CCTV cameras, video monitors, in-wall speakers, PA amplifiers and megaphones

President: Todd Keller
Marketing Manager: Peter Botelho
Catalog Cost: Free
Mailing List Information: Names for rent
In Business: 50 years
Number of Employees: 40
Sales Volume: $8.5 Million

1988 Tiger Direct
Tiger Direct, Inc.
7795 W Flagler St.
Suite 35
Miami, FL 33144-2367   305-415-2201
800-800-8300
Fax: 305-415-2202
www.tigerdirect.com

Audio electronics, blank media tapes, books, software, computer accessories and supplies

VP: Charles Steinberg
Sales Manager: Jeff Green
Credit Cards: AMEX; MasterCard; Visa
Catalog Cost: Free
In Business: 20 years
Number of Employees: 60
Sales Volume: $ 6 Million

1989 Vinten
Camera Dynamics, Inc.
709 Executive Blvd
Valley Cottage, NY 10989-2024   845-268-2113
Fax: 845-268-9324
www.vinten.com

Television camera support equipment, including studio pedestals, pan/tilt heads, tripod systems and more

President: Eric Falkenberg
CFO: Nick Piscitelli
Marketing Manager: Stephen Savitt
Production Manager: Kenneth Schwartz
CEO: Jansen Joop
International Marketing Manager: Nick Kent
Catalog Cost: Free
Catalog Circulation: Mailed 52 time(s) per year to 5M
Average Order Size: $2500
Printing Information: 26 pages in 4 colors on Glossy Stock
Press: Letterpress
Binding: Saddle Stitched
Mailing List Information: Names for rent
List Manager: Joanne Snider
In Business: 102 years
Number of Employees: 60
Sales Volume: $40 Million

1990 Wireless Emporium Catalog
Wireless Emporium
1375 S. Acacia Ave.
Fullerton, CA 92831-1930   714-278-1930
                                800-305-1106
service@wirelessemporium.com
www.wirelessemporium.com

Accessories for cellphones, tablets, smartphones, etc

Marketing Manager: John Wang
Co-Founder: Gene Ku
Co-Founder: Tony Lee
In Business: 10 years
Number of Employees: 15
Sales Volume: $ 5 Million

Disability Products
General Aids

1991 Ablenet
Ablenet Inc
2625 Patton Road
Roseville, MN 55113-1308   651-294-2200
                                800-322-0956
Fax: 651-294-2259
customerservice@ablenetinc.com
www.ablenetinc.com

Products for educators, physical therapists, occupational therapists and other providers to help persons with disabilities reach their remarkable potential

Chairman: Bill Sproull
President: Jennifer Thalhuber
CFO: Paul Sugden
Credit Cards: AMEX; MasterCard; Visa
Catalog Cost: Free
In Business: 30 years
Sales Volume: $900,000

1992 Access to Recreation
Access to Recreation, Inc.
8 Sandra Ct
Newbury Park, CA 91320-4302   805-498-7535
                                800-634-4351
Fax: 805-498-8186
dkrebs@accesstr.com
www.accesstr.com

Recreation/exercise equipment that has been adapted specifically for use by the elderly & disabled; large-print playing cards, rehabilitational pool lifts, fishing equipment & golf clubs

President: Don Krebs
dkrebs@accesstr.com
Credit Cards: AMEX; MasterCard; Visa
Catalog Cost: Free
Catalog Circulation: to 100,0
Average Order Size: $100
Printing Information: 52 pages in 4 colors on Glossy Stock
Press: Web Press
Binding: Saddle Stitched
Mailing List Information: Names for rent
In Business: 24 years
Number of Employees: 2
Sales Volume: $499,000

1993 Age Comfort
130 Great Gulf Drive
Concord, ON L4K-5W1   800-520-3259
Fax: 905-738-6479
info@agecomfort.com
www.agecomfort.com

Home goods and aids for the disabled or elderly.

Credit Cards: MasterCard

1994 Alzheimer's Store Catalog
Healthcare Products, LLC
420 Osierfield Drive
Fitzgerald, GA 31750   678-947-4001
                                800-752-3238
Fax: 678-947-8411
contact@alzstore.com
www.alzstore.com

Unique products and information for those caring for someone with Alzheimer's

Partner: Bruce Barnet
Credit Cards: AMEX; MasterCard
Catalog Cost: Free
In Business: 12 years
Number of Employees: 7
Sales Volume: $500,000 - $1 Million

1995 Attainment Company IEP Resources
Attainment Company, Inc.
504 Commerce Parkway
PO Box 930160
Verona, WI 53593-160   608-845-7880
                                800-327-4269
Fax: 800-942-3865
info@attainmentcompany.com
www.attainmentcompany.com

Life skills training and special education materials

President: Don Bastian
Production Manager: Susan Lockard
Founder & CEO: Don Bastian
Director of Software Development: Scott Meister
scott@attainmentcompany.com
Senior Trainer/Manager: Autumn Mueller-Garza
autumn@attainmentcompany.com
Credit Cards: MasterCard; Visa
Catalog Cost: Free
Printing Information: 90 pages
In Business: 36 years
Number of Employees: 23
Sales Volume: $ 4.5 Million

1996 Beyond Sight
Beyond Sight
5650 S. Windermere Street
Littleton, CO 80120   303-795-6455
Fax: 303-795-6425
www.beyondsight.com

President: Scott Chaplick
Credit Cards: AMEX; MasterCard
In Business: 26 years

1997 Cane & Able
Cane & Able
169 W. Lincoln Hwy.
Langhorne PA   215-757-2263
canenable@gmail.com
www.canenable.com

President: David E. Farre

1998 Community Playthings
Community Playthings
PO Box 2
Ulster Park, NY 12487   845-658-7720
                                800-777-4244
Fax: 845-658-8065
sales@communityplaythings.com
www.communityplaythings.com

Maple furniture, shelving, desks, cribs, cots, changing tables, high chairs, mats, art equipment and toys

President: John Rhodes
CFO: Marcus Mommsen
Credit Cards: AMEX; MasterCard; Visa
Printing Information:
Press: Web Press
In Business: 65 years
Number of Employees: 10

1999 Electro Medical Equipment
Electro Medical Equipment
PO Box 670893
Marietta, GA 30066   800-235-2952
Fax: 770-926-4022
info@electro-medical.com
www.electro-medical.com

In Business: 34 years

2000 EnableMart
EnableMart
865 Muirfield Drive
Hanover Park, IL 60133   801-281-7644
                                888-640-1999
Fax: 800-235-1305
www.enablemart.com

Assistive technology and assistive living devices from over 200 manufacturers

President: Kay Lillquist
Marketing Manager: Bradford Bond
Credit Cards: AMEX; MasterCard
Number of Employees: 14
Sales Volume: $ 10 Million

2001 Fashionable Canes & Walking Sticks
Fashionable Canes
12399 S Belcher Rd
Ste 160
Largo, FL 33773   800-887-5185
questions@fashionablecanes.com
www.fashionablecanes.com

Hand carved canes and walking sticks

President: Stephen Carroll
Credit Cards: AMEX; MasterCard; Visa
Catalog Cost: Free
In Business: 13 years

2002 Harris Communications
Harris Communications
15155 Technology Drive
Eden Prairie, MN 55344-2273   800-825-6758
Fax: 952-906-1099
info@harriscomm.com
www.harriscomm.com

Books, videos, telecommunications and assistive devices for the deaf and hard of hearing

President: Robert Harris PhD
Marketing Manager: Lori Foss
Buyers: Dave Motes
Credit Cards: AMEX; MasterCard; Visa
Catalog Cost: Free
Printing Information: 200 pages in 4 colors on Matte Stock
Press: Web Press
Binding: Perfect Bound
Mailing List Information: Names for rent
In Business: 30 years
Number of Employees: 30

2003 Headsets.com
Headsets
211 Austin Street
San Francisco, CA 94109-5473   415-474-1106
                                800-432-3738
Fax: 800-457-0467
info@headsets.com
www.headsets.com

Headsets for cell phones, telephones and computers

President: Mike Faith
Production Manager: Chris Hicken
CEO: Mike Faith
Shipping Manager: Jake Cohen
jake@headsets.com
Credit Cards: AMEX; MasterCard
Catalog Cost: Free
Catalog Circulation: to 12M
Printing Information: 48 pages in 4 colors on Glossy Stock
Binding: Saddle Stitched
In Business: 15 years
Sales Volume: $ 10-20 Million

2004 Hear More
HEAR MORE
42 Executive Blvd
Farmingdale, NY 11735-4710   631-752-0738
800-881-4327
Fax: 631-752-0689
www.hearmore.com

Products for independent living for the hard of hearing and deaf

Credit Cards: AMEX; MasterCard; Visa
Printing Information: 244 pages
Sales Volume: $500,000 - 1 Million

2005 HumanWare
HumanWare
1800, Michaud street
Drummondville, CN 12919   819-471-4818
888-723-7273
Fax: 819-471-4828
ca.info@humanware.com
www.humanware.com

Devices for the learning disabled, blind and visually impaired

Chairman: Real Goulet
President: Phil Rance
Corporate Director: Michel Côté
CEO: Gilles Pepin
Corporate Director: Georges Morin
Buyers: Sharon Spiker
Credit Cards: MasterCard; Visa
Catalog Cost: Free
175 Mason Circle
Concord, CA 94520
9256807100
In Business: 10 years
Number of Employees: 25
Sales Volume: $ 5-10 Million

2006 LS&S
LS & S
145 River Rock Drive
Buffalo, NY 14207   716-348-3500
800-468-4789
Fax: 877-498-1482
lssgrp@aol.com
www.lssproducts.com

Products for the blind, deaf, visually and hearing impaired including: TTY's; computer adaptive devices; CCTV's; talking blood pressure, blood glucose and talking scales

President: Melissa Balbach
CFO: John Bace
Executive Vice President: John K. Bace
Credit Cards: AMEX; MasterCard; Visa
Catalog Cost: Free
In Business: 27 years
Number of Employees: 23
Sales Volume: $ 4 Million

2007 Maxi Aids
Maxi-Aids, Inc.
42 Executive Blvd
Farmingdale, NY 11735-4710   631-752-0521
800-522-6294
Fax: 631-752-0689
khimf@maxiaids.com
www.maxiaids.com

Aids, appliances and home health care products for the arthritic, visually impaired, hearing impaired, physically challenged, and mature adult

President: Elliot Zaretsky
Marketing Manager: Paul Weingarten
Executive Director: Larry Di Blasi
Chief Technology Officer: Mitchell Zaretsky
Buyers: Iz Belski
Ursula Izurieta
Credit Cards: AMEX; MasterCard; Visa
Catalog Cost: Free
Mailing List Information: Names for rent
Number of Employees: 77
Sales Volume: $11.3 MM

2008 Meyer Physical Therapy
Meyer Physical Therapy
6333 Hudson Crossing Pkwy
Hudson, OH 44236   866-528-2144
Fax: 800-577-4632
www.meyerpt.com

2009 PHC Wheelchair Catalog
PHC
35 Soaring Bird Court
Las Vegas, NV 89135   866-722-4581
Fax: 702-666-9018
service@phc-online.com
www.phc-online.com

Manual wheelchairs and mobility supplies

President: Dylan Fugitt
CFO: Deanne Fugitt
Credit Cards: AMEX; MasterCard
In Business: 18 years
Number of Employees: 10

2010 Relief & Remedies
Relief & Remedies
412 Dream Lane
Van Nuys, CA 91496   800-530-2689
www.reliefandremedies.com
In Business: 25 years

2011 ScripHessco 2015 Catalog
ScripHessco
360 Veterans Parkway
Suite 115
Bolingbrook, IL 60440-4607   630-771-7400
800-747-3488
Fax: 888-674-4380
www.scriphessco.com

2012 Sportaid
Sportaid
78 Bay Creek Rd.
Loganville, GA 30052   770-554-5130
800-743-7203
Fax: 770-554-5944
webmaster@sportaid.com
www.sportaid.com

Wheelchairs and related products.

In Business: 50 years

2013 SunMate & Pudgee Orthopedic Cushions
Dynamic Systems, Inc.
104 Morrow Branch
Leicester, NC 28748   828-683-3523
855-786-6283
Fax: 844-270-6478
dsi@sunmatecushions.com
www.sunmatecushions.com

Orthopedic foam cushion material

President: Robin Yost
CFO: Melinda Garrett
Marketing Manager: Susan Yost
Production Manager: Andrew Biebinger
Buyers: Stacy Miller
Credit Cards: AMEX; MasterCard; Visa
Catalog Circulation: Mailed 12 time(s) per year
Printing Information: 8 pages in 4 colors on Matte Stock
Press: Sheetfed Press
Binding: Saddle Stitched
Mailing List Information: Names for rent
In Business: 50 years
Number of Employees: 18
Sales Volume: $ 1-3 Million

2014 The Wright Stuff Daily Living Aids
The Wright Stuff
111 Harris Street
Crystal Springs, MS 39059   601-892-3115
877-750-0376
Fax: 601-892-3116
info@thewrightstuff.com
www.wrightstuff.biz

Specialty mobility aids, caregiver products, arthritis supplies, and helpful ADL equipment

President: Christopher Wright
Credit Cards: AMEX; MasterCard; Visa
Printing Information: 40 pages in 4 colors
In Business: 16 years
Sales Volume: Under $500,000

2015 eSpecial Needs
11704 Lackland Industrial Drive
St. Louis, MO 63146   314-692-2424
877-664-4565
Fax: 314-692-2428
www.especialneeds.com

Special needs products and therapeutic devices

Automobile Aids

2016 Advantage Medical
360 Veterans Parkway
Suite 115
Bolingbrook, IL 60440   630-771-7400
800-577-5694
Fax: 800-390-0162
www.advantagemedical.com

Rehabilitation equipment and supplies

2017 Allman Products
9755 Independence Avenue
Chatsworth, CA 91311   818-715-0093
800-223-6889
Fax: 818-715-9629
allmanproducts.com

Home medical supplies

2018 Coach Lift Catalog
S&S Products Inc
1951 E Myrna Lane
Tempe, AZ 85284-3451   480-456-5438
888-224-1425
Fax: 480-456-3722
sales@coachlift.com
www.coachlift.com

Person lifts that are designed to help an individual easily gain access into a vehicle, bus, RV or airplane

President: Susan Lucking
Marketing Manager: Thomas Finklea
Catalog Cost: Free
In Business: 7 years
Number of Employees: 15
Sales Volume: $720,000

2019 Gresham Driving Aids
Gresham Driving Aids
30800 Wixom Road
Wixom, MI 48393-334   248-624-1533
800-521-8930
Fax: 248-624-6358
gpersons@greshamdrivingaids.com
www.greshamdrivingaids.com

Driving aids, handicap equipment

President: William Dillon
General Manager: David Ohrt
dave@greshamdrivingaids.com
Sales Consultant: Craig Wigginton
craig@greshamdrivingaids.com
Service Manager: Dexter Jackson
dex@greshamdrivingaids.com
Credit Cards: MasterCard; Visa
Catalog Cost: Free
In Business: 54 years
Number of Employees: 21
Sales Volume: $ 1-3 Million

2020 Maddak
661 Route 23 South
Wayne, NJ 07470   973-628-7600
800-443-4926
Fax: 973-305-0841
custservice@maddak.com
www.maddak.com

Home healthcare for seniors or people with disabilities

2021 Wright Way Catalog
Wright Way Inc
175 E Interstate 30
Garland, TX 75043-4021   972-240-8839
877-669-0961
Fax: 972-240-0412
www.wrightwayinc.com

Driving aids
President: Thomas Wright
Credit Cards: AMEX; MasterCard; Visa
Catalog Cost: Free
In Business: 44 years
Number of Employees: 22
Sales Volume: $ 3-5 Million

Clothing

2022 Buck & Buck
3111 27th Ave S
Seattle, WA 98144-6502   800-458-0600
Fax: 800-317-2182
info@buckandbuck.com
www.buckandbuck.com

Adaptive clothing

2023 Clothes for Seniors
302 Town Center Boulevard
Easton, PA 18040   800-252-0584
www.clothesforseniors.com

Traditional and adaptive clothing for senior citizens

2024 Clothing Solutions
Clothing Solutions
849 Performance Drive
Stockton, CA 95206   714-427-0781
800-445-1981
Fax: 888-709-8709
icareclothingsolutions@gmail.com
www.clothingsolutions.com

Clothing and accessories for individuals with disabilities
President: Jim Lechner
Catalog Cost: Free
In Business: 10 years
Sales Volume: $500,000

2025 Fossil
Fossil
901 S. Central Expressway
Richardson, TX 75080-4412   972-234-2525
800-449-3056
Fax: 972-234-4669
www.fossil.com

Men's and Women's clothing, shoes, watches, handbags and jewelry
President: Michael Barnes
Chairman/CEO: Kosta Kartsotis
Credit Cards: AMEX; MasterCard
In Business: 61 years

2026 Hatch Corporation
Hatch
3120 E. Mission Blvd.
Suite A
Ontario, CA 91761-3445   805-486-6489
800-347-1200
Fax: 909-923-7400
www.safariland.com

Gloves for the wheelchair users and edema protective gloves featuring cut resistance and anti-vibration
President: Robert Hatch
Credit Cards: AMEX; MasterCard; Visa
Average Order Size: $100
Mailing List Information: Names for rent
Number of Employees: 30
Sales Volume: $3MM to $5MM

2027 Maddak
661 Route 23 South
Wayne, NJ 07470   973-628-7600
800-443-4926
Fax: 973-305-0841
custservice@maddak.com
www.maddak.com

Home healthcare for seniors or people with disabilities

2028 Resident Essentials
65 Mathewson Drive
Suite A
Weymouth, MA 02189   888-543-2566
Fax: 781-803-3046
info@residentessentials.com
www.residentessentials.com

Clothing, accessories and furniture to assist the elderly or disabled
Owner/ Founder: Donald Bookstein

2029 Spec-L
Spec-L, Inc.
849 Performance Drive
Stockton, CA 95206   209-465-1981
800-445-1981
Fax: 888-709-8709

Adaptive clothing and accessories
President: Roger Fortun
CFO: Betty Fortun
Manager: Jemmie Minor
Credit Cards: AMEX; MasterCard; Visa
Catalog Cost: Free
Printing Information: 50 pages in 4 colors on Glossy Stock
Binding: Saddle Stitched
In Business: 30+ years
Number of Employees: 7
Sales Volume: $680,000

Lifts, Ramps & Elevators

2030 Advantage Medical
360 Veterans Parkway
Suite 115
Bolingbrook, IL 60440   630-771-7400
800-577-5694
Fax: 800-390-0162
www.advantagemedical.com

Rehabilitation equipment and supplies

2031 Allman Products
9755 Independence Avenue
Chatsworth, CA 91311   818-715-0093
800-223-6889
Fax: 818-715-9629
allmanproducts.com

Home medical supplies

2032 Easy Stand Catalog
Altimate Medical Inc
262 West 1st Street
PO Box 180
Morton, MN 56270   507-697-6393
800-342-8968
Fax: 507-697-6900
info@easystand.com
www.easystand.com

Standing equipment for mobility impaired children and adults, rehab equipment

President: Alan Tholkes
Marketing Manager: Mark Schmitt
Cio, Cto, Cso, Vp Of Tech, It Direc: Todd Tholkes
International Marketing Manager: Andrew Gardeen
Catalog Cost: Free
Mailing List Information: Names for rent
In Business: 28 years
Number of Employees: 35

2033 Garaventa Lift
Garaventa Lift
PO Box 1769
Blaine, WA 98231-1769   604-594-0422
800-663-6556
Fax: 604-594-9915
productinfo@garaventa.ca
www.garaventa.ca

Wheelchair lifts, vertical lifts, and emergency evacuation chairs
President: Mark Townsend
Marketing Manager: Norm Cooper
Catalog Cost: Free
In Business: 25 years
Number of Employees: 130

2034 Handi-Ramp
Handi-Ramp
510 North Ave
Libertyville, IL 60048-2025   847-680-7700
800-876-7267
Fax: 847-816-8866
info@handiramp.com
www.Handiramp.Com

Ramps and safety products for personal or business needs - portable ramps, permanent ramps, non slip treads for stairs and ramps available for purchase or rental
President: Thom Disch
Marketing Manager: Roberta Pierce
CEO: Thom Disch
Credit Cards: AMEX; MasterCard; Visa
Catalog Cost: Free
Catalog Circulation: to 5000
Mailing List Information: Names for rent
In Business: 57 years
Number of Employees: 30
Sales Volume: $5,000,000-$10,000,000

2035 Inclinator Company of America
Inclinator
601 Gibson Boulevard
Harrisburg, PA 17104-1557   717-939-8420
800-343-9007
Fax: 717-939-8075
www.inclinator.com

Stair lifts and home elevators
President: William M. Stratton
Marketing Manager: Mark Crispen
Sales Manager: Brad Rose
Plan Manager: John Groft
Human Resources/Accounting: Marcia Cleland
Catalog Cost: Free
In Business: 92 years
Number of Employees: 52
Sales Volume: $5MM to $10MM

2036 Maddak
661 Route 23 South
Wayne, NJ 07470   973-628-7600
800-443-4926
Fax: 973-305-0841
custservice@maddak.com
www.maddak.com

Home healthcare for seniors or people with disabilities

2037 Mohawk Lifts
Mohawk lifts
65 Vrooman Avenue
PO BOX 110
Amsterdam, NY 12010-110   518-842-1431
800-833-2006
Fax: 518-842-1289
sperlstein@mohawklifts.com
www.mohawklifts.com

Mohawk manufactures two post lifts, scissor lifts, turf lifts, four post lifts, mobile column lifts, parallelogram lifts, and lift accessories
President: Steve Perlstein
Marketing Manager: Steve Perlstein
Director of Operations: Patrick O'Farrell
patricko@mohawklifts.com
HR Department: Pam Smith
psmith@mohawklifts.com
Sales: Ray Pedrick
rpedrick@mohawklifts.com
Credit Cards: MasterCard; Visa
Catalog Cost: $2
Catalog Circulation: to 200M
Printing Information: 10 pages
In Business: 34 years
Number of Employees: 70
Sales Volume: $10.9 MM

2038 Prime Engineering
Prime Engineering
4202 W Sierra Madre Ave
Fresno, CA 93722-3932   559-276-0991
800-827-8263
Fax: 800-800-3355
info@primeengineering.com
www.primeengineering.com

Supplier of personal and clinical standing devices including lifts, walkers, and coasters
President: Mary Boegel
mary@primeengineering.com
CFO: Bruce Boegel
bruce@primeengineering.com
Marketing Manager: David Moore
davem@primeengineering.com
Credit Cards: AMEX; MasterCard
Catalog Cost: Free
In Business: 31 years
Number of Employees: 26
Sales Volume: $ 3 Million

2039 Rifton Equipment
PO Box 260
Rifton, NY 12471-260   845-658-7750
800-571-8198
Fax: 845-658-7751
sales@rifton.com
www.rifton.com

Furniture and equipment for early childhood settings

Wheelchairs

2040 Advantage Bags
Advantage Bag Company
22633 Ellinwood Dr
Torrance, CA 90505-3323   800-556-6307
Fax: 310-316-2561
advantagebag@verizon.net
www.advantagebag.com

Bags for wheelchairs, walkers, scooters, strollers and crutches
President: Deborah V Frane
Credit Cards: MasterCard; Visa
Catalog Cost: Free
In Business: 27 years
Number of Employees: 2
Sales Volume: $120,000

2041 Advantage Medical
360 Veterans Parkway
Suite 115
Bolingbrook, IL 60440   630-771-7400
800-577-5694
Fax: 800-390-0162
www.advantagemedical.com

Rehabilitation equipment and supplies

2042 Bound Tree Medical
PO Box 8023
Dublin, OH 43016-2023   800-533-0523
Fax: 800-257-5713
www.boundtree.com

Emergency medical supplies

2043 Med-Plus
39 Mayfield Avenue
Edison, NJ 08837   732-512-1222
888-277-0282
www.medpluspro.com

Medical supplies

2044 Resident Essentials
65 Mathewson Drive
Suite A
Weymouth, MA 02189   888-543-2566
Fax: 781-803-3046
info@residentessentials.com
www.residentessentials.com

Clothing, accessories and furniture to assist the elderly or disabled
Owner/ Founder: Donald Bookstein

Educational Products
General

2045 A&D Bookstore & Supply Educational
A&D Bookstore & Supply
2401 Paramount Blvd
Amarillo, TX 79109-5949   806-463-1545
800-858-4017
Fax: 806-463-1593
www.aanddbookstore.com

Teaching aids for kids.
President: Elanor Dennis
Credit Cards: MasterCard; Visa
In Business: 47 years
Number of Employees: 6
Sales Volume: $500M to $1MM

2046 ABC Feelings
Adage Publications/ABC Feelings
PO Box 7280
Ketchum, ID 83340   208-788-5399
Fax: 208-788-4195
info@abcfeelings.com
www.abcfeelings.com

Catalog of children's books, tapes, cards and games to increase their self esteem and build a strong foundation for character.
President: Alexandra Delis Abrams
Catalog Cost: Free
Mailing List Information: Names for rent
In Business: 20 years
Sales Volume: Under $500M

2047 ACE Educational Supplies
ACE Educational Supplies
5595 S. University Drive
Davie, FL 33328   954-434-2773
800-432-0213
Fax: 954-434-2783
orders@ACEeducational.com
www.aceeducational.com

Credit Cards: AMEX; MasterCard
Printing Information: 408 pages
In Business: 41 years

2048 Academic Superstore
Academic Superstore
5212 Tennyson Pkwy.
Ste. 130
Plano, TX 75024   512-450-1199
800-876-3507
Fax: 866-947-4525
contact@academicsuperstore.com
www.academicsuperstore.com

Academic software, hardware, and electronics for students, teachers, and schools; and home school materials
Marketing Manager: Natalie Jones
CEO: Mike Fishler
Owner/CEO: Nathan Jones
Credit Cards: AMEX; MasterCard
Catalog Cost: Free
Printing Information: in 4 colors
In Business: 17 years
Number of Employees: 50
Sales Volume: $4.6 million

2049 Agricultural Sciences
Nasco Arts & Crafts Store
901 Janesville Avenue
PO Box 901
Fort Atkinson, WI 53538-901   920-563-2446
800-558-9595
Fax: 920-563-6044
custserv@enasco.com
www.enasco.com

Instructional aids for all areas of agriculture; agriculture, horticulture, agronomy, and farm supplies
President: Andrew Reinen
Marketing Manager: Phil Niemeyer
Manager, Data Processing: Mike Wagner
Catalog Cost: Free
Catalog Circulation: to 25000
In Business: 74 years
Number of Employees: 540

2050 American Educational Products
American Educational Products
401 W Hickory St
PO Box 2121
Fort Collins, CO 80522   970-484-7445
800-289-9299
Fax: 970-484-1198
custserv@amep.com
www.amep.com

Educational materials including math and science manipulatives and kits
President: Michael Anderson
CFO: Dean Johnson
Buyers: Joel Sumearall
Credit Cards: AMEX; MasterCard; Visa
Catalog Cost: Free
Average Order Size: $50
Mailing List Information: Names for rent
In Business: 35 years
Number of Employees: 80

2051 Anderson's Middle School
Anderson's
4875 White Bear Parkway
White Bear Lake, MN 55110   800-338-3346
Fax: 800-213-8166
service@andersons.com
www.andersons.com

Products for middle school
President: Troy Ethan
Credit Cards: AMEX; MasterCard; Visa
Catalog Cost: Free

2052 Asia for Kids
Asia for Kids
PO Box 9096
Cincinnati, OH 45209
513-563-3100
800-888-9681
Fax: 513-563-3105
info@afk.com
www.afk.com

Resource materials for teaching Asian languages.
In Business: 22 years

2053 Assessments Catalog
Pro Ed
8700 Shoal Creek Boulevard
Austin, TX 78757-6897
512-451-3246
800-897-3202
Fax: 800-397-7633
info@proedinc.com
www.proedinc.com

Assessments and related materials for disabilities
President: Donald D Hammill
Credit Cards: AMEX; MasterCard; Visa
Catalog Cost: Free
In Business: 32 years
Sales Volume: $20MM to $50MM

2054 At Risk Resources
Standard Deviants School
1661 Tennessee St.
Suite 3-D
San Francisco, CA 94107
415-541-9901
866-386-0253
Fax: 805-426-8136
www.sdteach.com

Publisher of life-skills educational media for the K-12 market programs of which include intervention with children and young adults
President: Thomas Slagle
CFO: David Vander Ploeg
Marketing Manager: David Johnson
Credit Cards: AMEX; MasterCard; Visa
Catalog Cost: Free
Mailing List Information: Names for rent
In Business: 11 years

2055 Atlas Greenhouse Systems
Atlas Manufacturing, Inc.
PO Box 558
Alapaha, GA 31622-558
229-532-2905
800-346-9902
Fax: 229-532-4600
www.atlasgreenhouse.com

Commercial, educational and hobby greenhouses, as well as carports and agricultural buildings
President: Mark Davis
Office Manager: Billy Stewart
Sales Manager: Bill Mathis
Shipping Coordinator: Tommie Ann Stone
Credit Cards: MasterCard; Visa
Catalog Cost: Free
In Business: 29 years

2056 CBD Home School
Christian Book Distributors
140 Summit St.
Peabody, MA 01960
800-247-4784
customer.service@christianbook.com
www.christianbook.com

Textbooks, curriculum, resources, tools and projects for teaching a child at home.
President: Ray Hendrickson
Catalog Cost: Free
Mailing List Information: Names for rent
In Business: 39 years
Number of Employees: 500

2057 Calloway House Elementary Edition
Calloway House
451 Richardson Drive
Lancaster, PA 17603-4098
717-299-5703
800-233-0290
Fax: 717-299-6754
service@callowayhouse.com
www.callowayhouse.com

Designed and selected storage, organization, presentation and timesaving tools
President: Monica Knarr
Marketing Manager: April Wheatley
CEO: Dustin Knarr
VP, Operations: Kim McCall
Director, Purchasing & Customer Ser: Sabina Barr
Catalog Cost: Free
In Business: 47 years
Number of Employees: 25
Sales Volume: $1.5 Million

2058 Calloway House Middle School/High School Catalog
Calloway House
451 Richardson Drive
Lancaster, PA 17603-4098
717-299-5703
800-233-0290
Fax: 717-299-6754
service@callowayhouse.com
www.callowayhouse.com

A wide selection of products to help secondary-level educators better manage their classroom environment and ever-increasing workload
President: Monica Knarr
CEO: Dustin Knarr
VP, Operations: Kim McCall
Director, Purchasing & Customer Ser: Sabina Barr
Catalog Cost: Free
In Business: 47 years

2059 Carson-Dellosa Publishing
Carson-Dellosa Publishing Group
P.O. Box 35665
Greensboro, NC 27425-5665
336-632-0084
800-321-0943
Fax: 336-632-0087
webhelp@carsondellosa.com
www.carsondellosa.com

Full line of supplemental teaching aids including math manipulative and print materials, science, early learning and language arts materials in the Pre-K through Grade 6 range
Chairman: Lindsay Sparks
President: Stefan Carlson
CFO: Thomas Purcell
Credit Cards: AMEX; MasterCard
Catalog Cost: Free
Catalog Circulation: Mailed 1 time(s) per year
Printing Information: 48 pages in 4 colors on Glossy Stock
Press: Web Press
Binding: Saddle Stitched
In Business: 40 years
Number of Employees: 100
Sales Volume: $33 Million

2060 Childcraft Education
School Specialty
PO Box 1579
Appleton, WI 54912-1579
888-388-3224
Fax: 888-388-6344
orders@schoolspecialty.com
www.childcraft.com

Quality toys designed to entertain and educate
Chairman: James R. Henderson
President: Joseph M. Yorio
CFO: Kevin Baehler
EVP, Distribution: Patrick T. Collins
EVP, Educators Publishing Service: Rick

Holden
Catalog Cost: Free

2061 Chime Time
PO Box 369
Landisville, PA 17538-369
800-784-5717
Fax: 800-219-5253
service@e-c-direct.com
www.chimetime.com

Movement and musical products for children designed to promote increased brain development in infants through children age eight
Printing Information: 202 pages in 4 colors

2062 Chinaberry
Chinaberry
6655 Shelburne Road
Suite 100
Shelburne, VT 05482
802-860-1300
888-481-6744
service@chinaberry.com
www.chinaberry.com

Books, audio books, toys, games and crafts
Credit Cards: AMEX; MasterCard
Catalog Cost: Free
Printing Information: 120 pages in 3 colors on Glossy Stock
Binding: Folded
Mailing List Information: Names for rent
In Business: 36 years
Number of Employees: 45
Sales Volume: $11.5 Million

2063 Classroom Direct
Classroom Direct
PO Box 1579
Appleton, WI 54942
800-248-9171
Fax: 800-628-6250
customercare@classroomdirect.com
https://store.schoolspecialty.com/OA_HTML/ib
eCCtpSctDspRte.j

School supplies, teaching aids, early childhood materials and computer software
President: Roger Smith
CFO: David Vander Ploeg
Marketing Manager: David Johnson
Credit Cards: AMEX; MasterCard; Visa
Catalog Cost: Free

2064 Classroom Supplymart Catalog
Quality Products, Inc.
129 Wilkins Wise Road
PO Box 564
Columbus, MS 39703
800-647-1057
Fax: 800-824-8510
bsmith@classroomsupply.com

School supplies and fundraising products for Elementary, Middle and High School
President: Beth Smith
Vice President: Bethea Jones
Manager: Sandra Murray
Secretary: Hunter Gholson
Credit Cards: AMEX; MasterCard
Catalog Cost: Free
Catalog Circulation: to 50000
Printing Information: 132 pages in 4 colors on Glossy Stock
Binding: Saddle Stitched
Mailing List Information: Names for rent
In Business: 52 years
Number of Employees: 19
Sales Volume: $14.52 MM

2065 Constructive Playthings
Constructive Playthings
13201 Arrington Rd.
Grandview, MO 64030
816-761-5900
www.constructiveplaythings.com

Educational toys, classroom materials and teaching supplies.

Catalog Cost: Free
Printing Information: in 4 colors
In Business: 63 years

2066 Constructive Playthings Playground Catalog
Constructive Playthings
13201 Arrington Rd.
Grandview, MO 64030   816-761-5900
www.constructiveplaythings.com

Playground equipment

Catalog Cost: Free
Printing Information: in 4 colors
In Business: 63 years

2067 Corwin
Corwin
2455 Teller Road
Thousand Oaks, CA 91320   805-499-9734
                              800-233-9936
                         Fax: 800-417-2466
                         order@corwin.com
                         www.corwin.com

Learning resources

President: Mike Soules
Marketing Manager: Elena Nikitina
Vice President, Publishing: Lisa Shaw
Director of Professional Learning: Kristin Anderson
Sales: Brian Roy
Brian.Roy@corwin.com

2068 Courage To Change
Courage To Change
PO Box 486
Wilkes-Barre, PA 18703-486   800-440-4003
                         Fax: 800-772-6499
customerservice@guidance-group.com
www.couragetochange.com

Books, videos and board games for organizations, mental health professionals, and individuals who help others

President: Brenda Milton
CFO: Carmine Russo
Catalog Cost: Free

2069 Creative Learning Institute
The Creative Learning Institute
7 Indian Hill Avenue
Portland, CT 06480   860-342-3952
                   Fax: 860-342-2582
www.thecreativelearninginstitute.com

Books, tapes, software to encourage learning through unconventional methods

President: Edward Smith

2070 Curriculum Associates
Curriculum Associates Massachusetts
382 North Smith
North Billerica, MA 01862-9914   800-366-1158
                                     800-225-0248
                               Fax: 800-366-1158
                    www.curriculumassociates.com

Educational instructional materials

Chairman: Frank E Ferguson
fferguson@curriculumassociates.com
President: Renee Foster
rwaldron@curriculumassociates.com
CFO: Dave Caron
ppayette@curriculumassociates.com
Marketing Manager: Renee Foster
rfoster@curriculumassociates.com
Production Manager: Tricia McCarthy
tmccarthy@curriculumassociates.com
CEO: Rob Waldron
Credit Cards: MasterCard; Visa
Catalog Cost: Free
Mailing List Information: Names for rent
In Business: 42 years
Number of Employees: 150
Sales Volume: Under $500M

2071 Davis Publications
Davis
50 Portland Street
Worcester, MA 01608   508-754-7201
                         800-533-2847
                    Fax: 508-753-3834
                    vsullivan@davisart.com
                    www.davisart.com

School supplies including quality textbook programs, ancillary materials, and supplemental books

Chairman: Mark W Davis
President: Wyatt Wade
CFO: Thomas Lucci
Marketing Manager: Toni Henneman
Credit Cards: AMEX; MasterCard; Visa
Catalog Cost: Free
Printing Information: 52 pages
In Business: 53 years
Number of Employees: 35
Sales Volume: $8 Million

2072 Didax Educational Resources
Didax
395 Main Street
Rowley, MA 01969-1207   978-948-2340
                           800-458-0024
                      Fax: 800-350-2345
                      info@didax.com
                      www.didax.com

Math, language arts, fun games and character education resources

President: Brian Scarlett
Credit Cards: AMEX; MasterCard
Catalog Cost: Free
Printing Information: 132 pages
In Business: 35 years
Number of Employees: 17
Sales Volume: $2.9 Million

2073 Different Roads to Learning
Different Roads to Learning
121 West 27th Street
Suite 1003B
New York, NY 10001   212-604-9637
                        800-853-1057
                   Fax: 212-206-9329
                   info@difflearn.com
                   www.difflearn.com

Over 500 products for children with Autism

President: Julie Azuma
Marketing Manager: Abigail Schlaifer
Credit Cards: AMEX; MasterCard
Catalog Cost: Free
Printing Information: 98 pages
In Business: 20 years
Number of Employees: 5
Sales Volume: $2.9 Million

2074 Discount School Supply
Discount School Supply
PO Box 6013
Carol Stream, IL 60197-6013   800-627-2829
                            Fax: 800-879-3753
customerservice@discountschoolsupply.com
www.discountschoolsupply.com

Thousands of arts and crafts materials, school supplies and educational toys

President: Ron Elliott
CFO: Kelly Crampton
Credit Cards: AMEX; MasterCard
Catalog Circulation: Mailed 6 time(s) per year to 2.6M
Printing Information: 500 pages
In Business: 25 years

2075 Early Advantage
Early Advantage
PO Box 743
Fairfield, CT 06824-9853   888-248-0480
                         Fax: 800-301-9268
customerservice@early-advantage.com
www.early-advantage.com

Learning programs for young children, includes the Early Advantage family of programs, such as MUZZY, BBC Language Course for Children

President: David Ward
Credit Cards: AMEX; MasterCard
Catalog Cost: Free

2076 Educational Insights
Educational Insights
152 W Walnut St.
Suite 201
Gardena, CA 90248   800-995-4436
                  Fax: 888-498-8670
                  www.educationalinsights.com

Educational toys and games.

Catalog Circulation: Mailed 1 time(s) per year
Printing Information: 166 pages in 4 colors
In Business: 10 years
Number of Employees: 20
Sales Volume: $2 Million

2077 Edupress Catalog
Highsmith, LLC
PO Box 8610
4810 Forest Run Road
Madison, WI 53708-8610   608-241-1201
                            800-694-5827
                       Fax: 800-835-2329
                  www.highsmith.com/edupress

Standards-based language arts, math, science and social studies materials for PreK through eighth grade

Catalog Cost: Free

2078 Environments
Environments
PO Box 1348
Beaufort, SC 29901-1348   800-342-4453
                        Fax: 800-343-2987
                        care@environments.com
                        www.eichild.com

Early childhood equipment, learning materials and educational toys

President: Beecher M Hoogenboom
General Manager: Robert Williams
Credit Cards: AMEX; MasterCard; Visa
Catalog Cost: Free
In Business: 40 years
Number of Employees: 103
Sales Volume: $14.6 Million

2079 Fat Brain Toys
Fat Brain Toys, LLC
1405 N. 205th Street
Ste 120
Elkhorn, NE 68022   402-779-3181
                       800-590-5987
                  Fax: 402-779-3253
                  cs@fatbraintoys.com
                  www.fatbraintoys.com

Open-ended toys, gifts and games that educate and entertain

CFO: Dean Giesselmann
Co-Founder: Mark Carson
Co-Founder: Karen Carson
Credit Cards: AMEX; MasterCard
Catalog Cost: Free
Printing Information: 30 pages in 4 colors on Glossy Stock
Press: Sheetfed Press
Binding: Folded
In Business: 12 years
Number of Employees: 100-
Sales Volume: $ 5-10 Million

2080 Foothills Adult Education
Education Connection
355 Goshen Road
PO Box 909
Litchfield, CT 06759-909   860-567-0863
   800-300-4781
Fax: 860-567-3381
info@educationconnection.org
www.educationconnection.org

Educational materials, adult education

President: John Howard
Director of Human Resources: Laurene Pesce
Transportation Manager: Bert Hughes
Technology Coordinator: Lynn Barton
Credit Cards: MasterCard; Visa
Catalog Cost: Free
Mailing List Information: Names for rent

2081 Future Horizons
Future Horizons
721 W. Abram Street
Arlington, TX 76013   817-277-0727
   800-489-0727
Fax: 817-277-2270
www.fhautism.com

DVD's and books on Asperger's Syndrome and Autism

President: R. Wayne Gilpin
Marketing Manager: Kim Fritschen
Fulfillment: Dennis Schoenwald
Vice President: Jennifer Gilpin Yacio
Conference Administrator: Teresa Corey
Marketing Assistant: Maddie Coe
Credit Cards: MasterCard; Visa
Catalog Cost: Free
Printing Information: 30 pages on Glossy Stock
Press: Letterpress
In Business: 18 years
Number of Employees: 20

2082 Gould and Goodrich
Gould and Goodrich
709 E McNeil Street
Lillington, NC 27546   910-893-2071
   800-277-0732
Fax: 910-893-4742
service@gouldusa.com
www.gouldusa.com

Law enforcement duty gear, including leather and nylon belts, holsters and accessories

President: Scott Nelson
Marketing Manager: Phyllis Gould
Credit Cards: MasterCard; Visa
Printing Information: 30 pages
In Business: 33 years
Number of Employees: 67
Sales Volume: $ 5-10 Million

2083 Greenhaven Press
Gale
10650 Toebben Drive
Independence, KY 41051-5501   800-877-4253
Fax: 877-363-4253
order.samples@cengage.com

Educational materials

President: Ronald G Dunn
Credit Cards: AMEX; MasterCard; Visa
Catalog Cost: Free
Printing Information: 102 pages
Mailing List Information: Names for rent
Number of Employees: 45

2084 Heathkit Educational Systems
Heathkit Company Inc
PO Box 3115
Santa Cruz, CA 95063   269-925-6000
   800-253-0570
Fax: 269-925-2898
www.heathkit.com

Classroom and home electronics courses

Catalog Cost: Free
Printing Information: 59 pages
In Business: 84 years
Number of Employees: 75

2085 Highlights
Highlights for Children
1800 Watermark Drive
P.O. Box 269
Columbus, OH 43216-0269   888-372-6433
Fax: 614-487-2700
www.highlights.com

Children's books and fun with a purpose, including toys, games, puzzles, and activity kits

Marketing Manager: Shelly Stotzer
Production Manager: Sarah Bergman
CEO: Kent Johnson
Editor in Chief: Christine French Cully
Buyers: Lisa Hess
Erin Fogarty
Credit Cards: MasterCard; Visa
Catalog Circulation: Mailed 6 time(s) per year
Average Order Size: $60
Printing Information: 52 pages in 4 colors on Glossy Stock
Press: Web Press
Binding: Saddle Stitched
In Business: 69 years
Sales Volume: $10MM to $20MM

2086 Highlights Toy Catalog
Highlights for Children
1800 Watermark Drive
PO Box 269
Columbus, OH 43216-0269   888-372-6433
Fax: 614-487-2700
www.highlights.com

Kids games, puzzles, and toys for ages 4 to 12

Marketing Manager: Shelly Stotzer
CEO: Kent Johnson
Editor in Chief: Christine French Cully
Credit Cards: AMEX; MasterCard
Catalog Cost: Free
In Business: 69 years
Number of Employees: 400
Sales Volume: $10MM to $20MM

2087 KidSafety of America
KidSafety of America
6288 Susana Street
Chino, CA 91710   909-627-8700
   800-524-1156
Fax: 909-627-8777
info@kidsafetystore.com
www.kidsafetystore.com

Educational books and videos to promote the health and safety of children and their families

President: Peter D Osilaja
Buyers: Virginia Anorade
Credit Cards: AMEX; MasterCard; Visa
Catalog Cost: Free
Mailing List Information: Names for rent
In Business: 23 years
Number of Employees: 10
Sales Volume: $930,000

2088 KinderMark
KinderMark
7324 Amberwood Lane
Savage, MN 55378   888-281-9440
Fax: 952-892-3524
www.kindermark.com

Toys, children's furnishings

In Business: 18 years

2089 Lakeshore Learning Materials
Lakeshore
2695 E Dominguez Street
Carson, CA 90895   310-537-8600
   800-778-4456
Fax: 800-537-5403
lakeshore@lakeshorelearning.com
www.lakeshorelearning.com

Early learning materials for preschools, day care programs, headstart program, public and private schools

Chairman: Michael Kaplan
President: Bo Kaplan
Marketing Manager: Maxine Davis
Purchasing Manager: Jeff Cummins
Credit Cards: AMEX; MasterCard; Visa
Catalog Cost: Free
In Business: 62 years
Number of Employees: 1800
Sales Volume: $50MM to $100MM

2090 Learning Resources
Learning Resources Inc
380 N Fairway Drive
Vernon Hills, IL 60061   847-573-8400
   800-333-8281
Fax: 888-892-8731
info@learningresources.com
www.learningresources.com

Educational toys, games and puzzles

Chairman: Richard Woldenberg
CFO: Mike Dost
Marketing Manager: Lisa Guili
CEO: Eitenne Veber
Purchasing Director: Cathy Parrish
Credit Cards: AMEX; MasterCard; Visa
Catalog Cost: Free
In Business: 27 years
Number of Employees: 122
Sales Volume: $13.6 Million

2091 Love to Learn
Love to Learn
741 North State Road 198
Salem, UT 84653-9299   801-423-2009
Fax: 801-423-9188
CustomerService@LoveToLearn.net
www.lovetolearn.net

Homeschool resources and homeschool supplies.

President: Richard Hopkins
Credit Cards: AMEX; MasterCard
Number of Employees: 25
Sales Volume: $1.6 Million

2092 Map, Globe and Atlas Catalog
Nystrom
4719 W. 62nd Street
Indianapolis, IN 46268-2593   800-621-8086
Fax: 317-329-3305
cram@maps-globes.com
www.herffjonesnystrom.com

Globes and maps

President: Joe Slaughter
CFO: Michael Parrett
Marketing Manager: Brent Douthit
Director, Sales & Marketing: Richard Bramhill
Catalog Cost: Free
Mailing List Information: Names for rent
In Business: 107 years
Number of Employees: 200

2093 MindWare
MindWare
P.O. Box 45307
Omaha, NE 68145   651-582-0555
   800-999-0398
Fax: 888-299-9273
custserv@mindware.com
www.Mindwareonline.Com

Toys and games for children

President: Matt Reutiman
Founder: Jeanne Voigt
Credit Cards: AMEX; MasterCard; Visa
Catalog Cost: Free
In Business: 18 years
Sales Volume: $1MM to $3MM

2094 Muggins Math Series
Old Fashioned Products Inc
4860 Burnt Mountain Road
Ellijay, GA 30536-8317   800-962-8849
                                Fax: 706-635-7611
muggins@mugginsmath.com
mugginsmath.com

Math board games

President: Alan Schuler
CFO: Sue Schuler
Marketing Manager: Alan Schuler
Production Manager: Ruth Babcock
Fulfillment: Melissa Walton
Credit Cards: MasterCard; Visa
Catalog Circulation: Mailed 1 time(s) per year
to 1000
Average Order Size: $50
Printing Information: 2 pages in 4 colors on
Glossy Stock
Press: Sheetfed Press
Binding: Folded
Mailing List Information: Names for rent
In Business: 12 years
Number of Employees: 5
Sales Volume: Under $500M

2095 National Archives-Pub. & Distribution
National Archives Records Administration
8601 Adelphi Road
College Park, MD 20740-6001   301-837-1600
                                866-272-6272
                                Fax: 301-837-0483
mpr.status@nara.gov
www.archives.gov

Aids for genealogical research

President: John M Carlin
Catalog Cost: Free
Printing Information: 30 pages
In Business: 71 years

2096 National Geographic Society
National Geographic Society
1145 17th Street
NW (17th and M)
Washington, DC 20036   202-857-7700
                                888-557-4450
                                Fax: 513-341-2755
ngtickets@ngs.org
www.nationalgeographic.com

Nature and geography multimedia

Chairman: Gilbert M Grosvenor
President: John Fahey
Credit Cards: AMEX; MasterCard; Visa
Catalog Cost: Free
Printing Information: 71 pages in 4 colors on
Glossy Stock
Binding: Saddle Stitched
Number of Employees: 1050

2097 Nature Company Catalog
The Discovery Channel
PO Box 788
Florence, KY 41022   800-938-0333
                                Fax: 606-342-0633
www.store.discovery.com

Educational toys

2098 Nature Watch
Nature Watch
5312 Derry Avenue
Unit R
Agoura Hills, CA 91301   818-735-3555
                                800-228-5816
                                Fax: 818-735-3566
info@nature-watch.com
www.nature-watch.com

Educational products and activity kits

President: Harold Gordon
Catalog Cost: Free
In Business: 27 years
Number of Employees: 6
Sales Volume: $1.1 Million

2099 Nienhuis Educational Catalog
Nienhuis Montessori USA
150 South Whisman Road
Mountain View, CA 94041-1512   650-964-2735
                                800-942-8697
                                Fax: 650-964-8162
info@nienhuis-usa.com
www.nienhuis.com

**Books by and about Dr. Maria Montessori
and her method, books for teachers and parents, and for reference**

President: Dick K P Luijendijk
Founder: Albert Nienhuis
Credit Cards: AMEX; MasterCard; Visa
Catalog Cost: Free
In Business: 86 years

2100 PCI Education
PRO-ED Inc.
8700 Shoal Creek Boulevard
Austin, TX 78757-6897   512-451-3246
                                800-897-3202
                                Fax: 512-451-8542
general@proedinc.com
www.proedinc.com

**Special education and ELL materials, lesson
plans and resources**

President: Jeff McLane
Marketing Manager: Randy Pennington
Production Manager: Jill Haney
President/CEO: Lee Wilson
Credit Cards: AMEX; MasterCard; Visa
Catalog Cost: Free
In Business: 20 years
Number of Employees: 95
Sales Volume: $8.9 Million

2101 Pearson Clinical
Pearson Clinical
P.O. Box 599700
San Antonio, TX 78259   800-627-7271
                                Fax: 800-232-1223
clinicalcustomersupport@pearson.com
www.pearsonclinical.com

**PreK-16 special education resources and as-
sistance, psychology services, speech and
language services, occupational and physical therapy, early childhood development
services, and talent assessments**

Catalog Cost: Free
In Business: 80 years

2102 Perfection Learning
Perfection Learning
1000 North Second Avenue
1000 North Second Avenue
Logan, IA 51546-500   800-831-4190
                                Fax: 800-543-2745
orders@perfectionlearning.com
www.perfectionlearning.com

**Teacher and student curriculum materials
for grades Pre-K through 12**

Chairman: Dave Wurst
President: Steven J Keay
Sr. VP Sales and Marketing: David Irons
VP, National Sales Manager: Caryl Collins
Credit Cards: AMEX; MasterCard
Catalog Cost: Free
In Business: 89 years
Sales Volume: $10MM to $20MM

2103 Performance Education
Performance Education
3700 Millington Road
Free Union, VA 22940   434-249-0082
                                877-588-1085
                                Fax: 434-823-2832
www.performance-education.com

**Educational resources for teachers, parents
and kids**

2104 Performance Zone
Abatron, Inc.
5501 - 95th Avenue
Kenosha, WI 53144-4529   262-653-2000
                                800-445-1754
                                Fax: 262-653-2019
info@abatron.com
www.abatron.com

**Books, directories, apparel and other refer-
ence items and merchandise for the concrete and masonry construction fields**

Credit Cards: AMEX; MasterCard
Catalog Circulation: Mailed 2 time(s) per year
to 500M
Printing Information: 20 pages in 4 colors
Press: Web Press
Binding: Saddle Stitched
In Business: 58 years
Number of Employees: 40
Sales Volume: $10,000,000 - $25,000,000

2105 Prestwick House
Prestwick House
PO Box 658
Clayton, DE 19938   800-932-4593
                                Fax: 888-718-9333
info@prestwickhouse.com
www.prestwickhouse.com

**Language and learning books, teaching liter-
ature and reference books**

Catalog Cost: Free
In Business: 35 years

2106 Red Ribbon Resources
Red Ribbon Resources
303 Crossway Park Drive
Woodbury, NY 18703-1246   888-433-8368
                                Fax: 800-262-1886
info@redribbonresources.com
www.redribbonresources.com

**Educational resources including activity
books, banners, bracelets, buttons, games,
poster charts, ribbons, stickers, and t-shirts**

President: Ed Werz
Credit Cards: AMEX; MasterCard; Visa
Catalog Cost: Free
In Business: 10 years
Number of Employees: 3
Sales Volume: $900,000

**2107 Resources For Struggling Learners
Spring 2015 Wies**
Wieser Educational
20722 Linear Lane
Lake Forest, CA 92630   800-880-4433
                                Fax: 800-949-0209
service@wiesereducational.com
www.wiesereducational.com

Education materials

In Business: 37 years

2108 Road Scholar
Road Scholar
11 Avenue de Lafayette
Boston, MA 02111   800-454-5768
                                roadscholar.org

**Not-for-profit alternative educational travels
in 150 countries across the world**

President: Jim Moses
CFO: Lowell Partridge
Marketing Manager: Kristin Moore

SVP, Program Development: JoAnne Bell
SVP, Chief Information Officer: Eric Bird
VP, Programs: Maeve Hartney
Catalog Cost: Free
In Business: 42 years

2109 Special Needs
Pro-Ed Inc
8700 Shoal Creek Boulevard
Austin, TX 78757-6897   512-451-3246
                            800-397-7633
                       Fax: 800-397-7633
                    info@proedinc.com
                    www.proedinc.com

Instructional and therapy materials for people of all ages and levels of ability

President: Donald D Hammill
Credit Cards: AMEX; MasterCard; Visa
Catalog Cost: Free
In Business: 30 years
Sales Volume: $20MM to $50MM

2110 Speech and Language
Pro-Ed Inc
8700 Shoal Creek Blvd
Austin, TX 78757-6897   512-451-3246
                            800-397-7633
                       Fax: 512-451-8542
                    info@proedinc.com
                    www.proedinc.com

Useful tools for the Speech-Language Pathologist

President: Donald D Hammill
Credit Cards: AMEX; MasterCard; Visa
Catalog Cost: Free
In Business: 30 years
Sales Volume: $20MM to $50MM

2111 Summit Learning
Summit Learning
755 Rockwell Avenue
PO Box 755
Fort Atkinson, WI 53538-755   800-558-9595
                       Fax: 800-317-2194

Products for learning Math and Science in the PreK to Middle School classrooms

Catalog Cost: Free

2112 Super Duper Publications
Super Duper Publications
P.O. Box 24997
Greenville, SC 29616   864-288-3536
                            800-277-8737
                       Fax: 864-288-3380
              customerhelp@superduperinc.com
                    www.superduperinc.com

Learning materials for kids with special needs

President: Thomas Webber
CFO: M T Webber
Purchasing: Jason Derbyshire
Credit Cards: AMEX; MasterCard
Catalog Cost: Free
Catalog Circulation: Mailed 1 time(s) per year
Printing Information: 288 pages in 4 colors
In Business: 31 years
Number of Employees: 115
Sales Volume: $22 Million

2113 Sycamore Tree Curriculum
Sycamore Academy
PO Box 565
Keene, TX 76059   714-668-1343
                            817-645-0895
                       Fax: 714-668-1344
                info@SycamoreAcademy.com
                    www.sycamoretree.com

Over 3000 items to supplement home-school curriculums; Includes books, games, puzzles, craft kits and art supplies, models, cassettes and videos, computer accessories, science projects and music

President: William B Gogel
Credit Cards: AMEX; MasterCard; Visa
Catalog Cost: Free
Printing Information: 26 pages
In Business: 32 years
Number of Employees: 10

2114 The Great Courses
The Great Courses
4840 Westfields blvd.
Suite 500
Chantilly, VA 20151   800-832-2412
                    www.thegreatcourses.com

Offers a variety of courses and methods of teaching by top educators.

President: Paul Suijk
Marketing Manager: Scott Ableman
Founder: Thomas Rollins
Chief Brand Officer: Ed Leon
VP, Operations: Jason Smigel
In Business: 25 years

2115 Trainer's Warehouse
Trainer's Warehouse
89 Washington Ave
Suite K
Natick, MA 01760-3441   800-299-3770
                       Fax: 508-651-2674
                info@trainerswarehouse.com
                    www.trainerswarehouse.com

Tools, tips and toys for trainers and teachers

President: Susan Doctoroff Landay
susan@trainerswarehouse.com
Marketing Manager: John Neuhauser
VP: Honey Doctoroff
honey@trainerswarehouse.com
Founder: Michael Doctoroff
Credit Cards: AMEX; MasterCard; Visa
Catalog Cost: Free
In Business: 22 years
Number of Employees: 18
Sales Volume: $2 Million

2116 Twin Sister's Productions LLC
Twin Sister's Productions LLC
4710 Hudson Drive
Stow, OH 44224   800-248-8946
                       Fax: 800-480-8946
                    www.twinsisters.com

Children's educational music on cd's

CEO: Karen M Hilderbrand
Operations Purchasing Manager: Nikki Schmitt
Catalog Cost: Free
In Business: 9 years
Number of Employees: 40
Sales Volume: $5 Million

2117 U.S. School Supply
U.S. School Supply
3361 West Hospital Ave
Chamblee, GA 30341-3419   877-780-8900
                       Fax: 877-780-8901
                support@usschoolsupply.com
                    www.usschoolsupply.com

School supply

2118 Visual Education
Vis-Ed
581 West Leffel Lane
P.O. Box 1666
Springfield, OH 45501   937-325-5503
                            800-243-7070
                       Fax: 937-324-5697
                    sales@vis-ed.com
                    www.vis-ed.com

Study aids in the form of flash cards for high school and college level individuals, subjects include titles in math, science, social studies, foreign languages, S.A.T., religion and business

President: Jeanne A Lampe
Credit Cards: AMEX; MasterCard; Visa
Catalog Cost: Free
Mailing List Information: Names for rent
In Business: 52 years
Number of Employees: 30
Sales Volume: $500M to $1MM

2119 Young Explorers
Young Explorers
2 BITS Trail
PO Box 3338
Chelmsford, MA 01824-0938   877-756-5058
                       Fax: 800-866-3235
                help@youngexplorers.com
                    www.youngexplorers.com

Educational toys

President: John Fleischman
Credit Cards: AMEX; MasterCard; Visa
Catalog Cost: Free
In Business: 52 years

Scientific Equipment & Supplies

2120 AIMS Education Foundation
AIMS Education Foundation
1595 S Chestnut Ave
Fresno, CA 93702   559-255-4094
                            888-733-2467
                       Fax: 559-255-6396
                    www.aimsedu.org

Books, magazine, workshops, sciences

President: Richard Thiessen
Executive Director: Lori Hamada
lhamada@aimsedu.org
Senior Researcher: Chris Brownell
cbrownell@aimsedu.org
Senior Researcher: Tiffany Friesen, Ph.D.
tiffanyFY@aimsedu.org
Credit Cards: MasterCard; Visa
Catalog Cost: Free
In Business: 33 years
Number of Employees: 220
Sales Volume: $4.2 Million

2121 Abbeon Cal Plastic Working Tools
Abbeon Cal, Inc.
123 Gray Ave
Santa Barbara, CA 93101-1809   805-966-0810
                            800-922-0977
                       Fax: 805-966-7659
                    abbeoncal@abbeon.com
                    www.abbeon.com

Scientific instruments and industrial equipment, tools and equipment, plastic working tools for cutting bending and welding

President: Alice Wertheim
Marketing Manager: Bob Brunsman
VP: Kathering Wertheim
Founder: Jared Abbeon
Credit Cards: AMEX; MasterCard; Visa
Catalog Circulation: to 250M
Average Order Size: $500
Printing Information: 128 pages in 4 colors on Newsprint
Press: Web Press
Binding: Folded
In Business: 41 years
Number of Employees: 8
Sales Volume: $1.89 Million

2122 American 3B Scientific
3B Scientific
2189 Flintstone Drive
Unit O
Tucker, GA 30084   770-492-9111
                            888-326-6335
                       Fax: 770-492-0111
                    info@3bscientific.com
                    www.a3bs.com

Anatomical models & charts, mannequins, biology supplies and books for schools, universities and physicians

Marketing Manager: Jennifer Wilson Flynn
jennifer.flynn@3bs.com
VP/General Manager: Miles Sprott
miles.sprott@a3bs.com
Managing Director: Otto H. Gies
Managing Director: Manfred Kurland
Credit Cards: MasterCard
Catalog Cost: Free
In Business: 19 years
Number of Employees: 20

2123 American Educational Products
American Educational Products
401 W Hickory St
PO Box 2121
Fort Collins, CO 80522   970-484-7445
                                800-289-9299
                           Fax: 970-484-1198
                          custserv@amep.com
                             www.amep.com

Educational materials including math and science manipulatives and kits

President: Michael Anderson
CFO: Dean Johnson
Buyers: Joel Sumearall
Credit Cards: AMEX; MasterCard; Visa
Catalog Cost: Free
Average Order Size: $50
Mailing List Information: Names for rent
In Business: 35 years
Number of Employees: 80

2124 American Geological Institute
American Geosciences Institute
4220 King St
Alexandria, VA 22302-1502   703-379-2480
                           Fax: 703-379-7563
                    agi@americangeosciences.org
                             www.agiweb.org

Geologic posters, glossary of geology, data pages, glossary of hydrology, environmental awareness series, georef and Geotimes magazine

Chairman: Roger Pinkerton
President: Peter Scholle
CFO: Walter R. Sisson
wsisson@americangeosciences.org
Marketing Manager: John Rasanen
jr@americangeosciences.org
Executive Director: P. Patrick Leahy
pleahy@americangeosciences.org
Education and Outreach: Edward C. Robeck
ecrobeck@americangeosciences.org
GeosciencePolicy: Maeve Boland
mboland@americangeosciences.org
Credit Cards: MasterCard; Visa
Catalog Cost: Free
Mailing List Information: Names for rent
In Business: 67 years
Number of Employees: 60

2125 American Institute of Chemical Engineers
AIChE
120 Wall Street
FL 23
New York, NY 10005-4020   800-242-4363
                           Fax: 203-775-5177
                             heaty@aiche.org
                             www.aiche.org

Contains engineering books and journals, technical manuals, symposia proceedings and directories

President: T. Bond Calloway
President-Elect: Christine Seymour
Secretary: Freeman E. Self
Treasurer: Joseph Smith
Catalog Cost: Free
Catalog Circulation: Mailed 1 time(s) per year to 50M
In Business: 109 years
Number of Employees: 150
Sales Volume: $10 million

2126 American Weather Enterprises
American Weather Enterprises
PO Box 14381
San Francisco, CA 94114   415-401-8553
                                800-293-2555
                           Fax: 415-401-8480
                    fogcity@americanweather.com

Weather instruments: hygrometers, thermometers, barometers, anemometers, recording equipment, sundials, weathervanes etc.

President: Robert Sanders
General Manager: Dillon Sanders
Credit Cards: MasterCard; Visa
Catalog Cost: Free
In Business: 6 years
Number of Employees: 3
Sales Volume: $270,000

2127 Animal, Organ & Cell Physiology
Harvard Apparatus
84 October Hill Rd
Holliston, MA 01746-1388   508-893-8999
                                800-232-2380
                           Fax: 508-429-5732
                 webmaster@harvardapparatus.com
                       www.harvardapparatus.com

Research and laboratory equipment and supplies

President: Walter DiGiusto
CFO: Thomas McNaughton
Marketing Manager: Mara Potter
Production Manager: Michael Mailman
Buyers: John Stearns
Credit Cards: AMEX; MasterCard; Visa
Catalog Cost: Free
Catalog Circulation: to 36000
Average Order Size: $2000
Printing Information: 950 pages in 4 colors
Mailing List Information: Names for rent
In Business: 114 years
Number of Employees: 90

2128 Arbor Scientific
Arbor Scientific
PO Box 2750
Ann Arbor, MI 48106-2750   734-477-9370
                                800-367-6695
                           Fax: 734-477-9373
                             www.arborsci.com

Educational science equipment, science supplies and physics lab equipment

President: C. Peter Rea
peter@arborsci.com
Credit Cards: AMEX; MasterCard
Catalog Cost: Free
Mailing List Information: Names for rent
Number of Employees: 10-J

2129 Astrographics
Astrographics
539 Concord Road
Warminster, PA 18974   888-817-8768
                           Fax: 215-364-3154
                       mail@astrographics.com
                        www.astrographics.com

Collection of format photo reproductions of telescope images, astronomical pictures, microscopic studies and other scientific images

Principal: Tony Lanzetta
Credit Cards: AMEX; MasterCard; Visa
Catalog Cost: Free
Printing Information: 28 pages
In Business: 17 years

2130 Bel-Art Products
Bel-Art Products
661 Route 23 South
Wayne, NJ 07470-1994   973-694-0500
                                800-423-5278
                           Fax: 973-694-7199
                          cservice@belart.com
                             www.belart.com

Bel-Art Products is a manufacturer of essential & unique problem-solving items for scientific, industrial & educational markets worldwide, over 4,000 items from wash bottles to fume hoods

President: David Landsberger
Marketing Manager: Shirley Miller
International Marketing Manager: Joe Kelly
Credit Cards: AMEX; MasterCard; Visa
Catalog Cost: Free
Printing Information: 480 pages
Mailing List Information: Names for rent
In Business: 69 years
Number of Employees: 300
Sales Volume: $10MM to $20MM

2131 Chem Scientific
Chem Scientific, LLC
478 Walpole Street
Norwood, MA 02062-4028   781-440-0900
                                888-527-5827
                           Fax: 781-440-0088
                       info@chemscientific.com

Education and scientific materials and supplies

President: Gerald Deban
Credit Cards: MasterCard; Visa
Catalog Cost: $6
Average Order Size: $400
In Business: 37 years
Number of Employees: 8
Sales Volume: $3MM to $5MM

2132 Citizen America Corporation
Citizen America Corporation
363 Van Ness Way
Suite 404
Torrance, CA 90501-6282   310-781-1460
                                800-421-6516
                           Fax: 310-781-9152
                customerservice_us@citizenwatch.com
                       www.citizen-america.com

Dot matrix printers, bar code printers, LCD, FDD, crystals, IC packaging and oscillators

President: Maso Yamasaki
CFO: Lee Chin
VP: G Gallagher
In Business: 42 years
Number of Employees: 1700
Sales Volume: $ 3 Million

2133 Crystal Art Resources
Crystal Productions
5320 Carpinteria Ave
Suite K
Carpinteria, CA 93013-2107   847-657-8144
                                800-255-8629
                           Fax: 847-657-8149
                       www.crystalproductions.com

Art education resources materials for Pre-K, Elementary, Seondary, and College

President: Dennis Cavaliere
Owner: Amy Woodworth
Credit Cards: MasterCard; Visa
Catalog Cost: Free
Catalog Circulation: Mailed 2 time(s) per year
Printing Information: 56 pages in 4 colors
Binding: Perfect Bound
Mailing List Information: Names for rent
In Business: 42 years
Number of Employees: 15
Sales Volume: $1.2 Million

2134 Daigger & Company Lab Supply
A. Daigger & Company
620 Lakeview Parkway
Vernon Hills, IL 60061-1828   847-816-5060
800-621-7193
Fax: 800-320-7200
daigger@daigger.com
www.daigger.com

Laboratory supplies
President: Jim Woldenberg
CFO: Mike Dost
Regional Account Manager: Meghan O'Connell
Senior Account Manager: Michael Bledsoe
International Sales Director: Jim Woldenberg
In Business: 121 years
Number of Employees: 215

2135 Delta Pre-K - 6 Science and Math
Delta Education LLC
80 Northwest Blvd
PO Box 3000
Nashua, NH 03061-3000   800-258-1302
Fax: 800-282-9560
www.delta-education.com

Hands-on science curriculum, kits, and innovative educational programs and materials
President: Steve Korte
Credit Cards: AMEX; MasterCard; Visa
Catalog Cost: Free
Printing Information: 288 pages
In Business: 38 years
Number of Employees: 300
Sales Volume: $20MM to $50MM

2136 Dissection Materials Catalog
Nasco Arts & Crafts Store
901 Janesville Avenue
PO Box 901
Fort Atkinson, WI 53538-901   920-563-2446
800-558-9595
Fax: 920-563-6044
custserv@enasco.com
www.enasco.com

Safe specimens and high-quality materials; also offers apparatus for dissection, microscopes, and teacher resource materials
President: Andrew Reinen
Marketing Manager: Phil Niemeyer
Manager, Data Processing: Mike Wagner
Credit Cards: AMEX; MasterCard
Catalog Cost: Free
Catalog Circulation: to 25000
In Business: 74 years
Number of Employees: 540

2137 Elementary STEM Catalog
Pitsco Education
P.O. Box 1708
Pittsburg, KS 66762-1708   620-231-0010
888-835-0686
Fax: 800-533-8104
orders@pitsco.com
www.pitsco.com

Science, Technology, Engineering and Math teaching resources
President: Harvey R. Dean
Production Manager: Kyle Bailey
Chief Operating Officer: Lisa Paterni
Catalog Cost: Free
Catalog Circulation: Mailed 1 time(s) per year
Printing Information: 112 pages in 4 colors
In Business: 46 years
Number of Employees: 200
Sales Volume: $50MM to $100MM

2138 Fotodyne
FOTODYNE Incorporated
950 Walnut Ridge Dr
Hartland, WI 53029-9388   262-369-7000
800-362-3686
Fax: 262-369-7017
info@fotodyne.com
www.fotodyne.com

Innovative products for molecular biology research and molecular biology for the classrooom
President: Brian Walsh
Credit Cards: MasterCard; Visa
Catalog Cost: Free
Mailing List Information: Names for rent
In Business: 30 years
Number of Employees: 25
Sales Volume: $3MM to $5MM

2139 Genesis
Genesis, Inc.
PO Box 2242
Mount Vernon, WA 98273   360-422-6764
800-473-5538
Fax: 360-422-6765
info@pellet.com
www.pellet.com

Owl pellets and owl pellet kits and teaching aids
President: David Carter
Credit Cards: AMEX; MasterCard
Catalog Cost: Free
In Business: 28 years
Number of Employees: 2
Sales Volume: under 500,000

2140 HEMCO Corporation
HEMCO
711 S Powell Rd
Independence, MO 64056-2602   816-796-2900
800-779-4362
Fax: 816-796-3333
info@hemcocorp.com
www.hemcocorp.com

Laboratory fume hoods, furniture and engineered enclosures
President: Ronald E Hill
Marketing Manager: David Campbell
VP: Sue Hill
Catalog Cost: Free
In Business: 56 years
Number of Employees: 30
Sales Volume: $1.9 Million

2141 Hach Company
Hach Company
PO Box 389
Loveland, CO 80539-389   970-669-3050
800-227-4224
Fax: 970-669-2932
www.hach.com

Test kits and laboratory instruments
President: Kathryn Hach-Darrow
Catalog Cost: Free
In Business: 81 years
Number of Employees: 800

2142 Hampden Engineering
Hampden Engineering Corporation
PO Box 563
East Longmeadow, MA 01028-563413-525-3981
800-253-2133
Fax: 413-525-4741
sales@hampden.com
www.hampden.com

Educational materials, equipment and training programs
President: Burton Thomas
CFO: John Flynn
Office Manager: Donna Kelly
Catalog Cost: Free
In Business: 61 years

Number of Employees: 85
Sales Volume: $14 Million

2143 Hawkhill Science Catalog
Hawkhill Associates, Inc.
125 E Gilman St
Madison, WI 53703-1498   608-467-7003
800-422-4295
Fax: 608-467-7003
customerservice@hawkhill.com
www.Hawkhill.Com

Science videos, CD-roms, and DVDs for schools and home schools
President: Bill Stonebarger
Credit Cards: AMEX; MasterCard; Visa
Catalog Cost: Free
Average Order Size: $250
Mailing List Information: Names for rent
In Business: 30 years
Number of Employees: 4
Sales Volume: Under $500M

2144 Health Edco
HEALTH EDCO
PO Box 21207
Waco, TX 76702-1207   254-981-5001
855-510-6720
Fax: 254-751-0221
www.healthedco.com

Health education materials
Marketing Manager: Cathi Davis
Owner/CEO: Scott Salmans
President/COO: Gary Hutchison
Catalog Cost: Free
In Business: 42 years
Number of Employees: 138
Sales Volume: $14 Million

2145 Heathrow Scientific
620 Lakeview Parkway
Vernon Hills, IL 60061   847-816-5070
Fax: 847-816-5072
info@heatsci.com
www.heathrowscientific.com

Laboratory supplies
Global Sales Director: Mark Shelton
National Sales Manager: Jeff Maris

2146 Herbach & Rademan Company
Herbach & Rademan Company
353 Crider Avenue
Moorestown, NJ 08057   856-802-0422
800-848-8001
Fax: 856-802-0465
sales@herbach.com
www.herbach.com

Scientific equipment
President: Frank Lobascio
Credit Cards: MasterCard; Visa
Catalog Cost: Free
In Business: 81 years
Number of Employees: 8
Sales Volume: $374,000

2147 Insect Lore
Insect Lore
PO Box 1535
Shafter, CA 93263-1535   800-548-3284
Fax: 661-746-0334
livebug@insectlore.com
www.insectlore.com

Books and supplies for bug catching
President: Carlos White PhD
Marketing Manager: John White
Credit Cards: MasterCard; Visa
Catalog Cost: Free
In Business: 40 years
Number of Employees: 48
Sales Volume: $10 Million

2148 Kelvin
Kelvin
280 Adams Blvd
Farmingdale, NY 11735
631-756-1750
800-535-8469
Fax: 631-756-1763
kelvin@kelvin.com
www.kelvin.com

New and innovative products for technology education, science, robotics, and pre-engineering
President: Avi Hadar
avi@kelvin.com
Purchasing Manager: Joseph Chu
CEO: Avi Hadar
Credit Cards: AMEX; MasterCard; Visa
Catalog Cost: Free
In Business: 66 years
Number of Employees: 20
Sales Volume: $2.3 Million

2149 Ken-A-Vision Manufacturing Company
Ken-a-vision
5615 Raytown Road
Kansas City, MO 64133
816-353-4787
800-501-7366
Fax: 816-358-5072
info@ken-a-vision.com
www.ken-a-vision.com

Microprojectors, microscopes, video flex (flexible camera), vision viewer
President: Steven Dunn
CFO: Karen Dunn
Marketing Manager: Mary Mitchell
VP: Michael Mathews
Marketing & Promotions Manager: Lesa Brownell
International Marketing Manager: Steven Dunn
Catalog Cost: Free
Mailing List Information: Names for rent
In Business: 61 years
Number of Employees: 25
Sales Volume: $3.3 Million

2150 Kewaunee Scientific Corporation
Kewaunee
2700 West Front Street
PO Box 1842
Statesville, NC 28677-1842
704-873-7202
Fax: 704-873-5160
KSCMarketing@Kewaunee.Com
www.Kewaunee.Com

Science laboratory furniture, fume hoods and accessories
President: David M. Rausch
CFO: D Michael Parker
Marketing Manager: Dana L Dahlgren
Production Manager: Keith D. Smith
Managing Director of International: B. Sathyamurthy
Vice President, Human Resources: Elizabeth D. Phillips
Vice President, Engineering and Pro: Kurt P. Rindoks
Catalog Cost: Free
In Business: 109 years
Number of Employees: 572

2151 LaMotte Environmental Science Products
LaMotte Company
802 Washington Avenue
PO Box 329
Chestertown, MD 21620
410-778-3100
800-344-3100
Fax: 410-778-6394
tech@lamotte.com
www.lamotte.com

Equipment for students of water, soil and air chemistry for hands on testing
Marketing Manager: Sue Byerly
Printing Information: 24 pages
In Business: 96 years

2152 MarketLab
6850 Southbelt Dr
Caledonia, MI 49316
866-237-3722
Fax: 616-656-2475
service@marketlabinc.com
www.marketlab.com

Laboratory supplies

2153 McMillan Optical Company
McMillan Optical Company
1155 Market Circle
Port Charlotte, FL 33953
941-627-0100
Fax: 941-629-7810
moc1103@outlook.com
www.mcmillanoptical.com/

Optical components and electronics
President: Jeanette Mc Millan
General Manager / Sales: Ed Walton
In Business: 58 years
Number of Employees: 8
Sales Volume: $500,000 - $1,000,000

2154 Mettler-Toledo International
Mettler Toledo
1900 Polaris Parkway
Columbus, OH 43240-4035
614-438-4511
800-638-8537
Fax: 614-438-4646
www.Us.Mt.Com

Precision lab equipment, balances, titigators, thermal analysis, PH makers, DO meters, DE, KE
President: Oliver Filliol
CFO: William P Donnelly
CEO: Olivier Filliol
Head of Human Resources: Christian Magloth
Head of Laboratory Division: Thomas Caratsch
Credit Cards: AMEX; MasterCard; Visa
Catalog Cost: Free
Number of Employees: 5400

2155 NSTA
NSTA
1840 Wilson Blvd
Arlington, VA 22201-3000
703-243-7100
800-722-6782
Fax: 703-243-7177
executive@nsta.org
www.Nsta.Org

Posters and other curriculum-enhancing materials for science educators
President: Dr. Carolyn Hayes
Executive Director: Dr. David L. Evans
President-Elect: Mary Gromko
msgromko@q.com
Operations and Membership: Moira Baker
Credit Cards: AMEX; MasterCard; Visa
Catalog Cost: Free
In Business: 71 years

2156 Nebraska Scientific
3823 Leavenworth Street
Omaha, NE 68105-1180
402-346-7214
800-228-7117
Fax: 402-346-2216
staff@NebraskaScientific.com
www.nebraskascientific.com

Laboratory supplies and equipment

2157 Parco Scientific Company
Parco Scientific Company
PO Box 851559
Westland, MI 48185
330-637-2849
877-592-5837
Fax: 877-592-5838
info@parcoscientific.com
www.parcoscientific.com

Microscopes, laboratory supplies and aids, meters and kits, for the educational, medical and industrial markets

President: Brian Martorana
Credit Cards: MasterCard; Visa
Catalog Cost: Free
In Business: 50 years
Number of Employees: 12
Sales Volume: 5MM-10MM

2158 Pitsco Big Book Catalog
Pitsco Education
P.O. Box 1708
Pittsburg, KS 66762-1708
620-231-0010
800-835-0686
Fax: 800-533-8104
orders@pitsco.com
www.pitsco.com

Science, Technology, Engineering and Math teaching resources
President: Harvey R Dean PhD
Production Manager: Kyle Bailey
Chief Operating Officer: Lisa Paterni
Credit Cards: AMEX; MasterCard
Catalog Cost: Free
Catalog Circulation: Mailed 1 time(s) per year
Average Order Size: $400
Printing Information: 404 pages in 4 colors
In Business: 46 years
Number of Employees: 200
Sales Volume: $50MM to $100MM

2159 Pitsco Maker Space Catalog
Pitsco Education
P.O. Box 1708
Pittsburg, KS 66762-1708
620-231-0010
800-835-0686
Fax: 800-533-8104
orders@pitsco.com
www.pitsco.com

Activities, project kits, supplies, furniture, and storage to create maker spaces for robobits and other science activities.
President: Harvey R. Dean
Production Manager: Kyle Bailey
Chief Operating Officer: Lisa Paterni
Catalog Cost: Free
Catalog Circulation: Mailed 1 time(s) per year
Printing Information: 64 pages in 4 colors
In Business: 46 years
Number of Employees: 200
Sales Volume: $50MM to $100MM

2160 Premiere Products
Premiere Products
PO Box 944
Columbus, NE 68602
402-564-4909
800-323-2799
Fax: 402-564-3703
customerservice@premiereproducts.biz
www.premiereproducts.biz

Weather instruments for home and business, radio controlled clocks and watches, outdoor furniture, specialty gifts
President: Georgia Behlen
Credit Cards: AMEX; MasterCard
Catalog Cost: Free
Mailing List Information: Names for rent
In Business: 25 years
Number of Employees: 3
Sales Volume: Under $500M

2161 Prufrock Press
Prufrock Press
PO Box 8813
Waco, TX 76714-8813
254-756-3337
800-998-2208
Fax: 254-756-3339
info@prufrock.com
www.prufrock.com

Activity books, teaching resources, identification instruments, journals and magazines for teaching and educating gifted children
General Manager: Ginny Bates
Marketing Assistant: Elizabeth Harp
Credit Cards: AMEX; MasterCard

Catalog Cost: Free
In Business: 23 years
Number of Employees: 7
Sales Volume: $660,000

2162 RobotiKitsDirect Catalog
OWI Inc.
17141 Kingsview Avenue
Carson, CA 90808
310-515-6800
Fax: 310-515-0927
info@owirobot.com
www.owirobot.com

Robot kits for beginners, intermediate and advanced experimenters, teacher resource kits, and study guides

President: Craig Morioka
Chief Executive Officer: Ned Morioka
Vice President: Joseph Martinez
Credit Cards: MasterCard
Catalog Cost: Free
Printing Information:
Press: Web Press
Binding: Folded
In Business: 34 years
Number of Employees: 13
Sales Volume: $2 Million

2163 Robotics
Pitsco Education
P.O. Box 1708
Pittsburg, KS 66762-1708
620-231-0010
800-835-0686
Fax: 800-533-8104
orders@pitsco.com
www.pitsco.com

science, Technology, Engineering, Math, and Robotics teaching resources

President: Harvey R Dean
Production Manager: Kyle Bailey
Chief Operating Officer: Lisa Paterni
Catalog Cost: Free
Catalog Circulation: Mailed 1 time(s) per year
Printing Information: 68 pages in 4 colors
In Business: 46 years
Number of Employees: 200
Sales Volume: $50MM to $100MM

2164 Scientific Chemical & Biological Catalog
Flinn Scientific Inc
PO Box 219
Batavia, IL 60510
800-452-1261
Fax: 866-452-1436
flinn@flinnsci.com
www.flinnsci.com

Chemical storage and disposabl procedures, solution preparation recipes, lab technique how to boxes

Chairman: Margaret Flinn
President: Lawrence Flinn
CFO: Bill Wolford
Marketing Manager: Kevin McNulty
Production Manager: Tony Leben
VP Purchasing: Sharon Barr
CEO: Pat Flinn
Credit Cards: AMEX; MasterCard; Visa
Catalog Cost: Free
In Business: 34 years
Number of Employees: 65
Sales Volume: $11.6 Million

2165 Sipco Products
SIPCO Products, Inc.
4301 Prospect Road
Peoria Heights, IL 61603-3411
309-682-5400
Fax: 309-637-5120
terry@sipcoproducts.com
www.sipcoproducts.com

Safety products, fire protection devices, head protection, safety signs, storage containers, fire safety equipment, lifting devices, spill clean up equipment, safety auditing services

President: Eileen Grawey
CFO: Eileen Grawey
Marketing Manager: Terry Grawey
In Business: 69 years
Number of Employees: 8
Sales Volume: $500,000 - $1,000,000

2166 Skulls Unlimited International
Skulls Unlimited International, Inc
10313 S Sunnylane
Okhlama City, OK 73160
405-794-9300
800-659-7585
Fax: 405-794-6985
info@skullsunlimited.com
www.skullsunlimited.com

Leading supplier of osteological specimens, supplying the educational community with over 350 varieties of human and animal skulls from around the world

President: Jay Villemarette
Marketing Manager: Kim Villemarette
Production Manager: Eric Humphries
Owner: Christian Zylinski
Co-Owner:
Credit Cards: AMEX; MasterCard
Catalog Cost: 9.95
Average Order Size: $267
Mailing List Information: Names for rent
In Business: 29 years
Number of Employees: 7
Sales Volume: $1 million

2167 Summit Learning
Summit Learning
755 Rockwell Avenue
PO Box 755
Fort Atkinson, WI 53538-755
800-558-9595
Fax: 800-317-2194

Products for learning Math and Science in the PreK to Middle School classrooms

Catalog Cost: Free

2168 Thomas Scientific
PO Box 99
Swedesboro, NJ 08085
856-467-2000
Fax: 856-467-3087
www.thomassci.com

Laboratory supplies

2169 XUMP Science Toys
XUMP & Innovation Frontier Inc
3710 Industry Avenue
Suite 206
Lakewood, CA 90712
562-492-9560
888-438-8986
Fax: 562-492-9580
www.xump.com

Science supplies, educational kits, toys and gifts

President: Anton Skorucak
Credit Cards: AMEX; MasterCard
Catalog Cost: Free

2170 Young Naturalist Company Catalog
Young Naturalist Company
835 Oakcrest Street
Iowa City, IA 52246
563-299-6128
Fax: 515-223-0899
info@youngnaturalistcompany.com
www.youngnaturalistcompany.com

Nature education kits, teacher lesson plans and dried specimens

President: Miles Coady
Credit Cards: MasterCard; Visa
Catalog Cost: Free
Mailing List Information: Names for rent
In Business: 26 years
Number of Employees: 5

Software

2171 AAVIM
Amn. Assoc. for Vocational Instructional
220 Smithonia Rd.
Winterville, GA 30683
706-742-5355
800-228-4689
Fax: 706-742-7005
sales@aavim.com
www.aavim.com

Instructional materials for vocational education.

President: Marion Fletcher
CFO: Jimmy McCully
Production Manager: Kim Butler
Fulfillment: Kim Butler
Vice President: Brad Bryant
Catalog Cost: Free
Catalog Circulation: to 10000
Mailing List Information: Names for rent
List Manager: Karen Seabaugh
List Company: Market Data Retrieval
In Business: 67 years
Number of Employees: 3
Sales Volume: $400K

2172 Academic Superstore
Academic Superstore
5212 Tennyson Pkwy.
Ste. 130
Plano, TX 75024
512-450-1199
800-876-3507
Fax: 866-947-4525
contact@academicsuperstore.com
www.academicsuperstore.com

Academic software, hardware, and electronics for students, teachers, and schools; and home school materials

Marketing Manager: Natalie Jones
CEO: Mike Fishler
Owner/CEO: Nathan Jones
Credit Cards: AMEX; MasterCard
Catalog Cost: Free
Printing Information: in 4 colors
In Business: 17 years
Number of Employees: 50
Sales Volume: $4.6 million

2173 Cambridge Soft Products Catalog
PerkinElmer Inc.
940 Winter Street
Waltham, MA 02451
203-925-4602
800-315-7300
Fax: 781-663-8080
informatics.customer_service@perkinelmer.com
www.cambridgesoft.com

Chemistry information and teaching tools on CD-ROMs and computer software

President: Michael G Tomasic
CFO: James T Reilly
Marketing Manager: Robert S Joseph
Credit Cards: MasterCard; Visa
Catalog Cost: Free
In Business: 10 years

2174 Cheng & Tsui Company
Cheng and Tsui Company
25 West Street
Boston, MA 02111-1213
617-988-2400
800-554-1963
Fax: 617-426-3669
service@cheng-tsui.com
www.Cheng-Tsui.Com

Asian language-learning materials, literature in translation, computer software and other products that introduce East Asian languages and cultures to the Western world

President: Jill Cheng
Marketing Manager: J D Willson
Production Manager: Sandry Korinchak
Catalog Circulation: to 10000

Printing Information: 80 pages in 4 colors on Newsprint
Press: Sheetfed Press
Binding: Saddle Stitched
In Business: 36 years
Sales Volume: $3MM to $5MM

2175 Christy's Editorial Film Supply
Christy's Editorial
3625 West Pacific Ave
Burbank, CA 91505-1451   818-845-1755
                                800-556-5706
                                Fax: 818-845-1756
                                info@christys.net
                                www.christys.net

Film editing supplies
President: Craig Christy
Marketing Manager: Julie Kramer
Credit Cards: MasterCard; Visa
Printing Information: 30 pages
In Business: 45 years
Number of Employees: 10

2176 Classroom Complete Press
Classroom Complete Press
P.O. Box 19729
San Diego, CA 92159   613-389-6792
                             800-663-3609
                             Fax: 800-663-3608
                             www.ccpinteractive.com

Interactive study lessons
Credit Cards: AMEX; MasterCard
Printing Information: 22 pages

2177 Discovery Channel
Discovery Store
300 California Street
3rd Floor
San Francisco, CA 94104   800-938-0333
                                 Fax: 276-670-2121
                                 www.discoverystore.com

Gifts from shows on the Discovery Channel; Great ideas and fun items for all
Chairman: John Hendricks
President: David Zaslav
CFO: Bradley E. Singer (Brad)
Marketing Manager: Lori McFarling
Credit Cards: AMEX; MasterCard
Catalog Cost: Free

2178 Essential Skills Software
Essential Skills Software
5614 Connecticut Ave NW
#150
Washington, DC 20015-2604   800-753-3727
                                   Fax: 800-723-7718
                                   info@essentialskills.net
                                   essentialskills.net

CD & Web-based Educational Software
In Business: 15+ years

2179 Health Care Educational Materials
Nasco Arts & Crafts Store
901 Janesville Avenue
PO Box 901
Fort Atkinson, WI 53538-901   920-563-2446
                                     800-558-9595
                                     Fax: 920-563-6044
                                     custserv@enasco.com
                                     www.enasco.com

DVDs, games, computer software and a variety of anatomical models, charts and replicas
President: Andrew Reinen
Marketing Manager: Phil Niemeyer
Manager, Data Processing: Mike Wagner
Contract Sales Manager: Dave Johnson
Director: Tim Taggart
ttaggart@eNasco.com
Catalog Cost: Free
Catalog Circulation: to 25000

In Business: 74 years
Number of Employees: 540

2180 Hotronic, Inc.
Hotronic, Inc.
1875 Winchester Blvd
Suite 100
Campbell, CA 95008-1168   408-378-3883
                                 Fax: 408-378-3888
                                 sales@hotronics.com
                                 www.hotronics.com

Digital effects audio/video mixer
President: Andy Ho
CEO, Manager: Linda Chang
In Business: 33 years
Number of Employees: 25
Sales Volume: $2.5M

2181 Learning Services
Learning Services
P.O. Box 10636
Eugene, OR 97440   800-877-9378
                          Fax: 800-815-5154
                          www.learningservicesus.com
Printing Information: 16 pages

2182 Lynx Media
Lynx Media
12501 Chandler Blvd
Suite 202
Valley Village, CA 91607   818-761-5859
                                  800-451-5969
                                  Fax: 818-761-7099
                                  sales@lynxmedia.com
                                  www.lynxmedia.com

Developer of circulation and product fulfillment software
President: Len Latimer
Marketing Manager: Len Latimer
In Business: 29 years
Sales Volume: $500,000- 1 Million

2183 MacConnection
PC Connection Inc.
730 Milford Road
Route 101A
Merrimack, NH 03054-4631   603-355-6005
                                  888-213-0607
                                  Fax: 603-423-5748
                                  customerservice@pcconnection.com
                                  www.pcconnection.com

Office supplies and software programs
Chairman: Patricia Gallup
President: Timothy McGrath
CFO: Jack Ferguson
CEO: Timothy McGrath
Credit Cards: AMEX; MasterCard; Visa
Printing Information: 62 pages
In Business: 32 years
Number of Employees: 1556
Sales Volume: Over $1 Billion

2184 MacMall
PC Mall Sales
1940 E. Mariposa Ave
El Segundo, CA 90245   310-354-5600
                              800-700-1000
                              Fax: 310-225-4030
                              customerservice@pcm.com
                              www.pcm.com

Hardware, software and accessories for Macintosh
Chairman: Frank K. Khulusi
President: Robert (Jay) Miley
CFO: Brandon H. LaVerne
Marketing Manager: Kristin Rogers
Director: Ronald B. Beck
EVP, Chief Legal Officer & Secretar: Robert I. Newton
EVP- IT, Operations & Commercial Sa: Simon M. Abuyounes
Credit Cards: AMEX; MasterCard; Visa

Catalog Cost: $3
Printing Information: 132 pages
In Business: 27 years
Number of Employees: 2657
Sales Volume: Over $1 Billion

2185 National Instruments
National Instruments Corporation
11500 N Mopac Expwy
Austin, TX 78759-3504   512-683-0100
                               800-531-5066
                               Fax: 512-683-8411
                               www.ni.com

Computer interfaces and software
President: James Truchard
Marketing Manager: Dirk Mol
Credit Cards: MasterCard; Visa
In Business: 38 years
Number of Employees: 7100
Sales Volume: $ 15 Million

2186 Stages Learning Materials
Stages Learning Materials
PO Box 1770
Pacific Pasilades, CA 90272   530-892-1112
                                     888-501-8880
                                     Fax: 888-735-7791
                                     info@stageslearning.com
                                     www.stageslearning.com
In Business: 18 years

Videos & Tapes

2187 At Risk Resources
Standard Deviants School
1661 Tennessee St.
Suite 3-D
San Francisco, CA 94107   415-541-9901
                                 866-386-0253
                                 Fax: 805-426-8136
                                 www.sdteach.com

Publisher of life-skills educational media for the K-12 market programs of which include intervention with children and young adults
President: Thomas Slagle
CFO: David Vander Ploeg
Marketing Manager: David Johnson
Credit Cards: AMEX; MasterCard; Visa
Catalog Cost: Free
Mailing List Information: Names for rent
In Business: 11 years

2188 Brookes Publishing
Brookes Publishing
PO Box 10624
Baltimore, MD 21285-624   800-638-3775
                                 Fax: 410-337-8539
                                 custserv@brookespublishing.com
                                 www.brookespublishing.com

Books and videos on education, developmental disabilities, early childhood, early interaction, literacy, mental health, communication and language and related subjects
Chairman: Paul H. Brookes
President: Jeffrey D. Brookes
EVP: Melissa A Behm
Vice President & Publisher: George S. Stamathis
Credit Cards: AMEX; MasterCard; Visa
Catalog Cost: Free
Mailing List Information: Names for rent
In Business: 35 years
Number of Employees: 50

2189 Bureau for At-Risk Youth
The Bureau for At-Risk Youth
PO Box 170
Farmingville, NY 11738   800-999-6884
                                Fax: 800-262-1886
                                info@at-risk.com
                                www.at-risk.com

Health and educational books and videos on topics including drugs, self-esteem, safe schools, parenting and professional development

President: James Werz
Credit Cards: MasterCard; Visa
Catalog Cost: Free
Printing Information: 48 pages

2190 CBD Home School
Christian Book Distributors
140 Summit St.
Peabody, MA 01960   800-247-4784
customer.service@christianbook.com
www.christianbook.com

Textbooks, curriculum, resources, tools and projects for teaching a child at home.

President: Ray Hendrickson
Catalog Cost: Free
Mailing List Information: Names for rent
In Business: 39 years
Number of Employees: 500

2191 Christy's Editorial Film Supply
Christy's Editorial
3625 West Pacific Ave
Burbank, CA 91505-1451   818-845-1755
800-556-5706
Fax: 818-845-1756
info@christys.net
www.christys.net

Film editing supplies

President: Craig Christy
Marketing Manager: Julie Kramer
Credit Cards: MasterCard; Visa
Printing Information: 30 pages
In Business: 45 years
Number of Employees: 10

2192 Disc Makers
Disc Makers
150 West 25th St., Suite #402
New York, NY 10001   800-468-9353
Fax: 856-661-3450
www.discmakers.com

CD and DVD manufacturer, services, blank media, duplicators, and supplies

President: Tony van Veen
Catalog Cost: Free
In Business: 69 years

2193 Educational Activities
Educational Activities
P.O. Box 87
Baldwin, NY 11510   800-797-3223
Fax: 516-623-9282
www.edact.com

Credit Cards: AMEX; MasterCard
Printing Information: 40 pages

2194 English as a Second Language
AudioForum
175 Copse Road
Madison, CT 06443-2272   203-245-0195
800-243-1234
Fax: 888-453-4329
www.audioforum.com

Self-instructional and classroom audio and video materials for learning to speak English as another language

President: Jeffrey Norton
CFO: Bruce Salendar
Marketing Manager: Arthur Townes
Production Manager: Elizabeth Lockwood
Buyers: Janis Yates, VP
Credit Cards: AMEX; MasterCard; Visa; Discover
Catalog Cost: Free
Catalog Circulation: Mailed 4 time(s) per year
Printing Information: 23 pages in 2 colors on Glossy Stock
Press: Web Press

Binding: Folded
Mailing List Information: Names for rent
List Company: Statistics
In Business: 32 years
Number of Employees: 30
Sales Volume: $1MM to $3MM

2195 Fred Pryor Seminars
Pryor Learning Solutions
5700 Broadmoor Street
Suite 300
Mission, KS 66202-2219   913-967-8849
800-780-8476
customerservice@pryor.com
www.pryor.com

Training sessions/seminars for professional trainers and business managers

President: Michael Hays
Credit Cards: AMEX; MasterCard
In Business: 47 years
Sales Volume: $10MM to $20MM

2196 Hearlihy Drafting
Pitsco, Inc.
P.O. Box 1708
Pittsburg, KS 66762-1708   800-835-0686
Fax: 800-533-8104
orders@pitsco.com
www.pitsco.com

Drafting supplies: pens, printers, and tutorials to hands-on projects, modeling supplies, and construction kits

President: Patrick Hearlihy
President: Harvey Dean
Credit Cards: AMEX; MasterCard; Visa
Catalog Cost: Free
In Business: 44 years
Number of Employees: 8
Sales Volume: $5 Million

2197 Human Relations Media
Human Relations Media
41 Kensico Drive
Mt. Kisco, NY 10549   800-431-2050
letters@hrmvideo.com
www.hrmvideo.com

Educational programs

In Business: 35+ years

2198 Palm Kids Calatog
Music for Little People
30 Amberwood Parkway
Ashland, OH 44805   707-923-3991
800-409-2457
Fax: 707-923-3241

Audio and video recordings, games, toys and musical instruments

Chairman: Maureen Mccready
www.maureenmccready.com
President: Leib Ostrow
Marketing Manager: Sherry Smiley
Fulfillment: Gayle Peterson
Credit Cards: AMEX; MasterCard; Visa
Catalog Cost: Free
Catalog Circulation: Mailed 2 time(s) per year to 20000
Average Order Size: $45
Printing Information: 47 pages in 4 colors on Matte Stock
Press: Web Press
Binding: Saddle Stitched
Mailing List Information: Names for rent
List Company: DJ & Associates
PO Box 2048
Ridgefield, CT 06877
203-431-8777
In Business: 20 years
Number of Employees: 8
Sales Volume: $1MM to $3MM

2199 Performance Resource Press
Amplified Life Network, LLC
7791 Byron Center Ave, SW
Byron Center, MI 49315-2843   248-588-7733
800-453-7733
Fax: 616-499-2077
contact@amplifenet.com
amplifenet.com

Viedo tapes for students

President: Lyle Labardee
Founder: Lyle Labardee
Director: Susan Labardee
VP of Engagement: Tyler Higley
In Business: 3 years
Sales Volume: $3MM to $5MM

2200 Physical Education & Health
Films Media Group
132 West 31st Street
17th Floor
New York, NY 10001-2053   800-322-8755
Fax: 800-678-3633
custserv@films.com
www.films.com

Video and multimedia for academic, vocational and life-skills conent

CFO: Jason McClure
Marketing Manager: Melinda Ball
Production Manager: Kim Keiffer
Buyers: Vickie Meadows
Credit Cards: AMEX; MasterCard
Catalog Circulation: Mailed 12 time(s) per year to 30000
Average Order Size: $100
Printing Information: 48 pages in 4 colors on Matte Stock
Press: Web Press
Binding: Saddle Stitched
Mailing List Information: Names for rent
List Company: Stevens-Knox
In Business: 17 years
Number of Employees: 40
Sales Volume: $5MM to $10MM

2201 Red Ribbon Resources
Red Ribbon Resources
303 Crossway Park Drive
Woodbury, NY 18703-1246   888-433-8368
Fax: 800-262-1886
info@redribbonresources.com
www.redribbonresources.com

Educational resources including activity books, banners, bracelets, buttons, games, poster charts, ribbons, stickers, and t-shirts

President: Ed Werz
Credit Cards: AMEX; MasterCard; Visa
Catalog Cost: Free
In Business: 10 years
Number of Employees: 3
Sales Volume: $900,000

2202 The Hair Factory
The Hair Factory
116 Pleasant Street, Suite 229
Easthampton, MA 00102   413-585-9666
800-999-9328
Fax: 413-585-8902
customerservice@hairfactory.com
www.hairfactory.com

Supplies consumers with 100% natural human hair for hair pieces and extensions—also supplies how to books, videos, and hair care products

Catalog Cost: Free
In Business: 30 years

2203 Tom Thumb Kids Catalog
Rhythms Productions
PO Box 34485
Los Angeles, CA 90034-485   310-836-4678
800-544-7244
Fax: 310-837-1534
www.rhythmproductions.com

Educational cassettes and cd's, and Tom Thumb Music products
Mailing List Information: Names for rent
In Business: 60 years
Number of Employees: 4

2204 Video Learning Library
ArtVideo Productions
5777 Azalea Dr
Grants Pass, OR 97526-8229   541-479-7140
800-576-1482
Fax: 541-476-8728
www.artvideo.com

Rent or purchase art videos, over 1,200 titles
President: Gail Newcomb
Printing Information: 16 pages in 2 colors on Matte Stock
Binding: Folded
Mailing List Information: Names for rent
In Business: 30 years

2205 Video/Entertainment
Specialty Store Services
454 Jarvis Ave
Des Plaines, IL 60018-1912   888-441-4440
Fax: 888-368-8001
www.specialtystoreservices.com

Shelving, video and DVD cases and supplies
Chairman: Malcolm Finke
Credit Cards: MasterCard
In Business: 26 years

2206 Wavelength Catalog
Wavelength Inc
4753 N Broadway St # 818
Suite 818
Chicago, IL 60640-4992   773-784-1012
877-528-4472
Fax: 773-784-1079
info@wavelengthinc.com
www.Wavelength.Biz

Videos for professionals within the fields of edcuation and business
President: Jim Winter
Artistic Director: Rochelle Richelieu, M.S.W.
Credit Cards: MasterCard; Visa
Catalog Cost: Free
In Business: 35 years
Sales Volume: $1MM to $3MM

Electronics
Products & Equipment

2207 Accu-Tech Cable
Accu-Tech
660 Hembree Parkway
Suite 100
Roswell, GA 30076-3890   770-751-9473
800-221-4767
Fax: 770-475-4659
sales@accu-tech.com
www.accu-tech.com

Fiber optic cables and connectivity products, surge protection products, tools and accessories
President: Ed Ellis
CFO: Alison Santoro
Marketing Manager: Alice Milihram
Production Manager: Claire Scannell
Branch Manager: Todd Delavie
Regional Vice President: Butch Flynt
Ops. Contact: Carlos Deere
Credit Cards: AMEX; MasterCard; Visa
In Business: 30 years

2208 All Pro Sound
AP Sound, Inc.
806 Beverly Parkway
Pensacola, FL 32505   850-432-5780
800-925-5776
Fax: 850-432-0844
www.allprosound.com

Musical instruments, products and accessories for audio, video, and lighting
Credit Cards: AMEX; MasterCard
Catalog Cost: Free
In Business: 30+ years

2209 BEAR-COM Motorola Affordable Communication Systems
BEARCOM
P.O. Box 559001
Dallas, TX 75355   214-680-9750
800-252-1691
Fax: 214-349-8950
www.bearcom.com

Paging, radio, CCTV, and nextel equipment
Chairman: John Watson
President: Jerry Denham
CFO: Jerry Noonan
Marketing Manager: Kent H. Huffman
Executive Vice President & Founder: Brent Bisnar
Vice President of Sales: Nader Mortazavi
Vice President of Operations: Ken Nixon
Credit Cards: AMEX; MasterCard
Catalog Cost: Free
Printing Information: 48 pages in 4 colors on Glossy Stock
Binding: Saddle Stitched
In Business: 34 years

2210 Barksdale Control Products
Barksdale Inc.
3211 Fruitland Avenue
PO Box 58843
Los Angeles, CA 90058-843   323-589-6181
800-835-1060
Fax: 323-589-3463
sales@barksdale.com
www.Barksdale.Com

Manufacturer of electronic controls for industrial applications specializing in the measurement of fluids, including valves, switches, transducers, and regulators
Chairman: Robert S Evans
President: Ian Dodd
CFO: Timothy J MacCarrick
Catalog Cost: Free
In Business: 66 years
Number of Employees: 100-

2211 Burst Electronics
Burst Electronics
PO Box 65947
Albuquerque, NM 87193   505-898-1455
Fax: 505-898-0159
sales@burstelectronics.com
www.burstelectronics.com

Audio/video equipment

2212 Business Boosters Catalog
Atlas Pen & Pencil Corporation
1204 E Nakoma Street
Hollywood, FL 33020-1310   954-920-4444
888-672-1240
Fax: 800-342-8889
ljoyal@atlaspen.com
www.atlaspencil.com

Print name and logos on hats, t-shirts, pens, keychains, calendars, calculators and mugs
President: Eric Schneider
Credit Cards: AMEX; MasterCard; Visa
Catalog Cost: Free
Printing Information: 45 pages
In Business: 68 years

2213 Cablescan
Cablescan
3022 Inland Empire Boulevard
Ontario, CA 91764-4803   909-483-2436
800-898-5783
Fax: 909-483-2463
sales@cablescan.com
www.cablescan.com

Electronic instruments for assembly and testing of wire harnesses, cables, back planes, circuit boards, and on-board wiring systems
President: David Eubanks
Catalog Cost: Free
In Business: 46 years
Number of Employees: 7
Sales Volume: $1,000,000 - $5,000,000

2214 Canare Catalog 13
Canare Corporation of America
45 Commerce Way
Unit C
Totowa, NJ 07512   973-837-0070
Fax: 973-837-0080
canare@canare.com
www.canare.com

Audio and video cable, 75 Ohm BNC, F and RCA connectors, patchbays, cable reels, snake systems, assemblies, crimp tools, cable strippers and more
President: Kazuo Urata
CFO: Gary Pagliocca
CEO: Woody Urata
VP: Patrick Gallager
Catalog Cost: Free
Mailing List Information: Names for rent
In Business: 45 years
Number of Employees: 25
Sales Volume: $4 Million

2215 Clinton Electronics
Clinton Electronics
6701 Clinton Road
Loves Park, IL 61111   800-447-3306
800-549-6393
Fax: 815-633-8712
www.clintonelectronics.com

Clinton's product line include Cameras, DVRs, PVMs, LCDs, Monitor Mounts, Power Supplies, Lenses, Cable, Installation Tools, and more.
Founder: Tom Clinton Sr.
In Business: 52 years

2216 Communications Electronics Journal
Communications Electronics Inc.
PO Box 1045
Ann Arbor, MI 48106-1045   734-996-8888
800-297-1023
Fax: 734-663-8888

Electronic shortwave radios, scanners, CB radios phones
President: Ken Ascher
Marketing Manager: Sam Ascher
Credit Cards: AMEX; MasterCard; Visa Discover Optima
Catalog Circulation: to 800M
Printing Information: 64 pages
In Business: 24 years
Number of Employees: 25
Sales Volume: $ 1-3 Million

2217 Crutchfield
Crutchfield Corporation
1 Crutchfield Park
Charlottesville, VA 22911-9097   434-817-1000
844-347-7281
Fax: 434-817-1010
support@crutchfield.com
www.crutchfield.com

Audio and video components, home theater, car stereos, telephones, pagers and digital satellite systems

CEO: William G Crutchfield Jr
Founder and CEO: Bill Crutchfield
Credit Cards: AMEX; MasterCard
Catalog Cost: Free
Catalog Circulation: Mailed 6 time(s) per year
Average Order Size: $275
Printing Information: 52 pages in 4 colors
Mailing List Information: Names for rent
List Manager: The Specialists
In Business: 43 years
Number of Employees: 550
Sales Volume: $50MM to $100MM

2218 Crystek

Crystek Corporation
12730 Commonwealth Drive
Fort Myers, FL 33913-6135
239-561-3311
800-237-3061
Fax: 239-561-1025
sales@crystek.com
www.Crystek.Com

Frequency control devices

President: Anthony Mastropole
Printing Information: 152 pages
In Business: 57 years
Sales Volume: $10MM to $20MM

2219 Deluxe Small Business Services

New England Business Service, Inc. (NEBS
500 Main St
Groton, MA 01471-1
888-823-6327
Fax: 978-449-3419
www.nebs.com

Small business management and marketing solutions

President: Dave Saunders
Number of Employees: 8000

2220 EZAutomation

EZAutomation.net
4140 Utica Ridge Road
Bettendorf, IA 52722
877-774-EASY
Fax: 877-775-EASY
sales@ezautomation.net
ezautomation.net

Computer parts

President: Vikram Kumar
Credit Cards: AMEX; MasterCard
Catalog Cost: Free
In Business: 16 years

2221 Eaton

Eaton Corporation
1111 Superior Ave E # 19
Cleveland, OH 44114-2535
440-523-4400
800-386-1911
Fax: 216-523-4787
www.eaton.com

Electrical control products for industrial use including aerospace, automotive, filtration, and hydraulics

Chairman: Alexander M Cutler
CFO: Richard M Fearon
Vice Chairman and COO: Craig Arnold
Senior Vice President and CIO: William W. Blausey Jr.
Executive Vice President, Chief HR: Cynthia K. Brabander
Catalog Cost: Free
Average Order Size: $150
Mailing List Information: Names for rent
In Business: 119 years
Number of Employees: 7300
Sales Volume: $500M to $1MM

2222 Electro Enterprises

Electro Enterprises
3601 N. I-35 Service Road
Oklahoma, OK 73111
405-427-6591
800-324-6591
www.electroenterprises.com

Electro Enterprises is your Franchised/Authorized stocking distributor of interconnect, electro-mechanical, wire/cable, and wire harness management products.

Printing Information: 45 pages
In Business: 45 years
Number of Employees: 150

2223 Electronix Express

Electronix Express
900 Hart Street
Rahway, NJ 7065
800-972-2225
Fax: 732-381-1572
sales@elexp.com
www.elexp.com

GW Instek is the largest manufacturer and developer of test and measurement instruments in Taiwan. Instek has more than 300 product items, ranging from oscilloscopes, spectrum analyzers, signal source

Credit Cards: AMEX; MasterCard
Printing Information: 368 pages

2224 Fairgate Rule

Stamp Inc
Saw Kill Industrial Park
Rhinebeck, NY 12572-391
845-876-3063
800-431-2180
Fax: 845-876-7039
stampinc@infionline.net
www.stampinc.com

Stamping, electro mechanical assemblies, resistance welding, equipment reconditioning, tools and dies

President: Gary Hosey
Catalog Circulation: Mailed 1 time(s) per year
Printing Information: in 1 color on Matte Stock
In Business: 50 years
Number of Employees: 15
Sales Volume: $1,000,000 - $5,000,000

2225 Falcon Fine Wire and Wire Products

Falcon Fine Wire and Wire Products
2401 Discovery Boulevard
Rockwall, TX 75032
214-771-3441
800-874-7230
falconwire@aol.com
www.falconfinewire.com

Wiring and cabling products

President: William D LeCount
Chief Operating Officer: Annette V. LeCount
VP of Manufacturing: James Bunt
Office Manager: Diane Dewald
Catalog Cost: Free
Number of Employees: 50-1
Sales Volume: $10,000,000 - $25,000,000

2226 FirstSTREET for Boomers & Beyond

FirstSTREET
1998 Ruffin Mill Road
Colonial Heights, VA 23834-5913
804-524-9888
800-958-8324
Fax: 866-889-9960
customerservice@firststreetonline.com
www.firststreetonline.com

Innovative products for Boomers and Beyond

President: Mark Gordon
CFO: Kevin Miller
Credit Cards: AMEX; MasterCard
Catalog Cost: Free
Catalog Circulation: Mailed 1 time(s) per year
Printing Information: in 4 colors
Number of Employees: 200

2227 Fluke Corporation

Fluke Corporation
PO Box 9090
Everett, WA 98206-9090
425-347-6100
800-443-5853
Fax: 425-446-5116
fluke-info@fluke.com
www.fluke.com

Electronic test and measurement equipment

President: Wes Pringle
CFO: Monti Ackerman
VP, Global Operations: Paul Caldarazzo
Vice President, Engineering: Paul Heydron
Vice President, Sales: Ernie Lauber
Catalog Cost: Free
In Business: 66 years
Number of Employees: 2400

2228 Focus Camera

Focus Camera Inc
895 McDonald Ave
Brooklyn, NY 11218-2017
718-431-7900
800-221-0828
Fax: 718-438-4263
cs@focuscamera.com
focuscamera.com

Cameras, video, telescopes, and binoculars

Chairman: Abe Berkowitz
President: Abe Berkowitz
Credit Cards: AMEX; MasterCard
In Business: 49 years
Number of Employees: 60
Sales Volume: $500M to $1MM

2229 GC Electronics

GC Electronics
1801 Morgan Street
Rockford, IL 61102-2690
815-316-9080
Fax: 815-316-9081
corp@gcelectronics.com
www.gcelectronics.com

Product lines with DVI, HDMI, USB and IEEE-1394 "FireWire™" cables, Home Theater products, Surge Protectors, Raceway products and more. GC Electronics continues to bring new products to its Electrica

In Business: 85 years

2230 Gadget Universe

Gravity Defyer
10643 Glenoaks Blvd
Pacoima, CA 91331
818-833-4860
800-429-0039
www.gravitydefyer.com

Gifts, gadgets, toys and hobbies, clocks and watches, electronics

Marketing Manager: Jared Tracy
Credit Cards: AMEX; MasterCard; Visa
Catalog Cost: Free

2231 HMC Electronics

Hisco Corporate
6650 Concord Park Drive
P.O. Box 526
Houston, TX 77040-4098
844-807-1901
Fax: 781-821-4133
cs@hmcelectronics.com
www.hisco.com

Products for electronic assembly and repair

President: Stan Goldberg
VP/General Manager: Howard Chase
Catalog Cost: Free
In Business: 40 years
Number of Employees: 18
Sales Volume: $9 Million

2232 Hagstrom Electronics
Hagstrom Electronics
1986 Junction Road
Starsburg, VA 22657 540-465-4677
888-690-9080
Fax: 540-465-4678
sales@hagstromelectronics.com
www.hagstromelectronics.com
Keyboard Encoder Modules, Protocol Converters, Special Interfaces, Single Chip Encoders, Accessories,
Credit Cards: AMEX; MasterCard
In Business: 21 years

2233 Hammond Electronics
Hammond Electronics
1230 West Central Blvd
Orlando, FL 32805 407-849-6060
800-929-2677
Fax: 407-872-0826
webmaster@hammondelec.com
www.hammondelec.com
Electronic components including connectors, wire & cable, capacitors, resistors, test equipment, digital oscilloscopes, relays and switches. Production equipment including soldering and de-soldering s
Founder: Grattan Hammond Jr
In Business: 68 years

2234 Hard-Style
Dragon Door
800-899-5111
www.dragondoor.com
Kettlebells, Strength, Conditioning, Flexibility, and Advanced Fitness Resources
Catalog Cost: Free

2235 Have Inc
350 Power Avenue
Hudson, NY 12534-2448 518-828-2000
800-999-4283
Fax: 518-828-2008
have@haveinc.com
Audio, video and data cable and cable related products, complete DVD duplication, complete IT investment management
President: Nancy Gordon

2236 Ideal Industries
The Electricity Forum
Ste. 302
One Franklin Square
Geneva, NY 14456 315-789-8323
Fax: 315-789-8940
forum1@verizon.net
www.electricityforum.com
Produces electrical test equipment and electrical transformers
President: R.W. Hurst
randy@electricityforum.com
VP, Print/Digital Advertising: Barbara John
forum1@verizon.net

2237 Inca TV Lifts
Inca
1648 West 134th Street
Gardena, CA 90249-2014 310-808-0001
877-961-4622
Fax: 310-808-9092
inca@inca-tvlifts.com
tvlifts-inca.com
TV and projector lifts, plasma screen lifts, automatic and manual swivels, pullout and swivels, door openers, infrared controls
President: George Roberts
In Business: 46 years
Number of Employees: 35
Sales Volume: $20MM to $50MM

2238 Jameco Electronics
Jameco Electronics
1355 Shoreway Road
Belmont, CA 94002 650-592-8097
800-831-4242
Fax: 650-592-2503
Sales@jameco.com
www.jameco.com
Electronic & computer parts and components
President: Phil Greeves
CFO: Ester Baldovino
Marketing Manager: Greg Harris
CEO: James Farrey
VP: Gil Orozco
Director of Information Technology: Matt Smith
Catalog Cost: Free
In Business: 35 years
Number of Employees: 100
Sales Volume: $5 million

2239 KGS Electronics
KGS Electronics
418 East Live Oak Avenue
Arcadia, CA 91006-5619 626-574-1175
Fax: 626-574-0553
info@kgselectronics.com
www.kgselectronics.com
line of airborne 400Hz and 50/60Hz static inverters, voltage/frequency converters, DC to DC power converters, light dimming power supplies and AC to KGS Electronics has full line of airborne 400Hz and
In Business: 56 years
Number of Employees: 120

2240 Kanson Electronics
Kanson Electronics
245 Forrest Avenue
Hohenwald, TN 38462-1120 931-796-3050
800-233-9354
Fax: 931-796-3956
www.issc-kanson.com
Electronic assembly and subassembly systems; industrial solid state controls (ISSC); injection molding (modor)
President: Arthur Filson
Production Manager: Jennifer McDonald
Credit Cards: AMEX; MasterCard; Visa
Catalog Cost: Free
Printing Information: 25 pages on Glossy Stock
Mailing List Information: Names for rent
In Business: 51 years
Number of Employees: 17
Sales Volume: Under $500M

2241 Keithley Instruments
Keithley Instruments
28775 Aurora Road
Cleveland, OH 44139-1891 440-248-0400
800-935-5595
Fax: 440-248-6168
info@keithley.com
www.Keithley.Com
Instruments for electronic measuring testing; Counters, timers, digital multimeters, distortion meters, voltmeters, electrometers, picoammeters, source measure units and more
Chairman: Joseph P Keithley
President: Joseph P Keithley
CFO: Mark J Plush
Marketing Manager: Ellen Modock
VP: Mark J. Plush
CEO: Joseph P Keithley
Mailing List Information: Names for rent
In Business: 55 years
Number of Employees: 698
Sales Volume: Under $500M

2242 Kepco, Inc.
Kepco, Inc.
131-38 Sanford Avenue
Flushing, NY 11355-4245 718-461-7000
Fax: 718-767-1102
hq@kepcopower.com
www.kepcopower.com
Regulated DC power supplies
Chairman: Max Kupferberg
President: Martin Kupferberg
Production Manager: Mark Kupforberg
Catalog Cost: Free
Mailing List Information: Names for rent
In Business: 71 years
Number of Employees: 200
Sales Volume: $26 Million

2243 MECA ELECTRONICS
MECA ELECTRONICS
459 East Main Street
Denville, NJ 7834 973-625-0661
866-444-6322
Fax: 973-625-9277
sales@e-MECA.com
www.rfpartsondemand.com
RF/Microwave equipment including D.A.S. Equipment, Low PIM Products, mmWave, Power Dividers & Combiners, Directional & Hybrid Couplers, Fixed & Variable Attenuators, RF Terminations, Circulators/Isola
Credit Cards: AMEX; MasterCard
Printing Information: 104 pages
In Business: 54 years

2244 Methode Electronics
Methode Electronics
7401 West Wilson Ave
Chicago, IL 60706-4548 708-867-6777
877-316-7700
Fax: 708-867-6999
info@methode.com
www.Methode.Com
Global manufacturer of component and subsystem devices
President: Donald W Duda
Number of Employees: 2876

2245 Mouser Electronics
Mouser Electronics
1000 North Main Street
Mansfield, TX 76063 800-346-6873
817-804-3888
Fax: 817-804-3899
www.mouser.com
Mouser Electronics is a worldwide leading authorized distributor of semiconductors and electronic components and offering includes semiconductors, interconnects, passives, and electromechanical compon
Chairman: Warren Buffett
President: Glenn Smith
Marketing Manager: Kevin Hess
Senior Vice President: Mark Burr-Lonnon
Senior Vice President: Barry McConnell
Vice President: Todd McAtee
Printing Information: 2965 pages
In Business: 42 years

2246 NTE Electronics
NTE ELECTRONICS
44 Farrand Street
Bloomfield, NJ 07003-2597 866-285-3959
Fax: 973-748-6224
custserv@ntepartsdirect.com
www.ntepartsdirect.com
Hookup lines, fusers, capacitors, power cords, cables, wires, transformers and other electronic supplies
President: Andrew Licari
In Business: 36 years

Number of Employees: 50-1
Sales Volume: $20MM to $50MM

2247 Office Access Catalog
Eye Communication Systems Inc
PO Box 620
455 E. Industrial Dr.
Hartland, WI 53029-620   262-367-1240
800-558-2153
Fax: 262-367-1362
www.eyecom.com

Digital retrieval systems, toner, ribbons and
print cartridges

President: John Bessent
Credit Cards: MasterCard; Visa
Catalog Cost: Free
Catalog Circulation: Mailed 4 time(s) per year
to 140M
Average Order Size: $75
Printing Information: 12 pages in 4 colors on
Glossy Stock
Mailing List Information: Names for rent
In Business: 35 years
Number of Employees: 15
Sales Volume: $3MM to $5MM

2248 Office Electronics Buyers Guide
19300 Janacek Court
Brookfield, WI 53045   414-297-9709

Variety of electronics
President: John DeGlopper

2249 Phoenix Contact USA
Phoenix Contact USA
586 Fulling Mill Road
Middletown, PA 17057   717-944-1300
Fax: 717-944-1625
info@phoenixcon.com
www.phoenixcontact.com

Innovative technology and electronics
VP & General Manager: Spencer Bolgard
Director of Information Technology: Betsy
Clark
Director of Supply Chain: Louis Paioletti
In Business: 36 years
Number of Employees: 500
Sales Volume: $10MM to $20MM

2250 Print Products International
Pace Incorporated
255 Air Tool Drive
Southern Pines, NC 28387   910-695-7223
Fax: 910-695-1594
www.paceworldwide.com

Products for the assembly, rework, repair
and testing of printed circuit boards
In Business: 57 years

2251 Pro Sound & Stage Lighting
Pro Sound & Stage Lighting
10743 Walker Street
Cypress, CA 90630-5247   714-891-5914
800-268-5520
Fax: 888-777-5329
www.pssl.com

Pro audio equipment, DJ gear and lighting,
accessories, karaoke and video gear
President: Dave Rice
Credit Cards: AMEX; MasterCard
Catalog Cost: Free
Catalog Circulation: Mailed 1 time(s) per year
Printing Information: 132 pages in 4 colors
Binding: Perfect Bound

2252 R&L Electronics
R&L Electronics
1315 Maple Ave
Hamilton, OH 45011   800-221-7735
Fax: 513-868-6574
sales@randl.com
www.randl.com

Amplifiers Preamps, Antenas, Antenas Accessory, Antenna Mounts, Antena Tuners,
Books, Cable Coax, Radios and many more.

2253 RBE Electronics
RBE Electronics of SD, Inc.
714 Corporation Street
Aberdeen, SD 57401   605-226-2448
800-342-1912
Fax: 605-226-0710
info@rbeelectronics.com

Electronic controls, sensors and timers
President: Roger Ernst
Engineer: Steve Wolff
Credit Cards: MasterCard; Visa
Catalog Cost: Free
In Business: 34 years
Number of Employees: 28
Sales Volume: $1,000,000 - $5,000,000

2254 Renco Electronics
Renco Electronics, Inc.
595 International Place
Rockledge, FL 32955-4200   321-637-1000
800-645-5828
Fax: 321-637-1600
www.rencousa.com

Transformers, inductors, chokes and coils
President: Edward Rensing
Catalog Cost: Free
In Business: 62 years
Number of Employees: 110
Sales Volume: $10,000,000 - $25,000,000

2255 Security Cameras Direct
Security Cameras Direct
11000 N Mopac Expressway
Building 300
Austin, TX 78759   830-401-7000
877-797-7377
Fax: 830-875-9010
www.securitycamerasdirect.com

Complete line of security cameras, CCTV,
Video Security, and IP Surveillance
President: Aaron James
CFO: Laura Parsons
Production Manager: Norman Ragland
VP Sales: Robert Dugan
Regional Sales Manager: Brian Barnhart
Catalog Cost: Free
Printing Information: in 3 colors
In Business: 15 years
Number of Employees: 35
Sales Volume: $6 million

2256 Shakespeare Electronic Products Group
Shakespeare LLC
6111 Shakespeare Road
Columbia, SC 29223   803-227-1590
Fax: 803-419-3099
shakespeare-ce.com/marine

Electronics including antennas, cell phone
products, connectors, adapters, cables and
accessories
President: Jim Bennett
Marketing Manager: Craig Woods
Catalog Cost: Free
Printing Information: in 3 colors
In Business: 118 years

2257 Skyvision
Skyvision
1010 Frontier Dr
Fergus Falls, MN 56537-1023   218-739-5231
800-500-9275
Fax: 218-739-4879
www.skyvision.com

Home security, electronics, communication,
atomic weather stations
President: Del Jose
Catalog Cost: Free
In Business: 31 years

Number of Employees: 25
Sales Volume: $2.2 Million

2258 Smoky Mountain Knife Works
Smoky Mountain Knife Works, Inc.
2320 Winfield Dunn Parkway
P.O. Box 4430
Sevierville, TN 37864   865-453-5871
800-251-9306
Fax: 865-428-5991
help@smkw.com

Knives and accessories for hunting, tacti-
cal-military, cutlery, martial arts, and
camping
President: Kevin Pipes
Catalog Cost: Free
In Business: 45 years

2259 Sony Creative Software
Sony Creative Software Inc
8215 Greenway Blvd
Suite 400
Middleton, WI 53562   608-203-7620
800-577-6642
www.sonycreativesoftware.com

Multimedia creation and production tools;
video and audio, editing, delivery, accesso-
ries
President: Brad Reinke
CFO: Curtis Palmer
Vice President: Bob Phelan
Credit Cards: AMEX; MasterCard
Catalog Cost: Free
Printing Information: 20 pages
In Business: 12 years
Number of Employees: 90
Sales Volume: $35 Million

2260 Stanton Video Services
Stanton Video Services Inc.
2223 E Rose Garden Loop
Phoenix, AZ 85024-4442   602-493-9505
Fax: 602-493-2468
jim@jimmyjib.com
www.jimmyjib.com

Video supplies
President: Jim Stanton
Owner: Lori Stanton
Credit Cards: MasterCard
In Business: 29 years
Number of Employees: 3
Sales Volume: 350K

2261 Sterling Production Control Units
Production Control Units, Inc.
2280 W Dorothy Lane
Dayton, OH 45439-1892   937-299-5594
866-840-2144
Fax: 937-299-3843

Electronic production control units for re-
frigerant and fluid processing systems in a
broad range of industries
President: Thomas H Hodge
Service: Alan Walker
Technicalservice@pcuinc.com
Catalog Cost: Free
In Business: 68 years
Number of Employees: 100
Sales Volume: $10,000,000 - $25,000,000

2262 Strongbox
Strongbox
2234 Wellesley Avenue
Blvd. #198
Los Angeles, CA 90064-2726   310-305-8288
Fax: 310-402-8000
sales@strongboxmarketing.com
www.Rackmountchassis.Com

Rack-mounted enclosures for electronics
Credit Cards: AMEX; MasterCard; Visa
Catalog Cost: Free
Mailing List Information: Names for rent

List Manager: L Martinek
In Business: 16 years
Number of Employees: 4
Sales Volume: Under $500,000

2263 TOMAR Electronics
TOMAR Electronics
2100 W. Obispo Avenue
Gilbert, AR 85233
800-338-3133
480-497-4400
Fax: 800-688-6627
www.tomar.com

Tomar Electronics. Inc. products line inludes lightbars, lightstick and traffic directors, lightheads, controllers and sirens, self-contained systems, vehcile system, scene lights, traffic control, tl

Printing Information: 86 pages
In Business: 47 years

2264 TRS RenTelco
TRS-Ren Telco
1830 West Airfield Drive
PO Box 619260
DFW Airport, TX 75261
972-456-4000
800-874-7123
Fax: 972-456-4002
trs@trs-rentelco.com
www.Trs-Rentelco.Com

Electronic test, measurement and computer equipment

President: Susan Boutwell
CFO: Keith E Pratt
Catalog Cost: Free
In Business: 30 years
Number of Employees: 100-

2265 Transcat
Transcat, Inc.
35 Vantage Point Drive
Rochester, NY 14624
800-828-1470
sales@transcat.com
www.transcat.com

Test, measurement and calibration instruments

Chairman: Carl Sassano
President: Charles Hadeed
Chief Executive Officer: Lee Rudow
Credit Cards: MasterCard
Catalog Cost: Free
Catalog Circulation: Mailed 1 time(s) per year
Printing Information: 169 pages in 4 colors on Glossy Stock
In Business: 52 years
Number of Employees: 313
Sales Volume: $91 Million

2266 WTSmedia Catalog
Wholesale Tape & Supply Company
2841 Hickory Valley Rd
Chattanooga, TN 37421
423-894-9427
888-987-6334
Fax: 423-894-7281
sales@wtsmedia.com
www.wtsmedia.com

CD & DVD recordable media, duplicators, blank audio cassettes, video tapes and a variety of pro audio products

President: Tom Plemons
Marketing Manager: Greg Callaham
President/Finance Executive: Michael Salley
Owner/VP: Diane Salley
Credit Cards: AMEX; MasterCard
Catalog Cost: Free
In Business: 38 years
Number of Employees: 45
Sales Volume: $4.4 Million

Environmental Products
Green Products

2267 Adaptive Seeds
Adaptive Seeds
25079 Brush Creek Rd
Sweet Home, OR 97386
888-900-5235
www.adaptiveseeds.com

Seed varieties.

Credit Cards: AMEX; MasterCard
In Business: 6 years

2268 Alfa Aesar
Alfa Aesar
26 Parkridge Rd
Ward Hill, MA 01835
978-521-6300
Fax: 978-521-6350
info@alfa.com
www.alfa.com

Chemical compounds, pure elements, alloys, analytical products, and precious metal compounds and catalysts

President: Jerry Nenby
Marketing Manager: Fernand Lopes
CEO: Barry Singleif
Purchasing Agent: Patti Ranta
Catalog Cost: Free
In Business: 22 years
Number of Employees: 99
Sales Volume: $18.5 Million

2269 Amazon Exotic Hardwoods
Amazon Exotic Hardwoods
328 Commercial St
Casselberry, FL 32707
407-339-9590
866-339-9596
Fax: 407-339-9906
info@amazonexotichardwoods.com
www.amazonexotichardwoods.com

Domestic and exotic hardwoods, specially cut and prepared for cabinetmakers, carvers, knife makers, musical instrument makers and wood turners

President: James Lie
Credit Cards: AMEX; MasterCard
Catalog Cost: Free
In Business: 12 years
Number of Employees: 1
Sales Volume: $250,000

2270 Ben Meadows
Ben Meadows
P.O. Box 5277
Janesville, WI 53547-5277
608-373-2796
800-241-6401
Fax: 800-628-2068
productpros@benmeadows.com
www.benmeadows.com

Forestry supplies and equipment, fire and rescue gear, safety equipment, outdoor clothing and footwear, soil, weather and mapping equipment, outdoor gear

Customer Service Supervisor: Lynette Erickson
Credit Cards: AMEX; MasterCard
Catalog Cost: Free
Catalog Circulation: Mailed 1 time(s) per year
Printing Information: 572 pages in 4 colors
In Business: 61 years

2271 Caig Laboratories
CAIG Laboratories, Inc.
12200 Thatcher Court
Poway, CA 92064-6876
858-486-8388
800-224-4123
Fax: 858-486-8398
info@caig.com
www.Caig.Com

Environmentally safe contact cleaners, degreasers, contact lubricants

President: Mark Lohkemper
In Business: 59 years
Sales Volume: $10MM to $20MM

2272 Complete Environmental Products
Complete Environmental Products
3500 Pasadena Freeway
Pasadena, TX 77503
713-921-7900
800-444-4237
Fax: 713-921-7967
customer_service@cepsorbents.com
www.cepsorbents.com

Quality absorbents, secondary containment, spill kits and more.

In Business: 21 years

2273 Davis Instruments
Davis
3465 Diablo Ave
Hayward, CA 94545-2778
510-732-9229
800-678-3669
Fax: 510-670-0589
sales@davisnet.com
www.davisnet.com

Weathering monitoring stations, vehicle monitoring stations, marine products

President: Bob Selig
CFO: Susan Tatum
Credit Cards: MasterCard; Visa
Catalog Cost: Free
Average Order Size: $700
Mailing List Information: Names for rent
In Business: 52 years
Number of Employees: 100
Sales Volume: $12.30

2274 Erik Organic Dining Table Catalog
Erik Organic
3125 East 78th Street
Inver Grove Heights, MN 55076
888-900-5235
Fax: 877-365-7372
www.erikorganic.com

Furniture created from genuine Midwestern hardwoods.

Credit Cards: AMEX; MasterCard

2275 Gaiam Living
Gaiam
833 W. South Boulder Road
P.O. Box 3095
Louisville, CO 80027-2452
303-222-3719
877-989-6321
Fax: 303-222-3750
customerservice@gaiam.com
www.gaiam.com

Organic/natural fiber bedding, bath and clothing; energy-saving products; earth-friendly cleaners; air & water filters; eco-conscious furnishings; fair trade decor & jewelry; natural wellness tools

President: Lynn Powers
CFO: Janet Mathews
CEO: Jirka Rysavy
Manager: Kraig Corbin
Director of Customer Relations: Christopher Fisher
Credit Cards: AMEX; MasterCard; Visa
Catalog Cost: Free
Catalog Circulation: Mailed 4 time(s) per year
Printing Information: in 4 colors
In Business: 20 years

2276 Heifer International
Heifer International
One World Avenue
PO Box 8058
Little Rock, AR 72202
855-948-6437
Fax: 501-907-2902
info@heifer.org
www.heifer.org

Contribute to sustainable development by helping to send a heifer, llama, water buffalo, pigs, rabbits, chicks or other gifts that will assist in moving a community from poverty to self-reliance

Founder: Dan West
Credit Cards: AMEX; MasterCard
Printing Information: in 4 colors on Glossy Stock

2277 Indigo Wild
Indigo Wild
3125 Wyandotte Street
Kansas City, MO 64111   800-361-5686
                              Fax: 816-221-4035
                              www.indigowild.com

All natural bath and body products such as soaps, bath salts, lotions, balms, and oils

Catalog Cost: Free

2278 Lehman's Non Electric Catalog
Lehman's
PO Box 270
Kidron, OH 44636   330-828-8828
                             888-438-5346
                             Fax: 330-828-8270
                             info@lehmans.com
                             www.lehmans.com

Non-electric appliances, oil lamps, gas refrigerators, wood stoves, old fashioned toys, kitchenware, butchering, cheese making, water pumps, butter making, water filters, camping, gardening, farming

Chairman: Jay Lehman
President: Galen Lehman
Marketing Manager: Glenda Lehman Ervin
Credit Cards: MasterCard; Visa; Discover
Catalog Cost: $3
Mailing List Information: Names for rent
In Business: 59 years
Number of Employees: 90

2279 Lesman Instrument
Lesman
135 Bernice Dr
Bensenville, IL 60106-3366   630-595-8400
                               800-953-7626
                               Fax: 630-595-2386
                               sales@lesman.com
                               www.lesman.com

Temperature instruments, thermometers and environmental and wastewater level instruments

President: Michael De Lacluyse
CFO: Mike Heatherly
Marketing Manager: Beth Rose
Catalog Cost: Free
In Business: 50 years
Number of Employees: 33
Sales Volume: $12.5 Million

2280 PCS Catalog
Perma-Chink Systems
17635 NE 67th Ct
Redmond, WA 98052   888-838-5070
                            Fax: 425-869-0107
                            www.pcsproducts.com

Complete line of environmentally conscious sealants, stains and preservatives available; uniquely designed for log homes

President: Rich Dunstan
Production Manager: Tony Huddleston
General Manager/Operations Manager: Terry Hofrichter
Credit Cards: MasterCard; Visa
Catalog Cost: Free
Catalog Circulation: to 10M+
Printing Information: 20 pages in 4 colors on Matte Stock
Mailing List Information: Names for rent
In Business: 34 years

Number of Employees: 50
Sales Volume: $6.6 Million

2281 Seeds from Italy
Seeds from Italy
PO Box 3908
Lawrence, KS 66046   785-748-0959
                            Fax: 785-748-0609
                            www.growitalian.com

Packaged vegetable seeds.

In Business: 14 years

2282 Sequoyah Soaps
Sequoyah Soaps
PO Box 292
Washington, NY 11050   516-767-1740
                            www.sequoyahsoaps.com

2283 Sun-Mar Corporation
Sun-Mar Corp.
600 Main Street
Tonawanda, NY 14150   905-332-1314
                            800-461-2461
                            Fax: 905-332-1315
                            compost@sun-mar.com
                            www.sun-mar.com

Composting toilet systems

Manager: Dennis Forster
Credit Cards: AMEX; MasterCard; Visa
Catalog Cost: Free
Printing Information: on Glossy Stock
In Business: 44 years
Number of Employees: 30
Sales Volume: $8 Million

2284 Tomorrow's World Catalog
Organic Comfort Zone
201 W Ocean View Ave.
Norfolk, VA 23503-1504   757-480-8500
                            800-229-7571
                            Fax: 757-480-3148
                            www.tomorrowsworld.Com

Natural fashions, men and women, organic cotton, hemp, wool and flax

Chairman: Richard Hahn
President: Cheryl Hahn
Credit Cards: AMEX; MasterCard; Visa
Catalog Cost: $2
Catalog Circulation: Mailed 12 time(s) per year to 1M
Average Order Size: $85
Printing Information: 64 pages in 4 colors on Matte Stock
Press: Web Press
Binding: Saddle Stitched
In Business: 24 years
Number of Employees: 6
Sales Volume: $500,000- 1 Million

2285 Water Quality Testing Products
LaMotte Company
802 Washington Ave
PO Box 329
Chestertown, MD 21620   410-778-3100
                            800-344-3100
                            Fax: 410-778-6394
                            mkt@lamotte.com
                            www.lamotte.com

Waste plant treatment products; test kits, instruments and reagants for water analysis

President: David LaMotte
Marketing Manager: James Moore
Production Manager: Libby Woolever
Catalog Circulation: Mailed 1 time(s) per year to 5000
Printing Information: 100 pages in 4 colors on Glossy Stock
Press: Sheetfed Press
Binding: Perfect Bound
Mailing List Information: Names for rent
In Business: 96 years
Number of Employees: 120

2286 Worms Way Catalog
Worms Way
7850 North State Road 37
Bloomington, IN 47404   812-876-6450
                            800-274-9676
                            Fax: 800-466-0795
                            sales@wormsway.com

Organic fertilizers, pest control products and greenhouses

President: Martin Heydt
Credit Cards: AMEX; MasterCard
Catalog Cost: Free
In Business: 29 years
Sales Volume: $20MM to $50MM

Film, Video & Recordings
CDs, Audio Cassettes & Records

2287 2015 Music Catalog
Concordia Publishing House
3558 South Jefferson
St. Louis, MO 63118   314-268-1000
                            800-325-3040
                            www.cph.org

Concordia Publishing House will develop, produce, market and distribute products and services that are faithful to the Scriptures and the Lutheran Confessions and which will effectively serve such pro

President: Dr. Bruce G. Kintz
Vice President & Corporate Counsel: Jonathan D. Schultz
jonathan.schultz@cph.org
Director of Graphic Design: Tim Agnew
tim.agnew@cph.org
In Business: 146 years

2288 APSCO Catalog
Antique Phonograph Supply Company
PO Box 123
7994 CR 10
Davenport Center, NY 13751   607-278-6218
                               Fax: 607-278-6218
                               apsco@antiquephono.com
                               www.antiquephono.com

Repairs, rebuilds and parts of antique phonographs

President: Patricia Valente
Credit Cards: MasterCard
Catalog Cost: $7

2289 Acoustic Sounds
Acoustic Sounds, Inc.
605 W. North Street
PO Box 1905
Salina, KS 67402-1905   785-825-8609
                            888-926-2564
                            Fax: 785-825-0156
                            www.acousticsounds.com

LPs, CDs, DVDs

President: Chad Kassem
Credit Cards: AMEX; MasterCard
Catalog Cost: Free
Catalog Circulation: Mailed 4 time(s) per year to 50000
Printing Information: 129 pages in 4 colors on Glossy Stock
Press: Web Press
Binding: Saddle Stitched
In Business: 20 years
Number of Employees: 18

2290 Arcal
Arcal LLC
PO Box 3397
Fullerton, CA 92834   800-272-2591
                            Fax: 714-871-0453
                            info@cvcaudiovideo.com
                            www.arcal.com

Recording and duplicating supplies

Credit Cards: MasterCard
In Business: 55 years

2291 At Peace Media
At Peace Media LLC
1117 E Putnam Avenue #246
Riverside, CT 06878   914-481-5250
                            800-619-1410
                        Fax: 914-840-1344
john@atpeacemedia.com
www.atpeacemedia.com

Music, DVDs, yoga and massage enhancing oils

President: John Gelb
john@atpeacemedia.com
Executive Producer: Sherry Donovan
Assistant Producer: Stephanie Carbino
Catalog Cost: Free

2292 Bible Study Planning Guide
Precept Ministries International
7324 Noah Reid Road
P.O. Box 182218
Chattanooga, TN 37422   423-892-6814
                            800-763-8280
                        Fax: 423-894-2449
info@precept.org
www.precept.org

Bible study materials and Christian recordings

President: David Arthur
Executive VP: Kay Arthur
Credit Cards: AMEX; MasterCard
Catalog Cost: Free
Catalog Circulation: Mailed 2 time(s) per year to 15000
Average Order Size: $9
Printing Information: 40 pages in 4 colors on Glossy Stock
Press: Web Press
Binding: Saddle Stitched
Mailing List Information: Names for rent
In Business: 47 years
Number of Employees: 130
Sales Volume: $5MM to $10MM

2293 Cambridge Educational Catalog
Films Media Group
132 West 31st Street
17th Floor
New York, NY 10001   800-322-8755
                        Fax: 800-678-3633
custserv@films.com
www.films.com

Business videos, software, cd-rom, books and posters

Credit Cards: MasterCard; Visa
Catalog Circulation: to 160m
Printing Information: 48 pages
In Business: 17 years
Number of Employees: 40

2294 Canyon Records
Canyon Records
3131 West Clarendon Avenue
Phoenix, AZ 85017   602-279-5941
                            800-268-1141
                        Fax: 602-279-9233
canyon@canyonrecords.com
www.canyonrecords.com

Production and distribution of traditional and contemporary native american music

President: Robert Doyle
Sales Volume: $1MM to $3MM

2295 Collectibles Records
Oldies.com
P.O. Box 77
Narberth, PA 19072   610-649-7565
                            800-336-4627
                        Fax: 610-649-0315
www.oldies.com

Rhythm and blues records from the 1970's

President: Jerry Greene
Credit Cards: AMEX; MasterCard; Visa
Catalog Cost: Free
Catalog Circulation: Mailed 2 time(s) per year
Average Order Size: $200
Printing Information: 42 pages in 2 colors on Matte Stock
Binding: Folded
In Business: 37 years
Sales Volume: $20MM to $50MM

2296 Country Music Greats
Catalog Music Corporation
PO Box 159297
Nashville, TN 37215-9297   615-298-4338
                            800-774-8204
www.purecountrymusic.com

Hard to find classic country music

President: Martin Davis
Credit Cards: AMEX; MasterCard
Catalog Cost: Free
Number of Employees: 30
Sales Volume: $4.3 Million

2297 Critics' Choice Music
Critics' Choice Music
17822 Gillette Avenue
Suite A
Irvine, CA 92614   630-919-2247
                            800-923-1122
www.ccmusic.com

Classic and modern music on CD, vinyl, DVD and Blur-ray

Chief Executive Officer: Jeff Walker
Credit Cards: AMEX; MasterCard
Catalog Cost: Free

2298 Critics' Choice Video
Critics' Choice Video
17822 Gillette Avenue
Suite A
Irvine, CA 92614   630-919-2246
                            800-367-7765
www.ccvideo.com

Classic film and television series on DVD and Blu-ray, books and music

Chief Executive Officer: Jeff Walker
Credit Cards: AMEX; MasterCard
Catalog Cost: Free

2299 Disc Makers
Disc Makers
150 West 25th St., Suite #402
New York, NY 10001   800-468-9353
                        Fax: 856-661-3450
www.discmakers.com

CD and DVD manufacturer, services, blank media, duplicators, and supplies

President: Tony van Veen
Catalog Cost: Free
In Business: 69 years

2300 Edward R Hamilton Bookseller
Edward R Hamilton Bookseller
PO Box 15
Falls Village, CT 06031-15   800-677-3483
comments@edwardrhamilton.com
www.edwardrhamilton.com

Books and audio cassettes on history, politics, religion, travel, sports, wildlife and pets, gardening, art and architecture, fiction, cookbooks, computer, children's books and more at bargain prices

President: Edward R Hamilton
Catalog Cost: Free
Catalog Circulation: Mailed 4 time(s) per year
Printing Information: 98 pages in 1 color on Newsprint
Press: Web Press
Binding: Perfect Bound

2301 Effective Learning Systems
ELS Audio Publishing, LLC
5108 W 74th Street
#390160
Minneapolis, MN 55439   952-943-1660
                            800-966-0443
                        Fax: 952-943-1665
info@effectivelearning.com
www.effectivelearning.com

Self-help and relaxation books and audio cassettes

President: Jeffrey Griswold
Credit Cards: MasterCard; Visa
Catalog Cost: Free
Printing Information: 32 pages in 4 colors
Mailing List Information: Names for rent
In Business: 26 years
Number of Employees: 10
Sales Volume: $500M to $1MM

2302 Gentle Wind
Gentle Wind
PO Box 3103
Albany, NY 12203-103   518-482-9023
                            888-386-7664
hello@gentlewind.com
www.gentlewind.com

Children's audiotapes

President: Jill Person
Credit Cards: MasterCard; Visa
Catalog Circulation: Mailed 1 time(s) per year to 10000
Average Order Size: $45
Printing Information: 16 pages in 4 colors on Glossy Stock
Binding: Saddle Stitched
Number of Employees: 3
Sales Volume: Under $500M

2303 Harvard Square Records
Harvard Square Records
PO Box 19517
Austin, TX 78760   877-465-7669
lpnow@yahoo.com
www.lpnow.com

Lp's and cassettes

President: Barry D Mayer
Credit Cards: MasterCard; Visa
Catalog Cost: $2
Catalog Circulation: Mailed 2 time(s) per year to 100
Average Order Size: $40
Printing Information: 56 pages in 2 colors on Newsprint
Press: Web Press
Binding: Perfect Bound
Mailing List Information: Names for rent
List Company: George Mann
609-443-1330
In Business: 20 years
Number of Employees: 2
Sales Volume: $500M to $1MM

2304 Island Cases
Island Cases
1121-20 Lincoln Avenue
Holbrook, NY 11741-2264   631-563-0633
                            800-343-1433
                        Fax: 631-563-1390
www.islandcases.com

Cases and custom cases for CD's & LP's, single mixer and rack mixer cases

President: Frank Maiella
Credit Cards: AMEX; MasterCard; Visa
Printing Information: 82 pages
Sales Volume: $ 1-3 Million

2305 Kimbo Educational

Kimbo
P.O. Box 477
Long Branch, NJ 07740
732-229-4949
800-631-2187
service@kimboed.com
www.kimboed.com

Educational cds and videos for early childhood

President: Jim Kimble
Marketing Manager: Elaine Murphy
Vice President: Jeffrey Kimble
Founder: Bob Kimble
Founder: Gert Kimble
Buyers: Amy Laufer
Credit Cards: MasterCard; Visa
Catalog Cost: Free
Catalog Circulation: Mailed 4 time(s) per year to 400K
Average Order Size: $60
Printing Information: 32 pages in 4 colors on Glossy Stock
Press: Web Press
Binding: Saddle Stitched
Mailing List Information: Names for rent
In Business: 59 years
Number of Employees: 25
Sales Volume: $3MM to $5MM

2306 Lots and Lots of DVD Gifts for Kids

Marshall Publishing & Promotions Inc
123 S Hough Street
Barrington, IL 60010
224-238-3530
888-300-3455
Fax: 224-238-3531
info@marshallpublishinginc.com
www.marshallpublishinginc.com

Kid's videos, DVDs, CDs and books

Credit Cards: AMEX; MasterCard
Catalog Cost: Free
Catalog Circulation: Mailed 1 time(s) per year
Average Order Size: $50
Printing Information: 10 pages in 4 colors on Glossy Stock
Press: Web Press
Binding: Folded
Mailing List Information: Names for rent
List Manager: Glaser Direct
In Business: 8 years
Number of Employees: 1
Sales Volume: $500M to $1MM

2307 Music Direct

Music Direct
1811 W Bryn Mawr Ave
Chicago, IL 60660
312-433-0200
800-449-8333
Fax: 312-433-0011
www.musicdirect.com

Audio equipment, record albums, and accessories

President: Jim Davis
Sales Volume: $3MM to $5MM

2308 National Association of Printers & Lithographers

Epicomm
One Meadowlands Plaza
Suite 1511
East Rutherford, NJ 07073
201-634-9600
800-642-6275
Fax: 201-634-0324
epicomm.org

Information on books and products produced by NAPL to assist printers and print salespeople

Chairman: Tom Duchene
President: Ken Garner
kgarner@epicomm.org
CFO: Dean D'Ambrosi
Marketing Manager: Samantha Lake
SVP/Managing Director: Mike Philie
mphilie@epicomm.org

SVP/Chief Economist: Andrew D. Paparozzi
apaparozzi@epicomm.org
Director of Marketing: Samantha Lake
slake@epicomm.org
Printing Information: 6 pages in 2 colors
In Business: 1 years

2309 Native American Collection

Cherokee Publications
PO Box 430
Cherokee, NC 28719
828-488-8856
800-948-3161
Fax: 828-488-6934
www.cherokeepublications.net

Videos, tapes and books on Native Americana

Credit Cards: MasterCard; Visa
Catalog Cost: $1
In Business: 58 years
Number of Employees: 4
Sales Volume: Under $500M

2310 Power & Music

Power & Music
380 North 200 West
Suite 105
Bountiful, UT 84010-3030
801-292-2418
800-777-2328
Fax: 801-292-2462
www.powermusic.com

Professional fitness, mind and body, dance and cheer music

President: Richard Petty
Production Manager: Michial Piptone
Credit Cards: AMEX; MasterCard
Catalog Cost: Free
Printing Information: 64 pages
Number of Employees: 18
Sales Volume: $1MM to $3MM

2311 Qualiton Imports

Qualiton Imports
2402 40th Ave
Long Island City, NY 11101-3908 718-937-8515
Fax: 718-729-3239
www.Qualiton.Com

Rare music on lps and cds

President: Otto Quittner
Marketing Manager: Angela Cuciniello
Credit Cards: MasterCard
Catalog Circulation: Mailed 1 time(s) per year
Printing Information: 16 pages
Binding: Saddle Stitched
Mailing List Information: Names for rent
Number of Employees: 30
Sales Volume: $5MM to $10MM

2312 Radio Spirits

Radio Spirits
PO Box 3107
Wallingford, CT 06492
203-265-8044
www.radiospirits.com

Old-time pre-recorded audio and video products

President: Carl Amari

2313 Record Roundup

Rounders
One Rounder Way
Burlington, MA 01803
617-354-0700
800-768-6337
Fax: 617-354-4840
info@rounder.com
www.rounder.com

Compact discs, LP's, and cassettes

President: Dennis MacDonald
Marketing Manager: Mike Annis
Credit Cards: MasterCard
Catalog Cost: $2
Catalog Circulation: Mailed 1 time(s) per year
Printing Information: 58 pages

Binding: Saddle Stitched
In Business: 45 years

2314 Rediscover Music

Rediscover Music
705 S Washington Street
Suite 3
Naperville, IL 60540
630-305-0770
800-232-7328
Fax: 630-305-0782

Classic rock, jazz and folk music cds and dvds

President: Allan Shaw
allan@folkera.com
Production Manager: Allan Shaw
Fulfillment: Kerry Loudon
International Marketing Manager: Allan Shaw
Credit Cards: AMEX; MasterCard
Catalog Cost: Free
Catalog Circulation: Mailed 26 time(s) per year to 500M
Printing Information: 80 pages in 1 color on Newsprint
Binding: Saddle Stitched
Mailing List Information: Names for rent
List Manager: Allan Shaw
In Business: 20 years
Number of Employees: 4
Sales Volume: $500M to $1MM

2315 Rego Irish Records and Tapes

Rego Irish Records
PO Box 1515
Green Island, NY 12183
289-002-5020
800-458-7346
www.regorecords.com

Irish records and tapes

Credit Cards: AMEX; MasterCard; Visa
Catalog Cost: Free
Catalog Circulation: Mailed 2 time(s) per year to 500
Average Order Size: $40
Printing Information: 64 pages in 4 colors on Glossy Stock
Press: Web Press
Binding: Perfect Bound
Mailing List Information: Names for rent
In Business: 46 years
Number of Employees: 15
Sales Volume: $1MM to $3MM

2316 SISU Home Entertainment/Sifriyat Ami

Kol Ami, Inc.
22-19 41st Avenue
Suite 509
Long Island City, NY 11101
212-947-7888
800-223-7478
Fax: 212-947-8388
sisu@sisuent.com
www.sisuent.com

Jewish and Israeli music, videos, DVDs, books and CD-roms

President: Haim Scheininger
Credit Cards: AMEX; MasterCard
Catalog Circulation: Mailed 4 time(s) per year to 250M
Average Order Size: $60
Printing Information: 32 pages in 4 colors on Matte Stock
Press: Web Press
Binding: Saddle Stitched
Mailing List Information: Names for rent
In Business: 27 years
Number of Employees: 6
Sales Volume: $500,000

2317 Self Healing Through Mind Body Medicine

Emmett Miller MD
P.O. 803
Nevada City, CA 95959
530-478-1807
800-528-2737
Fax: 530-478-0160
www.drmiller.com

Self healing tapes, CDs, books and training materials

President: Emmett Miller, MD
Production Manager: Susan McGuire
productmanager@drmiller.com
Fulfillment: Dr. Miller
General Manager: Aeron Miller
Client/Patient Services: Lisa Gorbet
Social Media Manager: Cabrina Channing
Credit Cards: MasterCard
Catalog Cost: Free
Printing Information: 16 pages in 3 colors
Press: Web Press
Mailing List Information: Names for rent
In Business: 40 years
Sales Volume: Under $500M

2318 Sounds True
Sounds True inc
413 S Arthur Avenue
Louisville, CO 80027   303-665-3151
                         800-333-9185
                    Fax: 303-665-5292
                 support@soundstrue.com
                    www.soundstrue.com

Original spokenword, audio programs, instruction, video, world music, spirituality, health, psychology, meditation and yoga

President: Tami Simon
Electronic Producer: Evan Bartholomew
Physian: Rachel Cariton Abrams
Forecaster: Patricia Aburdene
Buyers: Matt Licata
Credit Cards: MasterCard; Visa
Catalog Cost: Free
Catalog Circulation: Mailed 6 time(s) per year to 15000
Printing Information: 48 pages in 4 colors on Glossy Stock
Press: Web Press
Binding: Saddle Stitched
Mailing List Information: Names for rent
List Company: Pacific Lists
In Business: 30 years
Number of Employees: 80
Sales Volume: $3MM to $5MM

2319 The Video Collection
The Video Collection
17822 Gillette Avenue
Suite A
Irvine, CA 92614   630-919-2248
                      800-538-5856
              www.videocollection.com

Classic film and TV series on DVD and Blu-ray

Chief Executive Officer: Jeff Walker
Credit Cards: AMEX; MasterCard
Catalog Cost: Free

2320 VAI Direct
Video Artists International
109 Wheeler Avenue
Pleasantville, NY 10570   914-769-3691
                            800-477-7146
                       Fax: 914-769-5407
                  inquiries@vaimusic.com
                      www.vaimusic.com

Rare repertoire, historic performances, great singers and famous instrumentalists on CD and video; opera, vocal and instrumental recitals; dance on video

President: Ernest Gilbert
Catalog Cost: Free
Catalog Circulation: Mailed 1 time(s) per year to 10000
Average Order Size: $30
Printing Information: 32 pages in 4 colors on Newsprint
Press: Sheetfed Press
Binding: Folded
Mailing List Information: Names for rent
In Business: 32 years

Number of Employees: 7
Sales Volume: $500M to $1MM

2321 Whole World Music Catalog
Cafe Lango
2351 Boston Post Rd #101
Guilford, CT 06437   203-453-1456
                        800-243-1234
                   Fax: 203-453-5110
                    www.audioforum.com

Audio and video cassettes of children's music and other music from around the world

President: Jeffrey Norton
CFO: Bruce Salender
Marketing Manager: Sharon Eaton
Production Manager: Elizabeth Lockwood
Buyers: Janis Yates
Credit Cards: AMEX; MasterCard; Visa; Discover
Catalog Cost: Free
Catalog Circulation: Mailed 2 time(s) per year
Printing Information: 52 pages in 4 colors on Glossy Stock
Press: Web Press
Binding: Saddle Stitched
Mailing List Information: Names for rent
List Company: Allan Drey
330 N Michigan Avenue
Chicago, IL 60601
In Business: 30 years
Number of Employees: 30
Sales Volume: $1MM to $3MM

Video Cassettes & Discs

2322 ABC Feelings
Adage Publications/ABC Feelings
PO Box 7280
Ketchum, ID 83340   208-788-5399
                   Fax: 208-788-4195
                 info@abcfeelings.com
                    www.abcfeelings.com

Catalog of children's books, tapes, cards and games to increase their self esteem and build a strong foundation for character.

President: Alexandra Delis Abrams
Catalog Cost: Free
Mailing List Information: Names for rent
In Business: 20 years
Sales Volume: Under $500M

2323 Aging Resources
Attainment Company Inc
504 Commerce Parkway
PO Box 930160
Verona, WI 53593-160   608-845-7880
                          800-327-4269
                     Fax: 608-845-8040
          customerservice@attainmentcompany.com
                 www.attainmentcompany.com

Senior education books and DVDs to improve mental health

President: Don Bastian
Director of Software Development: Scott Meister
scott@attainmentcompany.com
Administrative Supervisor: Theresa O'Connor
theresa@attainmentcompany.com
Graphic Designer: Sherry Pribbenow
sherry@attainmentcompany.com
Credit Cards: MasterCard; Visa
Catalog Cost: Free
In Business: 36 years
Number of Employees: 23

2324 Art Video Productions
Art Video Productions
5777 Azalea Drive
Grants Pass, OR 97526   541-479-7140
                           800-576-1482
                  support@artvideo.com
                     www.artvideo.com

Art video tapes

President: Harold Reed
Credit Cards: AMEX; MasterCard; Visa
Catalog Cost: Free
Catalog Circulation: Mailed 4 time(s) per year
Printing Information: 10 pages in 1 color
In Business: 30 years
Number of Employees: 2
Sales Volume: Under $500M

2325 Baby-Go-To-Sleep Parenting Resources
Audio-Therapy Innovations, Inc
PO Box 550
Colorado Springs, CO 80901   719-473-0100
                                800-537-7748
                       terry@audiotherapy.com
                       www.babygotosleep.com

Music therapy recordings to help baby stop crying and sleep all night, soothes colic

President: Terry R Woodford
Credit Cards: AMEX; MasterCard
Catalog Cost: Free
Average Order Size: $28
Printing Information: 12 pages in 4 colors on Glossy Stock
Binding: Saddle Stitched
Mailing List Information: Names for rent
In Business: 30 years
Number of Employees: 9

2326 CBD Kid's
Christian Book Distributors
140 Summit St.
Peabody, MA 01960   800-247-4784
           customer.service@christianbook.com
                    www.christianbook.com

Toys, games, DVDs, books, crafts and activities.

President: Ray Hendrickson
Catalog Cost: Free
Mailing List Information: Names for rent
In Business: 39 years
Number of Employees: 500

2327 CQ VHF Ham Radio Magazine
CQ VHF
25 Newbridge Road
Hicksville, NY 11801-2887   516-681-2922
                               800-853-9797
                          Fax: 516-681-2926
         cqcomm.com/cq_portal_corp_contact.html

A wide selection of radio books, videos, CDs and CQ calendars

President: Richard Ross
Marketing Manager: Don Allen, Advertising Manager
Business Manager: Dorothy Kehrwieder
Editorial Director: Richard S. Moseson
Art Director: Elizabeth Ryan
Catalog Circulation: Mailed 4 time(s) per year
Printing Information: in 4 colors
In Business: 30 years
Sales Volume: $10MM to $20MM

2328 Captain Bijou
Captain Bijou
PO Box 7307
Houston, TX 77248-7307   713-864-8101
                       Fax: 713-863-1467
                  info@captainbijou.com
                    www.captainbijou.com

Videos of old shows and movies

President: Earl Blair
Marketing Manager: Leigh Steovall
Catalog Circulation: to 50000
Printing Information: 180 pages in 4 colors on Matte Stock
Press: Offset Press
In Business: 20 years

2329 English as a Second Language
AudioForum
175 Copse Road
Madison, CT 06443-2272   203-245-0195
                                800-243-1234
                            Fax: 888-453-4329
                            www.audioforum.com

Self-instructional and classroom audio and video materials for learning to speak English as another language

President: Jeffrey Norton
CFO: Bruce Salendar
Marketing Manager: Arthur Townes
Production Manager: Elizabeth Lockwood
Buyers: Janis Yates, VP
Credit Cards: AMEX; MasterCard; Visa; Discover
Catalog Cost: Free
Catalog Circulation: Mailed 4 time(s) per year
Printing Information: 23 pages in 2 colors on Glossy Stock
Press: Web Press
Binding: Folded
Mailing List Information: Names for rent
List Company: Statistics
In Business: 32 years
Number of Employees: 30
Sales Volume: $1MM to $3MM

2330 Entertainment You Can Believe In
CCC of America
102 Decker Court Suite #204
Irving, TX 75062   800-935-2222
       customerservice@cccofamerica.com
       www.cccofamerica.com

Wholesome family entertainment videos

President: Mario Skertchly
Credit Cards: AMEX; MasterCard; Visa
Catalog Circulation: Mailed 2 time(s) per year to 50000
Printing Information: 4 pages in 4 colors on Glossy Stock
Press: Web Press
Binding: Saddle Stitched
Mailing List Information: Names for rent
Number of Employees: 35
Sales Volume: $5MM to $10MM

2331 Homespun Music Instruction
Homespun Tapes
Woodstock NY   800-338-2737
                  Fax: 845-246-5282
                  www.homespun.com

Instructional books, CDs, DVDs, and supplies to learn how to play a variety of instruments

President: Happy Traum
Co-Founder/Vice President: Jane Traum
Office Manager: Susan Robinson
Customer Service/Production Assoc.: Joyce Rado
Catalog Cost: Free
In Business: 48 years

2332 JMJ Religious Books
JMJ Religious Books
227 S Main St
PO Box 15
Necedah, WI 54646   608-565-2516
                       Fax: 608-565-8045
                       jmjbookco@tds.net
                       stores.jmjrelbooks.com

Bible, religious books, cd, dvds, books, and many more.

2333 Kultur Performing Arts DVD's
Kultur Films
195 Highway 36
PO Box 755
Forked River, NJ 08731   888-329-2580
                         support@kultur.com
                         www.kulturvideo.com

Performing arts, visual arts, history and literature videos

Chairman: Dennis M Hedlund
Marketing Manager: John Winfrey
Credit Cards: AMEX; MasterCard
Catalog Cost: Free
Catalog Circulation: Mailed 2 time(s) per year
Printing Information: 32 pages in 4 colors on Glossy Stock
Press: Web Press
Binding: Saddle Stitched
Mailing List Information: Names for rent
In Business: 26 years
Number of Employees: 25

2334 Malaco Records
Malaco Records
3023 West Northside Drive
Jackson, MS 38213   601-982-4522
                        800-272-7936
                    Fax: 601-982-4528
                    www.malaco.com

In Business: 47 years

2335 Military Video
PO Box 4470
Cave Creek, AZ 85327-4470   480-488-1377
                            Fax: 480-488-1316

Military videos ￼

Catalog Cost: $2
Printing Information: 60 pages

2336 Monastery Store
Dharma Communications
831 Plank Road
PO Box 156
Mount Tremper, NY 12457   845-688-7993
                          Fax: 845-688-7995
                          support@dharma.net

Meditation cushions, clothing, books, DVDs, CDs, MP3s and artwork

2337 Movies Unlimited
Movies Unlimited
3015 Darnell Road
Philadelphia, PA 19154-3201   215-637-4444
                              800-668-4344
                          Fax: 215-637-2350
               movies@moviesunlimited.com
               www.moviesunlimited.com

Catalog describes virtually every movie available on video from early silent classics to new releases

President: Jerry Frebowitz
Credit Cards: AMEX; MasterCard; Visa
Catalog Cost: 9.95
Catalog Circulation: Mailed 8 time(s) per year
Printing Information: 800 pages in 2 colors on Newsprint
Press: Web Press
Binding: Perfect Bound
Mailing List Information: Names for rent
List Company: The Specialists
In Business: 36 years
Number of Employees: 60
Sales Volume: $500,000

2338 OPTP Tools for Fitness Catalog
OPTP
3800 Annapolis Lane
Suite 165 PO Box 47009
Minneapolis, MN 55447-9   763-553-0452
                          888-819-0121
                      Fax: 763-553-9355
               customerservice@optp.com
               www.optp.com

Books on strengthening, stretching and rehabilitation

President: Shari Schroeder
Marketing Manager: Cathy Lindvall
Owner: Mark Bookhout
VP Administration: Gloria Woog
Business, Finance & Purchasing Dir.: Paul

Youleau
Buyers: Michelle Braun
Credit Cards: AMEX; MasterCard
Catalog Cost: Free
Average Order Size: $50
Printing Information: 100 pages in 4 colors
Binding: Perfect Bound
Mailing List Information: Names for rent
In Business: 42 years
Number of Employees: 23
Sales Volume: $2.9 MM

2339 Pegasus Auto Racing Supplies
Pegasus Auto Racing Supplies
2475 S 179th Street
New Berlin, WI 53146   262-317-1234
                          800-688-6946
                      Fax: 262-317-1201
               CustSvc@PegasusAutoRacing.com
               www.pegasusautoracing.com

Auto racing books and supplies, items for the racer including many unique and hard to find products

Personnel Director: Carla Heitman
Warehouse Manager: Joel Webber
Treasurer: Christopher Heitman
Buyers: Michael Marmurowicz
Credit Cards: AMEX; MasterCard
Catalog Cost: Free
Catalog Circulation: Mailed 1 time(s) per year to 120M
Average Order Size: $170
Printing Information: 164 pages in 1 color on Matte Stock
Press: Web Press
Binding: Perfect Bound
Mailing List Information: Names for rent
In Business: 40 years
Number of Employees: 15
Sales Volume: $5.3 Million

2340 Pelican Publishing
Pelican Publishing Company
1000 Burmaster St
Gretna, LA 70053-2246   504-368-1175
                          800-843-1724
                      Fax: 504-368-1195
               sales@pelicanpub.com
               www.pelicanpub.com

Books and audiocasettes, including the Maverick Guide Series, recent releases, and children's books including Christmas books from the past

President: Milburn Calhoun
Marketing Manager: Kathleen Calhoun
Credit Cards: MasterCard
Catalog Cost: Free
Catalog Circulation: Mailed 3 time(s) per year
Printing Information: 48 pages in 4 colors on Matte Stock
Press: Web Press
Binding: Saddle Stitched
Mailing List Information: Names for rent
In Business: 89 years
Number of Employees: 35
Sales Volume: $5MM to $10MM

2341 Polyline
Polyline Corp.com
845 N Church Ct
Elmhurst, IL 60126-1036   630-993-2700
                          800-701-7689
                      Fax: 800-816-3330
               sales@polylinecorp.com
               www.Polylinecorp.Com

Duplicating, packaging supplies for audio video and cds

President: Michael Schlobohm
Catalog Circulation: Mailed 2 time(s) per year
Printing Information: 40 pages in 2 colors on Glossy Stock
Binding: Saddle Stitched
In Business: 43 years
Number of Employees: 50

2342 Scholar's Bookshelf
The Scholar's Bookshelf
110 Melrich Rd # 5
Cranbury, NJ 08512-3524 609-395-6933
Fax: 609-395-0755
www.Scholarsbookshelf.Com

Books and videos: military, history, fine arts, literature, philosophy, religion, music

President: Abbot Friedland
Fulfillment: Ginny Goss
Buyers: John Breenberg
Loren Hoeuzen
Credit Cards: MasterCard; Visa
Catalog Cost: Free
Catalog Circulation: Mailed 18 time(s) per year to 2.5MM
Average Order Size: $55
Printing Information: 64 pages in 2 colors on Newsprint
Press: Web Press
Binding: Saddle Stitched
Mailing List Information: Names for rent
List Manager: Jeanne Mael
List Company: Conrad Direct
300 Knicker Bocker Road
Cresskill, NJ 07526
In Business: 30 years
Number of Employees: 25
Sales Volume: $1MM to $3MM

2343 VIEW Video
VIEW Video
PO Box 77
Saugerties, NY 12477-4499 845-246-9955
800-843-9843
Fax: 845-246-9966
info@view.com
www.View.Com

Live concerts, documentaries and rare films of jazz musicians and concerts, opera, dance, sports

President: Bob Karcy
CFO: Debbie Foster
Marketing Manager: Joe Knipes
Production Manager: Bob Karcy
bob@view.com
Founder: Bob Karcy
Credit Cards: AMEX; MasterCard; Visa
Catalog Circulation: to 50000
Printing Information: 40 pages on Glossy Stock
Mailing List Information: Names for rent
In Business: 20 years
Number of Employees: 20
Sales Volume: $3MM to $5MM

Fishing & Hunting Products
Ammunition

2344 2015 Nosler Upfront
Nosler Inc
107 SW Columbia St
Bend, OR 97702 800-285-3701
catalog@nosler.com
www.nosler.com

Bullets, rifles, ammunition, brass

Printing Information: 59 pages
In Business: 67 years

2345 Ballistic Products
Ballistic Products
20015 75th Avenue N
Corcoran, MN 55340 763-494-9237
888-273-5623
Fax: 763-494-9236
info@ballisticproducts.com
www.ballisticproducts.com

Shotgun reloading components, information and hunting supplies

President: K D Fackler
Chief Operating Officer: Grant Fackler
General Manager: Shannon Swahn

Credit Cards: AMEX; MasterCard; Visa
Catalog Circulation: Mailed 4 time(s) per year to 200
Average Order Size: $110
Printing Information: 64 pages in 4 colors on Newsprint
Press: Web Press
Binding: Saddle Stitched
Mailing List Information: Names for rent
In Business: 32 years
Number of Employees: 12
Sales Volume: $1.3 Million

2346 Corbin Manufacturing & Supply
Corbin
600 Industrial Circle
PO Box 2659
White City, OR 97503 541-826-5211
Fax: 541-826-8669
sales@corbins.com
www.corbins.com

Bullet making tools and supplies

President: David Corbin
Manager; Treasurer: Katherine Corbin
Credit Cards: MasterCard; Visa
Catalog Circulation: to 25M
Printing Information: 300 pages
In Business: 36 years
Number of Employees: 5
Sales Volume: $450,000

2347 Gamaliel Shooting Supply
Gamaliel Shooting Supply
1497 Fountain Run Road
Gamaliel, KY 42140 270-457-2825
800-356-6230
Fax: 270-457-3974
info@Gamaliel.com
www.Gamaliel.com

Shooting supply

Credit Cards: AMEX; MasterCard

2348 Hornady
Hornady Manufacturing
3625 West Old Potash Highway
Grand Island, NE 68803 308-382-1390
800-338-3220
Fax: 308-382-5761
www.hornady.com

Ammunition and bullets

President: Steve Hornady
Director of Sales: Jason Hornady
Credit Cards: AMEX; MasterCard
Catalog Cost: Free
Catalog Circulation: Mailed 1 time(s) per year
Printing Information: 132 pages in 4 colors
In Business: 68 years

2349 Hunter Dan
Creative Outdoor Products, Inc.
PO Box 103
Greencastle, IN 46135 888-241-HUNT
hunterdan.com

Hunting toys

Printing Information: 6 pages

2350 Lazzeroni
Lazzeroni
P.O. Box 26696
Tucson, AZ 85726 888-492-7247
Fax: 520-624-6202
arms@lazzeroni.com
www.lazzeroni.com

Rifles, ammunition

2351 Midway USA Master
Midway USA Master
5875 W Van Horn Tavern Rd
Columbia, MO 65203-9004 573-445-6363
800-243-3220
Fax: 800-992-8312
larrypotterfield@midwayusa.com
www.midwayusa.com

Ammunition and reloading supplies and equipment

President: Larry W Potterfield
CEO: Larry Potterfield
Credit Cards: AMEX; MasterCard; Visa
Catalog Cost: Free
Catalog Circulation: Mailed 12 time(s) per year
Printing Information: 970 pages in 4 colors on Newsprint
Press: Web Press
Binding: Saddle Stitched
Mailing List Information: Names for rent
In Business: 31 years
Number of Employees: 140

2352 Military & Law Enforcement Product Catalog
Smith & Wesson
2100 Roosevelt Avenue
Springfield, MA 01104 413-781-8300
800-331-0852
Fax: 413-747-3317
www.smith-wesson.com

Firearms and firearm safety/security products

President: P. James Debney
CFO: Jeffrey Buchanan
Credit Cards: AMEX; MasterCard
Catalog Cost: Free
Printing Information: 84 pages in 4 colors
In Business: 165 years

2353 Precision Reloading
Precision Reloading
1700 W Cedar Ave
Suite B
Mitchell, SD 57301 605-996-9984
605-223-0900
Fax: 605-996-9987
sales@precisionreloading.com
www.precisionreloading.com

Hunting and reloading components, shooting supplies and accessories

President: Peter Maffei
Marketing Manager: Cindy Maffei
Credit Cards: MasterCard
Catalog Cost: Free
Catalog Circulation: Mailed 1 time(s) per year to 40m
Average Order Size: $100
Printing Information: 56 pages in 4 colors on Matte Stock
Press: Web Press
Binding: Saddle Stitched
Mailing List Information: Names for rent
In Business: 25 years
Number of Employees: 5
Sales Volume: $280,000

2354 TriStar
TriStar Arms
1816 Linn St.
North Kansas City, MO 64116 816-421-1400
Fax: 816-421-4182
www.tristararms.com

Firearms

In Business: 40+ years

Fishing Equipment & Supplies

2355 2015 Rollie & Helen's Musky Shop
Rollie & Helen's Musky Shop
7542 Hwy. 51 South
Minocqua, WI 54548
715-356-6011
800-453-5224
Fax: 715-356-5719
info@muskyshop.com
www.muskyshop.com

Fishing equipment

2356 Abel
Abel
165 Aviador St.
Camarillo, CA 93010
805-484-8789
info@abelreels.com
www.abelreels.com

Fishing tools, fly reels
Printing Information: 15 pages
In Business: 35 years

2357 Al's Goldfish Lure Company
Al's Goldfish Lure Company
40 Main St
Suite 40-113
Biddeford, ME 4005
Fax: 413-543-3153
www.alsgoldfish.com

Lures
Credit Cards: MasterCard
In Business: 61 years

2358 Anglers Catalog
Silver Creek Press
P.O. Box 993
Eagle, ID 83616
208-378-9536
800-657-8040
Fax: 208-378-9532
sales@silvercreekpress.com
www.anglers-catalog.com

Art and sculptures, clothing, calendars, gift ideas for the fly fisherman and dining and kitchen accessories
Production Manager: Chris Petrilli
Credit Cards: AMEX; MasterCard
In Business: 21 years

2359 Baitmasters of South Florida
Baitmasters
6911 NE 3rd Ave
Miami, FL 33138-5511
305-751-7007
800-639-2248
Fax: 305-758-8074
www.baitmasters.com

Quality Baits: ballyhoo, mackerel, mullet, squid, rigged, unrigged
President: Mark Pumo
Catalog Cost: Free
In Business: 18 years
Number of Employees: 2
Sales Volume: $300,000

2360 Barlow's Fishing Tackle
Barlow's Tackle
451 N Central Expressway
Richardson, TX 75080
972-231-5982
800-707-0208
Fax: 972-690-4044
goodfishing@barlowstackle.com
www.barlowstackle.com

Fishing tackle including rods, reels, lures, hooks, and fly tying materials
President: William Barlow
Credit Cards: AMEX; MasterCard; Visa
Catalog Cost: Free
Printing Information: 110 pages
Sales Volume: $1,000,000

2361 Boston Whaler
Boston Whaler
100 Whaler Way
Edgewater, FL 32141
877-294-5645
www.bostonwhaler.com

Sport fishing boats, pleasure boats, yacht tenders and dingies

2362 CRKT Mid Year Catalog
Columbia River Knife & Tool
18348 SW 126th Place
Tualatin, OR 97062
503-685-5015
800-891-3100
Fax: 503-682-9680
info@crkt.com
www.crkt.com

Multi-tools and knives designed especially for firefighters, EMTs, police and water rescue teams.
Founder: Rod Bremer
Printing Information: 96 pages in 4 colors
In Business: 21 years

2363 CRKT Product Catalog
Columbia River Knife & Tool
18348 SW 126th Place
Tualatin, OR 97062
503-685-5015
800-891-3100
Fax: 503-682-9680
info@crkt.com
www.crkt.com

Multi-tools and knives designed especially for firefighters, EMTs, police and water rescue teams.
Founder: Rod Bremer
Printing Information: 96 pages in 4 colors
In Business: 21 years

2364 Cabela's Fall Master
Cabela's Inc.
One Cabela Dr.
Sidney, NE 69160
www.cabelas.com

Gear for fall.
CFO: Ralph Castner
CEO: Thomas Millner
COO: Michael Copeland
Catalog Cost: Free
Catalog Circulation: Mailed 4 time(s) per year
Printing Information: in 4 colors
List Company: Chilcutt Direct
In Business: 55 years
Sales Volume: $3 Billion

2365 Cabela's Fly Fishing
Cabela's Inc.
One Cabela Dr.
Sidney, NE 69160
www.cabelas.com

Gear, tackle and clothing for fly fishing.
CFO: Ralph Castner
CEO: Thomas Millner
COO: Michael Copeland
Catalog Cost: Free
Catalog Circulation: Mailed 4 time(s) per year
Printing Information: in 4 colors
List Company: Chilcutt Direct
In Business: 55 years
Sales Volume: $3 Billion

2366 Cabela's Saltwater
Cabela's Inc.
One Cabela Dr.
Sidney, NE 69160
www.cabelas.com

Gear, tackle and clothing for saltwater fishing.
CFO: Ralph Castner
CEO: Thomas Millner
COO: Michael Copeland
Catalog Cost: Free

Catalog Circulation: Mailed 4 time(s) per year
Printing Information: in 4 colors
List Company: Chilcutt Direct
In Business: 55 years
Sales Volume: $3 Billion

2367 Cabela's Spring Master
Cabela's Inc.
One Cabela Dr.
Sidney, NE 69160
www.cabelas.com

CFO: Ralph Castner
CEO: Thomas Millner
COO: Michael Copeland
Catalog Cost: Free
Catalog Circulation: Mailed 4 time(s) per year
Printing Information: in 4 colors
List Company: Chilcutt Direct
In Business: 55 years
Sales Volume: $3 Billion

2368 Cannon Downriggers
Johnson Outdoors
121 Power Dr.
Mankato, MN 56001
800-227-6433
Fax: 800-527-4464
cannondownriggers.com

Electronic fishing equipment and trackers.
Chair & CEO: Helen Johnson-Leipold
Catalog Cost: Free
Printing Information: 24 pages in 4 colors
Mailing List Information: Names for rent
In Business: 46 years
Number of Employees: 1300
Sales Volume: $400 Million

2369 Captain Harry's Fishing Supply
Capt. Harry's Fishing Supply
8501 NW 7th Avenue
Miami, FL 33150-2503
305-374-4661
800-327-4088
Fax: 305-374-3713
sales@captharry.com
www.captharry.com

Fishing equipment, supplies and gear
President: Harry Vernon
Credit Cards: AMEX; MasterCard; Visa
Catalog Cost: Free
Catalog Circulation: Mailed 1 time(s) per year
Printing Information: 92 pages in 4 colors
Press: Web Press
Binding: Saddle Stitched
Mailing List Information: Names for rent
In Business: 45 years
Number of Employees: 20

2370 Carolina Skiff
Carolina Skiff LLC
3231 Fulford Rd.
Waycross, GA 31503
912-287-0547
800-422-7282
www.carolinaskiff.com

Skiff boats

2371 Clear Creek Fishing Gear
Clear Creek
501 North State St.
Denver, IA 50622
319-984-6180
800-894-0483
Fax: 319-984-6403
www.clearcreek.net

Fly fishing gear

2372 Creme Lure Company
Creme Lure Company
5401 Kent Drive
P.O. Box 6162
Tyler, TX 75711-1947
info@cremelure.com
www.cremelure.com

Fishing lures
President: Wayne Kent
Plant Manager, VP Finance: Christopher Kent
Office Manager: Leslie Thompson

Secretary/Treasurer: Zella Reed
Credit Cards: MasterCard; Visa
Catalog Cost: Free
Catalog Circulation: Mailed 1 time(s) per year
Printing Information: 20 pages in 4 colors on
Glossy Stock
Binding: Saddle Stitched
In Business: 54 years
Number of Employees: 50
Sales Volume: $4.7 Million

2373 Dr. Slick
Dr. Slick Co.
105 Pollywog Lane
Belgrade, MT 59714-9106   406-388-8109
800-462-4474
Fax: 800-420-2468
info@drslick.com
www.drslick.com

Surgical grade instruments for anglers
President: Kenneth High MD
Marketing Manager: Steve Fournier
Credit Cards: AMEX; MasterCard
Catalog Cost: Free
Printing Information: 20 pages
In Business: 26 years

2374 Dyna King
Dyna-King, Inc.
597 Santana Drive
A
Cloverdale, CA 95425-4250   707-894-5566
800-396-2546
Fax: 707-894-5990
info@dyna-king.com
www.dyna-king.com

Handcrafted fly-tying vises and accessories
President: Ron Abby
CFO: Karen Hall
Manager: Shannon Langevein
Credit Cards: AMEX; MasterCard
Printing Information: 12 pages
In Business: 30 years
Number of Employees: 12
Sales Volume: $800,000

2375 EZ-Dock
EZ-Dock, Inc.
878 Hwy 60
Monett, MO 65708   800-654-8168
www.ez-dock.com

Customizable docking material for personal ponds and lakes

2376 Elmer Hinckley
Elmer Hinkley Fishing Tackle
15343 Edgewater Road NE
Pine City, MN 55063-4784   320-629-6393
Fax: 320-629-6506
ehfish@hotmail.com
www.elmerhinckley.com

Fishing lures and tackle
President: Charles Misel
Manager: Bill Swanberg
In Business: 28 years
Number of Employees: 2
Sales Volume: $76,000

2377 Erie Dearie Lure Company
Erie Dearie Lure Inc
2252 Greenville Road
Cortland, OH 44410   330-638-6675
Fax: 330-393-3601
connie@eriedearie.com
www.eriedearie.com

Fishing lures
President: Cathy Brunstetter
Marketing Manager: Mary Galbincea
mo@eriedearie.com
Dan Galbincea III:
dannyg@eriedearie.com
Office Manager: Connie Sanfrey
conie@eriedearie.com

Director of Sales: Richard J Kovacs
hogman@eriedearie.com, FishingLures
Credit Cards: MasterCard; Visa
Catalog Cost: Free
Catalog Circulation: Mailed 1 time(s) per year
to 20000
Printing Information: 15 pages in 4 colors on
Glossy Stock
Binding: Perfect Bound
Mailing List Information: Names for rent
In Business: 56 years
Number of Employees: 27
Sales Volume: $500,000

2378 Fall Angler
Bass Pro Shops
2500 E Kearney
Springfield, MO 65898   417-873-5000
800-227-7776
Fax: 417-873-5060
www.basspro.com

Fishing gear and apparel.
President & CEO: James Hagale
Catalog Cost: Free
Catalog Circulation: Mailed 1 time(s) per year
Printing Information: 76 pages in 4 colors
Mailing List Information: Names for rent
List Company: Eddie Woods, Domestic
In Business: 45 years
Number of Employees: 2200
Sales Volume: $4.45 Billion

2379 Feather Craft Fly Fishing
National Feather Craft Co., Inc.
8307 Manchester Rd
PO Box 440128
St. Louis, MO 63144   314-963-7876
800-659-1707
Fax: 314-963-0324
orders@feather-craft.com
www.feather-craft.com

Fly fishing rods, reels, waders, flies and fly tying materials
President: Ed Story
Executive Director: Brian Flinchpaugh
Vice President: Robert Story
Treasurer: Janel Story
Printing Information: 100 pages in 4 colors on
Glossy Stock
Binding: Saddle Stitched
In Business: 33 years
Number of Employees: 31
Sales Volume: $3.3 MM

2380 Final Flight Outfitters
Final Flight Outfitters
5933 Martin Hwy
Union City, TN 38261   731-885-5056
Fax: 731-885-5337
sales@finalflight.net
www.finalflight.net

Archery accessories and duck hunting equipment

2381 Fishing Components Catalog
Hagen's
3150 W Havens Street
Mitchell, SD 57301-6220   800-541-4586
Fax: 605-996-8946
hagensfish@santel.net
www.hagensfish.com

Fishing tackle, rods and lures
President: Kevin Hagen
Credit Cards: AMEX; MasterCard; Visa
Catalog Cost: Free
Catalog Circulation: Mailed 1 time(s) per year
to 40000
Printing Information: 176 pages in 4 colors on
Matte Stock
Press: Web Press
Binding: Perfect Bound
Mailing List Information: Names for rent
In Business: 25 years

Number of Employees: 65
Sales Volume: Under $500M

2382 Fishing Hot Spots, Inc.
Fishing Hot Spots, Inc.
1853 N Stevens Street
PO Box 1167
Rhinelander, WI 54501-2163   715-365-5555
800-ALL-MAPS
Fax: 715-365-5575
customerservice@fishinghotspots.com
www.fishinghotspots.com

Fishing publications and maps
President: George Swierczynski
CFO: Dawn Richter
Production Manager: Steve Swierczynski
Fulfillment: Nicole Stein
Credit Cards: AMEX; MasterCard; Visa
Catalog Cost: Free
Catalog Circulation: Mailed 2 time(s) per year
to 2000
Printing Information: 10 pages in 4 colors on
Matte Stock
Press: Offset Press
Binding: Saddle Stitched
In Business: 40 years
Number of Employees: 20
Sales Volume: $2 MM

2383 Fly Shop
Fly Shop
4140 Churn Creek Rd
Redding, CA 96002-3629   530-222-3555
800-669-3474
Fax: 530-222-3572
info@theflyshop.com
www.flyshop.com

Fly fishing equipment, supplies and vacation packages
President: Mike Michalak
mike@theflyshop.com
Manager: Timothy Fox
Vice President: Bertha Michalack
Owner: Milton Milleman
Buyers: Cory Williams
Credit Cards: AMEX; MasterCard; Visa
Catalog Cost: Free
Catalog Circulation: Mailed 2 time(s) per year
to 400M
Average Order Size: $150
Printing Information: 172 pages in 4 colors on
Glossy Stock
Press: Web Press
Binding: Saddle Stitched
Mailing List Information: Names for rent
List Manager: Eric Fields
In Business: 37 years
Number of Employees: 21
Sales Volume: $1.5 MM

2384 G Loomis
G.Loomis
1 Holland Drive
Irvine, CA 92618-2597   949-951-5003
877-577-0600
Fax: 360-225-7169
www.gloomis.com

Fishing rods, reels and accessories
President: Yozo Shimano
CFO: Jim L Force
Marketing Manager: Penina Bush
Chief Information Officer: Mike Holland
Vice President, Operations: Keiji Kakutani
SEVP, Chief Manufacturing Officer: Shinji
Wada
Buyers: Jerry Beaber
Credit Cards: AMEX; MasterCard; Visa
Catalog Cost: Free
Catalog Circulation: Mailed 1 time(s) per year
to 90000
Printing Information: 120 pages in 4 colors on
Glossy Stock
Press: Web Press
Binding: Perfect Bound
Mailing List Information: Names for rent

In Business: 53 years
Number of Employees: 100
Sales Volume: $32.6 MM

2385 Gator Grip
Gator Grip
3147 WEST US 40
Greenfield, IN 46140-8320   317-789-9103
                                    Fax: 317-789-9105
                                    brook@gatorgrip.com
                                    www.gatorgrip.com

Fishing tackle and accessories

President: Brook Johnson
Buyers: Brook Johnson
Credit Cards: MasterCard; Visa
Catalog Cost: Free
Catalog Circulation: Mailed 1 time(s) per year
to 4000
Average Order Size: $78
Printing Information: 8 pages in 4 colors on
Glossy Stock
Binding: Saddle Stitched
Mailing List Information: Names for rent
In Business: 20 years
Number of Employees: 6
Sales Volume: $499,000

2386 HOVER-LURE
HOVER-LURE
631 N.E. 18th Ave
Fort Lauderdale, FL 33304   954-351-2222
                                    866-BAS- FLY
                                    info@hover-lure.com
                                    www.kingofbass.com

2387 Hook & Hackle Company
Hook & Hackle Company
607 Ann Street Rear
Homestead, PA 15120   412-476-8620
                                    800-552-8342
                                    Fax: 412-476-8639
                                    ron@hookhack.com
                                    www.hookhack.com

Fly fishing equipment, rods and lures at discount prices

President: Ron Weiss
Credit Cards: AMEX; MasterCard; Visa
Catalog Cost: Free
Catalog Circulation: Mailed 1 time(s) per year
to 50 M
Average Order Size: $80
Printing Information: 96 pages in 1 color on
Newsprint
Press: Web Press
Binding: Saddle Stitched
Mailing List Information: Names for rent
In Business: 40 years
Number of Employees: 6

2388 JB Tackle Co.
JB Tackle Co.
25 Smith Avenue
Niantic, CT 6357   860-739-7419
                                    Fax: 860-739-9208
                                    Sales@jbtackle.com
                                    www.jbtackle.com

Fishing equipment

President: Capt. Kerry Douton
Printing Information: 116 pages
In Business: 35+ years

2389 K&K Flyfishers
KKFlyfisher
8643 Grant Street
Overland Park, KS 66212   913-341-8118
                                    800-795-8118
                                    Fax: 913-341-1252
                                    sales@kkflyfisher.com
                                    www.kkflyfisher.com

Fly fishing and fly typing products

President: Kevin Kurz
General Manager: Katherine Hale
Credit Cards: AMEX; MasterCard

Catalog Cost: Free
Catalog Circulation: Mailed 2 time(s) per year
to 60000
Average Order Size: $100
Printing Information: 60 pages in 4 colors on
Glossy Stock
Press: Web Press
Binding: Saddle Stitched
Mailing List Information: Names for rent
In Business: 31 years
Number of Employees: 12
Sales Volume: $790,000

2390 L.L.Bean Fishing
L.L.Bean Inc.
15 Casco St.
Freeport, ME 04033   207-552-2000
                                    www.llbean.com

Fishing clothing, accessories, supplies and equipment.

Chairman: Shawn Gorman
President: Stephen Smith
Catalog Cost: Free
Printing Information: 52 pages in 4 colors
Mailing List Information: Names for rent
List Company: Millard Group
In Business: 105 years
Number of Employees: 5000
Sales Volume: $1.6 Billion

2391 Loop Fly Fishing
Fly Rod and Reel Distributors LLC
998 W Flagler Street
Miami, FL 33130   541-673-9810
                                    Fax: 541-673-3810
                                    flyfish2@bellsouth.net
                                    www.loopusa.com

Fly fishing supplies

President: Jeff Gidney

2392 Mack's Prairie Wing
Mack's Prairie Wing
2335 US-63
Stuttgart, AR 72160   870-673-6960
                                    877-622-5779
                                    customerservice@macksprairiewings.com
                                    www.mackspw.com
President: Marion McCollum

2393 Madison River Fishing Company
Madison River Fishing Company
109 Main St.
PO Box 627
Ennis, MT 59729   406-682-4293
                                    800-227-7127
                                    Fax: 406-682-4744
                                    mrfc@3rivers.net
                                    www.mrfc.com

Trout fishing supplies

2394 Marine Catalog
Bass Pro Shops
2500 E Kearney
Springfield, MO 65898   417-873-5000
                                    800-227-7776
                                    Fax: 417-873-5060
                                    www.basspro.com

Boats and boating accessories.

President & CEO: James Hagale
Catalog Cost: Free
Catalog Circulation: Mailed 1 time(s) per year
Printing Information: 124 pages in 4 colors
In Business: 45 years
Number of Employees: 2200
Sales Volume: $4.45 Billion

2395 Melton Tackle
Melton International Tackle, Inc.
1375 S. State College Blvd.
Anaheim, CA 92806   714-507-4177
                                    800-372-3474
                                    Fax: 714-978-9299
                                    www.meltontackle.com

Lures, reels, rods, gamefishing accessories, boat accessories, clothing and gifts

2396 Memphis Net & Twine Company
Memphis Net & Twine Company
P.O. Box 80331
Memphis, TN 38108-0331   901-458-2656
                                    888-674-7638
                                    Fax: 901-458-1601
                                    fishinfo@memphisnet.net
                                    www.memphisnet.net

Fish nets, seine nets, gill nets, trammel nets, cast nets, fish netting, trawls, rope and twine

Chairman: William McCorkle
President: Albert Caruthers
Marketing Manager: Bryan Denley
General Manager: Frank A Gibson
Vice President Sales: William Raiford
Credit Cards: AMEX; MasterCard; Visa
Catalog Cost: Free
Catalog Circulation: Mailed 2 time(s) per year
to 50000
Printing Information: 64 pages in 2 colors on
Newsprint
Press: Web Press
Binding: Saddle Stitched
Mailing List Information: Names for rent
In Business: 52 years
Number of Employees: 33
Sales Volume: $4.6 Million

2397 Mepps Fishing Guide
Sheldon's Inc
626 Center Street
Antigo, WI 54409-2496   715-623-2382
                                    Fax: 715-623-3001
                                    shep@mepps.com
                                    www.mepps.com

Fishing lures, Mepps spinners and spoons

President: J M Sheldon
CFO: Robert Bender
Marketing Manager: Michael Sheldon
Production Manager: Dan Sheldon
Credit Cards: AMEX; MasterCard
Printing Information: in 4 colors on G
Press: W
Binding: S
Mailing List Information: Names for rent
In Business: 53 years
Number of Employees: 70

2398 Minn Kota
Johnson Outdoors
121 Power Dr.
Mankato, MN 56001   800-227-6433
                                    Fax: 800-527-4464
                                    www.minnkotamotors.com

Electric trolling motors and accessories.

Chair & CEO: Helen Johnson-Leipold
Catalog Cost: Free
Printing Information: 42 pages in 4 colors
Mailing List Information: Names for rent
In Business: 84 years
Sales Volume: $262 Million

2399 Mister Twister Tackle
Sheldon's Inc
626 Center Street
Antigo, WI 54409-2496   715-623-2382
                                    Fax: 715-623-3001
                                    shep@mepps.com
                                    www.mepps.com

Fishing lures, Mepps spinners and spoons

President: J M Sheldon
CFO: Robert Bender
Marketing Manager: Michael Sheldon
Production Manager: Dan Sheldon
Credit Cards: AMEX; MasterCard
Printing Information: in 4 colors on G
Press: W
Binding: S
Mailing List Information: Names for rent
In Business: 55 years
Number of Employees: 70

2400 Mud Hole Custom Tackle

866-790-7637
www.mudhole.com

Custom tackle

2401 Murrays Fly Shop
Murrays Fly Shop
121 S Main Street
PO Box 156
Edinburg, VA 22824   540-984-4212
Fax: 540-984-4895
info@murraysflyshop.com
www.murraysflyshop.com

Fly fishing accessories and supplies, on-the-stream schools and guide service, books and video by Harry Murray, maps and local information
Founder: Harry Murray
Credit Cards: AMEX; MasterCard
Catalog Cost: Free
Catalog Circulation: Mailed 1 time(s) per year to 6000
Printing Information: 40 pages in 1 color
Mailing List Information: Names for rent
In Business: 53 years
Number of Employees: 8
Sales Volume: $1MM to $3MM

2402 Northern Angler
Bass Pro Shops
2500 E Kearney
Springfield, MO 65898   417-873-5000
800-227-7776
Fax: 417-873-5060
www.basspro.com

Rods and reels, boat accessories, blades and lures.
President & CEO: James Hagale
Catalog Cost: Free
Printing Information: 148 pages in 4 colors
In Business: 45 years
Number of Employees: 2200
Sales Volume: $4.45 Billion

2403 NuCanoe Fishing Kayaks
NuCanoe, Inc.
2125 Humboldt St.
Bellingham, WA 98225   360-543-9019
888-226-6310
Fax: 360-483-5613
info@nucanoe.com
www.nucanoe.com

Fishing and hybrid kayaks

2404 Nylon Net Company
Nylon Net Company
845 N Main Street
Memphis, TN 38101-2311   901-526-6500
800-238-7529
Fax: 901-526-6538
nylonnet@nylonnet.com

Commercial fishing nets, rope and twine
President: Stephen Christides
VP: Tommy Slaughter
Director of Sales: Rob Ayres
Manager: Robert Alba, Jr.
Credit Cards: MasterCard; Visa
Catalog Cost: Free
Catalog Circulation: to 75M
Printing Information: 45 pages
In Business: 60 years
Number of Employees: 30
Sales Volume: $2.5 MM

2405 Orvis Fly Fishing
The Orvis Company Inc.
178 Conservation Way
Sunderland, VT 05250-4465   802-362-1300
888-235-9763
Fax: 802-362-0141
www.orvis.com

Fly fishing gear and equipment.

CEO: Leigh H. Perkins Jr.
Catalog Cost: Free
In Business: 160 years
Number of Employees: 1700
Sales Volume: $340 Million

2406 Orvis Gifts for Men
The Orvis Company Inc.
178 Conservation Way
Sunderland, VT 05250-4465   802-362-1300
888-235-9763
Fax: 802-362-0141
www.orvis.com

Hunting and fishing equipment and clothing.
CEO: Leigh H. Perkins Jr.
Catalog Cost: Free
In Business: 160 years
Number of Employees: 1700
Sales Volume: $340 Million

2407 Patagonia Fish
Patagonia
259 W Santa Clara St.
Ventura, CA 93001   805-643-8616
www.patagonia.com

Outdoor apparel for men and women.
CEO: Rose Marcario
Catalog Cost: Free
Catalog Circulation: Mailed 1 time(s) per year
Printing Information: in 4 colors
In Business: 43 years
Number of Employees: 2000
Sales Volume: $600 Million

2408 Saltwater Specialist Catalog - Master Edition
Bass Pro Shops
2500 E Kearney
Springfield, MO 65898   417-873-5000
800-227-7776
Fax: 417-873-5060
www.basspro.com

Saltwater gear and tackle.
President & CEO: James Hagale
Catalog Cost: Free
Catalog Circulation: Mailed 1 time(s) per year
Printing Information: in 4 colors
In Business: 45 years
Number of Employees: 2200
Sales Volume: $4.45 Billion

2409 Spring Fishing Master
Bass Pro Shops
2500 E Kearney
Springfield, MO 65898   417-873-5000
800-227-7776
Fax: 417-873-5060
www.basspro.com

Fishing gear and apparel.
President & CEO: James Hagale
Catalog Cost: Free
Catalog Circulation: Mailed 1 time(s) per year
Printing Information: in 4 colors
Mailing List Information: Names for rent
List Company: Eddie Woods, Domestic
In Business: 45 years
Number of Employees: 2200
Sales Volume: $4.45 Billion

2410 Summer Angler
Bass Pro Shops
2500 E Kearney
Springfield, MO 65898   417-873-5000
800-227-7776
Fax: 417-873-5060
www.basspro.com

Fishing gear and apparel.
President & CEO: James Hagale
Catalog Cost: Free
Catalog Circulation: Mailed 1 time(s) per year
Printing Information: in 4 colors
Mailing List Information: Names for rent

List Company: Eddie Woods, Domestic
In Business: 45 years
Number of Employees: 2200
Sales Volume: $4.45 Billion

2411 Terminal Tackle Co.
Terminal Tackle Co.
120 Main Street
Kings Park, NY 11754   631-269-6005
Fax: 631-269-3920
hooks@terminaltackleco.com
www.terminaltackleco.com
Printing Information: 72 pages

2412 The Sportsman's Guide
The Sportsman's Guide
PO Box 239
411 Farwell Ave.
South St. Paul, MN 55075-0239   800-882-2962
www.sportsmansguide.com

A wide variety of outdoor apparel, hunting accessories, fishing and camping equipment.
In Business: 46 years
Sales Volume: $500MM to $1 Billion

2413 Thomas Lures
Thomas Spinning Lures, Inc.
316 Wayne Ave.
Hawley, PA 18428   570-226-4011
800-724-6768
Fax: 570-226-8518
info@thomaslures.com
www.thomaslures.com

Fishing lures

2414 Warrior Lures
Warrior Lures
Traverse City MI   231-421-3372
www.warriorlures.com

Fishing spoons, blades, lures and tackle

2415 Westbank Anglers Catalog
Westbank Anglers
3670 North Moose Wilson Road
PO Box 523
Teton Village, WY 83014   307-733-6483
800-922-3474
Fax: 307-733-9382
custserv@westbank.com
www.westbank.com

Fishing tackle and accessories for salt and fresh water
President: Baker Salisbury
Credit Cards: AMEX; MasterCard
Catalog Cost: Free
Catalog Circulation: Mailed 1 time(s) per year to 50000
Printing Information: 64 pages in 4 colors on Glossy Stock
Press: Web Press
Binding: Folded
Mailing List Information: Names for rent
In Business: 25 years
Number of Employees: 8
Sales Volume: $1.5 MM

2416 White River Fly Shop Fly Fishing
Bass Pro Shops
2500 E Kearney
Springfield, MO 65898   417-873-5000
800-227-7776
Fax: 417-873-5060
www.basspro.com

Fly fishing tools, accessories and apparel.
President & CEO: James Hagale
Catalog Cost: Free
Catalog Circulation: Mailed 1 time(s) per year
Printing Information: in 4 colors
Mailing List Information: Names for rent
List Company: Eddie Woods, Domestic
In Business: 45 years

Number of Employees: 2200
Sales Volume: $4.45 Billion

2417 Wing Supply Catalog
Wing Supply
6771 Chrisphalt Drive
Bath, PA 18014-1762   270-338-5866
800-388-9464
Fax: 270-338-0057
service@wingsupply.com
www.wingsupply.com

Hunting and sporting equipment and accessories

President: Walter L Fauntleroy
Director, Human Resources: Joey Steele
Vice President: Angie Whitmer
Credit Cards: AMEX; MasterCard
In Business: 38 years
Number of Employees: 80
Sales Volume: $12 MM

2418 Worden's Lures Catalog
Yakima Bait Company Inc
P.O. Box 310
Granger, WA 98932   509-854-1311
Fax: 509-854-2263
ybcinc@yakimabait.com
www.yakimabait.com

Fishing lures, lines and leaders

Chairman: Karl Staudinger
President: Mark Masterson
CFO: Karen Blankenship
Marketing Manager: Paul Bates
Plant Manager: Linda Morrow
Safety Director: Curtis Willey
Credit Cards: MasterCard; Visa
Catalog Cost: Free
Catalog Circulation: Mailed 1 time(s) per year to 10000
Printing Information: 84 pages in 4 colors on Glossy Stock
Binding: Perfect Bound
In Business: 83 years
Number of Employees: 175
Sales Volume: $13.8 MM

Guns & Gun Equipment

2419 American Technologies Network
American Technologies Network
1341 San Mateo Avenue
South San Francisco, CA 94080   650-989-5100
800-910-2862
Fax: 650-875-0129
info@atncorp.com
www.atncorp.com

Night vision equipment and scopes, security equipment

President: James Munn
CEO: Marc Vayn
Vice President, Sales: Lowell Stacy
Vice President: Lenny Gaber
Printing Information: in 4 colors on Glossy Stock
Binding: Saddle Stitched
Mailing List Information: Names for rent
In Business: 20 years
Number of Employees: 51
Sales Volume: $8,800,000

2420 Beretta Product Guide
Beretta USA
17601 Beretta Dr.
Accokeek, MD 20607   www.berettausa.com

Pistols and tactical products.

CFO: Steve Biondi
Catalog Cost: Free
Catalog Circulation: Mailed 1 time(s) per year
Printing Information: in 4 colors
In Business: 44 years
Number of Employees: 400
Sales Volume: $100MM to $500MM

2421 Beretta Rifle Product Guide
Beretta USA
17601 Beretta Dr.
Accokeek, MD 20607   www.berettausa.com

Rifles and accessories.

CFO: Steve Biondi
Catalog Cost: Free
Catalog Circulation: Mailed 1 time(s) per year
Printing Information: in 4 colors
In Business: 44 years
Number of Employees: 400
Sales Volume: $100MM to $500MM

2422 Birchwood Casey
Birchwood Casey LLC
7887 Fuller Road
Suite 100
Eden Prairie, MN 55344-2138   952-388-6717
800-746-6862
Fax: 952-388-6718
customerservice@birchwoodcasey.com
www.birchwoodcasey.com

Gun cleaning products, gun refinishing products and targets

President: Dan Brooks
VP: Mike Wenner
Human Resources Director: Amy Shero
Human Resources Director: Beth Fredrickson
Credit Cards: AMEX; MasterCard; Visa
Catalog Cost: Free
Printing Information: 47 pages
In Business: 23 years
Number of Employees: 80
Sales Volume: $99,000,000

2423 Brownells
Brownells
200 South Front St.
Montezuma, IA 50171   641-623-5401
800-741-0015
Fax: 800-264-3068
www.brownells.com

Archery products, firearm accessories, gunsmithing tools

2424 Browning
One Browning Place
Morgan, UT 84050   801-876-2711
800-333-3288
www.browning.com

Hunting and shooting products

2425 Cabela's Fall Master
Cabela's Inc.
One Cabela Dr.
Sidney, NE 69160   www.cabelas.com

Gear for fall.

CFO: Ralph Castner
CEO: Thomas Millner
COO: Michael Copeland
Catalog Cost: Free
Catalog Circulation: Mailed 4 time(s) per year
Printing Information: in 4 colors
List Company: Chilcutt Direct
In Business: 55 years
Sales Volume: $3 Billion

2426 Cabela's Spring Master
Cabela's Inc.
One Cabela Dr.
Sidney, NE 69160   www.cabelas.com

CFO: Ralph Castner
CEO: Thomas Millner
COO: Michael Copeland
Catalog Cost: Free
Catalog Circulation: Mailed 4 time(s) per year
Printing Information: in 4 colors
List Company: Chilcutt Direct
In Business: 55 years
Sales Volume: $3 Billion

2427 Centerfire Systems
Centerfire Systems
102 Fieldview Dr
Versailles, KY 40383-1464   859-873-2352
800-950-1231
Fax: 859-873-1842
info@centerfiresystems.com
www.centerfiresystems.com

Various guns, ammunition and gun equipment

President: Shane Coe
Credit Cards: AMEX; MasterCard; Visa
Catalog Cost: Free
Catalog Circulation: to 47500
Printing Information: 70 pages in 4 colors on Newsprint
Press: Web Press
Binding: Folded
Mailing List Information: Names for rent
In Business: 16 years
Number of Employees: 18

2428 Crimson Trace
Crimson Trace
9780 SW Freeman Drive
Wilsonville, OR 97070-9221   800-442-2406
800-442-2406
Fax: 503-783-5334
customer@crimsontrace.com
www.crimsontrace.com

Laser sights for guns

President: Lewis Danielson
CFO: Mark Avolio
Marketing Manager: Lane Tobiassen
VP Sales: Pegi Labbe
Director, Public Relations: Travis Noteboom
Director, Global Sales: Lance Giammanco
Buyers: June Howes
Jack Woodward
Lane Tobiassen
Credit Cards: MasterCard; Visa
Catalog Cost: Free
In Business: 19 years
Number of Employees: 90
Sales Volume: $12.3 Million

2429 DeSantis Holster
DeSantis Gunhide
431 Bayview Ave
Amityville, NY 11701-2638   631-841-6300
800-424-1236
Fax: 631-841-6320
sales@desantisholster.com
www.desantisholster.com

Complete line of leather and nylon holsters and related accessories; belts, slings, concealment bags including pocketbooks, briefcases, Gunny Sack hip pouch

President: Gene Desantis
Credit Cards: AMEX; MasterCard; Visa
Catalog Cost: $5
Catalog Circulation: to 75M
Printing Information: 60 pages
Number of Employees: 60
Sales Volume: $1,000,000 - $5,000,000

2430 Delta Force
Delta Group
215 S Washington Ave
El Dorado, AR 71730-5927   870-862-3811
Fax: 870-862-9671
info@deltapress.com
www.deltapress.com

Shooting/sporting accessories and reading material

Credit Cards: MasterCard
Catalog Cost: $5
Catalog Circulation: Mailed 2 time(s) per year
Average Order Size: $80
Printing Information: 72 pages in 4 colors on Glossy Stock
Press: Web Press
Binding: Saddle Stitched

Mailing List Information: Names for rent
In Business: 15 years
Number of Employees: 18

2431 E.M.F Company

EMF Company, Inc.
1900 East Warner Ave.
Suite 1-D
Santa Ana, CA 92705-5549   949-261-6611
   800-430-1310
Fax: 949-756-0133
www.emf-company.com

Muzzle loader replica rifles and handguns

President: Boyd Davis
Credit Cards: AMEX; MasterCard
Catalog Cost: $5
Printing Information: 32 pages
In Business: 59 years
Number of Employees: 10
Sales Volume: $1.5 Million

2432 EAA Corporation

European American Armory Corp.
411 Hawk Street
PO Box 560746
Rockledge, FL 32956-746   321-639-4842
Fax: 321-639-7006
eaacorp@eaacorp.com
www.eaacorp.com

Gun accessories

President: Keith Bernkrant
CFO: Janet Helms
Vice President: Paul Richter
Credit Cards: AMEX; MasterCard
Catalog Circulation: to 40000
Printing Information: 12 pages in 4 colors on Glossy Stock
Binding: Saddle Stitched
In Business: 21 years
Number of Employees: 4
Sales Volume: $540,000

2433 Henry Repeating Arms

Henry
59 East 1st Street
Bayonne, NJ 07002   201-858-4400
Fax: 201-858-4435
info@henryrepeating.com
www.henryrepeating.com

Henry Repeating rifles

President: Anthony Imperato
Customer Service Supervisor: Thomas Kotz
Instructor / Wildlife: Charlie Volkmann
Customer Service: Kathy Scarpa
Credit Cards: AMEX; MasterCard; Visa
Catalog Cost: Free
Printing Information: in 4 colors
In Business: 157 years
Number of Employees: 85
Sales Volume: $7 MM

2434 Hogue Grip

Hogue, Inc.
P.O. Box 91360
Hendersones, NV 89009   800-438-4747
Fax: 805-239-2553
www.getgrip.com

Handgun grips for rifles

President: Aaron Hogue
Vice President: Patrick Hogue
Vice President: Jim Bruhns
Vice President: Neil Hogue
Catalog Circulation: Mailed 1 time(s) per year
Printing Information: 52 pages in 4 colors
In Business: 50 years
Number of Employees: 36
Sales Volume: $3.8 MM

2435 Hornady

Hornady Manufacturing
3625 West Old Potash Highway
Grand Island, NE 68803   308-382-1390
   800-338-3220
Fax: 308-382-5761
www.hornady.com

Ammunition and bullets

President: Steve Hornady
Director of Sales: Jason Hornady
Credit Cards: AMEX; MasterCard
Catalog Cost: Free
Catalog Circulation: Mailed 1 time(s) per year
Printing Information: 132 pages in 4 colors
In Business: 68 years

2436 J&G Sales

440 Miller Valley Road
Prescott, AZ 86301   928-445-9650
Fax: 928-445-9658
info@jgsales.com
www.jgsales.com

Guns

2437 Jonathan Arthur Ciener

Jonathan Arthur Ciener
8700 Commerce St
Cape Canaveral, FL 32920   321-868-2200
Fax: 321-868-2201
www.22lrconversions.com

.22 caliber conversions for various firearms

President: Jonathan Ciener
Director of Manufacturing: William Reynolds
Director: Emanuel Ciener
Catalog Cost: $5
Catalog Circulation: to 1.2M
Printing Information: 5 pages
In Business: 37 years
Number of Employees: 25
Sales Volume: $3,000,000

2438 Kirkpatrick Leather

Kirkpatrick Leather Company
1910 San Bernardo Avenue
PO Box 677
Laredo, TX 78040-4840   956-723-6893
   800-451-9394
Fax: 956-725-0672
support@kirkpatrickleather.com
www.kirkpatrickleather.com

Gunbelts and holsters

President: Joe W Kirkpatrick
Marketing Manager: Olga Vearreal
Production Manager: Mike Kirkpatrick
VP: G Michael Rigler
VP: Christina Kirkpatrick
VP, Secretary, Treasurer: Maria C Kirkpatrick
Catalog Cost: $5
Catalog Circulation: to 5M
Printing Information: 24 pages
In Business: 65 years
Number of Employees: 18
Sales Volume: $1,000,000

2439 Legacy Sports International

4750 Longley Lane
Suite 209
Reno, NV 89502   775-828-0555
Fax: 775-828-0565
nfsales@legacysports.com
www.legacysports.com

Guns and hunting equipment

President: Andy McCormick
CFO: Doug Miller

2440 Leupold & Stevens

Leupold & Stevens
14400 NW Greenbrier Parkway
Beaverton, OR 97006   800-538-7653
www.leupold.com

Hunting and shooting products and accessories, tactical, observation and golf gear.

2441 Marlin Firearms

Marlin
P.O. Box 1871
Madison, NC 27025   800-544-8892
www.marlinfirearms.com

Sporting rifles

Chairman: Frank Kenna III
CFO: Pamela Griffin
Credit Cards: MasterCard; Visa
Catalog Cost: Free
Catalog Circulation: Mailed 1 time(s) per year to 5000
Printing Information: 34 pages in 4 colors on Glossy Stock
Press: Web Press
Binding: Saddle Stitched
Mailing List Information: Names for rent
In Business: 147 years
Number of Employees: 575
Sales Volume: $36.4 MM

2442 Midway USA Master

Midway USA Master
5875 W Van Horn Tavern Rd
Columbia, MO 65203-9004   573-445-6363
   800-243-3220
Fax: 800-992-8312
larrypotterfield@midwayusa.com
www.midwayusa.com

Ammunition and reloading supplies and equipment

President: Larry W Potterfield
CEO: Larry Potterfield
Credit Cards: AMEX; MasterCard; Visa
Catalog Cost: Free
Catalog Circulation: Mailed 12 time(s) per year
Printing Information: 970 pages in 4 colors on Newsprint
Press: Web Press
Binding: Saddle Stitched
Mailing List Information: Names for rent
In Business: 31 years
Number of Employees: 140

2443 Military & Law Enforcement Product Catalog

Smith & Wesson
2100 Roosevelt Avenue
Springfield, MA 01104   413-781-8300
   800-331-0852
Fax: 413-747-3317
www.smith-wesson.com

Firearms and firearm safety/security products

President: P. James Debney
CFO: Jeffrey Buchanan
Credit Cards: AMEX; MasterCard
Catalog Cost: Free
Printing Information: 84 pages in 4 colors
In Business: 165 years

2444 Mossberg Catalog

O.F. Mossberg & Sons
7 Grasso Avenue
North Haven, CT 06473   203-230-5300
Fax: 203-230-5420
www.mossberg.com

Firearms, parts, accessories, hunting apparel and gear

Chief Executive Officer: Alan Iver Mossberg Jr
Director of Media Relations: Linda Powell
Credit Cards: AMEX; MasterCard
Catalog Cost: Free
Catalog Circulation: Mailed 1 time(s) per year
Printing Information: 92 pages in 4 colors
In Business: 98 years
Sales Volume: $24.6 Million

2445 NIC Law Enforcement Supply
NIC Law Enforcement Supply
1403 Highway 313
Building A
Algodones, NM 87001   318-688-1365
                             888-642-0007
                       Fax: 318-688-1367
                       orders@nles.com
                       www.nles.com

Law enforcement equipment custom badges, wallets, and ID systems

President: Dana McCommon
CFO: Chales Tooraen
Catalog Cost: Free
Catalog Circulation: to 200M
Average Order Size: $65
Printing Information: 82 pages in 4 colors on Glossy Stock
Press: Web Press
Binding: Saddle Stitched
Mailing List Information: Names for rent
In Business: 30 years
Number of Employees: 2
Sales Volume: $120,000

2446 Natchez Shooters Supply
Natchez Shooters Supply
2600 Walker Road
PO Box 182212
Chattanooga, TN 37422   423-889-0499
                              800-251-7839
                        Fax: 423-892-4482
                        orders@natchezss.com
                        www.natchezss.com

Hunting supplies

CFO: David Dodson
Owner: Jeff Hamm
Information Technology Manager: Andy Lee
President, Sales: Brian Hall
Credit Cards: MasterCard
Printing Information: 104 pages
Number of Employees: 1
Sales Volume: $62,000

2447 Navy Arms Company
Navy Arms Company
54 Dupont Road
Martinsburg, WV 25404-5009   304-274-0004
                        Fax: 304-274-0006
                        info@ows-ammo.com
                        www.navyarms.com

Historical guns, replica fire arms and swords

President: Val Forgett III
Catalog Cost: $2
Printing Information: 36 pages
In Business: 24 years
Number of Employees: 8
Sales Volume: $ 1 Million

2448 Para USA
Para USA, LLC
1816 Remington Circle
Huntsville, AL 35824-7381   704-930-7600
                              888-999-9386
                        Fax: 256-327-2852
                        contact@para-usa.com
                        www.para-usa.com

Pistols

CFO: Thanos Polyzos
Director Finance & Human Resources: Roxeanne Copegog
Catalog Cost:
In Business: 26 years
Number of Employees: 60
Sales Volume: $10.98 MM

2449 Pyramyd Air
Pyramyd Air Ltd.
5135 Naiman Parkway
Solon, OH 44139-7771   888-262-4867
                        Fax: 216-896-0896
                        sales@pyramydair.com
                        www.pyramydair.com

Air rifles

President: Val Gamerman
CEO: Joshua D. Uniger
Director, Human Resources: Pat Ferry
Assistant Warehouse Manager: David Haller
Credit Cards: MasterCard; Visa
Catalog Cost: Free
Catalog Circulation: Mailed 3 time(s) per year to 300M
Printing Information: 24 pages in 4 colors on Newsprint
Press: Web Press
Mailing List Information: Names for rent
In Business: 20 years
Number of Employees: 52
Sales Volume: $14.23 Million

2450 RedHead Hunting Master
Bass Pro Shops
2500 E Kearney
Springfield, MO 65898   417-873-5000
                              800-227-7776
                        Fax: 417-873-5060
                        www.basspro.com

Top-quality gear for hunting, camping, boating, fishing and other outdoor activities.

President & CEO: James Hagale
Catalog Cost: Free
Catalog Circulation: Mailed 1 time(s) per year
Printing Information: 600 pages in 4 colors
In Business: 45 years
Number of Employees: 2200
Sales Volume: $4.45 Billion

2451 STI International
STI International, Inc.
114 Halmar Cove
Georgetown, TX 78628-2331   512-819-0656
                        Fax: 512-819-0465
                        info@stiguns.com
                        www.stiguns.com

Frame kits, short blocks, complete guns

President: David Skinner
Vice President Engineering: Ed Minshew
Finance Executive: Karen Fuessel
Sales Executive: Pauletta Skinner
Printing Information: in 1 color
In Business: 24 years
Number of Employees: 65
Sales Volume: $6.9 Million

2452 Safariland Master Catalog
Safariland
13386 International Pkwy.
Jacksonville, FL 32218   800-347-1200
                        www.safariland.com

Body armor and other gun accessories.

Printing Information: 252 pages in 4 colors
In Business: 52 years
Number of Employees: 1400
Sales Volume: $200 Million

2453 Safariland Shooting Gear Catalog
Safariland
13386 International Pkwy.
Jacksonville, FL 32218   800-347-1200
                        www.safariland.com

Shooting accessories including gloves, belts and holsters.

Printing Information: 196 pages in 4 colors
In Business: 52 years
Number of Employees: 1400
Sales Volume: $200 Million

2454 Smith & Alexander
Smith & Alexander, Inc.
PO Box 299
Copeville, TX 75121   972-853-0008
                              800-722-1911
                        Fax: 972-853-0526
                        www.smithandalexander.com

Mag Guides and grips with screws and bushings

President: Dr.Alan Smith
Customer Service: Barbara Smith
Credit Cards: MasterCard
Printing Information: in 4 colors

2455 Stoeger Airguns
901 Eighth Street
Pocomoke, MD 21851   301-283-6981
                        usa.stoegerairguns.com

Airguns

2456 TenPoint Crossbows
TenPoint Crossbows
1325 Waterloo Road
Mogadore, OH 44260   330-628-9245
                        www.tenpointcrossbows.com

Crossbows and crossbow accessories

President: Richard L. Bednar
Director of Sales & Service: Randy Wood
Service Manager: Bryan Zabitski
Customer Service Supervisor: Amber Vandegrift
Credit Cards: AMEX; MasterCard
Catalog Cost: Free
Catalog Circulation: Mailed 1 time(s) per year
Printing Information: 31 pages in 4 colors
In Business: 23 years

2457 Waterfowl Hunting
Bass Pro Shops
2500 E Kearney
Springfield, MO 65898   417-873-5000
                              800-227-7776
                        Fax: 417-873-5060
                        www.basspro.com

Gear and apparel for waterfowlers.

President & CEO: James Hagale
Catalog Cost: Free
Catalog Circulation: Mailed 1 time(s) per year
Printing Information: 68 pages in 4 colors
In Business: 45 years
Number of Employees: 2200
Sales Volume: $4.45 Billion

2458 Weatherby
1605 Commerce Way
Paso Robles, CA 93446   805-227-2600
                        Fax: 805-237-0427
                        www.weatherby.com

Guns and gun equipment

Hunting Equipment & Supplies

2459 3Rivers Archery
3Rivers Archery
607 HL Thompson Jr Dr
PO Box 517
Ashley, IN 46705-517   260-587-9501
                              866-732-8783
                        Fax: 888-329-9872
                        info@3riversarchery.com
                        www.3riversarchery.com

Archery supplies for bow hunting and target shooting.

President: Dale Karch
CFO: Sandie Karch
Marketing Manager: Jonathan Karch
Production Manager: Matt Karch
Fulfillment: Kim
VP Operations: Teresa Williams
Inventory Manager: Ashley Sunday
Creative Specialist: Wil Radcliffe
Credit Cards: AMEX; MasterCard
Catalog Cost: Free
Printing Information: 75 pages in 4 colors
In Business: 30 years
Number of Employees: 22
Sales Volume: $1.9 Million

2460 API Outdoors
API Outdoors
PO Box 24
Windom, MN 56101
507-832-8282
888-393-9611
Fax: 507-832-8205
customer.service@apioutdoors.com
www.apioutdoors.com

Tree stands and hunting accessories

President: Paul Meeks
Marketing Manager: Jim Jones
Sales Director: Howard Lutz
Information Technology Director: George Davidson
Director, Human Resources: Jonathan Knight
Buyers: Cammi Skeldon
Credit Cards: AMEX; MasterCard; Visa
Catalog Cost: Free
Catalog Circulation: Mailed 1 time(s) per year to 50000
Printing Information: 16 pages in 4 colors on Glossy Stock
In Business: 29 years
Number of Employees: 125
Sales Volume: $8,100,000

2461 AllPredatorCalls.com
1517 E. 3850 S.
St. George, UT 84790
435-628-8993
888-826-9683
Fax: 435-628-8633
allpredatorcalls@gmail.com
www.allpredatorcalls.com

Predator hunting products

2462 American Technologies Network
American Technologies Network
1341 San Mateo Avenue
South San Francisco, CA 94080
650-989-5100
800-910-2862
Fax: 650-875-0129
info@atncorp.com
www.atncorp.com

Night vision equipment and scopes, security equipment

President: James Munn
CEO: Marc Vayn
Vice President, Sales: Lowell Stacy
Vice President: Lenny Gaber
Printing Information: in 4 colors on Glossy Stock
Binding: Saddle Stitched
Mailing List Information: Names for rent
In Business: 20 years
Number of Employees: 51
Sales Volume: $8,800,000

2463 Archery
Eder, Inc.
85 Forest Ave
PO Box 774
Locust Valley, NY 11560-774
516-656-0808
Fax: 516-656-3312
cs@eders.com
www.eders.com

Archery and bowhunting equipment

President: David Eder
Vice President: Leonard Eder
Founder, Vice President: Robert Eder
Credit Cards: AMEX; MasterCard
Catalog Cost: Free
In Business: 16 years
Number of Employees: 6
Sales Volume: $2,000,000

2464 Browning
One Browning Place
Morgan, UT 84050
801-876-2711
800-333-3288
www.browning.com

Hunting and shooting products

2465 Burris Optics Catalog
Burris Company
331 E 8th Street
Greeley, CO 80631
888-440-0244
customerservice@burrisoptics.com
www.burrisoptics.com

Gun sights, telescopic, binoculars and mounts

Marketing Manager: Ryan Hennig
General Manager: Dale Pratt
Buyers: Melody Harpster
Credit Cards: MasterCard; Visa
Catalog Cost: Free
Catalog Circulation: Mailed 1 time(s) per year to 100M
Printing Information: 80 pages in 4 colors on Glossy Stock
Press: Web Press
Binding: Saddle Stitched
In Business: 41 years
Number of Employees: 100
Sales Volume: $20,000,000

2466 CRKT Mid Year Catalog
Columbia River Knife & Tool
18348 SW 126th Place
Tualatin, OR 97062
503-685-5015
800-891-3100
Fax: 503-682-9680
info@crkt.com
www.crkt.com

Multi-tools and knives designed especially for firefighters, EMTs, police and water rescue teams.

Founder: Rod Bremer
Printing Information: 96 pages in 4 colors
In Business: 21 years

2467 CRKT Product Catalog
Columbia River Knife & Tool
18348 SW 126th Place
Tualatin, OR 97062
503-685-5015
800-891-3100
Fax: 503-682-9680
info@crkt.com
www.crkt.com

Multi-tools and knives designed especially for firefighters, EMTs, police and water rescue teams.

Founder: Rod Bremer
Printing Information: 96 pages in 4 colors
In Business: 21 years

2468 Cabela's Fall Master
Cabela's Inc.
One Cabela Dr.
Sidney, NE 69160
www.cabelas.com

Gear for fall.

CFO: Ralph Castner
CEO: Thomas Millner
COO: Michael Copeland
Catalog Cost: Free
Catalog Circulation: Mailed 4 time(s) per year
Printing Information: in 4 colors
List Company: Chilcutt Direct
In Business: 55 years
Sales Volume: $3 Billion

2469 Cabela's Spring Master
Cabela's Inc.
One Cabela Dr.
Sidney, NE 69160
www.cabelas.com

CFO: Ralph Castner
CEO: Thomas Millner
COO: Michael Copeland
Catalog Cost: Free
Catalog Circulation: Mailed 4 time(s) per year
Printing Information: in 4 colors
List Company: Chilcutt Direct
In Business: 55 years
Sales Volume: $3 Billion

2470 Cabela's Spring Turkey
Cabela's Inc.
One Cabela Dr.
Sidney, NE 69160
www.cabelas.com

CFO: Ralph Castner
CEO: Thomas Millner
COO: Michael Copeland
Catalog Cost: Free
Catalog Circulation: Mailed 4 time(s) per year
Printing Information: in 4 colors
List Company: Chilcutt Direct
In Business: 55 years
Sales Volume: $3 Billion

2471 Centerfire Systems
Centerfire Systems
102 Fieldview Dr
Versailles, KY 40383-1464
859-873-2352
800-950-1231
Fax: 859-873-1842
info@centerfiresystems.com
www.centerfiresystems.com

Various guns, ammunition and gun equipment

President: Shane Coe
Credit Cards: AMEX; MasterCard; Visa
Catalog Cost: Free
Catalog Circulation: to 47500
Printing Information: 70 pages in 4 colors on Newsprint
Press: Web Press
Binding: Folded
Mailing List Information: Names for rent
In Business: 16 years
Number of Employees: 18

2472 Crimson Trace
Crimson Trace
9780 SW Freeman Drive
Wilsonville, OR 97070-9221
800-442-2406
800-442-2406
Fax: 503-783-5334
customer@crimsontrace.com
www.crimsontrace.com

Laser sights for guns

President: Lewis Danielson
CFO: Mark Avolio
Marketing Manager: Lane Tobiassen
VP Sales: Pegi Labbe
Director, Public Relations: Travis Noteboom
Director, Global Sales: Lance Giammanco
Buyers: June Howes
Jack Woodward
Lane Tobiassen
Credit Cards: MasterCard; Visa
Catalog Cost: Free
In Business: 19 years
Number of Employees: 90
Sales Volume: $12.3 Million

2473 Cumberland's Northwest Trappers Supply
PO Box 408
Owatonna, MN 55060
507-451-7607
Fax: 507-451-5869
trapper@nwtrappers.com
www.nwtrappers.com

Hunting and fishing supplies and equipment

2474 Deer & Deer Hunting Catalog
Krause Publications
700 E State Street
Iola, WI 54990-1
715-445-2214
800-258-0929
Fax: 715-445-4087
zielkec@krause.com
www.krausebooks.com

Fine gifts for deer hunters

Marketing Manager: David Mueller
Production Manager: Cheryl Hayburn
Chairman & CEO: David B Nussbaum
Director, Public Relations: Stacie Berger
SVP Manufacturing: Phil Graham
Credit Cards: AMEX; MasterCard; Visa

Catalog Cost: $1
Catalog Circulation: Mailed 2 time(s) per year to 40000
Average Order Size: $30
Printing Information: 20 pages in 4 colors on Glossy Stock
Press: Web Press
Binding: Saddle Stitched
List Company: The Other List Company
PO Box 286
Matawan, NJ 07747
201-591-1180
In Business: 63 years
Number of Employees: 450

2475 Deershack
The Deer Shack
7155 Highway B
Belgium, WI 53004-905
920-994-9818
800-443-3337
Fax: 920-994-4099
www.deershack.com

Unique gifts and field tested gear for the sportsman including black powder, scent-lok, hunting gear, limited edition prints, sport T's, cedar log furniture, rustic accents for the lodge and more

President: Joseph O'Connell
CFO: Bruce Comdohr
Treasurer: Patricia O'Connell
Credit Cards: AMEX; MasterCard
Catalog Cost: $2
Catalog Circulation: Mailed 3 time(s) per year to 400M
Average Order Size: $75
Printing Information: 64 pages in 4 colors on Matte Stock
Press: Web Press
Binding: Saddle Stitched
Mailing List Information: Names for rent
List Company: The Other List
In Business: 42 years
Number of Employees: 12
Sales Volume: $990,000

2476 Fall Hunting II
Bass Pro Shops
2500 E Kearney
Springfield, MO 65898
417-873-5000
800-227-7776
Fax: 417-873-5060
www.basspro.com

Hunting gear, tools and clothing.

President & CEO: James Hagale
Catalog Cost: Free
Catalog Circulation: Mailed 1 time(s) per year
Printing Information: 220 pages in 4 colors
In Business: 45 years
Number of Employees: 2200
Sales Volume: $4.45 Billion

2477 Field Outfitting
3006 Brownells Parkway
Grinnell, IA 50112
866-277-3920
concierge@thefieldoutfitting.com

Clothing and accessories

2478 Forster Products
Forster Products
310 East Lanark Avenue
Lanark, IL 61046-9704
815-493-6360
Fax: 815-493-2371
tech@forsterproducts.com
www.forsterproducts.com

Gunsmithing tools and accessories

President: Rodney P Hartman
CFO: Robert R Ruch
Officer: Diane Haverland
Credit Cards: AMEX; MasterCard; Visa
Catalog Cost: Free
Catalog Circulation: Mailed 1 time(s) per year to 20M
Printing Information: 36 pages in 4 colors on Glossy Stock

Press: Web Press
Mailing List Information: Names for rent
In Business: 79 years
Number of Employees: 16
Sales Volume: $1.1 MM

2479 Henry Repeating Arms
Henry
59 East 1st Street
Bayonne, NJ 07002
201-858-4400
Fax: 201-858-4435
info@henryrepeating.com
www.henryrepeating.com

Henry Repeating rifles

President: Anthony Imperato
Customer Service Supervisor: Thomas Kotz
Instructor / Wildlife: Charlie Volkmann
Customer Service: Kathy Scarpa
Credit Cards: AMEX; MasterCard; Visa
Catalog Cost: Free
Printing Information: in 4 colors
In Business: 157 years
Number of Employees: 85
Sales Volume: $7 MM

2480 Hoosier Trapper Supply
Hoosier Trapper Supply, Inc.
1155 North Mathews Rd.
Greenwood, IN 46143
317-881-3075
Fax: 317-881-3325
info@hoosiertrappersupply.com
www.hoosiertrappersupply.com

Taxidermy, coyote tracking and hunting supplies and products

2481 Kimber
Kimber
555 Taxter Road
Suite 235
Elmsford, NY 10523
406-758-2222
888-243-4522
Fax: 914-964-9340
catalog@kimberamerica.com
www.kimberamerica.com

Pistols, rifles, shotguns and accessories

President: Leslie Edelman
CFO: James Cox
Purchasing Manager: Tom Overacker
Chief Operating Officer: Raplh Karanian
Credit Cards: AMEX; MasterCard; Visa
Catalog Cost: Free
Number of Employees: 220
Sales Volume: $24.5 MM

2482 L.L.Bean Hunting
L.L.Bean Inc.
15 Casco St.
Freeport, ME 04033
207-552-2000
www.llbean.com

Hunting gear and apparel.

Chairman: Shawn Gorman
President: Stephen Smith
Catalog Cost: Free
Printing Information: 60 pages in 4 colors
In Business: 105 years
Number of Employees: 5000
Sales Volume: $1.6 Billion

2483 Leupold & Stevens
Leupold & Stevens
14400 NW Greenbrier Parkway
Beaverton, OR 97006
800-538-7653
www.leupold.com

Hunting and shooting products and accessories, tactical, observation and golf gear.

2484 Marlin Firearms
Marlin
P.O. Box 1871
Madison, NC 27025
800-544-8892
www.marlinfirearms.com

Sporting rifles

Chairman: Frank Kenna III
CFO: Pamela Griffin
Credit Cards: MasterCard; Visa
Catalog Cost: Free
Catalog Circulation: Mailed 1 time(s) per year to 5000
Printing Information: 34 pages in 4 colors on Glossy Stock
Press: Web Press
Binding: Saddle Stitched
Mailing List Information: Names for rent
In Business: 147 years
Number of Employees: 575
Sales Volume: $36.4 MM

2485 Midwest TurkeyCall Supply
PO Box 16
Sullivan, IL 61951
217-797-5550
customerservice@midwestturkeycall.com
www.midwestturkeycall.com

Hunting and fishing equipment

2486 Mossberg Catalog
O.F. Mossberg & Sons
7 Grasso Avenue
North Haven, CT 06473
203-230-5300
Fax: 203-230-5420
www.mossberg.com

Firearms, parts, accessories, hunting apparel and gear

Chief Executive Officer: Alan Iver Mossberg Jr
Director of Media Relations: Linda Powell
Credit Cards: AMEX; MasterCard
Catalog Cost: Free
Catalog Circulation: Mailed 1 time(s) per year
Printing Information: 92 pages in 4 colors
In Business: 98 years
Sales Volume: $24.6 Million

2487 NIC Law Enforcement Supply
NIC Law Enforcement Supply
1403 Highway 313
Building A
Algodones, NM 87001
318-688-1365
888-642-0007
Fax: 318-688-1367
orders@nles.com
www.nles.com

Law enforcement equipment custom badges, wallets, and ID systems

President: Dana McCommon
CFO: Chales Tooraen
Catalog Cost: Free
Catalog Circulation: to 200M
Average Order Size: $65
Printing Information: 82 pages in 4 colors on Glossy Stock
Press: Web Press
Binding: Saddle Stitched
Mailing List Information: Names for rent
In Business: 30 years
Number of Employees: 2
Sales Volume: $120,000

2488 Nite-Lite Company
NLC Products, Inc.
3801 Woodland Hgts Road, Suite 100
PO Box 8300
Little Rock, AR 72222
501-227-9050
800-332-6968
Fax: 479-754-5669
www.huntsmart.com

Hunting and dog supplies

Chairman: Henry Mariani
President: Tim Mariani
Marketing Manager: J McCay
Finance: Gina Terry
Human Resources: Tricia Mariani
Business Manager: John Carlton
Credit Cards: MasterCard; Visa
Catalog Cost: Free
Catalog Circulation: Mailed 2 time(s) per year
Printing Information: 96 pages in 1 color
In Business: 5 years

Number of Employees: 70
Sales Volume: $13 MM

2489 Orvis Hunting
The Orvis Company Inc.
178 Conservation Way
Sunderland, VT 05250-4465   802-362-1300
                              888-235-9763
                        Fax: 802-362-0141
                              www.orvis.com

Hunting gear and accessories.

CEO: Leigh H. Perkins Jr.
Catalog Cost: Free
In Business: 160 years
Number of Employees: 1700
Sales Volume: $340 Million

2490 Para USA
Para USA, LLC
1816 Remington Circle
Huntsville, AL 35824-7381   704-930-7600
                              888-999-9386
                        Fax: 256-327-2852
                   contact@para-usa.com
                        www.para-usa.com

Pistols

CFO: Thanos Polyzos
Director Finance & Human Resources:
Roxeanne Copegog
Catalog Cost:
In Business: 26 years
Number of Employees: 60
Sales Volume: $10.98 MM

2491 Precision Reloading
Precision Reloading
1700 W Cedar Ave
Suite B
Mitchell, SD 57301   605-996-9984
                              800-223-0900
                        Fax: 605-996-9987
              sales@precisionreloading.com
                 www.precisionreloading.com

Hunting and reloading components, shooting supplies and accessories

President: Peter Maffei
Marketing Manager: Cindy Maffei
Credit Cards: MasterCard
Catalog Cost: Free
Catalog Circulation: Mailed 1 time(s) per year
to 40m
Average Order Size: $100
Printing Information: 56 pages in 4 colors on
Matte Stock
Press: Web Press
Binding: Saddle Stitched
Mailing List Information: Names for rent
In Business: 25 years
Number of Employees: 5
Sales Volume: $280,000

2492 Red Saltbox
503 South Brady Street
Attica, IN 47918   765-762-6292
                 wendy@theredsaltbox.com
                    www.theredsaltbox.com

Knives

2493 RedHead Archery
Bass Pro Shops
2500 E Kearney
Springfield, MO 65898   417-873-5000
                             800-227-7776
                       Fax: 417-873-5060
                             www.basspro.com

Bows, arrows and accessories, treestands, optics, scents, feeders, targets, blinds, rugged hunting boots, camo and more.

President & CEO: James Hagale
Catalog Cost: Free
Printing Information: 148 pages in 4 colors
In Business: 45 years

Number of Employees: 2200
Sales Volume: $4.45 Billion

2494 RedHead Hunting Master
Bass Pro Shops
2500 E Kearney
Springfield, MO 65898   417-873-5000
                             800-227-7776
                       Fax: 417-873-5060
                             www.basspro.com

Top-quality gear for hunting, camping, boating, fishing and other outdoor activities.

President & CEO: James Hagale
Catalog Cost: Free
Catalog Circulation: Mailed 1 time(s) per year
Printing Information: 600 pages in 4 colors
In Business: 45 years
Number of Employees: 2200
Sales Volume: $4.45 Billion

2495 STI International
STI International, Inc.
114 Halmar Cove
Georgetown, TX 78628-2331   512-819-0656
                       Fax: 512-819-0465
                        info@stiguns.com
                           www.stiguns.com

Frame kits, short blocks, complete guns

President: David Skinner
Vice President Engineering: Ed Minshew
Finance Executive: Karen Fuessel
Sales Executive: Pauletta Skinner
Printing Information: in 1 color
In Business: 24 years
Number of Employees: 65
Sales Volume: $6.9 Million

2496 Smoky Mountain Knife Works
Smoky Mountain Knife Works, Inc.
2320 Winfield Dunn Parkway
P.O. Box 4430
Sevierville, TN 37864   865-453-5871
                             800-251-9306
                       Fax: 865-428-5991
                          help@smkw.com

Knives and accessories for hunting, tactical-military, cutlery, martial arts, and camping

President: Kevin Pipes
Catalog Cost: Free
In Business: 45 years

2497 Summit Stands Catalog
Summit Treestands LLC
715 Summit Drive
Decatur, AL 35601   256-353-0634
                             800-353-0634
                       Fax: 256-353-9818
                    info@summitstands.com
                     www.summitstands.com

Treestands

President: John Woller
Marketing Manager: Jason Gordon
Chief Information Officer: Tim Brewer
Purchasing Agent: Karen Rogers
Credit Cards: MasterCard; Visa
Catalog Cost: Free
Printing Information: 10 pages
In Business: 27 years
Number of Employees: 35
Sales Volume: $500M to $1MM

2498 TenPoint Crossbows
TenPoint Crossbows
1325 Waterloo Road
Mogadore, OH 44260   330-628-9245
                      www.tenpointcrossbows.com

Crossbows and crossbow accessories

President: Richard L. Bednar
Director of Sales & Service: Randy Wood
Service Manager: Bryan Zabitski
Customer Service Supervisor: Amber

Vandegrift
Credit Cards: AMEX; MasterCard
Catalog Cost: Free
Catalog Circulation: Mailed 1 time(s) per year
Printing Information: 31 pages in 4 colors
In Business: 23 years

2499 The Snare Shop
The Snare Shop
330 S. Main St.
PO Box 70
Lidderdale, IA 51452   712-822-5780
                     sshop@snareshop.com
                        www.snareshop.com

Trapping and snare supplies

2500 The Sportsman's Guide
The Sportsman's Guide
PO Box 239
411 Farwell Ave.
South St. Paul, MN 55075-0239   800-882-2962
                        www.sportsmansguide.com

A wide variety of outdoor apparel, hunting accessories, fishing and camping equipment.

In Business: 46 years
Sales Volume: $500MM to $1 Billion

2501 Thompson/Center Arms
Thompson/Center Arms
2100 Roosevelt Ave.
Springfield, MA 01104-4351   603-330-5700
                             866-730-1614
                       Fax: 603-330-8614
              tca_customerservice@tcarms.com
                             www.tcarms.com

Hunting apparel and equipment

President: Michael Golden
Marketing Manager: Eric Brooker
Production Manager: Tyler Stone
In Business: 48 years
Sales Volume: $ 1-3 Million

2502 Waterfowl Hunting
Bass Pro Shops
2500 E Kearney
Springfield, MO 65898   417-873-5000
                             800-227-7776
                       Fax: 417-873-5060
                             www.basspro.com

Gear and apparel for waterfowlers.

President & CEO: James Hagale
Catalog Cost: Free
Catalog Circulation: Mailed 1 time(s) per year
Printing Information: 68 pages in 4 colors
In Business: 45 years
Number of Employees: 2200
Sales Volume: $4.45 Billion

Food & Beverage Products
Miscellaneous

2503 A La Zing
Omaha Steaks
10909 John Galt Blvd.
PO Box 3300
Omaha, NE 68103   800-228-9872

Quality delivered meals that can be prepared in less than 30 minutes at home.

Chairman: Alan Simon
President: Bruce Simon
CFO: David Hershiser
Marketing Manager: Vickie Hagen
Credit Cards: AMEX; MasterCard; Visa
Catalog Cost: Free
Printing Information: 52 pages
In Business: 98 years

2504 American Gourmet
American Gourmet
6698 Orchard Lake Rd
West Bloomfield Township, MI 48322 248-851-4450
800-966-7263
Fax: 248-737-3669
americangourmet@aol.com
www.agourmet.com

Hospitality gifts, Godiva-dipped fresh strawberries, cookies, chocolates, and gift baskets by the occassion

Owner: Herbert Sayers
Credit Cards: AMEX; MasterCard; Visa
Catalog Cost: Free
In Business: 34 years

2505 Archival Products
Archival Products
P.O. Box 1413
Des Moines, IA 50306-1413 800-526-5640
Fax: 888-220-2397
info@archival.com
www.archival.com

Handcrafted products and the development of solutions for preserving items

Account Representative: Phet Louvan
phetl@archival.com
Division Manager: Janice Comer
janicec@archival.com
Catalog Cost: Free

2506 Aunt Sally's Gift Catalog
Aunt Sally's Praline Shops Inc
750 St Charles Ave.
New Orleans, LA 70117-7315 504-524-3373
800-642-7257
Fax: 504-944-5925
service@auntsallys.com
www.AuntSallys.Com

Pralines and Creole food gift baskets from Louisiana

President: Bethany Gex
Marketing Manager: Cherie Cunningham
Production Manager: Karl Schmidt
Fulfillment: Bethany Gex
Credit Cards: AMEX; MasterCard; Visa
Catalog Cost: Free
In Business: 80 years
Number of Employees: 36
Sales Volume: $10MM to $20MM

2507 Azure Standard
Azure Standard
79709 Dufur Valley Rd.
Dufur, OR 97021 971-200-8350
Fax: 971-645-4759
www.azurestandard.com

Organic and natural food distributor.

Founder & CEO: David Stelzer
In Business: 44 years

2508 Bear Creek Smokehouse
Bear Creek Smokehouse
10857 State Hwy 154
Marshall, TX 75670 903-935-5217
800-950-2327
Fax: 903-935-2871
www.bearcreeksmokehouse.com

Premium Smoked Meats, smoked beef, pork and poultry items

In Business: 70+ years

2509 Carlisle Food Service Products
Carlisle Food Service Products
P.O. Box 53006
Oklahoma City, OK 73152-3066 405-475-5600
800-654-8210
Fax: 800-872-4701
customerservice@carlislefsp.com
www.carlislefsp.com

Global manufacturer of over 16,000 innovative, versatile and durable product solutions for the global food market from food bars & accesories to washing rackets and accessories

President: Dave Shannon
CFO: Carolyn Ford
Marketing Manager: Todd Mauer
Production Manager: Rich McDonagh
International Marketing Manager: Jim Calamito
Buyers: Susan Wortham
Catalog Circulation: Mailed 1 time(s) per year to 200M
Printing Information: 344 pages in 4 colors on Glossy Stock
Press: Web Press
Binding: Perfect Bound
Mailing List Information: Names for rent
In Business: 60 years
Number of Employees: 420
Sales Volume: $50,000,000

2510 Challah Connection
Challah Connection
66 Fort Point Street
Norwalk, CT 06855 866-242-5524
Fax: 203-222-0400
www.challahconnection.com

Gourmet foods, kosher gift baskets, baked goods and pastries

President: Jane Moritz
Catalog Cost: Free
In Business: 15 years

2511 Dean & DeLuca
Dean & DeLuca, Inc.
2526 E 36th Circle North
Wichita, KS 67219 316-821-3200
800-221-7714
Fax: 800-781-4050
customercare@deandeluca.com
www.deandeluca.com

Cheese, wines & spirits, seafood & shellfish, herbs & spices, oils & vinegars, hors d'ouvres & appetizers, coffee, tea & beverages, bakery, candy, confections & sweets

Chairman: Leslie G Rudd
CFO: Justin P Seamonds
Marketing Manager: Cristin Coats
CEO: Mark Daley
Credit Cards: AMEX; MasterCard; Visa
Catalog Cost: Free
Catalog Circulation: Mailed 4 time(s) per year to 40000
Average Order Size: $100
Printing Information: 24 pages in 1 color on Matte Stock
Press: Web Press
Mailing List Information: Names for rent
List Company: Action List
1 Kalisa Way
Paramus, NJ 07652
201-261-1500
In Business: 34 years
Number of Employees: 400
Sales Volume: $10MM to $20MM

2512 Earth & Vine Provisions
Earth & Vine Provisions
P.O. Box 1637
Loomis, CA 95650 888-723-8463
customerservice@earthnvine.com
www.earthnvine.com
In Business: 18 years

2513 Frontier Soups
Frontier Soups
2001 Swanson Ct.
Gurnee, IL 60031 847-688-1200
800-300-7687
Fax: 847-688-1206
info@frontiersoups.com
www.frontiersoups.com

Soup mixes
In Business: 28+ years

2514 Hodgson Mill
Hodgson Mill
1100 Stevens Ave
Effingham, IL 62401 800-525-0177
Fax: 217-347-0198
customerservice@hodgsonmill.com
www.hodgsonmill.com

Stone ground, whole grain and organic foods: flours, cornmeals, cereals, baking mixes, pastas and more

Chairman: Cathy Goldstein
President: Robert Goldstein
Marketing Manager: Paul Kirby
Credit Cards: AMEX; MasterCard; Visa
Catalog Cost: Free
In Business: 178 years
Number of Employees: 106
Sales Volume: $26 Million

2515 House of Webster
House of Webster
1013 N 2nd St
PO Box 1988
Rogers, AR 72756-1988 479-636-4640
800-369-4641
Fax: 479-636-2974
info@houseofwebster.com
www.houseofwebster.com

Gift packages and gourmet food items

CFO: Craig Castrellon
Marketing Manager: Denny Fletcher
Production Manager: Craig Duncan
Fulfillment: Chris Humphreys
Credit Cards: AMEX; MasterCard; Visa
Printing Information: 32 pages
In Business: 81 years

2516 Jed's Maple
Jed's Maple
259 Derby Pond Road
Derby, VT 5829 802-766-2700
866-4PU-EVT
Fax: 802-766-2702
www.jedsmaple.com

Maple products

2517 King Arthur Flour & The Bakers
King Arthur Flour & The Bakers
135 US Route 5 South
Norwich, VT 05055-9430 802-649-3361
800-827-6836
Fax: 802-649-3365
bakers@kingarthurflour.com
www.kingarthurflour.com

Flour, baking mixes and specialty baking supplies

Chairman: Frank E Sands II
President: Steve Voigt
CFO: Susan Renaud
Marketing Manager: Tom Payne
Production Manager: Sue Gray
Buyers: PJ Hamel
Credit Cards: AMEX; MasterCard; Visa
Catalog Cost: Free
Catalog Circulation: Mailed 12 time(s) per year to 6M
Printing Information: 56 pages in 4 colors on Matte Stock
Press: Web Press
Binding: Saddle Stitched
List Company: Direct Media
200 Pemberwick Road
Greenwich, CT 06830
203-532-3713
In Business: 225 years
Number of Employees: 150
Sales Volume: $20MM to $50MM

2518 Lucero Olive Oil
Lucero Olive Oil
2120 Loleta Avenue
Coming, CA 96021   877-330-2190
hello@lucerooliveoil.com
www.lucerooliveoil.com

Food - olives

Trade Inquiries/New Accounts: Claude Weiller
claude@lucerooliveoil.com
Program Development : Kimberly Connell
kimberly.connell@lucerooliveoil.com
Reorders: Trisha
sales@lucerooliveoil.com
In Business: 10 years

2519 McIlhenny Company
McIlhenny Company
Highway 329
Avery Island, LA 70513   337-365-8173
800-634-9599
Fax: 504-596-6442
countrystore@tabasco.com
www.tabasco.com

Sauces & specialty foods, gifts, bar accessories, etc.

Chairman: Edward Simmons
President: Paul McIlhenny
CFO: Michael Terrell
Marketing Manager: Martin Manion
Production Manager: Raymond Boudreaux
Purchasing Agent: Ricky Venable
International Marketing Manager: Stephen C Romero
Credit Cards: AMEX; MasterCard; Visa
Catalog Cost: Free
In Business: 146 years
Number of Employees: 200

2520 Monastery Greetings
Monastery Greetings
540 East 105th Street #115
Cleveland, OH 44108   800-472-0425
Fax: 216-249-3387
info@monasterygreetings.com
www.monasterygreetings.com

Gourmet treats and gifts from monasteries around the world

President: Will Keller
Founder: Will Keller
Credit Cards: MasterCard
Catalog Cost: Free
In Business: 18 years
Number of Employees: 2
Sales Volume: $76,000

2521 NapaStyle
NapaStyle
360 Industrial Court
Suite A
Benicia, CA 94510   866-776-1600
Fax: 707-252-1470
customerservice@napastyle.com
www.napastyle.com

Food products and kitchen delights

President: Michael Chiarello
Marketing Manager: Eileen Gordon
Founder: Michael Chiarello
Catalog Cost: Free
Printing Information: 67 pages in 4 colors on Glossy Stock
Binding: Saddle Stitched
Mailing List Information: Names for rent
In Business: 5 years
Number of Employees: 20

2522 Nelson Jameson
Nelson Jameson
2400 E 5th Street
Marshfield, WI 54449   715-837-1151
800-826-8302
Fax: 800-472-0840
sales@nelsonjameson.com
www.nelsonjameson.com

Supplier of products used by food, dairy, and beverage processing facilities

Chairman: Adam Nelson
President: Jerry Lippert
Production Manager: Kyle Willfahrt
VP of Branch/Warehouse Operations: Carl Hamann
Credit Cards: AMEX; MasterCard
Catalog Cost: Free
Catalog Circulation: Mailed 1 time(s) per year
Printing Information: 846 pages in 2 colors
In Business: 70 years
Number of Employees: 102
Sales Volume: $98 Million

2523 Olive Press
Olive Press
Jacuzzi Family Winery
24724 Highway 121 (Arnold Drive)
Sanoma, CA 95476   707-939-8900
800-965-4839
Fax: 707-939-1203
www.theolivepress.com

Extra virgin olive oil, citrus olive oil, dipping and flavored oils and cookbooks, bath and body collections and gifts

Marketing Manager: Debra Rogers
Owner: Tony Williams
Founder: Ed Stoleman
Catalog Cost: Free
In Business: 18 years
Number of Employees: 12
Sales Volume: $950,000

2524 The Lighter Side Catalog
The Lighter Side Co.
P.O. Box 25600
Bradenton, FL 34206-5600   800-244-9116
800-232-0963
Fax: 800-551-4406
CustomerService@lighterside.com

Novelties, gifts, and practical jokes

Catalog Cost: Free
In Business: 110 years

2525 Things You Never Knew Existed
Johnson Smith Company
P.O. Box 25600
Bradenton, FL 34206-5600   800-853-9490
customerservice@thingsyouneverknew.com
www.thingsyouneverknew.com

Funmakers, jokes, hobbies and novelties

CFO: David Crofoot
Marketing Manager: Kim Boyd
Founder: Alfred Johnson Smith
Credit Cards: AMEX; MasterCard; Visa
Catalog Cost: Free
Printing Information: in 4 colors on Matte Stock
Press: Web Press
Binding: Saddle Stitched
Mailing List Information: Names for rent
List Manager: Kris Temple
In Business: 110 years
Sales Volume: $20MM to $50MM

2526 Trophy Nut
Trophy Nut
320 N 2nd Street
Tipp City, OH 45371-1912   937-667-8478
800-219-9004
Fax: 937-667-4656
bwilke@trophynut.com
www.trophynut.com

Candy, chocolate, cookies and nut gifts

President: Jeff Bollinger
Purchasing: Jill Larger
jlarger@trophynut.com
VP, Sales: Bob Wilke
bwilke@trophynut.com
Export: Dave Ramirez
dramirez@trophynut.com
Credit Cards: AMEX; MasterCard; Visa

Catalog Cost: Free
Catalog Circulation: Mailed 3 time(s) per year
Printing Information: 40 pages in 4 colors on Glossy Stock
Press: Web Press
Binding: Saddle Stitched
Mailing List Information: Names for rent
In Business: 50 years
Number of Employees: 66
Sales Volume: $24 Million

2527 UVC Gourmet
Fireworks Popcorn
101 West Grand Ave
Port Washington, WI 53074   414-449-2000
877-668-4800
Fax: 414-449-5200
popcornlovers.com

Naturally grown, GMO free, gourmet popping corns; 12 varieties, sample packs, 8oz to 25lbs, gift packs, baskets, gift bowls, poppers and accessories

President: Rob Hercules
Owner: Wayne Chrusciel
Printing Information: 10 pages in 4 colors
In Business: 15 years

2528 Walden Foods
Walden Farms, Inc.
1209 West St. Georges Avenue
Linden, NJ 07036-6117   540-622-2800
800-229-1706
Fax: 540-622-2840
customerservice@waldenfarms.com
www.waldenfarms.com

100% applewood smoked seafood and poultry; trout, salmon, mousse, smoked chicken breast, catfish, nova lox, free of pesticides, chemicals, artificial preservatives, sweeteners and dyes

President: John P. Good Jr
Marketing Manager: Christina Hyre, VP
Production Manager: Connie Reed
Credit Cards: MasterCard; Visa; Discover
Catalog Cost: Free
Catalog Circulation: Mailed 1 time(s) per year
Average Order Size: $50
Printing Information: 1 pages in 4 colors on Glossy Stock
Press: Sheetfed Press
In Business: 42 years
Number of Employees: 20
Sales Volume: ? 2,400,000

2529 Wild Thymes Farm
Wild Thymes Farm
245 County Route 351
Medusa, NY 12120   845-266-8387
800-492-6949
Fax: 845-266-8395
info@wildthymes.com
www.wildthymes.com

BBQ sauces, chutneys, cranberry sauces, dipping sauces, marinades, salad refreshers, vinaigrettes

CFO: Maggie Moyer
Owner: Enid Stettner
Catalog Cost: Free
In Business: 22 years
Number of Employees: 15
Sales Volume: $1.3 Million

2530 Zapp's Potato Chips
Zapp's Potato Chips
PO Box 1533
Gramercy, LA 70052-1533   888-744-7889
Fax: 225-869-9779
www.zapps.com

Kettle cooked potato chips in a variety of flavors

President: Ron Zappe
Marketing Manager: Richard Gaudry
In Business: 30 years

2531 Zingerman's Mail Order Cupboard
Zingerman's Catering & Events
422 Detroit St
Ann Arbor, MI 48104-1118   734-663-3400
                                888-636-8162
                           Fax: 734-477-6988
                   service@zingermans.com
                   www.Zingermanscatering.Com

Fine traditional foods and gifts

President: Ari Weinzweig
CFO: M Frechette
Marketing Manager: M Frechette
Credit Cards: AMEX; MasterCard; Visa
Catalog Cost: Free
Catalog Circulation: Mailed 3 time(s) per year
Average Order Size: $65
Printing Information: 47 pages in 3 colors on Newsprint
Press: Web Press
Binding: Saddle Stitched
Mailing List Information: Names for rent
In Business: 32 years
Number of Employees: 3
Sales Volume: $1,000,000

Breads & Grains

2532 Beatrice Bakery
Beatrice Bakery Co
201 S 5th St
PO Box 457
Beatrice, NE 68310-4408   402-223-2358
                               800-228-4030
           customerservice@beatricebakery.com
                   www.beatricebakery.com

Hand-crafted dessert cakes made especially with fruit and nuts; dessert toppings

President: Greg Leach
Marketing Manager: Rebecca Brown
Production Manager: Robin Dickinson
Catalog Cost: Free
In Business: 98 years
Number of Employees: 43
Sales Volume: $1.4 Million

2533 Bread Alone
Bread Alone
2121 Ulster Ave
Lake Katrine, NY 1244   845-657-6057
                               800-769-3328
                          Fax: 845-657-6228
                   info@breadalone.com
                   www.breadalone.com

Whole grain hearth loaf and sourdough breads

Chairman: Sharon Leader
President: Daniel M Leader
Vice President: Nels Leader
General Manager: Melissa Beck
Office Mnager: Heather Berman Waner
Credit Cards: MasterCard; Visa
Catalog Circulation: to 1000
Printing Information: 1 pages in 1 color on Matte Stock
In Business: 32 years
Number of Employees: 40
Sales Volume: $20,000,000

2534 DiCamillo Bakery
DiCamillo
811 Linwood Avenue
Niagara Falls, NY 14305-2584   800-634-4363
                          Fax: 816-282-7236
                   info@dicamillobakery.com
                   www.dicamillobakery.com

Biscotti, cookies, confections, breads, holiday cakes, gourmet coffees and gift items

President: David Di Camillo
Credit Cards: AMEX; MasterCard
Catalog Cost: Free
In Business: 95 years
Number of Employees: 40
Sales Volume: $20MM to $50MM

2535 K-Y Farms
K-Y Farms
25691 Altas Palmas Rd
Harlingen, TX 78552   956-412-8066
                               800-255-1486
                          Fax: 956-423-1897
                   orders@k-yfarms.com
                   www.k-yfarms.com

2536 Kenyon's Grist Mill
Kenyon's Grist Mill
21 Glen Rock Road
PO Box 221
West Kingston, RI 02892-1706   401-783-4054
                               800-753-6966
                          Fax: 401-782-3564
                   www.kenyonsgristmill.com

Stone ground corn meal and flour; Jams, marmalades, syrups and clam or corn chowders

President: Paul Drumm III
Marketing Manager: Karen Cooke
General Manager: Russell Spencer
Facilities Manager: Richard Thibodeau
Labeling & Packing: Rana Anjum
Credit Cards: MasterCard; Visa
Catalog Cost: Free
Catalog Circulation: to 1000
In Business: 318 years
Number of Employees: 7
Sales Volume: $500,000

2537 O&H Danish Bakery
O&H Danish Bakery
5910 Washington Avenue
Racine, WI 53406   262-504-7000
                               800-709-4009
                   store.ohdanishbakery.com/home

Bakery, cakes

In Business: 66 years

2538 Pelican Bay Ltd
Pelican Bay Ltd
150 Douglas Ave
Dunedin, FL 34698-7908   727-733-8399
                               800-826-8982
                          Fax: 727-734-5860
                   sales@pelicanbayltd.com
                   www.pelicanbayltd.com

Bread mixes, cookie mixes, seasoning blends, dip mixes, cool drink and hot drinks

President: Linda Pfaelzer
CFO: Paul Whitman
Catalog Cost: Free
Printing Information: 35 pages
In Business: 33 years
Number of Employees: 30
Sales Volume: $4.8 Million

2539 Strawberry Hill Povitica
Strawberry Hill Povitica
7226 W Frontage Road
Merriam, KS 66203   913-631-1002
                               800-634-1002
                          Fax: 913-631-9442
                   Bakers@Povitica.com
                   www.povitica.com

Printing Information: 11 pages

2540 Sunrise Bakery & Gourmet Foods
Sunrise Bakery & Gourmet Foods
2810 Diane Lane
Hibbing, MN 55746   218-262-1219
                               800-782-6736
                          Fax: 218-263-4305
                   sales@sunrisebakery.com
                   www.sunrisegourmet.com

Specially baked items, walnut potica, strudel, biscotti, antipasto, fruitcake, chocolate fruitcake and much more

President: Donna Anthony
Catalog Cost: Free

In Business: 102 years
Number of Employees: 12
Sales Volume: $630,000

2541 True Brands
True Brands
154 N 35th Street
Seattle, WA 98103   800-750-8783
                   www.truefabrications.com

Restaurant supplies for liquor, beer and wine

President: Dhruv Agarwal
Credit Cards: AMEX; MasterCard
Catalog Circulation: Mailed 4 time(s) per year
Printing Information: 52 pages in 4 colors
Press: Web Press
Binding: Saddle Stitched
In Business: 13 years
Sales Volume: $5MM to $10MM

2542 Wolferman's
Wolferman's
2500 S Pacific Highway
PO Box 9100
Medford, OR 97501-700   800-798-6241
                          Fax: 800-999-7548
                   service@wolfermans.com
                   www.wolfermans.com

English muffins, scones, tea breads and crumpets, toppings, elegant desserts, premiun teas and specially blended coffee

President: Brian Hubbard
CFO: Tim Anderson
Marketing Manager: Margaret Hartnett
Buyers: Susan Brown
Credit Cards: AMEX; MasterCard; Visa
Catalog Cost: Free
Catalog Circulation: Mailed 11 time(s) per year to 10000
Average Order Size: $60
Printing Information: 32 pages in 4 colors on Glossy Stock
Press: Web Press
Binding: Saddle Stitched
Mailing List Information: Names for rent
List Company: Mokrynski & Associates Hackensack, NJ
In Business: 127 years
Number of Employees: 25
Sales Volume: $10MM to $20MM

2543 Zehnder's
Zehnder's
730 S. Main Street
Frankenmuth, MI 48734   800-863-7999
                               844-207-7309
                   webmaster@zehnders.com
                   www.zehnders.com

Candy & Snacks

2544 Alethea's Chocolates
Alethea's Chocolates
8301 Main St
Williamsville, NY 14221-6139   716-633-8620
                   www.aletheas.com

Chocolates, toffees, nuts and truffles

President: Dean Tassy
CFO: Ge Tassy
Credit Cards: MasterCard; Visa
Catalog Circulation: to 2500
Printing Information: 4 pages in 2 colors on Newsprint
Press: Sheetfed Press
Binding: Folded
In Business: 47 years
Number of Employees: 50
Sales Volume: $3,000,000

2545 American Gourmet

American Gourmet
6698 Orchard Lake Rd
West Bloomfield Township, MI 48322   248-851-4450
   800-966-7263
Fax: 248-737-3669
americangourmet@aol.com
www.agourmet.com

Hospitality gifts, Godiva-dipped fresh strawberries, cookies, chocolates, and gift baskets by the occassion

Owner: Herbert Sayers
Credit Cards: AMEX; MasterCard; Visa
Catalog Cost: Free
In Business: 34 years

2546 Aplets & Cotlets

Liberty Orchards Co., Inc.
117 Mission Ave.
PO Box C
Cashmere, WA 98815
   509-782-1000
   800-888-5696
Fax: 509-782-4776
service@libertyorchards.com
www.libertyorchards.com

Manufacturer of America's favorite fruit and nut candy, chocolates, baked goods and food gifts

President: Gregory A. Taylor
Catalog Cost: Free
Printing Information: 24 pages in 4 colors
In Business: 95 years
Number of Employees: 80
Sales Volume: $9 Million

2547 Bates Nut Farm

Bates Nut Farm
15954 Woods Valley Rd
Valley Center, CA 92082
   760-749-3333
   800-642-0348
Fax: 760-749-9499
info@batesnutfarm.biz
www.batesnutfarm.biz

Nuts, dried fruits, candies, chocolates, fudge and gift boxes

President: Walter Bates
Credit Cards: MasterCard; Visa
Printing Information: 4 pages
In Business: 94 years
Number of Employees: 28

2548 Biscoff Gourmet Catalog

Lotus Bakeries North America, Inc.
50 Francisco Street
Suite 115
San Francisco, CA 94133
   855-415-0077
Fax: 415-956-4922
customerservice@biscoff.com
www.biscoff.com

Biscoff gourmet cookies, chocolates and pastries, gift baskets and gift tins

Marketing Manager: Ignace Heyman
CEO: Jan Boone
COO: Jan Vander Stichele
Catalog Cost: Free
Printing Information: 24 pages in 4 colors on Glossy Stock
Binding: Saddle Stitched
In Business: 82 years

2549 Bissinger French Confectioners

Bissinger French Confectioners
97 Plaza Frontenac
St Louis, MO 63131
   314-367-9750
   800-325-8881
Fax: 314-367-9751
orders@bissingers.com
www.Bissingers.Com

Handmade, gourmet chocolate, chocolate-dipped fruits, truffles and caramels

President: Ken Kellerhals
CFO: Francine Nicholson
Marketing Manager: Gina Mantovani
Business Gifts Contact: Maureen Bassett-Baran
maureen@bissingers.com
Media Contact: Rosemary Sturm
rosemary@bissingers.com
Special Events Contact: Jessica Aubuchon
jaubuchon@bissingers.com
Credit Cards: MasterCard
Catalog Cost: Free
Printing Information: 23 pages in 4 colors on Glossy Stock
Binding: Saddle Stitched
In Business: 148 years
Number of Employees: 80
Sales Volume: $10.5 million

2550 Bridgewater Chocolate

Bridgewater Chocolate
559 Federal Rd.
Brookfield, CT 06804
   203-775-2286
   800-888-8742
Fax: 203-775-9369
www.bridgewaterchocolate.com

Gourmet chocolates, nuts, pretzels, toffee and gift baskets.

Founder: Erik Landegren
Partner: Andrew Blauner
Catalog Cost: Free
Printing Information: 11 pages in 4 colors
In Business: 21 years

2551 Cakes by Jane

Cakes by Jane, LLC
9 Burnsville Hill Rd
Suite #3
Asheville, NC 28804-3140
   828-285-9292
   888-834-9981
Fax: 828-281-2597
info@cakesbyjane.com
www.cakesbyjane.com

Mouthwatering cream cheese poundcakes in different flavors

President: Melissa Kreidler
Catalog Cost: Free
Catalog Circulation: Mailed 1 time(s) per year to 10000
Printing Information: 8 pages in 6 colors on Glossy Stock
Press: Sheetfed Press
Binding: Folded
In Business: 39 years
Number of Employees: 3
Sales Volume: $300,000

2552 Candy & Craft Molds Catalog

Candyland Crafts
201 West Main Street
Somerville, NJ 08876-2811
   908-685-0410
   877-487-4289
Fax: 908-575-1640
orders@candylandcrafts.com
www.Candylandcrafts.Com

Cake & candy molds, cake decorating sets and molds, cake display stands, levelers and accessories, turntables, pillars, bridges, icings and fondant, soap making kits and molds

President: Diane Stephan
Credit Cards: AMEX; MasterCard
Catalog Cost: $11.95
Printing Information: 200 pages in 2 colors on Glossy Stock
In Business: 32 years
Sales Volume: $1MM to $3MM

2553 Candy Crate Catalog

Candy Crate
12520 Business Center Dr.
Bldg D
Victorville, CA 92395
   760-949-0467
customerservice@candycrate.com
www.candycrate.com

Retro and modern candy and snacks as well as assorted baskets and arrangements.

2554 Carson Wrapped Hershey's Chocolates

WhCandy
3115 Homeward Way
Fairfield, OH 45014-4255
   513-874-7414
   800-995-2288
Fax: 513-870-4822
www.wrappedhersheys.com

Custom wrapped Hershey bars with personalized wrappers

President: Scott J Frederick
Marketing Manager: Sharon Frederick
Credit Cards: AMEX; MasterCard; Visa
Catalog Cost: Free
Printing Information: 25 pages in 4 colors on Glossy Stock
Mailing List Information: Names for rent
In Business: 20 years
Number of Employees: 55
Sales Volume: $5MM to $10MM

2555 Challah Connection

Challah Connection
66 Fort Point Street
Norwalk, CT 06855
   866-242-5524
Fax: 203-222-0400
www.challahconnection.com

Gourmet foods, kosher gift baskets, baked goods and pastries

President: Jane Moritz
Catalog Cost: Free
In Business: 15 years

2556 Chocolate Catalogue

Bissinger
1600 North Broadway
Saint Louis, MO 63102
   314-615-2400
   800-325-8881
Fax: 314-534-2419
orders@bissingers.com
www.bissingers.com

Gourmet chocolate, gourmet candy, chocolate gifts

CFO: Francine Nicholson
COO: Bill Bremmer
Credit Cards: AMEX; MasterCard; Visa
Catalog Cost: Free
Catalog Circulation: Mailed 4 time(s) per year to 1MM
Printing Information: 24 pages in 4 colors
Press: Web Press
Mailing List Information: Names for rent
Sales Volume: $6 Million

2557 Chocolate Inn

Chocolate Inn
110 Buffalo Avenue
Freeport, NY 11520-2802
   516-377-8370
   800-526-3437
Fax: 516-377-7190
customerservice@chocolateinn.com
www.taylor-grant.com/

Custom molded chocolates

President: David Miller
Production Manager: Kurt Boehringer
Credit Cards: AMEX; MasterCard; Visa
Catalog Cost: Free
Catalog Circulation: to 14000
Printing Information: 71 pages
Number of Employees: 8
Sales Volume: $1MM to $3MM

2558 Chocolate by Design
Chocolate by Design, Inc.
700-4 Union Parkway
Ronkonkoma, NY 11779-7427   631-737-0082
                             800-536-3618
                             chocobd@aol.com
                             www.chocolatebydesigninc.com

Processor of gourmet chocolate novelties and coins, also, custom molding available

President: Richard Motlin
CFO: Ellen Motlin
Catalog Cost: Free
Catalog Circulation: to 2000
Average Order Size: $250
Printing Information: 12 pages in 4 colors on Glossy Stock
Mailing List Information: Names for rent
In Business: 36 years
Number of Employees: 10
Sales Volume: $1MM to $3MM

2559 Cookie Garden
The Cookie Garden
362 Beinoris Drive
Wood Dale Il, IL 60191   800-582-9191
                          webmaster@cookiegarden.com
                          www.cookiegarden.com

Gourmet cookies, fruit baskets, holiday, themed and special occasion gifts and corporate gift baskets

President: Dave Anfuson
In Business: 28 years

2560 Country Kitchen SweetArt
Country Kitchen SweetArt, Inc.
4621 Speedway Drive
Fort Wayne, IN 46825-5236   260-482-4835
                             800-497-3927
                         Fax: 260-483-4091
                         mail@countrykitchensa.com
                         www.countrykitchensa.com

Specializing in cake, candy, cookie, pastry supplies as well as quality kitchen products

Marketing Manager: Autumn Carpenter
General Manager: Leslie Myers
Credit Cards: MasterCard; Visa
Catalog Cost: Free
Catalog Circulation: Mailed 1 time(s) per year to 5000
Average Order Size: $40
Printing Information: 352 pages in 4 colors on Glossy Stock
Press: Web Press
Binding: Perfect Bound
In Business: 47 years
Number of Employees: 20
Sales Volume: $1.9 Million

2561 Cryer Creek Kitchens
Collin Street Bakery
401 West 7th Avenue
Corsicana, TX 75110   903-872-8411
                       800-353-7437
                  Fax: 903-654-6725
                  www.cryercreek.com

Texas pecan cakes, old fashioned favorites cookie assortment, blueberry cheesecake, golden rum cake

President: Robert Means
Marketing Manager: Robert Means
Credit Cards: Visa
Catalog Cost: Free
Catalog Circulation: Mailed 1 time(s) per year to 60000
Printing Information: 15 pages in 4 colors on Glossy Stock
Number of Employees: 4
Sales Volume: $500M to $1MM

2562 Cummings Studio Chocolates
Cummings Studio Chocolates
679 East 900 South
Salt Lake City, UT 84105-1101   801-328-4858
                                 800-537-3957
                            Fax: 801-328-4801
                            www.Cummingsstudiochocolates.Com

Chocolates, brittle and roasted nuts

President: Marion Cummings
Credit Cards: AMEX; MasterCard; Visa
Catalog Cost: Free
Catalog Circulation: Mailed 1 time(s) per year to 6500
Printing Information: 2 pages in 4 colors on Glossy Stock
Mailing List Information: Names for rent
In Business: 90 years
Number of Employees: 40
Sales Volume: $5MM to $10MM

2563 Dale and Thomas Popcorn
Dale and Thomas Popcorn
One Cedar Lane
Englewood, NJ 07631   800-767-4444
                       800-767-4444

Gourmet flavored popcorn and gift baskets

President: Sean Orr
VP Purchasing: Richard Riordan
COO: Glenn Flook
Credit Cards: AMEX; MasterCard; Visa
Catalog Cost: Free
Catalog Circulation: Mailed 4 time(s) per year
Printing Information: in 4 colors
In Business: 9 years
Number of Employees: 200
Sales Volume: $9.4 million

2564 Davidson of Dundee
Dundee Groves
PO Box 829
Dundee, FL 33838-800   800-294-2266
                        www.dundeegroves.com

Citrus candies, marmalades and fresh fruit

President: Tom Davidson
Marketing Manager: Tom Davidson
Credit Cards: AMEX; MasterCard
Catalog Cost: Free
Catalog Circulation: Mailed 2 time(s) per year to 20000
Printing Information: 32 pages in 4 colors on Glossy Stock
Press: Web Press
Binding: Saddle Stitched
Mailing List Information: Names for rent
In Business: 44 years
Number of Employees: 100-
Sales Volume: $3MM to $5MM

2565 Edible Arrangements
Edible Arrangements
95 Barnes Road
Wallingford, CT 06492-1800   203-774-8000
                              877-363-7848
                         Fax: 203-774-0531
                         www.ediblearrangements.com

Fresh fruit bouquets for every special occasion

Marketing Manager: Stephen Thomas
Founder and CEO: Tariq Farid
COO: Kamran Farid
EVP: Kristy Ferguson
Credit Cards: AMEX; MasterCard
In Business: 12 years
Number of Employees: 75
Sales Volume: $18.47MM

2566 Empress Chocolates Company
Empress Chocolates Company
5518 Avenue N
Brooklyn, NY 11234   718-951-2251
                      800-793-3809
                 Fax: 718-951-2254

Chocolates, truffles, dipped fruits; special occassion and corporate gift boxes available

President: Ernest Grunhut
CFO: Jack Grunhut
Credit Cards: AMEX; MasterCard
Catalog Cost: Free
In Business: 27 years
Number of Employees: 35
Sales Volume: $2.8 Million

2567 Enstrom Candies
Enstrom Candies
701 Colorado Ave.
PO Box 1088
Grand Junction, CO 81501   800-367-8766
                       Fax: 970-683-1011
                            www.enstrom.com

Classic chocolate assortments, toffees, chocolate turtles, gift baskets, tins, boxes and corporate gifts

President: Douglas S Simons
Marketing Manager: Bob Jackson
General Manager: Emery Dorsey
Credit Cards: AMEX; MasterCard; Visa
Catalog Cost: Free
Printing Information: 9 pages
Mailing List Information: Names for rent
In Business: 51 years
Number of Employees: 52
Sales Volume: $5MM to $10MM

2568 Fannie May
Fannie May
2457 W North Ave.
Melrose Park, IL 60160   800-333-3629
                          www.fanniemay.com

Assorted chocolates

Catalog Cost: Free
Printing Information: 36 pages in 4 colors
In Business: 96 years

2569 Fran's Chocolates
Fran's Chocolates, Ltd.
5900 Airport Way
Seattle, WA 98122-4083   206-322-0233
                          800-422-3726
                     Fax: 206-322-0452
                     orders@franschocolates.com
                     www.franschocolates.com

Chocolates, caramels, fruits and nuts, truffles, sauces, gift baskets and boxes of chocolates

President: Fran Bigelow
Marketing Manager: Sean Seedlock
Production Manager: Dylan Bigelow
Credit Cards: AMEX; MasterCard
Catalog Cost: Free
Catalog Circulation: Mailed 1 time(s) per year to 60000
Average Order Size: $26
Printing Information: 16 pages in 4 colors on Matte Stock
Press: Sheetfed Press
Binding: Saddle Stitched
Mailing List Information: Names for rent
In Business: 29 years
Number of Employees: 40
Sales Volume: $6 Million

2570 Godiva Chocolatier
Godiva
139 Mill Rock Rd East
Old Saybrook, CT 06475-4201   860-510-7300
                               800-946-3482
                          Fax: 860-510-7331
                          letters@godiva.com
                          www.godiva.com

Chocolates, and Godiva special roast coffee

Principal: Kenneth Seale
Credit Cards: AMEX; MasterCard; Visa
Catalog Cost: Free
Catalog Circulation: Mailed 8 time(s) per year

Printing Information: 32 pages in 4 colors on Glossy Stock
Binding: Saddle Stitched
Mailing List Information: Names for rent
List Company: AZ Marketing Services
31 River Road
Cos Cob, CT 06807
203-629-8088
Number of Employees: 6
Sales Volume: Under $500M

2571 Good Fortunes
Good Fortunes
5190 Lake Worth Road
Greenacres, FL 33463-2813   561-439-8813
                                 800-644-9474
                          Fax: 561-641-2764
                     sales@goodfortunes.com
                       www.goodfortunes.com

Chocolate dipped and decorated fortune cookies and oreos, special cookies for weddings

Credit Cards: AMEX; MasterCard
Catalog Cost: Free
Printing Information: 6 pages in 4 colors on Matte Stock
In Business: 22 years

2572 Gourmet Honey Candies from Queen Bee Gardens
Queen Bee Gardens
262 East Main Street
Lovell, WY 82401   307-548-2543
                                 800-225-7553
                          Fax: 307-548-7994
                   queenbee@queenbeegardens.com
                     www.queenbeegardens.com

Hand-dipped, hand-crafted, low-sugar and sugar-free honey candies

President: Gene B Zeller
Marketing Manager: Sidney Pitt
Catalog Cost: Free
Catalog Circulation: Mailed 2 time(s) per year to 2.5M
Average Order Size: $250
Printing Information: 12 pages in 4 colors
Mailing List Information: Names for rent
In Business: 35 years
Number of Employees: 12
Sales Volume: $480,000

2573 Harbor Candy Shop
Harbor Candy Shop
248 Main Street
Ogunquit, ME 03907   800-331-5856
                       www.harborcandy.com

Candy, fudge and other confections, handmade chocolates from Maine

President: Eugenie Sotiropoulos
CFO: Jean Sotiropoulos
Marketing Manager: Colleen Osselaer
Credit Cards: MasterCard; Visa
Catalog Cost: Free
Catalog Circulation: Mailed 2 time(s) per year to 10000
Average Order Size: $50
Printing Information: 44 pages in 4 colors on Glossy Stock
Press: Letterpress
Binding: Saddle Stitched
In Business: 58 years
Number of Employees: 20
Sales Volume: $1.9 Million

2574 Harbor Sweets
Harbor Sweets
85 Leavitt Street
Salem, MA 01970-5599   978-745-7648
                                 800-243-2115
                          Fax: 978-741-7811
                      info@harborsweets.com
                        www.harborsweets.com

Handmade chocolates and candies

President: Phyllis Le Blanc
CFO: Jon Blake
Marketing Manager: Billie Phillips
Credit Cards: MasterCard; Visa
Catalog Cost: Free
Catalog Circulation: Mailed 4 time(s) per year to 34000
Printing Information: 16 pages in 6 colors on Glossy Stock
Press: Web Press
Binding: o
Mailing List Information: Names for rent
List Company: D-J Associates
77 Danbury Road
Ridgefield, CT 06877
203-431-8777
In Business: 42 years
Number of Employees: 50
Sales Volume: $50MM to $100MM

2575 Harry London's Candies
Fannie May
2457 W. North Avenue
Melrose Park, IL 60160   800-333-3629
            customerservice@harrylondon.com
                        www.fanniemay.com

Chocolates, buckeyes, joys, chocolate covered pretzels

President: Terry Mitchell
CFO: Matt Anderson
VP, Sales & Marketing: Ed Seibolt
Credit Cards: MasterCard; Visa
Catalog Cost: Free
Printing Information: 12 pages in 4 colors
In Business: 95 years
Number of Employees: 200
Sales Volume: $10 Million

2576 Indian Wells Date Gardens & Chocolatier
Sea View brand
86-235 Avenue 52
PO Box 818
Coachella, CA 92236   760-398-8850
                          Fax: 760-398-8851
                    Info@SeaViewSales.com
                      www.seaviewsales.com

Dates, chocolates, apricots, etc

President: Dennis Jensen
SVP: Roya Jensen
Plant Manager: Hugo Barajas
Field Agronomist: Dennis Maroney
Catalog Cost: Free
Printing Information: 10 pages
Number of Employees: 10

2577 James and Fralinger's Catalog
James Candy Company
1519 Boardwalk
Atlantic City, NJ 08401-7287   800-441-1404
                 comments@jamescandy.com
                       www.jamescandy.com

Salt water taffy, chocolates, fudge, macaroons, nuts, gift towers, gift baskets and corporate gifts

President: Frank Glaser
Marketing Manager: Lisa Glaser Whitley
EVP Sales and Marketing: Lisa Glaser Whitley
VP Internet Technology: Art Gager
Controller: Rose Gedicke
Credit Cards: AMEX; MasterCard; Visa
Catalog Cost: Free
Catalog Circulation: Mailed 1 time(s) per year
Printing Information: 1 pages in 4 colors
Number of Employees: 4
Sales Volume: Under $500M

2578 Jer's Chocolates
Jer's Chocolates
437 S. Highway 101
Suite 105
Solana Beach, CA 92075   800-540-7265
                              info@jers.com
                            www.jers.com

Gourmet chocolates.

2579 Jo's Candies
Jo's Candies
2530 W 237th St
Torrance, CA 90505   310-257-0260
                                 800-770-1946
                    Sales@JosCandies.com
                       www.joscandies.com

Chocolates, candies, cookies

In Business: 69 years

2580 Lammes Candies
Lammes Candies
PO Box 1885
Austin, TX 78767-1885   512-310-2223
                                 800-252-1885
                          Fax: 512-238-2019
                            www.lammes.com

Pralines, Signature chocolates, taffies and toffee, assorted chocolates and sugar free

Chairman: David L Teich
CFO: Pam Teich
Purchasing Agent: Marina Guadiano
Founder: William Wirt Lamme
Credit Cards: MasterCard; Visa
Catalog Cost: Free
Catalog Circulation: to 120
Printing Information: 6 pages in 4 colors on Glossy Stock
Binding: Folded
In Business: 136 years
Number of Employees: 95
Sales Volume: $11.6 Million

2581 Linda's Lollies Company
Linda's Lollies Company
1 International Blvd Ste 208
Mahwah, NJ 07495-20   201-252-8765
                                 800-347-1545
                          Fax: 201-252-8768
                      info@lindaslollies.com
                        www.lindaslollies.com

Gourmet lollipops and hard candies

President: Linda Harkavy
In Business: 31 years

2582 Marshall's Fudge & Homemade Candies
Marshall's Fudge Candy Company
308 East Central
Mackinaw City, MI 49701-639   231-436-5082
                                 800-343-8343
                          Fax: 231-436-5107
                       www.Marshallsfudge.Com

Homemade candies, fudge, gourmet caramel apples, caramel corn, popcorn, bark, taffy, nuts and toppings

President: Patrick Frohoff
Marketing Manager: John E Montgomery
Production Manager: Gerald Herholz Jr
Credit Cards: AMEX; MasterCard; Visa Discover Optima
Catalog Cost: Free
Catalog Circulation: Mailed 1 time(s) per year to 15000
Average Order Size: $36
Printing Information: 12 pages in 4 colors on Glossy Stock
Press: Web Press
Binding: Saddle Stitched
Mailing List Information: Names for rent
In Business: 127 years
Number of Employees: 15
Sales Volume: $5MM to $10MM

2583 Monastery Candy
Monastery Candy
8318 Abbey Hill Lane
Dubuque, IW 52003   563-556-6330
                                 866-556-3400
                 questions@monasterycandy.com
                      www.monasterycandy.com

Candy

In Business: 50 years

2584 Mother Myrick's Confectionery
Mother Myrick
Mother Myrick's
PO Box 1142
Manchester Center, VT 05255-1142 802-362-1560
888-669-7425
Fax: 802-362-6001
callmom@mothermyricks.com
www.mothermyricks.com

Handmade chocolates, buttercrunch, hot fudge and award-winning desserts

President: Jacqueline Baker
Marketing Manager: Ron Mancini
Credit Cards: AMEX; MasterCard; Visa
Catalog Cost: Free
Catalog Circulation: Mailed 4 time(s) per year to 30M
Printing Information: 11 pages in 4 colors on Matte Stock
Press: Sheetfed Press
Mailing List Information: Names for rent
In Business: 38 years

2585 Mrs. Kimball's Candy Shoppe
Miles Kimball
250 City Center
Oshkosh, WI 54906   855-202-7394
www.mileskimball.com

Candy

Catalog Cost: Free
In Business: 81 years
Sales Volume: $10 Million

2586 Original Juan Specialty Foods
Original Juan Specialty Foods
111 Southwest Boulevard
Kansas City, KS 66103   913-432-5228
800-568-8468
Fax: 913-432-5880
www.originaljuan.com

Specialty sauces, salsas, snacks and dips

President: Joe R Polo Sr
Marketing Manager: Lindsay Howerton
Production Manager: Valerie Lewellen
VP Operations: Tom Clark
Purchasing Manager: Jason Erickson
Bookkeeper: Ruth Becker
Catalog Cost: Free
In Business: 17 years
Number of Employees: 25
Sales Volume: $4.6 Million

2587 Paradigm Foodworks
Paradigm Foodworks,Inc
5875 Lakeview Blvd
Suite 102
Lake Oswego, OR 97035-7047   503-595-4360
800-234-0250
Fax: 503-595-4234
Sales@ParadigmFoodworks.com
www.paradigmfoodworks.com

Specialty foods and chocolate

President: Lynne Barra
Credit Cards: AMEX; MasterCard; Visa
Catalog Circulation: Mailed 1 time(s) per year
Average Order Size: $30
Printing Information: 4 pages in 1 color on Matte Stock
Press: Letterpress
Mailing List Information: Names for rent
In Business: 35 years
Number of Employees: 10
Sales Volume: $10MM to $20MM

2588 Perfectly Sweet
Perfectly Sweet, Inc.
7292 NW 25th Street
PO BOX 522626
Miami, FL 33152-2626   800-815-0009
Fax: 844-272-8343
orders@perfectlysweet.com
www.perfectlysweet.com

Sugar free candy and chocolates

President: David Taks
Credit Cards: AMEX; MasterCard
Catalog Cost: Free
In Business: 20 years
Number of Employees: 5
Sales Volume: $650,000

2589 Plumbridge Confections & Gifts
Plumbridge
99 Huntingtown Road
PO Box 219
Newtown, CT 06470-2637   212-744-6640
customerservice@plumbridge.com
www.plumbridge.com

Candy gifts

President: Roseanne Beck
Production Manager: Donald Beck
Credit Cards: AMEX; MasterCard
Catalog Cost: Free
Catalog Circulation: Mailed 4 time(s) per year to 4000
Printing Information: 4 pages in 2 colors on Glossy Stock
Press: Letterpress
In Business: 129 years
Number of Employees: 10-J
Sales Volume: Under $500M

2590 Priester's Pecans
Priester's Pecan Company
208 Old Fort Road East
Fort Deposit, AL 36032   866-477-4736
800-277-3226
Fax: 334-227-4294
customerservice@priesters.com
www.priesters.com

Premium shelled pecans and homemade candies and desserts that incorporate pecans

Manager: Thomas Ellis
Manager: Ellen Ellis Burkett
Credit Cards: AMEX; MasterCard
Catalog Cost: Free
Catalog Circulation: Mailed 3 time(s) per year to 10000
Printing Information: 32 pages in 4 colors on Glossy Stock
Press: Web Press
Binding: Saddle Stitched
Mailing List Information: Names for rent
List Company: Moran Direct
713-880-3725
In Business: 80 years
Number of Employees: 75
Sales Volume: 20MM-50MM

2591 Revival Confections
Revival Confections, Inc.
1332 S Genesee Avenue
Los Angeles, CA 90019   323-936-4241
info@revivalconfections.com
www.revivalconfections.com

Chocolate covered raisins, chocolate toffee almonds, dark chocolate covered apricots

President: Gail Asch
Catalog Cost: Free
Mailing List Information: Names for rent
In Business: 17 years
Number of Employees: 2
Sales Volume: $150,000

2592 River Street Sweets
River Street Sweets
13 East River Street
Savannah, GA 31402   912-234-4608
800-793-3876
Fax: 912-234-1584
megan@riverstreetsweets.com
www.riverstreetsweets.com

Savannah pralines, chocolate bear claws, glazed pecans, pecan pies, praline pound cake and fudge

CFO: Jennifer Strickland
Owner: Pam Strickland
CEO: Tim Strickland
Credit Cards: AMEX; MasterCard
Catalog Cost: Free
In Business: 40 years
Number of Employees: 70
Sales Volume: $3 Million

2593 Rocky Mountain Chocolate Factory
Rocky Mountain Chocolate Factory, Inc.
265 Turner Dr
Durango, CO 81303-7941   970-259-0554
888-525-2462
Fax: 970-259-5895
customerservice@rmcf.com
rockymountainchocolatefactory.com

Handmade chocolate gifts

President: Franklin E Crail
CFO: Bryan Merryman
Marketing Manager: Ed Dudley
SVP Franchise Support/Operations: Gregory L. Pope
Credit Cards: AMEX; MasterCard
Printing Information: 23 pages in 4 colors on Glossy Stock
Press: Web Press
Binding: Saddle Stitched
In Business: 30 years
Number of Employees: 250
Sales Volume: $28.4 Million

2594 Savannah's Candy Kitchen
Savannah's Candy Kitchen
225 E River Street
Savannah, GA 31401-1220   912-233-8411
800-433-7884
support@savannahcandy.com
www.savannahcandy.com

Candy

Catalog Cost: Free

2595 See's Candies
See's Candy Shops, Inc.
20600 S Alameda St
Carson, CA 90810   310-604-6200
800-347-7337
Fax: 310-604-6255
SeesCandiesCustomerCare@sees.com
www.sees.com

Candies

President: Richard Fitzgerald
test@test.com
CFO: Verne Fitzgerald
verne_f@seesinc.com
Catalog Cost: Free
Printing Information: 32 pages in 3 colors
In Business: 94 years
Sales Volume: $10MM to $20MM

2596 Senor Murphy Candymaker
Senor Murphy Candymaker
1904 Chamisa Street
Santa Fe, NM 87505   505-988-4311
877-988-4311
Fax: 505-988-2050
chocolate@senormurphy.com
www.senormurphy.com

Handmade gourmet chocolates, brittles, toffees, jellies and nuts, many unique to the Southwest

President: Rand Levitt
Credit Cards: MasterCard; Visa
Catalog Cost: Free
Catalog Circulation: Mailed 1 time(s) per year
Printing Information: 6 pages in 4 colors on Glossy Stock
Press: Web Press
Binding: Saddle Stitched
Mailing List Information: Names for rent
In Business: 44 years
Number of Employees: 22
Sales Volume: $990,000

2597 Southern Season
Southern Season
University Mall
201 S Estes Drive
Chapel Hill, NC 27514 877-929-7133
866-253-5317
Fax: 919-942-9274
customerservice@southernseason.com
www.southernseason.com

Gourmet foods and gifts with a southern flair

kvanleer@southernseason.com
Catalog Cost: Free
Catalog Circulation: Mailed 1 time(s) per year
In Business: 40 years
Number of Employees: 250
Sales Volume: $25 Million

2598 Stahmanns Pecans
Stahmanns Pecans
22505 S. Highway 28
La Mesa, NM 88055 575-526-2453
800-654-6887
Fax: 575-526-7824
Pecans@Stahmanns.com
stahmannpecan.com

Gourmet chocolate gift baskets, mail order pecan gifts, flavored pecans

Credit Cards: AMEX; MasterCard; Visa
Catalog Cost: Free
In Business: 81 years
Number of Employees: 180

2599 Sweet Tooth Candies
Sweet Tooth Candies
125 West 11th Street
Newport, KY 41071-2129 859-581-4663
877-581-5132
www.sweettoothchocolates.com

Candy

President: Robert Schneider
Credit Cards: MasterCard; Visa
Catalog Cost: Free
Catalog Circulation: Mailed 2 time(s) per year
to 3000
Printing Information: 9 pages in 4 colors on
Matte Stock
In Business: 100 years
Number of Employees: 7
Sales Volume: $500M to $1MM

2600 Trappistine Quality Candy
Trappistine Quality Candy
300 Arnold Street
Wrentham, MA 02093 508-520-9139
866-549-8929
Fax: 215-922-1335
info@trappistinecandy.com
www.trappistinecandy.com

Candy

In Business: 61 years

2601 World's Finest Chocolate
World's Finest Chocolate
4801 S. Lawndale
Chicago, IL 60632 888-821-8452
Fax: 877-256-2685
www.worldsfinestchocolate.com

Chocolate of all varieties used for fundraising by children and schools, also suitable for gifts and personal use

CEO: Eddie Opler
Credit Cards: AMEX; MasterCard; Visa
In Business: 107 years

Cheese

2602 Calef's Country Store
Calef's Country Store
606 Franklin Pierce Highway
Barrington, NH 03825-57 603-664-2231
800-462-2118
Fax: 603-664-5857
info@calefs.com
www.calefs.com

Cheeses, maple syrup and candies

President: Lindy Horton
Credit Cards: MasterCard; Visa
Catalog Circulation: Mailed 1 time(s) per year
to 10000
Average Order Size: $45
Printing Information: 8 pages in 2 colors on
Matte Stock
Press: Sheetfed Press
Binding: Saddle Stitched
Mailing List Information: Names for rent
In Business: 146 years
Number of Employees: 21
Sales Volume: $1MM to $3MM

2603 Cheese Box
The Cheese Box
801 South Wells Street
Lake Geneva, WI 53147-2445 262-248-3440
800-345-6105
info@cheesebox.com
www.cheesebox.com

Wisconsin cheese and sausage gift boxes

President: Edward Schwinn
Credit Cards: AMEX; MasterCard; Visa
Catalog Circulation: Mailed 1 time(s) per year
to 25000
Printing Information: 20 pages in 4 colors on
Glossy Stock
Press: Sheetfed Press
Binding: Saddle Stitched
In Business: 60 years
Number of Employees: 3
Sales Volume: $500M to $1MM

2604 Eichten's Hidden Acres Cheese Farm
Eichten's Market & Grill
16440 Lake Blvd
US Highway 8
Center City, MN 55012-9637 651-257-1566
800-657-6572
Fax: 651-257-6286
eichtens@frontiernet.net
www.specialtycheese.com

European-style cheeses and American Bison meat

President: Eileen Eichten
Credit Cards: MasterCard; Visa
Catalog Cost: Free
Catalog Circulation: Mailed 2 time(s) per year
to 10000
Printing Information: 15 pages in 4 colors on
Glossy Stock
Binding: Saddle Stitched
Mailing List Information: Names for rent
In Business: 39 years
Number of Employees: 15
Sales Volume: $450,000

2605 Gifts of Distinction
Marin French Cheese Co.
7500 Red Hill Road
Petaluma, CA 94952-9438 707-762-6001
800-292-6001
Fax: 707-762-0430
cheesefactory@marinfrenchcheese.com
www.marinfrenchcheese.com

Camembert, brie, breakfast and schloss cheeses

President: James Boyce
Production Manager: Candice Millhouse, General Manager
Credit Cards: MasterCard; Visa

Catalog Cost: Free
Catalog Circulation: to 1000
Printing Information: 2 pages in 4 colors on
Glossy Stock
Binding: Folded
In Business: 150 years
Number of Employees: 18
Sales Volume: $10MM to $20MM

2606 Grafton Village Cheese Company
Grafton Village Cheese
400 Linden Street
Brattleboro, VT 05301 800-472-3866
Fax: 802-246-2210
info@graftonvillagecheese.com
www.graftonvillagecheese.com

Handmade, all natural Vermont cheddars and Vermont specialty products, bacon and ham

CFO: Peter Mohn
Marketing Manager: Meri Spicer
Plant Manager: Richard Woods
Credit Cards: MasterCard; Visa
Catalog Cost: Free
Catalog Circulation: to 10000
Printing Information: 8 pages
Number of Employees: 18

2607 Guggisberg Cheese
Guggisberg Cheese
5060 SR 557
Millersburg, OH 44654 330-893-2500
800-262-2505
Fax: 330-893-3240
info@babyswiss.com
www.guggisberg.com

Cheese, spreads and meats

President: Richard Guggisberg
Vice president/ treasurer: Diane Melloe
Office Manager: Linda Kaiser
Credit Cards: MasterCard; Visa
In Business: 44 years

2608 Harman's Cheese and Country Store
Harman's Cheese & Country Store
1400 Route 117
PO Box 624
Sugar Hill, NH 03586 603-823-8000
cheese@harmanscheese.com
www.harmanscheese.com

Aged cheddar cheese and cheese spreads, many varieties of jams and jellies, soldier beans, common crackers, maple products, pancake mixes, salad dressings and other gourmet condiments

President: Maxine Aldrich
Catalog Cost: Free
Catalog Circulation: to 8000
Printing Information: 10 pages in 2 colors on
Glossy Stock
Press: Offset Press
Binding: Folded
Mailing List Information: Names for rent
In Business: 60 years
Number of Employees: 5
Sales Volume: $550,000

2609 Maytag Dairy Farms
Maytag Dairy Farms, Inc.
PO Box 806
Newton, IA 50208-806 641-792-1133
800-247-2458
Fax: 641-792-1567
www.maytagdairyfarms.com

Blue cheese, wheels, wedges, white cheddar, swiss

Chairman: Kenneth Maytag
President: Myrna Ploeg
President/CEO/Executive Director: James W
Stevens
Credit Cards: AMEX; MasterCard; Visa
Catalog Cost: Free
Catalog Circulation: Mailed 4 time(s) per year

to 300M
Printing Information: 24 pages in 4 colors on Glossy Stock
Press: Sheetfed Press
Binding: Saddle Stitched
Mailing List Information: Names for rent
In Business: 73 years
Number of Employees: 50
Sales Volume: $5.4 Million

2610 Mission Orchards of Hickory Farms
Hickory Farms
PO Box 219
Maumee, OH 43537-2157   419-893-7611
                          800-776-4111
                     Fax: 419-893-0164
                 www.Hickoryfarms.Com

Cheese and sausage gifts

Chairman: John J Langdon
President: James O'Neill
CFO: Mark J Wagner
Founder: Richard Ransom
Credit Cards: AMEX; MasterCard; Visa
Printing Information: 36 pages in 4 colors on Glossy Stock
Binding: Saddle Stitched
Mailing List Information: Names for rent
List Company: Gnames Enterprises
In Business: 64 years
Number of Employees: 125

2611 Nueske's Applewood Smoked Meats
Nueske's
203 N Genesee Street
Wittenberg, WI 54499   800-720-1153
                          800-392-2266
                     Fax: 800-962-2266
                 info@nueske.com
                 www.nueske.com

A complete line of applewood smoked specialty meats, poultry, cheese, desserts, soups and quiches

President: Robert D Nueske
CFO: Gary Ashenbrenner
Marketing Manager: Megan Dorsch
Production Manager: Jeff Bushman
Contact: Bob Nueske
Credit Cards: AMEX; MasterCard; Visa
Catalog Cost: Free
Catalog Circulation: Mailed 5 time(s) per year to 30000
Average Order Size: $85
Printing Information: 35 pages in 4 colors on Glossy Stock
Press: Web Press
Binding: Saddle Stitched
In Business: 82 years
Number of Employees: 120
Sales Volume: $25 Million

2612 Paoli Cheese
Paoli Cheese
657 2nd Street
Monroe, WI 53566   608-328-3355
                      800-762-4644
                 Fax: 608-845-8025
             info@paolicheese.com

Wisconsin cheeses and sausage

President: Willam Hastings
Catalog Cost: Free
In Business: 30 years
Number of Employees: 3
Sales Volume: $150,000

2613 Pittman & Davis
Southern Fulfillment Services
801 N Expressway 77
Harlingen, TX 78552-5105   800-289-7829
                         Fax: 866-329-7829
                     fruit@pittmandavis.com
                     www.pittmandavis.com

Citrus fruits, dried fruits, cheeses, baked treats and gift baskets

President: Frank Davis
EVP/General Manager: Andy Graham
Credit Cards: AMEX; MasterCard
Catalog Cost: Free
Catalog Circulation: Mailed 3 time(s) per year
Printing Information: 45 pages in 4 colors on Glossy Stock
Press: Web Press
Binding: Saddle Stitched
Mailing List Information: Names for rent
In Business: 85 years
Number of Employees: 21
Sales Volume: $1.9 Million

2614 Plymouth Artisan Cheese
Plymouth Artisan Cheese
106 Messer Hill Road
Plymouth Notch, VT 05056-1   802-672-3650
                 www.plymouthartisancheese.com

Cheese

President: Steve Lidle
Catalog Cost: Free
Catalog Circulation: to 13000
Printing Information: 2 pages in 1 color
In Business: 113 years
Number of Employees: 5
Sales Volume: $3MM to $5MM

2615 Shelburne Farms
Shelburne Farms
1611 Harbor Rd
Shelburne, VT 05482-7671   802-985-8686
                         Fax: 802-985-8123
                     info@shelburnefarms.org
                     www.shelburnefarms.org

Cheddar cheese, hams, maple syrup, vermont products and gift packages

President: Alec Webb
awebb@shelburnefarms.org
Owner: William Webb
Development Assistant: Jane Boisvert
jboisvert@shelburnefarms.org
VP And Program Director: Megan Camp
mcamp@shelburnefarms@.org
Credit Cards: AMEX; MasterCard; Visa
Catalog Cost: Free
Printing Information: 7 pages in 4 colors on Glossy Stock
Binding: Saddle Stitched
In Business: 43 years
Number of Employees: 40
Sales Volume: $3.6 Million

2616 Sonoma Cheese Factory
Sonoma Cheese Factory
2 Spain Street
On the Plaza
Sonoma, CA 95476   707-996-1931
                      800-535-2855
                 Fax: 707-935-8846
         retailstore@sonomacheesefactory.com
             www.sonomacheesefactory.com

Cheeses

President: David Viviani
interviewer: mike
mike@sonomachessefactory.com
Credit Cards: AMEX; MasterCard
In Business: 85 years

2617 Sugarbush Farm
Sugarbush Farm, Inc.
591 Sugarbush Farm Road
Woodstock, VT 05091   802-457-1757
                          800-281-1757
                     Fax: 802-457-3269
             contact@sugarbushfarm.com
                 www.sugarbushfarm.com

Cheese, vermont maple syrup and food gift boxes

President: Elizabeth Luce
Credit Cards: AMEX; MasterCard; Visa
Catalog Cost: Free
Catalog Circulation: Mailed 5 time(s) per year to 65000

Average Order Size: $84
Printing Information: 6 pages in 4 colors on Glossy Stock
Press: Web Press
Binding: Folded
Mailing List Information: Names for rent
In Business: 70 years
Number of Employees: 7
Sales Volume: $1.5 Million

2618 Swiss Colony
The Swiss Colony, LLC
1112 7th Ave.
Monroe, WI 53566-1364   800-914-1459
                           800-913-0743

Cheese, meats, pastries and gift packs

Chairman: Chairman
President: John Baumann
CFO: Donald R Hughes
Credit Cards: AMEX; MasterCard; Visa
Catalog Cost: Free
Catalog Circulation: to 20000
Printing Information: 66 pages
In Business: 87 years
Number of Employees: 1000

2619 WSU Creamery
WSU Creamery
Washington State University
PO Box 641122
Pullman, WA 99164-1122   509-335-4014
                            800-457-5442
                       Fax: 800-572-3289
                     creamery@wsu.edu
                     www.wsu.edu/creamery

Natural cheeses

President: Marc Bates
Marketing Manager: Jill Whelchel
Direct Marketing: David Dean
creamery@wsu.edu
Asst. Manager: John Haugen
jfhaugen@wsu.edu
ferdinands@wsu.edu
Credit Cards: MasterCard; Visa
Catalog Circulation: Mailed 1 time(s) per year to 20000
Average Order Size: $60
Printing Information: 8 pages in 4 colors on Matte Stock
Press: Letterpress
In Business: 90 years
Number of Employees: 70
Sales Volume: $1MM to $3MM

2620 Wisconsin Cheeseman
The Wisconsin Cheeseman
1112 7th Ave.
Monroe, WI 53566-1364   800-693-0834
         customerservice@wisconsincheeseman.com

Cheese, sausage, chocolates, candies, fruit cakes and more.

Catalog Cost: Free
Catalog Circulation: Mailed 4 time(s) per year
Printing Information: 54 pages in 4 colors
Mailing List Information: Names for rent
In Business: 70 years
Sales Volume: $20MM to $50MM

Coffee & Tea

2621 Alaska Herb Tea Company
Alaska Herb Tea Company
6710 Weimer Dr
Anchorage, AK 99502-2054   907-245-3499
                               800-654-2764
                          Fax: 907-245-3499
                     herbtea@alaska.net
                     www.Alaskaherbtea.Com

Teas and tea accesories

President: Charles Walsh
Credit Cards: AMEX; MasterCard
In Business: 36 years
Sales Volume: $1 million

2622 Barnie's Coffee & Tea Company

Barnie's Coffee & Tea Company
2420 Lakemont Avenue
#160
Orlando, FL 32814-8249   407-854-6626
                                800-284-1416
                           Fax: 407-854-6636
customerservice@barniescoffee.com
www.barniescoffee.com

Coffee, tea, cocoa, brewing equipment and mugs

President: Phil Jones
CFO: Tricia Relvini
Marketing Manager: Shannon Kidd
Production Manager: Jamie McLaughlin
Chief Operating Officer: Sonya Hardy
Senior Vice President of Sales: Scott Uguccioni
Credit Cards: AMEX; MasterCard
Catalog Circulation: to 10000
Printing Information: 28 pages
In Business: 33 years
Number of Employees: 50
Sales Volume: $1,000,000

2623 Baronet Coffee

Baronet Coffee
77 Weston Street
PO Box 987
Hartford, CT 06143-987   800-227-6638
info@baronetcoffee.com
www.baronetcoffee.com

Flavored, decaffeinated and specialty coffees

President: Leon Goldsmith
Credit Cards: AMEX; MasterCard; Visa
Printing Information: 15 pages
In Business: 68 years
Number of Employees: 12
Sales Volume: $500,000

2624 Bean Bag Deli & Catering Co.

The Bean Bag
1605 E. Gude Drive
Rockville, MD 20850   301-251-4794
                        Fax: 301-340-7149
coffee@thebeanbag.com
www.thebeanbag.com

Sandwiches, teas and coffees

President: Sandra Wool
Credit Cards: MasterCard; Visa
Catalog Circulation: to 10000
Printing Information: 4 pages
Number of Employees: 5
Sales Volume: $500,000

2625 Cafe Du Monde

Cafe Du Monde
800 Decatur Street
New Orleans, LA 70116-3306   504-525-4544
                                    800-772-2927
                               Fax: 504-587-0847
www.cafedumonde.com

Cafe Du Monde coffee and beignets

President: Scott Escarra
CFO: Jay Roman
Credit Cards: AMEX; MasterCard; Visa
Catalog Cost: Free
Printing Information: 16 pages in 4 colors on Glossy Stock
Press: Offset Press
Binding: Saddle Stitched
In Business: 153 years
Number of Employees: 300

2626 Cafe La Semeuse

Cafe La Semeuse
PO BOX 1404
Southampton, NY 11968   844-736-3873
                          Fax: 215-425-1496
john@cafelasemeuse.com
www.cafelasemeuse.com

Cafe La Semeuse coffee available in Soleil Levant, Classique, water processed decaf, espresso, costa rican, and Ethiopian

President: Marc Greenberg
Credit Cards: AMEX; MasterCard; Visa
Catalog Cost: Free
Printing Information: 2 pages in 2 colors
In Business: 115 years

2627 Cajun Creole Products

Cajun Creole Products, Inc.
5610 Daspit Road
New Iberia, LA 70563   337-229-8464
                              800-946-8688
                         Fax: 337-229-4814
info@cajuncreole.com
www.cajuncreole.com

Specialty Cajun Creole coffee, Cajun Creole hot nuts and Cajun spices

President: Velvet Guidry
Catalog Cost: Free
Catalog Circulation: Mailed 2 time(s) per year
Average Order Size: $55
Printing Information: 4 pages in 4 colors on Glossy Stock
Mailing List Information: Names for rent
In Business: 37 years
Number of Employees: 6
Sales Volume: $3MM to $5MM

2628 Coffee Bean Direct

PO Box 538
Stockton, NJ 08559   888-232-6711
contactus@coffeebeandirect.com
www.coffeebeandirect.com

Roasted coffee beans and products

2629 Community Coffee Company

Community Coffee Company
PO Box 2311
Baton Rouge, LA 70821   800-884-5282
                               800-525-5583
                          Fax: 800-643-8199
customerservice@communitycoffee.com
www.communitycoffee.com

Louisiana coffee, gourmet food, tea and chocolate

Chairman: H Norman Saurage III
President: Matthew C Saurage
CFO: Annette L Vaccaro
Marketing Manager: Austin Wilcox
COO: David G Belanger Sr
General Manager of Purchasing: Aaron Savoie
Catalog Cost: Free
In Business: 94 years
Number of Employees: 1000

2630 Davidson's Organics

Davidson's Organics
PO Box 11214
Reno, NV 89510-1214   800-882-5888
                         Fax: 775-356-3713
info@davidsonstea.com
www.davidsonstea.com

Organic teas, cocoa, herbs, spices, accessories and gifts

President: Sharon Davidson
Owner: John Davidson
Credit Cards: AMEX; MasterCard
Catalog Cost: Free
Printing Information: 44 pages
In Business: 39 years

2631 Espresso Gourmet

Espresso Gourmet
10991 Bellbrook Circle
Highlands Ranch, CO 80130   303-683-3646
                                   866-683-3646

Espresso beans

President: Sharon Hart
In Business: 13 years

2632 Espresso Supply

1123 NW 51st Street
Seattle, WA 98107   206-782-6670
                           800-782-6671
                      Fax: 206-789-8221
info@espressosupply.com
www.espressosupply.com

Espresso smallwares and accessories

2633 Espresso Zone

Espresso Zone
1206 Lake Avenue
Ashtabula, OH 44004   440-964-7400
                             800-345-8945
                        Fax: 440-964-7440
support@espressozone.com
www.espressozone.com

Gourmet products for the coffee enthusiast, including espresso makers, coffee makers, coffee grinders, cups, barista tools and supplies

President: George Collins
Credit Cards: AMEX; MasterCard
Catalog Cost: Free
Catalog Circulation: to 100M
In Business: 11 years
Number of Employees: 8
Sales Volume: $5 Million

2634 Frontier Natural Products Co-Op

Frontier Natural Products Co-Op
3021 78th St
PO Box 299
Norway, IA 52318-9520   800-669-3275
                          Fax: 800-717-4372
customercare@frontiercoop.com
www.frontiercoop.com

A wholesale supplier of organic coffee, bottled spices, baking flavors, aromatherapy items, natural items and other manufacturers' products

President: Nancy Hinkel
CFO: Bill Kooistra
Marketing Manager: Clint Landis
Production Manager: Andrea Weiss
Purchasing Manager: Kai Stark
Credit Cards: AMEX; MasterCard
Catalog Cost: Free
In Business: 39 years
Number of Employees: 225
Sales Volume: $20MM to $50MM

2635 Gevalia Coffee

Gevalia Kaffe
Holmparken Square
PO Box 6276
Dover, DE 19905-6275   800-438-2542
                              800-438-2542
                         Fax: 302-430-7279
customer_service@gevalia.com
www.gevalia.com

Coffee and coffee accessories, gift baskets, confectionaries, housewares

Credit Cards: AMEX; MasterCard
Catalog Cost: Free
Catalog Circulation: Mailed 2 time(s) per year
Printing Information: 36 pages in 4 colors on Glossy Stock
Press: Web Press
Binding: Saddle Stitched
In Business: 150 years

2636 Grace Tea Company

Grace Tea Company
14-A Craig Road
Acton, MA 1720   978-635-9500
                   Fax: 978-635-9701
customerservice@gracetea.com
gracetea.com

Tea

Credit Cards: AMEX; MasterCard
In Business: 56 years

2637 Harney & Sons Fine Teas
Harney & Sons Fine Teas
5723 Route 22
Millerton, NY 12546 518-789-2100
888-745-9354
Fax: 800-832-8463
customerservice@harneyteas.com
www.harney.com

An assortment of gourmet teas, supplies and accessories, books and gifts
President: Andy Clarke
CFO: John Harney
Catalog Cost: Free
Catalog Circulation: Mailed 3 time(s) per year to 5M
Average Order Size: $50
Printing Information: 39 pages on Matte Stock
Press: Letterpress
Binding: Perfect Bound
In Business: 28 years
Number of Employees: 100
Sales Volume: $20 Million

2638 Hawaii Coffee Company
Lion Coffee
1555 Kalani Street
Honolulu, HI 96817 808-847-3600
800-338-8353
info@hicoffeeco.com
www.lioncoffee.com

Hawaiian coffee, tropical teas and accesories, lion coffee, royal kona coffee, Hawaiian islands tea
President: James M Wayman
Operations Director: Roy Wong
Credit Cards: MasterCard
Catalog Cost: Free
Catalog Circulation: Mailed 3 time(s) per year to 15000
Average Order Size: $60
Printing Information: 10 pages in 4 colors on Matte Stock
Binding: Folded
Mailing List Information: Names for rent
List Manager: Eriko Fong
In Business: 154 years
Number of Employees: 120
Sales Volume: $24.2 Million

2639 International Tea Importers
International Tea Importers
8551 Loch Lomond Dr.
Pico Rivera, CA 90660 562-801-9600
877-TEA-AND
Fax: 562-801-9601
iti@teavendor.com
www.teavendor.com

Tea

2640 Luzianne Coffee Company
Luzianne Coffee Company
640 Magazine Street
New Orleans, LA 70130 504-524-6131
800-535-1961
Fax: 504-539-5427
service@reilyproducts.com
www.luzianne.com

Coffee, tea, brownie mixes, cake flour, chili's, chicken and seafood coating mixes and condiments
Chairman: William B Reily III
President: C James McCarthy III
CFO: Harold Herrmann Jr
Catalog Cost: Free
In Business: 111 years
Number of Employees: 1454

2641 Market Spice
Market Spice
85 A Pike Place
Seattle, WA 98101 206-622-6340
800-735-7198
Fax: 206-622-6340
retail@marketspice.com
www.marketspice.com

Teas and spices including world famous market spice tea, new products, candles, cookies, BBQ sauce, breath mints
Manager: Nancy Duette
Buyers: Steve Rivas
Judy Dawson
Credit Cards: AMEX; MasterCard; Visa
Catalog Cost: Free
Catalog Circulation: Mailed 2 time(s) per year to 1000
Average Order Size: $10
Printing Information: 10 pages in 3 colors on Matte Stock
Press: Letterpress
Binding: Folded
Mailing List Information: Names for rent
In Business: 103 years
Number of Employees: 10
Sales Volume: $10MM to $20MM

2642 McNulty's Tea and Coffee Company
McNulty's Tea & Coffee Co., Inc.
109 Christopher Street
New York, NY 10014 212-242-5351
800-356-5200
info@mcnultys.com
www.McNultys.Com

Coffees, rare teas, tea pots, infusers and strainers
President: David Wong
Credit Cards: AMEX; MasterCard; Visa
Catalog Cost: Free
Catalog Circulation: Mailed 1 time(s) per year
Printing Information: 22 pages in 2 colors
In Business: 119 years
Number of Employees: 3
Sales Volume: Under $500M

2643 Mountain Rose Herbs
Mountain Rose Herbs
P.O. Box 50220
Eugene, OR 97405 541-741-7307
800-879-3337
Fax: 510-217-4012
support@mountainroseherbs.com
www.mountainroseherbs.com

Organic herbal products, all natural body care products, essential oils and bulk ingredients for those crafting and formulating their own products
President: Julie Bailey
CFO: Cameron Stearns
Marketing Manager: Irene Wolansky
Production Manager: Julie Debord
Vice President: Shawn Donnille
Executive Director of Operations: Jennifer Gerrity
Product Manager: Christine Rice
Catalog Cost: Free
Catalog Circulation: Mailed 2 time(s) per year to 12000
Printing Information: 84 pages in 4 colors on Matte Stock
Press: Web Press
Binding: Saddle Stitched
In Business: 26 years
Number of Employees: 84
Sales Volume: $ 13 Million

2644 New Mexico Pinon Coffee 2014 Catalog
New Mexico Pinon Coffee
4431 Anaheim Avenue
Northeast Albuquerque, NM 87113 505-298-1964
customercare@nmpinoncoffee.com
nmpinoncoffee.com

Gourmet Coffee &Tea

Credit Cards: AMEX; MasterCard
In Business: 20+ years

2645 Northwestern Coffee Mills
Northwestern Coffee Mills
30950 Nevers Road
Washburn, WI 54891 715-373-2122
800-243-5283
Fax: 715-373-0072
www.northwesterncoffeemills.com

Coffee, tea, spices, seasonings and coffee filters
President: Harry Demorest
Credit Cards: AMEX; MasterCard; Visa
Catalog Cost: Free
Catalog Circulation: Mailed 1 time(s) per year to 6000
Average Order Size: $48
Printing Information: 16 pages in 1 color on Matte Stock
Press: Web Press
Binding: Saddle Stitched
Mailing List Information: Names for rent
In Business: 138 years
Number of Employees: 3
Sales Volume: $500M to $1MM

2646 Peet's Coffee & Tea
Peet's Coffee & Tea
PO Box 12509
Berkeley, CA 94712-3509 510-594-2100
800-999-2132
Fax: 510-594-2180
webmail@peets.com
www.peets.com

Specialty coffee
President: Pat O'Dea
CFO: Tom Cawley
Marketing Manager: Alisha Chan
Production Manager: Donnell Albert
Printing Information: 12 pages on Matte Stock
Binding: Saddle Stitched
In Business: 49 years

2647 S&D Coffee & Tea
S&D Coffee & Tea
300 Concord Parkway South
PO Box 1628
Concord, NC 28027 800-933-2210
Fax: 800-950-4378
www.sdcoffeetea.com

Coffee and tea company
Marketing Manager: John Buckner
Production Manager: Brent Hall
VP, Culinary & Innovation: Eric Nakata
VP, Strategic Initiatives: Tracy Ging
VP, Global Sourcing: Kyle Newkirk
In Business: 88 years

2648 San Francisco Herb & Natural Food
San Francisco Herb & Natural Food Compan
47444 Kato Road
Fremont, CA 94538 510-770-1215
800-227-2830
Fax: 510-770-9021
customerservice@herbspicetea.com

Botanicals, herbs, teas, spices, spa, oils and extracts
COO: Fahimeh Niroomand
Finance Manager: Miranda Mill
Catalog Cost: Free
Printing Information: in 2 colors
Binding: Saddle Stitched
Mailing List Information: Names for rent
In Business: 42 years
Number of Employees: 85
Sales Volume: $13.5 Million

2649 Seelect Tea
Seelect Tea
833 N. Elm St.
Orange, CA 92867   714-771-3317
          Fax: 714-771-2424
          www.seelecttea.com

Tea, coffee, soda, syrups.

2650 Simpson & Vail
Simpson & Vail, Inc.
3 Quarry Road
PO Box 765
Brookfield, CT 06804   203-775-0240
          800-282-8327
          Fax: 203-775-0462
          info@svtea.com
          www.svtea.com

Coffees, teas, brewing accessories, gourmet foods, china and gifts

President: James F Harron, Jr
VP: Joan Harron
Credit Cards: AMEX; MasterCard
Catalog Cost: Free
Catalog Circulation: Mailed 6 time(s) per year
Average Order Size: $100
Printing Information: 32 pages in 4 colors on Glossy Stock
Press: Web Press
Binding: Saddle Stitched
Mailing List Information: Names for rent
In Business: 86 years
Number of Employees: 9
Sales Volume: $1 Million

2651 Stash Tea
Stash Tea Company
16655 SW 72nd Avenue
Suite 200
Tigard, OR 97224   503-684-4482
          800-547-1514
          Fax: 503-684-4424
          mailorder@stashtea.com
          www.stashtea.com

Specialty teas, tea gifts, accessories and baked goods

President: Thomas D Lisicki
Marketing Manager: Dorothy Arnold
Buyers: Barbara Thomas
Dorothy Arnold
Credit Cards: MasterCard; Visa
Catalog Cost: Free
Catalog Circulation: Mailed 10 time(s) per year to 40000
Printing Information: 36 pages in 4 colors on Glossy Stock
Press: Web Press
Binding: Saddle Stitched
Mailing List Information: Names for rent
In Business: 40 years
Number of Employees: 49
Sales Volume: $8.7 Million

2652 The Republic of Tea
The Republic of Tea
5 Hamilton Landing
Suite 100
Novato, CA 94949   800-298-4832
          www.republicoftea.com

Tea

In Business: 23 years

2653 True Brands
True Brands
154 N 35th Street
Seattle, WA 98103   800-750-8783
          www.truefabrications.com

Restaurant supplies for liquor, beer and wine

President: Dhruv Agarwal
Credit Cards: AMEX; MasterCard
Catalog Circulation: Mailed 4 time(s) per year
Printing Information: 52 pages in 4 colors
Press: Web Press
Binding: Saddle Stitched

In Business: 13 years
Sales Volume: $5MM to $10MM

2654 Upton Tea Imports
Upton Tea Imports
100 Jeffrey Avenue #1
Holliston, MA 01746   508-474-6840
          800-234-8327
          Fax: 508-429-0918
          cservice@uptontea.com
          www.uptontea.com

Over 420 varieties of loose teas and accessories

President: Thomas Eck
Catalog Cost: Free
Printing Information: 56 pages
In Business: 25 years
Number of Employees: 14
Sales Volume: $1.70 Million

2655 Visions Espresso Service
Visions Espresso Service, Inc.
2737 First Avenue South
Seattle, WA 98134   800-277-7277
          Fax: 206-623-6710
          info@visionsespresso.com
          www.visionsespresso.com

Espresso machine parts, cleaning supplies and accessories

President: Dawn Loraas
Operations Manager: Luke Green
Credit Cards: AMEX; MasterCard; Visa
Catalog Cost: Free
Catalog Circulation: to 10000
Printing Information: 32 pages on Glossy Stock
Binding: Saddle Stitched
Mailing List Information: Names for rent
In Business: 29 years
Number of Employees: 19
Sales Volume: $2.5 Million

2656 William's Brewing Company Catalog
William's Brewing Company
2088 Burroughs Avenue
San Leandro, CA 94577   510-895-2739
          800-759-6025
          Fax: 510-895-2745
          service@williamsbrewing.com
          www.williamsbrewing.com

Home brewing, wine making and coffee roasting products

President: William Moore
Catalog Cost: Free
In Business: 36 years
Number of Employees: 5
Sales Volume: $310,000

Desserts

2657 Beatrice Bakery Company
Beatrice Bakery Company
201 S 5th Street
PO Box 457
Beatrice, NE 68310-4408   402-223-2358
          800-228-4030
          Fax: 402-223-4465
          customerservice@beatricebakery.com
          www.beatricebakery.com

Gourmet fruit cakes and dessert cakes made from premium fruits and nuts, brandies, rum and bourbon

President: Greg Leach
Marketing Manager: Rebecca Brown
Production Manager: Robin Dickinson
Credit Cards: AMEX; MasterCard; Visa
Catalog Cost: Free
Catalog Circulation: to 30000
Printing Information: 4 pages
In Business: 98 years
Number of Employees: 43
Sales Volume: $1.4 Million

2658 Bellows House Bakery
Bellows House Bakery
117 Church Street
North Walpole, NH 03609   603-445-1974
          800-358-6302
          Fax: 603-445-1973
          info@bellowshouse.com
          www.bellowshouse.com

Brownies, cookies, breakfast treats, and gift items

President: Lois Ford
Catalog Cost: Free
Printing Information: 2 pages
In Business: 29 years
Number of Employees: 12
Sales Volume: $440,000

2659 Biscoff Gourmet Catalog
Lotus Bakeries North America, Inc.
50 Francisco Street
Suite 115
San Francisco, CA 94133   855-415-0077
          Fax: 415-956-4922
          customerservice@biscoff.com
          www.biscoff.com

Biscoff gourmet cookies, chocolates and pastries, gift baskets and gift tins

Marketing Manager: Ignace Heyman
CEO: Jan Boone
COO: Jan Vander Stichele
Catalog Cost: Free
Printing Information: 24 pages in 4 colors on Glossy Stock
Binding: Saddle Stitched
In Business: 82 years

2660 Brownie Points
Brownie Points Inc.
5712 Westbourne Avenue
Columbus, OH 43213   614-860-8470
          800-427-9643
          Fax: 614-860-8477
          info@BrowniePointsInc.com
          www.browniepointsinc.com

Brownies,popcorn gifts,confections,gourmet gift baskets

President: Lisa Rothstein
Credit Cards: AMEX; MasterCard
Catalog Cost: Free
Printing Information: in 4 colors on Glossy Stock
Press: d
Binding: Folded
In Business: 24 years
Number of Employees: 5
Sales Volume: $470,000

2661 Byrd Cookie Company
Byrd Cookie Company
PO Box 13086
Savannah, GA 31416   912-355-1716
          800-291-2973
          Fax: 912-355-4431
          info@byrdcookiecompany.com
          www.byrdcookiecompany.com

Gourmet cookies and cocktail snacks, key lime coolers, raspberry tarts, Benne wafers and chocolate mint cookies

President: Benny H Curl
Production Manager: Max Cruze
Operations/Purchasing Director: Shawn Curl
Credit Cards: AMEX; MasterCard; Visa
Catalog Cost: Free
Catalog Circulation: Mailed 31 time(s) per year to 50000
Printing Information: 20 pages in 4 colors on Matte Stock
Press: Sheetfed Press
Binding: Saddle Stitched
Mailing List Information: Names for rent
List Manager: Colleen Ballance
In Business: 91 years

Number of Employees: 40
Sales Volume: $2.7 Million

2662 Carolina Cookie Company

Carolina Cookie Company
1010 Arnold Street
Greensboro, NC 27405   336-294-2100
800-447-5797
Fax: 336-294-9537
www.carolinacookie.com

Gourmet cookies

President: Gary Smith
Production Manager: Mark Adkins
Credit Cards: AMEX; MasterCard
Catalog Cost: Free
Catalog Circulation: Mailed 2 time(s) per year
In Business: 27 years
Number of Employees: 20
Sales Volume: $3 Million

2663 Chocolate Catalogue

Bissinger
1600 North Broadway
Saint Louis, MO 63102   314-615-2400
800-325-8881
Fax: 314-534-2419
orders@bissingers.com
www.bissingers.com

Gourmet chocolate, gourmet candy, chocolate gifts

CFO: Francine Nicholson
COO: Bill Bremmer
Credit Cards: AMEX; MasterCard; Visa
Catalog Cost: Free
Catalog Circulation: Mailed 4 time(s) per year to 1MM
Printing Information: 24 pages in 4 colors
Press: Web Press
Mailing List Information: Names for rent
Sales Volume: $6 Million

2664 Claxton Bakery, Inc.

Claxton Bakery, Inc.
203 West Main Street
PO Box 367
Claxton, GA 30417-367   912-739-3441
800-841-4211
Fax: 912-739-3097
service@claxtonfruitcake.com
www.claxtonfruitcake.com

Claxton fruit cakes

President: Delorease Parker
CFO: Paul Parker
Marketing Manager: Dale Parker
Sales Executive: Charles Tanner
Credit Cards: AMEX; MasterCard; Visa
Catalog Cost: Free
Printing Information: 2 pages in 4 colors on Glossy Stock
Press: Offset Press
Binding: Folded
In Business: 103 years
Number of Employees: 120
Sales Volume: $8.6 Million

2665 Collin Street Bakery

Collin Street Bakery
P.O. Box 79
Corsicana, TX 75151   800-267-4657
Fax: 903-872-6879
www.collinstreetbakery.com

Fruit cakes, cheesecakes, cookies, pies, breads and muffins

President: Robert P McNutt
Production Manager: Sandy Watson
Credit Cards: AMEX; MasterCard; Visa
Catalog Cost: Free
Catalog Circulation: Mailed 2 time(s) per year
Average Order Size: $35
Printing Information: 8 pages in 4 colors on Matte Stock
Press: Web Press
Binding: Folded
Mailing List Information: Names for rent

List Company: Sara Nelson
In Business: 116 years
Number of Employees: 78
Sales Volume: $25,000,000 - $50,000,000

2666 Cookie Bouquets

Cookie Bouquets Inc
6665-H Huntley Rd
Columbus, OH 43229-1045   614-888-2171
800-233-2171
Fax: 614-841-3950
chips@cookiebouquets.com
www.Cookiebouquets.Com

Floral-like bouquets of freshly baked, colorfully wrapped chocolate chip cookies for all occasions

President: Dinene Clark
Credit Cards: AMEX; MasterCard
Catalog Cost: Free
Catalog Circulation: Mailed 2 time(s) per year
Average Order Size: $30
Printing Information: 8 pages in 4 colors on Glossy Stock
Press: Web Press
Binding: Saddle Stitched
Mailing List Information: Names for rent
In Business: 30 years
Number of Employees: 20-O
Sales Volume: $1MM to $3MM

2667 Cookies by Design's Cookie Gift Book

Cookies by Design
1865 Summit Ave
Suite 605
Plano, TX 75074   972-398-9536
888-675-1453
Fax: 972-398-9542
customerservice@cookiesbydesign.com
www.cookiesbydesign.com

Cookie bouquets made for any occasion

CFO: David Patterson
Owner: Julie Clifford
Owner: Linda Stoker
Owner: John Downey
Catalog Cost: Free
In Business: 30 years
Number of Employees: 25
Sales Volume: $920,000

2668 Country Home Creations

Country Home Creations
P.O. Box 126
Goodrich, MI 48438   810-244-7348
800-457-3477
info@chcdips.com
www.countryhomecreations.com

Dips, soup, bread, spread mixes etc.

Credit Cards: AMEX; MasterCard
In Business: 30+ years

2669 Dancing Deer Baking Company

Dancing Deer Baking Company, Inc.
65 Sprague Street
West A
Boston, MA 2136   617-442-7300
888-699-3337
Fax: 617-442-8118
info@dancingdeer.com
www.dancingdeer.com

Cookies, brownies, cakes, shortbread cookies, pancake and waffle mix

President: Frank Carpenito
Marketing Manager: Laura Stanton
Consumer Sales: Andrew Hoberman
Catalog Cost: Free
Catalog Circulation: to 50000
In Business: 21 years

2670 David's Cookies

David's Cookies
11 Cliffside Drive
Cedar Grove, NJ 07009   973-227-2800
800-500-2800
Fax: 973-882-6998
custserv@davidscookies.com
www.davidscookies.com

Cookies and cookie gift baskets, frozen cookie dough

President: David Liederman
Credit Cards: AMEX; MasterCard; Visa
Catalog Cost: Free
In Business: 29 years
Number of Employees: 95
Sales Volume: $13.8 Million

2671 Desserts by David Glass

Desserts by David Glass
400 Chapel Road Unit 2D
Bissell Commons
South Windsor, CT 06002-5304   860-462-7520
800-328-4399
Fax: 860-242-4408
david@davidglass.com

Gourmet desserts

President: David Glass
Credit Cards: AMEX; MasterCard
Catalog Cost: Free
Catalog Circulation: Mailed 1 time(s) per year
Average Order Size: $60
Printing Information: 8 pages in 4 colors on Glossy Stock
Number of Employees: 20
Sales Volume: $5MM to $10MM

2672 Dinkel's Bakery

Dinkel's Bakery
3329 North Lincoln Avenue
Chicago, IL 60657   773-281-7300
800-822-8817
Fax: 773-281-6169
cakes@dinkels.com
www.dinkels.com

Stollen, strudels, cakes and cookies

President: Norman J Dinkel
General Manager: Luke Karl
Credit Cards: AMEX; MasterCard
Catalog Cost: Free
In Business: 93 years
Number of Employees: 25
Sales Volume: $870,000

2673 Divine Delights

Divine Delights
1250 Holm Road
Petaluma, CA 94954-1106   800-443-2836
Fax: 707-559-7098
customerservice@divinedelights.com
www.divinedelights.com

Chocolates, petits fours, cakes, cookies and tarts

President: William Fry
CFO: Angelique Fry
Buyers: Angelique Fry
Credit Cards: AMEX; MasterCard
Catalog Cost: Free
Catalog Circulation: Mailed 2 time(s) per year
Average Order Size: $85
Printing Information: 16 pages in 4 colors on Glossy Stock
Press: Web Press
Mailing List Information: Names for rent
List Company: George Mann Associates Hightstown, NJ
In Business: 30 years
Number of Employees: 6
Sales Volume: $830,000

2674 Dr. Cookie Gourmet Cookies
Dr Cookie
6335 1st Avenue S
Seattle, WA 98108-3258   206-767-2812
                                 800-247-4259
                            Fax: 206-767-2815
                            www.drcookie.com

Low fat and high fiber cookies

Credit Cards: MasterCard
Printing Information: 2 pages in 4 colors on Glossy Stock
Binding: Folded
In Business: 19 years

2675 Dufour Pastry Kitchens
Dufour Pastry Kitchens, Inc.
251 Locust Avenue
Bronx, NY 10454   212-929-2800
                                 800-439-1282
                     info@dufourpastrykitchens.com
                     www.dufourpastrykitchens.com

Horsd'oeuvres, puff pastry dough and tart shells

President: Judith Arnold
Credit Cards: AMEX; MasterCard
Catalog Circulation: Mailed 1 time(s) per year
Average Order Size: $100
Printing Information: 1 pages in 1 color
Mailing List Information: Names for rent
In Business: 31 years
Number of Employees: 20-O

2676 Eilenberger Bakery
Eilenberger Bakery
512 N John St
Palestine, TX 75801   903-729-2176
                                 800-788-2996
                            Fax: 903-723-2889
                     www.eilenbergerbakery.com

Wide assortment of baked goods

VP Marketing/General Manager: Sarah Pryor
VP: Stephen K Smith
Catalog Cost: Free
Printing Information: 34 pages in 4 colors on Glossy Stock
Binding: Saddle Stitched
In Business: 117 years
Number of Employees: 25
Sales Volume: $710,000

2677 Eli's Cheesecake
The Eli's Cheesecake Company
6701 W. Forest Preserve Drive
Chicago, IL 60634-1405   800-354-2253
                            Fax: 773-736-1169
                     info@elicheesecake.com
                     www.elicheesecake.com

Cheesecake, specialty desserts and branded merchandise

CFO: Marc Zawicki
Marketing Manager: Debbie Marchok
Production Manager: Jeff Anderson
Catalog Cost: Free
Printing Information: 20 pages in 4 colors on Glossy Stock
Binding: Folded
Mailing List Information: Names for rent
In Business: 31 years
Number of Employees: 220
Sales Volume: n/a

2678 Fairytale Brownies Bakery
Fairytale Brownies Bakery
4610 E Cotton Center Blvd
Suite 100
Phoenix, AZ 85040-8898   602-489-5100
                                 800-324-7982
                            Fax: 602-489-5122
                            www.brownies.com

Gourmet brownie gifting company

President: David Kravetz
Marketing Manager: Mary Howard

Catalog Cost: Free
In Business: 19 years
Number of Employees: 35
Sales Volume: $8 Million

2679 Figi's Gifts in Good Taste
Figi's Gifts in Good Taste
3200 S Central Avenue
Marshfield, WI 54404   608-324-8080
                                 866-855-0203
                            Fax: 715-384-1129
                            www.figis.com

Fancy foods and gifts

President: Dolores Aue
CFO: Rick Golz
Marketing Manager: Louis Donnell
Purchasing: Lynn Kelnhofer
Buyers: George Douma
Craig Steinkraus
Credit Cards: AMEX; MasterCard; Visa
Catalog Cost: Free
Catalog Circulation: Mailed 6 time(s) per year to 30000
Printing Information: 96 pages in 4 colors on Glossy Stock
Press: Web Press
Binding: Saddle Stitched
Mailing List Information: Names for rent
In Business: 70 years
Number of Employees: 180

2680 Figi's Sugar Free & More
Figi's Gifts in Good Taste
3200 S Central Avenue
Marshfield, WI 54404   608-324-8080
                                 866-855-0203
                            Fax: 715-384-1129
                            www.figis.com

Sugar free desserts

President: Dolores Aue
CFO: Rick Golz
Marketing Manager: Louis Donnell
Purchasing: Lynn Kelnhofer
Buyers: George Douma
Craig Steinkraus
Credit Cards: AMEX; MasterCard; Visa
Catalog Cost: Free
Catalog Circulation: Mailed 6 time(s) per year to 30000
Printing Information: 96 pages in 4 colors on Glossy Stock
Press: Web Press
Binding: Saddle Stitched
Mailing List Information: Names for rent
In Business: 70 years
Number of Employees: 180

2681 Haydel's Bakery
Haydel's Bakery
4037 Jefferson Hwy
New Orleans, LA 70121-1643   504-837-0190
                                 800-442-1342
                            Fax: 504-837-5512
                     info@haydelbakery.com
                     www.haydelbakery.com

King Cakes, cookies, pastries, coffees, wedding cakes and gifts

President: David Haydel
Credit Cards: AMEX; MasterCard; Visa
Catalog Cost: Free
In Business: 54 years
Number of Employees: 20
Sales Volume: $1MM to $3MM

2682 Heartwarming Treasures
Heartwarming Treasures
3843 Fremont Ave N
Seattle, WA 98103-8755   206-547-2623
                                 866-332-6904
                heartwarmingtreasures@yahoo.com
                www.heartwarmingtreasures.com

Northwest food and wine gourmet gift baskets

President: Sue Wolf
Credit Cards: AMEX; MasterCard; Visa
Catalog Cost: Free
In Business: 19 years
Number of Employees: 2
Sales Volume: $79,000

2683 Honey Baked Ham
Honey Baked Ham
P.O. Box 370
Carrollton, GA 30117   800-367-7720
                            Fax: 800-728-4426
                     catalogservice@hbham.com
                     www.honeybakedonline.com

Hams, turkey, turkey breasts, BBQ ribs, desserts, baskets and more

President: Kim Hunter
Founder: Harry J. Hoenselaar
Credit Cards: AMEX; MasterCard; Visa
Catalog Cost: Free
Catalog Circulation: Mailed 10 time(s) per year to 750M
Printing Information: 16 pages in 4 colors on Glossy Stock
Press: Web Press
Mailing List Information: Names for rent
In Business: 58 years
Number of Employees: 15
Sales Volume: $1MM to $3MM

2684 HoneyBaked Ham Company
Honey Baked Ham Company
P.O. Box 370
Carrollton, GA 30117-8430   800-367-7720
                            Fax: 419-867-3860
                     www.honeybakedonline.com

Hams, beef, poultry, side dishes, desserts, fruit, chocolate and nuts, cookies and seafood

VP: Louis Schmidt, Jr.
Founder: Harry J. Hoenselaar
Credit Cards: AMEX
Catalog Cost: Free
Catalog Circulation: Mailed 5 time(s) per year
Printing Information: 32 pages in 4 colors on Glossy Stock
Binding: Perfect Bound
In Business: 58 years

2685 Hunt Country Foods
Hunt Country Foods Inc.
PO Box 876
Middleburg, VA 20118-876   540-364-2622
                            Fax: 540-364-3112
                     info@send-best-of-luck.com
                     www.send-best-of-luck.com

Best of Luck, Shortbread cookies, Horseshoes, Nails, Horseshoe chocolates, jazz bars and luscious lips chocolates

President: Maggi Castelloe
Credit Cards: MasterCard; Visa
Catalog Cost: Free
Printing Information: 2 pages
In Business: 28 years
Number of Employees: 12

2686 Jaarsma Bakery
Jaarsma Bakery, Inc.
727 Franklin Street
Pella, IA 50219-1619   641-628-2940
                                 641-628-9148
                            Fax: 641-628-9148
                     sales@jaarsmabakery.com
                     www.jaarsmabakery.com

A taste of Holland delivered to your door

President: Kristi Balk
Catalog Cost: Free
Catalog Circulation: Mailed 2 time(s) per year
Printing Information: 1 pages in 1 color
Mailing List Information: Names for rent
In Business: 117 years
Number of Employees: 40
Sales Volume: $1MM to $3MM

2687 Mary of Puddin Hill
Mary of Puddin Hill
512 N John Street
Palestine, TX 75801 903-455-2651
800-545-8889
Fax: 903-723-2889
customerservice@puddinhill.com
www.puddinhill.com

Fruit cakes, chocolates, fudge, caramels, nut brittle and more

In Business: 175 years
Number of Employees: 30

2688 Matthews 1812 House
Matthews 1812 House, Inc.
250 Kent Road South
Cornwall Bridge, CT 06754-15 860-672-0230
800-662-1812
Fax: 860-672-1812
cynthia@1812house.com
www.matthews1812house.com

Fruit cakes, tortes, Chocolate Explosion brownies, candies, nuts, cakes and cookies

President: Deanna Matthews
Marketing Manager: Blaine Matthews
Founder: Deanna Matthews
Credit Cards: AMEX; MasterCard; Visa Discover Optima
Catalog Cost: Free
Catalog Circulation: Mailed 1 time(s) per year to 170M
Average Order Size: $50
Printing Information: 48 pages in 4 colors on Glossy Stock
Press: Web Press
Binding: Saddle Stitched
Mailing List Information: Names for rent
In Business: 33 years
Number of Employees: 15
Sales Volume: $1.3 Million

2689 Mrs Fields Gourmet Gifts
Mrs. Fields
2855 E Cottonwood Parkway
Suite 400
Salt Lake City, UT 84121-7050 800-266-5437
www.mrsfields.com

Cookies and brownies; Gift baskets, tins and cookie jars

President: Neil Courtney
Credit Cards: AMEX; MasterCard
Catalog Cost: Free
Catalog Circulation: Mailed 6 time(s) per year
Printing Information: 22 pages in 4 colors on Glossy Stock
Press: Web Press
Binding: Saddle Stitched
Mailing List Information: Names for rent
In Business: 40 years
Number of Employees: 200
Sales Volume: $60 Million

2690 Mrs Hanes Moravian Cookies
Mrs. Hanes' Moravian Cookie Crisps
4643 Friedberg Church Road
Clemmons, NC 27012-6882 336-764-1402
888-764-1402
Fax: 336-764-8637
hanes@hanescookies.com
www.hanescookies.com

Hand rolled, cut and packed Moravian cookies made from an old family recipie dating back to the 1700s — no preservatives or additives

President: Ramona Templin
Production Manager: Mike Hanes
Credit Cards: MasterCard; Visa
Catalog Cost: Free
Catalog Circulation: Mailed 1 time(s) per year
Average Order Size: $35
Printing Information: 8 pages in 4 colors on Glossy Stock
Press: Web Press

Binding: Saddle Stitched
Mailing List Information: Names for rent
Number of Employees: 45
Sales Volume: $20MM to $50MM

2691 My Grandma's of New England
My Grandma's of New England
1636 Hyde Park Avenue
Boston, MA 02136-2458 617-364-9900
800-847-2636
Fax: 617-364-0505
customerservice@mygrandma.com
www.mygrandma.com

Coffee cakes

President: Robert Katz
CFO: Seth Anapolle
Production Manager: Will Weeks
EVP, General Sales: Bruce Mills
sales@MyGrandma.com
Controller, Accounting: Seth Anapolle
sanapolle@MyGrandma.com
Sales Manager: Victor Otero
votero@MyGrandma.com
Credit Cards: AMEX; MasterCard; Visa
Catalog Cost: Free
Average Order Size: $50
Printing Information: 4 pages in 4 colors on Glossy Stock
Press: Web Press
Binding: Folded
Mailing List Information: Names for rent
In Business: 24 years
Number of Employees: 40
Sales Volume: 8 Million

2692 Original YA-HOO Cake Company
MK Commercial Kitchens
5302 Texoma Pkwy
Sherman, TX 75090-2112 903-868-9665
888-869-2466
Fax: 903-893-5036
customerservice@yahoocake.com
www.yahoocake.com

Cakes, cookies, brownies, teacakes, fruitcakes, other gourmet desserts and confections

President: Geoff Crowley
Buyers: Monette Wible
Credit Cards: AMEX; MasterCard; Visa; Discover
Catalog Cost: Free
Catalog Circulation: Mailed 1 time(s) per year to 10000
Average Order Size: $60
Printing Information: 15 pages in 4 colors on Glossy Stock
Press: Web Press
Binding: Folded
Mailing List Information: Names for rent
List Company: Moran Direct
2299 White Street
Houston, TX 77007
In Business: 71 years
Number of Employees: 102
Sales Volume: Under $500M

2693 Pecans.com Catalog
Pecan Producers Inc
1020 W Front St
Goldthwaite, TX 76844 325-648-2200
800-473-2267
Fax: 325-938-5490
retail@pecans.com
www.pecans.com

Fresh Texas pecans, pecan gifts, dressings, sauces and rubs

President: Martin Mount
Owner: DeWayne McCasland
Credit Cards: AMEX; MasterCard; Visa
Catalog Cost: Free
In Business: 44 years
Number of Employees: 6
Sales Volume: $2.8 Million

2694 Penn Street Bakery
Penn Street Bakery
900 Hynes Avenue SW
Grand Rapids, MI 49507 616-241-2583
800-84 -CAKE
Fax: 616-241-6332
www.pennstreetbakery.com

Gourmet gift collection featuring world famous Penn Street cakes, hand dipped chocolates and homemade cookies available in designer tins and gift baskets

President: Dan Abraham
Marketing Manager: Dave Benge
Purchasing Manager: Yvonne Michell
Credit Cards: AMEX; MasterCard; Visa
Catalog Cost: Free
Catalog Circulation: Mailed 4 time(s) per year
Average Order Size: $25
Printing Information: 12 pages in 4 colors on Glossy Stock
Press: Letterpress
Binding: Saddle Stitched
Mailing List Information: Names for rent
In Business: 21 years
Number of Employees: 55
Sales Volume: $5.1 million

2695 Plaza Sweets
Plaza Sweets Inc.
521 Waverly Ave
Mamaroneck, NY 10543-2235 914-698-0233
800-816-8416
Fax: 914-698-3712
customerservice@plazasweetsbakery.com
www.plazasweetsbakery.com

Gourmet desserts and sweet breads

Chairman: James Ward
President: Rodney Holder
Marketing Manager: Nina Dosett
Production Manager: Ricardo Mendoza
Credit Cards: AMEX; MasterCard
Catalog Cost: Free
Printing Information: 17 pages on Glossy Stock
Binding: Folded
Mailing List Information: Names for rent
In Business: 32 years
Number of Employees: 50
Sales Volume: $5.7 Million

2696 Priester's Pecans
Priester's Pecan Company
208 Old Fort Road East
Fort Deposit, AL 36032 866-477-4736
800-277-3226
Fax: 334-227-4294
customerservice@priesters.com
www.priesters.com

Premium shelled pecans and homemade candies and desserts that incorporate pecans

Manager: Thomas Ellis
Manager: Ellen Ellis Burkett
Credit Cards: AMEX; MasterCard
Catalog Cost: Free
Catalog Circulation: Mailed 3 time(s) per year to 10000
Printing Information: 32 pages in 4 colors on Glossy Stock
Press: Web Press
Binding: Saddle Stitched
Mailing List Information: Names for rent
List Company: Moran Direct
713-880-3725
In Business: 80 years
Number of Employees: 75
Sales Volume: 20MM-50MM

2697 Sunrise Bakery & Gourmet Foods
Sunrise Bakery & Gourmet Foods
2810 Diane Lane
Hibbing, MN 55746 218-262-1219
800-782-6736
Fax: 218-263-4305
sales@sunrisebakery.com
www.sunrisegourmet.com

Specially baked items, walnut potica, strudel, biscotti, antipasto, fruitcake, chocolate fruitcake and much more
President: Donna Anthony
Catalog Cost: Free
In Business: 102 years
Number of Employees: 12
Sales Volume: $630,000

2698 The Fruit Company
The Fruit Company
2900 Van Horn Dr.
Hood River, OR 97031 541-387-3100
800-387-3100
Fax: 541-387-3104
customerservice@thefruitcompany.com
www.thefruitcompany.com

Fruit baskets, desserts, and chocolates for all occasions
Catalog Cost: Free
In Business: 72 years

2699 Tortuga Rum Cake Company
Tortuga Rum Cake Company
14202 SW 142 Ave
Miami, FL 33186 305-378-6668
877-486-7884
Fax: 305-378-0990
customerservice@tortugaimports.com
www.tortugarumcakes.com

Rum Cakes, Coffee, Chocolates.

In Business: 31 years

2700 Willa's Shortbread
Willa's Shortbread
1249 Northgate Bsn Pkwy #1
Suite 1
Madison, TN 37115-2487 615-868-6130
855-364-3844
Fax: 615-868-6132
info@willas-shortbread.com
www.willas-shortbread.com

Shortbread and cheese biscuit
Chairman: Eric Rion
President: Teresa Rion
Marketing Manager: Eugenia Shealy, General Manager
Credit Cards: MasterCard; Visa
Catalog Circulation: Mailed 1 time(s) per year
Printing Information: in 1 color on Matte Stock
Press: Letterpress
Binding: Folded
Mailing List Information: Names for rent
Number of Employees: 4018
Sales Volume: Under $500M

2701 William Greenberg Desserts
William Greenberg Desserts
1100 Madison Ave
New York, NY 10028-327 212-861-1340
www.wmgreenbergdesserts.com

Cookies, cakes brownies and pies
President: Carol Becker
Credit Cards: AMEX; MasterCard; Visa
In Business: 50 years
Number of Employees: 40
Sales Volume: $1MM to $3MM

2702 Yellow Awning Fold Out Brochure
Caroline's Cakes
1580 Whitehall Road
Annapolis, MD 21409 410-349-2212
888-801-2253
www.carolinescakes.com

Nut free bakery, gluten free cakes

Ethnic & International Foods

2703 Cibolo Junction
Chimayo To Go/Cibolo Junction
500 Broadway SE
Albuquerque, NM 87102 800-683-9628
info@chimayotogo.com
www.cibolojunction.com

High quality mexican food products - chiles and salsas
President: Terry Cordes
Marketing Manager: Mary Cordes
In Business: 17 years

2704 Clancy's Fancy
Clancy's Fancy
401 E. Stadium
Ann Arbor, MI 48104 734-663-4338
Fax: 734-663-0056
clancysorders@gmail.com
www.clancysfancy.com

Irish hot sauce
President: Colleen Clancy
Catalog Circulation: to 200
In Business: 25 years
Number of Employees: 2
Sales Volume: $100,000

2705 Ferrara Foods & Confections
Ferrara Cafe
195 Grand St
New York, NY 10013-3717 212-226-6150
Fax: 212-226-0667
www.Ferraracafe.Com

Italian gourmet foods, coffees, cakes and syrups
President: Ernest Lepore
Marketing Manager: Philip Marhuggi
Credit Cards: AMEX; MasterCard
Catalog Cost: Free
Printing Information: 32 pages in 4 colors
In Business: 123 years
Number of Employees: 100
Sales Volume: $10MM to $20MM

2706 House of Spices
House of Spices
127-40 Willets Point Blvd.
Flushing, NY 11368-1506 718-507-4900
Fax: 718-507-4798
hosindia@aol.com
www.Hosindia.Com

Indian grocery and spices, pickles, chutneys, snack food and frozen foods
President: G L Soni
CFO: Neil Soni
Marketing Manager: George Aasar
Production Manager: G L Soni
Buyers: GL Soni
Catalog Cost: Free
Catalog Circulation: to 1000
Printing Information: 27 pages
Mailing List Information: Names for rent
In Business: 45 years
Number of Employees: 100
Sales Volume: $5MM to $10MM

2707 Kosher Connection
TES, Inc.
343 Spook Rock Road
Suffern, NY 97225 845-362-6340
800-950-7227
Fax: 845-357-5720
www.kosherconnection.com

Kosher gourmet food/gifts
Credit Cards: AMEX; MasterCard; Visa
Number of Employees: 2

2708 Lou Malnati's Tastes Of Chicago
Lou Malnati's Pizzeria
3685 Woodhead Dr
Northbrook, IL 60062-1816 847-562-1814
800-568-8646
Fax: 847-562-1950
meck@loumalnatis.com
www.loumalnatis.com

Chicago style deep-dish pizza
President: Marc Malnati
Credit Cards: AMEX; MasterCard; Visa
Catalog Cost:
Printing Information: 4 pages in 4 colors
In Business: 42 years
Sales Volume: $500M to $1MM

2709 Pendery's
Pendery's
1221 Manufacturing St
Dallas, TX 75207 817-924-3434
214-741-1870
email@penderys.com
www.penderys.com

Mexican chilies
President: Pat Haggerty
VP: Mary P Haggerty
General Manager: Clint C Haggerty
Credit Cards: MasterCard; Visa
Catalog Cost: Free
Catalog Circulation: Mailed 4 time(s) per year to 60000
Printing Information: 79 pages in 6 colors on Glossy Stock
Binding: Folded
In Business: 145 years
Number of Employees: 7
Sales Volume: Under $500M

2710 Polana
POLANA INC
3512 N. Kostner Ave
Chicago, IL 60641-3807 773-545-4900
888-765-2621
Fax: 773-545-6800
info@polana.com
www.polana.com

Authentic Polish sausages, breads, soups, cakes, pierogies, stuffed cabbage, gift baskets
President: Mary Machnicki
Marketing Manager: Mario Malanicki
Credit Cards: AMEX; MasterCard
Catalog Cost: Free
Catalog Circulation: Mailed 3 time(s) per year
Average Order Size: $110
Printing Information: 26 pages in 4 colors on Glossy Stock
Press: Web Press
Binding: Saddle Stitched
Mailing List Information: Names for rent
In Business: 15 years
Sales Volume: $1MM to $3MM

2711 Rossi Pasta
Rossi Pasta, Ltd.
PO Box 930
Marietta, OH 45750 800-227-6774
info@rossipasta.com
www.rossipasta.com

Gourmet pasta and sauces

President: Frank L Christy
Marketing Manager: Lori Sweezy
Buyers: John Rossi
Credit Cards: AMEX; MasterCard; Visa
Catalog Cost: Free
Catalog Circulation: Mailed 8 time(s) per year to 80000
Average Order Size: $100
Printing Information: 16 pages in 4 colors on Glossy Stock
Press: Web Press
Binding: Saddle Stitched
Mailing List Information: Names for rent
In Business: 30 years
Number of Employees: 15
Sales Volume: $1.85 Million

2712 Schaller & Weber
Schaller Manufacturing Corp.
22-35 46th St
Astoria, NY 11105   718-721-5480
                          800-847-4115
                     Fax: 718-956-9157
info@schallerweber.com
www.schallerweber.com

Sausages, liverwurst, cold cuts, special smoked meats, salami and servelat, sooked and smoked meats, poultry, pickles and mustard

President: Ralph Schaller
Plant Manager: Harold Nagel
Credit Cards: MasterCard; Visa
Catalog Cost: Free
Printing Information: 8 pages in 3 colors
In Business: 97 years
Number of Employees: 75
Sales Volume: $12 Million

2713 Scottish Gourmet USA
Scottish Gourmet USA
1908 Fairfax Road
Suite B
Greensboro, NC 27407   336-663-7467
                          877-814-3663
info@scottishgourmetusa.com
www.scottishgourmetusa.com

Scottish and gourmet food specialties

President: Anne Robinson
Catalog Cost: Free
Printing Information: 36 pages in 4 colors on Glossy Stock
Binding: Saddle Stitched
Mailing List Information: Names for rent
In Business: 12 years
Number of Employees: 10

2714 Todaro Brothers
Todaro Brothers
555 2nd Avenue
New York, NY 10016-6346   212-532-0633
Eat@TodaroBros.com
www.todarobros.com

Imported gourmet specialty foods from the Mediterranean

President: Luciano Todaro
CFO: Lucian Todaro
Marketing Manager: Mary Todaro
Credit Cards: AMEX; MasterCard; Visa
Catalog Circulation: Mailed 1 time(s) per year
Printing Information: 25 pages
Mailing List Information: Names for rent
List Manager: James Todaro
In Business: 97 years
Number of Employees: 50
Sales Volume: $5MM to $10MM

Fish & Seafood

2715 A Taste of Juneau
Taku Nature's Fish Store
550 S Franklin Street
Juneau, AK 99801-1330   907-463-3474
                          800-582-5122
mailorder@takusmokeries.com
www.takustore.com

Alaskan fresh, frozen and smoked seafood, king crabs and salmon.

Marketing Manager: Sendro Lane
Production Manager: Jeremy LaPierre
Chief Financial Officer: Dan Pardee
Credit Cards: AMEX; MasterCard
Catalog Circulation: Mailed 1 time(s) per year
Printing Information: 6 pages in 4 colors on Matte Stock
Press: Web Press
Mailing List Information: Names for rent
Number of Employees: 35
Sales Volume: $10MM to $20MM

2716 Allen Brothers
Allen Brothers
3737 S Halsted St.
Chicago, IL 60609-1689   800-548-7777
                     Fax: 800-890-9146
www.allenbrothers.com

Steak, poultry and seafood.

Chairman: Christopher Pappas
Catalog Cost: Free
In Business: 123 years
Sales Volume: $80 Million

2717 Blue Crab Bay: Tastes & Traditions
Blue Crab Bay Company
29368 Atlantic Dr
Accomack Airport Industrial Park
Melfa, VA 23410-3354   757-787-3602
                          800-221-2722
                     Fax: 757-787-3430
sales@bluecrabbay.com
www.Bluecrabbay.Com

Specialty foods and gifts from the Chesapeake Bay region, including Sting Ray Bloody Mary Mixer, the Crab Cake Kit and seafood soups

President: Pamela Barefoot
CFO: Dawn Colana
Marketing Manager: Bev Turner
Credit Cards: AMEX; MasterCard
Catalog Cost: Free
Catalog Circulation: Mailed 1 time(s) per year to 30000
Average Order Size: $50
Printing Information: 22 pages in 4 colors on Matte Stock
Press: Web Press
Binding: Saddle Stitched
Mailing List Information: Names for rent
List Manager: Paula Atkinson
In Business: 28 years
Number of Employees: 25
Sales Volume: $1,000,000

2718 Chesapeake Bay Crab Cakes & More
Chesapeake Bay Crab Cakes & More
10711 Red Run Boulevard
Suite 113
Owings Mills, MD 21117   800-282-2722
                     Fax: 800-858-6547
info@cbcrabcakes.com
www.cbcrabcakes.com

Crabcakes, lobster, seafood, chicken & turkey entrees, side dishes, and appetizers, desserts such as chocolate cakes, bread puddings, pies and fruit bars

CFO: Gary Lueck
General Manager: Steve Cohen
Credit Cards: AMEX; MasterCard; Visa
Catalog Cost: Free
Printing Information: 32 pages

In Business: 25 years
Number of Employees: 27
Sales Volume: $4 Million

2719 East Coast Gourmet
East Coast Gourmet
101 Phoenix Avenue
Lowell, MA 01852-1580   888-424-6932
charlie@eastcoastgourmet.com
www.eastcoastgourmet.com

Lobster, chowders, seafood and gift baskets

Catalog Cost: Free

2720 Ekone Oyster Company
Ekone Oyster Company
378 Bay Center Rd.
Bay Center, WA 98527-9042 360-875-5494
                          888-875-5494
                     Fax: 360-875-6058
info@ekoneoyster.com
www.ekoneoyster.com

Fresh smoked oysters for Oregon, Washington and California and canned smoked oysters

President: Nick Jambor
Marketing Manager: Kevin Funkhouser
Catalog Cost: Free
Printing Information: 1 pages in 1 color
Mailing List Information: Names for rent
In Business: 33 years
Number of Employees: 35
Sales Volume: $3MM to $5MM

2721 Fairbury Steaks
Fairbury Steaks
504 D Street
Fairbury, NE 68352   402-729-3364
                          877-316-9266
                     Fax: 402-729-5449
www.fairburysteaks.com

Beef, pork, poultry and seafood

President: Dennis Brown
Credit Cards: AMEX; MasterCard
Catalog Cost: Free
Catalog Circulation: Mailed 4 time(s) per year
In Business: 71 years

2722 Hansen Caviar Company
Hansen Caviar Company
881 State Route 28
Kingston, NY 12401-7216   845-895-2296
                          845-895-1196
                     Fax: 845-331-8075
hcaviar@aol.com

Caviar, imported smoked fish, foie gras, pate's, caviar service and spoons

President: Michael Hansen-Sturm
Buyers: Andrea Dreyfus
Credit Cards: AMEX; MasterCard
Catalog Cost: Free
Catalog Circulation: Mailed 1 time(s) per year
Average Order Size: $5000
Printing Information: 1 pages in 4 colors on Glossy Stock
Binding: Folded
Mailing List Information: Names for rent
In Business: 108 years
Number of Employees: 5
Sales Volume: $3MM to $5MM

2723 Joe's Goes Direct
Joe's Stone Crab
11 Washington Avenue
Miami Beach, FL 33139-7395 305-673-0365
                          800-780-2722
privatedining@joesstonecrab.com

Stone crabs, key lime pie, cole slaw, cream spinach clam chowder and various merchandise

President: Steve Sawitz
CFO: Marc Fine
Production Manager: Lori Kahn

Director, Manufacturing/Operations: James McClendon
Credit Cards: AMEX; MasterCard; Visa
Catalog Circulation: to 2000
Average Order Size: $150
Printing Information: 10 pages
Mailing List Information: Names for rent
In Business: 102 years
Number of Employees: 320
Sales Volume: $9 Million

2724 Josephsons Smokehouse & Specialty Seafood
Josephsons
106 Marine Drive
PO Box 412
Astoria, OR 97103   503-325-2190
                         800-772-3474
                  sales@josephsons.com
                   www.josephsons.com

Specialty smoked seafood

President: Michael Josephson
Marketing Manager: Linda Josephson
Credit Cards: AMEX; MasterCard; Visa
Catalog Circulation: to 100
Mailing List Information: Names for rent
In Business: 95 years
Number of Employees: 10
Sales Volume: $1MM to $3MM

2725 Legal Sea Foods
Legal Sea Foods, LLC
One Seafood Way
Boston, MA 02210-2702   617-530-9000
                           800-343-5804
                      Fax: 617-530-9021
                   www.legalseafoods.com

Maine lobsters, New England clambakes and many other seafood specialties

President: Roger Berkowitz
Marketing Manager: Lisa Landry
CEO: Roger Berkowitz
Credit Cards: AMEX; MasterCard; Visa
Catalog Cost: Free
Catalog Circulation: Mailed 1 time(s) per year to 1000
Printing Information: 23 pages in 4 colors on Glossy Stock
Mailing List Information: Names for rent
In Business: 65 years
Number of Employees: 3000
Sales Volume: $65 Million

2726 Lobster Gram
Lobster Gram
4664 N Lowell Ave
Chicago, IL 60630   773-777-4123
                         800-548-3562
                    Fax: 773-427-5174
         customerservice@lobstergram.com
                    www.livelob.com

Live lobster, steaks, seafood, side dishes, appetizers and more

President: Dan Zawacki
CFO: Karen Zawacki
Marketing Manager: Nikki Pingrey
Catalog Cost: Free
In Business: 28 years
Number of Employees: 30
Sales Volume: $3.7 Million

2727 LobsterAnywhere.com
LobsterAnywhere.com
101 Phoenix Ave.
Lowell, MA 01852   888-85 -aine
                       Fax: 603-251-2427
         feedback@lobsteranywhere.com
               www.lobsteranywhere.com

Maine lobster and fresh seafood, chowders, desserts, seasonal specials and gift packages

President: Joe Bowab
Credit Cards: AMEX; MasterCard; Visa
Catalog Cost: Free

2728 Louisiana Fish Fry Products
Louisiana Fish Fry Products, Ltd.
5267 Plank Rd
Baton Rouge, LA 70805-2730   225-356-2905
                               800-356-2905
                          Fax: 225-356-8867
                     www.louisianafishfry.com

Fish & chicken seasonings, frys & mixes, sauces, spices, seasonings and gift boxes

President: Cliff Pizzolato
Marketing Manager: John Deutschman
Sales Operations Manager : Jolyn Gatlin
National Sales Manager : Patrick Murray
Marketing Brand Manager : Richard Rees
Buyers: Brad Burkett
Credit Cards: AMEX; MasterCard; Visa
Catalog Cost: Free
Average Order Size: $25
Printing Information: 5 pages in 4 colors on Matte Stock
Mailing List Information: Names for rent
In Business: 55 years
Number of Employees: 65
Sales Volume: $20MM to $50MM

2729 Phillips Harborplace
Philips World Headquarters
3761 Commerce Drive
Suite 413
Baltimore, MD 21227-1037   443-263-1200
                              888-234-1200
                         Fax: 410-837-8526
                    www.phillipsseafood.com

Fresh seafood, seasonings and gift cards

President: Stephen Phillip
Catalog Circulation: Mailed 1 time(s) per year
Printing Information: 2 pages
In Business: 59 years
Sales Volume: Under $500M

2730 SeaBear Smokehouse
SeaBear Smokehouse
605-30th Street
Anacortes, WA 98221   360-293-4661
                           800-645-3474
                      Fax: 888-487-6427
              smokehouse@seabear.com
                    www.seabear.com

Halibut, Crab, Prawns, Lobster, Tuna, Cod, Sole, Oysters, Mussels, and Smoked wild salmon, desserts and cooking tools

President: Michael Mondello
mikem@seabear.com
CFO: Dan Jondal
Marketing Manager: Barbara Hoenselaar
Production Manager: Cathy Hayward-Hughes
VP Direc to Consumer: Patti Fisher
patti@seabear.com
Credit Cards: AMEX; MasterCard; Visa
Catalog Circulation: Mailed 5 time(s) per year
Printing Information: 24 pages in 4 colors on Glossy Stock
Press: Web Press
Binding: Saddle Stitched
Mailing List Information: Names for rent
In Business: 58 years
Number of Employees: 45
Sales Volume: Under $500M

2731 Shuckman's Fish Company and Smokery
Shuckman's Fish Company and Smokery
3001 W Main St
Louisville, KY 40212   502-775-6478
                            888-990-8990
                       Fax: 502-775-6373
             shuckmans@kysmokedfish.com
                   www.kysmokedfish.com

Smoked trout, salmon, catfish, spoonfish, caviar, bass

President: Lewis Shuckman
Buyers: Lewis Shuckman
Credit Cards: AMEX; MasterCard
Catalog Cost: Free
Catalog Circulation: Mailed 1 time(s) per year to 1000
Average Order Size: $1200
Printing Information: 2 pages on Newsprint
Press: Letterpress
Binding: Perfect Bound
Mailing List Information: Names for rent
In Business: 94 years
Number of Employees: 12
Sales Volume: $3MM to $5MM

2732 Tsar Nicoulai Caviar
TNC Holding Company, LLC
3018 Willow Pass Road
Suite 200
Concord, CA 94519-1807   415-543-3007
                            800-952-2842
                       Fax: 415-543-5172
            concierge@tsarnicoulai.com
                  www.tsarnicoulai.com

Farmed California American white sturgeon caviar, also smoked fish, infused whitefish roes, caviar accessories and accoutrements and trout roe and salmon roe

Chairman: Dafne Engstom
President: Tom Trauger
Marketing Manager: Stephanie Mann
Buyers: D Engstrom
Credit Cards: AMEX; MasterCard; Visa
Catalog Cost: Free
Catalog Circulation: Mailed 12 time(s) per year
Average Order Size: $500
Printing Information: 1 pages in 4 colors on Matte Stock
Press: Web Press
Binding: Saddle Stitched
Mailing List Information: Names for rent
In Business: 36 years
Number of Employees: 15
Sales Volume: $7,50,000

2733 Weathervane Seafoods
Weathervane Seafoo
31 Badgers Island West
Kittery, ME 03904-5504   207-439-0335
                             800-914-1774
                        Fax: 207-439-7754
        shipping@weathervaneseafoods.com
               www.weathervaneseafoods.com

Seafood - lobsters, scallops, clams and more

President: Terry Gagner
CFO: Bill Kurkel
Marketing Manager: Sue Paquette
Buyers: Jim Collins
Catalog Cost: Free
Catalog Circulation: to 75000
Printing Information: 6 pages in 4 colors on Glossy Stock
Press: Offset Press
Binding: Folded
In Business: 46 years
Number of Employees: 20-5
Sales Volume: Under $500M

Fruit Spreads, Honey & Syrups

2734 American Spoon Foods
American Spoon Foods
1668 Clarion Avenue
PO Box 566
Petoskey, MI 49770-566   231-347-9030
                            888-735-6700
                       hello@spoon.com
                      www.spoon.com

Jams, jellies, salsas and condiments

President: Justin Rashid
Purchasing Director: John Kafer
Plant Manager: Paul Ramey
Credit Cards: AMEX; MasterCard; Visa; Discover

Catalog Cost: Free
Catalog Circulation: Mailed 2 time(s) per year to 30000
Printing Information: 32 pages in 4 colors on Matte Stock
Press: Web Press
Binding: Saddle Stitched
Mailing List Information: Names for rent
In Business: 33 years
Number of Employees: 45

2735 Beatrice Bakery
Beatrice Bakery Co
201 S 5th St
PO Box 457
Beatrice, NE 68310-4408   402-223-2358
                             800-228-4030
customerservice@beatricebakery.com
www.beatricebakery.com

Hand-crafted dessert cakes made especially with fruit and nuts; dessert toppings

President: Greg Leach
Marketing Manager: Rebecca Brown
Production Manager: Robin Dickinson
Catalog Cost: Free
In Business: 98 years
Number of Employees: 43
Sales Volume: $1.4 Million

2736 Beth's Farm Kitchen
Beth's Farm Kitchen
504 County Route 46
PO Box 113
Stuyvesant Falls, NY 12174-113   518-799-3414
                                  800-331-5267
                         Fax: 518-799-2042
bfk@bethsfarmkitchen.com
www.bethsfarmkitchen.com

Jams, chutneys and pickled products made from regional fruit in small batches with the homemade touch

President: Beth Linskey
Production Manager: Liz Beals
Credit Cards: MasterCard; Visa
Catalog Circulation: to 6000
Printing Information: 6 pages
In Business: 34 years
Number of Employees: 6
Sales Volume: $400,000

2737 Bread Dip Company
Bread Dip Company
PO Box 607
Maple Valley, WA 98038   425-358-7386
                     Fax: 425-413-2104
Jim@breaddipcompany.com
www.breaddipcompany.com

Manufacturer of gourmet spreads

President: Laura Sterbenz
In Business: 21 years

2738 Butternut Mountain Farm
The Vermont Maple Sugar Company
37 Industrial Park Drive
Morrisville, VT 05661-8533   802-888-3491
                                800-828-2376
                         Fax: 802-888-5909
sales@butternutmountainfarm.com
www.butternutmountainfarm.com

Maple products

President: David R Marvin
CFO: John Kingston
Credit Cards: MasterCard; Visa
Catalog Cost: Free
Catalog Circulation: Mailed 1 time(s) per year
Printing Information: 15 pages in 4 colors on Matte Stock
In Business: 40 years
Number of Employees: 65
Sales Volume: $6.4 Million

2739 CS Steen Syrup Mill
Steen's Syrup Mill
119 N. Main Street
PO Box 339
Abbeville, LA 70510-339   337-893-1654
                             800-725-1654
                      Fax: 337-893-2478
steens@steensyrup.com
www.steensyrup.com

Pure cane syrup

President: Albert Steen
Production Manager: Charley Steen
Credit Cards: MasterCard; Visa
Catalog Cost: Free
In Business: 105 years
Sales Volume: $3MM to $5MM

2740 Callaway Gardens Country Store
Callaway Gardens
17800 US Hwy 27
Pine Mountain, GA 31822-2000   706-663-6799
                                800-852-3810
                         Fax: 706-663-6812
info@callawaygardens.com
www.Callawaygardens.Com

Callaway gardens speckled heart grits, muscadine jelly, preserves and sauce

President: Bob Sykora
CFO: David Bean
Marketing Manager: Kathy Tilley
Production Manager: Rita Joyner
Director of Conference Services: Pat Kiel
pkiel@callawaygardens.com
Credit Cards: AMEX; MasterCard; Visa
Catalog Cost: Free
Printing Information: 12 pages in 4 colors on Matte Stock
Binding: Folded
Mailing List Information: Names for rent
In Business: 63 years
Number of Employees: 500

2741 Champlain Valley Apiaries
Champlain Valley Apiaries
504 Washington Street
PO Box 127
Middlebury, VT 05753-127   802-388-7724
                              800-841-7334
                       Fax: 802-388-1653
cva@together.net
www.champlainvalleyhoney.com

Honey, tea, maple syrup, candles, wax, bath & body products, books

President: Charles Mraz
Catalog Cost: Free
Printing Information: on Glossy Stock
Press: Sheetfed Press
Binding: Folded
Mailing List Information: Names for rent
In Business: 82 years
Number of Employees: 4
Sales Volume: $150,000

2742 Clearbrook Farms
Clearbrook Farms
3015 East Kemper Road
Sharonville, OH 45241-1514   513-771-2000
                                800-222-9966
                         Fax: 513-771-8381
mailorders@clearbrookfarms.com
www.clearbrookfarms.com

Fruit preserves, spreads, dessert sauces, fruit-tart, and fruit drizzel

Chairman: Stanley Liscow
President: Andy Liscow
CFO: Joe Heinrich
Marketing Manager: Dan Cohen
dan@clearbrookfarms.com
Production Manager: Scott Smith
Catalog Cost: Free
Catalog Circulation: Mailed 1 time(s) per year to 2000
Printing Information: 8 pages in 7 colors on

Glossy Stock
Press: Letterpress
Binding: Folded
Mailing List Information: Names for rent
In Business: 91 years
Number of Employees: 18
Sales Volume: $1.8 Million

2743 Cold Hollow Cider Mill
Cold Hollow Cider Mill
3600 Waterbury-Stowe Road
Waterbury Center, VT 05677   802-244-8771
                                800-327-7537
                         Fax: 802-244-7212
martia@coldhollow.com
www.coldhollow.com

Maple products, cheddar cheese, apple products, jams, jellies, mustards and gift packages

Production Manager: Greg Spina
gregs@coldhollow.com
Owner, Accounts Payable: Paul Brown
paulb@coldhollow.com
Retail Store Manager: Marti Austin
martia@coldhollow.com
Production & Wholesale Cider Sales:
MarkCasavant
markc@coldhollow.com
Credit Cards: AMEX; MasterCard
Catalog Cost: Free
Catalog Circulation: Mailed 4 time(s) per year
Printing Information: 23 pages in 4 colors on Glossy Stock
Press: Web Press
Binding: Folded
Mailing List Information: Names for rent
In Business: 39 years
Number of Employees: 20
Sales Volume: $2.5 Million

2744 Country Store
Reiman Publications
5400 S 60th Street
Greendale, WI 53129   414-423-0100
                       Fax: 414-423-8463
www.rda.com

Gourmet food and one of a kind gifts

Chairman: Richard Walker
President: Bonnie Kintzer
Marketing Manager: Lisa Karpinski
In Business: 22 years
Number of Employees: 400

2745 Das Peach Haus
Fischer & Wieser Specialty Foods
411 South Lincoln Street
Fredericksburg, TX 78624-4502   877-861- 026
                                   800-369-9257
                            Fax: 830-997-0455
info@jelly.com
www.jelly.Com

Jams, jellies, pie fillings, salsa's, salad dressings and cooking sauces

Chairman: Mark B. Wieser
President: Case D. Fischer
CFO: Dave Lewis
Marketing Manager: Jonathan D. Pehl
Director of Sales: Mary Llanes Guevera
Chief Operating Officer: Jenny Wieser, Ph.D
Director of Retail: Deanna Fischer
Credit Cards: AMEX; MasterCard; Visa
Catalog Cost: Free
Catalog Circulation: Mailed 2 time(s) per year
Printing Information: 10 pages on Glossy Stock
In Business: 40 years
Number of Employees: 75
Sales Volume: $15 Million

2746 Doyle's Thornless Blackberry
Doyle's Thornless Blackberry
1600 Bedford Road
Washington, IN 47501   812-254-2654
                    Fax: 812-254-2655
              doyle@fruitsandberries.com
                  www.fruitsandberries.com

Blackberry plants, gardening accessories, animal and insect repellents, organic growth stimulants and fertilizers
President: Tom Doyle
Credit Cards: AMEX; MasterCard
Catalog Cost: Free
In Business: 40 years

2747 Green Mountain Sugar House
Green Mountain Sugar House
Rte 100N
820 Route
Ludlow, VT 05149   800-643-9338
                    Fax: 802-228-2298
                  gmsh@ludl.tds.net
                    www.gmsh.com

Maple syrup, maple products, cheese and Vermont bacon jams
Co-Owner: Ann Rose
Co-Owner: Doug Rose
Credit Cards: AMEX; MasterCard; Visa
Catalog Cost: Free
Catalog Circulation: Mailed 1 time(s) per year to 14000
Printing Information: 16 pages
In Business: 60 years
Number of Employees: 3
Sales Volume: $300,000

2748 Honeyville
Honeyville
33633 Hwy 550
Durango, CA 81301   800-676-7690
                    Fax: 970-403-0022
                www.honeyvillecolorado.com

Honey, sauces, toppings, jams, jellies

2749 Huckleberry Haven
Huckleberry Haven, Inc.
PO Box 5160
Kalispell, MT 59903-5160   406-756-5525
                            800-774-8257
                    Fax: 406-756-5526
                huckhavn@cyberport.net
                www.huckleberryhaven.com

Wild berry products; jams, syrups, toppings and honey
Production Manager: Edward Springman
Credit Cards: MasterCard; Visa
Catalog Cost: Free
Catalog Circulation: Mailed 2 time(s) per year to 6000
Printing Information: 16 pages in 4 colors on Glossy Stock
Press: Sheetfed Press
Binding: Saddle Stitched
Mailing List Information: Names for rent
In Business: 20 years
Number of Employees: 10

2750 Knott's Berry Farm Food
Knott's Berry Farm
1 Strawberry Lane
Orville, OH 44667-280   866-828-5502
                            800-877-6887
                    Fax: 714-579-2490
                www.knottsberryfarmfoods.com

Jams, jellies, preserves, cheeses, candy and baked goods
President: Cynthia Geborkian
Credit Cards: AMEX; MasterCard; Visa
Catalog Cost: Free
Catalog Circulation: Mailed 1 time(s) per year to 10000
Printing Information: 16 pages in 4 colors on

Glossy Stock
Press: Web Press
Binding: Saddle Stitched
Mailing List Information: Names for rent
In Business: 95 years

2751 Kozlowski Farms
Kozlowski Farms
5566 Highway 116
Forestville, CA 95436   707-887-1587
                            800-473-2767
                    Fax: 707-887-9650
                  koz@kozlowskifarms.com
                  www.kozlowskifarms.com

Preserves, chutney, sauces, wines and gift baskets
President: Carmen Kozlowski
CFO: Cindy Hayworth
President: Carol Kozlowski
Credit Cards: AMEX; MasterCard; Visa
Catalog Cost: Free
Mailing List Information: Names for rent
In Business: 65 years
Number of Employees: 20
Sales Volume: $2.8 Million

2752 Linn's of Cambria
Linn's of Cambria
2325 Village Lane
Suite A
Cambria, CA 93428   805-927-1499
                    www.linnsfruitbin.com

Bakery, fruits, gifts

2753 Mad River Farm Kitchen
Mad River Farm
100 Ericson Ct
140
Arcata, CA 95521   707-822-0248
                    Fax: 707-822-4441
                contact@mad-river-farm.com
                    www.mad-river-farm.com

Jams and jellies, also barbecue sauces
President: Marika Myrick
Production Manager: Cary Bartlett
Administration: Marika Myrick
Administration: Robin Bartlett
Catalog Cost: Free
In Business: 25 years
Number of Employees: 2
Sales Volume: $1MM to $3MM

2754 McCutcheon's Apple Products
McCutcheon Apple Products, Inc.
13 S Wisner St
PO Box 243
Frederick, MD 21701   301-662-3261
                            800-888-7537
                    Fax: 301-663-6217
                    www.bobmccutcheon.com

Preserves, jellies and jams, dressings, relishes, and juice sweetened spreads
President: Robert J Mc Cutcheon
Marketing Manager: Vanessa Smith
Credit Cards: MasterCard; Visa
Catalog Cost: Free
Catalog Circulation: Mailed 2 time(s) per year to 10000
Average Order Size: $38
Printing Information: 8 pages in 4 colors on Glossy Stock
Binding: Saddle Stitched
Mailing List Information: Names for rent
In Business: 72 years
Number of Employees: 24
Sales Volume: $10MM to $20MM

2755 Moon Shine Trading Company
Z Specialty Food, LLC
1250-A Harter Avenue
Woodland, CA 95776-6134   530-668-0660
                            800-678-1226
                    Fax: 530-668-6061
                  tasty@zspecialtyfood.com
                    zspecialtyfood.com

Honey, fruit spreads, chocolate nut spreads, honey straws, gift boxes, nut butters, bee pollen, fresh royal jelly, beeswax, propolis, gum
President: Ishai Zeldner
Customer Service Representative: Amina Harris
Lead Drone: Ishai Zeldner
Nectar Director: Josh Zeldner
Credit Cards: MasterCard; Visa
Catalog Cost: Free
Catalog Circulation: Mailed 1 time(s) per year
Printing Information: 2 pages in 4 colors on Glossy Stock
Mailing List Information: Names for rent
In Business: 32 years
Number of Employees: 4
Sales Volume: $190,000

2756 Party Kits Unlimited
Party Kits & Equestrian Gifts
10920 Plantside Drive
Suite C
Louisville, KY 40299-8659   502-425-2126
                            800-993-3729
                    Fax: 502-719-9200
                    info@partykits.com
                    www.derbygifts.com

Kentucky Derby party supplies and fine equestrian gifts
President: Rebecca Biesel
CEO: Becky Biesel
Credit Cards: AMEX; MasterCard; Visa
Catalog Circulation: Mailed 2 time(s) per year
Sales Volume: $3MM to $5MM

2757 RB Swan & Son
SHOWMELOCAL Inc.
25 Prospect St
Brewer, ME 04412-2627   207-989-7803
                    info@ShowMeLocal.com
                    www.showmelocal.com

Maine honey and beeswax candles
President: Harold Swan
CFO: Karen Sennett
Credit Cards: MasterCard; Visa
Catalog Cost: Free
Catalog Circulation: Mailed 1 time(s) per year
Printing Information: 2 pages
Binding: Folded
Mailing List Information: Names for rent
In Business: 50 years
Number of Employees: 7
Sales Volume: $1MM to $3MM

2758 Rocky Top Farms
Rocky Top Farms
11486 Essex Rd
Ellsworth, MI 49729   231-599-2251
                            800-862-9303
                    Fax: 231-599-2352
                  sales@rockytopfarms.com
                    www.rockytopfarms.com

Fruit preserves, toppings and butters sold in handcrafted gift boxes
President: Tom Cooper
Credit Cards: MasterCard; Visa
Catalog Cost: Free
Mailing List Information: Names for rent
In Business: 40 years
Number of Employees: 6
Sales Volume: $3MM to $5MM

2759 Smucker's Catalog
The J.M. Smucker Company
1 Strawberry Ln
Orrville, OH 44667-280
144-667-0280
888-550-9555
Fax: 330-684-6410
www.Smuckers.Com

Jams, jellies, syrups and gift baskets

Chairman: Richard P Smucker
President: Timothy P Smucker
CFO: Mark Belgya
Director Of Investor Relations: Aaron Broholm
aaron.broholm@jmsmucker.com
Credit Cards: AMEX; MasterCard; Visa
Catalog Cost: Free
Printing Information: 32 pages in 4 colors on Glossy Stock
Binding: Saddle Stitched
In Business: 118 years
Number of Employees: 4700

2760 Sticky Fingers Bakeries
Sticky Fingers Bakeries
P.O. Box 8128
Spokane, WA 99203
509-922-1985
800-458-5826
Fax: 509-922-7102
www.stickyfingersbakeries.com

Bakeries, scone mixes, muffin mixes, irish soda bread mix, fruit spreads including curds, jams, jellies and fruit butters

In Business: 28 years

2761 True Brands
True Brands
154 N 35th Street
Seattle, WA 98103
800-750-8783
www.truefabrications.com

Restaurant supplies for liquor, beer and wine

President: Dhruv Agarwal
Credit Cards: AMEX; MasterCard
Catalog Circulation: Mailed 4 time(s) per year
Printing Information: 52 pages in 4 colors
Press: Web Press
Binding: Saddle Stitched
In Business: 13 years
Sales Volume: $5MM to $10MM

2762 Vermont Maple Outlet
Vermont Maple Outlet
3929 Vermont Route 15
Jeffersonville, VT 05464-9806
802-644-5482
800-858-3121
Fax: 802-644-5038
info@vermontmapleoutlet.com
www.vermontmapleoutlet.com

Maple syrup, maple cream, maple sugar, maple candy, Vermont specialty foods and gift boxes

President: Diane Marsh
Credit Cards: MasterCard
Catalog Cost: Free
Catalog Circulation: Mailed 1 time(s) per year to 6000
Printing Information: 8 pages in 4 colors on Glossy Stock
Binding: Folded
Mailing List Information: Names for rent
In Business: 95 years
Number of Employees: 3
Sales Volume: $170,000

2763 Wood Prairie Farm
Wood Prairie Farm
49 Kinney Road
Bridgewater, ME 04735
800-829-9765
Fax: 800-300-6494
orders@woodprairie.com
www.woodprairie.com

Organically grown vegetables and vegetable seeds, cheese, gift baskets, baking mixes, maple syrup

President: Jim Gerritsen
Owner: Megan Gerritsen
Catalog Cost: Free
In Business: 39 years
Number of Employees: 12
Sales Volume: $1.7 million

2764 Wood's Cider Mill
Wood's Cider Mill
1482 Weathersfield Ctr Rd
Springfield, VT 05156-9648
802-263-5547
Fax: 802-263-9674
orders@woodscidermill.com
www.woodscidermill.com

Cider products and maple syrup

President: Willis Wood
Credit Cards: MasterCard; Visa
Catalog Cost: Free
Catalog Circulation: Mailed 1 time(s) per year
Printing Information: 1 pages in 1 color on Matte Stock
Binding: Folded
Mailing List Information: Names for rent
In Business: 12 years
Number of Employees: 7
Sales Volume: $500M to $1MM

Fruits & Vegetables

2765 Albritton Fruit Company
Albritton Fruit Company
5430 Proctor Rd
Sarasota, FL 34233
941-923-2573
800-237-3682
Fax: 941-925-1098
www.albrittonfruit.com

Citrus, fresh squeezed orange and grapefruit juice, candy and marmalades

President: John M Albritton
CFO: Laura Albritton
General Manager: Tom Houser
Buyers: Amber Albritton
Credit Cards: AMEX; MasterCard; Visa
Catalog Cost: Free
Catalog Circulation: Mailed 1 time(s) per year to 17500
Average Order Size: $27
Printing Information: 24 pages in 4 colors on Glossy Stock
Press: Web Press
Binding: Saddle Stitched
In Business: 135 years
Number of Employees: 6
Sales Volume: $340,000

2766 Apricot Farm
Marra Brothers Distributing
550 Monterey Road
Morgan Hill, CA 95037
408-718-0307
800-233-4413
www.apricot-farm.com

Dried fruits, nuts and mixes and gift packages

President: Kevin Perry
Credit Cards: MasterCard; Visa
Catalog Circulation: Mailed 4 time(s) per year to 50000
Printing Information: 16 pages in 4 colors on Glossy Stock
Binding: Saddle Stitched
In Business: 5 years
Number of Employees: 10

2767 Avocado of the Month Club
Avocado of the Month Club
4606 Snapdragon Way
San Luis Obispo, CA 93401
805-277-7452
lblume@avocadoofthemonthclub.com
www.avocadoofthemonthclub.com

Variety of avocados, artichokes, gourmet oils, guacamole recipes and gift baskets

Chairman: Lori Blume
President: Greg Blume
Credit Cards: AMEX; MasterCard

Catalog Cost: Free
In Business: 11 years

2768 Bountiful Fruit
Bountiful Fruit
3615 US-97-ALT
Wenatchee, WA 98801
800-315-2306
customerservice@bountifulfruit.com
www.bountifulfruit.com

Washington State's apples, pears, cherries and fruit baskets

President: Tom Mathison
Credit Cards: MasterCard; Visa
Catalog Cost: Free

2769 Citrus Country Groves
Southern Fulfillment Services
1650 90th Avenue
PO Box 691208
Vero Beach, FL 32966
772-226-3500
800-891-2120
Fax: 877-329-4253
www.southernfulfillment.com/

Citrus fruits, fruit baskets and gourmet gifts

President: Alex Brown
CFO: Keith Tyson
Executive VP: Don Wright
Executive VP & GM - P&D: Andy Graham
VP-Marketing: Bob Daberkow
Credit Cards: MasterCard; Visa
Catalog Cost: Free
Catalog Circulation: Mailed 1 time(s) per year
Average Order Size: $90
Printing Information: 40 pages in 4 colors on Glossy Stock
Press: Web Press
Binding: Saddle Stitched
In Business: 9 years
Sales Volume: $3MM

2770 Delicious Orchards
Delicious Orchards
315 Route 537
Colts Neck, NJ 07722
732-462-1989
800-624-1893
Fax: 732-542-2111
customerservice@deliciousorchardsnjonline.com
www.deliciousorchardsnjonline.com

Quality fruit baskets and bakery products

President: Bill McDonald
Bakery Sales Manager: Carol Chojnacki
Credit Cards: AMEX; MasterCard
Catalog Cost: Free
In Business: 102 years
Number of Employees: 250
Sales Volume: $50MM to $100MM

2771 Edible Arrangements
Edible Arrangements
95 Barnes Road
Wallingford, CT 06492-1800
203-774-8000
877-363-7848
Fax: 203-774-0531
www.ediblearrangements.com

Fresh fruit bouquets for every special occasion

Marketing Manager: Stephen Thomas
Founder and CEO: Tariq Farid
COO: Kamran Farid
EVP: Kristy Ferguson
Credit Cards: AMEX; MasterCard
In Business: 12 years
Number of Employees: 75
Sales Volume: $18.47MM

2772 Florida Gold Fruit Co.
Florida Gold Fruit Co.
P.O. Box 829
Dundee, FL 33838
800-987-8667
Fax: 863-439-4694
www.floridagoldfruit.com

Citrus fruits, gifts

In Business: 47 years

2773 Food Catalog
Kansas Wind Power
13569 214th Rd
Holton, KS 66436-8138   785-364-4407
Fax: 785-364-5123
www.kansaswindpower.net

Over 1300 freeze dried, dehydrated and bulk items for grains, beans, mixes, salads, soups, breakfasts, snacks, flours, vegetable, fruits, meats, TVP, eggs, dairy, desserts, meat or meatless entrees

President: Bob Mc Broom
Catalog Cost: $4
Printing Information: 100 pages in 1 color on Matte Stock
Binding: Saddle Stitched
Mailing List Information: Names for rent
In Business: 40 years
Sales Volume: $500M to $1MM

2774 Hale Groves
Hale Groves
9250 US Highway 1
PO Box 691237
Wabasso, FL 32970   772-581-9915
800-562-4502
Fax: 877-329-4253
customercare@halegroves.com
www.halegroves.com

Oranges, grapefruit and fruit gift baskets

President: Don Wright
CFO: Keith Tyson
Chairman: Keith Morgan
EVP of Strategy: Alex Brown
Sales Manager: Mike Lore
Buyers: John Todd
Credit Cards: AMEX; MasterCard
Catalog Cost: Free
Catalog Circulation: Mailed 1 time(s) per year
Printing Information: 40 pages in 4 colors on Glossy Stock
Press: Web Press
Binding: Saddle Stitched
Mailing List Information: Names for rent
In Business: 68 years
Number of Employees: 1000
Sales Volume: $20MM

2775 Hale Indian River Groves
Hale Groves
9250 US Highway 1
PO Box 691237
Wabasso, FL 32970   772-581-9915
800-562-4502
Fax: 877-326-4253
customercare@halegroves.com
www.halegroves.com

Gift food baskets, jams and jellies

Credit Cards: AMEX; MasterCard; Visa
Catalog Cost: Free
Catalog Circulation: Mailed 1 time(s) per year to 10000
Printing Information: 35 pages
Mailing List Information: Names for rent
In Business: 68 years
Number of Employees: 175

2776 Happy Valley Ranch
Happy Valley Ranch
16577 W 327th St
Paola, KS 66071   913-849-3103
Fax: 913-849-3104
www.happyvalleyranch.com

Cider and fruit presses and accessories

President: Wanda Stagg
Owner: Ray Stagg
Credit Cards: AMEX; MasterCard; Visa
Catalog Cost: Free
Catalog Circulation: Mailed 1 time(s) per year
Printing Information: 16 pages in 4 colors on Glossy Stock

Press: Web Press
Binding: Saddle Stitched
Mailing List Information: Names for rent
In Business: 44 years
Number of Employees: 7
Sales Volume: $710,000

2777 Hyatt Fruit
Hyatt Fruit
PO Box 639
Vero Beach, FL 32961   866-991-8889
Fax: 863-439-4694
www.hyattfruitco.com

Oranges, grapefruits and other citrus fruits

President: Thomas R Jones
Credit Cards: AMEX; MasterCard; Visa; Discover
Catalog Cost: Free
Catalog Circulation: Mailed 2 time(s) per year to 10000
Average Order Size: $61
Printing Information: 16 pages in 4 colors on Glossy Stock
Binding: Saddle Stitched
In Business: 69 years
Number of Employees: 5
Sales Volume: 1MM-3MM

2778 Maine Potato Catalog
Wood Prairie Farm
49 Kinney Road
Bridgewater, ME 04735   207-425-7741
800-829-9765
Fax: 800-300-6494
orders@woodprairie.com
www.woodprairie.com

Organic potato samplers, double-certified organic seed potatoes, organic gift baskets; organic herb and vegetable seeds and gifts

President: Jim Gerritsen
CFO: Megan Gerritsen
Buyers: Jim Gerritsen
Catalog Cost: Free
Catalog Circulation: Mailed 2 time(s) per year to 100M
Average Order Size: $47
Printing Information: 40 pages in 4 colors on Matte Stock
Press: Sheetfed Press
Binding: Saddle Stitched
Mailing List Information: Names for rent
List Manager: Megan Gerritsen
In Business: 30 years
Number of Employees: 8
Sales Volume: $5,50,000

2779 Manhattan Fruitier
Manhattan Fruitier
2109 Borden Avenue
7th Fl.
Long Island City, NY 11101   212-686-0404
800-841-5718
Fax: 212-686-0479
customerservice@mfruit.com
www.Manhattanfruitier.Com

Fruit baskets, flowers and fine foods

President: Jehv Gold
In Business: 27 years
Sales Volume: $1MM to $3MM

2780 Mixon Fruit Farms
Mixon Fruit Farms
2525 27th St E
Bradenton, FL 34208   941-748-5829
800-608-2525
Fax: 941-748-1085
info@mixon.com
www.mixon.com

Oranges, grapefruit, cheeseballs, and other citrus gifts

President: William Mixon
General Manager / Owner : Dean Mixon
deanm@mixon.com

Operations Manager - Fundraising /: Jay Ellis
fundraising@mixon.com
Office Manager : Jody Wilcox
jodyw@mixon.com
Catalog Cost: Free
In Business: 72 years
Number of Employees: 20
Sales Volume: $3.4 Million

2781 Pato's Dream
Pato's Dream Date Gardens
60499 Highway 86
Thermal, CA 92274-9742   patozdrm@aol.com
www.patosdategardens.com

Dates

2782 Pittman & Davis
Southern Fulfillment Services
801 N Expressway 77
Harlingen, TX 78552-5105   800-289-7829
Fax: 866-329-7829
fruit@pittmandavis.com
www.pittmandavis.com

Citrus fruits, dried fruits, cheeses, baked treats and gift baskets

President: Frank Davis
EVP/General Manager: Andy Graham
Credit Cards: AMEX; MasterCard
Catalog Cost: Free
Catalog Circulation: Mailed 3 time(s) per year
Printing Information: 45 pages in 4 colors on Glossy Stock
Press: Web Press
Binding: Saddle Stitched
Mailing List Information: Names for rent
In Business: 85 years
Number of Employees: 21
Sales Volume: $1.9 Million

2783 Poinsettia Groves
Poinsettia Groves
PO Box 1388
Vero Beach, FL 32961-1388   772-562-3356
800-327-8624
Fax: 772-562-3629
customer.service@poinsettiagroves.com
www.poinsettiagroves.com

Indian River gift fruit

President: Jeb Hudson
Marketing Manager: Jeb Hudson
Credit Cards: AMEX; MasterCard
Catalog Cost: Free
Catalog Circulation: Mailed 6 time(s) per year
Printing Information: 24 pages in 4 colors on Glossy Stock
Press: Letterpress
In Business: 68 years
Number of Employees: 50
Sales Volume: $20MM to $50MM

2784 Red Cooper
Red Cooper
PO Box 3089
Mission, TX 78573   800-289-7829
Fax: 866-329-7829
fruit@pittmandavis.com
www.pittmandavis.com/red-cooper.html

Oranges, Sweet grapefruit and other citrus

President: Red Cooper
Credit Cards: AMEX; MasterCard; Visa
Catalog Cost: Free
In Business: 89 years

2785 Ruma's Fruit & Gift Basket World
Ruma's Fruit & Gift Basket World
210 Beacham Street
Everett, MA 02149   617-389-8090
800-252-8282
Fax: 617-387-7894
sales@rumasfruit.com
www.rumasfruit.com

Fancy fruits and New England themed gift baskets

President: Jim Ruma
Catalog Cost: Free
Sales Volume: $1MM to $3MM

2786 Seeds Trust
Seeds Trust
5870 S Long Lane
Littleton, CO 80121   720-335-3436
Fax: 877-686-7524
support3@seedstrust.com
www.seedstrust.com

Vegetables, tomoatoes, wildflowers, wild-flower mixes, native grasses, herbs

President: Bill McDorman
Marketing Manager: Belle McDorman
Catalog Cost:
In Business: 25 years

2787 Shari's Berries
Shari's Berries
4840 Eastgate Mall
San Diego, CA 92121   877-237-7437
wecare@customercare.berries.com
www.berries.com

Gifts baskets specializing in strawberries, berries, as well as other fruits and delights

President: Kevin Beresford
Catalog Cost: Free
Printing Information: 16 pages
In Business: 28 years
Sales Volume: Under $500M

2788 Sphinx Date Ranch & Southwest Market
Sphinx Ranch LLC
3039 N Scottsdale Rd
Scottsdale, AZ 85251   480-941-2261
800-482-3283
info@sphinxdateranch.com
www.sphinxdateranch.com

Medjool dates, dried fruit, nuts and gift baskets

President: Jason Heetland
Credit Cards: AMEX; MasterCard; Visa
Catalog Cost: Free
In Business: 62 years
Number of Employees: 9
Sales Volume: $404,000

2789 W Atlee Burpee and Company
W Atlee Burpee & Company
300 Park Avenue
Warminster, PA 18974-4818   215-674-4900
800-888-1447
Fax: 215-674-4170
www.Burpee.Com

Vegetables, annual and perennial flowers, herbs, flowering bulbs, seed starting, and gardening supplies

President: George Ball
In Business: 139 years
Sales Volume: $20MM to $50MM

Gourmet & Gift Baskets

2790 American Gourmet
American Gourmet
6698 Orchard Lake Rd
West Bloomfield Township, MI 48324   248-851-4450
800-966-7263
Fax: 248-737-3669
americangourmet@aol.com
www.agourmet.com

Hospitality gifts, Godiva-dipped fresh strawberries, cookies, chocolates, and gift baskets by the occassion

Owner: Herbert Sayers
Credit Cards: AMEX; MasterCard; Visa
Catalog Cost: Free
In Business: 34 years

2791 Aunt Sally's Gift Catalog
Aunt Sally's Praline Shops Inc
750 St Charles Ave.
New Orleans, LA 70117-7315   504-524-3373
800-642-7257
Fax: 504-944-5925
service@auntsallys.com
www.AuntSallys.Com

Pralines and Creole food gift baskets from Louisiana

President: Bethany Gex
Marketing Manager: Cherie Cunningham
Production Manager: Karl Schmidt
Fulfillment: Bethany Gex
Credit Cards: AMEX; MasterCard; Visa
Catalog Cost: Free
In Business: 80 years
Number of Employees: 36
Sales Volume: $10MM to $20MM

2792 Basket Works
BasketWorks
2384 Dehne Road
Northbrook, IL 60062   847-559-9379
888-794-4387
Fax: 847-239-7766
info@79gifts.com
www.79gifts.com

Gift basket company, variety of gifts & gift baskets built to order

President: Lise Schleicher
Credit Cards: AMEX; MasterCard; Visa
Catalog Cost: $1
In Business: 18 years

2793 Biscoff Gourmet Catalog
Lotus Bakeries North America, Inc.
50 Francisco Street
Suite 115
San Francisco, CA 94133   855-415-0077
Fax: 415-956-4922
customerservice@biscoff.com
www.biscoff.com

Biscoff gourmet cookies, chocolates and pastries, gift baskets and gift tins

Marketing Manager: Ignace Heyman
CEO: Jan Boone
COO: Jan Vander Stichele
Catalog Cost: Free
Printing Information: 24 pages in 4 colors on Glossy Stock
Binding: Saddle Stitched
In Business: 82 years

2794 Bridgewater Chocolate
Bridgewater Chocolate
559 Federal Rd.
Brookfield, CT 06804   203-775-2286
800-888-8742
Fax: 203-775-9369
www.bridgewaterchocolate.com

Gourmet chocolates, nuts, pretzels, toffee and gift baskets.

Founder: Erik Landegren
Partner: Andrew Blauner
Catalog Cost: Free
Printing Information: 11 pages in 4 colors
In Business: 21 years

2795 Challah Connection
Challah Connection
66 Fort Point Street
Norwalk, CT 06855   866-242-5524
Fax: 203-222-0400
www.challahconnection.com

Gourmet foods, kosher gift baskets, baked goods and pastries

President: Jane Moritz
Catalog Cost: Free
In Business: 15 years

2796 Chukar Cherry Company
Chukar Cherry Company
320 Wine Country Road
P.O. Box 510
Prosser, WA 99350   800-624-9544
Fax: 509-786-2591
customerservice@chukar.com
www.chukar.com

Chocolates and gifts.

Catalog Cost: Free
Mailing List Information: Names for rent
Sales Volume: $3MM to $5MM

2797 Clubs of America
Clubs of America
484 Wegner Road
Lakemoor, IL 60051-3000   815-363-4000
800-800-9122
Fax: 815-363-4677
info@greatclubs.com
www.greatclubs.com

Leader in mail order clubs - select from clubs in beer, wine, flowers, cigars, pizza, coffee and chocolates of the month

President: Doug Doretti
CFO: Dirk J Doretti
Credit Cards: AMEX; MasterCard
Catalog Cost: Free
Catalog Circulation: Mailed 1 time(s) per year
Average Order Size: $120
Printing Information: 16 pages in 4 colors on Matte Stock
Press: Web Press
Binding: Saddle Stitched
Mailing List Information: Names for rent
In Business: 21 years
Number of Employees: 15
Sales Volume: $1 million

2798 Country Store
Reiman Publications
5400 S 60th Street
Greendale, WI 53129   414-423-0100
Fax: 414-423-8463
www.rda.com

Gourmet food and one of a kind gifts

Chairman: Richard Walker
President: Bonnie Kintzer
Marketing Manager: Lisa Karpinski
In Business: 22 years
Number of Employees: 400

2799 Creative Irish Gifts
ShopIrish.com
PO Box 8300
Little Rock, AR 72222   866-851-7918
Fax: 877-213-3660
www.shopirish.com

Irish and Celtic gifts, jewelry and foods

President: Diane O'Connor
Credit Cards: AMEX; MasterCard
Catalog Cost: Free
Number of Employees: 40

2800 Edible Arrangements
Edible Arrangements
95 Barnes Road
Wallingford, CT 06492-1800   203-774-8000
877-363-7848
Fax: 203-774-0531
www.ediblearrangements.com

Fresh fruit bouquets for every special occasion

Marketing Manager: Stephen Thomas
Founder and CEO: Tariq Farid
COO: Kamran Farid
EVP: Kristy Ferguson
Credit Cards: AMEX; MasterCard
In Business: 12 years
Number of Employees: 75
Sales Volume: $18.47MM

2801 Eilenberger Bakery
Eilenberger Bakery
512 N John St
Palestine, TX 75801
903-729-2176
800-788-2996
Fax: 903-723-2889
www.eilenbergerbakery.com

Wide assortment of baked goods

VP Marketing/General Manager: Sarah Pryor
VP: Stephen K Smith
Catalog Cost: Free
Printing Information: 34 pages in 4 colors on Glossy Stock
Binding: Saddle Stitched
In Business: 117 years
Number of Employees: 25
Sales Volume: $710,000

2802 Fairytale Brownies Bakery
Fairytale Brownies Bakery
4610 E Cotton Center Blvd
Suite 100
Phoenix, AZ 85040-8898
602-489-5100
800-324-7982
Fax: 602-489-5122
www.brownies.com

Gourmet brownie gifting company

President: David Kravetz
Marketing Manager: Mary Howard
Catalog Cost: Free
In Business: 19 years
Number of Employees: 35
Sales Volume: $8 Million

2803 Farm Basket
The Farm Basket
2008 Langhorne Rd
Lynchburg, VA 24501-1446
434-528-1107
800-432-1107
Fax: 434-847-8622
customercare@thefarmbasket.com
www.thefarmbasket.com

Gift and gourmet food shop, apples

President: Betty Brown
Production Manager: Mollie Snead
Guardian (GM): Kerry Giles
Chief Ambassador: Trey
Garden Manager: Katy
Credit Cards: AMEX; MasterCard
Catalog Cost: Free
Catalog Circulation: Mailed 1 time(s) per year to 15000
Average Order Size: $55
Printing Information: 8 pages in 4 colors on Glossy Stock
Binding: Saddle Stitched
Number of Employees: 30
Sales Volume: $3MM to $5MM

2804 Figi's Gifts in Good Taste
Figi's Gifts in Good Taste
3200 S Central Avenue
Marshfield, WI 54404
608-324-8080
866-855-0203
Fax: 715-384-1129
www.figis.com

Fancy foods and gifts

President: Dolores Aue
CFO: Rick Golz
Marketing Manager: Louis Donnell
Purchasing: Lynn Kelnhofer
Buyers: George Douma
Craig Steinkraus
Credit Cards: AMEX; MasterCard; Visa
Catalog Cost: Free
Catalog Circulation: Mailed 6 time(s) per year to 30000
Printing Information: 96 pages in 4 colors on Glossy Stock
Press: Web Press
Binding: Saddle Stitched
Mailing List Information: Names for rent
In Business: 70 years
Number of Employees: 180

2805 Figi's Sugar Free & More
Figi's Gifts in Good Taste
3200 S Central Avenue
Marshfield, WI 54404
608-324-8080
866-855-0203
Fax: 715-384-1129
www.figis.com

Sugar free desserts

President: Dolores Aue
CFO: Rick Golz
Marketing Manager: Louis Donnell
Purchasing: Lynn Kelnhofer
Buyers: George Douma
Craig Steinkraus
Credit Cards: AMEX; MasterCard; Visa
Catalog Cost: Free
Catalog Circulation: Mailed 6 time(s) per year to 30000
Printing Information: 96 pages in 4 colors on Glossy Stock
Press: Web Press
Binding: Saddle Stitched
Mailing List Information: Names for rent
In Business: 70 years
Number of Employees: 180

2806 Goodies from Goodman
Goodies from Goodman
11390 Grissom Ln
Dallas, TX 75229
972-484-3236
800-535-3136
cust_svc@goodiesfromgoodman.com
www.goodiesfromgoodman.com

Gift basket

In Business: 99 years

2807 Gourmet Fantasy
Gourmet Fantasy
42 Angeles St., Buting Pasig
Mill Neck, NY 11765
922-819-8220
Fax: 516-624-6776
gourmet_fantasies@yahoo.com
www.gourmet-fantasies.com

Gift baskets

President: Sharyne Wolf
Credit Cards: MasterCard; Visa
Catalog Cost: Free
Catalog Circulation: Mailed 1 time(s) per year to 10000
Average Order Size: $75
Printing Information: 4 pages in 4 colors on Glossy Stock
Mailing List Information: Names for rent

2808 Gourmet Food Store
Gourmet Food Store
3212 NW 64th St
Suite 340
Boca Raton, FL 33496-5621
201-263-0900
877-220-4181
Fax: 201-781-6706
support@GourmetFoodStore.com
www.gourmetfoodstore.com

Caviar, cheese, foie gras and pate, gourmet chocolates, oils and vinegars, smoked salmon, specialty meats, teas, fresh truffles

Marketing Manager: Jon Knigin
Catalog Cost: Free
Sales Volume: $500M to $1MM

2809 Gourmet Market Place
Hickory Farms
1505 Holland Road
Maumee, OH 43537-75
800-753-8558
www.hickoryfarms.com

Cheese and sausage gifts

President: Robert Dyer
CFO: John Brenholt
Marketing Manager: Lisa Caldwell
Credit Cards: AMEX; MasterCard; Visa
Printing Information: 31 pages in 4 colors on Glossy Stock

Binding: Saddle Stitched
Mailing List Information: Names for rent
List Company: Gnames Enterprises
Number of Employees: 125

2810 Harry & David
Harry & David
2500 S Pacific Hwy.
Medford, OR 97501
877-322-1200
Fax: 800-648-6640
service@harryanddavid.com
www.harryanddavid.com

Fruit and food gifts.

Catalog Cost: Free
Printing Information: 32 pages in 4 colors
In Business: 82 years

2811 Holiday Foods Catalogue Division
The Schwann Food Company
115 West College Drive
Marshall, MN 56258-3119
877-302-7426
800-877-7434
Fax: 954-921-5425
info@holidayfoods.com
www.schwansfoodservice.com

Quiche Lorraine with seafood or mushrooms, Hors d'Oeuvres, Canape's and finger sandwiches, mini dessert assortments

Marketing Manager: Bill Flack, Sr.
Bill.Flack@Schwans.com
General Manager: Scott Meter
Credit Cards: AMEX; MasterCard; Visa
Catalog Cost: Free
Catalog Circulation: Mailed 1 time(s) per year
Printing Information: 30 pages
Number of Employees: 75

2812 Horchow Catalog
Horchow Catalog
PO Box 650589
Dallas, TX 75265-589
888-888-4757
Fax: 972-401-6542
www.horchow.com

Gourmet foods, furniture and home decor

President: Karen Katz
CFO: James Skinner
Marketing Manager: Jessica Weiland, VP
Production Manager: Donna Denise
Product Design Manager: Lauren Hunter
Credit Cards: AMEX; MasterCard; Visa
Catalog Cost: $5.5
Catalog Circulation: Mailed 15 time(s) per year
Printing Information: 40 pages in 4 colors
Mailing List Information: Names for rent
Number of Employees: 5
Sales Volume: 500M-1MM

2813 Impromptu Gourmet
Impromptu Gourmet
10711 Red Run Blvd
Suite 113
Owings Mills, MD 21117
877-632-5766
Fax: 800-858-6547
info@impromptugourmet.com
www.impromptugourmet.com

Food

2814 Liberty Orchards
Liberty Orchards
117 Mission Avenue
P.O. Box C
Cashmere, WA 98815
509-782-1000
800-888-5696
Fax: 509-782-4776
service@libertyorchards.com
www.libertyorchards.com

Fruit & Nut Candies and Gifts.

2815 Mackenzie Limited

Mackenzie Limited
10711 Red Run Blvd
Ste 113
Owings Mills, MD 21117 877-867-6851
Fax: 800-858-6547
info@mackenzieltd.com
www.mackenzieltd.com

Products include gourmet seafood and meat products, cheeses, coffees and teas, in addition to a selection of pastry items such as cookies, cakes, and pies

President/Marketing Director: Lori McManus
Credit Cards: AMEX; MasterCard; Visa
Catalog Cost: Free
Printing Information: 44 pages
Number of Employees: 6
Sales Volume: $3,00,000

2816 Monastery Greetings

Monastery Greetings
540 East 105th Street #115
Cleveland, OH 44108 800-472-0425
Fax: 216-249-3387
info@monasterygreetings.com
www.monasterygreetings.com

Gourmet treats and gifts from monasteries around the world

President: Will Keller
Founder: Will Keller
Credit Cards: MasterCard
Catalog Cost: Free
In Business: 18 years
Number of Employees: 2
Sales Volume: $76,000

2817 Mrs Fields Gourmet Gifts

Mrs. Fields
2855 E Cottonwood Parkway
Suite 400
Salt Lake City, UT 84121-7050 800-266-5437
www.mrsfields.com

Cookies and brownies; Gift baskets, tins and cookie jars

President: Neil Courtney
Credit Cards: AMEX; MasterCard
Catalog Cost: Free
Catalog Circulation: Mailed 6 time(s) per year
Printing Information: 22 pages in 4 colors on Glossy Stock
Press: Web Press
Binding: Saddle Stitched
Mailing List Information: Names for rent
In Business: 40 years
Number of Employees: 200
Sales Volume: $60 Million

2818 Oakville Grocery

Oakville Grocery, Napa Valley
7856 St. Helena Highway
Oakville, CA 94562-86 707-944-8802
800-736-6602
Fax: 707-944-1844
cateringnv@oakvillegrocery.com
www.oakvillegrocery.com

Specialty products, elegant gift baskets

President: Steve Carlin
Credit Cards: AMEX; MasterCard; Visa
Catalog Cost: Free
Printing Information: 8 pages in 4 colors on Glossy Stock
Binding: Saddle Stitched
Mailing List Information: Names for rent
Number of Employees: 250
Sales Volume: $5MM to $10MM

2819 Pemberton Farms

Pemberton Farms
2225 Massachusetts Ave
Cambridge, MA 02140 617-491-2244
800-551-7327
Fax: 617-876-5748
customerservice@pembertonfarms.com
www.pembertonfarms.com

Fruit baskets, chocolate gifts and gourmet food assortments

President: Thomas Saidnawey
Marketing Manager: Mark Saidnawey
Credit Cards: MasterCard
Catalog Cost: Free
Printing Information: 62 pages in 4 colors on Glossy Stock
In Business: 85 years
Number of Employees: 65
Sales Volume: $2.4 Million

2820 Pittman & Davis

Southern Fulfillment Services
801 N Expressway 77
Harlingen, TX 78552-5105 800-289-7829
Fax: 866-329-7829
fruit@pittmandavis.com
www.pittmandavis.com

Citrus fruits, dried fruits, cheeses, baked treats and gift baskets

President: Frank Davis
EVP/General Manager: Andy Graham
Credit Cards: AMEX; MasterCard
Catalog Cost: Free
Catalog Circulation: Mailed 3 time(s) per year
Printing Information: 45 pages in 4 colors on Glossy Stock
Press: Web Press
Binding: Saddle Stitched
Mailing List Information: Names for rent
In Business: 85 years
Number of Employees: 21
Sales Volume: $1.9 Million

2821 Rowena's Kitchen

Rowena's Kitchen
758 West 22nd Street
Norfolk, VA 23517 757-627-8699
800-627-8699
info@rowenas.com
www.rowenas.com

Gourmet foods from baked goods to jams to confections and more.

Catalog Cost: Free
In Business: 32 years
Number of Employees: 18

2822 Schaul's Signature Gourmet Foods

Schaul's Signature Gourmet Foods
520 Lively Boulevard
Elk Grove Village, IL 60007 847-593-7500
800-562-5660
Fax: 847-647-6406
www.schauls.com

Beef, poultry, hams, pork, seafood, lamb, veal, gift baskets, fancy nuts, gourmet chocolates

VP/Manager: Thomas Schaul
Catalog Cost: Free
In Business: 92 years
Number of Employees: 25

2823 Scottish Gourmet USA

Scottish Gourmet USA
1908 Fairfax Road
Suite B
Greensboro, NC 27407 336-663-7467
877-814-3663
info@scottishgourmetusa.com
www.scottishgourmetusa.com

Scottish and gourmet food specialties

President: Anne Robinson
Catalog Cost: Free

Printing Information: 36 pages in 4 colors on Glossy Stock
Binding: Saddle Stitched
Mailing List Information: Names for rent
In Business: 12 years
Number of Employees: 10

2824 Shari's Berries

Shari's Berries
4840 Eastgate Mall
San Diego, CA 92121 877-237-7437
wecare@customercare.berries.com
www.berries.com

Gifts baskets specializing in strawberries, berries, as well as other fruits and delights

President: Kevin Beresford
Catalog Cost: Free
Printing Information: 16 pages
In Business: 28 years
Sales Volume: Under $500M

2825 Sieco USA Corporation

Sieco USA Corporation
9014 Ruland Dr.
Houston, TX 77055-4612 713-464-1726
800-325-9443
Fax: 713-457-5169
sales@sieco-usa.com
www.sieco-usa.com

Olive oil, Balsamic vinegar, private label, gift sets, and bulk.

President: Diann Chemam
Marketing Manager: Sherif Chemam
Production Manager: S.M. Chemam
Buyers: Sherif Chemam
Credit Cards: MasterCard; Visa
Catalog Circulation: Mailed 2 time(s) per year
Printing Information: 3 pages in 4 colors on Glossy Stock
Press: Sheetfed Press
Binding: Folded
Mailing List Information: Names for rent
In Business: 25 years
Number of Employees: 3
Sales Volume: $300,000

2826 Stonewall Kitchen

Stonewall Kitchen
2 Stonewall Ln
York, ME 03909-1662 207-351-2712
800-826-1752
Fax: 207-351-2715
guestservices@stonewallkitchen.com
www.stonewallkitchen.com

Gourmet foods, gifts, kitchenware and baking supplies

President: Thom Rindt
CFO: Lori King
Marketing Manager: Sheri Tripp
Credit Cards: MasterCard
Catalog Cost: Free
In Business: 23 years
Number of Employees: 120
Sales Volume: $34 million

2827 Sunnyland Farms

Sunnyland Farms, Inc.
2314 Wilson Road
P.O. Box 8200
Albany, GA 31706-8200 800-999-2488
Fax: 229-317-4949
www.sunnylandfarms.com

Specialty nuts and fruits, cakes, candies and miscellaneous other food items

President: Jane Willson
Co-Owner: Larry Willson
Co-Owner: Beverly Willson
Credit Cards: AMEX; MasterCard
Catalog Cost: Free
Catalog Circulation: to 1000
Average Order Size: $80
Printing Information: 48 pages in 4 colors on Glossy Stock
Press: Web Press

Binding: Saddle Stitched
Mailing List Information: Names for rent
In Business: 69 years
Number of Employees: 200
Sales Volume: $10MM to $20MM

2828 The Fruit Company
The Fruit Company
2900 Van Horn Dr.
Hood River, OR 97031

541-387-3100
800-387-3100
Fax: 541-387-3104
customerservice@thefruitcompany.com
www.thefruitcompany.com

Fruit baskets, desserts, and chocolates for all occasions

Catalog Cost: Free
In Business: 72 years

2829 Van's Gifts
Van's Gifts, Inc.
PO Box 5532
Fullerton, CA 92838

800-822-7538
Fax: 714-869-0840
customerservice@vansgifts.com
www.vansgifts.com

Wine gift baskets

President: Reva Colover
Marketing Manager: Sophanara Choeum
Credit Cards: AMEX; MasterCard
Catalog Cost: Free
In Business: 31 years
Number of Employees: 25
Sales Volume: $3.5 Million

2830 Wisconsin Cheese Mart
Wisconsin Cheese Mart
215 W. Highland Avenue
Milwaukee, WI 53203

888-482-7700
www.wisconsincheesemart.com

Cheese, gourmet food, gifts

Credit Cards: AMEX; MasterCard
Printing Information: 17 pages

2831 Wisconsin Cheeseman
The Wisconsin Cheeseman
1112 7th Ave.
Monroe, WI 53566-1364

800-693-0834
customerservice@wisconsincheeseman.com

Cheese, sausage, chocolates, candies, fruit cakes and more.

Catalog Cost: Free
Catalog Circulation: Mailed 4 time(s) per year
Printing Information: 54 pages in 4 colors
Mailing List Information: Names for rent
In Business: 70 years
Sales Volume: $20MM to $50MM

2832 Wood Prairie Farm
Wood Prairie Farm
49 Kinney Road
Bridgewater, ME 04735

800-829-9765
Fax: 800-300-6494
orders@woodprairie.com
www.woodprairie.com

Organically grown vegetables and vegetable seeds, cheese, gift baskets, baking mixes, maple syrup

President: Jim Gerritsen
Owner: Megan Gerritsen
Catalog Cost: Free
In Business: 39 years
Number of Employees: 12
Sales Volume: $1.7 million

2833 Zabar's Catalog
Zabar's
2245 Broadway
New York, NY 10024

212-787-2000
800-697-6301
Fax: 212-580-4477
info@zabars.com
www.zabars.com

Gourmet food and gift baskets

President: Saul Zabar
Credit Cards: AMEX; MasterCard; Visa
Catalog Cost: Free
Catalog Circulation: Mailed 2 time(s) per year
Average Order Size: $10
Printing Information: 20 pages in 4 colors on Glossy Stock
Press: Web Press
Binding: Saddle Stitched
Number of Employees: 200
Sales Volume: $20MM to $50MM

Health Foods

2834 Beans Without the Bang
CRM Farms Inc
Po Box 237
Gooding, ID 83330

208-934-4527
800-648-4851
Fax: 208-934-5969
fartless@fartless.com
www.fartless.com

Chili, popcorn and easy-to-digest beans

Credit Cards: MasterCard
Printing Information: 14 pages
In Business: 24 years

2835 Bickford Flavors
Bickford Flavors
19007 Saint Clair Ave
Cleveland, OH 44117-1001

216-531-6006
800-283-8322
Fax: 216-531-2006
orders@bickfordflavors.com
www.BickfordFlavors.com

Flavorings, extracts and oils for special dietary needs, baking, ice cream and candy making

President: Barbara Sofer
VP: Scott Sofer
Credit Cards: AMEX; MasterCard
Printing Information: 1 pages
In Business: 98 years
Number of Employees: 5
Sales Volume: $3 million

2836 Bouchard Family Farm
Bouchard Family Farms
3 Strip Rd
Fort Kent, ME 04743-1550

207-834-3237
800-239-3237
Fax: 207-834-7422
bouchard@ployes.com
www.ployes.com

Gluten free, cholesterol free and sugar free products

President: Joseph Bouchard
Catalog Cost: Free
Catalog Circulation: to 5000
Printing Information: 2 pages
In Business: 142 years
Number of Employees: 5
Sales Volume: $125,000

2837 Cuprem Premium Products
Cuprem Inc
202 N. Smith Avenue
P.O. Box 147
Kenesaw, NE 68956

402-752-3322
800-228-4253
Fax: 402-752-3397
info@cuprem.com
www.cuprem.com

Animal health products; personal health products

President: Arwin V Mulford
Secretary: Carol Mulford
Credit Cards: AMEX; MasterCard
Catalog Cost: Free
Average Order Size: $86
Printing Information: 32 pages in 4 colors on Glossy Stock
Press: Sheetfed Press
Mailing List Information: Names for rent
In Business: 50 years
Number of Employees: 11
Sales Volume: $1,000,000

2838 Dale and Thomas Popcorn
Dale and Thomas Popcorn
One Cedar Lane
Englewood, NJ 07631

800-767-4444
800-767-4444

Gourmet flavored popcorn and gift baskets

President: Sean Orr
VP Purchasing: Richard Riordan
COO: Glenn Flook
Credit Cards: AMEX; MasterCard; Visa
Catalog Cost: Free
Catalog Circulation: Mailed 4 time(s) per year
Printing Information: in 4 colors
In Business: 9 years
Number of Employees: 200
Sales Volume: $9.4 million

2839 EatRaw
EatRaw
140 58th Street
Suite 6E
Brooklyn, NY 11220

718-210-0048
Fax: 718-439-7302
sales@eatraw.com
www.eatraw.com

Raw and organic living food

2840 Ener-G-Foods
Ener-G-Foods, Inc.
5960 1st Ave S
Seattle, WA 98108

206-767-3928
800-331-5222
Fax: 206-764-3398
customerservice@ener-g.com
www.ener-g.com

Dietary foods for allergies, celiac sprue, PKU, kidney failure, wheat-free, gluten-free, and dairy free, kosher

President: Sam Wylde III
CFO: James Smiley Williamson
Marketing Manager: Jerry Colburn
Purchasing Director: Sabina Milovic
Buyers: Sabina Milovic
Credit Cards: AMEX; MasterCard
Catalog Cost: Free
Catalog Circulation: Mailed 1 time(s) per year
Printing Information: 28 pages in 1 color on Newsprint
Press: Web Press
Binding: Saddle Stitched
Mailing List Information: Names for rent
In Business: 63 years
Number of Employees: 47
Sales Volume: $4 Million

2841 George Chiala Farms
George Chiala Farms
15500 Hill Road
Morgan Hill, CA 95037

408-778-0562
Fax: 408-779-4034
www.gcfarmsinc.com

Agricultural food products

President: George Chiala, Sr.
CFO: Alice Chiala
Marketing Manager: George Chiala, Jr.
Production Manager: Pat Connelly
Dir. of Fresh Market Sales & Procur: Tim Chiala

Farm Manager: Ian Teresi
Plant Engineer: Rusty McMillan

2842 GloryBee Natural Foods and Crafts

GloryBeeFoods, Inc
29548 B Airport Rd
Eugene, OR 97402   541-689-0913
     800-456-7923
Fax: 541-689-9692
info@glorybeefoods.com
www.glorybeefoods.com

Candlemaking and candymaking supplies, beekeeping supplies, soapmaking supplies, nutritional supplements, aromatherapy supplies, honey and honey stix

President: Richard Turanski
CFO: Richard Shaneyfelt
Purchasing Manager: Randy Djonne
International Marketing Manager: Daniel Shaneyfelt
Buyers: Darren Miller
Credit Cards: MasterCard
Catalog Cost: Free
Catalog Circulation: Mailed 1 time(s) per year to 60M
Average Order Size: $75
Printing Information: 70 pages in 4 colors on Glossy Stock
Press: Web Press
Binding: Saddle Stitched
Mailing List Information: Names for rent
List Manager: Shannon Arch
In Business: 40 years
Number of Employees: 100
Sales Volume: $50 Million

2843 Gold Mine Natural Food Company Winter 2010/2011

Gold Mine Natural Food Company
13200 Danielson Street
Suite A-1
Poway, CA 92064   858-537-9830
     800-475-3663
Fax: 858-695-0811
customerservice@goldminenaturalfoods.com
shop.goldminenaturalfoods.com
Founder, Owner: Jean Richardson
In Business: 30 years

2844 Hallelujah Diet

Hallelujah Diet
916 Cox Road
Suite 210
Gastonia, NC 28054   704-481-1700
     800-915-9355
www.myhdiet.com

Diet program

President: Paul Malkmus
CEO: Paul Malkmus
Chief Education Officer: Ann Malkmus
Vice President of Health: Olin Idol
In Business: 30+ years

2845 Harvest Direct

Harvest Direct
61 Accord Park Drive
Norwell, MA 02061-906   865-539-6305
     800- 73- 21
Fax: 865-539-2737
info@harvestdirect.com
www.harvestdirect.com

Vegetarian products and meat alternatives

President: Cynthia Holzapfel
Marketing Manager: Cynthia Holzapfel
Catalog Cost: Free
Catalog Circulation: Mailed 5 time(s) per year
Printing Information: 32 pages in 1 color on Newsprint
Mailing List Information: Names for rent
Number of Employees: 10

2846 Healthy Eating

The Mail Order Catalog
413 Farm Road
PO Box 180
Summertown, TN 38483-8008   931-964-2241
     800-695-2241
Fax: 931-964-2291
info@healthy-eating.com
www.healthy-eating.com

Vegetarian food products and cook books, sprouting seeds, meat and dairy substitutes

Marketing Manager: Cynthia Holzapfel
Co-owner: Robert Holzapfel
Credit Cards: AMEX; MasterCard
Catalog Cost: Free
Catalog Circulation: Mailed 2 time(s) per year
Printing Information: 7 pages in 1 color on Newsprint
Binding: Folded
In Business: 25 years
Number of Employees: 10
Sales Volume: $610,000

2847 Hodgson Mill

Hodgson Mill
1100 Stevens Ave
Effingham, IL 62401   800-525-0177
Fax: 217-347-0198
customerservice@hodgsonmill.com
www.hodgsonmill.com

Stone ground, whole grain and organic foods: flours, cornmeals, cereals, baking mixes, pastas and more

Chairman: Cathy Goldstein
President: Robert Goldstein
Marketing Manager: Paul Kirby
Credit Cards: AMEX; MasterCard; Visa
Catalog Cost: Free
In Business: 178 years
Number of Employees: 106
Sales Volume: $26 Million

2848 J.R. Watkins

J.R. Watkins
150 Liberty Street
P.O. Box 5570
Winona, MN 55987-0570   507-457-3300
     800-243-9423
Fax: 507-452-6723
webhelp@jrwatkins.com
www.jrwatkins.com

Remedies and vitamins made from all natural ingredients, spices, soaps and detergents

Catalog Cost: Free
In Business: 146 years

2849 Jaffe Brothers Natural Foods

Jaffe Bros., Inc.
28560 Lilac Road
Valley Center, CA 92082   760-749-1133
     877-975-2333
Fax: 760-749-1282
jaffebros@att.net
www.organicfruitsandnuts.com

Organic, untreated natural foods, dried fruits, nuts, pasta and coffee

President: Emma Jaffe
International Marketing Manager: Larry Jaffe
Credit Cards: AMEX; MasterCard; Visa
Catalog Cost: Free
Catalog Circulation: Mailed 1 time(s) per year to 20000
Average Order Size: $100
Printing Information: 27 pages in 4 colors on Newsprint
Press: Web Press
Mailing List Information: Names for rent
In Business: 69 years
Number of Employees: 8
Sales Volume: $5MM to $10MM

2850 Living Tree Community Foods

Living Tree Community Foods
PO Box 10082
Berkeley, CA 94709   510-526-7106
     800-260-5534
Fax: 510-526-9516
info@livingtreecommunity.com
www.livingtreecommunity.com

Raw organic almond butter, cashew butter, olive oil, olives, almonds, cashews and dried fruit

President: Jesse Schwartz
Catalog Cost: Free
Catalog Circulation: to 2000
Printing Information: 15 pages on Newsprint
Press: Sheetfed Press
Mailing List Information: Names for rent
In Business: 36 years
Number of Employees: 12
Sales Volume: $600,000

2851 MagicKitchen.Com

My Magic Kitchen, Inc.
118 Bentley Square
Mountain View, CA 94040   650-941-2260
     877-516-2442
Fax: 650-941-2255
orders@magickitchen.com
www.magickitchen.com

Prepared meals, soups, sides, main courses and desserts. Also diabetic, gluten free and weight loss meals, as well as meals for seniors.

President: Michelle Tayler
CEO: Greg Miller
Catalog Cost: Free
Printing Information: 16 pages in 4 colors
In Business: 11 years
Number of Employees: 16
Sales Volume: $10 Million

2852 Maine Coast Sea Vegetables

Maine Coast Sea Vegetables
430 Washington Junction Rd.
Hancock, ME 04640   207-412-0094
Fax: 207-412-0639
info@seaveg.com
www.Seaveg.Com

Organically certified sea vegetables, sea seasonings, sea chips, maine coast crunch and natural foods

President: Shep Erhart
International Marketing Manager: Craig Hoke
Credit Cards: MasterCard; Visa
Average Order Size: $45
Printing Information: in 2 colors on Matte Stock
Press: Letterpress
Mailing List Information: Names for rent
In Business: 43 years
Number of Employees: 10
Sales Volume: $5 million

2853 Northwest Wild Foods

Northwest Wild Foods
12535 Pulver Rd
Burlington, WA 98233   360-757-7940
     866-945-3232
Fax: 360-757-0437
thebear@nwwildfoods.com
www.nwwildfoods.com

Organic wild harvest food

Credit Cards: AMEX; MasterCard

2854 Sechlers Fine Pickles

Sechler's Pickles, Inc.
5686 SR 1
St Joe, IN 46785   260-337-5461
     800-332-5461
Fax: 260-337-5771
showroom@sechlerspickles.com
www.sechlerspickles.com

Forty varieties of gourmet pickles

Owner: David Sechler
General Manager: Max Troyer
Credit Cards: MasterCard; Visa
Catalog Cost: Free
Catalog Circulation: Mailed 2 time(s) per year to 18000
Printing Information: 4 pages in 2 colors on Matte Stock
Binding: Folded
Mailing List Information: Names for rent
In Business: 85 years
Number of Employees: 32
Sales Volume: $4 Million

2855 Something Better Natural Foods
Something Better Natural Foods
22201 Capital Avenue NE
Battle Creek, MI 49017   269-965-1199
Fax: 269-965-8500
orders@somethingbetternaturalfoods.com
www.somethingbetternaturalfoods.com/in-dex.html

Natural and organic foods

Credit Cards: MasterCard
Printing Information: 94 pages
In Business: 28+ years

2856 Wildseed Reference Guide & Seed Catalog
Wildseed Farms
100 Legacy Drive
PO Box 3000
Fredericksburg, TX 78624   800-848-0078
Fax: 830-990-8090
orders1@wildseedfarms.com
www.wildseedfarms.com

Wildflower seeds, specialty foods, home and garden, gourmet gift baskets

President: John Thomas
CFO: Kerry Fisher
Marketing Manager: Tom Kramer
Catalog Cost: Free
Number of Employees: 45
Sales Volume: $6 Million

2857 eDietShop
eDietShop
PO Box 1037
Evanston, IL 60204-1397   847-679-5409
800-325-5409
Fax: 847-869-2170
edietshop@edietshop.com
www.edietshop.com

Diet foods

President: Steven Bernard
Catalog Cost: Free
In Business: 33 years

Herbs, Spices & Sauces

2858 Atlantic Spice
Atlantic Spice Company
2 Shore Road
North Truro, MA 02652   508-487-6100
800-316-7965
Fax: 508-487-2550
weborders@atlanticspice.com
www.atlanticspice.com

Culinary herbs and spices, teas, dehydrated vegetables, nuts, seeds, botanicals, essential oils, spice blends, potpourri ingredients and fragrance oils

Buyers: Cory Chapman
Credit Cards: AMEX; MasterCard
Catalog Cost: Free
Catalog Circulation: Mailed 2 time(s) per year
Average Order Size: $300
Printing Information: 17 pages in 2 colors on Matte Stock
Press: Letterpress
Binding: Saddle Stitched

Mailing List Information: Names for rent
In Business: 10 years
Number of Employees: 8
Sales Volume: $10MM to $20MM

2859 Attar Herbs & Spices
Attar Herbs & Spices
5 Sargent Camp Road
Harrisville, NH 03450   603-924-2210
800-541-6900
Fax: 603-924-2211
info@attarherbs.com
www.attarherbs.com

Herbs and spices

President: Richard Martin
Credit Cards: MasterCard; Visa
Catalog Cost: $1
Catalog Circulation: Mailed 1 time(s) per year
Printing Information: 8 pages in 2 colors
In Business: 41 years
Number of Employees: 3
Sales Volume: $340,000

2860 Fiorella's Jack Stack Barbecue
Fiorella's Jack Stack Barbecue
13441 Holmes Rd
Kansas City, MO 64145-1445   816-942-9141
877-419-7427
Fax: 816-942-5166
www.jackstackbbq.com

Kansas City barbeque ribs to beef brisket, sauces and rubs

President: Case Dorman
Operations Director: Rod Toelkes
Credit Cards: AMEX; MasterCard
Catalog Cost: Free
Sales Volume: $5MM to $10MM

2861 Frontier Wholesale Price Guide
Frontier Natural Products Co-Op
3021 78th St
PO Box 299
Norway, IA 52318-9520   319-227-7996
800-669-3275
Fax: 319-227-7966
customercare@frontiercoop.com
www.Frontiercoop.Com

Frontier herbs, organic coffee, essential oils, herbal extracts, shampoo and more

President: Tony Bedard
Credit Cards: AMEX; MasterCard
Catalog Circulation: Mailed 1 time(s) per year
Printing Information: 238 pages in 2 colors
Binding: Perfect Bound
In Business: 39 years
Sales Volume: $20MM to $50MM

2862 HealthWatchers System
Puritan's Pride
1233 Montauk Highway
PO Box 9001
Oak Dale, AZ 11769-9001   800-645-9584
800-645-1030
Fax: 800-948-8150
www.puritan.com

Multi-vitamins, supplements, hearbal products

President: Arthur Rudolph
Credit Cards: AMEX; MasterCard
Catalog Cost: Free
Catalog Circulation: Mailed 4 time(s) per year
Printing Information: 95 pages in 5 colors
In Business: 40 years

2863 J.R. Watkins
J.R. Watkins
150 Liberty Street
P.O. Box 5570
Winona, MN 55987-0570   507-457-3300
800-243-9423
Fax: 507-452-6723
webhelp@jrwatkins.com
www.jrwatkins.com

Remedies and vitamins made from all natural ingredients, spices, soaps and detergents

Catalog Cost: Free
In Business: 146 years

2864 Kozlowski Farms
Kozlowski Farms
5566 Highway 116
Forestville, CA 95436   707-887-1587
800-473-2767
Fax: 707-887-9650
koz@kozlowskifarms.com
www.kozlowskifarms.com

Preserves, chutney, sauces, wines and gift baskets

President: Carmen Kozlowski
CFO: Cindy Hayworth
President: Carol Kozlowski
Credit Cards: AMEX; MasterCard; Visa
Catalog Cost: Free
Mailing List Information: Names for rent
In Business: 65 years
Number of Employees: 20
Sales Volume: $2.8 Million

2865 Magic Seasonings Catalog
Magic Seasonings Blends
720 Distributors Row
PO Box 23342
New Orleans, LA 70183-0342   504-731-3590
800-457-2857
Fax: 504-731-3576
info@chefpaul.com
www.chefpaul.com

Seasonings, cookbooks, gift packs, smoked meats, cookware and recipes from Chef Paul Prudhomme

President: Chef Paul Prudhomme
CFO: Jack Eumont
jeumont@chefpaul.com
International Marketing Manager: Anna Zuniga
Credit Cards: MasterCard
Catalog Cost: Free
Catalog Circulation: Mailed 2 time(s) per year to 300M
Average Order Size: $40
Printing Information: 15 pages in 4 colors on Glossy Stock
Press: Web Press
Binding: Saddle Stitched
Mailing List Information: Names for rent
List Manager: Anna Zuniga
In Business: 30 years
Number of Employees: 60
Sales Volume: $1MM to $3MM

2866 Maurice's Piggie Park Barbeque
Maurice's Piggie Park Barbeque
1600 Charleston Highway
West Columbia, SC 29169   803-796-0220
800-628-7423
Fax: 803-791-8707
mail@piggiepark.com
www.piggiepark.com

Gourmet barbeque sauce

President: Lloyd M. Bessinger, II
Credit Cards: AMEX; MasterCard; Visa
Catalog Cost: Free
Printing Information: 1 pages in 4 colors
In Business: 75 years

2867 MiFarmMarket.com
MiFarmMarket.com
9525 Center Street
Ellsworth, MI 49729
231-753-8682
866-544-1088
mifarmmarket.com

Food products, gift items

In Business: 20+ years

2868 Mo Hotta Mo Betta
Mo Hotta Mo Betta
2822 Limerick Street
Savannah, GA 31404
912-748-2766
800-462-3220
Fax: 912-748-1364
mohotta@mohotta.com
www.mohotta.com

Hot sauces, bbq, salsas and sauces, snacks and spices

President: James M Kelly
Credit Cards: AMEX; MasterCard
Catalog Cost: Free
In Business: 26 years
Number of Employees: 6
Sales Volume: $680,000

2869 Mustard Museum and Gourmet Foods
Mustard musem
7477 Hubbard Avenue
Middleton, WI 53562-468
608-831-2222
800-438-6878
customerservice@mustardmuseum.com
www.Mustardmuseum.Com

Mustard products

Chairman: Barry Levenson, Curator
President: Barry Levenson
Marketing Manager: Patti Levenson
plevenson@mustardmuseum.com
Founder/Curator: Barry Levenson
curator@mustardmuseum.com
Director of Marketing & Tours: Patti Levenson
plevenson@mustardmuseum.com
Credit Cards: MasterCard
Catalog Cost: Free
Catalog Circulation: Mailed 1 time(s) per year
to 55000
Printing Information: 20 pages in 4 colors on
Glossy Stock
Binding: Saddle Stitched
In Business: 21 years

2870 Natures Flavors
Natures Flavors
833 N. Elm St.
Orange, CA 92867
714-744-3700
Fax: 714-771-2424
www.naturesflavors.com

Natural food products

2871 Olde Westport Spice & Trading Company
Olde Westport Spice & Trading Company
1218 Main St.
Goodland, KS 67735
785-899-2020
800-537-6470
Fax: 785-899-2021
oldebill@oldewestportspice.com
www.oldewestportspice.com

Seasonings and soup mixes

President: Judy Petersen
Marketing Manager: Ann Myers
Catalog Cost: Free
Printing Information: 29 pages
Mailing List Information: Names for rent
In Business: 34 years
Number of Employees: 4
Sales Volume: $500M to $1MM

2872 Original Juan Specialty Foods
Original Juan Specialty Foods
111 Southwest Boulevard
Kansas City, KS 66103
913-432-5228
800-568-8468
Fax: 913-432-5880
www.originaljuan.com

Specialty sauces, salsas, snacks and dips

President: Joe R Polo Sr
Marketing Manager: Lindsay Howerton
Production Manager: Valerie Lewellen
VP Operations: Tom Clark
Purchasing Manager: Jason Erickson
Bookkeeper: Ruth Becker
Catalog Cost: Free
In Business: 17 years
Number of Employees: 25
Sales Volume: $4.6 Million

2873 PS Seasoning and Spices
PS Seasoning and Spices
216 W. Pleasant Street
Iron Ridge, WI 53035
800-328-8313
Fax: 920-387-2204
csr@psseasoning.com
www.psseasoning.com

Seasonings, spices, smoking and cooking supplies

Credit Cards: AMEX; MasterCard
Catalog Cost: Free
In Business: 31 years

2874 Pacific Botanicals
Pacific Botanicals
4840 Fish Hatchery Road
Grants Pass, OR 97527
541-479-7777
Fax: 541-479-7780
sherlee@pacificbotanicals.com
www.pacificbotanicals.com

Organic medicinal herbs, spices, green foods and seaweed

President: Mark Wheeler
General Operations: Toni Corrent-Evans
Purchasing & Sales Manager: Nate Brennan
Operations Manager: Mike Moran
Credit Cards: MasterCard; Visa
Catalog Cost: Free
Catalog Circulation: Mailed 2 time(s) per year
to 25K
Printing Information: 8 pages in 2 colors on
Matte Stock
Press: Web Press
Binding: Folded
Mailing List Information: Names for rent
In Business: 34 years
Number of Employees: 22
Sales Volume: $1 Million

2875 Pelican Bay Ltd
Pelican Bay Ltd
150 Douglas Ave
Dunedin, FL 34698-7908
727-733-8399
800-826-8982
Fax: 727-734-5860
sales@pelicanbayltd.com
www.pelicanbayltd.com

Bread mixes, cookie mixes, seasoning blends, dip mixes, cool drink and hot drinks

President: Linda Pfaelzer
CFO: Paul Whitman
Catalog Cost: Free
Printing Information: 35 pages
In Business: 33 years
Number of Employees: 30
Sales Volume: $4.8 Million

2876 Penn Herb Company
Penn Herb Company Ltd
1061 Decatur Road
Suite 2
Philadelphia, PA 19154-3293
215-632-6100
800-523-9971
Fax: 215-632-7945
www.pennherb.com

Medicinal and culinary herbs, rare essential oils, herbal extracts, homeopathic preparations and ginseng, herbal capsules, herbal blends, vitamins minerals and health products

CFO: Ronald Betz
Marketing Manager: Karen Page
General Manager/Purchasing Agent: Jerome Hannah
Buyers: Karl C Ruch
Jerome C Hannah
Credit Cards: MasterCard; Visa
Catalog Cost: Free
Catalog Circulation: Mailed 1 time(s) per year
to 10300
Average Order Size: $75
Printing Information: 88 pages in 4 colors on
Matte Stock
Press: Web Press
Binding: Saddle Stitched
In Business: 91 years
Number of Employees: 32
Sales Volume: $3.5 Million

2877 Penzeys Spices
Penzeys Spices
12001 W Capitol Drive
Wauwatosa, WI 53222
414-760-7337
800-741-7787
Fax: 414-760-7317
www.penzeys.com

Herbs, spices and seasonings

Credit Cards: MasterCard; Visa
Catalog Cost: Free
Catalog Circulation: Mailed 6 time(s) per year
to 4.5MM
Printing Information: 48 pages in 4 colors on
Matte Stock
Press: Web Press
Binding: Saddle Stitched
Number of Employees: 8
Sales Volume: $1MM to $3MM

2878 Piggie Park Enterprises
Maurice's Gourmet Barbeque
PO Box 6847
West Columbia, SC 29171
803-791-5887
800-628-7423
Fax: 803-791-8707
mail@mauricesbbq.com
www.mauricesbbq.com

Gourmet heirloom barbeque sauces

President: Maurice Bessinger
Buyers: Lloyd M Bessinger, II
Credit Cards: AMEX; MasterCard
Catalog Circulation: to 35000
Average Order Size: $60
Printing Information: 4 pages in 4 colors on
Glossy Stock
Press: Web Press
Binding: Perfect Bound
In Business: 76 years

2879 Rafal Spice
Rafal Spice
2521 Russell Street
Detroit, MI 48207-2632
313-259-6373
800-228-4276
Fax: 313-259-6220

Herbs, spices, coffee, tea, flavorings and cookbooks

President: Donald Rafal
Credit Cards: MasterCard; Visa
Catalog Cost: Free
Catalog Circulation: to 50000
Printing Information: 102 pages

In Business: 45 years
Number of Employees: 12

2880 Riley's Seasoning and Spices
Riley Seasoning Inc
PO Box 321
Pittsfield, IL 62363-321   217-833-2207
                                             800-690-7720
www.rileys-seasonings.com

Seasonings and spices

Catalog Cost: Free
Catalog Circulation: to 4000
Printing Information: 3 pages in 1 color
In Business: 41 years

2881 San Francisco Herb & Natural Food
San Francisco Herb & Natural Food Compan
47444 Kato Road
Fremont, CA 94538   510-770-1215
                                             800-227-2830
Fax: 510-770-9021
customerservice@herbspicetea.com

Botanicals, herbs, teas, spices, spa, oils and extracts

COO: Fahimeh Niroomand
Finance Manager: Miranda Mill
Catalog Cost: Free
Printing Information: in 2 colors
Binding: Saddle Stitched
Mailing List Information: Names for rent
In Business: 42 years
Number of Employees: 85
Sales Volume: $13.5 Million

2882 San Francisco Herb Catalog
250 14th St
San Francisco, CA 94103   800-227-4530
info@sfherb.com
www.sfherb.com

Culinary herbs, spices, potpourri ingredients, teas, extracts and essential oils

Owner: Neil Hanscomb
Credit Cards: MasterCard; Visa
Catalog Cost: Free
Catalog Circulation: Mailed 2 time(s) per year
Printing Information: in 2 colors on Matte Stock
Binding: Folded
Mailing List Information: Names for rent
Number of Employees: 12
Sales Volume: $5MM to $10MM

2883 Sandy Mush Herb Nursery
The Sandy Mush Herb Nursery
316 Surrett Cove Rd
Leicester, NC 28748   828-683-2014
info@sandymushherbs.com
www.sandymushherbs.com

Herbs, seeds, books, perennials, trees, shrubs and rare plants

Chairman: Kate Jane
President: Fairman Jane
Buyers: Kate Jayne
Fairman Jayne
Credit Cards: MasterCard; Visa
Catalog Cost: $5
Catalog Circulation: to 6000
Printing Information: 84 pages in 1 color
Press: Letterpress
Binding: Saddle Stitched
Mailing List Information: Names for rent
In Business: 31 years
Number of Employees: 2
Sales Volume: Under $500M

2884 Seeds Trust
Seeds Trust
5870 S Long Lane
Littleton, CO 80121   720-335-3436
Fax: 877-686-7524
support3@seedstrust.com
www.seedstrust.com

Vegetables, tomatoes, wildflowers, wildflower mixes, native grasses, herbs

President: Bill McDorman
Marketing Manager: Belle McDorman
Catalog Cost:
In Business: 25 years

2885 Sound of Mustard
National Mustard Museum
7477 Hubbard Avenue
Middleton, WI 53562-7477   608-831-2222
                                800-438-6878
customerservice@mustardmuseum.com
www.Mustardmuseum.Com

Mustards, gourmet foods and souvenirs

President: Barry Levenson
curator@mustardmuseum.com
Marketing Manager: Patti Levenson
plevson@mustardmuseum.com
Buyers: Joy Haubrich
Credit Cards: MasterCard
Catalog Cost: Free
Catalog Circulation: Mailed 1 time(s) per year to 15000
Average Order Size: $55
Printing Information: 36 pages in 4 colors on Glossy Stock
Press: Web Press
Binding: Saddle Stitched
Mailing List Information: Names for rent
List Manager: Michael Carr
In Business: 29 years
Number of Employees: 10
Sales Volume: $500M to $1MM

2886 Soupbase.com
Soupbase.com
4145 Mayfield Rd.
Cleveland, OH 44121   216-381-9916
                                800-827-8328
Fax: 216-381-7170
cooking@soupbase.com
www.soupbase.com

Professional cooking ingredients available to the home cook, bases, sauce preps, soups and gravies

Credit Cards: MasterCard
Catalog Cost: Free
Catalog Circulation: Mailed 1 time(s) per year
Mailing List Information: Names for rent
In Business: 21 years
Number of Employees: 5
Sales Volume: Under $500M

2887 Spice Hunter
Spice Hunter, Inc
PO Box 8110
2000 West Broad St.
Richmond, VA 23220   805-544-6632
                                800-444-3061
Fax: 805-544-9046
www.spicehunter.com

Spices, herbs, seasonings and flavors

President: Lucia Cleveland
CFO: William F Ulick
Marketing Manager: Robin Cegelski
Production Manager: Carol Lambert
Purchasing Manager: John Fiorenza
Buyers: Rod Gray
Catalog Cost: Free
In Business: 33 years
Number of Employees: 65
Sales Volume: $6.3 Million

2888 Spices Etc
Spices Etc
2822 Limerick Street
Savannah, GA 31404   800-827-6373
info@spicesetc.com
www.spicesetc.com

Herbs, spices, flavorings and extracts, as well as cooking accessories

Buyers: Jim Kelly
Credit Cards: MasterCard; Visa
Catalog Circulation: Mailed 8 time(s) per year to 425M
Printing Information: 40 pages in 4 colors on Glossy Stock
Press: Web Press
Binding: Saddle Stitched
Mailing List Information: Names for rent
In Business: 23 years
Number of Employees: 6
Sales Volume: $1MM to $3MM

2889 Terrapin Ridge Farms
Terrapin Ridge Farms
1208 S. Myrtle Ave
Clearwater, FL 33767   800-999-4052
www.terrapinridge.com

Gourmet products

In Business: 13+ years

2890 Up The Country Creations
Up The Country Creations
42 Maggie Drive
P.O. Box 34
Perham, ME 4766   207-227-7562
www.upthecountycreations.com

Jams, Pickles, Whoopie pies, Fiddle Heads

2891 War Eagle Mill Product & Gift
War Eagle Mill
11045 War Eagle Road
Rogers, AR 72756-7544   479-789-5343
                                866-492-7324
Fax: 479-789-2146
info@wareaglemill.com
www.wareaglemill.com

Fish fry coating mix, flours, meals, mixes, old-fashioned graniteware, jellies, honey and cookbooks

Credit Cards: MasterCard; Visa
Catalog Cost: Free
Catalog Circulation: Mailed 1 time(s) per year to 15000
Average Order Size: $20
Printing Information: 16 pages in 4 colors on Glossy Stock
Press: Web Press
Binding: Saddle Stitched
Mailing List Information: Names for rent
In Business: 182 years
Number of Employees: 22
Sales Volume: $500M to $1MM

2892 Wild Thymes Farm
Wild Thymes Farm
245 County Route 351
Medusa, NY 12120   845-266-8387
                                800-492-6949
Fax: 845-266-8395
info@wildthymes.com
www.wildthymes.com

BBQ sauces, chutneys, cranberry sauces, dipping sauces, marinades, salad refreshers, vinaigrettes

CFO: Maggie Moyer
Owner: Enid Stettner
Catalog Cost: Free
In Business: 22 years
Number of Employees: 15
Sales Volume: $1.3 Million

Meats & Poultry

2893 Allen Brothers
Allen Brothers
3737 S Halsted St.
Chicago, IL 60609-1689   800-548-7777
Fax: 800-890-9146
www.allenbrothers.com

Steak, poultry and seafood.

Chairman: Christopher Pappas
Catalog Cost: Free
In Business: 123 years
Sales Volume: $80 Million

2894 Amana Meat Shop & Smokehouse

Amana Meat Shop & Smokehouse
4513 F Street
Amana, IA 52203   800-373-6328
info@amanameatshop.com
www.amanameatshop.com

Smoked meats, hams, bacon and fresh meats

Production Manager: Greg Hergert
Credit Cards: MasterCard; Visa
Catalog Cost: Free
Catalog Circulation: Mailed 1 time(s) per year to 10000
Printing Information: 17 pages in 4 colors
In Business: 162 years
Number of Employees: 20
Sales Volume: $1,000,000

2895 AppetizersUSA

AppetizersUSA
7750 E Redfield Rd. D-106
Scottsdale, AZ 85260   480-471-2601
sales@appetizersusa.com
www.appetizersusa.com

Gourmet appetizers, hors d'oeuvres, premium entrees and desserts.

2896 Bates Turkey Farm

Bates Turkey Farm Inc
45 Bates Rd
Fort Deposit, AL 36032   334-227-4505
888-249-4505
Fax: 334-227-4386
sales@batesturkey.com
www.batesturkey.com

Turkey

President: Willie Bates
CFO: Rebecca Sloane
Production Manager: John Bates
Catalog Cost: Free
In Business: 92 years
Number of Employees: 31
Sales Volume: $2 Million

2897 Broadbent Country Hams

Broadbent B & B Foods
257 Mary Blue Road
Kuttawa, KY 42055   800-841-2202
Fax: 270-388-0613
orders@broadbenthams.com
www.broadbenthams.com

Country ham, bacon, sausage, cheeses, honey, molasses, biscuits and pancake mix

President: Ronny Drennan
Owner: Ronny Drennan
Credit Cards: AMEX; MasterCard; Visa
Catalog Cost: Free
Catalog Circulation: Mailed 1 time(s) per year
Printing Information: 15 pages in 4 colors
Binding: Saddle Stitched
Mailing List Information: Names for rent
In Business: 47 years
Number of Employees: 6
Sales Volume: Under $500M

2898 Burge's Hickory Smoked Turkeys & Hams

Burge's Hickory Smoked Turkeys & Hams
PO Box 759
Lewisville, AR 71845   870-921-4292
800-921-4292
Fax: 870-921-4500
burges@smokedturkeys.com
www.smokedturkeys.com

Smoked turkeys and hams

President: Jack Burge
In Business: 62 years

2899 Burgers' Smokehouse

Burgers' Smokehouse
32819 Highway 87
California, MO 65018   800-345-5185
Fax: 573-796-3137
service@smokehouse.com
www.smokehouse.com

Cured and smoked meats and poultry

President: Philip H. Burger
Vice President: Chris Mouse
Credit Cards: AMEX; MasterCard; Visa
Catalog Cost: Free
Catalog Circulation: Mailed 2 time(s) per year
Average Order Size: $100
Printing Information: 67 pages in 4 colors on Matte Stock
Press: Web Press
Binding: Saddle Stitched
Mailing List Information: Names for rent
In Business: 65 years
Number of Employees: 250
Sales Volume: $20 MM

2900 Certified Steak and Seafood

Certified Steak and Seafood
1741 W Beaver Street
Suite A
Jacksonville, FL 32209   800-334-7428
www.certifiedsteakandseafood.com

Seafood, desserts

President: Mark Frisch
Partner, Buyer: Adam Frisch
Partner, Buyer: Steven Frisch

2901 Comeaux's Grocery

Comeaux's Incorporated
116 Alley 3
Lafayette, LA 70506   888-264-5460
Fax: 337-507-3343
ray@comeaux.com
www.comeaux.com

Comeaux's cajun sausage, boudin and andouille, tasso, and an unusual crawfish boudin

President: Ray Comeaux
Marketing Manager: Jenny McGuire
Credit Cards: AMEX; MasterCard; Visa
Catalog Cost: Free
In Business: 46 years
Number of Employees: 16
Sales Volume: $500M to $1MM

2902 Cozzini

Cozzini
4300 West Bryn Mawr Avenue
Chicago, IL 60646   773-478-9700
Fax: 773-478-8689
info@cozzini.com
www.cozzini.com

Meat slicers, sausage production equipment, pumping systems, loaders, conveyors and material handling equipment

President: Ivo Cozzini
CFO: Oscar Cozzini
Marketing Manager: Donna Nastaly
VP: Tom Spino
VP Marketing: Keith Shackalford
In Business: 26 years
Number of Employees: 160
Sales Volume: $10 Million

2903 Fine Foods & Accompaniments

Smithfield Catalog Group
8012 Hankins Industrial Park Road
Toano, VA 23168   800-926-8448
888-741-2221
Fax: 757-566-2991
info@smithfieldmarketplace.com
www.smithfieldhams.com

Dry cured aged Smithfield hams

Credit Cards: AMEX; MasterCard; Visa
Catalog Cost: Free

Mailing List Information: Names for rent
In Business: 77 years
Number of Employees: 1000

2904 Fiorella's Jack Stack Barbecue

Fiorella's Jack Stack Barbecue
13441 Holmes Rd
Kansas City, MO 64145-1445   816-942-9141
877-419-7427
Fax: 816-942-5166
www.jackstackbbq.com

Kansas City barbeque ribs to beef brisket, sauces and rubs

President: Case Dorman
Operations Director: Rod Toelkes
Credit Cards: AMEX; MasterCard
Catalog Cost: Free
Sales Volume: $5MM to $10MM

2905 Food Catalog

Kansas Wind Power
13569 214th Rd
Holton, KS 66436-8138   785-364-4407
Fax: 785-364-5123
www.kansaswindpower.net

Over 1300 freeze dried, dehydrated and bulk items for grains, beans, mixes, salads, soups, breakfasts, snacks, flours, vegetable, fruits, meats, TVP, eggs, dairy, desserts, meat or meatless entrees

President: Bob Mc Broom
Catalog Cost: $4
Printing Information: 100 pages in 1 color on Matte Stock
Binding: Saddle Stitched
Mailing List Information: Names for rent
In Business: 40 years
Sales Volume: $500M to $1MM

2906 Four Oaks Farm

Four Oaks Farm, Inc.
4856 Augusta Road
Lexington, SC 29071-9198   800-858-5006
www.fouroaksfarm.com

Smoked meats, condiments, jams and gift boxes

President: Fred Mathias Jr
Credit Cards: MasterCard; Visa
Catalog Cost: Free
Catalog Circulation: Mailed 2 time(s) per year to 45000
Printing Information: 16 pages in 2 colors on Matte Stock
Press: Letterpress
Binding: Folded
Mailing List Information: Names for rent
In Business: 81 years
Number of Employees: 11
Sales Volume: $1MM to $3MM

2907 Hantover

Hantover Inc.
PO Box 410646
Kansas City, MO 64141-646   816-761-7800
877-853-0230
Fax: 913-214-4995
contactus@hantover.com
www.hantover.com

Distributor of meat and other foods

President: Benard Huff
In Business: 75 years

2908 Harper's Country Hams

Harper's Country Hams
2955 U.S. Hwy. 51 N
PO Box 122
Clinton, KY 42031-122   888-427-7377
info@hamtastic.com
www.hamtastic.com

Country hams and ham products

Catalog Circulation: to 10000
Printing Information: 15 pages in 4 colors on

Glossy Stock
Binding: Saddle Stitched
In Business: 60 years

2909 Harrington's of Vermont
Harrington's of Vermont
210 Main Rd
PO Box 288
Richmond, VT 05477   802-434-3415
          Fax: 802-434-3166
info@harringtonham.com
www.harringtonham.com

Smoked meats and fine foods

President: Patrick Comstock
Catalog Cost: Free
Printing Information: 6 pages
In Business: 140 years
Sales Volume: Under $500M

2910 Heartland Steaks
Heartland Steaks
7501 Industrial Drive
Forest Park, IL 60130   800-365-5502
          Fax: 800-365-6396
www.heartlandsteaks.com

Steakhouse

President: Joe Miller
In Business: 12 years

2911 Hickory Farms
Hickory Farms
1505 Holland Road
PO Box 75
Maumee, OH 43537-75   800-442-5671
www.hickoryfarms.com

Cheese and sausage gifts

President: Tom Williamson
CFO: Marc Mucci
Credit Cards: AMEX; MasterCard; Visa
Catalog Cost: Free
Printing Information: 39 pages in 4 colors on
Glossy Stock
Binding: Saddle Stitched
Mailing List Information: Names for rent
List Company: Gnames Enterprises
In Business: 64 years
Number of Employees: 125

2912 High Plains Bison
High Plains Bison
1395 S Platte River Drive
Denver, CO 80223   877-526-7375
          Fax: 303-865-5966
customerservice@highplainsbison.com
www.highplainsbison.com

Grass-fed bison meat products

President: Curt Samson
Credit Cards: AMEX; MasterCard; Visa
Catalog Cost: Free
Number of Employees: 3
Sales Volume: $170,000

2913 Honey Baked Ham
Honey Baked Ham
P.O. Box 370
Carrollton, GA 30117   800-367-7720
          Fax: 800-728-4426
catalogservice@hbham.com
www.honeybakedonline.com

Hams, turkey, turkey breasts, BBQ ribs, desserts, baskets and more

President: Kim Hunter
Founder: Harry J. Hoenselaar
Credit Cards: AMEX; MasterCard; Visa
Catalog Cost: Free
Catalog Circulation: Mailed 10 time(s) per
year to 750M
Printing Information: 16 pages in 4 colors on
Glossy Stock
Press: Web Press
Mailing List Information: Names for rent
In Business: 58 years

Number of Employees: 15
Sales Volume: $1MM to $3MM

2914 HoneyBaked Ham Company
Honey Baked Ham Company
P.O. Box 370
Carrollton, GA 30117-8430   800-367-7720
          Fax: 419-867-3860
www.honeybakedonline.com

Hams, beef, poultry, side dishes, desserts, fruit, chocolate and nuts, cookies and seafood

VP: Louis Schmidt, Jr.
Founder: Harry J. Hoenselaar
Credit Cards: AMEX
Catalog Cost: Free
Catalog Circulation: Mailed 5 time(s) per year
Printing Information: 32 pages in 4 colors on
Glossy Stock
Binding: Perfect Bound
In Business: 58 years

2915 Jackson Hole Buffalo Meat
Jackson Hole Buffalo Meat
1325 U.S. 89
Jackson, WY 83001   307-733-4159
          800-543-6328
          Fax: 307-733-7244
info@jhbuffalomeat.com
www.jhbuffalomeat.com

Gift packs of smoked meats, steaks, salami, smoked trout, buffalo and elk gift packs and jerky

President: Dan Marino
Credit Cards: AMEX; MasterCard; Visa
Catalog Cost: Free
Catalog Circulation: Mailed 2 time(s) per year
to 10000
Average Order Size: $120
Printing Information: 24 pages in 4 colors on
Glossy Stock
Press: Web Press
Binding: Saddle Stitched
Mailing List Information: Names for rent
In Business: 68 years
Number of Employees: 15

2916 Kansas City Steak Company
Kansas City Steak Company
5140 Kansas Avenue
Kansas City, KS 66106   800-987-8325
customerservice@kansascitysteaks.com
www.kansascitysteaks.com

Fine cuts of meat

President: Edward Scavuzzo
Marketing Manager: Mauren Friedt
Credit Cards: MasterCard
Catalog Cost: Free
Catalog Circulation: Mailed 4 time(s) per year
Printing Information: 24 pages in 4 colors
Binding: Saddle Stitched
In Business: 85 years
Number of Employees: 9
Sales Volume: $50MM to $100MM

2917 Loveless Cafe
Loveless Cafe
8400 Highway 100
Nashville, TN 37221-4012   615-577-6690
          800-889-2432
info@LovelessCafe.com
www.lovelesscafe.com

Homemade preserves, smoked country hams, bacon, sausage and gift packages

President: Tom Morales
CFO: Robynne Napier
Credit Cards: AMEX; MasterCard
Catalog Cost: Free
Catalog Circulation: Mailed 2 time(s) per year
to 20000
Average Order Size: $75
Printing Information: 16 pages in 4 colors on
Glossy Stock
Press: Sheetfed Press

Binding: Saddle Stitched
Mailing List Information: Names for rent
In Business: 63 years
Number of Employees: 30
Sales Volume: $120,000

2918 Meacham Hams
Meacham Country Hams
705 O'Nan Dyer Road
Sturgis, KY 42459   800-552-3190
info@meachamhams.com

Smoked ham—dry cured and moist cured, plus bacon, turkey, cheese, desserts, etc.

President: Rodman Meacham
Secretary/Treasurer: Robert Shirel
In Business: 80 years

2919 Nebraska Famous Steaks
Nebraska Famous Steaks
1406 Veterans Dr.
Suite #215
Elkhorn, NE 68022-3685   402-884-7227
          888-463-8823
Info@FamousSteaks.com
www.famoussteaks.com

Steaks, chops, prime rib, smoked turkeys, ham, meat and cheese pies, seafood and desserts

President: Susan Gracey
Owner: Robert Gottsch
Catalog Cost: Free
Catalog Circulation: Mailed 2 time(s) per year
Average Order Size: $120
Printing Information: 16 pages in 4 colors on
Glossy Stock
Press: Web Press
Binding: Saddle Stitched
Mailing List Information: Names for rent
In Business: 21 years
Number of Employees: 20-O
Sales Volume: Under $500M

2920 New Braunfels Smokehouse
New Braunfels Smokehouse
PO Box 311159
New Braunfels, TX 78131-1159   830-625-7316
          800-537-6932
          Fax: 800-284-5330
help@nbsmokehouse.com
www.nbsmokehouse.com

Hickey smoked brisket, turkey, ribs, ham & sausages

President: Dudley Snyder
VP/General Manager: Mike Dietert
Plant Manager: Rocky Trays
Credit Cards: AMEX; MasterCard
Catalog Cost: Free
Catalog Circulation: Mailed 7 time(s) per year
to 50000
Printing Information: 36 pages in 4 colors on
Glossy Stock
Press: Web Press
Binding: Folded
Mailing List Information: Names for rent
In Business: 72 years
Number of Employees: 119
Sales Volume: $3MM to $5MM

2921 New Skete
New Skete
345 Ash Grove Rd
Cambridge, NY 12816-128   518-677-3810
          Fax: 518-677-3001
orders@newskete.com
www.newskete.com

Cheesecake, fruitcakes and cheese spreads, dog books, biscuits, beds, leashes and toys, spiritual books and liturgical music, CDs, crosses, books, cards, soaps and more

Fulfillment: Sister Cecelia
Credit Cards: MasterCard
Catalog Cost: Free
Catalog Circulation: Mailed 2 time(s) per year

Printing Information: 12 pages in 4 colors on Glossy Stock
Press: Offset Press
Binding: Folded
Mailing List Information: Names for rent
In Business: 49 years
Number of Employees: 12

2922 Nodine's Smokehouse
Nodine's Smokehouse
65 Fowler Avenue
P.O. Box 1787
Torrington, CT 06790   860-489-0132
                               800-222-2059
                          Fax: 860-496-9787
                  nodinesmoke@optonline.net
                     www.nodinesmokehouse.com

Smoked meats, poultry, cheese and fish
President: Ronald F Nodine
Vice President: Johanne H Nodine
VP of Operations: Calvin Nodine
Credit Cards: AMEX; MasterCard; Visa
Catalog Cost: Free
Catalog Circulation: Mailed 1 time(s) per year to 3000
Average Order Size: $75
Printing Information: 4 pages in 4 colors on Glossy Stock
Press: Letterpress
Binding: Folded
Mailing List Information: Names for rent
In Business: 48 years
Number of Employees: 32
Sales Volume: $5MM to $10MM

2923 Nueske's Applewood Smoked Meats
Nueske's
203 N Genesee Street
Wittenberg, WI 54499   800-720-1153
                               800-392-2266
                          Fax: 800-962-2266
                          info@nueske.com
                          www.nueske.com

A complete line of applewood smoked specialty meats, poultry, cheese, desserts, soups and quiches
President: Robert D Nueske
CFO: Gary Ashenbrenner
Marketing Manager: Megan Dorsch
Production Manager: Jeff Bushman
Contact: Bob Nueske
Credit Cards: AMEX; MasterCard; Visa
Catalog Cost: Free
Catalog Circulation: Mailed 5 time(s) per year to 30000
Average Order Size: $85
Printing Information: 35 pages in 4 colors on Glossy Stock
Press: Web Press
Binding: Saddle Stitched
In Business: 82 years
Number of Employees: 120
Sales Volume: $25 Million

2924 Oak Grove Smokehouse
Oak Grove Smokehouse Inc
17618 Old Jefferson Hwy
Prairieville, LA 70769-3931   225-673-6857
                               Fax: 225-673-5757
                        www.oakgrovemix.webs.com

Smoked meats
President: Robert H Schexnailder
In Business: 43 years
Sales Volume: $3MM to $5MM

2925 Oakwood Game Farm
Oakwood Game Farm,Inc
PO Box 274
30703 Hwy 169
Princeton, MN 55371   763-389-2031
                               800-328-6647
                          Fax: 763-389-2077
                  info@oakwoodgamefarm.com
                  www.oakwoodgamefarm.com

Fresh frozen pheasant, partidge, quail, mallard duck, smoked pheasant, pheasant sausage and jerky
President: James Meyer
CFO: Betty Meyer
Credit Cards: AMEX; MasterCard; Visa
Catalog Cost: Free
Catalog Circulation: Mailed 1 time(s) per year to 2.5M
Average Order Size: $50
Printing Information: 4 pages in 4 colors on Glossy Stock
Press: Web Press
In Business: 48 years
Number of Employees: 15
Sales Volume: $3MM to $5MM

2926 Omaha Steaks
Omaha Steaks
Omaha NE   800-228-9872
                  www.omahasteaks.com

Gourmet steaks, meats, seafood, poultry, desserts and specialty items
President: Bruce A Simon
CFO: David Hershiser
Marketing Manager: Vickie Hagen
Senior Vice President: Todd Simon
Credit Cards: AMEX; MasterCard; Visa
Catalog Cost: Free
Catalog Circulation: Mailed 3 time(s) per year
Printing Information: 40 pages in 4 colors on Glossy Stock
Press: Web Press
Binding: Saddle Stitched
In Business: 100 years
Number of Employees: 1800
Sales Volume: $32.7 Million

2927 Pfaelzer Brothers
Pfaelzer Brothers
1505 Holland Road
Maumee, OH 43537   800-621-0202
                          www.pfaelzer.com

Steaks, seafood and desserts
Credit Cards: AMEX; MasterCard
Catalog Cost: Free
Printing Information: 68 pages in 4 colors on Glossy Stock
Press: Web Press
Binding: Saddle Stitched
Mailing List Information: Names for rent
List Company: Gnames Enterprises
In Business: 92 years
Number of Employees: 125

2928 Poche's Meat Market & Restaurant
Poche's Meat Market & Restaurant
3015a Main Highway
Breaux Bridge, LA 70517-6347   337-332-2108
                               800-376-2437
                          Fax: 337-332-5051
                          www.poches.com

Meats and sausage available for shipping
President: Floyd Poche
CFO: Floyd Poche
Credit Cards: AMEX; MasterCard
Catalog Cost: Free
Catalog Circulation: to 1000
Printing Information: 7 pages in 4 colors on Matte Stock
Press: Offset Press
Binding: Folded
In Business: 53 years
Number of Employees: 40

2929 Poultry Catalog
Hoffman Hatchery, Inc
PO Box 129
Gratz, PA 17030   717-365-3694
                  info@hoffmanhatchery.com
                  www.hoffmanhatchery.com

Poultry
President: John Hoffman
Catalog Cost: Free

Catalog Circulation: to 4000
Printing Information: 15 pages in 2 colors on Newsprint
Binding: Saddle Stitched
Mailing List Information: Names for rent
In Business: 67 years
Number of Employees: 3
Sales Volume: $150,000

2930 Ralph's Packing
Ralphs Circle R Brand
PO Box 249
500 West Freeman Street
Perkins, OK 74059   405-547-2464
                               800-522-3979
                          Fax: 405-547-2364
                          www.ralphspacking.com

Sugar cured hams and bacon
Credit Cards: MasterCard; Visa
Catalog Cost: Free
Catalog Circulation: Mailed 4 time(s) per year
Printing Information: 5 pages in 2 colors
In Business: 56 years
Number of Employees: 30
Sales Volume: $10MM to $20MM

2931 Ranch House Mesquite Smoked Meats
Ranch House
PO Box 977
Menard, TX 76859   800-749-6329
                          Fax: 888-917-6328
                          sales@brisket.net
                          www.brisket.net

Beef, pork, poultry, sausages & snacks
Chairman: Marsha Stabel
marsha@brisket.net
President: Max Stabel
max@brisket.net
Owner: Marsha Stabel
Plant Manager: Bill Adams
Credit Cards: AMEX; MasterCard
Catalog Cost: Free
Catalog Circulation: to 30000
Average Order Size: $75
Printing Information: 20 pages in 7 colors on Glossy Stock
Press: Web Press
Binding: Folded
In Business: 37 years
Number of Employees: 13
Sales Volume: $1.1 Million

2932 Sausage Maker
The Sausage Maker, Inc.
1500 Clinton Street
Building 7
Buffalo, NY 14206   716-824-5814
                               888-490-8525
                          Fax: 716-824-6465
                  customerservice@sausagemaker.com
                          www.sausagemaker.com

Sausage making equipment and supplies
President: Kris Stanuscek
Marketing Manager: Norma Mathewson
International Marketing Manager: Wes Smyczynski
Buyers: John Wasinski
Credit Cards: AMEX; MasterCard
Catalog Cost: Free
Catalog Circulation: Mailed 3 time(s) per year to 15000
Printing Information: 55 pages in 4 colors on Matte Stock
Press: Web Press
Binding: Saddle Stitched
Mailing List Information: Names for rent
In Business: 45 years
Number of Employees: 30
Sales Volume: $5,000,000

2933 Schaul's Signature Gourmet Foods
Schaul's Signature Gourmet Foods
520 Lively Boulevard
Elk Grove Village, IL 60007   847-593-7500
   800-562-5660
Fax: 847-647-6406
www.schauls.com

Beef, poultry, hams, pork, seafood, lamb, veal, gift baskets, fancy nuts, gourmet chocolates

VP/Manager: Thomas Schaul
Catalog Cost: Free
In Business: 92 years
Number of Employees: 25

2934 Smithfield Ham Catalog
Smithfield Marketplace
8012 Hankins Industrial Park Road
Suite 201
Toano, VA 23168   605-274-0379
   888-741-2221
Fax: 757-566-2991
info@smithfieldmarketplace.com
www.smithfieldmarketplace.com

Spiral cut hams, country hams and bacon

Catalog Cost: Free
Printing Information: 16 pages on Glossy Stock

2935 Southern Season
Southern Season
University Mall
201 S Estes Drive
Chapel Hill, NC 27514   877-929-7133
   866-253-5317
Fax: 919-942-9274
customerservice@southernseason.com
www.southernseason.com

Gourmet foods and gifts with a southern flair

kvanleer@southernseason.com
Catalog Cost: Free
Catalog Circulation: Mailed 1 time(s) per year
In Business: 40 years
Number of Employees: 250
Sales Volume: $25 Million

2936 Stock Yards
Stock Yards
2500 S Pacific Highway
Medford, OR 97501-2675   888-842-6111
Fax: 888-700-9919
myorder@stockyards.com
www.stockyards.com

Complete line of gourmet foods, seafood, lamb, pork, appetizers and desserts

President: Mark Saviski
Chief Executive Officer: Daniel Pollack
Credit Cards: AMEX; MasterCard; Visa
Catalog Cost: Free
Catalog Circulation: Mailed 8 time(s) per year
Printing Information: 12 pages in 4 colors on Glossy Stock
Press: Web Press
Binding: Saddle Stitched
In Business: 124 years
Number of Employees: 25
Sales Volume: $10MM

2937 Swiss Colony
The Swiss Colony, LLC
1112 7th Ave.
Monroe, WI 53566-1364   800-914-1459
   800-913-0743

Cheese, meats, pastries and gift packs

Chairman: Chairman
President: John Baumann
CFO: Donald R Hughes
Credit Cards: AMEX; MasterCard; Visa
Catalog Cost: Free
Catalog Circulation: to 20000
Printing Information: 66 pages

In Business: 87 years
Number of Employees: 1000

2938 Today Gourmet Foods
Today Gourmet Foods
Morrisville NC   888-760-8632
webmaster@todaygourmetfoods.com
www.todaygourmetfoods.com

Steaks, poultry, seafood, pork, veal, lamb and other gourmet foods.

2939 Usinger's Famous Sausage
Fred Usinger, Inc.
1030 N Old World Third Street
Milwaukee, WI 53203   414-276-9105
   800-558-9998
www.usinger.com

German sausages, ham, certified angus beef steaks and wisconsin cheeses

President: Frederick Usinger IV
Marketing Manager: John Gabe
Plant Manager: Gary Anderson
Purchasing Manager: John Zizzo
Credit Cards: MasterCard; Visa
Catalog Cost: Free
Catalog Circulation: Mailed 1 time(s) per year to 300
Printing Information: 28 pages in 4 colors on Glossy Stock
Press: Web Press
Binding: Saddle Stitched
Mailing List Information: Names for rent
In Business: 137 years
Number of Employees: 140
Sales Volume: $20MM to $50MM

2940 Virginia Traditions
S Wallace Edwards & Sons, Inc.
PO Box 25
Surry, VA 23883   800-222-4267
   800-290-9213
Fax: 757-294-5378
www.edwardsvaham.com

Hams, bacon, sausage, poultry, soups, sides & seasonings, desserts, nuts & snacks, seafood

President: Samuel W Edwards III
Catalog Cost: Free
In Business: 89 years
Number of Employees: 5

2941 Vital Choice Wild Seafood & Organics
Vital Choice Wild Seafood & Organics
PO Box 4121
Bellingham, WA 98227   800-608-4825
www.vitalchoice.com

Seafood

President: Randy Hartnell

2942 Weaver's Catalog
Godshall's Quality Meats
675 Mill Rd
Tedford, PA 18969   215-256-8867
   888-463-7425
Fax: 215-256-4965
foodservicesales@godshalls.com
www.Godshalls.Com

Smoked meats, gift baskets, lebanon bologna, bacon and meat snacks

President: Jerry Landuyt
Credit Cards: AMEX; MasterCard; Visa; Discover
Catalog Circulation: Mailed 2 time(s) per year to 75k
Average Order Size: $50
Printing Information: 16 pages in 4 colors on Glossy Stock
Press: Web Press
Binding: Saddle Stitched
Mailing List Information: Names for rent
In Business: 68 years
Number of Employees: 45
Sales Volume: $10MM to $20MM

Nuts

2943 A Taste of the South
A Taste of the South
3827 Broad River Rd
Columbia, SC 29210-514   803-731-2843
   888-828-2783
Fax: 803-731-2845
info@atasteofthesouth.com
www.atasteofthesouth.com

Wide assortment of pecans, peanuts, nuts, chocolates and gift baskets.

President: Denise Sturkie
Catalog Cost: Free
Printing Information: 15 pages in 4 colors on Glossy Stock
Binding: Saddle Stitched
In Business: 28 years
Sales Volume: $500M to $1MM

2944 Aunt Ruby's Peanuts
Aunt Ruby's Peanuts
200 Halifax Street
Enfield, NC 27823   800-732-6887
www.auntrubyspeanuts.com

Peanut products

2945 Bates Nut Farm
Bates Nut Farm
15954 Woods Valley Rd
Valley Center, CA 92082   760-749-3333
   800-642-0348
Fax: 760-749-9499
info@batesnutfarm.biz
www.batesnutfarm.biz

Nuts, dried fruits, candies, chocolates, fudge and gift boxes

President: Walter Bates
Credit Cards: MasterCard; Visa
Printing Information: 4 pages
In Business: 94 years
Number of Employees: 28

2946 Buchanan Hollow Nut Company
Buchanan Hollow Nut Company
6510 Minturn Road
Le Grand, CA 95333-9710   209-389-4594
   800-532-1500
Fax: 209-389-4321
sharleen@bhnc.com
www.Bhnc.Com

Pistachios, almonds and gift baskets

President: Sharleen Robson
Credit Cards: MasterCard; Visa
Catalog Cost: Free
Catalog Circulation: Mailed 1 time(s) per year
Printing Information: 6 pages in 4 colors on Matte Stock
Press: Letterpress
Binding: Folded
Mailing List Information: Names for rent
In Business: 22 years
Number of Employees: 4
Sales Volume: $500,000

2947 Durey Libby Edible Nuts
Durey Libby Edible Nuts Inc.
100 Industrial Road
Carlstadt, NJ 07072-1614   201-939-2775
   800-332-6887
Fax: 201-939-0386
www.DureyLibby.Com

Edible nuts and seeds, dried fruit and candy

President: Wendy Dicker
Production Manager: Bill Dicker
Credit Cards: AMEX; MasterCard
Catalog Cost: Free
Catalog Circulation: Mailed 1 time(s) per year
Printing Information: 8 pages in 1 color on Matte Stock
Press: Sheetfed Press
Binding: Folded

Mailing List Information: Names for rent
In Business: 65 years
Number of Employees: 20
Sales Volume: $2,000,000

2948 Eilenberger Bakery
Eilenberger Bakery
512 N John St
Palestine, TX 75801 903-729-2176
800-788-2996
Fax: 903-723-2889
www.eilenbergerbakery.com

Wide assortment of baked goods

VP Marketing/General Manager: Sarah Pryor
VP: Stephen K Smith
Catalog Cost: Free
Printing Information: 34 pages in 4 colors on Glossy Stock
Binding: Saddle Stitched
In Business: 117 years
Number of Employees: 25
Sales Volume: $710,000

2949 Feridies
The Peanut Patch, Inc.
28285 Mill Creek Drive
PO Box 186
Courtland, VA 23837 800-544-0896
866-732-6883
Fax: 757-653-9530
customerservice@feridies.com
www.feridies.com

Gourmet Virginia peanuts and peanut candies, gift assortments, baskets, hams and gourmet foods

President: Judy S Riddick
CFO: Paul Shaffer
Buyers: Alice Shaffer
Credit Cards: AMEX; MasterCard
Catalog Cost: Free
Catalog Circulation: Mailed 3 time(s) per year
Printing Information: 20 pages in 4 colors on Glossy Stock
Mailing List Information: Names for rent
In Business: 42 years
Number of Employees: 25
Sales Volume: $3.8 Million

2950 Fiddyment Farms
Fiddyment Farms
563 Second Street, Suite 210
PO Box 245
Lincoln, CA 95648 916-645-7244
877-343-3276
Fax: 916-645-7825
info@fiddymentfarms.com
www.fiddymentfarms.com

Pistachios

Credit Cards: MasterCard
Catalog Cost: Free
Printing Information: 2 pages in 1 color
In Business: 46 years

2951 Finnottes
Finnottes
417 Main Street
La Crosse, WI 54601 608-782-3184
Laurie@Finnottes.com
www.finnottes.com

Nuts, gourmet chocolates and assorted candies

In Business: 29 years

2952 Fran's Gifts to Go
The Orchards Gourmet, LLC
707 S Main Street
PO Box 444
Wrens, GA 30833 706-547-2220
888-239-3649
Fax: 866-476-6887

Pecans, nuts of all kinds, chocolate coated fruits, cookies, gift baskets, hams, beef products, cakes, and turkeys

Owner: Jerry Dowdy
Credit Cards: MasterCard; Visa
Catalog Cost: Free
Catalog Circulation: Mailed 2 time(s) per year to 150K
Printing Information: 32 pages in 4 colors on Glossy Stock
Press: Web Press
Mailing List Information: Names for rent
In Business: 35 years
Number of Employees: 100

2953 Golden Kernel Pecan Company
Golden Kernel Pecan Company
5244 Cameron Road
Cameron, SC 29030 803-823-2311
800-845-2448
Fax: 803-823-2080
info@goldenkernel.com
www.goldenkernel.com

Shelled pecans, pecan candies, salted and honey roasted pecans and hams, fruitcakes

President: David K Summers Jr
Marketing Manager: Bill Summers
Production Manager: Jerry Fogle
Credit Cards: MasterCard; Visa
Catalog Cost: Free
Catalog Circulation: Mailed 1 time(s) per year to 25M
Average Order Size: $18
Printing Information: 20 pages in 4 colors on Glossy Stock
Press: Sheetfed Press
Binding: Folded
Mailing List Information: Names for rent
List Manager: Nancy Summers
In Business: 78 years
Number of Employees: 45
Sales Volume: $1MM to $3MM

2954 Hammons Pantry
Hammons Product Company
105 Hammons Drive
PO Box 140
Stockton, MO 65785 417-276-5187
888-429-6887
Fax: 417-276-5187
Info@black-walnuts.com
www.hammonsproducts.com

Black walnuts, other nutmeats, cakes, cookies, fudges and candies

President: Brian Hammons
Marketing Manager: Susan Zartman
Credit Cards: AMEX; MasterCard; Visa
Catalog Cost: $0
Catalog Circulation: Mailed 1 time(s) per year to 10000
Average Order Size: $40
Printing Information: 12 pages in 4 colors on Matte Stock
Press: Web Press
Binding: Saddle Stitched
Mailing List Information: Names for rent
In Business: 70 years
Number of Employees: 150
Sales Volume: $10MM to $20MM

2955 Harvey's Groves
Harvey's Groves
P.O. Box 560700
Rockledge, FL 32956 321-633-4132
800-327-9312
Fax: 321-636-6072
support@harveysgroves.com
www.harveysgroves.com

Fruits, gift baskets

In Business: 89 years

2956 Hubbard Peanut Company
Hubbard Peanut Company
30275 Sycamore Avenue
PO Box 94
Sedley, VA 23878 757-562-4081
800-889-7688
Fax: 757-562-2741
hubs@hubspeanuts.com
www.hubspeanuts.com

Peanuts from Virginia

President: Lynne H Rabi
Credit Cards: AMEX; MasterCard; Visa; Discover
Catalog Cost: Free
Catalog Circulation: Mailed 2 time(s) per year to 50000
Printing Information: 9 pages in 4 colors
In Business: 61 years
Number of Employees: 12
Sales Volume: $1MM to $3MM

2957 Joe C Williams
Joe C Williams
PO Box 640
Camden, AL 36726-640 334-682-4559
800-967-3226
Fax: 334-682-9580
www.joecwilliams.com/

Shelled pecans

President: Joe C Williams
Credit Cards: MasterCard; Visa
Catalog Cost: Free
Catalog Circulation: Mailed 1 time(s) per year to 20000
Printing Information: 2 pages in 2 colors
In Business: 62 years

2958 Koeze Company
Koeze Company
2555 Burlingame Avenue SW
P.O. Box 9470
Grand Rapids, MI 49509 844-814-8872
Fax: 866-817-0147
service@koezedirect.com
www.koeze.com

Cashews, mixed nuts and chocolate confections

President: Jeffrey Koeze
Production Manager: John Feenstra
Credit Cards: AMEX; MasterCard
Catalog Cost: Free
Catalog Circulation: Mailed 3 time(s) per year to 10000
Printing Information: 16 pages in 4 colors
Press: Web Press
Binding: Saddle Stitched
In Business: 16 years
Number of Employees: 35
Sales Volume: $10.4 Million

2959 Koinonia Partners
Koinonia Farm
1324 GA Highway 49 S
Americus, GA 31719-9599 229-924-0391
877-738-1741
Fax: 229-924-6504
info@koinoniapartners.org
www.koinoniapartners.org

Pecans, gift tins, chocolate, carob, granola, coffee, fruitcakes, peanuts, pine cones, books, tapes

Chairman: Phil Gillis
President: Jim Tyree
CFO: Kathy Doyle
Catalog Cost: Free
Catalog Circulation: Mailed 1 time(s) per year
Average Order Size: $30
Printing Information: 15 pages in 4 colors on Glossy Stock
Press: Letterpress
Binding: Saddle Stitched
Mailing List Information: Names for rent
In Business: 73 years

Number of Employees: 20-5
Sales Volume: $1MM to $3MM

2960 La Tienda

La Tienda
3601 La Grange Parkway
Toano, VA 23168
888-331-4362
800-710-4304
www.tienda.com

Spanish products, cheese, chorizo, wine etc.

In Business: 19 years

2961 Mascot Pecan Shelling Company

Mascot Pecan Shelling Co., Inc.
819 South Veterans Blvd
PO Box 760
Glennville, GA 30427
912-654-2195
800-841-3985
Fax: 912-654-2618
info@mascotpecan.com
www.mascotpecan.com

Pecans and pecan products

President: Kenny Traver
Office Manager: Danna Rogers
danna@mascotpecan.com
Customer Service: Janiece Martin
Janiece@mascotpecan.com
Catalog Cost: Free
Printing Information: 11 pages
In Business: 59 years
Number of Employees: 50
Sales Volume: Under $500M

2962 Merritt Pecan Company

Merritt Pecan Company
PO Box 39
Weston, GA 31832
800-762-9152
Fax: 229-828-2061
www.merritt-pecan.com

Pecans

President: Tammy Merritt
Marketing Manager: Tammy Merritt
Catalog Cost: Free
Printing Information: 12 pages
Mailing List Information: Names for rent
In Business: 35 years
Number of Employees: 30
Sales Volume: $3,000,000

2963 Minsky Pecan Market

Minsky Pecan Market
1214 Sparrow Street (Hwy. 65 South)
Lake Providence, LA 71254-3700
318-559-1339
800-646-7597
Fax: 318-559-1613
minsky@bayou.com
www.minskywearenuts.com

Pecans; fancy nuts; gourmets; gift boxes; and seafood

President: Reynold Minsky
Marketing Manager: Reynold Minsky
Treasurer, Secretary: Carleen Minsky
International Marketing Manager: Reynold Minsky
Buyers: Reynold Minsky
Printing Information: 3 pages on Glossy Stock
Press: Letterpress
In Business: 65 years
Number of Employees: 3
Sales Volume: $140,000

2964 Peanut Shop of Williamsburg

Peanut Shop of Williamsburg
8012 Hankins Industrial Park Road
Toano, VA 23618
800-831-1828
Fax: 757-566-2992
info@thepeanutshop.com
www.thepeanutshop.com

Home style peanuts-salted or unsalted

Production Manager: Larry Wcislo
Credit Cards: MasterCard; Visa
Catalog Cost: Free

Printing Information: 24 pages in 7 colors on Glossy Stock
Binding: Saddle Stitched
In Business: 17 years
Number of Employees: 15

2965 Pecans.com Catalog

Pecan Producers Inc
1020 W Front St
Goldthwaite, TX 76844
325-648-2200
800-473-2267
Fax: 325-938-5490
retail@pecans.com
www.pecans.com

Fresh Texas pecans, pecan gifts, dressings, sauces and rubs

President: Martin Mount
Owner: DeWayne McCasland
Credit Cards: AMEX; MasterCard; Visa
Catalog Cost: Free
In Business: 44 years
Number of Employees: 6
Sales Volume: $2.8 Million

2966 River Street Sweets

River Street Sweets
13 East River Street
Savannah, GA 31402
912-234-4608
800-793-3876
Fax: 912-234-1584
megan@riverstreetsweets.com
www.riverstreetsweets.com

Savannah pralines, chocolate bear claws, glazed pecans, pecan pies, praline pound cake and fudge

CFO: Jennifer Strickland
Owner: Pam Strickland
CEO: Tim Strickland
Credit Cards: AMEX; MasterCard
Catalog Cost: Free
In Business: 40 years
Number of Employees: 70
Sales Volume: $3 Million

2967 Schaul's Signature Gourmet Foods

Schaul's Signature Gourmet Foods
520 Lively Boulevard
Elk Grove Village, IL 60007
847-593-7500
800-562-5660
Fax: 847-647-6406
www.schauls.com

Beef, poultry, hams, pork, seafood, lamb, veal, gift baskets, fancy nuts, gourmet chocolates

VP/Manager: Thomas Schaul
Catalog Cost: Free
In Business: 92 years
Number of Employees: 25

2968 Shari's Berries

Shari's Berries
4840 Eastgate Mall
San Diego, CA 92121
877-237-7437
wecare@customercare.berries.com
www.berries.com

Gifts baskets specializing in strawberries, berries, as well as other fruits and delights

President: Kevin Beresford
Catalog Cost: Free
Printing Information: 16 pages
In Business: 28 years
Sales Volume: Under $500M

2969 Sherard Plantation

Sherard Plantation Pecan
PO Box 75
Sherard, MS 38669-75
662-627-7211
800-647-5518
Fax: 662-627-1629

In-shell and shelled pecans, white and milk chocolate coated, roasted pecans and fruitcakes

President: John H Sherard IV
CFO: John H Sherard IV
Credit Cards: AMEX; MasterCard; Visa
Catalog Cost: Free
Catalog Circulation: Mailed 1 time(s) per year to 15000
Printing Information: 1 pages in 4 colors on Glossy Stock
Press: Letterpress
Number of Employees: 10
Sales Volume: Under $500M

2970 Sphinx Date Ranch & Southwest Market

Sphinx Ranch LLC
3039 N Scottsdale Rd
Scottsdale, AZ 85251
480-941-2261
800-482-3283
info@sphinxdateranch.com
www.sphinxdateranch.com

Medjool dates, dried fruit, nuts and gift baskets

President: Jason Heetland
Credit Cards: AMEX; MasterCard; Visa
Catalog Cost: Free
In Business: 62 years
Number of Employees: 9
Sales Volume: $404,000

2971 Stahmanns

Stahmanns Pecans
22505 S. Highway 28
La Mesa, NM 88055-130
575-526-2453
800-654-6887
Fax: 575-526-7824
Pecans@Stahmanns.com
stahmannpecan.com

Pecans and other pecan products

President: Sally Stahmann
Catalog Cost: Free
In Business: 81 years
Sales Volume: $10MM to $20MM

2972 Stahmanns Pecans

Stahmanns Pecans
22505 S. Highway 28
La Mesa, NM 88055
575-526-2453
800-654-6887
Fax: 575-526-7824
Pecans@Stahmanns.com
stahmannpecan.com

Gourmet chocolate gift baskets, mail order pecan gifts, flavored pecans

Credit Cards: AMEX; MasterCard; Visa
Catalog Cost: Free
In Business: 81 years
Number of Employees: 180

2973 Sunnyland Farms

Sunnyland Farms, Inc.
2314 Wilson Road
P.O. Box 8200
Albany, GA 31706-8200
800-999-2488
Fax: 229-317-4949
www.sunnylandfarms.com

Specialty nuts and fruits, cakes, candies and miscellaneous other food items

President: Jane Willson
Co-Owner: Larry Willson
Co-Owner: Beverly Willson
Credit Cards: AMEX; MasterCard
Catalog Cost: Free
Catalog Circulation: to 1000
Average Order Size: $80
Printing Information: 48 pages in 4 colors on Glossy Stock
Press: Web Press
Binding: Saddle Stitched
Mailing List Information: Names for rent
In Business: 69 years
Number of Employees: 200
Sales Volume: $10MM to $20MM

2974 Trophy Nut
Trophy Nut
320 N 2nd Street
Tipp City, OH 45371-1912   937-667-8478
                                 800-219-9004
                                 Fax: 937-667-4656
                                 bwilke@trophynut.com
                                 www.trophynut.com

Candy, chocolate, cookies and nut gifts

President: Jeff Bollinger
Purchasing: Jill Larger
jlarger@trophynut.com
VP, Sales: Bob Wilke
bwilke@trophynut.com
Export: Dave Ramirez
dramirez@trophynut.com
Credit Cards: AMEX; MasterCard; Visa
Catalog Cost: Free
Catalog Circulation: Mailed 3 time(s) per year
Printing Information: 40 pages in 4 colors on Glossy Stock
Press: Web Press
Binding: Saddle Stitched
Mailing List Information: Names for rent
In Business: 50 years
Number of Employees: 66
Sales Volume: $24 Million

2975 Virginia Diner
Virginia Diner, Inc.
322 W Main Street
Wakefield, VA 23888-2940   888-823-4637
                                 custservice@vadiner.com
                                 www.vadiner.com

Virginia peanuts and peanut products

President: Christine Epperson
Marketing Manager: Scott Stephens
Credit Cards: AMEX; MasterCard; Visa; Discover
Catalog Circulation: to 20000
In Business: 88 years
Number of Employees: 150
Sales Volume: $10MM

2976 Wakefield Peanut Company
Wakefield Peanut Co., LLC
11253 General Mahone Highway (Route
PO Box 538
Wakefield, VA 23888   757-899-5481
                             800-803-1309
                             Fax: 757-899-7604
                             www.Wakefieldpeanutco.Com

Sells peanuts wholesale and retail to customers, other peanut businesses, farmers, mail order and fundraising activities

President: James Laine
In Business: 150 years
Sales Volume: $20MM to $50MM

2977 Whitley's Peanut Factory
Whitley's Peanut Factory
PO Box 647
Hayes, VA 23072-647   804-642-7688
                             800-470-2244
                             Fax: 804-642-7658
                             customercare@whitleyspeanut.com
                             www.whitleyspeanut.com

Larga variety of peanuts

In Business: 14 years

2978 Young Plantations
Young Plantations
2005 Babar Lane
Florence, SC 29501   800-729-8004
                            800-729-6003
                            www.youngplantations.com

Pecans

Credit Cards: AMEX; MasterCard; Visa
Catalog Cost: Free
Average Order Size: $75
Sales Volume: $50MM to $100MM

2979 Young Plantations Catalog
Young Plantations
551 W Lucas Street
PO Box 6709
Florence, SC 29501-2827   843-662-2452
                                 800-829-6864
                                 Fax: 843-664-2338
                                 www.youngpecanplantations.com

Sells fresh pecans & pecan gift items

President: James Swink
In Business: 57 years

Regional Foods

2980 AKA Gourmet
Wine.Com
2220 4th Street
Berkeley, CA 94710   510-704-8007
                            800-592-5870
                            berkeley@wine.com
                            www.wine.com

Wines, gourmet gift baskets, wine decanters, glasses and accessories

Chairman: Robert Manning
President: Michael Osborn
Marketing Manager: Peter Elarde
CEO: Rich Bergsund
Founder & VP Merchandising: Michael Osborn
VP Engineering: Greg Tatem
Credit Cards: AMEX; MasterCard; Visa
In Business: 17 years

2981 Chile Shop
The Chile Shop
109 E Water St
Santa Fe, NM 87501-2132   505-983-6080
                                 Fax: 505-984-0737
                                 info@thechileshop.com
                                 www.thechileshop.com

Southwest items; chile powders, herbs, Mimbreno China, petroglyph pottery, sand etched crystal, aprons, Seven Kilborn pottery

President: Jacque Beck
Credit Cards: MasterCard; Visa
Catalog Cost: Free
Catalog Circulation: Mailed 1 time(s) per year
Average Order Size: $75
Printing Information: 16 pages in 1 color on Matte Stock
Press: Web Press
Binding: Saddle Stitched
Mailing List Information: Names for rent
In Business: 26 years
Number of Employees: 6
Sales Volume: $150,000

2982 Crockett Farms
Crockett Farms
25691 Altas Palmas Road
Harlingen, TX 78552   956-412-1747
                             800-580-1900
                             Fax: 956-423-1897
                             texasfruit@crockettfarms.com
                             www.crockettfarms.com

Texas citrus fruits and smoked meats

President: Terrie Crockett
Production Manager: Terrie Crockett
Owner: Allan Crockett
Buyers: Terrie Crockett
Credit Cards: AMEX; MasterCard
Catalog Cost: Free
Catalog Circulation: Mailed 1 time(s) per year to 50000
Average Order Size: $79
Printing Information: 16 pages in 4 colors on Glossy Stock
Press: Web Press
Binding: Saddle Stitched
In Business: 50 years
Number of Employees: 4
Sales Volume: $450,000

2983 Dakin Farm
Dakin Farm
5797 Route 7
Ferrisburgh, VT 05456   800-993-2546
                               Fax: 802-425-2765
                               corporatesales@dakinfarm.com
                               www.dakinfarm.com

Vermont specialty foods: smoked meats, cheddar cheese, & maple syrup

President: Sam Cutting IV
General Manager: Sam Cutting III
Catalog Cost: Free
In Business: 55 years
Number of Employees: 17
Sales Volume: $3.6 Million

2984 Flying Noodle
Flying Noodle
84 West Park Place
5th floor
Stamford, CT 06901   800-566-0599
                            info@flyingnoodle.com
                            www.flyingnoodle.com

Gourmet pastas, sauces, oils and sweets

Catalog Cost: Free

2985 High Plains Bison
High Plains Bison
1395 S Platte River Drive
Denver, CO 80223   877-526-7375
                          Fax: 303-865-5966
                          customerservice@highplainsbison.com
                          www.highplainsbison.com

Grass-fed bison meat products

President: Curt Samson
Credit Cards: AMEX; MasterCard; Visa
Catalog Cost: Free
Number of Employees: 3
Sales Volume: $170,000

2986 Jardine Foods
Jardine's
#1 Chisholm Trail
PO Box 153
Buda, TX 78610-3350   512-295-4600
                             800-544-1880
                             Fax: 512-295-3020
                             customerservice@jardinefoods.com
                             www.jardinefoods.com

Texas food products including salsas, chili, condiments, drink mixes, snacks and gift sets

President: Jay Kemper
CFO: Kelly Allen
Marketing Manager: Garth Gardner
Production Manager: Robert Espinoza
Owner: Byron Severence
Purchasing Manager: Eddie Ochoa
Catalog Cost: Free
Printing Information: 12 pages in 7 colors on Glossy Stock
Binding: Saddle Stitched
Mailing List Information: Names for rent
In Business: 35 years
Number of Employees: 45
Sales Volume: $5.5 Million

2987 Los Chileros De Nuevo Mexico
Los Chileros de Nuevo Mexico
309 Industrial Ave NE
Albuquerque, NM 87107   505-768-1100
                               888-EAT-CHIL
                               Fax: 505-242-7513
                               www.loschileros.com/

Southwestern ingredients

President: Terrie Lucero
Credit Cards: MasterCard; Visa
Catalog Cost: Free
Catalog Circulation: Mailed 1 time(s) per year
Printing Information: 2 pages
In Business: 33 years

Number of Employees: 7
Sales Volume: $5MM to $10MM

2988 Maple Grove Farms of Vermont
Maple Grove Farms of Vermont
1052 Portland St
St Johnsbury, VT 05819-2815   920-682-0161
800-525-2540
Fax: 920-683-7589
www.Maplegrove.Com

Maple syrup and other maple products

Chairman: Glen Tellock
President: Stephen Jones
CEO: Glen Tellock
Credit Cards: AMEX; MasterCard; Visa
Catalog Cost: Free
Catalog Circulation: Mailed 5 time(s) per year
to 1M
Average Order Size: $53
Printing Information: 24 pages in 4 colors on
Glossy Stock
Press: Web Press
Binding: Saddle Stitched
Mailing List Information: Names for rent
List Manager: Marianne Jancaitis
In Business: 85 years
Number of Employees: 115

2989 Moonlite Food & Gift Magazine
MoonLite BAN-B-Q
2840 W Parrish Ave
Owensboro, KY 42301-3312   270-684-8143
800-322-8989
Fax: 270-684-8105
PBosley@moonlite.com
www.Moonlite.Com

**Barbequed meats, hams and sauces in the
kentucky tradition**

President: Fred Bosley
International Marketing Manager: Pat Bosley
Buyers: Tracy Philips
Credit Cards: AMEX; MasterCard; Visa
Catalog Cost: Free
Catalog Circulation: to 10000
Average Order Size: $40
Printing Information: 32 pages in 4 colors on
Glossy Stock
Press: Sheetfed Press
Binding: Saddle Stitched
Mailing List Information: Names for rent
List Manager: Pat Bosley
In Business: 40 years
Number of Employees: 125
Sales Volume: $5MM to $10MM

2990 Rao's Specialty Foods
Rao's Specialty Foods
17 Battery Place
New York, NY 10004   800-466-3623
www.raos.com

Recipes, gift sets, and food products

In Business: 20 years

2991 Rent Mother Nature
Rent Mother Nature
PO Box 380193
Cambridge, MA 02238   800-232-4048
800-232-4048
Fax: 617-868-5861
orders@rentmothernature.com
www.rentmothernature.com

**Products from family farms such as, maple
syrup, honey, pancake mix and more**

Credit Cards: AMEX; MasterCard
Catalog Cost: $0
Catalog Circulation: to 500k
Average Order Size: $84
Printing Information: 16 pages in 4 colors on
Matte Stock
Binding: Perfect Bound
Mailing List Information: Names for rent
List Manager: Richard Hill
In Business: 36 years

Number of Employees: 5
Sales Volume: Under $500M

2992 Simonton's Cheese & Gourmet House
Simonton's Cheese & Gourmet House
2278 US-127 # 101
Crossville, TN 38572   931-484-5193
888-819-3226
www.simontonscheese.com

Gift basket company

Credit Cards: AMEX; MasterCard
In Business: 68 years

Wines & Spirits

2993 1-877-Spirits.com
1-877-Spirits.com Inc
99 Powerhouse Road
Suite 200
Roslyn Heights, NY 11577   516-626-4150
877-774-7487
Fax: 516-626-4164
info@1877spirits.com
www.1-877-spirits.com

**A world-wide gift delivery service of cham-
pagnes, fine wines, spirits and gourmet gift
baskets.**

President: Harvey Ishofsky
Credit Cards: AMEX; MasterCard; Visa
Catalog Cost: Free
Average Order Size: $100
Printing Information: 40 pages
In Business: 30 years
Number of Employees: 20
Sales Volume: $5MM to $10MM

2994 Bounty Hunter Rare Wine & Provisions
Bounty Hunter Rare Wine & Provisions
975 First Street
Napa, CA 94559   707-255-0622
800-943-9463
Fax: 707-257-2202
info@bountyhunterwine.com
www.bountyhunterwine.com

**Winery and winemaker products and equip-
ment**

Founder and CEO: Mark Steven Pope
Winemaker: Timothy Milos
Wine Director: Rhett Gadke
In Business: 20 years

2995 Capalbo's Gift Baskets
Capalbo's Gift Baskets
350 Allwood Rd.
Clifton, NJ 7012   973-667-6262
800-252-6262
Fax: 973-450-1199
sales@capalbosonline.com
www.capalbosonline.com

Gift basket

Credit Cards: AMEX; MasterCard
In Business: 109 years

2996 Double A Vineyards
Double A Vineyards
10277 Christy Road
Fredonia, NY 14063   716-672-8493
Fax: 716-679-3442
www.doubleavineyards.com

**Various types of grapevines, berries and rhu-
barb plants, books and accessories.**

2997 EC Kraus Home Wine Making
EC Kraus Home Wine Making
733 S Northern Blvd
PO Box 7850
Independence, MO 64054   800-353-1906
Fax: 816-254-7051
customerservice@eckraus.com
www.eckraus.com

Wine and beer making supplies

President: Ed Kraus
Credit Cards: AMEX; MasterCard
Catalog Cost: Free
In Business: 47 years
Number of Employees: 7
Sales Volume: $630,000

2998 Heartwarming Treasures
Heartwarming Treasures
3843 Fremont Ave N
Seattle, WA 98103-8755   206-547-2623
866-332-6904
heartwarmingtreasures@yahoo.com
www.heartwarmingtreasures.com

**Northwest food and wine gourmet gift bas-
kets**

President: Sue Wolf
Credit Cards: AMEX; MasterCard; Visa
Catalog Cost: Free
In Business: 19 years
Number of Employees: 2
Sales Volume: $79,000

2999 Holiday Gift Basket
Gift Basket Village
Ocala FL   800-563-8890
Fax: 352-489-8750
www.giftbasketvillage.com

Gift basket

3000 Home Brewery
Home Brewery
1967 W Boat St
PO Box 730
Ozark, MO 65721   417-581-0963
800-321-2739
Fax: 417-485-4107
brewery@homebrewery.com
www.homebrewery.com

**Wine making supplies, beer equipment, wine
equipment, beer & wine ingredients**

President: Todd Frye
Credit Cards: AMEX; MasterCard
Catalog Cost: Free
Printing Information: 52 pages
In Business: 31 years
Sales Volume: $500M to $1MM

3001 IWA
International Wine Accessories
1445 N. McDowell Blvd
Petaluma, CA 94954   707-794-8000
800-527-4072
Fax: 800-781-4050
customerservice@iwawine.com
www.iwawine.com

Wine cellar plans, kits and accessories

President: Ben Argov
Credit Cards: AMEX; MasterCard
Catalog Cost: Free
Catalog Circulation: Mailed 12 time(s) per
year to 40000
Average Order Size: $100
Printing Information: 36 pages in 4 colors
Press: Web Press
Binding: Saddle Stitched
Mailing List Information: Names for rent
In Business: 21 years
Number of Employees: 30
Sales Volume: $170,000

3002 Jim's Supply Co., Inc.
Jim's Supply Co., Inc.
3530 Buck Owens Blvd.
Bakersfield, CA 93308   800-423-8016
Fax: 661-324-6566
info@jimssupply.com
www.jimssupply.com

Bird netting for vineyards

3003 Morrell & Company
Morrell
1 Rockefeller Plaza
New York, NY 10020
212-688-9370
800-969-4637
Fax: 212-223-1846
customerservice@morrellwine.com
www.morrellwine.com

Fine wines and spirits

President: Roberta Morrell
CEO, Morrell & Company Retail & Auc:
Jeremy Noye
Chief Operating Officer and Wine &: Tom
Stanley
Credit Cards: AMEX; MasterCard; Visa; Discover
Catalog Cost: Free
Catalog Circulation: Mailed 5 time(s) per year
to 35000
Average Order Size: $300
Printing Information: 40 pages in 4 colors on
Glossy Stock
Press: Letterpress
Mailing List Information: Names for rent
In Business: 68 years
Number of Employees: 20-5
Sales Volume: $1MM to $3MM

3004 Presque Isle Wine Cellars
9440 West Main Rd.
North East, PA 16428
814-725-1314
800-488-7492
Fax: 814-725-2092
www.piwine.com

Wine making and beer brewing equipment

Vice President: Doug Moorhead
Secretary/ Company Director: Marlene
Moorhead

3005 Sherry Lehmann Wine & Spirits
Sherry-Lehman Wine And Spirits
505 Park Avenue
New York, NY 10022
212-838-7500
Fax: 212-838-9285
inquiries@sherry-lehmann.com
www.sherry-lehmann.com

Fine wines and spirits, gift baskets, samplers and accessories

Credit Cards: AMEX; MasterCard; Visa
Catalog Cost: Free
Catalog Circulation: Mailed 5 time(s) per year
to 800M
Average Order Size: $100
Printing Information: 60 pages in 4 colors on
Glossy Stock
Press: Web Press
Binding: Saddle Stitched
Mailing List Information: Names for rent
List Manager: Sara Weinberg
List Company: MSGI Metro List Manager
333 Seventh Avenue
New York, NY 10001
212-594-7688
In Business: 80 years
Number of Employees: 75
Sales Volume: 20MM-50MM

3006 Stew Leonard's
Stew Leonard's
111 Glover Ave
Norwalk, CT 6851
800-729-7839
www.stewleonardsgifts.com

Gift basket

In Business: 46 years

3007 Vinotemp
Vinotemp International
16782 Von Karman Avenue
Suite 15
Irvine, CA 92606
800-777-8466
Fax: 310-886-3310
info@vinotemp.com
www.Vinotemp.Com

Wine cellars and cigar humidors

President: Francis Ravel
Credit Cards: AMEX; MasterCard; Visa
Catalog Cost: Free
Printing Information: 81 pages in 4 colors
In Business: 30 years
Sales Volume: $5MM to $10MM

3008 Vintage Cellars
Vintage Cellars
904 Rancheros Dr
Suite G
San Marcos, CA 92069-3045
760-735-9946
800-876-8789
Fax: 760-735-9956
sales@vintagecellars.com
www.Vintagecellars.Com

Custom wine cellars, cooling systems, wine openers, wine storage cabinets and walk in wine cellars

President: Gene Walder
Credit Cards: AMEX; MasterCard
In Business: 25 years
Sales Volume: $1MM to $3MM

3009 VintageView
VintageView Wine Storage Systems
10645 E 47th Avenue
Denver, CO 80239
303-504-9463
866-650-1500
Fax: 866-650-1501
info@vintageview.com
vintageview.com

Wine storage equipment, including racks, cooling units, and accessories

President: Doug McCain
Credit Cards: AMEX; MasterCard
Catalog Cost: Free
Catalog Circulation: Mailed 1 time(s) per year
Printing Information: 22 pages in 4 colors
In Business: 16 years
Number of Employees: 20

3010 William's Brewing Company Catalog
William's Brewing Company
2088 Burroughs Avenue
San Leandro, CA 94577
510-895-2739
800-759-6025
Fax: 510-895-2745
service@williamsbrewing.com
www.williamsbrewing.com

Home brewing, wine making and coffee roasting products

President: William Moore
Catalog Cost: Free
In Business: 36 years
Number of Employees: 5
Sales Volume: $310,000

3011 Wine Cellar Innovations Catalog
Wine Cellar Innovations
4575 Eastern Ave
Cincinnati, OH 45226-1805
513-321-3733
800-229-9813
Fax: 513-979-5280
forms@winecellarinnovations.com
www.winecellarinnovations.com

Wood wine racks, wine racks, commercial wine racks, wine cellar refrigeration, wine cellar doors and wine art

President: James Deckenbach
Marketing Manager: Erin Chamberlain
Purchasing Manager: Sandy Smith
Catalog Cost: Free
Printing Information: 13 pages
In Business: 41 years
Number of Employees: 157
Sales Volume: $16.5 Million

3012 Wine Country Gift Baskets Catalog
Wine Country Gift Baskets
4225 N Palm Street
Fullerton, CA 92835
800-394-0394
Fax: 714-525-0746
www.winecountrygiftbaskets.com

Variety of gift baskets

President: John Brian
Marketing Manager: Bill Martin
Credit Cards: AMEX; MasterCard
Catalog Cost: Free
In Business: 29 years
Number of Employees: 72
Sales Volume: $3.7 Million

3013 Wine Enthusiast Catalog
Wine Enthusiast
200 Summit Lane Drive
4th Floor
Valhalla, NY 10595
914-345-9463
800-356-8466
custserv@wineenthusiast.net
www.wineenthusiast.com

Wine cellars, racks, glasses, decanters and china

President: Adam Strum
Marketing Manager: Judith Roberts
Buyers: Margaret White
Credit Cards: AMEX; MasterCard
Catalog Cost: Free
Catalog Circulation: Mailed 5 time(s) per year
Average Order Size: $250
Printing Information: 64 pages in 4 colors on
Glossy Stock
Press: Web Press
Binding: Saddle Stitched
Mailing List Information: Names for rent
In Business: 39 years
Number of Employees: 100
Sales Volume: $20MM to $50MM

3014 Wine Express Catalog
Wine Enthusiast Company
333 N Bedford Road
Mount Kisco, NY 10549
914-345-9463
800-356-8466
Fax: 800-833-8466
custserv@wineenthusiast.net
www.wineenthusiast.com

Fine wines

President: Adam Strum
Marketing Manager: Judith Roberts
Credit Cards: AMEX; MasterCard; Visa
Catalog Cost: $4
Printing Information: 16 pages in 4 colors
Binding: Saddle Stitched
In Business: 36 years

3015 Wine Merchant Catalog
D Sokolin Company
PO Box 755
PO Box 1206
Bridgehampton, NY 11932
631-537-4434
800-946-3947
Fax: 631-537-4435
sales@sokolin.com
www.sokolin.com

Fine wines

Catalog Circulation: to 1000
Printing Information: 18 pages
Binding: Saddle Stitched
In Business: 72 years

3016 Wine.com - Holiday Catalog
Wine.Com
2220 4th Street
Berkley, CA 94710
800-592-5870
www.wine.com

Wine selections from around the world

CEO: Rich Bergsund
Founder & VP Merchandising: Michael Osborn
VP Engineering: Greg Tatem

Credit Cards: AMEX; MasterCard; Visa
Catalog Cost: Free
Catalog Circulation: Mailed 1 time(s) per year
Printing Information: 24 pages
In Business: 17 years

Garden & Lawn Products
Equipment

3017 A.M. Leonard Gardeners Edge
A.M. Leonard, Inc.
241 Fox Drive
P.O. Box 816
Piqua, OH 45356   888-556-5676
                          Fax: 800-433-0633
              custserv@gardenersedge.com
                  www.gardenersedge.com

Gardening tools and supplies.
President: Gregory Stephens
CFO: Shirley Reiber
Production Manager: Beth Marshall
Marketing Operations Manager: Melissa Shea
Credit Cards: AMEX; MasterCard
Catalog Cost: Free
In Business: 12 years
Number of Employees: 90
Sales Volume: $28.42 Million

3018 AeroGarden
AeroGrow International Inc.
PO Box 18450
Boulder, CO 80308   303-444-7755
                            800-476-9669
                       Fax: 303-444-0406
            customerservice@aerogrow.com
                      www.aerogarden.com

Indoor herb garden, kit and seeds
Chairman: Jack J Walkers
President: Mike Wolfe
CFO: H MacGregor Clarke
Marketing Manager: John K Thompson
Credit Cards: AMEX; MasterCard; Visa
Catalog Cost: Free
In Business: 9 years
Number of Employees: 34
Sales Volume: $11.31MM

3019 American Arborist Supplies
American Arborist Supplies
882 S Matlack Street
Unit A
West Chester, PA 19382   610-430-1214
                                800-441-8381
                           Fax: 610-430-8560
                      info@arborist.com
                      www.arborist.com

Tools and equipment for tree workers as well as books on arboriculture
President: Dave Francis
International Marketing Manager: Steff Haymen
Credit Cards: AMEX; MasterCard
Catalog Circulation: Mailed 1 time(s) per year to 15000
Printing Information: 86 pages in 4 colors on Glossy Stock
Press: Web Press
Binding: Perfect Bound
Mailing List Information: Names for rent
In Business: 34 years
Number of Employees: 5
Sales Volume: $3MM

3020 American Tank Company
Water Tanks.com
2804 West Admiral Doyle Drive
New Iberia, LA 70560   707-535-1400
                              877-655-1100
                         Fax: 707-535-1450
              sales@americantankco.com
                    www.watertanks.com

Water, chemical, fire, septic, pumps and equipment
President: Mark D. Luzaich
Marketing Manager: Jim M. Kinley
Vice President: Guy Giordanego
Printing Information: 16 pages
In Business: 28 years
Number of Employees: 20
Sales Volume: $1MM

3021 BC Greenhouse Builders
BC Greenhouse Builders Limited
1685 H Street
#27245
Blaine, WA 98230   604-882-8408
                          888-391-4433
                     Fax: 604-882-8491
                www.bcgreenhouses.com

Greenhouses
President: Rick Heinen
Credit Cards: AMEX; MasterCard
Catalog Cost: Free
In Business: 66 years

3022 BlueStone Garden
BlueStone Garden
5017 Boone Ave.
Suite 200
Minneapolis, MN 55428   866-543-1222
                          Fax: 763-746-7385
              info@bluestonegarden.com
                  www.bluestonegarden.com

Gardening tools and accessories.
Catalog Cost: Free
Printing Information: 10 pages on Glossy Stock
In Business: 20 years
Number of Employees: 14

3023 Bowie Industries
Bowie Industries, Inc.
1004 E. Wise Street
PO Box 931
Bowie, TX 76230   940-872-1106
                          800-433-0934
                     Fax: 940-872-4792
            tellmemore@bowieindustries.com
                  www.bowieindustries.com

Lawn and landscaping equipment and products
President: Gary Meyer
garymeyer@bowieindustries.com
CFO: Dean Myers
bowind@morgan.net
Controller: Robert Jones
bobjones@bowieindustries.com
VP: Carlotta Jones
cgm@bowieindustries.com
Catalog Cost: Free
Catalog Circulation: Mailed 1 time(s) per year to 1000
Printing Information: 7 pages on Glossy Stock
In Business: 66 years
Number of Employees: 47
Sales Volume: $5.40MM

3024 CADplans
CADPlans Corporation
PO Box 0606
Daleville, VA 24083-606   540-992-4758
                                 800-211-4255
                            Fax: 540-966-4714
                      cadplans@aol.com
                      www.cadplans.com

Build it yourself loaders, diggers, tractors
Production Manager: John Mikulus
Credit Cards: MasterCard; Visa
Catalog Cost: Free
Printing Information: 40 pages

3025 CF Struck Corporation
CF Struck Corporation
P.O Box 307
W51N545 Struck Lane
Cedarburg, WI 53012   262-377-3300
                             877-828-8323
                        Fax: 262-377-9247
                      info@struckcorp.com
                      www.struckcorp.com

Compact tractors/crawler-capabilities include: backhoe, loader, dozer blade, stone and soil rakes, log splitter, log forks, post-hole augers, and plow
President: Charles Struck
Credit Cards: MasterCard; Visa
Catalog Cost: Free
In Business: 58 years
Number of Employees: 10
Sales Volume: $1MM to $3MM

3026 CT Farm & Country
CT Farm & Country
1301 N 14th St.
Indianola, IA 50125   800-860-1799
                      www.ctfarmonline.com

Tractor, harvesting, mowing and tillage parts.
Catalog Cost: Free
Printing Information: 189 pages in 4 colors
In Business: 81 years

3027 Cable Design Guide
Carl Stahl Sava Industries Inc.
4 North Corporate Drive
P.O. Box 30
Riverdale, NJ 07457   973-835-0882
                          Fax: 973-835-0877
                      info@savacable.com
                      www.savacable.com

Manufacturing cable solutions in cable, cable assemblies, idler pulleys, and push and pull control assemblies
President: Marc E. Alterman
Production Manager: Ron Paras
Chief Executive Officer: Zdenek A Fremund
VP of Operations: Jack Maas
VP of Sales & Marketing: Bruce R. Staubitz
Catalog Cost: Free
Catalog Circulation: Mailed 1 time(s) per year to 7000
Printing Information: 36 pages in 2 colors on Glossy Stock
Binding: Folded
Mailing List Information: Names for rent
In Business: 42 years
Number of Employees: 85
Sales Volume: $ 20 Million

3028 Commodity Traders International
Commodity Traders International
101 E. Main Street
PO Box 6
Trilla, IL 62469-6   217-235-4322
                          Fax: 217-235-3246
              sales@commoditytraders.biz
                  www.commoditytraders.biz

Seed and grain equipment
President: Charles Stodden Sr
Marketing Manager: Charles Stodden Jr
Mailing List Information: Names for rent
In Business: 40 years
Number of Employees: 4
Sales Volume: Under $500M

3029 DAIDO Corporation
DAIDO Corporation of America
1031 Fred White Blvd
Portland, TN 37148   615-323-4020
                            866-219-9972
                       Fax: 615-323-4015
                      www.daidocorp.com

Rotary incremental shaft encoders, precision ground and roller ball screws, power transmission and various electronic instruments

CFO: Kakuko Scott
Owner: Toshi Horie
Manager: Jenni Anderson
Catalog Cost: Free
In Business: 64 years
Number of Employees: 40
Sales Volume: $27 Million

3030 DR Power Equipment

DR Power Equipment
75 Meigs Road
P.O. Box 25
Vergennes, VT 05491   802-870-1437
                             800-687-6575
                        Fax: 802-877-1213
                   websupport@drpower.com
                          www.drpower.com

Chippers, brush mowers, leaf vacs, power haulers, trimmers, splitters

President: Joe Perrotto
CFO: Christopher Knapp
Marketing Manager: Ned Van Woert
Production Manager: John Berlind
Fulfillment: Moe Matte
International Marketing Manager: Carl Eikenberg
Buyers: Carl Eikenberg
Credit Cards: MasterCard
Catalog Cost: Free
Average Order Size: $150
Printing Information: 48 pages in 4 colors
Press: Offset Press
Binding: Saddle Stitched
In Business: 32 years
Number of Employees: 250
Sales Volume: $20 Million

3031 Dixon Industries

Dixon Industries
9335 Harris Corners Parkway
Charlotte, NC 28269   info@dixon-ztr.com
                          www.dixon-ztr.com

Lawnmowers

President: John P Mowder
CFO: Ron Bryant
Marketing Manager: Mike Kadel
Production Manager: Charles Roger
Credit Cards: AMEX; MasterCard
Catalog Circulation: to 10K
Printing Information: 20 pages in 4 colors on Glossy Stock
Press: Sheetfed Press
Binding: Saddle Stitched
Mailing List Information: Names for rent
In Business: 32 years
Number of Employees: 200
Sales Volume: $25,000,000 - $50,000,000

3032 Doheny's

Doheny's Water Warehouse
6950 51 Street
Kenosha, WI 53144-1740   262-605-1060
                                800-574-7665
                           Fax: 262-605-1065
                     customercare@doheny.com
                            www.doheny.com

Supplier of discounted pool products

President: John Doheny
Credit Cards: AMEX; MasterCard
Catalog Cost: Free
In Business: 48 years

3033 Drip Irrigation

Submatic Irrigation Systems
3002 Upland Ave
Lubbock, TX 79407-246   806-799-0700
                                800-692-4100
                           Fax: 806-799-0722
                     submatic@sbcglobal.net
                           www.submatic.com

Drip irrigation products and sprinklers

President: Curry Blackwell
Credit Cards: MasterCard
Catalog Cost: Free
Catalog Circulation: Mailed 2 time(s) per year to 10M
Average Order Size: $150
Printing Information: 25 pages in 2 colors on Glossy Stock
Press: Letterpress
Binding: Perfect Bound
Mailing List Information: Names for rent
In Business: 10 years
Number of Employees: 4
Sales Volume: $500M to $1MM

3034 Early's Seed Catalog

Early's Farm & Garden Centre
2615 Lorne Avenue
Saskatoon, SK S7J-0S5   306-931-1982
                               800-667-1159
                          Fax: 306-931-7110
                        www.earlysgarden.com

Seeds, garden tools, pest control, wild bird supplies, pond supplies and more

General Manager: Derek Bloski
General Manager: Kevin Bloski
Catalog Cost: Free
In Business: 110 years
Number of Employees: 39

3035 FarmTek

FarmTek
1440 Field of Dreams Way
Dyersville, IA 52040   800-245-9881
                               800-327-6835
                          Fax: 800-457-8887
                            www.farmtek.com

Agricultural products

CEO: Barry Goldsher
Catalog Cost: Free
Printing Information: 356 pages in 4 colors
Mailing List Information: Names for rent
In Business: 34 years

3036 GEMPLER'S

GEMPLER'S
PO Box 5175
Janesville, WI 53547-5175   608-662-3301
                                800-382-8473
                           Fax: 800-551-1128
                   customerservice@gemplers.com
                            www.gemplers.com

Safety supplies, shop supplies, sprayers, tires, footwear, agriculture products etc.

3037 Garden Artisans

Garden Artisans
451 Defense Highway
Suite A
Annapolis, MD 21401   410-672-0082
                          Fax: 410-280-2184
                 info@gardenartisans.com
                       gardenartisans.com

Garden decor, garden planters, garden structures, garden trellises, arches and arbors, garden lighting, christmas ornaments

President: Janet Kirkpatrick
Catalog Cost: Free
Catalog Circulation: Mailed 1 time(s) per year to 40M
Average Order Size: $200
Printing Information: 64 pages in 4 colors
Mailing List Information: Names for rent
In Business: 19 years
Number of Employees: 2
Sales Volume: $499,000

3038 Garden Catalog

Lee Valley Tools Ltd.
PO Box 1780
Ogdensburg, NY 13669-6780   613-596-0350
                               800-267-8735
                          Fax: 800-513-7885
                 customerservice@leevalley.com
                           www.leevalley.com

Tools and supplies for both indoors and out

President: Robin C Lee
Credit Cards: AMEX; MasterCard; Visa
Catalog Cost: Free
Catalog Circulation: Mailed 1 time(s) per year
Printing Information: 272 pages in 4 colors
Press: Web Press
Binding: Saddle Stitched
In Business: 36 years

3039 Garden Tools by Lee Valley

Lee Valley Tools Ltd.
PO Box 1780
Ogdensburg, NY 13669-6780   613-596-0350
                               800-871-8158
                          Fax: 800-513-7885
                 customerservice@leevalley.com
                           www.leevalley.com

Woodworking and gardening hand tools and accessories

President: Leonard Lee
Marketing Manager: Robin Lee
Credit Cards: MasterCard; Visa
Catalog Cost: $5
Catalog Circulation: Mailed 12 time(s) per year
Printing Information: 245 pages in 4 colors
Press: Web Press
Binding: Saddle Stitched
In Business: 36 years

3040 Gardeners Edge Catalog

A M Leonard Inc
241 Fox Drive
P.O. Box 816
Piqua, OH 45356   888-556-5676
                          Fax: 800-433-0633
                 custserv@gardenersedge.com
                       www.gardenersedge.com

Gardening tools and supplies

President: Greg Stephens
Owner: Shirley Reiber
Chief Operating Officer: Wayne Roland
Credit Cards: AMEX; MasterCard
Catalog Cost: Free
Catalog Circulation: Mailed 6 time(s) per year
Printing Information: 72 pages in 4 colors on Matte Stock
Press: Web Press
Binding: Saddle Stitched
Mailing List Information: Names for rent
In Business: 12 years
Number of Employees: 100
Sales Volume: $28.42 Million

3041 Greenhouses & Horticultural Supply

Gothic Arch Greenhouses, Inc.
PO Box 1564
Mobile, AL 36633-1564   251-471-5238
                               800-531-4769
                          Fax: 251-471-5465
                 Info@gothicarchgreenhouses.net
                  www.gothicarchgreenhouses.com

Greenhouses and horticultural equipment and supplies

President: William H Buzz Sierke Jr
bsierke@comcast.net
Marketing Manager: Paul Sierke
Administrative & Sales Associate: Kim Brooks
Administrative & Sales Associate: Shasta Godwin
Sales Associate & Consultant: Zack Sierke
Catalog Cost: $5
Catalog Circulation: Mailed 1 time(s) per year
Average Order Size: $1000
Printing Information: 50 pages in 1 color on

Matte Stock
Press: Web Press
Binding: Saddle Stitched
Mailing List Information: Names for rent
In Business: 69 years
Sales Volume: $500M to $1MM

3042 Greenhouses Catalog

Corrugated Plas-Tech
3740 Brooklake Road NE
Salem, OR 97303-9728   503-393-3973
    800-825-1925
Fax: 503-393-3119
info@greenhousecatalog.com
www.greenhousecatalog.com

Greenhouses, gardening supplies, grow lights and heaters

President: Mike Perry
CFO: Kim Boes
Marketing Manager: Michelle Torres
Production Manager: Michelle Moore
Catalog Cost: Free
Catalog Circulation: to 10000
Printing Information: 28 pages in 4 colors on Glossy Stock
Press: Sheetfed Press
Binding: Saddle Stitched
Mailing List Information: Names for rent
In Business: 17 years
Number of Employees: 12
Sales Volume: $1MM to $3MM

3043 Growers Supply

Growers Supply
1440 Field of Dreams Way
Dyersville, IA 52040   563-875-2288
    800-245-9881
Fax: 800-457-8887
contactus@growerssupply.com
www.growerssupply.com

Greenhouses and green house supplies

President: Bob McClendon
CEO: Barry Goldsher
Credit Cards: AMEX; MasterCard; Visa
Catalog Cost: Free
Catalog Circulation: Mailed 12 time(s) per year
Printing Information: 352 pages in 4 colors on Matte Stock
Mailing List Information: Names for rent
In Business: 35 years

3044 Haigie Manufacturing

Haigie Manufacturing
PO Box 273
Clarion, IA 50525-273   515-532-2861
    800-247-4885
Fax: 515-532-3553
info@hagie.com
www.hagie.com

Agricultural sprayers

Interim Executive Director: Mike Maranell
Director of Human Resources: Dave Maxheimer
In Business: 68 years

3045 Imperial Sprinkler Supply

Imperial Sprinkler Supply
1485 N Manassero Street
Anaheim, CA 92807-1938   714-792-2925
Fax: 714-792-2921
info@imperialsprinkler.com
www.imperialsprinklersupply.com

Imperial sprinkler systems, install automatic irrigation systems, commercial and residential, sprinkler lines for small and large underground systems; including hydraulic, electric, and lake systems

President: Gabriel Moriel
Catalog Cost: Free
In Business: 37 years
Sales Volume: $20MM to $50MM

3046 Indco Catalog

Indco
PO Box 589
New Albany, IN 47151   812-945-4383
    800-942-4383
Fax: 812-944-9742
info@indco.com
www.indco.com

Industrial mixing equipment

Chairman: Kris Wilberding
President: C. Mark Hennis
Marketing Manager: Linda Potts
Production Manager: David Ruppe
Sales & Customer Service Manager: Tricia Thien
Catalog Cost: Free
Catalog Circulation: to 1M
Printing Information: 56 pages
In Business: 40 years
Number of Employees: 50

3047 Janco Greenhouses

Janco Greenhouses
138 Cathedral Street
Elkton, MD 21921   443-350-9631
    800-323-6933
Fax: 443-350-9639
info@jancoinc.com
www.jancogreenhouses.com

Greenhouses, solariums and atriums

President: Dominick Savo
Catalog Cost: Free
Printing Information: 34 pages in 1 color
In Business: 69 years
Sales Volume: $5,000,000 - $10,000,000

3048 Jim's Supply Co., Inc.

Jim's Supply Co., Inc.
3530 Buck Owens Blvd.
Bakersfield, CA 93308   800-423-8016
Fax: 661-324-6566
info@jimssupply.com
www.jimssupply.com

Bird netting for vineyards

3049 Loc-Line

Loc-Line
5615 Willow Lane
PO Box 1546
Lake Oswego, OR 97035-5338   503-635-8113
    800-423-1625
Fax: 503-635-2844
info@loc-line.com
www.loc-line.com

A wide selection of hose sizes, nozzles, connectors and accessories for you home and garden

Printing Information: 24 pages in 4 colors on Glossy Stock
Binding: Saddle Stitched
Mailing List Information: Names for rent
In Business: 20 years

3050 Loyal Catalog

Roth Manufacturing Company
314 E Elm Drive (Highway 98 E)
PO Box 40
Loyal, WI 54446   715-255-8515
    800-472-2341
Fax: 800-677-2341
info@loyal-roth.com
www.loyal-roth.com

ATV dump trailers, atv harrows, atv manure spreaders and seeders, barn grooming equipment, feed carts, feed handling systems, calf hutches & pens, and barn ventilation systems

Chairman: Thomas Roth
President: Anthony Roth
Marketing Manager: Thomas Roth
Catalog Cost: Free
Catalog Circulation: Mailed 1 time(s) per year

Printing Information: 80 pages
Mailing List Information: Names for rent
In Business: 58 years
Number of Employees: 8
Sales Volume: $680,000

3051 Mantis Catalog

Schiller-Pfeiffer Inc.
1028 Street Road
Southampton, PA 18966   215-355-9700
    800-366-6268
Fax: 215-357-1071
www.mantisgardentools.com

Garden Tillers

President: Stuart Bryan
CFO: Tom Schwarz
Marketing Manager: Robert Bell
Production Manager: Howard Kaplan
Credit Cards: AMEX; MasterCard; Visa
Catalog Cost: Free
Mailing List Information: Names for rent
List Manager: Stephen LePera
In Business: 25 years
Number of Employees: 75

3052 Palmer Electric Transporters

Palmer Industries
PO Box 5707
Endicott, NY 13763-5707   607-754-2957
    800-847-1304
Fax: 607-754-1954
palmer@palmerind.com
www.palmerind.com

Electric outdoor wheelchairs, electric 1,2,3 & 4 person vehicles, electric kits for bicycles and tricycles

President: J Palmer
Marketing Manager: Joe Martin
Production Manager: J Homer II
Credit Cards: MasterCard; Visa
Catalog Cost: Free
Catalog Circulation: to 15000
Printing Information: 4 pages in 4 colors on Glossy Stock
Press: Letterpress
Binding: Folded
Mailing List Information: Names for rent
In Business: 42 years
Number of Employees: 20
Sales Volume: $1MM to $3MM

3053 QCI Direct

QCI Direct
100 Beaver Rd
Churchville, NY 14624   800-810-2340
    888-488-3088
Fax: 585-889-8686

Organizing, cleaning, cooking, household and health/personal-care products

Printing Information: 36 pages
In Business: 32 years

3054 Reinco

Relinco Inc
PO Box 512
Plainfield, NJ 07061-512   908-755-0921
    800-526-7687
Fax: 908-755-6379
www.reinco.com

Mulching machines

In Business: 50 years
Number of Employees: 20-O
Sales Volume: $1,000,000 - $5,000,000

3055 Sporty's Preferred Living Catalog

Sportsman's Market Inc.
Clermont County/Sporty's Airport
2001 Sporty's Drive
Batavia, OH 45103   513-735-9000
    800-776-7897
Fax: 800-543-8633
www.sportys.com

Products for outdooor leisure, safety and security, automotive and garage, personal care, yard and garden, pool and games

Chairman: Harold Shevers
President: Michael Wolf
CFO: Daniel Robinson
Buyers: Howard Law
Credit Cards: AMEX; MasterCard; Visa
Catalog Cost: Free
Catalog Circulation: Mailed 4 time(s) per year to 20000
Printing Information: in 4 colors
Mailing List Information: Names for rent
List Company: Names & Addresses
In Business: 40 years
Number of Employees: 200
Sales Volume: $20MM to $50MM

3056 Stoneberry
Stoneberry
1356 Williams Street
Chippewa Falls, WI 54729   800-704-5480
www.stoneberry.com

Home furnishings and appliances, home entertainment, toys and games, gardening and yard maintenance equipment, sport and fitness products, health and beauty products

Credit Cards: AMEX; MasterCard
Catalog Cost: Free
Catalog Circulation: Mailed 2 time(s) per year
Printing Information: 200 pages in 4 colors
Sales Volume: $50MM to $100MM

3057 Sturdi-Built Greenhouse
Sturdi-built Greenhouse Manufacturing Co
11304 SW Boones Ferry Rd
Portland, OR 97219   503-244-4100
800-334-4115
sturdi@sturdi-built.com
www.sturdi-built.com

Greenhouse building kits complete with plans and materials

President: Richard Warner
Credit Cards: MasterCard; Visa
Catalog Cost: Free
Printing Information: 16 pages
In Business: 46 years
Sales Volume: $5MM to $10MM

3058 Turner Greenhouses
Turner Greenhouses
1500 Highway 117 S
PO Box 1260
Goldsboro, NC 27533   800-672-4770
sales@turnergreenhouses.com
www.turnergreenhouses.com

Pre-fabricated hobby greenhouses, fixtures and accessories

President: Gary Smithwick
Marketing Manager: Duffy Fleming
Credit Cards: MasterCard; Visa
Catalog Cost: Free
Mailing List Information: Names for rent
In Business: 57 years
Number of Employees: 42
Sales Volume: $5,00,000

3059 WW Grainger
Grainger
3240 Mannheim Road
Franklin Park, IL 60131-1532   800-472-4643
www.grainger.com

Industrial and lawn equipment, tools, motors and pumps

Chairman: James T. Ryan
President: Court Carruthers
Senior VP: D.G. Macpherson
Director: E. Scott Santi
Director: James D. Slavik
Catalog Cost: Free
Catalog Circulation: Mailed 3 time(s) per year
Printing Information: 795 pages
Mailing List Information: Names for rent

In Business: 88 years
Number of Employees: 1833
Sales Volume: $247.35 million

3060 Wafer Warehouse
Doheny's Water Warehouse
6950 51st Street
Kenosha, WI 53144-1740   800-574-7665
800-372-1318
Fax: 262-605-1065
www.doheny.com

Quality swimming pool supplies at discount prices

Credit Cards: AMEX; MasterCard
Catalog Cost: $2
In Business: 47 years

3061 Watts Heatway Catalog
Watts Radiant, Inc.
4500 E Progress Place
Springfield, MO 65803-8816   417-864-6108
800-276-2419
Fax: 417-864-8161
www.Wattsradiant.Com

Produces electric radiant heat systems, snowmelting systems, and domestic water systems

President: Rich Calloway
In Business: 141 years

3062 WeatherPort Shelter Systems
WeatherPort Shelter Systems
1860 1600 Road
Delta, CO 81416-8405   970-399-5909
866-984-7778
Fax: 970-874-5090
info@weatherport.com
www.weatherport.com

Tensioned fabric structures, greenhouses

Printing Information: 6 pages
In Business: 49 years
Number of Employees: 50
Sales Volume: $1,000,000 - $5,000,000

3063 White's Metal Detectors
White's Electronics Factory, U.S.A.
1011 Pleasant Valley Road
Sweet Home, OR 97386   541-367-6121
800-547-6911
Fax: 541-367-6629
sales@whiteselectronics.com
www.whiteselectronics.com

Manufactures metal detectors for recreation, security, and industry

President: Ken and Mary White
Catalog Cost: Free
In Business: 64 years

Fertilizers & Pest Control

3064 Arbico Organics
Arbico Organics
10831 N. Mavinee Dr.
Ste. 185
Oro Valley, AZ 85737-9531   520-825-9785
800-827-2847
Fax: 520-825-2038
info@arbico.com
www.arbico-organics.com

Beneficial insects, gardening supplies, books, pet products, soil amendments, fertilizers, natural household products

President: Rick Frey
Marketing Manager: Shen Frey
Buyers: Debbie Williams
Credit Cards: AMEX; MasterCard; Visa
Catalog Cost: Free
Catalog Circulation: Mailed 3 time(s) per year to 30000
Average Order Size: $75
Printing Information: 56 pages in 4 colors on

Glossy Stock
Press: Web Press
Binding: Saddle Stitched
Mailing List Information: Names for rent
List Manager: Shen Frey
In Business: 36 years
Number of Employees: 40
Sales Volume: $3,500,000

3065 BIRD-X
Bird-X, Inc.
300 N Oakley Blvd
Chicago, IL 60612   312-226-2473
800-662-5021
Fax: 312-226-2480
josh.p@bird-x.com
www.Bird-X.Com

Bird control products, goose repellers

President: Dennis Tillis
Owner: Glenn Steigbigel
Owner: Ronald Schwartz
Credit Cards: MasterCard; Visa
Catalog Cost: Free
Catalog Circulation: Mailed 2 time(s) per year to 200M
Printing Information: 6 pages in 4 colors on Glossy Stock
Binding: Folded
Mailing List Information: Names for rent
In Business: 51 years
Number of Employees: 35
Sales Volume: $13MM

3066 Dixondale Farms
Dixondale Farms
PO Box 129
Department WP15
Carrizo Springs, TX 78834-6129   877-367-1015
www.dixondalefarms.com
In Business: 102 years

3067 DripWorks
DripWorks
190 Sanhedrin Circle
Willits, CA 95490   800-522-3747
support@dripworks.com
www.dripworks.com

Drip irrigation supplies

Printing Information: 56 pages

3068 Fertrell Company
Fertrell
600 N Second Street
P.O. Box 265
Bainbridge, PA 17502   717-367-1566
800-347-1566
Fax: 717-367-9319
info@fertrell.com
www.fertrell.com

Organic fertilizers and custom blends

President: David Mattocks
Production Manager: Paul Douglass
paul@fertrell.com
Orders & Customer Service: Theresia Tredway
theresia@fertrell.com
Orders & Customer Service: Beth Knaub
beth@fertrell.com
Literature & General Inquiries: LynnHartman
info@fertrell.com
Buyers: Walter Gantz
Credit Cards: MasterCard; Visa
Catalog Cost: Free
Printing Information: on Matte Stock
Press: Letterpress
In Business: 71 years
Number of Employees: 20
Sales Volume: $10,000,000 - $25,000,000

3069 Gardens Alive!
Gardens Alive!
5100 Schenley Place
Lawrenceberg, IN 47025   513-354-1482

Lawn care, soil care, plant care, insect pest control, animal, pest control, disease control and weed control

President: Niles Knark
CFO: Bill Taulbee
Marketing Manager: Eric Hamant
VP Merchandising: Matt Wrhel
Credit Cards: AMEX; MasterCard
Catalog Cost: Free
In Business: 20 years
Number of Employees: 150
Sales Volume: $7.2 Million

3070 Hired Bugs
Nature's Control
205 Fern Valley Rd
Suite X
Phoenix, OR 97535   541-245-6033
                          Fax: 541-698-6250
info@naturescontrol.com
www.naturescontrol.com

Beneficial insects for organic gardening

President: Nathan Jackson
Credit Cards: AMEX; MasterCard
Catalog Cost: Free
Catalog Circulation: Mailed 2 time(s) per year
Printing Information: 25 pages in 1 color on Newsprint
Press: Web Press
Mailing List Information: Names for rent
In Business: 34 years
Number of Employees: 10-J
Sales Volume: $500M to $1MM

3071 Ohio Earth Food
Ohio Earth Food
5488 Swamp Street NE
Hartville, OH 44632   330-877-9356
                          Fax: 330-877-4237
info@ohioearthfood.com
www.ohioearthfood.com

Natural fertilizers including Re-Vita Compost Plus, Re-Vita Hi-K, Re-Vita Organic Lawn Fertilizer, phosphate, greensand, seaweed products, fish products, humates, Ful-Po-Mag and sulfate of potash

President: Larry Ringer
Production Manager: Cynthia L Ringer
Credit Cards: MasterCard
Catalog Cost: Free
Catalog Circulation: Mailed 1 time(s) per year to 5M
Printing Information: 32 pages in 4 colors
Mailing List Information: Names for rent
In Business: 43 years
Number of Employees: 2
Sales Volume: $1MM to $3MM

3072 OrchidLight.com
OrchidLight.com
27 Clover Lane
Burlington, VT 5408   800-261-3101
customerservice@orchidlight.com
www.orchidlight.com

Humidity trays, grow lights, watering globes, watering stakes, bulbs etc.

In Business: 21 years

3073 QA Supplies
QA Supplies LLC
1185 Pineridge Road
Norfolk, VA 23502   757-855-3094
                           800-472-7205
                          Fax: 757-855-4155
info@qasupplies.com
www.qasupplies.com

Pest control, temperature measurement, scales, weather monitoring, humidifiers, alarm and security systems

3074 SherrillTree
SherrillTree
200 Seneca Rd
Greensboro, NC 27406   800-525-8873
info@sherrilltree.com
www.sherrilltree.com

Tree gear

In Business: 55 years

3075 The Garden Dept.
The Garden Dept.
16 Acre Distribution Center   631-736-3378
                          Fax: 631-698-0404
www.gardendept.com

3076 Turf, Tree & Ornamental Catalog
Growth Products, Ltd
80 Lafayette Avenue
White Plains, NY 10603-1252   914-428-1316
                           800-648-7626
                          Fax: 914-428-2780
roberlander@growthproducts.com
www.growthproducts.com

Professional liquid fertilizers, micronutrients, natural organics and a new biological fungicide for the turf, horticulture and greenhouse markets

President: Clare Reinbergen
Marketing Manager: Nicole Campbell
Technical/Sales Staff, NY Metro Are: Howard Gold
Technical/Sales Staff, Florida: Mark White
Technical/Sales Staff, Plains: Paul Hoffmann
Printing Information:
Binding: Saddle Stitched
Mailing List Information: Names for rent
In Business: 20 years
Number of Employees: 25
Sales Volume: $10,000,000 - $25,000,000

3077 Wildlife Control Supplies
PO Box 538
East Granby, CT 06026   877-684-7262
                          Fax: 860-413-9831
sales@wildlifecontrolsupplies.com
www.wildlifecontrolsupplies.com

Bird and animal controls and traps.

Plants, Trees & Shrubs

3078 Adams County Nursery
Adams County Nursery
26 Nursery Road
PO Box 108
Aspers, PA 17304   717-677-8105
                          Fax: 717-677-4124
www.acnursery.com

Fruit trees

President: John Baugher
Marketing Manager: Tom Callahan
Vice President: Nadine Baugher
Sales Executive: Philip Baugher
Credit Cards: MasterCard; Visa
Catalog Cost: Free
Catalog Circulation: Mailed 1 time(s) per year
Printing Information: 28 pages in 4 colors
Mailing List Information: Names for rent
In Business: 110 years
Number of Employees: 45
Sales Volume: $10MM

3079 Aitken's Salmon Creek Garden
Aitken's Salmon Creek Garden
608 NW 119th St
Vancouver, WA 98685   360-573-4472
                          Fax: 360-576-7012
aitken@flowerfantasy.net
www.flowerfantasy.net

Wide variety of award-winning irises and orchids

President: J T Aitken
Credit Cards: AMEX; MasterCard
Catalog Cost: $4
Catalog Circulation: Mailed 1 time(s) per year
Printing Information: 48 pages in 1 color on Glossy Stock
Binding: Saddle Stitched
Mailing List Information: Names for rent
In Business: 45 years
Number of Employees: 2
Sales Volume: $500M

3080 Aloha Tropicals
Aloha Tropicals
PO Box 6042
Oceanside, CA 92054   760-631-2880
                          Fax: 760-631-2880
alohatrop@aol.com
www.alohatropicals.com

Exotic trees, tropical plants and flowers

President: Andrew Zuckwich
Credit Cards: AMEX; MasterCard
Catalog Cost: $5
In Business: 18 years
Sales Volume: $230,000

3081 Amador Flower Farm
Amador Flower Farm
22001 Shenandoah School Rd
Plymouth, CA 95669-9526   209-245-6660
                          Fax: 209-245-6648
daylilies@daylilyfarm.com
www.amadorflowerfarm.com

Specializing in daylilies, unusual perennials and grasses, and gardening items

President: Ken Deaver
Owner: Jeanne Deaver
Owner: Mary Deaver
Credit Cards: AMEX; MasterCard; Visa
Catalog Cost: $3.5
Catalog Circulation: Mailed 1 time(s) per year
Printing Information: 28 pages in 4 colors on Glossy Stock
Mailing List Information: Names for rent
In Business: 20 years
Number of Employees: 8
Sales Volume: $310,000

3082 Amaryllis Bulb Company
Amaryllis & Caladium Bulb Company
1231 E Magnolia St
Lakeland, FL 33801   863-802-0001
                           888-966-9866
                          Fax: 863-683-8479
contact@amaryllisandcaladiumbulbco.com
www.amaryllis.com

Amaryllis plants and pots

President: Shirley Henry
Credit Cards: AMEX; MasterCard
Catalog Cost: Free
Catalog Circulation: Mailed 1 time(s) per year
Printing Information: 9 pages in 4 colors
In Business: 8 years
Number of Employees: 4
Sales Volume: $170,000

3083 American Daylily & Perennials
American Daylily & Perennials
P.O. Box 210
Grain Valley, MO 64029-9297   816-224-2852
                           800-770-2777
                          Fax: 816-443-2849
www.americandaylily.com

Daylilies, lantanas, cannas and more

President: Robert Robertson
Vice President: Jo Roberson
Accountant: Ladonna Clevinger
Catalog Cost: Free
In Business: 37 years
Sales Volume: $1MM

3084 Arrowhead Alpines

Arrowhead Alpines
1310 N Gregory Road
P.O. Box 857
Fowlerville, MI 48836   517-223-3581
Fax: 517-223-8750
www.arrowheadalpines.com

Rare perennial plants and seeds

President: Robert Stewart
Owner: Vargitta Stewart
Credit Cards: MasterCard
Catalog Cost:
Printing Information: 64 pages
In Business: 20 years
Number of Employees: 12
Sales Volume: $333,000

3085 Avant Gardens

Avant Gardens
710 High Hill Road
Dartmouth, MA 02747-1363   508-998-8819
Fax: 508-998-9405
plants@avantgardensne.com
www.avantgardensne.com

Unusual shrubs, annuals, perennials along with common plants, rock garden selections

President: P. Buss
Catalog Cost: $3
In Business: 5 years
Number of Employees: 2
Sales Volume: $65,000

3086 Big Apple Florist

Big Apple Florist Inc
228 E 45th Street
New York, NY 10017   212-687-3434
800-554-0001
Fax: 212-337-7822
comments@bigapplelorist.com
www.bigapplelorist.com

Arrangements of flowers by floral designers who have won awards

President: Marc Rothkopf
Credit Cards: AMEX; MasterCard
Catalog Circulation: Mailed 1 time(s) per year
Printing Information: 8 pages in 4 colors
Binding: Saddle Stitched
In Business: 69 years
Number of Employees: 17
Sales Volume: $3MM

3087 Bigelow Nurseries

Bigelow Nurseries, Inc.
455 W Main Street
P.O. Box 718
Northboro, MA 01532-0718   508-845-2143
Fax: 508-842-9245
cs@bigelownurseries.com
www.bigelownurseries.com

Fruits, berries and nuts

President: Pat Bigelow
pat@bigelownurseries.com
Production Manager: Brad Bigelow
bbigelow@bigelownurseries.com
General Manager: Jay Flanigan
jay@bigelownurseries.com
Sales Manager: Jeff Dragon
jdragon@bigelownurseries.com
Catalog Cost: Free
Catalog Circulation: Mailed 1 time(s) per year
In Business: 102 years
Number of Employees: 35
Sales Volume: $50MM

3088 Blake Nursery Catalog

Blake Nursery
316 Otter Creek Rd
Big Timber, MT 59011   406-932-4195
Fax: 406-932-4193
info@blakenursery.com
www.blakenursery.com

Large selection of plants, many montana natives

President: Francis Blake
Retail Manager: Meghan Fenoglio
Maintenance Manager: Nora Melius
Landscape Foreman: Dave Melius
Catalog Cost: Free
In Business: 38 years
Number of Employees: 3
Sales Volume: $220,000

3089 Blossom Flower Shop

Blossom Flower Shop
275 Mamaroneck Ave
White Plains, NY 10605-4105   914-304-5374
888-415-0019
Fax: 914-237-3213
sales@blossomflower.com
www.Blossomflower.Com

Flowers, fruits and gourmet baskets

President: Kevin Kegan
Credit Cards: AMEX; MasterCard; Visa
Catalog Circulation: Mailed 24 time(s) per year
Printing Information: 6 pages in 4 colors
In Business: 90 years
Number of Employees: 20
Sales Volume: $500,000

3090 Bluestone Perennials

Bluestone Perennials
7211 Middle Ridge Road
Madison, OH 44057   800-852-5243
Fax: 800-852-5243
service@bluestoneperennials.com
www.bluestoneperennials.com

Perennial plants

President: Bill Boonstra
Credit Cards: AMEX; MasterCard; Visa
Catalog Cost: Free
Catalog Circulation: Mailed 1 time(s) per year
Printing Information: 72 pages in 4 colors on Glossy Stock
Press: Web Press
Binding: Saddle Stitched
Mailing List Information: Names for rent
In Business: 45 years
Number of Employees: 60
Sales Volume: $10MM

3091 Bob Wells Nursery

Bob Wells Nursery
17160 CR 4100
Lindale, TX 75771   903-882-3550
Fax: 903-882-8030
bobwellsnursery@gmail.com
www.bobwellsnursery.com

Citrus, shade, fruit and nut trees

President: Bob Wells
Credit Cards: MasterCard; Visa
Catalog Cost: Free
In Business: 38 years
Number of Employees: 4
Sales Volume: $190,000

3092 Bountiful Gardens

Ecology Action of the Mid-Peninsula
1712-D South Main Street
Willitts, CA 95490-4400   707-459-6410
Fax: 707-459-1925
www.bountifulgardens.org

Seeds, flowers, herbs, vegetables, tools, books and supplies

Chairman: Alejandro Glenn
President: John Jeavons
Head: Ed Glenn
Catalog Cost: Free
Catalog Circulation: Mailed 12 time(s) per year
Printing Information: in 4 colors
In Business: 30 years
Number of Employees: 15
Sales Volume: $1.44MM

3093 Bovees Nursery

The Bovees Nursery
1737 SW Coronado St
Portland, OR 97219-7654   503-244-9341
866-652-3219
info@bovees.com
www.bovees.com

Species and hybrid rhododendrons, semi tropical

President: Lucie Sorensen-Smith
Companion Plant Propagator: Janice Palmer
Customer Service: E. White Smith
Credit Cards: MasterCard; Visa
Catalog Cost: Free
Printing Information: 44 pages in 1 color
In Business: 62 years
Number of Employees: 3
Sales Volume: $50K

3094 Breck's Bulbs

Breck's
PO Box 65
Guilford, IN 47022-4180   513-354-1511
Fax: 513-354-1505
www.brecks.com

Dutch flower bulbs

Credit Cards: AMEX; MasterCard
Catalog Cost: Free
Printing Information: 52 pages in 4 colors
In Business: 196 years
Number of Employees: 850

3095 Brown's Omaha Plant Farms

Brown's Omaha Plant Farms
110 McLean Ave
PO Box 787
Omaha, TX 75571   903-884-2421
Fax: 903-884-2423
mail@bopf.com
www.bopf.com

Onion plants

President: Jim D Brown
Marketing Manager: Greg Brown
Catalog Cost: Free
Catalog Circulation: Mailed 1 time(s) per year
Printing Information: 4 pages in 1 color on Matte Stock
Press: Web Press
Binding: Saddle Stitched
Mailing List Information: Names for rent
In Business: 75 years
Number of Employees: 16
Sales Volume: $860M

3096 Brussel's Bonsai Nursery

Brussel's Bonsai Nursery
8125 Center Hill Road
Olive Branch, MS 38654   800-582-2593
Fax: 662-895-4157
service@brusselsbonsai.com
www.brusselsbonsai.com

Bonsai trees and nursery

President: Brussel Martin
Production Manager: Dana Quattlebaum
Number of Employees: 24
Sales Volume: $2 Million

3097 Burgess Seed and Plant Company

Burgess Seed and Plant Company
1804 E Hamilton Road
Bloomington, IL 61704-9609   309-662-7761
customercare@eburgess.com
www.eburgess.com

Fruits, berries, nuts, vegetable seeds, trees, perennials and plants

President: Richard Owen
Credit Cards: MasterCard
Catalog Cost:
Catalog Circulation: Mailed 3 time(s) per year
Average Order Size: $48
Printing Information: 39 pages in 4 colors on Newsprint

Binding: Saddle Stitched
Mailing List Information: Names for rent
In Business: 103 years
Sales Volume: $10MM to $20MM

3098 Burnt Ridge Nursery
Burnt Ridge Orchards, Inc.
432 Burnt Ridge Road
Onalaska, WA 98570-9446   360-985-2873
Fax: 360-985-0882
mail@burntridgenursery.com
www.burntridgenursery.com

Disease resistant trees and vines that produce edible fruits and nuts; Ornamental & useful trees and shrubs such as dogwoods and bamboo; Northwest natives

President: Michael Dolan
Marketing Manager: Carolyn Cerling-Dolan
Catalog Cost: Free
Catalog Circulation: Mailed 1 time(s) per year to 40000
Average Order Size: $150
Printing Information: 40 pages on Newsprint
Press: Sheetfed Press
Binding: Saddle Stitched
In Business: 35 years
Number of Employees: 4
Sales Volume: 700,000

3099 Bustani Plant Farm
Bustani Plant Farm
1313 East 44th Avenue
Stillwater, OK 74074   405-372-3379
Fax: 405-707-8697
info@bustaniplantfarm.com
www.bustaniplantfarm.com

Perennials, annuals, trees and shrubs, Some tropical color plants

President: Steve Owens
steve@bustaniplantfarm.com
Co-Owner: Steve Owens
steve@bustaniplantfarm.com
Co-Owner: Ruth Owens
ruth@bustaniplantfarm.com
Catalog Cost: Free
Printing Information: 48 pages
In Business: 3 years
Number of Employees: 2
Sales Volume: $50,000

3100 Caladium World
Caladium World
PO Box 629
Sebring, FL 33871-629   863-385-7661
Fax: 863-385-5836
sales@caladiumworld.com
www.caladiumworld.com

Quality Caladiums and Elephant Ear bulbs shipped direct to the homeowner

President: LE Selph
Credit Cards: MasterCard
Catalog Cost: Free
Catalog Circulation: Mailed 1 time(s) per year
Printing Information: 1 pages in 4 colors on Glossy Stock
Binding: Folded
Mailing List Information: Names for rent
In Business: 31 years
Number of Employees: 8
Sales Volume: $499,000

3101 Calyx Flowers
Calyx Flowers
6655 Shelburne Road
Shelburne, VT 05482   802-985-3001
800-800-7788
Fax: 802-985-1304
business@calyxflowers.com
www.calyxflowers.com

Fresh flowers

Marketing Manager: Irene Steiner
Credit Cards: AMEX; MasterCard
Catalog Cost: Free

Catalog Circulation: Mailed 6 time(s) per year
Printing Information: 32 pages in 4 colors on Glossy Stock
Binding: Saddle Stitched
In Business: 11 years
Number of Employees: 50

3102 Camellia Forest Nursery
Camellia Forest Nursery
620 Hwy 54 West
Chapel Hill, NC 27516   919-968-0504
Fax: 919-929-8971
camelliaforest@gmail.com
www.camforest.com

Mail order nursery specializing in Camellias as well as unusual trees and shrubs from Asia

President: Kai-Mei Parks
Credit Cards: MasterCard
Catalog Cost: Free
Catalog Circulation: Mailed 1 time(s) per year to 8000
Average Order Size: $100
Printing Information: 48 pages on Matte Stock
Press: Web Press
Binding: Saddle Stitched
Mailing List Information: Names for rent
In Business: 30 years
Number of Employees: 3
Sales Volume: $200,000

3103 Canadian Gardening Catalogue
Gardenimport.com
135 W Beaver Creek Road
Box 760
Richmond Hill, CN L4B 1   905-731-1950
800-339-8314
Fax: 905-731-3093

Bulbs, plants, vines and shrubs, sutton seeds

President: Duglad Cameron
Credit Cards: MasterCard; Visa
Catalog Cost: $5
Catalog Circulation: Mailed 2 time(s) per year
Printing Information: 48 pages
In Business: 30 years

3104 Canyon Creek Nursery
Plants Delight Nursery Inc
9241 Sauls Road
Raleigh, NC 27603-9113   919-772-4794
Fax: 919-662-0370
office@plantdelights.com
www.plantdelights.com/

Uncommon perennials

President: John Whittlesey
Business Manager: Heather Brameyer
Chief Admin Officer and Co-Owner: Anita Avent
Co-Owner: Tony Avent
Catalog Cost: $2
Catalog Circulation: Mailed 1 time(s) per year
Printing Information: 30 pages in 1 color
In Business: 27 years
Number of Employees: 2
Sales Volume: Under $500M

3105 Chestnut Hill Nursery
Chestnut Hill Tree Farm
15105 NW 94th Ave
Alachua, FL 32615-6709   386-462-2820
800-669-2067
Fax: 386-462-4330
chestnuthillnursery@gmail.com
www.chestnuthilltreefarm.com

Wholesale trees

President: Deborag Gaw
E-Business: Jolene King
Credit Cards: AMEX; MasterCard; Visa
Catalog Cost: Free
Catalog Circulation: Mailed 1 time(s) per year to 20M
Printing Information: 20 pages in 4 colors on Matte Stock

Mailing List Information: Names for rent
In Business: 14 years
Number of Employees: 14
Sales Volume: $950,000

3106 Clematis Specialty Nursery
Clematis Specialty Nursery
217 Argilla Road
Ipswich, MA 01938-2617   978-356-3197
Fax: 978-356-3197
info@clematisnursery.com
www.clematisnursery.com

Over 200 unusual and hard-to-find varieties small and large flowered, in pots

President: Austin Fusan
Catalog Cost: $3
Printing Information: 33 pages
In Business: 32 years

3107 Cloud Mountain Farm Center
Cloud Mountain Farm Center
6906 Goodwin Road
Everson, WA 98247   360-966-5859
Fax: 360-966-0921
info@cloudmountainfarmcenter.org
www.cloudmountainfarmcenter.org

Fruit trees, berries and ornamental plants, including natives, educational programs

Production Manager: Mark Thompson
Executive Director: Thomas Thornton
Catalog Cost: $2
Printing Information: 48 pages on Newsprint
Press: Web Press
In Business: 39 years
Number of Employees: 12
Sales Volume: $900,000

3108 Comstock, Ferre & Company
Baker Creek Heirloom seed Co.
2278 Baker Creek Road
Mansfield, MO 65704-1890   417-924-8917
860-571-6590
Fax: 417-924-8887
seeds@rareseeds.com
www.rareseeds.com

Quality vegetable, flower and herb seeds

President: Pierre Bennerup
Manager: Steve Hale
Credit Cards: AMEX; MasterCard
Catalog Cost: Free
Catalog Circulation: Mailed 1 time(s) per year
Average Order Size: $20
Printing Information: 212 pages in 1 color on Newsprint
Mailing List Information: Names for rent
In Business: 200 years
Number of Employees: 10
Sales Volume: $860,000

3109 Connell's Dahlias
K Connell Dahlias
10616 Waller Rd E
Tacoma, WA 98446-2231   253-620-0044
Fax: 253-536-7725
kercon6@msn.com
www.Connells-Dahlias.Com

Pom pons, waterlilies, dahlias, split petals and seeds

President: Kerry Connell
kercon6@msn.com
Catalog Cost: $2
Catalog Circulation: Mailed 1 time(s) per year
Average Order Size: $45
Printing Information: 28 pages in 4 colors on Glossy Stock
Binding: Folded
Mailing List Information: Names for rent
In Business: 35 years
Number of Employees: 6
Sales Volume: $1MM to $3MM

3110 Cricket Hill Garden
Cricket Hill Garden
670 Walnut Hill Road
Thomaston, CT 06787-1136   860-283-1042
www.treepeony.com

Chinese tree peonies, 50 varieties, Chinese herbaeous peonies

President: Kasha Furman
Co-Founder: David Furman
Credit Cards: AMEX; MasterCard
Catalog Cost: Free
Catalog Circulation: Mailed 1 time(s) per year to 10M
Average Order Size: $100
Printing Information: 16 pages in 4 colors on Glossy Stock
Press: Web Press
Binding: Saddle Stitched
Mailing List Information: Names for rent
In Business: 28 years
Sales Volume: $1MM to $3MM

3111 David Austin Handbook of Roses
David Austin Roses
15059 Highway 64 West
Tyler, TX 75704   800-328-8893
us@davidaustinroses.com
www.davidaustinroses.com

Roses over 50 varieties containing english roses, plus a wide range of interesting and unusual old fashioned, shurb, climing, and hybrid tea roses

President: David Austin II
Founder: David Austin
Credit Cards: AMEX; MasterCard; Visa
Catalog Cost: Free
Catalog Circulation: Mailed 1 time(s) per year
Average Order Size: $74
Printing Information: 80 pages in 7 colors on Glossy Stock
Binding: Folded
Mailing List Information: Names for rent
Number of Employees: 100
Sales Volume: 1,000,000

3112 Davidson Greenhouse & Nursery
Davidson Greenhouse & Nursery
3147 E Ladoga Rd
Crawfordsville, IN 47933   765-364-0556
877-723-6834
Fax: 800-276-3691
vicki@davidsongreenhouse.com
www.Davidsongreenhouse.Com

Scented geraniums, begonias, and impatiens; houseplants, herbs, and succulents

President: Mark Davidson
Credit Cards: AMEX; MasterCard; Visa
Catalog Cost: $3
Catalog Circulation: Mailed 1 time(s) per year to 11M
Average Order Size: $60
Printing Information: 40 pages in 4 colors on Glossy Stock
Press: Web Press
Binding: Saddle Stitched
Mailing List Information: Names for rent
In Business: 21 years
Number of Employees: 10
Sales Volume: $1MM to $3MM

3113 Digging Dog Nursery
Digging Dog Nursery
31101 Middle Ridge Rd.
Albion, CA 95410   707-937-1130
Fax: 707-937-2480
business@diggingdog.com
www.diggingdog.com

Perennials, trees, vines, shrubs, grasses, t-shirts and gifts

Fulfillment: Cherie Koss Waldo
Propagation Specialist: Lynn Chrysler
Nursery Care: Carol Clary
Mail-order Coordinator: Jessica Alexis

Friedland
Credit Cards: AMEX; MasterCard
Catalog Cost: $4
In Business: 20 years

3114 Direct Gardening
Direct Gardening
1704 Morrissey Drive
Bloomington, IL 61704-9249   309-662-7943
customercare@directgardening.com
www.directgardening.com

Roses, bulbs, perennials and ornamentals

President: Richard Owen
Credit Cards: MasterCard
Catalog Cost: $1.5
Sales Volume: $20MM to $50MM

3115 Donahue's Greenhouse
Donahue's Greenhouse
420 SW 10th Street
PO Box 366
Fairbault, MN 55021   507-334-8404
Fax: 507-334-0485
knass@donahuesgreenhouse.com
www.donahuesgreenhouse.com

Chrysanthemums

President: Kathy Donahue Nass
Credit Cards: MasterCard
Catalog Cost: Free
Catalog Circulation: to 1000
Printing Information: 3 pages in 1 color
In Business: 32 years
Number of Employees: 25

3116 Double A Vineyards
Double A Vineyards
10277 Christy Road
Fredonia, NY 14063   716-672-8493
Fax: 716-679-3442
www.doubleavineyards.com

Various types of grapevines, berries and rhubarb plants, books and accessories.

3117 Dutch Gardens
Dutch Gardens
144 Intervale Rd
Burlington, VT 05401-2804   802-863-1700
800-944-2250
Fax: 802-660-3501
www.dutchgardens.com

Flowers

President: Leo Vandervlugt
Credit Cards: AMEX; MasterCard
Sales Volume: $500M to $1MM

3118 Earthly Pursuits
Earthly Pursuits, Inc.
2901 Kuntz Road
Windsor Mill, MD 21244-1106   410-496-2523
Fax: 410-496-5894
mail@earthlypursuits.net
www.Earthlypursuits.Net

Large selection of ornamental grasses, perennials, ferns and bamboo

President: Monika Burwell
Credit Cards: AMEX; MasterCard
Printing Information: 50 pages on Matte Stock
Press: Web Press
Binding: Saddle Stitched
In Business: 46 years
Number of Employees: 2
Sales Volume: $400,000

3119 Eden Organic Nursery Services
E.O.N.S. Inc
P.O. Box 4604
Hallandale, FL 33008   954-382-8281
Fax: 954-382-8280
info@eonseed.com
www.eonseed.com

Gardening accessories and supplies, herbs and pure plant extracts, vines, tropicals, pest control

President: Anne V Foss
Marketing Manager: Anne V Foss
In Business: 20 years
Number of Employees: 3

3120 Edible Landscaping
Edible Landscaping
361 Spirit Ridge Lane
Afton, VA 22920   434-361-9134
Fax: 434-361-1916
info@ediblelandscaping.com
www.ediblelandscaping.com

Low maintenance edibles for your yard or garden, including kiwi, black currants, gooseberries, oriental persimmons, mulberries, jujubi, pawpaw, citrus, bush cherries, plums, and pears, figs

President: Michael McConkey
Marketing Manager: Michael McConkey
Fulfillment: Janet Dickie
Credit Cards: AMEX; MasterCard
Catalog Cost: $2
Catalog Circulation: Mailed 12 time(s) per year to 50000
Average Order Size: $100
Printing Information: 32 pages on Glossy Stock
Press: Web Press
Binding: Saddle Stitched
Mailing List Information: Names for rent
In Business: 38 years
Number of Employees: 8
Sales Volume: $1MM to $3MM

3121 Edmunds' Roses
Edmund Roses
335 S. High St
Randolph, WI 53956-9727   888-481-7673
www.edmundsroses.com

Large selection of modern hybrid tea, floribunda, grandiflora and climbing roses

President: Philip Edmunds
CFO: Kathy Edmunds
Credit Cards: MasterCard; Visa
Catalog Cost: Free
Catalog Circulation: Mailed 1 time(s) per year
Average Order Size: $90
Printing Information: 48 pages in 4 colors on Glossy Stock
Press: Web Press
Mailing List Information: Names for rent
In Business: 55 years
Number of Employees: 4
Sales Volume: $500M to $1MM

3122 Exotic Houseplants
Lynn Mckameys usual palms & Exotic Plant
PO Box 287
Gregory, TX 78359-287   361-643-2061
www.rarepalms.com

Rare, exotic houseplants, Japanese pottery and bonsai books

President: Lynn McKamey
Credit Cards: MasterCard; Visa
Catalog Cost: $2
Catalog Circulation: to 5M
Printing Information: 10 pages in 1 color
Number of Employees: 7
Sales Volume: $1MM to $3MM

3123 Farmer Seed & Nursery Company
Farmer Seed & Nursery
818 NW 4th Street
Faribault, MN 55021   507-334-1623
customercare@farmerseed.com
www.farmerseed.com

Vegetables, seeds, plants, trees and bulbs

President: Greg Mews
Credit Cards: MasterCard
Catalog Cost: Free

Catalog Circulation: Mailed 4 time(s) per year
Printing Information: 44 pages in 4 colors
In Business: 130 years
Number of Employees: 35
Sales Volume: $10MM to $20MM

3124 Fieldstone Gardens

Fieldstone Gardens
55 Quaker Ln
Vassalboro, ME 04989-3816   207-923-3836
                                    Fax: 207-923-3836
sales@fieldstonegardens.com
www.fieldstonegardens.com

Perennial plants, rock and garden plants siberian iris, asters, astible, campanulas, clematis, delphiniums, epimediums, hardy geraniums, herbaceous peonies, phlox and more

President: Steven Jones
Marketing Manager: Karen Mitchell
General Manager: Bob Milano
bob@fieldstonegardens.com
Credit Cards: MasterCard
Catalog Cost: $2.5
Catalog Circulation: Mailed 1 time(s) per year
Printing Information: 48 pages in 4 colors on Matte Stock
Press: Web Press
Binding: Saddle Stitched
Mailing List Information: Names for rent
In Business: 31 years
Number of Employees: 6
Sales Volume: $1MM to $3MM

3125 Flickinger's Nursery

Flickinger's Nursery
PO Box 245
Sagamore, PA 16250   724-783-6528
                             800-368-7381
                        Fax: 724-783-6528
www.flicknursery.com

Pines, spruce, fir, hemlock seedlings and transplants, free professional advice

President: Tom Flickinger
Credit Cards: MasterCard
Catalog Cost: Free
Catalog Circulation: Mailed 1 time(s) per year to 6000
Average Order Size: $200
Printing Information: 15 pages in 4 colors on Glossy Stock
Press: Web Press
Binding: Saddle Stitched
Mailing List Information: Names for rent
In Business: 68 years
Number of Employees: 12
Sales Volume: $499,000

3126 Foliage Gardens

Foliage Gardens
2003 128th Avenue SE
Bellevue, WA 98005   425-747-2998
                        Fax: 425-643-6886
foliageg@juno.com
www.foliagegardens.com

Spore grown ferns, Japanese maples

President: Sue Olson
Catalog Cost: $2
Printing Information: 12 pages
In Business: 48 years

3127 Forestfarm Catalog

Forest Farm At Pacifica
14643 Watergap Road
Williams, OR 97544   541-846-7269
                        Fax: 541-846-6963
plants@forestfarm.com
www.forestfarm.com

Hardy ornamental plants

President: Ray Prag
Marketing Manager: Jen Hardin-Tietjen
jen@forestfarm.com
Credit Cards: MasterCard
Catalog Cost: $5

Catalog Circulation: Mailed 2 time(s) per year to 80M
Printing Information: 250 pages in 1 color on Newsprint
Press: Web Press
Binding: Perfect Bound
In Business: 41 years
Number of Employees: 18
Sales Volume: Under $500M

3128 Four Season's Nursery

Four Season's Nursery
1706 Morrisey Drive
Bloomington, IL 61704   309-834-7200
customercare@4seasonsnurseries.com
www.4seasonsnurseries.com

Perrenials, seeds, ornamentals, bulbs, container pots, hedges, herbs, fruit and nut trees

Credit Cards: MasterCard
Catalog Cost: Free
In Business: 41 years
Number of Employees: 5

3129 Freedom Tree Farms

Freedom Tree Farms
PO Box 69
Pelham, TN 37366-69   931-467-3600
                             800-222-3062
                        Fax: 931-467-3062
info@freedomtreefarms.com
www.freedomtreefarms.com

Fruit trees, shade trees and ornamental trees

President: Dale Bryan
Catalog Circulation: Mailed 1 time(s) per year to 3000
Average Order Size: $1500
Printing Information: 8 pages in 2 colors on Glossy Stock
Press: Letterpress
Binding: Folded
Mailing List Information: Names for rent
In Business: 17 years
Number of Employees: 34

3130 G&B Orchid Laboratory

Orchid Source Laboratory & Nursing
2426 Cherimoya Drive
Vista, CA 92084-7812   760-727-2611
                        Fax: 760-727-0017
orchidsource@gmail.com
www.orchidsource.com

Phalaenopsis, cymbidium, dendrobium and species orchids

President: Barry Cohen
Credit Cards: AMEX; MasterCard
Catalog Cost: $1
Number of Employees: 5
Sales Volume: Under $500M

3131 Gardens of the Blue Ridge

Gardens of the Blue Ridge
PO Box 10
9056 Pittmans Gap Rd
Newland, NC 28662-10   828-733-2417
                        Fax: 828-733-8894
Contact@gardensoftheblueridge.com
www.gardensoftheblueridge.com

Wildflowers, ferns, orchids and native shrubs & trees

President: Katy R Fletcher
Marketing Manager: Paul Fletcher
Production Manager: Robyn Fletcher
Credit Cards: AMEX; MasterCard
Catalog Cost: $3
Catalog Circulation: Mailed 1 time(s) per year to 3M
Average Order Size: $70
Printing Information: 32 pages in 4 colors on Glossy Stock
Press: Letterpress
Binding: Folded
Mailing List Information: Names for rent
In Business: 118 years

Number of Employees: 4
Sales Volume: Under $500M

3132 Gary's Perennials

Gary's Perennials
1122 E Welsh Rd
Maple Glen, PA 19002   215-628-4070
                             800-898-6653
                        Fax: 215-628-0216
roots@garysperennials.com
www.garysperennials.com

Wholesale fieldgrown perennials with heavy root systems including: Asarum, Astilbe, Coreopsis, Ferns, Ornamental Grasses, Hemerocallis, Hosta, Iris, Liriope, Natives, Wetland Plants and more

President: Gary Steinberg
Marketing Manager: Andrea Steinberg
Production Manager: Andrea Steinberg
Credit Cards: MasterCard
Catalog Cost: Free
Catalog Circulation: Mailed 1 time(s) per year to 4000
Average Order Size: $1000
Printing Information: 20 pages in 4 colors on Glossy Stock
Press: Letterpress
Binding: Perfect Bound
Mailing List Information: Names for rent
In Business: 35 years
Number of Employees: 4
Sales Volume: $500,000 to $1,000,000

3133 Gilbert H Wild & Son

Gilbert H Wild & Son
2944 State Highway 37
Reeds, MO 64859   417-548-3514
                        Fax: 417-548-6831
www.gilberthwild.com

Daylilies, peonies and iris and bare root plants

President: Greg Jones
Credit Cards: AMEX; MasterCard
Catalog Cost:
Catalog Circulation: Mailed 1 time(s) per year to 55M
Average Order Size: $78
Printing Information: 52 pages in 2 colors on Matte Stock
Press: Web Press
Binding: Perfect Bound
Mailing List Information: Names for rent
List Company: ZED Marketing
In Business: 130 years
Number of Employees: 65
Sales Volume: $1MM to $3MM

3134 Going Bananas

Going Bananas
24401 SW 197 Ave
Homestead, FL 33031   305-247-0397
                        Fax: 305-247-7877
goingbananas@bellsouth.net
www.going-bananas.com

Banana plants

President: Katie Chafin
Catalog Cost: $1
Printing Information: 8 pages
In Business: 5 years
Sales Volume: $500M to $1MM

3135 Greenleaf Nursery Company

Greenleaf Nursery Company
28406 Highway 82
Park Hill, OK 74451-2845   918-457-5172
                                  800-331-2982
                             Fax: 918-457-5550
www.Greenleafnursery.Com

Shrubs, flowers, trees and more

President: Randy Davis
Marketing Manager: Larry Ahrens
Credit Cards: MasterCard; Visa
Printing Information: 92 pages in 4 colors
In Business: 30 years

Number of Employees: 600
Sales Volume: $20MM to $50MM

3136 Greenwood Daylily Gardens

Greenwood Daylily Gardens, Inc.
8000 Balcom Canyon Rd
Somis, CA 93066-2107
562-494-8944
Fax: 562-494-0486
info@greenwoodgarden.com
www.greenwooddaylily.com

Daylilies, Irises, Cannas and Geraniums

President: John Schoustra
Credit Cards: MasterCard
Catalog Cost: Free
Catalog Circulation: Mailed 1 time(s) per year
to 8M
Printing Information: 20 pages in 4 colors on
Glossy Stock
Press: Sheetfed Press
Binding: Folded
Mailing List Information: Names for rent
In Business: 16 years
Sales Volume: $1MM to $3MM

3137 Grimes Seeds

Grimes
11335 Concord Hambden Rd
Concord, OH 44077-9704
440-352-3333
800-241-7333
Fax: 440-352-1800
info@grimes-hort.com
www.grimesseeds.com

Seeds and plants

President: Rod LeDrew
Production Manager: Matt Gasper
CEO: Gary Grimes
VP: Rod LeDrew
Sales Director: Bill Watson
In Business: 74 years
Sales Volume: $20MM to $50MM

3138 Growbiz-Abco

Growbiz
1782 Heathrow Drive - N
Cookeville, TN 38506-3738
931-528-8539
rphillips@growbiz-abco.com
www.growbiz-abco.com

Grow expensive plants at home

President: Roy Phillips

3139 Growing Supplies

Violet Showcase
P. O. Box 300091
Denver, CO 80203-91
303-761-1770
Fax: 303-762-1808
www.violetshowcase.com

African violets

Catalog Cost: $2
Catalog Circulation: to 1000
Printing Information: 34 pages in 2 colors on
Matte Stock
Press: Letterpress
Binding: Folded
In Business: 45 years
Number of Employees: 3
Sales Volume: Under $500M

3140 Guide to Deer-Resistant Plants

Deer-Resistant Landscape Nursery
3200 Sunstone Ct.
Clare, MI 48617
800-595-3650
sales@deerxlandscape.com
www.deerresistantplants.com

Deer-resistant plants, deer repellents and deer fencing.

President: David Jensen
Catalog Cost: $3.85
In Business: 16 years
Number of Employees: 3
Sales Volume: $43K

3141 Hartman's Herb Farm

Hartman's Herb Farm
1026 Old Dana Rd
Barre, MA 01005-9445
978-355-2015
Fax: 978-355-0162
hartmansherb@hotmail.com
www.Hartmansherbfarm.Com

Herb and scented plants, dried flower crafts

President: Carissa Hartman
CFO: Lynn Hartman
Marketing Manager: Carissa Hartman
Production Manager: Carissa Hartman
Catalog Circulation: to 15000
Printing Information: 16 pages in 4 colors on
Matte Stock
Press: Offset Press
Binding: Folded
In Business: 58 years
Number of Employees: 3
Sales Volume: Under $500M

3142 Hawaii's Flowers Catalog

Island Tropicals
310 Ululani Street
PO Box 1601
Hilo, HI 96720-1546
808-961-0606
800-367-5155
Fax: 808-966-7684
www.islandtropicals.com

Hawaiian tropical flowers

President: Mike Goldstein
Marketing Manager: Mike Goldstein
Credit Cards: AMEX; MasterCard
Catalog Cost: Free
Catalog Circulation: to 150
Average Order Size: $40
Printing Information: 2 pages in 4 colors on
Glossy Stock
Press: Sheetfed Press
Binding: Folded
Mailing List Information: Names for rent
Will Trade Names: Yes
In Business: 48 years
Number of Employees: 4
Sales Volume: Under $500M

3143 Heirloom Roses

Heirloom Roses
24062 NE Riverside Drive
St Paul, OR 97137-9715
503-538-1576
800-820-0465
Fax: 503-538-5902
info@heirloomroses.com
www.heirloomroses.com

Old garden roses, David Austin English, landscape, ground cover, modern shrubs and hybrid tea roses, Heirloom's own hybrids, climbers, miniature roses

President: Louise Clements
General Manager: Cheryl Malone
Owners: Ben Hanna
Credit Cards: MasterCard; Visa
Catalog Cost:
Printing Information: 68 pages in 4 colors

3144 Heronswood Nursery

Heronswood
31912 Little Boston Rd NE
Kingston, WA 98346
360-297-4172
Fax: 360-297-8321
Heronswoodgardens@gmail.com
www.heronswood.com

Rare and unusual plants, perennials, grasses, shrubs and trees

Chairman: Jeromy Sullivan
CFO: Robert Jones
Marketing Manager: Robert Jones
Production Manager: Robert Jones
Garden Director: Daniel Hinkley
Garden Manager & Head Gardener: Celia Pedersen
Gardener Assistant: Bernie Folz
Catalog Cost: $5
Catalog Circulation: Mailed 1 time(s) per year

to 40000
Printing Information: 250 pages in 2 colors on
Glossy Stock
Press: Letterpress
Binding: Perfect Bound
Mailing List Information: Names for rent
In Business: 26 years
Number of Employees: 30

3145 High Country Gardens

High Country Gardens
223 Ave D
Suite 30
Williston, VT 05495
505-438-3031
800-925-9387
Fax: 505-438-9552
plants@highcountrygardens.com
www.Highcountrygardens.Com

Ornamental grasses, perennials, bulbs, groundcovers, tulips, alliums, crocus and muscari

President: David Salman
Marketing Manager: Ava Salman
Production Manager: David Salman
Catalog Circulation: to 10000
Average Order Size: $72
Printing Information: 83 pages in 7 colors
Press: Web Press
Mailing List Information: Names for rent
List Company: Millard Group
In Business: 31 years
Number of Employees: 3
Sales Volume: $500M to $1MM

3146 High Country Roses

High Country Roses
9122 E Highway 40
PO Box 148
Jensen, UT 84035
435-789-3371
800-552-2082
Fax: 435-789-5517
www.highcountryroses.com

Hardy roses including antique old garden roses, shrub and species roses

President: Day Delahunt
Credit Cards: MasterCard
Catalog Cost: Free
Catalog Circulation: Mailed 1 time(s) per year
to 6000
Printing Information: 24 pages in 4 colors on
Matte Stock
Press: Web Press
Mailing List Information: Names for rent
In Business: 43 years
Number of Employees: 5
Sales Volume: $160,000

3147 Hilltop Nurseries

Hilltop Fruit Trees
PO Box 578
Hartford, MI 49057-578
616-621-3135
800-253-2911
Fax: 616-621-2062
adam@hilltopfruittrees.com
www.hilltopfruittrees.com

Fruit trees

Marketing Manager: Larry Polec
Catalog Cost: $5
In Business: 104 years

3148 House of Wesley

House of Wesley
1704 Morrissey Drive
Bloomington, IL 61704-7107
309-664-7334
customercare@houseofwesley.com
www.houseofwesley.com

Mosquito shoo geraniums, ground cover daylilies and hardy amur privets

President: Richard Owen
Credit Cards: MasterCard
Catalog Cost: Free
Catalog Circulation: Mailed 4 time(s) per year
Average Order Size: $40

Printing Information: 67 pages in 4 colors on Newsprint
Binding: Saddle Stitched
Mailing List Information: Names for rent
In Business: 40 years
Number of Employees: 5
Sales Volume: 10MM-20MM

3149 Hydrangeas Plus
Hydrangeas Plus
PO Box 389
Aurora, OR 97002-389   503-651-2887
                         866-433-7896
                Fax: 503-651-2648
            info@hydrangeasplus.com
            www.hydrangeasplus.com

Rare and unusual hydrangeas

Catalog Cost: $5
Catalog Circulation: Mailed 1 time(s) per year to 10000
Average Order Size: $50
Printing Information: 40 pages in 4 colors on Glossy Stock
Press: Web Press
Mailing List Information: Names for rent
In Business: 17 years
Number of Employees: 5
Sales Volume: Under $500M

3150 Indiana Berry & Plant Company
Indiana Berry
2811 US 31
Plymouth, IN 46563   800-295-2226
                Fax: 574-784-2468
            info@indianaberry.com
            www.indianaberry.com

Small fruit plants, strawberries, blueberries; gardening books; tools and supplies; gardening containers

Credit Cards: MasterCard
Catalog Cost: Free

3151 Intermountain Cactus
Intermountain Cactus
1478 Ewe Turn
Kaysville, UT 84037-1256   801-546-2006
            www.intermountaincactus.com

Cactus plants

President: Robert Johnson
In Business: 39 years

3152 Ison's Nursery & Vineyards
Ison's Nursery & Vineyards
6855 Newnan Road (GA Highway 16)
PO Box 190
Brooks, GA 30205   770-599-6970
                         800-733-0324
                Fax: 770-599-1727
                ison@isons.com
                www.isons.com

Fruit trees, nut trees, specialty fruits, flowering trees and muscadines

President: Janet McClure
CFO: Greg Ison
Marketing Manager: Kim Harris
Production Manager: Greg Ison
Credit Cards: MasterCard
Catalog Cost: Free
Catalog Circulation: to 40000
Average Order Size: $50
Printing Information: 32 pages in 4 colors on Glossy Stock
Press: Letterpress
Binding: Perfect Bound
Mailing List Information: Names for rent
List Manager: Darlene Evans
In Business: 80 years
Number of Employees: 12
Sales Volume: $5MM to $10MM

3153 Johnson Nursery Fruit Trees & Small Fruit
Johnson Nursery, Inc.
1352 Big Creek Road
Ellijay, GA 30536-4534   706-276-3187
                         888-276-3187
                Fax: 706-276-3186
            sales@johnsonnursery.com
            www.johnsonnursery.com

Hardy fruit trees with antique and disease-resistant varieties, apple, peach, plum, cherry, fig, grapes, berries, orchard supplies

President: Elisa S Ford
Marketing Manager: Elisa S Ford
Production Manager: Bill Ford
Catalog Cost: Free
Mailing List Information: Names for rent
In Business: 31 years
Number of Employees: 7
Sales Volume: Under $500M

3154 Joy Creek Nursery
Joy Creek
20300 NW Watson Road
Scappoose, OR 97056   503-543-7474
                Fax: 503-543-6933
            catalogue@joycreek.com
                www.joycreek.com

Unique and unusual perennials and native plants

President: Mike Smith
Marketing Manager: Maurice Horn
VP: Scott Christy
Catalog Cost: $4
Printing Information: 117 pages
In Business: 22 years
Number of Employees: 15
Sales Volume: $900,000

3155 Just Fruits and Exotics
Just Fruits and Exotics
30 Saint Frances St
Crawfordville, FL 32327-4257   850-926-5644
                            888-926-7441
                Fax: 850-926-9885
            justfruits@hotmail.com
            www.justfruitsandexotics.com/

Wide range of fruits, nuts and berries for zone and butterfly-garden plants; Many unique varieties like Olive, Mayhaw, and Jujuba; Exotic or ornamentals; Collection of ginger lilies

President: Roxanne Cowley
CFO: Ted Cowly-Gilbert
Production Manager: Vicki Thomas
Catalog Cost: $3
Catalog Circulation: to 3000
Average Order Size: $100
Printing Information: 42 pages in 1 color on Matte Stock
Binding: Folded
Mailing List Information: Names for rent
In Business: 19 years
Number of Employees: 6
Sales Volume: $500M to $1MM

3156 Keith Keppel
Keith Keppel Irises
PO Box 18154
Salem, OR 97305-8154   503-391-9241
            plicataman@earthlink.net
            www.keithkeppeliris.com

Bearded iris plants

President: Keith Keppel
Catalog Circulation: Mailed 1 time(s) per year to 1200
Printing Information: 24 pages on Matte Stock
Binding: Saddle Stitched

3157 Kelly Brothers Nurseries
Kelly Nurseries
410 8th Avenue NW
Faribault, MN 55021   507-334-1623
            customercare@kellynurseries.com
            www.kellynurseries.com

Bulbs, daylilies, roses, houseplants, perennials, shrubs and vegetables

President: Richard Owen
Credit Cards: MasterCard
Catalog Cost: Free
Catalog Circulation: to 40000
Average Order Size: $55
Printing Information: 60 pages in 4 colors on Matte Stock
Press: Rotogravure
Binding: Saddle Stitched
Mailing List Information: Names for rent
Number of Employees: 2
Sales Volume: $130,000

3158 King's Mums
King's Mums
14115 West 56th Street S
Sand Springs, OK 74063-8749   503-656-2078
                Fax: 562-502-4318
                mums@kingsmums.com
                www.kingsmums.com

Rooted chrysanthemum plants

President: Ray Gray
CFO: Kim Gray
Catalog Cost: $2
Catalog Circulation: Mailed 1 time(s) per year to 1000
Average Order Size: $60
Printing Information: 31 pages in 4 colors on Glossy Stock
Press: Letterpress
Binding: Saddle Stitched
In Business: 40 years
Number of Employees: 2
Sales Volume: $500,000

3159 Klehm's Song Sparrow Perennial Farm
Klehm's Song Sparrow
13101 East Rye Road
Avalon, WI 53505   608-883-2356
                         800-553-3715
                Fax: 608-883-2257
            info@songsparrow.com
            www.songsparrow.com

Klehm peonies, hemerocallis, hosta, Siberian iris and companion plants, woody ornamentals, and tree peonies

President: Roy G Klehm
Marketing Manager: Renee Jaeger
Production Manager: Renee Jaeger
Credit Cards: AMEX; MasterCard; Visa
Catalog Cost: Free
Catalog Circulation: Mailed 1 time(s) per year to 50M
Printing Information: 100 pages in 4 colors on Glossy Stock
Press: Web Press
Mailing List Information: Names for rent
List Manager: Roy Klehm
In Business: 30 years

3160 Lawyer Nursery
Lawyer Nursery
6625 Montana Highway 200
Plains, MT 59859   406-826-3881
                         800-551-9875
                Fax: 406-826-5700
            trees@lawyernursery.com
            www.lawyernursery.com

Bareroot woody plants

President: John Lawyer
Founder: David Lawyer
Founder: Esther Lawyer
Credit Cards: MasterCard
Catalog Cost: Free
Catalog Circulation: Mailed 1 time(s) per year to 8000

Average Order Size: $500
Printing Information: 64 pages in 1 color on Matte Stock
Press: Web Press
Binding: Saddle Stitched
Mailing List Information: Names for rent
In Business: 58 years
Number of Employees: 100
Sales Volume: $3MM to $5MM

3161 Lazy K Nursery
Lazy K Nursery Inc.
705 Wright Road
Pine Mountain, GA 31822-3012   706-663-4991
Fax: 706-663-0939
info@lazyknursery.com
www.lazyknursery.com

Native American Azaleas and companion plants

President: Ernest Koone, III
Catalog Cost: Free
Catalog Circulation: Mailed 1 time(s) per year
Printing Information: 8 pages
In Business: 57 years

3162 Lee's Gardens
Lee's Gardens
25986 Sauder Road
Tremont, IL 61568   309-925-5262
Fax: 309-925-5010
sales@leesgardens.com
www.leesgardens.com

Perennials, hostas, daylilies, wildflowers and shade plants

President: Janis Lee
Marketing Manager: Janis Lee
Credit Cards: MasterCard; Visa
Catalog Cost: $2
Catalog Circulation: Mailed 1 time(s) per year to 5000
Printing Information: 54 pages in 2 colors on Matte Stock
Binding: Saddle Stitched
Mailing List Information: Names for rent
In Business: 17 years
Number of Employees: 10-J
Sales Volume: Under $500M

3163 Lilypons Water Gardens
Lilypons Water Gardens
6800 Lily Pons Road
Adamstown, MD 21710   800-999-5459
www.lilypons.com

Water gardens featuring water lilies, pond liners, pumps, filters, fish and more

President: Margaret Thomas Koogle
Marketing Manager: Suzanne Boom
Fulfillment: David Hoffman
Vice President: Richard Koogle
Office Manager: Melissa Richard
Buyers: Rick Roscoe
Credit Cards: AMEX; MasterCard; Visa
Catalog Cost: Free
Catalog Circulation: Mailed 5 time(s) per year to 85000
Average Order Size: $100
Printing Information: 45 pages in 4 colors on Glossy Stock
Press: Web Press
Binding: Saddle Stitched
Mailing List Information: Names for rent
In Business: 100 years
Number of Employees: 15
Sales Volume: $1.7 Million

3164 Logee's Greenhouses
Logee's Greenhouses
141 North Street
Danielson, CT 06239   888-330-8038
info@logees.com
www.logees.com

Rare plants and herbs, tropicals and sub-tropicals

President: Byron Martin
Production Manager: Amy Miller
Operations Manager: Sham Elshakhs
Merchandise Manager: Sheryl Felty
Credit Cards: MasterCard; Visa
Catalog Cost: Free
Catalog Circulation: Mailed 5 time(s) per year to 200m
Average Order Size: $40
Printing Information: 110 pages in 4 colors on Glossy Stock
Press: Web Press
Binding: Saddle Stitched
Mailing List Information: Names for rent
List Company: George Mann & Associates
609-443-1330
In Business: 123 years
Number of Employees: 25
Sales Volume: $1.6 Million

3165 Louisiana Nursery
Louisiana Nursery
8680 Perkins Road
Baton Rouge, LA 7081   225-766-0300
Fax: 337-942-6404
contact@louisiananursery.com
www.louisiananursery.com/

Magnolias and other garden aristocrats

President: Ken Durio
Marketing Manager: Dalton Durio
Founder: Roger Mayes
Credit Cards: MasterCard; Visa
Catalog Cost: $6
Printing Information: 276 pages in 4 colors
In Business: 31 years
Number of Employees: 6
Sales Volume: $100,000

3166 Lyndon Lyon Greenhouses
Lyndon Lyon Greenhouses Inc
PO Box 249
Dolgeville, NY 13329-0249   315-429-8291
Fax: 315-429-3820
info@lyndonlyon.com
www.lyndonlyon.com

African violets and exotic houseplants

President: Paul Sorano
VP: Sidney Sarano
Owner/Hybridizer: Paul Sorano
Manager/Hybridizer: Debbie DiCamillo
Credit Cards: MasterCard; Visa
Catalog Cost: $3
Catalog Circulation: Mailed 1 time(s) per year to 2000
Average Order Size: $50
Printing Information: 22 pages in 4 colors on Glossy Stock
Press: Sheetfed Press
Binding: Saddle Stitched
Mailing List Information: Names for rent
In Business: 60 years
Number of Employees: 3
Sales Volume: $200,000

3167 Mary's Plant Farm
Mary's Plant Farm
2410 Lanes Mill Road
Hamilton, OH 45013   513-894-0022
Fax: 513-892-2053
marysplantfarm@zoomtown.com
www.marysplantfarm.com

Perennials, flowering trees, shrubs, daylily, iris, hosta, ferns, ivies, herbs, old roses, wild flowers, and native plants

President: Mary E Harrison
Co-Owner: Mary Harrison
Co-Owner: Sherri Berger
Catalog Cost: $3
Catalog Circulation: Mailed 1 time(s) per year to 500
Printing Information: 50 pages in 2 colors
Press: Letterpress
Binding: Folded
Mailing List Information: Names for rent
In Business: 30 years

Number of Employees: 8
Sales Volume: $500M to $1MM

3168 Michigan Bulb Company
Michigan Bulb Company
PO Box 4180
Lawrenceburg, IN 47025-4180   812-260-2148
Fax: 513-354-1499
www.michiganbulb.com

Bulbs, perennials, trees, vines, hedges and tools

Marketing Manager: Jennifer Castro
CEO: Niles Kinerk
Credit Cards: MasterCard
Catalog Cost: Free
Printing Information: in 4 colors
Number of Employees: 7
Sales Volume: $50 Million

3169 Mini-Edition Iris Lover's
Schreiner's Garden
3625 Quinaby Road NE
Salem, OR 97303   503-393-3232
800-525-2367
Fax: 503-393-5590
iris@schreinersgardens.com
www.schreinersgardens.com

Tall bearded and dwarf iris

President: David Schreiner
Marketing Manager: Tom Abregg
Credit Cards: MasterCard; Visa
Catalog Cost:
Catalog Circulation: Mailed 1 time(s) per year to 45M
Printing Information: 72 pages in 4 colors on Glossy Stock
Press: Sheetfed Press
Binding: Saddle Stitched
Mailing List Information: Names for rent
List Manager: David Schreiner
In Business: 92 years
Number of Employees: 35
Sales Volume: $20MM to $50MM

3170 Mischel's Greenhouses
Mischel's Greenhouses Ltd
11660 Arrowhead Drive
Williamsburg, MI 49690   231-264-5489
800-830-8447
Fax: 231-264-0289
customerservice@mischelsgreenhouses.com
www.mischelsgreenhouses.com

Flowers, plants, flower boxes, flower pots and hanging baskets, garden supplies

President: John Mischel
CFO: Rachel Mischel
Credit Cards: MasterCard
Catalog Cost: Free
In Business: 29 years

3171 Musser Forests
Musser Forests, Inc.
1880 Route 119 Hwy N
Indiana, PA 15701-7341   724-465-5685
800-643-8319
Fax: 724-465-9893
info@musserforests.com
www.musserforests.com

Evergreen and hardwood seedlings, transplants, ornamental shrubs and groundcovers

Principal: Jeffrey A Musser
Principal: Kevin A Musser
Principal: Fred A Musser
Credit Cards: MasterCard; Visa
Catalog Cost: Free
Catalog Circulation: Mailed 2 time(s) per year to 500M
Average Order Size: $75
Printing Information: 16 pages in 4 colors
Press: Web Press
Binding: Saddle Stitched
Mailing List Information: Names for rent

In Business: 89 years
Number of Employees: 170
Sales Volume: $20MM to $50MM

3172 National Arbor Day Foundation

Arbor Day Foundation
100 Arbor Avenue
Nebraska City, NE 68410   888-448-7337
                                888-448-7337
                                www.arborday.org

Trees, books, audio visual products, balloons and educational items

In Business: 42 years

3173 Native Gardener's Companion

Prairie Moon Nursery
32115 Prairie Lane
Winona, MN 55987   507-452-1362
                          866-417-8156
                          Fax: 504-454-5238
                          info@prairiemoon.com
                          www.prairiemoon.com

North American native seeds and plants for restoration and gardening.

President: Kathy Christopherson
CFO: Gail Testor
Marketing Manager: Rebecca Klukas-Brewer
Catalog Cost: Free
Catalog Circulation: to 27000
Printing Information: 48 pages in 4 colors on Glossy Stock
Press: Web Press
Binding: Saddle Stitched
Mailing List Information: Names for rent
In Business: 35 years
Number of Employees: 30

3174 New England Bamboo Company

Greentop LLC
156R Granite Street
Rockport, MA 01966   978-546-3110
                           Fax: 978-546-1075
                           info@greentopllc.com
                           shop.greentopllc.com

Rare and unusual bamboo and grasses

Founder: Christopher DeRosa
Credit Cards:
Catalog Cost: $2
Catalog Circulation: to 20000
Printing Information: 45 pages in 5 colors on Glossy Stock
Binding: Saddle Stitched
In Business: 26 years

3175 Niche Gardens

Niche Gardens
1111 Dawson Road
Chapel Hill, NC 27516-8576   919-967-0078
                                 Fax: 919-967-4026
                                 mail@nichegardens.com
                                 www.nichegardens.com

Native plants and unusual ornaments, trees, shrubs & grasses

President: Blair Durant
Marketing Manager: Meg Sorrell
Credit Cards: MasterCard
Catalog Circulation: Mailed 1 time(s) per year to 10000
Average Order Size: $75
Printing Information: 40 pages in 4 colors on Glossy Stock
Press: Web Press
Binding: Saddle Stitched
Mailing List Information: Names for rent
In Business: 27 years
Number of Employees: 7
Sales Volume: $350,000

3176 Nolin River Nut Tree Nursery

Nolin River Nut Tree Nursery
797 Port Wooden Road
Upton, KY 42784-9218   270-369-8551
                             john.brittain@windstream.net
                             www.nolinnursery.com

Grafted nut trees, persimmons and pawpaws

President: John Brittain
Owner: John Brittain
Owner: Lisa Brittain
Catalog Cost: Free
Catalog Circulation: Mailed 1 time(s) per year to 3000
Printing Information: 10 pages in 1 color on Matte Stock
Press: Web Press
Binding: Folded
Mailing List Information: Names for rent
In Business: 30 years
Number of Employees: 2

3177 North Coast Native Nursery

Pacific Open Space
PO Box 660
Petaluma, CA 94953-660   707-769-1213
                               Fax: 707-769-1230
www.northcoastnativenursery.com

Plants from coastal, wetland, forest, woodland, riparian, grassland, and chaparral habitats

Planning, Installation & Management: Dave Kaplow
dave@pacificopenspace.com
Administration: Roanne Kaplow
roanne@northcoastnativenursery.com
Catalog Circulation: to 200
Printing Information: 6 pages in 1 color
In Business: 28 years

3178 Northern Climate Fruit & Nut Trees Catalog

St Lawrence Nurseries
325 State Highway 345
P.O. Box 957
Potsdam, NY 13676   315-261-1925
                          connor@sln.potsdam.ny.us
                          www.sln.potsdam.ny.us

Fruit and nut trees and edible landscaping plants

President: William Mackentley
Catalog Cost:
Catalog Circulation: Mailed 1 time(s) per year to 10K
Printing Information: 34 pages
In Business: 34 years
Number of Employees: 7

3179 Nourse Farms

Nourse
41 River Road
Whately, MA 01093-9754   413-665-2658
                              Fax: 413-665-7888
                              info@noursefarms.com
                              www.noursefarms.com

Strawberry, raspberry, blueberry, blackberry, currant and gooseberry plants, asparagus, rhubarb and horseradish

President: Tim Nourse
Marketing Manager: Anne Kowaleck
Buyers: Nate Nourse
Credit Cards: MasterCard
Catalog Cost: Free
Catalog Circulation: Mailed 1 time(s) per year to 45K
Printing Information: 32 pages in 4 colors on Glossy Stock
Press: Web Press
Binding: Saddle Stitched
Mailing List Information: Names for rent
List Manager: Nata Nourse
In Business: 87 years
Number of Employees: 60
Sales Volume: $50MM to $100MM

3180 Nuccio's Nurseries

Nuccio's Nurseries Incorporated
3555 Chaney Trl
Altadena, CA 91001-3811   626-794-3383
                               www.Nucciosnurseries.Com

Camellias and azaleas

President: Julius Nuccio
Printing Information: 55 pages
In Business: 80 years
Number of Employees: 12
Sales Volume: $1MM to $3MM

3181 Oak Hill Gardens

Oak Hill Gardens
37W550 Binnie Road
PO Box 25
Dundee, IL 60118-25   847-428-8500
                            Fax: 847-428-8527
                            www.oakhillgardens.com

Hybrid orchids and tropical plants

President: Liese Butler
Owner: Greg Butler
Credit Cards: MasterCard; Visa
Number of Employees: 7
Sales Volume: Under $500M

3182 Oakes Daylilies

Oakes Daylilies
8153 Monday Road
P.O. Box 268
Corryton, TN 37721   865-687-3770
                           800-532-9545
                           Fax: 865-688-8186
                           www.oakesdaylilies.com

Variety of daylilies

Marketing Manager: Kenneth Oakes
Owner: Stewart Oakes
Credit Cards: MasterCard; Visa; Discover
Catalog Cost: Free
Catalog Circulation: Mailed 1 time(s) per year to 100M
Average Order Size: $80
Printing Information: 48 pages in 4 colors on Glossy Stock
Press: Web Press
Binding: Saddle Stitched
In Business: 17 years
Number of Employees: 15
Sales Volume: $5MM to $10MM

3183 Office Scapes Direct

Office Scapes Direct
12021 Centron Place
Cincinnati, OH 45246   800-557-1997
                             Fax: 914-328-1959
                             service@officescapesdirect.com
                             www.officescapesdirect.com

Silk flowers, silk trees, silk plants and framed art and wall decor

3184 Oikos Tree Crops

Oikos Tree Crops
PO Box 19425
Kalamazoo, MI 40019-425   269-624-6233
                               Fax: 269-624-4019
                               customerservice@oikostreecrops.com
                               www.oikostreecrops.com

Trees, shrubs, perennials, rare plants, nuts, oaks, native fruits, bird plants and tubers

President: Ken Asmus
Credit Cards: MasterCard; Visa
Catalog Cost: Free
Catalog Circulation: Mailed 1 time(s) per year to 30000
Average Order Size: $100
Printing Information: 60 pages in 4 colors on Matte Stock
Press: Letterpress
Binding: Saddle Stitched
In Business: 19 years
Number of Employees: 10-J
Sales Volume: Under $500M

3185 Omni Farm
Omni Farm
1369 Calloway Gap Road
West Jefferson, NC 28694-9212 336-982-3475
800-873-3327
Fax: 336-982-4163
omnifarm@omnifarm.com
www.omnifarm.com

Christmas trees, wreaths and garlands

President: Hal F Gimlin
Printing Information: 12 pages in 4 colors on Glossy Stock
Press: Web Press
Binding: Saddle Stitched
Mailing List Information: Names for rent
In Business: 43 years
Number of Employees: 20-O
Sales Volume: Under $500M

3186 One Green World
One Green World
6469 SE 134th Avenue
Portland, OR 97236
877-353-4028
info@onegreenworld.com
www.onegreenworld.com

Fruits and unusual ornamentals, columnar apples, hardy kiwis, pawpaws, quince and passion flowers

Owner: James Gilbert
Catalog Cost: $2
Catalog Circulation: Mailed 1 time(s) per year to 70M
Printing Information: 72 pages in 4 colors on Glossy Stock
Press: Web Press
Mailing List Information: Names for rent
In Business: 25 years
Number of Employees: 4
Sales Volume: 30,000

3187 Peekskill Nurseries
Peekskill Nurseries
PO Box 428
Shrub Oak, NY 10588-428 914-245-5595
webmaster@peekskillnurseries.com
www.peekskillnurseries.com

Ground covers

Credit Cards: MasterCard; Visa
Catalog Cost: $1
Printing Information: 4 pages in 1 color
In Business: 78 years
Number of Employees: 8

3188 Perennial Pleasures Nursery
Perennial Pleasures
63 Brickhouse Road
PO Box 147
East Hardwick, VT 05836 802-472-5104
Fax: 802-472-3737
annex@perennialpleasures.net
www.perennialpleasures.net

Antique perennials

Catalog Cost: Free
Mailing List Information: Names for rent
In Business: 35 years
Number of Employees: 10-J
Sales Volume: $500M to $1MM

3189 Pike's Peak Nurseries
Pike's Peak Nurseries
8289 Route 222 Highway E
Penn Run, PA 15765
724-463-7747
800-787-6730
Fax: 724-463-0775
pikespak@sgi.net
www.pikespeaknurseries.net

Evergreen seedlings and transplants, northern hardy specialties and native wood plant material

Buyers: Sean Schwarts
Catalog Cost: Free
Catalog Circulation: Mailed 1 time(s) per year

to 25M
Average Order Size: $100
Printing Information: 32 pages in 4 colors on Glossy Stock
Press: Letterpress
Binding: Saddle Stitched
Mailing List Information: Names for rent
List Manager: Marcie Daugherty
In Business: 78 years
Number of Employees: 50
Sales Volume: 1.2M

3190 Pine Ridge Gardens
Pine Ridge Gardens
PO Box 200
London, AR 72847
479-293-4359
Fax: 479-293-4659
office@pineridgegardens.com
www.pineridgegardens.com

Plant and environmental books; mostly native plants

Catalog Cost: $5
Catalog Circulation: Mailed 1 time(s) per year
Average Order Size: $125
Printing Information: 55 pages in 1 color on Matte Stock
Mailing List Information: Names for rent
In Business: 21 years
Sales Volume: $500,000

3191 Plant Delights Nursery
Plant Delights Nursery,Inc
9241 Sauls Road
Raleigh, NC 27603
919-772-4794
Fax: 919-662-0370
office@plantdelights.com
www.plantdelights.com

New and rare perennials, ornamental grasses and vines

Administrative Assistant: Debbie Hamrick
Business Manager: Heather Brameyer
E-Commerce and Database Specialist: Robert Lawless
In Business: 27 years
Number of Employees: 14
Sales Volume: $1.2 million

3192 Plants of the Southwest
Plants of the Southwest
3095 Agua Fria Street
Santa Fe, NM 87507-5411
505-438-8888
800-788-7333
Fax: 505-438-8800
plantsofthesouthwest@gmail.com
plantsofthesouthwest.com

Southwestern native plants including berry and nut producing trees and shrubs, wildflowers, native grasses and ancient and drought tolerant vegetable seeds

Credit Cards: AMEX; MasterCard
Catalog Cost: Free
Mailing List Information: Names for rent
In Business: 27 years
Number of Employees: 20-5
Sales Volume: $1MM to $3MM

3193 Plants of the Wild
Plants of the Wild
123 State Line Rd
PO Box 866
Tekoa, WA 99033
509-284-2848
Fax: 509-284-6464
kathy@plantsofthewild.com
www.plantsofthewild.com

Plants native to the Pacific Northwest

Production Manager: Kathy Hutton
Assistant Manager: Carrie Garcia
Credit Cards: AMEX; MasterCard
Catalog Cost:
Catalog Circulation: Mailed 1 time(s) per year to 5M
Printing Information: 24 pages in 2 colors on Matte Stock

Press: Letterpress
Binding: Saddle Stitched
Mailing List Information: Names for rent
In Business: 36 years
Number of Employees: 20
Sales Volume: Under $500M

3194 Possum Trot Tropical Fruit Nursery
Possum Trot Tropical Fruit Nursery
14955 SW 214th Street
Miami, FL 33187-4602
305-251-5040

Tropical fruit

President: Robert Barnum

3195 Prairie Moon Nursery Catalog and Cultural Guide
Prairie Moon Nursery
32115 Prairie Lane
Winona, MN 55987
507-452-1362
866-417-8156
Fax: 504-454-5238
info@prairiemoon.com
www.prairiemoon.com

North American native seeds and plants for restoration and gardening.

President: Kathy Christopherson
CFO: Gail Testor
Marketing Manager: Rebecca Klukas-Brewer
Catalog Cost: Free
Catalog Circulation: to 27000
Printing Information: 48 pages in 4 colors on Glossy Stock
Press: Web Press
Binding: Saddle Stitched
Mailing List Information: Names for rent
In Business: 35 years
Number of Employees: 30

3196 ProFlowers
ProFlowers
5005 Wateridge Vista Drive
San Diego, CA 92121
800-580-2913
wecare@customercare.proflowers.com
www.proflowers.com

Flowers, plants, desserts and gifts

Credit Cards: AMEX; MasterCard
In Business: 15 years
Number of Employees: 175

3197 Raintree Nursery
Raintree Nursery
391 Butts Road
Morton, WA 98356-9700
800-391-8892
customerservice@raintreenursery.com
www.raintreenursery.com

Fruit, nut and berry trees and ornamentals, bamboo for backyard ecological growers, gardening supplies, fruit strainers, peelers and pitters

President: Sam Benowitz
Horticulturist: Katy Fraser
Garden Center Manager: Karen Fry
Field Manager: Carl Nelson
Credit Cards: MasterCard; Visa
Catalog Cost: Free
Catalog Circulation: Mailed 2 time(s) per year
Average Order Size: $65
Printing Information: 96 pages in 4 colors on Glossy Stock
Press: Web Press
Binding: Saddle Stitched
Mailing List Information: Names for rent
In Business: 45 years
Number of Employees: 25
Sales Volume: $1MM-$3MM

3198 Rare Fruiting Plants & Trees
Garden of Delights
14560 SW 14th Street
Davie, FL 33325-4217
954-370-9004
800-741-3103
Fax: 954-236-4588
godelights@aol.com
www.gardenofdelights.com

Sugar apple, chocolate, miracle fruit, rare fruiting, plants and tree oil palms, toddy palms, passion fruit, vanilla orchid, lemon grass, habanero pepper and black pepper

President: Murray Corman
Marketing Manager: Phil Croke
Average Order Size: $90
Printing Information: 8 pages in 1 color on Matte Stock
Binding: Folded
Mailing List Information: Names for rent
In Business: 27 years
Number of Employees: 3
Sales Volume: $250,000

3199 Reath's Nursery
Reath's Nursery
N-195 Hamilton Lake Rd
Vulcan, MI 49892
906-563-9777

Peonies

President: David Reath
In Business: 52 years
Number of Employees: 10-J
Sales Volume: $500M to $1MM

3200 Red's Rhodies
Red's Rhodies
15920 SW Oberst Lane
Sherwood, OR 97140-5020
503-625-6331
Fax: 503-625-8055
www.hardy-orchids.com

Hardy terrestrial orchids that will grow in the garden including Bletilla, Chinese Cymbidium, Cypripedium, Dactylorhiza and Pleionc

President: Karen Cavender
CFO: Richard Cavender
Catalog Cost: $1
Catalog Circulation: Mailed 1 time(s) per year
Average Order Size: $75
Printing Information: 6 pages in 2 colors on Newsprint
Press: Web Press
Binding: Folded
Mailing List Information: Names for rent
In Business: 31 years
Number of Employees: 5
Sales Volume: Under $500M

3201 Richard Owen Nursery
Richard Owen Nursery, Inc
1800 E Hamilton Drive
Bloomington, IL 61704
309-663-9553
customercare@excitinggardens.com
www.excitinggardens.com

Flowers, plants and trees

President: Richard Owen
Credit Cards: MasterCard
Catalog Cost: Free
Catalog Circulation: Mailed 2 time(s) per year
Printing Information: 56 pages in 4 colors on Newsprint
Binding: Saddle Stitched
In Business: 22 years
Number of Employees: 75
Sales Volume: under 500,000

3202 Ritchers Herbs
Ritchers
357 Highway 47
Goodwood, ON L0C-1A0
905-640-6677
800-668-4372
Fax: 905-640-6641
www.ritchers.com

Seeds, herbs, plants, flowers, vegetables, garden supplies

Catalog Cost: Free
In Business: 48 years

3203 Rock Spray Nursery
Rock Spray Nursery Inc.
PO Boc 2035
Truro, MA 02666
508-349-6769
Fax: 508-349-2732
www.gardens.com

Over 100 varieties of Heath and Heather plants and books

President: Mary Matwey
Credit Cards: AMEX; MasterCard; Visa
Catalog Cost: Free
Catalog Circulation: Mailed 1 time(s) per year to 40M
Average Order Size: $145
Printing Information: 28 pages in 4 colors on Glossy Stock
Press: Web Press
Binding: Saddle Stitched
Mailing List Information: Names for rent
In Business: 27 years
Number of Employees: 7
Sales Volume: Under $500M

3204 Roozengarde Tulips
Roozengarde
15867 Beaver Marsh Rd.
Mount Vernan, VA 98273
360-424-0419
866-488-5477
Fax: 360-424-3113
info@tulips.com
www.tulips.com

Largest growers of Tulips, Irises and Daffodils in the world

President: Leo Roozen
CFO: Mike Roozen
Credit Cards: AMEX; MasterCard
Catalog Cost: Free
Printing Information: in 3 colors
In Business: 30 years

3205 Rose Catalog/Rose Reference Guide
Heirloom Roses, Inc.
24062 Riverside Dr NE
St Paul, OR 97137
503-538-1576
800-820-0465
Fax: 503-538-5902
info@heirloomroses.com
www.heirloomroses.com

Roses, rose bushes, rose gardening, rose plants

President: Louise Clements
Credit Cards: MasterCard; Visa
Catalog Cost:
Catalog Circulation: Mailed 1 time(s) per year
Printing Information: 36 pages in 4 colors on Glossy Stock
Press: Web Press
Binding: Saddle Stitched
Mailing List Information: Names for rent

3206 Roses of Yesterday & Today
Roses of Yesterday and Today
803 Browns Valley Rd
Watsonville, CA 95076
831-728-1901
Fax: 805-227-4095
postmaster@rosesofyesterday.com
www.Rosesofyesterday.Com

Rare and unusual roses

President: Jennifer Wiley
Marketing Manager: Jack Wiley
Production Manager: Guinivere Wiley
Founder: Dorothy Stemle
Catalog Cost: $5
Catalog Circulation: Mailed 1 time(s) per year to 35M
Printing Information: 80 pages in 3 colors on Matte Stock
Press: Web Press

Binding: Saddle Stitched
In Business: 85 years
Number of Employees: 4
Sales Volume: $500,000

3207 Schreiners Gardens
Schreiner's Iris Gardens
3625 Quinaby Rd NE
Salem, OR 97303
503-393-3232
800-525-2367
Fax: 503-393-5590
iris@schreinersgardens.com
www.Schreinersgardens.Com

Tall bearded and dwarf iris

President: David Schreiner
Marketing Manager: Tom Abregg
VP: Raymond Schreiner
Catalog Circulation: Mailed 1 time(s) per year
Printing Information: 72 pages in 3 colors
In Business: 99 years

3208 Select Seeds
Select Seeds
180 Stickney Hill Road
Union, CT 06076-4617
860-684-9310
800-684-0395
Fax: 800-653-3304
info@selectseeds.com
www.selectseeds.com

Antique flowers, selection of unique, high-quality flower seeds and plants, flowering vines and rare cottage garden annuals

President: Marilyn Barlow
Catalog Cost:
Printing Information: 64 pages in 4 colors
Binding: Saddle Stitched
Mailing List Information: Names for rent
In Business: 50 years
Number of Employees: 5
Sales Volume: Under $500M

3209 Shady Oaks Nursery
PSI-Shady Oaks Nursery
1601 5th Street SE
PO Box 708
Waseca, MN 56093
507-835-5033
Fax: 507-835-8772
www.shadyoaks.com

Perennial plants and hostas

President: Gordon J Oslund
Buyers: Emily McCarthy
Credit Cards: MasterCard; Visa
Catalog Cost: Free
Catalog Circulation: Mailed 1 time(s) per year to 9000
Average Order Size: $90
Printing Information: 48 pages in 4 colors on Glossy Stock
Press: Sheetfed Press
Binding: Saddle Stitched
Mailing List Information: Names for rent
List Manager: Rickard List Marketing
List Company: Rickard List Marketing
Corporate Plaza, Suite 135
Farmingdale, NY 11735
In Business: 22 years
Number of Employees: 22
Sales Volume: $1MM to $3MM

3210 Spring Hill Nursery
Spring Hill Nurseries
P.O. Box 330
Harrison, OH 45030-9935
513-354-1509
Fax: 513-354-1504
service@springhillnursery.com
www.springhillnursery.com

Perennials, flowering shrubs, ground covers, roses, summer blooming bulbs and houseplants, gardening tools and accessories, bird houses and bird seeds.

Credit Cards: MasterCard; Visa
Catalog Cost: Free
Catalog Circulation: Mailed 20 time(s) per

year
Printing Information: 30 pages in 4 colors on Glossy Stock
Press: Web Press
Binding: Saddle Stitched
Mailing List Information: Names for rent
In Business: 166 years
Sales Volume: $50MM to $100MM

3211 Springbrook Gardens
Springbrook Gardens, Inc.
6676 Heisely Road
PO Box 388
Mentor, OH 44061-388   440-255-3059
    888-255-3059
Fax: 440-255-9535

Field grown perennials, ground covers and ornamental grasses
President: Glenn Anderson
Credit Cards: AMEX; MasterCard; Visa
Catalog Cost:
Catalog Circulation: Mailed 1 time(s) per year to 3.5M
Printing Information: 57 pages in 1 color on Matte Stock
Press: Web Press
Mailing List Information: Names for rent
In Business: 68 years
Number of Employees: 35
Sales Volume: $3MM to $5MM

3212 Spruce Gardens
Spruce It Up Garden Centre
777 - 210 Ave SE
Macleod Trail S & 210 Ave SE
Calgary, CN T2J 5   403-201-7525
Fax: 403-254-6959
info@siugc.ca
www.spruceitupgardencentre.com

Spruce varieties and other evergreen trees
President: Meryl Coombs
Store Manager and Buyer: Cathy Steele

3213 St. Lawrence Nurseries
Saint Lawrence Nurseries
325 State Highway 345
P.O. Box 957
Potsdam, NY 13676-3515   315-261-1925
connor@sln.potsdam.ny.us
www.sln.potsdam.ny.us

Cold-hardy fruit and nut trees
President: William Mackentley
Catalog Circulation: Mailed 1 time(s) per year to 5000
Printing Information: 30 pages in 1 color on Matte Stock
Press: Web Press
Binding: Saddle Stitched
In Business: 34 years
Sales Volume: $1MM to $3MM

3214 Stark Bro's
Stark Bro's Nurseries & Orchards Co.
P.O. Box 1800
Louisiana, MO 63353-8904   800-325-4180
Fax: 573-754-3701
info@starkbros.com
www.starkbros.com

Gardening supplies and dwarf fruit trees, roses, shade trees, small fruits, garden aids
President: John E Miller
Credit Cards: AMEX; MasterCard; Visa
Catalog Cost: Free
Catalog Circulation: Mailed 9 time(s) per year to 3.6MM
Average Order Size: $60
Printing Information: 60 pages in 4 colors on Glossy Stock
Press: Web Press
Binding: Saddle Stitched
Mailing List Information: Names for rent
In Business: 201 years
Number of Employees: 80
Sales Volume: $5MM to $10MM

3215 Stark Bro's Nurseries & Orchards Company
Stark Bro's Nurseries & Orchards
PO Box 1800
Louisiana, MO 63353   800-325-4180
Fax: 573-754-3701
info@starkbros.com
www.starkbros.com

Plants and flowers
Manager: Jenny Andrews
Credit Cards: AMEX; MasterCard; Visa
Catalog Cost: Free
Catalog Circulation: Mailed 5 time(s) per year to 13000
Printing Information: 36 pages in 4 colors on Newsprint
Binding: Saddle Stitched
Mailing List Information: Names for rent
List Company: Catalyst Direct Marketing
4640 Lankershin Blvd., Suite 515
North Hollywood, CA 91602
818-762-0036
In Business: 198 years
Number of Employees: 150
Sales Volume: 46MM

3216 Steele Plant Company
Steele Plant Company, LLC.
202 Collins St.
PO Box 191
Gleason, TN 38229   731-648-5476
Fax: 731-648-1946
plants@steeleplantcompany.com
www.sweetpotatoplant.com

Sweet potato and onion plants
President: Ken Sanders
Catalog Circulation: to 25000
Printing Information: 8 pages in 2 colors
Mailing List Information: Names for rent
In Business: 60 years
Number of Employees: 2

3217 Stokes Tropicals
Stokes Tropicals
4806 E Old Spanish Trail
Jeanerette, LA 70544   337-365-6998
    866-478-2502
Fax: 337-365-6991
info@stokestropicals.com
www.stokestropicals.com

Plumerias, gingers, bananas, tropical plants, tropical planting mix and fertilizer
President: Glenn M Stokes
Marketing Manager: Sondra Stokes
Credit Cards: AMEX; MasterCard
Catalog Cost: $4.95
Catalog Circulation: Mailed 1 time(s) per year to 50000
Average Order Size: $90
Printing Information: 98 pages in 4 colors on Glossy Stock
Press: Web Press
Binding: Saddle Stitched
Mailing List Information: Names for rent
In Business: 100 years
Number of Employees: 15
Sales Volume: $300,000

3218 Sunlight Gardens
Sunlight Gardens
174 Golden Ln
Andersonville, TN 37705-4024   865-494-8237
    800-272-7396
Fax: 865-494-7086
info@sunlightgardens.com
www.sunlightgardens.com

Wildflowers and perennials
President: Martin Zenni
Credit Cards: MasterCard; Visa
Catalog Cost: Free
Catalog Circulation: Mailed 1 time(s) per year to 20m
Printing Information: 16 pages in 4 colors on Glossy Stock

Press: Web Press
Binding: Saddle Stitched
In Business: 32 years
Number of Employees: 6
Sales Volume: $1MM to $3MM

3219 Sunshine Farm & Gardens Perennial Plants
Sunshine Farm and Gardens
696 Glicks Rd.
Renick, WV 24966   304-497-2208
Fax: 304-497-2698
barry@sunfarm.com
www.sunfarm.com

Rare and unusual plants and perennials
President: Barry Glick
barry@sunfarm.com
Marketing Manager: Zak Glick
Fulfillment: Abbey Glick
Buyers: Patty Wiley
Credit Cards: AMEX; MasterCard; Visa
Catalog Cost: $2
Catalog Circulation: Mailed 1 time(s) per year to 100M
Average Order Size: $165
Printing Information: 28 pages in 1 color on Matte Stock
Press: Web Press
Binding: Saddle Stitched
Mailing List Information: Names for rent
List Manager: Barry Glick
In Business: 32 years
Number of Employees: 16
Sales Volume: $1MM to $3MM

3220 Surry Gardens' Bedding Plant Catalog
Surry Gardens
1248 Surry Rd. (Route 172) Surry Vi
PO Box 145
Surry, ME 04684   207-667-4493
Fax: 207-667-5532
mail@surrygardens.com
www.surrygardens.com

Bird, deer resistant, shade and native plants
President: James Dickinson
Credit Cards: MasterCard; Visa
Catalog Cost: $1
Printing Information: 89 pages in 1 color on Matte Stock
Binding: Saddle Stitched
Mailing List Information: Names for rent
In Business: 30 years
Number of Employees: 20
Sales Volume: Under $500M

3221 Swan Island Dahlias
Swan Island Dahlias
995 NW 22nd Avenue
PO Box 700
Canby, OR 97013   503-266-7711
    800-410-6540
Fax: 503-266-8768
info@dahlias.com
www.dahlias.com

Dahalias
President: Nicholas Gitts
Marketing Manager: Nicholas Gitts
Credit Cards: AMEX; MasterCard
Catalog Cost: Free
Printing Information: 43 pages
In Business: 86 years
Sales Volume: $3MM to $5MM

3222 Trees of Antiquity
Trees of Antiquity
20 Wellsona Road
Paso Robles, CA 93446   805-467-9909
Fax: 805-467-9909
www.treesofantiquity.com

Organic heritage apples, peaches, pears, plums, figs and grape vines
President: Neil Collins
Credit Cards: MasterCard; Visa
Catalog Cost: Free

Catalog Circulation: Mailed 1 time(s) per year
to 1mm
Printing Information: 62 pages in 1 color
Mailing List Information: Names for rent
In Business: 30 years
Number of Employees: 5
Sales Volume: Under $500M

3223 Van Bourgondien Brothers
K. Van Bourgondien & Sons, Inc.
PO Box 289
Cleves, OH 45002-2000   800-622-9997
                                800-552-9996
                           Fax: 800-327-4268
                         blooms@dutchbulbs.com
                          www.dutchbulbs.com

Dutch bulbs and perennials
President: Jan Van Dyck
Credit Cards: AMEX; MasterCard
Catalog Cost: Free
Printing Information: 68 pages

3224 Vans Pines Nursery
Vans Pines Nursery
14731 Baldwin Street
West Olive, MI 49460-9708   616-399-1620
                                800-888-7337
                           Fax: 616-399-1652
                      info@vanspinesnursery.com
                       www.Vanspinesnursery.Com

Evergreen, deciduous seedlings and transplants
President: Gary Van Slooten
CFO: Gary Van Slooten
Credit Cards: MasterCard; Visa
Catalog Cost: Free
Catalog Circulation: Mailed 1 time(s) per year
to 14000
Average Order Size: $1030
Printing Information: 24 pages in 4 colors on
Newsprint
Press: Web Press
Binding: Saddle Stitched
In Business: 81 years
Number of Employees: 30
Sales Volume: $5MM to $10MM

3225 Vanwell Nursery
VanWell Nursery
2821 Grant Road
East Wenatchee, WA 98802   509-886-8189
                                800-572-1553
                           Fax: 509-886-0294
                         vanwell@vanwell.net
                           www.vanwell.net

Fruit trees
President: Pete VanWell
CFO: Tom Van Well
Operations Manager: Dick Van Well
International Affairs: Suzanne Van Well
Information Systems: Joe Adams
Credit Cards: MasterCard
Catalog Cost:
Catalog Circulation: Mailed 1 time(s) per year
to 20000
Average Order Size: $80
Printing Information: 32 pages in 4 colors on
Glossy Stock
Press: Web Press
Binding: Saddle Stitched
Mailing List Information: Names for rent
In Business: 71 years
Number of Employees: 60
Sales Volume: $5,000,000

3226 Violet Showcase
The Violet Showcase
PO Box 300091
Denver, CO 80203-0091   303-204- 59
                           Fax: 303-762-1808
                       violetshowcase@yahoo.com
                       www.Violetshowcase.Com

African violets

President: Douglas Crispin
Printing Information: 34 pages in 2 colors
In Business: 44 years

3227 Wayside Gardens Catalog
Wayside Gardens
1 Garden Lane
Hodges, SC 29653   864-330-2004
                                800-845-1124
                           Fax: 800-817-1124
                      info@waysidegardens.com
                       www.waysidegardens.com

Perennials, bulbs, roses, trees, and shrubs
President: Charlees Fox
Catalog Cost: Free
Printing Information: 132 pages in 4 colors
In Business: 96 years
Sales Volume: $1MM to $3MM

3228 Well-Sweep Herb Farm Catalog
Well-Sweep Herb Farm Inc
205 Mount Bethel Rd
Port Murray, NJ 07865-4147   908-852-5390
                           Fax: 908-852-1649
                           herbs@goes.com
                         www.Wellsweep.Com

Herbs, perennials and rare plants, as well as seeds, dried flowers, books and wreaths
President: Louise Hyde
Marketing Manager: David Hyde
Credit Cards: MasterCard; Visa
Catalog Circulation: Mailed 1 time(s) per year
Average Order Size: $25
Printing Information: 84 pages in 7 colors
Mailing List Information: Names for rent
In Business: 44 years
Number of Employees: 8
Sales Volume: $500M to $1MM

3229 White Flower Farm Catalog
White Flower Farm
Route 63
PO Box 50
Litchfield, CT 06759   860-496-9624
                                800-503-9624
                           Fax: 860-496-1418
                   michelle@whiteflowerfarm.com
                     www.whiteflowerfarm.com

Perennials, unusual annuals, bulbs, roses, shrubs and gifts
President: Lorraine Calder
Production Manager: Tom Cooper
Fulfillment: Melissa Jack-Benjamin
Buyers: Nancy McCarthy, Plants
Keen Fisher, Hardgoods
Credit Cards: AMEX; MasterCard
Catalog Cost: Free
Catalog Circulation: Mailed 3 time(s) per year
Average Order Size: $90
Printing Information: 98 pages in 4 colors on
Glossy Stock
Mailing List Information: Names for rent
List Manager: Millard Group
List Company: Millard Group
10 Vose Road
Peterborough, NH 03458
603-924-9262
In Business: 65 years
Number of Employees: 120

3230 Whitman Farms Catalog
White Farms
3995 Gibson Rd NW
Salem, OR 97304-9527   503-585-8728
                           Fax: 503-363-5020
                      lucile@whitmanfarms.com
                       www.Whitmanfarms.Com

Small fruits, gooseberries, currants, mulberries and unsual trees in rootcontrol bags
President: Lucile Whitman
Catalog Cost: Free
Catalog Circulation: Mailed 1 time(s) per year
to 1000

Average Order Size: $30
Printing Information: 16 pages in 1 color on
Matte Stock
Press: Web Press
Binding: Folded
Mailing List Information: Names for rent
In Business: 35 years
Number of Employees: 3
Sales Volume: $1MM to $3MM

3231 Whitney Gardens & Nursery Catalog
Whitney Gardens & Nursery
306264 Highway 101
PO Box 170
Brinnon, WA 98320   360-796-4411
                                800-952-2404
                           Fax: 360-796-3556
                      info@whitneygardens.com
                       www.whitneygardens.com

Hybrid and species rhododendrons, azaleas, maples, camellias, kalmias, ground covers, perennial, magnolias and conifers
President: Anne Sather
Marketing Manager: Ellie Sather
Credit Cards: AMEX; MasterCard
Catalog Cost:
Catalog Circulation: Mailed 1 time(s) per year
to 5000
Average Order Size: $35
Printing Information: 112 pages in 4 colors on
Matte Stock
Press: Web Press
Binding: Saddle Stitched
Mailing List Information: Names for rent
360-796-4411
In Business: 50 years
Number of Employees: 6
Sales Volume: $1MM to $3MM

3232 Wholesale Nursery Catalog of Native Wetland Plants
Environmental Concern, Inc.
201 Boundary Lane
PO Box P
St. Michaels, MD 21663   410-745-9620
                           Fax: 410-745-3517
                           www.wetlands.org

Wholesale wetland plant nursery.

3233 Wicklein's Water Gardens
Wicklein's Water Gardens
1820 Cromwell Bridge Rd
Baltimore, MD 21234   410-823-1335
                                800-382-6716
                           Fax: 410-823-1427
                    sales@wickleinaquatics.com
                     www.wickleinaquatics.com

Water lilies, lotus and aquatic plants
President: Eric Wicklein
Catalog Circulation: to 2500
Printing Information: 36 pages in 1 color on
Newsprint
Press: Sheetfed Press
Binding: Saddle Stitched
In Business: 51 years
Number of Employees: 10
Sales Volume: $1MM to $3MM

3234 Wildflower Gardening The Vermont Wildflower Farm G
Vermont Wildflower Farm
3488 Ethan Allen Highway
P.O. Box 96
Charlotte, VT 5445   802-425-3641
                                855-846-9453
                 vermontwildflowerfarm@yahoo.com
                  www.vermontwildflowerfarm.com

Gardening, farms, planting, seeds, herbs
Credit Cards: AMEX; MasterCard
Printing Information: 36 pages
In Business: 34 years

3235 Wilkerson Mill Gardens Catalog
Wilkerson Mill Gardens
9595 Wilkerson Mill Rd
Chattahoochee Hills, GA 30268-1807 770-463-2400
Fax: 770-463-9717
edean007@gmail.com
www.hydrangea.com

Hydrangea plants
President: Elizabeth Dean
Catalog Cost: $3
Sales Volume: $500M to $1MM

3236 William Tricker Catalog
William Tricker, Inc.
7125 Tanglewood Drive
Independence, OH 44131-3489 800-524-3492
williamtricker@prodigy.net
www.tricker.com

Plants, fish, pond supplies, water lilies, and water gardening supplies
President: Richard Lee
Catalog Cost: $2
Catalog Circulation: Mailed 1 time(s) per year
Printing Information: 60 pages in 4 colors on Glossy Stock
Binding: Saddle Stitched
In Business: 124 years
Number of Employees: 15
Sales Volume: 3MM-5MM

3237 Womack's Nursery Catalog
Womack's Nursery
2551 State Highway 6
De Leon, TX 76444-6333 254-893-6497
254-893-3400
Fax: 254-893-3400
pecan@womacknursery.com
www.womacknursery.com

Fruits, pecan trees, blackberries and grapevines
President: Larry Don Womack
Catalog Cost: Free
Printing Information: 36 pages
Mailing List Information: Names for rent
In Business: 33 years
Number of Employees: 12
Sales Volume: $3MM to $5MM

3238 Yucca Do Nursery Catalog
Yucca Do Nursery Inc
PO Box 1039
Giddings, TX 78942-907 979-542-8811
info@yuccado.com
www.yuccado.com

Native texas plants and mexican/asian plants, rare and unusual plants from around the world
Credit Cards: MasterCard
Catalog Cost: $4
Catalog Circulation: Mailed 1 time(s) per year
Printing Information: 10 pages in 4 colors on Glossy Stock
Press: Web Press
Binding: Saddle Stitched
Mailing List Information: Names for rent
In Business: 14 years
Number of Employees: 6
Sales Volume: Under $500M

Seeds & Bulbs

3239 Allen, Sterling, & Lothrop
Allen, Sterling & Lothrop
191 Us Route 1
Falmouth, ME 04105-1385 207-781-4142
Fax: 207-781-4143
shirley@allensterlinglothrop.com
www.allensterlinglothrop.com

Vegetable, flower and herb seeds as well as top quality lawn, garden, and greenhouse supplies
President: Shirley Brannigan
Seed-Room Manager: Jenn Herring
General Manager: Shawn Brannigan
Credit Cards: MasterCard; Visa
Catalog Cost: $1
Catalog Circulation: Mailed 1 time(s) per year to 25000
Printing Information: 32 pages in 1 color on s
Binding: Folded
Mailing List Information: Names for rent
In Business: 104 years
Number of Employees: 11
Sales Volume: $5MM-$10MM

3240 Alpines Seed Catalog
Alplains Seed Catalog
PO Box 489
Kiowa, CO 80117-489 *Fax:* 303-621-2864
alandean7@msn.com
www.alplains.com

Rare and wild-collected seed from native alpines
President: Alan D. Bradshaw
Proprietor: Alan D. Bradshaw
Catalog Cost: Free
In Business: 21 years
Number of Employees: 2
Sales Volume: $100,000

3241 Applewood Seed Company
Applewood Seed Company
5380 Vivian Street
Arvada, CO 80002 303-431-7333
Fax: 303-467-7886
sales@applewoodseed.com
www.applewoodseed.com

Horticultural gift products and flower pot baking kit
General Manager: Norm Poppe
Ecologist: Diane Wilson
Sales Specialist: Evan Mawe
Credit Cards: AMEX; MasterCard; Visa
Catalog Cost: Free
In Business: 50 years
Sales Volume: $4MM

3242 Bamert Seed Company
Bamert Seed
1897 County Road 1018
Muleshoe, TX 79347-7221 806-272-5506
800-262-9892
Fax: 806-272-3114
natives@bamertseed.com
www.Bamertseed.Com

Over 40 species of native grasses, legumes and forbs for prairie restoration, wildlife habitat, wildlife food plots, reclamation and conservation reserve programs
President: Nick Bamert
Production Manager: Rayniel Bamert
Owner: Carl Bamert
Credit Cards: AMEX; MasterCard
Catalog Circulation: Mailed 1 time(s) per year
Printing Information: 10 pages in 1 color on Matte Stock
In Business: 63 years
Number of Employees: 15
Sales Volume: $700M

3243 Bulb Catalog
RoozenGaarde
15867 Beaver Marsh Rd.
Mount Vernon, WA 98273 360-424-8531
866-488-5477
Fax: 360-424-3113
info@tulips.com
www.tulips.com

Flowers
President: Jeanne Gerde
Credit Cards: AMEX; MasterCard
In Business: 30 years

3244 Burpee Garden Catalog
W Atlee Burpee & Company
300 Park Avenue
Warminster, PA 18974 800-888-1447
www.burpee.com

Flower bulbs, vegetable seeds and plants, herb seeds and plants
Chairman: George Ball Jr
Marketing Manager: Don Zeidler
Chief Operating Officer: Chris Romas
Credit Cards: AMEX; MasterCard; Visa
Catalog Cost: Free
Catalog Circulation: Mailed 1 time(s) per year to 40000
Printing Information: in 4 colors
Binding: Saddle Stitched
Mailing List Information: Names for rent
In Business: 136 years
Number of Employees: 350
Sales Volume: $20,000,000

3245 Caladium World
Caladium World
PO Box 629
Sebring, FL 33871-629 863-385-7661
Fax: 863-385-5836
sales@caladiumworld.com
www.caladiumworld.com

Quality Caladiums and Elephant Ear bulbs shipped direct to the homeowner
President: LE Selph
Credit Cards: MasterCard
Catalog Cost: Free
Catalog Circulation: Mailed 1 time(s) per year
Printing Information: 1 pages in 4 colors on Glossy Stock
Binding: Folded
Mailing List Information: Names for rent
In Business: 31 years
Number of Employees: 8
Sales Volume: $499,000

3246 Collector's Nursery
Collector's Nursery
16804 NE 102nd Avenue
Battle Ground, WA 98604 360-690-5732
Fax: 360-571-8540
dianar@collectorsnursery.com
www.collectorsnursery.com

Rare and unique plants - conifers, perennials and variegated
President: Diana Reeck
Catalog Cost: $2
In Business: 16 years
Number of Employees: 1
Sales Volume: $10,000

3247 Color by the Yard
Roozengaarde
15867 Beaver Marsh Rd.
PO Box 1248
Mount Vernon, WA 98273 360-424-0419
866-488-5477
Fax: 360-424-3113
info@tulips.com
www.tulips.com

Tulips, daffodils and irises flower bulbs
President: Leo Roozen
Credit Cards: AMEX; MasterCard; Visa
Catalog Cost: Free
Printing Information: in 4 colors
In Business: 30 years

3248 Colorblends Catalog
Colorblends
747 Barnum Avenue
Bridgeport, CT 06608 203-338-0776
888-847-8637
Fax: 203-338-0744
info@colorblends.com
www.colorblends.com

Spring flowering bulbs and tulip combinations for your garden

President: Timothy P Schipper
Marketing Manager: Tim Schipper
Credit Cards: AMEX; MasterCard
Catalog Cost: Free
Catalog Circulation: Mailed 1 time(s) per year
Average Order Size: $70
Printing Information: 152 pages in 4 colors on Glossy Stock
Binding: Saddle Stitched
Mailing List Information: Names for rent
In Business: 103 years

3249 Cook's Garden
PO Box C5030
Warminster, PA 18974-574   215-674-4900
                                800-457-9703
                        www.cooksgarden.com

Vegetable, flower and herb seeds, kitchen supplies, garden supplies, plants and bulbs

Buyers: Shepherd & Ellen Ogden
Catalog Cost: Free
Catalog Circulation: Mailed 1 time(s) per year
Printing Information: in 4 colors on Matte Stock
Press: Web Press
Mailing List Information: Names for rent

3250 Daylily Discounters
Pinecliffe Gardens
6745 Foster Road
Philpot, KY 42366   270-281-9791
                                800-329-5459
                        Fax: 270-281-4160
                www.daylily-discounters.com

Variety of lilies and similar flowering bulbs

President: Tom Allin
Catalog Cost: $9

3251 Early's Seed Catalog
Early's Farm & Garden Centre
2615 Lorne Avenue
Saskatoon, SK S7J-0S5   306-931-1982
                                800-667-1159
                        Fax: 306-931-7110
                    www.earlysgarden.com

Seeds, garden tools, pest control, wild bird supplies, pond supplies and more

General Manager: Derek Bloski
General Manager: Kevin Bloski
Catalog Cost: Free
In Business: 110 years
Number of Employees: 39

3252 Ecoseeds Catalog
Redwood City Seed Company
PO Box 361
Redwood City, CA 94064   650-325-7333
                        Fax: 650-325-4056
                    www.ecoseeds.com

Heirloom non hybrid vegetables, hot peppers and herb seeds

President: Sue Dremann
Marketing Manager: Craig Dremann
Credit Cards: AMEX; MasterCard
Catalog Cost: Free
Catalog Circulation: Mailed 1 time(s) per year
Printing Information: 28 pages in 1 color on Matte Stock
Press: Sheetfed Press
Binding: Saddle Stitched
In Business: 35 years
Number of Employees: 2

3253 Ernst Conservation Seeds
Ernst Conservation Seeds
8884 Mercer Pike
Meadville, PA 16335   814-336-2404
                                800-873-3321
                        Fax: 814-336-5191
                    sales@ernstseed.com
                    www.ernstseed.com

Plants and seeds

President: Calvin Ernst
Marketing Manager: Marcia Ernst
Production Manager: Robin Ernst
VP: Andy Ernst
Biomass Manager: Dan Arnett
VP: Michael Ernst
Credit Cards: MasterCard; Visa
Catalog Cost: Free
Catalog Circulation: Mailed 1 time(s) per year to 6000
Printing Information: 74 pages in 1 color on Glossy Stock
Binding: Saddle Stitched
In Business: 51 years
Number of Employees: 20
Sales Volume: $20MM to $50MM

3254 Ethnobotanical Catalog of Seeds
J.L. Hudson, Seedsman
P.O. Box 337
La Honda, CA 94020-337   jlog@jlhudsonseeds.net
                        www.jlhudsonseeds.net

Rare and exotic seeds

Catalog Cost: $1
Printing Information: 96 pages
Mailing List Information: Names for rent
In Business: 104 years

3255 FW Schumacher Company
F. W. Schumacher Co., Inc.
36 Spring Hill Road
P.O. Box 1023
Sandwich, MA 02563-1023   508-888-0659
                        Fax: 508-833-0322
                    info@treeshrubseeds.com
                    www.treeshrubseeds.com

Variety of tree and shrub trees

President: Donald Allen
Catalog Cost: Free
Catalog Circulation: Mailed 2 time(s) per year
Printing Information: 26 pages
Mailing List Information: Names for rent
In Business: 87 years
Number of Employees: 4

3256 Fedco Seeds
Fedco Co-op Garden Supplies
PO Box 520
Waterville, ME 04903-520   207-426-9900
                        Fax: 207-692-1022
                    questions@fedcoseeds.com
                    www.fedcoseeds.com

Untreated vegetable, herb and flower seeds, soil amendments, fertilizers, cover crops, garden tools, bulbs, seed potatoes, onion sets, garlic, fruit trees, ornamentals, perennials, and tender bulbs

President: CR Lawn
Executive Director: Russell Libby
Catalog Cost: Free
Catalog Circulation: Mailed 3 time(s) per year to 90M
Printing Information: 107 pages in 1 color on Newsprint
Press: Web Press
Binding: Saddle Stitched
Mailing List Information: Names for rent
In Business: 32 years
Number of Employees: 50
Sales Volume: Under $500M

3257 Fedco Trees
Fedco Co-op Garden Supplies
PO Box 520
Waterville, ME 04903-520   207-426-9900
                        Fax: 207-692-1022
                    questions@fedcoseeds.com
                    www.fedcoseeds.com

Fedco trees offers fruit trees, berry bushes, ornamental trees & bulbs, perennials and spring planted bulbs

President: CR Lawn
Executive Director: Russell Libby
Catalog Cost: Free

Catalog Circulation: Mailed 1 time(s) per year to 30M
Printing Information: 72 pages in 1 color on Newsprint
Press: Web Press
Binding: Saddle Stitched
Mailing List Information: Names for rent
In Business: 32 years
Number of Employees: 50
Sales Volume: Under $500M

3258 Field and Forest Products
Field and Forest Products
N3296 Kozuzek Road
Peshtigo, WI 54157-9590   715-582-4997
                                800-792-6220
                        Fax: 715-582-0181
                fieldandforest@centurytel.net
                        www.fieldforest.net

Mushroom spawn and growing supplies

President: Mary Kozak
Marketing Manager: Joseph H Krawczyk
Credit Cards: MasterCard
Catalog Cost: Free
Catalog Circulation: Mailed 2 time(s) per year to 30000
Average Order Size: $80
Printing Information: 32 pages in 4 colors on Matte Stock
Press: Web Press
Binding: Folded
Mailing List Information: Names for rent
In Business: 35 years
Number of Employees: 5
Sales Volume: $500M to $1MM

3259 Filaree Farms Seed Garlic Catalog
Filaree Garlic Farm
83 Epley Road
Omak, WA 98841   509-422-6940
                    info@filareefarm.com
                    www.filareefarm.com

Variety of garlic seeds

President: Maya W Woods
Catalog Circulation: to 12000
Printing Information: 44 pages in 2 colors on Newsprint
Binding: Folded
Mailing List Information: Names for rent
In Business: 27 years
Sales Volume: $3MM to $5MM

3260 Flower & Herb Exchange
Graphics Lacerosse
3094 N Winn Road
Decorah, IA 52101-7776   563-382-5990
                        Fax: 563-382-6511
                    www.seedsavers.org

Vegetables, herbs, flowers, transplants, prairie plants, potatoes and garlic seeds

Chairman: Keith Crotz
President: John Torgrimson
CFO: Diane Ott Whealy
Vice-Chair of the Board: Neil Hamilton
Secretary/Treasurer of the Board: Larry Grimstad
Deputy Director - Administration: Lynne Rilling
Credit Cards: AMEX; MasterCard
Printing Information: 84 pages in 7 colors on Newsprint
Binding: Saddle Stitched
In Business: 40 years

3261 Four Season's Nursery
Four Season's Nursery
1706 Morrisey Drive
Bloomington, IL 61704   309-834-7200
            customercare@4seasonsnurseries.com
                www.4seasonsnurseries.com

Perrenials, seeds, ornamentals, bulbs, container pots, hedges, herbs, fruit and nut trees

Credit Cards: MasterCard
Catalog Cost: Free

In Business: 41 years
Number of Employees: 5

3262 Fungi Perfecti
Fungi Perfecti LLC
P.O. Box 7634
Olympia, WA 98507   360-426-9292
      800-780-9126
      info@fungi.com
      www.fungi.com

Mushroom spawn, growing kits, supplies and books for the home and commercial grower

President: Paul Stamets
Credit Cards: MasterCard; Visa
Catalog Cost: Free
Catalog Circulation: Mailed 1 time(s) per year
Average Order Size: $75
Printing Information: 82 pages in 4 colors on Glossy Stock
Press: Web Press
Binding: Saddle Stitched
Mailing List Information: Names for rent
In Business: 20 years
Number of Employees: 10
Sales Volume: $1MM to $3MM

3263 Garden City Seeds
Irish Eyes Garden Seeds
5045 Robinson Canyon Road
Ellensburg, WA 98926-9096   509-933-7150
      877-733-3001
      Fax: 800-964-9210
customerservice@irisheyesgardenseeds.com
      www.irisheyesgardenseeds.com

Vegetable, flower and herb seeds

President: Greg Lutousky
greg@irisheyesgardenseeds.com
CFO: Sue Lutousky
sue@irisheyesgardenseeds.com
Marketing Manager: Greg Lutousky
Production Manager: Greg Lutousky
Buyers: John Schneeberger, Seeds
Karen Coombs, Garden Supplies
Credit Cards: MasterCard; Visa; Discover
Catalog Cost: $2
Catalog Circulation: Mailed 1 time(s) per year
Average Order Size: $45
Printing Information: 88 pages in 4 colors on Newsprint
Press: Web Press
Binding: Folded
Mailing List Information: Names for rent
List Company: Chilcott Direct
In Business: 13 years
Number of Employees: 10

3264 Goodwin Creek Gardens
Goodwin Creek Gardens
PO Box 83
Williams, OR 97544   800-846-7359
      Fax: 541-846-7357
      info@goodwincreekgardens.com
      www.goodwincreekgardens.com

Herb plants and seeds

President: Jim Becker
Catalog Circulation: to 20000
Printing Information: 68 pages in 2 colors on Newsprint
Press: Web Press
Binding: Saddle Stitched
Mailing List Information: Names for rent
In Business: 40 years
Number of Employees: 2

3265 Greenworld Project
Greenworld Project
26309 Blackwater Rd.
PO Box 177
Cohasset, MN 55721   218-328-5744
      800-825-5122
      Fax: 877-257-6221
      www.greenworldproject.net

Sells seed packets or trees that have started to grow

Credit Cards: AMEX; MasterCard

3266 Gurney's Seeds & Nursery
Gurney's Seeds & Nursery Company
PO Box 4178
Greendale, IN 47025-4178   513-354-1492
      812-260-2153
      Fax: 513-354-1493
      www.gurneys.com

Seeds, plants and bulbs

Director of Research and Developmen: Felix Cooper
Credit Cards: MasterCard
Catalog Cost: Free

3267 Henry Field's Seed & Nursery
Henry Field's Seed & Nursery
PO Box 397
Aurora, IN 47001-397   513-354-1494
      Fax: 513-354-1496
      www.henryfields.com

Shrubs, seed starter, mail order plants, potato, vegetable seeds, flower bulbs, tomato seed, apple trees, garlic, perennial plants, onion sets, tulip bulbs, fruit tree, daylily, strawaberry plants

Credit Cards: MasterCard
Catalog Cost: Free

3268 High Mowing Organic Seeds
76 Quarry Rd.
Wolcott, VT 05680   802-472-6174
      866-735-4454
      Fax: 802-472-3201
      www.highmowingseeds.com

Seeds

Founder/ Head Seedsman: Tom Stearns
Co-Owner/ Director: Meredith Davis

3269 Holland Bulb Farms
Holland Bulb Farms
8480 North 87th Street
Milwaukee, WI 53224   800-689-2852
      Fax: 888-508-3762
      info@hollandbulbfarms.com
      www.hollandbulbfarms.com

Flower bulbs

Credit Cards: MasterCard
Catalog Cost: Free

3270 Home Gardener's Vegetable, Flower & Supplies
Harris Seeds
355 Paul Road
PO Box 24966
Rochester, NY 14624-966   800-544-7938
      Fax: 877-892-9197
      gardeners@harrisseeds.com
      www.harrisseeds.com

Vegetable seeds, annual and perennial flower seeds, garden ready transplants, flower bulbs and tubers

President: Richard Chamberlin
Ornamentals Manager: Vicky Rupley
Credit Cards: AMEX; MasterCard
Catalog Cost: Free
Catalog Circulation: Mailed 1 time(s) per year
Average Order Size: $300
Printing Information: 120 pages in 4 colors on Glossy Stock
Press: Web Press
Binding: Saddle Stitched
Mailing List Information: Names for rent
In Business: 135 years
Number of Employees: 38
Sales Volume: $10MM to $20MM

3271 Horticultural Products & Services
Horticultural Products & Services
334 W Stroud Street
Suite 1
Randolph, WI 53956-1341   800-322-7288
      Fax: 888-477-7333
      info@hpsseed.com
      www.hpsseed.com

Flower, vegetable and herb seeds

Catalog Cost: Free
Printing Information: 136 pages

3272 Hudson Valley Seed Library
484 Mettacahonts Rd.
Accord, NY 12404   845-204-8769
      mail@seedlibrary.org
      www.seedlibrary.org

Seeds and plants, garden supplies and accessories

Managing/ Creative Director: Ken Greene
Technical and Financial Manager: Doug Muller

3273 Irish Eyes
Irish Eyes Garden Seeds
5045 Robinson Canyon Rd
Ellensburg, WA 9892-307   509-933-7150
      Fax: 509-962-4830
      customerservice@irisheyesgardenseeds.com
      www.irisheyesgardenseeds.com

Seed potatoes, garlic, and shallots, vegetable seeds, flower seeds, fertilizers, books, garden supplies and specialty foods

President: Greg A Lutovsky
greg@irisheyesgardenseeds.com
CFO: Sue Lutovsky
sue@irisheyesgardenseeds.com
Catalog Cost: Free
Catalog Circulation: Mailed 1 time(s) per year to 50M
Average Order Size: $52
Printing Information: 26 pages in 1 color on Newsprint
In Business:
Number of Employees: 40
Sales Volume: $500M to $1MM

3274 J L Hudson Seeds
J. L. Hudson, Seedsman
PO Box 337
La Honda, CA 94020-337   jlhry@jlhudsonseeds.net
      www.jlhudsonseeds.net

Uncommon seeds, hard-to-find ornamentals, unusual perennials, etc

Catalog Cost:
In Business: 103 years

3275 Jackson & Perkins
Jackson & Perkins
2 Floral Avenue
Hodges, SC 29653   800-292-4769
      Fax: 800-242-0329
      service@jacksonandperkins.com
      www.jacksonandperkins.com

Roses, bulbs, perennials and gifts

Buyers: Scott Anderson
Credit Cards: AMEX; MasterCard
Catalog Cost: Free
Average Order Size: $94
Printing Information: 44 pages
Press: Web Press
List Company: American List Counsel
In Business: 142 years
Number of Employees: 5000

3276 John Scheeper's Beauty from Bulbs
John Scheeper's Inc
23 Tulip Drive
PO Box 638
Bantam, CT 06750-1631   860-567-0838
Fax: 860-567-5323
customerservice@johnscheepers.com
www.johnscheepers.com

Tulips, narcissi, lilies, amaryllis and rare and
unusual Dutch bulbs

President: Jo-Anne van den Berg-Ohms
Credit Cards: MasterCard
Sales Volume: $10MM to $20MM

3277 Johnny's Selected Seeds
Johnny's Selected Seeds
13 Main Street
Fairfield, ME 04901   877-564-6697
www.johnnyseeds.com

Vegetable, herb and flower seeds as well as
accessories, including roots, tubers, seed
cultivation supplies and books

Chairman: Rob Johnston, Jr
Territory Sales Representative, CA: John
Bauer
jbauer@johnnyseeds.com
International Marketing Manager: Chris Siladi
Catalog Circulation: Mailed 1 time(s) per year
Average Order Size: $42
Printing Information: in 4 colors on Glossy
Stock
Press: Web Press
Binding: Saddle Stitched
Mailing List Information: Names for rent
List Manager: Bob Milano
In Business: 40 years
Sales Volume: $20MM to $50MM

3278 Jordan Seeds Inc.
Jordan Seeds Inc.
6400 Upper Afton Rd.
Woodbury, MN 55125-1146   651-739-9578
Fax: 651-731-7690
seeds@jordanseeds.com
www.jordanseeds.com

Vegetable seeds

President: Jacob Jordan
CFO: Dan Jordan
Production Manager: Dan Jordan
Catalog Circulation: to 8000
Average Order Size: $300
Printing Information: 32 pages in 2 colors
In Business: 25 years
Number of Employees: 3
Sales Volume: Under $500M

3279 Jung Seeds & Plants
Jung
335 S High Street
Randolph, WI 53956   800-297-3123
info@jungseed.com
www.jungseed.com

Seeds and nursery stock

President/Marketing: Richard Zondag
Finance Director: David Wild
Catalog Cost: Free
Printing Information: 112 pages
In Business: 106 years
Number of Employees: 450

3280 Kester's Wild Game Food Nurseries
Kester's Wild Game Food Nurseries Inc
PO Box 516
Omro, WI 54963-516   920-685-2929
Fax: 920-685-6727
pkester@vbe.com
www.kestersnursery.com

Seeds and aquatic plants for wildlife feeding

President: David Kester
Owner: Patricia Kester
Credit Cards: MasterCard; Visa
Catalog Cost:

Catalog Circulation: Mailed 1 time(s) per year
to 2.5M
Printing Information: 40 pages in 4 colors on
Matte Stock
Press: Web Press
Binding: Saddle Stitched
Mailing List Information: Names for rent
In Business: 80 years
Number of Employees: 7
Sales Volume: $500M to $1MM

3281 Kitchen Garden Seeds
23 Tulip Drive
PO Box 638
Bantam, CT 06750   860-567-6086
Fax: 860-567-5323
Customerservice@kitchengardenseeds.com
www.kitchengardenseeds.com

Seeds

Managing Director: Jo-Anne van den
Berg-Ohms

3282 Liberty Seed Company
Stokes
2495 Walden Avenue
Buffalo, NY 14225   800-396-9238
Fax: 800-272-5560
stokes@stokeseeds.com
www.stokeseeds.com

Vegetable, flower seeds and gardening supplies

President: Wayne Gale
Credit Cards: MasterCard
Catalog Cost: Free
Catalog Circulation: Mailed 1 time(s) per year
to 10000
Average Order Size: $23
Printing Information: 36 pages in 4 colors on
Glossy Stock
Press: Web Press
Binding: Perfect Bound
PO Box 548
Buffalo, NY 14240
716.695.6980
In Business: 136 years
Number of Employees: 20
Sales Volume: $1MM to $3MM

3283 McClure & Zimmerman
McClure & Zimmerman
335 S High Street
Randolph, WI 53956   800-546-4053
www.mzbulb.com

Bulbs, seeds and supplies

Catalog Cost: Free

3284 Meyer Seed
Meyer Seed Company of Baltimore, Inc
600 S Caroline Street
Baltimore, MD 21231-2813   410-342-4224
800-458-SEED
Fax: 410-327-1469
info@meyerseedco.com
www.meyerseedco.com/

Seeds, garden supplies and tools

Credit Cards: AMEX; MasterCard
Catalog Cost: Free
Catalog Circulation: Mailed 1 time(s) per year
Printing Information: 40 pages in 4 colors
Binding: Saddle Stitched
Mailing List Information: Names for rent
In Business: 105 years
Number of Employees: 30
Sales Volume: Under $500M

3285 Native Seeds
Native Seeds
3061 N. Campbell Avenue
Tucson, AZ 85719   520-622-5561
866-622-5561
Fax: 520-622-5591
info@nativeseeds.org
www.nativeseeds.org

Southwestern U.S. indigenous heirloom
food and wildflower seeds; Made to order gift
baskets with native foods, unique bake
mixes, native crafts, herbs, seeds and books

President: Bryan Jones
CFO: Tracy Martineau
Marketing Manager: Julie Evans, Market-
ing/Operations
Executive Director: Bill McDorman
Deputy Director: Belle Starr
Director of Finance and Operations: Leilani M.
Rothrock
Catalog Circulation: Mailed 1 time(s) per year
Printing Information: 20 pages in 4 colors on
Newsprint
Press: Web Press
Binding: Saddle Stitched
Mailing List Information: Names for rent
In Business: 31 years
Number of Employees: 15
Sales Volume: $3MM to $5MM

3286 Nature Hills Nursery
Nature Hills Nursery, Inc.
9910 N. 48th Street
Suite 200
Omaha, NE 68152   402-934-8116
888-864-7663
Fax: 402-991-0778
info@naturehills.com
www.naturehills.com

Tree and shrub products, perennials, rose
bushes and other plants, flower bulbs and
seeds

President: Jeffrey J Dinslage
Credit Cards: AMEX; MasterCard
In Business: 13 years
Number of Employees: 20
Sales Volume: $1.2 Million

3287 Nichols Garden Nursery
Nichols Garden Nursery
1190 Old Salem Road NE
Albany, OR 97321-4580   800-422-3985
Fax: 800-231-5306
www.nicholsgardennursery.com

Herb seeds and plants

President: Rose Marie McGee
Credit Cards: AMEX; MasterCard
Catalog Cost: Free
Catalog Circulation: Mailed 1 time(s) per year
to 250M
Printing Information: 55 pages in 4 colors
Mailing List Information: Names for rent
List Manager: Keane McGee
In Business: 65 years
Number of Employees: 20
Sales Volume: $1MM to $3MM

3288 Otis S Twilley Seed Company
Otis S. Twilley Seed Co., Inc.
121 Gary Road
Hodges, SC 29653-9168   864-227-5117
800-622-7333
Fax: 864-227-5108
twilley@twilleyseed.com
www.twilleyseed.com

Seeds, vegetables and flowers

President: George Park
Credit Cards: AMEX; MasterCard
Catalog Cost: Free
Catalog Circulation: Mailed 1 time(s) per year
to 15000
Printing Information: 88 pages in 4 colors
Press: Web Press
Binding: Saddle Stitched
Mailing List Information: Names for rent
In Business: 100 years

3289   Park Seed Company
Park Seed Company
3507 Cokesbury Road
Hodges, SC 29653   864-330-2003
                                     800-845-3369
                                     info@parkseed.com
                                     www.parkseed.com

Plants, seeds and bulbs, and herbs.

President: Rik Binet
Catalog Circulation: Mailed 4 time(s) per year
Printing Information: 36 pages in 4 colors
Mailing List Information: Names for rent
In Business: 149 years
Number of Employees: 1000
Sales Volume: $50MM

3290   Pepper Gal
Pepper Gal
400 NW 20th St.
Fort Lauderdale, FL 33311   954-537-5540
                                peppergal@bellsouth.net
                                www.peppergal.com

Capsicum (pepper) seeds, hot, sweet, ornamental, gourds, herbs, tomatos, pepper design items for home and garden, clothing and books.

President: Betty Payton
Catalog Cost: Free
Catalog Circulation: to 10000
Printing Information: 4 pages
Mailing List Information: Names for rent
In Business: 23 years
Number of Employees: 2

3291   Pinetree Garden Seeds
Pinetree Garden Seeds
P.O. Box 300
New Gloucester, ME 04260   207-926-3400
                               hello@superseeds.com
                               www.superseeds.com

Flower, vegetable, herb and houseplant seeds, tools, garden equipment and books

President: Richard Meiners
Marketing Manager: Jef Wright
Credit Cards: AMEX; MasterCard
Catalog Cost: Free
Catalog Circulation: Mailed 1 time(s) per year to 575M
Average Order Size: $35
Printing Information: 164 pages in 4 colors on Newsprint
Press: Web Press
Binding: Saddle Stitched
Mailing List Information: Names for rent
In Business: 38 years
Number of Employees: 45
Sales Volume: $2,000,000

3292   Pleasant Valley Glads & Dahlias
Pleasant Valley Glads & Dahlias
PO Box 213
West Suffield, CT 06093-494   860-798-8189
                                860-668-7868
                                pleasantvalleyglads@cox.net
                                www.gladiola.com

Gladiolas & dahlias

President: Gary Adams
Credit Cards: AMEX; MasterCard
In Business: 55 years

3293   Prairie Nursery
Prairie Nursery
P.O. Box 306
Westfield, WI 53964   800-476-9453
                                Fax: 608-296-2741
                                www.prairienursery.com

Native flowers and grasses for prairies and woodlands - plants and seeds

President: Neil Diboll
Credit Cards: AMEX; MasterCard
Catalog Cost: Free
Catalog Circulation: Mailed 1 time(s) per year

to 2500
Average Order Size: $125
Printing Information: 74 pages in 4 colors on Matte Stock
Press: Web Press
Binding: Saddle Stitched
Mailing List Information: Names for rent
In Business: 45 years
Number of Employees: 25
Sales Volume: $1MM to $3MM

3294   RH Shumway
RH Shumway
334 W Stroud St
Randolph, WI 53956   800-342-9461
                                Fax: 888-437-2733
                                info@rhshumway.com
                                www.rhshumway.com

Seeds, nursery stock and horticultural supplies

President: RH Shumway
Credit Cards: MasterCard; Visa
Catalog Cost:
Catalog Circulation: Mailed 1 time(s) per year to 1MM
Printing Information: 64 pages in 4 colors
Press: Web Press
Binding: Saddle Stitched
In Business: 11 years
Number of Employees: 100

3295   Rare Fruiting Plants & Trees
Garden of Delights
14560 SW 14th Street
Davie, FL 33325-4217   954-370-9004
                                800-741-3103
                                Fax: 954-236-4588
                                godelights@aol.com
                                www.gardenofdelights.com

Sugar apple, chocolate, miracle fruit, rare fruiting, plants and tree oil palms, toddy palms, passion fruit, vanilla orchid, lemon grass, habanero pepper and black pepper

President: Murray Corman
Marketing Manager: Phil Croke
Average Order Size: $90
Printing Information: 8 pages in 1 color on Matte Stock
Binding: Folded
Mailing List Information: Names for rent
In Business: 27 years
Number of Employees: 3
Sales Volume: $250,000

3296   Redwood City Seed Company
Redwood City Seed Company
PO Box 361
Redwood City, CA 94064   650-325-7333
                                Fax: 650-325-4056
                                ecoseeds.com

Heirloom, non-hybrid vegetables, hot peppers and herb seeds

President: Craig Dremann
Buyers: Craig Dremann
Credit Cards: AMEX; MasterCard
Catalog Cost:
Catalog Circulation: Mailed 1 time(s) per year
Printing Information: 28 pages in 1 color on Matte Stock
Press: Web Press
Binding: Saddle Stitched
Mailing List Information: Names for rent
In Business: 41 years

3297   Ritchers Herbs
Ritchers
357 Highway 47
Goodwood, ON L0C-1A0   905-640-6677
                                800-668-4372
                                Fax: 905-640-6641
                                www.ritchers.com

Seeds, herbs, plants, flowers, vegetables, garden supplies

Catalog Cost: Free
In Business: 48 years

3298   Robert's Seeds
Roberts Seed, Inc.
982 22 Rd
Axtell, NE 68924   308-743-2565
                                Fax: 541-926-8159
                                www.robertsseed.com

Large variety of seeds

President: Walter Bryant

3299   Rocky Mountain Rare Plants
Karmaloop
1706 Deerpath Road
Franktown, CO 80116-9462   303-688-6645
                                Fax: 970-663-7938
                                staff@rmrp.com
                                www.rmrp.com

Seeds of alpines and rock garden plants grown in the Rocky Mountains

President: Rebecca Skowron
Credit Cards: MasterCard; Visa
Catalog Cost:

3300   Rohrer Seeds
Rohrer & Brothers Inc
2472 Old Philadephia Pike
P.O. Box 250
Smoketown, PA 17576   717-299-2571
                                info@rohrerseeds.com
                                www.rohrerseeds.com

Over 1000 varieties of seed which include vegetables, flowers, herbs, cover crops, wildlife grazing crops and lawn grass

President: Doug Rohrer
CFO: Gordon Rohrer
Marketing Manager: James Carpenter
Buyers: Jeff Watson
Credit Cards: MasterCard
Catalog Cost: Free
Catalog Circulation: Mailed 1 time(s) per year to 18000
Average Order Size: $50
Printing Information: 64 pages in 1 color on Glossy Stock
Press: Web Press
Binding: Saddle Stitched
Mailing List Information: Names for rent
In Business: 98 years
Number of Employees: 25
Sales Volume: $5MM to $10MM

3301   Rupp Seeds
Rupp Seeds Inc
17919 County Road B
Wauseon, OH 43567-9458   419-337-1841
                                800-700-1199
                                Fax: 419-337-5491
                                www.Ruppseeds.Com

Sweet corn seeds

President: Roger Rupp
Credit Cards: MasterCard; Visa
Catalog Circulation: to 15000
Printing Information: 60 pages on Matte Stock
Binding: Folded
In Business: 69 years
Number of Employees: 25
Sales Volume: $10MM to $20MM

3302   Seed Savers Exchange
Seed Savers Exchange
3094 N Winn Rd
Decorah, IA 52101-7776   563-382-5990
                                Fax: 563-382-6511
                                customerservice@seedsavers.org
                                www.Seedsavers.org

Heirloom seeds, gardening books and gifts

Chairman: Keith Crotz
President: John Torgrimson
Marketing Manager: Kelly Tagtow
Vice-Chair Of the Board: Neil Hamilton, J.D.

Secretary: Larry Grimstad
Treasurer: Larry Grimstad
Catalog Cost:
Catalog Circulation: Mailed 1 time(s) per year to 75000
Printing Information: 101 pages in 3 colors
Press: Letterpress
Binding: Saddle Stitched
Mailing List Information: Names for rent
In Business: 40 years
Number of Employees: 10
Sales Volume: $3MM to $5MM

3303 Seeds Trust

Seeds Trust
5870 S Long Lane
Littleton, CO 80121   720-335-3436
                          Fax: 877-686-7524
            support3@seedstrust.com
                www.seedstrust.com

Vegetables, tomoatoes, wildflowers, wildflower mixes, native grasses, herbs

President: Bill McDorman
Marketing Manager: Belle McDorman
Catalog Cost:
In Business: 25 years

3304 Seeds of Change

Seeds of Change
PO Box 4908
Rancho
Dominguez, CA 90220-5700   505-438-8080
                          888-762-7333
                   Fax: 505-438-7052
          gardener@seedsofchange.com
               www.seedsofchange.com

Organic seeds

President: Stephen Badger
Marketing Manager: Scott Vlaun
Catalog Cost: Free
Printing Information: 72 pages in 3 colors on Matte Stock
Press: Letterpress
Binding: Folded
In Business: 24 years
Number of Employees: 10
Sales Volume: 500M-1MM

3305 Select Seeds Antique Flowers

Select Seeds
180 Stickney Hill Rd
Union, CT 06076   860-684-9310
                          800-684-0395
                   Fax: 860-684-9224
            info@selectseeds.com
               www.Selectseeds.com

Cottage garden and heirloom flowers seeds and plants

President: Marilyn Barlow
Credit Cards: MasterCard; Visa
Catalog Circulation: to 40000
Average Order Size: $28
Printing Information: 64 pages in 3 colors on Newsprint
Mailing List Information: Names for rent
In Business: 50 years
Number of Employees: 8
Sales Volume: $5MM to $10MM

3306 Shepard Iris Garden

Shepard Iris Garden
3342 W Orangewood Avenue
Phoenix, AZ 85051-7453   602-841-1231
                          800-548-0625
                   Fax: 602-841-1231
        davesgarden.com/products/gwd/c/1574/

Collection of iris bulbs and plants

President: Don/Bobbie Shepard
Marketing Manager: Bobbie Shepard

3307 Southern Exposure Seed Exchange

Southern Exposure Seed Exchange
PO Box 460
Mineral, VA 23117   540-894-9480
                     Fax: 540-894-9481
          gardens@southernexposure.com
               www.southernexposure.com

Over 700 varieties of open-pollinated, heirloom and traditional varieties of vegetables, flowers and herb seeds

Chairman: Paul Blundell
President: Ira Wallace
CFO: Douglas Steven Hall
Production Manager: Ken Bezilla
International Marketing Manager: Brian Rakita
Buyers: Hanz Hammar
Credit Cards: MasterCard
Catalog Cost:
Catalog Circulation: to 10000
Average Order Size: $31
Printing Information: 84 pages in 4 colors on Newsprint
Binding: Saddle Stitched
Mailing List Information: Names for rent
In Business: 43 years
Number of Employees: 15
Sales Volume: Under $500M

3308 Stock Seed Farms

Stock Seed Farms
28008 Mill Rd
Murdock, NE 68407   402-867-3771
                          800-759-1520
                   Fax: 402-867-2442
            prairie@stockseed.com
                www.stockseed.com

Seed of prairie wildflowers and native Midwest grasses, turf type buffalo grasses, coby and bowie

President: David Stock, Praire Grasses/Wflwr
Catalog Cost: Free
Catalog Circulation: Mailed 1 time(s) per year
Printing Information: 22 pages in 4 colors on Glossy Stock
Press: Web Press
Binding: Saddle Stitched
Mailing List Information: Names for rent
In Business: 50 years
Number of Employees: 7
Sales Volume: $3MM to $5MM

3309 Stokes Seeds

Stokes Seeds
PO Box 548
Buffalo, NY 14240-548   716-695-6980
                          800-396-9238
                   Fax: 888-831-3334
            stokes@stokeseeds.com
                www.stokeseeds.com

Flower garden and vegetable garden seeds

President: Wayne Gale
Credit Cards: AMEX; MasterCard
In Business: 133 years

3310 Territorial Seed Company

Territorial Seed Company
P.O. Box 158
Cottage Grove, OR 97424   541-942-9547
                          800-626-0866
                   Fax: 888-657-3131
            info@territorialseed.com
               www.territorialseed.com

Complete line of vegetable, flower and herb seeds and plants, tools, garlic and organic gardening supplies

President: Tom Johns
Fulfillment: Kathy Ledserwood
Founder: Steve Solomon
Owner: Julie Johns
Credit Cards: MasterCard; Visa
Catalog Cost: Free
Catalog Circulation: Mailed 2 time(s) per year to 700M

Printing Information: 95 pages in 4 colors on Newsprint
Press: Web Press
Binding: Saddle Stitched
Mailing List Information: Names for rent
In Business: 32 years
Number of Employees: 24
Sales Volume: $1MM to $3MM

3311 Thompson & Morgan Seedsmen

Thmpson & Morgan Seeds
P.O. Box 397
Aurora, IN 47001-397   800-274-7333
                     Fax: 888-466-4769
                www.tmseeds.com

Flower and vegetable seeds

Buyers: Burt Garris
Catalog Cost: Free
In Business: 160 years
Number of Employees: 25
Sales Volume: $5MM to $10MM

3312 Tomato Growers Supply

PO Box 60015
Fort Myers, FL 33906   239-768-1119
                          888-478-7333
                   Fax: 239-768-3476
        customerservice@tomatogrowers.com
               www.tomatogrowers.com

Seeds

3313 Totally Tomatoes

Totally Tomatoes
334 W Stroud Street
Randolph, WI 53956-1274   800-345-5977
                     Fax: 888-477-7333
            info@totallytomato.com
               www.totallytomato.com

Varieties of tomato and pepper seeds

Catalog Cost: Free
Printing Information: 72 pages
In Business: 8 years
Number of Employees: 100

3314 Urban Farmer Seeds

Urban Farmer Seeds
120 E 161st Street
Westfield, IN 46074   317-600-2807
                www.ufseeds.com

Vegetables, herbs, flowers, fruits, and supplies

Catalog Cost: Free
In Business: 9 years

3315 Van Dyck's Flower Farm

K. Van Bourgondien & Sons, Inc.
P.O. Box 289
Cleves, OH 45002-2000   800-552-9996
                          800-552-9916
                   Fax: 800-327-4268
            blooms@dutchbulbs.com
               www.dutchbulbs.com

Dutch flower bulbs

President: Jan Van Dyck
Credit Cards: AMEX; MasterCard
Catalog Cost: Free
Catalog Circulation: Mailed 2 time(s) per year to 1.5MM
Average Order Size: $100
Printing Information: 68 pages in 4 colors on Glossy Stock
Binding: Saddle Stitched
Number of Employees: 15
Sales Volume: $1,000,000

3316 Van Engelen
Van Engelen, Inc.
23 Tulip Drive
PO Box 638
Bantam, CT 06750   860-567-8734
                          Fax: 860-567-5323
customerservice@vanengelen.com
www.vanengelen.com

Flower bulbs

Chairman: Jo-Anne van den Berg-Ohms
President: Jan S. Ohms
Owner: Jan S. Ohms
Credit Cards: MasterCard; Visa
Catalog Cost: Free
Catalog Circulation: Mailed 1 time(s) per year
Printing Information: 52 pages in 1 color
Mailing List Information: Names for rent

3317 Veldheer Tulip Gardens
Veldheers
12755 Quincy St
Holland, MI 49424   616-399-1900
                          619-399-1803
                          Fax: 616-399-1270
twingoose1@aol.com
www.Veldheer.Com

Fall and spring bulbs, domestic and import

President: Jim Veldheer
Marketing Manager: James L Veldheer
Founder: Vern Veldheer
Credit Cards: MasterCard; Visa
Catalog Circulation: Mailed 2 time(s) per year
to 30000
Printing Information: 18 pages in 4 colors on
Glossy Stock
Press: Web Press
Binding: Perfect Bound
In Business: 65 years
Number of Employees: 16
Sales Volume: $20MM to $50MM

3318 Vermont Bean Seed Company
Vermont Bean Seed Company
334 W Stroud Street
Randolph, WI 53956   800-349-1071
                            800-349-1071
                            Fax: 888-500-7333
info@vermontbean.com
www.vermontbean.com

**Untreated heirloom bean, pea and corn seed,
herb, vegetable, green and flower seeds**

Credit Cards: MasterCard; Visa
Catalog Circulation: Mailed 1 time(s) per year
to 500M
Printing Information: 79 pages in 4 colors
Press: Web Press
Binding: Saddle Stitched
Number of Employees: 100

3319 Vesey's Seeds
Veseys
411 York Road, Highway 25
PO Box 9000
York, PE C0A 1   902-368-7333
                        800-363-7333
                        Fax: 800-686-0329
customerservice@veseys.com
www.veseys.com

Vegetable and flower seeds

President: Bev Simpson
Marketing Manager: John Barrett
Founder: Arthur Vesey
Catalog Cost: Free
Printing Information: 72 pages in 4 colors on
Glossy Stock
Press: Web Press
Binding: Saddle Stitched
In Business: 76 years
Sales Volume: $200,000

3320 W Atlee Burpee and Company
W Atlee Burpee & Company
300 Park Avenue
Warminster, PA 18974-4818   215-674-4900
                                   800-888-1447
                                   Fax: 215-674-4170
www.Burpee.Com

**Vegetables, annual and perennial flowers,
herbs, flowering bulbs, seed starting, and
gardening supplies**

President: George Ball
In Business: 139 years
Sales Volume: $20MM to $50MM

3321 Wild Garden Seed
Wild Garden Seed
PO Box 1509
Philomath, OR 97370   541-929-4068
karen@wildgardenseed.com
www.wildgardenseed.com

Vegetable seeds

President: Frank Morton
Credit Cards: MasterCard
Catalog Cost: Free

**3322 Wildflower Reference Guide & Seed
Catalog**
Wildseed Farms
100 Legacy Drive
PO Box 3000
Fredericksburg, TX 78624   800-848-0078
                                  Fax: 830-990-8090
orders1@wildseedfarms.com
www.wildseedfarms.com

**Over 90 varieties of wildflowers, grasses,
herbs and exotic gardent variety seeds**

President: John R Thomas
CFO: Kerry Fisher
Marketing Manager: Tom Kramer
Credit Cards: AMEX; MasterCard; Visa
Catalog Cost: Free
Catalog Circulation: Mailed 1 time(s) per year
to 80000
Printing Information: 49 pages in 4 colors on
Glossy Stock
Press: Web Press
Binding: Saddle Stitched
Mailing List Information: Names for rent
In Business: 20 years
Number of Employees: 50

3323 Wildflower Seed Company Catalog
Wildflower Seed Company
PO Box 406
Saint Helena, CA 94574-406   707-963-3359
                                    800-456-3359
                                    Fax: 707-253-2582
sales@wildflower-seed.com
www.wildflower-seed.com

**Wildflowers and specific landscape seed
mixes**

Catalog Circulation: to 3000
Printing Information: in 4 colors
Binding: Folded
In Business: 20 years
Number of Employees: 5
Sales Volume: under 500,000

3324 Willhite Seed Catalog
Coffey Seed Company
199 Sparks Street
PO Box 23
Poolville, TX 76487-23   817-599-8656
                                800-828-1840
                                Fax: 817-599-5843
info@willhiteseed.com
www.willhiteseed.com

Over 450 varieties of vegetable seeds

Owner: Robyn Coffey
Manager: Don Dobbs
Credit Cards: MasterCard; Visa
Catalog Cost: Free

Catalog Circulation: Mailed 1 time(s) per year
Printing Information: 64 pages in 4 colors
In Business: 85+ years

3325 Wood Prairie Farm
Wood Prairie Farm
49 Kinney Road
Bridgewater, ME 04735   800-829-9765
                               Fax: 800-300-6494
orders@woodprairie.com
www.woodprairie.com

**Organically grown vegetables and vegetable
seeds, cheese, gift baskets, baking mixes,
maple syrup**

President: Jim Gerritsen
Owner: Megan Gerritsen
Catalog Cost: Free
In Business: 39 years
Number of Employees: 12
Sales Volume: $1.7 million

Supplies & Accessories

3326 AeroGarden
AeroGrow International Inc.
PO Box 18450
Boulder, CO 80308   303-444-7755
                           800-476-9669
                           Fax: 303-444-0406
customerservice@aerogrow.com
www.aerogarden.com

Indoor herb garden, kit and seeds

Chairman: Jack J Walkers
President: Mike Wolfe
CFO: H MacGregor Clarke
Marketing Manager: John K Thompson
Credit Cards: AMEX; MasterCard; Visa
Catalog Cost: Free
In Business: 9 years
Number of Employees: 34
Sales Volume: $11.31MM

3327 Amish Country Gazebos
Amish Country Gazebos
340 Hostetter Road
Manheim, PA 17545   800-700-1777
www.amishgazebos.com

Amish gazebos

President: Chet Beiler
Dan Osborne:
CEO
Treasurer: Sharon Beiler
Credit Cards: AMEX; MasterCard; Visa
Catalog Cost: Free
Catalog Circulation: Mailed 1 time(s) per year
Printing Information: 60 pages
In Business: 23 years
Sales Volume: $460,000

3328 Apple Gate Furniture
Apple Gate Furniture
4200 Boardman Canfield Rd
Canfield, OH 44406-9044   330-533-3464
                                 888-633-4305
                                 Fax: 330-533-3548
sales@applegatefurniture.com
www.Applegatefurniture.Com

**Amish handmade furniture; porch swings,
gliders, adirondack chairs, benches, rocking chairs, picnic tables, wooden arbors,
rocking horses and cedar chests and more**

President: Gail Tomasic
Credit Cards: MasterCard
Catalog Cost: Free
In Business: 30 years
Sales Volume: $200,000

3329 Audubon Workshop
Spring Hill Nurseries
110 West Elm St.
Tipp City, OH 45371-1699   513-354-1509
                         Fax: 513-354-1504
service@springhillnursery.com
www.springhillnursery.com

Bird feed, houses, feeders and accessories
President: Niles Kinerk
Credit Cards: AMEX; MasterCard
Catalog Cost: Free
Sales Volume: $1MM to $3MM

3330 Avant Gardens
Avant Gardens
710 High Hill Road
Dartmouth, MA 02747-1363   508-998-8819
                         Fax: 508-998-9405
plants@avantgardensne.com
www.avantgardensne.com

Unusual shrubs, annuals, perennials along with common plants, rock garden selections
President: P. Buss
Catalog Cost: $3
In Business: 5 years
Number of Employees: 2
Sales Volume: $65,000

3331 Barco Products Company
Barco Products
24 N. Washington Ave
Batavia, IL 60510   630-879-0084
                         800-338-2697
                         Fax: 630-879-8687
sales@barcoproducts.com
www.barcoproducts.com

Picnic tables, park benches, trash receptacles, safety products, parking lot products
President: Robert Runke
Marketing Manager: Susan Ross
Production Manager: Kim Vallone
CEO: Cyril Matter
Catalog Cost: Free
In Business: 30 years
Sales Volume: $6MM

3332 Bartlett Arborist Supply & Manufacturing Company
Bartlett Manufacturing Company
7876 S. Van Dyke
Marlette,, MI 48453   989-635-8900
                         800-331-7101
                         Fax: 989-635-8902
della@bartlettman.com
www.bartlettman.com

Arborist equipment, tree care supplies, cabling and bracing hardware, tree climbing gear, pole saws, pole pruners and more
President: John Nelson
VP: Dorothy Nelson
Credit Cards: MasterCard; Visa
Catalog Cost: Free
Printing Information: 38 pages in 1 color on Glossy Stock
Mailing List Information: Names for rent
In Business: 99 years
Number of Employees: 6
Sales Volume: $1,000,000 - $5,000,000

3333 Bustani Plant Farm
Bustani Plant Farm
1313 East 44th Avenue
Stillwater, OK 74074   405-372-3379
                         Fax: 405-707-8697
info@bustaniplantfarm.com
www.bustaniplantfarm.com

Perennials, annuals, trees and shrubs, Some tropical color plants
President: Steve Owens
steve@bustaniplantfarm.com
Co-Owner: Steve Owens
steve@bustaniplantfarm.com

Co-Owner: Ruth Owens
ruth@bustaniplantfarm.com
Catalog Cost: Free
Printing Information: 48 pages
In Business: 3 years
Number of Employees: 2
Sales Volume: $50,000

3334 Capital Cresting
Capital Cresting
104 Ironwood Court
PO Box 126
Milford, PA 18337-126   570-296-7722
                         800-442-4766
                         Fax: 570-296-4766
www.capitalcrestings.com/

Custom and reproduction roof crestings, finials, snow guards, window grilles, room dividers
Customer Service Manager: Don Quick
Credit Cards: MasterCard; Visa
Catalog Cost: $2
Catalog Circulation: Mailed 4 time(s) per year
Average Order Size: $2400
Printing Information: 24 pages in 2 colors on Glossy Stock
In Business: 19 years
Number of Employees: 10

3335 Carlin Horticultural Supplies
Carlin Horticultural Supplies
8170 N Granville Woods Road
Milwaukee, WI 53223   800-657-0745
                         Fax: 414-355-3107
www.carlinsales.com

Gardening supplies
President: Dan Groh
CFO: Jim Moore
Marketing Manager: Jenny Mitchell
CEO: Mark Maletzke
Credit Cards: MasterCard; Visa
Catalog Cost: $15
In Business: 30 years

3336 Charleston Battery Bench
Geo. C. Birlant & Company
191 King Street
Charleston, SC 29401-3132   843-722-3842
                         888-247-5268
                         Fax: 843-722-3846
birlant@aol.com
www.birlant.com

Iron and wood garden benches and reproduction benches, commercial, ornamental, using South Carolina cypress and cast iron ends from original 19th century molds
President: Phil H Slotin
CFO: Andrew Birlant Slotin
Catalog Cost: Free
Catalog Circulation: to 1000
Average Order Size: $300
Printing Information: 136 pages in 2 colors on Glossy Stock
Binding: Folded
Mailing List Information: Names for rent
In Business: 93 years
Number of Employees: 7
Sales Volume: $1MM to $3MM

3337 Cloud Mountain Farm Center
Cloud Mountain Farm Center
6906 Goodwin Road
Everson, WA 98247   360-966-5859
                         Fax: 360-966-0921
info@cloudmountainfarmcenter.org
www.cloudmountainfarmcenter.org

Fruit trees, berries and ornamental plants, including natives, educational programs
Production Manager: Mark Thompson
Executive Director: Thomas Thornton
Catalog Cost: $2
Printing Information: 48 pages on Newsprint
Press: Web Press

In Business: 39 years
Number of Employees: 12
Sales Volume: $900,000

3338 Collections Etc.
Collections Etc.
PO Box 7985
Elk Grove Village, IL 60009-7985 620-584-8000
                         Fax: 847-350-5701
www.collectionsetc.com

Home essentials, unique gifts and garden accessories all under $20
President: Shelley Nandkeolyar
Marketing Manager: Karl Steigerwald
Fulfillment: Bruce Getowicz
CEO/Founder: Todd Lustbader
COO: Paul Klassman
Credit Cards: AMEX; MasterCard; Visa
Catalog Cost: Free
In Business: 18 years
Number of Employees: 200
Sales Volume: 12.7M

3339 Commercial Hydroponic Catalog
Cropking
134 West Drive
Lodi, OH 44254   330-302-4203
                         Fax: 330-302-4204
cropking@cropking.com
www.cropking.com

Greenhouses and supplies and equipment for hydroponic growers; rockwool, books and videos
President: Paul Brentlinger
General Manager & Partial Owner: Marilyn Brentinger
mbrent@cropking.com
Credit Cards: MasterCard; Visa
Catalog Cost: Free
Catalog Circulation: Mailed 1 time(s) per year
Printing Information: 72 pages in 4 colors
In Business: 35 years
Number of Employees: 30
Sales Volume: $3MM to $5MM

3340 DBS
Dorothy Biddle Service
348 Greeley Lake Rd.
Greeley, PA 18425   570-226-3239
                         888-712-3239
                         Fax: 570-226-0349
lynne@dorothybiddle.com
www.dorothybiddle.com

Flower arranging supplies and equipment; gardening and houseplant accessories; gifts for the gardener; cutting tools, and flower arranging equipment including flower holders of all types
President: Lynne Dodson
Manager: Karen Bolton
Catalog Cost: $1
Catalog Circulation: Mailed 1 time(s) per year to 20000
Printing Information: 28 pages in 4 colors on Glossy Stock
Mailing List Information: Names for rent
In Business: 80 years
Number of Employees: 5
Sales Volume: $900K

3341 Dramm Professional Watering Tools
Dramm Corporation of Manitowoc
2000 North 18th Street
PO Box 1960
Manitowoc, WI 54220-1857   920-684-0227
                         800-258-0848
                         Fax: 920-684-4499
information@dramm.com
www.dramm.com

Watering tools for high velocity water
President: Kurt Dramm
CFO: Theresa Krejcarek
Production Manager: Kurt Dramm

Executive Director: Robert Echter
VP: Charles Bohman
Human Resource Manager: Howard Zimmerman
Buyers: Cathy Brunner
Credit Cards: AMEX; MasterCard
Catalog Circulation: Mailed 1 time(s) per year to 25K
Printing Information: 16 pages in 4 colors
Press: Sheetfed Press
Binding: Saddle Stitched
In Business: 68 years
Number of Employees: 48
Sales Volume: $5.4 MM

3342 Earthbox

Earthbox
1330 Loop Road
Lancaster, PA 17601   888-917-3908
800-442-7336
Fax: 717-392-0734
customerservice@earthbox.com
www.earthbox.com

Complete growing kits, including containers, watering systems and components, live plants, seeds, greenhouses and garden accessories

President: Blake Whisenant
Marketing Manager: Kathy Sponenberg
General Manager: Frank DiPaolo
Operations Manager: Mark Tokash
Marketing Associate/ Graphic Design: Stephanie E. Youngs Seese
Credit Cards: AMEX; MasterCard
In Business: 21 years

3343 Escort Lighting

Escort Lighting
51 North Elm Street
Wernersville, PA 19565-1209   800-856-7948
Fax: 800-398-7661
info@escortlighting.com
www.escortlighting.com

Garden lighting fixtures

President: Michael Hartman
Marketing Manager: Mike Hartman
Credit Cards: AMEX; MasterCard
Catalog Cost: Free
Printing Information: 25 pages
In Business: 25 years
Number of Employees: 8

3344 Everything for the Lilypool

Slocum Water Gardens
1101 Cypress Gardens Boulevard
Winter Haven, FL 33883   863-293-7151
Fax: 800-322-1896
www.slocumwatergardens.com

Complete garden pool products, water lilies, lotus, aquatics, goldfish, pumps, filters, pools, liners and books on water gardening

President: Peter D Slocum
Credit Cards: MasterCard; Visa
Catalog Cost: $3
Catalog Circulation: Mailed 1 time(s) per year to 10M
Printing Information: 60 pages in 4 colors on Glossy Stock
Press: Web Press
Binding: Saddle Stitched
Mailing List Information: Names for rent
In Business: 6 years
Number of Employees: 6
Sales Volume: Under $500M

3345 Fall Planting

Peaceful Valley Farm Supply, Inc.
125 Clydesdale Court
P.O. Box 2209
Grass Valley, CA 95945   530-272-4769
888-784-1722
helpdesk@groworganic.com
www.groworganic.com

Vegetable/herb/flower seed packs or in bulk, propagating, water and irrigation, greenhouse, composting supplies, natural weed control, garden equipment and more

President: Eric Boudier
Vice President: Patricia Boudier
General Manager: Lee Dickerson
Catalog Cost: Free
Catalog Circulation: Mailed 1 time(s) per year
Printing Information: 35 pages in 4 colors
In Business: 41 years
Number of Employees: 60
Sales Volume: $7.2 Million

3346 Fan Fair

Fan Fair
2233 Wisconsin Avenue NW
Washington, DC 20007-4104   202-342-6290

Casablanca and Hunter ceiling fans as well as Fanimation; table and floor lamps

President: C Philip Mitchell
CFO: Charles H Betts
Credit Cards: MasterCard
Catalog Circulation: Mailed 6 time(s) per year
Printing Information: 30 pages
In Business: 20 years
Number of Employees: 12
Sales Volume: $1MM to $3MM

3347 Fischer & Jirouch Company

Fischer & Jirouch Company
4821 Superior Avenue
Cleveland, OH 44103-1295   216-361-3840
Fax: 216-361-0650
fischerjirouch@att.net
www.fischerandjirouch.com

Hand crafted plaster ornaments and custom reproduction

President: Robert Mattei
Catalog Cost: $10
Printing Information: 145 pages
In Business: 115 years
Number of Employees: 11
Sales Volume: $5MM to $10MM

3348 Florentine Craftsmen

Florentine Craftsmen
114 Willenbrock Road
Oxford, CT 06478   203-264-2831
Fax: 203-264-2833
maria@klynchandsons.com
www.florentinecraftsmen.com

Handcrafted garden ornaments, statuary, fountains, furniture

President: Graham Brown
Marketing Manager: Skip Brown
Vice President of Manufacturing: Maria Lynch Dumoulin
Credit Cards: AMEX; MasterCard; Visa
Catalog Cost: $5
Catalog Circulation: to 10K
Average Order Size: $2000
Printing Information: 48 pages in 4 colors on Glossy Stock
Press: Letterpress
Binding: Saddle Stitched
Mailing List Information: Names for rent
In Business: 90 years
Number of Employees: 12
Sales Volume: $500M to $1MM

3349 Flutterbye Garden

Fiutterby Garden Landscaping LLC
2350 Hill Road Boise
Boise, ID 83702   208-571-2170
flutterbygardens@earthlink.net
www.goflutterby.com

Garden accessories

3350 Garden Book

White Flower Farm
Route 63
P.O. Box 50
Litchfield, CT 06759-50   860-496-9624
800-503-9624
Fax: 860-496-1418
www.whiteflowerfarm.com

Gardening supplies

President: Elliot Bradsworth II
CFO: Bruce Bjork
Credit Cards: AMEX; MasterCard
In Business: 65 years

3351 Garden Carts

Norway Co
E9237 Highway O
Sauk City, WI 53583   608-544-5000
norway@norwaycarryall.com
www.norwaycarryall.com

Carry-All Carts

Credit Cards: MasterCard
Catalog Cost: Free
Catalog Circulation: to 2000
Printing Information: 3 pages in 1 color on Glossy Stock
Press: Offset Press
Binding: Folded
Mailing List Information: Names for rent
In Business: 35 years
Number of Employees: 2
Sales Volume: 100,000

3352 GardenTalk Catalog

Garden Talk LLC
PO Box 433
Topsfield, MA 01983   978-887-3388
800-822-4114
Fax: 978-887-9395
CustomerService@GardenTalk.com
www.gardentalk.com

Domestic and imported gardening tools and accessories

Chairman: Robert A. Iger
President: Katrina Neefus
CFO: James A. Rasulo
EVP, Corporate Strategy and Busines: Kevin A. Mayer
EVP, Chief Communications Officer: Zenia B. Mucha
EVP, Chief Human Resources Officer: Jayne Parker
Credit Cards: MasterCard; Visa
Average Order Size: $70
Printing Information: 64 pages on Matte Stock
Press: Web Press
Binding: Folded
Mailing List Information: Names for rent
In Business: 48 years
Number of Employees: 6
Sales Volume: $500M to $1MM

3353 Gardener's Catalog

Kinsman Company
PO Box 428
Pipersville, PA 18947   800-733-4129
800-733-4146
kinsco@kinsmangarden.com
www.kinsmangarden.com

Garden supplies, especially unusual items from England

President: Graham Kinsman
Credit Cards: MasterCard
Catalog Cost: Free
Catalog Circulation: Mailed 2 time(s) per year to 750K
Average Order Size: $90
Printing Information: 112 pages in 4 colors on Glossy Stock
Press: Web Press
Binding: Saddle Stitched
Mailing List Information: Names for rent
In Business: 36 years

Number of Employees: 40
Sales Volume: $5MM to $10MM

3354 Gardener's Supply
Gardener's Supply Company
128 Intervale Road
Burlington, VT 05401-2850   800-876-5520
888-833-1412
info@gardeners.com
www.gardeners.com

Garden tools and supplies, composters, seedstarting, greenhouses, fertilizers, statuary, furniture, organic pest controls, natural home and health products

Marketing Manager: John White
Chief Operating Officer: Cindy Turcot
Buyers: Mark Hurziger
Steve Kovarie
Frank Oliver
Credit Cards: AMEX; MasterCard
Catalog Cost: Free
Catalog Circulation: Mailed 52 time(s) per year to 20000
Printing Information: 65 pages in 4 colors on Matte Stock
Press: Web Press
Binding: Saddle Stitched
Mailing List Information: Names for rent
List Company: AZ Marketing
Cos Cob, CT
In Business: 34 years
Number of Employees: 200
Sales Volume: $20MM to $50MM

3355 Gardening with Kids
Gardening with Kids
237 Commerce Street
Suite 101
Williston, VT 05495-8000   802-863-5251
800-538-7476
Fax: 802-864-6889
customerservice@garden.org

Educational gardening products

President: Mike Metallo
mikem@garden.org
CFO: Tony Vargo
Marketing Manager: Susan Robbins
IT Director: Dan Cristelli
danc@garden.org
Director of Finance: Jean Tedeschi
jennt@garden.org
Research Director: Bruce Butterfield
bruceb@garden.org
Catalog Circulation: Mailed 2 time(s) per year to 500M
Printing Information: 56 pages in 4 colors on Glossy Stock
Press: Web Press
Binding: Perfect Bound
Mailing List Information: Names for rent
In Business: 30 years
Number of Employees: 14
Sales Volume: $3MM to $5MM

3356 Good Scents
Davidson Greenhouse & Nursery, Inc.
3147 E Ladoga Road
Crawfordsville, IN 47933   765-364-0556
Fax: 800-276-3691
vicki@davidsongreenhouse.com
www.davidsongreenhouse.com

Plants and flowers

President: Mark Davidson
Marketing Manager: Mark Davidson
Credit Cards: AMEX; MasterCard
Catalog Cost: $3
In Business: 35 years

3357 Great Gardens
Troy-Bilt
102nd Street 9th Avenue
Troy, NY 12180   518-391-7000
Fax: 518-233-0311
www.troy-bilt.com

Garden supplies

3358 Greenhouse Catalog
The Greenhouse Catalog
3740 Brooklake Road NE
Salem, OR 97303   503-393-3973
800-825-1925
Fax: 503-393-3119
info@greenhousecatalog.com
www.greenhousecatalog.com

Greenhouses and gardening

Chairman: Beverly Perry, Owner
President: Michael Perry
Marketing Manager: Michelle Torres
michelle@Sulexx.com
In Business: 27 years
Number of Employees: 15

3359 Greenhouse Kits Catalog
Charley's Greenhouse & Garden
17979 State Route 536
Mt. Vernon, WA 98273   360-428-2626
800-322-4707
Fax: 360-873-8264
customerservice@charleysgreenhouse.com
www.charleysgreenhouse.com

Greenhouse and garden supplies

3360 Guide to Deer-Resistant Plants
Deer-Resistant Landscape Nursery
3200 Sunstone Ct.
Clare, MI 48617   800-595-3650
sales@deerxlandscape.com
www.deerresistantplants.com

Deer-resistant plants, deer repellents and deer fencing.

President: David Jensen
Catalog Cost: $3.85
In Business: 16 years
Number of Employees: 3
Sales Volume: $43K

3361 Hangouts
CSD
2525 Arapahoe
Suite E4-447
Boulder, CO 80302   303-444-1671
800-426-4688
Fax: 303-443-0808
info@csdco.com
www.csd.net

Hammocks and hanging chairs

President: Beto Goldberg
Catalog Cost: Free
Printing Information: 20 pages in 4 colors on Glossy Stock
Press: Web Press
Binding: Saddle Stitched
Mailing List Information: Names for rent
In Business: 25 years
Number of Employees: 4
Sales Volume: Under $500M

3362 Harmony Farm Supply & Nursery
Harmony Farm Supply & Nursery
3244 Gravenstein Hwy North
Sebastopol, CA 95472-460   707-823-9125
Fax: 707-823-1734
www.harmonyfarm.com

Organic farm and garden supply

In Business: 35 years
Sales Volume: $5MM to $10MM

3363 Harvesting & Country Living
Peaceful Valley Farm Supply, Inc.
125 Clydesdale Court
P.O. Box 2209
Grass Valley, CA 95945   530-272-4769
888-784-1722
helpdesk@groworganic.com
www.groworganic.com

Vegetable/herb/flower seed packs or in bulk, propagating, water and irrigation, greenhouse, composting supplies, natural weed control, garden equipment and more

President: Eric Boudier
Vice President: Patricia Boudier
General Manager: Lee Dickerson
Catalog Cost: Free
Catalog Circulation: Mailed 1 time(s) per year
Printing Information: 68 pages in 4 colors
In Business: 41 years
Number of Employees: 60
Sales Volume: $7.2 Million

3364 Home Place Products
Home Place Products.com
111 Conn Terrace
Lexington, KY 40508-4042   859-621-5511
800-230-8199
Fax: 859-296-0650
info@neilsulier.com
www.neilsuliershopmall.com

Garden tools, BBQ turner, couch caddy, pet pick up tool

President: Neil Sulier
Credit Cards: AMEX; MasterCard; Visa
Average Order Size: $25
Printing Information: 2 pages in 1 color on Matte Stock
Press: Letterpress
Binding: Folded
Mailing List Information: Names for rent
Number of Employees: 5
Sales Volume: $500M to $1MM

3365 Hudson Valley Seed Library
484 Mettacahonts Rd.
Accord, NY 12404   845-204-8769
mail@seedlibrary.org
www.seedlibrary.org

Seeds and plants, garden supplies and accessories

Managing/ Creative Director: Ken Greene
Technical and Financial Manager: Doug Muller

3366 Hydro-Farm West
Hydro-Farm West
2249 S McDowell Ext
Petaluma, CA 94954   800-634-9990
www.hydrofarm.com

Suppliers of hydroponic systems, supplies and books

Reception/Information: Carolyn Andrews
Credit Cards: MasterCard
Catalog Cost: Free
Printing Information: 308 pages
In Business: 37 years

3367 John Deere Construction Equipment
John Deere
One John Deere Place
Moline, IL 61265   309-765-8000
www.deere.com

Agriculture, construction, forestry, lawn and grounds care products and equipment

Chairman: Samuel R. Allen
President: Pierre E Leroy
CFO: Rajesh Kalathur
Marketing Manager: Xenya Mucha
SVP and General Counsel: Mary K. W. Jones
SVP and Chief Financial Officer: Rajesh Kalathur
VP and Deputy Financial Officer: Marie Z. Ziegler
In Business: 178 years
Number of Employees: 760
Sales Volume: $57 MM

3368 Kenneth Lynch & Sons
Kenneth Lynch & Sons
114 Willenbrock Road
Oxford, CT 06478 203-264-2831
info@klynchandsons.com
www.klynchandsons.com

Garden ornaments and statues
President: Timothy Lynch
Sales Manager: Maria Lynch Dumoulin
Sales Assistant: Melody Sonntag
Catalog Circulation: to 3000
Printing Information: 350 pages in 1 color on Matte Stock
Press: Web Press
Binding: Perfect Bound
Mailing List Information: Names for rent
In Business: 82 years
Number of Employees: 12
Sales Volume: $1MM to $3MM

3369 Lilypons Water Gardens
Lilypons Water Gardens
6800 Lily Pons Road
Adamstown, MD 21710 800-999-5459
www.lilypons.com

Water gardens featuring water lilies, pond liners, pumps, filters, fish and more
President: Margaret Thomas Koogle
Marketing Manager: Suzanne Boom
Fulfillment: David Hoffman
Vice President: Richard Koogle
Office Manager: Melissa Richard
Buyers: Rick Roscoe
Credit Cards: AMEX; MasterCard; Visa
Catalog Cost: Free
Catalog Circulation: Mailed 5 time(s) per year to 85000
Average Order Size: $100
Printing Information: 45 pages in 4 colors on Glossy Stock
Press: Web Press
Binding: Saddle Stitched
Mailing List Information: Names for rent
In Business: 100 years
Number of Employees: 15
Sales Volume: $1.7 Million

3370 Long Hungry Creek Nursery
Long Hungry Creek Nursery
P.O. Box 163
Red Boiling Springs, TN 37150 615-699-2493
barefootfarmer@gmail.com
www.barefootfarmer.com/

Gardening supplies and plants
President: Jeff Poppen

3371 Mailboxes Catalog
Mailboxes.com
1010 East 62nd Street
Los Angeles, CA 90001 323-846-6700
800-624-5299
Fax: 323-846-6800
customerservice@mailboxes.com
www.mailboxes.com

Mailboxes, lockers, signs and postal specialties
President: Dennis Fraher
CFO: Mike Lobasso
Marketing Manager: Brian Fraher
Credit Cards: AMEX; MasterCard
Catalog Cost: Free
Catalog Circulation: Mailed 2 time(s) per year to 100M
Printing Information: 121 pages in 4 colors on Glossy Stock
Press: Web Press
Binding: Saddle Stitched
Mailing List Information: Names for rent
In Business: 81 years
Number of Employees: 100
Sales Volume: $5MM to $10MM

3372 Marugg Company
Marugg Company
PO Box 1418
Tracy City, TN 37387 931-592-5042
marugg@blomand.net
www.themaruggcompany.com

European scythes
Co-Owner: Amy Wilson
Co-Owner: Allen Wilson

3373 Michigan Bulb Company
Michigan Bulb Company
PO Box 4180
Lawrenceburg, IN 47025-4180 812-260-2148
Fax: 513-354-1499
www.michiganbulb.com

Bulbs, perennials, trees, vines, hedges and tools
Marketing Manager: Jennifer Castro
CEO: Niles Kinerk
Credit Cards: MasterCard
Catalog Cost: Free
Printing Information: in 4 colors
Number of Employees: 7
Sales Volume: $50 Million

3374 Midlothian
Midlothian Inc
4 Devonshire Lane
Greenville, SC 29617 800-806-1983
Fax: 678-817-9969
www.realteak.com

Teak Benches, Teak dining tables and chair ensembles, and Teak occasional tables and chairs
President: Valerie Terry
Credit Cards: AMEX; MasterCard; Visa
Catalog Cost: Free
Catalog Circulation: to 3000
Printing Information: 20 pages in 4 colors on Glossy Stock
Press: Web Press
Binding: Saddle Stitched
In Business: 8 years

3375 Midwest Supplies
Midwest Supplies
5825 Excelsior Blvd
Minneapolis, MN 55416 952-562-5300
888-449-2739
Fax: 952-925-9867
www.midwesthydroponics.com

Organic, and Hydroponic gardening supplies
Printing Information: 64 pages
In Business: 20 years

3376 Natural & Organic Fertilizers
Peaceful Valley Farm Supply, Inc.
125 Clydesdale Court
P.O. Box 2209
Grass Valley, CA 95945 530-272-4769
888-874-1722
helpdesk@groworganic.com
www.groworganic.com

Vegetable/herb/flower seed packs or in bulk, propagating, water and irrigation, greenhouse, composting supplies, natural weed control, garden equipment and more
President: Eric Boudier
Vice President: Patricia Boudier
General Manager: Lee Dickerson
Catalog Cost: Free
Catalog Circulation: Mailed 1 time(s) per year
Printing Information: 68 pages in 4 colors
In Business: 41 years
Number of Employees: 60
Sales Volume: $7.2 Million

3377 Oly-Ola Sales
Oly-Ola Edgings, Inc
124 E Saint Charles Rd
Villa Park, IL 60181-2414 630-833-3033
800-334-4647
Fax: 630-833-0816
edgings@olyola.com
www.Olyola.Com

Paver restraints, landscape edging, edging for ponds/water grooves
President: Sandra Hechler
Credit Cards: AMEX; MasterCard; Visa
Catalog Cost: Free
Printing Information: 16 pages on Glossy Stock
Mailing List Information: Names for rent
In Business: 3 years
Number of Employees: 10
Sales Volume: $1,000,000 - $5,000,000

3378 Organic Gardening Essentials
Peaceful Valley Farm Supply, Inc.
125 Clydesdale Court
P.O. Box 2209
Grass Valley, CA 95945 530-272-4769
888-784-1722
helpdesk@groworganic.com
www.groworganic.com

Vegetable/herb/flower seed packs or in bulk, propagating, water and irrigation, greenhouse, composting supplies, natural weed control, garden equipment and more
President: Eric Boudier
Vice President: Patricia Boudier
General Manager: Lee Dickerson
Catalog Cost: Free
Printing Information: 168 pages in 4 colors
Press: Web Press
In Business: 41 years
Number of Employees: 60
Sales Volume: $7.2 Million

3379 Organic Seeds
Peaceful Valley Farm Supply, Inc.
125 Clydesdale Court
P.O. Box 2209
Grass Valley, CA 95945 530-272-4769
888-784-1722
helpdesk@groworganic.com
www.groworganic.com

Vegetable/herb/flower seed packs or in bulk, propagating, water and irrigation, greenhouse, composting supplies, natural weed control, garden equipment and more
President: Eric Boudier
Vice President: Patricia Boudier
General Manager: Lee Dickerson
Catalog Cost: Free
Catalog Circulation: Mailed 1 time(s) per year
Printing Information: 68 pages in 4 colors
In Business: 41 years
Number of Employees: 60
Sales Volume: $7.2 Million

3380 Paradise Water Gardens & Landscape
Paradise Water Gardens Ltd.
803 Old County Road
San Carlos, CA 94070 408-520-8960
info@paradisewatergardens.org
www.paradisewatergardens.org

Fiberglass pools and liners, aquatic plants including waterlilies and lotus, fancy goldfish and Japanese Koi
mauricio@paradisewatergardens.org
joe@paradisewatergardens.org
Credit Cards: MasterCard
Catalog Cost: Free
Catalog Circulation: Mailed 1 time(s) per year to 50M
Printing Information: 90 pages in 4 colors on Glossy Stock
Press: Web Press
Binding: Saddle Stitched

Mailing List Information: Names for rent
In Business: 67 years
Number of Employees: 15
Sales Volume: 3MM-5MM

3381 Paw Paw Everlast Label Company
Paw Paw Everlast Label Company
PO Box 93
Paw Paw, MI 49079-93   616-657-4921
www.everlastlabel.com

Permanent metal garden labels and garden markers with 11 designs available for any gardening requirements

President: Arthur Arens
Marketing Manager: Dorothy Arens
Catalog Circulation: to 20000
In Business: 78 years
Number of Employees: 25

3382 Permaloc Aluminum Edging
Permaloc Corporation
13505 Barry Street
Holland, MI 49424   616-399-9600
800-356-9660
Fax: 616-399-9770
info@permaloc.com
www.permaloc.com

Aluminum landscape edging and paving restraints

President: Daniel G Zwier
Marketing Manager: Dave Bareman
Credit Cards: AMEX; MasterCard
Catalog Cost: Free
Catalog Circulation: Mailed 1 time(s) per year to 10M
Printing Information: 10 pages in 4 colors on Glossy Stock
Press: Web Press
Mailing List Information: Names for rent
In Business: 25 years
Number of Employees: 12
Sales Volume: $500M to $1MM

3383 Pest & Weed Control
Peaceful Valley Farm Supply, Inc.
125 Clydesdale Court
P.O. Box 2209
Grass Valley, CA 95945   530-272-4769
888-874-1722
helpdesk@groworganic.com
www.groworganic.com

Vegeatable/herb/flower seed packs or in bulk, propagating, water and irrigation, greenhouse, composting supplies, natural weed control, garden equipment and more

President: Eric Boudier
Vice President: Patricia Boudier
General Manager: Lee Dickerson
Catalog Cost: Free
Catalog Circulation: Mailed 1 time(s) per year
Printing Information: 68 pages in 4 colors
In Business: 41 years
Number of Employees: 60
Sales Volume: $7.2 Million

3384 Plow & Hearth
Plow & Hearth
130 Commerce Lane #B
Rochelle, VA 22738   540-948-3659
800-494-7544
info@plowhearth.com
www.plowhearth.com

Products for country living, home, garden, pets and gifts

President: John Haydock
CFO: Dana Pappas
Manager: Roxanne Dobson
Credit Cards: AMEX; MasterCard
Catalog Cost: Free
Catalog Circulation: Mailed 4 time(s) per year
Printing Information: 132 pages in 4 colors on Glossy Stock
Binding: Saddle Stitched

In Business: 37 years
Number of Employees: 200
Sales Volume: $50MM to $100MM

3385 Pond Guy
15425 Chets Way
Armada, MI 48005   866-766-3435
Fax: 586-589-8600
pondhelp@thepondguy.com
www.thepondguy.com

Garden and residential pond products

Owner: Jason G. Blake

3386 Pond Guy, Inc.
Pond Guy, Inc.
15425 Chets Way
Armada, MI 48005-1402   810-765-7400
Fax: 586-589-8600
pondhelp@thepondguy.com
www.thepondguy.com

Pond and lake supplies; decorative pond supplies

President: J Blake
In Business: 17 years
Number of Employees: 20
Sales Volume: $3.8 Million

3387 PoolSupplyWorld
PoolSupplyWorld
3725 Cincinnati Ave 200
Rocklin, CA 95765   800-722-0467
866-556-0224
Fax: 866-556-3552
sales@poolsupplyworld.com
www.poolsupplyworld.com

Manufacturers of spa and swimming pool supplies

Credit Cards: AMEX; MasterCard
Catalog Cost: Free

3388 Prima Bead
Prima Bead
12333 Enterprise Blvd.
Largo, FL 33773   800-366-2218
customerservice@primabead.com
www.primabead.com

Supplies to create handmade jewelry—also provides free projects, and how-to-videos

Catalog Cost: Free

3389 QC Supply
PO Box 581
574 Road 11
Schuyler, NE 68661-581   402-352-3167
800-433-6340
Fax: 402-352-8825
www.qcsupply.com

Garden supplies

3390 Quality Tools & Drip Irrigation Supplies
Peaceful Valley Farm Supply, Inc.
125 Clydesdale Court
P.O. Box 2209
Grass Valley, CA 95945   530-272-4769
888-784-1722
helpdesk@groworganic.com
www.groworganic.com

Vegetable/herb/flower seed packs or in bulk, propagating, water and irrigation, greenhouse, composting supplies, natural weed control, garden equipment and more

President: Eric Boudier
Vice President: Patricia Boudier
General Manager: Lee Dickerson
Catalog Cost: Free
Catalog Circulation: Mailed 1 time(s) per year
Printing Information: 68 pages in 4 colors
In Business: 41 years
Number of Employees: 60
Sales Volume: $7.2 Million

3391 Sandifer Sculpture
Sandifer Sculpture
1217 Bishops Lodge Rd
Santa Fe, NM 87501-6900   505-984-3049
Fax: 505-984-0768
www.sandifersculpture.com

Sculptures

President: Rosie Sandifer
studio@rosiesandifer.com
Production Manager: Nina Fresquez
Manager: Alexis Ehrgott
Catalog Cost: $15
Catalog Circulation: Mailed 1 time(s) per year
Printing Information: 40 pages in 3 colors

3392 Santa Barbara Greenhouses
Santa Barbara Greenhouses
721 Richmond Ave
Oxnard, CA 93030-7229   805-483-4288
800-544-5276
Fax: 805-483-0229
robsbg@aol.com
www.Sbgreenhouse.Com

Greenhouses and supplies

President: Robert West
Catalog Cost: Free
Catalog Circulation: Mailed 1 time(s) per year
Printing Information: 16 pages in 4 colors
Press: Web Press
Binding: Saddle Stitched
In Business: 41 years
Number of Employees: 6
Sales Volume: $500M to $1MM

3393 Sculpture in Contemporary Garden
Contempary Art Center
44 East Sixth Street
Cincinnati, NY 45202-1153   513-345-8400
513-345-8405
Fax: 513-721-7418
www.contemporaryartscenter.org

Garden sculptures and fountains in marble and bronze

Chairman: James A. Miller
President: David P. Osborn
VP: Matthew Fischer
Treasurer: Ron Bates
Secretary: Elizabeth T. Olson
Catalog Cost: $10
Catalog Circulation: to 500+
Printing Information: 72 pages in 1 color on Glossy Stock
In Business: 79 years
Number of Employees: 10-J
Sales Volume: Under $500M

3394 Siebert & Rice
Seibert & Rice
PO Box 365
Short Hills, NJ 07078-365   973-467-8266
Fax: 973-379-2536
terracotta@seibert-rice.com
www.seibert-rice.com

Terra cotta planters by top American designers handmade in Italy

Chairman: Lenore Rice, VP
President: Mara Seibert
Catalog Cost: $5
Printing Information: in 4 colors
In Business: 20 years

3395 Smith & Hawken
Smith & Hawken
PO Box 8690
Pueblo, CO 81008-9998   800-940-1170
800-940-1170
customerservice@smithandhawken.com
www.target.com

Garden related home accessories, plants, clothing, furniture

Chairman: Gordon Erickson, CEO
President: Gordon Erickson, CEO

Marketing Manager: Felix Carbullido
Fulfillment: Brian Waddle
Buyers: David McCreight
Credit Cards: MasterCard
Catalog Circulation: Mailed 12 time(s) per year
Printing Information: 72 pages in 4 colors on Glossy Stock
Binding: Saddle Stitched
Mailing List Information: Names for rent
In Business: 30 years

3396 Stone Forest

Stone Forest
PO Box 2840
Santa Fe, NM 87504-2840

505-986-8883
888-682-2987
Fax: 505-982-2712
info@stoneforest.com
www.stoneforest.com

Hand carved granite fountains, benches and lanterns; Stone, bronze, copper and bamboo bath & kitchen sinks

President: Michael Zimber
Marketing Manager: Cameron Johnson
Production Manager: Michael Cahill
Catalog Cost: $4
Mailing List Information: Names for rent
In Business: 25 years
Sales Volume: $1MM to $3MM

3397 Sweetbrier Waterfalls & Ponds

Smyth Jewelers
2020 York Road
Timonium, MD 21093-8696

410-252-6666
800-638-3333
www.smythjewelers.com

Waterfalls, ponds and hollow log planters

President: Greg Sweet
Catalog Cost: Free
Printing Information: 81 pages
In Business: 101 years
Number of Employees: 8
Sales Volume: Under $500M

3398 Sycamore Creek

Sycamore Creek
PO Box 16
Ancram, NY 12502

518-398-6393
Fax: 518-398-7697
sycamorecreek@taconic.net
www.sycamorecreek.com

Handcrafted copper garden furnishings, specializing in trellises and arbors, custom designs and bluestone tables

President: Carol Smillie
Credit Cards: MasterCard
Catalog Cost: Free
Catalog Circulation: Mailed 1 time(s) per year to 10000
Average Order Size: $300
Printing Information: 16 pages in 4 colors on Glossy Stock
Binding: Folded
Mailing List Information: Names for rent
In Business: 9 years
Sales Volume: Under $500M

3399 Texas Iron Fence & Gate Company

Texas Iron Fence & Gate Co.
1807 North Business Highway 287
Decatur, TX 76234

940-627-2718
Fax: 940-627-7184
info@texasironfence.com
www.texasironfence.com

Iron fencing, gates, beds and garden borders

Credit Cards: AMEX; MasterCard
Catalog Circulation: to 2000
Printing Information: 92 pages in 2 colors
Press: Web Press
Binding: Folded
In Business: 9 years

3400 The Lighter Side Catalog

The Lighter Side Co.
P.O. Box 25600
Bradenton, FL 34206-5600

800-244-9116
800-232-0963
Fax: 800-551-4406
CustomerService@lighterside.com

Novelties, gifts, and practical jokes

Catalog Cost: Free
In Business: 110 years

3401 Things You Never Knew Existed

Johnson Smith Company
P.O. Box 25600
Bradenton, FL 34206-5600

800-853-9490
customerservice@thingsyouneverknew.com
www.thingsyouneverknew.com

Funmakers, jokes, hobbies and novelties

CFO: David Crofoot
Marketing Manager: Kim Boyd
Founder: Alfred Johnson Smith
Credit Cards: AMEX; MasterCard; Visa
Catalog Cost: Free
Printing Information: in 4 colors on Matte Stock
Press: Web Press
Binding: Saddle Stitched
Mailing List Information: Names for rent
List Manager: Kris Temple
In Business: 110 years
Sales Volume: $20MM to $50MM

3402 Tidewater Workshop

Tidewater Workshop
P.O. Box 456
Oceanville, NJ 08231

609-241-8916
800-666-8433
Fax: 609-241-8892
customers@tidewaterworkshop.com
www.tidewaterworkshop.com

Manufacturer and direct marketer of cedar outdoor furnishings nationwide

Chairman: Nadine Caporilli, Company Director
President: Peter Caporilli
Credit Cards: AMEX; MasterCard; Visa
Catalog Cost: $2
Printing Information: 28 pages in 4 colors
Press: Web Press
Binding: Saddle Stitched
Mailing List Information: Names for rent
Will Trade Names: Yes
In Business: 58 years
Number of Employees: 130
Sales Volume: $10MM to $20MM

3403 Town 'n Country Cart

Vermont Ware
399 Barber Road
St George, VT 05495-8064

877-488-9273
877-488-9273
Fax: 802-482-4226
www.vermontware.com

2 wheel carts for gardening; super sized King Cart, rugged Model A, versatile Model B, compact Model C, innovative Work 'n Rest, Scoop-All and accessories

Credit Cards: MasterCard; Visa
Catalog Cost: Free

3404 Urban Farmer Seeds

Urban Farmer Seeds
120 E 161st Street
Westfield, IN 46074

317-600-2807
www.ufseeds.com

Vegetables, herbs, flowers, fruits, and supplies

Catalog Cost: Free
In Business: 9 years

3405 Violet House of Pots

Violet Pots
PO Box 393
Evinston, FL 32633-393

352-622-6989
800-377-8466
www.violethouse.com

Plastic flower pots, hanging baskets, seeds and soil

President: Bebe Edwards
Catalog Cost: Free
Catalog Circulation: Mailed 1 time(s) per year
Printing Information: in 1 color
Number of Employees: 2
Sales Volume: Under $500M

3406 Vixen Hill Gazebos

Vixen Hill Manufacturing Co.
69 E Main St.
PO Box 389
Elverson, PA 19520

610-286-0909
800-423-2766
Fax: 610-286-2099
sales@vixenhill.com
www.vixenhill.com

Cedar modular gazebos, screened garden houses, porch systems and exterior shutters

President: Christopher Peeples
Marketing Manager: Andrea
Production Manager: Robert Brown
Credit Cards: MasterCard; Visa
Catalog Circulation: Mailed 52 time(s) per year
Average Order Size: $5000
Printing Information: 10 pages in 4 colors on Matte Stock
Binding: Folded
Mailing List Information: Names for rent
In Business: 33 years
Number of Employees: 30
Sales Volume: $1MM to $3MM

3407 Walpole Woodworkers Fence Master Catalog

Walpole Woodworkers
767 East Street
Rt. 27
Walpole, MA 02081-151

508-668-2800
800-343-6948
Fax: 508-668-7301
sales@walpolewoodworkers.com
www.walpolewoodworkers.com

Fence styles, outdoor structures including arbors, pergolas, small buildings, tennis courts and more

President: Louis Maglio
Marketing Manager: Rita Collins
Credit Cards: AMEX; MasterCard
Catalog Cost: $10
Catalog Circulation: to 10000
Printing Information: 160 pages in 4 colors on Glossy Stock
Press: Web Press
Binding: Saddle Stitched
In Business: 80 years
Number of Employees: 350
Sales Volume: $36 Million

3408 Water Visions

Van Ness Water Gardens
2460 N Euclid Avenue
Upland, CA 91784-1199

909-982-2425
800-205-2425
Fax: 909-949-7217
kristen@vnwg.com
www.vnwg.com

Aquatic plants and related filters, pumps, and setup charts, waterlillies, bogs, aquatic products, pond specialist

President: William G Uber
CFO: Carolyn Uber
Marketing Manager: William Uber
Credit Cards: MasterCard; Visa

Average Order Size: $75
Mailing List Information: Names for rent
In Business: 92 years
Number of Employees: 8

3409 Wind & Weather Catalog
Wind & Weather
7021 Wolftown Hood Road
Madison, VA 22727 540-948-2272
877-255-3700
Fax: 800-843-2509
www.windandweather.com

Weather instruments for the home, rain gauges, garden statuary and decor, collectibles, gifts, and outdoor furniture

President: Peter Rice
Fulfillment: Peggy Rice
Credit Cards: AMEX; MasterCard; Visa
Catalog Cost: Free
Printing Information: 76 pages in 4 colors on f
Binding: Saddle Stitched
In Business: 30 years

3410 Womanswork
The Garden Group Inc.
412 E 55th Street
Suite 3C
New York, NY 10022 212-753-1086
800-639-2709
Fax: 212-753-1010

Women's work and gardening gloves; men's and children's styles also available, garden tools and accessories

President: Dorian Rogers Winslow
Fulfillment: Biz Rogers
Credit Cards: AMEX; MasterCard
Catalog Cost: Free
Catalog Circulation: Mailed 1 time(s) per year
Average Order Size: $50
Printing Information: 25 pages in 5 colors on Glossy Stock
Press: Sheetfed Press
Binding: Saddle Stitched
Mailing List Information: Names for rent
In Business: 19 years
Number of Employees: 5
Sales Volume: 500M-1MM

Gifts
General

3411 1-877-Spirits.com
1-877-Spirits.com Inc
99 Powerhouse Road
Suite 200
Roslyn Heights, NY 11577 516-626-4150
877-774-7487
Fax: 516-626-4164
info@1877spirits.com
www.1-877-spirits.com

A world-wide gift delivery service of champagnes, fine wines, spirits and gourmet gift baskets.

President: Harvey Ishofsky
Credit Cards: AMEX; MasterCard; Visa
Catalog Cost: Free
Average Order Size: $100
Printing Information: 40 pages
In Business: 30 years
Number of Employees: 20
Sales Volume: $5MM to $10MM

3412 AD Trophy
AD Trophy Manufacturing Corporation
248-44 Jericho Turnpike
Bellrose, NY 11001 516-352-6161
800-841-6790
Fax: 516-352-8502
www.adtrophy.com

Sports and academic plaques, awards and trophies.

Credit Cards: AMEX; MasterCard; Visa
Catalog Cost: Free
Printing Information: in 4 colors
In Business: 45 years

3413 Added Touch
The Added Touch
P.O. BOX 20029
West Lorne, ON N0L-2P0 905-338-6767
888-238-6824
Fax: 888-232-4049
customerservice@addedtouch.ca
www.addedtouch.ca

Offers a wide variety of gifts including books, gourmet food and treats, home accents, novelty items, office gadgets and more

President: Garrett Hall
Manager: Barbara Bidwell
Credit Cards: MasterCard; Visa
Catalog Cost: Free
Mailing List Information: Names for rent
In Business: 54 years
Number of Employees: 25
Sales Volume: 79K

3414 Alberene Royal Mail
Alberene Royal Mail
5173 Alberene Rd
North Garden, VA 22959 800-843-9078
Fax: 434-971-7411
info@alberene.com
www.alberene.com

Scottish items, cashmere sweaters, pottery, castles, teas, tapestries, jewelry, coins, clocks, posters, art and signs

President: Jim Joyner
Manager: Coleen Stewart
Credit Cards: AMEX; MasterCard; Visa
Catalog Cost: Free
Printing Information: 64 pages
In Business: 33 years
Number of Employees: 4
Sales Volume: $170,000

3415 American Acrylic Awards & Gifts
American Acrylic Awards & Gifts
121 Brent Circle
Walnut, CA 91789 909-598-8889
800-899-3346
Fax: 909-598-9066
info@americanacrylicaward.com
www.americanacrylicaward.com

Engraved clocks, gifts, frames, paper weights and plaques

President: Lawrence Fu
Catalog Cost: Free
Number of Employees: 9
Sales Volume: $700,000

3416 American Stationery
American Stationery Company
100 N Park Avenue
Peru, IN 46970 800-822-2577
Fax: 800-253-9054
www.americanstationery.com

Stationery, holiday cards and personalized gifts

President: Michael Bakehorn
Credit Cards: AMEX; MasterCard
Catalog Cost: Free
Mailing List Information: Names for rent
In Business: 98 years
Number of Employees: 250
Sales Volume: $50MM to $100MM

3417 Basket Works
BasketWorks
2384 Dehne Road
Northbrook, IL 60062 847-559-9379
888-794-4387
Fax: 847-239-7766
info@79gifts.com
www.79gifts.com

Gift basket company, variety of gifts & gift baskets built to order

President: Lise Schleicher
Credit Cards: AMEX; MasterCard; Visa
Catalog Cost: $1
In Business: 18 years

3418 Before & After
Before & After, LLC
1981 Moreland Pkwy
Bldg 3 Ste 3
Annapolis, MD 21401 410-672-3399
Fax: 410-695-6066
info@courageinstone.com
www.courageinstone.com

Word stones and pocket tokens, inspiration and motivational gifts

President: Brenda
Catalog Circulation: Mailed 1 time(s) per year
Printing Information: 24 pages in 4 colors on Matte Stock
Binding: Saddle Stitched
Mailing List Information: Names for rent
In Business: 9 years
Number of Employees: 3
Sales Volume: Under $500M

3419 Besame Cosmetics Inc.
Besame Cosmetics Inc.
3505 W Magnolia Blvd
Burbank, CA 91505 818-558-1558
besamecosmetics.com
In Business: 69 years

3420 Brookstone
Brookstone
One Innovation Way
Merrimack, NH 03054 www.brookstone.com

Consumer products from bedding to massage chairs.

CEO: Tom Via
Catalog Cost: Free
Printing Information: in 4 colors
In Business: 43 years
Sales Volume: 0

3421 Bunnies by the Bay and Friends
Bunnies by the Bay
3115 V Place
PO Box 1630
Anacortes, WA 98221-1630 360-293-8037
877-467-7248
Fax: 360-293-4729
customerservice@bunniesbythebay.com
www.bunniesbythebay.com

Baby gifts including plush animals, apparel, books, teethers and toys.

President: Jeanne Hayes
Marketing Manager: Anne Callaghan
Production Manager: Jeanne Hayes
Fulfillment: Patty Richardson
International Marketing Manager: Jeanne Hayes
Buyers: Suzanne Knutson
Catalog Cost: Free
Catalog Circulation: to 20000
Printing Information: 60 pages in 4 colors on Matte Stock
Press: Web Press
Binding: Saddle Stitched
Mailing List Information: Names for rent
In Business: 30 years
Number of Employees: 27
Sales Volume: $1 Million

3422 **Carol Wright Gifts**
Carol Wright Gifts
PO Box 7823
Edison, NJ 08818-7821   732-225-0100
800-267-5750
Fax: 732-572-2118
www.carolwrightgifts.com

Gifts, personal care, apparel, household helps, kitchen items, and outdoor and garden

President: Gary Giesler
Credit Cards: AMEX; MasterCard
Catalog Cost: Free
Average Order Size: $32
Printing Information: 63 pages in 4 colors on Glossy Stock
Binding: Saddle Stitched
In Business: 43 years
Number of Employees: 650

3423 **Catalog Favorites**
Catalog Favorites
PO Box 3335
Chelmsford, MA 01824-93   877-754-7430
800-221-1133
Fax: 800-866-3235
help@catalogfavorites.com
www.catalogfavorites.com

Gifts for the home and garden, kids and infants, jewelry, apparel and accessories, pet products

President: Bob Piro
Credit Cards: AMEX; MasterCard
Catalog Cost: Free
Printing Information: 55 pages on Glossy Stock
Binding: Saddle Stitched
In Business: 17 years

3424 **Celebrate the Wonder**
Amber Lotus Publishing
5018 Ne 22nd Ave Studio A
PO Box 11329
Portland, OR 97211-329   503-284-6400
800-326-2375
Fax: 503-284-6417
info@amberlotus.com
www.amberlotus.com

A collection of Christian books, Bibles, music and gifts

VP: Leslie Gignilliat-Day
VP: Tim Campbell
Credit Cards: AMEX; MasterCard; Visa
Printing Information: 24 pages
5018 NE 22nd Avenue Studio A
Portland, OR 97211
503.284.6400
In Business: 27 years
Number of Employees: 7
Sales Volume: 1.3M

3425 **Cheryl's**
Cheryl's
646 McCorkle Blvd.
Westerville, OH 43082-8708   800-443-8124
www.cheryls.com

Gourmet cookie gifts.

President: Chris McCann
Printing Information: 44 pages in 4 colors
In Business: 35 years

3426 **Christian Brands Gifts**
Christian Brands Gifts
5226 South 31st Place
Phoenix, AZ 85040   800-572-5780
Fax: 800-525-7959
www.cb-gift.com

Christian products.

3427 **Collections Etc.**
Collections Etc.
PO Box 7985
Elk Grove Village, IL 60009-7985   620-584-8000
Fax: 847-350-5701
www.collectionsetc.com

Home essentials, unique gifts and garden accessories all under $20

President: Shelley Nandkeolyar
Marketing Manager: Karl Steigerwald
Fulfillment: Bruce Getowicz
CEO/Founder: Todd Lustbader
COO: Paul Klassman
Credit Cards: AMEX; MasterCard; Visa
Catalog Cost: Free
In Business: 18 years
Number of Employees: 200
Sales Volume: 12.7M

3428 **Comfort House**
Comfort House
189-V Frelinghuysen Ave.
Newark, NJ 07114-1595   973-242-8080
800-359-7701
Fax: 973-242-0131
customerservice@comforthouse.com
www.comforthouse.com

Bed, bath, kitchen, furniture, garden, pet, gifts, personal and health care items

President: Jeffrey Gornstein
jeff@comforthouse.com
Buyers: Jeffrey Gornstein
Credit Cards: AMEX; MasterCard
Catalog Cost: $2
Catalog Circulation: Mailed 1 time(s) per year
Printing Information: 28 pages
Mailing List Information: Names for rent
In Business: 24 years
Sales Volume: $5MM to $10MM

3429 **Computer Gear**
Computer Gear
19510 144th Ave NE
Suite E-5
Woodinville, WA 98072-8429   425-487-3600
800-373-6353
Fax: 425-487-3699
service@computergear.com
www.computergear.com

Fun computer stuff for the truly addicted, from jewelry to chocolates, and all in between

President: Terry Powers
VP of Operations: Mark Mackaman
Credit Cards: AMEX; MasterCard; Visa
Printing Information: 48 pages in 4 colors on Glossy Stock
Press: Web Press
Binding: Saddle Stitched
Mailing List Information: Names for rent
In Business: 22 years
Number of Employees: 9
Sales Volume: 770K

3430 **Cottage Shop**
The Cottage Shop
PO Box 4836
Stamford, CT 06897   203-762-1777
800-965-7467
Fax: 203-762-0888
thecottageshop@aol.com
www.thecottageshop.com

Fine collectibles, upscale gifts, Limoges

Catalog Cost: Free
In Business: 30 years

3431 **Current**
Current USA
1005 E Woodmen Rd.
Colorado Springs, CO 80920   800-848-2848
Fax: 800-993-3232
www.currentcatalog.com

Gifts, gift wrap and cards.

Catalog Cost: Free
In Business: 66 years
Number of Employees: 1200
Sales Volume: $200 Million

3432 **Dream Products**
Dream Products
412 Dream Lane
Van Nuys, CA 91496-1   800-410-2153
Fax: 818-206-8061
customerservice@dreamproducts.net
www.dreamproductscatalog.com

Unique items at affordable prices; General merchandies product line includes: housewares, jewelry, footwear, lingerie, health and beauty, apparel, handbags, wallets, and more

President: Linda Denniger
Credit Cards: AMEX; MasterCard
Catalog Cost: Free
Mailing List Information: Names for rent
In Business: 35 years
Sales Volume: $500M to $1MM

3433 **Ephemera Magnets Button & Stickers**
Ephemera, Inc.
PO Box 490
Phoenix, OR 97535-490   541-535-4195
800-537-7226
Fax: 800-316-9488
mail@ephemera-inc.com
www.ephemera-inc.com

Provocative, irreverent & outrageously funny novelty buttons, magnets, stickers and coasters

Credit Cards: MasterCard; Visa
Catalog Cost: $4
Catalog Circulation: Mailed 1 time(s) per year to 10M
Average Order Size: $200
Printing Information: 38 pages in 4 colors on Glossy Stock
Press: Sheetfed Press
Binding: Folded
Mailing List Information: Names for rent
In Business: 35 years
Number of Employees: 7
Sales Volume: $500M to $1MM

3434 **Events by Paper Direct**
PaperDirect
1005 E Woodmen Road
Colorado Springs, CO 80920   800-272-7377
Fax: 800-443-2973
customerservice@paperdirect.com
www.paperdirect.com

Offers themed papers for all occasions and events

President: Wendy Huxta
Marketing Manager: Alice Munro
Production Manager: Vanessa Apodaca
Credit Cards: AMEX; MasterCard; Visa
Catalog Cost: Free
In Business: 23 years
Number of Employees: 25
Sales Volume: $1 Million

3435 **First Frost**
Coldwater Creek
1176 E Dayton Yellow Springs Rd.
Fairborn, OH 45324   888-678-5576
www.coldwatercreek.com

Women's apparel, jewelry, accessories and gifts.

CEO: Dave Walde
President: Brenda Koskinen
Catalog Cost: Free
Printing Information: 88 pages in 4 colors
In Business: 32 years
Number of Employees: 100
Sales Volume: $780 Million

3436 First Street Catalog
First Street for Boomers and Beyond
1998 Ruffin Mill Rd
Colonial Heights, VA 23834-5909   800-704-1209
800-958-8324
Fax: 866-889-9960
customerservice@firststreetonline.com
www.firststreetonline.com

Electronic gifts and gadgets and other unusual items for those who like technology

President: Mark Gordon
CFO: Kevin Miller
Credit Cards: AMEX; MasterCard; Visa
Catalog Cost: Free
Printing Information: 55 pages in 4 colors on Glossy Stock
Binding: Saddle Stitched
Sales Volume: $1MM to $3MM

3437 Frontgate
Frontgate
5566 West Chester Rd
West Chester, OH 45069-2914   513-603-1000
888-263-9850
Fax: 800-436-2105
service@frontgate.com
www.frontgate.com

Indoor furnishings, bed and bath essentials, kitchen and entertaining, home care and storage, electronic innovations, outdoor living; holiday gifts.

Chairman: John O'Steen
President: Paul Tarvin
CFO: James Pekarek
CEO: Mark Ethier
Catalog Cost: Free
Printing Information: 88 pages
In Business: 24 years
Number of Employees: 130
Sales Volume: $25.9 MM

3438 Gadget Universe
Gravity Defyer
10643 Glenoaks Blvd
Pacoima, CA 91331   818-833-4860
800-429-0039
www.gravitydefyer.com

Gifts, gadgets, toys and hobbies, clocks and watches, electronics

Marketing Manager: Jared Tracy
Credit Cards: AMEX; MasterCard; Visa
Catalog Cost: Free

3439 GaelSong
GaelSong
PO Box 15388
Seattle, WA 98115   800-205-5790
800-207-4256
Fax: 206-729-0183
gaelsong@gaelsong.com
www.gaelsong.com

Celtic gifts and jewelry imported from Ireland, Scotland and Wales

President: Colleen Connell
Credit Cards: AMEX; MasterCard; Visa
Catalog Cost: Free

3440 Gaiam Living
Gaiam
833 W. South Boulder Road
P.O. Box 3095
Louisville, CO 80027-2452   303-222-3719
877-989-6321
Fax: 303-222-3750
customerservice@gaiam.com
www.gaiam.com

Organic/natural fiber bedding, bath and clothing; energy-saving products; earth-friendly cleaners; air & water filters; eco-conscious furnishings; fair trade decor & jewelry; natural wellness tools

President: Lynn Powers
CFO: Janet Mathews
CEO: Jirka Rysavy
Manager: Kraig Corbin
Director of Customer Relations: Christopher Fisher
Credit Cards: AMEX; MasterCard; Visa
Catalog Cost: Free
Catalog Circulation: Mailed 4 time(s) per year
Printing Information: in 4 colors
In Business: 20 years

3441 Gift Box
Gift Box Corp of America
305 Veterans Blvd
Carlstadt, NJ 07072-2708   201-933-9777
800-GIF-TBOX
Fax: 201-933-5316
info@800giftbox.com
www.800giftbox.com

Gift boxes, bags, ribbon, wraps and more

President: Clyde Brownstone
Marketing Manager: Peter Shore
Production Manager: Dave Spendiff
Credit Cards: AMEX; MasterCard
Catalog Cost: Free
Catalog Circulation: to 35000
Printing Information: in 4 colors on Glossy Stock
Binding: Saddle Stitched
In Business: 71 years
Number of Employees: 2

3442 Gift Tree
Gift Tree
1800 W Fourth Plain Boulevard
Suite 120-B
Vancouver, WA 98660   800-379-4065
www.gifttree.com

Gift baskets for all occasions

President: Craig Bowen
Credit Cards: AMEX; MasterCard
In Business: 12 years

3443 Gimbel & Sons
PO Box 8008
Stevens Point, WI 54481-9910   888-633-1463
customerservice@gimbelscollectibles.com
gimbelscollectibles.com

Clocks, dolls and miniature collectibles

Credit Cards: AMEX; MasterCard; Visa
Catalog Cost: Free
Printing Information: 64 pages in 4 colors on Glossy Stock
Binding: Saddle Stitched

3444 Greenfield Basket Factory
Greenfield Basket Factory
11423 Wilson Rd
North East, PA 16428-6121   814-725-3419
800-227-5385
Fax: 814-725-9090
greenfieldbasket@juno.com
www.greenfieldbasket.com

Stapled veneer baskets, and specialty baskets

President: David Foster
Credit Cards: MasterCard; Visa
In Business: 81 years
Sales Volume: $3MM to $5MM

3445 Guy Gifter
19510 144th Avenue NE #E-5
Woodinville, WA 98072   425-486-0500
888-650-4438
Fax: 425-487-3699
www.guygifter.com

Men's gifts for all occasions

President: Mark Mackaman
Credit Cards: AMEX; MasterCard; Visa
Catalog Cost: Free
In Business: 18 years

3446 Hapco
Hapco, Inc.
353 Circuit St
Hanover, MA 02339-2018   781-826-8801
877-729-4272
Fax: 781-826-9544
info@hapcoweb.com
www.Hapcoweb.Com

Meter-mix dispensing equipment and thermoset polymers

President: Steve Aronson
Marketing Manager: Dan McClelland
daniel_mcclelland@hapcoweb.com
Sales Manager: Fred DeSimone
fred_desimone@hapcoweb.com
Ordering/Pricing: Jennie Schell
jennie_schell@hapcoweb.com
Quality Manager/Purchasing: Michael Bundock
michael_bundock@hapcoweb.com
Credit Cards: AMEX; MasterCard; Visa
In Business: 44 years
Number of Employees: 35
Sales Volume: $4.2 Million

3447 Happy Kids Personalized Catalog
Happy Kids Productions Inc
247 Route 100
Suite 1010
Somers, NY 10589-3241   800-543-7687
Fax: 914-242-5941
www.happykidspersonalized.com

Personalized children's gifts including books, music, CDs, party favors and more

Chairman: Cindy Rosenbaum
President: Michael Rosenbaum
Credit Cards: MasterCard
Catalog Cost: Free

3448 Health Care Logistics
Health Care Logistics
PO Box 25
Circleville, OH 43113   800-848-1633
Fax: 800-447-2923
www.healthcarelogistics.com

Bins & accessories, security seals, infection prevention items, cabinets and shelving

President: Gary Sharpe
Catalog Cost: Free
In Business: 36 years

3449 Heartland America
Heartland America
8085 Century Blvd
Chaska, MN 55318-3056   800-229-2901
info@heartlandamerica.com
www.heartlandamerica.com

General consumer products and gifts including electronics, home and office, auto, hardware, and fashion accessories

President: Bruce Brekke
Credit Cards: AMEX; MasterCard
Catalog Cost: Free
In Business: 30 years
Sales Volume: $ 20-50 Million

3450 Heartland Music
Heartland Music
17822 Gillette Avenue
Suite A
Irvine, CA 92614   630-919-2287
888-339-0001
www.heartlandmusic.com

Vinyl records, CDs, DVDs and Blu-rays

Chief Executive Officer: Jeff Walker
Credit Cards: AMEX; MasterCard
Catalog Cost: Free

3451 Hitching Post Supply
Hitching Post Supply
10312 210th ST SE
Snohomish, WA 98296-1809   360-668-2349
800-689-9971
Fax: 360-668-0721
vickie@hitchingpostsupply.com
www.hitchingpostsupply.com

Cowboy and western music, books and gear, horsehair by the pound

President: Vickie Mullen
In Business: 27 years

3452 Horchow Mail Order
Horchow Catalog
PO Box 650589
Dallas, TX 75265   888-888-4757
www.horchow.com

Complete gift guide of all Horchow products, including linens, gifts, foods and unique kitchen items

President: Karen Katz
CFO: James Skinner
Marketing Manager: Jessica Weiland
Production Manager: Donna Denise
Credit Cards: AMEX; MasterCard; Visa
Catalog Cost: Free
Catalog Circulation: Mailed 1 time(s) per year
Printing Information: 64 pages in 4 colors on Glossy Stock
Press: Web Press
Binding: Saddle Stitched
Mailing List Information: Names for rent
Sales Volume: $500M to $1MM

3453 House of Webster
House of Webster
1013 N 2nd St
PO Box 1988
Rogers, AR 72756-1988   479-636-4640
800-369-4641
Fax: 479-636-2974
info@houseofwebster.com
www.houseofwebster.com

Gift packages and gourmet food items

CFO: Craig Castrellon
Marketing Manager: Denny Fletcher
Production Manager: Craig Duncan
Fulfillment: Chris Humphreys
Credit Cards: AMEX; MasterCard; Visa
Printing Information: 32 pages
In Business: 81 years

3454 Indiana Berry & Plant Company
Indiana Berry
2811 US 31
Plymouth, IN 46563   800-295-2226
Fax: 574-784-2468
info@indianaberry.com
www.indianaberry.com

Small fruit plants, strawberries, blueberries; gardening books; tools and supplies; gardening containers

Credit Cards: MasterCard
Catalog Cost: Free

3455 Islands Tropicals
Island Tropicals
PO Box 1989
Keaau, HI 96749   800-367-5155
Fax: 808-966-7684
www.hawaii2u.com

Hawaiian flowers and gifts

Credit Cards: AMEX; MasterCard; Visa
In Business: 48 years

3456 JC Penney Holiday Catalog
JC Penney
PO Box 10001
Plano, TX 75301-7311   972-431-3400
800-842-9470
jcpinvestorrelations@jcpenney.com
www.jcpenney.com

Holiday catalog of toys, gifts, apparel and holiday clothing

Chairman: Thomas Engibous
President: Ken C Hicks
CFO: Edward Record
Marketing Manager: Debra Berman
Chief Executive Officer: Mike Ullman
EVP, General Counsel and Secretary: Janet Dhillon
EVP, Chief Information Officer: Scott Laverty
Credit Cards: AMEX; MasterCard; Visa
Catalog Cost: Free
Mailing List Information: Names for rent

3457 JC Penney Wedding Catalog
JC Penney
6501 Legacy Dr
Plano, TX 75024-3612   972-431-3400
800-842-9470
Fax: 972-591-9322
jcpinvestorrelations@jcpenney.com
www.jcpenney.com

Wedding gifts and registry

Chairman: Thomas Engibous
CFO: Edward Record
Marketing Manager: Debra Berman
Chief Executive Officer: Mike Ullman
EVP, General Counsel and Secretary: Janet Dhillon
EVP, Chief Information Officer: Scott Laverty
Credit Cards: AMEX; MasterCard; Visa
Catalog Cost: Free

3458 John & Kira's
John & Kira's Chocolates
163 W. Wyoming Avenue
Philadelphia, PA 19140   800-747-4808
support@johnandkiras.com
www.johnandkiras.com

Chocolates.

3459 KP Creek Gifts
KP Creek Gifts
PO Box 30964
Gahanna, OH 43230   800-391-1521
Fax: 800-955-5915
www.kpcreek.com

In Business: 13 years

3460 Lakeside Collection
The Lakeside Collection
PO Box 3088
Northbrook, IL 60065-3088   847-444-3150
Fax: 847-735-9711
www.lakeside.com

Unique gifts for any occasion

President: John Lewis
Credit Cards: AMEX; MasterCard; Visa
Catalog Cost: Free
Printing Information: 196 pages in 4 colors on Glossy Stock
Binding: Perfect Bound

3461 Lang
The Lang Company
PO Box 1605
Waukesha, WI 53187   800-967-3399
Fax: 262-523-2883
www.lang.com

Calendars, cards and stationery, decor.

Credit Cards: AMEX; MasterCard; Visa
Catalog Cost: Free
In Business: 33 years

3462 Leanin' Tree
Trumble Greetings Inc
PO Box 9800
Boulder, CO 80301   303-530-7768
800-525-0656
Fax: 800-777-4770
info@leanintree.com
www.leanintree.com

Cards for all occassions

Chairman: Ed Trumble
President: Tom Trumble
Founder: Ed Trumble
Credit Cards: MasterCard; Visa
Catalog Cost: Free
Printing Information: 24 pages in 4 colors
Binding: Saddle Stitched
Mailing List Information: Names for rent
In Business: 55 years

3463 Levenger
The Levenger Store
420 South Congress Ave
Delray Beach, FL 33445-4696   561-276-2436
800-544-0880
Fax: 800-544-6910
Cservice@levenger.com
www.Levenger.Com

Collection of furnishings and accessories created to enhance your well-read life, you'll find bookcases, halogen lighting, desks, chairs, leather goods, plus personal and corporate gifts

President: Steve Leveen
CFO: Lori Leveen
Marketing Manager: Susan Devito
Production Manager: Lee Passarella
Fulfillment: Gerald Patterson
Founder: Steve Leveen
Founder: Lori Leveen
Buyers: Denise Tedaldi
Credit Cards: AMEX; MasterCard; Visa
Catalog Cost: Free
Catalog Circulation: Mailed 12 time(s) per year to 20MM
Average Order Size: $130
Printing Information: 76 pages in 4 colors on Glossy Stock
Press: Web Press
Binding: Saddle Stitched
Mailing List Information: Names for rent
List Manager: Susan Devito
List Company: Mokrynski & Associates
401 Hackensack Avenue
Hackensack, NJ 07601
2014885656
In Business: 28 years
Number of Employees: 270
Sales Volume: $20MM to $50MM

3464 Lillian Vernon
Lillian Vernon Corporation
P.O. Box 35022
Colorado Springs, CO 80935-3522 800-545-5426
www.lillianvernon.com

Clothing and accessories; housewares; holiday decor; toys

President: Tom Arland
Credit Cards: AMEX; MasterCard
Catalog Cost: Free
Catalog Circulation: Mailed 6 time(s) per year
Printing Information: 80 pages in 4 colors on Glossy Stock
Press: Web Press
Binding: Folded
In Business: 66 years
Number of Employees: 175
Sales Volume: $ 10-20 Million

3465 Lillian Vernon Personalized Gifts
Lillian Vernon Corporation
P.O. Box 35980
Colorado Springs, CO 80935-5980 800-545-5426
800-545-5426
Fax: 800-852-2365
custserv@lillianvernon.com
www.lillianvernon.com

Finest selection of personalized gifts

In Business: 66 years
Sales Volume: $10MM to $20MM

3466 Lillian Vernon Sales & Bargains
Lillian Vernon Corporation
PO Box 35980
Colorado Springs, CO 80935-5980 800-545-5426
800-545-5426
Fax: 800-852-2365
custserv@lillianvernon.com
www.lillianvernon.com

Savings on sale items including home and office producs, kitchen and dining, bath, accessory, outdoor and garden products

In Business: 64 years

3467 Massage Warehouse & Spa Essentials
Massage Warehouse & Spa Essentials
360 Veterans Parkway
Suite 115
Bolingbrook, IL 60440-4607 630-771-7400
800-910-9955
Fax: 888-674-4380
support@massagewarehouse.com
www.massagewarehouse.com

Apparel and fitness, gifts, massage and spa, treatment supplies, books, videos, yoga and fitness

President: Robert Cooper
Marketing Manager: Heather Zdan
Credit Cards: AMEX; MasterCard; Visa
Printing Information: 12 pages
In Business: 52 years
Number of Employees: 126
Sales Volume: $ 13 Million

3468 Miles Kimball Christmas Cards
Miles Kimball
250 City Center
Oshkosh, WI 54906 855-202-7394
www.mileskimball.com

Christmas cards

Catalog Cost: Free
In Business: 81 years
Sales Volume: $10 Million

3469 Monticello Catalog
The Shop Monticello
PO Box 318
Charlottesville, VA 22902-318 800-243-0743
800-243-1743
catalog@monticello.org
www.monticellocatalog.org

Wide selection of gift ideas selected to reflect Thomas Jefferson's taste for elegance and quality

Marketing Manager: Liesel Nowak
Founder: Thomas Jefferson
Credit Cards: AMEX; MasterCard
Catalog Cost: Free
Catalog Circulation: Mailed 2 time(s) per year
Printing Information: 48 pages in 4 colors on Glossy Stock
Binding: Saddle Stitched
In Business: 90 years

3470 Nature by Design
Nature by Design of Vermont
PO Box 499
Barton, VT 05822-466 802-754-6400
888-552-3747
Fax: 802-754-2626
sales@naturebydesign.com
www.naturebydesign.com

Great gifts for nature and animal lovers

President: Peter R Leblanc
Catalog Cost: Free

3471 New England Office Supply
New England Office Supply
135 Lundquist Dr.
Braintree, MA 00218 support@neosusa.com
www.neosusa.com

Office products and supplies

3472 Nordic Shop
The Nordic Shop
111 S Broadway
Skyway Level
Rochester, MN 55904-6511 507-285-9143
800-282-6673
Fax: 507-285-5573
www.nordicshop.net

Scandinavian gifts

President: Louise Hanson
Marketing Manager: Louise Hanson
Credit Cards: AMEX; MasterCard; Visa
Catalog Circulation: Mailed 3 time(s) per year
Average Order Size: $75
Printing Information: 8 pages in 1 color on Glossy Stock
Binding: Saddle Stitched
Mailing List Information: Names for rent
In Business: 32 years
Number of Employees: 10
Sales Volume: $1MM to $3MM

3473 Northern Sun
Northern Sun
2916 E Lake St
Minneapolis, MN 55406-2065 612-729-2001
800-258-8579
Fax: 612-729-0149
info@northernsun.com
www.Northernsun.Com

T-shirts, bumper stickers, buttons, posters, magnets and mugs on a wide variety of social issues, from a progressive point of view

President: Scott Cramer
Credit Cards: AMEX; MasterCard
Catalog Cost: $1
Catalog Circulation: Mailed 2 time(s) per year
Average Order Size: $45
Printing Information: 32 pages in 4 colors
Press: Web Press
Binding: Saddle Stitched
Mailing List Information: Names for rent
List Company: Names in the News
415-989-3350
In Business: 36 years
Number of Employees: 20
Sales Volume: $1MM to $3MM

3474 Old Durham Road
Pickering & Simmons
115 Campus Drive
Edison, NJ 08837 732-516-1616
866-298-1627
Fax: 732-516-1617

English country living products including gifts, books and more

Chairman: Arline Friedman
President: Craig Weidenheimer
Credit Cards: AMEX; MasterCard; Visa
Catalog Cost: Free

3475 Olive Press
Olive Press
Jacuzzi Family Winery
24724 Highway 121 (Arnold Drive)
Sanoma, CA 95476 707-939-8900
800-965-4839
Fax: 707-939-1203
www.theolivepress.com

Extra virgin olive oil, citrus olive oil, dipping and flavored oils and cookbooks, bath and body collections and gifts

Marketing Manager: Debra Rogers
Owner: Tony Williams
Founder: Ed Stoleman
Catalog Cost: Free
In Business: 18 years
Number of Employees: 12
Sales Volume: $950,000

3476 On Sale
Airline International Luggage
8701 Montana Avenue
El Paso, TX 79925-1220 915-778-1234
855-565-1818
Fax: 915-778-1533
www.airlineintl.com

Luggage, pens, gifts, backpacks and travel accessories

President: Edward Kallman
Catalog Cost: Free
Printing Information: 6 pages in 4 colors
Number of Employees: 30

3477 One World Projects
One World Projects, Inc.
43 Ellicott Ave
Batavia, NY 14020-2030 585-343-4490
Fax: 585-344-3551
sales@oneworldprojects.com
www.oneworldprojects.com

Puzzles, gift baskets, photo albums, ceramic animals, soapstone carvings, jewelry

President: Phil Smith
Credit Cards: AMEX; MasterCard; Visa
In Business: 23 years
Sales Volume: $3MM to $5MM

3478 Orvis Home & Gift
The Orvis Company Inc.
178 Conservation Way
Sunderland, VT 05250-4465 802-362-1300
888-235-9763
Fax: 802-362-0141
www.orvis.com

Home furnishings and gifts.

CEO: Leigh H. Perkins Jr.
Catalog Cost: Free
In Business: 160 years
Number of Employees: 1700
Sales Volume: $340 Million

3479 PaperDirect
PaperDirect
P.O. Box 1151
Minneapolis, MN 55440-1151 800-272-7377
Fax: 800-443-2973
volumesales@paperdirect.com
www.paperdirect.com

Paper for all laser printer copier and desktop publishing needs

President: Tim Arland
CFO: Kirby Heck
Credit Cards: AMEX; MasterCard; Visa
Catalog Cost: Free
Catalog Circulation: Mailed 5 time(s) per year
Printing Information: 95 pages in 4 colors on Glossy Stock
Press: Web Press
Binding: Saddle Stitched
In Business: 29 years
Number of Employees: 1200
Sales Volume: $ 78 Million

3480 Personal Creations Gift Catalog
Personal Creations
4840 Eastgate Mall
San Diego, CA 92121   866-834-7695
888-527-1404
wecare@customercare.personalcreations.com
www.personalcreations.com

Personalize gifts for holidays, weddings, anniversaries, birthdays, babies and kids

Customer Service Manager: Geri Fosnaugh
Catalog Cost: Free
Printing Information: 72 pages in 4 colors
In Business: 7 years
Sales Volume: $3MM to $5MM

3481 Petals Catalog
Petals Decorative Accents
12021 Centron Place Cincinnati
Ridgefield, OH 45246   203-431-3300
800-783-9966
Fax: 914-328-1959
service@petals.com
www.petals.com

Silk flowers and arrangements for your home

Chairman: Stephen M Hicks
President: Stephen M Hicks
CFO: Gregory Powell
Buyers: Tom C Corelli
Credit Cards: AMEX; MasterCard
Catalog Cost: Free
Mailing List Information: Names for rent
In Business: 60 years
Number of Employees: 350
Sales Volume: $20MM to $50MM

3482 Pink House Studios
Pink House Studios,Inc
35 Bank Street
Saint Albans, VT 05478   802-524-7191
Fax: 802-524-7191
mark@pinkhouse.com
www.pinkhouse.com

Sculpture supplies and restoration services

President: Mark Prent
Buyers: Mark Prent
Credit Cards: MasterCard
Catalog Cost: $5
Average Order Size: $100
Mailing List Information: Names for rent
List Manager: Mark Prent
In Business: 11 years
Sales Volume: Under $500M

3483 Plow & Hearth
Plow & Hearth
130 Commerce Lane #B
Rochelle, VA 22738   540-948-3659
800-494-7544
info@plowhearth.com
www.plowhearth.com

Products for country living, home, garden, pets and gifts

President: John Haydock
CFO: Dana Pappas
Manager: Roxanne Dobson
Credit Cards: AMEX; MasterCard
Catalog Cost: Free
Catalog Circulation: Mailed 4 time(s) per year
Printing Information: 132 pages in 4 colors on Glossy Stock
Binding: Saddle Stitched
In Business: 37 years
Number of Employees: 200
Sales Volume: $50MM to $100MM

3484 Plumeria Bay
Plumeria Bay
37960 Theo Lane
Birdsview, WA 98237-9256   360-826-3600
877-722-9266
www.plumeriabay.com

Down comforters, down pillows, blankets and throws, gifts and feather beds

President: Stephen Clay
Credit Cards: AMEX; MasterCard
Catalog Cost: Free
Printing Information: 31 pages in 4 colors on Glossy Stock
Binding: Saddle Stitched
In Business: 13 years
Sales Volume: $500M to $1MM

3485 Polart by Mail
Polart Distribution (USA) Inc.
5700 Sarah Avenue
Sarasota, FL 34233-3446   941-927-8983
800-278-9393
Fax: 941-927-8239
www.polandbymail.com

Giftware, stoneware, ceramics, crystal, videos, CDs, books, armoury replicas of over 4000 items from Poland, wholesale sales available

President: Jarek Zaremba
Marketing Manager: Maciek Zaremba
Credit Cards: AMEX; MasterCard
Catalog Cost: $2
Average Order Size: $90
Printing Information: 16 pages in 4 colors on Glossy Stock
Press: Web Press
Binding: Saddle Stitched
Mailing List Information: Names for rent
Number of Employees: 7
Sales Volume: $1MM to $3MM

3486 Quality Merchandise Direct
Quality Merchandise Direct
630 West Prien Lake Road
Suite B113
Lake Charles, LA 70601   337-564-4712
Fax: 337-564-4712
qualitymerchandisedirect@live.com

Candles, collectibles, Garden decor, bath and body

President: Myer Spector
Credit Cards: AMEX; MasterCard
In Business: 49 years

3487 Serengeti
Serengeti
PO Box 3349
Chelmsford, MA 01824-949   800-426-2852
Fax: 800-866-3235
help@serengeticatalog.com
www.serengeticatalog.com

Line of womens clothing and accessories

Chairman: Jack Rosenfeld
President: John Fleischman
CFO: Steven Steiner
Credit Cards: AMEX; MasterCard; Visa
Catalog Cost: Free
Printing Information: 63 pages in 4 colors on Glossy Stock
Binding: Saddle Stitched
In Business: 27 years

3488 Share the Spirit!
Coldwater Creek
1176 E Dayton Yellow Springs Rd.
Fairborn, OH 45324   888-678-5576
www.coldwatercreek.com

Women's apparel, jewelry, accessories and gifts.

CEO: Dave Walde
President: Brenda Koskinen
Catalog Cost: Free
Printing Information: 96 pages in 4 colors
In Business: 32 years
Number of Employees: 100
Sales Volume: $780 Million

3489 Sharper Image
Sharper Image
27725 Stansbury
Suite 175
Farmington Hills, MI 48334   248-741-5100
877-206-7862
www.sharperimage.com

Products for the home, travel, auto and outdoors.

Managing Partner: David Katzman
Catalog Cost: Free
Printing Information: 76 pages in 4 colors
In Business: 39 years

3490 Shelburne Farms
Shelburne Farms
1611 Harbor Rd
Shelburne, VT 05482-7671   802-985-8686
Fax: 802-985-8123
info@shelburnefarms.org
www.shelburnefarms.org

Cheddar cheese, hams, maple syrup, vermont products and gift packages

President: Alec Webb
awebb@shelburnefarms.org
Owner: William Webb
Development Assistant: Jane Boisvert
jboisvert@shelburnefarms.org
VP And Program Director: Megan Camp
mcamp@shelburnefarms@.org
Credit Cards: AMEX; MasterCard; Visa
Catalog Cost: Free
Printing Information: 7 pages in 4 colors on Glossy Stock
Binding: Saddle Stitched
In Business: 43 years
Number of Employees: 40
Sales Volume: $3.6 Million

3491 Shop at Home Catalog Directory
ShopAtHome.Com
7100 E Belleview Ave # 208
Greenwood Vlg, CO 80111-1636   303-741-1971
800-315-1995
Fax: 303-843-0377
sales@belcarogroup.com

350 catalogs to order, all of which cost money to obtain

President: Marc Braunstein
Credit Cards: MasterCard; Visa
Catalog Cost: Free
Printing Information: 48 pages in 4 colors on Glossy Stock
Press: Web Press
Binding: Saddle Stitched
In Business: 28 years
Number of Employees: 100
Sales Volume: $500M to $1MM

3492 Simply Charming Fine Wedding Accessories
Simply Charming
2741 Plaza Del Amo
Suite 203
Torrance, CA 90503   310-328-0418
800-222-9530
Fax: 310-328-4152
scharming@aol.com
www.simplycharming.com

Wedding, shower, bachelorette, prom and first communion accessories and gifts

President: William White
CFO: Gregory White
Marketing Manager: Barbara White
Buyers: Barbara White
Printing Information: 35 pages
In Business: 20 years

3493 Solutions Catalog
PO Box 127
Jessup, PA 18434 877-718-7901
800-342-9988
Fax: 800-821-1282
www.solutionscatalog.com

Storage and organizing solutions, home furnishings, kitchen equipment, outdoor living, pet products, pest control and practical gifts

President: John Emrick
Credit Cards: AMEX; MasterCard; Visa
Catalog Cost: Free
Catalog Circulation: Mailed 1 time(s) per year
Printing Information: 72 pages in 4 colors on Glossy Stock
Press: Web Press
Binding: Saddle Stitched
Mailing List Information: Names for rent
List Manager: Patty Davis
In Business: 29 years
Number of Employees: 500

3494 St. Jude Gift Shop
St. Jude Gift Shop
501 St. Jude Place
Memphis, TN 38105 800-746-1539
giftshop.stjude.org

3495 Sun Harvest Citrus
Sun Harvest Citrus
14601 Six Mile Cypress Parkway
Fort Myers, FL 33912-4463 239-768-2686
800-743-1480
Fax: 239-768-9255
info@sunharvestcitrus.com
www.sunharvestcitrus.com

Gourmet foods, fruit baskets, gifts and fresh picked fruit

President: David McKenzie
Catalog Cost: Free
In Business: 26 years
Sales Volume: $50MM to $100MM

3496 Sundance Company
Sundance Company
3865 West 2400 South
Salt Lake City, UT 84120-7212 800-422-2770
Fax: 800-843-9445
service@sundance.net
www.Sundancecatalog.Com

Home and garden decor, furniture, gifts, apparel, jewelry, accessories, footwear, with a flavor of the American West and native cultures of the world

Chairman: Robert Redforth
President: Stephen J Gordon
CFO: Polly Boe
Marketing Manager: David Brown
Production Manager: Matey Erdos
Buyers: Gary Beer
Brent Beck
Credit Cards: AMEX; MasterCard; Visa
Catalog Cost: Free
Catalog Circulation: Mailed 7 time(s) per year to 11000
Printing Information: 75 pages in 7 colors on Glossy Stock
Press: Web Press
Binding: Saddle Stitched
Mailing List Information: Names for rent
List Company: AZ Marketing
Cos Cob, CT
In Business: 45 years
Number of Employees: 100
Sales Volume: $10MM

3497 Taylor Gifts
Taylor Gifts
600 Cedar Hollow Rd
Paoli, PA 19301-1753 610-725-1100
800-868-6169
Fax: 610-725-1144
tgcustomerservice@taylorgifts.com
www.Taylorgifts.Com

Gifts, housewares and novelties

President: Bl Taylor Jr
Marketing Manager: Frank Ruthkosky
Founder: B.L. Taylor
Buyers: J Reed Taylor
Margo Firebaugh
Credit Cards: AMEX; MasterCard; Visa
Catalog Cost: Free
Printing Information: 25 pages
Mailing List Information: Names for rent
Will Trade Names: Yes
In Business: 62 years
Number of Employees: 100
Sales Volume: $5MM to $10MM

3498 Terra Sancta Guild
Terra Sancta Guild
2031 Stout Dr.
Unit 1
Warminster, PA 18974-339 215-675-8472
800-523-5155
Fax: 215-643-9258
sales@terrasanctaguild.com
www.terrasanctaguild.com

Christian and inspirational gifts, crosses, lapel pins, faith medals and plaques

President: Frank Cleary
Printing Information: 150 pages
Sales Volume: $500M to $1MM

3499 Terrys Village
Terrys Village
PO Box 2778
Omaha, NE 68103-2778 800-535-9917
Fax: 800-723-9000
www.terrysvillage.com

Decor and gifts for home and garden with country charm

Marketing Manager: Betty Camenzind
Buyers: Shelly Cunningham, Terry's Village
Curt Weber, Oriental Trading Co.
Credit Cards: AMEX; MasterCard; Visa; Discover
Catalog Cost: Free
Catalog Circulation: Mailed 8 time(s) per year to 30000
Average Order Size: $50
Printing Information: 60 pages in 4 colors on Glossy Stock
Press: Web Press
Binding: Saddle Stitched
Mailing List Information: Names for rent
List Company: Mokrynski & Associates
In Business: 20 years
Number of Employees: 100
Sales Volume: 30MM

3500 The Popcorn Factory
The Popcorn Factory
PO Box 5043
Lake Forest, IL 60045-5043 800-541-2676
Fax: 888-333-4595
thepopcornfactory.com

Gourmet popcorn gifts.

President: Chris McCann
Printing Information: 44 pages in 4 colors
In Business: 35 years

3501 Tipton & Hurst
Tipton & Hurst
1801 N Grant
Little Rock, AR 72207 501-666-3333
800-666-3333
Fax: 501-666-4205
comments@tiptonhurst.com
www.Tiptonhurst.Com

Florist that offers flower arrangements, corporate gifts, plants, and gourmet food baskets

President: Howard Hurst
Credit Cards: AMEX; MasterCard; Visa
Catalog Cost: Free

In Business: 129 years
Number of Employees: 110

3502 TouchStone Catalog
TouchStone Catalog
P.O. Box 760
Harrison, OH 45003 808-745-9195
Fax: 866-239-6770
www.touchstonecatalog.com
In Business: 26 years

3503 Tourneau Watch
Tourneau Time Machine
12 E. 57th Street
New York, NY 10022 212-758-7300
800-348-3332
www.tourneau.com

Men's & women's watches

President: Jim Seuss
VP, Marketing: Andrew Block
Credit Cards: AMEX; MasterCard
Catalog Cost: Free
Catalog Circulation: Mailed 1 time(s) per year
Printing Information: 24 pages in 4 colors
Binding: Saddle Stitched
In Business: 115 years

3504 UNICEF Catalog
United States Fund for UNICEF
125 Maiden Lane
New York, NY 10038 800-367-5437
www.unicefusa.org

Greeting cards, stationery and gifts

Chairman: Vince Hemmer
President: Caryl M. Stern
CFO: Edward G. Lloyd
Marketing Manager: Jose Carbonell
Production Manager: Laura Calassano
Senior Vice President, Development: Barron Segar
Vice President, HR: William B. Sherwood
VP, Finance & Budget: Richard Esserman
Credit Cards: AMEX; MasterCard; Visa
Catalog Circulation: Mailed 2 time(s) per year
Printing Information: in 4 colors
In Business: 69 years
Number of Employees: 100

3505 Vermont Christmas Company
Vermont Christmas Company
PO Box 1071
Burlington, VT 05402 802-893-1670
888-890-0005
info@vermontchristmasco.com
www.vermontchristmasco.com

Holiday advent calendars, Christmas card greetings and gifts

President: Andrew Kelly
Credit Cards: MasterCard; Visa
Catalog Cost: Free
Printing Information: in 4 colors
In Business: 29 years

3506 Walter Drake
Walter Drake
250 City Center
Oshkosh, WI 54906 920-231-3800
855-202-7393
www.wdrake.com

Bakeware, food storage, kitchen decor accessories, closet & bed accessories, storage organizers, small appliances, gadgets and tools.

Catalog Cost: Free
In Business: 69 years

3507 Way Out Wax Catalog
Way Out Wax Inc
76 Deer Run Lane
PO Box 175
North Hyde Park, VT 05665   802-730-8069
                              888-727-1903
                         Fax: 802-730-8164
                         info@wayoutwax.com
                         www.Wayoutwax.Com

Clean, pure and natural aromatherapy, soy and container candles

President: James Rossiter
Credit Cards: MasterCard; Visa
Catalog Cost: Free
In Business: 23 years
Sales Volume: $1MM to $3MM

3508 Weekender
PO Box 1499
Burnsville, MN 55337-499   800-438-5480
                         Fax: 952-882-6927

Clothing, cooking accessories and high-tech electronic gifts

3509 Welcome to the Best of Lillian Vernon
Lillian Vernon
P.O. Box 35980
Colorado Springs, CO 80935-5980 914-949-1979
                              800-545-5426
                         Fax: 914-949-2685
                         www.lillianvernon.com

Gifts, household, gardening, children's and holiday items

Chairman: Lillian Vernon
President: Howard Goldberg
CFO: Robert Mednick
Marketing Manager: Kevin Green, VP Marketing
Production Manager: Laura Zambano, VP Merchandising
Buyers: Norma Zambano
Credit Cards: AMEX; MasterCard; Visa
Catalog Cost: Free
Catalog Circulation: Mailed 10 time(s) per year to 10000
Average Order Size: $45
Printing Information: 108 pages in 4 colors on Glossy Stock
Binding: Saddle Stitched
Mailing List Information: Names for rent
Will Trade Names: Yes
In Business: 64 years
Number of Employees: 150

3510 Whales & Friends Catalog
Whales & Friends
2060 Lincoln Ave. at Willow
Alameda, CA 94501   510-769-8500
                      800-234-1024
                 Fax: 860-767-4381
                 whalesandfriends@gmail.com
                 www.whalesandfriends.biz

Nature oriented catalog offering marine, bird and mammal products

Chairman: Thomas Romano
President: Caroll Romano
CFO: Robert Braumann
Buyers: Trisha Braumann
Susan Miller
Credit Cards: AMEX; MasterCard
Catalog Cost: Free
Catalog Circulation: Mailed 6 time(s) per year to 40000
Average Order Size: $60
Printing Information: 48 pages in 4 colors on Glossy Stock
Press: Web Press
Binding: Saddle Stitched
Mailing List Information: Names for rent
Will Trade Names: Yes
List Company: Direct Media
200 Pemberwick Road
Greenwich, CT
In Business: 20 years

Number of Employees: 30
Sales Volume: $3MM to $5MM

3511 White Pass Railroad
White Pass & Yukon Route Railroad
231 Second Avenue
PO Box 435
Skagway, AK 99840-435   907-983-9813
                          800-343-7373
                     Fax: 983-273- 231
                     info@wpyr.com
                     www.wpyr.com

Apparel, calendars, collectibles and more

President: John Finlayson
Marketing Manager: Eleanor Davenport
Chief Mechanical Officer: Glenn Sullivan
gsullivan@wpyr.com
Director of Safety & Labor Rel: Tyler Rose
trose@wpyr.com
Director of Passenger Operations: Vickey Moy
vmoy@wpyr.com

3512 World's Largest Party Superstore Catalog
World's Largest Party Superstore
One Party Place
South Whitley, IN 46787   800-314-8736
                            csr@shindigz.com
                            www.shindigz.com

Party supplies for birthdays, holidays and weddings

In Business: 89 years

3513 Your Breed
Your Breed Clothing Company
128 A South Walnut Circle
Greensboro, NC 3046   855-849-7213
                        info@yourbreed.com
                        www.yourbreed.com

Unique gifts for dog lovers

President: Nancy D Holloway
Credit Cards: AMEX; MasterCard

Business & School

3514 ABC Distributing
LTD Commodities
2800 Lakeside Dr
Bannockburn, IL 60015-1280   847-295-5532
                               847-295-6058
                          Fax: 847-604-7600
                          www.ltdcommodities.com

Furniture, garden accessories, jewelry, purses, electronics, gifts and collectibles.

President: Cathy Bauer
Marketing Manager: Karen Wallace
Catalog Circulation: Mailed 1 time(s) per year
Printing Information: 200 pages in 4 colors
In Business: 56 years
Number of Employees: 10
Sales Volume: $400,000

3515 Advertising Specialties & Business Gifts
Promotion Plus, Inc.
4104 Vachell Ln
San Luis Obispo, CA 93401-8113 805-541-5730
                                800-943-9494
                           Fax: 805-541-4795
                           alyssa@promoplus.com
                           www.promoplus.com

Complete line of premium and incentive gifts

Chairman: Ernie Roide
eroide@promoplus.com
President: Bill Luffee
bill@promoplus.com
Production Manager: Michelle Roberts
michelle@promoplus.com
Account Executive: Rob Fagot
robpromo@comcast.net
Credit Cards: AMEX; MasterCard; Visa
Catalog Cost: Free
Catalog Circulation: Mailed 1 time(s) per year
Printing Information: 148 pages in 4 colors

Binding: Perfect Bound
In Business: 26 years
Number of Employees: 16
Sales Volume: 5.8M

3516 Alphabet U
Anderson's Alphabet U
4875 White Bear Parkway
White Bear Lake, MN 55110   800-338-3346
                         Fax: 800-213-8166
                         service@andersons.com
                         www.andersons.com

Preschool and kindergarten personalized school supplies, graduation apparel, award and recognition and classroom accessories

President: Troy Ethan
Credit Cards: AMEX; MasterCard; Visa
Catalog Cost: Free
Printing Information: 31 pages in 4 colors
In Business: 45 years

3517 Anderson's Prom Catalog
Andersons.Com
4875 White Bear Pkwy
White Bear Lake, MN 55110-3325 651-426-1084
                              800-338-3346
                         Fax: 800-213-8166
                         service@andersons.com
                         www.andersons.com

Prom decorations, supplies, favors and gifts

President: Charles B Anderson
Credit Cards: AMEX; MasterCard; Visa
Catalog Cost: Free
In Business: 43 years
Number of Employees: 20
Sales Volume: $3MM to $5MM

3518 Asprey
Asprey New York
853 Madison Ave
New York, NY 10021-4908   212-688-1811
                       Fax: 212-688-2749
                       enquiries@asprey.com
                       www.Asprey.Com

High quality gifts, jewelry, executive gifts, china and glass

Chairman: Philip Warner
President: Robert Donofriol
Credit Cards: AMEX; MasterCard; Visa
Catalog Cost: $16
Printing Information: 46 pages in 4 colors on Glossy Stock
Press: Web Press
Binding: Saddle Stitched
Mailing List Information: Names for rent
In Business: 28 years
Number of Employees: 15
Sales Volume: $3MM to $5MM

3519 Atlas Pen Catalog
Atlas Pen & Pencil Corporation
342 Shelbyville Mills Road
Shelbyville, TN 37160-189   866-900-7367
                              800-900-7367
                         Fax: 877-286-3039
                         CustomerCare@pens.com
                         www.pens.com

Print name and logos on hats, t-shirts, pens, keychains, calendars, calculators and mugs

President: Eric Schneider
Credit Cards: AMEX; MasterCard; Visa
Catalog Cost: Free
Catalog Circulation: Mailed 1 time(s) per year
Printing Information: 51 pages in 4 colors
In Business: 49 years
Number of Employees: 200
Sales Volume: $10,000,000 - $25,000,000

3520 Awards.com
Awards.com
2915 S. Congress Ave
Delray Beach, FL 33445   407-265-2001
                                 800-429-2737
                            Fax: 561-952-4097
                    ContactUs@awards.com
                    www.awards.com

Awards, trophies, medals, plaques, corporate gifts, logo apparel
President: Aaron Itzkowitz
VP/GM: Jim Nelson
Controller: Lars Wiksten
Director of Operations: Tracee Ferguson
Credit Cards: AMEX; MasterCard
Printing Information: on Glossy Stock
Binding: Perfect Bound
In Business: 10 years
Number of Employees: 70
Sales Volume: 8.3M

3521 Bale Awards
Bale
                                 800-822-5350
                            Fax: 401-831-5500
                                 www.bale.com

Award medals, pins, plaques, trophies, and school jewelry.
Catalog Cost: Free

3522 Baudville
Baudville
5380 52nd St SE
Grand Rapids, MI 49512   616-698-0889
                                 800-728-0888
                            Fax: 616-698-0554
                    service@baudville.com
                    www.baudville.Com

Trophies, recognition items, lapel pins, event paper, seals & embosers, certificate papers, ID accessories, folders & frames and more
President: David Pezzato
Marketing Manager: Jack Fisher
VP: Kristy Sherlund
Credit Cards: AMEX; MasterCard
Catalog Cost: Free
Printing Information: 80 pages in 4 colors on Matte Stock
Binding: Perfect Bound
In Business: 30 years
Number of Employees: 85
Sales Volume: 9.5M

3523 Big Little Fudge
Big Little Fudge
18417 Hwy 105 W
Suite 5
Montgomery, TX 77356   888-543-8343
                            Fax: 936-582-7958
                    robin@biglittlefudge.com
                    www.biglittlefudge.com

Fudges

3524 Bluegrass Playgrounds
1056 Fedde Lane
Ashland, NE 68003   800-828-9690
                            Fax: 866-271-4011
              quotations@bluegrassplaygrounds.com
                    www.bluegrassplaygrounds.com

Traditional and modern playground equipment

3525 BrittenMedia
Britten Banners Inc.
2322 Cass Rd.
Traverse City, MI 49684   231-941-8200
                                 855-763-8204
                            Fax: 231-941-8299
                    sales@brittenmedia.com
                    www.brittenstudios.com

Digitally printed and screen printed banners and signs; banner display accessories, backdrops, mural, flags, tradeshow accessories, museum and zoo exhibit accessories
Chairman: Liz Keegan
President: Paul Britten
Marketing Manager: Jenn Ryan
Production Manager: Peter White
Catalog Cost: Free
Printing Information: 16 pages in 4 colors
In Business: 30 years
Number of Employees: 90
Sales Volume: $25 Million

3526 Call One
Call One Inc
400 Imprial Blvd.
Cape Canaveral, FL 32920-9002   321-783-2400
                                 800-749-3160
                            Fax: 321-799-9222
                    www.calloneonline.com

Telephones, headset bases and amplifiers, headsets and accessories
VP: Raymond Hirsch
VP, Director - Sales/Marketing: William Mays
Sales Manager: Danny Hayasaka
Credit Cards: AMEX; MasterCard
In Business: 26 years
Number of Employees: 80

3527 Carron Net
Carron Net
1623 17th St.
PO Box 177
Two Rivers, WI 54241-0177   800-558-7768
                    sales@carronnet.com
                    www.carronnet.com

Custom and standard sports netting for baseball batting cages, soccer nets, golf range nets, windscreens, tennis and volleyball nets

3528 Collection Book
International Watch Company
3325 Las Vegas Boulevard S
Suite 1702
Las Vegas, NV 89109-5910   702-650-0817
                                 800-432-9330
                            Fax: 702-650-0725
                    boutique.vegas@iwc.com
                         www.iwc.com

Timepieces
CEO: Georges Kern
Mailing List Information: Names for rent

3529 Custom-Printed Promotional Items
Larry Fox and Company Ltd
PO Box 729
Valley Stream, NY 11582-729   516-791-7929
                                 800-397-7923
                            Fax: 516-791-1022
                    ellen@larryfox.com
       promo-web.com/d/d32.asp?d=larryfox&pg=32

Promotional gifts and imprinted products for businesses, organizations, schools, camps, fire departments, EMS, paramedics
President: Ellen Ingber
Marketing Manager: Ellen Ingber
CEO: Larry Fox
Credit Cards: MasterCard
Catalog Cost: Free
Catalog Circulation: Mailed 1 time(s) per year to 20000
Printing Information: 64 pages in 1 color on Matte Stock
Press: Web Press
Binding: Perfect Bound
Mailing List Information: Names for rent
In Business: 54 years
Number of Employees: 2
Sales Volume: $500M to $1MM

3530 Direct Promotions
Direct Promotions
29395 Agoura Road
Suite 207
Agoura Hills, CA 91301   818-591-9010
                                 800-444-7706
                            Fax: 818-591-2071
                    sales@directpromotions.net
                    www.directpromotions.net

Custom printed promotional products and business gifts
President: Randy Perry
Credit Cards: AMEX; MasterCard
Catalog Cost: Free
Catalog Circulation: Mailed 1 time(s) per year
Printing Information: 24 pages in 4 colors on Glossy Stock
Press: Web Press
Binding: Saddle Stitched
In Business: 12 years
Number of Employees: 4
Sales Volume: $500M to $1MM

3531 Discovery Channel
Discovery Store
300 California Street
3rd Floor
San Francisco, CA 94104   800-938-0333
                            Fax: 276-670-2121
                    www.discoverystore.com

Gifts from shows on the Discovery Channel; Great ideas and fun items for all
Chairman: John Hendricks
President: David Zaslav
CFO: Bradley E. Singer (Brad)
Marketing Manager: Lori McFarling
Credit Cards: AMEX; MasterCard
Catalog Cost: Free

3532 Eastern Emblem
Eastern Emblem Mfg Corp
509 18th Street
PO Box 828
Union City, NJ 07087-828   201-854-0338
                                 800-344-5112
                            Fax: 201-867-7248
                    jnsboyscouts@gmail.com
                    www.easternemblem.com

Emblems and insignia for advertising or groups; custom embroidery and metal pins; custom work for embroidery-metal logo pins, stickers, garments
President: S Lefkowitz
Production Manager: Len
Credit Cards: AMEX; MasterCard
Catalog Cost: Free
In Business: 55 years
Number of Employees: 7
Sales Volume: $1MM-$3MM

3533 Emedco Buyer's Guide
Emedco, Inc.
PO Box 369
Buffalo, NY 14240   866-222-4743
                                 866-509-1976
                            Fax: 800-344-2578
                    customerservice@emedco.com
                    www.emedco.com

Engraved signs, frames and graphic communication products
President: Jonathan Sayers
Marketing Manager: Scott Wardour
Credit Cards: AMEX; MasterCard; Visa
Catalog Cost: Free
Printing Information: 154 pages in 4 colors
In Business: 60 years
Number of Employees: 160
Sales Volume: $10MM to $20MM

3534 Engraving Connection
Engraving Connection
1205 S Main St
Plymouth, MI 48170-2215   734-459-3180
                                 877-829-2737
                            Fax: 734-455-6040
etched@engravecon.com
www.engravecon.com

Personalized gifts, awards, badges and desk nameplates
President: Rex Tubbs
In Business: 37 years
Number of Employees: 6
Sales Volume: $500,000 - $1,000,000

3535 Flemington Aluminum & Brass
Flemington Aluminum and Brass Inc
24 Junction Rd
Flemington, NJ 08822-5721   908-782-6317
                            Fax: 908-782-8078
info@fabonline.net
www.Fabonline.Net

Traffic signal products, street lighting, aluminum poles, cabinets and enclosures, cast aluminum and brass plaques, custom castings
President: Jim Kozicki
Catalog Cost: Free
Printing Information: 50 pages in 2 colors on Glossy Stock
Mailing List Information: Names for rent
In Business: 74 years
Number of Employees: 25
Sales Volume: $1,000,000 - $5,000,000

3536 GameTime
GameTime
150 PlayCore Drive SE
Fort Payne, AL 35967   800-235-2440
                            Fax: 256-845-9361
www.gametime.com

Playground equipment

3537 Hartmann by Design
Hartmann
PO Box 550
Lebanon, TN 37088-550   615-444-5000
                                 800-621-5293
                            Fax: 615-443-4619
customerservice@pobox.hartmann.com
www.Hartmann.Com

Leather carry-on luggage, wheeled luggage, business cases, totes, garment bags, wallets, gift sets and travel accesories
President: David Herman
Credit Cards: AMEX; MasterCard; Visa
Catalog Cost: Free
In Business: 137 years
Number of Employees: 3750

3538 HomeRoom Direct
HomeRoom
PO Box 388
Centerbrook, CT 06409-388   860-767-4200
                                 800-234-1024
                            Fax: 860-767-4381
customerservice@homeroomdirect.com
www.homeroomdirect.com

School teacher gifts
President: Tom Romano
Credit Cards: AMEX; MasterCard; Visa
Catalog Cost: Free
Printing Information: 45 pages
In Business: 23 years

3539 Impact Gift Collection
Promotion Plus Inc
4104 Vachell Lane
San Luis Obispo, CA 93401-8113 805-541-5730
                                 800-943-9494
alyssa@promoplus.com
www.promoplus.com

Incentive gift ideas
Catalog Circulation: Mailed 2 time(s) per year
Printing Information: 106 pages in 4 colors
Binding: Perfect Bound
Number of Employees: 30

3540 Intercollegiate Designs
Intercollegiate Designs
1095 Broadhollow Rd
Farmingdale, NY 11735-4815   631-694-1130
                                 800-333-9822
                            Fax: 631-694-1142
bk55238@worldnet.att.net

Custom decorated ceramic mugs, beverageware, and plates for clubs, schools and organizations
President: David Goldsmith
Marketing Manager: Martin R Kaye
Production Manager: Brian McDonald
Catalog Cost: $4
Catalog Circulation: Mailed 4 time(s) per year
Printing Information: 24 pages in 4 colors on Glossy Stock
Press: Web Press
Binding: Saddle Stitched
In Business: 63 years
Number of Employees: 11

3541 International Bronze Manufacturers
International Bronze Manufacturers & Des
810 Willis Avenue
Albertson, NY 11507-1919   516-248-3080
                                 800-227-8752
                            Fax: 516-248-4047
sales@internationalbronze.com
www.internationalbronze.com

Bronze plaques, architectural sculptures, sign systems, name plates and monuments
President: Kenneth Klein
Catalog Cost: FREE
In Business: 79 years
Sales Volume: $3MM to $5MM

3542 Jones School Supply
Jones School Supply Company
PO Box 100197
Columbia, SC 29202   800-845-1807
                            Fax: 800-942-5421
customerservice@jonesawards.com
www.jonesawards.com

Academic awards, certificates, medals and pins
In Business: 95 years

3543 Koeze Direct
Koeze Direct
2555 Burlingame Ave SW
P.O.Box 9470
Grand Rapids, MI 49509   800-555-9688
                            Fax: 866-817-0147
service@koezedirect.com
koeze.com

Credit Cards: AMEX; MasterCard
In Business: 15 years

3544 Kogle Cards
Cordial Greetings
150 Kingswood Road
PO Box 8465
Mankato, MN 56002-8465   800-257-8276
                            Fax: 800-842-9371
customerservice@cordialgreetings.com
www.cordialgreetings.com

Greeting cards and promotional gifts for businesses
Marketing Manager: Michelle Johnson
Credit Cards: AMEX; MasterCard; Visa
Catalog Cost: Free
Catalog Circulation: Mailed 1 time(s) per year
Printing Information: 80 pages in 4 colors on Glossy Stock
Press: Web Press
Binding: Saddle Stitched
In Business: 26 years
Number of Employees: 50
Sales Volume: $1MM to $3MM

3545 Marquis Awards & Specialties
Marquis Awards & Specialties, Inc.
108 N Bent St
Powell, WY 82435   307-754-2272
                                 800-327-2446
                            Fax: 307-754-9577
marquisawards@bresnan.net
www.rushawards.com

Awards, sportswear and promotional gifts for businesses and consumers
President: John H Collins
Marketing Manager: Terry Collins
Founder: John Collins
Founder: Terry Collins
Credit Cards: AMEX; MasterCard; Visa; Discover
Catalog Cost: Free
Catalog Circulation: Mailed 12 time(s) per year
Printing Information: 97 pages in 4 colors on Matte Stock
Press: Web Press
Binding: Saddle Stitched
Mailing List Information: Names for rent
In Business: 31 years
Number of Employees: 5
Sales Volume: $500M to $1MM

3546 Medallic Art Company, Ltd
Medallic Art Company, Ltd
80 E. Airpark Vista Boulevard
Dayton, NV 89403   775-246-6000
                                 800-843-9854
                            Fax: 775-246-6006
minted@medallic.com
www.medallic.com

Commemorative and premium awards
President: Robert W Hoff
Printing Information: 16 pages
Number of Employees: 40
Sales Volume: $3MM to $5MM

3547 Nurses Station Catalog
CRT Associates
224 Birmingham Dr
#2b
Cardiff, CA 92007   760-550-9901
                                 800-227-1927
                            Fax: 860-767-4381
customerservice@nursesdirect.com

Gifts for individuals in the nursing profession
President: Tom Romano
Credit Cards: AMEX; MasterCard; Visa
Catalog Cost: Free
Printing Information: 45 pages
In Business: 25 years

3548 OnDeck Sports
OnDeck Sports
88 Spark St.
Brockton, MA 00230   800-365-6171
                            Fax: 508-580-0211
info@ondecksports.com
www.ondecksports.com

Netting, artificial turf, baseball equipment, batting cages and portable pitching mounds.

3549 Ostrich Baskets & Custom Gifts
Ostrich Baskets & Custom Gifts
2350 East Nichols Place
Centennial, CO 80122   800-858-6599
ostrichbaskets.com

Gifts

CFO: Connie Shammas
connie@ostrichbaskets.com
Marketing Manager: Carole Senn
carole@ostrichbaskets.com
Operations Manager: Toby Zellers
orders@ostrichbaskets.com
Realtor Basket Director: Robert M. Shammas
roberts@ostrichbaskets.com
I.T. Manager: CharlesHoskins
charles@ostrichbaskets.com
Credit Cards: AMEX; MasterCard

3550 Pacific Sportswear & Emblem Company
Pacific Sportswear Co.,Inc
Box 15211
San Diego, CA 92195-5211   619-281-6688
     800-872-8778
Fax: 619-281-6687
info@pacsport.com
www.Pacsport.Com

Custom embroidered Flag Patches and Pins, headwear, embroidered patches, rubber keychains and lapel pins

President: Rich Soergel
CFO: Cathy Mellies
Marketing Manager: Rich Roengel
Production Manager: Bob Bond
Credit Cards: MasterCard; Visa
Catalog Cost: Free
Catalog Circulation: Mailed 52 time(s) per year to 10M
Average Order Size: $5000
Printing Information: 10 pages in 1 color on Matte Stock
Press: Web Press
Binding: Saddle Stitched
Mailing List Information: Names for rent
List Manager: Rich Soergel
In Business: 28 years
Number of Employees: 8
Sales Volume: $1,000,000 - $5,000,000

3551 Pecco Premiums
Pecco, Inc.
8760 Orion Place, Suite 100,
Columbus, OH 43240-2911   201-461-0055
Fax: 201-461-5333
www.manta.com

Sales promotion novelties predominantly in the $1-$5 price range, including audios, calculators, clocks, watches, bags, accessories, etc

President: Patrick Lam
CFO: George Trotman
Marketing Manager: Andrew P Goranson
Production Manager: PW Lam
CEO: John Swanciger
COO: Dario Ambrosini
VP, Platform & Technology: Brad Warnick
Catalog Cost: Free
Catalog Circulation: to 15M
Printing Information: 26 pages in 4 colors on Matte Stock
Press: Sheetfed Press
Number of Employees: 15

3552 Pioneer Linens
Pioneer Linens
210 Clematis Street
West Palm Beach, FL 33401   561-655-8553
     800-207-5463
Fax: 561-655-8889
www.pioneerlinens.com

Home decor, gifts, candles, fragrances, table accessories, bedding and bath

President: Penny Murphy
Catalog Cost: Free
In Business: 103 years

Number of Employees: 25
Sales Volume: $5.03 Million

3553 Popcornopolis
Popcornopolis
1301 E. El Segundo Blvd.
El Segundo, CA 90245   310-414-6700
     800-767-2489
www.popcornopolis.com

Popcorn

Mayor: Wally Arnold

3554 Positive Impressions Idea Showcase
Positive Impression Inc
150 Clearbrook Rd
Elmsford, NY 10523-1143   914-592-4133
     800-895-5505
Fax: 914-592-0717
sales@positiveimpressions.com
www.positiveimpressions.com

Personalized incentives and awards

President: Jim Doyle
Credit Cards: AMEX; MasterCard
Catalog Cost: Free
Printing Information: 98 pages in 4 colors
Binding: Perfect Bound
In Business: 24 years
Number of Employees: 10-J
Sales Volume: $500M to $1MM

3555 Print Craft, Inc.
Print Craft Incorporated
315 5th Avenue N.W.
Minneapolis, MN 55112   651-633-8122
     800-217-8060
www.printcraft.com

Customized retail and commercial packaging, as well as printed products such as calendars, brochures, books, booklets, and reports

President: Mike Gallagher
Production Manager: Jon Riederer
Credit Cards: AMEX; MasterCard
Catalog Circulation: Mailed 2 time(s) per year
Printing Information: 60 pages in 4 colors on Glossy Stock
Press: Web Press
Binding: Saddle Stitched
In Business: 51 years
Number of Employees: 165

3556 Quill Full Line
Quill Corporation
P.O. Box 37600
Philadelphia, PA 19101-600   800-982-3400
Fax: 800-789-8955
imprints@quill.com
www.quill.com

Electronics to enhance incentive programs, office furniture and office supplies

President: Michael Patriarca
Marketing Manager: James Meyer
Catalog Cost: Free
Catalog Circulation: Mailed 1 time(s) per year
Printing Information: 16 pages in 4 colors
Binding: Saddle Stitched
In Business: 59 years
Number of Employees: 1400

3557 Rainbow Industries
Brand Builders
PO Box 1087
Tenafly, NJ 07670-5087   973-575-8383
     800-842-0527
Fax: 973-575-6001
jeffrey@brandbuildersllc.com
www.brandbuildersllc.com

Advertising specialties and executive gifts

President: Richard Brown
Marketing Manager: Jeffery Brown
Production Manager: Richard Brown
Catalog Cost: Free

Catalog Circulation: Mailed 10 time(s) per year to 10M
Average Order Size: $500
Printing Information: 20 pages in 4 colors on Glossy Stock
Press: Web Press
Binding: Folded
Mailing List Information: Names for rent
List Manager: R Brown
In Business: 21 years
Number of Employees: 15
Sales Volume: $3MM to $5MM

3558 Rebechini Studios
Rebechini Studios,Inc
680 Fargo Ave
Elk Grove Vlg, IL 60007-4701   847-437-9030
     800-229-6050
Fax: 847-437-0324
www.rsi-design.com

Architectural signage and castings

President: Glenn Rebechini
glenn.r@rsi-design.com
Production Manager: Vince Papp
vpapp@rsi-design.com
Credit Cards: MasterCard; Visa
Catalog Cost: Free
Catalog Circulation: Mailed 1 time(s) per year to 60M
Average Order Size: $1500
Printing Information: 18 pages in 1 color on Matte Stock
Press: Web Press
Binding: Saddle Stitched
Mailing List Information: Names for rent
In Business: 55 years
Number of Employees: 23
Sales Volume: $1,000,000 - $5,000,000

3559 Room It Up
All for Colors
1237 SE Indian Street
Suite 101
Stuart, FL 34997   800-240-3222
info@allforcolor.com
www.allforcolor.com

Backpacks, bags, lap desks and dorm room decor

President: Chauss Jamie
Credit Cards: AMEX; MasterCard
Catalog Cost: Free
In Business: 14 years
Number of Employees: 13
Sales Volume: $6 million

3560 Sales Promotion Tool Book
The Godfrey Group
1000 Centre Green Way
Ste 200
Cary, NC 27513-7659   919-544-6504
     800-789-9394
Fax: 919-544-6729
sales@godfreygroup.com
www.godfreygroup.com

Trade show exhibits and displays

President: H Glenn Godfrey
Principal: Will Daniel
VP: Ann Godfrey
Project Manager: Pete Smith
Credit Cards: AMEX; MasterCard
Catalog Cost: Free
Printing Information: 42 pages in 4 colors on Glossy Stock
In Business: 40 years

3561 Siegel Display
Siegel Display Products
300 Display Drive
Moody, AL 35004   800-626-0322
Fax: 501-525-7716
sales@siegeldisplay.com
www.siegeldisplay.com

Displays for books, novelities, and trade show displays

President: Jeannette Beck
Credit Cards: AMEX; MasterCard
Catalog Cost: Free
Catalog Circulation: Mailed 1 time(s) per year to 50M
Printing Information: 76 pages in 4 colors
Press: Sheetfed Press
Binding: Saddle Stitched
Mailing List Information: Names for rent
In Business: 46 years
Number of Employees: 20-5
Sales Volume: $1,000,000 - $5,000,000

3562 Sportime Catalog
School Specialty Inc
PO Box 1579
Appleton, WI 54912-1579 888-388-3224
 800-283-5700
 Fax: 888-388-6344
 orders@schoolspecialty.com
 www.schoolspecialty.com

Innovative audio/video products for physical education & recreation, sensory solutions, school supplies, early childhood and special needs products and equipment

Chairman: James R. Henderson
President: Joseph M. Yorio
CFO: Kevin Baehler
Principal: Justin Lu
Portfolio Manager: Madhu Satyanarayana
EVP, Distribution: Patrick T. Collins
Credit Cards: AMEX; MasterCard
Catalog Cost: Free
Catalog Circulation: Mailed 1 time(s) per year
Printing Information: 400 pages

3563 Things Remembered
Things Remembered
5043 Tuttle Crossing Blvd.
Dublin, OH 43016 614-760-8891
 866-902-4438
 Fax: 440-473-2018
 customerservice@thingsremembered.com
 www.thingsremembered.com

Recognition and incentive gifts - personalized

President: Michael Anthony
CFO: David Stefko
Buyers: Jeanette Brewster
Credit Cards: AMEX; MasterCard; Visa
Catalog Cost: Free
Catalog Circulation: Mailed 3 time(s) per year to 2.7MM
Printing Information: 32 pages in 4 colors on Glossy Stock
Press: Web Press
Binding: Saddle Stitched
Mailing List Information: Names for rent
In Business: 40 years
Number of Employees: 200

3564 Thumb Things
Thumb Things, Inc.
1022 Robert St S
Saint Paul, MN 55118-1447 651-457-8900
 Fax: 651-457-7049
 lucyatbw@aol.com
 www.thumbthings.com

Lapel pins, wedding invitations, promotional gifts

President: Lucy Baker
lucyatbw@aol.com
In Business: 36 years
Number of Employees: 4
Sales Volume: $500M to $1MM

3565 Trophyland USA
Trophyland USA Inc
7001 West 20th Avenue
Hialeah, FL 33014-4496 305-823-4830
 800-327-5820
 Fax: 305-823-4836
 info@trophyland.com
 www.trophyland.com

Trophies, plaques, medals and awards

President: Tony Mendez
Marketing Manager: Clara Diaz
Fulfillment: Julio Gonzales
International Marketing Manager: Julio Gonzales
Buyers: Paul Fields
Julio Gonzales
Credit Cards: AMEX; MasterCard; Visa
Catalog Cost: Free
Catalog Circulation: Mailed 2 time(s) per year to 25M
Printing Information: 88 pages
Mailing List Information: Names for rent
List Manager: Clara Diaz
In Business: 38 years
Number of Employees: 75
Sales Volume: $1,000,000 - $5,000,000

3566 Union Pen Company Full Line Catalog
Amsterdam Printing
166 Wallins Corners Road
Amsterdam, NY 12010 800-203-9917
 Fax: 518-843-5204
 www.unionpen.com

Direct marketer of imprinted promotional products

President: Morton Tenny
CFO: R Rosenthal
Credit Cards: AMEX; MasterCard
Catalog Cost: Free
Catalog Circulation: Mailed 6 time(s) per year to 15000
Average Order Size: $350
Printing Information: 48 pages in 4 colors on Matte Stock
Press: Web Press
Binding: Saddle Stitched
Mailing List Information: Names for rent
Will Trade Names: Yes
In Business: 116 years
Number of Employees: 150
Sales Volume: $10,000,000 - $25,000,000

3567 Windjammer Promotions
Windjammer Promotions Inc
PO Box 1669
Framingham, MA 01701-1669 877-596-2505
 800-721-5050
 Fax: 508-877-1819

Promotional products to help generate sales, thank your customers or reward your valued employees

President: Anthony Nasch
Credit Cards: AMEX; MasterCard
Catalog Cost: Free
Catalog Circulation: Mailed 2 time(s) per year
Printing Information: 32 pages in 4 colors
Binding: Saddle Stitched
Number of Employees: 5
Sales Volume: 3MM-5MM

3568 Woodland Smoky Bear Catalog
Woodland Enterprises
310 N Main St
Moscow, ID 83843-2629 208-882-4767
 Fax: 208-882-0373
 smokey@smokeybeargifts.com
 www.smokeybeargifts.com

Smoky the Bear gifts and collectibles

President: Dawn Fazio
Production Manager: Jim Fazio
Credit Cards: MasterCard; Visa
Catalog Cost: Free
Printing Information: on Glossy Stock
Binding: Saddle Stitched
In Business: 30 years
Sales Volume: Under $500M

Home Furnishings

3569 Acacia
Acacia
PO Box 8310
West Chester, OH 45069-8310 800-944-0474
 customerservice@acacialifestyle.com
 www.acacialifestyle.com

Clothing, shoes, jewelry, accessories, home decor and garden sculptures

President: Mark Stevens
CEO: Miguel Penella
Rozanne Hakala
Catalog Cost: Free
Printing Information: 47 pages in 4 colors on Glossy Stock
Binding: Saddle Stitched

3570 B Lazarus
Lazarus Manufacturing
10140 NW South River Drive
Medley, FL 33178-4416 305-885-8904
 Fax: 305-885-8940
 www.lazarusmanufacturing.com/

Curtains, draperies, window hardware, bedspreads and upholstery fabrics

President: Deborah Lazarus
deborah@lazarusmanufacturing.com
CFO: Andra Lazarus
alma@lazarusmanufacturing.com
Marketing Manager: Eric Lazarus
eric@lazarusmanufacturing.com
Production Manager: Michael Yunis
Fulfillment: Michael Lazarus
VP and Partner: Alma Franqui
alma@lazarusmanufacturing.com
VicePresident, Sales and Marketing: Eric Lazarus
eric@lazarusmanufacturing.com
Catalog Cost: Free
Printing Information: 26 pages
In Business: 75 years
Number of Employees: 60
Sales Volume: $5,000,000 - $10,000,000

3571 Baccarat
Baccarat
625 Madison Ave
New York, NY 10022-1801 212-826-4130
 800-215-1300
 Fax: 212-826-5043
 us.baccarat.com

Baccarat crystal

President: F Minitte
Credit Cards: AMEX; MasterCard; Visa
Catalog Cost: Free
Number of Employees: 8
Sales Volume: Under $500M

3572 Beverly Bremer Silver Shop
Beverly Bremer Silver Shop
3164 Peachtree Rd NE
Atlanta, GA 30305-1827 404-261-4009
 800-270-4009
 Fax: 404-261-9708
 sterlingsilver@beverlybremer.com
 www.beverlybremer.com

New and estate silver flatware, holloware and gifts

President: Beverly Bremer
Secretary: Charles D'Huyvetter
Credit Cards: AMEX; MasterCard; Visa
In Business: 40 years
Number of Employees: 14
Sales Volume: $900,000

3573 Brass Bed Shoppe
A Brass Bed Shoppe
13800 Miles Avenue
Cleveland, OH 44105 216-371-0400
 Fax: 216-292-0026
 info@brassbedshoppe.com
 www.brassbedshoppe.com

Brass beds, iron beds, cribs, twin beds and daybeds

Printing Information: 12 pages on Glossy Stock
Press: Web Press
Mailing List Information: Names for rent
In Business: 37 years
Number of Employees: 4
Sales Volume: 400K

3574 Calico Corners

Calico Corners
203 Gale Lane
Kennett Square, PA 19348-1735   800-213-6366
www.calicocorners.com

Decorative fabric, trimmings and furniture

President: Roy Simpson
Catalog Cost: Free
Catalog Circulation: Mailed 4 time(s) per year
Printing Information: 40 pages in 4 colors on Glossy Stock
Binding: Perfect Bound
In Business: 67 years
Sales Volume: Under $500M

3575 Chapman

Chapman Manufacturing Company
481 West Main Street
Avon, MA 02322-359   508-588-3200
Fax: 508-587-7592
info@chapmanco.com
www.Chapmanco.Com

Lighting and furniture accessories

President: Thomas Ruskin
Catalog Cost: $100
Printing Information: 40 pages
Number of Employees: 110

3576 Charleston Gardens

Charleston Gardens
183 Madison Avenue
Suite 1415
New York, NY 10016   646-560-5244
877-422-9688
Fax: 800-532-5140
staff@charlestongardens.com
www.charlestongardens.com

Classic furniture and accessories for the home and garden

President: Leeda Marting
CFO: Tom Feagin
Marketing Manager: David Aldrich
Catalog Cost: Free
Catalog Circulation: Mailed 12 time(s) per year to 2 M
Average Order Size: $300
Printing Information: 64 pages in 4 colors on G
Press: W
Binding: S
Mailing List Information: Names for rent
In Business: 17 years
Number of Employees: 15
Sales Volume: 2M

3577 Collections Etc

Winston Brands Incorporated
P.O. Box 7985
Elk Grove Village, IL 60009-7985   620-584-8000
www.collectionsetc.com

Gifts, housewares and novelties

President: Todd Lustbader
Credit Cards: AMEX; MasterCard
Catalog Cost: Free
Catalog Circulation: Mailed 5 time(s) per year to 20000
Printing Information: 68 pages in 4 colors on Glossy Stock
Press: Web Press
Binding: Saddle Stitched
Mailing List Information: Names for rent
Will Trade Names: Yes
In Business: 20 years

Number of Employees: 50
Sales Volume: $20MM to $50MM

3578 Colonial Williamsburg

Colonial Williamsburg Foundation
201 Fifth Avenue
Williamsburg, VA 23185   800-446-9240
shop@cwf.org
shop.colonialwilliamsburg.com

Reproduction home furnishings and gifts

Chairman: Henry C. Wolf
President: Mitchell B. Reiss
Marketing Manager: Tammy Kersey
Production Manager: Cathleen Moore
Fulfillment: Marie Lapetina
Buyers: Bob Keroack
Credit Cards: AMEX; MasterCard; Visa; Discover
Catalog Cost: Free
Average Order Size: $135
Printing Information: 68 pages in 4 colors on G
Press: W
Binding: S
Mailing List Information: Names for rent
List Company: Mokrynski & Associates
401 Hackensack Avenue
Hackensack, NJ 07601
2014885656
In Business: 30 years
Number of Employees: 60
Sales Volume: $20,000,000

3579 Country Door

Through the Country Door
1112 7th Avenue
Monroe, WI 53566-1364   800-341-9477
www.countrydoor.com

Casual and timeless home decor and furnishings.

3580 Country House

Country House
2420 West Zion Road
Salisbury, MD 21801   800-331-3602
800-596-4666
Fax: 800-721-6023
web@thecountryhouse.com
www.thecountryhouse.com

Antique reproductions, primitive country collectibles, home furnishings, tinware, candles, lighting, old toys, dolls, country fixin's, and garden accessories

President: Mike Delano
Marketing Manager: Norma Delano
Catalog Cost: Free
Catalog Circulation: to 50000
Average Order Size: $58
Printing Information: 54 pages in 4 colors on Glossy Stock
Press: Web Press
Binding: Saddle Stitched
Mailing List Information: Names for rent
In Business: 30 years
Number of Employees: 70
Sales Volume: 6M

3581 Crystal Classics

Crystal Classics
6185-K Huntley Road
Columbus, OH 43229-1094   614-430-8180
800-999-0655
Fax: 614-430-8728
info@crystalclassics.com
www.crystalclassics.com

Crystal stemware collections, lamps, barware, wedding gifts, ornaments

President: Maxine Stotler
Marketing Manager: Bruno Bergman
Credit Cards: AMEX; MasterCard; Visa
Catalog Cost: Free
In Business: 19 years
Number of Employees: 26
Sales Volume: 1.2M

3582 Danforth Pewter

Danforth Pewter
52 Seymour Street
PO Box 828
Middlebury, VM 5753   800-222-3142
Fax: 802-388-0099
info@danforthpewter.com
www.danforthpewter.com

3583 Emerald Collection

Emerald Collection
100 Cummings Ctr
Beverly, MA 01915-6115   800-334-3750
Fax: 978-524-8585
info@emerald-collection.com
www.emerald-collection.com

China, crystal and collectibles

Credit Cards: AMEX; MasterCard; Visa
Catalog Cost: Free
Catalog Circulation: Mailed 2 time(s) per year
Printing Information: 48 pages in 4 colors on Glossy Stock
Press: Web Press
Binding: Saddle Stitched
Mailing List Information: Names for rent
In Business: 26 years
Number of Employees: 12

3584 Fan Man

Fan Man
1914 Abrams Pkwy
Dallas, TX 75214-6218   214-826-7700
Fax: 214-826-7700
fanmanusa3@aol.com
www.fanmanusa.com

Electric fans from the 1890's to 1990's sales, restorations, parts and rentals

President: Jim De Noyer
Marketing Manager: Linda Denoyer
Catalog Cost: $2
Catalog Circulation: Mailed 6 time(s) per year
Printing Information: 12 pages in 2 colors on Matte Stock
Binding: Folded
In Business: 30 years
Sales Volume: Under $500M

3585 Ferdco Corporation

Hoffman Brothers
1795 Birchwood Avenue
PO Box 65
Des Plaines, IL 60018-3005   800-323-9120
Fax: 847-671-1320
hoffmanbrothers1@aol.com
www.ferdco.com

Sewing machines and accessories for light to heavy stitching needs

President: Cheryl Mathis
Sales Volume: $3MM to $5MM

3586 FirstSTREET for Boomers & Beyond

FirstSTREET
1998 Ruffin Mill Road
Colonial Heights, VA 23834-5913 804-524-9888
800-958-8324
Fax: 866-889-9960
customerservice@firststreetonline.com
www.firststreetonline.com

Innovative products for Boomers and Beyond

President: Mark Gordon
CFO: Kevin Miller
Credit Cards: AMEX; MasterCard
Catalog Cost: Free
Catalog Circulation: Mailed 1 time(s) per year
Printing Information: in 4 colors
Number of Employees: 200

3587 **Fran's Wicker & Rattan Furniture**
Fran's Wicker & Rattan Furn
1050 Route 46
Ledgewood, NJ 07876-1321   973-927-8530
800-372-6799
Fax: 973-584-7446
www.Dfwicker.Com

Wicker and Rattan furniture
President: David Gruber
Credit Cards: AMEX; MasterCard
Printing Information: 96 pages
Sales Volume: $10MM to $20MM

3588 **Frye's Measure Mill**
Frye's Measure Mill
12 Frye Mill Rd
Wilton, NH 03086-5010   603-654-6581
Fax: 603-654-6103
www.fryesmeasuremill.com

Antique wooden ware, shaker boxes, round, oval and square colonial boxes, trays and folk art
President: Harley Savage
Credit Cards: MasterCard; Visa
Catalog Cost: $3.75
Catalog Circulation: Mailed 1 time(s) per year to 10000
Average Order Size: $75
Printing Information: 24 pages in 4 colors on Glossy Stock
Press: Letterpress
Binding: Saddle Stitched
In Business: 157 years
Number of Employees: 5
Sales Volume: Under $500M

3589 **Griffith Pottery House**
Griffith Pottery House Inc
100 Lorraine Ave
Oreland, PA 19075-1799   215-887-2222
800-760-8147
Fax: 215-884-0676
info@gphprint.com
www.gphprint.com

Custom decorators of glassware, china and sporting goods
President: B Kevin Griffith
Catalog Cost: Free
Catalog Circulation: Mailed 2 time(s) per year
Printing Information: 36 pages
In Business: 70 years
Number of Employees: 4
Sales Volume: $1MM to $3MM

3590 **Hall's Merchandising**
Hallmark Cards, Inc.
P.O. Box 419034
Mail Drop 216
Kansas City, MO 64141-2509   816-274-8346
888-425-5722
Fax: 816-274-4471
www.hallmark.com

China, glassware and home furnishings
President: Kelly Cole
Production Manager: Debbie Robinson
Printing Information: 26 pages in 4 colors on Glossy Stock
Binding: Saddle Stitched
Number of Employees: 5700

3591 **Heart of Vermont**
Heart of Vermont
131 South Main Street
PO Box 612
Barre, VT 05641-612   800-639-4123
Fax: 802-479-5395
info@heartofvermont.com
www.heartofvermont.com

Flannel sheets, satin sheets, pillows & pillow cases, blankets, comforters, matress toppers, mattress sets, furniture

3592 **House Parts**
House Parts
479 Whitehall St SW
Atlanta, GA 30303-3750   404-577-5584
Fax: 404-525-6708
sales@houseparts.com
www.houseparts.com

Antique, historical and architectural reproductions, home and garden decor, drapery hardware
Chairman: Rachel Conway
President: Rachel Conway
Catalog Cost: Free
In Business: 36 years
Number of Employees: 150
Sales Volume: $3MM to $5MM

3593 **Irvins Country Tinware**
Irvins Country Tinware
115 Cedar Lane
Mt Pleasant Mills, PA 17853-8016 570-539-8200
800-800-4846
Fax: 570-539-2721
service@irvins.com
www.irvins.com

Tinware, Custom Furniture, and home accents
President: Irvin Hoover
Catalog Cost: Free
Printing Information: 44 pages in 4 colors on Glossy Stock
Binding: Saddle Stitched
In Business: 55 years
Sales Volume: $5MM to $10MM

3594 **Kings Chandelier**
Kings Chandelier
729 South Van Buren Road
Eden, NC 27288   336-623-6188
Fax: 336-627-9935
crystal@chandelier.com
www.chandelier.com

Crystal chandeliers, candelabra's and sconces
President: Nancy Daniel
Credit Cards: AMEX; MasterCard; Visa
Catalog Cost: $6
Printing Information: 42 pages
In Business: 80 years
Sales Volume: $1MM to $3MM

3595 **Kraftsman Playground and Park Equipment**
Kraftsman Commercial Playgrounds & Water
19535 Haude Road
Spring, TX 77388-5233   281-353-9599
800-451-4869
Fax: 281-353-2265
info@kraftsmanplaygrounds.com
www.kraftsmanplaygrounds.com

Playground equipment and aquatic playground and pool equipment
President: Michelle Soderberg
Marketing Manager: Kris Soderberg
Credit Cards: MasterCard
Catalog Cost: Free
In Business: 33 years
Sales Volume: $3MM to $5MM

3596 **Lighter Side**
Lighter Side
PO Box 25600
Bradenton, FL 34206-5600   800-244-9116
CustomerService@lighterside.com
www.lighterside.com

Apparel, accessories, children's items, decor, games, books, housewares, and novelties

President: Reid Lawson
Sales Volume: $500M to $1MM

President: David Crofoot
Marketing Manager: Kim Boyd
Founder: Alfred Johnson Smith
Credit Cards: AMEX; MasterCard; Visa
Catalog Cost: Free
Printing Information: 64 pages in 4 colors on Glossy Stock
Press: Web Press
Binding: Saddle Stitched
Mailing List Information: Names for rent
List Manager: Kris Temple
In Business: 110 years
Sales Volume: $20MM to $50MM

3597 **Marvin Windows & Doors**
Marvin Windows and Doors
PO Box 100
Warroad, MN 56763   218-386-1430
888-537-7828
international@marvin.com
www.marvin.com

Custom windows and doors
Printing Information: 163 pages in 4 colors on Glossy Stock
In Business: 60 years

3598 **Michael C Fina**
Michael C Fina
500 Park Avenue
New York, NY 10022   212-557-2500
800-289-3462
Fax: 718-937-7193
www.michaelcfina.com

Jewelry, tableware, silver and giftware
President: Amy Chuckerman
Credit Cards: AMEX; MasterCard; Visa
Catalog Cost: Free
In Business: 80 years
Number of Employees: 100
Sales Volume: Under $500M

3599 **Mountaine Meadows Pottery**
Mountaine Meadows Pottery
187 Stoneshead Road
South Ryegate, VT 05069-163   802-584-3164
800-639-6790
Fax: 802-584-3193
custservice@mountainemeadows.com
www.mountainemeadows.com

Handmade stoneware; lamps, plaques, and clocks
Catalog Cost: Free
Printing Information: 4 pages in 1 color on Matte Stock
Binding: Folded
In Business: 41 years
Number of Employees: 10-J
Sales Volume: $500M to $1MM

3600 **National Wildlife Federation**
National Wildlife Federation
1 Stationery Place
Rexburg, ID 83441-5000   800-756-3752
Fax: 800-525-5562
www.shopnwf.org

Nature-related and educational gifts, including home accessories, clothing and toys
President: Larry J Schweiger
Credit Cards: MasterCard; Visa
Catalog Cost: Free
Catalog Circulation: Mailed 4 time(s) per year
Printing Information: 60 pages
Number of Employees: 35
Sales Volume: 5MM-10MM

3601 **Plain & Fancy Custom Cabinetry**
Plain & Fancy Custom Cabinetry
2550 Stiegel Pike
Schaefferstown, PA 17088   717-949-6571
800-447-9006
sales@plainfancycabinetry.com
www.plainfancycabinetry.com

Country, traditional and contemporary cabinets

President: John Achey
Catalog Cost: $20
Printing Information: 90 pages
In Business: 44 years
Number of Employees: 185

3602 Pretty Personal

Pretty Personal Gifts
1143 Leesome Lane
Altamount, NY 12209 516-203-7594
   Fax: 518-438-9738
shop@prettypersonalgifts.com
www.prettypersonalgifts.com

Unique and personalized gifts for family and friends; jewelry, decor for children, apparel & more

President: Janine Jerominek
Marketing Manager: Nancy Smith
Production Manager: Carol Markowitz
Buyers: Janine Jerominek
Credit Cards: AMEX; MasterCard
Catalog Cost: Free
Catalog Circulation: Mailed 2 time(s) per year to 20m
Printing Information: in 4 colors on Glossy Stock
Press: Sheetfed Press
Binding: Saddle Stitched
Mailing List Information: Names for rent
In Business: 14 years
Number of Employees: 10
Sales Volume: $500M to $1MM

3603 Silver Queen

Silver Queen
1350 W Bay Drive
Largo, FL 33770 727-581-6827
   800-262-3134
   Fax: 727-586-0822
sales@silverqueen.com
www.silverqueen.com

Sterling flatware, china, crystal, baby gifts, wedding gifts and ornaments

President: Greg Arbutine
Catalog Cost: Free
Catalog Circulation: Mailed 2 time(s) per year
Average Order Size: $150
Printing Information: in 4 colors on Glossy Stock
Press: Web Press
Binding: Saddle Stitched
Mailing List Information: Names for rent
In Business: 42 years
Number of Employees: 19
Sales Volume: $4.76 MM

3604 Soapstone

Woodstock Soapstone Company
66 Airpark Rd
West Lebanon, NH 03784-1683 603-298-5955
   800-866-4344
   Fax: 603-298-5958
info@woodstove.com
www.woodstove.Com

Wood stoves, gas stoves, countertops, sinks

President: Tom Morrissey
Credit Cards: MasterCard
In Business: 36 years
Sales Volume: $5MM to $10MM

3605 Sporty's Tool Shop Catalog

Sportsman's Market Inc.
Clermont County/Sporty's Airport
2001 Sporty's Drive
Batavia, OH 45103 513-735-9000
   800-776-7897
   Fax: 800-543-8633
www.sportys.com

Home items, lawn care, organization, tools/maintenance

Chairman: Harold Shevers
President: Michael Wolf
CFO: Daniel Robinson
Marketing Manager: Howard Law
Buyers: Howard Law
Credit Cards: AMEX; MasterCard; Visa
Catalog Cost: Free
Catalog Circulation: Mailed 4 time(s) per year to 20000
Printing Information: 80 pages in 4 colors
Mailing List Information: Names for rent
List Company: Names & Addresses
Number of Employees: 200
Sales Volume: $20MM to $50MM

3606 Sturbridge Yankee Workshop

Sturbridge Yankee Workshop
90 Blueberry Road
Portland, ME 04102-1989 207-774-9045
   800-343-1144
www.sturbridgeyankee.Com

Country furnishings, Shaker-style designs and Victorian accents; Maine-made items, unique folk art and many exclusives

President: Bill Binnie
Buyers: Joseph Mango
Jennifer Anderson
Credit Cards: AMEX; MasterCard
Catalog Cost: Free
Catalog Circulation: Mailed 5 time(s) per year
Average Order Size: $125
Printing Information: 48 pages in 4 colors on Glossy Stock
Binding: Saddle Stitched
Mailing List Information: Names for rent
List Company: Diane Brackett
In Business: 64 years
Number of Employees: 75
Sales Volume: $20MM to $50MM

3607 Through the Country Door

Through the Country Door
1112 7th Avenue
Monroe, WI 53566-1364 800-240-6878
   800-341-9477

Kitchen & dining, bed & bath, home accents, furniture, rugs & curtains, seasonal, gifts

President: Ann Bush
Catalog Cost: Free
In Business: 11 years
Number of Employees: 3
Sales Volume: $1,70,000

3608 Trias Flowers, Weddings & Events

Trias Flowers, Weddings & Events
6520 SW 40th St
Miami, FL 33155 305-749-0316
   800-877-6573
www.triasflowers.com

In Business: 103 years

3609 Unison Fall 2015

Unison
2000 West Fulton Street
Chicago, IL 60612 312-492-7960
info@unisonhome.com
www.unisonhome.com

3610 United Force Products

United Force Products
7470 Allison Place
PO Box 3491
Chilliwack, WA 98295-3491 800-741-1344
   Fax: 800-742-8250
www.unitedforce.com

Antique reproductions to accent your home and wooden signs

Credit Cards: MasterCard; Visa
Catalog Circulation: Mailed 52 time(s) per year
Printing Information: 8 pages in 4 colors on Matte Stock
Press: Web Press
Binding: Saddle Stitched

Mailing List Information: Names for rent
In Business: 8 years
Number of Employees: 4
Sales Volume: $500M to $1MM

3611 Vivre

Voyager Spirit
11 E 26th St
15th Floor
New York, NY 10010-1421 212-739-6193
   800-411-6515
   Fax: 212-739-1736

Women, men and kids footwear, outerwear and accessories; home furnishings and gifts

Chairman: James Robinson
President: Eva Jeanbart-Lorenzotti
Marketing Manager: Eileen Shulock
EVP: Meg Galea
mgalea@vivre.com
Credit Cards: AMEX; MasterCard
Catalog Cost: $10
Catalog Circulation: Mailed 2 time(s) per year to 1.5MM
Average Order Size: $600
Printing Information: 80 pages
In Business: 17 years
Number of Employees: 25
Sales Volume: $ 1-3 Million

3612 What on Earth

What on Earth
5581 Hudson Industrial Parkway
PO Box 2599
Hudson, OH 44236 800-441-2242
   800-945-2552
   Fax: 800-950-9569
shop@whatonearthcatalog.com
www.whatonearthcatalog.com

Catalog full of great gifts, from t-shirts to home decor

President: Jared Florian
Buyers: Karyn Vajner
Credit Cards: AMEX; MasterCard; Visa
Catalog Cost: Free
Catalog Circulation: Mailed 12 time(s) per year
Printing Information: 63 pages in 4 colors on Glossy Stock
Press: Web Press
Binding: Saddle Stitched
Mailing List Information: Names for rent
List Company: Mokrynski & Associates
401 Hackensack Avenue
Hackensack, NJ 07601
In Business: 125 years
Number of Employees: 75
Sales Volume: $ 10-20 Million

3613 Whatever Works Catalog

Whatever Works
PO Box 3339
Chelmsford, MA 01824-939 877-756-5053
   800-499-6757
   Fax: 800-866-3235
help@whateverworks.com
www.whateverworks.com

Solutions for the home, office and garden

President: David Krings
Catalog Cost: Free
Printing Information: in 3 colors
In Business: 17 years

3614 Wimpole Street Creations

Wimpole Street, Inc.
445 N 700 W
Ste 110
North Salt Lake, UT 84054-2603 801-298-0504
   800-765-0504
   Fax: 801-298-1333
friends@wimpolestreet.com
www.Wimpolestreet.Com

Table linens for special occasions and everyday, dishtowels, napkins and table accessories, lace and lace details, gifts, items for baby and wedding celebrations, home decor

President: Jeen Brown
Marketing Manager: Christi Parry
Fulfillment: Jeen Brown
Credit Cards: MasterCard
Catalog Cost: $3
Catalog Circulation: Mailed 12 time(s) per year
Average Order Size: $80
Printing Information: on Glossy Stock
Press: Sheetfed Press
Mailing List Information: Names for rent
In Business: 21 years
Number of Employees: 20
Sales Volume: $1MM to $3MM

3615   Woodbury Pewterers
Woodbury Pewterers, Inc.
860 Main Street S
Woodbury, CT 06798-3706   203-263-2668
                                800-648-2014
info@woodburypewter.com
www.woodburypewter.com

Pewter gifts, including collectibles, housewares and decorative accessories

President: Paul Titcomb
Credit Cards: MasterCard; Visa
Catalog Cost: Free
Printing Information: 12 pages in 4 colors on Glossy Stock
Press: Web Press
In Business: 64 years
Number of Employees: 20
Sales Volume: $1MM to $3MM

Luggage

3616   Airline International Luggage & Gifts
Airline International
8701 Montana Ave
El Paso, TX 79925-1220   915-778-1234
                               855-565-1818
Fax: 915-778-1533
orders@airlineintl.com
www.AirlineIntl.Com

Luggage, handbags, business cases, fine writing instruments and gifts

Chairman: Edward Kallman
President: Jerry Kallman
CFO: Bob Hanson
GM, Sales Executive: Steve Geller
Buyers: Stephen Geller, Gifts
Jerry Kallman, Luggage
Edward Kallman, Gifts/Electronics
Credit Cards: AMEX; MasterCard; Visa
Catalog Cost: Free
Catalog Circulation: Mailed 3 time(s) per year to 10000
Printing Information: 48 pages in 4 colors on Glossy Stock
Press: Web Press
Binding: Saddle Stitched
In Business: 33 years
Number of Employees: 30
Sales Volume: $5,000,000

3617   Ebags
eBags, Inc.
5500 Greenwood Plaza Blvd.
Suite 160
Greenwood Village, CO 80111   303-694-1933
                                 800-820-6126
Fax: 303-694-9491
info@ebags.com
www.ebags.com

Handbags, luggage, backpacks, carry-ons, computer cases, wallets and purses and travel accessories

Chairman: Jon Nordmark
President: Mike Edwards
CFO: Mark DeOrio

Marketing Manager: Keith Bristol
CEO & Director: Vince Jones
Credit Cards: AMEX; MasterCard; Visa
Catalog Cost: Free
Printing Information: 32 pages in 4 colors
Binding: Perfect Bound
In Business: 16 years
Number of Employees: 72
Sales Volume: $4.6 Million

3618   Irv's Luggage
Irv's Luggage
2200 S Busse Road
Mount Prospect, IL 60056   847-437-4787
                                 888-300-4787
Fax: 847-437-4895
sales@irvsluggage.com
www.irvsluggage.com

United States and International providers of luggage, business and travel products

Catalog Cost: Free
In Business: 68 years

3619   Jeffers Handbell Supply
Jeffers Handbell Supply
455 Western Lane, PO Box 1728
Irmo, SC 29063-1728   803-781-0555
                            800-547-2355
www.handbellworld.com

Handchime and Handbell Sheet Music.

In Business: 40 years

3620   Justin Charles
Justin Charles
312 Crosstown Rd. Box 312
Peachtree City GA   770-213-1630
                 Fax: 678-815-0972
www.justincharles.com

Technically innovative clothing.

Chief Executive: JohnMark Conklin

3621   Mori Luggage & Gifts
Mori Luggage & Gifts
3595 McCall Place
Atlanta, GA 30340   800-678-6674
                      www.moriluggage.com

Appealing merchandise.

In Business: 39 years

3622   Tumi, Inc.
Tumi, Inc.
1001 Durham Ave
South Plainfield, NJ 07080-2300   908-756-4400
                                   800-299-8864
Fax: 908-756-5878
info@tumi.com
www.tumi.com

Luggage, backpacks, handbags, wallets, cosmetic cases, belts, key chains, laptop covers, umbrellas

President: Jerome Griffith
CFO: Michael Mardy
Credit Cards: AMEX; MasterCard; Visa
Mailing List Information: Names for rent
In Business: 40 years
Number of Employees: 100
Sales Volume: $ 20-50 Million

3623   Weaver West
Weaver Leather, LLC
7540 CR 201
PO Box 68
Mt Hope, OH 44660-68   330-674-1782
                             800-932-8371
Fax: 330-674-0330
info@weaverleather.com
www.Weaverleather.Com

Complete line of luggage materials

President: Paul Weaver
Marketing Manager: Susan Reynolds

Production Manager: Myron Stutzman
COO: Chris Weaver
Printing Information: 256 pages
In Business: 42 years
Sales Volume: $20MM to $50MM

3624   eBags Catalog
eBags Inc
5500 Greenwood Plaza Blvd.
Suite 160
Greenwood Village, CO 80111-480 303-694-1933
                                 800-820-6126
Fax: 303-694-9491
info@ebags.com
www.Ebags.Com

Handbags, luggage, backpacks, carry-ons, computer cases, wallets and purses and travel accessories

President: Mike Edwards
CFO: Mark DeOrio
Marketing Manager: Peter Cobb
EVP Marketing: Peter Cobb
EVP Financial Planning: Steve Neptune
SVP, Technology: Mike Frazzini
Credit Cards: AMEX; MasterCard
Catalog Cost: Free
Printing Information: 32 pages in 4 colors
Binding: Perfect Bound
In Business: 15 years
Sales Volume: $500M to $1MM

Museum

3625   Art Institute of Chicago
The Art Institute of Chicago
111 S Michigan Ave # 1
Michigan Avenue at Adams Street
Chicago, IL 60603-6488   312-443-3533
                               855-301-9612
Fax: 312-443-0849
artinstituteshop@artic.edu
www.artinstituteshop.org

Books, home furnishings, jewelry, stationery and wall art

President: Carol Becker

3626   Concession Equipment Depot
Concession Equipment Depot
1690 SE Village Green Drive
Port Saint Lucie, FL 34952   877-536-6615
                    www.concessionequipmentdepot.com

3627   Heirloom European Tapestries
Heirloom European Tapestries
P.O. Box 539
Dobbins, CA 95935   800-699-6836
info@heirloomtapestries.com
www.heirloomtapestries.com

12th to 19th century museum tapestry reproductions loomed in France, Belgium and Italy, plus handwoven tapestries, carpets and accessories

President: James Waite
CFO: Alla Marinow
Credit Cards: AMEX; MasterCard
Catalog Cost: Free
Catalog Circulation: Mailed 1 time(s) per year
Mailing List Information: Names for rent
In Business: 16 years
Sales Volume: $1MM to $3MM

3628   International Spy Museum
Spy Museum Store
800 F Street, NW
Washington, DC 20004-1505   202-393-7798
                                  877-SPY-BUYS
Fax: 202-393-7797
customerservice@spymuseumstore.org
www.spymuseumstore.org

Spy-related accessories, gadgets, books, gifts, apparel, toys, and collectibles

President: Mike Devine
Marketing Manager: Jodi Zeppelin
Executive Director: Peter Earnest
Catalog Cost: Free
Printing Information: 8 pages
Mailing List Information: Names for rent
In Business: 6 years
Number of Employees: 33
Sales Volume: $ 1-3 Million

3629 Museum Replicas Limited

Museum Replicas Limited
2147 Gees Mill Road
PO Box 840
Conyers, GA 30013

770-922-7500
800-883-8838
Fax: 770-388-0246
custserv@museumreplicas.com
www.museumreplicas.com

Swords, daggers, axes, period clothing and museum replicas

President: Pradeer Windlass
Marketing Manager: Terry Moss
Credit Cards: AMEX; MasterCard
Catalog Cost: Free
Catalog Circulation: Mailed 5 time(s) per year to 1.5MM
Printing Information: 76 pages in 4 colors on Glossy Stock
Press: Web Press
Binding: Saddle Stitched
Mailing List Information: Names for rent
In Business: 44 years
Number of Employees: 45
Sales Volume: $5MM to $10MM

3630 Museum Shop Catalog

Art Institute of Chicago
111 South Michigan Avenue
Chicago, IL 60603-6404

800-518-4214
885-301-9612
Fax: 312-849-4981
mshop@artic.edu
www.artinstituteshop.org

Museum gifts, stationery and apparel

President: Thomas Ahn
Credit Cards: AMEX; MasterCard; Visa
Catalog Cost: Free
Catalog Circulation: Mailed 1 time(s) per year
Printing Information: 44 pages in 4 colors on Glossy Stock
List Company: Walter Karl
1 Blue Hill Plaza
Pear River, NY 10965
Number of Employees: 1000

3631 Nowetah's American Indian Store & Museum

Nowetah's American Indian Museum & Store
#59 State House Station
Augusta, ME 04333-0059

207-628-4981
888-624-6345
www.visitmaine.com

12 separate catalogs featuring genuine American Indian hand-woven rugs, arts, baskets, moccasins, footware, crafts, gifts, clothing, pottery, boots, dolls, toys, jewelry and more

President: Nowetah Wirick
Marketing Manager: Nowetah Wirick
Catalog Cost: Free
Catalog Circulation: to 1000
Average Order Size: $50
Printing Information: 30 pages in 4 colors on Glossy Stock
Press: Web Press
Binding: Folded
Mailing List Information: Names for rent
Will Trade Names: Yes
In Business: 38 years
Number of Employees: 4
Sales Volume: $500M to $1MM

3632 Panther Primitives

Panther Primitives
P.O. Box 32
Normantown, WV 25267

304-462-7718
800-487-2684
Fax: 304-462-7755
info@pantherprimitives.com
www.pantherprimitives.com

Historical camp gear, supplier of reproduction tents and supplies for re-enactors and collectors

Catalog Cost:
Printing Information: 135 pages

3633 Smithsonian

Smithsonian Institution
PO Box 8005
Martinsburg, WV 25402-8005

866-945-6897
Fax: 866-707-4717
www.smithsonianstore.com

Gifts, reproductions, jewelry and American items

Credit Cards: AMEX; MasterCard
Catalog Cost: Free
Catalog Circulation: Mailed 5 time(s) per year
Printing Information: 100 pages in 4 colors on Glossy Stock
Press: Web Press
Binding: Saddle Stitched
Mailing List Information: Names for rent
List Company: Millard Group
10 Vose Farm Road
Peterborough, NH 03458
603-924-9262
Number of Employees: 4
Sales Volume: $500M to $1MM

3634 The Noble Collection

The Noble Collection
PO Box 1476
Sterling, VA 20167

800-866-2538
customerservice@noblecollection.com
www.noblecollection.com

Licensed merchandise, specializing in movie props and collectibles.

Novelty

3635 A Taste of Indiana

A Taste of Indiana
6404 Rucker Road
Indianapolis, IN 46220

317-252-5850
800-289-2758
Fax: 317-257-5983
www.atasteofindiana.com

Credit Cards: AMEX; MasterCard

3636 Abbey Press

Abbey Press Trade Marketing
One Hill Drive
Customer Service Plant 1
St. Meinrad, IN 47577-1004

812-357-8290
800-621-1588
Fax: 812-357-8353
service@abbeytrade.com
www.abbeytrade.com

Religious and novelty gifts

President: Garold Wilhite
Marketing Director: Townes Osborn
Marketing Director: Tami Freson
VP Development: Michael Ziemianski
Credit Cards: AMEX; MasterCard; Visa
Catalog Circulation: Mailed 1 time(s) per year
Printing Information: 63 pages in 4 colors on Glossy Stock
Binding: Saddle Stitched
Mailing List Information: Names for rent
Will Trade Names: Yes
List Company: Direct Media
PO Box 4565
Greenwich, CT 06830
203-532-1000

In Business: 148 years
Number of Employees: 306
Sales Volume: $18.9MM

3637 Airplane Shop

The Airplane Shop
24 Stewart Place
Unit 4
Fairfield, NJ 07004

973-244-1203
800-752-6346
Fax: 973-882-4566
info@airplaneshop.com
www.airplaneshop.com

Military and commercial aviation toys, models and collectibles

President: Ronald Marks
Credit Cards: AMEX; MasterCard
In Business: 22 years
Number of Employees: 16
Sales Volume: 1M

3638 Alaska Wild Berry Products

Alaska Wild Berry Products, Inc.
5225 Juneau St
Anchorage, AK 99518-1483

907-562-8858
800-280-2927
Fax: 907-562-5467
info@akwbp.com
alaskawildberryproducts.com

Wild berry products including jams and jellies, chocolates, candies, caramels, corporate gifts and gift baskets

President: Peter G. Eden
CFO: Thomas Purcell
Marketing Manager: Drew Hamilton
Production Manager: William McDonald
Vice President: Mercedes Eden
Credit Cards: AMEX; MasterCard; Visa
Catalog Cost: Free
Printing Information: 16 pages in 4 colors
Binding: Saddle Stitched
Mailing List Information: Names for rent
In Business: 69 years
Number of Employees: 40
Sales Volume: 4M

3639 American Flag and Gift Catalog

American Flag and Gift
1101 Highland Way
Suite B
Grover Beach, CA 93433

805-473-0395
800-448-3524
Fax: 805-473-0126
flags@anyflag.com
www.anyflag.com

Flags and flag poles

Chairman: John Solley
President: Bridgett Solley
Catalog Cost: $5
Mailing List Information: Names for rent
In Business: 23 years
Number of Employees: 8

3640 Archie McPhee

Archie McPhee & Company
10915 47th Ave. W
Mukilteo, WA 98275

425-349-3009
Fax: 425-349-5188
mcphee@mcphee.com
www.mcphee.com

For the jokester in the family

President: Mark Pahlow
Catalog Circulation: Mailed 1 time(s) per year
In Business: 28 years
Number of Employees: 45
Sales Volume: 60K

3641 Aunt Vera's Attic

Aunt Vera's Attic
15692 Summer Lake Dr
Chesterfield, MO 63017-5136

636-532-5242
800-513-7041

Handmade mailbox decorations, door decorations and mailbox flags

President: Don Davis
Credit Cards: MasterCard; Visa
Catalog Circulation: Mailed 2 time(s) per year to 10000
Printing Information: 4 pages in 4 colors on Glossy Stock
Press: Web Press
Will Trade Names: Yes
In Business: 28 years
Number of Employees: 5
Sales Volume: 250K

3642 Before & After
Before & After, LLC
1981 Moreland Pkwy
Bldg 3 Ste 3
Annapolis, MD 21401   410-672-3399
                          Fax: 410-695-6066
info@courageinstone.com
www.courageinstone.com

Word stones and pocket tokens, inspiration and motivational gifts

President: Brenda
Catalog Circulation: Mailed 1 time(s) per year
Printing Information: 24 pages in 4 colors on Matte Stock
Binding: Saddle Stitched
Mailing List Information: Names for rent
In Business: 9 years
Number of Employees: 3
Sales Volume: Under $500M

3643 Betty's Attic
Betty's Attic
PO Box 25600
Bradenton, FL 34206-5600   941-747-5566
                             800-311-0733
                          Fax: 800-551-4406
customerservice@bettysattic.com
www.bettysattic.com

Nostalgic items and collectibles from the 1920s to the 1970s

President: Ralph Hoenle
CFO: David Crofoot
Marketing Manager: Kim Boyd
Buyers: Tom Ronzi
Catalog Cost: Free
Catalog Circulation: Mailed 52 time(s) per year
Printing Information: 64 pages
Mailing List Information: Names for rent
List Manager: Carolyn Foley
In Business: 101 years
Number of Employees: 100
Sales Volume: $500M to $1MM

3644 Bronner's Christmas Favorites
Bronner's Christmas Wonderland
25 Christmas Lane
PO Box 176
Frankenmuth, MI 48734-0176   989-652-9931
                            Fax: 989-652-3466
customerservice@bronner.com
www.bronners.com

Indoor and outdoor Christmas ornaments and decorations.

Catalog Cost: Free
Printing Information: 64 pages in 4 colors
In Business: 71 years

3645 Brookhollow Collection
Brookhollow
12750 Merit Drive
Suite 700
Dallas, TX 75251   208-359-1000
                             800-272-4182
                          Fax: 800-822-0256
service@brookhollowcards.com
www.brookhollowcards.com

All occasion, holiday and profession specific customizable cards and calendars

Chairman: Michael Johnson
President: Erv Wiebe
Marketing Manager: Collette Rinehart
Credit Cards: AMEX; MasterCard; Visa
Catalog Cost: Free
Catalog Circulation: Mailed 1 time(s) per year
Printing Information: 32 pages in 4 colors on Glossy Stock
Press: Web Press
Binding: Saddle Stitched
Mailing List Information: Names for rent
In Business: 50 years
Number of Employees: 650
Sales Volume: $5MM to $10MM

3646 Celebriducks
Celebriducks
28 Mountain View Ave.
San Rafael, CA 94901-1346   415-456-3452
info@celebriducks.com
www.celebriducks.com

Celebrity rubber ducks of the greatest icons of film, music, history and athletics.

President: Craig Wolfe
CFO: Laura Appel
Production Manager: Chris Howes
International Marketing Manager: Matthew Wong
Catalog Cost: Free
Mailing List Information: Names for rent
In Business: 25 years
Number of Employees: 50
Sales Volume: $3MM to $5MM

3647 Creative Irish Gifts
ShopIrish.com
PO Box 8300
Little Rock, AR 72222   866-851-7918
                          Fax: 877-213-3660
www.shopirish.com

Irish and Celtic gifts, jewelry and foods

President: Diane O'Connor
Credit Cards: AMEX; MasterCard
Catalog Cost: Free
Number of Employees: 40

3648 Current
Current USA
1005 E Woodmen Rd.
Colorado Springs, CO 80920   800-848-2848
                          Fax: 800-993-3232
www.currentcatalog.com

Gifts, gift wrap and cards.

Catalog Cost: Free
In Business: 66 years
Number of Employees: 1200
Sales Volume: $200 Million

3649 Discovery Channel
Discovery Store
300 California Street
3rd Floor
San Francisco, CA 94104   800-938-0333
                          Fax: 276-670-2121
www.discoverystore.com

Gifts from shows on the Discovery Channel; Great ideas and fun items for all

Chairman: John Hendricks
President: David Zaslav
CFO: Bradley E. Singer (Brad)
Marketing Manager: Lori McFarling
Credit Cards: AMEX; MasterCard
Catalog Cost: Free

3650 Expressions
Expressions
222 Mill Rd
P.O. Box 6529
Chelmsford, MA 01824-929   877-756-6837
                             800-388-2699
                          Fax: 800-866-3235
help@expressionscatalog.com
www.expressionscatalog.com

Gifts and decorative accessories

Chairman: Mark A Kirk
Marketing Manager: William Knowles
Production Manager: Edward Knowles
Fulfillment: Nick Parrinelli
Credit Cards: AMEX; MasterCard; Visa
Catalog Cost: Free
Catalog Circulation: Mailed 6 time(s) per year
Printing Information: 60 pages in 4 colors on Glossy Stock
Press: Web Press
Mailing List Information: Names for rent
In Business: 27 years
Number of Employees: 175
Sales Volume: $13 Million

3651 Fat Brain Toys
Fat Brain Toys, LLC
1405 N. 205th Street
Ste 120
Elkhorn, NE 68022   402-779-3181
                             800-590-5987
                          Fax: 402-779-3253
cs@fatbraintoys.com
www.fatbraintoys.com

Open-ended toys, gifts and games that educate and entertain

CFO: Dean Giesselmann
Co-Founder: Mark Carson
Co-Founder: Karen Carson
Credit Cards: AMEX; MasterCard
Catalog Cost: Free
Printing Information: 30 pages in 4 colors on Glossy Stock
Press: Sheetfed Press
Binding: Folded
In Business: 12 years
Number of Employees: 100-
Sales Volume: $ 5-10 Million

3652 Franklin Mint
The Franklin Mint
801 Springdale Dr
Suite 200
Exton, PA 19341   800-843-6468
                          Fax: 610-459-6880
info@franklinmint.com
www.franklinmint.com

Die-cast cars and airplanes, precision modeling, collectibles, jewelry, seasonal giftware

Chairman: Moshe Malamud
President: Steven Sisskind
CFO: Noah Becker
Credit Cards: AMEX
Catalog Cost: Free
Catalog Circulation: Mailed 4 time(s) per year
Printing Information: 60 pages
In Business: 49 years
Number of Employees: 42
Sales Volume: $6.2MM

3653 Funny Side Up
Funny Side Up
425 Stump Road
Montgomeryville, PA 18936-9631   215-361-5100
                             800-247-3747
                          Fax: 215-368-3595
www.funnysideup.com

Novelties and gag items

President: Ronald P Lassin
CFO: Gary Lassin
Marketing Manager: Mary J Reeves
Production Manager: Peggy Hunter
Buyers: Gerri Sassa
Credit Cards: AMEX; MasterCard; Visa; Discover Optima
Printing Information: 64 pages in 4 colors on Glossy Stock
Press: Web Press
Binding: Saddle Stitched
Will Trade Names: Yes
Number of Employees: 475

3654 Garfield
Garfield.com
5440 E. County Rd 450 N.
Albany, IN 47320 765-287-2222
888-274-7297
Fax: 765-287-2329
cliff@pawsinc.com
www.garfield.com

Garfield gifts and collectibles

Chairman: Kim Campbell
kim@pawsinc.com
President: Jim Davis
jill@pawsinc.com
CFO: Thomas Greiwe
Production Manager: Madelyn Ferris Sr
Art Director: Brad Hill
brad@pawsinc.com
Brand Manager: Ted Chmura III
ted@milestoneevents.org
Dir. of Education: Bob Levy
bobl@pawsinc.com

3655 Golden Cockerel
Golden Cockerel
1651 Nc Highway 194 N # 2
Boone, NC 28607-6788 828-297-4653
800-892-5409
Fax: 828-297-4653
service@goldencockerel.com
www.goldencockerel.com

Russian nesting dolls gifts and collectibles

President: Walton Conway
Catalog Cost: Free
Catalog Circulation: Mailed 1 time(s) per year
Average Order Size: $75
Printing Information: 32 pages in 4 colors on
Glossy Stock
Press: Sheetfed Press
Mailing List Information: Names for rent
In Business: 21 years
Number of Employees: 3
Sales Volume: $500,000

3656 Good Fortune
Pacific Spirit
1334 Pacific Avenue
Forest Grove, OR 97116-2315 503-357-1566
800-634-9057
Fax: 503-357-1669
csrservice@mystictrader.com
www.pacificspiritcatalogs.com

A source of fun for bringing good luck and fortune into the home or office and an ideal resource as you set about creating prosperity and abundance in your life

3657 Graceland Gifts
Graceland/Elvis Presley Enterprises, Inc
3734 Elvis Presley Blvd
Memphis, TN 38116-4106 901-332-3322
800-238-2000
Fax: 901-344-3222
www.Elvis.Com

Elvis products

President: Jack Soden
Credit Cards: AMEX; MasterCard
Catalog Cost: Free
Catalog Circulation: Mailed 2 time(s) per year
Printing Information: 16 pages in 4 colors
Number of Employees: 300
Sales Volume: $10MM to $20MM

3658 Harriet Carter Gifts, Inc.
Harriet Carter Gifts Inc.
425 Stump Road
North Wales, PA 19454-427 215-361-5122
800-377-7878
Fax: 215-361-5344
customerservice@harrietcarter.com
www.harrietcarter.com

Gifts, apparel, home decor, lawn & garden items, bed & bath items, health and beauty aids

President: Ronald P Lassin
Buyers: Gerri Sassa
Credit Cards: AMEX; MasterCard; Visa
In Business: 56 years
Number of Employees: 475

3659 Hodges Badge Company
Hodges Badge Company, Inc.
1170 E Main Road
Portsmouth, RI 02871 401-682-2000
800-556-2440
Fax: 800-292-7377
info@hodgesbadge.com
www.hodgesbadge.com

Awards, ribbons, rosettes, athletic medals, and celluloid buttons, silver, crystal and much more.

President: Rick Hodges
Catalog Cost: Free
In Business: 97 years
Sales Volume: $20MM to $50MM

3660 Holiday Cards for Businesses
National Wildlife Federation
11100 Wildlife Center Drive
Reston, VA 20190-5362 800-822-9919
Fax: 800-525-5562
www.nwf.org

Christmas cards, calendars and apparel with a wildlife theme

Chairman: Deborah Spalding
President: Collin O'Mara
Marketing Manager: Al Lamson
Production Manager: Robin Clark
EVP/COO: Jaime Matyas
CEO: Collin O'Mara
Buyers: Lynn Piper, Gift Accessories
Mary Lamer, Greeting Cards
Robin Clark, Apparel
Credit Cards: MasterCard; Visa
Catalog Cost: Free
Catalog Circulation: Mailed 6 time(s) per year
to 20MM
Printing Information: 48 pages in 4 colors on
Glossy Stock
Press: Web Press
Binding: Saddle Stitched
Mailing List Information: Names for rent
In Business: 63 years
Number of Employees: 675

3661 Kelli's Gift Shop Suppliers
Kelli's Gift Shop Suppliers
3311 Boyington Drive
#400
Carrollton, TX 75006 972-759-7000
888-609-8860
Fax: 888-609-8861
websupport@kellisgifts.com
www.kellisgifts.com

Credit Cards: AMEX; MasterCard
In Business: 15 years

3662 Kipp
Kipp Toys
491 W. Muskegon Drive
Greenfield, IN 46140 800-428-1153
Fax: 800-832-5477
www.kipptoys.com

Toys, novelties, and party supplies

Catalog Cost: Free
In Business: 134 years

3663 Kron Chocolatier
Kron Chocolatier
24 Middle Neck Rd.
Great Neck, NY 11021 516-829-5550
800-564-kron
Fax: 516-829-9322
www.kronchocolatier.com

Hand dipped fresh fruit, the famous Budapest Crème Truffle and a large variety of hand molded chocolate sculptures.

3664 Lighter Side
Lighter Side
PO Box 25600
Bradenton, FL 34206-5600 800-244-9116
CustomerService@lighterside.com
www.lighterside.com

Apparel, accessories, children's items, decor, games, books, housewares, and novelties

President: David Crofoot
Marketing Manager: Kim Boyd
Founder: Alfred Johnson Smith
Credit Cards: AMEX; MasterCard; Visa
Catalog Cost: Free
Printing Information: 64 pages in 4 colors on
Glossy Stock
Press: Web Press
Binding: Saddle Stitched
Mailing List Information: Names for rent
List Manager: Kris Temple
In Business: 110 years
Sales Volume: $20MM to $50MM

3665 Lime Green
9452 Telephone Road #226
Ventura, CA 93004-2600 888-414-9158
800-591-5245
Fax: 805-672-2666

Toys, games, book sets, magnetic toys, music, arts & crafts, and science and nature projects

Catalog Cost: Free

3666 Living Grace Catalog
Living Grace Catalog
5226 South 31st Place
Phoenix, AZ 85040 800-572-5258
Fax: 800-582-1166
www.livinggracecatalog.com

3667 Magic Cabin
Magic Cabin
7021 Wolftown-Hood Rd.
Madison, VA 22727 888-623-3655
www.magiccabin.com

Children's toys, games, craft kits, and other accessories

3668 Midwest Volleyball Warehouse
Midwest Volleyball Warehouse
14050 Judicial Road
Burnsville, MN 55337 952-808-0100
800-876-8858
www.midwestvolleyball.com

3669 NA Information and Trade Center
National Native American Cooperative
PO Box 27626
Tucson, AZ 85726-7626 520-622-4900
Fax: 520-292-0779
info@usaindianinfo.com
www.usaindianinfo.com

Authentic American Indian crafts, books and music, also coordinates American Indian special events, Pow Wows

President: Fred Synder
Catalog Circulation: Mailed 4 time(s) per year
to 10000
Printing Information: 16 pages
Press: Web Press
In Business: 46 years
Sales Volume: $1MM to $3MM

3670 Now & Forever
PO Box 203
Bastesville, IN 47006 800-521-0584
Fax: 800-421-3965

Wedding invitations, gifts and stationery

Credit Cards: AMEX; MasterCard; Visa
Catalog Cost: Free

3671 Oriental Trading Crafts!
Oriental Trading Company
P.O. Box 2308
Omaha, NE 68103-2308   800-348-6483
www.orientaltrading.com
Holiday crafts
CEO: Sam Taylor
Catalog Cost: Free
Printing Information: in 4 colors
In Business: 84 years
Number of Employees: 2000

3672 Oriental Trading Holiday
Oriental Trading Company
P.O. Box 2308
Omaha, NE 68103-2308   800-348-6483
www.orientaltrading.com
Gifts and novelties
CEO: Sam Taylor
Catalog Cost: Free
Printing Information: in 4 colors
In Business: 84 years
Number of Employees: 2000

3673 Oriental Trading Party!
Oriental Trading Company
P.O. Box 2308
Omaha, NE 68103-2308   800-348-6483
www.orientaltrading.com
Holiday party supplies
CEO: Sam Taylor
Catalog Cost: Free
Printing Information: in 4 colors
In Business: 84 years
Number of Employees: 2000

3674 Our Designs
Our Designs, Inc.
314 E. McLoughlin Blvd.
Suite 200
Vancouver, WA 98663   360-567-2530
800-382-5252
Fax: 800-347-3367
sales@ourdesigns.com
www.ourdesigns.com
Great gifts for your favorite EMT's, firefighters, paramedics
President: Tony Johnson
Founder: Ralph Daugherty
Credit Cards: AMEX; MasterCard
Catalog Cost: Free
Printing Information: 56 pages in 4 colors on Glossy Stock
Press: Web Press
Binding: Saddle Stitched
Mailing List Information: Names for rent
List Manager: Tony Johnson
In Business: 38 years
Number of Employees: 25
Sales Volume: $ 3 Million

3675 Palmer Sales
B Palmer Sales Company, Inc.
3510 Highway 80,East
Mesquite, TX 75149   972-288-1026
Fax: 972-288-1362
www.apartmentcities.com
Trinkets, charms, holiday decorations, party supplies
Credit Cards: AMEX; MasterCard; Visa
Printing Information: 52 pages
Number of Employees: 10
Sales Volume: $500M to $1MM

3676 Party Kits Equestrian Gifts
Party Kits & Equestrian Gifts
10920 Plantside Drive
Suite C
Louisville, KY 40299-8659   502-261-7111
800-993-3729
Fax: 502-719-9200
info@partykits.com
www.Equinegifts.Com
Equestrian party supplies, tins, gifts and Kentucky foods for horse lovers of all ages
President: Becky Biesel
Credit Cards: AMEX; MasterCard; Visa
Catalog Circulation: Mailed 1 time(s) per year to 50000
Printing Information: 28 pages on Glossy Stock
Press: Web Press
Binding: Saddle Stitched
Mailing List Information: Names for rent
Number of Employees: 20
Sales Volume: $3MM to $5MM

3677 Past Times
4545 Bishop Ln
Louisville, KY 40218-4531   502-361-8863
866-877-4281
service@past-times.com
Fine Christmas gifts from Great Britain inspired by the past
Credit Cards: AMEX; MasterCard; Visa; Discover
Catalog Cost: Free
Catalog Circulation: Mailed 1 time(s) per year
Printing Information: 70 pages in 4 colors on Glossy Stock
Press: Web Press
Binding: Saddle Stitched

3678 Personal Creations Gift Catalog
Personal Creations
4840 Eastgate Mall
San Diego, CA 92121   866-834-7695
888-527-1404
wecare@customercare.personalcreations.com
www.personalcreations.com
Personalize gifts for holidays, weddings, anniversaries, birthdays, babies and kids
Customer Service Manager: Geri Fosnaugh
Catalog Cost: Free
Printing Information: 72 pages in 4 colors
In Business: 7 years
Sales Volume: $3MM to $5MM

3679 Pioneer National Latex
Pioneer National Latex
246 E 4th St
Ashland, OH 44805-2412   419-289-3300
800-537-6723
Fax: 419-289-7118
MassSales@natlatex.com
www.pioneernational.com
Balloons, punch balls and playballs
President: Vic Webby
Catalog Circulation: Mailed 1 time(s) per year
Printing Information: 40 pages in 4 colors
Binding: Saddle Stitched
Number of Employees: 250-
Sales Volume: $25,000,000 - $50,000,000

3680 Polart: Poland by Mail
Polart Distribution USA Inc
5700 Sarah Ave
Sarasota, FL 34233-3446   941-927-8983
800-278-9393
Fax: 941-927-8239
www.polandbymail.com
Polish gifts and collectibles
President: Jarek Zaremba
Credit Cards: AMEX; MasterCard
Catalog Cost: Free
Catalog Circulation: Mailed 12 time(s) per

year
Printing Information: in 4 colors on Glossy Stock
Press: Web Press
Binding: Saddle Stitched
Mailing List Information: Names for rent
In Business: 10 years
Sales Volume: Under $500,000

3681 Prestons - Ships & Sea
S.T. Preston & Son, Inc.
102 Main Street
P.O. Box 2115
Greenport, NY 11944-967   800-836-1165
Fax: 631-477-8541
www.prestons.com
Decorative nautical items
President: Peter Rowsom
Credit Cards: AMEX; MasterCard
Printing Information: 55 pages in 4 colors
In Business: 125 years
Sales Volume: $ 3-5 Million

3682 Pretty Personal
Pretty Personal Gifts
1143 Leesome Lane
Altamount, NY 12209   516-203-7594
Fax: 518-438-9738
shop@prettypersonalgifts.com
www.prettypersonalgifts.com
Unique and personalized gifts for family and friends; jewelry, decor for children, apparel & more
President: Janine Jerominek
Marketing Manager: Nancy Smith
Production Manager: Carol Markowitz
Buyers: Janine Jerominek
Credit Cards: AMEX; MasterCard
Catalog Cost: Free
Catalog Circulation: Mailed 2 time(s) per year to 20m
Printing Information: in 4 colors on Glossy Stock
Press: Sheetfed Press
Binding: Saddle Stitched
Mailing List Information: Names for rent
In Business: 14 years
Number of Employees: 10
Sales Volume: $500M to $1MM

3683 Prints of Peace Rubber Stamps
Prints of Peace Rubber Stamps
3850 Meyers Rd
Camino, CA 95709-9552   530-644-7044
Fax: 530-644-7044
design@printsofpeace.com
www.printsofpeace.com
Rubber stamps, Christian note cards
President: Warren Dayton
Marketing Manager: Martha Dayton
Production Manager: Warren Dayton
Buyers: Martha Dayton
Credit Cards: AMEX; MasterCard
Catalog Cost: $2
Average Order Size: $30
Printing Information: 32 pages in 4 colors on Matte Stock
Press: Web Press
Binding: Saddle Stitched
Mailing List Information: Names for rent
Number of Employees: 2
Sales Volume: $500,000

3684 Pyramid Collection
Pyramid Collection
PO Box 3333
Chelmsford, MA 01824-933   800-333-4220
Fax: 800-866-3235
help@pyramidcollection.com
www.pyramidcollection.com
New age gifts, clothing, jewelry and accessories
Chairman: Jack Rosenfeld
President: John Fleischman

CFO: Steven Steiner
Marketing Manager: Robert Webb
Production Manager: Edward Knowles
Fulfillment: Nick Parrinelli
Credit Cards: AMEX; MasterCard
Catalog Cost: Free
In Business: 40 years
Number of Employees: 200
Sales Volume: $20MM to $50MM

3685 Raymond Geddes & Company
Raymond Geddes & Company
7110 Belair Road
Suite 200
Baltimore, MD 21206   888-431-1722
                    Fax: 800-533-3359
service@raymondgeddes.com
www.raymondgeddes.com

Imaginative and affordable pens, pencils, mechanical pencils, erasers and other school supplies designed for school stores, classrooms, and education fundraising.

3686 Rhode Island Novelty
Rhode Island Novelty
350 Commerce Drive
Fall River, MA 02720   508-675-9400
                    800-528-5599
sales@rinovelty.com
www.rinovelty.com

Distributor of novelty toys, hats, bracelets, stickers and candy

President: Bob Nowak
Catalog Cost: Free
Catalog Circulation: Mailed 12 time(s) per year
Printing Information: 54 pages in 4 colors on Glossy Stock
Binding: Perfect Bound
In Business: 29 years
Sales Volume: $50MM to $100MM

3687 SQP
SQP Inc
PO Box 248
Columbus, NJ 08022-4554   609-298-5111
                    800-648-4789

Fantasy and science fiction gifts, erotic art books, t-shirts and fantasy books

President: Sal Quartuccio
Production Manager: Bob Keenan
Credit Cards: AMEX; MasterCard; Visa
Catalog Cost: Free
Catalog Circulation: Mailed 3 time(s) per year to 12500
Printing Information: 32 pages in 3 colors on Matte Stock
Press: Web Press
Binding: Saddle Stitched
In Business: 35 years
Number of Employees: 6
Sales Volume: $500,000

3688 ScripHessco
ScripHessco
360 Veterans Parkway
Suite 115
Bolingbrook, IL 60440-4607   630-771-7400
                    800-747-3488
                    Fax: 888-674-4380
www.scriphessco.com

3689 Shades of Color
Shades of Color LLC
20850 Leapwood Ave
Unit #K/L
Carson, CA 90746   310-329-1090
                    800-924-1811
                    Fax: 323-296-2010
orders@shadescalendars.com
www.shadescalendars.com

African-American calendars, figurines, checkbook planners, christmas cards, magnets, journals, address books, note pads and mugs

President: Adrian Woods
Credit Cards: AMEX; MasterCard
Catalog Cost: Free
Catalog Circulation: Mailed 1 time(s) per year
Printing Information: 26 pages in 4 colors
Mailing List Information: Names for rent
In Business: 22 years
Number of Employees: 15
Sales Volume: $5MM to $10MM

3690 Sharper Image
Sharper Image
27725 Stansbury
Suite 175
Farmington Hills, MI 48334   248-741-5100
                    877-206-7862
www.sharperimage.com

Products for the home, travel, auto and outdoors.

Managing Partner: David Katzman
Catalog Cost: Free
Printing Information: 76 pages in 4 colors
In Business: 39 years

3691 She Plays Sports, Inc.
She Plays Sports, Inc.
801 Easton Road
Suite 6
Willow Grove, PA 19090   877-743-529
CustomerCare@ShePlaysSports.com
www.sheplayssports.com

Apparel.
In Business: 18 years

3692 ShindigZ
ShindigZ
One Party Place
South Whitley, TN 46787-305   800-235-3272
                    Fax: 260-723-6976
csr@celebrationfantastic.com
www.celebrationfantastic.com

Party supplies for graduations, baby showers, bridal showers/weddings/anniversaries, school events, fundraisers and office parties

Chairman: Shep Moyle
President: Wendy Moyle
Buyers: Cindy Peppin
Credit Cards: AMEX; MasterCard; Visa
Catalog Cost: Free
Catalog Circulation: Mailed 12 time(s) per year
Printing Information: 56 pages in 4 colors on Glossy Stock
Press: Web Press
Binding: Saddle Stitched
Mailing List Information: Names for rent
In Business: 83 years

3693 SmileMakers
SmileMakers
PO Box 2543
Spartanburg, SC 29304-2543   888-800-7645
                    Fax: 877-567-7645
customer.service@smilemakers.com
www.smilemakers.com

Stickers, balloons, buttons and colored pencils

Credit Cards: MasterCard; Visa
Catalog Circulation: Mailed 1 time(s) per year
Printing Information: 30 pages in 4 colors on Glossy Stock
Binding: Saddle Stitched
Mailing List Information: Names for rent
List Company: Millard Group
10 Vose Farm Road
Peterborough, NH 03458
603-924-9261
In Business: 39 years

Number of Employees: 68
Sales Volume: $5MM to $10MM

3694 Speak to Me
Speak To Me Catalog
PMB 154
330 SW 43rd Street Suite K
Renton, WA 98057-4900   425-227-6608
                    800-248-9965
www.speaktomecatalog.com

Unique talking gifts and novelties

President: Seth Russell
Credit Cards: AMEX; MasterCard; Visa
Catalog Cost: Free
Printing Information: 40 pages in 4 colors
In Business: 20 years

3695 Stumps
Stumps Prom & Party
1 Party Place
PO Box 305
South Whitley, IN 46787-305   800-348-5084
                    Fax: 260-723-6976
csr@stumpsparty.com
www.stumpsparty.com

Prom, wedding and party items

President: Shep Moyle
Credit Cards: AMEX; MasterCard; Visa
Catalog Cost: Free
Catalog Circulation: Mailed 1 time(s) per year
Printing Information: 500 pages
In Business: 89 years
Number of Employees: 200

3696 Surma Book & Music
Surma Book & Music Company Inc
11 E 7th St
New York, NY 10003-8094   212-477-0729
                    Fax: 212-473-0439
surma@brama.com
www.surmastore.com

Ukranian gifts

President: Markian Surmach
Credit Cards: AMEX; MasterCard; Visa
Catalog Cost: Free
Catalog Circulation: Mailed 1 time(s) per year
Printing Information: 5 pages in 2 colors
In Business: 97 years
Number of Employees: 3
Sales Volume: Under $500M

3697 TecArt Industries
Tec Art Industries Inc.
28059 Center Oaks Court
Wixom, MI 48393-3654   248-624-8880
                    800-446-7609
                    Fax: 248-624-8066
sales@tecartinc.com
www.Tecartinc.Com

Illuminated pop signage, banners and stands

President: Bernie Lash
Catalog Cost: Free
Catalog Circulation: to 500
Average Order Size: $189
Printing Information: 4 pages in 4 colors on Glossy Stock
Mailing List Information: Names for rent
In Business: 24 years
Number of Employees: 20
Sales Volume: $1,000,000 - $5,000,000

3698 The English Company, Inc. 2012 - 13 Catalog Knight
The English Company, Inc.
P.O. Box 811
Jefferson Valley, NY 10535   800-444-5632
                    Fax: 914-528-0166
www.kofcsupplies.com

Credit Cards: AMEX; MasterCard
In Business: 65 years

3699 The Lighter Side Catalog
The Lighter Side Co.
P.O. Box 25600
Bradenton, FL 34206-5600   800-244-9116
                             800-232-0963
                       Fax: 800-551-4406
        CustomerService@lighterside.com
Novelties, gifts, and practical jokes
Catalog Cost: Free
In Business: 110 years

3700 Things You Never Knew Existed
Johnson Smith Company
P.O. Box 25600
Bradenton, FL 34206-5600   800-853-9490
     customerservice@thingsyouneverknew.com
          www.thingsyouneverknew.com
Funmakers, jokes, hobbies and novelties
CFO: David Crofoot
Marketing Manager: Kim Boyd
Founder: Alfred Johnson Smith
Credit Cards: AMEX; MasterCard; Visa
Catalog Cost: Free
Printing Information: in 4 colors on Matte
Stock
Press: Web Press
Binding: Saddle Stitched
Mailing List Information: Names for rent
List Manager: Kris Temple
In Business: 110 years
Sales Volume: $20MM to $50MM

3701 Tres Charmant
Simply Charming
PO Box 3184
Torrance, CA 90503   310-328-0441
                            800-598-8375
                       Fax: 310-328-4152
              scharming@aol.com
Wedding, baby keepsake accessories
President: William White
CFO: Gregory White
Marketing Manager: Barbara White
Buyers: Barbara White
Credit Cards: MasterCard
Catalog Cost: Free
Average Order Size: $60
Printing Information: in 4 colors on Matte
Stock
Press: Sheetfed Press
Binding: Perfect Bound
Mailing List Information: Names for rent
In Business: 18 years
Number of Employees: 6
Sales Volume: Under $500M

3702 U.S. Toy
U.S. Toy
13201 Arrington Rd.
Grandview, MO 64030   816-761-5900
                    www.ustoy.com
Novelty toys, gifts and party supplies.
Catalog Cost: Free
In Business: 63 years

3703 Veon Creations
Austin Bead Society
P. O. Box 656
Austin, TX 78767-656   636-586-5377
                       Fax: 636-586-5377
         austinbeadsociety@yahoo.com
             www.austinbeadsociety.org
Beads, beadworking supplies, jewelry findings, bead and crafts how to books, American Indian heritage books and Indian craft supplies
President: Nora Pero
Vice President: Danielle Baker
Secretary: Marsha Cekaj
Treasurer: Connie White
treasurer@austinbeadsociety.org
Credit Cards: MasterCard
Catalog Cost: $4

Catalog Circulation: Mailed 12 time(s) per
year to 1000
Printing Information: 48 pages in 1 color on
Matte Stock
Press: Web Press
Binding: Saddle Stitched
Mailing List Information: Names for rent
In Business: 25 years
Sales Volume: $500M to $1MM

3704 Vermont Life Green Mountain Gifts
Vermont Life Magazine
One National Life Dr 6th Floor
6th Floor
Montpelier, VT 05620-501   800-455-3399
                            800-455-3399
                       Fax: 802-828-3366
              subs@vtlife.com
           www.vermontlifecatalog.com
Vermont Life calendars, Vermont books, foods, videos, gifts
President: Tom Slayton
Marketing Manager: Andrew Jackson
Production Manager: David Goodman
david.goodman@state.vt.us
Publisher: Steve Cook
Editor: Mary Hegarty Nowlan
Credit Cards: AMEX; MasterCard
Catalog Cost: Free
Catalog Circulation: Mailed 1 time(s) per year
Average Order Size: $30
Printing Information: 16 pages in 4 colors on
Glossy Stock
Press: Web Press
Binding: Saddle Stitched
Mailing List Information: Names for rent
Number of Employees: 10
Sales Volume: $500M to $1MM

3705 Wandering Star Astrology Jewelry
Wandering Star Designs
1627 NE Alberta St
Ste B
Portland, OR 97211   503-209-3956
                            800-978-2725
           www.wanderingstarjewelry.com
Custom astrology horoscope jewelry and zodiac gifts; aromatherapy and astrology books
President: Alicia C Katz
Credit Cards: AMEX; MasterCard; Visa
Catalog Cost: Free
Catalog Circulation: Mailed 1 time(s) per year
Printing Information: 16 pages in 4 colors
In Business: 19 years

3706 Weddingstar Catalog
Weddingstar Inc.
2032 Bullshead Road
Dunmore, CN T1B-0K9   403-529-1110
                            800-661-8096
                       Fax: 403-529-6841
         customerservice@weddingstar.com
             www.weddingstar.com
Wedding accessories; stationery, party favors, cake toppers and much more
President: Rick Brink
Secretary, Treasurer: Helle Bertram Brink
Credit Cards: AMEX; MasterCard
Catalog Cost: 9.99
Catalog Circulation: Mailed 4 time(s) per year
Printing Information: 400 pages in 4 colors on
Glossy Stock
Press: Sheetfed Press
Binding: Perfect Bound
In Business: 27 years
Number of Employees: 30
Sales Volume: $5.2M

3707 Wild Horsefeathers Catalog
Wild Horsefeathers
113 School House Lane
Portsmouth, RI 02871   401-683-4998
                            800-298-4998
                       Fax: 401-682-1848
         pony@wildhorsefeathers.com
             www.wildhorsefeathers.com
Annual catalog for horse lovers
President: Carol Manchester
Owner: Kimberly Dunn
Credit Cards: AMEX; MasterCard; Visa
Catalog Cost: Free
Catalog Circulation: Mailed 1 time(s) per year
Mailing List Information: Names for rent
In Business: 19 years
Number of Employees: 16
Sales Volume: $ 1-3 Million

3708 WinCraft
WinCraft, Inc.
960 East Mark St.
PO Box 888
Winona, MN 55987-0888   507-454-5510
                            800-533-8006
                       Fax: 507-453-0690
         contact@wincraft.com
             www.wincraft.com
Banners, flags, poms, pennants, magnets, seat cushions, popcorn tins, clocks, mats, puzzles, wastebaskets, ribbons, bumper strips, car flags, hemo boards, pins.
Chairman & CEO: Dick Pope
President & COO: John Killen
Catalog Cost: Free
Catalog Circulation: Mailed 1 time(s) per year
Printing Information: 58 pages in 4 colors
Mailing List Information: Names for rent
In Business: 55 years
Sales Volume: $100MM to $500MM

3709 Windy City Novelties Catalog
Windy City Novelties
300 Lakeview Pkwy.
Vernon Hills, IL 60061-1800   847-403-0000
                               800-442-9722
                       Fax: 847-680-9250
           www.windycitynovelties.com
Line of party supplies and accessories
President: Mike Schrimmer
Credit Cards: AMEX; MasterCard
In Business: 32 years
Sales Volume: $5MM to $10MM

3710 Wireless
Wireless Catalog
5581 Hudson Industrial Parkway
P.O. Box 2599
Hudson, OH 44236   844-250-3397
                            800-687-9250
                       Fax: 800-950-9569
           www.thewirelesscatalog.com
Audio cassettes, clothing, books and unique gifts for fans of the public radio
Credit Cards: AMEX; MasterCard; Visa
Catalog Circulation: Mailed 5 time(s) per year
Printing Information: 47 pages in 4 colors on
Glossy Stock
Press: Web Press
Binding: Saddle Stitched
Will Trade Names: Yes
In Business: 34 years
Sales Volume: $5MM to $10MM

3711 Your Breed
Your Breed Clothing Company
128 A South Walnut Circle
Greensboro, NC 3046   855-849-7213
              info@yourbreed.com
              www.yourbreed.com
Unique gifts for dog lovers

President: Nancy D Holloway
Credit Cards: AMEX; MasterCard

Handicrafts
General Equipment & Supplies

3712 AccuCut Craft
AccuCut Systems
8843 S. 137th Circle
Attn: Customer Service Center
Omaha, NE 68138   402-934-1070
                        888-317-0093
                   Fax: 402-939-0304
info@accucutcraft.com
www.accucutcraft.com

Hand-operated machines, die cutting machines, equipment and tools for embossing, fabric crafts and home decor crafts

President: Greg Gaggini

3713 Art Impressions
Art Impressions
PO Box 20085
Salem, OR 97307   800-393-2014
                   Fax: 503-393-7956
feedback@artimpressions.com
www.artimpressions.com

Stamps and accessories

President: Bonnie Krebs
Credit Cards: AMEX; MasterCard; Visa
Catalog Cost: $14.7
In Business: 35 years

3714 Art Tech Casting Company
Arttech Casting Company
82 Main St
PO Box 54
Scottsville, NY 14546-1249   585-889-9187
                        800-418-9970
                   Fax: 585-889-9187
arttechcastingco@gmail.com
www.Arttech.Org

General hobby equipment and supplies

President: Jeffery Pyle
Credit Cards: AMEX; MasterCard; Visa
In Business: 32 years
Sales Volume: $1 million

3715 Badge-A-Minit
Badge-A-Minit
345 N Lewis Avenue
Oglesby, IL 61348-9776   815-883-8822
                        800-223-4103
                   Fax: 815-883-9696
questions@badgeaminit.com
www.badgeaminit.com

Button-making equipment and accessories

President: Cindy Kurkowski
Marketing Manager: Teresa Urban, VP Marketing
Credit Cards: AMEX; MasterCard; Visa
Catalog Cost: Free
Printing Information: 47 pages in 4 colors
Mailing List Information: Names for rent
In Business: 40 years
Number of Employees: 80

3716 Bag Making Accessories
H.A. Kidd & Co
5 Northline Road
Toronto, ON M4B-3P2   416-364-6451
                        800-387-1753
                   Fax: 888-236-8204
info1@hakidd.com
www.hakidd.com

Supplies and tools for handmade bags and accessories

Marketing Manager: Lynda Macham
VP, Chief Operating Officer: Jim Thielen
Controller, Human Resources: Amir Mirza

Credit Cards: MasterCard
Catalog Cost: Free
Catalog Circulation: Mailed 1 time(s) per year
Printing Information: 32 pages in 4 colors on Matte Stock
In Business: 93 years
Sales Volume: $20MM to $50MM

3717 Blue Ridge Machinery and Tools
Blue Ridge Machinery and Tools
PO Box 536
Hurricane, WV 25526-536   304-562-3538
                        800-872-6500
                   Fax: 304-562-5311
blueridgemachine@att.net
www.blueridgemachinery.com

Lathes, milling machines, machine shop supplies, how to books and videos, cutting tools, measuring tools, abrasives, bandsaws

President: Paul Stonestreet
paul@blueridgemachinery.com
Marketing Manager: Linda Stonestreet
Production Manager: Linda Stonestreet
Director Advertising and Marketing: Linda Stonestreet
linda@blueridgemachinery.com
Purchasing Contact: Gene Griffith
gene@blueridgemachinery.com
Inside Sales Contact: TimAlford
tim@blueridgemachinery.com
Credit Cards: AMEX; MasterCard; Visa; Discover
Catalog Cost: Free
Catalog Circulation: Mailed 12 time(s) per year to 1200
Average Order Size: $100
Printing Information: 80 pages in 1 color on Glossy Stock
Press: Web Press
Binding: Saddle Stitched
Mailing List Information: Names for rent
In Business: 33 years
Number of Employees: 20-D
Sales Volume: $500,000

3718 Button Basics
H.A. Kidd & Company Limited
5 Northline Road
Toronto, ON M4B-3P2   416-364-6451
                        800-387-1753
                   Fax: 888-236-8204
info1@hakidd.com
www.hakidd.com

Buttons for sewing and craft projects

Marketing Manager: Lynda Macham
VP, Chief Operating Officer: Jim Thielen
Controller, Human Resources: Amir Mirza
Credit Cards: MasterCard
Catalog Cost: Free
Printing Information: 8 pages in 4 colors
In Business: 93 years

3719 Buttons Galore & More
Buttons Galore
250 Pinedge Drive
West Berlin, NJ 08091   856-753-6700
service@buttonsgaloreandmore.com
www.buttonsgaloreandmore.com/

Crafting supplies

President: Lisa Bearnson
Credit Cards: AMEX; MasterCard
Catalog Cost: Free
Catalog Circulation: Mailed 1 time(s) per year
Printing Information: in 4 colors
In Business: 15 years

3720 Cheap Joe's Art Stuff
374 Industrial Park Dr.
Boone, NC 28607   828-262-0793
                        888-771-9509
                   Fax: 800-257- 087
info@cheapjoes.com
www.cheapjoes.com

Paints, brushes, canvas, papers, easels, drawing tools, other art supplies

Owner: Joe Miller

3721 Cheryl Oberle Designs
Cheryl Oberle Designs
3315 Newton Street
Denver, CO 80211-3138   303-433-9205
                   Fax: 303-477-5645
cheryl@cheryloberle.com
www.cheryloberle.com

Hand-painted knitting kits for sweaters, vests, shawls and socks; also books, patterns

President: Cheryl Oberle
Credit Cards: MasterCard; Visa
Catalog Cost: $10
In Business: 20 years
Number of Employees: 3
Sales Volume: $140K

3722 Colophon Book Arts Supply
Colophon Book Arts Supply
3611 Ryan Street SE
Lacey, WA 98503   360-459-2940
                   Fax: 360-459-2945
nancy@colophonbookarts.com
www.colophonbookarts.com

Craft supplies

President: Nancy Morains
Contact Person: Nancy Morains
nancy@colophonbookarts.com
Credit Cards: MasterCard; Visa
In Business: 27 years

3723 Costumakers Zippers & Accessories
H.A. Kidd & Company Limited
5 Northline Road
Toronto, ON M4B-3P2   416-364-6451
                        800-387-1753
                   Fax: 888-236-8104
info1@hakidd.com
www.hakidd.com

Zippers and accessories

Marketing Manager: Lynda Macham
VP, Chief Operating Officer: Jim Thielen
Controller, Human Resources: Amir Mirza
Credit Cards: MasterCard
Catalog Cost: Free
Printing Information: 16 pages in 4 colors
In Business: 93 years
Sales Volume: $20MM to $50MM

3724 Crafts, Needlework and Hobbies
Dover Publications
31 E 2nd Street
Mineola, NY 11501-3852   516-294-7000
                   Fax: 516-742-6953
www.doverpublications.com

Needlecraft and knitting books as well as stained glass, beading, cooking and woodworking

President: Christopher J Kuppig
Marketing Manager: Kristine Anderson
Acquisitions Editor: Nora Rawn
Account Manager: Christopher Higgins
Credit Cards: MasterCard; Visa
Catalog Cost: Free
In Business: 76 years
Number of Employees: 150
Sales Volume: 40MM

3725 Cranberry Junction Designs
Cranberry Junction Designs
535 W 7th S
PO Box 68
Rexburg, ID 83440-9681   208-313-0359
                   Fax: 208-356-8924
cranjd@cranberryjunction.com
www.cranberryjunction.com

Gift Tags labels over 250 gift hang tags designs perforated, foldover etc., also a line of rustic painted patterns for stitching needle punch and dolls, santas, craft supplies from our pattern catalog

President: Steve Danielson
Credit Cards: MasterCard
Catalog Cost: $3
Printing Information: in 2 colors on s
Mailing List Information: Names for rent
In Business: 13 years
Number of Employees: 6

3726 DJ Inkers

DJ Inkers
PO Box 1999
Mt. Dora, FL 32757
435-714-7007
800-325-4890
Fax: 801-880-7509
smiles@djinkers.com
www.djinkers.com

Design doodles: clip art, scrapbooking supplies, fonts, stamps and more

President: Dianne J Hook
In Business: 25 years
Number of Employees: 20
Sales Volume: $15 Million

3727 Definitely Decorative

Stampin' Up
P.O. Box 550
Riverton, UT 84065
800-STA-MPUP
ds@stampinup.com
www.stampinup.com

Stamps and card making supplies

Chairman: Shelli Gardner
President: Dale Fillmore
CFO: Scott Nielsen
Marketing Manager: Cori Hancock
Fulfillment: Kris Fiedler
Public Relations Specialist: Rachel Jensen
rajensen@stampinup.com
Credit Cards: AMEX; MasterCard; Visa
Catalog Cost: Free
In Business: 25 years
Sales Volume: $29.9 Milliom

3728 Discount School Supply

Discount School Supply
PO Box 6013
Carol Stream, IL 60197-6013
800-627-2829
Fax: 800-879-3753
customerservice@discountschoolsupply.com
www.discountschoolsupply.com

Thousands of arts and crafts materials, school supplies and educational toys

President: Ron Elliott
CFO: Kelly Crampton
Credit Cards: AMEX; MasterCard
Catalog Circulation: Mailed 6 time(s) per year to 2.6M
Printing Information: 500 pages
In Business: 25 years

3729 Eccentricks

CR Management
488 7th Avenue
#5-B
New York, NY 10018
646-285-7406
800-987-4257
Fax: 800-548-0839
chris@chrisrittermanagement.com
www.chrisrittermanagement.com/index.htm

Rubber stamps

Chairman: Stephen R. Hardis

3730 Economy Handicrafts 99 Cents Catalog

Economy Handicrafts, Inc.
29 Riverside Ave. Bldg # 2
Newark, NJ 07104-2331
718-431-9300
800-216-1601
Fax: 877-216-1604
customerservice@econocrafts.com
www.economyhandicrafts.com

99 cent crafting supplies. Basketry, beads and jewelry, candles, craft tools, frames, bags, drawing supplies and fabric

President: Eric Schwedock
Manager: Sam Tyberg
Credit Cards: AMEX; MasterCard
Catalog Cost: Free
Printing Information: in 4 colors on Glossy Stock
In Business: 59 years
Number of Employees: 2
Sales Volume: $110,000

3731 Economy Handicrafts Annual Catalog

Economy Handicrafts, Inc.
29 Riverside Ave. Bldg # 2
Newark, NJ 07104-2331
718-431-9300
800-216-1601
Fax: 877-216-1604
customerservice@econocrafts.com
www.economyhandicrafts.com

Handicraft supplies

President: Eric Schwedock
Manager: Sam Tyberg
Credit Cards: AMEX; MasterCard
Catalog Cost: Free
Printing Information: 267 pages in 4 colors on Glossy Stock
In Business: 59 years
Number of Employees: 2
Sales Volume: $110,000

3732 Elan Buttons

H.A. Kidd & Company Limited
5 Northline Road
Toronto, ON M4B-3P2
416-364-6451
800-387-1753
Fax: 888-236-8204
info1@hakidd.com
www.hakidd.com

Buttons for sewing and other crafting projects

Marketing Manager: Lynda Macham
VP, Chief Operating Officer: Jim Thielen
Controller, Human Resources: Amir Mirza
Credit Cards: MasterCard
Catalog Cost: Free
Catalog Circulation: Mailed 4 time(s) per year
Printing Information: 102 pages in 4 colors
In Business: 93 years
Sales Volume: $20MM to $50MM

3733 Engraving Arts Custom Branding Irons

Engraving Arts
PO Box 787
Laytonville, CA 95454-9026
575-421-0072
800-422-4509
Fax: 707-984-8045
clem@brandingirons.net
www.brandingirons.net

Branding Irons, custom electric and torch heated heavy duty hand held or drill press type also branding presses

President: Clem Wilkes
Printing Information: 4 pages in 1 color on Matte Stock
Press: Sheetfed Press
Binding: Folded
Mailing List Information: Names for rent
In Business: 33 years
Number of Employees: 1
Sales Volume: Under $500M

3734 Eureka Stamps

Eureka Stamps
19522 High Park Road
Cedaredge, CO 81413
303-717-1223
800-679-8740
Fax: 970-856-7454
sales@eurekastamps.com
www.eurekastamps.com

Rubber stamps

3735 Fair Oak Workshops

PO Box 5578
River Forest, IL 60305
800-341-0597
Fax: 708-386-3162
www.fairoak.com

Arts and crafts supplies

3736 Fire Protection Products

Fire End & Croker Corporation
7 Westchester Plaza
Elmsford, NY 10523-1678
914-592-3640
800-759-3473
Fax: 914-592-3892
info@croker.com
www.croker.com

Nozzles, valves and extinguishers, hose cabinets

Credit Cards: AMEX; MasterCard
Printing Information: 32 pages
In Business: 104 years

3737 GloryBee Natural Foods and Crafts

GloryBeeFoods, Inc
29548 B Airport Rd
Eugene, OR 97402
541-689-0913
800-456-7923
Fax: 541-689-9692
info@glorybeefoods.com
www.glorybeefoods.com

Candlemaking and candymaking supplies, beekeeping supplies, soapmaking supplies, nutritional supplements, aromatherapy supplies, honey and honey stix

President: Richard Turanski
CFO: Richard Shaneyfelt
Purchasing Manager: Randy Djonne
International Marketing Manager: Daniel Shaneyfelt
Buyers: Darren Miller
Credit Cards: MasterCard
Catalog Cost: Free
Catalog Circulation: Mailed 1 time(s) per year to 60M
Average Order Size: $75
Printing Information: 70 pages in 4 colors on Glossy Stock
Press: Web Press
Binding: Saddle Stitched
Mailing List Information: Names for rent
List Manager: Shannon Arch
In Business: 40 years
Number of Employees: 100
Sales Volume: $50 Million

3738 Gold's Artworks

Gold's Artworks Inc
2100 N Pine Street
Lumberton, NC 28358-3938
800-356-2306
Fax: 910-739-9605
goldsartworks.20m.com

Papermaking supplies

Credit Cards: MasterCard

3739 Holiday Mini Catalog

Stampin' Up
12907 S 3600 W
Riverton, UT 84065
801-257-5400
800-782-6787
Fax: 801-257-5207
ds@stampinup.com
www.stampinup.com

Stamp sets, new accessories and exciting samples you can re-create

Chairman: Shelli Gardner
President: Dale Fillmore
CFO: Scott Nielsen
Marketing Manager: Pam Morgan
Production Manager: Jerry Day
Credit Cards: AMEX; MasterCard; Visa
Printing Information: 40 pages
In Business: 21 years
Number of Employees: 560
Sales Volume: $19.3 Million

3740 Howard Decorative Packaging

Howard Decorative Packaging
3462 W Touhy Avenue
Skokie, IL 60076   800-323-1609
                         888-772-9821
info@howardpkg.com
www.howardpkg.com

Custom printed packaging, offers packaging programs to fit your need and budget

President: Ron Watson
rwatson@howardpkg.com
C.S. Manager: Debbie Brazier
csmanager@howardpkg.com
Credit and Receivables: Susan Malinowski
smalinowski@howardpkg.com
Shipping and Receiving: Dean Voss
dvoss@howardpkg.com
Catalog Cost: Free
Printing Information: 28 pages
In Business: 58 years
Sales Volume: $20MM to $50MM

3741 Idea Book & Catalog

Stampin' Up
12907 S 3600 W
Riverton, UT 84065   801-257-5400
                         800-782-6787
                    Fax: 801-257-5207
ds@stampinup.com
www.stampinup.com

Stampin' Up stamp sets, accessories, and product ideas

Chairman: Shelli Gardner
President: Rich Jutkins
CFO: Scott Nielsen
Marketing Manager: Pam Morgan
Production Manager: Jerry Day
Human Resources VP: Julie Gandy
CEO: Shelli Gardner
Credit Cards: AMEX; MasterCard; Visa
Printing Information: 212 pages
In Business: 25 years
Number of Employees: 560
Sales Volume: $19.3 Million

3742 Inspire

H.A. Kidd & Company Limited
5 Northline Road
Toronto, ON M4B-3P2   416-364-6451
                         800-387-1753
                    Fax: 888-236-8204
info1@hakidd.com
www.hakidd.com

Buttons for sewing and other crafting projects

Marketing Manager: Lynda Macham
VP, Chief Operating Officer: Jim Thielen
Controller, Human Resources: Amir Mirza
Credit Cards: MasterCard
Catalog Cost: Free
Catalog Circulation: Mailed 4 time(s) per year
Printing Information: 20 pages in 4 colors
In Business: 93 years
Sales Volume: $20MM to $50MM

3743 J&R Industries: Craft Supplies

J&R Industries, Inc.
PO Box 4221
Shawnee Mission, KS 66204   913-362-6667
                        Fax: 913-362-7421
www.jandrind.com

Craft supplies

President: Jeffery Moualim
In Business: 43 years

3744 Judi-Kins Rubber Stamps

Judi-Kins
17803 S Harvard Blvd
Gardena, CA 90248-3629   310-515-1115
                    Fax: 310-323-6619
customerservice@judikins.com
www.judikins.com

Rubber stamps

President: Charles R Bostick
CFO: Brian Kay
Catalog Cost: $7
Catalog Circulation: Mailed 52 time(s) per year to 5000
Average Order Size: $50
Printing Information: 44 pages in 4 colors on Glossy Stock
Binding: Saddle Stitched
Mailing List Information: Names for rent
In Business: 27 years
Number of Employees: 20
Sales Volume: $3MM to $5MM

3745 Lake City Craft Company

Lake City Craft Company
1209 Eaglecrest Street
PO Box 2009
Nixa, MO 65714   417-725-8444
                    Fax: 417-725-8448
questions@quilling.com
www.quilling.com

Craft supplies

President: Sandy Wrasin
Credit Cards: MasterCard; Visa
In Business: 35 years
Number of Employees: 14
Sales Volume: $500M to $1MM

3746 Meer Image Craft

Meer Image
1720 Victor Blvd.
Arcata, CA 95521   707-268-0436
steven@meerimage.com
www.meerimage.com

Rubber stamps

President: Steven Vander Meer
Credit Cards: AMEX; MasterCard; Visa
In Business: 21 years

3747 Mega Hobby

Megahobby.com Inc.
901 E Clements Bridge Road
Suite 3C
Runnemede, NJ 08078   888-642-0093
                         888-642-0093
                    Fax: 856-312-8386
info@megahobby.com
www.megahobby.com

Plastic and wooden model kits, paint tools, toys and games

President: Peter Vetri
Credit Cards: AMEX; MasterCard; Visa

3748 Micro Mark

Micro Mark
340 Snyder Avenue
Berkeley Heights, NJ 07922-1505 908-464-2984
                         800-225-1066
                    Fax: 908-665-9383
info@micromark.com
www.micromark.com

Model building tools and supplies

President: Tom Piccirillo
Credit Cards: AMEX; MasterCard
Catalog Cost: Free
Average Order Size: $85
Mailing List Information: Names for rent

In Business: 87 years
Number of Employees: 25

3749 My Sentiments Exactly

My Sentiments Exactly
633 Elkton Drive
Colorado Springs, CO 80907   719-373-2885
                        Fax: 719-522-0797
www.sentiments.com

Rubber stamps for and supplies for scrapbooking and special projects

President: Amy L Kennedy
Catalog Cost: $4
Catalog Circulation: Mailed 1 time(s) per year
Printing Information: 25 pages in 4 colors
Mailing List Information: Names for rent
In Business: 10 years
Number of Employees: 98
Sales Volume: $500M to $1MM

3750 National Artcraft Craft Supplies

National Artcraft Co.
300 Campus Dr.
Aurora, OH 44202   888-937-2723
                    Fax: 800-292-4916
sales@nationalartcraft.com
www.nationalartcraft.com

Creative components for crafts, ceramics, art and hobbies.

Catalog Cost: Free
Printing Information: 60 pages in 2 colors
In Business: 66 years
Sales Volume: $5MM to $10MM

3751 Non Sequitur Rubber Stamps

Non Sequitur Stamps
2602 Florence Avenue
Pasadena, TX 77502-8246 @de-stempelwinkel.nl
www.nonsequiturstamps.com

Rubber stamps

President: Lisette Cannedy
Credit Cards: AMEX; MasterCard; Visa
Catalog Cost: $5
In Business: 14 years

3752 Origami USA

Origami USA
15 W 77th Street
New York, NY 10024-5192   212-769-5635
                    Fax: 212-769-5668
admin@origami-usa.org
www.origami-usa.org

Origami supplies

Chairman: Jan Polish
President: Wendy Zeichner
wendy.zeichner@origamiusa.org
CFO: Shrikant Iyer
Treasurer: Jean Baden-Gillette
Secretary: Marcio Noguchi
Local VP: Marc Kirschenbaum
marc.kirschenbaum@origamiusa.org
Printing Information: 10 pages in 2 colors
Binding: Saddle Stitched
In Business: 25 years

3753 Paper Crafts Magazine

Paper Crafts Subscriber Services
PO Box 420235
Palm Coast, FL 32142-235   303-215-5600
                         800-269-5959
                    Fax: 386-447-2321
customerservice@creativecraftsgroup.com
www.scrapandpapershop.com

Handmade decorations, invitations, recipes, games

Catalog Cost: $5.99
Printing Information: 84 pages

3754 Paper Parachute
Paper Parachute Art Design Co., LLC
16630 SW Shaw Street
Suite G
Beaverton, OR 97007 503-533-4513
Fax: 503-533-8243
paperparachute@aol.com
www.paperparachute.com

Rubber stamps and paper

President: Beth Thompson
Marketing & Design Consultant: Brad Anderson
Credit Cards: AMEX; MasterCard; Visa
In Business: 25 years

3755 Patternworks
Patternworks
12 Main Street
PO Box 1618
Center Harbor, NH 03226 603-253-8148
800-723-9210
Fax: 603-253-8346
customerservice@patternworks.com
www.patternworks.com

Yarns, yarn samples, books and patterns

President: Judy Sabanek
Credit Cards: AMEX; MasterCard; Visa
Catalog Cost: Free
Printing Information: 52 pages in 4 colors
In Business: 36 years
Number of Employees: 30
Sales Volume: 2.9MM

3756 Pink House Studios
Pink House Studios,Inc
35 Bank Street
Saint Albans, VT 05478 802-524-7191
Fax: 802-524-7191
mark@pinkhouse.com
www.pinkhouse.com

Sculpture supplies and restoration services

President: Mark Prent
Buyers: Mark Prent
Credit Cards: MasterCard
Catalog Cost: $5
Average Order Size: $100
Mailing List Information: Names for rent
List Manager: Mark Prent
In Business: 11 years
Sales Volume: Under $500M

3757 Pippin's Hollow Dollmaking
National Artcraft Co.
300 Campus Drive
Aurora, OH 44202 330-562-3500
888-937-2723
Fax: 800-292-4916
sales@nationalartcraft.com
www.nationalartcraft.com

Creative components for crafts, ceramics, art and hobbies

President: Jon Berrie
CFO: Robert Wiece
Production Manager: Harve Eisenberg
Credit Cards: MasterCard
Catalog Cost: $3
Catalog Circulation: Mailed 1 time(s) per year
Printing Information: 48 pages in 2 colors
In Business: 66 years
Number of Employees: 30
Sales Volume: $5MM to $10MM

3758 Posh Impressions
Posh Impressions
34231 Camino Capistrano
Suite 202
Capistrano Beach, CA 92624 949-542-7707
800-401-8644
Fax: 949-542-7711
contact@poshimpressions.com
www.poshimpressions.com

Rubber stamps

In Business: 36 years

3759 Pro Chemical & Dye
Pro Chemical & Dye
126 Shove St.
Fall River, MA 02724 508-676-3838
Fax: 508-676-3980
promail@prochemical.com
www.prochemical.com

Dyes and paints

President: Adelle Wiener
Marketing Manager: Mark Chaves
Credit Cards: AMEX; MasterCard
In Business: 45 years

3760 Purebred & Wild Animal Rubber Stamps
Clacritter Designs by Leslie
1406 Triple S Trail
Johnson City, TX 78636 512-426-6236
Fax: 830-868-4272
Leslie@clacritter.com
www.clacritter.com

Rubber stamps

President: Leslie Falteisek
Credit Cards: AMEX; MasterCard
Printing Information: in 1 color on Matte Stock
Binding: Saddle Stitched
Mailing List Information: Names for rent
In Business: 40 years
Number of Employees: 1
Sales Volume: Under $500M

3761 Rainbow Meadow
Rainbow Meadow, Inc.
4494 Brooklyn Rd
Jackson, MI 49201 517-764-9765
800-207-4047
Fax: 517-764-9766
www.rainbowmeadow.com

Essential oils for aromatherapy, cosmetics and pharmaceuticals

President: Melody Upham
CFO: Timothy Upham
CEO: Melody Upham
Credit Cards: AMEX; MasterCard
Mailing List Information: Names for rent
In Business: 18 years
Sales Volume: $580,000

3762 Rynne China Company
Rynne China Company
222 W 8 Mile Road
Hazel Park, MI 48030-2432 248-542-9400
800-468-1987
Fax: 248-542-0047
info@rynnechina.com

Blank china for painters and jewelry

President: Kathy Damaska
Credit Cards: MasterCard; Visa
Catalog Cost: Free
Mailing List Information: Names for rent
Number of Employees: 20
Sales Volume: $1MM to $3MM

3763 Sally Distributors
S&S Worldwide
75 Mill Street
PO Box 513
Colochester, CT 06415 860-537-3451
800-288-9941
Fax: 800-566-6678
cservice@ssww.com
www.ssww.com

Arts and crafts kits and activities

Marketing Manager: Roger Morine
Printing Information: in 3 colors
In Business: 109 years

3764 Sax Arts & Crafts
School Specialty, Inc
PO Box 1579
Appleton, WI 54912-1579 888-388-3224
800-558-6696
Fax: 888-388-6344
orders@schoolspecialty.com
www.schoolspecialty.com

Artist's supplies, full line of weaving looms and aids, basketry and batik supplies

Chairman: James R. Henderson
President: Joseph M. Yorio
CFO: Kevin Baehler
Principal: Justin Lu
Portfolio Manager: Madhu Satyanarayana
EVP, Distribution: Patrick T. Collins
Printing Information: 600 pages in 7 colors
Binding: Perfect Bound

3765 Serrv Handcrafts
Serrv
532 Baltimore Boulevard
Suite 409
Westminster, MD 21157 800-422-5915
888-294-9660
Fax: 888-294-6376
orders@serrv.org
www.serrv.org

Handcrafted gifts and imported clothing

Chairman: Cathy Dowdell
President: Loreen Epp
International Marketing Manager: Bob Chase
Buyers: Linda Jacobson
Credit Cards: MasterCard; Visa
Catalog Cost: Free
Catalog Circulation: Mailed 2 time(s) per year
Printing Information: 68 pages in 4 colors
In Business: 68 years
Number of Employees: 35
Sales Volume: $3MM to $5MM

3766 Soap Saloon
The Soap Salon
3716 30th Street
Sacramento, CA 95820 916-376-7390
Fax: 916-921-9464
info@soapsalon.net

Soap molds and soap making supplies in addition to a product line of handcrafted soaps, body oils, bath salts and other bath and skin care products

Credit Cards: AMEX; MasterCard
Catalog Cost: Free
Mailing List Information: Names for rent
Number of Employees: 8
Sales Volume: Under $500M

3767 Stamp of Excellence
Stamp of Excellence Inc
1105 Main Street
Canon City, CO 81212-46 719-275-8422
Fax: 719-275-7950
www.stampofexcellence.com

Rubber stamps

President: Judi Lynn
Marketing Manager: Judi Lynn
Catalog Cost: $4
Printing Information: 48 pages in 4 colors on Matte Stock
Binding: Folded
Mailing List Information: Names for rent
In Business: 24 years
Number of Employees: 3

3768 Stampin' Place
The Stampin' Place
PO Box 43
Big Lake, MN 55309-43 763-263-6646
800-634-3717
Fax: 763-263-6463
info@stampin.com
www.stampin.com

Rubber stamps

President: Cathy Booth
Credit Cards: MasterCard; Visa
Catalog Cost: $9
Catalog Circulation: to 10000
Printing Information: 204 pages in 1 color on Newsprint
Binding: Perfect Bound
In Business: 34 years

3769 Stampin' Up
Stampin' Up
P.O. Box 550
Riverton, UT 84065   800-STA-MPUP
ds@stampinup.com
www.stampinup.com

Stamps and card making supplies

Chairman: Shelli Gardner
President: Dale Fillmore
CFO: Scott Nielsen
Marketing Manager: Cori Hancock
Fulfillment: Kris Fiedler
Public Relations Specialist: Rachel Jensen
rajensen@stampinup.com
Credit Cards: AMEX; MasterCard; Visa
Catalog Cost: Free
Catalog Circulation: Mailed 1 time(s) per year
Printing Information: 236 pages in 4 colors
In Business: 23 years
Number of Employees: 470
Sales Volume: $29.9 Milliom

3770 Stamps N' More
Stamps N' More
109 E Main Street
Schuylkill Haven, PA 17972   570-294-9886
866-385-4877
Fax: 570-385-4876
contact@stampsnmore.com
www.stampsnmore.com

Stamps and accessories

President: Ann Stevenson
Catalog Circulation: to 5000
Printing Information: 65 pages in 1 color on Matte Stock
Binding: Folded
In Business: 15 years

3771 Standard Hobby Supply
Standard Hobby Supply
806 State Rt 17
Ramsey, NJ 07446-1608   201-825-2211
800-223-1355
Fax: 201-512-0882
www.standardhobby.com

Railroad model equipment

Credit Cards: MasterCard
Catalog Cost: $3

3772 Sunshine Discount Crafts
Sunshine Discount Crafts
12335 62nd St W
Largo, FL 33773-3715   727-538-2878
888-552-7238
Fax: 727-531-2739
customer_service@consumercrafts.com,
www.sunshinecrafts.com

Contains over 14,000 craft supply items

President: David Rothschild
Credit Cards: AMEX; MasterCard
Catalog Cost: $5
Printing Information: 136 pages in 4 colors on Newsprint
Press: Web Press
Binding: Saddle Stitched
Mailing List Information: Names for rent
List Manager: Jordan Direct
In Business: 34 years
Number of Employees: 12

3773 The Bee Lee Company
The Bee Lee Company
2714 Bomar Ave
PO Box 36108
Dallas, TX 75235   214-351-2091
800-527-5271
Fax: 214-351-2131
pearlsnap@thebeeleecompany.com
www.thebeeleecompany.com

Snap Fasteners and sewing supplies

Catalog Cost: Free
In Business: 58 years

3774 Times to Cherish
Current, Usa Inc.
1005 E Woodmen Road
Colorado Springs, CO 80941-1   800-848-2848
800-525-7170
Fax: 800-993-3232
CurrentLargeQuantity@CurrentInc.com
www.currentcatalog.com

Scrapbooking supplies

President: Miriam Loo
Credit Cards: MasterCard
Catalog Cost: Free
In Business: 65 years

3775 Touche Rubber Stamps
Touche Rubber Stamps
1827 16 1/2 Street NW
Rochester, MN 55901-234   507-288-2317
800-241-8497
Fax: 507-286-1428
www.touchestamps.com

Artistic rubber stamps for the holidays and every day, hundreds of verses & tiny stamps

President: Susan Tollers
Marketing Manager: Susan Tollers
Credit Cards: MasterCard; Visa
Catalog Cost: $6
Printing Information: 132 pages
Mailing List Information: Names for rent
In Business: 19 years
Number of Employees: 5
Sales Volume: Under $500M

3776 Triarco Arts & Crafts
Triarco Companies
9909 S. Shore Dr.
Suite 1015
Plymouth, MN 55441-5037   763-559-5590
800-328-3360
Fax: 763-559-2215

Arts & crafts supplies

President: Merle Munsterman
Catalog Cost: Free
Printing Information: 400 pages
In Business: 68 years
Number of Employees: 14
Sales Volume: $10,00,000

3777 Twinrocker Handmade Paper
Twinrocker Handmade Paper
100 East Third Street
PO Box 413
Brookston, IN 47923   765-563-3119
800-757-8946
Fax: 765-563-8946
twinrocker@twinrocker.com
www.twinrocker.com

Paper making and bookart supplies

President: Travis Becker
Marketing Manager: Kathryn Clark
Production Manager: Howard Clark
Owner: Travis Becker
twinrocker@twinrocker.com
Customer Service: Fran Lacy
info@twinrockerhandmadepaper.com
Papermaker: Gerald McVay
Catalog Circulation: to 100M
Average Order Size: $75
Printing Information: 31 pages on Matte Stock

Press: Sheetfed Press
Binding: Folded
In Business: 44 years
Sales Volume: $500M to $1MM

3778 Woodcreek Drieds Inc
Woodcreek Drieds Inc
10824 Pemberville Road
Wayne, OH 43466-9765   419-288-0802
800-664-1630
Fax: 419-288-8203
sales@woodcreekdrieds.com
www.woodcreekdrieds.com

Dried flowers, herbs, wreaths, swags, assorted supplies, preserved foliage, eucalyptus

President: Jody Bryant
Credit Cards: AMEX; MasterCard
Catalog Circulation: to 1000
Printing Information: 10 pages in 2 colors
In Business: 16 years

3779 X-Stamper
X-Stamper Online
PO Box 14133
Pinedale, CA 93650   559-233-7894
800-234-0893
Fax: 559-233-1518
sales@xstamperonline.com
www.xstamperonline.com

Stamps and stamp supplies

Credit Cards: AMEX; MasterCard; Visa
Catalog Cost: Free
Catalog Circulation: Mailed 1 time(s) per year
Printing Information: 20 pages in 4 colors
Binding: Perfect Bound

Basketry & Caning

3780 Arnie's Arts & Crafts
Arnie's Arts & Crafts
3741 West Houghton Lake Drive
Houghton Lake, MI 48629   989-366-8794
800-563-2356
Fax: 989-366-5931
www.basketpatterns.com

Basket making kits and supplies, gourd patterns and tools, lamp and leather kits, weaving tools

Chairman: Roberta Goupil
President: Arnold Goupil
Catalog Cost: Free
In Business: 29 years
Number of Employees: 5
Sales Volume: $300,000

3781 Atkinson's Country House
Sandra Atkinson
2775 Riniel Road
Lennon, MI 48449-9334   810-208-6987
810-280-6987
Fax: 810-621-3058
sandy@sandyatkinson.com
www.sandyatkinson.com

Basketweaving supplies, natural fibers, reed dyes and stains, basket bases, handles, hoops, wire handles and hangers, patterns and books, dryweed and seagrass, seagrass classes

President: Sandy Atkinson
Production Manager: Steve Atkinson
Catalog Cost: Free
Average Order Size: $80
Printing Information: 34 pages in 4 colors
Mailing List Information: Names for rent
In Business: 31 years
Number of Employees: 32
Sales Volume: Under $500M

3782 Basket Basics
Basket Basics
8303 West Crum Road
Bloomington, IN 47403   812-854-4447
Fax: 812-825-4447
sherry@basketbasics.com
www.basketbasics.com

Baskets and basket making supplies
Credit Cards: AMEX; MasterCard
In Business: 24 years

3783 Basket Maker's
GH Productions Inc.
521 E Walnut Street
PO Box 621
Scottsville, KY 42164   270-237-4821
800-447-7008
mail@basketmakerscatalog.com
www.basketmakerscatalog.com

Flat reed, round reed, basket kits, chair seating supplies, books and more
President: Scott Gilbert, Founder
Credit Cards: AMEX; MasterCard
Catalog Cost: Free
Printing Information: 24 pages
In Business: 32 years

3784 BasketPatterns.com
3741 W Houghton Lake Dr
Houghton Lake, MI 48629   800-563-2356
Fax: 989-366-5931
www.basketpatterns.com

Basketting, caning, weaving
Author: Linda Allen
Author: Ruth Andre

3785 Cane & Basket Supply
Cane & Basket Supply Co.
1283 S Cochran Avenue
Los Angeles, CA 90019-2846   323-939-9644
800-468-3966
Fax: 323-939-7237
info@caneandbasket.com
www.caneandbasket.com

Caning and basketry supplies
President: William Fimpler
Secretary, Treasurer: Audrey J Fimpler
Credit Cards: AMEX; MasterCard; Visa
Catalog Cost: Free
Catalog Circulation: to 3000
Printing Information: 25 pages in 1 color on Matte Stock
Press: Letterpress
Binding: Folded
Mailing List Information: Names for rent
In Business: 81 years
Number of Employees: 6
Sales Volume: $800,000

3786 Caning Shop
The Caning Shop
926 Gilman Street
Berkeley, CA 94710   510-527-5010
800-544-3373
Fax: 510-527-7718
jim@caning.com
www.caningshop.com

Gourd craft, chair caning & basketry
President: Jim Widess
Credit Cards: AMEX; MasterCard; Visa
Printing Information: 20 pages
In Business: 46 years
Number of Employees: 6
Sales Volume: $370K

3787 Connecticut Cane & Reed Company
Connecticut Cane & Reed Company
85 Hilliard Street
PO Box 762
Manchester, CT 06045   860-646-6586
800-227-8498
Fax: 860-649-2221
help@caneandreed.com
www.caneandreed.com

Chair seating materials, wicker repair, basketry supplies, Nantucket basketry accessories
President: K C Parkinson
Production Manager: Alana Parkinson
Credit Cards: AMEX; MasterCard; Visa
Catalog Cost: Free
Printing Information: 14 pages in 2 colors on Matte Stock
Press: Sheetfed Press
Binding: Saddle Stitched
Mailing List Information: Names for rent
In Business: 25 years
Number of Employees: 10-J
Sales Volume: $500M to $1MM

3788 English Basketry Willows
English Basketry Willows
412 County Road 31
Norwich, NY 13815-3149   607-336-9031
Fax: 607-336-9031
bonwillow@frontiernet.net
www.englishbasketrywillows.com

Resource for willow basketry and living willow structures
President: Bonnie Gale
Credit Cards: MasterCard
Catalog Cost: $1
Catalog Circulation: Mailed 1 time(s) per year
Printing Information: 24 pages on Matte Stock
Binding: Saddle Stitched
Mailing List Information: Names for rent
In Business: 23 years
Sales Volume: Under $500M

3789 Frank's Cane and Rush Supply
Frank's Cane and Rush Supply
7252 Heil Avenue
Huntington Beach, CA 92647-4466 714-847-0707
Fax: 714-843-5645
orders@frcrs.com
www.franksupply.com

Chair caning, wicker repair and upholstery, wood parts and wood furniture kits, and basketry and fiber arts supplies
President: Michael Frank
Credit Cards: AMEX; MasterCard; Visa
Catalog Cost: Free
Printing Information: 40 pages in 1 color
Mailing List Information: Names for rent
In Business: 37 years
Number of Employees: 10
Sales Volume: $950K

3790 H H Perkins
H H Perkins
370 State Street
North Haven, CT 06473   800-462-6660
Fax: 203-787-1161
www.hhperkins.com

Materials and tools for seat and basket weaving, caning and webbing for chairs, stools and frames
President: Ray DeFrancesco
VP: Stephen DeFrancesco
Treasurer: Mark DeFrancesco
Credit Cards: AMEX; MasterCard
Catalog Cost: Free
In Business: 96 years
Number of Employees: 18
Sales Volume: $2 million

3791 Hardware of the Past
405 N Main St
Saint Charles, MO 63301   800-562-5855
hopinfo@hardwareofthepast.com
www.hardwareofthepast.com

Antique hardware and furnishings

3792 John C. Campbell Folk School
One Folk School Road
Brasstown, NC 28902   828-837-2775
Fax: 828-837-8637
www.folkschool.org

Handmade crafts
Director: Jan Davidson
Program Manager: Karen Beaty

3793 Nate's Nantuckets
Nate's Nantuckets, Inc.
979 Kimmins Street
Hohenwald, TN 38462   931-295-3213
Fax: 931-295-3213
www.basketshop.com

Tools and equipment to make Shaker baskets; authentic Nantucket baskets, reproductions of original wooden basket molds
President: Nathan Taylor
Founder: Nathan Taylor
Credit Cards: MasterCard; Visa
Catalog Cost: $3
Catalog Circulation: Mailed 1 time(s) per year
Printing Information: 35 pages
Number of Employees: 10-J

3794 NorEsta Cane and Reed
The NorEsta Cane & Reed
329 Water Street
Allegan, MI 49010   269-673-3249
800-667-3782
Fax: 269-673-7372
sales@noresta.com
www.noresta.com

Basketry supplies including press cane, hank cane, rush, splint, wicker, flat and round hoops, handles, dyes, tools and books
President: Esther Grisby
Marketing Manager: Cris Green
Production Manager: Jill Grisby
Owner: Esther Grigsby
Owner: Norm Grisby
Mailing List Information: Names for rent

3795 North Carolina Basketworks
Suzanne Moore's NC Basketworks
130 Main Street
PO Box 744
Vass, NC 28394-744   910-245-3049
800-338-4972
Fax: 910-245-3243
sales@ncbasketworks.com
www.ncbasketworks.com

Large selection of basketweaving supplies including reed handles, patterns, books, embellishments, tools and more
President: Suzanne Moore
Credit Cards: AMEX; MasterCard
Catalog Cost: Free
Printing Information: on Matte Stock
Binding: Folded
Mailing List Information: Names for rent
In Business: 34 years
Number of Employees: 6

3796 Royalwood Basket Weaving & Caning Supply
Royalwood, Ltd.
517 Woodville Road
Mansfield, OH 44907
419-526-1630
800-526-1630
Fax: 419-526-1618
Orders@RoyalwoodLtd.com
www.royalwoodltd.com

Basket weaving and chair caning supplies, Irish waxed linen thread, beads, kits, patterns

President: Kathy Halter
Credit Cards: MasterCard
Catalog Cost: $2
Catalog Circulation: Mailed 1 time(s) per year
Printing Information: 46 pages
Mailing List Information: Names for rent
In Business: 33 years
Number of Employees: 9
Sales Volume: $500M to $1MM

3797 Sarah's Baskets
Sarah's Baskets
8204 Highway 117 S
Po Box 6935
Rocky Point, VA 24142
800-831-8295
srsbasket1@aol.com
www.jim-minick.com

Supplies for basketmaking

President: Vicki Warrell
Owner: Sarah Minick
sarahminick@hughes.net
Catalog Cost: Free
Catalog Circulation: Mailed 2 time(s) per year
Average Order Size: $150
Printing Information: 24 pages in 1 color on Matte Stock
Press: Letterpress
Binding: Folded
Mailing List Information: Names for rent
In Business: 8 years
Number of Employees: 10-J
Sales Volume: $500M to $1MM

3798 The Country Seat
The Country Seat, Inc.
1013 Old Philly Pike
Kempton, PA 19529-9321
610-756-6124
Fax: 610-756-0088
weaving@countryseat.com
www.countryseat.com

Basketry supplies, gourd weaving and chair seat supplies

President: Donna Longenecker
CFO: Bill Longenecker
Catalog Cost: Free
Printing Information: 23 pages
In Business: 40 years
Number of Employees: 3
Sales Volume: $20,000

3799 VI Reed and Cane
V.I. Reed & Cane, Inc.
3602 D Street
Omaha, NE 68107-7364
479-789-2639
800-852-0025
Fax: 561-828-5968
info@seatweaving.org
www.Seatweaving.Org

Basket and seat weaving supplies, patterns (BasketryStudio A), Linda Hebert instructional videos, webbing, reed, seagrass, custom T shirts for guilds

President: Roger Hebert
Production Manager: Roger Hebert
Credit Cards: AMEX; MasterCard
Catalog Cost: Free
Catalog Circulation: Mailed 1 time(s) per year
Printing Information: 16 pages on Matte Stock
Binding: Saddle Stitched
Mailing List Information: Names for rent

In Business: 34 years
Sales Volume: Under $500M

3800 West Virginia Basketry Supply
West Virginia Basketry Supply
Route 71
PO Box 26A
Glenville, WV 26351
304-462-7638
basketmakingsuppliers.com

Basketry materials, including honeysuckle, cattails and yucca

3801 Willowes Basketry & Yarn
Willowes Basketry & Yarn
226 West Main Street
Greenfield, IN 46140
317-462-2026
800-230-3195
Fax: 317-467-1995
contact@willowes.com
www.willowes.com

Caning and basket supplies, yarns, stains and dyes

President: Margaret Harness
Catalog Cost: Free
Number of Employees: 2
Sales Volume: $100,000

Candlemaking

3802 Beeswax Candle Works
Beeswax Candle Works Inc
P.O.Box 1450
Cottage Grove, OR 97424-60
541-942-7061
beeswaxcandleworks@gmail.com
www.beeswaxcandleworks.com

Beeswax candles and supplies

President: Christine I Barth
Marketing Manager: Christine Barth
VP Operations: Edwin G Barth
Credit Cards: AMEX; MasterCard
Catalog Cost: Free
Mailing List Information: Names for rent
In Business: 35 years
Number of Employees: 2
Sales Volume: $125,000

3803 Brushy Mountain Bee Farm
610 Bethany Church Road
Moravian Falls, NC 28654
336-921-3640
Fax: 336-921-2681
www.brushymountainbeefarm.com

Candlemaking and beekeeping

3804 Cake and Candle
Hearth & Home Traditions Ltd.
102 Sundale Rd.
Norwich, OH 43767
740-872-3248
888-444-CAKE
Fax: 740-872-3312
customerservice@lumi-lite.com
www.cakecandle.com/

Candles, trim ring sets, potpourri products, candle holders

President: George Pappas
Credit Cards: AMEX; MasterCard
Catalog Cost: Free
Average Order Size: $15
Mailing List Information: Names for rent
Number of Employees: 2
Sales Volume: Under $500M

3805 Cementex Latex Corporation
Holden's Latex Corp.
121 Varick Street
New York, NY 10013-1408
212-741-1770
800-782-9056
Fax: 212-627-2770
info@HoldensLatex.com
www.holdenslatex.com

Mold making supplies for architectural restoration, stones, bricks and ornamentals, and candle making

President: Arthur Gononsky
Catalog Cost: $5
Printing Information: 108 pages
In Business: 79 years
Number of Employees: 10
Sales Volume: $1.2 Million

3806 Colonial Candle
Colonial Candle
41 W 8th Avenue
PO Box 3645
Oshkosh, WI 54903
866-445-9993
CustomerService@mwcbk.com
www.colonialcandle.com

Candles and potpourri

President: Miles Kimball
Marketing Manager: Michele Redmon
Credit Cards: AMEX; MasterCard
Catalog Cost: Free
Catalog Circulation: to 300T
Average Order Size: $50
Printing Information: 16 pages on Glossy Stock
Binding: Perfect Bound
In Business: 106 years

3807 Honeywax / Candle-Flex Molds
Mann Lake
501 S. 1st St.
Hackensack, MN 56452-2526
800-880-7694
Fax: 218-675-6156
beekeeper@mannlakeltd.com
www.mannlakeltd.com

Books and magazines, candle making equipment and supplies, clothing, comb honey, containers, extractors, feeds, feeders and more

President: Jack and Betty Thomas
Credit Cards: AMEX; MasterCard; Visa
Catalog Cost: Free
Printing Information: 171 pages in 4 colors on Glossy Stock
Mailing List Information: Names for rent
In Business: 31' years

3808 Illuminations
Illuminations
1736 Corporate Circle
Petaluma, CA 94954
707-769-2700
888-987-0789
Fax: 707-769-8700
www.candleshop.com

Candles

President: Wallis D Arnold
Credit Cards: AMEX; MasterCard; Visa
Printing Information: 35 pages in 4 colors on Glossy Stock
Press: Web Press
Binding: Saddle Stitched

3809 Soap Saloon
The Soap Salon
3716 30th Street
Sacramento, CA 95820
916-376-7390
Fax: 916-921-9464
info@soapsalon.net

Soap molds and soap making supplies in addition to a product line of handcrafted soaps, body oils, bath salts and other bath and skin care products

Credit Cards: AMEX; MasterCard
Catalog Cost: Free
Mailing List Information: Names for rent
Number of Employees: 8
Sales Volume: Under $500M

3810 Wicks Unlimited
Wicks Unlimited
1515 SW 13th Court
Pompano Beach, FL 33069   631-472-2010
Fax: 954-545-7427
sales@wicksunlimited.com
www.wicksunlimited.com

Wicks, wax and candles

3811 Yankee Candle
The Yankee Candle Company, Inc.
16 Yankee Candle Way
PO Box 110
South Deerfield, MA 01373-110   413-665-8306
800-243-1776
Fax: 413-665-4815
info@yankeecandle.com
www.yankeecandle.com

Candles

Chairman: Craig W Rydin
President: Harlan Kent
CFO: Bruce Hartman
Marketing Manager: Richard R Ruffolo
Credit Cards: AMEX; MasterCard
Catalog Cost: Free
Catalog Circulation: Mailed 4 time(s) per year
Printing Information: in 4 colors
In Business: 36 years

3812 Yankee Candle Catalog
The Yankee Candle, Company, Inc.
16 Yankee Candle Way
PO Box 110
South Deerfield, MA 00137-0110   413-665-8306
800-243-1776
info@yankeecandle.com
www.yankeecandle.com

Candles and accessories

Catalog Cost: Free

Ceramics

3813 AIM Kilns
Aim Kiln Manufacturing Company
2516 Business Parkway Unit #E
Minden, NV 89423-1619   775-267-2607
800-246-5456
Fax: 775-267-2002
aimkilns@yahoo.com
www.aimkiln.com

Kilns, furnaces, controllers; custom designed kilns and kiln/controller setups

President: Graydon Gannam
Credit Cards: AMEX; MasterCard; Visa
Catalog Circulation: to 3000
Average Order Size: $300
Printing Information: 6 pages in 2 colors on Matte Stock
Press: Web Press
Binding: Saddle Stitched
In Business: 30 years
Number of Employees: 14
Sales Volume: $1,000,000

3814 ART Studio Clay Company
A.R.T. Studio Clay Company, Inc.
9320 Michigan Ave
Sturtevant, WI 53177-2435   262-884-4278
877-278-2529
Fax: 262-884-4343
www.Artclay.Com

Ceramic and pottery supplies and equipment: clay, glazes, chemicals, stains, kilns, potter's wheels, mixers, pug-mills, slabrollers and videos

President: Tim Haggerty
CFO: Bea Black
Production Manager: Ron Craft
Buyers: Beatrize Black
Credit Cards: MasterCard; Visa
Catalog Cost: $5
Catalog Circulation: Mailed 1 time(s) per year

Average Order Size: $250
Printing Information: 137 pages in 2 colors on Glossy Stock
Press: Web Press
Binding: Perfect Bound
Mailing List Information: Names for rent
Will Trade Names: Yes
Number of Employees: 25

3815 Aftosa
Aftosa
1776 Wright Ave
Richmond, CA 94804-3841   510-233-0334
800-231-0397
Fax: 510-233-3569
customerservice@aftosa.com
www.aftosa.Com

Ceramic supplies, metal clay, glass, books and jewelry

President: Arnie Bernstein
Credit Cards: AMEX; MasterCard; Visa
Catalog Cost: Free
In Business: 32 years
Number of Employees: 10
Sales Volume: $5MM to $10MM

3816 Aim Kilns
Aim Kiln Manufacturing Co.
2516 Business Parkway Unit #E
Minden, NV 89423   775-267-2607
800-246-5456
Fax: 775-267-2002
aimkiln@msn.com
www.aimkiln.com

Ceramic items and accessories

3817 Biordi Art Imports
Biordi's Art Imports
412 Columbus Ave
San Francisco, CA 94133-3902   415-392-8096
Fax: 415-392-2608
info@biordi.com
www.biordi.com

Italian majolica ceramics such as dinnerware, countertop and serving pieces, decorative items, vases, planters, gift items and jewelry

President: Giovanni Savio
Catalog Cost: Free
Catalog Circulation: Mailed 1 time(s) per year
In Business: 69 years
Number of Employees: 8

3818 Brickyard Ceramics & Crafts
Brickyard Ceramics and Crafts
6060 Guion Rd
Indianapolis, IN 46254-1222   317-244-5230
800-677-3289
Fax: 317-429-5319
brickyardorders@amaco.com
www.Brickyardceramics.Com

Ceramic and craft supplies

President: Cheri Schupp
Credit Cards: AMEX; MasterCard; Visa
Catalog Cost: Free
In Business: 4 years
Number of Employees: 1
Sales Volume: $38K

3819 Ceramic Bug Supplies
Autumn Drive
16105 Garden Valley Rd.
Woodstock, IL 60098-9155   815-568-7663
www.autumndrive.net

Ceramic supplies

President: Karen Schneider
Sales Volume: Under $500M

3820 Ceramic Kilns
Evenheat Kiln, Inc.
6949 Legion Road
PO Box 399
Caseville, MI 48725-399   989-856-2281
Fax: 989-856-4040
www.evenheat-kiln.com

Ceramic kilns

President: Mike Kelly
In Business: 67 years
Sales Volume: $3MM to $5MM

3821 Chinese Porcelain Company
The Chinese Porcelain Company
232 East 59th Street
5th Floor
New York, NY 10022-1669   212-838-7744
Fax: 212-838-4922
chineseporcelainco@gmail.com
www.Chineseporcelainco.Com

Chinese export porcelain

President: Conor Mahony
Store Manager: Michelle Cheng
Credit Cards: MasterCard; Visa
Catalog Cost: $50
Catalog Circulation: Mailed 2 time(s) per year
Printing Information: 116 pages in 4 colors
In Business: 30 years
Number of Employees: 9
Sales Volume: $650K

3822 Continental Clay Company
Continental Clay Company
1101 Stinson Blvd NE
Minneapolis, MN 55413-1572   612-331-9332
800-432-2529
Fax: 612-331-8564
www.Continentalclay.Com

Clay, glaze, accessories and equipment

President: Michael Swartout
Marketing Manager: David Gamble
Credit Cards: MasterCard
Catalog Cost: Free
Catalog Circulation: Mailed 1 time(s) per year
Printing Information: 48 pages in 4 colors
Binding: Saddle Stitched
Number of Employees: 15
Sales Volume: $3MM to $5MM

3823 Creative Hobbies
Creative Hobbies, Inc.
900 Creek Road
Bellmawr, NJ 08031-1676   856-933-2540
800-THE-KILN
Fax: 856-931-1240
www.creative-hobbies.com

Ceramics supplies

President: George Strassner
In Business: 41 years
Sales Volume: $3MM to $5MM

3824 Duncan Enterprises
Duncan Enterprises
5673 E Shields Avenue
Fresno, CA 93727-7886   559-291-4444
800-438-6226
Fax: 559-291-9444
www.ilovetocreate.com

Ceramic products

Chairman: Larry R Duncan
President: Mark Peters
CFO: Douglas A Morgan
Chief Creative Officer: Valerie Marderosian
VP of Operations: Keith Martino
Credit Cards: AMEX; MasterCard
In Business: 69 years
Sales Volume: $20MM to $50MM

3825 Duralite
Duralite Inc.
15 School Street
PO Box 188
Riverton, CT 06065-1013   860-379-3113
                            888-432-8797
                       Fax: 860-379-5879
                            sales@duralite.com
                            www.Duralite.Com

Electrical elements for kilns
President: Mark Jessen
Credit Cards: AMEX; MasterCard
In Business: 65 years
Number of Employees: 10
Sales Volume: $920K

3826 Evenheat Kilns & Ovens
Evenheat Kiln
6949 Legion Road
PO Box 399
Caseville, MI 48725-399   989-856-2281
                       Fax: 989-856-4040
                            infor@evenheat-kiln.com
                            www.Evenheat-Kiln.Com

Kilns, ovens, controls and accessories
President: Mike Kelly
In Business: 67 years
Number of Employees: 12
Sales Volume: $3MM to $5MM

3827 Florida Clay Art Company
Florida Clay Art Company
1645 Hangar Rd
Sanford, FL 32773-6803   407-330-1116
                           800-211-7713
                      Fax: 407-330-5058
                           orders@flclay.com
                           www.Flclay.Com

Pottery and ceramic supplies, wheels, kilns, tile making, new and used equipment
President: Carol Tague
Catalog Circulation: to 3000
Average Order Size: $100
Printing Information: 112 pages in 3 colors on Matte Stock
Press: Sheetfed Press
Binding: Perfect Bound
Mailing List Information: Names for rent
In Business: 19 years
Number of Employees: 1
Sales Volume: $1MM to $3MM

3828 Gainey Ceramics
1200 Arrow Highway
La Verne, CA 91750   909-593-3533
                  Fax: 909-593-0488

Ceramics and pottery
Founder: John Gainey

3829 Georgies Ceramic & Clay Company
Georgies Ceramic & Clay Company
756 NE Lombard St
Portland, OR 97211-3502   503-283-1353
                            800-999-2529
                       Fax: 503-283-1387
                            info@georgies.com
                            www.Georgies.Com

Carry products, equipment and more, make clays, glazes, molds and bisque
President: Linda Mazer
Credit Cards: MasterCard
In Business: 40 years
Sales Volume: $5MM to $10MM

3830 L&L Kiln Manufacturing
L&L Kiln Mfg Inc
505 Sharptown Road
Swedesboro, NJ 08085-3163   856-294-0077
                              800-750-8350
                         Fax: 856-294-0070
                              sales@hotkilns.com
                              www.hotkilns.com

Electric kilns
President: Stephen Lewicki
Catalog Cost: Free
Average Order Size: $3000
Printing Information: 90 pages
Mailing List Information: Names for rent
In Business: 65 years
Number of Employees: 20
Sales Volume: $3MM to $5MM

3831 MacKenzie-Childs
Aurora, NY 13026   888-665-1999
customerservice@mackenzie-childs.com
www.mackenzie-childs.com

Ceramics

3832 Olympia Enterprises
Olympia Enterprise Inc.
715 McCartney Road
Youngstown, OH 44505-5038   330-746-2726
                         Fax: 330-746-1156
                              sales@olympiadecals.com

Decals and other ceramic supplies
Credit Cards: AMEX; MasterCard; Visa
Catalog Cost: $22
Printing Information: 327 pages in 4 colors
In Business: 36 years

3833 READE
Reade Advanced Materials
850 Waterman Avenue
East Providence, RI 02915   401-433-7000
                         Fax: 401-433-7001
                              info@reade.com
                              www.reade.com

Listing of specialty chemical solids (metal, mineral, ceramic, composite, alloy, polymer, natural fiber, powder, foil, sheet, wire, tube, nanoparticle, conductive, magnetic, fillers, additives)
Chairman: Charles Reade
President: Emily Reade
Marketing Manager: Elisabeth Law
Sales & Marketing Manager: Charles Reade
Catalog Cost: Free
Catalog Circulation: Mailed 4 time(s) per year to 200m
Average Order Size: $275
Printing Information: in 2 colors
Mailing List Information: Names for rent
In Business: 128 years
Number of Employees: 45
Sales Volume: $3MM to $5MM

3834 RiverView Ceramic Molds
RiverView Molds
172 Country Club Road
Williamsburg, IA 52361   319-668-9800
                      Fax: 319-668-9800
                           riverview@iowatelecom.net
                           www.riverviewmolds.com

Molds for ceramics
Credit Cards: AMEX; MasterCard; Visa
Printing Information: 119 pages
Mailing List Information: Names for rent
Sales Volume: Under $500M

3835 Sacred Source
Sacred Source
1394 Blair Park Rd
PO Box 163WW
Crozet, VA 22932-2828   434-823-1515
                          800-290-6203
                     Fax: 434-823-7665
                          spirit@sacredsource.com
                          www.sacredsource.com

Ancient deity images
President: Liana Kowalzik
CFO: Peter Kowalzik
Catalog Cost: Free
In Business: 37 years
Sales Volume: Under $500M

3836 Silver Falcon Brushes
Silver Falcon Brushes
1167 N. Service Road E.
Sullivan, MO 63080-2630   573-468-8355
                            877-443-2526
                       Fax: 573-468-5385
                            order@silverfalcon.com
                            www.silverfalcon.com

Paint brushes for arts & crafts, ceramics and porcelain
President: German Lopez
International Marketing Manager: Larry Flesher
Credit Cards: AMEX; MasterCard

3837 Yozie Mold
Yozie Mold Co.
124 College Ave
Dunbar, PA 15431-4204   724-628-3693
                     Fax: 724-628-3693
                          yozie@cvzoom.net
                          www.yoziemold.com

Ceramic molds
President: Kent M Yozie
Printing Information: 81 pages
Mailing List Information: Names for rent
Sales Volume: $500M to $1MM

Clocks

3838 American Time & Signal Company
American Time & Signal Company
140 3rd St. S.
PO Box 707
Dassel, MN 55325-707   320-275-2101
                         800-328-8996
                    Fax: 800-789-1882
                         theclockexperts@atsclock.com
                         www.Atsclock.Com

Manufacturer and distributor of institutional and industrial clocks, parts and accessories
President: Karen Sipola
Owner/CEO: Jeff Baumgartner

3839 Clockparts.com
Clockparts.Com
11869 Teale Street
Suite 302
Culver City, CA 90230   888-827-2387
                     Fax: 310-482-3480
                          customerservice@clockparts.com
                          www.clockparts.com

Clock movements, clock kits and plans, pendulums, batteries, accessories, cases, dials, hands, and hardware
Chairman: Leon Pearl
President: Eddie Blau
Marketing Manager: Michael Delbucchia
Production Manager: Laura Pastrana
VP & Technical Support: Mike Brosman
Manager: Alejandra Castillo
Customer Service: Omar Botello
Credit Cards: MasterCard
Catalog Cost: Free
Printing Information: 52 pages

In Business: 44 years
Number of Employees: 80

3840 Decor Time Products
Decor Time Products
PO Box 277698
Sacramento, CA 95827-7698   916-383-9338
                                   800-653-3267
                              Fax: 888-383-8982
customerservice@decortime.com
www.decortime.com

Clock parts and accessories
Credit Cards: AMEX; MasterCard
In Business: 30 years

3841 Electric Time Company
Electric Time Company, Inc.
97 West Street
Medfield, MA 02052-466   508-359-4396
                           Fax: 508-359-4482
salese@electrictime.com
www.Electrictime.Com

Handcrafted clock manufacture and design
President: Thomas D Erb
Printing Information: 16 pages
In Business: 85 years
Number of Employees: 30
Sales Volume: $5MM to $10MM

3842 Emperor Clock, LLC
Emperor Clock, LLC
340 Industrial Park Drive
PO Box 960
Amherst, VA 24521-960   800-642-0011
                               800-642-0011
                          Fax: 434-946-1420
service@emperorclock.com
www.emperorclock.com

Clock and furniture kits, mechanical and quartz movements, clock plans, assembled clocks
President: Gerd Hermle
Marketing Manager: Julie George
Production Manager: Debbie Vaughn
Credit Cards: AMEX; MasterCard; Visa
Catalog Cost: Free
Printing Information: 36 pages
Mailing List Information: Names for rent
Will Trade Names: Yes
In Business: 40 years
Number of Employees: 25

3843 KlockIt
KlockIt
N3211 County Road H
PO Box 636
Lake Geneva, WI 53147   800-556-2548
                          Fax: 262-248-9899
klockit@klockit.com
www.klockit.com

Clock kits, pland and components including quartz movements, clock inserts, clock dials, hour & minute hands, mechanical movements, clock pendulums and more
Marketing Manager: Sherrie Bittner
Catalog Cost: Free
In Business: 39 years
Number of Employees: 2
Sales Volume: $120,000

3844 Masterclock
Masterclock
2484 West Clay St.
Saint Charles, MO 63301   636-724-3666
                                 800-940-2248
                            Fax: 636-724-3776
www.masterclock.com

Highly synchronized clocks

3845 PTI Pyramid Technologies
PTI Pyramid Technologies
45 Gracey Avenue
Meriden, CT 06451   203-238-0550
                           888-479-7264
                      Fax: 203-634-1696
www.pyramidtimesystems.com

Time and attendance clocks and accessories.
President: John Augustyn
Marketing Manager: Brad Burton
Production Manager: John Ekegren
Vice President of Engineering: George Bucci
Vice President of Finance: Marlowe Gronbeck
Vice President of Sales and Marketi: Bob Lennon
Catalog Circulation: to 20M
Printing Information: 12 pages
In Business: 20 years
Number of Employees: 65
Sales Volume: $5,000,000 - $10,000,000

3846 Premiere Products
Premiere Products
PO Box 944
Columbus, NE 68602   402-564-4909
                            800-323-2799
                       Fax: 402-564-3703
customerservice@premiereproducts.biz
www.premiereproducts.biz

Weather instruments for home and business, radio controlled clocks and watches, outdoor furniture, specialty gifts
President: Georgia Behlen
Credit Cards: AMEX; MasterCard
Catalog Cost: Free
Mailing List Information: Names for rent
In Business: 25 years
Number of Employees: 3
Sales Volume: Under $500M

3847 Turncraft Clocks
Meisel Hardware Specialties
PO Box 70
Mound, MN 55364-70   952-746-2379
                            800-441-9870
                       Fax: 952-471-8579
Office@Meiselwoodhobby.com
www.MeiselwoodHobby.com

Clock plans, kits, clock movements, dials and clock hardware
President: Paul Meisel
Catalog Cost: Free
Catalog Circulation: Mailed 2 time(s) per year
Printing Information: 32 pages in 4 colors on Glossy Stock
Mailing List Information: Names for rent
In Business: 20 years
Number of Employees: 45

3848 Woodcraft Supply Catalog
Woodcraft Supply LLC
P.O. Box 1686
Parkersburg, WV 26102-1686   304-422-5412
                                    800-535-4486
                               Fax: 304-422-5417
custserv@woodcraft.com
www.woodcraft.com

Woodworking supplies and books, clock parts, musical movements, glass domes, specialty tools and plans
Chairman: Samuel Ross
President: Jeffrey Forbes
International Marketing Manager: Tim Rinehart
Catalog Cost: Free
Catalog Circulation: Mailed 12 time(s) per year
Printing Information: 176 pages in 4 colors
In Business: 89 years
Number of Employees: 75
Sales Volume: $ 38 Million

3849 Crazy Crow Trading Post
Crazy Crow Trading Post
1801 Airport Road
PO Box 847
Pottsboro, TX 75076   903-786-2287
                             800-786-6210
                        Fax: 903-786-9059
orders@crazycrow.com
www.crazycrow.com

Complete line of Native American Indian and American Mountain Man crafts and craft supplies
President: Cecelia Floyd
Owner: Rex Reddick
Owner: Ginger Reddick
Credit Cards: MasterCard; Visa
Catalog Cost: $5
Catalog Circulation: Mailed 1 time(s) per year
Printing Information: 140 pages
In Business: 45 years

3850 Four Winds Indian Auction
Four Winds Indian Trading Post
PO Box 580
Saint Ignatius, MT 59865-580   406-745-4336
                                 Fax: 406-745-3595
www.fourwindsindiantradingpost.com

Indian crafts and frontier collectibles
President: Preston Miller
Credit Cards: AMEX; MasterCard; Visa
Catalog Cost: $3
Printing Information: 12 pages in 1 color
In Business: 50 years
Number of Employees: 10-J
Sales Volume: Under $500M

3851 HOME
HOME
PO Box 10
Orland, ME 04472-10   207-469-7961
                             207-469-7962
                        Fax: 207-469-1023
info@homecoop.net
www.homecoop.net

Handcrafted gifts and wreaths from Maine, Native American local crafters
Chairman: Millie Grimes
President: Lucy Poulin
Marketing Manager: Lorraine Mooers
Credit Cards: AMEX; MasterCard; Visa
Catalog Cost: $1
Catalog Circulation: Mailed 1 time(s) per year to 700
Printing Information: 14 pages in 1 color on Matte Stock
Press: Web Press
Mailing List Information: Names for rent
In Business: 43 years
Number of Employees: 56
Sales Volume: Under $500M

3852 Pipestone Indian Shrine Association
Pipestone National Monument
PO Box 727
Pipestone, MN 56164-727   507-825-5463
                                 888-209-0418
                            Fax: 507-825-2903
sales@authenticpipestone.com
www.authenticpipestone.com

Indian handicrafts
President: Mike Morgan
CFO: Charles Draper
Credit Cards: MasterCard
Catalog Cost: Free
Catalog Circulation: Mailed 1 time(s) per year
Printing Information: 2 pages in 1 color
Mailing List Information: Names for rent
In Business: 85 years
Number of Employees: 4
Sales Volume: $184,000

3853 Supernaw's Oklahoma Indian Supply
Supernaw's Oklahoma Indian Supply
303 E Rogers Boulevard
Box 216
Skiatook, OK 74070-1205 918-396-1713
888-720-1967
Fax: 918-396-1711
supernaw@flash.net
www.supernaw.com

Indian crafts and supplies

President: Kugee Supernaw
Credit Cards: AMEX; MasterCard
Catalog Cost: $1
Catalog Circulation: Mailed 1 time(s) per year
Printing Information: 25 pages
In Business: 46 years
Number of Employees: 10-J
Sales Volume: Under $500M

3854 Veon Creations
Austin Bead Society
P. O. Box 656
Austin, TX 78767-656 636-586-5377
Fax: 636-586-5377
austinbeadsociety@yahoo.com
www.austinbeadsociety.org

Beads, beadworking supplies, jewelry findings, bead and crafts how to books, American Indian heritage books and Indian craft supplies

President: Nora Pero
Vice President: Danielle Baker
Secretary: Marsha Cekaj
Treasurer: Connie White
treasurer@austinbeadsociety.org
Credit Cards: MasterCard
Catalog Cost: $4
Catalog Circulation: Mailed 12 time(s) per year to 1000
Printing Information: 48 pages in 1 color on Matte Stock
Press: Web Press
Binding: Saddle Stitched
Mailing List Information: Names for rent
In Business: 25 years
Sales Volume: $500M to $1MM

Jewelry

3855 AA Clouet
Salvadore Tool & Findings, Inc.
24 Althea St
Providence, RI 02907-2802 401-272-4100
Fax: 401-273-9758
info@salvadoretool.com
www.salvadoretool.Com

Component parts for jewelry.

President: David Salvadore
CFO: Clare Salvadore
Catalog Circulation: to 500
Printing Information: 3 pages in 1 color on Newsprint
Binding: Folded
Mailing List Information: Names for rent
In Business: 55 years
Sales Volume: $5MM to $10MM

3856 AU-RUS Wax Patterns
Au-Rus Wax Patterns
302 Main Street
Kellogg, ID 83837 208-786-9301
888-769-7003
Fax: 208-786-9301
www.auruswaxpatterns.com

Over 5,000 wax patterns for a variety of decorative uses

Catalog Cost: $15
Catalog Circulation: to 5000
Printing Information: 182 pages in 2 colors on Matte Stock
Binding: Perfect Bound
In Business: 23 years

3857 Alpine Casting Company
Alpine Casting Company, Inc.
3530 Chelton Loop North
Suite C
Colorado Springs, CO 80909 719-358-2234
888-391-5028
Fax: 888-618-0187
mail@alpinecasting.com
www.alpinecasting.com

Jewelry making supplies, custom metal castings

President: Marilyn Benedict
mail@alpinecasting.com
CEO: Andy Benedict
andy@alpinecasting.com
Catalog Circulation: to 1000
Printing Information: 10 pages in 2 colors on Matte Stock
Binding: Folded
In Business: 30 years
Sales Volume: $500,000

3858 Arhaus Jewels
Arhaus Jewels
7700 Northfield Rd
Walton Hills, OH 44146 877-857-4158
www.arhausjewels.com

Jewelry, clothing, accessories, and footwear

Catalog Cost: Free
In Business: 25+ years

3859 Bead Warehouse
Artbeads.com
11901 137th Avenue Ct KPN
Gig Harbor, WA 98329-6312 253-857-3433
866-715-2323
Fax: 253-857-2385
support@artbeads.com
www.artbeads.com

Beads, stones, books, tools, findings

President: Devin Kimura
Credit Cards: AMEX; MasterCard
Catalog Cost: $2
Printing Information: 80 pages
In Business: 14 years

3860 Beadalon
Beadalon
440 Highlands Boulevard
Valley Twp., PA 19320 610-466-6000
866-423-2325
Fax: 610-384-7260
sales@beadalon.com
www.beadalon.com

Products to make jewelry, and beads

President: James Clark
Product Manager: Wyatt White

3861 Beadcats
Beadcats
PO Box 2840
Wilsonville, OR 97070-2840 503-625-2323
Fax: 503-625-4329
catalogs@beadcats.com
www.beadcats.com

Seed beads (11/0 - 22/0), bugle beads, Czech pressed glass beads in a variety of shapes. Bead sample cards available, supplies, tools, books

Credit Cards: AMEX; MasterCard
Catalog Cost: $4
Printing Information: 60 pages in 2 colors on Newsprint
Binding: Folded
In Business: 20 years
Number of Employees: 5

3862 Best Brushes
321 South Main St
Yerington, NV 89447 888-463-9177
Fax: 775-463-1582
thebestbrushes.com

Jewelry

3863 Diamond Pacific Tool
Diamond Pacific Tool Corporation
2620 W Main Street
Barstow, CA 92311 760-255-1030
800-253-2954
Fax: 760-255-1077
diamondpacific@aol.com
www.diamondpacific.Com

Lapidary equipment

President: Bill Depue
CFO: Stacy Depue
Buyers: Jill Durbin
Credit Cards: AMEX; MasterCard
Catalog Cost: Free
Catalog Circulation: Mailed 1 time(s) per year
Printing Information: 124 pages in 1 color
Mailing List Information: Names for rent
In Business: 43 years
Number of Employees: 26
Sales Volume: $10MM to $20MM

3864 Drumbeat Indian Arts
Drumbeat Indian Arts, Inc.
4143 North 16th Street
Phoenix, AZ 85016 602-266-4823
800-895-4859
Fax: 602-265-2402
info@drumbeatindianarts.com
www.drumbeatindianarts.com

Beads in a variety of types and sizes, seeds, recailles, bugles, crow, hexagon, metal and bone, threads, quills furs, shells, feathers, findings and shawl fringes

President: Robert L Nuss
Credit Cards: AMEX; MasterCard
Printing Information: 150 pages in 1 color
In Business: 31 years
Sales Volume: $1MM to $3MM

3865 Easy Leaf Products
Neuberg & Neuberg Importers Group, Inc.
6001 Santa Monica Blvd
Los Angeles, CA 90038-1807 323-769-4822
800-569-5323
Fax: 877-386-1489
info@nnigroup.com
www.easyleaf.com

Edible gold & silver leaf and recipes

President: Larry Neuberg
CFO: Sam Neuberg
Marketing Manager: Scot Holland
Vice President: Rommel Villa
rommelvilla@nnigroup.com
Food & Beverage Manager: Lynn Neuberg
lynnneuberg@nnigroup.com
Founder: Sam Neuberg
samneuberg@nnigroup.com
Catalog Circulation: Mailed 1 time(s) per year to 4M
Printing Information: 20 pages in 2 colors
Mailing List Information: Names for rent
In Business: 7 years
Number of Employees: 50
Sales Volume: $7.2 Million

3866 Elvee Rosenberg
Elvee/Rosenberg Inc.
PO BOX 4583
New York, NY 10163-4583 212-575-0767
Fax: 212-575-0931
sales@elveerosenberg.com
www.elveerosenberg.com

Simulated pearls and fashion beads, glass, plastic, naturals, sterling silver, electroplated beads, cabachons and findings

President: Chester Hochbaum
Marketing Manager: Melanie Holzberg
Credit Cards: AMEX; MasterCard
In Business: 101 years
Number of Employees: 13
Sales Volume: $2.6 Million

3867 Findings & Metals
Swest Inc.
11090 N Stemmons Freeway
PO Box 59389
Dallas, TX 75229-4520   214-350-4011
                                  Fax: 800-441-5162
                             swest@mindspring.com
                                www.swestinc.com

Jewelry making and metalwork
President: FW Ward
Marketing Manager: Gary Fuller

3868 Fire Mountain Gems & Beads Jewelry Maker's Catalog
Fire Mountain Gems and Beads
1 Fire Mountain Way
Grants Pass, OR 97526-2373   800-355-2137
                                 800-423-2319
                              Fax: 800-292-3473
                           www.firemountaingems.com

Jewelry making supplies, beads, seed beads, findings, gem stones, mountings, tools, earrings.
Catalog Cost: Free
Printing Information: 327 pages in 4 colors
In Business: 43 years

3869 Frei & Borel Findings
Otto Frei
126 2nd St
Oakland, CA 94607-4514   510-832-0355
                                 800-772-3456
                              Fax: 510-834-6217
                               info@ottofrei.com
                                 www.ottofrei.com

Jewelry tools and findings
President: Steve Frei
Marketing Manager: John J Frei
Co-Owner: Bob Frei
Credit Cards: AMEX; MasterCard; Visa
Catalog Cost: $10
Catalog Circulation: to 20000
Printing Information: 134 pages in 4 colors on Glossy Stock
Press: Sheetfed Press
Binding: Perfect Bound
Mailing List Information: Names for rent
In Business: 85 years
Number of Employees: 40
Sales Volume: $6.9 Million

3870 Gampel Supply
Elvee Rosen Berge Inc
11 W 37th St
New York, NY 10163-4583   212-575-0767
                              Fax: 212-575-0931
                          sales@elveerosenberg.com
                            www.elveerosenberg.com

Bead stringing and jewelry making supplies, tools, adhesives, findings, wire, needles, threads, cording, beads, bead boards, and much more
President: Chet Hochbaum
Credit Cards: MasterCard
Printing Information: in 4 colors on Glossy Stock
Press: Offset Press
Binding: Folded
In Business: 101 years
Sales Volume: $10MM to $20MM

3871 Garden of Beadin'
Garden of Beadin'
752 Redwood Drive
Garberville, CA 95542   707-923-9120
                                 800-232-3588
                              Fax: 707-923-9160
                                 beads@asis.com
                            www.gardenofbeadin.com

Beads and beading supplies in a wide array of colors
President: Charlotte Silverstein
Credit Cards: AMEX; MasterCard; Visa
Catalog Cost: Free
Catalog Circulation: Mailed 1 time(s) per year to 50000
Average Order Size: $56
Printing Information: 88 pages in 4 colors
Mailing List Information: Names for rent
In Business: 29 years
Number of Employees: 5

3872 Gems & Minerals Catalog
Gem Center USA Inc.
4100 Alameda Avenue
El Paso, TX 79905-2601   877-533-7153
                             gemcenter@sbcglobal.net
                              www.gemcenterusa.com

Stone beads, stone cabochons, crystals and minerals, rough rock cutting material, silver jewelry, rock spheres
President: Jeanette B Carrillo
Marketing Manager: Hector Carillo Jr
Credit Cards: MasterCard; Visa
Catalog Cost: Free
In Business: 47 years
Number of Employees: 6
Sales Volume: $500,000

3873 Ghirelli Rosaries
Ghirelli USA, Inc.
990 Green Bay Road-Suite 2A
Winnetka, IL 60093   847-446-5121
                                 usa@ghirelli.com
                               www.ghirellishop.com

Rosaries, religious bracelets, pendants, sculptures, etc.
Catalog Cost: Free
In Business: 27 years

3874 Gryphon Corporation
Gryphon Corporation
12417 Foothill Blvd
Sylmar, CA 91342-6005   818-890-7770
                               www.gryphoncorp.com

Books and supplies for jewelry making
President: Mel Jones
In Business: 54 years
Sales Volume: $3MM to $5MM

3875 Guildcraft Arts and Crafts
100 Fire Tower Drive
Tonawanda, NY 14150   800-345-5563
                              Fax: 800-550-3555
                            service@guildcraftinc.com
                              www.guildcraftinc.com

Crafting supplies and materials

3876 HHH Enterprises
HHH Enterprises
301 East South 11th Street
Abilene, TX 79602-4002   325-672-8746
                                 800-777-0218
                              Fax: 325-673-5435
                           customer@hhhenterprises.com
                             www.hhhenterprises.com

Beads, jewelry components, findings
President: Homer H Hillis
CFO: David Flowers
Credit Cards: AMEX; MasterCard; Visa
Catalog Cost: $10
Catalog Circulation: to 10000

Printing Information: 200 pages in 4 colors on Glossy Stock
Press: Sheetfed Press
Binding: Saddle Stitched
In Business: 30 years
Number of Employees: 100

3877 Halstead Bead
650 Inter-Cal Way
Prescott, AZ 86301   928-778-6776
                              Fax: 928-776-1158
                               www.halsteadbead.com

Beads, jewelry
Customer Service: Barb
Customer Service: Linda

3878 House of Onyx
House of Onyx
120 North Main Street
Greenville, KY 42345-1504   270-338-2363
                                 800-844-3100
                              Fax: 270-338-9605
                            sales@houseofonyx.Com
                             www.HouseofOnyx.Com

Gemstones, jewelry, carvings, minerals, gift items, and cloisonne lamps, vase, decorator items
President: Shirley Rowe
Production Manager: Betsy Smith
Credit Cards: MasterCard; Visa
Catalog Cost: Free
Catalog Circulation: Mailed 12 time(s) per year to 750m
Average Order Size: $100
Printing Information: 36 pages in 4 colors on Newsprint
Press: Web Press
Binding: Folded
Mailing List Information: Names for rent
In Business: 47 years
Number of Employees: 17
Sales Volume: $3MM to $5MM

3879 James Avery Craftsman
James Avery Craftsman, Inc
145 Avery Road
Kerrville, TX 78028-7603   800-283-1770
                                 800-283-1770
                              Fax: 830-895-6601
                          customerservice@jamesavery.com
                               www.jamesavery.com

Handcrafted silver and gold jewelry
Chairman: James Avery
President: Chris Avery
EVP: Paul Avery
CEO: Chris Avery
Credit Cards: AMEX; MasterCard; Visa
Catalog Cost: Free
Catalog Circulation: Mailed 4 time(s) per year
Printing Information: 48 pages in 4 colors on Glossy Stock
Binding: Saddle Stitched
In Business: 70 years
Number of Employees: 1000
Sales Volume: $20MM to $50MM

3880 Jewel of the Isle
Jewel of the Isle
6 Straight Wharf
Nantucket, MA 02554-3537   508-228-2448
                                 800-927-2148
                              Fax: 508-374-0448
                               trainor3@gmail.com
                             www.Jeweloftheisle.Com

Handcrafted Nantucket themed jewelry, fine jewelry
President: Gary Trainor
CFO: Kelly Trainor
Credit Cards: AMEX; MasterCard; Visa
Printing Information: 33 pages
In Business: 26 years
Sales Volume: $500M to $1MM

3881 Jewelry Maker's Catalog
Tripp's Manufacturing
PO Box 1369
Socorro, NM 87801
575-835-2465
800-545-7962
Fax: 505-835-2848
tripps@tripps.com
www.tripps.com

Rings, earrings, and pendants, chains, findings and beads; Diamonds, Rubies, Amethyst, Sapphire, Topaz, Opal, Pearls and more

Fulfillment: Antoinette Matlins
Credit Cards: AMEX; MasterCard; Visa
Catalog Cost:
Printing Information: 228 pages
In Business: 37 years

3882 John C. Campbell Folk School
One Folk School Road
Brasstown, NC 28902
828-837-2775
Fax: 828-837-8637
www.folkschool.org

Handmade crafts

Director: Jan Davidson
Program Manager: Karen Beaty

3883 Kassoy
Kassoy
101 Commercial Street
Suite 200
Plainview, NY 11803
516-942-0560
800-452-7769
Fax: 516-942-0402
sales@kassoy.com
www.kassoy.com

Tools, equipment and supplies for jewelers

President: Joanne Slawitsky
CFO: Joann Slawitsky
Manager: Joe Regal
Credit Cards: AMEX; MasterCard
Catalog Cost: Free
Catalog Circulation: Mailed 1 time(s) per year
Printing Information: 162 pages in 4 colors on Glossy Stock
Press: Web Press
Binding: Perfect Bound
Mailing List Information: Names for rent
In Business: 75 years
Number of Employees: 18
Sales Volume: $2.60 Million

3884 Kingsley North Jewelry Supply
Kingsley North, Inc.
910 Brown Street
P.O. Box 216
Norway, MI 49870
906-563-9228
800-338-9280
Fax: 906-563-7143
sales@kingsleynorth.com
www.kingsleynorth.com

Jewelry making tools, gemology, findings, beeds, rough rock, cabochons and more

President: Dan Paupore
Vice President: Mark Paupore
Treasurer: David Paupore
Credit Cards: MasterCard
Catalog Cost: Free
Catalog Circulation: Mailed 1 time(s) per year to 200M
Average Order Size: $215
Printing Information: 164 pages in 1 color on Newsprint
Press: Web Press
Binding: Saddle Stitched
In Business: 78 years
Number of Employees: 8
Sales Volume: $3 Million

3885 Kingsley North Lapidary Supply
Kingsley North, Inc.
910 Brown Street
P.O. Box 216
Norway, MI 49870
906-563-9228
800-338-9280
Fax: 906-563-7143
sales@kingsleynorth.com
www.kingsleynorth.com

Jewelry making tools, gemology, lapidary supplies, findings, beads, rough rock, cabochons

President: Dan Paupore
Vice President: Mark Paupore
Treasurer: David Paupore
Credit Cards: MasterCard; Visa
Catalog Cost: Free
Catalog Circulation: Mailed 1 time(s) per year to 200M
Average Order Size: $215
Printing Information: 164 pages in 1 color on Newsprint
Press: Web Press
Binding: Saddle Stitched
Mailing List Information: Names for rent
List Manager: Dan Paupore
In Business: 78 years
Number of Employees: 8
Sales Volume: $3 Million

3886 Margola Corporation
Margola Corporation
232 South Van Brunt Street
Englewood, NJ 07631
201-816-9500
Fax: 201-816-0051
info@margola.com
www.margola.com

Czech beads, seed, 2 and 3 cut, bugle, druk, firepolish, crystal, glass beads, glass and crystal quality rhinestones, jewelry findings, nailheads, settings, pearl varieties, puff and fabric trim plus

President: Neil Chalfin
VP: Bernard Chalfin
Credit Cards: MasterCard
Catalog Cost: varies
In Business: 92 years
Number of Employees: 25
Sales Volume: $5 Million

3887 Max & Chloe
Max & Chloe
646-290-6446
888-629-2456
www.maxandchloe.com

Fashion and fine jewelry.

3888 Minnesota Lapidary Supply
Minnesota Lapidary Supply
201 N Rum River Drive
Princeton, MN 55371-1616
763-631-0405
888-612-3444
Fax: 763-631-0405
sales@lapidarysupplies.com
www.lapidarysupplies.com

Stones for jewelry making

President: Val B Carver
Credit Cards: MasterCard
Catalog Cost: Free
Catalog Circulation: Mailed 52 time(s) per year to 3000
Printing Information: 55 pages in 1 color on Matte Stock
Press: Web Press
Binding: Folded
Mailing List Information: Names for rent
In Business: 50 years
Number of Employees: 2
Sales Volume: Under $500M

3889 Morion Company
Morion Company
60 Leo Birmingham Parkway
Suite 111
Brighton, MA 02135
617-787-2133
Fax: 617-787-4628
labgems@morioncompany.com
www.morioncompany.com

Lab created minerals for wholesale and retail, for hobbyists, crafters, collectors, jewelers and jewelry manufacturers

Chairman: Uriah Pritchard, MS
President: Leonid Pride, PhD
Founder: Leonid Pride, Ph.D.
Catalog Cost: Free
Catalog Circulation: Mailed 3 time(s) per year to 780
Average Order Size: $400
Printing Information: 6 pages in 1 color on Matte Stock
Press: Web Press
Binding: Folded
Mailing List Information: Names for rent
In Business: 22 years
Number of Employees: 2
Sales Volume: Under $500M

3890 Morning Light Emporium
Morning Light Emporium
Roxy Grinnell
PO Box 1155
Paonia, CO 81428
970-527-4493
800-392-0365
Fax: 970-527-4493
rgrinnell2010@yahoo.com

Glass beads, including crow, pony, 11/0 and 14/0 seed beads, bugles,chevrons, metal and bone

President: Roxy Grinnell
Credit Cards: MasterCard
Catalog Cost: Free
Printing Information: in 1 color

3891 Nature's Jewelry
Nature's Jewelry
P.O. Box 3387
Chelmsford, MA 01824-987
877-755-5747
800-333-3235
Fax: 800-866-3235
help@naturesjewelry.com
www.naturesjewelry.com

Earrings, necklaces, chains, watches and pins.

Credit Cards: AMEX; MasterCard; Visa
Catalog Cost: Free
In Business: 37 years

3892 Oriental Crest
Oriental Crest limited edition
6161 Savoy Dr
Suite 958
Houston, TX 77036-3323
713-780-2425
800-367-3954
Fax: 713-367-3954
info@orientalcrest.com
www.Orientalcrest.Com

Jewelry-making supplies and tools

President: Wilson Lin
Credit Cards: AMEX; MasterCard
Catalog Cost: Free
Catalog Circulation: to 3000
Printing Information: 80 pages in 7 colors on Glossy Stock
Press: Letterpress
Binding: Folded
In Business: 20 years
Number of Employees: 20
Sales Volume: $4.5 Million

3893 Ornamental Resources

Ornamental Resources
5712 W.38th Ave
Wheat Ridge, CO 80212   303-567-2222
                               800-876-6762
                          Fax: 303-567-4245
                          orna@ornabead.com
                          www.ornabead.com

Complete lines of glass beads, faceted, cut, foiled, decorated, fancy, metal, natural, bugles, pony, and seed beads in all sizes

Credit Cards: AMEX; MasterCard; Visa
Catalog Cost: $15
Printing Information: in 4 colors
In Business: 44 years

3894 Pickens Minerals

Pickens Minerals
610 N Martin Avenue
Waukegan, IL 60085-3436   847-623-2823
                          Fax: 847-623-2865
                          www.pickensminerals.com

Stones for making jewelry

President: Reo Pickens
Catalog Cost: $5
Printing Information: 54 pages in 4 colors on Glossy Stock
Press: Offset Press
In Business: 61 years
Number of Employees: 1
Sales Volume: $180,000

3895 Precious Metal Jewelry Findings

New York Findings Corp
72 Bowery
New York, NY 10013-4638   212-925-5745
                               888-925-5745
                          Fax: 212-925-5870
                          nyfindings@aol.com
                          www.newyorkfindings.com

Precious metal findings for the jewelry trade

President: Don King
Marketing Manager: Tuna
Average Order Size: $100
Printing Information: in 4 colors
Press: Web Press
Binding: Perfect Bound
Mailing List Information: Names for rent
In Business: 62 years
Number of Employees: 100
Sales Volume: $10,000,000

3896 Precious Metals and Refining Services

David H Fell & Company, Inc.
PO Box 910952
Los Angeles, CA 90091-952   323-722-9992
                               800-822-1996
                          Fax: 323-722-6567
                          info@dhfco.com
                          www.dhfco.com

Supplies for jewelry-making

President: Larry Fell
CFO: David Fell
Marketing Manager: Kevin Haras
Production Manager: Ken Rose
Catalog Cost: Free
Printing Information: 28 pages
In Business: 35 years
Number of Employees: 25
Sales Volume: $2.73 Million

3897 Prima Bead

Prima Bead
12333 Enterprise Blvd.
Largo, FL 33773   800-366-2218
                          customerservice@primabead.com
                          www.primabead.com

Supplies to create handmade jewelry—also provides free projects, and how-to-videos

Catalog Cost: Free

3898 Reactive Metals Studio

Reactive Metals Studio, Inc.
PO Box 890
Clarkdale, AZ 86324-890   928-634-3434
                               800-876-3434
                          Fax: 928-634-6734
                          info@reactivemetals.com
                          www.reactivemetals.com

Niobium and titanium, jewelry findings,anodizing supplies, mokume-gane shakudo, shibuichi

President: Bill Seeley
Credit Cards: AMEX; MasterCard
Catalog Cost: Free
Catalog Circulation: Mailed 1 time(s) per year
Printing Information: 42 pages in 1 color on Matte Stock
Press: Web Press
Binding: Saddle Stitched
Mailing List Information: Names for rent
In Business: 21 years
Number of Employees: 3
Sales Volume: $500M to $1MM

3899 Rishashay

Rishashay
PO Box 8271
Missoula, MT 59807-8271   406-721-0580
                               800-517-3311
                          Fax: 406-549-3467
                          inquire@rishashay.com
                          www.rishashay.com

Sterling silver beads, clasps, earwires, posts, headpins and components

President: John P Anderson
Secretary/Treasurer: David Anderson
Credit Cards: AMEX; MasterCard; Visa
Catalog Cost: $7
Catalog Circulation: to 20000
Average Order Size: $100
Printing Information: 100 pages in 4 colors on Glossy Stock
Press: Letterpress
Binding: Perfect Bound
In Business: 36 years
Number of Employees: 6
Sales Volume: $720,000

3900 Roussels

Roussels
330 East Main Street
PO Box 901
Gramercy, LA 70052-52   225-869-9097
                          Fax: 978-443-8888
                          www.roussels.com

Craft supplies and jewelry findings

Catalog Cost: $0.5
Printing Information: 2 pages in 2 colors on Glossy Stock
Press: Offset Press
Binding: Folded
In Business: 30 years

3901 Sadigh Gallery Ancient Art

Sadigh Gallery Ancient Art Inc
303 5th Ave # 1603
Suite 1603
New York, NY 10016-6636   212-725-7537
                               800-426-2007
                          Fax: 212-545-7612
                          info@sadighgallery.com
                          www.sadighgallery.Com

Genuine Egyptian, Mid Eastern Classical and Pre-Columbian artifacts, jewelry and collectibles,and more

President: Mehrdad Sadigh
Credit Cards: AMEX; MasterCard; Visa
Catalog Cost: Free
Printing Information: in 3 colors
Mailing List Information: Names for rent
In Business: 37 years
Number of Employees: 5
Sales Volume: Under $500,000

3902 Scottsdale Bead Supply & Imports

Scottsdale Bead Supply
3625 N Marshall Way
Scottsdale, AZ 85251-5515   480-945-5988
                          Fax: 480-945-4248
                          support@scottsdalebead.com
                          www.scottsdalebead.com

Direct importers of Balinese silver beads, Czech, Indian, Japanese beads, assortment of custom lamp beads, manufacturers of dichroic glass donuts and pendants, cabochons and charms

President: Mike Charveaux
CFO: Kelly Charveaux
Credit Cards: AMEX; MasterCard
Catalog Cost: $5
Printing Information: 46 pages
In Business: 22 years
Sales Volume: $1,000,000

3903 Simply Whispers

Roman Research, Inc.
800 Franklin St.
Hanson, MA 00234   800-451-5700
                          Fax: 781-447-0995
                          custserv@romanresearch.com
                          www.simplywhispers.com

Nickel-free jewelry.

President: Dale Southworth
In Business: 45 years

3904 Special Request

A Special Request
PO Box 681036
Park City, UT 84060   435-640-3252
                               800-695-7519
                          Fax: 435-655-9999
                          bethmoon@bethmoon.biz
                          www.specialrequest.net

Jewelry findings, mountings, bola slides, baroque stones in over 500 varieties

Catalog Cost: $3
Average Order Size: $50
Printing Information: 28 pages in 4 colors on Matte Stock
Press: Letterpress
P.O. Box 681036
Park City, UT 84060
435-645-7519
In Business: 30 years
Sales Volume: Under $500M

3905 Spiegel

Spiegel LLC
110 William St
11th Fl.
New York City, NY 10038-5367   800-222-5680
                               800-253-4742
                          customerservice@spiegel.com
                          www.spiegel.com

General merchandise, clothing and jewelry

President: Geralynn Madonna
CFO: Thomas C Pacelli, VP Finance
Credit Cards: AMEX; MasterCard; Visa
Catalog Cost: $5
Catalog Circulation: to 10000
Printing Information: 96 pages
In Business: 149 years
Number of Employees: 1000
Sales Volume: 769MM

3906 Starstruck

Star Struck, LLC.
8 FJ Clarke Circle
PO Box 308
Bethel, CT 06801-2853   203-778-4925
                               800-243-6144
                          Fax: 203-778-6938
                          cs@starstruckllc.com
                          www.starstruck.com

Jewelry distributor of gold testers, precision jewelery gauges, microscopes, magnifiers, loupes etc.

Chairman: Peter Nisselson
President: Kenneth Karlan
CFO: Barry Curtis
Marketing Manager: David Sable
Credit Cards: AMEX; MasterCard
Catalog Cost: $2
Printing Information: 64 pages
In Business: 32 years
Number of Employees: 35
Sales Volume: $ 1.7 Million

3907 Toro Imports
1007 Oakmead Drive
Arlington, TX 76011   817-652-0404
                Fax: 817-652-0467
           toroimports@aol.com
           www.mazbot-tools.com

Tools for jewelry making

3908 Wax Patterns
Legacy Designs
PO Box 9895
Springfield, MO 65801-1899   417-833-8071
                Fax: 863-603-9372
           waxpatterns@gmail.com
           www.waxpatterns.com

Jeweler's tools, supplies and equipment

President: FW Ward
Marketing Manager: Gary Fuller
Buyers: Tom Rush
Credit Cards: MasterCard; Visa
Catalog Cost: $10
Catalog Circulation: Mailed 1 time(s) per year
Printing Information: 344 pages

3909 Wire Wizard
Wire Wizard
12201 SE 25th Street Bellevue
Bellevue, WA 98005-312   425-644-1009
                866-881-9698
           beadlady@thewirewizard.com

Supplies for making jewelry

President: Corrine Gurry
Catalog Circulation: to 10000
Printing Information: 6 pages in 4 colors on Matte Stock
Press: Letterpress
Binding: Folded
In Business: 23 years

3910 Zarlene Imports
Zarlene Imports
1550 E Oakland Park Blvd
Ft. Lauderdale, FL 33334-4446   954-566-4081
                800-223-7999
           Fax: 954-566-4206
           sales@zarlene.com
           www.zarlene.com

Wholesale Semi-Precious Stones and Findings

President: Joseph Zerger
VP: Danielle Zerger
Catalog Cost: $10
In Business: 49 years
Number of Employees: 10
Sales Volume: $2,000,000

Metal & Leatherwork

3911 Arnie's Arts & Crafts
Arnie's Arts & Crafts
3741 West Houghton Lake Drive
Houghton Lake, MI 48629   989-366-8794
                800-563-2356
           Fax: 989-366-5931
           www.basketpatterns.com

Basket making kits and supplies, gourd patterns and tools, lamp and leather kits, weaving tools

Chairman: Roberta Goupil
President: Arnold Goupil
Catalog Cost: Free
In Business: 29 years
Number of Employees: 5
Sales Volume: $300,000

3912 CS Osborne Tools
CS Osborne & Company
125 Jersey Street
Harrison, NJ 07029-1798   973-483-3232
                Fax: 973-484-3621
           cso@csosborne.com
           www.csosborne.com

Industrial hand tools, upholstery tools and leather working tools

President: Ralph D Osborne III
Catalog Cost: Free
In Business: 191 years
Number of Employees: 145
Sales Volume: $16M

3913 Campbell Tool Company
Campbell Tool Company
2100 Selma Rd
Springfield, OH 45505-4718   937-322-8562
                Fax: 937-882-6648
           www.campbelltools.com

Lathes, mills, metals, steam engine kits, books, videos and precision instruments for hobbyists and industrial use

President: Renee L. Morningstar
Marketing Manager: Lanny G. Wallace
Credit Cards: AMEX; MasterCard; Visa
Catalog Circulation: Mailed 1 time(s) per year to 5M
Printing Information: 94 pages in 1 color on Newsprint
Press: Web Press
Binding: Saddle Stitched
In Business: 44 years
Number of Employees: 6

3914 Castings
Castings
PO Box 298
Eastsound, WA 98245-298   360-376-3266
                800-346-0567
           Fax: 888-429-1707
           castings@miniaturemolds.com
           www.webmolds.com

Miniature figure molds, melting pots and casting supplies

President: Robert Blanc
VP: Enid Blanc
Credit Cards: AMEX; MasterCard
Catalog Cost: $3
Catalog Circulation: to 11000
Mailing List Information: Names for rent
In Business: 40 years
Number of Employees: 3
Sales Volume: $250K

3915 Country Accents
Country Accents
615 Dunwoody Road
Williamsport, PA 17701   570-478-4127
                Fax: 570-478-2007
           sales@piercedtin.com
           www.piercedtin.com

Tools for tin-piercing, made to order pierced tin inserts for cabinetry, custom designs and sizes

President: James Palotas
Marketing Manager: Theresa Sullivan
Credit Cards: MasterCard
Catalog Cost: $5
Catalog Circulation: to 3000+
Average Order Size: $150
Printing Information: 80 pages in 4 colors
Binding: Saddle Stitched
Mailing List Information: Names for rent
In Business: 36 years

Number of Employees: 4
Sales Volume: $190,000

3916 East West DyeCom
East West DyeCom
PO Box 12294
Roanoke, VA 24024-2294   540-362-1489
                800-407-6371
           Fax: 540-362-7425

Metal working tools, anodized aluminum for industry and art

President: Ben Lawhorn
CFO: Tamea Franco
VP: Betsy Hairston
Credit Cards: AMEX; MasterCard
In Business: 26 years
Number of Employees: 10
Sales Volume: $610,000

3917 Findings & Metals
Swest Inc.
11090 N Stemmons Freeway
PO Box 59389
Dallas, TX 75229-4520   214-350-4011
                Fax: 800-441-5162
           swest@mindspring.com
           www.swestinc.com

Jewelry making and metalwork

President: FW Ward
Marketing Manager: Gary Fuller

3918 Gallery Leather
Gallery Leather Company, Inc.
27 Industrial Way
Trenton, ME 00460   877-811-7901
           service@galleryleather.com
           www.galleryleather.com

Handcrafted leather goods, specially designed planners, journals, albums, and organizers

Catalog Cost: Free
In Business: 30 years

3919 Guildcraft Arts and Crafts
100 Fire Tower Drive
Tonawanda, NY 14150   800-345-5563
                Fax: 800-550-3555
           service@guildcraftinc.com
           www.guildcraftinc.com

Crafting supplies and materials

3920 HE Goldberg & Company
HE Goldberg & Company
9050 Martin Luther King Jr Way
Seattle, WA 98118-5097   206-722-8200
                800-722-8201
           Fax: 206-722-0435
           hegcofur@aol.com
           www.hegoldbergfur.com

Furskins

President: Erwin Goldberg
Credit Cards: AMEX; MasterCard
Catalog Cost: Free
Catalog Circulation: Mailed 4 time(s) per year
Printing Information: 6 pages on Glossy Stock
Mailing List Information: Names for rent
In Business: 103 years
Sales Volume: $10MM to $20MM

3921 Hermes
Hermes
691 Madison Ave
New York, NY 10065-8002   212-751-3181
                800-441-4488
           Fax: 212-751-8143
           www.Hermes.Com

Fine leather goods

President: Anthony Fuccillo

3922 John C. Campbell Folk School
One Folk School Road
Brasstown, NC 28902   828-837-2775
Fax: 828-837-8637
www.folkschool.org

Handmade crafts

Director: Jan Davidson
Program Manager: Karen Beaty

3923 Klise Manufacturing Company
601 Maryland Ave NE
Grand Rapids, MI 49505   616-459-4283
klise@klisemfg.com
www.klisemfg.com

Lineal wood mouldings and metalwork

3924 Langlitz Leathers
2443 SE Division
Portland, OR 97202   503-235-0959
Fax: 503-235-0049
catalog@langlitz.com
www.langlitz.com

Leathers and hides

Owner: Jackie
General and Technical Manager: Judy

3925 Ohio Travel Bag
6481 Davis Industrial Parkway
Solon, OH 44139-3547   800-800-1941
Fax: 800-989-5559
info@ohiotravelbag.com
www.ohiotravelbag.com

Bags and baggage

3926 Prima Bead
Prima Bead
12333 Enterprise Blvd.
Largo, FL 33773   800-366-2218
customerservice@primabead.com
www.primabead.com

Supplies to create handmade jewelry—also provides free projects, and how-to-videos

Catalog Cost: Free

3927 Schlaifer's Enameling Supplies
Schlaifer's Enameling Supplies, LLC
PO Box 6776
Gardnerville, NV 89460   800-525-5959
Fax: 775-265-3284
ses@enameling.com
www.enameling.com

Products for copper enamelists, price of catalog applied to first order

President: Joan Schlaifer
Catalog Cost: $7
Catalog Circulation: to 250
Average Order Size: $100
Printing Information: 46 pages in 2 colors on Glossy Stock
Press: Sheetfed Press
Binding: Perfect Bound
In Business: 20 years
Number of Employees: 1
Sales Volume: Under $500M

3928 Swiss Precision Instruments
Swiss Precision Instrument, Inc.
11450 Markon Drive
Garden Grove, CA 92841-3135   888-774-8200
Fax: 800-842-5164
sales@swissprec.com
www.swissprec.com

Machinists/metalwork instruments and tools

President: Allan Newman
CFO: Marc Serlin
Credit Cards: MasterCard
Catalog Cost: Free
Catalog Circulation: Mailed 1 time(s) per year
Printing Information: 432 pages in 1 color

In Business: 58 years
Number of Employees: 22

3929 Veteran Leather Corporation
Veteran Leather Co., Inc.
3614 35th Street
Long Island City, NY 11106-1302   718-786-0935
800-221-7565
Fax: 718-786-0701
www.veteranleather.com

Leather craft equipment

President: Andrew Sapienza
Marketing Manager: Vincent Sapienza
Founder: Salvatore Sapienza
Credit Cards: MasterCard; Visa
Catalog Cost: $2
Catalog Circulation: Mailed 1 time(s) per year
Printing Information: 56 pages in 1 color
In Business: 69 years
Number of Employees: 45
Sales Volume: $1MM to $3MM

3930 Victor Machinery Exchange
Victor Machinery Exchange Inc
33-53 62nd St.
Woodside, NY 11377-3817   718-899-1502
800-723-5359
Fax: 718-899-0556
sales@victornet.com
www.victornet.com

Metal working tools

President: Marc Freidus
Credit Cards: AMEX; MasterCard; Visa
Catalog Cost: Free
Catalog Circulation: Mailed 1 time(s) per year to 70000
Printing Information: 136 pages in 4 colors on Glossy Stock
Binding: Saddle Stitched
Mailing List Information: Names for rent
In Business: 97 years
Number of Employees: 10
Sales Volume: $1MM to $3MM

3931 Weaver Leather
Weaver Leather, LLC
7540 CR 201
PO Box 68
Mt Hope, OH 44660-68   330-674-1782
800-932-8371
Fax: 330-674-0330
info@weaverleather.com
www.Weaverleather.Com

Leather and leatherworking/saddlery supplies, parts, and tools

President: Paul Weaver
Marketing Manager: Molly Wagner
Production Manager: Myron Stutzman
COO: Chris Weaver
International Marketing Manager: Chris Weaver
Buyers: Chris Miller
Credit Cards: MasterCard; Visa
Catalog Cost: Free
Catalog Circulation: Mailed 2 time(s) per year
Printing Information: 256 pages in 4 colors on Glossy Stock
Press: Web Press
Binding: Perfect Bound
Mailing List Information: Names for rent
List Manager: Suzette M Frank
In Business: 42 years
Number of Employees: 160
Sales Volume: $20MM to $50MM

Needlework

3932 A Child's Dream
A Child's Dream
214-A Cedar St.
Sand Point, ID 83864   208-255-1664
800-359-2906
Fax: 208-255-2656
info@achildsdream.com
www.achildsdream.com

100% wool felt; felting fibers and kits, Waldorf doll and toy making supplies, patterns and kits, dyes, natural yarns.

Credit Cards: MasterCard
Catalog Cost: $3
Catalog Circulation: Mailed 1 time(s) per year
Printing Information: 30 pages in 4 colors

3933 Annie's Attic Needlecraft
Annie's catalog
PO Box 8000
Big Sandy, TX 75755-2446   903-636-4303
800-282-6643
Fax: 800-882-6643
Customer_Service@AnniesCatalog.com
www.anniescatalog.com

Patterns and supplies for crochet, plastic canvas, cross-stitch, knitting, tatting and other needlecrafts

Manager: Tammie Godfrey
Buyers: Claudie Claussen
Credit Cards: AMEX; MasterCard
Catalog Circulation: Mailed 8 time(s) per year
Average Order Size: $25
Printing Information: 40 pages in 4 colors on Matte Stock
Press: Web Press
Binding: Saddle Stitched
Mailing List Information: Names for rent
In Business: 39 years
Number of Employees: 90
Sales Volume: $130,000

3934 Atlanta Thread & Supply
WAWAK Sewing
1059 Powers Road
Conklin, NY 13748   800-654-2235
Fax: 800-298-0403
customerservice@wawak.com
www.wawak.com

Sewing supplies, notions and pressing equipment

CFO: Allen Wootton
VP: Kirk Goggans
Credit Cards: AMEX; MasterCard; Visa
Catalog Cost: $1
In Business: 108 years
Number of Employees: 25
Sales Volume: $4,000,000

3935 Baglady Press
BagLady, Inc.
PO Box 240
Solon Springs, WI 54873-2409   303-670-2177
888-222-4523
Fax: 303-670-2179
support@shopatron.com
www.baglady.com

All the materials needed to create your own beaded handbag and evening size handbags

President: Jeffrey Williams
CFO: Theresa Williams
Credit Cards: MasterCard; Visa
Catalog Cost: Free
In Business: 8 years

3936 Basket Case Needlework Therapy
Creations
1013 Main Street
Kerrville, TX 78028   830-896-8088
creations@creations-online.com
www.creations-online.com

Needlework supplies

President: Nancy Huggins
Credit Cards: MasterCard; Visa
Catalog Cost: $3
Printing Information: 20 pages
In Business: 37 years
Number of Employees: 1

3937 Boutique Trims
Boutique Trims
21200 Pontiac Trail
South Lyon, MI 48178-9406   248-437-2017
                               Fax: 248-437-9463
                               info@btcrafts.com
                               www.Boutiquetrims.Com

Notions

President: Kevin Williams
In Business: 46 years
Sales Volume: $10MM to $20MM

3938 Brewer Sewing Supplies
Brewer Quilting & Sewing Supplies
3702 Prairie Lake Court
Aurora, IL 60504   630-820-5695
                                 800-676-6543
                               Fax: 630-851-2136
                               info@brewersewing.com
                               www.brewersewing.com

A wholesale/distributor of sewing machine parts, notions, fabrics, quilting supplies, and books

President: Jerry Smith
In Business: 101 years
Sales Volume: $10MM to $20MM

3939 Bucilla Stocking Kits
MerryStockings
160 1st St. SE
#5
New Brighton, MN 55112   888-764-2271
                               info@merrystockings.com
                               www.merrystockings.com

Bucilla felt Christmas stocking kits

3940 Busy Thimble Quilt Shop
Busy Thimble Quilt Shop
1213 E Nakoma Street
Litchfield, ME 04350-3836   207-268-4581
                               Fax: 207-268-2564
                               bsythmbl@fairpoint.net

Needlepoint yarn, fabrics, wool and felt materials, books, patterns, rug hooking supplies, and accessories

President: Cindy Black
Catalog Cost:

3941 Butterick
Butterick
120 Broadway
34th Floor
New York, NY 10271   butterick.mccall.com

Sewing patterns

President & CEO: Frank Rizzo
Catalog Cost: $30
Catalog Circulation: Mailed 4 time(s) per year
Printing Information: in 4 colors
Mailing List Information: Names for rent
List Company: Lake Group, The
411 Theodore Freund Avenue
Rye, NY 10580
914-925-2400
In Business: 146 years
Sales Volume: $40 Million

3942 Catherine Knits
Catherine Knits
544 77th Street
Brooklyn, NY 11209-3308   718-836-6439
                               www.catherineknits.com

Specializes in quality products for knitters and crocheters including books, buttons, crochet hooks, knitting needles, kits, patterns and yarn packs

President: Catherine Conrad
Credit Cards: MasterCard
Catalog Cost: $3

3943 Cedarburg Woolen Mill
Cedarburg Woolen Mill
W62 N580 Washington Avenue
Cedarburg, WI 53012-1926   262-377-5000
                               kaywltrs@gmail.com
                               www.cedarburgwoolenmill.com/

Custom wool processing and carding, as well as a large line of spinning, weaving, basketry, quilting and knitting supplies and equipment

President: Kay Walters
Credit Cards: MasterCard; Visa
Catalog Cost: Free
In Business: 151 years
Number of Employees: 10

3944 Clotilde, LLC
Annie's Catalog
PO Box 7500
Big Sandy, TX 75755-7500   903-636-4094
                                 800-545-4002
                               Fax: 800-863-3191
                               www.anniescatalog.com/

Sewing supplies and books

President: Nancy Laman
Credit Cards: AMEX; MasterCard
Catalog Cost: Free
Catalog Circulation: Mailed 5 time(s) per year
Printing Information: 100 pages in 4 colors
In Business: 40 years
Number of Employees: 5

3945 Clover
H.A. Kidd & Company Limited
5 Northline Road
Toronto, ON M4B-3P2   416-364-6451
                                 800-387-1753
                               Fax: 888-236-8204
                               info1@hakidd.com
                               www.hakidd.com

Knitting, crafing and embroidery supplies

Marketing Manager: Lynda Macham
VP, Chief operating Officer: Jim Thielen
Controller, Human Resources: Amir Mirza
Credit Cards: MasterCard
Catalog Cost: Free
Catalog Circulation: Mailed 1 time(s) per year
Printing Information: 48 pages in 4 colors
In Business: 93 years
Sales Volume: $20MM to $50MM

3946 Crafty Needle
Crafty Needle
PO Box 916010
Longwood, FL 32791-6010   321-214-4379
                                 800-345-3332
                               Fax: 321-206-3143
                               shop@craftyneedle.com
                               www.craftyneedle.com

Jewish needle crafts

President: Judy Rosenbaum
Production Manager: Dora Soulema
Credit Cards: AMEX; MasterCard; Visa
Catalog Circulation: Mailed 2 time(s) per year to 100
Average Order Size: $65
Printing Information: 40 pages in 4 colors on Newsprint
Press: Web Press
Binding: Saddle Stitched
Mailing List Information: Names for rent
List Company: AB Data
414-352-4404
Number of Employees: 8
Sales Volume: Under $500M

3947 Dana Marie Design Company
Dana Marie Design Company
2337 Hillview Ct.
Clarkston, WA 99403   360-653-0901
                                 888-455-5143
                               Fax: 360-653-0932
                               info@danamarie.com
                               www.danamarie.com

Artistic garment patterns, multisize from XS to 5XL, art stamps, sewing notions, fabrics

President: Dana Bontrager
Production Manager: Lynn Karn
Credit Cards: MasterCard
Catalog Cost:
Average Order Size: $40
Printing Information: 120 pages in 1 color on Glossy Stock
Binding: Perfect Bound
Mailing List Information: Names for rent
In Business: 31 years
Sales Volume: Under $500M

3948 Designs by Joan Green
Joan Green Designs
3897 Indian Ridge Woods
P.O.Box 715
Oxford, OH 45056   513-523-2690
                               Fax: 513-523-1520
                               info@joangreendesigns.com
                               www.joangreendesigns.com

Pattern books, kits and supplies for plastic canvas needle work

President: Joan L Green
Credit Cards: AMEX; MasterCard
Catalog Cost: Free
Catalog Circulation: Mailed 2 time(s) per year
Printing Information: 6 pages in 1 color
In Business: 30 years
Number of Employees: 1
Sales Volume: $60,000

3949 Dos De Tejas Patterns
Dos de Tejas / The Pattern Co.
PO Box 1636
Sherman, TX 75091-1636   800-883-5278
                                 800-883-5278
                               www.dosdetejas.com

Over 40 fashion patterns sized 6-24, instructional videos of classes, complete garment kits, Charlatan button kits

President: Karen Odam
Credit Cards: MasterCard
Catalog Cost: $2

3950 Ehrman Tapestry
Ehrman Tapestry
207 S. Cross Street
Suite 104
Chestertown, MD 21620-1510   410-810-3032
                                 888-826-8600
                               Fax: 410-810-3034
                               www.ehrmantapestry.com

Needlepoint kits from Britain

President: Marjorie Adams
Marketing Manager: US Branch, CEO
Credit Cards: AMEX; MasterCard
Catalog Cost: $5
Catalog Circulation: Mailed 1 time(s) per year
Average Order Size: $150
Printing Information: 31 pages in 4 colors on Glossy Stock
Binding: Perfect Bound
Mailing List Information: Names for rent
In Business: 30 years
Number of Employees: 2
Sales Volume: $82K

3951 Examplarery
The Examplarery
PO Box 2554
Dearborn, MI 48123-2554   313-278-3282
                               Fax: 910-892-3024

Reproduction samplers, crewel designs, fabrics and needlework accessories and books

President: Joanne Harvey
Catalog Cost: $4

3952 Folkwear

Folkwear
The Old Fire Station
Box 189
Barnardsville, NC 28709-189   828-626-3100
                                888-200-9099
                           Fax: 828-626-3030
                           mail@folkwear.com
                           www.folkwear.com

Sewing patterns adapted from traditional ethnic costumes and vintage fashions from around the world, multi-size patterns for men, women and children, with instructions and lore regarding embellishment

President: Kate Mathews
Production Manager: Val Anderson
Cover Illustrator: Gretchen Sheilds
Pattern Designer: Lisa Sanders
Pattern Tester: Elizabeth George
Credit Cards: MasterCard; Visa
Catalog Cost: $3
Printing Information: 28 pages
In Business: 44 years

3953 Fry Designs of Plastic Canvas Patterns

Fry Designs
PO Box 1079
Winchester, OR 97495-1079   541-672-5863
                              888-753-2339
                         Fax: 780-753-3512

Over 250 original plastic-canvas needle-point patterns: tissue box covers, toothpick holders, samplers

President: Gail Fry
Marketing Manager: Vicki Fry
Mailing List Information: Names for rent
In Business: 25 years
Number of Employees: 2

3954 Ghee's

Ghee's
P.O. Box 4424
Shreveport, LA 71134-2479   318-226-1701
                         Fax: 318-226-1781
                              bags@ghees.com
                              www.Ghees.Com

Handbag making supplies, metal frames in a variety of sizes and shapes, magnetic closures, chains, handbag accessories, handbag and vest patterns, books on fabric manipulation

President: Linda Mc Gehee
Credit Cards: MasterCard
Catalog Cost: $1
In Business: 20 years

3955 Graham Embroidery

Graham Embroidery
300 South Valley Mills Drive
Waco, TX 76710   888-996-8678
                        Fax: 888-996-8693
                        grahamembroidery.com

Embroidered products.

3956 GⅢTermann Creative

H.A. Kidd & Company Limited
5 Northline Road
Toronto, ON M4B-3P2   416-364-6451
                              800-387-1753
                         Fax: 888-236-8204
                              info1@hakidd.com
                              www.hakidd.com

Thread, embroidery floss, tools and supplies

Marketing Manager: Lynda Macham
VP, Chief Operating Officer: Jim Thielen

Controller, Human Resources: Amir Mirza
Credit Cards: MasterCard
Catalog Cost: Free
Printing Information: 36 pages in 4 colors
In Business: 93 years
Sales Volume: $20MM to $50MM

3957 Harriets

Harriets
1 N Nabby Road
Danbury, CT 06811-3320   203-730-2122
                          Fax: 203-599-1863
                          tcs.info@harriets.com
                          www.harriets.com

Over 200 vintage patterns for men, women and children, XL sizes available; Circa 1300-1945, 8 styles of hoops, corsets, boning, fabric, 100% polished cotton and silks, rentals and accessories

President: Harriet A Engler
Business Manager and Webmaster: Lynda Engler
Credit Cards: AMEX; MasterCard
Catalog Cost: $16

3958 Heirloom Lace

Knitted Heirloom Lace
109 W 4th St
Hermann, MO 65041-1001   573-486-2162
                          knitlace@mchsi.com
                          www.knitlacepatterns.com

Lace knitting patterns and knitted outfits for bears; pattern search service

President: Gloria Penning
In Business: 0 years

3959 Herrschners

Herrschners
2800 Hoover Road
Stevens Point, WI 54481   800-713-1239
                          Fax: 715-341-2250
                          customerservice@herrschners.com
                          www.herrschners.com

Needlecraft kits and supplies

President: Theodore Hesemann
CFO: Jeff Hesemann
Production Manager: Gloriann Doyle
VP, Operations: James Cisewski
Manager: Gretchen Trautman
Credit Cards: AMEX; MasterCard; Visa
Catalog Cost: Free
Printing Information: 64 pages
In Business: 114 years
Number of Employees: 200
Sales Volume: $25,000,000

3960 Home Sew

Home Sew, Inc.
1825 W Market Street
P.O. Box 4099
Bethlehem, PA 18018   610-867-3833
                              800-344-4739
                          Fax: 610-867-9717
                          customerservice@homesew.com
                          www.homesew.com

Sewing and crafts supplies with dicounts up to 60% off retail; Threads, zippers, lace, trims, elastic, quilting supplies, buttons, doll accessories and more

President: Mark A. Dammeyer
Marketing Manager: Allen Dammeyer
Production Manager: Mary Seng
Fulfillment: Ashley Morin
Buyers: Mark Dammeyer
Average Order Size: $30
Printing Information: in 4 colors
Mailing List Information: Names for rent
In Business: 50 years
Number of Employees: 25
Sales Volume: $1MM to $3MM

3961 Just Needlin'

Just Needlin'
PO Box 3805
Olathe, KS 66063-1900   913-709-9080
                          www.justneedlin.com/

3962 Keepsake Needle Arts

PO Box 1618
Center Harbor, NH 03226   800-852-7338
                          Fax: 800-340-1757
                          customerservice@keepsakeneedlearts.com
                          www.keepsakeneedlearts.com

Needlepoint and cross stitch kits and patterns.

Customer Service: Maggie Fuentes

3963 Klass,

H.A. Kidd & Company Limited
5 Northline Road
Toronto, ON M4B-3P2   416-364-6451
                              800-387-1753
                         Fax: 888-236-8104
                              info1@hakidd.com
                              www.hakidd.com

Pins and sewing machine needles

Marketing Manager: Lynda Macham
VP, Chief Operating Officer: Jim Thielen
Controller, Human Resources: Amir Mirza
Credit Cards: MasterCard
Catalog Cost: Free
Printing Information: 16 pages in 4 colors
In Business: 93 years
Sales Volume: $20MM to $50MM

3964 Knit Picks

Knit Picks
13118 NE 4th Street
Vancouver, WA 98684   360-260-8900
                              800-574-1323
                         Fax: 360-260-8877
                          customerservice@knitpicks.com
                          www.knitpicks.com

Luxury knitting yarn, needles, books, kits and patterns

President: Bob Petkun
CFO: Carla Salazar
Marketing Manager: Jenny K
Production Manager: Diane Miller
Fulfillment: Kara Tripp
CEO: Matt
Purchasing Director: Diedre
Graphic Designer: Emily G
Catalog Circulation: to 1.3M
Average Order Size: $50
Printing Information: 38 pages in 4 colors on Glossy Stock
Press: Sheetfed Press
Binding: Folded
Mailing List Information: Names for rent
List Manager: Bob Petkun
In Business: 7 years
Number of Employees: 100
Sales Volume: $10MM to $20MM

3965 Knitting Basket

Knitting Basket
5611 Grove Avenue
Richmond, VI 23226   804-282-2909
                              800-252-YARN
                          www.knittingbasket.com

Packaged yarns and patterns

President: Irene York
Catalog Cost: Free
In Business: 32 years

3966 Kwik Sew

Kwik Sew
120 Broadway
34th Floor
New York, NY 10271   kwiksew.mccall.com

Sewing patterns

President & CEO: Frank Rizzo
Catalog Cost: $36
Printing Information: in 4 colors
Mailing List Information: Names for rent
List Company: Lake Group, The
411 Theodore Freund Avenue
Rye, NY 10580
914-925-2400
In Business: 146 years
Sales Volume: $40 Million

3967 Lacis
Lacis
3163 Adeline St
Berkeley, CA 94703-2401   510-843-7178
Fax: 510-843-5018
www.lacis.com

Books, tools and materials for the textile arts with emphasis on the crafts of lace, embroidery, tatting, braiding, weaving, beadwork and costume

President: Jules Kliot
General Manager: Perrin Kliot
Manager: Erin Algeo
Buyers: Kaethe Kliot
Credit Cards: MasterCard; Visa
Catalog Circulation: Mailed 1 time(s) per year to 6000
Average Order Size: $60
Printing Information: 90 pages in 4 colors on Matte Stock
Press: Letterpress
Binding: Folded
Mailing List Information: Names for rent
In Business: 48 years
Number of Employees: 9
Sales Volume: $346,000

3968 Mary Maxim
Mary Maxim
2001 Holland Avenue
P.O. Box 5019
Port Huron, MI 48061-5019   810-987-2000
800-962-9504
Fax: 810-987-5056
info@marymaxim.com
www.marymaxim.com

Crochet, knitting and needlework patterns and supplies

President: Rusty McPhedrain
CFO: Tom Jackson
Credit Cards: AMEX; MasterCard; Visa
Catalog Cost: Free
Printing Information: in 4 colors
In Business: 61 years
Number of Employees: 128
Sales Volume: $36.5 Million

3969 McCall's
McCall's
120 Broadway
34th Floor
New York, NY 10271 mccallpattern.mccall.com

Sewing patterns

President & CEO: Frank Rizzo
Catalog Cost: $30
Printing Information: in 4 colors
Mailing List Information: Names for rent
List Company: Lake Group, The
411 Theodore Freund Avenue
Rye, NY 10580
914-925-2400
In Business: 146 years
Sales Volume: $40 Million

3970 McCall's Patterns
McCall Pattern Company
120 Broadway
34th Floor
New York, NY 10271   800-782-0323
Fax: 212-465-6814
www.mccallpattern.com

Textiles and patterns

President: Robin Davies
CFO: John Kobiskie
Marketing Manager: Joe Anselmo
Credit Cards: MasterCard; Visa
Catalog Cost: $30
Catalog Circulation: Mailed 6 time(s) per year
Printing Information: 64 pages in 4 colors
Binding: Perfect Bound
In Business: 140 years
Number of Employees: 200

3971 Nancy's Notions
Nancy's Notions
333 Beichl Ave
PO Box 683
Beaver Dam, WI 53916-683   920-887-0391
800-833-0690
Fax: 920-887-2133
custserv@nancysnotions.com
www.nancysnotions.com

Sewing supplies, quilting supplies, machine embroidery supplies and designs, patterns, books, DVDs, fabrics, and kits

President: Katherine Johnson
Production Manager: Kathy Gittus
Fulfillment: John Nickel
Owner/President: Nancy L Zieman
Buyers: Chris Stam
Credit Cards: AMEX; MasterCard
Catalog Cost: Free
Catalog Circulation: Mailed 13 time(s) per year
Printing Information: 70 pages in 4 colors on Matte Stock
Press: Web Press
Binding: Saddle Stitched
Mailing List Information: Names for rent
List Company: Zed Marketing
416 Autmnwood Court
Edmond, OK 73003
405-348-8145
In Business: 35 years
Sales Volume: $10MM to $20MM

3972 Nordic Needle
Nordic Needle, Inc
1314 Gateway Drive SW
Fargo, ND 58103-3596   701-235-5231
800-433-4321
Fax: 701-235-0952
info@nordicneedle.com
www.nordicneedle.com

Catalog of Hardanger embroidery, cross stitch, blackwork, tatting, huck embroidery, Brazilian embroidery and all other needlecraft supplies, kits and patterns

President: Susan Meier
CFO: Roz Watnem
Operations Manager: Duane Hill
Product Ordering And Management: Diane
Marketing Coordinator: Debi
Credit Cards: MasterCard; Visa
Catalog Cost: Free
Catalog Circulation: Mailed 3 time(s) per year to 180K
Printing Information: 48 pages in 4 colors on Glossy Stock
Press: Web Press
Binding: Saddle Stitched
Mailing List Information: Names for rent
In Business: 37 years
Number of Employees: 21
Sales Volume: $3.5 Million

3973 Ribbon Factory Outlet
The Ribbon Factory
600 North Brown Street
PO Box 405
Titusville, PA 16354-405   814-827-6431
866-827-6431
Fax: 814-827-4191
ribbon@ribbonfactory.com
www.ribbonfactory.com

Ribbons galore

President: David Steinbuhler
Marketing Manager: Chris Barrett
Production Manager: Chase Steinbuhler
Credit Cards: AMEX; MasterCard; Visa
Catalog Cost: Free
Printing Information: in 3 colors
In Business: 116 years
Number of Employees: 30
Sales Volume: $3.90 Million

3974 Richard the Thread
Richard The Thread
1960 S. La Cienega Blvd.
Los Angeles, CA 90034   310-837-4997
800-473-4997
Fax: 310-836-4996
www.richardthethread.com

Specialty sewing and costume supplies

President: Herb Braha
Manager: Lois Munera
Catalog Cost: $3
Printing Information: 30 pages in 4 colors on Glossy Stock
Mailing List Information: Names for rent
In Business: 58 years
Number of Employees: 5
Sales Volume: Under $500M

3975 Robison-Anton Textile
Robison-Anton Textile Company
24 American Street
PO Box 507
Mount Holly, NC 28120   704-827-4311
800-847-3235
Fax: 800-847-3236
salesRA@amefird.com
www.robison-anton.com

Decorative thread and yarn for embroidery and monogramming

Printing Information: in 4 colors
In Business: 115 years

3976 Roclith Creations
Roclith Blankets
238 Crimson Lane
Petersburgh, WV 26847-9409   304-749-7754
800-240-5484
Fax: 304-749-7654
roclith@roclith.com

Keyto Knitlite knitting machine light, adjustable clamp on, with triphosphor fluorescent tube, output equivalent to 250W incandescent bulb

In Business: 15 years

3977 Rose Brand
Rose Brand
4 Emerson Lane
Secaucus, NJ 07094-2661   201-809-1730
800-223-1624
Fax: 201-809-1851
info@rosebrand.com
www.rosebrand.com

Fabrics and custom draperies for theaters, churches, school, events and entertainment venues

President: George Jacobson
CFO: Peter Finder
Marketing Manager: Mary Vandaver
Production Manager: Bob Betrand
Product Manager: Mark O'Brien
Graphic Designer: Kelly Salvadore
General Manager: Tina Carlin
International Marketing Manager: Vicki Williamson
Catalog Cost: Free
Printing Information: 96 pages in 4 colors on Glossy Stock
Press: Web Press
Binding: Saddle Stitched
Mailing List Information: Names for rent
In Business: 102 years

Number of Employees: 150
Sales Volume: Under $500M

3978 Sailrite Home Catalog
Sailrite Enterprises, Inc.
2390 E 100 S
Columbia City, IN 46725   260-244-4647
                            800-348-2769
                            Fax: 260-818-2005
                            info@sailrite.com
                            www.sailrite.com

Home sewing machines, fabrics, and supplies

President: Matt Grant
Co-Owner: Hallie Grant
Catalog Cost: Free
Catalog Circulation: Mailed 1 time(s) per year
Printing Information: 260 pages in 4 colors
In Business: 48 years
Number of Employees: 12

3979 Scarlet Letter
Scarlet Letter company
4640 Lankershim Blvd
Suite 120
N. Hollywood, CA 91602-397   262-593-8470
                               818-760-9595
                    Info@scarletletterstitles.com

Reproduction sampler kits, Books, Lines, Antiques and accessories

President: Marsha Van Valin
Owner: Marsha Parker
Credit Cards: AMEX; MasterCard; Visa
Catalog Cost: $10
Catalog Circulation: Mailed 2 time(s) per year
Printing Information: in 4 colors
In Business: 31 years
Number of Employees: 2
Sales Volume: Under $500M

3980 Schmetz Nadeln
H.A. Kidd & Company Limited
5 Northline Road
Toronto, ON M4B-3P2   416-364-6451
                        800-387-1753
                        Fax: 888-236-8204
                        info1@hakidd.com
                        www.hakidd.com

Pins and needles for sewing and quilting projects

Marketing Manager: Lynda Macham
VP, Chief operating Officer: Jim Thielen
Controller, Human Resources: Amir Mirza
Credit Cards: MasterCard
Catalog Cost: Free
Printing Information: 28 pages in 4 colors
In Business: 93 years
Sales Volume: $20MM to $50MM

3981 Stitchery Catalog
Laurel's Stitchery
P.O. Box 3332
Suite 203
Chelmsford, MA 01824-0932   800-388-9662
                              877-758-6946
                              Fax: 800-866-3235
                              help@thestitchery.com
                              www.stitchery.com

Cross stitch kits, needlepoint stitchery kits, embroidery kits, projects and needlecraft tools

Buyers: Mariann Rand
Credit Cards: AMEX; MasterCard; Visa
Catalog Cost: Free
Mailing List Information: Names for rent
Will Trade Names: Yes
List Company: Old Colony Advertising
120 N Meadows Road
Medfield, MA 02052
508-359-4649
In Business: 0 years
Number of Employees: 42
Sales Volume: $10MM to $20MM

3982 Sudberry House
Sudberry House, LLC
323 Boston Post Road #3
Old Saybrook, CT 06475   860-388-9045
                    sales@sudberry.com
                    www.sudberry.com

Fine wood accessories for displaying needlework - trays, footstools, clocks, mirrors and many boxes, including New England shaker and new music jewelry

President: Judy Beers
CFO: David Beers
Catalog Cost: $2.5
Catalog Circulation: to 300
Printing Information: 20 pages in 4 colors on Glossy Stock
Binding: Saddle Stitched
Mailing List Information: Names for rent
In Business: 48 years
Number of Employees: 7
Sales Volume: $500,000

3983 Vogue Patterns
Vogue Patterns
120 Broadway
34th Floor
New York, NY 10271 voguepatterns.mccall.com

Designer sewing patterns

President & CEO: Frank Rizzo
Catalog Cost: $36
Printing Information: in 4 colors
Mailing List Information: Names for rent
List Company: Lake Group, The
411 Theodore Freund Avenue
Rye, NY 10580
914-925-2400
In Business: 146 years
Sales Volume: $40 Million

3984 WEBS - America's Yarn Store
WEBS-America's Yarn Store
75 Service Center Road
Northampton, MA 01060   800-367-9327
                          Fax: 413-584-1603
                    customerservice@yarn.com
                          www.yarn.com

Yarns, weaving looms & equipment, spinning wheels, fibers and books

In Business: 41 years

3985 Web-Sters
The Websters
11 N Main Street
Ashland, OR 97520-2725   541-482-9801
                           800-482-9801
                    www.yarnatwebsters.com

Extensive line of yarns, looms, spinning wheels, raw materials, books, dyes and tools for handweavers, knitters and spinners

President: Annette Dahlquist
CFO: Dona Zimmerman
Credit Cards: AMEX; MasterCard
Catalog Cost: Free
Printing Information: 40 pages
In Business: 31 years
Number of Employees: 5

3986 Wimpole Street Creations
Wimpole Street, Inc.
445 N 700 W
Ste 110
North Salt Lake, UT 84054-2603   801-298-0504
                                 800-765-0504
                                 Fax: 801-298-1333
                    friends@wimpolestreet.com
                    www.Wimpolestreet.Com

Table linens for special occasions and everyday, dishtowels, napkins and table accessories, lace and lace details, gifts, items for baby and wedding celebrations, home decor

President: Jeen Brown
Marketing Manager: Christi Parry
Fulfillment: Jeen Brown
Credit Cards: MasterCard
Catalog Cost: $3
Catalog Circulation: Mailed 12 time(s) per year
Average Order Size: $80
Printing Information: on Glossy Stock
Press: Sheetfed Press
Mailing List Information: Names for rent
In Business: 21 years
Number of Employees: 20
Sales Volume: $1MM to $3MM

3987 Yarn Basket
Yarn Basket
150 Falling Spring Rd
Chambersburg, PA 17202-9001   717-263-3236
                              888-976-2758
                    sales@yarnbasketpa.com
                    www.Yarnbasketpa.Com

Yarn

President: S Yeager
Sales Volume: $500M to $1MM

Pottery

3988 Axner Company
Axner Pottery Supply
490 Kane Ct
Oviedo, FL 32765-7851   407-365-2600
                          800-843-7057
                          Fax: 407-365-5573
                          axner@axner.com
                          www.axner.Com

Kilns & furnaces, potters wheels, tools and brushes

President: Howard Axner
Marketing Manager: Rosanne Sloane
In Business: 37 years
Sales Volume: $3MM to $5MM

3989 Bailey Ceramic Supply & Pottery Equipment
Bailey Pottery Equipment Corporation
62-68 Tenbroeck Avenue
Kingston, NY 12402   845-339-3721
                       800-431-6067
                       Fax: 845-339-5530
                       info@baileypottery.com
                       www.baileypottery.com

Pottery equipment, kilns, glazes and clay

President: Jim Bailey
CFO: Anne Bailey
Credit Cards: MasterCard; Visa
Catalog Cost: Free
Printing Information: 186 pages
In Business: 39 years

3990 Cedar Mesa Pottery
Cedar Mesa Products Co.
333 South Main St.
Blanding, UT 84511   800-235-7687
                       www.cmpottery.com

Native American style pottery

3991 Ceramic Supply of New York & New Jersey
Ceramic Supply, Inc.
7 Route 46 West
Lodi, NJ 07644-1317   800-723-7264
                        Fax: 973-340-0089
                    orders@eceramicsupply.com
                        www.7ceramic.Com

Ceramic and pottery supplies and equipment: kilns, wheels, tools, glazes, bruchers, lamp parts, clay, etc

President: Mariam Vogelman
VP: Turnbull Crham
Programming Director: Craig Nutt
Buyers: Miriam Vogelman, Hobby Supplies

Judy Noe, Pottery Supplies
Credit Cards: MasterCard; Visa
Catalog Cost: Free
Catalog Circulation: Mailed 1 time(s) per year
Printing Information: 136 pages in 1 color on Matte Stock
Press: Web Press
Binding: Perfect Bound
Mailing List Information: Names for rent
In Business: 27 years
Number of Employees: 20-O
Sales Volume: $160,000

3992 Cheap Joe's Art Stuff
374 Industrial Park Dr.
Boone, NC 28607   828-262-0793
     888-771-9509
Fax: 800-257- 087
info@cheapjoes.com
www.cheapjoes.com

Paints, brushes, canvas, papers, easels, drawing tools, other art supplies

Owner: Joe Miller

3993 Chile Shop
The Chile Shop
109 E Water St
Santa Fe, NM 87501-2132   505-983-6080
Fax: 505-984-0737
info@thechileshop.com
www.thechileshop.com

Southwest items; chile powders, herbs, Mimbreno China, petroglyph pottery, sand etched crystal, aprons, Seven Kilborn pottery

President: Jacque Beck
Credit Cards: MasterCard; Visa
Catalog Cost: Free
Catalog Circulation: Mailed 1 time(s) per year
Average Order Size: $75
Printing Information: 16 pages in 1 color on Matte Stock
Press: Web Press
Binding: Saddle Stitched
Mailing List Information: Names for rent
In Business: 26 years
Number of Employees: 6
Sales Volume: $150,000

3994 Clay Factory of Escondido
Clay Factory Inc
PO Box 460598
Escondido, CA 92046-598   760-741-3242
     877-728-5739
Fax: 760-741-5436
info@clayfactory.net
www.clayfactory.net

Sculpy products, Granitex, Elasticlay, Cernit, Pearl Powders, Kemper tools and videos by Maureen Carlson, Marie Segal, Tory Hughes and Donna Kato

President: Howard Segal
Credit Cards: AMEX; MasterCard
Catalog Cost: Free
In Business: 34 years
Number of Employees: 2
Sales Volume: $1,000,000

3995 Clay In Motion
Clay In Motion, Inc.
85301 Hwy 11
Milton-Freewater, OR 97862   541-938-3316
Fax: 541-938-3004
www.clayinmotion.com

Hand-made pottery.

3996 Compleat Sculptor
The Compleat Sculptor, Inc.
90 Vandam Street
New York, NY 10013-1007   212-243-6074
     800-972-8578
Fax: 212-243-6374
tcs@sculpt.com
www.Sculpt.Com

Largest selection of stone, wood, clay molding and casting materials, backup services, mold-making/casting, finishing and mounting, show installation and photography

President: Marc Fields
CFO: David Fields
Marketing Manager: Heather Droak
Production Manager: Heather Droak
COO: Marc
Inventory Manager: Brandon
Sales Associate: Evelyn
Buyers: Kenard Kosima
Credit Cards: AMEX; MasterCard
Catalog Cost: $5
Catalog Circulation: Mailed 1 time(s) per year
Average Order Size: $150
Printing Information: 118 pages in 4 colors on Glossy Stock
Press: Web Press
Binding: Perfect Bound
Mailing List Information: Names for rent
In Business: 20 years
Number of Employees: 12
Sales Volume: $1MM to $3MM

3997 Deneen Pottery
Deneen Pottery
2325 Endicott St.
St. Paul, MN 55114   651-646-0238
     888-646-0238
Fax: 651-646-8605
www.deneenpottery.com

High quality, custom, hand-made mugs.

3998 Easy Fire Kilns
L&L Kiln Mfg., Inc.
505 Sharptown Rd.
Swedesboro, NJ 08085   856-294-0077
     800-750-8350
Fax: 856-294-0070
service@hotkilns.com
www.hotkilns.com

Electric kilns for schools, hobbyists and artists.

President: Stephen Lewicki
Catalog Cost: Free
Printing Information: 8 pages
Mailing List Information: Names for rent
In Business: 56 years
Number of Employees: 25

3999 Ephraim Pottery
Ephraim Pottery
203 W. Lake St.
Lake Mills, WI 53551   920-648-5269
     888-704-7687
Fax: 920-648-5357
ephriam.office@gmail.com
www.ephraimpottery.com

Heirloom-quality, arts and crafts style art pottery and decorative accessories.

4000 Gainey Ceramics
1200 Arrow Highway
La Verne, CA 91750   909-593-3533
Fax: 909-593-0488

Ceramics and pottery

Founder: John Gainey

4001 Heat Treating & America's Finest
Cress Mfg. Company
4736 Convair Drive
Carson City, NV 89706-493   775-884-2777
     800-423-4584
Fax: 775-884-2991
info@cressmfg.com
www.cressmfg.com

Heat treating furnaces and kilns for ceramics, glass, pottery, etc

President: Steve Cress
Mailing List Information: Names for rent
In Business: 42 years

4002 Paragon Kilns
Paragon Industries L.P.
2011 South Town East Blvd.
Mesquite, TX 75149   972-288-7557
     888-222-6450
Fax: 972-222-0646
info@paragonweb.com
www.paragonweb.com

Electric kilns and furnaces for commerical and hobby applications

4003 Potting Shed
Hareloom,Inc
PO Box 1287
Concord, MA 01742-1287   978-369-1382
     800-RAB-BITS
Fax: 978-369-1416
theoldgrayhare@harelooms.com
www.harelooms.com

19th century pottery

President: Richard Starr
Credit Cards: AMEX; MasterCard
Catalog Cost: $6
In Business: 119 years
Number of Employees: 50
Sales Volume: $3MM to $5MM

4004 Tait Farm Foods
Tait Farm Foods
179 Tait Road
Centre Hall, PA 16828   814-466-2386
info@taitfarmfoods.com
www.taitfarmfoods.com

Gifts from the Land, including local foods, works of local artisans, and inspirations for the kitchen, home and garden.

In Business: 65 years

4005 The Potters Shed
The Potter's Shed
260 Industrial Blvd.
Shell Lake, WI 54871   715-468-4122
     800-850-8880
Fax: 715-468-4123
spoonercreek@centurytel.net
www.thepottersshed.com

Pottery, make your own mosaic, paint your own pottery.

4006 Westerwald Pottery
Westerwald Pottery
40 Pottery Lane
Scenery Hill, PA 15360   724-945-6000
Fax: 724-945-5139
potterywest@yahoo.com
www.westerwaldpottery.com

Westerwald offered potential customers the opportunity to order products that could be inscribed with specific names, dates, images etc

In Business: 42 years

Quilting

4007 Airtex Consumer Products
Airtex
150 Industrial Park Road
Cokato, MN 55321-4271 800-851-8887
Fax: 320-286-2428
customerservice@airtex.com
www.airtex.com

Filling products, polyester fiberfill, quilt batting, pillow forms, and foam and cotton quilt batting

President: Dale Kautz
Credit Cards: MasterCard
In Business: 71 years
Number of Employees: 350
Sales Volume: $155 million

4008 Bella Taylor
Victorian Heart Company, Inc.
P.O. Box 17
Kirbyville, MO 65679 888-334-3099
Fax: 417-973-0423
info@vhcbrands.com
www.vhcbrands.com

Quilted handbags, purses, and backpacks

Chairman: Billy Kline
President: Kenneth Kline
Key Accont Manager: Josh Ellig
Mid-Atlantic Central Account: David Brown
dbrown@vhcbrands.com
Sales Manager: Joe Morimoto
jmorimoto@vhcbrands.com
Catalog Cost: Free
Catalog Circulation: Mailed 1 time(s) per year
Printing Information: 78 pages in 4 colors
In Business: 21 years
Number of Employees: 25
Sales Volume: $3.3 Million

4009 Buffalo Batt & Felt Company
Polyester Fibres
3307 Walden Avenue
Depew, NY 14043-2347 716-683-4100
Fax: 716-683-8928
info@poly-fibers.com
www.Buffalobatt.Com

Quilt batting and pillow inserts

Plant Manager: Jeff Horvatits
Nancy Karaszweski
Credit Cards: MasterCard; Visa
Catalog Cost: $2
Printing Information: 2 pages in 1 color
In Business: 100 years
Number of Employees: 550

4010 Button Basics
H.A. Kidd & Company Limited
5 Northline Road
Toronto, ON M4B-3P2 416-364-6451
800-387-1753
Fax: 888-236-8204
info1@hakidd.com
www.hakidd.com

Buttons for sewing and craft projects

Marketing Manager: Lynda Macham
VP, Chief Operating Officer: Jim Thielen
Controller, Human Resources: Amir Mirza
Credit Cards: MasterCard
Catalog Cost: Free
Printing Information: 8 pages in 4 colors
In Business: 93 years

4011 Clover
H.A. Kidd & Company Limited
5 Northline Road
Toronto, ON M4B-3P2 416-364-6451
800-387-1753
Fax: 888-236-8204
info1@hakidd.com
www.hakidd.com

Knitting, crafing and embroidery supplies

Marketing Manager: Lynda Macham
VP, Chief operating Officer: Jim Thielen
Controller, Human Resources: Amir Mirza
Credit Cards: MasterCard
Catalog Cost: Free
Catalog Circulation: Mailed 1 time(s) per year
Printing Information: 48 pages in 4 colors
In Business: 93 years
Sales Volume: $20MM to $50MM

4012 Connecting Threads
Connecting Threads
13118 NE 4th Street
Vancouver, WA 98684 360-260-8900
800-574-6454
Fax: 360-260-8877
customerservice@connectingthreads.com
www.connectingthreads.com

Quilting fabrics, thread, tools, books, and kits

Chairman: Bob Petkun
President: Matt Petkun
VP & Creative Director: Kelley Petkun
Credit Cards: AMEX; MasterCard; Visa
Catalog Cost: Free
Catalog Circulation: Mailed 12 time(s) per year to 2M
Average Order Size: $50
Printing Information: 64 pages in 4 colors on Glossy Stock
Press: Sheetfed Press
Binding: Folded
Mailing List Information: Names for rent
List Manager: Bob Petkun
In Business: 21 years
Number of Employees: 80
Sales Volume: $8.8 Million

4013 Fabrics Catalog
H.A. Kidd & Company Limited
5 Northline Road
Toronto, ON M4B-3P2 416-364-6451
800-387-1753
Fax: 888-236-8104
info1@hakidd.com
www.hakidd.com

Assorted fabrics

Marketing Manager: Lynda Macham
VP, Chief Operating Officer: Jim Thielen
Controller, Human Resources: Amir Mirza
Credit Cards: MasterCard
Catalog Cost: Free
Catalog Circulation: Mailed 4 time(s) per year
Printing Information: 28 pages in 4 colors
In Business: 93 years
Sales Volume: $20MM to $50MM

4014 Fairfield Processing
Fairfield
PO Box 1157
88 Rose Hill Avenue
Danbury, CT 06813-1157 203-744-2090
800-243-0989
Fax: 203-792-9710
sales@fairfieldworld.com
www.fairfieldworld.com

Products for home sewing, quilt and craft industries, Poly-fil, Soft Touch, and Crafters Choice brand fiberfill plus quilt pattern books, batting and more

President: Jordan Young
Marketing Manager: Judy Novella
CEO: Robert Young
Credit Cards: MasterCard
In Business: 75 years

4015 Inspire
H.A. Kidd & Company Limited
5 Northline Road
Toronto, ON M4B-3P2 416-364-6451
800-387-1753
Fax: 888-236-8204
info1@hakidd.com
www.hakidd.com

Buttons for sewing and other crafting projects

Marketing Manager: Lynda Macham
VP, Chief Operating Officer: Jim Thielen
Controller, Human Resources: Amir Mirza
Credit Cards: MasterCard
Catalog Cost: Free
Catalog Circulation: Mailed 4 time(s) per year
Printing Information: 20 pages in 4 colors
In Business: 93 years
Sales Volume: $20MM to $50MM

4016 Keepsake Quilting
Keepsake Quilting
P.O. Box 1618
Center Harbor, NH 03226 603-253-8731
800-525-8086
Fax: 603-253-8731
customerservice@keepsakequilting.com
www.keepsakequilting.com

Cotton fabric, notions, books, patterns, etc., for quilting

President: Rob O'Brian
CFO: Nancy Joyce
Marketing Manager: Melissa Howley
Credit Cards: MasterCard; Visa
Catalog Cost: Free
Printing Information: 66 pages in 4 colors
Mailing List Information: Names for rent
In Business: 31 years
Number of Employees: 12
Sales Volume: $10MM to $20MM

4017 Klass,
H.A. Kidd & Company Limited
5 Northline Road
Toronto, ON M4B-3P2 416-364-6451
800-387-1753
Fax: 888-236-8104
info1@hakidd.com
www.hakidd.com

Pins and sewing machine needles

Marketing Manager: Lynda Macham
VP, Chief Operating Officer: Jim Thielen
Controller, Human Resources: Amir Mirza
Credit Cards: MasterCard
Catalog Cost: Free
Printing Information: 16 pages in 4 colors
In Business: 93 years
Sales Volume: $20MM to $50MM

4018 Nustyle Quilting Machines and Supplies
Nustyle
309 W 4th St, Stover
Stover, MO 65078 573-377-2244
800-821-7490
Fax: 573-377-2833
info@nustylequilting.com
www.nustylequilting.com

Long arm quilting machines and frames, hand quilting frames, large rolls Dacron and cotton batt, sewing and quilting books, supplies, tools, over 4,000 bolts of fabric

Owner: Tom Dale
Owner: Lora Dale
Credit Cards: MasterCard
Average Order Size: $70
Printing Information: 12 pages in 1 color on Newsprint
Press: Sheetfed Press
Mailing List Information: Names for rent
In Business: 139 years
Number of Employees: 4
Sales Volume: Under $500M

4019 Oklee Quilting
Oklee Quilting
128 S Main Street
PO Box 279
Oklee, MN 56742-279   218-796-5151
                             800-777-7403
                        Fax: 218-796-4601
                  okleequilt@gvtel.com
                  www.okleequiltinginc.com

Quilt batting, broadcloth, pillow forms and stuffing, quilting prints and notions

President: Toni Johnson
Credit Cards: MasterCard; Visa
Catalog Cost: Free
Catalog Circulation: Mailed 2 time(s) per year to 6000
Printing Information: 1 pages in 7 colors on Matte Stock
Binding: Folded
In Business: 22 years
Number of Employees: 5
Sales Volume: Under $500M

4020 Quilt Kit Catalog
Hearthside Quilts
207 E Depot St
PO Box 864
Bedford, VA 24523-610   802-482-7800
                             800-451-3533
                        Fax: 802-482-7803
                  hearthsidequilts@att.net
                  www.hearthsidequilts.com

Assortment of quilt kits, fabrics and quilting frames

President: George Wachob
Credit Cards: AMEX; MasterCard
Catalog Cost: $2
Catalog Circulation: Mailed 1 time(s) per year to 12500
Printing Information: 32 pages in 4 colors on Glossy Stock
Press: Offset Press
Binding: Folded
Mailing List Information: Names for rent
In Business: 34 years
Number of Employees: 15

4021 Schmetz Nadeln
H.A. Kidd & Company Limited
5 Northline Road
Toronto, ON M4B-3P2   416-364-6451
                             800-387-1753
                        Fax: 888-236-8204
                  info1@hakidd.com
                  www.hakidd.com

Pins and needles for sewing and quilting projects

Marketing Manager: Lynda Macham
VP, Chief operating Officer: Jim Thielen
Controller, Human Resources: Amir Mirza
Credit Cards: MasterCard
Catalog Cost: Free
Printing Information: 28 pages in 4 colors
In Business: 93 years
Sales Volume: $20MM to $50MM

4022 The Electric Quilt Company
The Electric Quilt Company
419 Gould St.
Suite 2
Bowling Green, OH 43402-3047 419-352-1134
                        Fax: 419-352-4332
                  customerservice@electricquilt.com
                  www.electricquilt.com

Software, books and printables for quilters.

4023 VHC Brands
Victorian Heart Company, Inc.
P.O. Box 17
Kirbyville, MO 65679   888-334-3099
                        Fax: 417-973-0423
                  info@vhcbrands.com
                  www.vhcbrands.com

Wholesale imported quilts, throws and linens

Chairman: Billy Kline
President: Kenneth Kline
Key Account Manager: Josh Ellig
Mid-Atlantic Central Account Manage: David Brown
dbrown@vhcbrands.com
Sales Manager: Joe Morimoto
jmorimoto@vhcbrands.com
Credit Cards: AMEX; MasterCard; Visa
Catalog Cost: Free
Catalog Circulation: Mailed 4 time(s) per year
Printing Information: 292 pages in 4 colors on Glossy Stock
Press: Letterpress
Binding: Saddle Stitched
Mailing List Information: Names for rent
In Business: 21 years
Number of Employees: 25
Sales Volume: $3.3 Million

Rughooking

4024 Family Heir-Loom Weavers
Family Heir-Loom Weavers
775 Meadowview Dr
Red Lion, PA 17356-8608   717-873-6314
                        Fax: 717-246-7439
                  pathfhw@gmail.com
                  www.Familyheirloomweavers.Com

Jacquard woven ingrain carpet, table runners and coverlets and historically accurate 19th century fabrics

President: Patrick Kline
Credit Cards: MasterCard
Catalog Cost: $4
Printing Information: in 4 colors
Mailing List Information: Names for rent
Number of Employees: 25
Sales Volume: $1MM to $3MM

4025 Great Northern Weaving
Great Northern Weaving
451 E D Ave
Kalamazoo, MI 49009-6312   269-341-9752
                             800-370-7235
                        Fax: 269-341-9525
                  www.greatnorthernweaving.com

Supplies for rug weavers including rag coil, rug warps, cotton loopers, selvedge and yarns for weaving, looms, shuttles, etc

President: Emma Schering
Catalog Cost: $2.5
Catalog Circulation: to 1000
Average Order Size: $150
Printing Information: 12 pages in 4 colors on Matte Stock
Press: Sheetfed Press
Binding: Folded
Mailing List Information: Names for rent
In Business: 10 years
Number of Employees: 10-J
Sales Volume: $3MM to $5MM

4026 Halcyon Yarn
Halcyon Yarn
12 School Street
Bath, ME 04530   207-442-7909
                             800-341-0282
                        Fax: 207-442-0633
                  service@halcyonyarn.com
                  www.halcyonyarn.com

Yarns, fibers, books, equipment and supplies for knitting, weaving, spinning, crochet, felting, rug hooking and many other fiber crafts

Chairman: Will Blake
President: Halcyon Blake
Marketing Manager: Gretchen Jaeger
Production Manager: Amos Wright
Fulfillment: Susan Upham
Orders, Product Management, Wholesa: Susan

slu@halcyonyarn.com
Catlogs: Beth
request@halcyonyarn.com
Buyers: Susan Upham
Credit Cards: AMEX; MasterCard
Catalog Cost: Free
Catalog Circulation: Mailed 2 time(s) per year to 85000
Average Order Size: $58
Printing Information: 96 pages in 4 colors on Glossy Stock
Press: Web Press
Binding: Saddle Stitched
Mailing List Information: Names for rent
List Manager: Will Blake
In Business: 42 years
Number of Employees: 20
Sales Volume: $1MM to $3MM

4027 Jacqueline Designs 1840 House
Jacqueline Designs 1840 House
237 Pine Point Road
Scarborough, ME 04074-8822   207-883-5403
                  designs1840@maine.rr.com
                  www.rughookersnetwork.com/jacqueline-designs/index.htm

Rughooking supplies, patterns and kits

President: Jacqueline Hansen
Catalog Cost: $5.5
Catalog Circulation: Mailed 1 time(s) per year
Printing Information: 40 pages in 4 colors on Matte Stock
Press: Letterpress
Binding: Perfect Bound
In Business: 20 years
Sales Volume: Under $500M

4028 Lion Brand Yarn
Lion Brand Yarn
135 Kero Road
Carlstadt, NJ 07072   212-243-8995
                             800-258-9276
                        Fax: 212-627-8154
                  www.lionbrand.com

Yarn, knitting supplies, and knitting and crochet patterns

President: David Blumenthal
EVP/COO: Dean Blumenthal
CEO: David Blumenthal
Credit Cards: MasterCard
Catalog Cost: Free
In Business: 137 years

Stained Glass

4029 Black Forest Decor
PO Box 297
Jenks, OK 74037-297   800-605-0915
                  info@blackforestdecor.com
                  www.blackforestdecor.com

Home decor

4030 C&R Loo
C&R Loo Inc
1732 Wright Avenue
Richmond, CA 94804-2112   510-232-0276
                             800-227-1780
                        Fax: 510-232-7810
                  sales@crloo.com
                  www.Crloo.Com

Products include supplies for stained glass, beadmaking, flameworking, lampworking, glass casting/fusing/blowing

President: Patrick Loo
Sales Volume: $1MM to $3MM

4031 Carolyn Kyle Enterprises
CKE Publications
PO Box 12869
Olympia, WA 98512-6197   360-352-4427
                                 800-428-7402
                            Fax: 360-943-3978
                  ckepublications@comcast.net
                       www.ckepublications.com

Books and full size patterns for glass crafts

Marketing Manager: Marge Mix
Production Manager: Nancy Hembraff
Fulfillment: Marge Mix
Credit Cards: MasterCard
Catalog Cost: Free
Catalog Circulation: Mailed 1 time(s) per year
to 2000
Printing Information: 40 pages in 1 color on
Matte Stock
Press: Letterpress
Binding: Folded
Mailing List Information: Names for rent
In Business: 19 years
Number of Employees: 3
Sales Volume: $400,000

4032 Delphi's Annual Supply Catalog
Delphi Glass Corporation
3380 East Jolly Rd.
Lansing, MI 48910-8539   517-394-4631
                                 800-248-2048
                            Fax: 517-394-5364
                      sales@delphiglass.com
                        www.delphiglass.com

**Stained glass, mosaic patterns and jewelry
supplies**

President: Daniel Daniels
CFO: Dennis Fattaleh
Executive Director: Lisa Parks
Credit Cards: AMEX; MasterCard; Visa
Catalog Cost: Free
Printing Information: 419 pages in 4 colors
In Business: 43 years
Number of Employees: 25
Sales Volume: $2.30 Million

4033 GGI LLC
Glass Graphics Imaging LLC
PO Box 279
578 Washington Blvd, #371
Marina Del Rey, CA 53092   310-822-2365
                            Fax: 262-268-9811
                          info@ggi-llc.com
                           www.ggillc.com

**Custom stained glass designs, collectibles,
and gifts**

Mailing List Information: Names for rent
Number of Employees: 16

4034 Glass Craft
Glass Craft
411 Violet Street
Golden, CO 80401-4047   888-272-3830
                            Fax: 303-278-4672
                        www.glasscraftinc.com

Stained glass supplies

President: Dave Winship
CFO: Jon Roberts
Production Manager: Shannon Spencer
Purchasing & Marketing : Ariel & Nico Schulze
Customer Service: Shawn Quine
Human Resource Manager: Suzanne Box
Credit Cards: MasterCard
In Business: 44 years

4035 Guildcraft Arts and Crafts
100 Fire Tower Drive
Tonawanda, NY 14150   800-345-5563
                            Fax: 800-550-3555
                      service@guildcraftinc.com
                        www.guildcraftinc.com

Crafting supplies and materials

4036 Houston Stained Glass Supply
Houston Glass Craft Supply
2002 Brittmoore Rd
Houston, TX 77043-2209   713-690-8844
                            Fax: 713-690-0009
                     supplyinfo@glasscraft.net
                         www.glasscraft.net

Supplies for stained glass making

President: John Plummer
Printing Information: 70 pages
In Business: 36 years
Sales Volume: $20MM to $50MM

4037 Jax Chemical Company
Jax Chemical Company
640 South Fulton Avenue
Mount Vernon, NY 10550-1313   914-668-1818
                            Fax: 914-668-8490
                       www.jaxchemicals.com/

President: Jack Simons
In Business: 40 years
Sales Volume: $3MM to $5MM

4038 Premium Products of Louisiana
Premium Products of Louisiana Inc.
1813 Bertrand Drive
Lafayette, LA 70506-2748   337-234-1642
                            Fax: 337-234-1646

Glass for stained glass making

President: Al Chauvin
In Business: 27 years

4039 Rayer's Bearden SG Supply
Rayer's Bearden Stained Glass Supply
6205 W Kellogg Dr
Wichita, KS 67209-2346   316-942-2929
                                 800-228-4101
                            Fax: 316-945-2929
                      rayersinc@sbcglobal.net
                         www.Rayersinc.Com

Stained glass supplies

President: Randy Rayer
In Business: 35 years
Sales Volume: $3MM to $5MM

4040 Warner-Crivellaro
Warner Stained Glass
603 8th Street
Suite A
Whitehall, PA 18052-9427   610-264-1100
                                 800-523-4242
                            Fax: 800-523-5012
                  info@warnerstainedglass.com
                        www.warner-criv.com

Stained glass supplies

President: Marianne Warner
Marketing Manager: Eric Lenner
Credit Cards: AMEX; MasterCard; Visa; Dis-
cover Optima
Catalog Cost: $3
Catalog Circulation: Mailed 1 time(s) per year
Printing Information: 96 pages in 4 colors on
Glossy Stock
Press: Letterpress
Binding: Perfect Bound
Mailing List Information: Names for rent
In Business: 30 years
Number of Employees: 35
Sales Volume: $1MM to $3MM

4041 Wild Wings Collection
2101 South Highway 61
Lake City, MN 55041   800-445-4833
                            Fax: 651-345-2981
                       info@wildwings.com
                        www.wildwings.com

Canvas and crafting supplies

4042 Worden System
HL Worden Company
PO Box 519
Granger, WA 98932-519   509-854-1557
                                 800-541-1103
                            Fax: 509-854-2021
                      info@wordensystem.com
                       www.wordensystem.com

**Patterns and kits for stained glass
lampshades**

President: Howard Worden
Marketing Manager: David Leech
Credit Cards: MasterCard; Visa
Catalog Cost: $1
Catalog Circulation: Mailed 1 time(s) per year
Printing Information: 8 pages in 4 colors
Mailing List Information: Names for rent
In Business: 31 years
Number of Employees: 9
Sales Volume: Under $500M

Stencil Art

4043 American Carnival Mart Key Items
1317 Lindbergh Plaza Center
Saint Louis, MO 63132-1911   314-991-6818
                        info@funcarnival.com
                         www.funcarnival.com

Carnival and picnic supplies

4044 Crafts Manufacturing Company
Crafts Manufacturing Company
72 Massachusetts Ave
Lunenburg, MA 01462-1212   724-532-2702
                            Fax: 330-562-3507
                         info@craftmfg.com
                          www.craftmfg.com

Tinware for stencilers and tole painting

President: William Hardy
Catalog Cost: Free
Printing Information: 16 pages
Number of Employees: 2
Sales Volume: Under $500M

4045 Designer Culinary Stencils
Designer Stencils
2503 Silverside Road
Wilmington, DE 19810-3707   302-475-7300
                                 800-822-7836
                            Fax: 302-475-8644
               customerservice@designerstencils.com
                      www.designerstencils.com

Custom stencils

President: Helen Walker
CFO: Jim Walker
Manager: Carol Walker
Credit Cards: AMEX; MasterCard
Catalog Cost: $3
Printing Information: 75 pages
In Business: 36 years
Number of Employees: 4
Sales Volume: $140K

4046 Epoch Designs
Epoch Designs
PO Box 4033
Elwyn, PA 19063-7033   610-565-9180
                          www.epochdesigns.com

Repro Victorian stencil designs

Credit Cards: AMEX; MasterCard
Catalog Cost: $2.75
In Business: 23 years

4047 Great Tracers
Great Tracers
8760 Orion Place,
Ste. 100
Columbus, OH 43240   847-255-0436
                          blustein@yahoo.com
                           www.manta.com

Custom cut stencils and metal social security cards

President: Joshua Blustein
Marketing Manager: Tami Blustein
Production Manager: David Blustein
Catalog Cost: $1
Catalog Circulation: Mailed 1 time(s) per year to 5000
Printing Information: 5 pages in 2 colors
Press: Sheetfed Press
Binding: Saddle Stitched
In Business: 21 years
Number of Employees: 6
Sales Volume: Under $500M

4048 LA Stencilworks

LA Stencilworks
115 Hawley Street
Wilmington, DE 19805   818-989-0262
                               877-989-0262
                          Fax: 818-989-0405
                          www.lastencil.com

Stencils for murals, innovative borders, classical stencil work, furniture sized designs and more, Catalog has over 750 designs, 22 fully stenciled murals and handbook

President: Barbara Robins
Catalog Cost: $13.5
Catalog Circulation: Mailed 1 time(s) per year
Average Order Size: $50
Printing Information: 100 pages in 4 colors on Glossy Stock
Mailing List Information: Names for rent
Sales Volume: Under $500M

4049 Natural Accents

Lynn Brehm Designs
6827 Caminito Sueno
Carlsbad, CA 92009-4100   760-845-6989
                          Fax: 760-845-6989
              LSBDesigns@natural-accents.com
                      www.natural-accents.com

Stencils for home, childrens rooms and office

President: Lynn Brehm
Credit Cards: AMEX; MasterCard
Catalog Cost: $10
Printing Information: in 4 colors
In Business: 13 years
Number of Employees: 1
Sales Volume: $49,000

4050 Nature's Vignettes

Nature's Vignettes
205 W Meeker St
Kent, WA 98032-5820   253-813-2593
                               877-813-2593
                          Fax: 253-854-9298
                  www.naturesvignettes.com

Over 100 beautiful, detailed stencil designs, lasercut on 5 mil mylar with instructions included

President: Sarah Mitchell
Owner: Sarah Mitchell
Credit Cards: AMEX; MasterCard
Catalog Cost: Free
Catalog Circulation: to 750
Average Order Size: $45
Printing Information: 13 pages in 4 colors on Glossy Stock
Press: Web Press
Binding: Saddle Stitched
Mailing List Information: Names for rent
In Business: 15 years
Number of Employees: 5

4051 P.J.'s Decorative Stencils

Decorative Painting by P.J.!
21 Carter Street
Newburyport, MA 01950   978-358-8555
                          pj@pjstencils.com
                          www.pjstencils.com

Stencils, stencil cutting tools and supplies

President: PJ Goddard
Credit Cards: MasterCard; Visa
Catalog Cost: $5
Printing Information: 6 pages in 4 colors
In Business: 28 years
Number of Employees: 1
Sales Volume: $44K

4052 Paper Source

                               312-906-9678
              customerservice@paper-source.com
                          www.papersource.com

Stationery and labels, cards envelopes and gifts

CEO: Sally Pofcher

4053 Peg Hall Studios

Infogroup
1020 E 1st Street
Papillion, NE 68046-3001   402-836-5290
              contentfeedback@infogroup.com
                       www.expressupdate.com

Tinware and furniture decorating patterns and designs

Chairman: Michael Laccarino
President: David B Hall
CFO: John Hofmann
Assitant General Counsel: Jeffrey Tooley
Credit Cards: MasterCard; Visa
Catalog Cost: Free
Catalog Circulation: Mailed 1 time(s) per year
Printing Information: 4 pages in 1 color

4054 Royal Design Studio

Royal Design Studio
3517 Main Street
Suite 302
Chula Vista, CA 91911-6653   619-934-9062
                               800-747-9767
                          Fax: 619-271-1472
                 sales@royaldesignstudio.com
                      www.royaldesignstudio.com

Extraordinary stencils, elegant, classically-inspired designs

President: Melanie Royals
Design Consultant/Customer Service: Natalie Serhan
natalie@modellodesigns.com
Credit Cards: AMEX; MasterCard; Visa
Catalog Cost: $15
Average Order Size: $56
Printing Information: 32 pages in 4 colors
In Business: 26 years
Number of Employees: 3
Sales Volume: $110,000

4055 Stencil Ease International

Stencil Ease
P.O. Box 1127
Old Saybrook, CT 06475   860-395-0150
                               800-334-1776
                          Fax: 860-395-0166
                          info@stencilease.com
                          www.stencilease.com

Stencils, home decor stencils, stencil paints, stencil brushes

Chairman: Earl Greenho
President: Brian Greenho
Credit Cards: AMEX; MasterCard
Catalog Cost: $3.50
Average Order Size: $25
Printing Information: 48 pages in 4 colors on Glossy Stock
Press: Sheetfed Press
Will Trade Names: Yes
In Business: 27 years
Number of Employees: 18
Sales Volume: $1.4 Million

4056 Stencil Planet

Stencil Planet
18 William Street
1st Floor
Summit, NJ 07901   908-771-8967
                               877-836-2457
                          Fax: 908-517-9104
                       support@stencilplanet.com
                          www.stencilplanet.com

Custom stencil lettering and designs

Credit Cards: AMEX; MasterCard
Catalog Cost: $5
Printing Information: 91 pages

4057 Stencils by Nancy

Stencils by Nancy
19115 Relay Road
Humble, TX 77346   281-686-1226
                          Fax: 281-446-2162
                 custsvc@stencilsbynancy.net
                      www.stencilsbynancy.net

Stencils, paints, brushes, and related supplies

President: Nancy Tribolet
Credit Cards: AMEX; MasterCard
In Business: 25 years
Sales Volume: Under $500M

4058 Yowler & Shepps Stencils

Yowler and Shepps Stencils
3529 Main St.
Conestoga, PA 17516-9608   717-872-2820
                               800-292-5060
                          Fax: 717-872-5890
                       ys.stencils@gmail.com
                  www.yowlersheppsstencils.com

English country, classical, Victorian, childrens, garden motifs, and more

President: Lori Shepps
CFO: Bonnie Yowler
Credit Cards: MasterCard; Visa
Catalog Cost: $3
Printing Information: 40 pages in 4 colors on Glossy Stock
Binding: Saddle Stitched
In Business: 24 years
Number of Employees: 2
Sales Volume: $140,000

Taxidermy

4059 Creations and Collections

Creations and Collections
Po Box 8300
Little Rock, AR 72222   800-575-9255
                          Fax: 877-213-3660
              www.creationsandcollections.com

Gifts, collectibles, taxidermy, home decor, sculptures

4060 Foster Taxidermy Supply

Foster Taxidermy Supply
5124 Troy Highway L
Montgomery, AL 36116   334-281-7676
                               800-848-5602
                          Fax: 334-281-7676
         customerservice@fostertaxidermysupply.com
                  www.fostertaxidermysupply.com

Taxidermy supplies including small animal forms, antelope forms and ready to paint reproductions

President: Danny Foster
Owner: Debbie Foster
Credit Cards: MasterCard
Catalog Cost: Free
In Business: 38 years
Number of Employees: 4
Sales Volume: $300K

4061 Head Quarters Taxidermy Supply
Head Quarters Taxidermy Supply
900 Freedom Drive
PO Box 1449
Raleigh, NC 27610   866-365-0130
info@BigRockSports.com
www.hqtaxidermy.com

Taxidermy supplies including forms of all sizes
CFO: Pat Harvey
CEO: Ed Small
SVP, Human Resources: Jay Samuels
Catalog Cost: Free

4062 Hoosier Trapper Supply
Hoosier Trapper Supply, Inc.
1155 North Mathews Rd.
Greenwood, IN 46143   317-881-3075
Fax: 317-881-3325
info@hoosiertrappersupply.com
www.hoosiertrappersupply.com

Taxidermy, coyote tracking and hunting supplies and products

4063 Jetz Taxidermy Supply Company
Jetz Taxidermy Supply Company
204 Peterson Drive
Kerrville, TX 78028   830-792-4694
www.jetztaxidermysupply.com

Sculpted taxidermy forms
Credit Cards: AMEX; MasterCard
Printing Information: 16 pages

4064 Jim Allred Taxidermy Supply
Jim Allred Taxidermy Supply
1309 Ozone Drive
Saluda, NC 28773   828-749-5800
800-624-7507
Fax: 828-749-5890
www.jimallred.com

Taxidermy supplies including antler mounts, wall mounts, casting materials, and tools
President: Jim Allred
Interim Executive Director: Joe Kulis
Credit Cards: MasterCard
Catalog Cost: Free
Number of Employees: 4

4065 Jonas Supply Company
Jonas Supply Company
1850 Dogwood Street
Louisville, CO 80027   303-466-3377
800-279-7985
Fax: 303-466-1111
claudia@jonastaxidermy.com
www.jonas-supply.com

Taxidermy forms, tools, and supplies
President: Rocco Lasasso
Production Manager: Bill Zlupco
CEO: Claudia Padillo
claudia@jonastaxidermy.com
Catalog Cost: Free
In Business: 100 years
Number of Employees: 50
Sales Volume: $5 million

4066 Matuska Taxidermy Supply Company 2015 Catalog
Matuska Taxidermy
3735 Highway 71
PO Box 293
Spirit Lake, LW 51360   712-336-3256
800-488-3256
Fax: 712-336-2069
matuskataxidermy.com
In Business: 39 years

4067 McKenzie Taxidermy Supply
McKenzie Taxidermy Supply
PO Box 480
Granite Quarry, NC 28072   800-279-7985
taxidermy@mckenziesp.com
www.McKenziesp.Com

Taxidermy and wildlife art supplies and instruction
CFO: Dave Sachs
VP, Sales & Marketing: Tom Powell
Credit Cards: AMEX; MasterCard; Visa
Printing Information: 770 pages in 3 colors
In Business: 30 years
Number of Employees: 125

4068 Quality Taxidermy Supply Company
Quality Texidermy Supply Company
2186 Southwood Road
Kingston, NC 28501   252-527-8722
888-527-8722
Fax: 252-527-8722
www.qualitytaxidermysupply.com

Taxidermy forms and accessories
President: Terry Lipscomb
CFO: Tammy Lipscomb
Credit Cards: AMEX; MasterCard
Catalog Cost: Free

4069 Research Mannikins
Research Mannikins
PO Box 315
Lebanon, OR 97355   541-451-1538
800-826-0654
Fax: 541-451-5455
www.rmi-online.com

Taxidermy supplies, including life-size forms and videos
President: David Rogers
CFO: Dennis Middleton
Production Manager: Greg Hogan
Taxidermist: Mark McLair
markm@rmi-online.com
Credit Cards: MasterCard
Catalog Cost: Free
Printing Information: 423 pages
In Business: 32 years
Number of Employees: 50
Sales Volume: $6 million

4070 Second 2 Nature
Second 2 Nature Texidermy Supply
13599 Blackwater Road
Baker, LA 70714-6800   225-261-3795
800-535-8220
Fax: 225-261-5526
info@second2nature.com
www.second2nature.com

Taxidermy supplies
President: Dan Chase
VP Sales: Jeff Martin
Manager: Janet Tucker
Secretary/Treasurer: Lilly Chase
Credit Cards: MasterCard; Visa
Catalog Cost: Free
In Business: 42 years
Number of Employees: 100
Sales Volume: $9.10 Million

4071 Trufitt Life Form Mannikins
Trufitt Life Form Mannikins
1744 South Redwood
Salt Lake City, UT 84104   800-874-7660
Fax: 801-973-2455
Webmaster@trufitt.net
www.trufitt.net

Taxidermy supplies.
Catalog Cost: $49.5
In Business: 20 years

4072 Van Dyke's
Van Dyke's Supply Co.
Po Box 480
Granite Quarry, NC 28072   704-279-7985
800-279-7985
Fax: 704-279-8958
vandykes@mckenziesp.com
www.vandykestaxidermy.com

Taxidermy supplies
President: Dick Zabela
CFO: Dave Goodwin
Marketing Manager: Jerry Hanson
Production Manager: Susan Kalb
Catalog Cost: Free
In Business: 66 years

4073 WASCO
McKenzie Taxidermy Supply
P.O.Box 480
Granite Quarry, NC 28072-1759   704-279-7985
800-279-7985
Fax: 770-267-8970
taxidermy@mckenziesp.com
www.taxidermy.com

Taxidermy supplies, books, kits, videos and accessories
President: Eddie Ray
CFO: Sallie Dahmes
CEO, VP: Ken Edwards
Credit Cards: AMEX; MasterCard; Visa
Catalog Cost: Free
Printing Information: 324 pages in 4 colors
In Business: 33 years
Number of Employees: 30
Sales Volume: $4.7 Million

Weaving

4074 Autumn House Farm
Autumn House Farm
1001 Locust Road
Rochester Mills, PA 15771-7413   724-286-9596
Fax: 724-286-9596
autumnhousefarminfo@gmail.com
www.autumnhousefarm.com

Carded wools and exotic fibers for handspinning
President: Harriet Knox
Credit Cards: AMEX; MasterCard; Visa
Catalog Cost: $1
Printing Information: 4 pages in 4 colors on Matte Stock
Press: Web Press
Binding: Saddle Stitched
In Business: 25 years
Number of Employees: 10-J

4075 Black Pines Sheep
Black Pines Sheep
12535 Weld Co. Road 80
Eaton, CO 80615-8405   970-834-2629
www.blackpinessheep.com

Large selection of covered and heavily-skirted handspinning fleeces available in white and natural colors
President: Gwen Perinn
Catalog Cost: $1.5
In Business: 51 years

4076 Bluster Bay Woodworks
Bluster Bay Woodworks
P.O. Box 1891
Sandpoint, ID 83864   208-263-4600
blusterbay@gmail.com
www.blusterbaywoodworks.com/

Weaving shuttles, bentwood boxes
President: Terry Lavallee, Owner
Catalog Cost: Free
In Business: 30 years

4077 Detta's Spindle
Detta's Spindle
209 9th Street NW
Buffalolain, MN 55313   763-682-4389
dettasspindle@yahoo.com
www.dettasspindle.net

Weaving and spinning supplies, custom spinning of dog hair yarn

President: Detta Juusola
Credit Cards: AMEX; MasterCard
Catalog Cost: $3
Catalog Circulation: Mailed 1 time(s) per year to 700
Average Order Size: $80
Printing Information: 28 pages in 1 color on Matte Stock
Binding: Saddle Stitched
Mailing List Information: Names for rent
In Business: 25 years
Number of Employees: 10-J
Sales Volume: $1MM to $3MM

4078 Fireside Fiberarts
Fireside Looms for Fiber Artists
380 Dodds Road
Butler, PA 16002   724-283-0575
www.firesidelooms.com

Handcrafted oak, cherry or walnut jack-type looms, tapestry looms and benches

President: Gary Swett
Credit Cards: AMEX; MasterCard
Catalog Cost: $3
In Business: 35 years
Number of Employees: 10-J

4079 For Small Hands Family Resource Catalog
Montessori Services
11 West 9th Street
Santa Rosa, CA 95401   800-214-8959
Fax: 707-579-1604
www.montessoriservices.com

Polishing, cleaning and woodworking products

Founder: Jane Mills Campbell

4080 Glimakra Looms & Weaving Equipment
Glimakra USA LLC
1471 Railroad Blvd.
Eugene, OR 97402   406-442-0354
866-890-7314
Fax: 406-442-4892
info@glimakrausa.com
www.glimakrausa.com

Largest importer of Scandinavian weaving equipment in the US, specialty books for textile industry

President: Joanne Hall
joanne@glimakrausa.com
Marketing Manager: Edwin Hall
ed@glimakrausa.com
Production Manager: mary@glimakrausa.com
Credit Cards: MasterCard; Visa
Catalog Cost: Free
Catalog Circulation: to 900
Average Order Size: $200
Printing Information: 32 pages in 4 colors on Matte Stock
Press: Sheetfed Press
Binding: Folded
In Business: 40 years
Sales Volume: $500,000

4081 Gowdey Reed Company
Gowdey Reed Company
325 Illinois St
Central Falls, RI 02863-1935   401-723-6114
Fax: 401-727-0720
gowdeyreed@msn.com
www.Gowdeyreed.Com

Oldest weaving reed manufacturer in the US, supplying loom reeds in a variety of lengths and epi's

President: James Wilson
Printing Information: 1 pages in 1 color
Binding: Folded
In Business: 181 years
Number of Employees: 10-J
Sales Volume: $1MM to $3MM

4082 Halcyon Yarn
Halcyon Yarn
12 School Street
Bath, ME 04530   207-442-7909
800-341-0282
Fax: 207-442-0633
service@halcyonyarn.com
www.halcyonyarn.com

Yarns, fibers, books, equipment and supplies for knitting, weaving, spinning, crochet, felting, rug hooking and many other fiber crafts

Chairman: Will Blake
President: Halcyon Blake
Marketing Manager: Gretchen Jaeger
Production Manager: Amos Wright
Fulfillment: Susan Upham
Orders, Product Management, Wholesa: Susan
slu@halcyonyarn.com
Catlogs: Beth
request@halcyonyarn.com
Buyers: Susan Upham
Credit Cards: AMEX; MasterCard
Catalog Cost: Free
Catalog Circulation: Mailed 2 time(s) per year to 85000
Average Order Size: $58
Printing Information: 96 pages in 4 colors on Glossy Stock
Press: Web Press
Binding: Saddle Stitched
Mailing List Information: Names for rent
List Manager: Will Blake
In Business: 42 years
Number of Employees: 20
Sales Volume: $1MM to $3MM

4083 Macomber Looms
Macomber Looms
130 Beech Ridge Road
PO Box 186
York, ME 03909   207-363-2808
Fax: 207-363-2808
www.macomberloom.com

Hand looms and accessories

President: Rick Hart
Production Manager: Ed Carbone
Credit Cards: MasterCard; Visa
Catalog Cost: Free
Catalog Circulation: to 1200
Printing Information: 20 pages in 2 colors
Binding: Saddle Stitched
In Business: 77 years
Number of Employees: 5
Sales Volume: $500M to $1MM

4084 Pepperell Braiding Company
Pepprell Braiding Company
22 Lowell St
PO Box 1487
Pepperell, MA 01463-1703   978-433-2133
800-343-8114
Fax: 978-433-9048
info@pepperell.com
www.pepperell.com

Plastic lacing, pom poms, macrame chair patterns

President: W P Slivinski
Credit Cards: AMEX; MasterCard
In Business: 98 years
Sales Volume: $1MM to $3MM

4085 Schacht Spindle Co.
6101 Ben Place
Boulder, CO 80301   303-442-3212
Fax: 303-447-9273
info@schachtspindle.com
www.schachtspindle.com

Specialty looms

4086 Web-Sters
The Websters
11 N Main Street
Ashland, OR 97520-2725   541-482-9801
800-482-9801
www.yarnatwebsters.com

Extensive line of yarns, looms, spinning wheels, raw materials, books, dyes and tools for handweavers, knitters and spinners

President: Annette Dahlquist
CFO: Dona Zimmerman
Credit Cards: AMEX; MasterCard
Catalog Cost: Free
Printing Information: 40 pages
In Business: 31 years
Number of Employees: 5

Woodworking

4087 Amana Tool
Amana Tool
120 Carolyn Blvd.
Farmingdale, NY 11756   631-752-1300
800-445-0077
Fax: 631-752-1674
tools@amanatool.com
www.amanatool.com

Tungsten carbide woodworking tools for woodworking industry, sawshops, cabinet makers & hobbyists

President: Michael Ciccarelli
Printing Information: in 4 colors
In Business: 42 years
Number of Employees: 52
Sales Volume: $7.7MM

4088 American Furniture Design
American Furniture Design Co.
PO Box 300100
Escondido, CA 92030-100   760-743-6923
Fax: 760-743-0707
americanfurniture@cox.net
www.americanfuredsgn.com

Woodworking plans, tools, brushes, hardware

President: Brian Murphy
CFO: Nancy Murphy
Marketing Manager: Chris Murphy
Production Manager: Kelly Krueger
Credit Cards: MasterCard
Catalog Cost: Free
Average Order Size: $25
Printing Information: 68 pages in 1 color on Matte Stock
Press: Web Press
Binding: Saddle Stitched
Mailing List Information: Names for rent
In Business: 17 years
Number of Employees: 5
Sales Volume: $400,000

4089 Artistic Woodworking Products
Artistic Woodworking, Inc
PO Box 789
Imperial, NE 69033   308-882-4873
800-621-3992
Fax: 308-882-5507
artistic@chase3000.com
www.artwood.com/

Accent trim mouldings, carved rosettes, embossed carvings and more

President: Jim L. Sorge

4090 Badger Hardwoods of Wisconsin
Badger Hardwoods of Wisconsin, Ltd
N1517 Us Highway 14
Walworth, WI 53184-5528   262-275-1162
                                 800-252-2373
                          Fax: 262-275-9855
badgerwood@badgerwood.com
www.badgerwood.com

Aromatic cedar, ash, aspen, basswood, birch, butternut, cherry, mahogany, hickory, hackberry, hard and soft maples, Northern white pine, poplar, red elm, red oak quartersawn, red, white oak and more

President: Bob Hansen
Credit Cards: MasterCard
Mailing List Information: Names for rent
In Business: 20 years
Number of Employees: 3
Sales Volume: $350,000

4091 Catalog of Fine Woodworking Tools
Japan Woodworker
406 Airport Industrial Park
P.O. Box 1686
Parkersburg, WV 26104-9778   304-428-4866
                                800-537-7820
                          Fax: 304-428-8271
support@thejapanwoodworker.com
www.japanwoodworker.com

Japanese woodworking tools, gardening tools and cutlery

President: Fred Damsen
VP: Sally Damsen
Office Manager: Connie Harper
Credit Cards: AMEX; MasterCard; Visa
Catalog Cost: Free
Catalog Circulation: Mailed 4 time(s) per year to 100
Average Order Size: $98
Printing Information: 80 pages in 4 colors on Glossy Stock
Press: Web Press
Binding: Saddle Stitched
In Business: 35 years
Number of Employees: 15
Sales Volume: $1.80 Million

4092 Cherry Tree Toys
Cherry Tree Toys
12446 W State Road 81
Beloit, WI 53511   608-302-4675
                                800-848-4363
www.cherrytreetoys.com

Woodworking toys, plans, clock parts, kits, tools and supplies

President: Cindy Stewart
Credit Cards: MasterCard; Visa
Catalog Cost: $1
Catalog Circulation: Mailed 2 time(s) per year
Average Order Size: $50
Printing Information: 112 pages in 4 colors on Glossy Stock
Press: Web Press
Binding: Folded
Mailing List Information: Names for rent
Will Trade Names: Yes
List Company: Names & Addresses
4096 Commercial Avenue
Northbrook, IL 60062
708-272-7938
In Business: 35 years
Sales Volume: $5,000,000

4093 Christian J Hummul
Christian J Hummul Company
12446 W State Rd 81
Beloit, WI 53511   608-302-4680
                                800-762-0235
                          Fax: 608-302-4677
mail@hummul.com
www.hummul.com

Woodcarving and woodburning supplies

President: Cynthia Kryshak
CFO: Jean Llefke
Catalog Cost: Free
Catalog Circulation: Mailed 1 time(s) per year to 27000
Printing Information: 88 pages on Glossy Stock
Press: Web Press
Binding: Saddle Stitched
Mailing List Information: Names for rent
In Business: 35 years
Number of Employees: 8
Sales Volume: $120K

4094 Cinderwhit & Company
Cinderwhit & Company
733 Eleventh Avenue South
Wahpeton, ND 58075-4868   701-642-9064
                                800-527-9064
                          Fax: 701-642-4204
info@cinderwhit.com
www.cinderwhit.com

Wood turnings for porches and stairways: replica, custom or stock designs of porch posts, newel parts, balusters and spindles

President: Cynthia Schreiber-Beck
Credit Cards: MasterCard; Visa
Catalog Cost: Free
Average Order Size: $1200
Printing Information: 1 pages on Matte Stock
Press: Letterpress
Mailing List Information: Names for rent
Number of Employees: 7
Sales Volume: $500M to $1MM

4095 Colonial Hardwoods
Colonial Hardwoods, Inc.
7953 Cameron Brown Ct
Springfield, VA 22153-2809   703-451-9217
                                800-466-5451
www.Colonialhardwoods.Com

Over 120 species of lumber custom cut to size: Burls, woodworking supplies and veneers

President: Jiri Otmar
Fulfillment: Marie Otmar
Credit Cards: MasterCard
Sales Volume: $1MM to $3MM

4096 Craft Supplies USA
Craft Supplies USA
1287 E 1120 S
Provo, UT 84606-6322   801-373-0917
                                800-551-8876
                          Fax: 801-377-7742
service@woodturnerscatalog.com
www.woodturnerscatalog.com

Products, tools and supplies for woodworking

President: Darrel Nish
Treasurer: Brenda Nish
General Manager: Ben Williams
Credit Cards: AMEX; MasterCard
Catalog Cost: Free
Printing Information: 144 pages in 4 colors
In Business: 33 years
Number of Employees: 25
Sales Volume: $3 Million

4097 Cupboard Distributing
Cupboard Distributing
1463 South US Hwy 68
Urbana, OH 43078-8405   937-652-3338
                          Fax: 937-652-3898
info@cdwood.com
www.Cdwood.Com

Unfinished wood products, craft items and woodworking supplies

President: Chris Haughey
Credit Cards: MasterCard
Catalog Cost: Free
Catalog Circulation: Mailed 1 time(s) per year
Average Order Size: $25

Printing Information: 58 pages in 2 colors on Newsprint
Press: Web Press
Binding: Saddle Stitched
Mailing List Information: Names for rent
In Business: 26 years
Number of Employees: 10
Sales Volume: $400,000

4098 Dust Collection
Penn State Industries
9900 Global Road
Philadelphia, PA 19115   215-676-7606
                                800-377-7297
                          Fax: 215-676-7603
psind@pennstateind.com
www.pennstateind.com

Tools specializing in dust collection: mini lathes, lathe projects and supplies

President: Ed Levy
Credit Cards: AMEX; MasterCard
Catalog Cost: Free
Printing Information: 24 pages in 4 colors
In Business: 79 years

4099 Eagle America
Eagle America
2381 Philmont Ave
Suite 107
Huntingdon Valley, PA 19006   888-872-7637
                                800-872-2511
                          Fax: 800-872-9471
eagle@eagleamerica.com
www.eagleamerica.com

Router bits, woodworking accessories

President: Dan Walter
Buyers: Dave Swartz
Credit Cards: AMEX; MasterCard
Catalog Cost: Free
Catalog Circulation: Mailed 9 time(s) per year
Printing Information: 88 pages in 4 colors on Glossy Stock
Press: Web Press
Binding: Saddle Stitched
Mailing List Information: Names for rent
In Business: 26 years
Number of Employees: 20-5

4100 Econ-Abrasives
Econ-Abrasives
117 Austin St.
PO Box 1628
Garland, TX 75040-1628   972-335-9234
                                800-367-4101
                          Fax: 972-377-2248
www.econabrasives.com

Abrasive belts, router bits, woodworking supplies

President: William Clarkson
Credit Cards: AMEX; MasterCard
Catalog Cost: Free
Printing Information: 32 pages
Number of Employees: 40

4101 Fein Power Tools
Fein Power Tools Inc.
1000 Omega Drive
Suite 1180
Pittsburgh, PA 15205   412-922-8886
                                800-441-9878
                          Fax: 412-922-8767
info@feinus.com
www.feinus.com

Portable power tools

President: Chris Cable
CFO: Mary Wilkie
Marketing Manager: Robert Hillard
Catalog Cost: Free
Mailing List Information: Names for rent
In Business: 140 years
Number of Employees: 40

4102 Flexcut Carving Tools
Flexcut Tool Company.
8105 Hawthorne Dr
Erie, PA 16509-4653   814-864-7855
                            800-524-9077
                            Fax: 814-866-7312
                            www.Flexcut.Com

Wood carving tools, Flexcut chisels and mallet tools and accessories, manufacturer of wood carving tools

President: Stephen Vain
Credit Cards: MasterCard
In Business: 28 years
Sales Volume: $5MM to $10MM

4103 For Small Hands Family Resource Catalog
Montessori Services
11 West 9th Street
Santa Rosa, CA 95401   800-214-8959
                            Fax: 707-579-1604
                            www.montessoriservices.com

Polishing, cleaning and woodworking products

Founder: Jane Mills Campbell

4104 Garrett Wade
Garrett Wade
5389 E Provident Drive
Cincinnati, OH 45246   800-221-2942
                            www.garrettwade.com

Woodworking, gardening and outdoor tools, home & office supplies and accessories

President: Garretson W Chinn
Credit Cards: AMEX; MasterCard
Catalog Cost: Free
Catalog Circulation: Mailed 12 time(s) per year to 1.8M
Average Order Size: $150
Printing Information: 100 pages in 4 colors on Glossy Stock
Press: Web Press
Binding: Saddle Stitched
Mailing List Information: Names for rent
In Business: 42 years
Number of Employees: 50
Sales Volume: $10,000,000

4105 Home Lumber
HomeTops
499 W Whitewater St
Whitewater, WI 53190-1986   262-473-3538
                            800-211-8665
                            Fax: 262-473-6908
                            tooltime@idcnet.com
                            www.hometops.com

Power tools including Makita, Bosch, Bostich, Paslode, Panasonic Power Tools, Amana carbide blades and router bits, free shipping on orders over $50, same day service

President: Geoff Hale
Marketing Manager: Jay Savignac
Fulfillment: Geoff Hale
Buyers: Craig Seefeldt
Credit Cards: MasterCard
Catalog Cost: Free
Catalog Circulation: Mailed 3 time(s) per year to 35000
Average Order Size: $175
Printing Information: 28 pages in 2 colors on Glossy Stock
Press: Sheetfed Press
Binding: Saddle Stitched
Mailing List Information: Names for rent
In Business: 111 years
Number of Employees: 35
Sales Volume: $10MM to $20MM

4106 Hood Finishing Products
Hood Finishing Products
9 Factory Lane
PO Box 97
Middlesex, NJ 08846-97   732-805-0088
                            800-229-0934
                            Fax: 732-805-4042
                            info@hoodfinishing.com
                            www.hoodfinishing.com

Line of products for wood finishing and refinishing from surface preparation to wood care

President: Erick Kasner
ekasner@hoodfinishing.com
Director: Joan Goldberg
General Manager: Erick Kasner
Credit Cards: MasterCard; Visa
Catalog Cost: Free
Printing Information: 36 pages in 3 colors on Newsprint
Binding: Saddle Stitched
In Business: 34 years
Number of Employees: 10
Sales Volume: $2,000,000

4107 Hot Tools
M.M. Newman Corporation
24 Tioga Way
PO Box 615
Marblehead, MA 01945-1575   781-631-7100
                            800-777-6309
                            Fax: 781-631-8887
                            sales@mmnewman.com
                            www.Mmnewman.Com

Woodburning tools, hot knife, library marker, lacquer burn in knife and stencil maker

President: Charles Loutrell
CFO: Charles Loutrel
Credit Cards: MasterCard
Catalog Cost: Free
Catalog Circulation: Mailed 1 time(s) per year to 100
Average Order Size: $50
Printing Information: 12 pages in 4 colors on Matte Stock
Mailing List Information: Names for rent
In Business: 59 years
Number of Employees: 12
Sales Volume: $1MM to $3MM

4108 Industrial Abrasives
Industrial Abrasives
642 N. 8th Street
PO Box 14955
Reading, PA 19601-4955   610-378-1861
                            800-428-2222
                            Fax: 610-378-4868
                            sandyiac@comcast.net
                            www.industrialabrasives.com

Sandpaper and other coated abrasive products, such as belts, rolls and discs

President: Sandra a Reese
Credit Cards: AMEX; MasterCard
In Business: 68 years
Sales Volume: $5MM to $10MM

4109 Intarsia Times
Intarsia
Roberts Studio
2620 Heather Road
Seymour, TN 37865-5422   865-428-8875
                            800-316-9010
                            Fax: 865-428-7870
                            judy@intarsia.com
                            www.intarsia.com

Intarsia patterns, scroll saw pattern books, Intarsia woodworking how-to books and videos, scroll saw blades, hardware items, varnish, specialty tools

President: Jerry Booher
Marketing Manager: Jerry Booher
Fulfillment: Jerry Boooher

Catalog Circulation: Mailed 2 time(s) per year
Printing Information: 16 pages in 4 colors on Glossy Stock
Press: Web Press
Binding: Saddle Stitched
In Business: 15 years
Number of Employees: 5
Sales Volume: $500M to $1MM

4110 Japan Woodworker
Japan Woodworker
406 Airport Industrial Park Road
P.O. Box 1686
Parkersburg, WV 26104-9778   800-537-7820
                            support@thejapanwoodworker.com
                            www.japanwoodworker.com

Japanese woodworking, garden tools, and cutlery

President: Fred Damsen
Catalog Cost: $2
Catalog Circulation: Mailed 52 time(s) per year
Average Order Size: $105
Printing Information: 80 pages in 1 color on Matte Stock
Press: Web Press
Binding: Saddle Stitched
Mailing List Information: Names for rent
In Business: 30 years
Number of Employees: 20-O
Sales Volume: $5MM to $10MM

4111 Jennings Decoy Company
Jennings Decoy Company
601 Franklin Ave NE
St Cloud, MN 56304-256   320-253-2253
                            800-331-5613
                            Fax: 320-253-9537
                            info@jenningsdecoycompany.com
                            www.Jenningsdecoycompany.Com

Over 1,400 products for carvers: basswood, butternut cutouts and cutout kits; wildfowl and other figures, offers eyes, other accessories, patterns cork decoy kits, books and paints

President: Jim Russell
Production Manager: Harry Patton
Fulfillment: Donna Alourd
Buyers: Steve Ree
Credit Cards: MasterCard
Catalog Cost: Free
Catalog Circulation: Mailed 3 time(s) per year to 30000
Average Order Size: $55
Printing Information: 18 pages in 4 colors on Glossy Stock
Press: Web Press
Binding: Saddle Stitched
Mailing List Information: Names for rent
List Manager: Steve Ree
In Business: 21 years
Number of Employees: 4
Sales Volume: $500M to $1MM

4112 Klingspor's Woodworking Shop
Klingspor's Woodworking Shop
856 21st St Dr SE
Hickory, NC 28602-3737   800-228-0000
                            828-327-4634
                            Fax: 800-872-2005
                            sales@woodworkingshop.com
                            www.woodworkingshop.com

Woodworking tools and supplies

Manager: Tom Ferone
Manager: Paul Rolfe
Credit Cards: AMEX; MasterCard; Visa
Catalog Cost: Free
Catalog Circulation: Mailed 2 time(s) per year
Printing Information: 50 pages in 4 colors on Glossy Stock
Binding: Saddle Stitched
Number of Employees: 4

4113   Lee Valley Tools
Lee Valley Tools
PO Box 1780
Ogdensburg, NY 13669-6780   800-871-8158
Fax: 800-513-7885
customerservice@leevalley.com
www.leevalley.com

Gardening and woodworking hand tools and accessories

President: Iain Campbell
Marketing Manager: Robin Lee
VP, Customer Service: Lucy Robitaille
Director, Research & Development: Rick Blaiklock
Credit Cards: AMEX; MasterCard
Catalog Cost: Free
Printing Information: 260 pages in 4 colors
Mailing List Information: Names for rent
In Business: 37 years
Number of Employees: 4

4114   Lie-Nielsen Toolworks
264 Stirling Road
Warren, ME 04864   800-327-2520
Fax: 207-273-2657
Toolworks@lie-nielsen.com
www.lie-nielsen.com

Tools and woodworking equipment

4115   MLCS-Router Bits & Professional Woodworking
MLCS
PO Box 165
Huntingdon Valley, PA 19006-0165 215-938-5060
800-533-9298
Fax: 215-938-5070
sawdust@mlcswoodworking.com
www.mlcswoodworking.com

Woodworking machines, tools, supplies and hobby center

Credit Cards: AMEX; MasterCard
Printing Information: 60 pages on Matte Stock

4116   Meisel Hardware Specialties
Meisel Hardware Specialties
PO Box 70
Mound, MN 55364-70   952-746-2379
800-441-9870
Fax: 952-471-8579
office@meiselwoodhobby.com
www.meiselwoodhobby.com

Over 850 woodworking plans including country, storage and outdoor furniture, kitchen items, child's furniture and toys, lamps, music boxes, holiday cutouts and more

President: Paul Meisel
CFO: Patricia Meisel
Marketing Manager: Eric Meisel
Production Manager: Greg Meisel
Credit Cards: MasterCard
Catalog Cost: $2
Catalog Circulation: Mailed 3 time(s) per year to 10000
Printing Information: 100 pages in 4 colors on Glossy Stock
Press: Web Press
Binding: Saddle Stitched
Mailing List Information: Names for rent
List Company: List Locators & Managers
In Business: 29 years
Number of Employees: 50
Sales Volume: $5MM to $10MM

4117   Midwest Dowel Works
Midwest Dowel Works
320 North State Street
Harrison, OH 45030-1146   513-367-5999
Fax: 513-202-0942
www.midwestdowel.com

Dowels, plugs and pegs, buttons, pins, decorative spindles, rope moulding, wood craft items, balls, blocks, split balls, shapes

President: Ruth Campbell
CFO: Peter Puttmann
Marketing Manager: Jim Oliverio
Fulfillment: Jim Oliverio
Buyers: Jim Oliverio
Catalog Cost: Free
Catalog Circulation: to 6mm
Printing Information: 22 pages in 4 colors on Glossy Stock
Mailing List Information: Names for rent
List Manager: Peter Puttmann
In Business: 14 years
Number of Employees: 3
Sales Volume: $5MM to $10MM

4118   Mountain Woodcarvers
Mountain Woodcravers.com
PO Box 3485
Estes Park, CO 80517   800-292-6788
mtncarvers@aol.com
www.mountainwoodcarvers.com

Woodcarving supplies including books, tools, woodburners, wood, videos, roughouts, eyes & feet for bird mallets and many more accessories

President: Pam Johnson
Credit Cards: AMEX; MasterCard; Visa
Catalog Cost: Free
Catalog Circulation: Mailed 1 time(s) per year
Printing Information: 48 pages in 1 color on Newsprint
Press: Web Press
Binding: Saddle Stitched
Mailing List Information: Names for rent
In Business: 15 years
Number of Employees: 4
Sales Volume: $400,000

4119   Newfound Woodworks
67 Danforth Brook Road
Bristol, NH 03222   603-744-6872
info@newfound.com
www.newfound.com

Woodworkd, canoes, kayaks

4120   Packard Woodworks
Packward Woodworks Inc.
215 S. Trade Street
Tryon, NC 28782   828-859-6762
800-683-8876
Fax: 828-859-5551
sales@packardwoodworks.com
www.packardwoodworks.com

Woodturning tools and supplies, Books, Videos

President: Bradford Packard
CFO: Debra Packard
Credit Cards: AMEX; MasterCard
Catalog Circulation: Mailed 2 time(s) per year
Printing Information: 60 pages in 4 colors on Glossy Stock
Press: Web Press
Binding: Folded
Mailing List Information: Names for rent
In Business: 20 years
Number of Employees: 6
Sales Volume: $50,000

4121   Penn State Industries
Penn State Industries
9900 Global Road
Philadelphia, PA 19115   215-676-7606
800-377-7297
Fax: 215-676-7603
www.pennstateind.com

Woodworking plans, projects, tools, mini lathes and lathe accessories

President: Marvin Levy
CFO: Ed Levy
Printing Information: 24 pages
In Business: 79 years

4122   RapidStart
PO Box 506
Rittman, OH 44270   330-927-2743
Fax: 330-927-2744
info@rapidstartusa.com
www.rapidstartusa.com

Screws, nails and hardware

4123   Razor Tools
Rayer's Bearden Stained Glass
6205 W. Kellogg
Wichita, KS 67209   316-942-2929
800-228-4101
Fax: 813-875-5430
sales@razorwoodworks.com
www.rayersinc.com

Router bits, sawblades, shaper cutters, planer knives and woodworking accessories

President: Gerald Davich
Marketing Manager: Alan Goodsell
Catalog Cost: Free
Catalog Circulation: Mailed 12 time(s) per year
Printing Information: 64 pages in 4 colors on Glossy Stock
Press: Web Press
Binding: Saddle Stitched
Mailing List Information: Names for rent
In Business: 35 years

4124   Red Hill
Red Hill Corporation
1540 Biglerville Road
PO Box 4234
Gettysburg, PA 17325-4234   717-337-3038
800-822-4003
Fax: 717-337-0732
laura@supergrit.com
www.Supergrit.Com

Sanding belts, discs, sheets, woodworking accessories, abrasives for metalworking and automotive refinishing

President: Arturo Ottolenghi
Buyers: Arturo Ottolenghi
Catalog Cost: Free
Catalog Circulation: Mailed 1 time(s) per year
Average Order Size: $90
Printing Information: 46 pages in 4 colors on G
Press: W
Binding: S
Mailing List Information: Names for rent
In Business: 36 years
Number of Employees: 5
Sales Volume: $1MM to $3MM

4125   Rockler Woodworking & Hardware
Rockler Woodworking and Hardware
4365 Willow Dr
Medina, MN 55340-4522   763-478-8201
800-279-4441
Fax: 763-478-8395
info@rockler.com
www.rockler.com

Woodworking projects and power tools

President: Ann Rockler Jackson
Marketing Manager: Scott Ekman
VP Product Development: Steve Krohmer
Director Marketing Executive: Ellen Manderfield
Editor-in-Chief: Rob Johnstone
Credit Cards: AMEX; MasterCard
Catalog Cost: Free
Printing Information: 156 pages in 4 colors on Glossy Stock
In Business: 61 years
Sales Volume: $500,000

4126 Shaker Workshops
Shaker Workshops
14 South Pleasant Street
Ashburnham, MA 01430-1649   978-827-9900
800-840-9121
Fax: 978-827-6554
service@shakerworkshops.com
www.shakerworkshops.com

Reproductions of Shaker furniture, oval boxes and gift items

President: Thomas Williams
Credit Cards: AMEX; MasterCard; Visa
Catalog Cost: Free
Printing Information: in 3 colors on Glossy Stock
Press: Web Press
Binding: Saddle Stitched
In Business: 44 years
Number of Employees: 35

4127 Sherwood Creations
Sherwood Creations Inc.
1459 N Leroy St
Fenton, MI 48430-2763   810-629-0907
800-843-2571
info@sherwoodonline.com

Offers plans, patterns, and supplies for woodworking

President: Fred Bender
Catalog Cost: Free
In Business: 16 years
Sales Volume: $500M to $1MM

4128 Shop Solutions
Affinity Tool Works, LLC
1161 Rankin Drive
Troy, MI 48083   248-588-0395
800-624-2027
Fax: 248-588-0623
info@affinitytool.com
www.boratool.com

Woodworking supports, mitre saw stands, mobile bases, workshop accessories, saw guards

President: Tim Hewitt
Marketing Manager: Mark Cross
Catalog Cost: Free
Catalog Circulation: Mailed 6 time(s) per year to 300M
Printing Information: 36 pages in 4 colors on Glossy Stock
Press: Web Press
Binding: Saddle Stitched
Mailing List Information: Names for rent
In Business: 31 years

4129 Sugar Pine Woodcarving Supplies
Sugarpine Woodcarving Supplies, Inc.
315 W. Sherman
PO Box 859
Lebanon, OR 97355   800-452-2783
Fax: 541-451-5455
customerservice@sugarpinewoodcarving.com
www.sugarpinewoodcarving.com

Wood carving supplies

President: David Rogers
Operations Manager: Greg Hogan
greg@sugarpinewoodcarving.com
Credit Cards: MasterCard
Catalog Cost: Free
Printing Information: 104 pages in 4 colors

4130 Sunhill Insider
Sunhill Machinery
1208 Andover Park E
Seattle, WA 98188-3905   206-575-4131
800-929-4321
Fax: 206-575-3617
www.sunhillmachinery.com

Woodworking machinery and accessories

Credit Cards: AMEX; MasterCard
Printing Information: 6 pages in 2 colors
Number of Employees: 15

4131 Traditional Woodworker
885 E. Collins Blvd
Suite 104
Richardson, TX 75081   800-509-0081
Fax: 972-480-0582

Woodworking supplies and materials

4132 Veneering Catalog
Bob Morgan Woodworking Supplies, Inc.
6521 Jacob Drive
Westport, KY 40077   502-265-0954
www.morganwood.com

Woodworking supplies, vaneers and supplies, chair caning supplies

President: Bob Morgan
Catalog Cost: Free
In Business: 41 years

4133 Vesterheim Norwegian American Museum
Vesterheim
523 W Water St
PO Box 379
Decorah, IA 52101-1733   563-382-9681
Fax: 563-382-8828
info@vesterheim.org
www.vesterheim.com

Collection of artefacts, large samplings of fine decorative folk arts, tools & machinery of early agriculture

Credit Cards: AMEX; MasterCard
In Business: 136 years

4134 Viking Woodcrafts Inc
Viking Woodcrafts, Inc.
1317 8th St SE
Waseca, MN 56093   507-835-8043
800-328-0116
Fax: 507-835-3895
viking@vikingwoodcrafts.com
www.vikingwoodcrafts.com

Paper, paint, stamps, stencils, paint brushes, wood surfaces, tools and glass & porcelain surfaces

President: Robert Reese
Credit Cards: AMEX; MasterCard
Catalog Cost: $6
Catalog Circulation: Mailed 1 time(s) per year to 10K
Printing Information: 32 pages in 1 color on Newsprint
Binding: Perfect Bound
Mailing List Information: Names for rent
In Business: 32 years
Number of Employees: 15
Sales Volume: $ 3-5 Million

4135 WL Fuller
W.L. Fuller Co., Inc.
7 Cypress St
PO Box 8767
Warwick, RI 02888-767   401-467-2900
Fax: 401-467-2905
info@wlfuller.com
www.wlfuller.com

Countersinks, counterbores, plug cutters, taper point drills, brad point drills and step drills, also specials

President: Diane Nobel
CFO: Gary Fuller
Marketing Manager: Debbie Fuller
Production Manager: Andrew Henninger
Fulfillment: Debbie Fuller
Buyers: Sandy Fuller
Credit Cards: MasterCard; Visa; Discover
Catalog Cost: Free
Printing Information: 152 pages on Matte Stock
Press: Web Press

Binding: Perfect Bound
Mailing List Information: Names for rent
In Business: 63 years
Number of Employees: 60
Sales Volume: $10MM to $20MM

4136 West Penn Hardwoods
West Penn Hardwoods, Inc.
1405 Deborah Herman Rd
Olean, NY 28613-3512   828-322-9663
888-636-9663
Fax: 828-322-2369
Support@westpennhardwoods.com
www.westpennhardwoods.com

Hardwoods

President: Rocky Mehta
Office Assistant: Lynn Graves
Office Manager: Pam Cammeyer
Catalog Cost: Free
In Business: 20 years
Number of Employees: 5

4137 Williams & Hussey Machine Co.
70 Powers Street
Milford, NH 03055   603-732-0219
Fax: 603-732-4048
customerservice@williamsnhussey.com
www.williamsnhussey.com

Custom knives

4138 Winfield Collection
The Winfield Collection
8350 Silver Lake Rd
Linden, MI 48451-9061   810-735-2480
800-946-3435
Fax: 810-735-2481
cserv@thewinfieldcollection.com
www.thewinfieldcollection.com

Woodcraft patterns, toys and country furniture

President: Mike Easler
CFO: Brandon Easler
Marketing Manager: Becky Wakenan
Production Manager: Tracy Bowlby
Credit Cards: MasterCard; Visa
Catalog Cost: Free
Catalog Circulation: Mailed 4 time(s) per year to 10000
Printing Information: 68 pages in 4 colors
Binding: Folded
In Business: 45 years

4139 Wood Carvers Supply Catalog
Wood Carvers Supply, Inc.
PO Box 7500
Englewood, FL 34295-7500   941-698-0123
800-284-6229
Fax: 941-460-9433
teamwcs@yahoo.com
www.woodcarverssupply.com

Color catalog with over 2,000 items, including hand and power woodcarving tools, books, knives, and more

President: Timothy Effrem
CFO: Deborah Effrem
Production Manager: Chris Effram
Fulfillment: Timothy Effram
Credit Cards: AMEX; MasterCard
Catalog Cost: Free
Printing Information: 52 pages
In Business: 72 years
Number of Employees: 4
Sales Volume: $250,000

4140 Wood Classics
Greenlife Llc
6060 Kells Lane
Milford, OH 45150   800-982-3880
Fax: 888-316-5461
www.arthurlauer.com

Indoor and outdoor furniture, patio & garden furniture, tables and accessories

President: Jeremy Smith
Marketing Manager: Sue Hamel
Credit Cards: MasterCard
Catalog Cost: Free
Printing Information:
Binding: Perfect Bound
In Business: 31 years

4141   Woodhaven
Woodhaven Inc
501 W 1st Ave
Durant, IA 52747-9729   563-785-0107
                                800-344-6657
                           Fax: 563-785-6813
                           info@woodhaven.com
                           www.woodhaven.com

Woodworking tools and accessories

President: Brad Witt
Credit Cards: MasterCard
Catalog Cost: Free
Printing Information: in 4 colors
Binding: Perfect Bound
In Business: 52 years
Number of Employees: 50
Sales Volume: $1MM to $3MM

4142   Woodline USA
Woodline USA
111 Wheeler St
La Vergne, TN 37086-3119   615-793-0474
                                 800-472-6950
                            Fax: 615-793-0565
                            techsupport@woodline.com
                            www.woodline.com

Router bits and shaper cutters

President: Mickey Thompson
CFO: Bill Thompson
Credit Cards: AMEX; MasterCard
Catalog Cost: Free
Number of Employees: 10
Sales Volume: $850,000

4143   Woodplay
Woodplay
817 Maxwell Avenue
Evansville, IN 47711   800-966-3752
                           www.swingsets.com

Wooden swings, seesaws and tree houses

President: Jim Sally
Credit Cards: MasterCard
Catalog Cost: Free
Catalog Circulation: Mailed 52 time(s) per
year to 10000
Average Order Size: $2500
Printing Information: 60 pages in 4 colors on
Glossy Stock
Press: Web Press
Binding: Saddle Stitched
Mailing List Information: Names for rent
In Business: 38 years
Number of Employees: 20
Sales Volume: $10,000,000

4144   Woodturning Catalog
Penn State Industries
9900 Global Road
Philadelphia, PA 19115   215-676-7606
                                 800-377-7297
                            Fax: 215-676-7603
                            www.pennstateind.com

**Woodworking and wood turning equipment,
kits and accessories**

President: Ed Levy
Credit Cards: AMEX; MasterCard
Catalog Cost: Free
In Business: 79 years

4145   Woodworker's Supply
Woodworker's Supply Inc
1108 N Glenn Road
Casper, WY 82601-1635   307-237-5354
                                 800-645-9292
                            Fax: 800-853-9663
                            sales@woodworker.com
                            www.woodworker.com

Woodworking tools and supplies

President: John Wirth, Jr.
john@woodworker.com
International Sales: Clay Taylor
clayt@woodworker.com
Website Manager: Robert Tyrrell
rtyrrell@woodworker.com
Customer Service: Lisa Weesner
lisaw@woodworker.com
Credit Cards: AMEX; MasterCard
Catalog Cost: Free
Printing Information: 78 pages
In Business: 45 years
Sales Volume: $5MM to $10MM

**4146   Woodworkers Source -
Scottsdale/Corporate**
Woodworkers Source
5111 N Scottsdale Road
#206
Scottsdale, AZ 85250   480-344-1020
                                 800-713-3418
                            Fax: 480-344-1023
                            cust.support@woodworkerssource.com
                            www.woodworkerssource.com

**Domestic and imported hardwood lumber,
veneer and turning stock, rare, specialty,
and hard-to-find exotic woods**

President: Keith Stephens
Marketing Manager: Betty Stephens
Operations Manager: John Porter
nphx@woodworkerssource.com
Credit Cards: AMEX; MasterCard
Catalog Cost: Free
Catalog Circulation: Mailed 2 time(s) per year
to 60000
Average Order Size: $150
Printing Information: 4 pages on Glossy Stock
Press: Sheetfed Press
Binding: Folded
In Business: 37 years
Number of Employees: 15

4147   Woodworkers Supply
Woodworkers Supply, Inc
1108 N Glenn Rd
Casper, WY 82601-1635   307-237-5528
                                 800-645-9292
                            Fax: 800-853-9663
                            comments@woodworker.com
                            www.woodworker.com

Woodworking tools and supplies

President: John Wirth, Jr.
john@woodworker.com
CFO: Joe McQuade
Marketing Manager: Ken Pollitt
kenp@woodworker.com
Production Manager: Dean Cannon
Operations Manager: Darrell Feldman
darrellf@woodworker.com
International Marketing Manager: Jay Sanger
Buyers: Cynthia Quintana
Credit Cards: AMEX; MasterCard
Catalog Cost: Free
Catalog Circulation: Mailed 12 time(s) per
year to 6M
Average Order Size: $100
Printing Information: 220 pages in 4 colors on
Glossy Stock
Press: Web Press
Binding: Perfect Bound
Mailing List Information: Names for rent
List Manager: Mike Gilb
In Business: 43 years
Number of Employees: 76

4148   2JP Ranch
2JP Ranch
150 Scenic Drive
Mountain Home, TX 78058   775-750-2433
                            Fax: 830-866-3304
                            www.2jpranch.com

**Sheep wool, fleeces, roving and yarns avail-
able in white or natural.**

President: Pauline Holmes
Pauline@2JPRanch.com

4149   Alexandra's Homespun Textiles
The Seraph
5606 State Route 37 E
Delaware, OH 43015-9642   740-369-1817
                            Fax: 740-363-0664
                            www.theseraph.com

Authentic homespun reproduction textiles

Catalog Cost: $9

4150   America's Yarn Store
WEBS - America's Yarn Store
75 Service Center Road
Northampton, MA 01060   800-367-9327
                            Fax: 413-584-1603
                            customerservice@yarn.com
                            www.yarn.com

**Knitting, weaving, spinning and crocheting
yarns and supplies**

President: Steve Elkins
Marketing Manager: Kathy Elkins
Credit Cards: AMEX; MasterCard
Catalog Cost: Free
Mailing List Information: Names for rent
In Business: 41 years
Number of Employees: 50
Sales Volume: $1,000,000+

4151   Aurora Silk
Aurora Silk
5806 N Vancouver Avenue
Portland, OR 97217   503-286-4149
                            dyer@aurorasilk.com
                            www.aurorasilk.com

**silk fabrics, yarns and fibre. Speciality:
Peace, wild and Ahimsa silks. Natural Dyes
all 100% Organic or wildcrafted. 100% natural Hemp fabrics.**

President: Cheryl Kolander
Fulfillment: Phoebe Holland
Catalog Cost: $15
In Business: 49 years

4152   Bartlett Yarns
Bartlettyarns Inc
20 Water Street
PO Box 36
Harmony, ME 04942-36   207-683-2251
                            Fax: 207-683-2261
                            info@bartlettyarns.com
                            www.bartlettyarns.com

**Wool knitting yarns, rovings, warp yarns,
blankets, patterns and knitting accessories**

President: Lindsey Rice
Credit Cards: MasterCard; Visa
Catalog Circulation: Mailed 1 time(s) per year
to 3000
Printing Information: 4 pages in 1 color
Press: Sheetfed Press
Binding: Folded
Mailing List Information: Names for rent
In Business: 193 years
Number of Employees: 1
Sales Volume: $30,000

4153 Blackberry Ridge Woolen Mill
Blackberry Ridge Woolen Mill
3776 Forshaug Road
Mt Horeb, WI 53572-1012   608-437-3762
anne@blackberry-ridge.com
www.blackberry-ridge.com

Wonderfully soft yarns, kits and patterns
President: Anne Bosch
Director: David Byers
Credit Cards: MasterCard; Visa
Catalog Cost: Free
Catalog Circulation: to 2000
Printing Information: 36 pages in 4 colors on
Glossy Stock
Binding: Saddle Stitched
In Business: 16 years
Number of Employees: 10
Sales Volume: $130,000

4154 Blue Mountain Wall Coverings
Blue Mountain Wall Coverings
15 Akron Road
Toronto, CN M8W 1   216-464-3700
866-563-9872
Fax: 216-378-5529
info@blmtn.com
www.blmtn.com

Fabric collections
Chairman: Dick Lappin
President: Suzanne Taylor
President: James P Toohey
In Business: 25 years

4155 Bonnie Triola Yarns
Knit it Now
1001 Avenida Pico C274
San Clemente, CA 92673   949-940-8868
Fax: 440-628-5188
info@btyarns.com
www.knititnow.com/

Surplus yarns for machine knitting - manufacturers' closeouts, books and original patterns
President: Bonnie Triola
Credit Cards: MasterCard
Catalog Cost: $10
Catalog Circulation: to 200
Printing Information: 30 pages in 2 colors on
Matte Stock
In Business: 25 years
Number of Employees: 2

4156 Bucilla Stocking Kits
MerryStockings
160 1st St. SE
#5
New Brighton, MN 55112   888-764-2271
info@merrystockings.com
www.merrystockings.com

Bucilla felt Christmas stocking kits

4157 Calico Corners
Calico Corners
203 Gale Lane
Kennett Square, PA 19348-1735   800-213-6366
www.calicocorners.com

Decorative fabric, trimmings and furniture
President: Roy Simpson
Catalog Cost: Free
Catalog Circulation: Mailed 4 time(s) per year
Printing Information: 40 pages in 4 colors on
Glossy Stock
Binding: Perfect Bound
In Business: 67 years
Sales Volume: Under $500M

4158 Camela Nitschke Ribbonry
The Ribbonry
119 Lousianna Ave.
Perrysburg, OH 43551   419-872-0073
Fax: 419-872-0073
info@ribbonry.com
www.ribbonry.com

Ribbons
President: Camela Mithchke
Credit Cards: AMEX; MasterCard
Printing Information: 5 pages in 2 colors on
Matte Stock
Binding: Folded
In Business: 15 years

4159 Castlegate Farm
Castlegate Farm
424 Kingwood-Locktown Road
Flemington, NJ 08822-4708   908-996-6152
Fax: 908-996-2416
nan@castlegatefarm.com
www.Castlegatefarm.Com

Fleece, handspun and millspun yarns, breeding stock and sheepskins, handmade wool boxes, sheep-shaped coat racks and key holders
President: Nancy Clarke
Catalog Cost: $2.5
Sales Volume: Under $500M

4160 Cotton Clouds
Cotton Clouds, Inc.
5176 S. 14th Avenue
Safford, AZ 85546-9252   928-428-7000
800-322-7888
Fax: 928-428-6630
info@cottonclouds.com
www.cottonclouds.com

Yarn, patterns, books, videos, kits for weaving crochet, knitting and spinning, spinning wheels, knitting machines and exclusive kits
President: Irene Schmoller
Representatives: Jodi Ybarra
Credit Cards: AMEX; MasterCard
Catalog Cost: $2.5
Catalog Circulation: Mailed 1 time(s) per year
Printing Information: in 4 colors
Press: Web Press
Binding: Saddle Stitched
In Business: 37 years
Sales Volume: Under $500M

4161 Country Textiles
Judy Robinson's Country Textiles
3350 Chicken Coop Hill Road
Lancaster, OH 43130-8286   740-746-9602
Fax: 740-746-0409
jrobinson@fairfieldi.com
www.judyrobinsonscountrytextiles.com

Patterns, rugs and textiles
President: Judy Robinson
Catalog Cost: $4
In Business: 26 years
Number of Employees: 3
Sales Volume: $1MM to $3MM

4162 Createx Colors
Createx Colors
14 Airport Park Road
PO Box 120
East Granby, CT 06026-9523   860-653-5505
800-243-2712
Fax: 860-653-0643
info@createxcolors.com
www.createxcolors.com

Airbrush colors for automobiles, acrylic colors for use on wood, canvas, textiles, leather, fiberglass, and vinyl
President: Vincent Kennedy
VP Operations: Dennis Deloranzo
VP, Finance: Craig Kennedy
Office Manager: Cory Roberts

Credit Cards: MasterCard; Visa
Printing Information: 11 pages in 4 colors
In Business: 37 years
Number of Employees: 17
Sales Volume: $300,000

4163 Dazian Fabrics
Dazian Fabrics
18 Central Boulevard
South Hackensack, NJ 07606   201-549-1000
877-232-9426
Fax: 201-549-1055
info@dazian.com
www.dazian.com

Fabrics, drapes, home theatre and projection screen materials
President: Jon Weingarten
CFO: Chris Diaz
Marketing Manager: Karen Loftus
Production Manager: Wade Wesson
Credit Cards: AMEX; MasterCard; Visa
Catalog Cost: Free
In Business: 173 years
Number of Employees: 80
Sales Volume: $16.2 Million

4164 Edinburgh Imports
Edinburgh Imports
3551 Voyager Street
Unit B
Torrance, CA 90503   310-370-5800
800-334-6274
Fax: 310-370-5802
info@edinburghimports.com
www.edinburghimports.com

Teddy bear fabrics and craft supplies
President: Elke Block
CFO: Ronald Block
Credit Cards: AMEX; MasterCard
Catalog Circulation: Mailed 1 time(s) per year
Printing Information: 32 pages in 1 color on
Matte Stock
Mailing List Information: Names for rent
In Business: 32 years
Number of Employees: 26

4165 Exotic Silks
Exotic Silks, Inc.
1959 Leghorn Street
Mountain View, CA 94043-1797   650-965-7760
800-845-7455
Fax: 650-965-0712
silks@exoticsilks.com
www.exoticsilks.com

Silk and cotton fabric, velvet silk rayon, brocades, 100% silk chiffon, silk prints, satin silks
President: Deanne Shute
Sales: Miki Cleveland
mikisilksgift@hotmail.com
Sales: Marvin Levine
mjL18Marvin@sbcglobal.net
Assistant Manager: Margie Mishito
Buyers: Mary Carter
Credit Cards: AMEX; MasterCard; Visa
Catalog Cost: Free
Catalog Circulation: Mailed 2 time(s) per year
Average Order Size: $400
Printing Information: 8 pages in 2 colors
Mailing List Information: Names for rent
In Business: 53 years
Number of Employees: 39
Sales Volume: $6 Million

4166 Fabrics Catalog
H.A. Kidd & Company Limited
5 Northline Road
Toronto, ON M4B-3P2   416-364-6451
800-387-1753
Fax: 888-236-8104
info1@hakidd.com
www.hakidd.com

Assorted fabrics

Marketing Manager: Lynda Macham
VP, Chief Operating Officer: Jim Thielen
Controller, Human Resources: Amir Mirza
Credit Cards: MasterCard
Catalog Cost: Free
Catalog Circulation: Mailed 4 time(s) per year
Printing Information: 28 pages in 4 colors
In Business: 93 years
Sales Volume: $20MM to $50MM

4167   Fancifuls

Fancifuls Inc.
1070 Leonard Rd
Marathon, NY 13803-3401   607-849-6870
                                    Fax: 607-849-6870
                              fancifuls@frontier.com
                              www.fancifulsinc.com

Brass charms, embellishments

Chairman: Vincent Pedini
President: Donna Pedini
Credit Cards: MasterCard
Catalog Cost: Free
Printing Information: 114 pages in 2 colors on Newsprint
In Business: 15 years
Number of Employees: 2
Sales Volume: $280,000

4168   Fashion Fabrics Club

Fashion Fabrics Club
10490 Baur Blvd.
St Louis, MO 63132-1907   314-993-4919
                                    800-468-0602
                              Fax: 314-993-5802
                        www.Fashionfabricsclub.Com

Dress fabrics

President: Tom Samson
Credit Cards: MasterCard
Catalog Cost: $10
Catalog Circulation: Mailed 12 time(s) per year
Number of Employees: 10
Sales Volume: $1MM to $3MM

4169   Fiber Arts Supplies Catalog

Dharma Trading Co.
1805 South McDowell Blvd. Ext.
Petaluma, CA 94954   707-283-0390
                                    800-542-5227
                              Fax: 707-283-0379
                        catalog@dharmatrading.com
                        www.dharmatrading.com

Fabric dyes, paints, clothing blanks, fabrics and information

President: Isaac Goff
Buyers: Isaac Goff
Credit Cards: AMEX; MasterCard
Catalog Cost: Free
Catalog Circulation: Mailed 2 time(s) per year
Printing Information: 144 pages in 1 color on Newsprint
Press: Web Press
Binding: Saddle Stitched
Mailing List Information: Names for rent
In Business: 42 years
Number of Employees: 65

4170   Field's Fabrics

Field's Fabrics
3701 Plainfield Ave
Grand Rapids, MI 49525-5001   616-364-6505
                                    800-678-5872
                              Fax: 616-455-1052
                        www.Fieldsfabrics.com

Fabrics

President: Roger Veldman
Credit Cards: AMEX; MasterCard
In Business: 62 years
Sales Volume: $3MM to $5MM

4171   Fiesta Yarns

Fiesta Yarns
5620 Venice Ave. NE
Suite J
Albuquerque, NM 87113-2548   505-892-5008
                                    877-834-3782
                        Customerservice@FiestaYarns.com
                        www.fiestayarns.com

Hand dyed yarns: mohair, rayon, cotton, silk, and wools, in a variety of plies, colors and textures, catalog/color cards available

Owner: Dye Pot Goddess
Catalog Cost: $10

4172   Fingerlakes Woolen Mill

Fingerlakes Woolen Mill
1193 Stewarts Corners Road
Genoa, NY 13071   315-497-1542
                                    800-441-9665
                        yarn@fingerlakes-yarns.com
                        www.fingerlakes-yarns.com

Fingerlake yarns: wools, angora/wool, silk/wool blends, brushed mohair and Unspun in 23 colors, sock, sweater and stocking kits

Catalog Cost: $4
In Business: 34 years

4173   Fox Hollow Farm & Fiber

Oregon Wool Growers Association
30781 Fox Hollow Road
Eugene, OR 97405   541-343-6596
                        kusiwarmi13@gmail.com
                        www.oregonwool.com

Natural colored fleeces, raw or washed mohair, yarns, exotic fibers, hot acid dye kits, spinning wheels and accessories

President: Rolly Thompson
In Business: 12 years

4174   Green Mountain Spinnery

Green Mountain Spinnery
PO Box 568
Putney, VT 05346-568   802-387-4528
                                    800-321-9665
                              Fax: 802-387-4841
                        spinnery@sover.net
                        www.spinnery.com

Knitting and weaving yarns of natural fiber blends: wool, mohair,cotton, alpaca

President: Claire Wilson
Catalog Cost: $8
Catalog Circulation: to 2000
Printing Information: 20 pages in 4 colors on Matte Stock
Press: Sheetfed Press
Binding: Saddle Stitched
Mailing List Information: Names for rent
In Business: 34 years
Number of Employees: 20-O
Sales Volume: Under $500M

4175   H.A. Kidd

H.A. Kidd & Company Limited
5 Northline Road
Toronto, ON M4B-3P2   416-364-6451
                                    800-387-1753
                              Fax: 888-236-8204
                        info1@hakidd.com
                        www.hakidd.com

Fabrics, yarn, needles and hooks, cutting tools, buttons and closures, zippers, batting and stabilizers

Marketing Manager: Lynda Macham
VP, Chief Operating Officer: Jim Thielen
Controller, Human Resources: Amir Mirza
In Business: 93 years
Sales Volume: $20MM to $50MM

4176   Hancock's of Paducah

Hancock's of Paducah
3841 Hinkleville Road
Paducah, KY 42001-9155   270-443-4410
                                    800-845-8723
                              Fax: 270-442-2164
                        customerservice@hancocks-paducah.com
                        www.hancocks-paducah.com

Quilting fabrics and notions; also home decorating fabrics, drapery and upholstery fabrics

Credit Cards: AMEX; MasterCard
Catalog Circulation: Mailed 4 time(s) per year
Printing Information: in 4 colors
In Business: 63 years

4177   Handy Hands

578 N. 1800 E
Paxton, IL 60957   217-379-3802
                              Fax: 217-379-3799
                        staff@hhtatting.com
                        www.hhtatting.com

Needle tatting

4178   Harriets

Harriets
1 N Nabby Road
Danbury, CT 06811-3320   203-730-2122
                              Fax: 203-599-1863
                        tcs.info@harriets.com
                        www.harriets.com

Over 200 vintage patterns for men, women and children, XL sizes available; Circa 1300-1945, 8 styles of hoops, corsets, boning, fabric, 100% polished cotton and silks, rentals and accessories

President: Harriet A Engler
Business Manager and Webmaster: Lynda Engler
Credit Cards: AMEX; MasterCard
Catalog Cost: $16

4179   JR Burrows

JR Burrows
393 Union Street
PO Box 522
Rockland, MA 02370-522   781-982-1812
                                    800-347-1795
                              Fax: 781-982-1636
                        merchant@burrows.com
                        www.Burrows.Com

Arts and crafts, wallpaper, fabric, carpet and lace

President: John Burrows
Marketing Manager: Dan Cooper
Catalog Cost: Free
Printing Information: 5 pages in 2 colors on Glossy Stock
Binding: Folded
In Business: 28 years
Number of Employees: 3
Sales Volume: $500M to $1MM

4180   JaggerSpun

JaggerSpun
PO Box 188
Springvale, ME 04083-188   207-324-4455
                              Fax: 207-490-2661
                        www.jaggeryarn.com/

Offers an assortment of natural fiber yarns suitable for weaving or knitting

President: Susan L Upham
Catalog Cost: $6
In Business: 117 years
Number of Employees: 75

4181 John Robshaw Textiles
John Robshaw Textiles
245 W. 29th St.
Suite 1501
New York, NY 10001   212-594-6006
Fax: 212-594-6116
info@johnrobshaw.com
www.johnrobshaw.com

Textiles, napkins, duvet covers, tabletop runners, window treatments, bedding.

4182 Knit Knack Shop
Knit Knack Shop, Inc.
3378 West 550 North
Peru, IN 46970-8293   765-985-3164
800-735-8266
Fax: 888-648-3902
kks@knitknackshop.com
www.Knitknackshop.Com

Machine knitting yarns, knitting machines, Hauge Linkens, machine knitting books, and machine knitting assembly

Chairman: Harold Shafer
President: Harold Shafer
Marketing Manager: Noel Shafer
Credit Cards: MasterCard
Number of Employees: 5
Sales Volume: $1MM to $3MM

4183 Knitting & Crochet Catalog
The Village Spinning & Weaving Shop
425 Alisal Road
Solvang, CA 93463-3704   805-686-1192
888-686-1192
inquiry@villagespinweave.com
www.villagespinweave.com

Knit and crochet tools, books, yarns, and supplies

President: John & Marsha Novak
Credit Cards: AMEX; MasterCard
Catalog Cost: Free
Printing Information: 16 pages in 1 color on Matte Stock
Mailing List Information: Names for rent
In Business: 22 years

4184 Lambspun
Lambspun of Colorado
1101 E Lincoln Ave
PO Box 320
Fort Collins, CO 80526   970-484-1998
800-558-5262
Fax: 970-484-1081
www.Lambspun.Com

Selection of natural fibers and yarns for knitting or weaving, kits, spinning fibers and more

President: Shirley Ellsworth
Catalog Cost: Free
Catalog Circulation: to 4500
Average Order Size: $75
Printing Information: 4 pages in 1 color on Glossy Stock
Binding: Saddle Stitched
In Business: 15 years
Number of Employees: 7
Sales Volume: $500M to $1MM

4185 Lion Brand Yarn
Lion Brand Yarn
135 Kero Road
Carlstadt, NJ 07072   212-243-8995
800-258-9276
Fax: 212-627-8154
www.lionbrand.com

Yarn, knitting supplies, and knitting and crochet patterns

President: David Blumenthal
EVP/COO: Dean Blumenthal
CEO: David Blumenthal
Credit Cards: MasterCard

Catalog Cost: Free
In Business: 137 years

4186 Logan Kits
Logan Kits
686 County Road 3053
Double Springs, AL 35553   205-486-7732
Fax: 205-486-7732
logankits@ala.nu

Cotton, velour, underwires, silver jewelry, lingerie kits, pounds and yard goods, tricot, cotton Lycra spandex, fleece, collars, thread, Sew Lovely patterns, and rib and free patterns

President: Evelyn Logan
Catalog Cost: $1.5
Catalog Circulation: Mailed 1 time(s) per year
Printing Information: 28 pages in 1 color on Newsprint
Binding: Folded
Mailing List Information: Names for rent
In Business: 20 years
Sales Volume: Under $500M

4187 Nancy's Notions
Nancy's Notions
333 Beichl Ave
PO Box 683
Beaver Dam, WI 53916-683   920-887-0391
800-833-0690
Fax: 920-887-2133
custserv@nancysnotions.com
www.nancysnotions.com

Sewing supplies, quilting supplies, machine embroidery supplies and designs, patterns, books, DVDs, fabrics, and kits

President: Katherine Johnson
Production Manager: Kathy Gittus
Fulfillment: John Nickel
Owner/President: Nancy L Zieman
Buyers: Chris Stam
Credit Cards: AMEX; MasterCard
Catalog Cost: Free
Catalog Circulation: Mailed 13 time(s) per year
Printing Information: 70 pages in 4 colors on Matte Stock
Press: Web Press
Binding: Saddle Stitched
Mailing List Information: Names for rent
List Company: Zed Marketing
416 Autmnwood Court
Edmond, OK 73003
405-348-8145
In Business: 35 years
Sales Volume: $10MM to $20MM

4188 Nordic Fiber Arts
Nordic Fiber Arts
4 Cutts Road
Durham, NH 03824-3101   603-868-1196
info@nordicfiberarts.com
www.nordicfiberarts.com

Original knitting patterns, Norwegian Rauma yarns, knitting needles and pewter buttons, clasps and knitting books from Scandinavia

President: Deborah Gremlitz
Credit Cards: MasterCard
Catalog Cost: Free
Printing Information: 30 pages in 4 colors
In Business: 21 years
Number of Employees: 1
Sales Volume: $86,000

4189 Norsk Fjord Fiber
Norsk Fjord Fiber
PO Box 219
Sapphire, NC 28774   352-682-3255
srm@norskfjordfiber.com
www.norskfjordfiber.com

Unique spinning fibers from Scandinavia and wools from primitive breeds of sheep

Credit Cards: MasterCard
Catalog Cost:
In Business: 30 years

4190 Nustyle Quilting Machines and Supplies
Nustyle
309 W 4th St, Stover
Stover, MO 65078   573-377-2244
800-821-7490
Fax: 573-377-2833
info@nustylequilting.com
www.nustylequilting.com

Long arm quilting machines and frames, hand quilting frames, large rolls Dacron and cotton batt, sewing and quilting books, supplies, tools, over 4,000 bolts of fabric

Owner: Tom Dale
Owner: Lora Dale
Credit Cards: MasterCard
Average Order Size: $70
Printing Information: 12 pages in 1 color on Newsprint
Press: Sheetfed Press
Mailing List Information: Names for rent
In Business: 139 years
Number of Employees: 4
Sales Volume: Under $500M

4191 Personal Threads Boutique
Personal Threads Boutique
8600 Cass Street
Omaha, NE 68114-3413   402-391-7733
800-306-7733
Fax: 402-391-0039
sales@personalthreads.com
www.personalthreads.com

Fine yarns, hand-painted needlepoints, knitting and needlecraft supplies

President: Julie Wynn
Founder: Carolyn Lewis
Credit Cards: AMEX; MasterCard
Catalog Cost: Free
Catalog Circulation: Mailed 2 time(s) per year
Average Order Size: $25
Printing Information: 50 pages in 2 colors on Glossy Stock
Press: Web Press
Binding: Saddle Stitched
Mailing List Information: Names for rent
In Business: 22 years
Number of Employees: 10-J

4192 Pinecreek Farm
Pinecreek Farm
2095 N Phillips Road
Deford, MI 48729-9765   989-872-5496
pinecreekfarm@pinecreekfarm.com

Offers everything mohair - raw hair, roving, yarns, t-shirts, notecards, dolls, throws, spinning wheels and more

President: Don and Debbie Krug
Catalog Cost: $1
In Business: 32 years

4193 Quest Outfitters
Quest Outfitters
4919 Hubner Circle
Sarasota, FL 34241-9224   941-923-5006
800-359-6931
Fax: 941-923-5006
info@questoutfitters.com
www.questoutfitters.com

Outdoor fabrics, patterns, fasteners and zippers, stretch binding for use on fleece fabrics, wear and gear patterns

President: Kay Anderson
Credit Cards: MasterCard
Catalog Cost: Free
Catalog Circulation: to 3000
Average Order Size: $50
Printing Information: 16 pages on Matte Stock
Binding: Folded
In Business: 22 years

Number of Employees: 2
Sales Volume: Under $500M

4194 Rose Brand
Rose Brand
4 Emerson Lane
Secaucus, NJ 07094-2661 201-809-1730
800-223-1624
Fax: 201-809-1851
info@rosebrand.com
www.rosebrand.com

Fabrics and custom draperies for theaters, churches, school, events and entertainment venues

President: George Jacobson
CFO: Peter Finder
Marketing Manager: Mary Vandaver
Production Manager: Bob Betrand
Product Manager: Mark O'Brien
Graphic Designer: Kelly Salvadore
General Manager: Tina Carlin
International Marketing Manager: Vicki Williamson
Catalog Cost: Free
Printing Information: 96 pages in 4 colors on Glossy Stock
Press: Web Press
Binding: Saddle Stitched
Mailing List Information: Names for rent
In Business: 102 years
Number of Employees: 150
Sales Volume: Under $500M

4195 Sailrite Home Catalog
Sailrite Enterprises, Inc.
2390 E 100 S
Columbia City, IN 46725 260-244-4647
800-348-2769
Fax: 260-818-2005
info@sailrite.com
www.sailrite.com

Home sewing machines, fabrics, and supplies

President: Matt Grant
Co-Owner: Hallie Grant
Catalog Cost: Free
Catalog Circulation: Mailed 1 time(s) per year
Printing Information: 260 pages in 4 colors
In Business: 48 years
Number of Employees: 12

4196 Sarah's Sewing Supplies
SewWithSarah.com
3412 Holt Circle Suite C
Pensacola, FL 32526 850-944-7570
800-883-2348
Fax: 800-558-3647
sarah@sewwithsarah.com
www.sewwithsarah.com

Sewing supplies, pattern books and sewing how-to videotapes

President: Sarah J Doyle
Marketing Manager: Denise Hemphill
Credit Cards: MasterCard; Visa
Catalog Circulation: Mailed 1 time(s) per year
Printing Information: 106 pages in 2 colors on Newsprint
Press: Web Press
Binding: Saddle Stitched
In Business: 40 years
Sales Volume: Under $500M

4197 Sawyer Brook Distinctive Fabrics
Sawyer Brook Distinctive Fabrics
P.O. Box 700
Clinton, MA 01510-700 978-368-3133
800-290-2739
Fax: 978-365-1775
service@sawyerbrook.com
www.sawyerbrook.com

Fine fabrics

President: Barbara Blom
Mailing List Information: Names for rent

In Business: 40 years
Number of Employees: 9

4198 Seraph's Full Color First Period Inclination
The Seraph
420 Main Street
PO Box 500
Sturbridge, MA 01566 508-347-2241
Fax: 508-347-9162
www.theseraph.com

Historic fabrics, furniture, stencils, lighting, paint, jewelry and accessories

President: Alexandra Pifer
Credit Cards: MasterCard
Catalog Cost: $3
Printing Information: in 4 colors on Matte Stock
Mailing List Information: Names for rent
Number of Employees: 5
Sales Volume: $1MM to $3MM

4199 Sewbaby
Sewbaby
1511 Sussex Court
Champaign, IL 61821 800-249-1907
Fax: 253-830-7840
sewbaby@sewbaby.com
www.sewbaby.com

Childrens' fabrics, unique patterns, snaps, novelty buttons, lace and bows, Fabric Club $25/year for 30 fabric samples

President: Ann Brodsky
Customer Service Representative: Shirley Robbins
Credit Cards: AMEX; MasterCard
Printing Information: in 3 colors
In Business: 20 years

4200 Shillcraft
Shillcraft
P.O. Box 325
Bonsall, CA 92003 951-674-4307
Fax: 951-674-4325
support@shillcraft.com
www.shillcraft.com

Latch hook kits, materials, and accessories

Catalog Cost:
In Business: 64+ years

4201 Solo Slide Fasteners
WAWAK Sewing
1059 Powers Road
Conklin, NY 13748-8589 800-654-2235
customerservice@wawak.com
www.Soloslide.Com

Drycleaning, tailoring and sewing supplies

President: Michael Flatto
Buyers: Mark Lubow
Credit Cards: MasterCard
Catalog Cost: Free
Catalog Circulation: Mailed 3 time(s) per year to 15000
Printing Information: 100 pages in 4 colors on Glossy Stock
Press: Sheetfed Press
Mailing List Information: Names for rent
In Business: 107 years

4202 Spinning & Felting Supply
Village Spinning & Weaving
425 Alisal Road
Solvang, CA 93463-3704 805-686-1192
888-686-1192
inquiry@villagespinweave.com
villagespinweave.com

Spinning tools, supplies, books, fibers, and felting

President: John & Marsha Novak
Credit Cards: AMEX; MasterCard
Catalog Cost: Free
Printing Information: 10 pages in 1 color on

Newsprint
Mailing List Information: Names for rent
In Business: 23 years

4203 Straw into Gold/Crystal Palace Yarns
Crystal Palace Yarns
160 23rd St
Richmond, CA 94804-1828 510-237-9988
Fax: 510-237-9809
cpyinfo@straw.com
www.Straw.Com

Yarns, books, fibers, and Ashford Spinning wheels

Chairman: Andy MacEwan
President: Susan Druding
In Business: 43 years
Sales Volume: $500M to $1MM

4204 Such a Deal Lace & Trim
SUCH-A-DEAL LACE & TRIM
7341 Winding Way
Fair Oaks, CA 95628-5503 916-966-5223
800-368-3186
Fax: 916-966-5213
info@such-a-deal.com
www.such-a-deal.com

Laces, ribbons, braids, bridal, etc.

Catalog Cost: $3
Printing Information: 30 pages
Press: Sheetfed Press
Binding: Saddle Stitched
Mailing List Information: Names for rent
In Business: 20 years
Number of Employees: 4
Sales Volume: $530,000

4205 Suedeshop.Com
Michiko's Creations
PO Box 4313
Napa, CA 94558-431 707-224-8546
Fax: 707-224-2246
michiko@suedeshop.com
www.suedeshop.com

Suede and synthetic suede fabrics

Credit Cards: MasterCard; Visa
In Business: 29 years
Number of Employees: 1
Sales Volume: $200,000

4206 Super Silk
Super Silk, Inc.
PO Box 527596
Flushing, NY 11352-7596 718-886-2606
800-432-7455
Fax: 718-886-2657
sales@supersilk.com

Silk fabrics

President: Anita Nadiadhara
Manager: Sharon Liang
Credit Cards: AMEX; MasterCard
Catalog Cost: Free
In Business: 24 years
Number of Employees: 3
Sales Volume: $390,000

4207 Testfabrics
Testfabrics, Inc.
415 Delaware Avenue
West Pittston, PA 18643-2105 570-603-0432
Fax: 570-603-0433
info@testfabrics.com
www.testfabrics.com

Textiles and fabrics for crafts and industrial use

President: W. Finley Klaas
Marketing Manager: Normandy Klaas
Warehouse & Shipping Manager: Brian Winslow
Accounts Manager: Jeremy Klaas
Quality Assurance: Miranda Klaas
Credit Cards: AMEX; MasterCard; Visa
Catalog Cost: Free

Catalog Circulation: Mailed 2 time(s) per year
Printing Information: 20 pages in 1 color on Matte Stock
Mailing List Information: Names for rent
In Business: 86 years
Number of Employees: 20
Sales Volume: $3MM to $5MM

4208 Textile Enterprises

Textile Enterprises Inc
216 Main Street
P O Box 154
Whitesburg, GA 30185-3203   770-834-2094
                              866-777-5273
                Fax: 770-834-2096
                textilenterprise@aol.com
                www.textilenterprises.com

Dried and painted floral products, Spanish moss, excelsior, wreaths and others.;Floral supplies, bells, beads, novelties, baskets, macrame cord, craft cords and supplies. Rope, purse handles, rings

President: Martha Arnold
marthaqarnold@bellsouth.net
Printing Information: on Matte Stock
Binding: Folded
In Business: 37 years
Sales Volume: $5,00,000

4209 The Country Seat

The Country Seat, Inc.
1013 Old Philly Pike
Kempton, PA 19529-9321   610-756-6124
                Fax: 610-756-0088
                weaving@countryseat.com
                www.countryseat.com

Basketry supplies, gourd weaving and chair seat supplies

President: Donna Longenecker
CFO: Bill Longenecker
Catalog Cost: Free
Printing Information: 23 pages
In Business: 40 years
Number of Employees: 3
Sales Volume: $20,000

4210 The Fiber Loft

The Fiber Loft
9 Massachusetts Avenue (Rte. 111)
Harvard, MA 01451-327   978-456-8669
                yarn@TheFiberLoft.com
                www.thefiberloft.com

Natural fiber yarns for machine/hand crochet/knitting and weaving

President: Reba Maisel
Founder: Reba Maisel
Credit Cards: MasterCard
Printing Information: 64 pages
In Business: 40 years
Sales Volume: Under $500M

4211 Tinsel Trading Company

Tinsel Trading Company
828 Lexington Avenue
New York, NY 10065-5361   212-730-1030
                Fax: 212-768-8823
                www.Tinseltrading.Com

Trim, tussels, flowers, ribbon, fringers, cord, specializing in vintage metallic tassels

President: Marcia Ceppos
Printing Information: 47 pages
Mailing List Information: Names for rent
In Business: 82 years
Number of Employees: 8
Sales Volume: $5MM to $10MM

4212 Upholstery Supplies

Baer Fabrics
515 E Market Street
Louisville, KY 40202-1114   502-583-5521
                              800-769-7779
                Fax: 502-569-7030
                stuart.sewingman@gmail.com
                www.baerfabrics.com

Full line of upholstery fabrics and supplies for furniture, automotive and marine, plus retractable Awnings and Awning fabrics

President: Stuart S Goldberg
CFO: Stuart S Goldberg
Catalog Cost: $6
Printing Information: 100 pages in 1 color on Matte Stock
Press: Sheetfed Press
Binding: Perfect Bound
Mailing List Information: Names for rent
In Business: 38 years

4213 W.D. Lockwood

W.D. Lockwood & Company, Inc.
49 Walker Street
1st Floor
New York, NY 10013-3443   212-966-4046
                              866-293-8913
                Fax: 212-274-9616
                sales@wdlockwood.com
                www.wdlockwood.com

Wood stains and dyes

President: Herb Lockwood
Credit Cards: AMEX; MasterCard; Visa
Printing Information: 7 pages
Binding: Folded
In Business: 134 years

4214 WEBS - America's Yarn Store

WEBS-America's Yarn Store
75 Service Center Road
Northampton, MA 01060   800-367-9327
                Fax: 413-584-1603
                customerservice@yarn.com
                www.yarn.com

Yarns, weaving looms & equipment, spinning wheels, fibers and books

In Business: 41 years

4215 Warm Company

The Warm Company
5529 186th Place Sw
Lynnwood, WA 98037   425-248-2424
                       800-234-9276
                Fax: 206-320-0974
                info@warmcompany.com
                www.warmcompany.com

Warm Window insulated fabric, with 4 layers quilted together for energy saving, warm and natural needled cotton batting for quilts, crafts and wearable art, Steam-a-Seam fabric fusing web and more

In Business: 35 years

4216 Willow Yarns

2800 Hoover Road
Stevens Point, WI 54492   855-279-4701
                CustomerService@WillowYarns.com
                www.willowyarns.com

Yarns

4217 Willowes Basketry & Yarn

Willowes Basketry & Yarn
226 West Main Street
Greenfield, IN 46140   317-462-2026
                         800-230-3195
                Fax: 317-467-1995
                contact@willowes.com
                www.willowes.com

Caning and basket supplies, yarns, stains and dyes

President: Margaret Harness
Catalog Cost: Free
Number of Employees: 2
Sales Volume: $100,000

4218 Wool Gathering

Wool Gathering
6899 Cary Bluff
Pittsville, WI 54466   715-884-2799
                         800-968-5648
                Fax: 715-884-2829
                info@schoolhousepress.com
                www.schoolhousepress.com

100% wool, 200 books, instructional videos, needles, buttons, and an assortment of knitting tools

President: Meg Swansen
Marketing Manager: Eleanor Haase
Credit Cards: MasterCard
Catalog Cost: $3
Catalog Circulation: Mailed 2 time(s) per year to 3000
Printing Information: 12 pages in 1 color on Matte Stock
Press: Letterpress
Binding: Saddle Stitched
Mailing List Information: Names for rent
In Business: 57 years
Number of Employees: 3
Sales Volume: $10MM to $20MM

4219 Woolery

The Woolery
315 St. Clair St
Frankfort, KY 40601   502-352-9800
                        800-441-9665
                Fax: 502-352-9802
                info@woolery.com
                www.woolery.com

Spinning wheels, looms, fibers, yarns (wool, angora, silk, cotton), felting, rug hooking, handknitting, braiding, spinning & weaving supplies, dyes, books, videos, gifts

President: Nancy Miller
Marketing Manager: Marianne DeSalle
Production Manager: Tim Horchler
Fulfillment: Denise Smith
International Marketing Manager: Marianne Horchler
Buyers: Marianne Horchler
Credit Cards: MasterCard
Catalog Cost: Free
Catalog Circulation: Mailed 2 time(s) per year to 30000
Average Order Size: $60
Printing Information: 96 pages in 4 colors on Glossy Stock
Binding: Perfect Bound
Mailing List Information: Names for rent
List Manager: Tim Horchler
In Business: 34 years
Number of Employees: 5
Sales Volume: Under $500M

4220 Wooly West

The Wooly West
PO Box 58306
Salt Lake City, UT 84158   801-581-9812
                             888-487-9665
                catalog@woolywest.com
                www.woolywest.com

Natural fiber yarns, supplies, patterns, pewter buttons, books, knitting needles and more

President: Nancy Bush
Credit Cards: AMEX; MasterCard
Catalog Cost: $5
In Business: 35 years

4221 Yarn Barn's DVD & Video Catalog
Yarn Barn of Kansas, Inc.
930 Massachusetts St
Lawrence, KS 66044-2868   785-842-4333
800-468-0035
Fax: 785-842-0794
info@yarnbarn-ks.com
www.yarnbarn-ks.com

How to craft videos cover beading, weaving, spinning, dyeing, knitting, crochet, basketry, sewing, quilting, needlework, lacemaking and more

President: Susan Bateman
Marketing Manager: Susan Bateman
Credit Cards: MasterCard; Visa
Catalog Cost: Free
Catalog Circulation: to 10K
Printing Information: 50 pages
In Business: 35 years
Number of Employees: 7
Sales Volume: $1,500,000

4222 Yarn Barn's Weaving, Spinning & Dyeing Catalog
Yarn Barn of Kansas, Inc.
930 Massachusetts Street
Lawrence, KS 66044   785-842-4333
800-468-0035
info@yarnbarn-ks.com
www.yarnbarn-ks.com

Supplies for weaving, spinning, dyeing, papermaking, crochet, looms, spinning wheels, spinning fibers, raw fibers, knitting tools, and more

President: Susan Bateman
Credit Cards: MasterCard; Visa
Catalog Cost: Free
Catalog Circulation: Mailed 2 time(s) per year
Average Order Size: $50
Printing Information: 60 pages in 4 colors on Glossy Stock
Press: Web Press
Binding: Saddle Stitched
Mailing List Information: Names for rent
In Business: 37 years
Number of Employees: 7
Sales Volume: $1.5 Million

4223 Yarn by Mills
Yarn by Mills
1769 Camp Run Road
Wallback, WV 25285-28   304-587-2561
Fax: 304-587-2561
yarnbymills@yahoo.com
www.yarnbymills.com

Handspun, hand-dyed knitting or weaving yarns

President: Margy Mills
Catalog Cost: Free
Printing Information: 2 pages

4224 Yarn-it-All
Yarn-it-All
1 Bank St.
No. Attleboro, MA 02760-4810   215-362-3300
508-695-3331
Fax: 215-412-3656
info@yarnitallonline.com
www.yarnitallonline.com

Brother knitting machines - electric and fine needle, bulky punch card and all accessories, name brand yarns, videos, pattern books and instructional books available

President: Katherine Beals
Credit Cards: MasterCard
Sales Volume: Under $500M

Health & Personal Care Products
Apparatus & Exercise Equipment

4225 ASHA
American Speech-Language-Hearing Assoc.
2200 Research Boulevard
Rockville, MD 20850-3289   800-498-2071
800-638-8255
Fax: 301-296-8580
www.asha.org

Products and educational resources

Chairman: Margot L. Beckerman
President: Gail J. Richard
CFO: Judy Rich
Chief Executive Officer: Arlene A. Pietranton
Catalog Cost: Free
Catalog Circulation: Mailed 1 time(s) per year
Printing Information: 120 pages in 4 colors
In Business: 92 years
Number of Employees: 300
Sales Volume: Under $500M

4226 AliMed Operating Room Products
AliMed, Inc
297 High Street
Dedham, MA 02026   781-329-2900
800-437-2966
Fax: 781-329-8392
customerservice@alimed.com
www.alimed.com

Medical and home healthcare equipment

President: Julian Cherubini
Production Manager: Fred Smith
Credit Cards: AMEX; MasterCard; Visa
Catalog Cost: Free
Catalog Circulation: Mailed 1 time(s) per year to 60K
Printing Information: 260 pages in 4 colors
Binding: Perfect Bound
In Business: 37 years
Sales Volume: $20-50 Million

4227 Armstrong Medical Industries
Armstrong Medical Industries, Inc.
575 Knightsbridge Parkway
PO Box 700
Lincolnshire, IL 60069-700   847-913-0101
800-323-4220
Fax: 847-913-0138
csr@armstrongmedical.com
www.armstrongmedical.com

Medical equipment, medical carts and CPR manikins

President: Warren Armstrong
CFO: Rose West
Marketing Manager: Corinne Walker
International Marketing Manager: Mikki Erickson
Credit Cards: AMEX; MasterCard; Visa
Catalog Cost: Free
Catalog Circulation: Mailed 1 time(s) per year to 150M
Printing Information: 180 pages in 4 colors on Glossy Stock
Press: Web Press
Binding: Perfect Bound
Mailing List Information: Names for rent
In Business: 58 years
Number of Employees: 95
Sales Volume: $13 Million

4228 Atlantic Fitness Products
Atlantic Fitness Products
PO Box 300
Linthicum, MD 21090-300   410-859-3538
800-445-1855
Fax: 410-859-3907
www.atlanticfitnessproducts.com/

Equipment for weightlifting and fitness

President: Faye Miller
CFO: Ronald E Overby

Production Manager: Donald White
International Marketing Manager: Richard Stone
Buyers: Gary Edwards
Printing Information: 26 pages in 4 colors on Glossy Stock
Press: Letterpress
Binding: Folded
Mailing List Information: Names for rent
List Manager: John Barnhauser
In Business: 33 years
Number of Employees: 10
Sales Volume: $3MM to $5MM

4229 Back Be Nimble
Back Be Nimble
90 W 500 S
Suite 215
Bountiful, UT 84010   800-639-3746
sales@backbenimble.com
www.backbenimble.com

Online back store and self-care catalogue specializing in products to help reduce back pain, neck pain and stress

President: Brad Lustick
Printing Information: 1000 pages in 1 color
Mailing List Information: Names for rent
In Business: 21 years
Sales Volume: $1MM to $3MM

4230 Bowflex Home Fitness
Bowflex
17750 SE 6th Way
Vancouver, WA 98683   800-628-8458
www.bowflex.com

Home gyms, treadmills, elliptical, benches, exercise bikes, stairs and steppers.

CEO: Bruce Cazenave
Catalog Cost: Free
Printing Information: in 4 colors
In Business: 30 years
Number of Employees: 300
Sales Volume: $218 Million

4231 CWI Medical
CWI Medical
200 Allen Boulevard
Farmingdale, NY 11735-5637   631-753-8390
877-929-4633
Fax: 631-753-8394
info@cwimedical.com
www.cwimedical.com

Quality medical and rehabilitation supplies and equipment

President: Shirley Lam
Marketing Manager: Dan Dunleavy
Fulfillment: Maritza Rivera
Credit Cards: AMEX; MasterCard; Visa
Number of Employees: 25
Sales Volume: $ 2 Million

4232 Clientele
Clientele
14101 NW Fourth Street
Sunrise, FL 33325   954-845-9500
800-327-4660
Fax: 954-845-9505
customerservice@clientelebeauty.com
www.clientele.org

Exercise equipment and vitamins

President: Patricia Riley
CFO: Gordan Bowman
CEO and Founder: Pat Riley
Credit Cards: AMEX; MasterCard; Visa
Catalog Cost: Free
Catalog Circulation: Mailed 4 time(s) per year
Printing Information: 20 pages in 2 colors
Binding: Saddle Stitched
In Business: 28 years
Number of Employees: 150
Sales Volume: $ 26 Million

4233 ETS Home Tanning Beds
ETS Tan
7445 Company Drive
Indianapolis, IN 46237
317-554-3500
800-553-9590
Fax: 800-358-7947
www.etstan.com

Tanning beds, tanning products and tanning bed accessories

President: Steven Bloomer
CFO: Edna Gray
Marketing Manager: John Keiffner
CEO: Bill Pipp
Credit Cards: AMEX; MasterCard
Catalog Circulation: to 10000
Printing Information: 68 pages in 4 colors on Glossy Stock
Press: Web Press
Binding: Saddle Stitched
In Business: 30 years
Number of Employees: 500
Sales Volume: $720,000

4234 Endless Pools
Endless Pools
1601 Dutton Mill Road
Aston, PA 19014-2931
484-768-1865
800-910-2714
Fax: 610-497-9328
swim@endlesspools.com
www.endlesspools.com

Home pools

President: James Murdock
CFO: Dan Harshbarger
Marketing Manager: Mark Langan
Production Manager: Kevin Kurtz
In Business: 27 years
Number of Employees: 100
Sales Volume: $ 11 Million

4235 Ergonomics/Occupational Health & Safety
AliMed, Inc.
297 High Street
Dedham, MA 02026-2852
781-329-2900
800-225-2610
Fax: 781-329-8392
info@alimed.com
www.alimed.com

Ergonomic products and accessories

President: Julian Cherubini
Marketing Manager: Jackie Stansbury
Credit Cards: AMEX; MasterCard; Visa
Catalog Cost: Free
Catalog Circulation: Mailed 12 time(s) per year
Printing Information: 168 pages in 4 colors on Glossy Stock
Binding: Saddle Stitched
In Business: 30 years
Number of Employees: 100

4236 Fitness Factory Outlet
Fitness Factory
1900 S Des Plaines Ave
Forest Park, IL 60130-2512
708-427-3599
800-383-9300
Fax: 708-427-3556
sales@fitnessfactory.com
www.fitnessfactory.com

Fitness and exercise equipment

President: Stewart Glenn
Credit Cards: AMEX; MasterCard; Visa
Catalog Cost: Free
Printing Information: 48 pages
Sales Volume: $ 5-10 Million

4237 Full Of Life
Full Of Life
P.O. Box 25600
Bradenton, FL 34206-5600
800-558-6967
800-521-7638
CustomerService@fulloflife.com
www.fulloflife.com

Health aids, hobbies, gifts, fitness products, and personal care

Catalog Cost: Free
In Business: 101 years

4238 Golden Ratio Woodworks
Golden Ratio
11300 Minnetonka Mills Rd
Minnetonka, MN 55305
952-460-3644
body.mechanics@hotmail.com
www.goldenratio.com

Massage tables, part and repairs

President: Timothy Sweeney
Marketing Manager: George Makris

4239 Gravity Plus
Yourback.com
PO Box 1166
La Jolla, CA 92038-1166
858-454-1626
800-383-8056
Fax: 858-964-4532
gravity@san.rr.com
www.yourback.com

Back care and related exercise equipment

President: Gerhard Gessner
Credit Cards: AMEX; MasterCard
Catalog Cost: Free
Catalog Circulation: Mailed 1 time(s) per year to 30000
Average Order Size: $100
Printing Information: 16 pages in 4 colors
Binding: Folded
In Business: 20 years
Sales Volume: Under $500,000

4240 Hard-Style
Dragon Door
800-899-5111
www.dragondoor.com

Kettlebells, Strength, Conditioning, Flexibility, and Advanced Fitness Resources

Catalog Cost: Free

4241 Healthy Living
AmeriMark Direct
6864 Engle Rd.
Cleveland, OH 44130
866-345-1388
www.amerimark.com

Exercise, diet, weight loss and general health.

CFO: Joe Albanese
CEO & President: Gareth Giesler
Catalog Cost: Free
Printing Information: in 4 colors
In Business: 47 years
Number of Employees: 700
Sales Volume: $400 Million

4242 InnerBalance
Gaiam, Inc
833 W. South Boulder R.
PO Box 3095
Boulder, CO 80307-3095
303-464-3600
877-989-6321
Fax: 303-464-3700
customerservice@gaiam.com
www.gaiam.com

Provides the tools people need to achieve total health, naturally

President: Lynn Powers
Credit Cards: AMEX; MasterCard; Visa
Printing Information: 64 pages in 4 colors
Binding: Saddle Stitched

4243 Integrated Medical
Integrated Medical
7012 S. Revere Parkway
Suite 140
Centennial, CO 80112
303-792-0069
800-333-7617
Fax: 303-799-3516
sales@integratedmedicalonline.com
www.integratedmedicalonline.com

Products for Physical Therapy and Rehabilitation market.

In Business: 35 years

4244 IronMind
IronMind
P. O. Box 1228
Nevada City, CA 9595
530-272-3579
Fax: 530-272-3095
sales@ironmind.com
www.ironmind.com

4245 Life Fitness Products
Life Fitness
9525 Bryn Mawr Avenue
Rosemont, IL 60018-1075
847-288-3300
800-351-3737
Fax: 800-216-8893
customersupport@lifefitness.com
www.lifefitness.com

Weightlifting machines and equipment

Chairman: Augustine Nieto
President: John Stransky
CEO: Andy Maduza
Credit Cards: MasterCard; Visa
Catalog Cost: Free
Catalog Circulation: Mailed 1 time(s) per year
Printing Information: 24 pages in 4 colors
Binding: Saddle Stitched
In Business: 13 years
Sales Volume: $ 1-3 Million

4246 NZ Manufacturing
Nz manufacturing,inc.
412 Commerce St.
Tallmadge, OH 44278
330-634-0271
800-886-6621
Fax: 855-387-0214
info@nzmfg.com
www.nzmfg.com

Workout equipment and clothing

Marketing Manager: Maureen Petrasko
Credit Cards: AMEX; MasterCard
Catalog Cost: Free
Mailing List Information: Names for rent
In Business: 30 years

4247 New Life Systems
Scrip Companies
360 Veterans Parkway
Suite 115
Boilingbrook, IL 60440-4607
630-771-7400
800-852-3082
Fax: 888-674-4380
support@newlifesystems.com
www.scripcompanies.com

Spa, salon and massage supplies and equipment

President: Kray Kibler, CPA
CFO: Kray Kibler, CPA
Marketing Manager: Julie Lohmeier
VP Sales for Chiropractic & Physica: Steve Keller
Vice President IT: John Matusiewicz
In Business: 49 years
Number of Employees: 126
Sales Volume: $ 13 Million

4248 Promolife
Promolife
PO Box 385
Fayetteville, AR 72702   479-442-3404
    888-742-3404
Fax: 479-444-6422
info@promolife.com
www.promolife.com

Alternative health and fitness products

President: Gerry Segal
Credit Cards: AMEX; MasterCard
Catalog Cost: Free
In Business: 13 years
Number of Employees: 3
Sales Volume: $170,000

4249 Sportsmith
Sportsmith, LLC
5925 S 118th East Ave
Tulsa, OK 74146   918-307-2446
    888-713-2880
Fax: 918-307-0216
www.sportsmith.net

Supplier of fitness equipment parts

President: Brad Schupp
Marketing Manager: Troy Mosley
Credit Cards: AMEX; MasterCard
Catalog Cost: Free
In Business: 20 years
Number of Employees: 38
Sales Volume: $12.5 Million

4250 Stronglite
Stronglite, LLC
369 Orange St # 7
Salt Lake City, UT 84104-3516   801-886-1616
    800-289-5487
Fax: 801-886-1411
slcustserv@stronglite.com
www.stronglite.com

Portable massage tables, chairs and body-work equipment

President: John Lloyd
Marketing Manager: Flora Bond
In Business: 20 years
Number of Employees: 5
Sales Volume: Under $500,000

4251 TruMedical Solutions
TruMedical Solutions
PO Box 1869
Collegedale, TN 37315   423-910-0100
    877-882-7844
Fax: 877-882-7845
info@tru-medical.com
www.tru-medical.com

4252 WaterRower
WaterRower US
560 Metacom Ave
Warren, RI 02885-2826   401-247-7742
    800-852-2210
Fax: 401-247-7743
info@waterrower.com
www.waterrower.com

Rowing machine

President: Peter King
Marketing Manager: Steve DaSilva
Production Manager: Mark Sinclair
In Business: 27 years
Sales Volume: $ 2 Million

4253 Y Catalog
The Y Catalog
8325 Linda Vista Av
Atascadero, CA 93422   805-460-6342
Fax: 310-460-1719
infotheYcatalog@gmail.com
www.theycatalog.com

Yoga, eco-minded clothing, accessories, apparel, equipment and health products

President: Keri Lassalle
Credit Cards: AMEX; MasterCard
Catalog Circulation: Mailed 4 time(s) per year to 200M
Average Order Size: $80
Printing Information: 44 pages

4254 Yopa Bags
Lucky Star Sales, LLC
PO Box 711911
Salt Lake City, UT 84171   801-944-9672
    888-944-9555
sales@yopa.us
www.yopabag.com

Bags for Yoga/Pilates and sports accessories

4255 Yukon Fitness Equipment
Yukon Fitness Equipment
23700 Aurora Road
Bedford Heights, OH 44146-1714   440-439-0000
    800-799-8566
Fax: 440-439-0030
customerservice@yukon-fitness.com
www.yukon-fitness.com

Premium line of fitness equipment; built stable, durable and effective

President: Rory Haehn
Sarah Kirsch:
Finance Manager
Credit Cards: AMEX; MasterCard
Catalog Cost: Free
Catalog Circulation: Mailed 1 time(s) per year
Printing Information: 40 pages in 4 colors
In Business: 17 years
Number of Employees: 10
Sales Volume: $ 1-3 Million

Fragrances

4256 Beauty Boutique
AmeriMark Direct
6864 Engle Rd.
Cleveland, OH 44130   866-345-1388
www.amerimark.com

Women's and men's fragrances, cosmetics and personal care products.

CFO: Joe Albanese
CEO & President: Gareth Giesler
Catalog Cost: Free
Printing Information: in 4 colors
In Business: 47 years
Number of Employees: 700
Sales Volume: $400 Million

4257 Caswell-Massey
Caswell-Massey
29 Northfield Avenue
Edison, NJ 08837   800-326-0500
info@caswellmassey.com
www.caswellmassey.com

Natural bath and body products, essential oils, fragrances and gift sets

Marketing Manager: Donna Chamberlin
Owner: Elizabeth Alvarez
Credit Cards: AMEX; MasterCard; Visa
Catalog Cost: Free
Printing Information: 48 pages in 4 colors on Matte Stock
Press: Web Press
Binding: Saddle Stitched
In Business: 265 years
Number of Employees: 70
Sales Volume: $ 4 Million

4258 DHC Care
DHC USA
555 Montgomery Street
Suite 1400
San Francisco, CA 94111   800-342-2273
customercare@dhccare.com
www.dhccare.com

Marketing Manager: Florence Schweinberg
Communications Manager: Amanne Sharif
COO & General Counsel: Darcy Manning
Catalog Cost: Free
Catalog Circulation: Mailed 4 time(s) per year
Printing Information: in 4 colors
In Business: 22 years
Number of Employees: 150

4259 Easy Comforts
Easy Comforts
250 City Center
Oshkosh, WI 54906   920-231-3800
    855-202-7391
Fax: 888-252-8462
www.easycomforts.com

Value-priced personal and health care merchandise for the mature consumer.

Catalog Cost: Free

4260 Elizabeth Van Buren Aromatherapy
Elizabeth Van Buren Essential Oil Therap
303 Potrero St
33
Santa Cruz, CA 95061-7542   831-425-8218
    800-710-7759
Fax: 831-425-8258
sales@elizabethvanburen.com
www.elizabethvanburen.com

Aromatherapy essential oils and blends

President: Larry Jones
Production Manager: Lawrence Jones
Operations Manager: Larry J. Machado, Jr.
Sales Representative: Patty Jacobsen
Sales Representative: Katie Novak
Credit Cards: AMEX; MasterCard; Visa
Catalog Cost: Free
Catalog Circulation: Mailed 2 time(s) per year to 10000
Printing Information: 10 pages in 4 colors
Will Trade Names: Yes
In Business: 32 years
Number of Employees: 9
Sales Volume: $ 1 Million

4261 Erbaviva
Erbaviva
18203 Parthenia Street
Northridge, CA 91325   818-998-7773
    877-372-2848
Fax: 818-998-7112
info@erbaviva.com
www.erbaviva.com

All-natural, organic skincare products

Production Manager: Grace Prestidge
Founder: Robin Brown
Founder: Anna Cirronis
Catalog Cost: Free
In Business: 16 years
Number of Employees: 18
Sales Volume: $2 Million

4262 Essential Oil Company
The Essential Oil Company
8225 SE 7th Ave
Portland, OR 97202-6428   503-872-8772
    800-729-5912
Fax: 503-872-8767
orders@essentialoil.com
www.essentialoil.com

Incense catalog specializes in aromatherapy supplies and essential oils, soap molds and supplies, potpourri and frangrance oils, and incense amterials

President: Robert Seidel
Credit Cards: AMEX; MasterCard
Catalog Circulation: to 1000
Printing Information: 19 pages in 2 colors on Matte Stock
Binding: Saddle Stitched
In Business: 38 years
Sales Volume: $630,000

4263 Frette
Frette Madison
850 Third Ave
10th Floor
New York, NY 10022
212-299-0400
800-353-7388
Fax: 347-862-9309
assistance@frette.com

Luxury linens, bath items and gifts; cashmere, silk, velvet, mink fabrics

CFO: Anna Ermakova
EVP: Rico Merenelli
Credit Cards: AMEX; MasterCard
Catalog Circulation: Mailed 2 time(s) per year
Printing Information: on Glossy Stock
In Business: 155 years
Number of Employees: 75

4264 Frontier Natural Products Co-Op
Frontier Natural Products Co-Op
3021 78th St
PO Box 299
Norway, IA 52318-9520
800-669-3275
Fax: 800-717-4372
customercare@frontiercoop.com
www.frontiercoop.com

A wholesale supplier of organic coffee, bottled spices, baking flavors, aromatherapy items, natural items and other manufacturers' products

President: Nancy Hinkel
CFO: Bill Kooistra
Marketing Manager: Clint Landis
Production Manager: Andrea Weiss
Purchasing Manager: Kai Stark
Credit Cards: AMEX; MasterCard
Catalog Cost: Free
In Business: 39 years
Number of Employees: 225
Sales Volume: $20MM to $50MM

4265 Garden Botanika
Ziddle
8500 Valcour Avenue
Saint Louis, MO 63123
800-724-7227
Fax: 314-633-4804
www.ziddle.com

Skin care, cosmetic products and fragrances

Production Manager: Lisa Springer
Credit Cards: AMEX; MasterCard
Catalog Cost: Free
Catalog Circulation: Mailed 8 time(s) per year
Number of Employees: 2
Sales Volume: Under $500,000

4266 House of Fragrances
House of Fragrances
2618-A Battleground Avenue #127
Department 4
Greensboro, NC 27408
336-273-7097
888-516-8387
Fax: 336-273-7002
www.thehouseoffragrances.com

Wholesale fragrances, oils, lotions and more

VP: Teretha Jones
Catalog Cost: Free
Mailing List Information: Names for rent
In Business: 10 years
Number of Employees: 4
Sales Volume: Under $500,000

4267 Hove Parfumeur
Hove Parfumeur
434 Chartres Street
New Orleans, LA 70130
504-525-7827
Fax: 504-525-7994
hove@bellsouth.net
www.hoveparfumeur.com

Perfume, cologne and bath-oil soap

President: Amy VanCalsem
Marketing Manager: Bill Wendel

Credit Cards: AMEX; MasterCard; Visa
Catalog Cost: Free
Catalog Circulation: Mailed 1 time(s) per year to 20000
Printing Information: 21 pages in 1 color on Glossy Stock
Mailing List Information: Names for rent
In Business: 84 years
Number of Employees: 4
Sales Volume: Under $500,000

4268 Key West Aloe
Key West Aloe
416 Greene Street
Key West, FL 33040
305-735-4927
800-445-2563
Fax: 305-883-3185
cs@keywestaloe.com
www.keywestaloe.com

Skin care, suntan, bath and fragrance products for men and women

President: Nalin Patel
VP of Sales: Nancy Begin
Credit Cards: AMEX; MasterCard; Visa
Catalog Cost: Free
Catalog Circulation: Mailed 5 time(s) per year to 60000
Printing Information: 40 pages in 4 colors on Glossy Stock
Binding: Saddle Stitched
In Business: 47 years
Number of Employees: 25
Sales Volume: $ 3 Million

4269 La-Tee-Da
La-Tee-Da
P.O Box 740
, Sc TX-7568
903-927-3502
800-246-1826
Fax: 903-935-8007
www.ltdfragrance.com

Home fragrance products.

4270 Liza & Rose
AmeriMark Direct
6864 Engle Rd.
Cleveland, OH 44130
866-345-1388
www.amerimark.com

Fashion jewelry, fragrances, cosmetics, casual wear and footwear.

CFO: Joe Albanese
CEO & President: Gareth Giesler
Catalog Cost: Free
Printing Information: in 4 colors
In Business: 47 years
Number of Employees: 700
Sales Volume: $400 Million

4271 Luzier Personalized Cosmetics
Luzier
5601 E 135th St
Grandview, MO 64030
816-531-8338
800-821-6632
Fax: 816-531-6979
customerservice@luzier.com
www.luzier.com

Rejuvenating skincare treatments, cosmetics rich in pure color, bath products and personalized signature fragrances

Chairman: Kathleen Craven Grissom
CEO: Kathleen Grissom
In Business: 91 years
Number of Employees: 4000

4272 Maine Balsam Fir Products
Maine Balsam Fir Products
PO Box 9
West Paris, ME 04289
207-674-5094
800-5 B-lsam
Fax: 207-674-5094
info@mainebalsam.com
www.mainebalsam.com

All-natural fragrant balsam fir filled pillows, sachets, draft stoppers, trivets and other scented items

President: Wendy Newmeyer
Production Manager: Jack Newmeyer
Catalog Cost: Free
Average Order Size: $250
Printing Information: 32 pages in 4 colors on Glossy Stock
Press: Sheetfed Press
Binding: Perfect Bound
Mailing List Information: Names for rent
In Business: 30 years
Number of Employees: 10
Sales Volume: $3,00,000

4273 Monroe and Main
Monroe and Main
1112 7th Avenue
Monroe, WI 53566
800-727-9496

Wear to Work collection.

4274 My Sweet Victoria
My Sweet Victoria
4356 Biddeford Cir
Doylestown, PA 18901
267-354-1362
Fax: 215-348-8021
mysweetvictoria@hotmail.com
www.sentiments.com

Perfumes and colognes

President: Nancy Booth
In Business: 32 years

4275 Newport Flavours and Fragrances
Newport Flavours
833 N. Elm St.
Orange, CA 92867
714-771-2200
Fax: 714-771-2424
www.newportflavours.com

In Business: 25 years

4276 Old Durham Road
Pickering & Simmons
115 Campus Drive
Edison, NJ 08837
732-516-1616
866-298-1627
Fax: 732-516-1617

English country living products including gifts, books and more

Chairman: Arline Friedman
President: Craig Weidenheimer
Credit Cards: AMEX; MasterCard; Visa
Catalog Cost: Free

4277 Palm Beach Jewelry Signature Collection
Palm Beach
6400 E Rogers Circle
Boca Raton, FL 33499
561-994-2660
866-804-3745
Fax: 561-994-1710
customerservice@palmbeachjewelry.com
www.palmbeachjewelry.com

Women's and men's jewelry, fragrances

President: Anthony Seta
Marketing Manager: Daniel DeYoung
Credit Cards: AMEX; MasterCard; Visa
Catalog Cost: Free
Catalog Circulation: Mailed 4 time(s) per year
Printing Information: 3 pages in 4 colors
In Business: 63 years
Number of Employees: 90
Sales Volume: $ 9 Million

4278 Perfumax
Perfumax
Blythourne Station
P.O. Box 191213
Brooklyn, NY 11219
718-854-6136
800-300-7800
Fax: 888-755-7373
www.perfumax.com

Name brand fragrances, skin, bath and body care products

Catalog Cost: Free

4279 Rainbow Meadow
Rainbow Meadow, Inc.
4494 Brooklyn Rd
Jackson, MI 49201   517-764-9765
                          800-207-4047
                     Fax: 517-764-9766
                  www.rainbowmeadow.com

Essential oils for aromatherapy, cosmetics and pharmaceuticals

President: Melody Upham
CFO: Timothy Upham
CEO: Melody Upham
Credit Cards: AMEX; MasterCard
Mailing List Information: Names for rent
In Business: 18 years
Sales Volume: $580,000

4280 Spray Advantage
Spray Advantage
130 Gateway Drive
Grand Forks, ND 58203   701-775-8089
                          866-775-8089
                     Fax: 701-775-8217
                  www.sprayadvantage.com/

4281 Touch America
Touch America
1403 S Third St Ext
PO Box 1304
Mebane, NC 27302   919-732-6968
                          800-678-6824
                     Fax: 919-732-1173
                  info@touchamerica.com
                   www.touchamerica.com

Massage and spa equipment

President: Stewart Griffith
Marketing Manager: Lianne De Moya
Finance Executive: Chris Owens
International Marketing Manager: Valerie Rawlings
Credit Cards: AMEX; MasterCard
Catalog Cost: Free
Catalog Circulation: Mailed 2 time(s) per year to 25000
Average Order Size: $200
Printing Information: 40 pages in 4 colors on Glossy Stock
Press: Sheetfed Press
Binding: Saddle Stitched
Mailing List Information: Names for rent
In Business: 32 years
Sales Volume: Under $500,000

Home Health Care

4282 Achievement Products for Special Needs
Achievement Products For Children
PO Box 6013
Carol Stream, IL 60197-6013   800-373-4699
                           Fax: 800-766-4303
                  info@achievement-products.com
                   www.achievement-products.com

Therapy, exercise and special education products for children with special needs

Production Manager: Scott Russo
Buyers: Julie Fraser
Credit Cards: AMEX; MasterCard; Visa
Catalog Cost: Free
In Business: 32 years

4283 Active Forever
Active Forever
9299 N. Olive Ave
Peoria, AZ 85345   480-767-6800
                     Fax: 602-296-0297
                  www.activeforever.com

4284 Allergy Asthma Technology
Allergy Asthma Technology
8145 N Austin Avenue
Morton Grove, IL 60053-3204   800-621-5545
                           Fax: 847-966-3068
                  support@allergyasthmatech.com
                   www.allergyasthmatech.com

Preventive equipment, alergy & asthma products, enviromental products

President: Rich Shear
Credit Cards: MasterCard
Catalog Cost: Free
Printing Information: 38 pages in 4 colors on Glossy Stock
Press: Web Press
Binding: Saddle Stitched
Mailing List Information: Names for rent
In Business: 43 years
Sales Volume: $3 Million

4285 Alzheimer's Store Catalog
Healthcare Products, LLC
420 Osierfield Drive
Fitzgerald, GA 31750   678-947-4001
                          800-752-3238
                     Fax: 678-947-8411
                  contact@alzstore.com
                   www.alzstore.com

Unique products and information for those caring for someone with Alzheimer's

Partner: Bruce Barnet
Credit Cards: AMEX; MasterCard
Catalog Cost: Free
In Business: 12 years
Number of Employees: 7
Sales Volume: $500,000 - $1 Million

4286 Ames Walker Support Hosiery
Ames Walker International
300 Industrial Park Avenue
PO Box 1027
Asheboro, NC 27204   336-625-3979
                          877-525-7224
                     Fax: 336-629-0632
                  customerservice@ameswalker.com
                   www.ameswalker.com

Support hosiery, foot care products and accessories

President: Ken Walker
Production Manager: Ryan Zell
Credit Cards: AMEX; MasterCard
Catalog Cost: Free
Printing Information: 88 pages
In Business: 11 years
Number of Employees: 11

4287 As We Change
As We Change
250 City Center
Oshkosh, WI 54901   855-202-7392
                     Fax: 888-534-8469
                  help@aswechange.com
                   www.aswechange.com

Nutrition, beauty, skin care, exercise, personal care and lifestyle products for women ages 40-50+ years.

Catalog Cost: Free
In Business: 20 years

4288 Atlantic Tan
Atlantic Tan Distributors
5251 Z-Max Blvd
Harrisburg, NC 28075   704-455-7840
                          800-831-7649
                     Fax: 704-455-7846
                  info@atlantictan.com
                   www.atlantictan.com

Tanning beds, body wraps and salon supplies

President: Charles Boss Jr
Owner: Angela Boss
Credit Cards: AMEX; MasterCard; Visa

Catalog Cost: Free
In Business: 25 years
Number of Employees: 5
Sales Volume: $1.6 Million

4289 Bedwetting Store
Bedwetting Store
11840 West Market Place
Suite H
Fulton, MD 20759   301-776-0715
                          800-214-9605
                     Fax: 301-776-0716

Waterproof bedding, mattress covers and matress pads, undergarments, spot removers, books and accessories

President: Renee Mercer
In Business: 15 years

4290 Biomagnetics
Biomagnetics USA
PO Box 358701
Gainesville, FL 32635-295   352-377-0704
                              800-922-1744
                         Fax: 937-456-9897
                      magnetage@att.net

Health and personal care items that incorporate magnetic therapy

Catalog Cost: Free
Printing Information: on Matte Stock
Press: Web Press
Binding: Folded
Mailing List Information: Names for rent
In Business: 79 years
Number of Employees: 3

4291 CWI Medical
CWI Medical
200 Allen Boulevard
Farmingdale, NY 11735-5637   631-753-8390
                               877-929-4633
                          Fax: 631-753-8394
                       info@cwimedical.com
                        www.cwimedical.com

Quality medical and rehabilitation supplies and equipment

President: Shirley Lam
Marketing Manager: Dan Dunleavy
Fulfillment: Maritza Rivera
Credit Cards: AMEX; MasterCard; Visa
Number of Employees: 25
Sales Volume: $ 2 Million

4292 Caregiver Education Catalog
ActiveForever
9299 W. Olive Avenue
Suite 604
Peoria, AZ 85345   480-767-6800
                          800-377-8033
                     Fax: 623-215-8471
                  customerservice@activeforever.com
                   www.activeforever.com

Products designed to make daily life and rehabilitation needs easier and more attainable

President: Erika Feinberg
CEO & Chief Happiness Officer: Erika Feinberg
Credit Cards: AMEX; MasterCard; Visa
Catalog Cost: Free
Printing Information: in 4 colors
In Business: 22 years

4293 Comfort House
Comfort House
189-V Frelinghuysen Ave.
Newark, NJ 07114-1595   973-242-8080
                          800-359-7701
                     Fax: 973-242-0131
                  customerservice@comforthouse.com
                   www.comforthouse.com

Bed, bath, kitchen, furniture, garden, pet, gifts, personal and health care items

President: Jeffrey Gornstein
jeff@comforthouse.com
Buyers: Jeffrey Gornstein
Credit Cards: AMEX; MasterCard
Catalog Cost: $2
Catalog Circulation: Mailed 1 time(s) per year
Printing Information: 28 pages
Mailing List Information: Names for rent
In Business: 24 years
Sales Volume: $5MM to $10MM

4294 Directory of Life Extension Nutrients and Drugs
Life Extension
PO Box 229120
Hollywood, FL 33022-9120   800-841-5433
                                Fax: 954-761-9199
                                www.lef.org

High-tech products and therapies, to improve health and performance

Credit Cards: AMEX; MasterCard
Catalog Circulation: Mailed 1 time(s) per year
Printing Information: 134 pages in 4 colors
Binding: Perfect Bound
In Business: 34 years

4295 Discover Magnetics
Discover Magnetics
4901 E 215th St
Belton, MO 64012   816-618-3499
                         800-497-9391
                www.discovermagnetics.com

Magnetic products for pain relief

Owner: Cherry Kelly
Credit Cards: MasterCard
Catalog Cost: Free
Printing Information: 14 pages in 2 colors
Binding: Saddle Stitched
In Business: 12 years
Number of Employees: 2
Sales Volume: Under $500,000

4296 Dr Leonard's
Dr Leonard's Healthcare Corporation
PO Box 7821
Edison, NJ 08818-7821   732-225-0100
                              800-455-1918
                         Fax: 732-572-2118
                         www.drleonards.com

Discount health products such as exercise equipment, personal care products, mobility aids, diet supplements, and more

President: Gary Giesler
CFO: Joe Albanese
Marketing Manager: Marissa Cozzo
VP Operations: Gary Porto
Credit Cards: AMEX; MasterCard
Catalog Cost: Free
In Business: 35 years
Number of Employees: 600

4297 Dr. Leonard's Healthcare
Dr Leonard's Healthcare Corporation
P.O.Box 7821
Edison, NJ 08818-7821   800-455-1918
                         www.drleonards.com

Health products along with clothing, exercise equipment, home furnishing, housewares and shoes

President: Gary Giesler
CFO: Joe Albanese
VP Operations: Gary Porto
Buyers: Pyna Van Der Veer
Credit Cards: AMEX; MasterCard
Catalog Cost: Free
List Company: Mokrynski & Associates
In Business: 37 years
Number of Employees: 250
Sales Volume: $ 50-100 Million

4298 Drug Package
Drug Package
901 Drug Package Lane
O'Fallon, MO 63366   800-325-6137
                          Fax: 800-600-6137
                     sales@drugpackage.com
                     www.drugpackage.com

4299 Dutchguard
Dutchguard
412 W 10th Street
PO Box 411687
Kansas City, MO 64105-1687   816-221-3581
                                   800-821-5157
                              Fax: 816-842-9344
                            sales@dutchguard.com
                            www.dutchguard.com

A variety of products including: canes and walking sticks; clocks and watches; toys; pet products; flashlights; cleaning supplies; jewelry; books; tools; health and nutrition

Owner: Earl Kaufman
Credit Cards: AMEX; MasterCard
Catalog Cost: Free
Catalog Circulation: Mailed 2 time(s) per year
Printing Information: 64 pages
In Business: 23 years
Number of Employees: 15
Sales Volume: $740,000

4300 DynaPro International
DynaPro International
451 N Main St
Kaysville, UT 84123   801-621-1413
                           800-877-1413
                      Fax: 801-593-0911
                 sales@dynaprointernational.com
                 www.dynaprointernational.com

Home health care products and vitamins

President: Bailey Hall
Buyers: Beverly Roybal
Credit Cards: AMEX; MasterCard
Catalog Cost: Free
Catalog Circulation: to 2500
Printing Information: 60 pages in 2 colors on Matte Stock
Binding: Folded
In Business: 31 years
Sales Volume: Under $500,000

4301 Easy Comforts
Easy Comforts
250 City Center
Oshkosh, WI 54906   920-231-3800
                          855-202-7391
                     Fax: 888-252-8462
                     www.easycomforts.com

Value-priced personal and health care merchandise for the mature consumer.

Catalog Cost: Free

4302 Edgepark Continence Catalog
Edgepark Medical Supplies
1810 Summit Commerce Park
Twinsburg, OH 44087   888-394-5375
                       Fax: 330-425-4355
                       www.edgepark.com

Continence supplies including catheters and adult briefs.

Catalog Cost: Free
Catalog Circulation: Mailed 1 time(s) per year
Printing Information: 116 pages in 4 colors
In Business: 88 years

4303 Edgepark Diabetes Catalog
Edgepark Medical Supplies
1810 Summit Commerce Park
Twinsburg, OH 44087   888-394-5375
                       Fax: 330-425-4355
                       www.edgepark.com

Diabetes care products including blood glucose monitors and testing supplies.

Catalog Cost: Free
Catalog Circulation: Mailed 1 time(s) per year
Printing Information: 52 pages in 4 colors
In Business: 88 years

4304 Edgepark Full-line Catalog
Edgepark Medical Supplies
1810 Summit Commerce Park
Twinsburg, OH 44087   888-394-5375
                       Fax: 330-425-4355
                       www.edgepark.com

Ostomy, diabetes, urological, incontinence and wound care products.

Catalog Cost: Free
Catalog Circulation: Mailed 1 time(s) per year
Printing Information: 268 pages in 4 colors
In Business: 88 years

4305 Edgepark Ostomy Catalog
Edgepark Medical Supplies
1810 Summit Commerce Park
Twinsburg, OH 44087   888-394-5375
                       Fax: 330-425-4355
                       www.edgepark.com

Ostomy supplies including all major brands.

Catalog Cost: Free
Catalog Circulation: Mailed 1 time(s) per year
Printing Information: 150 pages in 4 colors
In Business: 88 years

4306 Ferno Physical Therapy & Sports Equipment
Ferno-Washington, Inc
70 Weil Way
Wilmington, OH 45177-9371   937-382-1451
                                  877-733-0911
                             Fax: 937-382-1191
                             www.fernoems.com

Physical therapy and sports equipment

Chairman: Elroy Bourgraf
CFO: Paul Riordan
Printing Information: 82 pages in 4 colors
Binding: Perfect Bound
In Business: 56 years
Number of Employees: 440
Sales Volume: $ 34 Million

4307 Four Corners
Four Corners
PO Box 4800
Sarasota, FL 34230-4800   800-560-6100
                           www.fourcorners.com

In Business: 30 years

4308 Full Of Life
Full Of Life
P.O. Box 25600
Bradenton, FL 34206-5600   800-558-6967
                                 800-521-7638
                      CustomerService@fulloflife.com
                      www.fulloflife.com

Health aids, hobbies, gifts, fitness products, and personal care

Catalog Cost: Free
In Business: 101 years

4309 Full of Life
Full of Life
PO Box 25600
Bradenton, FL 34206-5600   800-521-7638
                                 800-558-6967
                            Fax: 800-551-4406
                      customerservice@fulloflife.com
                      www.fulloflife.com

Health aids

Credit Cards: AMEX; MasterCard; Visa
In Business: 101 years

4310 Fuller Brush Company

Fuller Brush Company
One Fuller Way
Great Bend, KS 67530

620-792-1711
Fax: 620-792-1906
info@fuller.com
www.fuller.com

Cleaning supplies and personal care products

CFO: Brady Gros
Marketing Manager: Dennis Roncace
Catalog Cost: Free
In Business: 109 years
Number of Employees: 350

4311 Get Motivated

KRS Edstrom
PO Box 2755
Toluca Lake, CA 91610-755

323-851-8623
contactus@askkrs.com
www.askkrs.com

Products for personal growth and healing including stress, fear of flying, pain, insomnia, guided meditation, diet, exercise, motivation, weight loss, nutrition, healthy living

President: Kris Edstrom
Mailing List Information: Names for rent
In Business: 20 years
Sales Volume: Under $500,000

4312 HDIS Catalog

Home Delivery Incontinent Supplies
9385 Dielman Industrial Dr
Olivette, MO 63132

314-997-8771
800-269-4663
custcare@hdis.com
www.hdis.com

Variety of incontinence supplies, urological supplies, aids for daily living, bathroom safety items and mobility aids

President: Marla Paterson
CFO: Brian Flint
Marketing Manager: Mark Nedvin
Credit Cards: AMEX; MasterCard; Visa
Catalog Cost: Free
In Business: 28 years
Number of Employees: 19
Sales Volume: $2.4 Million

4313 Healthcare Innovations

ActiveForever
10799 N 90th Street
Scottsdale, AZ 85260

480-767-6800
800-377-8033
Fax: 602-296-0297
customerservice@activeforever.com
www.activeforever.com

Offers solutions for any physical challenge

Chairman: Erika Feinberg
President: Erika Feinberg
CEO: Erika Feinberg
Credit Cards: AMEX; MasterCard; Visa
Catalog Cost: Free
Printing Information: in 4 colors
In Business: 21 years

4314 Healthy Back

Healthy Back
10300 Southard Drive
Beltsville, MD 20705-1296

703-339-7100
888-469-2225
Fax: 703-339-4288
www.healthyback.com

Furniture for Healthy Backs

President: Anthony Mazlish
CEO: Anthony Mazlish
Printing Information: 22 pages
In Business: 17 years
Number of Employees: 100

4315 Healthy Living

AmeriMark Direct
6864 Engle Rd.
Cleveland, OH 44130

866-345-1388
www.amerimark.com

Exercise, diet, weight loss and general health.

CFO: Joe Albanese
CEO & President: Gareth Giesler
Catalog Cost: Free
Printing Information: in 4 colors
In Business: 47 years
Number of Employees: 700
Sales Volume: $400 Million

4316 Herbal Healer Academy

HHA Inc.
127 McCain Drive
Mountain View, AR 72560-7576

870-269-4177
Fax: 870-269-5424
www.herbalhealer.com

Thousands of natural health care supplies

President: Marijah McCain
VP: Stephen McCain
Executive Sales Manager: Jeff McCain
Credit Cards: AMEX; MasterCard
Catalog Cost: Free
Catalog Circulation: Mailed 1 time(s) per year
Printing Information: 128 pages
Binding: Saddle Stitched
Mailing List Information: Names for rent
In Business: 24 years
Number of Employees: 15
Sales Volume: $760,000

4317 Homeopathic Reference Catalog

Hyland's Inc
PO Box 61067
Los Angeles, CA 90061-67

310-768-0700
800-624-9659
Fax: 310-516-8579
info@hylands.com
www.hylands.com

Homeopathic medicines

Chairman: John P. Borneman
President: Dan Krombach
CFO: Dan Krombach
President/Chief Strategy Officer: Margot Murphy Moore
CEO: John P. Borneman
President, Hyland's, Inc.: Dale S. Nepsa
Credit Cards: MasterCard
Catalog Circulation: to 10000
Printing Information: 22 pages in 4 colors
Press: Letterpress
Binding: Saddle Stitched
Mailing List Information: Names for rent
In Business: 110 years
Sales Volume: Under $500,000

4318 Independent Living Aids

Independent Living Aids
137 Rano Rd
Buffalo, NY 14207

800-537-2118
Fax: 516-937-3906
barbara@independentliving.com
www.independentliving.com

Products for people with blindness or low vision

President: Irwin Schneidmill
Marketing Manager: Janice Grimm
Director of Operations: Michael Gutierrez
Director of Merchandising: Ursula Izurieta
International Accounts Manager: Cesar Gomez
Credit Cards: AMEX; MasterCard; Visa
Catalog Cost: Free
Catalog Circulation: Mailed 1 time(s) per year
In Business: 35 years
Sales Volume: $ 1-3 Million

4319 Independent Living Aids Low Vision Catalog

Independent Living Aids
137 Rano Rd
Buffalo, NY 14207

800-537-2118
Fax: 516-937-3906
barbara@independentliving.com
www.independentliving.com

Low vision products to assist in daily life

President: Irwin Schneidmill
Marketing Manager: Janice Grimm
Director of Operations: Michael Gutierrez
Director of Merchandising: Ursula Izurieta
International Accounts Manager: Cesar Gomez
Credit Cards: AMEX; MasterCard; Visa
Catalog Cost: Free
Catalog Circulation: Mailed 1 time(s) per year
In Business: 35 years
Sales Volume: $ 1-3 Million

4320 Interactive Therapeutics

AliMed
297 High Street
Dedham, MA 02026-805

781-329-2900
800-225-2610
Fax: 781-329-8392
info@alimed.com
www.alimed.com

Teaching tools to help with orthopedic therapy

President: Len Ivins
Credit Cards: AMEX; MasterCard
In Business: 35 years
Sales Volume: $440,000

4321 Internatural Health & Wellness

Internatural
PO Box 489
Twin Lakes, WI 53181-489

800-905-6887
800-643-4221
Fax: 262-889-8591
www.internatural.com

Natural personal care products, cosmetics and dietary supplements

President: Santosh Krinsky
Buyers: Laura Parker
Catalog Cost: Free
Catalog Circulation: Mailed 52 time(s) per year to 30000
Average Order Size: $40
Printing Information: 36 pages in 4 colors on Matte Stock
Press: Sheetfed Press
Binding: Folded
Mailing List Information: Names for rent
In Business: 23 years
Sales Volume: $ 500,000- 1 Million

4322 Isabella

Isabella
120 Graham Way #200
Suite B
Shelburne, VT 05482

619-670-5200
800-777-5205
Fax: 619-670-5203
service@isabellacatalog.net
www.isabellacatalog.com

Books, gifts and other inspirational products for inner peace

Founder: Ann Ruethling
Founder: Patti Pitcher
Catalog Cost: Free
In Business: 20 years

4323 J.R. Watkins
J.R. Watkins
150 Liberty Street
P.O. Box 5570
Winona, MN 55987-0570   507-457-3300
   800-243-9423
Fax: 507-452-6723
webhelp@jrwatkins.com
www.jrwatkins.com

Remedies and vitamins made from all natural ingredients, spices, soaps and detergents

Catalog Cost: Free
In Business: 146 years

4324 Janice Corporation
Janice's, LLC
30 Arbor Street South
Hartford, CT 06106-1215   860-523-4479
   800-526-4237
Fax: 860-523-4178
dlerner@janices.com
www.janices.com

Bedding, clothing, soaps and grooming products, notions and other products that provide comfort and relief to persons who suffer from sensitivities, allergies and dermatological problems

President: David Lerner
Marketing Manager: Lucille Werner
Production Manager: Audrey Dorman
In Business: 9 years
Number of Employees: 20
Sales Volume: $ 1 Million

4325 Lotus Press Alternative Health Publisher
Lotus Press
1100 Lotus Drive, Building 3
P.O. Box 325
Twin Lakes, WI 53181   262-889-8561
   800-824-6396
Fax: 262-889-8591
lotuspress@lotuspress.com
www.lotuspress.com

Alternative health publisher of books on ayurveda, reiki, herbalism, alternative health and wellness, and spirituality

President: Santosh Krinsky
Credit Cards: MasterCard; Visa
Catalog Cost: Free
Catalog Circulation: Mailed 2 time(s) per year to 5000
Printing Information: 58 pages in 4 colors on Glossy Stock
Press: Sheetfed Press
Binding: Saddle Stitched
Mailing List Information: Names for rent
In Business: 25 years
Number of Employees: 50
Sales Volume: $ 8 Million

4326 Low Vision/Hearing Loss Catalog
ActiveForever
10799 N 90th Street
Scottsdale, AZ 85260   480-767-6800
   800-377-8033
Fax: 602-296-0297
www.activeforever.com

Low vision aids such as the Quickloom Zoom Portable Video Magnifier and hearing loss aids such as the TV Ears

Chairman: Erika L Feinberg
Erika@ActiveForever.com
Chief Outcomes Officer: Erika Feinberg
Credit Cards: AMEX; MasterCard; Visa
Catalog Cost: Free
Printing Information: in 4 colors
In Business: 21 years

4327 Moore Norman Technology Center
Moore Norman Technology Center
South Penn Campus
13301 S. Pennsylvania
Oklahoma City, OK 73170   405-364-5763
Fax: 405-809-3548
www.mntc.edu

In Business: 43 years

4328 Movement Disorder
ActiveForever
9299 W. Olive Avenue
Suite 604
Peoria, AZ 85345   480-767-6800
   800-377-8033
Fax: 602-296-0297
customerservice@activeforever.com
www.activeforever.com

Offers solutions for transfer and mobility issues

President: Erika Feinberg
Credit Cards: AMEX; MasterCard; Visa
Catalog Cost: Free
Printing Information: in 4 colors
In Business: 21 years

4329 Practica
Paragon
PO Box 4068
Westerly, RI 02891-3637   866-752-3714
Fax: 513-354-1294
customerservice@paragongifts.com
www.paragongifts.com

Unusual items for everyday living; From the kitchen and bath, to personal items

President: Steve Rawley
CFO: Bruce Caldwell
Marketing Manager: Gary Smith
Credit Cards: AMEX; MasterCard
Catalog Circulation: Mailed 5 time(s) per year
Average Order Size: $50
Printing Information: 60 pages in 4 colors on Glossy Stock
Press: Web Press
Binding: Saddle Stitched
Mailing List Information: Names for rent
In Business: 41 years
Sales Volume: $ 3-5 Million

4330 Pro-Med Products
Pro-Med
360 Veterans Parkway
Suite 115
Bolingbrook, IL 60440-4607   770-777-8237
   800-542-9297
Fax: 888-674-4380
www.promedproducts.com

Health care products

Credit Cards: AMEX; MasterCard
Catalog Cost: Free
In Business: 22 years
Sales Volume: $ 1 Million

4331 Puritan's Pride
Puritan's Pride
PO Box 9001
Oakdale, NY 11769-9001   631-244-1290
   800-645-1030
Fax: 631-471-5693
vitamins@puritan.com
www.puritan.com

Discount health products including vitamins, minerals, food supplements, herbs, amino acids, natural pet products, skin and health care.

President: Steve Cahillane
Director, Catalog Marketing: Michelle Davis
Catalog Cost: Free
Printing Information: 112 pages in 4 colors
Press: Web Press
Binding: Saddle Stitched
Mailing List Information: Names for rent

List Company: Rifkin Direct
64 Appletree Lane
Roslyn Heights, NY 11577
516-621-1076
In Business: 50 years
Sales Volume: $20MM to $50MM

4332 Red Line
Red Line, Research Company Inc
10845 Wheatlands Ave
Suite C
Santee, CA 92071-2865   619-562-7591
Fax: 619-449-7244
sales@redlineresearch.com
www.redlineresearch.com

RF Heat Sealed products such as medical components & devices, orthopedic bags and straps

President: Steve Leiserson
VP: Nancy Byrd
Catalog Circulation: Mailed 1 time(s) per year
In Business: 31 years
Number of Employees: 8
Sales Volume: $ 1 Million

4333 Relax the Back
Relax The Back Corporation
6 Centerpointe Drive
Suite 350
La Palma, CA 90623   714-523-2870
   800-222-5728
Fax: 714-523-2980
info@relaxtheback.com
www.relaxtheback.com

Products to relieve back pain

President: Richard Palfreyman
CFO: Robert McMillan
Marketing Manager: Leanne Mattes
Catalog Cost: Free
In Business: 31 years
Number of Employees: 8
Sales Volume: $ 1.2 Million

4334 Sammons Preston
Patterson Medical
28100 Torch Parkway
Suite 700
Warrenville, IL 60555-3938   630-393-6000
   800-475-5036
Fax: 630-393-7600
www.pattersonmedical.com

Healthcare products to lighten chores, increase comfort and adapt household items for easier use

President: David Sproat
CEO: Scott Anderson
Credit Cards: AMEX; MasterCard
Printing Information: in 3 colors
Sales Volume: $ 9 Million

4335 Shaklee
Shaklee Corporation
4747 Willow Road
#2110
Pleasanton, CA 94588   925-924-2000
Fax: 925-924-2862
www.shaklee.com

Air source best water foundations products, cinch inch loss plan, building blocks, immune support, cardo health, joint & muscles, digestive health, mind & spirit, advance health, women health

Chairman: Roger Barnett
President: Dan Rajczak
CFO: Mike Batesole
Marketing Manager: Jennifer Steeves-kiss
Chief Supply Officer: Rong Xue
Chief Information Officer: Rich Libby
Chief Innovation Officer: Emanuel Fakoukakis
Catalog Cost: $5
Printing Information: 96 pages
Mailing List Information: Names for rent

In Business: 100 years
Sales Volume: $3MM to $5MM

4336 SoundBytes
SoundBytes
137 Rano Rd
Buffalo, NY 14207-137   855-746-7452
800-537-2118
Fax: 516-937-3906

Hearing enhancement devices
President: Irwin Schneidmill
Credit Cards: AMEX; MasterCard
Catalog Cost: Free
In Business: 35 years

4337 Support Hose Store
Support House Store
906 South Jefferson St
Suite 100
Amarillo, TX 79101-4632   800-515-4271
800-515-4271
Fax: 888-235-8257
customerservice@supporthosestore.com
www.supporthosestore.com

Support stockings by Jobst, Sigvaris and Mediven
President: Vanda Lancour
CFO: Rod Lancour
Credit Cards: AMEX; MasterCard
Catalog Cost: Free
In Business: 10 years
Number of Employees: 10
Sales Volume: $ 1-3 Million

4338 Touch America
Touch America
1403 S Third St Ext
PO Box 1304
Mebane, NC 27302   919-732-6968
800-678-6824
Fax: 919-732-1173
info@touchamerica.com
www.touchamerica.com

Massage and spa equipment
President: Stewart Griffith
Marketing Manager: Lianne De Moya
Finance Executive: Chris Owens
International Marketing Manager: Valerie Rawlings
Credit Cards: AMEX; MasterCard
Catalog Cost: Free
Catalog Circulation: Mailed 2 time(s) per year to 25000
Average Order Size: $200
Printing Information: 40 pages in 4 colors on Glossy Stock
Press: Sheetfed Press
Binding: Saddle Stitched
Mailing List Information: Names for rent
In Business: 32 years
Sales Volume: Under $500,000

4339 Walter Drake
Walter Drake
250 City Center
Oshkosh, WI 54906   920-231-3800
855-202-7393
www.wdrake.com

Bakeware, food storage, kitchen decor accessories, closet & bed accessories, storage organizers, small appliances, gadgets and tools.
Catalog Cost: Free
In Business: 69 years

4340 Waterwise
Waterwise Inc
2460 North Euclid Avenue
Upland, CA 91784-1199   909-982-2425
800-205-2425
Fax: 909-949-7217
kristen@vnwg.com
www.vnwg.com

Water and air purification systems for home and office
President: Jack Barber
CFO: Bob Barber
Marketing Manager: Greg Barber
Buyers: Mike Lane
Credit Cards: AMEX; MasterCard
Catalog Cost: Free
Catalog Circulation: Mailed 6 time(s) per year to 15000
Average Order Size: $200
Printing Information: 36 pages in 4 colors on Glossy Stock
Press: Web Press
Binding: Saddle Stitched
Mailing List Information: Names for rent
List Manager: Greg Barber
In Business: 93 years
Number of Employees: 32
Sales Volume: $4,000,000

4341 Weleda
Weleda North America
1 Bridge St.
Suite 42
Irvington, NY 10533   845-268-8599
800-241-1030
Fax: 800-280-4899
info@weleda.com
www.weleda.com

Natural personal care products
President: Jasper Van Brakel
Marketing Manager: Hamish Cook
Finance Manager: Patricia Masterson
Credit Cards: MasterCard
In Business: 94 years
Number of Employees: 34
Sales Volume: $ 14 Million

4342 Youcan Toocan Catalog
Youcan Toocan
6460 E Yale Avenue
Suite E10
Denver, CO 80222   303-759-9525
888-663-9396
www.youcantoocan.com

Hotel and home health products
President: Martha Hansen
Production Manager: Micky Kapelkee
Credit Cards: AMEX; MasterCard
Catalog Cost: Free
In Business: 18 years
Number of Employees: 12
Sales Volume: $ 1 Million

Medical Supplies

4343 AlcoPro
AlcoPro
2547 Sutherland Ave.
Knoxville, TN 37919   865-525-4900
800-227-9890
Fax: 865-525-4935
info@alcopro.com
www.alcopro.com

On-site drug and alcohol testing products for professional use
President: Jack Singleton
Marketing Manager: Greg Clark
Special Projects Coordinator: Sam Smithey
Customer Service Manager: Shannan Kennedy
Production Manager: Lorraine Jenkins
Credit Cards: MasterCard; Visa
Catalog Circulation: to 60M
Printing Information: 16 pages in 2 colors
In Business: 33 years
Number of Employees: 7
Sales Volume: $1.1 Million

4344 Alimed
AliMed, Inc
297 High St
Dedham, MA 02026-2898   781-329-2900
800-437-2966
Fax: 781-329-8392
info@alimed.com
www.alimed.com

Medical and ergonomic products for health care, business, and home
President: Julian Cherubini
CEO: John Snowden
Operations Manager: Frank Wilson
Director of Sales: Rob Weiner
Credit Cards: AMEX; MasterCard; Visa
Catalog Cost: Free
Sales Volume: $ 10-20 Million

4345 American Health & Safety
American Health & Safety
325 Industrial Circle
Stoughton, WI 53589   608-273-4000
800-522-7554
Fax: 800-522-7554
american@ahsafety.com
www.ahsafety.com

Safety equipment and first aid supplies
Chairman: Kurt Christensen
President: John Cronkrak
Buyers: Becky Kasmeder
Credit Cards: MasterCard; Visa
Catalog Cost: Free
Printing Information: 112 pages in 4 colors on Glossy Stock
Press: Web Press
Binding: Saddle Stitched
Mailing List Information: Names for rent
In Business: 30 years
Sales Volume: $ 5-10 Million

4346 Anatomical Chart Company
Wolters Kluwer Health
16522 Hunters Green Parkway
Hagerstown, MD 21740   301-223-2300
800-621-7500
Fax: 301-223-2400
orders@lww.com
www.anatomical.com

Anatomical charts and related products for human health markets
President: Diana Nole
CFO: Susan Yules
Marketing Manager: Marilyn Lack
President & CEO, Health Learning, R: Cathy Wolfe
President & CEO, Clinical Effective: Denise S. Basow, MD
President & CEO, Clinical Software: David A. Del Toro
In Business: 179 years
Sales Volume: $ 1-3 Million

4347 Arbill Safety Products
Arbill
10450 Drummond Road
Philadelphia, PA 19154   800-523-5367
info@arbill.com
www.arbill.com

Personal protective clothing, eye and hearing protection, head gear, respiratory equipment, back supports, ergonomic equipment, fall protection equipment, confined space protection, spill clean-up
President: Robyn Zlotkin
CFO: Keith Daviston
Production Manager: Bill Gabriele
Chief Executive Officer: Julie Copeland
Director of Operations: Bill Keay
Credit Cards: AMEX; MasterCard
Catalog Cost: Free
In Business: 72 years
Number of Employees: 55
Sales Volume: $ 10 Million

4348 Arista Surgical Supply Company
AliMed, Inc.
297 High Street
Dedham, MA 02026
781-329-2900
800-225-2610
Fax: 781-329-8392
info@alimed.com
www.alimed.com

Surgical supplies, surgical instruments, homecare, sutures, dressings, lab glasswares, stethoscopes, scalpel blades, spnygmomanometer, etc

President: Irving Horowitz
Credit Cards: AMEX; MasterCard; Visa
Catalog Cost: Free
Catalog Circulation: Mailed 6 time(s) per year
Printing Information: 80 pages on Matte Stock
Press: Letterpress
Binding: Saddle Stitched
Mailing List Information: Names for rent
In Business: 59 years
Number of Employees: 15
Sales Volume: $1MM to $3MM

4349 Bosom Buddy Breast Forms
B & B Company
PO Box 5731
Boise, ID 83705-731
208-343-9696
800-262-2789
Fax: 208-343-9266
www.bosombuddy.com

All- fabric, external breast prostheses

President: Stacie Neely
Credit Cards: AMEX; MasterCard
Catalog Cost: Free
Catalog Circulation: Mailed 3 time(s) per year to 15000
Average Order Size: $80
Printing Information: 2 pages in 4 colors on Matte Stock
Binding: Folded
Mailing List Information: Names for rent
In Business: 37 years
Number of Employees: 23
Sales Volume: $739,000

4350 Bruce Medical Supply
Bruce Medical Supply
411 Waverley Oaks Road
Suite 154
Waltham, MA 02452
781-894-6262
800-225-8446
Fax: 781-894-9519
sales@brucemedical.com
www.brucemedical.com

Health and medical supplies

President: Richard A. Najarian
Credit Cards: AMEX; MasterCard; Visa
Catalog Cost: Free
Catalog Circulation: Mailed 4 time(s) per year
Printing Information: 64 pages in 4 colors on Glossy Stock
Press: Web Press
Binding: Saddle Stitched
In Business: 35 years
Sales Volume: $ 3-5 Million

4351 CCR Medical
CCR Medical
967 43 Avenue NE
St. Petersburg, FL 33703
727-822-1420
888-883-7331
Fax: 727-894-6650
info@ccrmed.com
www.ccrmed.com

Nerve Stimulators widely used by CRNAs and Anesthesiologists nationwide.

4352 Claflin Medical Equipment
Claflin Medical Equipment
1206 Jefferson Blvd.
Warwick, RI 2886
401-732-9150
800-338-2372
Fax: 888-685-5455
customerservice@claflinequip.com
www.claflinequip.com

Medical equipment specialist company serving hospitals, clinics, surgical centers, and general practices.

Credit Cards: AMEX; MasterCard
In Business: 198 years

4353 Conney Safety
Conney Safety
3202 Latham Drive
P.O. Box 44190
Madison, WI 53744-4190
888-356-9100
Fax: 800-845-9095
safety@conney.com
www.conney.com

Products and equipment that keep people safe in the workplace

President: Bruce Hagan
CFO: Steven Boyack
CEO: Michael Wessner
Credit Cards: AMEX; MasterCard; Visa
Catalog Cost: Free
Printing Information: 72 pages in 4 colors on Glossy Stock
Press: Web Press
Binding: Perfect Bound
Mailing List Information: Names for rent
List Manager: Carl Sieg
In Business: 68 years
Number of Employees: 150
Sales Volume: $60 Million

4354 Duke Medical Supply
Duke Medical Supply
300 Biltmore Drive
Suite 350
Fenton, MO 63026
888-678-6692
Fax: 888-550-7663
www.dukemedicalsupply.com

4355 Edgepark Continence Catalog
Edgepark Medical Supplies
1810 Summit Commerce Park
Twinsburg, OH 44087
888-394-5375
Fax: 330-425-4355
www.edgepark.com

Continence supplies including catheters and adult briefs.

Catalog Cost: Free
Catalog Circulation: Mailed 1 time(s) per year
Printing Information: 116 pages in 4 colors
In Business: 88 years

4356 Edgepark Diabetes Catalog
Edgepark Medical Supplies
1810 Summit Commerce Park
Twinsburg, OH 44087
888-394-5375
Fax: 330-425-4355
www.edgepark.com

Diabetes care products including blood glucose monitors and testing supplies.

Catalog Cost: Free
Catalog Circulation: Mailed 1 time(s) per year
Printing Information: 52 pages in 4 colors
In Business: 88 years

4357 Edgepark Full-line Catalog
Edgepark Medical Supplies
1810 Summit Commerce Park
Twinsburg, OH 44087
888-394-5375
Fax: 330-425-4355
www.edgepark.com

Ostomy, diabetes, urological, incontinence and wound care products.

Catalog Cost: Free
Catalog Circulation: Mailed 1 time(s) per year
Printing Information: 268 pages in 4 colors
In Business: 88 years

4358 Edgepark Ostomy Catalog
Edgepark Medical Supplies
1810 Summit Commerce Park
Twinsburg, OH 44087
888-394-5375
Fax: 330-425-4355
www.edgepark.com

Ostomy supplies including all major brands.

Catalog Cost: Free
Catalog Circulation: Mailed 1 time(s) per year
Printing Information: 150 pages in 4 colors
In Business: 88 years

4359 Emergency Medical Products
Emergency Medical Products, Inc
5235 International Drive
Suite B
Cudahy, WI 53110
262-513-5753
800-558-6270
Fax: 800-558-1551
service@buyemp.com
www.buyemp.com

Emergency and medical supplies for your home or office, EMS, rescue campus & safety infection, pandemic control, hospital & clinic supplies, first aid

Chairman: Ronald Reed
President: Timothy Helz
Credit Cards: AMEX; MasterCard; Visa
Catalog Cost: Free
Catalog Circulation: Mailed 3 time(s) per year
Average Order Size: $400
Printing Information: 600 pages in 4 colors
Press: Web Press
Binding: Perfect Bound
In Business: 43 years
Number of Employees: 60

4360 Express Medical Supply, Inc
Express Medical Supply, Inc
218 Seebold Spur
Fenton, MO 63026
800-633-2139
800-633-9188
sales@exmed.net
www.exmed.net

In Business: 21 years

4361 Gall's
Gall's
1340 Russell Cave Road
Lexington, KY 40505
866-673-7643
888-831-9824
help-desk@galls.com
www.galls.com

Public safety equipment

President: Calvin Johnston
CFO: Larry Kinney
Marketing Manager: Jenny Super
Credit Cards: AMEX; MasterCard; Visa
Catalog Cost: Free
Catalog Circulation: Mailed 5 time(s) per year to 1MM
Average Order Size: $130
Printing Information: 284 pages in 4 colors
Binding: Perfect Bound
Mailing List Information: Names for rent
List Company: Chilcutt Direct
In Business: 48 years
Number of Employees: 350
Sales Volume: $ 54.5 Million

4362 HMI Marketing
Medical Arts Press
8500 Wyoming Ave N
Brooklyn Park, MN 55445-1825
800-982-3400
Fax: 800-499-8805
taxexempt@medicalartspress.com
www.quill.com

Marketing eyecare, dental materials to doctors, dentists, optometrists, and chiropracters

President: Elaine Ralls
Catalog Cost: Free
In Business: 64 years
Number of Employees: 600

4363 Hopkin's Medical Products

Hopkin's Medical Products
5 Greenwood Place
Baltimore, MD 21208-2763   410-484-2036
800-835-1995
Fax: 410-484-4036
customerservice@hopkinsmedical.net
www.hopkinsmedicalproducts.com

Complete line of medical products for doctors and nurses

President: Philip M. Kenney
CFO: Charles Goldberg
VP: Lou Klug
CEO: Philip M. Kenney
Credit Cards: MasterCard; Visa
Catalog Cost: Free
Catalog Circulation: Mailed 1 time(s) per year
Printing Information: 48 pages in 1 color
In Business: 70 years
Sales Volume: $ 1-3 Million

4364 Latest Products Corporation

Latest Products Corporation
PO Box 190
Syosset, NY 11791   516-367-4700
800-288-3547
Fax: 516-367-4714
info@latestproducts.net

Specialty items for nursing homes, government, state agencies, and hospitals primarily for use in laundry and housekeeping departments

VP: Aaron Hermen
Credit Cards: AMEX; MasterCard
Catalog Cost: Free
Catalog Circulation: Mailed 4 time(s) per year to 75K
Printing Information: 96 pages in 2 colors
Press: Web Press
Binding: Saddle Stitched
In Business: 43 years
Sales Volume: $500,000

4365 Medco Sports Medicine

Masune First Aid & Safety
500 Fillmore Avenue
Tonawanda, NY 14150   716-695-3244
800-831-0894
Fax: 800-222-1934
customersupport@masune.com
www.masune.com

Distributor of first aid, safety sports medicine for athletic physical therapy

President: Paul De Martinis
Sales Volume: $ 20-50

4366 MediRest, Inc

MediRest, Inc
233 Oxmoor Circle
Birmingham, AL 35209   205-942-1616
Fax: 205-942-1008
www.medirestinc.com

Rehab and bariatric equipment.

4367 Medical Supplies Depot

Medical Supplies Depot
1515 University Blvd. South
Mobile, AL 36609   800-879-6863
Fax: 800-329-2987
www.msdepot.com

Medical supplies and equipment.

4368 Moore Medical Corporation

Moore Medical LLC
1690 New Britain Avenue
PO Box 4066
Farmington, CT 06032-4066   860-826-3600
800-234-1464
Fax: 877-881-0710
e-support@mooremedical.com

Medical supplies and medical equipment

President: Rick Frey
Manager Vendor Promotions: Ryan Stefanski
Credit Cards: MasterCard; Visa
Catalog Cost: Free
Catalog Circulation: Mailed 3 time(s) per year
Printing Information: 180 pages in 2 colors
List Company: Direct Media
In Business: 63 years
Number of Employees: 305
Sales Volume: $ 16 Million

4369 National Hospitality Supply

National Hospitality Supply, Inc.
10660 N Executive Ct
Mequon, WI 53092   800-526-8224
Fax: 262-478-0229
cs@nathosp.com
www.nathosp.com

Accessories and furniture for hotels and motels

Chairman: Dan Crimmins
Credit Cards: AMEX; MasterCard
Catalog Cost: Free
Catalog Circulation: Mailed 4 time(s) per year
Printing Information: 116 pages in 4 colors
Binding: Perfect Bound
In Business: 24 years

4370 Pharmaceutical Systems, Inc

Pharmaceutical Systems, Inc
8240 S Lewis Ave
Tulsa, OK 74137   800-998-8558
Fax: 800-745-2476

4371 ProMed Products Xpress

ProMed Products Xpress
360 Veterans Parkway
Suite 115
Bolingbrook, IL 60440-4607   630-771-7400
800-542-9297
Fax: 888-674-4380
www.promedxpress.com

Physical therapy equipment and supplies for chiropractors, physical therapists, occupational therapists, massage therapists and athletic trainers

VP of Sales: Steve Keller
Director: Angela Anderson
Credit Cards: AMEX; MasterCard
In Business: 46 years
Number of Employees: 126
Sales Volume: $ 13 Million

4372 Redding Medical

Redding Medical
152 Westminster Rd
Reisterstown, MD 21136-1027   410-526-9755
800-733-2796
Fax: 410-526-9759
info@reddingmedical.com
www.reddingmedical.com

Medical supplies, medical equipment and instruments

President: Sharon Shipe
VP: David Shipe
Credit Cards: AMEX; MasterCard
Catalog Cost: Free
Catalog Circulation: Mailed 14 time(s) per year
Printing Information: 14 pages in 2 colors on Matte Stock
Press: Sheetfed Press
Mailing List Information: Names for rent

In Business: 39 years
Sales Volume: $ 1.5 Million

4373 School Health Sports Medicine

School Health Corporation
865 Muirfield Dr
Hanover Park, IL 60133-5461   630-582-0024
866-323-5465
Fax: 800-235-1305
info@schoolhealth.com
www.schoolhealth.com

Medicine and health supplies and equipment/acccessories for school athletic departments

Chairman: Veda Johnson
President: Susan Rogers
CFO: Scott Cormack
Marketing Manager: John Rooney
VP/COO: Robert Rogers
In Business: 65 years
Number of Employees: 70
Sales Volume: $ 10-20 Million

4374 School Kids Healthcare

School Kids Healthcare
5235 International Drive
Suite B
Cudahy, WI 53110   866-558-0686
Fax: 800-558-1551
service@schoolkidshealthcare.com
www.schoolkidshealthcare.com

School health products and nurse supplies; nursing education, emergency supplies, first air, anatomical models, displays & posters, infection & flu control

Marketing Manager: Michael Margolies
Credit Cards: AMEX; MasterCard; Visa
Catalog Cost: Free
Catalog Circulation: Mailed 1 time(s) per year
Average Order Size: $350
Printing Information: 300 pages in 4 colors
Press: Web Press
Binding: Perfect Bound
In Business: 9 years

4375 Silicones

Silicones, Inc.
211 Woodbine Street
PO Box 363
High Point, NC 27261-363   336-886-5018
800-533-8709
Fax: 336-886-7122
info@silicones-inc.com
www.silicones-inc.com

Silicone manufacturers servicing electrical contractors, medical suppliers, furniture suppliers and more

President: Gerald B Swanson
CFO: Don Griffin
Marketing Manager: Tori Swanson
Sales Executive: Myra Bungardner
In Business: 41 years
Number of Employees: 17
Sales Volume: $6.7MM

4376 Support Plus

Support Plus
5581 Hudson Industrial Parkway
Hudson, OH 44236-0099   844-276-2020
www.supportplus.com

Medical hosiery, comfort shoes and aids to daily living

President: Ed Janos
Buyers: Marilyn Mygan
Credit Cards: AMEX; MasterCard
Catalog Cost: Free
Catalog Circulation: Mailed 10 time(s) per year to 8MM
Average Order Size: $70
Printing Information: 80 pages in 4 colors on Glossy Stock
Press: Web Press
Binding: Saddle Stitched

Mailing List Information: Names for rent
List Manager: The Other List Companny
In Business: 45 years
Sales Volume: $ 10-20 Million

4377 The Parthenon Company
The Parthenon Company, Inc.
3311 West 2400 South
Salt Lake City, UT 84119   801-972-5184
    800-453-8898
Fax: 801-972-4734
info@parthenoninc.com
www.parthenoninc.com

Ostonomy products, wound care, skin care, and urological products
President: Nicholas Mihalopoulos
Founder & CEO : Nick Mihalopoulos, R.Ph., Ph.D.
President : Jason Mihalopoulos, MPH, MBA, MS Nu
Credit Cards: AMEX; MasterCard; Visa
Catalog Cost: Free
Printing Information: 100 pages
In Business: 54 years
Number of Employees: 8
Sales Volume: $ 1.3 Million

4378 Veridian Healthcare
Veridian Healthcare
1175 Lakeside Drive
Gurnee, IL 60031   866-736-3330
Fax: 866-480-1717
www.veridianhealthcare.com
In Business: 50 years

4379 Zymo Research
Zymo Research
17062 Murphy Avenue
Irvine, CA 92614   949-679-1190
    888-882-9682
Fax: 949-266-9452
info@zymoresearch.com
www.zymoresearch.com

Medical supplies, devices and instruments
Chairman: Larry Jia
Catalog Cost: Free
Catalog Circulation: Mailed 1 time(s) per year
Printing Information: 228 pages in 4 colors
In Business: 23 years

Nutrition

4380 Azure Standard
Azure Standard
79709 Dufur Valley Rd.
Dufur, OR 97021   971-200-8350
Fax: 971-645-4759
www.azurestandard.com

Organic and natural food distributor.
Founder & CEO: David Stelzer
In Business: 44 years

4381 Botanic Choice
Indiana Botanic Gardens, Inc
3401 W 37th Avenue
Hobart, IN 46342-1751   800-644-8327
Fax: 219-947-4148
info@botanichealth.com
www.botanicchoice.com

Herbal supplements and natural remedies
President: Tim Cleland
Sales: Gail Thomas
Credit Cards: MasterCard; Visa
Catalog Cost: Free
Catalog Circulation: Mailed 15 time(s) per year
Average Order Size: $40
Printing Information: 32 pages in 4 colors on Glossy Stock
Press: Web Press
Binding: Saddle Stitched
Mailing List Information: Names for rent
In Business: 107 years

Number of Employees: 157
Sales Volume: $25 Million

4382 Bronson Vitamins
Bronson Laboratories
350 South 400 West
Suite 102
Lindon, UT 84042-1931   801-443-3005
    800-235-3200
Fax: 800-596-4242
help@bronsonsupport.com
www.bronsonvitamins.com/

Vitamins
President: Derek Price
Credit Cards: AMEX; MasterCard; Visa
Catalog Cost: Free
Printing Information: 72 pages
In Business: 55 years
Sales Volume: $ 10-20 Million

4383 Carol Bond Health Foods
Carol Bond Health Foods, Inc.
334 Main Street
Liberty, TX 77575-47   936-336-9001
    800-833-8282
Fax: 936-336-6226
customerservice@carolbond.com
www.carolbond.com

Vitamin and nutritional supplements
President: Phillip Gerber
CEO/Owner: Carol Bond
Credit Cards: AMEX; MasterCard; Visa
Catalog Cost: Free
Catalog Circulation: Mailed 2 time(s) per year to 50M
Printing Information: 32 pages in 1 color on Glossy Stock
Press: Web Press
Binding: Saddle Stitched
In Business: 35 years
Sales Volume: Under $500,000

4384 Easy Comforts
Easy Comforts
250 City Center
Oshkosh, WI 54906   920-231-3800
    855-202-7391
Fax: 888-252-8462
www.easycomforts.com

Value-priced personal and health care merchandise for the mature consumer.
Catalog Cost: Free

4385 Eden Ranch
Betty Lee Vitamins
22155 Eden Rd
Topanga, CA 90290-3804   310-455-2065
    877-825-9558
Fax: 310-455-2067
www.bettyleevitamins.com

Vitamins
President: Patricia Moore
Credit Cards: MasterCard; Visa
Catalog Cost: Free
Printing Information: 6 pages in 4 colors
Number of Employees: 6
Sales Volume: Under $500M

4386 Fitness Systems
Fitness Systems Manufacturing Corporatio
104 Evans Avenue
PO Box 2073
Sinking Spring, PA 19608-73   610-670-0135
    800-967-1827
Fax: 610-670-0135
vitaminout@aol.com
fitness-systems.net

Athletic/sports proteins, amino acids, vitamins and supplements at wholesale prices
President: David Hoffman
Credit Cards: MasterCard
Catalog Cost: Free

Printing Information:
Press: Web Press
Mailing List Information: Names for rent
In Business: 26 years
Number of Employees: 15

4387 Fruitful Yield
Fruitful Yield
229 W Roosevelt Rd
Lombard, IL 60148-4403   630-705-0313
    800-469-5552
Fax: 630-629-9244
sales@fruitfulyielddirect.com
www.fruitfulyield.com

Affordable nutritional, dietary supplements and vitamins
President: Elwood Richard
Production Manager: Catherine Dickenscheidt
In Business: 53 years
Sales Volume: $ 1-3 Million

4388 Full Of Life
Full Of Life
P.O. Box 25600
Bradenton, FL 34206-5600   800-558-6967
    800-521-7638
CustomerService@fulloflife.com
www.fulloflife.com

Health aids, hobbies, gifts, fitness products, and personal care
Catalog Cost: Free
In Business: 101 years

4389 Hammer Nutrition
Hammer Nutrition
4952 Whitefish Stage Rd.
Whitefish, MT 59937   800-336-1977
Fax: 406-862-4543
www.hammernutrition.com

Products, knowledge and service to health conscious athletes all over the world.
In Business: 28 years

4390 Health Management Resources
Health Management Resources
99 Summer Street
Suite 1200
Boston, MA 02110-1346   617-357-9876
    800-418-1367
Fax: 617-357-9690
www.hmrprogram.com

Weight and health management programs
President: Lawrence Stifler
Program Manager: Karen Handy
Catalog Cost: Free
In Business: 31 years
Number of Employees: 135
Sales Volume: $ 7 Million

4391 Healthy America
Healthy America
2973 Harbor Blvd
#566
Costa Mesa, CA 92626   800-783-0023
Fax: 866-645-2005
info@healthy-america.com
www.ha-nutrition.com

Vitamins and supplements
In Business: 23 years

4392 Healthy Living
AmeriMark Direct
6864 Engle Rd.
Cleveland, OH 44130   866-345-1388
www.amerimark.com

Exercise, diet, weight loss and general health.
CFO: Joe Albanese
CEO & President: Gareth Giesler
Catalog Cost: Free

Printing Information: in 4 colors
In Business: 47 years
Number of Employees: 700
Sales Volume: $400 Million

4393 Herbal Actives
Nature's Plus
548 Broadhollow Rd.
Melville, NY 11747-1719   800-645-9500
     800-645-9500
www.naturesplus.com

Herbal remedies and supplements

President: James Gibbons
In Business: 40 years

4394 Institute for Vibrant Living
Naturmed, Inc.
661 E Howards Rd
Ste C
Camp Verde, AZ 86322   928-567-2991
     800-720-1245
Fax: 928-567-6487
www.ivlproducts.com

Antioxidants, detoxification formulas, energy formulas, homeopathic products and weight management

Chairman: Don Elgie
President: Bill Ruble
CFO: Larry Zic
Marketing Manager: Gina Lascano
Production Manager: Patrick Heffernan
EVP, Health Research: Jay White
Shipping Manager: Monica Johnson
Art Director: Kathy Williams
Credit Cards: AMEX; MasterCard; Visa
Catalog Cost: Free
In Business: 7 years
Number of Employees: 40
Sales Volume: $ 1.8 Million

4395 Internatural Health & Wellness
Internatural
PO Box 489
Twin Lakes, WI 53181-489   800-905-6887
     800-643-4221
Fax: 262-889-8591
www.internatural.com

Natural personal care products, cosmetics and dietary supplements

President: Santosh Krinsky
Buyers: Laura Parker
Catalog Cost: Free
Catalog Circulation: Mailed 52 time(s) per year to 30000
Average Order Size: $40
Printing Information: 36 pages in 4 colors on Matte Stock
Press: Sheetfed Press
Binding: Folded
Mailing List Information: Names for rent
In Business: 23 years
Sales Volume: $ 500,000- 1 Million

4396 Kava Kauai
Kava Kauai
PO Box 1202
Kapaa, HI 96746-7202   800-626-0883
Fax: 800-626-0883
info@realkava.com
www.realkava.com

Kava root, Kava products, Shamanic herbs and seeds

President: Gary Mack
Catalog Cost: Free
In Business: 18 years
Sales Volume: Under $500,000

4397 Learning ZoneXpress
Learning ZoneXpress
667 E Vine St
PO Box 1022
Owatonna, MN 55060   507-455-9076
     888-455-7003
Fax: 507-455-3380
www.learningzonexpress.com

4398 Mountain Naturals of Vermont
Mountain Naturals
20 New England Drive
Essex Junction, VT 05452   802-878-5508
     800-874-9444
Fax: 802-878-0549
info@mountainnaturals.com

Vitamins, supplements and multivitamins for people and pets

President: Dom Orlandi, Jr.
CFO: Tricia Wunsch
Chief Operating Officer: Bill O'Connor
Buyers: Tina Abentroth
Credit Cards: AMEX; MasterCard; Visa
Catalog Cost: Free
Catalog Circulation: Mailed 2 time(s) per year to 10000
Printing Information: 60 pages in 4 colors on Glossy Stock
Press: Sheetfed Press
Binding: Folded
Mailing List Information: Names for rent
In Business: 39 years
Number of Employees: 115
Sales Volume: $32 MM

4399 Nashua Nutrition
Nashua Nutrition
522 Amherst Street
Suite 1
Nashua, NH 3063   800-649-1374
Fax: 800-649-1374
Info@NashuaNutrition.com
www.nashuanutrition.com

Credit Cards: AMEX; MasterCard

4400 Pain & Stress Center Products
Pain & Stress Center Products
8650 Bandera Road
San Antonio, TX 78250   210-614-7246
     800-669-2256
Fax: 210-614-4336
mailpsctr@painstresscenter.com
www.painstresscenter.com

Products for pain, stress, anxiety, hyperactivity/ADD, fibromyalgia and Specialty amino acids/nutrient formulas for IBS support; decaffeinated green tea extract; special mineral formulas

President: Billie J Sahley
CFO: Camille Boyd
Marketing Manager: Laura Boyd
VP of operations: Katherine Birkner
Credit Cards: MasterCard
Catalog Cost: Free
Catalog Circulation: Mailed 2 time(s) per year to 60MM
Average Order Size: $65
Printing Information: 64 pages in 4 colors on Matte Stock
Press: Web Press
Binding: Saddle Stitched
Mailing List Information: Names for rent
In Business: 38 years
Number of Employees: 8
Sales Volume: $2,000,000

4401 Power Shack
Power Shack, Inc.
273 Covenant Square Drive
Biloxi, MS 39531-6752   228-388-0155
     800-359-4792
Fax: 228-388-2548
tom@powershack.com
www.powershack.com

Health and fitness products

Sales: Mike Banisch
Purchasing: Tom Banisch
Buyers: Tom Banisch
Credit Cards: AMEX; MasterCard
Average Order Size: $99
Printing Information: 120 pages in 4 colors on Glossy Stock
Binding: Saddle Stitched
Mailing List Information: Names for rent
In Business: 24 years
Number of Employees: 24
Sales Volume: $ 1.7 Million

4402 Puritan's Pride
Puritan's Pride
PO Box 9001
Oakdale, NY 11769-9001   631-244-1290
     800-645-1030
Fax: 631-471-5693
vitamins@puritan.com
www.puritan.com

Discount health products including vitamins, minerals, food supplements, herbs, amino acids, natural pet products, skin and health care.

President: Steve Cahillane
Director, Catalog Marketing: Michelle Davis
Catalog Cost: Free
Printing Information: 112 pages in 4 colors
Press: Web Press
Binding: Saddle Stitched
Mailing List Information: Names for rent
List Company: Rifkin Direct
64 Appletree Lane
Roslyn Heights, NY 11577
516-621-1076
In Business: 50 years
Sales Volume: $20MM to $50MM

4403 Quantum Medicine
Quantum, Inc.
PO Box 2791
Eugene, OR 97402-331   541-345-5556
     800-448-1448
Fax: 541-345-4825
orders@quantumhealth.com
www.quantumhealth.Com

Nutritional products and vitamins

President: Eve McClure
Marketing Manager: David Shaw
Credit Cards: MasterCard
Catalog Cost: Free
Catalog Circulation: Mailed 2 time(s) per year to 70000
In Business: 34 years
Number of Employees: 24
Sales Volume: $ 4 Million

4404 Ron Teeguarden's Dragon Herbs
Ron Teeguarden Enterprises, Inc.
315 Wilshire Blvd
Santa Monica, CA 90401-1311   310-917-2288
     888-558-6642
Fax: 310-917-1164
www.dragonherbs.com

Chinese tonic, herbs and superfoods

President: Ron Teeguarden
Marketing Manager: Heather Cook
CEO: Yanlin Teeguarden
Catalog Cost: Free
Catalog Circulation: Mailed 1 time(s) per year
Mailing List Information: Names for rent
In Business: 18 years
Number of Employees: 20
Sales Volume: $ 1-3 Million

4405 TNVitamins
TNVitamins
75 BI-COUNTY BLVD.
FARMINGDALE, NY 11735   631-694-7358
customerservice@tnvitamins.com
www.tnvitamins.com

Nutritional supplements.

In Business: 36 years

4406 TriVita
TriVita, Inc.
16100 N Greenway Hayden Lp.
Suite #950
Scottsdale, AZ 85260
561-514-5758
800-991-7116
Fax: 877-432-4829
www.trivita.com/Web/US/content/products/cat-
egory.aspx?id=300

Nutritional supplements and snacks

CFO: Don Kurtenbach
Marketing Manager: Marcus Ellison
Founder: Michael R. Ellison
Director of Legal Affairs: Judy Beal
Catalog Cost: Free
Catalog Circulation: Mailed 12 time(s) per
year
Printing Information: 64 pages in 4 colors
In Business: 24 years
Number of Employees: 35
Sales Volume: $ 5.5 Million

4407 Uckele
Uckele
PO Box 160
Blissfield, MI 49228
800-248-0330
customerservice@uckele.com
www.uckele.com

In Business: 50 years

4408 Valley Naturals
Valley Naturals
1118 Pony Express Highway
Marysville, KS 66508
866-373-2175
Fax: 866-373-2112
Service@ValleyNaturals.com
www.valleynaturals.com

**Men's and women's vitamins for nutrition to
diet supplements**

Credit Cards: AMEX; MasterCard; Visa
Catalog Cost: Free

4409 Vitamin Direct
Vitamin Direct Inc
PO Box 1983
San Marcos, CA 92079-1983
760-738-4940
800-468-4027
Fax: 760-738-1150
diana_vitamindirect@yahoo.com

**Quality vitamins, minerals, herbs, and spe-
cialty supplements capules**

President: Diana Sprowl
CFO: Jon Sprowl
Fulfillment: James Sprowl
Catalog Cost: Free
Catalog Circulation: Mailed 4 time(s) per year
to 3000
Average Order Size: $50
Printing Information: in 1 color on Matte Stock
Press: Sheetfed Press
Binding: Folded
Mailing List Information: Names for rent
In Business: 25 years
Sales Volume: Under $500,000

4410 Vitamin Research Products
Vitamin Research Products
4610 Arrowhead Drive
Carson City, NV 89706
817-785-4652
888-362-1699
Fax: 775-884-1331
customerservice@vrp.com
www.vrp.com

Anti-aging supplements

President: Robert Watson
CFO: Ted Johnson
Marketing Manager: Maria Watson
Production Manager: Tom Lomax
Credit Cards: AMEX; MasterCard
Catalog Circulation: Mailed 2 time(s) per year
Printing Information: 100 pages in 4 colors

Mailing List Information: Names for rent
In Business: 36 years
Sales Volume: Under $500,000

**4411 Wysong Products for Thinking People
Catalog**
Wysong
7550 Eastman Avenue
Midland, MI 48642-7779
989-631-0009
800-748-0188
Fax: 989-631-9280
wysong@wysong.net
www.wysong.net

**Healthy natural products for people and their
companion animals**

President: Randy Wysong
Marketing Manager: Lucas Wysong
Buyers: Joyce Morton
Credit Cards: AMEX; MasterCard
Catalog Cost: Free
Mailing List Information: Names for rent
In Business: 36 years
Number of Employees: 20
Sales Volume: $ 3.5 Million

4412 Zahler
Zahler
50 Lawrence Avenue
Brooklyn, NY 11230
212-444-9936
info@zahlers.com
www.zahlers.com

Natural antidotes.
Catalog Cost: Free

Pharmaceuticals

4413 D&E Pharmaceuticals
DNE Nutraceuticals
700 Central Avenue
Farmingdale, NJ 07727
212-235-5200
800-221-1833
Fax: 212-235-5243
info@dnenutra.com
www.dnenutra.com

**Pharmaceutical products, health aids, fit-
ness aids and over the counter drugs**

President: Eric Organ
Credit Cards: AMEX; MasterCard; Visa
Catalog Cost: Free
Catalog Circulation: Mailed 4 time(s) per year
to 500,0
Average Order Size: $55
Printing Information: 115 pages in 4 colors
Mailing List Information: Names for rent
List Company: D&E Belgium
Number of Employees: 25
Sales Volume: $ 20-50 Million

4414 Life-Assist.com
11277 Sunrise Park Drive
Rancho Cordova, CA 95742
800-824-6016
Fax: 800-290-9794

Assistment aides for the elderly or disabled

4415 Merit Pharmaceutical
2611 N. San Fernando Road
Los Angeles, CA 90065
323-227-4831
800-421-9657
Fax: 323-227-4833
solutions@meritpharm.com
www.meritpharm.com

Pharmaceuticals

Skin & Hair Care

4416 Absolutely Natural
Absolutely Natural
640 Atlantis Road
Melbourne, FL 32904
321-728-7191
800-848-7623
Fax: 321-951-2037
info@absolutely-natural.com
www.absolutely-natural.com

In Business: 23 years

4417 As We Change
As We Change
250 City Center
Oshkosh, WI 54901
855-202-7392
Fax: 888-534-8469
help@aswechange.com
www.aswechange.com

**Nutrition, beauty, skin care, exercise, per-
sonal care and lifestyle products for women
ages 40-50+ years.**

Catalog Cost: Free
In Business: 20 years

4418 Aubrey Organics
Aubrey Organics, Inc.
5046 W. Linebaugh Avenue
Tampa, FL 33624
813-877-4186
800-282-7394
Fax: 813-876-8166
www.aubrey-organics.com

**Certified organic, includes natural hair, skin
and body care products**

President: Aubrey Hampton
Marketing Manager: Patrycia Siewert
Production Manager: Pat Basin
VP Sales: Karen Ress
Credit Cards: MasterCard; Visa; Discover
Catalog Cost: $3.5
Catalog Circulation: Mailed 4 time(s) per year
Printing Information: 51 pages in 4 colors on
Matte Stock
Press: Web Press
Binding: Folded
Mailing List Information: Names for rent
In Business: 48 years
Number of Employees: 52
Sales Volume: $8.2 Million

4419 Auromere Ayurvedic Products
Auromere Ayurvedic Imports
2621 W Highway 12
Lodi, CA 95242-9200
209-339-3710
800-735-4691
Fax: 209-339-3715
www.auromere.com

**Ayurvedic body care & aromatherapy in-
cense from India: toothpaste, soap, massage oil, shampoo, lotion, mudbath,
incense; all cruelty-free environmentally
friendly, pure, authentic and effective**

President: Dakshina Vanzetti
Marketing Manager: Vishnu Eschner
Credit Cards: AMEX; MasterCard
Average Order Size: $25
In Business: 25 years
Number of Employees: 4
Sales Volume: $370,000

4420 Azida
Aazida, Inc.
4078 S Hohokam Drive
Sierra Vista, AZ 85650-8590
520-803-8872
800-603-6601
Fax: 520-803-7449
info@azid.com
www.azida.com

Hemp oil body care products

President: Andy West
Credit Cards: AMEX; MasterCard
In Business: 19 years

4421 BUYnail.com
BUYnail.com
13891 Nautilus Dr
Garden Grove, CA 92843   714-265-6106
bncs@buynail.com
www.buynail.com

4422 Baar
Baar
PO Box 60
Downingtown, PA 19335   610-873-4591
800-269-2502
Fax: 610-873-7945
www.baar.com
Credit Cards: AMEX; MasterCard

4423 Badger
Badger
768 Route 10
Gilsum, NH 3448   603-357-2958
800-603-6100
Fax: 603-352-4818
custserv@badgerbalm.com
www.badgerbalm.com
In Business: 20 years

4424 Baudelaire
Baudelaire
12 Business Center Drive
Swanzey, NH 03446-2121   603-352-9234
800-327-2324
Fax: 603-352-9239
www.baudelairesoaps.com

Fine imported soaps and assorted bath products
President: Joe Marks
CFO: Joanne Finn
VP: David Blistein
Credit Cards: AMEX; MasterCard; Visa; Discover Optima
Catalog Cost: Free
Catalog Circulation: Mailed 2 time(s) per year to 20M
Average Order Size: $40
Printing Information: 24 pages in 4 colors on Matte Stock
Press: Sheetfed Press
Binding: Saddle Stitched
Mailing List Information: Names for rent
In Business: 28 years
Number of Employees: 20
Sales Volume: $ 3.4 Million

4425 Beauty Book
The Industry Source
29683 W K Smith Drive
New Hudson, MI 48165-2601   248-347-7700
800-362-6245
Fax: 248-347-7734
sales@theindustrysource.com
www.theindustrysource.com/

Beauty salon supplies
President: Larry Gaynor
CFO: Brad Kellett
Marketing Manager: Lisa Phillion
Credit Cards: AMEX; MasterCard
Printing Information: 283 pages in 7 colors on Glossy Stock
Binding: Folded
In Business: 30 years
Number of Employees: 275
Sales Volume: $ 19 Million

4426 Beauty Boutique
AmeriMark Direct
6864 Engle Rd.
Cleveland, OH 44130   866-345-1388
www.amerimark.com

Women's and men's fragrances, cosmetics and personal care products.
CFO: Joe Albanese
CEO & President: Gareth Giesler
Catalog Cost: Free

Printing Information: in 4 colors
In Business: 47 years
Number of Employees: 700
Sales Volume: $400 Million

4427 Beauty Naturally
Beauty Naturally
850 Stanton Road
Burlingame, CA 94010   650-697-1809
800-432-4323
Fax: 650-697-1941
sales@beautynaturally.com
www.beautynaturally.com

Marketer of unique cosmetics, hair and skin products
President: Janet C Wong
jwong@ksystem.com
Printing Information: in 1 color on Matte Stock
Binding: Folded
Mailing List Information: Names for rent
In Business: 35 years
Number of Employees: 3
Sales Volume: $270,000

4428 Beehive Botanicals
Beehive Botanicals
16297 W Nursery Rd
Hayward, WI 54843-7138   715-634-4274
800-233-4483
Fax: 715-634-3523
beehive.shopmaster@beehivebotanicals.com
www.beehivebotanicals.com

Skin care, hair care, oral care and health supplements
President: Linda Graham
Credit Cards: AMEX; MasterCard; Visa
Catalog Cost: Free
Catalog Circulation: Mailed 3 time(s) per year to 50000
Average Order Size: $50
Printing Information: 4 pages in 4 colors on Glossy Stock
Binding: Saddle Stitched
In Business: 42 years
Number of Employees: 38
Sales Volume: $6.5 Million

4429 Botanic Gardens
Indiana Botanic Gardens, Inc.
3401 W 37th Avenue
Hobart, IN 46342-1751   800-644-8327
Fax: 219-947-4148
info@botanichealth.com
www.botanicchoice.com

Herbs, vitamins and minerals
President: Tim Cleland
Catalog Cost: Free
In Business: 106 years
Number of Employees: 157
Sales Volume: $ 25 Million

4430 DHC
DHC USA Inc.
5021 Louise Drive
Mechanicsburg, PA 17055-6916   800-342-2273
Fax: 888-650-7118
www.dhccare.com

Provides beauty products including skincare, body care, and makeup items
Catalog Cost: Free
In Business: 20 years

4431 DHC Care
DHC USA
555 Montgomery Street
Suite 1400
San Francisco, CA 94111   800-342-2273
customercare@dhccare.com
www.dhccare.com
Marketing Manager: Florence Schweinberg
Communications Manager: Amanne Sharif
COO & General Counsel: Darcy Manning
Catalog Cost: Free

Catalog Circulation: Mailed 4 time(s) per year
Printing Information: in 4 colors
In Business: 22 years
Number of Employees: 150

4432 GA Labs
Spiral Energetics
60 E Ashley Ave
Suite B
Driggs, ID 83422-5166   208-787-2153
888-425-2250
Fax: 208-201-3143
HelpDesk@galabs.com
www.spiralenergetics.com

Personal care products for the entire family, specializing in hard-to-find products
Average Order Size: $50
Printing Information: 5 pages on Matte Stock
Press: Web Press
In Business: 37 years

4433 Gold Medal Hair Products
Gold Medal Hair
330 Conklin Street
Farmingdale, NY 11735   631-465-0202
800-324-7136
Fax: 631-465-0207
www.goldmedalhair.com

Black hair care products and wigs
President: Richard Laban
ricklaban@aol.com
Marketing Manager: Rick Laban
Sales Manager: Florence Robinson
Buyers: Cary Shapiro
Gloria Rivers
Credit Cards: MasterCard; Visa
Catalog Cost: Free
Catalog Circulation: Mailed 12 time(s) per year to 20000
Average Order Size: $47
Printing Information: 16 pages in 4 colors on Glossy Stock
Press: Web Press
Binding: Saddle Stitched
Mailing List Information: Names for rent
List Company: JAMI Marketing
914-620-0700
In Business: 75 years
Number of Employees: 40
Sales Volume: $ 5 Million

4434 Green Book of Natural Beauty
Yves Rocher
PO Box 1701
Champlain, NY 12919-1701   888-909-0771
Fax: 800-321-4909
info@yvesrocherusa.com
www.yvesrocherusa.com

Skin and body care products, fragrances and cosmetics

4435 Hobe Laboratories
Hobe Laboratories Inc
6479 S Ash Ave
Tempe, AZ 85283   480-413-1950
800-528-4482
Fax: 480-413-2005
hobelabs@aol.com
www.hobelabs.com

All-natural health and beauty products
President: Bill Robertson
Marketing Manager: Brenda Martin
Production Manager: Peter Samuell
Credit Cards: AMEX; MasterCard
Catalog Cost: Free
Average Order Size: $75
Printing Information: 20 pages in 4 colors on Glossy Stock
Press: Letterpress
Binding: Perfect Bound
Mailing List Information: Names for rent
In Business: 40 years
Number of Employees: 12
Sales Volume: $1 Million

4436 Indiana Botanic Gardens

Indiana Botanic Gardens, Inc
3401 W 37th Ave
Hobart, IN 46342-1751   800-644-8327
Fax: 219-947-4148
info@botanichealth.com
www.botanicchoice.com

Herbs, vitamins and minerals

President: Tim Cleland
CEO: Tim Cleland
In Business: 104 years
Number of Employees: 157
Sales Volume: $25 Million

4437 Indigo Wild

Indigo Wild
3125 Wyandotte Street
Kansas City, MO 64111   800-361-5686
Fax: 816-221-4035
www.indigowild.com

All natural bath and body products such as soaps, bath salts, lotions, balms, and oils

Catalog Cost: Free

4438 Jojoba

KSA Jojoba
19025 Parthenia Street
Dept DOM
Northridge, CA 91324-4820   818-701-1534
Fax: 818-993-0194
jojoba99@hotmail.com
www.jojoba-ksa-jojoba.com

Cosmetics, toiletries, haircare products, oils, skin care and pet skin care products

President: Kathie Aamodt
Marketing Manager: Tina Newton
Credit Cards: MasterCard; Visa
Catalog Cost: Free
Catalog Circulation: Mailed 1 time(s) per year to 10M
Average Order Size: $15
Printing Information: 5 pages in 1 color on Matte Stock
Press: Letterpress
Mailing List Information: Names for rent
List Manager: Kathie Aamodt
In Business: 26 years
Number of Employees: 5
Sales Volume: $5MM to $10MM

4439 Just for Redheads Beauty Products

Just for Redheads
16622 North 91st Street
Building B Suite 101
Scottsdale, AZ 85260   480-361-6066
800-831-8240
Fax: 480-361-6076
Info@Justforredheads.com
www.justforredheads.com

Beauty and skin care products for redheads

President: Paula Pennypacker
Founder: Paula Pennypacker
Credit Cards: MasterCard
Catalog Cost: Free
Sales Volume: Under $500,000

4440 Kettle Care-Pure Herbal Body Care

Kettle Care Inc
3575 Highway 93 North
Kalispell, MT 59901   406-257-6622
888-556-2316
Fax: 406-551-4930
office@kettlecare.com
www.kettlecare.com

Pure herbal body care products for people with dry and/or sensitive skin

President: Lynn Wallingford
Production Manager: Ben
Lab Manager: James
Shipping & Lab Assistant: Jean
Office/Production Assistant: Deborah
Catalog Cost: $1

Catalog Circulation: Mailed 2 time(s) per year to 20000
Average Order Size: $30
Printing Information: 18 pages in 4 colors on Glossy Stock
Binding: Saddle Stitched
In Business: 28 years
Number of Employees: 5
Sales Volume: $320,000

4441 Lipsense Catalog

Diva Beauty Products
K Lewis Enterprises
Warren NJ   908-598-5209
karole@divabeautyproducts.com
www.divabeautyproducts.com

4442 Lucky Heart Cosmetics

Lucky Heart Cosmetics
390 Mulberry Street
Memphis, TN 38103   901-526-7658
800-283-1014
www.luckyheart.com

Cosmetics

President: Tom Colturi
VP: Chandra Stockren
Buyers: Chandra Miller
Catalog Cost: Free
Catalog Circulation: Mailed 2 time(s) per year
Average Order Size: $50
Printing Information: 31 pages in 4 colors on Matte Stock
Press: Web Press
Binding: Perfect Bound
In Business: 77 years
Number of Employees: 4
Sales Volume: $320,000

4443 Miracle of Aloe

Miracle Of Aloe
PO Box 612688
Dallas, TX 75261-2688   972-790-7033
800-966-2563
Fax: 972-986-5337
info@miracleofaloe.com
www.miracleofaloe.com

Specializing in health and beauty aids made with pure aloe vera gel

President: JC Clarke
Founder: Jess F. Clarke Jr.
Catalog Cost: Free
In Business: 34 years

4444 Mountain Rose Herbs

Mountain Rose Herbs
P.O. Box 50220
Eugene, OR 97405   541-741-7307
800-879-3337
Fax: 510-217-4012
support@mountainroseherbs.com
www.mountainroseherbs.com

Organic herbal products, all natural body care products, essential oils and bulk ingredients for those crafting and formulating their own products

President: Julie Bailey
CFO: Cameron Stearns
Marketing Manager: Irene Wolansky
Production Manager: Julie Debord
Vice President: Shawn Donnille
Executive Director of Operations: Jennifer Gerrity
Product Manager: Christine Rice
Catalog Cost: Free
Catalog Circulation: Mailed 2 time(s) per year to 12000
Printing Information: 84 pages in 4 colors on Matte Stock
Press: Web Press
Binding: Saddle Stitched
In Business: 26 years
Number of Employees: 84
Sales Volume: $ 13 Million

4445 NYR Organic

NYR Organic
490 Virginia Road
Concord , MA 1742   888-NYR-0909
inquiries.us@nyrorganic.com
us.nyrorganic.com

4446 New Life Systems

Scrip Companies
360 Veterans Parkway
Suite 115
Boilingbrook, IL 60440-4607   630-771-7400
800-852-3082
Fax: 888-674-4380
support@newlifesystems.com
www.scripcompanies.com

Spa, salon and massage supplies and equipment

President: Kray Kibler, CPA
CFO: Kray Kibler, CPA
Marketing Manager: Julie Lohmeier
VP Sales for Chiropractic & Physica: Steve Keller
Vice President IT: John Matusiewicz
In Business: 49 years
Number of Employees: 126
Sales Volume: $ 13 Million

4447 Ole Henriksen Face and Body Day Spa

Ole Henriksen
8622 W Sunset Blvd # A
Los Angeles, CA 90069-2302   310-854-7700
800-327-0331
Fax: 310-854-1869
ole@olehenriksen.com
www.olehenriksen.com

Skin care products

President: Ole Henriksen
Marketing Manager: Stacey Webb
Credit Cards: AMEX; MasterCard; Visa
In Business: 30 years
Number of Employees: 20
Sales Volume: Under $500,000

4448 Paula's Choice Skincare

Paula's Choice
705 5th Ave S, Suite 200
Seattle, WA 98104   800-831-4088
www.paulaschoice.com

Skin care products

President: Paula Begoun
Research and Content Director: Bryan Barron
Catalog Cost: Free
In Business: 19 years

4449 Pedifix Footcare Products

PediFix, Inc.
281 Fields Lane
Suite 1
Brewster, NY 10509-2651   845-277-2850
800-733-4349
Fax: 845-277-2851
sales@pedifix.com
www.pedifix.com

Complete over the counter line of unique and innovative products

President: Dennis Case
CFO: John Barrows
Marketing Manager: Caroline Bochnia
Production Manager: Frank Brenna
Fulfillment: Richard Ovadeck
Buyers: Richard Ovadek
Credit Cards: MasterCard; Visa
Catalog Cost: Free
Catalog Circulation: Mailed 3 time(s) per year to 100
Average Order Size: $80
Printing Information: 45 pages in 4 colors on Glossy Stock
Press: Web Press
Binding: Saddle Stitched
Mailing List Information: Names for rent
List Company: Stevens Knox

In Business: 121 years
Number of Employees: 30
Sales Volume: $ 5-10 Million

4450 PharmaSkinCare
Pharma Skin Care
10443 Arminta Street
Sun Valley, CA 91352   800-266-9506
www.pharmaskincare.com

Unique and balanced skin care formulations for all skin types

4451 Pretty Baby Naturals
Pretty Baby Naturals
PO Box 555
China Grove, NC 28023   704-209-0669
704-209-0669
Fax: 704-209-0226
soapshop@prettybabysoap.com
www.prettybabysoap.com

All natural, handcrafted, herbal soaps, salts, oils and bath products

President: Terrianne Taylor
Marketing Manager: James Taylor
Credit Cards: AMEX; MasterCard
Catalog Cost: Free
Catalog Circulation: Mailed 1 time(s) per year to 2000
Printing Information: 12 pages in 4 colors on Glossy Stock
Press: Sheetfed Press
Binding: Saddle Stitched
Mailing List Information: Names for rent
In Business: 58 years

4452 Pure Herbal Body Care
Kettle Care Organics
3575 US Highway 93 North
Kalispell, MT 59901   406-257-6622
888-556-2316
office@kettlecare.com
www.kettlecare.com

Pure, all-natural skin and body care products for people who have sensative skin

President: Lyne Wallingford
Owner
Production Manager: Ben
Lab Manager: Jim
Shipping & Lab Assistant: Jean
Office/Production Assistant: Deborah
Credit Cards: AMEX; MasterCard
In Business: 28 years

4453 Puritan's Pride
Puritan's Pride
PO Box 9001
Oakdale, NY 11769-9001   631-244-1290
800-645-1030
Fax: 631-471-5693
vitamins@puritan.com
www.puritan.com

Discount health products including vitamins, minerals, food supplements, herbs, amino acids, natural pet products, skin and health care.

President: Steve Cahillane
Director, Catalog Marketing: Michelle Davis
Catalog Cost: Free
Printing Information: 112 pages in 4 colors
Press: Web Press
Binding: Saddle Stitched
Mailing List Information: Names for rent
List Company: Rifkin Direct
64 Appletree Lane
Roslyn Heights, NY 11577
516-621-1076
In Business: 50 years
Sales Volume: $20MM to $50MM

4454 Reviva Labs
Reviva Labs Inc.
705 Hopkins Rd
Haddonfield, NJ 08033-3096   856-428-3885
800-257-7774
Fax: 856-429-0767
annamarie.hamp@revivalabs.com
www.revivalabs.com

Natural skin care collection - cleansers, toners, moisturizers, night creams, ampules, beauty masks, aromatherapy oils, acne and anti-aging products

President: Stephen Strassler
VP: Judy Strassler
International Marketing Manager: Farin Greber
Buyers: Fred Barth
Paul Barris
Credit Cards: MasterCard; Visa
Catalog Cost: Free
Catalog Circulation: Mailed 1 time(s) per year
Printing Information: 20 pages in 2 colors on Newsprint
Press: Web Press
Binding: Saddle Stitched
Mailing List Information: Names for rent
List Manager: Anna Marie Hamp
In Business: 42 years
Number of Employees: 40
Sales Volume: $5 Million

4455 Rodale's
Rodale's
4300 Glendale Milford Road
Cincinnati, OH 45242   888-891-8900
www.rodales.com

Publisher.

In Business: 73 years

4456 Rush Industries
Rush Industries, Inc.
263 Horton Highway
Mineola, NY 11501   516-741-0346
Fax: 516-741-0348
www.rushindustries.com

Health and beauty aids

President: Sheena Esra
General Manager: Howard Peckard
Credit Cards: AMEX; MasterCard
Printing Information: 8 pages in 4 colors
In Business: 35 years
Number of Employees: 11
Sales Volume: $1 Million

4457 SkinStore.com Catalog
SkinStore.com
11344 Coloma Rd
Suite 725
Gold River, CA 95670   916-475-1400
888-586-7546
Fax: 800-893-9868
customerservice@skinstore.com
www.skinstore.com

Skin care products

Chairman: Jim Steeb
President: Jim Steeb
CFO: John Crisan
Marketing Manager: Marc Cawdrey
COO: Steve Brown
Credit Cards: AMEX; MasterCard
Catalog Cost: Free
In Business: 18 years
Sales Volume: $10 Million

4458 Songline Emu Farm
Songline Enterprises LLC
66 French King Hwy
Gill, MA 01354   413-772-0700
866-539-2996
deedee@allaboutemu.com
www.allaboutemu.com

Emu products for skin care

President: Diane Mares
Production Manager: Stanley Johnson
Credit Cards: AMEX; MasterCard
Catalog Cost: Free
In Business: 18 years
Number of Employees: 5
Sales Volume: $67,000

4459 SunFeather Natural Soap Company
Sunfeather
1551 State Highway 72
Potsdam, NY 13676   315-265-3648
800-276-1365
Fax: 800-276-4873
customerservice@sunfeather.com
www.sunfeather.com

Handcrafted soaps and gifts, herbal homekeeping, oil and waxes, soap colorants, soap supplies and utensils, books, professional soapmaking equipment

President: Sandy Maine
CFO: Bob Dwyer
Marketing Manager: Cathy Whalen
Production Manager: Bonnie Wilson
Fulfillment: Wyona Crump
VP: Louis Maine
Buyers: Sandy Maine
Susan Hewittson
Credit Cards: AMEX; MasterCard; Visa
Catalog Cost: Free
Average Order Size: $50
List Manager: Amy Dougan
In Business: 34 years
Number of Employees: 8
Sales Volume: $ 1 Million

4460 Sunco Tanning
Sunco, Inc.
876 Holliston Mills Rd
Church Hill, TN 37642-4502   423-357-0680
800-382-8932
Fax: 423-357-9837
email@suncotanning.com
www.suncotanning.com

Distributor of tanning beds, lotions and accessories

President: Bo Carter
In Business: 24 years
Number of Employees: 6
Sales Volume: $ 3 Million

4461 Tova
QVC, Inc.
1200 Wilson Drive
Westchester, PA 19380-4262   800-852-9999
michele@tova90210.com
www.beautybytova.com

Skin care, bath, fragrance and hair products

President: Emila Tova
Founder: Tova Borgnine
Catalog Cost: $2
Printing Information: 12 pages
In Business: 30 years

4462 Universal Companies
Universal Companies, Inc.
18260 Oak Park Drive
Abingdon, VA 24210   276-466-9110
800-558-5571
Fax: 800-237-7199
info@universalcompanies.com
www.universalcompanies.com

Spa supplies, products and equipment

President: Brenda Gilbert
CFO: Minette Bruce
Marketing Manager: Karen Short
Senior VP, Sales and Marketing: Karen Short
VP Product Development: Kelly Wilson
Senior VP, Operations: Manuel Lopez
In Business: 33 years
Number of Employees: 81
Sales Volume: $12 Million

4463 Vitacost
Vitacost
840 Pilot Road
Las Vegas, NV 89119   702-263-7193
                          800-381-0759
                          www.vitacost.com

Organic and natural vitamins, supplements, nutraceuticals; health and kosher specialty foods; health and beauty; herbs and more

President: Allen Josephs
Production Manager: Danny Scott
Credit Cards: AMEX; MasterCard
Catalog Cost: Free

4464 W.S. Badger Company
W.S. Badger Company
PO Box 58
Gilsum, NH 03448   603-357-2958
                    Fax: 603-352-4818
                          www.badgerbalm.com

Hair care

Chief Operating Officer: Katie Schwerin
Head Badger & CEO: Bill Whyte

4465 Wonder Laboratories
Wonder Laboratories
115 SCT Court
PO Box 820
White House, TN 37188   800-992-1672
                    Fax: 877-992-0820
                          www.wonderlabs.com

Vitamin store and vitamin supplements

Credit Cards: AMEX; MasterCard
Catalog Cost: Free
Printing Information: 116 pages
Binding: Folded
Mailing List Information: Names for rent
In Business: 53 years

4466 Yves Rocher
Yves Rocher
PO Box 1701
Champlain, NY 12919-1701   888-909-0771
                    Fax: 800-321-4909
                    customer_services@yrnet.com
                          www.Yvesrocherusa.com

Beauty and health products for women

Credit Cards: AMEX; MasterCard; Visa
Catalog Cost: Free
Number of Employees: 75

4467 Zia Natural Skincare
Zia Natural Skincare
4600 Sleepytime Dr
Boulder, CO 80301-3284   303-530-5300
                          800-434-4246
                    Fax: 303-581-1249
                          www.zianatural.com

Natural cosmetics and skincare

President: Fran Strachan
Catalog Cost: Free
Printing Information: 15 pages
In Business: 31 years

Wigs

4468 Afro World Hair Company
Afro World Hair and Fashion Company
7276 Natural Bridge Rd
St Louis, MO 63121-5024   314-389-5194
                          800-229-4247
                    Fax: 314-389-8508
                          www.afroworld.com

All-natural human hair for weaving, braiding, bonding, and all types of hair extensions, plus Afrocentric clothing, art, skincare preparations and hair care items

President: Sheila Forrest
In Business: 45 years

4469 BeautyTrends
BeautyTrends
10725 Midwest Industrial Blvd
St Louis, MO 63132   314-785-0221
                          800-268-7210
                    Fax: 314-785-0224
                    4service@beautytrends.com
                          www.beautytrends.com

Wigs and hair add ons

President: KaySong Lee
CFO: David Rubin
Marketing Manager: A Rong Perzan
Credit Cards: MasterCard; Visa; Discover
Catalog Cost: Free
Mailing List Information: Names for rent
In Business: 25 years
Number of Employees: 150

4470 Clary's Wig
Clary's Wig
1373 55th Street
Brooklyn, NY 11219   718-854-6552
                    Fax: 718-854-1541
                    info@claryswigs.com
                          www.claryswigs.com

4471 Especially Yours
Especially Yours
PO Box 105
South Easton, MA 02375   800-952-5926
                    Fax: 508-238-1965
                    customerservice@especiallyyours.com
                          www.especiallyyours.com

African American wigs, hairpieces, hair extensions, hair weaves and stylish clothing for the fashion-concious black woman.

Catalog Cost: Free
Printing Information: in 4 colors

4472 Jean Paree Wigs
Jean Paree Weegs Inc
4041 S 700 E # 2
Suite 2
Salt Lake City, UT 84107-2187   801-328-9756
                          800-422-9447
                    Fax: 801-261-2047
                          www.jeanparee.com

Wigs and hairpieces for men, women and children; 41 different styles; over 10,000 in stock

President: Gloria Van Woerkon
Buyers: Gloria Van Woerkom
Credit Cards: MasterCard; Visa
Catalog Cost: Free
Catalog Circulation: Mailed 1 time(s) per year to 10M
Printing Information: 21 pages in 4 colors on Glossy Stock
Press: Letterpress
Binding: Saddle Stitched
Mailing List Information: Names for rent
List Manager: Julie Van Woerkom
In Business: 40 years
Number of Employees: 8
Sales Volume: $500M to $1MM

4473 Paula Young
Paula Young
P.O. Box 483
Brockton, MA 02303   800-343-9695
                    Fax: 508-238-1965
                    customerservice@paulayoung.com
                          www.paulayoung.com

Eva Gabor and Paula Young wigs and wig accessories

President: Stephen O'Hara
Marketing Manager: David Freeman
Production Manager: Robert Sanford
Credit Cards: MasterCard; Visa
Catalog Cost: Free
Catalog Circulation: Mailed 12 time(s) per year to 12000
Printing Information: 32 pages in 4 colors on

Glossy Stock
Press: Web Press
Mailing List Information: Names for rent
List Company: RMI Direct Marketing
Number of Employees: 250
Sales Volume: $20MM to $50MM

4474 Paula Young Catalog
Paula Young
PO Box 483
Brockton, MA 02303-483   800-364-9060
                    Fax: 508-238-1965
                    Customerservice@paulayoung.com
                          www.paulayoung.com

Wigs and hairpieces

President: Joe Grabowski
Credit Cards: AMEX; MasterCard
Catalog Cost: Free
Catalog Circulation: to 12000
Printing Information: 32 pages in 4 colors on Glossy Stock
Press: Web Press
Binding: Saddle Stitched
In Business: 30 years

4475 TLC
TLC
PO Box 395
Louisiana, MO 63353-395   800-850-9445
                    customerservice@tlcdirect.org
                          https://www.tlcdirect.org

Wigs and other hair loss products.

In Business: 19 years

4476 TWC Wig Company
TWC
1387 McLaughlin Run Road
Pittsburgh, PA 15241-950   412-221-4790
                          800-245-6288
                    Fax: 412-257-8181
                    custserv@twcwigs.com
                          www.thewigcompany.com

Various lines of wigs and hairpieces for women

President: Vincent De Carlucci
CFO: James McCaffrey
In Business: 55 years
Number of Employees: 36
Sales Volume: $3.8 Million

4477 The Hair Factory
The Hair Factory
116 Pleasant Street, Suite 229
Easthampton, MA 00102   413-585-9666
                          800-999-9328
                    Fax: 413-585-8902
                    customerservice@hairfactory.com
                          www.hairfactory.com

Supplies consumers with 100% natural human hair for hair pieces and extensions—also supplies how to books, videos, and hair care products

Catalog Cost: Free
In Business: 30 years

4478 The Wig Company
The Wig Company
1387 McLaughlin Run Road
Pittsburgh, PA 15241   412-257-4790
                          800-568-3499
                    Fax: 412-257-8181
                          www.thewigcompany.com

Wigs and hairpieces.

In Business: 53 years

4479 Wig America
Wig America Co.
27317 Industrial Blvd
Hayward, CA 94545
510-887-9579
800-338-7600
Fax: 510-887-9574
sales@wigamerica.com
www.wigamerica.com

Wigs and hairpieces for both men and women

CEO: Wallace Lee
Credit Cards: MasterCard; Visa
Catalog Circulation: Mailed 1 time(s) per year to 5000
Printing Information: 20 pages in 4 colors
Press: Web Press
Binding: Saddle Stitched
In Business: 40 years
Number of Employees: 10
Sales Volume: $500M to $1MM

Hobbies
General Supplies

4480 Ames & Rollinson
The Award Group
132 Nassau St # 11
11th Floor
New York, NY 10038-2427
212-473-7000
888-753-9483
Fax: 212-566-2600
www.Theawardgroup.Com

Calligraphy - products include plaques, trophies, certificates, embedments, medallions

President: Stuart Levine
COO: Henry Richman
Catalog Cost: Free
Catalog Circulation: Mailed 1 time(s) per year
Printing Information: 8 pages in 4 colors
Mailing List Information: Names for rent
Number of Employees: 30
Sales Volume: $ 2 Million

4481 Bill Cole Enterprises
Bill Cole Enterprises Inc
PO Box 60
Randolph, MA 02368-60
781-986-2653
800-225-8249
Fax: 781-986-2656
sales@bcemylar.com
www.bcemylar.com

Mylar sleeves for paper collectibles

President: Bill Cole
Credit Cards: MasterCard
Printing Information: 28 pages
In Business: 41 years

4482 Caprine Supply
Caprine Supply
P. O. Box Y
De Soto, KS 66018
913-585-1191
800-646-7736
Fax: 800-646-7796
info@caprinesupply.com
www.caprinesupply.com
In Business: 37 years

4483 Clover
H.A. Kidd & Company Limited
5 Northline Road
Toronto, ON M4B-3P2
416-364-6451
800-387-1753
Fax: 888-236-8204
info1@hakidd.com
www.hakidd.com

Knitting, crafing and embroidery supplies

Marketing Manager: Lynda Macham
VP, Chief operating Officer: Jim Thielen
Controller, Human Resources: Amir Mirza
Credit Cards: MasterCard
Catalog Cost: Free

Catalog Circulation: Mailed 1 time(s) per year
Printing Information: 48 pages in 4 colors
In Business: 93 years
Sales Volume: $20MM to $50MM

4484 Historic Rail Product Catalog
Historic Rail
640 Taft Street NE
Minneapolis, MN 55413-2815
612-206-3200
800-261-5922
Fax: 621-877-3160
info@historicrail.com
www.historicrail.com

Books, videos, art, models & kits, puzzels and games, calendars & holiday, audio, home decor, accessories and more

Catalog Cost: Free

4485 Horizon Dart Supply
Horizon Darts
2415 South 50th Street
Kansas City, KS 66106-3498
913-236-9111
800-542-3278
Fax: 913-236-8829
darts@horizondarts.com
www.horizondarts.com

Darts and dart supplies

President: Terry Maness
Catalog Cost: $10
Catalog Circulation: Mailed 1 time(s) per year to 5M
Average Order Size: $100
Printing Information: 108 pages in 4 colors on Glossy Stock
Binding: Perfect Bound
Mailing List Information: Names for rent
In Business: 30 years
Number of Employees: 7
Sales Volume: $3 Million

4486 Keepsake NeedleArts
Keepsake NeedleArts
PO Box 1618
Center Harbor, NH 3226
800-526-1148
Fax: 603-253-8346
customerservice@keepsakeneedlearts.com
www.keepsakeneedlearts.com

Quilting supplies

In Business: 28 years

4487 Kellyco Metal Detector Superstore
Kellyco Metal Detector Superstore
1085 Belle Avenue
Winter Springs, FL 32708-2921
407-699-8700
888-535-5926
Fax: 407-695-6671
info@kellycodetectors.com
www.kellycodetectors.com

Metal detectors, coin detectors, treasure locators, security systems, metal detecting equipment for land-beach-water-coins-jewelery and gold

President: Stuart Auerbach
stu@kellycodetectors.com
CFO: Maureen Walker
Marketing Manager: David Auerbach
Production Manager: Curt Dorn
Fulfillment: Jim Nielsen
Sales: Gene
Sales: Brad
Sales: James
International Marketing Manager: Margaret Schellange
Buyers: John Fetner
Catalog Cost: Free
Catalog Circulation: Mailed 2 time(s) per year to 100K
Average Order Size: $500
Printing Information: 40 pages in 4 colors on Newsprint
Press: Sheetfed Press
Binding: Folded
Mailing List Information: Names for rent

In Business: 59 years
Sales Volume: $ 20-50 Million

4488 Kolo
Kolo Retail LLC
1224 Mill Street, Bldg B
East Berlin, CT 06023-1515
800-833-5979
Fax: 860-547-0598
www.kolo-usa.com

Albums, binders, accessories, storage boxes, archival quality storage/display, scrapbooking supplies, wedding; retail or wholesale

President: Keith Horner
Catalog Cost: Free
In Business: 12 years
Number of Employees: 15
Sales Volume: $20-50 Million

4489 Squadron
Squadron
1115 Crowley Dr
Carrollton, TX 75006-1312
972-242-8663
877-414-0434
Fax: 972-242-3775
customercare@mmd-squadron.com
www.squadron.com

Hobby and craft kits and accessories

President: Jerry Campbell
Director: Macky Sue
Catalog Cost: $5
Catalog Circulation: Mailed 1 time(s) per year
Printing Information: 108 pages in 4 colors on Glossy Stock
Press: Sheetfed Press
Binding: Folded
In Business: 47 years
Sales Volume: Under $500,000

4490 The Grace Company
The Grace Company
2225 South
3200 West
Salt Lake City, UT 84119
800-264-0644
info@graceframe.com
www.graceframe.com

Frame models, quilting hoops and quilting accessories.

In Business: 28 years

4491 Warren Tool Catalog
Warren Cutlery
3584 Rt. 9
Rhinebeck, NY 12572-289
845-876-3444
Fax: 845-876-5664
warrencutlery@frontiernet.net
www.warrencutlery.com

A specialty catalog for woodcarvers' needs

President: James Zitz
Credit Cards: MasterCard
Catalog Cost: $1
Catalog Circulation: Mailed 1 time(s) per year to 5000
Printing Information: 24 pages in 4 colors on Matte Stock
Press: Sheetfed Press
Binding: Folded
In Business: 88 years
Number of Employees: 10
Sales Volume: $ 1 Million

Beekeeping

4492 Betterbee
Betterbee
8 Meader Road
Greenwich, NY 12834-2734
518-314-0575
800-632-3379
www.betterbee.com

Candle making supplies and bee keeping supplies

President: Margaret Stevens
Credit Cards: MasterCard
Catalog Cost: Free
Catalog Circulation: Mailed 1 time(s) per year to 60000
Average Order Size: $150
Printing Information: 72 pages in 1 color on Matte Stock
Press: Web Press
In Business: 34 years
Number of Employees: 32
Sales Volume: $1.4 Million

4493 Brushy Mountain Bee Farm
610 Bethany Church Road
Moravian Falls, NC 28654   336-921-3640
Fax: 336-921-2681
www.brushymountainbeefarm.com

Candlemaking and beekeeping

4494 Draper's Super Bee Apiaries
32 Avonlea Lane
Millerton, PA 16936   800-233-4273
Fax: 570-537-2727
sales@draperbee.com
www.draperbee.com

Beekeeping

4495 Gold Star Honeybees
PO Box 313
Gardiner, ME 04345   207-449-1121
Fax: 207-449-1121
info@GoldStarHoneybees.com
www.goldstarhoneybees.com

Beekeeping and honey

4496 Walter T Kelley Company
Walter T Kelley Bee Co.
807 W Main Street
Clarkson, KY 42726   270-242-6002
800-233-2899
sales@kelleybees.com
www.kelleybees.com

Beekeeping equipment and supplies
President: Sarah Manion
CEO: Shane Burgess
Credit Cards: MasterCard; Visa
Catalog Cost: Free
Catalog Circulation: Mailed 1 time(s) per year to 50000
Printing Information: 64 pages in 4 colors on Matte Stock
Press: Letterpress
Binding: Folded
In Business: 93 years
Number of Employees: 57
Sales Volume: $5.2 Million

Fireworks

4497 Big Country Fireworks
16903 482nd Avenue
Revillo, SD 57259   888-388-2264
Fax: 605-623-4561
del@bigcountryfw.com
www.bigcountryfw.com

Fireworks
President: Del Mulder

4498 Phantom Fireworks
Phantom Fireworks
555 Martin Luther King Jr Blvd
Youngstown, OH 44502-1102   330-746-1064
800-777-1699
Fax: 330-746-4410
info@fireworks.com
www.fireworks.com

Fireworks and fireworks accessories
President: Bruce Zoldan
Buyers: Alan Zoldan
Credit Cards: AMEX; MasterCard
Catalog Cost: Free

Catalog Circulation: Mailed 1 time(s) per year
Printing Information: 32 pages in 4 colors on Glossy Stock
Press: Web Press
Binding: Saddle Stitched
In Business: 32 years
Number of Employees: 60
Sales Volume: $ 8 Million

4499 Premier Pyrotechnics
25255 Hwy K
Richland, MO 65556   888-647-6863
Fax: 417-453-6339
www.premierpyro.com

Fireworks
President: Matt Sutcliffe
Magazine Manager: Chris Sanderson

4500 Pyro Direct
PO Box 52
Dingmans Ferry, PA 18328   570-296-1790
Fax: 845-230-6693
www.pyrodirect.com

Fireworks

4501 Sky King Fireworks
info@skykingfireworks.com
www.skykingfireworks.com

Fireworks

4502 TNT Fireworks
TNT Fireworks
PO Box 1318
Florence, AL 35630   253-764-6131
866-868-3953
Fax: 256-760-0154
info@tntfireworks.com
www.tntfireworks.com

Complete line of Class C consumer fireworks
President: Tommy Glasgow
Catalog Circulation: Mailed 2 time(s) per year
Printing Information: 36 pages in 4 colors on Glossy Stock
Binding: Saddle Stitched
Mailing List Information: Names for rent
In Business: 50 years
Number of Employees: 100
Sales Volume: $ 10-20 Million

4503 Xtreme Fireworks
2720 West 5 Mile Road
Caledonia, WI 53108   888-887-2264
Fax: 262-835-9015
www.xfireworks.com

Fireworks

Kites

4504 IntoTheWind Catalog
Into The Wind Inc.
1408 Pearl Street
Boulder, CO 80302   303-449-5356
800-541-0314
Fax: 303-449-7315
kites@intothewind.com
www.intothewind.com

Kites of all shapes and sizes
President: George Emmons
Sales Executive: Paul Kusler
Catalog Cost: Free
Printing Information: 64 pages
In Business: 31 years
Number of Employees: 23
Sales Volume: 1.3M

4505 Kitty Hawk Kites
PO Box 1839
Nags Head, NC 27959   252-441-4127
Fax: 252-441-2498
office@kittyhawk.com
www.kittyhawk.com

Kites
Marketing Director: Jeff Schwartzenberg

4506 Skydog Kites
220 Westchester Rd
Colchester, CT 06415   256-308-0988
Fax: 860-365-0214
www.skydogkites.com

Kites

Models

4507 American Marine Model Gallery
American Marine Model Gallery Inc
20 Pleasant Street
PO Box 6102
Gloucester, MA 01930   978-281-1166
Fax: 978-281-2166
wall@shipmodel.com
www.shipmodel.com

Fully documented, one of a kind ship models by internationally acclaimed professional marine model artists; restorations, conservation, appraisals
President: R Michael Wall
Credit Cards: AMEX; MasterCard; Visa
Printing Information: 80 pages
Mailing List Information: Names for rent
In Business: 40 years
Sales Volume: $ 500,000- 1 Million

4508 Atlas Model Railroad Company
Atlas O, LLC
378 Florence Ave
Hillside, NJ 07205   908-687-9590
Fax: 908-687-6282
smillenbach@atlasrr.com
www.atlaso.com

Model trains and supplies for the serious train buff
Sales, R&D & Product: Jerry Kimble
jkimble@atlaso.com
Dealer Orders/Cust. Serv.: Jorge Rosado
jrosado@atlasrr.com
Repair Tech./Parts: Bill Serratelli
bserratelli@atlaso.com
Credit Cards: AMEX; MasterCard; Visa; Discover
Printing Information: 76 pages
In Business: 62 years
Number of Employees: 50
Sales Volume: $3 Million

4509 Authentic Models Holland
888 Garfield Street
Eugene, OR 97402-2705   541-686-4666
800-888-1992
Fax: 541-686-5111
sales@am-usa.com
www.authenticmodels.com

Nautical replicas
President: Alfons Woudstra
CFO: Boyd Piebenga
Credit Cards: MasterCard; Visa
Catalog Cost: Free
Catalog Circulation: Mailed 2 time(s) per year
Printing Information: 88 pages in 4 colors
In Business: 23 years
Number of Employees: 65
Sales Volume: $ 10 Million

4510 Central Valley
Central Valley Model Works
1203 Pike Lane
Oceano, CA 93445-9403   805-489-8586
sales@cvmw.com
www.cvmw.com

Supplies and materials needed for making models
President: Jeff Parker
CFO: Jeff Parker

Hobbies / Models

Credit Cards: AMEX; MasterCard
Catalog Circulation: to 1000
Printing Information: 12 pages in 4 colors on Matte Stock
Press: Offset Press
Binding: Folded
In Business: 68 years
Number of Employees: 2
Sales Volume: Under $500,000

4511 Charles Ro Supply Company
Charles Ro Supply Company
662 Cross Street
Malden, MA 02148   customerservice@charlesro.com
www.charlesro.com

Lionel model trains

President: Charles Ro
Credit Cards: AMEX; MasterCard; Visa
Catalog Circulation: Mailed 2 time(s) per year to 25000
Printing Information: 32 pages in 2 colors
In Business: 44 years
Number of Employees: 14
Sales Volume: $ 1.8 Million

4512 Dee's Delights
Dee's Delight Inc
3150 State Line Road
North Bend, OH 45052-9731   513-353-3390
Fax: 513-353-3933
www.deesdelights.com

Model and doll making supplies and accessories

President: Jerry Hacker
Printing Information: 650 pages in 4 colors
Press: Offset Press
Binding: Perfect Bound
In Business: 43 years
Number of Employees: 25
Sales Volume: $ 3 Million

4513 Green Frog Railroad Catalog
Green Frog Productions Limited
189 Waterbury Way
Douglasville, GA 30134   770-977-3555
800-227-1336
Fax: 770-949-3727
greenfrogproduct@bellsouth.net
www.greenfrog.com

All railroad products for the rail fan and model railroader; Video & audio, DVDs, CDs, VHS

President: John G. Koch
Vice President: James T. Koch
Vice President: Robert J. Koch
Catalog Cost: Free
Catalog Circulation: Mailed 4 time(s) per year
Printing Information: 5 pages in 1 color
Mailing List Information: Names for rent
In Business: 34 years
Number of Employees: 6
Sales Volume: $500M to $1MM

4514 HO Reference Book
Wm. K. Walthers, Inc.
5619 W Florist Avenue
Milwaukee, WI 53218-1622   414-527-0770
800-487-2467
Fax: 800-807-2467
custserv@walthers.com

HMO model railroading information

President: J Philip Walthers
CFO: Kathy Schmidt
Credit Cards: AMEX; MasterCard
Catalog Cost: $19.98
Catalog Circulation: Mailed 1 time(s) per year
Printing Information: 64 pages in 4 colors on Glossy Stock
Press: Web Press
Binding: Perfect Bound
In Business: 80 years
Number of Employees: 124

4515 Hobbytyme
64C Oakland Ave.
East Hartford, CT 06108   860-528-9854
800-441-3302
Fax: 860-291-9814
friends@hobbytyme.com
www.hobbytyme.com

Models, wooden ships, crafting supplies

4516 International Hobby Corporation
IHC Hobby Texas
19519 Suncove Lane
Humble, TX 77346-2322   215-426-2873
800-875-1600
Fax: 215-634-2122
ihc-hobby@earthlink.net
www.ihc-hobby.com

Model trains, cars, airplanes and toys

President: Bernard Paul
Marketing Manager: Ray Harris
Production Manager: Judy Rupinski
Fulfillment: Chris Spiers
International Marketing Manager: Ray Garcia
Buyers: Ron Moyer
Credit Cards: MasterCard; Visa
Catalog Cost: $3.98
Catalog Circulation: Mailed 3 time(s) per year to 10000
Average Order Size: $44
Printing Information: 17 pages in 4 colors on Glossy Stock
Press: Web Press
Binding: Saddle Stitched
Mailing List Information: Names for rent
In Business: 25 years
Number of Employees: 40
Sales Volume: $ 3-5 Million

4517 Military Issue
640 Taft St. NE
Minneapolis, MN 55413-2815   612-206-3200
800-989-1945
Fax: 612-877-3160
info@militaryissue.com
www.militaryissue.com

Military models

4518 Mission Supply House
Collect-US.com
PO Box 950427-N
Lake Mary, FL 32795-427   407-328-7669
800-320-7669
Fax: 407-328-9222
inquiries@collect-us.com
www.collect-us.com

Model horses

President: Joseph Rosier
Catalog Cost: Free
Catalog Circulation: Mailed 1 time(s) per year
Printing Information: 12 pages in 4 colors
Mailing List Information: Names for rent
In Business: 57 years
Sales Volume: $150,000

4519 Model Empire
7116 W. Greenfield Avenue
West Allis, WI 53214   414-453-4610
Fax: 414-453-8180
info@modelempireusa.com
modelempireusa.com

Models

4520 Model Expo
Model Expo
3850 N 29th Terrace
Suite 106
Hollywood, FL 33020-1018   954-925-5551
800-222-3876
Fax: 800-742-7171
www.modelexpo-online.com

Historic model ship kits, hobby tools and ship modeling books

President: Mark Mosko
Credit Cards: AMEX; MasterCard
Catalog Cost: Free
Catalog Circulation: to 1M
Printing Information: 32 pages on Glossy Stock
Press: Web Press
Binding: Saddle Stitched
Mailing List Information: Names for rent
In Business: 36 years
Number of Employees: 20
Sales Volume: $ 3-5 Million

4521 MotorStyles
640 Taft St. NE
Minneapolis, MN 55413-2815   612-206-3200
800-961-1861
Fax: 612-877-3160
info@motorstyles.com
www.motorstyles.com

Automotive model kits, books, DVDs, posters and apparel

4522 Plastruct
Plastruct
1020 S Wallace Place
City of Industry, CA 91748   626-912-7017
800-666-7015
Fax: 626-965-2036
plastruct@plastruct.com
www.plastruct.com

Plastic scale model parts

President: John Wanderman
Production Manager: Darlene Carriaga
Credit Cards: AMEX; MasterCard
Catalog Cost: $5
Printing Information: 155 pages in 4 colors
In Business: 44 years
Number of Employees: 57
Sales Volume: $ 5-10 Million

4523 Reaper Miniatures
PO Box 2107
Lake Dallas, TX 75065-2107   940-484-6464
Fax: 940-484-0096
business@reapermini.com
www.reapermini.com

Pewter miniature figurines

Reaper Game Store Manager: Gus Landt

4524 Replicarz
166 Spruce St.
Rutland, VT 05701   802-747-7151
800-639-1744
Fax: 802-775-1981
sales@replicarz.com
www.replicarz.com

Model cars

President: Mark Fothergill
Vice President/ Director: Brian Fothergill

4525 Shell Valley Companies
Shell Valley Classic Wheels, Inc.
23119 287th Street
Platte Center, NE 68653-5055   402-246-2355
888-246-0900
Fax: 402-246-3710
svm@megavision.com
www.shellvalley.com

Replicas of popular and rare historically nostalgic cars

President: Travis Roth
Catalog Cost: Free
In Business: 45 years

4526 Smooth-On
2000 Saint John Street
Easton, PA 18042   610-252-5800
800-762-0744
Fax: 610-252-6200
www.smooth-on.com

Models

4527 Tower Hobbies
Tower Hobbies
1608 Interstate Drive
P.O. Box 9078
Champaign, IL 61826-9078   217-398-3636
                                   800-637-6050
                              Fax: 800-637-7303
                              info@towerhobbies.com
                              www.towerhobbies.com

Radio controlled models

President: Bruce Holecek
Marketing Manager: Kevin Hisel
Buyers: Bruce Holecek, Special merchandise
Al Green, Imported merchandise
Marsha Osterbur, Domestic
Credit Cards: MasterCard; Visa
Catalog Cost: $3
Catalog Circulation: Mailed 1 time(s) per year
Printing Information: 244 pages in 4 colors
Mailing List Information: Names for rent
In Business: 44 years
Number of Employees: 10
Sales Volume: $ 1-3 Million

4528 Warplanes
Actionjetz LLC
4626 E Janice Way
Phoenix, AZ 85032   480-991-1841
                                   800-579-1207
                              Fax: 480-991-1853

Hand crafted model war planes

President: Graeme Warring
Credit Cards: AMEX; MasterCard; Visa
Catalog Circulation: Mailed 1 time(s) per year
Printing Information: 35 pages in 4 colors
Number of Employees: 4
Sales Volume: $160,000

4529 Woodland Scenics
Woodland Scenics
PO Box 98
Linn Creek, MO 65052   573-346-5555
                              Fax: 573-346-3768
                              sales@woodlandscenics.com
                              www.woodlandscenics.com

Model landscapes

President: Dwayne Fulton
Catalog Cost: $5
Printing Information: 146 pages in 4 colors on Glossy Stock
Binding: Folded
In Business: 30 years
Sales Volume: $1 Million

Winemaking & Brewing

4530 All World Scientific
17120 Tye Street SE
Suite D
Monroe, WA 98272   360-453-2090
                                   800-289-6753
                              Fax: 360-453-2091

Wine testing supplies

4531 Beer, Beer & More Beer
MoreFlavor
995 Detroit Ave
Suite G
Concord, CA 94518-2526   925-671-4958
                                   800-600-0033
                              Fax: 925-671-4978
                              info@moreflavor.com
                              www.morewinemaking.com

All supplies needed for wine making, beer making, coffee roasting

President: Chris Graham
CFO: Chris Graham
Fulfillment: Ryan Barto
CEO/Founder: Olin Schultz
COO: Dan Lipscomb

CMO/CO/Founder: Darren Schleth
Credit Cards: AMEX; MasterCard; Visa
In Business: 20 years
Sales Volume: $ 4 Million

4532 EC Kraus Wine & Beermaking Supplies
EC Kraus
733 S. Northern Blvd.
PO Box 7850
Independence, MO 64054   816-254-7448
                                   800-353-1906
                              Fax: 816-254-7051
                              customerservice@eckraus.com
                              www.eckraus.com

Complete line of home wine and beer making supplies and equipment

President: Ed Kraus
Credit Cards: AMEX; MasterCard
Catalog Cost: Free
Catalog Circulation: to 13000
Printing Information: 28 pages in 1 color on Matte Stock
Press: Web Press
Binding: Saddle Stitched
Mailing List Information: Names for rent
In Business: 46 years
Number of Employees: 7
Sales Volume: $630,000

4533 Fall Bright
Fall Bright Winemakers Shop
10110 Hyatt Hill Rd
Dundee, NY 14837-9600   607-292-3995
                              winemaking@fallbright.com
                              www.fallbright.com

Winemaking kits and supplies

President: Tom Mitchell
Co-owner: Marcy Mitchell
Credit Cards: MasterCard; Visa
Catalog Cost: Free
Printing Information: 17 pages
In Business: 34 years
Sales Volume: Under $500,000

4534 Grapestompers
Grapestompers
102 Thistle Meadow
Laurel Springs, NC 28644   336-359-2322
                                   800-233-1505
                              Fax: 413-803-9850
                              www.grapestompers.com

Wine kits and wine making equipment

President: Tom Burgiss
Production Manager: Jimmy Benge
Winemaker: Don Mabe
Credit Cards: MasterCard; Visa
Catalog Cost: Free
In Business: 16 years
Sales Volume: Under $500,000

4535 International Wine Accessories
International Wine Accessories
1445 N. McDowell Blvd
Petaluma, CA 94954   707-794-8000
                                   800-527-4072
                              customerservice@iwawine.com
                              www.iwawine.com

Refrigerated wine storage and racking systems, corkscrews, wine books, videos, software, Riedel glassware

President: Robert Orenstein
Marketing Manager: Larry Lynch
Credit Cards: AMEX; MasterCard; Visa
Catalog Circulation: Mailed 14 time(s) per year
Average Order Size: $185
Printing Information: 36 pages in 4 colors on Glossy Stock
Press: Web Press
Binding: Saddle Stitched
Mailing List Information: Names for rent
Will Trade Names: Yes
Sales Volume: $170,000

4536 Midwest Homebrewing and Winemaking
Midwest Supplies Homebrewing and Winemak
5825 Excelsior Blvd
Minneapolis, MN 55416   952-562-5300
                                   888-449-2739
                              Fax: 952-925-9867
                              service@midwestsupplies.com
                              www.midwestsupplies.com

Homebrewing and winemaking supplies

Owner: David Turbenson
Catalog Cost: Free
Printing Information: 88 pages
In Business: 15 years
Number of Employees: 7
Sales Volume: $340,000

4537 MoreBeer!
MoreBeer!
701 Willow Pass Rd.
Suite 1
Pittsburg, CA 94565   800-600-0033
                              Fax: 925-671-4978
                              info@moreflavor.com
                              www.morebeer.com

Homebrewing equipment.

Founder & CEO: Olin Schultz
Catalog Cost: Free
Printing Information: 80 pages in 4 colors
In Business: 21 years

4538 Northern Brewer
2221 Highway 36 West
Roseville, MN 55113   651-291-8849
                                   800-681-2739
                              brewmaster@northernbrewer.com
                              www.northernbrewer.com

Home beer brewing equipment

4539 Retail Winemaking
Gino Pinto Inc
373 S White Horse Pike
Hammonton, NJ 08037   609-561-8199
                              Fax: 609-561-3429
                              makewine@comcast.net
                              www.ginopinto.com

Winemaking equipment

President: Karoll Pinto
Manager: Michael Pinto
makewine@comcast.net
Winery & Commercial Sales: John Falcone
johnfalcone@ginopinto.com
Catalog Cost: Free
In Business: 44 years
Sales Volume: $ 1 Million

4540 The Home Brewery
The Home Brewery
1967 W Boat Street
Ozark, MO 65721   417-581-0963
                                   800-321-2739
                              Fax: 417-485-4107
                              www.homebrewery.com

Winemaking supplies

President: Sam Wammack
Catalog Cost: Free
Printing Information: 24 pages in 1 color
In Business: 32 years
Number of Employees: 9
Sales Volume: $3MM to $5MM

4541 William's Brewing Company Catalog
William's Brewing Company
2088 Burroughs Avenue
San Leandro, CA 94577   510-895-2739
                                   800-759-6025
                              Fax: 510-895-2745
                              service@williamsbrewing.com
                              www.williamsbrewing.com

Home brewing, wine making and coffee roasting products

President: William Moore
Catalog Cost: Free
In Business: 36 years
Number of Employees: 5
Sales Volume: $310,000

4542 WindRiver Brewing Company
WindRiver Brewing Company
861 10th Avenue
Barron, WI 54812   715-357-3125
                                 800-266-4677
                                 windrvr@bitstream.net
                                 www.windriverbrew.com

Beer and winemaking supplies

Production Manager: Ken Bushinski
Co-Founder: Will Holoway
Co-Founder: Scott Law
In Business: 22 years
Sales Volume: $200,000

4543 Wine Appreciation Guild Store
Wine Appreciation Guild Store
450 Taraval Street
San Francisco, CA 94116   650-866-3020
                                 800-231-9463
                          Fax: 650-866-3029
                                 info@wineappreciation.com
                                 www.wineappreciation.com

Complete catalog of crockscrews, openers, glasware, wine racks, cellars, gifts, speciality items and wine books

President: James Mackey
Marketing Manager: Alex Shaw
VP of Marketing: Elliott Mackey
International Marketing Manager: Maurice Sullivan, VP
Buyers: Maurice Sullivan
Catalog Cost: Free
Catalog Circulation: Mailed 2 time(s) per year
Printing Information: 48 pages in 4 colors on Matte Stock
Press: Web Press
Binding: Saddle Stitched
Mailing List Information: Names for rent
In Business: 44 years
Number of Employees: 47
Sales Volume: $ 6 Million

Holidays & Celebrations
Birthdays

4544 Broadway Basketeers
520 James Street
Suite 1A
Lakewood, NJ 8701   888-599-4438
                          Fax: 866-886-9212
                                 info@bbbaskets.com
                                 www.broadwaybasketeers.com

Gift baskets

Credit Cards: AMEX; MasterCard

4545 Chelsea Market Baskets
75 Ninth Avenue
New York, NY 10011   212-727-1111
                                 888-727-7887
                          Fax: 212-727-1778
                                 www.chelseamarketbasket.com

Pantry, gifts etc.

Owner: David Porat
Printing Information: 16 pages
In Business: 22 years

4546 Clifford's
86 Liberty Street
P.O. Box 692399
Quincy, MA 2169   888-441-8884
                                 www.cliffords.com

Flowers

In Business: 60+ years

4547 Graphics 3
Graphics 3 Inc
1400 W Indiantown Road
P.O. Box 937
Jupiter, FL 33468-7998   561-746-6746
                          Fax: 561-746-6922
                                 pop-ups@graphics3inc.com
                                 www.graphics3inc.com

Three dimensional cards and calendars for promotions

Credit Cards: AMEX; MasterCard
Catalog Cost: Free
Catalog Circulation: Mailed 1 time(s) per year
Printing Information: in 4 colors
Binding: Saddle Stitched
In Business: 39 years
Number of Employees: 20
Sales Volume: $1,000,000 - $5,000,000

4548 John & Kira's 2014-2015 Catalog
163 W. Wyoming Avenue
Philadelphia, PA 19140   215-324-9222
                                 800-747-4808
                                 support@johnandkiras.com
                                 www.johnandkiras.com

Chocolates

Printing Information: 23 pages

4549 Oriental Trading Birthdays
Oriental Trading Company
P.O. Box 2308
Omaha, NE 68103-2308   800-348-6483
                                 www.orientaltrading.com

Birthday party supplies

CEO: Sam Taylor
Catalog Cost: Free
Printing Information: in 4 colors
In Business: 84 years
Number of Employees: 2000

4550 Peanut Shop of Williamsburg, The
8012 Hankins Industrial Park Road
Toano, VA 23168   800-637-3268
                          Fax: 757-566-2992
                                 info@thepeanutshop.com
                                 www.thepeanutshop.com

In Business: 40+ years

4551 Shamrock Paper
Shamrock Corporation
422 N Chimney Rock Road
Greensboro, NC 27410-9448   800-334-8982
                          Fax: 800-325-1651
                                 orders@shamrock1.com
                                 www.shamrockwraps.com

Custom printed gift wraps

Chairman: David Worth
President: Rob Hadgraft
Catalog Cost: Free
Catalog Circulation: Mailed 1 time(s) per year
Printing Information: 132 pages in 4 colors on Glossy Stock
Press: Web Press
Binding: Saddle Stitched
In Business: 60 years
Number of Employees: 5
Sales Volume: 50MM-100MM

Christmas

4552 Bronner's Christmas Favorites
Bronner's Christmas Wonderland
25 Christmas Lane
PO Box 176
Frankenmuth, MI 48734-0176   989-652-9931
                          Fax: 989-652-3466
                                 customerservice@bronner.com
                                 www.bronners.com

Indoor and outdoor Christmas ornaments and decorations.

Catalog Cost: Free
Printing Information: 64 pages in 4 colors
In Business: 71 years

4553 Cheryl's
Cheryl's
646 McCorkle Blvd.
Westerville, OH 43082-8708   800-443-8124
                                 www.cheryls.com

Gourmet cookie gifts.

President: Chris McCann
Printing Information: 44 pages in 4 colors
In Business: 35 years

4554 Christmas
Bass Pro Shops
2500 E Kearney
Springfield, MO 65898   417-873-5000
                                 800-227-7776
                          Fax: 417-873-5060
                                 www.basspro.com

Toys, casual wear and gifts.

President & CEO: James Hagale
Catalog Cost: Free
Catalog Circulation: Mailed 1 time(s) per year
Printing Information: 220 pages in 4 colors
In Business: 45 years
Number of Employees: 2200
Sales Volume: $4.45 Billion

4555 Graphics 3
Graphics 3 Inc
1400 W Indiantown Road
P.O. Box 937
Jupiter, FL 33468-7998   561-746-6746
                          Fax: 561-746-6922
                                 pop-ups@graphics3inc.com
                                 www.graphics3inc.com

Three dimensional cards and calendars for promotions

Credit Cards: AMEX; MasterCard
Catalog Cost: Free
Catalog Circulation: Mailed 1 time(s) per year
Printing Information: in 4 colors
Binding: Saddle Stitched
In Business: 39 years
Number of Employees: 20
Sales Volume: $1,000,000 - $5,000,000

4556 L.L.Bean Christmas
L.L.Bean Inc.
15 Casco St.
Freeport, ME 04033   207-552-2000
                                 www.llbean.com

Christmas decorations and men's and women's casual apparel.

Chairman: Shawn Gorman
President: Stephen Smith
Catalog Cost: Free
Printing Information: 204 pages in 4 colors
In Business: 105 years
Number of Employees: 5000
Sales Volume: $1.6 Billion

4557 Lenox Holiday Decor & Gifts
Lenox
P.O. Box 735
Bristol, PA 19007-0806   800-223-4311
                                 www.lenox.com

Kitchen collectibles, figurines and gifts, dishes and crystal.

CEO: Katrina Helmkamp
Catalog Cost: Free
Printing Information: in 4 colors
In Business: 127 years

4558 Miles Kimball Christmas Cards
Miles Kimball
250 City Center
Oshkosh, WI 54906   855-202-7394
                                 www.mileskimball.com

Christmas cards

Catalog Cost: Free
In Business: 81 years
Sales Volume: $10 Million

4559   Monastery Icons
P.O. Box 1429
West Chester, OH 45071-1429   800-729-4952
                                Fax: 800-969-1251
                          www.monasteryicons.com

Sacred arts

Printing Information: 56 pages
In Business: 27+ years

4560   Neil Holiday Catalog
Neil Enterprises
450 E Bunker Ct
Vernon Hills, IL 60061   847-549-7627
                              800-621-5584
                        Fax: 847-549-0349
info@neilenterprises.com
www.neilenterprises.com

**Promotional product/photo novelty manu-
facturer and supplier/distributor of instant
photographic equipment serving the photographic, printing/screenprint, craft, education and ad specialty industries**

President: Jerry Fine
Catalog Cost: Free
Catalog Circulation: Mailed 1 time(s) per year
Printing Information: 12 pages in 4 colors on
Glossy Stock
Press: Web Press
Binding: Perfect Bound
In Business: 56 years
Number of Employees: 25
Sales Volume: $50-100 Million

4561   Oriental Trading Beading & More!
Oriental Trading Company
P.O. Box 2308
Omaha, NE 68103-2308   800-348-6483
                        www.orientaltrading.com

Christmas beading

CEO: Sam Taylor
Catalog Cost: Free
Printing Information: in 4 colors
In Business: 84 years
Number of Employees: 2000

4562   Oriental Trading Crafts!
Oriental Trading Company
P.O. Box 2308
Omaha, NE 68103-2308   800-348-6483
                        www.orientaltrading.com

Holiday crafts

CEO: Sam Taylor
Catalog Cost: Free
Printing Information: in 4 colors
In Business: 84 years
Number of Employees: 2000

4563   Oriental Trading Education
Oriental Trading Company
P.O. Box 2308
Omaha, NE 68103-2308   800-348-6483
                        www.orientaltrading.com

Teaching supplies

CEO: Sam Taylor
Catalog Cost: Free
Printing Information: in 4 colors
In Business: 84 years
Number of Employees: 2000

4564   Oriental Trading Fun & Faith
Oriental Trading Company
P.O. Box 2308
Omaha, NE 68103-2308   800-348-6483
                        www.orientaltrading.com

Holiday accessories

CEO: Sam Taylor
Catalog Cost: Free

Printing Information: in 4 colors
In Business: 84 years
Number of Employees: 2000

4565   Oriental Trading Holiday
Oriental Trading Company
P.O. Box 2308
Omaha, NE 68103-2308   800-348-6483
                        www.orientaltrading.com

Gifts and novelties

CEO: Sam Taylor
Catalog Cost: Free
Printing Information: in 4 colors
In Business: 84 years
Number of Employees: 2000

4566   Oriental Trading Party!
Oriental Trading Company
P.O. Box 2308
Omaha, NE 68103-2308   800-348-6483
                        www.orientaltrading.com

Holiday party supplies

CEO: Sam Taylor
Catalog Cost: Free
Printing Information: in 4 colors
In Business: 84 years
Number of Employees: 2000

4567   Personal Creations Gift Catalog
Personal Creations
4840 Eastgate Mall
San Diego, CA 92121   866-834-7695
                            888-527-1404
wecare@customercare.personalcreations.com
www.personalcreations.com

**Personalize gifts for holidays, weddings, an-
niversaries, birthdays, babies and kids**

Customer Service Manager: Geri Fosnaugh
Catalog Cost: Free
Printing Information: 72 pages in 4 colors
In Business: 7 years
Sales Volume: $3MM to $5MM

4568   RH Holiday
Restoration Hardware
15 Koch Rd.
Corte Madera, CA 94925   800-762-1005
                        www.restorationhardware.com

Apparel, decorations, toys and accessories.

CEO: Gary Friedman
Printing Information: 380 pages in 4 colors
In Business: 37 years
Number of Employees: 2900
Sales Volume: $1.5 Billion

4569   Shamrock Paper
Shamrock Corporation
422 N Chimney Rock Road
Greensboro, NC 27410-9448   800-334-8982
                            Fax: 800-325-1651
orders@shamrock1.com
www.shamrockwraps.com

Custom printed gift wraps

Chairman: David Worth
President: Rob Hadgraft
Catalog Cost: Free
Catalog Circulation: Mailed 1 time(s) per year
Printing Information: 132 pages in 4 colors on
Glossy Stock
Press: Web Press
Binding: Saddle Stitched
In Business: 60 years
Number of Employees: 5
Sales Volume: 50MM-100MM

4570   The Christmas Book
Neiman Marcus
1618 Main St.
Dallas, TX 75201   214-741-6911
                        www.neimanmarcus.com

Women's apparel, shoes and handbags; jewelry and accessories; men's apparel; electronics; beauty and fragrance; home and
entertaining; and various gifts

President: Karen Katz
Printing Information: 300 pages in 4 colors
Mailing List Information: Names for rent
Sales Volume: Over $1 Billion

Easter

4571   Cane River Pecan Company
1415 Easy Street
New Iberia, LA 70560   800-293-8710
                        Fax: 337-365-4137
info@caneriverpecan.com
www.caneriverpecan.com

Pecan specialties

Chief Nut Officer: Jady Regard
Chief Operating Officer : Sonja Fredieu
Chief Administration Officer: Vicki Bazer
In Business: 46 years

4572   Lake Champlain Chocolates
750 Pine Street
Burlington, VT 5401   800-465-5909
                        Fax: 802-864-1806
info@lakechamplainchocolates.com
www.lakechamplainchocolates.com

Chocolates

In Business: 32 years

4573   Lee Sims Chocolates
743 Bergen Avenue
Jersey City, NJ 7306   201-433-1308
                        Fax: 201-433-0288
leesims743@aol.com
www.leesimschocolates.com

Chocolates

4574   Sarris Candies Easter
511 Adams Avenue
Canonsburg, PA 15317   724-745-4042
                            800-255-7771
                        Fax: 724-745-5642
www.sarriscandies.com

Candies

Founder: Frank Sarris
Printing Information: 19 pages

4575   Vermont Nut Free Chocolates
10 Island Circle
Grand Isle, VT 5458   802-372-4654
                            888-468-8373
                        Fax: 802-372-4654
customerservice@vermontnutfree.com
www.vermontnutfree.com

Chocolates

Halloween

4576   Gardners Candies
30 W. 10th St
Tyrone, PA 16686   814-684-0857
                        www.gardnerscandies.com

Candies

Printing Information: 19 pages
In Business: 118 years

4577   Light Up Your Holidays
P.O. Box 965
Oswego, IL 60543   800-722-2501
sales@templedisplay.com
www.templedisplay.com

Holiday decoration equipments

Printing Information: 64 pages
In Business: 30+ years

4578 Olive & Cocoa
3030 Directors Row
Salt Lake City, UT 84104
800-538-5404
Fax: 801-433-5008
customerservice@oliveandcocoa.com
www.oliveandcocoa.com
In Business: 6 years

4579 RSH Catalog
PO Box 117
Cleves, OH 45002
888-264-2592
www.rshcatalog.com

4580 Russell Stover Candies
4900 Oak Street
Kansas City, MO 64112-2702
800-477-8683
800-777-4004
customerservice@russellstover.com
www.russellstover.com

Candies

In Business: 37+ years

4581 See's Candy
20600 South Alameda Street
Carson, CA 90810
310-604-6200
800-347-7337
Fax: 800-930-7337
SeesCandiesCustomerCare@sees.com
www.sees.com

Candies

Printing Information: 28 pages
In Business: 90+ years

Weddings

4582 Action Lighting Holiday Catalog
Action Lighting
310 Ice Pond Road
Bozeman, MT 59715
406-586-5105
800-248-0076
Fax: 406-585-3078
action@actionlighting.com
www.actionlighting.com
Marketing Manager: Allan Kottwitz
allan@actionlighting.com
Sales & Tech Support: Don Smith
don@actionlighting.com
General Manager: Robert Stone
bob@actionlighting.com
Credit Cards: AMEX; MasterCard
Printing Information: 60 pages
In Business: 28 years

4583 Belk Wedding Catalog
Belk
2801 W Tyvola Road
Charlotte NC
800-669-6550
care@belk.com
www.belk.com

Home furnishings, accessories, and appliances

President: Lisa Harper
CFO: Scott Hurd
Marketing Manager: Barb Pellegrino
Chief Operating Officer: Don Hendricks
Chief Stores Officer: Randy Whitaker
Product Sourcing & Technical Design: Tanya Cauren
Catalog Cost: Free
Catalog Circulation: Mailed 1 time(s) per year
Printing Information: 31 pages in 4 colors
In Business: 129 years

4584 Boston Coffee Cake
351 Willow Street South
North Andover, MA 1845
800-434-0500
customerservice@bostoncoffeecake.com
www.bostoncoffeecake.com

Cakes

Founder: Mark Forman
In Business: 23 years

4585 Dante Zeller Tuxedo & Menswear
277 West St George Ave
Linden, NJ 7036
908-486-2829
Fax: 908-486-1642
www.dantezeller.com

Tuxedos, Menswear

4586 Dunkin's Diamonds
11500 S. Cleveland Ave.
Fort Myers, FL 33907
239-277-1011
877-343-4883
customerservice@dunkins.net
www.dunkinsdiamonds.com

Diamond jewelery

General Manager: Sherelyn Mora

4587 Graphics 3
Graphics 3 Inc
1400 W Indiantown Road
P.O. Box 937
Jupiter, FL 33468-7998
561-746-6746
Fax: 561-746-6922
pop-ups@graphics3inc.com
www.graphics3inc.com

Three dimensional cards and calendars for promotions

Credit Cards: AMEX; MasterCard
Catalog Cost: Free
Catalog Circulation: Mailed 1 time(s) per year
Printing Information: in 4 colors
Binding: Saddle Stitched
In Business: 39 years
Number of Employees: 20
Sales Volume: $1,000,000 - $5,000,000

4588 Joshua's Jewelry
412 W. 6th St., #1215
Los Angeles, CA 90014
213-489-4788
888-489-JOSH
www.joshuasjewelry.com

Jewellery

Credit Cards: AMEX; MasterCard
In Business: 26 years

4589 KD Bridal Collection
17887 Redmond Way
Suite 110
Redmond, WA 98052
425-898-0704
Fax: 425-285-9075
info@kdbridalcollection.com
www.kdbridalcollection.com

Jewellery- necklaces, earrings, rings, anklets, bracelets

4590 Kolick's Jewelers
29560 Center Ridge Road
Emerald Square
Westlake, OH 44145
440-871-5111
info@kolickjewelers.com
www.kolickjewelers.com

Jewellery

In Business: 66 years

4591 Shamrock Paper
Shamrock Corporation
422 N Chimney Rock Road
Greensboro, NC 27410-9448
800-334-8982
Fax: 800-325-1651
orders@shamrock1.com
www.shamrockwraps.com

Custom printed gift wraps

Chairman: David Worth
President: Rob Hadgraft
Catalog Cost: Free
Catalog Circulation: Mailed 1 time(s) per year
Printing Information: 132 pages in 4 colors on Glossy Stock
Press: Web Press
Binding: Saddle Stitched
In Business: 60 years

Number of Employees: 5
Sales Volume: 50MM-100MM

4592 Bare Root Fruit Trees
Peaceful Valley Farm Supply, Inc.
125 Clydesdale Court
P.O. Box 2209
Grass Valley, CA 95945
530-272-4769
888-784-1722
helpdesk@groworganic.com
www.groworganic.com

Vegetable/herb/flower seed packs or in bulk, propagating, water and irrigation, greenhouse, composting supplies, natural weed control, garden equipment and more

President: Eric Boudier
Vice President: Patricia Boudier
General Manager: Lee Dickerson
Catalog Cost: Free
Catalog Circulation: Mailed 1 time(s) per year
Printing Information: 68 pages in 4 colors
In Business: 41 years
Number of Employees: 60
Sales Volume: $7.2 Million

Home Building & Repair
General Supplies

4593 A.M. Leonard Master Guide
A.M. Leonard
241 Fox Drive
P.O. Box 816
Piqua, OH 45356
800-543-8955
Fax: 800-433-0633
info@amleo.com
www.amleo.com

Hand tools, power equipment, greenhouses, work apparel and fertilizers

President: Gregory Stephens
CFO: Shirley Reiber
Production Manager: Beth Marshall
Marketing Operations Manager: Melissa Shea
Credit Cards: AMEX; MasterCard
Catalog Cost: Free
Printing Information: 380 pages in 4 colors
In Business: 132 years
Number of Employees: 100
Sales Volume: $28.42 Million

4594 ABC Supply Co., Inc.
ABC Supply Co., Inc.
1 ABC Pkwy.
Beloit, WI 53511
608-362-7777
www.abcsupply.com

Roofing, siding, windows, gutters, tools and accessories.

President: Ken Rozolis
Catalog Cost: Free
Catalog Circulation: Mailed 12 time(s) per year
Printing Information: 2 pages in 4 colors
In Business: 34 years
Sales Volume: $6 Billion

4595 ALP Lighting
A.L.P. Lighting Components, Inc.
6333 Gross Point Rd
Niles, IL 60714-3915
773-774-9550
877-257-5841
Fax: 773-594-3874
kurtpuffpaff@billbrownsales.com
www.alplighting.com

Lighting and lighting supplies

Chairman: William Brown
President: Jeff Benton
CFO: Jim Grady
CEO: Steve Brown
VP/Business Manager: Tom Barnes
Chief Operating Officer: David Brown
In Business: 43 years
Number of Employees: 1000
Sales Volume: $100,000

4596 Accurate Metal Weather Strip Company

Accurate Metal Weatherstrip Co.
725 S Fulton Avenue
Mount Vernon, NY 10550-5013   914-668-6042
                                800-536-6043
                           Fax: 914-668-6062
info@accurateweatherstrip.com
www.accurateweatherstrip.com

Metal weather strips, interlocking weather stripping and tools for doors and windows

President: Fred O Kammerer
CFO: Ronald Kammerer
Catalog Circulation: Mailed 1 time(s) per year
Printing Information: 30 pages
In Business: 119 years
Number of Employees: 7
Sales Volume: $17.5 Million

4597 Addison Products Company

Addison
7050 Overland Rd
Orlando, FL 32810-3404   407-292-4400
                      Fax: 407-299-6178
info@addison-hvac.com
www.addison-hvac.com

Heat pumps 1-30 h.p., air conditioning 1-40 h.p.

President: Don Peck
Marketing Manager: Joseph Allegra
Production Manager: James Benjamin
Number of Employees: 200
Sales Volume: $25,000,000 - $50,000,000

4598 Amazing Gates

Amazing Gates
8617 Paseo Alamede NE
Albuquerque, NM 87113   877-313-8901
                      Fax: 505-771-8999
ask@amazinggates.com
www.amazinggates.com

Driveway gates, garden gates, custom gates, sliding gates, security gates, gate openers, access controls, accessories, fencing

President: Ken Helfer
Executive Officer: Bruce Brantley
Credit Cards: AMEX; MasterCard; Visa
In Business: 28 years
Number of Employees: 6
Sales Volume: $820,000

4599 American Homeowners Foundation

American Homeowners Foundation
6776 Little Falls Rd
Arlington, VA 22213-1213   703-536-7776
                         800-489-7776
                    Fax: 703-536-7079
AHGA@AmericanHomeowners.org
www.americanhomeowners.org

Books, model contracts and other products and services for home buyers, sellers, investors, remodelers and builders

President: Beth Hahn
Production Manager: Jeff Griffith
Credit Cards: AMEX; MasterCard; Visa
Average Order Size: $2
Printing Information: in 4 colors on Glossy Stock
Binding: Folded
Mailing List Information: Names for rent
In Business: 20 years
Number of Employees: 3
Sales Volume: Under $500M

4600 Aqua Supercenter

Aqua Supercenter
1990 Main St
Suite 750
Sarasota, FL 34236   941-487-2775
                   888-404-2782
              Fax: 941-487-2774
help@aquasupercenter.com
www.aquasupercenter.com

Discount swimming pools and supplies, patio furniture, charcoal grills and pond supplies

President: Chris Smith
Vice President: Nick Figueroa
Vice President, Internet Operations: Tina Jowers
Vice President, Customer Service: Fernando Frometa

4601 Architectural Components

Architectual Components, Inc
26 North Leverett Rd
Montague, MA 01351-9538   413-367-9441
                        Fax: 413-367-9461
ceb@architecturalcomponentsinc.com
www.Architecturalcomponentsinc.Com

Architectural entryways

President: Chris James
cj@architecturalcomponentsinc.com
Office Manager: Kathy Warner
kw@architecturalcomponentsinc.com
Project Manager / Estimating: Scott Milewski
sm@architecturalcomponentsinc.com
Designer: CarlWorden
cww@architecturalcomponentsinc.com
Catalog Circulation: to 100
Printing Information: 20 pages in 1 color on Glossy Stock
Binding: Perfect Bound
In Business: 20 years
Number of Employees: 10
Sales Volume: $3,000,000

4602 Arsco Manufacturing Company

Arsco Manufacturing Company
5313 Robert Avenue
Cincinnati, OH 45248   513-385-0555
                     800-543-7040
                Fax: 513-741-6292
arsco@arscomfg.com
www.Arscomfg.Com

Radiator enclosures, metal covers for steam and hot water heating systems, baseboard convector covers, pipe covers and fan coil enclosures, custom cabinetry and shelving

President: Gregory Hemmert
Marketing Manager: Edward D Hemmert
Buyers: Pam Hopkins
Credit Cards: MasterCard; Visa; Discover
Catalog Cost: Free
Catalog Circulation: to 10000
Printing Information: 6 pages in 4 colors on Glossy Stock
Press: Sheetfed Press
Binding: Folded
Mailing List Information: Names for rent
In Business: 81 years
Number of Employees: 11

4603 Artisan Design

Artisan Design
2208 South Elder Circle
Broken Arrow, OK 74012-1015   918-251-9795
                            800-747-8263
artdes3192@aol.com
www.artisandesign.com

Floor, tabletop and lap stands, accessories, lighting and magnification for decorative needlepoint enthusiasts

President: Sheldon Padawer
Production Manager: Laura Padawer
In Business: 20 years
Sales Volume: $500M to $1MM

4604 Astrup Company

Trivantage
18401 Sheldon Road
Suite A
Middleburg Heights, OH 44130-5392   216-696-2800
                                800-786-7601
                           Fax: 216-696-0914
www.trivantage.com

Fabric, hardware - industrial supplies

Chairman: John Kirk
President: J W Kirk
In Business: 123 years
Number of Employees: 160
Sales Volume: $10,000,000 - $25,000,000

4605 Atlas Greenhouse Systems

Atlas Manufacturing, Inc.
PO Box 558
Alapaha, GA 31622-558   229-532-2905
                      800-346-9902
                 Fax: 229-532-4600
www.atlasgreenhouse.com

Commercial, educational and hobby greenhouses, as well as carports and agricultural buildings

President: Mark Davis
Office Manager: Billy Stewart
Sales Manager: Bill Mathis
Shipping Coordinator: Tommie Ann Stone
Credit Cards: MasterCard; Visa
Catalog Cost: Free
In Business: 29 years

4606 Atomizing Systems

Atomizing Systems Inc.
1 Hollywood Ave # 1
Ho Ho Kus, NJ 07423-1433   201-447-1222
                         888-265-3364
                    Fax: 201-447-6932
info@coldfog.com
www.Coldfog.Com

High pressure fog systems for water and chemicals for HVAC, cooling, effects, dust and odor suppression

President: Michael Elkas
Production Manager: Tom Pagliaroni
International Marketing Manager: Michael V. Elkas
Buyers: Michael Farrelly
Catalog Circulation: Mailed 1 time(s) per year
Mailing List Information: Names for rent
In Business: 22 years
Number of Employees: 16
Sales Volume: $1,500,000

4607 BJB Enterprises

BJB Enterprises, Inc.
14791 Franklin Ave
Tustin, CA 92780-7215   714-734-8450
                      Fax: 714-734-8929
info@bjbenterprises.com
www.Bjbenterprises.Com

Supplies liquid resin systems

President: Brian Stransky
Marketing Manager: Jill Spilker
Production Manager: Fred Vandorp
Catalog Circulation: to 500
Printing Information: 40 pages in 7 colors on Glossy Stock
In Business: 44 years
Sales Volume: $5,000,000

4608 BMI Supply

BMI Supply
571 Queensbury Ave
Queensbury, NY 12804-7613   518-793-6706
                          800-836-0524
                     Fax: 518-793-6181
bminy@bmisupply.com
www.bmisupply.com

Home accessories such as hardware, fabrics, lighting and electrical supplies

President: Cindy Barber
cindy@bmisupply.com
Marketing Manager: Steve Roudebush
steve@bmisupply.com
Senior Sales Manager: Matt Williams
matt.williams@bmisupply.com
Project Manager: Greg Faust
greg.faust@bmisupply.com
Project Manager: Kris Nutting
kris.nutting@bmisupply.com
Buyers: Carl Spaulding
Average Order Size: $150
Printing Information: 2 pages on l
Press: f
Mailing List Information: Names for rent
In Business: 0 years
Number of Employees: 28
Sales Volume: $3MM to $5MM

4609 Berea Hardwoods
The Berea Hardwoods Company Inc
18745 Sheldon Rd
Middleburgh Heights, OH 44130-2426   216-898-8956
877-736-5487
Fax: 216-898-8962
customerservice@bereahardwoods.com
www.Bereahardwoods.Com

Quality pen kits and turning kits

President: Jim Heusinger
Catalog Cost: Free
Catalog Circulation: Mailed 1 time(s) per year
Printing Information: 54 pages in 4 colors on Glossy Stock
Press: Sheetfed Press
Binding: Perfect Bound
Mailing List Information: Names for rent
In Business: 34 years
Sales Volume: $1MM to $3MM

4610 Blue Ox Millworks
Blue Ox Millworks & Historic Park
One X Street
Eureka, CA 95501-847   707-444-3437
800-248-4259
Fax: 707-444-0918
info@blueoxmill.com
www.Blueoxmill.Com

Durable building materials

President: Viviana Hollenbeck
In Business: 42 years
Number of Employees: 2
Sales Volume: Under $500M

4611 Bostitch
Stanley Fastening Systems,L.P.
701 E Jopra RD.
Towson, MD 21286-700   401-884-2500
800-556-6696
Fax: 800-842-9360
www.bostitch.com

Hardware and supplies

Chairman: Nolan Archibald
President: John Lundgren
CFO: Donald Allan, Jr.
EVP and COO: James M. Loree
SVP and CIO/SFS:
Credit Cards: MasterCard
Catalog Circulation: Mailed 2 time(s) per year
Printing Information: 16 pages
Binding: Saddle Stitched
In Business: 118 years

4612 Brusso Hardware
Brusso Hardware
67-69 Greylock Ave
Belleville, NJ 7109   212-337-8510
Fax: 212-337-9840
info@brusso.com
www.brusso.com

B&M has built a reputation for supplying the aerospace, industrial, and fine hardware markets with high quality standards, timely order fulfillment, and professional customer service.

4613 Ciro C Coppa
Coppa Woodworking Inc
1231 Paraiso Street
San Pedro, CA 90731-1334   310-548-4142
Fax: 310-548-6740
info@coppawoodworking.com
www.coppawoodworking.com

Wood screen doors, window screen, hardware, screen embroidery, adirondack chairs

President: Ciro Coppa
Catalog Cost: Free
In Business: 35 years

4614 Conklin's Authentic Antique Barnwood
Conklin's Auth Barnwood & Hand Hewn Beam
18 Conklin Road
Susquehanna, PA 18847-7261   570-465-3832
Fax: 570-465-3835
info@conklinsbarnwood.com
www.Uniquecountry.Com

Barnwood, hand hewn beams, flooring, rustic, reclaimed lumber

President: Sandra Conklin
Credit Cards: MasterCard; Visa
Catalog Cost: $5
Catalog Circulation: to 3000
Printing Information: in 4 colors on Glossy Stock
Binding: Folded
Mailing List Information: Names for rent
In Business: 39 years
Number of Employees: 4
Sales Volume: $500M to $1MM

4615 Creative Openings
Creative Openings
929 N State St
Bellingham, WA 98225-5071   360-671-6420
212-563-6852
Fax: 360-671-0207
bikedog53@yahoo.com
www.Creativeopenings.Com

Victorian Style screen doors, hardwood doors, cabinetry and stairway

President: Tom Anderson
In Business: 36 years
Number of Employees: 10-J
Sales Volume: Under $500M

4616 Crown Heritage
Crown Heritage
2 Grandview Street
P.O. Box 130
North Wilesboro, NC 28659-130   828-728-8402
800-745-5931
Fax: 828-728-0022
crownheritageinfo@ecmd.com
www.Crownheritage.Com

Antique crowns and moldings

President: Susan Bates
Sales Volume: $5MM to $10MM

4617 Custom Hardware by Kayne & Son
Custom Harware by Kayne & Son Inc
100 Daniel Ridge Road
Candler, NC 28715   828-667-8868
Fax: 828-665-8303
kaynehdwe@charter.net
www.customforgedhardware.com

Custom hardware for doors, windows, gates, builders and architects

President: Shirley Kayne
CFO: Shirley Kayne
Marketing Manager: Shirley Kayne
Production Manager: David Kayne
Credit Cards: AMEX; MasterCard
Catalog Cost: $8
Mailing List Information: Names for rent
In Business: 35 years
Number of Employees: 3

4618 Fine Architectural Metalsmiths
Fine Architectural Metalsmiths
44 Jayne Street
Florida, NY 10921   845-651-7550
888-862-9577
Fax: 845-651-7857
info@iceforge.com
www.iceforge.com

Architectural metalwork and home accessories

President: Eduard Mack
Marketing Manager: Rhoda Mack
Production Manager: Rhoda Mack
Catalog Cost: $5
Catalog Circulation: Mailed 1 time(s) per year to 5M
Printing Information: 10 pages in 1 color on Matte Stock
Press: Letterpress
Mailing List Information: Names for rent
In Business: 33 years
Number of Employees: 8
Sales Volume: $500,000 - $1,000,000

4619 Flanders
Flanders/CSC Corporation
531 Flanders Filter Rd
Washington, NC 27889-7805   252-946-8081
800-637-2803
Fax: 252-644-1215
customerservice@flanderscorp.com
www.flanders-csc.com

High efficiency air filters and filtration systems

President: Tom Morse
CFO: Steve Clark
Marketing Manager: Knox Oakley
Production Manager: Elwood Jefferson
Mailing List Information: Names for rent
In Business: 48 years
Number of Employees: 307
Sales Volume: $10MM to $20MM

4620 Fraser-Johnston Heating/Air Conditioning
Unitary Products
5005 York Drive
Norman, OK 73069   405-364-4040
877-874-7378
cg-upgconsumerrelations@jci.com
www.fraserjohnston.com

Residential and commercial furnaces,controls and services,heat pumps and air conditioning, refrigeration and security systems for buildings

President: R Barnett
Marketing Manager: RN Morrison

4621 Friedrich Air Conditioning
Friedrich Air Conditioning
10001 Reunion Place,Ste 500
San Antonio, TX 78216   210-546-0500
800-541-6645
Fax: 210-357-4432
www.friedrich.com

Air conditioning, dehumidifiers, heat pumps

President: Georgr Vanhoomisen
Marketing Manager: J Deming
Fulfillment: Jennifer Graham
Catalog Cost: Free
Printing Information: 4 pages in 4 colors on Glossy Stock
Press: Sheetfed Press
Binding: Folded
Mailing List Information: Names for rent
In Business: 131 years
Number of Employees: 600
Sales Volume: $20MM to $50MM

4622 General Shale Brick
General Shale Brick, Inc.
3015 Briston Hwy
Johnson City, TN 37601 276-783-8161
800-414-4661
Fax: 276-782-3238
www.generalshale.com

Over 250 styles and types of brick, building stones, concrete products and hardscapes

President: Richard Green
Production Manager: Kim Daugherty
VP, Sales: Randy Smith
Printing Information: in 2 colors
In Business: 86 years
Number of Employees: 2000

4623 Granville Manufacturing
Granville Manufacturing Company
Route 100
Granville, VT 05747 802-767-4747
800-828-1005
Fax: 802-767-3107
woodsiding@woodsiding.com
www.woodsiding.com

Clapboards, wooden bowls and wooden kitchenware

President: Robert Fuller
International Marketing Manager: Cindy Fuller
Credit Cards: MasterCard; Visa
Catalog Cost: Free
Printing Information: 9 pages in 9 colors
Mailing List Information: Names for rent
List Manager: Robert Fuller
In Business: 157 years
Number of Employees: 35
Sales Volume: $1,000,000 - $5,000,000

4624 Home Improvements
Improvements
5568 West Chester Road
West Chester, OH 45069-2914 800-634-9484
Fax: 800-757-9997
custserv@improvementscatalog.com
www.improvementscatalog.com

items for home upkeep and improvement

Credit Cards: AMEX; MasterCard
Catalog Circulation: Mailed 4 time(s) per year
Printing Information: 56 pages in 4 colors
Binding: Saddle Stitched
In Business: 18 years

4625 Leisure Living
Pool Supplies.com
574 Main Street
Tonawanda, NY 14150 800-356-3025
Fax: 800-460-6830
info@leisureliving.com
www.poolsupplies.com

Above ground pools, in ground pools, alarms, diving boards and pool supplies

President: Paul Gerspach
Founder: Richard Gerspach
Credit Cards: AMEX; MasterCard
In Business: 57 years

4626 Lumber Liquidators
Lumber Liquidators, Inc.
3000 John Deere Rd
Customer Care Dept.
Toano, VA 23168 757-259-4280
800-366-4204
Fax: 757-524-9461
www.Lumberliquidators.Com

Assortment of hardwood flooring

Chairman: Tom Sullivan
chairman@lumberliquidators.com
President: Jeffrey W Griffiths
Catalog Cost: Free
In Business: 21 years
Number of Employees: 788

4627 National Manufacturing Co
National Manufacturing Co
P.O.Box 577
Sterling, IL 61081 800-346-9445
Fax: 800-346-9448
www.natman.com

Home and builders' hardware

Chairman: Keith Benson
President: Matthew L Minnick
CFO: Charles R Phillips
Marketing Manager: Doug Sandberg, Director Marketing
Production Manager: John Benson, VP Production
Catalog Cost: Free
Catalog Circulation: Mailed 1 time(s) per year
Mailing List Information: Names for rent
In Business: 115 years
Number of Employees: 1000
Sales Volume: $50,000,000 - $100,000,00

4628 Outdoor Fun Store
Outdoor Fun Store
P.O. Box 6089
Plymouth, MI 48170-2003 734-728-2200
877-386-1700
Fax: 734-728-3430
www.Outdoorfunstore.Com

Installs, sells and services swing sets, wooden play systems, playground equipment, gazebos, sheds, and most other items related to outdoor fun

President: Dan Wright
In Business: 14 years
Sales Volume: $1MM to $3MM

4629 Phyllis Kennedy
Kennedy Hardware LLC
10655 Andrade Dr
Zionsville, IN 46077-9230 317-873-1316
Fax: 317-873-8662
philken@kennedyhardware.com
www.kennedyhardware.com

President: Phyllis Kennedy
In Business: 26 years
Sales Volume: $500M to $1MM

4630 ProTech Systems
M&G DuraVent, Inc
10 Jupiter Ln
Albany, NY 12205-1912 518-649-9700
800-835-4429
Fax: 519-463-5271
info@duravent.com
www.Protechinfo.Com

Ventinox Chimney lining systems and TherMix prepackaged masonry insulation material

President: Martin J Wawrla
Buyers: Michael Zoglia
Credit Cards: AMEX; MasterCard
In Business: 85 years
Number of Employees: 30
Sales Volume: $5MM to $10MM

4631 Professional Equipment
Grainger
600 N. Lynndale Dr.
Appleton, WI 54914-3021 631-348-3780
800-472-4643
Fax: 888-776-3187
info@professionalequipment.com
www.grainger.com

Tools and testing equipment for the electrical, inspection, HVAC and engineering and building professionals

President: Patrick Norton
Credit Cards: AMEX; MasterCard
Catalog Circulation: Mailed 12 time(s) per year to 1m
Printing Information: 90 pages
Press: Web Press

Binding: Perfect Bound
In Business: 27 years

4632 Putnam Rolling Ladder Company
Putnam Rolling Ladder Co Inc
32 Howard Street
New York, NY 10013 212-226-5147
Fax: 212-941-1836
putnam1905@aol.com
www.putnamrollingladder.com

Step, straight and extension ladders; rolling ladder

Credit Cards: AMEX; MasterCard
Catalog Cost: Free
Printing Information: 5 pages on Glossy Stock
Binding: Folded
Mailing List Information: Names for rent
In Business: 105 years
Number of Employees: 44

4633 RBC Industries
RBC Industries,Inc
80 Cypress St
Warwick, RI 02888-2119 401-941-3000
888-722-3769
Fax: 401-941-0150
support@rbcepoxy.com
www.Rbcepoxy.Com

Epoxy

Credit Cards: MasterCard
Catalog Cost: Free
In Business: 39 years
Sales Volume: $20MM to $50MM

4634 Rainhandler
Rainhandler
2710 North Ave
Bridgeport, CT 06604-2352 203-382-2992
800-942-3004
Fax: 800-606-2028
rainhandle@aol.com
www.rainhandler.com

Rainhandler replaces conventional gutters to protect your home from the harmful effects of rain and snow - 3/4 inch wide aluminum louvers similar to opened Venetian blinds

President: Donna Buckenmaier
Credit Cards: AMEX; MasterCard
In Business: 25 years
Sales Volume: $1MM to $3MM

4635 Rare Earth Hardwood
Rare Earth Hardwood
6778 E Traverse Hwy
Traverse City, MI 49684-8364 231-946-0043
800-968-0074
Fax: 231-946-6221
Sales@rehwood.net
www.Rare-Earth-Hardwoods.Com

Hardwood flooring and decks, interior and exterior grade plywood

President: Rick Paid
Marketing Manager: Don Chamberlin
Production Manager: Austin Garno
Credit Cards: MasterCard
Catalog Circulation: to 1000
Printing Information: 8 pages in 3 colors
Press: Sheetfed Press
Binding: Saddle Stitched
Mailing List Information: Names for rent
In Business: 33 years
Number of Employees: 40
Sales Volume: $1,000,000 - $5,000,000

4636 Rosenzweig Lumber Corporation
Rosenzweig Lumber & Plywood Corp.
801 E 135th St # 1
Bronx, NY 10454-3583 718-585-8050
800-228-7674
Fax: 718-292-8611
www.Rosenzweiglumber.Com

Lumber

President: George Goldstein
Executive: John Jensen
Credit Cards: MasterCard
In Business: 213 years
Sales Volume: $10MM to $20MM

4637 ShadeTree Canopies

Shade Tree
6317 Busch Blvd
Columbus, OH 43229-1802
614-844-5990
800-894-3801
Fax: 614-844-5991
inquiries@shadetreecanopies.com
www.Shadetreecanopies.Com

Canopies and awning shade systems for decks and patios

President: Marvin Williams
Printing Information: in 3 colors
Sales Volume: $5MM to $10MM

4638 Shuttercraft

Shuttercraft, Inc.
15 Orchard Park
Madison, CT 06443
203-245-2608
Fax: 203-245-5969
all@shuttercraft.com
www.shuttercraft.com

Interior and exterior house shutters and hardware; authentic styles in cedar, mahogany, cypress for exterior, catalog mailed daily

President: Colleen Murdock
Credit Cards: AMEX; MasterCard
Catalog Cost: Free
Average Order Size: $2000
Printing Information: 20 pages in 4 colors on Glossy Stock
Press: Sheetfed Press
Binding: Saddle Stitched
Mailing List Information: Names for rent
In Business: 22 years
Number of Employees: 25
Sales Volume: $499,000

4639 Somerset Door & Column Company

Somerset Door & Column Company
PO Box 755
174 Sagamore Street Somerset
Somerset, PA 15501-328
814-444-9427
800-242-7916
Fax: 814-443-1658
www.doorandcolumn.com

Wood columns, doors and windows

General Manager: Bob McVicker
bob@doorandcolumn.com
Office Administrator: Tmara Shaffer
tmara@doorandcolumn.com
CAD Operator: Derrick Walker
derrick@doorandcolumn.com
Credit Cards: MasterCard; Visa
Catalog Cost: Free
Catalog Circulation: Mailed 1 time(s) per year to 65000
Printing Information: 8 pages in 1 color
In Business: 107 years

4640 Strongwell

Strongwell Corporation
400 Commonwealth Ave.
PO Box 580
Bristol, VA 24203-0580
276-645-8000
Fax: 276-645-8132
webmaster@strongwell.com
www.strongwell.com

Architectural and industrial metal decking systems, studs and nuts

Chairman: John D. Tickle
President: G. David Oakley, Jr.
CFO: John E. Delaney
Production Manager: Rusty Short
VP,Business Development and Marketi: Glenn Barefoot
VP, Sales and Engineering: David Gibbs
Difector of Sales: Mike Carr
In Business: 90 years

4641 Technical Manufacturing Corporation

Techical Manufacturing Corporation
15 Centennial Drive
Peabody, MA 01960-7993
978-532-6330
800-542-9725
Fax: 978-531-8682
sales@techmfg.com
www.Techmfg.Com

Solutions to problems caused by ambient building floor vibration

President: Ulf B Heide

4642 Teksupply Catalog

TekSupply
1440 Field Of Dreams Way
Dyersville, IA 52040
860-528-5626
800-835-7877
Fax: 800-457-8887
contactus@teksupply.com
www.teksupply.com

Building, maintainance and storage supplies

President: Barry Goldsher
Catalog Cost: Free
Catalog Circulation: Mailed 12 time(s) per year
Printing Information: in 4 colors on Matte Stock
Mailing List Information: Names for rent
In Business: 36 years

4643 Touchstone Woodworks

Touchstone Woodworks
PO Box 112
Ravenna, OH 44266-112
330-297-1313
Fax: 330-297-1313
tinawalters@touchstonewoodworks.com
www.touchstonewoodworks.com

Custom mahogany screen-storm doors

President: Tina Walters
Credit Cards: AMEX; MasterCard
Catalog Cost: $3
Printing Information: 16 pages in 2 colors on Matte Stock
Binding: Saddle Stitched
In Business: 25 years
Number of Employees: 2

4644 Trellis Structures

Trellis Structures, Inc.
25 North Main St. Rear
PO Box 408
E. Templeton, MA 01438-408
978-630-8787
888-285-4624
Fax: 978-630-8725
sales@trellisstructures.com
www.trellisstructures.com

Arbors, trellises, pergolas and garden furniture in western red cedar

President: David Valcovic
CFO: David Valcovic
Marketing Manager: Patricia Cormell
Production Manager: David Valcovic
Founder: David Valcovic
Founder: Patricia Cornell
Average Order Size: $600
Printing Information: 42 pages in 4 colors on Glossy Stock
Press: Letterpress
Binding: Folded
Mailing List Information: Names for rent
In Business: 20 years
Number of Employees: 12
Sales Volume: $1MM to $3MM

4645 Tri-Boro Construction Supplies

Tri-Boro Construction Supplies
465 Locust Street
Dallastown, PA 17313-8
717-246-3095
800-632-9018
Fax: 717-246-3506
www.tri-borosupplies.com

Building supplies

CFO: Linda Rexroth
Founder: Glenn
Founder: Linda
Management Team: JR
Catalog Cost: Free
In Business: 39 years
Number of Employees: 75
Sales Volume: $10,000,000 - $25,000,000

4646 Victoriana East

Victoriana East
3011 Centre St
Merchantville, NJ 08109-2526
856-910-1887
www.Victorianaeast.Com

Victorian storm doors

President: Rick Tamburo, Jr.
Credit Cards: MasterCard
Catalog Cost: Free
Sales Volume: Under $500M

4647 Wallis Stained Glass, Doors, Cabinets, Art, Glass

Jack Wallis Stained Glass & Doors
2985 Butterworth Rd
Murray, KY 42071-8217
270-489-2613
Fax: 270-489-2187
wallis@wk.net
www.jackwallisdoors.com

Cabinet art glass, stained glass, stained glass house doors

President: Jack Wallis
Marketing Manager: Jeremy Speight
Credit Cards: AMEX; MasterCard
Catalog Cost: Free
Catalog Circulation: to 400
Average Order Size: $5000
Printing Information: 12 pages in 4 colors on Glossy Stock
Mailing List Information: Names for rent
In Business: 43 years
Number of Employees: 6
Sales Volume: $400,000

4648 Water Warehouse

Doheny's Water Warehouse
6950 51st Street
Kenosha, WI 53144-1740
262-605-1060
800-574-7665
Fax: 262-605-1065
customercare@doheny.com
www.doheny.com

Swimming pool supplies and equipment

Credit Cards: AMEX; MasterCard
Catalog Cost: $2
Printing Information: 52 pages

4649 Waterwise

Waterwise Inc
2460 North Euclid Avenue
Upland, CA 91784-1199
909-982-2425
800-205-2425
Fax: 909-949-7217
kristen@vnwg.com
www.vnwg.com

Water and air purification systems for home and office

President: Jack Barber
CFO: Bob Barber
Marketing Manager: Greg Barber
Buyers: Mike Lane
Credit Cards: AMEX; MasterCard
Catalog Cost: Free
Catalog Circulation: Mailed 6 time(s) per year to 15000

Average Order Size: $200
Printing Information: 36 pages in 4 colors on Glossy Stock
Press: Web Press
Binding: Saddle Stitched
Mailing List Information: Names for rent
List Manager: Greg Barber
In Business: 93 years
Number of Employees: 32
Sales Volume: $4,000,000

4650 Weather Shield Windows and Doors
Weather Shield
One Weather Shield Plaza
P.O. Box 309
Medford, WI 54451-309   715-748-2100
                               877-452-5535
                          Fax: 715-748-2441
                    www.Weathershield.Com

Offers project planning guides for remodeling or new home projects

President: Edward Schield
VP: Kevin Shield
VP: Mark Shield
Sales Manager: Bill Stannert
Catalog Cost: Free
In Business: 60 years
Number of Employees: 5000

4651 Wood Screen Doors
Coppa Woodworking Inc
1231 Paraiso Street
San Pedro, CA 90731   310-548-4142
                          Fax: 310-548-6740
             info@coppawoodworking.com
             www.coppawoodworking.com

Wood screen and storm doors

Credit Cards: MasterCard; Visa
In Business: 35 years

4652 Wood Window Workshop
Wood Window Workshop
839 Broad Street
Utica, NY 13501-1401   315-724-3619
                               800-724-3081
                          Fax: 315-733-0933
             mike@woodwindowworkshop.com
             www.woodwindowworkshop.com

Windows and restoration

President: Mike Kershaw
Number of Employees: 15
Sales Volume: $3MM to $5MM

4653 Wood Workers Store Catalog
Rockler Woodworking and Hardware
4365 Willow Drive
Medina, MN 55340   763-478-8201
                               800-279-4441
                          Fax: 800-865-1229
                        www.rockler.com

Hardware, trim and woodworking supplies

Credit Cards: AMEX; MasterCard
In Business: 61 years

4654 Wrisco Industries
Wrisco Industries,Inc
355 Hiatt Dr # B
Suite B
Palm Beach Gdns, FL 33418-7199561-626-5700
                               800-627-2646
                          Fax: 561-627-3574
                        www.wrisco.com

Pre-finished aluminum in choice of color/finishes for roofing, awnings, flashing, walls, gutters, patios, insulated roof and wall panels

President: Jim Monastra
Marketing Manager: AJ Monastra
Catalog Circulation: Mailed 4 time(s) per year to 10M
Average Order Size: $3000
Printing Information: 15 pages in 2 colors on

Glossy Stock
Press: Letterpress
Binding: Folded
In Business: 98 years
Number of Employees: 104
Sales Volume: $10MM to $20MM

4655 York Ladder
York Ladder
37-20 12th St
Long Island City, NY 11101-6098 718-784-6666
                               800-640-YORK
                          Fax: 718-482-9016
                    info@yorkscaffold.com
                    www.yorkscaffold.com

Ladders-all varieties ans sizes

President: John Ottulich
In Business: 81 years
Sales Volume: $3MM to $5MM

4656 Yukon/Eagle Furnace
Alpha American Co
10 Industrial Boulevard
PO Box 20
Palisade, MN 56469   218-845-2124
                               800-358-0060
                          Fax: 800-440-1994
                 sales@yukon-eagle.com
                 www.yukon-eagle.com

wood furnaces-wood/oil, wood/gas, wood/electric, warm air furnaces

President: David Tjosvold
CFO: Terri Olsen
Marketing Manager: Lisa Johnson
Production Manager: Ron Prince
International Marketing Manager: Keith Nelson
Buyers: Lisa Johnson
Credit Cards: AMEX; MasterCard
Catalog Cost: Free
Catalog Circulation: to 3000
Printing Information: 8 pages on Glossy Stock
In Business: 45 years
Number of Employees: 25
Sales Volume: $3MM to $5MM

Alternative Energy

4657 AltE Catalog
altE Store
330 Codman Hill Road
Boxborough, MA 01719   978-562-5858
                               877-878-4060
                          Fax: 978-263-7081
                        www.altestore.com

Solar, wind, and other alternative energy resources

President: Sascha Deri
Credit Cards: AMEX; MasterCard
Catalog Cost: $5
Printing Information: 88 pages
In Business: 16 years
Number of Employees: 12
Sales Volume: 5.8MM

4658 Appalachian Stove
Appalachian Stove
329 Emma Rd
Asheville, NC 28806-3885   828-253-0164
                          Fax: 828-254-7803
                 sales@gandwenergy.com
                 www.Appalachianstove.Com

Quality Stoves, Fireplaces & Mantels

President: James Rice
In Business: 38 years
Number of Employees: 70
Sales Volume: $5,000,000 - $10,000,000

4659 Aqua-Therm
Aqua-Therm, LLC
310 Oak St.
PO Box 262
New London, MN 56273   320-346-2264
                               800-325-2760
                          Fax: 320-354-3275
                 kbenjamin@aqua-therm.com
                    www.aqua-therm.com

Outside wood burning furnace

President: Olav Isane
Credit Cards: MasterCard; Visa
In Business: 16 years
Number of Employees: 7
Sales Volume: $500M to $1MM

4660 Backwoods Solar Electric Systems
Backwoods Solar Electric Systems
1589 Rapid Lightning Creek Rd
Sandpoint, ID 83864-4754   208-263-4290
                          Fax: 208-265-4788
                 info@backwoodssolar.com
                 www.Backwoodssolar.Com

Solar electric power systems for remote homes where power lines are not available

President: Scott Gentleman
Catalog Cost: $3
Catalog Circulation: Mailed 1 time(s) per year to 30M
Average Order Size: $2000
Printing Information: 177 pages in 1 color on Glossy Stock
Press: Sheetfed Press
Binding: Perfect Bound
Mailing List Information: Names for rent
In Business: 37 years
Number of Employees: 6
Sales Volume: $1,000,000

4661 Big Frog Mountain Corporation
Big Frog Mountain Corporation
3821 Hixson Pike
Chattanooga, TN 37415   423-265-0307
                               877-232-1580
                          Fax: 423-265-9030
                    www.bigfrogmountain.com

Design and sell solar and wind electric power systems

President: T Tripp
Credit Cards: AMEX; MasterCard
In Business: 26 years

4662 Environmental Geothermal Houses
Enertia Building Systems, Inc.
PO Box 845
Youngsville, NC 27596-845   919-556-2391
                 enertia@mindspring.com
                    www.enertia.com

Solar-kit homes designed using new inertial technology

President: Michael Sykes
Credit Cards: MasterCard; Visa
Catalog Cost: $15
Catalog Circulation: Mailed 1 time(s) per year to 5000
Printing Information: 50 pages on Matte Stock
Press: Offset Press
Mailing List Information: Names for rent
In Business: 18 years
Number of Employees: 4
Sales Volume: Under $500,000

4663 Hardy Diesels
Hardy Diesels
15749 Lyons Valley Road
Jamul, CA 91935-3503   619-669-1995
                               800-341-7027
                          Fax: 619-669-4829
                 sales@hardydiesel.com
                    www.hardydiesel.com

Small diesel generators and diesel tractors, tractor implements, farm tractors, diesel marine engines, solar panels, wind generators, inverters, water pumps

Credit Cards: MasterCard

4664 HearthStone Catalog: Wood & Pellet Products
HearthStone
317 Stafford Avenue
Morrisville, VT 05661-8695   877-877-2113
warm@hearthstonestoves.com
www.Hearthstonestoves.Com

Wood and gas-fired stoves

President: David Kuhfahl
Credit Cards: MasterCard; Visa
Catalog Cost: Free
Printing Information: in 4 colors
In Business: 37 years
Number of Employees: 45
Sales Volume: $1,000,000 - $5,000,000

4665 Heatmor
Heatmor
105 Industrial Park Court NE
PO Box 787
Warroad, MN 56763   218-386-2769
800-834-7552
Fax: 218-386-2947
woodheat@heatmor.com
www.heatmor.com

Outdoor stainless steel furnaces

President: Gerry Reed
Marketing Manager: Darrell Shaugabay
darrell@heatmor.com
VP of Operations: Keith Astrup
kastrup@heatmor.com
Accounting: Brenda Nieman
brenda@heatmor.com
Services: Mike Galusha
mgalusha@heatmor.com
In Business: 31 years
Number of Employees: 36
Sales Volume: $5MM to $10MM

4666 New England Solar Electric
New England Solar Electric, Inc.
401 Huntington Road
PO Box 435
Worthington, MA 01098-9551   413-238-5974
800-914-4131
Fax: 413-238-0203
spschulze@newenglandsolar.com
www.Newenglandsolar.Com

Solar electric kits, components, gas appliances and wind mills

President: Steve Schulze
Credit Cards: MasterCard; Visa; Discover
Catalog Cost: $3
Catalog Circulation: Mailed 2 time(s) per year to 20M+
Printing Information: 83 pages in 1 color on Newsprint
Press: Web Press
Binding: Saddle Stitched
Mailing List Information: Names for rent
In Business: 15 years
Number of Employees: 3
Sales Volume: $1MM to $3MM

4667 Solar Flare
Sierra Solar Systems
563-C Idaho Maryland Road
Grass Valley, CA 95945   530-273-6754
888-667-6527
Fax: 530-273-1760
info@sierrasolar.com
www.sierrasolar.com

Solar electric systems and components

President: Jonathan Hill
Credit Cards: AMEX; MasterCard; Visa; Discover
Catalog Cost: Free

Catalog Circulation: Mailed 2 time(s) per year to 50M
Average Order Size: $500
Printing Information: 68 pages in 4 colors on Newsprint
Press: Web Press
Binding: Saddle Stitched
Mailing List Information: Names for rent
List Manager: Jonathan Hill
In Business: 34 years
Number of Employees: 10
Sales Volume: 1MM

4668 SunDog Solar
SunDog Solar
PO Box 348
Chatham, NY 12037   518-392-4000
518-392-8191
info@sundogsolar.net
www.sundogsolar.net

Residential and commercial renewable energy systems and services.

4669 Sunelco
Sunelco, Inc.
620 Fish Hatchery Road
Suite 130
hamilton, MT 59840-9209   406-642-6422
888-786-3526
Fax: 406-642-9768
info@sunelco.com
www.sunelco.com

Renewable energy equipment

President: Tom Bishop
CFO: Nilda Bishop
Catalog Cost: Free
Catalog Circulation: to 2000
Printing Information: 112 pages in 1 color on Matte Stock
Binding: Perfect Bound
Mailing List Information: Names for rent
In Business: 30 years
Number of Employees: 5
Sales Volume: $95,000

4670 Vermont Castings
Vermont Castings
PO Box 501
Bethel, VT 05032-501   802-234-2300
Fax: 802-234-2340
www.vermontcastings.com

Stoves and fireplaces

President: Dennis Dillon
Production Manager: Jason Perry
Credit Cards: MasterCard; Visa
Catalog Circulation: Mailed 2 time(s) per year to 30000
Printing Information: 48 pages in 4 colors on Glossy Stock
Press: Web Press
Binding: Saddle Stitched
List Company: Brigar
Albany, NY
Number of Employees: 61
Sales Volume: $5MM to $10MM

4671 Yellow Jacket Solar
Ritchie Engineering Company, Inc
10950 Hampshire Avenue South
PO Box 60
Bloomington, MN 55438-60   952-943-1300
800-769-8370
Fax: 952-943-1300
custserv@yellowjacket.com
www.yellowjacket.com

Alternative energy components and systems

President: Tom Ritchie
tritchie@yellowjacket.com
EVP, International Sales: Brian Flynn
bflynn@yellowjacket.com
VP, Domestic Sales & Marketing: Michael Lanners
mlanners@yellowjacket.com

VP, Finance and Operations: Phil Hayne
phayne@yellowjacket.com
Credit Cards: MasterCard; Visa
Catalog Cost: $2
Catalog Circulation: Mailed 2 time(s) per year
Printing Information: 40 pages in 1 color
Number of Employees: 5
Sales Volume: 500M-1MM

Antique & Recycled Materials

4672 Balsam Hill
Balsam Hill
1561 Adrian Rd.
Burlingame, CA 94010   650-863-5466
888-552-2572
customerservice@balsamhill.com
www.balsamhill.com

Luxurious artificial trees.

4673 Bartley Collection
Bartley Collection
65 Engerman Ave # 2
Denton, MD 21629-2004   410-479-4480
800-787-2800
Fax: 410-479-4514
www.bartleycollection.com

Fine antique reproduction furniture kits

President: Bob Stenecker
Credit Cards: MasterCard
Catalog Circulation: to 70000
Printing Information: 70 pages
In Business: 43 years
Sales Volume: $1,000,000

4674 Berridge Manufacturing Company
Berridge Manufacturing Company
6515 Fratt Road
San Antonio, TX 78218-7199   210-650-3050
800-669-0009
Fax: 210-650-0379
info@berridge.com
www.berridge.com

Metal roofing products

President: Joel Jesse
Catalog Cost: Free
Catalog Circulation: Mailed 1 time(s) per year to 10M
Printing Information: 23 pages in 4 colors
In Business: 47 years
Number of Employees: 175
Sales Volume: $3,000,000

4675 Brass Knob
The Brass Knob Architectural Antiques
2311 18th St NW
Washington, DC 20009-1814   202-332-3370
Fax: 202-332-5594
info@thebrassknob.com
www.thebrassknob.com

Architectural antiques

President: Donetta George
Co-Founder: Donetta George
Sales Staff: Taylor Jenkins
In Business: 34 years
Number of Employees: 4
Sales Volume: $500M to $1MM

4676 Campbellsville Industries, Inc
Campbellsville Industries, Inc
P.O. Box 278-W
Campbellsville, KY 42719   270-465-8135
800-467-8135
Fax: 270-465-6839
steeple@cvilleindustries.com
www.cvilleindustries.com

Repro Victorian roof parts; cupolas, steeples, clocks, columns, cornices, louvers and balustrade railings

President: Rick Moon
Marketing Manager: David England
Production Manager: Burr Hendron

production@cvilleindustries.com
Fulfillment: Donna Grammer
Engineer: Hasan El-Amouri
hasan@cvilleindustries.com
Controller/Human Relations Director: Glenda
Britton
glenda@cvilleindustries.com
Accts Payable/Accts Receivable: Jessica
Hunt
jessica@cvilleindustries.com
Buyers: Terry Lawson, Materials
Catalog Cost: Free
Catalog Circulation: to 3000
Average Order Size: $1200
Mailing List Information: Names for rent
In Business: 60 years
Number of Employees: 125
Sales Volume: $20MM to $50MM

4677 Cape Cod Cupola Company
Cape Cod Cupola Co, Inc.
78 State Road
North Dartmouth, MA 02747-2922 508-994-2119
Fax: 508-997-2511
capecodcupola@gmail.com
www.capecodcupola.com

Cupolas, weathervanes, finials, lanterns, home accents

President: John E Bernier Jr
Production Manager: Brian R Chabot
Credit Cards: MasterCard; Visa
Catalog Cost: Free
Catalog Circulation: Mailed 52 time(s) per year
Printing Information: 20 pages in 4 colors on Matte Stock
Press: Web Press
Binding: Saddle Stitched
Mailing List Information: Names for rent
In Business: 76 years
Number of Employees: 6
Sales Volume: $530,000

4678 Charles W Jacobsen
Jacobsen Rugs
225 Wilkinson Street
Syracuse, NY 13204-1719 315-422-7832
Fax: 315-422-6909
rugpeople@jacobsenrugs.com
www.Jacobsenrugs.Com

New and antique Oriental rugs

President: Brent Goodsell
Marketing Manager: Patty O'Day, Advertising
Agent
Credit Cards: AMEX; MasterCard; Visa
Printing Information: 34 pages
In Business: 90 years
Number of Employees: 32

4679 Cirecast
CIRECAST, INC.
1790 Yosemite Avenue
San Francisco, CA 94124-2622 415-822-3030
Fax: 415-822-3004
www.Cirecast.Com

Doorknobs and antique hardware

President: Peter Morenstein
Credit Cards: MasterCard
Catalog Cost: Free
Catalog Circulation: Mailed 2 time(s) per year
Printing Information: 6 pages
In Business: 49 years
Number of Employees: 20
Sales Volume: $1MM to $3MM

4680 Mountain Lumber Company
Mountain Lumber Company
6812 Spring Hill Rd.
Ruckersville, VA 22968 434-985-3646
800-445-2671
Fax: 434-885-4105
ales@mountainlumber.com
www.mountainlumber.com

Flooring and rough lumber.

In Business: 41 years

4681 Vintage Wood Works
Vintage Woodworks
9195 Hwy 34 S
PO Box 39
Quinlan, TX 75474-39 903-356-2158
Fax: 903-356-3023
mail@vintagewoodworks.com
www.vintagewoodworks.com

Manufacturer of architectural details direct to consumers for interior and exterior in various wood and cellular PVC

President: Gregory Tatsch
Buyers: Roland Tatsch, Raw Materials
Credit Cards: AMEX; MasterCard; Visa
Catalog Cost: $3
Printing Information: 144 pages in 1 color
Press: Web Press
Mailing List Information: Names for rent
In Business: 37 years
Number of Employees: 60
Sales Volume: $1,000,000 - $5,000,000

4682 Williamsburg Blacksmiths
Williamsburg Blacksmiths
26 Williams Street
Williamsburg, MA 01096-9427 413-268-7341
Fax: 413-268-9317
williamsburgblacksmiths@gmail.com
www.williamsburgblacksmith.com

Reproduction Early American wrought-iron hardware

President: Elizabeth Tiley
Credit Cards: AMEX; MasterCard; Visa
Catalog Cost: Free
Mailing List Information: Names for rent
In Business: 48 years
Number of Employees: 5
Sales Volume: $1MM to $3MM

Furniture Plans & Kits

4683 Adams Wood Products
Adam Wood Products
PO Box 728
Morristown, TN 37815-0728 423-587-2942
Fax: 423-586-2188
adamswoodproducts.com

Furniture components from table legs, beds and hardware.

President: Larry Swinson
Catalog Cost: Free
In Business: 41 years
Number of Employees: 80

4684 Bartley Collection
Bartley Collection
65 Engerman Ave # 2
Denton, MD 21629-2004 410-479-4480
800-787-2800
Fax: 410-479-4514
www.bartleycollection.com

Fine antique reproduction furniture kits

President: Bob Stenecker
Credit Cards: MasterCard
Catalog Circulation: to 70000
Printing Information: 70 pages
In Business: 43 years
Sales Volume: $1,000,000

4685 Consumer Brochure
Wood-Mode Fine Custom Cabinetry
One Second Street
Kreamer, PA 17833 570-374-2711
877-635-7500
Fax: 570-374-2700
www.wood-mode.com

Brief guide to dealers and custom-built cabinetry

Chairman: Robert Gronlund
President: Fred Richetia
CFO: John Fairis
Catalog Cost: Free
Printing Information: 12 pages in 4 colors
Binding: Folded

4686 Emperor Clock, LLC
Emperor Clock, LLC
340 Industrial Park Drive
PO Box 960
Amherst, VA 24521-960 800-642-0011
800-642-0011
Fax: 434-946-1420
service@emperorclock.com
www.emperorclock.com

Clock and furniture kits, mechanical and quartz movements, clock plans, assembled clocks

President: Gerd Hermle
Marketing Manager: Julie George
Production Manager: Debbie Vaughn
Credit Cards: AMEX; MasterCard; Visa
Catalog Cost: Free
Printing Information: 36 pages
Mailing List Information: Names for rent
Will Trade Names: Yes
In Business: 40 years
Number of Employees: 25

4687 HomePortfolio Insider
HomePortfolio, Inc.
2625 Kotter Avenue
Evansville, IN 47715 617-965-0565
Fax: 615-965-4082
info@homeportfolio.com
www.homeportfolio.com

Closet systems, wall-units, beds and dining room furniture

President: Cinzia Henolucci
Catalog Cost: Free
Number of Employees: 15
Sales Volume: 5MM-10MM

4688 Osborne Wood Products
Osborne Wood Products, Inc.
4618 GA Hwy 123 N
Toccoa, GA 30577-8327 706-886-1065
800-849-8876
Fax: 888-777-4304
www.osbornewood.com

Wood turnings, table legs, bed posts, island legs, hardware

President: Leon Osborne
Marketing Manager: Jody Griffith
Production Manager: Janice Osborne
Credit Cards: AMEX; MasterCard; Visa
Catalog Cost: Free
Catalog Circulation: Mailed 40 time(s) per year to 40000
Average Order Size: $200
Printing Information: 60 pages in 4 colors on Glossy Stock
Binding: Saddle Stitched
Mailing List Information: Names for rent
In Business: 38 years
Number of Employees: 9
Sales Volume: $5MM to $10MM

4689 Rojek Woodworking Machinery
Rojek Woodworking Machinery
7901 Industry Drive
North Little Roc, AR 72117 800-787-6747
Fax: 501-945-0312
info@tech-mark.com
www.rojekusa.com

In Business: 25 years

4690 Woodcraft Plans Catalog
Furniture Designs
300 Warren St
Dayton, OH 45402-2806 937-224-7526
800-296-6256

Plans for making furniture

President: Matt Jones
Credit Cards: MasterCard; Visa
Catalog Cost: $2
Catalog Circulation: to 15000
Printing Information: 64 pages in 1 color on Matte Stock
Binding: Saddle Stitched
Mailing List Information: Names for rent
In Business: 25 years
Number of Employees: 4
Sales Volume: Under $500M

Home Plans & Kits

4691   ASL Associates
A.S.L. & Associates
302 N Last Chance Gulch # 410
Helena, MT 59601-5028   406-443-3389
                                    Fax: 406-443-3303
                                asl@asl-associates.com
                                www.Asl-Associates.Com

Gazebo blueprints

President: Dr. Allen S. Lefohn
Catalog Circulation: Mailed 6 time(s) per year to 10000
Printing Information: 2 pages
In Business: 34 years
Sales Volume: Under $500M

4692   Acorn Deck House
Acorn Deck House Company
852 Main Street
Acton, MA 01720-5811   978-263-6800
                                    800-727-3325
                                Fax: 978-635-9923
                                info@deckhouse.com
                                www.deckhouse.com

Custom built post and beam homes

President: Tom Trudeau
CFO: Anne Trudeau
General Manager: Paul Buraczynski
Credit Cards: MasterCard; Visa
Catalog Cost: $20
Catalog Circulation: Mailed 52 time(s) per year to 7000
Average Order Size: $20
Printing Information: 60 pages in 4 colors on Glossy Stock
Press: Web Press
Binding: Saddle Stitched
In Business: 56 years
Number of Employees: 5
Sales Volume: $300,000

4693   Deltec Homes
Deltec Homes
69 Bingham Road
Asheville, NC 28806-3824   800-642-2508
                                www.deltechomes.com

Custom panelized round houses

President: Steve Linton
Senior Project Manager: Chad Moore
Project Manager: Kerry Watkins
Director of Purchasing and Manufact: John Nicholson
Catalog Cost: Free
Printing Information: 20 pages in 4 colors
In Business: 69 years
Sales Volume: $10MM to $20MM

4694   Four Seasons Sunrooms
Four Seasons Sunrooms, Llc
5005 Veterans Memorial Hwy
Holbrook, NY 11741-4507   631-563-4000
                                    800-368-7732
                                Fax: 631-563-4010
                                info@fourseasonssunrooms.com
                                www.fourseasonssunrooms.com

Sunrooms, conservatories, patio rooms, patio and deck enclosures, skylights

President: Patrick Marron
Catalog Cost: Free

Printing Information: in 4 colors
In Business: 39 years
Number of Employees: 300

4695   Habitat Post & Beam
Habitat Post & Beam
21 Elm Street
South Deerfield, MA 01373-1005 413-665-4006
                                    800-992-0121
                                Fax: 413-665-4008
                                info@postandbeam.com
                                www.postandbeam.com

Timber frame and additions

President: Peter May
Marketing Manager: Sandy Reohmski
Production Manager: D Bagdon
Head of the Engineer: Donald Gibavic
Designer: Casey Goddard
Administration: Peter May
Credit Cards: MasterCard; Visa
Catalog Cost: $15
Catalog Circulation: Mailed 1 time(s) per year
Printing Information: 76 pages in 4 colors
Mailing List Information: Names for rent
In Business: 45 years
Number of Employees: 20
Sales Volume: $5MM to $10MM

4696   Historical Replications
Authentic Historical Designs, Llc
3908 North State Street
Jackson, MS 39206   601-981-8743
                                    800-426-5628
                                Fax: 601-981-8185
                                cecilia@historicaldesigns.com
                                www.historicaldesigns.com

Blueprints and plans for historical homes

President: Cecilia Reese Bullock
Catalog Cost: $20
Catalog Circulation: Mailed 52 time(s) per year
Average Order Size: $800
Printing Information: 48 pages in 2 colors on Matte Stock
Press: Offset Press
Mailing List Information: Names for rent
In Business: 38 years
Number of Employees: 10-J
Sales Volume: Under $500M

4697   Homes by Vanderbuilt
Homes by Vanderbuilt
3300 Jefferson Davis Hwy.
Sanford, NC 27332   919-718-2760
                                    800-537-2448
                                sales@ncmodulars.com
                                www.ncmodulars.com

Modular home plans.

President: Tom Van de Riet
tomv@ncmodulars.com
Sales Mnager: Rick Key
rickk@ncmodulars.com
Sales Assistant: Becky Davis
beckyd@ncmodulars.com
Service: Julie Childress
hbvservice@ncmodulars.com
In Business: 31 years

4698   Hoop House Greenhouse Kits
Hoop House Greenhouse Kits
PO Box 2430
Mashpee, MA 02649   800-760-5192
                                Fax: 508-539-1108
                                www.hoophouse.com

From 10'W x 8'L up to 10' W x 100' L, galvanized steel hoops, 6 mil commercial poly film

President: Ralph H Bartlett
Credit Cards: AMEX; MasterCard
Printing Information: 6 pages on Glossy Stock
Mailing List Information: Names for rent
In Business: 30 years
Number of Employees: 5
Sales Volume: $500M to $1MM

4699   Jim Barna Log & Timber Homes
Homestead Communications Corp
22459 Alberta Street
Oneida, TN 37841-4529   423-569-2180
                                    800-962-4734
                                Fax: 423-569-5903
                                info@jimbarna.com
                                www.logcabins.com

Log home floor plans, materials packages, and services

Chairman: Joe Varda
President: Tim Parsons
CFO: Joy Mulkern
Marketing Manager: Shellie Valentine
Credit Cards: MasterCard; Visa
Catalog Cost: $15
Printing Information: in 4 colors on Glossy Stock
Press: Web Press
Binding: Saddle Stitched
Mailing List Information: Names for rent
In Business: 22 years
Number of Employees: 79

4700   Meisel Hardware Specialties
Meisel Hardware Specialties
PO Box 70
Mound, MN 55364-70   952-746-2379
                                    800-441-9870
                                Fax: 952-471-8579
                                office@meiselwoodhobby.com
                                www.meiselwoodhobby.com

Over 850 woodworking plans including country, storage and outdoor furniture, kitchen items, child's furniture and toys, lamps, music boxes, holiday cutouts and more

President: Paul Meisel
CFO: Patricia Meisel
Marketing Manager: Eric Meisel
Production Manager: Greg Meisel
Credit Cards: MasterCard
Catalog Cost: $2
Catalog Circulation: Mailed 3 time(s) per year to 10000
Printing Information: 100 pages in 4 colors on Glossy Stock
Press: Web Press
Binding: Saddle Stitched
Mailing List Information: Names for rent
List Company: List Locators & Managers
In Business: 29 years
Number of Employees: 50
Sales Volume: $5MM to $10MM

4701   Natural Spaces Domes
Natural Spaces Domes
37955 Bridge Rd
North Branch, MN 55056-5398 651-674-4292
                                    800-733-7107
                                Fax: 651-674-5005
                                nsd@naturalspacesdomes.com
                                www.Naturalspacesdomes.Com

Design, manufacture and construction of geodesic domes used for homes, cabins, businesses, churches

President: Dennis Johnson
Credit Cards: AMEX; MasterCard; Visa
Catalog Cost: Free
Catalog Circulation: Mailed 1 time(s) per year
Printing Information: 50 pages in 4 colors on Matte Stock
Binding: Saddle Stitched
In Business: 17 years
Number of Employees: 7
Sales Volume: $500,000 - $1,000,000

4702   Nomadics Tipi Makers
Nomadics Tipi Makers
17671 Snow Creek Road
Bend, OR 97701-9149   541-389-3980
                                Fax: 541-389-3980
                                nomadics@tipi.com
                                www.Tipi.Com

Authentic Sioux style tipis, with hand painted designs 4x6 southwest design rugs, pillows, backrest chairs; made tipis for Dances with Wolves, the movie

President: Jeb Barton
Credit Cards: MasterCard; Visa
Catalog Cost: $5
Catalog Circulation: to 3000
Average Order Size: $1200
Printing Information: 40 pages in 4 colors on Glossy Stock
Binding: Folded
Mailing List Information: Names for rent
In Business: 45 years
Number of Employees: 2
Sales Volume: under 500,000

4703 Shelter Systems

Shelter Systems Ltd.
224 Walnut Street
Menlo Park, CA 95003-3003   831-464-2002
866-777-1066
eleanor@shelter-systems.com
www.shelter-systems.com

Portable domes and greenhouses

President: Bob Gillis
Manager: Eleanor Hamner
Production Manager: Jeffrey Devitt
Printing Information: in 3 colors
In Business: 38 years

4704 Shelter-Kit

Shelter-Kit, Inc.
1 East Main Street
P.O. Box 111
Warner, NH 03278-5003   603-456-3801
Fax: 603-456-3353
shelterkit@gmail.com
www.shelter-kit.com

Pre-cut, owner buildable cabins, barns, garages and houses

President: David Kimball
Catalog Cost: $1
Catalog Circulation: to 4000
Printing Information: on Matte Stock
Press: Letterpress
Binding: Saddle Stitched
In Business: 44 years
Number of Employees: 3
Sales Volume: $1MM to $3MM

4705 Timberlane Woodcrafters

Timberlane, Inc.
150 Domorah Drive
Montgomeryville, PA 18936-9633   800-250-2221
Fax: 215-616-0749
customerservice@timberlane.com
www.timberlaneshutters.com

Custom exterior wood shutters

President: Richard Skidmore
Marketing Manager: Rich Heggs
Production Manager: Wayne Kuser
Catalog Cost: Free
Average Order Size: $500
Printing Information: 64 pages in 1 color on Glossy Stock
Press: Web Press
Binding: Saddle Stitched
Mailing List Information: Names for rent
In Business: 22 years
Number of Employees: 30
Sales Volume: $3MM to $5MM

4706 Timberline Geodesics

Timberline Geodesics
2015 Blake Street
Berkeley, CA 94704-2603   510-849-4481
800-366-3466
info@domehome.com
www.domehome.com

Designer and manufacturer of geodesic dome kits used for housing and commercial applications

President: Robert Singer
rsinger@domehome.com
Credit Cards: MasterCard; Visa; Discover
Catalog Cost: $14
Catalog Circulation: Mailed 1 time(s) per year to 5000
Printing Information: 100 pages in 4 colors on Glossy Stock
Press: Web Press
Binding: Saddle Stitched
Mailing List Information: Names for rent
In Business: 37 years
Number of Employees: 5
Sales Volume: $1MM to $3MM

4707 US Buildings

US Buildings Direct
1182 E Newport Center Dr
Deerfield Beach, FL 33442-7702   954-281-2100
800-463-6062
Fax: 954-281-2083
usbuildingsdirect.com

Steel buildings including, commercial, recreational, residential, agricultural

President: Gary Rack
Catalog Cost: Free
In Business: 25 years
Sales Volume: $20MM to $50MM

4708 Vermont Log Buildings

Real Log Homes
61 Plains Road
Claremont, NH 03743-202   603-542-5407
800-732-5564
Fax: 802-436-2128
info@realloghomes.com
www.realloghomes.com

Log home, barn and commercial building kits

President: Jay Foster
Marketing Manager: Andy Lafreniere
Production Manager: Paul White
Regional Manager: Kirk Allaire
kallaire@realloghomes.com
Credit Cards: AMEX; MasterCard; Visa
Catalog Cost: $10
Catalog Circulation: Mailed 1 time(s) per year
Printing Information: 83 pages in 4 colors on Matte Stock
Binding: Saddle Stitched
Mailing List Information: Names for rent
In Business: 50 years
Number of Employees: 40

4709 Ward Log Homes

Ward Cedar Log Homes
P.O. Box 72
Houlton, ME 04730   207-532-6531
800-341-1566
Fax: 207-532-7806
info@wardcedarloghomes.com
www.wardcedarloghomes.com

Manufacturer and seller of pre-cut log homes

Sales: Ron Silliboy
r.silliboy@wardcedarloghomes.com
Credit Cards: MasterCard; Visa
Mailing List Information: Names for rent
In Business: 94 years
Number of Employees: 55
Sales Volume: $5MM to $10MM

4710 Where's Home For You?

International Homes of Cedar
PO Box 886
Woodinville, WA 98072-886   360-668-8511
800-767-7674
Fax: 360-668-5562
ihc@ihoc.com
www.cedarleader.com

Pre-cut engineered home building material packages

President: Rodney Robertson
CFO: Rodney Robertson

Marketing Manager: Pamela Anderson
Production Manager: Tom Warren
Credit Cards: AMEX; MasterCard; Visa
Catalog Cost: $15
Catalog Circulation: to 50000
Average Order Size: $100
Printing Information: 40 pages in 4 colors on Glossy Stock
Binding: Perfect Bound
Mailing List Information: Names for rent
In Business: 48 years
Number of Employees: 20-5

4711 Wisconsin Log & Cedar Homes

Wisconsin Log & Cedar Homes
2390 Pamperin Road
Green Bay, WI 54313-8900   920-434-3010
800-678-9107
Fax: 920-434-2140
info@wisconsinloghomes.com
www.wisconsinloghomes.com

Manufacturer of custom log and cedar home packages, plan book includes log home plans, price list and materials list

President: Dave Janczak
Marketing Manager: Laura Burke
Production Manager: Steve Klaubauf
Credit Cards: MasterCard; Visa
Catalog Cost: $14.95
Printing Information: 145 pages in 4 colors on Glossy Stock
Press: Web Press
Mailing List Information: Names for rent
In Business: 39 years
Number of Employees: 33
Sales Volume: $20MM to $50MM

4712 Woodcraft Plans Catalog

Furniture Designs
300 Warren St
Dayton, OH 45402-2806   937-224-7526
800-296-6256

Plans for making furniture

President: Matt Jones
Credit Cards: MasterCard; Visa
Catalog Cost: $2
Catalog Circulation: to 15000
Printing Information: 64 pages in 1 color on Matte Stock
Binding: Saddle Stitched
Mailing List Information: Names for rent
In Business: 25 years
Number of Employees: 4
Sales Volume: Under $500M

Interior & Decorative Supplies

4713 2015 Security & Builder's Hardware Catalog

HBC Home & Hardware Products
324 Cranbury Half Acre Rd
Cranbury, NJ 8512   800-523-1268
www.hberger.com

Security & builder's hardware, plumbing products, paint applicators and home environment products.

In Business: 43 years

4714 Adams Wood Products

Adam Wood Products
PO Box 728
Morristown, TN 37815-0728   423-587-2942
Fax: 423-586-2188
adamswoodproducts.com

Furniture components from table legs, beds and hardware.

President: Larry Swinson
Catalog Cost: Free
In Business: 41 years
Number of Employees: 80

4715 Aged Woods
Aged Woods, Inc.
4065 Deerhill Drive
Suite V101
York, PA 17406
717-840-0330
800-233-9307
Fax: 717-840-0330
info@agedwoods.com
www.agedwoods.com

Antique wood flooring
President: Jeff Horn
CFO: Donald Sprenkle, Jr.
Secretary: Denise Horn
In Business: 32 years
Number of Employees: 3
Sales Volume: $410,000

4716 Albany Woodworks
Albany Woodworks, Inc.
30380 Payne Alley Road
Tickfaw, LA 70466
225-567-1155
www.albanywoodworks.com

Wide plank hardwood flooring, antique heart pine flooring, timber floors, exposed beams, millwork and doors
CEO: Richard Woods
Catalog Cost: Free
Catalog Circulation: Mailed 1 time(s) per year
Average Order Size: $5000
Printing Information: 24 pages in 4 colors on Glossy Stock
Press: Letterpress
Binding: Saddle Stitched
Mailing List Information: Names for rent
In Business: 41 years
Number of Employees: 17
Sales Volume: $1.4 Million

4717 B Lazarus
Lazarus Manufacturing
10140 NW South River Drive
Medley, FL 33178-4416
305-885-8904
Fax: 305-885-8940
www.lazarusmanufacturing.com/

Curtains, draperies, window hardware, bedspreads and upholstery fabrics
President: Deborah Lazarus
deborah@lazarusmanufacturing.com
CFO: Andra Lazarus
alma@lazarusmanufacturing.com
Marketing Manager: Eric Lazarus
eric@lazarusmanufacturing.com
Production Manager: Michael Yunis
Fulfillment: Michael Lazarus
VP and Partner: Alma Franqui
alma@lazarusmanufacturing.com
VicePresident, Sales and Marketing: Eric Lazarus
eric@lazarusmanufacturing.com
Catalog Cost: Free
Printing Information: 26 pages
In Business: 75 years
Number of Employees: 60
Sales Volume: $5,000,000 - $10,000,000

4718 B&W Tile Company
B&W Tile Company
14600 S Western Ave
Gardena, CA 90249-3399
310-538-9579
Fax: 310-538-2190
bandwtile@yahoo.com
www.Bwtile.Com

Ceramic bisque and glazed tiles for craft and home decorative use
President: Ralph R Logan
CFO: Ralph R Logan
Production Manager: Deborah Pfahler
Buyers: Joseph Logan
Catalog Cost: $1
Catalog Circulation: to 1000
Printing Information: 13 pages in 4 colors on Glossy Stock
Press: Sheetfed Press
Binding: Perfect Bound

Mailing List Information: Names for rent
In Business: 62 years
Number of Employees: 49
Sales Volume: $10MM to $20MM

4719 Benjamin Moore & Co.
Benjamin Moore & Co.
101 Paragon Drive
Montvale, NJ 07645-8299
855-724-6802
info@benjaminmoore.com
www.benjaminmoore.com

Restoration and renovation hardware
President: Mike Searles
Catalog Cost: Free
In Business: 134 years
Sales Volume: $10MM to $20MM

4720 Blind Butler
Blind Buster
23052 Alicia Pkwy # H202
Mission Viejo, CA 92692-1661
949-768-6695
888-922-5463
Fax: 949-768-6599
www.blindbutler.com

Blind cleaner using special wax and wax system
President: Steven Dale
Credit Cards: MasterCard
Sales Volume: $500M to $1MM

4721 Brass Center
The Brass Center
248 E 58th St
New York, NY 10022-2001
212-421-0090
Fax: 212-371-7088
info@thebrasscenter.com
www.Thebrasscenter.Com

Plumbing accessories
President: Mark Glick
Printing Information: in 4 colors on Glossy Stock
In Business: 25 years
Sales Volume: $1MM to $3MM

4722 Capital Balconettes
Capital Balconettes
104 Ironwood Court
PO Box 126
Milford, PA 18337-126
570-296-7722
800-442-4766
Fax: 570-296-4766
www.balconettes.com

Ornamental iron window boxes, crestings, finials, snowguards, balconettes, mailbox surrounds, firewood and planter boxes
Customer Service Manager: Don Quick
Credit Cards: MasterCard; Visa
Catalog Cost: $2
Catalog Circulation: Mailed 4 time(s) per year
Average Order Size: $875
Printing Information: 24 pages in 2 colors on Glossy Stock
In Business: 19 years
Number of Employees: 20

4723 Carpet Hardware Systems
Bedlam Architectural Metalworks LLC.
202 12th Ave
Paterson, NJ 07501
973-523-7323
800-233-5261
Fax: 800-233-5262
bedlamusa@aol.com
www.bedlamarchitectural.com

Solid-brass carpet hardware for stairway runners
President: Dick Grabowsky
CFO: Marleen Grabowsky
Marketing Manager: Jayne Kaine
Production Manager: Paul Rainey
Buyers: Dick Grabowsky
Jayne Kaine
Credit Cards: AMEX; MasterCard; Visa

Catalog Cost: Free
Printing Information: in 4 colors on Glossy Stock
Mailing List Information: Names for rent
In Business: 31 years
Number of Employees: 15
Sales Volume: $1MM to $3MM

4724 Charles Lubin Company
Charles Lubin Company Inc
145 Saw Mill River Road
Yonkers, NY 10701-6631
914-968-5700
Fax: 914-968-5723
info@lubinflowers.com
www.Lubinflowers.Com

Silk flowers
President: Dorothy L Bordin
Printing Information: in 4 colors
Press: Web Press
Mailing List Information: Names for rent
In Business: 105 years
Sales Volume: $1MM to $3MM

4725 Chelsea Decorative Metal Company
Chelsea Decorative Metal Company
8212 Braewick Drive
Houston, TX 77074-7814
713-721-9200
Fax: 713-776-8661
info@thetinman.com
www.thetinman.com

Pressed tin for walls and ceilings
President: Glenn Eldridge
Credit Cards: AMEX; MasterCard
Catalog Cost: Free
Catalog Circulation: to 500
Average Order Size: $1500
Printing Information: 8 pages in 1 color on Glossy Stock
Binding: Folded
Mailing List Information: Names for rent
In Business: 40 years
Number of Employees: 5
Sales Volume: Under $500M

4726 Columns Catalog
Chadsworth Incorporated
277 North Front Street
Wilmington, NC 28401-3907
800-265-8667
Fax: 910-763-3191
sales@columns.com
shop.columns.com

Architectural columns
President: Jeffrey Davis
Marketing Manager: Raye Frazelle
Printing Information: 68 pages in 4 colors on M
Binding: S
Mailing List Information: Names for rent
In Business: 30 years
Number of Employees: 51
Sales Volume: $5MM-$10MM

4727 Copperbeech Millwork
Copper Beech Millwork : A Main Street Mi
47 Silvio O. Conte Drive
P.O. Box 253
Greenfield, MA 01320-718
413-584-3003
800-532-9110
Fax: 413-582-0164
sales@copperbeech.com
www.copperbeech.com

Wood moldings, decking, doors, floors, plywoods, stair parts, mantels
President: David Short
Marketing Manager: Karen Laverdiere
Credit Cards: MasterCard; Visa
Catalog Cost: $5
Catalog Circulation: Mailed 1 time(s) per year to 3000
Average Order Size: $250
Printing Information: 44 pages in 4 colors on Matte Stock
Press: Web Press
Binding: Saddle Stitched

Mailing List Information: Names for rent
In Business: 28 years
Number of Employees: 50
Sales Volume: $3MM to $5MM

4728 Custom Service Hardware
Custom Service Hardware
1170 N Wauwatosa Rd
Cedarburg, WI 53012   800-882-0009
                            www.cshardware.com
Credit Cards: AMEX; MasterCard
Printing Information: 204 pages
In Business: 38 years

4729 Decor by Dobry
Decor by Dobry
2152 Poplar Ridge Rd
Pasadena, MD 21122-3820   410-437-0297
                            800-648-8856
                       Fax: 410-437-9200
            clair.dobry@decorbydobry.com
                www.decorbydobry.com

Instuction books on custom draperies, cloud shades, no-sew drapery swags and jabots
President: Clair Dobry
Mailing List Information: Names for rent
Number of Employees: 2
Sales Volume: Under $500M

4730 Decorators Supply Corporation
Decorators Supply Corporation
3610 S Morgan Street
Rear Building
Chicago, IL 60609-1587   773-847-6300
                            888-689-7339
                       Fax: 773-847-6357
            www.decoratorssupply.com

Wood ornaments, plaster ornament and capitals
President: Steve Grage
Credit Cards: AMEX; MasterCard; Visa
Catalog Cost: $25
Printing Information: in 1 color
In Business: 127 years
Number of Employees: 40
Sales Volume: $20MM to $50MM

4731 Driwood Moulding Company
Driwood Moulding Company
623 W. Lucas St.
PO Box 1729
Florence, SC 29503-1729   843-669-2478
                            888-245-9663
                       Fax: 843-669-4874
                sales@driwood.com
                www.driwood.com

Plain and embossed hardwood mouldings, over 400 different profiles in stock & custom architecture woodwork
Credit Cards: MasterCard
Catalog Cost: $8
Printing Information: 75 pages in 4 colors on Glossy Stock
Mailing List Information: Names for rent
In Business: 50 years
Number of Employees: 35

4732 Ercole
Ercole, Inc.
142 W 26 Street
Room 803
New York, NY 10001-1160   212-675-2218
                       Fax: 212-929-6059
                ercole@ercolehome.com
                www.Ercolehome.Com

pedestals, finishes
President: Ornella Pisano
In Business: 29 years
Sales Volume: $3MM to $5MM

4733 Excalibur Collection
Excalibur Collection
309 Starr St
Brooklyn, NY 11237-2611   718-366-3444
                       Fax: 718-366-7927
            CService@EXcaliburBronzeNY.com
                www.excaliburbronze.com

Bronze interior furnishings
President: William Gold
CFO: Eleanor Brown
Marketing Manager: Joan Bennefiel
Production Manager: Roger Bukowski
Buyers: Joan Benefiel
Credit Cards: MasterCard; Visa
Catalog Cost: $50
Printing Information: 75 pages in 4 colors on Matte Stock
Press: Sheetfed Press
Mailing List Information: Names for rent
In Business: 48 years
Number of Employees: 35
Sales Volume: $500M to $1MM

4734 Exposures
Exposures
1 Memory Lane
PO Box 3690
Oshkosh, WI 54903-3690   855-202-7390
                       Fax: 800-699-6993
            csr@exposuresonline.com
                www.exposuresonline.com

Picture frames, photo albums, photo-related gifts, curio cabinets, and photograph storage systems.
Catalog Cost: Free
Printing Information: in 4 colors

4735 FAST Corporation
F.A.S.T. Corporation
P.O.Box 258
Sparta, WI 54656-258   608-269-7110
                       Fax: 608-269-7514
            info@fastkorp.com
                www.Fastkorp.Com

Fiberglass statues and amusements
President: Darren Schauf
Printing Information: 35 pages in 4 colors on Glossy Stock
Binding: Saddle Stitched
Mailing List Information: Names for rent
In Business: 37 years
Number of Employees: 16
Sales Volume: $10MM to $20MM

4736 Felber Ornamental Plastering
Felber Ornamental Plastering Corporation
1000 West Washington Street
PO Box 57
Norristown, PA 19404-57   610-275-4713
                            800-392-6896
                       Fax: 610-275-6636
                info@felber.net
                www.Felber.Net

Plaster ceiling medallions, mouldings, domes and brackets
President: James Kuryloski
CFO: Ted Ottey
Catalog Cost: $3
Catalog Circulation: to 6000
Printing Information: 60 pages in 1 color on Matte Stock
Binding: Saddle Stitched
Mailing List Information: Names for rent
In Business: 30 years
Sales Volume: $1MM to $3MM

4737 Fypon
Fypon, Ltd.
1750 Indian Wood Circle
Maumee, OH 43537   800-446-3040
                www.fypon.com

Molded millwork, builing materials, lumber and wood production

President: Tom Riscli
Marketing Manager: Kathy Ziprik
Catalog Cost: Free
Average Order Size: $2500
In Business: 48 years
Number of Employees: 550
Sales Volume: $41.1 Million

4738 Gregor's Studios
Gregor's Studios
1511 Dragon St.
Dallas, TX 75207-3906   214-744-3385
                            866-845-5732
                       Fax: 214-748-4864
            rich@gregorsstudios.com
                www.gregorsstudios.com

Hand carved mantels and architectural pieces in 18th century tradition
President: Gregor Schragin Jr
Credit Cards: MasterCard; Visa
Catalog Cost: $12
In Business: 40+ years
Number of Employees: 20-O
Sales Volume: Under $500M

4739 HA Guden Company
HA Guden Company Inc
99 Raynor Avenue
Ronkonkoma, NY 11779-6649   631-737-2900
                            800-3HI-NGES
                       Fax: 631-737-2933
                info@guden.com
                www.guden.com

Hinges, handles, gas springs, dampers, industrial hardware
Chairman: Al Guden
President: Al Guden
CFO: Carol Fitzpatrick
Marketing Manager: Doug Graham
Quality Manager: Jay Goehring
Catalog Cost: Free
Catalog Circulation: Mailed 1 time(s) per year to 15000
Average Order Size: $325
Printing Information: 52 pages in 2 colors on Glossy Stock
Press: Web Press
Binding: Saddle Stitched
Mailing List Information: Names for rent
In Business: 95 years
Number of Employees: 35
Sales Volume: $5MM to $10MM

4740 Harristone Product Guide
G.S. Harris Co., Inc. USA
2810 Pennsylvania Ave.
Ogden, UT 84401   801-621-1380
                            888-878-6631
            info@harristone.com
                harristone.com

In Business: 50 years

4741 Homecraft Veneer & Woodworker's Supplies
Homecraft Veneer & Woodworker's Supplies
PO Box 776
Youngstown, PA 15696-776   724-537-8435
                            800-796-6348
                       Fax: 724-537-0543
            woodman@homecraftveneer.com
                www.homecraftveneer.com

Veneer and veneer supplies, longwoods, burls, crotches & swirls
President: Alan J McCullough
Credit Cards: MasterCard; Visa
Catalog Cost: $1
Catalog Circulation: Mailed 2 time(s) per year
Printing Information: 8 pages in 2 colors on Glossy Stock
Press: Letterpress
Binding: Folded
Mailing List Information: Names for rent
In Business: 40 years

Number of Employees: 2
Sales Volume: Under $500M

4742 Howard Miller Clock Company
Howard Miller Clock Company
860 East Main Avenue
Zeeland, MI 49464-1300   616-772-9131
                                     Fax: 616-772-1670
                              www.howardmiller.com

Weather and marine instruments and clocks of all styles and types

President: Howard Miller
Marketing Manager: Robert S Lehocky
Phil Miller:
CEO
VP Finance: Dennis Palasek
Credit Cards: MasterCard; Visa
Catalog Cost: $5
Catalog Circulation: to 30K
Printing Information: 92 pages in 4 colors
In Business: 91 years
Number of Employees: 500
Sales Volume: $50 Million

4743 Iron Shop
The Iron Shop
400 Reed Road
PO Box 547
Broomall, PA 19008-547   610-544-7100
                                     800-523-7427
                               Fax: 610-544-7297
                              www.TheIronShop.com

Spiral staircases available in metal, oak, victorian cast aluminum, and all welded units

President: Allen Cohen
Director of Marketing: Michele Cohen
Credit Cards: AMEX; MasterCard
Catalog Cost: Free
Printing Information: in 4 colors
In Business: 82 years
Number of Employees: 75
Sales Volume: 20MM-50MM

4744 J Sussman
J Sussman Inc.
109-10 180th Street
Jamaica, NY 11433-2622   718-297-0228
                                     Fax: 718-297-3090
                           sales@jsussmaninc.com
                              www.Jsussmaninc.Com

Designers and manufacturers of commercial, residential and church windows, skylights, sunbilt sunrooms, metal and glass bending

President: David Sussman
CFO: Steven Sussman
Marketing Manager: Mel Wachsstock
Production Manager: Mario Ortiz
Bookkeeper, Office Manager: Bibi
Purchase, Research and Development: Jake
Head of Engineering: Mario
International Marketing Manager: Mel Wachsstock
Buyers: David Sussman
Catalog Cost: Free
Catalog Circulation: Mailed 1 time(s) per year to 40M
Printing Information: 12 pages in 4 colors on Glossy Stock
Press: Sheetfed Press
Binding: Saddle Stitched
Mailing List Information: Names for rent
List Manager: Mel Wachsstock
In Business: 109 years
Number of Employees: 55
Sales Volume: $10MM to $20MM

4745 JP Weaver Company
Jp Weaver Co.
941 Air Way
Glendale, CA 91201-3001   818-500-1740
                                     Fax: 818-500-1798
                              info@jpweaver.com
                                 www.Jpweaver.Com

Segments, in larger interchangeable parts, for walls, doors, ceilings and fireplaces, that form European design composites

President: Mayra Gomez
CFO: Lenna Tyler-Kast
Marketing Manager: Marya Gomez
Production Manager: Marya Gomez
Credit Cards: MasterCard; Visa
Catalog Cost: $130
Average Order Size: $1000
Printing Information: 530 pages in 1 color
Binding: Saddle Stitched
Mailing List Information: Names for rent
In Business: 100 years
Number of Employees: 20
Sales Volume: $10MM to $20MM

4746 LH Selman Ltd
LH Selman Ltd
410 S. Michigan Ave.
Suite # 207
Chicago, IL 60605-3907   312-583-1177
                                     800-538-0766
                               Fax: 312-583-0111
                              info@selman.com
                          www.theglassgallery.com

Paperweights and art glass

President: Larry Selman
In Business: 40 years

4747 Lafayette Venetian Blind
Lafayette Interior Fashions Inc.
3000 Klondike Rd.
PO Box 2838
West Lafayette, IN 47996-2838   765-464-2500
                                            800-342-5523
                                      Fax: 765-423-2402
                                    inquiry@lafvb.com
                                       www.Lafvb.Com

One source for Lafayette Interior Fashions products including, Woodland Harvest custom shutters, Marquis shutters, Wood Venetians, Heartland Woods, Klondike Woods, Wonder Wood

President: Joe Morgan
Marketing Manager: Tom Robinson
In Business: 52 years
Number of Employees: 850

4748 Landmark Creations
Landmark Creations
819A N Barlow Lane
Bishop, CA 93514   760-873-1134
                              800-588-3844
             CustomerService@Landmark-Creations.com
                   www.landmark-creations.com

Exceptional European blown glass ornaments depicting landmarks from around the world

Founder & Designer: Jo Ellen Church
Artist & Author: Michael Storrings
Catalog Cost: Free
Printing Information: in 4 colors on Glossy Stock
Binding: Saddle Stitched
Mailing List Information: Names for rent
819A North Barlow Lane
Bishop, CA 93514
760-873-1134
In Business: 12 years
Number of Employees: 11
Sales Volume: $730,000

4749 Mad River Woodworks
Mad River Woodworks
PO Box 1067
Blue Lake, CA 95525-1067   707-668-5671
                                       800-446-6580
                                  Fax: 707-668-5673
                       info@madriverwoodworks.com
                          www.madriverwoodworks.com

Victorian millwork, porch parts, gable ornaments, custom moldings, brackets, corbels

President: Tim Thornton
Marketing Manager: Kathy Marks
Owner: Tim Thornton
Credit Cards: MasterCard; Visa
Catalog Cost: $3
Catalog Circulation: Mailed 1 time(s) per year
Average Order Size: $2000
Printing Information: 32 pages in 1 color
Press: Web Press
Binding: Saddle Stitched
Mailing List Information: Names for rent
In Business: 33 years
Number of Employees: 4
Sales Volume: Under $500M

4750 Milton W Bosley Company
Bosley mouldings
151 8th Avenue N.W
Glen Burnie, MD 21061-576   410-761-7727
                                        800-638-5010
                                  Fax: 410-553-0575
                           www.bosleymouldings.com/

Architectural and picture frame moldings; wood, metal and laminate

President: Bosley Wright
Founder: Milton W. Bosley
In Business: 102 years
Number of Employees: 27
Sales Volume: $1,000,000 - $5,000,000

4751 NextMonet
Mill Pond Press
91 Armstrong Avenue
Unit A
Georgetown, ON L7G 4-5548   905-702-9116
                                        800-387-6645
                                  Fax: 905-702-0615
                              sales@millpond.com
                                 www.millpond.com

Fine art for your home and office

President: Steven Coles
stevecoles@naturesscene.com
Vice President: Brandon Cole
brandoncoles@naturesscene.com
Sales: Peter Coles
colespeter@naturesscene.com
Credit Manager: Gina Hockin
ginahockin@naturesscene.com
Credit Cards: AMEX; MasterCard; Visa
In Business: 41 years
Sales Volume: $ 3-5 Million

4752 Nostalgic Warehouse Door Hardware
Nostalgic Warehouse Door Hardware
4661 Monaco Street
Denver, CO 80216-3304   303-355-2344
                                    800-522-7336
                               Fax: 800-322-7002
                         www.nostalgicwarehouse.com

Decorative Door Hardware, Decorative Cabinet Hardware

President: Larry Broderick
CFO: Dennis Cross
Marketing Manager: Darcy Barton
Production Manager: Michael Weis
Credit Cards: MasterCard; Visa
Printing Information: 30 pages in 2 colors on Glossy Stock
Press: Web Press
Binding: Folded
Mailing List Information: Names for rent
In Business: 35 years
Number of Employees: 30

4753 Old World Mouldings
Old World Mouldings,Inc
821 Lincoln Ave
Bohemia, NY 11716-4103   631-563-8660
                                 Fax: 631-563-8815
                         mouldings@optonline.net
                          www.Oldworldmouldings.Com

Sells interior wood mouldings, both wholesale and retail

President: Alan D Havranek
Sales Volume: $3MM to $5MM

4754 Pagliacco Turning and Milling
Pagliacco Turning & Milling
PO Box 229
Woodacre, CA 94973-229   415-488-4333
Fax: 415-488-9372
pagliacco@comcast.net
www.pagliacco.com

Exterior and interior decorating materials

President: Steve Evans
Catalog Cost: $6
Average Order Size: $2000
Printing Information: 31 pages in 1 color on Matte Stock
Number of Employees: 5
Sales Volume: Under $500M

4755 Phylrich International
Phylrich International
1261 Logan Avenue
Costa Mesa, CA 92626   714-361-4830
800-749-5742
Fax: 866-800-9774
customer.service@phylrich.com
www.Phylrich.Com

Interior design products

President: Alfred Dubin
CFO: Carlos Griffouliere
Marketing Manager: Checole Acuina-Dubin
Production Manager: John Pellez
Catalog Cost: $25
Printing Information: in 4 colors
In Business: 54 years
Number of Employees: 60

4756 Plaster Gallery
Plaster Gallery
2756 Coney Island Ave
Brooklyn, NY 11235-5016   718-769-1007
Fax: 718-490-6321
plastergalleryinc@yahoo.com

colums, pedestals, plaster figurines

President: Harvey Dinim
Sales Volume: Under $500M

4757 Reggio Register Company
Reggio Register Co LLC
31 Jytek Rd.
Leominster, MA 01453-5933   978-870-1020
800-880-3090
Fax: 978-870-1030
reggio@reggioregister.com
www.Reggioregister.Com

Cast iron, brass, aluminum and wood decorative grilles and registers

President: Mike Reggio
Marketing Manager: Bill Licata
Production Manager: Cheryl Costley
Founder: Giacomo Abbate
Credit Cards: AMEX; MasterCard
Catalog Cost: $1
Catalog Circulation: Mailed 5 time(s) per year to 35000
Average Order Size: $200
Printing Information: 48 pages in 4 colors on Glossy Stock
Press: Web Press
Binding: Saddle Stitched
Mailing List Information: Names for rent
List Company: Leon Henry
In Business: 37 years
Number of Employees: 8
Sales Volume: $5MM to $10MM

4758 Schroeder Log Home Supply
Schroeder Log Home Supply
1101 SE 7th Ave
Grand Rapids, MN 55744   218-326-4434
800-359-6614
Fax: 800-755-3249
www.loghelp.com

Credit Cards: AMEX; MasterCard
In Business: 29 years

4759 Siteworks
Siteworks, Inc.
363 W Canino Road
Houston, TX 77037-3713   281-931-1000
800-599-5463
Fax: 281-931-1044
reception@siteworkstone.com
www.chateaustone.com

Fireplaces, mantels, filler panels, hearths

President: Alex Newton
Catalog Cost: Free
Printing Information: 193 pages in 4 colors
In Business: 22 years
Sales Volume: $5MM to $10MM

4760 Specification Chemicals
Specification Chemicals, Inc.
824 Keeler Street
PO Box 709
Boone, IA 50036-2728   515-432-8256
800-247-3932
Fax: 515-432-8366
sales@spec-chem.com
www.spec-chem.com

Materials to restore cracked plaster walls and ceilings, roofing material for low-slope roofs, basement waterproofing, polyester fabric convertors

President: Suzanne Salter
Director: Johnnie L Ball
VP, Treasurer: Clarence E Ball
Catalog Cost: Free
In Business: 40 years
Number of Employees: 10
Sales Volume: $499,000

4761 Stair Specialist
Stair Specialist Inc.
2257 West Columbia Ave
Battle Creek, MI 49015-8639   269-964-2351
269-964-3450
Fax: 269-964-4824
www.StairSpecialistinc.Com

Circular stairs

President: Ted Goff
Catalog Cost: $5
Catalog Circulation: to 10000
Printing Information: 16 pages in 4 colors on Matte Stock
Binding: Saddle Stitched
In Business: 42 years
Number of Employees: 2
Sales Volume: Under $500M

4762 Stencilworks
Stencilwerks
1918 Tilghman
Allentown, PA 18104-4158   610-433-7776
800-357-4954
Fax: 610-289-7792
Stencilwerks@gmail.com

Designer stencils for the discriminate stenciler. pre-cut stencils of the highest quality, natural brushes, stencil sleeves, American Paints and other stencil accessories

President: Carolyn Blahosky
Catalog Cost: $5
Catalog Circulation: Mailed 1 time(s) per year to 500
Average Order Size: $45
Printing Information: 48 pages in 7 colors on Glossy Stock
Press: Sheetfed Press
Binding: Saddle Stitched
Mailing List Information: Names for rent
In Business: 30 years
Number of Employees: 6
Sales Volume: $1MM to $3MM

4763 Stonewall Kitchen
Stonewall Kitchen
2 Stonewall Ln
York, ME 03909-1662   207-351-2712
800-826-1752
Fax: 207-351-2715
guestservices@stonewallkitchen.com
www.stonewallkitchen.com

Gourmet foods, gifts, kitchenware and baking supplies

President: Thom Rindt
CFO: Lori King
Marketing Manager: Sheri Tripp
Credit Cards: MasterCard
Catalog Cost: Free
In Business: 23 years
Number of Employees: 120
Sales Volume: $34 million

4764 Tile Restoration Center
Tile Restoration Center
2464 NE Stapleton Rd.#4
Vancouver, WA 98661   206-633-4866
Fax: 206-633-3489
trc@tilerestorationcenter.com
www.tilerestorationcenter.com

Historic reproductions of period tile, wainscot

President: Steve Moon
Founder: Marie Glasse Tapp
Catalog Cost: $5
Catalog Circulation: Mailed 1 time(s) per year
Average Order Size: $800
Printing Information: 26 pages in 4 colors on Matte Stock
In Business: 35 years
Number of Employees: 7
Sales Volume: Under $500M

4765 US Bells
US Bells
P.O.Box 73
Prospect Harbor, ME 04669-73   207-963-7184
866-963-7184
rtfisher@usbells.com
www.Usbells.Com

Cast bronze windbells & door bells

President: Richard Fisher
Credit Cards: MasterCard; Visa
In Business: 43 years
Sales Volume: $1MM to $3MM

4766 Urban Archeology
Urban Archaeology
239 East 58th Street
New York, NY 10022-2915   212-431-4646
Fax: 212-371-1601
NYuptown@urbanarchaeology.com
www.Urbanarchaeology.Com

Interior and exterior bath, lighting and tile collections.

President: Gil Shapiro
Creative Director: Judith Stockman
Founder: Gil Shapiro
Credit Cards: AMEX; MasterCard; Visa
Catalog Cost: Free
Catalog Circulation: to 3000
Printing Information: 5 pages in 4 colors
In Business: 43 years
Number of Employees: 50
Sales Volume: $10MM to $20MM

4767 Vesterheim Norwegian American Museum
Vesterheim
523 W Water St
PO Box 379
Decorah, IA 52101-1733   563-382-9681
Fax: 563-382-8828
info@vesterheim.org
www.vesterheim.com

Collection of artefacts, large samplings of fine decorative folk arts, tools & machinery of early agriculture

Credit Cards: AMEX; MasterCard
In Business: 136 years

4768 Viking Folk Art Publications
Viking Folk Art Publications, Inc.
301 16th Ave SE
Waseca, MN 56093-3134   507-835-8009
Fax: 507-835-8541
books@vikingpub.com
www.Viking-Publications.Com

Decorative painting instructional books, wide range of subject matter from American, Norwegian, Russian, Bavarian, and Spanish to Japanese folk art, home decor, florals and landscape on canvas

President: Jan Draheim
Credit Cards: AMEX; MasterCard
Printing Information: 30 pages in 4 colors
Binding: o
In Business: 20 years
Sales Volume: $1MM to $3MM

4769 WF Norman Corporation
W.F. Norman Corp.
214 N Cedar
P.O. Box 323
Nevada, MO 64772   417-667-5552
800-641-4038
Fax: 417-667-2708
info@wfnorman.com
www.wfnorman.com

Metal ceilings, wainscotting and cornices

President: Annette J Quitno
Marketing Manager: Mark Quitno
Founder: William Franklin Norman
Credit Cards: AMEX; MasterCard; Visa
Catalog Cost: $3
Printing Information: 72 pages in 1 color
In Business: 119 years
Number of Employees: 40
Sales Volume: $5MM to $10MM

4770 Wood Factory
Wood Factory
111 S Railroad St
Navasota, TX 77868-3529   936-825-7233
Fax: 936-825-1791
www.Woodfactory.Com

Woodwork, mouldings, screen doors, entry doors and ornamental trim, stock and custom matched porch posts, turnings and finials

President: Dean Arnold
CFO: Kathy Arnold
Credit Cards: MasterCard; Visa
Catalog Cost: $2
Catalog Circulation: to 3000
Printing Information: 40 pages in 1 color on Matte Stock
Number of Employees: 6
Sales Volume: $500M to $1MM

4771 Woodhouse
Woodhouse
3295 Route 549
PO Box 219
Mansfield, PA 16933   570-549-6232
800-227-4311
Fax: 570-549-6233
sales@timberframe1.com
www.timberframe1.com

Old fashioned, wide, country plank or quartersawn flooring of antique heart pine, oak, chestnut and other fine woods

President: Patrick Seaman
VP, Sales: Jeff Baker
Purchasing Manager: Todd Davey
Financial Manager: Mary Dimouro

Catalog Cost: Free
In Business: 35 years

4772 Worthington Architectural Details Catalog
Worthington Millwork, LLC
17842 Ashley Drive
Suite C
Panama City Beach, FL 32413   904-281-1485
800-872-1608
Fax: 904-281-1488
sales@worthingtonmillwork.com
www.worthingtonmillwork.com

Columns, balusters, molding, ceiling medallions, niches, window heads, pediments pilasters, louvers and many other architectural details

President: Kyle Boatwright
Credit Cards: AMEX; MasterCard; Visa
Catalog Circulation: Mailed 1 time(s) per year
Printing Information: 72 pages in 1 color on Matte Stock
Press: Web Press
Binding: Saddle Stitched
Mailing List Information: Names for rent
In Business: 30 years
Number of Employees: 2
Sales Volume: $130,000

4773 YesterYear's Vintage Doors
YesterYear's Vintage Doors
66 South Main Street
Hammond, NY 13646   315-324-5250
800-787-2001
Fax: 315-324-6531
info@vintagedoors.com
www.vintagedoors.com

Fine woodworking and craftsmanship supplies.

In Business: 25 years

Paints, Finishes & Removers

4774 Daly's
Daly's
3525 Stone Way North
Seattle, WA 98103-8923   206-633-4200
800-735-7019
Fax: 206-632-2565
info@dalyspaint.com
www.dalyspaint.com

Wood finishing products

President: Robin Daly
robin@dalyspaint.com
CFO: Amanda Timm
Marketing Manager: Terri Parke
Credit Cards: AMEX; MasterCard; Visa
Catalog Cost: Free
Catalog Circulation: Mailed 54 time(s) per year
Average Order Size: $50
Printing Information: 2 pages in 2 colors on Glossy Stock
Press: Web Press
Mailing List Information: Names for rent
Number of Employees: 55
Sales Volume: $500M to $1MM

4775 Fox Valley Systems
Fox Valley Systems, Inc.
640 Industrial Dr
Dept.Ws
Cary, IL 60013-1944   847-639-5744
800-323-4700
Fax: 847-639-8190
info@foxvalleysystems.com
www.foxpaint.com

Aerosol paints, stripping and marking equipment

President: Thomas Smrt
Credit Cards: MasterCard; Visa
Catalog Cost: Free
Catalog Circulation: Mailed 30 time(s) per year

Printing Information: 4 pages
Number of Employees: 100
Sales Volume: $25,000,000 - $50,000,000

4776 Gold Leaf and Metallic Powders
Gold Leaf and Metallic Powders
6001 Santa Monica Blvd
Los Angeles, CA 90038-1807   323-769-4888
888-465-3716
Fax: 877-386-1489
info@glandmp.com
www.nnigroup.com/glandmp/default.aspx

Frames, mouldings, liners, bronzing and mica powders, metal leafing, wood care and touch formulas, faux finishing specialties

President: Larry Neuberg
Marketing Manager: Scot Halland, Managing Director
Credit Cards: AMEX; MasterCard
Sales Volume: $20MM to $50MM

4777 Old-Fashioned Milk Paint Company
The Old Fashioned Milk Paint Co.,Inc.
436 Main Street
Po Box 222
Groton, MA 01450-222   978-448-6336
866-350-6455
Fax: 978-448-2754
questions@milkpaint.com
www.milkpaint.com

Milk based paint

President: Anne Thibeau
anne@milkpaint.com
Marketing Manager: Anne Thibeau
Credit Cards: MasterCard; Visa
Catalog Cost: Free
Catalog Circulation: to 5000
Printing Information: in 4 colors on Glossy Stock
Binding: Folded
Mailing List Information: Names for rent
In Business: 41 years
Number of Employees: 5
Sales Volume: $3MM to $5MM

4778 Preserva-Products
Preserva Products Ltd
12860 Earhart Avenue
Suite 102
Auburn, CA 95602-9000   530-887-0177
800-797-2537
Fax: 530-887-0187
info@preservaproducts.com
www.preservaproducts.com

Penetrating natural finishes for wood (exterior and interior), masonry, decks, fences, siding, shingles, log homes, concrete, brick, stucco, stone, grout, tile

President: Greg Riecks
CFO: Cindy Riecks
In Business: 44 years
Number of Employees: 10
Sales Volume: 1.3M

4779 Sepp Leaf Products
Sepp Leaf Products, Inc.
381 Park Ave S # 1301
New York, NY 10016-8819   212-683-2840
800-971-7377
Fax: 212-725-0308
sales@seppleaf.com
www.Seppleaf.Com

Gilder's source for leaf, supplies, tools, venetian plaster

President: Peter Sepp
Printing Information: in 3 colors
Sales Volume: $1MM to $3MM

4780 Silkpaint Corporation
Silkpaint Corporation
18220 Waldron Drive
PO Box 18
Waldron, MO 64092-18   816-891-7774
                             800-563-0074
                        Fax: 816-891-7775
                        art@silkpaint.com
                        www.Silkpaint.Com

Airpen dispensing tools, Silkpaint brand water-soluble resist, fiber-etch fiber remover, sugarveil confectionary mix, sugarveil icing dispenser
President: Michele Hester
Credit Cards: MasterCard
Catalog Cost: Free
Mailing List Information: Names for rent
In Business: 12 years
Number of Employees: 10-J
Sales Volume: $1MM to $3MM

4781 US Bronze Powders
United States Bronze Powders, Inc.
408 Route 202 N.
Flemington, NJ 08822-31   908-782-5454
                         Fax: 908-782-3489
                    inquiry@usbronzepowders.com
                    www.usbronzepowders.com

Bronze powders for paint
President: Kenneth C Ramsey
In Business: 95 years
Sales Volume: $20MM to $50MM

4782 Wishbook
Magic Brush Inc.
PO Box 1123
Lockhart, TX 78644   520-558-2285
                         Fax: 520-558-2285
                    orders@sherrycnelson.com
                    www.sherrycnelson.com

Patterns/instruction books for decorative painting, by Sherry C. Nelson, MDA, how to paint realistic birds, butterflies and animals on wood, reverse glass or canvas
President: Sherry C Nelson
Production Manager: Deborah A Galloway
Credit Cards: MasterCard
Mailing List Information: Names for rent
In Business: 27 years
Number of Employees: 2
Sales Volume: Under $500M

Plumbing Supplies

4783 2015 Spring/Summer HBC Catalog
HBC Home & Hardware Products
324 Cranbury Half Acre Rd
Cranbury, NJ 8512   800-523-1268
                        www.hberger.com

Security & builder's hardware, plumbing products, paint applicators and home environment products.
In Business: 43 years

4784 Chem Tainer Industries
Chem Tainer Industries
361 Neptune Avenue
West Babylon, NY 11704-5800 631-661-8300
                              800-275-2436
                         Fax: 631-661-8209
                    sales@chemtainer.com
                    www.Chemtainer.Com

Water storage tanks, poly tanks, underground water tanks
President: James B Glen

4785 Farmer Boy AG
Farmer Boy AG
50 West Stoever Avenue
Myerstown, PA 17067   800-845-3374
                        www.farmerboyag.com

Agricultural supplies, building materials, animal housing, and animal handling
In Business: 20 years

4786 Faucet Outlet
Build.Com, Inc.
402 Otterson Dr.
Chico, CA 95928   800-444-5783
                         Fax: 845-294-9626
                         cs@faucet.com
                         www.faucet.com

Wholesale discounts on major name brand faucets, sinks, toilets, whirlpools, claw-foot tubs, sterling shower doors and more
President: Daniel Auer
Credit Cards: AMEX; MasterCard
Catalog Cost: $4
Catalog Circulation: Mailed 2 time(s) per year to 50000
Average Order Size: $350
Printing Information: 64 pages in 4 colors on Glossy Stock
Press: Web Press
Mailing List Information: Names for rent
Number of Employees: 5
Sales Volume: $1MM to $3MM

4787 Nicholson Steam Trap
Spence Engineering Company,Inc.
150 Coldenham Road
Walden, NY 12586-2909   845-778-5566
                              800-398-2493
                         Fax: 845-778-1072
                    sales@spenceengineering.com
                    www.spenceengineering.com

Steam traps, temp control and muffler products
Catalog Circulation: Mailed 1 time(s) per year
Printing Information: 60 pages in 2 colors

4788 Plast-O-Matic Valves
Plast-O-Matic Valves, Inc.
1384 Pompton Ave
Cedar Grove, NJ 07009-1095   973-256-3000
                         Fax: 973-256-4745
                    info@plastomatic.com
                    www.Plastomatic.Com

Plastic valves
President: Bob Sinclair
CFO: Daniel Anderio
Marketing Manager: Rick Bolgre
Production Manager: Parry Lunno
Inside Sales Manager: Erin Mulder
Catalog Cost: Free
Printing Information: 40 pages in 3 colors
In Business: 48 years
Sales Volume: $20MM to $50MM

4789 Saniflo
SFA Saniflo, Inc.
105 Newfield Ave # B
Raritan Center, Suite B
Edison, NJ 08837-3825   732-225-6070
                              800-571-8191
                         Fax: 732-225-6072
                         www.saniflo.com

Macerating toilets, water pumps
In Business: 50 years
Sales Volume: Under $500M

4790 The Part-Works Inc. Backflow Prevention
The Part-Works, Inc.
2900 4th Ave S
Seattle, WA 98134   800-336-8900
                         Fax: 866-553-7981
                    customerservice@thepartworks.com
                    www.thepartworks.com

Plumbing and industrial replacement parts.
President: Katie Parris
Marketing Manager: Oly Welke

Production Manager: Larry Farley
Operation Mnager: LeAndra Sharp

4791 The Part-Works Inc. CHG Faucets
The Part-Works, Inc.
2900 4th Ave S
Seattle, WA 98134   800-336-8900
                         Fax: 866-553-7981
                    customerservice@thepartworks.com
                    www.thepartworks.com

Plumbing and industrial replacement parts.
President: Katie Parris
Marketing Manager: Oly Welke
Production Manager: Larry Farley
Operation Mnager: LeAndra Sharp

4792 The Part-Works Inc. Hydrants
The Part-Works, Inc.
2900 4th Ave S
Seattle, WA 98134   800-336-8900
                         Fax: 866-553-7981
                    customerservice@thepartworks.com
                    www.thepartworks.com

Plumbing and industrial replacement parts.
President: Katie Parris
Marketing Manager: Oly Welke
Production Manager: Larry Farley
Operation Mnager: LeAndra Sharp

4793 Watercolors Inc
Watercolors Inc
High Ridge Road
Garrison, NY 10524   845-424-3327
                         Fax: 845-424-3169
                    watercolorsinc@earthlink.net
                    www.watercolorsinc.com

English, Edwardian, Italian and French bathroom fixtures, other traditional and contemporary faucet and accessory designs, also tubs, whirl pools, saunas, lighting
President: Joyce Blum
CFO: Larry Fleischer
Marketing Manager: Lisa Olmstead
Production Manager: Paul Gerwirtz
Fulfillment: Lisa Olmstead
International Marketing Manager: Joyce Blum
Buyers: Joyce Blun
Catalog Cost: $35
Catalog Circulation: Mailed 52 time(s) per year to 1000
Average Order Size: $500
Printing Information: 250 pages in 4 colors on Glossy Stock
Press: Sheetfed Press
Binding: Saddle Stitched
Mailing List Information: Names for rent
List Manager: Lisa Olmstead
In Business: 40 years
Number of Employees: 5

Home Furnishings
General

4794 A Great Idea to Hang Onto
Walker Display, Inc.
4000 Airpark Blvd
Duluth, MN 55811   218-624-8990
                              800-234-7614
                         Fax: 218-624-8991
                    wdinc@walkerdisplay.com
                    www.walkerdisplay.com

Picture, exhibit and artwork hanging systems.
President: Richard Levey
Credit Cards: AMEX; MasterCard
Catalog Cost: Free
Printing Information: 10 pages in 4 colors on Matte Stock
Binding: Saddle Stitched

4795 American Postal Manufacturing
Postal Products Unlimited Inc
500 W Oklahoma Avenue
Milwaukee, WI 53207-2649   414-290-1067
800-229-4500
Fax: 800-570-0007
info@mailproducts.com
www.mailproducts.com

Mailboxes

Credit Cards: AMEX; MasterCard
In Business: 3 years
Number of Employees: 5
Sales Volume: $300,000

4796 April Cornell
April Cornell
131 Battery Street
Burlington, VT 5401   802-448-3281
888-332-7745
customerservice@aprilcornell.com
www.aprilcornell.com

4797 Asi Home
ASI Home
CS1 36 Gumbletown Raod
Paupack, PA 18451   800-263-8608
Fax: 570-576-0007
sales@asihome.com
www.asihome.com

Products and solutions for the intelligent home

President: Richard Scholl
Marketing Manager: Leo Soderman
Buyers: Leo Soderman
Credit Cards: AMEX; MasterCard
Catalog Circulation: Mailed 2 time(s) per year
Printing Information: 32 pages in 4 colors on Matte Stock
Press: Web Press
Binding: Saddle Stitched
Mailing List Information: Names for rent
In Business: 5 years
Number of Employees: 50
Sales Volume: Under $500M

4798 Ballard Designs
Ballard Designs
5568 West Chester Road
West Chester, OH 45069   800-536-7551
Fax: 800-989-4510
custserv@ballarddesigns.net
www.ballarddesigns.com

Home furnishings

President: Ryan McKelvey
Marketing Manager: Laura Daily
Vice President of Marketing: Jean Jones
VP of Finance: Sam Touchstone
Vice President of Customer Care: Lisa Barnes
Number of Employees: 10

4799 Belfort Furniture
Belfort Furniture
22250 Shaw Rd
Dulles, VA 20166   703-406-7600
www.belfortfurniture.com

Furniture.

4800 Belk New Directions
Belk
2801 W Tyvola Road
Charlotte NC   800-669-6550
care@belk.com
www.belk.com

Casualwear for women, men, and children, jewelry, footwear, home furnishings and appliances

President: Lisa Harper
CFO: Scott Hurd
Marketing Manager: Barb Pellegrino
Chief Operating Officer: Don Hendricks
Chief Stores Officer: Randy Whitaker
Product Sourcing & Technical Design: Tanya

Cauren
Catalog Cost: Free
Printing Information: 12 pages in 4 colors
In Business: 129 years

4801 Belk Wedding Catalog
Belk
2801 W Tyvola Road
Charlotte NC   800-669-6550
care@belk.com
www.belk.com

Home furnishings, accessories, and appliances

President: Lisa Harper
CFO: Scott Hurd
Marketing Manager: Barb Pellegrino
Chief Operating Officer: Don Hendricks
Chief Stores Officer: Randy Whitaker
Product Sourcing & Technical Design: Tanya Cauren
Catalog Cost: Free
Catalog Circulation: Mailed 1 time(s) per year
Printing Information: 31 pages in 4 colors
In Business: 129 years

4802 Bella Coastal Décor
Bella Coastal Décor
PO Box 297
Jenks, OK 74037-297   877-436-9098
www.bellacoastaldecor.com

Fine bedding essentials including beach bed sets, nautical bed sets, inspired coastal bedding and exotic tropical bedding.

4803 Berry Hill Limited
Berry Hill Ltd
75 Burwell Road
St Thomas ON, CN N5P-3R5   519-631-0480
800-668-3072
Fax: 519-631-8935
customerservice@berryhill.ca
www.berryhilllimited.com

For the home, kitchenware, farm supplies, outdoor living, pet supplies, gifts and holidays and books

President: Ann Foster
Credit Cards: MasterCard
Catalog Cost: $6
In Business: 69 years
Number of Employees: 12
Sales Volume: $1.38 Million

4804 Blair Home
Blair
220 Hickory St.
Warren, PA 16366   800-821-5744
www.blair.com

Home furnishings for the whole home.

President: Marisa Smith
Catalog Cost: Free
Printing Information: in 4 colors
In Business: 106 years
Number of Employees: 2000
Sales Volume: $1 Billion

4805 Bluestem Brands
Bluestem Brands, Inc.
7075 Flying Cloud Drive
Eden Prairie, MN 55344   r@bluestembrands.com
www.bluestem.com

Consumer electronics, bedding, furniture and general merchandise

President: Steve Nave
CFO: Pete Michielutti, EVP
EVP, COO, & Chief Digital Officer: Vince Jones
EVP & President of Credit Services: Jim Slavik
Credit Cards: AMEX; MasterCard
Mailing List Information: Names for rent
In Business: 15 years
Number of Employees: 2900
Sales Volume: Over $1 Billion

4806 BrylaneHome
BrylaneHome
One New York Plaza
New York, NY 10004   www.brylanehome.com

Home furnishings, decor indoor and outdoor furniture.

CEO: Paul Tarvin
Catalog Cost: Free
In Business: 105 years
Number of Employees: 6400
Sales Volume: Over $1 Billion

4807 CB2
CB2
1860 W Jefferson Avenue
Naperville, IL 60540   630-388-4555
800-606-6252
Fax: 630-527-1448
www.cb2.com

Modern home and office furniture and accessories]

Chief Executive Officer: Neela Montgomery
Credit Cards: AMEX; MasterCard
Catalog Cost: Free
Catalog Circulation: Mailed 12 time(s) per year
Printing Information: 92 pages in 4 colors
In Business: 17 years
Sales Volume: $10MM to $20MM

4808 Check-All Valve
Check-All Valve Mfg. Co.
1800 Fuller Road
West Des Moines, IA 50265-5526 515-224-2301
Fax: 515-224-2326
sales@checkall.com
www.Checkall.Com

Manufacturer of spring loaded check valves; 1/8 inch to 20 inch; various materials and end connections available

President: Tom Jensen
Marketing Manager: Connie Eller
Production Manager: Joe Offenburger
Quality Control Director: Steve Bock
Data Processing Manager: Richard Sabelka
Sales Manager: Brian Strait
Credit Cards: AMEX; MasterCard
Catalog Cost: Free
Printing Information: 63 pages
In Business: 59 years
Number of Employees: 33
Sales Volume: $5.3 Million

4809 Christmas Tree Shops
877-463-1549
www.christmastreeshops.com

Gifts, home decor, accessories

4810 Clean Report
Don Aslett's Cleaning Center
210 West Halliday Street
Pocatello, ID 83204   208-232-6212
800-451-2402
Fax: 208-232-6286
info.website@cleanreport.com
www.cleanreport.com

Professional cleaning products for the home

President: Don Aslett
CFO: Dave Hermansen
Marketing Manager: Kim Williams
Production Manager: Kim Williams
Credit Cards: MasterCard
Catalog Cost: Free
Catalog Circulation: Mailed 52 time(s) per year to 75000
Average Order Size: $75
Printing Information: 32 pages in 4 colors on Matte Stock
Press: Web Press
Binding: Folded
Mailing List Information: Names for rent
In Business: 18 years

Number of Employees: 12
Sales Volume: $1MM to $3MM

4811 Comfortex Blindcrafter Center

Comfortex Corporation
21 Elm Street
Maplewood, NY 12189
800-843-4151
info@comfortex.com
www.comfortex.com

Custom built shades and blinds

President: Tom Marusak
Executive Vice President: John Fitzgerald
Export Sales Manager: Meinrad Rickenbacher
Director of Human Resources: Patricia Gaglianese
Catalog Cost: Free
In Business: 31 years
Number of Employees: 750
Sales Volume: $20MM to $50MM

4812 Crate & Barrel

Crate & Barrel
1860 W Jefferson Avenue
Naperville, IL 60540-3918
630-357-1155
800-967-6696
Fax: 630-527-1404
www.crateandbarrel.com

Home furnishings and kitchenware

Chief Executive Officer: Neela Montgomery
Credit Cards: AMEX; MasterCard; Visa
Catalog Cost: Free
Catalog Circulation: Mailed 12 time(s) per year
Printing Information: 80 pages in 4 colors
In Business: 55 years
Number of Employees: 5000
Sales Volume: $10MM to $20MM

4813 Decorative Home

Neiman Marcus
5th Avenue At 58th Street
New York, NY 10019
800-558-1855
888-774-2424
www.bergdorfgoodman.com

Vintage and unique home items

Chairman: Nicholas Manville, VP
President: Bergdorf Goodman
Printing Information: 16 pages

4814 DwellStudio

DwellStudio
New York NY
877-993-9355
www.dwellstudio.com

Home furnishings

Catalog Cost: Free
Printing Information: in 4 colors
In Business: 16 years

4815 Easy Closets.Com

EasyClosets
20 Stone House Road
Millington, NJ 07946-1352
800-910-0129
www.easyclosets.com

Closets, pantries, laundry rooms and garages

In Business: 7 years

4816 Exair Corporation

Exair Corporation
11510 Goldcoast Drive
Cincinnati, OH 45249-1621
513-671-3322
800-903-9247
Fax: 513-671-3363
techelp@exair.com
www.exair.com

Compressed air products and controls for use in industrial plants

President: Roy Sweeney
Marketing Manager: Gary Gunkel
Production Manager: Bryan Peters
Chief Executive Officer : Roy O. Sweeney

Credit Cards: AMEX; MasterCard
Catalog Cost: Free
Catalog Circulation: to 50000
Printing Information: 80 pages
In Business: 32 years
Number of Employees: 36
Sales Volume: $5,000,000 - $10,000,000

4817 First Frost

Coldwater Creek
1176 E Dayton Yellow Springs Rd.
Fairborn, OH 45324
888-678-5576
www.coldwatercreek.com

Women's apparel, jewelry, accessories and gifts.

CEO: Dave Walde
President: Brenda Koskinen
Catalog Cost: Free
Printing Information: 88 pages in 4 colors
In Business: 32 years
Number of Employees: 100
Sales Volume: $780 Million

4818 Freedom Outdoor Furniture

Freedom Outdoor Furniture
PO Box 87
Sugar Grove, IL 60554
703-406-7600
866-441-3733
sales@freedomoutdoorfurniture.com
www.freedomoutdoorfurniture.com

4819 Fresh Finds

Fresh Finds, LLC
425 Stump Road
PO Box 2800
North Wales, PA 19454-2800
215-361-5352
800-860-6022
customerservice@freshfinds.com
www.freshfinds.com

Affordable kitchen and home solutions

Catalog Cost: Free

4820 Frontgate

Frontgate
5566 West Chester Rd
West Chester, OH 45069-2914
513-603-1000
888-263-9850
Fax: 800-436-2105
service@frontgate.com
www.frontgate.com

Indoor furnishings, bed and bath essentials, kitchen and entertaining, home care and storage, electronic innovations, outdoor living; holiday gifts.

Chairman: John O'Steen
President: Paul Tarvin
CFO: James Pekarek
CEO: Mark Ethier
Catalog Cost: Free
Printing Information: 88 pages
In Business: 24 years
Number of Employees: 130
Sales Volume: $25.9 MM

4821 Geary's

Geary's
351 N Beverly Drive
Beverly Hills, CA 90210
310-273-4741
800-793-6670
www.gearys.com

A world-class showcase of fine jewelry, tableware, and giftware for the home

President: Darrell S Ross
Credit Cards: AMEX; MasterCard; Visa
Catalog Cost: Free
Mailing List Information: Names for rent
List Company: Mokrynski & Associates
401 Hackensack Avenue
Hackensack, NJ 07601
2014885656
In Business: 84 years
Number of Employees: 130
Sales Volume: $10MM to $20MM

4822 Grandin Road

Grandin Road
5566 W Chester Rd
West Chester, OH 45069
513-603-1492
866-668-5962
Fax: 800-491-5193
service@grandinroad.com
www.grandinroad.com

Quality home decor

President: Paul Tarvin
Catalog Circulation: to 28.5M
In Business: 3 years
Sales Volume: $500M to $1MM

4823 Gudrun Sjoden

Gudrun Sj"d,n
50 Greene Street
New York, NY 10013
212-219-2510
877-574-1486
customerservice@gundrunsjoden.com
www.durunsjoden.com

Clothing and home furnishings

President: Gudron Sj"d,n
Credit Cards: MasterCard
Catalog Cost: Free
In Business: 41 years

4824 Hammacher Schlemmer

Hammacher Schlemmer
147 E 57th St
New York, NY 10022-2101
212-421-9000
800-321-1484
customerservice@hammacher.com
www.hammacher.com

Electronics, home living, apparel, toys & games, gifts, home office, sports & leisure, home care and more

President: Linda Drummond
CFO: Jeff Kuznitsky
Marketing Manager: Fred Berns
Production Manager: Jack Mc Carthy
Buyers: Ray Moore
Katie Kaspar
Credit Cards: AMEX; MasterCard
Printing Information: 87 pages in 4 colors on Glossy Stock
Binding: Saddle Stitched
Mailing List Information: Names for rent
Will Trade Names: Yes
List Company: Names & Addresses
In Business: 88 years
Number of Employees: 100
Sales Volume: 100MM

4825 Home Decorators Collection

Home Decorators Collection
3074 Chastain Meadows Parkway
Marietta, GA 30066
800-245-2217
www.homedecorators.com

Rugs, bar stools, bookshelves, coffe tables, mirrors, bathroom vanities, book cases and storage benches.

Catalog Cost: Free
Printing Information: 148 pages in 4 colors
Sales Volume: $300 Million

4826 Home at Five

1112 7th Avenue
Monroe, WI 53566
800-487-9025

Kitchen, dining, bed and bathroom furnishings and accessories

4827 Hyde Tools

Hyde
54 Eastford Road
Southbridge, MA 01550-1875
800-872-4933
Fax: 508-765-5250
info@hydetools.com
www.hydetools.com

Painting, wallcovering.

Chairman: Richard Hardy
President: Rob Scoble
CFO: Ronald Carlson
Marketing Manager: Corey Talbot
CEO: Rick Clemence
COO: Rob Scoble
Printing Information: 63 pages in 4 colors
Binding: Perfect Bound
In Business: 39 years
Number of Employees: 546

4828 I.O. Metro
PO Box 3417
Bentonville, AR 72712   888-223-5628
                               www.iometro.com

Modern ecclectic furniture, art and accessories

CEO: Lou Spagna

4829 IKEA
IKEA
420 Alan Wood Road
Conshohocken, PA 19428   www.ikea.com

Furniture, accessories and gifts for the home

President: Peter Agnefjall
Catalog Cost: Free
Printing Information: 374 pages in 4 colors on Glossy Stock
Binding: Perfect Bound
In Business: 74 years
Sales Volume: $500MM to $1 Billion

4830 JC Penney Casual Home Furnishings
JC Penney
6501 Legacy Drive
Plano, TX 75024   972-431-3400
                             800-842-9470
                        Fax: 972-591-9322
jcpinvestorrelations@jcpenney.com
www.jcpenney.com

Comfortable, current home furnishings that fit effortlessly into your casual lifestyle

Chairman: Myron E Ullman III
President: Ken C Hicks
CFO: Edward Record
Marketing Manager: Debra Berman
Chief Executive Officer: Mike Ullman
EVP, General Counsel and Secretary: Janet Dhillon
EVP, Chief Information Officer: Scott Laverty
Credit Cards: AMEX; MasterCard; Visa
Catalog Cost: Free

4831 Kotula's
2800 Southcross Drive W
Burnsville, MN 55306   800-685-4845
                        Fax: 952-882-6927
commerce@kotulas.com
www.kotulas.com

Games, toys, gifts, remote control toys, electronics, garage and auto supplies, home & outdoor living accessories, sports and recreation

Chairman: Donald Kotula
President: Chuck Albrecht
CFO: Tom Erickson
Marketing Manager: Wade Mattson
VP Operations: Rich Flogstad
Credit Cards: AMEX; MasterCard
Catalog Cost: Free
In Business: 30 years
Number of Employees: 300

4832 Lands' End Home
Lands' End, Inc.
1 Lands' End Lane
Dodgeville, WI 53595   800-963-4816
                        Fax: 800-332-0103
                             www.landsend.com

Indoor and outdoor items for the home, includes bath, bedding and luggage.

Co-interim CEO: James Gooch
Co-interim CEO: James Boitano
Catalog Cost: Free
Printing Information: in 4 colors
Mailing List Information: Names for rent
List Company: Millard Group
In Business: 53 years
Number of Employees: 5300
Sales Volume: $1.42 Billion

4833 Lazy Hill Farm Designs
Lazy Hill Farm Designs
20 Commerce Drive
Danbury, CT 06810   Fax: 203-743-5226
contact@gooddirections.com
www.lazyhill.com

Bird houses, feeders and garden furniture

Credit Cards: AMEX; MasterCard; Visa
Catalog Cost: Free
Catalog Circulation: Mailed 52 time(s) per year to 4000
Average Order Size: $75
Printing Information: 16 pages in 7 colors on Glossy Stock
Press: Web Press
Binding: Saddle Stitched
Mailing List Information: Names for rent
In Business: 35 years
Number of Employees: 20
Sales Volume: $500M to $1MM

4834 Lillian Vernon Big Sale
Lillian Vernon Corporation
PO Box 35980
Colorado Springs, CO 80935-5980 800-545-5426
                             800-545-5426
                        Fax: 757-427-7819
custserv@lillianvernon.com
www.lillianvernon.com

Lillian Vernon's best selling products

President: Tom Arland
CFO: Kirby Heck
Marketing Manager: John Buleza
Credit Cards: AMEX; MasterCard
Catalog Cost: Free
Catalog Circulation: Mailed 4 time(s) per year
Printing Information: in 4 colors on Glossy Stock
Press: Web Press
In Business: 64 years
Sales Volume: $10MM to $20MM

4835 Lone Star Western D,cor
PO Box 297
Jenks, OK 74037-297   877-493-3779
info@lonestarwesterndecor.com
www.lonestarwesterndecor.com

Western furniture collection set and western lighting

4836 Matt McGhee
Matt McGhee
445 Warren Street
Hudson, NY 10014   518-822-1700
mattmcghee@verizon.net
www.mattmcghee.com

Christmas tree ornaments

4837 Miles Kimball
Miles Kimball
250 City Center
Oshkosh, WI 54906   855-202-7394
                             www.mileskimball.com

Kitchen gadgets, home decor, storage & organization, books, jewelry, apparel, health, beauty, home office supplies and gift items.

Catalog Cost: Free
In Business: 81 years
Sales Volume: $10 Million

4838 Ornaments to Remember
Ornaments 2 Remember
PO Box 3440
Wilsonville, OR 97070-3440   503-638-1536
                                800-330-3382
                           Fax: 503-210-0832
www.ornaments2remember.com

Asian, Hawaii, Mexican, travel, garden, food and drink ornaments

President: Sarah Stanley
Sales Volume: $3MM to $5MM

4839 Orvis Home & Gift
The Orvis Company Inc.
178 Conservation Way
Sunderland, VT 05250-4465   802-362-1300
                               888-235-9763
                          Fax: 802-362-0141
                               www.orvis.com

Home furnishings and gifts.

CEO: Leigh H. Perkins Jr.
Catalog Cost: Free
In Business: 160 years
Number of Employees: 1700
Sales Volume: $340 Million

4840 Panaram International Trading Company
USATOWEL
126 Greylock Ave
Belleville, NJ 07109-3324   973-751-1100
                               800-872-8695
                          Fax: 973-751-2231
julie@usatowl.com
www.Usatowl.Com

Towels, bed linens, table linens, polishes, waxes, cleaners, washers, dryers

President: Ira Feinberg
Marketing Manager: Juliette H Silver
Fulfillment: Ira Feinberg
International Marketing Manager: H. Nelson
Mailing List Information: Names for rent
In Business: 15+ years
Number of Employees: 8
Sales Volume: $500M to $1MM

4841 Piper Classics
Piper Classics
1806 Deep Run Road
Unit H
Pipersville, PA 18947   888-766-7925
                          Fax: 215-766-2830
e.shopping@piperclassics.com
www.piperclassics.com

French country decor, rustic lodge decorations and country prints for your home

President: David Chittick
In Business: 34 years
Number of Employees: 13
Sales Volume: $1.4 Million

4842 Polart Distribution
Polart Distribution
5700 Sarah Avenue
Sarasota, FL 34233-3446   941-927-8983
                               800-278-9393
                          Fax: 941-927-8239
                               www.polandbymail.com

Home accessories.

President: Jarek Zaremba
In Business: 21 years
Number of Employees: 7
Sales Volume: $1.5 Million

4843 Pottery Barn
Pottery Barn
3250 Van Ness Ave.
San Francisco, CA 94109   415-421-7900
                               www.potterybarn.com

Home furnishings and accessories.

President: Sandra Stangl
Catalog Cost: Free

Printing Information: 156 pages in 4 colors
Mailing List Information: Names for rent
In Business: 67 years
Sales Volume: $3 Billion

4844 Promolife
Promolife
PO Box 385
Fayetteville, AR 72702   479-442-3404
888-742-3404
Fax: 479-444-6422
info@promolife.com
www.promolife.com

Alternative health and fitness products
President: Gerry Segal
Credit Cards: AMEX; MasterCard
Catalog Cost: Free
In Business: 13 years
Number of Employees: 3
Sales Volume: $170,000

4845 RH Baby & Child
Restoration Hardware
15 Koch Rd.
Corte Madera, CA 94925   800-762-1005
www.rhbabyandchild.com

Distinctive and unique items for the home, including furniture, lighting, cabinet hardware, gardenware, fixtures, tools, books, devices and amusements.
CEO: Gary Friedman
Printing Information: 296 pages in 4 colors
Mailing List Information: Names for rent
In Business: 37 years
Number of Employees: 2900
Sales Volume: $1.5 Billion

4846 RH Holiday
Restoration Hardware
15 Koch Rd.
Corte Madera, CA 94925   800-762-1005
www.restorationhardware.com

Apparel, decorations, toys and accessories.
CEO: Gary Friedman
Printing Information: 380 pages in 4 colors
In Business: 37 years
Number of Employees: 2900
Sales Volume: $1.5 Billion

4847 RH Interiors
Restoration Hardware
15 Koch Rd.
Corte Madera, CA 94925   800-762-1005
www.restorationhardware.com

Home furnishings.
CEO: Gary Friedman
Printing Information: 668 pages in 4 colors
In Business: 37 years
Number of Employees: 2900
Sales Volume: $1.5 Billion

4848 RH Modern
Restoration Hardware
15 Koch Road
Corte Madera, CA 94925   800-762-1005
www.restorationhardware.com

Home furnishings and d,cor
Chief Executive Officer: Gary Friedman
Catalog Cost: Free
Catalog Circulation: Mailed 4 time(s) per year
Printing Information: 730 pages in 4 colors
In Business: 37 years
Number of Employees: 2900
Sales Volume: $1.5 Billion

4849 RH Outdoor
Restoration Hardware
15 Koch Rd.
Corte Madera, CA 94925   800-762-1005
www.restorationhardware.com

Distinctive and unique gardenware, fixtures, tools, books, devices and amusements.

CEO: Gary Friedman
Printing Information: 380 pages in 4 colors
In Business: 37 years
Number of Employees: 2900
Sales Volume: $1.5 Billion

4850 RH Teen
Restoration Hardware
15 Koch Rd.
Corte Madera, CA 94925   800-762-1005
www.rhteen.com

Furniture, bedding and accessories for teens.
CEO: Gary Friedman
Printing Information: 192 pages in 4 colors
In Business: 37 years
Number of Employees: 2900
Sales Volume: $1.5 Billion

4851 Ressler Importers
Ressler Importers, Inc.
63 Flushing Ave
Unit 250
Brooklyn, NY 11205   718-488-3902
Fax: 718-488-3905
info@resslerimporters.com
www.resslerimporters.com

Furniture parts and supplies
Owner/Chairman/President/CEO: Rudolph Ressler
In Business: 87 years
Number of Employees: 10
Sales Volume: $1.2 Million

4852 Room & Board
Room & Board
4600 Olson Memorial Hwy.
Minneapolis, MN 55422   800-301-9720
www.roomandboard.com

Home furnishings inspired by the Shaker, Asian, Danish, Arts & Crafts and Modern design movements.
Catalog Cost: Free
Printing Information: 240 pages
Mailing List Information: Names for rent
In Business: 36 years
Number of Employees: 715
Sales Volume: $400 Million

4853 School Fix Supply
School Fix
    800-930-6299
Fax: 800-964-4629
www.schoolfix.com

Supplies, furniture and hardware for school classrooms and buildings.

4854 Share the Spirit!
Coldwater Creek
1176 E Dayton Yellow Springs Rd.
Fairborn, OH 45324   888-678-5576
www.coldwatercreek.com

Women's apparel, jewelry, accessories and gifts.
CEO: Dave Walde
President: Brenda Koskinen
Catalog Cost: Free
Printing Information: 96 pages in 4 colors
In Business: 32 years
Number of Employees: 100
Sales Volume: $780 Million

4855 Sierra Home and Gift
Sierra Trading Post
5025 Campstool Rd
Cheyenne, WY 82007-1898   037-775-8000
800-713-4534
Fax: 800-378-8946
customerservice@sierratradingpost.com
www.sierratradingpost.com

Home furnishings, daily essentials for him and her, slippers, gifts, outdoor gear and camping equipment & supplies
President: Keith Richardson
CFO: Gary Imig
Production Manager: Sheila Russell
Fulfillment: Robin Jahnke
Credit Cards: AMEX; MasterCard
Catalog Cost: Free
Mailing List Information: Names for rent
In Business: 20 years
Number of Employees: 135
Sales Volume: $20-50 Million

4856 Silkflowers.Com
Silkflowers.Com
12021 Centron Place
Cincinatti, OH 45246   800-783-9966
Fax: 914-328-1959
service@petals.com
www.silkflowers.com

Silf flowers, plants, trees, decorative potpourri and scented candles
Managing Director: Chris Corelli
In Business: 30 years

4857 Stoneberry
Stoneberry
1356 Williams Street
Chippewa Falls, WI 54729   800-704-5480
www.stoneberry.com

Home furnishings and appliances, home entertainment, toys and games, gardening and yard maintenance equipment, sport and fitness products, health and beauty products
Credit Cards: AMEX; MasterCard
Catalog Cost: Free
Catalog Circulation: Mailed 2 time(s) per year
Printing Information: 200 pages in 4 colors
Sales Volume: $50MM to $100MM

4858 Sunland Home
Sunland Home
PO Box 17053
Tucson, AZ 85731-7053   520-917-0342
888-786-8876
www.sunlandhomedecor.com

Southwestern style decor and furnishings, Contemporary Rustic style, encompassing modern lodge, Western and uniquely American designs
Credit Cards: AMEX; MasterCard
In Business: 18 years

4859 Sunshine Rooms
Sunshine Rooms, Inc.
3333 N Mead Street
Wichita, KS 67219-4059   316-838-0033
800-222-1598
Fax: 316-838-0839
staff@sunshinerooms.com
www.sunshinerooms.com

Solariums, greenhouses, pool enclosures, conservatories, etc.
Chairman: Wade Griffith
President: L Griffith
CFO: Buddy Frenz
VP Sales: Geoff Graves
Purchasing Manager: Eddie Banelos
Director: Eric Griffith
Credit Cards: AMEX; MasterCard
Printing Information: in 3 colors
In Business: 35 years
Number of Employees: 20
Sales Volume: $1,000,000 - $5,000,000

4860 Through the Country Door
Through the Country Door
1112 7th Avenue
Monroe, WI 53566-1364   800-240-6878
800-341-9477

Kitchen & dining, bed & bath, home accents, furniture, rugs & curtains, seasonal, gifts

President: Ann Bush
Catalog Cost: Free
In Business: 11 years
Number of Employees: 3
Sales Volume: $1,70,000

4861 Touch of Class
Touch of Class
709 W 12th Street
Huntingburg, IN 47542 812-683-3707
800-457-7456
Fax: 812-683-5921
customerservice@touchofclass.com
www.touchofclass.com

Bedding ensembles, giftware, home decorative, loungewear and slippers

Chairman: Carla Parke-Bell
President: Fred Bell
Buyers: Brenda Phelps, Giftware/Home
Barbara Krodel, Bath, rugs, pillows
Credit Cards: AMEX; MasterCard; Visa
Catalog Cost: Free
Average Order Size: $140
Mailing List Information: Names for rent
In Business: 26 years
Number of Employees: 250
Sales Volume: $20MM to $50MM

4862 Touchstone
Touchstone
PO Box 760
Harrison, OH 45030 800-962-6890
Fax: 866-239-6770
service@touchstonecatalog.com
www.touchstonecatalog.com

Home furnishing and decor

In Business: 26 years

4863 Urban Outfitters
UrbanOutfitters.com
30 Industrial Park Blvd
Trenton, SC 29847 800-282-2200
800-988-7726
Fax: 800-959-8795
www.urbanoutfitters.com

Men and women's clothing, shoes and accessories an home furnishing

Marketing Manager: Teresa Lee
Credit Cards: AMEX; MasterCard
Catalog Circulation: Mailed 12 time(s) per year
Number of Employees: 29

4864 Viridian Bay
Viridian Bay
377 Swift Avenue
South San Francisco, CA 94080 844-847-4229
info@viridianbay.com
viridianbay.com

Home d,cor, cutlery and serveware, dinnerware, patio furniture and d,cor, garden sculptures, and more

Head Designer: Oana Alupoaie
Credit Cards: AMEX; MasterCard
Catalog Cost: Free
Catalog Circulation: Mailed 2 time(s) per year
Printing Information: in 4 colors
In Business: 2 years
Sales Volume: $1MM to $3MM

4865 VivaTerra
VivaTerra
7021 Wolftown-Hood Road
Madison, VA 22727 800-247-6799
Fax: 719-948-1905
customerservice@vivaterra.com
www.vivaterra.com

Eco friendly home furnishings and garden decorations

Credit Cards: AMEX; MasterCard
In Business: 11 years

4866 Walter Drake
Walter Drake
250 City Center
Oshkosh, WI 54906 920-231-3800
855-202-7393
www.wdrake.com

Bakeware, food storage, kitchen decor accessories, closet & bed accessories, storage organizers, small appliances, gadgets and tools.

Catalog Cost: Free
In Business: 69 years

4867 Wayfair
Wayfair
4 Copley Place
7th Floor
Boston, MA 02116 844-690-4149
www.wayfair.com

Home furnishings, kitchen & bathroom appliances

Chairman: Steve Conine
President: Niraj Shah
CFO: Michael Fleisher
Marketing Manager: Ed Macri
General Cousel: Enrique Colbert
Chief Merchandising Officer: Steve Oblak
VP of Sales & Service: Liz Graham
Catalog Cost: Free
In Business: 15 years

4868 West Elm
Williams-Sonoma, Inc.
3333 Bear St.
Space 231
Costa Mesa, CA 92626 714-662-1960
888-922-4119
Fax: 702-363-2541
customerservice@westelm.com
www.westelm.com

Furniture, bedding and bath for modern living

Chairman: Andrew Bellamy
President: Laura Alber
CFO: Sharon L McCollam
Marketing Manager: Patrick J Connolly
SVP & CIO: John Strain
Credit Cards: AMEX; MasterCard
Catalog Cost: Free
Catalog Circulation: Mailed 2 time(s) per year
Printing Information: 52 pages in 4 colors on Glossy Stock
Binding: Saddle Stitched
In Business: 13 years
Number of Employees: 80
Sales Volume: $4.3 MM

4869 Whispering Pines
Whispering Pines Catalog
43 Ruane Street
Fairfield, CT 06824-5837 203-307-5431
800-836-4662
spanian@whisperingpinescatalog.com
www.whisperingpinescatalog.com

Apparel, housewares, home furnishings, and decorative items with a rustic look; rustic wedding collection; rustic lifestyle collection; rustic holiday collection; rustic home collection

Chairman: Susan Kelly Panian
President: Mickey Kelly
theboss@whisperingpinescatalog.com
Credit Cards: AMEX; MasterCard
Catalog Cost: Free
Printing Information: 52 pages in 4 colors

4870 Wisteria
Wisteria
13780 Benchmark Drive
Farmers Branch, TX 75234 800-320-9757
Fax: 214-358-2953
customerservice@wisteria.com
www.wisteria.com

Home furnishing, nursery and garden supplies

Marketing Manager: Trisha Irwin
Credit Cards: AMEX; MasterCard; Visa
Catalog Cost: Free
Catalog Circulation: Mailed 12 time(s) per year
Printing Information: in 4 colors
In Business: 9 years
Number of Employees: 75
Sales Volume: 5.9MM

4871 World Art Group
World Art Group
8080 Villa Park Drive
Richmond, VI 23228 804-213-0600
Fax: 804-213-0700
orders@theworldartgroup.com
www.theworldartgroup.com

Wall décor.

In Business: 40 years

4872 Xander Blue
PO Box 798
Skaneateles, NY 13152 315-685-1092
Fax: 315-685-0267
info@xanderblue.com

Home furnishings

Appliances

4873 A Liss & Company
A Liss & Company Inc
51-55 59th Place
Woodside, NY 11377-7408 718-728-0600
800-221-0938
Fax: 718-728-1227
sales@alissco.com
www.alissco.com

Fire extinguishers, appliances, projection screens, lockers, bathroom accessories, shelving and toilet partitions.

President: Jeffrey Liss
Mailing List Information: Names for rent
In Business: 79 years
Number of Employees: 20

4874 AVAC Corporation
AVAC Corporation
2575 Fairview Ave. N
Suite 180
Roseville, MN 55113 651-222-0763
800-328-9430
Fax: 651-224-2674
info@avacorp.com
www.avaccorp.com

Vacuum cleaners, related parts and supplies

President: Russ Battisto
In Business: 39 years
Sales Volume: $10 Million

4875 Allergy Buyers Club
Allergy Buyers Group LLC
45 Braintree Hill Office Park
Suite 300
Braintree, MA 02184 781-419-5500
888-236-7231
Fax: 781-843-2163
www.allergybuyersclub.com

The leading retailer of air purifiers, bedding, dehumidifiers, furniture, humidifiers, lighting, steam cleaners, vacuum cleaners and water filters

President: Mercia Tapping
Credit Cards: AMEX; MasterCard; Visa
Catalog Cost: Free
In Business: 16 years
Sales Volume: Under $500M

4876 BrylaneHome

BrylaneHome
One New York Plaza
New York, NY 10004   www.brylanehome.com

Home furnishings, decor indoor and outdoor furniture.

CEO: Paul Tarvin
Catalog Cost: Free
In Business: 105 years
Number of Employees: 6400
Sales Volume: Over $1 Billion

4877 Earthstone Wood-Fire Ovens

Earthstone Wood-Fire Ovens
6717 San Fernando Rd
Glendale, CA 91201-1704   818-553-1134
                                           800-840-4915
              Fax: 818-553-1133
    info@earthstoneovens.com
    www.Earthstoneovens.Com

Wood and gas fired ovens for commercial and residential uses

Credit Cards: AMEX; MasterCard
In Business: 28 years
Sales Volume: $3MM to $5MM

4878 Feller US Corporation

Feller LLC
9100 Industrial Blvd NE
Leland, NC 28451-9037   910-383-6920
                                      800-736-7333
              Fax: 910-383-6921
    sales@feller-us.com
    www.feller-us.net

International and domestic power cords, cord set assemblers, appliance couplers and power entry modules

President: Gregor Kysely
CFO: Douglas Fox
Production Manager: Rod Linville
Regional Sales Manager: Rick Wilhelm
rick@feller-us.com
Senior Buyer/Planner: Adriana Kysely
adriana@feller-us.com
Quality Control: Ana Jimenez
ana@feller-us.com
Printing Information: 55 pages
In Business: 152 years
Number of Employees: 30
Sales Volume: $ 6 Million

4879 Gast Manufacturing Corporation

Gast Manufacturing, Inc.
2300 M-139 Highway
P.O. Box 97
Benton Harbor, MI 49023-0097   269-926-6171
              Fax: 269-927-0808
    www.gastmfg.com

Compressors, vacuum pumps

President: Warren E Gast
Marketing Manager: K Gast
In Business: 95 years
Number of Employees: 600
Sales Volume: $50MM to $100MM

4880 Good Time Stove

Good Time Stove Co.
188A Cape Street
PO Box 306
Goshen, MA 01032-306   413-268-3677
    Stoveprincess@GoodTimeStove.com
    www.goodtimestove.com

Restored antique ranges and stoves

President: Richard Richardson
In Business: 42 years

Number of Employees: 10
Sales Volume: $750,000

4881 Lehman's Non Electric Catalog

Lehman's
PO Box 270
Kidron, OH 44636   330-828-8828
                             888-438-5346
    Fax: 330-828-8270
    info@lehmans.com
    www.lehmans.com

Non-electric appliances, oil lamps, gas refrigerators, wood stoves, old fashioned toys, kitchenware, butchering, cheese making, water pumps, butter making, water filters, camping, gardening, farming

Chairman: Jay Lehman
President: Galen Lehman
Marketing Manager: Glenda Lehman Ervin
Credit Cards: MasterCard; Visa; Discover
Catalog Cost: $3
Mailing List Information: Names for rent
In Business: 59 years
Number of Employees: 90

4882 Parts and Supply Catalog

V&V Appliance Parts Inc.
27 W Myrtle Ave
Youngstown, OH 44507-1115   330-743-5144
                                              800-321-2704
              Fax: 800-743-3682
    info@vvapplianceparts.com
    www.vvapplianceparts.com

Appliance parts and testing equipment

Catalog Circulation: Mailed 1 time(s) per year
Printing Information: 382 pages on Newsprint
Binding: Perfect Bound

4883 Pure 'n Natural Systems

Pure n Natural Systems, Inc.
PO Box 1137
Streamwood, IL 60107-3332   630-372-9681
                                              800-237-9199
              Fax: 630-736-0542
    info@purennatural.com
    www.purennatural.com

Air and water purification systems

President: Joseph A Roy Jr
Credit Cards: AMEX; MasterCard
Catalog Circulation: to 200K
Average Order Size: $250
Printing Information: 30 pages in 4 colors on Glossy Stock
Press: Web Press
Binding: Saddle Stitched
Mailing List Information: Names for rent
P.O. Box 1137
Streamwood, IL 60107
In Business: 13 years
Number of Employees: 6

4884 Rada Cutlery

Rada Manufacturing Co.
P.O. Box 838
Waverly, IA 50611   319-352-5454
                            800-311-9691
              Fax: 800-311-9623
    customerservice@radamfg.com
    www.radacutlery.com

Cutlery and other cookware, cookbooks

President: Gary Nelson
Catalog Cost: Free
Printing Information: 32 pages in 4 colors
In Business: 69 years

4885 Wayfair

Wayfair
4 Copley Place
7th Floor
Boston, MA 02116   844-690-4149
    www.wayfair.com

Home furnishings, kitchen & bathroom appliances

Chairman: Steve Conine
President: Niraj Shah
CFO: Michael Fleisher
Marketing Manager: Ed Macri
General Cousel: Enrique Colbert
Chief Merchandising Officer: Steve Oblak
VP of Sales & Service: Liz Graham
Catalog Cost: Free
In Business: 15 years

4886 Wittus

Wittus, Inc.
40 Westchester Avenue
P.O. Box 120
Pound Ridge, NY 10576   914-764-5679
              Fax: 914-764-0465
    info@wittus.com
    www.wittus.com

European contemporary stoves, fireplaces and accessories

President: Niels Wittus
nw@wittus.com
Production Manager: Mark Fischer
Fulfillment: Joan Martin
Catalog Cost: Free
Catalog Circulation: to 25000
Average Order Size: $4
Printing Information: 20 pages in 4 colors on Glossy Stock
Press: Web Press
Mailing List Information: Names for rent
In Business: 39 years
Number of Employees: 5
Sales Volume: $2.11 Million

Bathroom

4887 American Standard

American Standard
1 Centennial Plaza
PO Box 6820
Piscataway, NJ 08855-6820   800-442-1902
                                              800-442-1902
    www.americanstandard-us.com

Fine porcelain bath tubs, toilet bowls, basins and accessories

Marketing Manager: Jeannette Long
CEO: Donald C. Devine
In Business: 140 years

4888 Coco Bidets Catalog

Bio Life Technologies
103 N Grand
Enid, OK 73701   580-977-2077
                          888-502-0375
              Fax: 580-701-4965
    support@biolifetechnologies.com
    www.biolifetechnologies.com

Bidets, bathroom vanities, electric bidet faucet, bidet toilet seats, and bathroom fixures

Credit Cards: AMEX; MasterCard; Visa
Catalog Cost: Free

4889 Home Decorators Collection

Home Decorators Collection
3074 Chastain Meadows Parkway
Marietta, GA 30066   800-245-2217
    www.homedecorators.com

Rugs, bar stools, bookshelves, coffe tables, mirrors, bathroom vanities, book cases and storage benches.

Catalog Cost: Free
Printing Information: 148 pages in 4 colors
Sales Volume: $300 Million

4890 Home Trends
Home Trends
Operations Center, 100 Beaver Rd.
PO Box 20403
Rochester, NY 14602-403   888-815-0814
                                 800-810-2340
                            Fax: 585-889-8686
customercare@qcidirect.com
www.shophometrends.com

Home care products and household cleaning products including the complete Fuller Brush line of cleaning products

President: Jane L Glazer
Marketing Manager: Larry Glazer
Production Manager: Scott Constantino
Buyers: Stacy Bershod
Credit Cards: AMEX; MasterCard; Visa; Discover
Catalog Cost: Free
Catalog Circulation: Mailed 12 time(s) per year to 60000
Average Order Size: $50
Printing Information: 76 pages in 4 colors on Glossy Stock
Press: Offset Press
Binding: Saddle Stitched
Mailing List Information: Names for rent
Will Trade Names: Yes
List Company: JAMI
New York, NY
In Business: 32 years
Number of Employees: 150
Sales Volume: $20MM to $50MM

4891 Indigo Wild
Indigo Wild
3125 Wyandotte Street
Kansas City, MO 64111   800-361-5686
                          Fax: 816-221-4035
                          www.indigowild.com

All natural bath and body products such as soaps, bath salts, lotions, balms, and oils

Catalog Cost: Free

4892 Kentwood Manufacturing
Kentwood Manufacturing
4849 Barden Court SE
Grand Rapids, MI 49512   616-698-6370
                          Fax: 616-698-6832
customerservice@kentwoodmfg.com
www.kentwoodmfg.com

Bathroom mirrors and decorative wood, lacquered and frameless wall mirrors

Marketing Manager: Doug West
Catalog Circulation: Mailed 1 time(s) per year
Printing Information: 36 pages in 2 colors on Matte Stock
Press: Web Press
Binding: Saddle Stitched
In Business: 58 years
Number of Employees: 25
Sales Volume: $2 Million

4893 Lands' End Home
Lands' End, Inc.
1 Lands' End Lane
Dodgeville, WI 53595   800-963-4816
                         Fax: 800-332-0103
                         www.landsend.com

Indoor and outdoor items for the home, includes bath, bedding and luggage.

Co-interim CEO: James Gooch
Co-interim CEO: James Boitano
Catalog Cost: Free
Printing Information: in 4 colors
Mailing List Information: Names for rent
List Company: Millard Group
In Business: 53 years
Number of Employees: 5300
Sales Volume: $1.42 Billion

4894 Mac the Antique Plumber
Mac the Antique Plumber
6325 Elvas Avenue
Sacramento, CA 95819   916-454-4507
                         800-916-BATH
                    Fax: 916-454-4150
                    www.antiqueplumber.com

Antique plumbing, bath accessories, lighting, hardware

President: Bryan Mc Intire
Credit Cards: MasterCard
Catalog Cost: $10
Catalog Circulation: Mailed 1 time(s) per year to 10000
Average Order Size: $225
Printing Information: 200 pages in 4 colors on Glossy Stock
Binding: Saddle Stitched
In Business: 25 years
Number of Employees: 7
Sales Volume: $500M to $1MM

4895 Madison Industries
Hostess Brands
279 5th Ave Floor 2
New York, NY 10016-6501   212-679-5110
                            800-223-1808
                       Fax: 212-779-0426
hostess@pwpartners.com
www.oldhbinc.info

Bath rugs and towels

Chairman: Robert Weinstein
President: Robert Weinstein
CEO: Gregory F. Rayburn
Number of Employees: 14

4896 Mallory Lane
Collections Etc., Inc.
PO Box 7985
Elk Grove Village, IL 60009-7985 620-584-8000
                            888-468-1666
                       Fax: 847-350-5701
www.collectionsetc.com

Home decor for the bedroom, bathroom and kitchen. Also available outdoor living accessories

President: Shelley Nandkeolyar
Marketing Manager: Karl Steigerwald
Fulfillment: Bruce Getowicz
CEO/Founder: Todd Lustbader
COO: Paul Klassman
Credit Cards: AMEX; MasterCard; Visa
Catalog Cost: Free
In Business: 40 years
Number of Employees: 200
Sales Volume: 12.7M

4897 Myson Towel Warmers
Myson, Inc.
45 Krupp Drive
Williston, VT 05495   802-654-7500
                         800-698-9690
                    Fax: 802-654-7022
info@mysoninc.com
www.Mysoninc.Com

Many styles of towel warmers

President: Neil MacPherson
Marketing Manager: Ron Ferrara
ron.ferrara@mysoninc.com
President/General Manager: Ray Farley
Technical Director: Bob Meekins
bob.meekins@mysoninc.com
Controller: Ryan Wasi
ryan.wasi@mysoninc.com
Catalog Circulation: Mailed 1 time(s) per year
Printing Information: 16 pages in 4 colors
Binding: Saddle Stitched
Sales Volume: $6 Million

4898 P.E. Guerin
P.E. Guerin
23 Jane Street
New York, NY 10014   212-243-5270
                        Fax: 212-727-2290
info@peguerin.com
www.peguerin.com

Bathroom fixtures, plumbing, cabinetry

President: Andrew F Ward
Catalog Cost: $40
Printing Information: 125 pages in 1 color on Glossy Stock
Press: Offset Press
In Business: 160 years
Number of Employees: 75
Sales Volume: 1MM-3MM

4899 PBteen
PBteen
3250 Van Ness Ave.
San Francisco, CA 94109   415-421-7900
www.pbteen.com

Furniture, bedding and decor for teens.

President: Sandra Stangl
Printing Information: 64 pages in 4 colors
In Business: 13 years
Sales Volume: $3 Billion

4900 Pioneer Linens
Pioneer Linens
210 Clematis Street
West Palm Beach, FL 33401   561-655-8553
                              800-207-5463
                         Fax: 561-655-8889
www.pioneerlinens.com

Home decor, gifts, candles, fragrances, table accessories, bedding and bath

President: Penny Murphy
Catalog Cost: Free
In Business: 103 years
Number of Employees: 25
Sales Volume: $5.03 Million

4901 Pottery Barn Bed and Bath
Pottery Barn
3250 Van Ness Ave.
San Francisco, CA 94109   415-421-7900
www.potterybarn.com

Home furnishings and accents for bed and bath.

President: Sandra Stangl
Catalog Cost: Free
Printing Information: 80 pages in 4 colors
Mailing List Information: Names for rent
Sales Volume: $3 Billion

4902 Pottery Barn Kids
Pottery Barn Kids
3250 Van Ness Ave.
San Francisco, CA 94109   415-421-7900
www.potterybarnkids.com

Children's furnishings, textiles, toys and accessories.

President: Sandra Stangl
Catalog Cost: Free
Printing Information: 132 pages in 4 colors
In Business: 17 years
Sales Volume: $3 Billion

4903 Simon's Kitchen & Bath
Simon's Hardware and Bath
421 3rd Avenue
New York, NY 10016-8151   212-532-9220
                            888-274-6667
                       Fax: 212-481-0564
www.simonsny.com

Decorative and industrial hardware, fixtures and accessories for bathroom and kitchen

President: Elias Chahine
elias@simonsny.com
Credit Cards: AMEX; MasterCard; Visa

In Business: 111 years
Number of Employees: 70
Sales Volume: $5MM to $10MM

4904 Sun-Mar Corporation
Sun-Mar Corp.
600 Main Street
Tonawanda, NY 14150 905-332-1314
800-461-2461
Fax: 905-332-1315
compost@sun-mar.com
www.sun-mar.com

Composting toilet systems

Manager: Dennis Forster
Credit Cards: AMEX; MasterCard; Visa
Catalog Cost: Free
Printing Information: on Glossy Stock
In Business: 44 years
Number of Employees: 30
Sales Volume: $8 Million

4905 Wayfair
Wayfair
4 Copley Place
7th Floor
Boston, MA 02116 844-690-4149
www.wayfair.com

Home furnishings, kitchen & bathroom appliances

Chairman: Steve Conine
President: Niraj Shah
CFO: Michael Fleisher
Marketing Manager: Ed Macri
General Cousel: Enrique Colbert
Chief Merchandising Officer: Steve Oblak
VP of Sales & Service: Liz Graham
Catalog Cost: Free
In Business: 15 years

Bedroom

4906 Charles P Rogers
Charles P. Rogers Bed Direct
26 West 17 Street
New York, NY 10011-5513 212-675-4400
800-582-6229
Fax: 212-675-6495
info@charlesprogers.com
www.Charlesprogers.Com

Handcrafted, solid wrought iron and brass beds

President: Linda Allen
Credit Cards: MasterCard; Visa
Catalog Cost: $3
Printing Information: 50 pages in 7 colors on Glossy Stock
Binding: Folded
In Business: 160 years
Number of Employees: 6
Sales Volume: $1MM to $3MM

4907 Company Store
The Company Store
500 Company Store Road
La Crosse, WI 54601-4477 800-323-8000
Fax: 800-238-0271
custserv@thecompanystore.com
www.thecompanystore.com

Comforters, duvets, pillows and more.

President: John Schomer
VP: David Pipkorn
Catalog Cost: Free
In Business: 104 years
Number of Employees: 300
Sales Volume: $7.4 Million

4908 Country Bed Shop
Country Bed Shop
328 Richardson Road
Ashby, MA 01431 978-386-7550
Fax: 978-386-7263
alan@countrybed.com
www.countrybed.com

Reproduction beds

President: Alan Pease
Chief Information Officer: David Wood
Catalog Cost: $4
Catalog Circulation: Mailed 2 time(s) per year to 400
Average Order Size: $2000
Printing Information: 32 pages in 1 color on Matte Stock
Press: Web Press
Binding: Saddle Stitched
Mailing List Information: Names for rent
In Business: 40 years
Number of Employees: 3
Sales Volume: $250,000

4909 Cuddledown
Cuddledown
14 Yarmouth Junction
Yarmouth, ME 04096 800-323-6793
800-323-6793
Fax: 207-761-1948
www.cuddledown.com

Down comforters, pillows and featherbeds

President: Chris Bradley
Marketing Manager: Debra Dyer
Production Manager: Gerhard Gross
In Business: 42 years

4910 DwellStudio
DwellStudio
New York NY 877-993-9355
www.dwellstudio.com

Home furnishings

Catalog Cost: Free
Printing Information: in 4 colors
In Business: 16 years

4911 High Fashion Home
3100 Travis Street
Houston, TX 77006 713-528-3838
888-685-3838
info@highfashionhome.com
www.highfashionhome.com

Furniture, fabric, drapery, lighting, accessories and gifts

4912 Kentwood Manufacturing
Kentwood Manufacturing
4849 Barden Court SE
Grand Rapids, MI 49512 616-698-6370
Fax: 616-698-6832
customerservice@kentwoodmfg.com
www.kentwoodmfg.com

Bathroom mirrors and decorative wood, lacquered and frameless wall mirrors

Marketing Manager: Doug West
Catalog Circulation: Mailed 1 time(s) per year
Printing Information: 36 pages in 2 colors on Matte Stock
Press: Web Press
Binding: Saddle Stitched
In Business: 58 years
Number of Employees: 25
Sales Volume: $2 Million

4913 Lands' End Home
Lands' End, Inc.
1 Lands' End Lane
Dodgeville, WI 53595 800-963-4816
Fax: 800-332-0103
www.landsend.com

Indoor and outdoor items for the home, includes bath, bedding and luggage.

Co-interim CEO: James Gooch
Co-interim CEO: James Boitano
Catalog Cost: Free
Printing Information: in 4 colors
Mailing List Information: Names for rent
List Company: Millard Group
In Business: 53 years

Number of Employees: 5300
Sales Volume: $1.42 Billion

4914 Lifekind Products
Lifekind
1415 Whispering Pines Lane
Suite 100
Grass Valley, CA 95945 530-477-5395
800-284-4983
Fax: 530-477-5399
www.lifekind.com

Organic mattresses and bedding

President: Walt Bader
Credit Cards: AMEX; MasterCard; Visa
Catalog Cost: Free
In Business: 19 years

4915 LittleMissMatched
MissMatched Inc
307 7th Avenue
Suite 501
New York, NY 10001 201-902-0056
customerservice@littlemissmatched.com
www.littlemissmatched.com

Mismatched girls socks, bedding, pajamas, accessorise, clothing and more

Co-Founder/CEO: Jonah Staw
Catalog Cost: Free

4916 Mallory Lane
Collections Etc., Inc.
PO Box 7985
Elk Grove Village, IL 60009-7985 620-584-8000
888-468-1666
Fax: 847-350-5701
www.collectionsetc.com

Home decor for the bedroom, bathroom and kitchen. Also available outdoor living accessories

President: Shelley Nandkeolyar
Marketing Manager: Karl Steigerwald
Fulfillment: Bruce Getowicz
CEO/Founder: Todd Lustbader
COO: Paul Klassman
Credit Cards: AMEX; MasterCard; Visa
Catalog Cost: Free
In Business: 40 years
Number of Employees: 200
Sales Volume: 12.7M

4917 PBteen
PBteen
3250 Van Ness Ave.
San Francisco, CA 94109 415-421-7900
www.pbteen.com

Furniture, bedding and decor for teens.

President: Sandra Stangl
Printing Information: 64 pages in 4 colors
In Business: 13 years
Sales Volume: $3 Billion

4918 Perfect Fit Industries
Perfect Fit
8501 Tower Point Drive
Charlotte, NC 28227-7851 704-815-2200
800-864-7618
Fax: 704-815-2460
custserv@pfisleep.com

Bedspreads, comforters and top treatments

President: Daniel A. Hammer
CFO: Jeffrey Kies
Marketing Manager: Carmen Waite
Senior Sourcing Manager: Terri Zagorski
Customer Care: Kim Holmes
Senior Graphic Designer: Angie Kendall
In Business: 83 years
Number of Employees: 23

4919 Pioneer Linens
Pioneer Linens
210 Clematis Street
West Palm Beach, FL 33401   561-655-8553
800-207-5463
Fax: 561-655-8889
www.pioneerlinens.com

Home decor, gifts, candles, fragrances, table accessories, bedding and bath

President: Penny Murphy
Catalog Cost: Free
In Business: 103 years
Number of Employees: 25
Sales Volume: $5.03 Million

4920 Pottery Barn
Pottery Barn
3250 Van Ness Ave.
San Francisco, CA 94109   415-421-7900
www.potterybarn.com

Home furnishings and accessories.

President: Sandra Stangl
Catalog Cost: Free
Printing Information: 156 pages in 4 colors
Mailing List Information: Names for rent
In Business: 67 years
Sales Volume: $3 Billion

4921 Pottery Barn Bed and Bath
Pottery Barn
3250 Van Ness Ave.
San Francisco, CA 94109   415-421-7900
www.potterybarn.com

Home furnishings and accents for bed and bath.

President: Sandra Stangl
Catalog Cost: Free
Printing Information: 80 pages in 4 colors
Mailing List Information: Names for rent
Sales Volume: $3 Billion

4922 Pottery Barn Kids
Pottery Barn Kids
3250 Van Ness Ave.
San Francisco, CA 94109   415-421-7900
www.potterybarnkids.com

Children's furnishings, textiles, toys and accessories.

President: Sandra Stangl
Catalog Cost: Free
Printing Information: 132 pages in 4 colors
In Business: 17 years
Sales Volume: $3 Billion

4923 RH Baby & Child
Restoration Hardware
15 Koch Rd.
Corte Madera, CA 94925   800-762-1005
www.rhbabyandchild.com

Distinctive and unique items for the home, including furniture, lighting, cabinet hardware, gardenware, fixtures, tools, books, devices and amusements.

CEO: Gary Friedman
Printing Information: 296 pages in 4 colors
Mailing List Information: Names for rent
In Business: 37 years
Number of Employees: 2900
Sales Volume: $1.5 Billion

4924 Room & Board
Room & Board
4600 Olson Memorial Hwy.
Minneapolis, MN 55422   800-301-9720
www.roomandboard.com

Home furnishings inspired by the Shaker, Asian, Danish, Arts & Crafts and Modern design movements.

Catalog Cost: Free
Printing Information: 240 pages
Mailing List Information: Names for rent

In Business: 36 years
Number of Employees: 715
Sales Volume: $400 Million

4925 Seventh Avenue Catalog
Seventh Avenue
1112 7th Ave
Monroe, WI 53566-1364   608-328-8400
800-356-9090
Fax: 608-328-8400

Bed, bath, home store.

Chairman: Raymond Kubly
President: John Baumann
CFO: Donald R Hughes
VP, Merchandising and Inventory: Ann Bush
VP, Global Sourcing: Chris Finley
Credit Cards: AMEX; MasterCard; Visa
Catalog Cost: Free
Catalog Circulation: Mailed 4 time(s) per year
Printing Information: 120 pages in 4 colors on Glossy Stock
Binding: Saddle Stitched
Mailing List Information: Names for rent
In Business: 30 years
Number of Employees: 600
Sales Volume: $56 MM

4926 Shades of Light
Shades of Light
14001 Justice Road
Midlothian, VA 23113   804-288-3235
Fax: 804-288-5029
info@shadesoflight.com
www.shadesoflight.com

Lighting, rugs, curtains and bedding

CFO: Denise McCarney
Catalog Cost: Free
Catalog Circulation: Mailed 1 time(s) per year
Printing Information: 74 pages in 4 colors on Glossy Stock
Binding: Saddle Stitched
In Business: 31 years
Number of Employees: 55
Sales Volume: $5MM to $10MM

4927 Snug Fleece Woolens
SnugFleece Woollens, Inc.
2740 Pole Line Rd
Pocatello, ID 83201-6112   208-233-9622
800-824-1177
Fax: 208-234-0936
www.snugfleece.com

Wool mattress covers and pillow shams

President: Frank Holden
Marketing Manager: Chase Rich
Production Manager: Chase Rich
In Business: 30 years
Number of Employees: 7
Sales Volume: $1,000,000 - $5,000,000

4928 The Company Store
The Company Store
500 Company Store Road
La Crosse, WI 54601-4477   608-791-6000
800-323-8000
Fax: 800-238-0271
CustServ@TheCompanyStore.com
www.thecompanystore.com

Linens, home decor, apparel, bath

President: John DiFrancesco
Catalog Cost: Free
Printing Information: 103 pages in 4 colors on Glossy Stock
Binding: Saddle Stitched
In Business: 103 years
Number of Employees: 120
Sales Volume: $6 Million

4929 The Electric Quilt Company
The Electric Quilt Company
419 Gould St.
Suite 2
Bowling Green, OH 43402-3047   419-352-1134
Fax: 419-352-4332
customerservice@electricquilt.com
www.electricquilt.com

Software, books and printables for quilters.

4930 Viridian Bay
Viridian Bay
377 Swift Avenue
South San Francisco, CA 94080   844-847-4229
info@viridianbay.com
viridianbay.com

Home d,cor, cutlery and serveware, dinnerware, patio furniture and d,cor, garden sculptures, and more

Head Designer: Oana Alupoaie
Credit Cards: AMEX; MasterCard
Catalog Cost: Free
Catalog Circulation: Mailed 2 time(s) per year
Printing Information: in 4 colors
In Business: 2 years
Sales Volume: $1MM to $3MM

4931 Wake Up Frankie
Wake Up Frankie
12717 Barrow Lane
Suite 14
Plainfield, IL 60585   630-420-2332
866-925-3872
Fax: 630-420-2202

Bedding and furniture for bedrooms

President: Frankie Trull
In Business: 14 years

Draperies & Wallpaper

4932 AL Ellis
A.L. Ellis, Inc.
113 Griffin Street
Fall River, MA 02724-4399   508-672-4799
Fax: 508-672-4808
customerservice@elliscurtain.com
www.elliscurtain.com

Curtains, draperies, chair pads, bedding & dust ruffles

President: A Linnwood Ellis III
Catalog Circulation: Mailed 2 time(s) per year
Printing Information: 60 pages
In Business: 97 years
Number of Employees: 25
Sales Volume: $1,000,000 - $5,000,000

4933 American Blind & Wallpaper Factory
American Blinds Wallpaper And More
1302 Waugh Drive
#943
Houston, TX 77019   800-575-8016
customerserviceteam@americanblinds.com
www.americanblinds.com

Rugs, wall art, lighting, curtains, home decor, shutters, paint, and more

Chairman: Dan Gilmartin
President: Steven Katzman
Marketing Manager: Monica Hardin
Production Manager: John Norris
Credit Cards: AMEX; MasterCard
Catalog Cost: Free
In Business: 50+ years
Number of Employees: 500-

4934 Arts & Crafts Textiles
Ann Wallace
PO Box 79341
Los Angeles, CA 90079   213-614-1757
info@annwallace.com
www.annwallace.com

Custom and stock home textiles in arts and crafts styles; curtains, shades, bedding, table linens, kits, period appropriate window hardware, fabric, hand embroidery and applique patterns

President: Ann Wallace
Catalog Cost: $10
Catalog Circulation: Mailed 52 time(s) per year to 5000
Average Order Size: $300
Printing Information: 20 pages in 4 colors on Matte Stock
Binding: Folded
Mailing List Information: Names for rent
In Business: 17 years
Number of Employees: 2
Sales Volume: $200,000

4935 Astrup Company
Trivantage
18401 Sheldon Road
Suite A
Middleburg Heights, OH 44130-5392 216-696-2800
800-786-7601
Fax: 216-696-0914
www.trivantage.com

Fabric, hardware - industrial supplies

Chairman: John Kirk
President: J W Kirk
In Business: 123 years
Number of Employees: 160
Sales Volume: $10,000,000 - $25,000,000

4936 Bella Coastal D‚cor
PO Box 297
Jenks, OK 74037-297 877-208-6215
info@bellacoastaldecor.com
www.bellacoastaldecor.com

Home decor

4937 Black Forest Decor
PO Box 297
Jenks, OK 74037-297 800-605-0915
info@blackforestdecor.com
www.blackforestdecor.com

Home decor

4938 Christmas Tree Shops
877-463-1549
www.christmastreeshops.com

Gifts, home decor, accessories

4939 Country Curtains
Country Curtains
705 Pleasant St.
Lee, MA 01238 413-243-1474
www.countrycurtains.com

Curtains in various lengths and widths, rods and hardware, top treatments, bedding, fabrics, pillows and home accents.

Catalog Cost: Free
Printing Information: 64 pages in 4 colors
In Business: 20 years
Number of Employees: 175
Sales Volume: $79 Million

4940 Country Ruffles
Village Discount Drapery
215 Raytheon Road
Bristol, TN 37620 423-968-9531
800-488-9531
contactus@countryruffles.com
www.countryruffles.com

Curtains, drapes and bedding

President: Dennis Houser
Credit Cards: AMEX; MasterCard
Catalog Cost: Free
Catalog Circulation: Mailed 1 time(s) per year
Printing Information: 55 pages in 4 colors
190 N. 7th St.
New Castle, CO 81647
In Business: 44 years

Number of Employees: 12
Sales Volume: $500M to $1MM

4941 Great Windows
Great Windows
8251 Preston Ct
Jessup, MD 20794 800-556-6632
Fax: 877-208-1051
support@greatwindows.com
www.greatwindows.com

Window treatments

President: Steve Freishtat
Number of Employees: 2
Sales Volume: $110,000

4942 High Fashion Home
3100 Travis Street
Houston, TX 77006 713-528-3838
888-685-3838
info@highfashionhome.com
www.highfashionhome.com

Furniture, fabric, drapery, lighting, accessories and gifts

4943 Hunter Douglas Window Fashions
Hunter Douglas
P.O.Box 740
Upper Saddle Rvr, NJ 07458-740 201-327-8200
800-789-0331
Fax: 201-327-7938
consumer@hunterdouglas.com
www.Hunterdouglas.Com

Window fashions

President: Marvin B Hopkins
Number of Employees: 7044

4944 Jayson Home
1885 N Clybourn Ave
Chicago, IL 60614 773-248-8180
800-472-1885
info@jaysonhome.com
www.jaysonhome.com

Furnishings and home accessories

4945 Paper White
Paper White
2915 Kerner Boulevard
Suite F
San Rafael, CA 94901 415-482-9989
Fax: 415-482-0990
pwlinens@paperwhitelifestyle.com
www.paperwhitelifestyle.com

Luxury linens for the bed, bath, table and window

President: Jan Dutton
Number of Employees: 15
Sales Volume: $1,000,000 - $5,000,000

4946 RH Modern
Restoration Hardware
15 Koch Road
Corte Madera, CA 94925 800-762-1005
www.restorationhardware.com

Home furnishings and d‚cor

Chief Executive Officer: Gary Friedman
Catalog Cost: Free
Catalog Circulation: Mailed 4 time(s) per year
Printing Information: 730 pages in 4 colors
In Business: 37 years
Number of Employees: 2900
Sales Volume: $1.5 Billion

4947 Rowley Company
230 Meek Road
Gastonia, NC 28056 800-343-4542
Fax: 704-868-9787
support@rowleycompany.com
www.rowleycompany.com

Home decor

Chief Executive Officer: William J. Taylor
EVP, Sales & Marketing: Kathy Hall

4948 Smith and Noble Windoware
Smith & Noble
1181 California Avenue
Corona, CA 92881-7233 800-248-8888
www.smithnoble.com

An exclusive selection of blinds, draperies, panels, and accessories

President: Ken Constable
Credit Cards: MasterCard; Visa
Catalog Cost: Free
Catalog Circulation: Mailed 11 time(s) per year
Printing Information: 44 pages in 4 colors
In Business: 30 years
Sales Volume: $20MM to $50MM

4949 Steve's Blinds & Wallpaper
Steve's Blinds & Wallpaper
6615 19 1/2 Mile Road
Sterling Heights, MI 48314-1408 586-262-5555
800-627-1572
Fax: 586-262-5603
irmak@stevesblinds.com
www.stevesblindsandwallpaper.com

Blinds, wallpaper, draperies and curtains

President: Steve Katzman
Credit Cards: AMEX; MasterCard
In Business: 28 years
Number of Employees: 25
Sales Volume: $1.5 Million

4950 Stevenson & Vestalury
Stevenson Vestal
2347 W Hanford Road
Burlington, NC 27215-6765 336-226-2183
800-535-3636
Fax: 800-533-6881
customerservice@stevensonvestal.com
www.stevensonvestal.com

Custom window and bed coverings, draperies, valences, shades, swags, cornices, bedspreads, screens, pillows, headboards

President: Dave Stevenson, Bill Vestal
Marketing Manager: Dave Gude
Director of Customer Service: Terri Yarbrough
Information Systems: Brian Jones
Personnel Department: Marian Hill
Catalog Cost: $100
Catalog Circulation: Mailed 2 time(s) per year
Average Order Size: $600
Printing Information: 350 pages in 1 color on Glossy Stock
Binding: Saddle Stitched
Mailing List Information: Names for rent
In Business: 32 years
Number of Employees: 100

4951 Z Gallerie
1855 West 139th Street
Gardena, CA 90249 800-358-8288
customerservice@zgallerie.com
www.zgallerie.com

Furniture, art, tableware and home decor

Fireplace Accessories

4952 Bella Coastal D‚cor
PO Box 297
Jenks, OK 74037-297 877-208-6215
info@bellacoastaldecor.com
www.bellacoastaldecor.com

Home decor

4953 Charmaster Products
Charmaster Products
2307 Highway 2 West
Grand Rapids, MN 55744 218-326-6786
Fax: 218-326-1065

Wood burning furnaces - forced air and hot water

President: Larry Lessin
Marketing Manager: Andrea Lessin
Credit Cards: MasterCard
Catalog Cost: Free
Average Order Size: $5000
Printing Information: 30 pages in 4 colors on Glossy Stock
Press: Web Press
Binding: Saddle Stitched
Mailing List Information: Names for rent
In Business: 43 years
Number of Employees: 12
Sales Volume: $499,000

4954 Country Iron Foundry
The Country Iron Foundry
1200 Rosemary Lane
Naples, FL 34103

800-233-9945
800-233-9945
Fax: 239-434-7207
info@firebacks.com
www.firebacks.com

Antique and contemporary design firebacks

President: Wendy Stoughton
Credit Cards: MasterCard; Visa
Catalog Cost: $3
Catalog Circulation: Mailed 2 time(s) per year
Average Order Size: $350
Printing Information: 36 pages in 4 colors on Matte Stock
Press: Web Press
Mailing List Information: Names for rent
In Business: 39 years
Number of Employees: 3
Sales Volume: $500M to $1MM

4955 Woodstock Soapstone Company
Woodstock Soapstone Company
66 Airpark Rd
West Lebanon, NH 03784-1683

603-298-5955
800-866-4344
Fax: 603-298-5958
info@woodstove.com
www.woodstove.com

woodstoves

President: Tom Morrissey
Sales Volume: $5MM to $10MM

Flags & Banners

4956 Armstrong Flag
American Made Flag Store
228 Andover Street
Wilmington, MA 01887

978-658-8077
888-553-5247
Fax: 978-658-8233
customerservice@americanmadeflagstore.com
www.americanmadeflagstore.com

State flags, flags of the world, sports flags and flag poles

President: Walter Armstrong III
Director; Treasurer: Jennifer F Armstrong
Credit Cards: AMEX; MasterCard
In Business: 16 years

4957 Flag-Works
Flag-Works over America, LLC
16 Kennedy Lane
Concord, NH 03301

603-225-2530
800-580-0009
Fax: 603-225-0071
customerservice@flag-works.com
www.flag-works.com

American flags, state, country, message, military flags and custom flags and banners; also flag poles and flag pole accessories

Owner: Patrick Page
Credit Cards: AMEX; MasterCard
Mailing List Information: Names for rent

In Business: 19 years
Number of Employees: 4
Sales Volume: $280,000

4958 Gorham Flag Center
Gorham Flag Center
376 Main St
Gorham, ME 04038-1314

207-839-4675
800-345-2999
Fax: 207-839-3952
flaginfo@gorhamflag.Com
www.GorhamFlag.Com

Flags and poles

President: Paul Auclair
Credit Cards: MasterCard; Visa
Catalog Cost: $4
Catalog Circulation: Mailed 1 time(s) per year to 5000
Printing Information: 50 pages in 4 colors
Number of Employees: 10-J
Sales Volume: Under $500M

4959 Handcrafted Applique Flags
Flag Fables Inc.
1472 Riverdale Road
Suite 4
West Springfield, MA 01089-4673

413-747-0525
800-257-1025
Fax: 800-214-4773
info@flagfables.com
www.flagfables.com

Decorative flags

Production Manager: Debbie Kogut
debbie@flagfables.com
Owner: Wendy Diamond
wendy@lagfables.com
Credit Cards: AMEX; MasterCard
Catalog Cost: $24
Catalog Circulation: Mailed 6 time(s) per year to 100M
Average Order Size: $50
Printing Information: in 4 colors on Matte Stock
Press: Web Press
Binding: Saddle Stitched
Mailing List Information: Names for rent
In Business: 30 years
Number of Employees: 20
Sales Volume: $500M to $1MM

4960 Praise Banners
Praise Banners
2810 Azalea Place
Nashville, TN 37204

615-298-3152
800-226-6377
Fax: 615-298-9231
customerservice@praisebanners.com
www.praisebanners.com

Church banners and flags

President: Drew Trotman
Credit Cards: AMEX; MasterCard
Printing Information: 68 pages
In Business: 24 years
Number of Employees: 15
Sales Volume: $1.6 Million

4961 Printed Products
FlagFables
1472 Riverdale Road
Suite 4
West Springfield, MA 01089-4673

413-747-0525
800-257-1025
Fax: 800-214-4773
info@flagfables.com
www.flagfables.com

Flags, mail wraps, yard decoration signs and more

Production Manager: Debbie Kogut
debbie@flagfables.com
Owner: Wendy Diamond
wendy@lagfables.com
Credit Cards: AMEX; MasterCard
Catalog Cost: $24

Catalog Circulation: Mailed 6 time(s) per year to 100M
Average Order Size: $50
Printing Information: in 4 colors on Matte Stock
Press: Web Press
Binding: Saddle Stitched
Mailing List Information: Names for rent
In Business: 31 years
Number of Employees: 20
Sales Volume: $500M to $1MM

4962 Quinn Flags
Quin Flag
581 W. CHESTNUT ST.
Hanover, PA 17331

717-630-8040
800-353-2468
Fax: 717-630-2661
info@quinnflags.com
www.quinnflags.com

Full range of United States flags, world flags, checkered flags and huge selection of digitally printed custom flags

President: Matt Quinn
CFO: Peter Comly
Production Manager: Sandy Rosewag
COO: Ryan Halvorsen
VP Sales: Bruce Kolbrener
Office Manager: Valerie Cromer
Credit Cards: AMEX; MasterCard; Visa
Catalog Cost: Free
In Business: 21 years

Furniture

4963 Available Plastics
Preproduction Plastics Inc.
210 N Teller St.
Corona, CA 92879

951-340-9680
Fax: 951-340-1048
sales@apiplastics.com
www.ppiplastics.com

Plastic furniture, PBC pipe and fittings, custom extruded, bent or fabricated PVC pipe and connectors, WetStuff patio, pool and spa accessory line, PVC furniture, FlowMax Gold Vacuum pipe

President: Steven Brown
Marketing Manager: Dana Gecker
Credit Cards: AMEX; MasterCard; Visa
Catalog Circulation: Mailed 3 time(s) per year
Average Order Size: $400
Printing Information: 6 pages in 4 colors on Glossy Stock
Press: Sheetfed Press
Binding: Folded
Mailing List Information: Names for rent
In Business: 26 years
Number of Employees: 85
Sales Volume: $10.7 Million

4964 Ball and Ball
Ball and Ball
463 W Lincoln Hwy
Exton, PA 19341

610-363-7330
800-257-3711
Fax: 610-363-7639
bill@ballandball.com
www.ballandball.com

Quality reproduction door locks, lighting, and hardware

General Manager: Billl Ball
Catalog Cost: $7
Printing Information: 108 pages in 1 color
In Business: 83 years
Number of Employees: 50
Sales Volume: $5MM to $10MM

4965 Brigger Furniture
99 Sadler Street
Gloucester, MA 01930

978-281-5276
800-451-7247
Fax: 978-282-0344
www.briggerfurniture.com

Furniture

4966 Brumbaugh's Furniture & Rug Catalog
Brumbaughs Fine Home Furnishings
I-30 West @ Linkcrest
West Fort Worth, TX 76008   817-244-9346
info@brumbaughs.com
www.brumbaughs.com

Fine home furnishings

4967 BrylaneHome
BrylaneHome
One New York Plaza
New York, NY 10004   www.brylanehome.com

Home furnishings, decor indoor and outdoor furniture.
CEO: Paul Tarvin
Catalog Cost: Free
In Business: 105 years
Number of Employees: 6400
Sales Volume: Over $1 Billion

4968 CB2
CB2
1860 W Jefferson Avenue
Naperville, IL 60540   630-388-4555
800-606-6252
Fax: 630-527-1448
www.cb2.com

Modern home and office furniture and accessories]
Chief Executive Officer: Neela Montgomery
Credit Cards: AMEX; MasterCard
Catalog Cost: Free
Catalog Circulation: Mailed 12 time(s) per year
Printing Information: 92 pages in 4 colors
In Business: 17 years
Sales Volume: $10MM to $20MM

4969 Cape Cod Treasure Chest
PO Box 185, N
Truro, MA 02652   888-381-5300
Fax: 866-538-9053
info@capecodtreasurechest.com
www.capecodtreasurechest.com

Decorative tiles, teak and cedar furniture

4970 Classic Designs by Matthew Burak
Classic Designs by Matthew Burak
84 Central Street
St Johnsbury, VT 05819-2329   802-748-9378
800-748-3480
Fax: 802-748-4350
legs@tablelegs.com
www.tablelegs.com

Turned and carved furniture parts from solid wood, table legs, bed posts, bun feet, table base kits and hardware
President: Matthew Burak
CFO: Mark Desrochers
Marketing Manager: Mark Desrochers
Catalog Cost: Free
Catalog Circulation: Mailed 12 time(s) per year to 400K
Average Order Size: $200
Printing Information: 54 pages in 4 colors on Glossy Stock
Press: Web Press
Binding: Saddle Stitched
Mailing List Information: Names for rent
In Business: 9 years
Number of Employees: 25
Sales Volume: $5MM to $10MM

4971 Cohasset Colonials
Cohasset Colonials
14 South Pleasant St.
Po Box 548
Ashburnham, MA 00143   978-827-3001
800-288-2389
Fax: 978-827-3227
cohassetcolonials.custservice@gmail.com
www.cohassetcolonials.com

Furniture, lighting and home accessories

4972 Country Casual
Country Casual
7601 Rickenbacker Drive
Gaithersburg, MD 20879   301-296-9195
800-289-8325
Fax: 301-296-9198
www.countrycasual.com

Comprehensive selection of high quality outdoor English style, solid teak garden furniture including benches, chairs, tables, trash receptacles, swings, planters, umbrellas and wicker furniture
President: Bobbie Goldstein
Credit Cards: AMEX; MasterCard; Visa
Mailing List Information: Names for rent
In Business: 40 years
Number of Employees: 30
Sales Volume: $3MM to $5MM

4973 Crow's Nest Trading Company
Crow's Nest Trading Company
3205 Airport Blvd
Wilson, NC 27896   800-900-8558
Fax: 800-900-3136
ldolliver@thecrowsnesttrading.com
www.thecrowsnesttrading.com

Rustic furniture, southwestern decor and women's western apparel
President: Doug Tennis
CFO: Gary Tennis
Catalog Cost: Free
Catalog Circulation: Mailed 4 time(s) per year
Printing Information: 84 pages in 4 colors on Glossy Stock
Press: Web Press
Binding: Saddle Stitched
In Business: 16 years
Number of Employees: 20
Sales Volume: $3MM to $5MM

4974 Demco Furniture Catalog
DEMCO
P.O. Box 7488
Madison, WI 53707-7336   608-210-8993
877-449-1797
Fax: 800-245-1329
international@demco.com
www.demco.com

Office, school, library supplies and furniture
Chairman: John Wall
President: Ed Muir
Credit Cards: AMEX; MasterCard; Visa
Catalog Cost: Free
Catalog Circulation: Mailed 1 time(s) per year
Printing Information: 600 pages in 4 colors
Mailing List Information: Names for rent
List Manager: Jeff McLaughlin
Number of Employees: 250
Sales Volume: $20MM to $50MM

4975 Design Toscano
Design Toscano
1400 Morse Ave
Elk Grove Village, IL 60007   847-952-0100
800-525-5141
Fax: 847-952-8992
www.designtoscano.com

Garden statues, indoor statues, home accents, furniture, jewelry and gifts
President: Michael Stopka
CFO: David Jones

Marketing Manager: Kim Hansen
COO: Kathleen Matej
Credit Cards: AMEX; MasterCard
In Business: 25 years
Number of Employees: 100
Sales Volume: $20MM to $50MM

4976 Design Within Reach
Design Within Reach
711 Canal St. 3rd Floor
Stamford, CT 06902   203-614-0750
800-944-2233
Fax: 203-614-0845
www.dwr.com

Well designed furniture usually found in designer showrooms to businesses, design professionals and consumers
Chairman: Rob Forbes
President: Kelly Spain
CFO: Ken La Honta
Credit Cards: AMEX; MasterCard
Catalog Cost: Free
Sales Volume: $1MM to $3MM

4977 Eldred Wheeler
Eldred Wheeler
199 Winter Street
Hanover, MA 02043   508-330-4182
800-779-5310
email@eldredwheeler.com
www.eldredwheeler.com

18th century handcrafted American reproduction furniture
President: Emmet Eldred
Catalog Cost: $1
Catalog Circulation: to 3M
Printing Information: 30 pages on Glossy Stock
Binding: Saddle Stitched
Mailing List Information: Names for rent
Will Trade Names: Yes
In Business: 40 years
Number of Employees: 70
Sales Volume: $3MM to $5MM

4978 Fine Wood Source Book
Hickory Printing Company
37 9th Street Place SE
Hickory, NC 28602-1215   828-328-1801
800-349-HKRY
Fax: 828-328-8954
info@hickorychair.com
www.hickorychair.com

Fine wood furnishings
President: Jay Reardon
CFO: Jeff Anderson
Marketing Manager: Laura Poland
Catalog Cost: $25
Catalog Circulation: to 3000
Printing Information: 200 pages in 4 colors on Glossy Stock
Binding: Perfect Bound
In Business: 93 years

4979 Ginny's
1112 7th Ave.
Monroe, WI 53566-1364   800-290-9514

Home products and furniture for bed and bath

4980 Green Design Furniture
Green Design Furniture
P.O. Box 17796
Portland, ME 04112   207-775-4324
800-853-4234
info@greendesigns.com
www.greendesigns.com

Wood furniture
Credit Cards: AMEX; MasterCard; Visa
Catalog Cost: $10
Catalog Circulation: Mailed 1 time(s) per year to 30000

Printing Information: 35 pages in 4 colors on Matte Stock
Press: Letterpress
Binding: Folded
Mailing List Information: Names for rent
In Business: 19 years
Number of Employees: 14
Sales Volume: $1.6 Million

4981 Guardian Custom Products
Guardian Custom Products
PO Box 10010
Perrysburg, OH 43552-9932   419-872-6400
800-444-0778
Fax: 419-872-4774
sales@guardian-tablepad.com
www.guardian-tablepad.com

Custom-fit table pads, fabric care products, storage bags and related accessories
Credit Cards: AMEX; MasterCard
In Business: 92 years

4982 I.O. Metro
PO Box 3417
Bentonville, AR 72712   888-223-5628
www.iometro.com

Modern ecclectic furniture, art and accessories
CEO: Lou Spagna

4983 Improvements
HSN Improvements LLC
5568 West Chester Road
West Chester, OH 45069-2914   800-634-9484
custserv@improvementscatalog.com
www.improvementscatalog.com

Furniture and decor, small appliances, shelving, electronics, pet supplies and home security items
President: Paul Tarvin
Credit Cards: AMEX; MasterCard; Visa
Catalog Cost: Free
Printing Information: 72 pages in 4 colors on Glossy Stock
Binding: Saddle Stitched
Mailing List Information: Names for rent
In Business: 16 years

4984 Land of Nod
8135 River Drive
Morton Grove, IL 60053   800-933-9904
Fax: 847-656-4750
customerservice@landofnod.com
www.landofnod.com

Furniture, beding, gear, toys, books and holiday decorations

4985 Levenger
The Levenger Store
420 South Congress Ave
Delray Beach, FL 33445-4696   561-276-2436
800-544-0880
Fax: 800-544-6910
Cservice@levenger.com
www.Levenger.Com

Collection of furnishings and accessories created to enhance your well-read life, you'll find bookcases, halogen lighting, desks, chairs, leather goods, plus personal and corporate gifts
President: Steve Leveen
CFO: Lori Leveen
Marketing Manager: Susan Devito
Production Manager: Lee Passarella
Fulfillment: Gerald Patterson
Founder: Steve Leveen
Founder: Lori Leveen
Buyers: Denise Tedaldi
Credit Cards: AMEX; MasterCard; Visa
Catalog Cost: Free
Catalog Circulation: Mailed 12 time(s) per year to 20MM

Average Order Size: $130
Printing Information: 76 pages in 4 colors on Glossy Stock
Press: Web Press
Binding: Saddle Stitched
Mailing List Information: Names for rent
List Manager: Susan Devito
List Company: Mokrynski & Associates
401 Hackensack Avenue
Hackensack, NJ 07601
2014885656
In Business: 28 years
Number of Employees: 270
Sales Volume: $20MM to $50MM

4986 Magnolia Hall
Magnolia Hall
49A Bryant Street
Jasper, GA 30143   404-351-1910
866-410-2755
Fax: 706-692-4068
belvedere@magnoliahall.com
www.magnoliahall.com

Victorian reproduction furniture and accessories
President: Barry Nerli
Co-Owner: Becky Nerli
Co-Owner: Barry Nerli
Credit Cards: MasterCard; Visa
Catalog Cost: Free
Catalog Circulation: Mailed 3 time(s) per year to 30000
Average Order Size: $400
Printing Information: 80 pages in 4 colors on Glossy Stock
Press: Web Press
Binding: Saddle Stitched
Mailing List Information: Names for rent
In Business: 52 years
Number of Employees: 5
Sales Volume: $7,50,000

4987 PBteen
PBteen
3250 Van Ness Ave.
San Francisco, CA 94109   415-421-7900
www.pbteen.com

Furniture, bedding and decor for teens.
President: Sandra Stangl
Printing Information: 64 pages in 4 colors
In Business: 13 years
Sales Volume: $3 Billion

4988 Pompanoosuc Mills
Pompanoosuc Mills
PO Box 238
Route 5
East Thetford, VT 05043   802-785-4851
800-757-4061
Fax: 802-785-4485
customerservice@pompy.com
www.pompy.com

Hardwood furniture
President: Dwight Sargent
Marketing Manager: Robert Chapin
Credit Cards: AMEX; MasterCard
Printing Information: on Glossy Stock
In Business: 42 years
Number of Employees: 150

4989 Pottery Barn
Pottery Barn
3250 Van Ness Ave.
San Francisco, CA 94109   415-421-7900
www.potterybarn.com

Home furnishings and accessories.
President: Sandra Stangl
Catalog Cost: Free
Printing Information: 156 pages in 4 colors
Mailing List Information: Names for rent
In Business: 67 years
Sales Volume: $3 Billion

4990 Pottery Barn Kids
Pottery Barn Kids
3250 Van Ness Ave.
San Francisco, CA 94109   415-421-7900
www.potterybarnkids.com

Children's furnishings, textiles, toys and accessories.
President: Sandra Stangl
Catalog Cost: Free
Printing Information: 132 pages in 4 colors
In Business: 17 years
Sales Volume: $3 Billion

4991 RH Modern
Restoration Hardware
15 Koch Road
Corte Madera, CA 94925   800-762-1005
www.restorationhardware.com

Home furnishings and d,cor
Chief Executive Officer: Gary Friedman
Catalog Cost: Free
Catalog Circulation: Mailed 4 time(s) per year
Printing Information: 730 pages in 4 colors
In Business: 37 years
Number of Employees: 2900
Sales Volume: $1.5 Billion

4992 Room & Board
Room & Board
4600 Olson Memorial Hwy.
Minneapolis, MN 55422   800-301-9720
www.roomandboard.com

Home furnishings inspired by the Shaker, Asian, Danish, Arts & Crafts and Modern design movements.
Catalog Cost: Free
Printing Information: 240 pages
Mailing List Information: Names for rent
In Business: 36 years
Number of Employees: 715
Sales Volume: $400 Million

4993 Scully & Scully
Scully & Scully
504 Park Avenue
New York, NY 10022-2298   212-755-2590
800-223-3717
customerservice@scullyandscully.com
www.scullyandscully.com

Gifts and home furnishings, fine china and crystal, reproduction antique furniture
President: Michael Scully
Credit Cards: AMEX; MasterCard; Visa
Catalog Cost: $4
Catalog Circulation: Mailed 4 time(s) per year
Printing Information: 72 pages in 4 colors on Glossy Stock
Mailing List Information: Names for rent
In Business: 83 years
Number of Employees: 20
Sales Volume: 10MM-20MM

4994 Seventh Avenue Catalog
Seventh Avenue
1112 7th Ave
Monroe, WI 53566-1364   608-328-8400
800-356-9090
Fax: 608-328-8400

Bed, bath, home store.
Chairman: Raymond Kubly
President: John Baumann
CFO: Donald R Hughes
VP, Merchandising and Inventory: Ann Bush
VP, Global Sourcing: Chris Finley
Credit Cards: AMEX; MasterCard; Visa
Catalog Cost: Free
Catalog Circulation: Mailed 4 time(s) per year
Printing Information: 120 pages in 4 colors on Glossy Stock
Binding: Saddle Stitched
Mailing List Information: Names for rent
In Business: 30 years

Number of Employees: 600
Sales Volume: $56 MM

4995 Sterling
ELK Group International
12 Willow Lane
Nesquehoning, PA 18240   800-613-3261
Fax: 866-613-3264
www.mysterlinghome.com

Lighting, accessories, wall decor and furniture

Chief Executive Officer: Bradford Smith

4996 Stickley
L & J G Stickley
One Stickley Drive
PO Box 480
Manlius, NY 13104   315-682-5500
Fax: 315-682-6306
www.stickley.com

Solid wood furniture

President: Aminy Audi
Credit Cards: MasterCard; Visa
Catalog Cost: $10
Printing Information: 84 pages
Number of Employees: 1600

4997 Sure Fit
Sure Fit Inc
8000 Quarry Road
Suite C
Alburtis, PA 18011   888-796-0500
Fax: 610-336-8995
customerservice@surefit.com
www.surefit.net

Machine washable, ready-made slipcovers

Marketing Manager: Kathleen Spero
CEO: Hugh R Rovit
VP Product Development: Nancy Cartisano
Credit Cards: AMEX; MasterCard
Catalog Circulation: Mailed 52 time(s) per year
Average Order Size: $144
Printing Information: 37 pages in 2 colors on Matte Stock
Press: Web Press
Binding: Saddle Stitched
Mailing List Information: Names for rent
Number of Employees: 100
Sales Volume: $500M to $1MM

4998 Telescope Casual Consumer Furniture
Telescope Casual Consumer Furniture
82 Church Street
Granville, NY 12832   800-451-0938
Fax: 800-458-3876
adv@telescopecasual.com
www.telescopecasual.com

Summer and casual furniture

Catalog Cost: Free
Catalog Circulation: Mailed 1 time(s) per year
to 25000
Printing Information: 60 pages in 4 colors on
Glossy Stock
Press: Letterpress
Binding: Saddle Stitched
In Business: 112 years

4999 Vanguard Furniture Company
Vanguard Furniture Company
109 Simpson Street
Conover, NC 28613   828-328-5601
Fax: 828-328-9816
info@vanguardfurniture.com
www.vanguardfurniture.com

**Stockist of Stetson Home Classics and many
more famous names in fine furniture**

5000 Victorian Furniture
Victorian Furniture Company
PO Box 241473
Montgomery, AL 36124   334-478-3365
877-356-6065
Fax: 334-478-3365
www.victorianfurnitureco.com

Victorian and French furniture reproductions

Credit Cards: AMEX; MasterCard; Visa
Catalog Cost: $7
Printing Information: 40 pages
Mailing List Information: Names for rent
In Business: 11 years

5001 Viridian Bay
Viridian Bay
377 Swift Avenue
South San Francisco, CA 94080   844-847-4229
info@viridianbay.com
viridianbay.com

Home d,cor, cutlery and serveware, dinnerware, patio furniture and d,cor, garden sculptures, and more

Head Designer: Oana Alupoaie
Credit Cards: AMEX; MasterCard
Catalog Cost: Free
Catalog Circulation: Mailed 2 time(s) per year
Printing Information: in 4 colors
In Business: 2 years
Sales Volume: $1MM to $3MM

5002 Warm Biscuit Bedding Catalog
Warm Biscuit Bedding
140 Fulton Street
4th Floor
New York, NY 10038-2562   800-231-4231
www.warmbiscuit.com

Vintage-inspired children's and nursery bedding, furniture, decor, and accessories

President: Vicki Bodwell
Catalog Circulation: Mailed 6 time(s) per year
Sales Volume: $1MM to $3MM

5003 Whitechapel Limited
Whitechapel Ltd.
PO Box 11719
Jackson, WY 83002-1719   307-739-9478
800-468-5534
Fax: 307-739-9458
info@whitechapel-ltd.com
www.whitechapel-ltd.com

Furniture maker; high quality hardware

President: Robert Dunstan
Credit Cards: AMEX; MasterCard
Catalog Cost: $5
Catalog Circulation: Mailed 1 time(s) per year
to 8000
Printing Information: 312 pages in 1 color on
Glossy Stock
Press: Web Press
Binding: Saddle Stitched
In Business: 28 years
Number of Employees: 6
Sales Volume: $500M to $1MM

5004 Wicker Furniture Catalog
Fran's Wicker & Rattan Furniture
295 State Route 10 E
Succasunna, NJ 07876   973-584-2230
800-372-6799
sales@franswicker.com
www.franswicker.com

Wicker furniture and accessories

VP/Treasurer: Fran Gruber
Credit Cards: AMEX; MasterCard
Catalog Circulation: Mailed 3 time(s) per year
Average Order Size: $150
Printing Information: 72 pages in 4 colors on
Matte Stock
Press: Web Press
Binding: Saddle Stitched

Mailing List Information: Names for rent
In Business: 50 years
Number of Employees: 50
Sales Volume: $5.3 Million

5005 Wicker Warehouse
Wicker Warehouse
195 S River St
Hackensack, NJ 07601   201-342-6709
800-274-8602
Fax: 201-342-1495
sales@wickerwarehouse.com
www.wickerwarehouse.com

Wicker and rattan furniture and gifts

President: Bob Ermillo
Operation Manager: Gary Pasquariello
Credit Cards: MasterCard
Catalog Cost: Free
Catalog Circulation: Mailed 1 time(s) per year
to 2MM
Printing Information: 72 pages in 4 colors on
Glossy Stock
Press: Web Press
Binding: Saddle Stitched
Mailing List Information: Names for rent
In Business: 37 years
Number of Employees: 10
Sales Volume: $5 Million

Hardware & Accessories

5006 AllMetal Manufacturing
AllMetal Manufacturing
25395 Pleasant Valley Road
Suite 145
Chantilly, VA 20152   703-850-1007
Fax: 703-563-9542
garys@allmetalman.com
www.allmetalman.com

Custom metal fabrication, sheet metal fabrication and laser cutting services

President: Paul Bickford
Catalog Cost: $5
Printing Information: 30 pages
Number of Employees: 4
Sales Volume: $270,000

5007 American Furniture Design
American Furniture Design Co.
PO Box 300100
Escondido, CA 92030-100   760-743-6923
Fax: 760-743-0707
americanfurniture@cox.net
www.americanfurnituredsgn.com

Woodworking plans, tools, brushes, hardware

President: Brian Murphy
CFO: Nancy Murphy
Marketing Manager: Chris Murphy
Production Manager: Kelly Krueger
Credit Cards: MasterCard
Catalog Cost: Free
Average Order Size: $25
Printing Information: 68 pages in 1 color on
Matte Stock
Press: Web Press
Binding: Saddle Stitched
Mailing List Information: Names for rent
In Business: 17 years
Number of Employees: 5
Sales Volume: $400,000

5008 Apollo: Your Packaging Expert
Apollo Technologies
1850 S Cobb Industrial Blvd
Smyrna, GA 30082-4908   770-433-0210
800-533-3548
Fax: 770-433-0132
customerservice@apolloind.com
www.Apolloind.Com

Aerosal products

President: Maria Callas
Printing Information: 22 pages
In Business: 43 years

5009 Bella Coastal D,cor
PO Box 297
Jenks, OK 74037-297   877-208-6215
info@bellacoastaldecor.com
www.bellacoastaldecor.com

Home decor

5010 Blaine Window Hardware
Blaine Window Hardware
17319 Blaine Dr.
Hagerstown, MD 21740   301-797-6500
800-678-1919
Fax: 888-250-3960
info@blainewindow.com
www.blainewindow.com

Replacement hardware for windows, doors, lockers, closet doors, custom screens, toilet compartments and components, patio door hardware; more than 20,000 parts; custom manufacturing

President: Margaret Blaine
Marketing Manager: Paula Ford
General Manager: Dave Crouse
Catalog Cost: Free
Printing Information: 80 pages in 1 color
Mailing List Information: Names for rent
In Business: 62 years
Number of Employees: 40
Sales Volume: $10MM to $20MM

5011 Decorative Hardware Studio
Decorative Hardware Studio
P.O. Box 627
Chappaqua, NY 10514-0627   914-238-5251
Fax: 914-238-4880
dhshardware@gmail.com
www.decorativehardwarestudio.com

Decorative hardware

President: Ron Prezner
Printing Information: 100 pages in 1 color
Number of Employees: 5
Sales Volume: $1MM to $3MM

5012 Delia's Contents
Delias
Po Box 6143
Westerville, OH 43086   866-293-3268
Fax: 800-335-4265
customerservice@deliasmerch.com
store.delias.com

Home accessories

Chairman: Chris Edgar
President: Steve Kahn
CFO: Evan Guillemin
Credit Cards: AMEX; MasterCard; Visa
Sales Volume: $500M to $1MM

5013 Erie Landmark
Erie Landmark Company
637 Hempfield Hill Road
Columbia, PA 17512   717-285-5853
800-874-7848
Fax: 717-285-9060
info@erielandmark.com
www.erielandmark.com

Custom designed plaques in cast bronze and aluminum

President: Paul W Zimmerman
Vice President: David L. Zimmerman
Secretary: Louise Harnish
General Manager: Andrea M. Zimmerman
Credit Cards: AMEX; MasterCard
Catalog Cost: Free
Average Order Size: $100
Printing Information: 8 pages in 4 colors on Matte Stock
Press: Sheetfed Press
Binding: Folded

Mailing List Information: Names for rent
In Business: 78 years
Number of Employees: 12
Sales Volume: $499,000

5014 Hardware Catalog
Lee Valley Tools
PO Box 1780
Ogdensburg, NY 13669-6780   613-596-0350
800-513-7885
Fax: 613-596-6030
customerservice@leevalley.com
www.leevalley.com

Router table insert plate, accessories.

President: Robin Lee
Marketing Manager: Paul Cathcart
Owner/President: Iain Campbell
In Business: 36 years

5015 Harwil Corporation
Harwil Corporation
541 Kinetic Dr
Oxnard, CA 93030   805-988-6800
800-562-2447
Fax: 805-988-6804
harwil@harwil.com
www.harwil.com

Complete line of fluid flow and liquid level switches, liquid level pump up/down controllers and pump emergency shutdown controllers for a wide range of industrial applications

VP and General Manager: Bruce Bowman
Credit Cards: AMEX; MasterCard; Visa
Catalog Cost: Free
In Business: 52 years
Number of Employees: 20-5
Sales Volume: $1,000,000 - $5,000,000

5016 Home & Garden
Whitehall Products
8786 Water Street
Montague, MI 49437   800-728-2164
Fax: 231-894-6235
www.whitehallproducts.com

Home and garden accents including weathervanes, bird feeders and more

President: Brad Bruns
CFO: Roger Buter
Marketing Manager: Jim Holz
President: Lorie Vanwerden
Credit Cards: AMEX; MasterCard; Visa
Catalog Cost: Free
Printing Information: 35 pages
In Business: 69 years
Number of Employees: 150
Sales Volume: $16.6 Million

5017 Horton Brasses
Horton Brasses, Inc.
49 Nooks Hill Road
Cromwell, CT 06416   860-635-4400
800-754-9127
Fax: 860-635-6473
contact@horton-brasses.com
www.horton-brasses.com

Brass and wrought iron reproduction hardware for furniture and cabinetry, handles, knobs, latches, hinges and slides

President: Barbara Rockwell
Credit Cards: MasterCard; Visa
Catalog Cost: $4
Printing Information: 64 pages in 4 colors on Glossy Stock
Press: Sheetfed Press
Binding: Saddle Stitched
Mailing List Information: Names for rent
In Business: 81 years
Number of Employees: 15
Sales Volume: $3MM to $5MM

5018 Kennedy Hardware
Kennedy Hardware, LLC
10655 Andrade Drive
Zionsville, IN 46077-9230   317-873-1316
800-621-1245
Fax: 317-873-8662
philken@kennedyhardware.com
www.kennedyhardware.com

Antique hardware and parts for Hoosier cabinets, general furniture hardware, keys, locks

President: Phyllis Kennedy
CFO: Philip D Kennedy
Credit Cards: MasterCard; Visa
Catalog Cost: $3
Catalog Circulation: to 2000
Average Order Size: $30
Printing Information: 72 pages in 1 color on Glossy Stock
Press: Sheetfed Press
Binding: Saddle Stitched
Mailing List Information: Names for rent
In Business: 31 years
Number of Employees: 3
Sales Volume: $750,000

5019 Personalized Plaques Catalog
Whitehall Products
8786 Water Street
Montague, MI 49437   800-728-2164
Fax: 231-894-6235
www.whitehallproducts.com

Personalized name and address plaques

President: Brad Bruns
CFO: Roger Buter
Marketing Manager: Jim Holz
President: Lorie Vanwerden
Credit Cards: AMEX; MasterCard
Catalog Cost: Free
Printing Information: 35 pages
In Business: 69 years
Number of Employees: 150
Sales Volume: $16.6 Million

5020 Pottery Barn Bed and Bath
Pottery Barn
3250 Van Ness Ave.
San Francisco, CA 94109   415-421-7900
www.potterybarn.com

Home furnishings and accents for bed and bath.

President: Sandra Stangl
Catalog Cost: Free
Printing Information: 80 pages in 4 colors
Mailing List Information: Names for rent
Sales Volume: $3 Billion

5021 Quality Saw & Knife Company
Quality Saw & Knife Company
115 Otis St
West Babylon, NY 11704-1429   631-491-4747
800-662-7297
Fax: 631-491-6740
techinfo@qualitysaw.com
www.qualitysaw.com

Custom made saw blades for the framer

President: Skip Luberto
Credit Cards: AMEX; MasterCard
In Business: 31 years
Number of Employees: 10
Sales Volume: $1-3 Million

5022 RH Baby & Child
Restoration Hardware
15 Koch Rd.
Corte Madera, CA 94925   800-762-1005
www.rhbabyandchild.com

Distinctive and unique items for the home, including furniture, lighting, cabinet hardware, gardenware, fixtures, tools, books, devices and amusements.

CEO: Gary Friedman
Printing Information: 296 pages in 4 colors

Mailing List Information: Names for rent
In Business: 37 years
Number of Employees: 2900
Sales Volume: $1.5 Billion

5023 RH Holiday

Restoration Hardware
15 Koch Rd.
Corte Madera, CA 94925   800-762-1005
www.restorationhardware.com

Apparel, decorations, toys and accessories.

CEO: Gary Friedman
Printing Information: 380 pages in 4 colors
In Business: 37 years
Number of Employees: 2900
Sales Volume: $1.5 Billion

5024 RH Lighting

Restoration Hardware
15 Koch Rd.
Corte Madera, CA 94925   800-762-1005
www.restorationhardware.com

Distinctive fixtures, from chandeliers to sconces.

CEO: Gary Friedman
Printing Information: 220 pages in 4 colors
In Business: 37 years
Number of Employees: 2900
Sales Volume: $1.5 Billion

5025 Reemay

Reemay
PO Box 511
Old Hickory, TN 37138-511   615-847-7000
Fax: 615-847-7068
www.fiberwebfiltration.com

Housewrap

President: Migo Nalbantyan
Number of Employees: 500
Sales Volume: $50MM to $100MM

5026 Relay Specialties

Relay Specialties,Inc
PO Box 7000
Oakland, NJ 07436-7000   201-337-1000
800-526-5376
Fax: 201-337-1862
sales@relayspec.com
www.relayspec.com

Indusrtial electronic components specializing in relays, switches, circuit breakers, terminal blocks, timers, sensors, controls and thousands ofother electromechanical components

President: Barry Sauer
Credit Cards: AMEX; MasterCard; Visa
Catalog Cost: Free
In Business: 41 years
Number of Employees: 45

5027 Rowley Company

230 Meek Road
Gastonia, NC 28056   800-343-4542
Fax: 704-868-9787
support@rowleycompany.com
www.rowleycompany.com

Home decor

Chief Executive Officer: William J. Taylor
EVP, Sales & Marketing: Kathy Hall

5028 START International

START International
4270 Airborn Drive
Addison, TX 75001   972-248-1999
800-259-1986
Fax: 972-248-1991
info@startinternational.com
www.startinternational.com

Optical inspection devices, tape and label dispensers, non-adhesive cutters and specialty items

Credit Cards: AMEX; MasterCard; Visa
Catalog Cost: Free
Printing Information: 24 pages
In Business: 34 years
Sales Volume: $1 million

5029 Salice

Salice America Inc.
2123 Crown Centre Dr
Charlotte, NC 28227-7701   704-841-7810
800-222-9652
Fax: 704-841-7808
info.salice@saliceamerica.com
www.Saliceamerica.Com

Concealed drawer slides, shock absorber for cabinets doors

President: Luciano Salice
CFO: Massimo Salice
Marketing Manager: Matteo Fregosi
IT Manager: Jeff Michelle
Controller: Lor Miller
Printing Information: 8 pages
In Business: 26 years
Number of Employees: 25

5030 Universal Fog Systems

Universal Fog Systems
2145 E Riverdale St.
Mesa, AZ 8521   602-254-9114
800-432-6478
Fax: 602-254-9191
info@unifog.com
www.unifog.com

High pressure misting pumps, nozzles, slip-lok fittings, tubing, solenoid valves and brass fittings

President: Tom Bontems
Founder: Tom Bontems
Catalog Cost: Free
Printing Information: 18 pages
In Business: 26 years
Number of Employees: 5
Sales Volume: $1,000,000

5031 Van Dyke's Restorers

Van Dykes Restorers
Po Box 52
Louisiana, MO 63353   800-237-8833
Fax: 573-754-8608
customerservice@vandykes.com
www.vandykes.com

Antique-style home remodeling products, decorative home accessories, very uniuqe product mix

President: Tim Judge
CFO: Ellen Judge
Buyers: Ellen & Tim Judge
Credit Cards: MasterCard; Visa; Discover
Catalog Cost: Free
Catalog Circulation: Mailed 1 time(s) per year
Printing Information: 80 pages in 4 colors on Glossy Stock
Press: Web Press
Binding: Saddle Stitched
Mailing List Information: Names for rent
Number of Employees: 20-O
Sales Volume: $1MM to $3MM

5032 Vintage Hardware

Vintage Hardware & Lighting
2000 W Sims Way
Port Townsend, WA 98368   360-379-9030
Fax: 360-379-9029
sales@vintagehardware.com
www.vintagehardware.com

Over 3000 reproduction hardware items, plus more than 200 reproduction lights from neo-rococo, victorian, art deco, and turn-of-the-century periods

President: Kenneth Kelly
Marketing Manager: Ian McDonald
Credit Cards: AMEX; MasterCard
Catalog Cost: Free

Printing Information: 135 pages in 4 colors
Mailing List Information: Names for rent
In Business: 37 years

5033 Whatever Works Catalog

Whatever Works
PO Box 3339
Chelmsford, MA 01824-939   877-756-5053
800-499-6757
Fax: 800-866-3235
help@whateverworks.com
www.whateverworks.com

Solutions for the home, office and garden

President: David Krings
Catalog Cost: Free
Printing Information: in 3 colors
In Business: 17 years

5034 Windmill Water Pump & Hand Pump Catalog

Kansas Wind Power
13569 214th Road
Holton, KS 66436-8138   785-364-4407
Fax: 785-364-4407
www.kansaswindpower.net

Cistern pumps, hand pumps, cylinders, windmill water pumps and replacement parts

Chairman: Roy Hallauer
Owner/President: Mike Eubanks
Finance Manager/Purchasing Exec: Doris Yonke
Credit Cards: MasterCard
Catalog Cost: $5
In Business: 39 years
Number of Employees: 1
Sales Volume: $200,000

5035 Woodwright Company

The Woodwright Company
5753 NC 58 North
Elm City, NC 27822   252-243-9663
877-887-9663
Fax: 252-237-5502
thewoodwrightco@gmail.com
www.thewoodwrightco.com

Wood lamp post

Credit Cards: MasterCard; Visa
Catalog Cost: Free
Average Order Size: $200
Number of Employees: 4
Sales Volume: $500M to $1MM

5036 Wooster Products

Wooster Products,Inc
1000 Spruce Street
PO Box 6005
Wooster, OH 44691-4654   330-264-2844
800-321-4936
Fax: 330-262-4151
tim@wooster-products.com
www.wooster-products.com

Safety products including anti-slip tread and tape, deck covering,etc.

President: G Arora
Marketing Manager: Kris Bennett
kris@wooster-products.com
Sales Manager (South): Chuck Hess
ceh@wooster-products.com
Sales Manager (Midwest, Northeast &: Tim Brennan
tim@wooster-products.com
*Sales Manager (Central):*Ben Geiser
ben@wooster-products.com
Credit Cards: AMEX; MasterCard
Catalog Cost: Free
In Business: 91 years
Number of Employees: 80
Sales Volume: $12 Million

Lighting

5037 All Pro Sound
AP Sound, Inc.
806 Beverly Parkway
Pensacola, FL 32505   850-432-5780
                            800-925-5776
                       Fax: 850-432-0844
www.allprosound.com

Musical instruments, products and accessories for audio, video, and lighting
Credit Cards: AMEX; MasterCard
Catalog Cost: Free
In Business: 30+ years

5038 American Light Source
American Light Source
215 Bobby Jones Expy
Martinez, GA 30907-3404   800-741-0571
                       Fax: 706-868-5083
service@americanlightsource.com
www.americanlightsource.com

Light fixtures and ceiling fans
Credit Cards: AMEX; MasterCard; Visa
Catalog Cost: $5
Printing Information: 170 pages in 4 colors

5039 Artful Home
Artful Home
931 E Main Street
Suite 9
Madison, WI 53703   608-257-2590
                            877-223-4600
                       Fax: 608-257-2690
info@artfulhome.com
www.artfulhome.com

Apparel, jewelry, gifts, ceramics, art glass, wall art, ornaments, lighting and furniture
Chairman: Scott Potter
President: Toni Sikes
CFO: Bill Lathrop
Marketing Manager: Terry Nelson
CEO: Lisa Bayne
VP of Finance: Bill Lathrop
Credit Cards: AMEX; MasterCard
Catalog Cost: Free
Catalog Circulation: Mailed 4 time(s) per year
Printing Information: 60 pages
In Business: 30 years
Number of Employees: 35
Sales Volume: $3.1 Million

5040 Aurora Decklights
Aurora Decklights
960 E. Milwaukee Street
Whitewater, WI 53190-1986   800-603-3520
                       Fax: 262-472-6268
customerservice@auroradecklighting.com
www.auroradecklighting.com

Assortment of post caps, post caps 12x12, high end fence & deck accessories, cadillac lighting for decks & fencing, decklighting for all size posts available in solar, low voltage and line voltage
President: Geoff Hale
Fulfillment: Geoff Hale
Buyers: Jay Savignac
Catalog Cost: Free
Catalog Circulation: Mailed 1 time(s) per year to 3000
Average Order Size: $350
Printing Information: 20 pages on Glossy Stock
Press: Letterpress
Mailing List Information: Names for rent
In Business: 11 years
Number of Employees: 20
Sales Volume: $1,000,000

5041 Brass Light Gallery
Brass Light Gallery
1101 W St Paul Avenue
Milwaukee, WI 53233   414-271-8300
                            800-243-9595
                       Fax: 800-505-9404
customerservice@brasslight.com
www.newclassicsbrasslight.com/Default.asp

Handcrafted architectural lighting made in Milwaukee for over 30 years in traditional and comtemporary styles with 18 metal finishes
President: Stephen Kaniewski
Marketing Manager: Margaret Howland
mhowland@brasslight.com
Credit Cards: MasterCard
Catalog Circulation: to 3000
In Business: 41 years
Number of Employees: 10
Sales Volume: $1 Million

5042 Bulbtronics
Bulbtronics
45 Banfi Plaza N
Farmingdale, NY 11735-1539   800-654-8542
                       Fax: 631-249-6066
custservdept@bulbtronics.com
www.bulbtronics.com

Light bulbs
President: Bruce Thaw
Marketing Manager: John Roberts
Catalog Cost: Free
In Business: 41 years
Sales Volume: $20MM to $50MM

5043 Classic Accents
Classic Accents
13631 Brest Street
Southgate, MI 48195-1702   734-284-7661
                            800-245-7742
                       Fax: 734-284-7185
classicaccents@bignet.net
www.classicaccents.net

Push button light switches, decorative and plain wall plates, dimmer single, and 3-way
President: Peter Brevoort
Marketing Manager: Ed Richter
Catalog Cost: $2
Mailing List Information: Names for rent
In Business: 11 years

5044 Cohasset Colonials
Cohasset Colonials
14 South Pleasant St.
Po Box 548
Ashburnham, MA 00143   978-827-3001
                            800-288-2389
                       Fax: 978-827-3227
cohassetcolonials.custservice@gmail.com
www.cohassetcolonials.com

Furniture, lighting and home accessories

5045 Copper House
The Copper House
1747 Dover Rd.
Rte. 4
Epsom, NH 03234-1   603-736-9798
                            800-281-9798
                       Fax: 603-736-9798
www.thecopperhouse.com

Brass and copper lighting, copper weathervanes
President: Tom Leclair
Buyers: Bruce L Coutu
Credit Cards: AMEX; MasterCard
Catalog Cost: $4
Average Order Size: $125
Printing Information: 33 pages in 4 colors
In Business: 40 years
Number of Employees: 10

5046 Crystal Farm
Crystal Farm
18 Antelope Drive
Redstone, CO 81623-9401   970-963-2350
crystalfarm@crystalfarm.com
www.crystalfarm.com

Antler chandeliers and furniture
President: Stephen Kent
Marketing Manager: Joan Benson
Catalog Cost: $25
Printing Information: 56 pages in 4 colors
Mailing List Information: Names for rent
Sales Volume: $1MM to $3MM

5047 Day-Ray Products
Day-Ray Products
1133 Mission Street
PO Box 189
South Pasadena, CA 91031-189 626-799-3549
                            800-432-9729
                       Fax: 626-799-3804
customer_service@day-ray.com
www.Day-Ray.Com

Fluorescent ballasts, lamps, work lights and inspection lamps
President: Peter Kingston
CFO: Linda Kingston
Marketing Manager: Rick Rice
In Business: 74 years
Number of Employees: 38
Sales Volume: $1,000,000 - $5,000,000

5048 Dazor Manufacturing Corporation
Dazor Manufacturing Corporation
2079 Congressional Dr.
St Louis, MO 63146   314-652-2400
                            800-345-9103
                       Fax: 314-652-2069
info@dazor.com
www.dazor.com

Lighting, magnifiers, video microscopes
Chairman: Herbert Hogrebe
President: Stan Hogrebe
CFO: Karen Kyle
CEO: Mark Hogrebe
Marketing Executive: Kirk Cressey
Buyers: Richard Harding
Credit Cards: MasterCard; Visa
Catalog Cost: Free
Catalog Circulation: Mailed 1 time(s) per year to 20M
Printing Information: 8 pages in 1 color on Matte Stock
Binding: Saddle Stitched
Mailing List Information: Names for rent
List Manager: Tony Roldan
List Company: Roldan Marketing International
In Business: 77 years
Number of Employees: 25
Sales Volume: $4.9 Million

5049 Full Spectrum Lighting
Full Spectrum Solutions, Inc.
PO Box 1087
Jackson, MI 49204   517-783-3800
                            888-574-7014
                       Fax: 517-783-3802
sales@fullspectrumsolutions.com
www.fullspectrumsolutions.com

Lamps and light fixtures for home and office
President: Michael Nevins
Marketing Manager: Joelle Kalhagen
Credit Cards: AMEX; MasterCard
In Business: 18 years

5050 Hammerworks
Lighting By Hammerworks
6 Fremont St
Worcester, MA 01603   603-279-7352
                            888-499-5519
                       Fax: 603-279-7352
hwhg@comcast.net
www.hammerworks.com

Primitive chandeliers, lanterns, arts and crafts

Partner: Mark Rochefor
Partner: Thomas Sauriol
Catalog Cost: $5
Printing Information: 56 pages
In Business: 36 years
Number of Employees: 23

5051 Havis Inc

Havis Inc
75 Jacksonville Road
Warminster, PA 18974   215-957-0720
800-524-9900
Fax: 215-957-0729
sales@havis.com
www.customers.havis.com

Lighting equipment

President: Joseph Bernert Sr
CFO: Steve Ferraro
Marketing Manager: Heather Miller
CEO: Joe Bernert
Director of Engineering: Bruce Jonik
Director of Operations: Pete Spera
Number of Employees: 80
Sales Volume: Under $500M

5052 Historic Housefitters Company

Historic Housefitters Co., Inc.
287 New Milford Turnpike (Rte 202)
PO Box 2305
New Preston, CT 06777-1606   860-619-0400
800-247-4111
Fax: 860-619-0243
historic@historichousefitters.com
www.historichousefitters.com

Eighteenth century period hardware and light fixtures, authentic hand-forged iron thumb latches, strap hinges, hand H-L hinges, fireplace tools, and hearth cooking equipment

President: David Sposato
Credit Cards: MasterCard; Visa
Catalog Cost: $5
Catalog Circulation: Mailed 1 time(s) per year to 20000
Average Order Size: $200
Printing Information: 60 pages in 4 colors on Glossy Stock
Press: Sheetfed Press
Binding: Saddle Stitched
In Business: 30 years
Number of Employees: 4
Sales Volume: 1,000,000 - 3,000,000

5053 House of Troy

House of Troy
902 Silver Ridge Road
Hyde Park, VT 05655-9396   802-888-7984
800-428-5367
Fax: 888-881-7952
customerservice@houseoftroy.com
www.houseoftroy.com

Handcrafted lighting products such as piano and desk lamps, floor and table lamps, wall sconces, cabinet lighting, task and specialty lamps

Chairman: Everett Bailey
President: Malcolm Tripp
CFO: Chuck Hogan
COO: William Brown
Director: Kipp Lykins
Catalog Cost: $15
Printing Information: 180 pages
In Business: 67 years
Number of Employees: 34
Sales Volume: $3.6 Million

5054 Hurley Patentee Manor Lighting

Hurley Patentee Lighting
464 Old Route 209
Hurley, NY 12443-5926   845-331-5414
800-247-5414
Fax: 845-331-5414
www.Hurleypatenteelighting.Com

Authentic colonial lighting fixtures, hand-crafted on premises

President: Wayne Waligurski
Marketing Manager: Carolyn M Waligurski
Credit Cards: MasterCard; Visa
Catalog Cost: $3
Average Order Size: $300
Printing Information: 38 pages in 1 color on Matte Stock
Mailing List Information: Names for rent
In Business: 30 years
Number of Employees: 5
Sales Volume: 500M-1MM

5055 Idaho Wood Lighting

Idaho Wood Lighting
PO Box 488
258 McGhee Road
Sandpoint, ID 83864-488   208-263-9521
800-635-1100
Fax: 208-263-3102
www.idahowood.com

Landscape lighting

President: Leon Lewis
Marketing Manager: Leon Lewis
Production Manager: Leon Lewis
Credit Cards: MasterCard; Visa
Catalog Circulation: to 60K
Printing Information: 20 pages
In Business: 33 years
Number of Employees: 7

5056 JKL Components Corporation

JKL Components Corporation
13343 Paxton Street
Pacoima, CA 91331-2340   818-896-0019
800-421-7244
Fax: 818-897-3056
jkl@jkllamps.com
www.jkllamps.Com

Miniature lighting products

Chairman: Kent Koerting
President: Joe Belas
CFO: Bob Levine
Marketing Manager: Sherry Carpenter
Production Manager: Brian Woodruff
Fulfillment: Don Sonntag
Credit Cards: MasterCard; Visa
Printing Information: 64 pages
In Business: 43 years
Number of Employees: 40
Sales Volume: $ 17 Million

5057 King's Chandelier

King's Chandelier
729 South Van Buren Road
Highway 14 South
Eden, NC 27288   336-623-6188
Fax: 336-627-9935
crystal@chandelier.com
www.chandelier.com

Czech, Venetian, and Strass crystal chandeliers and lighting fixtures and Victorian gaslight reproductions

President: Franklin King Ricks
Marketing Manager: Nancy Talbert
Credit Cards: MasterCard; Visa
Catalog Cost: $5
Catalog Circulation: to 10M
Printing Information: 40 pages
In Business: 80 years
Number of Employees: 8
Sales Volume: $1,000,000 - $5,000,000

5058 Koehler Bright Star

Koehler Bright Star
380 Stewart Road
Hanover Twp, PA 18706-1459   570-825-1900
800-788-1696
Fax: 570-825-7108
sales@flashlight.com
www.Flashlight.Com

Personal, area and equipment lighting

President: Mark Dirsa
CFO: Lauria Cywinski
Marketing Manager: June Dutka
Production Manager: Mark Dirsa
Credit Cards: MasterCard; Visa
Catalog Circulation: to 4M
Printing Information: 32 pages
In Business: 92 years
Number of Employees: 110

5059 Lamp Glass

Lamp Glass
PO Box 1387
Arlington, MA 02474-22   617-497-0770
Fax: 617-497-2074
lamps@lampglass.nu
www.lampglass.nu

Specialists in replacement glass lamp shades including chimneys, student shades, ceiling globes, sconce glass, chandelier glass and prisms

Credit Cards: MasterCard; Visa
Catalog Cost: $1
Catalog Circulation: Mailed 1 time(s) per year
Average Order Size: $30
Printing Information: 5 pages in 4 colors on Glossy Stock
Press: Sheetfed Press
Binding: Folded
Mailing List Information: Names for rent
In Business: 34 years
Number of Employees: 10-J
Sales Volume: Under $500M

5060 Lamps Plus

Lamps Plus
20250 Plummer Street
Chatsworth, CA 91311   877-704-2425
800-782-1967
customerservice@lampsplus.com
www.lampsplus.com

Lighting fixtures

CFO: Clark Linstone
CEO: Dennis Swanson
Credit Cards: AMEX; MasterCard
Printing Information: 52 pages
In Business: 39 years
Number of Employees: 1200

5061 Lumenpulse

Lumenpulse
10 Post Office Square
Suite 900
Boston, MA 02109   617-307-5700
Fax: 617-350-9912
info@lumenpulse.com
www.lumenpulse.com

Energy efficient lighting products

Senior Vice President & CTO: Greg Campbell
Director of Sales: Anthony Sauce
Catalog Cost: Free
Catalog Circulation: Mailed 1 time(s) per year
Printing Information: 45 pages in 4 colors
In Business: 11 years
Number of Employees: 500

5062 O'Ryan Industries

O'Ryan Industries
12711 NE 95th Street
PO Box 1736
Vancouver, WA 98682-8978   360-892-0447
800-426-4311
Fax: 360-892-6742
www.oryanindustries.com

LED and incandescent lighting and power supplies for pools, spas and whirlpool baths; Dental composit curing lights, scalers and endo units, fiberoptic light sources for dental, medical industries

President: Rick Grant
Marketing Manager: Benson Perry
Production Manager: Benson Perry
Vice President: Sharon Grant
Buyers: Benson Perry
Printing Information: 12 pages in 2 colors on Matte Stock
Binding: Folded
Mailing List Information: Names for rent
In Business: 28 years
Number of Employees: 27
Sales Volume: $1MM to $3MM

5063 Old California Lantern Company
Old California Lantern Company
975 N Enterprise St
Orange, CA 92867-5448   714-771-5223
                             800-577-6679
                        Fax: 714-771-5714
                   ocsales@oldcalifornia.com
                       www.Oldcalifornia.Com

Bungalow lighting

President: Tom Richard
In Business: 26 years
Sales Volume: $3MM to $5MM

5064 P&H Crystalite
P&H Crystalite, Inc.
101 Palm Harbor Parkway #117
Palm Coast, FL 32137   561-330-8660
                             800-468-8673
                        Fax: 561-330-8665
                    phcrystalite@aol.com
                         www.flexalite.com

Rope lighting, Flex-A-Lite, Black Lights, Neon Signs, Strobes

President: Richard D Rubin
Marketing Manager: Anna Robin
Credit Cards: AMEX; MasterCard; Visa
Printing Information: 17 pages
Mailing List Information: Names for rent
In Business: 21 years
Number of Employees: 5
Sales Volume: $1MM to $3MM

5065 Packaged Lighting Systems
Packaged Lighting Systems
29 Grant Street
PO Box 285
Walden, NY 12586-285   845-778-3515
                             800-836-1024
                        Fax: 845-778-1286
                    www.Packagedlighting.Com

Stage lighting, special effects, decorative lighting and control systems for the stage, television, display and entertainment industries

President: Lee Daniels
Marketing Manager: Lois Meyer
Catalog Circulation: to 30000
Printing Information: 80 pages
In Business: 25 years
Number of Employees: 50
Sales Volume: $1,000,000 - $5,000,000

5066 Period Collection
American Period Lighting
3004 Columbia Avenue
Lancaster, PA 17603-4001   717-925-7035
                          Fax: 717-509-3127
                 www.americanperiodlighting.com

Handcrafted traditional and period lighting fixtures; lanterns, chandeliers, postlights of tin and brass

Catalog Cost: $2.5
Catalog Circulation: to 15M
Printing Information: 3 pages

In Business: 45 years
Number of Employees: 4

5067 Period Lighting Fixtures
Period Lighting
167 River Rd
North Adams, MA 01247-2147   413-664-7141
                                  800-828-6990
                             Fax: 413-664-7142
                     sales@periodlighting.com
                         www.periodlighting.com

Period-style American lighting fixtures, authentic handmade reproductions of early American lighting fixtures from 1620 to 1850

President: Christopher Burda
Credit Cards: AMEX; MasterCard
Catalog Cost: $10
Catalog Circulation: to 100
Printing Information: 90 pages
In Business: 41 years
Number of Employees: 10
Sales Volume: $638,000

5068 RH Lighting
Restoration Hardware
15 Koch Rd.
Corte Madera, CA 94925   800-762-1005
                    www.restorationhardware.com

Distinctive fixtures, from chandeliers to sconces.

CEO: Gary Friedman
Printing Information: 220 pages in 4 colors
In Business: 37 years
Number of Employees: 2900
Sales Volume: $1.5 Billion

5069 Rejuvenation Lamp & Fixture Company
Rejuvenation
2550 NW Nicolai Street
Portland, OR 97210   888-401-1900
                     Fax: 800-526-7329
            customerservice@rejuvenation.com
                    www.rejuvenation.com

Manufactures over 260 authentically reproduced lights including chandeliers, sconces, porch lights and lamps in Victorian, Arts and Crafts and Neoclassic styles

President: Alysa Rose
Founder/Owner: Jim Kelly
VP Operations: Dennis Conner
Credit Cards: MasterCard; Visa; Discover
Catalog Cost: Free
Catalog Circulation: Mailed 1 time(s) per year to 150
Average Order Size: $400
Printing Information: 88 pages in 4 colors on Glossy Stock
Press: Web Press
Binding: Saddle Stitched
Mailing List Information: Names for rent
In Business: 38 years
Number of Employees: 200
Sales Volume: $10MM to $20MM

5070 Shade Store
                          800-754-1455
                design@theshadestore.com
                    www.theshadestore.com

Shades, blinds and draperies

5071 Shades of Light
Shades of Light
14001 Justice Road
Midlothian, VA 23113   804-288-3235
                       Fax: 804-288-5029
                  info@shadesoflight.com
                     www.shadesoflight.com

Lighting, rugs, curtains and bedding

CFO: Denise McCarney
Catalog Cost: Free
Catalog Circulation: Mailed 1 time(s) per year
Printing Information: 74 pages in 4 colors on Glossy Stock

Binding: Saddle Stitched
In Business: 31 years
Number of Employees: 55
Sales Volume: $5MM to $10MM

5072 Silverjack Iron Works
Silverjack Iron Works
14 Main Street
PO Box 166
Baker, NV 89311   775-234-7111
                        888-716-8484
                   Fax: 775-234-7114
              www.silverjackironworks.com

Chandeliers, bar lights, pool table lights, wall sconces, lamps

Owner: Bill Roundtree
Owner: Katherine Roundtree
Credit Cards: MasterCard
In Business: 25 years

5073 Simkar Corporation
Simkar Corporation
700 Ramona Ave
Philadelphia, PA 19120-4691   215-831-7700
                                   215-831-7798
                              Fax: 215-831-7703
                                 www.simkar.com

Linear and compact fluorescent, exit and emergency and vandal resistant lighting fixtures for commercial, industrial and residential applications

President: Glen Grunewald
Catalog Cost: $25
In Business: 68 years
Number of Employees: 25
Sales Volume: $1MM

5074 Streamlight
Streamlight, Inc
30 Eagleville Road
Eagleville, PA 19403-1476   610-631-0600
                                 800-523-7488
                            Fax: 610-631-0712
                         cs@streamlight.com
                         www.streamlight.com

A complete line of standard and rechargeable battery flashlights, lanterns and accessories

President: Brad Penney
CFO: George Collier
Marketing Manager: Loring Grove
Raymon Sharrah:
COO
Buyers: Christine Brunner
Catalog Circulation: Mailed 1 time(s) per year
Printing Information: 20 pages in 4 colors on Glossy Stock
Press: Web Press
Binding: Saddle Stitched
Mailing List Information: Names for rent
List Manager: C Bradford Penney
In Business: 41 years
Number of Employees: 240
Sales Volume: $33 Million

5075 Verilux Healthy Lighting Products
Verilux Healthy Lighting Products
340 Mad River Park
Suite 1
Waitsfield, VT 05673   802-496-3101
                             800-786-6850
                        Fax: 802-496-3105
                         info@verilux.com
                            www.verilux.com

Full spectrum, light therapy, S.A.D. therapy, craft lighting, Natural Spectrum and HappyLite lighting, lamps, bulbs and lighting accessories

President: Nicholas Harmon
CFO: Joe Vincent
Marketing Manager: Jan Knutsen
CEO: Ryan Douglas
General Manager: Bill Abbott-Koch

VP Operations: David Tauscher
Credit Cards: AMEX; MasterCard
Catalog Cost: Free
Catalog Circulation: to 700M
Average Order Size: $100
Printing Information: 32 pages in 4 colors on Glossy Stock
Press: Web Press
Binding: Saddle Stitched
Mailing List Information: Names for rent
In Business: 59 years
Number of Employees: 28
Sales Volume: $10MM to $20MM

5076 Vermont Industries

Vermont Industries
PO Box 222
Po Box 301
N. Springfield, VT 05150   802-885-6690
800-639-1715
Fax: 802-492-3500
support@domain.com
www.vermontindustries.com

Wrought-iron lighting and home accessories

President: Linda Burnf
Credit Cards: MasterCard
Catalog Cost: $3
Catalog Circulation: Mailed 1 time(s) per year to 300
Printing Information: 100 pages in 4 colors on Glossy Stock
Press: Web Press
Binding: Saddle Stitched
In Business: 15 years

Linens & Textiles

5077 Black Forest Decor

PO Box 297
Jenks, OK 74037-297   800-605-0915
info@blackforestdecor.com
www.blackforestdecor.com

Home decor

5078 CB2

CB2
1860 W Jefferson Avenue
Naperville, IL 60540   630-388-4555
800-606-6252
Fax: 630-527-1448
www.cb2.com

Modern home and office furniture and accessories]

Chief Executive Officer: Neela Montgomery
Credit Cards: AMEX; MasterCard
Catalog Cost: Free
Catalog Circulation: Mailed 12 time(s) per year
Printing Information: 92 pages in 4 colors
In Business: 17 years
Sales Volume: $10MM to $20MM

5079 Chair Covers and Linens

Chair Covers and Linens
25914 John R Rd
Madison Heights, MI 48071-4022   855-269-4376
info@linenhero.com
www.linenhero.com

Chair covers and linens for special occassions

President: Todd Lloyd
Catalog Cost: Free
In Business: 19 years
Number of Employees: 25
Sales Volume: $500M to $1MM

5080 Cohasset Colonials

Cohasset Colonials
14 South Pleasant St.
Po Box 548
Ashburnham, MA 00143   978-827-3001
800-288-2389
Fax: 978-827-3227
cohassetcolonials.custservice@gmail.com
www.cohassetcolonials.com

Furniture, lighting and home accessories

5081 Frette

Frette Madison
850 Third Ave
10th Floor
New York, NY 10022   212-299-0400
800-353-7388
Fax: 347-862-9309
assistance@frette.com

Luxury linens, bath items and gifts; cashmere, silk, velvet, mink fabrics

CFO: Anna Ermakova
EVP: Rico Merenelli
Credit Cards: AMEX; MasterCard
Catalog Circulation: Mailed 2 time(s) per year
Printing Information: on Glossy Stock
In Business: 155 years
Number of Employees: 75

5082 Hancock's of Paducah

Hancock's of Paducah
3841 Hinkleville Road
Paducah, KY 42001-9155   270-443-4410
800-845-8723
Fax: 270-442-2164
customerservice@hancocks-paducah.com
www.hancocks-paducah.com

Quilting fabrics and notions; also home decorating fabrics, drapery and upolstery fabrics

Credit Cards: AMEX; MasterCard
Catalog Circulation: Mailed 4 time(s) per year
Printing Information: in 4 colors
In Business: 63 years

5083 Jayson Home

1885 N Clybourn Ave
Chicago, IL 60614   773-248-8180
800-472-1885
info@jaysonhome.com
www.jaysonhome.com

Furnishings and home accessories

5084 Kreiss Furniture Collections Folio

Kreiss Collection
8525 Camino Santa Fe
San Diego, CA 92121   310-282-8800
800-573-4771
Fax: 212-593-1901
concierge@kreiss.com
www.kreiss.com

Fine furniture and linens

President: Micheal Kriess
Catalog Cost: $5
Printing Information: 50 pages in 4 colors on Glossy Stock
Binding: Perfect Bound
In Business: 70 years

5085 Mallory Lane

Collections Etc., Inc.
PO Box 7985
Elk Grove Village, IL 60009-7985   620-584-8000
888-468-1666
Fax: 847-350-5701
www.collectionsetc.com

Home decor for the bedroom, bathroom and kitchen. Also available outdoor living accessories

President: Shelley Nandkeolyar
Marketing Manager: Karl Steigerwald

Fulfillment: Bruce Getowicz
CEO/Founder: Todd Lustbader
COO: Paul Klassman
Credit Cards: AMEX; MasterCard; Visa
Catalog Cost: Free
In Business: 40 years
Number of Employees: 200
Sales Volume: 12.7M

5086 Pratesi

Pratesi
381 Park Ave S # 1223
New York, NY 10016-8820   212-689-3150
800-332-6925
Fax: 212-889-6721
pratesiusa@pratesi.com
www.Pratesi.Com

Italian sheets, towels and linens

President: Antonio Dibari
Marketing Manager: Priscilla Von Muehlen
Credit Cards: AMEX; MasterCard
Catalog Cost: $2
Printing Information: 60 pages in 4 colors
Number of Employees: 4
Sales Volume: $1MM to $3MM

5087 Schweitzer Linen

Schweitzer Linen
1132 Madison Avenue
New York, NY 10028   212-249-8361
800-554-6367
Fax: 212-737-6328
www.schweitzerlinen.com

Fine bedding, linens and nightwear

Chairman/President/CEO: Elaina Schweitzer
Manager: Ileana Jovica
Credit Cards: AMEX; MasterCard
Printing Information: 48 pages in 3 colors on Glossy Stock
Press: Web Press
Binding: Saddle Stitched
In Business: 40 years
Number of Employees: 8
Sales Volume: $1MM to $3MM

5088 Signals

Signals
5581 Hudson Industrial Parkway
PO Box 2599
Hudson, OH 44236-99   844-250-3393
Fax: 800-950-9569
www.signals.com

Home decor

5089 Swans Island Company

Swans Island Company
231 Atlantic Highway (Route 1)
Northport, ME 04849   207-338-9691
888-526-9526
Fax: 207-338-9166
info@swansislandcompany.com
swansislandcompany.com

Handwoven blankets and hand-dyed knitting yarns.

Chairman: Thomas Laurita
President: Bill Laurita
CFO: Justin Mazur
Marketing Manager: Caitlin MacRae
Partner & Knit Design Director: Michele Rose Orne
Catalog Cost: Free
In Business: 25 years
Number of Employees: 10

5090 VHC Brands

Victorian Heart Company, Inc.
P.O. Box 17
Kirbyville, MO 65679   888-334-3099
Fax: 417-973-0423
info@vhcbrands.com
www.vhcbrands.com

Wholesale imported quilts, throws and linens

Chairman: Billy Kline
President: Kenneth Kline
Key Account Manager: Josh Ellig
Mid-Atlantic Central Account Manage: David Brown
dbrown@vhcbrands.com
Sales Manager: Joe Morimoto
jmorimoto@vhcbrands.com
Credit Cards: AMEX; MasterCard; Visa
Catalog Cost: Free
Catalog Circulation: Mailed 4 time(s) per year
Printing Information: 292 pages in 4 colors on Glossy Stock
Press: Letterpress
Binding: Saddle Stitched
Mailing List Information: Names for rent
In Business: 21 years
Number of Employees: 25
Sales Volume: $3.3 Million

5091   Vermont Country Store
The Vermont Country Store
5650 Main Street
Manchester Center, VT 05255-9718 802-362-4667
800-564-4623
Fax: 802-362-8288
www.vermontcountrystore.com

Apothecary products, women's clothing, men's apparel, vermont maple syrup and home furnishings

Chairman: Lyman Orton
President: William Shouldice
Credit Cards: AMEX; MasterCard
Catalog Cost: Free
Catalog Circulation: Mailed 5 time(s) per year
Printing Information: 104 pages in 4 colors on Newsprint
Binding: Saddle Stitched
In Business: 69 years
Number of Employees: 600

5092   Warm Company
The Warm Company
5529 186th Place Sw
Lynnwood, WA 98037   425-248-2424
800-234-9276
Fax: 206-320-0974
info@warmcompany.com
www.warmcompany.com

Warm Window insulated fabric, with 4 layers quilted together for energy saving, warm and natural needled cotton batting for quilts, crafts and wearable art, Steam-a-Seam fabric fusing web and more

In Business: 35 years

5093   Warm Things
Warms Things
180 Paul Drive
San Rafael, CA 94903   415-472-2154
warmthings@msn.com
www.warmthingsonline.com

Bedding, comforters, slippers, robes and throws

President: Richard Smith-Allen
Credit Cards: MasterCard
Catalog Cost: Free
Catalog Circulation: Mailed 3 time(s) per year
Average Order Size: $200
Printing Information: 24 pages in 4 colors on Glossy Stock
Press: Web Press
Binding: Saddle Stitched
Mailing List Information: Names for rent
In Business: 44 years
Number of Employees: 10
Sales Volume: $3,000,000

Rugs & Floor Coverings

5094   Anji Mountain
1 First Missouri Center
Suite 214
Saint Louis, MO 63141   314-576-1000
888-344-5004
Fax: 314-576-3832
info@anjimountain.com
anjimountain.com

Rugs and chairmats

5095   Antique Art Carpets
Claremont Rug Company
6087 Claremont Avenue
Oakland, CA 94618   510-654-0816
800-441-1332
Fax: 510-654-8661
info@claremontrug.com
www.claremontrug.com

Antique carpets

President: Jan David Winitz
Marketing Manager: Christine Winitz

5096   Blair Home
Blair
220 Hickory St.
Warren, PA 16366   800-821-5744
www.blair.com

Home furnishings for the whole home.

President: Marisa Smith
Catalog Cost: Free
Printing Information: in 4 colors
In Business: 106 years
Number of Employees: 2000
Sales Volume: $1 Billion

5097   Canvasworks Floorcloths
CanvasWorks FloorCloths
326 Henry Gould Rd
Perkinsville, VT 05151-9419   802-263-5410
Fax: 866-469-4984
lisa@canvasworksfloorcloths.com
www.canvasworksfloorcloths.com

Colonial and folk art floorcloths

President: Lisa Curry-Mair
Credit Cards: AMEX; MasterCard
Catalog Cost: $5
Printing Information: in 6 colors on Matte Stock
Binding: Folded
Mailing List Information: Names for rent
In Business: 23 years
Number of Employees: 2
Sales Volume: Under $500M

5098   Charles W Jacobsen
Jacobsen Rugs
225 Wilkinson Street
Syracuse, NY 13204-1719   315-422-7832
Fax: 315-422-6909
rugpeople@jacobsenrugs.com
www.Jacobsenrugs.Com

New and antique Oriental rugs

President: Brent Goodsell
Marketing Manager: Patty O'Day, Advertising Agent
Credit Cards: AMEX; MasterCard; Visa
Printing Information: 34 pages
In Business: 90 years
Number of Employees: 32

5099   Coronet Carpets
Bliss
1502 Coronet Drive
PO BOX 1248
Dalton, GA 30722-1248   706-259-4511
800-241-4018
Fax: 706-259-4511
support@blissflooring.com
www.blissflooring.com

Carpets

President: Larry Swanson
Marketing Manager: Lloyd Bryson
Number of Employees: 1100
Sales Volume: $100MM

5100   Delia's
Delia's
50 W 23rd Street
New York, NY 10010   212-590-6200
866-293-3268
Fax: 212-590-6300
customerservice@deliasmerch.com
store.delias.com

Teen clothing, shoes, jewelry, and accessories

Chairman: Carter S Evans
President: Walter Killough
CFO: David J Dick
Marketing Manager: Douglas Sietsma
Credit Cards: AMEX; MasterCard; Visa
Catalog Cost: Free
Catalog Circulation: Mailed 1 time(s) per year to 65mm
Printing Information: 74 pages on Glossy Stock
Binding: Perfect Bound
In Business: 16 years
Number of Employees: 50
Sales Volume: $217MM

5101   DwellStudio
DwellStudio
New York NY   877-993-9355
www.dwellstudio.com

Home furnishings

Catalog Cost: Free
Printing Information: in 4 colors
In Business: 16 years

5102   Elizabeth Eakins
Elizabeth Eakins Inc.
654 Madison Avenue 14th Floor
New York, NY 10065   212-628-1950
Fax: 212-628-7696
inquires@elizabetheakins.com
www.elizabetheakins.com

Rugs and Fabrics in natural fibers

President: Elizabeth Eakins

5103   Elkes
Carpet One Floor & Home
1585 Gable Street
High Point, NC 27260-8474   336-899-7347
info@carpetone.com
www.carpetone.com

Carpets

President: Marty Elkes
Credit Cards: AMEX; MasterCard; Visa
Sales Volume: $3MM to $5MM

5104   Factory Direct Table Pad Company
Tablepads.com
1501 W Market Street
Indianapolis, IN 46222   800-737-4194
www.tablepads.com

Custom made table pads

President: David Berger
Marketing Manager: Ron Jukenick
Credit Cards: MasterCard; Visa
Catalog Cost: $1
Catalog Circulation: to 10300
Printing Information: 5 pages in 4 colors on Glossy Stock
Press: Web Press
Binding: Saddle Stitched
Mailing List Information: Names for rent
Number of Employees: 45
Sales Volume: Under $500M

5105 High Fashion Home
3100 Travis Street
Houston, TX 77006   713-528-3838
                            888-685-3838
info@highfashionhome.com
www.highfashionhome.com

Furniture, fabric, drapery, lighting, accessories and gifts

5106 Home Decorators Collection
Home Decorators Collection
3074 Chastain Meadows Parkway
Marietta, GA 30066   800-245-2217
www.homedecorators.com

Rugs, bar stools, bookshelves, coffe tables, mirrors, bathroom vanities, book cases and storage benches.

Catalog Cost: Free
Printing Information: 148 pages in 4 colors
Sales Volume: $300 Million

5107 InterfaceFlor
Interface Flooring Systems, Inc.
1503 Orchard Hill Road
Lagrange, GA 30240   706-882-1891
                            800-336-0225
Fax: 706-884-8340
www.Interfaceflooring.Com

Modular floor covering

President: John R Wells
CFO: Patrick Lynch
Credit Cards: AMEX; MasterCard
Catalog Circulation: to 17mm
In Business: 1 years
Number of Employees: 1000

5108 Jayson Home
1885 N Clybourn Ave
Chicago, IL 60614   773-248-8180
                            800-472-1885
info@jaysonhome.com
www.jaysonhome.com

Furnishings and home accessories

5109 Pace Stone Rugs
Pace Stone Inc
663 Washington Street
Eden, NC 27288   800-789-0236
Fax: 336-623-3347
pacestoneinc@yahoo.com
www.pacestone.com

Karastan carpets, contemporary, traditional and transitional rugs, and oriental weavers

President: William F Pace Sr
Owner/President/HR Executive: William Pace
Credit Cards: MasterCard; Visa
In Business: 91 years
Number of Employees: 21

5110 Peerless Imported Rugs
Peerless Imported Rugs
3033 N Lincoln Avenue
Chicago, IL 60657   773-525-0296
                            800-621-6573
Fax: 773-525-4055
customerservice@peerlessrugs.com
www.peerlessrugs.com

Rugs and tapestries

Credit Cards: AMEX; MasterCard; Visa
Catalog Cost: Free
Catalog Circulation: Mailed 2 time(s) per year to 10000
Printing Information: 88 pages in 4 colors on Newsprint
Binding: Folded
Mailing List Information: Names for rent
In Business: 79 years
Number of Employees: 20
Sales Volume: $3MM to $5MM

5111 RH Rugs
Restoration Hardware
15 Koch Rd.
Corte Madera, CA 94925   800-762-1005
www.restorationhardware.com

Traditional and contemporary rugs.

CEO: Gary Friedman
Printing Information: 260 pages in 4 colors
In Business: 37 years
Number of Employees: 2900
Sales Volume: $1.5 Billion

5112 Redbook Volume 5
White River Hardwoods-Woodworks, Inc.
1197 Happy Hollow Road
Fayetteville, AR 72701   479-442-6986
                                800-558-0119
Fax: 479-444-0406
info@whiteriver.com
www.whiteriver.com

Hardwood moldings

President: Joan Johnson
CFO: Roy Cain
Marketing Manager: Laura Johnson
Production Manager: Jesse Johnson
Fulfillment: Rose Diaz
Catalog Cost: $15
Catalog Circulation: to 75000
Printing Information: 175 pages
In Business: 36 years
Number of Employees: 51

5113 Renaissance Carpet & Tapestries
Renaissancecarpet
200 Lexington Ave # 1006
Suite 1006
New York, NY 10016-6255   212-696-0080
Fax: 212-696-4248
info@renaissancecarpet.com
www.Renaissancecarpet.Com

Renaissance Aubusson Collection and famous brands

President: Jan Soleimani
Vice President/Sales Manager: Jeffrey Soleimani
jeffrey@renaissancecarpet.com
Sales Volume: $10MM to $20MM

5114 Rugs Direct
Rugs Direct
116 Featherbed Ln
Winchester, VA 22601-4435   540-662-4142
                                    888-464-1447
Fax: 540-662-0063
info@rugsdirect.com
www.Rugs-Direct.Com

Rugs

President: David Craig
Credit Cards: AMEX; MasterCard
Catalog Cost: Free
Catalog Circulation: Mailed 2 time(s) per year
Printing Information: in 4 colors on Glossy Stock
In Business: 32 years
Sales Volume: $10MM to $20MM

5115 Rugs USA
Rugs USA
106 E Jericho Tpke
Mineola, NY 11501-3121   609-447-4515
                                800-982-7210
Fax: 866-681-8138
info@rugsusa.com
www.rugsusa.com

Rugs, tapestries, slipcovers, clocks, mirrors, lighting and art

Sales Volume: Under $500M

5116 Village Interiors Carpet One
Village Interiors Carpet One Floor & Hom
3203 Highway 70 SE
Newton, NC 28658   704-325-2304
Fax: 828-465-1864
sales@carpet-one.net
www.villageinteriorshickory.com

Quality carpet, hardwood, tile, vinyl and laminate flooring

President: Robert Norris
Catalog Cost: Free
Mailing List Information: Names for rent
Number of Employees: 8
Sales Volume: $1MM to $3MM

5117 Woodard Weave
Woodard & Greenstein
303 East 81st Street, West Store
5th Floor
New York, NY 10028   212-988-2906
                            800-332-7847
Fax: 212-734-9665
info@woodardandgreenstein.com
www.woodardweave.com

Rugs: Flat woven carpets, copied from antique American rug carpets, cotton rugs: reproduction of early American flat woven rugs

Owner/Officer: Thomas K Woodard
Principal: Blance Greenstein
Credit Cards: AMEX; MasterCard
Catalog Cost: $7
Average Order Size: $500
Printing Information: 65 pages in 4 colors on Glossy Stock
Press: Sheetfed Press
Binding: Saddle Stitched
Mailing List Information: Names for rent
In Business: 44 years
Number of Employees: 10
Sales Volume: $670,000

5118 Yankee Pride
Yankee Pride
29 Parkside Circle, Dept. Fw5
Braintree, MA 02184-3100   781-848-7611
                                  800-848-7610
Fax: 781-848-6218
customerservice@yankee-pride.com
www.Yankee-Pride.Com

Braided rugs, wool hand hooked rugs, rag, woven and oriental style rugs

President: Robert Packard
Credit Cards: MasterCard
Catalog Cost: Free
Catalog Circulation: Mailed 52 time(s) per year to 50000
Average Order Size: $234
Printing Information: 80 pages in 4 colors on Glossy Stock
Press: Web Press
Binding: Saddle Stitched
Will Trade Names: Yes
Number of Employees: 4
Sales Volume: Under $500M

Security Products

5119 Brooks Equipment
Brooks Equipment Company
10926 David Taylor Dr.
Suite 300
Charlotte, NC 28262   704-916-3448
                            800-826-3473
Fax: 800-433-9265
sales@brooksequipment.com
www.brooksequipment.com

Fire equipment and parts.

President: Tim Foughty
Printing Information: in 4 colors
In Business: 77 years

5120 C Crane
C. Crane Company, Inc.
172 Main Street
Fortuna, CA 95540-1816
707-725-9000
800-522-8863
Fax: 707-725-9060
www.ccrane.com

AM/FM/SW radios, AM/FM/SW antennas, flashlights, scanners, telephones, security products, radio controlled clocks and more

President: Bob Crane
Credit Cards: MasterCard
Catalog Cost: Free
Printing Information: 150 pages in 4 colors on Glossy Stock
Binding: Folded
In Business: 28 years
Sales Volume: $500M to $1MM

5121 Chief Supply
Chief Supply
1400 Executive Parkway
Eugene, OR 97401
888-588-8569
orders@chiefsupply.com
www.chiefsupply.com

Firefighting, law enforcement and emergency medical supplies, including apparel and gear bags, badges, flashlights, batteries and chargers, cases and antennas, specialty and close-out items

President: John Utley
In Business: 40 years
Sales Volume: $20MM to $50MM

5122 Dakota Alert
Dakota Alert, Inc.
32556 E. Main Street
PO Box 130
Elk Point, SD 57025
605-356-2772
Fax: 605-356-3662
www.dakotaalert.com

Wireless security equipment

President: Andrew Quam

5123 Handsome Rewards
19465 Brennan Ave.
Perris, CA 92599
800-522-0227
Fax: 951-943-5574
www.handsomerewards.com

Home furnishings

5124 Hidden Camera Surveillance Catalog
Saint Corporation
4720 Montgomery Lane
Suite 800
Bethesda, MD 20814
301-656-0521
800-596-2006
Fax: 301-656-4806
sales@saintcorporation.com
www.saintcorporation.com

Hidden cameras

Chairman: Ruchard S. Carson
President: Donna Ruginski
Production Manager: Randall Laudermilk
Chief Technical Officer: Mr. Sam Kline
VP of Security Services: Ms. Diane Reilly
Catalog Cost: $5
Printing Information: 39 pages
In Business: 17 years

5125 Improvements
HSN Improvements LLC
5568 West Chester Road
West Chester, OH 45069-2914
800-634-9484
custserv@improvementscatalog.com
www.improvementscatalog.com

Furniture and decor, small appliances, shelving, electronics, pet supplies and home security items

President: Paul Tarvin
Credit Cards: AMEX; MasterCard; Visa

Catalog Cost: Free
Printing Information: 72 pages in 4 colors on Glossy Stock
Binding: Saddle Stitched
Mailing List Information: Names for rent
In Business: 16 years

5126 Justrite Manufacturing Company
Justrite Mfg. Co
2454 E Dempster St
Suite 300
Des Plaines, IL 60016-5315
847-298-9250
800-978-9250
Fax: 847-298-9261
www.justritemfg.com

Flammable liquid safety equipment

Printing Information: 128 pages in 4 colors on Matte Stock
Press: Web Press
Binding: Perfect Bound
Mailing List Information: Names for rent
In Business: 97 years
Number of Employees: 200
Sales Volume: $3MM to $5MM

5127 Liberty Safe
1199 West Utah Avenue
Payson, UT 84651
800-247-5625
info@libertysafe.com
www.libertysafe.com

Full-sized residential safes

5128 SafeMart
LiveWatch Security LLC
512 W. Bertrand, Box 215
St. Mary, KS 94107-3515
888-796-0562
888-994-6028
Fax: 866-540-8158
www.livewatch.com

Security equipment

President: Chris Johnson
Marketing Manager: Mark Riddle
Director of Operations: Dave Riley
Director of Ecommerce: Joseph Mioni
Technical Services Manager: Joe Thomas
Printing Information: 8 pages in 3 colors
In Business: 13 years
Number of Employees: 8
Sales Volume: $1,000,000 - $5,000,000

5129 SafeShowroom.com
SafeShowroom
1865 Watson Blvd
Warner Robins, GA 31093-3631
424-261-5397
800-461-2864
sales@safeshowroom.com
www.safeshowroom.com

Safes and locks for homes or businesses

Credit Cards: AMEX; MasterCard
Catalog Cost: Free
In Business: 18 years

5130 Sirchie Product Catalog
Sirchie Finger Print Laboratories
100 Hunter Place
Youngsville, NC 27596-639
919-554-2244
800-356-7311
Fax: 919-554-2266
sirchieinfo@sirchie.com
www.sirchie.com

Law enforcement and security equipment

President: Paul Feldman
Buyers: Phillip Shusterman
Credit Cards: AMEX; MasterCard
Catalog Circulation: Mailed 1 time(s) per year to 8M
Printing Information: 80 pages in 1 color
In Business: 87 years
Number of Employees: 32
Sales Volume: $1,000,000 - $5,000,000

5131 Smarthome
Smarthome
16542 Millikan Avenue
Irvine, CA 92606-5027
949-221-9200
800-762-7846
Fax: 949-221-9240
custsvc@smarthome.com
www.smarthome.com

Home security, automation, wireless systems and much more are awaiting you in this great catalog

President: Mike Scharnagl
pr@smarthome.com
CFO: Charles McBrayer
CEO: Joe Dada
Credit Cards: AMEX; MasterCard
Catalog Cost: Free
Printing Information: 48 pages in 4 colors
In Business: 22 years

5132 Spy Gear Products
Spy Gear 4 U
PO Box 707
Kingsport, TN 37662
423-247-4390
877-943-2748
Fax: 423-378-4509
www.spygear4u.com

Providers of hi-tech spy and security products

President: Chris Dugger
Catalog Cost: Free
Printing Information: 40 pages
In Business: 10 years
Sales Volume: Under $500M

5133 Supercircuits
11000 N Mopac Expressway
Building 300
Austin, TX 78759
877-995-2288
www.supercircuits.com

Audio and video surveillance solutions

5134 White's Metal Detectors
White's Electronics Factory, U.S.A.
1011 Pleasant Valley Road
Sweet Home, OR 97386
541-367-6121
800-547-6911
Fax: 541-367-6629
sales@whiteselectronics.com
www.whiteselectronics.com

Manufactures metal detectors for recreation, security, and industry

President: Ken and Mary White
Catalog Cost: Free
In Business: 64 years

Jewelry
Costume

5135 AMC Sales
AMC Sales, Inc.
3241 Winpark Dr
New Hope, MN 55427-2023
763-545-0700
800-262-0332
Fax: 763-545-0480
www.amcsalesinc.com

Necklaces, earrings, armband tattoos, toys, sunglasses and candy

President: Aaron Crohn
VP: Mona Crohn
Credit Cards: AMEX; MasterCard; Visa
Catalog Cost: Free
Sales Volume: Under $500M

5136 Crossroads
Crossroads
12 State Street
Marblehead, MA 1945
781-315-4202
Fax: 781-325-1085
orders@crossroadsjewelry.com
www.crossroadsjewelry.com
Handcrafted jewelry and accessories.

5137 Exclusive Sports Jewelry
Exclusive Sports Jewelry
PO Box 686
Killingworth, CT 06419-2429
910-799-9200
800-533-3653
Fax: 203-778-4839
info@exclusivesportsjewelry.com
www.exclusivesportsjewelry.com

Sports related trophies and jewelry

Credit Cards: AMEX; MasterCard
Catalog Circulation: Mailed 1 time(s) per year
Printing Information: 30 pages in 4 colors
Binding: Saddle Stitched
In Business: 26 years

5138 Franklin Mint
The Franklin Mint
801 Springdale Dr
Suite 200
Exton, PA 19341
800-843-6468
Fax: 610-459-6880
info@franklinmint.com
www.franklinmint.com

Die-cast cars and airplanes, precision modeling, collectibles, jewelry, seasonal giftware

Chairman: Moshe Malamud
President: Steven Sisskind
CFO: Noah Becker
Credit Cards: AMEX
Catalog Cost: Free
Catalog Circulation: Mailed 4 time(s) per year
Printing Information: 60 pages
In Business: 49 years
Number of Employees: 42
Sales Volume: $6.2MM

5139 Fred Meyer Jewelers
Fred Meyer Jewelers
4350 24th Avenue
Suite 620
Fort Gradiot, MI 48059
810-385-7788
800-342-6663
www.fredmeyerjewelers.com

Jewelry

President: Fred Meyer
Credit Cards: AMEX; MasterCard
Catalog Cost: Free
Catalog Circulation: Mailed 4 time(s) per year
Printing Information: 17 pages in 4 colors
In Business: 44 years
Sales Volume: $100MM to $500MM

5140 Gavilan's
Gavilan's
Gavilan Hills, CA 92599
800-713-0493
800-777-0327
Fax: 951-940-1388
customerservice@gavilans.com
www.gavilans.com

General merchandise, jewelry, books, handbags, servingware, etc.

Credit Cards: AMEX; MasterCard
Catalog Cost: Free
In Business: 3 years
Number of Employees: 1
Sales Volume: $70,000

5141 Grangem Reg'd
Grangem Reg'd
PO Box 602
Derby Line, VT 05830-602
819-876-2998
Fax: 819-876-5979

Tourist and granite jewelry

President: Robert Murray
Credit Cards: MasterCard
Catalog Circulation: Mailed 1 time(s) per year to 500
Printing Information: 3 pages in 1 color
Press: Sheetfed Press
Binding: Saddle Stitched
In Business: 16 years

5142 Herb and Kay's
11320 Dumont Avenue
Norwalk, CA 90650-7406
562-868-1226
800-826-5906

Crystal jewelry with gold plating and filling

Printing Information: 28 pages
Binding: Saddle Stitched

5143 Holly Yashi
Holly Yashi
1300 9th St.
Arcata, CA 95221
877-607-8361
customerservice@hollyyashi.com
www.hollyyashi.com
In Business: 34 years

5144 JuJuBelle
JuJuBelle
307 S. Locust Street
Denton TX
940-387-2542
877-987-5858
www.jujubelle.com

Fashion jewelry.

In Business: 5 years

5145 Limoges Jewelry
Limoges Jewelry
3349 N. Elston Avenue
Chicago, IL 60618
847-375-1326
customerservice@limogesjewelry.com
www.limogesjewelry.com

Discount jewelry

Credit Cards: AMEX; MasterCard; Visa
Catalog Cost: Free
In Business: 113 years

5146 Liza & Rose
AmeriMark Direct
6864 Engle Rd.
Cleveland, OH 44130
866-345-1388
www.amerimark.com

Fashion jewelry, fragrances, cosmetics, casual wear and footwear.

CFO: Joe Albanese
CEO & President: Gareth Giesler
Catalog Cost: Free
Printing Information: in 4 colors
In Business: 47 years
Number of Employees: 700
Sales Volume: $400 Million

5147 Midnight Velvet
Midnight Velvet
1112 7th Avenue
Monroe, WI 53566-1364
608-324-6060
800-560-8151

Home accessories and gifts, jewelery

Credit Cards: AMEX; MasterCard; Visa
Catalog Cost: Free
Catalog Circulation: Mailed 2 time(s) per year
Printing Information: 116 pages in 4 colors
Binding: Saddle Stitched
In Business: 28 years
Number of Employees: 5

5148 Mignon Faget
Mignon Faget
3801 Magazine Street
New Orleans, LA 70115
800-375-7557
Fax: 500-891-2057
www.mignonfaget.com

Jewelry.

5149 Nordic Shop
The Nordic Shop
111 S Broadway
Skyway Level
Rochester, MN 55904-6511
507-285-9143
800-282-6673
Fax: 507-285-5573
www.nordicshop.net

Scandinavian gifts

President: Louise Hanson
Marketing Manager: Louise Hanson
Credit Cards: AMEX; MasterCard; Visa
Catalog Circulation: Mailed 3 time(s) per year
Average Order Size: $75
Printing Information: 8 pages in 1 color on Glossy Stock
Binding: Saddle Stitched
Mailing List Information: Names for rent
In Business: 32 years
Number of Employees: 10
Sales Volume: $1MM to $3MM

5150 NorthStyle
NorthStyle
Northwoods Trail
PO Box 6529
Chelmsford, MA 01824-929
877-756-4075
800-336-5666
Fax: 800-866-3235
help@northstyle.com
www.northstyle.com

Jewelry, clothing, homegoods and gifts.

President: Jack Rosenfeld
Buyers: Dawn Beausoleil
Credit Cards: AMEX; MasterCard
Catalog Cost: Free
Printing Information: 70 pages in 7 colors on Matte Stock
Binding: Saddle Stitched
In Business: 23 years
Number of Employees: 200
Sales Volume: $20-$50 Million

5151 Novel Box
Novel Box Company, Ltd.
659 Berriman Street
Brooklyn, NY 11208
718-965-2222
800-965-9192
Fax: 718-965-2235
sales@novelbox.com
www.novelbox.com

Jewelry boxes, displays, drawstring pouches and packaging

President: Moishe Sternhill
In Business: 68 years
Number of Employees: 25
Sales Volume: $3 Million

5152 Pyramid Collection
Pyramid Collection
PO Box 3333
Chelmsford, MA 01824-933
800-333-4220
Fax: 800-866-3235
help@pyramidcollection.com
www.pyramidcollection.com

New age gifts, clothing, jewelry and accessories

Chairman: Jack Rosenfeld
President: John Fleischman
CFO: Steven Steiner
Marketing Manager: Robert Webb
Production Manager: Edward Knowles
Fulfillment: Nick Parrinelli
Credit Cards: AMEX; MasterCard
Catalog Cost: Free
In Business: 40 years
Number of Employees: 200
Sales Volume: $20MM to $50MM

5153 Rings and Things
Rings & Things
304 E 2nd Ave
Spokane, WA 99202-450   509-252-2900
                             800-366-2156
                        Fax: 509-838-2602
                        www.rings-things.com

Costume jewelry and giftware

Chairman: Vic Phillips
President: Philip Versage
Catalog Circulation: Mailed 1 time(s) per year
In Business: 43 years

5154 Smithsonian Business Ventures
Smithsonian Institution
PO Box 37012
Washington, DC 20013-7012   866-945-6897
                        www.smithsonianstore.com

Toys and collectibles, jewelry, bookends, paperweights, furniture, clothing and desk accessories

5155 Sunshine Jewelry
Sunshine Jewelry
225 East Dania Beach Boulevard
Suite 217
Dania Beach, FL 33004   954-893-6767
                             800-767-4469
                        Fax: 954-961-3339
                        Soshiny800@aol.com
                        www.sunshinejewelry.com

Jewelry in 14K goldfilled, 10K goldfilled and sterling silver.

Credit Cards: AMEX; MasterCard; Visa
Catalog Cost: Free
Printing Information: 16 pages
In Business: 44 years
Number of Employees: 4
Sales Volume: $5MM to $10MM

5156 The Met Store
The Metropolitan Museum of Art
1000 Fifth Avenue
New York, NY 10028   800-468-7386
                customer.service@metmuseum.org
                        store.metmuseum.org

Jewelry, apparel, home d,cor, prints & posters, books, stationery & calendars inspired by the Metropolitan Museum of Art

Catalog Cost: Free
In Business: 96 years

5157 Vi Bella Jewelry
Vi Bella Jewelry
1275 7th Avenue NE
Sioux Center, IA 51250   712-722-4112
                        www.vibellajewelry.com
Credit Cards: AMEX; MasterCard
In Business: 4 years

5158 Windsor Collection
AmeriMark Direct
6864 Engle Rd.
Cleveland, OH 44130   866-345-1388
                        www.amerimark.com

Fashion jewelry

CFO: Joe Albanese
CEO & President: Gareth Giesler
Catalog Cost: Free
Printing Information: in 4 colors
In Business: 47 years
Number of Employees: 700
Sales Volume: $400 Million

Fine

5159 Adler's
Adler's
722 Canal Street
New Orleans, LA 70130   504-523-5292
                             800-925-7912
                        Fax: 504-568-0610
                        www.adlersjewelry.com
In Business: 100 years

5160 Ahee
edmund t. AHEE jewelers
20139 Mack Avenue
Grosse Pointe Woods, MI 48236   313-886-4600
                             800-987-AHEE
                        www.ahee.com

5161 Alan Furman & Company
Alan Furman & Co., Inc.
12250 Rockville Pike
2nd Floor, Suite 270
Rockville, MD 20852-1666   301-881-0234
                             800-654-7184
                        Fax: 301-881-0810
                        watches@alanfurman.com
                        www.alanfurman.com

Fine watches, jewelry and diamonds

President: Alan Furman
CFO: Jeffrey Griffin
Buyers: G Keith Douglas
Catalog Cost: Free
Catalog Circulation: Mailed 2 time(s) per year to 100M
Printing Information: 12 pages in 4 colors on Glossy Stock
Press: Web Press
In Business: 30 years
Number of Employees: 12
Sales Volume: $1,000,000

5162 American Diamond
American Diamond & American Pearl
579 5th Ave
Suite 455
New York, NY 10017-1917   212-446-6776
                             888-462-2369
                        Fax: 212-446-6777
                        www.americandiamondshop.com

Diamond jewelry

President: Joseph Bakhash
Credit Cards: AMEX; MasterCard; Visa
Catalog Cost: Free
In Business: 59 years
Number of Employees: 2
Sales Volume: Under $500M

5163 American Pearl
American Pearl & General Company
576 Fifth Avenue, Suite 1102
New York, NY 10036   212-764-1845
                             800-847-3275
                        Fax: 212-869-7473
                        www.americanpearl.com

Pearl jewelry

President: Edward Bakhash
Credit Cards: AMEX; MasterCard; Visa
In Business: 65 years
Number of Employees: 2

5164 Antique & Collectible Jewelry
PO Box 2978
Covington, LA 70434-2978   985-892-0014

Antiques and collectible jewelry

Catalog Cost: $3
Printing Information: 40 pages

5165 Ashley's Fine Equestrian Jewelry & Gifts
Ashley's
PO Box 306
Gwynedd, PA 19436-306   215-542-8820
                             800-843-3838
                        Fax: 215-542-0412
                        info@ashleysgifts.com
                        www.ashleyshorsejewelry.com

Ashley's signature jewelry, jewelry collections, crystal, art glass, table top and gifts

In Business: 21 years

5166 Baroni
Baroni
1049 Samoa Blvd
Arcata, CA 95521   707-822-8067
                             800-550-8942
                        Fax: 707-822- 779
                        sales@baronidesigns.com
                        www.baronidesigns.com

Jewelry.

In Business: 24 years

5167 Ben Bridge Jeweler
Ben Bridge Jeweler, Inc.
PO Box 1908
Seattle, WA 98111-1908   206-239-6802
                             888-448-1912
                        info@benbridge.com
                        www.benbridge.com

Fine jewelry and watches

President: Edward Bridge
CFO: Jerry Gronfein
Marketing Manager: Steve Davolt
Co-CEO: Herb Bridge
Co-CEO: Bob Bridge
Credit Cards: AMEX; MasterCard; Visa; Discover
Printing Information: 5 pages in 6 colors on Glossy Stock
Press: Web Press
Binding: Saddle Stitched
In Business: 12 years
Number of Employees: 50-1

5168 Blue Book
Tiffany & Co.
727 Fifth Ave.
New York, NY 10022   800-843-3269
                        www.tiffany.com

Fine jewelry.

CEO: Frederic Cumenal
Catalog Circulation: Mailed 1 time(s) per year
Printing Information: 122 pages in 4 colors
In Business: 179 years
Number of Employees: 1060
Sales Volume: $4.1 Billion

5169 Bridal / Anniversary Catalog 2012
Tenenbaum's Jewelry
219 East Bremer Avenue
Waverly, IA 50677   319-352-4112
                contactus@tenenbaumsjewelry.com
                        www.tenenbaumsjewelry.com

Jewelry.

In Business: 50 years

5170 Bridal / Anniversary Catalog 2013
Tenenbaum's Jewelry
219 East Bremer Avenue
Waverly, IA 50677   319-352-4112
                contactus@tenenbaumsjewelry.com
                        www.tenenbaumsjewelry.com

Jewelry.

In Business: 50 years

5171 Bridal Collection
Reeds Jewelers
2525 S 17th Street
PO Box 2229
Wilmington, NC 28402   910-350-3100
                                    877-406-3266
                              Fax: 910-350-3353
                        customer@reeds.com
                        www.reeds.com

Wedding and engagement jewelry
President: Alan M Zimmer
CFO: James R Rouse
Credit Cards: AMEX; MasterCard; Visa
Catalog Cost: Free
Catalog Circulation: Mailed 1 time(s) per year
In Business: 63 years
Number of Employees: 117

5172 Cartier
Cartier International Inc.
645 Fifth Avenue
8th Floor
New York, NY 10022-5902   212-446-3400
                                 800-227-8437
                           Fax: 212-446-2721
                        fifthavenue@cartier.com
                        www.Cartier.Com

Watches, jewelry, stationery, leather goods, and gifts by Cartier
President: Frederick Denart
Credit Cards: AMEX; MasterCard
Catalog Circulation: Mailed 1 time(s) per year
Printing Information: 80 pages in 4 colors
Binding: Saddle Stitched
Sales Volume: $1MM to $3MM

5173 Celtic Croft
Celtic Croft
8451 Xerxes Ave N.
Brooklyn Park, MN 55444   763-569-4373
                                 888-569-4373
                           Fax: 763-549-3583
                        sales@thecelticcroft.com
                        www.kilts-n-stuff.com

Scottish kilts, gifts and jewelry
President: Joseph Croft
Marketing Manager: Lorie Croft
Co-Owner: Joseph Croft
Co-Owner: Lorie Croft
Credit Cards: AMEX; MasterCard
Catalog Cost: Free
Catalog Circulation: Mailed 2 time(s) per year
Printing Information: in 4 colors
In Business: 8 years
Sales Volume: $500,000- 1 Million

5174 Diamond Essence
Diamond Essence
1115 Inman Ave.
Suite 333
Edison, NJ 08820   908-279-7986
                                 800-909-2525
                           Fax: 908-462-3881
                        info@diamondessence.com
                        www.diamond-essence.com

Simulated diamonds and cubic zirconia set in solid 14k gold.
Chairman: Raja Shah
President: Monali Shah
Marketing Manager: Raja Shah
Catalog Cost: Free
Printing Information: 52 pages in 4 colors
In Business: 37 years

5175 Drenon Jewelry Holiday
Drenon Jewelry
2314 Lee's Summit Road
Independence, MO 64055   816-252-8844
                        contactus@drenonjewelry.com
                        www.drenonjewelry.com

Jewelry.

Credit Cards: AMEX; MasterCard
In Business: 67 years

5176 Engagement
Tiffany & Co.
727 Fifth Ave.
New York, NY 10022   800-843-3269
                        www.tiffany.com

Engagement rings.
CEO: Frederic Cumenal
Catalog Circulation: Mailed 1 time(s) per year
Printing Information: 83 pages in 4 colors
In Business: 179 years
Number of Employees: 1060
Sales Volume: $4.1 Billion

5177 Family Crest Jewelry Catalog
Heraldica Imports, Inc
2 West 46th Street
Room 1208
New York, NY 10036   212-719-4204
                                800-782-0933
                          Fax: 212-719-4369
                        jcuchi@heraldica.com
                        www.heraldica.com

Family crest rings that are hand-engraved 14k gold
President: Jose A Cuchi
In Business: 48 years

5178 Fred Meyer Jewelers
Fred Meyer Jewelers
4350 24th Avenue
Suite 620
Fort Gradiot, MI 48059   810-385-7788
                                800-342-6663
                        www.fredmeyerjewelers.com

Jewelry
President: Fred Meyer
Credit Cards: AMEX; MasterCard
Catalog Cost: Free
Catalog Circulation: Mailed 4 time(s) per year
Printing Information: 17 pages in 4 colors
In Business: 44 years
Sales Volume: $100MM to $500MM

5179 GaelSong
GaelSong
PO Box 15388
Seattle, WA 98115   800-205-5790
                                800-207-4256
                          Fax: 206-729-0183
                        gaelsong@gaelsong.com
                        www.gaelsong.com

Celtic gifts and jewelry imported from Ireland, Scotland and Wales
President: Colleen Connell
Credit Cards: AMEX; MasterCard; Visa
Catalog Cost: Free

5180 Gray & Sons
Gray & Sons
9595 Harding Ave
Surfside, FL 33154   305-865-0999
                                800-918-2608
                          Fax: 305-865-9666
                        info@grayandsons.com
                        www.grayandsons.com

President: Keith Gray
keith@grayandsons.com
In Business: 35 years

5181 Heavenly Treasures
Heavenly Treasures
321 Main St
Allenhurst, NJ 07711-1037   732-531-7978
                                800-269-4637
                          Fax: 732-531-8044
                        www.heavenlytreasures.com

Fine jewlry and gems

President: Abraham Ades
VP, Marketing: Michael Ades
In Business: 17 years
Number of Employees: 8
Sales Volume: $1.1 Million

5182 I Do Collection
Tenenbaum's Jewelry
219 East Bremer Avenue
Waverly, IA 50677   319-352-4112
                        contactus@tenenbaumsjewelry.com
                        www.tenenbaumsjewelry.com

Jewelry.

In Business: 50 years

5183 Inspired Silver
Ecommerce Innovations
3245 Palm Center Drive
Las Vegas, NV 89103   866-547-4583
                        www.inspiredsilver.com

Sterling silver and Cubic Zirconia Jewelry; rings, earrings, bracelets, necklaces, wedding sets, accessories, and men's
Credit Cards: AMEX; MasterCard
Catalog Cost: Free

5184 JH Breakell & Company
JH Breakell & Co.
132 Spring Street
Newport, RI 02840   401-849-3522
                                800-767-6411
                        doris@breakell.com
                        www.breakell.com

Jewelry designed and made in Newport by James Breakell since 1972
President: Jim Breakell
Credit Cards: AMEX; MasterCard; Visa
Catalog Cost: Free
Catalog Circulation: Mailed 6 time(s) per year
Average Order Size: $100
Printing Information: 31 pages in 4 colors on Glossy Stock
Press: Web Press
Binding: Saddle Stitched
In Business: 43 years
Number of Employees: 10
Sales Volume: $1MM to $3MM

5185 Jensen Jewelers Current Bridal Catalog
Jensen Jewelers
1485 Pole Line Rd
Twin Falls, ID 83301   208-733-6309
                        www.jensen-jewelers.com

Jewelry.

In Business: 59 years

5186 Jensen Jewelers Elk Ivory Catalog
Jensen Jewelers
1485 Pole Line Rd
Twin Falls, ID 83301   208-733-6309
                        www.jensen-jewelers.com

Jewelry.

In Business: 59 years

5187 Jewelry Care
Tiffany & Co.
727 Fifth Ave.
New York, NY 10022   800-843-3269
                        www.tiffany.com

Jewelry care.
CEO: Frederic Cumenal
Printing Information: 18 pages in 2 colors
In Business: 179 years
Number of Employees: 1060
Sales Volume: $4.1 Billion

5188 John Christian
John Christian Company
14101 W Highway 290
Suite 900
Austin, TX 78737 512-858-2556
888-646-6466
jcinfo@john-christian.com
www.john-christian.com

Wedding & anniversary, special occasions, corporate gifts
President: Wesley P Weaver
Credit Cards: AMEX; MasterCard; Visa
In Business: 85 years
Number of Employees: 5
Sales Volume: $220,000

5189 Just the Thing
Tiffany & Co.
727 Fifth Ave.
New York, NY 10022 800-843-3269
www.tiffany.com

Fine jewelry and elegant gifts.
CEO: Frederic Cumenal
Catalog Circulation: Mailed 1 time(s) per year
Printing Information: 88 pages in 4 colors
In Business: 179 years
Number of Employees: 1060
Sales Volume: $4.1 Billion

5190 Kay Jewelers
Kay Jewelers
375 Ghent Road
Akron, OH 44999 330-668-5000
800-527-8029
Fax: 330-668-5052
www.kay.com

Engagement & wedding rings, diamond jewelry, color gemstones, gold, silver, and other jewelry
Chairman: Terry Burman
President: Mark Light
CFO: Robery Trabucco
Credit Cards: AMEX; MasterCard; Visa
Catalog Cost: Free
In Business: 99 years

5191 Kelly Herd
Kelly Herd
2713 Magnolia Court,
Cleveland, TE 37312 866-617-4653
Fax: 423-479-8607
Kelherd@aol.com
www.kellyherdjewelry.com

Jewelry.
In Business: 20 years

5192 Krout & Company
Krout & Company
Post Office Box 297
Lemont, PA 16851 814-883-9658
Todd@Kroutco.com
kroutco.com

Jewelry.

5193 Lee Michael's Fine Jewelry
Lee Michael's Fine Jewelry
7560 Corporate Blvd
Baton Rouge, LA 70809 225-926-4644
800-543-GEMS
Fax: 225-926-9600
bocage@lmfj.com
www.lmfj.com

Credit Cards: AMEX; MasterCard

5194 Littman Jewelers
Littman Jewelers
3800 SE 22nd Ave
Portland, OR 97202-2918 503-232-8844
800-342-6663
Fax: 503-797-7616
www.littmanjewelers.com

Engagement and wedding jewelry, as well as watches, rings, necklaces, and bracelets
President: Peter M Engel
Credit Cards: AMEX; MasterCard; Visa
Catalog Cost: Free

5195 Lovell Designs Earthsong Collection
Lovell Designs
26 Exchange St
PO Box 7130
Portland, ME 04112-7130 800-533-9685
Fax: 207-828-1067
april2@maine.rr.com
www.lovelldesigns.com

Nature-inspired jewelry, ornaments and tableware by Ken Kantro
President: Ken Kantro
Marketing Manager: April Kearney
Founder: Ken Kantro
Credit Cards: AMEX; MasterCard; Visa
Average Order Size: $60
Mailing List Information: Names for rent
In Business: 39 years
Number of Employees: 20

5196 Lux Bond & Green
Lux Bond & Green
46 Lasalle Road
West Hartford, CT 06107-2373 860-521-3015
800-524-7336
Fax: 860-521-8693
westhartford@lbgreen.com
www.Lbgreen.Com

Fine jewelry and gifts
President: Robert Green
Founder: Morris A. Green
Credit Cards: AMEX; MasterCard; Visa
Catalog Cost: Free
Printing Information: 10 pages in 4 colors on Glossy Stock
Press: Web Press
Binding: Saddle Stitched
In Business: 116 years
Number of Employees: 60
Sales Volume: $10MM to $20MM

5197 Maurice Badler Fine Jewelry
Maurice Badler Fine Jewelry Ltd
485 Park Avenue
New York, NY 10022 212-575-9632
800-622-3537
Fax: 212-575-9205
info@badler.com
www.badler.com

Fine jewelry
President: Jeffrey Badler
Credit Cards: AMEX; MasterCard; Visa
Catalog Cost: Free
Printing Information: 32 pages in 4 colors
Press: Web Press
Mailing List Information: Names for rent
In Business: 50 years
Number of Employees: 8

5198 Palm Beach Jewelry
Palm Beach
6400 E Rogers Circle
Boca Raton, FL 33499 866-804-3745
customerservice@palmbeachjewelry.com
www.palmbeachjewelry.com

Fine jewelry at discount prices
Credit Cards: AMEX; MasterCard
Catalog Cost: Free
Catalog Circulation: Mailed 10 time(s) per year
Average Order Size: $85
Printing Information: 48 pages in 4 colors on Glossy Stock
Press: Web Press
Binding: Saddle Stitched
In Business: 60 years
Number of Employees: 250
Sales Volume: $50MM to $100MM

5199 Ross Metals Corporation
Ross Metals Corporation
27 W 47th Street
New York, NY 10036 212-869-1407
800-654-7677
Fax: 212-768-3018
sales@rossmetals.com
www.rossmetals.com

Precious metals
President: Jack Ross
Executive Supervisor: Karin Zakarian
Sales Manager: Sally Singh
Refining Manager: Angela Diaz
Credit Cards: AMEX; MasterCard
Printing Information: 64 pages in 3 colors
Press: Web Press
Binding: Saddle Stitched
In Business: 28 years
Number of Employees: 25
Sales Volume: $5.4 Million

5200 Ross-Simons
Ross-Simons
9 Ross-Simons Drive
Cranston, RI 02920-4475 401-463-3100
800-521-7677
customerservice@ross-simons.com
www.ross-simons.com

Fine jewelry, and watches
President: Darrell Ross
CFO: David Pawlak
Credit Cards: AMEX; MasterCard; Visa
Catalog Circulation: Mailed 12 time(s) per year
Average Order Size: $170
Printing Information: 75 pages in 4 colors on Glossy Stock
Press: Web Press
Binding: Saddle Stitched
Mailing List Information: Names for rent
List Company: The Specialists
In Business: 65 years
Number of Employees: 500
Sales Volume: $50MM

5201 Slusher's Jewelry Holiday
Slusher's Jewelry
10276 State Route 118
Van Wert, OH 45891 416-232-3700
contactus@slushersjewelry.com
www.slushersjewelry.com

Jewelry.
In Business: 20 years

5202 Southwest Indian Foundation
Southwest Indian Foundation
100 West Coal Avenue
Gallup, NM 87301 505-863-4037
800-504-2723
customerservice@southwestindian.com
www.southwestindian.com

Southwest Indian jewelry
Chief Executive Officer: William McCarthy
Executive Director: Joseph Esparza
projectoffice@southwestindian.com
Credit Cards: MasterCard; Visa
Catalog Circulation: Mailed 4 time(s) per year
Printing Information: 64 pages on Matte Stock
In Business: 46 years
Number of Employees: 80
Sales Volume: $2.7 Million

5203 The Golden Bear
The Golden Bear
183 Gore Creek Drive, Ste 3A
PO Box 5060
Vail, CO 81657 970-476-4082
800-338-7782
Fax: 888-252-4759
tgb@thegoldenbear.com
www.thegoldenbear.com

Exclusive jewelry designs recognized around the world

Founder: Lee Kirch
Printing Information: 51 pages in 4 colors on Glossy Stock
Press: Web Press
In Business: 40 years
Number of Employees: 27

5204 This Is Tiffany
Tiffany & Co.
727 Fifth Ave.
New York, NY 10022   800-843-3269
www.tiffany.com

Engagement rings, jewelry, watches and gifts.

CEO: Frederic Cumenal
Catalog Circulation: Mailed 2 time(s) per year
Printing Information: 74 pages in 4 colors
Mailing List Information: Names for rent
List Company: Mokrynski & Associates
In Business: 179 years
Number of Employees: 1060
Sales Volume: $4.1 Billion

5205 Tiffany Watches
Tiffany & Co.
727 Fifth Ave.
New York, NY 10022   800-843-3269
www.tiffany.com

Fine watches.

CEO: Frederic Cumenal
Catalog Circulation: Mailed 1 time(s) per year
Printing Information: 82 pages in 4 colors
In Business: 179 years
Number of Employees: 1060
Sales Volume: $4.1 Billion

5206 Timepieces International
Timepieces International, Inc.
12800 N.W South River Drive
Medley, FL 33178   888-768-4468
800-733-8463
Fax: 888-675-3045
customerservices@timepiecesusa.com
www.timepiecesusa.com

Ladies' and mens' watches as well as fine jewelry

, Daniel Steiger, Zeitner, Klaus Kobec
Credit Cards: AMEX; MasterCard
Catalog Cost: Free
Printing Information: in 4 colors
In Business: 18 years

5207 Wandering Star Astrology Jewelry
Wandering Star Designs
1627 NE Alberta St
Ste B
Portland, OR 97211   503-209-3956
800-978-2725
www.wanderingstarjewelry.com

Custom astrology horoscope jewelry and zodiac gifts; aromatherapy and astrology books

President: Alicia C Katz
Credit Cards: AMEX; MasterCard; Visa
Catalog Cost: Free
Catalog Circulation: Mailed 1 time(s) per year
Printing Information: 16 pages in 4 colors
In Business: 19 years

5208 Windsor Collection
AmeriMark Direct
6864 Engle Rd.
Cleveland, OH 44130   866-345-1388
www.amerimark.com

Fashion jewelry

CFO: Joe Albanese
CEO & President: Gareth Giesler
Catalog Cost: Free
Printing Information: in 4 colors
In Business: 47 years
Number of Employees: 700
Sales Volume: $400 Million

Kitchenware
Equipment & Supplies

5209 AG Russell
AG Russell Knives, Inc.
2900 S 26th Street
Rogers, AR 72758-8571   479-631-0130
800-255-9034
Fax: 479-631-8493
ag@agrussell.com
www.agrussell.com

Knives and accessories

Chairman: Goldie Russell
President: A.G. Russell III
Credit Cards: MasterCard; Visa
Catalog Cost: Free
Catalog Circulation: Mailed 5 time(s) per year to 5M
Average Order Size: $139
Printing Information: 54 pages in 4 colors on Glossy Stock
Binding: Folded
In Business: 53 years
Number of Employees: 43
Sales Volume: $2.5M

5210 Bed Bath & Beyond
Bed Bath & Beyond Inc.
650 Liberty Avenue
Union, NJ 00708   800-462-3966
customer.service@bedbath.com
www.bedbathandbeyond.com

Bedding, bath, kitchen, home decor products and accessories, and gift registries

Co-Chairman: Warren Eisenberg
Co-Chairman: Leonard Feinstein
Chief Executive Officer: Steven Temares
Catalog Cost: Free
In Business: 43 years

5211 Bennington Potters
Bennington Potters
324 County Street
P.O. Box 199
Bennington, VT 05201   802-447-7531
800-205-8033
Fax: 802-442-6080
www.benningtonpotters.com

Dinner and cookware, bakeware, mixing bowls, pottery,

President: Gloria Gil
Owner/Marketing/Finance: Sheila Harden
General Manager: Paul Silberman
Credit Cards: AMEX; MasterCard; Visa
Catalog Cost: Free
Printing Information: 19 pages in 4 colors
In Business: 68 years
Number of Employees: 65
Sales Volume: $5MM to $10MM

5212 Bottles, Containers, & Bags
Consolidated Plastics
4700 Prosper Dr
Stow, OH 44224-2303   330-689-3000
800-362-1000
Fax: 800-858-5001
feedback@consolidatedplastics.com
www.consolidatedplastics.com

Bottles and caps, containers, jars, spray bottles and pumps, reclosable bags, beakers and weighing dishes, totes, etc.

President: Brenton Taussig
Buyers: Valarie Burgoyne
Credit Cards: AMEX; MasterCard; Visa
Catalog Cost: Free
Catalog Circulation: Mailed 1 time(s) per year
Printing Information: 28 pages in 4 colors on Matte Stock
Press: Web Press
Binding: Saddle Stitched
Mailing List Information: Names for rent
In Business: 34 years

Number of Employees: 14
Sales Volume: $10 MM

5213 BöKer
BöKer USA, Inc.
1550 Balsam Street
Lakewood, CO 80214-5917   800-835-6433
Fax: 303-462-0668
support@bokerusa.com
www.bokerusa.com

Knives and accessories

President: Dan Weidner
Sales Manager: Sammy Smith
Credit Cards: AMEX; MasterCard
Catalog Cost: Free
Catalog Circulation: Mailed 1 time(s) per year
Printing Information: 68 pages in 4 colors

5214 CUTCO
322 Houghton Avenue
Olean, NY 14760   800-828-0448
Fax: 716-790-7184
service@cutco.com
www.cutco.com

Knives

5215 Cashs of Ireland
Cashs of Ireland
6185-K Huntley Rd
Ste K
Columbus, OH 43229   614-430-8180
800-999-0655
Fax: 614-430-8728
info@crystalclassics.com
www.cashs.com

Irish and European clothing, crystal, china, gifts and tableware

President: Maxine Stotler
Marketing Manager: Bruno Bergman
Credit Cards: AMEX; MasterCard; Visa
Printing Information: 52 pages
In Business: 37 years
Number of Employees: 26
Sales Volume: $ 1.2 Million

5216 Ceramica Direct
CeramicaDirect.com
36 Main St
Chester, CT 06412   800-270-0900

Tabletop, dinnerware, kitchen, decorative accents and gifts

President: Carol Le Witt
Credit Cards: AMEX; MasterCard; Visa
Catalog Cost: Free
Sales Volume: $5MM to $10MM

5217 Commercial Mats and Matting
Consolidated Plastics
4700 Prosper Drive
Stow, OH 44224-2303   800-362-1000
800-362-1000
Fax: 800-858-5001
feedback@consolidatedplastics.com
www.consolidatedplastics.com

Entryway mats (indoor and outdoor), custom logo mats, anti-fatigue and rubber mats, grip strips, safety track tape

President: Brenton Taussig
Buyers: Valarie Burgoyne
Credit Cards: AMEX; MasterCard; Visa
Catalog Cost: Free
Catalog Circulation: Mailed 1 time(s) per year
Printing Information: 24 pages in 4 colors on Matte Stock
Press: Web Press
Binding: Saddle Stitched
Mailing List Information: Names for rent
In Business: 34 years
Number of Employees: 14
Sales Volume: $10 MM

5218 Cooking Enthusiast
Cooking Enthusiast
242 Branford Road
North Branford, CT 06471   800-625-1866
                                   800-792-6650
                            Fax: 800-296-8039
custserv@unoallavolta.com
www.unoallavolta.com

Kitchen cutlery, cookware and cook books, home decor, coffee and tea, pottery

President: Terri Alpert
Credit Cards: MasterCard; Visa
Catalog Cost: Free
Catalog Circulation: Mailed 5 time(s) per year
Average Order Size: $120
Printing Information: 37 pages in 2 colors on Matte Stock
Press: Web Press
Binding: Saddle Stitched
In Business: 30 years
Number of Employees: 40
Sales Volume: $3.30M

5219 Crystal Classics
Crystal Classics
6185-K Huntley Road
Columbus, OH 43229-1094   614-430-8180
                                  800-999-0655
                           Fax: 614-430-8728
info@crystalclassics.com
www.crystalclassics.com

Crystal stemware collections, lamps, barware, wedding gifts, ornaments

President: Maxine Stotler
Marketing Manager: Bruno Bergman
Credit Cards: AMEX; MasterCard; Visa
Catalog Cost: Free
In Business: 19 years
Number of Employees: 26
Sales Volume: 1.2M

5220 Fancy Flours
Fancy Flours
705 Osterman Drive
Suite E
Bozeman, MT 59715   406-587-0118
                          Fax: 406-522-0668
info@fancyflours.com
www.fancyflours.com

Bakeware, cake and cookie decorating supplies, oils, extracts and flavorings, premium vanillas, collector's copper tin cookie cutters, table and partyware

Credit Cards: AMEX; MasterCard
Catalog Cost: Free
Sales Volume: $1MM to $3MM

5221 Foodcrafter's Supply Catalog
Kitchen Krafts, Inc.
PO Box 442
Waukon, IA 52172-442   563-535-8000
                                 800-298-5389
                          Fax: 563-535-8001
service@kitchenkrafts.com
www.kitchenkrafts.com

Direct merchant of speciality foodcrafting supplies for cake decorating, baking, candymaking, canning and more, full range equipment, tools, ingredients, books, packaging and other supplies

President: Lynn Sorensen
Marketing Manager: Dean Sorensen
Credit Cards: AMEX; MasterCard; Visa
Catalog Cost: Free
Printing Information: 56 pages in 4 colors
Mailing List Information: Names for rent
In Business: 25 years
Number of Employees: 20
Sales Volume: $1MM-$3MM

5222 Fresh Finds
Fresh Finds, LLC
425 Stump Road
PO Box 2800
North Wales, PA 19454-2800   215-361-5352
                                 800-860-6022
customerservice@freshfinds.com
www.freshfinds.com

Affordable kitchen and home solutions

Catalog Cost: Free

5223 Grill Lovers Catalog
Bradley Direct
P.O. Box 1240
Columbus, GA 31902-1240   706-565-2100
                                 800-241-8981
                          Fax: 706-565-2119
www.grilllovers.com

Grills, cooking accessories, and outdoor entertaining products

President: Constance Warner
CFO: Len Lyons
Marketing Manager: Connie Warner
Production Manager: Amy Wilkerson
Buyers: Sonny Jones
Credit Cards: MasterCard
Catalog Cost: Free
Catalog Circulation: Mailed 6 time(s) per year to 9M
Average Order Size: $55
Printing Information: 48 pages in 4 colors on Matte Stock
Press: Web Press
Binding: Saddle Stitched
Mailing List Information: Names for rent
In Business: 25 years
Number of Employees: 400
Sales Volume: $10MM to $20MM

5224 Keen Ovens
Keen Ovens
PO Box 1322
Hammond, LA 70404   985-345-2171
                                 888-512-2870
                          Fax: 985-345-5653
sales@keenovens.com
www.keenovens.com

Outdoor cookers, welding consumable storage ovens,

President: Rich Freedman
Manager/Office Manager: Glenva Crawford
Credit Cards: MasterCard; Visa
Catalog Cost: Free
Printing Information: 4 pages
In Business: 88 years
Number of Employees: 16
Sales Volume: $1.2 Million

5225 King Arthur Flour & The Bakers
King Arthur Flour & The Bakers
135 US Route 5 South
Norwich, VT 05055-9430   802-649-3361
                                 800-827-6836
                          Fax: 802-649-3365
bakers@kingarthurflour.com
www.kingarthurflour.com

Flour, baking mixes and specialty baking supplies

Chairman: Frank E Sands II
President: Steve Voigt
CFO: Susan Renaud
Marketing Manager: Tom Payne
Production Manager: Sue Gray
Buyers: PJ Hamel
Credit Cards: AMEX; MasterCard; Visa
Catalog Cost: Free
Catalog Circulation: Mailed 12 time(s) per year to 6M
Printing Information: 56 pages in 4 colors on Matte Stock
Press: Web Press
Binding: Saddle Stitched
List Company: Direct Media
200 Pemberwick Road

Greenwich, CT 06830
203-532-3713
In Business: 225 years
Number of Employees: 150
Sales Volume: $20MM to $50MM

5226 Knife Merchant
Knife Merchant
7887 Dunbrook Rd
Suite H
San Diego, CA 92126   858-578-9007
                                 800-714-8226
                          Fax: 888-463-3117
customerservice@knifemerchant.com
www.knifemerchant.com

Kitchen knives and cutlery, cookware, coffee makers and grinders, countertop appliances, baking and pastry, flatware, cutting boards, kitchen tools and student supplies and more

President: David J Holly
Owner: David Holly
Credit Cards: AMEX; MasterCard
Catalog Cost: Free
Average Order Size: $100
Mailing List Information: Names for rent
In Business: 14 years
Number of Employees: 4
Sales Volume: $300,000

5227 Kraftware
Kraftware
270 Cox Street
Roselle, NJ 07203-1704   800-221-1728
twanna@k-ware.com
www.kraftwarecorp.com

Home entertaining accessories and barware

President: Randall Grant
National VP of Sales: Don Williams
donw@k-ware.com
Mailing List Information: Names for rent
Sales Volume: $5MM to $10MM

5228 Lansky Sharpeners
Lansky Sharpeners
PO Box 800
Buffalo, NY 14231   716-877-7511
                                 800-825-2675
                          Fax: 716-877-6955
customerservice@lansky.com
www.lansky.com

Knife and tool sharpeners

President: Edward Schwartz
Controller/Personnel Manager: Bonnie Maron
Credit Cards: AMEX; MasterCard; Visa
Catalog Cost: Free

5229 Miles Kimball
Miles Kimball
250 City Center
Oshkosh, WI 54906   855-202-7394
www.mileskimball.com

Kitchen gadgets, home decor, storage & organization, books, jewelry, apparel, health, beauty, home office supplies and gift items.

Catalog Cost: Free
In Business: 81 years
Sales Volume: $10 Million

5230 Oneida Air Systems
Oneida Air Systems
1001 W Fayette Street
Syracuse, NY 13204-2873   800-732-4065
                          Fax: 315-476-5044
info@oneida-air.com
www.oneida-air.com

Dust collection, air filtration, custom engineering, complete duct work packages, cyclones and filter media

President: Robert Witter
Credit Cards: AMEX; MasterCard
Mailing List Information: Names for rent

In Business: 24 years
Number of Employees: 25
Sales Volume: $20MM to $50MM

5231 Pfaltzgraff
Pfaltzgraff
PO Box 21769
York, PA 17402-190   717-852-2211
                            800-999-2811
                      Fax: 800-717-2481
              service@pfaltzgraff.com
              www.pfaltzgraff.com

Dinnerware, flatware, glassware, cutlery, bakeware, gifts, linen and more

President: Marsha M Everton
Credit Cards: AMEX; MasterCard
Catalog Cost: Free
In Business: 204 years
Number of Employees: 1000

5232 R & R Mill Company
Area Knowledge
48 W 100 S
PO Box 187
Smithfield, UT 84335   435-563-3333
                      Fax: 435-563-4093
              www.areaknowledge.com

Unusual kitchen items, cheese slicers, manual grain mills, wheatgrass juicers and more

President: Ralph Roylance
Marketing Manager: Karen Phillips
Credit Cards: AMEX; MasterCard; Visa
Catalog Cost: Free
Mailing List Information: Names for rent
In Business: 30 years
Number of Employees: 5
Sales Volume: under 500,000

5233 Rada Cutlery
Rada Manufacturing Co.
P.O. Box 838
Waverly, IA 50611   319-352-5454
                            800-311-9691
                      Fax: 800-311-9623
              customerservice@radamfg.com
              www.radacutlery.com

Cutlery and other cookware, cookbooks

President: Gary Nelson
Catalog Cost: Free
Printing Information: 32 pages in 4 colors
In Business: 69 years

5234 Shepherd Hills Cutlery
Shepherd Hills
PO Box 909
Lebanon, MO 65536-909   800-727-4643
                                888-422-7399
                      Fax: 417-532-6044
              info@shephills.com
              www.shepherdhillscutlery.com

Collectible knives, books, belt buckles, tee shirts, license plates, caps and hat pins, kitchen cutlery, accessories

President: Ida Reid
Vice President: Rod Reid
Credit Cards: MasterCard; Visa
Catalog Cost: Free
Printing Information: 44 pages in 3 colors
In Business: 43 years
Number of Employees: 85
Sales Volume: $6M

5235 Sur la Table
Sur la Table
PO Box 840
Brownsburg, IN 46112   800-243-0852
                      Fax: 317-858-5521
              www.surlatable.com

Fine equipment for domestic and professional kitchens.

CEO: Diane Neal
Catalog Cost: Free

Printing Information: in 4 colors
Number of Employees: 2300
Sales Volume: $175 Million

5236 The Clean Team
The Clean Team
498 East Purnell Street
Suite 103
Lewisville, TX 75057   972-219-0400
                                800-717-2532
              inquire@thecleanteam.com
              www.thecleanteam.com

Speed cleaning supplies, clutter control, home maintenance products, and household cleaning products that are safe and fast

President: Steve Sardone
Marketing Manager: Debbie Sardone
Credit Cards: AMEX; MasterCard; Visa
Catalog Cost: Free
Catalog Circulation: Mailed 4 time(s) per year
Average Order Size: $70
Printing Information: 16 pages in 4 colors on Glossy Stock
Press: Web Press
Binding: Saddle Stitched
Mailing List Information: Names for rent
In Business: 25 years
Number of Employees: 4
Sales Volume: $5,00,000

5237 Tupperware
Tupperware Brands Corporation
14901 S Orange Blossom Trail
Orlando, FL 32837   www.tupperware.com

Food preparation, storage and serving products.

Chairman & CEO: Rick Goings
Printing Information: 80 pages in 4 colors
In Business: 70 years
Number of Employees: 1350
Sales Volume: $2.3 Billion

5238 Tupperware Fundraiser Brochure
Tupperware Brands Corporation
14901 S Orange Blossom Trail
Orlando, FL 32837   www.tupperware.com

Food preparation, storage and serving products.

Chairman & CEO: Rick Goings
Printing Information: 16 pages in 4 colors
In Business: 70 years
Number of Employees: 1350
Sales Volume: $2.3 Billion

5239 Tupperware Mid-Month Brochure
Tupperware Brands Corporation
14901 S Orange Blossom Trail
Orlando, FL 32837   www.tupperware.com

Food preparation, storage and serving products.

Chairman & CEO: Rick Goings
Printing Information: 14 pages in 4 colors
In Business: 70 years
Number of Employees: 1350
Sales Volume: $2.3 Billion

5240 Williams-Sonoma
Williams-Sonoma, Inc.
3250 Van Ness Ave.
San Francisco, CA 94109   415-421-7900
              www.williams-sonomainc.com

Tools for cooking and entertaining.

CEO: Laura Alber
Catalog Cost: Free
Catalog Circulation: Mailed 12 time(s) per year
Printing Information: 128 pages in 4 colors
In Business: 60 years
Number of Employees: 2680
Sales Volume: $4.4 Billion

5241 Williams-Sonoma Home
Williams-Sonoma, Inc.
3250 Van Ness Ave.
San Francisco, CA 94109   415-421-7900
              www.williams-sonomainc.com

Tools for cooking and entertaining.

CEO: Laura Alber
Catalog Cost: Free
Catalog Circulation: Mailed 12 time(s) per year
Printing Information: 76 pages in 4 colors
In Business: 60 years
Number of Employees: 2680
Sales Volume: $4.4 Billion

Motorcycles
General Products & Accessories

5242 Aerostich Rider Wearhouse
Aero Design & Mfg. Co., Inc.
8 South 18th Avenue West
Duluth, MN 55806   218-722-1927
                            800-222-1994
                      Fax: 218-720-3610
              service@aerostich.com
              www.aerostich.com

Motorcycle jackets, suits, helmets, boots, gloves, tools, bags and other accessories

President: Andrew Goldfine
Credit Cards: AMEX; MasterCard; Visa
Catalog Cost: Free
Catalog Circulation: Mailed 5 time(s) per year
Printing Information: 250 pages in 4 colors on G
Binding: S
Mailing List Information: Names for rent
In Business: 32 years
Number of Employees: 100

5243 BTO Sports
BTO Sports, Inc.
600 Via Alondra
Camarillo, CA 93012   805-777-7601
                                888-613-3393
                      Fax: 805-777-7201
              info@btosports.com
              www.btosports.com

Motorcross gear, parts and accessories

President: Vincent Arimitsu
General Manager: Joe Arimitsu
Credit Cards: AMEX; MasterCard
In Business: 16 years
Number of Employees: 35
Sales Volume: $15 Million

5244 Bed Bath & Beyond
Bed Bath & Beyond Inc.
650 Liberty Avenue
Union, NJ 00708   800-462-3966
              customer.service@bedbath.com
              www.bedbathandbeyond.com

Bedding, bath, kitchen, home decor products and accessories, and gift registries

Co-Chairman: Warren Eisenberg
Co-Chairman: Leonard Feinstein
Chief Executive Officer: Steven Temares
Catalog Cost: Free
In Business: 43 years

5245 Bob's BMW
Bob's BMW
10720 Guilford Rd
Jessup, MD 20794-9385   301-497-8949
                                888-BMW-BOBS
                      Fax: 301-776-2338
              www.bobsbmw.com

BMW motorcycle apparel, parts and accessories

President: Bob Henig
Marketing Manager: Hanna Creekmore
hanna.creekmore@bobsbmw.com

Owner: Suzanne Henig
Suzanne.henig@bobsbmw.com
Bookkeeper: Dana Tompkins
Custodian: Bucky Buchanan
Printing Information: 77 pages in 2 colors on Matte Stock
Press: Web Press
Binding: Saddle Stitched
Mailing List Information: Names for rent
In Business: 40 years
Number of Employees: 37
Sales Volume: $8.91 MM

5246 Capital Cycle Corporation

Capital Cycle Corporation
45891 Woodland Road
#110
Sterling, VA 20166   703-421-7861
                             800-642-5100
                        Fax: 703-421-7868
                   info@capitalcycle.com
                   www.capitalcycle.com

BMW motorcycle OEM original and aftermarket parts, motorcycle accessories

President: R Moore, Jr.
Credit Cards: AMEX; MasterCard
Catalog Cost: Free
Catalog Circulation: Mailed 1 time(s) per year to 40000
Printing Information: 26 pages in 1 color on Glossy Stock
Press: Web Press
Binding: Saddle Stitched
In Business: 40 years
Number of Employees: 2
Sales Volume: $160,000

5247 Casual Wear Catalog

Bob's Cycle Supply
65 Viking DR W
St Paul, MN 55117   651-482-8181
                            888-306-2627
                       Fax: 651-482-0974
                   bobs@bobscycle.com
                   www.bobscycle.com

Casual clothing

President: Scott Muellner
Marketing Manager: Leisha Olson
Purchasing: Josh Lane
Team Manager: David Pingree
Credit Cards: AMEX; MasterCard
Catalog Cost: Free
Catalog Circulation: Mailed 12 time(s) per year
In Business: 40 years
Number of Employees: 47
Sales Volume: $10 million

5248 Chaparral Motorspots Catalog

Chaparral Motorsports
555 South H Street
San Bernardino, CA 92410   909-889-2761
                             800-841-2960
                        Fax: 800-841-4261
               info@chaparralmotorsports.com
                   www.chaparral-racing.com

Motorcycle parts and accessories

President: David Damron
Marketing Manager: Crystal Ashby
Vice President: James Damron
Sales Manager: Andy Anaya
Purchasing: Greg Shearer
In Business: 51 years
Number of Employees: 17
Sales Volume: $3.7 MM

5249 Competition Accessories

Competition Accessories
343 W Leffel Ln
Springfield, OH 45506-3525   855-518-6681
                              800-543-8208
                         www.compacc.com

Motorcycle parts and accessories

President: Dan Conetta
Finance Executive: Rich Harris
Credit Cards: AMEX; MasterCard; Visa
Catalog Cost: Free
Mailing List Information: Names for rent
Number of Employees: 100

5250 Cruiser Catalog

J&P Cycles
13225 Circle Drive
Anamosa, IA 52205   319-462-4817
                            800-318-4823
                       Fax: 319-462-4283
                   jpcycles@jpcycles.com
                   www.jpcycles.com

Motorcycle parts and accessories for Cruiser

President: John Parham
VP: Jill Parham
Purchasing Manager: Trafferd Anderson
Credit Cards: AMEX; MasterCard
Catalog Cost: Free
Mailing List Information: Names for rent
In Business: 36 years
Number of Employees: 9
Sales Volume: $460,000

5251 CruzTOOLS

CruzTOOLS, Inc.
PO Box 250
Standard, CA 95373   209-536-0491
                             888-909-8665
                        Fax: 209-536-0463
                   contact@cruztools.com
                   www.cruztools.com

Tools and tool kits for motorcyclists and musicians

President: Daniel Parks
Vice President: Elizabeth Parks
In Business: 14 years
Number of Employees: 5
Sales Volume: $450,000

5252 Cycle Gear, Inc.

Cycle Gear, Inc.
4705 Industrial Way
Benicia, CA 94510   707-747-5053
                            800-292-5343
                customerservice@cyclegear.com
                   www.cyclegear.com

Motorcycle parts, accessories and apparel

President: David Bertram
CFO: Jeff Forgan
Marketing Manager: Christine Parsley
Controller: Rob Cherep
Rider Rep: Daniel Mates
Director of Training: George Gerstenberg
Credit Cards: AMEX; MasterCard
Printing Information: in 4 colors
In Business: 41 years
Number of Employees: 520

5253 Dennis Kirk Metric Motorcycle Catalog

Dennis Kirk
955 South Frandsen Avenue
Rush City, MN 55069   800-969-7501
                         Fax: 320-358-4019
                customerservice@denniskirk.com
                   www.denniskirk.com

Motorcycle riding apparel, protective gear, performance products and more

President: Robert Behan
Marketing Manager: Renita Twingstrom
VP of Finance: Heidi Scheffer
Operations Manager: Mac McKenzie
Credit Cards: AMEX; MasterCard
Catalog Cost: Free
Printing Information: 856 pages in 4 colors
In Business: 48 years
Sales Volume: $50MM to $100MM

5254 Dennis Kirk Off Road Catalog

Dennis Kirk
955 South Frandsen Avenue
Rush City, MN 55069   320-358-4791
                              800-969-7501
                         Fax: 320-358-4019
                customerservice@denniskirk.com
                   www.denniskirk.com

Dirt bikes and ATVs riding apparel, performance parts and accessories

President: Bob Behan
Marketing Manager: Renita Twingstrom
VP of Finance: Heidi Scheffer
Credit Cards: AMEX; MasterCard
Catalog Cost: Free
In Business: 46 years

5255 Easyriders Roadware Catalog

Paisano Publications
28210 Dorothy Drive
Agoura Hills, CA 91301-2605   818-889-8740
                               800-323-3484
                bulkmagazines@paisanopub.com
                   www.paisanopub.com

Motorcycle clothing and accessories

President: Gil Luna
Credit Cards: AMEX; MasterCard; Visa
Catalog Cost: Free
In Business: 47 years
Sales Volume: $20MM to $50MM

5256 Goldwing Catalog

J&P Cycles
13225 Circle Drive
Anamosa, IA 52205   800-318-4823
                       Fax: 319-462-4283
                   jpcycles@jpcycles.com
                   www.jpcycles.com

Parts and accessories for GoldWings

President: John Parham
VP: Jill Parham
Purchasing Manager: Trafferd Anderson
Credit Cards: AMEX; MasterCard
Catalog Cost: Free
Mailing List Information: Names for rent
In Business: 35 years
Number of Employees: 9
Sales Volume: $460,000

5257 J&P Cycles

J&P Cycles
651 Canyon Drive
Suite 100
Coppell, TX 75019   386-603-7090
                            800-318-4823
                       Fax: 386-615-6722
                   www.jpcycles.com

Motorcycle parts and accessories for Harley-Davidsons years 1936-2010

President: John Parham, Founder
Marketing Manager: Nicole Ridge
Founder: Jill Parham
Vice President: Zach Partham
Credit Cards: AMEX; MasterCard; Visa
Catalog Cost: Free
Mailing List Information: Names for rent
In Business: 39 years
Number of Employees: 100
Sales Volume: $20MM to $50MM

5258 JC Whitney Motorcycle

JC Whitney and Company
761 Progress Parkway
La Salle, IL 61301   312-431-6098
                             866-529-5530
                        Fax: 800-537-2700
                customerservice@jcwhitney.com
                   www.jcwhitney.com

Motorcycle parts, accessories, and tools

President: Tom West
Credit Cards: AMEX; MasterCard
Catalog Cost: Free

In Business: 108 years
Sales Volume: $20MM to $50MM

5259 Jardine Performance Products

Jardine Performance Products
4540 W. 160th Street
Cleveland, OH 44135-130   216-265-8400
Fax: 216-265-0130
Jardine@SuperTrapp.com
www.jardineproducts.com

Motorcycle exhaust systems, grips, footpegs, backrests, racks, forward controls, wheels, spark arrestors and more

Marketing Manager: Paul Harrington
Buyers: Judy Wan
Catalog Cost: $4
Catalog Circulation: Mailed 1 time(s) per year
Printing Information: 27 pages in 4 colors on Glossy Stock
Mailing List Information: Names for rent
In Business: 34 years
Number of Employees: 90
Sales Volume: $3MM to $5MM

5260 Jerry Greer's Indian Engineering

Jerry Greer's
1900 14th Ave NW
PO Box 1564
Watertown, SD 57201-6564   605-884-1050
800-307-9027
Fax: 605-884-1041
jge@jerrygreersengineering.com
www.jerrygreersengineering.com

Motorcycle parts for a 1936-1953 Chief, Indian Scout or Four motorcycles.

Catalog Cost: $28.5
Printing Information: 212 pages

5261 Kiwi Indian Motorcycle

Kiwi Indian Motorcycle
19510 Van Buren Blvd
Suite F-3#258
Riverside, CA 92507-5903   951-780-5400
Fax: 951-780-7722
bigchief@kiwiindian.com
www.kiwiindian.com

Indian motorcycle parts, supplies and accessories in addition to listing of used bikes for sale, also Harley-Davidson parts

President: Mike Kiwi Tomas
BigChief@KiwiIndian.com
Owner and Kiwi Tribe Mother: Carolyn Tomas
Carolyn@KiwiIndian.com
The Design Guy: Ronnie Martinez
Angie@KiwiIndian.com
Cash Counter & Chaos Coordinator:
AngieProffer
Angie@KiwiIndian.com
Credit Cards: MasterCard; Visa
Catalog Cost: $15
In Business: 20 years

5262 LEDGlow

444 Commerce Lane
Suite B
West Berlin, NJ 08091   856-768-5700
877-LED-GLOW
customerservice@LEDGlow.com
www.motorcycleledlights.com

LED lights for motorcycles

5263 Langlitz Leathers

2443 SE Division
Portland, OR 97202   503-235-0959
Fax: 503-235-0049
catalog@langlitz.com
www.langlitz.com

Leathers and hides

Owner: Jackie
General and Technical Manager: Judy

5264 Motosport, Inc.

Motosport Inc
15353 SW Sequoia Parkway
Portland, OR 97224   503-783-5776
866-333-8033
Fax: 503-783-5696
www.motosport.com

Motorcycle apparel, accessories, gear and parts.

President: Drew Lieberman
CFO: Martin Day
Marketing Manager: Phillip Bulebar
Operations Manager: Travis Staley
Credit Cards: AMEX; MasterCard
Catalog Cost: Free
In Business: 16 years
Number of Employees: 140

5265 Mustang Replacement Seats for Metric Cruisers

Mustang Motorcycle Products, Inc.
4 Springfield Street, Suite 1
PO Box 185
Three Rivers, MA 01080   413-668-1100
800-243-1392
Fax: 800-243-1399
questions@mustangseats.com
www.mustangseats.com

Full line of Mustang seats for Honda, Yamaha, Suzuki and Kawasaki cruiser models as well as sissy bar pads and tank or fender bibs

President: Al Simmons
Marketing Manager: Marilyn Simmons
Credit Cards: AMEX; MasterCard; Visa
Catalog Cost: Free
Catalog Circulation: Mailed 1 time(s) per year
Printing Information: 36 pages
In Business: 35 years
Number of Employees: 22
Sales Volume: $3.6 Million

5266 Mustang Replacement Seats for Victory

Mustang Motorcycle Products, Inc.
4 Springfield Street, Suite 1
PO Box 185
Three Rivers, MA 01080   413-668-1100
800-243-1392
Fax: 800-243-1399
questions@mustangseats.com
www.mustangseats.com

Full line of Mustang seats for Victory Vegas, Kingpin, 8-Ball, V92C and TC models

President: Al Simmons
Marketing Manager: Marilyn Simmons
Credit Cards: AMEX; MasterCard; Visa
Catalog Cost: Free
Catalog Circulation: Mailed 1 time(s) per year
Printing Information: 8 pages in 4 colors
In Business: 35 years
Number of Employees: 22
Sales Volume: $3.6 Million

5267 Niehaus Cycle

Niehaus Cycle Sales Inc
718 Old Route 66 N
Litchfield, IL 62056   217-324-6565
Fax: 217-324-6563
info@niehauscycle.com
www.niehauscycle.com

Accessories and apparel for Honda and Yamaha motorcycles and ATV's

President: Brad Niehaus
CFO: Scott Neihaus
Buyers: Dale Stamer
Catalog Cost: Free
Catalog Circulation: Mailed 2 time(s) per year
Average Order Size: $180
Printing Information: 56 pages on Newsprint
Press: Web Press
Binding: Folded
Mailing List Information: Names for rent
In Business: 46 years

Number of Employees: 25
Sales Volume: $4.5 Million

5268 Offroad Catalog

Bob's Cycle Supply
65 W Viking Drive
St Paul, MN 55117   651-482-8181
888-306-2627
Fax: 651-482-0974
www.bobscycle.com

Off-road riding gear from apparel to helmets, boots and more

President: Scott Muellner
Marketing Manager: Leisha Olson
Purchasing: Josh Lane
Credit Cards: AMEX; MasterCard
Catalog Cost: Free
In Business: 42 years
Number of Employees: 47
Sales Volume: $10 million

5269 Parts & Accessories for Harley-Davidson

Dennis Kirk Inc
955 S Field Avenue
Rush City, MN 55069   800-969-7501
Fax: 320-358-4019
customerservice@denniskirk.com
www.denniskirk.com

Harley Davidson parts, accessories and apparel

President: Robert Beham
Marketing Manager: Renita Twingstrom
Credit Cards: AMEX; MasterCard; Visa
Catalog Cost: Free
Printing Information: 964 pages in 4 colors
In Business: 46 years
Number of Employees: 3

5270 Parts Unlimited Offroad Catalog

Parts Unlimited
PO Box 5222
Janesville, WI 53547-5222   608-758-1111
Fax: 608-758-4677
www.parts-unlimited.com

Helmets, rider apparel, gloves, boots and accessories for offroad riding or racing

5271 Parts Unlimited Street Catalog

Parts Unlimited
PO Box 5222
Janesville, WI 53547-5222   608-758-1111
Fax: 608-758-4677
www.parts-unlimited.com

Motorcycle helmets, rider apparel, gloves, boots and accessories

5272 Pine Ridge Enterprise

Pine Ridge Enterprise
13165 Center Rd
Bath, MI 48808-8438   517-641-4881
800-522-7224
Fax: 517-641-6444
info@carbag.com
www.carbag.com

Manufacturer and distributor of motorcycle and car storage bags; carjacket, motojacket, omnibag, omnidry (drying agent) that keeps the inside of the bags dry

Chairman: Betty Schoepke
President: John Schoepke
Credit Cards: AMEX; MasterCard
Catalog Cost: Free
In Business: 30 years
Number of Employees: 2
Sales Volume: $600,000

5273 Pingel
Pingel Enterprise
2072 11th Ave
Adams, WI 53910
608-339-7999
Fax: 608-339-9164
info@pingelonline.com
www.pingelonline.com

Motorcycle supples and accessories
President: Donna Pingel
Credit Cards: MasterCard
Catalog Cost: $13
Catalog Circulation: to 10000
Printing Information: 99 pages in 7 colors on
Matte Stock
Binding: Folded
In Business: 32 years
Number of Employees: 24
Sales Volume: $3 Million

5274 QA1
QA1
21730 Hanover Avenue
Lakeville, MN 55044
952-985-5675
800-721-7761
Fax: 952-985-5679
sales@qa1.net
www.qa1.net

Parts and accessories for motorsports, including racing
Founder: Jim Jordan
Catalog Cost: Free
Catalog Circulation: Mailed 1 time(s) per year
Printing Information: 172 pages in 4 colors
In Business: 24 years

5275 Rocky Mountain MC
Rocky Mountain TV
1551 American Way
Payson, UT 84651-4651
801-465-3140
800-336-5437
Fax: 801-465-3457
sales@rockymountainatv.com
www.Rockymountainatv.Com

Motorcycle and ATV accessories
President: Dan Thomas
In Business: 31 years
Sales Volume: $50MM to $100MM

5276 Shade Tree Powersports Metric Bikes
15141 Kinsman Road
Middlefield, OH 44062
440-834-4395
888-742-3387
Fax: 440-834-4579
www.shadetreepowersports.com

Motorcycle riding apparel, protective gear and performance parts
Credit Cards: MasterCard
Catalog Cost: Free
Printing Information: in 3 colors
In Business: 23 years

5277 Street Catalog
Bob's Cycle Supply
65 W Viking Drive
St Paul, MN 55117
651-482-8181
888-306-2627
Fax: 651-482-0974
www.bobscycle.com

Aftermarket parts, apparel and accessories for ATV, Snowmobile, Street or Off-Road Motorcycle
President: Scott Muellner
Marketing Manager: Leisha Olson
Purchasing: Josh Lane
Credit Cards: AMEX; MasterCard
Catalog Cost: Free
In Business: 42 years
Number of Employees: 47
Sales Volume: $10 million

5278 Vance & Hines Dirtbike Catalog
Vance and Hines
13861 Rosecrans Ave
Santa Fe Springs, CA 90670
562-921-7461
800-592-2529
Fax: 562-802-0110
info@vanceandhines.com
www.vanceandhines.com

Exhaust systems, fuel injection management and air intake systems
President: Terry Vance
Marketing Manager: John Potts
President: Brian Etter
Founder: Byron Hines
Founder: Terry Vance
Printing Information: 25 pages on Glossy
Stock
Binding: Folded
In Business: 43 years
Number of Employees: 250
Sales Volume: $20MM to $50MM

5279 Vance & Hines Harley Davidson Catalog
Vance and Hines
13861 Rosecrans Ave
Santa Fe Springs, CA 90670
562-921-7461
800-592-2529
Fax: 562-802-0110
info@vanceandhines.com
www.vanceandhines.com

Exhaust systems, fuel injection management and air intake systems
President: Terry Vance
Marketing Manager: John Potts
President: Brian Etter
Founder: Byron Hines
Founder: Terry Vance
Printing Information: 25 pages on Glossy
Stock
Binding: Folded
In Business: 43 years
Number of Employees: 250
Sales Volume: $20MM to $50MM

5280 Vance & Hines Metric Cruiser Catalog
Vance and Hines
13861 Rosecrans Ave
Santa Fe Springs, CA 90670
562-921-7461
800-592-2529
Fax: 562-802-0110
info@vanceandhines.com
www.vanceandhines.com

Exhaust systems, fuel injection management and air intake systems
President: Terry Vance
Marketing Manager: John Potts
President: Brian Etter
Founder: Byron Hines
Founder: Terry Vance
Printing Information: 55 pages on Glossy
Stock
Binding: Folded
In Business: 43 years
Number of Employees: 250
Sales Volume: $20MM to $50MM

5281 Vance & Hines Sportbike Catalog
Vance and Hines
13861 Rosecrans Ave
Santa Fe Springs, CA 90670
562-921-7461
800-592-2529
Fax: 562-802-0110
info@vanceandhines.com
www.vanceandhines.com

Exhaust systems, fuel injection management and air intake systems
President: Terry Vance
Marketing Manager: John Potts
President: Brian Etter
Founder: Byron Hines
Founder: Terry Vance
Printing Information: 16 pages on Glossy
Stock

Binding: Folded
In Business: 43 years
Number of Employees: 250
Sales Volume: $20MM to $50MM

5282 Yoshimura Catalog
Yoshimura
5420 Daniels Street
Chino, CA 91710
909-628-4722
800-634-9166
Fax: 909-591-2198
sales@yoshimura-rd.com
www.yoshimura-rd.com

Motorcycle mufflers
President: Fujio Yoshimura
CFO: Suehiro Watanabe
President: Kim Lott
VP Operations: Brad Stephens
Catalog Cost: Free
In Business: 35 years
Number of Employees: 100
Sales Volume: $13.2 Million

Music Products
Instruments & Accessories

5283 Accordion-O-Rama
Accordion-O-Rama
236 N Stevens Ave
South Amboy, NJ 08879-1362
732-727-7715
bws@monmouth.com
www.accordion-o-rama.com

Accordions, new and rebuilt; expert tuning and repair
President: Peter Shearer
Marketing Manager: Barbara Shearer
Credit Cards: MasterCard; Visa
Catalog Cost: $1
Catalog Circulation: Mailed 2 time(s) per year
to 12000
Average Order Size: $1000
Printing Information: 12 pages in 4 colors on
Matte Stock
Binding: Folded
Mailing List Information: Names for rent
In Business: 60 years
Number of Employees: 4
Sales Volume: $370,000

5284 Alden Lee Company
Alden Lee Company, Inc.
PO Box 348761
Sacramento, CA 95834
916-641-0932
800-324-5200
rlee52@yahoo.com
www.aldenlee.com

Furniture for musicians
President: Richard Lee
Catalog Cost: Free
Printing Information: 24 pages in 4 colors
Mailing List Information: Names for rent
In Business: 30 years

5285 All Pro Sound
AP Sound, Inc.
806 Beverly Parkway
Pensacola, FL 32505
850-432-5780
800-925-5776
Fax: 850-432-0844
www.allprosound.com

Musical instruments, products and accessories for audio, video, and lighting
Credit Cards: AMEX; MasterCard
Catalog Cost: Free
In Business: 30+ years

5286 American Musical Supply
American Musical Supply
130 Lake Ave N
Spicer, MN 56288-9816   320-796-2088
800-458-4076
Fax: 320-796-6036
customerservice@americanmusical.com
www.americanmusical.com

Musical instruments and recording equipment

President: Diane Buzzeo
EVP: Chris Buzzeo
Credit Cards: AMEX; MasterCard; Visa
Catalog Cost: Free
Printing Information: 124 pages
Number of Employees: 45
Sales Volume: $ 3.4 Million

5287 B-52 Professional / E.T.I. Sound Systems
3383 Gage Ave
Huntington Park, CA 90255   323-277-4100
800-344-4384
Fax: 323-277-4108
Information@B-52PRO.com
www.b-52stealthseries.com

Guitar products

5288 Brasswinds
Woodwind & Brasswind
PO Box 7479
Westlake Village, CA 91359   574-251-3500
800-348-5003
Fax: 574-251-3501
woodwind@wwbw.com
www.wwbw.com

Reed instruments, stringed instruments and accessories.

President: Gregory Spretnjak
CFO: Dave Yoder
COO: Carl Turza
Senior Manager of Operations: Chris Purkey
Credit Cards: AMEX; MasterCard; Visa
Catalog Cost: Free
Mailing List Information: Names for rent
Will Trade Names: Yes
In Business: 30 years
Number of Employees: 170
Sales Volume: $ 4.5 Million

5289 Cascio Interstate Drums & Percussion Catalog
Cascio Music
13819 W National Avenue
New Berlin, WI 53151   262-789-7600
800-462-2263
Fax: 800-529-0382
customerservice@interstatemusic.com
www.interstatemusic.com

Drums and percussion, guitars and amplifiers, dj and lighting equipment, sheet music and books

President: Michael Cascio
CFO: Elwood Winn
Marketing Manager: Michael Houser
Printing Information: 190 pages in 4 colors on Glossy Stock
Binding: Perfect Bound
Number of Employees: 215

5290 Castiglione Accordions
Castiglione Accordions
13300 E 11 Mile
Suite A
Warren, MI 48089-1367   586-755-6050
800-325-1832
Fax: 586-755-6339
johncast@bignet.net
www.castiglioneaccordions.com

New and used accordions and concertinas

President: John Castiglione
Partner: Giovannine Castiglione
Catalog Cost: $5

Catalog Circulation: Mailed 1 time(s) per year to 15000
Average Order Size: $25
Printing Information: 4 pages on G Press: L
Mailing List Information: Names for rent
In Business: 80 years
Number of Employees: 2
Sales Volume: $500,000

5291 Charles Double Reeds
Charles Double Reeds
1976 White Mtn. Hwy.
North Conway, NH 03860   603-356-9890
800-733-3847
Fax: 603-356-9891
service@charlesmusic.com
www.charlesmusic.com

Services and products for professional oboe and bassoon players; reeds, cane, instruments, tools and accessories

Production Manager: John Cotter
Owner and Director: Brian Charles
Credit Cards: AMEX; MasterCard
Catalog Cost: Free
Catalog Circulation: Mailed 4 time(s) per year to 15000
Average Order Size: $75
Printing Information: 48 pages in 2 colors on Matte Stock
Press: Web Press
Binding: Saddle Stitched
Mailing List Information: Names for rent
In Business: 31 years
Number of Employees: 10
Sales Volume: Under $500,000

5292 Conklin Guitars
Conklinguitars and Bases
3600 Battlefield Road
PO Box 1394
Springfield, MO 65807   417-886-3525
Fax: 417-886-2934
conklin@conklinguitars.com
www.conklinguitars.com

Custom and hand-crafted guitars and basses

President: Bill Conklin
Catalog Cost: Free
Mailing List Information: Names for rent
In Business: 17 years
Number of Employees: 2
Sales Volume: $90,000

5293 Country Music Treasures
Music Barn
PO Box 1083
Niagara Falls, NY 14304   800-984-0047
Fax: 905-513-6918
www.countrymusictreasures.com

Old time country, fiddle, bluegrass, religious, polka, and popular music recording from the 1930s to the 1960s.

President: Robert Bell
Credit Cards: AMEX; MasterCard; Visa
Catalog Cost: Free
In Business: 25 years

5294 Deering Banjo Company
Deering
3733 Kenora Dr
Spring Valley, CA 91977   619-464-8252
800-845-7791
Fax: 619-464-0833
carolinabridges@deeringbanjos.com
www.deeringbanjos.com

Banjos and all banjo related accessories

President: Charles Deering
Credit Cards: AMEX; MasterCard; Visa
Catalog Cost: Free
Mailing List Information: Names for rent
In Business: 37 years

Number of Employees: 40
Sales Volume: $4.3 Million

5295 Dulcimer Shoppe
McSpadden Dulcimers
1104 Sylamore Ave
PO Box 1230
Mountain View, AR 72560   877-269-4422
Fax: 870-269-5283
mcspadden@mvtel.net
www.mcspaddendulcimers.com

Dulcimer instruments and kits

President: James Woods
CFO: Betty Woods
Credit Cards: AMEX; MasterCard
Catalog Cost: Free
Catalog Circulation: to 500+
Average Order Size: $250
Printing Information: 18 pages in 4 colors on Glossy Stock
Binding: Saddle Stitched
Mailing List Information: Names for rent
In Business: 53 years
Number of Employees: 10
Sales Volume: $580,000

5296 Elderly Instruments
Elderly Instruments
1100 N Washington
Lansing, MI 48906   517-372-7890
888-473-5810
Fax: 517-372-5155
web@elderly.com
www.elderly.com

Musical instruments, accessories, compact discs, books and videos

President: Stan Werbin
Credit Cards: MasterCard; Visa
Catalog Cost: Free
Mailing List Information: Names for rent
In Business: 47 years
Number of Employees: 75
Sales Volume: $ 10-20 Million

5297 Full Compass Systems
9770 Silicon Prairie Parkway
Madison, WI 53593   608-831-7330
800-356-5844
Fax: 608-831-6330
customerservice@fullcompass.com
www.fullcompass.com

Professional-grade audio and video equipment and software

5298 Guitar Salon International
1455 19th Street
Santa Monica, CA 90404   310-586-1100
877-771-4321
Fax: 310-586-1142
info@guitarsalon.com
www.guitarsalon.com

Guitars and guitar products and accessories

5299 Jean Larrivee Guitars
1070 Yarnell Place
Oxnard, CA 93033-2454   805-487-9980
www.larrivee.com

Musical instruments

5300 Johnson String Instrument
1029 Chestnut Street
Newton Upper Falls, MA 02464   617-964-0954
800-359-9351
Fax: 617-527-2684
info@johnsonstring.com
www.johnsonstring.com

String instruments and accessories

5301 Latin Percussion
Latin Percussion
160 Belmont Avenue
Garfield, NJ 07026-2344
805-919-2499
800-813-1634
Fax: 973-772-3568
www.lpmusic.com

Collection of percussion instruments and accessories

President: Martin Cohen
Marketing Manager: Jim Rockwell
Credit Cards: MasterCard; Visa
Catalog Cost: $4.99
Catalog Circulation: Mailed 1 time(s) per year
Printing Information: 140 pages in 4 colors on Glossy Stock
Binding: Saddle Stitched
In Business: 59 years
Number of Employees: 80
Sales Volume: $ 10 Million

5302 Lone Star Percussion
Lone Star Percussiosn
10611 Control Place
Dallas, TX 75238
214-340-0835
866-792-0143
Fax: 214-340-0861
www.lonestarpercussion.com

Percussion instruments

President: Jeff Nelson
Credit Cards: AMEX; MasterCard
Catalog Cost: Free
Printing Information: 48 pages
In Business: 36 years
Number of Employees: 8
Sales Volume: $720,000

5303 Metropolitan Music
Metropolitan Music
4861 Mountain Road
PO Box 1415
Stowe, VT 05672
802-253-4814
866-846-5461
Fax: 802-253-9834
sales@metmusic.com
www.metmusic.com

Stringed instruments and accessories, tools and wood

President: Robert Juzek
Credit Cards: MasterCard; Visa
Catalog Cost: Free
Average Order Size: $150
Mailing List Information: Names for rent
In Business: 95 years
Number of Employees: 6
Sales Volume: $ 500,000- 1 Million

5304 Music Catalog
Ashgate Publishing Company
110 Cherry Street
Suite 3-1
Burlington, VT 05401-3818
802-865-7641
800-535-9544
Fax: 802-865-7847
ashgate.online@ashgate.com
www.ashgate.com

Topics/titles include: Popular and Folk Music; Ethnomusicology; Eighteenth/Nineteenth/Twentieth Century Music; Baroque Music; Medieval and Renaissance Music; Critical Theory and Aesthetics; Research

Fulfillment: Suzanne Sprague
Catalog Circulation: Mailed 1 time(s) per year
Printing Information: 24 pages
Press: Web Press
Binding: Saddle Stitched

5305 Music is Elementary
Music is Elementary
5228 Mayfield Road
Lyndhurst, OH 44124
800-888-7502
Fax: 440-461-3631
info@musiciselementary.com
www.musiciselementary.com

Items such as books, CDs, instruments, and accessories for elementary music education, music therapy, and anyone with an interest in music

Music Consultant: BethAnn Hepburn
Credit Cards: AMEX; MasterCard
Catalog Cost: Free

5306 Musician's Friend
PO Box 7479
Westlake Village, CA 91359
801-501-8110
Fax: 801-501-9552
www.musiciansfriend.com

Musical instruments, accessories, books, videos and more

Average Order Size: $200

5307 Musicmaker's Kits
Music Maker's
14525 61st St Ct N
PO Box 2117
Stillwater, MN 55082
651-439-9120
800-432-5487
Fax: 651-439-9130
info@harpkit.com
www.harpkit.com

Kits for making musical instruments

President: Jeremy Brown
Credit Cards: AMEX; MasterCard; Visa
Catalog Cost: $5
Printing Information: 32 pages
Mailing List Information: Names for rent
In Business: 37 years
Number of Employees: 8
Sales Volume: $ 500,000- 1 Million

5308 Rhythm Band Instruments
Rhtym Band Instrument
PO Box 126
Fort Worth, TX 76102
800-424-4724
sales@rhythmband.com
www.rhythmband.com

Musical instruments for preschool and elementary school

President: Robert Bergin
Owner: Brad Kirkpatrick
VP Sales: Laura Bergin
Credit Cards: MasterCard
Catalog Cost: Free
Printing Information: 63 pages in 4 colors
Mailing List Information: Names for rent
In Business: 56 years
Number of Employees: 20
Sales Volume: $ 2.6 Million

5309 Shar Music Catalog
Shar Products Company
2465 S Industrial
Ann Arbor, MI 48104
800-248-7427
Fax: 734-665-0829
sharserv@sharmusic.com
www.sharmusic.com

Listing instruments, bows, strings, accessories, and more; and sheet music

President: Haig Avsharian
CFO: Michael Dear
Chief Executive Officer: Charles Avsharian
Executive Vice President: Michael Avsharian
Credit Cards: AMEX; MasterCard; Visa
Catalog Cost: Free
Catalog Circulation: Mailed 4 time(s) per year
Average Order Size: $110
Printing Information: 115 pages in 4 colors
Mailing List Information: Names for rent
List Manager: Val lackiewicz

In Business: 55 years
Number of Employees: 26
Sales Volume: $ 11 Million

5310 StewMac
Stewart-MacDonald
21 N Shafer Street
Athens, OH 45701
800-848-2273
Fax: 740-593-7922
www.stewmac.com

Tools and supplies for guitarmaking

President: Kay Tousley
Credit Cards: MasterCard
Catalog Cost: Free
Catalog Circulation: Mailed 12 time(s) per year
Printing Information: 104 pages in 4 colors
In Business: 49 years

5311 String Swing
PO Box 10
27515 State Hwy. 131
Ontario, WI 54651
608-435-6628
888-455-6628
Fax: 608-435-6120
contact@stringswing.com
www.stringswing.com

Musical instruments

5312 Sylvia Woods Harp Center
Sylvia Woods Harp Center
P.O. Box 223434
Princeville, HI 96722
808-212-9525
info@harpcenter.com
www.harpcenter.com

Harps, electronic tuners, harp and dulcimer recordings

President: Sylvia Woods
Credit Cards: AMEX; MasterCard; Visa
Catalog Circulation: Mailed 3 time(s) per year to 50000
Printing Information: 104 pages in 2 colors on Newsprint
Binding: Folded

5313 Woodwind Catalog
Woodwind & Brasswind
PO Box 7479
Westlake Village, CA 91359
574-251-3500
800-348-5003
Fax: 574-251-3501
woodwind@wwbw.com
www.wwbw.com

Flutes and piccolos, Clarinets, Saxophones, Double Reed Instruments, Woodwind accessories and Woodwind care and cleaning

President: Gregory Spretnjak
CFO: Dave Yoder
COO: Carl Turza
Credit Cards: AMEX; MasterCard; Visa
Catalog Cost: Free
Mailing List Information: Names for rent
In Business: 34 years
Number of Employees: 170
Sales Volume: $ 4.5 Million

5314 Yamaha Music Corporation
Yamaha Music Corporation
6600 Orangethorpe Avenue
Buena Park, CA 90620-1186
mation@yamaha.com
us.yamaha.com

Electronic keyboards

President: Takuya Nakata
Managing Executive Officer: Motoki Takahashi
Senior Executive Officer: Masao Kondo
Senior Executive Officer: Masato Oike
In Business: 130 years
Number of Employees: 1000
Sales Volume: 410,304 million yen

5315 zZsounds Music Catalog
zZsounds Music
8 Thornton Road
Oakland, NJ 07436
Fax: 312-276-0186
800-996-8637
www.zzsounds.com

Complete dj systems, bass guitars, amps, keyboards, drums, computer music and accessories

President: Mark Schoenhals
Credit Cards: AMEX; MasterCard
In Business: 10 years
Number of Employees: 99

Sheet Music

5316 Guitar Addict
Guitar Addict
760 Meridian Way
San Jose, CA 95126
888-977-9998
info@guitaraddict.com
www.guitaraddict.com

vintage guitars, music instruments, and accessories

Credit Cards: AMEX; MasterCard

5317 Lemur Music
Lemur Music
32240 Paseo Adelanto
Suite A
San Juan Capistrano, CA 92675   949-493-8323
800-246-2277
Fax: 949- 49- 856
lemur@lemurmusic.com
www.lemurmusic.com

Lemur Exclusive Sunrise Basses, wonderful basses from E. Wilfer, E.M. Pöllmann, B. Stoll plus Vintage & Historic Basses.

5318 Lyon & Healy Harps, Inc.
Lyon & Healy Harps, Inc.
168 North Ogden Avenue
Chicago, IL 60607-1465
312-786-1881
800-621-3881
Fax: 312-226-1502
musicsales@lyonhealy.com
www.lyonhealy.com

Harps

In Business: 125 years

5319 Malaco
Malaco
P.O. Box 9287
Jackson, MS 39286
601-982-4522
800-272-7936
Fax: 601-982-4528
www.malaco.com

Songwriting and copyrighting

President: Thomas Couch
Production Mnager: Paul Timbiln
Executive Director: Louise Black
Vice President: Gerald Wolf Stephenson
In Business: 47 years

5320 Music Books & Scores
Dover Publications
31 E 2nd Street
Mineola, NY 11501-3852
516-294-7000
Fax: 516-742-6953
www.doverpublications.com

Books on music

President: Christopher J Kuppig
Marketing Manager: Kristine Anderson
Acquisitions Editor: Nora Rawn
Account Manager: Christopher Higgins
Catalog Cost: Free
In Business: 76 years
Number of Employees: 135
Sales Volume: 40MM

5321 Musica Russica
Musica Russica
7925 Silverton Ave.
Ste. 501
San Diego, CA 92126-6350
858-536-9989
800-326-3132
Fax: 858-536-9991
rusmuscat@musicarussica.com
www.musicarussica.com

Sheet music, Russian choral music

In Business: 28 years

5322 RDG Woodwinds
RDG Woodwinds
589 North Larchmont Blvd.
2nd Floor
Los Angles, CA 90004
303-463-4930
888-RDG-REED
www.rdgwoodwinds.com

Woodwind instruments, sheet music, and accessories

Credit Cards: MasterCard

5323 Resources for Children and Youth Choirs
Choristers Guild
12404 Park Central Drive
Suite 100
Dallas, TX 75251-1802
469-398-3606
800-246-7478
Fax: 469-398-3611
customerservice@mailcg.org
www.choristersguild.org

Sacred music and materials for children and youth choirs

President: Patricia Evans
Marketing Manager: Ellen Yost
Executive Director: Jim Rindelaub
Office Manger: Liann Harris
Administrative Assistant: Kiira Russell
Credit Cards: MasterCard; Visa
Catalog Cost: Free
Printing Information: 55 pages in 1 color
Mailing List Information: Names for rent
In Business: 66 years
Number of Employees: 10
Sales Volume: $629,000

Office Products
Furniture & Equipment

5324 ATD-American Catalog
ATD-AMERICAN
93 Old York Road
Suite 310
Jenkintown, PA 19046
866-523-2300
888-283-2378
Fax: 954-323-1853
website@atd.com
www.atd.com

Bookcases, displays, computer workstations, desks, filing, storage, partitions and tables

President: Arnie Zaslow
Marketing Manager: Irvin Greenberg
Director of Sales: Bill McDonough
Credit Cards: AMEX; MasterCard; Visa
Catalog Cost: Free
Catalog Circulation: Mailed 2 time(s) per year
Printing Information: 85 pages
List Company: Direct Media
In Business: 86 years
Number of Employees: 90
Sales Volume: $35 Million

5325 ATD-American School Catalog
ATD-American
93 Old York Road
Suite 310
Jenkintown, PA 19046
866-523-2300
888-283-2378
Fax: 954-323-1853
website@atd.com
www.atd.com

Bookcases, displays, computer workstations, desks, filing, storage units, partitions, and tables for classroom use

President: Arnie Zaslow
Marketing Manager: Irvin Greenberg
Director of Sales: Bill McDonough
Credit Cards: AMEX; MasterCard
Catalog Cost: Free
Catalog Circulation: Mailed 1 time(s) per year
Printing Information: 167 pages in 4 colors on Glossy Stock
Binding: Saddle Stitched
List Company: Direct Media
In Business: 86 years
Number of Employees: 90
Sales Volume: $35 Million

5326 Alfax Furniture
Dallas Midwest
4100 Alpha Road
Dallas, TX 75244
800-527-2417
Fax: 800-301-8314
www.alfaxfurniture.com

Furniture for schools, churches, and government agencies

Chairman: George Gayer
Chairman: Felix Zimmerman
General Manager: Teresa Darden
Credit Cards: AMEX; MasterCard
Catalog Cost: Free
In Business: 66 years
Sales Volume: $12 Million

5327 Benton Thomas
Benton Thomas
408 Edmunds Street
South Boston, VA 24592
434-572-3577
800-888-3577
Fax: 434-572-1322
www.bentonthomas.com

President: Mike Benton
mbenton@duffiegraphics.com

5328 Closeout City Office Furniture
309 Office Furniture
1711 Bethlehem Pike (Route 309)
Hatfield, PA 19440-1303
215-822-3333
888-822-3333
Fax: 215-997-7798
info@309officefurniture.com
www.309officefurniture.com

Office furniture

President: Wallace Rosenthal
Production Manager: Margie Dudley
Catalog Cost: Free
Printing Information: 160 pages
In Business: 24 years
Number of Employees: 20
Sales Volume: $ 2.7 Million

5329 Crest Office Furniture
Crest Office Furniture
2840 N. Lima St.
#110
Burbank, CA 91504
818-333-3160
www.crestoffice.com

In Business: 61 years

5330 DEMCO Library Supplies & Equipment
Demco imagine whats possible
PO BOX 7488
Madison, WI 53707   608-241-1201
                          Fax: 608-241-0666
                          president@demco.com
                          www.demco.com

Office, school, library supplies and furniture

Chairman: John Wall
President: Trevor Taylor
CFO: Don Rogers
Fulfillment: Bill Erickson
Credit Cards: AMEX; MasterCard; Visa
Catalog Cost: Free
Catalog Circulation: Mailed 1 time(s) per year
Printing Information: 880 pages in 4 colors on
Glossy Stock
Press: Web Press
Mailing List Information: Names for rent
List Manager: Jeff McLaughlin
In Business: 95 years
Number of Employees: 10
Sales Volume: $830,000

5331 Dallas Midwest
Dallas Midwest
4100 Alpha Road
Suite 111
Dallas, TX 75244-4333   972-866-0101
                           800-527-2417
                           Fax: 800-301-8314
                           sales@dallasmidwest.com
                           www.dallasmidwest.com

Furniture for the office, church, school, and daycare, including podiums, lockers, bulletin/whiteboard, partitions, filing cabinets and organizers

Chairman: Felix Zimmerman
CFO: Eileen Baus
Sales Manager: David Jenkins
Credit Cards: AMEX; MasterCard; Visa
Catalog Cost: Free
Catalog Circulation: Mailed 11 time(s) per year
Printing Information: 92 pages in 4 colors on
Glossy Stock
Press: Web Press
Binding: Perfect Bound
Mailing List Information: Names for rent
Number of Employees: 9
Sales Volume: $10.5 Million

5332 Dallek, Inc.
Dallek
269 Madison Ave
New York, NY 10016-982   212-684-4848
                          800-876-8786
                          Fax: 212-576-1036

Office seating, workstations, tables, storage and accessories

President: Neil Schwartzberg
Credit Cards: AMEX; MasterCard; Visa
Catalog Cost: Free
In Business: 90 years
Sales Volume: $5MM to $10MM

5333 Demco
Demco
P.O. Box 7488
Madison, WI 53707-7488   800-356-1200
                          Fax: 800-245-1329
                          www.demco.com

Library supplies, AV supplies, and equipment, singage & display, furniture, library promotions, learning materials, and more

President: Mike Grasee
Credit Cards: AMEX; MasterCard; Visa
Catalog Cost: Free
Printing Information: 1000 pages in 4 colors
on Matte Stock
Press: Web Press
Binding: Perfect Bound
Mailing List Information: Names for rent
In Business: 107 years

Number of Employees: 250
Sales Volume: $ 50-100 Million

5334 Everything Office Furniture
Everything Furniture
244 5th Ave
Suite 200
New York, NY 10001   877-209-7908
                          855-956-3929
                          Fax: 951-372-8099
                          www.everythingofficefurniture.com

Office furniture and equipment

In Business: 11 years

5335 Fordham Equipment Company
Fordham Equipment Company
3308 Edison Avenue
Bronx, NY 10469-2623   718-379-7300
                          800-249-5922
                          Fax: 718-379-7312

Library funiture and shelving, solid oak and all steel adjustable, high density shelving systems for medical records, open shelf filing, video and DVD shelving, computer stations, circulation and refe

President: Al Robbins
CFO: Florence Robbins
Credit Cards: MasterCard
Catalog Cost: Free
Catalog Circulation: Mailed 2 time(s) per year
to 40000
Printing Information: 16 pages in 2 colors on
Glossy Stock
Press: Web Press
Binding: Folded
Mailing List Information: Names for rent
In Business: 61 years
Number of Employees: 8
Sales Volume: $ 1 Million

5336 Furniture for Teaching & Technology
Smith Systems Manufacturing, Inc.
P.O. Box 860415
Plano, TX 75086   800-328-1061
                          Fax: 972-398-4051
                          www.smithsystem.com

Classroom, teacher/office and library furniture that's ergonomically sound and functional module design with optional accessories

President: Charles Risdall
CFO: Garth Shipley
Marketing Manager: Bill Risdall
Production Manager: Rick Taylor
Credit Cards: AMEX; MasterCard; Visa
Catalog Cost: Free
Catalog Circulation: Mailed 1 time(s) per year
Printing Information: 287 pages in 4 colors
Binding: Saddle Stitched
In Business: 112 years
Number of Employees: 125
Sales Volume: $ 10-20 Million

5337 GS Direct
GS Direct Inc.
6490 Carlson Drive
Eden Prairie, MN 55436-1729 952-942-6115
                            800-234-3729
                            Fax: 952-942-0216
                            info@gs-direct.com
                            www.gsdirect.net

Graphic supplies, software, organizers and furniture for architects, engineers and designers

President: Chuck Ehlers
Credit Cards: AMEX; MasterCard; Visa
Catalog Cost: Free
Catalog Circulation: Mailed 4 time(s) per year
to 300K
Printing Information: 68 pages in 4 colors on
Glossy Stock
Press: Web Press
Mailing List Information: Names for rent

In Business: 26 years
Number of Employees: 8
Sales Volume: $1,500,000

5338 Gaylord Archival
Gaylord Archival
P.O. Box 4901
Syracuse, NY 13221-4901   800-448-6160
                          Fax: 800-272-3412
                          customerservice@gaylord.com
                          www.gaylord.com

Exhibit and gallery display, storage and handling equipment

President: Guy Marhewka
Marketing Manager: Coleen Gagliardo
VP of Operations: Keith George
VP of Business Development: Henry Orr
Credit Cards: AMEX; MasterCard; Visa
Catalog Circulation: to 20000
Printing Information: on Glossy Stock
Press: Web Press
Binding: Perfect Bound
In Business: 116 years
Number of Employees: 300
Sales Volume: $ 50-100 Million

5339 Global Industrial
Global Industrial
11 Harbor Park Dr
Port Washington, NY 11050-4646 516-625-3663
                               800-806-5984
                               Fax: 888-381-2868
                               sales@globalindustrial.com
                               www.globalindustrial.com

Platform trucks, radios, computer work stations, lockers and bins

President: Richard Leeds
Credit Cards: AMEX; MasterCard
Catalog Cost: Free
Printing Information: 48 pages
In Business: 30 years
Number of Employees: 260
Sales Volume: $ 17 Million

5340 Global Industrial Catalog
Global Industrial
11 Harbor Park Dr.
Port Washington, NY 11050 *Fax:* 888-381-2868
                          www.globalindustrial.com

Industrial equipment and business supplies.

President: Bob Dooley
In Business: 67 years
Sales Volume: $180 Million

5341 Golden State Office Furniture
Golden State Office Furniture
2510 Tarmac Rd.
Suite A
Redding, CA 96003   530-229-9296
                          Fax: 530-229-9294
                          www.goldenstatefurniture.com

Furniture.

Credit Cards: AMEX; MasterCard

5342 Heartland America
Heartland America
8085 Century Blvd
Chaska, MN 55318-3056   800-229-2901
                          info@heartlandamerica.com
                          www.heartlandamerica.com

General consumer products and gifts including electronics, home and office, auto, hardware, and fashion accessories

President: Bruce Brekke
Credit Cards: AMEX; MasterCard
Catalog Cost: Free
In Business: 30 years
Sales Volume: $ 20-50 Million

5343 Miles Kimball
Miles Kimball
250 City Center
Oshkosh, WI 54906   855-202-7394
www.mileskimball.com

Kitchen gadgets, home decor, storage & organization, books, jewelry, apparel, health, beauty, home office supplies and gift items.

Catalog Cost: Free
In Business: 81 years
Sales Volume: $10 Million

5344 Modern Office Furniture
Modern Office Furniture
6900 Shady Oak Road
Eden Prairie, MN 55344   952-941-2837
                                800-443-5117
Fax: 952-949-9816
customersvc@modernofficefurniture.com
www.modernofficefurniture.com

Book cases, computer desks, desks, display cases, file cabinets, panels, carts, chairs and seating

Credit Cards: AMEX; MasterCard; Visa
Catalog Cost: Free
In Business: 36 years
Sales Volume: $ 3-5 Million

5345 National Business Furniture
National Business Furniture
770 S 70th Street
Milwaukee, WI 53214   800-558-1010
Fax: 800-329-9349
www.nationalbusinessfurniture.com

Office, school and healthcare furniture, desks, file cabinets, bookcases, chairs, storage and tables.

President: Kent Anderson
General Manager: Rick Wachowiak
Branch Manager: David Favro
Credit Cards: AMEX; MasterCard; Visa
Catalog Cost: Free
Catalog Circulation: Mailed 52 time(s) per year to 14MM
Average Order Size: $500
Printing Information: on Glossy Stock
Press: Web Press
Binding: Perfect Bound
Mailing List Information: Names for rent
List Company: Direct Media
Stamford, CT
In Business: 41 years
Number of Employees: 150
Sales Volume: $ 50-100 Million

5346 National Office Furniture
National Office Furniture
1610 Royal Street
Jasper, IN 47549   800-482-1717
Fax: 812-482-8800
www.nationalofficefurniture.com

Furniture.

In Business: 35 years

5347 Norsons Industries
Norsons Industries
169 Main Street
Suite 201
Matawan, NJ 07747   718-522-6060
                           800-438-6776
Fax: 732-862-2476
www.norsonsindustries.com

Genuine wood bookcases, files, cabinets, wall systems, computer consoles and desks

President: Irwin Kumer
Catalog Cost: Free
Average Order Size: $500
Printing Information: on Matte Stock
Press: Letterpress
In Business: 42 years
Number of Employees: 30
Sales Volume: $ 5 Million

5348 Office Center
The Office Center Inc
1500 S Avenue D
Portales, NM 88130-6840   575-356-4477
Fax: 575-356-8320
info@officecenterinc.com
www.officecenterinc.com

Sharp brand copiers, fax machines and calculators

President: Dorven King
Number of Employees: 7
Sales Volume: $ 500,000- 1 Million

5349 Office Furniture Concepts
Office Furniture Concepts Ltd.
PO Box 428
Phoenixville, PA 19460-3588   610-933-3036
                                     888-632-8480
Fax: 610-935-1728
info@ofconcepts.com
www.Ofconcepts.Com

Computer furniture, desks and workcenters, filing and storage, tables, partitions and cubicles and other office essentials

President: Frank Small
frank@ofconcepts.com
Vice President: Catharine Small
Manager: Jeremy Coffee
Credit Cards: AMEX; MasterCard
Catalog Cost: Free
Mailing List Information: Names for rent
In Business: 24 years
Number of Employees: 2
Sales Volume: $290,000

5350 OfficeDesigns.com
OfficeDesigns.com
722 Landwehr Road
Northbrook, IL 60062   877-696-3342
Fax: 847-504-1700
customercare@officedesigns.com
www.officedesigns.com

Office and home furniture

President: Rich Burke
Marketing Manager: Michi Kustra
Owner/President: Mark Levin
Credit Cards: AMEX; MasterCard
Catalog Cost: Free
In Business: 14 years
Number of Employees: 48
Sales Volume: $4.6 Million

5351 Photo Materials Company
Martin Yale Industries Inc
251 Wedcor Avenue
Wabash, IN 46992   260-563-0641
                          800-225-5644
Fax: 260-563-4575
www.martinyale.com

Shredders, folding machines, paper cutters, paper trimmers and mailroom equipment

President: Dawn Dials
Marketing Manager: Greg German
Production Manager: Brad Bozarth
Product Manager: David Parkhill
Catalog Cost: Free
Catalog Circulation: Mailed 1 time(s) per year
Printing Information: 52 pages in 4 colors
In Business: 75 years
Number of Employees: 129

5352 Repromat Catalog
ACM Technologies Inc
2535 Research Drive
Corona, MA 09288-7607   951-738-9898
                               800-722-7745
Fax: 951-273-2174
askacm@acmtech.com
www.acmtech.com

Digital copiers, printers, fax machines, toner, thermal transfer ribbons and machinery parts

President: Shue-Shang Lin
Credit Cards: AMEX; MasterCard
Catalog Cost: Free
Catalog Circulation: Mailed 1 time(s) per year to 5M
Printing Information: 215 pages in 1 color on Matte Stock
Press: Letterpress
In Business: 22 years
Number of Employees: 52
Sales Volume: $ 15 Million

5353 The Big Book
Office Depot
6600 N Military Trail
Boca Raton, FL 33496   800-463-3768
www.officedepot.com

Binders, calendars, planners, ink, toner, filing & storage, labels, pens, pencils, desktop & notebook computers, printers, copiers, shredders and office furniture

Chairman & CEO: Roland C. Smith
Catalog Cost: Free
Catalog Circulation: Mailed 1 time(s) per year
Printing Information: 868 pages in 4 colors
In Business: 30 years
Number of Employees: 4900
Sales Volume: $14.5 Billion

5354 The Hon Company
The Hon Company
200 Oak Street
Muscatine, LO 52761   563-272-7100
                             800-833-3964
honcustomersupport@honcompany.com
www.hon.com

5355 Thrifty
Thrifty
6321 Angus Drive
Raleigh, NC 27617   919-598-8454
www.thriftyofficefurniture.com

5356 USI Inc.
USI Inc.
98 Fort Path Road
Suite A
Madison, CT 06443   800-282-9290
Fax: 203-245-8619
techassist@usi-corp.com
www.usi-laminate.com

Laminating machines, roll, pouch, cold roll & tape laminating film, trimmers, blades, binding machines, paper folding machines, shredders, phone accessories and office furniture

President: Travis Merry
Marketing Manager: Garth Bertini
Owner: Frederick Franco
Finance Director: Sherri Montminy
Credit Cards: AMEX; MasterCard; Visa
Catalog Cost: Free
Printing Information: 32 pages
In Business: 42 years
Sales Volume: $3MM to $5MM

5357 Upbeat
Upbeat Site Furnishings
211 N Lindbergh Boulevard
St Louis, MO 63141   314-535-5005
                            800-325-3047
Fax: 314-535-4419
www.upbeat.com

Benches, bike and skate racks, cigarette waste receptacles, entryway, events, facility maintenance, floor mats, office and lobby, park furnishings, picnic tables, pool and patio furnishings and trash

Manager: Scott Glenn
Manager: Sherry Miller
Credit Cards: AMEX; MasterCard
Catalog Cost: Free
Catalog Circulation: Mailed 6 time(s) per year

to 4MM
Printing Information: 60 pages in 4 colors on Glossy Stock
Press: Web Press
Binding: Saddle Stitched
In Business: 33 years
Number of Employees: 50
Sales Volume: $11 Million

Organizers

5358   Charnstrom
Charnstrom
5391 12th Avenue East
5391 12th Avenue Eas
Shakopee, MN 55379-1896   800-328-2962
mail@charnstrom.com
www.charnstrom.com

5359   Colonial Redi Record Corporation
Colonial Bronze Company
511 Winsted Road
Torrington, CT 06790-0207   860-489-9233
Fax: 800-355-7903
sales@colonialbronze.com
www.colonialbronze.com

Calendars, boards, paper pads, diaries, easel boards, appointment books, planners, presentation books and desk accessories for purchase by distributors only

President: Joe Berkovits
Credit Cards: MasterCard
Catalog Cost: Free
Printing Information: 53 pages in 4 colors
Mailing List Information: Names for rent
In Business: 90 years
Number of Employees: 25
Sales Volume: $3MM to $5MM

5360   Dacasso
Dacasso
2350 NW 71st Pl
Gainesville, FL 32653   352-331-4710
866-322-2776
Fax: 352-331-5994
sales@dacasso.com
www.dacasso.com

Leather desk sets and conference room accessories.

5361   Day Runner Direct
Day Runner
101 Oneil Road
Sidney, NY 13838   800-936-9814
www.dayrunner.com

Personal organizers, planners, calendars, refills and accessories

5362   Day Timer
Day Timer
1 Willow Lane
East Texas, PA 18046   610-398-1151
800-457-5702
Fax: 800-452-7398
www.daytimer.com

Planners, planner covers, planner calendars, organizers, bags, briefcases, car organizers, desk accessories and sationery

President: Joe Winters
CFO: Danette Gerbino
Marketing Manager: Martha Curren
Production Manager: Glenn Large
International Marketing Manager: Pat Straubel
Credit Cards: AMEX; MasterCard; Visa
Catalog Cost: Free
Catalog Circulation: Mailed 2 time(s) per year
Mailing List Information: Names for rent
List Manager: Jerry Curran
List Company: Direct Media
In Business: 65 years
Number of Employees: 400

5363   Franklin Planner Holiday Gift Guide
FranklinCovey Co.
2200 W Parkway Blvd.
Salt Lake City, UT 84119   800-654-1776
franklinplanner.fcorgp.com

Planners, binders, planner refills, planner software, totes, laptop bags, messenger bags, books, pens, pencils, desk organizers, file folders, notepads, books and motivational seminars.

Chair & CEO: Robert Whitman
Catalog Cost: Free
Catalog Circulation: Mailed 1 time(s) per year
Printing Information: 44 pages in 4 colors
In Business: 19 years
Number of Employees: 1500
Sales Volume: $200 Million

5364   Franklin Planner Resolutions
FranklinCovey Co.
2200 W Parkway Blvd.
Salt Lake City, UT 84119   800-654-1776
franklinplanner.fcorgp.com

Planners, binders, planner refills, planner software, totes, laptop bags, messenger bags, books, pens, pencils, desk organizers, file folders, notepads, books and motivational seminars.

Chair & CEO: Robert Whitman
Catalog Cost: Free
Catalog Circulation: Mailed 1 time(s) per year
Printing Information: 68 pages in 4 colors
In Business: 19 years
Number of Employees: 1500
Sales Volume: $200 Million

5365   Gold Violin
Gold Violin
PO Box 126
Jessup, PA 18434   877-648-8466
800-361-3336
Fax: 800-821-1282
www.goldviolin.com

Medical organizers, compact pill boxes, cell phones, office supplies and kitchenware

President: Connie Hallquist
In Business: 19 years

5366   Magna Visual
Magna Visual
9400 Watson Road
St Louis, MO 63126-1596   800-472-3226
Fax: 314-843-0000
www.magnavisual.com

Magnetic steel & porcelain boards, custom color boards, double sided boards, grid/scheduling boards, magnetic accessories, chart tape, dry erase markers and water soluble pens

Chairman: Phillip Cady
President: William Cady
CFO: Diane Crews
Marketing Manager: John Winkler
Buyers: Chris Brown
Catalog Cost: Free
Catalog Circulation: Mailed 1 time(s) per year to 50M
Average Order Size: $100
Printing Information: 32 pages in 4 colors on Glossy Stock
Press: Web Press
Binding: Folded
Mailing List Information: Names for rent
List Manager: Matt Brown, Associates
In Business: 52 years
Number of Employees: 50
Sales Volume: $6 Million

5367   Solutions Catalog
PO Box 127
Jessup, PA 18434   877-718-7901
800-342-9988
Fax: 800-821-1282
www.solutionscatalog.com

Storage and organizing solutions, home furnishings, kitchen equipment, outdoor living, pest control and practical gifts

President: John Emrick
Credit Cards: AMEX; MasterCard; Visa
Catalog Cost: Free
Catalog Circulation: Mailed 1 time(s) per year
Printing Information: 72 pages in 4 colors on Glossy Stock
Press: Web Press
Binding: Saddle Stitched
Mailing List Information: Names for rent
List Manager: Patty Davis
In Business: 29 years
Number of Employees: 500

5368   The Big Book
Office Depot
6600 N Military Trail
Boca Raton, FL 33496   800-463-3768
www.officedepot.com

Binders, calendars, planners, ink, toner, filing & storage, labels, pens, pencils, desktop & notebook computers, printers, copiers, shredders and office furniture

Chairman & CEO: Roland C. Smith
Catalog Cost: Free
Catalog Circulation: Mailed 1 time(s) per year
Printing Information: 868 pages in 4 colors
In Business: 30 years
Number of Employees: 4900
Sales Volume: $14.5 Billion

5369   The Elegant Office
The Elegant Office
5200 NW 43rd Street
Suite 102-256
Gainesville, FL 32606   866-433-7573
sales@TheElegantOffice.com
www.theelegantoffice.com
In Business: 16 years

5370   The Land of Nod
The Land of Nod
8135 River Drive
Morton Grove, IL 60053   847-656-4750
customerservice@landofnod.com
www.landofnod.com

5371   Ultimate Office
Ultimate Office
PO Box 688
Farmingdale, NJ 07727-9701   732-780-6911
800-631-2233
Fax: 732-780-9833
customerservice@ultoffice.com
www.ultoffice.com

Binders & notebooks, binder storage carousels, clipboards, forms storage, desktop organizers, literature displays, reference organizers, workspace solutions and furniture

President: Craig W. Nelson
Production Manager: Dorris Gethard
Credit Cards: AMEX; MasterCard; Visa
Catalog Cost: Free
Catalog Circulation: Mailed 3 time(s) per year to 100M
Printing Information: 21 pages in 4 colors on Glossy Stock
Press: Web Press
Binding: Saddle Stitched
Mailing List Information: Names for rent
List Company: Direct Media
200 Pemberwick Road
Greenwich, CT 06830
203-531-1000

In Business: 25 years
Number of Employees: 25

5372 WA Charnstrom Mail Center Solutions
Charnstrom
5391 12th Avenue E
Shakopee, MN 55379-1896   800-328-2962
Fax: 800-916-3215
customerservice@charnstrom.com
www.charnstrom.com

Mailroom and mailing equipment and furniture

President: Greg Hedlund
Credit Cards: AMEX; MasterCard; Visa
Catalog Cost: Free
Printing Information: 52 pages in 4 colors
In Business: 57 years
Sales Volume: $5MM to $10MM

Supplies

5373 ACA Corporate Awards
Award Company of America
3200 Rice Mine Road NE
PO Box 2029
Tuscaloosa, AL 35406-1510   205-248-1621
800-633-2021
customerservice@awardcompany.com
www.awardcompany.com

Awards, plaques, trophies, ribbons, specialized greeting cards, promotional and specialty items.

President: Michael Reilly
CFO: Shane Elmore
Credit Cards: AMEX; MasterCard; Visa
Catalog Cost: Free
Mailing List Information: Names for rent
In Business: 40 years
Number of Employees: 200
Sales Volume: $ 10-20 Million

5374 ACA For Churches Only
Award Company of America
3200 Rice Mine Road NE
PO Box 2029
Tuscaloosa, AL 35406-1510   205-248-1621
800-633-2021
customerservice@awardcompany.com
www.awardcompany.com

Awards, plaques, trophies, ribbons, specialized greeting cards, promotional and specialty items.

President: Michael Reilly
CFO: Shane Elmore
Credit Cards: AMEX; MasterCard; Visa
Catalog Cost: Free
Mailing List Information: Names for rent
In Business: 40 years
Number of Employees: 200
Sales Volume: $ 10-20 Million

5375 ACA School Essentials
Award Company of America
3200 Rice Mine Road NE
PO Box 2029
Tuscaloosa, AL 35406-1510   205-248-1621
800-633-2021
customerservice@awardcompany.com
www.awardcompany.com

Awards, plaques, trophies, ribbons, specialized greeting cards, promotional and specialty items.

President: Michael Reilly
CFO: Shane Elmore
Credit Cards: AMEX; MasterCard; Visa
Catalog Cost: Free
Mailing List Information: Names for rent
In Business: 40 years
Number of Employees: 200
Sales Volume: $ 10-20 Million

5376 American Thermoplastic Company
American Thermoplastic Company
One Looseleaf Lane
P. O. Box 29
Vincent, AL 35178-0029   412-967-0900
800-245-6600
Fax: 800-344-8939
atc@binders.com
www.binders.com

Binders, index tabs and related loose-leaf products, especially custom imprinted

President: Steven Silberman
Marketing Manager: Joseph Sprumont
Credit Cards: AMEX; MasterCard
Catalog Cost: Free
Catalog Circulation: Mailed 1 time(s) per year
Printing Information: 20 pages in 4 colors on Glossy Stock
Binding: Saddle Stitched
Mailing List Information: Names for rent
In Business: 60 years

5377 Art Brown's International Pen
ST-DUPONT-NYC, INC
The N Y Jewelry exchange
20 West 47th street, #20R
New York, NY 10036   212-921-1144
800-341-7003
Fax: 212-575-5825
CustomerService@ST-Dupont-NYC.com
www.savingspros.com

Finest writing instruments, desk utensils and accessories

President: B Warren Brown
Credit Cards: AMEX; MasterCard; Visa
Catalog Cost: Free
Printing Information: 72 pages in 4 colors on Glossy Stock
Press: Web Press
Binding: Saddle Stitched
In Business: 143 years
Number of Employees: 25

5378 Associated Bag
Associated Bag Company
400 W Boden Street
Milwaukee, WI 53207-6276   800-926-6100
Fax: 800-926-4610
www.associatedbag.com

Packaging & shipping supplies including bags, boxes, bubble wrap, bubble mailers, labeling products, pallet wrap, shrink wrap and zipper bags

President: Herb Rubenstein
Credit Cards: AMEX; MasterCard; Visa
Catalog Cost: Free
Printing Information: 240 pages
Mailing List Information: Names for rent
In Business: 66 years
Number of Employees: 180
Sales Volume: $25,000,000 - $50,000,000

5379 Augusta Office Solutions
Augusta Office Solutions
3070 Damascus Rd
Suite C
Augusta, GA 30909   706-305-3971
Fax: 706-305-3972
customerservice@augustaofficesolutions.com
www.augustaofficesolutions.com
In Business: 20 years

5380 Betty Mills Catalog
The Betty Mills Company
2121 S El Camino Real
Suite C-120
San Mateo, CA 94403-1848   650-344-8228
800-238-8964
Fax: 650-341-1888
www.bettymills.com

Cleaning & janitorial products including brooms, brushes, floor & carpet care, cleaning chemicals, mops, buckets, recycling containers, vacuums and waste receptacles

President: Ofer Sabadosh
Managing Director: Steven Cinelli
Credit Cards: AMEX; MasterCard; Visa
Catalog Cost: $1.5
Catalog Circulation: to 100K
Average Order Size: $200
Printing Information: 250 pages on Glossy Stock
Press: Letterpress
Binding: Perfect Bound
Mailing List Information: Names for rent
In Business: 10 years
Number of Employees: 16
Sales Volume: $1.4 Million

5381 BrownCor BC Advantage
BrownCor
500 W Oklahoma Avenue
Milwaukee, WI 53207   414-443-1700
800-327-2278
Fax: 800-343-9228
www.browncor.com

Complete line of shipping, packing and warehouse supplies

President: Phil Arredia
Marketing Manager: Michael Smith
Production Manager: Poppy Payne
In Business: 7 years
Number of Employees: 17
Sales Volume: $ 18 Million

5382 CBD Supply
Christian Book Distributors
140 Summit St.
Peabody, MA 01960   800-247-4784
customer.service@christianbook.com
www.christianbook.com

Bibles, music, pastoral resources, outreach materials and more.

President: Ray Hendrickson
Catalog Cost: Free
Mailing List Information: Names for rent
In Business: 39 years
Number of Employees: 500

5383 Displays2Go
Displays2Go
55 Broadcommon Road
Bristol, RI 02809   401-247-0333
800-572-2194
Fax: 401-247-0392
info@displays2go.com
www.displays2go.com

Brochure/literature displays, magazine holders, sign and photo frames, display cases, poster hangers

President: Thomas Patton
CEO: Chris Patton
Credit Cards: AMEX; MasterCard
Catalog Cost: Free
In Business: 41 years
Number of Employees: 180
Sales Volume: $ 21.3Million

5384 Drawing Board
Drawing Board Printing
101 East Ninth Street
Waynesboro, PA 17268   800-527-9530
Fax: 800-253-1838
customerservice@drawingboard.com
www.drawingboard.com

Imprinted products such as labels, envelopes, stationery, forms, checks and promotional products

Credit Cards: AMEX; MasterCard
Catalog Cost: Free
Catalog Circulation: Mailed 12 time(s) per year
Printing Information: 100 pages in 4 colors on

Newsprint
Press: Web Press
Binding: Saddle Stitched
Number of Employees: 250

5385 Ellis Office Supply

Ellis Office Supply
1640 E. Pleasant Blvd.
Altoona, PA 16602 814-943-1660
888-943-1660
Fax: 814-942-4858
sales@ellisofficesupply.com
www.ellisofficesupply.com
Credit Cards: AMEX; MasterCard

5386 Epson Accessories

Epson America, Inc.
3840 Kilroy Airport Way
Long Beach, CA 90806-2452 562-981-3840
800-463-7766
Fax: 562-782-5220
www.epson.com

Printers, paper and imaging products

President: John Lang
In Business: 37 years
Number of Employees: 832
Sales Volume: $ 44 Million

5387 Fahrney's Pens

Fahrney's Pens
1317 F Street
Washington, NW 20004 202-628-9525
800-624-7367
Fax: 301-736-2926
custserv@fahrneyspens.com
www.fahrneyspens.com

Fine name brand and limited edition writing instruments including rollerball pens, ballpens, fountain pens, pen sets, pencils, pen refills, stationery and corporate gifts

President: Christopher Sullivan
Operations Director: Stephanie Watson
VP: Donna Korper
Buyers: Jon Sullivan
Chris Sullivan
Credit Cards: AMEX; MasterCard
Catalog Cost: Free
Catalog Circulation: Mailed 5 time(s) per year to 250M
Printing Information: 48 pages in 4 colors on Glossy Stock
Press: Web Press
Binding: Saddle Stitched
Mailing List Information: Names for rent
In Business: 85 years
Number of Employees: 24
Sales Volume: $ 1-3 Million

5388 Filing Supplies from A-Z

Medical Arts Press
8500 Wyoming Ave N
Minneapolis, MN 55445-1825 763-493-7300
800-328-2179
Fax: 800-328-0023
www.quill.com

Office supplies, medical ID tags, filing systems and more

President: Steven M Wexler
CFO: Mike Kasner
Marketing Manager: Barb Boyer
Production Manager: Terry Schwarting
Credit Cards: MasterCard; Visa
Catalog Circulation: Mailed 4 time(s) per year to 6000
Printing Information: 76 pages in 4 colors on Glossy Stock
Press: Web Press
Binding: Saddle Stitched
In Business: 53 years
Number of Employees: 460
Sales Volume: $ 32 Million

5389 Fountain Pen Hospital

Fountain Pen Hospital
10 Warren Street
New York, NY 10007-2218 212-964-0580
800-253-7367
Fax: 212-227-5916
info@fountainpenhospital.com
www.fountainpenhospital.com

All types of fine writing instruments-fountain pens, ball pens, rollerballs, pencils, and computer data pens plus accessories

President: Steve Wiederlight
Office Manager: Terry Woederlight
Credit Cards: AMEX; MasterCard; Visa
Catalog Cost: Free
Catalog Circulation: Mailed 12 time(s) per year
Printing Information: 92 pages in 2 colors on Glossy Stock
Press: Web Press
Binding: Saddle Stitched
Mailing List Information: Names for rent
In Business: 69 years
Number of Employees: 15
Sales Volume: $ 7 Million

5390 G Neil Direct Mail

HR direct
PO Box 452049
Sunrise, FL 33345-2049 877-968-7471
800-888-4040
Fax: 954-846-0777
questions@hrdirect.com
www.hrdirect.com

HR recordkeeping products and computer software, employee training and motivational products

President: Susan Drenning

5391 Hello Direct

Hello Direct
77 Northeastern Boulevard
Nashua, NH 03062 800-435-5634
xpressit@hellodirect.com
www.hellodirect.com

Phones, headsets, conferencing, recording and mobile equipment

VP of Business Development: Stephen Mays
Credit Cards: AMEX; MasterCard; Visa
Catalog Cost: Free
Printing Information: 23 pages in 4 colors on Newsprint
Press: Web Press
Binding: Saddle Stitched
Northeastern Boulevard
Nashua, NH 03062
In Business: 30 years
Number of Employees: 60
Sales Volume: $ 20-50 Million

5392 Homespun Music Instruction

Homespun Tapes
Woodstock NY 800-338-2737
Fax: 845-246-5282
www.homespun.com

Instructional books, CDs, DVDs, and supplies to learn how to play a variety of instruments

President: Happy Traum
Co-Founder/Vice President: Jane Traum
Office Manager: Susan Robinson
Customer Service/Production Assoc.: Joyce Rado
Catalog Cost: Free
In Business: 48 years

5393 Information Packaging

Information Packaging
1670 N Wayneport Road
Macedon, NY 14502-9160 315-986-5793
800-776-7633
Fax: 315-986-4585
www.infopkg.com

Paper and accessories for the business industry

Chairman: Jim Sellar
President: Mike Hogan
VP, Sales: David Young
Accounting Manager: Theresa Ange
Office Manager/Accounting: Deb Ludolph
In Business: 30 years
Sales Volume: $ 20-50 Million

5394 Kudos by Paper Direct

Paper Direct
Customer Service Department
1005 E. Woodmen Road
Colorado Springs, CO 80920-3570800-272-7377
Fax: 719-534-1741
customerservice@paperdirect.com
www.paperdirect.com

Offers an extensive line of products to reward, recognize and motivate employees

President: Wendy Huxta
CFO: Kirby Heck
Credit Cards: AMEX; MasterCard; Visa
Catalog Cost: Free
Catalog Circulation: Mailed 4 time(s) per year
Printing Information: in 4 colors
Binding: Saddle Stitched
In Business: 26 years
Number of Employees: 850

5395 Laser Labels Technology

LLT Products
4560 Darrow Road
Stow, OH 44224 800-842-4050
Fax: 800-395-4721
sales@lltproducts.com
www.lltproducts.com

Laser & impact labels, bar code systems, specialty labels, thermal printing supplies, pressure sensitive solutions and inventory systems

Credit Cards: AMEX; MasterCard; Visa
Catalog Cost: Free
Printing Information: 23 pages in 4 colors on Glossy Stock
Number of Employees: 32
Sales Volume: Under $500,000

5396 Leslie Company

Leslie Company
PO Box 610
Olathe, KS 66051 800-255-6210
Fax: 800-708-7066
info@leslieco.com
www.leslieco.com

Binders, calendars, index tabs, pocket folders, product templates and book binding & printing

President: Jerald Byrd
Marketing Manager: Michael Byrd
Credit Cards: AMEX; MasterCard; Visa
Catalog Cost: Free
Catalog Circulation: Mailed 1 time(s) per year to 40M
Printing Information: 84 pages in 4 colors on Glossy Stock
Press: Letterpress
Binding: Perfect Bound
Mailing List Information: Names for rent
In Business: 38 years
Number of Employees: 100
Sales Volume: $10.3 Million

5397 Merchandising Solutions

M F Blouin
710 Main Street
PO Box 10
Rollinsford, NH 03869 603-742-0104
800-394-1632
Fax: 603-742-9539
info@mfblouin.com
www.mfblouin.com

Banking office supplies & equipment including sign holders, compliance signs, nameplates, security pens, cash handling supplies, currency envelopes, ATM drive up items, check desks and teller stools

President: David Zoia
CFO: Linda White
Credit Cards: AMEX; MasterCard; Visa
Catalog Cost: Free
Catalog Circulation: Mailed 12 time(s) per year
Printing Information: 64 pages in 4 colors on Glossy Stock
Press: Web Press
Binding: Saddle Stitched
Mailing List Information: Names for rent
In Business: 63 years
Number of Employees: 40
Sales Volume: $ 4 Million

5398 Monarch Accounting Supplies
Monarch
750 Main Street
Holyoke, MA 01040   413-536-3444
800-828-6718
Fax: 413-536-3477
www.monarchtaxforms.com

Tax forms, accounting, auditing and bookkeeping supplies

President: William Grierson
Credit Cards: AMEX; MasterCard; Visa
Catalog Cost: Free
Catalog Circulation: Mailed 1 time(s) per year
Printing Information: 18 pages in 2 colors on Newsprint
Binding: Folded
Mailing List Information: Names for rent
List Manager: William Grierson
In Business: 62 years

5399 Namifiers
Namify, LLC
280 W 900 N
Springville, UT 84663   801-491-8068
800-470-6970
Fax: 801-489-7538
orders@namify.com
www.namify.com

Nametags, magnetic nametags, laynards, custom printed lanyards, vinyl banners, badge holders and reels, apparel and accessories, key rings, office name plates

Chairman: Bryan L. Welton Jr
President: Bryan L Welton Jr
Marketing Manager: Brad Gasaway
Owner: Jeff Edwards
CEO: Chris Jensen
Sales Executive: Brian Coltharp
brian@badgeboss.com
Catalog Cost: Free
Printing Information: 15 pages
In Business: 10 years
Number of Employees: 112
Sales Volume: $8 Million

5400 National Pen
National Pen Company
12121 Scripps Summit Dr.
San Diego, CA 92131   866-907-7367
www.nationalpen.com

Pens, pencils, electronics, executive gifts, greeting cards, office/desk accessories, bags and totes and apparel.

President & CEO: Peter Kelly
Catalog Cost: Free
In Business: 50 years
Sales Volume: $300 Million

5401 Office Penny
Office Penny
One Gateway Center
Suite 2600
Newark, NJ 7104   973-362-0062
855-997-3669
Fax: 855-997-3669
Cs@Officepenny.com

Office Products.
Credit Cards: AMEX; MasterCard

5402 Office Specialists, Inc
Office Specialists, Inc
143 E Ferris St
Galesburg, IL 61401   800-747-0071
www.osi.biz

5403 Omaha Fixture International
Omaha Fixture International
10320 J Street
Omaha, NE 68127   402-592-3720
800-637-2257
Fax: 402-593-5716
Service@OmahaFixture.com
www.omahafixture.com

Fixtures, displays and forms for businesses

President: Joel Alperson
Credit Cards: AMEX; MasterCard
In Business: 60 years

5404 PaperDirect
PaperDirect
P.O. Box 1151
Minneapolis, MN 55440-1151   800-272-7377
Fax: 800-443-2973
volumesales@paperdirect.com
www.paperdirect.com

Paper for all laser printer copier and desktop publishing needs

President: Tim Arland
CFO: Kirby Heck
Credit Cards: AMEX; MasterCard; Visa
Catalog Cost: Free
Catalog Circulation: Mailed 5 time(s) per year
Printing Information: 95 pages in 4 colors on Glossy Stock
Press: Web Press
Binding: Saddle Stitched
In Business: 29 years
Number of Employees: 1200
Sales Volume: $ 78 Million

5405 Pengad
Pengad,Inc
55 Oak Street
P.O.Box 99
Bayonne, NJ 07002-99   201-436-5625
800-631-6989
Fax: 201-436-9550
customerservice@pengad.com
www.pengad.com

Paper products and court reporter supplies

President: Tom Pierson
Owner: Jules Penn
Credit Cards: AMEX; MasterCard
Catalog Cost: Free
Catalog Circulation: Mailed 1 time(s) per year
Printing Information: 12 pages in 4 colors
In Business: 79 years
Sales Volume: $ 10-20 Million

5406 Piedmont Office Suppliers
Piedmont Office Suppliers
3206 Rehobeth Church Rd.
Greensboro, NC 27406   336-856-0100
Fax: 336-856-1101
wecare@piedmontoffice.com
www.piedmontoffice.com

In Business: 71 years

5407 Plastic Bag and Packaging
International Plastics, Inc.
185 Commerce Center
Greenville, SC 29615-5817   864-297-8000
800-820-4722
Fax: 864-297-7186
www.interplas.com

Plastic bags and packaging supplies for businesses

President: Steve McClure
CFO: Carolyn Robinson
Marketing Manager: Mark McClure
Production Manager: Mark McClure
Credit Cards: MasterCard
Catalog Cost: Free
Catalog Circulation: Mailed 12 time(s) per year
Average Order Size: $250
Printing Information: 48 pages in 4 colors on Glossy Stock
Press: Web Press
Binding: Saddle Stitched
Mailing List Information: Names for rent
In Business: 49 years
Number of Employees: 36
Sales Volume: $20,000,000-$50,000,000

5408 Prime Packaging Corp
Prime Packaging Corp
1290 Metropolitan Ave
Brooklyn, NY 11237   718-417-1116
Fax: 718-417-3348
cs@primepackaging.com
www.primepackaging.com

Wholesale packaging products

President: Arnold Kohn
In Business: 37 years
Number of Employees: 45
Sales Volume: $8.2 Million

5409 Quill.com
Quill Lincolnshire
100 Schelter Rd.
Lincolnshire, IL 60069   847-634-6690
www.quill.com

Furniture, filing, storage, ink, toner, printers, computer monitors and hard drives.

Catalog Cost: Free
In Business: 60 years
Number of Employees: 500
Sales Volume: $1 Billion

5410 Richter
Richter
757 Rte 113
PO Box 64288
Souderton, PA 18964   215-173-3900
888-258-7911
Fax: 215-723-6803
Sales@RichterOnline.com
www.richteronline.com

5411 Signs Plus Banners
Signs Plus Banners
20195 S Diamond Lake Road
Suite 100
Rogers, MN 55374   763-428-9405
800-635-6897
Fax: 763-428-6095
sales@signsplusbanners.com
www.signsplusbanners.com

Sign making supplies and wholesale

President: Bill Wallner
Operations Coordinator: Julie Melander
julieh@signsplusbanners.com
CEO: Don Kotula
Department Manager: Craig Morse
Credit Cards: AMEX; MasterCard; Visa
Catalog Cost: Free
Catalog Circulation: Mailed 26 time(s) per year
Printing Information: 24 pages

In Business: 34 years
Number of Employees: 32

5412 Specialty Store Services
Speciality Store Services
454 Jarvis Ave
Des Plaines, IL 60018   888-441-246
888-441-4440
Fax: 888-368-8001
www.specialtystoreservices.com

Bags, boxes, retail fixtures, gift wrap, labelers, price guns, cash handling equipment, shelving, counters and signage

President: Malcom Finke
Marketing Manager: Rudy Pichietti
VP Finance: Richard Robinson
Credit Cards: AMEX; MasterCard; Visa
Catalog Cost: Free
In Business: 30 years
Number of Employees: 85
Sales Volume: $15.4 Million

5413 Storesmart
StoreSMART
180 Metro Park
Rochester, NY 14623-2610   585-424-5300
800-424-1011
Fax: 585-424-1064
CS@storesmart.com
www.storesmart.com

Plastic folders, file jackets, hanging folders, paperwork organizers, portfolios, menu covers, sheet protectors, tag holders and magnetic plastic pockets

President: Reenie Feingold
Credit Cards: AMEX; MasterCard; Visa
Catalog Cost: Free
Catalog Circulation: to 10000
Average Order Size: $69
Mailing List Information: Names for rent
In Business: 44 years
Number of Employees: 14
Sales Volume: $ 1.3 Million

5414 Styles Checks
The Styles Check Company
8245 N Union Blvd
Colorado Springs, CO 80935-4456501-455-1600
866-449-8804
Fax: 410-676-8269
customerservice@styleschecks.com
www.styleschecks.com

Personal checks, business checks and other custom-printed products under multiple check brands

Catalog Cost: Free
In Business: 10 years

5415 Successories
Successories
2915 S. Congress Ave
Building B / Unit
Delray Beach, FL 33445   754-220-2942
800-535-2773
Fax: 561-952-4097
ContactUs@successories.com
www.successories.com

Office inspirational products: framed prints, desk accessories

President: Warren Struhl
Credit Cards: AMEX; MasterCard
Catalog Cost: Free
Printing Information: in 4 colors
In Business: 29 years

5416 The Big Book
Office Depot
6600 N Military Trail
Boca Raton, FL 33496   800-463-3768
www.officedepot.com

Binders, calendars, planners, ink, toner, filing & storage, labels, pens, pencils, desktop & notebook computers, printers, copiers, shredders and office furniture

Chairman & CEO: Roland C. Smith
Catalog Cost: Free
Catalog Circulation: Mailed 1 time(s) per year
Printing Information: 868 pages in 4 colors
In Business: 30 years
Number of Employees: 4900
Sales Volume: $14.5 Billion

5417 The Office Shop
The Office Shop
131 Batesville Shopping Village
Batesville, IN 47006   800-742-9760
Fax: 800-642-9760
info@officeshop.net
www.officeshop.net

In Business: 37 years

5418 Uline Shipping Supply Specialists
Uline
12575 Uline Drive
Pleasant Prairie, WI 53158   262-612-4200
800-295-5510
Fax: 800-295-5571
customer.service@uline.com
www.uline.com

Uline offers over 20,000 boxes, plastic poly bags, mailing tubes, warehouse supplies and bubble wrap for storage, packaging, or shipping supplies

President: Liz Uihlein
CEO: Dick Uihlein
Vice President: Duke Uihlein
Vice President: Steve Uihlein
Buyers: Brian Uihlein
Phil Hunt
Credit Cards: AMEX; MasterCard; Visa
Catalog Cost: Free
Catalog Circulation: Mailed 2 time(s) per year
Printing Information: 664 pages in 4 colors on Glossy Stock
Press: Web Press
Binding: Saddle Stitched
Mailing List Information: Names for rent
In Business: 35 years
Number of Employees: 250
Sales Volume: $ 20-50 Million

5419 WA Charnstrom Mail Center Solutions
Charnstrom
5391 12th Avenue E
Shakopee, MN 55379-1896   800-328-2962
Fax: 800-916-3215
customerservice@charnstrom.com
www.charnstrom.com

Mailroom and mailing equipment and furniture

President: Greg Hedlund
Credit Cards: AMEX; MasterCard; Visa
Catalog Cost: Free
Printing Information: 52 pages in 4 colors
In Business: 57 years
Sales Volume: $5MM to $10MM

5420 Yazoo Mills Catalog
Yazoo Mills Inc
305 Commerce St
P.O.Box 369
New Oxford, PA 17350-369   717-624-8993
800-242-5216
Fax: 717-624-4420
sales@yazoomills.com
www.yazoomills.com

High quality paper cores and tubes made form 100% recycled paperboard

President: Troy Eckerd
Production Manager: Steve McMaster
Credit Cards: AMEX; MasterCard; Visa
Catalog Cost: Free
Mailing List Information: Names for rent

In Business: 113 years
Number of Employees: 85
Sales Volume: $ 17 Million

Optical Products
Eyeware & Accessories

5421 Debbie Burk Optical
Debbie Burk Optical
7 Overlook Lane
Plainview, NY 11803-3227   516-935-4584
800-789-6322
Fax: 516-932-5628
help@debspecs.com
www.debspecs.com

Redy-to-wear designer reading glawsses and accompanying eyeglasses accessories; sunglasses, computer glasses, and low-vision eyewear

President: Debby Burk
Credit Cards: AMEX; MasterCard
Catalog Cost: Free
Printing Information: in 4 colors
Sales Volume: $500M to $1MM

5422 Focusers
Focusers, Inc.
1101 Market Street
Aramark Tower Suite 2700
Philadelphia, PA 19107   800-332-3534
information@focusers.com
www.focusers.com

Reading glasses, prescription glasses, sunglasses, frames, and opthalmic lenses

Credit Cards: AMEX; MasterCard
Catalog Cost: Free
In Business: 20 years

5423 Hidalgo
6507 Shreveport Hwy.
Pineville, LA 71360   318-641-7700
Fax: 318-641-9700
pilotseyewear.com

Eyeglasses

5424 Independent Living Aids Comprehensive Catalog
Independent Living Aids
137 Rano Rd
Buffalo, NY 14207   800-537-2118
Fax: 516-937-3906
barbara@independentliving.com
www.independentliving.com

Hearing products and low vision products to assist in daily life

President: Irwin Schneidmill
Credit Cards: AMEX; MasterCard; Visa
Catalog Cost: Free
Catalog Circulation: Mailed 1 time(s) per year
Printing Information: 125 pages in 4 colors on Glossy Stock
Binding: Saddle Stitched
In Business: 35 years

5425 See More Vision
See More Vision
PO Box 3413
Farmingdale, NY 11735-0686   800-428-6673
Fax: 631-752-0689

Low vision producst.

5426 SeeMoreVision.com
PO Box 3413
Farmingdale, NY 11735-686   800-428-6673
Fax: 631-752-0689
barryg@seemorevision.com
seemorevision.com

Vision products

5427 Sellstrom Manufacturing Company
Sellstrom Manufacturing Co.
2050 Hammond Drive
Schaumburg, IL 60173-355   847-358-2000
800-323-7402
Fax: 847-358-8564
sellstrom@sellstrom.com
www.sellstrom.com

Protective face shields, protective goggles, emergency eye/face wash units, welding helmets and goggles, spill control, emergency showers

President: David Peters
david.peters@sellstrom.com
CFO: Lawrence Schmidt
larry.schmidt@sellstrom.com
Marketing Manager: Rusty Franklin
rusty.franklin@sellstrom.com
Customer Service: Jason Suarez
Manager Engineering: Ken Lemke
Marketing Coordinator: Beverly Bensen
Catalog Circulation: to 30000
Printing Information: 64 pages in 3 colors
In Business: 92 years
Number of Employees: 100
Sales Volume: $20MM

5428 Sport Rx
Sport Rx Inc
5076 Santa Fe Street
Suite A
San Diego, CA 92109   888-831-5817
Fax: 858-571-0580
info@sportrx.com
www.sportrx.com

Prescription goggles and sunglasses for the motorcycle and action sports enthusiast

Credit Cards: AMEX; MasterCard
Catalog Cost: Free
Printing Information: in 4 colors
In Business: 18 years

5429 Titmus Optical
Serian Protection Optical, Inc.
15801 Woods Edge Road
Colonial Heights, VA 23834-2742   800-446-1802
800-446-1802
Fax: 800-544-0346
www.titmus.com

Prescription protective eyewear, vision screening instruments, street designs dress eyewear and accessories

President: Thomas Boeltz
In Business: 107 years
Number of Employees: 500
Sales Volume: $25,000,000 - $50,000,000

Telescopes, Binoculars & Microscopes

5430 Alpen Outdoor
10329 Dorset Street
Rancho Cucamonga, CA 91730   909-987-8370
877-987-8370
Fax: 909-987-8661
alpenoptics.com

Binoculars and telescopes

5431 Barska
Barska
855 Towne Center Dr.
Pomona, CA 91767   909-445-8168
888-666-6769
Fax: 909-445-8169
sales@barska.com
www.barska.com

Binoculars, sport optics products ranging from riflescopes and sporting scopes to telescopes

President: Johnson Yang
Marketing Manager: Joe Romero

Business Development Manager: Joanne Tan
Sales Manager: Harry Bajwa
Information Technology Manager: Jack Tan
Credit Cards: AMEX; MasterCard
In Business: 19 years
Number of Employees: 20
Sales Volume: $11,000,000

5432 Berger Brothers Camera Video Digital
Berger Bros.
22 Clinton Ave.
Huntington, NY 11743   631-421-2200

Film and digital cameras and accessories, darkroom supplies, lenses, memory, tripods, scanners and projectors, telescopes, video and voice recorders

President: Brad Berger
Professional Photographer: Yvonne Berger
Credit Cards: MasterCard
Catalog Cost: Free
In Business: 64 years
Number of Employees: 28
Sales Volume: $6,000,000+

5433 Eagle Optics
Eagle Optics
2120 W Greenview Dr
Middleton, WI 53562   800-289-1132
Fax: 608-836-4416
info@eagleoptics.com
www.eagleoptics.com

Binoculars, momoculars, spotting scopes, tripods & mounts, rengefinders and night vision binoculars

President: Dan Hamilton
Manager: Ben Lizdas
Credit Cards: AMEX; MasterCard
Catalog Cost: Free
Printing Information: 39 pages
In Business: 29 years
Sales Volume: $5MM to $10MM

5434 Haverhill's
Haverhills
16911 Grays Bay Blvd.
Wayzata, MN 55391   952-476-2006
800-797-7367
Fax: 952-476-5999
customerservice@haverhills.com
www.haverhills.com

Optics, hearing aids, microscopes, pest control, radios, watches

President: Paul Harris
Buyers: Nick Ranks
Printing Information: 16 pages in 4 colors
Mailing List Information: Names for rent
In Business: 42 years
Number of Employees: 4
Sales Volume: $1MM to $3MM

5435 Meadows Medical Supply
PO Box 2
62 Old Country Road
Quogue, NY 11959   800-645-3585
Fax: 888-989-8881
www.meadowsmedical.com

Resources for healthcare education

President: Brian Gallagher
Vice President: Sean Gallagher

5436 Olden Lighting
Olden Camera & Lens Co Inc
1263 Broadway # 4
New York, NY 10001-3593   212-725-1234
Fax: 212-725-1325

Lighting

President: Robert Olden
Sales Volume: $1MM to $3MM

5437 Optical Systems & Aspherics
Space Optics Research Labs
7 Stuart Road
Chelmsford, MA 01824   978-250-8640
800-552-7675
Fax: 978-256-5605
sorl@sorl.com
www.sorl.com

Telescope systems, mirror mounts, flat & shperical mirrors and laser beam expanders

Credit Cards: AMEX; MasterCard; Visa
Catalog Cost: Free
Number of Employees: 10

5438 Orion Telescopes & Binoculars
Orion Telescopes & Binoculars
89 Hangar Way
Watsonville, CA 95076   831-763-7000
800-676-1343
Fax: 831-763-7024
sales@telescope.com
www.telescope.com

Telescopes, microscopes, binoculars, mounts, tripods, books, cases, covers, eyepieces and atomic clocks

Credit Cards: AMEX; MasterCard
Catalog Cost: Free
In Business: 40 years
Sales Volume: $20MM to $50MM

5439 Semrock
3625 Buffalo Road
Suite 6
Rochester, NY 14624   585-594-7050
866-736-7625
Fax: 585-594-7095
semrock@idexcorp.com
www.semrock.com

Engineered products for optical systems

Strategic Account Manager: Amanda Savas
Strategic Account Manager: Brian O'Flaherty, PhD

5440 Spectrum Technologies
3600 Thayer Court
Aurora, IL 60504   815-436-4440
800-248-8873
Fax: 815-436-4460
info@specmeters.com
www.specmeters.com

Binoculars

5441 Ward's Science
5100 West Henrietta Road
PO Box 92912
Rochester, NY 14692-9102   800-962-2660
Fax: 800-635-8439
wardscs@vwr.com
www.wardsci.com

Scientific supplies and materials

5442 Woodland Hills Camera
Woodland Hills Camera & Telescopes
5348 Topanga Canyon Boulevard
Woodland Hills, CA 91364   818-347-2270
888-427-8766
Fax: 818-992-4486
telescopes.net

High quality cameras and parts & accessories

Credit Cards: AMEX; MasterCard
Catalog Cost: Free
Printing Information: on N
Press: W
Binding: F
Mailing List Information: Names for rent
In Business: 63 years
Number of Employees: 10
Sales Volume: under $500M

Performing Arts Products
Dance

5443 All About Dance
All About Dance
800-775-0578
info@allaboutdance.com
www.allaboutdance.com

Name brand dance clothing, shoes, and accessories

Catalog Cost: Free
In Business: 18 years

5444 Anyone Can Dance
DanceVision.com
9081 W Sahara Avenue
Las Vegas, NV 89117-5826   702-256-3830
800-851-2813
Fax: 702-256-4227
info@dancevision.com
www.dancevision.com

Learn to dance videos

President: James Hicks
Business Analyst: Wayne Eng
Credit Cards: AMEX; MasterCard
Catalog Cost: Free
Printing Information: 1 pages in 4 colors on Glossy Stock
Number of Employees: 9
Sales Volume: $950,000

5445 Art Stone the Competitor
Art Stone/ The Competitor
PO Box 2345
Cinnaminson, NJ 08077   631-582-9500
800-522-8897
Fax: 631-582-9541
customerservice@artstonecostumes.com
www.artstonecostumes.com

Dancewear

President: Art Stone
Credit Cards: AMEX; MasterCard
Catalog Cost: Free
In Business: 55 years
Number of Employees: 40
Sales Volume: $3MM to $5MM

5446 Butterfly Video
Wayne Green Book
PO Box 184
Antrim, NH 03440   603-588-2105
800-433-2623
Fax: 603-588-3205
info@kathyblake.com
www.butterflyvideo.com

Learn how to dance videos, tango, waltz and foxtrot

President: Sherry Smythe Green
Producer: Sherry Green
Credit Cards: AMEX; MasterCard; Visa
Catalog Cost:
Catalog Circulation: to 50000
Printing Information: 16 pages in 1 color on Matte Stock
Press: Sheetfed Press
Binding: Folded
Mailing List Information: Names for rent
Number of Employees: 5
Sales Volume: $400,000

5447 Dance Equipment International
Dance Equipment International
2103 Lincoln Avenue
Suite C
San Jose, CA 95125-3541   408-267-1446
800-626-9258
Fax: 408-265-7290
info@danceequipmentintl.com
www.danceequipmentintl.com

Dance equipment, dance floors, ballet barres, glassless mirrors, gym mats

President: Joseph Reinke
Catalog Cost: Free
Catalog Circulation: Mailed 1 time(s) per year to 20000
Printing Information: 12 pages in 1 color
Mailing List Information: Names for rent
In Business: 79 years
Number of Employees: 5

5448 Dansant Boutique
6623 Old Dominion Drive
McLean, VA 22101-4516   703-847-0736
www.loopnet.com

Ballet and other dance supplies

Printing Information: 26 pages

5449 Glamour Costumes
Glamour Costumes
3 Commercial St.
Hicksville, NY 11801   516-719-0996
855-203-0005
Fax: 516-719-0997
info@glamourcostumes.com
www.glamourcostumes.com

Dance wear

Credit Cards: AMEX; MasterCard

5450 Kultur Performing Arts DVD's
Kultur Films
195 Highway 36
PO Box 755
Forked River, NJ 08731   888-329-2580
support@kultur.com
www.kulturvideo.com

Performing arts, visual arts, history and literature videos

Chairman: Dennis M Hedlund
Marketing Manager: John Winfrey
Credit Cards: AMEX; MasterCard
Catalog Cost: Free
Catalog Circulation: Mailed 2 time(s) per year
Printing Information: 32 pages in 4 colors on Glossy Stock
Press: Web Press
Binding: Saddle Stitched
Mailing List Information: Names for rent
In Business: 26 years
Number of Employees: 25

5451 Laylas Dance Costumes
Laylas Dance Costumes
759 Bloomfield Ave
Suite 162
West Caldwell, NJ 7006   844-452-9527
Fax: 855-452-9527
Info@LaylasDanceCostumes.com
www.laylasdancecostumes.com

Dance costumes

Credit Cards: AMEX; MasterCard

5452 Showtime Dance Shoes
Showtime Dance Shoes
4458 Peachtree Lake Drive
Suite B
Duluth, GA 30096-3254   678-812-3000
800-433-5541
Fax: 678-812-3010
info@showtimedanceshoes.com
www.Showtimedanceshoes.Com

Hand lasted ballroom and Latin dance shoes

President: Don Dibble
Credit Cards: AMEX; MasterCard
Catalog Cost: Free
Catalog Circulation: Mailed 1 time(s) per year
In Business: 35 years
Number of Employees: 8
Sales Volume: $1MM to $3MM

5453 Spiritual Expressions
6750 Manchester Avenue
St. Louis, MO 63139   888-776-5533
Fax: 877-773-5175
www.spirtualexpressions.com

Skirts, pants, tops & tunics, dresses, tights, dance shoes and accessories

Credit Cards: AMEX; MasterCard; Visa

5454 Star Styled Dancewear
Star Styled Dancewear
P.O. Box 090490
Hallandale Beach, FL 33009   800-458-2549
Fax: 888-928-2282
www.starstyled.com

Women's dance clothing and supplies

President: Phillip D Giberson
CFO: Bonnie Felipe
Catalog Cost: Free
In Business: 55 years
Sales Volume: $7MM

5455 Supreme Audio
Supreme Audio, Inc.
155 Troy Rd.
PO Box 550
Marlborough, NH 03455-550   603-876-3636
800-445-7398
Fax: 603-876-4001
info@supremeaudio.com
www.supremeaudio.com

Specialists in dance & fitness sound systems & headsets

President: Peggy Heyman
Credit Cards: AMEX; MasterCard
Printing Information: 49 pages
In Business: 40 years

5456 Tic-Tac-Toes
Tic-Tac-Toes
1 Hamilton Street
PO Box 953
Gloversville, NY 12078   800-648-8126
contact@tictactoes.com
www.tictactoes.com

Contra Shoes, Square Dance Shoes, Shagging Shoes, Organist Shoes, Choir Shoes, Chorus Shoes, Latin Dancing Shoes, Ballroom Shoes, Mens Dancing Shoes and Theatrical Shoes

5457 Tosca Catalog - 2009
TOSCA Dancewear
2061 N.Los Robles # 209
Pasadena, CA 91104   626-345-1338
azita@toscafashion.com
www.toscafashion.com

Dance wear

5458 Trienawear
Trienawear
PO Box 20225
Columbus Circle
New York, NY 10023   212-877-4868
800-745-7613
Fax: 815-550-2124
info@trienawear.com
www.trienawear.com

5459 Xtreme Rhythmic
GymDivas
3214 Bart Conner Drive
Norman, OK 73072   877-GYM-DIVA
Fax: 405-321-7229
www.gymdivas.com

Gymnastics and dance sportswear

5460 danzia
danzia
797 Ames Ave
Milpitas, CA 95035   888-857-9118
                     Fax: 408-912-2881
                     www.danzia.com

Dance wear
Credit Cards: AMEX; MasterCard
Printing Information: 76 pages

Theater

5461 ALPHA Sound & Lighting Co.
ALPHA Sound & Lighting Co.
174 Baldwin Road
Satsuma, AL 36572   251-675-3358
                     Fax: 251-675-7572
                     sales@aslgc.com
                     www.aslgc.com

Sound and lighting systems
Vice President, Engineering: Mike Evans
Projects Manager: Kenny Stewart
Office Administrator: Thea Evans
Printing Information: 64 pages
In Business: 30+ years

5462 Alcone Company
Alcone LIC
5-45 49th Avenue
Long Island City, NY 11101   718-361-8373
                          800-466-7446
                     Fax: 718-729-8296
                     thepros@alconeco.com
                     www.alconeco.com

Makeup, lipstick, eye colors, removers, brushes, brush cleaners & brush holders, makeup chairs and attachments, prosthetics, rubber masks, bald caps, face paints and more
President: Vincent Mallardi
Credit Cards: AMEX; MasterCard; Visa
In Business: 65 years

5463 ArtFox Lighting
ArtFox Lighting
14836 Valley Blvd
City of Industry
Los Angeles, CA 91746   323-545-3995
                     sales@artfox.net
                     www.artfoxlighting.com

Moving Head Series, LED Moving heads, DJ Lighting, LED Par Lights, LED Wash Light

5464 Denny Manufacturing Company
The Denny Manufacturing Company, Inc.
PO Box 7200
Mobile, AL 36670-200   251-457-2388
                          800-844-5616
                     Fax: 251-452-4630
                     info@dennymfg.com
                     www.dennymfg.com

Backdrop and prop catalog
Credit Cards: AMEX; MasterCard
Catalog Cost: Free
Printing Information: 198 pages
In Business: 44 years
Number of Employees: 70
Sales Volume: $9,200,000

5465 Eliminator Lighting
Eliminator Lighting
4295 Charter Street
Los Angeles, CA 90058   323-948-0480
                     Fax: 323-583-6082
                     info@eliminatorlighting.com
                     www.eliminatorlighting.com

DJ Lighting

5466 Graftobian Beauty Catalog 2012 Print Version
Graftobian
510 Tasman Street
Madison, WI 53714   608-222-7849
                     Fax: 608-222-7893
                     www.graftobian.com

Makeup, Face Painting Make-Up, Color and Glitter Hairsprays and Gels, Graftobian Theatrical Make-Up and accessories
President: Eric G. Coffman
In Business: 37 years

5467 Hatcrafters
Hat Cap Exchange / Hatcrafters
20 N Springfield Rd
Clifton Heights, PA 19018-1497   302-478-9338
                          302-409-0117
                     Fax: 866-270-7668
                     info@hatcrafters.com
                     www.Hatcrafters.Com

Hats and accessories for theater
President: John Scott
john.hatcap@outlook.com
Number of Employees: 6
Sales Volume: Under $500M

5468 J Hats
Jacobson Hat Company, Inc.
1301 Ridge Row
Scranton, PA 18510-1429   800-233-4690
                     Fax: 800-882-5428
                     www.jhats.com

Hat and accessories for theatrical productions
President: Howard Jacobson
Catalog Cost: Free
In Business: 82 years
Sales Volume: $20MM to $50MM

5469 Norcostco
Norcostco
333-A Route 46 West
Fairfield, NJ 07004-2427   973-575-3503
                          800-220-6940
                     Fax: 973-575-2563
                     newjersey@norcostco.com
                     www.norcostco.com

Theatrical costumes, lighting and stage equipment
President: Steven Schweer
Credit Cards: MasterCard; Visa
Catalog Cost: Free
Catalog Circulation: Mailed 1 time(s) per year
Printing Information: 120 pages in 4 colors on Glossy Stock
Press: Web Press
Binding: Perfect Bound
In Business: 131 years
Number of Employees: 60
Sales Volume: Under $500M

5470 Southco
Southco
P.O.Box 116
P.O. Box 0116
Concordville, PA 19331-116   610-459-4000
                     Fax: 610-459-4012
                     info@southco.com
                     www.Southco.Com

Innovative engineered access hardware solutions
President: Brian McNeil
In Business: 116 years
Number of Employees: 800

5471 The Makeup Book: Catalog and Product Guide 2015-20
Graftobian
510 Tasman Street
Madison, WI 53714   608-222-7849
                     Fax: 608-222-7893
                     www.graftobian.com

Makeup, Face Painting Make-Up, Color and Glitter Hairsprays and Gels, Graftobian Theatrical Make-Up and accessories
President: Eric G. Coffman
In Business: 37 years

Photography Products
Accessories

5472 APR Prop and Background
American Photographic Resource
PO Box 820127
Fort Worth, TX 76182   817-595-9100
                          800-657-5213
                     Fax: 817-595-2300

Lighting equipment, photo albums, frames, fabric backgrounds, Artistic Series backgrounds and Silfondo backgrounds
President: Natalie Osborne
Catalog Cost: Free
Printing Information: 40 pages in 4 colors
In Business: 19 years

5473 B&H Photo Video Pro-Audio
B&H Photo Video
420 9th Avenue
New York, NY 10001   212-444-6615
                          800-606-6969
                     www.bhphotovideo.com

Photographic, video and digital imaging products, cameras, lenses, accessories, home theater components, binoculars, telescopes and much more
Chairman: Herman Schreiber
President: Sam Goldstein
CFO: Isreal Lebovits
Credit Cards: AMEX; MasterCard; Visa
Catalog Cost: Free
Catalog Circulation: Mailed 3 time(s) per year
Printing Information: 332 pages in 4 colors
In Business: 43 years
Number of Employees: 1100
Sales Volume: 85MM

5474 Backdrop Outlet
Backdrop Outlet
3540 Seagate Way
Oceanside, CA 92056   760-547-2900
                          800-466-1755
                     Fax: 760-547-2899
                     cs@backdropoutlet.com
                     www.backdropoutlet.com

A full line of backgrounds, props, sets, studio stands and studio props
President: Jay Gupta
Credit Cards: AMEX; MasterCard
Catalog Cost: Free
Catalog Circulation: Mailed 1 time(s) per year to 75000
Printing Information: 60 pages in 4 colors on Glossy Stock
In Business: 24 years
Number of Employees: 25
Sales Volume: $1-3 Million

5475 Buggies Unlimited
Buggies Unlimited
3510 Port Jacksonville Pkwy
Jacksonville, FL 32226   888-444-9994
                     Fax: 888-444-6364
                     support@buggiesunlimited.com
                     www.buggiesunlimited.com

Golf cart parts and accessories

Catalog Cost: Free

5476 Cases By Source
Cases By Source
215 Island Road
Mahwah, NJ 7430   888-515-5255
www.casesbysource.com

Stock Cases, Customized Stock Cases, Custom Engineered Case Solutions
Credit Cards: AMEX; MasterCard
In Business: 30 years

5477 Century Photo Products
Century Photo Products
2340 Brighton Henrietta Town Line R
Rochester, NY 14623   800-975-6429
Fax: 866-592-8642
help@fdmbrands.com
www.centuryphoto.com

Products for organizing and protecting photos
Marketing Manager: Bill Martin
Production Manager: Emily Lehrer
Credit Cards: AMEX; MasterCard
Catalog Cost: Free
Average Order Size: $90
Mailing List Information: Names for rent
List Company: Direct Media (Lisa Hamilton)
200 Pemberwick Road
Greenwich, CT 06830
203-532-3710
In Business: 61 years
Number of Employees: 250
Sales Volume: 450,000

5478 Custom Brackets
Custom Brackets
32 Alpha Park
Cleveland, OH 44143   440-446-0819
800-530-2289
info@custombrackets.com
www.custombrackets.com

Camera mount accessories
President: Michael Muzila
Printing Information: 29 pages

5479 Edmund Industrial Optics
Edmund Optics
101 East Gloucester Pike
Barrington, NJ 08007-1380   856-547-3488
800-363-1992
Fax: 856-573-6295
sales@edmundoptics.com
www.Edmundoptics.Com

Optical components, multi element lenses, camera lenses, lens coatings and imaging systems
Chairman: Robert M. Edmund
President: Samuel Sadoulet
CFO: Jason Mulliner
Marketing Manager: Marisa Edmund
Sr. Director, Global HR: Susan Tunney
Executive VP of Manufacturing: Susan O'Keefe
Executive VP of Asian Operations: Jeremy Chang
Printing Information: 460 pages
Number of Employees: 400
Sales Volume: $88,000,000

5480 Fuji Photo Film USA
Fuji Photo Film USA
200 Summit Lake Dr
Fl 2
Valhalla, NY 10595-1356   914-747-9538
Fax: 914-789-8295
www.fujifilmusa.com

Film and photo accessories
Chairman: Shigetaka Komori
President: Shigehiro Nakajima
Senior Vice Presidents: Yuzo Toda
Executive Vice President: Kouichi Tamai

Corporate Vice Presidents: Keiji Mihayashi
Sales Volume: $400,000

5481 Master Mount
Master Mount
23-21 College Point Boulevard
College Point, NY 11356   718-353-3297
800-424-1118
Fax: 718-353-4500
www.mastermount.com

Cards, albums, folders, proofbooks, and folios in stock
President: Margery Koleman
Credit Cards: AMEX; MasterCard; Visa
Catalog Cost: Free
Number of Employees: 5
Sales Volume: 3MM-5MM

5482 Porter's Photo Video Digital Catalog
Porter's Cedar Falls
323 W Viking Rd
Cedar Falls, IA 50613-6930   319-268-0303
Fax: 319-277-5254
www.porters.com

Digital photo accessories
President: Jeff Schmitt
Marketing Manager: Lisa Hawkins
Sales Volume: $10MM to $20MM

5483 Vinten
Camera Dynamics, Inc.
709 Executive Blvd
Valley Cottage, NY 10989-2024   845-268-2113
Fax: 845-268-9324
www.vinten.com

Television camera support equipment, including studio pedestals, pan/tilt heads, tripod systems and more
President: Eric Falkenberg
CFO: Nick Piscitelli
Marketing Manager: Stephen Savitt
Production Manager: Kenneth Schwartz
CEO: Jansen Joop
International Marketing Manager: Nick Kent
Catalog Cost: Free
Catalog Circulation: Mailed 52 time(s) per year to 5M
Average Order Size: $2500
Printing Information: 26 pages in 4 colors on Glossy Stock
Press: Letterpress
Binding: Saddle Stitched
Mailing List Information: Names for rent
List Manager: Joanne Snider
In Business: 102 years
Number of Employees: 60
Sales Volume: $40 Million

Cameras & Projectors

5484 Berger Brothers Camera Video Digital
Berger Bros.
22 Clinton Ave.
Huntington, NY 11743   631-421-2200

Film and digital cameras and accessories, darkroom supplies, lenses, memory, tripods, scanners and projectors, telescopes, video and voice recorders
President: Brad Berger
Professional Photographer: Yvonne Berger
Credit Cards: MasterCard
Catalog Cost: Free
In Business: 64 years
Number of Employees: 28
Sales Volume: $6,000,000+

5485 Cambridge Camera Exchange
Cambridgeworld.com
1284 E Nakoma Street
New York, NY 10011-5401   212-675-8600
800-221-2253
Fax: 718-858-5437
bestdeal@cambridgeworld.com
www.cambridgeworld.com

Camera and photography equipment
President: Thomas Black
Credit Cards: AMEX; MasterCard

5486 Focus Camera
Focus Camera Inc
895 McDonald Ave
Brooklyn, NY 11218-2017   718-431-7900
800-221-0828
Fax: 718-438-4263
cs@focuscamera.com
focuscamera.com

Cameras, video, telescopes, and binoculars
Chairman: Abe Berkowitz
President: Abe Berkowitz
Credit Cards: AMEX; MasterCard
In Business: 49 years
Number of Employees: 60
Sales Volume: $500M to $1MM

5487 Haverhill's
Haverhills
16911 Grays Bay Blvd.
Wayzata, MN 55391   952-476-2006
800-797-7367
Fax: 952-476-5999
customerservice@haverhills.com
www.haverhills.com

Optics, hearing aids, microscopes, pest control, radios, watches
President: Paul Harris
Buyers: Nick Ranks
Printing Information: 16 pages in 4 colors
Mailing List Information: Names for rent
In Business: 42 years
Number of Employees: 4
Sales Volume: $1MM to $3MM

5488 Ikegami Electronics, Inc.
Ikegami Electronics, Inc.
37 Brook Ave
Maywood, NJ 07607-1130   201-368-9171
Fax: 201-569-1626
general@ikegami.com
www.ikegami.com

Video cameras
President: Akira Harada
Executive Director: Yosuke Kiyomori
CEO: Akira Harada
In Business: 49 years
Sales Volume: $ 20-50 Million

5489 KEH Camera Brokers
Keh Camera
4900 Highlands Parkway SE
Smyrna, GA 30082-5132   770-333-4200
800-342-5534
Fax: 770-333-4242
sales@KEH.com
www.keh.com

Large used camera dealer, new equipment
President: King Grant Jr
Credit Cards: AMEX; MasterCard; Visa
Catalog Cost: Free
In Business: 35 years
Sales Volume: $10MM to $20MM

5490 Woodland Hills Camera
Woodland Hills Camera & Telescopes
5348 Topanga Canyon Boulevard
Woodland Hills, CA 91364   818-347-2270
                                   888-427-8766
                              Fax: 818-992-4486
                                   telescopes.net

High quality cameras and parts & accessories

Credit Cards: AMEX; MasterCard
Catalog Cost: Free
Printing Information: on N
Press: W
Binding: F
Mailing List Information: Names for rent
In Business: 63 years
Number of Employees: 10
Sales Volume: under $500M

Film, Paper & Processing

5491 B&H Photo Video Pro-Audio
B&H Photo Video
420 9th Avenue
New York, NY 10001   212-444-6615
                             800-606-6969
                        www.bhphotovideo.com

Photographic, video and digital imaging products, cameras, lenses, accessories, home theater components, binoculars, telescopes and much more

Chairman: Herman Schreiber
President: Sam Goldstein
CFO: Isreal Lebovits
Credit Cards: AMEX; MasterCard; Visa
Catalog Cost: Free
Catalog Circulation: Mailed 3 time(s) per year
Printing Information: 332 pages in 4 colors
In Business: 43 years
Number of Employees: 1100
Sales Volume: 85MM

5492 Heidelberg News
Heidelberg USA
1000 Gutenberg Drive
Kennesaw, GA 30144-7028   770-419-6600
                        Fax: 770-419-6550
                   hus.webmaster@heidelberg.com
                        www.Heidelberg.com

Printing presses, machinery and related equipment including prepress equipment such as scanners, proofing systems and film and plate output devices, and postpress finishing equipment.

Chairman: Rainer Hunds"rfer
Credit Cards: MasterCard
Catalog Circulation: Mailed 2 time(s) per year
Printing Information: 60 pages in 4 colors on Glossy Stock
Binding: Saddle Stitched
Mailing List Information: Names for rent
In Business: 152 years
Number of Employees: 1400
Sales Volume: $50MM to $100MM

5493 Kodak Professional Photographic Catalog
Kodak
343 State St
Rochester, NY 14650-1   585-724-4000
                             800-242-2424
                        Fax: 585-781-5400
                             www.kodak.com

Papers, chemicals, films and publications

President: Douglas J. Edwards, PhD
CFO: John N. McMullen
Marketing Manager: Steven Overman
CEO: Jeffrey J. Clarke
Chief Human Resources Officer & Sen: Mark Green
Chief Accounting Officer and Corpor: Eric H. Samuels
Catalog Cost: $1
Catalog Circulation: Mailed 1 time(s) per year

to 25000
Printing Information: 126 pages in 1 color
Mailing List Information: Names for rent
In Business: 127 years
Number of Employees: 100

5494 Light Impressions
Light Impressions
100 Carlson Raod
Rochester, NY 14610   800-975-6429
                        Fax: 866-592-8642
                     help@fdmbrands.com
                  www.lightimpressionsdirect.com

Archival storage, display & presentation materials for negatives, transparencies, CDs, photographs, artwork, & documents

President: Gabe Bristol
Credit Cards: AMEX; MasterCard
Catalog Cost: Free
Catalog Circulation: Mailed 52 time(s) per year
Printing Information: 116 pages in 4 colors on Glossy Stock
Press: Web Press
Binding: Saddle Stitched
Mailing List Information: Names for rent
List Manager: MSGi
In Business: 48 years
Number of Employees: 80
Sales Volume: $36 Million

5495 National Coating Corporation
National Coating Corporation
105 Industrial Way
Rockland, MA 02370   781-878-2781
                             800-979-9332
                        Fax: 781-871-4955
                     sales@natcoat.com
                        www.natcoat.com

Contract manufacturing: Custom coating and saturation services

President: Paul Stefanutti
Marketing Manager: Jon Platz
Customer & Process Development Mgnr: Bob Harrington
In Business: 66 years
Number of Employees: 42
Sales Volume: $5,000,000 - $10,000,000

5496 Neil Enterprises
Neil Enterprises
450 E Bunker Ct
Vernon Hills, IL 60061   847-549-7627
                             800-621-5584
                        Fax: 847-549-0349
                   info@neilenterprises.com
                   www.neilenterprises.com

Promotional product/photo novelty manufacturer and supplier/distributor of instant photographic equipment serving the photographic, printing/screenprint, craft, educational and ad specialty industries

President: Jerry Fine
Catalog Cost: Free
Catalog Circulation: Mailed 1 time(s) per year
Printing Information: 52 pages in 4 colors on Glossy Stock
Press: Web Press
Binding: Perfect Bound
Mailing List Information: Names for rent
In Business: 56 years
Number of Employees: 25
Sales Volume: $50-100 Million

5497 Neil Holiday Catalog
Neil Enterprises
450 E Bunker Ct
Vernon Hills, IL 60061   847-549-7627
                             800-621-5584
                        Fax: 847-549-0349
                   info@neilenterprises.com
                   www.neilenterprises.com

Promotional product/photo novelty manufacturer and supplier/distributor of instant photographic equipment serving the photographic, printing/screenprint, craft, education and ad specialty industries

President: Jerry Fine
Catalog Cost: Free
Catalog Circulation: Mailed 1 time(s) per year
Printing Information: 12 pages in 4 colors on Glossy Stock
Press: Web Press
Binding: Perfect Bound
In Business: 56 years
Number of Employees: 25
Sales Volume: $50-100 Million

5498 Photo Warehouse
Photo Warehouse
121 Lombard Street
Oxnard, CA 93030   805-485-9654
                             800-922-5484
                        Fax: 805-988-0213
                     www.ultrafineonline.com

Photo market, graphic arts

In Business: 36 years

5499 Photographer's Formulary
Photographer's Formulary
7079 Highway 83 N
PO Box 950
Condon, MT 59826-950   406-754-2891
                             800-922-5255
                        Fax: 406-754-2896
                   formulary@blackfoot.net
                   www.photoformulary.com

Photograde chemistry in small quantities, bulk chemicals, alternative processes, toners, holography and intensifiers, 30-second archival rapid fix, workshops and kits, labware and alternative papers

President: William G Wilson
Fulfillment: Lynn Wilson
Credit Cards: AMEX; MasterCard
Catalog Cost: Free
Printing Information: 31 pages
Mailing List Information: Names for rent
In Business: 34 years
Number of Employees: 6
Sales Volume: $500M to $1MM

5500 Regal/Arkay
Regal Photo Products, Inc
2769 S 34th Street
Milwaukee, WI 53215-3541   414-645-2050
                             800-695-2055
                        Fax: 414-645-9515

Photographic darkroom equipment - laboratory casework

President: Anthony Mlinar
CFO: Laurance Mlinar
Production Manager: Joe Gottlieb
Credit Cards: AMEX; MasterCard
Catalog Cost: Free
Catalog Circulation: Mailed 1 time(s) per year to 10000
Printing Information: 50 pages in 1 color on Glossy Stock
Press: Web Press
Binding: Saddle Stitched
Mailing List Information: Names for rent
In Business: 12 years
Number of Employees: 8
Sales Volume: $5MM to $10MM

Scientific Products
Equipment & Supplies

5501 2015 Sper Scientific Catalog
Sper Scientific Direct
8281 E. Evans Rd.
Suite #103
Scottsdale, AZ 85260   480-348-0278
Fax: 480-348-0279
support@sperdirect.com
www.sperdirect.com
Printing Information: 43 pages
In Business: 30+ years

5502 ABP/Pharmex
PDC Healthcare
27770 N. Entertainment Drive
Suite 200
Valencia, CA 91355   661-257-0233
800-435-4242
Fax: 800-321-4409
info@pdchealthcare.com
www.pdchealthcare.com/en-us/pharmex-phar-
macy-labeling-soluti

Pharmaceutical and laboratory supplies.

President: Robert Case
CFO: Michelle Wen
Finance Director
Marketing Manager: John Park
VP, North American Healthcare Sales: Rudy
Neal
Director, Research & Development: Richard
Kapusniak
Director of Human Resources: Fabian Grijalva
Catalog Cost: Free
Printing Information: 76 pages
Sales Volume: $5MM to $10MM

5503 Aerco International
AERCO
100 Oritani Drive
Blauvelt, NY 10913-2095   845-580-8000
800-526-0288
www.aerco.com

**Temperature regulators, gas fired heaters,
steam generators and heat exchangers**

President: Fred F Campagna
CFO: Tim Buhl
Catalog Cost: Free
In Business: 68 years
Number of Employees: 100
Sales Volume: $25,000,000 - $50,000,000

5504 All Weather Inc
All Weather Inc
1165 National Dr
Sacramento, CA 95834-1901   916-928-1000
800-824-5873
Fax: 916-928-1165
info@allweatherinc.com
www.Allweatherinc.Com

Weather monitoring instruments

President: Jason Hall
CFO: David Rigby
Production Manager: Adam Thomas
Director of Manufacturing
Chief Technology Officer: Neal Dillman
EVP, Engineering & Customer Service: Bob
Perrin
Director of Human Resources: Michelle
Chapmon
Catalog Circulation: Mailed 1 time(s) per year
Printing Information: 250 pages in 4 colors
Number of Employees: 35

5505 Allometrics
Allometrics
PO Box 15825
Baton Rouge, LA 70895-5825   225-303-0419
800-528-2246
Fax: 225-272-0844
info@allometrics.com
www.allometrics.com

**Specialty laboratory equipment and sup-
plies**

President: Ashton Stagg
Credit Cards: AMEX; MasterCard; Visa
In Business: 37 years
Number of Employees: 20
Sales Volume: $5MM to $10MM

5506 American Educational Products
American Educational Products
401 W Hickory St
PO Box 2121
Fort Collins, CO 80522   970-484-7445
800-289-9299
Fax: 970-484-1198
custserv@amep.com
www.amep.com

**Educational materials including math and
science manipulatives and kits**

President: Michael Anderson
CFO: Dean Johnson
Buyers: Joel Sumearall
Credit Cards: AMEX; MasterCard; Visa
Catalog Cost: Free
Average Order Size: $50
Mailing List Information: Names for rent
In Business: 35 years
Number of Employees: 80

5507 American Science & Surplus
American Science & Surplus
PO Box 1030
Skokie, IL 60076   888-724-7587
Fax: 800-934-0722
service@sciplus.com
www.sciplus.com

**Toys, arts and crafts, lab supplies and equip-
ment and electrical parts**

President: Philip Cable
President: Scott Causland
Operations manager: Carl Krueger
Credit Cards: MasterCard
In Business: 78 years
Number of Employees: 60

5508 Analytical Measurements
Analytical Measurements
22 Mountain View Drive
Chester, NJ 07930   908-955-7170
800-635-5580
Fax: 908-955-7170
phmeter@verizon.net
www.analyticalmeasurements.com

**PH meters, controllers and recorders; ORP
meters, controllers and recorders**

President: W Richard Adey
Marketing Manager: Theresa Scarinzi
Catalog Cost: Free
Printing Information: on Glossy Stock
Press: Web Press
Mailing List Information: Names for rent
In Business: 49 years
Number of Employees: 40
Sales Volume: Under $500M

5509 Ash-Dome
Ash Manufacturing Company
PO Box 312
Plainfield, IL 60544   815-436-9403
Fax: 815-436-1032
ashdome@ameritech.net
ashdome.com

**Observatory domes and tracking instrument
shelters.**

Catalog Cost: Free

5510 At-Mar Glass
At-Mar Glass
611 West State Street
Kennet Square, PA 19348   610-444-5903
800-317-7173
Fax: 610-444-1868
orders@atmarglass.com
www.atmarglass.com

5511 BrandTech Scientific
BrandTech Scientific
11 Bokum Road
Essex, CT 6426-1506   860-767-2562
888-522-2726
Fax: 860-767-2563
www.brandtech.com
Printing Information: 129 pages

5512 City Chemical
City Chemical LLC
139 Allings Crossing Road
West Haven, CT 06516-7521   203-932-2489
800-248-2436
Fax: 203-937-8400
sales@citychemical.com
www.citychemical.com

**Chemicals, inorganic chemicals and com-
pounds**

President: Peter Wolpert
pwolpert@citychemical.com
Number of Employees: 9
Sales Volume: $1,700,000

5513 Cole-Parmer
Cole-Parmer
625 East Bunker Court
Vernon Hills, IL 60061-1830   841-549-7600
800-323-4340
Fax: 847-549-1700
info@coleparmer.com
www.coleparmer.com

**Products for electrochemistry, fluid han-
dling, industrial process, laboratory research and more**

President: Alan Malus
CFO: Steven Gozdziewski
Marketing Manager: Larry Vanbogaerts
VP/General Manager: Monica Manotas
Director, Finance: Joe Straczek
VP, Human Resources: Wanda McKenny
Credit Cards: AMEX; MasterCard
Printing Information: 2600 pages
In Business: 60 years
Number of Employees: 320

5514 Cole-Parmer Instruments Product Catalog
Cole-Parmer
625 East Bunker Court
Vernon Hills, IL 60061-1830   847-549-7600
800-323-4340
Fax: 847-549-1700
info@coleparmer.com
www.coleparmer.com

**Instruments for measurement and control,
laboratory equipment and supplies**

President: John Palmer
VP/General Manager: Monica Manotas
Director, Finance: Joe Straczek
VP, Human Resources: Wanda McKenny
Catalog Cost: Free
Catalog Circulation: Mailed 1 time(s) per year
Printing Information: 999 pages in 4 colors
Binding: Perfect Bound
In Business: 60 years

5515 Continental Lab Products

NEPTUNE
9880 Mesa Rim Road
Suite 220
San Diego, CA 92121-4701   858-875-7696
                            888-330-2396
                      Fax: 858-875-5496
CSR@neptunescientific.com
www.neptunescientific.com

Laboratory products

President: Dave Barth
CFO: Tony Altig
COO: Ron Perkins
Vice President, Human Resources: Celia Reyes
Chief Executive Officer: Paul Nowak
6190 Corner Stone Ct East Suite 220
San Diego, CA 92121
858.279.5000
Number of Employees: 30

5516 Daigger Scientific

Daigger Scientific
620 Lakeview Parkway
Vernon Hills, IL 60061   847-816-5060
                          800-621-7193
                    Fax: 800-320-7200
daigger@daigger.com
www.daigger.com

Lab equipment and supplies

In Business: 121 years

5517 Dickson Company

Dickson Company
930 S Westwood Avenue
Addison, IL 60101-4917   630-543-3747
                          800-757-3747
                    Fax: 800-676-0498
www.dicksondata.com

Weather recording equipment

President: Michael Unger
CFO: Mark Kohlmeier
Marketing Manager: Chris Sorensen
Production Manager: Elaine Campion
VP of Manufacturing and Engineering: Fred Kirsch
Human Resources: Sue Madison
Inside Sales Consultant: Teresa Tomaszewski
Credit Cards: AMEX; MasterCard
Catalog Circulation: Mailed 12 time(s) per year
Printing Information: 21 pages in 4 colors
In Business: 94 years
Number of Employees: 50-1
Sales Volume: $10,000,000 - $25,000,000

5518 Dwyer

Dwyer Instruments International
102 Indiana Hwy 212
Michigan City, IN 46360   219-879-8000
                     Fax: 219-872-9057
www.dwyer-inst.com

Manufacturer of pressure, flow, level, temperature, air velocity, and humidity instrumentation, test equipment

Manager: Pranab Biswas
Catalog Cost: Free
Catalog Circulation: Mailed 1 time(s) per year
Printing Information: 548 pages in 4 colors
In Business: 86 years
Number of Employees: 600

5519 Elemental Scientific

Elemental Scientific, LLC
80 Minnesota Street
Little Canada, MI 55117   651-646-5339
                     Fax: 920-882-1277
info@elementalscientific.net
www.elementalscientific.net

Scientific and laboratory supplies

President: W. VanRyzin
Marketing Manager: C. VanRyzin
Production Manager: A. vanRyzin
Catalog Cost: $2
Catalog Circulation: Mailed 3 time(s) per year to 11M
Average Order Size: $50
Printing Information: 99 pages in 2 colors on Matte Stock
Press: Web Press
Binding: Saddle Stitched
Mailing List Information: Names for rent
In Business: 62 years
Number of Employees: 3
Sales Volume: Under $500M

5520 Excel Technologies

Excel Technologies Inc
99 Phoenix Avenue
PO Box 1258
Enfield, CT 06083-1258   860-741-3435
                          800-543-9832
                    Fax: 860-745-7212
www.extec.com

Laboratory supplies

President: J Ronald Rinaldi
In Business: 25 years
Number of Employees: 15
Sales Volume: $5MM to $10MM

5521 Extech Instruments

Extech Instruments
9 Townsend West
Nashua, NH 03063   877-239-8324
               Fax: 603-324-7864
sales@extech.com
www.extech.com

Test measurements calibration, datalogging and control instruments and customized catalogs for catalog distributors

President: Jerry Blakeley
CFO: Scott Black
Marketing Manager: Lois Corley
VP of Sales and Marketing: Arpineh Mullaney
Sales Manager: Joe Rocchio
joseph.rocchio@extech.com
Regional Sales Director: Travis Curtis
travis.curtis@flir.com
Buyers: Carolyn Simoko
In Business: 45 years
Number of Employees: 79
Sales Volume: $5,000,000 - $10,000,000

5522 Fisher Science Education

Fisher Science Education
300 Industry Drive
Pittsburgh, PA 15275   877-885-2081
                        800-766-7000
                  Fax: 800-926-1166
www.fishersci.com

General and safety supplies for science teachers

Printing Information:
Press: Web Press
Binding: Perfect Bound
Number of Employees: 30

5523 Glas-Col

Glas-Col
711 Hulman Street
PO Box 2128
Terre Haute, IN 47802-128   812-235-6167
                             800-452-7265
                       Fax: 812-234-6975
pinnacle@glascol.com
www.glascol.com

Laboratory products including heating, mixing and evaporation equipment for chemical, biotech, environmental and pharmaceutical use

President: Steve Sterrett
International Marketing Manager: Karen Elliott
Buyers: Patti Moore
Credit Cards: AMEX; MasterCard; Visa
Catalog Cost: Free

Mailing List Information: Names for rent
List Manager: Jenny Samm
In Business: 75 years
Number of Employees: 75
Sales Volume: $20MM to $50MM

5524 High School Science Catalog

PASCO Scientific, Inc.
10101 Foothills Boulevard
Roseville, CA 95747-7100   916-786-3800
                            800-772-8700
                      Fax: 916-786-7565
www.pasco.com

Teaching supplies for high school level science

President: Paul A. Stokstad
Catalog Cost: Free
Catalog Circulation: Mailed 1 time(s) per year
Printing Information: 192 pages in 4 colors
In Business: 53 years
Number of Employees: 160
Sales Volume: $50MM to $100MM

5525 HunterLab

Hunter Associates Laboratory, Inc,
11491 Sunset Hills Road
Reston, VA 20190-5280   703-471-6870
                    Fax: 703-471-4237
info@hunterlab.com
www.hunterlab.com

Laboratory supplies, testing equipment

Chairman: Phil Hunter
President: Phil Hunter
CFO: Teresa Demangos, Controller
Marketing Manager: Lore Potoker
CEO: Phil Hunter
Customer Service: Alex
Service Department: Linda
In Business: 71 years
Number of Employees: 49
Sales Volume: $10,000,000 - $25,000,000

5526 Industrial Lab & Plastics

Consolidated Plastics
4700 Prosper Dr
Stow, OH 44224   330-425-3900
                  800-362-1000
            Fax: 800-858-5001
www.consolidatedplastics.com

Laboratory plastics

President: Brent Harland
Credit Cards: MasterCard; Visa
Catalog Cost: Free
Catalog Circulation: Mailed 2 time(s) per year
Printing Information: 54 pages in 7 colors on Glossy Stock
Press: Letterpress
Binding: Saddle Stitched
In Business: 34 years
Number of Employees: 100-
Sales Volume: $5MM to $10MM

5527 Jump USA

Jump USA
1290 Lawrence Station Rd.
Sunnyvale, CA 94089   408-470-4320
                       800-586-7872
                 Fax: 650-967-6680
sales@jumpusa.com
www.jumpusa.com

Jumpsoles, speed, strength and vertical jump training equipment, products and accessories

5528 LabMart Catalog

The Labmart
4111 South Clinton Avenue
PO Box 310
South Plainfield, NJ 07080-310   908-561-1234
                                  800-684-1234
                            Fax: 908-561-3002
www.labmart.com

Scientific equipment and lab supplies

President: Steven Krupp
Catalog Cost: Free
Catalog Circulation: Mailed 4 time(s) per year
Printing Information: 96 pages in 4 colors
Sales Volume: $5MM to $10MM

5529 Laboratory Equipment for the Life Sciences Catalog
World Precision Instruments
175 Sarasota Center Blvd.
Sarasota, FL 34240
941-371-1003
866-606-1974
Fax: 941-377-5428
wpi@wpiinc.com
www.wpiinc.com

Laboratory equipment

Printing Information: 220 pages
In Business: 48 years

5530 Laboratory Glassware and Supplies Catalog
World Precision Instruments
175 Sarasota Center Blvd.
Sarasota, FL 34240
941-371-1003
866-606-1974
Fax: 941-377-5428
wpi@wpiinc.com
www.wpiinc.com

Laboratory equipment

Printing Information: 44 pages
In Business: 48 years

5531 MMS Medical Supply
MMS Medical Supply
2229 East Magnolia St.
Phoenix, AZ 85034
602-306-1722
800-777-2634
Fax: 602-306-1787
general@mmsmedical.com
www.mmsmedical.com

Laboratory and medical supplies

President: Gary Reeve
CFO: David Evans
Marketing Manager: Gina Marchese
EVP: Tom Harris
SVP - Business Systems: Dan Rieman
VP, Operations & GM: Kevin McDonnell
Buyers: Sue Shearin
Credit Cards: MasterCard; Visa
Catalog Circulation: Mailed 1 time(s) per year
Mailing List Information: Names for rent
In Business: 44 years
Number of Employees: 19
Sales Volume: $5MM to $10MM

5532 Magnets and Industrial Magnetic Equipment
Bunting Magnetics Co.
500 S Spencer Road
Newton, KS 67114
316-284-2020
800-835-2526
Fax: 316-283-4975
bmc@buntingmagnetics.com
www.buntingmagnetics.com

Magnets, magnetic equipment, and metal detection equipment

Chairman: June Bunting
President: Robert J. Bunting, Sr.
rjb@buntingmagnetics.com
CFO: Jana L. Davis
jdavis@buntingmagnetics.com
Marketing Manager: Charles Witt
Director of Sales: Rod Henricks
rhenricks@buntingmagnetics.com
Division Controller: Molly Taiclet
mtaiclet@buntingmagnetics.com
Product Manager: Barry Voorhees
bvoorhees@buntingmagnetics.com
Catalog Cost: Free
Catalog Circulation: to 10000
Printing Information: 56 pages in 2 colors on Glossy Stock
Press: Sheetfed Press

Binding: Saddle Stitched
Mailing List Information: Names for rent
In Business: 58 years
Number of Employees: 160
Sales Volume: $20,000,000

5533 Middle School Science Catalog
PASCO Scientific, Inc.
10101 Foothills Boulevard
Roseville, CA 95747-7100
916-786-3800
800-772-8700
Fax: 916-786-7565
www.pasco.com

Teaching supplies for middle school grades

President: Paul A. Stokstad
Catalog Cost: Free
Catalog Circulation: Mailed 1 time(s) per year
Printing Information: 56 pages in 4 colors
In Business: 53 years
Number of Employees: 160
Sales Volume: $50MM to $100MM

5534 Midland Scientific
Midland Scientific
1202 South 11th Street
Omaha, NE 68108-3611
402-346-8352
800-642-5263
Fax: 402-346-7694
orders@midlandsci.com
www.midlandsci.com

laboratory products such as chemicals, instrumentation, general lab supplies, glassware, lab consumables, media, measurement equipment, plasticware, reagents

Founder: John Gondring
Current Owner: Vivian Pappel

5535 Midwest Scientific
Midwest Scientific
280 Vance Rd
Valley Park, MO 63088-1521
636-225-9997
800-227-9997
Fax: 636-225-9998
custserv@Midsci.com
www.Midsci.com

Biotechnology and molecular biology supplies for research and development laboratory use

President: Mike Degenhart
Founder: Larry Degenhart
Credit Cards: AMEX; MasterCard; Visa
Catalog Cost: Free
Printing Information: 240 pages in 4 colors on Matte Stock
Press: Web Press
Binding: Saddle Stitched
In Business: 32 years
Number of Employees: 25
Sales Volume: $5MM to $10MM

5536 Newcomer Supply
Newcomer Supply
2505 Parview Road
Middleton, WI 53562-2579
800-383-7799
Fax: 608-831-0866
newly@newcomersupply.com
www.newcomersupply.com

Slides, cover slips, chemicals, reagents

Printing Information: 96 pages

5537 Parsons Manufacturing
1055 Obrien Dr
Menlo Park, CA 94025-1476
650-324-4726
800-221-0823
Fax: 650-324-3051

Scientific equipment and teaching aids

President: Alan Parsons
In Business: 35 years
Number of Employees: 29
Sales Volume: $2,800,000

5538 Perfection Distributing
Perfection Distributing
2189 Abraham Lane
Oshkosh, WI 54904-2066
920-230-0220
800-558-5830
Fax: 920-232-1225
sales@perfectiondistributing.com
www.perfectiondistributing.com

Supplies for studios, professional photographers and framers

President: Robert Paulick
Credit Cards: AMEX; MasterCard
Catalog Cost: Free
In Business: 77 years
Sales Volume: $3-5 Million

5539 Physics & Engineering Catalog
PASCO Scientific, Inc.
10101 Foothills Boulevard
Roseville, CA 95747-7100
916-786-3800
800-772-8700
Fax: 916-786-7565
www.pasco.com

Teaching supplies

President: Paul A. Stokstad
Credit Cards: MasterCard; Visa
Catalog Cost: Free
Catalog Circulation: Mailed 1 time(s) per year
Printing Information: 384 pages in 3 colors
In Business: 53 years
Number of Employees: 160
Sales Volume: $50MM to $100MM

5540 Pierce Biotechnology
Thermofisher,Inc
3747 N Meridian Rd
PO Box 117
Rockford, IL 61105-117
815-968-0747
800-874-3723
Fax: 800-842-5007
indiacs@lifetech.com
www.piercenet.com

Life science research kits and reagents

President: Robb Anderson
Marketing Manager: Sheila Burns
Production Manager: Holly Schubert
Mailing List Information: Names for rent
In Business: 51 years
Number of Employees: 150

5541 Quark Glass
Quark Glass
P.O. Box 2396
Vineland, NJ 8362
856-455-0376
800-955-0376
Fax: 856-455-3373
sales@quarkglass.com
www.quarkglass.com

Laboratory glassware, accessories

Credit Cards: AMEX; MasterCard
In Business: 32 years

5542 Reagents
Reagents, Inc.
PO Box 240746
4710 Sweden Rd.
Charlotte, NC 28224-5936
704-554-7474
800-732-8484
Fax: 888-843-4384
info@reagents.com
www.Reagents.Com

Laboratory reagents and chemicals

President: Charles Waits
In Business: 46 years
Number of Employees: 20-5
Sales Volume: $10MM to $20MM

5543 Rocket Age Enterprises
Rocket Age Enterprises
9 Lance Road
Lebanon, NJ 08858-5007 908-439-3559
Fax: 908-439-2140
rocketage@comcast.net
www.merchantcircle.com

Model rockets, engines and kits

President: Chris Mancini
Marketing Manager: Rudd Lipincott
Owner: Jeffrey Charney
CFO: Sharmila Patel
VP Business Development: Kevin Hunt
Printing Information: in 3 colors
In Business: 20 years
Number of Employees: 5
Sales Volume: $1 million

5544 Rousseau Company
Rousseauco
1392 Port Drive
Clarkston, WA 99403-3005 509-758-3954
800-635-3416
Fax: 509-758-4991
salesinfo@rousseauco.com
www.rousseauco.com

Router accessories

Catalog Cost: Free
In Business: 35 years

5545 Safariland Forensics Source Catalog
Safariland
13386 International Pkwy.
Jacksonville, FL 32218 800-347-1200
www.safariland.com

Supplies and equipment for forensics professionals.

Printing Information: 196 pages in 4 colors
In Business: 52 years
Number of Employees: 1400
Sales Volume: $200 Million

5546 Schoolmasters Science Catalog
School-Tech Inc
745 State Circle
Ann Arbor, MI 48108 800-521-2832
Fax: 800-654-4321
www.schoolmasters.com

Science equipment, teaching aids, safety equipment and videos

President: Donald B Canham
Marketing Manager: SW Canham
Credit Cards: MasterCard; Visa
Catalog Circulation: to 350M
Average Order Size: $130
Printing Information: on Glossy Stock
Press: Web Press
Binding: Perfect Bound
Mailing List Information: Names for rent
In Business: 54 years
Number of Employees: 50-1
Sales Volume: $50MM to $100MM

5547 Spex Certiprep
SPEX CertiPrep
203 Norcross Ave
Metuchen, NJ 08840-1253 732-549-7144
800-LAB-SPEX
Fax: 732-603-9647
crmsales@spex.com
www.spexcsp.com

Sample prep grinders, mixers and fluxors

President: Ralph Obenauf
Marketing Manager: Melanie Samko
Production Manager: Nimi Kocherlakota
International Marketing Manager: Suzanne Lepore
Catalog Circulation: Mailed 1 time(s) per year to 30000
Average Order Size: $600
Printing Information: 300 pages in 2 colors on Glossy Stock

Press: Letterpress
Binding: Perfect Bound
Mailing List Information: Names for rent
In Business: 60 years
Number of Employees: 200
Sales Volume: $10,000,000 - $25,000,000

5548 Stackhouse Athletic
Stackhouse Athletic
1450 McDonald St. NE
Salem, OR 97301 503-363-1840
800-285-3604
Fax: 503-363-0511
www.stackhouseathletic.com

Team or individual athletic and sporting equipment and accessories

5549 Tempo Glove
Tempo Glove
3820 W Wisconsin Ave
Milwaukee, WI 53208-3154 414-344-1100
800-558-8520
Fax: 414-344-4084
mmandlman@gmail.com
www.Tempoglove.Com

Modular wall/shield non-asbestos hand protection

President: Michael Mandlman
Marketing Manager: Richard Mandlman
Credit Cards: MasterCard; Visa
Catalog Cost: Free
Printing Information: 30 pages in 1 color
In Business: 64 years
Number of Employees: 20-5
Sales Volume: $1MM to $3MM

5550 Tesseract
Tesseract
Box 151
Hastings On Hudson, NY 10706 914-478-2594
mail@etesseract.com
www.etesseract.com

Scientific instruments

In Business: 33 years

5551 USA Scientific
USA Scientific
PO Box 3565
Ocala, FL 34478-3565 352-237-6288
800-522-8477
Fax: 352-351-2057
infoline@usascientific.com
www.usascientific.com

Racks, boxes, equipment, plates, sealing film

Credit Cards: AMEX; MasterCard
Printing Information: 204 pages

5552 Vantage PRO Wireless Weather Station Catalog
Davis Instruments Corp.
3465 Diablo Ave
Hayward, CA 94545-2746 510-732-9229
800-678-3669
Fax: 510-670-0589
sales@davisnet.com
www.davisnet.com

weather stations for business or home use

President: Jim Acquistapace
Printing Information: 32 pages

5553 Wheaton Science Products Catalog
Wheaton Science Products
1501 N 10th St
Millville, NJ 08332-2093 856-825-1100
800-225-1437
Fax: 856-825-1368
www.wheatonsci.com

Laboratory products, glassware and plastics

President: Wayne L. Brinster
wayne.brinster@wheaton.com
CFO: Thomas E. Kohut
tom.kohut@wheaton.com
Marketing Manager: Jackie Williams
VP, Quality Mgmt. Systems: Gregory W. Bianco
gregory.bianco@wheaton.com
VP, North American Sales: Chris Gildea
chris.gildea@wheaton.com
Director, Global Marketing: TracyNeri-Luciano
tracy.neri-luciano@wheaton.com
Catalog Circulation: Mailed 1 time(s) per year to 100M
Printing Information: 338 pages in 4 colors
In Business: 125 years
Number of Employees: 204
Sales Volume: $19.8 Million

5554 Wilkens-Anderson Company Catalog
Wilkens-Anderson Company
4525 W Division Street
Chicago, IL 60651-1674 800-847-2222
Fax: 773-384-6260
waco@wacolab.com
www.wacolab.com

Laboratory equipment, supplies, and chemicals for industrial quality control laboratories

Credit Cards: AMEX; MasterCard; Visa
Catalog Cost: Free
Printing Information: 700 pages in 4 colors
Press: Web Press
Binding: Perfect Bound
Mailing List Information: Names for rent
In Business: 98 years
Number of Employees: 30
Sales Volume: $3MM to $5MM

Shoes
General Styles

5555 Aerosoles
Aerogroup International, LLC
201 Meadow Road
PO Box 1916
Edison, NJ 08817-1916 732-985-6900
800-798-9478
Fax: 732-985-3697
customerservice@aerosoles.com
www.aerosoles.com

Women's footwear

Chairman: Andrew Scott
President: Jules Schneider
CFO: Richard Morris
Marketing Manager: Liz Morris
Managing Director: Jim Brownlee
Director of Technology: Dan Silvestro
Director, Budgeting & Planning: Karen Caster
Credit Cards: AMEX; MasterCard; Visa
Catalog Cost: Free
Catalog Circulation: Mailed 12 time(s) per year
Printing Information: 65 pages in 4 colors on Glossy Stock
Binding: Saddle Stitched
Mailing List Information: Names for rent
In Business: 27 years
Number of Employees: 1572

5556 Allen Edmonds
Allen Edmonds Shoe Corporation
201 E Seven Hills Road
Port Washington, WI 53074 262-235-6512
877-817-7615
cacmail@allenedmonds.com
www.allenedmonds.com

Dress and casual shoes, shoe care, belts

Chairman: John Stollenwerk
President: Paul Grangaard
Catalog Cost: Free
Printing Information: 23 pages
In Business: 93 years
Number of Employees: 600

5557 Arthur Beren Shoes
Arthur Beren
88 Kearny St
Suite 1450
San Francisco, CA 94108   415-365-9393
800-886-9797
Fax: 415-371-0162

High fashion designer shoes and boots in men's and women's styles; and accessories

President: David Beren
CFO: Rosalie Beren
Marketing Manager: Sharon Kuwatani
Credit Cards: AMEX; MasterCard; Visa
Catalog Cost: Free
Printing Information: in 4 colors
In Business: 27 years
Number of Employees: 60

5558 Auditions
Auditions Shoes
1251 1st Avenue
Suite 115
Chippewa Falls, WI 54774   800-462-7739
service@auditionsshoes.com
www.auditionsshoes.com

Women's shoes

Catalog Cost: Free
Printing Information: in 4 colors on Glossy Stock
Binding: Folded

5559 Aussie Dogs
Aussie Dogs
1315 N El Camino Real
San Clemente, CA 92672-4658   949-366-6727
800-359-7079
Fax: 949-366-0899
aussiedogs@sbcglobal.net
www.Aussie-Dogs.Com

Sheepskin footwear

President: Chris Watt
Mailing List Information: Names for rent
In Business: 22 years
Number of Employees: 3
Sales Volume: $2,000,000

5560 BA Mason
B.A. Mason
1251 1st Avenue
Chippewa Falls, WI 54729-8000   715-723-1871
800-422-1000
Fax: 715-720-4245
service@bamason.com
www.bamason.com

Men's and women's dress, work and casual footwear

President: John Lubs
Buyers: Matt Sullivan
Credit Cards: AMEX; MasterCard; Visa
Catalog Cost: Free
Catalog Circulation: Mailed 10 time(s) per year
Printing Information: 76 pages in 4 colors
Press: Web Press
Binding: Saddle Stitched
Mailing List Information: Names for rent
Will Trade Names: Yes
List Company: Names & Addresses
Wheeling, IL
Number of Employees: 200

5561 Bedford Fair
Bedford Fair Lifestyles
108 Telegraph Road
Bedford, PA 15522-6558   800-964-9030
international@blair.com
www.bedfordfair.blair.com

Women's clothing apparel and shoes

President: Steve Nave
CFO: Pete Michielutti
EVP, COO, & Chief Digital Officer: Vince Jones

EVP & President of Credit Services: Jim Slavik
Credit Cards: AMEX; MasterCard
Catalog Cost: Free
In Business: 19 years
Sales Volume: $ 50-100 Million

5562 Belgian Shoes
Belgian Shoes
110 E 55th Stree
New York, NY 10022-4540   212-755-7372
Fax: 212-755-7627
information@belgianshoes.com
www.belgianshoes.com

Shoes and accessories for men and women

President: John Bendel
Credit Cards: AMEX; MasterCard; Visa
Catalog Circulation: Mailed 1 time(s) per year
Printing Information: 30 pages in 4 colors on Newsprint
Binding: Saddle Stitched
Mailing List Information: Names for rent
In Business: 53 years
Number of Employees: 7
Sales Volume: $1,000,000

5563 Birkenstock Express
Birkenstock Usa Lp
6 Hamilton Landing
Suite #250
Novato, CA 94949   800-867-2475
INFO@birkenstockusa.com
www.Birkenstockusa.Com

Birkenstock footwear

President: Peter Wendel
CFO: Dee Wendel
Marketing Manager: Laney Barteen
Production Manager: Peter Rabenold
Buyers: Dee Wendel
Credit Cards: AMEX; MasterCard; Visa
Catalog Cost: Free
Catalog Circulation: Mailed 2 time(s) per year
Printing Information: 60 pages in 5 colors on Glossy Stock
Binding: Saddle Stitched
Mailing List Information: Names for rent
In Business: 40 years
Number of Employees: 15
Sales Volume: $5MM to $10MM

5564 Brooks
3400 Stone Way North
5th Floor
Seattle, WA 98103   800-2 B-OOKS
www.brooksrunning.com

Running accessories

5565 Charles Tyrwhitt
Charles Tyrwhitt
377 Madison Ave
New York, NY 10017-2543   212-286-8988
866-797-2701
Fax: 212-370-7302
madison@ctshirts.com
www.ctshirts.com

Mens & womens dress shirts, jackets, suits & separates, casual wear, shoes, accessories and cufflinks

President: Nick Wheeler
Marketing Manager: Valerie Sharrin
Partner: Peter Higgins
Credit Cards: AMEX; MasterCard
Catalog Cost: Free
In Business: 29 years
Number of Employees: 8
Sales Volume: $500,000- 1 Million

5566 Church's English Shoes
Church's English Shoes
689 Madison Ave
New York, NY 10065-8042   212-758-5200
Fax: 212-625-1379
church.madison@church-footwear.com
www.Church-footwear.com

English men's shoes

Credit Cards: AMEX; MasterCard; Visa
Catalog Cost: Free
Catalog Circulation: Mailed 2 time(s) per year
Printing Information: 15 pages
In Business: 132 years
Number of Employees: 35
Sales Volume: $500M to $1MM

5567 Cinderella of Boston
Cindrella of Boston
6452A Industry Way
Westminster, CA 92683-8511   714-899-2020
800-274-3338
Fax: 714-899-2024
info@cinderellaofboston.com
www.cinderellaofboston.com

Petite fashionable shoes for ladies

President: Charles Cohem
CFO: Lourie White
Credit Cards: MasterCard
Catalog Cost: Free
Catalog Circulation: to 80000
Printing Information: 32 pages in 7 colors on Matte Stock
Binding: Folded
In Business: 65 years
Number of Employees: 5
Sales Volume: $820,000

5568 Complements by Anthony Richards
AmeriMark Direct
6864 Engle Rd.
Cleveland, OH 44130   866-345-1388
www.amerimark.com

Casual, dress and athletic shoes, boots, slippers and sandals.

CFO: Joe Albanese
CEO & President: Gareth Giesler
Catalog Cost: Free
Printing Information: in 4 colors
In Business: 47 years
Number of Employees: 700
Sales Volume: $400 Million

5569 Duluth Trading Catalog for Men
Duluth Trading Company
PO Box 409
Belleville, WI 53508-409   608-424-1544
866-300-9719
Fax: 888-950-3199
customerservice@duluthtrading.com
www.duluthtrading.com

Men's work clothes, footwear and accessories

President: Steve Schecht
Production Manager: Dan Moeller
VP, Product Development: Mike Hollenstein
VP, Marketing: Peggy Langenfeld
Credit Cards: AMEX; MasterCard
Catalog Cost: Free
Printing Information: 116 pages
In Business: 24 years
Number of Employees: 150
Sales Volume: $ 15.6 Million

5570 Duluth Trading Catalog for Women
Duluth Trading Company
PO Box 409
Belleville, WI 53508-409   608-424-1544
866-300-9719
Fax: 888-950-3199
customerservice@duluthtrading.com
www.duluthtrading.com

Women's work clothes, footwear and accessories

President: Steve Schecht
VP, Product Development: Mike Hollenstein
VP, Marketing: Peggy Langenfeld
Credit Cards: AMEX; MasterCard
Catalog Cost: Free
Printing Information: 72 pages
In Business: 24 years

Number of Employees: 150
Sales Volume: $ 15.6 Million

5571 Eastbay
Eastbay
111 S First Ave.
Wausau, WI 54401   715-845-5538
asktheexperts@eastbay.com
www.eastbay.com

Athletic footwear and apparel.

President & CEO: Dowe Tillema
Catalog Cost: Free
In Business: 36 years
Number of Employees: 1500
Sales Volume: $200 Million

5572 Especially Yours
Especially Yours
PO Box 105
South Easton, MA 02375   800-952-5926
Fax: 508-238-1965
customerservice@especiallyyours.com
www.especiallyyours.com

African American wigs, hairpieces, hair extensions, hair weaves and stylish clothing for the fashion-concious black woman.

Catalog Cost: Free
Printing Information: in 4 colors

5573 Footprints
Footprints
1339 Massachusetts St
Lawrence, KS 66044-3431   785-841-7027
800-488-8316
Fax: 785-832-0087
info@footprints.com
www.Footprints.Com

Birkenstock shoes

President: Mick Ranney
Catalog Circulation: to 75000
Printing Information: 34 pages in 4 colors on Glossy Stock
Press: Web Press
Binding: Saddle Stitched
In Business: 22 years
Number of Employees: 7
Sales Volume: $500M to $1MM

5574 Footwear by Footskins
Footwear by Footskins
110 E. Main Street
P.O. Box 146
Spring Grove, MN 55974   507-498-3707
888-720-3131
Fax: 507-498-3707
service@footwearbyfootskins.com
www.footwearbyfootskins.com

Leather moccasins, slippers, shoes, boots, knee boots, baby booties, and coin purses

Credit Cards: MasterCard
Catalog Cost: Free
Catalog Circulation: Mailed 1 time(s) per year
Printing Information: 28 pages in 4 colors on Glossy Stock
Binding: Saddle Stitched
Mailing List Information: Names for rent
In Business: 19 years

5575 Footwise
Footwise
301 SW Madison Ave
Corvallis, OR 97333-4703   541-757-0875
800-451-1459
Fax: 541-752-6313
footwisecorvallis@footwise.com
www.footwise.com

Birkenstock shoes and sandals for men, women, and children

President: Peter Wendel
Credit Cards: AMEX; MasterCard; Visa
Catalog Circulation: Mailed 2 time(s) per year
Printing Information: 16 pages in 4 colors on

Glossy Stock
Binding: Saddle Stitched
Number of Employees: 20
Sales Volume: Under $500M

5576 Giordano's Petite Shoes
Giordano's Shoes Sales Inc
1150 2nd Avenue
New York, NY 10065-8572   212-688-7195
Fax: 212-688-7199
Giordanoshoes@aol.com
www.petiteshoes.com

Women's shoes, sizes 4-5 1/2 medium, with a vast collection of flats, heels, loafers, boots, and sandals from favorite designers

President: Allen Gonzalez
Catalog Circulation: Mailed 4 time(s) per year
Printing Information: 36 pages in 4 colors on Glossy Stock
Binding: Saddle Stitched
Mailing List Information: Names for rent
In Business: 35 years
Number of Employees: 10-J

5577 Johnston & Murphy Catalog
Genesco
1415 Murfreesboro Road
Suite 190
Nashville, TN 37217   615-367-7168
800-424-2854
Fax: 800-654-2371
JMInternational@genesco.com
www.Johnstonmurphy.Com

Footwear, outerwear, and accessories for men and women

President: Jonathan D Caplan
Catalog Cost: Free
Catalog Circulation: Mailed 1 time(s) per year
Printing Information: 52 pages in 4 colors on Glossy Stock
Press: Web Press
Binding: Saddle Stitched
In Business: 165 years
Number of Employees: 700

5578 Just Justin Catalog
Justin Brands Inc
610 W Daggett Ave
Fort Worth, TX 76104-1103   800-292-2668
800-548-1021
www.justinbrands.com

casual, work, cowboy boots and more for men, women, and children

President: Randy Watson
Credit Cards: AMEX; MasterCard; Visa
Catalog Cost: Free
Catalog Circulation: Mailed 2 time(s) per year
Printing Information: 12 pages in 4 colors on Glossy Stock
Press: Web Press
Binding: Saddle Stitched
In Business: 129 years
Number of Employees: 310
Sales Volume: $500M to $1MM

5579 K. Jordan
K Jordan
913 First Avenue
Chippewa Falls, WI 54774   800-944-4803
Fax: 800-446-2329
service@kjordan.com
www.kjordan.com

Womens clothing, shoes and accessories

Credit Cards: AMEX; MasterCard; Visa
Catalog Cost: Free
Printing Information: 48 pages in 4 colors on Glossy Stock
Binding: Saddle Stitched

5580 Maryland Square
Maryland Square
1350 Williams Street
Chippewa Falls, WI 54729-1500   715-723-5501
800-274-7196
Fax: 715-720-4247
service@marylandsquare.com
www.marylandsquare.com

Brand name women's footwear in regular and hard to find sizes

Credit Cards: AMEX; MasterCard; Visa
Catalog Cost: Free
Catalog Circulation: Mailed 12 time(s) per year
Average Order Size: $85
Printing Information: 48 pages in 4 colors on Glossy Stock
Press: Web Press
Binding: Saddle Stitched
Mailing List Information: Names for rent
List Company: Mokrynski & Associates
401 Hackensack Avenue
Hackensack, NJ 07601
2014885656
Number of Employees: 300

5581 Mason Shoes
B.A.Mason
1251 1st Avenue
Chippewa Falls, WI 54729-1408   715-723-1871
800-422-1000
Fax: 800-446-2329
service@bamason.com
www.bamason.com

Casual, dress, and athletic shoes for men and women

President: Dan Hunt
Founder: Bert Mason
Founder: August Mason
Buyers: Matt Sullivan
Credit Cards: AMEX; MasterCard; Visa
Catalog Cost: Free
Catalog Circulation: Mailed 10 time(s) per year
Printing Information: 76 pages in 4 colors
Press: Web Press
Binding: Saddle Stitched
Mailing List Information: Names for rent
Will Trade Names: Yes
List Company: Names & Addresses
Wheeling, IL
In Business: 110 years
Number of Employees: 500

5582 Massey's
Massey's
1251 1st Avenue
Chippewa Falls, WI 54729   866-229-2316
service@masseys.com
www.masseys.com

Women's footwear

Credit Cards: AMEX; MasterCard; Visa
Catalog Cost: Free
Catalog Circulation: Mailed 16 time(s) per year to 20000
Average Order Size: $90
Printing Information: 48 pages in 4 colors on Glossy Stock
Press: Web Press
Binding: Saddle Stitched
Mailing List Information: Names for rent
Will Trade Names: Yes
Number of Employees: 250
Sales Volume: $20MM to $50MM

5583 Masseys
1251 1st Avenue
Chippewa Falls, WI 54729   866-229-2316
service@masseys.com
www.masseys.com

Sporting goods

5584 Men's Catalog
Friedman's Shoes
209 Mitchell Street
Atlanta, GA 30303
404-524-1311
800-886-3668
Fax: 404-524-3831
www.Largefeet.Com

Fine men's shoes, in difficult to find sizes

President: Bruce Teilhaber
Catalog Cost: Free
Catalog Circulation: Mailed 2 time(s) per year
Printing Information: 25 pages in 4 colors on Glossy Stock
Binding: Folded
Number of Employees: 40

5585 Minnetonka Moccasins
Naples Creek Leather
Route 202 and Route 263
Suite #68
Lahaska, PA 18931
585-586-9070
877-418-6627
Fax: 585-586-9189
info@minnetonkamoccasinshop.com

Moccasins for the family

President: Robert Manzella
Marketing Manager: Robert Manzella
In Business: 69 years

5586 Nike Footwear
Nike USA Inc
P.O.Box 4027
Beaverton, OR 97076-4027
503-671-6453
800-344-6453
Fax: 503-671-6374
www.Nike.Com

Men's women's and children's athletic footwear and apparel

Chairman: Philip H Knight
President: Mark G Parker
CFO: Donald W Blair
Marketing Manager: Adam S Helfant
Credit Cards: AMEX; MasterCard; Visa
Catalog Cost: Free
Catalog Circulation: Mailed 4 time(s) per year
Printing Information: 25 pages in 4 colors on Glossy Stock
Press: Web Press
Binding: Saddle Stitched
Mailing List Information: Names for rent
Number of Employees: 3430
Sales Volume: $20MM to $50MM

5587 Noat at leathersandals.com
Sole Survivor
7312 Manchester Rd.
Maplewood, MO 63143
314-932-1475
800-950-6268
Fax: 618-234-0072
www.solesurvivorleather.com

Men's and women's leather sandals and casual shoes, featuring a unique anatomical footbed

Catalog Cost: Free
In Business: 64 years
Number of Employees: 160

5588 Rainbow Sandals
Rainbow Sandals
326 Calle de los Molinos
San Clemente, CA 92672
949-492-4930
800-762-7635
Fax: 949-493-8322
sales@rainbowsandals.com
www.rainbowsandals.com

Hand crafted sandals

President: Jay Longley
Credit Cards: MasterCard; Visa
In Business: 41 years

5589 Richlee Shoe
Richlee Shoe Company
7311-K Grove Rd.
Frederick, MD 21704-3566
301-663-5111
800-343-3810
Fax: 301-663-1066
richlee@elevatorshoes.com
www.Elevatorshoes.Com

Men's elevator shoes

President: Robert Martin
Credit Cards: AMEX; MasterCard; Visa
Catalog Cost: Free
Catalog Circulation: Mailed 10 time(s) per year
Printing Information: 56 pages in 4 colors
Binding: Folded
In Business: 76 years
Number of Employees: 16
Sales Volume: under 500,000

5590 Russell Moccasin
Russell Moccasin Company
285 SW Franklin Street
P.O. Box 309
Berlin, WI 54923-0309
920-361-2252
Fax: 920-361-3274
www.russellmoccasin.com

Handmade and custom moccasin shoes and boots, and accessories

President: Ralph Fabricius
Buyers: Ralph Fabricius
Credit Cards: MasterCard; Visa
Catalog Cost: Free
Catalog Circulation: Mailed 1 time(s) per year to 20000
Average Order Size: $250
Printing Information: 36 pages in 4 colors on Glossy Stock
Press: Sheetfed Press
Binding: Saddle Stitched
Mailing List Information: Names for rent
In Business: 119 years
Number of Employees: 37
Sales Volume: $1MM to $3MM

5591 Sexy Shoes Catalog
Leslie Shoe Company Inc
480 N 2nd St
Rogers City, MI 49779-1367
989-734-4030
800-716-8617
Fax: 989-734-4337
info@sexyshoes.com
www.sexyshoes.com

Ladie's high heel dress shoes, hand bags, jewelry and lingerie

President: Jeff Hopp
Buyers: Sandy Ruttan
Credit Cards: AMEX; MasterCard
Catalog Cost: $4
Catalog Circulation: Mailed 2 time(s) per year to 400M
Printing Information: 48 pages in 4 colors on Glossy Stock
Press: Web Press
Binding: Saddle Stitched
Mailing List Information: Names for rent
In Business: 20 years
Number of Employees: 5
Sales Volume: $1MM

5592 Shape-Ups Men's Catalog
Skechers USA, Inc.
228 Manhattan Beach Boulevard
Manhattan Beach, CA 90266
310-318-3100
800-746-3411
Fax: 310-318-5019
info@skechers.com
www.skechers.com

Men's athletic work-out footwear

Chairman: Robert Greenberg
President: Michael Greenberg
CFO: David Weinberg
Marketing Manager: Leonard Armato
EVP Business Affairs: Phillip Paccione

EVP Product Development: Mark Nason
SVP International: Harry Bernstein
Printing Information: in 3 colors
In Business: 22 years

5593 Shape-Ups Women's Catalog
Skechers USA, Inc.
228 Manhattan Beach Boulevard
Manhattan Beach, CA 90266
310-318-3100
800-746-3411
Fax: 310-318-5019
info@skechers.com
www.skechers.com

Women's athletic work-out footwear

Chairman: Robert Greenberg
President: Michael Greenberg
CFO: David Weinberg
Marketing Manager: Leonard Armato
EVP Business Affairs: Phillip Paccione
EVP Product Development: Mark Nason
SVP International: Harry Bernstein
Printing Information: in 3 colors
In Business: 22 years

5594 Shoes XL
Shoes XL
555 Turnpike Street
Canton, MA 02021
781-828-9300
800-690-7377
Fax: 781-575-9866
www.shoesxl.com

Bigger, wider men's shoes

Credit Cards: AMEX; MasterCard
Catalog Cost: Free

5595 Shoes for Crews
Shoes For Crews Corp.
250 S Australian Ave
West Palm Beach, FL 33401-7402
561-683-5090
800-523-4448
Fax: 888-647-4637
info@shoesforcrews.com
www.shoesforcrews.com

Slip-resistant footwear for the workplace

President: Stanley Smith
Credit Cards: AMEX; MasterCard
Catalog Cost: Free
Printing Information: 24 pages in 4 colors on Glossy Stock
Press: Letterpress
Binding: Saddle Stitched
Mailing List Information: Names for rent
In Business: 31 years

5596 Sierra Shoes
Sierra Trading Post
5025 Campstool Rd
Cheyenne, WY 82007-1898
307-775-8000
800-713-4534
Fax: 800-378-8946
customerservice@sierratradingpost.com
www.sierratradingpost.com

Footwear and accessories

President: Keith Richardson
CFO: Gary Imig
Production Manager: Shelia Russell
Fulfillment: Robin Jahnke
Credit Cards: AMEX; MasterCard
Catalog Cost: Free
Mailing List Information: Names for rent
In Business: 28 years
Number of Employees: 135
Sales Volume: 20MM-50MM

5597 Skechers
Skechers
707-624-772
ukinfo@eu.skechers.com
www.skechers.com

Casual and athletic footwear

Catalog Cost: Free
Printing Information: in 4 colors

5598 Soccer.com
Soccer.com
431 US Highway 70A E
Hillsborough, NC 27278　919-644-6800
　　　　800-950-1994
custserv@sportsendeavors.com
www.soccer.com

Footwear, apparel, equipment and uniforms.

In Business: 32 years

5599 TimsBoots.com
TimsBoots.com
15460 Ryan Wesley
El Paso, TX 79938　915-921-8396
　　　800-771-4214
Fax: 575-824-0354
sales@timsboots.com
www.timsboots.com

Cowboy and Cowgirl boots, Western boots and Western belts; Also Alligator boots, Ostrich boots, Crocodile boots, Caiman boots, Stingray boots, Elephant boots, Lizard boots and more

President: Tim Urling
Founder: Tim Urling
Credit Cards: AMEX; MasterCard
Catalog Cost: Free
In Business: 13 years

5600 VS Athletics Cross Country
Venue Sports Athletics
3474 Empresa Drive
Suite 120
San Luis Obispo, CA 93401-7704　805-781-3790
　　　888-415-5212
Fax: 805-781-6092
sales@vsathletics.com
www.vsathletics.com

Cross country and track & field athletic equipment: shoes, training information, throwing and timing equipment, track equipment.

President: Rich Benoy
IT Manager, Webmaster, Intl Sales: Doug Lynch
doug@vsathletics.com
Accounting/HR: Mary Inlow
mary@vsathletics.com
Buyers: David Ulibarri
Credit Cards: AMEX; MasterCard
Catalog Cost: Free
Catalog Circulation: Mailed 4 time(s) per year
Printing Information: 70 pages in 4 colors
In Business: 22 years
Number of Employees: 20
Sales Volume: $3MM to $5MM

5601 Vivre
Voyager Spirit
11 E 26th St
15th Floor
New York, NY 10010-1421　212-739-6193
　　　800-411-6515
Fax: 212-739-1736

Women, men and kids footwear, outerwear and accessories; home furnishings and gifts

Chairman: James Robinson
President: Eva Jeanbart-Lorenzotti
Marketing Manager: Eileen Shulock
EVP: Meg Galea
mgalea@vivre.com
Credit Cards: AMEX; MasterCard
Catalog Cost: $10
Catalog Circulation: Mailed 2 time(s) per year to 1.5MM
Average Order Size: $600
Printing Information: 80 pages
In Business: 17 years
Number of Employees: 25
Sales Volume: $ 1-3 Million

5602 2015 Perform Better Facility Design Calendar
M-F Athletic / Everything Track & Field
1600 Division Rd.
West Warwick, RI 2893　401-942-9363
　　　888-556-7464
Fax: 401-942-7645
mfathletic@mfathletic.com
www.everythingtrackandfield.com

Track & Field Equipment.

President: Eric Falk
ericf@mfathletic.com
Founder: Bill Falk
billf@mfathletic.com
General Manager: Mark Strawderman
marks@mfathletic.com
Contact: Nick Stebenne
nicks@mfathletic.com

5603 All Pro Team Sports
All Pro Team Sports
11615 Crossraods Circle
Suite H
Baltimore, MD 21220　410-335-9804
contacts@allproteamsports.com
www.allproteamsports.com

Sportswear, sporting equipment, gear, and uniforms

President: Steve Bottcher
steve@allproteamsports.com
Credit Cards: AMEX; MasterCard
Catalog Cost: Free
In Business: 8 years

5604 Athletic Connection
Athletic Connection
1901 Diplomat Drive
Farmers Branch, TX 75234　800-527-0871
Fax: 885-858-8337
www.athleticconnection.com

Sportswear, sporting equipment, gear, and uniforms

Credit Cards: AMEX; MasterCard
Catalog Cost: Free
Catalog Circulation: Mailed 1 time(s) per year
Printing Information: 364 pages in 4 colors

5605 BIKE Football
BIKE
3330 Cumberland Blvd SE # 3330
Atlanta, GA 30339-5995　770-933-6232
Fax: 678-742-8132

Football uniforms and protective equipment

President: Paul Gross
Credit Cards: AMEX; MasterCard; Visa
Catalog Cost: Free
Catalog Circulation: Mailed 1 time(s) per year
Printing Information: 50 pages in 4 colors
Binding: Saddle Stitched

5606 BSN Sports Athletic Performance
BSN Sports
PO Box 7726
Dallas, TX 75209　800-856-3488
Fax: 800-899-0149
www.bsnsports.com

Exercise equipment.

Chair & CEO: Adam Blumenfeld
President, COO & General Counsel: Terry Babilla
Catalog Cost: Free
Printing Information: 48 pages in 4 colors
In Business: 44 years
Number of Employees: 1200
Sales Volume: $500 Million

5607 BSN Sports Direct
BSN Sports
PO Box 7726
Dallas, TX 75209　800-856-3488
Fax: 800-899-0149
www.bsnsports.com

Equipment for team sports, facilities and physical education.

Chair & CEO: Adam Blumenfeld
President, COO & General Counsel: Terry Babilla
Catalog Cost: Free
Printing Information: 184 pages in 4 colors
In Business: 44 years
Number of Employees: 1200
Sales Volume: $500 Million

5608 BSN Sports Equipment
BSN Sports
PO Box 7726
Dallas, TX 75209　800-856-3488
Fax: 800-899-0149
www.bsnsports.com

Team apparel and equipment for team sports, facilities and physical education.

Chair & CEO: Adam Blumenfeld
President, COO & General Counsel: Terry Babilla
Catalog Cost: Free
Printing Information: 412 pages in 4 colors
In Business: 44 years
Number of Employees: 1200
Sales Volume: $500 Million

5609 BSN Sports Gear Pro-Tec
BSN Sports
PO Box 7726
Dallas, TX 75209　800-856-3488
Fax: 800-899-0149
www.bsnsports.com

Gear for elite athletes.

Chair & CEO: Adam Blumenfeld
President, COO & General Counsel: Terry Babilla
Catalog Cost: Free
Printing Information: 32 pages in 4 colors
In Business: 44 years
Number of Employees: 1200
Sales Volume: $500 Million

5610 BSN Sports League
BSN Sports
PO Box 7726
Dallas, TX 75209　800-856-3488
Fax: 800-899-0149
www.bsnsports.com

Team sports apparel and equipment.

Chair & CEO: Adam Blumenfeld
President, COO & General Counsel: Terry Babilla
Catalog Cost: Free
Printing Information: 388 pages in 4 colors
In Business: 44 years
Number of Employees: 1200
Sales Volume: $500 Million

5611 BSN Sports Middle School-Junior High
BSN Sports
PO Box 7726
Dallas, TX 75209　800-856-3488
Fax: 800-899-0149
www.bsnsports.com

Team sports apparel and equipment.

Chair & CEO: Adam Blumenfeld
President, COO & General Counsel: Terry Babilla
Catalog Cost: Free
Printing Information: 68 pages in 4 colors
In Business: 44 years
Number of Employees: 1200
Sales Volume: $500 Million

5612 Bart's Watersports
Bart's Water Sports
7581 E. 800 North
PO Box 294
North Webster, IN 46555-294   574-834-7666
                                  800-348-5016
                                  info@barts.com
                                  www.bartswatersports.com

Marketer of water sports equipment & accessories

President: Bart Culver
In Business: 43 years
Sales Volume: $3MM to $5MM

5613 Basketball Express
Team Express Distributing LLC
5750 Northwest Parkway
Suite 100
San Antonio, TX 78249-3374   210-348-7000
                                 877-411-0849
                          Fax: 210-525-9339
                  customer.service@basketballexpress.com
                        www.basketballexpress.com

Basketball supplies

President: Pat Cawles
VP Merchandising: Jamie Morey
Store Manager: Eddie Benavides
Credit Cards: AMEX; MasterCard
Catalog Cost: Free
In Business: 25 years
Number of Employees: 195

5614 Benchmade Catalog
Benchmade
300 Beavercreek Road
Oregon City, OR 97045   503-496-1853
                                 800-800-7427
                          www.benchmade.com

Knives, including custom orders and accessories

President: Les de Asis
Catalog Cost: Free
Catalog Circulation: Mailed 1 time(s) per year
Printing Information: 102 pages in 4 colors
In Business: 29 years
Number of Employees: 10

5615 CRKT Mid Year Catalog
Columbia River Knife & Tool
18348 SW 126th Place
Tualatin, OR 97062   503-685-5015
                                 800-891-3100
                          Fax: 503-682-9680
                                 info@crkt.com
                                 www.crkt.com

Multi-tools and knives designed especially for firefighters, EMTs, police and water rescue teams.

Founder: Rod Bremer
Printing Information: 96 pages in 4 colors
In Business: 21 years

5616 CRKT Product Catalog
Columbia River Knife & Tool
18348 SW 126th Place
Tualatin, OR 97062   503-685-5015
                                 800-891-3100
                          Fax: 503-682-9680
                                 info@crkt.com
                                 www.crkt.com

Multi-tools and knives designed especially for firefighters, EMTs, police and water rescue teams.

Founder: Rod Bremer
Printing Information: 96 pages in 4 colors
In Business: 21 years

5617 Campmor
Campmor
400 Corporate Drive
PO Box 680
Mahwah, NJ 07430   201-335-9064
                                 800-525-4784
                          Fax: 201-445-3151
                                 www.campmor.com

Camping gear and equipment, outerwear, sporting gear, etc.

Chairman: Morton Jarashow
President: Daniel Jarashow
Credit Cards: AMEX; MasterCard
In Business: 36 years
Number of Employees: 100
Sales Volume: $ 14 Million

5618 Cane Masters
Cane Masters Inc.
288 Village Blvd.
PO Box 5151
Incline Village, NV 89451   755-832-6560
                                 800-422-2263
                          Fax: 775-831-8440
                          info@canemasters.com
                          www.canemasters.com

Custom-made canes for self-defense, sport and fitness, how-to video packages

President: Mark Shuey Sr.
Catalog Cost: Free
Catalog Circulation: to 5000
Average Order Size: $125
Printing Information: 10 pages in 4 colors on Matte Stock
Press: Sheetfed Press
Binding: Folded
Mailing List Information: Names for rent
In Business: 10 years
Number of Employees: 5
Sales Volume: $275,000

5619 Cannon Sports
Cannon Sports
PO Box 11179
Burbank, CA 91510-1179   818-683-1000
                                 800-223-0064
                          Fax: 800-388-1993
                          csi@cannonsports.com
                          www.cannonsports.com

Sporting goods including aerobics, archery, apparel, badminton, baseball, softball and basketball

President: Jon Warner
Buyers: Jon Warner
Credit Cards: MasterCard; Visa
Catalog Cost: Free
Catalog Circulation: to 40000
Printing Information: 25 pages in 4 colors on Newsprint
Press: Web Press
Binding: Saddle Stitched
In Business: 19 years
Number of Employees: 30
Sales Volume: $10MM to $20MM

5620 Cascade Outfitters
Cascade Outfitters
604 E 45th Street
Boise, ID 83714   208-322-4411
                                 800-223-7238
                          Fax: 208-322-5016
                          www.cascadeoutfitters.com

Rafts, kayaks and boating accessories, whitewater equipment, rivercamping and clothing, paddles, oars, repairs and pumps, rescue and saftey, camping and cooking, gift ideas

President: Doug Tims
Credit Cards: AMEX; MasterCard; Visa
Catalog Cost: Free
In Business: 27 years
Number of Employees: 8
Sales Volume: Under $500,000

5621 Court Products
Court Products Inc.
3935 Grove Ave
Gurnee, IL 60031-2118   847-662-9000
                                 800-323-9388
                          Fax: 847-662-9055
                          info@courtproducts.com
                          www.courtproducts.com

Sports equipment and accessories

President: Stephen F. Angel
Catalog Circulation: Mailed 1 time(s) per year
Printing Information: 8 pages in 4 colors
Binding: Saddle Stitched
Number of Employees: 6
Sales Volume: $810,000

5622 Crown Awards and Trophies
Crown Awards
9 Skyline Dr
Suite 3
Hawthorne, NY 10532-2100   914-347-7700
                                 800-227-1557
                          Fax: 914-347-7008
                          info@crowntrophy.com
                          www.crowntrophy.com

Trophies, medals, pins, patches, ribbons, plaques and pemstual products

President: Chuck Weisenfeld
CFO: Elyse Weisenfeld
Marketing Manager: Lori Weisenfeld
Production Manager: Elyse Weisenfeld
Credit Cards: MasterCard; Visa
Catalog Cost: Free
Printing Information: 40 pages
Mailing List Information: Names for rent
In Business: 37 years
Number of Employees: 187
Sales Volume: $1,400,000

5623 Dinn Brothers Trophies
Dinn Brothers
221 Interstate Drive
West Springfield, MA 01089   413-750-3466
                                 800-628-9657
                          Fax: 800-876-7497
                          sales@dinntrophy.com
                          www.dinntrophy.com

Trophies, awards and plaques

Chairman: Bill Dinn
President: Paul J. Dinn
Marketing Manager: Mike Dinn
Production Manager: Ed Dinn
Credit Cards: AMEX; MasterCard
In Business: 60 years

5624 Duluth Trading Company
Duluth Trading Company
PO Box 200
Belleville, WI 53508-9739   608-424-1544
                                 866-300-9719
                          Fax: 888-950-3199
                  customerservice@duluthtrading.com
                          www.duluthtrading.com

Women & men clothing & accessories

President: Steve Schlecht
Production Manager: Dan Moeller
Credit Cards: AMEX; MasterCard
Catalog Cost: Free
In Business: 24 years
Number of Employees: 150
Sales Volume: $ 15 Million

5625 Everlast Worldwide
Everlast Worldwide Inc
1900 Highway DD
Moberly, MO 65270   800-821-7930
                          Fax: 800-480-0348
                          orderpro@everlast.com
                          www.everlast.com

Sporting Goods

President: Seth Horowitz
In Business: 95 years

5626 Everything Track & Field - 2015
M-F Athletic / Everything Track & Field
1600 Division Rd.
West Warwick, RI 2893   401-942-9363
                         888-556-7464
             Fax: 401-942-7645
mfathletic@mfathletic.com
www.everythingtrackandfield.com

Track & Field Equipment.

President: Eric Falk
ericf@mfathletic.com
Founder: Bill Falk
billf@mfathletic.com
General Manager: Mark Strawderman
marks@mfathletic.com
Contact: Nick Stebenne
nicks@mfathletic.com

5627 First Position Dancewear
First Position Dancewear Inc.
1550 Altamont Avenue
Schenectady, NY 12303   518-356-6664
             www.superpages.com

Dancewear

President: Carol Hussey
In Business: 21 years

5628 FlagHouse Physical Education and Recreation
Flaghouse Inc
601 Flaghouse Drive
Hasbrouck Heights, NJ 07604   201-288-7600
                               800-793-7900
             Fax: 800-793-7922
             www.flaghouse.com

Physical education, recreation, team sports, gymnastics, fitness and games for all ages

President: George Carmel
CFO: Chris Moore
Fulfillment: Doug Carmel
Credit Cards: MasterCard; Visa
Printing Information: 300 pages in 4 colors on Matte Stock
Press: Web Press
Binding: Perfect Bound
Mailing List Information: Names for rent
In Business: 61 years
Sales Volume: $20MM-$50MM

5629 Football America
Team Express Distributing LLC
5750 Northwest Pky
Ste. 100
San Antonio, TX 78249-3374   210-348-7000
                               877-697-7678
             Fax: 210-525-9339
customer.service@footballamerica.com
             www.footballamerica.com

Football supplies and products

President: Pat Cawles
VP Merchandising: Jamie Morey
Network Manager: Jimmy Tuma
Credit Cards: AMEX; MasterCard
Catalog Cost: Free
In Business: 24 years
Number of Employees: 195

5630 Franklin Sports
Franklin Sports Inc.
17 Campanelli Parkway
Stoughton, MA 02072   781-344-1111
                        800-225-8647
             Fax: 781-341-0333
b2bcustomerservice@franklinsports.com
             franklinsports.com

Sporting goods and toys.

President: Adam Franklin
In Business: 70 years
Number of Employees: 250

5631 Gear Pro-Tec
Athletic Connection
1901 Diplomat Drive
Farmers Branch, TX 75234   800-527-0871
             Fax: 888-858-8337
             www.athleticconnection.com

Football gear, equipment, and uniforms

Credit Cards: AMEX; MasterCard
Catalog Cost: Free
Catalog Circulation: Mailed 1 time(s) per year
Printing Information: 32 pages in 4 colors

5632 Goal Sporting Goods
Goal Sporting Goods, Inc.
37 Industrial Park Road
P.O. Box 236
Essex, CT 06426-243   860-767-9112
                        800-334-4625
             Fax: 860-767-9121
goal@goalsports.com
www.goalsports.com

Basketball, football, and baseball equipment including goals, gymnasium equipment, nets and mats, bleachers, benches and soccer equipment, referee gear, field marking paint

President: Morton Reich
Marketing Manager: Jon Fishman
Credit Cards: AMEX; MasterCard; Visa; Discover
Catalog Cost: Free
Catalog Circulation: Mailed 4 time(s) per year to 50000
Average Order Size: $250
Printing Information: 120 pages in 4 colors on Glossy Stock
Press: Web Press
Binding: Saddle Stitched
Mailing List Information: Names for rent
Number of Employees: 60
Sales Volume: $5MM to $10MM

5633 Great River Outfitters
GRO Kayaks
9 Phillips st.
North Kingstown, RI 02852-5125   401-295-4400
             Fax: 401-667-2680
funn@kayakcentre.com
www.grokayaks.com

Sea kayaks and accessories

President: Jeffrey Shapiro
Catalog Circulation: Mailed 11 time(s) per year to 5000
Printing Information: 24 pages on Glossy Stock
Press: Letterpress
Binding: Saddle Stitched
Mailing List Information: Names for rent
One Phillips Street
North Kingstown, RI 02852
401.667.2670
In Business: 15 years
Number of Employees: 4
Sales Volume: Under $500M

5634 H. Christiansen Co
H. Christiansen Co
4976 Arnold Road
Duluth, MN 55803   218-724-5509
                     800-372-1142
             Fax: 218-724-5609
christiansennets.com

Founder: Warren F. Tischler
In Business: 129 years

5635 HYDRO-FIT Gear
Hydro-Fit, Inc
160 Madison St
Eugene, OR 97402-5031   541-484-4361
                          800-346-7295
             Fax: 541-484-1443
info@hydrofit.com
www.hydrofit.com

Water fitness and therapy gear, shoes, equipment, accessories, clothing and teaching/training tools

Chairman: David Sarett
President: Craig Stuart
Director: Craig Stuart
Catalog Circulation: Mailed 1 time(s) per year
In Business: 25 years
Number of Employees: 12
Sales Volume: $ 1.7 Million

5636 Hoops King
Hoops King
2943 260th Street
Marshalltown, IA 50158   877-569-2508
             Fax: 877-569-2508
helpdesk@hoopsking.com
www.hoopsking.com

Basketball training videos, books, and equipment

Credit Cards: AMEX; MasterCard
Catalog Cost: Free
In Business: 15 years

5637 Hot Off the Ice
Starstruck
725 Landwehr Road
Northbrook, IL 60062   800-776-8326

Sporting accessories for baseball, hockey and other various sports

5638 House
The House
200 S. Owasso Blvd E.
Saint Paul, MN 55117-1099   651-482-9995
                              800-409-7669
             Fax: 800-382-2416
info@the-house.com
www.The-House.Com

Windsurfing, snowboarding, in-line skating, and kayaking equipment

President: Jon Magnusson
Credit Cards: AMEX; MasterCard; Visa
Catalog Cost: Free
Printing Information: 40 pages
Number of Employees: 20
Sales Volume: $3MM to $5MM

5639 Hulme Sporting Goods & MFG Company
3735 Hwy 641 S
Paris, TN 38242   731-642-0561
hulmesinc@gmail.com
www.hulmesportinggoods.com

Sporting goods

President: Ronald Brown
Credit Cards: MasterCard; Visa
Catalog Cost: Free
Catalog Circulation: Mailed 1 time(s) per year
Printing Information: 47 pages in 4 colors
Number of Employees: 5
Sales Volume: Under $500M

5640 JW Hulmeco
JW Hulme Co.
678 West Seventh Street
St Paul, MN 55102   651-222-7359
                      800-442-8212
             Fax: 651-228-1181
sales@jwhulmeco.com
www.jwhulmeco.com

Handbags and totes, leather collections, canvas collections and sporting and hunting products

In Business: 110 years

5641 Jaypro Sports
Jaypro Corporation, LLC
976 Hartford Turnpike
Waterford, CT 06385-4037   860-447-3001
860-243-0533
Fax: 860-444-1779
info@jaypro.com
www.jaypro.com

Sporting equipment for volleyball, soccer, baseball, lacrosse, field hockey, football, tennis and physical education

President: Robert Ferrara
Marketing Manager: David Stumpo
Catalog Cost: Free
Catalog Circulation: Mailed 1 time(s) per year to 5M
Printing Information: 128 pages in 4 colors on Glossy Stock
Press: Web Press
Binding: Perfect Bound
In Business: 60 years
Number of Employees: 60
Sales Volume: $10MM to $20MM

5642 KYTEC Athletic Speed Equipment
2718 W. 84th Street
Bloomington, MN 55431-1738   952-884-3424
800-732-4883
Fax: 952-884-3427
www.kytec.us

Athletic speed equipment, parachutes and rehabilitation equipment

President: Jodi Michaelson
Marketing Manager: Ky Michaelson
Catalog Cost: Free
Catalog Circulation: Mailed 2 time(s) per year
Average Order Size: $150
Printing Information: 47 pages in 4 colors on Glossy Stock
Press: Sheetfed Press
Mailing List Information: Names for rent
Number of Employees: 20-O
Sales Volume: Under $500M

5643 League Direct
Bsn Sports League
PO Box 7726
Dallas, TX 75209   800-856-3488
Fax: 800-899-0149
www.leaguedirect.com

Sports equipment, coaching supplies, scoreboards, locks and lockers and audio equipment

Chairman: Adam Blumenfeld
In Business: 43 years

5644 League Outfitters 2015 Football Equipment & Unifor
League Outfitters
9375 Washington Blvd. N.
Laurel, MD 20723   301-575-9400
Fax: 301-575-9439
info@leagueoutfitters.com
www.leagueoutfitters.com

Sports euipments.

In Business: 16 years

5645 Lyman Products Corporation
Lyman Products Corp
475 Smith Street
Middletown, CT 06457   860-632-2020
800-225-9626
Fax: 860-632-1699
www.lymanproducts.com

Guns, calibers and bullets

President: J Mace Thompson
CFO: Tom Anderson
Marketing Manager: Rick Ranzinger
Credit Cards: MasterCard; Visa
Catalog Cost: $2
Catalog Circulation: Mailed 1 time(s) per year to 50000

Printing Information: 40 pages in 4 colors on Glossy Stock
Press: Web Press
Mailing List Information: Names for rent
Number of Employees: 107
Sales Volume: $10MM to $20MM

5646 Markers
Markers Inc.
33490 Pin Oak Parkway
Avon Lake, OH 44012   440-933-5927
866-617-6275
Fax: 440-933-7839
www.MarkersInc.Com

Golf course and athletic field equipment and supplies

President: Dale Halvin
In Business: 27 years
Sales Volume: $1MM to $3MM

5647 Mid-America Sports Advantage
Mid-America Sports Advantage
1413 S Meridian Rd
Jasper, IN 47546-3831   812-634-2100
800-264-4519
Fax: 812-634-2036
service@sportsadvantage.com
www.sportsadvantage.com

Sports training aids and field maintenance equipment

President: Mike Schmitt, Jr.
Marketing Manager: Denise Kemker
IT Manager: Mike
mkemker@masa.com
Operations Manager: Ken
kbrelage@masa.com
Accounting Manager: Debbie
dbutler@masa.com
Credit Cards: MasterCard; Visa
Catalog Circulation: Mailed 1 time(s) per year to 100M
Printing Information: 156 pages in 4 colors on Newsprint
Press: Web Press
Binding: Folded
In Business: 43 years
Number of Employees: 32
Sales Volume: $3MM to $5MM

5648 Mountain Gear
Mountain Gear
6021 E Mansfield
Spokane Valley, WA 99212-1300   509-340-1165
800-829-2009
Fax: 509-340-1170
info@mountaingear.com
www.mountaingear.com

Outdoor gear and clothing

President: Whitney Parsons
Credit Cards: AMEX; MasterCard
Catalog Cost: Free
Printing Information: 104 pages in 7 colors
Binding: Folded
In Business: 24 years
Sales Volume: $20MM to $50MM

5649 Mueller
Mueller
4825 S 16th St.
Lincoln, NE 68512   800-925-7665
www.muellers.com

In Business: 60 years

5650 Murray Wind & Water Sports
Murrays.com
6389 Rose Lane
Suite B
Carpinteria, CA 93013-2950   805-684-8393
800-786-7245
Fax: 805-684-8966
info@murrays.com
www.murrays.com

Sailing, windsurfing and kite surf accessories and surf, boards and accessories by Terra Sports

Buyers: Doug Murray
Catalog Cost: $2
Catalog Circulation: Mailed 2 time(s) per year
Average Order Size: $150
Printing Information: 100 pages in 4 colors on Glossy Stock
Press: Web Press
Binding: Perfect Bound
Mailing List Information: Names for rent
In Business: 46 years
Number of Employees: 12
Sales Volume: $1MM to $3MM

5651 NRS
NRS
2009 S Main St
Moscow, ID 83843-8913   208-882-2749
877-677-4327
Fax: 208-882-1744
service@nrs.com
www.Nrsweb.Com

Camping equipment, life jackets, canoes, kayaks, helmets, float tubes, paddles and oars

President: Bill Parks
Sales Volume: $10MM to $20MM

5652 Nevco Scoreboard
Nevco, Inc.
301 East Harris Avenue
Greenville, IL 62246-2193   618-664-0360
800-851-4040
Fax: 618-664-0398
sales@nevco.com
www.nevco.com

Scoreboards

President: G.D. Moore
Catalog Cost: Free
Catalog Circulation: Mailed 52 time(s) per year to 75000
Printing Information: 28 pages in 1 color on Matte Stock
Press: Web Press
Binding: Saddle Stitched
Mailing List Information: Names for rent
In Business: 81 years
Number of Employees: 95
Sales Volume: $17M

5653 No Fault Sports Products
No Fault Sports Products
2101 Briarglen Dr
Houston, TX 77027-3711   713-683-7101
800-462-7766
Fax: 713-683-7103
nofaultsports@comcast.net
www.Nofaultsports.Com

Distributor of baseball, basketball, volleyball, soccer & tennis equipment

President: Alfredo Trullenque
Sales Volume: Under $500M

5654 Notre Dame: BGI Sport Shop
Notre Dame
PO Box 1007
Notre Dame, IN 46556-1007   574-239-6611
800-385-9925
Fax: 610-532-9001

Fighting Irish licensed products

Printing Information: 64 pages

5655 Overton's
Overton's
111 Red Banks Rd
Greenville, NC 27858   252-355-2923
800-334-6541
Fax: 252-355-2923
www.overtons.com

Camping, hunting equipment, dog and horse supplies

President: Larry Carroll
CFO: Mark Metcalfe
Marketing Manager: Marisa Dore
Credit Cards: AMEX; MasterCard; Visa
Catalog Cost: Free
Catalog Circulation: Mailed 2 time(s) per year to 16000
Printing Information: 284 pages in 4 colors on Matte Stock
Binding: Perfect Bound
Mailing List Information: Names for rent
In Business: 45 years
Sales Volume: $ 13 Million

5656 Ozone Billiards
Ozone Billiards, Inc.
3400 Town Point Dr
Suite 120
Kennesaw, GA 30144-7830   770-874-6181
                    sales@ozonebilliards.com
                    www.ozonebilliards.com

Pool sticks, pool cues, pool ball racks, pool balls, pool table lights and billiards posters and signs

President: Shawn Gargano
Credit Cards: AMEX; MasterCard
Sales Volume: $3MM to $5MM

5657 Pacific Drive Mail Order
Pacific Drive
756 Thomas Ave
San Diego, CA 92109-3938   858-270-3361
                    Fax: 858-270-5212
                    info@pacificdrive.com
                    www.pacificdrive.com

Skateboards and related materials

President: Jim Ruonala
Number of Employees: 6
Sales Volume: $720,000

5658 Perform Better - Fitness Edition 2015
M-F Athletic / Everything Track & Field
1600 Division Rd.
West Warwick, RI 2893   401-942-9363
                    888-556-7464
                    Fax: 401-942-7645
                    mfathletic@mfathletic.com
                    www.everythingtrackandfield.com

Track & Field Equipment.

President: Eric Falk
ericf@mfathletic.com
Founder: Bill Falk
billf@mfathletic.com
General Manager: Mark Strawderman
marks@mfathletic.com
Contact: Nick Stebenne
nicks@mfathletic.com

5659 Physical Education & Recreation
Flaghouse
601 US-46
Hasbrouck Heights, NJ 07604   800-793-7900
                    sales@flaghouse.com
                    www.flaghouse.com

Equipment for physical education including baseball, football, basketball, and equipment for special needs patients including sensory, mobility and balance exercises and positioning products

President: George Carmel
CFO: Sheila Morrison
Credit Cards: AMEX; MasterCard
Catalog Cost: Free
Catalog Circulation: Mailed 6 time(s) per year to 2MM
Printing Information: 208 pages in 4 colors on Glossy Stock
Press: Web Press
Binding: Perfect Bound
Mailing List Information: Names for rent
List Company: Wilson Marketing Group

11924 W Washington Boulevard
Los Angeles, CA 90066
213-398-2754
In Business: 62 years
Number of Employees: 120
Sales Volume: $20MM to $50MM

5660 Pioneer Athletics
Pioneerr Manufacturing Company, Inc
4529 Industrial Parkway
Cleveland, OH 44135-4541   800-877-1500
                    Fax: 800-877-1511
                    www.pioneerathletics.com

Industrial maintenance, flooring and roofing supplies

President: James Schattinger
Marketing Manager: Jackie Robertson
Catalog Cost: Free
Catalog Circulation: Mailed 1 time(s) per year
Printing Information: 64 pages in 4 colors on Glossy Stock
Binding: Saddle Stitched
Mailing List Information: Names for rent
In Business: 94 years
Number of Employees: 120
Sales Volume: $10MM to $20MM

5661 PoolDawg
PoolDawg
PO Box 552
Lafayette, CO 80026   866-843-3294
                    Fax: 720-214-2668
                    info@pooldawg.com
                    www.pooldawg.com

Pool cues and billiards supplies

Marketing Manager: Mike Feiman

5662 Prize Possessions
Prize Possessions
340R Vanderbilt Ave
Norwood, MA 02062-5008   781-762-8235
                    800-283-1166
                    Fax: 781-762-1729
                    prize@prizepossessions.com
                    www.prizepossessions.com

Croquet trophies, golf trophies

President: Kevin Lynch
CFO: James Steely
Credit Cards: AMEX; MasterCard
Printing Information: 26 pages on Glossy Stock
Binding: Saddle Stitched
In Business: 36 years
Number of Employees: 10
Sales Volume: $3MM to $5MM

5663 Pro Tour Sports
Pro Tour Sports Equip Mfg
8760 Orion Place
Ste. 100
Columbus, OH 43240-1   330-494-4282
                    800-777-9876
                    Fax: 330-497-6858
                    www.manta.com

President: Ben Suarez
CFO: George Troutman
Marketing Manager: John White
Founder: George Jenkins
CEO: John Swanciger
Credit Cards: AMEX; MasterCard
Number of Employees: 1000
Sales Volume: $500M to $1MM

5664 Race Quip Safety Systems
RaceQuip and Safe-Quip
11705 Boyette Rd
Tampa, FL 33569   813-642-6644
                    Fax: 813-630-5577
                    sales@racequip.com
                    www.racequip.com

Auto racing safety gear.

Chairman: Bob Mantell
President: Patrick Utt

Exec Sales Director: Bob Mantell
Manufacturing: Tim Lee
Printing Information: 16 pages
In Business: 40 years

5665 Rainbow Racing System
Rainbow Racing Systems
814 W Rosewood
PO Box 18310
Spokane, WA 99228-510   509-326-5470
                    800-962-1011
                    Fax: 509-326-5795
                    sales@rainbowracing.com
                    www.rainbowracing.com

Race numbers and supplies

Catalog Cost: Free
Printing Information: 25 pages
In Business: 33 years
Number of Employees: 15
Sales Volume: $1MM to $3MM

5666 Recreonics
Recreonics
4200 Schmitt Ave
Louisville, KY 40213-1931   502-456-5706
                    800-428-3254
                    Fax: 502-458-9471
                    sales@recreonics.com
                    www.Recreonics.Com

Swimming pool equipment and supplies

President: Frank L Jones Jr
In Business: 39 years
Sales Volume: $5MM to $10MM

5667 Regent Sports Corporation
Regent Sports Corp
One Hedstrom Dr.
Ashland, OH 44805   631-234-2800
                    800-765-9665
                    Fax: 631-234-2948
                    customerservicebbsregent@hedstrom.com
                    www.regentsports.com

Team sporting goods

President: Carl Serraro
Catalog Cost: Free
Printing Information: 48 pages in 4 colors on Glossy Stock
Press: Web Press
Binding: Saddle Stitched
In Business: 70 years
Number of Employees: 100
Sales Volume: $20MM to $50MM

5668 Resilite
Resilite Sports Products, Inc.
PO Box 764
Sunbury, PA 17801   800-843-6287
                    Fax: 570-473-8988
                    resilite@resilite.com
                    www.resilite.com

Athletic mats and wall padding.

In Business: 55 years

5669 SNA Sports
SNA Sports
4180 44th St. SE
Suite B
Grand Rapids, MI 49512   616-554-4945
                    800-823-0182
                    info@snasportsgroup.com
                    www.snasportsgroup.com

Sporting goods.

President: Jim Peterson
VP, Operations: Amy Deschaine
Service Manager/Sales: John Connors
Customer Service Representative: Julie Gorter

5670 Sierra Trading Post
Sierra Trading Post
5025 Campstool Rd.
Cheyenne, WY 82007 www.sierratradingpost.com

Outdoor gear and apparel for men, women and kids.

CEO: Keith Richardson
President: Gary Imig
Catalog Cost: Free
In Business: 30 years
Sales Volume: $200 Million

5671 Softball Catalog
Team Express Distributing, LLC
5750 North West Pky
Ste 100
San Antonio, TX 78249-3374   210-348-7000
                               800-882-1166
                          Fax: 210-525-9339
customer.service@softball.com
www.softball.com

Softball supplies and products

President: Pat Cawles
VP Merchandising: Jamie Morey
Credit Cards: AMEX; MasterCard
Catalog Cost: Free
In Business: 25 years
Number of Employees: 195

5672 Stagestep
Stagestep, Inc.
4701 Bath Street #46
Philadelphia, PA 19137-2235   215-636-9000
                                800-523-0960
                           Fax: 267-672-2912
stagestep@stagestep.com
www.stagestep.com

Flooring supplier to dance studios, theaters and athletic facilities

President: Randy Schwartz
Sales Consultant: Karen Flanagan
Installation Expert: sam Jamison
Catalog Circulation: Mailed 1 time(s) per year
Printing Information: 40 pages in 4 colors
In Business: 42 years
Sales Volume: $1MM to $3MM

5673 The Craft Shop
The Craft Shop, Inc.
699 East 2nd Street
Brooklyn, NY 11218   718-431-0301
                  Fax: 718-436-5815
info@thecraftshoponline.com
www.thecraftshoponline.com

School supplies, creative Arts and Crafts, craft kits for schools, camps.

5674 Title Nine Sports
Title Nine
6201 Doyle St.
Emeryville, CA 94608   858-454-4666
                         800-609-0092
                    Fax: 510-655-9191
www.titlenine.com

Sportswear and accessories for women

President: Missy Park
Credit Cards: MasterCard; Visa
Catalog Circulation: Mailed 8 time(s) per year
Printing Information: 71 pages in 4 colors on Glossy Stock
Press: Web Press
Binding: Saddle Stitched
Mailing List Information: Names for rent
In Business: 23 years
Number of Employees: 170
Sales Volume: $ 1-3 Million

5675 Toledo Physical Education Supply
Toledo Physical Education Supply
5101 Advantage Dr
Toledo, OH 43612-3875   419-726-8122
                          800-225-7749
                     Fax: 419-726-8118
custser@tpesonline.com
www.Tpesonline.Com

Sporting goods and athletic equipment

President: Thomas Mc Nutt
Founder: Thomas Mc Nutt
Credit Cards: AMEX; MasterCard; Visa
Catalog Cost: Free
Average Order Size: $350
Printing Information: 196 pages in 2 colors on Glossy Stock
Press: Web Press
Mailing List Information: Names for rent
In Business: 40 years
Number of Employees: 15
Sales Volume: $3MM to $5MM

5676 US Games
PO Box 7726
Dallas, TX 75209   800-327-0484
                Fax: 800-899-0149
www.usgames.com

Health, fitness and gym equipment

5677 Vasa Trainers
Vasa
1 Allen Martin Drive
Essex Junction, VT 05452-3403   802-872-7101
                                  800-488-8272
                             Fax: 802-872-7104
info@vasatrainer.com
www.Vasatrainer.Com

Onland swim trainers

President: Rob Sleamaker
Founder: Rob Sleamaker
Printing Information: 4 pages in 4 colors on Glossy Stock
In Business: 26 years
Number of Employees: 10-J
Sales Volume: $1MM to $3MM

5678 Wolverine Sports
School-Tech, Inc.
745 State Circle
Ann Arbor, MI 48108   800-521-2832
                   Fax: 800-654-4321
www.schoolmasters.com

Supplies for school sports

President: Donald B. Canham
Marketing Manager: SW Canham
Catalog Circulation: Mailed 1 time(s) per year
Printing Information: 341 pages in 4 colors
In Business: 54 years
Number of Employees: 80
Sales Volume: $50MM to $100MM

5679 Worldwide Sport Supply Wrestling
Worldwide Sport Supply, Inc
145 N Jensen Road
Vestal, NY 13850   800-756-3555
                Fax: 800-550-6850
customercare@wwsport.com
www.wwsport.com

Apparel decorating and sporting goods, with a focus on volleyball and wrestling

In Business: 34 years

5680 Worldwide Sport Supply Wrestling Coach
Worldwide Sport Supply, Inc
145 N Jensen Road
Vestal, NY 13850   800-756-3555
                Fax: 800-550-6850
customercare@wwsport.com
www.wwsport.com

Apparel decorating and sporting goods, with a focus on volleyball and wrestling

In Business: 34 years

5681 Wrestler's Express
601 Packard Court
Safety Harbor, FL 34695   800-950-7744
                       Fax: 800-642-8614
www.wrestlersexpress.com

Wrestling equipment, t-shirts, bags and accessories

Credit Cards: MasterCard; Visa
Catalog Cost: Free
Catalog Circulation: Mailed 1 time(s) per year
Printing Information: 32 pages in 4 colors on Glossy Stock
Press: Web Press
Binding: Saddle Stitched
Sales Volume: $10MM to $20MM

Archery

5682 3Rivers Archery
3Rivers Archery
607 HL Thompson Jr Dr
PO Box 517
Ashley, IN 46705-517   260-587-9501
                         866-732-8783
                    Fax: 888-329-9872
info@3riversarchery.com
www.3riversarchery.com

Archery supplies for bow hunting and target shooting.

President: Dale Karch
CFO: Sandie Karch
Marketing Manager: Jonathan Karch
Production Manager: Matt Karch
Fulfillment: Kim
VP Operations: Teresa Williams
Inventory Manager: Ashley Sunday
Creative Specialist: Wil Radcliffe
Credit Cards: AMEX; MasterCard
Catalog Cost: Free
Printing Information: 75 pages in 4 colors
In Business: 30 years
Number of Employees: 22
Sales Volume: $1.9 Million

5683 Alpine Archery
Alpine Archery
3101 North-South Hwy
Lewiston, ID 83501   208-746-4717
                  Fax: 208-746-1635
info@alpinearchery.com
www.alpinearchery.com

Bows, quivers, accessories and apparel

5684 Apple Archery Products
Apple Archery
1230 Poplar Ave
Superior, WI 54880   717-767-1784
                       800-745-8190
                  Fax: 717-395-9959
support@applearchery.com
www.applearchery.com

Bow presses, string making kits, vises, bow and arrow tools and maintainense supplies, target stands, replacement parts, manuals, and DVDs

Credit Cards: AMEX; MasterCard
Catalog Cost: Free
Printing Information: 25 pages in 4 colors
In Business: 23 years

5685 Black Widow Bows
Black Widow Bows
PO Box 2100
Nixa, MO 65714   417-725-3113
              Fax: 417-725-3190
www.blackwidowbows.com

One-piece and take-down recurves and long-bows made to order

5686 Bob Lee Bows
Bob Lee Bows
1483 US Hwy 175 W.
Jacksonville, TX 75766   903-586-1877
sales@bobleebows.net
www.bobleebows.net

Traditional recurves and longbows.

5687 Brownells
Brownells
200 South Front St.
Montezuma, IA 50171   641-623-5401
800-741-0015
Fax: 800-264-3068
www.brownells.com

Archery products, firearm accessories, gunsmithing tools

5688 Cabela's Archery
Cabela's Inc.
One Cabela Dr.
Sidney, NE 69160   www.cabelas.com

Bow hunting equipment, quality outerwear and footwear, game calls, treestands and more.

CFO: Ralph Castner
CEO: Thomas Millner
COO: Michael Copeland
Catalog Cost: Free
Catalog Circulation: Mailed 4 time(s) per year
Printing Information: in 4 colors
List Company: Chilcutt Direct
In Business: 55 years
Sales Volume: $3 Billion

5689 Darton Archery
Darton Archery
3540 Darton Road
Hale, MI 48739-8500   989-728-9511
Fax: 989-728-2410
www.dartonarchery.com

Archery products

President: Rex Darlington
Sales Manager: Ted Harpham
Credit Cards: AMEX; MasterCard; Visa
Catalog Cost: Free
Printing Information: 16 pages in 4 colors on Glossy Stock
Binding: Saddle Stitched
Number of Employees: 32
Sales Volume: $5MM to $10MM

5690 Fall Hunting II
Bass Pro Shops
2500 E Kearney
Springfield, MO 65898   417-873-5000
800-227-7776
Fax: 417-873-5060
www.basspro.com

Hunting gear, tools and clothing.

President & CEO: James Hagale
Catalog Cost: Free
Catalog Circulation: Mailed 1 time(s) per year
Printing Information: 220 pages in 4 colors
In Business: 45 years
Number of Employees: 2200
Sales Volume: $4.45 Billion

5691 Final Flight Outfitters
Final Flight Outfitters
5933 Martin Hwy
Union City, TN 38261   731-885-5056
Fax: 731-885-5337
sales@finalflight.net
www.finalflight.net

Archery accessories and duck hunting equipment

5692 Howard Hill Archery
Howard Hill Archery
54 North Canyon Drive
Hamilton, MT 59840-9542   406-363-1359
email@howardhillarchery.com
www.HowardHillarchery.com

Handcrafted longbows, arrows, and archery accessories

President: Jason, Craig & Evie Ekin
Credit Cards: AMEX; MasterCard
Catalog Cost: Free
Mailing List Information: Names for rent
In Business: 50 years
Number of Employees: 4
Sales Volume: $500M to $1MM

5693 Kings Way Archery
Kings Way Archery
12555 Superior Court
Suite B
Holland, MI 49424   616-796-0063
Fax: 616-796-0063
info@kingswayarchery.com
www.kingswayarchery.com

Bow sights, bows, arrows and archery supplies

5694 Kustom King Archery
Kustom King Traditional Archery
5435 W. 75th Ave
Schererville, IN 46375   219-322-0790
877-566-4269
Fax: 219-322-079
info@KustomKingArchery.com
www.kustomkingarchery.com

Archery equipment.

In Business: 43 years

5695 Lancaster Archery
Lancaster Archery
21 Graybill Rd
Leola, PA 17540   717-656-7229
855-922-7769
Fax: 717-394-8635
www.lancasterarchery.com

Archery equipment, supplies, and products

5696 Mike's Archery
Mike's Archery Inc
2630 State Route 141
Ironton, OH 45638   740-532-0142
888-948-0142
Fax: 740-533-1141
www.mikesarchery.com

Manufactures and distributes wholesale archery equipment to retailers

Catalog Cost: Free
In Business: 45 years

5697 Mountain Archery
Mountain Archery
2630 S. 2000 W.
PO Box 67
Rexburg, ID 83440   877-745-9286
Fax: 208-656-8988
info.mtnarchery@gmail.com
www.mountain-archery.com

Archery equipment.

President: Gordon Smith
mtnarchery@cs.com
Director: Gordon Smith
Customer Service / Sales: Rashelle Schneiter
sales.mtnarchery@gmail.com
Contact: Hank Grover

5698 Neet Archery
Neet Products, Inc.
5875 East Highway 50
Sedalia, MD 65301   660-826-6762
Fax: 660-826-4942
neet@neet.com
www.neetarcheryproducts.com

Quivers, rigs, gloves, tabs, armguards, bow cases and accessories

5699 Parker Bows
Parker Bows
3022 Lee Jackson Hwy
Staunton, VA 24401   540-337-5426
Fax: 540-337-0887
www.parkerbows.com

Crossbows, Compound bows and bow accessories, made in America

5700 RedHead Archery
Bass Pro Shops
2500 E Kearney
Springfield, MO 65898   417-873-5000
800-227-7776
Fax: 417-873-5060
www.basspro.com

Bows, arrows and accessories, treestands, optics, scents, feeders, targets, blinds, rugged hunting boots, camo and more.

President & CEO: James Hagale
Catalog Cost: Free
Printing Information: 148 pages in 4 colors
In Business: 45 years
Number of Employees: 2200
Sales Volume: $4.45 Billion

5701 Specialty Arch
Specialty Arch, LLC
1211 38th Ave. W.
Spencer, IA 51301   712-580-5762
800-555-2856
Fax: 712-580-2020
technical@specialtyarch.com
www.specialtyarch.com

Archery sights

5702 Specialty Archery LLC
Specialty Archery LLC
1211 38th Avenue West
Spencer, IA 51301   712-580-5762
800-555-2856
Fax: 712-580-2020
technical@specialtyarch.com
www.specialtyarch.com

Archery products that are dependable, innovative, and reliable.

5703 Sure-Loc
CS Gibbs Corporation
1230 Poplar Avenue
Superior, WI 54880   877-322-9988
Fax: 715-395-9959
support@sureloc.com
www.sureloc.com

Archers gear, targets, sights, scopes, accessories, bows and presses

President: Dianne Gibbs
Catalog Cost: Free
Printing Information: 32 pages

5704 TenPoint Crossbows
TenPoint Crossbows
1325 Waterloo Road
Mogadore, OH 44260   330-628-9245
www.tenpointcrossbows.com

Crossbows and crossbow accessories

President: Richard L. Bednar
Director of Sales & Service: Randy Wood
Service Manager: Bryan Zabitski
Customer Service Supervisor: Amber Vandegrift

Credit Cards: AMEX; MasterCard
Catalog Cost: Free
Catalog Circulation: Mailed 1 time(s) per year
Printing Information: 31 pages in 4 colors
In Business: 23 years

5705 The Bohning Company
The Bohning Company Ltd.
7361 N. Seven Mile Rd.
Lake City, MI 49651   231-229-4247
                      Fax: 231-229-4615
                      info@bohning.com
                      www.bohning.com

Archery supplies and equipment

5706 Tru-Fire
Tru-Fire
217 E. Larsen Dr
N Fond Du Lac, WI 54937-1572 920-923-6866
                      Fax: 920-923-4051
                      score@feradyne.com
                      www.trufire.com

Releases and broadhead arrows
President: Steve Tentler
Catalog Cost: Free
Sales Volume: $5MM to $10MM

5707 Valley Traditional Archery
Valley Traditional Archery Supply, Inc.
30 Sunrise Blvd. Silt
Colorado, CO 81652   970-319-4252
                      Fax: 970-319-4252
                      vtas@valleytradarchery.com
                      www.valleytradarchery.com

Archery equipment.

Baseball

5708 American Athletic
American Athletic
200 American Ave
Jefferson, IA 50129-2800   515-386-3125
                      800-247-3978
                      Fax: 515-386-4566
                      contact@americanathletic.com
                      www.americanathletic.com

Baseball training equipment
President: Jeff Bramble
CFO: Erwin Johnson
Marketing Manager: Tara Meier
In Business: 61 years
Number of Employees: 160
Sales Volume: $10MM to $20MM

5709 BSN Sports Baseball-Fastpitch
BSN Sports
PO Box 7726
Dallas, TX 75209   800-856-3488
                      Fax: 800-899-0149
                      www.bsnsports.com

Team sports apparel and equipment.
Chair & CEO: Adam Blumenfeld
President, COO & General Counsel: Terry Babilla
Catalog Cost: Free
Printing Information: 136 pages in 4 colors
In Business: 44 years
Number of Employees: 1200
Sales Volume: $500 Million

5710 Baseball Direct
Baseball Direct
PO Box 7563
Charlottesville, VA 22906   800-558-6273
                      888-244-8837
                      Fax: 434-974-4986
                      baseball@cstone.net
                      www.baseballdirect.com

Baseball video tapes, books, CDs, DVDs, audio tapes, calendars and other nostalgic collectibles

President: Reuben Holden
Credit Cards: MasterCard; Visa
Catalog Cost: Free

5711 Baseball, Softball, Football Superstore
Baseball Express
5750 Northwest Parkway
Suite 100
San Antonio, TX 78249-3374   210-348-7000
                      800-937-4824
                      Fax: 210-525-9339
                      customer.service@teamexpress.com
                      www.baseballexpress.com

Footwear, apparel, accessories, uniforms and more
President: Pat Cawles
CFO: Geoff Westmoreland
VP Sales and Marketing: Dale Fujimoto
Credit Cards: AMEX; MasterCard
Catalog Cost: Free
Catalog Circulation: Mailed 3 time(s) per year
Printing Information: 84 pages in 4 colors
Binding: Perfect Bound
In Business: 25 years
Number of Employees: 7
Sales Volume: Under $500,000

5712 OnDeck Sports
OnDeck Sports
88 Spark St.
Brockton, MA 00230   800-365-6171
                      Fax: 508-580-0211
                      info@ondecksports.com
                      www.ondecksports.com

Netting, artificial turf, baseball equipment, batting cages and portable pitching mounds.

5713 Roger's USA
Rogers Sports Group
130 Market Place
Suite 287
San Ramon, CA 94583-346   925-999-9560
                      800-829-7311
                      Fax: 717-361-8925
                      sales@rogersusainc.com
                      www.rogersbreakawaybase.com

Break Away Base for softball and baseball
President: Roger Hall
Catalog Circulation: to 4000
Printing Information: 4 pages in 2 colors
Number of Employees: 5
Sales Volume: Under $500M

5714 San Sun Hat and Cap Group
Daystone International Corporation
1105 Stevenson Court
Suite 104
Roselle, IL 60172   630-295-8100
                      800-323-2360
                      Fax: 630-295-8110
                      chi@daystone.com
                      www.daystone.com

Baseball, golf, caps, tote bags and umbrellas
President: Sheng T Day
CFO: Pei Ling Yang
Executive Vice President Engineerin: Showy Perry
Credit Cards: MasterCard
Catalog Cost: Free
Catalog Circulation: to 40000
Printing Information: 44 pages in 3 colors on Matte Stock
Press: Letterpress
Binding: Saddle Stitched
In Business: 32 years
Number of Employees: 6
Sales Volume: $3MM to $5MM

5715 Stackhouse Athletic Equipment
PO Box 12276
Salem, OR 97309   503-363-1840
                      800-285-3604
                      Fax: 503-363-0511
                      www.stackhouseathletic.com

Athletic equipment

5716 Super-Net
3209 Air Park Road
Fuquay - Varina, NC 27526   919-567-3737
                      800-955-6387
                      Fax: 919-567-1144
                      info@supernetusa.com
                      www.supernetsusa.com

Netting for sports, volleyball, tennis

Bicycling

5717 American Cycle Express
American Cycle Express
275 Floral Ave
Johnson City, NY 13790   607-797-2700
                      Fax: 607-785-3514
                      sales@americancycle.com
                      www.americancycle.com

Bike parts, frames and accessories
President: Jalal Zuwiyya
Credit Cards: AMEX; MasterCard
Printing Information: 24 pages
Mailing List Information: Names for rent
Number of Employees: 10
Sales Volume: $490,000

5718 Bike Nashbar
Bike Nashbar
PO Box 1455
Crab Orchard, WV 25827   800-627-4227
                      877-688-8600
                      Fax: 877-778-9456
                      customerservice@bikenashbar.com
                      www.nashbar.com

Bicycling supplies and apparel
In Business: 42 years
Number of Employees: 2
Sales Volume: $90,000+

5719 Burley Design Cooperative
Burley Design Cooperative
1500 Westec Drive
Eugene, OR 97402-5408   541-687-1644
                      800-311-5294
                      Fax: 541-687-0436
                      burley@burley.com
                      www.burley.com

Tandem bicycles
President: Matt Pervis
Printing Information: 52 pages
Number of Employees: 97
Sales Volume: $10MM to $20MM

5720 Cambria Bicycle Outfitter
CBO, Inc
1422 Monterey Street
San Luis Obispo, CA 93401-3020 805-543-1148
                      888-937-4331
                      Fax: 805-927-5174
                      info@cambriabike.com
                      www.cambriabike.com

Road and Mountain bikes, parts and accessories
President: Steve Fleury
Credit Cards: MasterCard
Catalog Cost: Free
Catalog Circulation: Mailed 12 time(s) per year
Printing Information: on Glossy Stock
Mailing List Information: Names for rent
In Business: 27 years
Sales Volume: $500M to $1MM

5721 CycloSource
Adventure Cycling Association
150 East Pine Street
PO Box 8308
Missoula, MT 59807
406-721-1776
800-755-2453
Fax: 406-721-8754
info@adventurecycling.org
www.adventurecycling.org

Bicycles and accessories for bicycle riders

President: Wally Werner
Marketing Manager: Teri Maloughney
Executive Director: Jim Sayer
VP: Donna O'Neal
Treasurer: Andrew Huppert
In Business: 42 years

5722 Cyclosource
Adventure Cycling Association
150 East Pine Street
PO Box 8308
Missoula, MT 59807-4515
406-721-1776
800-755-2453
Fax: 406-721-8754
info@adventurecycling.org
www.adventurecycling.org

Bicycling touring maps and books

President: Wally Werner
CFO: Sheila Snyder
Marketing Manager: Teri Maloughney
Production Manager: Dan D'Ambrosio
Executive Director: Jim Sayer
VP: Donna O'Neal
Treasurer: Andrew Huppert
Credit Cards: MasterCard; Visa
Average Order Size: $65
Printing Information: 32 pages in 4 colors on Glossy Stock
Press: Sheetfed Press
Binding: Saddle Stitched
Mailing List Information: Names for rent
In Business: 42 years
Number of Employees: 28
Sales Volume: $3,000,000+

5723 Frankford Bicycle
Frankford Bicycle
964 N State St
Girard, OH 44420-1788
330-545-0392
800-621-3593
Fax: 330-545-0391
sales@frankfordbike.com
www.Frankfordbike.Com

Bicycle parts and accessories

President: Paul Frankford
Credit Cards: MasterCard
Catalog Cost: Free
Number of Employees: 4
Sales Volume: $1MM to $3MM

5724 Free Agent BMX
2840 E. Harcourt St.
Rancho Dominguez, CA 90221
310-632-7173
info@freeagentbmx.com
www.freeagentbmx.com

Biking and BMX gear

5725 HED Cycling Products
1665 9th Street
White Bear Lake, MN 55110-6717 888-246-3639
Fax: 651-653-0275
info@hedcycling.com
www.analyticcycling.com

Cycling products

5726 HMC
REI
Department N7100
Sumner, WA 98352-1
253-891-2500
800-426-4840
Fax: 253-891-2523
www.rei.com

Gear and clothing for cycling, hiking, camping and more

Chairman: John Hamlin
President: Jerry Stritzke
Vice Chair: Cheryl Scott
Catalog Cost: Free
Number of Employees: 350

5727 Hawk Racing
6060 28th Street East Unit 5
Bradenton, FL 34203-3660
941-209-1790
Fax: 888-799-8792
www.hawk-racing.com

Bike equipment

President: Jack Doherty
Number of Employees: 2
Sales Volume: $500M to $1MM

5728 Just Two Bikes
JTB, Inc.
1785 Stillwater St.
White Bear Lake, MN 55110
651-426-1548
800-499-1548
Fax: 651-653-9444

Lycra bicycle riding clothing

President: Julie Olson
Credit Cards: MasterCard; Visa
Printing Information: 3 pages
Number of Employees: 3
Sales Volume: 1MM-3MM

5729 KHS Bicycles
2840 E. Harcourt St.
Rancho Dominguez, CA 90221
310-632-7173
khsbicycles.com

Bicycles

5730 Lone Peak Designs
Lone Peak Designs
7225 78th Dr. NE
Marysville, WA 98270-3000
801-272-5217
800-777-7679
Fax: 801-272-5240
lonepeakpack@hotmail.com
www.Lonepeakpacks.Com

Bicycling bags and accessories

President: Scott R Sterrett
Production Manager: John Kramer
Credit Cards: MasterCard; Visa
Catalog Circulation: Mailed 1 time(s) per year to 500
Printing Information: 8 pages in 4 colors on Glossy Stock
Press: Letterpress
Binding: Folded
In Business: 35 years
Number of Employees: 22
Sales Volume: $3MM to $5MM

5731 Loose Screws Bicycle Small Parts
Loose Screws Bicycle Small Parts
12225 Highway 66
Ashland, OR 97520-9421
541-488-4800
Fax: 541-482-0080
ctp.inc2@gmail.com
www.loosescrews.com

10,000+ small parts to fix bicycles

President: Jeff Gilmore
Marketing Manager: Jeff Gilmore
Credit Cards: MasterCard; Visa
Catalog Cost: $3
Catalog Circulation: Mailed 1 time(s) per year to 50000
Average Order Size: $76
Printing Information: 152 pages in 2 colors on Newsprint
Press: Web Press
Binding: Saddle Stitched
Mailing List Information: Names for rent
List Manager: Jeff Gilmore
In Business: 8 years
Number of Employees: 8
Sales Volume: Under $500M

5732 O'Neal Azonic
O'Neal
5401 Tech Circle
Moorpark, CA 93021
805-426-3300
Fax: 805-426-3301
tech@oneal.com
www.oneal.com

Bicycling, racing equipment

President: Jim O'Neal
Sponsorship Director: Marc Shaer
Printing Information: 154 pages in 4 colors
Sales Volume: $20MM to $50MM

5733 Performance Bicycle
Performance Bike
PO Box 2741
Chapel Hill, NC 27515
800-727-2433
800-727-2453
Fax: 304-683-2001
customerservice@performanceinc.com
www.performancebike.com

Bicycles, bicycling gear and accessories

President: Garry Snook
Marketing Manager: Sharon Snook
Credit Cards: AMEX; MasterCard
In Business: 33 years

5734 Price Point Bicycle
Price Point
1442 W Walnut Parkway
Rancho Dominguez, CA 90220-2216
310-323-3473
800-774-2376
Fax: 800-888-3294
custservice@pricepoint.com
www.Pricepoint.Com

Bicycles, clothing, parts, frames and more

President: Avi Ivan
Catalog Cost: Free
Printing Information: 60 pages in 4 colors on Glossy Stock
Press: Web Press
Binding: Saddle Stitched
Mailing List Information: Names for rent
In Business: 20 years
Number of Employees: 30
Sales Volume: $500M to $1MM

5735 Rans Recumbents
Rans Designs,Inc
4600 Highway 183 Alternate
Hays, KS 67601
785-625-6346
Fax: 785-625-2795
michele@rans.com
www.rans.com

Recumbent bicycles and tandem hybrid bikes

President: Paula Schlitter
Production Manager: Jack Poliska
OFFICE MANAGER & SALES: Michele Shelly Miller
PURCHASING: Lisa Hendershott
AIRCRAFT SALES: Randy Schlitter
Catalog Cost: Free
Catalog Circulation: to 1000
Printing Information: 30 pages in 5 colors on Glossy Stock
Binding: Folded
In Business: 20 years

5736 Tandems, Ltd
Tandems Limited
2220 Vanessa Dr
Birmingham, AL 35242-4430
205-991-5519
Fax: 205-991-7766
info@tandemsltd.com
www.tandemsltd.com

Tandems, tandem parts and accessories, and recumbents

President: Jack Goertz
In Business: 23 years
Sales Volume: Under $500M

5737 White Brothers
Vance & Hines
24845 Corbit Pl
Yorba Linda, CA 92887-5533 562-921-7461
Fax: 714-692-3409
sdarrow@vanceandhines.com
www.whitebros.com

Parts and accessories for atv, and mx bikes
Catalog Cost: Free
Printing Information: 20 pages
Number of Employees: 175

5738 Yeti Cycles
Yeti Cycles
621 Corporate Circle
Golden, CO 80401 303-278-6909
888-576-9384
info@yeticycles.com
www.yeticycles.com

Mountain bikes
President: Chris Conroy
Catalog Cost: Free
Number of Employees: 35
Sales Volume: 5MM-10MM

Fencing

5739 American Fencers Supply
American Fencers Supply
P.O. Box 336
Pacifica, CA 94044 650-359-7911
Fax: 650-359-7913
www.amfence.com

Fencing supplies, clothing and equipment
President: Matthew Porter
Credit Cards: AMEX; MasterCard
Catalog Circulation: Mailed 1 time(s) per year
Printing Information: 20 pages in 4 colors on Glossy Stock
Press: Web Press
Binding: Saddle Stitched
In Business: 50 years
Number of Employees: 8

5740 Fence PBT
fencePBT.com, Inc.
2732 Picardy Place
Charlotte, NC 28209 800-422-4728
Fax: 704-625-3677
sales@fencepbt.com

PBT fencing equipment.
Contact: Peter Zay
peter@fencePBT.com

5741 Zivkovic Modern Equipment
Zivkovic Modern Fencing Equipment, Inc.
77 Arnold Rd
Wellesley Hills, MA 02481-2820 781-235-3324
Fax: 781-239-1224
bzivkovic@zivkovic.com
www.Zivkovic.Com

Fencing equipment
President: Branimir Zivkovic
Printing Information: 51 pages
Number of Employees: 10-J
Sales Volume: Under $500M

Golf

5742 Buggies Unlimited
Buggies Unlimited
3510 Port Jacksonville Pkwy
Jacksonville, FL 32226 888-444-9994
Fax: 888-444-6364
support@buggiesunlimited.com
www.buggiesunlimited.com

Golf cart parts and accessories
Catalog Cost: Free

5743 CSG
CSG
116 East Nora
Spokane, WA 99207-2334 509-325-5905
800-597-5241
Fax: 509-232-0474
sales@csggolf.com
www.csggolf.com

Custom made and component golf clubs
President: Dave Clarke
In Business: 24 years
Sales Volume: Under $500M

5744 Cobra Golf
Cobra Puma Golf
1818 Aston Avenue
Carlsbad, CA 92008-7306 760-710-3500
800-917-3300
customerservice@cobragolf.com
www.cobragolf.com

King Cobra golf products
President: Robert Dubiel
Credit Cards: AMEX; MasterCard; Visa
Catalog Circulation: Mailed 1 time(s) per year
Printing Information: 52 pages in 4 colors
In Business: 44 years
Number of Employees: 210
Sales Volume: $20MM to $50MM

5745 Component Golf Supplies
CSG, INC.
116 East Nora
Spokane, WA 99207-2334 800-597-5241
Fax: 509-232-0474
sales@csggolf.com
www.csggolf.com

Golf accessories

5746 Diamond Tour Golf
Diamond Tour Golf
203 E Lincoln Hwy
Dekalb, IL 60115-3206 815-787-2649
800-826-5340
Fax: 815-787-3720
sales@diamondtour.com
www.diamondtour.com

Golf accessories
President: Jason Hiland
CFO: Sean Ebert
Marketing Manager: Brandon Wilden
Production Manager: Dan Back
Director, Internet Development: John Davis
Sales Manager: Jeff Bushnell
Credit Cards: AMEX; MasterCard
Printing Information: 35 pages on Glossy Stock
Binding: Folded
In Business: 20 years
Sales Volume: $210,000

5747 Everything Carts
Everything Carts
3510-1 Port Jacksonville Pkwy
Jacksonville, FL 32226 888-312-7342
Fax: 800-676-0789
contact@everythingcarts.com
www.everythingcarts.com

Golf carts, parts and accessories

5748 Golf Around the World
Golf Around the World
1396 N Killian Drive
Ste B / Bay 1
West Palm Beach, FL 33403-1924 561-848-8896
800-367-4279
Fax: 561-848-8896
orders@golftrainingaids.com
www.golftrainingaids.com

Golf training products
President: Dr. Gary Wiren
CFO: George Robins

Credit Cards: AMEX; MasterCard
Catalog Cost: Free
Printing Information: in 4 colors
Mailing List Information: Names for rent
In Business: 25 years
Number of Employees: 8
Sales Volume: $500M to $1MM

5749 Golf Haus
700 N Pennsylvania Ave
Lansing, MI 48906-5319 517-482-8842
Fax: 517-482-8843

Pro-Line golf clubs and accessories at discounted prices
President: Jim Hornberger
Credit Cards: MasterCard; Visa
Catalog Cost: Free
Average Order Size: $300
Printing Information: 5 pages in 1 color on Newsprint
Press: Letterpress
Mailing List Information: Names for rent
Number of Employees: 6
Sales Volume: $500M to $1MM

5750 Golf Warehouse
The Golf Warehouse
8833 E 34th Street N
Wichita, KS 67226 316-858-0470
888-838-5551
Fax: 316-838-5557
cs@tgw.com
www.tgw.com

Golf clubs, golf balls, golf bags, golf shoes, sports apparel and accessories
President: R Marney
CFO: Marie Daley
Credit Cards: AMEX; MasterCard
Catalog Cost: Free
In Business: 12 years
Number of Employees: 225
Sales Volume: $13 Million

5751 Golf Works
The GolfWorks
4820 Jacksontown Road
Newark, OH 43058-3008 740-328-4200
800-848-8358
Fax: 800-800-3290
golfworks@golfworks.com
www.golfworks.com

Golf equipment
President: Mark McCormick
Credit Cards: AMEX; MasterCard
Catalog Circulation: Mailed 1 time(s) per year
Printing Information: 227 pages in 4 colors
In Business: 40 years
Number of Employees: 175
Sales Volume: 20MM-50MM

5752 Golfpac Golf Tours
Golfpac
PO Box 162366
483 Montgomery Place
Altamonte Springs, FL 32716-2366407-260-2288
888-848-8941
Fax: 407-260-8989
info@golfpactravel.com
www.golfpactravel.com

Golf trip packages for businesses
President: Jeff Hamilton
Credit Cards: AMEX; MasterCard
Catalog Cost: Free
Catalog Circulation: Mailed 1 time(s) per year to 30000
Printing Information: 56 pages in 4 colors
Binding: Saddle Stitched
In Business: 39 years
Number of Employees: 30

5753 Golfsmart
13100 Grass Valley Avenue
Grass Valley, CA 95945-9041   530-272-1422
Fax: 530-272-2133

Sporting goods supplies relating to golf
President: Guthrie Kraut

5754 Golfsmith Store
Golf Smith International
11000 N i H 35
Austin, TX 78753-3195   512-837-1810
800-813-6897
Fax: 512-837-1245
comments@golfsmith.com
www.golfsmith.com

Golfing equipment, apparel and accessories
President: Jim Thompson
CFO: Virgina Bunte
Marketing Manager: Lisa Zoellner
Production Manager: Ken Brugh
Buyers: Mickey Uhlaender, Books/Tapes
Susan Shade, Apparel
Jim Thompson, Giftware
Credit Cards: AMEX; MasterCard
Catalog Cost: Free
Catalog Circulation: Mailed 14 time(s) per
year
Average Order Size: $120
Printing Information: 68 pages in 4 colors on
Matte Stock
Press: Web Press
Mailing List Information: Names for rent
In Business: 40 years
Number of Employees: 1300
Sales Volume: $1MM to $3MM

5755 Heard Golf Academy
7800 Whipple Avenue NW
North Canton, OH 44767   330-494-5504
Fax: 330-497-6847

Golf equipment and supplies
President: Benjamin Suarez

5756 Highlander Golf
Highlander Logo Corp.
1072 Jacoby Road
Akron, OH 44321   330-666-6748
Fax: 330-666-4525
lobly@corporateimageworks.com

Golf supplies and equipment
President: Tom Deighan
Marketing Manager: Timothy Deighan

5757 Hireko Golf Products
Hireko Trading Company, Inc
16185 Stephens Street
City of Industry, CA 91745-1718   626-330-5525
800-367-8912
Fax: 626-330-5729
support@hirekogolf.com
www.Hirekogolf.Com

Golf club making components and accessories
President: Gloria Lin
Catalog Cost: Free
Catalog Circulation: Mailed 1 time(s) per year
Printing Information: 152 pages
Number of Employees: 75
Sales Volume: 5MM-10MM

5758 Lefties Only
Lefties Only
1972 Williston Road
P.O. Box 3264
South Burlington, VT 05403-6041   802-862-1114
800-LEF-TIES
Fax: 802-864-7701
leftiesonlygolf@msn.com
www.Leftiesonlygolf.Com

**Golf products, equipment and gifts for left
hand golfers**

President: Walter Tripovich
International Marketing Manager: Walt
Trapovich
Buyers: Walt Triprovich
Credit Cards: MasterCard
Catalog Cost: Free
Catalog Circulation: Mailed 5 time(s) per year
Average Order Size: $170
Printing Information: 4 pages in 1 color on
Matte Stock
Press: Web Press
Binding: Folded
Mailing List Information: Names for rent
In Business: 19 years
Number of Employees: 4
Sales Volume: $500M to $1MM

5759 Lomma Golf
Lomma Enterprises
305 Cherry St
Scranton, PA 18505-1505   570-346-5555
Fax: 570-346-5580
info@lommagolf.com
www.lommagolf.com

Golf equipment and accessories
President: R J Lomma
Catalog Cost: Free
Mailing List Information: Names for rent
In Business: 60 years
Sales Volume: $500M to $1MM

5760 Monark Golf Supply
Monark Golf Supply Inc.
P.O. Box 1263
Walnut, CA 91788-1263   909-598-5443
877-551-4653
Fax: 909-598-5444
monark@aol.com
www.monarkgolf.com

**Golf club components, custom golf clubs
and golf accessories.**
In Business: 17 years

5761 Par Aide
Par Aide Product Company
6800 Otter Lake Rd
Lino Lake, MN 55038   888-893-2433
Fax: 651-429-4519
www.paraide.com

Golfand golf course equipment.

5762 Par-Buster
Parbuster Inc.
1209 E 3rd St
Tulsa, OK 74120-2605   918-585-8542
800-933-6387
Fax: 918-585-8580
sales@parbuster.com
www.Parbuster.Com

Golf equipment
President: Catherine Nickels
In Business: 52 years
Number of Employees: 10
Sales Volume: $740,000

5763 Ralph Maltby's GolfWorks
The Golfworks
4820 Jacksontown Road
PO Box 3008
Newark, OH 43058-3008   800-848-8358
Fax: 800-800-3290
golfworks@golfworks.com
www.golfworks.com

**Golf club heads, kits or assembled, grips,
tools, schools and more**
President: Ralph Maltby
Marketing Manager: Steve Gilligan
Production Manager: Todd Humphreys
Catalog Cost: Free
Catalog Circulation: Mailed 4 time(s) per year
Average Order Size: $75
Printing Information: 164 pages in 4 colors on

Glossy Stock
Press: Web Press
Binding: Perfect Bound
Mailing List Information: Names for rent
In Business: 39 years
Number of Employees: 150
Sales Volume: $20MM to $50MM

5764 SGD Golf
SGH Golf Inc.
6805 Mt. Vernon Avenue
Cincinnati, OH 45227   513-984-0414
800-284-8884
Fax: 513-984-9648
sgh@sghgolf.com
www.sghgolf.com

**Planners of major golf events and golf desti-
nations**
President: Ian Jack
Credit Cards: MasterCard
Catalog Circulation: Mailed 1 time(s) per year
to 11K
Printing Information: 76 pages in 3 colors
Press: Web Press
Binding: Saddle Stitched
In Business: 28 years

5765 Turtleson
Turtleson
423-217-4950
888-602-0652
customercare@turtleson.com
www.turtleson.com

Menswear for on and off the golf course

5766 Wittek Golf Supply
Wittek Golf Supply Company Inc.
3865 Commercial Avenue
Northbrook, IL 60062   847-943-2399
800-869-1800
Fax: 847-412-9591
info@wittekgolf.com
www.wittekgolf.com

**Manufacturer and distributor of driving
range equipment, golf couse accessories,
display fixtures and miniature golf supplies.**

Gymnastics

5767 Gibson Athletic
4912 Lima St.
Denver, CO 80239   303-937-1012
800-275-5999
Fax: 303-937-1049
info@gibsonathletic.com
www.gibsonathletic.com

**Gymnastics, cheer, dance and fitness equip-
ment**

5768 Hasty Awards Gymnastics
1015 Enterprise St
Ottawa, KS 66067   785-242-5297
800-448-7714
www.hastyawards.com

Awards for all sports and age groups

5769 Jaypro Sports
Jaypro Corporation, LLC
976 Hartford Turnpike
Waterford, CT 06385-4037   860-447-3001
800-243-0533
Fax: 860-444-1779
info@jaypro.com
www.jaypro.com

**Sporting equipment for volleyball, soccer,
baseball, lacrosse, field hockey, football,
tennis and physical education**
President: Robert Ferrara
Marketing Manager: David Stumpo
Catalog Cost: Free
Catalog Circulation: Mailed 1 time(s) per year

to 5M
Printing Information: 128 pages in 4 colors on Glossy Stock
Press: Web Press
Binding: Perfect Bound
In Business: 60 years
Number of Employees: 60
Sales Volume: $10MM to $20MM

5770 Midwest Gym Supply
Midwest Gym Supply
775 Scott Court
Madison, IN 47250-1829   812-265-4099
                                 800-876-3194
                            Fax: 812-273-4875
                  www.midwestgymsupply.com

Floor systems and uneven bars

President: Paul Kemp
Credit Cards: MasterCard; Visa
In Business: 26 years
Number of Employees: 2
Sales Volume: $1MM to $3MM

5771 Rage Fitness Supply
4912 Lima Street
Denver, CO 80239   720-257-7769
                                 877-660-7243
                            Fax: 303-937-1049
                       info@ragefitness.com
                       www.ragefitness.com

Fitness equipment and supplies

5772 Ten.o
GMR Gymnastics Sales
6729 Marbut Rd.
Lithonia, GA 30058   800-241-9249
                            Fax: 800-243-2556
                            www.ten-o.com

Equipment and products for gymnastics

5773 Tiffin Athletic Mats
Tiffin Athletic Mats
PO Box 823
Elkton, MD 21922-823   800-843-3467
                            Fax: 410-398-7397
             customer_service@tiffinmats.com
                       www.tiffinmats.com

Athletic mats

Catalog Cost: Free
Catalog Circulation: Mailed 2 time(s) per year
In Business: 35 years
Number of Employees: 15
Sales Volume: 1MM

Hockey

5774 Action Sports Systems
Action Sports Systems Inc
PO Box 1442
Morganton, NC 28680-1442   828-584-8000
                                 800-631-1091
                            Fax: 828-584-8440
                 sales@actionsportsuniforms.com
                     actionsportsuniforms.com

Hockey uniforms, nets and leg guards

President: Nand Thapar
Credit Cards: AMEX; MasterCard
In Business: 34 years
Number of Employees: 20
Sales Volume: $1,200,000

5775 Great Skate Hockey Supply Company
Great Skate Hockey Supply Co.
3395 Sheridan Dr
Amherst, NY 14226-1543   716-838-5100
                                 800-828-7496
                            Fax: 716-838-5123
                       www.Greatskate.Com

Hockey equipment

President: Tom Farkas
Credit Cards: MasterCard; Visa

Catalog Circulation: Mailed 2 time(s) per year
Printing Information: 70 pages in 4 colors on Glossy Stock
Press: Web Press
Binding: Saddle Stitched
Number of Employees: 20
Sales Volume: $3MM to $5MM

5776 Longstreth
PO Box 475
28 Wells Road
Parker Ford, PA 19457   610-495-7022
                                 800-545-1329
                            Fax: 610-495-7023
                 generalinfo@longstreth.com
                     www.longstreth.com

Hockey and lacrosse products

5777 Maska USA
PO Box 381
Bradford, VT 05033-381   802-222-4751
                                 800-232-9226
                            Fax: 800-232-9226
                       www.ccmsports.com

Guards, pads, helmets and accessories

President: Matt O'Toole
Credit Cards: MasterCard; Visa
Catalog Circulation: Mailed 1 time(s) per year
Printing Information: 50 pages
In Business: 13 years
Number of Employees: 50
Sales Volume: $20MM to $50MM

5778 Ocean Hockey Supply Company
Ocean Hockey Supply Co.
197 Chambersbridge Rd
Brick, NJ 08723-3492   732-477-4411
                                 800-631-2159
                            Fax: 732-477-1167
                     info@oceanhockey.com
                     www.Oceanhockey.Com

Hockey equipment

President: Betty Smith
Credit Cards: MasterCard; Visa
In Business: 53 years
Number of Employees: 25
Sales Volume: $3MM to $5MM

Horseback Riding

5779 Back In The Saddle
Back In The Saddle
P.O. Box 3336
Chelmsford, MA 00182-0936   877-756-5068
                                 800-865-2478
                            Fax: 800-866-3235
                 help@BackInTheSaddle.com
                     www.backinthesaddle.com

Horseback riding gear, clothing, jewelry, and accessories for   horse lovers

Catalog Cost: Free
In Business: 22 years

5780 Big Sky Leatherworks
Big Sky Leatherworks
5421 US Hwy 93
Suite 3
Jerome, ID 83338-4946   541-672-4951
                                 800-488-0938
                 info@bigskyleatherworks.com
                     www.Bigskyleatherworks.Com

Leather supplies for horses

President: Beverly Huffman
Catalog Cost: $3
Printing Information: 22 pages
In Business: 35 years
Number of Employees: 10-J
Sales Volume: $130,000

5781 Casa Zia Saddlery
6935 Commerce
El Paso, TX 79915   800-750-5940
                     info@casaziasaddlery.com
                     www.casaziasaddlery.com

Saddles and horse accessories and products

General Manager: Luc Wells

5782 Chamisa Ridge
Chamisa Ridge, Inc.
PO Box 2858
Santa Fe, NM 87504   505-438-4811
                                 800-743-3188
                            Fax: 505-438-8205
                       www.chamisaridge.com

Featuring Hilton Herbs, books, audios, videos and accessories for horseback riders

President: David Kuncicky
Credit Cards: MasterCard; Visa
Catalog Cost: Free
Catalog Circulation: Mailed 5 time(s) per year
Printing Information: 40 pages in 4 colors on Glossy Stock
Press: Web Press
Binding: Perfect Bound
Mailing List Information: Names for rent
In Business: 8 years
Number of Employees: 7
Sales Volume: $1,800,000

5783 Chick's Harness & Supply
Chick Harness & Supply, Inc.
18011 South Dupont Highway
Harrington, DE 19952-59   302-398-4630
                                 800-444-2441
                            Fax: 302-398-3920
                 saddles@chicksaddlery.com
                     www.chicksaddlery.com

English and Western saddlery, tack horse supplies, riding clothing and gifts

President: Frank Chick
Marketing Manager: Bob Fleming
Credit Cards: MasterCard
Catalog Cost: Free
Catalog Circulation: Mailed 3 time(s) per year to 300K
Average Order Size: $100
Printing Information: 72 pages in 4 colors on Glossy Stock
Press: Web Press
Binding: Saddle Stitched
Mailing List Information: Names for rent
In Business: 42 years
Number of Employees: 50
Sales Volume: $3MM to $5MM

5784 Down Under Saddle Supply
2250 Airport Blvd.
#300
Aurora, CO 80011   720-975-9290
                                 800-395-8225
                            Fax: 720-975-9295
                     info@downunderweb.com
                     www.downunderweb.com

Saddles and other products for horses

5785 Horse Catalog
American Livestock Supply
4602 Domain Drive
Menomonie, WI 54751   608-223-3232
                                 800-356-0700
                            Fax: 608-223-3223
                 info@americanlivestock.com
                     www.americanlivestock.com

Horse and pet related products

President: Mary Bohne
mary.bohne@americanlivestock.com
Credit Cards: AMEX; MasterCard
Catalog Cost: Free
In Business: 43 years
Sales Volume: $1MM to $3MM

5786 Horse Lover's Gift Guide
Equestrian Enterprise Inc
204 Mayflower Drive
Woodstock, GA 30188   800-767-1452
Fax: 770-591-0199
info@horseloversgifts.com
www.horseloversgifts.com

Complete line of gifts for horse lovers

President: Ana Maria Collantes
Catalog Cost: $2
Catalog Circulation: Mailed 2 time(s) per year
Printing Information: 40 pages
Press: Web Press
Binding: Folded
Mailing List Information: Names for rent
204 Mayflower Dr.
Woodstock, GA 30188
In Business: 27 years
Number of Employees: 4
Sales Volume: $20MM to $50MM

5787 Horse Supply Catalog
American Livestock and Pet Supply
4602 Domain Drive
Menomonie, WI 54751   608-223-3232
800-356-0700
Fax: 608-223-3223
www.americanlivestock.com

Horse related products

President: Michael J Ripp, VP
Credit Cards: MasterCard
Catalog Cost: Free
Catalog Circulation: Mailed 4 time(s) per year
Printing Information: 60 pages in 4 colors
Binding: Saddle Stitched
In Business: 43 years

5788 Justin Carriage Works
Justin Carriage Works
7615 Michigan 66
Nashville, MI 49073-336   517-852-9743
Fax: 517-852-9743
www.Buggy.Com

Carriage parts and accessories

President: Roxie Andler
Catalog Cost: $5
Catalog Circulation: Mailed 1 time(s) per year
to 2000
Printing Information: 10 pages in 4 colors
Number of Employees: 5
Sales Volume: $1MM to $3MM

5789 New Miller Harness
Miller Harness Company L.L.C.
PO Box 406
Westford, MA 01886   201-460-1200
800-784-5831
Fax: 201-460-1200
www.millerharness.com

Saddlery, riding clothing, stable supplies, and saddles

President: Mike Burge
CFO: Dennis L Norman
Marketing Manager: Laurie Cerney
Production Manager: Thomas Fenwick
Buyers: ME Norman
P Norman
Credit Cards: AMEX; MasterCard; Visa
Catalog Cost: $5
Catalog Circulation: Mailed 1 time(s) per year
to 20000
Printing Information: 160 pages in 4 colors on
Glossy Stock
Press: Web Press
Binding: Saddle Stitched
Number of Employees: 50
Sales Volume: $5MM to $10MM

5790 Ortho-Flex Saddles
Ortho-Flex, LLC
815 East Commerce Street
Lewisburg, TN 37091   423-949-1035
800-251-3474
Fax: 423-949-1035
nbs@nationalbridle.com
www.ortho-flex.com

Various models of saddles as well as tack and accessories

President: Acie Johnson
CEO: Bobby Beech
Catalog Cost: Free
Printing Information: 8 pages in 4 colors on
Glossy Stock
Number of Employees: 80

5791 Personalized Products
Personalized Products
625 W Sumner St
Suite 100
Hartford, WI 53027-1403   262-673-6300
800-431-5257
Fax: 262-673-6707
info@pphorse.com
www.Pphorse.Com

Equipment and apparel for equine, canine and human

President: Curtis Gunst
Catalog Circulation: to 60000
Number of Employees: 11
Sales Volume: $920,000

5792 State Line Tack
State Line Talk
626 CAN DO Expressway
Suite 1
Hazle Township, PA 18202-9790   570-384-7656
888-809-0751
Fax: 570-384-2500
customerservice@statelinetack.com
www.Statelinetack.Com

Stable gear, harnesses

Chairman: Samuel Parker
President: Dover Saddlery
Credit Cards: AMEX; MasterCard; Visa
Catalog Circulation: Mailed 1 time(s) per year
Printing Information: in 4 colors on Glossy
Stock
Press: Web Press
Binding: Perfect Bound
In Business: 47 years
Number of Employees: 160

5793 Western Fashions & Gifts
Rod's Western Place
3099 Silver Dr
Columbus, OH 43224-3945   614-268-8200
866-326-1975
Fax: 614-268-8203
rods@rods.com
www.rods.com

Western apparel, tack and unique western gifts

Chairman: Rod Pressel
CFO: Dan Evans
Credit Cards: MasterCard
Catalog Cost: Free
Catalog Circulation: Mailed 2 time(s) per year
In Business: 20 years

5794 Whip N Spur
14434 North Dale Mabry Highway
Tampa, FL 33618   813-962-6610
800-944-7677
Fax: 813-962-8342
www.whipnspur.com

Products and accessories for horses

Lacrosse

5795 BSN Sports Lacrosse
BSN Sports
PO Box 7726
Dallas, TX 75209   800-856-3488
Fax: 800-899-0149
www.bsnsports.com

Gear, apparel and game equipment.

Chair & CEO: Adam Blumenfeld
President, COO & General Counsel: Terry
Babilla
Catalog Cost: Free
Printing Information: 82 pages in 4 colors
In Business: 44 years
Number of Employees: 1200
Sales Volume: $500 Million

5796 Great Atlantic Lacrosse Company
Sports Endeavors
431 US Highway 70A E
Hillsborough, NC 27278-9334   919-644-6800
800-999-4623
Fax: 919-644-6808
www.lacrosse.com

Lacrosse gear and accessories

President: Char Watson
CFO: Roger Parro
Marketing Manager: Jim Noonan
Buyers: Andy Logan
Credit Cards: AMEX; MasterCard; Visa
Catalog Circulation: to 30000
Printing Information: 60 pages in 4 colors on
Glossy Stock
Binding: Saddle Stitched
In Business: 20 years

5797 Kemp's Hockey Supply Company
Kemp's Hockey Supply Company
704 New Loudon Rd
Latham, NY 12110-4016   518-785-5297
800-223-8571
Fax: 518-785-6027
www.Kempshockey.Com

Street hockey and lacrosse equipment

President: Jerry Kemp
Number of Employees: 20
Sales Volume: $1MM to $3MM

5798 Lacrosse International
Lacrosse International
101 Robbins Road
Downingtown, PA 19335-4068   610-873-1450
800-333-5299
Fax: 610-873-7550
www.Laxzilla.Com

Lacrosse equipment

President: Mike Twohig
Printing Information: in 4 colors
In Business: 35 years
Number of Employees: 12
Sales Volume: $1MM to $3MM

5799 Longstreth
PO Box 475
28 Wells Road
Parker Ford, PA 19457   610-495-7022
800-545-1329
Fax: 610-495-7023
generalinfo@longstreth.com
www.longstreth.com

Hockey and lacrosse products

Martial Arts

5800 **Artistic Video**
Movements of Magic - Healing and Martial
87 Tyler Avenue
Sound Beach, NY 11789-2639   631-744-5999
                                 888-982-4244
                            Fax: 631-744-5993
info@movementsofmagic.com
www.movementsofmagic.com

Martial arts, fitness and environmental videos and alternative healing instructional videos and DVDs, many titles on Tai-Chai and Kung-fu, also the Movements of Magic series of books

President: Bob Klein
Credit Cards: AMEX; MasterCard
Catalog Cost: Free
Catalog Circulation: Mailed 3 time(s) per year to 15000
Printing Information: 32 pages in 4 colors on Matte Stock
Press: Sheetfed Press
Binding: Folded
Mailing List Information: Names for rent
In Business: 21 years
Sales Volume: $400,000

5801 **Bud K Worldwide**
1185 E Nakoma Street
Moultrie, GA 31776   866-246-7164
                        Fax: 877-428-3599
webcs@budk.com
www.budk.com

Producer of swords, bowies, daggers, medieval arms, folding knives, apparel and ninja & martial arts accessories

President: Clint H Kadel

5802 **Century Martial Art Supply**
Century Martial Art Supply, LLC
1000 Century Boulevard
Oklahoma City, OK 73110-7961   405-732-2226
                               800-626-2787
                          Fax: 405-426-4191
customerservice@centurymartialarts.com
www.centurymartialarts.com

Martial arts supplies, including training gear, uniforms, knives

Chairman: Michael Dillard
Marketing Manager: Joy Clymer
Credit Cards: MasterCard; Visa
Catalog Cost: Free
Catalog Circulation: Mailed 1 time(s) per year to 350
Printing Information: 171 pages in 4 colors
In Business: 41 years
Number of Employees: 300
Sales Volume: $59,000,000+

5803 **Competitive Edge Dynamics**
2908 Betz Court
Orefield, PA 18069   610-366-9752
                             888-628-3233
                        Fax: 610-366-9680
info@cedhk.com
www.cedhk.com

Shooting related products

5804 **International Taekwondo Association**
International Taekwondo Association
PO Box 281
Grand Blanc, MI 48480-281   810-232-6482
                        Fax: 810-235-8594
hq@itatkd.com
www.itatkd.com

Taw Kwon Do Korean martial arts videos, books and supplies also Hapkido, Korean sword and weapons videos

President: Dr. James S Benko
Credit Cards: MasterCard; Visa

Catalog Cost: $3
Catalog Circulation: Mailed 4 time(s) per year to 2M
Printing Information: 16 pages in 1 color on Glossy Stock
Press: Web Press
Binding: Saddle Stitched
Mailing List Information: Names for rent
In Business: 40 years
Number of Employees: 3
Sales Volume: Under $500M

5805 **Jukado International**
Jukado International LLC
1230 E Lexington Ave
Pomona, CA 91766-5500   909-591-9344
                             800-535-7573
                        Fax: 909-752-0200
sales@juka.com
www.juka.com

Martial arts clothing and supplies

President: Poku Chan
Credit Cards: AMEX; MasterCard; Visa
Catalog Cost: $2
Printing Information: 24 pages
In Business: 25 years
Number of Employees: 3
Sales Volume: Under $500M

5806 **Ringside**
Ringside, Inc.
15850 W 108th St
Lenexa, KS 66219-1152   913-888-7766
                             877-426-9464
                        Fax: 913-888-2198
www.Ringside.Com

Sports equipment manufacturing

President: John Brown
Marketing Manager: Dave Lubs
Production Manager: Albert Guardado Jr
General Manager: Joe Kelly
Credit Manager: Stan Washington
Credit Cards: MasterCard
Catalog Cost: Free
Catalog Circulation: Mailed 6 time(s) per year to 250m
Printing Information: 200 pages in 4 colors on Glossy Stock
Press: Web Press
Binding: Perfect Bound
Mailing List Information: Names for rent
In Business: 37 years
Number of Employees: 80
Sales Volume: $20MM to $50MM

5807 **S&P of New York Budo**
S&P Budo
6049 Transit Road
Depew, NY 14043-1513   716-681-7911

Martial arts equipment, uniforms, weapons and books

President: Hiroaki Kimura
Marketing Manager: So Kimura
Production Manager: Hiroaki Kimura
Buyers: H Kimura
Credit Cards: AMEX; MasterCard; Visa
Catalog Cost: $1
Catalog Circulation: Mailed 2 time(s) per year to 3000
Printing Information: 30 pages in 3 colors on Newsprint
Press: Web Press
Binding: Saddle Stitched
In Business: 27 years
Number of Employees: 2
Sales Volume: Under $500M

5808 **Ten.o**
GMR Gymnastics Sales
6729 Marbut Rd.
Lithonia, GA 30058   800-241-9249
                        Fax: 800-243-2556
www.ten-o.com

Equipment and products for gymnastics

Mountaineering

5809 **American Alpine Institute**
1515 12th Street
Bellingham, WA 98225   360-671-1505
                             800-424-2249
                        Fax: 360-734-8890
info@alpineinstitute.com
www.alpineinstitute.com

Mountain climbing gear and accessories

President: Dunham Gooding
Director of Adventure Consultant: Guy Cotter

5810 **Big Agnes**
PO Box 773072
735 Oak Street
Steamboat Springs, CO 80487 970-871-1480
                             877-554-8975
                        Fax: 970-879-8038
www.bigagnes.com

Camping equipment and gear

5811 **Black Diamond Equipment**
Black Diamond Equipment
1120 E Nakoma Street
Salt Lake City, UT 84124-1723 801-278-5552
                          Fax: 801-278-5544
bdmo@bdel.com
www.bdel.com

Rock climbing, mountaineering and back-country skiing equipment

Chairman: Peter Wilkening
President: Peter Metcalf
CFO: Robert Peay
Buyers: Jordan Margid, Ski Line Manager
Credit Cards: MasterCard; Visa
Catalog Cost: Free
Catalog Circulation: Mailed 2 time(s) per year
Printing Information: 60 pages in 4 colors on Glossy Stock
Press: Web Press
Binding: Perfect Bound
Mailing List Information: Names for rent
Will Trade Names: Yes
List Company: Chilcutt Direct Marketing
9301 Cedar Lake Avenue
Oklahoma City, OK 73114
405-478-7245
Number of Employees: 270
Sales Volume: $500M to $1MM

5812 **Eastern Mountain Sports**
Eastern Mountain Sports
1 Vose Farm Road
Peterborough, NH 03458-2128 603-924-4320
                             888-463-6367
customerservice@ems.com
www.ems.com

Outdoor gear and clothing

President: William Manzer
CFO: Robert Mayerson
Marketing Manager: Scott Barrett
Catalog Cost: Free
Catalog Circulation: to 650T
Printing Information: 180 pages in 4 colors
In Business: 47 years

5813 **Fieldline**
Outdoor Recreations Group
1919 Vineburn Avenue
Los Angeles, CA 90032-3704   323-226-0830
                             800-438-3353
                        Fax: 323-226-0831
info@outdoorproducts.com
www.outdoorproducts.com

Backpack, duffel, lifestyle accessories

President: Joel Altshule
Marketing Manager: Bryan Stewart
Catalog Cost: Free
In Business: 40 years

Number of Employees: 300
Sales Volume: $500M to $1MM

5814 La Sportiva
3850 Frontier Ave.
#100
Boulder, CO 80301   303-443-8710
                            www.sportiva.com

Outdoor and sporting shoes and footwear

5815 Mountain Gear
Mountain Gear
6021 E Mansfield
Spokane Valley, WA 99212-1300 509-340-1165
                            800-829-2009
                            Fax: 509-340-1170
                            info@mountaingear.com
                            www.mountaingear.com

Outdoor gear and clothing

President: Whitney Parsons
Credit Cards: AMEX; MasterCard
Catalog Cost: Free
Printing Information: 104 pages in 7 colors
Binding: Folded
In Business: 24 years
Sales Volume: $20MM to $50MM

5816 PMI
Pigeon Mountain Industries, Inc
PO Box 803
La Fayette, GA 30728-803   706-764-1437
                            800-282-7673
                            Fax: 706-764-1531
                            custserv@pmirope.com
                            www.pmirope.com

Life safety ropes, fall protection gear, rock climbing protective gear and devices

President: Steve Hudson
CFO: Andrew Jaeger
Marketing Manager: Loui McCurley
Production Manager: Elbert Keen
Buyers: Keith Wishon
Credit Cards: MasterCard; Visa
Catalog Cost: Free
Catalog Circulation: Mailed 8 time(s) per year
Average Order Size: $250
Printing Information: 112 pages in 4 colors
Binding: Saddle Stitched
Mailing List Information: Names for rent
Number of Employees: 68

5817 Patagonia
Patagonia
259 W Santa Clara St.
Ventura, CA 93001   805-643-8616
                            www.patagonia.com

Outdoor apparel for men and women.

CEO: Rose Marcario
Catalog Cost: Free
Catalog Circulation: Mailed 12 time(s) per year
Printing Information: in 4 colors
In Business: 43 years
Number of Employees: 2000
Sales Volume: $600 Million

5818 Peter Limmer & Sons
Peter Limmer & Sons
P.O.Box 340
Intervale, NH 03845-88   603-694-2668
                            Fax: 603-694-2950
                            www.limmerboot.com

Mountaineering equipment

President: Peter Limmer
CFO: Carl Limmer
Catalog Cost: Free
Catalog Circulation: to 5000
Printing Information: 12 pages in 4 colors on Glossy Stock
Binding: Folded
Mailing List Information: Names for rent
In Business: 50 years

Number of Employees: 5
Sales Volume: $200,000

5819 REI
REI
                            800-426-4840
                            www.rei.com

Recreational sporting and adventure equipment and clothing

Chairman: Cheryl Scott
President: Jerry Stritzke
CFO: Tracie Windigler
Marketing Manager: Craig Rowley
EVP, Chief Operating Officer: Eric Artz
SVP of Merchandising: Susan Viscon
VP of Supply Chain: Rick Bingle
Buyers: Martha Boyd, Camping
Julie Baxter, Clothing/Shoes
Candyce Johnson, Ski & Bike, Climbing/Paddling
Credit Cards: MasterCard; Visa
Catalog Cost: Free
Catalog Circulation: Mailed 4 time(s) per year
Printing Information: 100 pages in 4 colors on Glossy Stock
Press: Web Press
Binding: Saddle Stitched
Mailing List Information: Names for rent
List Company: Mark Gappa, International
In Business: 69 years
Number of Employees: 6000
Sales Volume: $50MM to $100MM

5820 Rock-N-Rescue
J.E. Weinel, Inc.
300 Delwood Road
Butler, PA 16001-213   724-256-8822
                            800-346-7673
                            Fax: 724-256-8888
                            info@rocknrescue.com
                            www.rocknrescue.com

Manufacturer and distributor of rescue equipment for high angle, confined space, trench, water rescue, building collapse, and more

President: John A Weinel
Marketing Manager: Robert Womer
Fulfillment: Butch Weinel
Manager: Bob Barbarini
Credit Cards: AMEX; MasterCard; Visa
Catalog Cost: Free
Catalog Circulation: Mailed 52 time(s) per year to 30M
Average Order Size: $500
Printing Information: 100 pages in 3 colors on Matte Stock
Press: Web Press
Binding: Saddle Stitched
Mailing List Information: Names for rent
List Manager: Butch Weinel
In Business: 75 years
Number of Employees: 9
Sales Volume: $2,500,000

Parachuting & Hang Gliding

5821 ChutingStar
ChutingStar Enterprises
1349 Old 41 Hwy NW
Suite 105
Marietta, GA 30060-7929   770-445-4000
                            Gear@ChutingStar.com
                            www.chutingstar.com

Parachuting and hang-gliding supplies and accessories

5822 KYTEC Athletic Speed Equipment
2718 W. 84th Street
Bloomington, MN 55431-1738 952-884-3424
                            800-732-4883
                            Fax: 952-884-3427
                            www.kytec.us

Athletic speed equipment, parachutes and rehabilitation equipment

President: Jodi Michaelson
Marketing Manager: Ky Michaelson
Catalog Cost: Free
Catalog Circulation: Mailed 2 time(s) per year
Average Order Size: $150
Printing Information: 47 pages in 4 colors on Glossy Stock
Press: Sheetfed Press
Mailing List Information: Names for rent
Number of Employees: 20-O
Sales Volume: Under $500M

5823 Para-Gear Equipment
Para-Gear Equipment Co.
3839 Oakton Street
Skokie, IL 60076-3438   847-679-5905
                            800-323-0437
                            Fax: 847-679-8644
                            sales@paragear.com
                            www.para-gear.com

Parachuting equipment and supplies

President: Jay Daly
Founder: Lowell Bachman
Credit Cards: AMEX; MasterCard; Visa; Discover
Catalog Cost: $5
Catalog Circulation: Mailed 1 time(s) per year
Printing Information: 232 pages in 2 colors
In Business: 57 years
Number of Employees: 10
Sales Volume: $760,000

5824 Perform Better
1600 Division Rd.
West Warwick, RI 02893   401-942-9363
                            888-556-7464
                            Fax: 800-682-6950
                            performbetter@mfathletic.com
                            www.performbetter.com

Functional training and sports equipment

5825 Rigging Innovations
Rigging Innovations
4910 N. Lear Dr. HGR 1,
Eloy Municipal Airport
Eloy, AZ 85131-1210   520-466-2655
                            Fax: 520-466-2656
                            www.rigginginnovations.com

Catalog of aircraft and aero activities, offering aircraft recovery systems and para-gear, specializes in skydiving equipment

5826 Six Chuter International LLC
Six Chuter International LLC
5700 NE 82nd Avenue
Vancouver, WA 98662   360-771-4047
                            888-727-1998
                            sixchuterinfo@comcast.net
                            www.sixchuter.com

Catalog of aircraft and aero activities, offering hang gliding and powered parachutes, specializes in sky-riding aero-chute for one and two-persons

Marketing Manager: Doug Maas
doug@sixchuter.com
Printing Information: 37 pages
In Business: 25 years
Sales Volume: Under $500M

Rowing

5827 Alden Rowing Shells
Alden Rowing Shells, LLC
227 Bakers Avenue
Concord, MA 01742   978-263-9010
                            800-477-1507
                            Fax: 978-948-7698
                            info@rowalden.com
                            www.rowalden.com

Rowing shells, rowing art and rowing accessories

President: Edward C. Jarvis
General Manager: Gary G. Piantedosi
Catalog Circulation: Mailed 2 time(s) per year
Printing Information: in 4 colors on Glossy Stock
Number of Employees: 4
Sales Volume: $400,000

5828 Durham Boat Company
Durham Boat Company
220 Newmarket Rd
(Route 108)
Durham, NH 03824-4203   603-659-7575
Fax: 603-659-2548
cfuerst@durhamboat.com
www.durhamboat.com

Rowing products
President: Coleen Fuerst
Credit Cards: AMEX; MasterCard
In Business: 33 years
Number of Employees: 10
Sales Volume: $1,000,000

5829 Shell Boats
561 Polly Hubbard Road
St Albans, VT 05478   802-524-9645
Fax: 802-524-9645
shellboats@gmail.com
www.shellboats.com

Sailboat and rowboat kits, boat plans and finished boats

Running

5830 Dick Pond Athletics
Dick Pond Athletics, Inc
26W515 St. Charles Road
Unit A
Carol Stream, IL 60188   877-813-4169
Fax: 630-665-3341
info@dickpondathletics.com
www.dickpondathletics.com

Track and field and wrestling gear, shoes, accessories and apparel.
In Business: 46 years

5831 National Running Center
National Running Center
318 Davis Street
Clarks Summit, PA 18411-1836   570-586-1620
800-541-1773
Fax: 570-587-8844
help@nationalrunningcenter.com
www.nationalrunningcenter.com

Running apparel and equipment
President: Timothy Ritchie
Founder: Tim Ritchie
Founder: Dennis McWhorter
Catalog Circulation: to 45000
Mailing List Information: Names for rent
In Business: 27 years

5832 Pro-Tec Athletics
Maverick Sport Medicine,Inc.
18080 NE 68th St.
Suite A-150
Redmond, WA 98052-5554   425-497-0887
800-779-3372
Fax: 425-497-9223
info@pro-tecathletics.com
www.injurybegone.com

Sports medicine products, orthepedic braces
Marketing Manager: Sayeh Jackson
Credit Cards: AMEX; MasterCard
Catalog Cost: Free
Catalog Circulation: to 10000
Printing Information: 4 pages in 4 colors on Glossy Stock
Binding: Folded
Mailing List Information: Names for rent

In Business: 24 years
Number of Employees: 2
Sales Volume: $1MM to $3MM

5833 Road Runner Sports
Road Runner Sports
5549 Copley Drive
San Diego, CA 92111-7904   858-636-7652
800-636-3560
www.roadrunnersports.com

Men and women's running apparel and footwear
President: Michael Gotfredson
Marketing Manager: Jeff Rohling
Retail General Manager: Bob Bell
Credit Cards: AMEX; MasterCard
Catalog Cost: Free
Catalog Circulation: Mailed 8 time(s) per year to 90000
Printing Information: 100 pages in 4 colors on Glossy Stock
Press: Web Press
Binding: Saddle Stitched
List Company: Fasano & Associates
In Business: 34 years
Number of Employees: 220
Sales Volume: 70MM

5834 Sporthill
Sporthill Direct Inc
725 McKinley St
Eugene, OR 97402-2756   541-345-9623
800-622-8444
info@sporthill.com
www.sporthill.com

Running, skiing and adventure wear for men and women
President: Jim Hill
Catalog Cost: Free
Printing Information: 24 pages in 4 colors
Mailing List Information: Names for rent
In Business: 21 years
Sales Volume: $ 1-3 Million

Scuba Diving

5835 Berry Scuba Company
Berry Scuba Company
1094 E Nakoma Street
Chicago, IL 60631-1306   773-763-1626
800-621-6019
Fax: 773-775-1815
www.berryscuba.com

Scuba equipment
President: Bob Croll
Marketing Manager: Richard Drew
Buyers: Angelo Tagler, Scuba Equipment
Credit Cards: AMEX; MasterCard; Visa
Catalog Cost: Free
Catalog Circulation: Mailed 2 time(s) per year
Printing Information: 60 pages in 1 color
Mailing List Information: Names for rent
Number of Employees: 8
Sales Volume: $500M to $1MM

5836 Divers Direct
Divers Direct
180 Gulfstream Way
Dania Beach, FL 33004   954-926-4455
800-348-3872
Fax: 954-719-4913
ksenecal@diversdirect.com
www.diversdirect.com

Scuba diving equipment and accessories
President: Kevin Senecal
Marketing Manager: Michael Kohner
Production Manager: Patty Collins
Credit Cards: AMEX; MasterCard
Average Order Size: $90
Printing Information: 112 pages in 4 colors on Glossy Stock
Press: Web Press
Binding: Saddle Stitched

Mailing List Information: Names for rent
Number of Employees: 80
Sales Volume: $10MM to $20MM

5837 Dry Goods for a Wet World
No Gills Required Inc.
411 E Huntington Drive
Suite 107, Department 390
Arcadia, CA 91106   877-664-4557
877-664-4557
Fax: 626-358-3413
www.nogills.com

Diving sportswear and accessories
Credit Cards: AMEX; MasterCard
Catalog Cost: Free

5838 Performance Diver
Holiday Driver Inc.
180 Gulfstream Way
Dania Beach, FL 33004   954-926-4455
800-348-3872
Fax: 954-719-4913
www.diversdirect.com

Latest scuba gear
President: Kevin Senacal
Credit Cards: AMEX; MasterCard
Catalog Cost: Free
Printing Information: 45 pages in 4 colors
Mailing List Information: Names for rent
Number of Employees: 80
Sales Volume: $500M to $1MM

5839 Underwater Equipment Guide
Leisure Pro
42 West 18th Street
New York, NY 10011-4621   212-645-1234
888-805-3600
Fax: 212-691-7286
govsales@leisurepro.com
www.leisurepro.com

Big selection of underwater photography equipment, dive lights, and watches
Dive Store Manager & Instructor: Ben T.
Sales Rep.: Aaron N.
Sales Rep.: Charlie K.
Credit Cards: AMEX; MasterCard; Visa
Catalog Cost: Free
Number of Employees: 20

Skating

5840 Active Ride Skate Shop
Active Ride Shop
12178 4th Street
Rancho Cucamonga, CA 91730   951-934-4200
800-588-3911
Fax: 951-727-9520
customerservice@activerideshop.com
www.Activerideshop.Com

Skateboards, gear, footwear, clothing, and accessories
President: John Wallace
Credit Cards: AMEX; MasterCard
Catalog Circulation: Mailed 4 time(s) per year
In Business: 26 years

5841 Dante Cozzi Sports
Dante Cozzi
1001 Stewart Ave
Bethpage, NY 11714-2200   516-783-0215
Fax: 516-719-5960
cozzisports@gmail.com
www.cozzisports.com

Hockey and figure skates
President: Dante Cozzi
Credit Cards: AMEX; MasterCard
In Business: 38 years
Number of Employees: 6
Sales Volume: $700,000

5842 Del Arbour Designs
Del Arbour Designs
152 Old Gate Lane
Milford, CT 06460-3651   203-882-8501
                              800-417-0773
                         Fax: 203-882-8503
                   service@delarbour.com
                       www.delarbour.com

Skating apparel

President: Del Arbour
Credit Cards: AMEX; MasterCard
Catalog Cost: Free
Number of Employees: 10
Sales Volume: $750,000

5843 Designs by Margarita
Margarita Designs
PO Box 8517
Warwick, RI 02888   401-467-2520
            margarita@margaritadesigns.com
                  www.margaritadesigns.com

Skating pins

Credit Cards: AMEX; MasterCard
Printing Information: 20 pages

5844 Plus Skate Shop
186 Miracle Strip Pkwy. S.E.
Fort Walton Beach, FL 32548   850-244-6525
                              800-448-7723
                  info@plusskateshop.com
                      plusskateshop.com

Skating products

Skiing & Snowboarding

5845 Active Ride Snow Shop
Active Ride Shop
12178 4th Street
Rancho Cucamonga, CA 91730   951-934-4200
                              800-588-3911
                         Fax: 951-727-9520
        customerservice@activerideshop.com
                   www.Activerideshop.Com

Snowboards, gear, footwear, clothing, and accessories

President: John Wallace
Credit Cards: AMEX; MasterCard
In Business: 26 years

5846 Active Ride Women's Shop
Active Ride Shop
12178 4th Street
Rancho Cucamonga, CA 91730   951-934-4200
                              800-588-3911
                         Fax: 951-727-9520
        customerservice@activerideshop.com
                   www.Activerideshop.Com

Women's boards, gear, footwear, clothing, and accessories

President: John Wallace
Credit Cards: AMEX; MasterCard
In Business: 26 years

5847 Akers Ski
Akers Ski, Inc.
PO Box 293
Andover, ME 04216-280   207-392-4582
                         Fax: 207-392-1225
                     sales@akers-ski.com
                       www.akers-ski.com

Cross country skis, ski equipment and clothing and waxes

President: Leon M. Akers
Credit Cards: MasterCard
Catalog Cost: Free
Catalog Circulation: Mailed 1 time(s) per year to 40000
Printing Information: 70 pages in 2 colors on Newsprint
Press: Web Press

Binding: Saddle Stitched
Mailing List Information: Names for rent
In Business: 49 years
Number of Employees: 6
Sales Volume: $600,000

5848 Any Mountain
Any Mountain Ltd
71 Tamal Vista Boulevard
Corte Madera, CA 94925-1145   415-927-0170
                   jcoghlan1@vailresorts.com
                        anymountain.net

Ski apparel for men and women

Credit Cards: MasterCard; Visa
Mailing List Information: Names for rent
List Company: Chilcutt Direct Marketing
9301 Cedar Lake Avenue
Oklahoma City, OK 73114
405-478-7245
In Business: 45 years
Number of Employees: 65
Sales Volume: $5MM to $10MM

5849 Burton Snowboards
80 Industrial Parkway
Burlington, VT 05401   800-881-3138
                         Fax: 802-660-3250
                      info@burton.com
                       www.burton.com

Skiing and snowboarding gear

5850 CCS
California Cheap Skates
1235 E Nakoma Street
Westerville, OH 43068   971-229-0871
                              800-875-1800
                         Fax: 800-317-8105
                       www.ccs.com

Skateboard and snowboard related products

Catalog Cost: Free
Printing Information: 56 pages
In Business: 30 years
Number of Employees: 150

5851 House Boardshop
The House
200 S. Owasso Blvd E.
Saint Paul, MN 55117-1082   651-482-9995
                              800-409-7669
                         Fax: 800-382-2416
                      info@the-house.com
                       www.the-house.com

Snowboards, boots, bindings, clothing, skateboards, skate shoes, wakeboards, windsurfing, sunglasses

Credit Cards: AMEX; MasterCard

5852 K2 Sports
K2 Sports
4201 6th Ave S.
Seattle, WA 98108-5232   877-412-7467
                              800-985-2189
                         Fax: 206-463-2861
                       www.K2ski.com

Snow sports equipment, apparel and accessories

President: Robert Marcovitch
Catalog Circulation: Mailed 26 time(s) per year
Printing Information: 9 pages
In Business: 45 years
Number of Employees: 200

5853 Mountain Gear
Mountain Gear
6021 E Mansfield
Spokane Valley, WA 99212-1300 509-340-1165
                              800-829-2009
                         Fax: 509-340-1170
                  info@mountaingear.com
                     www.mountaingear.com

Outdoor gear and clothing

President: Whitney Parsons
Credit Cards: AMEX; MasterCard
Catalog Cost: Free
Printing Information: 104 pages in 7 colors
Binding: Folded
In Business: 24 years
Sales Volume: $20MM to $50MM

5854 Obermeyer
Obermeyer
P.O.Box 7848
Aspen, CO 81612-7848   970-925-6006
                              800-525-4203
                         Fax: 970-925-9203
                       www.obermeyer.com

Ski outerwear

President: Klaus Obermeyer
In Business: 68 years
Number of Employees: 56
Sales Volume: $20MM to $50MM

5855 REI
REI
                              800-426-4840
                       www.rei.com

Recreational sporting and adventure equipment and clothing

Chairman: Cheryl Scott
President: Jerry Stritzke
CFO: Tracie Windigler
Marketing Manager: Craig Rowley
EVP, Chief Operating Officer: Eric Artz
SVP of Merchandising: Susan Viscon
VP of Supply Chain: Rick Bingle
Buyers: Martha Boyd, Camping
Julie Baxter, Clothing/Shoes
Candyce Johnson, Ski & Bike, Climbing/Paddling
Credit Cards: MasterCard; Visa
Catalog Cost: Free
Catalog Circulation: Mailed 4 time(s) per year
Printing Information: 100 pages in 4 colors on Glossy Stock
Press: Web Press
Binding: Saddle Stitched
Mailing List Information: Names for rent
List Company: Mark Gappa, International
In Business: 69 years
Number of Employees: 6000
Sales Volume: $50MM to $100MM

5856 Race Place
222 SE Reed Market Road
#200
Bend, OR 97702   541-382-4216
                              800-814-7223
                  info@the-raceplace.com
                    www.the-raceplace.com

Ski clothing and accessories

Owner: Scott
Sales Floor & Shipping Department: Paula

5857 Reliable Racing Winter Sports
Reliable Racing Supply, Inc
643 Upper Glen Street
Queensbury, NY 12804   518-793-5677
                              800-223-4448
                         Fax: 518-793-6491
          customerservice@reliableracing.com
                    www.reliableracing.com

Ski racing equipment and apparel for alpine and nordic skiers; back country and tele skis, snowshoes

President: Tom Jacobs
CFO: Marilyn Jacobs
Marketing Manager: Tim Mullin
Production Manager: Mike Sylvia
Credit Cards: AMEX; MasterCard; Visa
Catalog Cost: Free
Catalog Circulation: Mailed 4 time(s) per year to 500
Average Order Size: $150

Printing Information: 84 pages in 4 colors on Matte Stock
Press: Web Press
Binding: Saddle Stitched
Mailing List Information: Names for rent
Number of Employees: 60
Sales Volume: $500M to $1MM

5858 Scandinavian Ski Shops
Scandinavian Ski and Sports Shop
16 E 55th St
New York, NY 10022-3103   212-757-8524
                                 Fax: 212-757-8211
                                 www.Skishop.Com

Skiwear and equipment
President: Marilyn Elstroad
Number of Employees: 15
Sales Volume: $1MM to $3MM

5859 Sport-Rx
Sport-Rx
45 Plant Road
PO Box 2032
Hyannis, MA 02601   508-778-8100
                           jeff@sport-rx.com
                           www.sport-rx.com

Accessories for skiing
President: Jeff Handler
Co-Founder: Dan McGovern
Sport Psychology Coach: Adam Naylor EdD

5860 Tognar Ski & Snowboard Tools
Tognar Toolworks
280 E Hersey
Unit 4
Ashland, OR 97520   541-890-5627
                           800-299-9904
                           Fax: 541-535-7776
                           info@tognar.com
                           www.tognar.com

Ski, snowboard tuning tools and wax
President: Jack Moore
Founder: Jack Moore
Catalog Circulation: Mailed 1 time(s) per year to 10000
Printing Information: 64 pages in 2 colors on Newsprint
Press: Web Press
Binding: Saddle Stitched
Mailing List Information: Names for rent
In Business: 29 years
Number of Employees: 3
Sales Volume: Under $500M

5861 White Cloud Lodging
White Cloud Lodging Company
207 N Main Street
PO Box 2205
Breckenridge, CO 80424   970-453-1018
                                888-676-9977
                                Fax: 970-453-2347
                                reservations@summitrentals.com

Lodging for skiers
President: Sarah Dane

Soccer

5862 DB Enterprises
DB Enterprises
543 El Sombrero
Edgewater, FL 32141   386-478-6876
                             800-444-6387
                             Fax: 386-428-5815
                             info@golfnetkits.com
                             www.golfnetkits.com

Batting, golf and soccer cages, nets and mats
President: David Babe
Credit Cards: AMEX; MasterCard; Visa
Catalog Cost: Free
Mailing List Information: Names for rent

In Business: 27 years
Number of Employees: 2

5863 Rugby & Soccer Supply/Godek Rugby
Matt Godek Rugby & Soccer Supply
PO Box 565
Merrifield, VA 22116   703-560-1919
                              800-872-7842
                              Fax: 703-280-4543
                              admin@rugbystore.com
                              www.Rugbystore.Com

All equipment for rugby
President: Matt Godek
Marketing Manager: Simon Bowyer
Credit Cards: MasterCard
Catalog Cost: $2
Average Order Size: $85
Printing Information: in 4 colors on Matte Stock
Press: Web Press
Binding: Saddle Stitched
Mailing List Information: Names for rent
In Business: 37 years
Number of Employees: 15
Sales Volume: $1MM to $3MM

5864 Soccer Learning Systems
17610 Murphy Pkwy
Lathrop, CA 95330   209-858-4300
                           800-762-2376
                           Fax: 209-858-4500
                           shipping@soccervideos.com
                           www.soccervideos.com

Videos to improve Soccer skills

5865 Soccer.com
Soccer.com
431 US Highway 70A E
Hillsborough, NC 27278   919-644-6800
                                800-950-1994
                                custserv@sportsendeavors.com
                                www.soccer.com

Footwear, apparel, equipment and uniforms.
In Business: 32 years

5866 Stackhouse Athletic Equipment
PO Box 12276
Salem, OR 97309   503-363-1840
                         800-285-3604
                         Fax: 503-363-0511
                         www.stackhouseathletic.com

Athletic equipment

5867 TSI Soccer
Eurosport, The Fabled Soccer Traders
431 US 70-A E
Soccer.com Customer Service Support
Hillsborough, NC 27278   919-655-6800
                                800-950-1994
                                Fax: 919-644-6808
                                custserv@sportsendeavors.com
                                www.tsisoccer.com

Specializes in soccer apparel
President: John Pinto
Credit Cards: MasterCard; Visa
Catalog Cost: Free
Catalog Circulation: Mailed 12 time(s) per year
Printing Information: 72 pages in 4 colors on Glossy Stock
Press: Web Press
Binding: Saddle Stitched
Mailing List Information: Names for rent
In Business: 22 years
Number of Employees: 325
Sales Volume: $20MM to $50MM

Tennis & Racket Sports

5868 ATS Sports
ATS Sports
200 Waterfront Dr
Pittsburgh, PA 15222-4737   412-323-9612
                                   800-866-7071
                                   Fax: 412-323-1320
                                   ace@atssports.com
                                   www.Atssports.Com

Tennis racquets, strings and accessories
President: Harry Ferrari
Credit Cards: AMEX; MasterCard; Visa
Catalog Cost: Free
Catalog Circulation: Mailed 1 time(s) per year
Number of Employees: 50
Sales Volume: $3,600,000

5869 Black Knight
Black Knight Annzus LLC
3383 Dellwood Road
Cleveland, OH 44118   216-334-8087
                             800-535-3300
                             ray@blackknightusa.com
                             www.blackknightusa.com

Squash and badminton racquets and accessories
President: Ray Lindsay
Buyers: Ray Lindsay
Credit Cards: MasterCard; Visa
Catalog Circulation: Mailed 2 time(s) per year to 10M
Printing Information: 8 pages in 4 colors on Glossy Stock
Press: Web Press
Binding: Perfect Bound
Mailing List Information: Names for rent
Number of Employees: 3
Sales Volume: $1,000,000

5870 Center Court
Golfsmith
11000 North IH-35
Austin, TX 78753   512-837-4810
                          800-813-6897
                          www.tennis.golfsmith.com

Latest tennis fashion apparel, tennis racquets, gear, footwear and accessories
President: Jim Thompson
Chief Marketing Officer: Lisa Zoellner
Catalog Cost: Free
Printing Information: 119 pages in 4 colors

5871 Fromuth Tennis
Fromuth Tennis
1100 Rocky Drive
West Lawn, PA 19609-1156   610-288-5030
                                  800-523-8414
                                  Fax: 610-288-5040
                                  www.fromuth.com

Racquet sports equipment
President: Patrick Shields
Catalog Circulation: Mailed 1 time(s) per year to 20000
In Business: 40 years
Number of Employees: 30
Sales Volume: $10MM to $20MM

5872 Golfsmith
Golfsmith International
11000 North IH-35
Austin, TX 78753   800-813-6897
                          www.golfsmith.com

Latest in color and fashion apparel, tennis racquets, gear, footwear and accessories
President: Jim Thompson
Marketing Manager: Lisa Zoellner
Credit Cards: AMEX; MasterCard
Catalog Cost: Free
Printing Information: 68 pages in 4 colors

5873 Guterman International
Guterman International
603 Pleasant St
Paxton, MA 01612-1305   508-852-8206
                                800-343-6096
                           Fax: 508-856-0632
guterman-intl@worldnet.att.net
www.GutermanIntl.Com

Portable stringers
President: Peter Guterman
In Business: 27 years
Number of Employees: 14
Sales Volume: $1MM to $3MM

5874 Holabird Sports
Holabird Sports
9220 Pulaski Highway
Baltimore, MD 21220-2416   410-687-6400
                                866-860-1416
                           Fax: 410-687-7311
info@holabirdsports.com
www.Holabirdsports.Com

All racquet sport equipment (tennis, racquetball and squash) and all athletic footwear running, tennis, basketball, cross training, walking, aerobics, cleats at 20-50% off everyday, all major brands
President: David Holabird
Credit Cards: AMEX; MasterCard; Visa
Catalog Cost: Free
Catalog Circulation: Mailed 12 time(s) per year
Average Order Size: $90
Printing Information: 8 pages in 1 color on Glossy Stock
Press: Web Press
Mailing List Information: Names for rent
In Business: 34 years
Number of Employees: 48
Sales Volume: $10,000,000 - $25,000,000

5875 NetKnacks
NetKnacks
4855 Peachtree Industrial Blvd
Suite 235
Norcross, GA 30092   770-650-8418
                                800-374-6153
                           Fax: 770-368-8577
sales@netknacks.com
netknacks.com

Provides tennis awards, apparel and promotional items to the tennis industry
In Business: 25 years

5876 Pacific Sports Warehouse
RacquetWorld.com
35 Fuller Rd
Albany, NY 12205   619-596-2135
                                800-835-1055
                           Fax: 518-438-3935
info@racquetworld.com
store.racquetworld.com

Racquetball equipment
President: Jeff Lehrer
Credit Cards: MasterCard; Visa
Catalog Cost: Free
Catalog Circulation: Mailed 3 time(s) per year
Printing Information: 40 pages in 4 colors on Glossy Stock
Press: Sheetfed Press
Binding: Saddle Stitched
Mailing List Information: Names for rent
Number of Employees: 10
Sales Volume: $1MM to $3MM

5877 Tennis Express
Tennis Express
11022 Westheimer Rd
Houston, TX 77042-3206   713-435-4818
                                800-833-6615
                           Fax: 713-781-3933
www.tennisexpress.com

Tennis racquets, apparel, shoes, bags, accessories, tennis balls, books, DVD's and tennis memorabilia
President: Todd White
Catalog Cost: Free
Catalog Circulation: Mailed 4 time(s) per year
Printing Information: in 4 colors
Sales Volume: $3MM to $5MM

Sports Uniforms

5878 All Pro Team Sports
All Pro Team Sports
11615 Crossraods Circle
Suite H
Baltimore, MD 21220   410-335-9804
contacts@allproteamsports.com
www.allproteamsports.com

Sportswear, sporting equipment, gear, and uniforms
President: Steve Bottcher
steve@allproteamsports.com
Credit Cards: AMEX; MasterCard
Catalog Cost: Free
In Business: 8 years

5879 Athletic Connection
Athletic Connection
1901 Diplomat Drive
Farmers Branch, TX 75234   800-527-0871
                           Fax: 885-858-8337
www.athleticconnection.com

Sportswear, sporting equipment, gear, and uniforms
Credit Cards: AMEX; MasterCard
Catalog Cost: Free
Catalog Circulation: Mailed 1 time(s) per year
Printing Information: 364 pages in 4 colors

5880 BSN Sports TeamWear
BSN Sports
PO Box 7726
Dallas, TX 75209   800-856-3488
                           Fax: 800-899-0149
www.bsnsports.com

Team apparel
Chair & CEO: Adam Blumenfeld
President, COO & General Counsel: Terry Babilla
Catalog Cost: Free
Printing Information: 272 pages in 4 colors
In Business: 44 years
Number of Employees: 1200
Sales Volume: $500 Million

5881 Dunbrooke Sportswear Company
Dunbrooke Apparel Corp
4200 Little Blue Parkway
Suite 500
Independence, MO 64057-1791   800-641-3627
www.dunbrooke.com

Sportswear for the family
President: Matt Grey
CFO: Jay Jones
Marketing Manager: Pat Sandvig
Production Manager: David W Brandy, VP
Credit Cards: AMEX; MasterCard
In Business: 78 years
Number of Employees: 1602
Sales Volume: $5,600,000

5882 Excel Sports Products
Excel Sports Products
15545 Computer Lane
Huntington Beach, CA 92649-1605 714-898-7720
                                800-677-3669
info@excelsportsproducts.com
www.excelsportsproducts.com

Training aids for athletes and coaches
President: Cherry Blaine
Printing Information: 32 pages

In Business: 17 years
Number of Employees: 6
Sales Volume: $620,000

5883 Golf Balls & More
Golf Balls & More/Sport Towels, Inc.
1774 Pheasant Avenue NW
Grand Rapids, MI 49534-2322   616-735-0248
                                800-926-2649
                           Fax: 616-735-1513
info@golfballs-mi.com
www.golfballs-mi.com

Custom imprinted golf balls, tees, markers; embroidered/screen printed golf, bowling and rally towels, shirts, hats and more; also logo ornaments and baseballs
President: Mort Hendricks
Marketing Manager: Kathy Farhat
Production Manager: Kathy Farhat
Credit Cards: MasterCard
Mailing List Information: Names for rent
In Business: 26 years
Number of Employees: 4

5884 Varsity Spirit Corporation
Varsity Spirit Corporation
6745 Lenox Center Court
Suite 300
Memphis, TN 38115   901-213-5300
                                800-533-8022
                           Fax: 901-387-4345
varsitytv@varsity.com
www.varsity.com

Varsity and sports clothing
President: Jeffrey Webb
VP: Marlene Cota
mcota@varsity.com
VP, Public Relations: Sheila Noone
snoone@varsity.com
VP, Corp. Marketing & Comm.: Nicole Lauchaire
nlauchaire@varsity.com
Catalog Circulation: to 16000
Average Order Size: $100
Printing Information: 140 pages in 4 colors on Glossy Stock
Press: Web Press
Binding: Saddle Stitched
In Business: 41 years
Number of Employees: 320

Volleyball

5885 Carron Net
Carron Net
1623 17th St.
PO Box 177
Two Rivers, WI 54241-0177   800-558-7768
sales@carronnet.com
www.carronnet.com

Custom and standard sports netting for baseball batting cages, soccer nets, golf range nets, windscreens, tennis and volleyball nets

5886 Franklin Sports
Franklin Sports Inc.
17 Campanelli Parkway
Stoughton, MA 02072   781-344-1111
                                800-225-8647
                           Fax: 781-341-0333
b2bcustomerservice@franklinsports.com
franklinsports.com

Sporting goods and toys.
President: Adam Franklin
In Business: 70 years
Number of Employees: 250

5887 Girls Got Game Volleyball
Girls Got Game
133 Main St
Suite 1
Geneseo, NY 14454   877-577-0342
Fax: 877-243-5268
custserv@girlsgotgame.com
www.girlsgotgamevolleyball.com

Volleyball shoes, uniforms, accessories and equipment

5888 Great Lakes Sports
Great Lakes Sports
P.O. Box 447
Lambertville, MI 48144   419-726-8233
800-446-2114
Fax: 419-726-8118
www.greatlakessports.com

Sports products.
President: Thomas McNutt
In Business: 21 years

5889 GymRats
GymRats, Inc.
6923 Narcoossee Road
Suite 616
Orlando, FL 32822   407-925-6876
Fax: 877-560-5926
CustomerService@gymratsvolleyball.com
www.gymratsvolleyball.com

Volleyball shopping items.
In Business: 15 years

5890 Memphis Net & Twine Company-Sports
Memphis Net & Twine Company
P.O. Box 80331
Memphis, TN 38108-331   901-458-2656
888-674-7638
Fax: 901-458-1601
fishinfo@memphisnet.net
www.memphisnet.net

Nets for volleyball, weight room equipment, windscreens, track and field, etc.
Chairman: William McCorkle
President: Albert Caruthers
Marketing Manager: Bryan Denley
General Manager: Frank A Gibson
Vice President Sales: William Raiford
Credit Cards: AMEX; MasterCard; Visa
Catalog Cost: Free
Catalog Circulation: Mailed 2 time(s) per year to 50000
Printing Information: 64 pages in 2 colors on Newsprint
Press: Web Press
Binding: Saddle Stitched
Mailing List Information: Names for rent
In Business: 52 years
Number of Employees: 33
Sales Volume: $4.6 Million

5891 On Deck Sports
On Deck Sports
88 Spark St.
Brockton, MA 2302   800-365-6171
Fax: 508-580-0211
Info@OnDeckSports.com
www.ondecksports.com

Artificial turf, sports netting, and baseball & softball equipment.
In Business: 14 years

5892 Palos Sports
Palos Sports
11711 S. Austin Ave
Alsip, IL 60803   708-396-2555
800-233-5484
Fax: 877-800-5973
www.palossports.com

Fitness equipment.

GSA Contract Administrator: Mara Zelencik
In Business: 58 years

5893 SNA Sports
SNA Sports
4180 44th St. SE
Suite B
Grand Rapids, MI 49512   616-554-4945
800-823-0182
info@snasportsgroup.com
www.snasportsgroup.com

Sporting goods.
President: Jim Peterson
VP, Operations: Amy Deschaine
Service Manager/Sales: John Connors
Customer Service Representative: Julie Gorter

5894 SportRx
SportRx
5076 Santa Fe Street
Suite A
San Diego, CA 92109   888-831-5817
www.sportrx.com

Prescription sunglasses and prescription snow goggles for athletes in virtually every sport and prescription wrap around lenses.

5895 Ultimate Systems, Limited
Ultimate Systems Limited
4335 N. Santa Fe Drive
Kingman, AZ 86401-4501   928-692-6789
800-777-6387
Fax: 928-692-9882
www.Homecourt.Com

Portable and permanent volleyball systems
President: Keith Stettner
Marketing Manager: Sheri Maltese
Production Manager: Sheri Stettner
Credit Cards: AMEX; MasterCard
Catalog Cost: Free
Catalog Circulation: Mailed 1 time(s) per year to 10000
Printing Information: 12 pages in 4 colors on Glossy Stock
Press: Offset Press
Binding: Saddle Stitched
In Business: 30 years
Sales Volume: $500M to $1MM

5896 Volleyball America Catalog
Team Express Distributing LLC
5750 Northwest Pky
Ste. 100
San Antonio, TX 78249-3374   210-348-7000
877-697-7678
Fax: 210-525-9339
customer.service@footballamerica.com
www.footballamerica.com

Volleyball footwear, equipment and apparel
President: Pat Cawles
VP Merchandising: Jamie Morey
Credit Cards: AMEX; MasterCard
Catalog Cost: Free
In Business: 25 years
Number of Employees: 195

5897 Worldwide Sport Supply Volleyball
Worldwide Sport Supply, Inc
145 N Jensen Road
Vestal, NY 13850   800-756-3555
Fax: 800-550-6850
customercare@wwsport.com
www.wwsport.com

Apparel decorating and sporting goods, with a focus on volleyball and wrestling.
In Business: 34 years

5898 Worldwide Sport Supply Volleyball Coach
Worldwide Sport Supply, Inc
145 N Jensen Road
Vestal, NY 13850   800-756-3555
Fax: 800-550-6850
customercare@wwsport.com
www.wwsport.com

Apparel decorating and sporting goods, with a focus on volleyball and wrestling.
In Business: 34 years

Xtreme Sports

5899 Army Navy Store Catalog
Army Navy Store.com
P.O. Box 230515
Gravesend, NY 11223   718-345-2222
800-766-9691
info@ArmyNavyStore.com
www.galaxyarmynavy.com

Clothing, accessories
Printing Information: 250 pages
In Business: 64 years

5900 QA1
QA1
21730 Hanover Avenue
Lakeville, MN 55044   952-985-5675
800-721-7761
Fax: 952-985-5679
sales@qa1.net
www.qa1.net

Parts and accessories for motorsports, including racing
Founder: Jim Jordan
Catalog Cost: Free
Catalog Circulation: Mailed 1 time(s) per year
Printing Information: 172 pages in 4 colors
In Business: 24 years

5901 Ranger Joes
325 Farr Road
Columbus, GA 31907-6248   706-689-3455
800-247-4541
customerservice@rangerjoes.com
www.rangerjoes.com

Military and law enforcement gear
Credit Cards: AMEX; MasterCard
In Business: 52 years

5902 SherrillTree 2015 Master Catalog
SherrillTree
200 Seneca Road
Greensboro, NC 27406   800-525-8873
info@sherrilltree.com
www.sherrilltree.com

Arborist supplies, arbor equipment, arboriculture gear, and arborist gear
In Business: 55 years

Stationery & Forms
Business

5903 Accountant Stationers & Printers
Accountant Stationers & Printers
742 E Washington Boulevard
Los Angeles, CA 90021   213-749-9241
800-423-9717
Fax: 213-749-4505
www.asandp.com

Accounting forms, tax forms, laser & business checks, software, filing and preparation supplies
President: Robert Rothman
Credit Cards: AMEX; MasterCard; Visa
Catalog Cost: Free
Catalog Circulation: Mailed 1 time(s) per year
Printing Information: 55 pages in 1 color
In Business: 67 years

Number of Employees: 19
Sales Volume: $2,200,000

5904 Alpha Office Products
Alpha Office Products
201 Kelly Mill Road
Cumming, GE 30040   770-887-1218
    800-524-1085
    Fax: 770-781-8211
    www.alphaofficega.com
Credit Cards: AMEX; MasterCard
In Business: 25 years

5905 Artistic Labels
Artistic Labels
P.O.Box 331
Colorado Springs, CO 80901   800-845-3720
    webcs@artisticdirect.com
    www.artisticlabels.com

Personalized address labels, address stamps and stationery for personal and business use, and other gift items

Catalog Cost: Free
In Business: 89 years

5906 At-A-Glance
At-A-Glance
11013 W Broad St
Glen Allen, VA 23060   804-327-5200
    800-880-2472
    Fax: 804-897-6383
    www.ataglance.com

Appointment books, desk and wall calendars

Catalog Cost: Free

5907 Brookhollow Collection
Brookhollow
12750 Merit Drive
Suite 700
Dallas, TX 75251   208-359-1000
    800-272-4182
    Fax: 800-822-0256
    service@brookhollowcards.com
    www.brookhollowcards.com

All occasion, holiday and profession specific customizable cards and calendars

Chairman: Michael Johnson
President: Erv Wiebe
Marketing Manager: Collette Rinehart
Credit Cards: AMEX; MasterCard; Visa
Catalog Cost: Free
Catalog Circulation: Mailed 1 time(s) per year
Printing Information: 32 pages in 4 colors on Glossy Stock
Press: Web Press
Binding: Saddle Stitched
Mailing List Information: Names for rent
In Business: 50 years
Number of Employees: 650
Sales Volume: $5MM to $10MM

5908 Cardphile
Cardphile
333 South State Street
Ste. V, #124
Lake Oswego, OR 97034   800-774-5857
    info@cardphile.com
    www.cardphile.com

Business Greeting Cards, Personalized Corporate Holiday Cards, Personal Greetings

In Business: 26 years

5909 CardsDirect.com
Cards Direct
12750 Merit Drive
Suite 900
Dallas, TX 75251   866-700-5030
    Fax: 866-422-4005
    support@cardsdirect.com
    www.cardsdirect.com

Business, photo, christmas, thanksgiving and custom greeting cards

Founder & CEO: Ward Mahowald
Founder & CEO: Michael Bunger
Director of Customer Service: Dawn Mayo
In Business: 17 years

5910 Checksforless.Com
Checksforless.com
200 Riverside Industrial Parkway
Portland, ME 04103-1414   800-245-5775
    Fax: 800-893-0177
    info@checksforless.com
    www.checksforless.com

Laser checks, deposit slips, window envelopes, one write checks, and more

President: Christopher Lefevre
Credit Cards: AMEX; MasterCard; Visa
Catalog Cost: Free
Catalog Circulation: to 50000
Printing Information: 28 pages in 4 colors on Glossy Stock
Press: Offset Press
Binding: Saddle Stitched
In Business: 42 years
Number of Employees: 20
Sales Volume: $20MM to $50MM

5911 Cordial Greetings
Thayer Publishing
150 Kingswood Drive
P.O. Box 8465
Mankato, MN 56002-8465   507-388-8647
    800-257-8276
    Fax: 800-842-9371
    customerservice@cordialgreetings.com
    www.cordialgreetings.com

Personalized holiday greeting cards and calendars

President: Leslie Stoltenberg
Marketing Manager: Lisa Kunst
President: Ed Kristen
Credit Cards: AMEX; MasterCard; Visa
Catalog Cost: Free
Printing Information: 32 pages
In Business: 50 years
Number of Employees: 150

5912 Courage Kenny Cards Corporate Holiday Card Catalog
Courage Kenny Cards
1750 Tower Blvd.
North Mankato, MN 56003   800-992-6872
    Fax: 888-873-1771
    www.couragecards.org

Holiday cards featuring original, exclusive and museum-quality artwork, many by artists with disabilities.

In Business: 57 years

5913 EiPrinting
Checks for Business
200 Riverside Industrial Parkway
Portland, ME 04103   800-245-5775
    Fax: 800-893-0177
    info@checksforless.com
    www.checksforless.com

Checks, deposit tickets and banking supplies

President: Chris LeFevre
Credit Cards: AMEX; MasterCard; Visa
Catalog Cost: Free
Catalog Circulation: to 50000
Printing Information: 28 pages in 4 colors on Glossy Stock
Press: Offset Press
Binding: Saddle Stitched
In Business: 35 years
Number of Employees: 20

5914 First Choice
Rexcraft
PO Box 299
Sugar City, ID 83448-299   800-762-9524
    Fax: 800-826-2712

Personalized holiday cards

President: Norm Doering
Marketing Manager: Collette Rinehart
Printing Information: 23 pages
In Business: 17 years
Number of Employees: 600

5915 G. Neil
HR direct
PO Box 452049
Sunrise, FL 33345-2049   877-968-7471
    800-888-4040
    Fax: 954-846-0777
    questions@hrdirect.com
    www.hrdirect.com

Human resource organizers and business specialties

President: Gary Brown
CFO: Carl Drew
Marketing Manager: Kevin Embry
Production Manager: Michelle A Newsom
Fulfillment: Joe Basgall
Catalog Circulation: to 10MM
Average Order Size: $108
Printing Information: 136 pages in 4 colors on Glossy Stock
Press: Web Press
List Company: Direct Media
Greenwich, CT
Number of Employees: 250

5916 Graphique de France
Graphique Boutique
9 State St
Woburn, MA 01801-2050   781-935-3415
    800-444-1464
    Fax: 781-935-5145
    customersupport@graphiquedefrance.com
    www.graphiquedefrance.com

Calendars, holiday cards and stationery

President: Jean-Jacque Toulotte
Credit Cards: AMEX; MasterCard
Catalog Cost: Free
Catalog Circulation: Mailed 1 time(s) per year
Printing Information: 200 pages in 4 colors
In Business: 27 years
Number of Employees: 46
Sales Volume: $10MM to $20MM

5917 Holiday Cards for Businesses
National Wildlife Federation
11100 Wildlife Center Drive
Reston, VA 20190-5362   800-822-9919
    Fax: 800-525-5562
    www.nwf.org

Christmas cards, calendars and apparel with a wildlife theme

Chairman: Deborah Spalding
President: Collin O'Mara
Marketing Manager: Al Lamson
Production Manager: Robin Clark
EVP/COO: Jaime Matyas
CEO: Collin O'Mara
Buyers: Lynn Piper, Gift Accessories
Mary Lamer, Greeting Cards
Robin Clark, Apparel
Credit Cards: MasterCard; Visa
Catalog Cost: Free
Catalog Circulation: Mailed 6 time(s) per year to 20MM
Printing Information: 48 pages in 4 colors on Glossy Stock
Press: Web Press
Binding: Saddle Stitched
Mailing List Information: Names for rent
In Business: 63 years
Number of Employees: 675

5918 Kraftbilt

Kraftbilt
PO Box 800
Tulsa, OK 74101   800-331-7290
Fax: 866-547-6967
kbcustomerservice@kraftbilt.com
www.kraftbilt.com

Tax forms, check register systems, oil & gas forms and products, tagging products, accounting and office supplies

President: Debbie Rule
Credit Cards: AMEX; MasterCard; Visa
Catalog Cost: Free
Catalog Circulation: Mailed 1 time(s) per year
Printing Information: 40 pages in 4 colors on Matte Stock
Binding: Saddle Stitched
In Business: 50 years

5919 Paper Showcase

PO Box 8465
Mankato, MN 56002-8465   507-388-5256
800-287-8163
Fax: 800-842-3371
www.papershowcase.com

Preprinted laser paper designs

Credit Cards: AMEX; MasterCard; Visa
Printing Information: 48 pages
Number of Employees: 175

5920 PaperDirect Events

PaperDirect
P.O. Box 1151
Minneapolis, MN 55440-1151   800-272-7377
Fax: 800-443-2973
volumesales@paperdirect.com
www.paperdirect.com

Do-it-yourself stationery; themes for occasions and events

President: Tim Arland
CFO: Kirby Heck
Credit Cards: AMEX; MasterCard
Catalog Cost: Free
Printing Information: in 4 colors
In Business: 29 years
Number of Employees: 1200
Sales Volume: $78 MM

5921 Posty Cards

Posty Cards
1600 Olive Street
Kansas City, MO 64127-2500   816-231-2323
800-821-7968
Fax: 888-577-3800
customerservice@postycards.com
www.postycards.com

Greeting cards and calendars

Chairman: Lance Jessee
President: Erick Jessee
Credit Cards: AMEX; MasterCard
Catalog Cost: Free
Catalog Circulation: Mailed 3 time(s) per year to 10000
Average Order Size: $106
Printing Information: 24 pages in 4 colors
Press: Web Press
Binding: Saddle Stitched
Mailing List Information: Names for rent
In Business: 69 years
Number of Employees: 45
Sales Volume: $10MM to $20MM

5922 Promotional Ideabook

Drawing Board
101 E Ninth St
Waynesboro, PA 17268   860-379-9911
800-527-9530
Fax: 800-253-1838
customerservice@drawingboard.com
www.drawingboard.com

Office products

President: Lee Bracken
Credit Cards: AMEX; MasterCard
Catalog Cost: Free
Catalog Circulation: Mailed 8 time(s) per year
Printing Information: 100 pages
Mailing List Information: Names for rent
Number of Employees: 300

5923 Pronto Business Cards

Paradise Press Printing
2065 Range Road
Clearwater, FL 33765-1256   727-447-1871
877-746-8925
Fax: 727-447-1866
Info@paradisepressprinting.com
www.prontotradeprint.com

Raised letter business cards and stationery, full color business cards, postcards, announcements and invitations

President: Melissa Neipert
CEO: Cindy Butler
Senior Customer Service Rep: Charlie Legg
Customer Service Rep: Terry Lagano
Credit Cards: AMEX; MasterCard
Catalog Cost: Free
Catalog Circulation: to 520
Printing Information: 50 pages on Matte Stock
Press: Sheetfed Press
Binding: Perfect Bound
Mailing List Information: Names for rent
In Business: 14 years
Number of Employees: 5
Sales Volume: $500M to $1MM

5924 Seton Catalog

Seton
20 Thompson Rd.
PO Box 819
Branford, CT 06405-819   203-488-8059
855-544-7992
Fax: 800-345-7819
help@seton.com
www.seton.com

Signs, labels, tags, pipe markers, security, and work apparel

President: Valerie Pyrell
CFO: Barbara Bolens
Marketing Manager: Donna J Canestri
VP Administration: Garry Toulson
Buyers: Jeffrey Lublin
Credit Cards: AMEX; MasterCard
Catalog Cost: Free
Catalog Circulation: Mailed 2 time(s) per year
Printing Information: 188 pages in 3 colors
Mailing List Information: Names for rent
List Company: Direct Media
In Business: 59 years
Number of Employees: 270
Sales Volume: $25,000,000 - $50,000,000

5925 Stratford Hall

6253 W 74th Street
Bedford Park, IL 60499   800-446-4510
Fax: 800-325-8262
www.stratfordhall.com

Personalized holiday cards and calendars

Credit Cards: AMEX; MasterCard
Catalog Cost: Free
Catalog Circulation: Mailed 1 time(s) per year
Printing Information: 32 pages in 4 colors on Glossy Stock
Press: Web Press
Binding: Saddle Stitched
Mailing List Information: Names for rent
In Business: 25 years
Number of Employees: 300

5926 TRIMCO

Trimco Display LLC
152 West 25th Street
Brooklyn, NY 10001-1902   212-627-2809
800-874-6261
Fax: 212-627-1805
info@trimco-display.com
www.trimco-display.com

Christmas cards and decorations for businesses

President: Ken Stolls
kstolls@lfs-trimco.com
Creative Director: Sean Sager
ssager@lfs-trimco.com
Showroom/Marketing Support: Rebecca Marchetti
rmarchetti@lfs-trimco.com
Showroom/Sales Support: Nicole Rosenthal
nrosenthal@lfs-trimco.com
Credit Cards: AMEX; MasterCard; Visa
Catalog Circulation: Mailed 1 time(s) per year
Printing Information: 23 pages in 4 colors on Glossy Stock
Press: Web Press
Binding: Saddle Stitched
In Business: 40 years
Number of Employees: 50-1
Sales Volume: $1,000,000 - $5,000,000

5927 Tenenz

Tenenz, Inc.
9655 Penn Avenue South
Minneapolis, MN 55431   952-227-1713
800-888-5803
Fax: 800-638-0015
mail@tenenz.com
www.tenenz.com

Accounting supplies, presentation materials, tax forms, business checks, stationery and software

Credit Cards: AMEX; MasterCard; Visa
Catalog Cost: Free
Printing Information: on Glossy Stock
Press: Web Press
Binding: Saddle Stitched
Mailing List Information: Names for rent
List Manager: Lee Myers
In Business: 40 years
Sales Volume: Under $500,000

5928 Tuttle Printing & Engraving

Tuttle Printing & Engraving
414 Quality Lane
Rutland, VT 05701   802-773-9171
800-776-7682
Fax: 802-773-5785
info@tuttleprinting.com
www.Tuttleprinting.Com

Printed and engraved stationery products for businesses and business cards

President: Joanne Cillo
Regional Sales Manager: Joel Perry
jperry@tuttleprinting.com
Regional Sales Manager: Don Goodman
dgoodman@tuttleprinting.com
Customer Service Manager: Diane Haggerty
diane@tuttleprinting.com
In Business: 102 years
Sales Volume: $10MM to $20MM

5929 UNICEF Catalog

United States Fund for UNICEF
125 Maiden Lane
New York, NY 10038   800-367-5437
www.unicefusa.org

Greeting cards, stationery and gifts

Chairman: Vince Hemmer
President: Caryl M. Stern
CFO: Edward G. Lloyd
Marketing Manager: Jose Carbonell
Production Manager: Laura Calassano
Senior Vice President, Development: Barron Segar
Vice President, HR: William B. Sherwood

VP, Finance & Budget: Richard Esserman
Credit Cards: AMEX; MasterCard; Visa
Catalog Circulation: Mailed 2 time(s) per year
Printing Information: in 4 colors
In Business: 69 years
Number of Employees: 100

5930   Unicef Corporate Card Collection
UNICEF United States Fund
125 Maiden Lane
New York, NY 10038   212-686-5522
                          800-367-5437
                     Fax: 212-779-1679
      www.shopbusiness.unicefusa.org/

Seasonal cards that convey the Unicef message

Chairman: Vince Hemmer
President: Caryl M. Stern
CFO: Edward G. Lloyd
Marketing Manager: Sylvia Gonzales
SVP, Marketing and Communications:
Francesco De Flaviis
SVP, Development: Barron Segar
Vice President, Finance & Budget: Richard
Esserman
Credit Cards: AMEX; MasterCard; Visa
Catalog Cost: Free
Catalog Circulation: Mailed 1 time(s) per year
to 1MM
Printing Information: 20 pages in 4 colors
Press: Web Press
Binding: Saddle Stitched
Number of Employees: 175

Personal

5931   American Stationery
American Stationery Company
100 N Park Avenue
Peru, IN 46970   800-822-2577
                     Fax: 800-253-9054
       www.americanstationery.com

Stationery, holiday cards and personalized gifts

President: Michael Bakehorn
Credit Cards: AMEX; MasterCard
Catalog Cost: Free
Mailing List Information: Names for rent
In Business: 98 years
Number of Employees: 250
Sales Volume: $50MM to $100MM

5932   AnB Stationery
AnB Stationery
20755 Plummer St.
Chatsworth, CA 91311   818-760-0244
                          800-832-8909
                     Fax: 818-506-8210
       anb@anbstationery.com
       www.anbstationery.com

Stationery and office supplies

5933   B Shackman
B. Shackman Company, Inc
PO Box 247
Galesburg, MI 49053   844-505-3229
                          800-221-7656
                     Fax: 212-656-1903
       www.shackman.com

Paper novelties, greeting cards, childrens picture books, stickers and toys

President: Dan Durett

5934   Celestial Products
Celestial Products
PO Box 801
Middleburg, VA 20118-801 540-338-4040
                          800-235-3783
                     Fax: 540-338-4042
       info@celestialproducts.com
       www.celestialproducts.com

Books and distributes popular reference materials, calendars, charts, note cards, and gifts designed to stimulate an understanding of the universe

President: Larry Bohlayer
CFO: Barbara Bohlayer
Credit Cards: MasterCard; Visa
Catalog Circulation: Mailed 1 time(s) per year
Printing Information: 24 pages in 4 colors
Binding: Saddle Stitched
Number of Employees: 4
Sales Volume: $440,000

5935   City Stationers Corporation
City Stationers Corporation
17 WEST 24 STREET
New York, NY 10010   212-675-0724
                     Fax: 212-727-8568
       wb013.britlink.com

Personal stationery

President: Richard Fialkow

5936   Colorful Images
Colorful Images
PO Box 35022
Colorado Springs, CO 80935-3522800-272-9209
                          800-458-7999
                     Fax: 800-458-6999
       www.colorfulimages.com

Personalized stationery, gifts and home decor

Catalog Cost: Free
Average Order Size: $35
In Business: 28 years

5937   Custom Address Labels
Current Labels
1005 E. Woodmen Rd
P.O.Box 1041
Colorado Springs, CO 80901 719-594-4100
                             877-755-7940
                     Fax: 719-531-2283
       webcs@currentlabels.com
       www.currentlabels.com

Personalized labels, stationery and more

President: Tim Arland
CFO: Kirby Heck
Marketing Manager: John Buleza
In Business: 52 years
Number of Employees: 850

5938   DHC
DHC USA Inc.
5021 Louise Drive
Mechanicsburg, PA 17055-6916 800-342-2273
                     Fax: 888-650-7118
       www.dhccare.com

Provides beauty products including skincare, body care, and makeup items

Catalog Cost: Free
In Business: 20 years

5939   Fine Impressions
Fine Impressions
1680 Roe Crest Dr.
North Mankato, MN 56003   800-748-2959
                     Fax: 800-541-6309
       cs@fineimpressions.com
       www.fineimpressions.com

Holiday cards, greeting cards, envelopes, napkinds, social invitations, stationery, customized materials.

5940   GiftsForYouNow.com
GiftsForYouNow.com
109 Shore Drive
Burr Ridge, IL 60527   630-771-0095
                          866-443-8748
                     Fax: 630-771-0098
       service@giftsforyounow.com
       www.giftsforyounow.com

Personalized gifts, products, and accessories for all occasions

Catalog Cost: Free
In Business: 16 years

5941   Greenwoods Collection
Holiday Classics
PO Box 599
Sunman, IN 47041-599   866-700-5030
                     Fax: 800-446-4510
       www.greenwoodscollection.com

Holiday greeting cards, calendars and chocolates

Credit Cards: AMEX; MasterCard; Visa
Catalog Cost: Free
Catalog Circulation: Mailed 1 time(s) per year
Printing Information: 40 pages in 4 colors on
Glossy Stock
Press: Web Press
Binding: Saddle Stitched
In Business: 40 years

5942   Heart Thoughts Birth Announcements
Heart Thoughts Designs
1711 S Longfellow St
Wichita, KS 67207   316-688-5781
                          800-524-2229
                     Fax: 800-526-2846
       www.heart-thoughts.com

Birth announcements, parenting books, exercise videos for moms, gifts

President: Grant Goodvin
Credit Cards: AMEX; MasterCard; Visa
Number of Employees: 100
Sales Volume: $5MM to $10MM

5943   Holiday Collection
National Wildlife Federation
11100 Wildlife Center Drive
Reston, VA 20190   800-822-9919
                     Fax: 800-525-5562
       www.nwf.org

Christmas cards, calendars and apparel with a wildlife theme

Chairman: Deborah Spalding
President: Collin O'Mara
CFO: Dulce Zormelo
CEO: Collin O'Mara
Credit Cards: AMEX; MasterCard; Visa
Catalog Cost: Free
Catalog Circulation: Mailed 6 time(s) per year
to 20MM
Printing Information: 48 pages in 4 colors on
Glossy Stock
Press: Web Press
Binding: Saddle Stitched
Mailing List Information: Names for rent
In Business: 63 years
Number of Employees: 350

5944   Holiday Expressions
Deluxe For Business
3680 Victoria Street North
Shoreview, MN 55126   800-865-1913
       www.holidayexpressions.com

Holiday greeting cards

Credit Cards: AMEX; MasterCard
Catalog Cost: Free
Printing Information: 35 pages in 4 colors on
Glossy Stock
Binding: Saddle Stitched

5945   House of Conception Abbey
The Printery House
37112 State Highway VV
P.O. Box 12
Conception, MO 64433   660-944-3110
                          800-322-2737
                     Fax: 888-556-8262
       sales@printeryhouse.org
       www.printeryhouse.org

Religious books, greeting cards, stationery and gifts

President: Gerald Nelson
Marketing Manager: Ron Riggs
Creative Director: Steve Hess
shee@printeryhouse.org
Buyers: Don Sullivan
Credit Cards: MasterCard; Visa
Catalog Cost: Free
Catalog Circulation: Mailed 5 time(s) per year to 10000
Average Order Size: $38
Printing Information: 56 pages in 4 colors on Glossy Stock
Press: Web Press
Binding: Saddle Stitched
Mailing List Information: Names for rent
In Business: 47 years
Number of Employees: 38
Sales Volume: $3MM to $5MM

5946 Literary Calligraphy
Literary Calligraphy
5326 White House Road
Moneta, VA 24121   540-297-7938
                         800-261-6325
                    Fax: 540-297-1599
susanloy@literarycalligraphy.com
www.literarycalligraphy.com

Catalog of calligraphy text with illustrations, great wedding or special gifts

President: Ron Ayers
Catalog Cost: Free
Catalog Circulation: Mailed 1 time(s) per year
Average Order Size: $60
Printing Information: 16 pages in 4 colors on Glossy Stock
Press: Sheetfed Press
Binding: Saddle Stitched
In Business: 14 years
Number of Employees: 8
Sales Volume: Under $500M

5947 Merrimade
Merrimade
PO Box 207
Peru, IN 46970   800-344-4256
www.merrimade.com

Personalized paper products and personal stationery

Credit Cards: AMEX; MasterCard; Visa
Catalog Cost: Free
Catalog Circulation: Mailed 2 time(s) per year to 1000
Average Order Size: $150
Printing Information: 24 pages in 4 colors on Glossy Stock
Press: Web Press
Binding: Saddle Stitched
Mailing List Information: Names for rent
In Business: 94 years
Number of Employees: 25
Sales Volume: $1MM to $3MM

5948 Message!Products
Message!Products
8245 N Union Blvd
P.O. Box 40012
Colorado Springs, CO 80920-4456866-460-0099
                         800-243-2565
                    Fax: 410-676-8269
helpmp@messageproducts.com
www.messageproducts.com

Eco-friendly personal checks and products

Credit Cards: MasterCard; Visa
Catalog Cost: Free
In Business: 30 years

5949 Paula's Choice Skincare
Paula's Choice
705 5th Ave S, Suite 200
Seattle, WA 98104   800-831-4088
www.paulaschoice.com

Skin care products

President: Paula Begoun
Research and Content Director: Bryan Barron
Catalog Cost: Free
In Business: 19 years

5950 Perfumax
Perfumax
Blythourne Station
P.O. Box 191213
Brooklyn, NY 11219   718-854-6136
                         800-300-7800
                    Fax: 888-755-7373
www.perfumax.com

Name brand fragrances, skin, bath and body care products

Catalog Cost: Free

5951 Pipsqueak Productions
Pipsqueak Productions
817 Hancock Highway
P.O. Box 1005
Honesdale, PA 18431-9551   570-253-4330
                         888-747-9054
                    Fax: 570-253-4539
sales@pipsqueakproductions.com
www.pipsqueakproductions.com

Pet Lover greeting cards & gifts

President: Mary Badenhop
Printing Information: 82 pages
In Business: 30 years

5952 Printery House
Printery House
Po Box 12
Conception, MO 64433   660-944-3110
                         800-322-2737
                    Fax: 660-944-3116
shess@printeryhouse.org
www.printeryhouse.org

Chrisitan greeting cards and gifts

5953 Promo Direct
Promo Direct
931 American Pacific Dr
Suite 100
Henderson, NV 89014   800-748-6150
order@promodirect.com
www.promodirect.com

President: Dave Sarro
Credit Cards: AMEX; MasterCard
Catalog Cost: Free
In Business: 24 years

5954 Renton's
Renton's
637 Wyckoff Ave, Suite 280
Wyckoff NJ, NJ 07481-6411   303-865-7025
                         800-365-6644
                    Fax: 800-873-3060
info@rentons.com
www.Rentons.Com

Greeting cards and stickers

Chairman: Jack Renton
President: Dawn Goldwasser
Credit Cards: AMEX; MasterCard
Catalog Cost: Free
Catalog Circulation: Mailed 2 time(s) per year
In Business: 48 years
Sales Volume: $1MM to $3MM

5955 Rytex Catalog
Rytex
100 N Park Avenue
Peru, IN 46970   800-277-5458
                    Fax: 800-329-1669
press@theboatmangroup.com
theboatmangroup.com

Personalized stationery, luggage tags and correspondence cards

Printing Information: in 3 colors
In Business: 82 years

5956 School Life
School Life
1080 Avenida Acaso
Camarillo, CA 93012-8725   877-773-7705
                    Fax: 877-563-3616
www.schoollife.com

In Business: 19 years

5957 Script and Scribble
Script and Scribble
12700 Biscayne Blvd
Sut 300
North Miami, FL 33181   800-652-1260
www.scriptandscribble.com

Founder: Lourdes Reich

5958 Shop Wright
Shop Wright
209 S. LaSalle St.
Chicago, IL 60604   877-848-3559
info@shopwright.org
www.shopwright.org

5959 Sormani Calendars
Sormani Calendars
P.O. Box 6059
Chelsea, MA 02150-6   617-889-9300
                         800-321-9327
                    Fax: 617-889-9306
www.sormanicalendars.com

Calendars: Scenic, fine art, pets and animals, hobby's, sports, special subjects, religious

CFO: Judith Jenkins
Marketing Manager: Alex Jenkins
Co-Owner: Rich Mastrovich
Co-Owner: MJ Mastrovich
Credit Cards: AMEX; MasterCard
Catalog Cost: Free
Catalog Circulation: Mailed 2 time(s) per year to 33000
Average Order Size: $45
Printing Information: 36 pages in 4 colors on Glossy Stock
Press: Web Press
Binding: Saddle Stitched
Mailing List Information: Names for rent
In Business: 74 years
Number of Employees: 4
Sales Volume: $500M to $1MM

5960 Stork Avenue Catalog
1500 S Dixie Hwy # 300
Third Floor
Coral Gables, FL 33146-3033   305-669-4878
                         800-861-5437
                    Fax: 305-662-9009
www.Storkavenue.Com

Announcements, invitations, and note cards for baby showers

President: Robert J Hunter
Credit Cards: AMEX; MasterCard
Sales Volume: $5MM to $10MM

5961 The Hair Factory
The Hair Factory
116 Pleasant Street, Suite 229
Easthampton, MA 00102   413-585-9666
                         800-999-9328
                    Fax: 413-585-8902
customerservice@hairfactory.com
www.hairfactory.com

Supplies consumers with 100% natural human hair for hair pieces and extensions—also supplies how to books, videos, and hair care products

Catalog Cost: Free
In Business: 30 years

5962 The Met Store
The Metropolitan Museum of Art
1000 Fifth Avenue
New York, NY 10028   800-468-7386
customer.service@metmuseum.org
store.metmuseum.org

Jewelry, apparel, home d,cor, prints & posters, books, stationery & calendars inspired by the Metropolitan Museum of Art

Catalog Cost: Free
In Business: 96 years

5963 The Printery House
The Printery House
37112 State Highway VV
PO BOX 12
Conception, MO 64433   660-944-3110
800-322-2737
custom@printeryhouse.org
www.printeryhouse.org

Catalog Cost: $19.99
In Business: 142 years

5964 Trumble Greetings
Trumble Greetings, Inc.
PO Box 9800
Boulder, CO 80301-9800   303-530-7768
800-525-0656
Fax: 303-530-5124
info@leanintree.com
www.leanintree.com

Christmas cards, everyday greeting cards, mugs, magnets, stationery and gifts

Chairman: Ed Trumble
President: Thomas Trumble
CFO: Peter Mahlstedt
Marketing Manager: Dana Pauley
Founder: Ed Trumble
Buyers: Thomas Trumble
Credit Cards: MasterCard; Visa
Catalog Cost: Free
Catalog Circulation: Mailed 4 time(s) per year
Printing Information: 32 pages in 4 colors on Glossy Stock
Press: Web Press
Binding: Saddle Stitched
Mailing List Information: Names for rent
Number of Employees: 200

5965 Victorian Papers
Victorian Trading Company
15600 W. 99th Street
Lenexa, KS 66219-2900   844-724-2340
customercare@victoriantrading.com
www.victoriantradingco.com

Holiday greeting cards

President: Randy Rolston
CFO: Kathy Coombs
Marketing Manager: Sarah Rouchka
Founder: Randy Rolston
Founder: Melissa Rolston
Catalog Cost: Free
Printing Information: 25 pages
In Business: 30 years
Sales Volume: $20MM to $50MM

5966 Webway Album Catalog
PO Box 767
Saint Cloud, MN 56302-767   320-251-7524
800-543-2397
www.shopwebway.com

Photo albums and refills

Credit Cards: MasterCard; Visa
Catalog Cost: Free
Printing Information: 15 pages in 4 colors
Number of Employees: 175

5967 Willow Tree Lane
Invitation By Dawn
1985 Lookout Drive North
Mankato, MN 56003   800-257-9567
contact@invitationsbydawn.com
www.invitationsbydawn.com

Personalized stationery gifts, wedding invitations

Catalog Cost: Free
Printing Information: 60 pages

5968 Write Touch
PO Box 290366
Columbia, SC 29229   866-557-8661
www.writetouch.net

Personalized stationary and unique gifts

Printing Information: 64 pages
Number of Employees: 175

Wedding

5969 American Wedding
American Wedding
300 N Park Avenue
Peru, IN 46970-1701   800-428-0379
Fax: 800-864-8673
www.theamericanwedding.com

Wedding invitations, tableware, favors, party gifts, stationery

President: Michael Bakehorn
Marketing Manager: Kathy Calderbank
Production Manager: Guy Luttrell Jr
Credit Cards: MasterCard; Visa; Discover
Catalog Cost: Free
Catalog Circulation: Mailed 2 time(s) per year
Average Order Size: $150
Printing Information: 92 pages in 4 colors on Glossy Stock
Press: Web Press
Binding: Saddle Stitched
Mailing List Information: Names for rent
In Business: 96 years
Number of Employees: 300

5970 Ann's Bridal Bargains
Ann's Bridal Bargains
1985 Lookout Drive
North Mankato, MN 56003   800-821-7011
service@annsbridalbargains.com
www.annsbridalbargains.com

Save the dates and bridal shower invitations, wedding invitations, thank you notes, ceremony and reception accessories

Catalog Cost: Free

5971 Ann's Wedding Stationary
Invitations by Dawn
1985 Lookout Drive
1 Stationery Place
North Mankato, MN 56003   812-654-2548
800-257-9567
Fax: 800-626-3670
contact@invitationsbydawn.com
www.invitationsbydawn.com

Wedding stationery and supplies

Credit Cards: MasterCard; Visa
Catalog Cost: Free
Catalog Circulation: Mailed 2 time(s) per year
Printing Information: 48 pages in 4 colors on Glossy Stock
Binding: Saddle Stitched
Number of Employees: 25

5972 Bill Levkoff
Bill Levkoff Inc.
8 Westchester Plaza
Elmsford, NY 10523   914-345-2900
www.billlevkoff.com

Bridesmaid apparel and accessories

President: Jon Levkoff
In Business: 65 years

5973 Creations by Elaine
Creations by Elaine
6253 W 74th Street
Bedford Park, IL 60499   708-496-4900
800-323-1208
Fax: 800-388-0086
sales@creationengine.com
www.creationsbyelaine.com

Wedding invitations

President: Jim Motz
Marketing Manager: Dolores Milam
Catalog Cost: Free
Printing Information: 68 pages in 4 colors on Glossy Stock
Press: Web Press
Binding: Saddle Stitched
Mailing List Information: Names for rent
Number of Employees: 250

5974 Evangel Wedding Service
Wedding Wire
1 Stationery Place
Rexburg, ID 83441-202   800-257-9567
Fax: 800-626-3670
contact@invitationsbydawn.com
www.invitationsbydawn.com

Christian wedding invitations

President: Eugene Johansen
Credit Cards: MasterCard; Visa
Catalog Cost: Free
Printing Information: 40 pages in 4 colors

5975 Exclusively Weddings
Exclusively Weddings
2305 Soabar Street
Greensboro, NC 27406   800-759-7666
800-759-7666
Fax: 336-275-4165
corporate@EWeddings.com
www.exclusivelyweddings.com

Wedding invitations, wedding guest favors and bridal accessories

President: Bonnie Mcelveen Hunter
General Manager: R. David Stubbs
Director of Merchandising, Statione: Beth Vogel
Director of Marketing: Matt Mitchell
Credit Cards: AMEX; MasterCard
Catalog Cost: Free
Printing Information: 117 pages in 4 colors on Glossy Stock
Press: Web Press
Binding: Saddle Stitched
In Business: 23 years
Number of Employees: 87
Sales Volume: $3MM to $5MM

5976 Family Medallion
Clergy Services Inc
PO Box 32333
Kansas City, MO 64171-5333   816-753-3886
800-237-1922
rcoleman@clergyservices.com
www.familymedallion.com

The Family Medallion and related presentation materials provide resources for including children in the wedding when a parent remarries

President: Dr Roger Coleman
Catalog Cost: Free
Average Order Size: $110
Printing Information: 12 pages in 4 colors on Glossy Stock
Press: Web Press
Binding: Folded
Mailing List Information: Names for rent
In Business: 15 years
Number of Employees: 10-J
Sales Volume: Under $500M

5977 Forever & Always
Forever & Always Inc
4536 Apulia Road
Jamesville, NY 13078   315-492-4652
                              800-581-5845
                              Fax: 585-924-9238
custsvc@foreverandalways.com
www.foreverandalways.com

Wedding favors, bridal accessories, guestbooks, caketops, unity candles, ring pillows, flower girl baskets, bridal party gifts and jewelry

President: Debra Hogan
deb@foreverandalways.com
Credit Cards: AMEX; MasterCard
Catalog Cost: Free
Catalog Circulation: Mailed 52 time(s) per year to 30000
Printing Information: 32 pages in 4 colors on Glossy Stock
Press: Web Press
Binding: Saddle Stitched
Mailing List Information: Names for rent
In Business: 12 years
Number of Employees: 4
Sales Volume: Under $500M

5978 Gunther Gifts Wedding Catalog
Gunther Gifts Inc.
2717 Loker Ave. West
Carlsbad, CA 92010   760-476-9131
                            877-544-0814
                            Fax: 775-890-6571

Personalized gifts, products, accessories, and engravings

Catalog Cost: Free
In Business: 29+ years

5979 Hortense B. Hewitt Co.
1 Stationery Place
Rexburg, ID 83441   800-821-2504
                           Fax: 800-535-1033
cshbh@hbh.zgate.com
www.hbhwedding.com

5980 JC Penney-Gift Registry
JC Penney
PO Box 10001
Dallas, TX 75301-7311   972-431-3400
                               800-842-9470
jcpinvestorrelations@jcpenney.com
www.jcpenney.com

Wedding gifts

Chairman: Thomas Engibous
President: James Oesterreicher
CFO: Edward Record
Marketing Manager: Debra Berman
Chief Executive Officer: Mike Ullman
EVP, General Counsel and Secretary: Janet Dhillon
EVP, Chief Information Officer: Scott Laverty
Credit Cards: AMEX; MasterCard; Visa; Discover
Number of Employees: 4000

5981 Minted Wedding
Minted
                               888-828-6468
                               www.minted.com

Wedding invitations and accessories.

President: Melissa Kim
CEO: Mariam Naficy
VP: Charlie Rice
Chief People Officer: Mala Singh
In Business: 8 years

5982 Paper Access
Paper Access
23 W 18th St
New York, NY 10011-4601   212-463-7035
                                 Fax: 212-463-7022
info@paperpresentation.com
www.paperpresentation.com

Stationery and matching envelopes and printing software

President: Chris Brown
VP: Arthur Rejay
Credit Cards: AMEX; MasterCard; Visa
Catalog Cost: Free
Catalog Circulation: Mailed 2 time(s) per year to 20M
Printing Information: 64 pages in 4 colors
Mailing List Information: Names for rent
List Manager: Venture Communications
List Company: Venture Communications
60 Madison Avenue, 3rd Floor
New York, NY 10010
212-684-4800
In Business: 20 years
Number of Employees: 25
Sales Volume: $ 3.6 Million

5983 PaperDirect Events
PaperDirect
P.O. Box 1151
Minneapolis, MN 55440-1151   800-272-7377
                                    Fax: 800-443-2973
volumesales@paperdirect.com
www.paperdirect.com

Do-it-yourself stationery; themes for occasions and events

President: Tim Arland
CFO: Kirby Heck
Credit Cards: AMEX; MasterCard
Catalog Cost: Free
Printing Information: in 4 colors
In Business: 29 years
Number of Employees: 1200
Sales Volume: $78 MM

5984 Rexcraft
Rexcraft
1 Stationery Plaza
Rexburg, ID 83441-1   800-285-8938
                             Fax: 800-826-2712
                             www.rexcraft.com

Wedding invitations

President: Norm Doering
Credit Cards: MasterCard; Visa
Catalog Cost: Free
Catalog Circulation: Mailed 1 time(s) per year
Printing Information: 30 pages in 3 colors
Mailing List Information: Names for rent
In Business: 100 years

5985 The American Wedding
The American Wedding
300 N. Park Avenue
Peru, IN 46970   800-428-0379
www.theamericanwedding.com

Personalized stationery and related products.

In Business: 96 years

5986 Victorian Bride
Victorian Bride
7501 N 18th Avenue
Phoenix, AZ 85021-7909   602-997-7499
                                800-706-4050
                                Fax: 602-997-7499

Fresh flowers for the wedding day and always, Victorian and contemporary designs, custom work welcome

President: Laura Reeves
CFO: Scott Reeves
Marketing Manager: Laura Reeves
Production Manager: Laura Reeves
Catalog Cost: $8
Printing Information: 50 pages in 4 colors on Glossy Stock
Press: Sheetfed Press
Mailing List Information: Names for rent
In Business: 11 years
Number of Employees: 5
Sales Volume: Under $500M

Tobacco Products
Supplies & Accessories

5987 Anthony's Cigar Emporium
Anthony's Cigar Emporium
7866 N Oracle Rd.
Tucson, AZ 85704   844-424-4277
sales@anthonyscigars.com
anthonyscigars.com

Cigars.

In Business: 20 years

5988 Back In The Saddle
Back In The Saddle
P.O. Box 3336
Chelmsford, MA 00182-0936   877-756-5068
                                   800-865-2478
                                   Fax: 800-866-3235
help@BackInTheSaddle.com
www.backinthesaddle.com

Horseback riding gear, clothing, jewelry, and accessories for   horse lovers

Catalog Cost: Free
In Business: 22 years

5989 Cigar.com
Cigar.com
1911 Spillman Dr
Dept #26
Bethlehem, PA 18015   800-357-9800
                             Fax: 877-464-2872
                             service@cigar.com
                             www.cigar.com

Hard to find cigars

In Business: 10 years

5990 Cigars International
Cigars International
1911 Spillman Dr
Dept #26
Bethlehem, PA 18015   888-244-2790
                             Fax: 888-792-2442
www.cigarsinternational.com

Variety of brand name cigars and tobacco supplies

Chairman: John DeMarco
President: Keith Meier
Catalog Cost: Free
Printing Information: 52 pages
In Business: 19 years

5991 Cigars for Aficionados
Cigars Aficionados
387 Park Avenue South
New York, NY 10016   212-684-4224
                            800-992-2442
                            Fax: 212-481-1540
cgacustserv@cdsfulfillment.com
www.cigaraficionado.com

Pipe and cigar catalogs

President: William Jefferson Clinton
Executive Director: J. Glynn Loope
Credit Cards: AMEX; MasterCard; Visa
Printing Information: 24 pages
In Business: 10 years
Number of Employees: 5
Sales Volume: $110,000

5992 Colibri Lighters
Colibri
100 Niantic Ave
Providence, RI 02907-3146   401-943-2100
                                   800-556-7354
                                   Fax: 401-943-4230
                                   www.colibri.com

Fine lighters, cigar accessories, table lighters and gifts

Chairman: Thomas Bendheim
President: Fredrick Levinger

CFO: Steve Silvia
Marketing Manager: Mike Relnolds
Credit Cards: AMEX; MasterCard; Visa
Catalog Cost: Free
Catalog Circulation: Mailed 1 time(s) per year
Printing Information: 22 pages in 4 colors on Glossy Stock
Press: Web Press
Binding: Saddle Stitched
In Business: 86 years
Number of Employees: 1
Sales Volume: $500M to $1MM

5993 Corona Cigar Company
Corona Cigar Company
7792 W Sand Lake Rd
Orlando, FL 32819
407-248-1212
888-70 -IGAR
Fax: 407-248-1211
www.coronacigar.com

Cigars.

President: Jeff Borysiewicz

5994 E.A. Carey's Smokeshop
E.A. Carey's Smokeshop
7090 Whipple Ave NW
North Canton, OH 44720
800-992-7427
custserv@eacarey.net
www.eacarey.com
Credit Cards: AMEX; MasterCard
In Business: 67 years

5995 Famous Smoke Shop
Famous Smoke Shop
90 Mort Drive
Easton, PA 18040-6657
610-559-8800
800-564-2486
info@famous-smoke.com
www.famous-smoke.com

Premium cigars, humidors, and accessories

Chairman: Stanford Newman
President: Arthur Zaretsky
Credit Cards: AMEX; MasterCard
Catalog Cost: Free
Printing Information: 68 pages in 4 colors
In Business: 76 years
Number of Employees: 48
Sales Volume: $2.8 Million

5996 Finck Cigar
Finck Cigar
414 Vera Cruz Street
San Antonio, TX 78207
210-226-4191
800-221-0638
Fax: 210-226-2825
custser@finckcigarcompany.com
www.finckcigarcompany.com

Cigars, pipes, tobacco, humidors, and smoking accessories

President: Bill Finck Jr
CFO: Felipe Gonzales
Marketing Manager: Lynn Michael
Production Manager: Olivia Chappa
Buyers: Bill Finck Jr
Credit Cards: MasterCard
Catalog Cost: Free
Catalog Circulation: Mailed 6 time(s) per year to 300M
Printing Information: 64 pages in 4 colors on Glossy Stock
Press: Web Press
Binding: Saddle Stitched
Mailing List Information: Names for rent
List Manager: Lynn Michael
In Business: 155 years
Number of Employees: 80
Sales Volume: $3MM to $5MM

5997 GiftsForYouNow.com
GiftsForYouNow.com
109 Shore Drive
Burr Ridge, IL 60527
630-771-0095
866-443-8748
Fax: 630-771-0098
service@giftsforyounow.com
www.giftsforyounow.com

Personalized gifts, products, and accessories for all occasions

Catalog Cost: Free
In Business: 16 years

5998 Gunther Gifts Wedding Catalog
Gunther Gifts Inc.
2717 Loker Ave. West
Carlsbad, CA 92010
760-476-9131
877-544-0814
Fax: 775-890-6571

Personalized gifts, products, accessories, and engravings

Catalog Cost: Free
In Business: 29+ years

5999 Holts Tobacconist
Holts Cigar Company
12270 Townsend Road
Philadelphia, PA 19154-1203
215-676-8778
800-523-1641
Fax: 215-676-9085
holts@holts.com
www.Holts.Com

Assortment of tobacco products, premium cigars and accessories

President: Robert Levin
Marketing Manager: Mike Pitkow
Production Manager: Karen Richardson
Credit Cards: AMEX; MasterCard; Visa
Catalog Cost: Free
Catalog Circulation: Mailed 8 time(s) per year
Printing Information: 32 pages in 4 colors on Glossy Stock
Press: Web Press
Binding: Saddle Stitched
Mailing List Information: Names for rent
In Business: 116 years
Number of Employees: 80
Sales Volume: $10MM to $20MM

6000 House of Oxford Wholesale Cigars
1122 Welling Court
Astoria, NY 11102-4023
718-721-5858
800-881-8893
Fax: 718-721-5828
www.momscigars.com

Premium cigars, tobaccos and accessories

President: Mark Goldman
Marketing Manager: Alex Goldman
Catalog Circulation: Mailed 2 time(s) per year
Printing Information: 32 pages in 4 colors on Glossy Stock
Press: Web Press
Binding: Saddle Stitched
Mailing List Information: Names for rent
In Business: 48 years
Number of Employees: 40
Sales Volume: $20MM to $50MM

6001 JR Cigars
JR Cigars
2589 Eric Lane
Burlington, NC 27215
800-572-4427
888-574-3576
Fax: 800-457-3299
customerservice@jrcigars.com
www.jrcigars.com

Large selection of cigars at discount prices.

President: Paul Gunther
Catalog Cost: Free
Printing Information: 90 pages in 4 colors on Matte Stock
Press: Web Press

Binding: Saddle Stitched
Number of Employees: 900
Sales Volume: $50MM to $100MM

6002 JR Tobacco
JR Cigars
2589 Eric Lane
Burlington, NC 27215
800-572-4427
888-574-3576
Fax: 800-457-3299
customerservice@jrcigars.com
www.jrcigars.com

Cigars and tobacco products

President: LW Rothman
Marketing Manager: Richard John
Credit Cards: AMEX; MasterCard; Visa
Catalog Cost: Free
Catalog Circulation: Mailed 4 time(s) per year
Printing Information: 140 pages in 4 colors

6003 Luis Martinez Gallery of Fine Cigars
Luis Martinez
2701 N 16th Street
Tampa, FL 33605
813-248-2124
800-822-4427
Fax: 813-248-4175
info@luismartinez.com
www.luismartinez.com

Tobacco products, tobacco accessories and coffee

Chairman: Shira Martin
President: Eric Newman
Marketing Manager: Shanda Lee
Sales & Service Coordinator: Heather Hill
heather@luismartinez.com
Catalog Cost: Free
Catalog Circulation: Mailed 4 time(s) per year
Printing Information: 39 pages in 4 colors
Mailing List Information: Names for rent
In Business: 138 years
Number of Employees: 130
Sales Volume: $ 950,000

6004 Mike's Cigars
Mike's Cigars
1030 Kane Concourse
Bay Harbor, FL 33154-2107
305-866-2277
800-962-4427
Fax: 305-866-7977
customerservice@mikescigars.com
www.mikescigars.com

Cigars and cigar merchandise

President: Oscar Boruchin
CFO: Rose Boruchin
Credit Cards: AMEX; MasterCard; Visa
Catalog Cost: Free
Printing Information: 16 pages in 4 colors
In Business: 30 years
Number of Employees: 29
Sales Volume: $17.3 Million

6005 Mom's Cigars
Mom's Cigars
344 Maple Ave West #110
Vienna, VA 22180
718-721-5858
800-831-8893
Fax: 718-721-5828
orders@momscigars.com
www.momscigars.com

Cigars, tobacco and smoker accessories

Chairman: Alex Goldman
Credit Cards: AMEX; MasterCard; Visa; Discover Optima
Catalog Cost: Free
Catalog Circulation: Mailed 3 time(s) per year to 10000
Average Order Size: $50
Printing Information: 40 pages in 4 colors on Glossy Stock
Press: Web Press
Binding: Saddle Stitched
Mailing List Information: Names for rent
List Company: George Mann Associates

Number of Employees: 40
Sales Volume: $20MM to $50MM

6006 Nat Sherman
Nat Sherman
12 East 42nd Street at Fifth Avenue
New York, NY 10017-6901   212-764-5000
800-MY -IGAR
Fax: 201-735-9099
www.Natsherman.Com

Pipes, cigars, cigarettes, tobacco and lighters

President: Joel Sherman
CFO: Louis Carbone
Marketing Manager: Bill Sherman
Production Manager: Peter Jenko
Buyers: William Mickey
Credit Cards: AMEX; MasterCard; Visa
Catalog Cost: Free
Catalog Circulation: Mailed 2 time(s) per year to 25000
Printing Information: 32 pages in 4 colors on Glossy Stock
Press: Web Press
Number of Employees: 35
Sales Volume: 5MM-10MM

6007 Nick's Cigar World
Nick's Cigar World
2705 Hwy 17 South
North Myrtle Beach, SC 29582   888-311-9826
Fax: 843-361-9058
www.nickscigarworld.net

Cigars.

6008 Pipes and Cigars
Pipes and Cigars
1911 Spillman Dr.
Dept #26
Bethlehem, PA 18015   610-297-9053
800-494-9144
Fax: 800-494-9144
www.pipesandcigars.com

Online retailer of pipes and pipe tobacco.

In Business: 16 years

6009 Thompson Cigar Company
Thompson Cigar Company
5401 Hangar Court
Tampa, FL 33634   800-573-9099
800-237-2559
Fax: 813-882-4605
www.thompsoncigar.com

Cigars, pipes, tobacco, humidors, gifts and accessories.

President: Robert Franzblau
CFO: Colm Conway
Marketing Manager: Steven Cobden
Credit Cards: AMEX; MasterCard; Visa
Catalog Cost: Free
Catalog Circulation: Mailed 12 time(s) per year
Printing Information: 47 pages in 4 colors
In Business: 101 years
Number of Employees: 450
Sales Volume: $83.2 Million

6010 Worldwide Cigar Club Catalog
Worldwide Cigar Club
484 Wegner Road
Lakemoor, IL 60051-3001   815-363-4000
800-800-9122
Fax: 815-363-4677
info@greatclubs.com
www.greatclubs.com

Mail order cigar club

President: Douglas M Doretti
CFO: Dirk J Doretti
Credit Cards: AMEX; MasterCard
Catalog Circulation: Mailed 3 time(s) per year to 20000
Printing Information: 6 pages in 4 colors on Glossy Stock

Press: Web Press
Binding: Saddle Stitched
In Business: 21 years
Number of Employees: 10
Sales Volume: $5MM to $10MM

Tools & Machinery
General Products

6011 3M Accessories for Abrasive Products
Contract Production Services/CPS
1936 Lyndale Avenue South
Minneapolis, MN 55403   612-767-2978
800-843-0619
Fax: 612-872-0189
sales@contactcps.com

Disc accessories, wheel, belt and hand-sanding accessories, dispensers, spindles and mandrels. Finesse-It system accessories, packs and kits, Scotch-Brite Radial Bristle product accessories.

Catalog Cost: Free
Catalog Circulation: Mailed 1 time(s) per year
Printing Information: 56 pages in 4 colors on Glossy Stock
In Business: 55 years

6012 A&H Abrasives
A&H Abrasives
1108 N Glenn Rd
Casper, WY 82601-1635   307-237-5354
800-831-6066
Fax: 307-237-4122
sales@woodworker.com

Abrasive tools, clothing, chemicals, hand tools and hardware.

President: John Wirth, Jr.
john@woodworker.com
General Manager: Steve Ford
stevef@woodworker.com
Customer Service Manager: Lisa Holthus
presales@woodworker.com
Website Manager: Robert Tyrrell
rtyrrell@woodworker.com
Credit Cards: AMEX; MasterCard; Visa
Catalog Cost: Free
Catalog Circulation: Mailed 4 time(s) per year
Printing Information: 16 pages in 4 colors on Glossy Stock
Press: Web Press
Binding: Saddle Stitched
In Business: 29 years
Number of Employees: 10
Sales Volume: $10MM

6013 Accu Trak Tool
Accu Trak Tool Corporation
490 Stafford St
Cherry Valley, MA 01611-3307   508-892-1787
800-433-4933
Fax: 508-892-1789
eng@accu-trak.com
www.accu-trak.com

Knurling tools, dies and holders for turning machines

President: Roland Mason
Marketing Manager: Ron Klaucke
Production Manager: Jon Mason
Buyers: Jon Mason
Credit Cards: AMEX; MasterCard; Visa
Catalog Circulation: Mailed 1 time(s) per year
Printing Information: 28 pages on Matte Stock
Binding: Folded
In Business: 29 years
Number of Employees: 17
Sales Volume: $3,000,000

6014 AccuCut Craft
AccuCut Systems
8843 S. 137th Circle
Attn: Customer Service Center
Omaha, NE 68138   402-934-1070
888-317-0093
Fax: 402-939-0304
info@accucutcraft.com
www.accucutcraft.com

Hand-operated machines, die cutting machines, equipment and tools for embossing, fabric crafts and home decor crafts

President: Greg Gaggini

6015 Ace Tank
Ace Tank & Equipment Company
18340 Andover Park W.
Tukwila, WA 98188   206-281-5000
800-426-2880
Fax: 888-475-1418
sales.800@acetank.com
www.acetank.com

Fuel tanks, oil tanks, fueling nozzles

Chairman: R.A. Reese
President: Robert Thompson
CFO: Jack Bruton
VP: Bill Durkin
Purchasing Manager: Ron Radach
Credit Cards: MasterCard; Visa
Catalog Cost: Free
Catalog Circulation: Mailed 26 time(s) per year
Printing Information: 250 pages
Binding: Perfect Bound
In Business: 78 years
Number of Employees: 60

6016 Acme Manufacturing
Acme Manufacturing
4240 N Atlantic Blvd
Auburn Hills, MI 48326-1578   248-393-7300
800-383-6993
Fax: 248-393-4060
www.Acmemfg.Com

Robotic and centerless belt grinding plus deburring systems

Chairman: Glen A Carlson Jr
President: G.A. Carlson III
Marketing Manager: Joe Saad
Production Manager: Dave Meredith
Credit Cards: AMEX; MasterCard; Visa
Mailing List Information: Names for rent
In Business: 105 years
Number of Employees: 60
Sales Volume: $9,000,000

6017 Acme Tools
Acme Tools
1603 12th Avenue N.
Grand Forks, ND 58203   877-345-ACME
support@acmetools.com
www.acmetools.com

Retailers of tools and equipment.

Credit Cards: AMEX; MasterCard
Catalog Cost: Free
In Business: 65 years

6018 Adjustable Clamp
Pony Tools Incorporated
404 N Armour St
Chicago, IL 60642-6397   312-666-0640
Fax: 312-666-2723
jorgensenponyclamp.com

Woodworking clamps, tape measures & pliers

President: Joe Krueger
Catalog Cost: Free
Printing Information: in 4 colors
In Business: 112 years
Number of Employees: 400
Sales Volume: $50,000,000 - $100,000,00

6019 Advanced Machinery

Advanced Machinery
PO Box 430
New Castle, DE 19720
302-322-2226
800-727-6553
Fax: 866-686-1615
wolfgang@advmachinery.com
www.advmachinery.com

Specialty woodworking tools

President: Wolfgang Derke
Credit Cards: AMEX; MasterCard; Visa
Catalog Cost: Free
Catalog Circulation: to 50000
Average Order Size: $53
Printing Information: 24 pages in 4 colors on Glossy Stock
Press: Web Press
Binding: Saddle Stitched
Mailing List Information: Names for rent
In Business: 23 years
Number of Employees: 11
Sales Volume: $1,500,000

6020 Aerial Lift

Altec NUECO
571 Plains Rd
Milford, CT 06461-1796
203-878-0694
866-617-1569
Fax: 203-878-2661
steve.weikart@nueco.com
www.nueco.com/articles/aerial-lift-of-connecti-cut

Aerial lifts, truck mounts and other types of machinery

President: Cheryl Depiero
CFO: David Walker
Credit Cards: AMEX; MasterCard; Visa
In Business: 41 years
Number of Employees: 48
Sales Volume: $10,000,000

6021 Air Tools, Hand Tools, Sheet Metal Tools

US Industrial Tool & Supply Company
14083 S Normandie Avenue
Gardena, CA 90249
310-464-8400
800-521-7394
Fax: 310-464-8880
info@ustool.com
www.ustool.com

Construction and hardware tools

General Manager: Ked Armstrong
Senior Accountant: Mike Hill
CEO: Tom Brotz
Credit Cards: MasterCard
Catalog Cost: Free
Printing Information: 151 pages in 2 colors
Binding: Perfect Bound
In Business: 59 years
Number of Employees: 47
Sales Volume: $10MM to $20MM

6022 Aircraft Tool Supply Company

Aircraft Tool Supply Company
1000 Old US 23
PO Box 370
Oscoda, MI 48750-370
989-739-1447
800-248-0638
Fax: 989-739-1448
info@aircraft-tool.com
www.aircraft-tool.com

Sheet metal tools, riveting equipment and aircraft engine repair and maintenance tools

President: Desmond Lynch
Production Manager: Bryan MacDonald
General Manager: Gaye Pappas
Catalog Cost: Free
Printing Information: 176 pages
In Business: 41 years
Number of Employees: 30
Sales Volume: $6 MM

6023 Albion Engineering

Albion Engineering
1250 N Church St
Moorestown, NJ 08057-1102
856-235-6688
800-841-7132
Fax: 856-235-9460
service@albioneng.com
www.Albioneng.Com

Small hand tools

President: Mark C. Schneider
Director: Frederick Van Cott
Director: Josh McCaully
Catalog Cost: Free
In Business: 86 years
Number of Employees: 40
Sales Volume: $5,000,000 - $10,000,000

6024 Albion Industries Full Line Catalog

Albion Industries
800 N Clark St
Albion, MI 49224-1455
517-629-9441
800-835-8911
Fax: 517-629-9501
customerservice@albioninc.com
www.albioncasters.com/

Casters, wheels and ergonomic floor locks

President: William Winslow
Marketing Manager: Barry Miller
VP: Mike Thorne
Manager: Ronald Hasse
Sales Executive: John Brumbaugh
Catalog Cost: Free
Catalog Circulation: Mailed 1 time(s) per year
Printing Information: 104 pages in 4 colors
In Business: 68 years
Number of Employees: 120
Sales Volume: $10MM to $20MM

6025 Amana Tool

Amana Tool
120 Carolyn Blvd.
Farmingdale, NY 11756
631-752-1300
800-445-0077
Fax: 631-752-1674
tools@amanatool.com
www.amanatool.com

Tungsten carbide woodworking tools for woodworking industry, sawshops, cabinet makers & hobbyists

President: Michael Ciccarelli
Printing Information: in 4 colors
In Business: 42 years
Number of Employees: 52
Sales Volume: $7.7MM

6026 American Rotary Tools Company

American Rotary Tools Company
250 West Duarte Road
#E
Monrovia, CA 91016-7464
626-358-8466
800-624-2212
Fax: 626- 35- 007
www.artcotools.com

Tools for the Screw Machining, Tool and Die Making, Precision Deburring, Plastic and Rubber Molding, Die Casting, Extrusion Die, Forge Die, Investment Mold, Jewelry, and Engraving industries.

In Business: 80 years

6027 American Safety Razor Company

Personna American Safety Razor Company
240 Cedar Knolls Rd # 401
Cedar Knolls, NJ 07927-1691
973-753-3000
888-254-2126
Fax: 973-326-9004
PBGInquiries@Energizer.com
www.personna.com

Industrial blades

President: Mario Soussou
CFO: Andy Bolt
Marketing Manager: Cris Anderson

Production Manager: Don Beaver
In Business: 140 years
Number of Employees: 2516
Sales Volume: $5,800,000

6028 American Saw & Manufacturing

Lenox
301 Chestnut St
East Longmeadow, MA 01028-2824
413-525-3961
800-628-3030
Fax: 800-223-7906
custserv@lenoxsaw.com
www.lenoxtools.com

Lenox saw blades and hand tools

President: Dave Pirkle
Marketing Manager: Tim Barry
Catalog Cost: Free
Catalog Circulation: Mailed 1 time(s) per year
Printing Information: 40 pages in 2 colors
In Business: 100 years
Number of Employees: 900
Sales Volume: $50,000,000 - $100,000,00

6029 Ames Taping Tool System

AMES Taping Tools
1380 Beverage Drive
Suite W
Stone Mountain, GA 30083
770-243-2637
800-303-1827
Fax: 770-243-2649
answers@amestools.com
www.amestools.com

Automatic taping and finishing tools

President: Mike Schaepper
In Business: 75 years

6030 Atkinson Dynamics

Atkinson Dynamics
2645 Federal Signal Drive
University Park, IL 60484-3167
708-534-3400
888-751-1500
Fax: 708-534-4852
atkinson-support@atkinsondynamics.com
www.atkinsondynamics.com

Heavy duty industrial intercoms, wall mount, panel mount, desk top intercoms

President: Bill Osborn
Marketing Manager: Bob Patnaude
bpatnaude@federalsignal.com
Production Manager: Traci Barron
tbarron@federalsignal.com
Catalog Cost: Free
Catalog Circulation: Mailed 1 time(s) per year
Printing Information: 2 pages in 4 colors
In Business: 57 years
Number of Employees: 25
Sales Volume: $1,000,000 - $5,000,000

6031 Bailey's Master Catalog

Bailey's
1210 Commerce Ave.
Suite 8
Woodland, CA 95776
707-984-6133
800-322-4539
Fax: 530-406-0895
baileys@baileysonline.com

Books, DVDs, chainsaws, grinders, outdoor power equipment and tree care supplies

President: Judith Baileys
CFO: Janet Peper
Marketing Manager: John Conroy
Credit Cards: AMEX; MasterCard
Printing Information: 266 pages
In Business: 40 years
Number of Employees: 50
Sales Volume: $19,000,000

6032 Balance Technology
Balance Technology Inc.
7035 Jomar Drive
Whitmore Lake, MI 48189-8241   734-769-2100
Fax: 734-769-2542
survey@balancetechnology.com
www.balancetechnology.com

Manufactures a complete line of industrial precision measurement and testing equipment
President: Tom Plunkett
In Business: 47 years

6033 Ballymore
Ballymore
501 Gunnard Carlson Drive
Coatesville, PA 19320   610-593-5062
800-762-8327
Fax: 610-593-8615
www.ballymore.com

Steel, aluminum and stainless steel safety ladders; work platforms, and lifts
President: William Frame
Marketing Manager: Thomas Richardson
Production Manager: Ron Bernard
Catalog Cost: Free
Catalog Circulation: Mailed 4 time(s) per year to 30000
Printing Information: 24 pages
Mailing List Information: Names for rent
In Business: 63 years
Number of Employees: 48
Sales Volume: $5MM to $10MM

6034 Bedlam Architectural Metal
Bedlam Architectural Metalworks LLC
202 12th Ave
Paterson, NJ 07501-1619   973-546-5000
800-233-5261
Fax: 800-233-5262
sales@bedlam.biz
www.bedlam.biz

Architectural metal accents
President: Larry Kaufman
Marketing Manager: Jayne Kaine
Sales Volume: $1MM to $3MM

6035 Ben Meadows
Ben Meadows
P.O. Box 5277
Janesville, WI 53547-5277   608-373-2796
800-241-6401
Fax: 800-628-2068
productpros@benmeadows.com
www.benmeadows.com

Forestry supplies and equipment, fire and rescue gear, safety equipment, outdoor clothing and footwear, soil, weather and mapping equipment, outdoor gear
Customer Service Supervisor: Lynette Erickson
Credit Cards: AMEX; MasterCard
Catalog Cost: Free
Catalog Circulation: Mailed 1 time(s) per year
Printing Information: 572 pages in 4 colors
In Business: 61 years

6036 Berg Precision Mechanical Components
WM Berg
5138 S. International Drive
PO Box 100558
Cudahy, WI 53110   414-747-5800
800-232-2374
Fax: 414-747-5801
wmbergcustomerservice@wmberg.com
www.wmberg.com

Gears, belts and sprockets
CFO: Peter Mantal
Marketing Manager: Kevin McBrien
Production Manager: Paul Maher
Manager: Bill Stocks
Buyers: John Sopp

Credit Cards: MasterCard; Visa
Catalog Cost: Free
Catalog Circulation: Mailed 1 time(s) per year to 110
Printing Information: 1400 pages in 4 colors on Matte Stock
Binding: Folded
In Business: 48 years
Number of Employees: 120
Sales Volume: $10,000,000

6037 Blackstone Industries
Blackstone Industries
16 Stony Hill Road
Bethel, CT 06801-1031   203-792-8622
800-272-2885
Fax: 203-796-7861
www.Foredom.Com

Unique saber saws
President: Willard Nelson
Marketing Manager: Eileen Olsen
Credit Cards: MasterCard; Visa
Catalog Cost: Free
Catalog Circulation: Mailed 1 time(s) per year to 20M
Printing Information: 4 pages in 4 colors
In Business: 93 years
Number of Employees: 50
Sales Volume: $15,000,000

6038 Blue Ridge Machinery and Tools
Blue Ridge Machinery and Tools
PO Box 536
Hurricane, WV 25526-536   304-562-3538
800-872-6500
Fax: 304-562-5311
blueridgemachine@att.net
www.blueridgemachinery.com

Lathes, milling machines, machine shop supplies, how to books and videos, cutting tools, measuring tools, abrasives, bandsaws
President: Paul Stonestreet
paul@blueridgemachinery.com
Marketing Manager: Linda Stonestreet
Production Manager: Linda Stonestreet
Director Advertising and Marketing: Linda Stonestreet
linda@blueridgemachinery.com
Purchasing Contact: Gene Griffith
gene@blueridgemachinery.com
Inside Sales Contact: TimAlford
tim@blueridgemachinery.com
Credit Cards: AMEX; MasterCard; Visa; Discover
Catalog Cost: Free
Catalog Circulation: Mailed 12 time(s) per year to 1200
Average Order Size: $100
Printing Information: 80 pages in 1 color on Glossy Stock
Press: Web Press
Binding: Saddle Stitched
Mailing List Information: Names for rent
In Business: 33 years
Number of Employees: 20-D
Sales Volume: $500,000

6039 Buck Brothers
Buck Brothers
14N937 Hwy 20
Hampshire, IL 60140   847-683-4440
Fax: 508-865-1172
info@buckbrosinc.com
www.buckbrosinc.com/

Tools
President: Sidney Jackoff
Store Manager-Hampshire IL: Ambrose Seyller
info@buckbrosinc.com
Parts Manager-Hampshire IL: Joe Seyller
parts@buckbrosinc.com
Service Manager-Hampshire IL: Dan Heidenreich
service@buckbrosinc.com

Credit Cards: MasterCard
Catalog Cost: Free
Printing Information: 2 pages

6040 CARL Manufacturing
CARL
1135 Tower Road
Schaumburg, IL 60173   847-884-2842
800-257-4771
Fax: 847-519-0533
carl@carlmfg.com
www.carlmfg.com

Precision cutting and paper punching systems
President: Richard Schultz
Credit Cards: MasterCard; Visa
Catalog Cost: Free
Catalog Circulation: Mailed 2 time(s) per year to 300M
Printing Information: 48 pages in 4 colors
Binding: Saddle Stitched
Mailing List Information: Names for rent
Will Trade Names: Yes
In Business: 86 years
Number of Employees: 5

6041 Charles GG Schmidt & Company
Charles G.G. Schmidt & Co., Inc.
301 W Grand Ave
Montvale, NJ 07645-1869   201-391-5300
800-724-6438
Fax: 201-391-3565
cggschmidt@aol.com
www.cggschmidt.com

Laser cut saw blades, tooling for shapers, molders, planers, routers, tenoners and saws; machinery for custom woodworking
President: Richard Paul
Executive Director: Jim McDermott
Catalog Circulation: to 15000
Printing Information: 60 pages in 4 colors on Glossy Stock
Binding: Saddle Stitched
Number of Employees: 25
Sales Volume: $3MM to $5MM

6042 Check-Line
Check-Line
600 Oakland Avenue
Cedarhurst, NY 11516   516-295-4300
800-645-4330
Fax: 516-295-4399
info@checkline.com
www.checkline.com

Tools and precision instruments
Credit Cards: AMEX; MasterCard
In Business: 57 years
Number of Employees: 10
Sales Volume: $1MM to $3MM

6043 Coastal Tool & Supply
Coastal Tool & Supply
510 New Park Ave
West Hartford, CT 06110-1313   860-233-8213
877-551-8665
Fax: 860-233-6295
sales@coastaltool.com
www.coastaltool.com

Power tools and hand tools
President: Robert Ludgin
Credit Cards: AMEX; MasterCard; Visa
Catalog Cost: Free
Catalog Circulation: Mailed 2 time(s) per year
Average Order Size: $50
Printing Information: 32 pages in 2 colors on Newsprint
Press: Web Press
Mailing List Information: Names for rent
In Business: 34 years
Sales Volume: $5MM to $10MM

6044 Cutting Tools C
Xylem
100 Cummings Center Drive
Suite 535-N
Beverly, MA 1915   978-281-0440
Fax: 978-283-2619
www.xylemflowcontrol.com

Bandsaw, jigsaw, power hacksaw, reciprocator saw blades, mandrels, pumps, seal detectors and winches
Chairman: Markos I. Tambakeras
President: Patrick K. Decker
CFO: Shashank Patel
Marketing Manager: Joseph P. Vesey
SVP & Chief Human Resources Officer: Kairus Tarapore
SVP, General Counsel & Corporate Se: Claudia S. Toussaint
SVP & President, Dewatering: Colin R. Sabol
Catalog Circulation: Mailed 1 time(s) per year to 30M
Printing Information: 10 pages
Number of Employees: 1200

6045 Detwiler Tractor Parts
Detwiler Tractor Parts
200 S Division Street
P.O. Box 85
Colby, WI 54421-9231   715-659-4252
patdetwiler@gmail.com
www.detwilertractor.com

New and used two-cylinder tractor parts, rerimming and spoke wheels
President: Tom Detwiler
Credit Cards: AMEX; MasterCard
In Business: 30 years
Number of Employees: 2
Sales Volume: $220,000

6046 Diamond Machining Technology
Diamond Machining Technology
85 Hayes Memorial Drive
Marlborough, MA 01752   508-481-5944
800-666-4368
Fax: 508-485-3924
www.dmtsharp.com

Hand-held diamond sharpeners
President: Mark Brandon
Marketing Manager: Stacey Brandon
Production Manager: Mark Bettke
Credit Cards: AMEX; MasterCard
Printing Information: 17 pages in 4 colors on Glossy Stock
Binding: Folded
Mailing List Information: Names for rent
In Business: 39 years
Number of Employees: 45

6047 Diefenbacher Tools
Diefenbacher Tools
12132 Old Big Bend Rd
St Louis, MO 63122-6841   314-966-8147
800-326-5316
Fax: 314-966-4629
ron@diefenbacher.com
www.diefenbacher.com

European and domestic edge tools: bench chisels, firmer gouges, paring chisels, carving tools, bent parers, lathe tools
President: Ron Diefenbacher
Credit Cards: AMEX; MasterCard
Number of Employees: 2
Sales Volume: $150,000

6048 Discount Snow Plow Parts
Mill Supply Inc
19801 Miles Road
P.O. Box 28400
Cleveland, OH 44128   216-518-5072
800-888-5072
Fax: 216-518-2700
questions5@rustrepair.com
www.discountsnowplowparts.com

Replacements parts that fit Meyer, Western, Fisher, Diamond, Boss and Blizzard snow plows, also spreaders and lights
Marketing Manager: John Shega
Fulfillment: David Schuld
Credit Cards: MasterCard
Catalog Cost: Free
Catalog Circulation: Mailed 1 time(s) per year to 90000
Printing Information: 64 pages in 4 colors on Newsprint
Press: Web Press
Binding: Saddle Stitched
Mailing List Information: Names for rent
In Business: 66 years
Number of Employees: 30
Sales Volume: $1MM to $3MM

6049 Dremel
Dremel
PO Box 081126
Racine, WI 53408-1126   262-554-1390
800-437-3635
Fax: 262-554-7654
www.dremel.com

Power tools, attachments and accessories, including redesigned Multipro high speed rotary tools, flex shaft attachments, and drill presses, plus 2 speed scroll saws, disc belt sanders and 165 bits
President: Frank Honland
Marketing Manager: Andrea Ash
Product Manager: Tom Vasis
Credit Cards: AMEX; MasterCard; Visa
Number of Employees: 65
Sales Volume: $10MM to $20MM

6050 Eugene Ernst Products Company
Ernst Flow Industries
116 Main Street
Farmingdale, NJ 07727-1429   732-938-5641
800-992-2843
Fax: 732-938-9463
www.ernstflow.com

Machinery
President: Roger Ernst
Catalog Cost: Free
Catalog Circulation: Mailed 6 time(s) per year to 210K
Printing Information: 50 pages in 4 colors on Glossy Stock
Press: Web Press
Binding: Saddle Stitched
Mailing List Information: Names for rent
In Business: 13 years
Number of Employees: 13
Sales Volume: $1MM to $3MM

6051 Extrema
Extrema Machinery Co.
11420 US-190
Hammond, LA 70401   225-567-3867
877-398-7362
Fax: 225-567-2966
www.extremausa.com

Machines, equipment, and supplies designed for use in the cabinet, millwork, and lumber industry.

6052 FNT 2015 Product Catalog
Fiber Network Tools & Telecom Supplies,
4401 E. Baseline Road
Suite #110
Phoenix, AZ 85042   602- 28- 118
866-818-8050
Fax: 602-414-4677
info@fibernetworktools.com

Telecom products designed for installing, testing and maintaining fiber, copper and hybrid based networks.

6053 Festool Catalog
Tooltechnic Systems LLC
400 N Enterprise Boulevard
Lebanon, IN 46052   765-482-4500
888-337-8600
Fax: 765-483-0903
www.festoolusa.com

Tools, cordless drills, orbital sanders
President: Christian Oltzcher
Marketing Manager: Mark Johnson
Production Manager: Rick Bush

6054 Flexbar Machine Corporation
Flexbar Machine Corporation
250 Gibbs Rd
Islandia, NY 11749-2697   631-582-8440
800-879-7575
Fax: 631-582-8487
www.Flexbar.Com

Lathe guards, machine guards, video inspection and measurement, all types of dimensional gaging, metrology grade casting materials
President: Jon Adler
Marketing Manager: Larry Derrig
Production Manager: John Faraci
Sales Director: Lou Valenti
Purchasing Manager: Maria Blando
Manufacturing Manager: Rick Boone
Buyers: Mario Blando
Catalog Circulation: Mailed 1 time(s) per year to 30K
Average Order Size: $250
Printing Information: 400 pages in 2 colors on Matte Stock
Press: Web Press
Binding: Saddle Stitched
Mailing List Information: Names for rent
In Business: 35 years
Number of Employees: 25
Sales Volume: $1,000,000 - $5,000,000

6055 Foredom Electric Company Power Tool Catalog
Blackstone Industries, Inc.
16 Stony Hill Road
Bethel, CT 06801-1039   203-792-8622
800-272-2885
Fax: 203-796-7861
www.foredom.com

Flexible shaft rotary power tools, 21 handpieces and accessory tools to cut, grind, buff polish sand and deburr, handpiece holders and tools for crafts/jewelry making, manufacturer
President: Willard P Nelson
Marketing Manager: Eileen Olsen
Operations Manager: Rob Horton
VP of Engineering: Kevin Cheh
In Business: 95 years
Number of Employees: 75
Sales Volume: $15,000,000

6056 Foster Manufacturing Company
Foster Keencut
204 B Progress Drive
Montgomeryville, PA 18936   267-413-6220
800-523-4855
Fax: 267-413-6227
information@go-foster.com
www.go-foster.com

Pre-press equipment including inspection systems, filing (flat and vertical), cutters and trimmers, line-up tables, color-correct viewing booths, light tables
President: Ted Borowsky
Marketing Manager: Patty Peterson
Catalog Cost: Free
Catalog Circulation: to 100M
Printing Information: 40 pages in 4 colors on Glossy Stock
Press: Web Press
Binding: Saddle Stitched

Mailing List Information: Names for rent
In Business: 71 years
Number of Employees: 12
Sales Volume: $3MM to $5MM

6057 Fresno Oxygen

Fresno Oxygen
2825 S. Elm
#101
Fresno, CA 93706-5460   559-233-6684
800-404-9353
Fax: 559-233-4206
info@fresnooxygen.com
www.Fresnooxygen.Com

Hand tools, power tools and welding accessories

President: Mike Barnes
In Business: 65 years
Sales Volume: $1MM to $3MM

6058 Freud

Freud Tools
218 Feld Avenue
High Point, NC 27263   800-334-4107
Fax: 336-434-8333
customerservice@freudtools.com
www.freudtools.com

Router bits

President: Russell Kohl
Owner: Eric Savelle
Catalog Cost: Free
In Business: 42 years
Number of Employees: 35
Sales Volume: $20MM to $50MM

6059 Global Industrial Catalog

Global Industrial
11 Harbor Park Dr.
Port Washington, NY 11050 *Fax:* 888-381-2868
www.globalindustrial.com

Industrial equipment and business supplies.

President: Bob Dooley
In Business: 67 years
Sales Volume: $180 Million

6060 Granberg International

Granberg International
PO Box 2347
Bldg. 289 Pintado St.
Vallejo, CA 94592-347   707-562-2099
800-233-6499
Fax: 707-562-2091
info@granberg.com
www.granberg.com

Saw chain maintenance tools to repair and sharpen saw chain and attachments for your chain saw

Catalog Circulation: to 10000
Printing Information: 4 pages in 4 colors
In Business: 28 years

6061 Grand Tool Supply Corporation

Grand Tool Supply
650 Huyler Street
South Hackensack, NJ 07606-1744 800-922-0512
Fax: 800-866-5730
www.grandtool.com

Quality cutting tools, machine shop equipment and measuring instruments for the metalworking industry; hard-to-find items for classic tooling and today's cutting-edge technology

Catalog Cost: Free
Printing Information: 736 pages in 4 colors
In Business: 71 years
Sales Volume: 2.3MM

6062 Grifhold

Griffin Manufacturing Co, Inc
1656 Ridge Rd
Webster, NY 14580   585-265-1991
800-344-6445
Fax: 585-265-2621
grifhold@aol.com
www.grifhold.com

Knives, blades, knife kits, specialty tools, pounce wheels, compasses, magnifiers, burnisher hand tools for fine art, graphic arts, industrial use, woodcrafting, arts and crafts

Buyers: Mary Gormane
Catalog Cost: Free
Catalog Circulation: Mailed 1 time(s) per year
Printing Information: 30 pages in 1 color on Matte Stock
Press: Web Press
Binding: Saddle Stitched
Mailing List Information: Names for rent
In Business: 70 years
Number of Employees: 25
Sales Volume: $500M to $1MM

6063 Griot's Garage

Griot's Garage
3333 South 38th St
Tacoma, WA 98409-1728   253-922-2400
800-345-5789
Fax: 253-922-7500
www.Griotsgarage.Com

Tools and products for every garage

President: Richard Griot
Credit Cards: AMEX; MasterCard; Visa
Catalog Cost: Free
Catalog Circulation: Mailed 4 time(s) per year
Printing Information: 60 pages in 4 colors on Glossy Stock
Press: Web Press
Binding: Saddle Stitched
In Business: 23 years
Number of Employees: 35
Sales Volume: 3MM-5MM

6064 Grizzly Industrial

Grizzly Industrial
1815 W Battlefield St
Springfield, MO 65807-4111   570-546-9663
800-523-4777
csr@grizzly.com
www.grizzly.com

Line of woodworking and metalworking tools

President: Debbie Isner
Printing Information: 784 pages
In Business: 32 years
Sales Volume: $3MM to $5MM

6065 H Gerstner and Sons

H. Gerstner & Sons, Inc.
20 Gerstner Way
Dayton, OH 45402-8408   937-228-1662
Fax: 937-228-8557
gerstner@gerstnerusa.com
www.Gerstnerusa.Com

Tool chests, roller benches, sportsman/hobby chests and gun & knife display cases

President: John H Campbell
VP of Operations: Scott Campbell
Shipping Specialist & Customer Serv: Linda Waldrop
Executive Vice President: Nancy Campbell
Sales Volume: $3MM to $5MM

6066 HUT Products

Hut Products
4502 State Road J
Fulton, MO 65251-3404   573-642-3614
800-547-5461
Fax: 800-684-9371
hutpfw@aol.com
www.hutproducts.com

Small woodturning supplies, wood finishes and tools, lathes, pen kits, exotic wood blanks, custom logos for pens, glues, epoxy, duck call kits, deer call kits, books, color wood, dyhand wood

President: James Irvin
Catalog Cost: Free
Catalog Circulation: Mailed 2 time(s) per year
Printing Information: 40 pages on Glossy Stock
Binding: Saddle Stitched
Mailing List Information: Names for rent
In Business: 24 years
Number of Employees: 5
Sales Volume: $500M to $1MM

6067 Hand Torque Tools Catalog

Mountz Torque Tools
1080 N. 11th St.
San Jose, CA 95112   888-925-2763
Fax: 408-292-2733
sales@mountztorque.com
www.mountztorque.com

Torque tool solutions and metric fasteners.

In Business: 50 years

6068 Hanley-Wood

Hanley Wood, LLC
1 Thomas Cir NW # 600
Suite 600
Washington, DC 20005-5811   202-452-0800
Fax: 202-785-1974
www.hanleywood.com

Wood furniture and accessories

President: Dave Colford
CFO: Matthew Flynn
Marketing Manager: Sheila Harris
Production Manager: Cathy Underwood
Chief Executive Officer : Peter Goldstone
Chief Design Director: Gillian Berenson
General Manager: Rizwan Ali
In Business: 40 years

6069 Harbor Freight Tools

Harbor Freight Tools
26541 Agoura Rd.
Calabasas, CA 91302   818-836-5000
www.harborfreight.com

Hand, air, power and automotive tools and accessories.

CEO: Eric Smidt
Catalog Cost: Free
In Business: 39 years
Number of Employees: 1700
Sales Volume: $2 Billion

6070 Hartville Tool

Hartville Tool
13163 Market Ave N
Hartville, OH 44632-9065   330-877-4680
800-345-2396
Fax: 330-877-4682
www.Hartvilletool.Com

Woodworking tools and supplies

President: Jason Bare

6071 Her-Saf

4005 El Camino Real
Atascadero, CA 93422-2561   805-466-1563
800-553-9344
Fax: 805-466-1947
sales@hersaf.com
www.hersaf.com

Woodworking equipment

6072 Herrington
Herrington
3 Symmes Drive
Londonderry, NH 03053-2142   866-558-7467
800-903-2878
Fax: 603-437-3492
customerservice@herringtoncatalog.com
www.herringtoncatalog.com
Apparel, electronic gifts, tools and gadgets
President: Lee Herrington
Credit Cards: AMEX; MasterCard; Visa
Catalog Cost: Free
Catalog Circulation: Mailed 8 time(s) per year
Printing Information: 48 pages in 4 colors on Glossy Stock
Binding: Saddle Stitched
In Business: 35 years
Number of Employees: 160
Sales Volume: $ 10 Million

6073 High Quality Tools High Quality Import Catalog
High Quality Tools
8950 131st Ave N.
Largo, FL 33773   727-585-8555
Fax: 727-585-6555
hqtfl@hqtinc.com
hqtinc.com
Replacement parts, tools and accessories for vertical knee-type milling machines.
In Business: 32 years

6074 High Quality Tools Master Catalog
High Quality Tools
8950 131st Ave N.
Largo, FL 33773   727-585-8555
Fax: 727-585-6555
hqtfl@hqtinc.com
hqtinc.com
Replacement parts, tools and accessories for vertical knee-type milling machines.
In Business: 32 years

6075 Highland Hardware
Highland Woodworking
1045 North Highland Avenue NE
Atlanta, GA 30306-3550   404-872-4466
800-241-6748
Fax: 404-876-1941
customerservice@highlandwoodworking.com
www.Highlandwoodworking.Com
Provides detailed tool descriptions, useful techniques, as well as a schedule of seminars
President: Chris Bagby
CFO: Sharon Bagby
Sales and Education: Terry Chumbler
Sales and Purchasing: Sidney Dew
Assistant Manager : Phil Colson
Mailing List Information: Names for rent
In Business: 37 years
Number of Employees: 20-5
Sales Volume: $5MM to $10MM

6076 Horn USA
Horn, Inc.
320 Premier Court
Suite 205
Franklin, TN 37067   888-818-4676
Fax: 615-771-4101
www.hornusa.com
Tools and machinery
President: Paul Horn
Credit Cards: AMEX; MasterCard
Catalog Cost: Free
In Business: 20 years

6077 Hoss Tools
P.O. Box 429
Norman Park, GA 31771   229-769-3999
888-672-5536
custserv@hosstools.com
hosstools.com

6078 Hut Products
Hut Products
4502 State Road J
Fulton, MO 65251-3404   573-642-3614
800-547-5461
Fax: 800-684-9371
hutpfw@aol.com
www.hutproducts.com
Pens, project and game call kits, lathes, turning materials and fine finishes for woodworkers
President: James Irvin
Catalog Circulation: Mailed 28 time(s) per year to 28000
Printing Information: 56 pages in 4 colors on G
Press: W
Binding: S
In Business: 24 years
Sales Volume: $500M to $1MM

6079 H„fele
H„fele America Co.
3901 Cheyenne Drive
Archdale, NC 27263   336-434-2322
800-423-3531
www.hafele.com
Closet hardware, architectural hardware, kitchen cabinet hardware, decorative hardware, cabinet pulls, drawer slides, cam and bolt connectors, LED lighting
President: Paul Smith
Director of Operations: Jed Kilpatrick
Credit Cards: MasterCard
Catalog Cost: Free
In Business: 44 years
Number of Employees: 1000
Sales Volume: $10MM to $20MM

6080 International Wood Products
JELD-WEN, inc
440 S. Church Street
Suite 400
Charlotte, NC 28202   877-535-3462
800-535-3936
www.jeld-wen.com
Wood products and accessories
Number of Employees: 2000

6081 Irwin Tools
Irwin Tools
8936 Northpointe Executive Dr
Suite 200
Huntersville, NC 28078   800-464-7946
Fax: 800-866-5742
www.irwin.com
Hand tools and power tool accessories.
In Business: 130 years

6082 Jantz Supply
Jantz Supply
309 W Main
PO Box 584
Davis, OK 73030-584   580-369-2316
800-351-8900
Fax: 580-369-3082
jantz@jantzusa.com
www.Knifemaking.Com
Knifemaking products
President: Ken Jantz
Credit Cards: AMEX; MasterCard
Catalog Cost: $5
Sales Volume: $3MM to $5MM

6083 Jensen Tools Master Sourcebook
Stanley Supplies & Services Inc.
335 Willow Street
North Andover, MA 01845-5995   978-682-9844
800-225-5370
Fax: 800-743-8141
www.stanleysupplyservices.com
Tools
President: Kai Juel
Marketing Manager: Jeff Richardson

6084 Jesada Tools
Razor Tools
10360 72nd Street
Suite 811
Largo, FL 33777   813-875-5400
Fax: 813-875-5430
RazorToolsUSA@yahoo.com
www.jesada.com
Tools
President: Gerard W Davich
Marketing Manager: Alan Goodsell

6085 Jointech
5415 Bandera Road #504
San Antonio, TX 78238   210-348-6655
800-619-1288
Fax: 210-377-1282
Router table and tablesaw fence systems
Catalog Cost: Free
Printing Information: in 4 colors on Glossy Stock

6086 KBC Tools
KBC Tools
6300 18 Mile Road
Sterling Heights, MI 48314-8006   586-979-0500
Fax: 586-979-4292
sales@kbctools.com
www.kbctools.com
Metal cutting tools
President: Paula Bass
Vice President: John Earles
Credit Cards: MasterCard; Visa
Catalog Cost: Free
Catalog Circulation: Mailed 1 time(s) per year
Printing Information: 860 pages on Newsprint
In Business: 52 years
Number of Employees: 50
Sales Volume: $10MM to $20MM

6087 Kett Tool
Kett Tool Company
5055 Madison Road
Cincinnati, OH 45227-1494   513-271-0333
800-215-3210
Fax: 513-271-5318
info@kett-tool.com
www.Kett-Tool.Com
Electric and peumatic shears,saws and nibblers
President: Rowe Hoffman
Buyers: Michael Hampton
Credit Cards: MasterCard; Visa
Printing Information: 6 pages in 4 colors on Matte Stock
Binding: Folded
Mailing List Information: Names for rent
In Business: 75 years
Number of Employees: 30
Sales Volume: $10MM to $20MM

6088 Kitts Industrial Tools
Kitts Industrial Tools
27600 West 8 Mile Road
Farmington Hills, MI 48336-3147   248-476-2121
800-521-6579
Fax: 313-531-0300
kitindustrial@aol.com
kittstools.securesites.net/store/
Over 200 tons of tools

President: Neill Kitts
Credit Cards: AMEX; MasterCard; Visa
In Business: 36 years
Number of Employees: 22

6089 Knot Head Wood Crafts
PO Box 2007
Ada OK   580-332-5336

Wood craft supplies
President: Monte Law

6090 Komet of America
Komet of America
2050 Mitchell Blvd
Schaumburg, IL 60193-4544   847-923-8400
                                847-923-8480
                          Fax: 800-865-6638
customerservice.us@kometgroup.com
                            www.Komet.Com

Cutting tools
President: Hans Grandin
CEO: Hans Grandin
In Business: 97 years
Number of Employees: 275
Sales Volume: $10,000,000 - $25,000,000

6091 Kreg Tool Company
Kreg
201 Campus Drive
Huxley, IA 50124-9760   515-597-6400
                                800-447-8638
                          Fax: 515-597-6401
technicalsupport@kregtool.com
                          www.kregtool.com

Complete line of hand tools
President: Craig Sommerfeld
Catalog Cost: Free
Number of Employees: 20
Sales Volume: $10MM to $20MM

6092 Lortone
Lortone
12130 Cyrus Way
Mukilteo, WA 98275-5700   425-493-1600
                                800-426-6773
                          Fax: 425-493-9494
equipment@lortone.com
                          www.Lortone.Com

Lapidary equipment and tools
President: Doug Guthrie
Buyers: Sara Schinkel
Credit Cards: MasterCard; Visa
Catalog Circulation: Mailed 1 time(s) per year
Printing Information: 25 pages in 4 colors
In Business: 35 years
Number of Employees: 20
Sales Volume: $1,000,000 - $5,000,000

6093 Lumberjack Tools
Lumberjack Tools
925 W River St
STE 6
Chippewa Falls, WI 54729   715-720-4719
                          Fax: 715-720-4801
www.lumberjacktools.com
Credit Cards: AMEX; MasterCard

6094 MSC Industrial Supply Company
MSC Industrial Supply Company
75 Maxess Road
Melville, NY 11747-3151   888-880-2048
                          Fax: 800-255-5067
international@mscdirect.com
                          www.mscdirect.com

Hand tools, emergency preparedness supplies and facility maintenance supplies
President: Erik Gershwind
SVP, Gen. Counsel & Corporate Secre: Steve Armstrong
EVP & Chief Supply Chain Officer: Douglas

Jones
Senior Vice President & CIO: Charles Bonomo
Catalog Cost: Free
In Business: 60 years

6095 Masecraft Supply
Masecraft Supply Co.
254 Amity St
Meriden, CT 06450-2392   203-238-3049
                                800-682-5489
                          Fax: 203-238-2373
info@masecraftsupply.com
masecraftsupply-com.3dcartstores.com/

Specializes in natural materials, decorative synthetic materials and rigid composite laminates for knife handles, gun grips, pens, musical instrument inlays, pool cue inlays and many others
President: Marge Hartman
Credit Cards: AMEX; MasterCard
Sales Volume: $3MM to $5MM

6096 Material Control
Material Control, Inc.
130 Seltzer Road
Croswell, MI 48422   630-892-4274
                                800-926-0376
                          Fax: 630-892-4931
sales@materialcontrolinc.com
www.materialcontrolinc.com

Rubber wiper blade belt cleaners, flags and flagpoles and safety mats, speed responsive switch, alignment switch, aerators, flow swith, brush type conv belt cleaner, safety stop switch, akro-mils bins
President: Clinton F Stimpson III
Credit Cards: MasterCard
Catalog Cost: Free
Printing Information: 4 pages in 4 colors
Mailing List Information: Names for rent
In Business: 52 years
Number of Employees: 180

6097 McFeely's Square Drive Screws
McFeely's Square Drive Screws
PO Box 44976
Madison, WI 53744-4976   800-443-7937
                                800-443-7937
                          Fax: 800-847-7136
customerservice@mcfeelys.com
                          www.mcfeelys.com

Square drive screws, stainless steel, silicon, bronze, brass, aluminum and abrasives
Founder: William J. McFeely III
Credit Cards: MasterCard
Catalog Cost: $2
Catalog Circulation: Mailed 7 time(s) per year to 1.5MM
Average Order Size: $65
Printing Information: 96 pages in 4 colors on Glossy Stock
Press: Web Press
Binding: Saddle Stitched
Mailing List Information: Names for rent
List Company: List Locators & Managers
5750 W 95th Street, Suite #300
Overland Park, KS 66207
800-487-8700
In Business: 36 years
Number of Employees: 35
Sales Volume: $5MM to $10MM

6098 Modern Track Machinery
Modern Track Machinery
1415 Davis Road
Elgin, IL 60123   847-697-7510
                          Fax: 847-697-0136
geismar-mtm.com/index.html

Tools from hand-held machinery to heavy equipment for track works.
In Business: 40 years

6099 Nortel Machinery
Nortel Manufacturing Limited
1051 Clinton Street
Buffalo, NY 14206-2877   716-852-2685
                          Fax: 716-852-6374
info@nortelmfg.com
www.Nortelmfg.Com

Glass working machinery and equipment; air movers
President: Pat Blake
Marketing Manager: Pat Blake
Founder: Peter Norton
Customer Service, Sales: Jean Robichaud
Manager: Pat Blake
Mailing List Information: Names for rent
In Business: 48 years
Number of Employees: 5
Sales Volume: $1MM to $3MM

6100 Northern Tool & Equipment Master Catalog
Northern Tool & Equipment
2800 Southcross Dr. W
Burnsville, MN 55306   800-221-0516
www.northerntool.com

Power tools, automotive, lawn and garden equipment.
Founder and CEO: Donald L. Kotula
International Marketing Manager: Bill Perrizo
Catalog Cost: Free
Printing Information: in 4 colors
Number of Employees: 2200
Sales Volume: $1.5 Billion

6101 Northway's Machinery
Northway's Machinery, Inc.
500 E Livingston
Des Moines, IA 50315   515-243-1824
                                866-638-2597
                          Fax: 515-243-1941
sales@northwaysmachinery.com
www.northwaysmachinery.com

Sheet metal equipment, new and used
President: Ivan Northway
Credit Cards: AMEX; MasterCard; Visa
In Business: 34 years
Number of Employees: 6

6102 Outdoor Power Equipment
Foley-Belsaw Co.
1173 Benson Street
River Falls, WI 54022-1395   715-426-2275
                                800-821-3452
                          Fax: 715-426-2198
info@foley-belsaw.com
www.foley-belsaw.com

Wholesale locksmith, sharpening and outdoor power equipment
Credit Cards: MasterCard; Visa
Catalog Cost: Free
Catalog Circulation: Mailed 4 time(s) per year
Printing Information: 48 pages in 4 colors
Mailing List Information: Names for rent
In Business: 91 years
Sales Volume: $20MM to $50MM

6103 PJ Catalog
PJ Company
2410 S Sequoia Drive
Compton, CA 90220   800-421-2880
                          Fax: 310-639-8145
sales@pjcasters.com
www.pjcasters.com

Casters and wheels for transporting equipment
International Marketing Manager: Tai Chung
Buyers: Yung Wee
Catalog Cost: Free
Catalog Circulation: Mailed 1 time(s) per year to 4000
Printing Information: 80 pages in 4 colors on Glossy Stock

Binding: Perfect Bound
Mailing List Information: Names for rent
List Manager: Theresa Lakey
In Business: 39 years
Number of Employees: 40
Sales Volume: $20MM to $50MM

6104 POBCO Plastics & Hardwood

POBCO Inc
99 Hope Ave
Worcester, MA 01603-2298   508-791-6376
                             800-222-6376
                        Fax: 508-791-3247
pobco@pobcoplastics.com
www.pobcoplastics.com

Conveyor components and friction reducing components made from bearing grade and food compliant plastics, lube filled hardwood, includes guide rails chain guides, wear strip and bearings

President: Stephen Johnson
Marketing Manager: Tom Johnson
International Marketing Manager: Tom Johnson
Catalog Cost: Free
Catalog Circulation: Mailed 12 time(s) per year to 25M
Printing Information: 126 pages in 2 colors on Glossy Stock
Press: Letterpress
Binding: Saddle Stitched
Mailing List Information: Names for rent
In Business: 56 years
Number of Employees: 50
Sales Volume: $2,500,000

6105 Peck Tool Company

The Peck Tool Company
803 Floral Ave
Terrace Park, OH 45174-4744   303-440-5480
                                800-454-8665
                           Fax: 303-440-8771
www.pecktool.com

Tools

President: Alison Webster
Credit Cards: AMEX; MasterCard
Catalog Cost: $1
Catalog Circulation: to 5000
Printing Information: 20 pages in 1 color on Glossy Stock
Binding: Saddle Stitched
In Business: 86 years
Number of Employees: 1
Sales Volume: $53,000

6106 Pico Electronics

Pico Electronic,Inc.
143 Sparks Ave
Pelham, NY 10803-1837   914-738-1400
                          800-431-1064
                     Fax: 914-738-8225
info@picoelectronics.com
www.Picoelectronics.Com

AC-DC power supplies

President: Joe Sweeney
Catalog Cost: Free
Catalog Circulation: Mailed 2 time(s) per year
Printing Information: 64 pages in 1 color
In Business: 17 years
Number of Employees: 90
Sales Volume: $5,000,000 - $10,000,000

6107 PortaBrace

PortaBrace, Inc.
940 Water Street
PO Box 220
North Bennington, VT 05257-249 802-442-8171
                           Fax: 802-442-9118
info@portabrace.com
www.portabrace.com

Audio cases, camera cases, computers and iPad cases, etc.

Chairman: Thomas Stark
President: Gregg Haythorn
Marketing Manager: Chris Miceli
chris@portabrace.com
Shipping Manager: Craig O'Dell
Sales Manager: Casey Krugman
Credit Cards: MasterCard
Catalog Cost: Free
In Business: 39 years
Number of Employees: 100
Sales Volume: $7.9 MM

6108 Power Torque Tools Catalog

Mountz Torque Tools
1080 N. 11th St.
San Jose, CA 95112   888-925-2763
                       Fax: 408-292-2733
sales@mountztorque.com
www.mountztorque.com

Torque tool solutions and metric fasteners.

In Business: 50 years

6109 Proxxon

Proxxon
P.O. Box 1909
Hickory, NC 28603-1909   877-776-9966
sales.us@proxxon.com
www.proxxon.com

Handheld power tools, adaptors, accessories for rotary tools, bench top units, lathe and milling systems

Export Manager: Anja Gehrke
Catalog Cost: Free
Printing Information: 48 pages
In Business: 40 years

6110 QTC Metric Gears

QTC Metric Gears
250 Duffy Avenue
Hicksville, NY 11801   516-437-6700
                            646-396-GEAR
qtcsupport@qtcgears.com
www.qtcgears.com

Minature Mechanical Components and metric gears

Production Manager: Fred Spitzenberger
Catalog Cost: Free
Catalog Circulation: Mailed 1 time(s) per year
Printing Information: 600 pages in 4 colors
In Business: 57 years
Number of Employees: 150

6111 Rabbit Tool USA

Rabbit Tool USA
105 9th St
Rock Island, IL 61201-8353 309-793-4375
                            800-451-8665
                       Fax: 309-793-4375
info@rabbittool.com
www.rabbittool.com

Precision tools for pipe finishing

President: O J Birkestrand
Catalog Circulation: Mailed 1 time(s) per year
Printing Information: 6 pages on Matte Stock
In Business: 10 years
Number of Employees: 10
Sales Volume: $500M to $1MM

6112 Ray Baker Classics

Ray Baker Classics
1030 E. Washington St.
Indianapolis, IN 46202-2142   616-847-5000
                                888-944-5478
                           Fax: 616-837-9652
www.angieslist.com

Oil pans, fuel pumps, fuel logs and rollerized pushrods

President: Raymond Baker
Credit Cards: MasterCard
Catalog Circulation: to 2m+
Printing Information: 6 pages in 2 colors

6113 Red Devil

Red Devil, Inc
4175 Webb St
Pryor, OK 74361-6741   918-825-5744
                            800-4AD-EVIL
                       Fax: 918-825-5761
info@reddevil.com
www.RedDevil.Com

Hand, tile tools, paint mixing and tinting equipment

President: Craig Cartwright
Credit Cards: AMEX; MasterCard
Catalog Cost: Free
Catalog Circulation: Mailed 1 time(s) per year to 25M
Printing Information: 36 pages in 2 colors on Matte Stock
Press: Web Press
Binding: Saddle Stitched
Mailing List Information: Names for rent
In Business: 141 years
Number of Employees: 125
Sales Volume: $20MM to $50MM

6114 Ridge Tool Company

Ridge Tool Company
400 Clark St
Elyria, OH 44035   632-214-804
ridgidfareast@emerson.com
www.ridgid.com

Tools.

6115 Rocker Shop

Classic Woodworks Inc.
1421 White Cir NW
Marietta, GA 30060   770-424-4741

Rocking chairs as well as parts and kits

President: Carole Melson

6116 Rutland Tool and Supply Catalog

Lawson Products, Inc.
2225 Workman Mill Rd
Whittier, CA 90601-1437   562-566-5010
                            800-289-4787
                       Fax: 562-566-5001
inquiry@rutlandtool.com
www.shoprutlandtool.com

Products for metalworking and maintenance

Chairman: Ronald B. Port
President: Andrew Verey
CFO: Ronald J. Knutson
Marketing Manager: Dave Adamek
Executive Vice President and COO: Harry Dochelli
Sales Account Manager: Jahenea Janay Wardell
Printing Information: 1832 pages in 3 colors
In Business: 55 years

6117 Saint Louis Slot Machines

Saint Louis Slot Machines
9617 Dielman Rock Island Drive
St Louis, MO 63132-2149   314-432-1699
                       Fax: 314-961-3846
stlslot@earthlink.net
www.Stlouisslot.Com

Antique slot machines, neon signs, old soda machines and jukeboxes

President: Tom Kolbrener
Production Manager: Marty Wilke
Sales Volume: Under $500M

6118 Seven Corners Ace Hardware

216 7th St W
St Paul, MN 55102-2521   651-224-4859
                            800-328-0457
                       Fax: 651-224-8263
info@7corners.com
www.7corners.com

Ladders, tools, hardware abrasives, and accessories

President: William Walsh
Printing Information: 736 pages in 3 colors
In Business: 77 years
Sales Volume: $5MM to $10MM

6119 Shorty's Tooling & Equipment
Shorty's Tooling & Equipment, Inc.
7531 Holland Road
Taylor, MI 48180   313-291-5200
                                800-443-6666
                           Fax: 313-291-4524

New and surplus tooling, attachments and replacement parts for American made automatic screw machines
President: Carl Sherman
Credit Cards: MasterCard
Catalog Cost: $15
Catalog Circulation: Mailed 1 time(s) per year
Printing Information: 66 pages
Binding: Saddle Stitched
In Business: 46 years

6120 Smithy Machine Tools and Accessories
Smithy Industries
170 Aprill Drive
Ann Arbor, MI 48103-1517   734-913-6700
                                800-476-4849
                           Fax: 734-913-6663
                         sales@smithy.com
                         www.smithy.com

Machine shop tools for metal work and automotive repair
Marketing Manager: Kerry Ballard
Credit Cards: AMEX; MasterCard
Catalog Cost: Free
In Business: 28 years
Number of Employees: 15

6121 Sommerfeld's Tools for Wood
Sommerfeld Tools for Wood
1408 Celebrity Road
Remsen, IA 51050-1045   712-786-2717
                                888-228-9268
                           Fax: 712-786-2770
                      ml@sommerfeldtools.com
                      www.Sommerfeldtools.Com

Woodworking machinery, tools, and bits
President: Marc Sommerfeld
In Business: 24 years
Sales Volume: $500M to $1MM

6122 Stanley Supply & Services
Stanley Supply &Services, Inc.
335 Willow Street
North Andover, MA 01845-5995   978-682-9844
                               800-225-5370
                           Fax: 800-743-8141
                  www.Stanleysupplyservices.Com

Tool kits, cases, test instruments, tools and equipment for technicians and service personnel in electronics and communications
President: Ken Lyon
Marketing Manager: Jeff Richardson
Credit Cards: AMEX; MasterCard; Visa
Catalog Cost: Free
Mailing List Information: Names for rent
In Business: 50 years
Number of Employees: 75
Sales Volume: $3MM to $5MM

6123 Swiss Precision Instruments
Swiss Precision Instrument, Inc.
11450 Markon Drive
Garden Grove, CA 92841-3135   888-774-8200
                           Fax: 800-842-5164
                         sales@swissprec.com
                         www.swissprec.com

Machinists/metalwork instruments and tools
President: Allan Newman
CFO: Marc Serlin
Credit Cards: MasterCard

Catalog Cost: Free
Catalog Circulation: Mailed 1 time(s) per year
Printing Information: 432 pages in 1 color
In Business: 58 years
Number of Employees: 22

6124 TP Tools and Equipment
TP Tools & Equipment
7075 State Route 446
PO Box 649
Canfield, OH 44406-649   330-533-3384
                                800-321-9260
                           Fax: 330-533-2876
                         www.tptools.com

Abrasive blasting cabinets, turbines, air compressors, air tools, auto tools and equipment, paint spray guns, and safety items
Credit Cards: AMEX; MasterCard
Printing Information: 156 pages

6125 Tecra Tools
Tecra Tools
2925 S. Umatilla Street
Englewood, CO 80110   303-338-9224
                                800-284-0808
                           Fax: 303-338-9289
                      info@tecratools.com
                      www.Tecratools.Com

Tools, cases and kits for service technicians
President: Terry Tautz
In Business: 40 years
Sales Volume: $1MM to $3MM

6126 Telpro
Telpro
7251 S 42nd St
Grand Forks, ND 58201-9163   701-775-0551
                                800-448-0822
                           Fax: 701-775-0629
                      telpromktg@telproinc.com
                      www.Telproinc.Com

Produces a variety of lifts for construction and industrial equipment and work platforms
President: Rolland Young
Sales Volume: $5MM to $10MM

6127 Time Motion Tools
Time and Motion
PO Box 547
Mittagong, CA 92064-6810   024-861-7265
                                800-779-8170
                           Fax: 028-246-6624
                      info@timemotion.com.au
                      www.Timemotion.Com

Quality tools and voice data telecom test equipment
President: Edward Durfey
Buyers: Shelda Auditett
Credit Cards: AMEX; MasterCard; Visa
Catalog Cost: Free
Catalog Circulation: Mailed 6 time(s) per year to 800K
Average Order Size: $275
Printing Information: 200 pages in 4 colors on Glossy Stock
Press: Web Press
Binding: Perfect Bound
Mailing List Information: Names for rent
List Manager: Ofelia Pereira
In Business: 40 years
Number of Employees: 50
Sales Volume: $20MM to $50MM

6128 Tool Supplies & Equipment
Swestinc.com
11090 N Stemmons Freeway
Dallas, TX 75229   972-247-7744
                           Fax: 800-441-5162
                         www.swestinc.com

Tools and equipment

President: Chuck Weismuller
Marketing Manager: Gary Fuller

6129 Torque Analyzer & Test Measurement Catalog
Mountz Torque Tools
1080 N. 11th St.
San Jose, CA 95112   888-925-2763
                           Fax: 408-292-2733
                      sales@mountztorque.com
                      www.mountztorque.com

Torque tool solutions and metric fasteners.
In Business: 50 years

6130 Tru Grit
Tru Grit
760 E Francis
Unit N
Ontario, CA 91761-5549   909-923-4116
                                800-532-3336
                           Fax: 909-923-9932
                         www.trugrit.com

Abrasives and knifemaking supplies
President: Scott Sharpe
Credit Cards: AMEX; MasterCard
Sales Volume: $1MM to $3MM

6131 WM Berg
WM Berg
5138 S International Dr
PO Box 100558
Cudahy, WI 53110-1226   414-747-5800
                                800-232-2374
                           Fax: 414-747-5801
                wmbergcustomerservice@wmberg.com
                         www.Wmberg.Com

Precisions mechanical components and engineering tools
President: Joe Amendolara
WMBergpresident@WMBerg.com
Credit Cards: MasterCard; Visa
Catalog Circulation: Mailed 1 time(s) per year
Printing Information: 616 pages in 4 colors on Glossy Stock
Press: 1
Binding: Perfect Bound
In Business: 48 years
Number of Employees: 150
Sales Volume: $20MM to $50MM

6132 Westhoff Machine Catalog
Westhoff Machine
9462 Watson Industrial Park
St Louis, MO 63126-1523   314-963-7130
                                800-364-0280
                           Fax: 800-324-1942
                  customerservice@westhoffinc.com
                         www.westhoffinc.com

Precision tools, cutting tools, abbrasives, hand tools, clamps and vises
President: Allen Johnson
Sales Volume: $1MM to $3MM

6133 Whirlwind
Whirlwind
99 Link Road
Dallas, TX 14612-1021   585-663-8820
                                800-733-9473
                           Fax: 585-865-8930
                      techsupport@whirlwindusa.com
                         www.whirlwindusa.com

Cut-off saws, measuring system, edge belt sander and digital stop systems
President: Michael Laiacona
michael@whirlwindusa.com
Marketing Manager: Robert Ramsden
GM/Customer Support: Al Keltz
alk@whirlwindusa.com
Marketing Director/Artist Relations: Will Young
willy@whirlwindusa.com

Disital/Southeast Sales: JoeBarnes
joeb@whirlwindusa.com
Printing Information: in 4 colors on Glossy
Stock
Mailing List Information: Names for rent
In Business: 22 years
Number of Employees: 10
Sales Volume: $1,000,000 - $5,000,000

6134 Wholesale Tool Catalog
Wholesale Tool Co Inc
12155 Stephens Dr.
PO Box 68
Warren, MI 48090-68   586-754-9270
                                     800-521-3420
                              Fax: 800-521-3661
                                    wtmich@aol.com
                                    www.Wttool.Com

Industrial distribution of cutting tools, precision tools, machinery, machine tool accesories, hand tools and power tools

President: Mark Dowdy
Buyers: Dan Knecht
Credit Cards: AMEX; MasterCard
Catalog Cost: $3
Catalog Circulation: Mailed 1 time(s) per year
to 55 K
Printing Information: 804 pages in 2 colors on
Matte Stock
Press: Web Press
Binding: Perfect Bound
Mailing List Information: Names for rent
In Business: 169 years
Number of Employees: 110
Sales Volume: $10MM to $20MM

6135 Wood Write Catalog
Wood Write
296 Ford Hampton Rd.
Winchester, KY 40391   717-646-0102
                                    866-641-8064
                              Fax: 717-646-0104
                              sales@WoodWriteLtd.com
                                    www.woodwriteltd.com

Precision mini lathes, one lathes, wood turning supplies, wood and pen kits

Credit Cards: MasterCard; Visa
Average Order Size: $350
In Business: 21 years
Number of Employees: 5

6136 Wood-Mizer Products Catalog
Wood-Mizer Products Inc
8180 W 10th St
Indianapolis, IN 46214-2430   317-271-1542
                                    800-553-0182
                              Fax: 317-273-1011
                              infocenter@woodmizer.com
                                    www.woodmizer.com

Saw mills, tools and edges

President: Dave Mann
In Business: 33 years
Number of Employees: 344
Sales Volume: $20MM to $50MM

6137 Woodcarvers Supply Catalog
Woodcarvers Supply
PO Box 7500
Englewood, FL 34295-7500   941-460-0123
                                    800-284-6229
                              Fax: 941-460-9433
                              teamwcs@yahoo.com
                                    www.woodcarverssupply.com

Woodcarving tools and equipment

Credit Cards: AMEX; MasterCard
Printing Information: 52 pages

6138 Woodline/Japan Woodworker Catalog
Woodline/Japan Woodworker
406 Airport Industrial Park
Parkersburg, WV 26104-9778   510-521-1810
                                    800-537-7820
                              Fax: 304-428-8271
                                    www.thejapanwoodworker.com

Tools for woodworking and gardening

Printing Information: 120 pages
Sales Volume: $3MM to $5MM

6139 Woodmaster Tools Catalog
Woodmaster Tools
1431 N Topping Ave
Kansas City, MO 64120-1219   816-483-0078
                                    800-821-6651
                              Fax: 816-483-7203
                              info@woodmastertools.com
                                    www.Woodmastertools.Com

Power tools, molding and sanders

President: John E Miller
Credit Cards: MasterCard; Visa
Catalog Cost: Free
Printing Information: 30 pages in 4 colors
In Business: 30 years
Number of Employees: 30
Sales Volume: $20MM to $50MM

6140 Woodturners Catalog
Craft Supplies USA
1287 E 1120 S
Provo, UT 84606   801-373-0917
                                    800-551-8876
                              Fax: 801-377-7742
                          service@woodturnerscatalog.com
                                www.woodturnerscatalog.com

Woodturning tools, abrasives and other craft supplies

President: Darrel Nish
Credit Cards: MasterCard; Visa
Catalog Circulation: Mailed 2 time(s) per year
Printing Information: 122 pages
In Business: 35 years
Number of Employees: 25
Sales Volume: 5MM-10MM

6141 Wyco Sales
Wyco Sales
1310 Garlington Road, Suite L
PO Box 26646
Greenville, SC 29615   864-458-8000
                              Fax: 864-458-8256
                                    sales@wyconet.com
                                    www.wyconet.com

Technical sales agency specializing in automation components and equipment

President: Tim Weiss
Marketing Manager: Anne Daniel
In Business: 24 years

Toys & Games
General

6142 ABaby
A Baby Inc.
1958-59th Street
Brooklyn, NY 11204   877-552-2229
                              Fax: 718-972-0397
                                    info@ababy.com
                                    www.ababy.com

Nursery furniture, bedding, accessories, cradles, bassinets, gifts toys, and decor.

President: Issac Greenfeld
Catalog Cost: Free
Printing Information: 46 pages
In Business: 13 years
Number of Employees: 16
Sales Volume: $1,000,000

6143 Al's Farm Toys
Al's Farm Toys & The Toy Box
Northgate Shopping Center
1208 7th St. N. W.
Rochester, MN 55901   651-402-5188
                              Fax: 952-858-9142
                                    alsfarmtoy@yahoo.com
                                    www.alsfarmtoys.com

Farm machinery and equipment for collectors and children

President: Alan L Batzel
Credit Cards: AMEX; MasterCard
Catalog Cost: Free
Average Order Size: $70
Mailing List Information: Names for rent
In Business: 17 years
Number of Employees: 10-J
Sales Volume: $500,000

6144 Alphabet Alley
Alphabet Alley
5739 Kanan Road
Ste 309
Agoura Hills, CA 91301-3358   703-860-1581
                              Fax: 818-337-1943
                                    www.alphabetalley.com

In Business: 11 years

6145 American Playground
American Playground
505 E 31st St # X
Anderson, IN 46016-5375   765-642-0288
                                    800-541-1602
                              Fax: 765-649-7162
                          cherrie@american-playground.net
                                www.American-Playground.net

Playground and recreational equipment

President: Peadar Oscanaill
CFO: Linda Greenlee
Marketing Manager: Dave Schweisthal
Catalog Circulation: Mailed 1 time(s) per year
Printing Information: 72 pages in 4 colors on
Glossy Stock
Press: Web Press
Binding: Saddle Stitched
In Business: 103 years
Number of Employees: 35
Sales Volume: $4,600,000

6146 American Science & Surplus
American Science & Surplus
PO Box 1030
Skokie, IL 60076   888-724-7587
                              Fax: 800-934-0722
                                    service@sciplus.com
                                    www.sciplus.com

Toys, arts and crafts, lab supplies and equipment and electrical parts

President: Philip Cable
President: Scott Causland
Operations manager: Carl Krueger
Credit Cards: MasterCard
In Business: 78 years
Number of Employees: 60

6147 Annalee Dolls
Annalee Dolls
339 Daniel Webster Highway
Meredith, NH 03253   603-279-3333
                                    800-433-6557
                              Fax: 603-279-6659
                          customerservice@annalee.com
                                    www.annalee.com

Felt dolls

President: Jason Ray
Marketing Manager: Betsey Pelletier
Credit Cards: AMEX; MasterCard; Visa
Catalog Cost: Free
Catalog Circulation: Mailed 1 time(s) per year
Printing Information: 32 pages in 4 colors on
Glossy Stock
Press: Sheetfed Press
Binding: Saddle Stitched

In Business: 83 years
Number of Employees: 15

6148 Archie McPhee Catalog
Archie McPhee
10915 47th Ave. W
Mukilteo, WA 98275   425-349-3009
Fax: 425-349-5188
mcphee@mcphee.com
www.mcphee.com

Toys, gifts and novelties
President: Mark McPhee

6149 Are You Game.Com
Are You Game.Com
2030 Harrison St
San Francisco, CA 94110-1310   415-503-0092
800-471-0641
Fax: 415-503-0085
orders@areyougame.com
www.areyougame.com

Great games for the family
President: Cris Lehman
In Business: 17 years
Sales Volume: $1MM to $3MM

6150 Aristoplay
Talicor, Inc.
901 Lincoln Parkway
Plainwell, MI 49080-1452   269-685-2345
800-433-4263
Fax: 269-685-6789
orders@talicor.com
www.talicor.com

Manufacturer of high quality board games, card games, and puzzles
President: Nicole Hancock
Treasurer: Cheryl Sidhu
In Business: 39 years
Number of Employees: 3

6151 Bay Tek Games
Bay Tek Games
1077 East Glenbrook Drive
Pulaski, WI 54162   920-822-3851
Fax: 920-822-8936
www.baytekgames.com

In Business: 38 years

6152 Best of Cards
U.S. Games Systems, Inc.
179 Ludlow Street
Stamford, CT 06902   203-353-8400
Fax: 203-353-8431
cservice@usgamesinc.com
www.usgamesinc.com

Variety of cards for all occasions
President: Stuart R Kaplan
Marketing Manager: Yvette Romero
Credit Cards: AMEX; MasterCard
In Business: 47 years

6153 Bits & Pieces
Bits & Pieces
P.O. BOX 4150
Lawrenceburg, IN 47025   866-503-6395
Fax: 513-354-1290
customersersvice@bitsandpieces.com
www.bitsandpieces.com

Puzzles and unique gifts
President: James Seward
Credit Cards: AMEX; MasterCard; Visa
Catalog Cost: Free
In Business: 31 years

6154 Boomerang Man
The Boomerang Man
1149 E Nakoma Street
Monroe, LA 71201-4222   318-323-2356
Fax: 318-329-1095
boomerangman@centurytel.net
www.theboomerangman.com

Boomerangs
President: Richard Harrison
Credit Cards: AMEX; MasterCard; Visa
Catalog Cost: Free
Catalog Circulation: Mailed 2 time(s) per year
Printing Information: 4 pages in 2 colors
Press: Offset Press
In Business: 35 years
Number of Employees: 2
Sales Volume: Under $500M

6155 CBD Kid's
Christian Book Distributors
140 Summit St.
Peabody, MA 01960   800-247-4784
customer.service@christianbook.com
www.christianbook.com

Toys, games, DVDs, books, crafts and activities.
President: Ray Hendrickson
Catalog Cost: Free
Mailing List Information: Names for rent
In Business: 39 years
Number of Employees: 500

6156 Cedar Works Playsets
CedarWorks
799 Commercial Street
PO Box 990
Rockport, ME 04856-990   207-596-1010
800-462-3327
Fax: 207-596-7900
info@cedarworks.com
www.cedarworks.com

Children's wooden playsets and accessories
Chairman: Duncan Brown
President: Barrett Brown
CFO: Kirby Kramer
Credit Cards: MasterCard; Visa
Catalog Cost: Free
Catalog Circulation: Mailed 1 time(s) per year to 30000
Printing Information: 60 pages in 4 colors on Glossy Stock
Press: Web Press
Binding: Saddle Stitched
Mailing List Information: Names for rent
Number of Employees: 50

6157 Celebrate Express
Celebrate Express
11220 120 Avenue NE
Kirkland, WA 98033-4535   425-250-1064
800-247-8432
Fax: 425-828-6252
customerservice@celebrateexpress.com
www.celebrateexpress.com

Party supplies and items including: holidays, graduation, theme parties, etc
President: Jalem Getz
CFO: Nancy Neilsen
Marketing Manager: Stacey Kaye
Production Manager: Travis Roberts
Credit Cards: AMEX; MasterCard
In Business: 18 years
Number of Employees: 332
Sales Volume: $ 18 Million

6158 Chasing Fireflies
Chasing Fireflies
5568 West Chester Rd
West Chester, OH 45069   206-574-4500
888-700-9474
Fax: 800-989-4510
customerservice@chasing-fireflies.com
www.chasing-fireflies.com

Children's, newborn and infant's clothes, toys and accessories
President: Dina Alhadeff
Co-Owner: Lori Liddle
Co-Owner: Amy Grealish
Credit Cards: AMEX; MasterCard
Catalog Cost: Free
Number of Employees: 100
Sales Volume: $10 Million

6159 Childlife
ChildLife
817 Maxwell Avenue
Evansville, IN 47711-2010   800-966-3752
www.childlife.com

Backyard play equipment, including swing sets, swings, slides, treehouses, jungle gyms, mountain climbing walls, many other add-ons, and sandboxes
Chairman: Robert Griffin
CFO: Debra Meinert
Credit Cards: AMEX; MasterCard; Visa
Catalog Cost: Free
Printing Information: 48 pages in 4 colors on Glossy Stock
Press: Web Press
Binding: Saddle Stitched
In Business: 72 years
Number of Employees: 600
Sales Volume: $116,000,000

6160 Childswork/Childsplay
Childswork/Childsplay
303 Crossways Park Drive
Woodbury, NY 11797   516-496-4863
800-962-1141
Fax: 800-262-1886
info@childswork.com
www.childswork.com

Books, games and playtime activities for childhood development
President: Lawrence Shapiro
Credit Cards: AMEX; MasterCard; Visa
Catalog Cost: $25
Printing Information: 57 pages
Mailing List Information: Names for rent
In Business: 10 years
Number of Employees: 25

6161 Chime Time
PO Box 369
Landisville, PA 17538-369   800-784-5717
Fax: 800-219-5253
service@e-c-direct.com; www.chimetime.com

Movement and musical products for children designed to promote increased brain development in infants through children age eight
Printing Information: 202 pages in 4 colors

6162 Christmas
Bass Pro Shops
2500 E Kearney
Springfield, MO 65898   417-873-5000
800-227-7776
Fax: 417-873-5060
www.basspro.com

Toys, casual wear and gifts.
President & CEO: James Hagale
Catalog Cost: Free
Catalog Circulation: Mailed 1 time(s) per year
Printing Information: 220 pages in 4 colors
In Business: 45 years
Number of Employees: 2200
Sales Volume: $4.45 Billion

6163 Constructive Playthings
Constructive Playthings
13201 Arrington Rd.
Grandview, MO 64030   816-761-5900
www.constructiveplaythings.com
Educational toys, classroom materials and teaching supplies.
Catalog Cost: Free
Printing Information: in 4 colors
In Business: 63 years

6164 Constructive Playthings Playground Catalog
Constructive Playthings
13201 Arrington Rd.
Grandview, MO 64030   816-761-5900
www.constructiveplaythings.com
Playground equipment
Catalog Cost: Free
Printing Information: in 4 colors
In Business: 63 years

6165 Costume Express
Costume Express
5915 S. Moorland Rd.
New Berlin, WI 53151-4535   262-901-2324
800-695-9668
Fax: 425-828-6252
customerservice@celebrateexpress.com
www.costumeexpress.com
Halloween costume catalog
President: Jalem Getz
CFO: Nancy Neilsen
Marketing Manager: Stacey Kaye
Production Manager: Travis Roberts
Credit Cards: AMEX; MasterCard
In Business: 18 years
Number of Employees: 332
Sales Volume: $ 18 Million

6166 Creative Kidstuff
Creative Kidstuff
One Union Square
600 University St., Suite 1000
Seattle, WA 98101-3906   206-268-5400
888-811-5271
Fax: 612-929-6770
customerservice@greatergood.com
www.creativekidstuff.com
Creative, innovative playthings
President: Roberta Bonoff
rbonoff@creativekidstuff.com
Marketing Manager: Happi Olson
holson@creativekidstuff.com
Merchandise Manager: Jennifer Dunne
jdunne@creativekidstuff.com
Art Director: Denise Womeldorff
dwomeldorff@creativekidstuff.com
Events and Special Sales: Sue Katsiotis
skatsiotis@creativekidstuff.com
Buyers: Libby Colburn
Credit Cards: MasterCard; Visa
Catalog Cost: Free
Sales Volume: $3MM to $5MM

6167 Creative Playthings
Creative Playthings
17 Reaville Avenue
Flemington, NJ 08822   800-598-4997
www.creativeplaythings.com
Wooden swing sets and creative playthings for children
President: Donald E Hoffman
Credit Cards: MasterCard; Visa
Catalog Cost: Free
Catalog Circulation: Mailed 1 time(s) per year
Printing Information: 23 pages
In Business: 66 years
Sales Volume: $20MM to $50MM

6168 Dakotah Toys
Dakotah Toys
44718 SD HWY 34
Madison, SD 57042-6601   605-256-6676
Fax: 605-256-9093
daktoys@yahoo.com
www.dakotahtoyparts.com
Farm toy and pedal tractor parts
President: Roger Ayers
Catalog Cost: $3.5
In Business: 20 years
Number of Employees: 4
Sales Volume: $400,000

6169 Dart Mart
Minnesota Fats' All Fun and Games
160 W 26th Street
New York, NY 10001   212-366-6981
Fax: 212-206-6491
www.mnfats.com
Dart equipment and supplies
President: Paul Giegerich

6170 Design Group
Design Group Pattern
PO Box 827
Milford, OH 45150   *Fax:* 513-248-1880
salvillano@gmail.com
www.designgroupweb.com
Patterns and books for games, toys and furniture
Credit Cards: AMEX; MasterCard
Catalog Cost: $2
Printing Information: 36 pages
In Business: 77 years
Number of Employees: 5

6171 Detailed Play Systems
Detailed Play Systems
PO Box 633
Manahawkin, NJ 8050   973-912-9440
800-398-7565
Fax: 973-710-3087
playsets@detailedplay.com
www.detailedplay.com
Playground equipment
President: Karl Jessen
Credit Cards: AMEX; MasterCard
Catalog Cost: Free

6172 Diecast Direct
Diecast Direct
3005 Old Lawrenceburg Road
Frankfort, KY 40601-9351   502-227-8697
800-718-1866
Fax: 502-227-9484
www.diecastdirect.com
Collectible die cast metal cars, trucks, buses, planes and other vehicles
President: Kevin Black
Controller: Beth McFarland
Credit Cards: MasterCard
Catalog Cost: Free
In Business: 30 years
Number of Employees: 15
Sales Volume: $ 1-3 Million

6173 Discovery Corner
Discovery Corner
Lawrence Hall Of Science
One Centennial Drive #5200
Berkeley, CA 94720-5200   510-642-5132
Fax: 510-642-1055
lhsstore@berkeley.edu
www.lawrencehallofscience.org
Toys and games
President: Judy Timmel
Marketing Manager: Linda Schneider
Director: Elizabeth K. Stage
Resource Development: Susan Gregory
Resource Management: Florencia Ramos

Credit Cards: MasterCard
Printing Information: 30 pages in 2 colors on Newsprint
Binding: Folded
In Business: 47 years

6174 Doll Lover Catalog
All About Dolls
937 Bonita Loop
Myrtle Beach, SC 29579-1310   843-742-5182
800-645-3655
Fax: 973-398-6338
sales@allaboutdolls.com
www.allaboutdolls.com
Doll making supplies for porcelain, vinyl and soft body dolls
President: Diane Stec
CFO: Rita McClosky
Credit Cards: AMEX; MasterCard
Catalog Cost: $6.95
In Business: 32 years
Number of Employees: 2
Sales Volume: Under $500M

6175 ELMS Jigsaw Puzzles
ELMS Puzzles
49 Hobbs Hill Lane
PO Box 537
Harrison, ME 04040-537   207-583-6262
800-353-3567
Fax: 207-583-6534
info@elmspuzzles.com
www.elmspuzzles.com
Wooden jigsaw puzzles
President: Fred Stuart
Credit Cards: AMEX; MasterCard
Catalog Cost: Free
Catalog Circulation: Mailed 1 time(s) per year
Average Order Size: $500
Printing Information: 24 pages in 4 colors on Glossy Stock
Press: Web Press
Mailing List Information: Names for rent
In Business: 27 years
Number of Employees: 10
Sales Volume: $500,000

6176 Educational Insights
Educational Insights
152 W Walnut St.
Suite 201
Gardena, CA 90248   800-995-4436
Fax: 888-498-8670
www.educationalinsights.com
Educational toys and games.
Catalog Circulation: Mailed 1 time(s) per year
Printing Information: 166 pages in 4 colors
In Business: 10 years
Number of Employees: 20
Sales Volume: $2 Million

6177 Entertainment Earth
Entertainment Earth Inc
61 Moreland Rd.
Simi Valley, CA 93065   818-255-0095
800-370-2320
Fax: 818-255-0091
cs@entertainmentearth.com
www.entertainmentearth.com
Action figures, toys, gifts, and collectibles
President: Jason Labowitz
Production Manager: Adam Lieber
CEO: Aaron Labowitz
Chief Technology Officer: Aaron Lipman
Chief Human Resources Officer: Adam Lieber
Credit Cards: AMEX; MasterCard
Catalog Cost: Free
Average Order Size: $85
Printing Information: 50 pages in 4 colors on Glossy Stock
Press: Web Press
Binding: Saddle Stitched
In Business: 20 years

Number of Employees: 31
Sales Volume: $10MM to $20MM

6178 Ertl Toy Catalog
RC2 Corp
2021 9th Street SE
Dyersville, IA 52040
563-875-5995
Fax: 563-875-8263
www.ertltoys.com

Toys and model kits

President: Boyd Meyer
Marketing Manager: Del Jorgerson
Production Manager: Pete Henseler
Buyers: John O'Neill, Model Kits
Credit Cards: MasterCard; Visa
Catalog Circulation: Mailed 1 time(s) per year
Printing Information: 50 pages in 4 colors
Number of Employees: 1000

6179 First Wishes
Birthday Express
5915 S.Moorland Rd.
New Berlin, WI 53151
866-255-3556
800-247-8432
Fax: 425-828-6252
customerservice@celebrateexpress.com
www.birthdayexpress.com

Party supplies for a child's first birthday

President: Mark Gordon
CFO: Nancy Neilson
Marketing Manager: Steve Parker
Production Manager: Travis Roberts
CEO: Mark Gordon
VP Finance: Kevin Miller
General Counsel & Secretary: Stacy Hackney
Credit Cards: AMEX; MasterCard; Visa
In Business: 18 years
Number of Employees: 332
Sales Volume: $ 18 Million

6180 Fisher-Price
Fisher-Price
636 Girard Avenue
East Aurora, NY 14052
716-687-3000
Fax: 716-687-3636
customerservice@fisher-pricestore.com
www.fisher-price.com

Toys, layette items

Chairman: Christopher A. Sinclair
President: Margaret Georgiadis
CFO: Joseph J. Euteneuer
Chief Operating Officer: Richard Dickson
Chief Technology Officer: Sven Gerjets
Chief Supply Chain Officer: Peter D. Gubbons
Credit Cards: AMEX; MasterCard; Visa
Catalog Cost: Free
Catalog Circulation: Mailed 5 time(s) per year
Printing Information: 41 pages in 4 colors on Glossy Stock
Press: Web Press
Binding: Saddle Stitched
In Business: 87 years
Number of Employees: 830
Sales Volume: $47.8 MM

6181 Folktale & Story Catalog
August House Publishers
3500 Piedmont Road
Suite 310
Atlanta, GA 30305
404-442-4420
800-284-8784
Fax: 404-442-4435
www.augusthouse.com

Books, spoken word cd's and audiocassettes

President: Steve Floyd
steve@augusthouse.com
Marketing Manager: Steve Floyd
steve@augusthouse.com
Production Manager: Graham Anthony
Publisher: Liz Parkhurst
Director of Development: Robe Cleveland
Director: August House
Average Order Size: $100

Printing Information: 61 pages in 4 colors on Matte Stock
Binding: Saddle Stitched
Mailing List Information: Names for rent
In Business: 25 years
Number of Employees: 5
Sales Volume: $260,000

6182 Giggletime Toy Company
Giggletime Toy Co.
PO Box 1759
Bishop, CA 93515
800-423-5198
Fax: 800-873-1758
info@jrousek.com
www.giggletimetoys.com

Kids toys and prizes for dental and medical offices; party favors, noise makers and wedding bubbles

President: Joseph L Rousek
Credit Cards: AMEX; MasterCard
Number of Employees: 19
Sales Volume: $2.4 Million

6183 Hearth Song
Hearth Song Inc
PO Box 5000
7021 Wolftown-Hood Rd
Madison, VA 22727-1500
540-948-2272
800-533-4397
Fax: 540-948-3544
www.hearthsong.com

Age-appropriate, wholesome, quality playthings: toys & games, arts & crafts, costumes and hobbies

President: Tim Hopkins
Catalog Cost: Free
Catalog Circulation: Mailed 6 time(s) per year
Printing Information: 80 pages in 4 colors
In Business: 31 years
Number of Employees: 425

6184 Historic Rail Product Catalog
Historic Rail
640 Taft Street NE
Minneapolis, MN 55413-2815
612-206-3200
800-261-5922
Fax: 621-877-3160
info@historicrail.com; www.historicrail.com

Books, videos, art, models & kits, puzzels and games, calendars & holiday, audio, home decor, accessories and more

Catalog Cost: Free

6185 Intelligent Outfitters
401 Broadkill Rd
Milton, DE 19968-1013
302-684-1547
Fax: 302-684-1593
www.Terrifictoys.Com

Jigsaw puzzles, science toys, activity toys, skill toys, pet themed toys, board games, card games, action games and brainteaser puzzles

President: Dirk Grove
Sales Volume: Under $500M

6186 Kapla USA
Kapla USA LP
PO Box 8185
Savannah, GA 31402-8185
912-944-6296
Fax: 912-525-3175
www.kaplatoys.com

Toy wood building blocks for children

Catalog Cost: Free

6187 Kaplan Early Learning Company
Kaplan
1310 Lewisville Clemmons Rd
Lewisville, NC 27023-609
336-766-7374
800-334-2014
Fax: 800-452-7526
info@kaplanco.com
www.Kaplanco.Com

Educational toys

President: Hal Kaplan
CFO: Hal Kaplan
CEO: Hal Kaplan
Credit Cards: AMEX; MasterCard; Visa
Catalog Cost: Free
Catalog Circulation: Mailed 12 time(s) per year
Average Order Size: $250
Printing Information: 233 pages in 4 colors on Glossy Stock
Press: Web Press
Binding: Saddle Stitched
Mailing List Information: Names for rent
In Business: 63 years
Number of Employees: 300
Sales Volume: $20MM to $50MM

6188 Kid Stuff Marketing
Kid Stuff Marketing
929 SW University Blvd., Suite B-1
PO Box 19235
Topeka, KS 66619
785-862-3707
800-677-4712
Fax: 785-862-0070
sales@kidstuff.com
www.kidstuff.com

Kids toys, cups, place mats, cartons and cups

President: John Woodward
johnwoodward@kidstuff.com
CFO: John Woodward
Marketing Manager: Joe Tindall
joetindall@kidstuff.com
Production Manager: Mark Larson
mark@kidstuff.com
Fulfillment: Carol Roush
carol@kidstuff.com
CEO: Joe Tindall
Marketing Coordinator: Hallie Schwartz
hallie@kidstuff.com
Catalog Cost: Free
Printing Information: 84 pages
Mailing List Information: Names for rent
In Business: 33 years
Number of Employees: 40
Sales Volume: $5.7 Million

6189 Kotula's
2800 Southcross Drive W
Burnsville, MN 55306
800-685-4845
Fax: 952-882-6927
commerce@kotulas.com; www.kotulas.com

Games, toys, gifts, remote control toys, electronics, garage and auto supplies, home & outdoor living accessories, sports and recreation

Chairman: Donald Kotula
President: Chuck Albrecht
CFO: Tom Erickson
Marketing Manager: Wade Mattson
VP Operations: Rich Flogstad
Credit Cards: AMEX; MasterCard
Catalog Cost: Free
In Business: 30 years
Number of Employees: 300

6190 LEGO Shop at Home
Lego
555 Taylor Road
P.O. Box 1138
Enfield, CT 06083-1138
800-835-4386
www.lego.com

Construction and educational toys

Chairman: Jorgen Vig Knustorp
CFO: Marjorie Lao

Marketing Manager: Julia Goldin
Chief Executive Officer: Niels B Christiansen
Chief Operations Officer: Carsten Rasmussen
Chief Commercial Officer: Loren I Shuster
Credit Cards: AMEX; MasterCard; Visa
Catalog Cost: Free
In Business: 85 years
Number of Employees: 1300
Sales Volume: $1MM to $3MM

6191 Lilliput
Lilliput Motor Company
321 South Main St
Yerington, NV 89447-2545   775-463-5181
                                                    800-846-8697
                                   Fax: 775-463-1582
                       www.lilliputmotorcompany.com

Toys, games, puzzles and gifts

President: Justus Bauschinger
Catalog Circulation: Mailed 12 time(s) per year to 10000
Average Order Size: $320
Printing Information: 46 pages in 1 color on Newsprint
Press: Web Press
Binding: Saddle Stitched
Mailing List Information: Names for rent
In Business: 22 years
Number of Employees: 16
Sales Volume: $500M to $1MM

6192 Mary Meyer Corporation
Mary Meyer Corporation
1 Teddy Bear Lane, Route 30
PO Box 275
Townshend, VT 05353   802-365-7793
                                                    800-451-4387
                                   Fax: 802-365-4233
                            info@marymeyer.com
                              www.marymeyer.com

Stuffed teddy bears, bunnies, frogs, penguins, and stuffed animals for babies and baby gifts

President: Kevin Meyer
Marketing Manager: Patricia Williams
VP: Michael Meyer
National Sales Manager: Tara Rubino
Credit Cards: MasterCard; Visa
Catalog Cost: Free
Catalog Circulation: Mailed 6 time(s) per year to 15000
Printing Information: 72 pages in 4 colors on Glossy Stock
Binding: Saddle Stitched
In Business: 75 years
Number of Employees: 55
Sales Volume: $8.4 Million

6193 Maukilo European Toys
Maukilo
4407 Jordan Road
Skaneateles, NY 13152   866-628-5456
                                   Fax: 866-628-5456
                        info@maukilo.com; www.maukilo.com

European children's toys and games

President: Alexandra Goedrich
Credit Cards: AMEX; MasterCard
Catalog Cost: Free

6194 Meadow View Imports
Meadow View Imports
81 Kingstown Road
PO Box 407
Wyoming, RI 02898   401-539-9090
                                                    800-249-9090
                                   Fax: 401-539-7199
                      toys@meadowviewimports.com
                       www.Meadowviewimports.Com

Ostheimer wooden toys, figures and collectibles imported from Germany

President: James Mathews
Production Manager: James Mathews
Credit Cards: MasterCard; Visa

Catalog Cost: Free
Catalog Circulation: Mailed 1 time(s) per year to 10000
Average Order Size: $200
Printing Information: 32 pages in 4 colors on Glossy Stock
Press: Web Press
Binding: Saddle Stitched
Mailing List Information: Names for rent
In Business: 20 years
Number of Employees: 3
Sales Volume: $500M to $1MM

6195 Met Kids Catalog
The Metropolitan Museum of Art Store
1000 Fifth Avenue
New York, NY 10028   800-468-7386
                   customer.service@metmuseum.org
                              store.metmuseum.org

Books, activity books, puzzles, toys, clothing, and collectables inspired by the collections at the Metropolitan Museum of Art

Credit Cards: AMEX; MasterCard; Visa
Catalog Cost: Free
In Business: 96 years

6196 Moolka
Moolka Toys
9960 Glenoa
Sun Valley, CA 91352   888-505-5455
                                        www.moolka.com

Toys and decor for children

President: Levon Shahbaghyan
Catalog Cost: Free
In Business: 3 years
Number of Employees: 4
Sales Volume: Under $500M

6197 National Wildlife Federation
National Wildlife Federation
1 Stationery Place
Rexburg, ID 83441-5000   800-756-3752
                                   Fax: 800-525-5562
                                        www.shopnwf.org

Nature-related and educational gifts, including home accessories, clothing and toys

President: Larry J Schweiger
Credit Cards: MasterCard; Visa
Catalog Cost: Free
Catalog Circulation: Mailed 4 time(s) per year
Printing Information: 60 pages
Number of Employees: 35
Sales Volume: 5MM-10MM

6198 Nova Natural Toys & Crafts
Nova Natural Toys & Crafts Llc
120 Graham Way #200
Shelburne, VT 05482-7513   802-860-1300
                                                    877-668-2111
                       support@novanatural.com
                              www.novanatural.com

Toys that encourage growth, imagination, creativity, and values

President: Jason Miller
Credit Cards: AMEX; MasterCard
Catalog Cost: Free
Printing Information: 64 pages
In Business: 9 years
Number of Employees: 6
Sales Volume: $1MM to $3MM

6199 Official US Chess Federation Catalog
United States Chess Federation
PO Box 3967
Crossville, TN 38557   931-787-1234
                                                    800-388-5464
                                   Fax: 913-787-1200
                                        www.uschess.org

Chess boards & sets from inexpensive to collector series; computer software, videos, books & more

President: Gary Walters
CFO: Allen Priest
Fulfillment: Traci Pond
Executive Director: Jean Hoffman
Senior Accountant: Debra Robison
Director of Affiliate Relations: Joan DuBois
Buyers: Joan DuBois
Credit Cards: AMEX; MasterCard; Visa
Catalog Cost: $4
Catalog Circulation: Mailed 3 time(s) per year
Average Order Size: $175
Printing Information: 80 pages in 4 colors on Glossy Stock
Press: Web Press
Binding: Saddle Stitched
Mailing List Information: Names for rent
Number of Employees: 45
Sales Volume: $500M to $1MM

6200 One Step Ahead
One Step Ahead
1112 7th Ave.
Monroe, WI 53566-1364   888-557-3851
                                   Fax: 847-615-7236
                              www.onestepahead.com

One stop shopping for moms and kids, from clothing to books and toys

President: Karen Scott
CFO: Susan O'Malley
Marketing Manager: Bob Patton
Credit Cards: AMEX; MasterCard
Catalog Cost: Free
Catalog Circulation: Mailed 12 time(s) per year to 10M
Average Order Size: $65
Printing Information: 48 pages in 4 colors on Glossy Stock
Press: Web Press
Binding: Saddle Stitched
Mailing List Information: Names for rent
List Manager: ALCNY
In Business: 23 years
Number of Employees: 150
Sales Volume: $ 9 Million

6201 Oompa Toys
Oompa Enterprises Inc
3 Gordon Dr.
Rockland, ME 04841-2303   844-883-3300
                                   Fax: 774-388-0234
                       hello@oompa.com; www.oompa.com

Educational toys, European toys, wooden puzzles, games & more

President: Milanie Cleere
Credit Cards: AMEX; MasterCard
Catalog Cost: Free
In Business: 8 years
Number of Employees: 20-5
Sales Volume: $1,000,000 to $4,999,999

6202 Ostheimer Toys
Meadow View Imports, LLC
81 Kingstown Road
PO Box 407
Wyoming, RI 02898-407   401-539-9090
                                                    800-249-9090
                                   Fax: 401-539-7199
                      toys@meadowviewimports.com
                       www.meadowviewimports.com

Toys and games

President: James Mathews
Number of Employees: 5
Sales Volume: $300,000

6203 Palumba Natural Toys and Crafts
Palumba
221 Felch Street, #2C
Ann Arbor, MI 48103-3353   734-995-5414
                                                    866-725-7122
                       hello@palumba.com; www.palumba.com

Natural wood toys, organic kids clothing, organic toys and furniture

President: Judy Alexander
Marketing Manager: Mickey Dean

Credit Cards: AMEX; MasterCard
Catalog Cost: Free
Sales Volume: Under $500,000

6204   Paragon-Gifts
The Paragon
P.O. BOX 4068
Lawrenceburg, IN 47025-4068   855-557-4658
Fax: 513-354-1294
customerservice@theparagon.com
www.theparagon.com

Unusual gifts and toys

President: Coy Clement
Marketing Manager: Doug Brown
Credit Cards: AMEX; MasterCard; Visa; Discover
Catalog Cost: Free
Catalog Circulation: Mailed 8 time(s) per year to 44000
Average Order Size: $50
Printing Information: 66 pages in 4 colors on Glossy Stock
Press: Web Press
Binding: Saddle Stitched
Mailing List Information: Names for rent
List Company: NRL
100 Union Avenue
Cresskill, NJ 07626
In Business: 46 years
Number of Employees: 400
Sales Volume: $20MM to $50MM

6205   Plushland
Plushland,Inc
4300 Union Pacific Ave.
Los Angeles, CA 90023   888-500-8697
Fax: 213-626-7256
www.plushland.com

High quality, hand crafted plush animals

President: Tony Weber
Credit Cards: AMEX; MasterCard
Printing Information: 22 pages
Number of Employees: 23
Sales Volume: $3.9 Million

6206   Polka Dots
Polka Dots
5227 Willing St
Milton, FL 32570-4969   850-564-4313
888-700-3687
Fax: 850-626-3570
cservice@mypolkadots.com
www.Mypolkadots.Com

Toy, kid's sleeping bags and children's products

President: Deb Pruitt
Sales Volume: $500M to $1MM

6207   Prime Time Toys
Prime Time Toys
P.O. Box 256
Pompton Lakes, NJ 7442   615-866-1052
www.primetimetoys.com

Toys & Games

6208   Rosie Hippo
Rosie Hippo Inc
30 Haddonfield Road
Short Hills, NJ 07078   570-497-3337
877-574-4776
Fax: 917-522-9733
Service@RosieHippo.com
www.rosiehippo.com

Natural, earth-friendly toys

President: Kim Bloom
Catalog Cost: Free
Printing Information: in 3 colors
In Business: 16 years
Number of Employees: 2
Sales Volume: $500,000

6209   Sensational Beginnings
GreaterGood stores
One Union Square
600 University St., Suite 1000
Seattle, WA 98101-4227   734-242-2147
888-811-5271
Fax: 734-242-8278
customerservice@greatergood.com
www.sensationalbeginnings.com

Educational toys, costume and dress-up and furniture

President: Debra Shah
Credit Cards: AMEX; MasterCard; Visa
Catalog Circulation: Mailed 12 time(s) per year to 5000
Average Order Size: $65
Printing Information: 48 pages in 4 colors on Glossy Stock
Press: Web Press
Binding: Saddle Stitched
Mailing List Information: Names for rent
In Business: 26 years
Number of Employees: 25
Sales Volume: $10MM to $20MM

6210   Stoneberry
Stoneberry
1356 Williams Street
Chippewa Falls, WI 54729   800-704-5480
www.stoneberry.com

Home furnishings and appliances, home entertainment, toys and games, gardening and yard maintenance equipment, sport and fitness products, health and beauty products

Credit Cards: AMEX; MasterCard
Catalog Cost: Free
Catalog Circulation: Mailed 2 time(s) per year
Printing Information: 200 pages in 4 colors
Sales Volume: $50MM to $100MM

6211   Talicor
Talicor
901 Lincoln Pkwy
Plainwell, MI 49080-1452   269-685-2345
800-433-GAME
Fax: 269-685-6789
orders@talicor.com
www.talicor.com

Intellectual board games

President: Nicole Hancock
Credit Cards: AMEX; MasterCard; Visa
Catalog Cost: Free
Catalog Circulation: Mailed 1 time(s) per year to 10000
Average Order Size: $40
Printing Information: 16 pages in 4 colors on Matte Stock
Press: Web Press
Binding: Saddle Stitched
Number of Employees: 10
Sales Volume: $500M to $1MM

6212   The Toy Network Fall Catalog 2015
The Toy Network
350 Commerce Dr
Fall River, MA 2720   508-675-9400
888-988-2244
Fax: 508-675-9401
info@thetoynetwork.com
www.thetoynetwork.com

Toys, Games, Accessories & Gifts.

6213   Toy Connection
Toy Connection, Inc.
22 Lawrence Lane
Lawrence, NY 11559-1137   516-371-9206
877-869-8691
Fax: 888-562-8697
sales@toyconnection.com
www.Toyconnection.Com

Toys, novelties, jewelry, stationery, stickers, tatoos, candy, holiday

President: Sharon Hecht
Credit Cards: AMEX; MasterCard
In Business: 60 years
Sales Volume: Under $500M

6214   Toy Soldier Catalog
Imprints Publication
100 Riverside Drive
Suite 1B, Department IN
New York, NY 10024-4822   212-721-6394
888-825-8697
Fax: 201-792-2626
jdelson@toysoldierco.com
www.ToysSoldierco.Com

Plastic and lead toy soldiers

President: James Delson
Catalog Cost: $3
Catalog Circulation: Mailed 12 time(s) per year to 40000
Printing Information: 88 pages in 2 colors on Newsprint
Press: Web Press
Binding: Saddle Stitched
Mailing List Information: Names for rent
In Business: 31 years
Sales Volume: Under $500M

6215   Toys to Grow On
Toys to Grow On
2695 E Dominguez St
Carson, CA 90895-1000   800-874-4242
800-987-4454
Fax: 800-537-5403
toyinfo@toystogrowon.com

Toys for all ages

President: Michael Kaplan
Credit Cards: AMEX; MasterCard
In Business: 60 years
Number of Employees: 75
Sales Volume: $7.8 Million

6216   Toysmith
Toysmith
3101 West Valley Hwy East
Sumner, WA 98390-1714   253-859-4343
800-356-0474
Fax: 253-859-2774
info@toysmith.com
www.toysmith.com

Toys and gift products

Catalog Cost: Free
Printing Information: 274 pages in 4 colors
In Business: 3 years

6217   U.S. Toy
U.S. Toy
13201 Arrington Rd.
Grandview, MO 64030   816-761-5900
www.ustoy.com

Novelty toys, gifts and party supplies.

Catalog Cost: Free
In Business: 63 years

6218   US Games Systems Inc
US Games Systems Inc
179 Ludlow Street
Stamford, CT 06902   800-544-2637
cservice@usgamesinc.com
www.usgamesinc.com

Publishes more than 400 proprietary products encompassing the world of tarot in deck and book form, specialty playing cards, informational card decks, and educational games for the entire family

President: Stuart Kaplan
CFO: Ricardo Cruz
Marketing Manager: Carole Vignoli
Production Manager: Paula Palmer
International Marketing Manager: Bobbie Bensaid
Buyers: Bobbie Bensaid
Credit Cards: AMEX; MasterCard

Catalog Cost: $2
Catalog Circulation: Mailed 2 time(s) per year
Average Order Size: $100
Printing Information: 60 pages in 4 colors on Glossy Stock
Press: Sheetfed Press
Binding: Saddle Stitched
Mailing List Information: Names for rent
In Business: 49 years
Number of Employees: 35
Sales Volume: $5MM to $10MM

6219 US Toy Company
US Toy Catalog
13201 Arrington Road
Grandview, MO 64030-2886   800-255-6124
Fax: 816-761-9295
www.ustoy.com

Carnival/party and seasonal decorations, novelty toys, stuffed animals and balloons

President: Michael Klein
Credit Cards: MasterCard
Catalog Cost: Free
In Business: 64 years
Sales Volume: $50MM to $100MM

6220 Vermont Teddy Bear Company
Vermont Teddy Bear Company
6655 Shelburne Road
Shelburne, VT 05482-965   802-985-3001
                                  800-829-BEAR
Fax: 802-985-1304
www.Vermontteddybear.Com

Teddy bears

President: John Gilbert
CFO: Mark Fleeper
Marketing Manager: Irene Steiner
Production Manager: Kathleen Straube
Credit Cards: MasterCard
Catalog Circulation: Mailed 3 time(s) per year
Printing Information: 25 pages in 4 colors on Glossy Stock
Binding: Saddle Stitched
Number of Employees: 300

6221 White Cap Industries
White Cap Industries
408 E University Drive
Phoenix, AZ 85004-2923   602-256-6900
                                 800-944-8322
Fax: 602-256-6067
www.whitecapdirect.com

Wholesale contractor and supplies company, full line of all contruction equipment, hardware, tools and materials

Credit Cards: AMEX; MasterCard
Catalog Cost: Free
In Business: 38 years
Number of Employees: 24

6222 White Mountain Puzzles
White Mountain Puzzles
PO Box 818
Jackson, NH 3846   800-548-8009
Fax: 603-383-4572
info@puzzlemaps.com
www.whitemountainpuzzles.com

Puzzles.

In Business: 37 years

6223 Wimmer-Ferguson
The Manhattan Toy Company
300 First Avenue North
Suite 200
Minneapolis, MN 55401-1738   612-337-9600
                                800-542-1345
Fax: 612-337-3896
support@shopatron.com
www.manhattantoy.com

Visual preference of infants in bold black and white graphics in baby toys

Printing Information: 2 pages in 2 colors

6224 Wisconsin Wagon Company
Wisconsin Wagon Company
300 North River Street
Janesville, WI 53548-3604   608-754-0026
Fax: 608-741-9404
Britten@wisconsinwagon.com
www.wisconsinwagon.com

Children's durable toys

President: Karen Ferguson
Credit Cards: MasterCard; Visa
Number of Employees: 4
Sales Volume: $1MM to $3MM

6225 Yesteryear Toys & Books Catalog
Yesteryear Toys & Books
PO Box 537
Alexandria Bay, NY 13607   613-475-1771
                                800-481-1353
Fax: 613-475-3748
info@yesteryeartoys.com
www.yesteryeartoys.com

Over 130 different models of steam engines and accessories

President: Frank VanMeeuwen
Catalog Cost: $6.95
Printing Information: 43 pages in 4 colors
In Business: 41 years
Number of Employees: 6

Travel & Leisure Products
Trips & Products

6226 2016 Trip Planner
Trek Travel
613 Williamson Street
Suite 207
Madison, WI 53703   608-255-8735
                            866-464-8735
Fax: 608-441-8733
trektravel.com

6227 Access to Recreation
Access to Recreation, Inc.
8 Sandra Ct
Newbury Park, CA 91320-4302   805-498-7535
                                 800-634-4351
Fax: 805-498-8186
dkrebs@accesstr.com; www.accesstr.com

Recreation/exercise equipment that has been adapted specifically for use by the elderly & disabled; large-print playing cards, rehabilitational pool lifts, fishing equipment & golf clubs

President: Don Krebs
dkrebs@accesstr.com
Credit Cards: AMEX; MasterCard; Visa
Catalog Cost: Free
Catalog Circulation: to 100,0
Average Order Size: $100
Printing Information: 52 pages in 4 colors on Glossy Stock
Press: Web Press
Binding: Saddle Stitched
Mailing List Information: Names for rent
In Business: 24 years
Number of Employees: 2
Sales Volume: $499,000

6228 American Map
Kappa Map Group, LLC
6198 Butler Pike
Blue Bell, PA 19422   386-873-3010
                              800-432-6277
Fax: 386-873-3011
info@kappamapgroup.com
www.Americanmap.Com

Maps, atlases, travel guides, language learning print & software, dictionaries and world atlases

Chairman: Andreas Langenscheidt
President: K Langenscheidt

Credit Cards: AMEX; MasterCard; Visa
Catalog Cost: Free
Catalog Circulation: Mailed 1 time(s) per year
Printing Information: 60 pages in 4 colors on Glossy Stock
Binding: Saddle Stitched
Mailing List Information: Names for rent
In Business: 98 years
Number of Employees: 267
Sales Volume: $10MM to $20MM

6229 Arta River Trips
ARTA River Trips
24000 Casa Loma Rd
Groveland, CA 95321-9302   209-962-7873
                                   800-323-2782
Fax: 209-962-4819
arta@arta.org; www.arta.org

Whitewater rafting trips

President: Steve Welch
Credit Cards: MasterCard; Visa
Catalog Circulation: Mailed 1 time(s) per year to 30000
Printing Information: 12 pages in 3 colors on Matte Stock
Binding: Folded
In Business: 41 years
Number of Employees: 44
Sales Volume: $2,600,000

6230 Asia Transpacific Journeys
Asia Transpacific Journeys
2995 Center Green Ct # C
Boulder, CO 80301-5421   303-443-6789
                                 800-642-2742
Fax: 303-443-7078
travel@asiatranspacific.com
www.asiatranspacific.com

Specializing in extraordinary journeys to Thailand, Indonesia, Burma, Cambodia, Laos, Vietnam, Malaysia, Philippines, Papua, New Guinea and Nepal

President: Marilyn Staff
Marketing Manager: Marilyn D Staff
Catalog Cost: Free
Catalog Circulation: Mailed 1 time(s) per year
Printing Information: 84 pages in 4 colors on Newsprint
Press: Letterpress
Binding: Saddle Stitched
In Business: 18 years
Number of Employees: 20
Sales Volume: $3MM to $5MM

6231 Backroads-Bicycling Vacations
Backroads
801 Cedar Street
Berkeley, CA 94710-1800   510-527-1555
                                  800-462-2848
goactive@backroads.com
www.backroads.com

Bicycle tours and vacation spots

President: Tom Hale
CFO: Karen Bennett
Marketing Manager: Lee Micheaux
Credit Cards: AMEX; MasterCard; Visa
Catalog Cost: Free
Catalog Circulation: Mailed 4 time(s) per year to 10000
Average Order Size: $1750
Printing Information: 194 pages in 4 colors on Matte Stock
Press: Web Press
List Company: Chilcutt Direct Marketing
In Business: 27 years
Number of Employees: 400
Sales Volume: $20,000,000

6232 Best Rafting Vacations in the West
Western River Expeditions
7258 Racquet Club Drive
Salt Lake City, UT 84121-4557   801-942-6669
                                   866-904-1160
Fax: 801-942-8514
www.westernriver.com

Professionally guided rafting vacations on the Colorado River through the Grand Canyon, Westwater and Cataract Canyons and Utah's Green River

President: Bill George
Marketing Manager: Brandon Lake
Credit Cards: AMEX; MasterCard; Visa
Catalog Cost: Free
Catalog Circulation: Mailed 2 time(s) per year to 6000
Printing Information: 34 pages
Mailing List Information: Names for rent
In Business: 54 years
Number of Employees: 72
Sales Volume: $500,000

6233 Country Heritage Tours
Country Heritage Tours
PO Box 59
Amherst, NH 3031   603-673-0604
800-346-9820
Fax: 603-673-5839
info@countryheritagetours.com
countryheritagetours.com

6234 Country Walkers
Country Walkers
PO Box 180
Waterbury, VT 05676-180   802-244-1387
800-234-6900
Fax: 802-244-5661
info@countrywalkers.com
www.countrywalkers.com

Walking vacations countryside worldwide in Europe, Africa, North and South America and the South Pacific

President: Robert Ellfasser
CFO: Cindy Maymard
Marketing Manager: Carolyn Walters Fox
Buyers: Tricia Dowon
Catalog Cost: Free
Catalog Circulation: Mailed 1 time(s) per year
Printing Information: 108 pages in 4 colors on Matte Stock
Press: Web Press
Binding: Perfect Bound
In Business: 35 years
Number of Employees: 18
Sales Volume: $5MM to $10MM

6235 Eagle Creek Travel Gear
Eagle Creek
5935 Darwin Court
Carlsbad, CA 92008-8347   760-431-6400
800-874-1048
Fax: 800-874-1038
info@eaglecreek.ie; www.Eaglecreek.Com

Travel gear

President: Steve Barker
CFO: Burt Fenenga
Marketing Manager: Connie McDonald
Production Manager: Richard Martin
International Marketing Manager: Kevin Carr
Credit Cards: AMEX; MasterCard
In Business: 40 years
Number of Employees: 200

6236 Ecotour Expeditions
Amazon Nature Tours
PO Box 128
Jamestown, RI 02835-128   401-423-3377
800-688-1822
info@naturetours.com
www.naturetours.com

Nature trips in Central and South America

President: Mark Baker
In Business: 26 years

6237 Edelweiss
Edelweiss Bike Travel
PO Box 1974
Wrightwood, CA 92397-1974   435-264-5690
800-582-2263
Fax: 760-249-3857
www.edelweissbiketravel.com

Motorcycle touring

Marketing Manager: Karin Gritsch
Marketing & Communications
Managing Director: Rainer Buck
Founder & Owner: Werner Wachter
Founder & Owner: Coral Wachter
Printing Information: 70 pages
In Business: 34 years

6238 Escape Adventures
Escape Adventures
10575 Discovery Dr
Suite 101
Las Vegas, NV 89135-9029   702-596-2953
800-596-2953
Fax: 702-838-6968
info@escapeadventures.com
www.Escapeadventures.Com

North American bicycling, hiking, climbing and rafting tours

President: Heather Fisher
Production Manager: Jared Fisher
Tour Director: Jared Fisher
Tour Leader: Zephyr Sylvester
Tour Leader: Eric Boxrud
Printing Information: 113 pages
Sales Volume: $1MM to $3MM

6239 Euro Bike & Walking
Austin Adventures
PO Box 81025
Billings, MT 59108-1025   815-758-8851
800-575-1540
www.eurobike.com

Experience Ireland's southwest coast and discover cycling at its best

Catalog Circulation: Mailed 1 time(s) per year
Printing Information: 124 pages in 4 colors

6240 Global Expedition Catalog
Jermy International
107 Aprill Drive
Suite 3
Ann Arbor, MI 48103-1956   734-665-4407
800-255-8735
Fax: 734-665-2945
info@journeysinternational.com
www.journeys-intl.com

Nature and outdoor expeditions

President: Robin Weber Pollak
robin@journeysinternational.com
CFO: Florine Herendeen
Marketing Manager: Sally Grimes
sally@journeysinternational.com
Production Manager: Pat Ballard
Senior Director: Will Weber
will@journeysinternational.com
Accounts and Special Trips: Florine Herendeen
florine@journeysinternational.com
Graphics and IT Services: Tom Osburn
tom@journeysinternational.com
Credit Cards: MasterCard; Visa
Catalog Circulation: to 5000
Printing Information: 72 pages in 4 colors on Glossy Stock
Mailing List Information: Names for rent
Number of Employees: 14

6241 Go Ahead Vacations
Go Ahead Tours
2 Education Circle
Cambridge, MA 02141-1833   617-252-6000
800-590-1170
Fax: 617-619-1001
www.goaheadvacations.com

Outdoor tours and travel plans

President: Louise Jillian
Catalog Cost: Free
Catalog Circulation: Mailed 12 time(s) per year
Printing Information: 15 pages in 4 colors on Glossy Stock
Press: Web Press
Binding: Saddle Stitched
Sales Volume: $1MM to $3MM

6242 Himalayan Institute
Himalayan Institute
952 Bethany Turnpike
Honesdale, PA 18431   570-253-5551
800-822-4547
Fax: 570-253-9078
info@himalayaninstitute.org
www.himalayaninstitute.org

Yoga and meditation instructional books, DVDs, tapes and retreats, botanicals, gifts, health products, and jewelry

Chairman: Irene Pertyszak
President: Rolf Fovik
Marketing Manager: Alena Miles
Founder: Swami Rama
Catalog Cost: Free
In Business: 44 years
Number of Employees: 60

6243 In the Swim
In the Swim
320 Industrial Dr.
West Chicago, IL 60185   630-876-0040
800-288-7946
Fax: 800-448-7329
drpool@intheswim.com; www.intheswim.com

Pool equipment and supplies.

VP, Marketing: Christine Matson
Director of Marketing: Erin Bayer
International Marketing Manager: Erin Bayer
Catalog Cost: Free
Printing Information: 52 pages
Binding: Saddle Stitched
In Business: 33 years

6244 Journeys International
Journey's International
107 Aprill Drive Suite 3
Ann Arbor, MI 48103-1893   734-665-4407
800-255-8735
Fax: 734-665-2945
info@journeysinternational.com
www.journeysinternational.com

Travel information and accessories

President: Will Weber
Sales Volume: $1MM to $3MM

6245 Just Cases
Just Cases
2925 S. Umatilla Street
Englewood, CO 80110-3845   303-283-0260
888-318-5878
Fax: 303-337-8232
info@justCASES.com
www.Justcases.Com

Custom carrying and transport cases; specialty shipping, cargo, and transport cases like: Pelican, Parker, Guardsman, SKB Military Spec cases, expo equipment, shock mount, rail, and flat screen cases

President: Terry Tautz
Credit Cards: AMEX; MasterCard
Catalog Cost: Free
In Business: 20 years
Sales Volume: $1MM to $3MM

6246 Kaehler Luggage
Kaehler Luggage Inc
1724 Sherman Avenue
Evanston, IL 60201   847-386-6730
                            800-314-2247
                        Fax: 847-480-1302
                     www.worldtraveler.com

Luggage
President: Wallace Kaehler
In Business: 95 years

6247 Moondance Adventures
Moondance Adventures
2 Gerber Rd
Suite 221
Asheville, NC 28803   828-350-1488
                              800-832-5229
          info@moondanceadventures.com
          www.moondanceadventures.com

6248 Mountain Travel-Sobek
Mountain Travel-Sobek
1266 66th Street
Suite 4
Emeryville, CA 94608-1117   510-594-6000
                              888-831-7526
                          Fax: 510-594-6001
          info@mtsobek.com; www.mtsobek.com
Offers a variety of outdoor adventures in Africa, Europe, North America, Asia, South America and more
President: Kevin Callaghan
CFO: Jim Kennick
Marketing Manager: Allie Roqueta
Director of Europe Programs: Anne Wood
Sales Manager: Alan Taylor
Art Director: Chris Bettencourt
Credit Cards: AMEX; MasterCard; Visa
Catalog Cost: Free
Catalog Circulation: Mailed 1 time(s) per year
Average Order Size: $3000
Printing Information: 132 pages in 4 colors on Glossy Stock
Press: Web Press
Binding: Saddle Stitched
1266 66th Street
Emeryville, CA 94608
In Business: 46 years
Number of Employees: 30
Sales Volume: $1MM to $3MM

6249 NE Camp
New England Camp Discounter
PO Box 7087
Dallas, TX 75209   888-909-8809
                          Fax: 888-909-5899
          feednec@sportssupplygroup.com
          www.newenglandcamp.com
Full line of camp and recreational equipment

6250 Northland Travel
Northland Travel
South 25th Street Suite A04
Ft Dodge, IA 50501   515-576-6494
                              877-694-8687
          www.northlandtravel.com

6251 Putney Student Travel
Putney Student Travel
345 Hickory Ridge Road
Putney, VT 5346   802-387-5000
                          Fax: 802-387-4276
                          info@goputney.com
                              goputney.com
In Business: 64 years

6252 Road Scholar
Road Scholar
11 Avenue de Lafayette
Boston, MA 02111   800-454-5768
                              roadscholar.org
Not-for-profit alternative educational travels in 150 countries across the world
President: Jim Moses
CFO: Lowell Partridge
Marketing Manager: Kristin Moore
SVP, Program Development: JoAnne Bell
SVP, Chief Information Officer: Eric Bird
VP, Programs: Maeve Hartney
Catalog Cost: Free
In Business: 42 years

6253 Smithsonian Journeys
Smithsonian Journeys
P.O. Box 23182
Washington, DC 20077-843   989-393-3218
          855-330-1542; Fax: 202-633-6088
              www.smithsonianjourneys.org
In Business: 45 years

6254 Sunrise Tours
Sunrise Tours
1819 Lynch Street
St. Louis, MO 63118   314-771-8300
                              travelsunrise.com
Manager: Brent Dalrymple
Tour Planner: Bruce Schwerdt
Tour Manager: Carol Pauk

6255 Travel Catalog
Duluth Trading Company
PO Box 200
Belleville, WI 53508-200   866-300-9719
                          Fax: 888-950-3199
          customerservice@duluthtrading.com
              www.duluthtrading.com
Travel tested clothing, luggage and accessories
Veterinary Surgeon: Liz
Dean of Students: Lori
Information Architect: Pat
In Business: 23 years

6256 Travel Video Store Catalog
TravelVideoStore.Com
5420 Boran Drive
Tampa, FL 33610   813-630-9778
                              800-288-5123
                          Fax: 813-627-0334
          customerservice@travelvideostore.com
              www.travelvideostore.com
Travel DVDs, CDs and videos on the Caribbean, Hawaii and Europe

Credit Cards: AMEX; MasterCard; Visa
In Business: 12 years

6257 VBT Delore Bicycling Vacations
VBT
614 Monkton Rd
Bristol, VT 05443-711   802-453-4811
                              800-245-3868
                          Fax: 802-453-4806
              info@vbt.com; www.vbt.com
Deluxe inn to inn bicycling vacation tours with first rate accommodations, dining, leader service and route selections
President: Gregg Marston
Marketing Manager: James Alden
Production Manager: Thomas Ziter
Credit Cards: MasterCard; Visa
Catalog Cost: $1.6
Catalog Circulation: Mailed 8 time(s) per year
Average Order Size: $2000
Printing Information: 164 pages in 4 colors on Glossy Stock
Press: Web Press
Binding: Saddle Stitched
Mailing List Information: Names for rent
In Business: 44 years
Number of Employees: 35
Sales Volume: $10MM to $20MM

6258 Vantage Deluxe World Travel
Vantage Deluxe World Travel
90 Canal Street
Boston, MA 2114-2031   617-878-6000
                              888-514-1845
                          Fax: 857-313-6400
              www.vantagetravel.com
Tours & travel.
Founder & Chief Executive Officer: Henry R. Lewis

6259 Wilderness Travel Journeys Catalog
Wilderness Travel
1102 9th St
Berkeley, CA 94710-1211   510-558-2488
                              800-368-2794
                          Fax: 510-558-2489
          info@wildernesstravel.com
              www.Wildernesstravel.Com
Adventure travel offers extraordinary cultural, hiking and wildlife adventures to over 50 countries
President: Bill Abbott
Marketing Manager: Barbara Banks
Production Manager: Barbara Banks
Catalog Circulation: Mailed 52 time(s) per year to 75K
Average Order Size: $2500
Printing Information: 128 pages in 4 colors on Matte Stock
Press: Sheetfed Press
Binding: Perfect Bound
Mailing List Information: Names for rent
List Manager: Ray Rodney
In Business: 36 years
Number of Employees: 20-5
Sales Volume: $3MM to $5MM

Business to Business Catalogs

Agriculture
Animal Care

6260 Agco
AGCO
4205 River Green Pkwy
Duluth, GA 30096-2584
770-813-9200
Fax: 770-813-6140
sales@agcofinance.com
www.agcocorp.com

Agricultural products

Chairman: Martin H. Richenhagen
President: Martin H. Richenhagen
CFO: Andrew H. Beck
VP/General Counsel/Corp Secretary: Roger N. Batkin
SVP Engineering: Helmut R. Endres
SVP/General Manager, Asia Pacific: Gary L. Collar
In Business: 113 years

6261 All About Dog Grooming
All About Dog Grooming
4720 Salisbury Rd.
Jacksonville, FL 32256
904-710-8318
888-800-1027
learntogroom@comcast.net
www.learntogroom.com

Health care and grooming supplies

Chairman: Carol Doggett
President: Richard Doggett
Co-Founder: Richard Doggett
Co-Founder: Carol Doggett
Credit Cards: AMEX; MasterCard
Catalog Cost: Free
In Business: 40 years

6262 Bean Farm
The Bean Farm
32514 NE 77th
Carnation, WA 98014-6701
425-861-7964
877-708-5882
Fax: 425-333-4205
beanfarm@beanfarm.com
www.beanfarm.com

Supply company specializing in reptile husbandry products

President: Giovanni Fagioli
Credit Cards: MasterCard

6263 Big Dee's Tack & Vet Supplies
Big Dee's Tack & Vet Supplies
9440 State Route 14
Streetsboro, OH 44241
330-626-5000
800-321-2142
sales@bigdweb.com
www.bigdweb.com

Standardbred & Thoroughbred racing, English & Western riding, horse blankets, custom stable wear & nameplates, vaccines, dewormers, nutritional supplements and more.

Catalog Cost: Free
In Business: 40 years

6264 Brinsea Products
Brinsea Products
704 N Dixie Avenue
Titusville, FL 32796
321-267-7009
888-667-7009
Fax: 321-267-6090
sales@brinsea.com
www.brinsea.com

Egg incubators, hatchers and brooders for parrot, falcon, poultry, chicken, duck, quail, pheasant and other birds or reptiles

President: Frank Pearce
Printing Information: in 4 colors
In Business: 39 years

Number of Employees: 5
Sales Information: Under $500M

6265 Cat Claws
Cat Claws
900 West Church Street
PO Box 1001
Morrilton, AR 72110
501-354-5015
800-783-0977
Fax: 501-354-4843
meow@catclaws.com
www.catclaws.com

Unique cat products including scratching pads, toys, treats and accessories

President: Bill Seliskar
Credit Cards: AMEX; MasterCard
Catalog Cost: Free
Average Order Size: $38
In Business: 23 years

6266 Central Metal Products: Dog Kennels
Central Metal Products, LLC
234 N Independence St
Tipton, IN 46072-1745
765-945-7677
800-874-3647
Fax: 765-945-7084

Dog kennels and accessories

President: Thomas Roseberry
In Business: 47 years
Sales Information: $3MM to $5MM

6267 Chamisa Ridge
Chamisa Ridge, Inc.
PO Box 2858
Santa Fe, NM 87504
505-438-4811
800-743-3188
Fax: 505-438-8205
www.chamisaridge.com

Featuring Hilton Herbs, books, audios, videos and accessories for horseback riders

President: David Kuncicky
Credit Cards: MasterCard; Visa
Catalog Cost: Free
Catalog Circulation: Mailed 5 time(s) per year
Printing Information: 40 pages in 4 colors on Glossy Stock
Press: Web Press
Binding: Perfect Bound
Mailing List Information: Names for rent
In Business: 8 years
Number of Employees: 7
Sales Information: $1,800,000

6268 Chilcutt Direct Marketing
Chilcutt Direct Marketing
813 East 33rd Street
Edmond, OK 73013
405-726-8780
Fax: 405-726-8799
info@cdmlist.com
www.cdmlist.com

List brokerage and management house

President: Matt Chilcutt
In Business: 20 years
Number of Employees: 26
Sales Information: $3MM to $5MM

6269 Dover Saddlery
Dover Saddlery
P.O. Box 1100
Littleton, MA 01460
800-406-8204
Fax: 978-952-6633
customerservice@doversaddlery.com
www.doversaddlery.com

Equipment for horse and rider

President: Stephen L Day
CFO: David R Pearce
Credit Cards: AMEX; MasterCard
Catalog Cost: Free
In Business: 38 years
Number of Employees: 497
Sales Information: $78 Million

6270 FarmTek
FarmTek
1440 Field of Dreams Way
Dyersville, IA 52040
800-245-9881
800-327-6835
Fax: 800-457-8887
www.farmtek.com

Agricultural products

CEO: Barry Goldsher
Catalog Cost: Free
Printing Information: 356 pages in 4 colors
Mailing List Information: Names for rent
In Business: 34 years

6271 Flexi USA, Inc.
Pet Adventures Worldwide
8494 Firebird Drive
West Chester, OH 45014-2273
513-874-5383
800-543-4921
Fax: 513-874-7269
custserv@petadventuresworldwide.com
www.petadventuresworldwide.com

Foods, products, supplies for pets

President: Ulrich Wuebker
CEO: Manfred Bogdahn
Credit Cards: AMEX; MasterCard
Catalog Cost: Free
Printing Information: 10 pages in 4 colors
Binding: Saddle Stitched
In Business: 26 years
Number of Employees: 20
Sales Information: $10MM to $20MM

6272 Hawthorne Horse Care Products
Hawthorne Products
16828 North State Road 167
PO Box 226
N. Dunkirk, IN 47336-226
765-768-6585
800-548-5658
Fax: 765-768-7672
kim@hawthorne-products.com
www.hawthorne-products.com

Horse care products

President: Kim Hobson
Marketing Manager: Pete Vollweiler
Production Manager: Kim Hubson
International Marketing Manager: Gary Bressier
Buyers: Debbie McCaffery
Catalog Circulation: to 500
Printing Information: 16 pages in 4 colors on Glossy Stock
Binding: Saddle Stitched
In Business: 37 years
Number of Employees: 10
Sales Information: $1MM to $3MM

6273 Heartland Veterinary Supply & Pharmacy
Heartland Veterinary Supply & Pharmacy
401 W 33rd Street
Hastings, NE 68901
800-934-9398
Fax: 888-424-0484
info@heartlandvetsupply.com
www.heartlandvetsupply.com

Horse, dog and cat products, supplements

President: David Behl
Catalog Cost: Free
In Business: 34 years

6274 Hoover's Hatchery
Hoover's Hatchery
PO Box 200
Rudd, IA 50471
641-395-2730
800-247-7014
Fax: 641-395-2208
hoovers@omnitelcom.com
www.hoovershatchery.com

Poultry equipment and medications

President: Mary Halstead
Credit Cards: MasterCard
Printing Information: in 4 colors

In Business: 71 years
Sales Information: $500M to $1MM

6275 Jeffers Livestock
Jeffers
310 W. Saunders Road
Dothan, AL 36301
334-793-6257
800-533-3377
Fax: 334-793-5179
customerservice@jefferspet.com
www.jefferspet.com

Livestock supplies

Chairman: Dorothy Jeffers
President: Jennifer Martin
CFO: Michael Hawke
Purchasing Director/VP Marketing: Ruth Jeffers
Catalog Cost: Free
In Business: 42 years
Number of Employees: 215
Sales Information: $55 Million

6276 Kennel-Aire
Petmate
2300 E Randol Mill Rd
PO Box 1246
Arlington, TX 76011-1246
888-367-5624
800-346-0134
Fax: 785-242-8383
kennelaire@aol.com
www.petmate.com

Dog cages, kennels and supplies

CFO: Trygve Pederson
VP: Robert Tyley
Manager: Jeff Schaper
Catalog Cost: Free
In Business: 53 years
Number of Employees: 45

6277 Lextron
Animal Health International
822 7th St
Ste 740
Greeley, CO 80631
970-353-2600
800-854-7664
Fax: 970-356-4623
webteam@animalhealthinternational.com
www.animalhealthinternational.com

Horse supplements

Chairman: Dr. Robert Hummel
President: John Adent
CFO: Dave Wagley
Marketing Manager: Kevin Pohlman
CEO: John Adent
Executive Vice President: Dave Wagley
Senior Vice President - Human Resou: Shelley Iwasaki
Catalog Circulation: Mailed 1 time(s) per year
Printing Information: 376 pages
In Business: 48 years
Number of Employees: 480

6278 Marine World Warehouse
Marine World Warehouse
PO Box 144353
Coral Gables, FL 33114-4353
305-443-7973
Fax: 305-447-0745
info@quantumleap.net
www.quantumleap.net

Livestock, dry goods, professional resource for aquarists

Co-Owner: Robin Burr
Co-Owner: Robert Burr

6279 Mason Company
Mason Company
P.O. Box 365
260 Depot Street
Leesburg, OH 45135
937-780-2321
800-543-5567
Fax: 937-780-6336
info@masonco.com
www.masonco.com

Modular dog cages and kennels

President: Greg Taylor
CEO: Greg Taylor
Founder: Henry Mason
Catalog Cost: Free
In Business: 122 years

6280 Milcare Company
Milcare Company
17683 250th Street
Fergus Falls, MN 56537-7444
218-736-2810
Fax: 218-736-5935
milcare@milcareco.com/
www.milcareco.com

Hoof trimmers

President: La Wayne Rogness
Catalog Cost: Free
Catalog Circulation: Mailed 2 time(s) per year
Mailing List Information: Names for rent
Number of Employees: 2
Sales Information: Under $500M

6281 Murray McMurray Hatchery
Murray McMurray Hatchery
191 Closz Drive
PO Box 458
Webster City, IA 50595
515-832-3280
800-456-3280
Fax: 515-832-2213
www.mcmurrayhatchery.com

Chickens and poultry supplies

President: Mike Lubbers
Owner/President: Murray J McMurray
Catalog Cost: Free
Printing Information: 108 pages
In Business: 94 years
Number of Employees: 15
Sales Information: $1.2 Million

6282 National Bridle Shop
National Bridle Shop
815 E Commerce Street
Lewisburg, TN 37091
800-251-3474
Fax: 931-359-8551
nbs@nationalbridle.com
www.nationalbridleshop.com

Horse saddles and horse health supplies, stable supplies, clothing & apparel, books, videos and gifts

President: Robert M Beech
Credit Cards: AMEX; MasterCard
Catalog Cost: Free
In Business: 66 years
Number of Employees: 27
Sales Information: $3.3 Million

6283 Omaha Vaccine Company/Pet Supplies Delivered
CSR Company Inc.
11701 Centennial Road
Suites 2 & 3
La Vista, NE 68128
800-367-4444
Fax: 800-242-9447
www.omahavaccine.com

Kennel and pet supplies for all animals

Chairman: Scott Remington
President: C. Remington
Credit Cards: MasterCard; Visa
Catalog Cost: Free
Catalog Circulation: Mailed 1 time(s) per year to 1.6MM
Printing Information: 150 pages in 4 colors
Mailing List Information: Names for rent

List Company: Total Media Concepts
222 Cedar Lane, Suite 201
Teaneck, NJ 07666
201-692-0018
In Business: 401 years
Number of Employees: 200

6284 PetEdge
PetEdge Inc.
PO Box 1000
Beverly, MA 01915-701
800-738-3343
800-638-5754
Fax: 800-329-6372
support@petedge.com
www.petedge.com

Pet care products and equipment for petcare professionals

President: Andrew S Katz
Founder: Loeb Katz
Credit Cards: AMEX; MasterCard
Catalog Cost: Free
In Business: 59 years
Sales Information: $10MM to $20MM

6285 Poultry & Gamebreeders Catalog
GQF Manufacturing Company
2343 Louisville Road
Savannah, GA 31415-1619
912-236-0651
Fax: 912-234-9978
sales@gqfmfg.com
www.gqfmfg.com

Incubators, feeders, waterers, medicine and supplies

President: Richard McGhee
Buyers: Steven McGhee
Credit Cards: AMEX; MasterCard
Catalog Cost: Free
Catalog Circulation: Mailed 2 time(s) per year
Printing Information: 24 pages in 1 color
In Business: 58 years
Number of Employees: 55
Sales Information: $10,000,000 - $25,000,000

6286 Rawhide Brand
Rawhide Brand
255 Keyes Avenue
PO Box 396
Hampshire, IL 60140
847-683-2288
800-323-6878
Fax: 847-683-2343
www.petag.com

Dog and cat pet snacks and store displays

President: Darlene Frudakis
EVP: Lew Sutton
Printing Information: 10 pages in 4 colors on Glossy Stock
Binding: Saddle Stitched
In Business: 25 years

6287 Risdon Rigs
Risdon Rigs, Inc.
PO Box 127
Laingsburg, MI 48848
517-651-6960
Fax: 517-651-6970
risdon3p@risdonrigs.com
www.risdonrigs.com

Dog sleds, rigs, harnesses, show hooks and dog bags

President: Patricia Risdon
Catalog Circulation: Mailed 1 time(s) per year to 1m
Printing Information: 8 pages in 1 color
In Business: 43 years
Number of Employees: 1

6288 Smith Brothers
Smith Brothers
PO Box 2700
Denton, TX 76202-2700
940-565-0886
800-784-5449
Fax: 940-565-8232
info@smithbrothers.com
www.smithbrothers.com

Show clothing and supplies for the Western horseman

President: Jim Smith
Credit Cards: AMEX; MasterCard
Catalog Cost: Free
Catalog Circulation: Mailed 1 time(s) per year
Printing Information: 184 pages
Binding: Perfect Bound
In Business: 37 years
Sales Information: Under $500M

6289 State Line Tack
State Line Talk
626 CAN DO Expressway
Suite 1
Hazle Township, PA 18202-9790   570-384-7656
888-809-0751
Fax: 570-384-2500
customerservice@statelinetack.com
www.Statelinetack.Com

Stable gear, harnesses

Chairman: Samuel Parker
President: Dover Saddlery
Credit Cards: AMEX; MasterCard; Visa
Catalog Circulation: Mailed 1 time(s) per year
Printing Information: in 4 colors on Glossy Stock
Press: Web Press
Binding: Perfect Bound
In Business: 47 years
Number of Employees: 160

6290 Stromberg's Chicks
Stromberg's Chicks & Game Birds
100 York Street
PO Box 400
Pine River, MN 56474   218-587-2222
800-720-1134
Fax: 218-587-4230
info@strombergschickens.com
www.strombergschickens.com

Baby chicks, poultry supplies, incubators and brooders

President: Loy Stromberg
VP: Janet Stromberg
Credit Cards: AMEX; MasterCard
Catalog Cost: Free
In Business: 94 years
Number of Employees: 6
Sales Information: $950,000

6291 UPCO Wholesale Pet Supplies
UPCO
3705 Pear Street
PO Box 969
St Joseph, MO 64503-969   816-233-8800
800-254-8726
Fax: 816-233-9696
sales@upco.com
www.upco.com

Supplies for dogs, cats, horses, reptiles, small animals and birds

Chairman: Frank J Evans
President: Walter J Evans
General Manager: Kyle Evans
Founder: Charles Evans
Credit Cards: AMEX; MasterCard
Catalog Cost: Free
Printing Information: 200 pages
Binding: Perfect Bound
In Business: 63 years
Number of Employees: 28
Sales Information: $2.9 Million

6292 Valley Vet Supply Catalog
Valley Vet Supply
1118 Pony Express Highway
Marysville, KS 66508   800-419-9524
Fax: 800-446-5597
service@valleyvet.com
www.valleyvet.com

Complete line of products and services for pets and livestock

President: Ray Schultz
Marketing Manager: Rebecca Pierce
Catalog Cost: Free
Mailing List Information: Names for rent
In Business: 31 years
Sales Information: $50MM to $100MM

6293 Vet Med Direct Catalog
Vet Med Direct, LLC
414 G Street
Fairbury, NE 68352-2640   402-729-5354
877-483-8633
Fax: 866-787-1185
monica@vetmeddirect.com

Complete line of pet meds, affordable vet supplies, animal care supplies and discount veterinary medications

Sales Information: Under $500M

6294 Vet-Vax, Inc.
Vet-Vax, Inc.
PO Box 400
Tonganoxie, KS 66086   913-845-3760
800-369-8297
Fax: 913-845-9472

Vaccines, medications, supplements and grooming equipment for pets and livestock; and a complete line of pet toys and training equipment including field and lap dog enthusiast's supplies

President: Bill Maritel
International Marketing Manager: Bud Moomau
Buyers: Scott Johnson
Credit Cards: AMEX; MasterCard; Visa
Catalog Cost: Free
Catalog Circulation: Mailed 2 time(s) per year to 50M
Average Order Size: $68
Printing Information: 191 pages in 1 color on Newsprint
Press: Web Press
Binding: Saddle Stitched
Mailing List Information: Names for rent
List Manager: Bud Moomau
In Business: 27 years
Number of Employees: 14

6295 Veterinary & Pet Care Reference Catalog
Medical Arts Press
8500 Wyoming Ave N
Brooklyn Park, MN 55445-1825   800-982-3400
Fax: 800-789-8955
taxexempt@medicalartspress.com
www.quill.com

Supplies for your veterinary and pet care practice

Credit Cards: AMEX; MasterCard; Visa
Catalog Cost: Free
Catalog Circulation: Mailed 2 time(s) per year
Printing Information: 750 pages in 4 colors
Mailing List Information: Names for rent
In Business: 59 years
Number of Employees: 600

Chemicals & Pest Control

6296 Atomizing Systems
Atomizing Systems Inc.
1 Hollywood Ave # 1
Ho Ho Kus, NJ 07423-1433   201-447-1222
888-265-3364
Fax: 201-447-6932
info@coldfog.com
www.Coldfog.Com

High pressure fog systems for water and chemicals for HVAC, cooling, effects, dust and odor suppression

President: Michael Elkas
Production Manager: Tom Pagliaroni
International Marketing Manager: Michael V. Elkas
Buyers: Michael Farrelly

Catalog Circulation: Mailed 1 time(s) per year
Mailing List Information: Names for rent
In Business: 22 years
Number of Employees: 16
Sales Information: $1,500,000

6297 Farnam Companies
Farnam Companies, Inc.
301 W. Osborn
Phoenix, AZ 85013   602-285-1660
800-234-2269
Fax: 602-285-1803
www.farnam.com

Fly bait

Chairman: Charles Duff
President: Chuck Duff
Marketing Manager: Steve LeVeau
Brand Manager: Alyssa Barngrover
Credit Cards: AMEX; MasterCard
Catalog Circulation: Mailed 1 time(s) per year to 10M+
Printing Information: 50 pages in 4 colors on Glossy Stock
In Business: 56 years
Number of Employees: 100

6298 Motomco
MOTOMCO
3699 Kinsman Blvd
Madison, WI 53704   608-244-2904
800-418-9242
Fax: 608-241-9631
www.motomco.com

Rodent bait

President: Joe Pluskota
VP Agriculture Sales: Kent Gutzmer
Territory Manager, Southern Region: Scott Miller
Territory Manager - Midwestern Regi: Steve Von Haden
Catalog Circulation: Mailed 2 time(s) per year
Number of Employees: 3
Sales Information: $3MM to $5MM

6299 Natural INSECTO Products
Natural INSECTO Products, Inc.
PO Box 12138
221 Sherwood Place
Costa Mesa, CA 92627   949-548-4275
800-332-2002
Fax: 949-548-4576
www.insecto.com

Grain insects insecticides (natural) INSECTO - an insecticide for control of grain insects

President: Jim Huber
Catalog Circulation: Mailed 1 time(s) per year
Printing Information: 4 pages in 1 color on Glossy Stock
Press: Web Press
Binding: Folded
Mailing List Information: Names for rent
Sales Information: $500M to $1MM

6300 Ohio Earth Food
Ohio Earth Food
5488 Swamp Street NE
Hartville, OH 44632   330-877-9356
Fax: 330-877-4237
info@ohioearthfood.com
www.ohioearthfood.com

Natural fertilizers including Re-Vita Compost Plus, Re-Vita Hi-K, Re-Vita Organic Lawn Fertilizer, phosphate, greensand, seaweed products, fish products, humates, Ful-Po-Mag and sulfate of potash

President: Larry Ringer
Production Manager: Cynthia L Ringer
Credit Cards: MasterCard
Catalog Cost: Free
Catalog Circulation: Mailed 1 time(s) per year to 5M
Printing Information: 32 pages in 4 colors

Mailing List Information: Names for rent
In Business: 43 years
Number of Employees: 2
Sales Information: $1MM to $3MM

6301 White Manufacturing Company
P H White Company
PO Box 155
Dyersburg, TN 38025-155   731-285-6202
   800-344-0115
   Fax: 731-287-1275
   phwhite@ecsis.net
   www.phwhite.com

Cattle rub

President: P H White
CFO: Sharon Horner
Catalog Circulation: Mailed 1 time(s) per year
Printing Information: in 4 colors on Glossy
Stock
Press: Web Press
Binding: Folded
Mailing List Information: Names for rent
In Business: 30 years
Number of Employees: 9
Sales Information: $1,000,000 - $5,000,000

Supplies & Equipment

6302 Aetna Bearing Company
Aetna
1081 Sesame St
Franklin Park, IL 60131   630-694-0024
   Fax: 630-694-0087
   info@aetnabearing.com
   www.aetnabearing.com

Ball thrust bearings, belt and precision idlers, rubber tire idlers, adapter bearings, and sprocket idlers for the automotive and agricultural industries

Chairman: Derick Marsh
President: James Trauscht
CFO: Mark Boozell
CEO: Richard Jenkins
Credit Cards: MasterCard; Visa
Catalog Circulation: Mailed 4 time(s) per year
In Business: 98 years
Number of Employees: 35
Sales Information: $3.7 Million

6303 Atlas Greenhouse Systems
Atlas Manufacturing, Inc.
PO Box 558
Alapaha, GA 31622-558   229-532-2905
   800-346-9902
   Fax: 229-532-4600
   www.atlasgreenhouse.com

Commercial, educational and hobby greenhouses, as well as carports and agricultural buildings

President: Mark Davis
Office Manager: Billy Stewart
Sales Manager: Bill Mathis
Shipping Coordinator: Tommie Ann Stone
Credit Cards: MasterCard; Visa
Catalog Cost: Free
In Business: 29 years

6304 Bass Equipment Company
Bass Equipment Company
PO Box 352
Monett, MO 65708   417-235-7557
   800-798-0150
   Fax: 417-235-4312
   sales@bassequipment.com
   www.bassequipment.com

Rabbit and kennel supplies

President: Gary Bass
Number of Employees: 20
Sales Information: $1.4 Million

6305 Brinsea Products
Brinsea Products
704 N Dixie Avenue
Titusville, FL 32796   321-267-7009
   888-667-7009
   Fax: 321-267-6090
   sales@brinsea.com
   www.brinsea.com

Egg incubators, hatchers and brooders for parrot, falcon, poultry, chicken, duck, quali, pheasant and other birds or reptiles

President: Frank Pearce
Printing Information: in 4 colors
In Business: 39 years
Number of Employees: 5
Sales Information: Under $500M

6306 CT Farm & Country
CT Farm & Country
1301 N 14th St.
Indianola, IA 50125   800-860-1799
   www.ctfarmonline.com

Tractor, harvesting, mowing and tillage parts.

Catalog Cost: Free
Printing Information: 189 pages in 4 colors
In Business: 81 years

6307 Carlin Horticultural Supplies
Carlin Horticultural Supplies
8170 N Granville Woods Road
Milwaukee, WI 53223   800-657-0745
   Fax: 414-355-3107
   www.carlinsales.com

Gardening supplies

President: Dan Groh
CFO: Jim Moore
Marketing Manager: Jenny Mitchell
CEO: Mark Maletzke
Credit Cards: MasterCard; Visa
Catalog Cost: $15
In Business: 30 years

6308 Circle K Industries
Circle K Industries
25563 N Gilmer Rd
Mundelein, IL 60060-9454   847-949-0363
   Fax: 847-566-7309
   sales@circle-k.com
   www.Circle-K.Com

Complete line of small animal equipment and equipment parts, from hamsters to dogs and cats, odor eliminator and relocation traps for wild animals

President: Emmet D Krist
Catalog Cost: Free
Catalog Circulation: Mailed 1 time(s) per year to 5000
Average Order Size: $125
Printing Information: 32 pages in 2 colors on Glossy Stock
Binding: Saddle Stitched
Mailing List Information: Names for rent
In Business: 31 years
Number of Employees: 15
Sales Information: $1,000,000 - $5,000,000

6309 Country Manufacturing
Country Manufacturing Inc
333 Salem Ave
PO Box 104
Fredericktown, OH 43019   740-694-9926
   800-335-1880
   Fax: 740-694-5088
   info@countrymfg.com
   www.countrymfg.com

Horse stalls and equipment

President: Joe Chattin
General Manager/VP: Chad Chattin
Credit Cards: AMEX; MasterCard
Catalog Cost: Free
Printing Information: on Glossy Stock

Mailing List Information: Names for rent
In Business: 33 years
Number of Employees: 15
Sales Information: $1.7 Million

6310 Discount Snow Plow Parts
Mill Supply Inc
19801 Miles Road
P.O. Box 28400
Cleveland, OH 44128   216-518-5072
   800-888-5072
   Fax: 216-518-2700
   questions5@rustrepair.com
   www.discountsnowplowparts.com

Replacements parts that fit Meyer, Western, Fisher, Diamond, Boss and Blizzard snow plows, also spreaders and lights

Marketing Manager: John Shega
Fulfillment: David Schuld
Credit Cards: MasterCard
Catalog Cost: Free
Catalog Circulation: Mailed 1 time(s) per year to 90000
Printing Information: 64 pages in 4 colors on Newsprint
Press: Web Press
Binding: Saddle Stitched
Mailing List Information: Names for rent
In Business: 66 years
Number of Employees: 30
Sales Information: $1MM to $3MM

6311 Dutton-Lainson Company Catalog
Dutton-Lainson Company
451 W. 2nd Street
Hastings, NE 68901   402-462-4141
   Fax: 402-460-4613
   dlsales@dutton-lainson.com
   www.dutton-lainson.com

Trailer accessories, hand and electric winches, couplers, tongue jacks, fuel tank filters, fence stretchers, air pumps, oilers

President: Charles Hermes
CFO: David Brandt
Marketing Manager: Mark Bliss
Production Manager: Mark Bliss
International Marketing Manager: Bruce Dillin
Credit Cards: AMEX; MasterCard
Catalog Cost: Free
Catalog Circulation: Mailed 1 time(s) per year to 10000
Average Order Size: $2000
Printing Information: 30 pages in 4 colors on Matte Stock
Press: Letterpress
Binding: Saddle Stitched
Mailing List Information: Names for rent
List Manager: Mark Bliss
In Business: 129 years
Number of Employees: 250

6312 EI Dupont De Nemours & Company
Du Pont
Barley Mill Plaza
Building 29
Wilmington, DE 19880   302-774-2866
   800-441-7515
   Fax: 302-774-7321
   www.dupont.com

Agricultural products

Chairman: Ellen Kullman
President: ES Woolard Jr
CFO: Nicholas C. Fanandakis
VP, Tax: Mary P. Van Veen
Vice President - Financial Strategi: Susan M. Stalnecker
Vice President and Treasurer: Donna H. Grier
Credit Cards: AMEX; MasterCard
Catalog Circulation: Mailed 1 time(s) per year

6313 EggCartons.Com
EggCartons.Com
9 Main Street, Suite 1F
PO Box 302
Manchaug, MA 01526-302   508-476-0084
                                888-852-5340
                           Fax: 508-476-7703
                           www.eggcartons.com

Discount supplier of egg cartons, poultry
supplies, egg baskets, feeders, laying nests,
incubator, gifs, and books

President: Paul Boutiette
Marketing Manager: Scott Stankus
Credit Cards: MasterCard
Catalog Circulation: Mailed 1 time(s) per year
to 45000
Printing Information: 12 pages in 4 colors on
Matte Stock
Press: Web Press
Binding: Saddle Stitched
Mailing List Information: Names for rent
In Business: 12 years
Number of Employees: 10
Sales Information: $1MM to $3MM

6314 FarmTek
FarmTek
1440 Field of Dreams Way
Dyersville, IA 52040   800-245-9881
                              800-327-6835
                         Fax: 800-457-8887
                         www.farmtek.com

Agricultural products

CEO: Barry Goldsher
Catalog Cost: Free
Printing Information: 356 pages in 4 colors
Mailing List Information: Names for rent
In Business: 34 years

6315 Farnam Horse & Livestock Equipment
Farnam Companies, Inc.
301 W. Osborn
Phoenix, AZ 85013   602-285-1660
                           800-234-2269
                      Fax: 602-285-1803
                      www.farnam.com

Livestock, farm and horse equipment, and
supplies

Chairman: Charles Duff
President: WR Remias
Marketing Manager: Martha Lefebvre
Brand Manager: Alyssa Barngrover
Credit Cards: AMEX; MasterCard
Catalog Circulation: Mailed 1 time(s) per year
to 150M
Printing Information: 76 pages in 4 colors
Press: Web Press
Binding: Saddle Stitched
In Business: 56 years

6316 Feterl Manufacturing Company
Feterl Manufacturing Corp
411 Center Ave
P.O. Box 398
Salem, SD 57058-398   885-524-1004
                             800-367-8660
                        Fax: 605-425-2183
                        trksales@feterl.com
                        www.feterl.com

Transport augers

President: Darrell Streff
Marketing Manager: Ken Streff
Catalog Circulation: Mailed 2 time(s) per year
Number of Employees: 100-
Sales Information: $25,000,000 - $50,000,000

6317 Global Pigeon Supplies
Global Pigeon Supplies
2301 Rowland Ave
Savannah, GA 31404-4447   912-356-1320
                                 800-562-2295
                            Fax: 912-356-1691
                            gpswo@aol.com
                            www.globalpigeon.com

Supplies for racing pigeon hobby including
lofts and medication

President: Bert Oostlander
Credit Cards: AMEX; MasterCard
Catalog Cost: Free
Catalog Circulation: Mailed 1 time(s) per year
to 20M
Average Order Size: $100
Printing Information: 88 pages in 2 colors on
Newsprint
Press: Web Press
Binding: Saddle Stitched
Mailing List Information: Names for rent
In Business: 25 years
Number of Employees: 7
Sales Information: $5MM to $10MM

6318 Great Plains All Product Catalog
Great Plains Manufacturing
1525 E North St.
Salina, KS 67401   785-823-3276
                     www.greatplainsmfg.com

Agricultural implement company

President: Linda Salem
Catalog Cost: Free
Printing Information: 72 pages in 4 colors
In Business: 40 years
Number of Employees: 1400
Sales Information: $100MM to $500MM

6319 Hardy Diesels
Hardy Diesels
15749 Lyons Valley Road
Jamul, CA 91935-3503   619-669-1995
                              800-341-7027
                         Fax: 619-669-4829
                         sales@hardydiesel.com
                         www.hardydiesel.com

Small diesel generators and diesel tractors,
tractor implements, farm tractors, diesel marine engines, solar panels, wind generators,
inverters, water pumps

Credit Cards: MasterCard

6320 Harmony Farm Supply & Nursery
Harmony Farm Supply & Nursery
3244 Gravenstein Hwy North
Sebastopol, CA 95472-460   707-823-9125
                             Fax: 707-823-1734
                             www.harmonyfarm.com

Organic farm and garden supply

In Business: 35 years
Sales Information: $5MM to $10MM

6321 Hasco Tag Company
Hasco Tag Company
1101 Second Avenue
Dayton, KY 41074-130   859-261-6000
                              800-860-6300
                         Fax: 859-261-6002
                         www.hascotag.com

Livestock identification tags

President: Tom V Haas
Marketing Manager: Mike Haas
Catalog Circulation: Mailed 1 time(s) per year
to 2M+
Printing Information: 11 pages on Glossy
Stock
In Business: 113 years
Number of Employees: 30
Sales Information: $1,000,000 - $5,000,000

6322 Hoffman Hatchery
Hoffman Hatchery
PO Box 129
Gratz, PA 17030   717-365-3694
                         info@hoffmanhatchery.com
                         www.hoffmanhatchery.com

Chicks, turkeys, ducklings, goslings, guineas, gamebirds, bantams, swans, equipment
and books

President: Anna Hoffman
In Business: 67 years

6323 Hoover's Hatchery
Hoover's Hatchery
PO Box 200
Rudd, IA 50471   641-395-2730
                        800-247-7014
                   Fax: 641-395-2208
                   hoovers@omnitelcom.com
                   www.hoovershatchery.com

Poultry equipment and medications

President: Mary Halstead
Credit Cards: MasterCard
Printing Information: in 4 colors
In Business: 71 years
Sales Information: $500M to $1MM

6324 Hubbard Milling Company
Hubbard Feeds
424 N. Riverfront Drive
Mankato, MN 56001-8500   507-388-9400
                                800-869-7219
                           Fax: 507-388-9453
                           info@hubbardfeeds.com
                           www.Hubbardfeeds.Com

Feed

President: Steve Van Roekel
Beef Specialist: Allen Stateler, Ph.D.
Dairy Specialist: Sarah Schuling, Ph.D.
Swine Specialist: Lori Stevermer
Catalog Circulation: Mailed 5 time(s) per year
Number of Employees: 1200

6325 Hypro Pressure
Pentair
375 5th Ave NW
New Brighton, MN 55112-3288   651-766-6300
                                     800-424-9776
                                Fax: 800-323-6496
                                www.Hypropumps.Com

Agricultural spraying supplies

President: Paul Meschke
Product Manager: Jared Krueger
Catalog Circulation: Mailed 1 time(s) per year
Printing Information: 24 pages in 4 colors on
Matte Stock
Binding: Saddle Stitched
In Business: 67 years

6326 Inpak-Systems
Inpak-Systems
540 Tasman Street
Madison, WI 53714-3162   937-642-5491
                           Fax: 608-221-4473
                           info@inpaksystems.com
                           www.inpaksystems.com

Portable baggers

President: Gerald Hoague
Catalog Circulation: Mailed 2 time(s) per year
In Business: 29 years
Number of Employees: 8
Sales Information: $5MM to $10MM

6327 Kent Feeds
Kent Nutrition Group.
2905 Highway 61 N
Muscatine, IA 52761-76   866-647-1212
                           Fax: 563-264-4289
                           www.kentfeeds.com

Kent preconditioner

President: Jack Nay
Catalog Circulation: Mailed 1 time(s) per year
In Business: 88 years
Number of Employees: 800

6328 Laboratory Sampling Products Catalog
Nasco Arts & Crafts Store
901 Janesville Avenue
PO Box 901
Fort Atkinson, WI 53538-901   920-563-2446
                              800-558-9595
                        Fax: 800-372-1236
                    custserv@enasco.com
                          www.enasco.com

Wide range of products used for sampling in the food, dairy, water, sewage, medical, pharmaceutical, veterinary, environmental, soil, forage, cosmetic and industrial markets

President: Andrew Reinen
Marketing Manager: Phil Niemeyer
Manager, Data Processing: Mike Wagner
Catalog Cost: Free
Catalog Circulation: to 25000
In Business: 74 years
Number of Employees: 540
Sales Information: Under $500M

6329 Marden Industries
Marden Industries
PO Box 796
Mulberry, FL 33860-0796   863-559-9548
                          800-881-0388
                    Fax: 863-428-1395
                  tom.king@supertrak.com
                       www.mardenind.com

Agricultural implements

President: Dave Sampson
Marketing Manager: Dale Broxton
VP: Tom Kin
Mailing List Information: Names for rent
In Business: 81 years
Number of Employees: 25
Sales Information: $1,000,000 - $5,000,000

6330 Mount Pulaski Products
The Andersons Cob Products
521 Illinois Avenue
Maumee, OH 43537-119   419-891-6511
                    Fax: 217-792-5040
              coborders@andersonsinc.com
                 www.andersonsmtpulaski.com

Air washed corn cob and nut shell products

President: R Scott Steinfort
Catalog Circulation: Mailed 1 time(s) per year
In Business: 58 years
Number of Employees: 3000
Sales Information: $5,000,000 - $10,000,000

6331 Musserforests
Musser Forests Inc
1880 Route 119 Hwy N
Indiana, PA 15701   724-465-5685
                     800-643-8319
               Fax: 724-465-9893
            info@musserforests.com
              www.musserforests.com

Agricultural equipment and supplies

President: Fred Musser Jr
Credit Cards: MasterCard; Visa
Catalog Circulation: Mailed 4 time(s) per year
Printing Information: in 4 colors on Glossy Stock
Press: Web Press
Binding: Saddle Stitched
In Business: 87 years
Number of Employees: 170
Sales Information: $10MM to $20MM

6332 Omaha Vaccine Company/Pet Supplies Delivered
CSR Company Inc.
11701 Centennial Road
Suites 2 & 3
La Vista, NE 68128   800-367-4444
                 Fax: 800-242-9447
              www.omahavaccine.com

Kennel and pet supplies for all animals

Chairman: Scott Remington
President: C. Remington
Credit Cards: MasterCard; Visa
Catalog Cost: Free
Catalog Circulation: Mailed 1 time(s) per year to 1.6MM
Printing Information: 150 pages in 4 colors
Mailing List Information: Names for rent
List Company: Total Media Concepts
222 Cedar Lane, Suite 201
Teaneck, NJ 07666
201-692-0018
In Business: 401 years
Number of Employees: 200

6333 Parker McCrory Manufacturing Company
Parker-McCrory Mfg.Co.
2000 Forest Ave
Kansas City, MO 64108-2800   816-221-2000
                              800-662-1038
                        Fax: 816-221-9879
                     info@parmakusa.com
                     www.Parmakusa.Com

Complete line of electric fence chargers and products

President: Ken Turner
Catalog Circulation: Mailed 3 time(s) per year
Printing Information: on Matte Stock
Binding: Folded
Mailing List Information: Names for rent
In Business: 94 years
Number of Employees: 115
Sales Information: $10,000,000 - $25,000,000

6334 Perry Company
The Perry Company
500 South Valley Mills Dr
PO Box 7187
Waco, TX 76711-7187   254-756-2139
                       800-792-3246
                 Fax: 254-756-2166
               info@perry-co.com
                  www.perry-co.com

Tractor canopies

President: Jeff Weaver
Catalog Circulation: Mailed 1 time(s) per year
In Business: 69 years
Number of Employees: 47
Sales Information: $5,000,000 - $10,000,000

6335 Pirelli Armstrong Tire Corporation
Pirelli Tire NA LLC
100 Pirelli Drive Rome
Rome, GA 30161-7000   706-368-5800
                       800-747-3554
                 Fax: 706-368-5832
                    www.us.pirelli.com

Farm tires

President: Hugh D Pace
Catalog Circulation: Mailed 1 time(s) per year
Number of Employees: 500

6336 Ramm Fence
Ramm and Horse Stalls and Horse Fencing
13150 Airport Highway
Swanton, OH 43558   419-825-2422
                     800-434-8456
               Fax: 419-825-2433
              ramm@rammfence.com
                 www.rammfence.com

Horsefencing, stalls and equipment

President: Debbie Disbrow
debbie@rammfence.com

CFO: Glen Johnson
glen@rammfence.com
CEO: Mike Disbrow
mike@rammfence.com
Catalog Cost: Free
In Business: 23 years
Number of Employees: 20
Sales Information: $15 Million

6337 Rubber Queen
Wooster Rubber, Ltd./Rubber Queen
1130 Riffel Road
Wooster, OH 44699-2260   330-345-5666
                     Fax: 330-345-5668
                  john@rubberqueen.com
                     www.rubberqueen.com

Utility mats

President: James Jones
Partner: Jerry Baker
VP of Manufacturing: Richard Berg
Purchasing Manager: Steve Croft
Catalog Circulation: Mailed 1 time(s) per year
Printing Information: in 3 colors

6338 Silver Springs Nursery
Silver Springs Nursery Inc
29751 SW Town Center Loop W
Wilsonville, OR 97070-8909   503-682-5089
                              800-342-6401
                        Fax: 503-682-5099
                       www.nurseryguide.com

Plants; Wholesale only; $100 minimum order

President: James Kraemer
Number of Employees: 2
Sales Information: Under $500M

6339 Slip-Ons Round Bale Covers
Bale Bonnet Slip Ons Round Bale Covers
PO Box 111
2525 St. Rt. 41
Cynthiana, OH 45624   740-634-2539
                       800-231-4242
                 Fax: 800-775-1727
           info@sliponsbalebonnets.com
                  www.balebonnets.com

Bale covers

President: Steve Chrisman
CFO: Helen Chrisman
Marketing Manager: LS Sowers
Buyers: Steve Chrisman
Credit Cards: MasterCard
Catalog Circulation: Mailed 1 time(s) per year
Printing Information: 12 pages in 1 color on Matte Stock
Press: Letterpress
Binding: Perfect Bound
In Business: 1 years
Number of Employees: 5
Sales Information: $1MM to $3MM

6340 Smith Brothers
Smith Brothers
PO Box 2700
Denton, TX 76202-2700   940-565-0886
                         800-784-5449
                   Fax: 940-565-8232
                info@smithbrothers.com
                  www.smithbrothers.com

Show clothing and supplies for the Western horseman

President: Jim Smith
Credit Cards: AMEX; MasterCard
Catalog Cost: Free
Catalog Circulation: Mailed 1 time(s) per year
Printing Information: 184 pages
Binding: Perfect Bound
In Business: 37 years
Sales Information: Under $500M

6341 Spraying Systems Company
Spraying Systems Company
N Avenue and Schmale Road
P.O. Box 7900
Wheaton, IL 60187-7901   630-665-5000
info@spray.com
www.spray.com

Sprayer calibrator
Catalog Circulation: Mailed 2 time(s) per year
In Business: 80 years
Number of Employees: 500

6342 Stanley Supplies and Services
Stanley Supply &Services, Inc.
335 Willow Street
North Andover, MA 01845-5995   978-682-9844
800-225-5370
Fax: 800-743-8141
www.stanleysupplyservices.com

Tool kits, cases, test instruments, tools and equipment for technicians and service personnel in electronics and communications
President: Ken Lyon
Marketing Manager: Jeff Richardson
Credit Cards: AMEX; MasterCard
Catalog Cost: Free
Catalog Circulation: Mailed 2 time(s) per year
Printing Information: 300 pages in 4 colors on Glossy Stock
Binding: Saddle Stitched
Mailing List Information: Names for rent
In Business: 48 years
Number of Employees: 75
Sales Information: $ 3-5 Million

6343 Stock Seed Farms
Stock Seed Farms
28008 Mill Rd
Murdock, NE 68407   402-867-3771
800-759-1520
Fax: 402-867-2442
prairie@stockseed.com
www.stockseed.com

Seed of prairie wildflowers and native Midwest grasses, turf type buffalo grasses, coby and bowie
President: David Stock, Praire Grasses/Wflwr
Catalog Cost: Free
Catalog Circulation: Mailed 1 time(s) per year
Printing Information: 22 pages in 4 colors on Glossy Stock
Press: Web Press
Binding: Saddle Stitched
Mailing List Information: Names for rent
In Business: 50 years
Number of Employees: 7
Sales Information: $3MM to $5MM

6344 Triple F Products
Insta-Pro International
4043 120th Street
Urbandale, IA 50323-600   515-254-1260
800-383-4524
Fax: 515-254-1650
info@insta-pro.com
www.Insta-Pro.Com

Processing Technologies for Food and Feed
President: Kevin Kacere
kkacere@insta-pro.com
Marketing Manager: Karl Arnold
karnold@insta-pro.com
VP, Engineering & Operations: Oz Grimm
oz@insta-pro.com
VP, Nutrition & Extrusion: Nabil Said
nsaid@insta-pro.com
Controller: Mike Williams
mwilliams@insta-pro.com
Catalog Circulation: Mailed 2 time(s) per year
In Business: 40 years
Number of Employees: 100
Sales Information: $20MM to $50MM

6345 Troy-Bilt
Troy-Bilt
1311 S Stemmons Fwy
Lewisville, TX 75067-6307   972-434-2214
800-828-5500
www.troybilt.com

Chipper and shredder
President: Mike Smith
Catalog Circulation: Mailed 1 time(s) per year
In Business: 78 years
Number of Employees: 300
Sales Information: $20MM to $50MM

6346 Vesey's Seeds
Veseys
411 York Road, Highway 25
PO Box 9000
York, PE C0A 1   902-368-7333
800-363-7333
Fax: 800-686-0329
customerservice@veseys.com
www.veseys.com

Vegetable and flower seeds
President: Bev Simpson
Marketing Manager: John Barrett
Founder: Arthur Vesey
Catalog Cost: Free
Printing Information: 72 pages in 4 colors on Glossy Stock
Press: Web Press
Binding: Saddle Stitched
In Business: 76 years
Sales Information: $200,000

6347 Weaver Leather
Weaver Leather, LLC
7540 CR 201
PO Box 68
Mt Hope, OH 44660-68   330-674-1782
800-932-8371
Fax: 330-674-0330
info@weaverleather.com
www.Weaverleather.Com

Leather and leatherworking/saddlery supplies, parts, and tools
President: Paul Weaver
Marketing Manager: Molly Wagner
Production Manager: Myron Stutzman
COO: Chris Weaver
International Marketing Manager: Chris Weaver
Buyers: Chris Miller
Credit Cards: MasterCard; Visa
Catalog Cost: Free
Catalog Circulation: Mailed 2 time(s) per year
Printing Information: 256 pages in 4 colors on Glossy Stock
Press: Web Press
Binding: Perfect Bound
Mailing List Information: Names for rent
List Manager: Suzette M Frank
In Business: 42 years
Number of Employees: 160
Sales Information: $20MM to $50MM

Arts & Graphic Arts
Frames & Framing Equipment

6348 A Great Idea to Hang Onto
Walker Display, Inc.
4000 Airpark Blvd
Duluth, MN 55811   218-624-8990
800-234-7614
Fax: 218-624-8991
wdinc@walkerdisplay.com
www.walkerdisplay.com

Picture, exhibit and artwork hanging systems.
President: Richard Levey
Credit Cards: AMEX; MasterCard
Catalog Cost: Free
Printing Information: 10 pages in 4 colors on

Matte Stock
Binding: Saddle Stitched

6349 Easy Leaf Products
Neuberg & Neuberg Importers Group, Inc.
6001 Santa Monica Blvd
Los Angeles, CA 90038-1807   323-769-4822
800-569-5323
Fax: 877-386-1489
info@nnigroup.com
www.easyleaf.com

Edible gold & silver leaf and recipes
President: Larry Neuberg
CFO: Sam Neuberg
Marketing Manager: Scot Holland
Vice President: Rommel Villa
rommelvilla@nnigroup.com
Food & Beverage Manager: Lynn Neuberg
lynnneuberg@nnigroup.com
Founder: Sam Neuberg
samneuberg@nnigroup.com
Catalog Circulation: Mailed 1 time(s) per year to 4M
Printing Information: 20 pages in 2 colors
Mailing List Information: Names for rent
In Business: 7 years
Number of Employees: 50
Sales Information: $7.2 Million

6350 Exposures
Exposures
1 Memory Lane
PO Box 3690
Oshkosh, WI 54903-3690   855-202-7390
Fax: 800-699-6993
csr@exposuresonline.com
www.exposuresonline.com

Picture frames, photo albums, photo-related gifts, curio cabinets, and photograph storage systems.
Catalog Cost: Free
Printing Information: in 4 colors

6351 General Shale Brick
General Shale Brick, Inc.
3015 Briston Hwy
Johnson City, TN 37601   276-783-8161
800-414-4661
Fax: 276-782-3238
www.generalshale.com

Over 250 styles and types of brick, building stones, concrete products and hardscapes
President: Richard Green
Production Manager: Kim Daugherty
VP, Sales: Randy Smith
Printing Information: in 2 colors
In Business: 86 years
Number of Employees: 2000

6352 Light Impressions
Light Impressions
100 Carlson Raod
Rochester, NY 14610   800-975-6429
Fax: 866-592-8642
help@fdmbrands.com
www.lightimpressionsdirect.com

Archival storage, display & presentation materials for negatives, transparencies, CDs, photographs, artwork, & documents
President: Gabe Bristol
Credit Cards: AMEX; MasterCard
Catalog Cost: Free
Catalog Circulation: Mailed 52 time(s) per year
Printing Information: 116 pages in 4 colors on Glossy Stock
Press: Web Press
Binding: Saddle Stitched
Mailing List Information: Names for rent
List Manager: MSGi
In Business: 48 years
Number of Employees: 80
Sales Information: $36 Million

6353 Milton W Bosley Company
Bosley mouldings
151 8th Avenue N.W
Glen Burnie, MD 21061-576   410-761-7727
                                                  800-638-5010
                                          Fax: 410-553-0575
                                www.bosleymouldings.com/

Architectural and picture frame moldings; wood, metal and laminate

President: Bosley Wright
Founder: Milton W. Bosley
In Business: 102 years
Number of Employees: 27
Sales Information: $1,000,000 - $5,000,000

6354 Ziabicki Import Company Catalog
Ziabicki Import Company
PO Box 081004
Racine, WI 53408-1004   262-633-7918
                                          Fax: 262-633-8711
                                          info@ziabicki.com
                                          www.ziabicki.com

Picture-hanging supplies

President: Tom Wolff
Credit Cards: AMEX; MasterCard
Printing Information: in 2 colors
Mailing List Information: Names for rent
In Business: 60 years
Number of Employees: 6
Sales Information: $300,000- 750,000

Materials & Supplies

6355 A Child's Dream
A Child's Dream
214-A Cedar St.
Sand Point, ID 83864   208-255-1664
                                                  800-359-2906
                                          Fax: 208-255-2656
                                info@achildsdream.com
                                www.achildsdream.com

100% wool felt; felting fibers and kits, Waldorf doll and toy making supplies, patterns and kits, dyes, natural yarns.

Credit Cards: MasterCard
Catalog Cost: $3
Catalog Circulation: Mailed 1 time(s) per year
Printing Information: 30 pages in 4 colors

6356 Ameri Stamp/Sign-A-Rama
AmeriStamp - Sign-A-Rama
1300 N Royal Avenue
Evansville, IN 47715   812-477-7763
                                                  800-223-3086
                                          Fax: 812-477-7898
                                websales@signsoveramerica.com
                                www.signsoveramerica.com

Full service sign company selling banners, outdoor signs, vehicle graphics, golf signs and more

President: Walter Valiant
VP of Public Relations: Grant Valiant
grant@signsoveramerica.com
Client Account Specialist: Sherri Hill
sherri@signsoveramerica.com
Account Executive: Matt Effinger
mteffinger@signsoveramerica.com
In Business: 57 years
Number of Employees: 17
Sales Information: $ 1 Million

6357 American Institute of Architects Press
The American Institute of Architects
1735 New York Ave NW
Washington, DC 20006-5292   202-626-7300
                                                  800-242-3837
                                          Fax: 202-626-7547
                                          infocentral@aia.org
                                          www.aia.org

Highly illustrated books on architects and architectual history, design and practice, reprints of rare architecture books, postcards, note cards and calendars

President: Elizabeth Chu Richter, FAIA
erichter@richterarchitects.com
CFO: Richard James
Marketing Manager: Philip Simon
Vice President: William J. Bates, AIA, NOMA
wbates@eatnpark.com
Vice President: James Easton Rains Jr., FAIA
jim@rainsstudio.com
Public Director: Julie D. Taylor, Hon. AIA/LA
julie@taylor-pr.com
Catalog Circulation: Mailed 1 time(s) per year
List Manager: Carol Madden
In Business: 158 years
Number of Employees: 200

6358 Art Supply Warehouse
Art Supply Wholesale Club
6104 Maddry Oaks Court
Raleigh, NC 27616   919-878-5077
                                                  800-995-6778
                                          Fax: 919-878-5075
                                www.aswexpress.com

Art supplies and materials

President: David Goldstein
Credit Cards: AMEX; MasterCard
Catalog Cost: Free
Catalog Circulation: Mailed 2 time(s) per year
Printing Information: 67 pages in 1 color on Newsprint
Press: Web Press
Binding: Saddle Stitched
In Business: 35 years
Number of Employees: 70
Sales Information: $1-3 Million

6359 Arts & Crafts
Nasco Arts & Crafts Store
901 Janesville Avenue
PO Box 901
Fort Atkinson, WI 53538-901   920-563-2446
                                                  800-558-9595
                                          Fax: 920-563-6044
                                custserv@enasco.com
                                www.enasco.com

Supplies and teaching materials for art history, sculpture, drawing, painting, tile work, leather crafts, ceramics, metal enameling, jewelry making, weaving, woodcraft, and stained glass

President: Andrew Reinen
Marketing Manager: Phil Niemeyer
Manager, Data Processing: Mike Wagner
Catalog Cost: Free
Catalog Circulation: to 25000
In Business: 74 years
Number of Employees: 540

6360 B&H Photo Video Pro-Audio
B&H Photo Video
420 9th Avenue
New York, NY 10001   212-444-6615
                                                  800-606-6969
                                www.bhphotovideo.com

Photographic, video and digital imaging products, cameras, lenses, accessories, home theater components, binoculars, telescopes and much more

Chairman: Herman Schreiber
President: Sam Goldstein
CFO: Isreal Lebovits
Credit Cards: AMEX; MasterCard; Visa
Catalog Cost: Free
Catalog Circulation: Mailed 3 time(s) per year
Printing Information: 332 pages in 4 colors
In Business: 43 years
Number of Employees: 1100
Sales Information: 85MM

6361 Baudville
Baudville
5380 52nd St SE
Grand Rapids, MI 49512   616-698-0889
                                                  800-728-0888
                                          Fax: 616-698-0554
                                          service@baudville.com
                                          www.baudville.Com

Trophies, recognition items, lapel pins, event paper, seals & embosers, certificate papers, ID accessories, folders & frames and more

President: David Pezzato
Marketing Manager: Jack Fisher
VP: Kristy Sherlund
Credit Cards: AMEX; MasterCard
Catalog Cost: Free
Printing Information: 80 pages in 4 colors on Matte Stock
Binding: Perfect Bound
In Business: 30 years
Number of Employees: 85
Sales Information: 9.5M

6362 Catalina Plastics & Coating
Catalina Graphic Films Incorporated
27001 Agoura Road
Suite 100
Calabasas Hills, CA 91301-5395   818-880-8060
                                                  800-333-3136
                                          Fax: 818-880-1144
                                sales@catalinagraphicfilms.com
                                www.Catalinagraphicfilms.Com

Distributor and converter of plastic sheet and film for the graphic arts trade

President: Jeff Dworman
Marketing Manager: Harold Kotkin
VP and General Manager: Kevin Yaezell
In Business: 47 years
Number of Employees: 18
Sales Information: $1,000,000 - $5,000,000

6363 Chesapeake Ceramic Supply
Chesapeake Ceramics, LLC
4706 Benson Ave
Baltimore, MD 21227-1411   410-247-1270
                                                  800-962-9655
                                          Fax: 410-247-1708
                                sales@chesapeakeceramics.com
                                www.ceramicsupply.com

Ceramic supplies and equipment

President: Jack Bitner
Owner: Steve Prichett
Sales: Diane Robinson
Education Specialist/Studio Potter: Bre Kathman
Credit Cards: AMEX; MasterCard
Catalog Circulation: Mailed 1 time(s) per year
Printing Information: 142 pages in 4 colors
Binding: Saddle Stitched
In Business: 30 years
Sales Information: $1MM to $3MM

6364 Complete Line of Architectural & Engineering
The Complete Line, LLC
15335 NE 95th Street
Redmond, WA 98052-5554   425-885-6360
                                                  800-447-3444
                                          Fax: 425-869-2988
                                sales@completeline.com
                                shop.completeline.com

Art and drafting supplies

President: Laura Harrison
Credit Cards: AMEX; MasterCard
Printing Information: 255 pages on Matte Stock
In Business: 37 years

6365 Continental Clay Company
Continental Clay Company
1101 Stinson Blvd NE
Minneapolis, MN 55413-1572   612-331-9332
                                800-432-2529
                                Fax: 612-331-8564
                                www.Continentalclay.Com

Clay, glaze, accessories and equipment

President: Michael Swartout
Marketing Manager: David Gamble
Credit Cards: MasterCard
Catalog Cost: Free
Catalog Circulation: Mailed 1 time(s) per year
Printing Information: 48 pages in 4 colors
Binding: Saddle Stitched
Number of Employees: 15
Sales Information: $3MM to $5MM

6366 Dharma Trading Company
Dharma Trading Company
1604 Fourth St.
PO Box 150916
San Rafael, CA 94915   707-283-0390
                          800-542-5227
                          Fax: 707-283-0379
                          service@dharmatrading.com
                          www.dharmatrading.com

Textile craft supplies and clothing blanks, tools, fabric markers,transfer paper, dyes, kits, and how to books

President: Isaac Goff
Credit Cards: AMEX; MasterCard
Catalog Cost: Free
Catalog Circulation: Mailed 2 time(s) per year to 150k
Printing Information: 120 pages in 1 color on Glossy Stock
Press: Web Press
Binding: Saddle Stitched
Mailing List Information: Names for rent
In Business: 31 years
Number of Employees: 50
Sales Information: $3-5 Million

6367 Dick Blick Art Materials
Dick Blick Art Materials
PO Box 1769
Galesburg, IL 61402-1267   309-343-6181
                              800-828-4548
                              Fax: 800-621-8293
                              info@dickblick.com
                              www.dickblick.com

America's widest selection of fine artist and craft materials and a tradition of service since 1911

Chairman: Jack Wyatt
President: Robert Buchsbaum
Credit Cards: AMEX; MasterCard
Catalog Cost: Free
Number of Employees: 575

6368 Dixie Art Airbrush
Dixie Art Airbrush
P.O. Box 6433
Metairie, LA 70009-6433   504-733-6509
                             800-783-2612
                             Fax: 504-733-0668
                             artdixie@aol.com
                             www.dixieart.com

Discount fine art supplies, free shipping

President: Don Aunoy
Credit Cards: AMEX; MasterCard
Catalog Cost: Free
Catalog Circulation: Mailed 1 time(s) per year
Printing Information: 42 pages in 2 colors on Matte Stock
In Business: 80 years
Number of Employees: 5
Sales Information: $1-3 Million

6369 GS Direct Graphic Supplies
GS Direct Inc.
6490 Carlson Dr
Eden Prairie, MN 55346-1729   952-942-6115
                                 800-234-3729
                                 Fax: 952-942-0216
                                 info@gs-direct.com
                                 www.gsdirect.net

Graphic supplies and drawing equipment including plotters, workstations, plotting media

President: Chuck Ehlers
Credit Cards: AMEX; MasterCard
Catalog Cost: Free
Catalog Circulation: Mailed 8 time(s) per year to 750M
Printing Information: 60 pages in 4 colors on Glossy Stock
Press: Web Press
Binding: Saddle Stitched
Mailing List Information: Names for rent
List Manager: Rich Trewilgas
In Business: 13 years
Number of Employees: 8
Sales Information: $1.5 Million

6370 Light Impressions
Light Impressions
100 Carlson Raod
Rochester, NY 14610   800-975-6429
                         Fax: 866-592-8642
                         help@fdmbrands.com
                         www.lightimpressionsdirect.com

Archival storage, display & presentation materials for negatives, transparencies, CDs, photographs, artwork, & documents

President: Gabe Bristol
Credit Cards: AMEX; MasterCard
Catalog Cost: Free
Catalog Circulation: Mailed 52 time(s) per year
Printing Information: 116 pages in 4 colors on Glossy Stock
Press: Web Press
Binding: Saddle Stitched
Mailing List Information: Names for rent
List Manager: MSGi
In Business: 48 years
Number of Employees: 80
Sales Information: $36 Million

6371 Morion Company
Morion Company
60 Leo Birmingham Parkway
Suite 111
Brighton, MA 02135   617-787-2133
                        Fax: 617-787-4628
                        labgems@morioncompany.com
                        www.morioncompany.com

Lab created minerals for wholesale and retail, for hobbyists, crafters, collectors, jewelers and jewelry manufacturers

Chairman: Uriah Pritchard, MS
President: Leonid Pride, PhD
Founder: Leonid Pride, Ph.D.
Catalog Cost: Free
Catalog Circulation: Mailed 3 time(s) per year to 780
Average Order Size: $400
Printing Information: 6 pages in 1 color on Matte Stock
Press: Web Press
Binding: Folded
Mailing List Information: Names for rent
In Business: 22 years
Number of Employees: 2
Sales Information: Under $500M

6372 Neil Enterprises
Neil Enterprises
450 E Bunker Ct
Vernon Hills, IL 60061   847-549-7627
                            800-621-5584
                            Fax: 847-549-0349
                            info@neilenterprises.com
                            www.neilenterprises.com

Promotional product/photo novelty manufacturer and supplier/distributor of instant photographic equipment serving the photographic, printing/screenprint, craft, educational and ad specialty industries

President: Jerry Fine
Catalog Cost: Free
Catalog Circulation: Mailed 1 time(s) per year
Printing Information: 52 pages in 4 colors on Glossy Stock
Press: Web Press
Binding: Perfect Bound
Mailing List Information: Names for rent
In Business: 56 years
Number of Employees: 25
Sales Information: $50-100 Million

6373 Neil Holiday Catalog
Neil Enterprises
450 E Bunker Ct
Vernon Hills, IL 60061   847-549-7627
                            800-621-5584
                            Fax: 847-549-0349
                            info@neilenterprises.com
                            www.neilenterprises.com

Promotional product/photo novelty manufacturer and supplier/distributor of instant photographic equipment serving the photographic, printing/screenprint, craft, education and ad specialty industries

President: Jerry Fine
Catalog Cost: Free
Catalog Circulation: Mailed 1 time(s) per year
Printing Information: 12 pages in 4 colors on Glossy Stock
Press: Web Press
Binding: Perfect Bound
In Business: 56 years
Number of Employees: 25
Sales Information: $50-100 Million

6374 Sax Arts & Crafts
School Specialty, Inc
PO Box 1579
Appleton, WI 54912-1579   888-388-3224
                             800-558-6696
                             Fax: 888-388-6344
                             orders@schoolspecialty.com
                             www.schoolspecialty.com

Artist's supplies, full line of weaving looms and aids, basketry and batik supplies

Chairman: James R. Henderson
President: Joseph M. Yorio
CFO: Kevin Baehler
Principal: Justin Lu
Portfolio Manager: Madhu Satyanarayana
EVP, Distribution: Patrick T. Collins
Printing Information: 600 pages in 7 colors
Binding: Perfect Bound

6375 Seton Catalog
Seton
20 Thompson Rd.
PO Box 819
Branford, CT 06405-819   203-488-8059
                            855-544-7992
                            Fax: 800-345-7819
                            help@seton.com
                            www.seton.com

Signs, labels, tags, pipe markers, security, and work apparel

President: Valerie Pyrell
CFO: Barbara Bolens
Marketing Manager: Donna J Canestri
VP Administration: Garry Toulson

Buyers: Jeffrey Lublin
Credit Cards: AMEX; MasterCard
Catalog Cost: Free
Catalog Circulation: Mailed 2 time(s) per year
Printing Information: 188 pages in 3 colors
Mailing List Information: Names for rent
List Company: Direct Media
In Business: 59 years
Number of Employees: 270
Sales Information: $25,000,000 - $50,000,000

6376 Solo Horton Brushes
Solo Horton Brushes, Inc.
151 Ella Grasso Avenue
Torrington, CT 06790   800-969-7656
                                 Fax: 800-899-4765
                               solo@snet.com
                            www.solobrushes.com

Art, wire, paint, power, tube and foam brushes

President: L Skeie
Secretary: Nan Skeie
Credit Cards: AMEX; MasterCard; Visa
Catalog Cost: Free
Catalog Circulation: Mailed 2 time(s) per year
Printing Information: 41 pages in 2 colors on Matte Stock
Press: Web Press
Binding: Saddle Stitched
In Business: 95 years
Number of Employees: 5
Sales Information: $500,000 - $1,000,000

6377 Stencil Ease International
Stencil Ease
P.O. Box 1127
Old Saybrook, CT 06475   860-395-0150
                                  800-334-1776
                                 Fax: 860-395-0166
                               info@stencilease.com
                            www.stencilease.com

Stencils, home decor stencils, stencil paints, stencil brushes

Chairman: Earl Greenho
President: Brian Greenho
Credit Cards: AMEX; MasterCard
Catalog Cost: $3.50
Average Order Size: $25
Printing Information: 48 pages in 4 colors on Glossy Stock
Press: Sheetfed Press
Will Trade Names: Yes
In Business: 27 years
Number of Employees: 18
Sales Information: $1.4 Million

6378 Testrite Visual Products
Testrite Visual
216 South Newman Street
Hackensack, NJ 07601   201-543-0240
                                  888-873-2735
                                 Fax: 201-543-2195
                               display@testrite.com
                            www.testrite.com

Easels, presentation products

Chairman: Harold Rubin
President: Larry Rubin
Vice President of Sales: Paula Goodelman
paula@testrite.com
VP, Retail Development: Ken Allen
ken@testrite.com
VP, Business Development: Mitchell Lewis
mitchell@testrite.com
Catalog Cost: Free
Catalog Circulation: Mailed 1 time(s) per year to 6.5M
Printing Information: 187 pages in 4 colors on Matte Stock
Binding: Saddle Stitched
In Business: 98 years
Number of Employees: 130
Sales Information: $16 Million

6379 Woodworkers Supply
Woodworkers Supply, Inc
1108 N Glenn Rd
Casper, WY 82601-1635   307-237-5528
                                  800-645-9292
                                 Fax: 800-853-9663
                            comments@woodworker.com
                               www.woodworker.com

Woodworking tools and supplies

President: John Wirth, Jr.
john@woodworker.com
CFO: Joe McQuade
Marketing Manager: Ken Pollitt
kenp@woodworker.com
Production Manager: Dean Cannon
Operations Manager: Darrell Feldman
darrellf@woodworker.com
International Marketing Manager: Jay Sanger
Buyers: Cynthia Quintana
Credit Cards: AMEX; MasterCard
Catalog Cost: Free
Catalog Circulation: Mailed 12 time(s) per year to 6M
Average Order Size: $100
Printing Information: 220 pages in 4 colors on Glossy Stock
Press: Web Press
Binding: Perfect Bound
Mailing List Information: Names for rent
List Manager: Mike Gilb
In Business: 43 years
Number of Employees: 76

Audio Visual
Duplication

6380 Dove Enterprises
Dove Multimedia Inc.
290 West Ave
Suite J
Tallmadge, OH 44278-1702   330-928-9160
                                  800-233-3683
                                 Fax: 330-928-9644
                               chris@dovecds.com
                            www.dovecds.com

Audio and video duplication

President: Larry Adams
Credit Cards: AMEX; MasterCard
Catalog Cost: Free
Catalog Circulation: Mailed 1 time(s) per year
Printing Information: 3 pages in 4 colors on Glossy Stock
Press: Web Press
Binding: Perfect Bound
In Business: 11 years
Number of Employees: 9
Sales Information: Under $500,000

6381 Maxell Corporation of America
Maxell Corporation of America
3 Garret Mountain Plaza
3rd Floor, Suite#300
Woodland Park, NJ 07424-3352   973-653-2400
                                  800-533-2836
                                 Fax: 201-796-8790
                               techsupp@maxell.com
                            www.Maxell.Com

Video duplication equipment and supplies

President: Don Patrician
Printing Information: in 2 colors
In Business: 45 years
Number of Employees: 118

Programs & Training Tapes

6382 American Management Association
American Management Association
1601 Broadway
New York, NY 10019   212-586-8100
                                  877-566-9441
                                 Fax: 518-891-0368
                            customerservice@amanet.org
                               www.amanet.org/

Professional training and development audio-cassette and Workbook Management Training materials through self-directed learning

Chairman: Charles R. Craig
President: Edward T. Reilly
CFO: Vivianna Guzman
Marketing Manager: Jeremey Donovan
Production Manager: Laurie Tiech
VP, Finance: Cathy Liberty
SVP/Chief Information Officer: Richard J. Barton
VP, Internal Audit: Robert Morales
Credit Cards: AMEX; MasterCard; Visa
Catalog Cost: Free
Catalog Circulation: Mailed 4 time(s) per year to 1.7MM
Printing Information: 80 pages in 2 colors
Press: Web Press
Binding: Saddle Stitched
Mailing List Information: Names for rent
List Manager: Connie Balandron
913-451-2700
In Business: 102 years
Number of Employees: 42

6383 Career Track
Career Track
5700 Broadmoor Street
Suite 300
Mission, KS 66202-2219   800-780-8476
                                 Fax: 913-967-8849
                            customerservice@pryor.com
                               www.careertrack.com

Audio and video training tapes covering a wide range of personal and professional development

Production Manager: David Allard
Credit Cards: AMEX; MasterCard; Visa; Discover
Catalog Cost: Free
Catalog Circulation: Mailed 4 time(s) per year
Printing Information: 22 pages in 4 colors on Glossy Stock
Press: Letterpress
Binding: Saddle Stitched
Mailing List Information: Names for rent
In Business: 43 years
Number of Employees: 425

6384 Novations Training Solutions Catalog
Novations Training Solutions
PO Box 1971
Waterloo, IA 50704   515-224-0919
                                 Fax: 515-327-2555

Training material on video, DVD, books e-commerce, e-learning and e-instructor-led

President: Tom Cantynger
Marketing Manager: Melssa Pollock
Catalog Circulation: Mailed 1 time(s) per year to 50000
Average Order Size: $695
Printing Information: 40 pages in 4 colors on Glossy Stock
Press: Web Press
Binding: Perfect Bound
Mailing List Information: Names for rent
In Business: 29 years
Number of Employees: 45

Supplies & Equipment

6385 Atlanta Cable Sales
ACS Solutions Inc.
495 Horizon Dr NE
Suite 200
Suwanee, GA 30024-7745   678-775-0208
                                  800-241-9881
                                 Fax: 678-775-0209
                               acs@acssolutions.com
                            acssolutions.com

Telecommunications and audio/video cables

Production Manager: Mark Keating
CEO: Bryan Glutting
Vice President: Dave Fox
Credit Cards: MasterCard; Visa
Catalog Cost: Free
In Business: 34 years
Sales Information: $ 5-10 Million

6386 Audio Accessories
Audio Accessories, Inc.
25 Mill Street
PO Box 360
Marlow, NH 03456   603-446-3335
                          Fax: 603-446-7543
audioacc@patchbays.com
www.patchbays.com

Audio accessories including jacks and panels, pre-wired patchbays, cords, holders, and cleaning tools

President: Robert Stofan
Production Manager: Tim Symonds
Credit Cards: MasterCard; Visa
In Business: 66 years
Number of Employees: 40
Sales Information: $ 5 Million

6387 B&H Photo Video Pro-Audio
B&H Photo Video
420 9th Avenue
New York, NY 10001   212-444-6615
                          800-606-6969
www.bhphotovideo.com

Photographic, video and digital imaging products, cameras, lenses, accessories, home theater components, binoculars, telescopes and much more

Chairman: Herman Schreiber
President: Sam Goldstein
CFO: Isreal Lebovits
Credit Cards: AMEX; MasterCard; Visa
Catalog Cost: Free
Catalog Circulation: Mailed 3 time(s) per year
Printing Information: 332 pages in 4 colors
In Business: 43 years
Number of Employees: 1100
Sales Information: 85MM

6388 Baseball, Softball, Football Superstore
Baseball Express
5750 Northwest Parkway
Suite 100
San Antonio, TX 78249-3374   210-348-7000
                          800-937-4824
                          Fax: 210-525-9339
customer.service@teamexpress.com
www.baseballexpress.com

Footwear, apparel, accessories, uniforms and more

President: Pat Cawles
CFO: Geoff Westmoreland
VP Sales and Marketing: Dale Fujimoto
Credit Cards: AMEX; MasterCard
Catalog Cost: Free
Catalog Circulation: Mailed 3 time(s) per year
Printing Information: 84 pages in 4 colors
Binding: Perfect Bound
In Business: 25 years
Number of Employees: 7
Sales Information: Under $500,000

6389 Bretford
Bretford
11000 Seymour Ave
Franklin Park, IL 60131-1230   847-678-2545
                          800-521-9614
                          Fax: 847-678-0852
www.bretford.com

AV computer carts, notebook carts, tables, workstations, seating, shelving and projection screens

Chairman: David Petrick
President: Mike Briggs
Marketing Manager: Trudy Brunot

CEO: Chris Petrick
Catalog Cost: Free
Catalog Circulation: Mailed 1 time(s) per year to 2MM
Printing Information: 76 pages in 4 colors on Matte Stock
Press: Web Press
Binding: Saddle Stitched
Mailing List Information: Names for rent
In Business: 46 years
Sales Information: $2 Million

6390 CCI Solutions
CCI Solutions
1247 85th Ave. SE
Olympia, WA 98501   360-943-5378
                          800-562-6006
                          Fax: 360-754-1566
info@ccisolutions.com
www.ccisolutions.com

Offers audio-visual consulting, products, technical systems and expertise.

Catalog Cost: Free
Printing Information: 72 pages in 4 colors
In Business: 40 years

6391 Catalog of Professional Audio/Video Services
WTS Media
2841 Hickory Valley Road
Chattanooga, TN 37421-6600   423-894-9427
                          888-987-6334
www.wtsmedia.com

Blank audio and video tape CD's, A/V equipment and duplication services

President: Tom Salley
Credit Cards: AMEX; MasterCard
Printing Information: 15 pages in 4 colors
Mailing List Information: Names for rent
In Business: 40 years
Number of Employees: 40
Sales Information: $5MM to $10MM

6392 Coleman Cable
Coleman Cable Inc.
1530 Shields Drive
Waukegan, IL 60085-8317   847-672-2300
                          800-323-9355
                          Fax: 847-689-1192
info@coleman-cable.com
www.Colemancable.Com

Wire and cable products

President: Gary Yetman
CFO: Alan Bergschneider
Marketing Manager: John Pappas
Executive VP, Distribution Group: Kathy Jo Van
Executive VP, CCI: Rich Carr
Executive VP, Operations: Kurt Hennelly
Credit Cards: MasterCard; Visa
Catalog Circulation: Mailed 2 time(s) per year to 15M
Printing Information: 37 pages in 4 colors on Glossy Stock
Press: Web Press
Binding: Saddle Stitched
Mailing List Information: Names for rent
In Business: 20 years
Number of Employees: 1180
Sales Information: $500M to $1MM

6393 Concept Catalog
AVI-SPL
6301 Benjamin Rd.
Suite 101
Tampa, FL 33634   866-708-5034
                          sales@avispl.com
                          www.avispl.com

AV system design and integration, consulting, creative show services, rental, event staging and production, sales, repair and extended warranty.

CEO: John Zettel
Printing Information: 58 pages in 4 colors
Mailing List Information: Names for rent
In Business: 37 years
Number of Employees: 1500
Sales Information: $577 Million

6394 Crutchfield
Crutchfield Corporation
1 Crutchfield Park
Charlottesville, VA 22911-9097   434-817-1000
                          844-347-7281
                          Fax: 434-817-1010
support@crutchfield.com
www.crutchfield.com

Audio and video components, home theater, car stereos, telephones, pagers and digital satellite systems

CEO: William G Crutchfield Jr
Founder and CEO: Bill Crutchfield
Credit Cards: AMEX; MasterCard
Catalog Cost: Free
Catalog Circulation: Mailed 6 time(s) per year
Average Order Size: $275
Printing Information: 52 pages in 4 colors
Mailing List Information: Names for rent
List Manager: The Specialists
In Business: 43 years
Number of Employees: 550
Sales Information: $50MM to $100MM

6395 Dukane Corporation
Dukane Corporation
2900 Dukane Drive
St Charles, IL 60174-3395   630-584-2300
                          800-676-2486
                          Fax: 630-797-4949
www.dukane.com

Multimedia projectors

President: Michael W Ritschdorff
VP of Administration: Terry Goldman
Credit Cards: AMEX; MasterCard
In Business: 93 years
Number of Employees: 150

6396 Knox Video
Knox Video Technologies
15875 Crabbs Branch Way
Suite A
Rockville, MD 20855-4121   301-840-5805
                          Fax: 301-840-2946
www.Knoxvideo.Com

Character generator

President: Ted Neiman
Catalog Circulation: Mailed 1 time(s) per year
In Business: 40 years
Number of Employees: 13
Sales Information: Under $500,000

6397 Lowel-Lighting Equipment
Lowel-Lighting Equipment
90 Oser Avenue
Hauppauge, NY 11788   631-273-2500
                          800-645-2522
                          Fax: 631-273-2557
techsupport@tiffen.com
www.lowel.com

Light systems, light controls, stands and mounts, cases and light kits

President: Ross Lowell
Manufacturing Engineer: Joseph Yu
Catalog Cost: Free
Catalog Circulation: Mailed 1 time(s) per year
Printing Information: 88 pages
In Business: 55 years
Number of Employees: 40
Sales Information: $10,000,000 - $25,000,000

6398 MCM Business to Business
MCM Business to Business
650 Congress Park Drive
Centerville, OH 45459-4000   877-626-3532
                                    888-235-4692
                               Fax: 800-765-6960
customerservice@mcmelectronics.com
www.mcmelectronics.com

Audio/video parts and accessories, computer hardware, security products, chemicals, technicians' aids

President: Phil Minix
pminix@mcmelectronics.com
Printing Information: 1164 pages
In Business: 38 years
Number of Employees: 120
Sales Information: 40 M

6399 MFJ Enterprises, Inc.
MFJ Enterprises, Inc.
PO Box 494
Mississippi State, MS 39762   662-323-5869
                                   800-647-1800
                              Fax: 662-323-6551
mfjcustserv@mfjenterprises.com
www.mfjenterprises.com

Ham radios and accessories

President: Martin F Jue
Founder: Martin F. Jue
Credit Cards: AMEX; MasterCard; Visa
Catalog Cost: Free
Catalog Circulation: Mailed 1 time(s) per year
Printing Information: 136 pages
In Business: 42 years
Number of Employees: 150
Sales Information: 12.6 M

6400 National AV Supply
National AV Supply
80 Little Falls Road
Fairfield, NJ 07004   800-686-0109
                                   800-825-4268
                              Fax: 800-453-6338
sales@valiantnational.com
www.valiantnational.com/

name-brand audio, video, imaging and projection products

Credit Cards: AMEX; MasterCard
Printing Information: 108 pages

6401 Pro Sound & Stage Lighting
Pro Sound & Stage Lighting
10743 Walker Street
Cypress, CA 90630-5247   714-891-5914
                                  800-268-5520
                             Fax: 888-777-5329
www.pssl.com

Pro audio equipment, DJ gear and lighting, accessories, karaoke and video gear

President: Dave Rice
Credit Cards: AMEX; MasterCard
Catalog Cost: Free
Catalog Circulation: Mailed 1 time(s) per year
Printing Information: 132 pages in 4 colors
Binding: Perfect Bound

6402 READE
Reade Advanced Materials
850 Waterman Avenue
East Providence, RI 02915   401-433-7000
                             Fax: 401-433-7001
info@reade.com
www.reade.com

Listing of specialty chemical solids (metal, mineral, ceramic, composite, alloy, polymer, natural fiber, powder, foil, sheet, wire, tube, nanoparticle, conductive, magnetic, fillers, additives)

Chairman: Charles Reade
President: Emily Reade
Marketing Manager: Elisabeth Law
Sales & Marketing Manager: Charles Reade

Catalog Cost: Free
Catalog Circulation: Mailed 4 time(s) per year to 200m
Average Order Size: $275
Printing Information: in 2 colors
Mailing List Information: Names for rent
In Business: 128 years
Number of Employees: 45
Sales Information: $3MM to $5MM

6403 Red Line
Red Line,Research Company Inc
10845 Wheatlands Ave
Suite C
Santee, CA 92071-2865   619-562-7591
                             Fax: 619-449-7244
sales@redlineresearch.com
www.redlineresearch.com

RF Heat Sealed products such as medical components & devices, orthopedic bags and straps

President: Steve Leiserson
VP: Nancy Byrd
Catalog Circulation: Mailed 1 time(s) per year
In Business: 31 years
Number of Employees: 8
Sales Information: $ 1 Million

6404 Source
Wholesale Tape and Supply Co.,Inc
2841 Hickory Valley Road
Chattanooga, TN 37421   423-894-9427
                                  888-987-6334
                             Fax: 423-894-7281
customerservice@wtsmedia.com
www.wtsmedia.com

Blank audio cassettes, blank video tapes, blank CD's, audio and video duplication services and equipment, including duplicators, microphones, mixing boards, CD burners, and other presentation products

President: Michael Salley
Marketing Manager: Greg Giordano
Sales Manager: Marianne Mankin
Credit Cards: AMEX; MasterCard
Catalog Cost: Free
Catalog Circulation: Mailed 4 time(s) per year to 12000
Average Order Size: $150
Printing Information: 64 pages in 4 colors on Glossy Stock
Press: Web Press
Binding: Saddle Stitched
Mailing List Information: Names for rent
In Business: 40 years
Number of Employees: 40
Sales Information: $5MM to $10MM

6405 Speco Audio Products
Speco Technologies
200 New Highway
Amityville, NY 11701   631-957-9142
                                  800-645-5516
                             Fax: 631-957-3880
sales@specotech.com
www.specotech.com

Residential and commercial audio and video security products specializing in CCTV cameras, video monitors, in-wall speakers, PA amplifiers and megaphones

President: Todd Keller
Marketing Manager: Peter Botelho
Catalog Cost: Free
Mailing List Information: Names for rent
In Business: 50 years
Number of Employees: 40
Sales Information: $8.5 Million

6406 Tiger Direct
Tiger Direct, Inc.
7795 W Flagler St.
Suite 35
Miami, FL 33144-2367   305-415-2201
                                 800-800-8300
                            Fax: 305-415-2202
www.tigerdirect.com

Audio electronics, blank media tapes, books, software, computer accessories and supplies

VP: Charles Steinberg
Sales Manager: Jeff Green
Credit Cards: AMEX; MasterCard; Visa
Catalog Cost: Free
In Business: 20 years
Number of Employees: 60
Sales Information: $ 6 Million

6407 Valiant IMC
Valiant National AV Supply
80 Little Falls Road
Fairfield, NJ 07004-1709   201-229-9800
                                 800-825-4268
                            Fax: 800-453-6338
sales@valiantnational.com
www.valiantaudiovisual.com

Audio-visual products and supplies at wholesale prices; video equipment, computer equipment and supplies

Chairman: Martin Siegel
President: Sheldon Goldstein
Managing Director: Scott Schaefer
Credit Cards: AMEX; MasterCard; Visa
Catalog Cost: Free
Catalog Circulation: Mailed 1 time(s) per year to 200M
Printing Information: 212 pages in 4 colors on Glossy Stock
Binding: Perfect Bound
Mailing List Information: Names for rent
In Business: 20 years
Number of Employees: 100
Sales Information: $ 13 Million

6408 Video Source
Aesthetic Video source
PO Box 188
West Jordan, UT 84084-188   801-282-2490
                                 800-414-2434
                            Fax: 801-282-9187
info@videoshelf.com
www.videoshelf.com

Industrial video equipment

President: Anil K Aggarwaz
Production Manager: Kurt Brochaussen
Catalog Cost: Free
Catalog Circulation: Mailed 3 time(s) per year
Printing Information: in 2 colors on Matte Stock
In Business: 6 years
Number of Employees: 20

6409 Vinten
Camera Dynamics, Inc.
709 Executive Blvd
Valley Cottage, NY 10989-2024   845-268-2113
                           Fax: 845-268-9324
www.vinten.com

Television camera support equipment, including studio pedestals, pan/tilt heads, tripod systems and more

President: Eric Falkenberg
CFO: Nick Piscitelli
Marketing Manager: Stephen Savitt
Production Manager: Kenneth Schwartz
CEO: Jansen Joop
International Marketing Manager: Nick Kent
Catalog Cost: Free
Catalog Circulation: Mailed 52 time(s) per year to 5M
Average Order Size: $2500
Printing Information: 26 pages in 4 colors on

Glossy Stock
Press: Letterpress
Binding: Saddle Stitched
Mailing List Information: Names for rent
List Manager: Joanne Snider
In Business: 102 years
Number of Employees: 60
Sales Information: $40 Million

6410 Wholesale Tape & Supply
Wholesale Tape & Supply
2841 Hickory Valley Rd
Chattanooga, TN 37421   423-894-9427
                              888-987-6334
                         Fax: 423-894-7281
                         www.Wtsmedia.Com

**Audio/visual supplies, recording and dupli-
cation equipment**

President: Michael Salley
Marketing Manager: Greg Callaham
Credit Cards: AMEX; MasterCard
Catalog Cost: Free
Printing Information: 50 pages in 4 colors on
Glossy Stock
Press: Web Press
Binding: Saddle Stitched
In Business: 38 years
Sales Information: $5MM to $10MM

6411 Woodhaven
Woodhaven Inc
501 W 1st Ave
Durant, IA 52747-9729   563-785-0107
                              800-344-6657
                         Fax: 563-785-6813
                         info@woodhaven.com
                         www.woodhaven.com

Woodworking tools and accessories

President: Brad Witt
Credit Cards: MasterCard
Catalog Cost: Free
Printing Information: in 4 colors
Binding: Perfect Bound
In Business: 52 years
Number of Employees: 50
Sales Information: $1MM to $3MM

Automotive
Accessories

6412 Advanced Graphics
Advanced Graphics Inc.
342 Williams Point Blvd
Cocoa, FL 32927-4828   321-632-0115
                              800-927-8247
              sales@advancedgraphicsinc.com
                 www.Advancedgraphicsinc.Com

**Airbrushed license plates & frames, signs,
magnets, stickers and clothing**

President: Rick Dean
Credit Cards: AMEX; MasterCard; Visa
In Business: 37 years
Number of Employees: 25
Sales Information: $5,000,000 - $10,000,000

6413 American Autowire
American Autowire, Inc.
150 Heller Pl #17W
Suite 17
Bellmawr, NJ 08031-2503   856-933-0805
                                 800-482-9473
                            Fax: 856-933-0805
                         www.americanautowire.com

**Wiring harnesses, accessories and parts for
GM restoration, modified original and custom street rods**

President: Michael Nanning
Marketing Manager: Dave McKelvey
Chief Operating Officer: Jim Cardona
Vice President: Frank Colonna
Vice President, I.T.: Jeff Moore
Credit Cards: AMEX; MasterCard

Catalog Cost: Free
In Business: 32 years
Sales Information: $1MM to $3MM

6414 Andy's Autosport
Andy's Auto Sport
15005 Concord Circle
Morgan Hill, CA 95037   800-419-1152
                         Fax: 408-762-4478
                      info@andysautosport.com
                      www.andysautosport.com

**Racing seats, exhaust systems, headlight,
body kits, exhaust systems and mufflers**

General Manager: Andy Ferguson
Credit Cards: AMEX; MasterCard
Catalog Cost: Free
Number of Employees: 100
Sales Information: $10 Million

6415 Auto Custom Carpets
Auto Custom Carpets, Inc
1429 Noble Street
P.O. Box 1350
Anniston, AL 36202-1350   800-352-8216
                            Fax: 256-236-7375
                            www.Accmats.Com

**Original replacement carpets for cars and
trucks from the 1940's to current models**

President: Ken Howell
Production Manager: Tim Gaskin
Credit Cards: AMEX; MasterCard; Visa
Catalog Circulation: Mailed 1 time(s) per year
to 10M
Printing Information: 50 pages in 4 colors on
Glossy Stock
Binding: Saddle Stitched
In Business: 38 years
Number of Employees: 180
Sales Information: $10 million

6416 Baudville
Baudville
5380 52nd St SE
Grand Rapids, MI 49512   616-698-0889
                                800-728-0888
                           Fax: 616-698-0554
                         service@baudville.com
                         www.baudville.Com

**Trophies, recognition items, lapel pins,
event paper, seals & embosers, certificate
papers, ID accessories, folders & frames and
more**

President: David Pezzato
Marketing Manager: Jack Fisher
VP: Kristy Sherlund
Credit Cards: AMEX; MasterCard
Catalog Cost: Free
Printing Information: 80 pages in 4 colors on
Matte Stock
Binding: Perfect Bound
In Business: 30 years
Number of Employees: 85
Sales Information: 9.5M

6417 Cable Organizer Office and Home
CableOrganizer.Com, Inc.
6250 NW 27th Way
Fort Lauderdale, FL 33309   954-861-2000
                                   866-222-0030
                              Fax: 954-861-2001
                         sales@cableorganizer.com
                         www.cableorganizer.com

**Cable covers, wire looms, cable tags and fire
protection for auto and marine wiring**

President: Valerie Holstein
Marketing Manager: Juan Ribero
Credit Cards: AMEX; MasterCard
Catalog Cost: Free
In Business: 13 years

6418 California Car Cover
California Car Cover
9525 DeSoto Avenue
Chatsworth, CA 91311   818-998-2100
                              800-423-5525
                         Fax: 818-998-2442
                         info@calcarcover.com
                         www.calcarcover.com

**Custom car & truck covers, accessories,
canopies, apparel, performance enhancement parts, motorcycle accessories, cleaning products and garage items/tools**

President: Jim DeFrank
Credit Cards: AMEX; MasterCard; Visa
Catalog Cost: Free

6419 Cambria Bicycle Outfitter
CBO, Inc
1422 Monterey Street
San Luis Obispo, CA 93401-3020 805-543-1148
                                888-937-4331
                           Fax: 805-927-5174
                         info@cambriabike.com
                         www.cambriabike.com

**Road and Mountain bikes, parts and acces-
sories**

President: Steve Fleury
Credit Cards: MasterCard
Catalog Cost: Free
Catalog Circulation: Mailed 12 time(s) per
year
Printing Information: on Glossy Stock
Mailing List Information: Names for rent
In Business: 27 years
Sales Information: $500M to $1MM

6420 Cerwin-Vega!
Cerwin-Vega! Inc
772 S Military Trail
Deerfield Beach, FL 33442   954-949-9600
                                   800-444-2766
                              Fax: 954-949-9590
                              www.cerwinvega.com

Home and professional speakers

President: Mike Quandt
CFO: Tim Dorwart
Credit Cards: AMEX; MasterCard
In Business: 52 years
Number of Employees: 246

6421 Comfort Products
Comfort Products inc.
122 Gayoso Avenue
Memphis, TN 38104   800-971-4630
                      Fax: 901-248-7196
              marketing@comfortproducts.net
                 www.comfortproducts.net

**Seat cushion and mats, including Kool
Kushion, Slumber Zone, Comfort Fit**

President: Gary Land
In Business: 96 years
Number of Employees: 120

6422 Creative Consumers Products
Creative Consumers Products
5630 Lassiter Rd
Las Cruces, NM 88001-7806   575-527-0018
                              Fax: 575-527-0227
                              www.musictote.com

Auto accessories and parts

President: James Carter
Marketing Manager: Mary Carter
Credit Cards: AMEX; MasterCard; Visa
Catalog Cost: Free
In Business: 5 years
Number of Employees: 4
Sales Information: Under $500M

6423 Custom Accessories
Custom Accessories
5900 Ami Drive
Richmond, IL 60071   815-678-1600
                              weborders@causa.com
                              www.causa.com

Auto accessories, car and wheel covers, mirrors, license frames

Catalog Cost: Free
Catalog Circulation: Mailed 1 time(s) per year
Printing Information: 124 pages in 4 colors
In Business: 43 years
Number of Employees: 100
Sales Information: $1,000,000 - $5,000,000

6424 Davis Instruments Corp.
Davis
3465 Diablo Ave
Hayward, CA 94545-2746   510-732-9229
                              800-678-3669
                         Fax: 510-670-0589
                              sales@davisnet.com
                              www.davisnet.com

A vehicle monitor which tracks speed, acceleration, deceleration and distance for a comprehensive driving record

Chairman: James Acquistapace
President: Bob Selig
CFO: Susan Tatum
Marketing Manager: Susan Foxall
Production Manager: Winston Wyckoff
International Marketing Manager: Russ Heihg
Credit Cards: MasterCard; Visa
Catalog Cost: Free
Catalog Circulation: Mailed 1 time(s) per year to 150M
Average Order Size: $300
Printing Information: 16 pages in 4 colors on Glossy Stock
Press: Web Press
Binding: Saddle Stitched
In Business: 52 years
Number of Employees: 100
Sales Information: $10,000,000 - $25,000,000

6425 Dayton Wheel Products
Dayton Wire Wheels
115 Compark Rd
Dayton, OH 45459-4803   937-438-0100
                              888-559-2880
                         Fax: 937-438-1215
                              www.Daytonwheel.Com

Wire wheels for cars, trucks and motorcycles

President: Charlie Schroeder
Credit Cards: AMEX; MasterCard; Visa
Catalog Cost: $10
Printing Information: 24 pages
In Business: 99 years
Sales Information: $5MM to $10MM

6426 Delta Truck Storage Solutions
Delta Consolidated Industries
14600 York Rd.
Suite A
Sparks, MD 21152   800-643-0084
                         Fax: 877-356-4081
                              www.deltatruckstorage.com

Truck storage containers, tanks and chests.

Printing Information: 64 pages in 4 colors
Number of Employees: 300

6427 Fremont Die Consumer Products
Fremont Die Consumer Products
1709A Endeavor Dr
Williamsburg, VA 23195-6239   757-872-6438
                               800-336-8847
                          Fax: 757-872-6958
                               cs@fremontdie.com
                               www.Fremontdie.Com

Automotive signs and novelties, NFL auto accessories

President: James Hotze
Credit Cards: AMEX; MasterCard; Visa
Catalog Cost: Free
In Business: 32 years
Number of Employees: 15
Sales Information: $3MM to $5MM

6428 Haynes Publications
Haynes
861 Lawrence Drive
Newbury Park, CA 91320-978   805-498-6703
                               800-442-9637
                          Fax: 805-498-2867
                               www.Haynes.Com

Automotive repair manuals

Chairman: John Haynes
President: Eric Oakley
Production Manager: Bill Kilduff
In Business: 53 years
Number of Employees: 37
Sales Information: $5,000,000 - $10,000,000

6429 Hecht Rubber Corporation
Hecht Rubber Corporation
6161 Philips Highway
Jacksonville, FL 32216   904-731-3401
                               800-872-3401
                          Fax: 888-340-3401
                               sales@hechtrubber.com
                               www.hechtrubber.com

Industrial rubber products for business, industry, government and safety

President: Larry Hecht
Credit Cards: MasterCard; Visa
Catalog Cost: Free
Catalog Circulation: Mailed 4 time(s) per year to 175K
Average Order Size: $150
Printing Information: 96 pages in 1 color on Newsprint
Press: Web Press
Mailing List Information: Names for rent
In Business: 73 years
Number of Employees: 33
Sales Information: $20MM to $50MM

6430 Hemming's Motor News
Hemming's
PO Box 100
Bennington, VT 05201   802-442-3101
                               800-227-4373
                          Fax: 802-447-9631
                               hmnmail@hemmings.com
                               www.hemmings.com

Automotive books, automobilia, calendars

Production Manager: Ed Heys
Manager: Perez Ehrich
Credit Cards: MasterCard; Visa
Catalog Cost: Free
Catalog Circulation: Mailed 2 time(s) per year to 400M
Printing Information: 12 pages in 4 colors on Matte Stock
Mailing List Information: Names for rent
List Manager: Marian Savage
In Business: 45 years
Number of Employees: 150
Sales Information: Under $500M

6431 Indiana Mills & Manufacturing
IMMI
18881 US 31 North
Westfield, IN 46074-9689   317-896-9531
                          Fax: 317-896-2142
                               info@imminet.com
                               www.imminet.com

Seat belts, slings, buckles and various car accessories

President: Tom Anthony
CFO: Kevin Boen
VP of Sales: James Johnson
Director of Program Management: Julia King
Chief Executive Officer: Larry Gray
Printing Information: 30 pages

In Business: 51 years
Number of Employees: 200
Sales Information: $10MM to $20MM

6432 JOBOX Premium Storage Solutions
Delta Consolidated Industries
14600 York Rd.
Suite A
Sparks, MD 21152   800-643-0084
                         Fax: 877-356-4081
                              www.deltatruckstorage.com

Truck storage containers, tanks and chests.

Printing Information: 56 pages in 4 colors
Number of Employees: 300

6433 MacNeil Automotive Products
MacNeil Automotive Products
841 Remington Blvd
Bolingbrook, IL 60440   630-769-1500
                              800-441-6287
                         Fax: 630-769-0300
                              sales@weathertech.com
                              www.weathertech.com

Automotive accessories including floor mats, cargo and floor liners, side window deflectors, and a variety of other functional automotive accessories

Credit Cards: AMEX; MasterCard
Catalog Cost: Free
Printing Information: 29 pages
Mailing List Information: Names for rent
In Business: 25 years

6434 Midland Radio Corporation
Midland
5900 Parretta Drive
Kansas City, MO 64120-2134   816-241-8500
                         Fax: 816-241-5713
                              mail@midlandradio.com
                              www.midlandradio.com

Consumer two-way communication products, including FRS and GMRS radios, CB radios, weather monitors, and accessories

President: Dan Devling
International Marketing Manager: Noe Tabaras
Credit Cards: AMEX; MasterCard
Catalog Cost: Free
Printing Information: 3 pages
Mailing List Information: Names for rent
In Business: 50 years
Number of Employees: 120
Sales Information: $20MM to $50MM

6435 Motorbooks
Quarto Knows
400 First Avenue North
Suite 400
Minneapolis, MN 55401   800-458-0454
                         Fax: 612-344-8691
                              customerservice@quartous.com
                              www.quartoknows.com

Automotive books, shop manuals and restoration books

Chairman: Tim Chadwick
President: Ken Fund
CFO: Michael Connole, FCA
Director, Quarto International Co-e: David Breuer
Group Director of Operations: Michael Clarke
Managing Director, Books & Gifts Di: Joe Craven
Credit Cards: AMEX; MasterCard; Visa
Catalog Circulation: Mailed 4 time(s) per year
Printing Information: 40 pages in 4 colors
In Business: 39 years
Number of Employees: 110

6436 Security Chain Company
Peerless Chain Company
PO Box 949
Clackamas, OR 97015-949   503-656-5400
Fax: 503-656-4836
custserv@peerlesschain.com
www.peerlesschain.com

Cable, tire and hardware chains, load straps, tow straps and other winter traction products

Catalog Circulation: Mailed 1 time(s) per year to 40M
Average Order Size: $2000
Printing Information: 48 pages in 2 colors on Glossy Stock
Press: Web Press
In Business: 98 years
Number of Employees: 120
Sales Information: $5,000,000 - $10,000,000

6437 Thunderbird Price and Accessory Catalog
Thunderbird Headquarters Inc
4020 Pike Lane
Concord, CA 94520-1227   925-825-9550
800-227-2174
Fax: 800-964-1957
parts@tbirdhq.com
www.tbirdhq.com

Ford licensed parts, including OEM and reproduction parts for classic Ford Thunderbirds

President: Don Johnson
Marketing Manager: Scott LeBean
Founder: Don Johnson
Founder: Sandy Johnson
Credit Cards: AMEX; MasterCard; Visa
Catalog Cost: Free
Average Order Size: $200
Printing Information: 99 pages in 1 color on Newsprint
Press: Web Press
Binding: Saddle Stitched
Mailing List Information: Names for rent
In Business: 36 years
Number of Employees: 23
Sales Information: $3MM to $5MM

6438 Yakima-Destination Hardware
Yakima Products, Inc.
15025 SW Koll Pkwy
Beaverton, OR 97006-6056   971-249-7500
888-925-4621
www.yakima.Com

Racks for cars

President: Jay Wilson
CFO: PJ Peacock, VP Finance
Marketing Manager: Dean Hart, VP Marketing
International Marketing Manager: Chris Chadwick, VP Sales
Printing Information: 40 pages in 4 colors on Matte Stock
Press: Sheetfed Press
Mailing List Information: Names for rent
In Business: 35 years
Number of Employees: 155
Sales Information: $20MM to $50MM

Car Care

6439 AMSOIL
AMSOIL
925 Tower Avenue
Superior, WI 54880-1582   715-399-8324
800-956-5695
Fax: 715-392-5225
www.amsoil.com

Manufactures premium synthetic lubricants for automotive, RV, marine, sport and heavy equipment applications for increased performance

President: Albert J. Amatuzio
CFO: Dean Alexander
EVP, Chief Operating Officer: Alan Amatuzio

Credit Cards: AMEX; MasterCard; Visa
Catalog Cost: Free
Catalog Circulation: to 1M
Average Order Size: $82
Printing Information: 48 pages on Glossy Stock
Press: Web Press
Binding: Saddle Stitched
Mailing List Information: Names for rent
In Business: 45 years
Number of Employees: 200
Sales Information: $35 Million

6440 Berkebile Oil Company
Berkebile Oil Company
PO Box 715
Somerset, PA 15501-715   814-443-1656
800-732-9235
Fax: 814-443-2873
info@berkebileoil.com
www.berkebileoil.com

2x2 antifreeze, power steering, brake fluids, degreasers, rust penetrant, and cleaners

President: Catherine Poorbaugh
In Business: 61 years
Number of Employees: 40
Sales Information: $10,000,000 - $25,000,000

6441 California Car Cover
California Car Cover
9525 DeSoto Avenue
Chatsworth, CA 91311   818-998-2100
800-423-5525
Fax: 818-998-2442
info@calcarcover.com
www.calcarcover.com

Custom car & truck covers, accessories, canopies, apparel, performance enhancement parts, motorcycle accessories, cleaning products and garage items/tools

President: Jim DeFrank
Credit Cards: AMEX; MasterCard; Visa
Catalog Cost: Free

6442 Car-Freshner Catalog
Car-Freshner Corporation
21205 Little Tree Drive
P.O. Box 719
Watertown, NY 13601-719   315-788-6250
800-545-5454
Fax: 315-788-7467
domestic@car-freshner.com
www.car-freshner.com

Air fresheners and car care products

President: Jody Lalone
CFO: Laura Tousant
Production Manager: Robert Swank
International Marketing Manager: Linda Frasher
Buyers: Dolly Bidwell
Catalog Circulation: Mailed 2 time(s) per year
Printing Information: 30 pages
Mailing List Information: Names for rent
Number of Employees: 130
Sales Information: $10MM to $20MM

6443 Castrol USA Catalog
BP Lubricants USA
P.O. Box 485
Lewiston, NY 14092-8427   973-633-2200
800-462-0835
Fax: 973-633-9867
Contactus@bp.com
www.Castrolusa.Com

Power steering and brake fluids, oils, transmission fluids

President: Stanley Mussington
Marketing Manager: Paul Giblett
Regional VP: Naveen Kshatriya
Regional Manage: Brian Gregory
Marketing Operations Manager: Lee Eng Han
In Business: 114 years
Number of Employees: 1200

6444 D&R Classic Automotive Camaro Catalog
D & R Classic Automotive
30 W 255 Calumet Avenue
Warrenville, IL 60555-1518   630-393-0009
888-226-2761
Fax: 630-393-1397
sales@drclassic.com
www.drclassic.com

Classic car parts for the following: Camaro, Firebird, Chevelle, Nova

President: Steve Drueck
Secretary: Dorothy Drueck
Credit Cards: MasterCard; Visa
Catalog Cost: $10
Catalog Circulation: Mailed 1 time(s) per year
Printing Information: 432 pages in 1 color on Matte Stock
Press: d
Mailing List Information: Names for rent
In Business: 28 years
Number of Employees: 12

6445 Header Parts
Headers By Ed, Inc
2710 - 16th Avenue South
Dept. WS-M
Minneapolis, MN 55407-1291   612-729-2802
Fax: 612-729-5638
info@headersbyed.com
www.headersbyed.com

V8 automotive and vertical exit exhaust headers, header kits, header parts for over 100 4, 6, V6, V8, V12, US made engines

President: Ed Henneman
Credit Cards: MasterCard
Catalog Cost: $4.5
Catalog Circulation: Mailed 3 time(s) per year to 5M
Average Order Size: $170
Printing Information: 32 pages in 1 color on Matte Stock
Press: Letterpress
Binding: Saddle Stitched
Mailing List Information: Names for rent
In Business: 52 years
Number of Employees: 3
Sales Information: $500,000 - $1,000,000

6446 ITW Automotive Products
ITW Consumer
10 Columbus Blvd
Hartford, CT 06106   561-845-2425
877-376-2839
Fax: 561-845-2504
info@itwconsumer.com
www.itwconsumer.com

Gasket sealants, chrome polish, rear view mirror adhesive

President: Walt Polcuyn
Credit Cards: AMEX; MasterCard; Visa
Catalog Cost: Free
Number of Employees: 200
Sales Information: $10,000,000 - $25,000,000

6447 Rightlook.com
Rightlook.com, Inc.
8525 Arjons Drive, Suite C
San Diego, CA 92126   858-271-4271
800-883-3446
Fax: 858-271-4303
www.rightlook.com

Offers the highest quality training, equipment, supplies, business consulting and marketing services for auto reconditioning and auto appearance

Catalog Cost: Free
In Business: 17 years

Cleaners, Compounds & Conditioners

6448 AVW Equipment Company
AVW Equipment Company, Inc.
105 S 9th Ave
Maywood, IL 60153-1340 708-343-7738
Fax: 708-343-9065
info@avwequipment.com
www.avwequipment.com

Car washing equipment
President: Milovan Vidakovich
Credit Cards: AMEX; MasterCard; Visa
Catalog Cost: Free
Printing Information: 40 pages
In Business: 27 years
Number of Employees: 15
Sales Information: $1,000,000 - $5,000,000

6449 Buffalo Industries
Buffalo Industries LLC
99 S Spokane Street
Seattle, WA 98134 206-682-9900
800-683-0052
Fax: 206-682-9907
office@buffaloindustries.com
www.buffaloindustries.com

Car wash towels, Chamois products, shop towels, sponges, detail towels, oil sorbents, spill kits & containment products
President: Mark Benezra
mark@buffaloindustries.com
Marketing Manager: Matt Benesch
International Marketing Manager: Larry Benezra
Catalog Cost: Free
Printing Information: 24 pages
In Business: 70 years
Number of Employees: 150
Sales Information: $10,000,000 - $25,000,000

6450 DQB Industries
DQB Industries
32165 Schoolcraft Rd
Livonia, MI 48150-1894 734-525-5660
800-722-3037
Fax: 734-525-0437
sales@dqb.com
www.Dqb.Com

Brushes for the automotive industry
President: Donald Weinbaum
Marketing Manager: John Avgoustis
Production Manager: Carl Lebamoff
In Business: 128 years
Number of Employees: 70
Sales Information: $10,000,000 - $25,000,000

6451 Nation/Ruskin
Nation/Ruskin, Inc.
206 Progress Drive
Montgomeryville, PA 18936 267-654-4000
800-523-2489
Fax: 267-654-4010
www.nationruskin.com

Buckets, car washing brushes, cloths, latex gloves, paint accessories, scouring pads, scrubbers, sponges, squeegees, towels
President: Raymond Adolf
In Business: 37 years
Number of Employees: 35
Sales Information: 5MM-10MM

6452 SM Arnold
S.M. Arnold Inc.
7901 Michigan Ave
St Louis, MO 63111-3594 314-544-4103
800-325-7865
Fax: 314-544-3159
info@smarnoldinc.com
www.Smarnoldinc.Com

Car brushes, cellulose and poly sponges, mitts, squeegees, polishing discs and bonnets
President: Joe Arnold
CFO: Gary Fox
Marketing Manager: Irv Speckmeyer
Production Manager: Sanford Arnold
Catalog Cost: Free
Catalog Circulation: Mailed 2 time(s) per year to 20M
Printing Information: 10 pages in 3 colors on Glossy Stock
Press: Web Press
Binding: Saddle Stitched
Mailing List Information: Names for rent
List Manager: Tracy Arnold
In Business: 87 years
Number of Employees: 60
Sales Information: $10,000,000

Lighting

6453 Pacer Performance
Pacer Performance
3901 Medford St
Los Angeles, CA 90063-1608 323-881-4311
800-423-2442
Fax: 323-263-3948
info@pacerperformance.com
www.pacerperformance.com

Truck lights and accessories
President: Bill Longo
Marketing Manager: Cathy Cripps
Printing Information: 20 pages
In Business: 50 years
Number of Employees: 4
Sales Information: $3MM to $5MM

6454 Philips Lighting Company
Philips Office solutions
501 Fulling Mill Road
Middletown, PA 8875-6800 732-667-4900
Fax: 732-563-3641
www.phillips.com

Headlamps and bulbs
Chairman: Edward Dolman
President: Michael McGinnis
Marketing Manager: James Gonedes
Credit Cards:
In Business: 219 years
Number of Employees: 500

Parts

6455 Acme
Acme Miami
1290 NW 74th St
Miami, FL 33147-6428 800-654-2154
Fax: 305-693-0045
bart@acmemiami.com
www.acmemiami.com

Fan blades, motor mounts and motor accessories
President: Chuck Levine
Marketing Manager: C Levine
Printing Information: 19 pages
Number of Employees: 11
Sales Information: $1,000,000

6456 American Autowire
American Autowire, Inc.
150 Heller Pl #17W
Suite 17
Bellmawr, NJ 08031-2503 856-933-0805
800-482-9473
Fax: 856-933-0805
www.americanautowire.com

Wiring harnesses, accessories and parts for GM restoration, modified original and custom street rods
President: Michael Nanning
Marketing Manager: Dave McKelvey

Chief Operating Officer: Jim Cardona
Vice President: Frank Colonna
Vice President, I.T.: Jeff Moore
Credit Cards: AMEX; MasterCard
Catalog Cost: Free
In Business: 32 years
Sales Information: $1MM to $3MM

6457 Ames Performance Engineering
Ames Performance Engineering
10 Pontiac Drive
P.O. Box 572
Spofford, NH 03462 800-421-2637
Fax: 603-363-7007
customer.service@amesperf.com
www.amesperformance.com

Pontiac parts and accessories
President: Don Emory
Buyers: Lee Selby
Credit Cards: AMEX; MasterCard; Visa
Catalog Cost: Free
Average Order Size: $175
Printing Information: 219 pages
Mailing List Information: Names for rent
In Business: 32 years
Number of Employees: 25
Sales Information: $5MM-$10MM

6458 Big Red Catalog
Taylor Wings, Inc.
3720 Omec Circle
Rancho Cordova, CA 95742-7303 916-851-9464
800-634-7757
Fax: 916-851-9466
terryt@taylorwings.com
www.taylorwings.com

Full range of wings with internal ram system available in all sizes
President: Terry Taylor
CFO: Terri Taylor
Marketing Manager: Linda Nieves
Production Manager: Chris Roberts
Fulfillment: Thomas Bridgham
Sales Contact: Terry Taylor
terryt@taylorwings.com
Production Contact: Chris Roberts
chrisr@taylorwings.com
Programming Contact: Scott Holden
srholden@taylorwings.com
Credit Cards: AMEX; MasterCard; Visa
Printing Information: 16 pages
In Business: 37 years

6459 Bill Hirsch Automotive
Bill Hirsch Auto
396 Littleton Avenue
Newark, NJ 07103 973-642-2404
800-828-2061
Fax: 973-642-6161
info@hirschauto.com
www.hirschauto.com

Antique, classic and exotic automotive restoration products
President: Bill Hirsch
Catalog Cost: Free
In Business: 40 years

6460 Bob's BMW
Bob's BMW
10720 Guilford Rd
Jessup, MD 20794-9385 301-497-8949
888-BMW-BOBS
Fax: 301-776-2338
www.bobsbmw.com

BMW motorcycle apparel, parts and accessories
President: Bob Henig
Marketing Manager: Hanna Creekmore
hanna.creekmore@bobsbmw.com
Owner: Suzanne Henig
Suzanne.henig@bobsbmw.com
Bookkeeper: Dana Tompkins
Custodian: Bucky Buchanan

Printing Information: 77 pages in 2 colors on Matte Stock
Press: Web Press
Binding: Saddle Stitched
Mailing List Information: Names for rent
In Business: 40 years
Number of Employees: 37
Sales Information: $8.91 MM

6461 Borgeson Universal Company
Borgeson Universal Company
91 Technology Park Drive
Torrington, CT 06790-3098   860-482-8283
Fax: 860-496-9320
sales@borgeson.com
www.borgeson.com

Steering universal joints and components for the automotive, military, and aerospace industries

President: Gerald Zordon
Catalog Cost: Free
In Business: 101 years

6462 Bradish Tractor Parts
George Bradish Tractor Parts
3865 State Route 982
Latrobe, PA 15650-3914   724-539-8386
Fax: 724-539-3808
info@georgebradishtractorparts.com
www.georgebradishtractorparts.com

Ford tractors and Dearborn implements parts

President: George Bradish
Credit Cards: MasterCard; Visa
In Business: 68 years

6463 Buick Parts Catalog
Bob's Automobilia
3352 S El Pomar
Templeton, CA 93465   805-434-2963
Fax: 805-434-2626
bob@bobsautomobilia.com
www.bobsautomobilia.com

New and used restoration parts for 1920-1958 era Buicks

President: Robert Carrubba Sr
CFO: Beverly Carrubba
Marketing Manager: Robert Carrubba Jr
Catalog Cost: $6
Catalog Circulation: to 3500
Average Order Size: $100
Printing Information: 112 pages on Matte Stock
Press: Letterpress
Binding: Perfect Bound
List Manager: Alvin Cable
In Business: 36 years
Number of Employees: 6
Sales Information: $1,000,000

6464 C & P 55-57 Chevy Passenger Cars
C & P Automotive
PO Box 348
Kulpsville, PA 19443   610-584-9105
800-235-2475
Fax: 610-584-9509
sales@cpchevy.com
www.cpchevy.com

Restoration supplies and customizing parts for 1955 thru 1957 Chevrolet passenger cars

Credit Cards: AMEX; MasterCard
Catalog Cost: $5
In Business: 25 years

6465 C & P 55-59 Chevrolet Trucks
C & P Automotive
PO Box 348
Kulpsville, PA 19443   610-584-9105
800-235-2475
Fax: 610-584-9509
sales@cpchevy.com
www.cpchevy.com

Restoration supplies and customizing parts for 1955 2nd series thru 1959 Chevrolet trucks

Credit Cards: AMEX; MasterCard
Catalog Cost: $3
In Business: 25 years

6466 Camaro Connection
Camaro Connection
250 Akron Street
Lindenhurst, NY 11757-3612   631-226-7982
Fax: 631-225-8824
shop@eastcoastrestorations.com
www.Camaroconnection.Com

Camaro parts, services and restorations

President: Tom Marcantonio
In Business: 28 years
Sales Information: $500M to $1MM

6467 Chicago Corvette Supply
Chicago Corvette Supply
7322 S Archer Road
Justice, IL 60458   800-872-2446
Fax: 708-458-2662
contact@chicagocorvette.net
www.chicagocorvette.net

Automotive parts and accessories for specific make and model corvettes as well as a large selection of carburetors for all cars

Credit Cards: MasterCard

6468 Classic Auto Air Manufacturing
Classic Auto Air Manufacturing
4901 Rio Vista Avenue
Tampa, FL 33634   813-251-2356
877-342-5526
Fax: 813-254-7419
sales@ClassicAutoAir.com
www.classicautoair.com

Air conditioning parts and systems for 1970's and older cars and trucks

President: Al Sedita
Catalog Cost: $5
Catalog Circulation: Mailed 2 time(s) per year
Printing Information: 56 pages in 1 color on Glossy Stock
Press: Sheetfed Press
Binding: Perfect Bound
Mailing List Information: Names for rent
In Business: 35 years
Number of Employees: 18
Sales Information: $1MM to $3MM

6469 Classic Parts of America
Classic Parts of America
1 Chevy Duty Drive
Riverside, MO 64150   816-741-8029
800-741-1678
Fax: 816-741-5255
customerservice@classicparts.com
www.classicparts.com

Parts and supplies for Chevy trucks

President: Mark S Jansen
Marketing Manager: Robert Mata
Credit Cards: AMEX; MasterCard
Catalog Cost: $3
Catalog Circulation: to 25M
Average Order Size: $150
Printing Information: 80 pages in 4 colors on Matte Stock
Press: Web Press
Binding: Saddle Stitched
Mailing List Information: Names for rent
In Business: 12 years
Number of Employees: 19
Sales Information: $3MM to $5MM

6470 Cliff's Classic Chevrolet
Cliff's Classic Chevrolet
619 S.E. 202nd Avenue
P.O. Box 1957
Portland, OR 97233   503-667-4329
Fax: 503-669-4268
clifchev@aol.com
www.cliffsclassicchevrolet.net

Quality used, new, and reproduction parts for your original, modified or hot rod, 1955-57 Chevrolet and 2nd series 55-59 truck parts

President: Cliff Waldron
Credit Cards: MasterCard
Catalog Cost: $5
In Business: 18 years
Sales Information: Under $500M

6471 Coast Distribution RV Catalog
The Coast Distribution System, Inc.
350 Woodview Ave
Suite 100
Morgan Hill, CA 95037-8105   408-782-6686
800-495-5858
Fax: 408-782-7790
customerservice@coastdist.com
www.coastdistribution.com

RV parts and accessories

Chairman: Thomas R. McGuire
President: James i Musbach
CFO: Sandra A. Knell
Executive VP - Operations: David A. Berger
Executive VP Manufacturing: Dennis A. Castagnola
Catalog Circulation: Mailed 1 time(s) per year
Printing Information: 220 pages
In Business: 52 years
Number of Employees: 300

6472 Corvette World
Corvette World
12491 Route 30
Irwin, PA 15642-1315   724-863-0410
800-327-0185
Fax: 724-863-5968
www.Corvettedept.Com

1953-2006 Covette restoration parts and accessories

President: Jared George
Credit Cards: AMEX; MasterCard
Catalog Cost: Free
Catalog Circulation: Mailed 1 time(s) per year to 10M
Average Order Size: $250
Printing Information: 120 pages in 2 colors on Glossy Stock
Press: Web Press
Binding: Saddle Stitched
Mailing List Information: Names for rent
In Business: 20 years
Number of Employees: 4
Sales Information: $500M to $1MM

6473 Dakotah Toys
Dakotah Toys
44718 SD HWY 34
Madison, SD 57042-6601   605-256-6676
Fax: 605-256-9093
daktoys@yahoo.com
www.dakotahtoyparts.com

Farm toy and pedal tractor parts

President: Roger Ayers
Catalog Cost: $3.5
In Business: 20 years
Number of Employees: 4
Sales Information: $400,000

6474 Danchuk Manufacturing

Danchuk Manufacturing
3201 South Standard Ave.
Santa Ana, CA 92705
714-751-1957
800-648-9554
Fax: 714-850-1957
custserv@danchuk.com
www.danchuk.com

Classic auto parts

President: Danny Danchuk
CFO: Steve Brown
Marketing Manager: Bill Roche
Production Manager: Sara Portillo
Credit Cards: AMEX; MasterCard
Catalog Cost: $5
Printing Information: 300 pages
In Business: 39 years
Number of Employees: 71
Sales Information: $11.10 Million

6475 Dennis Carpenter Ford Restoration

Dennis Carpenter
4140 Concord Parkway South
Concord, NC 28027
704-786-8139
800-476-9653
Fax: 704-786-8180
info@dennis-carpenter.com
www.dennis-carpenter.com

Ford restoration parts

President: Daniel Carpenter
Marketing Manager: Terry Rodenhuis
Owner: Dennis Carpenter
Credit Cards: AMEX; MasterCard

6476 Edelbrock Corporation

Edelbrock Corporation
2700 California Street
Torrance, CA 90503
310-781-2222
800-416-8628
Fax: 310-320-1187
www.edelbrock.com

A complete line of parts for Chevrolet, Ford, Pontiac, Oldsmobile and Harley-Davidson

Chairman: O Victor Edelbrock
President: O Victor Edelbrock
CFO: Norm Judd
Marketing Manager: Jason Snyder
Production Manager: Wayne P Murray
Director of Advertising: Eric Blakely
eblakely@edelbrock.com
Technical Sales Coordinator: Smitty Smith
smitty@edelbrock.com
Printing Information: 207 pages
In Business: 75 years

6477 Egge Machine Company

Egge Machine and Speed Shop
11707 Slauson Avenue
Santa Fe Springs, CA 90670-2217
562-945-3419
800-866-3443
Fax: 562-693-1635
info@egge.com
www.egge.com

Parts and services for nostalgic motors

President: Robert Egge
CFO: Ernie Silvers
Marketing Manager: Tony Colombini
Credit Cards: AMEX; MasterCard
Catalog Cost: Free
Printing Information: 190 pages
In Business: 100 years

6478 Ford Parts Specialists

JobLot Automotive, Inc.
98-11 211th Street
P.O. Box 75
Queens Village, NY 11429-1005
718-468-8585
Fax: 718-468-8686
www.joblotauto.com

Automotive parts and supplies covering 1928-1970 Ford cars, and 1928-1970 Ford trucks

President: Robert Schaeffer
CFO: Harold Brensilber
Credit Cards: MasterCard
Catalog Cost: $2
Catalog Circulation: Mailed 1 time(s) per year to 60M
Printing Information: 120 pages on Newsprint
Press: Web Press
In Business: 50 years

6479 Goodmark Retail Catalog

Goodmark
625 E. Old Norcross Road
Lawrenceville, GA 30045
770-339-8557
877-477-3577
Fax: 770-339-7562
www.goodmarkindustries.com

Restoration parts and accessories for classic cars and trucks

President: Anthony Frank
Credit Cards: AMEX; MasterCard
Catalog Cost: $5
In Business: 23 years
Sales Information: $3MM to $5MM

6480 Joblot Automotive

JobLot Automotive, Inc.
98-11 211th Street
P.O. Box 75
Queens Village, NY 11429
718-468-8585
Fax: 718-468-8686
www.joblotauto.com

Automotive parts and supplies

President: Robert Schaefer
CFO: Harold Brensilber
Catalog Cost: $2
Catalog Circulation: Mailed 1 time(s) per year to 60M
Printing Information: 120 pages on Newsprint
Press: Web Press
In Business: 52 years
Sales Information: $5MM to $10MM

6481 King Motorsports

King Motorsports Unlimited, Inc.
2130 South Danny Road
New Berlin, WI 53146-1601
262-522-7558
Fax: 262-522-7559
info@kingmotorsports.com
www.Kingmotorsports.Com

Automotive parts and accessories for specific makes and models, specializes in Acura parts and accessories

President: Scott Zellner
CEO: Scott Zellner
Founder: Jim Dentici
In Business: 34 years
Sales Information: $1MM to $3MM

6482 Korman Autoworks

Korman Autoworks
2629 Randleman Rd
Greensboro, NC 27406-5107
336-275-1494
Fax: 336-274-8003
service@kormanautoworks.com
www.Kormanautoworks.Com

High performance BMW auto parts

President: Ray Korman
Credit Cards: AMEX; MasterCard; Visa
Catalog Cost: Free
Average Order Size: $500
Printing Information: 15 pages
Mailing List Information: Names for rent
In Business: 37 years
Number of Employees: 10
Sales Information: $1MM to $3MM

6483 LMC Truck

LMC Truck
15450 W. 108th Street
Lenexa, KS 66219
913-541-0684
800-562-8782
Fax: 800-541-8525
customercare@longmotor.net
www.lmctruck.com

Chevy, Ford, GMC truck parts and accessories

President: Becky Hanrahan
Credit Cards: AMEX; MasterCard; Visa
Catalog Cost: Free
Printing Information: 124 pages
Number of Employees: 100
Sales Information: $50MM to $100MM

6484 Lokar Performance Products

Lokar Performance Products
2545 Quality Lane
Knoxville, TN 37931
865-824-9767
877-469-7440
Fax: 865-824-9761
tech@lokar.com
www.lokar.com

Automotive and truck performance parts

President: Van Walls
CFO: Deborah Walls
COO: Amanda Leblanc
Manager: Lawanda McClure
Credit Cards: MasterCard; Visa
Catalog Cost: Free
Printing Information: 84 pages
In Business: 22 years
Number of Employees: 40
Sales Information: $5.9 Million

6485 Long Island Corvette Supply

Long Island Corvette Supply
1445 S Strong Ave
Copiague, NY 11726-3227
631-225-3000
800-466-6367
Fax: 631-225-5030
www.licorvette.com

Automotive parts and accessories, offering parts for specific makes and models, specializing in 1963 to 1967 Corvette parts

Credit Cards: AMEX; MasterCard; Visa
Catalog Cost: $3
Printing Information: 87 pages in 1 color
Mailing List Information: Names for rent
In Business: 14 years
Number of Employees: 6
Sales Information: $1MM to $3MM

6486 Luttys Chevys - Warehouse Catalog

Luttys Chevys
2385 Saxonburg Blvd
Cheswick, PA 15024
724-265-2988
Fax: 724-265-4773
sales@luttyschevy.com
www.luttyschevy.com

1955 to 1957 Chevelle Monte Carlo, Camaro, Nova, Impala and 1947-1972 Chevy truck restoration parts and accessories

President: Darlene Lutty
International Marketing Manager: Chad Bevan
Buyers: Greg Jones
Credit Cards: AMEX; MasterCard; Visa
Catalog Cost: Free
Catalog Circulation: Mailed 1 time(s) per year to 30000
Mailing List Information: Names for rent
In Business: 33 years
Number of Employees: 12
Sales Information: $5MM to $10MM

6487 Mid America Motorworks Air-Cooled VW
Mid America Motorworks
17082 N US Highway 45
PO Box 1368
Effingham, IL 62401-6764   217-540-4200
                                 866-350-4543
                            Fax: 217-540-4425
                      mail@mamotorworks.com
                       www.mamotorworks.com

Parts and accessories for 1950-1979 air-cooled Volkswagons
President: Mike Yager
Mike.Yager@mamotorworks.com
Marketing Manager: Henk van Dongen
Production Manager: Scott Bohannon
Scott.Bohannon@mamotorworks.com
Fulfillment: Tim Curtis
Director of Information Technologie: Shannon Klein
shannon.klein@mamotorworks.com
Corporate Director: Laurie Yager
laurie.yager@mamotorworks.com
President Performance Choice: Steve Olson
Steve.Olson@performancechoice.com
Catalog Circulation: Mailed 8 time(s) per year
Average Order Size: $125
In Business: 41 years
Number of Employees: 150
Sales Information: $5MM to $10MM

6488 Motorsport Auto
Motorsport Auto
1139 W Collins Avenue
Orange, CA 92867   714-639-2620
                          800-633-6331
                     Fax: 714-639-7460
                 info@motorsportauto.com
                     www.zcarparts.com

Datsun Z/ZX and Nissan Z/ZX parts
President: Ken Smith
Marketing Manager: Joseph Carrubba
Administration: Sandra Smith
Sales Manager: Abraham DeGalicia
Marketing/Customer Service: Garrett Fleig
Credit Cards: AMEX; MasterCard
Catalog Cost: Free
Mailing List Information: Names for rent
In Business: 36 years

6489 National Parts Depot
National Parts Depot
900 SW 38th Avenue
Ocala, FL 34474   352-861-8700
                          800-874-7595
                     Fax: 352-861-8706
                        www.npdlink.com

Car parts: Mustang, T-Bird, Ford Bronco and trucks, Camaro, Chevelle, Malibu, El Camino, Firebird, Trans-AM
President: James A Schmidt
Printing Information: in 4 colors
In Business: 39 years

6490 Northern Hydraulics
Northern Tool & Equipment
2800 Southcross Drive West
Burnsville, MN 55306   952-894-9510
                              800-221-0516
                         Fax: 954-894-1020
            intlenglishsales@northerntool.com
                         www.northerntool.com

Hydraulic parts
President: Donald L. Kotula
Founder, CEO: Donald L. Kotula
In Business: 32 years

6491 Perry Company
The Perry Company
500 South Valley Mills Dr
PO Box 7187
Waco, TX 76711-7187   254-756-2139
                              800-792-3246
                         Fax: 254-756-2166
                          info@perry-co.com
                           www.perry-co.com

Tractor canopies
President: Jeff Weaver
Catalog Circulation: Mailed 1 time(s) per year
In Business: 69 years
Number of Employees: 47
Sales Information: $5,000,000 - $10,000,000

6492 Pirelli Armstrong Tire Corporation
Pirelli Tire NA LLC
100 Pirelli Drive Rome
Rome, GA 30161-7000   706-368-5800
                              800-747-3554
                         Fax: 706-368-5832
                          www.us.pirelli.com

Farm tires
President: Hugh D Pace
Catalog Circulation: Mailed 1 time(s) per year
Number of Employees: 500

6493 Raybuck Autobody Parts
Raybuck Autobody Parts, LLC
1723 W. North Ave
Pittsburgh, PA 15233   814-938-5248
                               800-334-0230
                          Fax: 814-938-4250
                        service@raybuck.com
                           www.raybuck.com

Aftermarket autobody parts and accessories for pickups, vans, SUVs and Jeeps
President: Lisa Raybuck
Marketing Manager: Randy Raybuck
Credit Cards: MasterCard
Catalog Cost: $3
Catalog Circulation: Mailed 12 time(s) per year to 25M
Printing Information: 50 pages in 1 color on Matte Stock
Press: Web Press
Binding: Saddle Stitched
Mailing List Information: Names for rent
In Business: 29 years
Number of Employees: 6
Sales Information: $1MM to $3MM

6494 Repco
Repco Inc.
6 Eves Drive
Marlton, NJ 08053   856-762-0172
                            800-822-9190
                       Fax: 800-424-9224
                      sales@repcoinc.com
                         www.repcoinc.com

A variety of automotive parts, supplies and accessories
President: John Lowlor
Credit Cards: AMEX; MasterCard; Visa
Catalog Cost: Free
Catalog Circulation: Mailed 2 time(s) per year
Printing Information: 25 pages in 2 colors on Newsprint
Press: Web Press
Binding: Saddle Stitched
In Business: 39 years
Number of Employees: 30
Sales Information: $3MM to $5MM

6495 Ron Francis Wiring
Wire Works
200 Keystone Road
Suite #1
Chester, PA 19013-1430   610-485-1981
                                 800-292-1940
                            www.ronfrancis.com

Wiring harnesses, fuel injection harnesses, wiring aids, grounding lighting and accessories for race cars
Chairman: Ronald Francis
President: Scott Bowers
Marketing Manager: Connie Francis
Production Manager: Gary DuRoss
Catalog Cost: $2
Catalog Circulation: Mailed 1 time(s) per year
Printing Information: 60 pages
In Business: 34 years
Number of Employees: 12
Sales Information: $1,000,000 - $5,000,000

6496 SLP Performance Parts
SLP Performance Parts
39555 Schoolcraft Rd
Plymouth Township, MI 48170   732-349-2109
                                      855-757-7373
                                 Fax: 732-244-0867
                                   www.slponline.com

Automotive supplies and parts
President: Edward Hamburger
Catalog Cost: $3
Printing Information: 52 pages in 4 colors on G
Mailing List Information: Names for rent
In Business: 28 years
Number of Employees: 75
Sales Information: $10MM-$20MM

6497 Sherman & Associates
Sherman & Associates, Inc.
61166 Van Dyke Road
Washington, MI 48094   586-677-6800
                               800-345-9487
                          Fax: 586-677-6801
                     info57@shermanparts.com
                        www.shermanparts.com

Automotive body parts, panel and accessories from 1949 to 2010 models for vintage, domestic and import cars and trucks
Credit Cards: AMEX; MasterCard
Catalog Cost: $12
In Business: 28 years

6498 Shorty's Tooling & Equipment
Shorty's Tooling & Equipment, Inc.
7531 Holland Road
Taylor, MI 48180   313-291-5200
                           800-443-6666
                      Fax: 313-291-4524

New and surplus tooling, attachments and replacement parts for American made automatic screw machines
President: Carl Sherman
Credit Cards: MasterCard
Catalog Cost: $15
Catalog Circulation: Mailed 1 time(s) per year
Printing Information: 66 pages
Binding: Saddle Stitched
In Business: 46 years

6499 Sinclair's
Sinclair's Impala Parts
508 Charming Road
Danville, VA 24541   434-685-2337
                       Fax: 434-685-3346
                     Info@impala-parts.com
                        www.impala-parts.com

Impala parts and accessories
Credit Cards: MasterCard
Catalog Cost: Free
Printing Information: 64 pages in 6 colors on Newsprint
Binding: Saddle Stitched
In Business: 20 years

6500 Springfield Rod & Custom
Springfield Rod & Custom
219 Buxton Ave
Springfield, OH 45505-1339   937-323-1932
                                  800-752-9763
                            Fax: 937-323-1973
                            fredyerkey@att.net

Vintage auto parts and accessories
President: Larry Chaney
Sales Information: Under $500M

6501 Steiner Tractor Parts
Steiner Tractor Parts
1660 S M-13
Lennon, MI 48449   810-621-3000
                               800-234-3280
                         Fax: 800-854-1373
                         sales@steinertractor.com
                         www.steinertractor.com

New replacement tractor parts: fenders, steering wheels, grills, emblems, maniforlds, battery boxes, magnetos
President: Daniel Steiner
VP: Jeniffer Steiner
Catalog Cost: $5
Printing Information: 482 pages
In Business: 38 years
Number of Employees: 28

6502 Stock Drive Products
Stock Drive Products / Sterling Instuume
2101 Jericho Turnpike
Box 5416
New Hyde Park, NY 11040-5416 516-328-3300
                              800-819-8900
                        Fax: 516-326-8827
                        sdp-sisupport@sdp-si.com
                        www.sdp-si.com

Engine and machine parts; small mechanical components
Marketing Manager: Herb Arum
Catalog Cost: Free
Catalog Circulation: Mailed 1 time(s) per year to 50m
Printing Information: 1200 pages in 2 colors on Glossy Stock
Press: Web Press
Binding: Perfect Bound
Mailing List Information: Names for rent
In Business: 50 years
Number of Employees: 350
Sales Information: $5,000,000 - $10,000,000

6503 Thunderbird Price and Accessory Catalog
Thunderbird Headquarters Inc
4020 Pike Lane
Concord, CA 94520-1227   925-825-9550
                               800-227-2174
                         Fax: 800-964-1957
                         parts@tbirdhq.com
                         www.tbirdhq.com

Ford licensed parts, including OEM and re-production parts for classic Ford Thunderbirds
President: Don Johnson
Marketing Manager: Scott LeBean
Founder: Don Johnson
Founder: Sandy Johnson
Credit Cards: AMEX; MasterCard; Visa
Catalog Cost: Free
Average Order Size: $200
Printing Information: 99 pages in 1 color on Newsprint
Press: Web Press
Binding: Saddle Stitched
Mailing List Information: Names for rent
In Business: 36 years
Number of Employees: 23
Sales Information: $3MM to $5MM

6504 Tomco
Tomco, Inc.
7208A Weil Avenue
St Louis, MO 63119   314-646-5300
                               800-325-9972
                         www.tomco-inc.com

Fuel and emission control parts
Catalog Cost: Free
Catalog Circulation: Mailed 1 time(s) per year to 20M
Printing Information: 46 pages in 1 color
In Business: 45 years
Number of Employees: 70
Sales Information: $10,000,000 - $25,000,000

6505 Torque Tech
Torque Tech & Co., Inc.
2632 Marine Way
Mountain View, CA 94043   888-465-1454
                         Fax: 229-242-5353
                         www.torquetechexh.com

Header and manifold applications, performance exhaust systems
Credit Cards: MasterCard; Visa
In Business: 27 years

6506 True Choice
Truechoice Motorsports
352 W Olentangy St
Powell, OH 43065   614-799-9530
                               800-388-8783
                         Fax: 614-799-9532
                         info@truechoice.com
                         www.truechoice.com

Parts and accessories for auto racing
Credit Cards: AMEX; MasterCard; Visa
Catalog Cost: Free
Printing Information: 140 pages
In Business: 10 years
Number of Employees: 20

6507 Tuff Country E-Z Ride Suspension
Tuff Country, Inc
4172 West 8370 South
West Jordan, UT 84088-5905   801-280-2777
                               800-288-2190
                         Fax: 801-280-2896
                         customerservice@tuffcountry.com
                         www.Tuffcountry.Com

Auto suspension lift kits, leveling kits, axle pivot brackets, leaf springs, shock absorbers, sharing and pitman arms
President: Troy Davis
Catalog Cost: $3
In Business: 27 years
Number of Employees: 18
Sales Information: $10MM to $20MM

6508 Two Brothers Racing
Two Brothers Racing
401 South Grand Ave.
Santa Ana, CA 92705-4102   714-550-6070
                               800-211-2767
                         Fax: 714-550-9661
                         www.twobros.com

Full line of TBR exhaust systems, custom accessories, performance clothing and parts, Ferodo pads and rotors, Goodridge brake lines, D.I.D. chain
Chairman: Jeff Whitten
President: Craig Erion
Credit Cards: AMEX; MasterCard; Visa
Catalog Cost: Free
Printing Information: 215 pages
In Business: 29 years
Number of Employees: 5
Sales Information: 5MM-10MM

6509 VDO Automotive Instruments
United Speedometer Service
2179 Macbeth Place
PO Box 51957
Riverside, CA 92507-1314   951-742-7117
                               800-877-4798
                         Fax: 951-742-7113
                         info@speedometershop.com
                         www.speedometershop.com

Speedometers, temperature gauges, clocks, tachometers, etc., for automobiles
President: Richard Workman
Printing Information: 44 pages
Binding: Saddle Stitched
In Business: 49 years
Number of Employees: 20-5

6510 Vintage Model Catalog
IPD
11744 NE Ainsworth Circle
Portland, OR 97220   503-257-7500
                               800-444-6473
                         Fax: 503-257-7596
                         info@ipdusa.com
                         www.ipdusa.Com

Aftermarket Volvo and Subaru accessories
President: Scott Hart
scott@ipdusa.com
CFO: David Precechtil
david@ipdusa.com
Marketing Manager: Bryan Cotrell
bryan@ipdusa.com
Production Manager: Cameron Daline
cdaline@ipdusa.com
CEO: Sue Hart
Sue@ipdusa.com
General Manager: Chris Delano
chris@ipdusa.com
Purchasing Manager: Michael Bernardi
mbernardi@ipdusa.com
Credit Cards: AMEX; MasterCard; Visa
Catalog Cost: Free
Catalog Circulation: Mailed 4 time(s) per year
Average Order Size: $130
Printing Information: 84 pages in 4 colors on Glossy Stock
Press: Sheetfed Press
Binding: Saddle Stitched
Mailing List Information: Names for rent
In Business: 52 years
Number of Employees: 20-5
Sales Information: $5,000,000 - $10,000,000

6511 Vintage Tire Hotline
Coker Tire Company
1317 Chestnut Street
Chattanooga, TN 37402   423-265-6368
                               866-516-3215
                         www.cokertire.com

Supplier of vintage and classic tires and wheels to the collector car hobbylist
Founder: Harold Coker
Credit Cards: AMEX; MasterCard; Visa
Catalog Cost: Free
Printing Information: 63 pages
In Business: 57 years

6512 Warner Electric
Warner Electric
449 Gardner Street
South Beloit, IL 61080-1326   815-825-6544
                               800-825-6544
                         Fax: 815-389-2582
                         info@warnerelectric.com
                         www.warnerelectric.com

Electric brakes, clutches and various auto parts
President: Carl Christenson
Production Manager: Shelley Smith
In Business: 70 years
Number of Employees: 800

6513 Willys & Jeep Parts Catalog
The Jeepsterman, Inc.
238 Ramtown Greenville Rd
Howell, NJ 07731-2788   732-458-3966
Fax: 732-458-9289
JeepstermanInc@AOL.com
www.thejeepsterman.com

Willys and Jeep parts 1942 to present - all hard to find parts, manuals, rubber parts, exhaust systems, sheet metal tops, side curtains, rugs, mats, etc

President: Morris Ratner
Marketing Manager: Shelley Ramhurst
Catalog Cost: Free
Catalog Circulation: Mailed 1 time(s) per year to 2000
Mailing List Information: Names for rent
In Business: 30 years
Number of Employees: 10-J
Sales Information: Under $500M

Supplies & Equipment

6514 Adcole Corporation
ADCOLE
669 Forest Street
Marlborough, MA 01752-3067   508-485-9100
Fax: 508-481-6142
info@adcole.com
www.adcole.com

Electro-optical instrumentation used in crankshafts, camshafts and pistons

President: Michael Foley, PhD
CFO: Doug Vandenberg
Marketing Manager: Daniel P. Harkins
VP, Software Development: William Smith
Vice President of Engineering: Stephen Corrado
Vice President of Aerospace: Tom MacDonald
In Business: 58 years
Number of Employees: 165
Sales Information: $10,000,000

6515 Air-Drive
Air Drive, Inc.
4070 Ryan Rd
Gurnee, IL 60031-1253   847-625-0226
Fax: 847-625-7422
sales@airdrive.com
www.airdrive.com

Aluminum and steel fan blades

President: James H. Gilford
Printing Information: 40 pages in 4 colors
In Business: 53 years
Number of Employees: 20
Sales Information: $5 million

6516 Alemite LLC
Alemite LLC
4010 Goodfellow Blvd
St. Louis, MO 63120   800-822-4579
Fax: 800-648-3917
yves.nys@skf.com
www.alemite.com

Industrial and automotive lubricating systems

President: Bart Aiken
Marketing Manager: Timothy Long
Production Manager: Americo Dos Santos
VP, Sales & Marketing: Paul Anderson
In Business: 97 years
Number of Employees: 35
Sales Information: $10,000,000

6517 American Van Equipment
American Van Equipment, Inc.
149 Lehigh Avenue
Lakewood, NJ 08701   800-526-4743
Fax: 800-833-8266
salesservice@amvanequip.com
www.americanvan.com

Van and truck equipment

President: Charles Richter
CFO: Joseph Fallon
Credit Cards: AMEX; MasterCard
Catalog Cost: Free
In Business: 36 years
Sales Information: $10MM to $20MM

6518 Andy's Autosport
Andy's Auto Sport
15005 Concord Circle
Morgan Hill, CA 95037   800-419-1152
Fax: 408-762-4478
info@andysautosport.com
www.andysautosport.com

Racing seats, exhaust systems, headlight, body kits, exhaust systems and mufflers

General Manager: Andy Ferguson
Credit Cards: AMEX; MasterCard
Catalog Cost: Free
Number of Employees: 100
Sales Information: $10 Million

6519 Automotive Airfilters
K&N Engineering, Inc.
1455 Citrus Street
Riverside, CA 92507-1329   951-826-4000
800-858-3333
tech@knfilters.com
www.knfilters.com

High performance air filters, exhaust (cat back systems)

President: Nate Shelton
CFO: Steve Rogers
Marketing Manager: Diane Camp
Credit Cards: Visa
Catalog Circulation: Mailed 1 time(s) per year to 150M
Printing Information: 100 pages in 6 colors on Glossy Stock
Press: Web Press
Binding: Perfect Bound
Mailing List Information: Names for rent
In Business: 28 years
Number of Employees: 400
Sales Information: $50MM to $100MM

6520 Backyard Buddy
Backyard Buddy
140 Dana St NE
Warren, OH 44483-3845   330-395-9372
800-837-9353
Fax: 330-392-9311
sales@backyardbuddy.com
www.backyardbuddy.com

Free-standing, electric four-post lifts and accessories for automobiles

President: Larry Gross
In Business: 27 years

6521 Bar's Leaks
Bar's Products, Inc.
Po Box 187
Holly, MI 48442   800-345-6572
800-521-7475
Fax: 810-603-1335
www.barsproducts.com

Power steering products, cooling system and engine products

President: Joseph Pasuit
CFO: William Christinsen
Marketing Manager: Welford Samuel
Production Manager: John Bovie
In Business: 67 years
Number of Employees: 10
Sales Information: $ 3-5 Million

6522 Citgo Petroleum Corporation
CITGO Petroleum Corporation
1293 Eldridge Parkway
P.O. Box 4689
Houston, TX 77210-4689   918-495-4000
800-992-4846
Fax: 918-495-4511
info@CITGO.com
www.citgo.com

Automotive anti-freeze and lubricants, oil and air filters

President: Alejandro Granado
Marketing Manager: WA DeVore
VP, Government and Public Affairs: Dario Merchan
VP Finance: Maritza Villanueva
VP Supply and Marketing: Gustavo Velasquez
Credit Cards: AMEX; MasterCard; Visa
In Business: 104 years
Number of Employees: 1300

6523 Cooper Industries
Eaton
600 Travis Street, Suite 5400
P. O. Box 4446
Houston, TX 77002-1001   713-209-8400
Fax: 636-527-1405
www.cooperindustries.com

Automotive fuseholders and fuses

Chairman: Alexander M. Cutler
President: John Monter
CFO: Richard H. Fearon
Marketing Manager: Scott Robinson
Production Manager: John Monter
Vice Chairman, COO: Craig Arnold
Vice Chairman, COO: Thomas S. Gross
SVP & Chief Information Officer: William W. Blausey Jr.
In Business: 114 years
Number of Employees: 850

6524 Deltran-Battery Tender
Deltran Corporation
801 Inernational Speedway Blvd.
Deland, FL 32724-2511   386-736-7900
Fax: 386-736-0379
service@batterytender.com
www.Batterytender.Com

Reliable advanced technology battery chargers that are available from distributors

President: Michael L Prelec Sr
CFO: mike prelec
CEO: Michael L. Prelec Sr.
VP: Michael Prelec Jr.
Manager of sales: John Ford
Credit Cards: AMEX; MasterCard
In Business: 50 years
Sales Information: $10MM to $20MM

6525 Dennis K Burk
Dennis K. Burk Inc.
284 Eastern Avenue
Chelsea, MA 02150-917   617-884-7800
800-289-2875
Fax: 617-884-7638
support@burkeoil.com
www.burkeoil.com

Petroleum products, gasoline and motor oil

Chairman: Ed Burke
President: Ted Burke
CFO: Joe Cote
Marketing Manager: Kelly Anderson
Director of Operations: Dan Hill
Executive Administrator: Meaghan Burke
Safety Director: Matthew Manoli
In Business: 54 years
Number of Employees: 52
Sales Information: $20MM to $50MM

6526 Detroit Body Products
Detroit Body Products
49750 Martin Drive
Wixom, MI 48393-159 800-521-8383
www.detroitbodyproducts.com
Synthetic and natural fiber fabrics
President: JP Kraft Sr
Credit Cards: AMEX; MasterCard

6527 Douglas Battery Manufacturing Company
Douglas Battery
500 Battery Drive
Winston Salem, NC 27107 336-650-7000
800-368-4527
Fax: 336-650-7072
www.Douglasbattery.Com
Batteries
Chairman: Tom S Douglas III
President: Charles Douglas
Marketing Manager: Tom Douglas
Production Manager: Stanley Turbeville
Credit Cards: AMEX; MasterCard
Printing Information: 26 pages
In Business: 94 years
Number of Employees: 250
Sales Information: $100MM-$500MM

6528 EFDYN
Efdyn Incorporated
7734 East 11th Street
Tulsa, OK 74112-5718 918-838-1170
800-950-1172
Fax: 918-835-3334
sales@efdyn.com
www.efdyn.com
Shock absorbers, recoil dampers, buffers
President: Carrie Wilkinson
Marketing Manager: Robert Walkerby
Credit Cards: AMEX; MasterCard
Printing Information: 40 pages
In Business: 59 years
Number of Employees: 36
Sales Information: $1,000,000 - $5,000,000

6529 Eagle Equipment-Automotive Equipment
Eagle Equipment
4810 Clover Road
Greensboro, NC 27405 800-336-2776
Fax: 800-590-9814
info@eagleequip.com
www.eagleequip.com
Above ground lifts, many models and styles include two post lifts, four post lifts, alignment lifts, scissor lifts, low and mid rise
CFO: Lisa Carlson
Marketing Manager: Marc DelChercolo
Credit Cards: AMEX; MasterCard
Catalog Cost: Free
Printing Information: 40 pages in 4 colors on Glossy Stock
Press: Web Press
Binding: Saddle Stitched
Mailing List Information: Names for rent
In Business: 61 years
Number of Employees: 70

6530 Eastwood Unique Automotive Tools & Supplies
The Eastwood Company
263 Shoemaker Road
Pottstown, PA 19464 866-759-2131
800-343-9353
www.eastwood.com
Unique automotive tools and supplies
Credit Cards: AMEX; MasterCard
Catalog Cost: Free
Catalog Circulation: Mailed 12 time(s) per year to 500T
Printing Information: 84 pages in 4 colors on Glossy Stock
Press: Offset Press

Binding: Saddle Stitched
In Business: 35 years

6531 Eaton Corporation World Headquarters
Eaton Corporation
1111 Superior Ave E # 19
Cleveland, OH 44114-2584 440-523-4400
800-386-1911
Fax: 216-523-4787
www.eaton.com
Automotive, appliance, energy, industrial controls and components
Chairman: Alexander M Cutler
CFO: J Carmont
Marketing Manager: Jeff Obrock
Vice Chairman and COO: Craig Arnold
Senior Vice President and CIO: William W. Blausey Jr.
Executive Vice President, Chief HR: Cynthia K. Brabander
Number of Employees: 7300
Sales Information: $20 million

6532 Force Control Industries
Force Control
PO Box 18366
3660 Dixie Highway
Fairfield, OH 45014-366 513-868-0900
800-829-3244
Fax: 513-868-2105
info@forcecontrol.com
www.forcecontrol.com
Clutches, brakes, transmission equipment and various auto parts
President: Michael Besl
Marketing Manager: R Kelly
In Business: 46 years
Number of Employees: 60
Sales Information: $5,000,000 - $10,000,000

6533 G.H. Meiser & Company
G.H. Meiser & Co.
2407 W. 140th Place
P.O. Box 315
Posen, IL 60469-315 708-388-7867
Fax: 708-388-4053
info@ghmeiser.com
www.ghmeiser.com
Tire gauges and cleaners
President: Brian Parduhn
Marketing Manager: Bruce Parduhn
Production Manager: Herman Parduhn
In Business: 106 years
Number of Employees: 35
Sales Information: $1,000,000 - $5,000,000

6534 Giant Industrial Corporation
Giant Industrial Corp
1 Baiting Place Rd
Farmingdale, NY 11735-6200 631-293-8282
Fax: 631-293-8132
www.Gicbrake.Com
Brake pads and shoes, filters, water pumps
President: Isaac Youssian
Marketing Manager: Eli Youssian
Catalog Cost: Free
Catalog Circulation: Mailed 2 time(s) per year to 5M
Printing Information: in 4 colors
Binding: Perfect Bound
In Business: 18 years
Number of Employees: 10
Sales Information: $5MM to $10MM

6535 Graphite Metalizing Corporation
Graphite Metalizing Corporation
1050 Nepperhan Ave
Yonkers, NY 10703-1421 914-968-8400
Fax: 914-968-8468
sales@graphalloy.com
www.graphalloy.com
Oil free bearings and bushings

President: Eben T Walker
Marketing Manager: Robert C Stowell
Catalog Cost: Free
Printing Information: in 2 colors on Matte Stock
Press: Web Press
Binding: Folded
Mailing List Information: Names for rent
In Business: 100 years
Number of Employees: 65
Sales Information: $5MM to $10MM

6536 Grove Gear Industrial Gear Drives
Grove Gear
1524 15th Avenue
Union Grove, WI 53182 262-878-1221
www.grovegear.com
Speed reducers and gear motors
President: Larry Minnich
Catalog Cost: Free
Catalog Circulation: Mailed 1 time(s) per year
Printing Information: in 1 color
In Business: 70 years
Number of Employees: 200
Sales Information: $25,000,000 - $50,000,000

6537 Header Parts
Headers By Ed, Inc
2710 - 16th Avenue South
Dept. WS-M
Minneapolis, MN 55407-1291 612-729-2802
Fax: 612-729-5638
info@headersbyed.com
www.headersbyed.com
V8 automotive and vertical exit exhaust headers, header kits, header parts for over 100 4, 6, V6, V8, V12, US made engines
President: Ed Henneman
Credit Cards: MasterCard
Catalog Cost: $4.5
Catalog Circulation: Mailed 3 time(s) per year to 5M
Average Order Size: $170
Printing Information: 32 pages in 1 color on Matte Stock
Press: Letterpress
Binding: Saddle Stitched
Mailing List Information: Names for rent
In Business: 52 years
Number of Employees: 3
Sales Information: $500,000 - $1,000,000

6538 High Performance Catalog
Auto Meter
413 W Elm Street
Sycamore, IL 60178 815-895-8141
866-248-6356
www.autometer.com
Tachometers, auto gage instruments, battery testers, LTM performance and charging system analyzers
President: Jeff Kingberg
Marketing Manager: Jeep Worthan
Credit Cards: AMEX; MasterCard; Visa
Catalog Cost: $5.95
Printing Information: 120 pages in 4 colors
In Business: 60 years
Number of Employees: 195
Sales Information: $20MM to $50MM

6539 Hitran Corporation
Hitran Corporation
362 Highway 31
Flemington, NJ 08822-5799 908-782-5525
Fax: 908-782-9733
www.hitrancorp.com
Transformers, chokes and reactors
President: John C Hindle Iii
In Business: 95 years
Number of Employees: 150
Sales Information: $25,000,000 - $50,000,000

6540 J-Mark
J-Mark
2790 Ranchview Lane
Plymouth, MN 55447-1996   763-559-3300
                                 800-328-6274
                            Fax: 763-559-4806
oem@j-markproducts.com
www.j-markproducts.com

Tailgate protectors, running boards, splash guards, bedliners, side bed caps

President: Gary Henriksen
Marketing Manager: Jerry Moore
Production Manager: Matt Henriksen
Buyers: Todd Slawson
Credit Cards:
Catalog Cost: $2
In Business: 35 years
Number of Employees: 35
Sales Information: $5,000,000 - $10,000,000

6541 Kent-Moore Automotive
SPX
13320 Ballantyne Corporate Place
Charlotte, NC 28277-5509   810-574-2332
                                 800-345-2233
                            Fax: 810-578-7375
www.spx.com

Special service tools for transportation industry

Chairman: Christopher J. Kearney
President: Christopher J. Kearney
Marketing Manager: N Robert Kindig
CEO: Christopher J. Kearney
EVP: Robert B. Foreman
SVP, Secretary and General Counsel: Kevin L. Lilly
Buyers: Patti Barone
Credit Cards: MasterCard
Catalog Cost: Free
Catalog Circulation: Mailed 1 time(s) per year to 50M
Printing Information: 200 pages
Press: Web Press
Binding: Perfect Bound
In Business: 113 years
Number of Employees: 150

6542 Lisle Corporation
Lisle Corporation
807 E. Main Street
PO Box 89
Clarinda, IA 51632-89   712-542-5101
                          Fax: 712-542-6591
info@lislecorp.com
www.lislecorp.com

Automotive specialty tools, lubrication & tire products and creepers

Chairman: John Lisle
President: William Lisle
Production Manager: Fred Lisle
EVP: Mary Landhuis
Advertising Mgr/Marketing Director: John Bielfeldt
Catalog Cost: Free
Printing Information: 64 pages
In Business: 112 years
Number of Employees: 248
Sales Information: $22.8 Million

6543 Mocal Oil Control Systems
BAT Inc.
7630 Matoaka Rd.
Sarasota, FL 34243-3119   941-355-0005
                            Fax: 941-355-4683
www.batinc.net/mocal.htm

Oil hoses, coolers, thermostats and fittings, for industrial, and racing applications

Credit Cards: AMEX; MasterCard
Catalog Circulation: Mailed 1 time(s) per year
Printing Information: 20 pages
In Business: 1 years

6544 Noco Company
The Noco Company
30339 Diamond Parkway #102
Glenwillow, OH 44139-5400   216-464-8131
                                  800-456-6626
                             Fax: 216-464-8172
info@noco-usa.com
www.noco-usa.com

Battery cables, testers, terminals and cleaners, booster cables and spark plug wire sets

Chairman: William Nook, Chairman/CEO
CFO: Fred Barr
Marketing Manager: Johnathan L Nook
In Business: 101 years
Number of Employees: 99
Sales Information: $20 to 50 million

6545 POBCO Plastics & Hardwood
POBCO Inc
99 Hope Ave
Worcester, MA 01603-2298   508-791-6376
                                 800-222-6376
                            Fax: 508-791-3247
pobco@pobcoplastics.com
www.pobcoplastics.com

Conveyor components and friction reducing components made from bearing grade and food compliant plastics, lube filled hardwood, includes guide rails chain guides, wear strip and bearings

President: Stephen Johnson
Marketing Manager: Tom Johnson
International Marketing Manager: Tom Johnson
Catalog Cost: Free
Catalog Circulation: Mailed 12 time(s) per year to 25M
Printing Information: 126 pages in 2 colors on Glossy Stock
Press: Letterpress
Binding: Saddle Stitched
Mailing List Information: Names for rent
In Business: 56 years
Number of Employees: 50
Sales Information: $2,500,000

6546 Prothane Motion Control
Dee Engineering
3560 Cadillac Avenue
Costa Mesa, CA 92626-1490   888-776-8426
prothane.com

Urethane performance products, sports seats, performance parts for Volkswagens

President: Rick Sadler
Catalog Circulation: Mailed 1 time(s) per year
Printing Information: 72 pages in 4 colors
In Business: 25 years
Sales Information: $20MM to $50MM

6547 Racer Wholesale
Racer Parts Wholesale
411 Dorman
Indianapolis, IN 46202   317-639-0725
                               800-397-7815
                          Fax: 678-832-1100
info@racerpartswholesale.com
www.racerwholesale.com

Auto racing safety equipment

Credit Cards: MasterCard
In Business: 15 years
Number of Employees: 10
Sales Information: $1MM to $3MM

6548 Repco
Repco Inc.
6 Eves Drive
Marlton, NJ 08053   856-762-0172
                          800-822-9190
                     Fax: 800-424-9224
sales@repcoinc.com
www.repcoinc.com

A variety of automotive parts, supplies and accessories

President: John Lowlor
Credit Cards: AMEX; MasterCard; Visa
Catalog Cost: Free
Catalog Circulation: Mailed 2 time(s) per year
Printing Information: 25 pages in 2 colors on Newsprint
Press: Web Press
Binding: Saddle Stitched
In Business: 39 years
Number of Employees: 30
Sales Information: $3MM to $5MM

6549 Springfield Rod & Custom
Springfield Rod & Custom
219 Buxton Ave
Springfield, OH 45505-1339   937-323-1932
                                   800-752-9763
                              Fax: 937-323-1973
fredyerkey@att.net

Vintage auto parts and accessories

President: Larry Chaney
Sales Information: Under $500M

6550 Stant
Stant Corporation
1620 Columbia Ave
Connersville, IN 47331-1696   765-825-3122
                                    800-822-3121
                               Fax: 765-962-6866
www.Stant.Com

Radiator caps, fuel caps, oil fliter caps, and thermostats

President: Marlin Bailey
Marketing Manager: John Blommel
Packaging: Noel Faulkender
nfaulkender@stantinc.com
Aftermarket: Gary Parks
gparks@stantinc.com
sdowning@stantinc.com: Steve Downing
Catalog Cost: Free
Catalog Circulation: Mailed 1 time(s) per year
Printing Information: 596 pages in 1 color
In Business: 116 years
Number of Employees: 7000
Sales Information: $50,000,000 - $100,000,00

6551 Touch America
Touch America
1403 S Third St Ext
PO Box 1304
Mebane, NC 27302   919-732-6968
                         800-678-6824
                    Fax: 919-732-1173
info@touchamerica.com
www.touchamerica.com

Massage and spa equipment

President: Stewart Griffith
Marketing Manager: Lianne De Moya
Finance Executive: Chris Owens
International Marketing Manager: Valerie Rawlings
Credit Cards: AMEX; MasterCard
Catalog Cost: Free
Catalog Circulation: Mailed 2 time(s) per year to 25000
Average Order Size: $200
Printing Information: 40 pages in 4 colors on Glossy Stock
Press: Sheetfed Press
Binding: Saddle Stitched
Mailing List Information: Names for rent
In Business: 32 years
Sales Information: Under $500,000

6552 Wilmar Corporation
Wilmar Corporation
PO Box 88259
Suite 115
Tukwila, WA 98138-2628   425-970-6970
                                800-426-1262
                            Fax: 206-394-2130
                            tools@wilmarcorp.com
                            www.wilmarcorp.com

Hand and air tools, car/truck covers, specialty and heavy duty equipment

President: William Bellando
International Marketing Manager: Mike Cantalini
Buyers: Dan Cantalini
Catalog Cost: Free
List Manager: Mike Cantalini
In Business: 43 years
Number of Employees: 25

6553 Woodworkers Supply
Woodworkers Supply, Inc
1108 N Glenn Rd
Casper, WY 82601-1635   307-237-5528
                                800-645-9292
                            Fax: 800-853-9663
                            comments@woodworker.com
                            www.woodworker.com

Woodworking tools and supplies

President: John Wirth, Jr.
john@woodworker.com
CFO: Joe McQuade
Marketing Manager: Ken Pollitt
kenp@woodworker.com
Production Manager: Dean Cannon
Operations Manager: Darrell Feldman
darrellf@woodworker.com
International Marketing Manager: Jay Sanger
Buyers: Cynthia Quintana
Credit Cards: AMEX; MasterCard
Catalog Cost: Free
Catalog Circulation: Mailed 12 time(s) per year to 6M
Average Order Size: $100
Printing Information: 220 pages in 4 colors on Glossy Stock
Press: Web Press
Binding: Perfect Bound
Mailing List Information: Names for rent
List Manager: Mike Gilb
In Business: 43 years
Number of Employees: 76

Aviation
Supplies & Equipment

6554 Adcoa Absorbents & Desicants
ADCOA
17000 S Vermont Ave
Gardena, CA 90247-5854   310-532-6086
                                800-228-4124
                            Fax: 310-532-5404
                            info@adcoa.net
                            www.adcoa.net

Drying and purification products

President: Tom Skillen
Catalog Circulation: Mailed 1 time(s) per year
Printing Information: 10 pages in 2 colors
Binding: Saddle Stitched
Sales Information: $1,000,000

6555 Aircraft Tool Supply Company
Aircraft Tool Supply Company
1000 Old US 23
PO Box 370
Oscoda, MI 48750-370   989-739-1447
                                800-248-0638
                            Fax: 989-739-1448
                            info@aircraft-tool.com
                            www.aircraft-tool.com

Sheet metal tools, riveting equipment and aircraft engine repair and maintenance tools

President: Desmond Lynch
Production Manager: Bryan MacDonald
General Manager: Gaye Pappas
Catalog Cost: Free
Printing Information: 176 pages
In Business: 41 years
Number of Employees: 30
Sales Information: $6 MM

6556 Allied-Signal & Aerospace Company
Honeywell
2525 W 190th Street
Torrance, CA 90504-6002   480-353-3020
                                877-841-2840
                            Fax: 310-512-2221
                            www.honeywell.com

Aircraft controls

Chairman: David M.Cote
President: Tim Mahoney
CFO: Tom Szlosek
Corporate VP, CSO & CMO: Rhonda Germany
SVP, General Counsel: Katherine L. Adams
SVP, HR, Procurement & Comm.: Mark R. James
In Business: 130 years
Number of Employees: 1270

6557 American Aerospace Controls
American Aerospace Controls
570 Smith St
Farmingdale, NY 11735-1115   631-694-5100
                                888-873-8559
                            Fax: 631-694-6739
                            info@a-a-c.com
                            www.A-A-C.Com

AC & DC current, voltage, power and frequency transducers for industrial, laboratory, rail transit, defense and space applications

President: Ruth Roberts
Credit Cards: MasterCard
Catalog Cost: Free
Printing Information: 30 pages in 4 colors
In Business: 50 years
Number of Employees: 30
Sales Information: $10MM to $20MM

6558 American Autoclave Company
American Autoclave Company
16541 Redmond Way
Suite 530-C
Redmond, WA 98052   253-863-5000
                                800-421-5161
                            Fax: 253-863-1770
                            rfstack@comcast.net
                            www.americanautoclave.com

Autoclaves, ovens, and oven control systems

President: Robert Stack
In Business: 47 years
Number of Employees: 12

6559 Aviator's Store
The Aviator's Store
225 Airport Circle
Suite C
Corona, CA 92880-3804   951-372-9555
                                877-477-7823
                            Fax: 951-372-0555
                            sales@aviationbook.com
                            www.aircraftspruce.com

Books, apparel, gifts and holiday items

Owner: Nancy Griffith
General Manager: Kristin Potter
In Business: 29 years
Number of Employees: 7
Sales Information: 1.6M

6560 Barnett Rotor Craft
Barnett Rotor Craft
4307 Olivehurst Ave
Olivehurst, CA 95961-4706   530-742-7416
                            Fax: 530-743-6866

Helicopter and gyroplane kits

President: Jerrie Barnett
Credit Cards: MasterCard; Visa
Catalog Cost: Free
In Business: 51 years
Sales Information: $1MM to $3MM

6561 California Power Systems
California Power Systems
225 Airport Circle Drive
Corona, CA 92880-3213   510-357-2403
                                800-247-9653
                            Fax: 951-372-0555
                            info@800-airwolf.com
                            www.cps-parts.com/

Ultralight and sport aircraft parts and accessories

President: Jim Irwin
Credit Cards: AMEX; MasterCard
Catalog Cost: $6.95
Printing Information: 160 pages
In Business: 34 years

6562 Courtaulds Aerospace
PPG industries
PO Box 1800
Glendale, CA 91209-1800   818-240-2060
                            Fax: 818-549-7989
                            corporate.ppg.com

Specializing in products for the aerospace industries

Chairman: Charles E. Bunch
President: Michele Hopper
CFO: Frank S. Sklarsky
Chairman/ CEO: John V. Faraci
Chairman/CEO: Hungh Grant
Catalog Circulation: Mailed 1 time(s) per year
Printing Information: 300 pages
Press: m
Number of Employees: 250

6563 Eaton Lighted Pushbutton Switches
Eaton Corporation
3184 Pullman St
Costa Mesa, CA 92626-3319   440-523-4400
                                800-300-9320
                            Fax: 949-957-6178
                            www.Eaton.Com

Sensing and controls for aeronautic purposes

Chairman: Alexander M Cutler
Vice Chairman and COO: Craig Arnold
Senior Vice President and CIO: William W. Blausey Jr.
Executive Vice President, Chief HR: Cynthia K. Brabander
Catalog Circulation: Mailed 1 time(s) per year
Printing Information: 22 pages
Binding: Saddle Stitched
Number of Employees: 7300
Sales Information: $20MM to $50MM

6564 GVS Industries
GVS Industries
P. O. Box 46947
Cincinnati,, OH 45246   513-851-3606
                            Fax: 513-648-0809
                            sales@gvsindustries.com
                            www.gvsindustries.com

Air craft hinges

President: Valencia Guiliermo

6565 Garsite Division of America
Garsite Aviation Refuelling Equipment
539 S 10th St
Kansas City, KS 66105-1201   913-342-5600
                                800-467-5600
                            Fax: 913-342-0638
                            sales@garsite.com
                            www.garsite.com

Designer and manufacturer of aviation refuelers and hydrant service equipment; complete line of aviation refuelers from 750 to 15,000 gallons, plus refurbished equipment

President: Steven Paul
Marketing Manager: John Bernard
Production Manager: John Fizer
International Marketing Manager: Susan Lee
Catalog Cost: Free
Catalog Circulation: to 500+
Printing Information: in 2 colors on Matte Stock
Mailing List Information: Names for rent
List Manager: Pete Hlavac
In Business: 63 years
Number of Employees: 90
Sales Information: $10,000,000 - $25,000,000

6566 Gibson & Barnes Flight Suits
Gibson & Barnes
1900 Weld Blvd
#140
El Cajon, CA 92020   619-440-2700
                            800-748-6693
                     Fax: 619-440-4618
                        store@ombps.com
                     www.gibson-barnes.com

High-quality, made-to-order flightsuits, uniforms, leather jackets and flying helmets for aviation, emergency medicine, and law enforcement

President: James A Wegge
Marketing Manager: Dan Longbrake
Catalog Circulation: to Weekl
In Business: 37 years

6567 Glass Goose Catalog
Quikkit Inc
9002 Summer Glen
Dallas, TX 75243-7445   214-349-0462
                     Fax: 214-349-0462
                      www.glassgoose.com

Catalog of aircraft and aero activities, offering aircraft kits-fixed wing powered, specializes in two-place amphibians

President: Tom Scott
Sec/Treasury: Toni Scott
Credit Cards: MasterCard; Visa
Catalog Cost: $25
In Business: 21 years
Number of Employees: 5
Sales Information: 590K

6568 Gulf Coast Avionics Products
Gulf Coast Avionics Corporation
3650 Drane Field Road
Lakeland Linder Regional Airport
Lakeland, FL 33811   863-709-9714
                            800-474-9714
                     Fax: 863-709-9736

Catalog of aircraft and aero activities, offering avionics and communications equipment, specializes in ready-to-install custom instrument panels for kit planes

Marketing Manager: Craig Jaroski
VP: Rick Garcia
Credit Cards: AMEX; MasterCard; Visa
Catalog Cost: Free
In Business: 29 years
Number of Employees: 22
Sales Information: 2.3M

6569 Habco
HABCO Industries LLC
172 Oak Street
Glastonbury, CT 06033-2443   860-682-6800
                              888-422-2647
                       Fax: 860-682-6804
                          sales@habco.biz
                          www.Habco.Biz

Aircraft equipment and supplies

President: Brian Montanari
brian.montanari@habco.biz
CFO: Paul Rocheleau
paul.rocheleau@habco.biz
Marketing Manager: K Backmann
VP Sales & Marketing: Jeff Kretzmer
jeff.kretzmer@habco.biz
V.P. of Operations: Nick Zandonella
nick.zandonella@habco.biz
Chief Technology Officer: David AlanPlis
david.plis@habco.biz
Credit Cards: AMEX; MasterCard
In Business: 45 years
Number of Employees: 27
Sales Information: $1,000,000 - $5,000,000

6570 Horberg Gage & Grinding Industries
Horberg
PO Box 6273
Bridgeport, CT 06606-273   203-334-9444
                            866-467-2374
                     Fax: 203-334-9445
                     precision@horberg.com
                        www.horberg.com

Aircraft machinery

President: Robert Leety
In Business: 80 years
Number of Employees: 15
Sales Information: $1,000,000 - $5,000,000

6571 ILC Data Device Corporation
Data Device Corporation
105 Wilbur Place
Bohemia, NY 11716-2482   631-567-5600
                            800-DDC-5757
                     Fax: 631-567-7358
                       service@ddc-web.com
                        www.ddc-web.com

Manufacturers of microelectronic components and environmental protective gear

President: Clifford Lane
Marketing Manager: Sean Sleicher
CEO: Clifford Lane
Catalog Cost: $5
Catalog Circulation: Mailed 1 time(s) per year to 100M
Printing Information: 600 pages
Press: Web Press
Binding: Perfect Bound
In Business: 49 years
Number of Employees: 500-

6572 Jane's Catalog
IHS Jane's 360 Inc.
110 N. Royal Street
Alexandria, VA 22314-1693   703-683-3700
                            800-447-2273
                     Fax: 703-836-0297
                   customerservice.us@janes.com
                          www.janes.com

Directories, books and magazines on aerospace, aviation, and militaria

President: Alfred Rolington
CFO: Michael Staton
Marketing Manager: Greg Wallace
Production Manager: Lois Smith
Operations Manager: Peter Baxter
Executive Director: Charles Cunningham
International Marketing Manager: Lynne Samuel
Credit Cards: AMEX; MasterCard; Visa
Catalog Cost: Free
Catalog Circulation: Mailed 2 time(s) per year to 60M
Average Order Size: $500
Printing Information: 60 pages in 4 colors on Glossy Stock
Press: Web Press
Binding: Saddle Stitched
Mailing List Information: Names for rent
List Manager: Lynne Samuel
List Company: Merkle Computer Systems
In Business: 30 years
Number of Employees: 70

6573 Leading Edge Air Foils
Leading Edge Air Foils
1216 North Road
PO Box 231
Lyons, WI 53148   262-763-4087
                            800-532-3462
                     Fax: 262-763-1920
                   info@leadingedge-airfoils.com
                   www.leadingedge-airfoils.com

Catalog of ultralight and aero activities, offering aircraft kits-fixed wing powered, specializes in one and two-place open-cockpit biplane

President: Bill Reed
CFO: Mary Myers
Catalog Cost: Free
Printing Information: 132 pages
Mailing List Information: Names for rent
In Business: 36 years
Number of Employees: 8
Sales Information: 910K

6574 Lockwood Aviation Supply
Lockwood Aviation Supply
1 Lockwood Lane
Sebring, FL 33870   863-655-5100
                            800-527-6829
                     Fax: 863-655-6225
                       Tisha@lockwood.aero
                   www.lockwood-aviation.com

Parts and accessories for light sport aircraft

President: Phillip Lockwood
General Manager: Tisha Lockwood
Tisha@lockwood.aero
Credit Cards: AMEX; MasterCard; Visa
Catalog Cost: Free
Printing Information: 205 pages
In Business: 25 years
Number of Employees: 3
Sales Information: 310K

6575 Metem Corporation
Metem Corporation
700 Parsippany Road
Parsippany, NJ 07054-3767   973-887-6635
                     Fax: 973-887-1755
                        expertise@metem.com
                          www.metem.com

Aerospace equipment and supplies

President: Steven Goldthwaite
Marketing Manager: Tom Ng
Production Manager: Nick Naumov
CEO: Steven Goldthwaite
Founder: duVal Goldthwaite
In Business: 53 years
Number of Employees: 125
Sales Information: $10,000,000 - $25,000,000

6576 Naugatuck Glass Company
FLABEG Technical Glass U.S. Corp.
Church & Bridge Street
Naugatuck, CT 06770-71   203-729-5227
                            800-533-3513
                     Fax: 203-729-8781
                         info@flabeg.com
                          www.flabeg.com

Aircraft instruments and systems

President: Jeffrey Witherwax
In Business: 85 years
Number of Employees: 112
Sales Information: $10MM to $20MM

6577 Northwestern Motor Company
Nmc-Wollard,Inc.
2021 Truax Boulevard
Eau Claire, WI 54703-9693   715-835-3151
                            800-656-6867
                     Fax: 715-835-6625
                        www.nmc-wollard.com

Aviation equipment

President: John Steingart
In Business: 21 years

Number of Employees: 125
Sales Information: $10,000,000 - $25,000,000

6578 PS Engineering
PS Engineering, Inc.
9800 Martel Road
Lenoir City, TN 37772   865-988-9800
                               800-427-2376
                          Fax: 865-988-6619
               contact@ps-engineering.com
               www.ps-engineering.com

Aircraft audio selector panels and components, intercoms, digital recorders, wire harnesses and modified headsets
President: Mark Scheuer
Credit Cards: AMEX; MasterCard; Visa
Catalog Cost: Free
Printing Information: 12 pages
In Business: 30 years

6579 Pacific Coast Avionics
Pacific Coast Avionics
Aurora State Airport
22783 Airport Road
Aurora, OR 97002   503-678-6242
                               800-353-0370
                          Fax: 503-678-6292
                         info@pca.aero
               www.pacificcoastavionics.com

Avionics instruments, communications equipment and accessories, kitpanels and GPS gear
VP/COO: Dewey Conroy
dewey@pca.aero
Sales Team Leader: Randy Wright
randay@pca.aero
Sales: Sergio Gemoets
sergio@pca.aero
Credit Cards: AMEX; MasterCard
Catalog Cost: Free
In Business: 24 years
Number of Employees: 19
Sales Information: 2M

6580 Poly Fiber Aircraft Coatings
Consolidated Aircraft Coatings
P.O. Box 3129
Riverside, CA 92519   951-684-4280
                               800-362-3490
                          Fax: 951-684-0518
               www.polyfiber.com

Aircraft fabric covering and painting
Credit Cards: MasterCard; Visa
Catalog Cost: Free
Printing Information: 151 pages
In Business: 40 years
Number of Employees: 20
Sales Information: $3MM to $5MM

6581 Poly-Fiber Aircraft Coatings Catalog
Poly-Fiber
7320 Rubidoux Boulevard
Riverside, CA 92519   909-684-4280
               www.polyfiber.com

Painting and covering fabric for aircraft
Printing Information: 16 pages
In Business: 40 years

6582 Ralmark Company
Ralmark Company
PO Box 1507
Kingston, PA 18704-507   570-288-9331
                          Fax: 570-288-0902
                         sales@ralmark.com
               www.ralmark.com

Aircraft pulleys
President: Gary Hozempa
In Business: 40 years
Number of Employees: 30
Sales Information: $1,000,000 - $5,000,000

6583 Rigging Innovations
Rigging Innovations
4910 N. Lear Dr. HGR 1,
Eloy Municipal Airport
Eloy, AZ 85131-1210   520-466-2655
                          Fax: 520-466-2656
               www.rigginginnovations.com

Catalog of aircraft and aero activities, offering aircraft recovery systems and para-gear, specializes in skydiving equipment

6584 Six Chuter International LLC
Six Chuter International LLC
5700 NE 82nd Avenue
Vancouver, WA 98662   360-771-4047
                               888-727-1998
               sixchuterinfo@comcast.net
               www.sixchuter.com

Catalog of aircraft and aero activities, offering hang gliding and powered parachutes, specializes in sky-riding aero-chute for one and two-persons
Marketing Manager: Doug Maas
doug@sixchuter.com
Printing Information: 37 pages
In Business: 25 years
Sales Information: Under $500M

6585 Starduster Catalog
Air Craft Spruce & Specialty Company
PO Box 4000
225 Airport Circle
Corona, CA 92880-4000   800-861-3192
                               877-477-7823
                          Fax: 951-372-0555
               info@aircraftspruce.com
               www.aircraftspruce.com

Aircraft and aero activities, offering aircraft kits-fixed wing powered, specializes in one and two-place biplanes
President: Jim Irwin
CFO: Nanci Irwin
Credit Cards: AMEX; MasterCard; Visa
In Business: 58 years
Number of Employees: 150

6586 Trans Lectric Corporation
Trans Lectric Corporation
349 West 168th Street
Gardena, CA 90248-4202   310-515-7600
                               855-235-3150
                          Fax: 310-464-8255
                         info@karrior.com
               www.translectric.com

Industrial vehicles for the airport industry
President: George Kettle
Marketing Manager: June
In Business: 41 years
Number of Employees: 24
Sales Information: $1,000,000 - $5,000,000

6587 Tronair
Tronair
1740 Eber Rd
Holland, OH 43528-9138   419-866-6301
                               800-426-6301
                          Fax: 419-867-0634
                         sales@tronair.com
               www.Tronair.Com

Aircraft ground support equipment
President: Ken Greene
Marketing Manager: P Barton
Production Manager: A Brubaker
Catalog Circulation: Mailed 1 time(s) per year
Printing Information: 104 pages in 2 colors on Glossy Stock
Binding: Perfect Bound
Mailing List Information: Names for rent
In Business: 44 years
Number of Employees: 80
Sales Information: $10,000,000 - $25,000,000

6588 USATCO
US Air Tool Company
60 Fleetwood Court
Ronkonkoma, NY 11779-6907   631-471-3300
                          Fax: 631-471-3308
                         info@usatco.com
               www.usatco.com

Manufactures and distributes riveting, pneumatic and metalworking tools to the aircraft, aerospace and metalworking industries
President: Geoff Perez
Founder: Joseph Percz
Credit Cards: AMEX; MasterCard
Catalog Cost: $7.5
Catalog Circulation: Mailed 1 time(s) per year to 15M
Printing Information: 200 pages in 1 color on Matte Stock
Press: Web Press
Binding: Perfect Bound
Mailing List Information: Names for rent
In Business: 66 years
Number of Employees: 20-5
Sales Information: $1,000,000 - $5,000,000

6589 Ultimate Hydroforming
Ultimate Hydroforming Inc.
42450 Yearego Drive
Sterling Heights, MI 48314-3262   586-254-2300
                          Fax: 586-254-3470
               info@ultimatehydroforming.com
               www.Ultimatehydroforming.Com

Aircraft equipment and accessories
Chairman: Shirley Klyn
President: Shirley A. Klyn
Vice President: Shane Klyn
Plant Manager: Dave Kopka
Technology Manager: Todd Chapman
In Business: 36 years
Number of Employees: 50
Sales Information: $5,000,000 - $10,000,000

6590 Van's Aircraft Accessories
Van's Aircraft, Inc.
14401 Keil Road NE
Aurora, OR 97002-9467   503-678-6545
                          Fax: 503-678-6560
                         info@vansaircraft.com
               www.Vansaircraft.Com

Catalog of aircraft and aero activities, offering aircraft kits-fixed wing powered, specializes in one- and two-place low-wing aircraft
Chairman: Richard VanGrunsven
President: Scott Risan
Credit Cards: MasterCard; Visa
Catalog Cost: Free
In Business: 43 years
Sales Information: $20MM to $50MM

6591 Wick's Aircraft Supply Catalog
Wick's Aircraft Supply
410 Pine Street
Highland, IL 62249   618-654-7447
                               800-221-9425
                          Fax: 888-440-5727
                         info@wicksaircraft.com
               www.wicksaircraft.com

Aircraft kits, parts and accessories
President: Scott Wick
General Manager: Eric Cleveland
Credit Cards: AMEX; MasterCard; Visa
Catalog Circulation: to 2000
Printing Information: 250 pages
In Business: 288 years
Number of Employees: 17
Sales Information: 3.50M

6592 Wicks Aircraft Supply
Wick's Aircraft Supply
410 Pine Street
Highland, IL 62249-1243   618-654-7447
                                 800-221-9425
                           Fax: 888-440-5727
                        info@wicksaircraft.com
                        www.wicksaircraft.com

Aircraft supplies, parts, equipment and accessories

Chairman: Rob Heer
President: Scott Wick
scottw@wicksaircraft.com
CFO: Mark Wick
Director: Jim Kaiser
Assistant Manager: Linda Haase
Credit Cards: AMEX; MasterCard; Visa
Printing Information: 450 pages
Binding: Perfect Bound
In Business: 37 years
Number of Employees: 17

6593 Zenith Aviation
Zenith Aviation
1321 Lafayette Boulevard
Fredericksburg, VA 22401   540-361-7700
                                 800-458-0454
                           Fax: 540-361-7800
                        rfq@zenithaviation.com
                        www.zenithaviation.com

Aviation literature and videos

President: Robert F. Stanford
rstanford@zenithaviation.com
CFO: Martin Coster
General Manager/Executive Vice Pres:
Angela Shawaryn
ashawaryn@zenithaviation.com
VP, Operations / Quality: Donald A. Capwell
dcapwell@zenithaviation.com
Director, Business Development:
ScottNordstrom
snordstrom@zenithaviation.com
Credit Cards: AMEX; MasterCard; Visa
Catalog Circulation: Mailed 1 time(s) per year
Printing Information: 24 pages in 4 colors
Mailing List Information: Names for rent
In Business: 33 years
Number of Employees: 90
Sales Information: $10,000,000 - $25,000,000

Book Publishers
General Business

6594 American Arbitration Association
American Arbitration Association
335 Madison Ave
Floor 10
New York, NY 10017-4611   212-716-5870
                                 800-778-7879
                           Fax: 212-716-5905
                        casefiling@adr.org
                        www.adr.org

Books on labor, industrial relations, subscription and mail order books, etc

President: William Slate
In Business: 19 years
Number of Employees: 300

6595 American Technical Publishers
American Technical Publishers
10100 Orland Parkway
Suite 200
Orland Park, IL 60467-5756   708-957-1100
                                    800-323-3471
                              Fax: 708-957-1101
                        service@americantech.net
                        www.atplearning.com/

Vocational/technical books and materials

President: Robert D Deisinger
Marketing Manager: J David Halloway
Production Manager: Chris Proctor
Editor In Chief: Jonathan F. Gosse

Credit Cards: AMEX; MasterCard; Visa
Catalog Circulation: Mailed 1 time(s) per year
to 80M
Printing Information: 40 pages in 4 colors on
Glossy Stock
Press: Web Press
Binding: Saddle Stitched
Mailing List Information: Names for rent
In Business: 117 years
Number of Employees: 32
Sales Information: $5,000,000 - $10,000,000

6596 Annual Reviews
Annual Reviews
P.O.Box 10139
Palo Alto, CA 94303-0139   650-493-4400
                                  800-523-8635
                            Fax: 650-855-9815
                        service@annualreviews.org
                        www.annualreviews.org

Publications for all sciences

Chairman: Richard Zare
rzare@annualreviews.org
President: Richard Gallagher
rgallagher@annualreviews.org
CFO: Steve Castro
scastro@annualreviews.org
Director of Technology: Paul Calvi
pcalvi@annualreviews.org
Director of Production: Jeniffer Jongsma
jjongsma@annualreviews.org
Editor-in-Chief/Corporate Secretary: Natalie
DeWitt
ndewitt@annualreviews.org
Credit Cards: AMEX; MasterCard
Catalog Circulation: Mailed 1 time(s) per year
Printing Information: on Matte Stock
In Business: 85 years
Number of Employees: 50-2
Sales Information: $5,000,000 - $10,000,000

6597 Aqua Quest Publications
Aqua Quest Publications, Incorporated
486 Bayville Road
Locust Valley, NY 11560-1209   516-759-0476
                                      800-933-8989
                                Fax: 516-759-4519
                        catalog@aquaquest.com
                        www.aquaquest.com

Books on scuba diving, including travel guides, underwater photography, shipwrecks and technical material

President: Anthony Bliss Jr
Fulfillment: Rosalie Dunne
Founder: Tony Bliss, Jr
Credit Cards: MasterCard
Catalog Cost: Free
Catalog Circulation: Mailed 2 time(s) per year
to 30M
Printing Information: 20 pages in 4 colors on
Glossy Stock
Press: Sheetfed Press
Binding: Saddle Stitched
Mailing List Information: Names for rent
In Business: 26 years
Number of Employees: 3
Sales Information: $400,000

6598 Art Brown's International Pen
ST-DUPONT-NYC, INC
The N Y Jewelry exchange
20 West 47th street, #20R
New York, NY 10036   212-921-1144
                            800-341-7003
                      Fax: 212-575-5825
             CustomerService@ST-Dupont-NYC.com
                      www.savingspros.com

Finest writing instruments, desk utensils and accessories

President: B Warren Brown
Credit Cards: AMEX; MasterCard; Visa
Catalog Cost: Free
Printing Information: 72 pages in 4 colors on
Glossy Stock
Press: Web Press

Binding: Saddle Stitched
In Business: 143 years
Number of Employees: 25

6599 Association for Information & Image Management
AIIM
1100 Wayne Avenue
Suite 1100
Silver Spring, MD 20910-5642   301-587-8202
                                      800-477-2446
                                Fax: 301-587-8202
                        aiim@aiim.org
                        www.aiim.org

Books

Chairman: Paul Engel
President: John F Mancini
CFO: Felicia Dillard
Chief Evangelist: Atle Skjekkeland
Chief Information Officer: Laurence Hart
VP and CMO: Peggy Winton
Catalog Circulation: Mailed 1 time(s) per year
Printing Information: 62 pages in 4 colors
Binding: Perfect Bound
Number of Employees: 100

6600 BBC Audiobooks America
AudioGo
42 Whitecap Drive
N Kingstown, RI 02852-7445   800-621-0182
                              Fax: 877-492-0873
                        www.audiogo-library.com/

Unabridged audiobooks and radio dramatizations for adults and children; direct to library sales; formats include CD, MP3, and Playaway

Marketing Manager: Michele Cobb
Principle: Jim Brannigan
Credit Cards: AMEX; MasterCard; Visa
Catalog Cost: Free
Catalog Circulation: Mailed 7 time(s) per year
to 18000
Printing Information: 65 pages
Mailing List Information: Names for rent
In Business: 20 years
Number of Employees: 40

6601 Battelle Press
Battelle
505 King Avenue
Columbus, OH 43201-2696   614-424-6424
                                 800-201-2011
                           Fax: 614-424-3819
                        solutions@battelle.org
                        www.Battelle.Org

Books on engineering, management and science

Chairman: John K. Welch
President: Dr Jeffrey Wadsworth
CFO: Dave Evans
EVP, Global Laboratory Operations: Ron
Townsend
SVP, General Counsel and Secretary: Russell
Austin
VP, Education: Aimee Kennedy
Credit Cards: AMEX; MasterCard; Visa
Catalog Cost: Free
Catalog Circulation: Mailed 3 time(s) per year
to 150M
Average Order Size: $100
Printing Information: 32 pages in 4 colors on
Glossy Stock
Press: Web Press
Binding: Saddle Stitched
Mailing List Information: Names for rent
In Business: 86 years
Number of Employees: 1000

6602 Bcc Research
Bcc Research
49 Walnut Park
Building 2
Wellesley, MA 02481   866-285-7215
info@bccresearch.com
www.bccresearch.com

Market research industry reports, newsletters and conferences

Senior Editor: Chris Spivey
Editorial Director: Kevin R. Fitzgerald
Catalog Circulation: Mailed 6 time(s) per year
to 200M
Printing Information: 32 pages in 2 colors on
Matte Stock
Binding: Saddle Stitched
In Business: 46 years
Number of Employees: 60
Sales Information: $1,000,000 - $5,000,000

6603 Bell Springs Publishing
Bell Springs Publishing
PO Box 1240
Willits, CA 95490-1240   707-459-6372
publisher@bellsprings.com
www.bellsprings.com/

Books for a small business

President: Bernard Kamoroff
Credit Cards: AMEX; MasterCard; Visa
Catalog Circulation: Mailed 1 time(s) per year
Printing Information: 16 pages in 2 colors on
Matte Stock

6604 Best of Blue Print
Springer
233 Spring Street
New York, NY 10013-1578   212-460-1507
Fax: 212-460-1581
service-ny@springer.com
www.springer.com

Reference and instructional print and media books

President: William Curtis
CFO: Ulrich Vest
Chief Executive Officer: Derk Haank
Chief Operating Officer: Martin Mos
Executive Vice President IT: Jan-Erik de Boer
Credit Cards: AMEX; MasterCard
Catalog Circulation: Mailed 1 time(s) per year
Printing Information: 6 pages
In Business: 51 years
Number of Employees: 550

6605 Brody Professional Development
Brody Professional Development
115 West Avenue
Ste 114
Jenkintown, PA 19046   215-886-1688
800-726-7936
Fax: 215-886-1699
info@brodypro.com
www.brodypro.com

Releases one new title each year in the business/self help categories; business communication skills books, self-help and career titles

President: Marjorie Brody
Marketing Manager: Laura Kemp
Account Manager: Tina Altman
Tina@BrodyPro.com
Account Manager: Tom Gill
TGill@BrodyPro.com
Operations Support: Suzanne P. Harkinson
Suzanne@BrodyPro.com
Mailing List Information: Names for rent
In Business: 30 years
Sales Information: Under $500M

6606 CAI's Bookstore
Community Associations Institute
6402 Arlington Blvd
Suite 500
Falls Church, VA 22402   703-970-9220
888-224-4321
Fax: 703-970-9558
CAldirect@caionline.org
www.caionline.org/Pages/Default.aspx

Home owners associations information, by-laws, forms and rules for your community

President: Andy Rand
Credit Cards: AMEX; MasterCard; Visa
Catalog Cost: Free
In Business: 35 years

6607 CCH Tax & Business Law Subscription
CCH
2700 Lake Cook Road
Riverwoods, IL 60015-3867   847-940-4600
800-739-9998
KnowledgeCenter@cch.com
www.Cch.Com

Publications on tax and business law

President: Karen Abramson
Credit Cards: AMEX; MasterCard
Catalog Circulation: Mailed 1 time(s) per year
Printing Information: 24 pages in 2 colors
Binding: Saddle Stitched
Number of Employees: 500-

6608 Career Works
Career Works
34 School Street
At Rear of Building
Brockton, MA 02301   508-513-3400
Fax: 508-513-3450
info@careerworks.org
www.careerworks.org

Publishers material relating to human resources, career development, job-search, training, professional improvement, software, books, audio/video and directories

Catalog Circulation: Mailed 4 time(s) per year
to 10M
Printing Information: 2 pages on Matte Stock
Press: Sheetfed Press
Number of Employees: 10

6609 Culinary & Hospitality Industry Publications
C.H.I.P.S.
10777 Mazoch Road
Weimar, TX 78962   979-263-5683
Fax: 979-263-5685
ordept@chipsbooks.com
www.chipsbooks.com

A source for professional resources in agricultural science and technology, architecture and design, cosmetic science and technology, and many more

6610 D & B Hoovers
Hoover's Inc.
7700 West Parmer Lane
Building A
Austin, TX 78729   512-374-4500
888-234-4567
Fax: 512-374-4501
customersupport@hoovers.com
www.hoovers.com

Handbooks, directories, electronic resources and other business related information

Chairman: Sara Mathew
President: Emanuele A. Conti
CFO: Richard H. Veldran
Marketing Manager: Michael Gallagher
CEO: Sara Mathew
SVP, Chief Data & Analytics Officer: Paul D.

Ballew
SVP/Chief HR Officer: Julian Prower
Credit Cards: AMEX; MasterCard
Catalog Circulation: Mailed 1 time(s) per year
Printing Information: 54 pages on Matte Stock
In Business: 171 years
Number of Employees: 400
Sales Information: $24 Million

6611 Directory Marketplace
Todd Publications
PO Box 1752
Boca Raton, FL 33429   561-910-0440
Fax: 561-910-0440
toddpub@aol.com

Offers reference books and directories in sales, marketing, advertising, computers, careers, internationsl trade, government, education, mail order, small and home business

President: Barry Klein
Marketing Manager: Berry Klein
Credit Cards: AMEX; MasterCard
Catalog Cost: Free
Catalog Circulation: Mailed 4 time(s) per year
to 25000
Average Order Size: $100
Printing Information: 8 pages in 2 colors on
Matte Stock
Press: Letterpress
Binding: Saddle Stitched
Mailing List Information: Names for rent
In Business: 35 years
Sales Information: Under $500M

6612 Empire Communications Corporation
Empire Communications Inc.
5818 N 7th Street
Suite 103
Phoenix, AZ 85014-5808   602-997-7707
800-223-7180
Fax: 602-269-3113

Books, manuals, audiotapes, courses and newsletters

President: Dan Kennedy
Credit Cards: AMEX; MasterCard; Visa
Catalog Cost: Free
Catalog Circulation: Mailed 2 time(s) per year
to 50M
Printing Information: 24 pages in 2 colors on
Newsprint
Press: Web Press
Binding: Saddle Stitched
Mailing List Information: Names for rent
In Business: 12 years
Number of Employees: 3
Sales Information: $500M to $1MM

6613 Entrepreneur Magazine
Entrepreneur Media, Inc.
2445 McCabe Way
Suite 400
Irvine, CA 92614-6234   949-261-2325
800-421-2300
Fax: 949-622-5274
press@entrepreneur.com
www.smallbizbooks.com

How-to business start-up books, tapes and software

Chairman: Peter Shea
President: Niel Perlman
CFO: Joe Goodman
Marketing Manager: Lori Gunnette
Credit Cards: AMEX; MasterCard; Visa
Catalog Cost: Free
Catalog Circulation: Mailed 2 time(s) per year
to 2MM
Average Order Size: $85
Printing Information: 16 pages in 4 colors on
Glossy Stock
Press: Web Press
Binding: Saddle Stitched
Mailing List Information: Names for rent
List Company: List Services
In Business: 20 years

Number of Employees: 150
Sales Information: $25,000,000 - $50,000,000

6614 Fraser Publishing Company
Fraser Publishing Company
PO Box 217
Flint Hill, VA 22627   540-675-9976

Financial and business related literature, as well as books dealing with crowd behavior and investment psychology and the contrary opinion approach to investing

President: James L Fraser
Marketing Manager: Karla Ferrelli
Production Manager: Karla Ferrelli
Fulfillment: Bonnie Mazza
International Marketing Manager: Bonnie Mazza
Credit Cards: MasterCard
Catalog Cost: Free
Catalog Circulation: Mailed 1 time(s) per year to 10M
Printing Information: 25 pages in 2 colors on Matte Stock
Binding: Saddle Stitched
Mailing List Information: Names for rent
In Business: 30 years
Number of Employees: 2
Sales Information: Under $500,000

6615 Great Potential Press
Great Potential Press
1650 North Kolb Road
Suite 200
Tucson, AZ 85715   520-777-6161
                         Fax: 520-777-6217
info@greatpotentialpress.com
www.greatpotentialpress.com

Quality books and materials to guide parents and educators through the world of giftedness

President: James T Webb, PhD
CFO: Janet L Gore, MEd
Marketing Manager: Kristina Grant
Fulfillment: Anne Morales
Catalog Cost: Free
Catalog Circulation: Mailed 2 time(s) per year to 12000
Printing Information: 32 pages in 4 colors on G
Binding: F
In Business: 32 years
Sales Information: $500M-$1MM

6616 Grey House Publishing
Grey House Publishing, Inc.
4919 Route 22
PO Box 56
Amenia, NY 12501   518-789-8700
                         800-562-2139
                         Fax: 518-789-0556
books@greyhouse.com
www.greyhouse.com

Reference directories in business, demographics, statistics, health and education as well as general reference encyclopedias

President: Richard Gottlieb
Marketing Manager: Jessica Moody
Production Manager: Kristen Hayes
Publisher: Leslie Mackenzie
Editorial Director: Laura Mars
Credit Cards: AMEX; MasterCard; Visa
Catalog Cost: Free
Catalog Circulation: Mailed 3 time(s) per year to 20M+
Average Order Size: $185
Printing Information: 12 pages in 4 colors on Glossy Stock
Press: Web Press
Binding: Saddle Stitched
In Business: 36 years
Number of Employees: 75

6617 HW Wilson Company
Grey House Publishing, Inc.
4919 Route 22
PO Box 56
Amenia, NY 12501   518-789-8700
                         844-630-6369
                         Fax: 518-789-0556
www.hwwilsoninprint.com

Library reference books

Marketing Manager: Jessica Moody
Production Manager: Kristen Hayes
Editorial Director: Laura Mars
Credit Cards: AMEX; MasterCard; Visa
Catalog Cost: Free
Catalog Circulation: Mailed 2 time(s) per year
Printing Information: 40 pages in 4 colors on Glossy Stock
Press: Web Press
Binding: Saddle Stitched
Mailing List Information: Names for rent
In Business: 117 years

6618 Harris InfoSource
Hoover's Inc.
5800 Airport Blvd.
Austin, TX 78752-1938   512-374-4500
                              888-234-4567
                              Fax: 512-374-4051
www.hoovers.com

Databases posting American manufacturers

Chairman: Sara Mathew
President: Emanuele A. Conti
CFO: Richard H. Veldran
Marketing Manager: E Layne Tosko
Production Manager: Fran Carlsen
Fulfillment: Gary Sowder
CEO: Sara Mathew
SVP, Chief Data & Analytics Officer: Paul D. Ballew
SVP and Chief HR Officer: Julian Prower
Buyers: Barb Atkinson
Credit Cards: AMEX; MasterCard; Visa
Catalog Circulation: Mailed 4 time(s) per year to 100M
Printing Information: 32 pages in 2 colors on Matte Stock
Press: Web Press
Binding: Saddle Stitched
Mailing List Information: Names for rent
List Manager: Susan Tully
In Business: 171 years
Number of Employees: 110
Sales Information: $10MM to $20MM

6619 Hart Publications
Hart Pub
4545 Post Oak Place Drive
Suite 210
Houston, TX 77027-3164   713-993-9320
                               800-874-2544
                               Fax: 713-840-8585
www.bigclearance.com

Directories, magazines and newsletters of the oil and gas industry

Fulfillment: Gina Acosta
Catalog Circulation: Mailed 1 time(s) per year to 103M
Printing Information: 15 pages in 1 color on Newsprint
Press: Web Press
Binding: Perfect Bound
In Business: 38 years
Number of Employees: 80

6620 Home Business Startup Handbook
HBM
20664 Jutland Place
Lakeville, MN 55044-8008   714-968-0331
                                 800-734-7042
                                 Fax: 714-388-3883
advertise@homebusinessmag.com
www.homebusinessmag.com

Contains information for the person who wishes to work from home, business selection, home office setup, raising money, sales, marketing and more

President: Richard Henderson
CFO: Richard Henderson
Fulfillment: UMRC, Inc
Catalog Cost: $3
Average Order Size: $3
Printing Information: 16 pages in 1 color on Newsprint
Press: Web Press
Binding: Saddle Stitched
Mailing List Information: Names for rent
In Business: 13 years
Number of Employees: 2

6621 International Wealth Success
International Wealth Success
PO Box 186
Merrick, NY 11566-186   516-766-5850
                              800-323-0548
                              Fax: 516-766-5919
admin@iwsmoney.com
www.iwsmoney.com

Newsletters on small business covering topics including finance, loans, venture capital, IPOs, and grants in the areas of real estate, import-export, e-commerce, etc

President: Tyler Hicks
Credit Cards: AMEX; MasterCard
Catalog Cost: $3
Catalog Circulation: Mailed 12 time(s) per year to 5000
Printing Information: 52 pages in 1 color on Matte Stock
Press: Web Press
Binding: Saddle Stitched
In Business: 49 years

6622 John Wiley & Sons Journals
John Wiley & Sons
111 River Street
Hoboken, NJ 07030-5774   201-748-6000
                               Fax: 201-748-6088
info@wiley.com
www.Wiley.Com

Business, chemistry, computer science, earth science, education, engineering, environmental management and sciences, law, life sciences, mathematics and statistics, medicine and psychology journals

Chairman: Peter Booth Wiley
President: Mark Allin
CFO: William B. Plummer
Managing Partner: Kalpana Raina
Mnager: Jese C. Wiley
Corporate Secretary: Edward J. May
Credit Cards: AMEX; MasterCard
Catalog Cost: Free
Catalog Circulation: Mailed 1 time(s) per year
Printing Information: 342 pages on Matte Stock
Binding: Perfect Bound
In Business: 208 years
Number of Employees: 5100

6623 Krames Health & Safety Education
Krames Health & Safety Education
280 Utah Ave
Suite 150
South San Francisco, CA 94080-3066   650-244-4333
                                           800-333-3032
                                           Fax: 650-244-4528
info@kramesstaywell.com
www.kramesstaywell.com

Health, wellness and safety information publications

President: George Parker
CFO: Mike Burnett
Marketing Manager: Frienelson
Production Manager: Ernesto Guzman
CEO: Bill Goldberg
Chief Medical Officer: David Gregg, M.D.

President, Strategic Partnerships D: Nancy Monahan
Buyers: Debbie Robinson
Noel Parker-Guerrero
Don Albert
Credit Cards: AMEX; MasterCard; Visa
Catalog Cost: Free
Catalog Circulation: Mailed 3 time(s) per year to 1.2M
Printing Information: 40 pages in 4 colors on Matte Stock
Press: Web Press
Binding: Saddle Stitched
Mailing List Information: Names for rent
In Business: 16 years
Number of Employees: 160
Sales Information: $25,000,000 - $50,000,000

6624 Krazy Duck Productions Catalog
Krazy Duck Productions
2227 Woods Creek Road
Liberty, KY 42539   606-787-2571
                         Fax: 606-787-8207
krazyduckproductions@msn.com
www.krazyduck.com

Self-publishers of fiction & non-fiction books including Tears and Tales: Stories of Animal and Human Rescue, Horse with the Golden Mane, Streetwise: Mafia Memoirs; Memoirs of the Street

President: Russell A Vassallo
Marketing Manager: Virginia G Vassallo
Production Manager: Virginia G Vassallo
Fulfillment: Virginia G Vassallo
Catalog Cost: Free
Average Order Size: $100
Printing Information: on Newsprint
Press: Letterpress
Binding: Perfect Bound
Mailing List Information: Names for rent
In Business: 7 years
Number of Employees: 2
Sales Information: $400,000

6625 Lawyers & Judges Publishing Company
Lawyers & Judges Publishing Company
917 North Swan Road
PO Box 30040
Tucson, AZ 85751-0040   520-323-1500
                              800-209-7109
                         Fax: 520-323-0055
sales@lawyersandjudges.com
www.Lawyersandjudges.Com

Professional aides for lawyers and insurance professionals

President: Steve Weintraub
Credit Cards: AMEX; MasterCard; Visa
Catalog Cost: Free
Catalog Circulation: Mailed 3 time(s) per year to 100M
Average Order Size: $95
Printing Information: 48 pages in 4 colors on Glossy Stock
Press: Web Press
Binding: Saddle Stitched
Mailing List Information: Names for rent
In Business: 52 years
Number of Employees: 4
Sales Information: $3MM to $5MM

6626 MIT Press
MIT Press
One Rogers Street
Cambridge, MA 02142-1209   617-253-5646
                                 800-405-1619
                            Fax: 617-258-6779
mitpress-order-inq@mit.edu
www.mitpress.mit.edu

Books published by Massachusetts Institute of Technology on a variety of subjects

Marketing Manager: Jill Rodgers
Production Manager: Janet Rossi
Director: Amy Brand
Director of Technology: Bill Trippe
Director of Finance: Brent Oberlin

Printing Information: 72 pages
Binding: Saddle Stitched
In Business: 52 years

6627 Maintenance Troubleshooting
Maintenance Troubleshooting
2917 Cheshire Road
Wilmington, DE 19810   302-738-0532
                              800-755-7672
                         Fax: 302-397-0248
mtbooks@pobox.com
www.mtroubleshooting.com

Literature, books and manual kits

President: Thomas Davis
In Business: 38 years
Number of Employees: 4

6628 Merchandising Solutions
M F Blouin
710 Main Street
PO Box 10
Rollinsford, NH 03869   603-742-0104
                              800-394-1632
                         Fax: 603-742-9539
info@mfblouin.com
www.mfblouin.com

Banking office supplies & equipment including sign holders, compliance signs, nameplates, security pens, cash handling supplies, currency envelopes, ATM drive up items, check desks and teller stools

President: David Zoia
CFO: Linda White
Credit Cards: AMEX; MasterCard; Visa
Catalog Cost: Free
Catalog Circulation: Mailed 12 time(s) per year
Printing Information: 64 pages in 4 colors on Glossy Stock
Press: Web Press
Binding: Saddle Stitched
Mailing List Information: Names for rent
In Business: 63 years
Number of Employees: 40
Sales Information: $ 4 Million

6629 National Association of Printers & Lithographers
Epicomm
One Meadowlands Plaza
Suite 1511
East Rutherford, NJ 07073   201-634-9600
                                  800-642-6275
                             Fax: 201-634-0324
epicomm.org

Information on books and products produced by NAPL to assist printers and print salespeople

Chairman: Tom Duchene
President: Ken Garner
kgarner@epicomm.org
CFO: Dean D'Ambrosi
Marketing Manager: Samantha Lake
SVP/Managing Director: Mike Philie
mphilie@epicomm.org
SVP/Chief Economist: Andrew D. Paparozzi
apaparozzi@epicomm.org
Director of Marketing: Samantha Lake
slake@epicomm.org
Printing Information: 6 pages in 2 colors
In Business: 1 years

6630 PSI Research
Publishing Services
PO Box 3727
Unit D
Central Point, OR 97502   541-855-5566
                                800-795-4059
                           Fax: 541-855-1360
www.psi-research.com

Business resource guides

President: Emmett Ramey
Credit Cards: AMEX; MasterCard; Visa

Catalog Cost: Free
Catalog Circulation: Mailed 2 time(s) per year to 2M
Printing Information: 32 pages in 2 colors on Glossy Stock
Press: Web Press
Binding: Saddle Stitched
In Business: 25 years
Number of Employees: 11

6631 Paper Clips
Baker & Taylor
2550 W Tyvola Road
Suite 300
Charlotte, NC 28217-4538   800-775-1800
                             Fax: 704-998-3100
btinfo@baker-taylor.com
www.btol.com

Paperback and audio titles list

Chairman: Thomas Morgan
President: George F. Coe
CFO: Jeff Leonard
Marketing Manager: Joanne Young
Executive VP: Amandeep Kochar
Managing Director: Raynier Picard
EVP, Chief Information Officer: Matt Carroll
Catalog Circulation: Mailed 12 time(s) per year
Printing Information: 50 pages
Press: Web Press
Binding: Saddle Stitched
In Business: 187 years

6632 Parlay International
Parlay International
712 Bancroft Rd
505
Walnut Creek, CA 94598   800-457-2752
                           Fax: 925-939-1414
info@parlay.com
www.parlay.com

Collection of reproducible resources: one-page handouts on a variety of topics for insurance companies, hospitals, military personnel

President: Robert Lester
In Business: 28 years
Sales Information: $500M to $1MM

6633 Rand McNally
Rand McNally & Company
9855 Woods Drive Skokie
Skokie, IL 60077-9915   847-329-8100
                              800-777-6277
                         Fax: 800-934-3479
ctsales@randmcnally.com
www.randmcnally.com

Business and marketing data books

President: Robert S Apatoff
Credit Cards: AMEX; MasterCard; Visa
Catalog Cost: Free
Catalog Circulation: Mailed 1 time(s) per year to 10M
Printing Information: 48 pages in 4 colors
In Business: 159 years
Number of Employees: 600

6634 Salem Press
Grey House Publishing, Inc.
4919 Route 22
PO Box 56
Amenia, NY 12501   518-789-8700
                         800-221-1592
                    Fax: 518-433-4739
sales@salempress.com
www.salempress.com

Award-winning history, literature, science and health titles that serve as excellent research tools for high school and undergraduate level students. Most titles include complementary online access.

Marketing Manager: Jessica Moody
Production Manager: Kristen Hayes

Editorial Director: Laura Mars
Sales Manager: Jim Wright
jwright@salempress.com
Catalog Cost: Free
Printing Information: 92 pages in 4 colors on Glossy Stock
Press: Web Press
Binding: Saddle Stitched
In Business: 66 years

6635 Small Business Development Catalog
Entrepreneur Media Inc.
18061 Fitch
Irvine, CA 92614-6234   949-261-2325
800-421-2300
Fax: 949-261-7729
press@entrepreneur.com
www.entrepreneur.com
Startup business guides, reference books, audio and videotape programs designed for small business owners and those planning an entrepreneurial venture

President: Peter Shea
Editor-in-Chief/VP: Amy Cosper
acosper@entrepreneur.com
Editorial Director, Entrepreneur.co: Raymond Hennessey
rhennessey@entrepreneur.com
Reprints Partner: Nick Lademarco
niademarco@wrightsmedia.com
Credit Cards: AMEX; MasterCard
Catalog Circulation: Mailed 2 time(s) per year to 12MM
Printing Information: 66 pages in 4 colors
Press: Web Press
Binding: Saddle Stitched

6636 The Original Privacy Catalog
Eden Press
PO Box 8410
Fountain Valley, CA 92728   714-968-8472
800-338-8484
edenpressinc@hotmail.com
www.edenpress.com
Books and videos that deal with privacy, money, home businesses, jobs, new identity, credit, degrees, cash business, foreign opportunities, residence and passports.

President: Barry Reid
Catalog Cost: Free
Printing Information: 16 pages on Newsprint
Press: Web Press
Binding: Saddle Stitched
Mailing List Information: Names for rent
In Business: 46 years
Sales Information: $410K

6637 TitleWaves Publishing
Follett Library Resources, Inc
1340 Ridgeview Dr.
McHenry, IL 60050-288   815-759-1700
888-511-5114
Fax: 815-759-9831
www.flr.follett.com
Books and software on personal finance, personal growth and legal issues

President: Rob Sanford
Marketing Manager: Layne Beck
Credit Cards: AMEX; MasterCard; Visa
Catalog Cost: Free
Catalog Circulation: Mailed 4 time(s) per year to 5M
Average Order Size: $63
Printing Information: 10 pages in 2 colors on Matte Stock
Press: Letterpress
Binding: Saddle Stitched
Mailing List Information: Names for rent
List Manager: Rob Sanford
In Business: 140 years
Number of Employees: 2

6638 Towers Club Book Store
Avid Reader
1600 Broadway
Sacramento, CA 95818-6801   916-441-4400
800-524-4045
Fax: 916-443-1345
avidreadertower.com
Books to help the neophyte or veteran mail order information merchant or home-based entrepreneur; hard-to-find titles of famous self-made entrepreneurs

President: Jerry Buchanan
Production Manager: Pam Powers
Credit Cards: MasterCard
Catalog Cost: Free
Catalog Circulation: Mailed 4 time(s) per year to 15M
Printing Information: 2 pages on Matte Stock
Press: Sheetfed Press
In Business: 27 years
Number of Employees: 5

6639 UN Publications
United Nations Publications Customer Ser
15200 NBN Way
PO Box 190
Blue Ridge Summit, PA 17214   800-254-4286
Fax: 800-338-4550
unpublications@nbnbooks.com
shop.un.org
Books published by the United Nations relating to international affairs, trade, business, development, disarmament, children's books and more

President: Susanna H Johnston
Marketing Manager: Fred Doulton
Credit Cards: MasterCard; Visa
Catalog Cost: Free
Catalog Circulation: Mailed 1 time(s) per year
Printing Information: 200 pages in 1 color on Matte Stock
Binding: Saddle Stitched
List Manager: Chris Woodthorpe
In Business: 68 years
Number of Employees: 1050

6640 US Department of Commerce
National Technical Information Service
5301 Shawnee Road
Alexandria, VA 22312-1   703-605-6000
800-553-6847
Fax: 703-605-6900
customerservice@ntis.gov
www.ntis.gov
Technological and scientific information

President: Ron Lawson
CFO: Alan Neuschatz
Marketing Manager: Wally Finch
Production Manager: Doug Campion
Director: Bruce Borzino
Credit Cards: AMEX; MasterCard; Visa
Catalog Cost: Free
Catalog Circulation: Mailed 1 time(s) per year to 70M
Average Order Size: $50
Printing Information: 60 pages in 2 colors on Matte Stock
Press: Letterpress
Binding: Saddle Stitched
Mailing List Information: Names for rent
List Manager: Lorraine Schrock
In Business: 5 years
Number of Employees: 350
Sales Information: $20MM to $50MM

6641 Wealth Unlimited
PO Box 6691
Jacksonville, FL 32236-6691   904-366-8068
www.wealth-unlimited.com
Wholesale book distributor, catalog and newsletter

President: Veronica Griffin

6642 Zig Ziglar Corporation
Zig Ziglar Corporation
5055 West Park Blvd
Suite 700
Plano, TX 75093-6480   972-233-9191
800-527-0306
Fax: 972-991-1853
customercare@ziglar.com
www.Ziglar.Com
Training materials, family resources and corporate training

President: Tom Ziglar
Marketing Manager: Steve Boyd
Production Manager: Chad Whitmeyer
Credit Cards: AMEX; MasterCard; Visa
Catalog Circulation: Mailed 1 time(s) per year to 300M
Printing Information: 16 pages in 4 colors on Matte Stock
Press: Web Press
Number of Employees: 35
Sales Information: 3MM-5MM

Building Supplies
General

6643 AME International
AME International
2324 Circuit Way
Brooksville, FL 34604   352-799-1111
877-755-4263
Fax: 352-799-1112
sales@ameintl.net
www.ameintl.net
Heavy duty tools, tools and tires for Passenger buses, tractor trailer trucks, construction, mining and forestry equipment, light trucks, motorcycles and ATV's

President: Keith Jarman
kjarman@ameintl.net
Marketing Manager: Wil Zufelt
wzufelt@ameintl.net
VP, Iinternational Sales: Luis Goyeneche
lgoyeneche@ameintl.net
VP, Domestic Sales: Brett Waggoner
bwaggoner@ameintl.net
Western USA/Asia Area Manager: ShaneWiley
swiley@ameintl.net
Printing Information: 104 pages
Number of Employees: 3
Sales Information: $140,000

6644 Abatron Building & Restoration
Abatron, Inc.
5501 95th Avenue
Kenosha, WI 53144-7499   262-653-2000
800-445-1754
Fax: 262-653-2019
info@abatron.com
www.abatron.com
Epoxy maintenance and restoration products

President: John Caporaso
Marketing Manager: M.J. Wohl
Director, Sales & Marketing: Richard Ahlstrom
Credit Cards: AMEX; MasterCard; Visa
Catalog Cost: Free
Printing Information: 36 pages in 4 colors
Binding: Saddle Stitched
Mailing List Information: Names for rent
In Business: 58 years
Number of Employees: 18
Sales Information: $2.10 Million

6645 Acrocrete
BASF Construction Chemicals, LLC
3550 St. Johns Bluff Road, South
Jacksonville, FL 32224-2614   904-996-6000
800-221-9255
Fax: 904-996-6300
www.acrocrete.basf.com

Interior and exterior synthetic acrylic stucco products and systems

President: Gary Hasbach
CFO: Howard L Ehler Jr
Production Manager: Robert E Brown
Catalog Circulation: to 2M
Printing Information: 200 pages in 1 color on Matte Stock
Press: Letterpress
List Manager: Lisa Brock
In Business: 27 years
Number of Employees: 15

6646 Barco Products Company
Barco Products
24 N. Washington Ave
Batavia, IL 60510   630-879-0084
                            800-338-2697
                       Fax: 630-879-8687
                sales@barcoproducts.com
                www.barcoproducts.com

Picnic tables, park benches, trash receptacles, safety products, parking lot products

President: Robert Runke
Marketing Manager: Susan Ross
Production Manager: Kim Vallone
CEO: Cyril Matter
Catalog Cost: Free
In Business: 30 years
Sales Information: $6MM

6647 Berridge Manufacturing Company
Berridge Manufacturing Company
6515 Fratt Road
San Antonio, TX 78218-7199   210-650-3050
                                800-669-0009
                           Fax: 210-650-0379
                           info@berridge.com
                           www.berridge.com

Metal roofing products

President: Joel Jesse
Catalog Cost: Free
Catalog Circulation: Mailed 1 time(s) per year to 10M
Printing Information: 23 pages in 4 colors
In Business: 47 years
Number of Employees: 175
Sales Information: $3,000,000

6648 Brass Knob
The Brass Knob Architectural Antiques
2311 18th St NW
Washington, DC 20009-1814   202-332-3370
                          Fax: 202-332-5594
               info@thebrassknob.com
               www.thebrassknob.com

Architectural antiques

President: Donetta George
Co-Founder: Donetta George
Sales Staff: Taylor Jenkins
In Business: 34 years
Number of Employees: 4
Sales Information: $500M to $1MM

6649 Bustin Safety Grating & Platforms
Bustin USA
401 Oak Street
East Stroudsburg, PA 18301-1415 570-424-6500
                                800-933-5166
                           Fax: 570-424-6453
                           www.bustin-usa.com

Steel, aluminum and fiberglass safety grating, platforms, ladders, stair treads, truck and trailer safety equipment

President: Karen Cramer
Marketing Manager: Michael Gutierrez
Truck & Trailer Product Support: Nan Maye
nmaye@bustin-usa.com
Industrial Product Support: Jeff Kovalick
jkovalick@bustin-usa.com
Industrial Product Manager: Stephen R. Lukas
slukas@bustin-usa.com
Catalog Circulation: Mailed 1 time(s) per year

Printing Information: 25 pages in 4 colors
Mailing List Information: Names for rent
In Business: 87 years
Number of Employees: 65
Sales Information: 6MM

6650 Chief Manufacturing
Chief
6436 City West Parkway
Suite 700
Eden Prairie, MN 55344-4540   952-894-6280
                                800-582-6480
                           Fax: 952-894-6918
                        chief@chiefmfg.com
                        www.Chiefmfg.Com

Bases, posts and shelves

President: Scott Gill
Director of Customer Service: Derek Derks
corey.chapek@milestone.com
Commercial Lead: Brandi Casebolt
brandi.casebolt@milestone.com
Technical: Jim Tesch
jim.tesch@milestone.com
Printing Information: 197 pages
In Business: 37 years
Number of Employees: 20
Sales Information: $1,000,000 - $5,000,000

6651 Cleveland Steel Specialty
Cleveland Steel Specialty Company
26001 Richmond Rd
Bedford Heights, OH 44146-1435 216-464-9400
                                 800-251-8351
                            Fax: 216-464-9404
                  info@clevelandsteel.com
                  www.Clevelandsteel.Com

Cast aluminum post bases

President: Robert W Ehrhardt
Marketing Manager: Dave Monhart
Credit Cards: MasterCard
Catalog Cost: Free
In Business: 91 years
Sales Information: $5MM to $10MM

6652 Detailed Play Systems Pro
Detailed Play Systems
PO Box 633
Manahawkin, NJ 8050   973-912-9440
                               800-398-7565
                          Fax: 973-710-3087
                  www.detailedplaypro.com

Playground equipment

President: Karl Jessen
Credit Cards: AMEX; MasterCard
Catalog Cost: Free

6653 Dome'l
Dome'l Inc.
3 Grunwald Street
Clifton, NJ 07013   973-641-1800
                          Fax: 973-614-8011
                        staff@domelinc.com
                        www.domelinc.com

Entry and walkway canopies

President: John Morse
Credit Cards: MasterCard
In Business: 43 years
Number of Employees: 130
Sales Information: $10,000,000 - $25,000,000

6654 EJ
EJ Group
301 Spring St.
East Jordan, MI 49727   800-874-4100
                        americas.ejco.com

Access solutions for water and telecommunications utilities.

6655 Enercept
Enercept
3100 9th Ave SE
Watertown, SD 57201-9170   605-882-2222
                               800-658-3303
                          Fax: 605-882-2753
                        info@enercept.com
                        www.enercept.com

Foam core structural insulated panels for residential, commercial and agricultural buildings

President: Alan Case
CFO: Barbara Hartley
Regional Sales Manager: Ron Gleysteen
rgleysteen@enercept.com
International Marketing Manager: Kermit Johnson
Printing Information: 16 pages
In Business: 30 years
Number of Employees: 40
Sales Information: $5,000,000 - $10,000,000

6656 Fine Architectural Metalsmiths
Fine Architectural Metalsmiths
44 Jayne Street
Florida, NY 10921   845-651-7550
                               888-862-9577
                          Fax: 845-651-7857
                        info@iceforge.com
                        www.iceforge.com

Architectural metalwork and home accessories

President: Eduard Mack
Marketing Manager: Rhoda Mack
Production Manager: Rhoda Mack
Catalog Cost: $5
Catalog Circulation: Mailed 1 time(s) per year to 5M
Printing Information: 10 pages in 1 color on Matte Stock
Press: Letterpress
Mailing List Information: Names for rent
In Business: 33 years
Number of Employees: 8
Sales Information: $500,000 - $1,000,000

6657 Garden State Brickface
Garden State Brickface, Windows & Siding
217 E Highland Pkwy
Roselle, NJ 07203-2688   908-241-5900
                               800-388-4472
                          Fax: 908-298-3890
                        www.Brickface.Com

Custom wall finishes

Chairman: David Moore
President: Cindy Lucas
Credit Cards: MasterCard
In Business: 62 years
Number of Employees: 100
Sales Information: $5MM to $10MM

6658 Gempler's Catalog
Gempler's
PO Box 5175
Madison, WI 53547-5175   608-662-3301
                               800-382-8473
                          Fax: 608-662-3360
                  customerservice@gemplers.com
                  www.gemplers.com

Contractor and industrial supplies

Marketing Manager: Karsten Sale
Credit Cards: AMEX; MasterCard
Printing Information: 12 pages

6659 Gosport Manufacturing Company
Gosport Manufacturing Company
P.O.Box 26
11 Louisa St.
Gosport, IN 47433-26   812-879-4224
                               800-457-4406
                          Fax: 812-879-4227
                        www.Gosportmfg.Com

Canvas, vinyl and polyethylene tarpaulins

President: Joe King
CFO: Mr Joe King
Marketing Manager: Mr Tom Rice
Production Manager: Mr Tom Rice
Mailing List Information: Names for rent
In Business: 54 years
Number of Employees: 55
Sales Information: $5,000,000 - $10,000,000

6660 Gupta Permold Corporation

Gupta Permold Corporation
234 Lott Road
Pittsburgh, PA 15235-4025   412-793-3511
                              Fax: 412-793-1055
                         info@guptapermold.com
                         www.guptapermold.com

Coatings and resistor assemblies

President: Lakshmi Gupta
In Business: 34 years
Number of Employees: 70
Sales Information: $5,000,000 - $10,000,000

6661 Haws Corporation

Haws
1455 Kleppe Ln
Sparks, NV 89431-6467   775-359-4712
                             888-640-4297
                        Fax: 775-359-7424
                          info@hawsco.com
                          www.Hawsco.Com

Drinking fountains and faucets, emergency drench showers and eye washers

Chairman: Michael Haws Traynos
President: Tom White
CFO: John Pettibone, VP Finance
Marketing Manager: Scott McLean, VP Sales
Production Manager: Tom White, VP Manufacturing
Fulfillment: Jim Hayes, VP Business Development
VP of Operations: Aaron Cross Jr.
VP of Business Development: Michael Markovsky
Mailing List Information: Names for rent
In Business: 108 years
Number of Employees: 100
Sales Information: $1,000,000 - $5,000,000

6662 Home Improvements

Improvements
5568 West Chester Road
West Chester, OH 45069-2914   800-634-9484
                              Fax: 800-757-9997
                    custserv@improvementscatalog.com
                    www.improvementscatalog.com

Items for home upkeep and improvement

Credit Cards: AMEX; MasterCard
Catalog Circulation: Mailed 4 time(s) per year
Printing Information: 56 pages in 4 colors
Binding: Saddle Stitched
In Business: 18 years

6663 IKG Industries

Harsco Industrial IKG
1514 Sheldon Rd
Channelview, TX 77530-2622   281-452-6637
                              Fax: 281-378-3987
                         salesikg@harsco.com
                         www.Ikgindustries.Com

Deck safety grating, metal bar grating, bridges, decks and highway drains

Chairman: Derek C Hathaway
President: Oscar Jarett
CFO: Salvatore D Fazzolari
Number of Employees: 35

6664 Industrial Abrasives

Industrial Abrasives
642 N. 8th Street
PO Box 14955
Reading, PA 19601-4955   610-378-1861
                              800-428-2222
                        Fax: 610-378-4868
                         sandyiac@comcast.net
                         www.industrialabrasives.com

Sandpaper and other coated abrasive products, such as belts, rolls and discs

President: Sandra a Reese
Credit Cards: AMEX; MasterCard
In Business: 68 years
Sales Information: $5MM to $10MM

6665 Jessup Manufacturing Company

Jessup Manufacturing Company
2815 West Route 120
PO Box 366
McHenry, IL 60051-366   815-918-4165
                              800-563-1681
                        Fax: 815-385-0079
                         sales@jessupmfg.com
                         www.jessupmfg.com

Non slip tapes, abrasive and non abrasive, available in rolls, sheets or custom die cut shapes

President: Robert Jessup
Marketing Manager: Al Carlson
Mailing List Information: Names for rent
In Business: 58 years
Number of Employees: 30

6666 LaMotte Soil Testing Products

LaMotte Soil Testing Products
802 Washington Avenue
PO Box 329
Chestertown, MD 21620-329   410-778-3100
                              800-344-3100
                        Fax: 410-778-6394
                         tech@lamotte.com
                         www.lamotte.com/soil.html

Equipment for testing PH and soil measurements

Marketing Manager: James Moore
Printing Information: 24 pages in 4 colors
In Business: 96 years

6667 Louisville Ladder

Louisville Ladder
7765 National Turnpike, Unit 190
Louisville, KY 40214   502-368-1785
                              800-666-2811
                        Fax: 800-274-4566
                         www.Louisvilleladder.Com

Industrial ladders, stages and accessories

President: Carlos Moreno
Marketing Manager: Santiago Veytia
In Business: 69 years
Number of Employees: 1500
Sales Information: $92 Million

6668 Macton Corporation

Macton Corporation
116 Willenbrock Road
Oxford, CT 06478   203-267-1500
                              Fax: 203-267-1555
                         dlouder@macton.com
                         www.Macton.Com

Turntables for architectural applications

President: Peter Mc Gonagle
Marketing Manager: John Curry
Mailing List Information: Names for rent
In Business: 5 years
Number of Employees: 30
Sales Information: $1,000,000 - $5,000,000

6669 Maintenance USA

Maintenance USA
3333 Lenox Avenue
Jacksonville, FL 32254   800-283-4000
                              888-803-4468
                        Fax: 800-288-2828
                         specialorder@e-musa.com
                         www.e-musa.com

Building supplies and fixtures

In Business: 28 years

6670 Master Catalogue

Wood-Mode Fine Custom Cabinetry
One 2nd Street
Kreamer, PA 17833   570-374-2711
                              877-635-7500
                        Fax: 570-374-2700
                         www.wood-mode.com

Custom-built cabinetry

Catalog Circulation: Mailed 1 time(s) per year to 100K
Printing Information: 65 pages in 4 colors

6671 Mavidon Catalog

Lord Corporation
3953 SW Bruner Terrace
Palm City, FL 34990-5549   877-275-5673
                              877-275-5673
                        Fax: 561-286-5885
                         www.lord.com

Adhesives, coatings and compounds

Chairman: Gen. James F. Amos, USMC (ret)
President: Edward L. Auslander
CFO: Tesa L. Oechsle
Marketing Manager: T Mascia
Director: Dr. Uma Chowdhury
Director: Dr. Delores M. Etter
Director: Richard L. McNeel
Number of Employees: 50
Sales Information: $10,000,000 - $25,000,000

6672 Musson Rubber Company

Musson
1320 East Archwood Ave.
PO Box 7038
Akron, OH 44306-2825   330-773-7651
                              800-321-2381
                        Fax: 330-773-3254
                         info@mussonrubber.com
                         www.Mussonrubber.Com

Vinyl mats and matting for commercial and industrial applications

President: Bennie D Segers
In Business: 70 years
Number of Employees: 46
Sales Information: $5MM to $10MM

6673 Natural Spaces Domes

Natural Spaces Domes
37955 Bridge Rd
North Branch, MN 55056-5398   651-674-4292
                              800-733-7107
                        Fax: 651-674-5005
                         nsd@naturalspacesdomes.com
                         www.Naturalspacesdomes.Com

Design, manufacture and construction of geodesic domes used for homes, cabins, businesses, churches

President: Dennis Johnson
Credit Cards: AMEX; MasterCard; Visa
Catalog Cost: Free
Catalog Circulation: Mailed 1 time(s) per year
Printing Information: 50 pages in 4 colors on Matte Stock
Binding: Saddle Stitched
In Business: 17 years
Number of Employees: 7
Sales Information: $500,000 - $1,000,000

6674 Niagara Fiberboard
Niagara Fiberboard, Inc.
PO Box 520
Lockport, NY 14095 716-434-8881
Fax: 716-434-8884
info@niagarafiberboard.com
www.niagarafiberboard.com

Recycled paperboard products

Chairman: Don Wolf
President: Dan Wilson
Marketing Manager: Richard Cain
Credit Cards: MasterCard
Mailing List Information: Names for rent
In Business: 25 years
Number of Employees: 35
Sales Information: $5,000,000 - $10,000,000

6675 Norton-Performance Plastics Catalog
Norton-Performance Plastics
1 Sealants Park
Granville, NY 12832-1652 518-642-2200
800-833-9693
Fax: 518-642-1792
www.nortonplastics.com

Log home foam

President: John Crawford
Marketing Manager: Sam Sher
In Business: 35 years
Number of Employees: 200
Sales Information: $25,000,000 - $50,000,000

6676 Omaha Fixture International
Omaha Fixture International
10320 J Street
Omaha, NE 68127 402-592-3720
800-637-2257
Fax: 402-593-5716
Service@OmahaFixture.com
www.omahafixture.com

Fixtures, displays and forms for businesses

President: Joel Alperson
Credit Cards: AMEX; MasterCard
In Business: 60 years

6677 Outwater Plastics Industries
Outwater Plastics Industries,Inc
24 River Road
P.O. Box 500
Bogota, NJ 07603 800-631-8375
Fax: 800-888-3315
www.outwater.com

Extrusions, furniture and cabinet components, knobs and pulls, injection molded parts, casters, store fixture components, lighting, engineering plastics, hardware, and architectural moulding/millwork.

President: Peter Kessler
Marketing Manager: Joey Shimm
Credit Cards: AMEX; MasterCard; Visa
In Business: 45 years
Number of Employees: 200
Sales Information: $10,000,000 - $25,000,000

6678 Palmer Products Corporation
Palmer Products Corporation
146 St. Matthews Avenue
P.O.Box 7155
Louisville, KY 40257-155 502-893-3668
800-431-6151
Fax: 502-895-9253
palmer@mirro-mastic.com
www.Mirro-Mastic.Com

Palmer Mirro-Mastics (adhesives for mirror)

President: Lawrence Palmer-Ball
CFO: Virginia Bronn
Marketing Manager: Missy Bush
Production Manager: Lawrence Palmer-Ball
Buyers: Adriane Koch
Catalog Circulation: to 5M
Printing Information: 6 pages in 4 colors on Glossy Stock
Press: Web Press

Mailing List Information: Names for rent
In Business: 104 years
Number of Employees: 18
Sales Information: $1,000,000 - $5,000,000

6679 Penco Products Catalog
Penco Products
1820 Stonehenge Drive
PO Box 158
Greenville, NC 27858-158 610-666-0500
800-562-1000
Fax: 800-248-1555
www.Pencoproducts.Com

Storage racks, steel shelving, lockers, storage cabinets, work benches and shop furniture

President: Greg Grogan
Marketing Manager: Philip Krugler
Production Manager: Philip Krugler
In Business: 145 years
Sales Information: $10MM to $20MM

6680 Permatex Industrial Catalog
Permatex
10 Columbus Boulevard
Hartford, CT 06106-4016 800-543-7500
877-376-2839
Fax: 860-543-6998
www.permatex.com

Adhesives, cleaners, coatings, hand cleaners and lubricants

VP/General Manager: Andy Robinson
Senior Director of Sales: Chris Crabill
Director of Technology: Claudia Britton
In Business: 106 years

6681 Polart by Mail
Polart Distribution (USA) Inc.
5700 Sarah Avenue
Sarasota, FL 34233-3446 941-927-8983
800-278-9393
Fax: 941-927-8239
www.polandbymail.com

Giftware, stoneware, ceramics, crystal, videos, CDs, books, armoury replicas of over 4000 items from Poland, wholesale sales available

President: Jarek Zaremba
Marketing Manager: Maciek Zaremba
Credit Cards: AMEX; MasterCard
Catalog Cost: $2
Average Order Size: $90
Printing Information: 16 pages in 4 colors on Glossy Stock
Press: Web Press
Binding: Saddle Stitched
Mailing List Information: Names for rent
Number of Employees: 7
Sales Information: $1MM to $3MM

6682 ProTech Systems
M&G DuraVent, Inc
10 Jupiter Ln
Albany, NY 12205-1912 518-649-9700
800-835-4429
Fax: 519-463-5271
info@duravent.com
www.Protechinfo.Com

Ventinox Chimney lining systems and TherMix prepackaged masonry insulation material

President: Martin J Wawrla
Buyers: Michael Zoglia
Credit Cards: AMEX; MasterCard
In Business: 85 years
Number of Employees: 30
Sales Information: $5MM to $10MM

6683 Products in, on and Around Concrete
Raw Equipment Building Materials Corp
2800 College Point Boulevard
Flushing, NY 11354-2512 718-461-2200
Fax: 718-762-3094
sales@rawequipment.com
www.rawequipment.com

Concrete accessories

Founder: Richard A. Wallace
Credit Cards: AMEX; MasterCard
Catalog Circulation: Mailed 1 time(s) per year
Printing Information: 35 pages in 2 colors
Binding: Saddle Stitched
In Business: 40 years

6684 Putnam Rolling Ladder Company
Putnam Rolling Ladder Co Inc
32 Howard Street
New York, NY 10013 212-226-5147
Fax: 212-941-1836
putnam1905@aol.com
www.putnamrollingladder.com

Step, straight and extension ladders; rolling ladder

Credit Cards: AMEX; MasterCard
Catalog Cost: Free
Printing Information: 5 pages on Glossy Stock
Binding: Folded
Mailing List Information: Names for rent
In Business: 105 years
Number of Employees: 44

6685 Quantum Composites Catalog
Quantum Composites
1310 S Valley Center Dr
Bay City, MI 48706-9798 989-922-3863
800-462-9318
Fax: 989-922-3915
www.Quantumcomposites.Com

High strength thermostat sheet moulding compounds

President: Gary Zellner
Credit Cards: AMEX; MasterCard
Number of Employees: 17
Sales Information: $5,000,000 - $10,000,000

6686 Scott Machine Development Corporation
Scott Machine Development Corp.
200 Prospect Avenue
P.O. Box 88
Walton, NY 13856-88 607-865-6511
800-227-2688
Fax: 607-865-7269
www.Scottmachinecorp.Com

Manufacturer of signmaking equipment and supplies; manual and computerized machines are available for engraving signs in plastic or for cutting letters in vinyl

President: Greg Waldron
Marketing Manager: Tim Moss
Catalog Cost: Free
Catalog Circulation: to 10M
Printing Information: 48 pages in 3 colors on Glossy Stock
Press: Web Press
Binding: Saddle Stitched
Mailing List Information: Names for rent
In Business: 53 years
Number of Employees: 45
Sales Information: $5,000,000 - $10,000,000

6687 Seals Eastern Catalog
Seals Eastern, Inc.
134 Pearl Street
Red Bank, NJ 07701-520 732-747-9200
Fax: 732-747-3647
www.sealseastern.com

Compounds and pre-production prototypes

President: Dan Hertz
Sales: Kris Solaas
sales@sealseastern.com
In Business: 50 years

Number of Employees: 100-
Sales Information: $10,000,000 - $25,000,000

6688 Shenango Steel Buildings
Shenango Steel Buildings, Inc.
33 Carbaugh St
PO Box 268
West Middlesex, PA 16159-4103   724-528-9925
800-548-0625
Fax: 724-528-2452
info@shenangosteelbuildings.com
www.Shenangosteelbuildings.Com

Manufacturers and erectors of pre-engineered steel buildings

President: James M Campbell
jmc@shenangosteelbuildings.com
Marketing Manager: J Bradley Campbell
jbc@shenangosteelbuildings.com
Catalog Circulation: Mailed 1 time(s) per year
Printing Information: 10 pages in 4 colors
Binding: Saddle Stitched
In Business: 50 years
Sales Information: $3MM to $5MM

6689 Somay Paint Factory Catalog
Somay Products, Inc.
4301 NW 35th Ave
Miami, FL 33142-4382   305-633-6333
888-247-6629
Fax: 305-638-5524
paint@somay.com
www.Somay.Com

Interior and exterior house paints and traffic paints, waterproofing coatings, roof paints, swimming pool paint, tennis court paint, epoxies, urethanes, fungistatic paints, underwater paints

Chairman: Lee Parker
President: Garth R Parker
CFO: George O Knapp III
Production Manager: William C Harper
Credit Cards: AMEX; MasterCard; Visa
Catalog Cost: $2.5
Printing Information: 12 pages in 4 colors on Glossy Stock
Binding: Saddle Stitched
Mailing List Information: Names for rent
In Business: 87 years
Number of Employees: 20
Sales Information: $5,000,000 - $10,000,000

6690 Standard Tar Products Catalog
Knight Chemicals, LLC
7320 W. Florist Ave.
Milwaukee, WI 53218-6294   414-461-0100
800-825-7650
Fax: 414-461-0903
greg@knightchemicals.com
www.standardtar.com

Wood protectors and finishes, Snomelt instant ice melters, and Natural Science Organic fertilization

President: Edward F Chouinard
CFO: Sharon A Chounard
Buyers: Marlis A Vlemm
Credit Cards: MasterCard; Visa
Catalog Cost: Free
Catalog Circulation: Mailed 6 time(s) per year to 10000
Average Order Size: $1000
Printing Information: 10 pages in 4 colors on Matte Stock
Press: Sheetfed Press
Binding: Folded
Mailing List Information: Names for rent
List Manager: EF Chouinard
In Business: 88 years
Number of Employees: 30
Sales Information: $10MM to $20MM

6691 Stuc-O-Flex, International
Stuc-O-Flex International, Inc.
17639 NE 67th Ct
Redmond, WA 98052-4944   425-885-5085
800-305-1045
Fax: 425-869-0107
www.Stucoflex.Com

Elastomeric acrylic wall systems, synthetic stucco

President: Richard Dunstan
Marketing Manager: Dan Johnson
Catalog Circulation: to 1M
Printing Information: in 2 colors on Matte Stock
Number of Employees: 10
Sales Information: $3MM to $5MM

6692 Tesa Tape
Tesa Tape, Inc.
5825 Carnegie Blvd
Charlotte, NC 28209-4633   800-426-2181
800-367-8825
Fax: 800-852-8831
customercare@tesatape.com
www.Tesatape.Com

Electrical, duct, masking, carpet and general purpose tape

President: Daniel Germain
CFO: Steve Jone
Marketing Manager: Thomas Barmann
Production Manager: Frank Pall
Catalog Cost: Free
Catalog Circulation: Mailed 4 time(s) per year to 2M
Average Order Size: $2400
Printing Information: 12 pages in 4 colors
List Manager: Frank Pall
In Business: 79 years
Number of Employees: 865
Sales Information: $20MM to $50MM

6693 Tiodize Catalog
Tiodize Company
5858 Engineer Drive
Huntington Beach, CA 92649-1569 714-898-4377
Fax: 714-891-7467
tiodize@tiodize.com
www.tiodize.com

Composites and advanced coatings for the prevention of friction, wear and corrosion; anodizing of titanium and aluminum

President: Thomas Adams
Marketing Manager: Wade Friedrichs
wade.friedrichs@tiodize.com
Purchasing: Tom Moore
tom.moore@tiodize.com
Technical Director: Gary Wittman
gary.wittman@tiodize.com
Controller: Patty Enna
patty.enna@tiodize.com
In Business: 49 years
Number of Employees: 55
Sales Information: $10,000,000 - $25,000,000

6694 Touch America
Touch America
1403 S Third St Ext
PO Box 1304
Mebane, NC 27302   919-732-6968
800-678-6824
Fax: 919-732-1173
info@touchamerica.com
www.touchamerica.com

Massage and spa equipment

President: Stewart Griffith
Marketing Manager: Lianne De Moya
Finance Executive: Chris Owens
International Marketing Manager: Valerie Rawlings
Credit Cards: AMEX; MasterCard
Catalog Cost: Free
Catalog Circulation: Mailed 2 time(s) per year to 25000
Average Order Size: $200

Printing Information: 40 pages in 4 colors on Glossy Stock
Press: Sheetfed Press
Binding: Saddle Stitched
Mailing List Information: Names for rent
In Business: 32 years
Sales Information: Under $500,000

6695 Tri-Boro Construction Supplies
Tri-Boro Construction Supplies
465 Locust Street
Dallastown, PA 17313-8   717-246-3095
800-632-9018
Fax: 717-246-3506
www.tri-borosupplies.com

Building supplies

CFO: Linda Rexroth
Founder: Glenn
Founder: Linda
Management Team: JR
Catalog Cost: Free
In Business: 39 years
Number of Employees: 75
Sales Information: $10,000,000 - $25,000,000

6696 Tubular Specialties Manufacturing
Tubular Specialities Manufacturing, Inc.
13011 South Spring Street
Los Angeles, CA 90061-262   310-515-5861
800-472-2227
Fax: 310-217-0653
tsm@calltsm.com
www.Calltsm.Com

ADA compliant shower seats, grab bars and handrailing

President: Arif Mansery
Marketing Manager: Pam Watts
Credit Cards: MasterCard; Visa
Catalog Cost: Free
Catalog Circulation: Mailed 1 time(s) per year to 25M
Printing Information: 36 pages in 1 color on Matte Stock
In Business: 49 years
Number of Employees: 60
Sales Information: $5,000,000 - $10,000,000

6697 Vermont Frames
Vermont Frames
22 Varney Hill Road
Starksboro, VT 05487-100   802-453-3727
800-545-6290
Fax: 802-453-2339
info@vermontframes.com
www.vermontframes.com

Post and beam frames

President: Jim Giroux
VP: Mark Driscroll
SIP's Projct Manager: Kyle Delabruere
Head Timber Frame Designer: Paul Gund
Printing Information: 12 pages
In Business: 39 years
Number of Employees: 8
Sales Information: $1,000,000 - $5,000,000

6698 Watercolors Inc
Watercolors Inc
High Ridge Road
Garrison, NY 10524   845-424-3327
Fax: 845-424-3169
watercolorsinc@earthlink.net
www.watercolorsinc.com

English, Edwardian, Italian and French bathroom fixtures, other traditional and contemporary faucet and accessory designs, also tubs, whirl pools, saunas, lighting

President: Joyce Blum
CFO: Larry Fleischer
Marketing Manager: Lisa Olmstead
Production Manager: Paul Gerwirtz
Fulfillment: Lisa Olmstead
International Marketing Manager: Joyce Blum
Buyers: Joyce Blun

Catalog Cost: $35
Catalog Circulation: Mailed 52 time(s) per year to 1000
Average Order Size: $500
Printing Information: 250 pages in 4 colors on Glossy Stock
Press: Sheetfed Press
Binding: Saddle Stitched
Mailing List Information: Names for rent
List Manager: Lisa Olmstead
In Business: 40 years
Number of Employees: 5

6699 Wrisco Industries
Wrisco Industries,Inc
355 Hiatt Dr # B
Suite B
Palm Beach Gdns, FL 33418-7199561-626-5700
   800-627-2646
Fax: 561-627-3574
www.wrisco.com

Pre-finished aluminum in choice of color/finishes for roofing, awnings, flashing, walls, gutters, patios, insulated roof and wall panels

President: Jim Monastra
Marketing Manager: AJ Monastra
Catalog Circulation: Mailed 4 time(s) per year to 10M
Average Order Size: $3000
Printing Information: 15 pages in 2 colors on Glossy Stock
Press: Letterpress
Binding: Folded
In Business: 98 years
Number of Employees: 104
Sales Information: $10MM to $20MM

Alternative Energy

6700 Appalachian Stove
Appalachian Stove
329 Emma Rd
Asheville, NC 28806-3885   828-253-0164
Fax: 828-254-7803
sales@gandwenergy.com
www.Appalachianstove.Com

Quality Stoves, Fireplaces & Mantels

President: James Rice
In Business: 38 years
Number of Employees: 70
Sales Information: $5,000,000 - $10,000,000

6701 Aqua-Therm
Aqua-Therm, LLC
310 Oak St.
PO Box 262
New London, MN 56273   320-346-2264
   800-325-2760
Fax: 320-354-3275
kbenjamin@aqua-therm.com
www.aqua-therm.com

Outside wood burning furnace

President: Olav Isane
Credit Cards: MasterCard; Visa
In Business: 16 years
Number of Employees: 7
Sales Information: $500M to $1MM

6702 Backwoods Solar Electric Systems
Backwoods Solar Electric Systems
1589 Rapid Lightning Creek Rd
Sandpoint, ID 83864-4754   208-263-4290
Fax: 208-265-4788
info@backwoodssolar.com
www.Backwoodssolar.Com

Solar electric power systems for remote homes where power lines are not available

President: Scott Gentleman
Catalog Cost: $3
Catalog Circulation: Mailed 1 time(s) per year to 30M
Average Order Size: $2000

Printing Information: 177 pages in 1 color on Glossy Stock
Press: Sheetfed Press
Binding: Perfect Bound
Mailing List Information: Names for rent
In Business: 37 years
Number of Employees: 6
Sales Information: $1,000,000

6703 Big Frog Mountain Corporation
Big Frog Mountain Corporation
3821 Hixson Pike
Chattanooga, TN 37415   423-265-0307
   877-232-1580
Fax: 423-265-9030
www.bigfrogmountain.com

Design and sell solar and wind electric power systems

President: T Tripp
Credit Cards: AMEX; MasterCard
In Business: 26 years

6704 Environmental Geothermal Houses
Enertia Building Systems, Inc.
PO Box 845
Youngsville, NC 27596-845   919-556-2391
enertia@mindspring.com
www.enertia.com

Solar-kit homes designed using new inertial technology

President: Michael Sykes
Credit Cards: MasterCard; Visa
Catalog Cost: $15
Catalog Circulation: Mailed 1 time(s) per year to 5000
Printing Information: 50 pages on Matte Stock
Press: Offset Press
Mailing List Information: Names for rent
In Business: 18 years
Number of Employees: 4
Sales Information: Under $500,000

6705 Hardy Diesels
Hardy Diesels
15749 Lyons Valley Road
Jamul, CA 91935-3503   619-669-1995
   800-341-7027
Fax: 619-669-4829
sales@hardydiesel.com
www.hardydiesel.com

Small diesel generators and diesel tractors, tractor implements, farm tractors, diesel marine engines, solar panels, wind generators, inverters, water pumps

Credit Cards: MasterCard

6706 HearthStone Catalog: Wood & Pellet Products
HearthStone
317 Stafford Avenue
Morrisville, VT 05661-8695   877-877-2113
warm@hearthstonestoves.com
www.Hearthstonestoves.Com

Wood and gas-fired stoves

President: David Kuhfahl
Credit Cards: MasterCard; Visa
Catalog Cost: Free
Printing Information: in 4 colors
In Business: 37 years
Number of Employees: 45
Sales Information: $1,000,000 - $5,000,000

6707 Heatmor
Heatmor
105 Industrial Park Court NE
PO Box 787
Warroad, MN 56763   218-386-2769
   800-834-7552
Fax: 218-386-2947
woodheat@heatmor.com
www.heatmor.com

Outdoor stainless steel furnaces

President: Gerry Reed
Marketing Manager: Darrell Shaugabay
darrell@heatmor.com
VP of Operations: Keith Astrup
kastrup@heatmor.com
Accounting: Brenda Nieman
brenda@heatmor.com
Services: Mike Galusha
mgalusha@heatmor.com
In Business: 31 years
Number of Employees: 36
Sales Information: $5MM to $10MM

6708 Kansas Wind Power
Kansas Wind Power
13569 214th Road
Holton, KS 66436-8138   785-364-4407
Fax: 785-364-4407
www.kansaswindpower.net

Solar electric, energy savers, pumps, solar cookers, grain mills, composting, toilets, propane appliances and telescopes

President: Bob Mc Broom
Catalog Cost: $4
Printing Information: 100 pages
In Business: 40 years

6709 New England Solar Electric
New England Solar Electric, Inc.
401 Huntington Road
PO Box 435
Worthington, MA 01098-9551   413-238-5974
   800-914-4131
Fax: 413-238-0203
spschulze@newenglandsolar.com
www.Newenglandsolar.Com

Solar electric kits, components, gas appliances and wind mills

President: Steve Schulze
Credit Cards: MasterCard; Visa; Discover
Catalog Cost: $3
Catalog Circulation: Mailed 2 time(s) per year to 20M+
Printing Information: 83 pages in 1 color on Newsprint
Press: Web Press
Binding: Saddle Stitched
Mailing List Information: Names for rent
In Business: 15 years
Number of Employees: 3
Sales Information: $1MM to $3MM

6710 Solar Flare
Sierra Solar Systems
563-C Idaho Maryland Road
Grass Valley, CA 95945   530-273-6754
   888-667-6527
Fax: 530-273-1760
info@sierrasolar.com
www.sierrasolar.com

Solar electric systems and components

President: Jonathan Hill
Credit Cards: AMEX; MasterCard; Visa; Discover
Catalog Cost: Free
Catalog Circulation: Mailed 2 time(s) per year to 50M
Average Order Size: $500
Printing Information: 68 pages in 4 colors on Newsprint
Press: Web Press
Binding: Saddle Stitched
Mailing List Information: Names for rent
List Manager: Jonathan Hill
In Business: 34 years
Number of Employees: 10
Sales Information: 1MM

6711 Sunelco

Sunelco, Inc.
620 Fish Hatchery Road
Suite 130
hamilton, MT 59840-9209   406-642-6422
   888-786-3526
Fax: 406-642-9768
info@sunelco.com
www.sunelco.com

Renewable energy equipment

President: Tom Bishop
CFO: Nilda Bishop
Catalog Cost: Free
Catalog Circulation: to 2000
Printing Information: 112 pages in 1 color on Matte Stock
Binding: Perfect Bound
Mailing List Information: Names for rent
In Business: 30 years
Number of Employees: 5
Sales Information: $95,000

6712 Wittus

Wittus, Inc.
40 Westchester Avenue
P.O. Box 120
Pound Ridge, NY 10576   914-764-5679
Fax: 914-764-0465
info@wittus.com
www.wittus.com

European contemporary stoves, fireplaces and accessories

President: Niels Wittus
nw@wittus.com
Production Manager: Mark Fischer
Fulfillment: Joan Martin
Catalog Cost: Free
Catalog Circulation: to 25000
Average Order Size: $4
Printing Information: 20 pages in 4 colors on Glossy Stock
Press: Web Press
Mailing List Information: Names for rent
In Business: 39 years
Number of Employees: 5
Sales Information: $2.11 Million

6713 Yellow Jacket Solar

Ritchie Engineering Company, Inc
10950 Hampshire Avenue South
PO Box 60
Bloomington, MN 55438-60   952-943-1300
   800-769-8370
Fax: 952-943-1300
custserv@yellowjacket.com
www.yellowjacket.com

Alternative energy components and systems

President: Tom Ritchie
tritchie@yellowjacket.com
EVP, International Sales: Brian Flynn
bflynn@yellowjacket.com
VP, Domestic Sales & Marketing: Michael Lanners
mlanners@yellowjacket.com
VP, Finance and Operations: Phil Hayne
phayne@yellowjacket.com
Credit Cards: MasterCard; Visa
Catalog Cost: $2
Catalog Circulation: Mailed 2 time(s) per year
Printing Information: 40 pages in 1 color
Number of Employees: 5
Sales Information: 500M-1MM

6714 Yukon/Eagle Furnace

Alpha American Co
10 Industrial Boulevard
PO Box 20
Palisade, MN 56469   218-845-2124
   800-358-0060
Fax: 800-440-1994
sales@yukon-eagle.com
www.yukon-eagle.com

wood furnaces-wood/oil, wood/gas, wood/electric, warm air furnaces

President: David Tjosvold
CFO: Terri Olsen
Marketing Manager: Lisa Johnson
Production Manager: Ron Prince
International Marketing Manager: Keith Nelson
Buyers: Lisa Johnson
Credit Cards: AMEX; MasterCard
Catalog Cost: Free
Catalog Circulation: to 3000
Printing Information: 8 pages on Glossy Stock
In Business: 45 years
Number of Employees: 25
Sales Information: $3MM to $5MM

Caulking, Chinking & Sealants

6715 Anti-Seize Technology

Anti-Seize Technology
2345 17th Avenue
Franklin Park, IL 60131-3432   847-455-2300
   800-991-1106
Fax: 847-455-2371
sales@antiseize.com
www.antiseize.com

Sealants lubricants, anti-seize compounds, thread sealers, instant gaskets penetrants, protectants, coatings greases, cleaners, degreasers, silicones

President: John Heydt
Marketing Manager: Kristy Rivera
VP, Research & Development: Allen Majeski
International Marketing Manager: Barbara Swanson
Buyers: Jim Michalewicz
Catalog Cost: Free
Catalog Circulation: Mailed 1 time(s) per year to 3M
Average Order Size: $4500
Printing Information: 32 pages
Mailing List Information: Names for rent
List Manager: Jeffery J Heydt
In Business: 46 years
Number of Employees: 15
Sales Information: $20,000,000

6716 Colorimetric Catalog

Dehco Inc.
58263 Charlotte Avenue
Elkhart, IN 46517-7292   574-294-2684
   800-621-2278
Fax: 574-296-7564
webmaster@dehco.com
www.Dehco.Com

Sealants, adhesives and coatings

President: Roy Strong
In Business: 59 years
Number of Employees: 45
Sales Information: $10,000,000 - $25,000,000

6717 Convenience Products

Clayton Corporation
866 Horan Drive
Fenton, MO 63026-2416   636-349-5855
   800-325-6180
Fax: 636-349-5335
www.convenienceproducts.com

Touch n' Seal Instant Sealant

President: Byron Lapin
Marketing Manager: Jane Leonard
Printing Information: 8 pages
Mailing List Information: Names for rent
In Business: 20 years
Number of Employees: 150
Sales Information: $10MM to $20MM

6718 Dunbar Sales & Manufacturing Company

Dunbar Sales
39 Avenue C First Floor
P.O.Box 8
Bayonne, NJ 07002-8   201-437-6500
   888-426-5765
Fax: 201-437-0366
sales@dunbarsales.com
www.Dunbarsales.Com

Adhesives, coatings, sealants, paints and lacquers

President: William Rubenstein
Credit Cards: AMEX; MasterCard; Visa
In Business: 55 years
Number of Employees: 20
Sales Information: $3MM to $5MM

6719 EV Roberts & Associates

E.V. Roberts
18027 Bishop Avenue
Carson, CA 90746-4019   310-204-6159
   800-374-3872
Fax: 310-202-7247
info@evroberts.com
evroberts.com

Epoxies, silicones, urethanes and adhesive coatings

President: Ronald Cloud
Credit Cards: AMEX; MasterCard
Number of Employees: 62
Sales Information: $10MM to $20MM

6720 Industrial Epoxies & Other Compounds Catalog

Abatron Inc
5501 - 95th Avenue
Kenosha, WI 53144-7499   262-653-2000
   800-445-1754
Fax: 262-653-2019
info@abatron.com
www.abatron.com

Resins, adhesives, coatings and sealants

President: Marsha Caporaso
Marketing Manager: MJ Wohl
Production Manager: SW West
Credit Cards: AMEX; MasterCard; Visa
Catalog Cost: Free
Catalog Circulation: Mailed 2 time(s) per year
Printing Information: 35 pages in 2 colors on Glossy Stock
Press: Letterpress
Mailing List Information: Names for rent
In Business: 56 years
Number of Employees: 450
Sales Information: $5MM to $10MM

6721 Magnolia Plastics Catalog

Magnolia Plastics
5547 Peachtree Blvd
Chamblee, GA 30341   770-451-2777
   800-831-8031
Fax: 770-451-5376
sales@magnolia-adv-mat.com
www.magnoliaplastics.com/

Custom epoxy compounds and sealants

President: Rick Wells
In Business: 89 years
Number of Employees: 27
Sales Information: $5,000,000 - $10,000,000

6722 PCS Catalog

Perma-Chink Systems
17635 NE 67th Ct
Redmond, WA 98052   888-838-5070
Fax: 425-869-0107
www.pcsproducts.com

Complete line of environmentally conscious sealants, stains and preservatives available; uniquely designed for log homes

President: Rich Dunstan
Production Manager: Tony Huddleston
General Manager/Operations Manager: Terry

Hofrichter
Credit Cards: MasterCard; Visa
Catalog Cost: Free
Catalog Circulation: to 10M+
Printing Information: 20 pages in 4 colors on Matte Stock
Mailing List Information: Names for rent
In Business: 34 years
Number of Employees: 50
Sales Information: $6.6 Million

6723 Pecora Catalog
Pecora Corporation
165 Wambold Road
Harleysville, PA 19438-2091   215-723-6051
                                 800-523-6688
                            Fax: 215-721-0286
                            www.pecora.com

Waterproofing and sealant products
President: Joseph F Virdone
Printing Information:
Sales Information: $50MM to $100MM

6724 Permabond International Catalog
Permabond International
14 Robinson St.
Pottstown, PA 19464-3355   732-868-1372
                              800-653-6523
                         Fax: 732-868-0267
            info.americas@permabond.com
                       www.permabond.com

Adhesives and sealants
President: Harold Ruchlin
In Business: 55 years
Number of Employees: 75
Sales Information: $5,000,000 - $10,000,000

6725 Preserva-Products
Preserva Products Ltd
12860 Earhart Avenue
Suite 102
Auburn, CA 95602-9000   530-887-0177
                           800-797-2537
                      Fax: 530-887-0187
            info@preservaproducts.com
              www.preservaproducts.com

Penetrating natural finishes for wood (exterior and interior), masonry, decks, fences, siding, shingles, log homes, concrete, brick, stucco, stone, grout, tile
President: Greg Riecks
CFO: Cindy Riecks
In Business: 44 years
Number of Employees: 10
Sales Information: 1.3M

6726 Sashco Sealants Catalog
Sashco Sealants
10300 E 107th Pl
Brighton, CO 80601-7176   303-286-7271
                             800-767-5656
                        Fax: 303-286-0400
                        www.Sashco.Com

Log Jam super-elastic home chinking
President: Lester Burch
CFO: Maryann Kozel
Marketing Manager: Walter Summons
VP Technical Director: Wayne Summons
VP Sales: Paul Shessler
VP of Macnufacturing: Bryan Hillsley
Printing Information: in 3 colors
In Business: 79 years
Number of Employees: 50-1
Sales Information: $10,000,000 - $25,000,000

6727 Sealers Catalog
Sealers
5017 S 38th Street
Saint Louis, MO 63116-4129   314-752-4667
                           Fax: 314-752-4035
              info@SealersInc.com
                 www.sealersinc.com

Butylog sealant for log homes
President: Jim Berger
Marketing Manager: Jim Berger
In Business: 40 years
Number of Employees: 15
Sales Information: $1,000,000 - $5,000,000

6728 Vimasco Catalog
Vimasco Corporation
280 West 19th Street, Republic way
Nitro, WV 25143-516   304-755-3328
                         800-624-8288
                    Fax: 304-755-7153
                    www.vimasco.com

LC-5 log chinking; flexible, textured coating for use in between the logs of a log home or for use as a standard architectural coating; water based elastomeric protective coatings, roof coatings, etc
President: William Pugh
Marketing Manager: Reid Pugh
Production Manager: Kathie Brown
kbrown@vimasco.com
Catalog Cost: Free
Catalog Circulation: to 500
Printing Information: 40 pages in 2 colors on Glossy Stock
Press: Web Press
Binding: Saddle Stitched
List Manager: Reid Pugh
In Business: 60 years
Number of Employees: 22
Sales Information: $1,000,000 - $5,000,000

6729 Weatherall Catalog
Weatherall Company, Inc
106 Industrial Way
Charlestown, IN 47111-1247   812-256-3378
                                800-367-7068
                           Fax: 812-256-2344
                           www.Weatherall.Com

Weatherflex Stucco latex acrylics
President: James McCain
Ranch Director: Bobby Lewis
Number of Employees: 11
Sales Information: $1,000,000 - $5,000,000

Construction

6730 Anthony Forest Products
Anthony Forest Products
P.O.Box 1877
309 N. Washington
El Dorado, AR 71731-1877   870-862-3414
                              800-856-2372
                         Fax: 870-863-0809
                         www.Anthonyforest.Com

Building materials
Chairman: Beryl Anthony
President: Aubra Anthony Jr
Marketing Manager: Kerlin Drake
Exec. Vice Pres.: Russ Anthony
VP, Forestry Mngmnt & Procurement: Steve Barham
VP, Finance & Treasurer: Ronnie Clay
In Business: 99 years
Number of Employees: 400

6731 Bon Tool
Bon Tool Company
4430 Gibsonia Road
Gibsonia, PA 15044-7945   800-444-7060
                        sales@bontool.com
                        www.bontool.com

Construction supplies and tools
President: John Bongiovanni
Credit Cards: MasterCard
Catalog Circulation: Mailed 4 time(s) per year
In Business: 59 years
Number of Employees: 60
Sales Information: $20MM to $50MM

6732 CID Associates
CID Associates, Inc
730 Ekastown Road
Route 228
Sarver, PA 16055-1143   724-353-0300
                      Fax: 724-353-0308
              sales@cidbuildings.com
              www.cidbuildings.com/

Interior design contractors
President: CD Docherty
Number of Employees: 20

6733 GE Modular Space
ModSpace
PO Box 1075
1200 Swedesford Rd.
Berwyn, PA 19312-1075   610-232-1200
                           800-523-7918
          more.info@modspace.com
                www.modspace.com

Mobile and modular structures for construction
In Business: 40 years

6734 Hanes Supply Company Catalog
Hanes Supply Company
55 James E Casey Drive
Buffalo, NY 14206-2361   888-426-3755
            sales@hanessupply.com
               www.hanessupply.com

Complete line of slings and rigging equipment as well as general contractor supplies
President: Bill Hanes
Catalog Cost: Free
In Business: 82 years
Sales Information: $50MM to $100MM

6735 Indco Pharma
Indco
4040 Earnings Way
New Albany, IN 47151-2275   812-945-4383
                               800-942-4383
                          Fax: 812-944-9742
                      info@indco.com
                      www.indco.com

Industrial mixing equipment and accessories
President: C. Mark Hennis
CFO: Jo Holt
Marketing Manager: Jo Holt
Production Manager: Mark Franco
Fulfillment: Jo Holt
International Marketing Manager: Tricia Groves
Credit Cards: AMEX; MasterCard; Visa
Catalog Cost: Free
Catalog Circulation: Mailed 3 time(s) per year to 150M
Average Order Size: $1250
Printing Information: 50 pages in 4 colors on Glossy Stock
Press: Web Press
Binding: Saddle Stitched
Mailing List Information: Names for rent
List Manager: Jo Holt
In Business: 40 years
Number of Employees: 50
Sales Information: $1MM-$3MM

6736 Louisiana-Pacific Corporation
LP
29 Industrial Park Drive
Binghamton, NY 13904-1818   503-225-5221
                               888-820-0325
                          Fax: 877-523-7192
                          www.lpcorp.com

Basic wood building materials
Chairman: Mark Suwyn
President: Mark Suwyn
CFO: Sallie B. Bailey
Marketing Manager: Rick Olszewski
EVP: Sallie B. Bailey

SVP and General Manager: Brad Southern
VP Human Resources: Tim Hartnett
Number of Employees: 110

6737 Master Builder
Sage
6561 Irvine Center Drive
Suite 200
Irvine, CA 92618-2301   707-829-8750
                              888-661-7281
                         Fax: 707-521-7380
productinfo.masterbuilder@sage.com
                              www.na.sage.com

Construction software

Chairman: Donald Brydon CBE
CFO: Steve Hare
Group CMO: Santiago Solanas
CEO: Stephen Kelly
Chief People Officer: Sandra Campopiano
Mailing List Information: Names for rent
In Business: 33 years
Number of Employees: 40
Sales Information: $1,000,000 - $5,000,000

6738 Metal Sales Manufacturing Corporation
Metal Sales Manufacturing Corporation
545 South 3rd Street
Suite 200
Louisville, KY 40202   502-855-4300
                              800-406-7387
                         Fax: 502-855-4200
www.metalsales.us.com

Manufacturer of steel panels and components for the building industry

Chairman: Craig Mackin
President: Jim Waldron
Production Manager: Dwayne Engle
Catalog Cost: Free
Catalog Circulation: Mailed 1 time(s) per year
Printing Information: 12 pages in 4 colors
Press: Letterpress
Binding: Saddle Stitched
In Business: 52 years
Number of Employees: 325

6739 MicroGroup Small Diameter Tubing Specialists
MicroGroup
7 Industrial Park Road
Medway, MA 02053-1750   508-533-4925
                              800-255-8823
                         Fax: 508-533-5691
info@microgroup.com
                         www.Microgroup.Com

Various types of small tubing made from a variety of metals

President: William J. Bergen
bbergen@microgroup.com
Credit Cards: MasterCard
Catalog Circulation: Mailed 1 time(s) per year
Printing Information: 142 pages on Matte Stock
Binding: Perfect Bound
In Business: 44 years
Number of Employees: 75

6740 Paslode Corporation
Paslode
888 Forest Edge Dr
Vernon Hills, IL 60061-4113   847-634-1900
                              800-222-6990
                         Fax: 847-634-6602
tech@paslode.com
                              www.Paslode.Com

Construction and industrial products

President: James Harris
Marketing Manager: Tom Dompke
In Business: 78 years
Number of Employees: 125

6741 Performance Zone
Abatron, Inc.
5501 - 95th Avenue
Kenosha, WI 53144-4529   262-653-2000
                              800-445-1754
                         Fax: 262-653-2019
info@abatron.com
                              www.abatron.com

Books, directories, apparel and other reference items and merchandise for the concrete and masonry construction fields

Credit Cards: AMEX; MasterCard
Catalog Circulation: Mailed 2 time(s) per year to 500M
Printing Information: 20 pages in 4 colors
Press: Web Press
Binding: Saddle Stitched
In Business: 58 years
Number of Employees: 40
Sales Information: $10,000,000 - $25,000,000

6742 Stockton Products
Stockton Products
4675 Vandenberg Drive
N Las Vegas, NV 89081-2709   702-651-1721
                              877-862-5866
                         Fax: 702-651-0948
office@stocktonproducts.com
                    www.stocktonproducts.com

Metal and wire products for the building industry

Catalog Cost: Free
Printing Information: 12 pages in 2 colors
Binding: Saddle Stitched
In Business: 65 years
Number of Employees: 5

6743 TRUSSFRAME-3
DesignandBuildwithMetal.com
92 Columbus Jobstown Rd.
PO Box 200
Columbus, NJ 08022   609-723-2600
                         Fax: 609-723-6700
www.designandbuildwithmetal.com

Steel framing for commercial, industrial, agricultural and recreational buildings up to 200 foot clear span

President: Emanuel A Coronis
CFO: Meg Coronis
Marketing Manager: Emanuel A Coronis
Production Manager: Ted Hierl
sales director: John Garvey
johng@designandbuildwithmetal.com
Editorial/Content Director: Bob Fittro
bobf@designandbuildwithmetal.com
Editorial/Content Director: Shawn Zuver
shawnz@designandbuildwithmetal.com
International Marketing Manager: Manny Coronis
Mailing List Information: Names for rent
In Business: 52 years
Number of Employees: 20
Sales Information: $1MM to $3MM

6744 Tools & Equipment Catalog
Bon Tool Co.
4430 Gibsonia Road
Gibsonia, PA 15044-7963   724-443-7080
                              800-444-7060
                         Fax: 724-443-7090
sales@bontool.com
                              www.bontool.com

Construction tools and equipment for all trowel trades, roofing and flooring work

President: Carl Bongiovanni
Marketing Manager: michelle brendor
Sales Representative: Bob Abbott
rabbott48@aol.com
Sales Representative: William Camp
williamcamp@bellsouth.net
Sales Representative: Billy Devitt
devittassociates@aol.com
Credit Cards: MasterCard

Catalog Cost: Free
Catalog Circulation: Mailed 4 time(s) per year
Printing Information: 116 pages
In Business: 57 years
Number of Employees: 20-5
Sales Information: $5,000,000 - $10,000,000

6745 Tri-Boro Construction Supplies
Tri-Boro Construction Supplies
465 Locust Street
Dallastown, PA 17313-8   717-246-3095
                              800-632-9018
                         Fax: 717-246-3506
www.tri-borosupplies.com

Building supplies

CFO: Linda Rexroth
Founder: Glenn
Founder: Linda
Management Team: JR
Catalog Cost: Free
In Business: 39 years
Number of Employees: 75
Sales Information: $10,000,000 - $25,000,000

6746 Waffle-Crete International
Waffle-Crete International, Inc.
2500 E 9th St
Hays, KS 67601-1008   785-625-3486
                              888-609-2900
                         Fax: 785-628-0677
info@global3darts.com
                              www.waffle-crete.com

Building systems, structural precast concrete for single and multi story buildings

Chairman: Jerry Kramer
President: Larry Lightman
Engineering Manager: Robert D. Disney
Operations Manager: Brandon Jacobs
Technology Advisor: David Van Doren
Credit Cards: AMEX; MasterCard
Printing Information: in 1 color on Glossy Stock
Press: Letterpress
Binding: Perfect Bound
Mailing List Information: Names for rent
In Business: 35 years
Number of Employees: 30
Sales Information: $1,000,000 - $5,000,000

6747 White Cap Industries
White Cap Industries
408 E University Drive
Phoenix, AZ 85004-2923   602-256-6900
                              800-944-8322
                         Fax: 602-256-6067
www.whitecapdirect.com

Wholesale contractor and supplies company, full line of all contruction equipment, hardware, tools and materials

Credit Cards: AMEX; MasterCard
Catalog Cost: Free
In Business: 38 years
Number of Employees: 24

6748 Wrisco Industries
Wrisco Industries,Inc
355 Hiatt Dr # B
Suite B
Palm Beach Gdns, FL 33418-7199   561-626-5700
                              800-627-2646
                         Fax: 561-627-3574
www.wrisco.com

Pre-finished aluminum in choice of color/finishes for roofing, awnings, flashing, walls, gutters, patios, insulated roof and wall panels

President: Jim Monastra
Marketing Manager: AJ Monastra
Catalog Circulation: Mailed 4 time(s) per year to 10M
Average Order Size: $3000
Printing Information: 15 pages in 2 colors on Glossy Stock

Press: Letterpress
Binding: Folded
In Business: 98 years
Number of Employees: 104
Sales Information: $10MM to $20MM

6749 York Industries Catalog
York Industries
303 Nassau Boulevard
Garden City Park, NY 11040-5213 516-746-3736
                                       800-354-8466
                              Fax: 516-746-3741
                              support@york-ind.com
                              www.york-ind.com

Stock Timing Pulleys, Custom Pulleys and Accessories, Tensioners, Timing Belts, Custom Gears/Assemblies, Pulley Stock and Flangers

President: Lee Smith
Credit Cards: AMEX; MasterCard
Catalog Cost: Free
Printing Information: 265 pages
In Business: 70 years
Number of Employees: 32
Sales Information: $6 Million

Flooring & Paneling

6750 Aged Woods
Aged Woods, Inc.
4065 Deerhill Drive
Suite V101
York, PA 17406   717-840-0330
                             800-233-9307
                       Fax: 717-840-0330
                       info@agedwoods.com
                       www.agedwoods.com

Antique wood flooring

President: Jeff Horn
CFO: Donald Sprenkle, Jr.
Secretary: Denise Horn
In Business: 32 years
Number of Employees: 3
Sales Information: $410,000

6751 Brown-Campbell Steel Corporation
Brown-Campbell Company
11800 Investment Drive
Shelby Township, MI 48315-1594 586-884-2116
                                 800-472-8464
                           Fax: 586-884-2181
                  websupport@brown-campbell.com
                       www.Brown-Campbell.Com

Industrial flooring and gratings

President: Mike Campbell
Catalog Cost: Free
Printing Information: 191 pages
In Business: 63 years
Number of Employees: 20
Sales Information: $1MM to $3MM

6752 CertainTeed Corporation
CertainTeed Corporations
750 East Swedesford Road
PO Box 860
Valley Forge, PA 19482-860   610-341-7000
                              800-233-8990
                        Fax: 610-341-7777
                        www.certainteed.com

Premium vinyl siding panel

Chairman: Pierre-André de Chalendar
President: John Crowe
Marketing Manager: Robert Clark
In Business: 111 years
Number of Employees: 600

6753 Elsro
Elsro Inc
114 37th St
Evans, CO 80620-2215   970-330-4844
                              800-252-0501
                        Fax: 970-330-5123
                        www.Elsroinc.Com

Asphalt plank flooring

President: Dennis Schulte
Marketing Manager: Dennis Schulte
In Business: 65 years
Number of Employees: 15
Sales Information: $1,000,000 - $5,000,000

6754 Fireslate-2
Fireslate-2
3065 Cranberry Hwy # A24
Unit 24-A
East Wareham, MA 02538-1325 508-273-0047
                              800-523-5902
                        Fax: 508-564-5448
                        tbw@fireslate.com

Fiber cement panels

President: Tom Worthen
In Business: 12 years
Number of Employees: 8
Sales Information: $1,000,000 - $5,000,000

6755 Foam Laminates of Vermont
Sovernet Communications
5 Canal Street
PO Box 495
Bellows Falls, VT 05101   802-463-2111
                              877-877-2120
                        Fax: 802-453-2339
                        www.sover.net

Manufacturer of stress-skin

President: Rich Kendall
Marketing Manager: Peter Stolley
CEO: Rich Kendall
Director of Finance: Michael Shuipis
Director of Regulatory Affairs: Lawrence Lackey
In Business: 20 years
Number of Employees: 3
Sales Information: Under $500,000

6756 Hardwood Flooring & Paneling
Sheoga
15320 Burton Windsor Road
Middlefield, OH 44062-9785   440-834-1710
                              800-834-1180
                        Fax: 440-834-9310
                        info@sheogaflooring.com
                        www.sheogaflooring.com

Manufacturer of 3/4 in. solid hardwood flooring and paneling; distributor of matching hardwood vents

President: Pete Miller
CFO: Barbara Titus
Marketing Manager: Pete C Miller
Printing Information: 6 pages in 4 colors on Matte Stock
Binding: Perfect Bound
Mailing List Information: Names for rent
In Business: 30 years
Number of Employees: 35
Sales Information: $1,000,000 - $5,000,000

6757 Pennwood Products Company
Pennwood Products Company
102 Locus Street
East Berlin, PA 17316-766   717-259-9551
                        Fax: 717-259-7560
                        www.tradeleads.at

Floorings and mouldings

President: NE Coxon Jr
Marketing Manager: Cynthia A Geesey
Managing Director: Brian Eche
In Business: 14 years
Number of Employees: 50
Sales Information: $1,000,000 - $5,000,000

6758 Pioneer Athletics
Pioneerr Manufacturing Company, Inc
4529 Industrial Parkway
Cleveland, OH 44135-4541   800-877-1500
                        Fax: 800-877-1511
                        www.pioneerathletics.com

Industrial maintenance, flooring and roofing supplies

President: James Schattinger
Marketing Manager: Jackie Robertson
Catalog Cost: Free
Catalog Circulation: Mailed 1 time(s) per year
Printing Information: 64 pages in 4 colors on Glossy Stock
Binding: Saddle Stitched
Mailing List Information: Names for rent
In Business: 94 years
Number of Employees: 120
Sales Information: $10MM to $20MM

6759 Rare Earth Hardwoods
Rare Earth Hardwood
6778 E Traverse Hwy
Traverse City, MI 49684-8364   231-946-0043
                                800-968-0074
                          Fax: 231-946-6221
                          Sales@rehwood.net
                          www.Rare-Earth-Hardwoods.Com

Importer and manufacturer of hardwood flooring and decks, offering interior and exterior grade plywood

President: Rick Paid
Marketing Manager: Don Chamberlin
Production Manager: Austin Gaines
Credit Cards: MasterCard
Catalog Cost: Free
Catalog Circulation: to 5.2M
Printing Information: 6 pages
Mailing List Information: Names for rent
In Business: 33 years
Number of Employees: 35
Sales Information: $1,000,000 - $5,000,000

6760 Rock-Tred Corporation
Rock-Tred II, LLC
405 N. Oakwood Avenue
Waukegan, IL 60085-4011   847-673-8200
                              888-762-5873
                        Fax: 847-679-6665
                        info@rocktred.com
                        www.rocktred.com

Heavy duty industrial and commercial floor protection

President: Chris O Brien
Marketing Manager: Colin Broadway
Plant Manager: Brian Wilson
Lab Technician: Sarah Marble
General Manager: Erik Sebby
Credit Cards: AMEX; MasterCard
Catalog Cost: Free
Catalog Circulation: Mailed 2 time(s) per year
Printing Information: 6 pages in 4 colors on Glossy Stock
Press: Web Press
In Business: 76 years
Number of Employees: 50
Sales Information: $10,000,000 - $25,000,000

6761 Stagestep
Stagestep, Inc.
4701 Bath Street #46
Philadelphia, PA 19137-2235   215-636-9000
                               800-523-0960
                         Fax: 267-672-2912
                         stagestep@stagestep.com
                         www.stagestep.com

Flooring supplier to dance studios, theaters and athletic facilities

President: Randy Schwartz
Sales Consultant: Karen Flanagan
Installation Expert: sam Jamison
Catalog Circulation: Mailed 1 time(s) per year
Printing Information: 40 pages in 4 colors

In Business: 42 years
Sales Information: $1MM to $3MM

6762 Weyerhaeuser
Weyerhaeuser Company
PO Box 9777
Federal Way, WA 98063-9777   253-924-2345
800-525-5440
Fax: 989-348-8226
www.Weyerhaeuser.Com

Flooring panels
President: Doyle R. Simons
CFO: Patricia M. Bedient
Marketing Manager: Michael Sekely
Senior Vice President, Human Resour: Denise M. Merle
enior Vice President, General Couns: Devin W. Stockfish
Senior Vice President, Cellulose Fi: Catherine I. Slater
Credit Cards: AMEX; MasterCard
In Business: 13 years
Number of Employees: 200
Sales Information: $25,000,000 - $50,000,000

Hardware

6763 Acorn Manufacturing Company
Acorn Manufacturing Company, Inc.
457 School Street
Mansfield, MA 02048-31   508-339-4500
800-835-0121
Fax: 508-339-0104
acorninfo@acornmfg.com
www.acornmfg.com

Hand forged iron items with hammer and anvil
President: Eric DeLong
In Business: 78 years
Number of Employees: 40
Sales Information: $5,000,000

6764 Air-Lec Industries
Air-Lec Industries
3300 Commercial Ave
Madison, WI 53714-1458   608-244-4754
Fax: 608-246-7676
info@air-lec.com
www.air-lec.com

Automatic pneumatic door operators, door hardware, track and accessories
President: John Lunenschloss
CFO: Laurie Lunenschloss
Marketing Manager: Harold Clute
General Manager: John Ganahl
jganahl@air-lec.com
Mailing List Information: Names for rent
In Business: 94 years
Number of Employees: 8
Sales Information: $50,000

6765 American Precision Glass Corporation
American Precision Glass Corporation
602 -604 Main St
Duryea, PA 18642-1326   570-457-9664
Fax: 570-457-9786
info@apgcorp.com
www.Apgcorp.Com

Small glass parts for optical systems
President: Jack Rowlands
Sales Information: $3MM to $5MM

6766 Androck Hardware Corporation
Androck Hardware Corporation
711 19th St
Rockford, IL 61104-3434   815-229-1144
800-397-2658
Fax: 815-229-1895
sales@androckhardware.com
www.Androckhardware.Com

Screws, hooks and hinges

President: Mark Maffei
Number of Employees: 20
Sales Information: $1,000,000 - $5,000,000

6767 Astrup Company
Trivantage
18401 Sheldon Road
Suite A
Middleburg Heights, OH 44130-5392   216-696-2800
800-786-7601
Fax: 216-696-0914
www.trivantage.com

Fabric, hardware - industrial supplies
Chairman: John Kirk
President: J W Kirk
In Business: 123 years
Number of Employees: 160
Sales Information: $10,000,000 - $25,000,000

6768 Brookfield Industries
Brookfield Industries
99 West Hillside Ave.
Thomaston, CT 06787-1433   860-283-6211
Fax: 860-283-6123
www.bfimfg.com/

Hinges and related hardware
President: Karl Kinzer
Number of Employees: 12
Sales Information: $1,000,000 - $5,000,000

6769 Cabinet Hardware from Cliffside Industries
Cliffside Industries Ltd
60 Wright Avenue
Lititz, PA 17543-9343   717-627-3286
800-873-9258
Fax: 800-926-3435
info@cliffsideind.com
www.cliffsideind.com

Distributers of solid brass hardware
President: Walter Zaleskie
Founder: Walter Zaleskie
Credit Cards: AMEX; MasterCard
Printing Information: 6 pages in 4 colors
Mailing List Information: Names for rent
In Business: 28 years

6770 Carey Manufacturing
Carey Manufacturing Company
5 Pasco Hill Road
Cromwell, CT 06416-1093   860-829-1803
866-813-0220
Fax: 860-829-1932
sales@careymfg.com
www.careymfg.com

Compression spring catches, heavy duty and light pulldown catches and handles for the aerospace, military, electronics, computer and automotive industries
President: John Carcy
CFO: Paul Sullivan
Marketing Manager: John Capece
Production Manager: Adam Wallace
General Manager: John Capece
jcapece@careymfg.com
Sales Coordinator: Alison Carey
acarey@careymfg.com
Human Resources Director: Peter Egan
pegan@careymfg.com
Catalog Cost: Free
Catalog Circulation: to 300
Printing Information: 176 pages in 2 colors on Glossy Stock
Press: Web Press
Binding: Saddle Stitched
Mailing List Information: Names for rent
In Business: 34 years
Number of Employees: 45
Sales Information: $6,000,000+

6771 Cirecast
CIRECAST, INC.
1790 Yosemite Avenue
San Francisco, CA 94124-2622   415-822-3030
Fax: 415-822-3004
www.Cirecast.Com

Doorknobs and antique hardware
President: Peter Morenstein
Credit Cards: MasterCard
Catalog Cost: Free
Catalog Circulation: Mailed 2 time(s) per year
Printing Information: 6 pages
In Business: 49 years
Number of Employees: 20
Sales Information: $1MM to $3MM

6772 Clark & Barlow Hardware Company
Clark & Barlow Hardware Company
353 West Grand Ave
Chicago, IL 60654-4596   312-726-3010
800-700-9485
Fax: 312-726-3016
info@clarkandbarlow.com
www.Clarkandbarlow.Com

Wholesale and decorative hardware
President: Joseph Sullivan
Buyers: Cliff Rehberg
Bob Olsen
Credit Cards: MasterCard; Visa
Catalog Cost: $12
Catalog Circulation: Mailed 1 time(s) per year
Printing Information: 500 pages in 1 color on Matte Stock
Press: Web Press
Mailing List Information: Names for rent
In Business: 120 years
Number of Employees: 55
Sales Information: $10MM to $20MM

6773 Colonial Bronze Company
Colonial Bronze Co
511 Winsted Road
Torrington, CT 06790-207   860-489-9233
Fax: 800-355-7903
www.Colonialbronze.Com

Manufacturers of solid brass hardware
President: Jamie Gregg
Printing Information: 53 pages
In Business: 88 years
Sales Information: $10MM to $20MM

6774 Daro Industries
Daro Industries
4099 White Bear Parkway
White Bear Lake, MN 55110-3511   651-483-2798
877-865-4154
Fax: 651-483-9221
sales@daro-ind.com
www.daro-ind.com

Heavy duty hinges for industrial and commercial doors
President: D Roberts
In Business: 38 years
Number of Employees: 20-5
Sales Information: $1,000,000 - $5,000,000

6775 Duro-Felt Products Catalog
Duro-Felt Products
6 White Aspen Court
Little Rock, AR 72212   501-225-2838
Fax: 501-219-9611
durofelt@att.net
www.durofelt.com

We offer felt & felt products in a wide variety of colors and sizes, product assortment includes PSA felt pads, strips, buffing wheels, polishing bobs, materials & wicking
President: Asha Sahita
Credit Cards: AMEX; MasterCard
Catalog Cost: Free
Average Order Size: $20
Printing Information: 8 pages on Matte Stock

Press: Letterpress
Mailing List Information: Names for rent
In Business: 16 years
Number of Employees: 3
Sales Information: $90,000

6776 Jacknor Corporation

Jacknob Corporation
290 Oser Avenue
PO Box 18032
Hauppauge, NY 11788-3610

631-546-6560
800-424-7495
Fax: 631-231-0330
custservice@jacknob.com
www.jacknob.com

Special hardware for toilet partitions

President: Jerry Loveless
In Business: 60 years
Number of Employees: 40
Sales Information: $3MM to $5MM

6777 Lewis Brass & Copper Company

Lewis Brass & Copper Company, INC
69-60 79th Street
Middle Village, NY 11379-67

718-894-1442
800-221-5579
Fax: 718-326-4032
sales@lewisbrass.com
www.lewisbrass.com

Brass, silver and stainless steel

President: Jay Horowitz
VP: Richard Bacharach
Inside Sales Manager: Sam Halon
Printing Information: 19 pages
In Business: 58 years
Number of Employees: 20
Sales Information: $5,000,000 - $10,000,000

6778 Micro-Mark, The Small Tool Specialists

Micro-Mark
340 Snyder Ave
Berkeley Heights, NJ 07922

908-464-2984
800-225-1066
Fax: 908-665-9383
info@micromark.com
www.micromark.com

Hard to find tools and supplies

President: Tom Piccirillo
Credit Cards: MasterCard
Catalog Cost: Free
Printing Information: 104 pages in 4 colors on Glossy Stock
In Business: 87 years

6779 Mr G's Fasteners

Mr. G's Enterprises
5613 Elliott Reeder Road
Fort Worth, TX 76117-6013

817-838-3131
817-831-3501
Fax: 817-838-5613
mrgs@mrgusa.com
www.mrgusa.com/

Screws, nuts, bolts, clips and other various hardware

President: Glenn Garrison
Credit Cards: AMEX; MasterCard; Visa
Catalog Cost: $5
Catalog Circulation: Mailed 3 time(s) per year to 20M
Printing Information: 226 pages in 1 color on Glossy Stock
Binding: Saddle Stitched
Mailing List Information: Names for rent
In Business: 15 years
Number of Employees: 11
Sales Information: $1MM to $3MM

6780 National Manufacturing Co

National Manufacturing Co
P.O.Box 577
Sterling, IL 61081

800-346-9445
Fax: 800-346-9448
www.natman.com

Home and builders' hardware

Chairman: Keith Benson
President: Matthew L Minnick
CFO: Charles R Phillips
Marketing Manager: Doug Sandberg, Director Marketing
Production Manager: John Benson, VP Production
Catalog Cost: Free
Catalog Circulation: Mailed 1 time(s) per year
Mailing List Information: Names for rent
In Business: 115 years
Number of Employees: 1000
Sales Information: $50,000,000 - $100,000,00

6781 Northeast Hinge Distributors Catalog

Northeast Hinge Distributors,Inc.
261 Proctor Hill Road
PO Box 891
Hollis, NH 03049-891

603-465-3244
800-882-0120
Fax: 603-465-3313
nehinge@nehinge.com
www.nehinge.com

Hinges, continuous, butt, spring and slip joint aluminum material, stainless steel, unplated steel, nickle plated, brass and brass plated, ball bearing, cabinet latching and various other hinges

President: Loren Valley
Marketing Manager: Martha Myers
Production Manager: Martha Myers
Fulfillment: Martha Myers
Credit Cards: AMEX; MasterCard
Catalog Cost: Free
Catalog Circulation: to 2000
Average Order Size: $100
Printing Information: 15 pages in 4 colors on Matte Stock
Press: Web Press
Binding: Folded
Mailing List Information: Names for rent
In Business: 25 years
Number of Employees: 6
Sales Information: $1MM to $3MM

6782 Peerless Hardware Manufacturing Company

Peerless Hardware
P.O.Box 351
210 Chestnut St.
Columbia, PA 17512-351

717-684-2889
800-233-3868
Fax: 717-684-3503
nwhite@peerlesshardware.com
www.Peerlesshardware.Com

Industrial and marine hardware

President: James P Speitel
CFO: Ann Speitel
In Business: 64 years
Number of Employees: 17
Sales Information: $1,000,000 - $5,000,000

6783 RKL Building Specialties Company

RKL Building Specialities Company Incorp
15-30 131st Street
College Point, NY 11356

718-728-7788
800-321-4755
Fax: 718-726-6836
rklbuilding.com

Specialty items such as anchor bolts, masonry accessories

President: Gary Kucich
In Business: 62 years
Number of Employees: 15
Sales Information: $1,000,000 - $5,000,000

6784 Rev-a-Shelf Specification Guide

Rev-A-Shelf, LLC
12400 Earl Jones Way
Louisville, KY 40299-585

502-499-5835
800-626-1126
Fax: 502-491-2215
rasmarketing@rev-a-shelf.com
www.Rev-A-Shelf.com

Wire accessories for the kitchen and bath

President: Craig Jones
Marketing Manager: Shari McPeek
smcpeek@rev-a-shelf.com
General Manager: David Noe
Director of Operations: Suzy Whatley
swhatley@rev-a-shelf.com
National Sales Assistant: Dee Baker
Catalog Cost: Free
Catalog Circulation: to 10000
Printing Information: 403 pages in 4 colors
In Business: 37 years
Sales Information: $20 million

6785 Rigidized Metals Corporation

Rigidized Metals Corporation
658 Ohio St
Buffalo, NY 14203-3185

716-849-4760
800-836-2580
Fax: 716-849-0401
hr@rigidized.com
www.Rigidized.Com

Building hardware

President: Richard S Smith
Marketing Manager: Louis Martin
Director: Frank Putnam Wilton
Architectural and Furniture: Kevin Porteus
kevinporteus@rigidized.com
Architectural and Furniture: Dave Miske
davemiske@rigidized.com
In Business: 75 years
Number of Employees: 38
Sales Information: $1,000,000 - $5,000,000

6786 Simon's Kitchen & Bath

Simon's Hardware and Bath
421 3rd Avenue
New York, NY 10016-8151

212-532-9220
888-274-6667
Fax: 212-481-0564
www.simonsny.com

Decorative and industrial hardware, fixtures and accessories for bathroom and kitchen

President: Elias Chahine
elias@simonsny.com
Credit Cards: AMEX; MasterCard; Visa
In Business: 111 years
Number of Employees: 70
Sales Information: $5MM to $10MM

6787 US Sky

U. S. Sky Sure SealGlazing System
2356 Fox Road
Suite 600
Santa Fe, NM 87507-5413

505-471-5711
800-323-5017
Fax: 505-471-5437
extremeglass@live.com
www.ussky.com

Glazing system

President: Kevin Sarr
Marketing Manager: Bill Yanda
Owner: Elizardo Avitia
extremeglass@live.com
In Business: 21 years
Number of Employees: 4
Sales Information: $3MM to $5MM

6788 WSI Distributors
WSI Distributors
405 N Main St
Saint Charles, MO 63301-1235   636-946-5811
                                    800-447-9974
                          Fax: 636-946-5832
talk2us@wsidistributors.com
www.wsidistributors.com

Brass hardware
President: Wayne Wolz
Credit Cards: MasterCard; Visa
Catalog Cost: Free
Catalog Circulation: Mailed 1 time(s) per year
to 500
Printing Information: 70 pages in 1 color
In Business: 37 years

6789 Williamsburg Blacksmiths
Williamsburg Blacksmiths
26 Williams Street
Williamsburg, MA 01096-9427   413-268-7341
                          Fax: 413-268-9317
williamsburgblacksmiths@gmail.com
www.williamsburgblacksmith.com

Reproduction Early American wrought-iron hardware
President: Elizabeth Tiley
Credit Cards: AMEX; MasterCard; Visa
Catalog Cost: Free
Mailing List Information: Names for rent
In Business: 48 years
Number of Employees: 5
Sales Information: $1MM to $3MM

Insulation

6790 Accurate Metal Weather Strip Company
Accurate Metal Weatherstrip Co.
725 S Fulton Avenue
Mount Vernon, NY 10550-5013   914-668-6042
                                    800-536-6043
                          Fax: 914-668-6062
info@accurateweatherstrip.com
www.accurateweatherstrip.com

Metal weather strips, interlocking weather stripping and tools for doors and windows
President: Fred O Kammerer
CFO: Ronald Kammerer
Catalog Circulation: Mailed 1 time(s) per year
Printing Information: 30 pages
In Business: 119 years
Number of Employees: 7
Sales Information: $17.5 Million

6791 Air Balance
Air Balance, Inc.
450 Riverside Drive
Wyalusing, PA 18853-9412   570-746-1888
                          Fax: 570-746-9286
elewis@mestek.com
www.airbalance.com

Shutters, louvers, fire and smoke dampers, air control dampers and access doors
President: Earl C Lewis
elewis@mestek.com
Marketing Manager: Carrie Covington
Production Manager: Eric Gohrang
VP, Operations: Kenneth D. Wahlers
kwahlers@mestek.com
Customer Service Manager: Diane Watson
Marketing/Product Assistant: Jay Huthmaker
In Business: 55 years
Number of Employees: 61
Sales Information: $5,000,000 - $10,000,000

6792 Albany International
Albany International
216 Airport Drive
Rochester, NH 03867-1122   603-330-5850
                          Fax: 603-994-3835
www.albint.com

Manufacturer of paper machine clothing and shoe presses used for making paper and heavyweight container boxes
President: Joseph G. Morone
CFO: John B. Cozzolino
President, Albany Engineered Compos: Ralph M. Polumbo
President - Machine Clothing: Daniel A. Halftermeyer
SVP & CTO: Robert A. Hansen
In Business: 120 years
Number of Employees: 4000
Sales Information: $745.3 million

6793 BNZ Materials
BNZ Materials
6901 S Pierce Street
Suite 260
Littleton, CO 80128-7205   303-978-1199
                                    800-999-0890
                          Fax: 303-978-0308
info@bnzmaterials.com
www.Bnzmaterials.Com

Insulating aggregates, cements, structural boards and insulating fire brick
Chairman: J Hulce
President: K W Hunter
In Business: 28 years
Number of Employees: 200
Sales Information: $3MM to $5MM

6794 Carlee Corporation
Carlee Corporation
28 Piermont Road
Rockleigh, NJ 07647-26   201-768-6800
                                    800-8 C-RLEE
                          Fax: 201-768-7614
sales@carlee.com
www.Carlee.Com

High-loft fiberfill batting, wadding, padding, insulation and filtration media
President: Bruce a Burgermaster
In Business: 64 years
Number of Employees: 50-1
Sales Information: $5,000,000 - $10,000,000

6795 Cornell Corporation
Cornell Corporation
PO Box 338
Cornell, WI 54732-338   888-439-6411
                          Fax: 800-267-8368
www.cornellcorporation.com

Vent-Top ThermaCal and ventilated nail base roof insulation
President: Neil Goodall
Marketing Manager: David Tonnancour
Mailing List Information: Names for rent
In Business: 61 years
Number of Employees: 20
Sales Information: $5,000,000 - $10,000,000

6796 FOMO Products
Fomo Products, Inc
2775 Barber Road
PO Box 1078
Norton, OH 44203-9478   330-753-4585
                                    800-321-5585
                          Fax: 330-753-5199
www.fomo.com

One/two component polyurethane foams and kits
President: Stefan Gantenbein
VP Marketing Development: Doug Caffoe
Printing Information: 28 pages
In Business: 40 years
Number of Employees: 75
Sales Information: $10,000,000 - $25,000,000

6797 Fi-Foil Company
Fi-Foil
612 Bridgers Avenue West
P.O. Box 800
Auburndale, FL 33823-800   863-965-1846
                                    888-315-9187
                          Fax: 863-967-0137
info@fifoil.com
www.fifoil.com

Reflective insulation and radiant barriers for residential. commercial and industrial building applications.
President: Bill Lippy
CFO: Tim Sheridan
Marketing Manager: Bill Lippy
Production Manager: Doug Kinninger
Mailing List Information: Names for rent
In Business: 30 years
Number of Employees: 18
Sales Information: $10,000,000 - $25,000,000

6798 Flexmaster USA
Flexmaster USA
5235 Ted St
Houston, TX 77040-6209   713-462-7694
                          Fax: 713-939-8441
info@flexmasterusa.com
www.Flexmasterusa.Com

Access doors, sheet metal fittings, flexible duct materials and accessories
President: Michael Jakobs
Vice President Sales & Marketing: Neil Silverman
neil@flexmasterusa.com
National Sales Manager: Shaun Griffith
shaun@flexmasterusa.com
Inside Sales, Marketing & Shipping: Angela Lewis
angela@flexmasterusa.com
In Business: 25 years
Number of Employees: 50
Sales Information: $5,000,000 - $10,000,000

6799 Reemay
Reemay
PO Box 511
Old Hickory, TN 37138-511   615-847-7000
                          Fax: 615-847-7068
www.fiberwebfiltration.com

Housewrap
President: Migo Nalbantyan
Number of Employees: 500
Sales Information: $50MM to $100MM

6800 Wrisco Industries
Wrisco Industries,Inc
355 Hiatt Dr # B
Suite B
Palm Beach Gdns, FL 33418-7199561-626-5700
                                    800-627-2646
                          Fax: 561-627-3574
www.wrisco.com

Pre-finished aluminum in choice of color/finishes for roofing, awnings, flashing, walls, gutters, patios, insulated roof and wall panels
President: Jim Monastra
Marketing Manager: AJ Monastra
Catalog Circulation: Mailed 4 time(s) per year
to 10M
Average Order Size: $3000
Printing Information: 15 pages in 2 colors on Glossy Stock
Press: Letterpress
Binding: Folded
In Business: 98 years
Number of Employees: 104
Sales Information: $10MM to $20MM

Ornamentation

6801 Campbellsville Industries, Inc
Campbellsville Industries, Inc
P.O. Box 278-W
Campbellsville, KY 42719   270-465-8135
800-467-8135
Fax: 270-465-6839
steeple@cvilleindustries.com
www.cvilleindustries.com

Repro Victorian roof parts; cupolas, steeples, clocks, columns, cornices, louvers and balustrade railings

President: Rick Moon
Marketing Manager: David England
Production Manager: Burr Hendron
production@cvilleindustries.com
Fulfillment: Donna Grammer
Engineer: Hasan El-Amouri
hasan@cvilleindustries.com
Controller/Human Relations Director: Glenda Britton
glenda@cvilleindustries.com
Accts Payable/Accts Receivable: Jessica Hunt
jessica@cvilleindustries.com
Buyers: Terry Lawson, Materials
Catalog Cost: Free
Catalog Circulation: to 3000
Average Order Size: $1200
Mailing List Information: Names for rent
In Business: 60 years
Number of Employees: 125
Sales Information: $20MM to $50MM

6802 Cape Cod Cupola Company
Cape Cod Cupola Co, Inc.
78 State Road
North Dartmouth, MA 02747-2922 508-994-2119
Fax: 508-997-2511
capecodcupola@gmail.com
www.capecodcupola.com

Cupolas, weathervanes, finials, lanterns, home accents

President: John E Bernier Jr
Production Manager: Brian R Chabot
Credit Cards: MasterCard; Visa
Catalog Cost: Free
Catalog Circulation: Mailed 52 time(s) per year
Printing Information: 20 pages in 4 colors on Matte Stock
Press: Web Press
Binding: Saddle Stitched
Mailing List Information: Names for rent
In Business: 76 years
Number of Employees: 6
Sales Information: $530,000

6803 Chelsea Decorative Metal Company
Chelsea Decorative Metal Company
8212 Braewick Drive
Houston, TX 77074-7814   713-721-9200
Fax: 713-776-8661
info@thetinman.com
www.thetinman.com

Pressed tin for walls and ceilings

President: Glenn Eldridge
Credit Cards: AMEX; MasterCard
Catalog Cost: Free
Catalog Circulation: to 500
Average Order Size: $1500
Printing Information: 8 pages in 1 color on Glossy Stock
Binding: Folded
Mailing List Information: Names for rent
In Business: 40 years
Number of Employees: 5
Sales Information: Under $500M

6804 Copper House
The Copper House
1747 Dover Rd.
Rte. 4
Epsom, NH 03234-1   603-736-9798
800-281-9798
Fax: 603-736-9798
www.thecopperhouse.com

Brass and copper lighting, copper weathervanes

President: Tom Leclair
Buyers: Bruce L Coutu
Credit Cards: AMEX; MasterCard
Catalog Cost: $4
Average Order Size: $125
Printing Information: 33 pages in 4 colors
In Business: 40 years
Number of Employees: 10

6805 Exclusively Weddings
Exclusively Weddings
2305 Soabar Street
Greensboro, NC 27406   800-759-7666
800-759-7666
Fax: 336-275-4165
corporate@EWeddings.com
www.exclusivelyweddings.com

Wedding invitations, wedding guest favors and bridal accessories

President: Bonnie Mcelveen Hunter
General Manager: R. David Stubbs
Director of Merchandising, Statione: Beth Vogel
Director of Marketing: Matt Mitchell
Credit Cards: AMEX; MasterCard
Catalog Cost: Free
Printing Information: 117 pages in 4 colors on Glossy Stock
Press: Web Press
Binding: Saddle Stitched
In Business: 23 years
Number of Employees: 87
Sales Information: $3MM to $5MM

6806 Ferro Weathervanes
Ferro Weathervanes
30 Cutler Street Mills
Studio 225
Warren, RI 02885   401-297-9560
Fax: 401-253-2830
coprguy@gmail.com
www.ferroweathervanes.com

World leader in weathervanes, finials and cupolas

Credit Cards: MasterCard
Catalog Circulation: Mailed 1 time(s) per year
Printing Information: on Newsprint
Mailing List Information: Names for rent
In Business: 9 years

6807 Heritage Fence Company
Heritage Fence Company
3890 Skippack Pike
PO Box 121
Skippack, PA 19474-121   610-584-6710
Fax: 610-584-2097
info@heritage-fence.com
www.Heritage-Fence.Com

Exterior decorating specialists

President: Rick Ross
Marketing Manager: Todd Clayton
Manager: Todd Clayton
In Business: 44 years
Number of Employees: 7
Sales Information: Under $500,000

6808 Milton W Bosley Company
Bosley mouldings
151 8th Avenue N.W
Glen Burnie, MD 21061-576   410-761-7727
800-638-5010
Fax: 410-553-0575
www.bosleymouldings.com/

Architectural and picture frame moldings; wood, metal and laminate

President: Bosley Wright
Founder: Milton W. Bosley
In Business: 102 years
Number of Employees: 27
Sales Information: $1,000,000 - $5,000,000

6809 Vintage Wood Works
Vintage Woodworks
9195 Hwy 34 S
PO Box 39
Quinlan, TX 75474-39   903-356-2158
Fax: 903-356-3023
mail@vintagewoodworks.com
www.vintagewoodworks.com

Manufacturer of architectural details direct to consumers for interior and exterior in various wood and cellular PVC

President: Gregory Tatsch
Buyers: Roland Tatsch, Raw Materials
Credit Cards: AMEX; MasterCard; Visa
Catalog Cost: $3
Printing Information: 144 pages in 1 color
Press: Web Press
Mailing List Information: Names for rent
In Business: 37 years
Number of Employees: 60
Sales Information: $1,000,000 - $5,000,000

Stains & Preservatives

6810 Basic Adhesives
Basic Adhesives
60 Webro Road
Clifton, NJ 07012   973-614-9000
800-394-9310
Fax: 973-614-9099
info@basicadhesives.com
www.basicadhesives.com

Adhesives and coatings: waterbased urethanes, latex, resins, PVA's, neoprenes, acrylics, solvent rubber; adhesive types: heat activated, pressure sensitive, laminating, cohesives

President: Yale Block
Marketing Manager: Myrna Block
Catalog Cost: Free
Catalog Circulation: Mailed 1 time(s) per year to 10M
Printing Information: 15 pages in 2 colors on Glossy Stock
Mailing List Information: Names for rent
List Company: Myrna Block
In Business: 27 years
Number of Employees: 70
Sales Information: $10,000,000 - $25,000,000

6811 ITW Philadelphia Resins Catalog
ITW Philadelphia Resins
130 Commerce Drive
Montgomeryville, PA 18936-9624   215-855-8450
Fax: 215-855-4688
info@itwcoatings.com
www.itwcoatings.com

Epoxy and urethane products

President: Dave Borzillo
Number of Employees: 6000

6812 Minwax Wood Finishing Products
Minwax
10 Mountainview Road
Upper Saddle River, NJ 07458-193201-818-7500
800-523-9299
Fax: 201-818-7605
www.minwax.com

Wood finishing products

Catalog Circulation: Mailed 1 time(s) per year
Printing Information: 18 pages in 4 colors
Binding: Saddle Stitched
In Business: 111 years

6813 **Preserva-Products**
Preserva Products Ltd
12860 Earhart Avenue
Suite 102
Auburn, CA 95602-9000 530-887-0177
800-797-2537
Fax: 530-887-0187
info@preservaproducts.com
www.preservaproducts.com

Penetrating natural finishes for wood (exterior and interior), masonry, decks, fences, siding, shingles, log homes, concrete, brick, stucco, stone, grout, tile

President: Greg Riecks
CFO: Cindy Riecks
In Business: 44 years
Number of Employees: 10
Sales Information: 1.3M

6814 **Velvit Products Catalog**
Velvit Products Company
2434 Progress Ct.
PO Box 1741
Appleton, WI 54913-1741 920-722-8355
Fax: 920-722-8456
sales@velvitproducts.com
www.velvitproducts.com

Fine wood finishes

President: Darla Bunno
Marketing Manager: Lee Neerhof
In Business: 43 years
Number of Employees: 6
Sales Information: $1,000,000 - $5,000,000

6815 **Weather-Bos Catalog**
Weather-Bos
316 California Avenue
Suite 1082
Reno, NV 89509-1650 702-278-8097
800-664-3978
Fax: 775-272-8098
info@weatherbos.com
www.weatherbos.com

Environmentally-safe wood preservatives and finishes for protecting surfaces

President: Charles Sins
Marketing Manager: Gary Wynn
Catalog Cost: Free
Catalog Circulation: to 10M
Printing Information: 30 pages in 4 colors on Glossy Stock
Press: Web Press
Binding: Perfect Bound
List Manager: Charles Sins
In Business: 27 years
Number of Employees: 85

Stairs

6816 **Iron Shop**
The Iron Shop
400 Reed Road
PO Box 547
Broomall, PA 19008-547 610-544-7100
800-523-7427
Fax: 610-544-7297
www.TheIronShop.com

Spiral staircases available in metal, oak, victorian cast aluminum, and all welded units

President: Allen Cohen
Director of Marketing: Michele Cohen
Credit Cards: AMEX; MasterCard
Catalog Cost: Free
Printing Information: in 4 colors
In Business: 82 years
Number of Employees: 75
Sales Information: 20MM-50MM

6817 **JG Braun Company**
J.G. Braun Company
PO Box 423
Bulter, WI 53007-423 414-214-0444
888-243-6914
Fax: 414-214-0450
info@mailwagner.com
www.wagnercompanies.com

Ornamental metal components and handrail systems in aluminum, bronze, brass, steel and stainless steel

President: Bob Wagner
Credit Cards: AMEX; MasterCard
Printing Information: 240 pages in 4 colors
Number of Employees: 11
Sales Information: $1MM to $3MM

6818 **Laitram Corporation**
Laitram Machinery, Inc.
220 Laitram Lane
Harahan, LA 70123-5308 504-733-6000
800-535-7631
Fax: 504-733-6111
lm.sales@laitram.com
www.laitram.com

Safety stairs

President: Mike Martin
Number of Employees: 1100
Sales Information: $10,000,000 - $25,000,000

Sunrooms & Greenhouses

6819 **Atlas Greenhouse Systems**
Atlas Manufacturing, Inc.
PO Box 558
Alapaha, GA 31622-558 229-532-2905
800-346-9902
Fax: 229-532-4600
www.atlasgreenhouse.com

Commercial, educational and hobby greenhouses, as well as carports and agricultural buildings

President: Mark Davis
Office Manager: Billy Stewart
Sales Manager: Bill Mathis
Shipping Coordinator: Tommie Ann Stone
Credit Cards: MasterCard; Visa
Catalog Cost: Free
In Business: 29 years

6820 **Contemporary Structures**
Contemporary Structures Inc.
1102 Center St
Ludlow, MA 01056-1199 413-589-0147
Fax: 413-589-1572
www.contemporarystructures.com

Sunspace components and packages

President: Bruce Libby
Marketing Manager: Carl F Libby
In Business: 40 years
Number of Employees: 4
Sales Information: Under $500,000

6821 **Greenhouse Catalog**
The Greenhouse Catalog
3740 Brooklake Road NE
Salem, OR 97303 503-393-3973
800-825-1925
Fax: 503-393-3119
info@greenhousecatalog.com
www.greenhousecatalog.com

Greenhouses and gardening

Chairman: Beverly Perry, Owner
President: Michael Perry
Marketing Manager: Michelle Torres
michelle@Sulexx.com
In Business: 27 years
Number of Employees: 15

6822 **Hoop House Greenhouse Kits**
Hoop House Greenhouse Kits
PO Box 2430
Mashpee, MA 02649 800-760-5192
Fax: 508-539-1108
www.hoophouse.com

From 10'W x 8'L up to 10' W x 100' L, galvanized steel hoops, 6 mil commercial poly film

President: Ralph H Bartlett
Credit Cards: AMEX; MasterCard
Printing Information: 6 pages on Glossy Stock
Mailing List Information: Names for rent
In Business: 30 years
Number of Employees: 5
Sales Information: $500M to $1MM

6823 **J Sussman**
J Sussman Inc.
109-10 180th Street
Jamaica, NY 11433-2622 718-297-0228
Fax: 718-297-3090
sales@jsussmaninc.com
www.Jsussmaninc.Com

Designers and manufacturers of commercial, residential and church windows, skylights, sunbilt sunrooms, metal and glass bending

President: David Sussman
CFO: Steven Sussman
Marketing Manager: Mel Wachsstock
Production Manager: Mario Ortiz
Bookkeeper, Office Manager: Bibi
Purchase, Research and Development: Jake
Head of Engineering: Mario
International Marketing Manager: Mel Wachsstock
Buyers: David Sussman
Catalog Cost: Free
Catalog Circulation: Mailed 1 time(s) per year to 40M
Printing Information: 12 pages in 4 colors on Glossy Stock
Press: Sheetfed Press
Binding: Saddle Stitched
Mailing List Information: Names for rent
List Manager: Mel Wachsstock
In Business: 109 years
Number of Employees: 55
Sales Information: $10MM to $20MM

6824 **Sunshine Rooms**
Sunshine Rooms, Inc.
3333 N Mead Street
Wichita, KS 67219-4059 316-838-0033
800-222-1598
Fax: 316-838-0839
staff@sunshinerooms.com
www.sunshinerooms.com

Solariums, greenhouses, pool enclosures, conservatories, etc.

Chairman: Wade Griffith
President: L Griffith
CFO: Buddy Frenz
VP Sales: Geoff Graves
Purchasing Manager: Eddie Banelos
Director: Eric Griffith
Credit Cards: AMEX; MasterCard
Printing Information: in 3 colors
In Business: 35 years
Number of Employees: 20
Sales Information: $1,000,000 - $5,000,000

6825 **Turner Greenhouses**
Turner Greenhouses
1500 Highway 117 S
PO Box 1260
Goldsboro, NC 27533 800-672-4770
sales@turnergreenhouses.com
www.turnergreenhouses.com

Pre-fabricated hobby greenhouses, fixtures and accessories

President: Gary Smithwick
Marketing Manager: Duffy Fleming
Credit Cards: MasterCard; Visa

Catalog Cost: Free
Mailing List Information: Names for rent
In Business: 57 years
Number of Employees: 42
Sales Information: $5,00,000

6826 WeatherPort Shelter Systems
WeatherPort Shelter Systems
1860 1600 Road
Delta, CO 81416-8405   970-399-5909
866-984-7778
Fax: 970-874-5090
info@weatherport.com
www.weatherport.com

Tensioned fabric structures, greenhouses

Printing Information: 6 pages
In Business: 49 years
Number of Employees: 50
Sales Information: $1,000,000 - $5,000,000

6827 Westview Products
Westview Products, Inc.
1350 SE Shelton Street
Dallas, OR 97338-569   503-623-5174
800-203-7557
Fax: 503-623-3382
www.westviewproducts.com

Sunrooms

President: Robert Ottaway
Marketing Manager: Terry Hurd
Mailing List Information: Names for rent
In Business: 43 years
Number of Employees: 20
Sales Information: $1,000,000 - $5,000,000

Vacuum Systems

6828 Guzzler Manufacturing
Guzzler
1621 S Illinois St
Streator, IL 61364-3945   815-672-3171
800-627-3171
Fax: 815-672-2779
sales@guzzler.com
www.Guzzler.Com

Vacuum systems

President: Dan Schueller
Marketing Manager: Kevin O'Brien
Production Manager: Tray Pritchard
Director of sales: Tony Fuller
Global Sales Manager: Joe Varca
International Sales Coordinator: Michael Ewald
Credit Cards: MasterCard; Visa
List Manager: John Ryan
In Business: 33 years
Number of Employees: 175
Sales Information: $10,000,000 - $25,000,000

6829 Vac-U-Max
VAC-U-MAX
69 William Street
Belleville, NJ 07109-3196   973-759-4600
800-822-8629
Fax: 973-759-6449
info@vac-u-max.com
www.Vac-U-Max.Com

Heavy duty industrial vacuum systems

President: Stevens Pendelton
Marketing Manager: John Bechtold
Mailing List Information: Names for rent
Number of Employees: 85
Sales Information: $10,000,000 - $25,000,000

6830 Vacuum Lifters for Materials Handling
Wood's Power-Grip Co., Inc.
908 West Main Street
PO Box 368
Laurel, MT 59044-2638   406-628-8231
888-769-7474
Fax: 406-628-8354
www.powrgrip.com

Vacuum equipment and tools for material handling and/or temporary mounts

President: K Wood
CFO: E Wood
Marketing Manager: Joe Landsverk
Production Manager: Brad Wood
Buyers: Lonnie Gradwohl
Credit Cards: MasterCard; Visa
Catalog Cost: Free
Catalog Circulation: Mailed 52 time(s) per year to 1000
Printing Information: 16 pages in 1 color on Matte Stock
Press: Sheetfed Press
Binding: Saddle Stitched
Mailing List Information: Names for rent
List Manager: Barry Wood
In Business: 68 years
Number of Employees: 95
Sales Information: $5,000,000 - $10,000,000

6831 Vacuum Parts Supply
Merchant Circle
385 Read Street
Santa Clara, CA 95050   408-727-9244
800-725-3535
Fax: 408-988-2206
www.merchantcircle.com

Vacuum systems and pumps

Chairman: Payam Zamani
President: Nancy Dusza
Marketing Manager: Chris Mancini
VP, MarketPlace: Tom Kelley
VP, Market place operations: Rudd Lippincott
VP, Marketing: Sunny Chang
Number of Employees: 4
Sales Information: $500M to $1MM

6832 William W Meyer & Sons
William W Meyer & Sons
1700 Franklin Boulevard
Libertyville, IL 60048-105   847-673-0312
847-918-8183
Fax: 847-673-5564
www.wmwmeyer.com

Industrial vacuums

President: William Meyer Jr
Production Manager: Wayne Burgard
In Business: 82 years
Number of Employees: 100
Sales Information: $10,000,000 - $25,000,000

Windows, Skylights & Doors

6833 American Metal Door Company
Door Engineering and Manufacturing
400 West Cherry Street
PO Box 5
Kasota, MN 56050-5   507-931-6910
800-959-1352
Fax: 507-931-9318
dooreng@doorengineering.com
www.doorengineering.com

Offering industrial, commerical, fire rated, aviation and specialty door solutions

President: Steve Saggau
Marketing Manager: Randy Dahl
rdahl@doorengineering.com
Product Manager: Chris Adams
cadams@doorengineering.com
Aviation Technical Sales Specialist: Dale Larson
dlarson@doorengineering.com
Ind/Comm Doors TechnicalSales Spec: Kevin Landgraff
klandgraff@doorengineering.com
Catalog Circulation: Mailed 1 time(s) per year
Printing Information: 2 pages in 4 colors
Binding: Saddle Stitched
In Business: 49 years

6834 Andersen Corporation
Andersen Corporation
100 4th Ave N
Bayport, MN 55003-1096   651-264-5150
800-426-4261
Fax: 651-264-5107
www.Andersenwindows.Com

Patio and exterior doors, windows

President: James E Humphrey
CFO: Fill Donaldson
Production Manager: Jay Lund
Printing Information: 250 pages
List Manager: Jay Lund(VP)
In Business: 112 years
Number of Employees: 9000

6835 Astrup Company
Trivantage
18401 Sheldon Road
Suite A
Middleburg Heights, OH 44130-539   216-696-2800
800-786-7601
Fax: 216-696-0914
www.trivantage.com

Fabric, hardware - industrial supplies

Chairman: John Kirk
President: J W Kirk
In Business: 123 years
Number of Employees: 160
Sales Information: $10,000,000 - $25,000,000

6836 Bennett Industries
Bennett Industries
1084 E Nakoma Street
Fort Lee, NJ 07024-5470   201-947-5340
Fax: 201-947-3908
www.bennett-ind.com

Oak door interiors, exteriors, bifolds and leaded glass; poplar, pine, mahogany doors; custom sizing; prehanging, prefinishing, patented kits for prehung doors

President: Laurence Evan Bennett
Catalog Circulation: to 500
Printing Information: 4 pages in 4 colors on Glossy Stock
In Business: 16 years
Number of Employees: 50

6837 Clopay Building Products
Cloplay
8585 Duke Blvd
Mason, OH 45040-3100   513-770-4800
800-225-6729
Fax: 513-770-3863
www.clopaydoor.com

Garage doors, window coverings, blinds and hardware

President: Steve Lynch
VP of Residential Marketing: Pat Lohse
In Business: 16 years
Number of Employees: 150

6838 Creative Openings
Creative Openings
929 N State St
Bellingham, WA 98225-5071   360-671-6420
212-563-6852
Fax: 360-671-0207
bikedog53@yahoo.com
www.Creativeopenings.Com

Victorian Style screen doors, hardwood doors, cabinetry and stairway

President: Tom Anderson
In Business: 36 years
Number of Employees: 10-J
Sales Information: Under $500M

6839 **Curtron Products**
Curtron Products
5350 Campbells Run Road
Pittsburgh, PA 15205   412-787-9750
                              800-888-9750
                         Fax: 412-787-3665
                   curtron@curtronproducts.com
                             www.tmi-pvc.com

Flexible transparent strip doors providing effective thermal, fly, bird barriers that you can see, walk or drive thru

President: Joseph Kleynjans
Marketing Manager: Steve Battaglia
Production Manager: Rick Poterni
International Marketing Manager: Mike Forber
Mailing List Information: Names for rent
In Business: 27 years
Number of Employees: 50
Sales Information: $1,000,000 - $5,000,000

6840 **Fox Lite**
Fox Lite
8300 Dayton Rd
Fairborn, OH 45324   937-864-1966
                            800-233-3699
                       Fax: 937-864-7010
                           www.Foxlite.Com

Quality skylights and roof windows

President: Douglas Hoy
CFO: Susan Davis
Marketing Manager: Mark W Hopkins
Production Manager: Jerry Korn
Fulfillment: Jill Fox
V.P. Sales/Warranty: Mark Hopkins
mark@foxlite.com
V.P. Engineering: Gary Cunagin
gary@foxlite.com
CAD Designer: John Duchesne
john@foxlite.com
Buyers: Laura Blair
Catalog Circulation: to 15M+
Printing Information: 6 pages in 2 colors on Glossy Stock
In Business: 39 years
Number of Employees: 50
Sales Information: $1,000,000 - $5,000,000

6841 **J Sussman**
J Sussman Inc.
109-10 180th Street
Jamaica, NY 11433-2622   718-297-0228
                           Fax: 718-297-3090
                       sales@jsussmaninc.com
                          www.Jsussmaninc.Com

Designers and manufacturers of commercial, residential and church windows, skylights, sunbilt sunrooms, metal and glass bending

President: David Sussman
CFO: Steven Sussman
Marketing Manager: Mel Wachsstock
Production Manager: Mario Ortiz
Bookkeeper, Office Manager: Bibi
Purchase, Research and Development: Jake
Head of Engineering: Mario
International Marketing Manager: Mel Wachsstock
Buyers: David Sussman
Catalog Cost: Free
Catalog Circulation: Mailed 1 time(s) per year to 40M
Printing Information: 12 pages in 4 colors on Glossy Stock
Press: Sheetfed Press
Binding: Saddle Stitched
Mailing List Information: Names for rent
List Manager: Mel Wachsstock
In Business: 109 years
Number of Employees: 55
Sales Information: $10MM to $20MM

6842 **Jamison Door Company**
Jamison Door Company
55 JV Jamison Drive
Hagerstown, MD 21740-70   240-313-7923
                              800-532-3667
                         Fax: 240-329-5155
                      sales@jamisondoor.com
                          www.jamisondoor.com

Cold storage doors

Chairman: John T. Williams
Marketing Manager: george
CEO: John T. Williams
Customer Service: Andy Lee
Purchasing: Don Wilson
Printing Information: 20 pages
Mailing List Information: Names for rent
In Business: 108 years
Number of Employees: 150
Sales Information: $10,000,000 - $25,000,000

6843 **Karp Associates**
KARP Associates, Inc.
260 Spagnoli Road
Melville, NY 11747   631-768-8300
                           800-888-4212
                      Fax: 631-768-8350
                        info@karpinc.com
                          www.Karpinc.Com

Access doors, walls, ceilings and floors

President: Adam Gold
In Business: 59 years
Number of Employees: 75
Sales Information: $5MM to $10MM

6844 **Omaha Fixture International**
Omaha Fixture International
10320 J Street
Omaha, NE 68127   402-592-3720
                         800-637-2257
                    Fax: 402-593-5716
               Service@OmahaFixture.com
                     www.omahafixture.com

Fixtures, displays and forms for businesses

President: Joel Alperson
Credit Cards: AMEX; MasterCard
In Business: 60 years

6845 **Pease Industries**
Peace Doors
4620 Burley Hills
Cincinnati, OH 45243   513-871-8907
                         Fax: 513-871-3375
                      info@peasedoors.com
                         www.peasedoors.com

Entry and patio doors

Chairman: David Pease
President: Leonard Cavens
Marketing Manager: Sue Calardo
Number of Employees: 320
Sales Information: $25,000,000 - $50,000,000

6846 **Simplex Strip Doors**
Simplex Isolation Systems
14500 Miller Avenue
Fontana, CA 92336-4265   909-429-0117
                              800-854-7951
                         Fax: 909-429-0217
                         info@simplexis.net
                    www.simplexstripdoors.com

Vinyl strip doors

President: David McKinnon
In Business: 36 years
Number of Employees: 18
Sales Information: $1MM to $3MM

6847 **Specialty Woodworks Company**
Speciality Woodworks Co.
212 Pennsylvania Ave
PO Box 450
Hamilton, MT 59840-450   406-363-6353
                         Fax: 406-363-6373
                  info@specialtywoodworksco.com
            www.montana.com/specialtywoodworks

Handcrafted solid wood doors and cabinets

President: Kent Olsen
Cabinet Designer: Zach Cheetham
Sales: Diana Machesky
Asst, General Manager: Dan Browning
Catalog Cost: $7
Catalog Circulation: to 540
Average Order Size: $45
Printing Information: 10 pages in 4 colors on Glossy Stock
Binding: Saddle Stitched
Mailing List Information: Names for rent
In Business: 30 years
Number of Employees: 25
Sales Information: $1,000,000 - $5,000,000

6848 **Starlight Skylights**
Starlight Skylights
P.O. Box 992
Hurlock, MD 21643-0992   800-776-1539
                         Fax: 410-943-8245
                  sales@starlightskylights.com
                     www.starlightskylights.com

Roof windows and skylights, residential enclosures and bus shelters

President: Ray Hollowell
ray@starlightskylights.com
Marketing Manager: Steven Naylor
Customer Service Rep.: Vickie
vickie@starlightskylights.com
Customer Service Rep.: Melissa
melissa@starlightskylights.com
Catalog Circulation: Mailed 1 time(s) per year to 10M
Printing Information: 6 pages in 4 colors on Glossy Stock
In Business: 20 years
Number of Employees: 10-J
Sales Information: $1,000,000 - $5,000,000

6849 **Vixen Hill Manufacturing**
Vixen Hill Manufacturing Co.
69 E Main St.
PO Box 389
Eiverson, PA 19520   610-286-0909
                            800-423-2766
                       Fax: 610-286-2099
                       sales@vixenhill.com
                           www.vixenhill.com

Cedar modular gazebos, screened gardenhouses, porch systems, cedar exterior shutters

President: Christopher Peeples
Marketing Manager: Andrea
Production Manager: Robert Brown
Credit Cards: MasterCard
Catalog Circulation: Mailed 52 time(s) per year
Average Order Size: $5000
Printing Information: 10 pages in 4 colors on Matte Stock
Binding: Folded
Mailing List Information: Names for rent
In Business: 33 years
Number of Employees: 30
Sales Information: $1MM to $3MM

6850 **Wallis Stained Glass, Doors, Cabinets, Art, Glass**
Jack Wallis Stained Glass & Doors
2985 Butterworth Rd
Murray, KY 42071-8217   270-489-2613
                          Fax: 270-489-2187
                            wallis@wk.net
                       www.jackwallisdoors.com

Cabinet art glass, stained glass, stained glass house doors

President: Jack Wallis
Marketing Manager: Jeremy Speight
Credit Cards: AMEX; MasterCard
Catalog Cost: Free
Catalog Circulation: to 400
Average Order Size: $5000
Printing Information: 12 pages in 4 colors on Glossy Stock
Mailing List Information: Names for rent
In Business: 43 years
Number of Employees: 6
Sales Information: $400,000

Business Information
Advertising & Promotions

6851 Above & Beyond Balloons
Above & Beyond
2400 Pullman St.
Santa Ana, CA 92705
949-586-8470
800-564-2234
Fax: 800-481-3299
sales@balloons.biz
www.advertisingballoons.com

Advertising and promotional balloons, inflatable product replicas,vinyl, helium and cold air inflatables

President: Mike Chaklos
Principal; Sales Manager: Pauls Chaklos
Credit Cards: AMEX; MasterCard; Visa
Catalog Circulation: Mailed 1 time(s) per year
Printing Information: 10 pages
Mailing List Information: Names for rent
In Business: 22 years
Number of Employees: 44
Sales Information: $4,000,000

6852 Badge-A-Minit
Badge-A-Minit
345 N Lewis Avenue
Oglesby, IL 61348-9776
815-883-8822
800-223-4103
Fax: 815-883-9696
questions@badgeaminit.com
www.badgeaminit.com

Button-making equipment and accessories

President: Cindy Kurkowski
Marketing Manager: Teresa Urban, VP Marketing
Credit Cards: AMEX; MasterCard; Visa
Catalog Cost: Free
Printing Information: 47 pages in 4 colors
Mailing List Information: Names for rent
In Business: 40 years
Number of Employees: 80

6853 Best Impressions
Best Impressions
345 North Lewis Avenue
Oglesby, IL 61348-9776
815-883-3532
800-635-2378
Fax: 815-883-8346
feedback@bestimpressions.com
www.bestimpressions.com

Promotional products and custom imprinted items for business

President: Cindy Kurkowski
Buyers: Shelly Smith
Credit Cards: AMEX; MasterCard; Visa
Catalog Cost: Free
In Business: 22 years
Number of Employees: 20-5
Sales Information: $20MM to $50MM

6854 BrittenMedia
Britten Banners Inc.
2322 Cass Rd.
Traverse City, MI 49684
231-941-8200
855-763-8204
Fax: 231-941-8299
sales@brittenmedia.com
www.brittenstudios.com

Digitally printed and screen printed banners and signs; banner display accessories, backdrops, mural, flags, tradeshow accessories, museum and zoo exhibit accessories

Chairman: Liz Keegan
President: Paul Britten
Marketing Manager: Jenn Ryan
Production Manager: Peter White
Catalog Cost: Free
Printing Information: 16 pages in 4 colors
In Business: 30 years
Number of Employees: 90
Sales Information: $25 Million

6855 Call One
Call One Inc
400 Imprial Blvd.
Cape Canaveral, FL 32920-9002
321-783-2400
800-749-3160
Fax: 321-799-9222
www.calloneonline.com

Telephones, headset bases and amplifiers, headsets and accessories

VP: Raymond Hirsch
VP, Director - Sales/Marketing: William Mays
Sales Manager: Danny Hayasaka
Credit Cards: AMEX; MasterCard
In Business: 26 years
Number of Employees: 80

6856 Cardinal Jackets
Cardinal Activewear
P.O. Box 1029
Grundy, VA 24614
800-647-7745
Fax: 276-935-4970
info@cardinalactivewear.com
www.cardinalactivewear.com

Nylon coach's windbreakers; Satin baseball jackets; Nylon baseball jackets; Nylon hooded pullover jacket; Mesh lined micro-twill windshirt

President: Mark Shortridge
CFO: Laura Barden
Marketing Manager: Mark Shortridge/Teresa Damron
Buyers: Teresa Damron
Credit Cards: AMEX; MasterCard; Visa
Catalog Cost: Free
Catalog Circulation: to 400m
Printing Information: 4 pages in 4 colors
Mailing List Information: Names for rent
In Business: 40 years
Number of Employees: 4
Sales Information: $110 Thousand

6857 Competitive Edge
Competitive Edge
3500 109th Street
Des Moines, IA 50322-8100
515-280-3343
800-458-3343
Fax: 515-288-3343
info@compet.com
www.Compet.Com

Advertising specialties/printing

Chairman: David M Greenspon
President: David Greenspon
CFO: Alice Bebruin
Marketing Manager: Michael Neary
Production Manager: Bob Rees
Fulfillment: Angie Mayo
International Marketing Manager: Michael Taylor
Buyers: Tau Gaobeag
Credit Cards: AMEX; MasterCard; Visa
Catalog Cost: Free

Catalog Circulation: Mailed 1 time(s) per year to 20000
Average Order Size: $350
Printing Information: 62 pages in 4 colors on Glossy Stock
Press: Web Press
Binding: Saddle Stitched
Mailing List Information: Names for rent
In Business: 15 years
Number of Employees: 94
Sales Information: $3MM to $5MM

6858 Corporate Service Center
Corporate Service Center
5605 Riggins Court
Suite 200
Reno, NV 89502-8535
866-411-2002
800-542-2077
Fax: 775-329-0852
info@corporateservicecenter.com
www.corporateservicecenter.com

Business and financial services

Executive V.P.: Trevor C. Rowley
Renewals Manager: Mike Fletcher
Renewal Team: Cathy Resytelo
Printing Information: 20 pages in 4 colors
In Business: 26 years
Sales Information: $5MM to $10MM

6859 Custom-Printed Promotional Items
Larry Fox and Company Ltd
PO Box 729
Valley Stream, NY 11582-729
516-791-7929
800-397-7923
Fax: 516-791-1022
ellen@larryfox.com
promo-web.com/d/d32.asp?d=larryfox&pg=32

Promotional gifts and imprinted products for businesses, organizations, schools, camps, fire departments, EMS, paramedics

President: Ellen Ingber
Marketing Manager: Ellen Ingber
CEO: Larry Fox
Credit Cards: MasterCard
Catalog Cost: Free
Catalog Circulation: Mailed 1 time(s) per year to 20000
Printing Information: 64 pages in 1 color on Matte Stock
Press: Web Press
Binding: Perfect Bound
Mailing List Information: Names for rent
In Business: 54 years
Number of Employees: 2
Sales Information: $500M to $1MM

6860 Deluxe Small Business Services
New England Business Service, Inc. (NEBS
500 Main St
Groton, MA 01471-1
888-823-6327
Fax: 978-449-3419
www.nebs.com

Small business management and marketing solutions

President: Dave Saunders
Number of Employees: 8000

6861 Direct Promotions
Direct Promotions
29395 Agoura Road
Suite 207
Agoura Hills, CA 91301
818-591-9010
800-444-7706
Fax: 818-591-2071
sales@directpromotions.net
www.directpromotions.net

Custom printed promotional products and business gifts

President: Randy Perry
Credit Cards: AMEX; MasterCard
Catalog Cost: Free
Catalog Circulation: Mailed 1 time(s) per year
Printing Information: 24 pages in 4 colors on

Glossy Stock
Press: Web Press
Binding: Saddle Stitched
In Business: 12 years
Number of Employees: 4
Sales Information: $500M to $1MM

6862 Eastern Emblem
Eastern Emblem Mfg Corp
509 18th Street
PO Box 828
Union City, NJ 07087-828   201-854-0338
                                   800-344-5112
                            Fax: 201-867-7248
jnsboyscouts@gmail.com
www.easternemblem.com

Emblems and insignia for advertising or groups; custom embroidery and metal pins; custom work for embroidery-metal logo pins, stickers, garments

President: S Lefkowitz
Production Manager: Len
Credit Cards: AMEX; MasterCard
Catalog Cost: Free
In Business: 55 years
Number of Employees: 7
Sales Information: $1MM-$3MM

6863 G&R Publishing Company
G&R Publishing Company
507 Industrial Rd
Waverly, IA 50677-1898   319-352-5391
                                  800-383-1679
                           Fax: 800-886-7496
books@gandrpublishing.com
www.Gandrpublishing.Com

Custom cookbook, a great fundraiser for your church, school, community, group or business

President: Thomas Scott
In Business: 36 years
Sales Information: $5MM to $10MM

6864 Glenncraft Corporation
Glenncraft Corporation
205 Fortin Drive
Woonsocket, RI 02895   401-769-0101
                                  800-553-9746
                           Fax: 401-766-1170
sales@glenncraft.com
www.glenncraft.com

Souvenirs, promotional products and gifts

Marketing Manager: Lou Inserra
Production Manager: Joe Arico
In Business: 33 years

6865 Graphics 3
Graphics 3 Inc
1400 W Indiantown Road
P.O. Box 937
Jupiter, FL 33468-7998   561-746-6746
                           Fax: 561-746-6922
pop-ups@graphics3inc.com
www.graphics3inc.com

Three dimensional cards and calendars for promotions

Credit Cards: AMEX; MasterCard
Catalog Cost: Free
Catalog Circulation: Mailed 1 time(s) per year
Printing Information: in 4 colors
Binding: Saddle Stitched
In Business: 39 years
Number of Employees: 20
Sales Information: $1,000,000 - $5,000,000

6866 Great Ideas Catalog
Larry Fox and Company, Ltd.
PO Box 729
Valley Stream, NY 11582-729   516-791-7929
                                  800-397-7923
                           Fax: 516-791-1022
ellen@larryfox.com
www.larryfox.com

Great promotional products all with your imprint or message, all prices are discounted and we have thousands of items

President: Ellen Ingber
Marketing Manager: Larry Fox
Fulfillment: Larry Fox
CEO: Larry Fox
Buyers: Ellen Ingber
Catalog Cost:
Catalog Circulation: Mailed 1 time(s) per year to 20000
Average Order Size: $500
Printing Information: 32 pages in 1 color on Matte Stock
Press: Web Press
Binding: Saddle Stitched
Mailing List Information: Names for rent
In Business: 52 years
Number of Employees: 2
Sales Information: Under $500M

6867 InfoUSA
InfoUSA
1020 East 1st St.
Papillion, NE 68046   800-835-5856
www.infousa.com

Business and consumer direct marketing list categories for direct mail, research and telemarketing campaigns.

Chair & CEO: Michael Iaccarino
Catalog Cost: Free
In Business: 47 years
Sales Information: $400 Million

6868 International Patterns
International Patterns
50 Inez Dr
Bay Shore, NY 11706-2238   631-952-2000
                                  800-394-9436
                           Fax: 516-938-1215
sales@internationalpatterns.com
www.Internationalpatterns.Com

Letter boards, advertising signs and products

President: Shelley Beckwith
Number of Employees: 120
Sales Information: $10,000,000 - $25,000,000

6869 Jay Group
Jay Group
700 Indian Springs Drive
Lancaster, PA 17601-9602   717-285-6200
                                  800-953-3572
                           Fax: 717-285-6274
information@jaygroup.com
www.Jaygroup.Com

Advertising specialties

President: Dana Chryst
CFO: Tom Smith
Marketing Manager: David Wood
Fulfillment: Doug Bushang
CEO: Dana Chryst
Center Manager: Dave Spendio
Information Technology: Mark Rambler
Printing Information: in 4 colors on Glossy Stock
Press: Web Press
Mailing List Information: Names for rent
In Business: 49 years
Number of Employees: 182
Sales Information: $20MM to $50MM

6870 JeweLite
Wagner Zip-Change Inc
3100 Hirsch
Melrose Park, IL 60160   708-681-4100
                                  800-323-0744
                           Fax: 800-243-4924
sales@wagnerzip.com
www.wagnerzip.com

Signage lettering trim: colored or metallic

VP: Georgene Bercier
VP of Operations: Gary Delaquila
In Business: 87 years

6871 Marquis Awards & Specialties
Marquis Awards & Specialties, Inc.
108 N Bent St
Powell, WY 82435   307-754-2272
                                  800-327-2446
                           Fax: 307-754-9577
marquisawards@bresnan.net
www.rushawards.com

Awards, sportswear and promotional gifts for businesses and consumers

President: John H Collins
Marketing Manager: Terry Collins
Founder: John Collins
Founder: Terry Collins
Credit Cards: AMEX; MasterCard; Visa; Discover
Catalog Cost: Free
Catalog Circulation: Mailed 12 time(s) per year
Printing Information: 97 pages in 4 colors on Matte Stock
Press: Web Press
Binding: Saddle Stitched
Mailing List Information: Names for rent
In Business: 31 years
Number of Employees: 5
Sales Information: $500M to $1MM

6872 Mo' Money Associates
Mo' Money Associates
3838 North Palafox Street
Pensacola, FL 32505-2591   850-432-6301
                                  800-874-7681
                           Fax: 850-434-5645
momoney@momoney.com
www.momoney.com/

Advertising novelties

Chairman: Wayne Mowe
President: Cliff Mowe
Marketing Manager: Cliff Mowe
VP Sales\Import: Travis Hall
VP Sales: Tom McVoy
Vice President, Sales: Emory Bell
In Business: 36 years
Number of Employees: 200
Sales Information: $10MM to $20MM

6873 Neil Enterprises
Neil Enterprises
450 E Bunker Ct
Vernon Hills, IL 60061   847-549-7627
                                  800-621-5584
                           Fax: 847-549-0349
info@neilenterprises.com
www.neilenterprises.com

Promotional product/photo novelty manufacturer and supplier/distributor of instant photographic equipment serving the photographic, printing/screenprint, craft, educational and ad specialty industries

President: Jerry Fine
Catalog Cost: Free
Catalog Circulation: Mailed 1 time(s) per year
Printing Information: 52 pages in 4 colors on Glossy Stock
Press: Web Press
Binding: Perfect Bound
Mailing List Information: Names for rent
In Business: 56 years

Number of Employees: 25
Sales Information: $50-100 Million

6874 Neil Holiday Catalog

Neil Enterprises
450 E Bunker Ct
Vernon Hills, IL 60061 847-549-7627
800-621-5584
Fax: 847-549-0349
info@neilenterprises.com
www.neilenterprises.com

Promotional product/photo novelty manufacturer and supplier/distributor of instant photographic equipment serving the photographic, printing/screenprint, craft, education and ad specialty industries

President: Jerry Fine
Catalog Cost: Free
Catalog Circulation: Mailed 1 time(s) per year
Printing Information: 12 pages in 4 colors on Glossy Stock
Press: Web Press
Binding: Perfect Bound
In Business: 56 years
Number of Employees: 25
Sales Information: $50-100 Million

6875 Pacific Sportswear & Emblem Company

Pacific Sportswear Co.,Inc
Box 15211
San Diego, CA 92195-5211 619-281-6688
800-872-8778
Fax: 619-281-6687
info@pacsport.com
www.Pacsport.Com

Custom embroidered Flag Patches and Pins, headwear, embroidered patches, rubber keychains and lapel pins

President: Rich Soergel
CFO: Cathy Mellies
Marketing Manager: Rich Roengel
Production Manager: Bob Bond
Credit Cards: MasterCard; Visa
Catalog Cost: Free
Catalog Circulation: Mailed 52 time(s) per year to 10M
Average Order Size: $5000
Printing Information: 10 pages in 1 color on Matte Stock
Press: Web Press
Binding: Saddle Stitched
Mailing List Information: Names for rent
List Manager: Rich Soergel
In Business: 28 years
Number of Employees: 8
Sales Information: $1,000,000 - $5,000,000

6876 Pecco Premiums

Pecco, Inc.
8760 Orion Place, Suite 100,
Columbus, OH 43240-2911 201-461-0055
Fax: 201-461-5333
www.manta.com

Sales promotion novelties predominantly in the $1-$5 price range, including audios, calculators, clocks, watches, bags, accessories, etc

President: Patrick Lam
CFO: George Trotman
Marketing Manager: Andrew P Goranson
Production Manager: PW Lam
CEO: John Swanciger
COO: Dario Ambrosini
VP, Platform & Technology: Brad Warnick
Catalog Cost: Free
Catalog Circulation: to 15M
Printing Information: 26 pages in 4 colors on Matte Stock
Press: Sheetfed Press
Number of Employees: 15

6877 Print Craft, Inc.

Print Craft Incorporated
315 5th Avenue N.W.
Minneapolis, MN 55112 651-633-8122
800-217-8060
www.printcraft.com

Customized retail and commercial packaging, as well as printed products such as calendars, brochures, books, booklets, and reports

President: Mike Gallagher
Production Manager: Jon Riederer
Credit Cards: AMEX; MasterCard
Catalog Circulation: Mailed 2 time(s) per year
Printing Information: 60 pages in 4 colors on Glossy Stock
Press: Web Press
Binding: Saddle Stitched
In Business: 51 years
Number of Employees: 165

6878 Promo Direct Catalog

Promo Direct, Inc
931 American Pacific Drive
Suite 100
Henderson, NV 89014 800-748-6150
Fax: 310-782-7660
info@promodirect.com
www.promodirect.com

Promotional products and items that can be customized with business or any information you would like

President: David Sarro
Credit Cards: AMEX; MasterCard
Catalog Cost: Free
Printing Information: 48 pages
In Business: 24 years

6879 Promo Unlimited

Promo Direct, Inc
931 American Pacific Drive
Suite 100
Henderson, NV 89014 310-782-9900
800-748-6150
Fax: 310-782-7660
info@promodirect.com
www.Promodirect.Com

Imprinted promotional products

President: David Sarro
Credit Cards: AMEX; MasterCard
Printing Information: 48 pages in 4 colors on Glossy Stock
Sales Information: $3MM to $5MM

6880 Promotional Ideabook

Drawing Board
101 E Ninth St
Waynesboro, PA 17268 860-379-9911
800-527-9530
Fax: 800-253-1838
customerservice@drawingboard.com
www.drawingboard.com

Office products

President: Lee Bracken
Credit Cards: AMEX; MasterCard
Catalog Cost: Free
Catalog Circulation: Mailed 8 time(s) per year
Printing Information: 100 pages
Mailing List Information: Names for rent
Number of Employees: 300

6881 Rainbow Industries

Brand Builders
PO Box 1087
Tenafly, NJ 07670-5087 973-575-8383
800-842-0527
Fax: 973-575-6001
jeffrey@brandbuildersllc.com
www.brandbuildersllc.com

Advertising specialties and executive gifts

President: Richard Brown
Marketing Manager: Jeffery Brown
Production Manager: Richard Brown
Catalog Cost: Free
Catalog Circulation: Mailed 10 time(s) per year to 10M
Average Order Size: $500
Printing Information: 20 pages in 4 colors on Glossy Stock
Press: Web Press
Binding: Folded
Mailing List Information: Names for rent
List Manager: R Brown
In Business: 21 years
Number of Employees: 15
Sales Information: $3MM to $5MM

6882 SGD Golf

SGH Golf Inc.
6805 Mt. Vernon Avenue
Cincinnati, OH 45227 513-984-0414
800-284-8884
Fax: 513-984-9648
sgh@sghgolf.com
www.sghgolf.com

Planners of major golf events and golf destinations

President: Ian Jack
Credit Cards: MasterCard
Catalog Circulation: Mailed 1 time(s) per year to 11K
Printing Information: 76 pages in 3 colors
Press: Web Press
Binding: Saddle Stitched
In Business: 28 years

6883 Sales Promotion Tool Book

The Godfrey Group
1000 Centre Green Way
Ste 200
Cary, NC 27513-7659 919-544-6504
800-789-9394
Fax: 919-544-6729
sales@godfreygroup.com
www.godfreygroup.com

Trade show exhibits and displays

President: H Glenn Godfrey
Principal: Will Daniel
VP: Ann Godfrey
Project Manager: Pete Smith
Credit Cards: AMEX; MasterCard
Catalog Cost: Free
Printing Information: 42 pages in 4 colors on Glossy Stock
In Business: 40 years

6884 Scott Sign Systems Catalog

Scott Sign Systems, Inc.
7525 Pennsylvania Av
Suite 101
Sarasota, FL 34243 941-355-5171
800-237-9447
Fax: 941-351-1787
www.Scottsigns.Com

Signs and sign systems including stock illuminated, illuminated open/business hours, illuminated custom, architectural sign systems, digital and complaince signs

President: Steve Evans
Marketing Manager: Jennifer Adkins
Production Manager: Maurice Aguinaldo
VP Sales: Carol Clarke
Sales: Kathy Hannon
kathyh@scottsigns.com
Account Manager: Lisa Pyrcz
lisa.pyrcz@identitygroup.com
Credit Cards: AMEX; MasterCard; Visa
Catalog Cost: Free
Printing Information: 64 pages in 3 colors on Glossy Stock
Press: Sheetfed Press
Binding: Saddle Stitched
Mailing List Information: Names for rent
In Business: 58 years
Number of Employees: 25
Sales Information: $1MM

6885 Shamrock Paper
Shamrock Corporation
422 N Chimney Rock Road
Greensboro, NC 27410-9448   800-334-8982
Fax: 800-325-1651
orders@shamrock1.com
www.shamrockwraps.com

Custom printed gift wraps

Chairman: David Worth
President: Rob Hadgraft
Catalog Cost: Free
Catalog Circulation: Mailed 1 time(s) per year
Printing Information: 132 pages in 4 colors on
Glossy Stock
Press: Web Press
Binding: Saddle Stitched
In Business: 60 years
Number of Employees: 5
Sales Information: 50MM-100MM

6886 Signcrafters
US Signcrafters
216 Lincolnway E
Osceola, IN 46561-2769   574-674-5055
800-659-6319
Fax: 574-674-5255
info@ussigncrafters.com
www.ussigncrafters.com

**Iluminated, architectural and commercial
signs**

President: Scott Franko
VP: Jenny Franko
Office Manager: Jackie Wade
Operations Manager: Jim Fields
In Business: 24 years
Sales Information: $1MM to $3MM

6887 Signs Plus Banners Catalog
Signs Plus Banners
20195 S Diamond Lake Road
Suite 100
Rogers, MN 55374   763-428-6090
800-635-6897
Fax: 763-428-6095
sales@signsplusbanners.com
www.signsplusbanners.com

**Wholesale vinyl signs, magnetic signs, ap-
plication products, banners & banner
stands, digital printing, sign frames, sign
blanks, storage products and software
graphics**

President: C Albrecht
Department Manager: Craig Morse
craig.morse@gnedi.com
Operations Coordinator: JulieMelander
julie.melander@gnedi.com
Customer Service Representative: Harold
Embry
harold.embry@gnedi .com
Credit Cards: AMEX; MasterCard; Visa
Catalog Cost: Free
Catalog Circulation: Mailed 26 time(s) per
year
Printing Information: 24 pages
In Business: 34 years

6888 Union Pen Company Full Line Catalog
Amsterdam Printing
166 Wallins Corners Road
Amsterdam, NY 12010   800-203-9917
Fax: 518-843-5204
www.unionpen.com

**Direct marketer of imprinted promotional
products**

President: Morton Tenny
CFO: R Rosenthal
Credit Cards: AMEX; MasterCard
Catalog Cost: Free
Catalog Circulation: Mailed 6 time(s) per year
to 15000
Average Order Size: $350
Printing Information: 48 pages in 4 colors on
Matte Stock

Press: Web Press
Binding: Saddle Stitched
Mailing List Information: Names for rent
Will Trade Names: Yes
In Business: 116 years
Number of Employees: 150
Sales Information: $10,000,000 - $25,000,000

6889 Wayne Industries
EBSCO Signs& Displays
1400 8th St N
Clanton, AL 35045-2400   205-755-5580
800-285-2504
Fax: 205-755-1516
www.WayneIndustries.Com

**Signs: Portable, outdoor, indoor, church,
school, bulletin boards, styrofoams,
A-frames**

President: Steve Hill
Founder: James Easterling
Credit Cards: AMEX; MasterCard; Visa
Catalog Cost: Free
Printing Information: 15 pages in 4 colors on
Glossy Stock
Press: Web Press
Binding: Saddle Stitched
In Business: 57 years
Number of Employees: 85
Sales Information: $5,000,000 - $10,000,000

Associations

**6890 AICPA Self-Study & On-Site Training
Catalog**
AICPA
1211 Avenue of the Americas
New York, NY 10036-8775   212-596-6200
888-777-7077
Fax: 212-596-6213
service@aicpa.org
www.aicpa.org

**Books for CPAs; self-study for professional
development**

Chairman: Tommye E. Barie, CPA
tbarie@aicpa.org
President: Barry C. Melancon, CPA, CGMA
bmelancon@aicpa.org
CFO: Tim LaSpaluto, CPA, CGMA, CITP
tlaspaluto@aicpa.org
Marketing Manager: Matty Carr
SVP, Strategy, People & Innovation: Lawson
Carmichael
lcarmichael@aicpa.org
SVP, Public Practice & Global Allia: Susan
Coffey, CPA, CGMA
scoffey@aicpa.org
Senior Vice President: JaniceMaiman, CAE
jmaiman@aicpa.org
In Business: 128 years

**6891 American Academy-Medical
Administrators**
American Academy-Medical Administrators
330 N Wabash Avenue
Suite 2000
Chicago, IL 60611-4516   312-321-6815
Fax: 312-673-6705
info@aameda.org
www.aameda.org

**Department heads and administrators in ar-
eas of food service management, nursing,
housekeeping and management**

Chairman: Mr. Eric Conde, MSA, CFAAMA
eric.conde@jax.ufl.edu
President: Renee S. Schleicher, CAE
renee@ameeda.org
CFO: Nancy L. Anderson, CPA, CAE
nanderson@aameda.org
Executive Director, Interim: David Schmahl
dschmahl@aameda.org
Education Director (interim): Christine Peck
cpeck@aameda.org
Program Coordinator: Jennifer Schap
jschap@aameda.org
Printing Information: 27 pages

In Business: 10 years
Number of Employees: 9

6892 CM Almy General
CM Almy
228 Sound Beach Avenue
Greenwich, CT 06870-2644   203-531-7600
800-225-2569
Fax: 203-531-9048
almyaccess@almy.com
www.almy.com

**Supplier of decorative furnishings, apparel,
worship related products and gifts to
churches, religious institutions, their clergy
and members**

President: Stephen Sendler
CFO: Mike Mc Gown
Credit Cards: MasterCard
Catalog Cost: Free
Printing Information: 208 pages in 4 colors on
Glossy Stock
In Business: 123 years
Sales Information: $5MM to $10MM

6893 Center for Creative Leadership
Center for Creative Leadership
PO Box 26300
One Leadership Place
Greensboro, NC 27410   336-545-2810
Fax: 336-282-3284
info@ccl.org
www.ccl.org/Leadership/

**An international, nonprofit educational insti-
tution devoted to behavioral science research, executive development and
leadership education**

Chairman: Odd Ingar Skaug
President: John R. Ryan
Marketing Manager: Hamish Madan
madanh@ccl.org
VP & Managing Director: Rudi Plettinx
plettinxr@ccl.org
Sales Director Open Enrollment: Philip Healy
healyp@ccl.org
Leadership Portfolio Director: Natalie Pothier
pothiern@ccl.org
In Business: 43 years
Number of Employees: 335

6894 Center for Management Effectiveness
Center for Management Effectiveness
P.O. Box 1202
Pacific Palisades, CA 90272-3612 310-459-6052
Fax: 310-459-6502
info@cmeinc.org
www.cmeinc.org

**Conducts programs for trainers on topics
such as stress management, resolution of
conflict and managing change**

President: Eric Herzog
Marketing Manager: Marilyn Ginsburg
Fulfillment: Dinah Breakell
VP: Jane Herzog
Catalog Cost: Free
Catalog Circulation: Mailed 2 time(s) per year
to 15M
Printing Information: 6 pages in 4 colors on
Glossy Stock
Press: Letterpress
Mailing List Information: Names for rent
In Business: 34 years
Number of Employees: 10
Sales Information: $400,000

6895 Christian Tools of Affirmation
Christian Tools of Affirmation
1625 Larkin Williams Rd
PO Box 1205
Fenton, MO 63026-1205   636-305-3100
800-999-1874
Fax: 800-315-8713
customerservice@ctainc.com
www.ctainc.com

Christian products and gifts such as bracelets, books, keychains, mugs, ornaments, stationery, videos, magnets and prayer journals

President: Terry Knoploh
CEO: Terry Knoploh
Credit Cards: MasterCard; Visa
Catalog Cost: Free
In Business: 15 years
Sales Information: $5MM to $10MM

6896 Institute of Certified Professional Managers
ICPM
James Madison University
MSC 5504
Harrisonburg, VA 22807-1   540-568-3247
Fax: 540-568-3587
info@icpm.biz
www.icpm.biz

Strives to recognize management as a profession, and provides opportunities for study in the field

President: Jackson Ramsey
Marketing Manager: Emily Benusa
Executive Director, Administration: Lynn Powell, MBA, CM
Instructional Designer: Jonathan Lutz, MET
Administration: Kimberley A. Foreman, MS, CPA
In Business: 41 years
Number of Employees: 5

6897 National Association of Printers & Lithographers
Epicomm
One Meadowlands Plaza
Suite 1511
East Rutherford, NJ 07073   201-634-9600
800-642-6275
Fax: 201-634-0324
epicomm.org

Information on books and products produced by NAPL to assist printers and print salespeople

Chairman: Tom Duchene
President: Ken Garner
kgarner@epicomm.org
CFO: Dean D'Ambrosi
Marketing Manager: Samantha Lake
SVP/Managing Director: Mike Philie
mphilie@epicomm.org
SVP/Chief Economist: Andrew D. Paparozzi
apaparozzi@epicomm.org
Director of Marketing: Samantha Lake
slake@epicomm.org
Printing Information: 6 pages in 2 colors
In Business: 1 years

6898 Support Services Alliance
Lifetime Benefit Solutions
115 Continuum Drive
Liverpool, NY 13088   315-448-9000
800-356-1029
Fax: 315-476-8440
info@ssamembers.com
www.lifetimebenefitsolutions.com

Multi-state membership organization that provides cost-savings services and legislative representation for small businesses and the self-employed

President: Robert Marquardt
In Business: 41 years
Number of Employees: 270

6899 World Confederation of Productivity
World Confederation of Productivity
2202 5th Street
Suite 1240
White Bear Lake, MN 55110-3038 651-429-3112
800-TOR-DAHL
Fax: 651-429-7951
info@tordahl.com
www.tordahl.com

Strives to promote productivity science, advance management techniques, and improve the quality of working life and environment

President: Tor Dahl
In Business: 41 years
Number of Employees: 8
Sales Information: $500M to $1MM

Seminars

6900 AICPA Self Study/Video Catalog
AICPA
1211 Avenue of the Americas
New York, NY 10036-8775   212-596-6200
888-777-7077
Fax: 212-596-6213
service@aicpa.org
www.aicpa.org

Self study videos and CAI continuing professional education courses

Chairman: Tommye E. Barie, CPA
tbarie@aicpa.org
President: Barry C. Melancon, CPA, CGMA
bmelancon@aicpa.org
CFO: Tim LaSpaluto, CPA, CGMA, CITP
tlaspaluto@aicpa.org
Marketing Manager: M Carr
Production Manager: L Moran
SVP, Strategy, People & Innovation: Lawson Carmichael
lcarmichael@aicpa.org
SVP, Public Practice & Global Allia: Susan Coffey, CPA, CGMA
scoffey@aicpa.org
Senior Vice President: JaniceMaiman, CAE
jmaiman@aicpa.org
Credit Cards: MasterCard; Visa
Catalog Circulation: to 60M
Printing Information: 72 pages in 4 colors on Matte Stock
Press: Web Press
Binding: Perfect Bound
List Manager: Julia Esposito
In Business: 128 years
Number of Employees: 781
Sales Information: $5,000,000

6901 Advanced Solutions Group
Advanced Solutions Group
Devine Street Research Center, Room
730 Devine Street, University of South C
Columbia, SC 29208   803-777-6431
Fax: 803-777-8833
www.asg.sc.edu

Multi-media, active web sites, computer based training, internet presentations

Marketing Manager: Randy Shelley
Director of the Advanced Solutions: Dr. Joseph E. Johnson, Ph.D.
jjohnson@sc.edu
Printing Information: 40 pages

6902 Bcc Research
Bcc Research
49 Walnut Park
Building 2
Wellesley, MA 02481   866-285-7215
info@bccresearch.com
www.bccresearch.com

Market research industry reports, newsletters and conferences

Senior Editor: Chris Spivey
Editorial Director: Kevin R. Fitzgerald

Catalog Circulation: Mailed 6 time(s) per year to 200M
Printing Information: 32 pages in 2 colors on Matte Stock
Binding: Saddle Stitched
In Business: 46 years
Number of Employees: 60
Sales Information: $1,000,000 - $5,000,000

6903 Fred Pryor Seminars
Pryor Learning Solutions
5700 Broadmoor Street
Suite 300
Mission, KS 66202-2219   913-967-8849
800-780-8476
customerservice@pryor.com
www.pryor.com

Training sessions/seminars for professional trainers and business managers

President: Michael Hays
Credit Cards: AMEX; MasterCard
In Business: 47 years
Sales Information: $10MM to $20MM

6904 NAED Education Foundation
NAED
1181 Corporate Lake Drive
St Louis, MO 63132   314-991-9000
888-791-2512
Fax: 314-991-3060
memberservices@naed.org
www.naed.org

Courses available to members of the National Association of Electrical Distributors to enhance their businesses

President: Tom Naber
tnaber@naed.org
Marketing Manager: Linda Thurman
lthurman@naed.org
Vice President of Gov't Affairs: Ed Orlet
eorlet@naed.org
SVP/Executive Director of NAED Foun: Michelle McNamara
mmcnamara@naed.org
Vice President Finance: TimDencker
tdencker@naed.org
In Business: 107 years
Number of Employees: 35

6905 Tapes And Seminars
National Seminars Training
6901 W. 63rd Street
P.O. Box 419107
Kansas City, KS 64141-6107   913-432-7755
800-258-7246
Fax: 913-432-0824
cstserv@natsem.com
www.nationalseminarstraining.com

Books, audiocassettes and other career development resources for business professionals who are serious about being the best they can be

Trainer: Beth Bednar
Trainer: Christopher Babson
Trainer: Gary Garner

Chemical Processing
Supplies & Equipment

6906 Aero Tec Laboratories
ATL
45 Spear Rd Industrial Park
Ramsey, NJ 07446-1251   201-825-1400
800-526-5330
Fax: 201-825-1962
atl@atlinc.com
www.atlinc.com

Water and chemical tanks, bulk-liquid transport bladders, collapsible air-lift drums and custom inflatable devices

President: Peter J Regna
Marketing Manager: Ian Marvuglio
Production Manager: Lou Damico
VP, Sales: David Dack
ddack@atlinc.com
VP, Contracts: Ingrid Janeiro
ijaneiro@atlinc.com
VP, Research & Development: Richard Clark
rclark@atlinc.com
In Business: 45 years
Number of Employees: 34
Sales Information: $6.7 Million

6907 American Chemical Society Publication Guide

ACS Publications
1155 Sixteenth Street N.W.
Washington, DC 20036-1   614-443-3600
                         Fax: 614-443-3713
www.pubs.acs.org/series/styleguide

Information on publications published by the American Chemical Society

Credit Cards: MasterCard
Printing Information: 13 pages in 2 colors on Matte Stock
In Business: 134 years

6908 American Institute of Chemical Engineers

AIChE
120 Wall Street
FL 23
New York, NY 10005-4020   800-242-4363
                         Fax: 203-775-5177
                         heaty@aiche.org
                         www.aiche.org

Contains engineering books and journals, technical manuals, symposia proceedings and directories

President: T. Bond Calloway
President-Elect: Christine Seymour
Secretary: Freeman E. Self
Treasurer: Joseph Smith
Catalog Cost: Free
Catalog Circulation: Mailed 1 time(s) per year to 50M
In Business: 109 years
Number of Employees: 150
Sales Information: $10 million

6909 BYK Gardner Catalog

BYK USA, Inc.
524 S Cherry Street
Wallingford, CT 06492-4453   203-265-2086
                         888-BYK-add1
                         Fax: 203-284-9158
                         cs.usa@byk.com
                         www.byk.com

Additives and instruments

President: Stephan Glander
CFO: Albert von Hebel
Catalog Cost: Free
In Business: 144 years
Number of Employees: 2000
Sales Information: $20MM to $50MM

6910 Blue White Industries

Blue-White Industries Ltd
5300 Business Drive
Huntington Beach, CA 92649-1226 714-893-8529
                         Fax: 714-894-9492
                         sales@blue-white.com
                         www.Blue-White.Com

Chemical metering pumps

President: Robin Gledhill
Marketing Manager: J Norman
Credit Cards: AMEX; MasterCard
In Business: 57 years
Number of Employees: 50
Sales Information: $5,000,000 - $10,000,000

6911 Environtronics

Weiss Envirotronics, Inc.
3881 N Greenbrooke Drive SE
Grand Rapids, MI 49512-5328   616-554-5020
                         800-368-4768
                         Fax: 616-554-5021
                         sales@envirotronics.com
                         www.envirotronics.com

Chemical environment test chambers

President: W Setchfield
Number of Employees: 100-
Sales Information: $10,000,000 - $25,000,000

6912 Fluid Metering

Fluid Metering, Inc
5 Aerial Way
Suite 500
Syosset, NY 11791-5593   516-922-6050
                         800-223-3388
                         Fax: 516-624-8261
                         pumps@fmipump.com
                         www.Fmipump.Com

Chemical processing pumps

President: Hank Pinkerton
Marketing Manager: David Peled
Printing Information: 32 pages in 2 colors
In Business: 40 years
Number of Employees: 50
Sales Information: $5,000,000 - $10,000,000

6913 G Neil Direct Mail

HR direct
PO Box 452049
Sunrise, FL 33345-2049   877-968-7471
                         800-888-4040
                         Fax: 954-846-0777
                         questions@hrdirect.com
                         www.hrdirect.com

HR recordkeeping products and computer software, employee training and motivational products

President: Susan Drenning

6914 Garrett Callahan

Garrett Callahan
50 Ingold Road
Burlingame, CA 94010-2206   650-697-5811
                         Fax: 650-692-6098
                         www.garrettcallahan.com

Water treatment chemicals

President: Jeffrey L. Garratt
CFO: Mansfield Garratt
Executive Vice-President: Matthew R. Garratt
In Business: 110 years
Number of Employees: 40
Sales Information: $10,000,000 - $25,000,000

6915 Goodway Technologies Catalog

Goodway Technologies Corporation
420 West Avenue
Stamford, CT 06902-6384   203-359-4708
                         800-333-7467
                         Fax: 203-359-9601
                         www.goodway.com

Commercial vacuums, pressure washers, vapor steam cleaners, floor scrubbers, drain cleaners, duct cleaners, filters, brushes and accessories

President: Per K Reichborn
Purchasing Manager: Marianne Winski
Credit Cards: AMEX; MasterCard
Catalog Cost: Free
Printing Information: 178 pages in 4 colors
In Business: 51 years
Sales Information: $10MM to $20MM

6916 Hockmeyer Equipment Corporation

Hockmeyer
6 Kitty Hawk Lane
Elizabeth City, NC 27909-1911   252-338-4705
                         Fax: 252-338-6540
                         sales@hockmeyer.com
                         www.hockmeyer.com

Chemical mixing and processing equipment

President: Herman H Hockmeyer
Marketing Manager: Cathy Strahan
Director of Marketing: Shawnacy McManus
In Business: 85 years
Number of Employees: 12
Sales Information: $5MM to $10MM

6917 Kano Laboratories

Kano Laboratories
PO Box 110098
#K
Nashville, TN 37222-98   615-833-4860
                         800-311-3374
                         Fax: 615-833-5790
                         www.Kanolabs.Com

Industrial specialty chemicals and lubricants

President: Peter J Zimmerman
In Business: 76 years
Number of Employees: 15
Sales Information: $10MM to $20MM

6918 Mech-Chem Associates

Mech-Chem Associates, Inc.
144 Main Street
Norfolk, MA 02056   508-528-5990
                         Fax: 508-528-8972
                         www.mech-chem.com

Chemical processing and mechanical engineering, pollution control systems, hazardous inspection and cleaning services and energy recovery systems

President: Ralph Cook
Number of Employees: 6
Sales Information: $500M to $1MM

6919 Oakwood Products

Oakwood Products,Inc
1741 Old Dunbar Rd
West Columbia, SC 29172-1901   803-739-8800
                         800-467-3386
                         Fax: 803-739-6957
                         www.Oakwoodchemical.Com

Research chemical processing company

President: Richard Tracey
Credit Cards: AMEX; MasterCard; Visa
Catalog Cost: Free
Catalog Circulation: Mailed 1 time(s) per year
Printing Information: 250 pages in 1 color on Matte Stock
Press: Web Press
Binding: Perfect Bound
Number of Employees: 15
Sales Information: $5,000,000 - $10,000,000

6920 Ohaus Corporation

Ohaus Corporation
7 Campus Drive
Suite 310
Parsippany, NJ 07054   973-377-9000
                         800-672-7722
                         Fax: 973-593-0359
                         sales@ohaus.com
                         www.ohaus.com

Manufacturer of electronic and mechanical scales, balances and accessories for the laboratory, education, and industrial markets

President: Jim Ohaus
CFO: Peter Mender
Catalog Cost: Free
In Business: 108 years
Number of Employees: 67
Sales Information: $11.6MM

6921 Phoenix Heat Treating
Phoenix Heat Treating
2405 W Mohave St
Phoenix, AZ 85009-6413   602-258-7751
                                Fax: 602-258-7767
                    www.Phoenix-Heat-Treating.Com

Processing services for heat treating and chemical metal finishing

President: Peter Hushek
In Business: 100 years
Number of Employees: 55
Sales Information: $1,000,000 - $5,000,000

6922 Raven Environmental Products
Raven Environmental Products,Inc
448 East Clinton Place
Suite B
Saint Louis, MO 63122-6400   314-822-1197
                                800-545-6953
                                Fax: 314-822-9968
                    dave@ravenep.com
                    www.ravenep.com

Manufacturer of waste and water plant control equipment

President: Dave Humann
Marketing Manager: Lynn Marshall
Catalog Cost: Free
Catalog Circulation: Mailed 1 time(s) per year
Printing Information: 4 pages in 2 colors on Matte Stock
Binding: Saddle Stitched
In Business: 32 years
Number of Employees: 3
Sales Information: $500M to $1MM

6923 Sauk Valley Equipment
The IFH Group, Inc.
3300 East Rock Falls Road
Rock Falls, IL 61071-1308   800-435-7003
                                Fax: 815-626-1438
                    tanks@ifhgroup.com
                    www.ifhgroup.com

Storage and dispensing systems for oils and lubricants

President: James King
CFO: John Nagy
Chief Operating Officer: Keith Ellefen
VP of Technology: Ed Wade
Director of Sales: Bryan McCarty
rmccarty@ifhgroup.com
Catalog Circulation: Mailed 1 time(s) per year
Printing Information: 16 pages in 3 colors
Binding: Saddle Stitched
In Business: 70 years

6924 Scott Equipment Company
Scott Equipment Company
605 4th Ave NW
New Prague, MN 56071-1121   952-758-2591
                                800-264-9519
                                Fax: 952-758-4377
                    info@scottequipment.com
                    www.Scottequipment.Com

Food, feed and chemical processing equipment

President: David J. Lucas
CFO: Jennifer O'Day
VP Production: James R Lucas
VP Human Resource & Finance: Terrance S. Lijewski
Lucas: Richard R.
VP Engineering
Printing Information: in 3 colors
Mailing List Information: Names for rent
In Business: 47 years
Number of Employees: 100
Sales Information: $20MM to $50MM

6925 Strem Chemicals
Srem Chemicals, Inc.
7 Mulliken Way
Newburyport, MA 01950-4098   978-499-1600
                                800-647-8736
                                Fax: 978-465-3104
                    info@strem.com
                    www.strem.com

Chemicals for research and commercial applications, bulk manufacturing and custom synthesis in GMP facilities

President: Dr. Michael E Strem
Marketing Manager: Dr. Ephraim Honig, COO
Credit Cards: AMEX; MasterCard; Visa
Catalog Cost: Free
In Business: 51 years
Number of Employees: 45

6926 Sun-Mar Corporation
Sun-Mar Corp.
600 Main Street
Tonawanda, NY 14150   905-332-1314
                                800-461-2461
                                Fax: 905-332-1315
                    compost@sun-mar.com
                    www.sun-mar.com

Composting toilet systems

Manager: Dennis Forster
Credit Cards: AMEX; MasterCard; Visa
Catalog Cost: Free
Printing Information: on Glossy Stock
In Business: 44 years
Number of Employees: 30
Sales Information: $8 Million

6927 Terra Universal
Terra Universal, Inc.
800 S. Raymond Avenue
Fullerton, CA 92831-2566   714-578-6100
                                Fax: 714-578-6020
                    info@TerraUniversal.com
                    www.TerraUniversal.com

Manufacturer of cleanroom equipment and supplies; humidity control systems, automated storage, laminar flows, glove boxes, hoods, static control, and semiconductor processing equipment

CFO: Ken Harms
Marketing Manager: Mike Buckwalter
Production Manager: Maria Papas
International Marketing Manager: Carl Higgins
Catalog Cost: Free
Catalog Circulation: Mailed 52 time(s) per year to 2000
Printing Information: 688 pages in 4 colors on Matte Stock
Press: Web Press
Binding: Perfect Bound
Mailing List Information: Names for rent
In Business: 38 years
Number of Employees: 200
Sales Information: $20MM to $50MM

6928 Titan Tool Supply Company
Titan Tool Supply
68 Comet Ave.
Buffalo, NY 14216-569   716-873-9907
                                Fax: 716-873-9998
                    info@titantoolsupply.com
                    www.Titantoolsupply.Com

Compasses, buffing and polishing compounds

President: Frank Menza
Catalog Circulation: Mailed 1 time(s) per year
Printing Information: 112 pages in 2 colors
Binding: Perfect Bound
In Business: 63 years
Sales Information: $1MM to $3MM

6929 US Testing Company
SGS North America, Inc.
201 Route 17 North
Rutherford, NJ 07070   201-508-3000
                                800-777-8378
                                Fax: 201-508-3183
                    www.us.sgs.com

Facilities in the field of chemical processing, metallurgy, microbiology, physical testing of materials and engineering

Chairman: Sergio Marchionne
President: Chris Kirk
Chief Operating Officer: Fred Herren
EVP, Mineral Services: Michael Belton
ExecutiveVP, Consumer Sevices: Malcolm Reid
In Business: 137 years

6930 Uvexs
UVEXS, Inc.
1260 Birchwood Drive
Sunnyvale, CA 94089-2205   408-734-4402
                                800-852-2911
                                Fax: 408-734-4502
                    customerservice@uvexs.com
                    www.Uvexs.Com

Ultraviolet exposure systems and photopolymer chemistries

President: Brent Puder
Marketing Manager: Charles Tucker
Production Manager: Doug Heinsohn
Catalog Cost: Free
Catalog Circulation: Mailed 1 time(s) per year to 500
Printing Information: 30 pages in 2 colors on Matte Stock
Press: Letterpress
Mailing List Information: Names for rent
In Business: 38 years
Number of Employees: 35
Sales Information: $1,000,000 - $5,000,000

6931 Water Quality Testing Products
LaMotte Company
802 Washington Ave
PO Box 329
Chestertown, MD 21620   410-778-3100
                                800-344-3100
                                Fax: 410-778-6394
                    mkt@lamotte.com
                    www.lamotte.com

Waste plant treatment products; test kits, instruments and reagants for water analysis

President: David LaMotte
Marketing Manager: James Moore
Production Manager: Libby Woolever
Catalog Circulation: Mailed 1 time(s) per year to 5000
Printing Information: 100 pages in 4 colors on Glossy Stock
Press: Sheetfed Press
Binding: Perfect Bound
Mailing List Information: Names for rent
In Business: 96 years
Number of Employees: 120

6932 Western States Machine Company
Western States Machine Company
625 Commerce Center Dr.
Fairfield, OH 45014-327   513-863-4758
                                Fax: 513-863-3846
                    sales@westernstates.com
                    www.Westernstates.Com

Chemical processing equipment, sugar processing equipment

President: Doug Buckner
CFO: Todd Hershberger
Marketing Manager: Bill Eckstein
Director of Sales & Marketing: Bob Sinnard
Operations Manager: Scott Kunkel
Director of Engineering: Don Meineke, Jr.
Mailing List Information: Names for rent
In Business: 98 years

Number of Employees: 130
Sales Information: $10MM to $20MM

6933 Zeller International
Zeller International
15261 State Highway 30
PO Box Z
Downsville, NY 13755   607-363-7792
Fax: 607-363-2071
contact@zeller-int.com
www.zeller-int.com

Specialty chemicals
Credit Cards: MasterCard
Mailing List Information: Names for rent
In Business: 51 years
Number of Employees: 10

Computers
Accessories

6934 B&B Electronics Manufacturing Company
B&B Electronics Manufacturing Company
707 Dayton Road
PO Box 1040
Ottawa, IL 61350   815-433-5100
800-346-3119
Fax: 815-433-5109
support@bb-elec.com
www.bb-elec.com

Data communication products
President: Don Wiencek
Credit Cards: AMEX; MasterCard; Visa
Catalog Cost: Free
Printing Information: 122 pages
In Business: 34 years
Number of Employees: 100

6935 B&R Industrial Automation Corporation
B&R Industrial Automation Corp.
1250 Northmeadow Parkway
Suite 100
Roswell, GA 30076   770-772-0400
Fax: 770-772-0243
office.us@br-automation.com
www.br-automation.com

Programmable controllers, industrial computers, software and support
Marketing Manager: Andreas Enzenbach
Credit Cards: MasterCard; Visa
In Business: 25 years
Sales Information: $ 3-5 Million

6936 Backdrop Outlet
Backdrop Outlet
3540 Seagate Way
Oceanside, CA 92056   760-547-2900
800-466-1755
Fax: 760-547-2899
cs@backdropoutlet.com
www.backdropoutlet.com

A full line of backgrounds, props, sets, studio stands and studio props
President: Jay Gupta
Credit Cards: AMEX; MasterCard
Catalog Cost: Free
Catalog Circulation: Mailed 1 time(s) per year to 75000
Printing Information: 60 pages in 4 colors on Glossy Stock
In Business: 24 years
Number of Employees: 25
Sales Information: $1-3 Million

6937 Baseball, Softball, Football Superstore
Baseball Express
5750 Northwest Parkway
Suite 100
San Antonio, TX 78249-3374   210-348-7000
800-937-4824
Fax: 210-525-9339
customer.service@teamexpress.com
www.baseballexpress.com

Footwear, apparel, accessories, uniforms and more
President: Pat Cawles
CFO: Geoff Westmoreland
VP Sales and Marketing: Dale Fujimoto
Credit Cards: AMEX; MasterCard
Catalog Cost: Free
Catalog Circulation: Mailed 3 time(s) per year
Printing Information: 84 pages in 4 colors
Binding: Perfect Bound
In Business: 25 years
Number of Employees: 7
Sales Information: Under $500,000

6938 CDW Solutions
CDW
200 N Milwaukee Ave.
Vernon Hills, IL 60061   847-371-6090
partnerrelations@cdw.com
www.cdw.com

Hardware, software and IT solutions.
Chairman: Thomas E. Richards
CFO: Ann E. Ziegler
SVP, Corporate Sales: Christina M. Corley
Catalog Cost: Free
In Business: 32 years
Number of Employees: 8600
Sales Information: $14 Billion

6939 CM Almy General
CM Almy
228 Sound Beach Avenue
Greenwich, CT 06870-2644   203-531-7600
800-225-2569
Fax: 203-531-9048
almyaccess@almy.com
www.almy.com

Supplier of decorative furnishings, apparel, worship related products and gifts to churches, religious institutions, their clergy and members
President: Stephen Sendler
CFO: Mike Mc Gown
Credit Cards: MasterCard
Catalog Cost: Free
Printing Information: 208 pages in 4 colors on Glossy Stock
In Business: 123 years
Sales Information: $5MM to $10MM

6940 Carey Manufacturing
Carey Manufacturing Company
5 Pasco Hill Road
Cromwell, CT 06416-1093   860-829-1803
866-813-0220
Fax: 860-829-1932
sales@careymfg.com
www.careymfg.com

Compression spring catches, heavy duty and light pulldown catches and handles for the aerospace, military, electronics, computer and automotive industries
President: John Carcy
CFO: Paul Sullivan
Marketing Manager: John Capece
Production Manager: Adam Wallace
General Manager: John Capece
jcapece@careymfg.com
Sales Coordinator: Alison Carey
acarey@careymfg.com
Human Resources Director: Peter Egan
pegan@careymfg.com
Catalog Cost: Free
Catalog Circulation: to 300

Printing Information: 176 pages in 2 colors on Glossy Stock
Press: Web Press
Binding: Saddle Stitched
Mailing List Information: Names for rent
In Business: 34 years
Number of Employees: 45
Sales Information: $6,000,000+

6941 GovConnection
GovConnection
7503 Standish Pl
Rockville, MD 20855-2731   301-340-1100
800-998-0009
Fax: 603-423-6192
customercare@govconnection.com
www.govconnection.com

IT solutions for government and education
President: Patricia Gallup
CFO: Jack Ferguson
Printing Information: in 4 colors
In Business: 32 years
Number of Employees: 180
Sales Information: $ 9 Million

6942 Network Access & Connectivity Product Line
Patton
7622 Rickenbacker Drive
Gaithersburg, MD 20879-4773   301-975-1000
Fax: 301-869-9293
support@patton.com
www.patton.com

Short range modems, converters, etc
President: Robert R Patton
Marketing Manager: Chris Christner
VP Finance/Administration: Bruce E Patton
VP Manufacturing: Steve Schrader
Sr. Director of Engineering: Joachim Wlotzka
Catalog Cost: Free
Printing Information: 150 pages
In Business: 33 years
Number of Employees: 175
Sales Information: $ 5-10 Million

6943 Osborne/McGraw-Hill
McGraw-Hill Education
2600 10th Street
P.O. Box 182605
Columbus, OH 43218-2522   800-338-3987
Fax: 609-308-4480
customer.service@mheducation.com
www.osborne.com

Computer books
President: Larry Levitsky
Marketing Manager: Kendal Andersen
Buyers: Allen Wyatt, Computers/Printers
Bill Emrick, Office Supp./Furn.
Credit Cards: AMEX; MasterCard; Visa
Catalog Cost: Free
Catalog Circulation: Mailed 5 time(s) per year to 500K
Printing Information: 44 pages in 4 colors on Glossy Stock
Press: Web Press
Mailing List Information: Names for rent
List Manager: Kendall Andersen
In Business: 15 years
Number of Employees: 55
Sales Information: $10,000,000 - $25,000,000

6944 Premise Wiring
Premise Wiring
565 Brea Canyon Road
Ste A
Walnut, CA 91789   626-964-7873
800-346-6668
Fax: 626-964-7880
info@unicomlink.com
www.unicomlink.com

Voice and data networking products
President: Jeffrey Lo
Marketing Manager: Brian Milliken

Production Manager: Chris Lin
Credit Cards: MasterCard
Catalog Cost: Free
Catalog Circulation: to 100M
Printing Information: 100 pages in 4 colors on Glossy Stock
Binding: Perfect Bound
Mailing List Information: Names for rent
In Business: 16 years
Number of Employees: 40
Sales Information: $ 3-5 Million

6945 Sealevel Systems
Sealevel Systems
PO Box 830
Liberty, SC 29657-3300   864-843-4343
Fax: 864-843-3067
support@sealevel.com
www.sealevel.com

Ports and products including PCI, USB and ISA Bus adapters, Windows COM

President: Ben O'Hanlan
beno@sealevel.com
Marketing Manager: Earle Foster
earlef@sealevel.com
CEO: Tom O'Hanlan
tom.ohanlan@sealevel.com
Human Resource Director: Nancy Gilreath
nancy.gilreath@sealevel.com
VP of Sales: Bill Hanrahan
bill.hanrahan@sealevel.com
In Business: 30 years

6946 Storesmart
StoreSMART
180 Metro Park
Rochester, NY 14623-2610   585-424-5300
800-424-1011
Fax: 585-424-1064
CS@storesmart.com
www.storesmart.com

Plastic folders, file jackets, hanging folders, paperwork organizers, portfolios, menu covers, sheet protectors, tag holders and magnetic plastic pockets

President: Reenie Feingold
Credit Cards: AMEX; MasterCard; Visa
Catalog Cost: Free
Catalog Circulation: to 10000
Average Order Size: $69
Mailing List Information: Names for rent
In Business: 44 years
Number of Employees: 14
Sales Information: $ 1.3 Million

6947 Viziflex Seels Computer Protection Products
Viziflex Seels, Inc.
406 N Midland Ave.
Saddle Brook, NJ 07663-6831   800-307-3357
800-627-7752
Fax: 201-487-3266
info@viziflex.com
www.viziflex.com

Computer accessories and static control products

President: Mike Glicksman
Production Manager: Sergio Gonzalez
VP: Andrea Glicksman
Buyers: Mike Dominguez, Computer Supplies
Catalog Circulation: Mailed 6 time(s) per year to 60M
Average Order Size: $850
Printing Information: 20 pages in 4 colors on Matte Stock
Press: Web Press
Binding: Perfect Bound
Mailing List Information: Names for rent
List Manager: Loretta Afif
In Business: 33 years
Sales Information: $ 3 Million

Graphics

6948 Astrographics
Astrographics
539 Concord Road
Warminster, PA 18974   888-817-8768
Fax: 215-364-3154
mail@astrographics.com
www.astrographics.com

Collection of format photo reproductions of telescope images, astronomical pictures, microscopic studies and other scientific images

Principal: Tony Lanzetta
Credit Cards: AMEX; MasterCard; Visa
Catalog Cost: Free
Printing Information: 28 pages
In Business: 17 years

6949 Data Translation Product Handbook
Data Translation, Inc.
100 Locke Drive
Marlborough, MA 01752-1192   508-481-3700
800-525-8528
Fax: 508-481-8620
www.Datx.Com

Data acquisition, machine vision and imaging products

President: Alfred a Molinari Jr
Credit Cards: AMEX; MasterCard; Visa
Catalog Cost: Free
Catalog Circulation: Mailed 1 time(s) per year
Printing Information: 250 pages in 4 colors
In Business: 42 years
Number of Employees: 85

Hardware

6950 Academic Superstore
Academic Superstore
5212 Tennyson Pkwy.
Ste. 130
Plano, TX 75024   512-450-1199
800-876-3507
Fax: 866-947-4525
contact@academicsuperstore.com
www.academicsuperstore.com

Academic software, hardware, and electronics for students, teachers, and schools; and home school materials

Marketing Manager: Natalie Jones
CEO: Mike Fishler
Owner/CEO: Nathan Jones
Credit Cards: AMEX; MasterCard
Catalog Cost: Free
Printing Information: in 4 colors
In Business: 17 years
Number of Employees: 50
Sales Information: $4.6 million

6951 B&R Industrial Automation Corporation
B&R Industrial Automation Corp.
1250 Northmeadow Parkway
Suite 100
Roswell, GA 30076   770-772-0400
Fax: 770-772-0243
office.us@br-automation.com
www.br-automation.com

Programmable controllers, industrial computers, software and support

Marketing Manager: Andreas Enzenbach
Credit Cards: MasterCard; Visa
In Business: 25 years
Sales Information: $ 3-5 Million

6952 BG Micro
BGMicro.com
3024 Lincoln Ct
Garland, TX 75041   972-205-9447
800-276-2206
Fax: 972-278-5105
bgmicro@bgmicro.com
www.bgmicro.com

IC's, crystals, eproms and RAMS for computers

President: John Gage
Owner: Jerry Gage
Credit Cards: MasterCard; Visa
Catalog Cost: Free
Catalog Circulation: Mailed 4 time(s) per year to 35M
Printing Information: 24 pages in 1 color on Matte Stock
Mailing List Information: Names for rent
In Business: 30 years
Number of Employees: 3
Sales Information: $500,000- 1 Million

6953 CDW Solutions
CDW
200 N Milwaukee Ave.
Vernon Hills, IL 60061   847-371-6090
partnerrelations@cdw.com
www.cdw.com

Hardware, software and IT solutions.

Chairman: Thomas E. Richards
CFO: Ann E. Ziegler
SVP, Corporate Sales: Christina M. Corley
Catalog Cost: Free
In Business: 32 years
Number of Employees: 8600
Sales Information: $14 Billion

6954 GovConnection
GovConnection
7503 Standish Pl
Rockville, MD 20855-2731   301-340-1100
800-998-0009
Fax: 603-423-6192
customercare@govconnection.com
www.govconnection.com

IT solutions for government and education

President: Patricia Gallup
CFO: Jack Ferguson
Printing Information: in 4 colors
In Business: 32 years
Number of Employees: 180
Sales Information: $ 9 Million

6955 MCM Business to Business
MCM Business to Business
650 Congress Park Drive
Centerville, OH 45459-4000   877-626-3532
888-235-4692
Fax: 800-765-6960
customerservice@mcmelectronics.com
www.mcmelectronics.com

Audio/video parts and accessories, computer hardware, security products, chemicals, technicians' aids

President: Phil Minix
pminix@mcmelectronics.com
Printing Information: 1164 pages
In Business: 38 years
Number of Employees: 120
Sales Information: 40 M

6956 Polywell Computers
Polywell Computers,Inc
1461 San Mateo Ave
S San Francisco, CA 94080-6553 650-583-7222
800-999-1278
Fax: 650-583-1974
info@polywell.com
www.Polywell.Com

IBM personal computers compatible 386, 486

President: Sam Chu
Marketing Manager: James Thomas
Production Manager: VP Sam Chu
Buyers: Eva Chu
Sam Chu
Credit Cards: AMEX; MasterCard
Catalog Cost: Free
Catalog Circulation: Mailed 4 time(s) per year to 50M
Printing Information: 8 pages in 4 colors on Glossy Stock
Press: Letterpress
Mailing List Information: Names for rent
List Manager: David Peters
In Business: 28 years
Number of Employees: 30
Sales Information: $10MM to $20MM

6957 ProVantage
ProVantage
7576 Freedom Avenue NW
North Canton, OH 44720-7143   330-494-8715
                                 800-336-1166
                            Fax: 330-494-5260
                      sales@provantage.com
                          www.provantage.com

Computer hardware

Chairman: Arno Zirngibl
President: Mike Colarik
Owner: Renee Ebert
Credit Cards: AMEX; MasterCard
Catalog Cost: Free
Catalog Circulation: Mailed 4 time(s) per year
Printing Information: in 4 colors
In Business: 31 years
Number of Employees: 50
Sales Information: $ 5-10 Million

6958 The Big Book
Office Depot
6600 N Military Trail
Boca Raton, FL 33496   800-463-3768
                          www.officedepot.com

Binders, calendars, planners, ink, toner, filing & storage, labels, pens, pencils, desktop & notebook computers, printers, copiers, shredders and office furniture

Chairman & CEO: Roland C. Smith
Catalog Cost: Free
Catalog Circulation: Mailed 1 time(s) per year
Printing Information: 868 pages in 4 colors
In Business: 30 years
Number of Employees: 4900
Sales Information: $14.5 Billion

6959 Twinhead Corporation
GammaTech Computer Corporation
48303 Fremont Blvd
Fremont, CA 94538-6510   510-492-0828
                               800-995-8946
                            Fax: 510-492-0820
                    sales@gammatechusa.com
                       www.gammatechusa.com

Computer systems and laptops

President: Bill Liu
Credit Cards: AMEX; MasterCard; Visa
Catalog Cost: Free
Catalog Circulation: Mailed 4 time(s) per year to 10M
Printing Information: 10 pages in 4 colors on Glossy Stock
Press: Letterpress
Mailing List Information: Names for rent
In Business: 10 years
Number of Employees: 26
Sales Information: $10MM to $20MM

6960 Valiant IMC
Valiant National AV Supply
80 Little Falls Road
Fairfield, NJ 07004-1709   201-229-9800
                               800-825-4268
                            Fax: 800-453-6338
                    sales@valiantnational.com
                    www.valiantaudiovisual.com

Audio-visual products and supplies at wholesale prices; video equipment, computer equipment and supplies

Chairman: Martin Siegel
President: Sheldon Goldstein
Managing Director: Scott Schaefer
Credit Cards: AMEX; MasterCard; Visa
Catalog Cost: Free
Catalog Circulation: Mailed 1 time(s) per year to 200M
Printing Information: 212 pages in 4 colors on Glossy Stock
Binding: Perfect Bound
Mailing List Information: Names for rent
In Business: 20 years
Number of Employees: 100
Sales Information: $ 13 Million

Peripherals & Systems

6961 CH Products
CH Products
970 Park Center Drive
Vista, CA 92081   760-598-2518
                               800-624-5804
                            Fax: 760-598-2524
                    Inquiries@chproducts.com
                         www.chproducts.com

High quality joysticks and peripherals for the PC Gaming Industry, fully programmable joysticks high-end flight simulation controllers

President: Charles Hayes
CEO: Fran Meyers
Credit Cards: MasterCard; Visa
Catalog Circulation: to 100M
Printing Information: 10 pages
In Business: 27 years
Number of Employees: 86
Sales Information: $ 11 Million

6962 Indus International
Indus
340 South Oak Street
West Salem, WI 54669-890   608-786-0300
                               800-843-9377
                            Fax: 608-786-0786
                      support@ventyx.com
                         www.indususa.com

Optical disk systems, micrographic readers and printers

President: Ameen Ayoob
Marketing Manager: Don Seawall
Owner: Sanober Ayoob
Credit Cards: MasterCard; Visa
Catalog Circulation: Mailed 12 time(s) per year
Mailing List Information: Names for rent
In Business: 29 years
Number of Employees: 21
Sales Information: $ 2 Million

6963 Maysteel
Maysteel LLC
6199 Highway W
PO Box 902
Allenton, WI 53002   262-251-1632
                               877-629-7833
                            Fax: 262-629-1612
                          www.maysteel.com

Computer and communication equipment and systems

President: Kevin Matkin
CFO: Randy Gromowski
Marketing Manager: Suzy Moody
Director of Program Management: Jeffrey Henn
Allenton Plant Manager: David Dembinski
VP, Business Development: Don Lawinger
In Business: 78 years
Number of Employees: 118
Sales Information: $10MM to $20MM

6964 PC Systems Handbook
CyberResearch, Inc.
25 Business Park Drive
Branford, CT 06405-2932   203-643-5000
                               800-341-2525
                            Fax: 203-643-5001
                    sales@cyberresearch.com
                       www.cyberresearch.com

Rugged industrial PC systems, data acquitions and motion control

President: Robert C. Molloy
Credit Cards: AMEX; MasterCard; Visa
Catalog Cost: Free
Catalog Circulation: Mailed 2 time(s) per year to 30M
Printing Information: 212 pages in 4 colors on Matte Stock
Press: Web Press
Mailing List Information: Names for rent
List Manager: Jerry Abramczyk
List Company: Edith Roman
In Business: 32 years
Number of Employees: 2225
Sales Information: $1,000,000 - $5,000,000

6965 Polywell Computers
Polywell Computers,Inc
1461 San Mateo Ave
S San Francisco, CA 94080-6553 650-583-7222
                                 800-999-1278
                            Fax: 650-583-1974
                        info@polywell.com
                          www.Polywell.Com

IBM personal computers compatible 386, 486

President: Sam Chu
Marketing Manager: James Thomas
Production Manager: VP Sam Chu
Buyers: Eva Chu
Sam Chu
Credit Cards: AMEX; MasterCard
Catalog Cost: Free
Catalog Circulation: Mailed 4 time(s) per year to 50M
Printing Information: 8 pages in 4 colors on Glossy Stock
Press: Letterpress
Mailing List Information: Names for rent
List Manager: David Peters
In Business: 28 years
Number of Employees: 30
Sales Information: $10MM to $20MM

6966 Server Management Products
Rose Electronics
10707 Stancliff Road
Houston, TX 77099-4306   281-933-7673
                               800-333-9343
                            Fax: 281-933-0044
                          sales@rose.com
                            www.rose.com

Data communication equipment and computer peripheral sharing equipment

President: David Rahvar
Marketing Manager: Dick Baker
Credit Cards: MasterCard; Visa
Catalog Cost: Free
Catalog Circulation: to 70K
Printing Information: 25 pages in 4 colors on Glossy Stock
Press: Web Press
Binding: Perfect Bound
Mailing List Information: Names for rent
In Business: 31 years
Number of Employees: 130
Sales Information: $10,000,000 - $25,000,000

6967 Twinhead Corporation
GammaTech Computer Corporation
48303 Fremont Blvd
Fremont, CA 94538-6510   510-492-0828
                                800-995-8946
                          Fax: 510-492-0820
                    sales@gammatechusa.com
                       www.gammatechusa.com

Computer systems and laptops

President: Bill Liu
Credit Cards: AMEX; MasterCard; Visa
Catalog Cost: Free
Catalog Circulation: Mailed 4 time(s) per year
to 10M
Printing Information: 10 pages in 4 colors on
Glossy Stock
Press: Letterpress
Mailing List Information: Names for rent
In Business: 10 years
Number of Employees: 26
Sales Information: $10MM to $20MM

6968 V-Infinity Power Quick Guide Catalog
CUI Inc
20050 SW 112th Avenue
Tualatin, OR 97062   503-612-2300
                            800-275-4899
                      Fax: 503-612-2383
                        sales@cui.com
                         www.cui.com

**An overview of the V-Infinity power supply
and dc-dc converter lines**

President: Matt McKenzie
CFO: Dan Ford
Senior VP: Mark Adams
VP Operations: John Hulden
Chief Technical Officer: Don Li
In Business: 25 years

Software

6969 Academic Superstore
Academic Superstore
5212 Tennyson Pkwy.
Ste. 130
Plano, TX 75024   512-450-1199
                         800-876-3507
                   Fax: 866-947-4525
            contact@academicsuperstore.com
                www.academicsuperstore.com

**Academic software, hardware, and electron-
ics for students, teachers, and schools; and
home school materials**

Marketing Manager: Natalie Jones
CEO: Mike Fishler
Owner/CEO: Nathan Jones
Credit Cards: AMEX; MasterCard
Catalog Cost: Free
Printing Information: in 4 colors
In Business: 17 years
Number of Employees: 50
Sales Information: $4.6 million

6970 Accu-Time Systems
Accu-Time Systems
420 Somers Road
Ellington, CT 06029-2629   860-870-5000
                                  800-355-4648
                            Fax: 860-872-1511
                          sales@accu-time.com
                             www.accu-time.com

Time clocks and data collection terminals

President: James Mchale
CFO: Lisa Gladysz
Marketing Manager: David Hopkins
Production Manager: Martin Seelig
Director of Human Resources: Karen Blovish
VP of Strategic Alliances: Jim Cox
VP of Strategic Alliance: Larry Dawson
International Marketing Manager: Karen
Parrott
Buyers: John Cappuccilli
Credit Cards: AMEX; MasterCard; Visa

Mailing List Information: Names for rent
List Manager: Karen Parrott
In Business: 24 years
Number of Employees: 40
Sales Information: $5.6 Million

6971 American Business Systems
American Business Systems
315 Littleton Road
Chelmsford, MA 01824-3392   800-356-4034
                             Fax: 978-250-8027
                        sales@abs-software.com
                           www.abs-software.com

**Business software for accounting, retail
point of sale, and wholesale distributors**

President: Jim Hamilton
Marketing Manager: Jim Hanlon
Catalog Cost: Free
Mailing List Information: Names for rent
In Business: 39 years
Number of Employees: 16
Sales Information: $3MM to $5MM

6972 B&R Industrial Automation Corporation
B&R Industrial Automation Corp.
1250 Northmeadow Parkway
Suite 100
Roswell, GA 30076   770-772-0400
                     Fax: 770-772-0243
              office.us@br-automation.com
                   www.br-automation.com

**Programmable controllers, industrial com-
puters, software and support**

Marketing Manager: Andreas Enzenbach
Credit Cards: MasterCard; Visa
In Business: 25 years
Sales Information: $ 3-5 Million

6973 Beyond.Com
Beyond.Com
1060 First Avenue
Suite 100
King of Prussia, PA 19406-1218   610-878-2800
                                 www.beyond.com

Software

Catalog Cost: Free

6974 CDW Solutions
CDW
200 N Milwaukee Ave.
Vernon Hills, IL 60061   847-371-6090
                      partnerrelations@cdw.com
                               www.cdw.com

Hardware, software and IT solutions.

Chairman: Thomas E. Richards
CFO: Ann E. Ziegler
SVP, Corporate Sales: Christina M. Corley
Catalog Cost: Free
In Business: 32 years
Number of Employees: 8600
Sales Information: $14 Billion

6975 CoLinear Systems
CoLinear Systems Inc
2650 Holcomb Bridge Road
Suite 610
Alpharetta, GA 30022-5008   770-643-0000
                                   800-265-4632
                             Fax: 770-643-0265
                          sales@colinear.com
                             www.Colinear.Com

Direct marketing software

President: Scott Weaver
Information Technologies Director: Rick
Harmon
Credit Cards: AMEX; MasterCard; Visa
Catalog Cost: Free
Printing Information: 6 pages in 4 colors on
Glossy Stock
Press: Web Press
Binding: Saddle Stitched

In Business: 29 years
Sales Information: $3MM to $5MM

6976 Complete Real Estate Software Catalog
Z-Law Software, Inc.
80 Upton Avenue
PO Box 40602
Providence, RI 02940-602   401-331-3002
                                  800-526-5588
                            Fax: 401-421-5334
                           Sales@z-law.com
                             www.z-law.com

**PC and MAC software for realtors, investors,
developers, property managers, and anyone
involved in real estate**

President: Gary L. Sherman, Esq.
Marketing Manager: William Sherman
Credit Cards: AMEX; MasterCard
Printing Information: 72 pages in 2 colors
Press: Sheetfed Press
Binding: Saddle Stitched
Mailing List Information: Names for rent
In Business: 22 years

6977 Computalabel
Computalabel International
80 Turkey Hill Road
Newburyport, MA 01950   800-289-0993
                               800-289-0993
                         Fax: 978-462-0303
                     info@computalabel.com
                        www.computalabel.com

**Barcoding software for macintosh and win-
dows, online barcode creator**

President: Simon Urquhart
Mailing List Information: Names for rent
In Business: 27 years

6978 Creation Engine
Creation Engine
425 North Whisman Road
Suite 300
Mountain View, CA 94043-4004   650-934-0176
                               800-431-8713
                         Fax: 650-934-3234
                  sales@creationengine.com
                     www.Creationengine.Com

Software for schools, faculty and students

President: Roberta Scherf
Credit Cards: AMEX; MasterCard
Catalog Cost: Free
Sales Information: $1MM to $3MM

6979 NewHaven Software
NewHaven Software
9840 Willows Rd Suite 102
P.O. Box 3456
Redmond, WA 98073-3456   425-861-7120
                          Fax: 425-861-7460
                   sales@newhavensoftware.com
                       www.newhavensoftware.com

**Mail Order Wizard, Mail List Monarch and
other software packages**

President: Tom Danner
CEO: Tom Danner
Credit Cards: MasterCard
Printing Information: 4 pages in 2 colors
In Business: 14 years
Number of Employees: 12

6980 PC/Nametag
PC/Nametag
124 Horizon Drive
Verona, WI 53593   888-354-7868
                    Fax: 800-233-9787
                  sales@pcnametag.com
                     www.pcnametag.com

Software equipment and supplies

President: Nick Topitzes
ntopitzes@pcnametag.com
International Marketing Manager: Darren

Walker
Credit Cards: AMEX; MasterCard
Catalog Circulation: Mailed 4 time(s) per year
Printing Information: 68 pages in 4 colors on Glossy Stock
Press: Web Press
Binding: Saddle Stitched
Mailing List Information: Names for rent
In Business: 29 years
Number of Employees: 25
Sales Information: $ 3-5 Million

6981 ProVantage
ProVantage
7576 Freedom Avenue NW
North Canton, OH 44720-7143   330-494-8715
                                 800-336-1166
                          Fax: 330-494-5260
                        sales@provantage.com
                          www.provantage.com

Computer hardware
Chairman: Arno Zirngibl
President: Mike Colarik
Owner: Renee Ebert
Credit Cards: AMEX; MasterCard
Catalog Cost: Free
Catalog Circulation: Mailed 4 time(s) per year
Printing Information: in 4 colors
In Business: 31 years
Number of Employees: 50
Sales Information: $ 5-10 Million

6982 RockWare
RockWare
2221 East St
Suite 1
Golden, CO 80401   303-278-3534
                                 800-775-6745
                          Fax: 303-278-4099
                        info@rockware.com
                          www.rockware.Com

Software products for earth science
President: Jim Reed
Marketing Manager: Amy Lunt
Credit Cards: AMEX; MasterCard
Catalog Circulation: Mailed 1 time(s) per year to 200K
Average Order Size: $300
Printing Information: 44 pages in 3 colors on Matte Stock
Press: Web Press
Binding: Saddle Stitched
Mailing List Information: Names for rent
In Business: 29 years
Sales Information: $5 million

6983 Storesmart
StoreSMART
180 Metro Park
Rochester, NY 14623-2610   585-424-5300
                                 800-424-1011
                          Fax: 585-424-1064
                        CS@storesmart.com
                          www.storesmart.com

Plastic folders, file jackets, hanging folders, paperwork organizers, portfolios, menu covers, sheet protectors, tag holders and magnetic plastic pockets
President: Reenie Feingold
Credit Cards: AMEX; MasterCard; Visa
Catalog Cost: Free
Catalog Circulation: to 10000
Average Order Size: $69
Mailing List Information: Names for rent
In Business: 44 years
Number of Employees: 14
Sales Information: $ 1.3 Million

6984 Valiant IMC
Valiant National AV Supply
80 Little Falls Road
Fairfield, NJ 07004-1709   201-229-9800
                                 800-825-4268
                          Fax: 800-453-6338
                        sales@valiantnational.com
                          www.valiantaudiovisual.com

Audio-visual products and supplies at wholesale prices; video equipment, computer equipment and supplies
Chairman: Martin Siegel
President: Sheldon Goldstein
Managing Director: Scott Schaefer
Credit Cards: AMEX; MasterCard; Visa
Catalog Cost: Free
Catalog Circulation: Mailed 1 time(s) per year to 200M
Printing Information: 212 pages in 4 colors on Glossy Stock
Binding: Perfect Bound
Mailing List Information: Names for rent
In Business: 20 years
Number of Employees: 100
Sales Information: $ 13 Million

Dental
Supplies & Equipment

6985 Almore International
Almore International, Inc.
PO Box 25214
Portland, OR 97298-214   503-643-6633
                                 800-547-1511
                          Fax: 503-643-9748
                        info@almore.com
                          www.almore.com

Dental equipment and supplies
President: Chuck Hastings
CFO: Michele Dupon
Buyers: Tammi Stadelman
Credit Cards: MasterCard
Catalog Cost: Free
Catalog Circulation: Mailed 3 time(s) per year to 24M
Printing Information: 48 pages in 4 colors on Glossy Stock
Press: Web Press
Binding: Saddle Stitched
Mailing List Information: Names for rent
List Manager: Dany Dupont
In Business: 67 years
Number of Employees: 15
Sales Information: $1,000,000 - $5,000,000

6986 American Dental Association
American Dental Association
211 E Chicago Avenue
Chicago, IL 60611-2678   312-440-2500
                          Fax: 312-440-3542
                        affiliates@ada.org
                          www.Ada.Org

Dental office supplies, including literature and videos
President: Dr. Maxine Feinberg
President-Elect: Dr. Carol Gomez Summerhays
Executive Director: Dr. Kathleen T. O'Loughlin
Catalog Circulation: Mailed 1 time(s) per year to 250M
Printing Information: 32 pages in 4 colors
Press: Web Press
Binding: Saddle Stitched
In Business: 156 years
Number of Employees: 300

6987 American Diamond Instruments
American Diamond Instruments
PO Box 130
Graeagle, CA 96103-5136   925-299-1415
                                 800-537-7474
                          Fax: 530-836-7455

Hand-held dental tools and supplies

President: Ron Verner
Credit Cards: MasterCard
Catalog Circulation: Mailed 2 time(s) per year
Printing Information: 12 pages
Binding: Saddle Stitched

6988 Gresco Products
Gresco Products, Inc.
13391 Murphy Road
Stafford, TX 77477-865   281-261-1811
                                 800-527-3250
                          Fax: 281-499-6515
                        info@grescoproducts.com
                          www.grescoproducts.com

Dental laboratory equipment and supplies
Credit Cards: AMEX; MasterCard
Catalog Cost: Free
Catalog Circulation: Mailed 1 time(s) per year
Printing Information: 12 pages in 2 colors on Glossy Stock
Binding: Saddle Stitched
In Business: 14 years
Number of Employees: 4

6989 Hello Direct
Hello Direct
77 Northeastern Boulevard
Nashua, NH 03062   800-435-5634
                        xpressit@hellodirect.com
                          www.hellodirect.com

Phones, headsets, conferencing, recording and mobile equipment
VP of Business Development: Stephen Mays
Credit Cards: AMEX; MasterCard; Visa
Catalog Cost: Free
Printing Information: 23 pages in 4 colors on Newsprint
Press: Web Press
Binding: Saddle Stitched
Northeastern Boulevard
Nashua, NH 03062
In Business: 30 years
Number of Employees: 60
Sales Information: $ 20-50 Million

6990 Lincoln Dental Supply
Lincoln Dental Supply
PO Box 2410
Cherry Hill, NJ 08034-3021   781-828-6440
                                 800-289-6678
                          Fax: 781-821-2212
                          www.lincolndental.com/

Dental lab supplies
President: Neal Breitman
Marketing Manager: Neal Breitman
Production Manager: Jeff Diblasi
VP: Jeff DiBlasi
Buyers: Guy Lennox
Credit Cards: MasterCard; Visa
Catalog Cost: Free
Catalog Circulation: Mailed 1 time(s) per year to 35M
Printing Information: 100 pages in 2 colors on Glossy Stock
Press: Letterpress
Binding: Perfect Bound
Mailing List Information: Names for rent
List Manager: Neal Breitman
In Business: 104 years
Number of Employees: 4
Sales Information: $1MM to $3MM

6991 Mailboxes Catalog
Mailboxes.com
1010 East 62nd Street
Los Angeles, CA 90001   323-846-6700
                                 800-624-5299
                          Fax: 323-846-6800
                        customerservice@mailboxes.com
                          www.mailboxes.com

Mailboxes, lockers, signs and postal specialties
President: Dennis Fraher
CFO: Mike Lobasso

Marketing Manager: Brian Fraher
Credit Cards: AMEX; MasterCard
Catalog Cost: Free
Catalog Circulation: Mailed 2 time(s) per year to 100M
Printing Information: 121 pages in 4 colors on Glossy Stock
Press: Web Press
Binding: Saddle Stitched
Mailing List Information: Names for rent
In Business: 81 years
Number of Employees: 100
Sales Information: $5MM to $10MM

6992 Mastercut Tool Corporation
Mastercut Tool Corporation
965 Harbor Lake Drive
Safety Harbor, FL 34695-2309   727-726-5336
800-343-8665
Fax: 727-725-2532
sales@mastercuttool.com
www.mastercuttool.com

Industrial and dental machinery and tools

President: Mike Shaluly
CEO: Mike Shaluly
In Business: 29 years
Number of Employees: 50
Sales Information: $1,000,000 - $5,000,000

6993 Mirage Dental Systems
Mirage Dental Systems
200 N 6th Street
Kansas City, KS 66101-3310   913-281-5552
800-366-0001
Fax: 913-621-7012
info@miragecdp.com
www.miragecdp.com/

Dental products

President: Tim Sigler
CFO: Tom Cooney
Marketing Manager: Kevin Pass
Production Manager: Fran Micek
Founder: Myron Sigler
Buyers: Dennis Goff
Credit Cards: AMEX; MasterCard; Visa
Catalog Cost: Free
Catalog Circulation: Mailed 1 time(s) per year to 10M
Average Order Size: $100
Printing Information: 25 pages in 4 colors on Glossy Stock
Press: Letterpress
Binding: Saddle Stitched
Mailing List Information: Names for rent
List Manager: Tom Carney
In Business: 79 years
Number of Employees: 20
Sales Information: $1MM to $3MM

6994 Northeast Dental Supplies
Northeast Dental & Medical Supply
2503 65th Street
Brooklyn, NY 11204   718-473-0151
800-724-0720
Fax: 866-633-3682
orders@nedental.com
www.nedental.com

Dental supplies

President: JR Agarwala
Catalog Cost: Free
Catalog Circulation: Mailed 4 time(s) per year to 20M
Printing Information: 50 pages in 2 colors on Matte Stock
Press: Letterpress
Binding: Saddle Stitched
Mailing List Information: Names for rent
In Business: 12 years
Number of Employees: 3
Sales Information: $1MM to $3MM

6995 Pollard Dental Products
Pollard Dental Products,Inc
15905 Greenway Hayden Loop
Suite 102
Scottsdale, AZ 85260-2638   805-235-1849
800-235-1849
Fax: 805-379-3273
info@pollarddentalproducts.com
www.pollarddentalproducts.com

Manufacturers of highest quality dental diamond drills and related products for Pollard's Advanced Restorative Procedures; in crown and bridge and 'suction-cup' dentures techniques

President: Jeff Pollard
CFO: Tess Pollard
Marketing Manager: Jeff Pollard
Production Manager: Martin Pollard
International Marketing Manager: Jeff Pollard
Buyers: Martin Pollard
Jeff Pollard, Raw Materials
Vic Pollard
Credit Cards: MasterCard; Visa
Catalog Cost: Free
Catalog Circulation: Mailed 3 time(s) per year to 15M
Average Order Size: $300
Printing Information: 10 pages in 2 colors on Matte Stock
Press: Letterpress
Binding: Folded
Mailing List Information: Names for rent
In Business: 55 years
Number of Employees: 11
Sales Information: $1,000,000 - $5,000,000

6996 Professional Products Company
Professional Products Company
12600 Daphne Ave
Hawthorne, CA 90250   323-306-5067
800-854-2770
Fax: 323-704-3682
www.professional-products.com

Dental products, pharmaceuticals, vitamins

President: Raymond D Spicer
Marketing Manager: Raymond D Spicer
Buyers: Raymond D Spicer
Credit Cards: AMEX; MasterCard
Catalog Circulation: Mailed 1 time(s) per year to 4000
Average Order Size: $30
Printing Information: in 2 colors on Matte Stock
Press: Letterpress
Binding: Folded
List Manager: Anne Spicer
In Business: 61 years
Number of Employees: 3
Sales Information: Under $500M

6997 Smart Practice
SmartPractice
3400 E. McDowell Rd
Phoenix, AZ 85008-7899   602-225-9090
800-522-0800
Fax: 800-522-8329
info@smartpractice.com
www.smartpractice.com

Dental supplies and equipment

President: Curt Hamann
Vice President: Beth Hamann
In Business: 40 years

6998 Sullivan Dental Products
Sullivan Dental Products, Inc.
10920 W Lincoln Avenue
Milwaukee, WI 53227-1130   414-321-8881
Fax: 414-321-8865

Dental products

President: Robert Sullivan
Catalog Circulation: Mailed 2 time(s) per year to 32M
Printing Information: 176 pages

Binding: Perfect Bound
Number of Employees: 175

6999 United Ad Label
RR Donnelly
35 West Wacker Drive
Chicago, IL 60601-2912   312-326-8000
800-423-4643
Fax: 312-326-8001
www.rrdonnelley.com

Tags, flags and labels designed for dentists

President: Thomas J. Quinlan III
CEO: Thomas J. Quinlan, III
Credit Cards: MasterCard
Catalog Circulation: Mailed 2 time(s) per year
Printing Information: in 4 colors
Binding: Saddle Stitched
In Business: 151 years
Number of Employees: 5500
Sales Information: $10.2 Billion

Disability Products
General

7000 Community Playthings
Community Playthings
PO Box 2
Ulster Park, NY 12487   845-658-7720
800-777-4244
Fax: 845-658-8065
sales@communityplaythings.com
www.communityplaythings.com

Maple furniture, shelving, desks, cribs, cots, changing tables, high chairs, mats, art equipment and toys

President: John Rhodes
CFO: Marcus Mommsen
Credit Cards: AMEX; MasterCard; Visa
Printing Information:
Press: Web Press
In Business: 65 years
Number of Employees: 10

7001 Easy Stand Catalog
Altimate Medical Inc
262 West 1st Street
PO Box 180
Morton, MN 56270   507-697-6393
800-342-8968
Fax: 507-697-6900
info@easystand.com
www.easystand.com

Standing equipment for mobility impaired children and adults, rehab equipment

President: Alan Tholkes
Marketing Manager: Mark Schmitt
Cio, Cto, Cso, Vp Of Tech, It Direc: Todd Tholkes
International Marketing Manager: Andrew Gardeen
Catalog Cost: Free
Mailing List Information: Names for rent
In Business: 28 years
Number of Employees: 35

7002 Handi-Ramp
Handi-Ramp
510 North Ave
Libertyville, IL 60048-2025   847-680-7700
800-876-7267
Fax: 847-816-8866
info@handiramp.com
www.Handiramp.Com

Ramps and safety products for personal or business needs - portable ramps, permanent ramps, non slip treads for stairs and ramps available for purchase or rental

President: Thom Disch
Marketing Manager: Roberta Pierce
CEO: Thom Disch
Credit Cards: AMEX; MasterCard; Visa
Catalog Cost: Free

Catalog Circulation: to 5000
Mailing List Information: Names for rent
In Business: 57 years
Number of Employees: 30
Sales Information: $5,000,000-$10,000,000

7003 HumanWare
HumanWare
1800, Michaud street
Drummondville, CN 12919   819-471-4818
                                 888-723-7273
                            Fax: 819-471-4828
                     ca.info@humanware.com
                          www.humanware.com

Devices for the learning disabled, blind and visually impaired

Chairman: Real Goulet
President: Phil Rance
Corporate Director: Michel Côté
CEO: Gilles Pepin
Corporate Director: Georges Morin
Buyers: Sharon Spiker
Credit Cards: MasterCard; Visa
Catalog Cost: Free
175 Mason Circle
Concord, CA 94520
9256807100
In Business: 10 years
Number of Employees: 25
Sales Information: $ 5-10 Million

7004 Kraftsman Playground and Park Equipment
Kraftsman Commercial Playgrounds & Water
19535 Haude Road
Spring, TX 77388-5233   281-353-9599
                                800-451-4869
                          Fax: 281-353-2265
                  info@kraftsmanplaygrounds.com
                  www.kraftsmanplaygrounds.com

Playground equipment and aquatic playground and pool equipment

President: Michelle Soderberg
Marketing Manager: Kris Soderberg
Credit Cards: MasterCard
Catalog Cost: Free
In Business: 33 years
Sales Information: $3MM to $5MM

7005 LinguiSystems Catalog
LinguiSystems Inc
8700 Shoal Creek Blvd
Austin, TX 78757-6897   309-755-2300
                                800-397-7633
                          Fax: 800-397-7633
                          info@proedinc.com
                       www.linguisystems.com

Materials for clinicians and teachers of students with special needs

Chairman: Rosemary Huisingh
President: Linda Bowers
CFO: Jeff Scherer
Credit Cards: AMEX; MasterCard; Visa
Average Order Size: $133
Printing Information: 170 pages
Mailing List Information: Names for rent
In Business: 34 years
Number of Employees: 42
Sales Information: $ 4.4 Million

7006 Sammons Preston
Patterson Medical
28100 Torch Parkway
Suite 700
Warrenville, IL 60555-3938   630-393-6000
                                     800-475-5036
                               Fax: 630-393-7600
                        www.pattersonmedical.com

Healthcare products to lighten chores, increase comfort and adapt household items for easier use

President: David Sproat
CEO: Scott Anderson

Credit Cards: AMEX; MasterCard
Printing Information: in 3 colors
Sales Information: $ 9 Million

7007 SunMate & Pudgee Orthopedic Cushions
Dynamic Systems, Inc.
104 Morrow Branch
Leicester, NC 28748   828-683-3523
                              855-786-6283
                        Fax: 844-270-6478
                   dsi@sunmatecushions.com
                    www.sunmatecushions.com

Orthopedic foam cushion material

President: Robin Yost
CFO: Melinda Garrett
Marketing Manager: Susan Yost
Production Manager: Andrew Biebinger
Buyers: Stacy Miller
Credit Cards: AMEX; MasterCard; Visa
Catalog Circulation: Mailed 12 time(s) per year
Printing Information: 8 pages in 4 colors on Matte Stock
Press: Sheetfed Press
Binding: Saddle Stitched
Mailing List Information: Names for rent
In Business: 50 years
Number of Employees: 18
Sales Information: $ 1-3 Million

Automobile Aids

7008 Corvette Central
Corvette Central
13550 Three Oaks Road
PO Box 16
Sawyer, MI 49125-9328   269-426-3342
                                800-345-4122
                          Fax: 269-426-4108
                   mail@corvettecentral.com
                     www.corvettecentral.com

Corvette parts and accessories

President: Jerry Kohen
CFO: Dan Baber
Credit Cards: MasterCard
Catalog Cost: Free
Printing Information: 14 pages in 4 colors
Binding: Perfect Bound
In Business: 40 years

7009 Gresham Driving Aids
Gresham Driving Aids
30800 Wixom Road
Wixom, MI 48393-334   248-624-1533
                              800-521-8930
                        Fax: 248-624-6358
             gpersons@greshamdrivingaids.com
                  www.greshamdrivingaids.com

Driving aids, handicap equipment

President: William Dillon
General Manager: David Ohrt
dave@greshamdrivingaids.com
Sales Consultant: Craig Wigginton
craig@greshamdrivingaids.com
Service Manager: Dexter Jackson
dex@greshamdrivingaids.com
Credit Cards: MasterCard; Visa
Catalog Cost: Free
In Business: 54 years
Number of Employees: 21
Sales Information: $ 1-3 Million

Lifts, Ramps & Elevators

7010 Acco Chain & Lifting Products
Peerless Industrial Group
401 Spring Valley Road
Jeannette, PA 15644   800-395-2445
                        Fax: 800-997-3192
                 custserv@peerlesschain.com
                    www.peerlesschain.com

Custom lifting devices for the disabled

President: Daniel Carmody
In Business: 98 years
Number of Employees: 20

7011 Garaventa Lift
Garaventa Lift
PO Box 1769
Blaine, WA 98231-1769   604-594-0422
                                800-663-6556
                          Fax: 604-594-9915
                    productinfo@garaventa.ca
                         www.garaventa.ca

Wheelchair lifts, vertical lifts, and emergency evacuation chairs

President: Mark Townsend
Marketing Manager: Norm Cooper
Catalog Cost: Free
In Business: 25 years
Number of Employees: 130

Wheelchairs

7012 Advantage Bags
Advantage Bag Company
22633 Ellinwood Dr
Torrance, CA 90505-3323   800-556-6307
                            Fax: 310-316-2561
                    advantagebag@verizon.net
                       www.advantagebag.com

Bags for wheelchairs, walkers, scooters, strollers and crutches

President: Deborah V Frane
Credit Cards: MasterCard; Visa
Catalog Cost: Free
In Business: 27 years
Number of Employees: 2
Sales Information: $120,000

Electronics
Parts & Supplies

7013 Accu-Tech Cable
Accu-Tech
660 Hembree Parkway
Suite 100
Roswell, GA 30076-3890   770-751-9473
                                 800-221-4767
                           Fax: 770-475-4659
                      sales@accu-tech.com
                        www.accu-tech.com

Fiber optic cables and connectivity products, surge protection products, tools and accessories

President: Ed Ellis
CFO: Alison Santoro
Marketing Manager: Alice Milihram
Production Manager: Claire Scannell
Branch Manager: Todd Delavie
Regional Vice President: Butch Flynt
Ops. Contact: Carlos Deere
Credit Cards: AMEX; MasterCard; Visa
In Business: 30 years

7014 Barksdale Control Products
Barksdale Inc.
3211 Fruitland Avenue
PO Box 58843
Los Angeles, CA 90058-843   323-589-6181
                                     800-835-1060
                               Fax: 323-589-3463
                        sales@barksdale.com
                          www.Barksdale.Com

Manufacturer of electronic controls for industrial applications specializing in the measurement of fluids, including valves, switches, transducers, and regulators

Chairman: Robert S Evans
President: Ian Dodd
CFO: Timothy J MacCarrick
Catalog Cost: Free

In Business: 66 years
Number of Employees: 100-

7015 Cablescan
Cablescan
3022 Inland Empire Boulevard
Ontario, CA 91764-4803   909-483-2436
                            800-898-5783
                        Fax: 909-483-2463
                    sales@cablescan.com
                    www.cablescan.com

Electronic instruments for assembly and testing of wire harnesses, cables, back planes, circuit boards, and on-board wiring systems

President: David Eubanks
Catalog Cost: Free
In Business: 46 years
Number of Employees: 7
Sales Information: $1,000,000 - $5,000,000

7016 Canare Catalog 13
Canare Corporation of America
45 Commerce Way
Unit C
Totowa, NJ 07512   973-837-0070
                  Fax: 973-837-0080
                  canare@canare.com
                  www.canare.com

Audio and video cable, 75 Ohm BNC, F and RCA connectors, patchbays, cable reels, snake systems, assemblies, crimp tools, cable strippers and more

President: Kazuo Urata
CFO: Gary Pagliocca
CEO: Woody Urata
VP: Patrick Gallager
Catalog Cost: Free
Mailing List Information: Names for rent
In Business: 45 years
Number of Employees: 25
Sales Information: $4 Million

7017 Carlton-Bates Company
Carlton-Bates
3600 W 69th St.
Little Rock, AR 72209   501-562-9100
                           866-600-6040
              customerservicecb@carltonbates.com
              www.carltonbates.com

Electronic components, devices, equipment, hardware, and accessories.

Catalog Cost: Free
In Business: 59 years

7018 Cole-Parmer-Temperature Measurement & Control
Cole-Parmer
625 East Bunker Court
Vernon Hills, IL 60061-1830   847-549-7600
                                 800-323-4340
                            Fax: 847-549-1700
                        info@coleparmer.com
                        www.coleparmer.com

Alarms, controllers, thermometers, thermistors, thermocouples and other instruments for use in temperature applications

President: John Palmer
VP/General Manager: Monica Manotas
Director, Finance: Joe Straczek
VP, Human Resources: Wanda McKenny
Catalog Circulation: Mailed 1 time(s) per year
Printing Information: 128 pages
In Business: 60 years

7019 Corvette Central
Corvette Central
13550 Three Oaks Road
PO Box 16
Sawyer, MI 49125-9328   269-426-3342
                           800-345-4122
                       Fax: 269-426-4108
                   mail@corvettecentral.com
                   www.corvettecentral.com

Corvette parts and accessories

President: Jerry Kohen
CFO: Dan Baber
Credit Cards: MasterCard
Catalog Cost: Free
Printing Information: 14 pages in 4 colors
Binding: Perfect Bound
In Business: 40 years

7020 Da-Lite Screen Company
Da-Lite Screen Company
3100 North Detroit Street
P.O. Box 137
Warsaw, IN 46582   574-267-8101
                      800-622-3737
                  Fax: 877-325-4832
                  info@da-lite.com
                  www.da-lite.com

Designers and manufacturers of projection screens - rear, manual or electric for permanent or portable applications

President: Richard Lundin
CFO: Jerry Young
Marketing Manager: Wendy Long
EVP: Judith D Loughran
Coordinator Bids & Quotations: Alisa Leek
Domestic Sales Partner: David Huntoon
International Marketing Manager: Adam Teevan
Catalog Circulation: Mailed 1 time(s) per year
Printing Information: 150 pages in 4 colors on Matte Stock
Press: Sheetfed Press
Binding: Perfect Bound
In Business: 105 years
Number of Employees: 415
Sales Information: $ 31 Million

7021 Dickson Company
Dickson Company
930 S Westwood Avenue
Addison, IL 60101-4917   630-543-3747
                            800-757-3747
                       Fax: 800-676-0498
                       www.dicksondata.com

Weather recording equipment

President: Michael Unger
CFO: Mark Kohlmeier
Marketing Manager: Chris Sorensen
Production Manager: Elaine Campion
VP of Manufacturing and Engineering: Fred Kirsch
Human Resources: Sue Madison
Inside Sales Consultant: Teresa Tomaszewski
Credit Cards: AMEX; MasterCard
Catalog Circulation: Mailed 12 time(s) per year
Printing Information: 21 pages in 4 colors
In Business: 94 years
Number of Employees: 50-1
Sales Information: $10,000,000 - $25,000,000

7022 Eaton
Eaton Corporation
1111 Superior Ave E # 19
Cleveland, OH 44114-2535   440-523-4400
                              800-386-1911
                         Fax: 216-523-4787
                         www.eaton.com

Electrical control products for industrial use including aerospace, automotive, filtration, and hydraulics

Chairman: Alexander M Cutler
CFO: Richard M Fearon

Vice Chairman and COO: Craig Arnold
Senior Vice President and CIO: William W. Blausey Jr.
Executive Vice President, Chief HR: Cynthia K. Brabander
Catalog Cost: Free
Average Order Size: $150
Mailing List Information: Names for rent
In Business: 119 years
Number of Employees: 7300
Sales Information: $500M to $1MM

7023 Electrosonic
Electrosonic
3320 North San Fernando Blvd.
Burbank, CA 91504   818-333-3604
                       800-328-6202
                   Fax: 818-566-4923
              techsupport@electrosonic.com
              www.electrosonic.com

Electronics

President: Kyle Carpenter
CFO: Scot Meyer
Marketing Manager: Chris Martatos
General Manager: Paul Brown
Sales Manager: Rob Smith
International Marketing Manager: celia garcia-hall
Mailing List Information: Names for rent
In Business: 51 years
Number of Employees: 200

7024 Encoder Line Card
Renco Encoders, Incorporated
595 International Place
Rockledge, FL 32955-4200   805-968-1525
                          Fax: 805-685-7965
                              www.Renco.Com

Complete range of optical encoders

President: Bob Setbacken
Printing Information: in 4 colors on Glossy Stock
Press: Sheetfed Press
Mailing List Information: Names for rent
In Business: 30 years
Number of Employees: 100
Sales Information: $20MM to $50MM

7025 Falcon Fine Wire and Wire Products
Falcon Fine Wire and Wire Products
2401 Discovery Boulevard
Rockwall, TX 75032   214-771-3441
                        800-874-7230
                    falconwire@aol.com
                    www.falconfinewire.com

Wiring and cabling products

President: William D LeCount
Chief Operating Officer: Annette V. LeCount
VP of Manufacturing: James Bunt
Office Manager: Diane Dewald
Catalog Cost: Free
Number of Employees: 50-1
Sales Information: $10,000,000 - $25,000,000

7026 Fluke Corporation
Fluke Corporation
PO Box 9090
Everett, WA 98206-9090   425-347-6100
                            800-443-5853
                       Fax: 425-446-5116
                       fluke-info@fluke.com
                       www.fluke.com

Electronic test and measurement equipment

President: Wes Pringle
CFO: Monti Ackerman
VP, Global Operations: Paul Caldarazzo
Vice President, Engineering: Paul Heydron
Vice President, Sales: Ernie Lauber
Catalog Cost: Free
In Business: 66 years
Number of Employees: 2400

7027 Kanson Electronics
Kanson Electronics
245 Forrest Avenue
Hohenwald, TN 38462-1120   931-796-3050
                             800-233-9354
                        Fax: 931-796-3956
                    www.issc-kanson.com

Electronic assembly and subassembly systems; industrial solid state controls (ISSC); injection molding (modor)
President: Arthur Filson
Production Manager: Jennifer McDonald
Credit Cards: AMEX; MasterCard; Visa
Catalog Cost: Free
Printing Information: 25 pages on Glossy Stock
Mailing List Information: Names for rent
In Business: 51 years
Number of Employees: 17
Sales Information: Under $500M

7028 Keithley Instruments
Keithley Instruments
28775 Aurora Road
Cleveland, OH 44139-1891   440-248-0400
                             800-935-5595
                        Fax: 440-248-6168
                     info@keithley.com
                     www.Keithley.Com

Instruments for electronic measuring testing; Counters, timers, digital multimeters, distortion meters, voltmeters, electrometers, picoammeters, source measure units and more
Chairman: Joseph P Keithley
President: Joseph P Keithley
CFO: Mark J Plush
Marketing Manager: Ellen Modock
VP: Mark J. Plush
CEO: Joseph P Keithley
Mailing List Information: Names for rent
In Business: 55 years
Number of Employees: 698
Sales Information: Under $500M

7029 Kepco, Inc.
Kepco, Inc.
131-38 Sanford Avenue
Flushing, NY 11355-4245   718-461-7000
                        Fax: 718-767-1102
                     hq@kepcopower.com
                     www.kepcopower.com

Regulated DC power supplies
Chairman: Max Kupferberg
President: Martin Kupferberg
Production Manager: Mark Kupforberg
Catalog Cost: Free
Mailing List Information: Names for rent
In Business: 71 years
Number of Employees: 200
Sales Information: $26 Million

7030 Keystone Electronics Corporation
Keystone Electronics Corp.
31-07 20th Road
Astoria, NY 11105-2055   718-956-8900
                           800-221-5510
                      Fax: 718-956-9040
                   kec@keyelco.com
                   www.keyelco.com

Electronic component hardware
President: Troy David
CFO: Richard David
Marketing Manager: Joe Rosenblum
joe@keyelco.com
Production Manager: Steve Israel
International Marketing Manager: Linda Vera
Buyers: Jim Magnusson
Catalog Circulation: Mailed 1 time(s) per year to 100M
Printing Information: 156 pages in 4 colors
Mailing List Information: Names for rent
In Business: 60 years

Number of Employees: 100
Sales Information: $1,000,000 - $5,000,000

7031 MilesTek Catalog
MilesTek
1506 Interstate 35 W
Denton, TX 76207-2402   940-484-9400
                          800-958-5173
                     Fax: 940-566-1047
              customerfirst@milestek.com
                     www.milestek.com

Complete line of electronic connectors
President: David B McCarthy
Credit Cards: AMEX; MasterCard
In Business: 34 years

7032 NTE Electronics
NTE ELECTRONICS
44 Farrand Street
Bloomfield, NJ 07003-2597   866-285-3959
                          Fax: 973-748-6224
                custserv@ntepartsdirect.com
                     www.ntepartsdirect.com

Hookup lines, fusers, capacitors, power cords, cables, wires, transformers and other electronic supplies
President: Andrew Licari
In Business: 36 years
Number of Employees: 50-1
Sales Information: $20MM to $50MM

7033 Phoenix Contact USA
Phoenix Contact USA
586 Fulling Mill Road
Middletown, PA 17057   717-944-1300
                     Fax: 717-944-1625
                info@phoenixcon.com
                www.phoenixcontact.com

Innovative technology and electronics
VP & General Manager: Spencer Bolgard
Director of Information Technology: Betsy Clark
Director of Supply Chain: Louis Paioletti
In Business: 36 years
Number of Employees: 500
Sales Information: $10MM to $20MM

7034 Plastruct
Plastruct
1020 S Wallace Place
City of Industry, CA 91748   626-912-7017
                           800-666-7015
                      Fax: 626-965-2036
                plastruct@plastruct.com
                     www.plastruct.com

Plastic scale model parts
President: John Wanderman
Production Manager: Darlene Carriaga
Credit Cards: AMEX; MasterCard
Catalog Cost: $5
Printing Information: 155 pages in 4 colors
In Business: 44 years
Number of Employees: 57
Sales Information: $ 5-10 Million

7035 Quality Thermistor
QTI Sensing Solutions
2108 Century Way
Boise, ID 83709-2862   208-377-3373
                         800-554-4784
                    Fax: 208-376-4754
               qtisales@thermistor.com
                    www.Thermistor.Com

Thermistors, printed circuits, assemblies, thermistor propes, and RV fan controls
President: Todd Ketlinski
Marketing Manager: Todd Ketlinski
Production Manager: Ron Ahrens
Credit Cards: AMEX; MasterCard
Catalog Cost: Free
Printing Information: 31 pages
Mailing List Information: Names for rent

In Business: 38 years
Number of Employees: 35
Sales Information: $1,000,000 - $5,000,000

7036 RBE Electronics
RBE Electronics of SD, Inc.
714 Corporation Street
Aberdeen, SD 57401   605-226-2448
                       800-342-1912
                  Fax: 605-226-0710
             info@rbeelectronics.com

Electronic controls, sensors and timers
President: Roger Ernst
Engineer: Steve Wolff
Credit Cards: MasterCard; Visa
Catalog Cost: Free
In Business: 34 years
Number of Employees: 28
Sales Information: $1,000,000 - $5,000,000

7037 Renbrandt-Flexible Couplings
Renbrandt,Inc
659 Massachusetts Ave
Boston, MA 02118-1821   617-445-8910
                          800-370-3539
                     Fax: 617-445-6032
                  info@renbrandt.com
                  www.Renbrandt.Com

HP flexible couplings
President: Raymond Renner
Catalog Cost: Free
Catalog Circulation: to 3000
Printing Information: 12 pages in 2 colors
Binding: Saddle Stitched
Mailing List Information: Names for rent
In Business: 64 years
Sales Information: $3MM to $5MM

7038 Renco Electronics
Renco Electronics, Inc.
595 International Place
Rockledge, FL 32955-4200   321-637-1000
                             800-645-5828
                        Fax: 321-637-1600
                        www.rencousa.com

Transformers, inductors, chokes and coils
President: Edward Rensing
Catalog Cost: Free
In Business: 62 years
Number of Employees: 110
Sales Information: $10,000,000 - $25,000,000

7039 Shakespeare Electronic Products Group
Shakespeare LLC
6111 Shakespeare Road
Columbia, SC 29223   803-227-1590
                     Fax: 803-419-3099
            shakespeare-ce.com/marine

Electronics including antennas, cell phone products, connectors, adapters, cables and accessories
President: Jim Bennett
Marketing Manager: Craig Woods
Catalog Cost: Free
Printing Information: in 3 colors
In Business: 118 years

7040 Sterling Production Control Units
Production Control Units, Inc.
2280 W Dorothy Lane
Dayton, OH 45439-1892   937-299-5594
                          866-840-2144
                     Fax: 937-299-3843

Electronic production control units for refrigerant and fluid processing systems in a broad range of industries
President: Thomas H Hodge
Service: Alan Walker
Technicalservice@pcuinc.com
Catalog Cost: Free
In Business: 68 years

Number of Employees: 100
Sales Information: $10,000,000 - $25,000,000

7041 Strongbox
Strongbox
2234 Wellesley Avenue
Blvd. #198
Los Angeles, CA 90064-2726   310-305-8288
Fax: 310-402-8000
sales@strongboxmarketing.com
www.Rackmountchassis.Com

Rack-mounted enclosures for electronics

Credit Cards: AMEX; MasterCard; Visa
Catalog Cost: Free
Mailing List Information: Names for rent
List Manager: L Martinek
In Business: 16 years
Number of Employees: 4
Sales Information: Under $500,000

7042 TRS RenTelco
TRS-Ren Telco
1830 West Airfield Drive
PO Box 619260
DFW Airport, TX 75261   972-456-4000
800-874-7123
Fax: 972-456-4002
trs@trs-rentelco.com
www.Trs-Rentelco.Com

Electronic test, measurement and computer equipment

President: Susan Boutwell
CFO: Keith E Pratt
Catalog Cost: Free
In Business: 30 years
Number of Employees: 100-

7043 Thermo ALKO
Thermo ALKO
500 Cummings Center
Beverly, MA 01915-6142   866-269-0070
Fax: 978-232-1068
thermoscientific.webhelp@thermofisher.com
www.thermo.com

Supplier of calibrators, electrodes, accessories and quality controls for use on over 120 instrument models

Printing Information: 11 pages

7044 Transcat
Transcat, Inc.
35 Vantage Point Drive
Rochester, NY 14624   800-828-1470
sales@transcat.com
www.transcat.com

Test, measurement and calibration instruments

Chairman: Carl Sassano
President: Charles Hadeed
Chief Executive Officer: Lee Rudow
Credit Cards: MasterCard
Catalog Cost: Free
Catalog Circulation: Mailed 1 time(s) per year
Printing Information: 169 pages in 4 colors on Glossy Stock
In Business: 52 years
Number of Employees: 313
Sales Information: $91 Million

7045 US Industrial Tool
US Industrial Tool & Supply Company
14083 S. Normandie Ave
Gardena, CA 90249   310-464-8400
800-521-7394
Fax: 310-464-8880
info@ustool.com
www.ustool.com

Aircraft tools, hand tools and sheetmetal tools

President: Mark Marinovich
Founder: William Marinovich
Credit Cards: MasterCard

Catalog Cost: Free
Catalog Circulation: to 30m
Printing Information: 188 pages in 4 colors on Glossy Stock
Binding: Saddle Stitched
Mailing List Information: Names for rent
In Business: 59 years
Number of Employees: 47
Sales Information: $5,000,000 - $10,000,000

7046 VECO Chip Thermistors
United Speedometer Service
2179 Macbeth Place
PO Box 51957
Riverside, CA 92507-1314   951-742-7117
800-877-4798
Fax: 951-742-7113
www.speedometershop.com

Thermistor chip technologies

Catalog Circulation: Mailed 1 time(s) per year
Printing Information: 4 pages in 2 colors
Binding: Saddle Stitched

7047 Viprofix
Vipro
3650 N Cicero Ave
Chicago, IL 60641-3641   773-545-7700
800-899-8111
Fax: 773-685-9229
prepress@viprofix.com
www.viprofix.com

Systems equipment for electronic publishing

President: Voitek Michalik
Marketing Manager: Greg Eagel
Sales Manager: Peter Warzecha
Director of Administration: Maria Michalik
Field Engineering: Andy Dankowski
Catalog Circulation: Mailed 1 time(s) per year
Printing Information: 4 pages in 4 colors
Binding: Saddle Stitched
In Business: 30 years
Sales Information: Under $500M

Exhibits
Displays & Materials

7048 Backdrop Outlet
Backdrop Outlet
3540 Seagate Way
Oceanside, CA 92056   760-547-2900
800-466-1755
Fax: 760-547-2899
cs@backdropoutlet.com
www.backdropoutlet.com

A full line of backgrounds, props, sets, studio stands and studio props

President: Jay Gupta
Credit Cards: AMEX; MasterCard
Catalog Cost: Free
Catalog Circulation: Mailed 1 time(s) per year to 75000
Printing Information: 60 pages in 4 colors on Glossy Stock
In Business: 24 years
Number of Employees: 25
Sales Information: $1-3 Million

7049 Bates Metal Products
Bates Metal Products
403 East Main Street
P.O. Box 68
Port Washington, OH 43837   740-498-8371
800-642-4372
Fax: 740-498-6315
jwbates@batesmetal.com
www.batesmetal.com

Metal racks, displays and exhibits

President: James Bates
VP: James W Bates
jbates@batesmetal.com
VP: Terry L Bates

tlbates@batesmetal.com
GM: Gene Peeper
sgpeeper@batesmetal.com
In Business: 59 years
Number of Employees: 50
Sales Information: $3MM to $5MM

7050 Baudville
Baudville
5380 52nd St SE
Grand Rapids, MI 49512   616-698-0889
800-728-0888
Fax: 616-698-0554
service@baudville.com
www.baudville.Com

Trophies, recognition items, lapel pins, event paper, seals & embosers, certificate papers, ID accessories, folders & frames and more

President: David Pezzato
Marketing Manager: Jack Fisher
VP: Kristy Sherlund
Credit Cards: AMEX; MasterCard
Catalog Cost: Free
Printing Information: 80 pages in 4 colors on Matte Stock
Binding: Perfect Bound
In Business: 30 years
Number of Employees: 85
Sales Information: 9.5M

7051 Benchmark Displays
Benchmark Displays
44-311 Monterey Avenue
Palm Dessert, CA 92260-2388   760-775-2424
800-600-2810
Fax: 760-284-6100
info@benchmarkdisplays.com
www.benchmarkdisplays.com

Plastic literature and product displays

CFO: Robert Stevens
Marketing Manager: Michael Rener
marketing@benchmarkdisplays.com
Production Manager: Bonnie Miller
Principle: Joanne Frohman
Credit Cards: MasterCard; Visa
Catalog Cost: Free
Catalog Circulation: Mailed 1 time(s) per year to 10M
Printing Information: 16 pages in 4 colors on Glossy Stock
Binding: Saddle Stitched
Mailing List Information: Names for rent
In Business: 30 years
Number of Employees: 9
Sales Information: $5,000,000

7052 Braeside Displays
Braeside Displays
795 Bartlett Avenue
Antioch, IL 60002-1819   847-395-8500
800-837-9888
Fax: 847-395-1743
info@braesidedisplays.com
www.Braesidedisplays.Com

Manufacturer of plastic pop displays: frames, table tents, brochure holders, signage and more; immediate delivery and in-house custom design

President: Susan Molloy
Marketing Manager: Laura Deligatti-Oravec
Credit Cards: AMEX; MasterCard; Visa
Catalog Cost: Free
Catalog Circulation: Mailed 1 time(s) per year
Printing Information: 20 pages in 4 colors on Glossy Stock
Press: Web Press
Binding: Saddle Stitched
Mailing List Information: Names for rent
In Business: 40 years
Number of Employees: 30
Sales Information: $1,000,000 - $5,000,000

7053 BrittenMedia
Britten Banners Inc.
2322 Cass Rd.
Traverse City, MI 49684
231-941-8200
855-763-8204
Fax: 231-941-8299
sales@brittenmedia.com
www.brittenstudios.com

Digitally printed and screen printed banners and signs; banner display accessories, backdrops, mural, flags, tradeshow accessories, museum and zoo exhibit accessories

Chairman: Liz Keegan
President: Paul Britten
Marketing Manager: Jenn Ryan
Production Manager: Peter White
Catalog Cost: Free
Printing Information: 16 pages in 4 colors
In Business: 30 years
Number of Employees: 90
Sales Information: $25 Million

7054 Church Identification Products
Lake Shore Industries Inc
1817 Poplar Street
PO Box 3427
Erie, PA 16508-427
800-458-0463
Fax: 814-453-4293
info@lsisigns.com
www.lsisigns.com

Books, plaques, architectural letters and recognition walls, as well as cemetery signs and markers

President: Leo Bruno
Marketing Manager: Shirley Bruno
Production Manager: David Mays
Credit Cards: MasterCard
Mailing List Information: Names for rent
In Business: 106 years
Number of Employees: 19
Sales Information: $1,400,000

7055 Crown Industries
Crown Industries, Inc.
155 N Park St
East Orange, NJ 07017-1790
973-672-2277
800-255-5678
Fax: 973-672-7536
customerservice@4rails.com
www.4rails.com

Exhibit booths

President: Hugh Loebner
Credit Cards: AMEX; MasterCard
Printing Information: 18 pages
Number of Employees: 15
Sales Information: $1,000,000 - $5,000,000

7056 Dealers Supply
Collectors House Co.
PO Box 3380
Jersey City, NJ 07303-717
201-432-6035
800-448-9298
Fax: 732-453-6390
dsi11@verizon.net
www.chdisplay.com

Tables, tabletop displayers, risers, display cases, lighting, personal security system items, cameras, alarms

President: Rob Eskew
Marketing Manager: David Smith
Outsides Sales: Jack Bonner
jbonner@delongequipment.com
Credit Cards: AMEX; MasterCard
In Business: 15 years

7057 Downing Displays
Downing Displays
550 Techne Center Dr
Milford, OH 45150-2785
513-248-9800
800-883-1800
Fax: 513-248-2605
www.Downingdisplays.Com

Portable and modular tradeshow exhibits

President: Michael Scherer
CFO: Robert Kerr
Production Manager: Ed Moore
Buyers: Tim Huth
Credit Cards: AMEX; MasterCard
Catalog Cost: Free
Catalog Circulation: Mailed 1 time(s) per year
Printing Information: 12 pages in 4 colors on Matte Stock
Mailing List Information: Names for rent
In Business: 50 years
Number of Employees: 110
Sales Information: $10,000,000 - $25,000,000

7058 Expo Displays & Exhibits Catalog
Expo Displays & Exhibits
3401 Mary Taylor Road
Birmingham, AL 35235
866-747-EXPO
800-367-3976
Fax: 205-439-8201
info@expodisplays.com
www.expodisplays.com

Commercial display and exhibit products

President: David Holladay
CEO: Jeff Culton
Business Development: Beverly Griffith
Office Administration: Leslie Mayo
In Business: 45 years
Number of Employees: 45
Sales Information: $3MM to $5MM

7059 Exponents
Exponents Insta USA Inc
1351 Air Wing Rd
Suite # 2
San Diego, CA 92154-4499
619-298-6473
800-451-4723
Fax: 619-374-2797
info@exponents.com
www.Exponents.Com

Exponents displays

President: Bruce Backer
CFO: Shravan Doshi
Marketing Manager: Mark Milden
Production Manager: Fred Presson
CEO: Rajnikant Kedia
Sr Customer Service Manager: Greg Turner
Customer Service Executive: Marquitta Moore
In Business: 33 years
Number of Employees: 64
Sales Information: $5,000,000 - $10,000,000

7060 Farmington Displays
Farmington Displays, Inc.
21 Hyde Road
Farmington, CT 06032-2801
860-677-2497
Fax: 860-677-1418
info@fdi-group.com
www.fdi-group.com

Trade show exhibits

President: Sebastian DiTommasu
Production Manager: Salvatore DiTommasu
List Manager: Paul Di Ttomanso
In Business: 42 years
Number of Employees: 52
Sales Information: $1,000,000 - $5,000,000

7061 Gallo Displays
Gallo
4922 E 49th St
Cleveland, OH 44125-1016
216-431-9500
800-422-4948
Fax: 216-431-1651
www.Gallodisplays.Com

Displays

President: Catherine Andre
Mailing List Information: Names for rent
In Business: 84 years
Number of Employees: 125
Sales Information: $10,000,000 - $25,000,000

7062 Handy Store Fixtures
Handy Store Fixtures
337 Sherman Avenue
Newark, NJ 07114
800-631-4280
Fax: 973-642-6222
www.handysf.com

Steel, wood, storage and warehouse fixtures including gondolas, wall units, end caps, display cases, checkout counters, shelving and merchandising accessories

President: Marc Kurland
Marketing Manager: Walter Pincus
Catalog Cost: Free
Catalog Circulation: Mailed 1 time(s) per year to 5M
Printing Information: 23 pages in 2 colors on Glossy Stock
Press: Web Press
Binding: Saddle Stitched
List Manager: Walter Pincus
In Business: 63 years
Number of Employees: 280
Sales Information: $10,000,000 - $25,000,000

7063 Houston Wire Works
Houston Wire Works
1007 Kentucky Street
South Houston, TX 77587-3220
713-946-2920
800-468-9477
Fax: 713-946-3579
info@houstonwire.com
www.houstonwire.com

Point of sale display racks, racks for bottled water and beverage industry.

President: Barbara Legler
CFO: Barbara Legler
Marketing Manager: Shelby Cruz
Production Manager: Donald Palermo
Buyers: Raquel Garza
Rusty Sandefur, Manufacturing
Credit Cards: AMEX; MasterCard
Catalog Cost: Free
Catalog Circulation: Mailed 5 time(s) per year to 25M
Printing Information: 4 pages in 4 colors on Glossy Stock
Press: Web Press
Mailing List Information: Names for rent
In Business: 53 years
Number of Employees: 40
Sales Information: $1,000,000 - $5,000,000

7064 International Crystal Company
International Crystal Co. Inc.
3008 34th Street
Lubbock, TX 79410
800-343-6657
800-343-6657
Fax: 806-791-1502
intcrysco@aol.com
www.internationalcrystal.com

Wholesale only: Jewelry in 500 original designs, sterling silver w/semi-precious stones

President: Michael Leach
Catalog Circulation: Mailed 52 time(s) per year
Average Order Size: $300
Printing Information: 20 pages in 4 colors on Glossy Stock
Press: Web Press
Binding: Saddle Stitched
Mailing List Information: Names for rent
In Business: 26 years
Number of Employees: 8

7065 Light Impressions
Light Impressions
100 Carlson Raod
Rochester, NY 14610
800-975-6429
Fax: 866-592-8642
help@fdmbrands.com
www.lightimpressionsdirect.com

Archival storage, display & presentation materials for negatives, transparencies, CDs, photographs, artwork, & documents

President: Gabe Bristol
Credit Cards: AMEX; MasterCard
Catalog Cost: Free
Catalog Circulation: Mailed 52 time(s) per year
Printing Information: 116 pages in 4 colors on Glossy Stock
Press: Web Press
Binding: Saddle Stitched
Mailing List Information: Names for rent
List Manager: MSGi
In Business: 48 years
Number of Employees: 80
Sales Information: $36 Million

7066 Mailboxes Catalog

Mailboxes.com
1010 East 62nd Street
Los Angeles, CA 90001

323-846-6700
800-624-5299
Fax: 323-846-6800
customerservice@mailboxes.com
www.mailboxes.com

Mailboxes, lockers, signs and postal specialties

President: Dennis Fraher
CFO: Mike Lobasso
Marketing Manager: Brian Fraher
Credit Cards: AMEX; MasterCard
Catalog Cost: Free
Catalog Circulation: Mailed 2 time(s) per year to 100M
Printing Information: 121 pages in 4 colors on Glossy Stock
Press: Web Press
Binding: Saddle Stitched
Mailing List Information: Names for rent
In Business: 81 years
Number of Employees: 100
Sales Information: $5MM to $10MM

7067 Manne-King Catalog

Manne-King
2000 S Dahlia St.
#300
Denver, CO 80222-4758

303-399-8712
800-779-1566
Fax: 303-399-8617
www.Manne-King.Com

Line of mannequins both new and used

President: Michael Davis
Co-Founder: Bill Davis
Co-Founder: Mike Davis
In Business: 25 years
Sales Information: $500M to $1MM

7068 Metro Shelving & Warehouse Products

Metro Shelving & Warehouse Products
4520 Mack Avenue, Unit H
Frederick, MD 21703

301-682-6797
800-827-7880
Fax: 301-231-0419

Shelving and warehouse equipment store fixtures

President: C John Liakos
Credit Cards:
Catalog Circulation: Mailed 2 time(s) per year
Printing Information: 180 pages
Binding: Perfect Bound
In Business: 43 years
Number of Employees: 5

7069 Moss

Moss Inc
2600 Elmhurst Rd.
Elk Grove Village, IL 60007-6312

847-238-4200
800-341-1557
Fax: 207-930-6044
moss@mossinc.com
www.Mossinc.Com

Lightweight tension fabric structures for exhibits and displays

President: Dan Patterson
CFO: Mark Ollinger
Marketing Manager: Shelly Alex
EVP, Sales: Dan Scandiff
EVP, R&D: Bob Frey
SVP, Operations: Sarah Browning
Number of Employees: 30
Sales Information: $1MM to $3MM

7070 Mossburg's Sign Products

Mossburg's Sign Products
631 Gossett Road
Spartanburg, SC 29307-340

864-699-2700
800-845-6140
Fax: 864-699-2515
sales@mossburgsign.com
www.Mossburgsign.Com

Sign products

President: Gary Mossburg
Credit Cards: MasterCard; Visa
Catalog Circulation: Mailed 1 time(s) per year
Printing Information: 22 pages in 2 colors
In Business: 33 years
Sales Information: $1MM to $3MM

7071 Multiplex Versatile Display Systems

The Miller Group
St. Louis Division
1610 Design Way
Dupo, IL 62239-1820

636-343-5700
800-325-3350
Fax: 618-286-6202
info@miller-group.com
www.multiplexdisplays.com

Professional displays and display systems for retailers, wholesalers, businesses, floor covering and art sellers, libraries, learning centers, and not-for-profit organizations

President: Randy Castle
Marketing Manager: Kathy Webster
kathywebster@miller-group.com
Credit Cards: AMEX; MasterCard; Visa
Catalog Cost: Free
Average Order Size: $750
Printing Information: 24 pages in 4 colors on Glossy Stock
Binding: Folded
Mailing List Information: Names for rent
Number of Employees: 150
Sales Information: $1MM to $3MM

7072 Nimlok Company

Nimlok Company
9033 Murphy Road
Woodridge, IL 60517-4024

630-226-1155
800-233-8870
Fax: 630-226-1133
info@nimlok.com
www.nimlok.com

Exhibit and display systems

Chairman: Gerald Perutz
President: Giles Douglas
In Business: 45 years
Number of Employees: 450
Sales Information: $10,000,000 - $25,000,000

7073 North American Plastic Manufacturing Company

North American Plastic Manufacturing Com
8 Parklawn Drive
Bethel, CT 06801

203-794-1310
800-934-7752
Fax: 203-598-0068
www.napcomfg.com

Display hangers

President: Robert La Perriere
Marketing Manager: Dean Kyburz
Catalog Circulation: Mailed 1 time(s) per year
Printing Information: in 4 colors
In Business: 29 years

Number of Employees: 10
Sales Information: Under $500,000

7074 OLEA Exhibits/Displays

Olea Kiosks,Inc
13845 Artesia Blvd.
Cerritos, CA 90703-2636

562-924-2644
800-927-8063
Fax: 562-924-2308
info@olea.com
www.Olea.Com

Customized displays

President: Fernando Olea
In Business: 40 years
Number of Employees: 40
Sales Information: $5MM to $10MM

7075 Perimeter Exhibits

Perimeter Exhibit Limited
1517 Hearthstone Drive
Plano, TX 75023-7843

972-943-9189
800-345-1356
www.perimeterexhibits.com

Nationwide dealer of portable, modular pop-up exhibit systems

President: Bob Drapeau
Marketing Manager: Dave Johnson
Manager: Jackie Kaiser
Credit Cards: AMEX; MasterCard
Catalog Cost: Free
Catalog Circulation: to 100
Average Order Size: $1500
Printing Information: 18 pages on Glossy Stock
Press: Letterpress
Binding: Saddle Stitched
Mailing List Information: Names for rent
In Business: 37 years
Number of Employees: 3
Sales Information: $210,000

7076 Plastruct

Plastruct
1020 S Wallace Place
City of Industry, CA 91748

626-912-7017
800-666-7015
Fax: 626-965-2036
plastruct@plastruct.com
www.plastruct.com

Plastic scale model parts

President: John Wanderman
Production Manager: Darlene Carriaga
Credit Cards: AMEX; MasterCard
Catalog Cost: $5
Printing Information: 155 pages in 4 colors
In Business: 44 years
Number of Employees: 57
Sales Information: $ 5-10 Million

7077 RPM Displays

RPM Displays
26 Aurelius Avenue
Auburn, NY 13021-2231

315-255-1105
800-669-3676
Fax: 315-252-1167
www.rpmdisplays.com

Various display stands for merchandisers

Catalog Circulation: Mailed 1 time(s) per year
Printing Information: 20 pages in 2 colors
In Business: 38 years

7078 Sales Promotion Tool Book

The Godfrey Group
1000 Centre Green Way
Ste 200
Cary, NC 27513-7659

919-544-6504
800-789-9394
Fax: 919-544-6729
sales@godfreygroup.com
www.godfreygroup.com

Trade show exhibits and displays

President: H Glenn Godfrey
Principal: Will Daniel
VP: Ann Godfrey
Project Manager: Pete Smith
Credit Cards: AMEX; MasterCard
Catalog Cost: Free
Printing Information: 42 pages in 4 colors on Glossy Stock
In Business: 40 years

7079 Salescaster Displays Corporation
Salescasterr Displays Corporation
2095 Protland Avenue
Scotch Plains, NJ 07076   800-346-4474
                              Fax: 908-322-3049
                      sales@salescaster.com
                      www.salescaster.com

Electronic visual displays

President: Dennis Tort
VP: Mark Tort
Printing Information: in 3 colors
In Business: 65 years

7080 ShowTopper Exhibits
Godfrey & Wing Inc.
220 Campus Drive
Aurora, OH 44202-249   330-562-1440
                              800-241-2579
                          Fax: 330-562-1510

Largest selection of systems, exhibits and planners

Credit Cards: AMEX; MasterCard; Visa
Catalog Cost: Free
Catalog Circulation: Mailed 1 time(s) per year
Printing Information: 5 pages in 2 colors on Glossy Stock
Press: Web Press
Binding: Perfect Bound
In Business: 65 years
Number of Employees: 35
Sales Information: $1,000,000 - $5,000,000

7081 Siegel Display
Siegel Display Products
300 Display Drive
Moody, AL 35004   800-626-0322
                      Fax: 501-525-7716
                  sales@siegeldisplay.com
                  www.siegeldisplay.com

Displays for books, novelities, and trade show displays

President: Jeannette Beck
Credit Cards: AMEX; MasterCard
Catalog Cost: Free
Catalog Circulation: Mailed 1 time(s) per year to 50M
Printing Information: 76 pages in 4 colors
Press: Sheetfed Press
Binding: Saddle Stitched
Mailing List Information: Names for rent
In Business: 46 years
Number of Employees: 20-5
Sales Information: $1,000,000 - $5,000,000

7082 Skyline Displays
Skyline International Design Center
3355 Discovery Rd
St Paul, MN 55121-2098   651-234-6592
                              800-328-2725
                          Fax: 651-234-6571
                          www.Skyline.Com

Attached self-contained tabletop and mirage displays

Chairman: Michael Vekich
President: Bill Dierberger
CFO: Jeff Meyer
Vice President, Sales & New Busines: Dave Bouquet
Senior Director: Paul Balus
Vice President, Operations: Tim Brengman
Credit Cards: AMEX; MasterCard; Visa
Catalog Cost: Free
Catalog Circulation: Mailed 1 time(s) per year
Printing Information: 3 pages in 4 colors on

Glossy Stock
Press: Web Press
Binding: Perfect Bound
In Business: 34 years
Number of Employees: 100
Sales Information: $20MM to $50MM

7083 Specialty Store Services
Speciality Store Services
454 Jarvis Ave
Des Plaines, IL 60018   888-441-246
                              888-441-4440
                          Fax: 888-368-8001
                  www.specialtystoreservices.com

Bags, boxes, retail fixtures, gift wrap, labelers, price guns, cash handling equipment, shelving, counters and signage

President: Malcom Finke
Marketing Manager: Rudy Pichietti
VP Finance: Richard Robinson
Credit Cards: AMEX; MasterCard; Visa
Catalog Cost: Free
In Business: 30 years
Number of Employees: 85
Sales Information: $15.4 Million

7084 Spectrum Corporation
Spectrum Corporation
10048 Easthaven Blvd
Houston, TX 77075-3298   713-944-6200
                              800-392-5050
                          Fax: 713-944-1290
                          www.Specorp.Com

Spectrum displays

President: Jim B Bishop
VP Sales & Marketing: Dan Boehm
In Business: 42 years
Number of Employees: 30
Sales Information: $1,000,000 - $5,000,000

7085 TecArt Industries
Tec Art Industries Inc.
28059 Center Oaks Court
Wixom, MI 48393-3654   248-624-8880
                              800-446-7609
                          Fax: 248-624-8066
                  sales@tecartinc.com
                  www.Tecartinc.Com

Illuminated pop signage, banners and stands

President: Bernie Lash
Catalog Cost: Free
Catalog Circulation: to 500
Average Order Size: $189
Printing Information: 4 pages in 4 colors on Glossy Stock
Mailing List Information: Names for rent
In Business: 24 years
Number of Employees: 20
Sales Information: $1,000,000 - $5,000,000

7086 Tobart Mannequins
Tobart Manican, Inc.
687 Lehigh Avenue
Union
New Jersey, NY 7083-5506   908-688-3888
                              800-221-2790
                          Fax: 908-687-1770
                  tobartitl@aol.com
                  www.tobart.com

Variety of mannequins and display alternatives

Fire Protection
Supplies & Equipment

7087 American Gas & Chemical Company
American Gas & Chemical Company
220 Pegasus Ave
Northvale, NJ 07647-1977   201-767-7300
                              800-288-3647
                          Fax: 201-767-1741
                  contact@amgas.com
                  www.amgas.com

Personal protection indicators

Chairman: Melanie Kershaw
President: Gerald Anderson
Sales Director: Chris Collins
Chief Sales Officer: John Blementhal
Credit Cards: AMEX; MasterCard; Visa
In Business: 62 years
Number of Employees: 30
Sales Information: $10MM to $20MM

7088 Apollo Valves Commercial Catalog
Apollo Valves
701 Matthews Mint Hill Road
Matthews, NC 28105-1706   704-841-6000
                          Fax: 843-672-1511
                  www.apollovalves.com

Various fire protection valves and breakers

President: Glenn Mosack
Catalog Circulation: Mailed 12 time(s) per year
Printing Information: 292 pages in 4 colors
Binding: Saddle Stitched
In Business: 89 years
Number of Employees: 250-
Sales Information: $10MM to $20MM

7089 Badger Fire Protection
Badger Fire Protection
944 Glenwood Station Lane
Suite 303
Charlottesville, VA 22901-1480   434-973-4361
                              800-446-3857
                          Fax: 800-248-7809
                          www.Badgerfire.Com

Fire extinguishers, dry chemical fire suppression systems, and Range Guard

President: Eric Moore
CFO: Steve Stone
Marketing Manager: Donna Deane, Sales Manager
Credit Cards: MasterCard; Visa
In Business: 22 years
Number of Employees: 228
Sales Information: $25,000,000 - $50,000,000

7090 Chief Supply
Chief Supply
1400 Executive Parkway
Eugene, OR 97401   888-588-8569
                  orders@chiefsupply.com
                  www.chiefsupply.com

Firefighting, law enforcement and emergency medical supplies, including apparel and gear bags, badges, flashlights, batteries and chargers, cases and antennas, specialty and close-out items

President: John Utley
In Business: 40 years
Sales Information: $20MM to $50MM

7091 Croker Fire Protection Products
Fire End & Croker Corporation
7 Westchester Plaza
Elmsford, NY 10523-1678   914-592-3640
                              800-759-3473
                          Fax: 914-592-3892
                          www.fire-end.com

Extinguishers, nozzles and valves, fire cabinets, fire department connections, hose reels

President: Paul Sposato
CFO: Shirley Loew
Marketing Manager: Larry Kaplan
Production Manager: Douglas Loew
International Marketing Manager: Larry Kaplan
Credit Cards: AMEX; MasterCard
Catalog Circulation: Mailed 1 time(s) per year
Printing Information: 120 pages in 4 colors
Mailing List Information: Names for rent
In Business: 106 years
Sales Information: $1,000,000 - $5,000,000

7092 Detex Corporation
Detex Corporation
302 Detex Drive
New Braunfels, TX 78130-3099   830-629-2900
800-729-3839
Fax: 830-620-6711
sales@detex.com
www.Detex.Com

Security control products

President: John Blodgett
Director of Manufacturing: Gene Boratko
Credit Cards: AMEX; MasterCard
Number of Employees: 150
Sales Information: $10MM to $20MM

7093 Flame Gard
Flame Gard
1890 Swarthmore Avenue
PO Box 2020
Lakewood, NJ 08701-1997   323-888-8707
800-526-3694
Fax: 732-364-8110
sales@flamegard.com
www.flamegard.com

Flame guard grease filters

President: Lawrence Capalbo
Number of Employees: 15
Sales Information: $5MM to $10MM

7094 Guardian Fire Equipment
Guardian Fire Equipment Inc.
3430 NW 38th St
Miami, FL 33142-5084   305-633-0361
800-327-6584
Fax: 305-638-4632
www.Guardianfire.Com

Fire equipment

President: Richard H Childress
CFO: Lisa C Petersen
Marketing Manager: Robert Petersen
Fulfillment: Ron Marsh
Buyers: Al Sanchez
Catalog Cost: Free
Printing Information: in 2 colors
Mailing List Information: Names for rent
List Manager: Robert Petersen
In Business: 37 years
Number of Employees: 35
Sales Information: $1,000,000 - $5,000,000

7095 HNU Systems
PID Analyzers
2 Washington Circle
Unit 4
Sandwich, MA 02563-2522   774-413-5281
800-724-5600
Fax: 774-413-5298
sales@hnu.com
www.hnu.com

Monitors

President: John Driscoll
In Business: 12 years
Number of Employees: 59
Sales Information: $5,000,000 - $10,000,000

7096 Hydro-Tempo
Hydro-Temp
PO Box 389
La Center, WA 98629   225-751-1200
www.hydro-tempinc.com

Early warning controls and detectors

President: Ken Myrick
Printing Information: on Glossy Stock
In Business: 44 years
Sales Information: Under $500M

7097 IFSTA
Fire Protection Publications (FPP)
930 N Willis Street
Stillwater, OK 74078-8045   405-744-5723
800-654-4055
Fax: 405-744-8204
customer.service@osufpp.org
www.ifsta.org

Curriculums, software, videos and books pertaining to fire training

Credit Cards: AMEX; MasterCard; Visa
Catalog Cost: Free
Catalog Circulation: Mailed 1 time(s) per year
Printing Information: 65 pages in 4 colors on Glossy Stock
In Business: 81 years

7098 Initial-Attack Firefighting
Owyhee Group Companies
1075 S Ancona Avenue
Eagle, ID 83616   208-938-6086
800-293-0405
Fax: 208-938-7829
sales@initial-attack.com
www.initial-attack.com

Firefighting Equipment

President: Mike Mclaughlin
Production Manager: Susan Lewis
Buyers: Edward W Smith
Credit Cards: AMEX; MasterCard
Catalog Cost: Free
Catalog Circulation: Mailed 1 time(s) per year to 2000
Printing Information: 110 pages in 2 colors on Glossy Stock
Press: Letterpress
In Business: 27 years
Number of Employees: 20
Sales Information: $500M to $1MM

7099 Interlogix Security & Life Safety Group
Interlogix
UTC Building & Industrial Systems
3211 Progress Drive
Lincolnton, NC 28092   855-286-8889
800-547-2556
Fax: 503-691-7566
orders@interlogix.com
www.interlogix.com

Designs, manufactures and distributes components, software, communication technologies and information for security, safety, and lifestyle enhancements

President: Brian McCarthy
CFO: Rick Falconer
Marketing Manager: David Tyler
Production Manager: Ali Saalabian
Buyers: Marc Koczwara
Catalog Cost: Free
Catalog Circulation: to 2000
Printing Information: 150 pages in 2 colors on Matte Stock
Binding: Perfect Bound
Mailing List Information: Names for rent
List Manager: Kim Benson
In Business: 34 years
Number of Employees: 700
Sales Information: $50MM to $100MM

7100 Justrite Manufacturing Company
Justrite Mfg. Co
2454 E Dempster St
Suite 300
Des Plaines, IL 60016-5315   847-298-9250
800-978-9250
Fax: 847-298-9261
www.justritemfg.com

Flammable liquid safety equipment

Printing Information: 128 pages in 4 colors on Matte Stock
Press: Web Press
Binding: Perfect Bound
Mailing List Information: Names for rent
In Business: 97 years
Number of Employees: 200
Sales Information: $3MM to $5MM

7101 Landrigan Corporation
Landrigan Corporation
2-12 Jeffries Street
PO Box 444
East Boston, MA 02128   617-567-2182
Fax: 617-569-6627
www.Landrigancorp.Com

Firefighting and lifesaving equipment

President: George Landrigan
Number of Employees: 4
Sales Information: $500,000 - $1,000,000

7102 Protection People
Dixon
800 High Street
Chestertown, MD 21620   877-712-6179
Fax: 410-778-9525
www.dixonvalve.com/division/dixon-fire

Valves, nozzles, adapters, nipples

Credit Cards: AMEX; MasterCard
Catalog Cost: Free
Printing Information: 16 pages
Binding: Saddle Stitched
In Business: 128 years

7103 Pyro-Chem
PYRO-CHEM
One Stanton Street
Marinette, WI 54143   715-732-3465
800-526-1079
Fax: 715-732-3569
ckakuk@tycoint.com
www.pyrochem.com

Extinguishing products

Marketing Manager: Bob Kroll
Product Manager: Katherine Adrian
kgordon@tycoint.com
Technical Services: Dennis Brohmer
dbrohmer@tycoint.com
Sr. Technical Services Specialist: Scott Wessely
swessely@tycoint.com
Credit Cards: AMEX; MasterCard
Number of Employees: 50
Sales Information: $5,000,000 - $10,000,000

7104 Rempac Foam Corporation
Rempac Foam LLC
370 W Passaic St
Rochelle Park, NJ 07662-3475   201-861-8880
Fax: 973-881-8880
www.rempac.com

Fire protection foam for commercial and military applications

President: R Bushell
Marketing Manager: Ralph Gallucio
In Business: 13 years
Number of Employees: 100
Sales Information: $10,000,000 - $25,000,000

7105 SES
Security Equipment Supply, Inc.
sales@sesonline.com
www.sesonline.com

Burglar and fire alarms, home automation, CCTV, access controls, protectors and supplies

President: Bob Van Dillen
bvandillen@sesonline.com
Marketing Manager: Jamie Roberston
Operations Manager: George Trussler
gtrussler@sesonline.com

Sales Manager: John Hill
Jhill@sesonline.com
Credit Cards: MasterCard; Visa
Catalog Cost: $15
Catalog Circulation: Mailed 3 time(s) per year
to 10000
Printing Information: 50 pages in 2 colors on
Glossy Stock
Binding: Saddle Stitched
In Business: 35 years
Number of Employees: 40
Sales Information: $10 million

7106   Specialty Store Services
Speciality Store Services
454 Jarvis Ave
Des Plaines, IL 60018   888-441-246
                                 888-441-4440
                        Fax: 888-368-8001
                www.specialtystoreservices.com

**Bags, boxes, retail fixtures, gift wrap, label-
ers, price guns, cash handling equipment,
shelving, counters and signage**

President: Malcom Finke
Marketing Manager: Rudy Pichietti
VP Finance: Richard Robinson
Credit Cards: AMEX; MasterCard; Visa
Catalog Cost: Free
In Business: 30 years
Number of Employees: 85
Sales Information: $15.4 Million

7107   Sportime Catalog
School Specialty Inc
PO Box 1579
Appleton, WI 54912-1579   888-388-3224
                                 800-283-5700
                        Fax: 888-388-6344
                orders@schoolspecialty.com
                www.schoolspecialty.com

**Innovative audio/video products for physi-
cal education & recreation, sensory solutions, school supplies, early childhood and
special needs products and equipment**

Chairman: James R. Henderson
President: Joseph M. Yorio
CFO: Kevin Baehler
Principal: Justin Lu
Portfolio Manager: Madhu Satyanarayana
EVP, Distribution: Patrick T. Collins
Credit Cards: AMEX; MasterCard
Catalog Cost: Free
Catalog Circulation: Mailed 1 time(s) per year
Printing Information: 400 pages

7108   Superior Signal Company
Superior Signal Company LLC
PO Box 96
Spotswood, NJ 08884-96   732-251-0800
                                 800-945-8378
                        Fax: 732-251-9442
                info@superiorsignal.com
                www.superiorsignal.com

Smoke generators

President: Jim Kovacs
Marketing Manager: Helen Kovacs
In Business: 55 years
Number of Employees: 25

7109   Survivair
Honeywell
900 Douglas Pike
Smithfield, RI 02917-6413   714-545-0410
                                 800-430-5490
                        Fax: 714-850-0299
                informationsp@honeywell.com
                www.honeywellsafety.com

Respiratory protection equipment

President: Jack Bell
CFO: Steve Wiser
Marketing Manager: Bob Hitchcock
Production Manager: Art Herbon
Fulfillment: Luci Rasmussen

International Marketing Manager: Rod Culwell
Buyers: Mike Rolle
Catalog Cost: Free
Printing Information: 9 pages in 4 colors on
Glossy Stock
Press: Web Press
Binding: Saddle Stitched
Mailing List Information: Names for rent
List Manager: Luci Rasmussen
In Business: 38 years
Number of Employees: 175
Sales Information: $25,000,000 - $50,000,000

7110   Ziamatic Corporation
Ziamatic Corporation
PO Box 337
10 West College Avenue
Yardley, PA 19067-8337   215-493-3618
                                 800-711-3473
                        Fax: 215-493-1401
                zservice@ziamatic.com
                www.ziamatic.com

Fire, safety, and marine products

President: Mike Ziaylek
Marketing Manager: Ron Larue
Credit Cards: AMEX; MasterCard
Catalog Cost: Free
Catalog Circulation: Mailed 1 time(s) per year
to 25M
Printing Information: 104 pages in 4 colors on
Matte Stock
Press: Web Press
Binding: Saddle Stitched
Mailing List Information: Names for rent
In Business: 41 years
Number of Employees: 25
Sales Information: 6MM

Furniture
Office & Institutional

7111   Alfax Furniture
Dallas Midwest
4100 Alpha Road
Dallas, TX 75244   800-527-2417
                        Fax: 800-301-8314
                www.alfaxfurniture.com

**Furniture for schools, churches, and govern-
ment agencies**

Chairman: George Gayer
Chairman: Felix Zimmerman
General Manager: Teresa Darden
Credit Cards: AMEX; MasterCard
Catalog Cost: Free
In Business: 66 years
Sales Information: $12 Million

7112   Autom Inspirational Gifts
Autom
5226 S 31st Place
Phoenix, AZ 85040   800-521-2914
                        Fax: 800-582-1166
                www.autom.com

**Catholic and Christian books and related
items**

President: Paul DiGiovanni
CFO: Thomas DiGiovanni
Credit Cards: AMEX; MasterCard
Catalog Cost: Free
Catalog Circulation: Mailed 1 time(s) per year
Printing Information: 56 pages
Binding: Perfect Bound
In Business: 65 years

7113   Barco Products Company
Barco Products
24 N. Washington Ave
Batavia, IL 60510   630-879-0084
                                 800-338-2697
                        Fax: 630-879-8687
                sales@barcoproducts.com
                www.barcoproducts.com

**Picnic tables, park benches, trash recepta-
cles, safety products, parking lot products**

President: Robert Runke
Marketing Manager: Susan Ross
Production Manager: Kim Vallone
CEO: Cyril Matter
Catalog Cost: Free
In Business: 30 years
Sales Information: $6MM

7114   Becker's School Supplies
Becker's School Supplies
1500 Melrose Highway
Pennsauken, NJ 08110-1410   800-523-1490
                        Fax: 856-792-4500
                customerservice@shopbecker.com
                www.shopbecker.com

School supplies, including art supplies

President: George Becker
Credit Cards: MasterCard
Catalog Cost: Free
Catalog Circulation: Mailed 1 time(s) per year
Printing Information: 272 pages in 4 colors
In Business: 89 years
Sales Information: $20-50 Million

7115   Charnstrom Company
Charnstrom Company
5391 12th Avenue East
Shakopee, MN 55379-1896   952-403-0303
                                 800-328-2962
                        Fax: 800-916-3215
                customerservice@charnstrom.com
                www.Charnstrom.Com

**Mailroom furniture and equipment for busi-
ness and government**

President: Greg Hedlund
Sales Manager: Kathy Lundy
Catalog Cost: Free
Printing Information: 52 pages
Sales Information: $5MM to $10MM

7116   Closeout City Office Furniture
309 Office Furniture
1711 Bethlehem Pike (Route 309)
Hatfield, PA 19440-1303   215-822-3333
                                 888-822-3333
                        Fax: 215-997-7798
                info@309officefurniture.com
                www.309officefurniture.com

Office furniture

President: Wallace Rosenthal
Production Manager: Margie Dudley
Catalog Cost: Free
Printing Information: 160 pages
In Business: 24 years
Number of Employees: 20
Sales Information: $ 2.7 Million

7117   DEMCO Library Supplies & Equipment
Demco imagine whats possible
PO BOX 7488
Madison, WI 53707   608-241-1201
                        Fax: 608-241-0666
                president@demco.com
                www.demco.com

Office, school, library supplies and furniture

Chairman: John Wall
President: Trevor Taylor
CFO: Don Rogers
Fulfillment: Bill Erickson
Credit Cards: AMEX; MasterCard; Visa
Catalog Cost: Free
Catalog Circulation: Mailed 1 time(s) per year
Printing Information: 880 pages in 4 colors on
Glossy Stock
Press: Web Press
Mailing List Information: Names for rent
List Manager: Jeff McLaughlin
In Business: 95 years
Number of Employees: 10
Sales Information: $830,000

7118 Demco Furniture Catalog
DEMCO
P.O. Box 7488
Madison, WI 53707-7336   608-210-8993
                               877-449-1797
                            Fax: 800-245-1329
                    international@demco.com
                         www.demco.com

Office, school, library supplies and furniture

Chairman: John Wall
President: Ed Muir
Credit Cards: AMEX; MasterCard; Visa
Catalog Cost: Free
Catalog Circulation: Mailed 1 time(s) per year
Printing Information: 600 pages in 4 colors
Mailing List Information: Names for rent
List Manager: Jeff McLaughlin
Number of Employees: 250
Sales Information: $20MM to $50MM

7119 Design Within Reach
Design Within Reach
711 Canal St. 3rd Floor
Stamford, CT 06902   203-614-0750
                           800-944-2233
                        Fax: 203-614-0845
                         www.dwr.com

Well designed furniture usually found in designer showrooms to businesses, design professionals and consumers

Chairman: Rob Forbes
President: Kelly Spain
CFO: Ken La Honta
Credit Cards: AMEX; MasterCard
Catalog Cost: Free
Sales Information: $1MM to $3MM

7120 Early Childhood Manufacturers' Direct
Early Childhood Manufacturers' Direct
PO Box 6013
Carol Stream, IL 60197-6013   800-896-9951
                            Fax: 800-879-3753
                customerservice@ecmdstore.com
                        www.ecmdstore.com

Furniture and equipment for schools, preschools and child care programs

Chairman: Ron Elliott
President: Paul Estep
Credit Cards: AMEX; MasterCard
Catalog Cost: Free
Catalog Circulation: to 150m
Average Order Size: $800
Printing Information: 260 pages in 4 colors
Binding: Perfect Bound
In Business: 19 years

7121 Hertz Furniture Systems Corporation
Hertz Furniture
170 Williams Dr Ramsey
Mahwah, NJ 07446-2105   888-286-3461
                              888-394-0594
                           Fax: 800-842-9290
                    info@hertzfurniture.com
                      www.Hertzfurniture.Com

Furniture for commercial, government, institutional and educational use

Chairman: Saul Wagner
President: David Mocton
CFO: Coleman Breger
VP of Sales and Business Developmen: David Azer
Customer Service Manager: Maralyn Ross
Buyers: Mandy Rose
Credit Cards: MasterCard; Visa
Catalog Cost: Free
Catalog Circulation: Mailed 8 time(s) per year
Printing Information: 356 pages in 4 colors on Glossy Stock
Press: Web Press
In Business: 63 years
Number of Employees: 65
Sales Information: $20MM to $50MM

7122 Inspired
American Hotel Register Company
100 S Milwaukee Ave.
Vernon Hills, IL 60061-4035   800-323-5686
                            Fax: 800-688-9108
                    ffe@americanhotel.com
                    www.americanhotel.com

Furniture, fixtures and equipment for the hospitality industry.

Chairman: James F. Leahy
President: Angela Korompilas
Catalog Cost: Free
Catalog Circulation: Mailed 1 time(s) per year
Printing Information: 122 pages in 4 colors
In Business: 151 years
Number of Employees: 1000
Sales Information: $850 Million

7123 KI Business Solutions
Krueger International
1330 Bellevue St.
Green Bay, WI 54308-8100   800-424-2432
                        info@ki.com
                        www.ki.com

Furniture solutions manufacturer for educational, university, business and government markets.

Chairman and CEO: Dick Resch
President: Brian Krenke
Catalog Cost: Free
Printing Information: 60 pages in 4 colors
In Business: 75 years
Number of Employees: 3000
Sales Information: $700 Million

7124 KI Government Solutions
Krueger International
1330 Bellevue St.
Green Bay, WI 54308-8100   800-424-2432
                        info@ki.com
                        www.ki.com

Furniture solutions manufacturer for educational, university, business and government markets.

Chairman and CEO: Dick Resch
President: Brian Krenke
Catalog Cost: Free
Printing Information: 2 pages in 4 colors
In Business: 75 years
Number of Employees: 3000
Sales Information: $700 Million

7125 KI Healthcare
Krueger International
1330 Bellevue St.
Green Bay, WI 54308-8100   800-424-2432
                        info@ki.com
                        www.ki.com

Furniture solutions manufacturer for educational, university, business and government markets.

Chairman and CEO: Dick Resch
President: Brian Krenke
Catalog Cost: Free
Printing Information: 101 pages in 4 colors
In Business: 75 years
Number of Employees: 3000
Sales Information: $700 Million

7126 KI Higher Education Solutions
Krueger International
1330 Bellevue St.
Green Bay, WI 54308-8100   800-424-2432
                        info@ki.com
                        www.ki.com

Furniture solutions manufacturer for educational, university, business and government markets.

Chairman and CEO: Dick Resch
President: Brian Krenke
Catalog Cost: Free
Printing Information: 108 pages in 4 colors

In Business: 75 years
Number of Employees: 3000
Sales Information: $700 Million

7127 KI K-12 Solutions
Krueger International
1330 Bellevue St.
Green Bay, WI 54308-8100   800-424-2432
                        info@ki.com
                        www.ki.com

Furniture solutions manufacturer for educational, university, business and government markets.

Chairman and CEO: Dick Resch
President: Brian Krenke
Catalog Cost: Free
Printing Information: 106 pages in 4 colors
In Business: 75 years
Number of Employees: 3000
Sales Information: $700 Million

7128 Kentwood Manufacturing
Kentwood Manufacturing
4849 Barden Court SE
Grand Rapids, MI 49512   616-698-6370
                           Fax: 616-698-6832
                customerservice@kentwoodmfg.com
                       www.kentwoodmfg.com

Bathroom mirrors and decorative wood, lacquered and frameless wall mirrors

Marketing Manager: Doug West
Catalog Circulation: Mailed 1 time(s) per year
Printing Information: 36 pages in 2 colors on Matte Stock
Press: Web Press
Binding: Saddle Stitched
In Business: 58 years
Number of Employees: 25
Sales Information: $2 Million

7129 Knape & Vogt
Knape & Vogt
2700 Oak Industrial Drive NE
Grand Rapids, MI 49505   800-253-1561
                        www.knapeandvogt.com

President: Peter Martin
CFO: Rick McQuigg
Marketing Manager: Peter Ross
Vice President, Operations: Gordon Kirsch
Vice President, Home and Commercial: Dan Pickett
Vice President, OEM Sales: Gary Ottenjan
Printing Information: in 4 colors
Binding: Perfect Bound

7130 Mailboxes Catalog
Mailboxes.com
1010 East 62nd Street
Los Angeles, CA 90001   323-846-6700
                              800-624-5299
                           Fax: 323-846-6800
                    customerservice@mailboxes.com
                         www.mailboxes.com

Mailboxes, lockers, signs and postal specialties

President: Dennis Fraher
CFO: Mike Lobasso
Marketing Manager: Brian Fraher
Credit Cards: AMEX; MasterCard
Catalog Cost: Free
Catalog Circulation: Mailed 2 time(s) per year to 100M
Printing Information: 121 pages in 4 colors on Glossy Stock
Press: Web Press
Binding: Saddle Stitched
Mailing List Information: Names for rent
In Business: 81 years
Number of Employees: 100
Sales Information: $5MM to $10MM

7131 National Business Furniture
National Business Furniture
770 S 70th Street
Milwaukee, WI 53214   800-558-1010
Fax: 800-329-9349
www.nationalbusinessfurniture.com

Office, school and healthcare furniture, desks, file cabinets, bookcases, chairs, storage and tables.

President: Kent Anderson
General Manager: Rick Wachowiak
Branch Manager: David Favro
Credit Cards: AMEX; MasterCard; Visa
Catalog Cost: Free
Catalog Circulation: Mailed 52 time(s) per year to 14MM
Average Order Size: $500
Printing Information: on Glossy Stock
Press: Web Press
Binding: Perfect Bound
Mailing List Information: Names for rent
List Company: Direct Media
Stamford, CT
In Business: 41 years
Number of Employees: 150
Sales Information: $ 50-100 Million

7132 National Hospitality Supply
National Hospitality Supply, Inc.
10660 N Executive Ct
Mequon, WI 53092   800-526-8224
Fax: 262-478-0229
cs@nathosp.com
www.nathosp.com

Accessories and furniture for hotels and motels

Chairman: Dan Crimmins
Credit Cards: AMEX; MasterCard
Catalog Cost: Free
Catalog Circulation: Mailed 4 time(s) per year
Printing Information: 116 pages in 4 colors
Binding: Perfect Bound
In Business: 24 years

7133 Northern Safety Company
Northern Safety Company
PO Box 4250
Utica, NY 13504-4250   315-793-4900
800-571-4646
Fax: 800-635-1591
customerservice@northernsafety.com
www.northernsafety.com

Safety and industrial supplies

Chairman: Sal Longo
President: Neil Sexton
CFO: Martha Moorehead
Marketing Manager: Robin Fostini
Founder, CEO: Sal Longo
slongoweb@northernsafety.com
Credit Cards: AMEX; MasterCard
Catalog Cost: Free
Printing Information: 532 pages
Binding: Perfect Bound
In Business: 32 years
Number of Employees: 75

7134 Physical Education & Recreation
Flaghouse
601 US-46
Hasbrouck Heights, NJ 07604   800-793-7900
sales@flaghouse.com
www.flaghouse.com

Equipment for physical education including baseball, football, basketball, and equipment for special needs patients including sensory, mobility and balance exercises and positioning products

President: George Carmel
CFO: Sheila Morrison
Credit Cards: AMEX; MasterCard
Catalog Cost: Free
Catalog Circulation: Mailed 6 time(s) per year to 2MM
Printing Information: 208 pages in 4 colors on

Glossy Stock
Press: Web Press
Binding: Perfect Bound
Mailing List Information: Names for rent
List Company: Wilson Marketing Group
11924 W Washington Boulevard
Los Angeles, CA 90066
213-398-2754
In Business: 62 years
Number of Employees: 120
Sales Information: $20MM to $50MM

7135 The Big Book
Office Depot
6600 N Military Trail
Boca Raton, FL 33496   800-463-3768
www.officedepot.com

Binders, calendars, planners, ink, toner, filing & storage, labels, pens, pencils, desktop & notebook computers, printers, copiers, shredders and office furniture

Chairman & CEO: Roland C. Smith
Catalog Cost: Free
Catalog Circulation: Mailed 1 time(s) per year
Printing Information: 868 pages in 4 colors
In Business: 30 years
Number of Employees: 4900
Sales Information: $14.5 Billion

7136 United Technologies Catalog
The University of Tennessee Chattanooga
615 McCallie Ave
Chattanooga, TN 37403-1355   423-425-4111
Fax: 317-240-5253
www.utc.edu

Molded storage equipment and plastic drawers

7137 Viking Acoustical Corporation
Viking Acoustical Corporation
21480 Heath Avenue
Lakeville, MN 55044-9105   952-469-3405
800-328-8385
Fax: 952-469-4503
webmaster@vikingusa.com
www.vikingusa.com

Adjustable computer furniture, office furniture and ergonomic accessories

President: Bret Starkweather
bstarkweather@vikingusa.com
Marketing Manager: James Thompson, VP Sales/Marketing
Sales Manager: Terry Kraft
tkraft@vikingusa.com
Customer Service: Kent Moberg
kmoberg@vikingusa.com
Controller: Mary Hixson
mhixson@vikingusa.com
Catalog Cost: Free
Catalog Circulation: to 20M
Printing Information: 40 pages
Mailing List Information: Names for rent
In Business: 29 years
Number of Employees: 90
Sales Information: $10,000,000 - $25,000,000

7138 WA Charnstrom Company
Charnstrom
5391 12th Ave E
Shakopee, MN 55379-1896   800-328-2962
Fax: 800-916-3215
customerservice@charnstrom.com
www.charnstrom.com

Mailroom and mailing equipment and furniture

President: Greg Hedlund
Marketing Manager: Kevin Huggett
Catalog Cost: Free
Catalog Circulation: Mailed 1 time(s) per year
Printing Information: 52 pages in 4 colors
In Business: 55 years
Number of Employees: 23
Sales Information: $2.8 Million

7139 Waterwise
Waterwise Inc
2460 North Euclid Avenue
Upland, CA 91784-1199   909-982-2425
800-205-2425
Fax: 909-949-7217
kristen@vnwg.com
www.vnwg.com

Water and air purification systems for home and office

President: Jack Barber
CFO: Bob Barber
Marketing Manager: Greg Barber
Buyers: Mike Lane
Credit Cards: AMEX; MasterCard
Catalog Cost: Free
Catalog Circulation: Mailed 6 time(s) per year to 15000
Average Order Size: $200
Printing Information: 36 pages in 4 colors on Glossy Stock
Press: Web Press
Binding: Saddle Stitched
Mailing List Information: Names for rent
List Manager: Greg Barber
In Business: 93 years
Number of Employees: 32
Sales Information: $4,000,000

Gifts
Corporate & Incentive

7140 1-877-Spirits.com
1-877-Spirits.com Inc
99 Powerhouse Road
Suite 200
Roslyn Heights, NY 11577   516-626-4150
877-774-7487
Fax: 516-626-4164
info@1877spirits.com
www.1-877-spirits.com

A world-wide gift delivery service of champagnes, fine wines, spirits and gourmet gift baskets.

President: Harvey Ishofsky
Credit Cards: AMEX; MasterCard; Visa
Catalog Cost: Free
Average Order Size: $100
Printing Information: 40 pages
In Business: 30 years
Number of Employees: 20
Sales Information: $5MM to $10MM

7141 ACA Corporate Awards
Award Company of America
3200 Rice Mine Road NE
PO Box 2029
Tuscaloosa, AL 35406-1510   205-248-1621
800-633-2021
customerservice@awardcompany.com
www.awardcompany.com

Awards, plaques, trophies, ribbons, specialized greeting cards, promotional and specialty items.

President: Michael Reilly
CFO: Shane Elmore
Credit Cards: AMEX; MasterCard; Visa
Catalog Cost: Free
Mailing List Information: Names for rent
In Business: 40 years
Number of Employees: 200
Sales Information: $ 10-20 Million

7142 ACA For Churches Only
Award Company of America
3200 Rice Mine Road NE
PO Box 2029
Tuscaloosa, AL 35406-1510   205-248-1621
800-633-2021
customerservice@awardcompany.com
www.awardcompany.com

Awards, plaques, trophies, ribbons, specialized greeting cards, promotional and specialty items.

President: Michael Reilly
CFO: Shane Elmore
Credit Cards: AMEX; MasterCard; Visa
Catalog Cost: Free
Mailing List Information: Names for rent
In Business: 40 years
Number of Employees: 200
Sales Information: $ 10-20 Million

7143 ACA School Essentials
Award Company of America
3200 Rice Mine Road NE
PO Box 2029
Tuscaloosa, AL 35406-1510   205-248-1621
                               800-633-2021
customerservice@awardcompany.com
www.awardcompany.com

Awards, plaques, trophies, ribbons, specialized greeting cards, promotional and specialty items.

President: Michael Reilly
CFO: Shane Elmore
Credit Cards: AMEX; MasterCard; Visa
Catalog Cost: Free
Mailing List Information: Names for rent
In Business: 40 years
Number of Employees: 200
Sales Information: $ 10-20 Million

7144 Advertising Specialties & Business Gifts
Promotion Plus, Inc.
4104 Vachell Ln
San Luis Obispo, CA 93401-8113 805-541-5730
                                 800-943-9494
                          Fax: 805-541-4795
alyssa@promoplus.com
www.promoplus.com

Complete line of premium and incentive gifts

Chairman: Ernie Roide
eroide@promoplus.com
President: Bill Luffee
bill@promoplus.com
Production Manager: Michelle Roberts
michelle@promoplus.com
Account Executive: Rob Fagot
robpromo@comcast.net
Credit Cards: AMEX; MasterCard; Visa
Catalog Cost: Free
Catalog Circulation: Mailed 1 time(s) per year
Printing Information: 148 pages in 4 colors
Binding: Perfect Bound
In Business: 26 years
Number of Employees: 16
Sales Information: 5.8M

7145 Archie McPhee & Company
Archie McPhee & Company
10915 47th Ave. W
Mukilteo, WA 98275-811   425-349-3009
                        Fax: 425-349-5188
mcphee@mcphee.com
www.mcphee.com

Retail gifts: popular culture, fun, science,
retro, lunch boxes, clocks and outer space

Credit Cards: MasterCard
Catalog Cost: Free
Catalog Circulation: Mailed 3 time(s) per year
Printing Information: 48 pages in 4 colors
In Business: 20 years
Number of Employees: 45

7146 Asprey
Asprey New York
853 Madison Ave
New York, NY 10021-4908   212-688-1811
                        Fax: 212-688-2749
enquiries@asprey.com
www.Asprey.Com

High quality gifts, jewelry, executive gifts,
china and glass

Chairman: Philip Warner
President: Robert Donofriol
Credit Cards: AMEX; MasterCard; Visa
Catalog Cost: $16
Printing Information: 46 pages in 4 colors on
Glossy Stock
Press: Web Press
Binding: Saddle Stitched
Mailing List Information: Names for rent
In Business: 28 years
Number of Employees: 15
Sales Information: $3MM to $5MM

7147 Awards.com
Awards.com
2915 S. Congress Ave
Delray Beach, FL 33445   407-265-2001
                             800-429-2737
                        Fax: 561-952-4097
ContactUs@awards.com
www.awards.com

Awards, trophies, medals, plaques, corporate gifts, logo apparel

President: Aaron Itzkowitz
VP/GM: Jim Nelson
Controller: Lars Wiksten
Director of Operations: Tracee Ferguson
Credit Cards: AMEX; MasterCard
Printing Information: on Glossy Stock
Binding: Perfect Bound
In Business: 10 years
Number of Employees: 70
Sales Information: 8.3M

7148 Bridgewater Chocolate
Bridgewater Chocolate
559 Federal Rd.
Brookfield, CT 06804   203-775-2286
                             800-888-8742
                        Fax: 203-775-9369
www.bridgewaterchocolate.com

Gourmet chocolates, nuts, pretzels, toffee
and gift baskets.

Founder: Erik Landegren
Partner: Andrew Blauner
Catalog Cost: Free
Printing Information: 11 pages in 4 colors
In Business: 21 years

7149 Bunnies by the Bay and Friends
Bunnies by the Bay
3115 V Place
PO Box 1630
Anacortes, WA 98221-1630   360-293-8037
                             877-467-7248
                        Fax: 360-293-4729
customerservice@bunniesbythebay.com
www.bunniesbythebay.com

Baby gifts including plush animals, apparel,
books, teethers and toys.

President: Jeanne Hayes
Marketing Manager: Anne Callaghan
Production Manager: Jeanne Hayes
Fulfillment: Patty Richardson
International Marketing Manager: Jeanne
Hayes
Buyers: Suzanne Knutson
Catalog Cost: Free
Catalog Circulation: to 20000
Printing Information: 60 pages in 4 colors on
Matte Stock
Press: Web Press
Binding: Saddle Stitched
Mailing List Information: Names for rent
In Business: 30 years
Number of Employees: 27
Sales Information: $1 Million

7150 CME Gifts
CircuitsMadeEasy.com
1250 E Nakoma Street
Dekalb, IL 60115-2414   815-756-1263
                        Fax: 815-758-4090
circuiteasy.com

Unique music, sports related products and
gift items

President: Michael Embrey
Production Manager: Chris Michaels
Credit Cards: MasterCard
Catalog Cost: $2
Catalog Circulation: Mailed 6 time(s) per year
to 400M
Printing Information: 32 pages in 2 colors on
Glossy Stock
Mailing List Information: Names for rent
In Business: 16 years
Number of Employees: 9

7151 Call One
Call One Inc
400 Imprial Blvd.
Cape Canaveral, FL 32920-9002 321-783-2400
                                800-749-3160
                           Fax: 321-799-9222
www.calloneonline.com

Telephones, headset bases and amplifiers,
headsets and accessories

VP: Raymond Hirsch
VP, Director - Sales/Marketing: William Mays
Sales Manager: Danny Hayasaka
Credit Cards: AMEX; MasterCard
In Business: 26 years
Number of Employees: 80

7152 Cardinal Jackets
Cardinal Activewear
P.O. Box 1029
Grundy, VA 24614   800-647-7745
                        Fax: 276-935-4970
info@cardinalactivewear.com
www.cardinalactivewear.com

Nylon coach's windbreakers; Satin baseball
jackets; Nylon baseball jackets; Nylon
hooded pullover jacket; Mesh lined micro-twill windshirt

President: Mark Shortridge
CFO: Laura Barden
Marketing Manager: Mark Shortridge/Teresa
Damron
Buyers: Teresa Damron
Credit Cards: AMEX; MasterCard; Visa
Catalog Cost: Free
Catalog Circulation: to 400m
Printing Information: 4 pages in 4 colors
Mailing List Information: Names for rent
In Business: 40 years
Number of Employees: 4
Sales Information: $110 Thousand

7153 Carlisle Company
Carlisle Company
PO Box 878
Roseville, CA 95678   800-233-3931

Science and nature gifts, wholesale and retail

President: Dave Carlisle
Credit Cards: AMEX; MasterCard
Catalog Cost: Free
Catalog Circulation: Mailed 1 time(s) per year
Printing Information: 31 pages in 4 colors
Binding: Saddle Stitched
Sales Information: $5MM to $10MM

7154 Chocolate Catalogue
Bissinger
1600 North Broadway
Saint Louis, MO 63102   314-615-2400
                             800-325-8881
                        Fax: 314-534-2419
orders@bissingers.com
www.bissingers.com

Gourmet chocolate, gourmet candy, chocolate gifts

CFO: Francine Nicholson
COO: Bill Bremmer
Credit Cards: AMEX; MasterCard; Visa

Catalog Cost: Free
Catalog Circulation: Mailed 4 time(s) per year to 1MM
Printing Information: 24 pages in 4 colors
Press: Web Press
Mailing List Information: Names for rent
Sales Information: $6 Million

7155 Cookie Bouquets
Cookie Bouquets Inc
6665-H Huntley Rd
Columbus, OH 43229-1045   614-888-2171
                                800-233-2171
                          Fax: 614-841-3950
                    chips@cookiebouquets.com
                    www.Cookiebouquets.Com

Floral-like bouquets of freshly baked, color-fully wrapped chocolate chip cookies for all occasions

President: Dinene Clark
Credit Cards: AMEX; MasterCard
Catalog Cost: Free
Catalog Circulation: Mailed 2 time(s) per year
Average Order Size: $30
Printing Information: 8 pages in 4 colors on Glossy Stock
Press: Web Press
Binding: Saddle Stitched
Mailing List Information: Names for rent
In Business: 30 years
Number of Employees: 20-O
Sales Information: $1MM to $3MM

7156 Deluxe Enterprise
Deluxe Enterprise
3680 Victoria St. N
Shoreview, MN 55126   800-865-1913
                            www.deluxe.com

Checks, business forms, office supplies and promotional products.

CEO: Lee Schram
Catalog Cost: Free
Mailing List Information: Names for rent
List Manager: Mel Reessi, Direct Media
List Company: Direct Media
In Business: 101 years
Number of Employees: 6000
Sales Information: $1.77 Billion

7157 Dinn Brothers Trophies
Dinn Brothers
221 Interstate Drive
West Springfield, MA 01089   413-750-3466
                                800-628-9657
                          Fax: 800-876-7497
                     sales@dinntrophy.com
                      www.dinntrophy.com

Trophies, awards and plaques

Chairman: Bill Dinn
President: Paul J. Dinn
Marketing Manager: Mike Dinn
Production Manager: Ed Dinn
Credit Cards: AMEX; MasterCard
In Business: 60 years

7158 Direct Promotions
Direct Promotions
29395 Agoura Road
Suite 207
Agoura Hills, CA 91301   818-591-9010
                                800-444-7706
                          Fax: 818-591-2071
                   sales@directpromotions.net
                     www.directpromotions.net

Custom printed promotional products and business gifts

President: Randy Perry
Credit Cards: AMEX; MasterCard
Catalog Cost: Free
Catalog Circulation: Mailed 1 time(s) per year
Printing Information: 24 pages in 4 colors on Glossy Stock
Press: Web Press

Binding: Saddle Stitched
In Business: 12 years
Number of Employees: 4
Sales Information: $500M to $1MM

7159 Eastern Emblem
Eastern Emblem Mfg Corp
509 18th Street
PO Box 828
Union City, NJ 07087-828   201-854-0338
                                800-344-5112
                          Fax: 201-867-7248
                   jnsboyscouts@gmail.com
                    www.easternemblem.com

Emblems and insignia for advertising or groups; custom embroidery and metal pins; custom work for embroidery-metal logo pins, stickers, garments

President: S Lefkowitz
Production Manager: Len
Credit Cards: AMEX; MasterCard
Catalog Cost: Free
In Business: 55 years
Number of Employees: 7
Sales Information: $1MM-$3MM

7160 Emedco Buyer's Guide
Emedco, Inc.
PO Box 369
Buffalo, NY 14240   866-222-4743
                                866-509-1976
                          Fax: 800-344-2578
                    customerservice@emedco.com
                         www.emedco.com

Engraved signs, frames and graphic communication products

President: Jonathan Sayers
Marketing Manager: Scott Wardour
Credit Cards: AMEX; MasterCard; Visa
Catalog Cost: Free
Printing Information: 154 pages in 4 colors
In Business: 60 years
Number of Employees: 160
Sales Information: $10MM to $20MM

7161 Empress Chocolates Company
Empress Chocolates Company
5518 Avenue N
Brooklyn, NY 11234   718-951-2251
                                800-793-3809
                          Fax: 718-951-2254

Chocolates, truffles, dipped fruits; special occasion and corporate gift boxes available

President: Ernest Grunhut
CFO: Jack Grunhut
Credit Cards: AMEX; MasterCard
Catalog Cost: Free
In Business: 27 years
Number of Employees: 35
Sales Information: $2.8 Million

7162 Engraving Connection
Engraving Connection
1205 S Main St
Plymouth, MI 48170-2215   734-459-3180
                                877-829-2737
                          Fax: 734-455-6040
                     etched@engravecon.com
                      www.engravecon.com

Personalized gifts, awards, badges and desk nameplates

President: Rex Tubbs
In Business: 37 years
Number of Employees: 6
Sales Information: $500,000 - $1,000,000

7163 First Street Catalog
First Street for Boomers and Beyond
1998 Ruffin Mill Rd
Colonial Heights, VA 23834-5909 800-704-1209
                                800-958-8324
                          Fax: 866-889-9960
              customerservice@firststreetonline.com
                    www.firststreetonline.com

Electronic gifts and gadgets and other unusual items for those who like technology

President: Mark Gordon
CFO: Kevin Miller
Credit Cards: AMEX; MasterCard; Visa
Catalog Cost: Free
Printing Information: 55 pages in 4 colors on Glossy Stock
Binding: Saddle Stitched
Sales Information: $1MM to $3MM

7164 Giggletime Toy Company
Giggletime Toy Co.
PO Box 1759
Bishop, CA 93515   800-423-5198
                          Fax: 800-873-1758
                         info@jrousek.com
                     www.giggletimetoys.com

Kids toys and prizes for dental and medical offices; party favors, noise makers and wedding bubbles

President: Joseph L Rousek
Credit Cards: AMEX; MasterCard
Number of Employees: 19
Sales Information: $2.4 Million

7165 Glenncraft Corporation
Glenncraft Corporation
205 Fortin Drive
Woonsocket, RI 02895   401-769-0101
                                800-553-9746
                          Fax: 401-766-1170
                       sales@glenncraft.com
                        www.glenncraft.com

Souvenirs, promotional products and gifts

Marketing Manager: Lou Inserra
Production Manager: Joe Arico
In Business: 33 years

7166 Global Industrial Catalog
Global Industrial
11 Harbor Park Dr.
Port Washington, NY 11050 *Fax:* 888-381-2868
                      www.globalindustrial.com

Industrial equipment and business supplies.

President: Bob Dooley
In Business: 67 years
Sales Information: $180 Million

7167 Gopromos
Amsterdam Printing
PO Box 698
166 Wallins Corners Road
Amsterdam, NY 12010   800-203-9917
                          Fax: 518-843-5204
                   cs@amsterdamprinting.com
                        www.gopromos.com

Promotional imprinted products

Credit Cards: AMEX; MasterCard
Catalog Cost: Free
In Business: 120 years

7168 Hawaii Wholesale Company
Ultimate Hawaii
155 Wailea Ike Pl
Apartment 109
Kihei, HI 96753-9528 info@ultimatehawaii.com
                        www.ultimatehawaii.com

General wholesale products

Catalog Cost: Free

7169 Holiday Cards for Businesses
National Wildlife Federation
11100 Wildlife Center Drive
Reston, VA 20190-5362 800-822-9919
Fax: 800-525-5562
www.nwf.org

Christmas cards, calendars and apparel with a wildlife theme

Chairman: Deborah Spalding
President: Collin O'Mara
Marketing Manager: Al Lamson
Production Manager: Robin Clark
EVP/COO: Jaime Matyas
CEO: Collin O'Mara
Buyers: Lynn Piper, Gift Accessories
Mary Lamer, Greeting Cards
Robin Clark, Apparel
Credit Cards: MasterCard; Visa
Catalog Cost: Free
Catalog Circulation: Mailed 6 time(s) per year to 20MM
Printing Information: 48 pages in 4 colors on Glossy Stock
Press: Web Press
Binding: Saddle Stitched
Mailing List Information: Names for rent
In Business: 63 years
Number of Employees: 675

7170 Holiday Gift Guide
alphabroder
6 Neshaminy Interplex
6th Floor
Trevose, PA 19053 800-523-4585
www.alphabroder.com

Imprintable apparel and accessories for the promotional industry.

CEO: Norman Hullinger
Catalog Cost: Free
Printing Information: 24 pages in 4 colors
Number of Employees: 2200
Sales Information: $1.5 Billion

7171 Honey Baked Ham
Honey Baked Ham
P.O. Box 370
Carrollton, GA 30117 800-367-7720
Fax: 800-728-4426
catalogservice@hbham.com
www.honeybakedonline.com

Hams, turkey, turkey breasts, BBQ ribs, desserts, baskets and more

President: Kim Hunter
Founder: Harry J. Hoenselaar
Credit Cards: AMEX; MasterCard; Visa
Catalog Cost: Free
Catalog Circulation: Mailed 10 time(s) per year to 750M
Printing Information: 16 pages in 4 colors on Glossy Stock
Mailing List Information: Names for rent
In Business: 58 years
Number of Employees: 15
Sales Information: $1MM to $3MM

7172 House of Webster
House of Webster
1013 N 2nd St
PO Box 1988
Rogers, AR 72756-1988 479-636-4640
800-369-4641
Fax: 479-636-2974
info@houseofwebster.com
www.houseofwebster.com

Gift packages and gourmet food items

CFO: Craig Castrellon
Marketing Manager: Denny Fletcher
Production Manager: Craig Duncan
Fulfillment: Chris Humphreys
Credit Cards: AMEX; MasterCard; Visa
Printing Information: 32 pages
In Business: 81 years

7173 Impact Gift Collection
Promotion Plus Inc
4104 Vachell Lane
San Luis Obispo, CA 93401-8113 805-541-5730
800-943-9494
alyssa@promoplus.com
www.promoplus.com

Incentive gift ideas

Catalog Circulation: Mailed 2 time(s) per year
Printing Information: 106 pages in 4 colors
Binding: Perfect Bound
Number of Employees: 30

7174 International Bronze Manufacturers
International Bronze Manufacturers & Des
810 Willis Avenue
Albertson, NY 11507-1919 516-248-3080
800-227-8752
Fax: 516-248-4047
sales@internationalbronze.com
www.internationalbronze.com

Bronze plaques, architectural sculptures, sign systems, name plates and monuments

President: Kenneth Klein
Catalog Cost: FREE
In Business: 79 years
Sales Information: $3MM to $5MM

7175 JanWay Company
JanWay Company
11 Academy Rd
Cogan Station, PA 17728-9351 570-494-1239
800-877-5242
Fax: 570-494-1350
janway@janway.com
www.Janway.Com

Promotional products, fund raisers, canvas and nylon bags and other supplies for libraries

President: Wayne G Stebbins
Catalog Circulation: to 20K
Printing Information: 6 pages
In Business: 32 years
Sales Information: $3MM to $5MM

7176 LTD Commodities
LTD Commodities
2800 Lakeside Drive
Bannockburn, IL 60015-735 847-295-5532
847-295-6058
Fax: 847-604-7600
www.Ltdcommodities.Com

Wholesale purchase of all kinds of gifts

President: Deren Smith
CFO: Michael Hara
VP: Juliana Furlong
Catalog Cost: Free
Catalog Circulation: Mailed 4 time(s) per year
Printing Information: 400 pages in 4 colors on Glossy Stock
Binding: Perfect Bound
In Business: 51 years
Sales Information: $20MM to $50MM

7177 Levenger
The Levenger Store
420 South Congress Ave
Delray Beach, FL 33445-4696 561-276-2436
800-544-0880
Fax: 800-544-6910
Cservice@levenger.com
www.Levenger.Com

Collection of furnishings and accessories created to enhance your well-read life, you'll find bookcases, halogen lighting, desks, chairs, leather goods, plus personal and corporate gifts

President: Steve Leveen
CFO: Lori Leveen
Marketing Manager: Susan Devito
Production Manager: Lee Passarella
Fulfillment: Gerald Patterson
Founder: Steve Leveen
Founder: Lori Leveen
Buyers: Denise Tedaldi
Credit Cards: AMEX; MasterCard; Visa
Catalog Cost: Free
Catalog Circulation: Mailed 12 time(s) per year to 20MM
Average Order Size: $130
Printing Information: 76 pages in 4 colors on Glossy Stock
Press: Web Press
Binding: Saddle Stitched
Mailing List Information: Names for rent
List Manager: Susan Devito
List Company: Mokrynski & Associates
401 Hackensack Avenue
Hackensack, NJ 07601
2014885656
In Business: 28 years
Number of Employees: 270
Sales Information: $20MM to $50MM

7178 Marquis Awards & Specialties
Marquis Awards & Specialties, Inc.
108 N Bent St
Powell, WY 82435 307-754-2272
800-327-2446
Fax: 307-754-9577
marquisawards@bresnan.net
www.rushawards.com

Awards, sportswear and promotional gifts for businesses and consumers

President: John H Collins
Marketing Manager: Terry Collins
Founder: John Collins
Founder: Terry Collins
Credit Cards: AMEX; MasterCard; Visa; Discover
Catalog Cost: Free
Catalog Circulation: Mailed 12 time(s) per year
Printing Information: 97 pages in 4 colors on Matte Stock
Press: Web Press
Binding: Saddle Stitched
Mailing List Information: Names for rent
In Business: 31 years
Number of Employees: 5
Sales Information: $500M to $1MM

7179 Mathews Wire Giftware Catalog
MATHEWS WIRE, INC.
654 West Morrison St.
Frankfort, IN 46041-1670 765-659-3542
800-826-9650
Fax: 765-659-1059
mwire@mathewswire.com
www.Mathewswire.Com

Wire reproductions, country and Victorian gifts and decorative accessories

President: Martin Mathews
CFO: Martin Mathews
Marketing Manager: Nikki Aughe
Production Manager: Martin Mathews
Fulfillment: Nikki Aughe
International Marketing Manager: Tracy Anderson
Buyers: Martin Mathews
Credit Cards: MasterCard; Visa
Catalog Circulation: Mailed 4 time(s) per year to 100K
Printing Information: 24 pages on G
Press: W
Mailing List Information: Names for rent
List Manager: Martin Mathews
In Business: 30 years
Number of Employees: 80
Sales Information: $1MM-$3MM

7180 Medallic Art Company, Ltd
Medallic Art Company, Ltd
80 E. Airpark Vista Boulevard
Dayton, NV 89403   775-246-6000
800-843-9854
Fax: 775-246-6006
minted@medallic.com
www.medallic.com
Commemorative and premium awards
President: Robert W Hoff
Printing Information: 16 pages
Number of Employees: 40
Sales Information: $3MM to $5MM

7181 Mrs Fields Gourmet Gifts
Mrs. Fields
2855 E Cottonwood Parkway
Suite 400
Salt Lake City, UT 84121-7050   800-266-5437
www.mrsfields.com
Cookies and brownies; Gift baskets, tins and cookie jars
President: Neil Courtney
Credit Cards: AMEX; MasterCard
Catalog Cost: Free
Catalog Circulation: Mailed 6 time(s) per year
Printing Information: 22 pages in 4 colors on Glossy Stock
Press: Web Press
Binding: Saddle Stitched
Mailing List Information: Names for rent
In Business: 40 years
Number of Employees: 200
Sales Information: $60 Million

7182 Nashville Wraps Catalog
Nashville Wraps
242 Molly Walton Drive
Hendersonville, TN 37075   615-338-3200
800-547-9727
Fax: 800-646-0046
www.nashvillewraps.com
Gift and storage packaging products
President: Pam Danziger
Credit Cards: AMEX; MasterCard
Printing Information: 76 pages
Press: Web Press
Binding: Saddle Stitched
Mailing List Information: Names for rent
In Business: 37 years

7183 National Pen
National Pen Company
12121 Scripps Summit Dr.
San Diego, CA 92131   866-907-7367
www.nationalpen.com
Pens, pencils, electronics, executive gifts, greeting cards, office/desk accessories, bags and totes and apparel.
President & CEO: Peter Kelly
Catalog Cost: Free
In Business: 50 years
Sales Information: $300 Million

7184 Oriental Trading Business Edition
Oriental Trading Company
P.O. Box 2308
Omaha, NE 68103-2308   800-348-6483
www.orientaltrading.com
Promotional products
CEO: Sam Taylor
Catalog Cost: Free
Printing Information: in 4 colors
In Business: 84 years
Number of Employees: 2000

7185 Pacific Sportswear & Emblem Company
Pacific Sportswear Co.,Inc
Box 15211
San Diego, CA 92195-5211   619-281-6688
800-872-8778
Fax: 619-281-6687
info@pacsport.com
www.Pacsport.Com
Custom embroidered Flag Patches and Pins, headwear, embroidered patches, rubber keychains and lapel pins
President: Rich Soergel
CFO: Cathy Mellies
Marketing Manager: Rich Roengel
Production Manager: Bob Bond
Credit Cards: MasterCard; Visa
Catalog Cost: Free
Catalog Circulation: Mailed 52 time(s) per year to 10M
Average Order Size: $5000
Printing Information: 10 pages in 1 color on Matte Stock
Press: Web Press
Binding: Saddle Stitched
Mailing List Information: Names for rent
List Manager: Rich Soergel
In Business: 28 years
Number of Employees: 8
Sales Information: $1,000,000 - $5,000,000

7186 Pioneer National Latex
Pioneer National Latex
246 E 4th St
Ashland, OH 44805-2412   419-289-3300
800-537-6723
Fax: 419-289-7118
MassSales@natlatex.com
www.pioneernational.com
Balloons, punch balls and playballs
President: Vic Webby
Catalog Circulation: Mailed 1 time(s) per year
Printing Information: 40 pages in 4 colors
Binding: Saddle Stitched
Number of Employees: 250-
Sales Information: $25,000,000 - $50,000,000

7187 Positive Impressions Idea Showcase
Positive Impression Inc
150 Clearbrook Rd
Elmsford, NY 10523-1143   914-592-4133
800-895-5505
Fax: 914-592-0717
sales@positiveimpressions.com
www.positiveimpressions.com
Personalized incentives and awards
President: Jim Doyle
Credit Cards: AMEX; MasterCard
Catalog Cost: Free
Printing Information: 98 pages in 4 colors
Binding: Perfect Bound
In Business: 24 years
Number of Employees: 10-J
Sales Information: $500M to $1MM

7188 Print Craft, Inc.
Print Craft Incorporated
315 5th Avenue N.W.
Minneapolis, MN 55112   651-633-8122
800-217-8060
www.printcraft.com
Customized retail and commercial packaging, as well as printed products such as calendars, brochures, books, booklets, and reports
President: Mike Gallagher
Production Manager: Jon Riederer
Credit Cards: AMEX; MasterCard
Catalog Circulation: Mailed 2 time(s) per year
Printing Information: 60 pages in 4 colors on Glossy Stock
Press: Web Press
Binding: Saddle Stitched
In Business: 51 years
Number of Employees: 165

7189 Promotional Ideabook
Drawing Board
101 E Ninth St
Waynesboro, PA 17268   860-379-9911
800-527-9530
Fax: 800-253-1838
customerservice@drawingboard.com
www.drawingboard.com
Office products
President: Lee Bracken
Credit Cards: AMEX; MasterCard
Catalog Cost: Free
Catalog Circulation: Mailed 8 time(s) per year
Printing Information: 100 pages
Mailing List Information: Names for rent
Number of Employees: 300

7190 Quill Full Line
Quill Corporation
P.O. Box 37600
Philadelphia, PA 19101-600   800-982-3400
Fax: 800-789-8955
imprints@quill.com
www.quill.com
Electronics to enhance incentive programs, office furniture and office supplies
President: Michael Patriarca
Marketing Manager: James Meyer
Catalog Cost: Free
Catalog Circulation: Mailed 1 time(s) per year
Printing Information: 16 pages in 4 colors
Binding: Saddle Stitched
In Business: 59 years
Number of Employees: 1400

7191 Rainbow Industries
Brand Builders
PO Box 1087
Tenafly, NJ 07670-5087   973-575-8383
800-842-0527
Fax: 973-575-6001
jeffrey@brandbuildersllc.com
www.brandbuildersllc.com
Advertising specialties and executive gifts
President: Richard Brown
Marketing Manager: Jeffery Brown
Production Manager: Richard Brown
Catalog Cost: Free
Catalog Circulation: Mailed 10 time(s) per year to 10M
Average Order Size: $500
Printing Information: 20 pages in 4 colors on Glossy Stock
Press: Web Press
Binding: Folded
Mailing List Information: Names for rent
List Manager: R Brown
In Business: 21 years
Number of Employees: 15
Sales Information: $3MM to $5MM

7192 Rebechini Studios
Rebechini Studios,Inc
680 Fargo Ave
Elk Grove Vlg, IL 60007-4701   847-437-9030
800-229-6050
Fax: 847-437-0324
www.rsi-design.com
Architectural signage and castings
President: Glenn Rebechini
glenn.r@rsi-design.com
Production Manager: Vince Papp
vpapp@rsi-design.com
Credit Cards: MasterCard; Visa
Catalog Cost: Free
Catalog Circulation: Mailed 1 time(s) per year to 60M
Average Order Size: $1500
Printing Information: 18 pages in 1 color on Matte Stock
Press: Web Press
Binding: Saddle Stitched
Mailing List Information: Names for rent
In Business: 55 years

Number of Employees: 23
Sales Information: $1,000,000 - $5,000,000

7193 Siskiyou Fine Pewter & Gifts
Siskiyou Gifts
3551 Avion Drive
Medford, OR 97504   541-858-3400
                            800-866-7475
                       Fax: 800-650-9926
customerservice@siskiyougifts.com
www.siskiyougifts.com

Pewter licensed sports products (NFL, NASCAR, MLB, NCAA, NHL) as well as non-licensed pewter gift items. Glassware, belt buckles, key rings, wallets and checkbook covers, pins, gift boxes and more

President: Ken Stringer
Credit Cards: MasterCard
Catalog Cost: $5
Catalog Circulation: Mailed 2 time(s) per year
Printing Information: 12 pages in 4 colors on Glossy Stock
Mailing List Information: Names for rent
In Business: 25 years
Number of Employees: 40
Sales Information: $5,000,000 - $10,000,000

7194 Sweet Impressions Catalog
Sweet Impressions
812 Calle Plano
Carmarillo, CA 93012   805-383-2525
                               800-323-8037
evemarie@sweetimpressions.com
www.sweetimpressions.com

Imprinted chocolate coins and boxes of candy, promotional gifts

President: Alejandro Verzoub
Catalog Circulation: Mailed 1 time(s) per year
Printing Information: 20 pages
In Business: 28 years

7195 Things Remembered
Things Remembered
5043 Tuttle Crossing Blvd.
Dublin, OH 43016   614-760-8891
                          866-902-4438
                     Fax: 440-473-2018
customerservice@thingsremembered.com
www.thingsremembered.com

Recognition and incentive gifts - personalized

President: Michael Anthony
CFO: David Stefko
Buyers: Jeanette Brewster
Credit Cards: AMEX; MasterCard; Visa
Catalog Cost: Free
Catalog Circulation: Mailed 3 time(s) per year to 2.7MM
Printing Information: 32 pages in 4 colors on Glossy Stock
Press: Web Press
Binding: Saddle Stitched
Mailing List Information: Names for rent
In Business: 40 years
Number of Employees: 200

7196 Things You Never Knew Existed
Johnson Smith Company
P.O. Box 25600
Bradenton, FL 34206-5600   800-853-9490
customerservice@thingsyouneverknew.com
www.thingsyouneverknew.com

Funmakers, jokes, hobbies and novelties

CFO: David Crofoot
Marketing Manager: Kim Boyd
Founder: Alfred Johnson Smith
Credit Cards: AMEX; MasterCard; Visa
Catalog Cost: Free
Printing Information: in 4 colors on Matte Stock
Press: Web Press
Binding: Saddle Stitched
Mailing List Information: Names for rent

List Manager: Kris Temple
In Business: 110 years
Sales Information: $20MM to $50MM

7197 Thumb Things
Thumb Things, Inc.
1022 Robert St S
Saint Paul, MN 55118-1447   651-457-8900
                           Fax: 651-457-7049
lucyatbw@aol.com
www.thumbthings.com

Lapel pins, wedding invitations, promotional gifts

President: Lucy Baker
lucyatbw@aol.com
In Business: 36 years
Number of Employees: 4
Sales Information: $500M to $1MM

7198 Tourneau Watch
Tourneau Time Machine
12 E. 57th Street
New York, NY 10022   212-758-7300
                            800-348-3332
www.tourneau.com

Men's & women's watches

President: Jim Seuss
VP, Marketing: Andrew Block
Credit Cards: AMEX; MasterCard
Catalog Cost: Free
Catalog Circulation: Mailed 1 time(s) per year
Printing Information: 24 pages in 4 colors
Binding: Saddle Stitched
In Business: 115 years

7199 Trophyland USA
Trophyland USA Inc
7001 West 20th Avenue
Hialeah, FL 33014-4496   305-823-4830
                                 800-327-5820
                            Fax: 305-823-4836
info@trophyland.com
www.trophyland.com

Trophies, plaques, medals and awards

President: Tony Mendez
Marketing Manager: Clara Diaz
Fulfillment: Julio Gonzales
International Marketing Manager: Julio Gonzales
Buyers: Paul Fields
Julio Gonzales
Credit Cards: AMEX; MasterCard; Visa
Catalog Cost: Free
Catalog Circulation: Mailed 2 time(s) per year to 25M
Printing Information: 88 pages
Mailing List Information: Names for rent
List Manager: Clara Diaz
In Business: 38 years
Number of Employees: 75
Sales Information: $1,000,000 - $5,000,000

7200 Union Pen Company Full Line Catalog
Amsterdam Printing
166 Wallins Corners Road
Amsterdam, NY 12010   800-203-9917
                         Fax: 518-843-5204
www.unionpen.com

Direct marketer of imprinted promotional products

President: Morton Tenny
CFO: R Rosenthal
Credit Cards: AMEX; MasterCard
Catalog Cost: Free
Catalog Circulation: Mailed 6 time(s) per year to 15000
Average Order Size: $350
Printing Information: 48 pages in 4 colors on Matte Stock
Press: Web Press
Binding: Saddle Stitched
Mailing List Information: Names for rent
Will Trade Names: Yes
In Business: 116 years

Number of Employees: 150
Sales Information: $10,000,000 - $25,000,000

7201 Windjammer Promotions
Windjammer Promotions Inc
PO Box 1669
Framingham, MA 01701-1669   877-596-2505
                                800-721-5050
                           Fax: 508-877-1819

Promotional products to help generate sales, thank your customers or reward your valued employees

President: Anthony Nasch
Credit Cards: AMEX; MasterCard
Catalog Cost: Free
Catalog Circulation: Mailed 2 time(s) per year
Printing Information: 32 pages in 4 colors
Binding: Saddle Stitched
Number of Employees: 5
Sales Information: 3MM-5MM

Healthcare
General

7202 Aesthetic Procedure & Treatment Guide
Henry Schein
135 Duryea Rd.
Melville, NY 11747   631-843-5500
www.henryschein.com

Surgical and spa supplies.

Chairman: Stanley M. Bergman
President: James P. Breslawski
Catalog Cost: Free
Printing Information: 48 pages in 4 colors
In Business: 84 years
Number of Employees: 1900
Sales Information: $10.6 Billion

7203 AlcoPro
AlcoPro
2547 Sutherland Ave.
Knoxville, TN 37919   865-525-4900
                             800-227-9890
                        Fax: 865-525-4935
info@alcopro.com
www.alcopro.com

On-site drug and alcohol testing products for professional use

President: Jack Singleton
Marketing Manager: Greg Clark
Special Projects Coordinator: Sam Smithey
Customer Service Manager: Shannan Kennedy
Production Manager: Lorraine Jenkins
Credit Cards: MasterCard; Visa
Catalog Circulation: to 60M
Printing Information: 16 pages in 2 colors
In Business: 33 years
Number of Employees: 7
Sales Information: $1.1 Million

7204 AliMed Operating Room Products
AliMed, Inc
297 High Street
Dedham, MA 02026   781-329-2900
                          800-437-2966
                     Fax: 781-329-8392
customerservice@alimed.com
www.alimed.com

Medical and home healthcare equipment

President: Julian Cherubini
Production Manager: Fred Smith
Credit Cards: AMEX; MasterCard; Visa
Catalog Cost: Free
Catalog Circulation: Mailed 1 time(s) per year to 60K
Printing Information: 260 pages in 4 colors
Binding: Perfect Bound
In Business: 37 years
Sales Information: $20-50 Million

7205 Allied Healthcare Products
Allied Healthcare Products
1720 Sublette Ave
St Louis, MO 63110-1927   314-771-2400
                                 800-444-3954
                            Fax: 314-771-4616
                 customerservice@alliedhpi.com
                           www.Alliedhpi.Com

Medical surgical equipment

President: Earl R Refsland
CFO: Dan Dunn
Printing Information: 25 pages
Number of Employees: 350

7206 Arista Surgical Supply Company
AliMed, Inc.
297 High Street
Dedham, MA 02026   781-329-2900
                          800-225-2610
                     Fax: 781-329-8392
                      info@alimed.com
                       www.alimed.com

Surgical supplies, surgical instruments, homecare, sutures, dressings, lab glasswares, stethoscopes, scalpel blades, spnygmomanometer, etc

President: Irving Horowitz
Credit Cards: AMEX; MasterCard; Visa
Catalog Cost: Free
Catalog Circulation: Mailed 6 time(s) per year
Printing Information: 80 pages on Matte Stock
Press: Letterpress
Binding: Saddle Stitched
Mailing List Information: Names for rent
In Business: 59 years
Number of Employees: 15
Sales Information: $1MM to $3MM

7207 Armstrong Medical Industries
Armstrong Medical Industries, Inc.
575 Knightsbridge Parkway
PO Box 700
Lincolnshire, IL 60069-700   847-913-0101
                                    800-323-4220
                               Fax: 847-913-0138
                         csr@armstrongmedical.com
                          www.armstrongmedical.com

Medical equipment, medical carts and CPR manikins

President: Warren Armstrong
CFO: Rose West
Marketing Manager: Corinne Walker
International Marketing Manager: Mikki Erickson
Credit Cards: AMEX; MasterCard; Visa
Catalog Cost: Free
Catalog Circulation: Mailed 1 time(s) per year to 150M
Printing Information: 180 pages in 4 colors on Glossy Stock
Press: Web Press
Binding: Perfect Bound
Mailing List Information: Names for rent
In Business: 58 years
Number of Employees: 95
Sales Information: $13 Million

7208 Athletics & Schools Sports Medicine Catalog
Henry Schein
135 Duryea Rd.
Melville, NY 11747   631-843-5500
                     www.henryschein.com

Medical supplies

Chairman: Stanley M. Bergman
President: James P. Breslawski
Catalog Cost: Free
Catalog Circulation: Mailed 1 time(s) per year
Printing Information: 450 pages in 4 colors
In Business: 84 years
Number of Employees: 1900
Sales Information: $10.6 Billion

7209 BSN Sports Athletic Performance
BSN Sports
PO Box 7726
Dallas, TX 75209   800-856-3488
                     Fax: 800-899-0149
                     www.bsnsports.com

Exercise equipment.

Chair & CEO: Adam Blumenfeld
President, COO & General Counsel: Terry Babilla
Catalog Cost: Free
Printing Information: 48 pages in 4 colors
In Business: 44 years
Number of Employees: 1200
Sales Information: $500 Million

7210 BSN Sports Direct
BSN Sports
PO Box 7726
Dallas, TX 75209   800-856-3488
                     Fax: 800-899-0149
                     www.bsnsports.com

Equipment for team sports, facilities and physical education.

Chair & CEO: Adam Blumenfeld
President, COO & General Counsel: Terry Babilla
Catalog Cost: Free
Printing Information: 184 pages in 4 colors
In Business: 44 years
Number of Employees: 1200
Sales Information: $500 Million

7211 Beck-Lee
Beck-Lee
PO Box 528
Stratford, CT 06607-528   203-332-7678
                                 888-599-5556
                            Fax: 800-525-4568
                            info@becklee.com
                             www.becklee.com

Cardiology and echo products

President: Bill Lichtenberger
Credit Cards: AMEX; MasterCard
Catalog Cost: Free
Catalog Circulation: Mailed 2 time(s) per year to 50000
Average Order Size: $200
Printing Information: in 4 colors on Glossy Stock
Binding: Saddle Stitched
Mailing List Information: Names for rent
In Business: 63 years
Number of Employees: 19
Sales Information: $5,000,000

7212 Bruce Medical Supply
Bruce Medical Supply
411 Waverley Oaks Road
Suite 154
Waltham, MA 02452   781-894-6262
                           800-225-8446
                      Fax: 781-894-9519
                sales@brucemedical.com
                  www.brucemedical.com

Health and medical supplies

President: Richard A. Najarian
Credit Cards: AMEX; MasterCard; Visa
Catalog Cost: Free
Catalog Circulation: Mailed 4 time(s) per year
Printing Information: 64 pages in 4 colors on Glossy Stock
Press: Web Press
Binding: Saddle Stitched
In Business: 35 years
Sales Information: $ 3-5 Million

7213 Bureau for At-Risk Youth
The Bureau for At-Risk Youth
PO Box 170
Farmingville, NY 11738   800-999-6884
                           Fax: 800-262-1886
                            info@at-risk.com
                             www.at-risk.com

Health and educational books and videos on topics including drugs, self-esteem, safe schools, parenting and professional development

President: James Werz
Credit Cards: MasterCard; Visa
Catalog Cost: Free
Printing Information: 48 pages

7214 CED Process Minerals-Engineering & Sales
CED Process Minerals
1653 Merriman Road
Suite 102
Akron, OH 44313-5278   330-869-0248
                         Fax: 330-869-0104
                 www.cedprocessminerals.com/

Applications and industries include high precision casting, dental appliances, abrasives and polishing media, coatings, and fillers

President: J Erwin
Printing Information: in 2 colors
In Business: 34 years

7215 CED Process Minerals-Manufacturing
CED Process Minerals
221 Sand Mine Road
PO Box 369
Gore, VA 22637-369   540-858-3224
                       Fax: 540-858-3227
                www.Cedprocessminerals.Com

Applications and industries include high precision casting, dental appliances, abrasives and polishing media, coatings, and fillers

President: Mark Basile
Printing Information: in 2 colors
In Business: 34 years
Sales Information: $3MM to $5MM

7216 CM Almy General
CM Almy
228 Sound Beach Avenue
Greenwich, CT 06870-2644   203-531-7600
                                  800-225-2569
                             Fax: 203-531-9048
                         almyaccess@almy.com
                              www.almy.com

Supplier of decorative furnishings, apparel, worship related products and gifts to churches, religious institutions, their clergy and members

President: Stephen Sendler
CFO: Mike Mc Gown
Credit Cards: MasterCard
Catalog Cost: Free
Printing Information: 208 pages in 4 colors on Glossy Stock
In Business: 123 years
Sales Information: $5MM to $10MM

7217 Chief Supply
Chief Supply
1400 Executive Parkway
Eugene, OR 97401   888-588-8569
                  orders@chiefsupply.com
                   www.chiefsupply.com

Firefighting, law enforcement and emergency medical supplies, including apparel and gear bags, badges, flashlights, batteries and chargers, cases and antennas, specialty and close-out items

President: John Utley
In Business: 40 years
Sales Information: $20MM to $50MM

7218   Clinical Health Products

Clinical Health Products
PO Box 425
Stratford, CT 06615-425   800-327-0235
Fax: 800-525-4568
info@chpmed.com
www.chpmed.com

Cardiology products

Printing Information: 180 pages
In Business: 35 years

7219   Complimentary Health Reference Catalog

Medical Arts Press® Corporation
PO Box 43200
Minneapolis, MN 55443-200   800-328-2179
Fax: 800-328-0023
www.medicalartspress.com

Chiropractic practice supplies, software and forms

Credit Cards: AMEX; MasterCard; Visa
Catalog Cost: Free
Catalog Circulation: Mailed 2 time(s) per year
Printing Information: 725 pages in 4 colors
Mailing List Information: Names for rent
In Business: 58 years
Number of Employees: 600

7220   Cone Instruments

Cone Instruments
6850 Southbelt Dr
Caledonia, MI 49316   440-248-1035
800-321-6964
Fax: 440-248-9477
service@coneinstruments.com
www.Coneinstruments.Com

Ultrasound systems, medical supplies and accessories for radiology, ultrasound and nuclear medicine, service and repair department

President: Patrick Beck
CEO: Matt Witzky
International Marketing Manager: Susan DeSantis
Catalog Circulation: Mailed 4 time(s) per year to 160M
Printing Information: 240 pages
Press: Web Press
Mailing List Information: Names for rent
In Business: 39 years
Number of Employees: 20
Sales Information: $5MM to $10MM

7221   D&E Pharmaceuticals

DNE Nutraceuticals
700 Central Avenue
Farmingdale, NJ 07727   212-235-5200
800-221-1833
Fax: 212-235-5243
info@dnenutra.com
www.dnenutra.com

Pharmaceutical products, health aids, fitness aids and over the counter drugs

President: Eric Organ
Credit Cards: AMEX; MasterCard; Visa
Catalog Cost: Free
Catalog Circulation: Mailed 4 time(s) per year to 500,0
Average Order Size: $55
Printing Information: 115 pages in 4 colors
Mailing List Information: Names for rent
List Company: D&E Belgium
Number of Employees: 25
Sales Information: $ 20-50 Million

7222   Dedicated Distribution

Dedicated Distribution
640 Miami Avenue
Kansas City, KS 66105-2140   913-371-2200
800-325-8367
Fax: 913-371-2252
ddinfo@dedicateddistribution.com
www.dedicateddistribution.com

Home medical products

President: Steven Cole
CFO: Gary Strub
Marketing Manager: Jennifer Cisneros
Credit Cards: AMEX; MasterCard
Catalog Cost: Free
Catalog Circulation: Mailed 1 time(s) per year
Printing Information: 74 pages
Binding: Perfect Bound
In Business: 25 years

7223   Enzymatic Natural Medicines

Enzymatic Therapy, Inc.
825 Challenger Drive
Green Bay, WI 54311-2310   920-469-1313
800-783-2286
Fax: 920-469-4444
www.enzy.com

Products for good health

Chairman: Charles Baird, Ira Brind
President: Randy Rose
CFO: Dick Danen
Credit Cards: MasterCard; Visa
Printing Information: 92 pages in 4 colors
Binding: Saddle Stitched

7224   Ergonomics/Occupational Health & Safety

AliMed, Inc.
297 High Street
Dedham, MA 02026-2852   781-329-2900
800-225-2610
Fax: 781-329-8392
info@alimed.com
www.alimed.com

Ergonomic products and accessories

President: Julian Cherubini
Marketing Manager: Jackie Stansbury
Credit Cards: AMEX; MasterCard; Visa
Catalog Cost: Free
Catalog Circulation: Mailed 12 time(s) per year
Printing Information: 168 pages in 4 colors on Glossy Stock
Binding: Saddle Stitched
In Business: 30 years
Number of Employees: 100

7225   Ferno Physical Therapy & Sports Equipment

Ferno-Washington, Inc
70 Weil Way
Wilmington, OH 45177-9371   937-382-1451
877-733-0911
Fax: 937-382-1191
www.fernoems.com

Physical therapy and sports equipment

Chairman: Elroy Bourgraf
CFO: Paul Riordan
Printing Information: 82 pages in 4 colors
Binding: Perfect Bound
In Business: 56 years
Number of Employees: 440
Sales Information: $ 34 Million

7226   Fluke Biomedical

Fluke Biomedical
6045 Cochran Road
Cleveland, OH 44139-3303   440-248-9300
800-850-4608
Fax: 440-349-2307
sales@flukebiomedical.com
www.flukebiomedical.com/rms

Medical and industrial imaging instruments and accessories

Marketing Manager: Susan Janney
Buyers: Frank Talbot
Credit Cards: AMEX; MasterCard
Catalog Cost: Free
Catalog Circulation: Mailed 1 time(s) per year to 15M
Average Order Size: $1000
Printing Information: 400 pages in 4 colors on Glossy Stock
Press: Web Press
Binding: Perfect Bound
Mailing List Information: Names for rent
In Business: 37 years
Number of Employees: 35
Sales Information: $10MM to $20MM

7227   Foot & Ankle Sports Medicine Catalog

Henry Schein
135 Duryea Rd.
Melville, NY 11747   631-843-5500
www.henryschein.com

Medical supplies

Chairman: Stanley M. Bergman
President: James P. Breslawski
Catalog Cost: Free
Catalog Circulation: Mailed 1 time(s) per year
Printing Information: 450 pages in 4 colors
In Business: 84 years
Number of Employees: 1900
Sales Information: $10.6 Billion

7228   Good-Lite Company

Good-Lite Company
1155 Jansen Farm Drive
Elgin, IL 60123   847-841-1145
800-362-3860
Fax: 847-841-1149
orders@good-lite.com
www.good-lite.com

Vision screening instruments and charts

In Business: 85 years

7229   Healthcare Supplies

American Healthcare Supply
100 S Milwaukee Ave.
Vernon Hills, IL 60061-4035   800-677-7180
Fax: 800-677-7190
healthcare@americanhotel.com
www.americanhealthcaresupply.com

Healthcare supplies

Chairman: James F. Leahy
President: Angela Korompilas
Catalog Cost: Free
Printing Information: 16 pages in 4 colors
In Business: 151 years
Number of Employees: 1000
Sales Information: $850 Million

7230   Henry Schein Medical Reference Guide

Henry Schein
135 Duryea Rd.
Melville, NY 11747   631-843-5500
www.henryschein.com

Medical supplies

Chairman: Stanley M. Bergman
President: James P. Breslawski
Catalog Cost: Free
Printing Information: 642 pages in 4 colors
In Business: 84 years
Number of Employees: 1900
Sales Information: $10.6 Billion

7231   Henry Schein and Preferred Brand Reference Guide

Henry Schein
135 Duryea Rd.
Melville, NY 11747   631-843-5500
www.henryschein.com

Medical supplies

Chairman: Stanley M. Bergman
President: James P. Breslawski
Catalog Cost: Free
Printing Information: 124 pages in 4 colors

In Business: 84 years
Number of Employees: 1900
Sales Information: $10.6 Billion

7232 Hopkin's Medical Products
Hopkin's Medical Products
5 Greenwood Place
Baltimore, MD 21208-2763   410-484-2036
800-835-1995
Fax: 410-484-4036
customerservice@hopkinsmedical.net
www.hopkinsmedicalproducts.com

Complete line of medical products for doctors and nurses

President: Philip M. Kenney
CFO: Charles Goldberg
VP: Lou Klug
CEO: Philip M. Kenney
Credit Cards: MasterCard; Visa
Catalog Cost: Free
Catalog Circulation: Mailed 1 time(s) per year
Printing Information: 48 pages in 1 color
In Business: 70 years
Sales Information: $ 1-3 Million

7233 Human Kinetics Academic & Professional Resources
Human Kinetics
1607 N Market Street
PO Box 5076
Champaign, IL 61820-5076   800-747-4457
Fax: 217-351-1549
info@hkusa.com
www.humankinetics.com

Information on physical activity success in sports

Facility Manager: Bill Squires
Sport Club Management: Matthew Robinson
Credit Cards: AMEX; MasterCard; Visa
Catalog Cost: Free
Printing Information: 57 pages in 4 colors on Glossy Stock
Binding: Saddle Stitched
In Business: 40 years
Number of Employees: 80

7234 Interactive Therapeutics
AliMed
297 High Street
Dedham, MA 02026-805   781-329-2900
800-225-2610
Fax: 781-329-8392
info@alimed.com
www.alimed.com

Teaching tools to help with orthopedic therapy

President: Len Ivins
Credit Cards: AMEX; MasterCard
In Business: 35 years
Sales Information: $440,000

7235 KidSafety of America
KidSafety of America
6288 Susana Street
Chino, CA 91710   909-627-8700
800-524-1156
Fax: 909-627-8777
info@kidsafetystore.com
www.kidsafetystore.com

Educational books and videos to promote the health and safety of children and their families

President: Peter D Osilaja
Buyers: Virginia Anorade
Credit Cards: AMEX; MasterCard; Visa
Catalog Cost: Free
Mailing List Information: Names for rent
In Business: 23 years
Number of Employees: 10
Sales Information: $930,000

7236 Latest Products Corporation
Latest Products Corporation
PO Box 190
Syosset, NY 11791   516-367-4700
800-288-3547
Fax: 516-367-4714
info@latestproducts.net

Specialty items for nursing homes, government, state agencies, and hospitals primarily for use in laundry and housekeeping departments

VP: Aaron Hermen
Credit Cards: AMEX; MasterCard
Catalog Cost: Free
Catalog Circulation: Mailed 4 time(s) per year to 75K
Printing Information: 96 pages in 2 colors
Press: Web Press
Binding: Saddle Stitched
In Business: 43 years
Sales Information: $500,000

7237 Medical-Diagnostic Specialty Gases
Medical-Diagnostic Specialty Gases
6141 Easton Road
Box 310
Plumsteadville, PA 18949   215-766-8860
877-715-8651
Fax: 215-766-2476
solutions.center@airliquide.com
www.scottgas.com

Gases and cylinders

Catalog Circulation: Mailed 1 time(s) per year
Printing Information: 34 pages
Binding: Saddle Stitched

7238 Moore Medical Corporation
Moore Medical LLC
1690 New Britain Avenue
PO Box 4066
Farmington, CT 06032-4066   860-826-3600
800-234-1464
Fax: 877-881-0710
e-support@mooremedical.com

Medical supplies and medical equipment

President: Rick Frey
Manager Vendor Promotions: Ryan Stefanski
Credit Cards: MasterCard; Visa
Catalog Cost: Free
Catalog Circulation: Mailed 3 time(s) per year
Printing Information: 180 pages in 2 colors
List Company: Direct Media
In Business: 63 years
Number of Employees: 305
Sales Information: $ 16 Million

7239 Ohaus Corporation
Ohaus Corporation
7 Campus Drive
Suite 310
Parsippany, NJ 07054   973-377-9000
800-672-7722
Fax: 973-593-0359
sales@ohaus.com
www.ohaus.com

Manufacturer of electronic and mechanical scales, balances and accessories for the laboratory, education, and industrial markets

President: Jim Ohaus
CFO: Peter Mender
Catalog Cost: Free
In Business: 108 years
Number of Employees: 67
Sales Information: $11.6MM

7240 Parlay International
Parlay International
712 Bancroft Rd
505
Walnut Creek, CA 94598   800-457-2752
Fax: 925-939-1414
info@parlay.com
www.parlay.com

Collection of reproducible resources: one-page handouts on a variety of topics for insurance companies, hospitals, military personnel

President: Robert Lester
In Business: 28 years
Sales Information: $500M to $1MM

7241 Physicians Laboratory Supply
Cen-Med Enterprises, Inc.
121 Jersey Ave
New Brunswick, NJ 08901   732-447-1100
800-470-3570
Fax: 732-249-0008
info@cenmed.com
www.cenmed.com

Laboratory supplies

President: Shakila Chaudhry
Catalog Circulation: Mailed 1 time(s) per year
Printing Information: 12 pages in 4 colors
Binding: Saddle Stitched
In Business: 23 years

7242 Polar Ware Health Care
Polar Ware Company
502 Highway 67
Kiel, WI 53042-3943   920-894-2293
800-237-3655
Fax: 920-459-5291
www.polarware.com

Medical ware bedpans, sinks, trays, etc

Catalog Circulation: Mailed 1 time(s) per year
Printing Information: 20 pages in 2 colors
Binding: Saddle Stitched
In Business: 105 years

7243 Precision Dynamics Corporation
PDC
27770 N. Entertainment Drive
Suite 200
Valencia, CA 91355-3490   818-897-1111
Fax: 818-899-4045
info@pdcorp.com
www.pdcorp.com

From ID bracelets and urinary bags to aprons and splints

President: Robert M. Case
Marketing Manager: Trish Ostroski
Vice President: Rudy Neal
Catalog Circulation: Mailed 1 time(s) per year
Printing Information: 56 pages in 4 colors
Binding: Saddle Stitched
In Business: 55 years

7244 Pro Supply Catalog
Oliver Outlet
15113 SW Barcelona Way
Bearverton, OR 97007-2195   877-652-0031
Fax: 860-432-7393
Sales@ProSupplyCo.Com
olivershardware.com

Medical imaging supplies and equipment

President: Amy Wheeler-Paige
Credit Cards: AMEX; MasterCard
Sales Information: $1MM to $3MM

7245 **Puritan Medical Products**
Puritan Medical
PO Box 149
Guilford, ME 04443-149
207-876-3311
800-321-2313
Fax: 207-876-3130
sales@puritanmedproducts.com
www.puritanmedproducts.com

Wooden tongue dispensers, cervical scrapers and applicators

CFO: Mark Brewer
Marketing Manager: Timothy L Templet
Credit Cards: AMEX; MasterCard
Catalog Cost: Free
Catalog Circulation: Mailed 1 time(s) per year
Printing Information: 35 pages in 4 colors on Glossy Stock
Mailing List Information: Names for rent
In Business: 86 years
Number of Employees: 340
Sales Information: $20MM to $50MM

7246 **Rad Care Products**
Red Care Products,Inc.
P.O.Box 60546
PO Box 60546
Sunnyvale, CA 94088-546
408-244-1818
800-882-4413
Fax: 408-244-1269
sales@radcare.net
www.radcare.net

Radiotherapy Treatment Accessories and Supplies, Dosimetry Supplies, Block Fabrication and Shop Hardware

Catalog Circulation: Mailed 1 time(s) per year
Printing Information: 112 pages
Binding: Perfect Bound
In Business: 25 years
Sales Information: $500M to $1MM

7247 **Redding Medical**
Redding Medical
152 Westminster Rd
Reisterstown, MD 21136-1027
410-526-9755
800-733-2796
Fax: 410-526-9759
info@reddingmedical.com
www.reddingmedical.com

Medical supplies, medical equipment and instruments

President: Sharon Shipe
VP: David Shipe
Credit Cards: AMEX; MasterCard
Catalog Cost: Free
Catalog Circulation: Mailed 14 time(s) per year
Printing Information: 14 pages in 2 colors on Matte Stock
Press: Sheetfed Press
Mailing List Information: Names for rent
In Business: 39 years
Sales Information: $ 1.5 Million

7248 **Sammons Preston**
Patterson Medical
28100 Torch Parkway
Suite 700
Warrenville, IL 60555-3938
630-393-6000
800-475-5036
Fax: 630-393-7600
www.pattersonmedical.com

Healthcare products to lighten chores, increase comfort and adapt household items for easier use

President: David Sproat
CEO: Scott Anderson
Credit Cards: AMEX; MasterCard
Printing Information: in 3 colors
Sales Information: $ 9 Million

7249 **School Health Corporation**
School Health Corporation
865 Muirfield Drive
Hanover Park, IL 60133-5461
866-323-5465
Fax: 800-235-1305
customerservice@schoolhealth.com
www.schoolhealth.com

Health supplies and equipment to schools

Senior Program Manager: Dr. Ray Heipp
Printing Information: in 3 colors
In Business: 65 years
Number of Employees: 70
Sales Information: $ 10-20 Million

7250 **School Kids Healthcare**
School Kids Healthcare
5235 International Drive
Suite B
Cudahy, WI 53110
866-558-0686
Fax: 800-558-1551
service@schoolkidshealthcare.com
www.schoolkidshealthcare.com

School health products and nurse supplies; nursing education, emergency supplies, first air, anatomical models, displays & posters, infection & flu control

Marketing Manager: Michael Margolies
Credit Cards: AMEX; MasterCard; Visa
Catalog Cost: Free
Catalog Circulation: Mailed 1 time(s) per year
Average Order Size: $350
Printing Information: 300 pages in 4 colors
Press: Web Press
Binding: Perfect Bound
In Business: 9 years

7251 **St. John Companies**
PDC Healthcare
27770 N. Entertainment Drive
Suite 200
Valencia, CA 91355
818-897-1111
800-435-4242
Fax: 818-686-9317
intl@pdcorp.com
www.pdchealthcare.com

Goods for mammography professionals

President: Robert Case
Production Manager: Donna Brooks
VP Healthcare Sales: Rudy Neal
Finance Director: Michelle Wen
Director, Research & Development: Richard Kapusniak
Printing Information: 156 pages
Press: Web Press
In Business: 55 years
Number of Employees: 35

7252 **Stephens Instruments**
Stephens Instruments
2500 Sandersville Rd
Lexington, KY 40511-1846
859-259-4924
800-354-7848
Fax: 859-259-4926
stephensinst@aol.com
www.Stephensinst.Com

Surgical and medical instruments

President: Dhaval K Shukla
Catalog Cost: $100
Catalog Circulation: Mailed 1 time(s) per year
Printing Information: 134 pages in 2 colors
In Business: 20 years
Sales Information: $10MM to $20MM

7253 **Support Plus**
Support Plus
5581 Hudson Industrial Parkway
Hudson, OH 44236-0099
844-276-2020
www.supportplus.com

Medical hosiery, comfort shoes and aids to daily living

President: Ed Janos
Buyers: Marilyn Mygan

Credit Cards: AMEX; MasterCard
Catalog Cost: Free
Catalog Circulation: Mailed 10 time(s) per year to 8MM
Average Order Size: $70
Printing Information: 80 pages in 4 colors on Glossy Stock
Press: Web Press
Binding: Saddle Stitched
Mailing List Information: Names for rent
List Manager: The Other List Companny
In Business: 45 years
Sales Information: $ 10-20 Million

7254 **Surgical Products Guide**
Surgical Solutions Group
5920 Longbow Drive
Boulder, CO 80301-3299
303-530-2300
800-255-8522
Fax: 303-530-6285
www.valleylabs.com

Surgical medical products

Printing Information: 77 pages
Binding: Saddle Stitched

7255 **The Parthenon Company**
The Parthenon Company, Inc.
3311 West 2400 South
Salt Lake City, UT 84119
801-972-5184
800-453-8898
Fax: 801-972-4734
info@parthenoninc.com
www.parthenoninc.com

Ostonomy products, wound care, skin care, and urological products

President: Nicholas Mihalopoulos
Founder & CEO : Nick Mihalopoulos, R.Ph., Ph.D.
President : Jason Mihalopoulos, MPH, MBA, MS Nu
Credit Cards: AMEX; MasterCard; Visa
Catalog Cost: Free
Printing Information: 100 pages
In Business: 54 years
Number of Employees: 8
Sales Information: $ 1.3 Million

7256 **Wine Country Gift Baskets Catalog**
Wine Country Gift Baskets
4225 N Palm Street
Fullerton, CA 92835
800-394-0394
Fax: 714-525-0746
www.winecountrygiftbaskets.com

Variety of gift baskets

President: John Brian
Marketing Manager: Bill Martin
Credit Cards: AMEX; MasterCard
Catalog Cost: Free
In Business: 29 years
Number of Employees: 72
Sales Information: $3.7 Million

Heating & Cooling
Fans & Ventilators

7257 **Ace Industrial Products**
Associated Equipment Corporation
5043 Farlin Ave
St Louis, MO 63115-1204
314-679-2540
800-949-1472
Fax: 314-385-3254
ace@associatedequip.com
www.aceindustrialproducts.com

Hoses, vents, dust collectors and other cleaning supplies

President: Tim Cronin
Catalog Cost: Free
Catalog Circulation: Mailed 1 time(s) per year to 2000
Printing Information: 8 pages in 4 colors on Glossy Stock

Binding: Folded
In Business: 48 years

7258 Air Filtronix

Air Filtronix
154 Huron Avenue
Clifton, NJ 07013-2949 973-779-5577
800-452-8510
Fax: 973-779-5954
TechnicalSupport@airfiltronix.com
www.airfiltronix.com

Portable ductless fume hoods

Credit Cards: MasterCard; Visa
Catalog Cost: Free
Catalog Circulation: Mailed 1 time(s) per year
Printing Information: 17 pages in 4 colors on Glossy Stock
Binding: Saddle Stitched
In Business: 36 years
Number of Employees: 12

7259 Air Handling Systems

Air Handling Systems
5 Lunar Dr
Woodbridge, CT 06525-2320 203-389-9595
800-367-3828
Fax: 203-389-8340
sales@airhand.com
www.airhand.com

Industrial air handling

President: David E Scott
DScott@airhand.com
Marketing Manager: Wayne Noron
Sales Manager: Curt Corum
Credit Cards: AMEX; MasterCard; Visa
In Business: 46 years
Number of Employees: 13
Sales Information: $2.19 Million

7260 Air-Jet

Air-Jet, Inc.
100 West Windsor Avenue
Elkhart, IN 46514 574-262-4511
800-735-5272
Fax: 574-262-2075
info@continentalindustries.com
www.continentalindustries.com

Air distribution products and venting systems

Chairman: Paul Leiter
President: David Leiter
CFO: Judy Leiter
Manager: Doug Gaugler
Catalog Cost: Free
Printing Information: 90 pages in 4 colors
In Business: 72 years
Number of Employees: 200
Sales Information: $50,000,000

7261 Airmaster Fan Company

Airmaster Fan Company
1300 Falahee Road
Suite 5
Jackson, MI 49203 517-764-2300
800-255-3084
Fax: 517-764-3838
sales@airmasterfan.com
www.airmasterfan.com

Commercial and industrial fans and air circulators

President: Richard Stone
CFO: Ron Johnson
Marketing Manager: Jane Hemer
jhemer@airmasterfan.com
VP of Sales & Marketing: Ed Laabs
elaabs@airmasterfan.com
Sales & Marketing - Marketing Assis: Megan Stevens
mstevens@airmasterfan.com
Credit Manager: KimKilgore
kkilgore@airmasterfan.com
International Marketing Manager: Lisa Kuntz
Buyers: Melinda Long

Catalog Cost: Free
Catalog Circulation: Mailed 2 time(s) per year to 20M
Average Order Size: $300
Printing Information: 30 pages
Mailing List Information: Names for rent
List Manager: MaryAnn Talbot
In Business: 129 years
Number of Employees: 60
Sales Information: $8.7 Million

7262 Aitken Products

Aitken Products
566 N. Eagle Street
PO Box 151
Geneva, OH 44041-151 440-466-5711
800-569-9341
Fax: 440-466-5716
www.aitkenproducts.com

Ceiling fans, electric and gas heating equipment

President: David Aitken
EVP: Sue Aitken
Manager: Jack Goellner
In Business: 58 years
Number of Employees: 10
Sales Information: $1,000,000

7263 American Coolair Corporation

American Coolair Corporation
PO Box 2300
Jacksonville, FL 32203-2300 904-389-3646
Fax: 904-387-3449
info@coolair.com
www.coolair.com

Commercial, industrial and greenhouse ventilation systems, ventilation systems for the dairy and poultry industry

President: Harry M Graves Jr
CFO: Cindy Rousis
Marketing Manager: Mark Fales
Sales: Terry Wimberly
Sales: Tyler Morrison
In Business: 87 years
Number of Employees: 20
Sales Information: $10,000,000

7264 EBM Industries

Ebm Papst Inc
100 Hyde Road
P.O. Box 4009
Farmington, CT 06034-2835 860-674-1515
Fax: 860-674-8536
sales@us.ebmpapst.com
www.ebmpapst.us

Blowers

President: Wesley A Roth
Advanced Technology Manager: Armin Hauer
Credit Cards: AMEX; MasterCard
Number of Employees: 150
Sales Information: $10,000,000 - $25,000,000

7265 Fantech

Fantech
10048 Industrial Blvd
Lenexa, KS 66215-2112 913-752-6000
800-747-1762
Fax: 913-752-6466
USsupport@fantech.net
www.Fantech.Net

Exhaust fans and inline centrifugal duct fans

President: Ola Wettergren
Marketing Manager: Glenn Thompson
In Business: 15 years
Number of Employees: 20
Sales Information: $5MM to $10MM

7266 Fasco Industries

Fasco
11206 Farm Road 2182
Cassville, MO 65625 517-663-2161
800-252-1182
Fax: 417-847-8273
fascohelp@regalbeloit.com
www.fasco.com

Motors, gear motors and blowers

President: Joesph Palazzi
In Business: 104 years
Number of Employees: 5000

7267 FloAire

Flo Aire National
1730 Walton Road
Suite # 203
Blue Bell, PA 19422 610-239-8405
800-726-5623
Fax: 610-239-8941
sales@floaire.com
www.floaire.com

Roof ventilators and exhaust fans

President: Ralph Kearney
Marketing Manager: L Collier
Number of Employees: 50
Sales Information: $5MM to $10MM

7268 Jennfan Commercial Products Group

Daikin Industries
13600 Industrial Park Boulevard
Minneapolis, MN 55441-3743 763-553-5330
800-432-1342
Fax: 763-553-5008
www.daikinmcquay.com

Commercial and industrial ventilating equipment

President: Charles Tambornino
In Business: 90 years
Number of Employees: 335
Sales Information: $25,000,000 - $50,000,000

7269 Kooltronic

Kooltronic, Inc.
30 Pennington Hopewell Road
Pennington, NJ 08534 609-466-3400
800-321-KOOL
Fax: 609-466-1114
sales@kooltronic.com
www.kooltronic.com

Compact fans, blowers, heat exchangers, air conditioners

Chairman: Jerry Freedman
President: Barry Freedman
Marketing Manager: Jeffrey Marcinowski
CEO: Anne Freedman
Catalog Circulation: Mailed 1 time(s) per year
Printing Information: 213 pages
Mailing List Information: Names for rent
In Business: 62 years
Number of Employees: 200
Sales Information: $25,000,000 - $50,000,000

Pumps & Compressors

7270 AAF-Environmental Commercial Product Group

Daikin Applied
13600 Industrial Park Boulevard
Minneapolis, MN 55441-3743 763-553-5330
800-432-1342
Fax: 763-553-5177
www.daikinmcquay.com

Air conditioning, heating, ventilation and refrigeration systems for industrial, commercial and institutional use.

Chairman: Robin Page
President: Eric Roberts
CFO: Barbara Salisbury
Marketing Manager: Don Winter
Production Manager: Hugh Crowther

VP, Sales and Marketing: Duane Rothstein
In Business: 141 years
Number of Employees: 450

7271 AJ Abrams Company
AJ Abrams company inc.
155 Post Road East
Suite 9
Westport, CT 06881-5171   203-226-3010
                                 800-842-3011
                    Fax: 203-226-8289
                    ajabramsco@ajabrams.com
                    www.ajabrams.com

Industrial hygiene/safety instruments

President: Russ Kraiterman
Manager: Bob Legrand
Credit Cards: AMEX; MasterCard
Catalog Cost: Free
Catalog Circulation: to 3M
Average Order Size: $1500
Printing Information: in 2 colors on Glossy Stock
Mailing List Information: Names for rent
In Business: 45 years
Number of Employees: 10

7272 Ace Pump Corporation
Ace Pump Corporation
1650 Channel Avenue
PO Box 13187
Memphis, TN 38113-187   901-948-8514
                    Fax: 901-774-6147
                    www.acepumps.com

Vacuum pumps and centrifugal water pumps

President: Andy Randle
CFO: Roy Bell
Manager: Annie Low
In Business: 68 years
Number of Employees: 96
Sales Information: $6.3 Million

7273 Ace Tank
Ace Tank & Equipment Company
18340 Andover Park W.
Tukwila, WA 98188   206-281-5000
                           800-426-2880
                    Fax: 888-475-1418
                    sales.800@acetank.com
                    www.acetank.com

Fuel tanks, oil tanks, fueling nozzles

Chairman: R.A. Reese
President: Robert Thompson
CFO: Jack Bruton
VP: Bill Durkin
Purchasing Manager: Ron Radach
Credit Cards: MasterCard; Visa
Catalog Cost: Free
Catalog Circulation: Mailed 26 time(s) per year
Printing Information: 250 pages
Binding: Perfect Bound
In Business: 78 years
Number of Employees: 60

7274 Acme Engineering & Manufacturing Corporation
Acme
PO Box 978
Muskogee, OK 74402   844-411-4761
                    Fax: 918-682-0134
                    marketing@acmefan.com
                    www.acmefan.com

Roof, wall and ceiling centrifugal exhausters

Chairman: Edward Buddrus
President: Lee Buddrus
CFO: Brian Combs
Marketing Manager: Rick Reeves
Production Manager: Michael Causey
Sales Manager: Ralph Kosir
In Business: 77 years
Number of Employees: 500
Sales Information: $50MM

7275 Addison Products Company
Addison
7050 Overland Rd
Orlando, FL 32810-3404   407-292-4400
                    Fax: 407-299-6178
                    info@addison-hvac.com
                    www.addison-hvac.com

Heat pumps 1-30 h.p., air conditioning 1-40 h.p.

President: Don Peck
Marketing Manager: Joseph Allegra
Production Manager: James Benjamin
Number of Employees: 200
Sales Information: $25,000,000 - $50,000,000

7276 Aftermarket Specialties
Aftermarket Specialties, Inc.
980 Cobb Place Blvd NW
Suite 100
Kennesaw, GA 30144-6801   678-819-2274
                                 800-438-5931
                    Fax: 678-819-2275
                    sales@aftermkt.com
                    www.aftermkt.com

Rotary and reciprocating compressors, dry metallized run capacitors, zone control systems, CF-20 internal coil line cleaner, CF-20 pump

President: Dallas Rohrer
CFO: Dion Rohrer
VP: Mary Anne Rohrer
Mailing List Information: Names for rent
In Business: 29 years
Number of Employees: 8

7277 Aircondex
Aircondex
5111 Mercantile Row
PO Box 560045
Dallas, TX 75356-45   214-634-0653
                    Fax: 214-634-9772

Refrigeration compressors and air conditioners

Chairman: Lee Ferrell
President: P. Lee Ferrell
lee@aircondexcompressors.com
Marketing Manager: RE Keith
Director of Manufacturing & QA: Larry Kelly
larry@aircondexcompressors.com
Controller and Assistant Treasurer: Don Loomis
don@aircondexcompressors.com
Administrative Assistant: CindyKeller
maryann@aircondexcompressors.com
In Business: 54 years
Number of Employees: 16
Sales Information: $1.5 Million

7278 Aquatic Eco-Systems
Pentair AES
2395 Apopka Boulevard
Apopka, FL 32703   407-886-3939
                          877-347-4788
                    Fax: 407-886-6787
                    PAES.General@Pentair.com
                    www.aquaticeco.com

Feed, feeders, fountains, tanks and electric pumps

President: Robert Heideman
In Business: 35 years

7279 Berry Metal Company
Berry Metal Company
2408 Evans City Road
Harmony, PA 16037   724-452-8040
                    Fax: 724-452-4115
                    www.berrymetal.com

Post combustion top and bottom blowing lances, gas burners, oxygen furnaces and related equipment

President: George J. Koenig
CFO: Thomas Gade

VP and General Manager: David R. Werner
VP Sales and Marketing: Robert A. D'Arrigo
Executive Director of Quality Assur: Robert A. Barthelemy
Number of Employees: 88
Sales Information: $5MM to $10MM

7280 Bowie Industries, Inc.
Bowie Industries, Inc.
1004 E. Wise St.
Bowie, TX 76230-931   940-872-1106
                             800-433-0934
                    Fax: 940-872-4792
                    tellmemore@bowieindustries.com
                    www.bowieindustries.com

Rotary pumps

CFO: Dean Myers
Director: Gary Meyer
Director: Carlotta Myers
Sales Executive: Carrie Davis
Printing Information: in 3 colors
Number of Employees: 50
Sales Information: $5,000,000 - $10,000,000

7281 Bristol Compressors
Bristol Compressors
15185 Industrial Park Road
Bristol, VA 24202   276-645-2458
                           855-601-0894
                    Fax: 276-645-2423
                    www.bristolcompressors.com/

Air conditioning, heat pump, refrigeration components and compressors

President: Ireland Smith
CFO: Vicky Kiser
Marketing Manager: B Guthrie
Production Manager: W Marino
CEO: Ed Gniewek
SVP of Global Sales and Marketing: Joel Moseley
Director of International Sales: Chris Robinson
Catalog Cost: Free
Printing Information: 89 pages
Number of Employees: 3
Sales Information: $3MM to $5MM

7282 CMP Corporation
CMP Corporation
4101 S.E. 85th Street
Oklahoma City, OK 73135   877-664-4743
                                 800-123-0408
                    Fax: 405-672-4547
                    brad@cmpcorp.com
                    www.cmpcorp.com

Replacement parts for air conditioning compressors

President: Brad Croy
brad@cmpcorp.com
VP: Darren Croy
darren@cmpcorp.com
Director of Marketing & Sales: Kelsey Poe
kelsey@cmpcorp.com
Director of Administration: Adam Harper
hr@cmpcorp.com
International Marketing Manager: Sherri Reeves
In Business: 46 years
Number of Employees: 90
Sales Information: $10MM to $20MM

7283 CPR Industries
CPR Industries
1501 N. Peck Road
South El Monte, CA 91733-4529   626-444-4521
                                800-334-4452
                    Fax: 626-454-8391
                    www.Cprindustries.Com

Compressors for the refrigeration and air conditioning industry

President: Keith Harwood
In Business: 54 years
Sales Information: $3MM to $5MM

7284 City Compressor Remanufacturers

City Compressor Remanufacturers
9750 Twin Lakes Parkway
Charlotte, NC 28269-7541   704-947-1811
800-392-4496
Fax: 704-947-1222
www.citycompressor.com

Semi hermetic and open drive compressor remanufacturers

President: Rusty Moreland
Number of Employees: 20
Sales Information: $1MM to $3MM

7285 Coastal Technologies

Coastal Technologies, Inc
78 Rentz Street
P.O. Box 624
Varnville, SC 29924-624   803-943-4822
Fax: 803-943-4744
sales@cti-sc.com
www.coastaltechnologiesinc.com

Mist eliminators and evaporators

President: John Hewlett
In Business: 28 years

7286 Copeland Corporation

Emerson Electric Co.
8000 West Florissant Avenue
P.O. Box 4100
St. Louis, MO 63136-2479   314-553-2000
Fax: 937-498-3307
www.emerson.com

Compressors and condensing units

Chairman: David N. Farr
President: Edward L. Monser
CFO: Frank J. Dellaquila
Marketing Manager: HL Lance
EVP: D. Scott Barbour
EVP: Mark J. Bulanda
EVP: Jay Geldmacher
In Business: 23 years
Number of Employees: 1350

7287 Doucette Industries

Doucette Industries
20 Leigh Drive
York, PA 17406-8474   717-845-8746
800-445-7511
Fax: 717-845-2864
info@doucetteindustries.com
www.doucetteindustries.com

Heat exchangers for air-conditioning, refrigeration and hydronic applications

President: John Lebo
Production Manager: Sam Miller
Buyers: Harry Tomes
Credit Cards: AMEX; MasterCard
Catalog Cost: Free
Catalog Circulation: Mailed 50 time(s) per year to 100
Average Order Size: $500
Printing Information: 16 pages in 1 color on Matte Stock
Mailing List Information: Names for rent
In Business: 26 years
Number of Employees: 35
Sales Information: $5,000,000 - $10,000,000

7288 FHP Bosch Group Catalog

FHP Bosch Group
601 NW 65th Court
Fort Lauderdale, FL 33309   866-642-3198
Fax: 954-776-5529
heatpump@fhp-mfg.com
www.fhp-mfg.com

Geothermal and water source heat pumps

President: Clifford Young
Pres; Ttnm-gm: Martin Kueper
In Business: 40 years

7289 Fraser-Johnston Heating/Air Conditioning

Unitary Products
5005 York Drive
Norman, OK 73069   405-364-4040
877-874-7378
cg-upgconsumerrelations@jci.com
www.fraserjohnston.com

Residential and commercial furnaces, controls and services, heat pumps and air conditioning, refrigeration and security systems for buildings

President: R Barnett
Marketing Manager: RN Morrison

7290 Friedrich Air Conditioning

Friedrich Air Conditioning
10001 Reunion Place, Ste 500
San Antonio, TX 78216   210-546-0500
800-541-6645
Fax: 210-357-4432
www.friedrich.com

Air conditioning, dehumidifiers, heat pumps

President: Georgr Vanhoomisen
Marketing Manager: J Deming
Fulfillment: Jennifer Graham
Catalog Cost: Free
Printing Information: 4 pages in 4 colors on Glossy Stock
Press: Sheetfed Press
Binding: Folded
Mailing List Information: Names for rent
In Business: 131 years
Number of Employees: 600
Sales Information: $20MM to $50MM

7291 Fuji Electric Corporation of America

Fuji Electric Corporation of America
50 Northfield Avenue
Edison, NJ 08837-5820   732-560-9410
800-327-3854
Fax: 201-368-8258
www.americas.fujielectric.Com

Ring compressors, blowers and devices for cooling

President: Michihiro Kitazawa
Marketing Manager: Shannon Elkins
Representative Director: Yoshio Okuno
Outside Director: Hiroaki Kurokawa
Director: Michio Abe
Catalog Cost: Free
Printing Information: in 2 colors
Mailing List Information: Names for rent
In Business: 92 years
Number of Employees: 2574
Sales Information: 810.7 billion

7292 Gast Manufacturing Corporation

Gast Manufacturing, Inc.
2300 M-139 Highway
P.O. Box 97
Benton Harbor, MI 49023-0097   269-926-6171
Fax: 269-927-0808
www.gastmfg.com

Compressors, vacuum pumps

President: Warren E Gast
Marketing Manager: K Gast
In Business: 95 years
Number of Employees: 600
Sales Information: $50MM to $100MM

7293 Great Plains Wholesale

Great Plains Wholesale
2800 Southcross Drive W
Burnsville, MN 55306-6936   612-885-0558
800-525-9716
Fax: 886-641-2568
gpcatalog@northerntool.com
www.gpcatalog.com

Pressure washers, water pumps, industrial generators and related power equipment

President: Alen Charles
Marketing Manager: Gerry Wright

Credit Cards: AMEX; MasterCard
Catalog Circulation: Mailed 3 time(s) per year to 1M+
Printing Information: 12 pages in 2 colors on Glossy Stock
Press: Web Press
Mailing List Information: Names for rent
In Business: 23 years
Number of Employees: 10

7294 Hannmann Machinery/Alyan Pump Company

Alyan Pump Company
1 Horne Dr
Folcroft, PA 19032-1807   610-583-6900
Fax: 610-583-1883
www.Alyanpump.Com

Pumps

President: Ralph Hannmann
In Business: 59 years
Sales Information: $10MM to $20MM

7295 Instech Laboratories

Instech Laboratories Inc.
5209 Militia Hill Rd
Plymouth Meeting, PA 19462-1237   610-941-0132
800-443-4227
Fax: 610-941-0134
www.Instechlabs.Com

Portable pumps, flow pumps and pumping tube assemblies

President: Michael Loughnane
Printing Information: 52 pages
In Business: 44 years
Number of Employees: 9
Sales Information: $1,000,000 - $5,000,000

7296 Madden Manufacturing

Madden Manufacturing
PO Box 387
Elkhart, IN 46515   574-295-4292
800-369-6233
Fax: 574-295-7562
www.maddenmfg.com

Pumps, continuous boiler blowdown control valves, chemical feed systems, coolers and heat recovery systems

President: Stuart Barb
Production Manager: Ed Wise
Buyers: Alice Baylor
Printing Information: 100 pages in 2 colors on Matte Stock
Press: Letterpress
Binding: Perfect Bound
In Business: 40+ years
Number of Employees: 13
Sales Information: $1,000,000 - $5,000,000

7297 Monitor Products

Monitor Products, Inc.
7 A Marlen Drive
Bangor, PA 18013   610-588-5367
609-584-0505
Fax: 610-588-5842
www.monitorproducts.com

Ductless room air conditioning and heat pumps

Marketing Manager: TM Tollinger
In Business: 30 years

7298 Pacer Pumps

Pacer Pumps
41 Industrial Cir
Lancaster, PA 17601-5927   717-656-2161
800-233-3861
Fax: 717-656-0477
sales@pacerpumps.com
www.pacerpumps.com

Self-priming centrifugal pumps for industry and agricultural manufactured from corrosion proof thermoplastics

President: Glenn Geist
Marketing Manager: Ron Hock
International Marketing Manager: Glenn Geist
Credit Cards: Visa
Catalog Cost: Free
Catalog Circulation: Mailed 1 time(s) per year to 10M+
Printing Information: 50 pages in 2 colors on Matte Stock
Press: Web Press
Mailing List Information: Names for rent
In Business: 41 years
Number of Employees: 70
Sales Information: $5MM to $10MM

7299   Sillair Corporation
Sullair
3700 E Michigan Blvd
Michigan City, IN 46360-6500   219-879-5451
                                                         800-348-2722
                                        Fax: 219-874-1273
sullaircompressors@sullair.com
                                  www.sullair.com

Rotary screw air compressors, air dryers and filters

President: Henry F Brooks
CFO: Gary Larson
Marketing Manager: R Stasyshan
General Manager & VP: Robert Lauson
robert.lauson@sullair.com
Customer Service Manager: Susan Donovan
susan.donovan@sullair.com
In Business: 50 years
Number of Employees: 2500
Sales Information: $100,000,000 - $500,000,0

7300   Thomas Industries
2414 Boston Post Rd.
Guilford, CT 00643-4855   203-458-0709
                                        Fax: 203-458-0727
gavel@thomasauction.com
                        www.thomasauction.com

Air compressors, vacuum pumps, air motors and spray equipment

President: John Novak
In Business: 68 years
Number of Employees: 500
Sales Information: $500M to $1MM

Purification Systems

7301   AGET Dust/Mist Collectors
Aget Manufacturing
1408 E. Church Street
P.O. Box 248
Adrian, MI 49221-248   517-263-5781
                                        800-832-2438
                                Fax: 517-263-7154
sales@agetmfg.com
                        www.agetmfg.com

Dust/mist collection systems, dustrop cyclones and filterunits

President: Ray Wakefield
Credit Cards: MasterCard; Visa
Catalog Circulation: Mailed 1 time(s) per year
Printing Information: 4 pages in 2 colors
Mailing List Information: Names for rent
In Business: 77 years
Number of Employees: 48
Sales Information: $3,000,000

7302   Air Filter Testing Laboratories
AFTL, Inc.
4632 Old LaGrange Road
Buckner, KY 40010   502-222-5720
                                Fax: 502-222-9881
Mmurphy562@aol.com
                        www.aftl.net

Air filtration, biological and environmental conditioning product testing

Chairman: Glenn Klausman
President: Jeanette Murphy
CFO: Michael Murphy

In Business: 47 years
Number of Employees: 5
Sales Information: $310,000

7303   Air Quality Engineering
Air Quality Engineering
7140 Northland Dr North
Minneapolis, MN 55428-1520   763-531-9823
                                                888-883-3273
                                        Fax: 763-531-9900
info@air-quality-eng.com
                        www.air-quality-eng.com

Electronic air cleaners

President: Heidi Oas
CFO: Debbie Tomala
VP, Engineering: Mark Schreiber
VP, Sales: Ira Golden
Finance/Office Manager: Joann Wentling
In Business: 42 years
Number of Employees: 50
Sales Information: $7.4 Million

7304   Air Rite Service Supply
Air Rite Service Supply
1290 W 117th St
Cleveland, OH 44107-3033   216-228-8200
                                                800-228-8209
                                        Fax: 216-228-5651
info@airrite-supply.com
                        www.airrite-supply.com

Air filters

President: Dave Harris
CFO: Marilyn Harris
Marketing Manager: Kenneth Rahm
Sales Manager: Don Andolek
In Business: 59 years
Number of Employees: 24
Sales Information: $3.5 Million

7305   Air-Dry Corporation of America
Air Dry Co. of America, LLC.
1740 Commerce Way
Paso Robles, CA 93446   805-238-2840
                                        Fax: 805-238-0241
infoairdry@sunbankcorp.com
                        www.airdrycompany.com

Purification systems

President: Jeff Watson
CFO: Ken Peterson
Marketing Manager: Kory Levoy
Production Manager: John Huntsberger
Catalog Cost: Free
Printing Information: 81 pages
In Business: 62 years
Number of Employees: 20
Sales Information: $10MM to $20MM

7306   Airguard Industries
CLARCOR Air Filtration Products
100 River Ridge Circle
Jeffersonville, IN 47130   502-969-2304
                                        866-247-4827
                                Fax: 866-601-1809
mailbag@airguard.com
                        www.clcair.com

Air filtration products

President: Bill Walker
Marketing Manager: Gary Heilmann
Customer Care Manager: Christy Robinson
crobinson@clcair.com
Career Development Trainer: Laura Whaley
lwhaley@clcair.com
Customer ServiceRepresentative: Carrie Deckard
cdeckard@clcair.com
Catalog Cost: Free
Printing Information: 15 pages
In Business: 51 years
Number of Employees: 75

7307   Airsan Corporation
Airsan Corporation
4554 W Woolworth Ave
Milwaukee, WI 53218-1497   414-353-5800
                                                800-558-5494
                                        Fax: 414-353-8402
inquiry@airsan.com
                        www.Airsan.Com

Air filters, acoustical products, moisture eliminators and grease filters

President: Arlin Ratajczak
In Business: 69 years
Number of Employees: 35
Sales Information: $1,000,000 - $5,000,000

7308   Allen Filters
Allen Global Companies
PO Box 747
Springfield, MO 65801   417-865-2844
                                        800-865-3208
                                Fax: 417-865-2469
www.allenfiltersinc.com

Fluid filtration and reclamation systems, oil conditioning and wastewater purification systems and tanks

President: Katherine Simon
Marketing Manager: Rob Simon
Managing Director: Michael Eisley
Sr. Design Engineer: Billy Angus
International Marketing Manager: R.J. Simon
Buyers: GL Eisey
Credit Cards: MasterCard
Printing Information: 20 pages
Mailing List Information: Names for rent
In Business: 65 years

7309   American Metal Products
Masco Corporation
21001 Van Born Road
Taylor, MI 48180   313-274-7400
                                Fax: 313-792-4177
irene_tasi@mascohq.com
                        www.masco.com

Vents, stacks, chimneys, humidifiers and air cleaners

Chairman: Richard A. Manoogian
President: Keith J. Alman
CFO: John G. Sznewajs
Marketing Manager: S Kruse
Production Manager: P Grandy
VP - Controller: John P. Lindow
Chief Human ResourceOofficer: Renee Straber
Group VP: Darius Padler
In Business: 86 years
Number of Employees: 170
Sales Information: $10,000,000 - $25,000,000

7310   Bergeman USA
Clyde Bergemann
4015 Presidential Parkway
Atlanta, GA 30340-3707   770-557-3600
                                        800-241-5996
                                Fax: 770-557-3651
www.Clydebergemann.Com

Sootblowers and controls

President: Hans Schwade
In Business: 103 years
Number of Employees: 3500

7311   Bioclimatic Air Systems
Bioclimatic Air Systems
600 Delran Parkway
Delran, NJ 08075-1269   856-764-4300
                                        800-962-5594
                                Fax: 856-764-4301
mail@bioclimatic.com
                        www.Bioclimatic.Com

Complete line of air purification systems for commercial and industrial applications; new design or retrofit

President: Michele Bottino
Printing Information: in 2 colors
In Business: 13 years
Number of Employees: 8
Sales Information: $500M to $1MM

7312 Calgon Carbon Corporation
Calgon Carbon Corporation
3000 GSK Drive
Moon Township, PA 15108   412-787-6700
                                800-4CA-BON
                          Fax: 412-787-6676
                          www.calgoncarbon.com

Water protection and purification systems
Chairman: Randy Dearth
President: Randall S. Dearth
CFO: Stevan R. Schott
Marketing Manager: John MacCrum
EVP and Chief Operating Officer: Robert P
O'Brien
SVP, Global Procurement: James C.
Coccagno
SVP, General Counsel and Secretary: Richard
D. Rose
Number of Employees: 350

7313 Clean Fuel
Clean Fuels
7364 Edgewood Road
Building A, Suite 100
Annapolis, MD 21403-3717   410-757-7576
                                888-320-3134
                          Fax: 804-262-1176
                    info@cleanfuelsassociates.com
                    www.cleanfuelsassociates.com/

Purification systems
President: William Hartman
VP of Operations: Christopher Hartman
Lead Technician and Field Superviso: Todd
Cook
HR Director (and Contracts Administ: David A.
Bishop
In Business: 29 years
Number of Employees: 10-J
Sales Information: Under $500M

7314 Coopermatics
BTI-Coopermatics Inc.
600 Held Drive
Northampton, PA 18067-450   610-262-7700
                                800-798-1679
                          Fax: 610-262-3384
                          www.coopermatics.com

Liquid filtration equipment
President: Thomas Joseph
General Manager: Abraham Thomas
Manager: Linda D. Cooper
Business Development Manager: Clay Cooper
Mailing List Information: Names for rent
In Business: 30 years
Number of Employees: 25
Sales Information: $1,000,000 - $5,000,000

7315 Everpure
Everpure
1040 Muirfield Drive
Hanover Park, IL 60133-5468   630-307-3000
                                800-323-7873
                          Fax: 630-307-3030
                    CSeverpure@pentair.com
                    www.everpure.pentair.com

Water filters and water treatment devices
President: Michael Madsen
In Business: 75 years
Number of Employees: 275
Sales Information: $50,000,000 - $100,000,00

7316 Laval Lakos Corporation
LAKOS Centrifugal Separators
1365 North Clovis Avenue
Fresno, CA 93727-2282   559-255-1601
                                800-344-7205
                          Fax: 559-255-8093
                          info@lakos.com
                          www.lakos.com/

Filtration devices
Chairman: Claude C. Laval III
President: Claude Laval
Number of Employees: 120
Sales Information: $10MM to $20MM

7317 MonlanGroup Division
PRAB
5944 East N Ave
Kalamazoo, MI 49048-9531   269-382-8200
                                800-968-7722
                          Fax: 269-382-8200
                          www.prab.com

**Coolant recycling equipment, Hyde tramp oil
separators, Hyde ultrafiltration systems,
evaporators, chemaperm magnetic slide
conveyors, solids filtration equipment in-
cluding Monlan vacumn filters**
President: Tim Hanna
CFO: David Mauer, VP
Marketing Manager: W Eschern
Production Manager: T Tripepi and R
Triesenberg
Fulfillment: R Triesenberg
Catalog Circulation: Mailed 1 time(s) per year
Printing Information: 50 pages in 4 colors
In Business: 65 years
Number of Employees: 75
Sales Information: $1,000,000 - $5,000,000

7318 Nalco Company
NALCO
1601 W Diehl Road
Naperville, IL 60563-1198   630-305-1000
                          Fax: 630-305-2900
                          www.Nalco.Com

**Water treatment chemicals and processing
equipment**
Chairman: William H. Joyce
President: J Erik Frywald
CFO: Bradley J. Bell
In Business: 87 years
Number of Employees: 47
Sales Information: $14 billion

7319 Nucon International
NUCON International,Inc
7000 Huntley Road
Columbus, OH 43229-2915   614-846-5710
                          Fax: 614-431-0858
                          sales@nucon-int.com
                          www.nucon-int.com

Solvent Vapor Recovery Systems
President: JL Kovach
Marketing Manager: Joseph Enneking
Buyers: SG Lee
Catalog Circulation: to 500
Printing Information: on Matte Stock
List Manager: Jack Jacox
In Business: 43 years
Number of Employees: 50
Sales Information: $5,000,000 - $10,000,000

7320 Research Products Corporation
Aprilaire
P.O.Box 1467
Madison, WI 53701-1467   608-257-8801
                                800-334-6011
                          Fax: 608-257-4357
                          www.Aprilaire.Com

**Air filters, cleaners, humidifiers and equip-
ment**
Chairman: V Hellenbrand
President: Vern Hellenbrand

Marketing Manager: Larry Olsen
In Business: 75 years
Number of Employees: 110
Sales Information: $10MM to $20MM

7321 Waterwise
Waterwise Inc
2460 North Euclid Avenue
Upland, CA 91784-1199   909-982-2425
                                800-205-2425
                          Fax: 909-949-7217
                          kristen@vnwg.com
                          www.vnwg.com

**Water and air purification systems for home
and office**
President: Jack Barber
CFO: Bob Barber
Marketing Manager: Greg Barber
Buyers: Mike Lane
Credit Cards: AMEX; MasterCard
Catalog Cost: Free
Catalog Circulation: Mailed 6 time(s) per year
to 15000
Average Order Size: $200
Printing Information: 36 pages in 4 colors on
Glossy Stock
Press: Web Press
Binding: Saddle Stitched
Mailing List Information: Names for rent
List Manager: Greg Barber
In Business: 93 years
Number of Employees: 32
Sales Information: $4,000,000

Refrigeration & Ice Makers

7322 Adrick Cooling Corporation
Adrick Marine Group
581 Cidco Road
Cocoa, FL 32926   321-631-0776
                          Fax: 321-631-0877
                          info@adrickmarine.com
                          www.adrickmarine.com

**Marine air conditioners, ice makers, refriger-
ators and freezers**
President: Thomas Vassallo
CFO: Richard Vassallo
Secretary/Treasurer: Susan Vassallo
In Business: 39 years
Number of Employees: 12
Sales Information: $2.10 Million

7323 Advance Energy Technology
Advance Energy Technologies, Inc.
One Solar Drive
Clifton Park, NY 12065-387   518-371-2140
                                800-724-0198
                          Fax: 518-371-0737
                          sales@advanceet.com
                          www.advanceet.com

**Walk in coolers, freezers, environmental en-
closures, cleanrooms, thermal panels and
engineered refrigeration systems**
President: Timothy Carlo
CFO: David Ohanlon
Senior Sales Engineer: Dave Weitz
sales@advanceet.com
General Manager: Michelle Horner
Catalog Cost: Free
Catalog Circulation: to 10M
Printing Information: 18 pages in 2 colors on
Glossy Stock
Mailing List Information: Names for rent
In Business: 45 years
Number of Employees: 27
Sales Information: $3.70 Million

7324 **Air Rover Company**
Air Rover, Inc.
PO Box 4850
Tyler, TX 75712
903-877-3430
800-858-6287
Fax: 903-877-2793
info@airrover.com
www.airrover.com

Air cooled and water cooled air conditioning systems

President: Francis Stiles
In Business: 29 years

7325 **American Panel Corporation**
American Panel Corporation
5800 SE 78th Street
Ocala, FL 34472-3412
352-245-7055
800-327-3015
sales@americanpanel.com
www.americanpanel.com

Walk-in/step-in coolers and freezers

President: Danny E Duncan
Production Manager: HS Lewis
Director Of Operations: Jeff Duncan
Purchasing Manager: Charlotte Towers
Catalog Cost: Free
Number of Employees: 130
Sales Information: $10,000,000 - $25,000,000

7326 **Bailey Refrigeration Company**
Bailey Refrigeration Company
2323 Randolph Ave
Avenel, NJ 07001-2493
732-382-1225
800-8BA-ILEY
Fax: 732-382-1048
sales@baileyco.com
www.Baileyco.Com

Refrigeration and air conditioning services and equipment

President: Benjamin Bailey
Number of Employees: 35
Sales Information: $10MM to $20MM

7327 **Baltimore Aircoil Company**
Baltimore Aircoil Company
7600 Dorsey Run Road
Jessup, MD 20794
410-799-6200
Fax: 410-799-6416
www.baltimoreaircoil.com/english/

Cooling towers, condensers, receivers and other refrigeration systems

President: Matthew J McKenna
Marketing Manager: Timothy Facius
In Business: 75 years
Number of Employees: 400

7328 **Bradleys' Hermetics**
Bradleys' Hermetics
6501 Robertson Drive
Corpus Christi, TX 78415-9720
361-854-9833
800-531-3120
Fax: 361-854-1440
ralejandre@bradleyshermetics.com
www.bradparts.com

Compressor parts for air conditioning and refrigerated compressors

President: Ramiro Alejandre
ralejandre@bradleyshermetics.com
CFO: Victor L. Reeves
vreeves@bradleyshermetics.com
VP: Maria Gargano-Reeves
Catalog Circulation: Mailed 2 time(s) per year to 350
Average Order Size: $1000
Printing Information: 125 pages on Matte Stock
Mailing List Information: Names for rent
In Business: 16 years
Number of Employees: 10
Sales Information: $5,000,000

7329 **Butcher Boy Door Company**
1214 E Nakoma Street
Jacksonville, TX 75766-4036
903-589-0929
Fax: 903-589-0338

Heavy duty doors and cold storage for industry

Printing Information: 28 pages in 2 colors

7330 **Eliason Corporation**
Eliason Corporation
9229 Shaver Rd
Portage, MI 49024-6799
269-327-7003
800-828-3655
Fax: 269-327-7006
doors@eliasoncorp.com
www.Eliasoncorp.Com

Double action doors for all service, traffic and convenience doorways in supermarkets, restaurants, retail stores, bars, taverns, convenience stores, hotels, hospitals

President: Edwanda Eliason
Marketing Manager: M Woolsey
Catalog Cost: Free
Catalog Circulation: to 8000
Printing Information: 50 pages in 1 color on Matte Stock
Mailing List Information: Names for rent
List Company: International Sales
In Business: 63 years
Number of Employees: 125
Sales Information: $5MM to $10MM

7331 **Entech Sales & Service**
Entech Sales And Services
3404 Garden Brook Dr
Dallas, TX 75234-2496
469-522-6000
855-247-3678
Fax: 972-243-1774
www.Entechsales.Com

Rebuilt chillers

President: Pat Rucker
Marketing Manager: J Mattes
Number of Employees: 150
Sales Information: $10MM to $20MM

7332 **Follett Corporation**
Follett Corporation
801 Church Lane
Easton, PA 18040
610-252-7301
800-523-9361
Fax: 610-250-0696
info@follettice.com
www.Follettice.Com

Ice storage bins and dispensers

President: Steven Follett
CFO: Tom Rohrbach
Marketing Manager: Lois Schnek
Production Manager: George Bauer
CEO: Steve Follett
In Business: 67 years
Number of Employees: 160
Sales Information: $10,000,000 - $25,000,000

7333 **Galileo Vacuum Systems**
Galileo Vacuum Systems
5950 Shiloh Road E
Suite M
Alpharetta, GA 30005-1763
678-513-0303
Fax: 678-513-0608
www.galileovacuum.com

Refrigerant charging equipment, vacuum pumps, gauges and vacuum pump repairs

Marketing Manager: Paolo Raugei
EVP & COO: Paolo Raugei
In Business: 151 years
Number of Employees: 7

7334 **Gem Refrigerator Company**
Gem Refrigerator Company
650 E Erie Ave
Philadelphia, PA 19134-1293
215-426-8700
Fax: 215-426-8731

Commercial refrigerators and freezers

President: Bruce Gruhler
CFO: Robert Gruhler
Marketing Manager: Tony Jacono
Mailing List Information: Names for rent
In Business: 80 years
Number of Employees: 30
Sales Information: $5MM to $10MM

7335 **Multistack**
Multistack
1065 Maple Ave.
PO BOX 510
Sparta, WI 54656-1710
608-366-2400
Fax: 608-366-2450
info@multistack.com
www.multistack.com

Modular water chillers

President: Richard Campbell
In Business: 26 years
Number of Employees: 24
Sales Information: $1,000,000 - $5,000,000

7336 **Rowald Refrigeration Systems Catalog**
Rowald Refrigeration Systems
515 Grable St
Rockford, IL 61109-2001
815-397-7733
Fax: 815-397-5936
info@rowald.com
www.Rowald.Com

Refrigeration systems

President: Robert W Rowald
Mailing List Information: Names for rent
In Business: 39 years
Number of Employees: 10
Sales Information: $1,000,000

7337 **Scientific Systems Corporation**
Scientific Systems Corporation
7924 Reco Avenue
Baton Rouge, LA 70814
225-926-6950
800-654-3857
Fax: 225-926-6973
sales@severeduty.com
www.severeduty.com

Air conditioning; Industrial and safety refrigeration and air conditioning

Production Manager: Charlie Cormier
Fulfillment: Henry I Townley
Average Order Size: $5000
In Business: 49 years
Number of Employees: 35
Sales Information: $5MM to $10MM

7338 **Spectronics Corporation Catalog**
Spectronics Corporation
956 Brush Hollow Road
Westbury, NY 11590-483
516-333-4840
800-274-8888
Fax: 516-333-4859
intlsales@spectroline.com
www.spectroline.com

Leak detection for air conditioning, refrigeration and fluid systems, diagnostic and preventative maintenance

President: Jonathan Cooper
Marketing Manager: Gary Fixel
Production Manager: Robert Reynolds
Owner: Gloria Blusk
VP: Lil Cooper
Sales Manager: Michael Newmark
International Marketing Manager: Gerri Curry
Catalog Cost: $0
In Business: 60 years
Number of Employees: 190
Sales Information: $23.1 MM

7339 Stulz-ATS
Stulz Air Technology Systems, Inc.
1572 Tilco Dr
Frederick, MD 21704-8378   301-620-2033
                                   888-592-1266
                              Fax: 301-662-5487
                              info@stulz-ats.com
                              www.stulz.com

Modular data processing air conditioners, chillers and console models
President: Mark Oliver Stulz
Production Manager: Shawn Cline
In Business: 63 years
Number of Employees: 10
Sales Information: $1,000,000 - $5,000,000

7340 VICI Valco Instruments
VICI, Inc.
8300 Waterbury
Houston, TX 77055   713-688-9345
                            800-367-8424
                       Fax: 713-688-7618
                       www.vici.com

Industrial refrigeration equipment
President: Stan Stearns
Marketing Manager: Laura Watson
In Business: 40 years
Number of Employees: 24
Sales Information: $1,000,000 - $5,000,000

7341 Zwick Energy Research
PO Box 2460
Huntington Beach, CA 92647-460 626-891-1640
                            Fax: 714-895-4117

Cryogenic pumps and compressors and gas vaporizers
President: Gene Zwick
CFO: Gil Courson
Number of Employees: 30
Sales Information: $5,000,000 - $10,000,000

Supplies & Controls

7342 A-J Manufacturing Company
A-J Manufacturing Company, Inc.
3601 E 18th Street
PO Box 270320
Kansas City, MO 64127-320   816-231-5522
                                    800-247-5746
                               Fax: 816-231-8437
                               www.ajmfg.com

Supply and return grilles, hinged filter grilles, bar grilles, ceiling diffusers and accessories.
President: Bob Haake
VP: Linda Haake
Treasurer/Sales Manager: Rob Haake
robhaake@ajmfg.us
General Manager: Tony Williams
tony@ajmfg.us
In Business: 84 years
Number of Employees: 25
Sales Information: $6,000,000

7343 ABB Drives
ABB
16250 W. Glendale Drive
New Berlin, WI 53151   262-785-3200
                               800-435-7365
                          Fax: 262-785-8525
                          www.abb.com

Motor speed controllers.
President: Charles Clark
CFO: Mike O'Donnell
VP Marketing: Eric Torseke
Sales Director: Doug Niebruegge
Catalog Cost: Free
Printing Information: 48 pages
In Business: 132 years
Number of Employees: 1400

7344 AMPCO Safety Tools
AMPCO Safety Tools
204 Barnes Drive
Garland, TX 75042   972-276-6181
                            800-580-9835
                       Fax: 972-276-5815
                       sales@ampcosafetytools.com
                       www.ampcosafetytools.com

Hazmat kits, wrenches, picks, hammers, axes, screwdrivers and pliers
President: Tate Pursell
Marketing Manager: K Hoyt
In Business: 101 years
Number of Employees: 150
Sales Information: $110,000

7345 Advanced Thermal Systems
Advanced Thermal Systems
15 Enterprise Dr
Lancaster, NY 14086-9773   716-681-1800
                                   800-443-9194
                              Fax: 716-681-0228
                              ats@advancedthermal.net
                              www.advancedthermal.net

Piping specialties: packed slip type expansion joints, ball joints, pipe anchors and guides
Chairman: Bill Kraus
President: Edward Patnode
CEO: Eugene Miliczky
Catalog Circulation: to 600
Printing Information: on Glossy Stock
Mailing List Information: Names for rent
In Business: 46 years
Number of Employees: 30
Sales Information: $6,500,000

7346 Air Conditioning Products Company
Air Conditioning Products Company
30350 Ecorse Rd
Romulus, MI 48174-3595   734-326-0050
                            Fax: 734-326-9632
                            www.Acpshutters.Com

Dampers and shutters
President: Phil Mebus
CFO: Christopher Mebus
Marketing Manager: W Melcher
Director: Mayhew Doeren
Catalog Cost: Free
Printing Information: 12 pages
In Business: 68 years
Number of Employees: 50
Sales Information: $10,000,000 - $25,000,000

7347 Air Monitor Corporation
Air Monitor Corporation
PO Box 6358
Santa Rosa, CA 95406-6358   707-544-2706
                                    800-247-3569
                               Fax: 707-526-9970
                               amcsales@airmonitor.com
                               www.airmonitor.com

Electronic and pneumatic air flow transmitters
President: Dean DeBaun
CFO: Sharon Hughes
Marketing Manager: Tim Bodemann
Manager: Jerry Cowan
In Business: 48 years
Number of Employees: 70
Sales Information: $10,000,000 - $25,000,000

7348 Altech Controls Corporation
Altech Controls Corporation
13203 Stafford Road
Suite 500
Missouri City, TX 77489   281-499-5697
                                  800-275-9266
                             Fax: 281-499-5504
                             www.altechcontrols.com/

Electronic expansion valves, refrigeration controls

President: Richard Alsenz
Marketing Manager: G Gertsen
Techical Support: Roger Ansted
Sales: Harold Washington
In Business: 41 years
Number of Employees: 30
Sales Information: $1,000,000 - $5,000,000

7349 American Tubing
American Tubing
2191 Ford Avenue
Springdale, AR 72764-4701   479-756-1291
                                    800-447-0284
                               Fax: 479-756-1346
                               www.americantubing.com

Copper tubing components and assemblies for refrigeration and air conditioning
President: Chuck Lewis
clewis@americantubing.com
Sales Engineer: James Laughter
jlaughter@americantubing.com
Service Representative: Kathy Franklin
kfranklin@americantubing.com
Quality Assurance Manager: BradGreathouse
bgreathouse@americantubing.com
Number of Employees: 115
Sales Information: $25,000,000 - $50,000,000

7350 Anderson Instrument Company
Anderson Instrument Company
156 Auriesville Road
Fultonville, NY 12072   518-922-5315
                           Fax: 518-922-8997
                           info@anderson-negele.com
                           www.anderson-negele.com

Temperature and pressure process controls
President: Lawrence Curtis
Quality & EHS Leader: Jessica Pharr
j.pharr@anderson-negele.com
In Business: 85 years
Number of Employees: $19B
Sales Information: $10,000,000 - $25,000,000

7351 Anderson-Snow Corporation
Anderson-Snow Corporation
9225 Ivanhoe Street
P.O. Box 2126
Schiller Park, IL 60176-2352   800-FIN-COIL
                                  Fax: 847-678-0413
                                  www.anscorcoils.com

Fin type coils
President: Ted Campbell
In Business: 63 years
Number of Employees: 33
Sales Information: $20MM to $50MM

7352 Apco/Valve & Primer Corporation
DeZurik
250 Riverside Avenue North
Sartell, MN 56377-4508   320-259-2000
                            Fax: 320-259-2227
                            www.dezurik.com/

Check valves, air release and air vacuum valves; metal seated ball and cone valves
President: George Christofidis
CFO: M Chris Dickson
Marketing Manager: Robert Mauriello
Catalog Circulation: Mailed 1 time(s) per year
In Business: 87 years
Number of Employees: 93
Sales Information: $10,000,000 - $25,000,000

7353 Atkins Technical
Atkins Technical Services
3401 SW 40th Boulevard
Gainesville, FL 32608-2389   919-539-9099
                                     800-284-2842
                                Fax: 352-335-6736
                                www.atkinstechnicalservices.com

Temperature and humidity instruments
President: Jeff Munnis
Credit Cards: AMEX; MasterCard; Visa

Catalog Cost: Free
Catalog Circulation: Mailed 6 time(s) per year to 150M
Printing Information: 10 pages in 4 colors on Glossy Stock
Press: Web Press
Mailing List Information: Names for rent
In Business: 28 years
Number of Employees: 110
Sales Information: $10,000,000 - $25,000,000

7354 B&B Electronics Manufacturing Company
B&B Electronics Manufacturing Company
707 Dayton Road
PO Box 1040
Ottawa, IL 61350   815-433-5100
                          800-346-3119
                    Fax: 815-433-5109
                support@bb-elec.com
                    www.bb-elec.com

Data communication products
President: Don Wiencek
Credit Cards: AMEX; MasterCard; Visa
Catalog Cost: Free
Printing Information: 122 pages
In Business: 34 years
Number of Employees: 100

7355 Cannon Technology
Cannon Boiler Works
510 Constitution Boulevard
New Kensington, PA 15068-6599 724-335-8541
                    Fax: 724-335-6511
            info@cannonboilerworks.com
            www.Cannonboilerworks.Com

Finned tube products
President: Arthur Skelley
Marketing Manager: Christopher Giron
Mailing List Information: Names for rent
In Business: 43 years
Number of Employees: 45
Sales Information: $5,000,000 - $10,000,000

7356 Cincinnati Sub-Zero Products
Cincinnati Sub-Zero Medicals
12011 Mosteller Rd
Cincinnati, OH 45241-1528   513-772-8810
                            800-989-7373
                      Fax: 513-772-9119
                 cszinc@cszinc.com
                 www.Cszmedical.Com

Temperature controlled products, environmental test chambers, burn-in units, thermal shock chambers, patient temperature, and controlled products for medical market
President: Steve Berke
Marketing Manager: Kristal Velton
In Business: 60 years
Number of Employees: 200
Sales Information: $10,000,000 - $25,000,000

7357 Cole-Parmer-Temperature Measurement & Control
Cole-Parmer
625 East Bunker Court
Vernon Hills, IL 60061-1830   847-549-7600
                            800-323-4340
                      Fax: 847-549-1700
                 info@coleparmer.com
                 www.coleparmer.com

Alarms, controllers, thermometers, thermistors, thermocouples and other instruments for use in temperature applications
President: John Palmer
VP/General Manager: Monica Manotas
Director, Finance: Joe Straczek
VP, Human Resources: Wanda McKenny
Catalog Circulation: Mailed 1 time(s) per year
Printing Information: 128 pages
In Business: 60 years

7358 Coolers/Freezers & Refrigeration Systems
Imperial Brown
2271 NE 194th
Portland, OR 97230-6833   503-665-5539
                            800-238-4093
                      Fax: 503-665-2929
               sales@imperial-brown.com
                    imperialmfg.com

Panels and electrical controls
President: Edward Brown
Marketing Manager: Linda Beers and Wayne Marin
VP: Paul Brown
VP, Sales and Marketing: Rio Giardinieri Joins
Sales Manager: Shah Named
Catalog Circulation: Mailed 1 time(s) per year
Printing Information: 416 pages in 4 colors
Binding: Perfect Bound
In Business: 100 years

7359 Davis & Warshow
Davis & Warshow
12500 Jefferson Avenue
PO Box 2778
Newport News, VA 23602-39   757-874-7795
                            888-937-9500
                      Fax: 757-989-2501
                first.last@ferguson.com
                    www.ferguson.com

Plumbing, heating and air conditioning supplies
President: Frank Finkel
CFO: J Sandberg
Marketing Manager: P Roland
Fulfillment: P Arenas
Buyers: F Sininsky
Credit Cards: AMEX; MasterCard
Catalog Circulation: Mailed 1 time(s) per year to 2M
Printing Information: 10 pages in 1 color on Matte Stock
Press: Web Press
Binding: Saddle Stitched
List Manager: R Jamarillo
In Business: 87 years
Number of Employees: 250
Sales Information: $20MM to $50MM

7360 De-Sta-Co
De-Sta-Co
691 N. Squirrel Road
Suite 250
Auburn Hills, MI 48326   248-836-6700
                            888-337-8226
                      Fax: 248-836-6740
               marketing@destaco.com
                    www.destaco.com

Toggle clamps, metal parts, blower wheel housings and various controls
President: Bob Leisure
Buyers: A Drake, Clamps
R Jarman, Valve Group
K Persaud, Blower Housings
In Business: 100 years
Number of Employees: 4
Sales Information: $1MM to $3MM

7361 EWC Controls
Autoflo
385 State Route 33
Manalapan, NJ 07726-8306   732-446-3110
                            800-446-3110
                      Fax: 732-446-5362
                colett@bestairpro.com
                    www.Autoflo.Com

Registers, diffusers, control panels for residential and light commercial systems, forced air zone controls for heating and cooling systems
President: Kevin Cyrano
Marketing Manager: M Reilly
Credit Cards: AMEX; MasterCard

Catalog Cost: Free
Catalog Circulation: Mailed 2 time(s) per year to 50M
Average Order Size: $2000
Printing Information: 16 pages in 4 colors on Glossy Stock
Press: Letterpress
Binding: Saddle Stitched
Mailing List Information: Names for rent
List Manager: M Reilly
In Business: 36 years
Number of Employees: 150
Sales Information: $20MM to $50MM

7362 Flow Design
Flow Design Inc.
8908 Governors Row
Dallas, TX 75247-3798   214-631-0011
                            800-999-3569
                      Fax: 214-631-0735
            customerservice@flowdesign.com
                    www.flowdesign.com

Flow control valves for commercial heating and air conditioning
President: Ed Clarke
Marketing Manager: B Weber
Production Manager: Mel Davis
VP: Mark Purcell,
mpurcell@flowdesign.com
Hydronic Training Manager: Bill England
bengland@flowdesign.com
International Sales: Wanda Burke
wanda.intl@flowdesign.com
Number of Employees: 1,50
Sales Information: $10,000,000 - $25,000,000

7363 Glenn Metalcraft
Glenn Metalcraft
1502 14th Street S
P.O. Box 446
Princeton, MN 55371-2317   763-389-5355
                            800-388-5355
                      Fax: 763-389-5356
                 www.glennmetalcraft.com

Custom metal spinnings and stampings
President: Dennis E Glenn
In Business: 66 years
Number of Employees: 30
Sales Information: $1,000,000 - $5,000,000

7364 Heatcraft
Luvata
1000 Heatcraft Drive
PO Box 1457
Grenada, MS 38901-1457   662-229-4000
                            800-225-4328
                      Fax: 662-229-4212
                 info@luvata.com
                 www.luvata.com

Commercial and industrial coils
Chairman: Finn Johnsson
President: John Peter Leesi
CFO: Jyrki Vesaluoma
Marketing Manager: D Anderson
CEO: John Peter Leesi
Senior VP of Communications: Justin Roux
Executive VP, Head of Special Produ: Jussi Helavirta
In Business: 7 years
Number of Employees: 6500

7365 HeatingHelp.com
HeatingHelp
63 North Oakdale Avenue
Bethpage, NY 11714-5234   800-853-8882
                      Fax: 888-486-9637
                 www.heatinghelp.com

Hydronic heating information and accessories for the plumber
Founder: Dan Holohan
Marketing Director: Erin Holohan Haskell
In Business: 18 years

7366 Hotwatt.com
Hotwatt, Inc.
128 Maple Street
Danvers, MA 01923-2096   978-777-0070
Fax: 978-774-2409
sales@hotwatt.com
www.hotwatt.com

Electric heaters-cartridge, air process, immersion, strip/finned strip, tubular/finned tubular, band, crankcase, foil, flexible glasrope, & ceramic heaters for industrial, medical, commercial & military

Chairman: Robert Lee
President: William Lee
CFO: Robert Cummings
Marketing Manager: Jim Gaines
Production Manager: Gary Rust
Human Resource Manager: Deb Vaillancourt
VP, Operations: Gary Vailancourt
International Marketing Manager: Jim Gaines
Buyers: Carole Ferguson
Credit Cards: MasterCard; Visa
Catalog Cost: Free
Catalog Circulation: to 1000
Printing Information: 172 pages in 4 colors on Glossy Stock
Binding: Perfect Bound
Mailing List Information: Names for rent
In Business: 63 years
Number of Employees: 120
Sales Information: $15 MM

7367 Industrial Pipe & Steel
Industrial Pipe & Steel
9936 Rush St
South El Monte, CA 91733-2684   626-443-9467
800-423-4981
Fax: 626-579-4602
info@ipstool.com
www.Ipstool.Com

Machinery, precision measuring instruments, power-air tools, abrasives, steel metals and other tools

President: Alejandro Melo
Marketing Manager: Tom Plumley
Production Manager: Kevin Chapman
Buyers: Dennis Montejo
Bob Entrikin
Gilbert Rojas
Credit Cards: AMEX; MasterCard; Visa
Catalog Cost: Free
Catalog Circulation: Mailed 6 time(s) per year to 150K
Average Order Size: $50
Printing Information: 16 pages in 4 colors on Newsprint
Press: Web Press
Mailing List Information: Names for rent
List Manager: Kevin Chapman
In Business: 43 years
Number of Employees: 70
Sales Information: $10,000,000 - $25,000,000

7368 JMF Company
JMF Company
2735 62nd Street Ct
Bettendorf, IA 52722-5599   563-332-9200
800-397-3739
Fax: 563-332-9880
jmf@jmfcompany.com
www.Jmfcompany.Com

Copper tubing, fittings and valves

President: Max Hansen
Marketing Manager: Max Hansen, National Sales Manager
Credit Cards: MasterCard; Visa
Catalog Cost: Free
In Business: 68 years
Number of Employees: 40
Sales Information: $20MM to $50MM

7369 MTM Molded Products
MTM Molded Products
3370 Obco Court
Dayton, OH 45414   937-890-7461
Fax: 937-890-1747
www.Mtmcase-Gard.Com

Plastic injection molded boxes and cases

President: Steve Minneman
In Business: 46 years
Number of Employees: 35
Sales Information: $1,000,000 - $5,000,000

7370 Marathon Special Products
Marathon Special Products
13300 Van Camp Road
PO Box 468
Bowling Green, OH 43402   419-352-8441
Fax: 419-352-0875
marketing@marathonsp.com
www.marathonsp.com

Fuseholders and terminal blocks

President: Larry Minnich, VP
Marketing Manager: Joe Campisi
Production Manager: Brian Mickich
Catalog Circulation: Mailed 2 time(s) per year
Printing Information: 120 pages on Glossy Stock
Binding: Perfect Bound
In Business: 60 years
Number of Employees: 220
Sales Information: $10,000,000 - $25,000,000

7371 McNeil Insulation Company
McNeil Inc.
15 Marlen Drive
Robbinsville, NJ 08691   609-890-7007
800-722-5538
Fax: 609-890-1414
sales@mcneilusa.com
www.McNeilusa.Com

Temperature gaskets and gasket materials

President: Jim Schuhl
In Business: 77 years
Number of Employees: 15
Sales Information: $3MM to $5MM

7372 National Controls Corporation
Ametek
1100 Cassatt Road
Berwyn, PA 19312-1880   610-647-2121
Fax: 215-323-9337
webmaster@ametek.com
www.ametek.com

Heavy-duty panel thermometers

Chairman: Frank S. Hermance
President: John W. Hardin
CFO: Robert R. Mandos
EVP, COO: David A. Zapico
Number of Employees: 275
Sales Information: $25,000,000 - $50,000,000

7373 Ohmic Instruments Company
Ohmic Instruments Co.
3081 Elm Point Industrial Dr
St. Charles, MO 63301   410-820-5111
Fax: 410-822-9633
www.Ohmicinstruments.Com

Humidity sensors, controls and measurement

President: Denes Roveti
Number of Employees: 20
Sales Information: $1,000,000 - $5,000,000

7374 Primore
Primore
PO Box 605
Adrian, MI 49221-605   517-265-6168
Fax: 517-265-6160
sales@sedco-prv.com
www.primore.com

Refrigeration and air conditioning shut-off valves

President: Robert Price
In Business: 55 years
Number of Employees: 14
Sales Information: $5MM to $10MM

7375 Quality Engineering Products Corporation
Quality
9400 NW 12th St
Doral, FL 33172-2804   305-599-2222
800-358-2014
Fax: 305-593-0069
qequality@qequality.com
www.Qequality.Com

Air conditioning and refrigeration accessories, components and controls

President: Luis Robaina
Credit Cards: AMEX; MasterCard
In Business: 36 years
Number of Employees: 16
Sales Information: $1,000,000 - $5,000,000

7376 Reliable Products
Hart & Cooley, Inc
5030 Corporate Exchange Blvd
Grand Rapids, MI 49512-580   800-433-6341
Fax: 800-223-8461
info@hartcool.com
www.hartandcooley.com

Registers, grilles, mechanical and architectural louvers

President: Bobbie Rae Cross
Marketing Manager: J Hicks
Production Manager: Clyde Cook
Number of Employees: 350
Sales Information: $25,000,000 - $50,000,000

7377 Sensitech
Sensitech Inc.
8801 148th Avenue N.E.
Redmond, WA 98052-599   425-883-7926
800-999-7926
Fax: 425-883-3766
info@sensitech.com
www.sensitech.com

Cold chain solutions for monitoring temperature-sensitive products

President: John Vache
Director Quality Assurance: David M. Ray
Facility Manger: Mato Sabino
Operations Manager: Ken Hibbard
Printing Information: in 2 colors
Mailing List Information: Names for rent
In Business: 77 years
Number of Employees: 90
Sales Information: $10,000,000 - $25,000,000

7378 Super Radiator Coils
Super Radiator Coils
104 Peavey Road
Chaska, MN 55318-2324   952-556-3330
800-394-2645
Fax: 952-556-3331
mnweb@superradiatorcoils.com
www.srcoils.com

Heat transfer coils for air conditioning

President: Jon R Holt
Marketing Manager: Chris Ruch, Midwest Sales Manager
In Business: 87 years
Number of Employees: 65
Sales Information: $5MM to $10MM

7379 Superior Valve Company
Am Cast, Inc.
2200 N Main Street
Washington, PA 15301-6150   724-222-3160
800-242-5500
Fax: 724-225-6188
www.amcast.com

Refrigeration and air conditioning valves, driers, filters, fittings and accessories

President: Mike Powell
Marketing Manager: SW Boyd
In Business: 14 years
Number of Employees: 350
Sales Information: $25,000,000 - $50,000,000

7380 Texas Instruments

Texas Instruments, Inc.
12500 TI Boulevard
P.O. Box 660199
Dallas, TX 75243-1245   972-995-2011
                              800-788-8861
                         Fax: 859-873-2614
                              www.Ti.Com

Pressure switches, thermostats and thermistors

Chairman: Rich Templeton
President: Rich Templeton
CFO: Kevin March
Marketing Manager: John Szczsponik
SVP, Analog: Steve Anderson
SVP, Human Resources: Darla Whitaker
EVP, Business Operations: Brian Crutcher
In Business: 80 years
Number of Employees: 800
Sales Information: $50,000,000 - $100,000,00

7381 Therm-O-Disc

Therm-O-Disc
1320 South Main Street
PO Box 3538
Mansfield, OH 44907-538   419-525-8500
                         Fax: 419-525-8344
                  TODSales-AMER@emerson.com
                         www.therm-o-disc.com

Temperature limiting and regulating controls, sensors and sequencers

President: James Kight
In Business: 68 years
Number of Employees: 1250

7382 Tridan Tool & Machine

Tridan Tool & Machine, Inc.
130 North Jackson Street
PO Box 537
Danville, IL 61834-537   217-443-3592
                         Fax: 217-443-3894
                              www.tridan.com/

Machinery and tooling for heat transfer coil production

President: Mike Ames
Manager, Sales: Ken Warren
kwarren@kaydon.com
In Business: 49 years
Number of Employees: 49
Sales Information: $10 Million - $49.9 Milli

7383 USA Manufacturing Corporation

U. S. Manufacturing Corp.
28201 Van Dyke
Warren, MI 48093-2713   586-467-1600
                         Fax: 586-467-1630
                              www.usmfg.com

Contactors, relays, transformers, electric motors, capacitors, air conditioners, furnaces and building materials

President: Jack Falcon
CFO: Mark Roll
VP, Sales, Marketing & Product Deve: Dr. Adel Khanfar
Director of Quality : Donald E. Ross
Founder: Joseph A. Simon, Sr.
Catalog Cost: Free
Catalog Circulation: Mailed 10 time(s) per year to 900M
Average Order Size: $500
Printing Information: 32 pages in 2 colors on Matte Stock
Press: Web Press
Binding: Saddle Stitched
Mailing List Information: Names for rent

List Manager: Anita Wolf, International
List Company: Bill Daniels, Domestic
In Business: 51 years
Number of Employees: 20
Sales Information: $5MM to $10MM

7384 Uniweld Products

Uniweld Products, Inc.
2850 Ravenswood Road
Fort Lauderdale, FL 33312   800-323-2111
                         Fax: 954-587-0109
                              uniweld.com

Test equipment and pressure gauges, welding and cutting equipment, flame tools for soldering and brazing, tubing tools

Chairman: David Pearl, Sr.
President: David S. Pearl II
International Marketing Manager: Richard Apodaca
Mailing List Information: Names for rent
In Business: 68 years
Number of Employees: 400
Sales Information: $50,000,000 - $100,000,00

7385 Victory Engineering VECO Thermistors

118 Victory Road
Springfield, NJ 07081-1314   973-379-5900
                         Fax: 973-379-5982
                  www.datasheetarchive.com

Flake thermistors

Catalog Circulation: Mailed 1 time(s) per year
Printing Information: 43 pages in 2 colors
Binding: Saddle Stitched

7386 Virginia KMP Corporation

VirginiaKMP Corp.
4100 Platinum Way
Dallas, TX 75237-1616   214-330-7731
                              800-285-8567
                         Fax: 214-337-8854
                         virginiakmpcorp.com/

Refrigeration components, cleaners, lubricants, sealants and water treatment chemicals

President: Brian Dillon
CFO: Masheka Allen
Marketing Manager: Ron Burge
Production Manager: Thomas Barmann
Catalog Cost: Free
Catalog Circulation: Mailed 1 time(s) per year to 25M
Printing Information: 28 pages in 4 colors on Matte Stock
Press: Web Press
Binding: Saddle Stitched
In Business: 85 years
Number of Employees: 600
Sales Information: $10MM to $20MM

7387 Visionary Solutions

Tempco Electric Heater Corporation
607 N Central Ave.
Wood Dale, IL 60191   630-350-2252
                              800-323-6859
                         Fax: 630-350-0232
                              info@tempco.com
                              www.tempco.com

Manufacturer of industrial and commercial electric heating elements.

President: Fermin A. Adames
CFO: Paul Wickland
Marketing Manager: Dennis Padlo
Production Manager: Richard Sachs
Operations Manager: Debbie Wiles
International Marketing Manager: Leo Adames
Catalog Cost: Free
Catalog Circulation: to 30000
Printing Information: 960 pages in 4 colors on Glossy Stock
Press: Web Press
Binding: Perfect Bound
Mailing List Information: Names for rent
In Business: 45 years

Number of Employees: 330
Sales Information: $20MM to $50MM

7388 Watlow Electric Manufacturing Company

Watlow
2800 Brookview Dr.
Burnsville, MN 55337-4039   408-776-6646
                              800-WAT-OW2
                         Fax: 314-878-6814
                              info@watlow.com
                              www.Watlow.Com

Thermal system components

President: Peter Desloge
CFO: Steve Desloge
Marketing Manager: Judy Simms-Brown
Catalog Cost: Free
Catalog Circulation: to 100M+
Average Order Size: $3
Printing Information: 331 pages in 4 colors on Matte Stock
Press: Web Press
Binding: Perfect Bound
Mailing List Information: Names for rent
In Business: 91 years
Number of Employees: 2000

7389 Wayne Products

Wayne Products, Inc.
888 Sussex Blvd
PO Box 788
Broomall, PA 19355-909   610-251-0933
                              800-255-5665
                         Fax: 610-251-0948
                  info@wayneproducts.com
                         www.wayneproducts.com

Cooling and dust protection equipment, industrial and oil skimmers

President: Richard L Segermark
Printing Information: 12 pages in 4 colors on Glossy Stock
Press: Letterpress
Binding: Saddle Stitched
In Business: 37 years
Number of Employees: 15
Sales Information: $1,000,000 - $5,000,000

7390 YSI Temperature

YSI
1700/1725 Brannum Lane
Yellow Springs, OH 45387-1107   937-767-7241
                              800-765-4974
                         Fax: 937-767-9353
                         environmental@ysi.com
                              www.ysi.com

Temperature sensing units

President: Rick Omlor
Catalog Circulation: Mailed 1 time(s) per year
Printing Information: 28 pages in 2 colors
Binding: Saddle Stitched
In Business: 66 years

Systems & Units

7391 ABCO Industries

Cleaver Brooks
221 Law Street
Thomasville, GA 31792   229-226-3024
                              800-250-5883
                  info@cleaverbrooks.com
                         www.cleaverbrooks.com

Water tube waste heat boilers

Chairman: P. Welch Goggins, Jr.
President: Bart A. Aitken
Marketing Manager: Paul M. Anderson
Production Manager: David Raymond
President, Packaged Boiler Systems: Earle Pfefferkorn
Senior Vice President, Operations: Matthew Blake
Buyers: John Davenport
Mailing List Information: Names for rent
List Manager: Bob Stemen
In Business: 88 years

Number of Employees: 1400
Sales Information: $15,000,000

7392 AEC

AEC, Inc.
2900 S. 160th St.
New Berlin, WI 53151
262-641-8600
800-423-3183
Fax: 262-641-8653
dazzarello@corpemail.com
www.acscorporate.com/aec

Air conditioners and heaters.

President: Bruce Freeman
CEO: Thomas Breslin
VP Operations: Lisa Dickson
In Business: 58 years
Number of Employees: 65
Sales Information: $7.6 Million

7393 Accutherm

Accutherm, Inc.
25 Industrial Drive
P.O. Box 249
Monroe City, MO 63456-249
573-735-1060
888-925-IDEA
Fax: 573-735-1066
heaters@accutherm.com
www.accutherm.com

Electric heating units and controls

President: Charles Bindemann
CFO: Marilyn Bindemann
Marketing Manager: Rich Stilley
Production Manager: Frank Cross
General Manager: Walter Tuley
Customer Service: Tracy Porter
Mailing List Information: Names for rent
In Business: 25 years
Number of Employees: 100

7394 Acra Electric Corporation

Delta Manufacturing Company, Inc.
PO Box 9889
Tulsa, OK 74157
918-224-6755
800-223-4328
Fax: 918-224-6866
info@deltamfg.com
www.deltamfg.com

Electrical heating elements for air conditioning and refrigeration, lab equipment and food service

President: Dick Housekeeper
CFO: Don Sallers
Marketing Manager: Gary Marschke
VP: Judy Housekeeper
Accounting Manager: Kathleen Cheesman
Credit Cards: AMEX; MasterCard
Mailing List Information: Names for rent
In Business: 65 years
Number of Employees: 16
Sales Information: $1.7 Million

7395 Adams Manufacturing Company

Adams Manufacturing Company
9790 Midwest Ave
Cleveland, OH 44125-2497
216-587-6801
Fax: 216-587-6807
adamsx@att.net
www.adamsmanufacturing.com

Oil and gas burners, humidifiers and electronic air cleaners, furnaces, unit heaters

President: Marty Schonberger Sr
VP: Ruth Schonberger
VP: Marty Schonberger, Jr.
Accounts: Sydney Schonberger
In Business: 70 years
Number of Employees: 50
Sales Information: $5,000,000

7396 Addison Products Company

Addison
7050 Overland Rd
Orlando, FL 32810-3404
407-292-4400
Fax: 407-299-6178
info@addison-hvac.com
www.addison-hvac.com

Heat pumps 1-30 h.p., air conditioning 1-40 h.p.

President: Don Peck
Marketing Manager: Joseph Allegra
Production Manager: James Benjamin
Number of Employees: 200
Sales Information: $25,000,000 - $50,000,000

7397 Aerco International

AERCO
100 Oritani Drive
Blauvelt, NY 10913-2095
845-580-8000
800-526-0288
www.aerco.com

Temperature regulators, gas fired heaters, steam generators and heat exchangers

President: Fred F Campagna
CFO: Tim Buhl
Catalog Cost: Free
In Business: 68 years
Number of Employees: 100
Sales Information: $25,000,000 - $50,000,000

7398 Aerofin Corporation

Aerofin
4621 Murray Place
P.O. Box 10819
Lynchburg, VA 24506
434-845-7081
800-237-6346
Fax: 434-528-6242
sales@aerofin.com
www.aerofin.com

Surface heating and cooling units

Chairman: Ernest Siddons
President: David L Corell
CFO: Gavin Divers
Marketing Manager: G Hagwood
Production Manager: Geoffrey Steadman
Manager: Paul Kavanaugh
In Business: 92 years
Number of Employees: 200

7399 Aggreko

Aggreko North America
15600 John F. Kennedy Blvd.
Suite 200
Houston, TX 77032-2343
281-985-8200
844-606-1672
Fax: 281-848-1399
www.aggreko.com

Generator rental power packages and systems, portable temperature control equipment, air conditioners, chillers and heaters

Chairman: Ken Hanna
President: Asterios Satrazemis
CFO: Carole Cran
Chief Executive Officer and Interim: Chris Weston
Director, Asia: Debajit Das
President, Rental Solutions: Asterios Satrazemis
In Business: 53 years
Number of Employees: 40
Sales Information: $500M

7400 Air Comfort

Air Comfort
2550 Braga Drive
Broadview, IL 60155
708-345-1900
800-466-3779
Fax: 708-345-2730
info@aircomfort.com
www.aircomfort.com

Manufactures heat pumps, air conditioners & electric furnaces

President: Tim Smerz
smerz@aircomfort.com
CFO: Lynette Mantey
manteyl@aircomfort.com
EVP: Jim Bartolotta
bartolottaj@aircomfort.com
VP, Service Operations: Mike Schmidt
schmidtm@aircomfort.com
VP: Blaz Lucas
lucasb@aircomfort.com
In Business: 80 years
Number of Employees: 110
Sales Information: $786,000

7401 Alfa-Laval Thermal

Alfa-Laval Thermal
5400 International Trade Drive
Richmond, VA 23231-231
804-222-5300
866-253-2528
Fax: 804-236-3276
customerservice.usa@alfalaval.com
www.Alfalaval.Us

Heat exchangers

President: Steven Pratt
Number of Employees: 1150

7402 Alhern Martin Industrial Furnace Company

Alhern Martin Industrial Furnace Company
2155 Austin Drive
Troy, MI 48083-2237
248-689-6363
Fax: 248-689-1344
sales@alhern-martin.com
www.alhern-martin.com/

Heat treating furnaces and boilers

President: James VanEtten
Credit Cards: AMEX; MasterCard
In Business: 70 years
Number of Employees: 15
Sales Information: $1,000,000 - $5,000,000

7403 Alloy Fabricators of New England

Alloy Fabricators of New England
39 York Ave
Randolph, MA 02368-1827
781-986-6400
800-343-1002
Fax: 781-986-2667
info@alloyfabne.com
www.alloyfabne.com/index.html

Heat treating equipment

President: Christian Dietz
Number of Employees: 18
Sales Information: $1,000,000 - $5,000,000

7404 Alstrom Corporation

Alstrom Corporation
1408 Seabury Ave
Bronx, NY 10461-3691
718-824-4901
800-223-4901
Fax: 718-409-3605
info@alstromcorp.com
www.Alstromcorp.Com

Industrial heat exchangers

President: Declan Power
In Business: 76 years
Number of Employees: 12
Sales Information: $1,000,000 - $5,000,000

7405 Amtrol

Amtrol
1400 Division Rd
West Warwick, RI 02893-2300
401-884-6300
Fax: 401-884-4773
info@amtrol.com
www.Amtrol.Com

Heat transfer products

Chairman: Larry T Guillemette
President: Larry T Guillemette
Marketing Manager: DH Ellis
CEO of Newport Global Advisors: Timothy T. Janszen

In Business: 69 years
Number of Employees: 800

7406 Application Engineering
AEC
2900 S. 160th St.
New Berlin, WI 53151 262-641-8600
800-423-3183
Fax: 262-641-8653
dazzarello@corpemail.com
www.aecinternet.com

Industrial water chilling systems

President: Bruce Freeman
Marketing Manager: Kevin Chubyk
In Business: 58 years
Number of Employees: 200
Sales Information: $500M to $1MM

7407 Atomizing Systems
Atomizing Systems Inc.
1 Hollywood Ave # 1
Ho Ho Kus, NJ 07423-1433 201-447-1222
888-265-3364
Fax: 201-447-6932
info@coldfog.com
www.Coldfog.Com

High pressure fog systems for water and chemicals for HVAC, cooling, effects, dust and odor suppression

President: Michael Elkas
Production Manager: Tom Pagliaroni
International Marketing Manager: Michael V. Elkas
Buyers: Michael Farrelly
Catalog Circulation: Mailed 1 time(s) per year
Mailing List Information: Names for rent
In Business: 22 years
Number of Employees: 16
Sales Information: $1,500,000

7408 Aztec Machinery Company
Aztec Machinery Company
960 Jacksonville Rd
Ivyland, PA 18974-1719 215-672-2600
Fax: 215-441-0289
www.aztecmachinery.com/

Heat processing machinery and drying systems

President: David Rattner
In Business: 54 years
Number of Employees: 65
Sales Information: $5,000,000 - $10,000,000

7409 Bock Water Heaters
Bock Water Heaters
110 S Dickinson Street
Madison, WI 53703-8632 608-257-2225
800-794-2491
Fax: 608-257-5304
info@bockwaterheaters.com
www.bockwaterheaters.com/

Oil, gas and electric water heaters

President: John C Bock
Marketing Manager: Donna Sheehan
In Business: 86 years
Number of Employees: 45
Sales Information: $10,000,000 - $25,000,000

7410 Brookside Group
Brookside Group
88 E. Main Street
Suite 436
Mendham, NJ 07945-1832 973-543-6765
800-336-0761
Fax: 973-543-6875
info@brooksidegroup.com
www.brooksidegroup.com

Air moving devices

President: CA Forth Jr
Marketing Manager: G Dunay
Founder and Principal: Michael (Mick) Sawka

Channel Program Development: Larry Lisser
Tech. Deve. & Client Services: Scott Bresnick

7411 Brown Fired Heater Division
Brown Fired Heater Division
300 Huron Street
Elyria, OH 44035-4829 440-323-7080
Fax: 440-323-5734
info@enerconsystems.com
www.enerconsystems.com

Fin tubed fired heaters, process fired heaters, superheaters and waste heat boilers

President: David A Hoecke
Catalog Cost: Free
Catalog Circulation: Mailed 50 time(s) per year
Average Order Size: $50
Printing Information: 6 pages in 2 colors on Glossy Stock
Binding: Saddle Stitched
Mailing List Information: Names for rent
In Business: 40 years
Number of Employees: 20
Sales Information: $1,000,000 - $5,000,000

7412 Burr Oak Tool & Gauge Company
Burr Oak Tool inc
405 W South Street
Sturgis, MI 49091-338 269-651-9393
Fax: 269-651-4324
sales@burroak.com
www.burroak.com

Return benders, condensors, evaporators and other air moving equipment

Chairman: N Franks
President: LA Franks
Sales Engineer: Bret Hamlin
bhamlin@burroak.com
Sales Engineer: Mark Hurley
mhurley@burroak.com
Sales Engineer: Rick Littlefield
rlittlefield@burroak.com
Number of Employees: 395
Sales Information: Under $500M

7413 Carlton-Bates Company
Carlton-Bates
3600 W 69th St.
Little Rock, AR 72209 501-562-9100
866-600-6040
customerservicecb@carltonbates.com
www.carltonbates.com

Electronic components, devices, equipment, hardware, and accessories.

Catalog Cost: Free
In Business: 59 years

7414 Chiller Rentals & Manufacturing
Johnson Controls
5757 N. Green Bay Avenue
PO Box 591
Milwaukee, WI 53201-2508 414-524-1200
Fax: 310-412-2809
www.johnsoncontrols.com

Air conditioners and cooling units

Chairman: Alex A. Molinaroli
President: Alex A. Molinaroli
CFO: Brian J. Stief
CEO: David Abney
VP/Secretary/General Counsel: Brian Cadwallader
EVP/Chief HR Officer: Susan F. Davis
In Business: 130 years
Number of Employees: 1680
Sales Information: Under $500M

7415 ClimateMaster
ClimateMaster
7300 S.W. 44th Street
Oklahoma City, OK 73179 405-745-6000
877-436-6263
Fax: 405-745-4102
www.climatemaster.com

Geothermal heating and cooling systems
President: Dan Ellis

7416 Compressors Unlimited
Compressors Unlimited Intl., LLC
2531 S Belt Line Road
P.O. Box 361027
Dallas, TX 75253-4602 972-286-2264
800-789-9890
Fax: 972-286-5545
gwen@cuillc.com
www.compressorsunlimited.com

Used and rebuilt air conditioning equipment

Marketing Manager: D Cline
Production Manager: Brian Robertson
brianr@cuillc.com
Manager: Gwen McCollum
gwen@cuillc.com
Manager: David Wilcox
davidw@cuillc.com
Manager: James McCollum
james@cuillc.com
In Business: 30 years

7417 Corbett Industries
Corbett Industries Inc.
39 Hewson Ave.
Waldwick, NJ 07463-212 201-445-6311
800-442-4028
Fax: 201-445-6316
info@corbettind.com
www.corbettind.com

Heat treating units

President: James F Corbett
In Business: 64 years
Number of Employees: 22
Sales Information: $1,000,000 - $5,000,000

7418 Correct Air Corporation
AirCorrect Inc.
17 Easton Road
Unit 7
Brantford, CN N3P 1 519-753-5333
800-231-3286
Fax: 519-753-0049
sales@aircorrectinc.com
www.aircorrectinc.com

Industrial air conditioning equipment

President: James H Rieghart
Credit Cards: MasterCard
Number of Employees: 20
Sales Information: $1,000,000 - $5,000,000

7419 Desert Aire Corporation
Desert Aire Corporation
N120 W18485 Freistadt Rd
Germantown, WI 53022-3844 262-946-7400
262-946-7401
Fax: 414-357-8501
sales@desert-aire.com
www.desert-aire.com

Industrial, refrigerated dehumidifiers

President: Keith Coursin
Marketing Manager: John Gregor
International Marketing Manager: Anton Bosch
Credit Cards: AMEX; MasterCard
Mailing List Information: Names for rent
In Business: 37 years
Number of Employees: 60
Sales Information: $5,000,000 - $10,000,000

7420 Dry Coolers
Dry Coolers Inc.
575 South Glaspie Street
Oxford, MI 48371-1638 248-969-3400
800-525-8173
Fax: 248-969-3401
info@drycoolers.com
www.Drycoolers.Com

Industrial cooling systems

Chairman: Margery Russell, VP
President: Brian Russell
CFO: Jessica Russell, Accounts Payable
Marketing Manager: David Russell, Sales Manager
Technical Sales: Armand Blake
armand@drycoolers.com
Plant Manager: Phillip Noel
pnoel@drycoolers.com
Chief Engineer: Matt Reed
matt.reed@drycoolers.com
Credit Cards: AMEX; MasterCard
In Business: 20 years
Number of Employees: 6
Sales Information: $3MM to $5MM

7421 Expanded Seal Tools
Curtiss Wright Flow control company EST
2701 Township Line Road
Hatfield, PA 19440-1770   215-721-1100
                                 800-355-7044
                           Fax: 215-721-1101
                     est-info@curtisswright.com
                         www.expansionseal.com

Heat exchangers

In Business: 47 years
Number of Employees: 20-5
Sales Information: $1,000,000 - $5,000,000

7422 Fostoria Industries
Fostoria Industries
114 Roscoe Fitz Road
Gray, TN 37615   419-435-9201
                                 800-495-4525
                           Fax: 419-435-0842

Portable, mounted and air forced electric heaters, infrared ovens

President: LE Dunlap
CFO: JL Donaldson
Marketing Manager: M Abell
VP: Steve Fruth
swfruth@tpicorp.com
Application Engineer: John Podach
jfpodach@tpicorp.com
Internet Marketing: Jamie Johns
jjohns@tpicorp.com
Number of Employees: 110
Sales Information: $20MM to $50MM

7423 Fraser-Johnston Heating/Air Conditioning
Unitary Products
5005 York Drive
Norman, OK 73069   405-364-4040
                                 877-874-7378
                  cg-upgconsumerrelations@jci.com
                        www.fraserjohnston.com

Residential and commercial furnaces, controls and services, heat pumps and air conditioning, refrigeration and security systems for buildings

President: R Barnett
Marketing Manager: RN Morrison

7424 Friedrich Air Conditioning
Friedrich Air Conditioning
10001 Reunion Place, Ste 500
San Antonio, TX 78216   210-546-0500
                                 800-541-6645
                           Fax: 210-357-4432
                          www.friedrich.com

Air conditioning, dehumidifiers, heat pumps

President: Georgr Vanhoomisen
Marketing Manager: J Deming
Fulfillment: Jennifer Graham
Catalog Cost: Free
Printing Information: 4 pages in 4 colors on Glossy Stock
Press: Sheetfed Press
Binding: Folded
Mailing List Information: Names for rent
In Business: 131 years
Number of Employees: 600
Sales Information: $20MM to $50MM

7425 Fuel Efficiency
Fuel Efficiency, LLC
101 Davis Industrial Park
P.O. Box 271
Clyde, NY 14433   315-923-2511
                                 800-448-9794
                           Fax: 315-923-9182
                      fuelefficiency@aol.com
            www.fuelefficiencyllc.com/location.html

Cast iron/fire tube boilers

President: H Knapp
In Business: 41 years
Number of Employees: 10-J
Sales Information: $1,000,000 - $5,000,000

7426 GC Broah Company
The G.C.Broach Company
7667 E 46th Pl
#B
Tulsa, OK 74145-6307   918-664-7420
                           Fax: 918-627-4083
                         broach@broach.com
                            www.broach.com

Process heaters, custom boilers, hot oil systems and propane vaporizers

Chairman: Clayton Broach
President: Roger Broach
VP: Brain Borach
In Business: 55 years
Number of Employees: 25
Sales Information: $5MM to $10MM

7427 Gas Fired Products
Gas Fired Products
PO Box 36485
305 Doggett Street
Charlotte, NC 28236-6485   704-372-3485
                                 800-830-3983
                           Fax: 704-332-5843
                  info@gasfiredproducts.com
                     www.gasfiredproducts.com

Industrial, commercial, residential radiant gas heating equipment, gas room heaters, tobacco curing equipment

President: Frank L Horne Jr
Mailing List Information: Names for rent
In Business: 66 years
Number of Employees: 50
Sales Information: $5,000,000 - $10,000,000

7428 Glo-Quartz Electric Heater Company
Glo-Quartz
7084 Maple St
Mentor, OH 44060   440-255-9701
                                 800-321-3574
                           Fax: 440-255-7852
                     tstrokes@gloquartz.com
                          www.Gloquartz.Com

Immersion heaters

President: George T Strokes
Credit Cards: MasterCard
In Business: 60 years
Number of Employees: 21
Sales Information: $1,000,000 - $5,000,000

7429 Grieve Corporation
Grieve
500 Hart Rd
Round Lake, IL 60073-2898   847-546-8225
                           Fax: 847-546-9210
                       sales@grievecorp.com
                          www.Grievecorp.Com

Industrial and laboratory ovens and furnaces

President: Dv Grieve
Marketing Manager: Lynn Niemi
Fulfillment: Frank Calabrese
Catalog Cost: Free
Printing Information: 100 pages in 4 colors on Glossy Stock
Mailing List Information: Names for rent
List Manager: Frank Calabrese

In Business: 65 years
Number of Employees: 140
Sales Information: $10,000,000 - $25,000,000

7430 Hansen Refrigeration Machinery Company
Hansen Refrigeration Machinery Company
415 Trowbridge Dr
Fond Du Lac, WI 54937-8620   920-922-4327
                           Fax: 920-922-0192
                   info@hansenrefrigeration.com
                     www.Hansenrefrigeration.Com

Liquid chillers for machine tools and industrial equipment

Chairman: JJ Julka
President: J R Julka
Production Manager: SB Wright
Mailing List Information: Names for rent
In Business: 58 years
Number of Employees: 20
Sales Information: $1,000,000 - $5,000,000

7431 Harper Electric Furnace Corporation
Harper International
4455 Genesee Street
Suite 123
Buffalo, NY 14225-1698   716-276-9900
                           Fax: 716-810-9460
                         info@harperintl.com
                          www.harperintl.com

Furnaces and kilns

Chairman: Waldron Bamford
President: Jeet Bhatia
Chief Executive: Wayne Robinson
Secretary: Jane Clemens
In Business: 24 years
Number of Employees: 100
Sales Information: $10,000,000 - $25,000,000

7432 Hayden
Hayden
1393 E. San Bernardino Ave.
San Bernardino, CA 92408-6901   951-736-2600
                                 800-854-4757
                           Fax: 951-736-2629
                        www.Haydenindustrial.Com

Heat exchangers

President: Jon Perry
CFO: Gil Leon
In Business: 25 years
Number of Employees: 150
Sales Information: $25,000,000 - $50,000,000

7433 Heat Treating & America's Finest
Cress Mfg. Company
4736 Convair Drive
Carson City, NV 89706-493   775-884-2777
                                 800-423-4584
                           Fax: 775-884-2991
                         info@cressmfg.com
                          www.cressmfg.com

Heat treating furnaces and kilns for ceramics, glass, pottery, etc

President: Steve Cress
Mailing List Information: Names for rent
In Business: 42 years

7434 Heatec
Heatec, Inc.
5200 Wilson Road
PO Box 72760
Chattanooga, TN 37410-5760   423-821-5200
                                 800-235-5200
                           Fax: 423-821-7673
                         heatec@heatec.com
                           www.heatec.com

Heating equipment for many industries

President: Tom Wilkey
twilkey@heatec.com
Production Manager: John Clayton
jclayton@heatec.com
Human Resources Director: Wesley Jones

wjones@heatec.com
Executive Vice President: Robert Wilfong
rwilfong@heatec.com
Advertising Director: Frank Eley
feley@heatec.com
Number of Employees: 130
Sales Information: $10,000,000 - $25,000,000

7435 Holland, RW
RW Holland Inc,
5004 S 101st East Ave
PO Box 472336
Tulsa, OK 74146-4919   918-664-7822
                              Fax: 918-665-1605
                              sales@rwholland.com
                              www.Rwholland.Com

Heat exchangers and heating coils

President: D J Eckenfels
Mailing List Information: Names for rent
In Business: 45 years
Number of Employees: 38
Sales Information: $1,000,000 - $5,000,000

7436 ITW BGK Finishing Systems
BGK Finishing Systems
4131 Pheasant Ridge Drive NE
Minneapolis, MN 55449-7102   763-784-0466
                              800-663-5498
                              Fax: 763-784-1362
                              information@finishingbrands.com
                              www.bgk.com

Infared airing equipment and finishing systems

President: Mark Rekucki
Operations Manager: Jim Sweeney
jsweeney@finishingbrands.com
Spare Parts: Gordie Markstrom
gmarkstrom@finishingbrands.com
Service: Scott Anderson
sanderson@finishingbrands.com
Mailing List Information: Names for rent
In Business: 18 years
Number of Employees: 65
Sales Information: $5,000,000 - $10,000,000

7437 Indeck Power Equipment Company
Indeck Power Equipment Company
1111 Willis Avenue
Wheeling, IL 60090-5841   847-541-8300
                              800-446-3325
                              Fax: 847-541-9984
                              info@indeck-power.com
                              www.Indeck.Com

Boilers and air cooled chillers

Chairman: Gerald R Forsythe
President: Marsha Fournier
CEO: Gerald R Forsythe
COO: Marsha Fournier
Number of Employees: 100
Sales Information: $20MM to $50MM

7438 Inductoheat
Inductoheat
32251 N Avis Dr
Madison Heights, MI 48071-5000 248-585-9393
                              800-624-6297
                              Fax: 248-589-1062
                              sales@inductoheat.com
                              www.Inductoheat.Com

Forge heating systems and equipment

Chairman: Gary Doyon
President: Doug Brown
Group VP: Gary Doyon
COO: Doug Brown
Number of Employees: 145
Sales Information: $10,000,000 - $25,000,000

7439 KH Huppert Company
KH Huppert Company
16808 S. Lathrop Ave.
Harvey, IL 60426-4800   708-339-2020
                              Fax: 708-339-2225
                              sales@huppert.com
                              www.huppert.com

Industrial heat treat furnaces and accessories

President: Norman K Huppert
Catalog Cost: Free
Catalog Circulation: to 1500
Average Order Size: $8000
Printing Information: in 2 colors on Glossy Stock
Press: Letterpress
Mailing List Information: Names for rent
In Business: 70 years
Number of Employees: 16
Sales Information: $1MM to $3MM

7440 Kim Kool
Kim Kool, Inc.
2619 Lena St
Sulphur, LA 70665-7439   337-527-5519
                              800-341-1109
                              Fax: 337-527-8809
                              www.Kimkool.Com

Industrial oil coolers and radiators

President: Dyrell K Stokes
CFO: Floy Stokes
Number of Employees: 18
Sales Information: $1,000,000 - $5,000,000

7441 Lattner Boilers Manufacturing
Lattner Boiler Company
1411 9th St. SW
Cedar Rapids, IA 52404-1527   319-366-0778
                              800-345-1527
                              Fax: 319-366-0770
                              info@lattner.com
                              www.lattner.com

Industrial steam and hot water boilers

President: Steven R Junge
In Business: 97 years
Number of Employees: 30
Sales Information: $1,000,000 - $5,000,000

7442 Lennox International
Lennox International
2140 Lake Park Blvd.
Richardson, TX 75080   972-497-5000
                              Fax: 972-497-5292
                              investor@lennoxintl.com
                              www.lennoxinternational.com/

Heating, ventilating, air conditioning and refrigeration products

Chairman: Todd M. Bluedorn
President: John W Norris Jr
CFO: Joseph W. Reitmeier
EVP: Joseph W. Reitmeier
EVP & Chief Technology Officer: Prakash Bedapudi
EVP & Chief Human Resources Officer: Daniel M. Sessa
In Business: 118 years
Number of Employees: 400

7443 Lindberg: A Unit of General Signal
SPX Thermal Product Solutions
2821 Old Route 15
New Columbia, PA 17856   570-538-7200
                              800-586-2473
                              Fax: 570-538-7391
                              info@thermalproductsolutions.com
                              www.thermalproductsolutions.com

Heat processing units

President: Kirit Patel
Number of Employees: 300
Sales Information: $25,000,000 - $50,000,000

7444 Lintern Corporation
Lintern Corporation
8685 Station Street
PO Box 90
Mentor, OH 44060-4336   440-255-9333
                              800-321-3638
                              Fax: 440-255-6427
                              solutions@lintern.com
                              www.lintern.com

Industrial air conditioners for heavy and severe duty environments

President: Richard Lintern
Marketing Manager: Mike Considder
Founder: William Lintern
Credit Cards: AMEX; MasterCard
Catalog Circulation: to 200
Printing Information: 20 pages in 4 colors on Glossy Stock
Mailing List Information: Names for rent
In Business: 123 years
Number of Employees: 40
Sales Information: $1,000,000 - $5,000,000

7445 Ludeca
Ludeca Inc.
1425 NW 88th Avenue
Doral, FL 33172   305-591-8935
                              Fax: 305-591-1537
                              info@ludeca.com
                              www.ludeca.com

Laser alignment, vibration analysis and balancing equpment, training and services

President: Frank Seidenthal
Marketing Manager: Anna Marie Delgado
VP: Alan Luedeking
In Business: 35 years
Number of Employees: 50
Sales Information: $10MM to $20MM

7446 M&W Systems
M&W Systems
2346 Tripaldi Way
Hayward, CA 94545   510-887-7008
                              Fax: 510-887-7220
                              Mandwsystems.com

Liquid cooling systems

President: Helga Price
Number of Employees: 5
Sales Information: 5MM-10MM

7447 M-E-C Company
M-E-C Company
1400 W. Main Street
PO Box 330
Neodesha, KS 66757-0330   620-325-2673
                              Fax: 620-325-2678
                              mec@m-e-c.com
                              www.m-e-c.com/

Air and direct heat dryers

President: David M Parker
Marketing Manager: Michael Hudson
V.P. of Sales: Stephen D. Rice
srice@m-e-c.com
Sales Executive: Michael R. Porter
mporter@m-e-c.com
Inside Sales: Zack A. Forslund
zforslund@m-e-c.com
In Business: 83 years
Number of Employees: 200
Sales Information: $25,000,000 - $50,000,000

7448 Magnat-Fairview
Maxcess International, Inc
222 West Memorial Rd.
Oklahoma City, OK 73114   405-755-1600
                              800-569-1286
                              Fax: 405-755-8425
                              sales@magnatfairview.com
                              www.magnatfairview.com

Engineered rolls, heating and cooling

President: Rhonda Barlow
In Business: 68 years

Number of Employees: 50
Sales Information: $5,000,000 - $10,000,000

7449 Matticks Industries
Matticks Industries
11232 Brittmoore Park Dr
Houston, TX 77041 832-243-0662
 800-383-8151
 Fax: 832-243-0660
 info@matticks.com
 www.matticks.com

Explosion proof air conditioners

President: Kevin Matticks
Inside Sales: Kevin A. Matticks
kevinm@matticks.com
Inside Sales: Philip A. Matticks
philipm@matticks.com
Inside Sales: David Masaryk
davem@matticks.com
In Business: 28 years
Number of Employees: 9
Sales Information: $1,000,000 - $5,000,000

7450 Memco Supply
Memco Supply
102 Main Street
PO Box 60
Jay, ME 04239 207-897-4100
 800-421-3123
 Fax: 207-897-4141
 memco@memcosupply.com
 www.memcosupply.com

Plumbing and heating systems and supplies

President: Norman St. Pierre
Marketing Manager: Morton A Melvin
Number of Employees: 5
Sales Information: Under $500,000

7451 Morton Machine Works
Morton Machine Works
125 Gearhart Street
Millersburg, PA 17061 800-441-2751
 Fax: 717-692-2120
 sales@mortonmachine.com
 www.mortonmachine.com

Stainless steel tanks, vessels, heat exchangers and heat recovery systems

Printing Information: 136 pages
In Business: 70 years
Number of Employees: 130
Sales Information: $10MM to $20MM

7452 Mountain States Equipment Company
Mountain States Equipment Company
1975 S Navajo Street
Denver, CO 80223-3845 303-934-5551
 800-886-5484
 Fax: 303-922-3709
 airexmse@aol.com
 www.airex-mse.com

Specialists in evaporation cooling systems; standard, custom and retrofit; manufacturers of Airex Evaporative Cooling Equipment

President: John Thomas Hobson Jr
Printing Information: 50 pages
In Business: 87 years
Number of Employees: 7
Sales Information: $1,000,000 - $5,000,000

7453 Nationwide Boiler Catalog
Nationwide Boiler, Inc.
42400 Christy Street
Fremont, CA 94538-4401 510-490-7100
 800-227-1966
 Fax: 510-490-0571
 info@nationwideboiler.com
 www.nationwideboiler.com

Boilers and related equipment, selective catalytic reduction systems, economizers, deaerators/feed water systems, heat recovery, and water treatment, rentals, sales and leasing

President: Jeffery Shallcross
CFO: James Hermerding
Marketing Manager: Larry Day
Sales Engineer: Tim McBride
Rental Sales Manager: Michael Medina
Controller: Michele Tomas
In Business: 47 years
Number of Employees: 35
Sales Information: $24.98 MM

7454 Nordic Air
HDT Engineering Services, Inc.
5455 Route 307 West
Geneva, OH 44041 440-466-6640
 800-533-5484
 Fax: 440-466-2012
 www.hdtglobal.com

Air and water cooled condensors

Chairman: R. Andrew Hove
President: R. Andrew Hove
CFO: Anthony DiLucente
Marketing Manager: Greg Miller
SVP of U.S. Business: Jack Custer
Vice President of Tax: Bob Demarchi
VP & Chief Information Officer: Todd Nelson
Number of Employees: 25
Sales Information: $1,000,000 - $5,000,000

7455 Parker Boiler Company
Parker Boiler Company
5930 Bandini Blvd
Los Angeles, CA 90040-2998 323-727-9800
 Fax: 323-722-2848
 sales@parkerboiler.com
 www.Parkerboiler.Com

Direct-fired hot water boilers, indirect-fired water heaters, thermal liquid heaters, low NOx steam and hot water boilers and burner systems

President: Sid Danenhauer
Marketing Manager: Michael J Leeming
Production Manager: Alex Cuilty
Accounting: Ed Marchak
Advertising & Marketing: Mike Leeming
Administration: Sid D. Danenhauer
International Marketing Manager: Michael J Leeming
Buyers: Robert Barnes
Credit Cards: MasterCard; Visa
Catalog Cost: $30
Catalog Circulation: to 400
Printing Information: 270 pages in 4 colors on Glossy Stock
Press: Letterpress
Binding: 3
Mailing List Information: Names for rent
In Business: 69 years
Number of Employees: 60
Sales Information: $5,000,000 - $10,000,000

7456 Professional Equipment
Grainger
600 N. Lynndale Dr.
Appleton, WI 54914-3021 631-348-3780
 800-472-4643
 Fax: 888-776-3187
 info@professionalequipment.com
 www.grainger.com

Tools and testing equipment for the electrical, inspection, HVAC and engineering and building professionals

President: Patrick Norton
Credit Cards: AMEX; MasterCard
Catalog Circulation: Mailed 12 time(s) per year to 1m
Printing Information: 90 pages
Press: Web Press
Binding: Perfect Bound
In Business: 27 years

7457 Ras Welding
RAS Process Equipment
324 Meadowbrook Rd
Robbinsville, NJ 08691-2503 609-371-1000
 Fax: 609-371-1200
 sales@ras-inc.com
 www.Ras-Inc.Com

Fabricating vessels, heat exchangers and reactors

President: John Bonacorda
In Business: 38 years
Sales Information: $5MM to $10MM

7458 Sentry Equipment Corporation
Sentry Equipment Corporation
966 Blue Ribbon Circle N
PO Box 12
Oconomowoc, WI 53066-127 262-567-7256
 Fax: 262-567-4523
 sales@sentry-equip.com
 www.Sentry-Equip.com

Boiler blowdown systems, steam and water sample analysis systems, sample coolers, process samplers, spiral, tube heat exchangers, plate and frame heat exchangers

Chairman: Brian Baker
President: Michael Farrell
CFO: Brian Baker
Marketing Manager: Myron Feldman
Production Manager: Scott Raether
Buyers: Margaret Dwyer
Credit Cards: MasterCard; Visa
Catalog Circulation: Mailed 1 time(s) per year to 6M
Mailing List Information: Names for rent
List Manager: Wendy Melby
In Business: 91 years
Number of Employees: 95
Sales Information: $5,000,000 - $10,000,000

7459 Skidmore
Skidmore Pump
1875 Dewey Ave
Benton Harbor, MI 49022-9608 269-925-8812
 Fax: 269-925-7888
 www.skidmorepump.Com

Pumps, boiler feed systems and accessories for heating systems

President: David Van Houten
Marketing Manager: Mark Hendrix
Mailing List Information: Names for rent
In Business: 90 years
Number of Employees: 40
Sales Information: $5,000,000 - $10,000,000

7460 Skuttle Manufacturing Company
Skuttle
101 Margaret St
Marietta, OH 45750-9052 740-373-9169
 800-848-9786
 Fax: 740-373-9565
 customerservice@skuttle.com
 www.skuttle.com

Steam, flow-through, drum, atomizing and hydronic humidifiers

President: Davis Powers
Marketing Manager: John Riley
In Business: 98 years
Number of Employees: 38
Sales Information: $5,000,000 - $10,000,000

7461 Solaronics
Solaronics, Inc.
704 Woodburn Avenue
PO Box 80217
Rochester, MI 48308-217 248-650-3824
 800-223-5335
 Fax: 248-651-0357
 sales@solaronicsusa.com
 www.Solaronicsusa.Com

Electric and gas infrared heaters for industrial space heating; also gas burners for commercial cooking and process heating
President: Richard F Rush Jr
Marketing Manager: TD Lester
Production Manager: Carl Moore
In Business: 53 years
Number of Employees: 45
Sales Information: $5,000,000 - $10,000,000

7462 Solid State Heating
SSHC, Inc.
PO Box 769
Old Saybrook, CT 06475   860-399-5434
                                 800-544-5182
                            Fax: 860-399-6460
                            info@sshcinc.com
                            www.sshcinc.com

Radiant heating for commercial, residential and industrial applications
President: Richard Watson
Marketing Manager: S Delise
Printing Information: on Glossy Stock
Press: Sheetfed Press
Mailing List Information: Names for rent
In Business: 20 years
Number of Employees: 31
Sales Information: $5MM to $10MM

7463 South-Port Systems
Southport Engineered Systems, LLC.
6919 51st Street
Kenosha, WI 53144   262-654-6630
                            Fax: 610-459-4012
                            info@southportengsys.com
                            www.southportengsys.com

Air conditioners, heating units, refrigeration units and explosion proof air conditioners
President: Robert Nuzzo , P.E.
Marketing Manager: J Landers
EVP: Tom Suchla , P.E.
VP of Engineering: Tim Pann, P.E.
In Business: 14 years
Number of Employees: 800
Sales Information: $3MM to $5MM

7464 Southwire Machinery Divison
Southwire Company ,LLC
one southwire drive
Carrollton, GA 30119-2   770-832-4242
                               800-444-1700
                            Fax: 770-832-5234
                            www.southwire.com

Aluminum furnaces and custom design equipment
President: Stu Thorn
CFO: Guyton Cochran
Executive VP, Human Resources: Mike Wiggins
Senior VP, Reseach & Development: Vince Kruse
Executive VP, Operations: Jeff Herrin
In Business: 76 years
Number of Employees: 200
Sales Information: $25,000,000 - $50,000,000

7465 Sta-Warm Electric Company
Sta-Warm Electric Co.
PO Box 150
Ravenna, OH 44266-150   330-296-6461
                            Fax: 330-296-9243
                            www.sta-warm.com

Electrically heated industrial equipment
President: Brian Borthwick
Mailing List Information: Names for rent
In Business: 94 years
Number of Employees: 10
Sales Information: $1,000,000 - $5,000,000

7466 Sussman Aquamatic Steam Products Corporation
Sussman Electric Boilers
43-20 34th Street
Long Island City, NY 11101-2321   718-937-4500
                                   800-238-3535
                            Fax: 718-937-4676
                            seb@sussmancorp.com
                            www.sussmanelectricboilers.com

Electric steam and hot water boilers
Chairman: Richard Sussman
President: Charles Monteverdi
Marketing Manager: Michael Pinkus
Printing Information: on Glossy Stock
Mailing List Information: Names for rent
In Business: 7 years
Number of Employees: 80
Sales Information: $25,000,000 - $50,000,000

7467 Thermal Engineering Company
Thermal Engineering Co.
2022 Adams St
Toledo, OH 43604-4488   419-244-7781
                            Fax: 419-244-1878
                            www.Thermal-Eng.Com

Refrigeration and heating testing equipment
President: Clarence Kamm
Number of Employees: 30
Sales Information: $1,000,000 - $5,000,000

7468 Thermal Transfer Corporation
Thermal Transfer Corporation
50 N Linden St
Duquesne, PA 15110-1067   412-460-4004
                            Fax: 412-466-2899
                            info.ttc@hamonusa.com
                            www.hamonusa.com

Heat exchangers
President: Shoun T. Kerbaugh
shoun.kerbaugh@hamonusa.com
EVP - BD: Timothy Ottie
tim.ottie@hamonusa.com
Sales Manager - Heat Recovery: Terry King
terry.king@hamonusa.com
Purchasing Manager: Paul R. Bo
paul.borland@hamonusa.com
In Business: 15 years
Number of Employees: 50
Sales Information: $1,000,000 - $5,000,000

7469 Thermo-Kinetics
Thermo Kinetics
6740 Invader Crescent
Mississauga, CN L5T 2   905-670-2266
                               800-268-0967
                            Fax: 905-670-8530
                            inquiries@thermo-kinetics.com
                            www.thermo-kinetics.com

Industrial heating and air conditioners
President: Joe Dello
Vice President: Jeff Dello
Central Region Manager: Peter Dello
In Business: 40 years
Number of Employees: 100
Sales Information: $10,000,000 - $25,000,000

7470 Tisdale Company
Tidsale Company, Inc.
5111 N. Frazier
P.O. Box 2728
Conroe, TX 77305-2728   936-856-1500
                            Fax: 936-856-1600
                            www.tisdalecompanyinc.com

Explosion proof, corrosion proof custom shillers and airconditioning units
President: Lloyd Tisdale
CFO: Brenda Tisdale
Founder: Paul Tisdale Jr
In Business: 47 years
Number of Employees: 30
Sales Information: $5,000,000 - $10,000,000

7471 Tocco
Ajax Tocco Magnethermic Corporation
30100 Stephenson Highway
Madison Heights, MI 48071-1630   248-399-8601
                                  800-468-4932
                            Fax: 248-399-8603
                            info@ajaxtocco.com
                            www.Ajaxtocco.Com

Heating equipment
President: George Pfaffmann
Number of Employees: 45
Sales Information: $10MM to $20MM

7472 Trol International
ZoneFirst
20 Bushes Lane
Elmwood Park, NJ 07407-3204   201-794-8004
                               877-604-1044
                            Fax: 201-794-1359
                            info@zonefirst.com
                            www.trolexcorp.com

Zone control systems and fresh air intake systems
President: Richard Foster
Marketing Manager: Marc Ivry
Mailing List Information: Names for rent
In Business: 50 years
Number of Employees: 50
Sales Information: $5,000,000 - $10,000,000

7473 Turbotec Products Catalog
Turbotec Products
1404 Blue Hills Ave.
Bloomfield, CT 06002-1348   860-731-4200
                               801-280-2777
                            Fax: 860-243-0085
                            info@turbotecproducts.com
                            www.Turbotecproducts.Com

Heat exchangers and flexible connector products, refrigeration, automotive, bio-medical, plumbing, water heating
President: Sunil Raina
sraina@turbotecproducts.com
CFO: Robert Lieberman
Marketing Manager: Craig Ellis
cingram@turbotecproducts.com
EVP: Chuck Ingram
cingram@turbotecproducts.com
Customer Service Manager: Donna Santomenno
dsantomenno@tubotecproducts.com
Sales Account Manager: RandyWright
rwright@turbotecproducts.com
Mailing List Information: Names for rent
In Business: 35 years
Number of Employees: 98

7474 US Radiator Corporation
U.S. Radiator Corp.
4423 District Blvd
Vernon, CA 90058-3111   323-826-0965
                            Fax: 323-826-0970
                            www.Usradiator.Com

Industrial radiators
President: Don Armstrong
Credit Cards: MasterCard; Visa
In Business: 40 years
Number of Employees: 35
Sales Information: $5,000,000 - $10,000,000

7475 Unist
UNIST, Inc.
4134 36th St SE
Grand Rapids, MI 49512-2903   616-949-0853
                               800-253-5462
                            Fax: 616-949-9503
                            salessupport@unist.com
                            www.Unist.Com

Equipment for micro-fluidization in manufacturing processes
President: Wallace Boelkins
Marketing Manager: Bryce Hoff

In Business: 58 years
Number of Employees: 28
Sales Information: $5,000,000 - $10,000,000

7476 Visionary Solutions
Tempco Electric Heater Corporation
607 N Central Ave.
Wood Dale, IL 60191   630-350-2252
                             800-323-6859
                        Fax: 630-350-0232
                        info@tempco.com
                        www.tempco.com

Manufacturer of industrial and commercial electric heating elements.

President: Fermin A. Adames
CFO: Paul Wickland
Marketing Manager: Dennis Padlo
Production Manager: Richard Sachs
Operations Manager: Debbie Wiles
International Marketing Manager: Leo Adames
Catalog Cost: Free
Catalog Circulation: to 30000
Printing Information: 960 pages in 4 colors on Glossy Stock
Press: Web Press
Binding: Perfect Bound
Mailing List Information: Names for rent
In Business: 45 years
Number of Employees: 330
Sales Information: $20MM to $50MM

7477 Vortec Corporation
Vortec
10125 Carver Rd
Blue Ash, OH 45242-4798   513-891-7485
                              800-441-7475
                         Fax: 513-891-4092
                         sales@vortec.com
                         www.vortec.com

Compressed air-operated products

President: Steve Vroerman
Marketing Manager: Mike Rawlings
General Manager: Barbara Stefl
Operations Manager: Stan Coley
Engineering Manager: Steve Broerman
In Business: 53 years
Number of Employees: 31
Sales Information: $1,000,000 - $5,000,000

7478 WAAGE Electric
WAAGE Electric, Inc.
720 Colfax Ave
Kenilworth, NJ 07033-337   908-245-9363
                              800-922-4365
                         Fax: 908-245-8477
                         info@waage.com
                         www.Waage.Com

Electrical industrial heating equipment

President: Mark Waage
Marketing Manager: Bruce Waage
In Business: 107 years
Number of Employees: 14
Sales Information: $1,000,000 - $5,000,000

7479 Water Systems
Water Systems, Inc.
501 Corporate Centre Drive
Suite 310
Franklin, TN 37067-9397   615-627-1965
                         Fax: 615-627-1981
                         info@watersystems.com
                         www.watersystems.com

Pressurized water cooling systems

President: Mike Heil
Number of Employees: 4
Sales Information: $3MM to $5MM

7480 Waterworks Technologies
Waterworks Technologies Inc
2024-12 Avenue NW
Calgary, CN T2N 1   403-289-3198
                         Fax: 403-289-3147
                         waterworks@waterworks.ca
                         www.waterworks.ca

Water cooling systems

President: Lee Borges
In Business: 29 years
Number of Employees: 5
Sales Information: Under $500M

7481 WeatherKing Air Conditioning
WeatherKing Heating & Air Conditioning
51 Meadow Lane
Suite E
Northfield, OH 44067-7010   330-908-0281
                              440-248-9100
                         Fax: 330-908-0270
                         www.weatherking1.com

Central heating and cooling equipment

President: D Foster
Production Manager: J Waters
Number of Employees: 5

7482 Yazaki Energy Systems
Yazaki Energy Systems,Inc
701 E Plano Parkway
Suite 305
Plano, TX 75074-6700   469-229-5443
                         Fax: 469-229-5448
                         www.yazakienergy.com

Gas fired air conditioning/absorbtion chillers for cogeneration systems

President: Trevor Judd
Production Manager: J Calverley
In Business: 64 years
Number of Employees: 6
Sales Information: $500M to $1MM

7483 Yula Corporation
Yula Corporation
330 Bryant Ave
Bronx, NY 10474-7113   718-991-0900
                         Fax: 718-842-4239
                         yula@yulacorp.com
                         www.Yulacorp.Com

Heat transfer equipment, process coolers, process heaters and heat exchangers

President: Fred Feldman
f.feldman@yulacorp.com
CFO: Larry Feldman
l.feldman@yulacorp.com
Production Manager: Jose Barcena
j.barcena@yulacorp.com
Lead Engineer: Jason Feldman
j.feldman@yulacorp.com
Purchasing Manager: Michael Feldman
m.feldman@yulacorp.com
Sales Manager: Matthew Feldman
matt.feldman@yulacorp.com
In Business: 89 years
Number of Employees: 55
Sales Information: $5,000,000 - $10,000,000

Interior Textiles
Bed & Bath

7484 Julien Shade Shop
Julien Shade Shop
403 East Saint Paul Avenue
Milwaukee, WI 53202-5804   414-271-3864
                              800-242-1551
                         Fax: 414-271-9802

Shower curtains and decorative accessories

President: Brian Julien
Credit Cards: MasterCard
Number of Employees: 20
Sales Information: $1,000,000 - $5,000,000

7485 Militex Industries Corporation
Carolina Center
Mebane, NC 27302   910-563-4755
                         Fax: 910-563-3155

Shower curtains, pillows and tablecloths

President: Michael Salim
Number of Employees: 100
Sales Information: $5MM to $10MM

7486 Newport
Newport Layton Home Fashions
295 Fifth Ave
Suite 1406
New York, NY 10016-7124   212-447-6777
                              800-888-6860
                         Fax: 212-447-6719
                         customerservice@newportlayton.com
                         www.newportlayton.com

Shower curtains, bedspreads and decorative pillows

President: Janine Bustamante
In Business: 61 years
Number of Employees: 3
Sales Information: $1MM to $3MM

7487 Paper White
Paper White
2915 Kerner Boulevard
Suite F
San Rafael, CA 94901   415-482-9989
                         Fax: 415-482-0990
                         pwlinens@paperwhitelifestyle.com
                         www.paperwhitelifestyle.com

Luxury linens for the bed, bath, table and window

President: Jan Dutton
Number of Employees: 15
Sales Information: $1,000,000 - $5,000,000

7488 Reliable Fabrics
Reliable Fabrics Inc
1691 Revere Beach Parkway
Everett, MA 02149-5909   617-387-5321
                              800-682-4567
                         Fax: 617-387-9352
                         info@reliablefabrics.com
                         www.reliablefabrics.com

Comforters and bed accessories

President: Charles Schultz
CFO: Cal Kobrin
In Business: 79 years
Number of Employees: 17
Sales Information: $1,000,000 - $5,000,000

7489 Snug Fleece Woolens
SnugFleece Woollens, Inc.
2740 Pole Line Rd
Pocatello, ID 83201-6112   208-233-9622
                              800-824-1177
                         Fax: 208-234-0936
                         www.snugfleece.com

Wool mattress covers and pillow shams

President: Frank Holden
Marketing Manager: Chase Rich
Production Manager: Chase Rich
In Business: 30 years
Number of Employees: 7
Sales Information: $1,000,000 - $5,000,000

7490 Springs Global
Springs Global
PO Box 70
Fort Mill, SC 29716   803-547-1500
                              888-926-7888
                         www.springs.com

Bed accessories

Chairman: Josue Christiano Gomes de Silva
President: Crandall Bowles
CFO: Pedro Garcia Bastos Neto
Marketing Manager: Kevin Jareck
Director of Investor Relations: Gustavo

Shimoda Kawassaki
Board Member: Josue Christiano Gomes da
Silva
Board Member: Daniel Platt Tredwell
In Business: 53 years
Number of Employees: 30
Sales Information: $20MM to $50MM

7491 Stevenson & Vestalury
Stevenson Vestal
2347 W Hanford Road
Burlington, NC 27215-6765   336-226-2183
                                  800-535-3636
                            Fax: 800-533-6881
customerservice@stevensonvestal.com
            www.stevensonvestal.com

Custom window and bed coverings, draperies, valences, shades, swags, cornices, bedspreads, screens, pillows, headboards

President: Dave Stevenson, Bill Vestal
Marketing Manager: Dave Gude
Director of Customer Service: Terri Yarbrough
Information Systems: Brian Jones
Personnel Department: Marian Hill
Catalog Cost: $100
Catalog Circulation: Mailed 2 time(s) per year
Average Order Size: $600
Printing Information: 350 pages in 1 color on
Glossy Stock
Binding: Saddle Stitched
Mailing List Information: Names for rent
In Business: 32 years
Number of Employees: 100

7492 Tomorrow's World Catalog
Organic Comfort Zone
201 W Ocean View Ave.
Norfolk, VA 23503-1504   757-480-8500
                                 800-229-7571
                            Fax: 757-480-3148
            www.tomorrowsworld.Com

Natural fashions, men and women, organic cotton, hemp, wool and flax

Chairman: Richard Hahn
President: Cheryl Hahn
Credit Cards: AMEX; MasterCard; Visa
Catalog Cost: $2
Catalog Circulation: Mailed 12 time(s) per
year to 1M
Average Order Size: $85
Printing Information: 64 pages in 4 colors on
Matte Stock
Press: Web Press
Binding: Saddle Stitched
In Business: 24 years
Number of Employees: 6
Sales Information: $500,000- 1 Million

7493 Wesco Fabrics
Wesco Fabrics Inc
4001 Forest St
Denver, CO 80216-4500   303-388-4101
                                 800-950-9372
                            Fax: 303-388-3908
            info@wescofabrics.com
            www.Wescofabrics.Com

Bed pillows and bedspreads

President: Marla Gentry
In Business: 69 years
Number of Employees: 100
Sales Information: $1,000,000 - $5,000,000

7494 West Point Pepperell
West Point Pepperell, Inc.
1185 Avenue of the Americas
New York, NY 10036-2601   212-278-0513
                            Fax: 212-930-3555
            www.west pointpepperell.com/

Bath rugs and towels

Chairman: Whitney Stevens
Marketing Manager: Risa Calmenson
Number of Employees: 400

Flooring

7495 Mystic Valley Traders
MysticValleyTraders
16 Sixth Road
Woburn, MA 01801-2128   781-995-2393
                                 800-922-0660
                            Fax: 800-928-7156
            info@mysticvalleytraders.com
            www.mysticvalleytraders.com

Floor coverings

President: Kyle Tager
Marketing Manager: Adam Tager
Production Manager: Karen Tager
Credit Cards: AMEX; MasterCard
In Business: 31 years
Number of Employees: 12
Sales Information: $3MM to $5MM

7496 Rug Market
The Rug Market America
4200 Sepulveda Blvd.
Culver City, CA 90320-3126   310-841-0111
                                 800-422-4354
                            Fax: 310-841-0126
            info@therugmarket.com
            www.therugmarket.com

Floor coverings

President: Mike Shabtai
Printing Information: 13 pages
In Business: 29 years
Number of Employees: 9
Sales Information: $1MM to $3MM

7497 Snug Fleece Woolens
SnugFleece Woollens, Inc.
2740 Pole Line Rd
Pocatello, ID 83201-6112   208-233-9622
                                 800-824-1177
                            Fax: 208-234-0936
            www.snugfleece.com

Wool mattress covers and pillow shams

President: Frank Holden
Marketing Manager: Chase Rich
Production Manager: Chase Rich
In Business: 30 years
Number of Employees: 7
Sales Information: $1,000,000 - $5,000,000

Windows & Walls

7498 AL Ellis
A.L. Ellis, Inc.
113 Griffin Street
Fall River, MA 02724-4399   508-672-4799
                            Fax: 508-672-4808
            customerservice@elliscurtain.com
                 www.elliscurtain.com

Curtains, draperies, chair pads, bedding & dust ruffles

President: A Linnwood Ellis III
Catalog Circulation: Mailed 2 time(s) per year
Printing Information: 60 pages
In Business: 97 years
Number of Employees: 25
Sales Information: $1,000,000 - $5,000,000

7499 Achim Importing Company
Achim Importing Company
58 2nd Avenue
Brooklyn, NY 11215-3132   718-369-2200
                                 800-54A-CHIM
            customerservice@achimonline.com
                 www.achimonline.com

Imported blinds, window coverings, and flooring

President: Marton B Grossman
Marketing Manager: Howard Siegal
In Business: 53 years
Number of Employees: 55
Sales Information: $1,000,000

7500 Anderson Fabrics
The Andersons Inc.
480 W. Dussel Drive
PO Box 119
Maumee, OH 43537-2137   419-893-5050
                                 800-537-3370
                            Fax: 218-835-4666
            hostmaster@andersonsinc.com
                 www.andersonsinc.com

Custom fabrics, curtains and draperies for the design and decorating industry

President: Rasesh Shah
emailthepresident@andersonsinc.com
Production Manager: Robert Gieryng
Credit Cards: AMEX; MasterCard; Visa
Mailing List Information: Names for rent
In Business: 50 years
Number of Employees: 3000
Sales Information: $1MM to $3MM

7501 Automatic Devices Company
Automatic Devices Company
2121 S 12th St
Allentown, PA 18103-4795   610-797-6000
                                 800-360-2321
                            Fax: 610-797-4088
            info@automaticdevices.com
                 www.Automaticdevices.Com

Shades, window hardware and accessories

President: John Samuels
Marketing Manager: Don Heller
Customer Service Manager: Stan Nemeth
sn@automaticdevices.com
Technical Sales: Robert Jones
rj@automaticdevices.com
Purchasing: Robert Buchman
rbuchman@automaticdevices.com
In Business: 96 years
Number of Employees: 50
Sales Information: $5,000,000 - $10,000,000

7502 Beauti-Vue Products Corporation
Beauti-Vue Products Corporation
8555 194th Avenue
Bristol, WI 53104-9543   262-857-2306
                                 800-558-9431
                            Fax: 800-329-9431
                 www.Beautivue.Com

Blinds, shades and shutters

President: Jim Grumbeck
Production Manager: Jim Grumbeck
Number of Employees: 100
Sales Information: $5,000,000 - $10,000,000

7503 C&M Shade Corporation
C&M Shade Corporation
53 Dwight Place
Fairfield, NJ 07004   973-808-2050
                                 800-486-1116
                            Fax: 973-808-2055
            customerservice@cmshade.com
                 www.Cmshade.Com

Shades, shutters, blinds, top treatments, window hardware and accessories

President: Allen Francus
Marketing Manager: Allen Frances
In Business: 58 years
Number of Employees: 47
Sales Information: $5,000,000 - $10,000,000

7504 Colonial Lace
Colonial Lace Company
2314 McDonald Ave
Brooklyn, NY 11223-4790   718-372-5757
                            Fax: 718-372-8605
            www.Colonial-Lace.Com

Curtains and draperies

President: Abraham Shamah
Marketing Manager: Sidney Shamah
Number of Employees: 20
Sales Information: $500,000 - $1,000,000

7505 Country Ruffles
Village Discount Drapery
215 Raytheon Road
Bristol, TN 37620

423-968-9531
800-488-9531
contactus@countryruffles.com
www.countryruffles.com

Curtains, drapes and bedding

President: Dennis Houser
Credit Cards: AMEX; MasterCard
Catalog Cost: Free
Catalog Circulation: Mailed 1 time(s) per year
Printing Information: 55 pages in 4 colors
190 N. 7th St.
New Castle, CO 81647
In Business: 44 years
Number of Employees: 12
Sales Information: $500M to $1MM

7506 Covoc Corporation
Covoc Corporation
1194 E. Valencia Drive
Fullerton, CA 92831-4691

714-879-0341
800-725-3266
Fax: 714-879-9365
info@covoc.com
www.Covoc.Com

Variety of curtains, draperies, blinds, window hardware and accessories, hospital cubicle curtains and track

Chairman: James Condon
President: Brad Condon
Mailing List Information: Names for rent
In Business: 51 years
Number of Employees: 11
Sales Information: $1,000,000 - $5,000,000

7507 Custom Laminations
The CLI Group
932 Market Street
Paterson, NJ 07513-2066

973-279-9174
Fax: 973-279-6916
info@thecligroup.com
www.thecligroup.com

Converts textiles, nonwovens, papers and films into custom-engineered products and materials

President: Daren Silverstein
Marketing Manager: Susan Andresen
marketing@thecligroup.com
CEO: Daren Silverstein
In Business: 53 years
Number of Employees: 20

7508 DSC Fabrics
DSC Window Fashions
5570 West 60th Avenue
Arvada, CO 80003-5710

800-873-0000
800-873-0000
Fax: 800-340-4380
cservice@dscwindowfashions.com
www.dscwindowfashions.com

Curtains, draperies, blinds and window hardware

President: Rick Robertson
Marketing Manager: Ken Rathke
Information Technology Manager: Mark Wissink
markw@dscwindowfashions.com
Sales Manager: Leslie Schneider
leslies@dscwindowfashions.com
Finance Department Manager: Carolyn Vogel
carolv@dscwindowfashions.com
Number of Employees: 20
Sales Information: $500,000

7509 Dan River
Dan River
3300 Kings Mountain Road
P.O. Box 7
Collinsville, VA 24078

276-634-2545
drba.va@danriver.org
www.danriver.org

Curtains and draperies

President: Allison Szuba
Executive Director: Tiffany Haworth
thaworth@danriver.org
Education Outreach & TIC Coordinato: Krista Hodges
khodges@danriver.org
Program Manager, Rockingham County: Jenny Edwards
jedwards@danriver.org
Number of Employees: 3500

7510 Decorator Industries
Decorator Industries
1400 E. Ash Street
Po Box 432
Abbotsford, WI 54405-9746

715-223-2384
800-678-5423
Fax: 715-223-3689
www.decoratorindustries.com

Bedspreads, curtains and draperies

President: Tony Kedrowski
Marketing Manager: Tony Kedrowski
Production Manager: Sandra Jakel
Printing Information: 100 pages in 4 colors on Glossy Stock
Binding: Saddle Stitched
Mailing List Information: Names for rent
In Business: 60 years
Number of Employees: 53
Sales Information: $1,000,000 - $5,000,000

7511 EKO
Eko
1237 Mile Creek Rd
Pickens, SC 29671-8703

864-868-4250
800-729-3461
Fax: 864-868-4250
ekochansky@gmail.com
www.ekochansky.com

Wall art

President: Ellen Kochansky
Credit Cards: AMEX; MasterCard
In Business: 32 years
Sales Information: Under $500M

7512 Ellie Dee Design
Elle Dee Designs
75 Runyan Avenue
Deal, NJ 07723-1231

732-531-6235
Fax: 718-338-0979
www.elledeedesign.com

Curtains and draperies

Marketing Manager: Jerry Dweck

7513 Fabric Quilters Unlimited
Fabric Quilters and Window Fashions,
1400 Shames Drive
Westbury, NY 11590-1759

516-333-2866
800-645-3498
Fax: 516-333-4016
karenb@fabricquilters.com
www.fabricquilters.com

Curtains, draperies, shades, blinds and top treatments

President: John W. Brunning Sr.
Marketing Manager: Karen Brunning
In Business: 57 years
Number of Employees: 22
Sales Information: $1,000,000 to $4,999,999

7514 Hunter Douglas
Hunter Douglas
P.O.Box 740
Upper Saddle Rvr, NJ 07458-740

201-327-8200
800-789-0331
Fax: 201-327-7938
www.Hunterdouglas.Com

Window fashions

President: Marvin B Hopkins
Marketing Manager: James Mathews
Catalog Cost: Free

Printing Information: 32 pages
Number of Employees: 7044

7515 Imperial Wallcoverings
Blue Mountain Wallcoverings
15 Akron Road
Toronto, CN M8W 1

216-464-3700
866-563-9872
Fax: 216-765-8648
www.ihdg.com

Wallcoverings

President: William Brucchieri
CFO: Keith McAslan
In Business: 24 years
Number of Employees: 400

7516 Kaslen Textiles
Kaslen Textiles
2140 E. 51st St.
Vernon, CA 90058-3642

323-588-7700
800-777-5789
Fax: 800-777-5401
custserv@kastex.com
www.Kaslentextiles.Com

Upholstery, drapery, lining, printed fabrics

President: Jack Cook
In Business: 35 years
Number of Employees: 50
Sales Information: $10MM to $20MM

7517 Laurel Manufacturing Company
Laurel Manufacturing Company
66-83 70th street
Queens, NY 11378-2421

718-894-9228
800-992-4624
Fax: 718-894-9529
laurelblinds@aol.com
www.laurelblinds.com

Blinds and shades, LogoDrape, specializing in 2 inch horizontal and vertical blinds

President: David Laurel
Credit Cards: MasterCard; Visa
Catalog Cost: Free
Catalog Circulation: Mailed 1 time(s) per year to 5M
Printing Information: 10 pages in 1 color
In Business: 81 years
Number of Employees: 4
Sales Information: Under $500,000

7518 Levelor Home Fashion
Levelor
4110 Premier Dr
High Point, NC 27265-8343

336-812-8181
800-752-9677
Fax: 336-881-5838
www.Levolor.Com

Blinds

President: Mark Carroll
CFO: Elton Potts
Marketing Manager: Bill Wright
In Business: 100 years
Number of Employees: 1000

7519 Levolor Kirsch Window Fashions
Levolor
4110 Premier Dr
High Point, NC 27265-8343

336-812-8181
800-752-9677
Fax: 336-881-5838
www.Levolor.Com

Window hardware and accessories

President: Mark Carroll
In Business: 100 years
Number of Employees: 1000

7520 Meyer Drapery Services
Meyer Drapery Services,Inc.
330 N Neil Street
Champaign, IL 61820-3614
217-352-5318
800-637-4885
Fax: 217-352-5615
david@meyerdrapery.com
www.meyerdrapery.com/

Custom curtains and draperies

President: David Meyer
Number of Employees: 13
Sales Information: $500M to $1MM

7521 Mitchellace
Sole Choice,Inc.
830 Murray Street
Portsmouth, OH 45662-89
740-354-2813
800-848-8696
Fax: 740-353-4669
sales@solechoiceinc.com
www.mitchellace.com

Braided cord and cordage, braiding and interior textiles

Chairman: Kerry Keating
President: Steve Keating
In Business: 113 years
Number of Employees: 350
Sales Information: $20MM to $50MM

7522 Morgan Manufacturing & Engineering Company
Morgan Manufacturing & Engineering Compa
1611 Fabricon Boulevard
Jeffersonville, IN 47130
812-288-4455
800-372-7379
Fax: 812-284-1518
www.1-800-drapery.com

Custom curtains and top treatments

President: Wade Morgan
CFO: Barbara Stewart
Printing Information: 30 pages
In Business: 25 years
Number of Employees: 12
Sales Information: $1,000,000 - $5,000,000

7523 Nanik
Graber
8467 Route 405 Highway South
PO Box 500
Montgomery, PA 17752
877-792-0002
windowfashions@springswindowfashions.com
www.graberblinds.com

Blinds and shutters

In Business: 70 years
Number of Employees: 300
Sales Information: $25,000,000 - $50,000,000

7524 Newell Window Furnishings
Newell Rubbermaid
29 E. Stephenson St.
Freeport, IL 61032-6037
770-418-7000
Fax: 815-233-8060
www.newellrubbermaid.com

Blinds, shutters and top treatments

Chairman: Michael T. Cowhig
President: Michael B. Polk
CFO: Douglas L. Martin
Marketing Manager: Greg Miles
Chief Operating Officer: William A. Burke III
Chief Human Resource Officer: James M. Sweet
Chief Legal Officer, Corporate Secr: John K. Stipancich
In Business: 112 years
Number of Employees: 375

7525 Office Scapes Direct
Office Scapes Direct
12021 Centron Place
Cincinnati, OH 45246
800-557-1997
Fax: 914-328-1959
service@officescapesdirect.com
www.officescapesdirect.com

Silk flowers, silk trees, silk plants and framed art and wall decor

7526 P Collins Fabrics
NC Textile Connect
1948 W Green Dr, High Point
High Point, NC 27260-2758
336-887-3086
800-333-8500
Fax: 336-883-8667
www.nctextileconnect.com

Window hardware and accessories

President: Steve Spillers
Contact: Shawn Dunning
Contact: Dr. Lori Rothenberg
Contact: Dr. Jim Watson
Number of Employees: 18
Sales Information: $3MM to $5MM

7527 PJ Hamilton Company
PJ Daly Contracting Ltd.
1320 StoneChurch Road East
Hamilton
Ontario, ON L8W 2
905-575-1525
800-844-9040
Fax: 905-575-8069
info@pjdalycontracting.com
www.pjdalycontracting.com

Window hardware and accessories

President: Peter Hamilton
In Business: 62 years

7528 Paper White
Paper White
2915 Kerner Boulevard
Suite F
San Rafael, CA 94901
415-482-9989
Fax: 415-482-0990
pwlinens@paperwhitelifestyle.com
www.paperwhitelifestyle.com

Luxury linens for the bed, bath, table and window

President: Jan Dutton
Number of Employees: 15
Sales Information: $1,000,000 - $5,000,000

7529 Payne Fabrics
Westgate Fabrics
1517 W N Carrier Parkway
Suite 116
Grand Prairie, TX 75050-1117
972-647-2323
800-527-2517
Fax: 972-602-8143

Wallcoverings

President: Val Blaugh
Number of Employees: 85
Sales Information: $10MM to $20MM

7530 RollEase
RollEase, Inc.
200 Harvard Ave
Stamford, CT 06902-6320
203-964-1573
800-552-5100
Fax: 203-358-5865
sales@rollease.com
www.Rollease.Com

Patented manual and motorized window covering systems for residential and commercial applications; including pleated shades, horizontal blinds, soft shades and roller shades

President: Derek Marsh
Marketing Manager: Cynthia Wittstock

Senior VP: Greg Farr
CFO: Tom Gilboy
Regional Sales Associate: Geremie Giancola
Credit Cards: MasterCard; Visa
Catalog Circulation: Mailed 1 time(s) per year to 5M
Printing Information: 10 pages in 2 colors on Glossy Stock
Mailing List Information: Names for rent
List Manager: Fred Ball
In Business: 35 years
Number of Employees: 90
Sales Information: $20MM to $50MM

7531 Source Window Coverings
Source Northwest Inc.
8329 216th Street SE
Woodinville, WA 98072-8060
360-668-2868
Fax: 360-668-1750

Blinds and shades including: cellular, pleated, roman, synergy, wood blinds, mini blinds, vertical blinds, woven woods, solar shades, shutters, motorization

President: Laron Olson
Marketing Manager: John Stickle
In Business: 35 years
Number of Employees: 50
Sales Information: $5,000,000 - $10,000,000

7532 Stevenson & Vestalury
Stevenson Vestal
2347 W Hanford Road
Burlington, NC 27215-6765
336-226-2183
800-535-3636
Fax: 800-533-6881
customerservice@stevensonvestal.com
www.stevensonvestal.com

Custom window and bed coverings, draperies, valences, shades, swags, cornices, bedspreads, screens, pillows, headboards

President: Dave Stevenson, Bill Vestal
Marketing Manager: Dave Gude
Director of Customer Service: Terri Yarbrough
Information Systems: Brian Jones
Personnel Department: Marian Hill
Catalog Cost: $100
Catalog Circulation: Mailed 2 time(s) per year
Average Order Size: $600
Printing Information: 350 pages in 1 color on Glossy Stock
Binding: Saddle Stitched
Mailing List Information: Names for rent
In Business: 32 years
Number of Employees: 100

7533 TDI Drapery Importing Corporation
TDI Drapery Importing Corp.
128 32nd Street
Fl. 3
Brooklyn, NY 11232-1833
718-832-2470
800-998-2470
Fax: 718-832-2475

Curtains and draperies

President: N Rosemberg
In Business: 26 years
Number of Employees: 6
Sales Information: $1MM to $3MM

7534 Tempo Decorative Fabrics
Kaslen Textiles
2140 E. 51st St.
Vernon, CA 90058-3642
323-588-7700
800-777-5789
Fax: 323-838-0346
custserv@kastex.com
www.kaslentextiles.com

Lensol fabrics, kas-tex, tempo decorative fabrics and draperies

President: David Hurmis
Marketing Manager: Kristine Cook
In Business: 35 years
Number of Employees: 10
Sales Information: $5MM to $10MM

7535 Window Imagination
Window Imagination
15 Union Street
Suite 420
Lawrence, MA 01840   978-655-4394
                                        Fax: 978-984-5019
Sales@Windowimagination.com
www.windowimagination.com

Window hardware and accessories

President: Thad Kallas
In Business: 20 years
Number of Employees: 5
Sales Information: $500M to $1MM

Laboratory
Supplies & Equipment

7536 ABP/Pharmex
PDC Healthcare
27770 N. Entertainment Drive
Suite 200
Valencia, CA 91355   661-257-0233
                                        800-435-4242
                                  Fax: 800-321-4409
info@pdchealthcare.com
www.pdchealthcare.com/en-us/pharmex-phar-
macy-labeling-soluti

Pharmaceutical and laboratory supplies.

President: Robert Case
CFO: Michelle Wen
Finance Director
Marketing Manager: John Park
VP, North American Healthcare Sales: Rudy
Neal
Director, Research & Development: Richard
Kapusniak
Director of Human Resources: Fabian Grijalva
Catalog Cost: Free
Printing Information: 76 pages
Sales Information: $5MM to $10MM

7537 Allometrics
Allometrics
PO Box 15825
Baton Rouge, LA 70895-5825   225-303-0419
                                        800-528-2246
                                  Fax: 225-272-0844
info@allometrics.com
www.allometrics.com

Specialty laboratory equipment and supplies

President: Ashton Stagg
Credit Cards: AMEX; MasterCard; Visa
In Business: 37 years
Number of Employees: 20
Sales Information: $5MM to $10MM

7538 Analytical Measurements
Analytical Measurements
22 Mountain View Drive
Chester, NJ 07930   908-955-7170
                                        800-635-5580
                                  Fax: 908-955-7170
phmeter@verizon.net
www.analyticalmeasurements.com

PH meters, controllers and recorders; ORP meters, controllers and recorders

President: W Richard Adey
Marketing Manager: Theresa Scarinzi
Catalog Cost: Free
Printing Information: on Glossy Stock
Press: Web Press
Mailing List Information: Names for rent
In Business: 49 years
Number of Employees: 40
Sales Information: Under $500M

7539 BEC Controls Corporation
BEC Controls Corporation
121 Water Street
Post Box 132
Mineral Point, WI 53565   608-987-4100
                                        800-677-8876
                                  Fax: 608-987-4300
sales@beccontrols.com
www.beccontrols.com

Controls

President: Robert Oberhauser
Credit Cards: AMEX; MasterCard
Mailing List Information: Names for rent
In Business: 57 years
Sales Information: $500M to $1MM

7540 BMA Environmental Chambers
Associated Environmental Systems
31 Willow Rd
Ayer, MA 01432-5510   978-772-0022
                                  Fax: 978-772-0644
sales@associatedenvironmental-bma.com
www.associatedenvironmentalsystems.com/

Ovens, walk-in rooms, and environmental test chambers

President: Jeff Aranjo
CEO: Beran Peter
Vice President: John O'Rourke
Aaron Robinson:
Vice President of Sales & Service
Catalog Circulation: to 5000
Printing Information: 24 pages
Mailing List Information: Names for rent
In Business: 56 years
Number of Employees: 18
Sales Information: $10,000,000

7541 Bel-Art Products
Bel-Art Products
661 Route 23 South
Wayne, NJ 07470-1994   973-694-0500
                                        800-423-5278
                                  Fax: 973-694-7199
cservice@belart.com
www.belart.com

Bel-Art Products is a manufacturer of essential & unique problem-solving items for scientific, industrial & educational markets worldwide, over 4,000 items from wash bottles to fume hoods

President: David Landsberger
Marketing Manager: Shirley Miller
International Marketing Manager: Joe Kelly
Credit Cards: AMEX; MasterCard; Visa
Catalog Cost: Free
Printing Information: 480 pages
Mailing List Information: Names for rent
In Business: 69 years
Number of Employees: 300
Sales Information: $10MM to $20MM

7542 Cole-Parmer
Cole-Parmer
625 East Bunker Court
Vernon Hills, IL 60061-1830   841-549-7600
                                        800-323-4340
                                  Fax: 847-549-1700
info@coleparmer.com
www.coleparmer.com

Products for electrochemistry, fluid handling, industrial process, laboratory research and more

President: Alan Malus
CFO: Steven Gozdziewski
Marketing Manager: Larry Vanbogaerts
VP/General Manager: Monica Manotas
Director, Finance: Joe Straczek
VP, Human Resources: Wanda McKenny
Credit Cards: AMEX; MasterCard
Printing Information: 2600 pages
In Business: 60 years
Number of Employees: 320

7543 Cole-Parmer Instruments Product Catalog
Cole-Parmer
625 East Bunker Court
Vernon Hills, IL 60061-1830   847-549-7600
                                        800-323-4340
                                  Fax: 847-549-1700
info@coleparmer.com
www.coleparmer.com

Instruments for measurement and control, laboratory equipment and supplies

President: John Palmer
VP/General Manager: Monica Manotas
Director, Finance: Joe Straczek
VP, Human Resources: Wanda McKenny
Catalog Cost: Free
Catalog Circulation: Mailed 1 time(s) per year
Printing Information: 999 pages in 4 colors
Binding: Perfect Bound
In Business: 60 years

7544 Conterra
Conterra, Inc
1600 Kentucky St
Suite A-3
Bellingham, WA 98229-4701   360-734-2311
                                  Fax: 360-738-2241
info@conterra-inc.com
www.conterra-inc.com

Medical backpacks/fanny paks

President: Rick Lipke
Credit Cards: AMEX; MasterCard
Catalog Cost: Free
Printing Information: 56 pages in 4 colors
Mailing List Information: Names for rent
Number of Employees: 28
Sales Information: 500M

7545 Continental Lab Products
NEPTUNE
9880 Mesa Rim Road
Suite 220
San Diego, CA 92121-4701   858-875-7696
                                        888-330-2396
                                  Fax: 858-875-5496
CSR@neptunescientific.com
www.neptunescientific.com

Laboratory products

President: Dave Barth
CFO: Tony Altig
COO: Ron Perkins
Vice President, Human Resources: Celia
Reyes
Chief Executive Officer: Paul Nowak
6190 Corner Stone Ct East Suite 220
San Diego, CA 92121
858.279.5000
Number of Employees: 30

7546 Daigger & Company Lab Supply
A. Daigger & Company
620 Lakeview Parkway
Vernon Hills, IL 60061-1828   847-816-5060
                                        800-621-7193
                                  Fax: 800-320-7200
daigger@daigger.com
www.daigger.com

Laboratory supplies

President: Jim Woldenberg
CFO: Mike Dost
Regional Account Manager: Meghan
O'Connell
Senior Account Manager: Michael Bledsoe
International Sales Director: Jim Woldenberg
In Business: 121 years
Number of Employees: 215

7547 Elemental Scientific
Elemental Scientific, LLC
80 Minnesota Street
Little Canada, MI 55117   651-646-5339
                                  Fax: 920-882-1277
info@elementalscientific.net
www.elementalscientific.net

Scientific and laboratory supplies

President: W. VanRyzin
Marketing Manager: C. VanRyzin
Production Manager: A. vanRyzin
Catalog Cost: $2
Catalog Circulation: Mailed 3 time(s) per year to 11M
Average Order Size: $50
Printing Information: 99 pages in 2 colors on Matte Stock
Press: Web Press
Binding: Saddle Stitched
Mailing List Information: Names for rent
In Business: 62 years
Number of Employees: 3
Sales Information: Under $500M

7548 Excel Technologies

Excel Technologies Inc
99 Phoenix Avenue
PO Box 1258
Enfield, CT 06083-1258   860-741-3435
    800-543-9832
Fax: 860-745-7212
www.extec.com

Laboratory supplies

President: J Ronald Rinaldi
In Business: 25 years
Number of Employees: 15
Sales Information: $5MM to $10MM

7549 Extech Instruments

Extech Instruments
9 Townsend West
Nashua, NH 03063   877-239-8324
Fax: 603-324-7864
sales@extech.com
www.extech.com

Test measurements calibration, datalogging and control instruments and customized catalogs for catalog distributors

President: Jerry Blakeley
CFO: Scott Black
Marketing Manager: Lois Corley
VP of Sales & Marketing: Arpineh Mullaney
Sales Manager: Joe Rocchio
joseph.rocchio@extech.com
Regional Sales Director: Travis Curtis
travis.curtis@flir.com
Buyers: Carolyn Simoko
In Business: 45 years
Number of Employees: 79
Sales Information: $5,000,000 - $10,000,000

7550 Glas-Col

Glas-Col
711 Hulman Street
PO Box 2128
Terre Haute, IN 47802-128   812-235-6167
    800-452-7265
Fax: 812-234-6975
pinnacle@glascol.com
www.glascol.com

Laboratory products including heating, mixing and evaporation equipment for chemical, biotech, environmental and pharmaceutical use

President: Steve Sterrett
International Marketing Manager: Karen Elliott
Buyers: Patti Moore
Credit Cards: AMEX; MasterCard; Visa
Catalog Cost: Free
Mailing List Information: Names for rent
List Manager: Jenny Samm
In Business: 75 years
Number of Employees: 75
Sales Information: $20MM to $50MM

7551 Hach Company

Hach Company
PO Box 389
Loveland, CO 80539-389   970-669-3050
    800-227-4224
Fax: 970-669-2932
www.hach.com

Test kits and laboratory instruments

President: Kathryn Hach-Darrow
Catalog Cost: Free
In Business: 81 years
Number of Employees: 800

7552 HunterLab

Hunter Associates Laboratory, Inc,
11491 Sunset Hills Road
Reston, VA 20190-5280   703-471-6870
Fax: 703-471-4237
info@hunterlab.com
www.hunterlab.com

Laboratory supplies, testing equipment

Chairman: Phil Hunter
President: Phil Hunter
CFO: Teresa Demangos, Controller
Marketing Manager: Lore Potoker
CEO: Phil Hunter
Customer Service: Alex
Service Department: Linda
In Business: 71 years
Number of Employees: 49
Sales Information: $10,000,000 - $25,000,000

7553 International Light

International Light
10 Technology Drive
Peabody, MA 01960-4014   978-818-6180
Fax: 978-818-6181
www.intl-lighttech.com

Light measurement instrumentation

President: Larry Schmutz
Marketing Manager: Suzanne Kavanagh
Buyers: Peter McKeough
Credit Cards: AMEX; MasterCard; Visa
Catalog Cost: Free
Catalog Circulation: Mailed 1 time(s) per year to 15M+
Printing Information: 36 pages in 2 colors on Glossy Stock
Press: Web Press
Binding: Saddle Stitched
Mailing List Information: Names for rent
List Manager: Robert A Angelo
In Business: 44 years
Number of Employees: 20
Sales Information: $1,000,000 - $5,000,000

7554 Jobmaster Magnets

Jobmaster Magnets
1420 Cornwall Road
Unit 1 & 2
Oakville, Ontario, CN L6J 7   905-337-8500
    800-642-1400
Fax: 905-337-8550
sales@jobmaster.com
www.jobmaster.com

Home science, industry and military magnets

President: Jeff Goldman
Catalog Cost: $25.95
Mailing List Information: Names for rent
In Business: 50 years
Number of Employees: 20
Sales Information: $1,000,000 - $5,000,000

7555 Ken-A-Vision Manufacturing Company

Ken-a-vision
5615 Raytown Road
Kansas City, MO 64133   816-353-4787
    800-501-7366
Fax: 816-358-5072
info@ken-a-vision.com
www.ken-a-vision.com

Microprojectors, microscopes, video flex (flexible camera), vision viewer

President: Steven Dunn
CFO: Karen Dunn
Marketing Manager: Mary Mitchell
VP: Michael Mathews
Marketing & Promotions Manager: Lesa Brownell
International Marketing Manager: Steven Dunn
Catalog Cost: Free
Mailing List Information: Names for rent
In Business: 61 years
Number of Employees: 25
Sales Information: $3.3 Million

7556 Kewaunee Scientific Corporation

Kewaunee
2700 West Front Street
PO Box 1842
Statesville, NC 28677-1842   704-873-7202
Fax: 704-873-5160
KSCMarketing@Kewaunee.Com
www.Kewaunee.Com

Science laboratory furniture, fume hoods and accessories

President: David M. Rausch
CFO: D Michael Parker
Marketing Manager: Dana L Dahlgren
Production Manager: Keith D. Smith
Managing Director of International: B. Sathyamurthy
Vice President, Human Resources: Elizabeth D. Phillips
Vice President, Engineering and Pro: Kurt P. Rindoks
Catalog Cost: Free
In Business: 109 years
Number of Employees: 572

7557 Lab Safety Supply Company

Grainger Industrial Supply
PO Box 1368
Janesville, WI 53547   608-754-7160
    800-472-4643
Fax: 800-543-9910
custsvc@labsafety.com
www.grainger.com

Products and equipment to promote safety in the laboratory

President: Larry J. Loizzo

7558 MMI Catalog

MMI Corporation
2950 Wyman Parkway
Baltimore, MD 21211   410-366-1222
Fax: 410-366-1222
mail@mmicorporation.com
www.Mmicorporation.Com

Astronomy materials for educators

President: Ralph Levy
In Business: 41 years
Sales Information: Under $500M

7559 MMS Medical Supply

MMS Medical Supply
2229 East Magnolia St.
Phoenix, AZ 85034   602-306-1722
    800-777-2634
Fax: 602-306-1787
general@mmsmedical.com
www.mmsmedical.com

Laboratory and medical supplies

President: Gary Reeve
CFO: David Evans
Marketing Manager: Gina Marchese
EVP: Tom Harris
SVP - Business Systems: Dan Rieman
VP, Operations & GM: Kevin McDonnell
Buyers: Sue Shearin
Credit Cards: MasterCard; Visa
Catalog Circulation: Mailed 1 time(s) per year
Mailing List Information: Names for rent

In Business: 44 years
Number of Employees: 19
Sales Information: $5MM to $10MM

7560 Medical-Diagnostic Specialty Gases
Medical-Diagnostic Specialty Gases
6141 Easton Road
Box 310
Plumsteadville, PA 18949   215-766-8860
                                                877-715-8651
                                Fax: 215-766-2476
              solutions.center@airliquide.com
                          www.scottgas.com

Gases and cylinders

Catalog Circulation: Mailed 1 time(s) per year
Printing Information: 34 pages
Binding: Saddle Stitched

7561 NEB Catalog
New England BioLabs, Inc.
240 Country Road
Ipswich, MA 01938   800-632-5227
                                    www.neb.com
Products and supply for scientic research

Marketing Manager: Stephanie Graber
Chief Information Officer: Sharon Kaiser
Catalog Cost: Free
In Business: 40 years
Number of Employees: 300

7562 National Hospitality Supply
National Hospitality Supply, Inc.
10660 N Executive Ct
Mequon, WI 53092   800-526-8224
                          Fax: 262-478-0229
                          cs@nathosp.com
                          www.nathosp.com

Accessories and furniture for hotels and motels

Chairman: Dan Crimmins
Credit Cards: AMEX; MasterCard
Catalog Cost: Free
Catalog Circulation: Mailed 4 time(s) per year
Printing Information: 116 pages in 4 colors
Binding: Perfect Bound
In Business: 24 years

7563 Oxford Biomedical Research
Oxford Biomedical Research
PO Box 522
Oxford, MI 48371-522   800-692-4633
                          Fax: 248-852-4466
                  info@oxfordbiomed.com
                  www.oxfordbiomed.com

Products for the biomedical and pharmaceutical research community

Founder: Denis M. Callewaert
In Business: 31 years

7564 Parco Scientific Company
Parco Scientific Company
PO Box 851559
Westland, MI 48185   330-637-2849
                                    877-592-5837
                          Fax: 877-592-5838
                  info@parcoscientific.com
                  www.parcoscientific.com

Microscopes, laboratory supplies and aids, meters and kits, for the educational, medical and industrial markets

President: Brian Martorana
Credit Cards: MasterCard; Visa
Catalog Cost: Free
In Business: 50 years
Number of Employees: 12
Sales Information: 5MM-10MM

7565 Physicians Laboratory Supply
Cen-Med Enterprises, Inc.
121 Jersey Ave
New Brunswick, NJ 08901   732-447-1100
                                                800-470-3570
                                Fax: 732-249-0008
                                info@cenmed.com
                                www.cenmed.com

Laboratory supplies

President: Shakila Chaudhry
Catalog Circulation: Mailed 1 time(s) per year
Printing Information: 12 pages in 4 colors
Binding: Saddle Stitched
In Business: 23 years

7566 Pierce Biotechnology
Thermofisher,Inc
3747 N Meridian Rd
PO Box 117
Rockford, IL 61105-117   815-968-0747
                                                800-874-3723
                                Fax: 800-842-5007
                          indiacs@lifetech.com
                          www.piercenet.com

Life science research kits and reagents

President: Robb Anderson
Marketing Manager: Sheila Burns
Production Manager: Holly Schubert
Mailing List Information: Names for rent
In Business: 51 years
Number of Employees: 150

7567 Spex Certiprep
SPEX CertiPrep
203 Norcross Ave
Metuchen, NJ 08840-1253   732-549-7144
                                          800-LAB-SPEX
                                Fax: 732-603-9647
                          crmsales@spex.com
                          www.spexcsp.com

Sample prep grinders, mixers and fluxors

President: Ralph Obenauf
Marketing Manager: Melanie Samko
Production Manager: Nimi Kocherlakota
International Marketing Manager: Suzanne Lepore
Catalog Circulation: Mailed 1 time(s) per year to 30000
Average Order Size: $600
Printing Information: 300 pages in 2 colors on Glossy Stock
Press: Letterpress
Binding: Perfect Bound
Mailing List Information: Names for rent
In Business: 60 years
Number of Employees: 200
Sales Information: $10,000,000 - $25,000,000

7568 Thermo ALKO
Thermo ALKO
500 Cummings Center
Beverly, MA 01915-6142   866-269-0070
                                Fax: 978-232-1068
          thermoscientific.webhelp@thermofisher.com
                                www.thermo.com

Supplier of calibrators, electrodes, accessories and quality controls for use on over 120 instrument models

Printing Information: 11 pages

7569 Wheaton Science Products Catalog
Wheaton Science Products
1501 N 10th St
Millville, NJ 08332-2093   856-825-1100
                                                800-225-1437
                                Fax: 856-825-1368
                                www.wheatonsci.com

Laboratory products, glassware and plastics

President: Wayne L. Brinster
wayne.brinster@wheaton.com
CFO: Thomas E. Kohut

tom.kohut@wheaton.com
Marketing Manager: Jackie Williams
VP, Quality Mgmt. Systems: Gregory W. Bianco
gregory.bianco@wheaton.com
VP, North American Sales: Chris Gildea
chris.gildea@wheaton.com
Director, Global Marketing: TracyNeri-Luciano
tracy.neri-luciano@wheaton.com
Catalog Circulation: Mailed 1 time(s) per year to 100M
Printing Information: 338 pages in 4 colors
In Business: 125 years
Number of Employees: 204
Sales Information: $19.8 Million

Landscaping
Chemicals

7570 American Tank Company
Water Tanks.com
2804 West Admiral Doyle Drive
New Iberia, LA 70560   707-535-1400
                                          877-655-1100
                                Fax: 707-535-1450
                  sales@americantankco.com
                  www.watertanks.com

Water, chemical, fire, septic, pumps and equipment

President: Mark D. Luzaich
Marketing Manager: Jim M. Kinley
Vice President: Guy Giordanego
Printing Information: 16 pages
In Business: 28 years
Number of Employees: 20
Sales Information: $1MM

7571 BIRD-X
Bird-X, Inc.
300 N Oakley Blvd
Chicago, IL 60612   312-226-2473
                                    800-662-5021
                          Fax: 312-226-2480
                          josh.p@bird-x.com
                          www.Bird-X.Com

Bird control products, goose repellers

President: Dennis Tillis
Owner: Glenn Steigbigel
Owner: Ronald Schwartz
Credit Cards: MasterCard; Visa
Catalog Cost: Free
Catalog Circulation: Mailed 2 time(s) per year to 200M
Printing Information: 6 pages in 4 colors on Glossy Stock
Binding: Folded
Mailing List Information: Names for rent
In Business: 51 years
Number of Employees: 35
Sales Information: $13MM

7572 Turf, Tree & Ornamental Catalog
Growth Products, Ltd
80 Lafayette Avenue
White Plains, NY 10603-1252   914-428-1316
                                                800-648-7626
                                Fax: 914-428-2780
                  roberlander@growthproducts.com
                  www.growthproducts.com

Professional liquid fertilizers, micronutrients, natural organics and a new biological fungicide for the turf, horticulture and greenhouse markets

President: Clare Reinbergen
Marketing Manager: Nicole Campbell
Technical/Sales Staff, NY Metro Are: Howard Gold
Technical/Sales Staff, Florida: Mark White
Technical/Sales Staff, Plains: Paul Hoffmann
Printing Information:
Binding: Saddle Stitched
Mailing List Information: Names for rent
In Business: 20 years

Number of Employees: 25
Sales Information: $10,000,000 - $25,000,000

Equipment

7573 American Arborist Supplies

American Arborist Supplies
882 S Matlack Street
Unit A
West Chester, PA 19382   610-430-1214
800-441-8381
Fax: 610-430-8560
info@arborist.com
www.arborist.com

Tools and equipment for tree workers as well as books on arboriculture

President: Dave Francis
International Marketing Manager: Steff Haymen
Credit Cards: AMEX; MasterCard
Catalog Circulation: Mailed 1 time(s) per year to 15000
Printing Information: 86 pages in 4 colors on Glossy Stock
Press: Web Press
Binding: Perfect Bound
Mailing List Information: Names for rent
In Business: 34 years
Number of Employees: 5
Sales Information: $3MM

7574 American Tank Company

Water Tanks.com
2804 West Admiral Doyle Drive
New Iberia, LA 70560   707-535-1400
877-655-1100
Fax: 707-535-1450
sales@americantankco.com
www.watertanks.com

Water, chemical, fire, septic, pumps and equipment

President: Mark D. Luzaich
Marketing Manager: Jim M. Kinley
Vice President: Guy Giordanego
Printing Information: 16 pages
In Business: 28 years
Number of Employees: 20
Sales Information: $1MM

7575 American Weather Enterprises

American Weather Enterprises
PO Box 14381
San Francisco, CA 94114   415-401-8553
800-293-2555
Fax: 415-401-8480
fogcity@americanweather.com

Weather instruments: hygrometers, thermometers, barometers, anemometers, recording equipment, sundials, weathervanes etc.

President: Robert Sanders
General Manager: Dillon Sanders
Credit Cards: MasterCard; Visa
Catalog Cost: Free
In Business: 6 years
Number of Employees: 3
Sales Information: $270,000

7576 Arbico Organics

Arbico Organics
10831 N. Mavinee Dr.
Ste. 185
Oro Valley, AZ 85737-9531   520-825-9785
800-827-2847
Fax: 520-825-2038
info@arbico.com
www.arbico-organics.com

Beneficial insects, gardening supplies, books, pet products, soil amendments, fertilizers, natural household products

President: Rick Frey
Marketing Manager: Shen Frey

Buyers: Debbie Williams
Credit Cards: AMEX; MasterCard; Visa
Catalog Cost: Free
Catalog Circulation: Mailed 3 time(s) per year to 30000
Average Order Size: $75
Printing Information: 56 pages in 4 colors on Glossy Stock
Press: Web Press
Binding: Saddle Stitched
Mailing List Information: Names for rent
List Manager: Shen Frey
In Business: 36 years
Number of Employees: 40
Sales Information: $3,500,000

7577 Atlas Greenhouse Systems

Atlas Manufacturing, Inc.
PO Box 558
Alapaha, GA 31622-558   229-532-2905
800-346-9902
Fax: 229-532-4600
www.atlasgreenhouse.com

Commercial, educational and hobby greenhouses, as well as carports and agricultural buildings

President: Mark Davis
Office Manager: Billy Stewart
Sales Manager: Bill Mathis
Shipping Coordinator: Tommie Ann Stone
Credit Cards: MasterCard; Visa
Catalog Cost: Free
In Business: 29 years

7578 Bartlett Arborist Supply & Manufacturing Company

Bartlett Manufacturing Company
7876 S. Van Dyke
Marlette,, MI 48453   989-635-8900
800-331-7101
Fax: 989-635-8902
della@bartlettman.com
www.bartlettman.com

Arborist equipment, tree care supplies, cabling and bracing hardware, tree climbing gear, pole saws, pole pruners and more

President: John Nelson
VP: Dorothy Nelson
Credit Cards: MasterCard; Visa
Catalog Cost: Free
Printing Information: 38 pages in 1 color on Glossy Stock
Mailing List Information: Names for rent
In Business: 99 years
Number of Employees: 6
Sales Information: $1,000,000 - $5,000,000

7579 Bowie Industries

Bowie Industries, Inc.
1004 E. Wise Street
PO Box 931
Bowie, TX 76230   940-872-1106
800-433-0934
Fax: 940-872-4792
tellmemore@bowieindustries.com
www.bowieindustries.com

Lawn and landscaping equipment and products

President: Gary Meyer
garymeyer@bowieindustries.com
CFO: Dean Myers
bowind@morgan.net
Controller: Robert Jones
bobjones@bowieindustries.com
VP: Carlotta Jones
cgm@bowieindustries.com
Catalog Cost: Free
Catalog Circulation: Mailed 1 time(s) per year to 1000
Printing Information: 7 pages on Glossy Stock
In Business: 66 years
Number of Employees: 47
Sales Information: $5.40MM

7580 CF Struck Corporation

CF Struck Corporation
P.O Box 307
W51N545 Struck Lane
Cedarburg, WI 53012   262-377-3300
877-828-8323
Fax: 262-377-9247
info@struckcorp.com
www.struckcorp.com

Compact tractors/crawler-capabilities include: backhoe, loader, dozer blade, stone and soil rakes, log splitter, log forks, post-hole augers, and plow

President: Charles Struck
Credit Cards: MasterCard; Visa
Catalog Cost: Free
In Business: 58 years
Number of Employees: 10
Sales Information: $1MM to $3MM

7581 Commodity Traders International

Commodity Traders International
101 E. Main Street
PO Box 6
Trilla, IL 62469-6   217-235-4322
Fax: 217-235-3246
sales@commoditytraders.biz
www.commoditytraders.biz

Seed and grain equipment

President: Charles Stodden Sr
Marketing Manager: Charles Stodden Jr
Mailing List Information: Names for rent
In Business: 40 years
Number of Employees: 4
Sales Information: Under $500M

7582 DR Power Equipment

DR Power Equipment
75 Meigs Road
P.O. Box 25
Vergennes, VT 05491   802-870-1437
800-687-6575
Fax: 802-877-1213
websupport@drpower.com
www.drpower.com

Chippers, brush mowers, leaf vacs, power haulers, trimmers, splitters

President: Joe Perrotto
CFO: Christopher Knapp
Marketing Manager: Ned Van Woert
Production Manager: John Berlind
Fulfillment: Moe Matte
International Marketing Manager: Carl Eikenberg
Buyers: Carl Eikenberg
Credit Cards: MasterCard
Catalog Cost: Free
Average Order Size: $150
Printing Information: 48 pages in 4 colors
Press: Offset Press
Binding: Saddle Stitched
In Business: 32 years
Number of Employees: 250
Sales Information: $20 Million

7583 Dixon Industries

Dixon Industries
9335 Harris Corners Parkway
Charlotte, NC 28269   info@dixon-ztr.com
www.dixon-ztr.com

Lawnmowers

President: John P Mowder
CFO: Ron Bryant
Marketing Manager: Mike Kadel
Production Manager: Charles Roger
Credit Cards: AMEX; MasterCard
Catalog Circulation: to 10K
Printing Information: 20 pages in 4 colors on Glossy Stock
Press: Sheetfed Press
Binding: Saddle Stitched
Mailing List Information: Names for rent
In Business: 32 years

Number of Employees: 200
Sales Information: $25,000,000 - $50,000,000

7584 Dramm Professional Watering Tools
Dramm Corporation of Manitowoc
2000 North 18th Street
PO Box 1960
Manitowoc, WI 54220-1857   920-684-0227
                                800-258-0848
                        Fax: 920-684-4499
information@dramm.com
www.dramm.com

Watering tools for high velocity water

President: Kurt Dramm
CFO: Theresa Krejcarek
Production Manager: Kurt Dramm
Executive Director: Robert Echter
VP: Charles Bohman
Human Resource Manager: Howard Zimmerman
Buyers: Cathy Brunner
Credit Cards: AMEX; MasterCard
Catalog Circulation: Mailed 1 time(s) per year to 25K
Printing Information: 16 pages in 4 colors
Press: Sheetfed Press
Binding: Saddle Stitched
In Business: 68 years
Number of Employees: 48
Sales Information: $5.4 MM

7585 Drip Irrigation
Submatic Irrigation Systems
3002 Upland Ave
Lubbock, TX 79407-246   806-799-0700
                             800-692-4100
                     Fax: 806-799-0722
submatic@sbcglobal.net
www.submatic.com

Drip irrigation products and sprinklers

President: Curry Blackwell
Credit Cards: MasterCard
Catalog Cost: Free
Catalog Circulation: Mailed 2 time(s) per year to 10M
Average Order Size: $150
Printing Information: 25 pages in 2 colors on Glossy Stock
Press: Letterpress
Binding: Perfect Bound
Mailing List Information: Names for rent
In Business: 10 years
Number of Employees: 4
Sales Information: $500M to $1MM

7586 Early Childhood Manufacturers' Direct
Early Childhood Manufacturers' Direct
PO Box 6013
Carol Stream, IL 60197-6013   800-896-9951
                           Fax: 800-879-3753
customerservice@ecmdstore.com
www.ecmdstore.com

Furniture and equipment for schools, preschools and child care programs

Chairman: Ron Elliott
President: Paul Estep
Credit Cards: AMEX; MasterCard
Catalog Cost: Free
Catalog Circulation: to 150m
Average Order Size: $800
Printing Information: 260 pages in 4 colors
Binding: Perfect Bound
In Business: 19 years

7587 Everything for the Lilypool
Slocum Water Gardens
1101 Cypress Gardens Boulevard
Winter Haven, FL 33883   863-293-7151
                      Fax: 800-322-1896
www.slocumwatergardens.com

Complete garden pool products, water lilies, lotus, aquatics, goldfish, pumps, filters, pools, liners and books on water gardening

President: Peter D Slocum
Credit Cards: MasterCard; Visa
Catalog Cost: $3
Catalog Circulation: Mailed 1 time(s) per year to 10M
Printing Information: 60 pages in 4 colors on Glossy Stock
Press: Web Press
Binding: Saddle Stitched
Mailing List Information: Names for rent
In Business: 6 years
Number of Employees: 6
Sales Information: Under $500M

7588 Fan Fair
Fan Fair
2233 Wisconsin Avenue NW
Washington, DC 20007-4104   202-342-6290

Casablanca and Hunter ceiling fans as well as Fanimation; table and floor lamps

President: C Philip Mitchell
CFO: Charles H Betts
Credit Cards: MasterCard
Catalog Circulation: Mailed 6 time(s) per year
Printing Information: 30 pages
In Business: 20 years
Number of Employees: 12
Sales Information: $1MM to $3MM

7589 Imperial Sprinkler Supply
Imperial Sprinkler Supply
1485 N Manassero Street
Anaheim, CA 92807-1938   714-792-2925
                      Fax: 714-792-2921
info@imperialsprinkler.com
www.imperialsprinklersupply.com

Imperial sprinkler systems, install automatic irrigation systems, commercial and residential, sprinkler lines for small and large underground systems; including hydraulic, electric, and lake systems

President: Gabriel Moriel
Catalog Cost: Free
In Business: 37 years
Sales Information: $20MM to $50MM

7590 International Irrigation Systems-Drip Irrigation
Irrigro
PO Box 360
Niagara Falls, NY 14304-360   905-688-4090
                             877-477-4476
                     Fax: 905-688-4093
info@irrigro.com
www.irrigro.com

Systems for drip irrigation and aeration

President: RL Neff
CFO: Gail I Neff
Buyers: RL Neff
Catalog Circulation: Mailed 1 time(s) per year
Mailing List Information: Names for rent
In Business: 25 years
Number of Employees: 5
Sales Information: $500M to $1MM

7591 MacKenzie Nursery Supply
Cherokke Manufacturing Llc
500 Malden Street
South Saint Paul, MN 55075   651-451-6568
                            800-798-9473
                    Fax: 651-451-1138
www.cherokeemfg.com

Wire tree baskets for the mechanical nursery tree trade

President: Bill Burr
In Business: 74 years
Sales Information: $5MM to $10MM

7592 Oly-Ola Sales
Oly-Ola Edgings, Inc
124 E Saint Charles Rd
Villa Park, IL 60181-2414   630-833-3033
                           800-334-4647
                   Fax: 630-833-0816
edgings@olyola.com
www.Olyola.Com

Paver restraints, landscape edging, edging for ponds/water grooves

President: Sandra Hechler
Credit Cards: AMEX; MasterCard; Visa
Catalog Cost: Free
Printing Information: 16 pages on Glossy Stock
Mailing List Information: Names for rent
In Business: 3 years
Number of Employees: 10
Sales Information: $1,000,000 - $5,000,000

7593 Paradise Water Gardens & Landscape
Paradise Water Gardens Ltd.
803 Old County Road
San Carlos, CA 94070   408-520-8960
info@paradisewatergardens.org
www.paradisewatergardens.org

Fiberglass pools and liners, aquatic plants including waterlilies and lotus, fancy goldfish and Japanese Koi

mauricio@paradisewatergardens.org
joe@paradisewatergardens.org
Credit Cards: MasterCard
Catalog Cost: Free
Catalog Circulation: Mailed 1 time(s) per year to 50M
Printing Information: 90 pages in 4 colors on Glossy Stock
Press: Web Press
Binding: Saddle Stitched
Mailing List Information: Names for rent
In Business: 67 years
Number of Employees: 15
Sales Information: 3MM-5MM

7594 Permaloc Aluminum Edging
Permaloc Corporation
13505 Barry Street
Holland, MI 49424   616-399-9600
                   800-356-9660
           Fax: 616-399-9770
info@permaloc.com
www.permaloc.com

Aluminum landscape edging and paving restraints

President: Daniel G Zwier
Marketing Manager: Dave Bareman
Credit Cards: AMEX; MasterCard
Catalog Cost: Free
Catalog Circulation: Mailed 1 time(s) per year to 10M
Printing Information: 10 pages in 4 colors on Glossy Stock
Press: Web Press
Mailing List Information: Names for rent
In Business: 25 years
Number of Employees: 12
Sales Information: $500M to $1MM

7595 PoolSupplyWorld
PoolSupplyWorld
3725 Cincinnati Ave 200
Rocklin, CA 95765   800-722-0467
                   866-556-0224
           Fax: 866-556-3552
sales@poolsupplyworld.com
www.poolsupplyworld.com

Manufacturers of spa and swimming pool supplies

Credit Cards: AMEX; MasterCard
Catalog Cost: Free

7596 Reinco
Relinco Inc
PO Box 512
Plainfield, NJ 07061-512
908-755-0921
800-526-7687
Fax: 908-755-6379
www.reinco.com

Mulching machines

In Business: 50 years
Number of Employees: 20-O
Sales Information: $1,000,000 - $5,000,000

7597 Revere
Revere Products
4529 Industrial Pkwy
Cleveland, OH 44135-311
800-321-1976
Fax: 800-877-1511
www.revereproducts.com

Facility Maintenance Repair Solutions

Credit Cards: MasterCard
Printing Information: in 3 colors on Matte
Stock
Binding: Saddle Stitched
In Business: 49 years

7598 Siebert & Rice
Seibert & Rice
PO Box 365
Short Hills, NJ 07078-365
973-467-8266
Fax: 973-379-2536
terracotta@seibert-rice.com
www.seibert-rice.com

Terra cotta planters by top American designers handmade in Italy

Chairman: Lenore Rice, VP
President: Mara Seibert
Catalog Cost: $5
Printing Information: in 4 colors
In Business: 20 years

7599 Sunlawn, Inc
Sunlawn, Inc.
325 Garfield Street
Fort Collins, CO 80524-3737
970-493-5284
Fax: 970-493-5202

Lawn equipment, mowers and tools

President: Terry Jarvis
Catalog Cost: Free
Mailing List Information: Names for rent
In Business: 16 years
Number of Employees: 2
Sales Information: Under $500M

Seeds

7600 Allen, Sterling, & Lothrop
Allen, Sterling & Lothrop
191 Us Route 1
Falmouth, ME 04105-1385
207-781-4142
Fax: 207-781-4143
shirley@allensterlinglothrop.com
www.allensterlinglothrop.com

Vegetable, flower and herb seeds as well as top quality lawn, garden, and greenhouse supplies

President: Shirley Brannigan
Seed-Room Manager: Jenn Herring
General Manager: Shawn Brannigan
Credit Cards: MasterCard; Visa
Catalog Cost: $1
Catalog Circulation: Mailed 1 time(s) per year
to 25000
Printing Information: 32 pages in 1 color on s
Binding: Folded
Mailing List Information: Names for rent
In Business: 104 years
Number of Employees: 11
Sales Information: $5MM-$10MM

7601 Applewood Seed Company
Applewood Seed Company
5380 Vivian Street
Arvada, CO 80002
303-431-7333
Fax: 303-467-7886
sales@applewoodseed.com
www.applewoodseed.com

Horticultural gift products and flower pot baking kit

General Manager: Norm Poppe
Ecologist: Diane Wilson
Sales Specialist: Evan Mawe
Credit Cards: AMEX; MasterCard; Visa
Catalog Cost: Free
In Business: 50 years
Sales Information: $4MM

7602 Bamert Seed Company
Bamert Seed
1897 County Road 1018
Muleshoe, TX 79347-7221
806-272-5506
800-262-9892
Fax: 806-272-3114
natives@bamertseed.com
www.bamertseed.Com

Over 40 species of native grasses, legumes and forbs for prairie restoration, wildlife habitat, wildlife food plots, reclamation and conservation reserve programs

President: Nick Bamert
Production Manager: Rayniel Bamert
Owner: Carl Bamert
Credit Cards: AMEX; MasterCard
Catalog Circulation: Mailed 1 time(s) per year
Printing Information: 10 pages in 1 color on
Matte Stock
In Business: 63 years
Number of Employees: 15
Sales Information: $700M

7603 Bare Root Fruit Trees
Peaceful Valley Farm Supply, Inc.
125 Clydesdale Court
P.O. Box 2209
Grass Valley, CA 95945
530-272-4769
888-784-1722
helpdesk@groworganic.com
www.groworganic.com

Vegetable/herb/flower seed packs or in bulk, propagating, water and irrigation, greenhouse, composting supplies, natural weed control, garden equipment and more

President: Eric Boudier
Vice President: Patricia Boudier
General Manager: Lee Dickerson
Catalog Cost: Free
Catalog Circulation: Mailed 1 time(s) per year
Printing Information: 68 pages in 4 colors
In Business: 41 years
Number of Employees: 60
Sales Information: $7.2 Million

7604 Breck's Bulbs
Breck's
PO Box 65
Guilford, IN 47022-4180
513-354-1511
Fax: 513-354-1505
www.brecks.com

Dutch flower bulbs

Credit Cards: AMEX; MasterCard
Catalog Cost: Free
Printing Information: 52 pages in 4 colors
In Business: 196 years
Number of Employees: 850

7605 Burgess Seed and Plant Company
Burgess Seed and Plant Company
1804 E Hamilton Road
Bloomington, IL 61704-9609
309-662-7761
customercare@eburgess.com
www.eburgess.com

Fruits, berries, nuts, vegetable seeds, trees, perennials and plants

President: Richard Owen
Credit Cards: MasterCard
Catalog Cost: Free
Catalog Circulation: Mailed 3 time(s) per year
Average Order Size: $48
Printing Information: 39 pages in 4 colors on
Newsprint
Binding: Saddle Stitched
Mailing List Information: Names for rent
In Business: 103 years
Sales Information: $10MM to $20MM

7606 Comstock, Ferre & Company
Baker Creek Heirloom seed Co.
2278 Baker Creek Road
Mansfield, MO 65704-1890
417-924-8917
860-571-6590
Fax: 417-924-8887
seeds@rareseeds.com
www.rareseeds.com

Quality vegetable, flower and herb seeds

President: Pierre Bennerup
Manager: Steve Hale
Credit Cards: AMEX; MasterCard
Catalog Cost: Free
Catalog Circulation: Mailed 1 time(s) per year
Average Order Size: $20
Printing Information: 212 pages in 1 color on
Newsprint
Mailing List Information: Names for rent
In Business: 200 years
Number of Employees: 10
Sales Information: $860,000

7607 Connell's Dahlias
K Connell Dahlias
10616 Waller Rd E
Tacoma, WA 98446-2231
253-620-0044
Fax: 253-536-7725
kercon6@msn.com
www.Connells-Dahlias.Com

Pom pons, waterlilies, dahlias, split petals and seeds

President: Kerry Connell
kercon6@msn.com
Catalog Cost: $2
Catalog Circulation: Mailed 1 time(s) per year
Average Order Size: $45
Printing Information: 28 pages in 4 colors on
Glossy Stock
Binding: Folded
Mailing List Information: Names for rent
In Business: 35 years
Number of Employees: 6
Sales Information: $1MM to $3MM

7608 Cook's Garden
PO Box C5030
Warminster, PA 18974-574
215-674-4900
800-457-9703
www.cooksgarden.com

Vegetable, flower and herb seeds, kitchen supplies, garden supplies, plants and bulbs

Buyers: Shepherd & Ellen Ogden
Catalog Cost: Free
Catalog Circulation: Mailed 1 time(s) per year
Printing Information: in 4 colors on Matte
Stock
Press: Web Press
Mailing List Information: Names for rent

7609 FW Schumacher Company
F. W. Schumacher Co., Inc.
36 Spring Hill Road
P.O. Box 1023
Sandwich, MA 02563-1023
508-888-0659
Fax: 508-833-0322
info@treeshrubseeds.com
www.treeshrubseeds.com

Variety of tree and shrub trees

President: Donald Allen
Catalog Cost: Free
Catalog Circulation: Mailed 2 time(s) per year
Printing Information: 26 pages
Mailing List Information: Names for rent
In Business: 87 years
Number of Employees: 4

7610 Fall Planting

Peaceful Valley Farm Supply, Inc.
125 Clydesdale Court
P.O. Box 2209
Grass Valley, CA 95945   530-272-4769
                                888-784-1722
helpdesk@groworganic.com
www.groworganic.com

Vegetable/herb/flower seed packs or in bulk, propagating, water and irrigation, greenhouse, composting supplies, natural weed control, garden equipment and more

President: Eric Boudier
Vice President: Patricia Boudier
General Manager: Lee Dickerson
Catalog Cost: Free
Catalog Circulation: Mailed 1 time(s) per year
Printing Information: 35 pages in 4 colors
In Business: 41 years
Number of Employees: 60
Sales Information: $7.2 Million

7611 Fedco Seeds

Fedco Co-op Garden Supplies
PO Box 520
Waterville, ME 04903-520   207-426-9900
                           Fax: 207-692-1022
questions@fedcoseeds.com
www.fedcoseeds.com

Untreated vegetable, herb and flower seeds, soil amendments, fertilizers, cover crops, garden tools, bulbs, seed potatoes, onion sets, garlic, fruit trees, ornamentals, perennials, and tender bulbs

President: CR Lawn
Executive Director: Russell Libby
Catalog Cost: Free
Catalog Circulation: Mailed 3 time(s) per year to 90M
Printing Information: 107 pages in 1 color on Newsprint
Press: Web Press
Binding: Saddle Stitched
Mailing List Information: Names for rent
In Business: 32 years
Number of Employees: 50
Sales Information: Under $500M

7612 Fedco Trees

Fedco Co-op Garden Supplies
PO Box 520
Waterville, ME 04903-520   207-426-9900
                           Fax: 207-692-1022
questions@fedcoseeds.com
www.fedcoseeds.com

Fedco trees offers fruit trees, berry bushes, ornamental trees & bulbs, perennials and spring planted bulbs

President: CR Lawn
Executive Director: Russell Libby
Catalog Cost: Free
Catalog Circulation: Mailed 1 time(s) per year to 30M
Printing Information: 72 pages in 1 color on Newsprint
Press: Web Press
Binding: Saddle Stitched
Mailing List Information: Names for rent
In Business: 32 years
Number of Employees: 50
Sales Information: Under $500M

7613 Fungi Perfecti

Fungi Perfecti LLC
P.O. Box 7634
Olympia, WA 98507   360-426-9292
                                800-780-9126
info@fungi.com
www.fungi.com

Mushroom spawn, growing kits, supplies and books for the home and commercial grower

President: Paul Stamets
Credit Cards: MasterCard; Visa
Catalog Cost: Free
Catalog Circulation: Mailed 1 time(s) per year
Average Order Size: $75
Printing Information: 82 pages in 4 colors on Glossy Stock
Press: Web Press
Binding: Saddle Stitched
Mailing List Information: Names for rent
In Business: 20 years
Number of Employees: 10
Sales Information: $1MM to $3MM

7614 Harvesting & Country Living

Peaceful Valley Farm Supply, Inc.
125 Clydesdale Court
P.O. Box 2209
Grass Valley, CA 95945   530-272-4769
                                888-784-1722
helpdesk@groworganic.com
www.groworganic.com

Vegetable/herb/flower seed packs or in bulk, propagating, water and irrigation, greenhouse, composting supplies, natural weed control, garden equipment and more

President: Eric Boudier
Vice President: Patricia Boudier
General Manager: Lee Dickerson
Catalog Cost: Free
Catalog Circulation: Mailed 1 time(s) per year
Printing Information: 68 pages in 4 colors
In Business: 41 years
Number of Employees: 60
Sales Information: $7.2 Million

7615 Johnny's Selected Seeds

Johnny's Selected Seeds
13 Main Street
Fairfield, ME 04901   877-564-6697
www.johnnyseeds.com

Vegetable, herb and flower seeds as well as accessories, including roots, tubers, seed cultivation supplies and books

Chairman: Rob Johnston, Jr
Territory Sales Representative, CA: John Bauer
jbauer@johnnyseeds.com
International Marketing Manager: Chris Siladi
Catalog Circulation: Mailed 1 time(s) per year
Average Order Size: $42
Printing Information: in 4 colors on Glossy Stock
Press: Web Press
Binding: Saddle Stitched
Mailing List Information: Names for rent
List Manager: Bob Milano
In Business: 40 years
Sales Information: $20MM to $50MM

7616 Jung Seeds & Plants

Jung
335 S High Street
Randolph, WI 53956   800-297-3123
info@jungseed.com
www.jungseed.com

Seeds and nursery stock

President/Marketing: Richard Zondag
Finance Director: David Wild
Catalog Cost: Free
Printing Information: 112 pages
In Business: 106 years
Number of Employees: 450

7617 Kester's Wild Game Food Nurseries

Kester's Wild Game Food Nurseries Inc
PO Box 516
Omro, WI 54963-516   920-685-2929
                           Fax: 920-685-6727
pkester@vbe.com
www.kestersnursery.com

Seeds and aquatic plants for wildlife feeding

President: David Kester
Owner: Patricia Kester
Credit Cards: MasterCard; Visa
Catalog Cost:
Catalog Circulation: Mailed 1 time(s) per year to 2.5M
Printing Information: 40 pages in 4 colors on Matte Stock
Press: Web Press
Binding: Saddle Stitched
Mailing List Information: Names for rent
In Business: 80 years
Number of Employees: 7
Sales Information: $500M to $1MM

7618 Meyer Seed

Meyer Seed Company of Baltimore, Inc
600 S Caroline Street
Baltimore, MD 21231-2813   410-342-4224
                                800-458-SEED
                           Fax: 410-327-1469
info@meyerseedco.com
www.meyerseedco.com/

Seeds, garden supplies and tools

Credit Cards: AMEX; MasterCard
Catalog Cost: Free
Catalog Circulation: Mailed 1 time(s) per year
Printing Information: 40 pages in 4 colors
Binding: Saddle Stitched
Mailing List Information: Names for rent
In Business: 105 years
Number of Employees: 30
Sales Information: Under $500M

7619 Natural & Organic Fertilizers

Peaceful Valley Farm Supply, Inc.
125 Clydesdale Court
P.O. Box 2209
Grass Valley, CA 95945   530-272-4769
                                888-874-1722
helpdesk@groworganic.com
www.groworganic.com

Vegetable/herb/flower seed packs or in bulk, propagating, water and irrigation, greenhouse, composting supplies, natural weed control, garden equipment and more

President: Eric Boudier
Vice President: Patricia Boudier
General Manager: Lee Dickerson
Catalog Cost: Free
Catalog Circulation: Mailed 1 time(s) per year
Printing Information: 68 pages in 4 colors
In Business: 41 years
Number of Employees: 60
Sales Information: $7.2 Million

7620 Nichols Garden Nursery

Nichols Garden Nursery
1190 Old Salem Road NE
Albany, OR 97321-4580   800-422-3985
                           Fax: 800-231-5306
www.nicholsgardennursery.com

Herb seeds and plants

President: Rose Marie McGee
Credit Cards: AMEX; MasterCard
Catalog Cost: Free
Catalog Circulation: Mailed 1 time(s) per year to 250M
Printing Information: 55 pages in 4 colors
Mailing List Information: Names for rent
List Manager: Keane McGee
In Business: 65 years
Number of Employees: 20
Sales Information: $1MM to $3MM

7621 Organic Gardening Essentials
Peaceful Valley Farm Supply, Inc.
125 Clydesdale Court
P.O. Box 2209
Grass Valley, CA 95945   530-272-4769
888-784-1722
helpdesk@groworganic.com
www.groworganic.com

Vegetable/herb/flower seed packs or in bulk, propagating, water and irrigation, greenhouse, composting supplies, natural weed control, garden equipment and more

President: Eric Boudier
Vice President: Patricia Boudier
General Manager: Lee Dickerson
Catalog Cost: Free
Printing Information: 168 pages in 4 colors
Press: Web Press
In Business: 41 years
Number of Employees: 60
Sales Information: $7.2 Million

7622 Organic Seeds
Peaceful Valley Farm Supply, Inc.
125 Clydesdale Court
P.O. Box 2209
Grass Valley, CA 95945   530-272-4769
888-784-1722
helpdesk@groworganic.com
www.groworganic.com

Vegetable/herb/flower seed packs or in bulk, propagating, water and irrigation, greenhouse, composting supplies, natural weed control, garden equipment and more

President: Eric Boudier
Vice President: Patricia Boudier
General Manager: Lee Dickerson
Catalog Cost: Free
Catalog Circulation: Mailed 1 time(s) per year
Printing Information: 68 pages in 4 colors
In Business: 41 years
Number of Employees: 60
Sales Information: $7.2 Million

7623 Perennial Pleasures Nursery
Perennial Pleasures
63 Brickhouse Road
PO Box 147
East Hardwick, VT 05836   802-472-5104
Fax: 802-472-3737
annex@perennialpleasures.net
www.perennialpleasures.net

Antique perennials

Catalog Cost: Free
Mailing List Information: Names for rent
In Business: 35 years
Number of Employees: 10-J
Sales Information: $500M to $1MM

7624 Pest & Weed Control
Peaceful Valley Farm Supply, Inc.
125 Clydesdale Court
P.O. Box 2209
Grass Valley, CA 95945   530-272-4769
888-874-1722
helpdesk@groworganic.com
www.groworganic.com

Vegeatable/herb/flower seed packs or in bulk, propagating, water and irrigation, greenhouse, composting supplies, natural weed control, garden equipment and more

President: Eric Boudier
Vice President: Patricia Boudier
General Manager: Lee Dickerson
Catalog Cost: Free
Catalog Circulation: Mailed 1 time(s) per year
Printing Information: 68 pages in 4 colors
In Business: 41 years
Number of Employees: 60
Sales Information: $7.2 Million

7625 Pinetree Garden Seeds
Pinetree Garden Seeds
P.O. Box 300
New Gloucester, ME 04260   207-926-3400
hello@superseeds.com
www.superseeds.com

Flower, vegetable, herb and houseplant seeds, tools, garden equipment and books

President: Richard Meiners
Marketing Manager: Jef Wright
Credit Cards: AMEX; MasterCard
Catalog Cost: Free
Catalog Circulation: Mailed 1 time(s) per year to 575M
Average Order Size: $35
Printing Information: 164 pages in 4 colors on Newsprint
Press: Web Press
Binding: Saddle Stitched
Mailing List Information: Names for rent
In Business: 38 years
Number of Employees: 45
Sales Information: $2,000,000

7626 Plants of the Southwest
Plants of the Southwest
3095 Agua Fria Street
Santa Fe, NM 87507-5411   505-438-8888
800-788-7333
Fax: 505-438-8800
plantsofthesouthwest@gmail.com
plantsofthesouthwest.com

Southwestern native plants including berry and nut producing trees and shrubs, wildflowers, native grasses and ancient and drought tolerant vegetable seeds

Credit Cards: AMEX; MasterCard
Catalog Cost: Free
Mailing List Information: Names for rent
In Business: 27 years
Number of Employees: 20-5
Sales Information: $1MM to $3MM

7627 Prairie Nursery
Prairie Nursery
P.O. Box 306
Westfield, WI 53964   800-476-9453
Fax: 608-296-2741
www.prairienursery.com

Native flowers and grasses for prairies and woodlands - plants and seeds

President: Neil Diboll
Credit Cards: AMEX; MasterCard
Catalog Cost: Free
Catalog Circulation: Mailed 1 time(s) per year to 2500
Average Order Size: $125
Printing Information: 74 pages in 4 colors on Matte Stock
Press: Web Press
Binding: Saddle Stitched
Mailing List Information: Names for rent
In Business: 45 years
Number of Employees: 25
Sales Information: $1MM to $3MM

7628 Quality Tools & Drip Irrigation Supplies
Peaceful Valley Farm Supply, Inc.
125 Clydesdale Court
P.O. Box 2209
Grass Valley, CA 95945   530-272-4769
888-784-1722
helpdesk@groworganic.com
www.groworganic.com

Vegetable/herb/flower seed packs or in bulk, propagating, water and irrigation, greenhouse, composting supplies, natural weed control, garden equipment and more

President: Eric Boudier
Vice President: Patricia Boudier
General Manager: Lee Dickerson
Catalog Cost: Free
Catalog Circulation: Mailed 1 time(s) per year

Printing Information: 68 pages in 4 colors
In Business: 41 years
Number of Employees: 60
Sales Information: $7.2 Million

7629 RH Shumway
RH Shumway
334 W Stroud St
Randolph, WI 53956   800-342-9461
Fax: 888-437-2733
info@rhshumway.com
www.rhshumway.com

Seeds, nursery stock and horticultural supplies

President: RH Shumway
Credit Cards: MasterCard; Visa
Catalog Cost:
Catalog Circulation: Mailed 1 time(s) per year to 1MM
Printing Information: 64 pages in 4 colors
Press: Web Press
Binding: Saddle Stitched
In Business: 11 years
Number of Employees: 100

7630 Redwood City Seed Company
Redwood City Seed Company
PO Box 361
Redwood City, CA 94064   650-325-7333
Fax: 650-325-4056
ecoseeds.com

Heirloom, non-hybrid vegetables, hot peppers and herb seeds

President: Craig Dremann
Buyers: Craig Dremann
Credit Cards: AMEX; MasterCard
Catalog Cost:
Catalog Circulation: Mailed 1 time(s) per year
Printing Information: 28 pages in 1 color on Matte Stock
Press: Web Press
Binding: Saddle Stitched
Mailing List Information: Names for rent
In Business: 41 years

7631 Seed Savers Exchange
Seed Savers Exchange
3094 N Winn Rd
Decorah, IA 52101-7776   563-382-5990
Fax: 563-382-6511
customerservice@seedsavers.org
www.Seedsavers.org

Heirloom seeds, gardening books and gifts

Chairman: Keith Crotz
President: John Torgrimson
Marketing Manager: Kelly Tagtow
Vice-Chair Of the Board: Neil Hamilton, J.D.
Secretary: Larry Grimstad
Treasurer: Larry Grimstad
Catalog Cost:
Catalog Circulation: Mailed 1 time(s) per year to 75000
Printing Information: 101 pages in 3 colors
Press: Letterpress
Binding: Saddle Stitched
Mailing List Information: Names for rent
In Business: 40 years
Number of Employees: 10
Sales Information: $3MM to $5MM

7632 Seeds of Change
Seeds of Change
PO Box 4908
Rancho
Dominguez, CA 90220-5700   505-438-8080
888-762-7333
Fax: 505-438-7052
gardener@seedsofchange.com
www.seedsofchange.com

Organic seeds

President: Stephen Badger
Marketing Manager: Scott Vlaun
Catalog Cost: Free
Printing Information: 72 pages in 3 colors on

Matte Stock
Press: Letterpress
Binding: Folded
In Business: 24 years
Number of Employees: 10
Sales Information: 500M-1MM

7633 Select Seeds Antique Flowers
Select Seeds
180 Stickney Hill Rd
Union, CT 06076   860-684-9310
                         800-684-0395
                    Fax: 860-684-9224
              info@selectseeds.com
              www.Selectseeds.com

Cottage garden and heirloom flowers seeds and plants

President: Marilyn Barlow
Credit Cards: MasterCard; Visa
Catalog Circulation: to 40000
Average Order Size: $28
Printing Information: 64 pages in 3 colors on Newsprint
Mailing List Information: Names for rent
In Business: 50 years
Number of Employees: 8
Sales Information: $5MM to $10MM

7634 Territorial Seed Company
Territorial Seed Company
P.O. Box 158
Cottage Grove, OR 97424   541-942-9547
                             800-626-0866
                        Fax: 888-657-3131
              info@territorialseed.com
              www.territorialseed.com

Complete line of vegetable, flower and herb seeds and plants, tools, garlic and organic gardening supplies

President: Tom Johns
Fulfillment: Kathy Ledserwood
Founder: Steve Solomon
Owner: Julie Johns
Credit Cards: MasterCard; Visa
Catalog Cost: Free
Catalog Circulation: Mailed 2 time(s) per year to 700M
Printing Information: 95 pages in 4 colors on Newsprint
Press: Web Press
Binding: Saddle Stitched
Mailing List Information: Names for rent
In Business: 32 years
Number of Employees: 24
Sales Information: $1MM to $3MM

7635 Thompson & Morgan Seedsmen
Thmpson & Morgan Seeds
P.O. Box 397
Aurora, IN 47001-397   800-274-7333
                        Fax: 888-466-4769
              www.tmseeds.com

Flower and vegetable seeds

Buyers: Burt Garris
Catalog Cost: Free
In Business: 160 years
Number of Employees: 25
Sales Information: $5MM to $10MM

7636 Van Dyck's Flower Farm
K. Van Bourgondien & Sons, Inc.
P.O. Box 289
Cleves, OH 45002-2000   800-552-9996
                             800-552-9916
                        Fax: 800-327-4268
              blooms@dutchbulbs.com
              www.dutchbulbs.com

Dutch flower bulbs

President: Jan Van Dyck
Credit Cards: AMEX; MasterCard
Catalog Cost: Free
Catalog Circulation: Mailed 2 time(s) per year to 1.5MM
Average Order Size: $100

Printing Information: 68 pages in 4 colors on Glossy Stock
Binding: Saddle Stitched
Number of Employees: 15
Sales Information: $1,000,000

7637 Van Engelen
Van Engelen, Inc.
23 Tulip Drive
PO Box 638
Bantam, CT 06750   860-567-8734
                        Fax: 860-567-5323
              customerservice@vanengelen.com
              www.vanengelen.com

Flower bulbs

Chairman: Jo-Anne van den Berg-Ohms
President: Jan S. Ohms
Owner: Jan S. Ohms
Credit Cards: MasterCard; Visa
Catalog Cost: Free
Catalog Circulation: Mailed 1 time(s) per year
Printing Information: 52 pages in 1 color
Mailing List Information: Names for rent

Shrubs & Plants

7638 Adams County Nursery
Adams County Nursery
26 Nursery Road
PO Box 108
Aspers, PA 17304   717-677-8105
                        Fax: 717-677-4124
              www.acnursery.com

Fruit trees

President: John Baugher
Marketing Manager: Tom Callahan
Vice President: Nadine Baugher
Sales Executive: Philip Baugher
Credit Cards: MasterCard; Visa
Catalog Cost: Free
Catalog Circulation: Mailed 1 time(s) per year
Printing Information: 28 pages in 4 colors
Mailing List Information: Names for rent
In Business: 110 years
Number of Employees: 45
Sales Information: $10MM

7639 Aitken's Salmon Creek Garden
Aitken's Salmon Creek Garden
608 NW 119th St
Vancouver, WA 98685   360-573-4472
                        Fax: 360-576-7012
              aitken@flowerfantasy.net
              www.flowerfantasy.net

Wide variety of award-winning irises and orchids

President: J T Aitken
Credit Cards: AMEX; MasterCard
Catalog Cost: $4
Catalog Circulation: Mailed 1 time(s) per year
Printing Information: 48 pages in 1 color on Glossy Stock
Binding: Saddle Stitched
Mailing List Information: Names for rent
In Business: 45 years
Number of Employees: 2
Sales Information: $500M

7640 Amaryllis Bulb Company
Amaryllis & Caladium Bulb Company
1231 E Magnolia St
Lakeland, FL 33801   863-802-0001
                             888-966-9866
                        Fax: 863-683-8479
              contact@amaryllisandcaladiumbulbco.com
              www.amaryllis.com

Amaryllis plants and pots

President: Shirley Henry
Credit Cards: AMEX; MasterCard
Catalog Cost: Free
Catalog Circulation: Mailed 1 time(s) per year
Printing Information: 9 pages in 4 colors
In Business: 8 years

Number of Employees: 4
Sales Information: $170,000

7641 Amazon Exotic Hardwoods
Amazon Exotic Hardwoods
328 Commercial St
Casselberry, FL 32707   407-339-9590
                             866-339-9596
                        Fax: 407-339-9906
              info@amazonexotichardwoods.com
              www.amazonexotichardwoods.com

Domestic and exotic hardwoods, specially cut and prepared for cabinetmakers, carvers, knife makers, musical instrument makers and wood turners

President: James Lie
Credit Cards: AMEX; MasterCard
Catalog Cost: Free
In Business: 12 years
Number of Employees: 1
Sales Information: $250,000

7642 Bigelow Nurseries
Bigelow Nurseries, Inc.
455 W Main Street
P.O. Box 718
Northboro, MA 01532-0718   508-845-2143
                        Fax: 508-842-9245
              cs@bigelownurseries.com
              www.bigelownurseries.com

Fruits, berries and nuts

President: Pat Bigelow
pat@bigelownurseries.com
Production Manager: Brad Bigelow
bbigelow@bigelownurseries.com
General Manager: Jay Flanigan
jay@bigelownurseries.com
Sales Manager: Jeff Dragon
jdragon@bigelownurseries.com
Catalog Cost: Free
Catalog Circulation: Mailed 1 time(s) per year
In Business: 102 years
Number of Employees: 35
Sales Information: $50MM

7643 Blake Nursery Catalog
Blake Nursery
316 Otter Creek Rd
Big Timber, MT 59011   406-932-4195
                        Fax: 406-932-4193
              info@blakenursery.com
              www.blakenursery.com

Large selection of plants, many montana natives

President: Francis Blake
Retail Manager: Meghan Fenoglio
Maintenance Manager: Nora Melius
Landscape Foreman: Dave Melius
Catalog Cost: Free
In Business: 38 years
Number of Employees: 3
Sales Information: $220,000

7644 Bluestone Perennials
Bluestone Perennials
7211 Middle Ridge Road
Madison, OH 44057   800-852-5243
                        Fax: 800-852-5243
              service@bluestoneperennials.com
              www.bluestoneperennials.com

Perennial plants

President: Bill Boonstra
Credit Cards: AMEX; MasterCard; Visa
Catalog Cost: Free
Catalog Circulation: Mailed 1 time(s) per year
Printing Information: 72 pages in 4 colors on Glossy Stock
Press: Web Press
Binding: Saddle Stitched
Mailing List Information: Names for rent
In Business: 45 years
Number of Employees: 60
Sales Information: $10MM

7645 Bovees Nursery
The Bovees Nursery
1737 SW Coronado St
Portland, OR 97219-7654   503-244-9341
866-652-3219
info@bovees.com
www.bovees.com

Species and hybrid rhododendrons, semi tropical

President: Lucie Sorensen-Smith
Companion Plant Propagator: Janice Palmer
Customer Service: E. White Smith
Credit Cards: MasterCard; Visa
Catalog Cost: Free
Printing Information: 44 pages in 1 color
In Business: 62 years
Number of Employees: 3
Sales Information: $50K

7646 Brown's Omaha Plant Farms
Brown's Omaha Plant Farms
110 McLean Ave
PO Box 787
Omaha, TX 75571   903-884-2421
Fax: 903-884-2423
mail@bopf.com
www.bopf.com

Onion plants

President: Jim D Brown
Marketing Manager: Greg Brown
Catalog Cost: Free
Catalog Circulation: Mailed 1 time(s) per year
Printing Information: 4 pages in 1 color on Matte Stock
Press: Web Press
Binding: Saddle Stitched
Mailing List Information: Names for rent
In Business: 75 years
Number of Employees: 16
Sales Information: $860M

7647 Burgess Seed and Plant Company
Burgess Seed and Plant Company
1804 E Hamilton Road
Bloomington, IL 61704-9609   309-662-7761
customercare@eburgess.com
www.eburgess.com

Fruits, berries, nuts, vegetable seeds, trees, perennials and plants

President: Richard Owen
Credit Cards: MasterCard
Catalog Cost:
Catalog Circulation: Mailed 3 time(s) per year
Average Order Size: $48
Printing Information: 39 pages in 4 colors on Newsprint
Binding: Saddle Stitched
Mailing List Information: Names for rent
In Business: 103 years
Sales Information: $10MM to $20MM

7648 Burnt Ridge Nursery
Burnt Ridge Orchards, Inc.
432 Burnt Ridge Road
Onalaska, WA 98570-9446   360-985-2873
Fax: 360-985-0882
mail@burntridgenursery.com
www.burntridgenursery.com

Disease resistant trees and vines that produce edible fruits and nuts; Ornamental & useful trees and shrubs such as dogwoods and bamboo; Northwest natives

President: Michael Dolan
Marketing Manager: Carolyn Cerling-Dolan
Catalog Cost: Free
Catalog Circulation: Mailed 1 time(s) per year to 40000
Average Order Size: $150
Printing Information: 40 pages on Newsprint
Press: Sheetfed Press
Binding: Saddle Stitched
In Business: 35 years
Number of Employees: 4
Sales Information: 700,000

7649 Calyx Flowers
Calyx Flowers
6655 Shelburne Road
Shelburne, VT 05482   802-985-3001
800-800-7788
Fax: 802-985-1304
business@calyxflowers.com
www.calyxflowers.com

Fresh flowers

Marketing Manager: Irene Steiner
Credit Cards: AMEX; MasterCard
Catalog Cost: Free
Catalog Circulation: Mailed 6 time(s) per year
Printing Information: 32 pages in 4 colors on Glossy Stock
Binding: Saddle Stitched
In Business: 11 years
Number of Employees: 50

7650 Camp Lot a Noise Tropicals
Camp Lot a Noise Tropicals
4084 47th Street
Sarasota, FL 34235-4402   941-351-2483
800-351-2483
Fax: 941-351-2483
www.Clanorchids.Com

Exotics, tropicals, supplies, fertilizer and orchids

President: Karen Sellers
In Business: 41 years
Sales Information: Under $500M

7651 Chestnut Hill Nursery
Chestnut Hill Tree Farm
15105 NW 94th Ave
Alachua, FL 32615-6709   386-462-2820
800-669-2067
Fax: 386-462-4330
chestnuthillnursery@gmail.com
www.chestnuthilltreefarm.com

Wholesale trees

President: Deborag Gaw
E-Business: Jolene King
Credit Cards: AMEX; MasterCard; Visa
Catalog Cost: Free
Catalog Circulation: Mailed 1 time(s) per year to 20M
Printing Information: 20 pages in 4 colors on Matte Stock
Mailing List Information: Names for rent
In Business: 14 years
Number of Employees: 14
Sales Information: $950,000

7652 Davidson Greenhouse & Nursery
Davidson Greenhouse & Nursery
3147 E Ladoga Rd
Crawfordsville, IN 47933   765-364-0556
877-723-6834
Fax: 800-276-3691
vicki@davidsongreenhouse.com
www.Davidsongreenhouse.Com

Scented geraniums, begonias, and impatiens; houseplants, herbs, and succulents

President: Mark Davidson
Credit Cards: AMEX; MasterCard; Visa
Catalog Cost: $3
Catalog Circulation: Mailed 1 time(s) per year to 11M
Average Order Size: $60
Printing Information: 40 pages in 4 colors on Glossy Stock
Press: Web Press
Binding: Saddle Stitched
Mailing List Information: Names for rent
In Business: 21 years
Number of Employees: 10
Sales Information: $1MM to $3MM

7653 Direct Gardening
Direct Gardening
1704 Morrissey Drive
Bloomington, IL 61704-9249   309-662-7943
customercare@directgardening.com
www.directgardening.com

Roses, bulbs, perennials and ornamentals

President: Richard Owen
Credit Cards: MasterCard
Catalog Cost: $1.5
Sales Information: $20MM to $50MM

7654 Edible Landscaping
Edible Landscaping
361 Spirit Ridge Lane
Afton, VA 22920   434-361-9134
Fax: 434-361-1916
info@ediblelandscaping.com
www.ediblelandscaping.com

Low maintenance edibles for your yard or garden, including kiwi, black currants, gooseberries, oriental persimmons, mulberries, jujubi, pawpaw, citrus, bush cherries, plums, and pears, figs

President: Michael McConkey
Marketing Manager: Michael McConkey
Fulfillment: Janet Dickie
Credit Cards: AMEX; MasterCard
Catalog Cost: $2
Catalog Circulation: Mailed 12 time(s) per year to 50000
Average Order Size: $100
Printing Information: 32 pages on Glossy Stock
Press: Web Press
Binding: Saddle Stitched
Mailing List Information: Names for rent
In Business: 38 years
Number of Employees: 8
Sales Information: $1MM to $3MM

7655 Exotic Houseplants
Lynn Mckameys usual palms & Exotic Plant
PO Box 287
Gregory, TX 78359-287   361-643-2061
www.rarepalms.com

Rare, exotic houseplants, Japanese pottery and bonsai books

President: Lynn McKamey
Credit Cards: MasterCard; Visa
Catalog Cost: $2
Catalog Circulation: to 5M
Printing Information: 10 pages in 1 color
Number of Employees: 7
Sales Information: $1MM to $3MM

7656 Farmer Seed & Nursery Company
Farmer Seed & Nursery
818 NW 4th Street
Faribault, MN 55021   507-334-1623
customercare@farmerseed.com
www.farmerseed.com

Vegetables, seeds, plants, trees and bulbs

President: Greg Mews
Credit Cards: MasterCard
Catalog Cost: Free
Catalog Circulation: Mailed 4 time(s) per year
Printing Information: 44 pages in 4 colors
In Business: 130 years
Number of Employees: 35
Sales Information: $10MM to $20MM

7657 Fiddyment Farms
Fiddyment Farms
563 Second Street, Suite 210
PO Box 245
Lincoln, CA 95648   916-645-7244
877-343-3276
Fax: 916-645-7825
info@fiddymentfarms.com
www.fiddymentfarms.com

Pistachios

Credit Cards: MasterCard
Catalog Cost: Free
Printing Information: 2 pages in 1 color
In Business: 46 years

7658 Fieldstone Gardens

Fieldstone Gardens
55 Quaker Ln
Vassalboro, ME 04989-3816   207-923-3816
Fax: 207-923-3836
sales@fieldstonegardens.com
www.fieldstonegardens.com

Perennial plants, rock and garden plants siberian iris, asters, astible, campanulas, clematis, delphiniums, epimediums, hardy geraniums, herbaceous peonies, phlox and more

President: Steven Jones
Marketing Manager: Karen Mitchell
General Manager: Bob Milano
bob@fieldstonegardens.com
Credit Cards: MasterCard
Catalog Cost: $2.5
Catalog Circulation: Mailed 1 time(s) per year
Printing Information: 48 pages in 4 colors on Matte Stock
Press: Web Press
Binding: Saddle Stitched
Mailing List Information: Names for rent
In Business: 31 years
Number of Employees: 6
Sales Information: $1MM to $3MM

7659 Forestfarm Catalog

Forest Farm At Pacifica
14643 Watergap Road
Williams, OR 97544   541-846-7269
Fax: 541-846-6963
plants@forestfarm.com
www.forestfarm.com

Hardy ornamental plants

President: Ray Prag
Marketing Manager: Jen Hardin-Tietjen
jen@forestfarm.com
Credit Cards: MasterCard
Catalog Cost: $5
Catalog Circulation: Mailed 2 time(s) per year to 80M
Printing Information: 250 pages in 1 color on Newsprint
Press: Web Press
Binding: Perfect Bound
In Business: 41 years
Number of Employees: 18
Sales Information: Under $500M

7660 G&B Orchid Laboratory

Orchid Source Laboratory & Nursing
2426 Cherimoya Drive
Vista, CA 92084-7812   760-727-2611
Fax: 760-727-0017
orchidsource@gmail.com
www.orchidsource.com

Phalaenopsis, cymbidium, dendrobium and species orchids

President: Barry Cohen
Credit Cards: AMEX; MasterCard
Catalog Cost: $1
Number of Employees: 5
Sales Information: Under $500M

7661 Gardens of the Blue Ridge

Gardens of the Blue Ridge
PO Box 10
9056 Pittmans Gap Rd
Newland, NC 28662-10   828-733-2417
Fax: 828-733-8894
Contact@gardensoftheblueridge.com
www.gardensoftheblueridge.com

Wildflowers, ferns, orchids and native shrubs & trees

President: Katy R Fletcher
Marketing Manager: Paul Fletcher

Production Manager: Robyn Fletcher
Credit Cards: AMEX; MasterCard
Catalog Cost: $3
Catalog Circulation: Mailed 1 time(s) per year to 3M
Average Order Size: $70
Printing Information: 32 pages in 4 colors on Glossy Stock
Press: Letterpress
Binding: Folded
Mailing List Information: Names for rent
In Business: 118 years
Number of Employees: 4
Sales Information: Under $500M

7662 Gary's Perennials

Gary's Perennials
1122 E Welsh Rd
Maple Glen, PA 19002   215-628-4070
800-898-6653
Fax: 215-628-0216
roots@garysperennials.com
www.garysperennials.com

Wholesale fieldgrown perennials with heavy root systems including: Asarum, Astilbe, Coreopsis, Ferns, Ornamental Grasses, Hemerocallis, Hosta, Iris, Liriope, Natives, Wetland Plants and more

President: Gary Steinberg
Marketing Manager: Andrea Steinberg
Production Manager: Andrea Steinberg
Credit Cards: MasterCard
Catalog Cost: Free
Catalog Circulation: Mailed 1 time(s) per year to 4000
Average Order Size: $1000
Printing Information: 20 pages in 4 colors on Glossy Stock
Press: Letterpress
Binding: Perfect Bound
Mailing List Information: Names for rent
In Business: 35 years
Number of Employees: 4
Sales Information: $500,000 to $1,000,000

7663 Gilbert H Wild & Son

Gilbert H Wild & Son
2944 State Highway 37
Reeds, MO 64859   417-548-3514
Fax: 417-548-6831
www.gilberthwild.com

Daylilies, peonies and iris and bare root plants

President: Greg Jones
Credit Cards: AMEX; MasterCard
Catalog Cost:
Catalog Circulation: Mailed 1 time(s) per year to 55M
Average Order Size: $78
Printing Information: 52 pages in 2 colors on Matte Stock
Press: Web Press
Binding: Perfect Bound
Mailing List Information: Names for rent
List Company: ZED Marketing
In Business: 130 years
Number of Employees: 65
Sales Information: $1MM to $3MM

7664 Going Bananas

Going Bananas
24401 SW 197 Ave
Homestead, FL 33031   305-247-0397
Fax: 305-247-7877
goingbananas@bellsouth.net
www.going-bananas.com

Banana plants

President: Katie Chafin
Catalog Cost: $1
Printing Information: 8 pages
In Business: 5 years
Sales Information: $500M to $1MM

7665 Greenleaf Nursery Company

Greenleaf Nursery Company
28406 Highway 82
Park Hill, OK 74451-2845   918-457-5172
800-331-2982
Fax: 918-457-5550
www.Greenleafnursery.Com

Shrubs, flowers, trees and more

President: Randy Davis
Marketing Manager: Larry Ahrens
Credit Cards: MasterCard; Visa
Printing Information: 92 pages in 4 colors
In Business: 30 years
Number of Employees: 600
Sales Information: $20MM to $50MM

7666 Greenwood Daylily Gardens

Greenwood Daylily Gardens, Inc.
8000 Balcom Canyon Rd
Somis, CA 93066-2107   562-494-8944
Fax: 562-494-0486
info@greenwoodgarden.com
www.greenwooddaylily.com

Daylilies, Irises, Cannas and Geraniums

President: John Schoustra
Credit Cards: MasterCard
Catalog Cost: Free
Catalog Circulation: Mailed 1 time(s) per year to 8M
Printing Information: 20 pages in 4 colors on Glossy Stock
Press: Sheetfed Press
Binding: Folded
Mailing List Information: Names for rent
In Business: 16 years
Sales Information: $1MM to $3MM

7667 Growbiz-Abco

Growbiz
1782 Heathrow Drive - N
Cookeville, TN 38506-3738   931-528-8539
rphillips@growbiz-abco.com
www.growbiz-abco.com

Grow expensive plants at home

President: Roy Phillips

7668 High Country Gardens

High Country Gardens
223 Ave D
Suite 30
Williston, VT 05495   505-438-3031
800-925-9387
Fax: 505-438-9552
plants@highcountrygardens.com
www.Highcountrygardens.Com

Ornamental grasses, perennials, bulbs, groundcovers, tulips, alliums, crocus and muscari

President: David Salman
Marketing Manager: Ava Salman
Production Manager: David Salman
Catalog Circulation: to 10000
Average Order Size: $72
Printing Information: 83 pages in 7 colors
Press: Web Press
Mailing List Information: Names for rent
List Company: Millard Group
In Business: 31 years
Number of Employees: 3
Sales Information: $500M to $1MM

7669 Hilltop Nurseries

Hilltop Fruit Trees
PO Box 578
Hartford, MI 49057-578   616-621-3135
800-253-2911
Fax: 616-621-2062
adam@hilltopfruittrees.com
www.hilltopfruittrees.com

Fruit trees

Marketing Manager: Larry Polec
Catalog Cost: $5
In Business: 104 years

7670 House of Wesley

House of Wesley
1704 Morrissey Drive
Bloomington, IL 61704-7107   309-664-7334
customercare@houseofwesley.com
www.houseofwesley.com

Mosquito shoo geraniums, ground cover daylilies and hardy amur privets

President: Richard Owen
Credit Cards: MasterCard
Catalog Cost: Free
Catalog Circulation: Mailed 4 time(s) per year
Average Order Size: $40
Printing Information: 67 pages in 4 colors on Newsprint
Binding: Saddle Stitched
Mailing List Information: Names for rent
In Business: 40 years
Number of Employees: 5
Sales Information: 10MM-20MM

7671 Intermountain Cactus

Intermountain Cactus
1478 Ewe Turn
Kaysville, UT 84037-1256   801-546-2006
www.intermountaincactus.com

Cactus plants

President: Robert Johnson
In Business: 39 years

7672 Just Fruits and Exotics

Just Fruits and Exotics
30 Saint Frances St
Crawfordville, FL 32327-4257   850-926-5644
888-926-7441
Fax: 850-926-9885
justfruits@hotmail.com
www.justfruitsandexotics.com/

Wide range of fruits, nuts and berries for zone and butterfly-garden plants; Many unique varieties like Olive, Mayhaw, and Jujuba; Exotic or ornamentals; Collection of ginger lilies

President: Roxanne Cowley
CFO: Ted Cowly-Gilbert
Production Manager: Vicki Thomas
Catalog Cost: $3
Catalog Circulation: to 3000
Average Order Size: $100
Printing Information: 42 pages in 1 color on Matte Stock
Binding: Folded
Mailing List Information: Names for rent
In Business: 19 years
Number of Employees: 6
Sales Information: $500M to $1MM

7673 Keith Keppel

Keith Keppel Irises
PO Box 18154
Salem, OR 97305-8154   503-391-9241
plicataman@earthlink.net
www.keithkeppeliris.com

Bearded iris plants

President: Keith Keppel
Catalog Circulation: Mailed 1 time(s) per year to 1200
Printing Information: 24 pages on Matte Stock
Binding: Saddle Stitched

7674 Klehm's Song Sparrow Perennial Farm

Klehm's Song Sparrow
13101 East Rye Road
Avalon, WI 53505   608-883-2356
800-553-3715
Fax: 608-883-2257
info@songsparrow.com
www.songsparrow.com

Klehm peonies, hemerocallis, hosta, Siberian iris and companion plants, woody ornamentals, and tree peonies

President: Roy G Klehm
Marketing Manager: Renee Jaeger
Production Manager: Renee Jaeger
Credit Cards: AMEX; MasterCard; Visa
Catalog Cost: Free
Catalog Circulation: Mailed 1 time(s) per year to 50M
Printing Information: 100 pages in 4 colors on Glossy Stock
Press: Web Press
Mailing List Information: Names for rent
List Manager: Roy Klehm
In Business: 30 years

7675 Lawyer Nursery

Lawyer Nursery
6625 Montana Highway 200
Plains, MT 59859   406-826-3881
800-551-9875
Fax: 406-826-5700
trees@lawyernursery.com
www.lawyernursery.com

Bareroot woody plants

President: John Lawyer
Founder: David Lawyer
Founder: Esther Lawyer
Credit Cards: MasterCard
Catalog Cost: Free
Catalog Circulation: Mailed 1 time(s) per year to 8000
Average Order Size: $500
Printing Information: 64 pages in 1 color on Matte Stock
Press: Web Press
Binding: Saddle Stitched
Mailing List Information: Names for rent
In Business: 58 years
Number of Employees: 100
Sales Information: $3MM to $5MM

7676 Lazy K Nursery

Lazy K Nursery Inc.
705 Wright Road
Pine Mountain, GA 31822-3012   706-663-4991
Fax: 706-663-0939
info@lazyknursery.com
www.lazyknursery.com

Native American Azaleas and companion plants

President: Ernest Koone, III
Catalog Cost: Free
Catalog Circulation: Mailed 1 time(s) per year
Printing Information: 8 pages
In Business: 57 years

7677 Logee's Greenhouses

Logee's Greenhouses
141 North Street
Danielson, CT 06239   888-330-8038
info@logees.com
www.logees.com

Rare plants and herbs, tropicals and sub-tropicals

President: Byron Martin
Production Manager: Amy Miller
Operations Manager: Sham Elshakhs
Merchandise Manager: Sheryl Felty
Credit Cards: MasterCard; Visa
Catalog Cost: Free
Catalog Circulation: Mailed 5 time(s) per year to 200m
Average Order Size: $40
Printing Information: 110 pages in 4 colors on Glossy Stock
Press: Web Press
Binding: Saddle Stitched
Mailing List Information: Names for rent
List Company: George Mann & Associates
609-443-1330
In Business: 123 years
Number of Employees: 25
Sales Information: $1.6 Million

7678 Louisiana Nursery

Louisiana Nursery
8680 Perkins Road
Baton Rouge, LA 7081   225-766-0300
Fax: 337-942-6404
contact@louisiananursery.com
www.louisiananursery.com/

Magnolias and other garden aristocrats

President: Ken Durio
Marketing Manager: Dalton Durio
Founder: Roger Mayes
Credit Cards: MasterCard; Visa
Catalog Cost: $6
Printing Information: 276 pages in 4 colors
In Business: 31 years
Number of Employees: 6
Sales Information: $100,000

7679 Maryland Aquatic Nurseries

Maryland Aquatic Nurseries
3427 N Furnace
Jarrettsville, MD 21084   410-692-4171
877-736-1807
Fax: 410-692-2837
info@marylandaquatic.com
www.Marylandaquatic.Com

Aquatic plants and water gardening products

President: Richard Schuck
Marketing Manager: Kelly Billing
Credit Cards: MasterCard; Visa
Catalog Cost: $5
Catalog Circulation: to 5000
Printing Information: 100 pages in 4 colors on Glossy Stock
Press: Web Press
Binding: Saddle Stitched
Mailing List Information: Names for rent
In Business: 15 years
Number of Employees: 15
Sales Information: $1MM to $3MM

7680 Mini-Edition Iris Lover's

Schreiner's Garden
3625 Quinaby Road NE
Salem, OR 97303   503-393-3232
800-525-2367
Fax: 503-393-5590
iris@schreinersgardens.com
www.schreinersgardens.com

Tall bearded and dwarf iris

President: David Schreiner
Marketing Manager: Tom Abregg
Credit Cards: MasterCard; Visa
Catalog Cost:
Catalog Circulation: Mailed 1 time(s) per year to 45M
Printing Information: 72 pages in 4 colors on Glossy Stock
Press: Sheetfed Press
Binding: Saddle Stitched
Mailing List Information: Names for rent
List Manager: David Schreiner
In Business: 92 years
Number of Employees: 35
Sales Information: $20MM to $50MM

7681 Musser Forests

Musser Forests, Inc.
1880 Route 119 Hwy N
Indiana, PA 15701-7341   724-465-5685
800-643-8319
Fax: 724-465-9893
info@musserforests.com
www.musserforests.com

Evergreen and hardwood seedlings, transplants, ornamental shrubs and groundcovers

Principal: Jeffrey A Musser
Principal: Kevin A Musser
Principal: Fred A Musser
Credit Cards: MasterCard; Visa
Catalog Cost: Free
Catalog Circulation: Mailed 2 time(s) per year

to 500M
Average Order Size: $75
Printing Information: 16 pages in 4 colors
Press: Web Press
Binding: Saddle Stitched
Mailing List Information: Names for rent
In Business: 89 years
Number of Employees: 170
Sales Information: $20MM to $50MM

7682   Natural & Organic Fertilizers
Peaceful Valley Farm Supply, Inc.
125 Clydesdale Court
P.O. Box 2209
Grass Valley, CA 95945   530-272-4769
                                 888-874-1722
helpdesk@groworganic.com
www.groworganic.com

Vegetable/herb/flower seed packs or in bulk, propagating, water and irrigation, greenhouse, composting supplies, natural weed control, garden equipment and more

President: Eric Boudier
Vice President: Patricia Boudier
General Manager: Lee Dickerson
Catalog Cost: Free
Catalog Circulation: Mailed 1 time(s) per year
Printing Information: 68 pages in 4 colors
In Business: 41 years
Number of Employees: 60
Sales Information: $7.2 Million

7683   Nichols Garden Nursery
Nichols Garden Nursery
1190 Old Salem Road NE
Albany, OR 97321-4580   800-422-3985
                                Fax: 800-231-5306
www.nicholsgardennursery.com

Herb seeds and plants

President: Rose Marie McGee
Credit Cards: AMEX; MasterCard
Catalog Cost: Free
Catalog Circulation: Mailed 1 time(s) per year
to 250M
Printing Information: 55 pages in 4 colors
Mailing List Information: Names for rent
List Manager: Keane McGee
In Business: 65 years
Number of Employees: 20
Sales Information: $1MM to $3MM

7684   Northern Climate Fruit & Nut Trees Catalog
St Lawrence Nurseries
325 State Highway 345
P.O. Box 957
Potsdam, NY 13676   315-261-1925
connor@sln.potsdam.ny.us
www.sln.potsdam.ny.us

Fruit and nut trees and edible landscaping plants

President: William Mackentley
Catalog Cost:
Catalog Circulation: Mailed 1 time(s) per year
to 10K
Printing Information: 34 pages
In Business: 34 years
Number of Employees: 7

7685   Nourse Farms
Nourse
41 River Road
Whately, MA 01093-9754   413-665-2658
                                 Fax: 413-665-7888
info@noursefarms.com
www.noursefarms.com

Strawberry, raspberry, blueberry, blackberry, currant and gooseberry plants, asparagus, rhubarb and horseradish

President: Tim Nourse
Marketing Manager: Anne Kowaleck
Buyers: Nate Nourse
Credit Cards: MasterCard

Catalog Cost: Free
Catalog Circulation: Mailed 1 time(s) per year
to 45K
Printing Information: 32 pages in 4 colors on Glossy Stock
Press: Web Press
Binding: Saddle Stitched
Mailing List Information: Names for rent
List Manager: Nata Nourse
In Business: 87 years
Number of Employees: 60
Sales Information: $50MM to $100MM

7686   Office Scapes Direct
Office Scapes Direct
12021 Centron Place
Cincinnati, OH 45246   800-557-1997
                                 Fax: 914-328-1959
service@officescapesdirect.com
www.officescapesdirect.com

Silk flowers, silk trees, silk plants and framed art and wall decor

7687   Oikos Tree Crops
Oikos Tree Crops
PO Box 19425
Kalamazoo, MI 40019-425   269-624-6233
                                 Fax: 269-624-4019
customerservice@oikostreecrops.com
www.oikostreecrops.com

Trees, shrubs, perennials, rare plants, nuts, oaks, native fruits, bird plants and tubers

President: Ken Asmus
Credit Cards: MasterCard; Visa
Catalog Cost: Free
Catalog Circulation: Mailed 1 time(s) per year
to 30000
Average Order Size: $100
Printing Information: 60 pages in 4 colors on Matte Stock
Press: Letterpress
Binding: Saddle Stitched
In Business: 19 years
Number of Employees: 10-J
Sales Information: Under $500M

7688   Organic Seeds
Peaceful Valley Farm Supply, Inc.
125 Clydesdale Court
P.O. Box 2209
Grass Valley, CA 95945   530-272-4769
                                 888-784-1722
helpdesk@groworganic.com
www.groworganic.com

Vegetable/herb/flower seed packs or in bulk, propagating, water and irrigation, greenhouse, composting supplies, natural weed control, garden equipment and more

President: Eric Boudier
Vice President: Patricia Boudier
General Manager: Lee Dickerson
Catalog Cost: Free
Catalog Circulation: Mailed 1 time(s) per year
Printing Information: 68 pages in 4 colors
In Business: 41 years
Number of Employees: 60
Sales Information: $7.2 Million

7689   Pike's Peak Nurseries
Pike's Peak Nurseries
8289 Route 222 Highway E
Penn Run, PA 15765   724-463-7747
                                 800-787-6730
                                 Fax: 724-463-0775
pikespak@sgi.net
www.pikespeaknurseries.net

Evergreen seedlings and transplants, northern hardy specialties and native wood plant material

Buyers: Sean Schwarts
Catalog Cost: Free
Catalog Circulation: Mailed 1 time(s) per year

to 25M
Average Order Size: $100
Printing Information: 32 pages in 4 colors on Glossy Stock
Press: Letterpress
Binding: Saddle Stitched
Mailing List Information: Names for rent
List Manager: Marcie Daugherty
In Business: 78 years
Number of Employees: 50
Sales Information: 1.2M

7690   Plants of the Southwest
Plants of the Southwest
3095 Agua Fria Street
Santa Fe, NM 87507-5411   505-438-8888
                                 800-788-7333
                                 Fax: 505-438-8800
plantsofthesouthwest@gmail.com
plantsofthesouthwest.com

Southwestern native plants including berry and nut producing trees and shrubs, wildflowers, native grasses and ancient and drought tolerant vegetable seeds

Credit Cards: AMEX; MasterCard
Catalog Cost: Free
Mailing List Information: Names for rent
In Business: 27 years
Number of Employees: 20-5
Sales Information: $1MM to $3MM

7691   Plants of the Wild
Plants of the Wild
123 State Line Rd
PO Box 866
Tekoa, WA 99033   509-284-2848
                                 Fax: 509-284-6464
kathy@plantsofthewild.com
www.plantsofthewild.com

Plants native to the Pacific Northwest

Production Manager: Kathy Hutton
Assistant Manager: Carrie Garcia
Credit Cards: AMEX; MasterCard
Catalog Cost:
Catalog Circulation: Mailed 1 time(s) per year
to 5M
Printing Information: 24 pages in 2 colors on Matte Stock
Press: Letterpress
Binding: Saddle Stitched
Mailing List Information: Names for rent
In Business: 36 years
Number of Employees: 20
Sales Information: Under $500M

7692   Quality Tools & Drip Irrigation Supplies
Peaceful Valley Farm Supply, Inc.
125 Clydesdale Court
P.O. Box 2209
Grass Valley, CA 95945   530-272-4769
                                 888-784-1722
helpdesk@groworganic.com
www.groworganic.com

Vegetable/herb/flower seed packs or in bulk, propagating, water and irrigation, greenhouse, composting supplies, natural weed control, garden equipment and more

President: Eric Boudier
Vice President: Patricia Boudier
General Manager: Lee Dickerson
Catalog Cost: Free
Catalog Circulation: Mailed 1 time(s) per year
Printing Information: 68 pages in 4 colors
In Business: 41 years
Number of Employees: 60
Sales Information: $7.2 Million

7693   Raintree Nursery
Raintree Nursery
391 Butts Road
Morton, WA 98356-9700   800-391-8892
customerservice@raintreenursery.com
www.raintreenursery.com

Fruit, nut and berry trees and ornamentals, bamboo for backyard ecological growers, gardening supplies, fruit strainers, peelers and pitters

President: Sam Benowitz
Horticulturist: Katy Fraser
Garden Center Manager: Karen Fry
Field Manager: Carl Nelson
Credit Cards: MasterCard; Visa
Catalog Cost: Free
Catalog Circulation: Mailed 2 time(s) per year
Average Order Size: $65
Printing Information: 96 pages in 4 colors on Glossy Stock
Press: Web Press
Binding: Saddle Stitched
Mailing List Information: Names for rent
In Business: 45 years
Number of Employees: 25
Sales Information: $1MM-$3MM

7694 Roses of Yesterday & Today

Roses of Yesterday and Today
803 Browns Valley Rd
Watsonville, CA 95076   831-728-1901
Fax: 805-227-4095
postmaster@rosesofyesterday.com
www.Rosesofyesterday.Com

Rare and unusual roses

President: Jennifer Wiley
Marketing Manager: Jack Wiley
Production Manager: Guinivere Wiley
Founder: Dorothy Stemle
Catalog Cost: $5
Catalog Circulation: Mailed 1 time(s) per year to 35M
Printing Information: 80 pages in 3 colors on Matte Stock
Press: Web Press
Binding: Saddle Stitched
In Business: 85 years
Number of Employees: 4
Sales Information: $500,000

7695 Shady Oaks Nursery

PSI-Shady Oaks Nursery
1601 5th Street SE
PO Box 708
Waseca, MN 56093   507-835-5033
Fax: 507-835-8772
www.shadyoaks.com

Perennial plants and hostas

President: Gordon J Oslund
Buyers: Emily McCarthy
Credit Cards: MasterCard; Visa
Catalog Cost: Free
Catalog Circulation: Mailed 1 time(s) per year to 9000
Average Order Size: $90
Printing Information: 48 pages in 4 colors on Glossy Stock
Press: Sheetfed Press
Binding: Saddle Stitched
Mailing List Information: Names for rent
List Manager: Rickard List Marketing
List Company: Rickard List Marketing
Corporate Plaza, Suite 135
Farmingdale, NY 11735
In Business: 22 years
Number of Employees: 22
Sales Information: $1MM to $3MM

7696 Spring Hill Nursery

Spring Hill Nurseries
P.O. Box 330
Harrison, OH 45030-9935   513-354-1509
Fax: 513-354-1504
service@springhillnursery.com
www.springhillnursery.com

Perennials, flowering shrubs, ground covers, roses, summer blooming bulbs and houseplants, gardening tools and accessories, bird houses and bird seeds.

Credit Cards: MasterCard; Visa
Catalog Cost: Free

Catalog Circulation: Mailed 20 time(s) per year
Printing Information: 30 pages in 4 colors on Glossy Stock
Press: Web Press
Binding: Saddle Stitched
Mailing List Information: Names for rent
In Business: 166 years
Sales Information: $50MM to $100MM

7697 Springbrook Gardens

Springbrook Gardens, Inc.
6676 Heisely Road
PO Box 388
Mentor, OH 44061-388   440-255-3059
    888-255-3059
Fax: 440-255-9535

Field grown perennials, ground covers and ornamental grasses

President: Glenn Anderson
Credit Cards: AMEX; MasterCard; Visa
Catalog Cost:
Catalog Circulation: Mailed 1 time(s) per year to 3.5M
Printing Information: 57 pages in 1 color on Matte Stock
Press: Web Press
Mailing List Information: Names for rent
In Business: 68 years
Number of Employees: 35
Sales Information: $3MM to $5MM

7698 St. Lawrence Nurseries

Saint Lawrence Nurseries
325 State Highway 345
P.O. Box 957
Potsdam, NY 13676-3515   315-261-1925
connor@sln.potsdam.ny.us
www.sln.potsdam.ny.us

Cold-hardy fruit and nut trees

President: William Mackentley
Catalog Circulation: Mailed 1 time(s) per year to 5000
Printing Information: 30 pages in 1 color on Matte Stock
Press: Web Press
Binding: Saddle Stitched
In Business: 34 years
Sales Information: $1MM to $3MM

7699 Stark Bro's

Stark Bro's Nurseries & Orchards Co.
P.O. Box 1800
Louisiana, MO 63353-8904   800-325-4180
Fax: 573-754-3701
info@starkbros.com
www.starkbros.com

Gardening supplies and dwarf fruit trees, roses, shade trees, small fruits, garden aids

President: John E Miller
Credit Cards: AMEX; MasterCard; Visa
Catalog Cost: Free
Catalog Circulation: Mailed 9 time(s) per year to 3.6MM
Average Order Size: $60
Printing Information: 60 pages in 4 colors on Glossy Stock
Press: Web Press
Binding: Saddle Stitched
Mailing List Information: Names for rent
In Business: 201 years
Number of Employees: 80
Sales Information: $5MM to $10MM

7700 Stock Seed Farms

Stock Seed Farms
28008 Mill Rd
Murdock, NE 68407   402-867-3771
    800-759-1520
Fax: 402-867-2442
prairie@stockseed.com
www.stockseed.com

Seed of prairie wildflowers and native Midwest grasses, turf type buffalo grasses, coby and bowie

President: David Stock, Praire Grasses/Wflwr
Catalog Cost: Free
Catalog Circulation: Mailed 1 time(s) per year
Printing Information: 22 pages in 4 colors on Glossy Stock
Press: Web Press
Binding: Saddle Stitched
Mailing List Information: Names for rent
In Business: 50 years
Number of Employees: 7
Sales Information: $3MM to $5MM

7701 Sunshine Farm & Gardens Perennial Plants

Sunshine Farm and Gardens
696 Glicks Rd.
Renick, WV 24966   304-497-2208
Fax: 304-497-2698
barry@sunfarm.com
www.sunfarm.com

Rare and unusual plants and perennials

President: Barry Glick
barry@sunfarm.com
Marketing Manager: Zak Glick
Fulfillment: Abbey Glick
Buyers: Patty Wiley
Credit Cards: AMEX; MasterCard; Visa
Catalog Cost: $2
Catalog Circulation: Mailed 1 time(s) per year to 100M
Average Order Size: $165
Printing Information: 28 pages in 1 color on Matte Stock
Press: Web Press
Binding: Saddle Stitched
Mailing List Information: Names for rent
List Manager: Barry Glick
In Business: 32 years
Number of Employees: 16
Sales Information: $1MM to $3MM

7702 Surry Gardens' Bedding Plant Catalog

Surry Gardens
1248 Surry Rd. (Route 172) Surry Vi
PO Box 145
Surry, ME 04684   207-667-4493
Fax: 207-667-5532
mail@surrygardens.com
www.surrygardens.com

Bird, deer resistant, shade and native plants

President: James Dickinson
Credit Cards: MasterCard; Visa
Catalog Cost: $1
Printing Information: 89 pages in 1 color on Matte Stock
Binding: Saddle Stitched
Mailing List Information: Names for rent
In Business: 30 years
Number of Employees: 20
Sales Information: Under $500M

7703 Trees of Antiquity

Trees of Antiquity
20 Wellsona Road
Paso Robles, CA 93446   805-467-9909
Fax: 805-467-9909
www.treesofantiquity.com

Organic heritage apples, peaches, pears, plums, figs and grape vines

President: Neil Collins
Credit Cards: MasterCard; Visa
Catalog Cost: Free
Catalog Circulation: Mailed 1 time(s) per year to 1mm
Printing Information: 62 pages in 1 color
Mailing List Information: Names for rent
In Business: 30 years
Number of Employees: 5
Sales Information: Under $500M

7704 Vermont Bean Seed Company
Vermont Bean Seed Company
334 W Stroud Street
Randolph, WI 53956
800-349-1071
800-349-1071
Fax: 888-500-7333
info@vermontbean.com
www.vermontbean.com

Untreated heirloom bean, pea and corn seed, herb, vegetable, green and flower seeds

Credit Cards: MasterCard; Visa
Catalog Circulation: Mailed 1 time(s) per year to 500M
Printing Information: 79 pages in 4 colors
Press: Web Press
Binding: Saddle Stitched
Number of Employees: 100

7705 White Flower Farm Catalog
White Flower Farm
Route 63
PO Box 50
Litchfield, CT 06759
860-496-9624
800-503-9624
Fax: 860-496-1418
michelle@whiteflowerfarm.com
www.whiteflowerfarm.com

Perennials, unusual annuals, bulbs, roses, shrubs and gifts

President: Lorraine Calder
Production Manager: Tom Cooper
Fulfillment: Melissa Jack-Benjamin
Buyers: Nancy McCarthy, Plants
Keen Fisher, Hardgoods
Credit Cards: AMEX; MasterCard
Catalog Cost: Free
Catalog Circulation: Mailed 3 time(s) per year
Average Order Size: $90
Printing Information: 98 pages in 4 colors on Glossy Stock
Mailing List Information: Names for rent
List Manager: Millard Group
List Company: Millard Group
10 Vose Road
Peterborough, NH 03458
603-924-9262
In Business: 65 years
Number of Employees: 120

7706 Whitman Farms Catalog
White Farms
3995 Gibson Rd NW
Salem, OR 97304-9527
503-585-8728
Fax: 503-363-5020
lucile@whitmanfarms.com
www.Whitmanfarms.Com

Small fruits, gooseberries, currants, mulberries and unsual trees in rootcontrol bags

President: Lucile Whitman
Catalog Cost: Free
Catalog Circulation: Mailed 1 time(s) per year to 1000
Average Order Size: $30
Printing Information: 16 pages in 1 color on Matte Stock
Press: Web Press
Binding: Folded
Mailing List Information: Names for rent
In Business: 35 years
Number of Employees: 3
Sales Information: $1MM to $3MM

7707 Womack's Nursery Catalog
Womack's Nursery
2551 State Highway 6
De Leon, TX 76444-6333
254-893-6497
254-893-3400
Fax: 254-893-3400
pecan@womacknursery.com
www.womacknursery.com

Fruits, pecan trees, blackberries and grapevines

President: Larry Don Womack
Catalog Cost: Free
Printing Information: 36 pages
Mailing List Information: Names for rent
In Business: 33 years
Number of Employees: 12
Sales Information: $3MM to $5MM

7708 Yucca Do Nursery Catalog
Yucca Do Nursery Inc
PO Box 1039
Giddings, TX 78942-907
979-542-8811
info@yuccado.com
www.yuccado.com

Native texas plants and mexican/asian plants, rare and unusual plants from around the world

Credit Cards: MasterCard
Catalog Cost: $4
Catalog Circulation: Mailed 1 time(s) per year
Printing Information: 10 pages in 4 colors on Glossy Stock
Press: Web Press
Binding: Saddle Stitched
Mailing List Information: Names for rent
In Business: 14 years
Number of Employees: 6
Sales Information: Under $500M

Law Enforcement
Supplies & Equipment

7709 Agricultural Sciences
Nasco Arts & Crafts Store
901 Janesville Avenue
PO Box 901
Fort Atkinson, WI 53538-901
920-563-2446
800-558-9595
Fax: 920-563-6044
custserv@enasco.com
www.enasco.com

Instructional aids for all areas of agriculture; agriculture, horticulture, agronomy, and farm supplies

President: Andrew Reinen
Marketing Manager: Phil Niemeyer
Manager, Data Processing: Mike Wagner
Catalog Cost: Free
Catalog Circulation: to 25000
In Business: 74 years
Number of Employees: 540

7710 AlcoPro
AlcoPro
2547 Sutherland Ave.
Knoxville, TN 37919
865-525-4900
800-227-9890
Fax: 865-525-4935
info@alcopro.com
www.alcopro.com

On-site drug and alcohol testing products for professional use

President: Jack Singleton
Marketing Manager: Greg Clark
Special Projects Coordinator: Sam Smithey
Customer Service Manager: Shannan Kennedy
Production Manager: Lorraine Jenkins
Credit Cards: MasterCard; Visa
Catalog Circulation: to 60M
Printing Information: 16 pages in 2 colors
In Business: 33 years
Number of Employees: 7
Sales Information: $1.1 Million

7711 American Technologies Network
American Technologies Network
1341 San Mateo Avenue
South San Francisco, CA 94080
650-989-5100
800-910-2862
Fax: 650-875-0129
info@atncorp.com
www.atncorp.com

Night vision equipment and scopes, security equipment

President: James Munn
CEO: Marc Vayn
Vice President, Sales: Lowell Stacy
Vice President: Lenny Gaber
Printing Information: in 4 colors on Glossy Stock
Binding: Saddle Stitched
Mailing List Information: Names for rent
In Business: 20 years
Number of Employees: 51
Sales Information: $8,800,000

7712 Bagmaster Quality Bags, Cases & Holsters
Bagmaster Manufacturing
4515 # 2 Miami Street
Saint Louis, MO 63116-3007
314-781-8002
800-950-8181
Fax: 314-771-8383
sales@bagmaster.com
www.bagmaster.com

Nylon weapon accessories, bags, gun cases, holsters and shooting accessories

President: Richard Kupferer
Marketing Manager: Modi Weiss
Buyers: Richard M Kupferer
Credit Cards: AMEX; MasterCard; Visa
Catalog Cost: Free
Catalog Circulation: Mailed 1 time(s) per year to 5M
Printing Information: 26 pages in 4 colors on Glossy Stock
Press: Letterpress
Mailing List Information: Names for rent
In Business: 30 years
Number of Employees: 30
Sales Information: $1,000,000 - $5,000,000

7713 Chief Supply
Chief Supply
1400 Executive Parkway
Eugene, OR 97401
888-588-8569
orders@chiefsupply.com
www.chiefsupply.com

Firefighting, law enforcement and emergency medical supplies, including apparel and gear bags, badges, flashlights, batteries and chargers, cases and antennas, specialty and close-out items

President: John Utley
In Business: 40 years
Sales Information: $20MM to $50MM

7714 DR Power Equipment
DR Power Equipment
75 Meigs Road
P.O. Box 25
Vergennes, VT 05491
802-870-1437
800-687-6575
Fax: 802-877-1213
websupport@drpower.com
www.drpower.com

Chippers, brush mowers, leaf vacs, power haulers, trimmers, splitters

President: Joe Perrotto
CFO: Christopher Knapp
Marketing Manager: Ned Van Woert
Production Manager: John Berlind
Fulfillment: Moe Matte
International Marketing Manager: Carl Eikenberg
Buyers: Carl Eikenberg
Credit Cards: MasterCard
Catalog Cost: Free
Average Order Size: $150
Printing Information: 48 pages in 4 colors
Press: Offset Press
Binding: Saddle Stitched
In Business: 32 years
Number of Employees: 250
Sales Information: $20 Million

7715 Gibson & Barnes Flight Suits
Gibson & Barnes
1900 Weld Blvd
#140
El Cajon, CA 92020   619-440-2700
                           800-748-6693
                      Fax: 619-440-4618
                     store@ombps.com
                  www.gibson-barnes.com

High-quality, made-to-order flightsuits, uniforms, leather jackets and flying helmets for aviation, emergency medicine, and law enforcement

President: James A Wegge
Marketing Manager: Dan Longbrake
Catalog Circulation: to Weekl
In Business: 37 years

7716 Greenhouse Catalog
The Greenhouse Catalog
3740 Brooklake Road NE
Salem, OR 97303   503-393-3973
                          800-825-1925
                     Fax: 503-393-3119
                info@greenhousecatalog.com
                   www.greenhousecatalog.com

Greenhouses and gardening

Chairman: Beverly Perry, Owner
President: Michael Perry
Marketing Manager: Michelle Torres
michelle@Sulexx.com
In Business: 27 years
Number of Employees: 15

7717 Hafner World Wide
Hafner World Wide Inc.
284 N.W. Falling Creek Road
PO Box 1987
Lake City, FL 32055-1987   386-755-6481
                        Fax: 386-755-6595
              HAFNER@HAFNERWORLDWIDE.COM
                    www.Hafnerworldwide.Com

Gun cases, holsters and duty bags, knife cases, knives, special purpose bags and hard cases

President: John Hafner
Buyers: John Hafner
Credit Cards: AMEX; MasterCard
Catalog Cost: Free
Catalog Circulation: to 2000
Printing Information: 30 pages in 1 color on Newsprint
Press: Web Press
Mailing List Information: Names for rent
In Business: 29 years
Number of Employees: 12
Sales Information: $500,000 - $1,000,000

7718 Hogue Grip
Hogue, Inc.
P.O. Box 91360
Hendersones, NV 89009   800-438-4747
                       Fax: 805-239-2553
                      www.getgrip.com

Handgun grips for rifles

President: Aaron Hogue
Vice President: Patrick Hogue
Vice President: Jim Bruhns
Vice President: Neil Hogue
Catalog Circulation: Mailed 1 time(s) per year
Printing Information: 52 pages in 4 colors
In Business: 50 years
Number of Employees: 36
Sales Information: $3.8 MM

7719 Marugg Company
Marugg Company
PO Box 1418
Tracy City, TN 37387   931-592-5042
                   marugg@blomand.net
                www.themaruggcompany.com

European scythes

Co-Owner: Amy Wilson
Co-Owner: Allen Wilson

7720 Midwest Supplies
Midwest Supplies
5825 Excelsior Blvd
Minneapolis, MN 55416   952-562-5300
                            888-449-2739
                       Fax: 952-925-9867
                 www.midwesthydroponics.com

Organic, and Hydroponic gardening supplies

Printing Information: 64 pages
In Business: 20 years

7721 Natchez Shooters Supply
Natchez Shooters Supply
2600 Walker Road
PO Box 182212
Chattanooga, TN 37422   423-889-0499
                            800-251-7839
                       Fax: 423-892-4482
                   orders@natchezss.com
                      www.natchezss.com

Hunting supplies

CFO: David Dodson
Owner: Jeff Hamm
Information Technology Manager: Andy Lee
President, Sales: Brian Hall
Credit Cards: MasterCard
Printing Information: 104 pages
Number of Employees: 1
Sales Information: $62,000

7722 Reliapon Police Products
Reliapon Police Products
4620 Calimesa Street
Suite D-1
Las Vegas, NV 89115   702-257-0145
                            800-423-0668
                       Fax: 702-293-0149
                     sales@reliapon.com
                       www.reliapon.com

Law enforcement, military, correctional, government, security products, non-lethal weapons and training; tactical technologies; training books/videos; high-tech surveillance; chemical decontamination

President: Vince Zucchero
Fulfillment: Kristie Bond
Credit Cards: MasterCard
Printing Information: 28 pages on Matte Stock
Binding: Saddle Stitched
In Business: 30 years
Sales Information: $3MM to $5MM

7723 World Guide to Gun Parts
World Guide to Gun Parts
226 Williams Lane
West Hurley, NY 12401   845-679-2417
                            866-686-7424
                       Fax: 877-486-7278
                  info@gunpartscorp.com
                     www.gunpartscorp.com

Firearms, parts, accessories, ammunition, gun smithing supplies, safety and surplus military equipment

President: Gregory M Jenks
Marketing Manager: Linda Munro
Buyers: Neill Amodeo
Credit Cards: AMEX; MasterCard
Catalog Cost: $12.95
Catalog Circulation: Mailed 1 time(s) per year to 100M+
Printing Information: 1152 pages in 1 color on Matte Stock
Press: Web Press
Binding: Perfect Bound
Mailing List Information: Names for rent
List Manager: Linda Munro
In Business: 65 years
Number of Employees: 100
Sales Information: $5MM to $10MM

Lighting
General

7724 ALP Lighting
A.L.P. Lighting Components, Inc.
6333 Gross Point Rd
Niles, IL 60714-3915   773-774-9550
                            877-257-5841
                       Fax: 773-594-3874
              kurtpuffpaff@billbrownsales.com
                      www.alplighting.com

Lighting and lighting supplies

Chairman: William Brown
President: Jeff Benton
CFO: Jim Grady
CEO: Steve Brown
VP/Business Manager: Tom Barnes
Chief Operating Officer: David Brown
In Business: 43 years
Number of Employees: 1000
Sales Information: $100,000

7725 Alert Stamping & Manufacturing Company
Alert Stamping & Manufacturing Company
24500 Solon Rd
Bedford Heights, OH 44146-4793 800-400-5020
                       Fax: 440-232-8417
                 Blanch.PS@alertstamping.com
                    www.alertstamping.com

Work lights, retractable extension cord reels, multi-plug reels and cord sets, multiple outlet hand crank reels for cord management

President: Paul S. Blanch
Blanch.PS@alertstamping.com
Marketing Manager: Ralph Technow
Technow.RJ@alertstamping.com
VP - Engineering, Production: James D. Kovacik
KovacikJD@prodigy.net
Office Manager, Customer Service: Georgene Javor
Javor.G@alertstamping.com
BusinessDevelopment Manager: Dave Collura
collura.d@alertstamping.com
Mailing List Information: Names for rent
In Business: 53 years
Number of Employees: 40
Sales Information: $4.10 Million

7726 American Scientific Lighting Corporation
American Scientific Lighting Corporation
25 12th Street
Brooklyn, NY 11215-3820   718-369-1100
                            800-369-1101
                       Fax: 800-552-3465
                      info@asllighting.com
                      www.Asllighting.Com

Fluorescent and low wattage HID lighting

President: Yaakov Singer
ysinger@asllighting.com
Catalog Circulation: to 10K
In Business: 36 years
Sales Information: $5,000,000

7727 Amglo Kemlite Laboratories
Amglo Kemlite Laboratories
215 Gateway Rd
Bensenville, IL 60106-1952 630-350-9470
                       Fax: 630-350-9474
                      info@amglo.com
                      www.amglo.com/

Flash tubes and lamps for use in warning and timing

President: James Hyland
Printing Information: 28 pages
In Business: 79 years
Number of Employees: 100
Sales Information: $500M to $1MM

7728 Carlton-Bates Company
Carlton-Bates
3600 W 69th St.
Little Rock, AR 72209   501-562-9100
                              866-600-6040
customerservicecb@carltonbates.com
www.carltonbates.com

Electronic components, devices, equipment, hardware, and accessories.

Catalog Cost: Free
In Business: 59 years

7729 Dazor Manufacturing Corporation
Dazor Manufacturing Corporation
2079 Congressional Dr.
St Louis, MO 63146   314-652-2400
                           800-345-9103
                      Fax: 314-652-2069
info@dazor.com
www.dazor.com

Lighting, magnifiers, video microscopes

Chairman: Herbert Hogrebe
President: Stan Hogrebe
CFO: Karen Kyle
CEO: Mark Hogrebe
Marketing Executive: Kirk Cressey
Buyers: Richard Harding
Credit Cards: MasterCard; Visa
Catalog Cost: Free
Catalog Circulation: Mailed 1 time(s) per year to 20M
Printing Information: 8 pages in 1 color on Matte Stock
Binding: Saddle Stitched
Mailing List Information: Names for rent
List Manager: Tony Roldan
List Company: Roldan Marketing International
In Business: 77 years
Number of Employees: 25
Sales Information: $4.9 Million

7730 Flemington Aluminum & Brass
Flemington Aluminum and Brass Inc
24 Junction Rd
Flemington, NJ 08822-5721   908-782-6317
                              Fax: 908-782-8078
info@fabonline.net
www.Fabonline.Net

Traffic signal products, street lighting, aluminum poles, cabinets and enclosures, cast aluminum and brass plaques, custom castings

President: Jim Kozicki
Catalog Cost: Free
Printing Information: 50 pages in 2 colors on Glossy Stock
Mailing List Information: Names for rent
In Business: 74 years
Number of Employees: 25
Sales Information: $1,000,000 - $5,000,000

7731 Havis Inc
Havis Inc
75 Jacksonville Road
Warminster, PA 18974   215-957-0720
                              800-524-9900
                         Fax: 215-957-0729
sales@havis.com
www.customers.havis.com

Lighting equipment

President: Joseph Bernert Sr
CFO: Steve Ferraro
Marketing Manager: Heather Miller
CEO: Joe Bernert
Director of Engineering: Bruce Jonik
Director of Operations: Pete Spera
Number of Employees: 80
Sales Information: Under $500M

7732 Lamp Glass
Lamp Glass
PO Box 1387
Arlington, MA 02474-22   617-497-0770
                           Fax: 617-497-2074
lamps@lampglass.nu
www.lampglass.nu

Specialists in replacement glass lamp shades including chimneys, student shades, ceiling globes, sconce glass, chandelier glass and prisms

Credit Cards: MasterCard; Visa
Catalog Cost: $1
Catalog Circulation: Mailed 1 time(s) per year
Average Order Size: $30
Printing Information: 5 pages in 4 colors on Glossy Stock
Press: Sheetfed Press
Binding: Folded
Mailing List Information: Names for rent
In Business: 34 years
Number of Employees: 10-J
Sales Information: Under $500M

7733 Levenger
The Levenger Store
420 South Congress Ave
Delray Beach, FL 33445-4696   561-276-2436
                              800-544-0880
                         Fax: 800-544-6910
Cservice@levenger.com
www.Levenger.Com

Collection of furnishings and accessories created to enhance your well-read life, you'll find bookcases, halogen lighting, desks, chairs, leather goods, plus personal and corporate gifts

President: Steve Leveen
CFO: Lori Leveen
Marketing Manager: Susan Devito
Production Manager: Lee Passarella
Fulfillment: Gerald Patterson
Founder: Steve Leveen
Founder: Lori Leveen
Buyers: Denise Tedaldi
Credit Cards: AMEX; MasterCard; Visa
Catalog Cost: Free
Catalog Circulation: Mailed 12 time(s) per year to 20MM
Average Order Size: $130
Printing Information: 76 pages in 4 colors on Glossy Stock
Press: Web Press
Binding: Saddle Stitched
Mailing List Information: Names for rent
List Manager: Susan Devito
List Company: Mokrynski & Associates
401 Hackensack Avenue
Hackensack, NJ 07601
2014885656
In Business: 28 years
Number of Employees: 270
Sales Information: $20MM to $50MM

7734 Lumenpulse
Lumenpulse
10 Post Office Square
Suite 900
Boston, MA 02109   617-307-5700
                     Fax: 617-350-9912
info@lumenpulse.com
www.lumenpulse.com

Energy efficient lighting products

Senior Vice President & CTO: Greg Campbell
Director of Sales: Anthony Sauce
Catalog Cost: Free
Catalog Circulation: Mailed 1 time(s) per year
Printing Information: 45 pages in 4 colors
In Business: 11 years
Number of Employees: 500

7735 Maintenance USA
Maintenance USA
3333 Lenox Avenue
Jacksonville, FL 32254   800-283-4000
                           888-803-4468
                      Fax: 800-288-2828
specialorder@e-musa.com
www.e-musa.com

Building supplies and fixtures

In Business: 28 years

7736 P&H Crystalite
P&H Crystalite, Inc.
101 Palm Harbor Parkway #117
Palm Coast, FL 32137   561-330-8660
                           800-468-8673
                      Fax: 561-330-8665
phcrystalite@aol.com
www.flexalite.com

Rope lighting, Flex-A-Lite, Black Lights, Neon Signs, Strobes

President: Richard D Rubin
Marketing Manager: Anna Robin
Credit Cards: AMEX; MasterCard; Visa
Printing Information: 17 pages
Mailing List Information: Names for rent
In Business: 21 years
Number of Employees: 5
Sales Information: $1MM to $3MM

7737 Rudd Lighting Catalog
Rudd Lighting Direct
9201 Washington Ave
Racine, WI 53406-3772   262-886-1900
                           800-236-7000
                      Fax: 800-236-7500
lighting.cree.com

Lighting fixtures directly marketed to electrical contractors

President: Daniel Wandler
Marketing Manager: Greg Mueller
Founder: Alan Ruud
EVP: Christopher Ruud
VP Sales: John Tennyek
Credit Cards: MasterCard
In Business: 29 years
Sales Information: $20MM to $50MM

7738 Shades of Light
Shades of Light
14001 Justice Road
Midlothian, VA 23113   804-288-3235
                         Fax: 804-288-5029
info@shadesoflight.com
www.shadesoflight.com

Lighting, rugs, curtains and bedding

CFO: Denise McCarney
Catalog Cost: Free
Catalog Circulation: Mailed 1 time(s) per year
Printing Information: 74 pages in 4 colors on Glossy Stock
Binding: Saddle Stitched
In Business: 31 years
Number of Employees: 55
Sales Information: $5MM to $10MM

7739 Streamlight
Streamlight, Inc
30 Eagleville Road
Eagleville, PA 19403-1476   610-631-0600
                              800-523-7488
                         Fax: 610-631-0712
cs@streamlight.com
www.streamlight.com

A complete line of standard and rechargeable battery flashlights, lanterns and accessories

President: Brad Penney
CFO: George Collier
Marketing Manager: Loring Grove
Raymon Sharrah:
COO

Buyers: Christine Brunner
Catalog Circulation: Mailed 1 time(s) per year
Printing Information: 20 pages in 4 colors on Glossy Stock
Press: Web Press
Binding: Saddle Stitched
Mailing List Information: Names for rent
List Manager: C Bradford Penney
In Business: 41 years
Number of Employees: 240
Sales Information: $33 Million

Mailing Lists & Fulfillment
General

7740 ALDATA
Symphony EYC
1040 Crown Pointe Parkway
Suite 905
Atlanta, GA 30338   404-355-3220
                           877-925-3282
                     Fax: 404-355-9956
                CustomerSupport@eyc.com
                           www.eyc.com

List brokers and consulting

Chairman: Dr. Romesh Wadhwani
President: Graeme Cooksley
CFO: Todd Sanders
Managing Director and Operating Par: Dr. Pallab Chatterjee
Managing Director: Bill Chisholm
Strategic Consultant and Advisor: Joan Lewis
Mailing List Information: Names for rent
In Business: 3 years
Number of Employees: 600
Sales Information: $1,000,000

7741 ALLMEDIA International
ALLMEDIA INC
5601 Democracy Dr.
Suite 255
Plano, TX 75024-5180   469-467-9100
                           800-466-4061
                     Fax: 214-291-5431
                brokerage@allmediainc.com
                       www.allmediainc.com

Provides thoroughly researched recommendations and services for international lists and media including list brokerage and list management

President: Laura McClendon Bogush
VP: Rick Becker
Vice President: Mary Loeffler
Account Manager: Joan Laufer
In Business: 34 years
Number of Employees: 21
Sales Information: $1,000,000

7742 American List Counsel
American List Counsel
750 College Road East
Suite 201
Princeton, NJ 08540-5219   609-580-2800
                           800-252-5478
                     Fax: 609-580-2888
                           info@alc.com
                           www.Alc.Com

Full service list company

Chairman: Donn Rappaport
Donn.Rappaport@alc.com
President: Susan Rice Rappaport
Susan.Rice.Rappaport@alc.com
CFO: Peter DeRosa
Peter.Derosa@alc.com
Marketing Manager: Elizabeth Perks
Elizabeth.Perks@alc.com
Production Manager: Mike Wilson
Chief Executive Officer: Susan Rice Rappaport
President, SMART Data Solutions: Fran Green
EVP, IT: Patricia Stecher
Credit Cards: AMEX; MasterCard; Visa

Catalog Cost: Free
Catalog Circulation: Mailed 10 time(s) per year to 100M
Printing Information: 48 pages in 2 colors on Matte Stock
Press: Web Press
Binding: Saddle Stitched
In Business: 37 years
Number of Employees: 90
Sales Information: $5,000,000

7743 Better Lists, Inc.
Better Lists, Inc.
64 Sunnyside Ave
Stamford, CT 06902-7641   203-324-4171
                     Fax: 203-358-0384
                        www.Betterlists.Com

List brokers, compilers, letter shop, fulfillment, computer service bureaus

President: George S Rath
Marketing Manager: Colin Rath
Mailing List Information: Names for rent
In Business: 51 years
Number of Employees: 15
Sales Information: $2MM

7744 CAS Marketing
CAS Marketing
12A Hart Street
Henley-on-Thames, Ox RG9 2   149-157-8888
                     Fax: 402-390-9497
             www.cas-marketing.com/cas-gets-social-boost-maison-blanc

Mailing lists for direct mail or telemarketing

Credit Cards: MasterCard
Printing Information: 18 pages on Matte Stock
Binding: Saddle Stitched
In Business: 23 years

7745 Chilcutt Direct Marketing
Chilcutt Direct Marketing
813 East 33rd Street
Edmond, OK 73013   405-726-8780
                     Fax: 405-726-8799
                          info@cdmlist.com
                           www.cdmlist.com

List brokerage and management house

President: Matt Chilcutt
In Business: 20 years
Number of Employees: 26
Sales Information: $3MM to $5MM

7746 Comco DataNet
Comco, Inc.
2884 Devils Glen Road
Suite 385
Bettendorf, IA 52722-5021   563-355-1212
                           800-432-8638
                     Fax: 563-355-4055
                      sales@comco-inc.com
                       www.Comco-Inc.Com

Hardware, software and supplies for mailing professionals

President: Brian Gillette
Credit Cards: AMEX; MasterCard
Catalog Circulation: Mailed 1 time(s) per year
Printing Information: in 2 colors
Binding: Saddle Stitched
Sales Information: $500M to $1MM

7747 Derf Electronics
Derf Electronics Corporation
253 North Grand Ave
Poughkeepsie, NY 12603-2204   845-790-9900
                           800-431-2912
                     Fax: 845-790-9915
                           sales@derf.com
                           www.derf.com

Broad line electronic component distributor

President: Al Derf
Credit Cards: MasterCard

In Business: 69 years
Number of Employees: 25

7748 Dirmark Group
Dirmark Data Group
Data Processing Division
306 W. 76th St. Suite 5A
New York, NY 10023   770-594-8695
                           888-395-6727
                     Fax: 800-318-8088
                     info@dmdatabases.com
                    www.Dirmarkdatagroup.Com

Mailing lists covering business to business, consumer and specialty markets

President: Linda Serpico
Credit Cards: AMEX; MasterCard
Printing Information: 48 pages in 2 colors on Matte Stock
Binding: Saddle Stitched
In Business: 29 years
Sales Information: Under $500M

7749 Dydacomp Development Corporation
Freestyle Solutions
9 Campus Drive
Parsippany, NJ 07054-1154   973-237-9415
                           800-858-3666
                     Fax: 973-237-9043
                       sales@dydacomp.com
                        www.Dydacomp.Com

Information on a variety of software and publications for direct marketers

President: John Healy
CFO: Paul Kincaid
Marketing Manager: Laura Hills
CEO: Fred Lizza
Senior VP of Product Development: Gary MacDougall
Vice President of Technology: Rick Bednarik
Credit Cards: AMEX; MasterCard
Catalog Circulation: Mailed 1 time(s) per year
Printing Information: 32 pages in 1 color on Matte Stock
Press: Web Press
Binding: Saddle Stitched
Number of Employees: 60
Sales Information: $500M to $1MM

7750 ELCOM Systems
Elcom International, Inc
50 Braintree Hill Office Park
Suite 309
Braintree, MA 02184-2601   781-501-4000
                     Fax: 781-501-4070
                          info@elcom.com
                           www.Elcom.Com

Personal electronic catalog and ordering systems for manufacturers and direct marketers

Chairman: William Lock
President: Greg King
Marketing Manager: Michael Rosemberg
Executive VP Sales: David Morton
Executive VP of Operations: Kevin Larnach
Executive VP of Finance: David Elliott
Credit Cards: AMEX; MasterCard
Printing Information: in 4 colors
Number of Employees: 200
Sales Information: $10MM to $20MM

7751 Fred Woolf List Company Catalog
Fred Woolf List Company
PO Box 346
Somers, NY 10589-346   914-694-4466
                           800-431-1557
                     Fax: 914-694-1710
                         info@woolflist.com
                         www.woolflist.com

Mailing lists compilers and brokers, compiled and proprietary business lists, residential and executive databases, special compilations, mail order buyers

President: Fred Woolf
Marketing Manager: Felicia Woolf DiBuono
Credit Cards: AMEX; MasterCard
List Manager: Sheila Wolf
In Business: 43 years

7752 Fulfillment America
Fulfillment America
17 Progress Rd
Billerica, MA 01821-5731   978-988-7576
800-662-5009
Fax: 978-988-7574
info@fulfillmentamerica.com
www.Faicentral.Com

Fulfillment services

President: John Barry Sr
Catalog Cost: Free
Printing Information: in 4 colors on Glossy Stock
Press: Web Press
Binding: Perfect Bound
In Business: 14 years
Number of Employees: 50
Sales Information: $20MM to $50MM

7753 InfoUSA
InfoUSA
1020 East 1st St.
Papillion, NE 68046   800-835-5856
www.infousa.com

Business and consumer direct marketing list categories for direct mail, research and telemarketing campaigns.

Chair & CEO: Michael Iaccarino
Catalog Cost: Free
In Business: 47 years
Sales Information: $400 Million

7754 Karol Media
Karol Fulfillment
375 Stewart Road
PO Box 7600
Wilkes Barre, PA 18706-7600   570-822-8899
800-526-4773
Fax: 570-822-8226
sales@karolmedia.com
karolfulfillmentservices.com

A customized fulfillment house that serves a variety of clients and has a product sales division

President: Mark Kincheloe
Marketing Manager: Michael Kincheloe
Founder: Carol Kincheloe
Founder: Mick Kincheloe
VP of Operations: Rob Costello
Catalog Cost: Free
Catalog Circulation: Mailed 2 time(s) per year
Printing Information: 16 pages in 2 colors on Glossy Stock
Press: Letterpress
Binding: Perfect Bound
Mailing List Information: Names for rent
In Business: 38 years
Number of Employees: 35
Sales Information: $1,000,000 - $5,000,000

7755 Leon Henry Catalog
Leon Henry Inc
210 North Central Avenue
Suite 320
Hartsdale, NY 10530-1940   914-285-3456
Fax: 914-285-3450
lh@leonhenryinc.com

Full service insert media/insert brokers and manager, mailing list, card deck and interactive media brokers/managers

Chairman: Leon Henry
President: Thelma Henry
Marketing Manager: Lynn Henry
Fulfillment: Gail Henry
EVP: Lynn Henry
EVP/General Manager: Gail Henry
EVP: Barbara Henry

Mailing List Information: Names for rent
List Manager: Jody Smith
In Business: 59 years
Number of Employees: 23

7756 List America
Market Development Group, Inc.
1832 Connecticut Avenue, NW
4th Floor
Washington, DC 20009-4124   202-298-8030
Fax: 202-244-4999
www.mdginc.org

Offers list management services, compilation, brokers and consultants

Chairman: John Alahouzo, Executive Vice Pres
President: Gerry Gretschel
CFO: C Ann Papp, SVP
Founder: Mike Gretschel
Founder: John Alahouzos
In Business: 37 years
Number of Employees: 10-J
Sales Information: $10MM to $20MM

7757 Market Data Retrieval
Market Data Retrieval
6 Armstrong Road
Suite 301
Shelton, CT 06484   203-926-4800
800-333-8802
Fax: 203-929-5253
mdrinfo@dnb.com
www.schooldata.com

Database covers education; preschool through college including public libraries in the US and Canada, extensive names, addresses and demographic information

Credit Cards: AMEX; MasterCard; Visa
Catalog Cost: Free
Catalog Circulation: Mailed 1 time(s) per year to 75M
Average Order Size: $350
Printing Information: 25 pages in 2 colors on Matte Stock
Press: Web Press
Binding: Saddle Stitched
In Business: 48 years
Number of Employees: 200
Sales Information: $10MM to $20MM

7758 Marketry
Marketry
4122 Factoria Blvd. S.E.
Suite #400
Bellevue, WA 98006   425-451-1262
Fax: 425-953-2957
info@marketry.com
www.marketry.com

Mailing lists

President: Norm Swent
CFO: Greg Swent
Credit Cards: MasterCard; Visa
Catalog Circulation: Mailed 4 time(s) per year
Printing Information: in 2 colors
In Business: 41 years

7759 Penton Lists
Penton Media, Inc.
1166 Avenue of the Americas/10th Fl
New York, NY 10036   212-204-4200
Fax: 216-696-1752
CorporateCustomerService@penton.com
www.penton.com

Business mailing lists

President: David B. Nussbaum
CFO: Nicola Allais
Nicola.Allais@penton.com
Marketing Manager: Sharon Beinecke
Fulfillment: Merit Direct
CEO: David Kieselstein
david.kieselstein@penton.com
Senior Vice President Human Resourc: Kurt E. Nelson

Kurt.Nelson@penton.com
Catalog Cost: Free
Catalog Circulation: to 7000
Printing Information: 104 pages in 4 colors on Glossy Stock
Press: Web Press
Binding: Perfect Bound
Mailing List Information: Names for rent
In Business: 31 years
Number of Employees: 1000
Sales Information: $3MM to $5MM

7760 Precision Response Corporation
Precision Response Corp.
1505 NW 167th St # 200
Miami, FL 33169-5133   305-474-5191
Fax: 305-626-4675
www.yellowpages.com

Fulfillment services

President: Mark J Gordon
CEO: David Krantz
Chief Information Office: Tyler Best
In Business: 14 years
Number of Employees: 600
Sales Information: Under $500M

7761 Reed Business Lists
Reed Business Information
230 Park Avenue
New York, NY 10169   212-309-8100
Fax: 646-746-7583
corporatecommunications@reedbusiness.com
www.reedbusiness.com

Business-to-Business publishers providing market-leading publications, webzines, directories, research and direct-marketing lists

President: Tad Smith, CEO
CFO: Stuart Whayman
VP: Andrew Rak
Mailing List Information: Names for rent
Number of Employees: 1200
Sales Information: 202 million

7762 Response Unlimited
Response Unlimited
284 Shalom Rd
Waynesboro, VA 22980-7349   540-943-6721
Fax: 540-943-0841
info@responseunlimited.com
www.responseunlimited.com

Conservative and Christian mailing lists

President: Philip Zodhiates
Marketing Manager: Mathew LaPorta
Production Manager: Joel Baugher
Catalog Cost: Free
Catalog Circulation: Mailed 1 time(s) per year to 15000
Average Order Size: $2000
Printing Information: 16 pages in 4 colors on Glossy Stock
Press: Sheetfed Press
Binding: Saddle Stitched
Mailing List Information: Names for rent
In Business: 36 years
Number of Employees: 10
Sales Information: $690,000

7763 SRDS Media Solutions
Standard Rate and Data Services, Inc.
5600 N. River Road
Suite 900
Rosemont, IL 60018   847-375-5000
800-851-7737
Fax: 847-375-5001
contact@srds.com
www.Srds.Com

Mailing lists, media rates and data, marketing information

CFO: Kevin McNally
Marketing Manager: David Kostolansky
Production Manager: Lorene Precht
VP Group Publisher: Steve Davis
Publisher Magazine Services: Joseph Hayes

Account Manager: Jacki Premak
Catalog Cost: Free
Catalog Circulation: Mailed 1 time(s) per year
Printing Information: in 3 colors on Matte Stock
Mailing List Information: Names for rent
In Business: 96 years
Number of Employees: 165

7764 US Monitor
US Monitor
86 Maple Ave
New City, NY 10956-5092   845-634-1331
                                 800-767-7967
                            Fax: 845-634-9618
                             www.Usmonitor.Com

Mail monitor protection service

President: Anita Sass
In Business: 41 years
Number of Employees: 30
Sales Information: $3MM to $5MM

7765 United Logistics
United Facilities
603 North Main Street
P.O. Box 559
East Peoria, IL 61651-2023   309-699-7271
                                 866-399-7271
                            Fax: 309-699-0228
                               www.unifac.com

Ongoing or episodic fulfillment, sales and marketing programs and mail management

President: Gary Morgan
Marketing Manager: Stan Savitz
Catalog Cost: Free
Printing Information: 15 pages in 2 colors on Glossy Stock
Press: Web Press
Binding: Saddle Stitched
In Business: 135 years
Number of Employees: 6
Sales Information: Under $500M

7766 Walter Karl Companies
Infogroup Targeting Solutions
1020 E 1st Street
Papillion, NE 68046   845-620-0700
                                 866-872-1313
                            Fax: 845-620-1885
                           ITSinfo@infogroup.com
                        www.infogrouptargeting.com

Mailing lists

Chairman: Mike Iaccarino
President: David McRae
CFO: John Hoffman
Marketing Manager: Lori Colantuono
Fulfillment: Barry Wood
Chief Technology Officer, Enterpris: Purandar Das
Chief Data Officer: Matt Graves
Senior Vice President, Sales: Andrea Haldeman
Credit Cards: MasterCard; Visa
In Business: 56 years
Number of Employees: 80

Metalwork
Supplies & Equipment

7767 A/C Fabricating Corporation
A/C Fabricating Corporation
1821 Century Drive
Goshen, IN 46528   574-534-1415
                            Fax: 574-533-5254
                         sales@acfabricating.com
                          www.acfabricating.com

Non-ferrous tube fabricating.

President: Gilbert Mast
Marketing Manager: D Mascarenas
Executive VP, Manager: Gerie Mast
In Business: 40 years

Number of Employees: 20
Sales Information: $200,000

7768 Alto Manufacturing Company
Alto Manufacturing Company, Inc.
2850 N Ashland Ave
Chicago, IL 60657-4089   773-935-7080
                            Fax: 773-935-7084
                         sales@altomfgco.com
                          www.altomfgco.com

Metal fabrication, frames, rolled frames, T posts, metal drawer slides

President: Russell Brandstetter
Printing Information: 20 pages in 2 colors
In Business: 96 years
Sales Information: $3,000,000-$5,000,000

7769 Anel Corpration
Anel Corpration
3244 Highway 51 South
PO Box 600
Winona, MS 38967   662-283-1540
                                 800-325-5089
                            Fax: 662-283-2949
                             www.anelcorp.com

Steel and aluminum fabrication

President: Charles B Holder
Credit Cards: MasterCard; Visa
In Business: 50 years
Number of Employees: 62
Sales Information: $5MM to $10MM

7770 Ardmore Textured Metals
Rimex Metals
2850 Woodbridge Avenue
Edison, NJ 08837-3616   732-549-3800
                            Fax: 732-549-6435
                          sales@rimexusa.com
                          www.rimexmetals.com

Decorative metals, back sheets and absorber plates

President: John Horbal
In Business: 56 years
Number of Employees: 20
Sales Information: $1,000,000 - $5,000,000

7771 Atlas Metal Industries
Atlas Metal Industries
1135 NW 159th Dr
Miami, FL 33169-5882   305-625-2451
                                 800-762-7565
                            Fax: 305-623-0475
                        sales@atlasfoodserv.com
                         www.Atlasfoodserv.Com

Metal fabricators

President: David Meade
Marketing Manager: R Nusbaum
In Business: 67 years
Number of Employees: 170
Sales Information: $25,000,000 - $50,000,000

7772 Buffalo Metal Fabricating
Buffalo Outfront Metalworks LP
50 Wicker Street
Buffalo, NY 14215-3897   716-892-7800
                            Fax: 716-892-8583
                             info@bofmw.com
                             www.bofmw.com/

Metal fabricators

President: Tony Van Es
CFO: Alfreda Moroczko
Owner: Tony Van Es
Director of Operations: Dave Myslinski
dave.myslinski@bofmw.com
Engineering/Project Management: Thomas Shiah
thomas.shiah@bofmw.com
In Business: 3 years
Number of Employees: 30
Sales Information: $1,000,000 - $5,000,000

7773 CFW/Precision Metal Components
Precision Metal Components
371-B Manhattan Avenue
P.O. Box 309
Grover Beach, CA 93433-1903   805-489-8750
                            Fax: 805-489-5270
                             info@cfwpmc.com
                             www.cfwpmc.com/

Metal components and machinery

President: Michael Greenelsh Jr
Sales Department: Don Burke
dburke@cfwpmc.com
In Business: 37 years
Number of Employees: 32
Sales Information: $3MM to $5MM

7774 Carl Stahl Sava Industries
Carl Stahl Sava Industries Inc.
4 North Corporate Drive
PO Box 30
Riverdale, NJ 07457-30   973-835-0882
                            Fax: 973-835-0877
                            info@savacable.com
                            www.Savacable.Com

Manufacturing cable solutions in cable, cable assemblies, idler pulleys and push pull control assemblies

President: Marc E. Alterman
Marketing Manager: Bruce Staubitz
Fulfillment: Bruce Staubitz
CEO: Zdenek A. Fremund
VP Operations: Jack Maas
VP Sales & Marketing: Bruce R. Staubitz
Buyers: Jim Hill
Catalog Cost: Free
Catalog Circulation: to 7500
Printing Information: 36 pages on Glossy Stock
Mailing List Information: Names for rent
List Manager: Bruce Staubitz
In Business: 35+ years
Number of Employees: 87
Sales Information: $5,000,000

7775 Central Sheet Metal Products
Central Sheet Metal Products, Inc.
7251 N. Linder
Skokie, IL 60077-3295   847-676-9650
                            Fax: 847-676-9677
                         sales@centralsheet.com
                          www.Centralsheet.Com

Metal fabricators

President: Robert Silverstein
In Business: 103 years
Number of Employees: 25
Sales Information: $1,000,000 - $5,000,000

7776 DeLong Equipment Company
DeLong Equipment Company
1216 Zonolite Road
Atlanta, GA 30306-2000   404-607-1234
                                 800-548-8233
                            Fax: 404-607-1000
                       sales@DeLongequipment.com
                        www.Delongequipment.Com

Metal finishing equipment

President: Rob Eskew
reskew@delongequipment.com
Service Manager: Tim Daniels
tdaniels@delongequipment.com
VP, Operations: Eddie Freeman
efreeman@delongequipment.com
Customer Service, Purchasing: Hal Freeman
hfreeman@delongequipment.com
Credit Cards: AMEX; MasterCard
In Business: 48 years
Number of Employees: 28
Sales Information: $1,000,000 - $5,000,000

7777 Findings & Metals
Swest Inc.
11090 N Stemmons Freeway
PO Box 59389
Dallas, TX 75229-4520   214-350-4011
                                   Fax: 800-441-5162
                                   swest@mindspring.com
                                   www.swestinc.com

Jewelry making and metalwork

President: FW Ward
Marketing Manager: Gary Fuller

7778 Flemington Aluminum & Brass
Flemington Aluminum and Brass Inc
24 Junction Rd
Flemington, NJ 08822-5721   908-782-6317
                                   Fax: 908-782-8078
                                   info@fabonline.net
                                   www.Fabonline.Net

Traffic signal products, street lighting, aluminum poles, cabinets and enclosures, cast aluminum and brass plaques, custom castings

President: Jim Kozicki
Catalog Cost: Free
Printing Information: 50 pages in 2 colors on Glossy Stock
Mailing List Information: Names for rent
In Business: 74 years
Number of Employees: 25
Sales Information: $1,000,000 - $5,000,000

7779 Girtz Industries
Girtz Industries
5262 N East Shafer Dr
Monticello, IN 47960-7313   574-278-7510
                                   Fax: 574-278-6221
                                   sales@girtz.com
                                   www.Girtz.Com

Metal fabricators

President: David Girtz
In Business: 51 years
Number of Employees: 125
Sales Information: $10,000,000 - $25,000,000

7780 Grand Tool Supply Corporation
Grand Tool Supply
650 Huyler Street
South Hackensack, NJ 07606-1744 800-922-0512
                                   Fax: 800-866-5730
                                   www.grandtool.com

Quality cutting tools, machine shop equipment and measuring instruments for the metalworking industry; hard-to-find items for classic tooling and today's cutting-edge technology

Catalog Cost: Free
Printing Information: 736 pages in 4 colors
In Business: 71 years
Sales Information: 2.3MM

7781 Hillside Wire Cloth Company
Hillside Wire Cloth Company
109 Roosevelt Avenue
Belleville, NJ 07109-1190   973-751-3131
                                   800-826-7395
                                   Fax: 973-470-8183
                                   sales@hillsidewirecloth.com
                                   www.hillsidewirecloth.com

Industrial wire cloth, metals, meshes and custom fabrications

President: Donald Metzinger
Marketing Manager: William Messinger
Production Manager: Joseph Librizzi
Buyers: Mary Murphy
Catalog Circulation: Mailed 2 time(s) per year to 10M
Average Order Size: $2000
Printing Information: 4 pages in 2 colors on Glossy Stock
Binding: Perfect Bound
Mailing List Information: Names for rent

In Business: 75 years
Number of Employees: 12
Sales Information: $1,000,000 - $5,000,000

7782 Humphrey Pneumatic Valves
Humphrey
PO Box 2008
Kalamazoo, MI 49003-2008   616-381-5500
                                   Fax: 616-381-4113
                                   www.humphrey-products.com

Patented stainless steel barrel pneumatic cylinders, single and double acting

Chairman: Randall Weber
President: Randall Webber
Marketing Manager: Rich McDonnell, Director Bus Dev
Production Manager: Pat Aldworth
Catalog Cost: Free
Catalog Circulation: Mailed 1 time(s) per year to 35M
Printing Information: 20 pages in 4 colors
Press: Web Press
Binding: Saddle Stitched
Mailing List Information: Names for rent
In Business: 100 years
Number of Employees: 600

7783 Johnson Bros Metal Forming Catalog
Johnson Bros Metal Forming Company
5744 McDermott Drive
Berkeley, IL 60163-1102   708-449-7050
                                   Fax: 708-449-0042
                                   www.johnsonrollforming.com

Custom roll formed: angles, channels, mouldings; special shapes in straight lenght and/or ring form; also lockseam and open buttseam tubing

President: Edwin O. Johnson
VP & General Manager: Brad Johnson
Catalog Cost: Free
Mailing List Information: Names for rent
In Business: 70 years

7784 Jones Metal Products
Jones Metal Products
3201 Third Avenue
Mankato, MN 56001-2725   507-625-4436
                                   800-967-1750
                                   Fax: 507-625-2994
                                   customercare@jonesmetalproducts.com
                                   www.Jonesmetalproducts.Com

Metal fabricators

President: Sarah Richards
CFO: Jennifer Thompson
Marketing Manager: Toby Begnaud
Purchasing Manager: David Richards
Purchasing Manager: Dale Kuyper
Director of Engineering: Dave Olson
In Business: 71 years
Number of Employees: 135
Sales Information: $10,000,000 - $25,000,000

7785 Magga Products
Magga Products
1512 State Ave, Suite A
Holly Hill, FL 32117   386-676-1080
                                   Fax: 386-672-6644
                                   sales@maggaproducts.com
                                   www.maggaproducts.com

Quartz, ceramic and metal fabricators

President: Maggie Morgan
Founder: Rick Morgan
Mailing List Information: Names for rent
In Business: 36 years
Number of Employees: 12
Sales Information: $500,000 - $1,000,000

7786 Marion Manufacturing Company
Marion Manufacturing Company
1675 Reinhard Road
Cheshire, CT 06410   203-272-5376
                                   Fax: 203-272-1792
                                   info@marionmfg.net
                                   www.marionmfg.com/

Wire forms, four-slide parts, progressive stampings and assemblies

President: Douglas Johnson
djohnson@marionmfg.net
Production Manager: Elizabeth Gerena
egerena@marionmfg.net
Plant Manager: David Dubois
ddubois@marionmfg.net
Purchasing & Sales Administration: Nancy Zawerton
nzawerton@marionmfg.net
Quality Assurance Manager: Patricia Stango
pstango@marionmfg.net
Number of Employees: 22
Sales Information: $1,000,000 - $5,000,000

7787 Martguild
Martguild
8563 Rte 10, Highway 46
PO Box 92
New Point, IN 47263   812-663-6311
                                   800-245-8978
                                   Fax: 812-663-5530
                                   www.newpointproducts.com/martguild/

Metal products

President: John H Tressler III
In Business: 45 years
Number of Employees: 18
Sales Information: $500,000 - $1,000,000

7788 Merrill Manufacturing Corporation
Merrill Manufacturing Corporation
236 South Genesee Street
PO Box 566
Merrill, WI 54452   715-536-5533
                                   888-662-9473
                                   Fax: 715-536-5590
                                   sales@merrill-mfg.com
                                   www.merrill-mfg.com/

Wire and flat metal parts for manufacturers

President: Richard L Taylor
Marketing Manager: James Stiles
Number of Employees: 160
Sales Information: $10,000,000 - $25,000,000

7789 Mica-Tron Products Corporation
Mica-Tron Products Corp.
275 Centre Street
Unit 13
Holbrook, MA 02343   781-961-5297
                                   Fax: 781-961-5492
                                   www.mica-tron.com

Precision metal machining

President: Paul Tassinari
Founder: Dino Tassinari
In Business: 56 years
Number of Employees: 8
Sales Information: $500M to $1MM

7790 Midwest Metal Products Company
Midwest Metal Products Company
800 66th Avenue SW
Cedar Rapids, IA 52404-4793   319-366-6264
                                   800-394-6474
                                   Fax: 319-366-6710
                                   rfq@mwestmp.com
                                   www.Mwestmp.Com

Metal fabricators

President: Kevin Urban
Production Manager: Randy Moyer
Founder: Ray Urban
Finance director: Dave Fritz
Sales manager: Adam Jelinek
In Business: 50 years

Number of Employees: 115
Sales Information: $10,000,000 - $25,000,000

7791 Myers Sheetmetal
Kampel Enterprises, Inc.
8390 Carlisle Rd
P.O.Box 157
Wellsville, PA 17365-157
717-432-9688
800-837-4971
Fax: 800-778-7006
info@kampelent.com
www.Kampelent.Com

Sheet metal fabricators

President: Judy Kampel
Marketing Manager: TE Kampel
Founder: Lawrence J.
Founder: Lawrence J. Kampel Jr.
Founder: Florence M.
In Business: 67 years
Number of Employees: 45
Sales Information: $1,000,000 - $5,000,000

7792 Norpin Manufacturing Company
Norpin Manufacturing Co. Inc
2342 Boston Road
P.O. Box 1031
Wilbraham, MA 01095-366
413-599-1627
800-795-1302
Fax: 413-599-1696
www.norpin.com

Deep drawn enclosures; aluminum, copper and brass

President: NT Pincinee
Marketing Manager: Lynne M Taylor
Production Manager: Wax Brackett
Fulfillment: Kenneth Pincince
Buyers: Martin Shepro
Catalog Cost: Free
Catalog Circulation: to 1M
Printing Information: 28 pages in 2 colors on Matte Stock
Mailing List Information: Names for rent
In Business: 58 years
Number of Employees: 20
Sales Information: $1,000,000 - $5,000,000

7793 Northern States Metals Corporation
Northern States Metals
3207 Innovation Place
PO Box 666
Youngstown, OH 44509-1926
330-799-1855
800-689-0666
Fax: 860-521-5204
sales@extrusions.com
www.Extrusions.Com

Aluminum extrusions, anodizing, painting, finishing, fabricating, die design

President: Paul Cusson
VP of Sales: Butch Ilievski
In Business: 43 years
Number of Employees: 20-O
Sales Information: $3MM to $5MM

7794 Olin Brass
GBC Metals, LLC
4801 Olympia Park Plaza
Suite 3500
Louisville, IL 40241-1197
502-873-3000
Fax: 502-327-3814
employment@olinbrass.com
www.olinbrass.com

Brass materials

President: William G. Toler
CFO: John Przybysz
CEO: John J. Wasz
Vice President, Marketing & Sales: Greg Keown
Vice President, Manufacturing: Dale R. Taylor
In Business: 123 years
Sales Information: $3MM to $5MM

7795 Onodi Tool & Engineering Company
Onodi Tool & Engineering
19150 Meginnity Avenue
Melvindale, MI 48122
313-386-6682
Fax: 313-386-8696
www.onoditool.com

Custom metal parts and assemblies

President: John Onodi
Catalog Circulation: Mailed 1 time(s) per year
Printing Information: 8 pages in 4 colors
Binding: Saddle Stitched
In Business: 38 years
Number of Employees: 50-1
Sales Information: $1,000,000 - $5,000,000

7796 Prentice Machine Work
Prentice Machine Work Inc.
310 E Butler Ave
Memphis, TN 38126-3306
901-529-1960
Fax: 901-521-9781
info@cylex-usa.com
www.cylex-usa.com

Custom fabrication and machine works

President: Johnny Prentice
Number of Employees: 18
Sales Information: $1,000,000 - $5,000,000

7797 Puritas Metal Products Company
Puritas Metal Products, Inc
7720 Race Rd North Ridgeville
Cleveland, OH 44135-140
440-353-1917
888-215-1745
Fax: 440-353-1918
info@puritasmetal.com
www.puritasmetal.com

Metal rings, screws and brackets

Credit Cards: AMEX; MasterCard
Catalog Circulation: Mailed 1 time(s) per year
Printing Information: 40 pages
Number of Employees: 10-J
Sales Information: $1,000,000 - $5,000,000

7798 Quest Technologies
Quest Technologies
1060 Corporate Center Dr
Oconomowoc, WI 53066-4828
262-567-9157
800-328-4630
Fax: 262-567-4047
quest.mail@mmm.com
www.questtechnologies.com

instrumentaion for monitoring noise, toxic gas, heat, indoor air quality, power, voltage, current and industrial hygiene dataloggers

President: Nick Eleftheriou
Number of Employees: 95
Sales Information: $1MM to $3MM

7799 RWC
RWC,Inc
2105 S Euclid Avenue
P.O. Box 920
Bay City, MI 48707-920
989-684-4030
Fax: 989-684-3960
www.rwcinc.com

Metal fabricating and assembly

President: Rich Glenn
In Business: 70 years
Number of Employees: 220
Sales Information: $20MM to $50MM

7800 Reid Tool Supply
Essentra Components
7400 West Industrial Drive
Forest Park, IL 60130-2684
231-777-3951
800-847-0486
Fax: 886-561-6617
us.essentracomponents.com

Industrial tooling and components, many hard-to-find items

President: Paul Reid
Corporate Affair Director: Joanna Speed

Credit Cards: MasterCard
Catalog Circulation: Mailed 4 time(s) per year
Printing Information: 300 pages on Matte Stock
Press: Web Press
Number of Employees: 75

7801 Ronson Technical Products
Ronson Technical Products Division
2146-B Flinstone Drive
PO Box 125
Tucker, GA 30084-800
770-414-8488
800-524-0698
Fax: 770-621-9660
contact@EnergyAndProcess.com
www.energyandprocess.com

Fasteners, tubing, steel plates and pipes

Marketing Manager: Tim Moravek
Catalog Circulation: Mailed 1 time(s) per year
Printing Information: 4 pages
In Business: 17 years

7802 Roof & Wall Systems
Metal Sales Manufacturing Corporation
545 South 3rd Street
Suite 200
Louisville, KY 40202
502-855-4300
800-406-7387
Fax: 502-855-4200
www.metalsales.us.com

Metal building component supplier

President: Jeffrey L. Mackin
CFO: Craig L. Mackin
Production Manager: David Cunningham
VP: Michael J. Mackin
VP: Jay L. Mackin
Catalog Circulation: Mailed 1 time(s) per year
Printing Information: 12 pages in 3 colors
Press: Letterpress
Binding: Saddle Stitched
In Business: 52 years

7803 Servo Products Company
Servo Products Co.
34940 Lakeland Boulevard
Eastlake, OH 44095-5226
440-942-9999
800-521-7359
Fax: 440-942-9100
mail@servoproductsco.com
www.servoproductsco.com

Power feeds, drill presses and machine tool accessories

Chairman: Mirko Cukelj
mcurelj@servoproductsco.com
President: Greg Heyen
gheyen@servoproducts.com
CFO: Ivanka Zovco
izovko@servoproductsco.com
Vice President: Bryan Heartz
bheartz@servoproductsco.com
Customer Service Specialist: Joseph Kugel
jkugel@servoproductsco.com
Customer Service Specialist: ElaineSkipper
eskipper@servoproductsco.com
In Business: 53 years
Number of Employees: 50-1
Sales Information: $5,000,000 - $10,000,000

7804 Sifco Forge Group
Sifco Industries, Inc.
970 E 64th St
Cleveland, OH 44103-1694
216-881-8600
Fax: 216-432-6281
Info@SIFCO.com
www.Sifco.Com

Forged metal parts

President: Greg Muniak
Marketing Manager: EJ Schmidt
In Business: 100 years
Number of Employees: 50-1
Sales Information: $10,000,000 - $25,000,000

7805 Skilcraft Sheetmetal
Skilcraft LLC.
5184 Limaburg Rd
PO Box 896
Burlington, KY 41005-9391 859-371-0799
800-888-2122
Fax: 859-371-2627
www.skilcraft.com

Sheetmetal fabricators and laser cutting services

President: Jim Berding
Marketing Manager: Tom Becker
In Business: 50 years
Number of Employees: 120
Sales Information: $5,000,000 - $10,000,000

7806 Stafford Manufacturing Corporation
Stafford Manufacturing Corp.
256 Andover St.
Wilmington, MA 01887-277 978-657-8000
800-695-5551
Fax: 978-657-4731
sales@staffordmfg.com
www.staffordmfg.com

Clamp-type shaft collars and couplings and related mechanical components to the power transmission industry

Marketing Manager: Laurie Mann
Production Manager: Jim Swiezynski
Catalog Cost: Free
Catalog Circulation: to 10K
Average Order Size: $15
Printing Information: 32 pages in 4 colors on Glossy Stock
Binding: Saddle Stitched
Mailing List Information: Names for rent
In Business: 39 years
Number of Employees: 40

7807 Stock Parts List
Buckeye Fasteners
5250 W 164th Street
Brook Park, OH 44142-1506 216-267-2240
800-437-1689
Fax: 216-267-3228
info@buckeyefasteners.com
buckeyefasteners.com

Weld nuts, weld screws, leg levelers, self-clinching fasteners, rivets and adjusting screws

Catalog Cost: Free
Catalog Circulation: Mailed 52 time(s) per year
Printing Information: 20 pages in 1 color on Matte Stock
Press: Web Press
Binding: Saddle Stitched
Mailing List Information: Names for rent
In Business: 33 years
Number of Employees: 26
Sales Information: Under $500M

7808 Stolle Corporation
Stolle Machinery Company, LLC
6949 S. Potomac Street
Sidney, OH 45365-8865 937-497-5400
Fax: 937-497-0409
www.stollemachinery.com

Metal fabricators

President: James H Hopkins
CFO: Denise Stasiak
Chief Operating & technology Office: Greg Butcher
Chief Executive Officer: Guss Reall
In Business: 144 years
Number of Employees: 2000
Sales Information: $50,000,000 - $100,000,00

7809 Tampa Sheet Metal Company
Tampa Sheet Metal Company
1402 West Kennedy Boulevard
Tampa, FL 33606-1847 813-251-1845
800-644-3120
Fax: 813-254-7399
sales@tampasheetmetal.com
www.Tampasheetmetal.Com

Metal fabricators

President: John L Jiretz
In Business: 94 years
Number of Employees: 21
Sales Information: $1,000,000 - $5,000,000

7810 Tuscarora Plastics
Tuscarora Plastics
880 5th Avenue
New Brighton, PA 15066-1922 724-843-8200
800-289-9966
Fax: 724-847-0807
www.tuscarora.com

Metal fabricators

Number of Employees: 20-5
Sales Information: $1,000,000 - $5,000,000

7811 USATCO
US Air Tool Company
60 Fleetwood Court
Ronkonkoma, NY 11779-6907 631-471-3300
Fax: 631-471-3308
info@usatco.com
www.usatco.com

Manufactures and distributes riveting, pneumatic and metalworking tools to the aircraft, aerospace and metalworking industries

President: Geoff Perez
Founder: Joseph Percz
Credit Cards: AMEX; MasterCard
Catalog Cost: $7.5
Catalog Circulation: Mailed 1 time(s) per year to 15M
Printing Information: 200 pages in 1 color on Matte Stock
Press: Web Press
Binding: Perfect Bound
Mailing List Information: Names for rent
In Business: 66 years
Number of Employees: 20-5
Sales Information: $1,000,000 - $5,000,000

7812 Victor Machinery Exchange
Victor Machinery Exchange Inc
33-53 62nd St.
Woodside, NY 11377-3817 718-899-1502
800-723-5359
Fax: 718-899-0556
sales@victornet.com
www.victornet.com

Metal working tools

President: Marc Freidus
Credit Cards: AMEX; MasterCard; Visa
Catalog Cost: Free
Catalog Circulation: Mailed 1 time(s) per year to 70000
Printing Information: 136 pages in 4 colors on Glossy Stock
Binding: Saddle Stitched
Mailing List Information: Names for rent
In Business: 97 years
Number of Employees: 10
Sales Information: $1MM to $3MM

7813 WL Fuller
W.L. Fuller Co., Inc.
7 Cypress St
PO Box 8767
Warwick, RI 02888-767 401-467-2900
Fax: 401-467-2905
info@wlfuller.com
www.wlfuller.com

Countersinks, counterbores, plug cutters, taper point drills, brad point drills and step drills, also specials

President: Diane Nobel
CFO: Gary Fuller
Marketing Manager: Debbie Fuller
Production Manager: Andrew Henninger
Fulfillment: Debbie Fuller
Buyers: Sandy Fuller
Credit Cards: MasterCard; Visa; Discover
Catalog Cost: Free
Printing Information: 152 pages on Matte Stock
Press: Web Press
Binding: Perfect Bound
Mailing List Information: Names for rent
In Business: 63 years
Number of Employees: 60
Sales Information: $10MM to $20MM

7814 Westfield Sheet Metal Works
Westfield Sheet Metal Works, Inc.
North 8th Street & Monroe Ave.
Kenilworth, NJ 07033-128 908-276-5500
Fax: 908-276-6808
info@westfieldsheetmetal.com
www.westfieldsheetmetal.com

Sheet metal fabrication

President: Campbell Johnstone
Production Manager: Thomas Johnstone
In Business: 87 years
Number of Employees: 100
Sales Information: $10,000,000 - $25,000,000

7815 Williams Lowbuck Tools
Williams Lowbuck Tools,Inc
4175 California Ave
Norco, CA 92860-1769 951-735-7848
800-735-7844
Fax: 951-735-1210
wlowbuck@aol.com
www.Lowbucktools.Com

Tube notchers and other metalworking tools

President: Dave Williams
Credit Cards: MasterCard
Catalog Cost: $3
Catalog Circulation: Mailed 1 time(s) per year to 10M
Printing Information: 32 pages in 2 colors
Press: Offset Press
Binding: Saddle Stitched
In Business: 37 years
Number of Employees: 10-J
Sales Information: $500,000 - $1,000,000

Models
Fabricators & Services

7816 Atlanta Models & Exhibits
Atlanta Models & Exhibits
6899 Peachtree Industrial Boulevard
Suite E
Norcross, GA 30092-3663 770-449-0800
800-449-0878
Fax: 770-242-6706
hamilton.models@gmail.com
www.atlantamodels.net/

Food, chemical and architectural model fabricators

President: Larry Hamilton
Marketing Manager: John Roberts
Contact Person for Models: Tim Lom
timlom@mindspring.com
contact Person for Exhibits: Larry Hamilton
lsham@mindspring.com
In Business: 39 years
Number of Employees: 2
Sales Information: Under $500M

7817 Kindt Collins Company
Kindt Collins Company
12651 Elmwood Ave
Cleveland, OH 44111-5994
216-252-4122
800-321-3170
Fax: 216-252-5639
www.Kindt-Collins.Com

Casting prototypes and accessory suppliers
President: Jon Lindseth
Marketing Manager: Len Principe
Number of Employees: 95
Sales Information: $10,000,000 - $25,000,000

7818 National Metal Fabricators
National Metal Fabricators
2395 Greenleaf Avenue
Elk Grove Village, IL 60007-5573
847-439-5321
800-323-8849
Fax: 847-439-4774
sales@nmfrings.com
www.Nmfrings.Com

Metal fabricators
President: W T Bonine Jr
In Business: 57 years
Number of Employees: 50
Sales Information: $1,000,000 - $5,000,000

7819 O'Brien Manufacturing
O'Brien Design and Manufacturing
2081 Knowles Road
Medford, OR 97501
541-773-2410
pop@obrienshowcases.com
obrienshowcases.com

Knockdown wood and glass fabrications, showcases, counters, wall cases and counter tops
Fulfillment: John M O'Brien
Catalog Cost: Free
Catalog Circulation: Mailed 2 time(s) per year
Average Order Size: $1000
Printing Information: 12 pages in 4 colors on Glossy Stock
Press: Sheetfed Press
Binding: Perfect Bound
In Business: 35 years
Number of Employees: 3
Sales Information: Under $500M

Office Products
Equipment

7820 Bostitch
Stanley Fastening Systems,L.P.
701 E Jopra RD.
Towson, MD 21286-700
401-884-2500
800-556-6696
Fax: 800-842-9360
www.bostitch.com

Hardware and supplies
Chairman: Nolan Archibald
President: John Lundgren
CFO: Donald Allan, Jr.
EVP and COO: James M. Loree
SVP and CIO/SFS:
Credit Cards: MasterCard
Catalog Circulation: Mailed 2 time(s) per year
Printing Information: 16 pages
Binding: Saddle Stitched
In Business: 118 years

7821 Comfort Telecommunications
Comfort Telecommunications
1407 SE 47th Terrace
Cape Coral, FL 33904
239-945-3224
800-399-3224
Fax: 239-945-0288
sales@comfortel.com
www.comfortel.com

New and reconditioned telephones and telephone headsets

President: Jon Minto
CFO: Sandy Laughing
Credit Cards: AMEX; MasterCard; Visa
Catalog Cost: Free
In Business: 28 years
Number of Employees: 50
Sales Information: $6 Million

7822 Dallas Midwest
Dallas Midwest
4100 Alpha Road
Suite 111
Dallas, TX 75244-4333
972-866-0101
800-527-2417
Fax: 800-301-8314
sales@dallasmidwest.com
www.dallasmidwest.com

Furniture for the office, church, school, and daycare, including podiums, lockers, bulletin/whiteboard, partitions, filing cabinets and organizers
Chairman: Felix Zimmerman
CFO: Eileen Baus
Sales Manager: David Jenkins
Credit Cards: AMEX; MasterCard; Visa
Catalog Cost: Free
Catalog Circulation: Mailed 11 time(s) per year
Printing Information: 92 pages in 4 colors on Glossy Stock
Press: Web Press
Binding: Perfect Bound
Mailing List Information: Names for rent
Number of Employees: 9
Sales Information: $10.5 Million

7823 Fahrney's Pens
Fahrney's Pens
1317 F Street
Washington, NW 20004
202-628-9525
800-624-7367
Fax: 301-736-2926
custserv@fahrneyspens.com
www.fahrneyspens.com

Fine name brand and limited edition writing instruments including rollerball pens, ballpens, fountain pens, pen sets, pencils, pen refills, stationery and corporate gifts
President: Christopher Sullivan
Operations Director: Stephanie Watson
VP: Donna Korper
Buyers: Jon Sullivan
Chris Sullivan
Credit Cards: AMEX; MasterCard
Catalog Cost: Free
Catalog Circulation: Mailed 5 time(s) per year to 250M
Printing Information: 48 pages in 4 colors on Glossy Stock
Press: Web Press
Binding: Saddle Stitched
Mailing List Information: Names for rent
In Business: 85 years
Number of Employees: 24
Sales Information: $ 1-3 Million

7824 H Wilson Company
H Wilson
2245 Delany Road
Waukegan, IL 60087-2065
708-339-5111
800-245-7224
Fax: 800-245-8224
info@hwilson.com
www.hwilson.com

Specialty furniture for the office, school, university, daycare or institution; full lifetime warranty on every product sold
President: Andy Tess, General Manager
Marketing Manager: Blake Olson
Fulfillment: Fob Factory
International Marketing Manager: Richard Arndt
Catalog Cost: Free
Printing Information: 44 pages in 4 colors on Glossy Stock

Press: Web Press
Binding: Saddle Stitched
Mailing List Information: Names for rent
In Business: 56 years
Number of Employees: 16

7825 Home Office Direct
Home Office Direct
8870 Darrow Road
Suite F106-Box 222
Twinsburg, OH 44087
877-709-9700
800-528-4144
Fax: 877-709-9700
info@homeofficedirect.com
www.HomeOfficeDirect.com

Office products
Chairman: Thomas Weisman
President: Jeffrey Aarons
Credit Cards: AMEX; MasterCard
In Business: 9 years

7826 Knoll Essentials
Knoll, Inc.
1235 Water Street
East Greenville, PA 18041
212-343-4190
800-343-5665
KNOLLTEXTILES@KNOLL.COM
www.Knoll.Com

Office furniture and systems
President: German Bosquez
Senior Vice President, Sales and Di: Pam Ahrens
pahrens@knoll.com
Divisional Vice President: Alan Howard
ahoward@knoll.com
Regional Director, New York: Doug Militzer
dmilitzer@knoll.com
Catalog Cost: Free
Printing Information: in 4 colors on Glossy Stock
Sales Information: $20MM to $50MM

7827 Levenger
The Levenger Store
420 South Congress Ave
Delray Beach, FL 33445-4696
561-276-2436
800-544-0880
Fax: 800-544-6910
Cservice@levenger.com
www.Levenger.Com

Collection of furnishings and accessories created to enhance your well-read life, you'll find bookcases, halogen lighting, desks, chairs, leather goods, plus personal and corporate gifts
President: Steve Leveen
CFO: Lori Leveen
Marketing Manager: Susan Devito
Production Manager: Lee Passarella
Fulfillment: Gerald Patterson
Founder: Steve Leveen
Founder: Lori Leveen
Buyers: Denise Tedaldi
Credit Cards: AMEX; MasterCard; Visa
Catalog Cost: Free
Catalog Circulation: Mailed 12 time(s) per year to 20MM
Average Order Size: $130
Printing Information: 76 pages in 4 colors on Glossy Stock
Press: Web Press
Binding: Saddle Stitched
Mailing List Information: Names for rent
List Manager: Susan Devito
List Company: Mokrynski & Associates
401 Hackensack Avenue
Hackensack, NJ 07601
2014885656
In Business: 28 years
Number of Employees: 270
Sales Information: $20MM to $50MM

7828 Photo Materials Company
Martin Yale Industries Inc
251 Wedcor Avenue
Wabash, IN 46992   260-563-0641
                         800-225-5644
                    Fax: 260-563-4575
                    www.martinyale.com

Shredders, folding machines, paper cutters, paper trimmers and mailroom equipment

President: Dawn Dials
Marketing Manager: Greg German
Production Manager: Brad Bozarth
Product Manager: David Parkhill
Catalog Cost: Free
Catalog Circulation: Mailed 1 time(s) per year
Printing Information: 52 pages in 4 colors
In Business: 75 years
Number of Employees: 129

7829 Platt Cases
Platt Luggage Inc
4051 W 51st Street
Chicago, IL 60632-4211   773-838-2000
                            800-222-1555
                       Fax: 773-838-2010
                 INFO@PLATTCASES.COM
                       www.plattcases.com

Professional cases for business and industry

President: Marc Platt
Marketing Manager: Allan Evavold
International Marketing Manager: Allan Evavold
Catalog Cost: Free
Catalog Circulation: to 50000
Printing Information:
Press: Web Press
Mailing List Information: Names for rent
In Business: 90 years
Number of Employees: 100

7830 Quill.com
Quill Lincolnshire
100 Schelter Rd.
Lincolnshire, IL 60069   847-634-6690
                            www.quill.com

Furniture, filing, storage, ink, toner, printers, computer monitors and hard drives.

Catalog Cost: Free
In Business: 60 years
Number of Employees: 500
Sales Information: $1 Billion

7831 Repromat Catalog
ACM Technologies Inc
2535 Research Drive
Corona, MA 09288-7607   951-738-9898
                            800-722-7745
                       Fax: 951-273-2174
                  askacm@acmtech.com
                       www.acmtech.com

Digital copiers, printers, fax machines, toner, thermal transfer ribbons and machinery parts

President: Shue-Shang Lin
Credit Cards: AMEX; MasterCard
Catalog Cost: Free
Catalog Circulation: Mailed 1 time(s) per year to 5M
Printing Information: 215 pages in 1 color on Matte Stock
Press: Letterpress
In Business: 22 years
Number of Employees: 52
Sales Information: $ 15 Million

7832 The Big Book
Office Depot
6600 N Military Trail
Boca Raton, FL 33496   800-463-3768
                       www.officedepot.com

Binders, calendars, planners, ink, toner, filing & storage, labels, pens, pencils, desktop & notebook computers, printers, copiers, shredders and office furniture

Chairman & CEO: Roland C. Smith
Catalog Cost: Free
Catalog Circulation: Mailed 1 time(s) per year
Printing Information: 868 pages in 4 colors
In Business: 30 years
Number of Employees: 4900
Sales Information: $14.5 Billion

7833 Upbeat
Upbeat Site Furnishings
211 N Lindbergh Boulevard
St Louis, MO 63141   314-535-5005
                            800-325-3047
                       Fax: 314-535-4419
                       www.upbeat.com

Benches, bike and skate racks, cigarette waste receptacles, entryway, events, facility maintenance, floor mats, office and lobby, park furnishings, picnic tables, pool and patio furnishings and trash

Manager: Scott Glenn
Manager: Sherry Miller
Credit Cards: AMEX; MasterCard
Catalog Cost: Free
Catalog Circulation: Mailed 6 time(s) per year to 4MM
Printing Information: 60 pages in 4 colors on Glossy Stock
Press: Web Press
Binding: Saddle Stitched
In Business: 33 years
Number of Employees: 50
Sales Information: $11 Million

7834 Whitaker Brothers
Whitaker Brothers
3 Taft Court
Rockville, MD 20850   301-230-2800
                            800-243-9226
                       Fax: 301-354-3034
              internet@whitakerbrothers.com
                  www.whitakerbrothers.com

Paper shredders

President: Joe Mitchell
Commercial Account Specialist: Eric
Govt. Account Specialist: Vivian
Customer Service Specialist: Liz
Credit Cards: AMEX; MasterCard
Printing Information: 4 pages
Binding: Perfect Bound
In Business: 69 years
Sales Information: $20MM to $50MM

7835 Wholesale Buyers Guide
Buyers Guide
6433 Topanga Canyon Ave
Suite 544
Canoga Park, CA 91331   818-342-5357
                       Fax: 818-343-0319
              sales@wholesalebuyersguide.com
                  www.wholesalebuyersguide.com

Business to business wholesale apparel, cell phones, toys, electronics, footwear, handbags, hats, health & beauty, jewelry, perfumes, tobacco & pipes, sporting goods, uniforms and dvd & video movies

President: Robin Zonte
Credit Cards: AMEX; MasterCard; Visa
Catalog Cost: Free
Catalog Circulation: Mailed 2 time(s) per year
Printing Information: 116 pages in 4 colors on Glossy Stock
Press: Web Press
Binding: Saddle Stitched
Mailing List Information: Names for rent
List Company: Direct Media
200 Pemberwick Road
Greenwich, CT 06830
203-532-3713
In Business: 117 years

Number of Employees: 120
Sales Information: $ 10-20 Million

Organizers

7836 Colonial Redi Record Corporation
Colonial Bronze Company
511 Winsted Road
Torrington, CT 06790-0207   860-489-9233
                       Fax: 800-355-7903
                 sales@colonialbronze.com
                   www.colonialbronze.com

Calendars, boards, paper pads, diaries, easel boards, appointment books, planners, presentation books and desk accessories for purchase by distributors only

President: Joe Berkovits
Credit Cards: MasterCard
Catalog Cost: Free
Printing Information: 53 pages in 4 colors
Mailing List Information: Names for rent
In Business: 90 years
Number of Employees: 25
Sales Information: $3MM to $5MM

7837 G. Neil
HR direct
PO Box 452049
Sunrise, FL 33345-2049   877-968-7471
                            800-888-4040
                       Fax: 954-846-0777
                  questions@hrdirect.com
                       www.hrdirect.com

Human resource organizers and business specialties

President: Gary Brown
CFO: Carl Drew
Marketing Manager: Kevin Embry
Production Manager: Michelle A Newsom
Fulfillment: Joe Basgall
Catalog Circulation: to 10MM
Average Order Size: $108
Printing Information: 136 pages in 4 colors on Glossy Stock
Press: Web Press
List Company: Direct Media
Greenwich, CT
Number of Employees: 250

7838 Magna Visual
Magna Visual
9400 Watson Road
St Louis, MO 63126-1596   800-472-3226
                       Fax: 314-843-0000
                       www.magnavisual.com

Magnetic steel & porcelain boards, custom color boards, double sided boards, grid/scheduling boards, magnetic accessories, chart tape, dry erase markers and water soluble pens

Chairman: Phillip Cady
President: William Cady
CFO: Diane Crews
Marketing Manager: John Winkler
Buyers: Chris Brown
Catalog Cost: Free
Catalog Circulation: Mailed 1 time(s) per year to 50M
Average Order Size: $100
Printing Information: 32 pages in 4 colors on Glossy Stock
Press: Web Press
Binding: Folded
Mailing List Information: Names for rent
List Manager: Matt Brown, Associates
In Business: 52 years
Number of Employees: 50
Sales Information: $6 Million

7839 Multiplex Versatile Display Systems
The Miller Group
St. Louis Division
1610 Design Way
Dupo, IL 62239-1820
636-343-5700
800-325-3350
Fax: 618-286-6202
info@miller-group.com
www.multiplexdisplays.com

Professional displays and display systems
for retailers, wholesalers, businesses, floor
covering and art sellers, libraries, learning
centers, and not-for-profit organizations

President: Randy Castle
Marketing Manager: Kathy Webster
kathywebster@miller-group.com
Credit Cards: AMEX; MasterCard; Visa
Catalog Cost: Free
Average Order Size: $750
Printing Information: 24 pages in 4 colors on
Glossy Stock
Binding: Folded
Mailing List Information: Names for rent
Number of Employees: 150
Sales Information: $1MM to $3MM

7840 Ultimate Office
Ultimate Office
PO Box 688
Farmingdale, NJ 07727-9701
732-780-6911
800-631-2233
Fax: 732-780-9833
customerservice@ultoffice.com
www.ultoffice.com

Binders & notebooks, binder storage carousels, clipboards, forms storage, desktop organizers, literature displays, reference
organizers, workspace solutions and
furniture

President: Craig W. Nelson
Production Manager: Dorris Gethard
Credit Cards: AMEX; MasterCard; Visa
Catalog Cost: Free
Catalog Circulation: Mailed 3 time(s) per year
to 100M
Printing Information: 21 pages in 4 colors on
Glossy Stock
Press: Web Press
Binding: Saddle Stitched
Mailing List Information: Names for rent
List Company: Direct Media
200 Pemberwick Road
Greenwich, CT 06830
203-531-1000
In Business: 25 years
Number of Employees: 25

Stationery & Forms

7841 Accountant Stationers & Printers
Accountant Stationers & Printers
742 E Washington Boulevard
Los Angeles, CA 90021
213-749-9241
800-423-9717
Fax: 213-749-4505
www.asandp.com

Accounting forms, tax forms, laser & business checks, software, filing and preparation supplies

President: Robert Rothman
Credit Cards: AMEX; MasterCard; Visa
Catalog Cost: Free
Catalog Circulation: Mailed 1 time(s) per year
Printing Information: 55 pages in 1 color
In Business: 67 years
Number of Employees: 19
Sales Information: $2,200,000

7842 American Stationery
American Stationery Company
100 N Park Avenue
Peru, IN 46970
800-822-2577
Fax: 800-253-9054
www.americanstationery.com

Stationery, holiday cards and personalized
gifts

President: Michael Bakehorn
Credit Cards: AMEX; MasterCard
Catalog Cost: Free
Mailing List Information: Names for rent
In Business: 98 years
Number of Employees: 250
Sales Information: $50MM to $100MM

7843 American Thermoplastic Company
American Thermoplastic Company
One Looseleaf Lane
P. O. Box 29
Vincent, AL 35178-0029
412-967-0900
800-245-6600
Fax: 800-344-8939
atc@binders.com
www.binders.com

Binders, index tabs and related loose-leaf
products, especially custom imprinted

President: Steven Silberman
Marketing Manager: Joseph Sprumont
Credit Cards: AMEX; MasterCard
Catalog Cost: Free
Catalog Circulation: Mailed 1 time(s) per year
Printing Information: 20 pages in 4 colors on
Glossy Stock
Binding: Saddle Stitched
Mailing List Information: Names for rent
In Business: 60 years

7844 Artistic Labels
Artistic Labels
P.O.Box 331
Colorado Springs, CO 80901
800-845-3720
webcs@artisticdirect.com
www.artisticlabels.com

Personalized address labels, address
stamps and stationery for personal and business use, and other gift items

Catalog Cost: Free
In Business: 89 years

7845 At-A-Glance
At-A-Glance
11013 W Broad St
Glen Allen, VA 23060
804-327-5200
800-880-2472
Fax: 804-897-6383
www.ataglance.com

Appointment books, desk and wall calendars

Catalog Cost: Free

7846 Brookhollow Collection
Brookhollow
12750 Merit Drive
Suite 700
Dallas, TX 75251
208-359-1000
800-272-4182
Fax: 800-822-0256
service@brookhollowcards.com
www.brookhollowcards.com

All occasion, holiday and profession specific customizable cards and calendars

Chairman: Michael Johnson
President: Erv Wiebe
Marketing Manager: Collette Rinehart
Credit Cards: AMEX; MasterCard; Visa
Catalog Cost: Free
Catalog Circulation: Mailed 1 time(s) per year
Printing Information: 32 pages in 4 colors on
Glossy Stock
Press: Web Press
Binding: Saddle Stitched
Mailing List Information: Names for rent
In Business: 50 years
Number of Employees: 650
Sales Information: $5MM to $10MM

7847 CEO Cards
CEO Cards
6712 Virgilia Ct.
Suite 101
Raleigh, NC 27616
972-712-9161
Fax: 972-712-2946
support@ceocards.com
www.ceocards.com

High quality, original greeting cards created
exclusively for business to business communications. CEO cards specializes in
All-Occasion, Thanksgiving, Holiday, and
New Year greeting cards.

Marketing Manager: Stephanie Warner
Owner & President: Paul Reiss
Credit Cards: AMEX; MasterCard
Catalog Cost: Free
Printing Information: in 4 colors
Mailing List Information: Names for rent
In Business: 5 years
Number of Employees: 9
Sales Information: $500,000

7848 Colonial Redi Record Corporation
Colonial Bronze Company
511 Winsted Road
Torrington, CT 06790-0207
860-489-9233
Fax: 860-355-7903
sales@colonialbronze.com
www.colonialbronze.com

Calendars, boards, paper pads, diaries, easel boards, appointment books, planners,
presentation books and desk accessories
for purchase by distributors only

President: Joe Berkovits
Credit Cards: MasterCard
Catalog Cost: Free
Printing Information: 53 pages in 4 colors
Mailing List Information: Names for rent
In Business: 90 years
Number of Employees: 25
Sales Information: $3MM to $5MM

7849 Day Timer
Day Timer
1 Willow Lane
East Texas, PA 18046
610-398-1151
800-457-5702
Fax: 800-452-7398
www.daytimer.com

Planners, planner covers, planner calendars, organizers, bags, briefcases, car organizers, desk accessories and sationery

President: Joe Winters
CFO: Danette Gerbino
Marketing Manager: Martha Curren
Production Manager: Glenn Large
International Marketing Manager: Pat Straubel
Credit Cards: AMEX; MasterCard; Visa
Catalog Cost: Free
Catalog Circulation: Mailed 2 time(s) per year
Mailing List Information: Names for rent
List Manager: Jerry Curran
List Company: Direct Media
In Business: 65 years
Number of Employees: 400

7850 Deluxe Small Business Services
New England Business Service, Inc. (NEBS)
500 Main St
Groton, MA 01471-1
888-823-6327
Fax: 978-449-3419
www.nebs.com

Small business management and marketing
solutions

President: Dave Saunders
Number of Employees: 8000

7851 Exclusively Weddings
Exclusively Weddings
2305 Soabar Street
Greensboro, NC 27406
800-759-7666
800-759-7666
Fax: 336-275-4165
corporate@EWeddings.com
www.exclusivelyweddings.com

Wedding invitations, wedding guest favors and bridal accessories

President: Bonnie Mcelveen Hunter
General Manager: R. David Stubbs
Director of Merchandising, Statione: Beth Vogel
Director of Marketing: Matt Mitchell
Credit Cards: AMEX; MasterCard
Catalog Cost: Free
Printing Information: 117 pages in 4 colors on Glossy Stock
Press: Web Press
Binding: Saddle Stitched
In Business: 23 years
Number of Employees: 87
Sales Information: $3MM to $5MM

7852 Farriers' Greeting Cards
Farriers' Greeting Cards-Hoofprints
13849 N 200 E
Alexandria, IN 46001
765-724-7004
800-741-5054
Fax: 765-724-4632
gina@hoofprints.com
www.hoofprints.com

Unique products for the Equine and Canine enthusiast

President: Gina Keesling
Catalog Cost: Free
In Business: 25 years
Number of Employees: 2
Sales Information: $97,000

7853 Folder Factory-Presentation Products
Folder Factory Inc.
5421 Main St. Suite 300
P.O. Box 308
Mount Jackson, VA 22842
540-984-8852
800-296-4321
Fax: 540-477-9677
admin@folders.com
www.folders.com

Pocket folders, binders, totes, folios, software & multi-media packaging, ridgid mailing envelopes, custom printing available in all products

President: Steve Gentile
Production Manager: Mack Gentile
Buyers: Alex McLeod
Credit Cards: AMEX; MasterCard
Catalog Circulation: Mailed 1 time(s) per year
Printing Information: 32 pages in 4 colors on Glossy Stock
Press: Sheetfed Press
Binding: Saddle Stitched
Mailing List Information: Names for rent
In Business: 42 years
Number of Employees: 35
Sales Information: $3MM to $5MM

7854 Gallery Collection Catalog
The Gallery Collection
65 Challenger Road
Ridgefield Park, NJ 07660
201-641-0070
800-950-7064
Fax: 800-772-1144
service@gallerycollection.com
www.gallerycollection.com

Personalized Christmas, holiday, and all occasion greeting cards

President: Alan Solow
Credit Cards: AMEX; MasterCard; Visa
Catalog Cost: Free
Catalog Circulation: Mailed 1 time(s) per year
Printing Information: 40 pages in 4 colors on

Glossy Stock
Press: Web Press
Binding: Saddle Stitched
Mailing List Information: Names for rent
List Company: Direct Media
200 Pemberwick Road
Greenwich, CT 06830
203-532-3713
In Business: 85 years
Number of Employees: 100-
Sales Information: $10,000,000 - $25,000,000

7855 Graphique de France
Graphique Boutique
9 State St
Woburn, MA 01801-2050
781-935-3415
800-444-1464
Fax: 781-935-5145
customersupport@graphiquedefrance.com
www.graphiquedefrance.com

Calendars, holiday cards and stationery

President: Jean-Jacque Toulotte
Credit Cards: AMEX; MasterCard
Catalog Cost: Free
Catalog Circulation: Mailed 1 time(s) per year
Printing Information: 200 pages in 4 colors
In Business: 27 years
Number of Employees: 46
Sales Information: $10MM to $20MM

7856 Greenwoods Collection
Holiday Classics
PO Box 599
Sunman, IN 47041-599
866-700-5030
Fax: 800-446-4510
www.greenwoodscollection.com

Holiday greeting cards, calendars and chocolates

Credit Cards: AMEX; MasterCard; Visa
Catalog Cost: Free
Catalog Circulation: Mailed 1 time(s) per year
Printing Information: 40 pages in 4 colors on Glossy Stock
Press: Web Press
Binding: Saddle Stitched
In Business: 40 years

7857 Henry Schein Office Supply Catalog
Henry Schein
135 Duryea Rd.
Melville, NY 11747
631-843-5500
www.henryschein.com

Office supplies including stationery, furniture and technology.

Chairman: Stanley M. Bergman
President: James P. Breslawski
Catalog Cost: Free
Printing Information: 190 pages in 4 colors
In Business: 84 years
Number of Employees: 1900
Sales Information: $10.6 Billion

7858 Holiday Cards for Businesses
National Wildlife Federation
11100 Wildlife Center Drive
Reston, VA 20190-5362
800-822-9919
Fax: 800-525-5562
www.nwf.org

Christmas cards, calendars and apparel with a wildlife theme

Chairman: Deborah Spalding
President: Collin O'Mara
Marketing Manager: Al Lamson
Production Manager: Robin Clark
EVP/COO: Jaime Matyas
CEO: Collin O'Mara
Buyers: Lynn Piper, Gift Accessories
Mary Lamer, Greeting Cards
Robin Clark, Apparel
Credit Cards: MasterCard; Visa
Catalog Cost: Free
Catalog Circulation: Mailed 6 time(s) per year to 20MM
Printing Information: 48 pages in 4 colors on

Glossy Stock
Press: Web Press
Binding: Saddle Stitched
Mailing List Information: Names for rent
In Business: 63 years
Number of Employees: 675

7859 Holiday Collection
National Wildlife Federation
11100 Wildlife Center Drive
Reston, VA 20190
800-822-9919
Fax: 800-525-5562
www.nwf.org

Christmas cards, calendars and apparel with a wildlife theme

Chairman: Deborah Spalding
President: Collin O'Mara
CFO: Dulce Zormelo
CEO: Collin O'Mara
Credit Cards: AMEX; MasterCard; Visa
Catalog Cost: Free
Catalog Circulation: Mailed 6 time(s) per year to 20MM
Printing Information: 48 pages in 4 colors on Glossy Stock
Press: Web Press
Binding: Saddle Stitched
Mailing List Information: Names for rent
In Business: 63 years
Number of Employees: 350

7860 Kogle Cards
Cordial Greetings
150 Kingswood Road
PO Box 8465
Mankato, MN 56002-8465
800-257-8276
Fax: 800-842-9371
customerservice@cordialgreetings.com
www.cordialgreetings.com

Greeting cards and promotional gifts for businesses

Marketing Manager: Michelle Johnson
Credit Cards: AMEX; MasterCard; Visa
Catalog Cost: Free
Catalog Circulation: Mailed 1 time(s) per year
Printing Information: 80 pages in 4 colors on Glossy Stock
Press: Web Press
Binding: Saddle Stitched
In Business: 26 years
Number of Employees: 50
Sales Information: $1MM to $3MM

7861 Kraftbilt
Kraftbilt
PO Box 800
Tulsa, OK 74101
800-331-7290
Fax: 866-547-6967
kbcustomerservice@kraftbilt.com
www.kraftbilt.com

Tax forms, check register systems, oil & gas forms and products, tagging products, accounting and office supplies

President: Debbie Rule
Credit Cards: AMEX; MasterCard; Visa
Catalog Cost: Free
Catalog Circulation: Mailed 1 time(s) per year
Printing Information: 40 pages in 4 colors on Matte Stock
Binding: Saddle Stitched
In Business: 50 years

7862 Leanin' Tree
Trumble Greetings Inc
PO Box 9800
Boulder, CO 80301
303-530-7768
800-525-0656
Fax: 800-777-4770
info@leanintree.com
www.leanintree.com

Cards for all occassions

Chairman: Ed Trumble
President: Tom Trumble
Founder: Ed Trumble

Credit Cards: MasterCard; Visa
Catalog Cost: Free
Printing Information: 24 pages in 4 colors
Binding: Saddle Stitched
Mailing List Information: Names for rent
In Business: 55 years

7863 Merrimade
Merrimade
PO Box 207
Peru, IN 46970 800-344-4256
www.merrimade.com

Personalized paper products and personal stationery

Credit Cards: AMEX; MasterCard; Visa
Catalog Cost: Free
Catalog Circulation: Mailed 2 time(s) per year to 1000
Average Order Size: $150
Printing Information: 24 pages in 4 colors on Glossy Stock
Press: Web Press
Binding: Saddle Stitched
Mailing List Information: Names for rent
In Business: 94 years
Number of Employees: 25
Sales Information: $1MM to $3MM

7864 Museum Shop Catalog
Art Institute of Chicago
111 South Michigan Avenue
Chicago, IL 60603-6404 800-518-4214
885-301-9612
Fax: 312-849-4981
mshop@artic.edu
www.artinstituteshop.org

Museum gifts, stationery and apparel

President: Thomas Ahn
Credit Cards: AMEX; MasterCard; Visa
Catalog Cost: Free
Catalog Circulation: Mailed 1 time(s) per year
Printing Information: 44 pages in 4 colors on Glossy Stock
List Company: Walter Karl
1 Blue Hill Plaza
Pear River, NY 10965
Number of Employees: 1000

7865 Paper Access
Paper Access
23 W 18th St
New York, NY 10011-4601 212-463-7035
Fax: 212-463-7022
info@paperpresentation.com
www.paperpresentation.com

Stationery and matching envelopes and printing software

President: Chris Brown
VP: Arthur Rejay
Credit Cards: AMEX; MasterCard; Visa
Catalog Cost: Free
Catalog Circulation: Mailed 2 time(s) per year to 20M
Printing Information: 64 pages in 4 colors
Mailing List Information: Names for rent
List Manager: Venture Communications
List Company: Venture Communications
60 Madison Avenue, 3rd Floor
New York, NY 10010
212-684-4800
In Business: 20 years
Number of Employees: 25
Sales Information: $ 3.6 Million

7866 PaperDirect Events
PaperDirect
P.O. Box 1151
Minneapolis, MN 55440-1151 800-272-7377
Fax: 800-443-2973
volumesales@paperdirect.com
www.paperdirect.com

Do-it-yourself stationery; themes for occasions and events

President: Tim Arland
CFO: Kirby Heck
Credit Cards: AMEX; MasterCard
Catalog Cost: Free
Printing Information: in 4 colors
In Business: 29 years
Number of Employees: 1200
Sales Information: $78 MM

7867 Pengad
Pengad,Inc
55 Oak Street
P.O.Box 99
Bayonne, NJ 07002-99 201-436-5625
800-631-6989
Fax: 201-436-9550
customerservice@pengad.com
www.pengad.com

Paper products and court reporter supplies

President: Tom Pierson
Owner: Jules Penn
Credit Cards: AMEX; MasterCard
Catalog Cost: Free
Catalog Circulation: Mailed 1 time(s) per year
Printing Information: 12 pages in 4 colors
In Business: 79 years
Sales Information: $ 10-20 Million

7868 Personalized Acknowledgement Cards
The Stationery Studio
3029 E Washington Street
Indianapolis, IN 46201-4279 317-262-3080
800-878-5223
Fax: 317-262-3088
customerservice@thestationerystudio.com
www.thestationerystudio.com

Engraved acknowledgement cards for funeral applications and nonpersonalized cards

Marketing Manager: Vickie Kashon
Production Manager: Mark Hurt
Owner: Renee Redman
Credit Cards: AMEX; MasterCard
Catalog Circulation: Mailed 1 time(s) per year
Printing Information:
Press: Web Press
In Business: 21 years

7869 Podiatry Reference Catalog
Medical Arts Press® Corporation
PO Box 43200
Minneapolis, MN 55443-200 800-982-3400
Fax: 800-789-8955
www.medicalartspress.com

Podiatry practice supplies, stationery and forms

Credit Cards: AMEX; MasterCard
Catalog Cost: Free
Catalog Circulation: Mailed 2 time(s) per year
Printing Information: 720 pages in 4 colors
Mailing List Information: Names for rent
In Business: 50 years
Number of Employees: 600

7870 Posty Cards
Posty Cards
1600 Olive Street
Kansas City, MO 64127-2500 816-231-2323
800-821-7968
Fax: 888-577-3800
customerservice@postycards.com
www.postycards.com

Greeting cards and calendars

Chairman: Lance Jessee
President: Erick Jessee
Credit Cards: AMEX; MasterCard
Catalog Cost: Free
Catalog Circulation: Mailed 3 time(s) per year to 10000
Average Order Size: $106
Printing Information: 24 pages in 4 colors
Press: Web Press
Binding: Saddle Stitched

Mailing List Information: Names for rent
In Business: 69 years
Number of Employees: 45
Sales Information: $10MM to $20MM

7871 TRIMCO
Trimco Display LLC
152 West 25th Street
Brooklyn, NY 10001-1902 212-627-2809
800-874-6261
Fax: 212-627-1805
info@trimco-display.com
www.trimco-display.com

Christmas cards and decorations for businesses

President: Ken Stolls
kstolls@lfs-trimco.com
Creative Director: Sean Sager
ssager@lfs-trimco.com
Showroom/Marketing Support: Rebecca Marchetti
rmarchetti@lfs-trimco.com
Showroom/Sales Support: Nicole Rosenthal
nrosenthal@lfs-trimco.com
Credit Cards: AMEX; MasterCard; Visa
Catalog Circulation: Mailed 1 time(s) per year
Printing Information: 23 pages in 4 colors on Glossy Stock
Press: Web Press
Binding: Saddle Stitched
In Business: 40 years
Number of Employees: 50-1
Sales Information: $1,000,000 - $5,000,000

7872 Tenenz
Tenenz, Inc.
9655 Penn Avenue South
Minneapolis, MN 55431 952-227-1713
800-888-5803
Fax: 800-638-0015
mail@tenenz.com
www.tenenz.com

Accounting supplies, presentation materials, tax forms, business checks, stationery and software

Credit Cards: AMEX; MasterCard; Visa
Catalog Cost: Free
Printing Information: on Glossy Stock
Press: Web Press
Binding: Saddle Stitched
Mailing List Information: Names for rent
List Manager: Lee Myers
In Business: 40 years
Sales Information: Under $500,000

7873 Thermographed Business Cards
J.B. Gray & Son, Inc.
19830 SW Stafford Road
West Linn, OR 97068-3852 503-673-0660
Fax: 503-673-0330

Various typestyles, logos and borders for business cards

President: Tom Farkas
Credit Cards: MasterCard
Catalog Cost: Free
Catalog Circulation: Mailed 1 time(s) per year
Printing Information: 40 pages in 2 colors
In Business: 70 years
Number of Employees: 6
Sales Information: $1MM to $3MM

7874 UNICEF Catalog
United States Fund for UNICEF
125 Maiden Lane
New York, NY 10038 800-367-5437
www.unicefusa.org

Greeting cards, stationery and gifts

Chairman: Vince Hemmer
President: Caryl M. Stern
CFO: Edward G. Lloyd
Marketing Manager: Jose Carbonell
Production Manager: Laura Calassano
Senior Vice President, Development: Barron Segar

Vice President, HR: William B. Sherwood
VP, Finance & Budget: Richard Esserman
Credit Cards: AMEX; MasterCard; Visa
Catalog Circulation: Mailed 2 time(s) per year
Printing Information: in 4 colors
In Business: 69 years
Number of Employees: 100

7875   Unicef Corporate Card Collection
UNICEF United States Fund
125 Maiden Lane
New York, NY 10038   212-686-5522
                                   800-367-5437
                          Fax: 212-779-1679
                 www.shopbusiness.unicefusa.org/

Seasonal cards that convey the Unicef message

Chairman: Vince Hemmer
President: Caryl M. Stern
CFO: Edward G. Lloyd
Marketing Manager: Sylvia Gonzales
SVP, Marketing and Communications:
Francesco De Flaviis
SVP, Development: Barron Segar
Vice President, Finance & Budget: Richard
Esserman
Credit Cards: AMEX; MasterCard; Visa
Catalog Cost: Free
Catalog Circulation: Mailed 1 time(s) per year
to 1MM
Printing Information: 20 pages in 4 colors
Press: Web Press
Binding: Saddle Stitched
Number of Employees: 175

Supplies

7876   ACA Corporate Awards
Award Company of America
3200 Rice Mine Road NE
PO Box 2029
Tuscaloosa, AL 35406-1510   205-248-1621
                                    800-633-2021
           customerservice@awardcompany.com
                      www.awardcompany.com

Awards, plaques, trophies, ribbons, specialized greeting cards, promotional and specialty items.

President: Michael Reilly
CFO: Shane Elmore
Credit Cards: AMEX; MasterCard; Visa
Catalog Cost: Free
Mailing List Information: Names for rent
In Business: 40 years
Number of Employees: 200
Sales Information: $ 10-20 Million

7877   ACA For Churches Only
Award Company of America
3200 Rice Mine Road NE
PO Box 2029
Tuscaloosa, AL 35406-1510   205-248-1621
                                    800-633-2021
           customerservice@awardcompany.com
                      www.awardcompany.com

Awards, plaques, trophies, ribbons, specialized greeting cards, promotional and specialty items.

President: Michael Reilly
CFO: Shane Elmore
Credit Cards: AMEX; MasterCard; Visa
Catalog Cost: Free
Mailing List Information: Names for rent
In Business: 40 years
Number of Employees: 200
Sales Information: $ 10-20 Million

7878   ACA School Essentials
Award Company of America
3200 Rice Mine Road NE
PO Box 2029
Tuscaloosa, AL 35406-1510   205-248-1621
                                    800-633-2021
           customerservice@awardcompany.com
                      www.awardcompany.com

Awards, plaques, trophies, ribbons, specialized greeting cards, promotional and specialty items.

President: Michael Reilly
CFO: Shane Elmore
Credit Cards: AMEX; MasterCard; Visa
Catalog Cost: Free
Mailing List Information: Names for rent
In Business: 40 years
Number of Employees: 200
Sales Information: $ 10-20 Million

7879   ATD-American Catalog
ATD-AMERICAN
93 Old York Road
Suite 310
Jenkintown, PA 19046   866-523-2300
                                    888-283-2378
                          Fax: 954-323-1853
                            website@atd.com
                               www.atd.com

Bookcases, displays, computer workstations, desks, filing, storage, partitions and tables

President: Arnie Zaslow
Marketing Manager: Irvin Greenberg
Director of Sales: Bill McDonough
Credit Cards: AMEX; MasterCard; Visa
Catalog Cost: Free
Catalog Circulation: Mailed 2 time(s) per year
Printing Information: 85 pages
List Company: Direct Media
In Business: 86 years
Number of Employees: 90
Sales Information: $35 Million

7880   Betty Mills Catalog
The Betty Mills Company
2121 S El Camino Real
Suite C-120
San Mateo, CA 94403-1848   650-344-8228
                                    800-238-8964
                          Fax: 650-341-1888
                            www.bettymills.com

Cleaning & janitorial products including brooms, brushes, floor & carpet care, cleaning chemicals, mops, buckets, recycling containers, vacuums and waste receptacles

President: Ofer Sabadosh
Managing Director: Steven Cinelli
Credit Cards: AMEX; MasterCard; Visa
Catalog Cost: $1.5
Catalog Circulation: to 100K
Average Order Size: $200
Printing Information: 250 pages on Glossy
Stock
Press: Letterpress
Binding: Perfect Bound
Mailing List Information: Names for rent
In Business: 10 years
Number of Employees: 16
Sales Information: $1.4 Million

7881   Bostitch
Stanley Fastening Systems,L.P.
701 E Jopra RD.
Towson, MD 21286-700   401-884-2500
                                    800-556-6696
                          Fax: 800-842-9360
                              www.bostitch.com

Hardware and supplies

Chairman: Nolan Archibald
President: John Lundgren
CFO: Donald Allan, Jr.
EVP and COO: James M. Loree

SVP and CIO/SFS:
Credit Cards: MasterCard
Catalog Circulation: Mailed 2 time(s) per year
Printing Information: 16 pages
Binding: Saddle Stitched
In Business: 118 years

7882   Church Identification Products
Lake Shore Industries Inc
1817 Poplar Street
PO Box 3427
Erie, PA 16508-427   800-458-0463
                          Fax: 814-453-4293
                            info@lsisigns.com
                             www.lsisigns.com

Books, plaques, architectural letters and recognition walls, as well as cemetery signs and markers

President: Leo Bruno
Marketing Manager: Shirley Bruno
Production Manager: David Mays
Credit Cards: MasterCard
Mailing List Information: Names for rent
In Business: 106 years
Number of Employees: 19
Sales Information: $1,400,000

7883   Comfort Telecommunications
Comfort Telecommunications
1407 SE 47th Terrace
Cape Coral, FL 33904   239-945-3224
                                    800-399-3224
                          Fax: 239-945-0288
                           sales@comfortel.com
                             www.comfortel.com

New and reconditioned telephones and telephone headsets

President: Jon Minto
CFO: Sandy Laughing
Credit Cards: AMEX; MasterCard; Visa
Catalog Cost: Free
In Business: 28 years
Number of Employees: 50
Sales Information: $6 Million

7884   DEMCO Library Supplies & Equipment
Demco imagine whats possible
PO BOX 7488
Madison, WI 53707   608-241-1201
                          Fax: 608-241-0666
                          president@demco.com
                              www.demco.com

Office, school, library supplies and furniture

Chairman: John Wall
President: Trevor Taylor
CFO: Don Rogers
Fulfillment: Bill Erickson
Credit Cards: AMEX; MasterCard; Visa
Catalog Cost: Free
Catalog Circulation: Mailed 1 time(s) per year
Printing Information: 880 pages in 4 colors on
Glossy Stock
Press: Web Press
Mailing List Information: Names for rent
List Manager: Jeff McLaughlin
In Business: 95 years
Number of Employees: 10
Sales Information: $830,000

7885   Deluxe Enterprise
Deluxe Enterprise
3680 Victoria St. N
Shoreview, MN 55126   800-865-1913
                              www.deluxe.com

Checks, business forms, office supplies and promotional products.

CEO: Lee Schram
Catalog Cost: Free
Mailing List Information: Names for rent
List Manager: Mel Reessi, Direct Media
List Company: Direct Media
In Business: 101 years
Number of Employees: 6000
Sales Information: $1.77 Billion

7886 **Deluxe Small Business Services**
New England Business Service, Inc. (NEBS
500 Main St
Groton, MA 01471-1 888-823-6327
Fax: 978-449-3419
www.nebs.com

Small business management and marketing solutions

President: Dave Saunders
Number of Employees: 8000

7887 **Dental Reference Catalog**
Medical Arts Press® Corporation
PO Box 43200
Minneapolis, MN 55443-200 800-328-2179
Fax: 800-328-0023
www.medicalartspress.com

Office supplies, furniture and forms

Credit Cards: AMEX; MasterCard
Catalog Cost: Free
Catalog Circulation: Mailed 2 time(s) per year
Printing Information: 825 pages in 4 colors
Mailing List Information: Names for rent
In Business: 54 years
Number of Employees: 600

7888 **Drawing Board**
Drawing Board Printing
101 East Ninth Street
Waynesboro, PA 17268 800-527-9530
Fax: 800-253-1838
customerservice@drawingboard.com
www.drawingboard.com

Imprinted products such as labels, envelopes, stationery, forms, checks and promotional products

Credit Cards: AMEX; MasterCard
Catalog Cost: Free
Catalog Circulation: Mailed 12 time(s) per year
Printing Information: 100 pages in 4 colors on Newsprint
Press: Web Press
Binding: Saddle Stitched
Number of Employees: 250

7889 **Emergency Medical Products**
Emergency Medical Products, Inc
5235 International Drive
Suite B
Cudahy, WI 53110 262-513-5753
800-558-6270
Fax: 800-558-1551
service@buyemp.com
www.buyemp.com

Emergency and medical supplies for your home or office, EMS, rescue campus & safety infection, pandemic control, hospital & clinic supplies, first aid

Chairman: Ronald Reed
President: Timothy Helz
Credit Cards: AMEX; MasterCard; Visa
Catalog Cost: Free
Catalog Circulation: Mailed 3 time(s) per year
Average Order Size: $400
Printing Information: 600 pages in 4 colors
Press: Web Press
Binding: Perfect Bound
In Business: 43 years
Number of Employees: 60

7890 **Eye Care Reference Catalog**
Medical Arts Press® Corporation
PO Box 43200
Minneapolis, MN 55443-200 800-328-2179
Fax: 800-328-0023
www.medicalartspress.com

Office supplies, specialized eye care products and stationery

Credit Cards: AMEX; MasterCard
Catalog Cost: Free
Catalog Circulation: Mailed 2 time(s) per year

Printing Information: 726 pages in 4 colors
Mailing List Information: Names for rent
In Business: 58 years
Number of Employees: 600

7891 **Folder Express Catalog**
Folder Express
11616 I Street
Omaha, NE 68137-1212 402-334-0788
800-322-1064
Fax: 402-330-8271
www.folderexpress.com

Presentation folders: sold through value added reseller, printers, marketing firms, advertising agencies, promotional products reseller

President: Jim Dswift
CFO: Michael J. Landis
Marketing Manager: Doug Boysen
Vice President Strategic Partners: Jeff Nraunstein
Chief Information Officer: Lix Devieb
General Manager: David Crysler
generalmanager@folderexpress.com
Credit Cards: AMEX; MasterCard
Catalog Cost: Free
Catalog Circulation: to 300M
Average Order Size: $750
Printing Information: 48 pages in 4 colors on Glossy Stock
Press: Sheetfed Press
Binding: Folded
Mailing List Information: Names for rent
List Manager: Doug Boysen
In Business: 88 years
Number of Employees: 200

7892 **Global Industrial Catalog**
Global Industrial
11 Harbor Park Dr.
Port Washington, NY 11050 Fax: 888-381-2868
www.globalindustrial.com

Industrial equipment and business supplies.

President: Bob Dooley
In Business: 67 years
Sales Information: $180 Million

7893 **H&L Biz'n Artz**
H&L Biz'n Artz
4712 Norma Drive NE
Albuquerque, NM 87109-1740 505-296-5805
800-854-2299
hlbiznartz@gmail.com
www.hlbiznartz.com

Home owned custom printing, design services and unusual gifts

President: Patricia Hostetter-Lopez
Credit Cards: AMEX; MasterCard
Catalog Cost: Free
Catalog Circulation: Mailed 2 time(s) per year to 20M
Printing Information: 20 pages in 4 colors on Glossy Stock
Mailing List Information: Names for rent
List Manager: Newt Paletz
In Business: 24 years
Number of Employees: 50
Sales Information: $5,000,000 - $10,000,000

7894 **Henry Schein Office Supply Catalog**
Henry Schein
135 Duryea Rd.
Melville, NY 11747 631-843-5500
www.henryschein.com

Office supplies including stationery, furniture and technology.

Chairman: Stanley M. Bergman
President: James P. Breslawski
Catalog Cost: Free
Printing Information: 190 pages in 4 colors
In Business: 84 years
Number of Employees: 1900
Sales Information: $10.6 Billion

7895 **Kudos by Paper Direct**
Paper Direct
Customer Service Department
1005 E. Woodmen Road
Colorado Springs, CO 80920-3570800-272-7377
Fax: 719-534-1741
customerservice@paperdirect.com
www.paperdirect.com

Offers an extensive line of products to reward, recognize and motivate employees

President: Wendy Huxta
CFO: Kirby Heck
Credit Cards: AMEX; MasterCard; Visa
Catalog Cost: Free
Catalog Circulation: Mailed 4 time(s) per year
Printing Information: in 4 colors
Binding: Saddle Stitched
In Business: 26 years
Number of Employees: 850

7896 **Leslie Company**
Leslie Company
PO Box 610
Olathe, KS 66051 800-255-6210
Fax: 800-708-7066
info@leslieco.com
www.leslieco.com

Binders, calendars, index tabs, pocket folders, product templates and book binding & printing

President: Jerald Byrd
Marketing Manager: Michael Byrd
Credit Cards: AMEX; MasterCard; Visa
Catalog Cost: Free
Catalog Circulation: Mailed 1 time(s) per year to 40M
Printing Information: 84 pages in 4 colors on Glossy Stock
Press: Letterpress
Binding: Perfect Bound
Mailing List Information: Names for rent
In Business: 38 years
Number of Employees: 100
Sales Information: $10.3 Million

7897 **Luckner Steel Shelving**
Karp Associates
260 Spagnoli Road
Melville, NY 11747 631-768-8300
800-888-4212
Fax: 631-768-8350
info@karpinc.com
www.Karpinc.Com

Steel shelving, access doors for walls, floors, and ceilings

President: Burt Gold
Printing Information: 20 pages
In Business: 58 years
Number of Employees: 75
Sales Information: $20MM to $50MM

7898 **Monarch Accounting Supplies**
Monarch
750 Main Street
Holyoke, MA 01040 413-536-3444
800-828-6718
Fax: 413-536-3477
www.monarchtaxforms.com

Tax forms, accounting, auditing and bookkeeping supplies

President: William Grierson
Credit Cards: AMEX; MasterCard; Visa
Catalog Cost: Free
Catalog Circulation: Mailed 1 time(s) per year
Printing Information: 18 pages in 2 colors on Newsprint
Binding: Folded
Mailing List Information: Names for rent
List Manager: William Grierson
In Business: 62 years

7899 Mossburg's Sign Products
Mossburg's Sign Products
631 Gossett Road
Spartanburg, SC 29307-340   864-699-2700
800-845-6140
Fax: 864-699-2515
sales@mossburgsign.com
www.Mossburgsign.Com

Sign products
President: Gary Mossburg
Credit Cards: MasterCard; Visa
Catalog Circulation: Mailed 1 time(s) per year
Printing Information: 22 pages in 2 colors
In Business: 33 years
Sales Information: $1MM to $3MM

7900 New England Etching Company
New England Etching Company
23 Spring St
Holyoke, MA 01040-5794   413-532-9482
Fax: 413-532-3359
info@newenglandetching.com
www.neetching.com

Name plates, labels and architectual signage and awards
Marketing Manager: Craig Foerster
Operations Manager: Walt Foerster Jr
Accounts Receivable: Jason Foerster
Customer Support: Joanne Marge
Catalog Cost: Free
Printing Information: 4 pages
In Business: 84 years
Number of Employees: 20-5
Sales Information: $1,000,000 to $4,999,999

7901 PaperDirect
PaperDirect
P.O. Box 1151
Minneapolis, MN 55440-1151   800-272-7377
Fax: 800-443-2973
volumesales@paperdirect.com
www.paperdirect.com

Paper for all laser printer copier and desktop publishing needs
President: Tim Arland
CFO: Kirby Heck
Credit Cards: AMEX; MasterCard; Visa
Catalog Cost: Free
Catalog Circulation: Mailed 5 time(s) per year
Printing Information: 95 pages in 4 colors on Glossy Stock
Press: Web Press
Binding: Saddle Stitched
In Business: 29 years
Number of Employees: 1200
Sales Information: $ 78 Million

7902 Pengad
Pengad,Inc
55 Oak Street
P.O.Box 99
Bayonne, NJ 07002-99   201-436-5625
800-631-6989
Fax: 201-436-9550
customerservice@pengad.com
www.pengad.com

Paper products and court reporter supplies
President: Tom Pierson
Owner: Jules Penn
Credit Cards: AMEX; MasterCard
Catalog Cost: Free
Catalog Circulation: Mailed 1 time(s) per year
Printing Information: 12 pages in 4 colors
In Business: 79 years
Sales Information: $ 10-20 Million

7903 Professional Insurance Agents
PIA
25 Chamberlain St
PO Box 997
Glenmont, NY 12077-997   800-424-4244
Fax: 888-225-6935
pia@pia.org
www.pia.org

Office supplies for insurance agents
President: Douglas Culkin
Credit Cards: AMEX; MasterCard
Catalog Cost: Free
Catalog Circulation: Mailed 1 time(s) per year
Printing Information: in 1 color
Number of Employees: 70

7904 Quill.com
Quill Lincolnshire
100 Schelter Rd.
Lincolnshire, IL 60069   847-634-6690
www.quill.com

Furniture, filing, storage, ink, toner, printers, computer monitors and hard drives.
Catalog Cost: Free
In Business: 60 years
Number of Employees: 500
Sales Information: $1 Billion

7905 Successories
Successories
2915 S. Congress Ave
Building B / Unit
Delray Beach, FL 33445   754-220-2942
800-535-2773
Fax: 561-952-4097
ContactUs@successories.com
www.successories.com

Office inspirational products: framed prints, desk accessories
President: Warren Struhl
Credit Cards: AMEX; MasterCard
Catalog Cost: Free
Printing Information: in 4 colors
In Business: 29 years

7906 Uline Shipping Supply Corporate Office Catalog
Uline Shipping Supply Specialists
12575 Uline Drive
Pleasant Prairie, WI 53158   847-473-3000
800-295-5510
Fax: 800-295-5571
customer.service@uline.com
www.uline.com

Shipping supplies including bags, bar code labels, scales, shrinkwrap, cushioning, mailers and moving supplies
President: Liz Uihlein
CEO: Dick Uihlein
Vice President: Duke Uihlein
Vice President: Steve Uihlein
Catalog Circulation: Mailed 2 time(s) per year
Printing Information: 664 pages in 4 colors
In Business: 35 years

7907 Uline Shipping Supply Specialists
Uline
12575 Uline Drive
Pleasant Prairie, WI 53158   262-612-4200
800-295-5510
Fax: 800-295-5571
customer.service@uline.com
www.uline.com

Uline offers over 20,000 boxes, plastic poly bags, mailing tubes, warehouse supplies and bubble wrap for storage, packaging, or shipping supplies
President: Liz Uihlein
CEO: Dick Uihlein
Vice President: Duke Uihlein
Vice President: Steve Uihlein

Buyers: Brian Uihlein
Phil Hunt
Credit Cards: AMEX; MasterCard; Visa
Catalog Cost: Free
Catalog Circulation: Mailed 2 time(s) per year
Printing Information: 664 pages in 4 colors on Glossy Stock
Press: Web Press
Binding: Saddle Stitched
Mailing List Information: Names for rent
In Business: 35 years
Number of Employees: 250
Sales Information: $ 20-50 Million

Optical
Eyewear & Accessories

7908 Arbill Safety Products
Arbill
10450 Drummond Road
Philadelphia, PA 19154   800-523-5367
info@arbill.com
www.arbill.com

Personal protective clothing, eye and hearing protection, head gear, respiratory equipment, back supports, ergonomic equipment, fall protection equipment, confined space protection, spill clean-up
President: Robyn Zlotkin
CFO: Keith Daviston
Production Manager: Bill Gabriele
Chief Executive Officer: Julie Copeland
Director of Operations: Bill Keay
Credit Cards: AMEX; MasterCard
Catalog Cost: Free
In Business: 72 years
Number of Employees: 55
Sales Information: $ 10 Million

7909 Ophthalmic Instrument Company
Opthalmic Instrument Co., Inc
378 Page Street
#5
Stoughton, MA 02072   781-341-2070
800-272-2070
Fax: 781-341-5060
www.oic2020.com

Ophthalmic testing and lab equipment for professionals
Marketing Manager: Geoffrey Sherrill
Credit Cards: MasterCard
Catalog Circulation: Mailed 1 time(s) per year
Printing Information: 303 pages on Matte Stock
In Business: 37 years
Number of Employees: 15

7910 Titmus Optical
Serian Protection Optical, Inc.
15801 Woods Edge Road
Colonial Heights, VA 23834-2742   800-446-1802
800-446-1802
Fax: 800-544-0346
www.titmus.com

Prescription protective eyewear, vision screening instruments, street designs dress eyewear and accessories
President: Thomas Boeltz
In Business: 107 years
Number of Employees: 500
Sales Information: $25,000,000 - $50,000,000

Supplies & Devices

7911 Abrisa Industrial Glass
ABRISA
200 S. Hallock Drive
Santa Paula, CA 93060-9646   805-525-4902
877-622-7472
Fax: 805-525-8604
info@abrisatechnologies.com
www.abrisa.com

Sight glasses, optical instruments and precision fabrication

President: Richard K Selfridge
CFO: Mark Grout
Marketing Manager: Jim Hooker
jhooker@abrisa.com
Production Manager: E Selfridge
VP, General Manager: Susan Hirst
shirst@abrisa.com
Quality Control: Marco Rojas
mrojas@abrisa.com
Credit Cards: AMEX; MasterCard
Catalog Cost: Free
Printing Information: 40 pages
In Business: 30 years
Number of Employees: 75
Sales Information: $5,000,000 - $10,000,000

7912 Bond Optics

Bond Optics
76 Etna Road
PO Box 422
Lebanon, NH 03766-422   603-448-2300
Fax: 603-448-5489
sales@bondoptics.com
www.Bondoptics.Com

Precision optical component fabrication

President: Leonard Guaraldi
VP and General Manager: Elliot Matteson
Mailing List Information: Names for rent
In Business: 56 years
Number of Employees: 60
Sales Information: $5,000,000 - $10,000,000

7913 Collimated Holes

Collimated Holes, Inc.
460 Division Street
Building 1
Campbell, CA 95008-6923   408-374-5080
Fax: 408-374-0670
contact@collimatedholes.com
www.Collimatedholes.Com

Optic products and engineering equipment

President: Richard W Mead
Marketing Manager: John Ellis
Production Manager: Wayne Wooley
Vice President: Daniel J. Dickerson
Sales Engineering: Matt Fate
Purchasing Agent : Patrick J. Davis
In Business: 40 years
Number of Employees: 30
Sales Information: $1,000,000 - $5,000,000

7914 Commercial Optical Manufacturing

Commercial Optical Manufacturing, Inc.
118 Bridge Street
Huntington, WV 25702-1520   304-523-0193
800-720-0193
Fax: 304-523-5873
info@commercialoptical.com
www.Comioptical.Com

Optical components

President: Kathy Runyon
CFO: Kathy Runyon
In Business: 69 years
Number of Employees: 25
Sales Information: $1,000,000 - $5,000,000

7915 Dominar

Dominar, Inc.
734 Aldo Avenue
Santa Clara, CA 95054-2210   408-496-0508
Fax: 408-496-0910
dominfo@dominar-inc.com
www.dominar-inc.com

Optical coatings

President: Dale Hansen
Founder: Dale Hansen
C.O.O.: John Ellis
Credit Cards: AMEX; MasterCard
In Business: 26 years
Number of Employees: 5
Sales Information: Under $500M

7916 Evaporated Coatings

Evaporated Coatings, Inc
2365 Maryland Road
Willow Grove, PA 19090-1708   215-659-3080
Fax: 215-659-1275
sales@evapcoat.com
www.evaporatedcoatings.com

Thin films for control of optical properties

President: Robert Schaffer
Marketing Manager: SL Schaffer
In Business: 50 years
Number of Employees: 42
Sales Information: $1MM to $3MM

7917 Force

EMCORE Corporation
2015 Chestnut Street
Alhambra, CA 91803   505-332-5000
800-732-5250
Fax: 505-332-3402
www.emcore.com

Fiber optics and electronic products

President: Hong Q. Hou Ph.D.
CFO: Mark B. Weinswig
Marketing Manager: Rod Ballard, VP Sales/Marketing
Production Manager: KB Vandyke, VP Operations
Chief Administrative Officer: Monica Van Berkel
General Counsel and Corporate Secre: Alfredo Gomez
EVP and General Manager: Brad Clevenger Ph.D.
Buyers: RB Snuffer
Credit Cards: MasterCard; Visa
Catalog Cost: Free
Printing Information: 16 pages in 4 colors on Glossy Stock
Press: Sheetfed Press
Binding: Saddle Stitched
Mailing List Information: Names for rent
In Business: 23 years
Number of Employees: 75
Sales Information: $10,000,000 - $25,000,000

7918 General Scientific Corporation

SurgiTEl
77 Enterprise Dr
Ann Arbor, MI 48103-9503   734-996-9200
800-959-0153
Fax: 734-662-0520
www.Surgitel.Com

Manufacturers of precision optics

President: Jin Chang
In Business: 82 years
Number of Employees: 40
Sales Information: $10MM to $20MM

7919 Hardin Optical Company

Hardin Optical Company
PO Box 219
Bandon, OR 97411-219   541-347-9467
800-394-3307
Fax: 541-347-8176
optics@hardinoptical.com
www.hardin-optical.com

Optical components

President: Larry Hardin
CFO: Joyce Hardin
In Business: 44 years
Number of Employees: 30
Sales Information: $1,000,000 - $5,000,000

7920 Headsets.com

Headsets
211 Austin Street
San Francisco, CA 94109-5473   415-474-1106
800-432-3738
Fax: 800-457-0467
info@headsets.com
www.headsets.com

Headsets for cell phones, telephones and computers

President: Mike Faith
Production Manager: Chris Hicken
CEO: Mike Faith
Shipping Manager: Jake Cohen
jake@headsets.com
Credit Cards: AMEX; MasterCard
Catalog Cost: Free
Catalog Circulation: to 12M
Printing Information: 48 pages in 4 colors on Glossy Stock
Binding: Saddle Stitched
In Business: 15 years
Sales Information: $ 10-20 Million

7921 Hornell Speedglas Catalog

3M
3M Center
St. Paul, MN 55144-1000   330-425-8880
888-364-3577
Fax: 330-425-4576
solutions.3m.com

Speedglas welding shield lens

Chairman: Inge Thulin
President: Inge Thulin
Marketing Manager: Jesse G. Singh
SVP, Business Transformation & IT: Julie L. Bushman
EVP, Health Care Business Group: Joaquin Delgado
SVP, Legal Affairs/General Counsel: Ivan K. Fong
Number of Employees: 8800
Sales Information: $30 Billion

7922 Incom

Incom
294 Southbridge Road
Charlton, MA 01507-528   508-909-2200
Fax: 508-765-0041
sales@incomusa.com
www.incomusa.com

Fiber optic plastics

President: Anthony Detarando
In Business: 38 years
Number of Employees: 200
Sales Information: $10,000,000 - $25,000,000

7923 Keystone View Company

Keystone View Company
2200 Dickerson Road
Reno, NV 89503-4906   775-324-5375
866-574-6360
Fax: 775-324-5375
sales@mastdev.com
www.keystoneview.com

Vision testers and vision training instruments

Credit Cards: MasterCard; Visa
Printing Information: 45 pages
Number of Employees: 5
Sales Information: 3MM-5MM

7924 Meller Optics

Meller Optics
120 Corliss Street
Providence, RI 02904   401-331-3717
800-821-0180
Fax: 401-331-0519
sales@melleroptics.com
www.melleroptics.com

Optical components

President: David Lydon
CFO: David Lydon
Marketing Manager: Steve Lydon
Production Manager: Ted Turnquist
Catalog Circulation: to 800
Printing Information: 3 pages in 4 colors on Glossy Stock
Press: Web Press
Binding: Folded
Mailing List Information: Names for rent

List Manager: Steve Lydon
In Business: 75 years
Number of Employees: 35
Sales Information: $1,000,000 - $5,000,000

7925 Newport Thin Film Laboratory
Newport Thin Film Laboratory, Inc.
13824 Magnolia Avenue
Chino, CA 91710-7027   909-591-0276
                              800-854-0089
                         Fax: 909-902-1638
                    sales@newportlab.com
                    www.Newportlab.Com

Optical products
President: Patrick Powers
General Manager: Ever Mata
Credit Cards: AMEX; MasterCard
In Business: 26 years
Number of Employees: 16
Sales Information: $1,000,000 - $5,000,000

7926 O&S Research
O&S Research Inc
1912 Bannard Street
POBox 221
Riverton, NJ 08077-221   856-829-2800
                          Fax: 856-829-0482
                     sales@osresearch.com
                     www.glassglobal.com

Optical coatings and glass products
President: Anderson L McCabe
Number of Employees: 35
Sales Information: $3MM to $5MM

7927 Ophthalmic Surgical Instruments
ASICO
26 Plaza Drive
Westmont, IL 60559-1130   630-986-8032
                              800-628-2879
                          Fax: 630-986-0065
                         info@asico.com
                         www.asico.com

Ophthalmic surgical instruments
Printing Information: 200 pages in 4 colors
In Business: 32 years

7928 Parco Scientific Company
Parco Scientific Company
PO Box 851559
Westland, MI 48185   330-637-2849
                              877-592-5837
                          Fax: 877-592-5838
                info@parcoscientific.com
                www.parcoscientific.com

Microscopes, laboratory supplies and aids, meters and kits, for the educational, medical and industrial markets
President: Brian Martorana
Credit Cards: MasterCard; Visa
Catalog Cost: Free
In Business: 50 years
Number of Employees: 12
Sales Information: 5MM-10MM

7929 Photon Technologies
Photon Technologies,Inc.
1960 E Interstate 30
Rockwall, TX 75087-6203   972-722-2522
                          Fax: 972-722-2422
                www.Photontechnologies.Com

Optical thin film coatings
President: Michael Brown
Marketing Manager: EC Curtis
Number of Employees: 9
Sales Information: $1MM to $3MM

7930 Precision Optics Corporation
Pro Chemical & Dye
22 East Broadway
Garner, MA 01440-7311   978-630-1800
                          Fax: 978-630-1487
                          info@poci.com
                          www.Poci.Com

High tech optics and optical thin films
President: Richard E Forkey
CFO: John Dreimiller
Printing Information: 35 pages
In Business: 30 years
Number of Employees: 51
Sales Information: $5,000,000 - $10,000,000

7931 Sirchie Product Catalog
Sirchie Finger Print Laboratories
100 Hunter Place
Youngsville, NC 27596-639   919-554-2244
                              800-356-7311
                          Fax: 919-554-2266
                     sirchieinfo@sirchie.com
                     www.sirchie.com

Law enforcement and security equipment
President: Paul Feldman
Buyers: Phillip Shusterman
Credit Cards: AMEX; MasterCard
Catalog Circulation: Mailed 1 time(s) per year to 8M
Printing Information: 80 pages in 1 color
In Business: 87 years
Number of Employees: 32
Sales Information: $1,000,000 - $5,000,000

7932 Stefan Sydor Optics
Sydor Optics
31 Jet View Dr
Rochester, NY 14624-4903   585-271-7300
                          Fax: 585-271-7309
                         sales@sydor.com
                         www.sydor.com

Manufacturer of precision optics for research, commercial, photgraphic, military and medical applications
President: Jim Sydor
Production Manager: Sam Ezzezew
sam@sydor.com
General Manager: Michael Naselaris
mike@sydor.com
Sales Engineer: Carol Corey
carol@sydor.com
Accounting: Jude Schnarr
jude@sydor.com
Credit Cards: MasterCard; Visa
Printing Information: 2 pages in 2 colors on Glossy Stock
Mailing List Information: Names for rent
In Business: 40 years
Number of Employees: 14
Sales Information: $1,000,000 - $5,000,000

7933 Surface Finishes Company
CMPC Surface Finishes
39 Official Rd.
Addison, IL 60101-4592   630-543-6682
                          Fax: 630-543-4013
          CustomerSupport@SurfaceFinishes.com
          www.surfacefinishes.com

Optical accessories
President: Mark Drzewiecki
Printing Information: 42 pages
In Business: 66 years
Number of Employees: 24
Sales Information: $1,000,000 - $5,000,000

7934 Technical Manufacturing Corporation
Techical Manufacturing Corporation
15 Centennial Drive
Peabody, MA 01960-7993   978-532-6330
                              800-542-9725
                          Fax: 978-531-8682
                         sales@techmfg.com
                         www.Techmfg.Com

Solutions to problems caused by ambient building floor vibration
President: Ulf B Heide

Telescopes & Binoculars

7935 B&H Photo Video Pro-Audio
B&H Photo Video
420 9th Avenue
New York, NY 10001   212-444-6615
                              800-606-6969
                     www.bhphotovideo.com

Photographic, video and digital imaging products, cameras, lenses, accessories, home theater components, binoculars, telescopes and much more
Chairman: Herman Schreiber
President: Sam Goldstein
CFO: Isreal Lebovits
Credit Cards: AMEX; MasterCard; Visa
Catalog Cost: Free
Catalog Circulation: Mailed 3 time(s) per year
Printing Information: 332 pages in 4 colors
In Business: 43 years
Number of Employees: 1100
Sales Information: 85MM

7936 Focus Camera
Focus Camera Inc
895 McDonald Ave
Brooklyn, NY 11218-2017   718-431-7900
                              800-221-0828
                          Fax: 718-438-4263
                     cs@focuscamera.com
                     focuscamera.com

Cameras, video, telescopes, and binoculars
Chairman: Abe Berkowitz
President: Abe Berkowitz
Credit Cards: AMEX; MasterCard
In Business: 49 years
Number of Employees: 60
Sales Information: $500M to $1MM

7937 Orion Telescopes & Binoculars
Orion Telescopes & Binoculars
89 Hangar Way
Watsonville, CA 95076   831-763-7000
                              800-676-1343
                          Fax: 831-763-7024
                     sales@telescope.com
                     www.telescope.com

Telescopes, microscopes, binoculars, mounts, tripods, books, cases, covers, eyepieces and atomic clocks
Credit Cards: AMEX; MasterCard
Catalog Cost: Free
In Business: 40 years
Sales Information: $20MM to $50MM

Packaging
Containers

7938 Akro-Mills
Akro-Mills
1293 S Main Street
Akron, OH 44301-1302   800-253-2467
                          Fax: 330-761-6348
                     www.akro-mils.com

Heavy duty polymer containers
President: Gary McDonald
Production Manager: Doug Popek
Managing Director: Joel Grant
Vice President and General Manager: Todd Smith
Catalog Cost: Free
Printing Information: 76 pages
In Business: 68 years
Number of Employees: 50
Sales Information: $10,000,000 - $25,000,000

7939 Allstate Can Corporation
Allstate Can Corporation
One Wood Hollow Road
Parsippany, NJ 07054-2821   973-828-0122
                             Fax: 973-560-9217
                             www.allstatecan.com

Standard and customized steel cans

President: Dave West
CFO: Gabe Papera
Marketing Manager: R Papera
Credit Cards: AMEX; MasterCard
Catalog Cost: Free
Printing Information: 28 pages
Number of Employees: 70
Sales Information: $25,000,000 - $50,000,000

7940 Althor Products
Althor Products
200 Old County Circle
Suite 116
Windsor Locks, CT 06096-640   860-386-6700
                               800-688-2693
                               Fax: 860-386-6705
                               althor640@aol.com
                               www.althor.com

Plastic boxes

President: H Shupak
Number of Employees: 5
Sales Information: $500,000 - $1,000,000

7941 Aluminum Case Company
Aluminum Case Company
3333 W 48th Place
Chicago, IL 60632-3098   773-247-4611
                          Fax: 773-247-8376
                          info@aluminumcaseco.com
                          www.aluminumcaseco.com

Alumium sample and carrying cases, mailing and shipping cases

President: George Kosinski
In Business: 68 years
Number of Employees: 7
Sales Information: $3MM to $5MM

7942 American Aluminum Company
American Aluminum Company
230 Sheffield Street
Mountainside, NJ 07092-2303   908-998-2592
                               Fax: 908-233-3241
                               info@amalco.com
                               www.amalco.com

Bottles, containers, cans and carrying cases

President: Robert Brucker
Marketing Manager: RJ King
In Business: 105 years
Number of Employees: 125
Sales Information: $5,000,000 - $10,000,000

7943 Anchor Box Company
Anchor Box Company
5889 S Gessner
Houston, TX 77036-2605   281-499-1900
                          800-522-8820
                          Fax: 281-499-1925
                          www.Anchorbox.Com

Boxes: gift, jewelry, apparel, die-cut, paper tubes, tissue paper, mailing tubes, bubble packaging, plastic bags, and all of your shipping and mailroom supplies

President: Dan Hansen
Credit Cards: AMEX; MasterCard
Catalog Cost: Free
In Business: 35 years
Number of Employees: 5
Sales Information: $500M to $1MM

7944 Association of Rotational Molders
Association of Rotational Molders
800 Roosevelt Road
Suite C-312
Glen-Ellyn, IL 60137-1804   630-942-6589
                             Fax: 630-790-3095
                             info@rotomolding.org
                             www.rotomolding.org/

Tanks and containers

President: Corey Claussen
Executive Director: Rick Church
Managing Director: Adam Webb
Legal Counsel: William C. Ives, Esq.
Number of Employees: 5

7945 Bristol Boarding
Bristol Case
1336 Culver Road
Rochester, NY 14609-1219   585-271-7860
                            800-343-3408
                            Fax: 716-271-3679
                            info@bristolcase.com
                            www.bristolcase.com

Shipping and carrying cases

President: Pat McDonald
Mailing List Information: Names for rent
Number of Employees: 7
Sales Information: $500,000 - $1,000,000

7946 Buckhorn
Buckhorn
55 West TechneCenter Drive
Milford, OH 45150-9779   513-831-4402
                          800-543-4454
                          Fax: 513-831-5474
                          sales@buckhorninc.com
                          www.Buckhorninc.Com

Reusable plastic storage and shipping containers, boxes and bins

President: Joel Grant
Marketing Manager: R Rothfuss
In Business: 82 years
Number of Employees: 50

7947 Caravan Protective Cases
Caravan Cases
25 Hawthorne St
Elyria, OH 44035-4007   440-366-9065
                         800-477-6780
                         Fax: 440-366-1809

Cases and containers

President: Charles Patton
Sales/Engineering Contact: Chuck Patton
chuck@caravancases.com
Number of Employees: 10
Sales Information: $1.1 MM

7948 Central Ohio Bag & Burlap
Central Ohio Bag & Burlap
1000 E. Fifth Avenue
Columbus, OH 43201   614-294-4495
                      800-798-9405
                      Fax: 614-294-4362
                      info@centralohiobagandburlap.com
                      www.centralohiobagandburlap.com

Specialty bags and packaging

President: James Stout
Credit Cards: AMEX; MasterCard
In Business: 82 years
Number of Employees: 5
Sales Information: $500M to $1MM

7949 Chem
Chem-Tainer Industries
361 Neptune Avenue
West Babylon, NY 11704-5818   631-661-8300
                               800-275-2436
                               Fax: 631-661-8209
                               sales@chemtainer.com
                               www.chemtainer.com

Tanks and containers for industrial storage

President: James Glen
Catalog Circulation: Mailed 12 time(s) per year
Average Order Size: $998
Printing Information: 900 pages
Mailing List Information: Names for rent
In Business: 52 years
Number of Employees: 300
Sales Information: $20MM to $50MM

7950 Container Salvage Company
Container Salvage Company
2724 Carner Avenue
PO Box 70902
North Charleston, SC 29415-902   843-554-0633
                                  Fax: 843-566-9782
                                  csalvage@earthlink.net
                                  www.container-salvage.com

Shipping containers, storage boxes and more

President: Anthony Rhoades
In Business: 34 years
Number of Employees: 10
Sales Information: $3MM to $5MM

7951 Crown Packaging International/Polycon Industries
Polycon Industries, Inc
8919 Colorado Street
Merrillville, IN 46410-7208   219-738-1000
                               800-621-4620
                               Fax: 219-738-1024
                               info@crownpolycon.com
                               www.crownpolycon.com

Glass and plastic bottles and jars

President: Berle Blitstein
In Business: 42 years
Number of Employees: 25
Sales Information: $3MM to $5MM

7952 Custom Bottle
CKS Packaging, Inc.
350 Great Southwest Parkway
Atlanta, GA 30336   404-691-8900
                     800-800-4257
                     Fax: 404-691-0086
                     www.ckspackaging.com

Blow molded bottles

Chairman: Charles K. Sewell
President: John R. Sewell
CFO: Dan Fischer
COO; Operations: Scott K. Sewell
EVP: Dewayne Phillips
COO; Administration: W. Drew Sewell
Number of Employees: 200
Sales Information: $25,000,000 - $50,000,000

7953 Fibre Container Company
Fleetwood-Fibre Packaging & Graphics, In
15250 Don Julian Rd
City of Industry, CA 91745-1031   626-968-8503
                                   Fax: 626-330-0870
                                   sales@fleetwood-fibre.com
                                   www.fleetwood-fibre.com

Corrugated boxes and folding cartons

Chairman: John Webb
President: Tony Pietrangelo
Marketing Manager: Jim Butz
In Business: 62 years
Number of Employees: 150
Sales Information: $10,000,000 - $25,000,000

7954 Fleisig Folding & Set-Up Paper Box
A. Fleisig Paper Box Corporation
525 Broadway
Suite 603
New York, NY 10012   212-226-7490
                      800-875-2244
                      Fax: 212-941-7840
                      afleisigbox@mindspring.com
                      www.afleisig.com

Shipping & display boxes, folding display boxes, hinged boxes

President: Robert Fleisig
Number of Employees: 100
Sales Information: $1,000,000 - $5,000,000

7955 Flexcon Container Corporation

Flexcon The Perfect Container Company
200 Connell Dr
Berkeley Heights, NJ 07922-2805 908-871-7000
Fax: 908-871-7171
info@flexconcontainer.Com
www.Flexconcontainer.Com

Tote boxes, bin boxes, packaging and shipping containers

President: Ken Beckerman
Marketing Manager: Ken Beckerman
Number of Employees: 80
Sales Information: $5,000,000 - $10,000,000

7956 Gary Plastic Packaging Corporation

Gary Plastic Packaging Corporation
1340 Viele Avenue
Bronx, NY 10474-7124 718-893-2200
Fax: 718-378-2141
sales@plasticboxes.com
www.plasticboxes.com

Plastic boxes, vials, containers and displays for collectibles

President: Gary Hellinger
Marketing Manager: Marilyn Hellinger
Buyers: Richard Hellinger
Credit Cards: AMEX; MasterCard
Catalog Cost: Free
Catalog Circulation: Mailed 1 time(s) per year
Printing Information: 92 pages in 2 colors
In Business: 37 years
Number of Employees: 400
Sales Information: $25,000,000 - $50,000,000

7957 Hoover Materials Handling Group

Hoover Ferguson
2135 Highway 6 S
Houston, TX 77077 281-870-8402
800-844-8683
www.hooverferguson.com

Bulk liquid handling containers

Chairman: Donald W. Young
President: Paul Lewis
CFO: Troy Carson
Chief Operating Officer: Jon Heyler
International Marketing Manager: Pete Brunn
Credit Cards: AMEX Visa
Catalog Circulation: Mailed 2 time(s) per year to 50M
Average Order Size: $250
Printing Information: 40 pages in 4 colors on Glossy Stock
Binding: Saddle Stitched
Mailing List Information: Names for rent
In Business: 106 years
Number of Employees: 350
Sales Information: $50MM to $100MM

7958 House of Cans

House of Cans
7060 N Lawndale Ave
Lincolnwood, IL 60712-2610 847-677-2100
Fax: 847-677-2103
www.Houseofcans.Com

Square, oblong and paint cans

President: Linda Worley
In Business: 40 years
Number of Employees: 7
Sales Information: $5MM to $10MM

7959 Howard Decorative Packaging

Howard Decorative Packaging
3462 W Touhy Avenue
Skokie, IL 60076 800-323-1609
888-772-9821
info@howardpkg.com
www.howardpkg.com

Custom printed packaging, offers packaging programs to fit your need and budget

President: Ron Watson
rwatson@howardpkg.com
C.S. Manager: Debbie Brazier
csmanager@howardpkg.com
Credit and Receivables: Susan Malinowski
smalinowski@howardpkg.com
Shipping and Receiving: Dean Voss
dvoss@howardpkg.com
Catalog Cost: Free
Printing Information: 28 pages
In Business: 58 years
Sales Information: $20MM to $50MM

7960 International Paper Company

International Paper Company
6400 Poplar Avenue
Memphis, TN 38197-1 203-541-8000
800-207-4003
www.internationalpaper.com

Bags, boxes, various containers and paper

Chairman: John V. Faraci
President: John T Dillon
CFO: Carol L. Roberts
Marketing Manager: Neil D Gluckin
SVP: Carol L. Roberts
CEO: John V. Faraci
SVP, Chief Information Officer: John N. Balboni
Number of Employees: 140

7961 Jewelry Packaging & Displays

Novel Box Company Ltd.
825 Lehigh Av
Union, NY 7083 908-686-7772
800-965-9192
Fax: 908-686-7774
sales@novelbox.com
www.novelbox.com

Paper, metal and plastic boxes for the jewelry trade, post boxes, pouches, jewelry displays

President: Moishe Sternhill
Marketing Manager: Abe Kwadrat
Catalog Cost: Free
Catalog Circulation: Mailed 2 time(s) per year to 20M
Average Order Size: $1000
Printing Information: 116 pages in 4 colors on Glossy Stock
Press: Web Press
Binding: Saddle Stitched
In Business: 60 years
Number of Employees: 20-5
Sales Information: $1,000,000 - $5,000,000

7962 Joe M Almand

Joe M. Alamand, Inc.
2440 Eastgate Place
Snellville, GA 30078-6132 770-979-5191
800-487-7044
Fax: 770-979-5432
info@almandbag.com
www.almandbag.com

Textiles and industrial packaging

President: Joe Almand
Credit Cards: MasterCard
In Business: 77 years
Number of Employees: 5
Sales Information: $1MM to $3MM

7963 Jonesville Paper Tube Company

Jonesville Paper Tube Corp.
540 Beck Street
PO Box 39
Jonesville, MI 49250-39 517-849-9963
Fax: 517-849-2229
mail@papertube.com
www.Papertube.Com

Paper tubes

Chairman: William Monnich
President: Rick Schaerer

Catalog Circulation: Mailed 1 time(s) per year to 500
Printing Information: in 4 colors
In Business: 60 years
Number of Employees: 100
Sales Information: $10,000,000 - $25,000,000

7964 Just Cases

Just Cases
2925 S. Umatilla Street
Englewood, CO 80110-3845 303-283-0260
888-318-5878
Fax: 303-337-8232
info@justCASES.com
www.Justcases.com

Custom carrying and transport cases; specialty shipping, cargo, and transport cases like: Pelican, Parker, Guardsman, SKB Military Spec cases, expo equipment, shock mount, rail, and flat screen cases

President: Terry Tautz
Credit Cards: AMEX; MasterCard
Catalog Cost: Free
In Business: 20 years
Sales Information: $1MM to $3MM

7965 Kal Plastics

Kal Plastics
2050 East 48th Street
Vernon, CA 90058-2022 323-581-6194
800-321-3925
Fax: 323-581-1805
www.Kal-Plastics.Com

Custom vacuum of thermo foamed plastic products

President: Juliet Goff
In Business: 50 years
Number of Employees: 14
Sales Information: $1MM to $3MM

7966 Macro Plastics

Macro Plastics, Inc.
2250 Huntington Drive
Fairfield, CA 94533-9732 707-437-1200
800-845-6555
Fax: 707-437-1201
info@macroplastics.com
www.Macroplastics.Com

Bins and pallets

Chairman: David A. Williams
President: Warren MacDonald
CFO: Greg Sutton
VP, Operations: Jeff Mitchell
VP, Ag Sales and Services: Peter Piccioli
VP, Automotive Sales: Wendell Smith
In Business: 10 years
Number of Employees: 80
Sales Information: $5,000,000 - $10,000,000

7967 Mason Box Catalog

Mason Box Company
P.O.Box 129
PO Box 129
North Attleboro, MA 02761-129 508-761-8576
800-225-2708
Fax: 508-695-3210
sales@masonbox.com
www.Masonbox.Com

Shipping and distribution boxes and cartons, etc.

President: Hugh Mason
Marketing Manager: Joe Winn
Production Manager: Ed Gagnon
Credit Cards: AMEX; MasterCard
Catalog Cost: Free
Catalog Circulation: Mailed 1 time(s) per year
Average Order Size: $350
Printing Information: 36 pages in 4 colors on Glossy Stock
Press: Sheetfed Press
Binding: Saddle Stitched
Mailing List Information: Names for rent
In Business: 117 years

Number of Employees: 100
Sales Information: $20MM to $50MM

7968 Material Flow & Conveyor Systems

Material Flow & Conveyor Systems
21150 Butteville Rd NE
P.O.Box 550
Donald,, OR 97020   503-684-1613
    800-338-1382
Fax: 503-684-5133
sales@materialflow.com
www.materialflow.com

Industrial containers, heaters, storage racks, casters, wheels, carts, ladders, lift equipment, pallet jacks, etc.

President: Randall Dozier
Credit Cards: AMEX; MasterCard
Printing Information: 155 pages in 2 colors on Newsprint
Press: Web Press
Binding: Saddle Stitched
Number of Employees: 77
Sales Information: $20MM to $50MM

7969 Mauser

Mauser USA, LLC.
35 Cotters Lane
East Brunswick, NJ 08816   732-353-7100
Fax: 732-651-9777
info.us@mausergroup.com
www.mausergroup.com

Industrial containers

President: Ronald M Litchkowski
CFO: Bjorn Kreiter
CEO: Hans-Peter Schaefer
SVP, Head of Global Key Accounts: Siegfried Weber
SBU Manager Asia: Stefan Wiedenhofer
In Business: 118 years
Number of Employees: 23
Sales Information: $3MM to $5MM

7970 Metal Edge International

Metal Edge International, Inc.
337 West Walnut Street
PO Box 1488
North Wales, PA 19454-488   215-699-8755
Fax: 215-699-6734
sales@metaledge.com
www.Metaledge.Com

Metal edged boxes and systems, tear edge systems and dispenser blades

President: John Russo
Marketing Manager: Paul Markert
Production Manager: Tom Javss
International Marketing Manager: Paul Markert
Buyers: Mark Anderson
Mailing List Information: Names for rent
In Business: 20 years
Number of Employees: 30
Sales Information: $1,000,000 - $5,000,000

7971 Nalpak Sales

NALPAK
1267 Vernon Way
El Cajon, CA 92020-1137   619-258-1200
    888-488-3372
Fax: 619-258-0925
service@nalpak.com
www.nalpak.com

Custom, stock, soft and rigid shipping carrying cases and material handling carts

President: RS Kaplan
Marketing Manager: David Northup
Credit Cards: AMEX; MasterCard; Visa
Catalog Circulation: Mailed 1 time(s) per year to 10M
Printing Information: 12 pages in 1 color on Glossy Stock
Mailing List Information: Names for rent
In Business: 34 years
Number of Employees: 3

7972 Packrite

PackRite
3026 Phillips Avenue
Racine, WI 53403-3585   262-635-6966
    800-248-6868
Fax: 262-634-0521
packrite@packrite.com
www.packrite.com

Band sealer pre-fab bags; Band Rite 6000, Robot Jaw Sealer, Thermo Jaw Sealer

Marketing Manager: Dave Bornhuetter
Production Manager: Dale Klinkhammer
International Marketing Manager: Eileen Pulice
Mailing List Information: Names for rent
In Business: 77 years
Number of Employees: 60
Sales Information: Under $500M

7973 Panoramic

Panoramic, Inc.
1500 N Parker Dr
Janesville, WI 53545-732   608-754-8850
    800-333-1394
Fax: 608-754-5703
sales@panoramicinc.com
www.panoramicinc.com

Designer and manufacturer of custom and stock thermo formed rigid plastic products for the Food, Consumer and Industrial markets

President: Rick Holznecht
Printing Information: 26 pages
Number of Employees: 300
Sales Information: $25,000,000 - $50,000,000

7974 Parkway Plastics

Parkway Plastics,Inc
561 Stelton Rd
Piscataway, NJ 08855-475   732-752-3636
    800-881-4996
Fax: 732-752-4097
www.parkwayjars.com

Jars, plastic vials and molded plastic

President: Edward W Rowan Jr
Marketing Manager: Roy Hemmingstad
Vice President of Operations: Ned Rowan
Secretary Treasurer: Kirstin Rowan Kelly
HR & Quality Assurance: Shirley Alvarez
In Business: 65 years
Number of Employees: 65
Sales Information: $5,000,000 - $10,000,000

7975 Poly Processing Company

Polytank,Inc
PO Box 4150
Monroe, LA 71211-4150   318-345-2600
Fax: 318-343-8795

Tanks and basins

President: Jerry France
Credit Cards: MasterCard
Number of Employees: 90
Sales Information: $10MM to $20MM

7976 SKB Corporation

SKB Corporation, Inc.
434 W Levers Pl
Orange, CA 92867-3605   714-637-1252
    800-654-5992
Fax: 714-283-0425
www.Skbcases.Com

Plastic cases and containers

President: Dave Sanderson
Printing Information: in 3 colors
In Business: 38 years
Number of Employees: 200
Sales Information: $10,000,000 - $25,000,000

7977 SLM Manufacturing Corporation

SLM Manufacturing Corporation
215 Davidson Avenue
P.O. Box 6722
Somerset, NJ 08873   732-469-7500
    800-526-3708
Fax: 732-469-5546
slminfo@slmcorp.com
www.SLmcorp.Com

Hot stamping containers, cartons, labeling and multipacks

President: Thomas Vajtay
Marketing Manager: Thomas Vajtay
Production Manager: Gabriel Zaha
In Business: 63 years
Number of Employees: 25
Sales Information: $1,000,000 - $5,000,000

7978 Semi-Bulk Systems

Semi-Bulk Systems, Inc.
159 Cassens Ct
St. Louis, MO 63026-2543   636-343-4500
    800-732-8769
Fax: 636-343-2822
info@semi-bulk.com
www.Semi-Bulk.Com

Container system for powders

Chairman: Craig Palubiax
President: Jeff Doherty
jdoherty@semi-bulk.com
CFO: Al Moresi
Marketing Manager: Ron Bentley
Rbentley@semi-bulk.com
CEO/COO: Charles Alack
Calack@semi-bulk.com
Director of Operations: Bernie Klipsch
bklipsch@semi-bulk.com
Vp, Engineering: Jeff Doherty
jdoherty@semi-bulk.com
In Business: 40 years
Number of Employees: 22
Sales Information: $3MM to $5MM

7979 Service Packaging

Service Packaging Design, Inc
6238 Lincoln Ave
Morton Grove, IL 60053-3348   847-966-6556
Fax: 847-966-6658
info@servicepackaging.com
www.Servicepackaging.Com

Corrugated boxes for packaging

President: Norman Croft
Marketing Manager: Norman F.Croft
In Business: 28 years
Number of Employees: 8
Sales Information: $3MM to $5MM

7980 Setco

Setco Automative Inc
565 Hwy. 77
Paris, TN 38242-808   731-642-4215
Fax: 731-642-7899
salesna@setcoauto.com
www.setcoauto.com

Custom plastic containers

President: Donald E Parodi
Marketing Manager: Tom Dunn
Number of Employees: 400
Sales Information: $25,000,000 - $50,000,000

7981 Sharpsville Container Corporation

Sharpsville Container
600 Main Street
Sharpsville, PA 16150-2058   724-962-1100
    800-645-1248
Fax: 724-962-1226
sales@scacon.com
www.sharpsvillecontainer.com

Tanks, containers and drums

President: Povl Jorgensen
CFO: Bill Sratos
Marketing Manager: Del Strandburg

Catalog Circulation: Mailed 1 time(s) per year
Printing Information: 16 pages
In Business: 155 years
Number of Employees: 40
Sales Information: $5,000,000 - $10,000,000

7982   Skydyne
The Skydyne Company
100 River Road
Port Jervis, NY 12771-5310   845-856-6655
                                   800-428-2273
                            Fax: 845-856-8378
                         cases@skydyne.com
                         www.skydyne.com

Protective transit cases and enclosures
President: Blair Gaida
In Business: 70 years
Number of Employees: 50
Sales Information: $3MM to $5MM

7983   Sonoco Products Company
Sonoco
1 N 2nd St
Hartsville, SC 29550-3305   843-383-7000
                                  800-377-2692
                            Fax: 843-383-7000
          corporate.communications@sonoco.com
                         www.sonoco.com

Paper and plastic cones, tubes and various packaging materials
Chairman: M. Jack Sanders
President: Harris Deloach
CFO: F Hill
VP, Marketing and Innovation: Names Thompson
In Business: 116 years
Number of Employees: 1000
Sales Information: $37.85 Million

7984   Super Box by Plant Service Corporation
Super Box by Plant Service Corporation
328 Tylers Mill Rd.
Sewell, NJ 08080-306   856-589-3336
                             800-257-7840
                       Fax: 856-589-0603
                  www.pscsuperbox.com

Portable storage containers
President: Dave Geserick
In Business: 45 years
Number of Employees: 25
Sales Information: $3MM to $5MM

7985   Superfos Packaging
RPC Superfos
411 Brooke Road
Winchester, VA 22603   540-504-7176
                             800-537-9242
                       Fax: 455-911-1180
                     usa@superfos.com
                     www.Superfos.Com

Open top containers
President: James Mason
CFO: Lars Hoeyer Tindbaek
lars.tindbaek@superfos.com
Production Manager: Birthe Bebe Nielsen
birthe.bebe.nielsen@superfos.com
Exective VP & Technology Director: Benny Nielsen
benny.nielsen@superfos.com
Divisional Product Manager, Sales &: Birthe Bebe Nielsen
birthe.bebe.nielsen@superfos.com
Divisional CRM Manager: Hanne Bloch Andreasen
hanne.bloch@superfos.com
Number of Employees: 2300
Sales Information: $10,000,000 - $25,000,000

7986   Tray-Pak Corporation
Tray-Pak Corporation
Tuckerton Road & Reading Crest Ave
PO Box 14804
Reading, PA 19612-4804   610-926-5800
                               888-926-1777
                         Fax: 610-926-9140
                       sales@traypak.com
                       www.traypak.com

Custom thermoformed products and integrated solutions in packaging for automated processes
President: Jack Rusnock, CEO
CFO: Scott Bestwick, Executive VP
Marketing Manager: Randy Simcox, VP Sales/Marketing
Production Manager: Joe Kijak, VP
Printing Information: 7 pages
Mailing List Information: Names for rent
In Business: 38 years
Number of Employees: 225
Sales Information: $20MM to $50MM

7987   Uline Shipping Supply Specialists
Uline
12575 Uline Drive
Pleasant Prairie, WI 53158   262-612-4200
                                   800-295-5510
                             Fax: 800-295-5571
                    customer.service@uline.com
                              www.uline.com

Uline offers over 20,000 boxes, plastic poly bags, mailing tubes, warehouse supplies and bubble wrap for storage, packaging, or shipping supplies
President: Liz Uihlein
CEO: Dick Uihlein
Vice President: Duke Uihlein
Vice President: Steve Uihlein
Buyers: Brian Uihlein
Phil Hunt
Credit Cards: AMEX; MasterCard; Visa
Catalog Cost: Free
Catalog Circulation: Mailed 2 time(s) per year
Printing Information: 664 pages in 4 colors on Glossy Stock
Press: Web Press
Binding: Saddle Stitched
Mailing List Information: Names for rent
In Business: 35 years
Number of Employees: 250
Sales Information: $ 20-50 Million

7988   VisiPak
Visipak
123 Manufacturers Dr
Arnold, MO 63010-5870   636-282-6800
                              800-949-1141
                        Fax: 636-282-6888
               customerservice@visipak.com
                        www.visipak.com

Extruded plastics and packaging
Chairman: Vincent Gorguze
President: Brad Stack
CFO: Vincent Gorgaze
Marketing Manager: Jennifer Bailie
Buyers: Susan Treuisano
Catalog Cost: Free
Catalog Circulation: to 5M
Printing Information: 17 pages in 4 colors on Glossy Stock
Press: Web Press
Binding: Perfect Bound
Mailing List Information: Names for rent
List Manager: Mark Forst
In Business: 50 years
Number of Employees: 99
Sales Information: $20MM to $50MM

7989   WB Bottle Supply Company
WB Bottle Supply Co., Inc
3400 S Clement Ave
Milwaukee, WI 53207-487   414-482-4300
                                800-738-3931
                          Fax: 414-482-2963
                         info@wbbottle.com
                         www.Wbbottle.Com

Glass and plastic bottles and containers
President: Bill Wing
Owner: Jerry Wing
Credit Cards: MasterCard; Visa
Catalog Cost: Free
In Business: 83 years
Number of Employees: 50
Sales Information: $20MM to $50MM

7990   Wisconsin Converting of Green Bay
Wisconsin Converting Inc
1689 Morrow St.
Green Bay, WI 54302-2357   920-437-6400
                                 800-544-1935
                           Fax: 920-436-4964
          cs-west@wisconsinconverting.com
                 www.wisconsinconverting.com

Eco-Shipper and Dura-Bag, utility shipping/mailing bags for fulfillment needs
President: John Brogan
Production Manager: Bob McGee
Catalog Circulation: Mailed 52 time(s) per year
Printing Information: in 2 colors on Matte Stock
Press: Letterpress
Mailing List Information: Names for rent
In Business: 28 years
Number of Employees: 40
Sales Information: $5,000,000 - $10,000,000

7991   Yazoo Mills Catalog
Yazoo Mills Inc
305 Commerce St
P.O.Box 369
New Oxford, PA 17350-369   717-624-8993
                                 800-242-5216
                           Fax: 717-624-4420
                      sales@yazoomills.com
                      www.yazoomills.com

High quality paper cores and tubes made form 100% recycled paperboard
President: Troy Eckerd
Production Manager: Steve McMaster
Credit Cards: AMEX; MasterCard; Visa
Catalog Cost: Free
Mailing List Information: Names for rent
In Business: 113 years
Number of Employees: 85
Sales Information: $ 17 Million

7992   Youngstown Barrel & Drum Company
Youngstown Barrel & Drum Company
1043 Marble St
Youngstown, OH 44502-1313   330-617-8044
                                  877-721-1264
                            Fax: 330-746-3288
                            www.Ybdco.Com

Industrial containers
President: Don Di Piero
Number of Employees: 12
Sales Information: $1MM to $3MM

Machinery

7993   Accu-Seal Corporation
Accu Seal Corporation
225 Bingham Drive
Suite B
San Marcos, CA 92069-1418   760-591-9800
                                  800-452-6040
                            Fax: 760-591-9117
                       info@accu-seal.com
                       www.accu-seal.com

Heat sealing machinery, vacuum sealers, medical and laboratory sealers

Chairman: Wayne Germain
President: Patti Germain
CFO: Linda Miller
Marketing Manager: Lesley Jensen
Office Manager: Elnora Murphy
Credit Cards: MasterCard
Catalog Circulation: Mailed 52 time(s) per year to 5M
Average Order Size: $2500
Printing Information: 10 pages in 4 colors on Glossy Stock
Binding: Folded
Mailing List Information: Names for rent
In Business: 40 years
Number of Employees: 19
Sales Information: $2.6 Million

7994 Air Fixtures
Air Fixtures, Inc.
1108 N. Sycamore Street
North Manchester, IN 46962-149 260-982-2169
800-303-5356
Fax: 260-982-7839
info@air-fixtures.com
www.air-fixtures.com

Air operated automatic tape dispensers for assembly line production and/or packaging

President: Leon L Bazzoni
Secretary: John Johnston
In Business: 63 years
Number of Employees: 15
Sales Information: $1.2 Million

7995 Aline Systems Corporation
Aline Systems Corporation
13700 South Broadway
Los Angeles, CA 90061-1032 310-715-6600
888-285-3917
Fax: 310-715-6606
alineinfo@sorbentsystems.com
www.Alinesys.Com

Designs and manufacturers vacuum sealing packaging equipment

President: Charles Schapira
Marketing Manager: Julio Gonzalez
Credit Cards: AMEX; MasterCard
In Business: 83 years
Number of Employees: 5
Sales Information: $500,000 - $1,000,000

7996 All Packaging Machinery & Supplies
All Packaging Machinery Corporation
90 13th Avenue
Unit 11
Ronkonkoma, NY 11779-6819 631-588-7310
800-637-8808
Fax: 631-467-4690
sales@apmpackaging.com
www.allpackagingmachinery.com

Table and drop sealers, heat sealing and band sealing machines for the food, medical, garment and toy industries

Chairman: Albert Bolla
President: John Bolla
Public Relations Director: Lynn Miranda
VP: Dan Wood
Manager: Irving Litt
International Marketing Manager: lynn miranda
In Business: 70 years
Number of Employees: 10
Sales Information: $1.85 Million

7997 All-Fill
All-Fill, Inc.
418 Creamery Way
Exton, PA 19341-2536 610-524-7350
866-334-1529
Fax: 610-363-2821
Info@All-Fill.com
www.all-fill.com

Packaging equipment and machinery, powder and liquid filling machines for the medical, food and pharmaceutical industries

President: Ryan Edginton
ryane@all-fill.com
CFO: Bill Egan
BillE@all-fill.com
Marketing Manager: Kyle Edginton
Kyle@all-fill.com
Vice President of Engineering: Ha Dinh
had@all-fill.com
Auger Fab VP Sales and Marketing: Eric Edginton
EricE@Auger-Fab.com
Director of Technology: Jerry Cupo
jerryc@all-fill.com
In Business: 46 years
Number of Employees: 80
Sales Information: $9.7 Million

7998 Altek Manufacturing Company
Precision Automation Company, Inc
1841 Old Cuthbert Road
Cherry Hill, NJ 08034-9151 856-428-7400
Fax: 856-428-1270
sales@precisionautomationinc.com
www.precisionautomationinc.com

Wrapping and packaging machinery

President: Glen Morris
Marketing Manager: Steve Fiscner
Founder: Fred Rexon, Sr
Mailing List Information: Names for rent
In Business: 69 years
Number of Employees: 30
Sales Information: $5MM to $10MM

7999 Auto Label
Auto Labe
3101 Industrial Avenue
Suite 2
Fort Pierce, FL 34946 772-465-4441
800-634-5376
Fax: 772-465-5177
info@autolabe.com
www.autolabe.com

Pressure sensitive labeling equipment

President: Robert N Smith
Marketing Manager: Mike Windle
Production Manager: Dean Stauffer
Credit Cards: MasterCard
Catalog Cost: Free
In Business: 48 years
Number of Employees: 50
Sales Information: $5,000,000 - $10,000,000

8000 Automated Conveyor Systems
Automated Conveyor Systems
3850 Southland Drive
West Memphis, AR 72301-6399 870-732-5050
Fax: 870-732-5191
info@automatedconveyors.com
www.automatedconveyors.com

Package conveyors and pallet conveyors

President: Charles Doty
Senior Vice-President: Geddes Self
gself@automatedconveyors.com
Senior Vice-President: Bill Henson
bhenson@automatedconveyors.com
Vice President - Finance: Jennifer Sager
jsager@automatedconveyors.com
Catalog Cost: Free
Printing Information: 100 pages in 4 colors
In Business: 44 years
Number of Employees: 175
Sales Information: $25,000,000 - $50,000,000

8001 BAG Corporation
BAG Corporation
1155 Kas Drive
Suite 170
Richardson, TX 75018-7212 214-340-7060
800-331-9200
Fax: 214-340-4598
estore@bagcorp.com
www.Bagcorp.Com

Packaging machinery and equipment

President: Jodi Simons
Marketing Manager: Cindy Finley
In Business: 46 years
Number of Employees: 40
Sales Information: $5MM to $10MM

8002 CCi Scale
Cci Scale Company
PO Box 1767
Clovis, CA 93613 559-325-7900
800-900- CCi
Fax: 888-693-2792
sales@cciscale.com
www.cciscale.com/

Microcomputer-based precision automated weighing, filling, and counting equipment

President: J Dishion
Printing Information: 16 pages in 2 colors
In Business: 35 years

8003 California Vibratory Feeders
California Vibratory Feeders
1725 Orangethorpe Park
Anaheim, CA 92801-1139 714-526-3359
800-354-0972
Fax: 714-526-3515
www.Calvibes.Com

S/S Vibratory gravity and horizontal in-line tracks feeder bowls and parts feeding

President: Donn Robinson
In Business: 43 years
Sales Information: $5MM to $10MM

8004 Campak/Tecnicam
Campak Inc.
119 Naylon Avenue
Livingston, NJ 07039-1005 973-597-1414
Fax: 973-992-4713
Info@campak.com
www.Campak.Com

Overwrappers, casepackers, bundlers and blister packers

President: Thomas Miller
In Business: 65 years
Number of Employees: 20
Sales Information: $5MM to $10MM

8005 Conflex Packaging
Conflex, Incorporated
W130 N10751 Washington Drive
Germantown, WI 53022-171 262-512-2665
800-225-4296
Fax: 262-512-1665
www.conflex.com

Packaging systems

In Business: 27 years
Number of Employees: 25
Sales Information: $1,000,000 - $5,000,000

8006 Elliott Manufacturing Company
Elliott Manufacturing Company
2664 S. Cherry Avenue
P.O.Box 11277
Fresno, CA 93772-1277 559-233-6235
Fax: 559-233-9833
elliottmfg@elliott-mfg.com
www.elliott-mfg.com

Case sealers, case erectors, cartoners, case packers, tray formers

President: Terry Aluisi
Marketing Manager: Richard Aubritton
President / CEO: Terry Aluisi
National Sales Manager: John M. Rea
jrea@elliott-mfg.com
Mailing List Information: Names for rent
In Business: 87 years
Number of Employees: 46
Sales Information: $ 5 Million

8007 Filamatic
Filamatic
4119 Fordleigh Rd
Baltimore, MD 21215-2292
410-764-0900
866-258-1914
Fax: 410-951-2093
info@filamatic.com
www.filamatic.com

Manufacturers of integrated liquid filling, capping, and monobloc systems for the pharmaceutical, cosmetic, personal care, food, household products, and chemical specialty industries

Chairman: Robert A Rosen
CFO: Denise Little
Marketing Manager: Daven Wlotko
Director, Sales & Marketing: Mark Bennett
Ken Himes
International Marketing Manager: Ignacio Mattos
Catalog Cost: Free
In Business: 62 years
Number of Employees: 110
Sales Information: $10,000,000 - $25,000,000

8008 Flexoveyor Industries
Flexoveyor Industries
3795 Paris St
Denver, CO 80239-2615
303-375-0200
800-466-1232
Fax: 303-373-5149
info@flexoveyor.com
www.flexoveyor.com

Conveyors and engineered conveying systems

President: Dave Huddleston
Credit Cards: AMEX; MasterCard
In Business: 74 years
Number of Employees: 25
Sales Information: $1,000,000 - $5,000,000

8009 Fres-Co System USA
Fres-Co System USA,Inc
3005 State Rd
Telford, PA 18969-1033
215-721-4600
Fax: 215-721-4414
www.fresco.com

Vacuum packaging equipment and printed flexible packaging materials

President: Tullio Vigano
In Business: 36 years
Number of Employees: 260
Sales Information: $25,000,000 - $50,000,000

8010 General Packaging Equipment Company
General Packaging Equipment Company
6048 Westview Dr
Houston, TX 77055-5499
713-686-4331
Fax: 713-683-3967
sales@generalpackaging.com
www.generalpackaging.com

Packaging equipment

President: Robert C Kelly
Director of Sales: Tom Wilson
sales@generalpackaging.com
Mailing List Information: Names for rent
In Business: 50 years
Number of Employees: 38
Sales Information: $5,000,000 - $10,000,000

8011 Glue-Fast Equipment Company
Glue-Fast Adhesive & Applicating Equipme
3535 State Route 66
Building #1
Neptune, NJ 07753
732-918-4600
800-242-7318
Fax: 732-918-4646
info@gluefast.com
www.gluefast.com

Labeling systems

President: Lester Mallet
Marketing Manager: Donna Budelman
VP: Amy Altman
General Manager: Joe Benenati
Office Manager: Laura Hincapie
In Business: 75 years
Number of Employees: 20
Sales Information: $5,000,000 - $10,000,000

8012 Heat & Control
Heat & Control
21121 Cabot Blvd.
Hayward, CA 94545-1132
510-259-0500
800-227-5980
Fax: 510-259-0600
www.heatandcontrol.com

Computerized combination weighers

President: Tony Caridis
CFO: George Lotti
Marketing Manager: Audry Waidelick
Plant Manager: Rich Garofolo
Printing Information: 10 pages in 4 colors
In Business: 63 years
Number of Employees: 200
Sales Information: $20MM to $50MM

8013 K&R Equipment
OK International Corp.
73 Bartlett Street
Suite 500
Marlborough, MA 01752-4427
508-303-8286
800-700-5677
Fax: 508-303-8207
sales@okcorp.com
www.okcorp.com

Automatic shipping case erector/poly bag insertion system

President: Fred Kruger
Marketing Manager: Don Ellinger
In Business: 33 years
Number of Employees: 43
Sales Information: $5,000,000 - $10,000,000

8014 Labels Catalog
Lancer Label
301 South 74th Street
Omaha, NE 68114-4618
800-288-7074
Fax: 800-344-9456
customerservice@lancerlabel.com
www.lancerlabel.com

Labels, decals, tags

Catalog Circulation: Mailed 1 time(s) per year to 60M
Printing Information: 48 pages in 4 colors
Binding: Saddle Stitched
Mailing List Information: Names for rent

8015 Lock Inspection Systems
Lock Inspection Systems
207 Authority Drive
Fitchburg, MA 01420-6044
978-343-3716
800-227-5539
Fax: 978-343-6278
sales@lockinspection.com
www.lockinspection.com

Inspection systems for processing, packaging industries; also metal detectors and checkweighers

President: Mark D'Onofrio
Mailing List Information: Names for rent
In Business: 65 years

Number of Employees: 30
Sales Information: $5,000,000 - $10,000,000

8016 Loeb Equipment & Appraisal Company
Loeb Equipment & Appraisal Company
4131 S State Street
Chicago, IL 60609
773-548-4131
800-560-LOEB
Fax: 773-548-2608
Sales@loebequipment.com
www.loebequipment.com

Processing and packaging equipment for food and chemical industries

President: Howard Newman, ASA, CEA
Marketing Manager: Sara Bogin
Principal, Loeb Term Solutions: Jim Newman
jimn@loebtermsolutions.com
Vice President of Finance & Operati: Sheldrick Holmes
sheldrickh@loebwinternitz.com
Vice President, BusinessDevelopmen: Jonathan Bloom
jonb@loebtermsolutions.com
Catalog Cost: Free
In Business: 135 years
Number of Employees: 99
Sales Information: $20MM to $50MM

8017 Marathon Equipment Company Catalog
Marathon Equipment Company
PO Box 1798
Vernon, AL 35592-1798
205-695-9105
800-269-7237
Fax: 205-695-8813
parts@marathonequipment.com
www.marathonequipment.com

Waste handling and recycling equipment including compactors, horizontal and verticalbalers, conveyor systems, transfer equipment, mobile scrap choppers and wire processors

President: Gordon Shaw
CFO: Gene Laminack
Marketing Manager: Shawnna Romans
Fulfillment: Renee Boman
International Marketing Manager: Fred Lauten
Mailing List Information: Names for rent
In Business: 47 years
Number of Employees: 500
Sales Information: $500M to $1MM

8018 Marq Packaging Systems
Marq Packaging Systems
3801 W. Washington Avenue
Yakima, WA 98903
509-966-4300
800-998-4301
Fax: 509-452-3307
www.Marq.Net

Computer adjustable machines

President: Rocky Marquis
Marketing Manager: Ted Marquis Jr
Sales Engineer: Mark Diddens
Service/Parts: Gene Barton
Service Manager: Trevor Dohrman
In Business: 49 years
Number of Employees: 120
Sales Information: $10,000,000 - $25,000,000

8019 Meyer Machine Company
Meyer Industries, Inc.
3528 Fredericksburg Rd.
PO Box 5460
San Antonio, TX 78201-0460
210-736-1811
Fax: 210-736-4662
sales@meyer-industries.com
www.Meyer-Industries.Com

Bulk material handling equipment and systems

President: Eugene W Teeter
CFO: Neomal Ratnayeke
Regional Sales Manager: Jim Lassiter
Number of Employees: 125
Sales Information: $10,000,000 - $25,000,000

8020 Moen Industries
Moen Industries
10330 Pioneer Blvd.,
Suite 230
Santa Fe Springs, CA 90670-2994 562-946-6381
800-723-7766
Fax: 562-946-3200
dkaz@moenindustries.com
www.Moenindustries.Com

Packaging equipment

President: Carl Moen
CFO: Carl Morlin
Marketing Manager: Iris Walker
Production Manager: Roy Cote
List Manager: Iris Walker
Number of Employees: 60
Sales Information: $5,000,000 - $10,000,000

8021 Ovalstrapping
Ovalstrapping Inc.
120 55th St NE
Fort Payne, AL 35967   256-845-1914
Fax: 256-845-1493
info@ovalstrapping.com
www.ovalstrapping.com

Automatic strapping machinery

President: Isabelle Lamb
In Business: 63 years
Number of Employees: 70
Sales Information: $10,000,000 - $25,000,000

8022 PDC International Corporation
PDC International Corporation
8 Sheehan Ave
Norwalk, CT 06854-4659   203-853-1516
Fax: 203-854-0834
sales@pdc-corp.com
www.pdc-corp.com

PDC manufactures a full line of machinery for applying heat shrinkable tamper evident seals and sleeve labels

President: Neal Konstantin
Marketing Manager: Rich Keenan
Catalog Cost: Free
Number of Employees: 45
Sales Information: $5,000,000 - $10,000,000

8023 Package Devices
Package Devices
PO Box 6262
Woodland Hills, CA 91365-6262   818-340-7866
Fax: 818-340-0168
www.packagedevices.com

Packing devices

President: Viney Sethi
Managing Partner: Mike Bruhns
Partner: Mike Kicherer
Associate: Aaron Arnold
In Business: 45 years
Number of Employees: 10-J
Sales Information: Under $500M

8024 Peabody Engineering
Peabody Engineering & Supply Inc.
13435 Estelle St
Corona, CA 92879-1877   951-734-7711
877-734-3759
Fax: 951-734-4111
sales@etanks.com
www.Etanks.Com

Fluid handling products and systems

President: Larry Peabody
Marketing Manager: M Peabody
In Business: 63 years
Number of Employees: 19
Sales Information: $10MM to $20MM

8025 Plas-Ties
PLAS-TIES,CO.
14272 Chambers Rd
Tustin, CA 92780-6994   714-542-4487
800-854-0137
Fax: 714-972-2978
info@plasties.com
www.Plasties.Com

Semi-automatic twist tying machinery and materials, digital coders

President: Lou Contreras
Production Manager: Jesse Garcia
In Business: 50 years
Number of Employees: 25
Sales Information: $1,000,000 - $5,000,000

8026 Pneumatic Scale
Pneumatic Scale Angelus
10 Ascot Parkway
Cuyahoga Falls, OH 44223   330-923-0491
Fax: 330-923-5570
kim.hutton@barry-wehmiller.com
www.psangelus.com

Packaging automation equipment and services for the pharmaceutical, household, cosmetic, food, and beverage industries

Chairman: Robert H. Chapman
President: William Morgan
CFO: Jim Lawson
Marketing Manager: Bethany Hilt
Average Order Size: $5000
Printing Information: 2 pages in 4 colors on Glossy Stock
Press: Web Press
List Manager: Stephen J Murphy
Number of Employees: 109
Sales Information: $70 Million

8027 Prab Conveyor
Prab
5944 East N Ave
Kalamazoo, MI 49048-2121   269-382-8200
800-968-7722
Fax: 269-349-2477
service@prab.com
www.prab.com

Conveyors, conveyor systems and processing equipment

President: Gary Herder
customer service manager: Tim Kamrowski
tim.kamrowski@prab.com
In Business: 65 years

8028 Prodo-Pak Corporation Catalog
Prodo-Pak Corporation
77 Commerce Street
PO Box 363
Garfield, NJ 07026   973-777-7770
Fax: 973-772-0471
sales@prodo-pak.com
www.prodo-pak.com

Form/fill/seal machinery

President: John Mueller
Marketing Manager: Bruce Teeling
Production Manager: Ralph Isler
Credit Cards: AMEX; MasterCard
Mailing List Information: Names for rent
In Business: 50 years
Number of Employees: 30

8029 Production Process
Production Process
61 Harvey Rd
Londonderry, NH 03053-7412 603-434-2300
Fax: 603-434-7851
www.Productionprocess.Com

Machine monitoring, process validation and production reporting

President: Karl Ritzinger
Credit Cards: AMEX; MasterCard
In Business: 37 years

Number of Employees: 12
Sales Information: $1,000,000 - $5,000,000

8030 Rol-Away Truck Manufacturing
Rol-Away Inc.
6143 SE Foster Rd
Portland, OR 97206-3797   503-777-3388
800-547-4548
Fax: 503-775-6639
sales@rol-away.com
www.Rol-Away.Com

Material handling equipment, aluminum carts, ladder trucks, stock picking equipment

President: James Cutler
Marketing Manager: John Devaney
Production Manager: Mike Morsman
Mailing List Information: Names for rent
In Business: 73 years
Number of Employees: 14
Sales Information: $1,500,000 - $3,500,000

8031 SJF Material Handling
SJF Material Handling Inc
211 Baker Ave
P.O.Box 70
Winsted, MN 55395-70   320-485-2824
800-598-5532
Fax: 320-485-2832
support@sjf.com
www.Sjf.Com

New, used or reconditioned rack, conveyor, shelving, storage, warehouse and other material handling equipment

President: Frank Sterner
CFO: Tina Goerish
Marketing Manager: Jason Dieter
VP Engineer: Jim Sterner
Engineer: Jim Laliberte
Facility Design and Layout: Matt Johnson
Catalog Cost: Free
Printing Information: 200 pages in 3 colors
In Business: 32 years
Sales Information: $5 million

8032 Scandia Packaging Machinery Company Catalog
Scandia Packaging Machinery Co.
15 Industrial Road
Fairfield, NJ 07004   973-473-6100
Fax: 973-473-7226
info@ScandiaPack.com
www.scandiapack.com

Packaging machinery

President: Bill Bronander III
CFO: Cecilia G Bronander
EVP: Pamela Bronander
Director Engineering: Arthur Goldberg
Sales Manager: James J. Brown
Printing Information: in 3 colors
Mailing List Information: Names for rent
In Business: 90 years
Number of Employees: 40
Sales Information: $5MM to $10MM

8033 Shorty's Tooling & Equipment
Shorty's Tooling & Equipment, Inc.
7531 Holland Road
Taylor, MI 48180   313-291-5200
800-443-6666
Fax: 313-291-4524

New and surplus tooling, attachments and replacement parts for American made automatic screw machines

President: Carl Sherman
Credit Cards: MasterCard
Catalog Cost: $15
Catalog Circulation: Mailed 1 time(s) per year
Printing Information: 66 pages
Binding: Saddle Stitched
In Business: 46 years

8034 Simplex
Simplex Filler company
640-A Airpark Rd.
Napa, CA 94558-7569

707-265-6801
800-796-7539
Fax: 707-265-6868
www.Simplexfiller.Com

Volumetric piston fillers, Pressure fillers, table-top series, accessories

President: G Donald Murray Iii
CFO: Edna Murray
Marketing Manager: Alden Murray
In Business: 40 years
Number of Employees: 23
Sales Information: $1,000,000 - $5,000,000

8035 Slautterback Products
Nordson Corporation
28601 Clemens Road
Westlake, OH 44145-1148

440-892-1580
Fax: 440-892-9507
www.nordson.com

Hotmelt applicator systems

President: Michael F. Hilton
CFO: Gregory A. Thaxton
Senior Vice President: John J. Keane
VP, Industrial Coating Systems: Douglas C. Bloomfield
VP, Human Resources: Shelly M. Peet
In Business: 60 years
Number of Employees: 145

8036 Stiles Rubber Company
Stiles Enterprises, Inc.
PO Box 92
Rockaway, NJ 07866-92

973-625-9660
800-325-4232
Fax: 973-625-9346
www.stilesenterprises.com

Packaging machinery replacement parts, fabricated belts and other parts and euipments

President: Richard Stiles
In Business: 81 years
Number of Employees: 10
Sales Information: $1,000,000 - $5,000,000

8037 Vertrod Corporation
PAC Machinery
25 Tiburon St.
San Rafael, CA 94901-3215

415-454-4868
800-985-9570
Fax: 415-454-6853
info@pacmachinery.com
www.pacmachinery.com

Packing Equipment

President: Louis Gross
Marketing Manager: Gerald Fener
Number of Employees: 50
Sales Information: $5MM to $10MM

8038 WA Charnstrom Mail Center Solutions
Charnstrom
5391 12th Avenue E
Shakopee, MN 55379-1896

800-328-2962
Fax: 800-916-3215
customerservice@charnstrom.com
www.charnstrom.com

Mailroom and mailing equipment and furniture

President: Greg Hedlund
Credit Cards: AMEX; MasterCard; Visa
Catalog Cost: Free
Printing Information: 52 pages in 4 colors
In Business: 57 years
Sales Information: $5MM to $10MM

8039 West-Link Corporation
West-Link Corp.
3467 Ocean View Blvd #F
Glendale, CA 91208-3508

818-249-4647
818-219-2121
Fax: 818-249-4951
www.West-Link.Com

Packaging machinery

President: Dennis R Ballere
In Business: 30 years
Number of Employees: 8
Sales Information: $10,000,000 - $25,000,000

8040 Winpak Lane
Winpak Ltd.
100 Saulteaux Crescent
Winnipeg, MB R3J-3T3

204-889-1015
800-804-4224
Fax: 204-889-7806
info@winpak.com
www.winpak.com

Food, cosmetic and pharmaceutical industrial machinery and equipment

President: Bill Lane Jr
Marketing Manager: Donald Kappen
In Business: 30 years
Number of Employees: 100
Sales Information: $10,000,000 - $25,000,000

8041 Woodworkers Supply
Woodworkers Supply, Inc
1108 N Glenn Rd
Casper, WY 82601-1635

307-237-5528
800-645-9292
Fax: 800-853-9663
comments@woodworker.com
www.woodworker.com

Woodworking tools and supplies

President: John Wirth, Jr.
john@woodworker.com
CFO: Joe McQuade
Marketing Manager: Ken Pollitt
kenp@woodworker.com
Production Manager: Dean Cannon
Operations Manager: Darrell Feldman
darrellf@woodworker.com
International Marketing Manager: Jay Sanger
Buyers: Cynthia Quintana
Credit Cards: AMEX; MasterCard
Catalog Cost: Free
Catalog Circulation: Mailed 12 time(s) per year to 6M
Average Order Size: $100
Printing Information: 220 pages in 4 colors on Glossy Stock
Press: Web Press
Binding: Perfect Bound
Mailing List Information: Names for rent
List Manager: Mike Gilb
In Business: 43 years
Number of Employees: 76

Materials, Supplies & Services

8042 A&M Industries
A&M Industries
3610 N. Cliff Avenue
Sioux Falls, SD 57104-868

605-332-4877
800-888-2615
Fax: 605-338-6015
amindustries@amindustries.com
www.amindustries.com

Gauges, hose fittings, valves, clamps.

President: Richard Miller
Printing Information: 43 pages
Mailing List Information: Names for rent
Number of Employees: 20
Sales Information: Under $500,000

8043 APS Packaging Systems
Advanced Paper Systems
499 Parrot Street
San Jose, CA 95112-4118

408-286-7770
800-526-2276
Fax: 408-286-3800
aps@apspackaging.com
www.apspackaging.com

Shrink-wrap plastic packaging systems

President: Henry Verbeke
Marketing Manager: Eric Verbeke
Mailing List Information: Names for rent
In Business: 38 years
Number of Employees: 15
Sales Information: $1,000,000 - $5,000,000

8044 Accu-line
Accu-line
PO Box 875
Hyannis, MA 02601-875

508-771-8022
800-363-7740
Fax: 508-771-8022
acculine@acculine.com
www.acculine.com

Surgical marking pens

President: Karleen Laviana
Director, Manufacturing/Operations: James Laviana
Partner: Nancy Donnelly
In Business: 32 years
Number of Employees: 6
Sales Information: $800,000

8045 Accurate Plastics
Accurate Plastics, Inc.
18 Morris Place
Yonkers, NY 10705-1929

914-476-0700
800-431-2274
Fax: 914-476-0533
sales@acculam.com
www.acculam.com

Sheets, rods, tapes and bags

President: Michael Stacey
In Business: 35 years

8046 Aceco Industrial Packaging Company
Ace Bag & Burlap Co
1601 Bronxdale Avenue
PO Box 93
Bronx, NY 10462-93

718-319-9300
800-328-7527
Fax: 718-319-9311
acebag@aol.com
www.ace-bag.com

Polyethylene bags, film and stretch wrap, multiwall paper bags, burlap bags and cloth, polypropylene bags and sandbags

President: R Sherman
CFO: Linda Sherman
Credit Cards: AMEX; MasterCard
In Business: 89 years
Number of Employees: 12
Sales Information: $2 Million

8047 Alameda Commons
Alameda Packaging
4445 Enterprise St
Fremont, CA 94538-6306

510-651-0277
Fax: 510-651-2396
info@alamedapackaging.com
www.Alamedapackaging.Com

Packaging products

President: Mike Beheshti
Director of Operations: Mike Beheshti
Mikeb@alamedapackaging.com
Account Executive: Ezra Gonzalez
csr2@alamedapackaging.com
Account Executive: Patrick van der Linde
csr1@alamedapackaging.com
Catalog Cost: Free
Catalog Circulation: Mailed 1 time(s) per year to 1M

Printing Information: 4 pages in 2 colors on Glossy Stock
Press: Letterpress
Mailing List Information: Names for rent
In Business: 6 years
Number of Employees: 3
Sales Information: $1,000,000 - $5,000,000

8048 Associated Bag
Associated Bag Company
400 W Boden Street
Milwaukee, WI 53207-6276   800-926-6100
Fax: 800-926-4610
www.associatedbag.com

Packaging & shipping supplies including bags, boxes, bubble wrap, bubble mailers, labeling products, pallet wrap, shrink wrap and zipper bags

President: Herb Rubenstein
Credit Cards: AMEX; MasterCard; Visa
Catalog Cost: Free
Printing Information: 240 pages
Mailing List Information: Names for rent
In Business: 66 years
Number of Employees: 180
Sales Information: $25,000,000 - $50,000,000

8049 Bearse Manufacturing Company
Bearse USA
3815 W. Cortland St.
Chicago, IL 60647-4601   773-235-8710
866-6BE-RSE
Fax: 773-235-8716
info@bearseusa.com
www.bearseusa.com/

Cotton bags, air line bags, canvas, coin, mailing and shipping containers

President: James Erickson
In Business: 94 years
Number of Employees: 150
Sales Information: $5MM to $10MM

8050 Becker's School Supplies
Becker's School Supplies
1500 Melrose Highway
Pennsauken, NJ 08110-1410   800-523-1490
Fax: 856-792-4500
customerservice@shopbecker.com
www.shopbecker.com

School supplies, including art supplies

President: George Becker
Credit Cards: MasterCard
Catalog Cost: Free
Catalog Circulation: Mailed 1 time(s) per year
Printing Information: 272 pages in 4 colors
In Business: 89 years
Sales Information: $20-50 Million

8051 Bib Pak
Bib Pak
1106 E Nakoma Street
Racine, WI 53403-3662   262-633-5803
Fax: 262-633-2606

Contract packagers

President: Jim Geshay
Number of Employees: 6
Sales Information: Under $500M

8052 Branson Ultrasonics Corporation
Branson Ultrasonics Corporation
41 Eagle Road
Danbury, CT 06810-1961   203-796-0400
Fax: 203-796-9838
Branson.Info@Emerson.com
www.emersonindustrial.com/en-US/branson/Pages/home.aspx

Package sealers

President: Ed M Boone
Marketing Manager: Edward Samuels
In Business: 69 years
Number of Employees: 1800

8053 Can-Do National Tape
Can-Do National Tape
195 Polk Avenue
Nashville, TN 37210-366   615-255-1775
800-643-5996
Fax: 615-256-6557
www.can-dotape.com

Pressure sensitive adhesive tape

Chairman: Bill Armested
President: Tim Douglas
CEO: Jerry Wethington
President: Rick Winkel
Catalog Circulation: Mailed 1 time(s) per year
Printing Information: 16 pages in 2 colors
Binding: Saddle Stitched
In Business: 43 years

8054 Consolidated Plastics Company
Consolidated Plastics
4700 Prosper Drive
Stow, OH 44224-1068   800-362-1000
Fax: 800-858-5001
www.consolidatedplastics.com

Bags, wraps, boxes and tapes for shipping

President: Brenton Taussig
Credit Cards: MasterCard
Catalog Circulation: Mailed 1 time(s) per year
Printing Information: 24 pages in 4 colors on Glossy Stock
Binding: Saddle Stitched
In Business: 36 years
Number of Employees: 100
Sales Information: $10MM

8055 Display Pack
Display Pack
1340 Monroe Ave. NW
Grand Rapids, MI 49505-4694   616-451-3061
Fax: 616-451-8907
info@displaypack.com
www.displaypack.com

Packaging services including printed, thermoformed and contract packaging

President: Victor Hansen
Marketing Manager: Roger Vander Zouwen
Production Manager: Jay Abbott
Credit Cards: AMEX; MasterCard
Catalog Circulation: to 30M
Printing Information: 8 pages in 4 colors on Glossy Stock
Press: Sheetfed Press
Binding: Folded
Mailing List Information: Names for rent
In Business: 48 years
Number of Employees: 400
Sales Information: $25,000,000 - $50,000,000

8056 Eastman Chemical Products
Eastman
200 South Wilcox Drive
PO Box 431
Kingsport, TN 37662-431   423-229-2000
800-327-8626
Fax: 423-229-1351
www.eastman.com

Adhesives, hot melt, films and resins

Chairman: Earnest Deavenport
President: James Rogers
CFO: Curtis Espeland
Marketing Manager: Alex Anderson
Chairman: J. Brian Ferguson
Executive Vice President: Brad A. Lich
Chief Operating Officer: Ronald C. Lindsay
Number of Employees: 5000

8057 Ecometics
Ecometics,Inc
19 Concord Street
P.O. Box 179
Norwalk, CT 06854-3706   203-853-7856
Fax: 203-853-6408
www.ecometics.com

Contract manufacturing

President: Mark G Lowenstein
CFO: Judith Lowenstein
Marketing Manager: Joanne Takacs
Production Manager: Kish Patel
Sales: Mark Lowenstein
sales@ecometics.com
Administration: Joanne Takacs
admin@ecometics.com
Research & Development: Kishor Patel
R&D@ecometics.com
Mailing List Information: Names for rent
In Business: 44 years
Number of Employees: 16
Sales Information: $5,000,000 - $10,000,000

8058 Enercon Industries Corporation
Enercon
W140 N9572 Fountain Blvd.
Menomonee Falls, WI 53051   262-255-6070
Fax: 262-255-7784
www.enerconind.com

Cap sealers

President: Don Nimmer
Number of Employees: 100
Sales Information: $10,000,000 - $25,000,000

8059 Filling Equipment Company
Filling Equipment Company ,Inc
15-39 130th St
College Point, NY 11356-2481   718-445-2111
800-247-7124
Fax: 718-463-6034
info@fillingequipment.com
www.Fillingequipment.Com

Fillers

President: Robert a Hampton
In Business: 55 years
Number of Employees: 15
Sales Information: $1,000,000 - $5,000,000

8060 Flex-O-Glass
Flex-O-Glass, Inc.
1100 N Cicero Ave # 1
Chicago, IL 60651-3214   773-379-7878
Fax: 773-261-5204
www.Flexoglass.Com

Films and plastic sheets

President: Harold Warp
Marketing Manager: Jeff Whittington
Mailing List Information: Names for rent
In Business: 49 years
Number of Employees: 15
Sales Information: $3MM to $5MM

8061 Flight Form Cases
Flight Form
6543 South Laramie Ave.
Bedford Park, IL 60638-8764   708-458-8989
800-657-1199
Fax: 708-458-9023
sales@caseguys.net

Reusable shipping cases and carrying cases

President: Dale Lorang
Marketing Manager: Glenn Stenson
International Marketing Manager: glenn stenson
Buyers: Glenn Stenson
Credit Cards: MasterCard; Visa
Catalog Cost: Free
Catalog Circulation: Mailed 1 time(s) per year to 5M
Printing Information: 20 pages in 4 colors on Glossy Stock
Mailing List Information: Names for rent
In Business: 52 years
Number of Employees: 50
Sales Information: $1,000,000 - $5,000,000

8062 GSS Gunter Shipping Supplies
Gunter Shipping Inc
1565 Bergen Street
Brooklyn, NY 11213stsvc@guntershipping.com
www.guntershipping.com

Packaging supplies

Credit Cards: AMEX; MasterCard
Catalog Circulation: Mailed 2 time(s) per year
Printing Information: 60 pages in 4 colors
Binding: Saddle Stitched
In Business: 16 years

8063 Glass, Plastic, Metal Packaging
All-Pac, Inc
4800 Quebec Ave. N.
New Hope, MN 55428   763-208-8155
                              Fax: 763-331-0546
                        pack@all-pac.com
                        www.all-pac.com

Glass, plastic, metal containers and closures

Chairman: Dennis Sipe
President: Dennis Crawford
CFO: Robert Petrini
Marketing Manager: Michael Lang
Production Manager: Jim Kramer
Credit Cards: MasterCard
Catalog Circulation: to 10M
Printing Information: 23 pages in 4 colors on Glossy Stock
Press: Sheetfed Press
Binding: Saddle Stitched
Mailing List Information: Names for rent
In Business: 45 years
Number of Employees: 170

8064 Huckster Packaging & Supply Catalog
Huckster Packaging & Supply Inc
6111 Griggs Rd.
PO Box 262327
Houston, TX 77207-2327   713-644-8277
                               800-255-1845
                          Fax: 713-644-1076
                         info1@huckster.com
                         www.Huckster.Com

Poly bag distributor in the Gulf Coast region, ancillary packaging products; tape, boxes, protective packaging, strapping

President: Gloria Terry
Marketing Manager: Bill Olson
Fulfillment: Brad Busey
Credit Cards: AMEX; MasterCard; Visa
Printing Information: 3 pages
Press: Letterpress
Mailing List Information: Names for rent
In Business: 51 years
Number of Employees: 25
Sales Information: $5MM to $10MM

8065 Industrial Packaging Supply
Industrial Packaging Supply, Inc.
108 Grove Street
Worcester, MA 01605   508-499-1600
                              800-233-5288
                          Fax: 508-987-2104
                     info@industrialpackaging.com
                     www.Industrialpackaging.Com

Supplies and equipment for the packaging industry

President: Matthew J Hogan
In Business: 53 years
Number of Employees: 25
Sales Information: $10MM to $20MM

8066 Iroquois Products Catalog
Iroquois Industries Corporation
2220 W 56th Street
Chicago, IL 60636-1047   773-436-4900
                               800-453-3355
                          Fax: 800-453-3344
                      sales@iroquoisproducts.com
                      www.iroquoisproducts.com

Packaging & shipping supplies, car cleaning/care supplies and marine cleaning/care supplies

President: Alan Gordon
Credit Cards: AMEX; MasterCard; Visa
Catalog Cost: Free

Catalog Circulation: Mailed 1 time(s) per year
Printing Information: 204 pages in 4 colors
In Business: 58 years
Number of Employees: 20
Sales Information: $10MM

8067 Keith Machinery Corporation
Keith Machinery Corporation
34 Gear Avenue
Lindenhurst, NY 11757-1078   631-957-1200
                          Fax: 631-957-9264
                     sales@keithmachinery.com
                     www.Keithmachinery.Com

Services

President: Jon Hatz
Number of Employees: 50
Sales Information: $1,000,000 - $5,000,000

8068 Machinery & Equipment Company
Machinery & Equipment Company, Inc.
PO Box 7632
San Francisco, CA 94120   415-467-3400
                               800-227-4544
                          Fax: 415-467-2639
                 info@machineryandequipment.com
                 www.machineryandequipment.com

Packaging equipment and supplies

Marketing Manager: Marisol Richardson
In Business: 76 years
Number of Employees: 24

8069 Magenta Closure Division
Magenta LLC
3800 N Milwaukee Ave
Chicago, IL 60641-2844   773-777-5050
                          Fax: 773-777-4055
                 customerfirst@magentallc.com
                 www.Magentacorp.Com

Closures

President: M C Illenberger
Number of Employees: 140
Sales Information: $10,000,000 - $25,000,000

8070 Marsh Shipping Supply Company
MSSC, LLC
926 McDonough Lake Rd
Collinsville, IL 62234   618-343-1006
                          Fax: 618-343-1016
                          www.msscllc.com/

Marsh produces tape machines, coders, stencil machines and stencil inks, oilboards and applicators, roller coders, markers and contact marking supplies

Marketing Manager: Rita Swettenham
In Business: 14 years
Number of Employees: 300
Sales Information: $3MM to $5MM

8071 Mid Atlantic Packaging
Mid Atlantic Packaging
14 Starlifter Avenue
Dover, DE 19901-9200   800-284-1332
                     www.midatlanticpackaging.com

Packaging supplies

President: Herb Glanden
Marketing Manager: Matt Rotuno
Customer Service: Dawn Carpenter
Credit Cards: AMEX; MasterCard
Printing Information: 34 pages in 4 colors on Matte Stock
Binding: Perfect Bound
In Business: 36 years
Number of Employees: 35
Sales Information: 20MM-50MM

8072 Mil-Spec Packaging Supply
5200 unruh avenue
Building B
Philadelphia, PA 19135-2921   800-728-8408
                          Fax: 215-335-7354

Military packaging supplies

In Business: 26 years

8073 Mil-Spec Packaging of Georgia
Mil-Spec Packaging of Georgia
8150 Industrial Highway
Macon, GA 31216-217   478-788-3454
                               800-216-3454
                          Fax: 478-781-5165
                     info@mil-specpkg.com
                     www.Mil-Specpkg.Com

Packaging materials certified to military specifications

President: Robert L Hentz
Credit Cards: MasterCard; Visa
Average Order Size: $2500
In Business: 49 years
Number of Employees: 12
Sales Information: $3MM to $5MM

8074 National Starch & Chemical Corporation
Ingredion
10 Finderne Ave
Bridgewater, NJ 08807-500   908-685-5082
                               800-743-6343
                          Fax: 908-685-5355
                     www.nationalstarch.com

Adhesives and coatings

Chairman: Mike Fenster
President: James Kennedy
In Business: 113 years
Number of Employees: 1200

8075 New Jersey Machine
Arlington Machine and Tool Co.
90 New Dutch Lane
Fairfield, NJ 07004-1684   973-276-1377
                          Fax: 973-276-1378
                     www.arlingtonmachine.com

Adhesive applicating, labels

President: James Starhar
Marketing Manager: TA Paul
Founder: John Staudinger
VP, Operations: John J. Staudinger
In Business: 52 years
Number of Employees: 65
Sales Information: $10,000,000 - $25,000,000

8076 Noteworthy Company
Noteworthy Company
100 Church Street
Amsterdam, NY 12010-4290   www.noteworthy.com

Packaging products for the photo finishing industry

President: Carol Constigino
Credit Cards: MasterCard
Catalog Cost: $1
Catalog Circulation: Mailed 1 time(s) per year to 40M
Printing Information: 68 pages in 4 colors
Press: Sheetfed Press
Binding: Saddle Stitched
Number of Employees: 275
Sales Information: $25,000,000 - $50,000,000

8077 Overnight Labels
Overnight Labels, Inc.
151-15 W Industry Court
Deer Park, NY 11729   631-242-4240
                               800-472-5753
                          Fax: 631-242-4385
                     info@overnightlabels.com
                     overnightlabels.com

Manufacturer specializing in a variety of packaging options, including labels, shrink sleeves, flexible packaging and more

President: Don Earl
Marketing Manager: Susan Cox
Mailing List Information: Names for rent
In Business: 28 years
Number of Employees: 50

8078 PAC/TEC Electronic Enclosures
PAC/TEC
One La France Way
Concordville, PA 19331   610-361-4286
                          Fax: 610-361-4378
moreinfo@pactecenclosures.com
www.PacTecEnclosures.com

Packaging and enclosures for electronic products

Credit Cards: AMEX; MasterCard
Catalog Circulation: Mailed 1 time(s) per year
Printing Information: 16 pages in 4 colors
Binding: Saddle Stitched
Mailing List Information: Names for rent
In Business: 38 years
Number of Employees: 1500

8079 Packaging Machinery Services
Packaging Machinery Services,Inc.
17877 St. Clair Ave.
Cleveland, OH 44110   216-451-7878
                          Fax: 216-451-4952
sales@packnow.com
www.Packnow.Com

Packaging machinery and services.

President: Ken Franklin
Marketing Manager: Ted Tate
Buyers: Ken Franklin
In Business: 25 years
Number of Employees: 44
Sales Information: $1,000,000 - $5,000,000

8080 Paket Contract Packaging
Packet Corporation
9165 S Harbor Ave
Chicago, IL 60617-4436   773-221-7300
                          Fax: 773-221-7316
www.Paketcorp.Com

Contract packaging

President: Mark O'Malley
MOmalley@paketcorp.com
CFO: Stella Diaz
SDiaz@paketcorp.com
Marketing Manager: Carvel Massengale
CMassengale@paketcorp.com
VP of Operations: David Alvarez
DAlvarez@paketcorp.com
VP of Product Development: Matt Zoeller
MZoeller@paketcorp.com
Customer Service Manager: DanO'Malley
DOmalley@paketcorp.com
In Business: 58 years
Number of Employees: 50
Sales Information: $3MM to $5MM

8081 Panef Corporation
Pack Logix, Inc.
5700 W Douglas Ave
Milwaukee, WI 53218-1691   414-464-7200
                          800-448-1247
                          Fax: 414-462-0980
info@pack-logix.com
www.Panef.Com

Contract packaging

Chairman: George Walker
President: Mike Smith
In Business: 67 years
Number of Employees: 30
Sales Information: $10,000,000 - $25,000,000

8082 Peacock Engineering Company
Peacock Engineering Co. LLC
1800 Averill Rd
Geneva, IL 60134-1684   630-845-9400
                          Fax: 630-845-9401
sales@peacockeng.com
www.Peacockeng.Com

Contract packaging and assembly

Chairman: Jerry Hayden
President: Michael a Bilder
CFO: Michael Wallach
Production Manager: Thomas McCaffer

In Business: 73 years
Number of Employees: 1700
Sales Information: $20MM to $50MM

8083 Perry Equipment Company
Perry Equipment Company
25 Mount Laurel Rd
Hainesport, NJ 08036-2711   609-267-1603
                          Fax: 609-267-4499
www.perry-equipment.co.uk

Packaging services

President: Gregg Epstein
In Business: 79 years
Number of Employees: 80
Sales Information: $500M to $1MM

8084 Plasteel Coporation
Plasteel Corporation
26970 Princeton Ave.
P.O.Box 555
Inkster, MI 48141-555   313-562-5400
                          Fax: 313-562-5402
customerservice@plasteelcorp.com
www.Plasteelcorp.Com

Foam specialists

President: William E Ohlsson Sr
Marketing Manager: W Olsen Jr
In Business: 74 years
Number of Employees: 23
Sales Information: $10,000,000 - $25,000,000

8085 Plastic Bag and Packaging
International Plastics, Inc.
185 Commerce Center
Greenville, SC 29615-5817   864-297-8000
                          800-820-4722
                          Fax: 864-297-7186
www.interplas.com

Plastic bags and packaging supplies for businesses

President: Steve McClure
CFO: Carolyn Robinson
Marketing Manager: Mark McClure
Production Manager: Mark McClure
Credit Cards: MasterCard
Catalog Cost: Free
Catalog Circulation: Mailed 12 time(s) per year
Average Order Size: $250
Printing Information: 48 pages in 4 colors on Glossy Stock
Press: Web Press
Binding: Saddle Stitched
Mailing List Information: Names for rent
In Business: 49 years
Number of Employees: 36
Sales Information: $20,000,000-$50,000,000

8086 Polyair Corporation
Polyair
330 Humberline Drive
Toronto, CN 60628-5150   416-679-6600
                          888-679-6600
                          Fax: 416-679-6610
marketing@polyair.com
www.Polyair.Com

Various sized sheets of air-bubbles for packaging needs

President: Carl Honaker
Production Manager: Lyn Vinicky
In Business: 11 years
Number of Employees: 100
Sales Information: $10,000,000 - $25,000,000

8087 Products Filling & Packaging Company Catalog
Products Filling & Packaging Company
1151 N Ellsworth Avenue
Villa Park, IL 60181   630-833-9700
                          800-559-1163
                          Fax: 630-833-9703
sales@profilpak.com
www.profilpak.com

Private label and contract packaging services of lubricants, adhesives and silicones

President: Betty B Graham
bbg@profilpak.com
Vice President: Anthony A. Graham
aag@profilpak.com
Manager: Earlene R. Graham
erg@profilpak.com
Credit Cards: AMEX; MasterCard
Mailing List Information: Names for rent
In Business: 67 years

8088 Raani Corporation
Raani Corporation
5202 70th Pl Chicago
Bedford Park, IL 60638-5637   708-594-2222
                          Fax: 708-496-8906

Contract packaging for private labels

President: Rashid Chaudary
Number of Employees: 200
Sales Information: $25,000,000 - $50,000,000

8089 Ryerson Wholesale Industrial Catalog
Ryerson Inc.
2621 W. 15th Place
Chicago, IL 60680-8000   773-762-2121
                          800-621-3309
                          Fax: 800-453-3684
www.ryerson.com

Material handling equipment and storage

President: Edward J. Lehner
CFO: Erich Schnaufer
Marketing Manager: Philip Areddia
Production Manager: Jennifer Pepping
Managing Director: Tony Gosse
Chief Operating Officer: Stephen Makarewicz
Chief Human Resources Officer: Roger W. Lindsay
Buyers: Jennifer Pepping
Catalog Cost: Free
Catalog Circulation: Mailed 3 time(s) per year to 1.5M
Printing Information: 188 pages in 3 colors on Glossy Stock
Press: Web Press
Binding: Perfect Bound
Mailing List Information: Names for rent
In Business: 169 years

8090 Servall Packaging Industries
Serv-All Packaging
3301 S. Harbor Blvd
Suite 105A
Santa Ana, CA 92704-1645   714-433-2210
                          Fax: 310-533-6077
www.serv-allpackaging.com

Packaging services

President: Scott Martineau
CFO: D Henry
In Business: 27 years
Number of Employees: 150
Sales Information: $10,000,000 - $25,000,000

8091 Shurtape
Shurtape Technologies, LLC
1712 8th StreetDrive SE
Hickory, NC 28602-1530   828-322-2700
                          888-442-8273
                          Fax: 828-322-4029
custservice@shurtape.com
www.shurtape.com

Pressure sensitive tapes for industrial and domestic applications

Credit Cards: MasterCard; Visa
Catalog Cost: Free
Catalog Circulation: Mailed 1 time(s) per year
Printing Information: 8 pages in 4 colors
Binding: Saddle Stitched
In Business: 60 years
Number of Employees: 1500

8092 Silgan Plastics
Silgn Plastics
14515 North Outer Forty
Suite 210
Chesterfield, MO 63017-1080   800-2 S-GLAN
                                800-274-5426
                           Fax: 314-469-5387
                       www.Silganplastics.Com

Packaging for personal care, household, industrial and food markets

President: Christoph Ganz
CFO: Stephen Lysik
Senior Vice President, Concrete: Mike Campion
EVP, Refurbishment: Rick Montani
EVP, Industry Division: Dan Hilliard
In Business: 104 years
Number of Employees: 4000
Sales Information: $25,000,000 - $50,000,000

8093 Simplimatic Engineering Company
PO Box 11709
Lynchburg, VA 24506-1709   434-582-1200
                         Fax: 434-582-1284
                      www.crown-simplimatic.com

Product handling and packaging equipment

President: Dennis Jaisle
Marketing Manager: JW Parker
Number of Employees: 450

8094 Sportime Catalog
School Specialty Inc
PO Box 1579
Appleton, WI 54912-1579   888-388-3224
                           800-283-5700
                      Fax: 888-388-6344
                  orders@schoolspecialty.com
                   www.schoolspecialty.com

Innovative audio/video products for physical education & recreation, sensory solutions, school supplies, early childhood and special needs products and equipment

Chairman: James R. Henderson
President: Joseph M. Yorio
CFO: Kevin Baehler
Principal: Justin Lu
Portfolio Manager: Madhu Satyanarayana
EVP, Distribution: Patrick T. Collins
Credit Cards: AMEX; MasterCard
Catalog Cost: Free
Catalog Circulation: Mailed 1 time(s) per year
Printing Information: 400 pages

8095 Tenco Assemblies
Tenco Assemblies, Inc
620 Nolan Avenue
Morrisville, PA 19067-7513   215-736-2746
                             855-888-3626
                        Fax: 215-736-2704
                    info@tencoassemblies.com
                     www.Tencoassemblies.Com

Contract packaging

President: Joseph Tentilucci
Marketing Manager: Joe Tentilucci
In Business: 37 years
Number of Employees: 100
Sales Information: $5MM to $10MM

8096 Uline Shipping Supply Specialists
Uline
12575 Uline Drive
Pleasant Prairie, WI 53158   262-612-4200
                             800-295-5510
                        Fax: 800-295-5571
                   customer.service@uline.com
                         www.uline.com

Uline offers over 20,000 boxes, plastic poly bags, mailing tubes, warehouse supplies and bubble wrap for storage, packaging, or shipping supplies

President: Liz Uihlein
CEO: Dick Uihlein

Vice President: Duke Uihlein
Vice President: Steve Uihlein
Buyers: Brian Uihlein
Phil Hunt
Credit Cards: AMEX; MasterCard; Visa
Catalog Cost: Free
Catalog Circulation: Mailed 2 time(s) per year
Printing Information: 664 pages in 4 colors on Glossy Stock
Press: Web Press
Binding: Saddle Stitched
Mailing List Information: Names for rent
In Business: 35 years
Number of Employees: 250
Sales Information: $ 20-50 Million

8097 Unette Corporation
Unette Corporation
1578 Sussex Turnpike
Building #5
Randolph, NJ 07869-1607   973-328-6800
                           973-584-4794
                      Fax: 973-584-4794
                      info@unette.com
                      www.Unette.Com

Packaging of liquids and semi-liquids

President: Carol Ann Hark
Sales Service Coordinator: Dawn Stone
info@unette.com
Sales Service Coordinator: Olia Teslenko
Sales Service Coordinator: Kara Weissman
In Business: 60 years
Number of Employees: 100-
Sales Information: $10MM to $20MM

8098 Unit Pack Company
Unit Pack Company, Inc.
7 Lewis Road
Cedar Grove, NJ 07009-1498   973-239-4112
                          Fax: 973-239-0429
                          info@unitpack.com
                          www.Unitpack.Com

Saran wrap film packaging

President: Ernest Loesser
Founder: Ernest Loesser Sr.
In Business: 51 years
Number of Employees: 25
Sales Information: $1,000,000 - $5,000,000

8099 United Resin Products
United Resin Corporation
4359 Normandy Court
Royal Oak, MI 48073   248-549-8200
                       800-521-4757
                  Fax: 248-549-9587
             urcepoxy@unitedresin.com
             www.unitedresincorp.com

Adhesive supplies

President: Pat Grande
In Business: 30 years
Number of Employees: 100
Sales Information: $10,000,000 - $25,000,000

8100 Vee Pak
Vee Pak, Inc.
6710 River Road
Hodgkins, IL 60525-4310   708-482-8881
                       Fax: 708-482-3343
                       info@veepak.com
                       www.Veepak.Com

Contract packaging

President: Ralph Vennetti
In Business: 11 years
Number of Employees: 50
Sales Information: $10,000,000 - $25,000,000

8101 Vinylweld
Blair Packaging
2011 W Hastings Street
Chicago, IL 60608   312-243-0606
                     800-444-4020
                Fax: 312-942-0693

Audio cassette packaging

Marketing Manager: Rick Galfano
Printing Information: 12 pages in 2 colors
Binding: Saddle Stitched
Number of Employees: 250-
Sales Information: $25,000,000 - $50,000,000

Plastics
General

8102 AIN Plastics of Michigan
ThyssenKrupp Materials NA, Inc.
22355 West 11 Mile Road
Southfield, MI 48033   248-233-5600
                        877-246-7700
                   Fax: 248-233-5699
www.tkmna.com/tkmna/TKMNADivisions/AINP
                        lastics/index.html

Plastic material manufacturers

Chairman: Joachim Limberg
President: Christian Dohr
CFO: Norbert Goertz
Chief Executive Officer: Christian Dohr
President: Werner Adamofsky
President: Brian Diephuis
In Business: 43 years
Number of Employees: 2900
Sales Information: $2.5 billion

8103 Abbeon Cal Plastic Working Tools
Abbeon Cal, Inc.
123 Gray Ave
Santa Barbara, CA 93101-1809   805-966-0810
                                800-922-0977
                           Fax: 805-966-7659
                        abbeoncal@abbeon.com
                           www.abbeon.com

Scientific instruments and industrial equipment, tools and equipment, plastic working tools for cutting bending and welding

President: Alice Wertheim
Marketing Manager: Bob Brunsman
VP: Kathering Wertheim
Founder: Jared Abbeon
Credit Cards: AMEX; MasterCard; Visa
Catalog Circulation: to 250M
Average Order Size: $500
Printing Information: 128 pages in 4 colors on Newsprint
Press: Web Press
Binding: Folded
In Business: 41 years
Number of Employees: 8
Sales Information: $1.89 Million

8104 Adapt Plastics
Adapt Plastics Inc
7949 Forest Hills Rd
Loves Park, IL 61111-2900   815-633-9263
                             800-633-9806
                        Fax: 815-654-2817
                    sales@adaptplastics.com
                      www.adaptplastics.com

Plastic fabricators

President: Larry Phippen
In Business: 36 years
Number of Employees: 40
Sales Information: $5,000,000 - $10,000,000

8105 Allied Plastic Supply
Allied Plastic Supply, Inc.
10828 Shady Trail
Dallas, TX 75220-1306   214-350-3990
                         888-838-2287
                    Fax: 214-350-3998
                 sales@alliedplastic.org
                  www.alliedplastic.org

Plastics and plastic products

President: Eddie Walker
Salesman: Aaron R Dennis
Salesman: Dan Benson
Catalog Cost: Free
Average Order Size: $50

Printing Information: on Glossy Stock
Mailing List Information: Names for rent
In Business: 36 years
Number of Employees: 60
Sales Information: $10MM to $20MM

8106 American Acrylics

American Acrylics
8124 Central Park Avenue
Skokie, IL 60076-4747   847-674-7800
                              Fax: 847-674-7888
americanacrylics@gmail.com
www.americanacrylics.com

Fabricators of plastic sheets, rods, tubes and rolls

President: Jim Scobie
Marketing Manager: James Luebke
In Business: 42 years
Number of Employees: 11
Sales Information: $1,000,000 - $5,000,000

8107 American Durafilm Company

American Durafilm
55 Boynton Road
PO Box 6770
Holliston, MA 01746-6770   508-429-8000
                              888-809-2314
                        Fax: 508-429-8500
info@americandurafilm.com
www.americandurafilm.com/

teflon coatings, high performance films

President: Jay Hendrick
In Business: 66 years
Sales Information: $5MM to $10MM

8108 Atlas Fibre Company

Atlas Fibre Company
3721 W Chase Avenue
Skokie, IL 60076-4008   847-674-1234
                              800-323-1408
                        Fax: 847-674-1723
sales@atlasfibre.com
www.atlasfibre.com/

Plastic fabricators

President: Mark L Grusin
Sales Engineer: Dan Kaczmarek
Sales Engineer: Deb Blanco
Sales Engineer: Darrell Booton
Mailing List Information: Names for rent
In Business: 56 years
Number of Employees: 100
Sales Information: $5,000,000 - $10,000,000

8109 Colvin-Friedman Company

Colvin Friedman Company
1311 Commerce Street
697 Morris Turnpike
Petaluma, CA 94954   707-769-4488
                              800-346-9296
                        Fax: 707-773-5844
sales@colvin-friedman.com
www.Colvin-Friedman.Com

Custom fabricating and die cutting

President: Mitchell Friedman
Marketing Manager: MA Friedman
In Business: 69 years
Number of Employees: 13
Sales Information: $1,000,000 - $5,000,000

8110 Comco Plastics

Nytef Plastics
9831 Jamaica Ave
Jamaica, NY 11421-2213   718-849-9000
                        Fax: 718-441-5361
www.Nytefplastics.Com

Fabricators of plastic parts

President: Slava Fishkin
EVP: M.R. French III
In Business: 43 years
Number of Employees: 120
Sales Information: $10,000,000 - $25,000,000

8111 Drytac

Drytac
34210 9th Avenue S
Suite 110
Federal Way, WA 98003   253-661-1020
                              800-562-6251
                        Fax: 800-622-8839
www.drytac.com

Overlaminating films, roller laminators, mounting adhesives, vacuum/drymount presses, specialty films/backers, precision cutters, display accessories, inkjet media, finishing accessories

Chairman: Richard Kelley
President: Marc Oosterhuis
Marketing Manager: Thomas Denstorff
Fulfillment: Mike Davis
VP: Jim Tatum
European Sales Director: Steve Broad
Manufacturing & Technical Manager: David Johnson
Credit Cards: AMEX; MasterCard
Catalog Circulation: Mailed 1 time(s) per year
Printing Information: 10 pages in 2 colors on Matte Stock
Binding: Saddle Stitched
In Business: 28 years

8112 Durham Manufacturing Company

The Durham Manufacturing Company
201 Main Street
Durham, CT 06422   860-349-3427
                              800-243-3774
                        Fax: 860-349-8235
info@durhammfg.com
www.durhammfg.com

Industrial storage bins, cabinets, material handling carts, trucks, work stations, work benches, shelving, first aid boxes & cabinets, safety products and literature & mail organizers

President: Richard Patterson
CFO: John Gowac
Credit Cards: AMEX; MasterCard
Catalog Cost: Free
Printing Information: 180 pages
In Business: 93 years
Number of Employees: 200
Sales Information: $ 20-50 Million

8113 Franklin Fibre-Lamitex Company

Franklin Fibre-Lamitex Corporation
903 East 13th Street
PO Box 1768
Wilmington, DE 19899   302-652-3621
                              800-233-9739
                        Fax: 302-571-9754
info@franklinfibre.com
www.Franklinfibre.Com

Plastics fabricators

President: James Vachris
Number of Employees: 41
Sales Information: $1,000,000 - $5,000,000

8114 Industrial Arts Supply Company

Industrial Arts Supply Company
5724 West 36th Street
Minneapolis, MN 55416-2594   952-920-2947
                              888-919-0899
sales@iasco-tesco.com
www.iasco-tesco.Com

Industrial art supplies; plastics, tools, molds, electronics and hobby items

Credit Cards: MasterCard; Visa
Catalog Cost: $3
Catalog Circulation: to 50M
Printing Information: 165 pages in 1 color
In Business: 39 years
Number of Employees: 20
Sales Information: $1-3 Million

8115 Leroy Plastics

LeRoy Plastics, Incorporated
20 Lent Avenue
Le Roy, NY 14482-1009   585-768-8158
                        Fax: 585-768-4283
Sales@LeRoyPlastics.com
www.LeroyPlastics.Com

Plastic fabricators

President: Keith Truax
Marketing Manager: E Truax
Printing Information: 14 pages
In Business: 45 years
Number of Employees: 25
Sales Information: $1,000,000 - $5,000,000

8116 M&T Plastics Industrial Products Catalog

M&T Industries, LLC
15210 Desman Road
La Mirada, CA 90638-1109   714-670-0700
                              800-234-0550
                        Fax: 714-670-0701

plastic pipes, fabricators pumps and etc

President: Mary Grey-Teska
Catalog Cost: Free
Catalog Circulation: to 50M
Printing Information: 244 pages in 2 colors on Newsprint
Binding: Perfect Bound
Number of Employees: 20

8117 Midwest Plastics

Midwest Plastics
6460 South 84th St.
Omaha, NE 68127-4101   402-339-1226
                              800-777-7910
                        Fax: 402-339-1277
mleahy@midwestplastics.com
www.Midwestplastics.Com

Plastics fabricators

President: Michael F Leahy
In Business: 31 years
Number of Employees: 14
Sales Information: $1,000,000 - $5,000,000

8118 Moore Fabrication

Moore Fabrication
5645 Northdale St
#A
Houston, TX 77087-4027   713-643-7477
                              800-624-7757
                        Fax: 713-643-9036
sales@moorefabrication.com
www.Moorefabrication.Com

Plastic fabricators

President: William i Moore Iii
Number of Employees: 20
Sales Information: $1,000,000 - $5,000,000

8119 POBCO Plastics & Hardwood

POBCO Inc
99 Hope Ave
Worcester, MA 01603-2298   508-791-6376
                              800-222-6376
                        Fax: 508-791-3247
pobco@pobcoplastics.com
www.pobcoplastics.com

Conveyor components and friction reducing components made from bearing grade and food compliant plastics, lube filled hardwood, includes guide rails chain guides, wear strip and bearings

President: Stephen Johnson
Marketing Manager: Tom Johnson
International Marketing Manager: Tom Johnson
Catalog Cost: Free
Catalog Circulation: Mailed 12 time(s) per year to 25M
Printing Information: 126 pages in 2 colors on Glossy Stock
Press: Letterpress
Binding: Saddle Stitched

Mailing List Information: Names for rent
In Business: 56 years
Number of Employees: 50
Sales Information: $2,500,000

8120 Pacific States Felt & Manufacturing Company
Pacific States Felt & Manufacturing Comp
23850 Clawiter Road Ste 20
Hayward, CA 94545-1723   510-783-0277
                          800-566-8866
                     Fax: 510-783-4725
              sales@pacificstatesfelt.net
              www.pacificstatesfelt.net

Gasket manufacturer, rubber fabricators, plastics fabricators

President: Walter L Perscheid Jr
Marketing Manager: K Gudjohnsen
Catalog Cost: Free
Catalog Circulation: to 2000
Printing Information: 4 pages in 2 colors on Glossy Stock
Binding: Folded
Mailing List Information: Names for rent
In Business: 93 years
Number of Employees: 25
Sales Information: $1,000,000 - $5,000,000

8121 Pawling Corporation
Pawling Corporation
32 Nelson Hill Road
P.O. Box 200
Wassaic, NY 12592-1188   845-373-9300
                          800-431-3456
                     sales@Pawling.com
                     www.pawling.com

Rubber and plastic products

CFO: Ralph Skokan
Catalog Cost: Free
Catalog Circulation: Mailed 1 time(s) per year
Printing Information: 76 pages in 4 colors
In Business: 72 years
Number of Employees: 350
Sales Information: $100,000,000 - $500,000,0

8122 Petra Manufacturing Company
Petra Manufacturing Company
6600 W Armitage Ave
Chicago, IL 60707-3908   773-622-1475
                          800-888-7387
                     Fax: 773-622-9448
              sales@petramanufacturing.com
              www.petramanufacturing.com

Heat sealed and sewn vinyl products, binders, CD Rom pics, and presentation products

President: Tom Cordena
Marketing Manager: Cheryl Visockis
Production Manager: Walther V
Mailing List Information: Names for rent
In Business: 82 years
Number of Employees: 80
Sales Information: $5,000,000 - $10,000,000

8123 Petro Plastics Company
Petro Plastics Company,Inc
450 South Avenue
P.O. Box 167
Garwood, NJ 07027-167   908-789-1200
                          800-486-4738
                     Fax: 908-789-1381
              petroquotes@petroplastics.com
              www.Petroplastics.Com

Plastic fabricators

President: Louis J Petrozziello
In Business: 63 years
Number of Employees: 55
Sales Information: $5,000,000 - $10,000,000

8124 Phoenix Plastics
Phoenix Plastics
5400 Jefferson Chemical Rd
Conroe, TX 77301-6836   866-760-2311
                     Fax: 936-760-2322
              phoenix@phoenixplastics.com
              www.Phoenixplastics.Com

Plastic fabricators

President: Rod Garcia
In Business: 19 years
Number of Employees: 62
Sales Information: $1,000,000 - $5,000,000

8125 Piper Plastics
Piper Plastics,Inc
1840 Enterprise Court
Libertyville, IL 60048-9731   847-367-0110
                          800-321-8787
                     Fax: 847-367-0566
              ILSales@piperplastics.com
              www.piperplastics.com

Plastics fabricators

President: Martin White
Number of Employees: 50
Sales Information: $1,000,000 - $5,000,000

8126 Plas-Tanks Industries
Plas-Tanks Industries,Inc.
39 Standen Dr
Hamilton, OH 45015-2209   513-942-3800
                     Fax: 513-942-3993
              www.Plastanks.Com

Plastics fabricators

President: J Kent Covey
In Business: 39 years
Sales Information: $10MM to $20MM

8127 Plastic Bag and Packaging
International Plastics, Inc.
185 Commerce Center
Greenville, SC 29615-5817   864-297-8000
                          800-820-4722
                     Fax: 864-297-7186
              www.interplas.com

Plastic bags and packaging supplies for businesses

President: Steve McClure
CFO: Carolyn Robinson
Marketing Manager: Mark McClure
Production Manager: Mark McClure
Credit Cards: MasterCard
Catalog Cost: Free
Catalog Circulation: Mailed 12 time(s) per year
Average Order Size: $250
Printing Information: 48 pages in 4 colors on Glossy Stock
Press: Web Press
Binding: Saddle Stitched
Mailing List Information: Names for rent
In Business: 49 years
Number of Employees: 36
Sales Information: $20,000,000-$50,000,000

8128 Plasticad Line
Abnote North America
225 Rivermoor Street
Boston, MA 02132-4905   800-776-7333
                     Fax: 617-327-1235
              marketing@abnotena.com
              www.abnote.com

Fabricators and converters of sheet plastics - custom printed plastic cards, tags, etc

Chairman: Steven Singer
President: David Kober
CFO: Stephen Sanford
Marketing Manager: Eric Blank
Production Manager: Larry Grant
Catalog Cost: Free
Printing Information: 4 pages in 2 colors
In Business: 220 years

Number of Employees: 100-
Sales Information: $10,000,000 - $25,000,000

8129 Pueblo Diversified Industries
PDI Pueblo
2828 Granada Blvd
Pueblo, CO 81005-3198   719-564-0000
                          800-466-8393
                     Fax: 719-564-3407
              www.pdipueblo.net

Plastics fabricators

President: Karen K Lillie
Marketing Manager: Mark Bunch
Credit Cards: AMEX; MasterCard
Number of Employees: 275
Sales Information: $1,000,000 - $5,000,000

8130 Rochling Engineered Plastics
Rochling
PO Box 2729
Gastonia, NC 28053-2729   704-922-7814
                          800-541-4419
                     Fax: 704-922-7651
              www.roechling.com

Plastics manufacturers and fabricators

President: Lewis Carter
CFO: Cletus O'Dell
Marketing Manager: Paul Krawczyk
Production Manager: Jack Ramsaur
Printing Information: 35 pages
Mailing List Information: Names for rent
In Business: 16 years
Number of Employees: 80
Sales Information: $5,000,000 - $10,000,000

8131 Space Age Plastic Fabricators
Space Age Plastic Fabricators, Inc.
4519 White Plains Road
Bronx, NY 10470-1608   718-324-6677
                          800-222-3240
                     Fax: 718-994-0582
              sapf@plastic64.com
              www.Plastic64.Com

Plastic fabricators, CNC milling and turning

President: Arthur Barsky
Production Manager: Joel Barsky
In Business: 51 years
Number of Employees: 35
Sales Information: $1,000,000 - $5,000,000

8132 T/C Press
Teachers College Press
P.O. Box 20
Williston, VT 05495-20   800-575-6566
                     Fax: 802-864-7626
              tcp.orders@aidcvt.com
              www.tcpress.com

Books on plastics and adhesives

President: George Epstein
Production Manager: Irene Stone
Director: Carole Saltz
Executive Acquisitions Editor: Brian Ellerbeck
ellerbeck@tc.edu.com
Subsidiary Rights Manager/ Special: Libby Powell
Catalog Cost: $40
Catalog Circulation: Mailed 4 time(s) per year
Printing Information: 20 pages in 2 colors on Matte Stock
Press: Sheetfed Press
Binding: Saddle Stitched
In Business: 100 years
Number of Employees: 5

8133 United States Plastic Corporation
United States Plastic Corporation
1390 Neubrecht Road
Lima, OH 45801-3196   800-769-1157
                          800-809-4217
                     Fax: 800-854-5498
              usp@usplastic.com
              www.usplastic.com

Distributor of industrial plastic products

President: Wesley A Lytle
CFO: D Olson
Founder: Dr. R. Stanley Tam
Credit Cards: MasterCard
Catalog Circulation: Mailed 1 time(s) per year
Printing Information: 300 pages in 4 colors on Matte Stock
Press: Web Press
Binding: Perfect Bound
In Business: 60 years

8134 Universal Plastics
Universal Plastic & Machine
7661 Freedom Ave
Canton, OH 44720-2086   330-433-2860
                              Fax: 330-433-2867
                  Plastics@UPLInternational.com
                  www.Universalplasticsmachine.Com

Plastics fabricators

President: Jeffrey Scarpitti
CFO: Karen Scarpitti
Marketing Manager: Wade Scarpitti
Production Manager: Pat Foster
International Marketing Manager: Jeff Scarpitti
Buyers: Jamie Hollard
Mailing List Information: Names for rent
In Business: 39 years
Number of Employees: 26
Sales Information: $1,000,000 - $5,000,000

8135 Whirl-Pak
Nasco International
901 Janesville Ave
P.O. Box 901
Fort Atkinson, WI 53538-901   920-563-2446
                                800-558-9595
                              Fax: 920-563-6044
                         custserv@enasco.com
                              www.enasco.com

Single use plastic containers

President: Andrew Reinen
Marketing Manager: Phil Niemeyer
Manager, Data Processing: Mike Wagner
Credit Cards: AMEX; MasterCard; Visa
Printing Information: 40 pages
In Business: 74 years
Number of Employees: 450
Sales Information: $ 10-20 Million

8136 Wilmington Fibre Specialty Company
Wilmington Fibre Specialty Company
700 Washington St New Castle
New Castle, DE 19720-192   302-328-7525
                                800-220-5132
                              Fax: 302-328-6630
                         sales@wilmfibre.com
                            www.wilmfibre.com

Plastics fabricators

President: B Scott-Morris
In Business: 111 years
Number of Employees: 25
Sales Information: $1,000,000 - $5,000,000

Printing
Equipment

8137 Brandtjen & Kluge
Brandtjen & Kluge
539 Blanding Woods Road
St Croix Falls, WI 54024-9001   715-483-3265
                                 800-826-7320
                              Fax: 715-483-1640
                             sales@kluge.biz
                              www.kluge.biz

Embossing, die cutting and foil stamping presses, folding and gluing equipment, blanking systems, UV coaters

Chairman: Michael Aumann, CEO
President: Hank Brandtjen
Marketing Manager: Scott Hansen
Production Manager: Don Kronschnable/Mutt Wilson

International Marketing Manager: Thomas Andersen
Buyers: Kevin Robbins
In Business: 96 years
Number of Employees: 30
Sales Information: $10,000,000 - $25,000,000

8138 Challenge Machinery
The Challenge Machinery Company
6125 Norton Center Drive
Norton Shores, MI 49441-6081   231-799-8484
                                800-866-7800
                              Fax: 231-798-1275
                        www.Challengemachinery.Com

Cutters, drills, folders and collators

President: Larry J Ritsema
Marketing Manager: Susan Hilliard
  shillard@challengemachinery.com
Production Manager: Wally Jones
Director-Marketing/Sales: Britt Cary
  bcary@challengmachinery.com
Manager - Marketing/Secretary: Susan Hilliard
  shillard@challengemachinery.com
In Business: 145 years
Number of Employees: 225
Sales Information: $10,000,000 - $25,000,000

8139 Douthitt Corporation
The Douthitt Corporation
245 Adair St
Detroit, MI 48207-4287   313-259-1565
                                800-368-8448
                              Fax: 313-259-6806
                          em@douthittcorp.com
                         www.Douthittcorp.Com

Exposure Units for Printed Circuit Boards, Flexographics, Offset Plates and Direct Method Screens, Olec Olite and Theimer Violux Metal Halide lights, bulbs and parts also available

Chairman: Robert Diehl
President: Robert Diehl
Co- president: Douglas Diehl
Co- president: John Diehl
Credit Cards: AMEX; MasterCard
Catalog Cost: Free
Catalog Circulation: Mailed 1 time(s) per year
Printing Information: 34 pages
In Business: 85 years
Number of Employees: 50-1
Sales Information: $5,000,000 - $10,000,000

8140 Fife Corporation
Maxcess
222 West Memorial Road
Oklahoma City, OK 73126-508   405-755-1600
                                800-639-3433
                              Fax: 405-755-8425
                             fife@fife.com
                       www.fife.maxcessintl.com

Automatic webguiding controls and web inspection systems

President: Chuck Mutter
CFO: Merlyn DeVries
Marketing Manager: Kimberly Auger
In Business: 60 years
Number of Employees: 200
Sales Information: $25,000,000 - $50,000,000

8141 Fox Valley Systems
Fox Valley Systems, Inc.
640 Industrial Dr
Dept.Ws
Cary, IL 60013-1944   847-639-5744
                                800-323-4700
                              Fax: 847-639-8190
                       info@foxvalleysystems.com
                            www.foxpaint.com

Aerosol paints, stripping and marking equipment

President: Thomas Smrt
Credit Cards: MasterCard; Visa
Catalog Cost: Free

Catalog Circulation: Mailed 30 time(s) per year
Printing Information: 4 pages
Number of Employees: 100
Sales Information: $25,000,000 - $50,000,000

8142 Gregstrom Corporation
Gregstrom Corporation
64 Holton St
PO Box 609
Woburn, MA 01801-5288   781-935-6600
                              Fax: 781-935-4905
                          info@gregstrom.com
                           www.Gregstrom.Com

Printing machinery

President: Paul Didonato
In Business: 70+ years
Number of Employees: 75
Sales Information: $5,000,000 - $10,000,000

8143 Harris Graphics
Heidelberger
121 Broadway
Dover, NH 03820-3299   603-749-6600
                              Fax: 603-749-0584
                           www.heidelberg.com

Web offset press systems

Chairman: Gerold Linzbach
President: Bob Brown
Marketing Manager: John M Hobby
Production Manager: Robert Brown
Number of Employees: 1100

8144 Heidelberg News
Heidelberg USA
1000 Gutenberg Drive
Kennesaw, GA 30144-7028   770-419-6600
                              Fax: 770-419-6550
                    hus.webmaster@heidelberg.com
                          www.Heidelberg.com

Printing presses, machinery and related equipment including prepress equipment such as scanners, proofing systems and film and plate output devices, and postpress finishing equipment.

Chairman: Rainer Hunds"rfer
Credit Cards: MasterCard
Catalog Circulation: Mailed 2 time(s) per year
Printing Information: 60 pages in 4 colors on Glossy Stock
Binding: Saddle Stitched
Mailing List Information: Names for rent
In Business: 152 years
Number of Employees: 1400
Sales Information: $50MM to $100MM

8145 Man Roland
Man Roland
800 East Oak Hill Drive
Westmont, IL 60559-5587   630-920-2000
                              Fax: 630-920-3582
                           www.manroland.us

Presses

President: Vincent H Lapinski
CFO: Brian Gott
Marketing Manager: Gerald J McConnell
CEO/Managing Director USA and Canad: Michael Mugavero
Vice President, Sheetfed Service Op: Jon Surch
Assistant Vice President of Used Eq: Chris Howes
Number of Employees: 800

8146 Neil Holiday Catalog
Neil Enterprises
450 E Bunker Ct
Vernon Hills, IL 60061   847-549-7627
                                800-621-5584
                              Fax: 847-549-0349
                        info@neilenterprises.com
                        www.neilenterprises.com

Promotional product/photo novelty manufacturer and supplier/distributor of instant
photographic equipment serving the photographic, printing/screenprint, craft, education and ad specialty industries

President: Jerry Fine
Catalog Cost: Free
Catalog Circulation: Mailed 1 time(s) per year
Printing Information: 12 pages in 4 colors on
Glossy Stock
Press: Web Press
Binding: Perfect Bound
In Business: 56 years
Number of Employees: 25
Sales Information: $50-100 Million

8147 Pierce Socbox
Pierce Equipment
1247 Northgate Business Parkway
Madison, TN 37115-3191   615-269-7272
800-828-3120
Fax: 615-292-4418
www.pierceusa.com

Printing equipment and supplies

President: Tom J. Ritter
Marketing Manager: Ron Hartman
In Business: 60 years
Number of Employees: 20-O
Sales Information: $1,000,000 - $5,000,000

8148 Pitman Company
Pitman
721 Union Blvd
Totowa, NJ 07512-2207   973-812-0400
888-274-8626
Fax: 973-812-1815
www.Pitman.Com

Supplies and equipment

President: Anthony Crupi
Number of Employees: 540
Sales Information: $20MM to $50MM

8149 Printers Parts Store
Printers Parts Store
82 Herman St
East Rutherford, NJ 07073-1211 201-935-9595
800-543-1117
Fax: 201-935-5333
info@ppsnj.com
www.Ppsnj.Com

Parts for printing presses

President: Barbara Tignato
Credit Cards: AMEX; MasterCard
Catalog Circulation: Mailed 1 time(s) per year
to 20000
Average Order Size: $100
Printing Information: 32 pages in 1 color on
Matte Stock
Press: Web Press
Binding: Saddle Stitched
Mailing List Information: Names for rent
In Business: 29 years
Sales Information: $1MM to $3MM

8150 Tec Systems
MEGTEC Systems, Inc.
830 Prosper Rd.
De Pere, WI 54115-30   920-336-5715
800-558-2884
Fax: 920-336-3404
www.megtec.com

**Web handling devices, dryers and pollution
control for printers**

President: Mohit Oberoi
CFO: Greg Lynn
Marketing Manager: Mary Vanvonderon
Printing Information: 400 pages
In Business: 40 years
Number of Employees: 500-
Sales Information: $50,000,000 - $100,000,00

8151 Tobias Associates
Tobias Associates, Inc.
50 Industrial Drive
PO Box 2699
Ivyland, PA 18974-347   215-322-1500
800-877-3367
Fax: 215-322-1504
Service@tobiasinc.com
www.densitometer.com

Pressroom equipment

President: Eric Tobias
Marketing Manager: William Bender
In Business: 56 years
Number of Employees: 50
Sales Information: $5,000,000 - $10,000,000

Paper

8152 Becker's School Supplies
Becker's School Supplies
1500 Melrose Highway
Pennsauken, NJ 08110-1410   800-523-1490
Fax: 856-792-4500
customerservice@shopbecker.com
www.shopbecker.com

School supplies, including art supplies

President: George Becker
Credit Cards: MasterCard
Catalog Cost: Free
Catalog Circulation: Mailed 1 time(s) per year
Printing Information: 272 pages in 4 colors
In Business: 89 years
Sales Information: $20-50 Million

8153 Custom Paper Group
FiberMark
70 Front Street
Po Box 498
West Springfield, MA 01089-7052 413-533-0699
800-843-1243
Fax: 413-532-4810
www.fibermark.com

Specialty papers for industrial use

President: Anthony MacLaurin
CFO: Craig Thiel
Marketing Manager: Jonathan Robson
Director of International Sales: Jeff Hopkins
VP of Performance Board: Les Eustace
VP of Customer Service: Robert Archbald
Number of Employees: 90
Sales Information: $10,000,000 - $25,000,000

8154 Georgia-Pacific
Georgia-Pacific
P.O.Box 105605
Atlanta, GA 30348-5605   404-652-4000
800-284-5347
Fax: 404-230-1675
www.Gp.Com

**Offset papers, business paper and uncoated
freesheet paper**

President: James Hannan
Marketing Manager: Frank Murray
SVP: Mike E. Adams
SVP - Human Resources: Julie Brehm
EVP - Packaging: Christian Fischer
Number of Employees: 6100

8155 National Coating Corporation
National Coating Corporation
105 Industrial Way
Rockland, MA 02370   781-878-2781
800-979-9332
Fax: 781-871-4955
sales@natcoat.com
www.natcoat.com

**Contract manufacturing: Custom coating
and saturation services**

President: Paul Stefanutti
Marketing Manager: Jon Platz
Customer & Process Development Mgnr: Bob
Harrington

In Business: 66 years
Number of Employees: 42
Sales Information: $5,000,000 - $10,000,000

8156 Roosevelt Paper
Roosevelt Paper
1 Roosevelt Dr
Mt Laurel, NJ 08054-6312   856-303-4100
800-523-3470
Fax: 856-642-1950
www.Rooseveltpaper.Com

**Distributor and converter of printing papers,
servicing the printing, direct mail and publishing industries; carries most coated and
uncoated grades of paper, as well as special
size rolls and sheets**

Chairman: Ted Kosloff
tkosloff@rooseveltpaper.com
President: David Kosloff
dkosloff@rooseveltpaper.com
CFO: Tony Janulewicz
tjanulewicz@rooseveltpaper.com
VP Sales: Eric Conine
econine@rooseveltpaper.com
Sales Manager: Dennis Carney
dcarney@rooseveltpaper.com
Founder: Irwing Kosloff
In Business: 75 years
Number of Employees: 100
Sales Information: $50MM

8157 Westvaco
MeadWestvaco Corporation
501 South 5th Street
Richmond, VA 23219-501   804-444-1000
Fax: 212-318-5104
www.mwv.com

**Paper products for catalogs, annual reports,
yearbooks, supplements and brochures**

Chairman: John A Luke Jr
President: Dr. Robert K. Beckler
CFO: William Beaver
Marketing Manager: Don Paul
Chief Executive Officer: Steve Voorhees
Chief Sustainability Officer: Nina Butler
Chief Communications Officer: Donna Owens
Cox
Number of Employees: 350
Sales Information: $3MM to $5MM

Services

8158 American Color Printing
American Color
3146 W. Montrose Avenue
Chicago, IL 60618   312-829-1090
866-706-5602
Fax: 312-829-1558
info@americancolor.net
www.americancolor.net

**Print brochures, catalog sheets, post cards,
posters, greeting cards, mouse pads,
menus, stickers, banner stands, vehicle
magnets and vehicle wraps,**

President: Dan Lincoln
Credit Cards: AMEX; MasterCard; Visa
Catalog Circulation: Mailed 1 time(s) per year
Printing Information: 26 pages in 4 colors
Binding: Perfect Bound
In Business: 7 years

8159 B&R Moll
B&R Moll
744 Nina Way
Warminster, PA 18974-1449   267-288-0282
866-438-4583
Fax: 267-288-0284
bmoll@mollbrothers.com
www.mollbrothers.com

**Leading manufacturer of folder/gluers and
specialized bindery/finishing equipment**

Chairman: Rick Moll
President: Bruce Moll

bmoll@mollbrothers.com
Director of Operations: Daniel Moll
dmoll@mollbrothers.com
Manager: Lorenzo Boscaino
lboscaino@mollbrothers.com
Manager Service Technician: Ron Brown
rbrown@mollbrothers.com
Number of Employees: 50
Sales Information: Under $500M

8160 Baldwin
Baldwin
3041 Woodcreek Drive
Suite 102
Downers Grove, IL 60515-4616 913-888-9800
800-654-4999
Fax: 913-888-4015
www.baldwintech.com

Printing services

President: Karl S Puehringer
VP Sales & Marketing: Don Gustafson
Number of Employees: 30
Sales Information: $3MM to $5MM

8161 Base-Line
Base-Line
4 Corporate Drive
Suite 186
Shelton, CT 06484-6206 203-925-0240
800-872-0075
Fax: 203-925-0239
www.base-line.com

Printing services

President: Howard E Harper
Marketing Manager: Roger Giza

8162 Count Numbering Machine
Count Machinery
2128 Auto Park Way
Escondido, CA 92029-1374 760-489-1400
800-468-6237
Fax: 760-489-1543
info114@countmachinery.com
www.Countmachinery.Com

Printing services, numbering, perforating, scoring, and folding equipment

President: Dave Gilbert
Marketing Manager: Sean
International Marketing Manager: Lydia K. Nastich
Credit Cards: AMEX; MasterCard
Printing Information: in 4 colors
Mailing List Information: Names for rent
In Business: 55 years
Number of Employees: 22
Sales Information: $1,000,000 - $5,000,000

8163 Diansupply
Diansuply, Inc.
4550 Commerce Avenue
High Ridge, MO 63049-7201 636-671-9600
800-331-6480
Fax: 636-671-9605
diansuply@diansuply.com
www.diansuply.com

Supplier of die making ejector rubber for the packaging industry

President: Jeremy Guest
Vice President: Christine Guest
Credit Cards: AMEX; MasterCard
Printing Information: 648 pages
Mailing List Information: Names for rent
In Business: 68 years
Number of Employees: 5
Sales Information: $500,000 - $1,000,000

8164 Dingley Press
The Dingley Press
119 Lisbon Street
Lisbon, ME 04250 207-353-4151
info@dingley.com
www.dingley.com

Catalog publications

President: Eric Lane
Marketing Manager: Mary Ann Schwanda
Credit Cards: AMEX; MasterCard
Catalog Circulation: to 200MM
In Business: 89 years
Number of Employees: 300
Sales Information: $25,000,000 - $50,000,000

8165 Foster Manufacturing Company
Foster Keencut
204 B Progress Drive
Montgomeryville, PA 18936 267-413-6220
800-523-4855
Fax: 267-413-6227
information@go-foster.com
www.go-foster.com

Pre-press equipment including inspection systems, filing (flat and vertical), cutters and trimmers, line-up tables, color-correct viewing booths, light tables

President: Ted Borowsky
Marketing Manager: Patty Peterson
Catalog Cost: Free
Catalog Circulation: to 100M
Printing Information: 40 pages in 4 colors on Glossy Stock
Press: Web Press
Binding: Saddle Stitched
Mailing List Information: Names for rent
In Business: 71 years
Number of Employees: 12
Sales Information: $3MM to $5MM

8166 Hadronics
Hadronics
4570 Steel Pl
Cincinnati, OH 45209-1189 513-321-9350
800-829-0826
Fax: 513-321-9377
www.Hadronics.Com

Printing services

President: Mike Green
Marketing Manager: Jeff McCarty
In Business: 28 years
Number of Employees: 60
Sales Information: $5,000,000 - $10,000,000

8167 Imagers
Imagers
1575 Northside Drive, Building 400
Suite 490
Atlanta, GA 30318-5411 404-351-5800
800-232-5411
Fax: 404-351-9020
www.Imagers.Com

Digital output and production services

President: Fred Lines
Vice President of Sales: Joe Edwards
Catalog Circulation: Mailed 1 time(s) per year
Printing Information: 19 pages in 4 colors on Glossy Stock
Press: Web Press
Binding: Saddle Stitched
Sales Information: $10MM to $20MM

8168 International Knife & Saw
International Knife & Saw
1435 North Cashua Dr.
P.O. Box 7588
Florence, SC 29501-7588 843-662-6345
800-354-9872
Fax: 843-684-1103
mkelly@iksinc.com
www.iksinc.com

Industrial knife and saw products

President: Don Weeks
VP, Finance & Manufacturing: Mike Gray
mgray@iksinc.com
VP, Metal & Printing Division: Jim Ranson
jranson@iksinc.com
Executive Vice President of Sales: Terry Isaacs

tisaacs@iksinc.com
Credit Cards: AMEX; MasterCard
Number of Employees: 360
Sales Information: 20MM-50MM

8169 Lubrication Equipment & Accessories
Balcrank Corporation
90 Monticello Rd.
Weaverville, NC 28787 828-645-4261
800-747-5300
Fax: 800-763-0840
www.balcrank.com

Lubrication equipment for automobile, commercial and industrial

President: C. Spackman
Marketing Manager: Paige Browning
VP, Sales & Marketing: Don Youman
dyouman@balcrank.com
Technical Support Specialist: Randy Watts
rwatts@balcrank.com
Technical Support Specialist: Daniel Wilson
dwilson@balcrank.com
Catalog Circulation: Mailed 3 time(s) per year
Printing Information: 100 pages in 2 colors on Glossy Stock
Press: Letterpress
Binding: Perfect Bound
Mailing List Information: Names for rent
In Business: 107 years
Number of Employees: 100
Sales Information: $10,000,000 - $25,000,000

8170 McNaughton & Gunn
McNaughton & Gunn
960 Woodland Drive
Saline, MI 48176 734-429-5411
info@bookprinters.com
www.bookprinters.com

Book manufacturers providing printing and other services for publishers

Chairman: Robert L. McNaughton
President: Julie McFarland
juliem@mcnaughton-gunn.com
CFO: Carlene Rogers
Regional Sales Manager: Chris Shore
chriss@mcnaughton-gunn.com
Regional Sales Manager: Marc Moore
marcm@mcnaughton-gunn.com
Exec. Dir. Of Sales/Marketing: Jonnie A. Bryant
jonnieb@mcnaughton-gunn.com
In Business: 42 years
Number of Employees: 250
Sales Information: $10,000,000 - $25,000,000

8171 Paul Leibinger Numbering Machine
Leibinger
221 Wilson Avenue
Norwalk, CT 06854-5026 203-853-0022
Fax: 203-853-3355
info@leibingerusa.com
leibinger-group.com

Printing services, numbering machines, marking and coding, high resolution ink jet, camera and monitoring

President: Paul Leibinger
Credit Cards: MasterCard; Visa
In Business: 67 years
Number of Employees: 200
Sales Information: $500M to $1MM

8172 Perretta Graphic
Perretta Graphics Corporation
46 Violet Ave
Poughkeepsie, NY 12601-1521 845-473-0550
800-537-0550
Fax: 845-454-7507
info@perretta.com
www.Perretta.Com

Printing services

President: Christopher Perretta
Marketing Manager: Bruce Quilliam
Vice President: Timothy Perretta
tperretta@perretta.com

In Business: 34 years
Number of Employees: 50
Sales Information: $20MM to $50MM

8173 Printing Industries of America
Printing Industries of America
301 Brush Creek Road
Warrendale, PA 15086-6302   412-741-6860
                                   800-910-4283
                              Fax: 412-741-2311
                          printingind@printing.org
                              www.printing.org

Printing and graphic arts

President: Mr Michael F. Makin
Assistant VP: Gary A. Jones
gjones@printing.org
Credit Cards: AMEX; MasterCard
Catalog Circulation: Mailed 1 time(s) per year
to 20M
Printing Information: 40 pages in 2 colors on
Matte Stock
Press: Sheetfed Press
Binding: Saddle Stitched
Number of Employees: 75

8174 Pronto Business Cards
Paradise Press Printing
2065 Range Road
Clearwater, FL 33765-1256   727-447-1871
                                   877-746-8925
                              Fax: 727-447-1866
                Info@paradisepressprinting.com
                          www.prontotradeprint.com

Raised letter business cards and stationery, full color business cards, postcards, announcements and invitations

President: Melissa Neipert
CEO: Cindy Butler
Senior Customer Service Rep: Charlie Legg
Customer Service Rep: Terry Lagano
Credit Cards: AMEX; MasterCard
Catalog Cost: Free
Catalog Circulation: to 520
Printing Information: 50 pages on Matte Stock
Press: Sheetfed Press
Binding: Perfect Bound
Mailing List Information: Names for rent
In Business: 14 years
Number of Employees: 5
Sales Information: $500M to $1MM

8175 Quick Draw & Machining
Quick Draw & Machining, Inc
4869 McGrath St # 130
Suite 130
Ventura, CA 93003-7767   805-644-6888
                                888-254-7797
                           Fax: 805-644-7884
                       info@QuickDraw.com
                          www.Quickdraw.Com

Deep drawings, stampings and impact extrusions, complex shapes from sheet metal for medical, AVS and commercial applications

President: Terry Ward-Llewellyn
Marketing Manager: Linda Luce
Production Manager: Jay Wolf
Fulfillment: Linda Luce
Quality Manager: Brandon Nichols
Accounts Manager: John Luce
Engineering Department: LeRoy Smith
Credit Cards: MasterCard
Catalog Cost: Free
Catalog Circulation: Mailed 52 time(s) per
year to 3M+
Average Order Size: $30
Printing Information: 4 pages in 4 colors
Mailing List Information: Names for rent
List Manager: Ron Boyd
In Business: 62 years
Number of Employees: 15
Sales Information: $1,000,000 - $5,000,000

8176 Rapidocolor Corporation
Rapidocolor Corporation
705 E Union Street
West Chester, PA 19382-4937   610-344-0506
                                     800-872-7436
                                Fax: 610-344-0506
                           csr@rapidocolor.com
                              www.rapidocolor.com

Printing services

President: John Powderly
Marketing Manager: Frank Sheldon
Credit Cards: MasterCard
Catalog Cost: Free
Catalog Circulation: Mailed 40 time(s) per
year to 40M
Printing Information: 30 pages in 4 colors on
Glossy Stock
Press: Letterpress
Binding: Saddle Stitched
Mailing List Information: Names for rent
In Business: 27 years
Number of Employees: 20-5
Sales Information: $1,000,000 - $5,000,000

8177 Rollem Corporation of America
Rollem Corporation of America Inc.
1650 S. Lewis Street
Anaheim, CA 92805-5434   714-935-9130
                                800-272-4381
                           Fax: 714-935-9131
                    dsherwood@rollemusa.com
                          www.Rollemusa.Com

Printing services

President: Larry Corwin
Marketing Manager: Susan Corwin
VP: Richard Nigro
In Business: 85 years
Number of Employees: 10
Sales Information: $5MM to $10MM

8178 Sprayway
Sprayway, Inc.
1005 S. Westgate Ave.
Addison, IL 60101-4421   630-628-3000
                                800-332-9000
                           Fax: 630-543-7797
                       info@spraywayinc.com
                          www.spraywayinc.com

Printing services

President: John Ferring
Marketing Manager: Jim Bright
Printing Information: 4 pages in 4 colors on
Glossy Stock
Binding: Folded
Mailing List Information: Names for rent
In Business: 68 years
Number of Employees: 75
Sales Information: $1,000,000 - $5,000,000

8179 Sun Process Converting
Sun Process Converting, Inc.
1660 Kenneth Dr
Mt Prospect, IL 60056-5515   847-593-0447
                                    800-323-0697
                               Fax: 847-593-0115
                           sales@sunprocess.com
                              www.Sunprocess.Com

Adhesive coating, laminating, converting, screen printing

President: Michael Moore
CFO: Bonnie Moravectz
Marketing Manager: Chris Moravectz
Production Manager: Tim Fitzgerald
Fulfillment: Denis Schauner
International Marketing Manager: Cameron
Griffiths
Buyers: Nilo Manasala
Catalog Cost: Free
Average Order Size: $5000
Printing Information: 35 pages in 4 colors on
Glossy Stock
Binding: Perfect Bound
Mailing List Information: Names for rent
In Business: 35 years

Number of Employees: 180
Sales Information: $25,000,000 - $50,000,000

8180 T/J Fabricators
T/J Fabricators, Inc.
2150 Executive Drive
Addison, IL 60101-1487   630-543-2293
                                800-292-3331
                           Fax: 630-543-0538
                         mail@tjfab.com
                          www.Tjfab.Com

Digital scanning inspection, punch presses, press brakes, painting and silk screening

President: Robert Wisniewski
In Business: 48 years
Number of Employees: 43
Sales Information: $1,000,000 - $5,000,000

8181 Therm-O-Type Corporation
THERM-O-TYPE Corp.
509 Church Street
P.O. Box 998
Nokomis, FL 34275-998   941-488-0123
                               800-237-9630
                          Fax: 941-485-6311
                     sales@thermotype.com
                          www.thermotype.com

Printing services

President: Ted Van Pelt
Number of Employees: 60
Sales Information: $5MM to $10MM

8182 Varn
Varn
905 S Westwood Avenue
Addison, IL 60101-4916   630-543-8600
                                800-336-8276
                           Fax: 630-543-8831
                              www.varn.com

Cleaning and chemical supplies for pressrooms

Marketing Manager: Jim Trisuzzi

8183 William Bonnell Company
William Bonnell Company
25 Bonnell Street
Newnan, GA 30263-428   770-253-2020
                         Fax: 800-846-8885
                   FinanceAR@bonlalum.com
                          www.bonlalum.com

Custom and stock dies, aluminum extrusions, electrostatic painting and powder coating

President: Douglas a Monk
In Business: 60 years
Number of Employees: 800
Sales Information: $100,000,000 - $500,000,0

8184 Z-Rite
X-Rite
4300 44th St. SE
Grand Rapids, MI 49512   616-803-2100
                                800-248-9748
                           Fax: 804-030-0400
                              www.x-rite.com

Printing services

President: Ted Thompson
CFO: Duane Kluting
Marketing Manager: Joan Andrew
Number of Employees: 500
Sales Information: $100,000,000 - $500,000,0

Supplies

8185 Baumfolder Corporation
Baumfolder Corporation
1660 Campbell Road
Sidney, OH 45365-728   937-492-1281
                              800-543-6107
                              Fax: 937-492-7280
baumfolder@baumfolder.com
www.Baumfolder.Com

folders, cutters, drills, perfect binders, genuine parts ask about our new ps creasers!

President: Ulrik T Nygaard
Marketing Manager: Mark Pellman
Production Manager: Sam Pryor
Fulfillment: Mike Hawkey
Buyers: Mike Scott
Larry Galinski
Catalog Circulation: Mailed 1 time(s) per year to 600
Printing Information: 38 pages in 1 color on Matte Stock
Press: Letterpress
Binding: Saddle Stitched
Mailing List Information: Names for rent
List Manager: Michael Grauel
In Business: 80 years
Number of Employees: 150
Sales Information: $10,000,000 - $25,000,000

8186 Blanks USA
Blanks USA
7700 68th Avenue N
Suite 7
Minneapolis, MN 55428   800-328-7311
                               Fax: 800-328-7312
customercare@blanksusa.com
www.blanksusa.com

Die cut paper products: tickets, door hangers, tags, folders, tab dividers and security paper tents

President: Andy Ogren
Marketing Manager: Brittany Schoenborn
Sales Representative: Carley Ogren
Credit Cards: AMEX; MasterCard
Catalog Cost: Free
Catalog Circulation: Mailed 1 time(s) per year
Printing Information: 40 pages in 4 colors on Glossy Stock
Press: Web Press
Binding: Saddle Stitched
Mailing List Information: Names for rent
In Business: 31 years
Sales Information: $5,000,000 - $10,000,000

8187 LifeStock Stock Photography Management
190 Pamassus Avenue
Apartment 5
San Francisco, CA 94117   951-244-8498
www.lifestockphotos.com

Stock photography of people in both business and lifestyle situations

Catalog Circulation: Mailed 1 time(s) per year

8188 Quality Business Cards
Quality Printing Group
2529 NW 74th Avenue
Miami, FL 33122   305-639-2848
                         800-222-9410
                         Fax: 800-224-9399
www.qualitypg.com

A for the trade only commercial printing specializing in; full color offset printing, short (100 to 5000) and medium size runs, foil stamping, embossing, diecutting, variable data printing service

President: Roberto Gramatges
Credit Cards: AMEX; MasterCard
Printing Information: 50 pages in 4 colors
In Business: 27 years
Number of Employees: 20
Sales Information: $1,000,000 - $5,000,000

8189 Support Products
Support Products, Inc.
309 W. Professional Park Avenue
Effingham, IL 62401-2940   217-536-6171
                                  800-367-3206
                                  Fax: 217-536-6828
sales@supportproducts.com
www.supportproducts.com

Printing supplies

President: Monica Kremer
CFO: Jim Calhoun
Marketing Manager: Tracee Bryant
Production Manager: Dennis Worman
Fulfillment: Tracee Bryant
Buyers: Angie Stremming
Credit Cards: AMEX; MasterCard; Visa
Catalog Cost: $1
Catalog Circulation: Mailed 1 time(s) per year to 20M
Average Order Size: $50
Printing Information: 64 pages in 1 color on Matte Stock
Press: Web Press
Binding: Saddle Stitched
Mailing List Information: Names for rent
List Manager: Ina Schlechte
In Business: 15 years
Number of Employees: 15
Sales Information: $1MM to $3MM

8190 Van Son Holland Ink Corporation of America
Van Son Ink Corporation
370 Turk Hill Park
Fairfort, NY 14450   800-645-4182
                            Fax: 800-442-8744
info@vansonink.com
www.vansonink.com

Printing press ink

President: Maurits Van Son
In Business: 143 years
Number of Employees: 100
Sales Information: $25,000,000 - $50,000,000

8191 Vijuk Equipment
G&-Vijuk Intern. Corp.
715 Church Road
Elmhurst, IL 60126-1415   630-530-2203
                                 Fax: 630-530-2245
info@guk-vijuk.com
www.vijukequip.com

Trimmers, die cutters, folders and in-line folders for web presses, 3-knife trimmers, die cutters, perfect binders, saddle stichers, collators, commercial and miniature folders, and in-line folders

President: Joseph Vijuk
CFO: Angie Rottinger
Marketing Manager: Roger Mattila
Mailing List Information: Names for rent
In Business: 67 years
Number of Employees: 40
Sales Information: $10MM to $20MM

Restaurants
Equipment

8192 Aztec Grill Corporation
Aztec Grill Corporation
PO Box 820037
Dallas, TX 75382-37   214-343-1897
                             800-346-8114
                             Fax: 214-034- 999
www.aztecgrill.com

Cooking and warming equipment

President: Dennis Whitting
In Business: 33 years
Number of Employees: 10-J
Sales Information: Under $500M

8193 B&J Peerless Restaurant Supply
B&J Food Service Equipment, Inc.
1616 Dielman Rd
St Louis, MO 63132-1516   314-428-1247
                                 Fax: 314-429-1035
www.bjfoodservice.com

Foodservice equipment

President: Mike Shade

8194 Bottles, Containers, & Bags
Consolidated Plastics
4700 Prosper Dr
Stow, OH 44224-2303   330-689-3000
                             800-362-1000
                             Fax: 800-858-5001
feedback@consolidatedplastics.com
www.consolidatedplastics.com

Bottles and caps, containers, jars, spray bottles and pumps, reclosable bags, beakers and weighing dishes, totes, etc.

President: Brenton Taussig
Buyers: Valarie Burgoyne
Credit Cards: AMEX; MasterCard; Visa
Catalog Cost: Free
Catalog Circulation: Mailed 1 time(s) per year
Printing Information: 28 pages in 4 colors on Matte Stock
Press: Web Press
Binding: Saddle Stitched
Mailing List Information: Names for rent
In Business: 34 years
Number of Employees: 14
Sales Information: $10 MM

8195 Commercial Mats and Matting
Consolidated Plastics
4700 Prosper Drive
Stow, OH 44224-2303   800-362-1000
                             800-362-1000
                             Fax: 800-858-5001
feedback@consolidatedplastics.com
www.consolidatedplastics.com

Entryway mats (indoor and outdoor), custom logo mats, anti-fatigue and rubber mats, grip strips, safety track tape

President: Brenton Taussig
Buyers: Valarie Burgoyne
Credit Cards: AMEX; MasterCard; Visa
Catalog Cost: Free
Catalog Circulation: Mailed 1 time(s) per year
Printing Information: 24 pages in 4 colors on Matte Stock
Press: Web Press
Binding: Saddle Stitched
Mailing List Information: Names for rent
In Business: 34 years
Number of Employees: 14
Sales Information: $10 MM

8196 Cookshack
Cookshack
2304 North Ash Street
Ponca City, OK 74601-1100   580-765-3669
                                   800-423-0698
                                   Fax: 580-765-2223
info@cookshack.com
www.Cookshack.Com

Sauces, bases, rubs, smoker ovens and bbq pits

President: Stuart Powell
s_powell@cookshack.com
Marketing Manager: Regina Bookout
r_bookout@cookshack.com
Production Manager: Jim Linnebur
j_linnebur@cookshack.com
Customer Service: Bill Vice
b_vice@cookshack.com
Inside Sales Manager: Terri Gordon
t_gordon@cookshack.com
Customer Service Manager: Tony Marlar
t_marlar@cookshack.com
Credit Cards: AMEX; MasterCard
Catalog Circulation: to 7000
Printing Information: in 4 colors

Binding: Folded
In Business: 50 years
Number of Employees: 35
Sales Information: $10MM to $20MM

8197 Cozzini

Cozzini
4300 West Bryn Mawr Avenue
Chicago, IL 60646   773-478-9700
Fax: 773-478-8689
info@cozzini.com
www.cozzini.com

Meat slicers, sausage production equipment, pumping systems, loaders, conveyors and material handling equipment

President: Ivo Cozzini
CFO: Oscar Cozzini
Marketing Manager: Donna Nastaly
VP: Tom Spino
VP Marketing: Keith Shackalford
In Business: 26 years
Number of Employees: 160
Sales Information: $10 Million

8198 Cozzini Knives

Cozzini Brothers, Inc.
4300 West Bryn Mawr Avenue
Chicago, IL 60646   773-478-9700
888-846-7785
Fax: 773-478-8689
www.cozzini.com

Knives, cutlery sharpening tools, food processor blade exchanges

President: Ivo Cozzini
CFO: Oscar Cozzini
Marketing Manager: John Maestranzi
jmaestranzi@cozzinibros.com
Sales Manager: Terry McCullough
tmccullough@cozzini.com
Field Sales Director: Jim Gaydusek
jgaydusek@cozzini.com
National Accounts Sales Manager:
RandyRhude
rrhude@cozzini.com
In Business: 26 years
Number of Employees: 48
Sales Information: $5,000,000 - $10,000,000

8199 Custom Sales & Service

Custom Mobile Food Equipment
275 South 2nd Road
Hammonton, NJ 08037-635   609-561-6900
800-257-7855
Fax: 609-567-9318
info@foodcart.com
www.Customsalesandservice.Com

Products include carts and kiosks, catering trucks, concession trailers and delivery vehicles, ice cream vans, mobile kitchens, scooters and street carts, disaster relief and emergency vehicles

President: William Sikora
Fulfillment: Cathy Chartier
In Business: 61 years
Number of Employees: 100
Sales Information: $10,000,000 - $25,000,000

8200 Gall's

Gall's
1340 Russell Cave Road
Lexington, KY 40505   866-673-7643
888-831-9824
help-desk@galls.com
www.galls.com

Public safety equipment

President: Calvin Johnston
CFO: Larry Kinney
Marketing Manager: Jenny Super
Credit Cards: AMEX; MasterCard; Visa
Catalog Cost: Free
Catalog Circulation: Mailed 5 time(s) per year to 1MM
Average Order Size: $130

Printing Information: 284 pages in 4 colors
Binding: Perfect Bound
Mailing List Information: Names for rent
List Company: Chilcutt Direct
In Business: 48 years
Number of Employees: 350
Sales Information: $ 54.5 Million

8201 Gold Medal

Gold Medal Products Co.
10700 Medallion Dr.
Cincinnati, OH 45241   800-543-0862
info@gmpopcorn.com
www.gmpopcorn.com

Concession equipment and supplies for making popcorn, sno-kones, shave ice, cotton candy, funnel cakes, hot dogs, caramel candy, apples, waffles, fried foods and more.

President: Greg Miller
Catalog Cost: Free
Mailing List Information: Names for rent
In Business: 97 years
Number of Employees: 350
Sales Information: $100 Million

8202 House of Winston

House of Winston
2345 Carton Drive
Louisville, KY 40299-2513   502-495-5400
800-234-5286
Fax: 502-495-5458
information@winstonind.com
www.Winstonind.Com

Food service equipment products

Chairman: Winston L Shelton
President: Valerie Shelton
CFO: Tina Thompson
Production Manager: Bob Leavitt
Brand Manager: Kerrie Clifford
IT Manager: Sonya Karmazin
COO: Paul Haviland
Credit Cards: MasterCard; Visa
Catalog Circulation: Mailed 1 time(s) per year to 50M
Printing Information: 50 pages in 4 colors on Glossy Stock
Press: Sheetfed Press
Binding: Perfect Bound
In Business: 45 years
Number of Employees: 150
Sales Information: $10,000,000 - $25,000,000

8203 Inspired

American Hotel Register Company
100 S Milwaukee Ave.
Vernon Hills, IL 60061-4035   800-323-5686
Fax: 800-688-9108
ffe@americanhotel.com
www.americanhotel.com

Furniture, fixtures and equipment for the hospitality industry.

Chairman: James F. Leahy
President: Angela Korompilas
Catalog Cost: Free
Catalog Circulation: Mailed 1 time(s) per year
Printing Information: 122 pages in 4 colors
In Business: 151 years
Number of Employees: 1000
Sales Information: $850 Million

8204 KaTom Catalog

KaTom Restaurant Supply Inc
305 KaTom Drive
Kodak, TN 37764   423-586-5877
800-541-8683
Fax: 800-821-9130
info@katom.com
www.katom.com

Restaurant equipment, kitchen supplies, bar supplies, furniture, buffet and catering supplies

President: Patricia Bible
VP: Paula Chesworth

CEO: Patricia Bible
Catalog Cost: Free
In Business: 28 years
Number of Employees: 4
Sales Information: $330,000

8205 KaTom Restaurant Supply

KaTom Restaurant Supply Inc
305 KaTom Drive
Kodak, TN 37764-55   423-586-5839
800-541-8683
Fax: 800-821-9130
info@katom.com
www.katom.com

All equipment for restaurants including ovens and shelving

President: Patricia Bible
VP: Paula Chesworth
CEO: Patricia Bible
Credit Cards: AMEX; MasterCard; Visa
Catalog Cost: Free
Printing Information: 48 pages
Binding: Saddle Stitched
In Business: 28 years

8206 Kitchen Krafts Catalog

Kitchen Krafts
PO Box 442
Waukon, IA 52172-442   563-535-8000
800-298-5389
Fax: 563-535-8001
service@kitchenkrafts.com
www.kitchenkrafts.com

Direct merchant of hard-to-find cooking tools, ingredients & supplies for creative cooks

President: Dean Sorensen
Credit Cards: AMEX; MasterCard; Visa
Catalog Cost: Free
Printing Information: 56 pages in 4 colors on Glossy Stock
Press: Web Press
Binding: Saddle Stitched
Mailing List Information: Names for rent
In Business: 20 years
Number of Employees: 12
Sales Information: $1MM to $3MM

8207 Merco/Savory

Merco
980 South Isabella Rd
PO Box 1229
Mt. Pleasant, MI 48858   989-773-7981
800-733-8821
Fax: 800-669-0619
www.mercoproducts.com

Food warmers, merchandisers, display and holding cabinets, hot food servers, slot toasters, conveyor toasters, cooking equipment

Chairman: Glen E. Tellock
President: Jeff From
CEO: Glen E. Tellock
Credit Cards: AMEX; MasterCard
Catalog Circulation: Mailed 1 time(s) per year
Number of Employees: 400
Sales Information: $25,000,000 - $50,000,000

8208 Moli-International

Moli-International
1150 W. Virginia Avenue
Denver, CO 80223-2026   303-777-0364
800-525-8468
Fax: 303-777-0658
sales@moliinternational.com
www.Moliinternational.Com

Food service equipment

President: Van Larson
Catalog Cost: Free
Catalog Circulation: to 250
Printing Information: 12 pages in 2 colors on Glossy Stock
Mailing List Information: Names for rent

In Business: 40 years
Number of Employees: 4
Sales Information: Under $500,000

8209 National Drying Machinery Company
Buhler
100 Aeroglide Drive
Cary, NC 27511-4202   919-851-2000
                             Fax: 919-851-6029
                             info@nationaldrying.com
                             www.aeroglide.com

A leading manufacturer of dryers, dehydrators, roasters and coolers for fruits, vegetables and processed foods

President: Richard Parkes
Mailing List Information: Names for rent
List Manager: Paul Branson
In Business: 80 years
Number of Employees: 120
Sales Information: $10,000,000 - $25,000,000

8210 Nemco Food Equipment
Nemco Food Equipment Inc.
301 Meuse Argonne
PO Box 305
Hicksville, OH 43526-305   419-542-7751
                             800-782-6761
                             Fax: 419-542-6690
                             jciecierski@nemcofoodequip.com
                             www.nemcofoodequip.com

Food preparation equipment, food warming equipment, food merchandising equipment, food cooking equipment, and waste disposers for restaurants, schools, and hospitals

President: Stan Guilliam
CFO: Richard Musser
Marketing Manager: Michelle Wibel
Production Manager: Jason Guilliam
jguilliam@nemcofoodequip.com
Sales Manager - East: Joe Ciecierski
jciecierski@nemcofoodequip.com
Sales Manager - Midwest: Joe Carcione, CFSP
jcarcione@nemcofoodequip.com
SalesManager - South: Jason Guilliam
jguilliam@nemcofoodequip.com
In Business: 39 years
Number of Employees: 51-2
Sales Information: $3 Million

8211 Nor-Lake
Nor-Lake
727 Second Street
Hudson, WI 54016-248   715-386-2323
                             800-477-5253
                             Fax: 715-386-4290
                             sales@norlake.com
                             www.norlake.com

Refrigeration equipment, walk-in coolers, freezers, cabinets, prep tables, merchandisers and refrigeration systems; Also laboratory refrigerators and freezers; environmental chambers

President: Charles Dullea
CFO: Johnny Manche
Marketing Manager: Barbara Belongia
Production Manager: Randy Clay
Buyers: Terry Clay
Catalog Cost: Free
Catalog Circulation: Mailed 1 time(s) per year
Printing Information: 75 pages in 2 colors on Glossy Stock
Press: Web Press
Mailing List Information: Names for rent
List Manager: Barbara Belongia
In Business: 68 years
Number of Employees: 250
Sales Information: $25,000,000 - $50,000,000

8212 Proprocess Corporation
ProLuxe
20281 Harvill Ave
Perris, CA 90723-4030   562-531-0305
                             800-594-5528
                             Fax: 951-657-4594
                             info@doughpro.com
                             www.proluxe.com

Pizza presses, tortilla presses, griddles, pan racks and accessories, ovens wood burning/gas

President: Eugene Raio
CFO: Daniel R Raio
Marketing Manager: Caroline DeJong
Production Manager: Steve Raio
Fulfillment: Caroline Sobrzano
Vice President: Glenn Fitzgerald
Director of Sales & Marketing: Michael Cole
Technical Support Manager: Kim Kitchin
International Marketing Manager: Mike Cervantes
Buyers: Amelia Fox
Credit Cards: AMEX; MasterCard
Catalog Cost: Free
Catalog Circulation: Mailed 10 time(s) per year to 100M
Printing Information: 40 pages in 4 colors on Glossy Stock
Press: Sheetfed Press
Binding: Saddle Stitched
Mailing List Information: Names for rent
In Business: 3 years
Sales Information: $3MM to $5MM

8213 Sausage Maker
The Sausage Maker, Inc.
1500 Clinton Street
Building 7
Buffalo, NY 14206   716-824-5814
                             888-490-8525
                             Fax: 716-824-6465
                             customerservice@sausagemaker.com
                             www.sausagemaker.com

Sausage making equipment and supplies

President: Kris Stanuscek
Marketing Manager: Norma Mathewson
International Marketing Manager: Wes Smyczynski
Buyers: John Wasinski
Credit Cards: AMEX; MasterCard
Catalog Cost: Free
Catalog Circulation: Mailed 3 time(s) per year to 15000
Printing Information: 55 pages in 4 colors on Matte Stock
Press: Web Press
Binding: Saddle Stitched
Mailing List Information: Names for rent
In Business: 45 years
Number of Employees: 30
Sales Information: $5,000,000

8214 Seco Mini Catalog
Piper Products Incorporated
300 S 84th Avenue
Wausau, WI 54401-8460   715-842-2724
                             800-544-3057
                             Fax: 715-842-3125
                             info@piperonline.net
                             www.piperonline.net

Variety of food service and restaurant equipment

Technical Service: Travis Nass
tnass@piperoline.net
Customer Service: Terri Bornheimer
terrib@piperoline.net
Catalog Circulation: Mailed 1 time(s) per year
Printing Information: 16 pages in 2 colors
Binding: Saddle Stitched
In Business: 55 years
Number of Employees: 175

8215 Uniflow Manufacturing Corporation
KDIndustries, Inc.
1525 East Lake Rd.
Erie, PA 16511-1088   814-453-6761
                             800-840-9577
                             Fax: 814-455-6336
                             info@kold-draft.com
                             www.kold-draft.com

Ice machines, ice bins and ice dispensers

President: Martin Gardner
CFO: Connie Mattis
Marketing Manager: Thomas O Martin
Production Manager: Joe Rumberger
Inside Sales: Katie Glass
katieg@kold-draft.com
Buyers: Kris Malee
Catalog Cost: Free
Catalog Circulation: to 1000
Printing Information: 15 pages in 2 colors on Glossy Stock
Mailing List Information: Names for rent
List Manager: Thomas O Martin
In Business: 95 years
Number of Employees: 35
Sales Information: $5,000,000 - $10,000,000

8216 Visions Espresso Service
Visions Espresso Service, Inc.
2737 First Avenue South
Seattle, WA 98134   800-277-7277
                             Fax: 206-623-6710
                             info@visionsespresso.com
                             www.visionsespresso.com

Espresso machine parts, cleaning supplies and accessories

President: Dawn Loraas
Operations Manager: Luke Green
Credit Cards: AMEX; MasterCard; Visa
Catalog Cost: Free
Catalog Circulation: to 10000
Printing Information: 32 pages on Glossy Stock
Binding: Saddle Stitched
Mailing List Information: Names for rent
In Business: 29 years
Number of Employees: 19
Sales Information: $2.5 Million

8217 West Elm
Williams-Sonoma, Inc.
3333 Bear St.
Space 231
Costa Mesa, CA 92626   714-662-1960
                             888-922-4119
                             Fax: 702-363-2541
                             customerservice@westelm.com
                             www.westelm.com

Furniture, bedding and bath for modern living

Chairman: Andrew Bellamy
President: Laura Alber
CFO: Sharon L McCollam
Marketing Manager: Patrick J Connolly
SVP & CIO: John Strain
Credit Cards: AMEX; MasterCard
Catalog Cost: Free
Catalog Circulation: Mailed 2 time(s) per year
Printing Information: 52 pages in 4 colors on Glossy Stock
Binding: Saddle Stitched
In Business: 13 years
Number of Employees: 80
Sales Information: $4.3 MM

Food Products

8218 Allen Brothers
Allen Brothers
3737 S Halsted St.
Chicago, IL 60609-1689   800-548-7777
                             Fax: 800-890-9146
                             www.allenbrothers.com

Steak, poultry and seafood.

Chairman: Christopher Pappas
Catalog Cost: Free
In Business: 123 years
Sales Information: $80 Million

8219 Beer, Beer & More Beer
MoreFlavor
995 Detroit Ave
Suite G
Concord, CA 94518-2526   925-671-4958
800-600-0033
Fax: 925-671-4978
info@moreflavor.com
www.morewinemaking.com

All supplies needed for wine making, beer making, coffee roasting

President: Chris Graham
CFO: Chris Graham
Fulfillment: Ryan Barto
CEO/Founder: Olin Schultz
COO: Dan Lipscomb
CMO/CO/Founder: Darren Schleth
Credit Cards: AMEX; MasterCard; Visa
In Business: 20 years
Sales Information: $ 4 Million

8220 Gold Medal
Gold Medal Products Co.
10700 Medallion Dr.
Cincinnati, OH 45241   800-543-0862
info@gmpopcorn.com
www.gmpopcorn.com

Concession equipment and supplies for making popcorn, sno-kones, shave ice, cotton candy, funnel cakes, hot dogs, caramel candy, apples, waffles, fried foods and more.

President: Greg Miller
Catalog Cost: Free
Mailing List Information: Names for rent
In Business: 97 years
Number of Employees: 350
Sales Information: $100 Million

8221 Hantover
Hantover Inc.
PO Box 410646
Kansas City, MO 64141-646   816-761-7800
877-853-0230
Fax: 913-214-4995
contactus@hantover.com
www.hantover.com

Distributor of meat and other foods

President: Benard Huff
In Business: 75 years

8222 Hospitality Mints
Hospitality Mints
213 Candy Lane
PO Box 3140
Boone, NC 28607-3140   828-264-3045
800-334-5181
Fax: 828-264-6933
contact@hospitalitymints.com
www.Hospitalitymints.Com

Candy mints and breath mints in 18 delicious flavors, including sugarfree; available in custom and stock wrappers and a variety of packaging options

President: Patrick Viancourt
CFO: Walter Kaudelka
Marketing Manager: Kathi Guy
Production Manager: Richard Townsend
Fulfillment: Kathi Guy
Catalog Cost: Free
Catalog Circulation: Mailed 6 time(s) per year to 20M
Printing Information: 24 pages in 4 colors on Glossy Stock
Mailing List Information: Names for rent
List Manager: Kathi Guy
In Business: 39 years
Number of Employees: 75
Sales Information: $3MM to $5MM

8223 Kikkoman International
KIKKOMAN SALES USA, INC
W-S P.O. Box 420784
San Francisco, CA 94142-784   415-956-7750
Fax: 415-956-7760
www.kikkoman.com

Breads, rolls, condiments, sauces and bases

Chairman: Yuzaburo Mogi
President: Noriaki Horikiri
CFO: Keiji Yamazaki
Marketing Manager: Shigaru Nemoto
CEO: Noriaki Horikiri
Honorary CEO: Yuzaburo Mogi
In Business: 96 years
Number of Employees: 44
Sales Information: $10,000,000 - $25,000,000

8224 King Arthur Flour & The Bakers
King Arthur Flour & The Bakers
135 US Route 5 South
Norwich, VT 05055-9430   802-649-3361
800-827-6836
Fax: 802-649-3365
bakers@kingarthurflour.com
www.kingarthurflour.com

Flour, baking mixes and specialty baking supplies

Chairman: Frank E Sands II
President: Steve Voigt
CFO: Susan Renaud
Marketing Manager: Tom Payne
Production Manager: Sue Gray
Buyers: PJ Hamel
Credit Cards: AMEX; MasterCard; Visa
Catalog Cost: Free
Catalog Circulation: Mailed 12 time(s) per year to 6M
Printing Information: 56 pages in 4 colors on Matte Stock
Press: Web Press
Binding: Saddle Stitched
List Company: Direct Media
200 Pemberwick Road
Greenwich, CT 06830
203-532-3713
In Business: 225 years
Number of Employees: 150
Sales Information: $20MM to $50MM

8225 Lamb-Weston
Lamb Weston
PO Box 1900
Pasco, WA 99302-1900   509-375-5810
800-766-7783
Fax: 509-736-0386
www.lambweston.com

Desserts and potatoes

In Business: 63 years
Number of Employees: 100-
Sales Information: $25,000,000 - $50,000,000

8226 Lobels of New York
Lobels
1501 East Avenue
Suite 210
Rochester, NY 14610-310   585-328-0420
800-556-2357
Fax: 585-328-0618
evan@lobels.com
www.lobels.com

Meats

President: Stanley Lobel
CFO: Steve Fraum
Production Manager: Evan Lobel
Buyers: Stanley Lobel
Credit Cards: AMEX; MasterCard; Visa
Catalog Cost: Free
Catalog Circulation: Mailed 1 time(s) per year to 10M
Average Order Size: $225
Printing Information: 40 pages in 4 colors on Glossy Stock
Press: Sheetfed Press

Binding: Folded
Mailing List Information: Names for rent
In Business: 47 years
Number of Employees: 12
Sales Information: $500M to $1MM

8227 MagicKitchen.Com
My Magic Kitchen, Inc.
118 Bentley Square
Mountain View, CA 94040   650-941-2260
877-516-2442
Fax: 650-941-2255
orders@magickitchen.com
www.magickitchen.com

Prepared meals, soups, sides, main courses and desserts. Also diabetic, gluten free and weight loss meals, as well as meals for seniors.

President: Michelle Tayler
CEO: Greg Miller
Catalog Cost: Free
Printing Information: 16 pages in 4 colors
In Business: 11 years
Number of Employees: 16
Sales Information: $10 Million

8228 McIlhenny Company
McIlhenny Company
Highway 329
Avery Island, LA 70513   337-365-8173
800-634-9599
Fax: 504-596-6442
countrystore@tabasco.com
www.tabasco.com

Sauces & specialty foods, gifts, bar accessories, etc.

Chairman: Edward Simmons
President: Paul McIlhenny
CFO: Michael Terrell
Marketing Manager: Martin Manion
Production Manager: Raymond Boudreaux
Purchasing Agent: Ricky Venable
International Marketing Manager: Stephen C Romero
Credit Cards: AMEX; MasterCard; Visa
Catalog Cost: Free
In Business: 146 years
Number of Employees: 200

8229 Mountain Rose Herbs
Mountain Rose Herbs
P.O. Box 50220
Eugene, OR 97405   541-741-7307
800-879-3337
Fax: 510-217-4012
support@mountainroseherbs.com
www.mountainroseherbs.com

Organic herbal products, all natural body care products, essential oils and bulk ingredients for those crafting and formulating their own products

President: Julie Bailey
CFO: Cameron Stearns
Marketing Manager: Irene Wolansky
Production Manager: Julie Debord
Vice President: Shawn Donnille
Executive Director of Operations: Jennifer Gerrity
Product Manager: Christine Rice
Catalog Cost: Free
Catalog Circulation: Mailed 2 time(s) per year to 12000
Printing Information: 84 pages in 4 colors on Matte Stock
Press: Web Press
Binding: Saddle Stitched
In Business: 26 years
Number of Employees: 84
Sales Information: $ 13 Million

8230 T Marzetti Company
T. Marzetti Company
P.O.Box 29163
Columbus, OH 43229-163   614-846-2232
800-999-1835
Fax: 614-848-8330
www.Marzetti.Com

Salad dressings, Dips, Slaw dressings, croutons

President: Bruce Rosa
In Business: 119 years
Number of Employees: 125

8231 Total Ultimate Foods
Total Ultimate Foods, Inc.
683 Manor Park Drive
Columbus, OH 43228-9522   614-870-0732
Fax: 614-870-1687

Dairy products, desserts, sauces and soups

President: David Belleau
Number of Employees: 55
Sales Information: $10,000,000 - $25,000,000

8232 Tyson Foods
Tyson Foods, Inc.
P.O.Box 2020
CP631
Springdale, AR 72765-2020   479-290-4000
800-233-6332
Fax: 479-290-4061
comments@tyson.com
www.Tysonfoodsinc.Com

Appetizers, beef, veal and various food products

President: Donnie Smith
CFO: Wayne Britt
Senior Director, Public Relations: Gary Mikelson
gary.mickelson@tyson.com
VP, Government Relations: Charles Penry
charlse.penry@tyson.com
Manager, Public Relations: Worth Sparkman
worth.sparkman@tyson.com
In Business: 83 years
Number of Employees: 1070

8233 Wisconsin Milk Marketing Board
Wisconsin Milk Marketing Board, Inc.
8418 Excelsior Dr
Madison, WI 53717-1931   608-836-8820
800-373-9662
Fax: 608-836-5822
info@EatWisconsinCheese.com
www.eatwisconsincheese.com

Beverages, cheeses and dairy products

President: James Robson
Number of Employees: 50

Maintenance & Sanitation

8234 APW Wyott Corporation
APW Wyott Corporation
1307 N. Watters Road
Suite 180
Allen, TX 75013   972-908-6100
800-527-2100
Fax: 214-565-0976
customercare@standexcsg.com
www.apwwyott.com

Charbroilers, conveyor ovens, toasters, countertop warming, foodwells, overhead warmers, holding drawers, plate dispensers for foodservice

President: Hilton L Jonas
Purchasing Manager: Joe Mullin
Credit Cards: MasterCard; Visa
In Business: 75 years
Number of Employees: 180
Sales Information: $10,000,000 - $25,000,000

8235 Daydots
Ecolab Center
370 N. Wabasha Street
St. Paul, MN 55121-7031   651-795-5800
800-321-3687
Fax: 800-458-7002
CustomerService@FoodSafetySolutions.com
foodsafety.ecolab.com

Products include temperature control, prep and handling items, protective apparel, material handling products, sanitation and cleaning products, in addition to office products

Chairman: Douglas M. Baker, Jr.
President: Thomas W. Handley
CFO: Daniel J. Schmechel
EVP, Human Resources: Laurie Marsh
SVP, Corporate Development: Angela Busch
SVP, Corporate Controller: Bryan Hughes
Credit Cards: AMEX; MasterCard; Visa
Catalog Cost: Free
Printing Information: 148 pages

8236 Electric-Eel Manufacturing Company
Electric-Eel
P.O.Box 419
Springfield, OH 45501-419   937-323-4644
800-833-1212
Fax: 937-323-3767
www.Electriceel.Com

Cleaning, sanitation and warewashing equipment

President: David Hale
Marketing Manager: Mark Speranza
Number of Employees: 40
Sales Information: $5,000,000 - $10,000,000

8237 Master Disposers
Somat Company
165 Independence Ct.
Lancaster, PA 17601   717-397-5100
800-237-6628
Fax: 717-291-0877
info@somatcompany.com
www.somatcompany.com/home/

Cleaning, sanitation and warewashing equipment

President: Mary G Grogan
Number of Employees: 12
Sales Information: $1,000,000 - $5,000,000

8238 McGlaughlin Company
The McGlaughlin Oil Company
3750 E Livingston Ave
Columbus, OH 43227   614-231-2518
800-839-6589
Fax: 614-231-7431
teresa@mcglaughlinoil.com
www.McGlaughlinoil.Com

Petrol-gel sanitary grease

President: Steve Theodor
Founder: William McGlaughlin Sr.
In Business: 77 years
Number of Employees: 11
Sales Information: $5,000,000 - $10,000,000

8239 Oakite Products
Chemetall Oakite Products
50 Valley Road
Berkeley Heights, NJ 07922-2712 908-665-8593
Fax: 908-464-4658
www.chemetallna.com

Materials for bottle washing, barrel finishing and cleaning

President: Earnst Molter
Number of Employees: 100

8240 Ridge Tool Company
Ridge Tool Company
400 Clark St
Elyria, OH 44035   632-214-804
ridgidfareast@emerson.com
www.ridgid.com

Tools.

8241 Witt Company
Witt Company
4600 N. Mason-Montgomery Rd
Mason, OH 45040-1135   800-543-7417
Fax: 877-891-8200
sales@witt.com
www.witt.com

Cleaning, sanitation and warewashing equipment

Chairman: Marcy Wydman
President: Mary W Wydman
CFO: Gregg Battaglia
Number of Employees: 200
Sales Information: $20MM to $50MM

Supplies

8242 Carlisle Food Service Products
Carlisle Food Service Products
P.O. Box 53006
Oklahoma City, OK 73152-3066 405-475-5600
800-654-8210
Fax: 800-872-4701
customerservice@carlislefsp.com
www.carlislefsp.com

Global manufacturer of over 16,000 innovative, versatile and durable product solutions for the global food market from food bars & accesories to washing rackets and accessories

President: Dave Shannon
CFO: Carolyn Ford
Marketing Manager: Todd Mauer
Production Manager: Rich McDonagh
International Marketing Manager: Jim Calamito
Buyers: Susan Wortham
Catalog Circulation: Mailed 1 time(s) per year to 200M
Printing Information: 344 pages in 4 colors on Glossy Stock
Press: Web Press
Binding: Perfect Bound
Mailing List Information: Names for rent
In Business: 60 years
Number of Employees: 420
Sales Information: $50,000,000

8243 Chefwear
Chefwear
2300 Windsor Ct
Suite C
Addison, IL 60101   630-396-8337
800-568-2433
Fax: 630-396-8393
carol.mueller@chefwear.com
www.chefwear.com

Clothing and accesories for chefs and home gourmets

President: Rochelle Huppin
Marketing Manager: Carol Mueller
carol.mueller@chefwear.com
VP-Sales & Marketing: Carol Mueller
carol.mueller@chefwear.com
Customer Service/Sales Manager: Michelle Schmuhl
mschmuhl@chefwear.com
Credit Cards: AMEX; MasterCard
Catalog Cost: Free
Printing Information: 40 pages in 4 colors
Press: Web Press
Binding: Saddle Stitched
Mailing List Information: Names for rent
In Business: 25 years

Number of Employees: 45
Sales Information: $ 3 Million

8244 Christian Tools of Affirmation
Christian Tools of Affirmation
1625 Larkin Williams Rd
PO Box 1205
Fenton, MO 63026-1205

636-305-3100
800-999-1874
Fax: 800-315-8713
customerservice@ctainc.com
www.ctainc.com

Christian products and gifts such as brace-lets, books, keychains, mugs, ornaments, stationery, videos, magnets and prayer journals

President: Terry Knoploh
CEO: Terry Knoploh
Credit Cards: MasterCard; Visa
Catalog Cost: Free
In Business: 15 years
Sales Information: $5MM to $10MM

8245 Fast Service For Food Service
Server Products, Inc.
3601 Pleasant Hill Road
PO Box 98
Richfield, WI 53076

262-628-5600
800-558-8722
Fax: 262-628-5110
spsales@server-products.com
www.server-products.com

Restaurant serving products

President: Paul Wickesberg
CFO: Jim Hollenhorst
Marketing Manager: Ron Ripple
Catalog Circulation: Mailed 1 time(s) per year
Printing Information: 16 pages in 4 colors
Binding: Saddle Stitched
In Business: 55 years
Number of Employees: 20-5

8246 Gold Medal
Gold Medal Products Co.
10700 Medallion Dr.
Cincinnati, OH 45241

800-543-0862
info@gmpopcorn.com
www.gmpopcorn.com

Concession equipment and supplies for making popcorn, sno-kones, shave ice, cotton candy, funnel cakes, hot dogs, caramel candy, apples, waffles, fried foods and more.

President: Greg Miller
Catalog Cost: Free
Mailing List Information: Names for rent
In Business: 97 years
Number of Employees: 350
Sales Information: $100 Million

8247 KaTom Catalog
KaTom Restaurant Supply Inc
305 KaTom Drive
Kodak, TN 37764

423-586-5877
800-541-8683
Fax: 800-821-9130
info@katom.com
www.katom.com

Restaurant equipment, kitchen supplies, bar supplies, furniture, buffet and catering supplies

President: Patricia Bible
VP: Paula Chesworth
CEO: Patricia Bible
Catalog Cost: Free
In Business: 28 years
Number of Employees: 4
Sales Information: $330,000

8248 King Arthur Flour & The Bakers
King Arthur Flour & The Bakers
135 US Route 5 South
Norwich, VT 05055-9430

802-649-3361
800-827-6836
Fax: 802-649-3365
bakers@kingarthurflour.com
www.kingarthurflour.com

Flour, baking mixes and specialty baking supplies

Chairman: Frank E Sands II
President: Steve Voigt
CFO: Susan Renaud
Marketing Manager: Tom Payne
Production Manager: Sue Gray
Buyers: PJ Hamel
Credit Cards: AMEX; MasterCard; Visa
Catalog Cost: Free
Catalog Circulation: Mailed 12 time(s) per year to 6M
Printing Information: 56 pages in 4 colors on Matte Stock
Press: Web Press
Binding: Saddle Stitched
List Company: Direct Media
200 Pemberwick Road
Greenwich, CT 06830
203-532-3713
In Business: 225 years
Number of Employees: 150
Sales Information: $20MM to $50MM

8249 Lancaster Colony Commercial Products
Lancaster Colony Commercial Products
2353 Westbrooke Dr
PO Box 630
Columbus, OH 43228-630

614-876-1026
800-528-2278
Fax: 614-876-1276
info@lccpinc.com
www.lccpinc.com

Hotel guestroom supplies and foodservice supplies; ice molds, coffee urns, glassware, candles, aluminum pots and pans, etc

President: Karl Evans
CFO: Mike Skinner
Marketing Manager: Vivian Khan
International Marketing Manager: Lois Marino
Buyers: Vivian Khan
Catalog Cost: Free
Catalog Circulation: Mailed 1 time(s) per year to 70M
Printing Information: 25 pages in 4 colors on Glossy Stock
Binding: Perfect Bound
Mailing List Information: Names for rent
List Manager: Ken Evans
In Business: 37 years
Number of Employees: 17
Sales Information: $10MM to $20MM

8250 Marshall Domestics
Marshall Domestics
12 Factory Street
West Warwick, RI 02893

401-821-8760
800-556-7440
Fax: 401-821-2230
marshalldomestics@verizon.net
www.marshalldomestics.net/

Institutional and restaurant textiles and supplies for food-service, hospitality, healthcare, janitorial supplies, and work clothing industries

President: David Greenstein
Marketing Manager: Lori Sovea
In Business: 44 years
Number of Employees: 15

8251 Milliken & Company
Milliken & Company
PO Box 1926
Spartanburg, SC 29304-1926

706-880-5511
800-241-4826
Fax: 864-503-2100
millikencarpet@milliken.com
www.Millikencarpet.Com

Napkins, tablemats and serving products

Chairman: Rodger Milliken
President: Joseph Salley
In Business: 150 years
Number of Employees: 1200

8252 Regency Service Cart
Regency Service Carts, Inc.
337 Carroll St
Brooklyn, NY 11231-5007

718-855-8304
Fax: 718-834-8507
regeastny@aol.com
www.regencynylv.com

Hotel & Restaurant equipment

President: Connie Pezulich
conpezulich@aol.com
regencywest2015@aol.com
In Business: 46 years
Sales Information: $20MM to $50MM

8253 Tablecraft Products Company
TableCraft
801 Lakeside Drive
Gurnee, IL 60031-2489

847-855-9000
800-323-8321
Fax: 800-323-8320
info@tablecraft.com
www.tablecraft.com

Fast food restaurant service and kitchen supplies

Founder: Adolf Davis
Printing Information: 94 pages in 4 colors
Binding: Saddle Stitched
In Business: 69 years
Number of Employees: 35

8254 True Brands
True Brands
154 N 35th Street
Seattle, WA 98103

800-750-8783
www.truefabrications.com

Restaurant supplies for liquor, beer and wine

President: Dhruv Agarwal
Credit Cards: AMEX; MasterCard
Catalog Circulation: Mailed 4 time(s) per year
Printing Information: 52 pages in 4 colors
Press: Web Press
Binding: Saddle Stitched
In Business: 13 years
Sales Information: $5MM to $10MM

Safety
Supplies & Equipment

8255 AAA Acme Rubber Company
AAA Acme Rubber Company
2003 E 5th Street
Building #1
Tempe, AZ 85281-3064

480-966-9311
800-AAA-ACME
Fax: 480-966-2273
info@acmerubber.com
www.acmerubber.com

Industrial rubber products.

President: Chuck Smith
Sales Information: $3MM to $5MM

8256 AK Ltd
AK Ltd
18412 NE Halsey St
Portland, OR 97230-7005
503-669-0986
800-742-1395
Fax: 503-661-4340
info@akltd.com
www.Akltd.Com

Standard and custom plastic fabrication products for use in safety and industrial markets, labs and cleanrooms
President: Carol Sparks
VP: Michele Sparks
michele@akltd.com
Credit Cards: MasterCard
In Business: 26 years
Number of Employees: 11
Sales Information: $3MM to $5MM

8257 Adaptive Micro Systems
Adaptive
7840 N 86th St
Milwaukee, WI 53224-3418
414-357-2020
800-558-7022
Fax: 414-357-2029
www.adaptivedisplays.com

Indoor and outdoor LED displays
President: Bill Latz
Marketing Manager: Bill Augustyne
Number of Employees: 150
Sales Information: $10,000,000 - $25,000,000

8258 Allied Glove & Safety Products Corporation
Allied Glove & Safety Products Corporati
8088 McCormick Boulevard
Skokie, IL 60076
800-621-3861
info@alliedglove.com

Protective clothing, footwear, eye protection and gloves
Chairman: Nathan Applebaum
President: Sol Applebaum
Credit Cards: MasterCard; Visa
Catalog Circulation: Mailed 2 time(s) per year
Printing Information: 21 pages
In Business: 97 years

8259 American Health & Safety
American Health & Safety
325 Industrial Circle
Stoughton, WI 53589
608-273-4000
800-522-7554
Fax: 800-522-7554
american@ahsafety.com
www.ahsafety.com

Safety equipment and first aid supplies
Chairman: Kurt Christensen
President: John Cronkrak
Buyers: Becky Kasmeder
Credit Cards: MasterCard; Visa
Catalog Cost: Free
Printing Information: 112 pages in 4 colors on Glossy Stock
Press: Web Press
Binding: Saddle Stitched
Mailing List Information: Names for rent
In Business: 30 years
Sales Information: $ 5-10 Million

8260 Arbill Safety Products
Arbill
10450 Drummond Road
Philadelphia, PA 19154
800-523-5367
info@arbill.com
www.arbill.com

Personal protective clothing, eye and hearing protection, head gear, respiratory equipment, back supports, ergonomic equipment, fall protection equipment, confined space protection, spill clean-up
President: Robyn Zlotkin
CFO: Keith Daviston

Production Manager: Bill Gabriele
Chief Executive Officer: Julie Copeland
Director of Operations: Bill Keay
Credit Cards: AMEX; MasterCard
Catalog Cost: Free
In Business: 72 years
Number of Employees: 55
Sales Information: $ 10 Million

8261 BP Barco Products
BP Barco Products
24 N. Washington Ave
Batavia, IL 60510
800-338-2697
Fax: 630-879-8687
sales@barcoproducts.com
www.barcoproducts.com

Safety barriers, traffic cones and posts, safety can liquid storage, pedestrian, traffic and parking signs, caution signs, sign posts; cleaning and sanitation products
President: Brian Barnes
CFO: Robin Sickafoose
CEO: Cyril Matter
Catalog Cost: Free
Printing Information: in 4 colors
In Business: 30 years
Number of Employees: 35
Sales Information: $6,000,000

8262 CEA Instruments
CEA Instruments
160 Tillman St.
Westwood, NJ 07675
201-967-5660
Fax: 201-967-8450
sales@ceainstruments.com
www.ceainstruments.com

Hazardous gas detection instrumentation
President: Steven Adelman
Printing Information: 3 pages
In Business: 43 years
Number of Employees: 3
Sales Information: $500M to $1MM

8263 CMC Rescue Equipment
CMC Rescue
6740 Cortona Drive
Goleta, CA 93117
805-562-9120
800-513-7455
Fax: 805-562-9870
info@cmcrescue.com
www.cmcrescue.com

Leading designer, manufacturer, trainer and distributor of rescue equipment
President: James Frank
VP: Steven Kirkman
Catalog Cost: Free
Printing Information: 180 pages
In Business: 37 years
Number of Employees: 45
Sales Information: $12 Million

8264 Calibrated Instruments
Calibrated Instruments
174 Brady Avenue
Hawthorne, NY 10532-2217
914-741-5700
888-779-2064
Fax: 914-741-5711
sales@calibrated.com
www.Calibrated.Com

Gas meters-wet test; air and gas sampling bags, gas analyzers, gas dilution instruments
President: John B Shroyer
Credit Cards: AMEX; MasterCard; Visa
Printing Information: 12 pages in 4 colors on Matte Stock
Press: Web Press
Binding: Folded
Mailing List Information: Names for rent
In Business: 30 years
Number of Employees: 50
Sales Information: $1,000,000 - $5,000,000

8265 Carlton Industries
Carlton Industries
PO Box 280
La Grange, TX 78945-280
979-242-5055
800-231-5988
Fax: 800-231-5934
sales@carltonusa.com
www.carltonusa.com/t-contact.aspx

Safety signs
President: Kay Carlton
In Business: 45 years
Number of Employees: 30
Sales Information: $1,000,000 - $5,000,000

8266 Castell Safety
Castell
150 N Michigan Avenue
Suite 800
Chicago, IL 60601-485
312-360-1516
Fax: 312-268-5174
ussales@castell.com
www.castell.com

Interlocks, switchgear, machine guarding, valving
President: Keith Allingham, Managing Director
CFO: Roy McKerracher, Financial Director
Marketing Manager: Mark Dornoff, Sales Manager
Production Manager: Keith Allingham, Operations Direct.
Quality Manager: Neil Partridge
npartridge@castell.com
Marketing Engineer: Adam Felton
afelton@castell.com
IT Manager: Darren Stewart
dstewart@castell.com
Printing Information: 72 pages
In Business: 91 years
Number of Employees: 20-O
Sales Information: $1,000,000 - $5,000,000

8267 Centryco
Centryco
300 West Broad Street
PO Box 250
Burlington, NJ 08016-250
609-386-6448
800-257-9537
Fax: 609-386-6739
info@centryco.com
www.centryco.com

Century covers for machinery
President: John Miller
Marketing Manager: Bill Hartman
Number of Employees: 40
Sales Information: $5,000,000 - $10,000,000

8268 Champion America
Champion America
PO Box 3092
Stony Creek, CT 06405-1692
877-242-6709
Fax: 800-336-3707
service@champion-america.com
www.champion-america.com

Traffic and parking signs
Credit Cards: AMEX; MasterCard
Catalog Cost: Free
Catalog Circulation: Mailed 4 time(s) per year
Printing Information: 111 pages in 4 colors on Newsprint
Press: Web Press
Binding: Saddle Stitched
In Business: 20 years
Number of Employees: 500
Sales Information: $1,000,000 - $5,000,000

8269 Champion America Safety Essentials
Champion America
PO Box 3092
Stony Creek, CT 06405-2803
877-242-6709
Fax: 800-336-3707
service@champion-america.com
www.champion-america.com

Safety products for eyes, hands, biohazards, spill control, electrical equipment, etc.

Credit Cards: AMEX; MasterCard
Catalog Cost: Free
Catalog Circulation: Mailed 4 time(s) per year
Printing Information: 60 pages in 4 colors
Binding: Saddle Stitched
In Business: 20 years

8270 Clarage

Clarage
202 Commerce Way
Pulaski, TN 38478-4745 931-424-2500
800-598-9234
sales@clarage.com
www.clarage.com

New custom centrifugal fans, multi-cyclone dust collectors, repair/rebuild of fans

Marketing Manager: Donna Elkins
Clarage Project Manager: John Hill
Catalog Cost: Free
In Business: 140 years
Number of Employees: 60

8271 Coastal Safety & Health Services

Desyne
6276 Sperryville Pike
Suite 143
Boston, VA 22713-6133 703-433-2710
800-368-0335
Fax: 800-360-2380
inquiries@desyne.com
www.coastalsafety.net

Mailing List Information: Names for rent
In Business: 17 years
Sales Information: Under $500M

8272 Cole-Parmer

Cole-Parmer
625 East Bunker Court
Vernon Hills, IL 60061-1830 841-549-7600
800-323-4340
Fax: 847-549-1700
info@coleparmer.com
www.coleparmer.com

Products for electrochemistry, fluid handling, industrial process, laboratory research and more

President: Alan Malus
CFO: Steven Gozdziewski
Marketing Manager: Larry Vanbogaerts
VP/General Manager: Monica Manotas
Director, Finance: Joe Straczek
VP, Human Resources: Wanda McKenny
Credit Cards: AMEX; MasterCard
Printing Information: 2600 pages
In Business: 60 years
Number of Employees: 320

8273 Conney Safety

Conney Safety
3202 Latham Drive
P.O. Box 44190
Madison, WI 53744-4190 888-356-9100
Fax: 800-845-9095
safety@conney.com
www.conney.com

Products and equipment that keep people safe in the workplace

President: Bruce Hagan
CFO: Steven Boyack
CEO: Michael Wessner
Credit Cards: AMEX; MasterCard; Visa
Catalog Cost: Free
Printing Information: 72 pages in 4 colors on Glossy Stock
Press: Web Press
Binding: Perfect Bound
Mailing List Information: Names for rent
List Manager: Carl Sieg
In Business: 68 years

Number of Employees: 150
Sales Information: $60 Million

8274 Cotton Goods Manufacturing Company

Cotton Goods Manufacturing Inc.
259 N California Ave
Chicago, IL 60612-1903 773-265-0088
Fax: 773-265-0096
www.Cottongoodsmfg.Com

Home safety products, shower curtains, table skirts

President: Edward Lewis
CFO: Kevin B Higgins
Mailing List Information: Names for rent
In Business: 50 years
Number of Employees: 20
Sales Information: $1,000,000 - $5,000,000

8275 Cyclope Industries

Cyclope Industries
432 3rd Avenue
PO Box 8614
South Charleston, WV 25303 304-744-9486
800-716-7506
Fax: 304-744-2505
info@cyclopswv.com
www.cyclopswv.com

Safety devices

President: Gene B Leroy
CFO: Julia Leroy
Number of Employees: 9
Sales Information: $1,000,000 - $5,000,000

8276 Dover Saddlery

Dover Saddlery
P.O. Box 1100
Littleton, MA 01460 800-406-8204
Fax: 978-952-6633
customerservice@doversaddlery.com
www.doversaddlery.com

Equipment for horse and rider

President: Stephen L Day
CFO: David R Pearce
Credit Cards: AMEX; MasterCard
Catalog Cost: Free
In Business: 38 years
Number of Employees: 497
Sales Information: $78 Million

8277 EMED Company

Emedco
PO Box 369
Buffalo, NY 14240 866-509-1976
Fax: 800-344-2578
customerservice@emedco.com
www.emedco.com

Offers security and safety communication and identification products

Credit Cards: AMEX; MasterCard
Catalog Cost: Free
Catalog Circulation: Mailed 4 time(s) per year
Printing Information: 75 pages in 4 colors on Matte Stock
Press: Web Press
Binding: Saddle Stitched
Number of Employees: 175
Sales Information: $10,000,000 - $25,000,000

8278 Ellwood Safety Appliance Company Catalog

Ellwood Safety Appliance Company
927 Beaver Avenue
PO Box 831
Ellwood City, PA 16117-1820 724-758-7538
800-486-7538
Fax: 724-758-0532
www.ellwoodsafety.com

Toe, foot and leg protective equipment; body armour for the toes, feet and legs; over the shoe foot protection

President: Richard Gray
VP: Christian Gray

Secretary, Treasurer: Cory Gray
Officer: Beverly Verone
Catalog Cost: Free
Printing Information: 3 pages in 2 colors on Glossy Stock
Binding: Folded
Mailing List Information: Names for rent
Number of Employees: 10
Sales Information: $1.5 MM

8279 Eriez Magnetics

Eriez Manufacturing Co.
2200 Asbury Road
Erie, PA 16506-608 814-835-6000
800-345-4946
Fax: 814-838-4960
eriez@eriez.com
www.eriez.com

Material handling equipment

Chairman: Richard Merwin
President: Tim Shuttleworth
Marketing Manager: Charlie Ingram
Production Manager: Fred Adams
V. P. Operations: Mike Mankosa, Ph.D.
V.P. International: Andy Lewis
CFO/Treasurer: Mark Mandel
In Business: 72 years
Number of Employees: 260
Sales Information: $25,000,000 - $50,000,000

8280 FabEnCo

FabEnCo, Inc.
2002 Karbach
Houston, TX 77092-8406 713-686-6620
800-962-6111
Fax: 713-688-8031
www.Safetygate.Com

Self-closing safety gate

President: David La Cook
Executive Director: Giovanni Coratolo
In Business: 43 years
Number of Employees: 17
Sales Information: $1,000,000 - $5,000,000

8281 Fall Protection & Confined Space Rescue Equipment

Gemtor
1 Johnson Avenue
Matawan, NJ 07747-2509 732-583-6200
800-405-9048
Fax: 732-290-9391
sales.info@gemtor.com
www.gemtor.com

Occupational safety products

President: Craig Neustater
Printing Information: in 4 colors on Matte Stock
Press: Web Press
Binding: Saddle Stitched
In Business: 2 years
Number of Employees: 30
Sales Information: $1,000,000 - $5,000,000

8282 Figaro USA

Figaro USA Inc.
121 S. Wilke Rd.
Suite 300
Arlington Heights, IL 60005 847-832-1701
Fax: 847-832-1705
figarousa@figarosensor.com
www.figarosensor.com

Gas sensing devices

President: Kazumi Uno
In Business: 38 years
Number of Employees: 4
Sales Information: $1MM to $3MM

8283 Gall's
Gall's
1340 Russell Cave Road
Lexington, KY 40505 866-673-7643
888-831-9824
help-desk@galls.com
www.galls.com

Public safety equipment
President: Calvin Johnston
CFO: Larry Kinney
Marketing Manager: Jenny Super
Credit Cards: AMEX; MasterCard; Visa
Catalog Cost: Free
Catalog Circulation: Mailed 5 time(s) per year to 1MM
Average Order Size: $130
Printing Information: 284 pages in 4 colors
Binding: Perfect Bound
Mailing List Information: Names for rent
List Company: Chilcutt Direct
In Business: 48 years
Number of Employees: 350
Sales Information: $ 54.5 Million

8284 Gordon Engineering Corporation
Gordon Products Incorporated
67 Del Mar Dr
Brookfield, CT 06804-2494 203-775-4501
Fax: 203-775-1162
sales@gordoneng.com
www.Gordoneng.Com

Presence sensing systems
President: Steven Weighart
In Business: 25 years
Number of Employees: 7
Sales Information: $500,000 - $1,000,000

8285 Grace Industries
Grace Industries
305 Bend Hill Road
Fredonia, PA 16154-167 724-962-9231
800-969-6933
Fax: 724-962-3611
www.Graceindustries.Com

Personal safety alarms, specialty lighting products, portable gas detection instruments, automatic signaling devices, 'man down' alarms
President: James Campman
CFO: James P Campman
Marketing Manager: Eric Schook
Production Manager: Paul Emmett
Catalog Cost: Free
Catalog Circulation: to 50K
Average Order Size: $3000
Printing Information: in 4 colors on Glossy Stock
Press: Letterpress
Binding: Folded
Mailing List Information: Names for rent
In Business: 40 years
Number of Employees: 40
Sales Information: $5,000,000 - $10,000,000

8286 Guard Rail Systems
Trinity Industries, Inc.
2525 N Stemmons Fwy
Dallas, TX 75207-2401 214-631-4420
800-631-4420
Fax: 214-589-8623
Customer.Service@trin.net
www.Trin.Net

Wide selection of barriers for any application
President: Tim Wallace
Marketing Manager: Steve Easton
Credit Cards: MasterCard; Visa
Catalog Cost: Free
Printing Information: 15 pages on Glossy Stock
Binding: Saddle Stitched
In Business: 40+ years

8287 Hanco International
Hanco International
1605 Waynesburg Dr SE
Canton, OH 44707-2137 330-456-4728
Fax: 330-456-3323
sales@hanco.com
www.Hanco.Com

Lineman's glove tester
President: Tim F Hannon
In Business: 60 years
Number of Employees: 68
Sales Information: $20MM to $50MM

8288 High Precision
High Precision
375 Morse Street
PO Box 6157
Hamden, CT 06517-157 203-777-5395
Fax: 203-773-1976
sales@highprecisioninc.com
www.highprecisioninc.com

Saf-T-Air blow guns
General Manager: Lloyd Ayer
In Business: 70 years
Number of Employees: 41
Sales Information: $5,000,000 - $10,000,000

8289 Honeywell Analytics
Honeywell Analytics, Inc.
405 Barclay Blvd
Lincolnshire, IL 60069 888-749-8878
Fax: 817-274-8321
detectgas@Honeywell.com
www.honeywellanalytics.com

Gas detection devices
President: Mark Levy
ACS Manager Communication: Lourdes Pena lourdes.pena@honeywell.com
Marketing Communications Supervisor: Donald P Galman don.galman@honeywell.com<R*Director of Sales, US Portables:* Kevin Boyle kevin.boyle@honeywell.com
In Business: 54 years
Number of Employees: 100
Sales Information: $10,000,000 - $25,000,000

8290 IFSTA
Fire Protection Publications (FPP)
930 N Willis Street
Stillwater, OK 74078-8045 405-744-5723
800-654-4055
Fax: 405-744-8204
customer.service@osufpp.org
www.ifsta.org

Curriculums, software, videos and books pertaining to fire training
Credit Cards: AMEX; MasterCard; Visa
Catalog Cost: Free
Catalog Circulation: Mailed 1 time(s) per year
Printing Information: 65 pages in 4 colors on Glossy Stock
In Business: 81 years

8291 IMSA Products & Services Catlog
IMSA
165 East Union Street
PO Box 539
Newark, NY 14513-539 315-331-2182
800-723-4672
Fax: 315-331-8205
sne@imsasafety.org
www.Imsasafety.Org

Certification and study guides offered in: traffic signals, fire alarm interior and municipal public safety dispatcher, workzone traffic control safety, signs and markings
Chairman: Lenny Addair
President: Marilyn Lawrence
CFO: Sharon Earl
Marketing Manager: Sharon Earl
Production Manager: Sharon Earl
Fulfillment: Sharon Earl
Managing Director: Christine Lagarde
Deputy Managing Director: Naoyuki Shinohara
Financial Counsellor: José Viñals
Credit Cards: MasterCard
Catalog Cost: Free
Catalog Circulation: to 70000
Printing Information: in 4 colors on Matte Stock
Press: Sheetfed Press
Binding: Saddle Stitched
Mailing List Information: Names for rent
In Business: 117 years
Number of Employees: 7
Sales Information: $1MM to $3MM

8292 Installations
Installations Inc.
25257 W 8 Mile Rd
Redford, MI 48240-1003 313-532-9000
800-442-2290
Fax: 313-532-0894
www.Installations.Org

Bullet proof doors, windows and bank tellers, bullet resistant barrier, CNC routing drilling cutting bullet resistant materials
President: Pearl Baltes
CFO: Lawrence Baltes
Mailing List Information: Names for rent
In Business: 30 years
Number of Employees: 20
Sales Information: $1,000,000 - $5,000,000

8293 Interlogix Security & Life Safety Group
Interlogix
UTC Building & Industrial Systems
3211 Progress Drive
Lincolnton, NC 28092 855-286-8889
800-547-2556
Fax: 503-691-7566
orders@interlogix.com
www.interlogix.com

Designs, manufactures and distributes components, software, communication technologies and information for security, safety, and lifestyle enhancements
President: Brian McCarthy
CFO: Rick Falconer
Marketing Manager: David Tyler
Production Manager: Ali Saalabian
Buyers: Marc Koczwara
Catalog Cost: Free
Catalog Circulation: to 2000
Printing Information: 150 pages in 2 colors on Matte Stock
Binding: Perfect Bound
Mailing List Information: Names for rent
List Manager: Kim Benson
In Business: 34 years
Number of Employees: 700
Sales Information: $50MM to $100MM

8294 International Sensor Technology
International Sensor Technology
3 Whatney # 100
Irvine, CA 92618-2824 949-452-9000
800-478-4271
Fax: 949-452-9009
jeff.lowe@intlsensor.com
www.intlsensor.com

Gas monitoring and detecting sensors
President: Danny Chou
Printing Information: 8 pages
In Business: 41 years
Number of Employees: 20-5
Sales Information: $1,000,000 - $5,000,000

8295 Interscan Corporation
Interscan Corporation
4590 Ish Drive
#110
Simi Valley, CA 93063-2496   818-882-2331
818-882-2331
800-458-6153
Fax: 818-341-0642
info@gasdetection.com
www.gasdetection.com

Toxic gas detector instrumentation

President: Manny Shaw
Marketing Manager: Michael Shaw
Number of Employees: 20
Sales Information: $5,000,000 - $10,000,000

8296 Justrite Manufacturing Company
Justrite Mfg. Co
2454 E Dempster St
Suite 300
Des Plaines, IL 60016-5315   847-298-9250
847-298-9250
800-978-9250
Fax: 847-298-9261
www.justritemfg.com

Flammable liquid safety equipment

Printing Information: 128 pages in 4 colors on
Matte Stock
Press: Web Press
Binding: Perfect Bound
Mailing List Information: Names for rent
In Business: 97 years
Number of Employees: 200
Sales Information: $3MM to $5MM

8297 Kelley Technical Coatings
Kelley Technical Coatings
1445 South 15th Street
PO Box 3726
Louisville, KY 40201-3726   502-636-2561
800-458-2842
Fax: 502-635-5170
www.kelleytech.com

Non-slip coatings

President: John R Kelley Jr
Marketing Manager: Brink Spruill
Production Manager: Art Sumner
In Business: 65 years
Number of Employees: 60
Sales Information: $10,000,000 - $25,000,000

**8298 Kemlon Products & Development
Corporation**
Kemlon Products Inc
1424 North Main Street
P.O. Box 2189
Pearland, TX 77581-4666   281-997-3300
Fax: 281-997-1300
sales@kemlon.com
www.kemlon.com/

**Compressors for handling corrosive, radio-
active and oil-free gas pumps**

President: Sandisford Ring
CEO: Avi Hadar
Number of Employees: 100
Sales Information: $10MM to $20MM

8299 Label Master
Labelmaster
5724 North Pulaski Road
Chicago, IL 60646-6724   773-478-0900
800-621-5808
Fax: 800-723-4327
webmaster@labelmaster.com
www.labelmaster.com/

**Hazardous waste labels and other
right-to-know and compliance products**

Chairman: Gary S. Mostow
President: Alan J. Schoen
Marketing Manager: Robert Finn
Production Manager: Michael J. Kaufman
Vice Chairman: Dwight E. Curtis
VP of Sales: Heidi Lohmann

VP of Software and Services: Forest
Himmelfarb

8300 Landauer
Landauer
2 Science Road
Glenwood, IL 60425-1586   708-755-7000
800-323-8830
Fax: 708-755-7016
custserv@landauer.com
www.Landauer.Com

**Dosimeters to measure x-ray, beta, gamma
radiation and neutrons**

President: Greg Groenke
CFO: Mark Zorko
Marketing Manager: Mike Kennedy
Fulfillment: Robert Greaney
Sr. Vice President of Global Techno: Craig
Yoder, PhD
VP, Global Sales: Amy Cosler
VP & Chief Information Officer: Doug King
Catalog Cost: Free
Catalog Circulation: to 8M
Printing Information: 1 pages in 4 colors on
Glossy Stock
Mailing List Information: Names for rent
List Manager: Joe Zlotnicki
In Business: 61 years
Number of Employees: 400
Sales Information: $25,000,000 - $50,000,000

8301 Lester L Brossard Company
Lester L. Brossard Co.
930 Dieckman Street
Woodstock, IL 60098-708   815-338-7825
800-222-7825
Fax: 815-338-7954
brossard@brossardmirrors.com
www.brossardmirrors.com

Safety and security mirrors

President: George Brossard
Marketing Manager: Dan Moran
Credit Cards: AMEX; MasterCard; Visa
Mailing List Information: Names for rent
In Business: 65 years
Number of Employees: 10
Sales Information: $1,000,000 - $5,000,000

8302 Life Support International
Life Support International Inc.
200 Rittenhouse Cir # 4-W
Bristol, PA 19007-1626   215-785-2870
Fax: 215-785-2880
www.Lifesupportintl.Com

Survival and rescue equipment

President: RA Brower

8303 Linemaster Switch Corporation
Linemaster
29 Plaine Hill Road
PO Box 238
Woodstock, CT 06281-238   860-974-1000
800-974-3668
Fax: 800-974-3668
info@linemaster.com
www.linemaster.com

**Anti-trip foot switch, complete line of foot
switches from duty to heavy duty, waterproof, dustproof and special application**

President: Joseph J Carlone
Catalog Circulation: to 8000
Printing Information: 38 pages in 4 colors on s
Mailing List Information: Names for rent
In Business: 19 years
Number of Employees: 175
Sales Information: $10,000,000 - $25,000,000

8304 Mallory Company
Mallory Company
PO Box 2068
1040 Industrial Waty
Longview, WA 98632   360-636-5750
Fax: 360-577-4244
www.Malloryco.Com

Safety supplies

President: Tim Loy
COO: Shawn Murray
CIO: Brian Loy
Operations Manager: Lorene Simmons
In Business: 40 years
Number of Employees: 200
Sales Information: $20MM to $50MM

8305 Mandall Armor Design & Manufacturing
Mandall BarrierWorks, LLC
7071 W. Frye Road
Chandler, AZ 85226   480-763-7340
800-944-1448
Fax: 480-763-6004
nick@mandall.com
www.Mandall.Com

**Specialty armor, armored systems and bal-
listic glass**

President: Michael Mandall
Engineering POC: Nick Mavrikos
nick@mandall.com
Sales Engineer POC: Jason Weed
jason@mandall.com
In Business: 24 years
Sales Information: $5MM to $10MM

8306 Marzetta Signs
Accuform
16228 Flight Path Drive
Brooksville, FL 34604   707-452-1630
800-237-1001
Fax: 800-394-4001
CustomerService@Accuform.com
www.accuform.com

Sensitive safety signs

Marketing Manager: Christina Murray
Account Manager: Nichole Tripp
Dir. Of Customer Service: John Murphy QSSP
Number of Employees: 25
Sales Information: $1,000,000 - $5,000,000

8307 Masune First Aid & Safety
Masune First Aid & Safety
500 Fillmore Avenue
Tonawanda, NY 14150   716-695-3244
800-831-0894
Fax: 800-222-1934
customersupport@masune.com
www.masune.com

**Offers a wide range of essential first aid and
safety products, including wound treatment,
personal protection, OTC Oral Medications,
medical equipment and instruments, and
biohazard response**

President: Mark LaDoucer
CFO: Jeff Millen
Marketing Manager: Don Laux
Production Manager: Kate Kennedy
Fulfillment: Tom Fischer
Buyers: Frank Sofia
Credit Cards: AMEX; MasterCard; Visa
Catalog Cost: Free
Catalog Circulation: Mailed 8 time(s) per year
to 6MM
Printing Information: 249 pages in 4 colors on
Newsprint
Press: Web Press
Binding: Perfect Bound
Mailing List Information: Names for rent
List Manager: Sue Barone
In Business: 35 years
Number of Employees: 172

8308 Miller Edge
MillerEdge
PO Box 159
West Grove, PA 19390   610-869-4422
                               800-220-3343
                          Fax: 610-869-4423
                          www.milleredge.com

Sensing switches for custom applications

President: Bearge Miller
Marketing Manager: Flossie Mohler
Founder: Norman K. Miller
VP Operations: Tim Castello
In Business: 79 years
Sales Information: $1MM to $3MM

8309 NGK Metals Corporation
NGK Berylco
917 Highway 11 S
Sweetwater, TN 37874-5730   423-337-5500
                               800-523-8268
                          Fax: 877-645-2328
                          marketing@ngkmetals.com
                          www.Ngkmetals.Com

Nonsparking safety tools

President: Glade Nelson
Number of Employees: 200
Sales Information: $1MM to $3MM

8310 National Draeger Detector Tube Products
Drager
101 Technology Dr
Pittsburgh, PA 15275-1005   412-787-8383
                               800-858-1737
                          Fax: 412-787-2207
                          www.Draeger.Com

Gas and alcohol detector tubes, respiratory protection gas monitoring instruments

President: Wes Kenneweg
CFO: Graeme Roberts
Marketing Manager: Dan Hirsch
Production Manager: Rob McCall
Catalog Circulation: Mailed 1 time(s) per year
Printing Information: 18 pages in 4 colors
Binding: Saddle Stitched
Mailing List Information: Names for rent
In Business: 25 years
Number of Employees: 200

8311 Northern Safety Company
Northern Safety Company
PO Box 4250
Utica, NY 13504-4250   315-793-4900
                               800-571-4646
                          Fax: 800-635-1591
                          customerservice@northernsafety.com
                          www.northernsafety.com

Safety and industrial supplies

Chairman: Sal Longo
President: Neil Sexton
CFO: Martha Moorehead
Marketing Manager: Robin Fostini
Founder, CEO: Sal Longo
slongoweb@northernsafety.com
Credit Cards: AMEX; MasterCard
Catalog Cost: Free
Printing Information: 532 pages
Binding: Perfect Bound
In Business: 32 years
Number of Employees: 75

8312 Panduit Electrical Group
Panduit
18900 Panduit Drive
Tinley Park, IL 60487-3091   800-777-3300
                          Fax: 708-532-1811
                          www.panduit.com

Safety tags

President: Jack E Caveney Sr
In Business: 60 years
Number of Employees: 3500

8313 Pendergast Safety
Pendergast
8400 Enterprise Ave
Philadelphia, PA 19153-3888   215-937-1900
                               800-551-1901
                          Fax: 215-365-7527
                          Sales@PendergastSafety.com
                          www.Pendergastsafety.Com

Supplier of industrial safety equipment

President: William F Grauer
CFO: David Grauer
Credit Cards: AMEX; MasterCard
In Business: 68 years
Number of Employees: 25
Sales Information: $1,000,000 - $5,000,000

8314 Personal Protection/Safety Products
Sellstrom Manufacturing Co
2050 Hammond Drive
Schaumburg, IL 60173-6260   847-358-2000
                               800-323-7402
                          Fax: 847-358-8564
                          sellstrom@sellstrom.com
                          www.sellstrom.com

Protective eyewear, fall protection, confined spaces; escape devices, welding gear and more

President: David W Peters
CFO: David W Peters
Marketing Manager: Thomas Barr
Fulfillment: Bill Spangler
Director of Business Development: Chris Gill
Buyers: Ellen Akerhaugen
Catalog Cost: Free
Catalog Circulation: to 30M
Printing Information: 15 pages in 4 colors on Glossy Stock
Binding: Saddle Stitched
List Manager: Janet Borello
In Business: 92 years
Number of Employees: 100
Sales Information: $10,000,000 - $25,000,000

8315 Positive Safety Manufacturing Company
Positive Safety Manufacturing Company
34099 Melinz Pkwy # A
UNIT A
EastLake, OH 44095-4001   440-951-2130
                          Fax: 440-951-2256
                          www.Positivesafetymfg.Com

Press guarding

President: Jeff Sloat
In Business: 91 years
Number of Employees: 25
Sales Information: $5MM to $10MM

8316 Promaco
Promaco Inc
3714 Runge Street
Franklin Park, IL 60131-1112 800-253-2866
                          Fax: 847-288-9999
                          info@promacoinc.com
                          www.promacoinc.com

Floor treads, cash drop boxes, safety signage, fire alarm pulls, key cabinets; cleaning supplies, bathroom supplies, gloves, janitorial products, brooms, mops, dust pans, waste bins; security cameras

Credit Cards: AMEX; MasterCard

8317 Protech Systems
Protech Systems
3100 E. Cedar Street
Suite #4
Ontario, CA 91761   909-590-9521
                               800-448-2737
                          Fax: 909-590-9921
                          info@protechsystems.com
                          www.Protechsystems.Com

Machinery safety systems

President: Tim Stephens
Marketing Manager: Jim Stephens

Credit Cards: AMEX; MasterCard
Mailing List Information: Names for rent
In Business: 21 years
Number of Employees: 13
Sales Information: $1,000,000 - $5,000,000

8318 Protection People
Dixon
800 High Street
Chestertown, MD 21620   877-712-6179
                          Fax: 410-778-9525
                          www.dixonvalve.com/division/dixon-fire

Valves, nozzles, adapters, nipples

Credit Cards: AMEX; MasterCard
Catalog Cost: Free
Printing Information: 16 pages
Binding: Saddle Stitched
In Business: 128 years

8319 R Stahl Automation Catalog
R Stahl,Inc
13259 N. Promenade Blvd
Stafford, TX 77477   713-792-9300
                               800-782-4357
                          Fax: 713-797-0105
                          info@stahl.de
                          www.rstahl.com

Saftey barriers, isolaters, fieldbus technology and operating & monitoring

Chairman: Martin Schomaker
President: Matthias Kuch
Marketing Manager: Craig Yoss
International Marketing Manager: Raina Naegle
Credit Cards: MasterCard; Visa
Printing Information: in 4 colors on Glossy Stock
In Business: 130 years
Number of Employees: 50
Sales Information: Under $500M

8320 R Stahl Explosion Proof/Protected Electrical
R Stahl,Inc
13259 N. Promenade Blvd
Stafford, TX 77477   713-792-9300
                               800-782-4357
                          Fax: 713-797-0105
                          info@stahl.de
                          www.rstahl.com

NEC and CEC explosion proof and explosion protected electrical products for US/Canada; enclosures, light fixtures, controls, plugs & receptacles, and distribution equipment

Chairman: Martin Schomaker
President: Matthias Kuch
Marketing Manager: Craig Yoss
International Marketing Manager: Raina Naegle
Credit Cards: MasterCard
Printing Information: 179 pages in 4 colors on Glossy Stock
Binding: Perfect Bound
In Business: 130 years
Number of Employees: 50
Sales Information: Under $500M

8321 Rock-N-Rescue
J.E. Weinel, Inc.
300 Delwood Road
Butler, PA 16001-213   724-256-8822
                               800-346-7673
                          Fax: 724-256-8888
                          info@rocknrescue.com
                          www.rocknrescue.com

Manufacturer and distributor of rescue equipment for high angle, confined space, trench, water rescue, building collapse, and more

President: John A Weinel
Marketing Manager: Robert Womer
Fulfillment: Butch Weinel

Manager: Bob Barbarini
Credit Cards: AMEX; MasterCard; Visa
Catalog Cost: Free
Catalog Circulation: Mailed 52 time(s) per year to 30M
Average Order Size: $500
Printing Information: 100 pages in 3 colors on Matte Stock
Press: Web Press
Binding: Saddle Stitched
Mailing List Information: Names for rent
List Manager: Butch Weinel
In Business: 75 years
Number of Employees: 9
Sales Information: $2,500,000

8322 SA-SO Catalog
SA-SO
525 N Great Southwest Parkway
Arlington, TX 76011-1299   972-641-4911
Fax: 972-660-3684
sales@sa-so.com
www.sa-so.com

Facility, traffic and safety products

Credit Cards: AMEX; MasterCard; Visa
Catalog Cost: Free
Mailing List Information: Names for rent
In Business: 69 years
Number of Employees: 300

8323 SES
Security Equipment Supply, Inc.
sales@sesonline.com
www.sesonline.com

Burglar and fire alarms, home automation, CCTV, access controls, protectors and supplies

President: Bob Van Dillen
bvandillen@sesonline.com
Marketing Manager: Jamie Roberston
Operations Manager: George Trussler
gtrussler@sesonline.com
Sales Manager: John Hill
Jhill@sesonline.com
Credit Cards: MasterCard; Visa
Catalog Cost: $15
Catalog Circulation: Mailed 3 time(s) per year to 10000
Printing Information: 50 pages in 2 colors on Glossy Stock
Binding: Saddle Stitched
In Business: 35 years
Number of Employees: 40
Sales Information: $10 million

8324 Saf-T-Gard
Saf-T-Gard International, Inc.
205 Huehl Rd
Northbrook, IL 60062-1972   847-291-1600
800-548-4273
Fax: 847-291-1610
safety@saftgard.com
www.Saftgard.Com

Protective clothing and safety supplies

President: Richard Rivkin
CFO: Robert A Diell
Marketing Manager: Loren Rivkin
Credit Cards: AMEX; MasterCard; Visa
Mailing List Information: Names for rent
In Business: 70 years
Sales Information: $10MM to $20MM

8325 Safe-Aire Radon Mitigation Products
Basement De-Watering Systems, Inc.
3100 N. Main St.
Canton, IL 61520-2769   309-647-0331
800-331-2943
Fax: 309-647-0498
info@bdws.com
www.bdws.com

Radon mitigation products

Chairman: Russell De Valois
President: Jerry Jarnagin
Marketing Manager: Lori McLouth

Production Manager: Chet Phillips
Manager: Jeff Puskarich
Credit Cards: MasterCard; Visa
Catalog Cost: Free
Catalog Circulation: Mailed 2 time(s) per year to 25M+
Printing Information: 32 pages in 2 colors on Newsprint
Press: Web Press
Mailing List Information: Names for rent
In Business: 39 years
Number of Employees: 30
Sales Information: $1,000,000 - $5,000,000

8326 Safety Premiums
The Reflectory
89 Broadway
Newburgh, NY 12550-5651   845-565-2037
800-654-1417
Fax: 845-565-2451
reflectory@msn.com
www.safetyreflectors.com

Reflector stickers, armbands, legbands, sashes and other items forpeople, pets and vehicles, including walking/jogging reflector wands and dangling pedestrian reflectors

President: Raymond Strakosch
Credit Cards: MasterCard
Catalog Cost: Free
Catalog Circulation: Mailed 1 time(s) per year to 2500
Average Order Size: $500
Printing Information: 8 pages in 4 colors on Glossy Stock
Binding: Perfect Bound
Mailing List Information: Names for rent
In Business: 40 years
Number of Employees: 3
Sales Information: Under $500,000

8327 SafetyWear
SafetyWear
P.O. Box 11283
Fort Wayne, IN 46857-2555   260-456-3630
800-877-3555
Fax: 260-459-4117
sales@safety-wear.com
www.safety-wear.com

Hand and wrist safety equipment

President: Daniel Brough
CFO: Brian Steele
Marketing Manager: Zac Brough
VP: Barbara Barron
Customer Service Manager: Kathleen Miller
Printing Information: 191 pages in 3 colors
In Business: 38 years
Number of Employees: 20
Sales Information: $10 million

8328 Schoolmasters Safety
School-Tech, Inc.
745 State Circle
Ann Arbor, MI 48108   800-521-2832
Fax: 800-654-4321
www.schoolmasters.com

School safety supplies

President: Donald B. Canham
Marketing Manager: SW Canham
Printing Information: 68 pages in 4 colors
In Business: 54 years
Number of Employees: 80
Sales Information: $50MM to $100MM

8329 Scientific Technologies
Omron Scientific Tehnologies, Inc.
2895 Greenspoint Parkway
Suite 200
Hoffman Estates, IL 60169   847-843-7900
800-556-6766
Fax: 847-843-7787
www.sti.com

Safety light curtains, factory automation products

President: James A Ashford
CFO: Akitsugu Kurahashi
SVP: James A Lazzara
VP Standards Developmen: L. Dwayne Townle
dtownley@severeduty.com
VP Finance & Administra: Carolyn Ray
Buyers: Russell Thomas
Catalog Cost: Free
Printing Information: 60 pages in 3 colors
Mailing List Information: Names for rent
In Business: 82 years
Number of Employees: 260
Sales Information: $25,000,000 - $50,000,000

8330 Scott Instruments
Scott Safety
4320 Goldmine Road
Monroe, NC 28110   704-291-8300
800-247-7257
Fax: 704-291-8330
domcustsrv.scotths.us@tycoint.com
www.scottsafety.com

Toxic gas detectors

Founder: Earl M, Scott
Printing Information: in 3 colors
In Business: 82 years
Number of Employees: 1100
Sales Information: $500 million

8331 See All
See All
3623 Sout Laflin Place
Chicago, IL 60609-1397   773-927-3232
800-873-1313
Fax: 773-927-7742
info@seeall.com
www.Seeall.Com

Quality convex mirrors, dome mirrors, magnifying mirrors, inspection mirrors, lighted mirrors, framedand speciality mirrors

President: Carmela Celenza
VP: Michelle Golubov
michelleg@seesinc.com
VP: Rich Fitzgerald
rich_f@seesinc.com
Printing Information: 11 pages in 3 colors
Number of Employees: 14
Sales Information: $1,000,000 - $5,000,000

8332 Sellstrom Manufacturing Company
Sellstrom Manufacturing Co.
2050 Hammond Drive
Schaumburg, IL 60173-355   847-358-2000
800-323-7402
Fax: 847-358-8564
sellstrom@sellstrom.com
www.sellstrom.com

Protective face shields, protective goggles, emergency eye/face wash units, welding helmets and goggles, spill control, emergency showers

President: David Peters
david.peters@sellstrom.com
CFO: Lawrence Schmidt
larry.schmidt@sellstrom.com
Marketing Manager: Rusty Franklin
rusty.franklin@sellstrom.com
Customer Service: Jason Suarez
Manager Engineering: Ken Lemke
Marketing Coordinator: Beverly Bensen
Catalog Circulation: to 30000
Printing Information: 64 pages in 3 colors
In Business: 92 years
Number of Employees: 100
Sales Information: $20MM

8333 Services & Materials Company
Select Safety Sales, LLC
PO Box 826
Clark, NJ 07066
866-864-3495
800-428-8185
Fax: 732-381-4365
sales@selectsafetysales.com
www.selectsafetysales.com

Highway and industrial safety products
President: Bill Howard
Marketing Manager: John Pappas
Number of Employees: 125
Sales Information: $10,000,000 - $25,000,000

8334 Seton Essentials
Seton
20 Thompson Rd.
PO Box 819
Branford, CT 06405-819
203-488-8059
855-544-7992
Fax: 800-345-7819
help@seton.com
www.seton.com

Safety, labeling and signage
President: Pascal Deman
Marketing Manager: Cassandra Goduti
Credit Cards: AMEX; MasterCard
In Business: 59 years
Number of Employees: 251

8335 Sierra Monitor Corporation
Sierra Monitor Corporation
1991 Tarob Ct
Milpitas, CA 95035-6840
408-262-6611
800-727-4377
Fax: 408-262-9042
info@sierramonitor.com
www.Sierramonitor.Com

Gas monitoring systems, communications bridge
President: Varun Nagaraj
CFO: Tamara Allen
Marketing Manager: Anders Axelsson
Director of Engineering: Bennie de Wet
Vice President of Operations: Michael C. Farr
Catalog Cost: Free
Catalog Circulation: Mailed 1 time(s) per year
Printing Information: 6 pages in 4 colors on Glossy Stock
Mailing List Information: Names for rent
In Business: 36 years
Number of Employees: 52
Sales Information: $1,000,000 - $5,000,000

8336 Sigalarm
Sigalarm
4150 ST. Johns Parkway
Suite 1002
Sanford, FL 32771
407-321-0722
800-589-3769
Fax: 407-321-0723
www.sigalarminc.com

Electronic safety systems
CEO: Lance Burney
In Business: 62 years

8337 Standard Safety Equipment Company
Standard Safety Equipment Company
1901 North Moore Street
Suite 808
Arlington, VA 22209-1762
703-525-1695
Fax: 703-528-2148
www.safetyequipment.org

Protective clothing and safety equipment
Chairman: Eric Beck
President: Daniel K. Shipp
dshipp@safetyequipment.org
Marketing Manager: BW Lyons
Vice Chairman: Sheila Eads
COO: John Kime
Office Services Manager: Ann M. Feder
afeder@safetyequipment.org

Printing Information: in 2 colors
Number of Employees: 35
Sales Information: $10MM to $20MM

8338 Stewart R Browne Manufacturing Company
Srewart R. Browne Manufacuring Company,
1165 Hightower Trl
PO Box 500008
Atlanta, GA 31150-2911
770-993-9600
Fax: 770-594-7758
info@srbrowne.com
www.StewartrBrowne.Com

Electrical safety equipment
President: Alan Browne
Marketing Manager: Mike Vaccaro
Sales Staff: Erik Browne
erik@srbrowne.com
Printing Information: in 4 colors on Glossy Stock
Mailing List Information: Names for rent
In Business: 95 years
Number of Employees: 11
Sales Information: $1,000,000 - $5,000,000

8339 Sun Precautions
Sun Precautions, Inc.
2815 Wetmore Ave
Everett, WA 98201-3517
425-303-8585
800-882-7860
Fax: 425-303-0836
www.sunprecautions.com

30+ SPF sun protective clothing and other products for people who are hypersensitive to the sun
President: Shaun Hughes
Catalog Cost: Free
Printing Information: 40 pages in 4 colors
In Business: 30 years
Sales Information: $ 500,000- 1 Million

8340 Syntechnics
Syntechnics
700 Terrace Lane
Paducah, KY 42003-9343
270-898-7303
Fax: 270-898-7306
michael.beott@trin.net
www.syntechnics.net

Barge covers, waste water treatments and safety devices
President: Teddy Holt
Sales: Mike Beott
michael.beott@trin.net
Technical: David E. Choat, P.E.
david.choat@trin.net
Number of Employees: 110
Sales Information: $10MM to $20MM

8341 TIF International
Rominar
655 Eisenhower Drive
Owatonna, MN 55060
507-455-7000
800-327-5060
Fax: 507-455-8354
inquiry@service-solutions.com
www.robinair.com

Offers leak detectors, charging meters, gauges and voltage detectors
President: Thomas Gerard
Marketing Manager: Adam Seymour
Sales Manager: Matt Fisher
In Business: 63 years
Number of Employees: 400
Sales Information: $25,000,000 - $50,000,000

8342 Tadiran Electronic Industries
Tadiran Batteries
2001 Marcus Ave
Suite 125 E.
Lake Success, NY 11042-4618
516-621-4980
800-537-1368
Fax: 516-621-4517
sales@tadiranbat.com
www.tadiranbat.com

Safety equipment, batteries and various devices
President: Sol Jacobs
Marketing Manager: E Shoval
Number of Employees: 11
Sales Information: $1MM to $3MM

8343 Tepromark International
Tepromark International, Inc.
249 5th Avenue SE
Osseo, MN 55369
763-273-8484
800-645-2622
Fax: 763-273-8486
sales@tepromark.com
www.tepromark.com

Wall protection systems
President: Joann Dee
In Business: 44 years
Number of Employees: 6
Sales Information: $500,000 - $1,000,000

8344 Thermadyne
Serian Protection Optical, Inc.
300 Lindenwood Drive
Suite 522
Malvern, PA 63126-8832
314-239-9183
Fax: 800-541-3193
info@flexolite.com
flexolite.com

Welding helmets
President: Robert Sandner
Production Manager: Bill Shaker
bill.shaker@flexolite.com
Global Commercial Manager: Mike Boeger
mike.boeger@flexolite.com
Govt. Sales/ Customer Service: Cliff Fisher
cliff.fisher@flexolite.com
Sales Manager: Ronald Boeger
ron.boeger@flexolite.com
Number of Employees: 300
Sales Information: $25,000,000 - $50,000,000

8345 Thermal Gas Systems
Thermal Gas systems, Inc.
11285 Elkins Rd.
Building H-1 Suite 110
Roswell, GA 30076-803
770-667-3865
800-896-2996
Fax: 770-667-3857
info@thermalgas.com
www.Thermalgas.Com

Electronic instruments for measuring toxic gases and oxygen depletion in closed spaces
President: Jay West
In Business: 27 years
Number of Employees: 6
Sales Information: $500,000 - $1,000,000

8346 Tigg Corporation
TIGG Corporate Headquarters
1 Willow Avenue
Oakdale, PA 15071
724-703-3020
800-925-0011
Fax: 724-703-3026
info@tigg.com
www.tigg.com

Activated carbon adsorption equipment
President: Georgiana N Riley
Production Manager: George Milantoni
Credit Cards: AMEX; MasterCard; Visa
In Business: 37 years

Number of Employees: 16
Sales Information: $10MM to $20MM

8347 Titmus Optical
Serian Protection Optical, Inc.
15801 Woods Edge Road
Colonial Heights, VA 23834-2742 800-446-1802
800-446-1802
Fax: 800-544-0346
www.titmus.com

Prescription protective eyewear, vision screening instruments, street designs dress eyewear and accessories

President: Thomas Boeltz
In Business: 107 years
Number of Employees: 500
Sales Information: $25,000,000 - $50,000,000

8348 Tomar Electronics
TOMAR Electronics, Inc.
2100 W Obispo Avenue
Gilbert, AZ 85233-3401   480-497-4400
800-338-3133
Fax: 480-497-4416
sales@tomar.com
www.Tomar.Com

Industrial and public safety strobe warning lights

President: Scott Sikora
CFO: Marilyn Sikora
Marketing Manager: Tracy Vanderkooi
Buyers: Sherry Kearney
Credit Cards: MasterCard; Visa
Catalog Circulation: Mailed 1 time(s) per year
Printing Information: 92 pages in 4 colors on Glossy Stock
Press: Letterpress
Mailing List Information: Names for rent
List Manager: Tracy Vanderkooi
In Business: 40 years
Number of Employees: 85
Sales Information: $5,000,000 - $10,000,000

8349 Town & Country Plastics
Town & Country Plastics, Inc.
10-B Timber Lane
P.O. BOX 269
Morganville, NJ 07746   732-780-5300
Fax: 732-294-0001
www.tandcplastics.net

Corrosion resistant products and pollution control/collection equipment and systems

President: Harold Mermel
CFO: Leslie Mermel
Marketing Manager: Harold Mermel
Production Manager: Kim Olsen
International Marketing Manager: Harold Mermel
Buyers: Leslie Mermel
Catalog Cost: Free
Catalog Circulation: Mailed 1 time(s) per year to 2M
Printing Information: 100 pages in 4 colors on Glossy Stock
Press: Web Press
In Business: 43 years
Number of Employees: 25
Sales Information: $1,000,000 - $5,000,000

8350 Tri-Mer Corporation
Tri-Mer Corporation
1400 Monroe Street
PO Box 730
Owosso, MI 48867-730   989-723-7838
800-688-7838
Fax: 989-723-7844
salesdpt@tri-mer.com
www.Tri-Mer.Com

Air pollution control systems

President: Eugene Ruess
Marketing Manager: JM Pardell, VP
Production Manager: Bret Ruess
Business Development Director: Kevin D.

Moss
kevin.moss@tri-mer.com
Director of Sales - Dry Dust Collec: Ron Doneff
rdoneff@tri-mer.com
Senior Technical Salesman: Darryl Haley
dhaley@tri-mer.com
Mailing List Information: Names for rent
In Business: 97 years
Number of Employees: 65
Sales Information: $5,000,000 - $10,000,000

8351 US Safety
US Safety
8101 Lenexa Drive
P.O. Box 95307
Lenexa, KS 66214   913-599-5555
800-821-5218
Fax: 800-252-5002
info@ussafety.com
www.ussafety.Com

Designs, develops and manufactures personal protective equipment to include prescription and non-prescription eyewear, respirators, goggles, faceshields and other miscellaneous products

President: Jp Sankpill
Credit Cards: MasterCard; Visa
Catalog Cost: Free
Mailing List Information: Names for rent
In Business: 66 years
Number of Employees: 350
Sales Information: $20MM to $50MM

8352 Unistrut Illinois
Unistrut Corporation
4205 Elizabeth St
Wayne, MI 48184-2091   734-721-9929
800-882-5543
Fax: 708-339-0615
www.Unistrut.Com

Fall arrest systems

President: Chuck Nehls
Marketing Manager: Madelyn Coleman
Director of Sales: Gorden Hunter
ghunter@unistrut.com
Product Engineer: Chad Zeilenga
Czeilenga@tyco-emp.com
Number of Employees: 50
Sales Information: $20MM to $50MM

8353 WH Salisbury & Company
Salisbury by Honeywell
101 E. Crossroads Pkwy
Suite A
Bolingbrook, IL 60440-3226   630-343-3800
877-406-4501
Fax: 630-343-3838
CSSD@honeywell.com
www.salisburybyhoneywell.com

Industrial products, line hose & covers, insulating blankets, plastic guards & covers.

President: Paul Dittmer
In Business: 160 years
Number of Employees: 70

8354 Whelen Engineering
Whelen
51 Winthrop Road
Chester, CT 06412-0684   860-526-9504
Fax: 860-526-4078
custserv@whelen.com
www.whelen.com

Visual and audible signaling products for vehicular applications

President: John Olson
Purchasing Manager: Norm Lowery
Catalog Cost: Free
Printing Information: 68 pages
In Business: 65 years
Number of Employees: 400
Sales Information: $50,000,000 - $100,000,00

8355 World Catalog of Oil Spill Response Products
World Catalog of Oil Spill Response Prod
200-1140 Morrison
Ottawa, ON K2H-8S9   613-232-1564
Fax: 613-232-6660
jake@slross.com
www.oilspillequipment.com

Oil spill response products from distributors and manufacturers worldwide

Catalog Cost: $275
Catalog Circulation: to 1500
Printing Information: 1000 pages
Binding: Perfect Bound
In Business: 37 years

8356 Safariland Master Catalog
Safariland
13386 International Pkwy.
Jacksonville, FL 32218   800-347-1200
www.safariland.com

Body armor and other gun accessories.

Printing Information: 252 pages in 4 colors
In Business: 52 years
Number of Employees: 1400
Sales Information: $200 Million

8357 Safariland Shooting Gear Catalog
Safariland
13386 International Pkwy.
Jacksonville, FL 32218   800-347-1200
www.safariland.com

Shooting accessories including gloves, belts and holsters.

Printing Information: 196 pages in 4 colors
In Business: 52 years
Number of Employees: 1400
Sales Information: $200 Million

Sanitation
General

8358 Aaladin Industries
Aaladin Cleaning Systems
32584 477th Avenue
Elk Point, SD 57025-6700   605-356-3325
800-356-3325
Fax: 605-356-2330
info@aaladin.com
www.aaladin.com

Steam cleaners, hot and cold pressure washers and industrial water heating systems

President: Pat Wingen
pwingen@aaladin.com
Director, Sales & Marketing: Randy Wheelock
randyw@aaladin.com
VP of Operations: Chris Wingen
cwingen@aaladin.com
Office Manager: Pam Hughes
phughes@aaladin.com
In Business: 34 years
Number of Employees: 75
Sales Information: $15,000,000

8359 Alconox
Alconox
30 Glenn Street
Suite 309
White Plains, NY 10603   914-948-4040
Fax: 914-948-4088
cleaning@alconox.com
www.alconox.com

Manufactures Alconox detergent for critical cleaning as required in health, educational, industrial, electronics and government institutions

President: Thomas Pasqualini
Marketing Manager: Malcolm McLaughlin
Credit Cards: AMEX; MasterCard
Catalog Cost: Free

Printing Information: 2 pages in 4 colors on Glossy Stock
In Business: 74 years

8360 Arbill Safety Products
Arbill
10450 Drummond Road
Philadelphia, PA 19154   800-523-5367
info@arbill.com
www.arbill.com

Personal protective clothing, eye and hearing protection, head gear, respiratory equipment, back supports, ergonomic equipment, fall protection equipment, confined space protection, spill clean-up

President: Robyn Zlotkin
CFO: Keith Daviston
Production Manager: Bill Gabriele
Chief Executive Officer: Julie Copeland
Director of Operations: Bill Keay
Credit Cards: AMEX; MasterCard
Catalog Cost: Free
In Business: 72 years
Number of Employees: 55
Sales Information: $ 10 Million

8361 BP Barco Products
BP Barco Products
24 N. Washington Ave
Batavia, IL 60510   800-338-2697
Fax: 630-879-8687
sales@barcoproducts.com
www.barcoproducts.com

Safety barriers, traffic cones and posts, safety can liquid storage, pedestrian, traffic and parking signs, caution signs, sign posts; cleaning and sanitation products

President: Brian Barnes
CFO: Robin Sickafoose
CEO: Cyril Matter
Catalog Cost: Free
Printing Information: in 4 colors
In Business: 30 years
Number of Employees: 35
Sales Information: $6,000,000

8362 BVS Samplers
BVS Inc
949 Poplar Road
PO Box 250
Honey Brook, PA 19344-250   610-273-2841
877-877-4821
Fax: 610-273-2843
info@bvssamplers.com
www.bvssamplers.com

Manufacturer of automatic samplers for water pollution surveillance and control

President: Robert M Blechman
Marketing Manager: U.S. Aparre
Production Manager: H.L. Lochmanner
Catalog Circulation: to 15000
Printing Information: 8 pages in 1 color on Glossy Stock
Press: Web Press
Binding: Saddle Stitched
Mailing List Information: Names for rent
In Business: 40 years
Number of Employees: 3
Sales Information: $1,000,000

8363 Barco Products Company
Barco Products
24 N. Washington Ave
Batavia, IL 60510   630-879-0084
800-338-2697
Fax: 630-879-8687
sales@barcoproducts.com
www.barcoproducts.com

Picnic tables, park benches, trash receptacles, safety products, parking lot products

President: Robert Runke
Marketing Manager: Susan Ross
Production Manager: Kim Vallone

CEO: Cyril Matter
Catalog Cost: Free
In Business: 30 years
Sales Information: $6MM

8364 Bete Fog Nozzle
Bete Fog Nozzle
50 Greenfield Street
Greenfield, MA 01301-1378   413-772-0846
800-235-0049
Fax: 413-772-6729
sales@bete.com
www.Bete.Com

Nozzles for dust, air, FGD, and water pollution control

President: Matthew Bete
Production Manager: Doug Dziadzio
Catalog Circulation: Mailed 1 time(s) per year to 15K
Printing Information: 72 pages in 4 colors on Glossy Stock
Binding: Perfect Bound
Mailing List Information: Names for rent
In Business: 65 years
Number of Employees: 130
Sales Information: $10,000,000

8365 Betty Mills Catalog
The Betty Mills Company
2121 S El Camino Real
Suite C-120
San Mateo, CA 94403-1848   650-344-8228
800-238-8964
Fax: 650-341-1888
www.bettymills.com

Cleaning & janitorial products including brooms, brushes, floor & carpet care, cleaning chemicals, mops, buckets, recycling containers, vacuums and waste receptacles

President: Ofer Sabadosh
Managing Director: Steven Cinelli
Credit Cards: AMEX; MasterCard; Visa
Catalog Cost: $1.5
Catalog Circulation: to 100K
Average Order Size: $200
Printing Information: 250 pages on Glossy Stock
Press: Letterpress
Binding: Perfect Bound
Mailing List Information: Names for rent
In Business: 10 years
Number of Employees: 16
Sales Information: $1.4 Million

8366 Carolina Brush Company
Carolina Brush Company
3093 Northwest Boulevard
PO Box 2469
Gastonia, NC 28052-2469   704-867-0286
800-822-1160
Fax: 704-861-0772
www.carolinabrush.com/index.php

Brushes and brooms

President: Barbara D Glenn
In Business: 96 years
Number of Employees: 65
Sales Information: $5MM to $10MM

8367 Coffin World Water Systems
Compass Water Solutions
15542 Mosher Ave
Tustin, CA 92780   949-222-5777
Fax: 949-222-5770
info@compasswater.com
www.Cworldwater.Com

Oil water separators, industrial waste separators, wastewater recyclers, reverse osmosis systems

President: Dan Grommesch
Marketing Manager: Kirk Brown
VP & General Manager: Robert K. Elders
Mailing List Information: Names for rent
In Business: 42 years

Number of Employees: 30
Sales Information: $1,000,000 - $5,000,000

8368 Cresswood Recycling Systems
Cresswood Shredding Machinery
55 W. Lincoln Hwy.
PO Box 489
Cortland, IL 60112   815-758-7171
800-962-7302
Fax: 815-758-0733
info@cresswood.com
www.cresswood.com

Manufacturers of grinders and shedders for wood and plastic industries

President: Jack Cress
Marketing Manager: J Cress
Mailing List Information: Names for rent
Number of Employees: 40
Sales Information: $3MM to $5MM

8369 DAWG, Inc.
DAWG, Inc.
Dawg Inc
P.O. Box 205
North Branford, CT 06471-205   860-540-0600
800-935-3294
Fax: 800-545-7297
www.dawginc.com

Line of cleaning products, spill kits and cans and cabinets

VP: Derek Yurgaitis
VP, Purchasing: John Galiatsato
Credit Cards: AMEX; MasterCard
Catalog Cost: Free
Printing Information: in 4 colors
In Business: 25 years
Sales Information: $500,000

8370 Decton Iron Works
Decton Iron Works Inc.
12850 W Silver Spring Drive
PO Box 314
Butler, WI 53007   262-781-5533
800-246-1478
Fax: 262-781-5593
dectoniron@sbcglobal.net
www.decton.com

Wood heating and incineration systems

President: Jeff Gullickson
In Business: 32 years
Number of Employees: 4
Sales Information: $500,000 - $1,000,000

8371 Elgee Power-Vac Sweeper
Elgee Mfg Company Inc
225 Stirling Road
Warren, NJ 07059-5238   908-647-4100
800-742-0400
Fax: 908-647-4242
sales@elgee.com
www.Elgee.Com

Power vacuums and sweepers

President: Steven Heinle
Marketing Manager: Debra Isselin
Production Manager: Wally Dury
Legal Secretary: Kelly Shannon
Credit Cards: MasterCard
Catalog Cost: Free
Average Order Size: $1700
Printing Information: 4 pages in 4 colors on Glossy Stock
Press: Web Press
Binding: Folded
Mailing List Information: Names for rent
List Manager: Debbie Isselin
In Business: 56 years
Number of Employees: 7
Sales Information: $500,000

8372 Harper Brush Industrial Catalog
Harper Brush Works, Inc.
400 N 2nd St
Fairfield, IA 52556-2416   641-472-5186
                                  800-223-7894
                              Fax: 641-472-3187
                         info@harperbrush.com
                         www.harperbrush.com

Commercial and industrial grade floor brooms and brushes, upright brooms, floor and window squeegees, window brushes, car/truck wash brushes, tire and wheel brushes, counter dusters, scrub brushes,

President: Barry Harper
CFO: Gary Wells
Marketing Manager: Candy Pfeifer
Fulfillment: Scott Reid
Catalog Cost: Free
Mailing List Information: Names for rent
In Business: 89 years
Number of Employees: 100
Sales Information: $5,000,000 - $10,000,000

8373 Hesco
Hesco
6633 N Milwaukee Ave
Niles, IL 60714-4483   847-647-6700
                              800-822-7467
                          Fax: 847-647-0534
                     sales@hescoinc.com
                     www.Hescoinc.Com

Cleaning and janitorial supplies for schools, municipalities, carpet care professionals and car wash facilities

President: Rory Gurson
CFO: Nancy Verdone
CEO: Gap Kovech
Credit Cards: AMEX; MasterCard; Visa
Catalog Cost: Free
In Business: 86 years
Number of Employees: 80
Sales Information: $ 14 Million

8374 Kamflex Corporation
KamFlex Corporation
1321 West 119th Street
Chicago, IL 60643-1835   630-682-1555
                                800-323-2440
                            Fax: 630-682-9312
                       kamflex@kamflex.com
                       www.kamflex.com

Stainless steel sanitary conveyors

President: Kirit Kamdar
Marketing Manager: John Tomaka
Mailing List Information: Names for rent
In Business: 41 years
Number of Employees: 36
Sales Information: $1,000,000 - $5,000,000

8375 LC Thomsen
Thomsen Group, LLC.
1303 43rd St.
Kenosha, WI 53140-219   262-652-3662
                               800-558-4018
                           Fax: 262-652-3526
                       www.Lcthomsen.Com

Sanitary stainless steel flow equipment, including pumps, valves, fittings, filters, specials, etc

President: Joyce Saftig
CFO: Paul Shemanske
Marketing Manager: Mike Dyutka
Production Manager: Jon Huges
Buyers: Robert Callan
Catalog Cost: Free
Catalog Circulation: Mailed 1 time(s) per year to 500+
Printing Information: 150 pages in 4 colors
Mailing List Information: Names for rent
List Manager: Robert Gapko
In Business: 82 years
Number of Employees: 40
Sales Information: $1,000,000 - $5,000,000

8376 Mars Air Door
Mars Air Systems
14716 South Broadway
Gardena, CA 90248   310-532-1555
                           800-421-1266
                       Fax: 310-324-3030
                   info@marsair.com
                   www.Marsair.Com

Air curtains that keep out insects, fumes and dust, also prevent loss of tempered air

President: Martin Smilo
Catalog Circulation: Mailed 1 time(s) per year to 5000
Printing Information: 4 pages in 2 colors
Press: Web Press
Mailing List Information: Names for rent
In Business: 43 years
Number of Employees: 50
Sales Information: $10MM to $20MM

8377 Micro-Brush Hand Scrub
ProSoap, Inc.
1830 Interstate 30
Rockwall, TX 75087-6201   972-722-1161
                                 800-776-7627
                             Fax: 972-722-1584
                        Clean@ProSoap.com
                        www.prosoap.com

Industrial hand cleaners

President: Scott Self
Credit Cards: MasterCard; Visa
Catalog Cost: Free
Printing Information: in 2 colors on Matte Stock
Press: Letterpress
Mailing List Information: Names for rent
In Business: 13 years
Number of Employees: 11

8378 Modern Chemical
BlueGold Cleaners
PO BOX 368
Jacksonville, AR 72078-368   501-988-1311
                                    800-366-8109
                    www.bluegoldcleaner.com

Industrial cleaners

President: Nancy Burger
In Business: 43 years
Number of Employees: 4
Sales Information: Under $500M

8379 Molded Fiber Glass Tray Company
MFG TRAY
6175 Route 6
Linesville, PA 16424   814-683-4500
                              800-458-6050
                          Fax: 814-683-4504
                      www.mfgtray.com

Maintenance and sanitation equipment

President: Thomas Levenhagen
Marketing Manager: Stephanie Goss
Production Manager: Bill Stanley
General Sales Manager: Mike Carr
Industrial/ESD Product Line Manager: Burt Hovis
Pharmaceutical Product Line Manager: Larry Acker
In Business: 63 years
Number of Employees: 250
Sales Information: $25,000,000 - $50,000,000

8380 Nikro Industries
Nikro Industries, Inc.
1115 N Ellsworth Ave
Villa Park, IL 60181-1040   630-530-0558
                                   800-875-6457
                               Fax: 630-530-0740
                          sales@nikro.com
                          www.Nikro.Com

Critical filtered cleaning systems for the removal of asbestos and hazardous waste

President: Jim Nicholson
In Business: 28 years
Number of Employees: 15
Sales Information: $1,000,000 - $5,000,000

8381 Panaram International Trading Company
USATOWEL
126 Greylock Ave
Belleville, NJ 07109-3324   973-751-1100
                                   800-872-8695
                               Fax: 973-751-2231
                          julie@usatowl.com
                          www.Usatowl.Com

Towels, bed linens, table linens, polishes, waxes, cleaners, washers, dryers

President: Ira Feinberg
Marketing Manager: Juliette H Silver
Fulfillment: Ira Feinberg
International Marketing Manager: H. Nelson
Mailing List Information: Names for rent
In Business: 15+ years
Number of Employees: 8
Sales Information: $500M to $1MM

8382 Petersen Products Company
Petersen
421 Wheeler Avenue
P.O.Box 340
Fredonia, WI 53021-340   262-692-2416
                                800-827-5275
                            Fax: 262-692-2418
                       sales@petersenproducts.com
                       www.petersenproducts.com

Drain and sewer cleaning equipment, inflatable pipe plugs

President: Philip L Lundman
Catalog Circulation: Mailed 1 time(s) per year
Printing Information: 6 pages in 2 colors on Glossy Stock
Mailing List Information: Names for rent
In Business: 99 years
Number of Employees: 10
Sales Information: $1,000,000 - $5,000,000

8383 Pressure Washer and Water Treatment Catalog
Landa
4275 NW Pacific Rim Boulevard
Camas, WA 98607-8801   306-833-9100
                              800-547-8672
                          Fax: 360-833-9200
                     info@landa.com
                     www.landa.com

Pressure cleaning equipment and wastewater treatment

President: Andy Gale
CFO: Bob Mazzacavallo
Marketing Manager: Crismon Lewis
Production Manager: Calvin Bishop
International Marketing Manager: Scott Linton
Buyers: Mike Hoikka
Credit Cards: AMEX; MasterCard
Catalog Cost: Free
Catalog Circulation: Mailed 1 time(s) per year to 33000
Printing Information: 160 pages in 4 colors on Matte Stock
Press: Web Press
Binding: Perfect Bound
Mailing List Information: Names for rent
In Business: 46 years
Number of Employees: 200
Sales Information: $10,000,000 - $25,000,000

8384 Promaco
Promaco Inc
3714 Runge Street
Franklin Park, IL 60131-1112   800-253-2866
                                  Fax: 847-288-9999
                             info@promacoinc.com
                             www.promacoinc.com

Floor treads, cash drop boxes, safety signage, fire alarm pulls, key cabinets; cleaning supplies, bathroom supplies, gloves, janitorial products, brooms, mops, dust pans, waste bins; security cameras

Credit Cards: AMEX; MasterCard

8385 Raven Environmental Products
Raven Environmental Products,Inc
448 East Clinton Place
Suite B
Saint Louis, MO 63122-6400   314-822-1197
800-545-6953
Fax: 314-822-9968
dave@ravenep.com
www.ravenep.com

Manufacturer of waste and water plant control equipment

President: Dave Humann
Marketing Manager: Lynn Marshall
Catalog Cost: Free
Catalog Circulation: Mailed 1 time(s) per year
Printing Information: 4 pages in 2 colors on Matte Stock
Binding: Saddle Stitched
In Business: 32 years
Number of Employees: 3
Sales Information: $500M to $1MM

8386 SA-SO Catalog
SA-SO
525 N Great Southwest Parkway
Arlington, TX 76011-1299   972-641-4911
Fax: 972-660-3684
sales@sa-so.com
www.sa-so.com

Facility, traffic and safety products

Credit Cards: AMEX; MasterCard; Visa
Catalog Cost: Free
Mailing List Information: Names for rent
In Business: 69 years
Number of Employees: 300

8387 Simple Green
Simple Green
15922 Pacific Coast Highway
Huntington Beach, CA 92649-1806562-795-6000
800-228-0709
Fax: 562-592-3830
www.simplegreen.com

Cleaning solvents

President: Bruce P. FaBrizio
Marketing Manager: Pat Sheehan
In Business: 40 years
Number of Employees: 40
Sales Information: $10,000,000 - $25,000,000

8388 Sun-Mar Corporation
Sun-Mar Corp.
600 Main Street
Tonawanda, NY 14150   905-332-1314
800-461-2461
Fax: 905-332-1315
compost@sun-mar.com
www.sun-mar.com

Composting toilet systems

Manager: Dennis Forster
Credit Cards: AMEX; MasterCard; Visa
Catalog Cost: Free
Printing Information: on Glossy Stock
In Business: 44 years
Number of Employees: 30
Sales Information: $8 Million

8389 Syntechnics
Syntechnics
700 Terrace Lane
Paducah, KY 42003-9343   270-898-7303
Fax: 270-898-7306
michael.beott@trin.net
www.syntechnics.net

Barge covers, waste water treatments and safety devices

President: Teddy Holt
Sales: Mike Beott
michael.beott@trin.net
Technical: David E. Choat, P.E.
david.choat@trin.net
Number of Employees: 110
Sales Information: $10MM to $20MM

8390 Tennant
Tennant Company
701 North Lilac Drive
PO Box 1452
Minneapolis, MN 55422   763-540-1200
800-553-8033
Fax: 763-513-2142
info@tennantco.com
www.Tennantco.Com

Industrial sweepers, scrubbers and coatings

Chairman: Roger Hale
President: H Chris Killingstad
CFO: Richard Snyder
Marketing Manager: William Strang
Founder: George H. Tennant
Printing Information: 12 pages in 4 colors
In Business: 144 years
Number of Employees: 3002

8391 The Clean Team
The Clean Team
498 East Purnell Street
Suite 103
Lewisville, TX 75057   972-219-0400
800-717-2532
inquire@thecleanteam.com
www.thecleanteam.com

Speed cleaning supplies, clutter control, home maintenance products, and household cleaning products that are safe and fast

President: Steve Sardone
Marketing Manager: Debbie Sardone
Credit Cards: AMEX; MasterCard; Visa
Catalog Cost: Free
Catalog Circulation: Mailed 4 time(s) per year
Average Order Size: $70
Printing Information: 16 pages in 4 colors on Glossy Stock
Press: Web Press
Binding: Saddle Stitched
Mailing List Information: Names for rent
In Business: 25 years
Number of Employees: 4
Sales Information: $5,00,000

8392 United Facilities
United Facilities
603 North Main Street
PO Box 559
East Peoria, IL 61651-2023   309-699-7271
866-699-7271
Fax: 309-699-0228
www.unifac.com

Steel, fiberglass and aluminum indoor and outdoor waste receptacles, recycling containers, smokers, urns, planters

President: Richard Weiss
CFO: Jim Minchhoff
Marketing Manager: John Knaut
Production Manager: Howard Nielson
Buyers: Ed Sedlock
Margaret Zimmerman
Credit Cards: MasterCard; Visa
Catalog Cost: Free
Catalog Circulation: Mailed 2 time(s) per year to 100M+
Printing Information: 36 pages in 4 colors on Glossy Stock
Press: Web Press
Binding: Saddle Stitched
List Manager: John Knaut, International
List Company: Trisha Walsh, Domestic
In Business: 134 years

Number of Employees: 200
Sales Information: $10MM to $20MM

8393 Universal Air Precipitator Corporation
Universal Air & Gas Products Corp.
1140 Kingwood Ave.
Norfolk, VA 23502-5603   757-461-0077
800-326-8406
Fax: 757-461-0808
info@uapc.com
www.Uapc.Com

Electronic air cleaner

President: Kurt Kondas
In Business: 53 years
Number of Employees: 26
Sales Information: $1,000,000 - $5,000,000

8394 Water Quality Testing Products
LaMotte Company
802 Washington Ave
PO Box 329
Chestertown, MD 21620   410-778-3100
800-344-3100
Fax: 410-778-6394
mkt@lamotte.com
www.lamotte.com

Waste plant treatment products; test kits, instruments and reagents for water analysis

President: David LaMotte
Marketing Manager: James Moore
Production Manager: Libby Woolever
Catalog Circulation: Mailed 1 time(s) per year to 5000
Printing Information: 100 pages in 4 colors on Glossy Stock
Press: Sheetfed Press
Binding: Perfect Bound
Mailing List Information: Names for rent
In Business: 96 years
Number of Employees: 120

8395 Wilden Pump & Engineering Company
PSG Dover
22069 Van Buren Street
Grand Terrace, CA 92313-5607   909-422-1700
Fax: 909-783-3440
wilden@psgdover.com
www.psgdover.com

Air-operated double diaphragm pumps for sewage sludge and mine dewatering, food, pharmeceuticals, semiconductor, parts, inks, dyes, metal finishing, chemicals and powder

President: Bruce Bartells
CFO: Daniel Anderson
Marketing Manager: Gary Bowan
Managing Director: Denny L. Buskirk
Director of Operations: Dwane Lamb
Director of Engineering: Greg Duncan
Catalog Cost: Free
Catalog Circulation: to 5m
Printing Information: in 1 color on Glossy Stock
Press: Web Press
Mailing List Information: Names for rent
In Business: 62 years
Number of Employees: 240
Sales Information: $50,000,000 - $100,000,00

8396 Wilen Brushworx
Continental Commercial Products
305 Rock Industrial Park Drive
Bridgeton, MO 63044   314-656-4301
800-325-1051
Fax: 314-327-5492
CustomerService@Contico.com
www.wilen.com

Cleaning supplies, including dust brooms and mops

Marketing Manager: Jack Hart
Catalog Circulation: Mailed 1 time(s) per year
Printing Information: in 4 colors
Binding: Saddle Stitched

In Business: 39 years
Number of Employees: 250-
Sales Information: $50,000,000 - $100,000,00

8397 World Catalog of Oil Spill Response Products
World Catalog of Oil Spill Response Prod
200-1140 Morrison
Ottawa, ON K2H-8S9 613-232-1564
Fax: 613-232-6660
jake@slross.com
www.oilspillequipment.com

Oil spill response products from distributors and manufacturers worldwide

Catalog Cost: $275
Catalog Circulation: to 1500
Printing Information: 1000 pages
Binding: Perfect Bound
In Business: 37 years

8398 World Dryer Corporation
World Dryer Corporation
5700 McDermott Drive
Berkeley, IL 60163-1102 708-449-6950
800-323-0701
Fax: 708-449-6958
sales@worlddryer.com
www.worlddryer.com

Hand dryers, hair dryers, and baby-changing stations

President: Tom Vic
Marketing Manager: Chris Berl
Catalog Cost: Free
Catalog Circulation: Mailed 2 time(s) per year
Printing Information: 4 pages
Mailing List Information: Names for rent
In Business: 56 years
Number of Employees: 60
Sales Information: $5,000,000 - $10,000,000

Security
Equipment

8399 B&B ARMR
B&B ARMR
2009 Chenault Drive
Suite 114
Carrollton, TX 75006-5920 972-385-7899
800-367-0387
Fax: 972-385-9887
info@bb-armr.com
www.Bb-Armr.Com

barriers, bollards, gate operators, crash beams, and traffic gates for perimeter security

President: Paul Matthews
Marketing Manager: Fred Pierce
Catalog Cost: Free
Printing Information: 100 pages in 4 colors on Glossy Stock
Mailing List Information: Names for rent
In Business: 90 years
Number of Employees: 30

8400 Best Access Systems
Stanley Security Solutions Inc.
6161 East 75th Street
Indianapolis, IN 46250-420 317-849-2250
855-365-2407
Fax: 317-845-7650
www.bestaccess.com/

Security equipment

President: Justin Boswell
CFO: Lee McChesney
VP and COO: Douglas McIntyre
Catalog Circulation: Mailed 1 time(s) per year
Printing Information: 140 pages in 4 colors

8401 Eagle Metal Products
Eagle Metal
802 N 3rd St
PO Box 1267
Mabank, TX 75147 903-887-3581
800-521-3245
Fax: 903-887-0443
www.eaglemetal.com

Fastrac walk-thru system parts

President: Thomas Whatley
Marketing Manager: Jerry Burney
Credit Cards: AMEX; MasterCard
Printing Information: 5 pages
In Business: 32 years

8402 Federal APD
Federal APD
42775 Nine Mile Rd.
Suite 200
Novi, MI 48375-4113 248-374-9600
800-521-9330
Fax: 248-374-9610
www.federalapd.com

Automatic parking control systems, gate opening devices, ticket dispensers, auto gates, security gates and various machinery

President: Joe Wilson
Marketing Manager: Thomas Bradfish, Sales Manager
Director: Matt Zaske
In Business: 60 years
Number of Employees: 300

8403 Federal Signal Corporation
Federal Signal
2645 Federal Signal Drive
University Park
Oak Brook, IL 60484 708-534-3400
Fax: 708-534-4774
lnoel@federalsignal.com
www.federalsignal.com

Explosion proof signals, safety signals, speakers, horns, bells and sirens

Chairman: James E.Goodwin
President: Peter Guile
CFO: Bonnie C. Lind
Marketing Manager: Joe Wilson
Director: Paul W.Jones
Director: Bonnie C.Lind
Director: Dennis J.Martin
Number of Employees: 620

8404 GuardAir Corporation
GuardAir
47 Veterans Drive
Chicopee, MA 01022-1062 413-594-4400
800-482-7324
Fax: 413-594-4884
info@guardaircorp.com
www.guardaircorp.com

Air guns

President: Thomas C Tremblay
In Business: 72 years
Number of Employees: 12
Sales Information: $1,000,000 - $5,000,000

8405 H-B Instrument Company
H-B Instrument Company
102 West Seventh Ave
PO Box 26770
Collegeville, PA 19426-770 610-489-5500
800-424-3292
Fax: 610-489-9100
info@hbinstrument.com
www.Hbinstrument.Com

Security equipment

President: Edward D Hiergesell
Marketing Manager: Deborah Poenisch
Production Manager: Richard Jackson
VP, Finance: Leslie Knorr Gall
VP, Sales: Darlyn Nash
Marketing/Sales: Laura Schlegel

Printing Information: 77 pages
In Business: 100 years
Number of Employees: 25
Sales Information: $1,000,000 - $5,000,000

8406 Identatronics
Identatronics
165 N. Lively Blvd.
Elk Grove Village, IL 60007-1319 847-437-2654
800-323-5403
Fax: 847-437-2660
www.Identatronics.Com

Photo ID cards

President: Mike Grzegorek
In Business: 41 years
Number of Employees: 40
Sales Information: $5,000,000 - $10,000,000

8407 Interlogix Security & Life Safety Group
Interlogix
UTC Building & Industrial Systems
3211 Progress Drive
Lincolnton, NC 28092 855-286-8889
800-547-2556
Fax: 503-691-7566
orders@interlogix.com
www.interlogix.com

Designs, manufactures and distributes components, software, communication technologies and information for security, safety, and lifestyle enhancements

President: Brian McCarthy
CFO: Rick Falconer
Marketing Manager: David Tyler
Production Manager: Ali Saalabian
Buyers: Marc Koczwara
Catalog Cost: Free
Catalog Circulation: to 2000
Printing Information: 150 pages in 2 colors on Matte Stock
Binding: Perfect Bound
Mailing List Information: Names for rent
List Manager: Kim Benson
In Business: 34 years
Number of Employees: 700
Sales Information: $50MM to $100MM

8408 Iris Limited
Iris Companies
901 Park Road
Fleetwwod, PA 19522 610-944-8588
800-453-4747
Fax: 866-432-2343
info@irisltd.com
www.irisltd.com

Polaroid films for ID cards and computer graphics

President: Susan Gehris
Printing Information: 36 pages
In Business: 34 years
Sales Information: $20MM to $50MM

8409 Isolation Technology
Isolation Technology Inc
PO Box 460T
Massapequa, NY 11758-460 631-253-3314
888-703-0403
Fax: 631-253-3316
www.isolationtech.com

Sound vibration equipment and sensors

President: R Grefe
Credit Cards: AMEX; MasterCard
In Business: 25 years

8410 JC Gury Company
JC Gury Company
530 East Jamie Avenue
La Habra, CA 90631-6842 714-738-6650
800-903-3385
Fax: 800-556-5576
info@jcgury.com
www.Jcgury.Com

Signs and decals for the security industry

President: Joe Kinda
In Business: 44 years
Number of Employees: 12
Sales Information: $3MM to $5MM

8411 Massa Products Corporation

Massa Products Corporation
280 Lincoln Street
Hingham, MA 02043-1796   781-749-4800
                                800-962-7543
                           Fax: 781-740-2045
                           sales@massa.com
                           www.Massa.Com

Ultrasonic air transducers, audible alarms and sonar systems

President: Don Massa
Marketing Manager: PA Shirley
Number of Employees: 75
Sales Information: $5,000,000 - $10,000,000

8412 Medeco Security Locks

Medeco
3625 Alleghany Drive
PO Box 3075
Salem, VA 24153-0330   540-380-5000
                                877-633-3261
                           Fax: 800-421-6615
                           support@medeco.com
                           www.medeco.com

Locks and lock cylinders

President: Bernd Wempen
Mailing List Information: Names for rent
Number of Employees: 250
Sales Information: $50,000,000 - $100,000,00

8413 Natchez Shooters Supply

Natchez Shooters Supply
2600 Walker Road
PO Box 182212
Chattanooga, TN 37422   423-889-0499
                                800-251-7839
                           Fax: 423-892-4482
                           orders@natchezss.com
                           www.natchezss.com

Hunting supplies

CFO: David Dodson
Owner: Jeff Hamm
Information Technology Manager: Andy Lee
President, Sales: Brian Hall
Credit Cards: MasterCard
Printing Information: 104 pages
Number of Employees: 1
Sales Information: $62,000

8414 National Bullet Proof

National Bullet Proof, Inc.
9855 S 78th Ave
Hickory Hills, IL 60457-2324   708-430-3200
                                800-323-2648
                           Fax: 708-430-3406
                           NBP@nationalbulletproof.com
                           www.Nationalbulletproof.Com

Bullet resistant security equipment, windows, doors and frames

President: Wally Newman
Marketing Manager: Wally Newman
Number of Employees: 28
Sales Information: $1,000,000 - $5,000,000

8415 Northern Specialty Supplies

Northern Specialty Supplies,Inc
48 Vienna Road
PO Box 248
Tillsonburg, CN N4G 4   519-688-0334
                                877-688-3834
                           Fax: 519-688-0329
                           www.nsscan.com

Security bags, boxes and sealing tape

President: John Mac Gregor
In Business: 29 years

Number of Employees: 12
Sales Information: $1MM to $3MM

8416 Professional Equipment

Grainger
600 N. Lynndale Dr.
Appleton, WI 54914-3021   631-348-3780
                                800-472-4643
                           Fax: 888-776-3187
                           info@professionalequipment.com
                           www.grainger.com

Tools and testing equipment for the electrical, inspection, HVAC and engineering and building professionals

President: Patrick Norton
Credit Cards: AMEX; MasterCard
Catalog Circulation: Mailed 12 time(s) per year to 1m
Printing Information: 90 pages
Press: Web Press
Binding: Perfect Bound
In Business: 27 years

8417 Promaco

Promaco Inc
3714 Runge Street
Franklin Park, IL 60131-1112   800-253-2866
                           Fax: 847-288-9999
                           info@promacoinc.com
                           www.promacoinc.com

Floor treads, cash drop boxes, safety signage, fire alarm pulls, key cabinets; cleaning supplies, bathroom supplies, gloves, janitorial products, brooms, mops, dust pans, waste bins; security cameras

Credit Cards: AMEX; MasterCard

8418 SES

Security Equipment Supply, Inc.
                           sales@sesonline.com
                           www.sesonline.com

Burglar and fire alarms, home automation, CCTV, access controls, protectors and supplies

President: Bob Van Dillen
bvandillen@sesonline.com
Marketing Manager: Jamie Roberston
Operations Manager: George Trussler
gtrussler@sesonline.com
Sales Manager: John Hill
Jhill@sesonline.com
Credit Cards: MasterCard; Visa
Catalog Cost: $15
Catalog Circulation: Mailed 3 time(s) per year to 10000
Printing Information: 50 pages in 2 colors on Glossy Stock
Binding: Saddle Stitched
In Business: 35 years
Number of Employees: 40
Sales Information: $10 million

8419 SafeMart

LiveWatch Security LLC
512 W. Bertrand, Box 215
St. Mary, KS 94107-3515   888-796-0562
                                888-994-6028
                           Fax: 866-540-8158
                           www.livewatch.com

Security equipment

President: Chris Johnson
Marketing Manager: Mark Riddle
Director of Operations: Dave Riley
Director of Ecommerce: Joseph Mioni
Technical Services Manager: Joe Thomas
Printing Information: 8 pages in 3 colors
In Business: 13 years
Number of Employees: 8
Sales Information: $1,000,000 - $5,000,000

8420 Security Cameras Direct

Security Cameras Direct
11000 N Mopac Expressway
Building 300
Austin, TX 78759   830-401-7000
                                877-797-7377
                           Fax: 830-875-9010
                           www.securitycamerasdirect.com

Complete line of security cameras, CCTV, Video Security, and IP Surveillance

President: Aaron James
CFO: Laura Parsons
Production Manager: Norman Ragland
VP Sales: Robert Dugan
Regional Sales Manager: Brian Barnhart
Catalog Cost: Free
Printing Information: in 3 colors
In Business: 15 years
Number of Employees: 35
Sales Information: $6 million

8421 Stranco Products

Stranco Inc.
1306 W US 20
Michigan City, IN 46360   219-874-5221
                                800-348-3217
                           Fax: 219-872-2835
                           sales@strancoinc.com
                           www.strancoinc.com

Pressure sensitive wire markers and industrial marking

President: John Gavin Sr
CFO: Kay Frank
Marketing Manager: Michelle Dee
Production Manager: Tom Barthmaier
Catalog Cost: Free
Catalog Circulation: to 30M
Printing Information: in 4 colors on Glossy Stock
Press: Web Press
Binding: Perfect Bound
Mailing List Information: Names for rent
In Business: 61 years
Number of Employees: 28
Sales Information: $5,000,000 - $10,000,000

8422 Syntechnics

Syntechnics
700 Terrace Lane
Paducah, KY 42003-9343   270-898-7303
                           Fax: 270-898-7306
                           michael.beott@trin.net
                           www.syntechnics.net

Barge covers, waste water treatments and safety devices

President: Teddy Holt
Sales: Mike Beott
michael.beott@trin.net
Technical: David E. Choat, P.E.
david.choat@trin.net
Number of Employees: 110
Sales Information: $10MM to $20MM

8423 Technical Furniture Systems

Winsted Corporation
10901 Hampshire Avenue South
Minneapolis, MN 55438-2351   952-944-9050
                                800-447-2257
                           Fax: 952-944-1546
                           info@winsted.com
                           www.winsted.com

CCTV and video consoles

President: Randy Smith
Marketing Manager: Bob Pep
Production Manager: Kent Lilja
Average Order Size: $800
Printing Information: 55 pages in 4 colors on Glossy Stock
Press: Web Press
Binding: Perfect Bound
Mailing List Information: Names for rent
In Business: 51 years
Number of Employees: 38
Sales Information: $5,000,000 - $10,000,000

8424 Telular Corporation
Telular Corporation
200 South Wacker Drive
Suite 1800
Chicago, IL 60606-1582   678-945-7770
                             800-835-8527
                             Fax: 312-379-8310
                             www.telular.com

Security products and wireless cellular technology

President: Daniel D Giacopelli
CFO: Bill Steckel
VP, Product Development: Christopher Bear
SVP, Manufacturing & Operations: Jerry Deutsch
CEO: Doug Milner
Credit Cards: MasterCard; Visa
In Business: 28 years
Number of Employees: 50
Sales Information: $5,000,000 - $10,000,000

8425 Toshiba CCTV
Toshiba America, Inc.
82 Totowa Rd
Wayne, NJ 07470-3114   973-305-0466
                             Fax: 973-628-1875
                             www.Toshiba.Com

Time-lapse VCRs, color and black and white cameras, monitors, video systems and accessories for the security industry

President: Toshihide Yasui
Marketing Manager: Takahiro Ishii
Catalog Circulation: Mailed 2 time(s) per year to 15000
Printing Information: 6 pages in 2 colors on Matte Stock
Number of Employees: 200
Sales Information: $5MM to $10MM

8426 Visonic
Visonic, Inc.
65 W. Dudley Town Rd.
Bloomfield, CT 06002-1911   860-243-0833
                             800-223-0020
                             Fax: 860-242-8094
                             info.us@visonic.com
                             www.visonic.com

Infrared detectors

President: Marc Freundlich
General Manager: Eli Gorovici
VP, Finance: Ofir Bar Levav
VP, Research & Development: Amir Gefen
In Business: 42 years
Number of Employees: 20
Sales Information: $5MM to $10MM

8427 WL Jenkins Company
The W.L. Jenkins Company
1445 Whipple Ave SW
Canton, OH 44710-1321   330-477-3407
                             Fax: 330-477-8404
                             info@wljenkinsco.com
                             www.Wljenkinsco.Com

Signals, alarms, bells and lights

President: Susan Jenkins
Founder: Wendell L. Jenkins
In Business: 97 years
Number of Employees: 60
Sales Information: $3MM to $5MM

8428 Wilson Safe Company
Wilson Safe Company
3031 Island Avenue
Philadelphia, PA 19142-310   215-492-7100
                             800-345-8053
                             Fax: 215-492-7104
                             info@wilsonsafe.com
                             www.Wilsonsafe.Com

Safes

President: Ray Wilson
In Business: 109 years

Number of Employees: 16
Sales Information: $5MM to $10MM

Systems

8429 Aeroflash Signal
Aeroflash Signal
1715 W Carroll Avenue
Chicago, IL 60612-2503   312-733-3513
                             800-322-2052
                             Fax: 312-733-0192
                             info@aeroflash.com
                             www.aeroflash.com

Strobe lights, kits and strobe warning systems for aircrafts, school buses, and vehicles

President: Cari Murray
CEO: Cari Murray
Plant Manager: Pat Garnica
Director, Quality Control: Lisa Gonzalez
In Business: 62 years
Number of Employees: 30
Sales Information: $5,000,000 - $10,000,000

8430 Alarm Controls Corporation
Alarm Controls Corporation
19 Brandywine Drive
Deer Park, NY 11729-280   631-586-4220
                             800-645-5538
                             Fax: 631-586-6500
                             info@alarmcontrols.com
                             www.alarmcontrols.com

Control panels, emergency door releases, push plates, push bars, under counter door release switches, vandal resistant push plates

President: Howard Berger
CFO: Arlene Berger
General Manager: John Benedetto
In Business: 44 years
Number of Employees: 20
Sales Information: $2 Million

8431 Alarm Monitoring Services
Alarm Monitoring Services, Inc.
4821 Fairfield Street
Metairie, LA 70001   504-456-8701
                             Fax: 504-456-8737
                             www.monitor1.com

Alarm monitoring services

President: Dera Deroche-Jolet
CFO: Dera DeRoche-Jolet
Marketing Manager: Sean Rockhold
Chief Executive Officer: Rick Jolet
VP-Operations: Carrie Badour
Administration: Sean Rockhold
In Business: 35 years
Number of Employees: 25
Sales Information: $1.5 Million

8432 Alarmax Distributors Inc.
Alarmax Distributors Inc.
381 Mansfield Avenue
Suite 205
Pittsburgh, PA 15220   412-921-8330
                             800-425-2760
                             Fax: 412-921-4333
                             www.alarmax.com

Electronic security, video and audio surveillance devices and equipment, police and protection equipment

President: Roger Graf
rgraf@alarmax.com
Sales: Greg Rosenberg
grosenberg@alarmax.com
Sales: Anthony Soricello
asoricello@alarmax.com
Sales: Kurt Christenson
kchristenson@alarmax.com
In Business: 25 years
Number of Employees: 4
Sales Information: $500,000

8433 Amcest
Amcest
1017 Walnut St
Roselle, NJ 07203-2098   800-631-7370
                             Fax: 908-241-7586
                             info@amcest.com
                             www.amcest.com

Emergency alarm monitoring service, wireless security systems

President: Leonard Rosenfeld
CFO: Roz Drucker
Marketing Manager: Fred Rosenfeld
Operations Manager: David Leria
Printing Information: 62 pages
In Business: 40 years
Number of Employees: 94
Sales Information: $6.6 Million

8434 Best Access Systems
Stanley Security Solutions Inc.
6161 East 75th Street
Indianapolis, IN 46250-420   317-849-2250
                             855-365-2407
                             Fax: 317-845-7650
                             www.bestaccess.com/

Security equipment

President: Justin Boswell
CFO: Lee McChesney
VP and COO: Douglas McIntyre
Catalog Circulation: Mailed 1 time(s) per year
Printing Information: 140 pages in 4 colors

8435 Dakota Alert
Dakota Alert, Inc.
32556 E. Main Street
PO Box 130
Elk Point, SD 57025   605-356-2772
                             Fax: 605-356-3662
                             www.dakotaalert.com

Wireless security equipment

President: Andrew Quam

8436 Delphian Corporation
Delphian Corporation
220 Pegasus Avenue
Northvale, NJ 07647-1900   201-767-7300
                             800-288-3647
                             Fax: 201-767-1741
                             www.Delphian.Com

Gas alarms, air monitors, gas detectors and gas sensors

President: Melanie Kershaw
Credit Cards: AMEX; MasterCard
Number of Employees: 20
Sales Information: $1,000,000 - $5,000,000

8437 Detcon
Detcon inc
4055 Technology Forest Blvd.
PO Box 8067
The Woodlands, TX 77381-8067 713-559-9200
                              888-367-4286
                              Fax: 281-292-2860
                              sales@detcon.com
                              www.detcon.com

Industrial gas detection products and systems

President: Dan Alpha
Marketing Manager: Tammy Bird-Scott
Sales Administration Manager: Monica Cano
VP of Sales & Marketing: Kevin McKeigue
kevinmckeigue@ist-group.com
Inside Technical Sales: Nelson Rubinstein
Credit Cards: AMEX; MasterCard
In Business: 32 years
Number of Employees: 50
Sales Information: $10,000,000 - $25,000,000

8438 GE Interlogix
GE Interlogix
2266 Second Street N
North St. Paul, MN 55109-2914   651-777-2690
800-777-5484
Fax: 651-779-4890
www.interlogix.com

Supervised wireless security systems

President: Ken Boyda
Number of Employees: 75

8439 Hirsch Electronics Corporation
Hirsch Identive
1900-B Carnegie Ave.
Santa Ana, CA 92705-5557   949-250-8888
888-809-8880
Fax: 949-250-7372
sales@identiv.com
www.hirsch-identive.com

Keypad based systems

Chairman: Steven Humphreys
President: Lawrence Midland
CFO: Brian Nelson
Director: Gary Kremen
CEO: Jason Hart

8440 K&H Industries
K&H Industries, Incorporated
160 Elmview Avenue
Hamburg, NY 14075-9697   716-312-0088
Fax: 716-312-0028
repairs@khindustries.com
www.Khindustries.Com

Portable fluorescent lighting for work or wide areas including hazardous location lighting for class I application, industrial and commercial cord reels and accessories, spotlights, quad lights

President: Joe Pinker
Marketing Manager: Bob Kickbush
Catalog Cost: Free
Catalog Circulation: Mailed 1 time(s) per year to 2000
Average Order Size: $500
Printing Information: 30 pages in 4 colors on Glossy Stock
Press: Letterpress
Binding: Folded
Mailing List Information: Names for rent
In Business: 55 years
Number of Employees: 40
Sales Information: $10MM to $20MM

8441 Norment Security Group
CompuDyne Corporation
14000 Highway 20
Madison, AL 35756   877-374-7311
www.normentsecurity.com

Security systems

President: Mitch Claborn
CFO: David Watts
Business Development and Services: Shannon Claborn
National Supply: Heather Lang
EVP, Administration & Manufacturing: Joe Hargrove
Catalog Cost: Free
Catalog Circulation: to 150
Printing Information: 40 pages in 3 colors on Glossy Stock
Mailing List Information: Names for rent
List Manager: Gary Hart
In Business: 18 years
Number of Employees: 500
Sales Information: $50MM to $100MM

8442 SECO-LARM USA
SECO-LARM U.S.A., Inc.
16842 Millikan Avenue
Irvine, CA 92606-5012   949-261-2999
800-662-0800
Fax: 949-261-7326
info@seco-larm.com
www.seco-larm.com

Hi-tech RF vehicle and burglar alarm systems with patented features such as electromagnetic shock detector that eliminates false alarms

President: Michael Block
Catalog Circulation: to 20M
Printing Information: 20 pages in 2 colors
Press: Sheetfed Press
Mailing List Information: Names for rent
In Business: 46 years
Sales Information: $10 million

8443 SafeMart
LiveWatch Security LLC
512 W. Bertrand, Box 215
St. Mary, KS 94107-3515   888-796-0562
888-994-6028
Fax: 866-540-8158
www.livewatch.com

Security equipment

President: Chris Johnson
Marketing Manager: Mark Riddle
Director of Operations: Dave Riley
Director of Ecommerce: Joseph Mioni
Technical Services Manager: Joe Thomas
Printing Information: 8 pages in 3 colors
In Business: 13 years
Number of Employees: 8
Sales Information: $1,000,000 - $5,000,000

8444 Sentrol Products
GE Security, Inc.
8985 Town Center Parkway
Bradentown, FL 34202-5129   914-739-4200
888-437-3287

Complete security systems

President: Dean S Seavers
CFO: Danie Gromko
Marketing Manager: Darren Nicholson
Production Manager: Ali Saalabian
President, EMEA: Bart A M Otten
President, Asia: Mohamed D Butt
President, Americas: Mark Barry
Printing Information: 160 pages
In Business: 30 years
Number of Employees: 500
Sales Information: $10MM to $20MM

8445 Sentronic International
Sentronic International
PO Box 815
Brunswick, OH 44212-815   440-225-3029
Fax: 330-225-3009
www.generalnucleonics-inc.com

Theft and pilferage control systems

President: Dr.D. W. Jones
c.peters@generalnucleonics-inc.com
l.barker@generalnucleonics-inc.com
r.charlton@generalnucleonics-inc.com
Number of Employees: 20-O
Sales Information: $1,000,000 - $5,000,000

8446 Siltron Emergency Systems
Siltron Emergency Systems
290 E Prairie Street
PO Box 518
Crystal Lake, IL 60014   815-459-7142
800-874-3392
Fax: 815-459-6126
info@siltron.com
www.siltron.com

Emergency and portable lighting, exit signs, inverters

President: Nick Shah
CFO: Steve Loria
Production Manager: Patricia A.Huber
International Marketing Manager: Patricia Huber
Credit Cards: MasterCard; Visa
Catalog Cost: Free
Printing Information: 70 pages
Mailing List Information: Names for rent
In Business: 48 years
Number of Employees: 65
Sales Information: Under $500M

Telecommunications
Supplies & Equipment

8447 Atkinson Dynamics
Atkinson Dynamics
2645 Federal Signal Drive
University Park, IL 60484-3167   708-534-3400
888-751-1500
Fax: 708-534-4852
atkinson-support@atkinsondynamics.com
www.atkinsondynamics.com

Heavy duty industrial intercoms, wall mount, panel mount, desk top intercoms

President: Bill Osborn
Marketing Manager: Bob Patnaude
bpatnaude@federalsignal.com
Production Manager: Traci Barron
tbarron@federalsignal.com
Catalog Cost: Free
Catalog Circulation: Mailed 1 time(s) per year
Printing Information: 2 pages in 4 colors
In Business: 57 years
Number of Employees: 25
Sales Information: $1,000,000 - $5,000,000

8448 Atlanta Cable Sales
ACS Solutions Inc.
495 Horizon Dr NE
Suite 200
Suwanee, GA 30024-7745   678-775-0208
800-241-9881
Fax: 678-775-0209
acs@acssolutions.com
acssolutions.com

Telecommunications and audio/video cables

Production Manager: Mark Keating
CEO: Bryan Glutting
Vice President: Dave Fox
Credit Cards: MasterCard; Visa
Catalog Cost: Free
In Business: 34 years
Sales Information: $ 5-10 Million

8449 Brooktrout Technology
Dialogic
15 Crawford Street
Needham, MA 02494-2815   781-449-4100
800-755-4444
Fax: 781-449-9009
insidesales@dialogic.com
www.dialogic.com

Electronic messaging systems, components, voice and fax

Chairman: Patrick S Jones
President: Bill Frank
CFO: Bob Dennerlein
Marketing Manager: Stephen Ide
EVP Corp Affairs & General Counsel: Anthony Housefather
SVP, Product Development & Operatio: Kevin Gould
VP, Human Resources: Guy F. Pedlini
Credit Cards: AMEX; MasterCard; Visa
Printing Information: 2 pages in 4 colors
In Business: 8 years
Number of Employees: 300
Sales Information: $500M to $1MM

8450 Electronic Tele-Communications
ETC
1915 MacArthur Road
Waukesha, WI 53188-5702   262-542-5600
                                 888-746-4382
                            Fax: 262-542-1524
                            www.Etcia.Com

Telephone systems and voice mail

President: Dean W Danner
CEO: Dean W. Danner
Treasurer: Bonita M. Danner
Director of Human Resources: Elizabeth
Danner
Catalog Circulation: Mailed 1 time(s) per year
Printing Information: 12 pages
Binding: Saddle Stitched
Number of Employees: 50-1

8451 Executive Systems
Executive Systems Inc
2113 Spencer Road
Richmond, VA 23230-2657   804-288-0041
                                 877-288-0041
                            Fax: 804-288-4731
                  www.Executivesystemsinc.Com

Telephone support systems

President: Nita Putnam
Vice President: Tom Steinmetz
Credit Cards: AMEX; MasterCard; Visa
Catalog Circulation: to 500
Printing Information: 100 pages in 2 colors on
Glossy Stock
Press: Letterpress
In Business: 45 years
Number of Employees: 18
Sales Information: $1MM to $3MM

8452 HB Distributors
HB Distributors
21612 Marilla St.
Chatsworth, CA 91311-4123   818-882-0000
                                 800-266-3478
                            Fax: 818-700-1808
                      info@hbdistributors.Com
                      www.Hbdistributors.Com

Telecommunication equipment

President: Pam Branner
CFO: Pam Branner
Marketing Manager: Sharon McAdams
Production Manager: Pam Branner
Credit Cards: AMEX; MasterCard; Visa
Catalog Circulation: Mailed 3 time(s) per year
to 10M
Printing Information: 69 pages in 2 colors on
Matte Stock
Press: Letterpress
Mailing List Information: Names for rent
In Business: 39 years
Number of Employees: 13
Sales Information: $1,000,000 - $5,000,000

8453 Jameson
Jameson
1451 Old North Main Street
PO Box 1030
Clover, SC 29710-4030   803-222-6400
                                 800-346-1956
                            Fax: 803-222-8470
                  salescero@jamesonllc.com
                        www.jamesonllc.com

**Products for the telecommunications, CATV,
power utility, tree care and military markets**

Printing Information: 24 pages
In Business: 59 years

8454 Lourdes Industries
Lourdes Industries Inc.
65 Hoffman Ave
Hauppauge, NY 11788-4798   631-234-6600
                            Fax: 631-234-7595
                        www.Lourdesinc.Com

Telecommunications systems

President: William Jakobsen
In Business: 60 years
Number of Employees: 100
Sales Information: $10,000,000 - $25,000,000

8455 Modular Devices
Modular Devices
35-D Wilson Drive
Sparta, NJ 07871-706   973-579-7220
                                 800-292-2201
                            Fax: 973-579-1820
                  modulardevices@optonline.net
                      www.modulardevices.biz/

Telephone, security and computer accessories

President: David Abo
Production Manager: Lonnie Horvath
Catalog Circulation: to 3M
Printing Information: 10 pages in 2 colors on
Glossy Stock
Press: Letterpress
Binding: Perfect Bound
In Business: 8 years
Number of Employees: 6

8456 National Communications
National Communications
69 Washington Street
West Orange, NJ 07052-5538   973-325-3151
                                 800-879-6240
                            Fax: 973-325-2690
                        ncisales@trynci.com
                            www.Trynci.Net

Cable and telecommunications equipment

President: Andrew Brooke
Marketing Manager: Darral Black
Fulfillment: Sheila Watson
Credit Cards: AMEX; MasterCard; Visa
Catalog Circulation: to 25M+
Printing Information: 130 pages in 4 colors on
Glossy Stock
Press: Web Press
Number of Employees: 14
Sales Information: $1,000,000 - $5,000,000

8457 Pro Video
Pro Video and Flim,Inc
2302 West Badger Road
Madison, WI 53713-4010   608-271-1226
                            Fax: 608-271-1226
                            www.provideo.com

**Video, audio, telecommunications, CCTV,
satellites and consumer electronics**

President: Jim Stiener
Marketing Manager: Jon Robbins
Production Manager: EB Hollin
Executive Producer: Jonas Dolkart
Buyers: Joseph Peca, Telecommunications
Jay Arnold, Pro Video
Gary Kaysew, Pro Video
Credit Cards: AMEX; MasterCard
Catalog Cost: Free
Catalog Circulation: Mailed 1 time(s) per year
to 50M
Printing Information: 200 pages in 4 colors on
Glossy Stock
Press: Web Press
Binding: Perfect Bound
Mailing List Information: Names for rent
In Business: 35 years
Number of Employees: 18
Sales Information: $3MM to $5MM

8458 Time Motion Tools
Time and Motion
PO Box 547
Mittagong, CA 92064-6810   024-861-7265
                                 800-779-8170
                            Fax: 028-246-6624
                  info@timemotion.com.au
                      www.Timemotion.Com

**Quality tools and voice data telecom test
equipment**

President: Edward Durfey
Buyers: Shelda Auditett
Credit Cards: AMEX; MasterCard; Visa
Catalog Cost: Free
Catalog Circulation: Mailed 6 time(s) per year
to 800K
Average Order Size: $275
Printing Information: 200 pages in 4 colors on
Glossy Stock
Press: Web Press
Binding: Perfect Bound
Mailing List Information: Names for rent
List Manager: Ofelia Pereira
In Business: 40 years
Number of Employees: 50
Sales Information: $20MM to $50MM

8459 Toner Cable Equipment
Toner Cable Equipment, Inc.
969 Horsham Road
Horsham, PA 19044-1378   215-675-2053
                                 800-523-5947
                            Fax: 215-675-7543
                        info@tonercable.com
                        www.tonercable.com

Cable TV equipment

President: BJ Toner
CFO: Bob Toner
bob@tonercable.com
Sales Manager: Steve Deasey
steve@tonercable.com
Government Sales, Broadcast Sales: Bob
Jenkins
bjenkins@tonercable.com
Director, Engineering: Ted Tozzi
ted@tonercable.com
Catalog Circulation: Mailed 1 time(s) per year
Printing Information: in 2 colors
In Business: 44 years
Sales Information: $10MM to $20MM

8460 UNESCO
UNESCO
7 place Fontenoy
Paris, 07 75352-2502   330-145-681
                                 800-776-1662
                            Fax: 305-825-3212
                            www.unesco.org

Office machines, phone systems and communications

Chairman: Mohamed Sameh Amr
President: Caryl M. Stern
CFO: Edward G. Lloyd
Senior VP, Strategic Partnerships: Rajesh
Anandan
Deputy Chief: Brian Meyers
Managing Director: Roberta Wallis
Buyers: Roxy Rodriguez
Credit Cards: MasterCard; Visa Discover Optima
Catalog Cost: Free
Catalog Circulation: Mailed 18 time(s) per
year to 5MM
Printing Information: 25 pages in 2 colors on
Matte Stock
Press: Letterpress
Mailing List Information: Names for rent
In Business: 70 years
Number of Employees: 10
Sales Information: $1MM to $3MM

Tools & Machinery
General

8461 3M Accessories for Abrasive Products
Contract Production Services/CPS
1936 Lyndale Avenue South
Minneapolis, MN 55403   612-767-2978
                                 800-843-0619
                            Fax: 612-872-0189
                      sales@contactcps.com

Disc accessories, wheel, belt and hand-sanding accessories, dispensers, spindles and mandrels. Finesse-It system accessories, packs and kits, Scotch-Brite Radial Bristle product accessories.

Catalog Cost: Free
Catalog Circulation: Mailed 1 time(s) per year
Printing Information: 56 pages in 4 colors on Glossy Stock
In Business: 55 years

8462 A&H Abrasives

A&H Abrasives
1108 N Glenn Rd
Casper, WY 82601-1635   307-237-5354
                           800-831-6066
                     Fax: 307-237-4122
                  sales@woodworker.com

Abrasive tools, clothing, chemicals, hand tools and hardware.

President: John Wirth, Jr.
john@woodworker.com
General Manager: Steve Ford
stevef@woodworker.com
Customer Service Manager: Lisa Holthus
presales@woodworker.com
Website Manager: Robert Tyrrell
rtyrrell@woodworker.com
Credit Cards: AMEX; MasterCard; Visa
Catalog Cost: Free
Catalog Circulation: Mailed 4 time(s) per year
Printing Information: 16 pages in 4 colors on Glossy Stock
Press: Web Press
Binding: Saddle Stitched
In Business: 29 years
Number of Employees: 10
Sales Information: $10MM

8463 ATSCO Alamo Transformer Supply Company

Alamo Transformer Supply Company (ATSCO)
4931 Space Center Dr
PO Box 39908
San Antonio, TX 78218-5394   210-661-8411
                           800-782-1313
                    Fax: 210-661-9268
               dsteward@alamotransformer.com
                www.alamotransformer.com

Manufacturing and repair of power transformers

President: Tom Zimmerman
Vice President: Eric Peter
Management Information Systems Mgr.: David Steward
dsteward@alamotransformer.com
Sales/Technical Support: Tom Zimmerman
tzimmerman@alamotransformer.com
In Business: 52 years
Number of Employees: 35

8464 Abbeon Cal Plastic Working Tools

Abbeon Cal, Inc.
123 Gray Ave
Santa Barbara, CA 93101-1809   805-966-0810
                              800-922-0977
                       Fax: 805-966-7659
                  abbeoncal@abbeon.com
                    www.abbeon.com

Scientific instruments and industrial equipment, tools and equipment, plastic working tools for cutting bending and welding

President: Alice Wertheim
Marketing Manager: Bob Brunsman
VP: Kathering Wertheim
Founder: Jared Abbeon
Credit Cards: AMEX; MasterCard; Visa
Catalog Circulation: to 250M
Average Order Size: $500
Printing Information: 128 pages in 4 colors on Newsprint
Press: Web Press
Binding: Folded
In Business: 41 years

Number of Employees: 8
Sales Information: $1.89 Million

8465 Accu Trak Tool

Accu Trak Tool Corporation
490 Stafford St
Cherry Valley, MA 01611-3307   508-892-1787
                              800-433-4933
                       Fax: 508-892-1789
                  eng@accu-trak.com
                    www.accu-trak.com

Knurling tools, dies and holders for turning machines

President: Roland Mason
Marketing Manager: Ron Klaucke
Production Manager: Jon Mason
Buyers: Jon Mason
Credit Cards: AMEX; MasterCard; Visa
Catalog Circulation: Mailed 1 time(s) per year
Printing Information: 28 pages on Matte Stock
Binding: Folded
In Business: 29 years
Number of Employees: 17
Sales Information: $3,000,000

8466 Accurate Industries Commercial Products

Accurate Industries
441 Carpenter Avenue
Wheeling, IL 60090   847-465-8990
                              800-977-8326
                       Fax: 847-465-8993
            customerservice@accurateindustries.com
                www.accurateindustries.com

Products for building commercial and residential saunas and steam rooms

President: Dave Sadowski
CFO: Lynda Ziemba
Marketing Manager: Dave Wigstone
Credit Cards: AMEX; MasterCard
Catalog Cost: Free
In Business: 46 years
Number of Employees: 13
Sales Information: $2.3 Million

8467 Acme Manufacturing

Acme Manufacturing
4240 N Atlantic Blvd
Auburn Hills, MI 48326-1578   248-393-7300
                              800-383-6993
                       Fax: 248-393-4060
                    www.Acmemfg.Com

Robotic and centerless belt grinding plus deburring systems

Chairman: Glen A Carlson Jr
President: G.A. Carlson III
Marketing Manager: Joe Saad
Production Manager: Dave Meredith
Credit Cards: AMEX; MasterCard; Visa
Mailing List Information: Names for rent
In Business: 105 years
Number of Employees: 60
Sales Information: $9,000,000

8468 Adjustable Clamp

Pony Tools Incorporated
404 N Armour St
Chicago, IL 60642-6397   312-666-0640
                       Fax: 312-666-2723
                jorgensenponyclamp.com

Woodworking clamps, tape measures & pliers

President: Joe Krueger
Catalog Cost: Free
Printing Information: in 4 colors
In Business: 112 years
Number of Employees: 400
Sales Information: $50,000,000 - $100,000,00

8469 Aerial Lift

Altec NUECO
571 Plains Rd
Milford, CT 06461-1796   203-878-0694
                              866-617-1569
                       Fax: 203-878-2661
              steve.weikart@nueco.com
        www.nueco.com/articles/aerial-lift-of-connecti-
                           cut

Aerial lifts, truck mounts and other types of machinery

President: Cheryl Depiero
CFO: David Walker
Credit Cards: AMEX; MasterCard; Visa
In Business: 41 years
Number of Employees: 48
Sales Information: $10,000,000

8470 Air Tools, Hand Tools, Sheet Metal Tools

US Industrial Tool & Supply Company
14083 S Normandie Avenue
Gardena, CA 90249   310-464-8400
                              800-521-7394
                       Fax: 310-464-8880
                  info@ustool.com
                    www.ustool.com

Construction and hardware tools

General Manager: Ked Armstrong
Senior Accountant: Mike Hill
CEO: Tom Brotz
Credit Cards: MasterCard
Catalog Cost: Free
Printing Information: 151 pages in 2 colors
Binding: Perfect Bound
In Business: 59 years
Number of Employees: 47
Sales Information: $10MM to $20MM

8471 Airmo Hydraulics

Airmo, Inc.
9445 Evergreen Boulevard NW
Minneapolis, MN 55433-5840   763-786-0000
                              800-394-0016
                       Fax: 763-786-4622
                  airmo@airmo.com
                    www.airmo.com

Tooling and systems for tube testing, forming and expansion systems used in Aerospace system testing, boiler retubing/sleeving and heat exchangers

President: Charles Smida
chucks@airmo.com
CFO: JJulie Campbell
juliec@airmo.com
Marketing Manager: Susanne M. Nelson
susannen@airmo.com
Chief Executive Officer/Owner: Judith Smida
judys@airmo.com
COO: Harry Moran
harrym@airmo.com
Inside Sales: Jim Benson
jimb@airmo.com
Mailing List Information: Names for rent
In Business: 68 years
Number of Employees: 12
Sales Information: $2 Million

8472 Albion Engineering

Albion Engineering
1250 N Church St
Moorestown, NJ 08057-1102   856-235-6688
                              800-841-7132
                       Fax: 856-235-9460
                  service@albioneng.com
                    www.Albioneng.Com

Small hand tools

President: Mark C. Schneider
Director: Frederick Van Cott
Director: Josh McCaully
Catalog Cost: Free
In Business: 86 years
Number of Employees: 40
Sales Information: $5,000,000 - $10,000,000

8473 Albion Industries Full Line Catalog
Albion Industries
800 N Clark St
Albion, MI 49224-1455   517-629-9441
                            800-835-8911
                       Fax: 517-629-9501
          customerservice@albioninc.com
                   www.albioncasters.com/

Casters, wheels and ergonomic floor locks

President: William Winslow
Marketing Manager: Barry Miller
VP: Mike Thorne
Manager: Ronald Hasse
Sales Executive: John Brumbaugh
Catalog Cost: Free
Catalog Circulation: Mailed 1 time(s) per year
Printing Information: 104 pages in 4 colors
In Business: 68 years
Number of Employees: 120
Sales Information: $10MM to $20MM

8474 Allied Engineering & Production Corporation
Allied Engineering & Production Corporat
2421 Blanding Avenue
Alameda, CA 94501-1503   510-522-1500
                       Fax: 510-522-2868

Large machining equipment

Chairman: Sylvia Salvador
President: Sharon Miller
Marketing Manager: Mike Kahn
General Manager: Dave Belcher
In Business: 63 years
Number of Employees: 36
Sales Information: $5.3 Million

8475 American Casting & Manufacturing Corporation
American Casting & Manufacturing, Corpor
51 Commercial Street
Plainview, NY 11803-2401   516-349-7010
                            800-342-0333
                       Fax: 516-349-8389
             info@americancasting.com
                   www.americancasting.com

Padlock seals, metal strap seals and etc

President: Normen Wenk
CFO: Chris Wenk
Marketing Manager: James Wenk
Production Manager: Joseph Wenk
In Business: 105 years

8476 American Machine & Hydraulics
American Machine & Hydraulics
1270 Avenida Acaso
Unit J
Camarillo, CA 93012-8748   805-388-2082
                       Fax: 805-388-3036
                   sammyg@a-m-h.com
                       www.A-M-H.Com

Hydraulic benders, swaggers, presses, tube pipe extenders and custom made equipment

President: Sam Grimaldo
Catalog Circulation: to 500K
Printing Information: 4 pages in 4 colors
Press: Web Press
Binding: Perfect Bound
Sales Information: $1,000,000

8477 American Safety Razor Company
Personna American Safety Razor Company
240 Cedar Knolls Rd # 401
Cedar Knolls, NJ 07927-1691   973-753-3000
                              888-254-2126
                       Fax: 973-326-9004
           PBGInquiries@Energizer.com
                       www.personna.com

Industrial blades

President: Mario Soussou
CFO: Andy Bolt
Marketing Manager: Cris Anderson
Production Manager: Don Beaver

In Business: 140 years
Number of Employees: 2516
Sales Information: $5,800,000

8478 American Saw & Manufacturing
Lenox
301 Chestnut St
East Longmeadow, MA 01028-2824   413-525-3961
                                 800-628-3030
                       Fax: 800-223-7906
                 custserv@lenoxsaw.com
                       www.lenoxtools.com

Lenox saw blades and hand tools

President: Dave Pirkle
Marketing Manager: Tim Barry
Catalog Cost: Free
Catalog Circulation: Mailed 1 time(s) per year
Printing Information: 40 pages in 2 colors
In Business: 100 years
Number of Employees: 900
Sales Information: $50,000,000 - $100,000,00

8479 BVS Samplers
BVS Inc
949 Poplar Road
PO Box 250
Honey Brook, PA 19344-250   610-273-2841
                             877-877-4821
                       Fax: 610-273-2843
                 info@bvssamplers.com
                       www.bvssamplers.com

Manufacturer of automatic samplers for water pollution surveillance and control

President: Robert M Blechman
Marketing Manager: U.S. Aparre
Production Manager: H.L. Lochmanner
Catalog Circulation: to 15000
Printing Information: 8 pages in 1 color on Glossy Stock
Press: Web Press
Binding: Saddle Stitched
Mailing List Information: Names for rent
In Business: 40 years
Number of Employees: 3
Sales Information: $1,000,000

8480 Bailey's Master Catalog
Bailey's
1210 Commerce Ave.
Suite 8
Woodland, CA 95776   707-984-6133
                             800-322-4539
                       Fax: 530-406-0895
                 baileys@baileysonline.com

Books, DVDs, chainsaws, grinders, outdoor power equipment and tree care supplies

President: Judith Baileys
CFO: Janet Peper
Marketing Manager: John Conroy
Credit Cards: AMEX; MasterCard
Printing Information: 266 pages
In Business: 40 years
Number of Employees: 50
Sales Information: $19,000,000

8481 Baker Hughes Mining Tools
Baker Hughes Incorporated
17021 Aldine Westfield
Houston, TX 77073   800-299-7447
                       www.bakerhughes.com

Mining equipment

Chairman: Martin Craighead
President: Maria Claudia Borras
CFO: Peter Ragauss
Marketing Manager: Alasdair Shiach
Catalog Cost: Free
Printing Information: on Glossy Stock
Binding: Saddle Stitched
Mailing List Information: Names for rent
In Business: 30 years
Number of Employees: 250-
Sales Information: $25,000,000 - $50,000,000

8482 Ballymore
Ballymore
501 Gunnard Carlson Drive
Coatesville, PA 19320   610-593-5062
                             800-762-8327
                       Fax: 610-593-8615
                       www.ballymore.com

Steel, aluminum and stainless steel safety ladders; work platforms, and lifts

President: William Frame
Marketing Manager: Thomas Richardson
Production Manager: Ron Bernard
Catalog Cost: Free
Catalog Circulation: Mailed 4 time(s) per year to 30000
Printing Information: 24 pages
Mailing List Information: Names for rent
In Business: 63 years
Number of Employees: 48
Sales Information: $5MM to $10MM

8483 Barnes Engineering Company
Barnes Engineering Company
2074 Aerotech Dr.
Colorado Springs, CO 80916   719-390-6500
                       Fax: 719-390-6700
                 sales@slim-track.com
                       www.slim-track.com

Roller bearing, solid bearing, ball, and all steel slides for military and industrial uses

President: George Barnes
Credit Cards: MasterCard
Printing Information: 16 pages in 2 colors
In Business: 52 years
Sales Information: $1MM to $3MM

8484 Bilt-Rite Conveyors
Bilt-Rite Conveyors
735 Industrial Loop Road
New London, WI 7026-3538   920-982-6600
                       Fax: 920-982-7750
                       www.bilt-rite.com

Conveyors

President: Jeffrey Billig
Catalog Cost: Free
Catalog Circulation: Mailed 1 time(s) per year
Printing Information: 34 pages
Mailing List Information: Names for rent
In Business: 40 years
Sales Information: $3MM to $5MM

8485 Blackstone Industries
Blackstone Industries
16 Stony Hill Road
Bethel, CT 06801-1031   203-792-8622
                             800-272-2885
                       Fax: 203-796-7861
                       www.Foredom.Com

Unique saber saws

President: Willard Nelson
Marketing Manager: Eileen Olsen
Credit Cards: MasterCard; Visa
Catalog Cost: Free
Catalog Circulation: Mailed 1 time(s) per year to 20M
Printing Information: 4 pages in 4 colors
In Business: 93 years
Number of Employees: 50
Sales Information: $15,000,000

8486 Blue Ridge Machinery and Tools
Blue Ridge Machinery and Tools
PO Box 536
Hurricane, WV 25526-536   304-562-3538
                             800-872-6500
                       Fax: 304-562-5311
             blueridgemachine@att.net
                   www.blueridgemachinery.com

Lathes, milling machines, machine shop supplies, how to books and videos, cutting tools, measuring tools, abrasives, bandsaws

President: Paul Stonestreet
paul@blueridgemachinery.com
Marketing Manager: Linda Stonestreet
Production Manager: Linda Stonestreet
Director Advertising and Marketing: Linda Stonestreet
linda@blueridgemachinery.com
Purchasing Contact: Gene Griffith
gene@blueridgemachinery.com
Inside Sales Contact: TimAlford
tim@blueridgemachinery.com
Credit Cards: AMEX; MasterCard; Visa; Discover
Catalog Cost: Free
Catalog Circulation: Mailed 12 time(s) per year to 1200
Average Order Size: $100
Printing Information: 80 pages in 1 color on Glossy Stock
Press: Web Press
Binding: Saddle Stitched
Mailing List Information: Names for rent
In Business: 33 years
Number of Employees: 20-D
Sales Information: $500,000

8487 Burton Press Company

Burton Press Company
2156 Avon Industrial Drive
Rochester Hills, MI 48309-3610   248-853-0212
800-394-0213
Fax: 248-853-2102
www.Burtonpress.Com

Pneumatic presses

President: Edward Lapierre
Catalog Circulation: to 110
Printing Information: 4 pages in 4 colors
Press: Offset Press
Binding: Saddle Stitched
Sales Information: $1,000,000

8488 C&C Tool Supply Company

C&C Tool Supply Company
833 Craghead Street
Danville, VA 24541-3347   434-799-9606
800-446-9113
Fax: 434-799-0893
sales@cctool.com
www.Cctool.Com

Complete line of manufacturing tools

President: Steve Clark
Credit Cards: AMEX; MasterCard
Printing Information: 16 pages
In Business: 38 years
Sales Information: $3MM to $5MM

8489 CARL Manufacturing

CARL
1135 Tower Road
Schaumburg, IL 60173   847-884-2842
800-257-4771
Fax: 847-519-0533
carl@carlmfg.com
www.carlmfg.com

Precision cutting and paper punching systems

President: Richard Schultz
Credit Cards: MasterCard; Visa
Catalog Cost: Free
Catalog Circulation: Mailed 2 time(s) per year to 300M
Printing Information: 48 pages in 4 colors
Binding: Saddle Stitched
Mailing List Information: Names for rent
Will Trade Names: Yes
In Business: 86 years
Number of Employees: 5

8490 CWS Parts Company

CWS Company
2608 Smithtown Road
Morgantown, WV 26508-2494   304-296-1736
800-327-6203
Fax: 304-291-5602
www.Swansonindustries.Com

Manufactures hydraulic cylinders and distributes hydraulic gear pumps, ball valves, motors, blowers, and directional control valves

President: Jeff Conaway
In Business: 52 years

8491 Cable Design Guide

Carl Stahl Sava Industries Inc.
4 North Corporate Drive
P.O. Box 30
Riverdale, NJ 07457   973-835-0882
Fax: 973-835-0877
info@savacable.com
www.savacable.com

Manufacturing cable solutions in cable, cable assemblies, idler pulleys, and push and pull control assemblies

President: Marc E. Alterman
Production Manager: Ron Paras
Chief Executive Officer: Zdenek A Fremund
VP of Operations: Jack Maas
VP of Sales & Marketing: Bruce R. Staubitz
Catalog Cost: Free
Catalog Circulation: Mailed 1 time(s) per year to 7000
Printing Information: 36 pages in 2 colors on Glossy Stock
Binding: Folded
Mailing List Information: Names for rent
In Business: 42 years
Number of Employees: 85
Sales Information: $ 20 Million

8492 Cambridge Metal Belts

Rexnord
105 Godwill Road
Cambridge, MD 21613   410-901-4979
800-638-9560
info@cambridge-intl.com
www.cambridge-intl.com

Metal belts

President: Duane Marshall
CFO: Duane Marshall/Len Janssen
Marketing Manager: Roger Crow
CEO: Joni Saj-nicole
Principal: Crystal Tanner
COO: Tom Ross
Catalog Circulation: Mailed 1 time(s) per year
Printing Information: 22 pages in 4 colors
Binding: Saddle Stitched
Mailing List Information: Names for rent
In Business: 17 years
Sales Information: $50MM to $100MM

8493 Campbell Tool Company

Campbell Tool Company
2100 Selma Rd
Springfield, OH 45505-4718   937-322-8562
Fax: 937-882-6648
www.campbelltools.com

Lathes, mills, metals, steam engine kits, books, videos and precision instruments for hobbyists and industrial use

President: Renee L. Morningstar
Marketing Manager: Lanny G. Wallace
Credit Cards: AMEX; MasterCard; Visa
Catalog Circulation: Mailed 1 time(s) per year to 5M
Printing Information: 94 pages in 1 color on Newsprint
Press: Web Press
Binding: Saddle Stitched
In Business: 44 years
Number of Employees: 6

8494 Check-Line

Check-Line
600 Oakland Avenue
Cedarhurst, NY 11516   516-295-4300
800-645-4330
Fax: 516-295-4399
info@checkline.com
www.checkline.com

Tools and precision instruments

Credit Cards: AMEX; MasterCard
In Business: 57 years
Number of Employees: 10
Sales Information: $1MM to $3MM

8495 Coastal Tool & Supply

Coastal Tool & Supply
510 New Park Ave
West Hartford, CT 06110-1313   860-233-8213
877-551-8665
Fax: 860-233-6295
sales@coastaltool.com
www.coastaltool.com

Power tools and hand tools

President: Robert Ludgin
Credit Cards: AMEX; MasterCard; Visa
Catalog Cost: Free
Catalog Circulation: Mailed 2 time(s) per year
Average Order Size: $50
Printing Information: 32 pages in 2 colors on Newsprint
Press: Web Press
Mailing List Information: Names for rent
In Business: 34 years
Sales Information: $5MM to $10MM

8496 Cutting Tools C

Xylem
100 Cummings Center Drive
Suite 535-N
Beverly, MA 1915   978-281-0440
Fax: 978-283-2619
www.xylemflowcontrol.com

Bandsaw, jigsaw, power hacksaw, reciprocator saw blades, mandrels, pumps, seal detectors and winches

Chairman: Markos I. Tambakeras
President: Patrick K. Decker
CFO: Shashank Patel
Marketing Manager: Joseph P. Vesey
SVP & Chief Human Resources Officer: Kairus Tarapore
SVP, General Counsel & Corporate Se: Claudia S. Toussaint
SVP & President, Dewatering: Colin R. Sabol
Catalog Circulation: Mailed 1 time(s) per year to 30M
Printing Information: 10 pages
Number of Employees: 1200

8497 Del-Tron Precision

Del-Tron Precision
5 Trowbridge Dr.
P.O.Box 505
Bethel, CT 06801-505   203-778-2727
800-245-5013
Fax: 203-778-2721
deltron@deltron.com
www.Deltron.Com

Ball slides, crossed roller slides, positioning tables, linear ball and roller slide assemblies

President: Ralph Mc Intosh
Marketing Manager: Ed Keane
Buyers: Shane Kelly
Credit Cards: MasterCard; Visa
Catalog Cost: Free
Catalog Circulation: Mailed 2 time(s) per year to 15M
Average Order Size: $1200
Printing Information: 70 pages in 4 colors on Glossy Stock
Press: Letterpress
Binding: Perfect Bound
Mailing List Information: Names for rent
List Manager: Ed Keane
In Business: 41 years
Number of Employees: 55
Sales Information: $5,000,000 - $10,000,000

8498 Detwiler Tractor Parts
Detwiler Tractor Parts
200 S Division Street
P.O. Box 85
Colby, WI 54421-9231   715-659-4252
patdetwiler@gmail.com
www.detwilertractor.com

New and used two-cylinder tractor parts, rerimming and spoke wheels

President: Tom Detwiler
Credit Cards: AMEX; MasterCard
In Business: 30 years
Number of Employees: 2
Sales Information: $220,000

8499 Diamond Machining Technology
Diamond Machining Technology
85 Hayes Memorial Drive
Marlborough, MA 01752   508-481-5944
800-666-4368
Fax: 508-485-3924
www.dmtsharp.com

Hand-held diamond sharpeners

President: Mark Brandon
Marketing Manager: Stacey Brandon
Production Manager: Mark Bettke
Credit Cards: AMEX; MasterCard
Printing Information: 17 pages in 4 colors on Glossy Stock
Binding: Folded
Mailing List Information: Names for rent
In Business: 39 years
Number of Employees: 45

8500 Differential Pressure Instruments
Orange research
140 Cascade Boulevard
Milford, CT 06460-2868   203-877-5657
800-989-5657
Fax: 203-783-9546
info@orangeresearch.com
www.orangeresearch.com

Instruments to control and measure differential pressure and flow

Chairman: Leslie Hoffman
President: Paul Hoffman
Marketing Manager: Jim Gill
Vice President, General Manager: Mike Donovan
Senior Sales Representative: Donald Malizia
Engineering Manager: Timothy McIntyre
Credit Cards: AMEX; MasterCard
Catalog Circulation: Mailed 1 time(s) per year to 10K
Printing Information: 16 pages in 4 colors
Binding: Saddle Stitched
In Business: 45 years

8501 Duniway Stockroom Corporation
Duniway Stockroom Corp
48501 Milmont Drive
Fremont, CA 94538   650-969-8811
800-446-8811
Fax: 650-965-0764
info@duniway.com
www.Duniway.Com

Vacuum equipment

President: Ralph Duniway
Sales Manager: Jana Crane
Customer Service Representative: Alan Ross
Customer Service Representative: Susan Gibes
Credit Cards: AMEX; MasterCard
Printing Information: 122 pages
In Business: 39 years
Sales Information: $10MM to $20MM

8502 EFD
Nordson EFD
40 Catamore Boulevard
East Providence, RI 02914   401-431-7000
800-556-3484
Fax: 401-431-7079
www.nordson.com

Automatic fluid dispensing components.

President: Michael F. Hilton
CFO: Gregory Thaxton
Senior Vice President: John J. Keane
VP, General Counsel and Secretary: Robert E. Veillette
Vice President, Human Resources: Shelly M. Peet
Credit Cards: AMEX; MasterCard
Catalog Cost: Free
Printing Information: in 4 colors
Mailing List Information: Names for rent
In Business: 54 years
Number of Employees: 205
Sales Information: $50MM to $100MM

8503 Eagle America
Eagle America
2381 Philmont Ave
Suite 107
Huntingdon Valley, PA 19006   888-872-7637
800-872-2511
Fax: 800-872-9471
eagle@eagleamerica.com
www.eagleamerica.com

Router bits, woodworking accessories

President: Dan Walter
Buyers: Dave Swartz
Credit Cards: AMEX; MasterCard
Catalog Cost: Free
Catalog Circulation: Mailed 9 time(s) per year
Printing Information: 88 pages in 4 colors on Glossy Stock
Press: Web Press
Binding: Saddle Stitched
Mailing List Information: Names for rent
In Business: 26 years
Number of Employees: 20-5

8504 Easy Picker Golf Products
Easy Picker Golf Products
415 Leonard Blvd N
Lehigh Acres, FL 33971-6302   239-368-6600
800-641-4653
Fax: 239-369-1579
salesdept@easypicker.com
www.Easypicker.Com

Products for golf course management

President: George Hedlin
Director: Bobby Brown
salesdept@easypicker.com
Catalog Circulation: Mailed 5 time(s) per year to 6M
Printing Information: 108 pages
In Business: 45 years
Number of Employees: 39
Sales Information: $20MM to $50MM

8505 Eaton Corporation World Headquarters
Eaton Corporation
1111 Superior Ave E # 19
Cleveland, OH 44114-2584   440-523-4400
800-386-1911
Fax: 216-523-4787
www.eaton.com

Automotive, appliance, energy, industrial controls and components

Chairman: Alexander M Cutler
CFO: J Carmont
Marketing Manager: Jeff Obrock
Vice Chairman and COO: Craig Arnold
Senior Vice President and CIO: William W. Blausey Jr.
Executive Vice President, Chief HR: Cynthia K. Brabander
Number of Employees: 7300
Sales Information: $20 million

8506 Ega Products
EGA Products ,Inc
4275 N. 127th St.
Brookfield, WI 53005-366   262-781-7899
800-937-3427
Fax: 262-781-3586
info@egaproducts.com
www.egaproducts.com

Rolling warehouse ladders and specialty ladders

President: David Young
Catalog Cost: Free
Catalog Circulation: Mailed 1 time(s) per year
Number of Employees: 75

8507 Emery Winslow Scale Company Catalog
Emery Winslow Scale Company
73 Cogwheel Lane
Seymour, CT 06483-3930   203-881-9333
Fax: 203-881-9477
www.emerywinslow.com

Truck, tank and floor bench seats, load cells and indicators

Chairman: Walter Young
President: William K Fischer
Marketing Manager: David Young
dmyoung@emerywinslow.com
Director of Operations: Mike Martella
Director of Manufacturing Developme: Frank Howell
International Marketing Manager: Walter Young
Mailing List Information: Names for rent
In Business: 147 years
Number of Employees: 85
Sales Information: $10MM to $20MM

8508 Eugene Ernst Products Company
Ernst Flow Industries
116 Main Street
Farmingdale, NJ 07727-1429   732-938-5641
800-992-2843
Fax: 732-938-9463
www.ernstflow.com

Machinery

President: Roger Ernst
Catalog Cost: Free
Catalog Circulation: Mailed 6 time(s) per year to 210K
Printing Information: 50 pages in 4 colors on Glossy Stock
Press: Web Press
Binding: Saddle Stitched
Mailing List Information: Names for rent
In Business: 13 years
Number of Employees: 13
Sales Information: $1MM to $3MM

8509 Fairchild Products
Fairchild Industrial Products Company
3920 Westpoint Boulevard
Winston Salem, NC 27103-6719   336-659-3400
us-ws-cs@rotork.com
www.fairchildproducts.com

Industrial pneumatic and electro-pneumatic controls and mechanical power transmission equipment

President: Hugh Steele
CFO: Ron Lowe
General Manager: Steve Juhasz
steve.juhasz@rotork.com
Inside Sales Manager: Andre Parra
andre.parra@rotork.com
Regional Sales Manager: Mike Weaver
mike.weaver@rotork.com
International Marketing Manager: Thomas McNichol
Buyers: Steve Baity
Catalog Cost: Free
Printing Information: 16 pages in 4 colors on Glossy Stock
Press: Web Press
Mailing List Information: Names for rent
In Business: 97 years

Number of Employees: 150
Sales Information: $25,000,000 - $50,000,000

8510 Fairgate Rule
Stamp Inc
Saw Kill Industrial Park
Rhinebeck, NY 12572-391
845-876-3063
800-431-2180
Fax: 845-876-7039
stampinc@infionline.net
www.stampinc.com

Stamping, electro mechanical assemblies, resistance welding, equipment reconditioning, tools and dies
President: Gary Hosey
Catalog Circulation: Mailed 1 time(s) per year
Printing Information: in 1 color on Matte Stock
In Business: 50 years
Number of Employees: 15
Sales Information: $1,000,000 - $5,000,000

8511 Feeny
Knape & Vogt Manufacturing Co.
2700 Oak Industrial Drive NE
Grand Rapids, MI 49505-191
765-288-8730
800-253-1561
Fax: 765-288-0851
www.knapeandvogt.com

Storage products
President: Peter Martin
CFO: Rick McQuigg
Marketing Manager: Peter Ross
VP of Operations: Gordon Kirsch
Vice President, Operations: Gordon Kirsch
Vice President, Home and Commercial: Dan Pickett
Catalog Cost: Free
Printing Information: 52 pages
Binding: Saddle Stitched

8512 Fein Power Tools
Fein Power Tools Inc.
1000 Omega Drive
Suite 1180
Pittsburgh, PA 15205
412-922-8886
800-441-9878
Fax: 412-922-8767
info@feinus.com
www.feinus.com

Portable power tools
President: Chris Cable
CFO: Mary Wilkie
Marketing Manager: Robert Hillard
Catalog Cost: Free
Mailing List Information: Names for rent
In Business: 140 years
Number of Employees: 40

8513 Felder USA
Fedler Group
2 Lukens Dr # 300
New Castle, DE 19720-2796
302-322-7732
866-792-5288
Fax: 302-322-9865
salesinfo@felderusa.com
www.felderusa.com

Machines and tools for woodworking
President: Hans-Georg Radel
Marketing Manager: Tom Van Alstine
Credit Cards: AMEX; MasterCard
Catalog Cost: Free
Mailing List Information: Names for rent
In Business: 58 years
Number of Employees: 12
Sales Information: $1MM to $3MM

8514 Festo Tooltecnic
DeLUCS Sales CO,.INC
2533 N Carson Street
Carson City, NV 89706-147
630-393-2000
888-337-8600
Fax: 630-393-9923
www.toolguide.com

Routers that work with or without patented guide system

8515 Fischer Technology
Fischer Measurement Technologies
750 Marshall Phelps Rd
Windsor, CT 06095-2199
860-683-0781
Fax: 860-688-8496
info@fischer-technology.com
www.helmut-fischer.com

Coating thickness measurement systems and material analysis instrumentation
President: Michael Haller
Marketing Manager: Christian Petrilli
Mailing List Information: Names for rent
In Business: 36 years
Number of Employees: 35
Sales Information: $1,000,000 - $5,000,000

8516 Flexbar Machine Corporation
Flexbar Machine Corporation
250 Gibbs Rd
Islandia, NY 11749-2697
631-582-8440
800-879-7575
Fax: 631-582-8487
www.Flexbar.Com

Lathe guards, machine guards, video inspection and measurement, all types of dimensional gaging, metrology grade casting materials
President: Jon Adler
Marketing Manager: Larry Derrig
Production Manager: John Faraci
Sales Director: Lou Valenti
Purchasing Manager: Maria Blando
Manufacturing Manager: Rick Boone
Buyers: Mario Blando
Catalog Circulation: Mailed 1 time(s) per year to 30K
Average Order Size: $250
Printing Information: 400 pages in 2 colors on Matte Stock
Press: Web Press
Binding: Saddle Stitched
Mailing List Information: Names for rent
In Business: 35 years
Number of Employees: 25
Sales Information: $1,000,000 - $5,000,000

8517 Forestry Suppliers 61 Catalog
Forestry Suppliers Inc
205 W Rankin Street
PO Box 8397
Jackson, MS 39201
601-354-3565
800-360-7788
Fax: 800-543-4203
fsi@forestry-suppliers.com
www.forestry-suppliers.com

Forestry, environmental and educational equipment
President: John Gwaltney
CFO: Bob Middleton
Marketing Manager: Clay Walker
Production Manager: Ken Peacock
International Marketing Manager: Charlie Rogers
Credit Cards: MasterCard; Visa
Catalog Cost: Free
Printing Information: 728 pages
Mailing List Information: Names for rent
List Manager: Brian Henry
In Business: 65 years
Number of Employees: 110

8518 G&N Gear
Rubricon Gear
225 Citation Circle
Corona, CA 92880-4308
951-356-3800
Fax: 714-973-0559
www.rubicon-gear.com

Custom gears for industrial, commercial and aircraft requirements

President: Ryan Edwards
redwards@rubicon-gear.com
Marketing Manager: N Edwards
Production Manager: Tom Cruse
Controller: Frank Salazar
fsalazar@rubicon-gear.com
Engineering/Custom Division: Steve Kisse
skissel@rubicon-gear.com
Quality: Jose Chavez Jr.
jchavez@rubicon-gear.com
In Business: 43 years
Number of Employees: 55
Sales Information: $5,000,000 - $10,000,000

8519 Garden Tools by Lee Valley
Lee Valley Tools Ltd.
PO Box 1780
Ogdensburg, NY 13669-6780
613-596-0350
800-871-8158
Fax: 800-513-7885
customerservice@leevalley.com
www.leevalley.com

Woodworking and gardening hand tools and accessories
President: Leonard Lee
Marketing Manager: Robin Lee
Credit Cards: MasterCard; Visa
Catalog Cost: $5
Catalog Circulation: Mailed 12 time(s) per year
Printing Information: 245 pages in 4 colors
Press: Web Press
Binding: Saddle Stitched
In Business: 36 years

8520 Garrett Wade
Garrett Wade
5389 E Provident Drive
Cincinnati, OH 45246
800-221-2942
www.garrettwade.com

Woodworking, gardening and outdoor tools, home & office supplies and accessories
President: Garretson W Chinn
Credit Cards: AMEX; MasterCard
Catalog Cost: Free
Catalog Circulation: Mailed 12 time(s) per year to 1.8M
Average Order Size: $150
Printing Information: 100 pages in 4 colors on Glossy Stock
Press: Web Press
Binding: Saddle Stitched
Mailing List Information: Names for rent
In Business: 42 years
Number of Employees: 50
Sales Information: $10,000,000

8521 Grand Tool Supply Corporation
Grand Tool Supply
650 Huyler Street
South Hackensack, NJ 07606-174 800-922-0512
Fax: 800-866-5730
www.grandtool.com

Quality cutting tools, machine shop equipment and measuring instruments for the metalworking industry; hard-to-find items for classic tooling and today's cutting-edge technology
Catalog Cost: Free
Printing Information: 736 pages in 4 colors
In Business: 71 years
Sales Information: 2.3MM

8522 Grant Industries
Grant Group
33415 Groesbeck Hwy
Fraser, MI 48026-4203
586-293-9200
800-394-5904
Fax: 586-293-9346
www.Grantgrp.Com

Machinery
President: Robert Grant
Number of Employees: 50
Sales Information: $5,000,000 - $10,000,000

8523 Griot's Garage
Griot's Garage
3333 South 38th St
Tacoma, WA 98409-1728   253-922-2400
                             800-345-5789
                        Fax: 253-922-7500
                        www.Griotsgarage.Com

Tools and products for every garage
President: Richard Griot
Credit Cards: AMEX; MasterCard; Visa
Catalog Cost: Free
Catalog Circulation: Mailed 4 time(s) per year
Printing Information: 60 pages in 4 colors on
Glossy Stock
Press: Web Press
Binding: Saddle Stitched
In Business: 23 years
Number of Employees: 35
Sales Information: 3MM-5MM

8524 H&H Exports
H&H Exports Inc.
1205 93rd Ave W
Duluth, MN 55808-1500   218-626-2715
                        Fax: 218-626-1801
                        solutions@hhexports.com
                        www.Hhexports.Com

Bearings and power transmittors
President: William J Howard
In Business: 38 years
Number of Employees: 15
Sales Information: $5MM to $10MM

8525 Hamilton Manufacturing Corporation
Hamilton Manufacturing Corporation
1026 Hamilton Dr
Holland, OH 43528-8210   419-867-4858
                             888-723-4858
                        Fax: 419-867-4850
                        www.Hamiltonmfg.Com

Manufacturer of currency changing machines
President: Robin Ritz
In Business: 94 years
Sales Information: $20MM to $50MM

8526 Hardy Diesels
Hardy Diesels
15749 Lyons Valley Road
Jamul, CA 91935-3503   619-669-1995
                             800-341-7027
                        Fax: 619-669-4829
                        sales@hardydiesel.com
                        www.hardydiesel.com

Small diesel generators and diesel tractors, tractor implements, farm tractors, diesel marine engines, solar panels, wind generators, inverters, water pumps
Credit Cards: MasterCard

8527 Herrington
Herrington
3 Symmes Drive
Londonderry, NH 03053-2142   866-558-7467
                             800-903-2878
                        Fax: 603-437-3492
                        customerservice@herringtoncatalog.com
                        www.herringtoncatalog.com

Apparel, electronic gifts, tools and gadgets
President: Lee Herrington
Credit Cards: AMEX; MasterCard; Visa
Catalog Cost: Free
Catalog Circulation: Mailed 8 time(s) per year
Printing Information: 48 pages in 4 colors on
Glossy Stock
Binding: Saddle Stitched
In Business: 35 years
Number of Employees: 160
Sales Information: $ 10 Million

8528 Hyde Tools
Hyde
54 Eastford Road
Southbridge, MA 01550-1875   800-872-4933
                        Fax: 508-765-5250
                        info@hydetools.com
                        www.hydetools.com

Painting, wallcovering.
Chairman: Richard Hardy
President: Rob Scoble
CFO: Ronald Carlson
Marketing Manager: Corey Talbot
CEO: Rick Clemence
COO: Rob Scoble
Printing Information: 63 pages in 4 colors
Binding: Perfect Bound
In Business: 39 years
Number of Employees: 546

8529 Inter-Lakes Bases
Inter-Lakes Bases Inc.
17480 Malyn Blvd
Fraser, MI 48026-1671   586-294-8120
                             800-448-7520
                        Fax: 586-294-8132
                        sales@interlakesbases.com
                        www.interlakesbases.com

Machine and robot bases, dial plates
President: Barbara Kasper
Printing Information: 25 pages in 2 colors on
Matte Stock
Press: Letterpress
Mailing List Information: Names for rent
In Business: 48 years
Number of Employees: 40
Sales Information: $1,000,000 - $5,000,000

8530 Irwin Industrial Tools
Irwin Industrial Tools
8936 Northpointe Executive Dr
Suite 200
Huntersville, NC 28078   800-464-7946
                        Fax: 800-866-5742
                        www.irwin.com

Hand tools and power tools
President: Neil Eibeler
Product Marketing Manager: Katy Vogl
Catalog Cost: Free
Catalog Circulation: Mailed 1 time(s) per year
Printing Information: 238 pages
Mailing List Information: Names for rent
In Business: 130 years
Number of Employees: 45
Sales Information: $5MM to $10MM

8531 Jackson Marking Products Catalog
Jackson Marking Products Company Inc
9105 N Rainbow Lane
Mt Vernon, IL 62864-6407   618-242-1334
                             800-782-6722
                        Fax: 618-242-7732
                        jmp@rubber-stamp.com
                        www.Rubber-Stamp.Com

Rubber stamps and stamping machinery including hot stamping, metal self inking, automatic numbering, hand die plate and logo stamps
President: Coy Jackson
Marketing Manager: Thomas Jackson
Credit Cards: AMEX; MasterCard; Visa
Catalog Cost: Free
Mailing List Information: Names for rent
In Business: 54 years
Number of Employees: 14
Sales Information: $1MM to $3MM

8532 Johnson Brass & Machine Foundry
Johnson Brass & Machine Foundry, Inc.
270 N. Mill Street
PO Box 219A
Saukville, WI 53080   262-377-9440
                        Fax: 262-284-7066
                        www.johnsoncentrifugal.com

Castings, gear blanks, bearings and more
President: Lance Johnson
Lance.Johnson@JohnsonCentrifugal.com
COO: Lance Johnson
Lance.Johnson@JohnsonCentrifugal.com
VP - Marketing and Sale: Tim Devine
Tim.Devine@JohnsonCentrifugal.com
Transportation Manager: Chris Morse
Chris.Morse@JohnsonCentrifugal.com
In Business: 100 years
Number of Employees: 100
Sales Information: $10,000,000 - $25,000,000

8533 KBC Tools
KBC Tools
6300 18 Mile Road
Sterling Heights, MI 48314-8006   586-979-0500
                        Fax: 586-979-4292
                        sales@kbctools.com
                        www.kbctools.com

Metal cutting tools
President: Paula Bass
Vice President: John Earles
Credit Cards: MasterCard; Visa
Catalog Cost: Free
Catalog Circulation: Mailed 1 time(s) per year
Printing Information: 860 pages on Newsprint
In Business: 52 years
Number of Employees: 50
Sales Information: $10MM to $20MM

8534 Kett Tool
Kett Tool Company
5055 Madison Road
Cincinnati, OH 45227-1494   513-271-0333
                             800-215-3210
                        Fax: 513-271-5318
                        info@kett-tool.com
                        www.Kett-Tool.Com

Electric and peumatic shears,saws and nibblers
President: Rowe Hoffman
Buyers: Michael Hampton
Credit Cards: MasterCard; Visa
Printing Information: 6 pages in 4 colors on
Matte Stock
Binding: Folded
Mailing List Information: Names for rent
In Business: 75 years
Number of Employees: 30
Sales Information: $10MM to $20MM

8535 Kitts Industrial Tools
Kitts Industrial Tools
27600 West 8 Mile Road
Farmington Hills, MI 48336-3147   248-476-2121
                             800-521-6579
                        Fax: 313-531-0300
                        kitindustrial@aol.com
                        kittstools.securesites.net/store/

Over 200 tons of tools
President: Neill Kitts
Credit Cards: AMEX; MasterCard; Visa
In Business: 36 years
Number of Employees: 22

8536 Komet of America
Komet of America
2050 Mitchell Blvd
Schaumburg, IL 60193-4544   847-923-8400
                             847-923-8480
                        Fax: 800-865-6638
                        customerservice.us@kometgroup.com
                        www.Komet.Com

Cutting tools
President: Hans Grandin
CEO: Hans Grandin
In Business: 97 years
Number of Employees: 275
Sales Information: $10,000,000 - $25,000,000

8537 Lansky Sharpeners
Lansky Sharpeners
PO Box 800
Buffalo, NY 14231   716-877-7511
                                        800-825-2675
                                  Fax: 716-877-6955
customerservice@lansky.com
www.lansky.com

Knife and tool sharpeners

President: Edward Schwartz
Controller/Personnel Manager: Bonnie Maron
Credit Cards: AMEX; MasterCard; Visa
Catalog Cost: Free

8538 LittleMachineShop.com Catalog
LittleMachineShop.com
396 W Washington Boulevard
Suite 500
Pasadena, CA 91103   626-797-7850
                                          800-981-9663
info@littlemachineshop.com
www.littlemachineshop.com

Premier source for tooling, parts, and accessories for bench top machinists

Marketing Manager: Carl Siechert
Catalog Cost: Free
Printing Information: 136 pages in 1 color
Mailing List Information: Names for rent
In Business: 12 years

8539 Lortone
Lortone
12130 Cyrus Way
Mukilteo, WA 98275-5700   425-493-1600
                                            800-426-6773
                                      Fax: 425-493-9494
equipment@lortone.com
www.Lortone.Com

Lapidary equipment and tools

President: Doug Guthrie
Buyers: Sara Schinkel
Credit Cards: MasterCard; Visa
Catalog Circulation: Mailed 1 time(s) per year
Printing Information: 25 pages in 4 colors
In Business: 35 years
Number of Employees: 20
Sales Information: $1,000,000 - $5,000,000

8540 M&C Specialties Company
M&C Specialties Co.
90 James Way
Southampton, PA 18966   215-322-1600
                                            800-441-6996
                                      Fax: 215-322-1620
info@mcspecialties.com
www.McSpecialties.Com

Pressure sensitive diecutting, converting and tapes

President: Donald Rauch
Marketing Manager: David Cornelison
Buyers: Jean Paluch
Catalog Cost: Free
Printing Information: 4 pages in 4 colors on Glossy Stock
Mailing List Information: Names for rent
In Business: 69 years
Number of Employees: 2000
Sales Information: $10,000,000 - $25,000,000

8541 Mac-It Corporation
Mac-It Corporation
275 East Liberty Street
Lancaster, PA 17602   717-397-3535
                                          800-394-6755
                                    Fax: 717-392-1843
info@macit.com
www.Macit.Com

Fasteners, screws and screw machine parts

President: Michael P Stillman
Marketing Manager: Terry Coonan
In Business: 92 years

Number of Employees: 50
Sales Information: $1,000,000 - $5,000,000

8542 McFeely's Square Drive Screws
McFeely's Square Drive Screws
PO Box 44976
Madison, WI 53744-4976   800-443-7937
                                            800-443-7937
                                      Fax: 800-847-7136
customerservice@mcfeelys.com
www.mcfeelys.com

Square drive screws, stainless steel, silicon, bronze, brass, aluminum and abrasives

Founder: William J. McFeely III
Credit Cards: MasterCard
Catalog Cost: $2
Catalog Circulation: Mailed 7 time(s) per year to 1.5MM
Average Order Size: $65
Printing Information: 96 pages in 4 colors on Glossy Stock
Press: Web Press
Binding: Saddle Stitched
Mailing List Information: Names for rent
List Company: List Locators & Managers
5750 W 95th Street, Suite #300
Overland Park, KS 66207
800-487-8700
In Business: 36 years
Number of Employees: 35
Sales Information: $5MM to $10MM

8543 Measurement Specialists
Measurement Specialists, Inc.
1000 Lucas Way
Hampton, VA 23666   757-766-1500
                                            800-745-8008
                                      Fax: 757-766-4297
www.meas-spec.com

Linear and angular displacement equipment

Chairman: Morton L Topfer
President: Frank D Guidone
CFO: Mark Thomson
EVP: Glen MacGibbon
VP - Finance and Treasurer: Jeffrey Kostelni
Chief Operating Officer: Joe Gleeson
Credit Cards: MasterCard
Catalog Circulation: Mailed 1 time(s) per year
Printing Information: 8 pages in 3 colors
Binding: Saddle Stitched
In Business: 30 years

8544 Meylan Corporation
Meylan Corporation
543 Valley Road
Suite 3
Upper Montclair, NJ 07043-1881   973-744-6400
                                                  888-769-9667
                                            Fax: 973-744-1011
meylan1@aol.com
www.meylan.com

Stopwatches, counters, loggers, tachometers, etc.

President: CM Prinaris
Marketing Manager: A Prinaris
Catalog Cost: Free
Catalog Circulation: Mailed 2 time(s) per year to 50K
Average Order Size: $100
Printing Information: 28 pages in 2 colors
Mailing List Information: Names for rent
In Business: 94 years
Number of Employees: 10-J
Sales Information: $500M to $1MM

8545 Micron Industries Corporation
Micron Industries Corporation
1211 22nd Street
Suite 200
Oak Brook, IL 60523   630-516-1222
                                          800-664-4660
                                    Fax: 630-516-1820
info@micronpower.com
www.micronpower.com

Power conversion equipment

President: Donald R Clark
Marketing Manager: Frank Bussa
Credit Cards: MasterCard
Printing Information: 30 pages
In Business: 49 years
Number of Employees: 140
Sales Information: $10,000,000 - $25,000,000

8546 Munroe
Munroe
1820 North Franklin Street
Pittsburgh, PA 15233-2253   412-231-0600
                                          Fax: 412-231-0647
rwoodings@munroeinc.com
www.munroeinc.com

Mill machinery, ASME code fabricator

President: Philip F Muck
Marketing Manager: Donald Capone
Production Manager: Michael Muck
Buyers: Daniel Travaglini
In Business: 165 years
Number of Employees: 250
Sales Information: $10MM to $20MM

8547 NANMAC Corporation
NANMAC
1657 Washington St., Bldg. 3
PO Box 6640
Holliston, MA 01746   508-872-4811
                                          800-786-4669
                                    Fax: 508-879-5450
info@nanmac.com
www.nanmac.com

Tools and machinery

8548 NELCO Wiring Accessory Specialists
NELCO
22 Riverside Drive
Pembroke, MA 02359-4931   781-826-3010
                                            800-346-3526
                                      Fax: 781-826-7344
info@nelcoproducts.com
www.Nelcoproducts.Net

Wiring accessories: cable ties and accessories, terminals and connectors, wiring routing products, identification products and tubing

President: Charles Nelson
Marketing Manager: M Abbondonzio
Production Manager: W Dalrymple
Buyers: B Ragazzini
Catalog Circulation: Mailed 52 time(s) per year
Printing Information: 16 pages in 1 color on Matte Stock
Press: Web Press
Binding: Saddle Stitched
Mailing List Information: Names for rent
In Business: 31 years
Number of Employees: 45
Sales Information: $10MM to $20MM

8549 NWL Transformers
NWL
312 Rising Sun Rd
#358
Bordentown, NJ 08505-9626   609-298-7300
                                          Fax: 609-298-1982
nwlinfo@nwl.com
www.Nwl.Com

Transformers

President: J David Seitz
In Business: 75 years
Sales Information: $20MM to $50MM

8550 **Neider Company**
Neider Company
1120 East Terrace Street
Suite 300
Seattle, WA 98122   206-325-0291
                          Fax: 206-325-6306
                          admin@neiders.com
                          www.neiders.com

Metal stampings
Founder & CEO: Karl Neiders
Operations Manager: Frank T. Hornung
Area Manager: Ingrid Powell-Wurgler
Catalog Cost: Free
Printing Information: 4 pages
In Business: 28 years

8551 **Neuhaus Corporation**
J.D. Neuhaus L.P.
9, Loveton Circle
Sparks, MD 21152   410-472-0500
                          800-331-2889
                          Fax: 410-472-2202
                          sales@jdneuhaus.com
                          www.jdngroup.com

Manufacturer of tools
In Business: 23 years

8552 **Norpin Deep Drawn Enclosures**
Norpin Manufacturing Co. Inc
2342 Boston Road
P.O. Box 1031
Wilbraham, MA 01095-366   413-599-1627
                          800-795-1302
                          Fax: 413-599-1696
                          www.norpin.com

All shapes of hardware, covers, and enclosures
Catalog Cost: Free
Printing Information: 30 pages in 2 colors
Binding: Saddle Stitched
In Business: 58 years

8553 **Nortel Machinery**
Nortel Manufacturing Limited
1051 Clinton Street
Buffalo, NY 14206-2877   716-852-2685
                          Fax: 716-852-6374
                          info@nortelmfg.com
                          www.Nortelmfg.Com

Glass working machinery and equipment; air movers
President: Pat Blake
Marketing Manager: Pat Blake
Founder: Peter Norton
Customer Service, Sales: Jean Robichaud
Manager: Pat Blake
Mailing List Information: Names for rent
In Business: 48 years
Number of Employees: 5
Sales Information: $1MM to $3MM

8554 **Norton Diamond Pressing Tools**
Norton
65 Beale Road
Arden, NC 28704-9213   800-438-4773
                          Fax: 828-684-1401
                          www.nortonindustrial.com

Diamond dressing and forming tools
Catalog Cost: Free
Catalog Circulation: Mailed 1 time(s) per year
In Business: 128 years

8555 **Nye**
Nye Lubricants, Inc
12 Howland Rd
Fairhaven, MA 02719-3453   508-996-6721
                          Fax: 508-997-5285
                          techhelp@nyelubricants.com
                          www.Nyelubricants.Com

Synthetic lubricants for automotive, power tool, appliance, telecommunications, office automation, corregation, aerospace, precision instruments, semiconductor manufacturing
President: George B. Mock, III
CFO: Gail Smith, CPA, CGMA
Marketing Manager: Brian Hollsy
Production Manager: Alden Pierce
Fulfillment: Ed Paar, Marketing/Communications
Vice President of Operations: Shaun J. Ensor
Director of Technology: Anthony V. Grossi
Director of Quality: Martin J Weinstein
Catalog Cost: Free
Printing Information: 8 pages in 4 colors
Binding: Saddle Stitched
In Business: 173 years

8556 **OPW Aboveground Storage Tank Equipment**
OPW, A Dover Company
9393 Princeton-Glendale Road
Hamilton, OH 45011   513-870-3315
                          800-422-2525
                          Fax: 800-421-3297
                          www.opwglobal.com

Equipment for gas and service stations
President: David Crouse
CFO: Susan Hathaway
VP, Global Marketing: Keith Moye
VP & General Manager, Retail Fuelin: Mike McCann
VP HR: Ann Miller
Catalog Circulation: Mailed 1 time(s) per year
Printing Information: 18 pages in 2 colors
Binding: Saddle Stitched
In Business: 123 years

8557 **OPW Service Station Equipment**
OPW Adover Company
9393 Princeton-Glendale Road
Hamilton, OH 45011   513-870-3315
                          800-422-2525
                          Fax: 513-870-3157
                          www.opwglobal.com

Pumps, nozzles, manholes and tanks
President: David Crouse
CFO: Susan Hathaway
VP, Global Marketing: Keith Moye
VP & General Manager, Retail Fuelin: Mike McCann
VP HR: Ann Miller
Catalog Circulation: Mailed 1 time(s) per year
Printing Information: 84 pages in 2 colors
Binding: Perfect Bound
In Business: 123 years

8558 **Ohio Nut & Bolt Company**
Ohio Nut & Bolt Company
5250 W 164th Street
Brook Park, OH 44142-1506 216-267-2240
                          800-437-1689
                          Fax: 216-267-3228
                          info@buckeyefasteners.com
                          www.buckeyefasteners.com

Resistance weld fasteners used in assembly plants, inccluding weld screws, weld nuts, tee nuts and weld pins, levelers and adjusting screws
Mailing List Information: Names for rent
In Business: 96 years
Number of Employees: 120

8559 **Oil-Rite Lubricating Equipment**
Oil-Rite Corparation
4325 Clipper Drive
PO Box 1207
Manitowoc, WI 54221-1207   920-682-6173
                          Fax: 920-682-7699
                          sales@oilrite.com
                          www.oilrite.com

A complete line of lubrication equipment

President: Donald G. Gruett
Credit Cards: MasterCard
Catalog Circulation: Mailed 1 time(s) per year to 10K
Printing Information: 94 pages in 4 colors
Binding: Saddle Stitched
In Business: 82 years

8560 **Oneida Air Systems**
Oneida Air Systems
1001 W Fayette Street
Syracuse, NY 13204-2873   800-732-4065
                          Fax: 315-476-5044
                          info@oneida-air.com
                          www.oneida-air.com

Dust collection, air filtration, custom engineering, complete duct work packages, cyclones and filter media
President: Robert Witter
Credit Cards: AMEX; MasterCard
Mailing List Information: Names for rent
In Business: 24 years
Number of Employees: 25
Sales Information: $20MM to $50MM

8561 **Osborn Manufacturing Corporation**
Osborn Manufacturing Corporation
960 N Lake St
PO Box 1650
Warsaw, IN 46580-1650   574-267-6156
                          Fax: 574-267-6527
                          NBell@mailosborn.com
                          www.osbornmfg.com

Industrial safety tools
President: Virgil I. Hagy
CFO: Vivian Kelly
Marketing Manager: Michael Hagy
Production Manager: Jerry Kelly
Buyers: Aimee Kintzel
Mailing List Information: Names for rent
In Business: 5 years
Number of Employees: 18
Sales Information: $1,000,000 - $5,000,000

8562 **Outdoor Power Equipment**
Foley-Belsaw Co.
1173 Benson Street
River Falls, WI 54022-1395 715-426-2275
                          800-821-3452
                          Fax: 715-426-2198
                          info@foley-belsaw.com
                          www.foley-belsaw.com

Wholesale locksmith, sharpening and outdoor power equipment
Credit Cards: MasterCard; Visa
Catalog Cost: Free
Catalog Circulation: Mailed 4 time(s) per year
Printing Information: 48 pages in 4 colors
Mailing List Information: Names for rent
In Business: 91 years
Sales Information: $20MM to $50MM

8563 **PJ Catalog**
PJ Company
2410 S Sequoia Drive
Compton, CA 90220   800-421-2880
                          Fax: 310-639-8145
                          sales@pjcasters.com
                          www.pjcasters.com

Casters and wheels for transporting equipment
International Marketing Manager: Tai Chung
Buyers: Yung Wee
Catalog Cost: Free
Catalog Circulation: Mailed 1 time(s) per year to 4000
Printing Information: 80 pages in 4 colors on Glossy Stock
Binding: Perfect Bound
Mailing List Information: Names for rent
List Manager: Theresa Lakey
In Business: 39 years

Number of Employees: 40
Sales Information: $20MM to $50MM

8564 PM Research
PM Research,Inc
4110 Niles Hill Rd
Wellsville, NY 14895-9608   585-593-3169
                                   800-724-3801
                              Fax: 585-593-5637
PMRgang@pmresearchinc.com
www.pmmodelengines.com

Model kits and finished models; steam and stirling engines, machine shop tools, boilers, accessories

President: Gary Bastian
Catalog Cost: $3
In Business: 39 years
Number of Employees: 18
Sales Information: $ 3 Million

8565 Parking Products
Parking Products Inc.
2517 Wyandotte Rd
Willow Grove, PA 19090-1219   215-657-7500
                              Fax: 215-657-4321
ppi@parkingproducts.com
www.Parkingproducts.Com

President: Holger Neibisch
Founder: Dieter Niebisch
In Business: 46 years
Sales Information: $1MM to $3MM

8566 Parks Repair Parts
The D.C. Morrison Company
201 Johnson Street
PO Box 586
Covington, KY 41011-586   859-581-7511
                                 888-246-6365
                              Fax: 859-581-9642
www.Dcmorrison.Com

Repair parts for parks planters

President: Henry E Reder
Sales: Donald Craig
Catalog Cost: $6.5
Printing Information: 10 pages
In Business: 26 years
Sales Information: Under $500M

8567 Patco Air Tool
PATCO Air Tools,Inc
100 Englewood Dr
Suite G
Orion, MI 48359-2518   248-648-8830
                                 800-727-2201
                              Fax: 248-648-8833
sales@patcoairtools.com
www.Patcoairtools.Com

Air tools and parts

President: Jon Kirsch
Catalog Circulation: Mailed 1 time(s) per year
Printing Information: 17 pages in 2 colors
In Business: 54 years
Sales Information: $5MM to $10MM

8568 PennTool
Penn Tool Co. Inc
1776
Springfield Avenue
Maplewood, NJ 07040   973-761-4343
                                 800-526-4956
                              Fax: 973-761-1494
info@penntoolco.com
www.penntoolco.com

Tools

President: Gene Elson
VP: Michael Elson

8569 Pennfield Feeds
Pennfield Corporation
2260 Erin Court
PO Box 4366
Lancaster, PA 17601-4366   717-299-2561
                                 800-732-0467
                              Fax: 717-295-8783
www.Pennfield.Com

Manufactures dairy, equine and specialty feeds

President: Ernest O Horn Iii
Catalog Circulation: Mailed 1 time(s) per year
Printing Information: 16 pages in 4 colors
Binding: Saddle Stitched
In Business: 93 years

8570 Pennsylvania Scale Company
Pennsylvania Scale Company
665 N. Reservoir Street
Lancaster, PA 17602-5606   717-295-6935
                                 800-233-0473
                              Fax: 800-768-6350
rsw@pascale.com
www.pascale.com

Commercial and industrial weighing scales, counting scales, counting and weighing indicators, process control indicators check weigh scales, bases, forklift scales, pallet jack scales, retail scales

President: Rob Woodward
CFO: Troy Frey
Marketing Manager: Robert Woodward
Catalog Circulation: Mailed 1 time(s) per year
Average Order Size: $1000
Printing Information: 4 pages in 4 colors on Glossy Stock
Mailing List Information: Names for rent
In Business: 107 years
Sales Information: $3MM to $5MM

8571 Petersen Products Co.
Petersen
421 Wheeler Avenue
P.O.Box 340
Fredonia, WI 53021-340   262-692-2416
                                 800-827-5275
                              Fax: 262-692-2418
sales@petersenproducts.com
www.petersenproducts.com

Mechanical and inflatable pipe plugs for most size, pressure and chemical requirements

President: Philip L Lundman
Production Manager: Chet Sowern
Credit Cards: AMEX; MasterCard
Catalog Cost: Free
Printing Information: 6 pages
Mailing List Information: Names for rent
In Business: 99 years
Number of Employees: 10
Sales Information: $1,000,000 - $5,000,000

8572 Pico Electronics
Pico Electronic,Inc.
143 Sparks Ave
Pelham, NY 10803-1837   914-738-1400
                                 800-431-1064
                              Fax: 914-738-8225
info@picoelectronics.com
www.Picoelectronics.Com

AC-DC power supplies

President: Joe Sweeney
Catalog Cost: Free
Catalog Circulation: Mailed 2 time(s) per year
Printing Information: 64 pages in 1 color
In Business: 17 years
Number of Employees: 90
Sales Information: $5,000,000 - $10,000,000

8573 Pipe End Finishing Equipment & Tooling
PHI
14955 Salt Lake Avenue
City Of Industry, CA 91746-3133   626-968-9680
                              Fax: 626-333-3610
info@phi-tulip.com
www.phi-tulip.com

Tube and pipe bending machines and handling equipment

Catalog Circulation: Mailed 1 time(s) per year
Printing Information: 24 pages in 2 colors
Binding: Saddle Stitched
Number of Employees: 100-
Sales Information: $5,000,000 - $10,000,000

8574 PortaBrace
PortaBrace, Inc.
940 Water Street
PO Box 220
North Bennington, VT 05257-249   802-442-8171
                              Fax: 802-442-9118
info@portabrace.com
www.portabrace.com

Audio cases, camera cases, computers and iPad cases, etc.

Chairman: Thomas Stark
President: Gregg Haythorn
Marketing Manager: Chris Miceli
chris@portabrace.com
Shipping Manager: Craig O'Dell
Sales Manager: Casey Krugman
Credit Cards: MasterCard
Catalog Cost: Free
In Business: 39 years
Number of Employees: 100
Sales Information: $7.9 MM

8575 Porter Punch Catalog
Porter Precision Products
2734 Banning Road
Cincinnati, OH 45253-5504   513-923-3777
                                 800-543-7041
                              Fax: 513-923-1111
porter@porterpunch.com
www.Porterpunch.Com

Die and punch products

President: John Cipriani Jr
CFO: Dale F. Werlaumont
Marketing Manager: Terry L. Wunder
Production Manager: Mike Webb
Catalog Circulation: Mailed 1 time(s) per year
Printing Information: 24 pages in 4 colors
Mailing List Information: Names for rent
In Business: 60 years
Number of Employees: 125
Sales Information: $10MM to $20MM

8576 Powermatic
Jet Tools North America
427 New Sanford Road
La Vergne, TN 37086   847-851-1000
                                 800-274-6848
                              Fax: 847-851-1045
www.jettools.com

Artesian table saw

Founder: Leslie P. Sussman
In Business: 57 years
Number of Employees: 250
Sales Information: $25,000,000 - $50,000,000

8577 Process Measurement Company
Process Measurement Company
5735 Lindsay St
Minneapolis, MN 55422-4655   855-544-0321
                                 800-328-1235
                              Fax: 763-544-5541
www.lakelandcompanies.com/companies/pmc

Instruments, controls and measurement meters

President: Jim Engebretsen
Credit Cards: MasterCard
Catalog Circulation: Mailed 1 time(s) per year

Printing Information: 48 pages in 2 colors
Binding: Saddle Stitched
In Business: 32 years
Sales Information: $3MM to $5MM

8578 Products in, on and Around Concrete

Raw Equipment Building Materials Corp
2800 College Point Boulevard
Flushing, NY 11354-2512 718-461-2200
Fax: 718-762-3094
sales@rawequipment.com
www.rawequipment.com

Concrete accessories

Founder: Richard A. Wallace
Credit Cards: AMEX; MasterCard
Catalog Circulation: Mailed 1 time(s) per year
Printing Information: 35 pages in 2 colors
Binding: Saddle Stitched
In Business: 40 years

8579 Professional Equipment

Grainger
600 N. Lynndale Dr.
Appleton, WI 54914-3021 631-348-3780
800-472-4643
Fax: 888-776-3187
info@professionalequipment.com
www.grainger.com

Tools and testing equipment for the electrical, inspection, HVAC and engineering and building professionals

President: Patrick Norton
Credit Cards: AMEX; MasterCard
Catalog Circulation: Mailed 12 time(s) per year to 1m
Printing Information: 90 pages
Press: Web Press
Binding: Perfect Bound
In Business: 27 years

8580 Protolab

Protolab Extractors
2570 Solano Rd
PO Box 165
Cameron Park, CA 95682-8921 530-677-5593
Fax: 530-677-6779
protolab@directcon.net
www.Protolabextractors.Com

Extracion tools

President: Dan Morris
Credit Cards: AMEX; MasterCard
Sales Information: Under $500M

8581 Pulva Corporation

Pulva Corporation
PO Box 427
Saxonburg, PA 16056-427 724-898-3000
800-878-5828
Fax: 724-898-3192
jenn@pulva.com
www.pulva.com

Impact pulverizers

Credit Cards: AMEX; MasterCard
Catalog Circulation: Mailed 1 time(s) per year
Printing Information: 4 pages in 2 colors
In Business: 77 years
Number of Employees: 20-5
Sales Information: $5,000,000 - $10,000,000

8582 RACO International

RACO International, LP
3350 Industrial Blvd
Bethel Park, PA 15102-2544 412-835-5744
888-289-7226
Fax: 412-835-0338
raco@racointernational.com
www.racointernational.com

Rodless linear actuators, electric linear actuators

President: Michael Bock
Marketing Manager: Paul Kuczma
Production Manager: Ken McGough

Catalog Circulation: Mailed 1 time(s) per year
Printing Information: 16 pages in 2 colors on Glossy Stock
Binding: Saddle Stitched
In Business: 51 years
Sales Information: $3MM to $5MM

8583 Rabbit Tool USA

Rabbit Tool USA
105 9th St
Rock Island, IL 61201-8353 309-793-4375
800-451-8665
Fax: 309-793-4375
info@rabbittool.com
www.rabbittool.com

Precision tools for pipe finishing

President: O J Birkestrand
Catalog Circulation: Mailed 1 time(s) per year
Printing Information: 6 pages on Matte Stock
In Business: 10 years
Number of Employees: 10
Sales Information: $500M to $1MM

8584 Ram Products

Ram Products, Inc.
182 Ridge Road
Suite D
Dayton, NJ 08816 732-651-5500
877-726-7763
Fax: 732-651-6688
ramprodinc@ramprodinc.com
www.ramprodinc.com

Products for manicure and pedicure professionals

In Business: 22 years

8585 Raven Environmental Products

Raven Environmental Products,Inc
448 East Clinton Place
Suite B
Saint Louis, MO 63122-6400 314-822-1197
800-545-6953
Fax: 314-822-9968
dave@ravenep.com
www.ravenep.com

Manufacturer of waste and water plant control equipment

President: Dave Humann
Marketing Manager: Lynn Marshall
Catalog Cost: Free
Catalog Circulation: Mailed 1 time(s) per year
Printing Information: 4 pages in 2 colors on Matte Stock
Binding: Saddle Stitched
In Business: 32 years
Number of Employees: 3
Sales Information: $500M to $1MM

8586 Red Devil

Red Devil, Inc
4175 Webb St
Pryor, OK 74361-6741 918-825-5744
800-4AD-EVIL
Fax: 918-825-5761
info@reddevil.com
www.Reddevil.Com

Hand, tile tools, paint mixing and tinting equipment

President: Craig Cartwright
Credit Cards: AMEX; MasterCard
Catalog Cost: Free
Catalog Circulation: Mailed 1 time(s) per year to 25M
Printing Information: 36 pages in 2 colors on Matte Stock
Press: Web Press
Binding: Saddle Stitched
Mailing List Information: Names for rent
In Business: 141 years
Number of Employees: 125
Sales Information: $20MM to $50MM

8587 Regitar USA

Regitar USA, Inc.
2575 Container Dr
Montgomery, AL 36109-1004 334-244-1885
Fax: 334-244-1901
info@regitar.com
www.Regitar.Com

Power tools, auto parts, ignition moduler, ignition, voltage reulators, rectifiers, ignitions coils, pick-up coils, distributor caps, rotors, diode trio, solenoids, condensers and more

President: Yu-Tueng Tsai
CFO: Chau L Tsai
Marketing Manager: Leo Manni
Production Manager: Ken Jimmerson
Fulfillment: Andrea Naranjo
Buyers: Chau Lee Tsai, Power Tools
Catalog Cost: $5
Catalog Circulation: Mailed 12 time(s) per year to 5000
Average Order Size: $250
Printing Information: 80 pages in 2 colors on Matte Stock
Press: Web Press
Binding: Saddle Stitched
Mailing List Information: Names for rent
List Manager: Yu-Tueng Tsai
In Business: 16 years
Number of Employees: 25
Sales Information: $1,000,000 - $5,000,000

8588 Renbrandt-Flexible Couplings

Renbrandt,Inc
659 Massachusetts Ave
Boston, MA 02118-1821 617-445-8910
800-370-3539
Fax: 617-445-6032
info@renbrandt.com
www.Renbrandt.Com

HP flexible couplings

President: Raymond Renner
Catalog Cost: Free
Catalog Circulation: to 3000
Printing Information: 12 pages in 2 colors
Binding: Saddle Stitched
Mailing List Information: Names for rent
In Business: 64 years
Sales Information: $3MM to $5MM

8589 Renton's

Renton's
637 Wyckoff Ave, Suite 280
Wyckoff NJ, NJ 07481-6411 303-865-7025
800-365-6644
Fax: 800-873-3060
info@rentons.com
www.Rentons.Com

Greeting cards and stickers

Chairman: Jack Renton
President: Dawn Goldwasser
Credit Cards: AMEX; MasterCard
Catalog Cost: Free
Catalog Circulation: Mailed 2 time(s) per year
In Business: 48 years
Sales Information: $1MM to $3MM

8590 Rice Hydro Equipment Manufacturing

Rice Hydro, Inc.
3500 Arrowhead Drive
Carson City, NV 89706 775-885-1280
800-245-4777
Fax: 775-885-1287
info@ricehydro.com
www.ricehydro.com

Hydrostatic test equipment that are designed for underground waterlines

President: Kenneth Alexander
Marketing Manager: Kristine Doherty
Manager: Duane Semon
Secreatry/Treasurer: Marietta Alexander
Catalog Circulation: Mailed 1 time(s) per year
Printing Information: 100 pages in 4 colors
Binding: Saddle Stitched
In Business: 39 years

8591 Ringfeder Arcusaflex Couplings
Ringfeder Power Transmission
165 Carver Ave # 1
PO Box 691
Westwood, NJ 07675-2617　　201-666-3320
　　　　　　　　　　　　　　800-245-2580
　　　　　　　　　　　　Fax: 201-664-6053
　　　　　　　　　　　sales@ringfeder.com
　　　　　　　　　　　www.Ringfeder.Com

Rubber disc couplings; torque Jimiters, friction springs; vibration dampening couplings; flexible disc couplings; rigid couplings
President: Carl W. Fenstermacher
carlf@ringfeeder.com
CEO: Thomas Moka
thomas.moka@ringfeder.com
Supply Chain Manager: Markus Fuchs
markus.fuchs@ringfeeder.com
Catalog Circulation: Mailed 1 time(s) per year
Printing Information: 16 pages in 2 colors
Binding: Saddle Stitched
In Business: 3+ years
Sales Information: $10MM to $20MM

8592 Roberts-Gordon
Roberts-Gordon LLC
P.O.Box 44
Buffalo, NY 14240-44　　　　716-852-4400
　　　　　　　　　　　　　　800-282-7450
　　　　　　　　　　　　Fax: 716-852-0854
　　　　　　　　　　　www.Rg-Inc.Com

Warm air and radiant heaters
Chairman: Paul A Dines
President: Mark J Dines
VP of Technology: Rob Hibbard
In Business: 26 years

8593 Robertshaw Industrial Instrumentation
Robertshaw Industrial Products
1602 Mustang Drive
Maryville, TN 37801-3311　　865-981-3100
　　　　　　　　　　　　　　800-228-7429
　　　　　　　　　　　　Fax: 865-981-3168
　　　　　　　　www.robertshawindustrial.com

Control instrumentation
Catalog Circulation: Mailed 1 time(s) per year
Printing Information: 30 pages in 2 colors
Binding: Perfect Bound

8594 Ronson Technical Products
Ronson Technical Products Division
2146-B Flinstone Drive
PO Box 125
Tucker, GA 30084-800　　　　770-414-8488
　　　　　　　　　　　　　　800-524-0698
　　　　　　　　　　　　Fax: 770-621-9660
　　　　　　　contact@EnergyAndProcess.com
　　　　　　　　www.energyandprocess.com

Fasteners, tubing, steel plates and pipes
Marketing Manager: Tim Moravek
Catalog Circulation: Mailed 1 time(s) per year
Printing Information: 4 pages
In Business: 17 years

8595 Rosedale Products
Rosdedale Products, Inc.
P.O.Box 1085
3730 West Liberty Road
Ann Arbor, MI 48106-1085　　734-665-8201
　　　　　　　　　　　　　　800-821-5373
　　　　　　　　　　　　Fax: 734-665-2214
　　　　　　　filters@rosedaleproducts.com
　　　　　　　　www.Rosedaleproducts.Com

Manufacturers of basket strainers and liquid bag filters
President: Nils Rosaen
Marketing Manager: Lori Petrill
VP Sales: Dan Morosky
General Sales: Michelle Berquist
Literature Representative: Tricia Rosen
Buyers: Rick Allen

Catalog Cost: Free
Catalog Circulation: Mailed 1 time(s) per year
Printing Information: 115 pages in 3 colors on Glossy Stock
Binding: Perfect Bound
In Business: 25 years
Number of Employees: 80
Sales Information: $10 million

8596 Rotor Clip Company
Rotor Clip Company, Inc.
187 Davidson Ave
Somerset, NJ 08873-4192　　732-469-7333
　　　　　　　　　　　　　　800-557-6867
　　　　　　　　　　　　Fax: 732-469-7898
　　　　　　　　　　　www.Rotorclip.Com

Standard internal and external retaining rings, constant section rings, hose clamps and installation tools
President: Robert Slass
Marketing Manager: Joe Cappello
Chief Information Officer: Robert Grinthal
VP of Technology: David Marvuglio
IT Director: David Kwiatkowski
Catalog Cost: Free
Printing Information: 168 pages in 2 colors on Matte Stock
Press: Web Press
Binding: Perfect Bound
Mailing List Information: Names for rent
In Business: 58 years
Number of Employees: 360
Sales Information: $20MM to $50MM

8597 Russell Industries
Russell Industries Inc
40 Horton Ave
Lynbrook, NY 11563　　　　516-536-5000
　　　　　　　　　　　　　　800-645-2202
　　　　　　　　　　　　Fax: 516-764-5747
　　　　　　　　　　　sales@russellind.com
　　　　　　　　　　　www.russellind.com

Rubber belts and custom belt designing, antennas, wire ties, bumpers, grommets, spiderless terminals, heat-shrink tubing, metric nuts and screws, flyback and accessories
President: Adam Russell
Marketing Manager: Neil Eiger
Manager: Stacey Russell
Catalog Cost: Free
Mailing List Information: Names for rent
In Business: 49 years
Number of Employees: 42
Sales Information: $1,000,000 - $5,000,000

8598 S&D Continuous Hinges
S & D Products, Inc.
1390 Schiferl Road
Bartlett, IL 60103-2219　　　630-766-6365
　　　　　　　　　　　　　　800-989-6365
　　　　　　　　　　　　Fax: 630-766-1483
　　　　　　　　　　　sales@sdproducts.com
　　　　　　　　　　　www.sdproducts.com

Hinges and assorted parts
President: David Guanci
VP Operations: Mark Guanci
Sales Manager: Cindy Flora
Secretary: Kathleen Guanci
Catalog Circulation: Mailed 1 time(s) per year
Printing Information: 8 pages in 1 color
Press: Web Press
Binding: Saddle Stitched

8599 SJF Material Handling
SJF Material Handling Inc
211 Baker Ave
P.O.Box 70
Winsted, MN 55395-70　　　320-485-2824
　　　　　　　　　　　　　　800-598-5532
　　　　　　　　　　　　Fax: 320-485-2832
　　　　　　　　　　　support@sjf.com
　　　　　　　　　　　www.Sjf.Com

New, used or reconditioned rack, conveyor, shelving, storage, warehouse and other material handling equipment
President: Frank Sterner
CFO: Tina Goerish
Marketing Manager: Jason Dieter
VP Engineer: Jim Sterner
Engineer: Jim Laliberte
Facility Design and Layout: Matt Johnson
Catalog Cost: Free
Printing Information: 200 pages in 3 colors
In Business: 32 years
Sales Information: $5 million

8600 SSP Product Catalog
SSP Corporation
8250 Boyle Pkwy
Twinsburg, OH 44087-2200　　330-425-4250
　　　　　　　　　　　　　Fax: 330-425-8106
　　　　　　　　　　　　　my-ssp-usa.com

Tube, pipe, hose fittings and valves
President: Raymond W King Jr
CFO: David King
Marketing Manager: Mark Hurt
VP: Richard Cordill
VP Operations: Johnny Keech
Controller: Tony Lucarell
Catalog Cost: Free
Catalog Circulation: to 10000
Printing Information: in 3 colors on Matte Stock
Binding: Perfect Bound
Mailing List Information: Names for rent
In Business: 82 years
Number of Employees: 200

8601 SafeWay Hydraulics
SafeWay Hydraulics, Inc.
5858 Centerville Road
St. Paul, MN 55127　　　　651-925-5620
　　　　　　　　　　　　　　800-222-1169
　　　　　　　　　　　　Fax: 651-653-0989
　　　　　　　　　　　info@safewayhyd.com
　　　　　　　　　　　www.Safewayhyd.Com

Hydraulic quick couplings
President: Daniel McKeown
Manager: Torbjorn Carlsen
Quality Control Manager: Paul Bennyhoff
Purchasing Agent: Cindy Sons
Catalog Circulation: Mailed 1 time(s) per year
Printing Information: 27 pages in 2 colors
Binding: Perfect Bound
In Business: 46 years
Sales Information: $20 million

8602 Slingmax
Slingmax, Inc.
205 Bridgewater Road
Aston, PA 19014-423　　　　610-485-8500
　　　　　　　　　　　　　　800-874-3539
　　　　　　　　　　　　Fax: 610-494-5835
　　　　　　　　　　　info@slingmax.com
　　　　　　　　　　　www.slingmax.com

All types of rigging gears and patented products
Credit Cards: MasterCard
Catalog Circulation: Mailed 1 time(s) per year
Printing Information: 130 pages
Binding: Perfect Bound
In Business: 29 years

8603 Snap-On Tools
Snap-on Incorporated
2801 80th Street
Kenosha, WI 53141　　　　877-762-7664
　　　　　　　　　　　　　877-777-8455
　　　　　　　　　　　store.snapon.com

Hand tools, auto tools
Chairman: Jack Michaels
President: Alan Biland
Marketing Manager: Andrew Ginger
Chief Information Officer: Jeanne Moreno
Vice President, Investor Relations: Leslie H.

Kratcoski
leslie.h.kratcoski@snapon.com
Credit Cards: AMEX; MasterCard; Visa
Catalog Circulation: Mailed 1 time(s) per year
Printing Information: 800 pages in 4 colors
In Business: 96 years
Number of Employees: 295
Sales Information: $51.90 MM

8604 Snyder Industries
Snyder Industries, Inc.
6940 O Street
Suite 100
Lincoln, NE 68504-583   402-467-5221
                               Fax: 402-465-1220
                               info@snydernet.com
                               www.Snydernet.Com

Manufacture rotational molded tanks and containers from cross linked polyolefin

President: Tom O'Connell
Catalog Circulation: Mailed 1 time(s) per year
Printing Information: 36 pages in 2 colors
Binding: Saddle Stitched
In Business: 58 years

8605 Solberg Manufacturers Catalog
Solberg Manufacturing, Inc
1151 Ardmore Ave
Itasca, IL 60143-1387   630-773-1363
                               Fax: 630-773-0727
                               sales@solbergmfg.com
                               www.Solbergmfg.Com

Manufacture filter silencers, filter breathers and filters for air compressors

President: Charles Solberg Jr
Printing Information: 60 pages
Sales Information: $20MM to $50MM

8606 Speed Tools
Swanson Tool Co., Inc.
211 Ontario Street
Frankfort, IL 60423-1662   815-469-9453
                               Fax: 815-469-4575
                               info@swansontoolco.com

Multi-function tools and accessories

Printing Information: 8 pages in 4 colors
In Business: 88 years

8607 Spokane Hardware Supply
Spokane Hardware Supply, Inc.
2001 E. Trent
PO Box 2664
Spokane, WA 99220-2664   509-535-1663
                               800-888-1663
                               Fax: 801-838-5179
                               www.spokane-hardware.com

Hardware

President: Steve Northrop
Marketing Manager: StephanieWiller
VP: Rick Reinbold
Operations Manager: Andrew Northrop
Controller: Alan Grimsrud
Catalog Cost: Free
In Business: 74 years

8608 Stafford Manufacturing Corporation
Stafford Manufacturing Corp.
256 Andover St.
Wilmington, MA 01887-277   978-657-8000
                               800-695-5551
                               Fax: 978-657-4731
                               sales@staffordmfg.com
                               www.staffordmfg.com

Clamp-type shaft collars and couplings and related mechanical components to the power transmission industry

Marketing Manager: Laurie Mann
Production Manager: Jim Swiezynski
Catalog Cost: Free
Catalog Circulation: to 10K
Average Order Size: $15
Printing Information: 32 pages in 4 colors on

Glossy Stock
Binding: Saddle Stitched
Mailing List Information: Names for rent
In Business: 39 years
Number of Employees: 40

8609 Standard Industrial Products Company
SIPCO-MLS
12610 Galveston Rd.
Webster
Houston, TX 77598-325   281-480-8711
                               Fax: 281-480-8656
                               sales@sipco-mls.com
                               www.Sipco.Com

Supplies gear reducers, speed drives, gear motors and eletric motors

President: Tom Jones
In Business: 29 years
Sales Information: $5MM to $10MM

8610 Standard Rubber Products
Standard Rubber Products Co.
120 Seegers Avenue
Elk Grove Vlg, IL 60007-797   847-593-5630
                               800-333-6322
                               Fax: 847-593-5634
                               info@srpco.com
                               www.Srpco.Com

Listing of rubbers products ranging from die cutting and molding to standard industrial products

President: Larry Gualano
In Business: 63 years
Sales Information: $20MM to $50MM

8611 Stephen Bader and Company
Stephen Bader Co., Inc.
10 Charles Street
Valley Falls, NY 12185-297   518-753-4456
                               Fax: 518-753-4962
                               www.Stephenbader.Com

Grinding and polishing machinery, contact wheels and accessories

President: Daniel Johnson
Printing Information: 6 pages in 2 colors
Binding: Folded
Mailing List Information: Names for rent
In Business: 45 years
Number of Employees: 15
Sales Information; $1MM to $3MM

8612 Stimpson Company
Stimpson Company
1515 SW 13th Court
Pompano Beach, FL 33069-4789 954-946-3500
                               877-765-0748
                               Fax: 954-545-7440
                               customer_service@stimpson.com
                               www.stimpsonco.com

Rivets, fasteners, hole plugs and attaching machines

President: Janice Hulbert
Catalog Cost: Free
Printing Information: 10 pages in 4 colors
In Business: 164 years
Number of Employees: 350
Sales Information: $25,000,000 - $50,000,000

8613 Subminiature Instruments Corporation
Subminiature Instruments Corp.
2147 N. Rulon White Blvd.
Suite 106
Ogden, UT 84404-3467   801-392-8557
                               Fax: 801-392-8624
                               subinstruments@gmail.com
                               www.subminiatureinstruments.com

Precision rotary and linear motion equipment

In Business: 56 years

8614 Sunhill Insider
Sunhill Machinery
1208 Andover Park E
Seattle, WA 98188-3905   206-575-4131
                               800-929-4321
                               Fax: 206-575-3617
                               www.sunhillmachinery.com

Woodworking machinery and accessories

Credit Cards: AMEX; MasterCard
Printing Information: 6 pages in 2 colors
Number of Employees: 15

8615 Super Shop
Superfuture Corporation
150 West 25th Street
Room 1002
New York, NY 10001-7458   646-480-0732
                               800-476-4849
                               super@superfuture.com
                               www.superfuture.com

Combination of woodworking tools

Producer: Wayne Berkowitz
Editorial: Simon Kristoph Harvey
Editor: Andreas Mueller
Printing Information: 24 pages
In Business: 16 years

8616 Superior Pneumatic Air Tools
Superior Pneumatic
PO Box 40420
Cleveland, OH 44140-420   440-871-8780
                               800-521-2282
                               Fax: 440-871-5127
                               airtools@superiorpneumatic.com
                               www.superiorpneumatic.com

Air hammers, needle scalers, Pittsburgh lock seam tools, grinders, drills and sanders

In Business: 83 years

8617 Swiss Precision Instruments
Swiss Precision Instrument, Inc.
11450 Markon Drive
Garden Grove, CA 92841-3135   888-774-8200
                               Fax: 800-842-5164
                               sales@swissprec.com
                               www.swissprec.com

Machinists/metalwork instruments and tools

President: Allan Newman
CFO: Marc Serlin
Credit Cards: MasterCard
Catalog Cost: Free
Catalog Circulation: Mailed 1 time(s) per year
Printing Information: 432 pages in 1 color
In Business: 58 years
Number of Employees: 22

8618 T&J Incorporated
T. J. Incorporated
24612 E. Colonial Drive
Christmas, FL 32709-3128   407-568-1112
                               Fax: 407-568-0455
                               www.tjinc-eng.com

Used machinery

President: Anthony Miniea
Printing Information: 32 pages in 4 colors
In Business: 21 years
Sales Information: $1MM to $3MM

8619 TP Tools & Equipment
TP Tools & Equipment
7075 State Route 446
PO Box 649
Canfield, OH 44406-649   330-533-3384
                               800-321-9260
                               Fax: 330-533-2876
                               www.tptools.com

Supplier of restoration and auto body repair tools

President: Robert Zwicker
Credit Cards: AMEX; MasterCard
Sales Information: $1MM to $3MM

8620 TP Tools and Equipment
TP Tools & Equipment
7075 State Route 446
PO Box 649
Canfield, OH 44406-649   330-533-3384
800-321-9260
Fax: 330-533-2876
www.tptools.com

Abrasive blasting cabinets, turbines, air compressors, air tools, auto tools and equipment, paint spray guns, and safety items

Credit Cards: AMEX; MasterCard
Printing Information: 156 pages

8621 TandemLoc
TANDEMLOC, Inc.
824 Highway 101
Havelock, NC 28532-3117   252-447-7155
800-258-7324
Fax: 800-892-3273
info@tandemloc.com
www.tandemloc.com

Container lift equipment and fittings

President: John M Di Martino Sr
Marketing Manager: John Di Martino
Founder: John 'Mike' DiMartino
Credit Cards: AMEX; MasterCard
Catalog Circulation: Mailed 1 time(s) per year
Printing Information: 16 pages in 2 colors
Binding: Saddle Stitched
In Business: 29 years
Sales Information: $3MM to $5MM

8622 Tapeswitch Corporation
Tapeswitch Corporation
100 Schmitt Blvd
Farmingdale, NY 11735-1482   631-630-0442
800-234-8273
Fax: 631-630-0454
sales@tapeswitch.com
www.Tapeswitch.Com

Manufacturer of presence sensing industrial switching mats, sensing edges and bumpers, press-at-any-point Controlflex ribbon switches, interface controllers and photo-electric curtain systems

President: Michael Steele
Marketing Manager: Nicole Allison
Production Manager: Marge Wisan
Founder: Robert Koening
Director of Finance: Marie Collins
Operations Manager: Frank Pitrelli
Mailing List Information: Names for rent
In Business: 55 years
Number of Employees: 90
Sales Information: $10,000,000 - $25,000,000

8623 Technical Manufacturing Corporation
Techical Manufacturing Corporation
15 Centennial Drive
Peabody, MA 01960-7993   978-532-6330
800-542-9725
Fax: 978-531-8682
sales@techmfg.com
www.Techmfg.Com

Solutions to problems caused by ambient building floor vibration

President: Ulf B Heide

8624 Technobrands
TMC-Ametek
15 Centennial Drive
Peabody, MA 01960-5913   978-532-6330
800-542-9725
Fax: 978-531-8682
sales@techmfg.com
www.Techmfg.Com

Gadgets, gizmos and high-tech products

8625 Terracon Corporation
Terracon Corporation
1376 West Central Street
Suite 130
Franklin, MA 02038-7100   508-429-9950
Fax: 508-429-8737
www.terracon-solutions.com

Tanks and related equipment

President: Richard Jewett
Catalog Cost: Free
Printing Information: 30 pages in 2 colors
In Business: 20 years
Sales Information: $5MM to $10MM

8626 Terramite Corporation
TerraQuip Construction Products, Inc.
600 Goff Mountain Rd
Cross Lanes, WV 25313-146   304-776-4231
800-428-3772
Fax: 304-776-4845
sales@terramite.com
www.terramite.com

Street sweepers, loaders, and compact tractor loader backhoes, concrete screeds

President: Bob Bristow
Marketing Manager: Barbara Cavender
Founder: Kelly G. Cunningham
Catalog Circulation: Mailed 52 time(s) per year
Printing Information: 468 pages in 4 colors
Binding: Saddle Stitched
In Business: 48 years
Number of Employees: 100
Sales Information: $25,000,000 - $50,000,000

8627 Time Motion Tools
Time and Motion
PO Box 547
Mittagong, CA 92064-6810   024-861-7265
800-779-8170
Fax: 028-246-6624
info@timemotion.com.au
www.Timemotion.Com

Quality tools and voice data telecom test equipment

President: Edward Durfey
Buyers: Shelda Auditett
Credit Cards: AMEX; MasterCard; Visa
Catalog Cost: Free
Catalog Circulation: Mailed 6 time(s) per year to 800K
Average Order Size: $275
Printing Information: 200 pages in 4 colors on Glossy Stock
Press: Web Press
Binding: Perfect Bound
Mailing List Information: Names for rent
List Manager: Ofelia Pereira
In Business: 40 years
Number of Employees: 50
Sales Information: $20MM to $50MM

8628 Timken Company
The Timken Company
4500 Mount Pleasant NW
North Canton, OH 44720   234-262-3000
800-223-1954
Fax: 330-458-6006
www.Timken.Com

Roller bearings

President: Richard G. Kyle
CFO: Philip D. Fracassa
Marketing Manager: Erik A Paulhardt
Vice President, Operations: Richard M. Boyer
Vice President, Quality: Ajay Das
EVP, Group President: Christopher A. Coughlin
In Business: 115 years
Number of Employees: 7000

8629 Titan Tool Supply Company
Titan Tool Supply
68 Comet Ave.
Buffalo, NY 14216-569   716-873-9907
Fax: 716-873-9998
info@titantoolsupply.com
www.Titantoolsupply.Com

Compasses, buffing and polishing compounds

President: Frank Menza
Catalog Circulation: Mailed 1 time(s) per year
Printing Information: 112 pages in 2 colors
Binding: Perfect Bound
In Business: 63 years
Sales Information: $1MM to $3MM

8630 Tocos America
TOCOS America, Inc.
1177 East Tower Road
Schaumburg, IL 60173-4305   847-884-6664
Fax: 847-884-6665
sales@tocos.com
www.Tocos.Com

Panel potentiometers, trimming potentiometers and related developmental equipment

President: John Shimizu
Catalog Circulation: Mailed 1 time(s) per year
Printing Information: 113 pages in 4 colors
Binding: Saddle Stitched
In Business: 58 years
Sales Information: $10MM to $20MM

8631 Tri-Motion Industrial
Tri-Motion Industries, Inc.
5688 West Crenshaw Street
Tampa, FL 33634-3043   813-884-6600
813-884-6600
Fax: 813-884-6800
sales@trimotionindustries.com
www.Trimotionindustries.Com

Pneumatic tool balances and lift assistants

President: Oliver Van Keuren
Marketing Manager: Don Skidmore
Credit Cards: AMEX; MasterCard; Visa
Catalog Cost: Free
Catalog Circulation: Mailed 1 time(s) per year
Printing Information: in 1 color
In Business: 35 years
Number of Employees: 27
Sales Information: $1,000,000 - $5,000,000

8632 Triad Controls
Triad Controls, Inc.
3715 Swenson Avenue
St. Charles, IL 60174-306   630-443-9320
800-851-2026
Fax: 630-443-9346
service@triadcontrols.com
www.triadcontrols.com

Machinery guards and controls

President: F Gary Kovac
Number of Employees: 30

8633 Tyler Machinery Company
Warsaw Machinery, Inc.
610 South Detroit Street
Warsaw, IN 46580-4407   574-267-5355
Fax: 574-267-5366
www.warsawmachinery.com

Industrial woodworking machinery

President: David Tyler
Number of Employees: 30
Sales Information: $1,000,000 - $5,000,000

8634 UMG Technologies, Inc.
UMG Technologies, Inc.
6A Electronics Avenue
Danvers, MA 01923-1008   978-739-1555
Fax: 978-739-1546
sales@umgtinc.com
www.Umgtinc.Com

Designs, manufactures and sells a variety of assembly interconnect machinery solutions

President: Ernest Roberts
Catalog Circulation: to 3000
Printing Information: 4 pages in 4 colors
Sales Information: $10MM to $20MM

8635 US Crane
United States Crane, Inc.
1155 Central Florida Parkway
P.O. Box 593290
Orlando, FL 32837-9258
407-859-6000
800-327-0300
Fax: 407-857-9146
information@supercage.com
www.Supercage.Com

Materials handling equipment and related supplies; Supercage/Superclamp

President: Julia Ames
Catalog Circulation: Mailed 1 time(s) per year to 1000
In Business: 49 years
Number of Employees: 36
Sales Information: $5MM to $10MM

8636 US Industrial Tool
US Industrial Tool & Supply Company
14083 S. Normandie Ave
Gardena, CA 90249
310-464-8400
800-521-7394
Fax: 310-464-8880
info@ustool.com
www.ustool.com

Aircraft tools, hand tools and sheetmetal tools

President: Mark Marinovich
Founder: William Marinovich
Credit Cards: MasterCard
Catalog Cost: Free
Catalog Circulation: to 30m
Printing Information: 188 pages in 4 colors on Glossy Stock
Binding: Saddle Stitched
Mailing List Information: Names for rent
In Business: 59 years
Number of Employees: 47
Sales Information: $5,000,000 - $10,000,000

8637 USABlue Book
USABlue Book
3781 Bur Wood Drive
Waukegan, IL 60085-9006
847-689-3000
800-548-1234
Fax: 847-689-3030
management@usabluebook.com
www.usabluebook.com

Supplies, equipment and parts used in water and sewer utilities

President: John Berry
Marketing Manager: Joyce Kendall
Production Manager: Kate Hall
International Marketing Manager: Bill Graham
Catalog Cost: Free
Catalog Circulation: Mailed 1 time(s) per year to 50000
Average Order Size: $350
Printing Information: 1760 pages in 4 colors on Newsprint
Press: Web Press
Binding: Perfect Bound
Mailing List Information: Names for rent
In Business: 24 years
Number of Employees: 65
Sales Information: $20MM to $50MM

8638 Ultimate HVAC and Door Products
Ultimate Supplies, LLC
2400 Alwin Court
Raleigh, NC 27604-1429
919-836-1627
800-542-7221
Fax: 919-834-4526
www.Ultimate-Products.Com

Car wash products, greenhouse heaters and equipment

President: Dean Debnam
CFO: Lou Boucher
Credit Cards: MasterCard; Visa
Catalog Cost: Free
Printing Information: 20 pages
Mailing List Information: Names for rent
In Business: 10 years
Number of Employees: 30
Sales Information: $5MM to $10MM

8639 United Testing Systems
United Calibration Corporation
5802 Engineer Drive
Huntington Beach, CA 92649-2954
714-638-2322
800-765-9997
Fax: 714-897-8496
infounited@tensiletest.com
www.Tensiletest.Com

Ten individual Bulletins of materials testing equipment

President: Bill Brown
Marketing Manager: Mark Shaffer
Printing Information: 16 pages in 4 colors
In Business: 51 years
Sales Information: $3MM to $5MM

8640 VOSSTechnologies SingleSample
Voss Technologies
4235 Centergate Street
San Antonio, TX 78217-4802
210-650-3124
800-247-6294
Fax: 210-650-8032
vosstec@aol.com
www.vosstech.com

Disposable bailers, coliwasas, and accessories

Printing Information: 10 pages
Binding: Saddle Stitched
In Business: 26 years

8641 Vacmasters of Denver
VACMASTERS
5879 W 58th Avenue
Arvada, CO 80002-2814
303-467-3801
800-466-7825
Fax: 303-420-3971
www.vacmasters.com

Vacuum digging technology

Catalog Circulation: Mailed 1 time(s) per year
Printing Information: 4 pages in 2 colors
Binding: Saddle Stitched
In Business: 60 years

8642 Van F Belknap
Van F. Belknap Co., Inc.
29164 Wall Street
Wixom, MI 48393-3524
248-348-7800
Fax: 248-348-9821
sales@belknaptools.com
www.belknaptools.com

Light and heavy duty torque control tools

President: MWThorn
Printing Information: 34 pages in 2 colors
In Business: 79 years

8643 Vanton Centrifugal/Rotary/Sump Pumps
Vanton Pump & Equipment Corp.
201 Sweetland Avenue
Hillside, NJ 07205-1756
908-688-4216
Fax: 908-686-9314
mkt@vanton.com
www.Vanton.Com

Centrifugal, rotary, and sump pumps

President: Gerald R Lewis
Catalog Circulation: Mailed 1 time(s) per year
Printing Information: 12 pages in 2 colors
Binding: Saddle Stitched
In Business: 65 years
Sales Information: $10MM to $20MM

8644 Ver Sales Catalog
Ver Sales, Inc.
2509 North Naomi St.
Burbank, CA 91504-3236
818-567-3000
800-229-0518
Fax: 818-567-3018
sales@versales.com
www.Versales.Com

Cable, chain and rope products

President: Gloria Ryan
Printing Information: 146 pages
Binding: Perfect Bound
Sales Information: $20MM to $50MM

8645 Vibrac Corporation Catalog
Vibrac, LLC
19 Columbia Drive
Amherst, NH 03031-2304
603-882-6777
Fax: 603-886-3857
sales@vibrac.com
www.Vibrac.Com

Precision torque measuring systems and sensors

President: Thomas Rogers
trogers@vibrac.com
Marketing Manager: Lisa Rogers
Production Manager: Scott Whipple
Production Manager: Scott Whipple
swhipple@vibrac.com
Operations/HR: Lisa Rogers
lrogers@vibrac.com
VP, Engineering: Bob Searle
rsearle@vibrac.com
Buyers: Paula Bouley
Mailing List Information: Names for rent
In Business: 55 years
Number of Employees: 16
Sales Information: $3MM to $5MM

8646 Victor Machinery Exchange
Victor Machinery Exchange Inc
33-53 62nd St.
Woodside, NY 11377-3817
718-899-1502
800-723-5359
Fax: 718-899-0556
sales@victornet.com
www.victornet.com

Metal working tools

President: Marc Freidus
Credit Cards: AMEX; MasterCard; Visa
Catalog Cost: Free
Catalog Circulation: Mailed 1 time(s) per year to 70000
Printing Information: 136 pages in 4 colors on Glossy Stock
Binding: Saddle Stitched
Mailing List Information: Names for rent
In Business: 97 years
Number of Employees: 10
Sales Information: $1MM to $3MM

8647 WESPUR
WesSpur Tree Equipment, Inc.
2121 Iron St
Bellingham, WA 98225-7602
360-734-5242
800-268-2141
Fax: 360-733-6311
www.Wesspur.Com

Climbing gear, chippers, stump grinders

President: Ryan Aarstol
Printing Information: 180 pages
In Business: 32 years
Sales Information: $3MM to $5MM

8648 WL Fuller
W.L. Fuller Co., Inc.
7 Cypress St
PO Box 8767
Warwick, RI 02888-767
401-467-2900
Fax: 401-467-2905
info@wlfuller.com
www.wlfuller.com

Countersinks, counterbores, plug cutters, taper point drills, brad point drills and step drills, also specials

President: Diane Nobel
CFO: Gary Fuller
Marketing Manager: Debbie Fuller
Production Manager: Andrew Henninger
Fulfillment: Debbie Fuller
Buyers: Sandy Fuller
Credit Cards: MasterCard; Visa; Discover
Catalog Cost: Free
Printing Information: 152 pages on Matte Stock
Press: Web Press
Binding: Perfect Bound
Mailing List Information: Names for rent
In Business: 63 years
Number of Employees: 60
Sales Information: $10MM to $20MM

8649 Water Quality Testing Products

LaMotte Company
802 Washington Ave
PO Box 329
Chestertown, MD 21620   410-778-3100
                                800-344-3100
                          Fax: 410-778-6394
                          mkt@lamotte.com
                          www.lamotte.com

Waste plant treatment products; test kits, instruments and reagants for water analysis

President: David LaMotte
Marketing Manager: James Moore
Production Manager: Libby Woolever
Catalog Circulation: Mailed 1 time(s) per year to 5000
Printing Information: 100 pages in 4 colors on Glossy Stock
Press: Sheetfed Press
Binding: Perfect Bound
Mailing List Information: Names for rent
In Business: 96 years
Number of Employees: 120

8650 Weltronic/Technitron

Welding Technology Corporation
24775 Crestview Court
Farmington Hills, MI 48335-2075   248-477-3900
                                   800-369-2502
                          Fax: 248-477-8897
                          www.weldtechcorp.com

Resistance welding controls

President: D Miller
Marketing Manager: M Defalco
In Business: 79 years
Number of Employees: 100
Sales Information: $10,000,000 - $25,000,000

8651 Whirlwind

Whirlwind
99 Link Road
Dallas, TX 14612-1021   585-663-8820
                                800-733-9473
                          Fax: 585-865-8930
                          techsupport@whirlwindusa.com
                          www.whirlwindusa.com

Cut-off saws, measuring system, edge belt sander and digital stop systems

President: Michael Laiacona
michael@whirlwindusa.com
Marketing Manager: Robert Ramsden
GM/Customer Support: Al Keltz
alk@whirlwindusa.com
Marketing Director/Artist Relations: Will Young
willy@whirlwindusa.com
Disital/Southeast Sales: JoeBarnes
joeb@whirlwindusa.com
Printing Information: in 4 colors on Glossy Stock
Mailing List Information: Names for rent
In Business: 22 years
Number of Employees: 10
Sales Information: $1,000,000 - $5,000,000

8652 White Cap Industries

White Cap Industries
408 E University Drive
Phoenix, AZ 85004-2923   602-256-6900
                                800-944-8322
                          Fax: 602-256-6067
                          www.whitecapdirect.com

Wholesale contractor and supplies company, full line of all contruction equipment, hardware, tools and materials

Credit Cards: AMEX; MasterCard
Catalog Cost: Free
In Business: 38 years
Number of Employees: 24

8653 Wholesale Tool Catalog

Wholesale Tool Co Inc
12155 Stephens Dr.
PO Box 68
Warren, MI 48090-68   586-754-9270
                              800-521-3420
                          Fax: 800-521-3661
                          wtmich@aol.com
                          www.Wttool.Com

Industrial distribution of cutting tools, precision tools, machinery, machine tool accesories, hand tools and power tools

President: Mark Dowdy
Buyers: Dan Knecht
Credit Cards: AMEX; MasterCard
Catalog Cost: $3
Catalog Circulation: Mailed 1 time(s) per year to 55 K
Printing Information: 804 pages in 2 colors on Matte Stock
Press: Web Press
Binding: Perfect Bound
Mailing List Information: Names for rent
In Business: 169 years
Number of Employees: 110
Sales Information: $10MM to $20MM

8654 Wood-Mizer Products Catalog

Wood-Mizer Products Inc
8180 W 10th St
Indianapolis, IN 46214-2430   317-271-1542
                                 800-553-0182
                          Fax: 317-273-1011
                          infocenter@woodmizer.com
                          www.woodmizer.com

Saw mills, tools and edges

President: Dave Mann
In Business: 33 years
Number of Employees: 344
Sales Information: $20MM to $50MM

8655 Woodcraft Supply Catalog

Woodcraft Supply LLC
P.O. Box 1686
Parkersburg, WV 26102-1686   304-422-5412
                                800-535-4486
                          Fax: 304-422-5417
                          custserv@woodcraft.com
                          www.woodcraft.com

Woodworking supplies and books, clock parts, musical movements, glass domes, specialty tools and plans

Chairman: Samuel Ross
President: Jeffrey Forbes
International Marketing Manager: Tim Rinehart
Catalog Cost: Free
Catalog Circulation: Mailed 12 time(s) per year
Printing Information: 176 pages in 4 colors
In Business: 89 years
Number of Employees: 75
Sales Information: $ 38 Million

Work Apparel & Uniforms
General

8656 5.11 Tactical

5.11 Inc.
4300 Spyres Way
Modesto, CA 95356-9259   209-527-4511
                                866-451-1726
                          Fax: 209-527-1511
                          www.511tactical.com

Tactical apparel for law enforcement, military, EMS and firefighters.

President: Francisco Morales
CFO: Jeff Hamilton
CEO: Dan Costa
Credit Cards: AMEX; MasterCard; Visa
Catalog Cost: Free
Printing Information: 180 pages
Number of Employees: 180
Sales Information: $ 8.7 Million

8657 Algy Team Collection

Algy
440 NE First Avenue
Hallandale, FL 33009   954-457-8100
                               800-458-2549
                          Fax: 888-928-2282
                          customerservice@algyteam.com
                          www.algyteam.com

Costumes and marching band uniforms

Chairman: Herbert Lieberman
President: Susan Gordon
CFO: Laurie Godbout
Chief Executive Officer: Sue Gordon
Credit Cards: AMEX; MasterCard
Catalog Cost: Free
Catalog Circulation: Mailed 2 time(s) per year to 50000
Printing Information: 102 pages in 4 colors on Glossy Stock
Press: Sheetfed Press
Binding: Perfect Bound
Mailing List Information: Names for rent
In Business: 75 years
Number of Employees: 55
Sales Information: $10-20 Million

8658 Alphabroder Buyer's Guide

alphabroder
6 Neshaminy Interplex
6th Floor
Trevose, PA 19053   800-523-4585
                          www.alphabroder.com

Imprintable apparel and accessories for the promotional industry.

CEO: Norman Hullinger
Catalog Cost: Free
Printing Information: 632 pages in 4 colors
Mailing List Information: Names for rent
Number of Employees: 2200
Sales Information: $1.5 Billion

8659 Ansell Protective Products

Ansell Healthcare
111 Wood Avenue South
Suite 210
Iselin, NJ 08830-4952   732-345-5400
                                800-800-0444
                          Fax: 800-800-0445
                          info@ansell.com
                          www.ansellpro.com

Protective aprons, sleeves, vests and rainwear

Marketing Manager: John Iachini
Production Manager: Terry Walker
Fulfillment: Susan Wilson
Catalog Circulation: Mailed 2 time(s) per year
Printing Information: in 4 colors
Mailing List Information: Names for rent
In Business: 20 years
Number of Employees: 100-
Sales Information: $10,000,000 - $25,000,000

8660 BSN Sports Equipment
BSN Sports
PO Box 7726
Dallas, TX 75209
800-856-3488
Fax: 800-899-0149
www.bsnsports.com

Team apparel and equipment for team sports, facilities and physical education.

Chair & CEO: Adam Blumenfeld
President, COO & General Counsel: Terry Babilla
Catalog Cost: Free
Printing Information: 412 pages in 4 colors
In Business: 44 years
Number of Employees: 1200
Sales Information: $500 Million

8661 BSN Sports Lacrosse
BSN Sports
PO Box 7726
Dallas, TX 75209
800-856-3488
Fax: 800-899-0149
www.bsnsports.com

Gear, apparel and game equipment.

Chair & CEO: Adam Blumenfeld
President, COO & General Counsel: Terry Babilla
Catalog Cost: Free
Printing Information: 82 pages in 4 colors
In Business: 44 years
Number of Employees: 1200
Sales Information: $500 Million

8662 BSN Sports League
BSN Sports
PO Box 7726
Dallas, TX 75209
800-856-3488
Fax: 800-899-0149
www.bsnsports.com

Team sports apparel and equipment.

Chair & CEO: Adam Blumenfeld
President, COO & General Counsel: Terry Babilla
Catalog Cost: Free
Printing Information: 388 pages in 4 colors
In Business: 44 years
Number of Employees: 1200
Sales Information: $500 Million

8663 BSN Sports Middle School-Junior High
BSN Sports
PO Box 7726
Dallas, TX 75209
800-856-3488
Fax: 800-899-0149
www.bsnsports.com

Team sports apparel and equipment.

Chair & CEO: Adam Blumenfeld
President, COO & General Counsel: Terry Babilla
Catalog Cost: Free
Printing Information: 68 pages in 4 colors
In Business: 44 years
Number of Employees: 1200
Sales Information: $500 Million

8664 BSN Sports Team-Work
BSN Sports
PO Box 7726
Dallas, TX 75209
800-856-3488
Fax: 800-899-0149
www.bsnsports.com/brandingsolutions

Corporate apparel, workwear and promotional items.

Chair & CEO: Adam Blumenfeld
President, COO & General Counsel: Terry Babilla
Catalog Cost: Free
Printing Information: 48 pages in 4 colors
In Business: 44 years
Number of Employees: 1200
Sales Information: $500 Million

8665 BSN Sports TeamWear
BSN Sports
PO Box 7726
Dallas, TX 75209
800-856-3488
Fax: 800-899-0149
www.bsnsports.com

Team apparel

Chair & CEO: Adam Blumenfeld
President, COO & General Counsel: Terry Babilla
Catalog Cost: Free
Printing Information: 272 pages in 4 colors
In Business: 44 years
Number of Employees: 1200
Sales Information: $500 Million

8666 Bates Leathers
Bates Leathers
3671 Industry Ave
Unit C5
Lakewood, CA 90712
562-426-8668
Fax: 562-426-4001
info@batesleathers.com
www.batesleathers.Com

Leather clothing accessories including hats and gloves

President: Dawn Grindle
Catalog Cost: $5
Catalog Circulation: Mailed 1 time(s) per year
Printing Information: 8 pages in 1 color on Glossy Stock
Binding: Saddle Stitched
Mailing List Information: Names for rent
In Business: 50 years
Number of Employees: 15
Sales Information: $ 3-5 Million

8667 Benchmark Industrial Supply
Benchmark Industrial Supply
1913 Commerce Road
Springfield, OH 45502-367
937-325-1001
877-975-2726
Fax: 937-328-6477
robin@benchmarkindustrial.com
www.Benchmarkindustrial.Com

Work gloves, disposable clothing and uniforms

President: Mary Walling
Marketing Manager: Daniel Lough
Production Manager: Samuel Shirey
Co-Founder: Patty Walling
Co-Founder: Claire Williamson
Printing Information: in 1 color
In Business: 12 years
Number of Employees: 4
Sales Information: $10MM to $20MM

8668 Bodek & Rhodes
alphabroder
6 Neshaminy Interplex
6th Floor
Trevose, PA 19053
800-523-4585
www.alphabroder.com

Imprintable apparel and accessories for the promotional industry.

CEO: Norman Hullinger
Catalog Cost: Free
Printing Information: 532 pages in 4 colors
Number of Employees: 2200
Sales Information: $1.5 Billion

8669 CC Filson Company
Filson
PO Box 34020
Seattle, WA 98124
866-860-8906
800-624-0201
www.filson.com

Rugged outdoor clothing and accessories

President: Stan Kohls
Marketing Manager: Amy Terai
Manager, Sales Department: Dan Drust
Credit Cards: AMEX; MasterCard; Visa

Catalog Cost: Free
Catalog Circulation: Mailed 2 time(s) per year
Printing Information: 103 pages in 4 colors
In Business: 115 years
Number of Employees: 150
Sales Information: $10 Million

8670 Cabela's Corporate Outfitter
Cabela's Inc.
One Cabela Dr.
Sidney, NE 69160
www.cabelas.com

CFO: Ralph Castner
CEO: Thomas Millner
COO: Michael Copeland
Catalog Cost: Free
Catalog Circulation: Mailed 6 time(s) per year
Printing Information: in 4 colors
List Company: Chilcutt Direct
In Business: 55 years
Sales Information: $3 Billion

8671 Cairns & Brother Fire Helmets
MSA Safety Company
1000 Cranberry Woods Drive
Cranberry Twp, PA 16066
877-672-3473
Fax: 877-672-3930
info.us@msasafety.com
us.msasafety.com/

Manufacturer of protective helmets and clothing for firefighters and general industrial protective clothing

President: William M. Lambert
CFO: Stacy McMahan
President, MSA North America: Nishan J. Vartanian
President, MSA International: Kerry M. Bove
VP, Global Operational Excellence: Steven C. Blanco
Catalog Cost: Free
In Business: 101 years
Number of Employees: 5300

8672 Cardinal Jackets
Cardinal Activewear
P.O. Box 1029
Grundy, VA 24614
800-647-7745
Fax: 276-935-4970
info@cardinalactivewear.com
www.cardinalactivewear.com

Nylon coach's windbreakers; Satin baseball jackets; Nylon baseball jackets; Nylon hooded pullover jacket; Mesh lined micro-twill windshirt

President: Mark Shortridge
CFO: Laura Barden
Marketing Manager: Mark Shortridge/Teresa Damron
Buyers: Teresa Damron
Credit Cards: AMEX; MasterCard; Visa
Catalog Cost: Free
Catalog Circulation: to 400m
Printing Information: 4 pages in 4 colors
Mailing List Information: Names for rent
In Business: 40 years
Number of Employees: 4
Sales Information: $110 Thousand

8673 Champaign Plastics Company
Champaign Plastics Company
PO Box 6413
Champaign, IL 61826-6413
217-359-3664
800-575-0170
Fax: 217-359-0091
products1@champaignplastics.com
www.champaignplastics.com

Aprons, disposable gloves and protective clothing

President: Donna Williams
Credit Cards: AMEX; MasterCard
Catalog Circulation: Mailed 12 time(s) per year
Printing Information: 5 pages

In Business: 32 years
Number of Employees: 10-J
Sales Information: Under $500,000

8674 Chefwear

Chefwear
2300 Windsor Ct
Suite C
Addison, IL 60101   630-396-8337
                          800-568-2433
                     Fax: 630-396-8393
          carol.mueller@chefwear.com
                    www.chefwear.com

Clothing and accesories for chefs and home gourmets

President: Rochelle Huppin
Marketing Manager: Carol Mueller
carol.mueller@chefwear.com
VP-Sales & Marketing: Carol Mueller
carol.mueller@chefwear.com
Customer Service/Sales Manager: Michelle Schmuhl
mschmuhl@chefwear.com
Credit Cards: AMEX; MasterCard
Catalog Cost: Free
Printing Information: 40 pages in 4 colors
Press: Web Press
Binding: Saddle Stitched
Mailing List Information: Names for rent
In Business: 25 years
Number of Employees: 45
Sales Information: $ 3 Million

8675 Continental Sports Supply

Continental Sports - CS-Vici
3981 South Decatur Street
Englewood, CO 80110-8637   720-833-0798
                            800-877-5053
                       Fax: 720-833-0814
              info@reuschusa.com
                   www.cs-vici.com

Soccer products and activewear

President: David Banning
Production Manager: David Dean
Buyers: David Dean
Credit Cards: AMEX; MasterCard
Catalog Cost: Free
Catalog Circulation: Mailed 1 time(s) per year to 35M
Printing Information: 28 pages in 4 colors on Glossy Stock
Press: Web Press
In Business: 22 years
Number of Employees: 10
Sales Information: $1MM to $3MM

8676 Copley's

Labwear.com
65-B Louis Street
Newington, CT 06111-111   860-666-4484
                           800-522-9327
                      Fax: 860-667-9559
                   www.labwear.com

Clothing and accessories for lab wear

President: Lee Blum
Credit Cards: AMEX; MasterCard
Catalog Circulation: Mailed 1 time(s) per year
Printing Information: 36 pages in 4 colors on Glossy Stock
Binding: Saddle Stitched
In Business: 35 years

8677 Corporate Outfitting Guide

alphabroder
6 Neshaminy Interplex
6th Floor
Trevose, PA 19053   800-523-4585
                   www.alphabroder.com

Corporate apparel.

CEO: Norman Hullinger
Catalog Cost: Free
Printing Information: 60 pages in 4 colors
Number of Employees: 2200
Sales Information: $1.5 Billion

8678 Dunbrooke Sportswear Company

Dunbrooke Apparel Corp
4200 Little Blue Parkway
Suite 500
Independence, MO 64057-1791   800-641-3627
                       www.dunbrooke.com

Sportswear for the family

President: Matt Grey
CFO: Jay Jones
Marketing Manager: Pat Sandvig
Production Manager: David W Brandy, VP
Credit Cards: AMEX; MasterCard
In Business: 78 years
Number of Employees: 1602
Sales Information: $5,600,000

8679 Ebbets Field Flannels

Ebbets Field Flannels
119 South Jackson Street
Seattle, WA 98104   506-382-7249
                           888-896-2936
                      Fax: 206-382-4411
           customerservice@ebbets.com
                      www.ebbets.com

Flannel baseball, hockey, and football clothing and accessories in authentic vintage styles; team uniforms and custom orders available

President: Jerry Cohen
Credit Cards: AMEX; MasterCard
Catalog Cost: Free
Catalog Circulation: Mailed 12 time(s) per year to 12500
Printing Information: 16 pages in 4 colors on Glossy Stock
Press: Web Press
Binding: Saddle Stitched
In Business: 25 years

8680 Exclusive Apparel

alphabroder
6 Neshaminy Interplex
6th Floor
Trevose, PA 19053   800-523-4585
                   www.alphabroder.com

Corporate, occupational and team apparel.

CEO: Norman Hullinger
Catalog Cost: Free
Printing Information: 284 pages in 4 colors
Number of Employees: 2200
Sales Information: $1.5 Billion

8681 Gibson & Barnes Flight Suits

Gibson & Barnes
1900 Weld Blvd
#140
El Cajon, CA 92020   619-440-2700
                           800-748-6693
                      Fax: 619-440-4618
              store@ombps.com
             www.gibson-barnes.com

High-quality, made-to-order flightsuits, uniforms, leather jackets and flying helmets for aviation, emergency medicine, and law enforcement

President: James A Wegge
Marketing Manager: Dan Longbrake
Catalog Circulation: to Weekl
In Business: 37 years

8682 Happy Chef

Happy Chef Inc
22 Park Place
Butler, NJ 07405   973-492-2525
                           800-347-0288
                      Fax: 973-492-0303
            www.happychefuniforms.com

Chef coats, pants and footwear, server pants and women's chefwear

Chairman: Joseph Nadler
President: Jim Nadler
CFO: Howard Curtain

Credit Cards: AMEX; MasterCard
Catalog Cost: Free
In Business: 47 years
Number of Employees: 45
Sales Information: $8 million

8683 Hard Hat Unique American Products

Hard Hat Knives & Flashlights
711 Leitchfield Road
Owensboro, KY 42303   270-683-1234
                      Fax: 270-683-1234
                   www.hardhatusa.com

Knives, flashlights, medallions, pins and keychains

President: Dan Clark
Credit Cards: AMEX; MasterCard
Catalog Cost: Free
Catalog Circulation: Mailed 2 time(s) per year to 1K
Printing Information: 48 pages in 4 colors
Binding: Saddle Stitched
In Business: 27 years
Number of Employees: 15
Sales Information: $1,000,000 - $5,000,000

8684 Head-To-Toe Catalog

Lion Apparel
7200 Poe Avenue
Suite 400
Dayton, OH 45414-2655   800-548-6614
                   www.lionprotects.com

Protective clothing

President: Stephen Schwartz
Sr. VP: Terry Smith
VP Military Programs: Dennis Dudek
VP Strategic Business Development: Jay Pavlick
Catalog Cost: Free
Catalog Circulation: Mailed 1 time(s) per year
Printing Information: 4 pages in 4 colors
In Business: 120 years
Sales Information: $50MM to $100MM

8685 Jaypro Sports

Jaypro Corporation, LLC
976 Hartford Turnpike
Waterford, CT 06385-4037   860-447-3001
                           800-243-0533
                      Fax: 860-444-1779
              info@jaypro.com
                   www.jaypro.com

Sporting equipment for volleyball, soccer, baseball, lacrosse, field hockey, football, tennis and physical education

President: Robert Ferrara
Marketing Manager: David Stumpo
Catalog Cost: Free
Catalog Circulation: Mailed 1 time(s) per year to 5M
Printing Information: 128 pages in 4 colors on Glossy Stock
Press: Web Press
Binding: Perfect Bound
In Business: 60 years
Number of Employees: 60
Sales Information: $10MM to $20MM

8686 Johnsey's Sporting Goods

Couchesonly
447 N Royal St
Jackson, TN 38301-5370   731-427-1082
                      Fax: 731-427-1083
                   www.Coachesonly.Com

School and team athletic supplies

President: Fred Johnsey Jr
Marketing Manager: Debra McDowell
Buyers: Debra McDowell
Fred Johnsay Jr
Fred Johnsay Sr
Credit Cards: MasterCard; Visa Discover Optima
Catalog Cost: Free
Printing Information: 114 pages in 2 colors on Matte Stock

Mailing List Information: Names for rent
List Manager: Debra McDowell
In Business: 46 years
Number of Employees: 10
Sales Information: Under $500M

8687 King Louie Sports
King Louie America
8788 Metcalf Ave
Overland Park, KS 66209-2039   913-648-2100
www.kinglouie.com

Bowling shirts, sweaters, activewear and hats

President: Brett Hackworth
Marketing Manager: Gary Ruhnke
CEO: Brett Hackworth
VP, Sales & Marketing: John McMillan
Catalog Cost: Free
Catalog Circulation: Mailed 1 time(s) per year to 200M
Printing Information: 64 pages in 4 colors on Glossy Stock
Press: Web Press
Binding: Saddle Stitched
In Business: 78 years
Number of Employees: 13
Sales Information: $1MM to $3MM

8688 Lands' End Business Outfitters
Lands' End, Inc.
1 Lands' End Lane
Dodgeville, WI 53595   800-963-4816
Fax: 800-332-0103
www.landsend.com

Business casual clothing and outerwear for men and women, including business accessories, gifts and business awards.

Co-interim CEO: James Gooch
Co-interim CEO: James Boitano
Catalog Cost: Free
Printing Information: in 4 colors
In Business: 53 years
Number of Employees: 5300
Sales Information: $1.42 Billion

8689 Lands' End School Outfitters
Lands' End, Inc.
1 Lands' End Lane
Dodgeville, WI 53595   800-963-4816
Fax: 800-332-0103
www.landsend.com

Uniforms in sizes to fit grades K-12

Co-interim CEO: James Gooch
Co-interim CEO: James Boitano
Catalog Cost: Free
Printing Information: in 4 colors
Mailing List Information: Names for rent
List Company: Millard Group
In Business: 53 years
Number of Employees: 5300
Sales Information: $1.42 Billion

8690 Leather Factory
Tandy Leather Factory, Inc.
1900 SE Loop 820
Fort Worth, TX 76140-4388   877-532-8437
tlfhelp@tandyleather.com
www.tandyleatherfactory.com

Offers retail and wholesale pricing on quality leather, and leathercraft supplies to individuals, institutions and businesses

President: Jon Thompson
CFO: Shannon Greene
Marketing Manager: Worth Jackson
Credit Cards: MasterCard
Catalog Cost: Free
Catalog Circulation: Mailed 6 time(s) per year to 178M
Printing Information: 188 pages in 2 colors on Matte Stock
Press: Sheetfed Press
Binding: Saddle Stitched
Mailing List Information: Names for rent
In Business: 37 years

Number of Employees: 466
Sales Information: $60 Million

8691 Mar Mac Manufacturing Company
Mar Mac Construction Products Inc.
PO Box 447
Mc Bee, SC 29101   843-335-5814
877-962-7622
Fax: 843-335-5909
info@marmac.com
www.marmac.com

Protective clothing for industrial, flame-retardant and chemical resistant applications, designed for mobility, protection and proper fit

President: John S McLeod Sr
CFO: Terry McQuire
Marketing Manager: David A Reischer
Printing Information: 20 pages in 4 colors on Glossy Stock
Press: Web Press
Mailing List Information: Names for rent
In Business: 61 years
Number of Employees: 300
Sales Information: $10,000,000 - $25,000,000

8692 Next Level
alphabroder
6 Neshaminy Interplex
6th Floor
Trevose, PA 19053   800-523-4585
www.alphabroder.com

Young contemporary apparel for the promotional industry.

CEO: Norman Hullinger
Catalog Cost: Free
Printing Information: 104 pages in 4 colors
Number of Employees: 2200
Sales Information: $1.5 Billion

8693 Nurses' Choice
Nurses Choice
6611 Amsterdam Way
Wilmington, NC 28405-4512   440-826-1900
800-747-7076
Fax: 910-452-2270
customerservice@nurses-choice.com
www.nurses-choice.com

Nurses' uniforms

President: Abbey Katz
Credit Cards: MasterCard; Visa
Catalog Cost: Free
Catalog Circulation: Mailed 4 time(s) per year to 200M
Printing Information: 30 pages in 4 colors
Mailing List Information: Names for rent
In Business: 26 years
Number of Employees: 200

8694 Putnam's
Putnam's Pub And Crooker
419 Myrtle Avenue
Brooklyn, NY 11205-295   347-799-2382
Fax: 603-654-5440
www.putnamspub.com

Work clothes, formal wear, career apparel, embroidery and screenprinting

President: Richard Putnam
Credit Cards: AMEX; MasterCard
Catalog Cost: Free
Printing Information: in 1 color on Matte Stock
In Business: 100 years
Number of Employees: 2
Sales Information: Under $500M

8695 Quartermaster
Quartermaster, LLC
17600 Fabrica Way
P.O. Box 4147
Cerritos, CA 90703   562-304-7300
866-673-7645
Fax: 562-304-7335
gsa@qmuniforms.com
www.qmuniforms.com

Public safety, security and military uniforms and equipment

Credit Cards: MasterCard
Catalog Cost: Free
Average Order Size: $75
Mailing List Information: Names for rent
List Company: Alan Drey Company
333 N Michigan Avenue
Chicago, IL 60601
312-236-8508
In Business: 37 years
Number of Employees: 90
Sales Information: $ 5-10 Million

8696 S&H Uniforms
S&H Uniforms
1 Aqueduct Rd
White Plains, NY 10606-1003   914-937-6800
800-210-5295
Fax: 914-937-0741
customerservice@sandhuniforms.com
www.sandhuniforms.com

Line of work uniforms and apparel

President: Glen Ross
Sales Manager: Patricia Kraft
Credit Cards: AMEX; MasterCard; Visa
Catalog Cost: Free
Catalog Circulation: Mailed 5 time(s) per year to 90MM
Average Order Size: $50
Printing Information: 96 pages in 1 color on Matte Stock
Press: Web Press
Binding: Perfect Bound
Mailing List Information: Names for rent
In Business: 54 years
Number of Employees: 65
Sales Information: $ 10 Million

8697 Sargent Welch
Sargent Welch
PO Box 92912
Rochester, NY 14692-9012   800-727-4368
Fax: 800-676-2540
customerservice@sargentwelch.com
www.sargentwelch.com

Science education equipment, supplies and lab furniture

In Business: 150 years

8698 Scrubs & Beyond
Scrubs & Beyond
PO Box 313
Louisiana, MO 63353   800-310-1580
866-972-2849
Fax: 800-313-5579
guestservice@scrubsandbeyond.com
www.scrubsandbeyond.com

Medical scrubs and accessories

President: Karla Bakersmith
Credit Cards: AMEX; MasterCard
Catalog Cost: Free
Catalog Circulation: Mailed 2 time(s) per year
Printing Information: 36 pages in 4 colors on Glossy Stock
Binding: Perfect Bound
In Business: 15 years

8699 Shoes for Crews
Shoes For Crews Corp.
250 S Australian Ave
West Palm Beach, FL 33401-7402 561-683-5090
800-523-4448
Fax: 888-647-4637
info@shoesforcrews.com
www.shoesforcrews.com

Slip-resistant footwear for the workplace

President: Stanley Smith
Credit Cards: AMEX; MasterCard
Catalog Cost: Free
Printing Information: 24 pages in 4 colors on
Glossy Stock
Press: Letterpress
Binding: Saddle Stitched
Mailing List Information: Names for rent
In Business: 31 years

8700 Sun Precautions
Sun Precautions, Inc.
2815 Wetmore Ave
Everett, WA 98201-3517   425-303-8585
800-882-7860
Fax: 425-303-0836
www.sunprecautions.com

**30+ SPF sun protective clothing and other
products for people who are hypersensitive
to the sun**

President: Shaun Hughes
Catalog Cost: Free
Printing Information: 40 pages in 4 colors
In Business: 30 years
Sales Information: $ 500,000- 1 Million

8701 Super Duper Publications
Super Duper Publications
P.O. Box 24997
Greenville, SC 29616   864-288-3536
800-277-8737
Fax: 864-288-3380
customerhelp@superduperinc.com
www.superduperinc.com

**Learning materials for kids with special
needs**

President: Thomas Webber
CFO: M T Webber
Purchasing: Jason Derbyshire
Credit Cards: AMEX; MasterCard
Catalog Cost: Free
Catalog Circulation: Mailed 1 time(s) per year
Printing Information: 288 pages in 4 colors
In Business: 31 years
Number of Employees: 115
Sales Information: $22 Million

8702 Team 365
alphabroder
6 Neshaminy Interplex
6th Floor
Trevose, PA 19053   800-523-4585
www.alphabroder.com

Team apparel colour guide.

CEO: Norman Hullinger
Catalog Cost: Free
Printing Information: 94 pages in 4 colors
Number of Employees: 2200
Sales Information: $1.5 Billion

8703 Tingley Rubber Corporation
Tingley Rubber Corporation
1551 S. Washington Ave.
Suite 403
Piscataway, NJ 08854-100   908-757-7474
800-631-5498
Fax: 866-757-9239
customerservice@tingleyrubber.com
www.tingleyrubber.com

Protective footwear and rainwear

Chairman: James McCollum
President: Bruce McCollum
CFO: Sophie Kye

Marketing Manager: James Towey
Production Manager: Don Mazzeo
Credit Cards: MasterCard; Visa
Printing Information: in 2 colors
In Business: 119 years
Number of Employees: 150
Sales Information: $10MM to $20MM

8704 Trenway Textiles
Trenway Textiles, Inc.
P.O. Box 681631
Ft. Payne, AL 35968   256-997-1857
800-251-7504
Fax: 800-441-8138
trenway@trenwaytextiles.com
www.trenwaytextiles.com

**Stirrup baseball hose, tube and soccer
socks, hockey socks**

President: Harlen Booth
CFO: Roger Cox
Catalog Cost: Free
Catalog Circulation: to 1800
Printing Information: 20 pages
Mailing List Information: Names for rent
In Business: 31 years
Number of Employees: 20
Sales Information: $1,000,000 - $5,000,000

8705 Turfer Sportswear
TURFER
530 Wood Street
Suite B
Bristol, RI 2809-2310   401-254-6125
800-222-1312
Fax: 401-223-9682
www.turfer.com

Jackets, vests and blankets

Chairman: Chris St Martin King, VP
President: Gary Goldberg
Credit Cards: MasterCard; Visa
Catalog Cost: Free
Catalog Circulation: Mailed 1 time(s) per year
Printing Information: 12 pages in 4 colors on
Glossy Stock
Press: Web Press
Mailing List Information: Names for rent
In Business: 65 years
Number of Employees: 65
Sales Information: $1,000,000 - $5,000,000

8706 US Cavalry
U.S. Cavalry
1222 East 38th St
Chattanooga, TN 37407-9000   270-351-1164
800-777-7172
Fax: 270-352-0266
service@uscav.com
www.uscav.com

**Army/navy surplus and military related
equipment; outdoor adventure equipment**

Chairman: Patrick Garvey
President: Wayne Weissler
Buyers: David Acton
Jeanine Mason
Credit Cards: AMEX; MasterCard; Visa
Catalog Cost: Free
Mailing List Information: Names for rent
List Manager: Carmen Shelton
In Business: 42 years
Number of Employees: 110
Sales Information: $ 28 Million

8707 UltraClub Corporate Outfitting
alphabroder
6 Neshaminy Interplex
6th Floor
Trevose, PA 19053   800-523-4585
www.alphabroder.com

Corporate apparel and accessories.

CEO: Norman Hullinger
Catalog Cost: Free
Printing Information: 72 pages in 4 colors
Number of Employees: 2200
Sales Information: $1.5 Billion

8708 UltraClub Performance Wear
alphabroder
6 Neshaminy Interplex
6th Floor
Trevose, PA 19053   800-523-4585
www.alphabroder.com

Imprintable casual and athletic apparel.

CEO: Norman Hullinger
Catalog Cost: Free
Printing Information: 60 pages in 4 colors
Number of Employees: 2200
Sales Information: $1.5 Billion

8709 Uniform Advantage Medical Uniforms
Uniform Advantage
150 South Pine Island Road
Suite 300
Plantation, FL 33324   954-626-2100
800-283-8708
Fax: 954-626-2112
www.uniformadvantage.com

Medical uniforms

President: Susan Fields
Production Manager: Melba Smith
Credit Cards: MasterCard
Catalog Cost: Free
Catalog Circulation: Mailed 1 time(s) per year
Printing Information: 64 pages in 4 colors
Binding: Perfect Bound
In Business: 30 years
Number of Employees: 33
Sales Information: $ 3 Million

8710 Vantage Apparel
Vantage Apparel
100 Vantage Dr
Avenel, NJ 07001-1080   732-340-3000
800-221-0020
Fax: 732-340-3165
customerservice@vantageapparel.com
www.vantageapparel.com

**Apparel of the names and logos of the coun-
try' leading corporations, resorts, golf
courses, colleges and casinos**

President: Ira Neaman
Catalog Cost: Free
In Business: 35 years
Sales Information: $ 20-50 Million

8711 Vista: Something for Everyone
B & F System, Inc.
3920 S Walton Walker
Dallas, TX 75236-1510   214-333-2111
Fax: 214-333-1511
service@bnfusa.com
www.bnfusa.com

**Offers products of nationally known whole-
salers and manufacturers that are made in af-
filiated offshore factories**

Chairman: Bill Meyer
President: John Meyer
CFO: Don Meyer
International Marketing Manager: John Meyer
Buyers: John Meyer
Credit Cards: MasterCard
Catalog Cost: $2
Catalog Circulation: Mailed 3 time(s) per year
to 1MM
Average Order Size: $250
Printing Information: 272 pages in 4 colors on
Glossy Stock
Press: Web Press
Binding: Perfect Bound
In Business: 67 years
Number of Employees: 112
Sales Information: $3MM to $5MM

8712   Wasserman Uniforms
Wasserman Uniforms
700 NW 57th Place
Fort Lauderdale, FL 33309   800-848-3576
                                                    Fax: 800-204-0416
            custserv@wassermanuniform.com
                www.wassermanuniform.com

Carries a large selection of uniforms and accessories for the postal industry.

Catalog Cost: Free
In Business: 46 years
Sales Information: $5MM to $10MM

8713   Western Promotion Sportswear
WestPro, Inc.
2294 Mountain Vista Lane
Provo, UT 84606-6206   801-373-2525
                                                    Fax: 801-373-8778
                    steve@westpro.net
                    www.westpro.net

Custom sportswear, including direct embroidery and screen printing

President: Steven Clement
CFO: John M Edmunds
Credit Cards: MasterCard
Catalog Cost: Free
Catalog Circulation: Mailed 1 time(s) per year to 2000
Average Order Size: $2000
Printing Information: 100 pages in 4 colors on Glossy Stock
Press: Web Press
Binding: Perfect Bound
Mailing List Information: Names for rent
In Business: 36 years
Number of Employees: 45
Sales Information: $ 3-5 Million

8714   What's New
alphabroder
6 Neshaminy Interplex
6th Floor
Trevose, PA 19053   800-523-4585
                www.alphabroder.com

Imprintable apparel and accessories for the promotional industry.

CEO: Norman Hullinger
Catalog Cost: Free
Printing Information: 52 pages in 4 colors
Number of Employees: 2200
Sales Information: $1.5 Billion

Classic Industries: Camaro, 473
Firewheel Classics, 503

Camellias
Nuccio's Nurseries, 3180

Camembert
Gifts of Distinction, 2605

Cameras
Adorama, 1972
Cambridge Camera Exchange, 5485
Edmund Industrial Optics, 5479
Focus Camera, 2228, 5486
KEH Camera Brokers, 5489
Vinten, 1989, 5483
Woodland Hills Camera, 5442, 5490
Digital
Berger Brothers Camera Video Digital, 5432, 5484
Security
Security Cameras Direct, 2255
Security Equipment
Hidden Camera Surveillance Catalog, 5124
Underwater
Underwater Equipment Guide, 5839

Camping Equipment & Supplies
American Tailgater, 389
Big Agnes, 5810
Cabela's Camping, 1228
Camping World, 391
Campmor, 1229, 5617
GCI Outdoor, 1234
Hot Deals, 1359
JM Cremps, 1236
Lance Camper Manufacturing, 397
NE Camp, 6249
NRS, 5651
New England Camp Discounter, 1239
Outfitters Supply, 1240
Panther Primitives, 1242, 3632
Pilot Rock Park, Street and Camp Site Products, 1244
Sierra Home and Gift, 1541, 4855
Sierra Trading Post, 1606, 5670
South Summit, 1247
US Patriot Tactical, 1225
Clothing
Adventure Edge, 1249, 1555
Ranger Joe's, 1223
Compasses
Brunton, 1227
Hunting Equipment
Overton's, 1241, 5655
Lanterns
Streamlight, 5074
Military
Quartermaster, 1222
Ranger Joe's, 1223
US Cavalry, 1224
Survival Gear
Ranger Joe's, 1223

Candelabra
Kings Chandelier, 3594

Candlemaking
Betterbee, 4492
Brushy Mountain Bee Farm, 3803, 4493
Cementex Latex Corporation, 3805
GloryBee Natural Foods and Crafts, 2842, 3737
Honeywax / Candle-Flex Molds, 3807
Wicks Unlimited, 3810

Candles
Beeswax Candle Works, 3802
Cake and Candle, 3804
Colonial Candle, 3806
Country House, 3580
Honeywax / Candle-Flex Molds, 3807
Illuminations, 3808
Pioneer Linens, 3552, 4900, 4919
Quality Merchandise Direct, 3486

Way Out Wax Catalog, 3507
Yankee Candle, 215, 3811
Accessories
Yankee Candle Catalog, 635, 3812

Candy
Aplets & Cotlets, 2546
Country Kitchen SweetArt, 2560
Enstrom Candies, 2567
Fannie May, 2568
Harbor Sweets, 2574
Harry London's Candies, 2575
Lammes Candies, 2580
Linda's Lollies Company, 2581
Mrs. Kimball's Candy Shoppe, 2585
Plumbridge Confections & Gifts, 2589
River Street Sweets, 2592, 2966
Savannah's Candy Kitchen, 2594
See's Candies, 2595
Senor Murphy Candymaker, 2596
Sweet Tooth Candies, 2599
Candy Molds
Candy & Craft Molds Catalog, 2552
Citrus
Davidson of Dundee, 2564
Fudge
Harbor Candy Shop, 2573
Marshall's Fudge & Homemade Candies, 2582
Taffy
James and Fralinger's Catalog, 2577

Candy Making
Foodcrafter's Supply Catalog, 5221

Canes
Dutchguard, 4299
Fashionable Canes & Walking Sticks, 2001
Handcarved
Fashionable Canes & Walking Sticks, 2001

Caning
Cane & Basket Supply, 3785
Caning Shop, 3786
H H Perkins, 3790
The Country Seat, 3798, 4209
Willowes Basketry & Yarn, 3801, 4217

Canoes
Clipper Canoes, 756
Perception Kayaks, 770
Shaw & Tenney, 738
Shearwater Boats, 781
Wenonah Canoe Catalog, 787
Accessories
Spring Creek Canoe Accessories, 744
Paddles
Spring Creek Canoe Accessories, 744

Canopies
ShadeTree Canopies, 4637
Teksupply Catalog, 4642
Tractor
Perry Company, 557

Canvas
SOAR Inflatables, Inc., 776

Car Accessories
Ranger Design, 421, 567

Car Care
Bar's Leaks, 455
International Auto Parts, 414, 431
Pit Pal Products, 320, 419, 562
Rightlook.com, 422
West Coast Corvettes, 425
Anti-freeze
Berkebile Oil Company, 407
Fluids
Berkebile Oil Company, 407
Castrol USA Catalog, 468
Oils
Castrol USA Catalog, 468

Sealants
ITW Automotive Products, 412

Car Parts
American Muscle, 283, 447
Good Vibrations Motorsports, 411, 512
Volkswagens
Prothane Motion Control, 420

Car Stereos
Custom Autosound, 298

Car Storage
Pine Ridge Enterprise, 5272

Caramels
Fran's Chocolates, 2569

Cards
Best of Cards, 6152
Leanin' Tree, 3462
Miles Kimball Christmas Cards, 3468, 4558
Pronto Business Cards, 5923
Rytex Catalog, 5955
Stork Avenue Catalog, 5960
Christmas
Cordial Greetings, 5911
Holiday Collection, 1432, 5943
TRIMCO, 5926
Greeting
B Shackman, 921, 5933
Bridge Building Images, 1039
CardsDirect.com, 5909
Current, 3431, 3648
Farriers' Greeting Cards, 8
HR Direct, 1953
Pipsqueak Productions, 5951
Renton's, 5954
UNICEF Catalog, 3504, 5929
Holiday
Holiday Expressions, 5944
Personalized
Cordial Greetings, 5911
Tarot
Hamilton New Age Mystical Arts Supplies, 1061

Carnival Supplies
American Carnival Mart Key Items, 4043

Carpeting
Elkes, 5103
Family Heir-Loom Weavers, 4024
Reproduction
Renaissance Carpet & Tapestries, 5113

Carts
Shopping
Garden Carts, 3351

Cases
Just Cases, 6245
PortaBrace, 6107

Cashmere
Frette, 4263, 5081
Schweitzer Nightwear, 1374, 1503

Cassettes
Folktale & Story Catalog, 6181
Harvard Square Records, 2303

Casters
Albion Industries Full Line Catalog, 6024
PJ Catalog, 6103

Caviar
Gourmet Food Store, 2808
Hansen Caviar Company, 2722
Tsar Nicoulai Caviar, 2732

Cellphones
Wireless Emporium Catalog, 1990

Celtic Gifts
Creative Irish Gifts, 2799, 3647
GaelSong, 3439, 5179

Ceramics
ART Studio Clay Company, 3814
Aftosa, 3815
Bailey Ceramic Supply & Pottery Equipment, 3989
Brickyard Ceramics & Crafts, 3818
Ceramic Kilns, 3820
Continental Clay Company, 3822
Creative Hobbies, 3823
Duncan Enterprises, 3824
Florida Clay Art Company, 3827
Gainey Ceramics, 3828, 4000
Georgies Ceramic & Clay Company, 3829
MacKenzie-Childs, 3831
Olympia Enterprises, 3832
RiverView Ceramic Molds, 3834
Yozie Mold, 3837
Bug
Ceramic Bug Supplies, 3819
Kilns
Aim Kilns, 3816
Duralite, 3825
Evenheat Kilns & Ovens, 3826
L&L Kiln Manufacturing, 3830
Majolica
Biordi Art Imports, 1732, 3817

Chains
Cable
Security Chain Company, 324

Chairs
Royalwood Basket Weaving & Caning Supply, 3796
Repairs
Connecticut Cane & Reed Company, 3787
Rocking
Rocker Shop, 6115

Champagne
1-877-Spirits.com, 2993, 3411

Chandeliers
Rejuvenation Lamp & Fixture Company, 5069

Checks
EiPrinting, 5913

Cheerleading
Anderson's School Spirit Catalog, 1411
Balance: Gymnastics & Cheerleading, 1412
Omni Cheer, 1438
Team Cheer, 1448
Dance
Team Leader Sports, 1294, 1614, 1654

Cheese
Calef's Country Store, 2602
Cheese Box, 2603
Cold Hollow Cider Mill, 2743
Eichten's Hidden Acres Cheese Farm, 2604
Gifts of Distinction, 2605
Gourmet Market Place, 2809
Guggisberg Cheese, 2607
Harman's Cheese and Country Store, 2608
Hickory Farms, 2911
Maytag Dairy Farms, 2609
Mission Orchards of Hickory Farms, 2610
Nodine's Smokehouse, 2922
Nueske's Applewood Smoked Meats, 2611, 2923
Paoli Cheese, 2612
Plymouth Artisan Cheese, 2614
Shelburne Farms, 2615, 3490
Usinger's Famous Sausage, 2939
WSU Creamery, 2619
Wisconsin Cheeseman, 2620, 2831

Cheesecakes
Collin Street Bakery, 2665

Chefware
Chef Works, 1628
Happy Chef, 1634

Chemicals
A&H Abrasives, 6012
City Chemical, 5512
Pro Chemical & Dye, 3759
READE, 3833
Reagents, 5542
Wilkens-Anderson Company Catalog, 5554
Inorganic
City Chemical, 5512

Cherries
Chukar Cherry Company, 2796

Chess
Official US Chess Federation Catalog, 6199

Chevrolet
Bob's Classic Chevy Catalog, 459
C & P 55-57 Chevy Passenger Cars, 353
C & P 55-59 Chevrolet Trucks, 354
Cheyenne Pick Up Parts, 469
Classic Chevrolet Parts, 472
Classic Industries: Chevrolet, 474
Classic Parts of America, 477
Cliff's Classic Chevrolet, 357
Dutchman 1955-1957 Chevy Car Catalog, 360
East Coast Chevy, 362
Eckler's Classic Chevy, 494
Filling Station, 366
Grumpy's Truck Parts, 518
Jim Carter's Antique Truck Parts, 368
LMC Truck, 533
Luttys Chevys - Warehouse Catalog, 371
Original Parts Group, 549
Parts & Accessories Catalog, 318
Pete's Fabrications, 375
Sinclair's, 576

Chilies
Pendery's, 2709

Chimes
Chime Time, 2061, 6161

China
Emerald Collection, 3583
Silver Queen, 3603

Chocolate
Alethea's Chocolates, 2544
American Gourmet, 2504, 2545, 2790
Biscoff Gourmet Catalog, 2548, 2659, 2793
Bissinger French Confectioners, 2549
Carson Wrapped Hershey's Chocolates, 2554
Chocolate Catalogue, 2556, 2663
Chocolate Inn, 2557
Chocolate by Design, 2558
Cummings Studio Chocolates, 2562
Divine Delights, 2673
Empress Chocolates Company, 2566
Fran's Chocolates, 2569
Godiva Chocolatier, 2570
Gourmet Food Store, 2808
Harbor Candy Shop, 2573
Harbor Sweets, 2574
Harry London's Candies, 2575
Indian Wells Date Gardens & Chocolatier, 2576
Mother Myrick's Confectionery, 2584
Paradigm Foodworks, 2587
Pemberton Farms, 2819
Perfectly Sweet, 2588
Revival Confections, 2591
Rocky Mountain Chocolate Factory, 2593
Stahmanns Pecans, 2598, 2972
Wisconsin Cheeseman, 2620, 2831
World's Finest Chocolate, 2601

Chocoolate Chip Cookies
Cookies
Cookie Bouquets, 2666

Chowder
East Coast Gourmet, 2719

Christmas
Bronner's Christmas Favorites, 3644, 4552
Christmas, 1264, 4554, 6162
L.L.Bean Christmas, 1275, 4556
Miles Kimball Christmas Cards, 3468, 4558
Mrs. Kimball's Candy Shoppe, 2585
Oriental Trading Beading & More!, 4561
Oriental Trading Crafts!, 3671, 4562
Oriental Trading Fun & Faith, 4564
Cards
Lang, 3461
Ornaments
Matt McGhee, 4836
Stockings
Bucilla Stocking Kits, 3939, 4156
Trees
Omni Farm, 3185

Chrysanthemums
Donahue's Greenhouse, 3115
King's Mums, 3158

Chutney
Sauces
Wild Thymes Farm, 2529, 2892

Cider
Wood's Cider Mill, 2764

Cigars
Cigar.com, 5989
Cigars International, 5990
Cigars for Aficionados, 5991
Colibri Lighters, 5992
Famous Smoke Shop, 5995
Finck Cigar, 5996
Holts Tobacconist, 5999
House of Oxford Wholesale Cigars, 6000
JR Cigars, 6001
JR Tobacco, 6002
Mike's Cigars, 6004
Mom's Cigars, 6005
Nat Sherman, 6006
Thompson Cigar Company, 6009
Worldwide Cigar Club Catalog, 6010

Citrus
Citrus Country Groves, 2769
Crockett Farms, 2982
Davidson of Dundee, 2564
Oranges
Hyatt Fruit, 2777

Clamps
Woodworking
Adjustable Clamp, 6018

Clapboards
Granville Manufacturing, 4623

Clay
Continental Clay Company, 3822

Cleaners
Betty Mills Catalog, 5380
Clean Report, 4810
Panaram International Trading Company, 4840
Liquid
Caig Laboratories, 2271
The Clean Team, 5236
Tire
G.H. Meiser & Company, 507

Clocks
American Acrylic Awards & Gifts, 3415
Decor Time Products, 3840
Gimbel & Sons, 3443
Masterclock, 3844
Mountaine Meadows Pottery, 3599
Premiere Products, 2160, 3846
Historical
Electric Time Company, 3841
Kits
Clockparts.com, 3839
Emperor Clock, LLC, 3842, 4686

KlockIt, 3843
Turncraft Clocks, 3847
Parts
Clockparts.com, 3839
Turncraft Clocks, 3847
Watches
Timepieces International, 5206

Closet Systems
HomePortfolio Insider, 4687

Clothing
Acacia, 671, 3569
Anthony Richards, 1305, 1679
Anthropologie, 1306, 1680
Arhaus Jewels, 672, 722, 3858
Balance: Gymnastics & Cheerleading, 1412
Beretta Seasonal Catalog, 1256
Blair Men's, 1356, 1517
Blair Women's, 1490, 1683
Budd Leather Company, 1479
Carhartt, 1261, 1523, 1627
Casual Wear Catalog, 1263, 5247
Chadwicks of Boston, 1313, 1687
Cheeks Cape May, 1688
Christmas, 1264, 4554, 6162
Clothing Solutions, 2024
Crazy Shirts, 1358
Dennis Kirk Snowmobile Catalog, 1315
Dream Products, 3432
Essentials by Anthony Richards, 1268
Field Outfitting, 2477
First Frost, 1696, 3435, 4817
Flirt, 1494, 1697
Gorsuch, 1582
Hanna Andersson, 1387
Herrington, 1271, 6072
Holiday Collection, 1432, 5943
J. Jill, 1700
J.Crew Style Guide, 1274, 1330, 1360
J.L. Powell The Sporting Life, 691, 1361, 1527
JC Penney Holiday Catalog, 3456
Jessica London, 1362, 1701
Jos. A. Bank Clothiers, 1332, 1528
KingSize, 1365, 1529
Ladies Collection 2, 1703
Lafayette 148 New York, 1704
Lands' End, 1278
Lands' End Kids, 1336, 1392
Lands' End Men, 1337, 1366, 1530
Lands' End Plus, 1338, 1367, 1705
Lands' End School Outfitters, 1393, 1636
Lillian Vernon, 1279, 3464
Max & Chloe, 3887
NASCAR Superstore, 1597
Offroad Catalog, 1282, 1599, 5268
Orvis Gifts for Men, 1370, 2406
Orvis Men, 1284, 1534
Orvis Women, 1285, 1371, 1711
Patagonia, 1600, 5817
Patagonia Fish, 1601, 2407
Patagonia Kids, 1602
Patagonia Surf, 1603
Peggy Lutz Plus, 1286, 1712
Pyramid Collection, 3684, 5152
Roaman's, 1372, 1716
Rochester Big and Tall Catalog, 1540
Romans, 705
Samantha's Style Shoppe, 1348, 1373, 1717
Share the Spirit!, 1718, 3488, 4854
Sierra Trading Post, 1606, 5670
Speedgear, 327
The Uniform Book, 1658
The Vermont Country Store, 1352
Turtleson, 1543, 1618, 5765
Ulla Popken, 1724
Urban Outfitters, 1296, 4863
Vantage Apparel, 1661
Vivre, 1545, 3611, 5601
West Marine Spring Waterlife, 812, 1620
Westport Big & Tall Catalog, 1546
Whatever Works Catalog, 3613, 5033
Whispering Pines, 4869
Wholesale Buyers Guide, 1300

Woman Within, 1381, 1725
Accessories
All About Dance, 607, 5443
Appleseed's, 1354
Arthur Beren Shoes, 5557
Bachrach, 1515
Bates Leathers, 1478
Bedford Fair, 1254, 5561
Bella Taylor, 1307, 4008
Bra Smyth, 1491
Chadwicks of Boston, 1313, 1687
Chico's, 1689
David Morgan, 1569
Donnelly/Colt Progressive Resources, 1318
Draper's & Damon's, 1694
Duluth Trading Catalog for Men, 1319, 5569
Fabulous-Furs, 1481
First Frost, 1696, 3435, 4817
Gavilan's, 1324, 5140
Gudrun Sjoden, 1270, 1325, 4823
Hangers.com, 1326
Hugger Mugger, 1329, 1464
J. Jill, 1700
J. Peterman Company, 1273
Jazzertogs, 1466
K. Jordan, 1334, 5579
Leather Coats Etc, 1483
OneStopPlus.com, 1710
Pure Collection, 1715
Rewards, 1345
Sahalie, 627, 1289, 1347
Share the Spirit!, 1718, 3488, 4854
Spec-L, 1445, 2029
Stauer, 1350, 1793
The Met Store, 914, 5156, 5962
The Vermont Country Store, 1352
Vineyard Vines, 1298
Vivre, 1545, 3611, 5601
Activewear
Athleta, 1454, 1559, 1682
CC Filson Company, 1566
Sahalie, 627, 1289, 1347
Tattoo Golf, 1613
West Marine Spring Waterlife, 812, 1620
Aquatic
HYDRO-FIT Gear, 1463, 5635
Army Navy
Big Ray's, 1217, 1355
Athletic
GK Men's Team Competitive, 688
GK Team Workout Wear Catalog, 1579
Automotive
HRP World, 519
Baby
Baby News, 673
Babystyle, 659, 1508
Garnet Hill, 664, 689, 1511
Olive Juice, 701
One Step Ahead, 948, 1397, 6200
Patagonia Kids, 1602
Big & Tall
KingSize, 1365, 1529
Bowling
King Louie Sports, 1591
Business
Jessica London, 1362, 1701
Roaman's, 1372, 1716
Camouflage
Beretta Seasonal Catalog, 1256
Day One Camouflage, 1218
Camouflage
Camo Trading, 1567
Cashmere
Alberene Royal Mail, 3414
Casual
Big Ray's, 1217, 1355
Coconut Telegraph, 1423
Crazy Shirts, 1358
Jos. A. Bank Clothiers, 1332, 1528
KingSize, 1365, 1529
L.L.Bean Christmas, 1275, 4556
Lafayette 148 New York, 1704

Antiquities
Faganarms, 1741
Sadigh Gallery Ancient Art, 1822, 3901

Bank Notes
Hard to Find US Coins & Bank Notes, 1788
Stamp & Collectibles, 1884

Baseball
Baseball Direct, 1125, 5710

Beatles
Fest for Beatles Fans, 1742

Coca-Cola Machines
Fun-Tronics, 1746

Coins
Air-Tite Holders, 1781
American Coin and Stamp Brokerage, 1782
Collectible America, 1784
Hard to Find US Coins & Bank Notes, 1788
Hoffman Mint, 1789
International Coins and Currency, 1790
Rare Coin & Currency, 1792
Sadigh Gallery Ancient Art, 1822, 3901
Village Coin Shop, 1794

Die Cast Toys
Diecast Direct, 1740, 6172

Documents
Cohasco, 1827

Dolls
American Girl, 1801
Antina's Doll Supply, 1802
Barbie Top 10 Holiday Picks, 1803
Dollmasters, 1806
Entertainment Earth, 6177
Golden Cockerel, 3655
Hobby Builder's Supply, 1855
Hobby House Press, 1165
House of Caron, 1810
Molds & Dollmaking Supplies, 1812
Paradise Galleries, 1813

Figurines
Precious Moments, 1756

Gemology
Ebersole Lapidary Supply, 1820
Graves Company, 1821

Glass Ornaments
Landmark Creations, 4748

Historical Documents
75th Historical Document Catalog, 1826

Maps
Geological Highway Maps, 1200
Raven Maps & Images, 1832

Militaria
Cotswold Collectibles, 1772, 1842
HJ Saunders/US Military Insignia, 1844
International Military Antiques, 1830, 1846
Medals of America, 1848
Sgt Grit's Marine Specialties, 1290, 1652

Miniatures
Gimbel & Sons, 3443

Paperweights
Collector's Paperweights, 1735

Pewter
Hampshire Pewter, 1750

Porcelain
Chinese Porcelain Company, 3821

Posters
Desperate Enterprises, 1773
Winn Devon Fine Art Collection Catalog, 243

Prints
Ducks, Ducks & More Ducks Catalog, 1873

Sports
Cruisin USA/Bowlingshirt, 1426

Stamps
American Coin and Stamp Brokerage, 1782
Clacritter Designs, 1871
Ducks, Ducks & More Ducks Catalog, 1873
Earl P L Apfelbaum, 1874
HE Harris & Company, 1876
Kenmore Stamp Company, 1878
Mystic Stamp, 1880
SAFE Collecting Supplies, 1883

Stamp & Collectibles, 1884
Whitman Publishing Catalog, 1885

Steins
Steinland Gifts & Collectibles, 1760

Toys
Cotswold Collectibles, 1772, 1842
Meadow View Imports, 6194

Worldwide
Worldwide Collectibles & Gifts Catalog, 1766

Columns
Columns Catalog, 4726
Somerset Door & Column Company, 4639
Worthington Architectural Details Catalog,
4772

Comic Books
Blue Line Pro, 184
Bud's Art Books, 1796
Comic Heaven Auction Catalog, 1797
Golden Age Comics, 1799
RTS Unlimited, 1179
Rip Off Press, 1180

Communication Aids
B&B Electronics Manufacturing Company,
813

Compact Discs
Acoustic Sounds, 2289
Audio Diversions Johnson, 857
Audio Editions, 858
Kimbo Educational, 2305
Polyline, 2341

Compasses
Pocket
Brunton, 1227

Computer Supplies & Equipment
Cablexpress Technologies, 1891
Conde Systems, 1893
GS Direct, 5337
Global Datacom, 1929
Global Industrial Catalog, 5340, 6059
HMC Electronics, 2231
HRO Catalog, 1896
Kolobags, 1902
MacConnection, 2183
Microbiz, 1903
Network Access & Connectivity Product Line,
1905
New England Business Service, 1906
Office City, 1907
Power Up!, 1936
ProStar, 1937
ProVantage, 1913
Quill.com, 5409
Sealevel Systems, 1919
TRS RenTelco, 2264
Valiant IMC, 273, 1970

Accessories
Computer Gear, 3429
Cyberguys.com, 1895
Jameco Electronics, 1930, 2238
Peace Frogs, 1442

Accounting
Rapid Forms, 1963

Audio Speaker
Parts Express, 1243, 1985

Communication Products
Maysteel, 1931

Computers
Hewlett Packard, 1897
Zones, 1971

Controllers
B&R Industrial Automation Corporation, 1887

Data Communication
Server Management Products, 1939

Desktop
PC Systems Handbook, 1934

Games
US Chess Federation, 1190

Hardware
PC Connection Express, 1909
Zones, 1971

Headsets
Headsets.com, 1981, 2003

IBM
Polywell Computers, 1935

Laptops
Twinhead Corporation, 1941

Macintosh
CDW, 1927
PC & MacConnection, 1933

Networking
Premise Wiring, 1911

Optics
Indus International, 1899

PC
Option PC, 1932

Peripherals
Rose Electronics, 1938
Tiger Direct Bussiness, 1968

Print Cartridges
Office Access Catalog, 2247

Printers
Repromat Catalog, 5352
Tape Resources, 271

Protection Products
Viziflex Seels Computer Protection Products,
1923

RAMS
BG Micro, 1888

Ribbons
Office Access Catalog, 2247

Software
Accountant Stationers & Printers, 5903
Baseball Overlay, 1126
Complete Real Estate Software Catalog,
1947
GovConnection, 1952
Health Education Services, 1954
International Marine Boating Books, 1169
NewHaven Software, 1958
PC/Nametag, 1959
Software Express Educators Catalog, 1966
Tape Resources, 271
Zones, 1971

Systems
Twinhead Corporation, 1941
V-Infinity Power Quick Guide Catalog, 1942

Tablets
Wireless Emporium Catalog, 1990

Toner
Office Access Catalog, 2247

Computers
Parts
EZAutomation, 1950, 2220

Condiments
American Spoon Foods, 2734

Mustard
Mustard Museum and Gourmet Foods, 2869

Conferences & Seminars
Deluxe Small Business Services, 2219

Conifers
Plants, Trees & Shrubs
Collector's Nursery, 3246

Construction
Equipment
White Cap Industries, 6221

Information Resources
Performance Zone, 2104

Supplies & Equipment
Tri-Boro Construction Supplies, 4645

Consumer Electronics
BestBuy, 1975
Brookstone, 3420
Crutchfield, 1977, 2217

First Street Catalog, 3436
Hammacher Schlemmer, 4824
Heartland America, 3449, 5342
Seventh Avenue Catalog, 4925, 4994
Sharper Image, 3489, 3690
Wireless Emporium Catalog, 1990

Antennas
Shakespeare Electronic Products Group,
2256

Audio Video
Tiger Direct, 1988

Radios
Haverhill's, 5434, 5487

Containers
Chests
Delta Truck Storage Solutions, 302
JOBOX Premium Storage Solutions, 307

Truck
Delta Truck Storage Solutions, 302
JOBOX Premium Storage Solutions, 307

Controls
Electronic
Barksdale Control Products, 2210
Fluke Corporation, 2227
RBE Electronics, 2253

Industrial
Eaton Corporation World Headquarters, 493
Sterling Production Control Units, 2261

Meters
Analytical Measurements, 5508
Keithley Instruments, 2241

Switches
Barksdale Control Products, 2210

Cookie Cutters
Fancy Flours, 5220

Cookies
Biscoff Gourmet Catalog, 2548, 2659, 2793
Byrd Cookie Company, 2661
Carolina Cookie Company, 2662
Cookie Garden, 2559
Cookies by Design's Cookie Gift Book, 2667
Cryer Creek Kitchens, 2561
David's Cookies, 2670
Dr. Cookie Gourmet Cookies, 2674
Haydel's Bakery, 2681
Mrs Fields Gourmet Gifts, 2689, 2817
William Greenberg Desserts, 2701

Cookware
Magic Seasonings Catalog, 2865
Sur la Table, 5235

Copper
Schlaifer's Enameling Supplies, 3927

Corn
Rupp Seeds, 3301

Corn Meal
Kenyon's Grist Mill, 2536

Corrals
Barnmaster, 111

Corvair
Clark's Corvair Parts, 355

Corvette
Corvette America, 294
Corvette Central, 481
Corvette Pacifica Motoring Accessories, 482
Corvette World, 483
Corvette/Volkswagen, 430
Eckler's 1953-2001 Corvette Parts and
Accessories, 363
Eckler's Corvette Parts, 495
Long Island Corvette Supply, 370
Mid America Motorworks, 311
Piper's Corvette Specialties, 560
Stoudt Auto Sales, 381
Vintage, 384

Mixon Fruit Farms, 2780
Red Cooper, 2784
Rocky Top Farms, 2758
Sun Harvest Citrus, 3495

German
Schaller & Weber, 2712

Gifts
Olive Press, 2523, 3475
Poinsettia Groves, 2783
Ruma's Fruit & Gift Basket World, 2785

Ginseng
Penn Herb Company, 2876

Gluten Free
MagicKitchen.Com, 2851
Vitacost, 4463

Gourmet
AKA Gourmet, 2980
AppetizersUSA, 2895
Bridgewater Chocolate, 2550, 2794
Dean & DeLuca, 2511
Gourmet Fantasy, 2807
Gourmet Food Store, 2808
Heartwarming Treasures, 2682, 2998
Horchow Catalog, 2812
House of Webster, 2515, 3453
Mackenzie Limited, 2815
Matthews 1812 House, 2688
Monastery Greetings, 2520, 2816
Schaul's Signature Gourmet Foods, 2822, 2933, 2967
Scottish Gourmet USA, 2713, 2823
Sechlers Fine Pickles, 2854
Sound of Mustard, 2885
Southern Season, 2597, 2935
Stock Yards, 2936
Stonewall Kitchen, 2826, 4763
UVC Gourmet, 2527
Zabar's Catalog, 2833
Zingerman's Mail Order Cupboard, 2531

Grits
Callaway Gardens Country Store, 2740

Hams
Amana Meat Shop & Smokehouse, 2894
Broadbent Country Hams, 2897
Burge's Hickory Smoked Turkeys & Hams, 2898
Harper's Country Hams, 2908
Meacham Hams, 2918
Moonlite Food & Gift Magazine, 2989
Ralph's Packing, 2930

Hawaiian
Penn Street Bakery, 2694

Health
eDietShop, 2857

Herbs
Attar Herbs & Spices, 2859
Davidson's Organics, 2630
Frontier Wholesale Price Guide, 2861
Herbal Actives, 4393
Herbal Healer Academy, 4316
Pacific Botanicals, 2874
Penn Herb Company, 2876
Penzeys Spices, 2877
Riley's Seasoning and Spices, 2880
San Francisco Herb Catalog, 2882
Sandy Mush Herb Nursery, 2883
Seeds Trust, 2786, 2884, 3303
Spices Etc, 2888
Vitacost, 4463

Honey
Champlain Valley Apiaries, 2741
GloryBee Natural Foods and Crafts, 2842, 3737
RB Swan & Son, 2757
Rent Mother Nature, 2991

Indian Food
House of Spices, 2706

International Teas
Upton Tea Imports, 2654

Irish
Clancy's Fancy, 2704

Italian
Ferrara Foods & Confections, 2705
Todaro Brothers, 2714

Jams
American Spoon Foods, 2734
Das Peach Haus, 2745
Knott's Berry Farm Food, 2750

Kentucky
Party Kits Equestrian Gifts, 3676

Lamb
Ranch House Mesquite Smoked Meats, 2931

Lobsters
Legal Sea Foods, 2725
LobsterAnywhere.com, 2727

Maple Syrup
Butternut Mountain Farm, 2738
Calef's Country Store, 2602
Cold Hollow Cider Mill, 2743
GloryBee Natural Foods and Crafts, 2842, 3737
Maple Grove Farms of Vermont, 2988
Rent Mother Nature, 2991
Vermont Maple Outlet, 2762

Marmalade
Moon Shine Trading Company, 2755

Meats
Bates Turkey Farm, 2896
Burge's Hickory Smoked Turkeys & Hams, 2898
Fairbury Steaks, 2721
Fine Foods & Accompaniments, 2903
Four Oaks Farm, 2906
Hantover, 2907
Harrington's of Vermont, 2909
High Plains Bison, 2912, 2985
Honey Baked Ham, 2683, 2913
Jackson Hole Buffalo Meat, 2915
Loveless Cafe, 2917
Nebraska Famous Steaks, 2919
New Braunfels Smokehouse, 2920
New Skete, 2921
Nodine's Smokehouse, 2922
Oakwood Game Farm, 2925
Poche's Meat Market & Restaurant, 2928
Smithfield Ham Catalog, 2934
Virginia Traditions, 2940

Medicinal
Kava Kauai, 4396

Mexican
Cibolo Junction, 2703

Mixes
King Arthur Flour & The Bakers, 2517, 5225
Pelican Bay Ltd, 2538, 2875
Rent Mother Nature, 2991
War Eagle Mill Product & Gift, 2891

Moravian
Mrs Hanes Moravian Cookies, 2690

Mustard
Sound of Mustard, 2885

Natural
Azure Standard, 2507, 4380
Horses Prefer, 128
Jaffe Brothers Natural Foods, 2849

Nuts
A Taste of the South, 2943
Hubbard Peanut Company, 2956
Koeze Company, 2958
Merritt Pecan Company, 2962
Sunnyland Farms, 2827, 2973
Trophy Nut, 2526, 2974
Virginia Diner, 2975
Wakefield Peanut Company, 2976
Whitley's Peanut Factory, 2977
Young Plantations Catalog, 2979

Oil
Flying Noodle, 2984

Olive Oil
Living Tree Community Foods, 2850
Olive Press, 2523, 3475

Onions
Mascot Pecan Shelling Company, 2961

Organic
Azure Standard, 2507, 4380
Frontier Natural Products Co-Op, 2634, 4264
Hodgson Mill, 2514, 2847
Jaffe Brothers Natural Foods, 2849
Maine Coast Sea Vegetables, 2852

Oysters
Ekone Oyster Company, 2720

Pasta
Flying Noodle, 2984
Rossi Pasta, 2711

Pastries
Dufour Pastry Kitchens, 2675

Peanuts
Feridies, 2949
Hubbard Peanut Company, 2956
Peanut Shop of Williamsburg, 2964
Whitley's Peanut Factory, 2977

Pecans
A Taste of the South, 2943
Fran's Gifts to Go, 2952
Golden Kernel Pecan Company, 2953
Joe C Williams, 2957
Koinonia Partners, 2959
Merritt Pecan Company, 2962
Pecans.com Catalog, 2693, 2965
Priester's Pecans, 2590, 2696
Sherard Plantation, 2969
Stahmans Pecans, 2598, 2972
Young Plantations, 2978

Petit Fours
Divine Delights, 2673

Pickles
Sechlers Fine Pickles, 2854

Pizza
Lou Malnati's Tastes Of Chicago, 2708

Polish
Polana, 2710

Popcorn
Dale and Thomas Popcorn, 2563, 2838

Poultry
Allen Brothers, 2716, 2893
Oakwood Game Farm, 2925
Omaha Steaks, 2926

Pralines
Aunt Sally's Gift Catalog, 2506, 2791

Prepared
A La Zing, 2503
AppetizersUSA, 2895

Prepared Meals
MagicKitchen.Com, 2851

Quiche
Holiday Foods Catalogue Division, 2811

Regional
Chile Shop, 2981, 3993
Green Mountain Sugar House, 2747
Jardine Foods, 2986
Maple Grove Farms of Vermont, 2988
Oakville Grocery, 2818
Ruma's Fruit & Gift Basket World, 2785

Salami
Jackson Hole Buffalo Meat, 2915

Salmon
Tsar Nicoulai Caviar, 2732

Salsa
Cibolo Junction, 2703
Mo Hotta Mo Betta, 2868

Sauces
Fiorella's Jack Stack Barbecue, 2860, 2904
Flying Noodle, 2984
Maurice's Piggie Park Barbeque, 2866
McIlhenny Company, 2519
Moonlite Food & Gift Magazine, 2989
Original Juan Specialty Foods, 2586, 2872
Pecans.com Catalog, 2693, 2965
Piggie Park Enterprises, 2878
Rossi Pasta, 2711
Soupbase.com, 2886

Sausage
Comeaux's Grocery, 2901
Mission Orchards of Hickory Farms, 2610
Pfaelzer Brothers, 2927
Usinger's Famous Sausage, 2939

Scottish
Hunt Country Foods, 2685
Scottish Gourmet USA, 2713, 2823

Seafood
Chesapeake Bay Crab Cakes & More, 2718
East Coast Gourmet, 2719
Fairbury Steaks, 2721
Legal Sea Foods, 2725
LobsterAnywhere.com, 2727
Omaha Steaks, 2926
Phillips Harborplace, 2729
War Eagle Mill Product & Gift, 2891
Weathervane Seafoods, 2733

Seasonings
Olde Westport Spice & Trading Company, 2871
PS Seasoning and Spices, 2873

Smoked
Amana Meat Shop & Smokehouse, 2894
Burgers' Smokehouse, 2899
Crockett Farms, 2982
Four Oaks Farm, 2906
Harrington's of Vermont, 2909
New Braunfels Smokehouse, 2920
Nodine's Smokehouse, 2922
Nueske's Applewood Smoked Meats, 2611, 2923
Oak Grove Smokehouse, 2924
Shuckman's Fish Company and Smokery, 2731
Walden Foods, 2528

Southern
Southern Season, 2597, 2935

Southwestern
Los Chileros De Nuevo Mexico, 2987

Spices
Atlantic Spice, 2858
Attar Herbs & Spices, 2859
Davidson's Organics, 2630
Mo Hotta Mo Betta, 2868
Olde Westport Spice & Trading Company, 2871
PS Seasoning and Spices, 2873
Pacific Botanicals, 2874
Penzeys Spices, 2877
Rafal Spice, 2879
Riley's Seasoning and Spices, 2880
San Francisco Herb Catalog, 2882
Spice Hunter, 2887

Spreads
Bread Dip Company, 2737
Kozlowski Farms, 2751, 2864

Steaks
Allen Brothers, 2716, 2893
Omaha Steaks, 2926
Stock Yards, 2936

Syrups
CS Steen Syrup Mill, 2739
Vermont Country Store, 1297, 5091

Tea
Frontier Natural Products Co-Op, 2634, 4264
San Francisco Herb Catalog, 2882

Trout
Walden Foods, 2528

Turkey
Bates Turkey Farm, 2896
Burge's Hickory Smoked Turkeys & Hams, 2898

Vegetables
Food Catalog, 2773, 2905
Jordan Seeds Inc., 3278
Maine Coast Sea Vegetables, 2852
Seeds Trust, 2786, 2884, 3303
W Atlee Burpee and Company, 2789, 3320

Vegetarian
Harvest Direct, 2845

Fertilizers
Fertrell Company, 3068
Ohio Earth Food, 3071
Stokes Tropicals, 3217
Turf, Tree & Ornamental Catalog, 3076

Flower Arranging
DBS, 3340

Fountains
Sculpture in Contemporary Garden, 3393

Furniture
Apple Gate Furniture, 3328
Country Casual, 4972
Sycamore Creek, 3398
Trellis Structures, 4644

Garden Markers
Paw Paw Everlast Label Company, 3381

Gardens
Avant Gardens, 3085, 3330
Bustani Plant Farm, 3099, 3333
Collector's Nursery, 3246
Guide to Deer-Resistant Plants, 3140, 3360

Gazebos
Vixen Hill Gazebos, 3406

Gloves
Womanswork, 3410

Greenhouses
Commercial Hydroponic Catalog, 3339
Earthbox, 3342
Greenhouses & Horticultural Supply, 3041
Growers Supply, 3043
Janco Greenhouses, 3047
Santa Barbara Greenhouses, 3392
Sturdi-Built Greenhouse, 3057
Turner Greenhouses, 3058

Hanging Baskets
Violet House of Pots, 3405

Hoses
Loc-Line, 3049

Hydroponic
Commercial Hydroponic Catalog, 3339

Indoor Kits
AeroGarden, 3018, 3326

Irrigation Systems
Imperial Sprinkler Supply, 3045

Lighting
Aurora Decklights, 5040
Escort Lighting, 3343

Organic
Fedco Seeds, 3256
Midwest Supplies, 3375

Ornaments
Florentine Craftsmen, 3348

Pavillions
Vixen Hill Gazebos, 3406

Pest Control
Gardens Alive!, 3069
Water Visions, 3408

Planters
Siebert & Rice, 3394

Ponds
Pond Guy, Inc., 3386
Sweetbrier Waterfalls & Ponds, 3397

Pools
Everything for the Lilypool, 3344
Paradise Water Gardens & Landscape, 3380
PoolSupplyWorld, 3387

Pots
Violet House of Pots, 3405

Sculptures
Sandifer Sculpture, 3391
Sculpture in Contemporary Garden, 3393

Seeds
Fedco Seeds, 3256

Supplies
Allen, Sterling, & Lothrop, 3239
Eden Organic Nursery Services, 3119
Gardeners Edge Catalog, 3040
Guide to Deer-Resistant Plants, 3140, 3360
Liberty Seed Company, 3282

Pond Guy, Inc., 3386
Stark Bro's, 3214

Tillers
Mantis Catalog, 3051

Tools & Equipment
A.M. Leonard Gardeners Edge, 3017
American Arborist Supplies, 3019
Bartlett Arborist Supply & Manufacturing Company, 3332
BlueStone Garden, 3022
CADplans, 3024
Dramm Professional Watering Tools, 3341
Garden Catalog, 3038
Gardener's Supply, 3354
Gardeners Edge Catalog, 3040
Marugg Company, 3372
Pinetree Garden Seeds, 3291

Trees
Fedco Trees, 3257
Spruce Gardens, 3212

Water Gardens
Lilypons Water Gardens, 3163, 3369

Water Lillies
Water Visions, 3408

Waterfalls
Sweetbrier Waterfalls & Ponds, 3397

Garden & Lawn Supplies
Quality Tools & Drip Irrigation Supplies, 3390

Garden Equipment
Greenhouse Kits Catalog, 3359

Garden Supplie
Seeds
Early's Seed Catalog, 3034, 3251

Garden Supplies
Greenhouses
BC Greenhouse Builders, 3021

Gardening
BlueStone Garden, 3022
Urban Farmer Seeds, 3314, 3404

Gardening Supplies
Ritchers Herbs, 3202, 3297

Gas Tanks
Ace Tank, 6015

Gates
Texas Iron Fence & Gate Company, 3399

Gauges
Tire
G.H. Meiser & Company, 507

Gazebos
ASL Associates, 4691
Amish Country Gazebos, 3327
Outdoor Fun Store, 4628

Gears
Berg Precision Mechanical Components, 6036

Gemstones
Diamond Essence, 5174
House of Onyx, 3878
Stone Age Industries, 1825
Zarlene Imports, 3910

Genealogy
National Archives-Pub. & Distribution, 2095

General Merchandise
Dream Products, 3432
Gavilan's, 1324, 5140
Good Fortune, 3656
Welcome to the Best of Lillian Vernon, 3509

Geraniums
Davidson Greenhouse & Nursery, 3112
Fieldstone Gardens, 3124
House of Wesley, 3148

Gift Baskets
Kosher
Challah Connection, 2510, 2555, 2795

Gifts
ABC Distributing, 3514
Alaska Wild Berry Products, 1728, 3638
American Acrylic Awards & Gifts, 3415
Archie McPhee Catalog, 6148
Asprey, 3518
Brookstone, 3420
CBD Clearance, 1042
CBD Gift, 1043
Cake and Candle, 3804
Carol Wright Gifts, 1262, 3422
Celebrate Express, 6157
Celestial Products, 5934
Cheryl's, 3425, 4553
Christian Tools of Affirmation, 1050
Christmas Tree Shops, 4809, 4938
Clay In Motion, 3995
Collection Book, 3528
Collections Etc., 3338, 3427
Comfort House, 3428, 4293
Computer Gear, 3429
Country Store, 2744, 2798
Creations and Collections, 1737, 4059
Current, 3431, 3648
FirstSTREET for Boomers & Beyond, 2226, 3586
Flemington Aluminum & Brass, 3535
GGI LLC, 4033
Gadget Universe, 2230, 3438
Harry & David, 2810
High Fashion Home, 4911, 4942, 5105
Home at Five, 4826
House of Webster, 2515, 3453
Impact Gift Collection, 3539
Jackson Hole Buffalo Meat, 2915
Jayson Home, 4944, 5083, 5108
Lillian Vernon Big Sale, 4834
Lillian Vernon Personalized Gifts, 3465
Lillian Vernon Sales & Bargains, 3466
Lone Star Western D,cor, 4835
Miles Kimball, 4837, 5229, 5343
Miles Kimball Christmas Cards, 3468, 4558
Mixon Fruit Farms, 2780
Mrs. Kimball's Candy Shoppe, 2585
National Artcraft Craft Supplies, 3750
Native Seeds, 3285
Nature's Expression, 1817
Oriental Trading Holiday, 3672, 4565
Orvis Home & Gift, 3478, 4839
Outfitters Supply, 1240
Paper Source, 4052
Paragon-Gifts, 6204
Personal Creations Gift Catalog, 3480, 3678, 4567
Pfaelzer Brothers, 2927
Pioneer National Latex, 3679
Pippin's Hollow Dollmaking, 3757
Plow & Hearth, 3384, 3483
Polart by Mail, 3485
Pyramid Collection, 3684, 5152
Quality Merchandise Direct, 3486
Rowley Company, 4947, 5027
Sharper Image, 3489, 3690
Shop at Home Catalog Directory, 3491
Speak to Me, 3694
The Popcorn Factory, 3500
Toysmith, 6216
Uncommon Goods, 1295
United Force Products, 3610
Vermont Christmas Company, 3505
Vivre, 1545, 3611, 5601
Walter Drake, 3506, 4339, 4866
What on Earth, 1380, 3612
Woodland Smoky Bear Catalog, 3568
Worldwide Collectibles & Gifts Catalog, 1766
Write Touch, 5968

Albums
Webway Album Catalog, 5966

American Indian
Nowetah's American Indian Store & Museum, 3631

Antique
Frye's Measure Mill, 3588

Awards
Alphabet U, 1409, 3516
Marquis Awards & Specialties, 3545

Baskets
Cheryl's, 3425, 4553
Figi's Gifts in Good Taste, 2679, 2804
Kozlowski Farms, 2751, 2864
Monastery Greetings, 2520, 2816
Pemberton Farms, 2819
Pittman & Davis, 2613, 2782, 2820
Sherry Lehmann Wine & Spirits, 3005
Smucker's Catalog, 2759
Sphinx Date Ranch & Southwest Market, 2788, 2970
Stahmanns Pecans, 2598, 2972
The Popcorn Factory, 3500
Van's Gifts, 2829
Weaver's Catalog, 2942
Wine Country Gift Baskets Catalog, 3012
Wood Prairie Farm, 2763, 2832, 3325
Zabar's Catalog, 2833

Birthdays
Personal Creations Gift Catalog, 3480, 3678, 4567

Boxes
Four Oaks Farm, 2906
Gift Box, 3441

Bridal
Bridal Collection, 5171
Exclusively Weddings, 5975

Bridge
Baron/Barclay Bridge Supplies, 1124

Business
Advertising Specialties & Business Gifts, 3515
Pecco Premiums, 3551
Positive Impressions Idea Showcase, 3554
Quill Full Line, 3556
Windjammer Promotions, 3567

Buttons
Badge-A-Minit, 3715
Ephemera Magnets Button & Stickers, 3433

Candy
Plumbridge Confections & Gifts, 2589

Cats
Custom Gifts & More, 83

Celtic
GaelSong, 3439, 5179

Childrens
Lilly's Kids, 1394

China
Emerald Collection, 3583
Griffith Pottery House, 3589
Hall's Merchandising, 3590

Christian
CBD Clearance, 1042
CBD Gift, 1043

Christmas
Past Times, 3677

Collectibles
Country House, 3580
Entertainment Earth, 6177

Consumer Electronics
Horchow Mail Order, 3452

Corporate
ACA Corporate Awards, 5373
Bridgewater Chocolate, 2550, 2794
Custom-Printed Promotional Items, 3529
Direct Promotions, 3530
Engraving Connection, 3534
Fahrney's Pens, 5387
Holiday Cards for Businesses, 3660, 5917
International Bronze Manufacturers, 3541
Kogle Cards, 3544
Medallic Art Company, Ltd, 3546
Pacific Sportswear & Emblem Company, 3550
Print Craft, Inc., 3555
Quill Full Line, 3556

Filters
Flanders, 4619

Furnaces
Fraser-Johnston Heating/Air Conditioning, 4620
Heat Treating & America's Finest, 4001

Regulators
Aerco International, 5503

Helicopters
Robinson Helicopter, 646

Kits
Barnett Rotor Craft, 638

Helmets
Fox Head, 1575

Herbs
AeroGarden, 3018, 3326
Attar Herbs & Spices, 2859
Botanic Gardens, 4429
Eden Organic Nursery Services, 3119
Frontier Wholesale Price Guide, 2861
Hartman's Herb Farm, 3141
Herbal Healer Academy, 4316
Kava Kauai, 4396
Logee's Greenhouses, 3164
Niche Gardens, 3175
Ritchers Herbs, 3202, 3297
San Francisco Herb & Natural Food, 2648, 2881
Spices Etc, 2888
Vitamin Direct, 4409
Woodcreek Drieds Inc, 3778

Chinese
Ron Teeguarden's Dragon Herbs, 4404

Seeds
Comstock, Ferre & Company, 3108
Garden City Seeds, 3263
Goodwin Creek Gardens, 3264
Horticultural Products & Services, 3271
Nichols Garden Nursery, 3287
Rohrer Seeds, 3300
Sandy Mush Herb Nursery, 2883
Southern Exposure Seed Exchange, 3307
Territorial Seed Company, 3310
Vermont Bean Seed Company, 3318
Wildflower Reference Guide & Seed Catalog, 3322

Hiking
Books
Appalachian Mountain Club Books & Maps, 1121

Hobbies
Art Tech Casting Company, 3714
Bill Cole Enterprises, 4481
Cabela's Fall Master, 2364, 2425, 2468
Cabela's Spring Master, 2367, 2426, 2469
Ecstasy Crafts, 191
Foredom Electric Company Power Tool Catalog, 6055
Mega Hobby, 3747
Smoky Mountain Knife Works, 1183, 2258, 2496
Squadron, 4489
Standard Hobby Supply, 3771

Beekeeping Supplies
Betterbee, 4492
Walter T Kelley Company, 4496

Boats
Sailrite Marine Catalog, 743, 778, 808

Calligraphy
Ames & Rollinson, 4480

Chess
US Chess Federation, 1190

Dolls
Hobby Builder's Supply, 1855

Fireworks
Phantom Fireworks, 4498
TNT Fireworks, 4502

General Supplies
Dick Blick Art Materials, 187

Paper Wishes, 206
Sunshine Discount Crafts, 3772

Jewelery
Crown Galleries, 729

Metal Detectors
Kellyco Metal Detector Superstore, 4487
White's Metal Detectors, 274, 3063, 5134

Miniatures
Hobby Builder's Supply, 1855

Models
Authentic Models Holland, 4509
Central Valley, 4510
Charles Ro Supply Company, 4511
Dee's Delights, 1805, 4512
Green Frog Railroad Catalog, 4513
Historic Rail Product Catalog, 4484, 6184
International Hobby Corporation, 4516
Mission Supply House, 4518
Plastruct, 4522
Tower Hobbies, 4527
Woodland Scenics, 4529

Sewing
Hancock's of Paducah, 4176, 5082

Ship Models
Model Expo, 4520

Supplies
Air-Tite Holders, 1781
Lion Brand Yarn, 4028, 4185
Mary Maxim, 3968
Times to Cherish, 3774

Tools
Crown Galleries, 729

Warplane Models
Warplanes, 4528

Winemaking
Retail Winemaking, 4539

Winemaking & Brewing
Beer, Beer & More Beer, 4531
EC Kraus Wine & Beermaking Supplies, 4532
Fall Bright, 4533
Grapestompers, 4534
International Wine Accessories, 4535
Midwest Homebrewing and Winemaking, 4536
MoreBeer!, 4537
The Home Brewery, 4540
WindRiver Brewing Company, 4542
Wine Appreciation Guild Store, 4543

Hobie Cat
Hobie Kayak Collection, 801

Hockey
Action Sports Systems, 5774
Dante Cozzi Sports, 5841
Great Skate Hockey Supply Company, 5775
Kemp's Hockey Supply Company, 5797
Maska USA, 5777
Ocean Hockey Supply Company, 5778

Holiday
Christmas
Graphics 3, 4547, 4555, 4587

Holiday Cards
Exposures, 161, 4734
Holiday Expressions, 5944

Corporate
Holiday Cards for Businesses, 3660, 5917

Home Appliances
Stoneberry, 3056, 4857, 6210

Home Building & Repair
Accurate Metal Weather Strip Company, 4596
BJB Enterprises, 4607
BMI Supply, 4608
Benjamin Moore & Co., 4719
Chelsea Decorative Metal Company, 4725
Crown Heritage, 4616
Daly's, 4774
Deltec Homes, 4693

Fox Valley Systems, 4775
Home Improvements, 4624
Homecraft Veneer & Woodworker's Supplies, 4741
Nostalgic Warehouse Door Hardware, 4752
Phyllis Kennedy, 4629
Phylrich International, 4755
Rainhandler, 4634
Rosenzweig Lumber Corporation, 4636
Specification Chemicals, 4760
Timberlane Woodcrafters, 4705
York Ladder, 4655

Alternative Energy
Backwoods Solar Electric Systems, 4660
HearthStone Catalog: Wood & Pellet Products, 4664
New England Solar Electric, 4666
Solar Flare, 4667
Sunelco, 4669
Vermont Castings, 4670
Yellow Jacket Solar, 4671

Architectural Antiques
Brass Knob, 4675

Awnings
Astrup Company, 4604, 4935

Blinds
Blind Butler, 4720

Building Materials
Blue Ox Millworks, 4610

Ceilings
WF Norman Corporation, 4769

Clapboards
Granville Manufacturing, 4623

Columns
Somerset Door & Column Company, 4639

Cupolas
Cape Cod Cupola Company, 4677

Doorknobs
Cirecast, 4679

Doors
Ciro C Coppa, 4613
Creative Openings, 4615
Touchstone Woodworks, 4643

Entryways
Architectural Components, 4601

Fences
Amazing Gates, 4598

Flooring
Aged Woods, 4715
Albany Woodworks, 4716
Woodhouse, 4771

Grilles
Reggio Register Company, 4757

Hardware
AllMetal Manufacturing, 5006
Ball and Ball, 4964
Custom Hardware by Kayne & Son, 4617
Decorative Hardware Studio, 5011
HA Guden Company, 4739
Shuttercraft, 4638
Vintage Hardware, 5032
Williamsburg Blacksmiths, 4682
Wood Workers Store Catalog, 4653

Hardwood
Badger Hardwoods of Wisconsin, 4090
Conklin's Authentic Antique Barnwood, 4614
Lumber Liquidators, 4626
Rare Earth Hardwood, 4635

House Kits
Habitat Post & Beam, 4695

Interior Design
American Blind & Wallpaper Factory, 4933
Pagliacco Turning and Milling, 4754

Kits
Shelter-Kit, 4704
US Buildings, 4707

Lighting
Ball and Ball, 4964
Classic Accents, 5043

Metalwork
Fine Architectural Metalsmiths, 4618

Millwork
Fypon, 4737
Mad River Woodworks, 4749

Mouldings
Copperbeech Millwork, 4727
Driwood Moulding Company, 4731
Old World Mouldings, 4753

Ornaments
Decorators Supply Corporation, 4730
JP Weaver Company, 4745

Paints/Finishes/Removers
Old-Fashioned Milk Paint Company, 4777

Paneling
Fan Fair, 3346

Plans
ASL Associates, 4691
Acorn Deck House, 4692
Historical Replications, 4696
Where's Home For You?, 4710

Plaster Ornaments
Felber Ornamental Plastering, 4736

Plumbing
Faucet Outlet, 4786
Urban Archeology, 4766
Watercolors Inc, 4793

Post & Beam
Acorn Deck House, 4692

Railings
Carpet Hardware Systems, 4723

Registers
Reggio Register Company, 4757

Roofing
ABC Supply Co., Inc., 4594
Berridge Manufacturing Company, 4674
Campbellsville Industries, Inc, 4676

Stairs
Iron Shop, 4743
Stair Specialist, 4761

Stencils
Stencilworks, 4762

Sunrooms
Four Seasons Sunrooms, 4694

Tile
Tile Restoration Center, 4764

Windows
Marvin Windows & Doors, 3597
Weather Shield Windows and Doors, 4650
Wood Window Workshop, 4652

Woodwork
Cinderwhit & Company, 4094
Wood Factory, 4770

Home Furnishing
Accessories
Wayfair, 4867, 4885, 4905

Home Furnishings
Acacia, 671, 3569
Anthropologie, 1306, 1680
Ballard Designs, 4798
Belk New Directions, 1255, 1384, 4800
Belk Wedding Catalog, 4583, 4801
Bella Coastal D,cor, 4936, 4952, 5009
Berry Hill Limited, 4803
Black Forest Decor, 4029, 4937, 5077
Blair Home, 4804, 5096
Brookstone, 3420
Brumbaugh's Furniture & Rug Catalog, 4966
BrylaneHome, 4806, 4876, 4967
CB2, 4807, 4968, 5078
Calico Corners, 3574, 4157
Christmas Tree Shops, 4809, 4938
Comfort House, 3428, 4293
Crate & Barrel, 4812
Deseret Book Company, 1053
Dr. Leonard's Healthcare, 4297
DwellStudio, 4814, 4910, 5101
Fresh Finds, 4819, 5222
Ginny's, 1786, 1808, 4979

BA Mason, 5560
Birkenstock Express, 5563
Cinderella of Boston, 5567
Complements by Anthony Richards, 5568
Coward Shoes, 1690
Delia's Contents, 5012
Giordano's Petite Shoes, 5576
K. Jordan, 1334, 5579
Maryland Square, 5580
Mason Shoes, 5581
Massey's, 5582
Naturalizer, 697
Nike Footwear, 5586
Shape-Ups Women's Catalog, 5593
SimplySoles, 1719
Work
Worker's Choice, 1666

Shortbread
Willa's Shortbread, 2700

Shrubs & Plants
Avant Gardens, 3085, 3330

Signs
BrittenMedia, 3525
Mailboxes Catalog, 3371
Rebechini Studios, 3558
Saint Louis Slot Machines, 6117
Seton Catalog, 5924
United Force Products, 3610
Automotive
Fremont Die Consumer Products, 305
Engraved
Emedco Buyer's Guide, 3533
Neon
P&H Crystalite, 5064

Silk
Clothing
Winter Silks Catalog, 1507

Silk Flowers
Petals Catalog, 3481
Silkflowers.Com, 4856

Silver
Jewelry
Michael C Fina, 3598

Skateboards
Active Ride Women's Shop, 5846
CCS, 5850
Pacific Drive Mail Order, 5657

Skating
National Running Center, 5831
Plus Skate Shop, 5844

Skiing
Akers Ski, 5847
Burton Snowboards, 5849
Obermeyer, 5854
Race Place, 5856
Scandinavian Ski Shops, 5858
Tognar Ski & Snowboard Tools, 5860
Racing
Reliable Racing Winter Sports, 5857
Skis
Sporthill, 1608, 5834

Skin & Beauty Products
DHC Care, 4258, 4431

Skin Care Products
As We Change, 1453, 4287, 4417
DHC, 1978, 4430, 5938
Hobe Laboratories, 4435
Paula's Choice Skincare, 4448, 5949
Perfumax, 1986, 4278, 5950
SkinStore.com Catalog, 4457
Tova, 4461
Child
Pretty Baby Naturals, 4451
Soaps
Indigo Wild, 2277, 4437, 4891
Soap Saloon, 3766, 3809

SunFeather Natural Soap Company, 4459

Skindiving
Berry Scuba Company, 5835
Performance Diver, 5838

Skydiving
Rigging Innovations, 5825

Sled Dog Equipment
Risdon Rigs, 107

Sleepwear
Time for Me, 1722

Sleeves
Mylar
Bill Cole Enterprises, 4481

Smoked Fish
Hansen Caviar Company, 2722

Smoked Oysters
Ekone Oyster Company, 2720

Smoked Salmon
SeaBear Smokehouse, 2730

Smoked Seafood
Walden Foods, 2528

Smoked Trout
Shuckman's Fish Company and Smokery, 2731

Snow Plows
Discount Snow Plow Parts, 6048

Snowboarding
Active Ride Women's Shop, 5846
Burton Snowboards, 5849
CCS, 5850

Snowboards
Active Ride Snow Shop, 5845

Soaps
Baudelaire, 4424
Soap Making Supplies
Soap Saloon, 3766, 3809

Soccer
Rugby & Soccer Supply/Godek Rugby, 5863
Soccer Learning Systems, 5864
Soccer.com, 1607, 5598, 5865
TSI Soccer, 5867

Softball
Softball Catalog, 5671

Software
Connection, 1894, 1948
Software Express Educators Catalog, 1966
Business
American Business Systems, 1945
Earth Science
RockWare, 1965
Printing
Paper Access, 1960, 5982
Real Estate
Complete Real Estate Software Catalog, 1947

Solar Energy
Big Frog Mountain Corporation, 4661
Environmental Geothermal Houses, 4662
New England Solar Electric, 4666
Solar Flare, 4667

Solariums
Aluminum
Sunshine Rooms, 4859

Special Education Software
Mayer-Johnson, 996, 1984

Special Needs
LS&S, 2006
Special Needs, 2109
Super Duper Publications, 2112

Special Occasion Foods
Cookie Garden, 2559

Specialty Food
Carson Wrapped Hershey's Chocolates, 2554
Dean & DeLuca, 2511
Schaul's Signature Gourmet Foods, 2822, 2933, 2967

Specimens
Dissection Materials Catalog, 2136
Skulls Unlimited International, 2166
Young Naturalist Company Catalog, 2170

Speech Language Materials
Speech and Language, 2110

Spices
Atlantic Spice, 2858
Market Spice, 2641
Olde Westport Spice & Trading Company, 2871
Rafal Spice, 2879
Riley's Seasoning and Spices, 2880
Spice Hunter, 2887
Spices Etc, 2888

Sporting Goods
Alden Rowing Shells, 5827
BSN Sports Athletic Performance, 5606
BSN Sports Baseball-Fastpitch, 5709
BSN Sports Direct, 5607
BSN Sports Equipment, 5608
BSN Sports Gear Pro-Tec, 5609
BSN Sports Lacrosse, 5795
BSN Sports League, 5610
BSN Sports Middle School-Junior High, 5611
BSN Sports TeamWear, 5880
Cannon Sports, 5619
Court Products, 5621
DB Enterprises, 5862
Everlast Worldwide, 5625
Franklin Sports, 5630, 5886
Goal Sporting Goods, 5632
House, 5638
Hulme Sporting Goods & MFG Company, 5639
League Direct, 5643
Memphis Net & Twine Company-Sports, 5890
OnDeck Sports, 3548, 5712
Perform Better, 5824
Pro Tour Sports, 5663
SGD Golf, 5764
SNA Sports, 5669, 5893
Sierra Trading Post, 1606, 5670
Softball Catalog, 5671
Stackhouse Athletic Equipment, 5715, 5866
Toledo Physical Education Supply, 5675
Yukon Fitness Equipment, 4255
Accessories
Smoky Mountain Knife Works, 1183, 2258, 2496
Archery
3Rivers Archery, 2459, 5682
Apple Archery Products, 5684
Cabela's Archery, 5688
Darton Archery, 5689
Mike's Archery, 5696
Baseball
Hot On the Ice, 5637
Mid-America Sports Advantage, 5647
No Fault Sports Products, 5653
Roger's USA, 5713
San Sun Hat and Cap Group, 5714
Basketball
Basketball Express, 5613
Hoops King, 5636
No Fault Sports Products, 5653
Pacific Sports Warehouse, 5876
Bicycling
American Cycle Express, 5717
Burley Design Cooperative, 5719
HED Cycling Products, 5725
HMC, 5726

Hawk Racing, 5727
Just Two Bikes, 5728
Lone Peak Designs, 5730
Loose Screws Bicycle Small Parts, 5731
Mountaineers Books, 1177
O'Neal Azonic, 5732
Performance Bicycle, 5733
Tandems, Ltd, 5736
Boxing
Ringside, 5806
Cheerleading
Stumps Spirit & Homecoming, 1447
Team Cheer, 1448
Childrens
FlagHouse Physical Education and Recreation, 5628
Clothing
Cloudveil, 1231, 1422
Dennis Kirk Snowmobile Catalog, 1315
Dennis Kirk Watercraft Catalog, 1571
Filson, 1573
REI, 5819, 5855
Croquet
Prize Possessions, 5662
Cross Country
VS Athletics Cross Country, 5600
Darts
Horizon Dart Supply, 4485
Equestrian
Big Sky Leatherworks, 5780
Chamisa Ridge, 5782
Chick's Harness & Supply, 5783
Horse.com, 12
Justin Carriage Works, 5788
New Miller Harness, 5789
Fencing
American Fencers Supply, 5739
Zivkovic Modern Equipment, 5741
General Products
BSN Sports Athletic Performance, 5606
BSN Sports Baseball-Fastpitch, 5709
BSN Sports Direct, 5607
BSN Sports Equipment, 5608
BSN Sports Gear Pro-Tec, 5609
BSN Sports Middle School-Junior High, 5611
Golf
Cobra Golf, 5744
Component Golf Supplies, 5745
Diamond Tour Golf, 5746
Golf Around the World, 5748
Golf Haus, 5749
Golfsmart, 5753
Golfsmith Store, 5754
Hireko Golf Products, 5757
Lefties Only, 5758
Lomma Golf, 5759
Par-Buster, 5762
Ralph Maltby's GolfWorks, 5763
Golf Accessories
Golf Balls & More, 5883
Gymnastics
Midwest Gym Supply, 5770
Hockey
Action Sports Systems, 5774
Great Skate Hockey Supply Company, 5775
Hot Off the Ice, 5637
Kemp's Hockey Supply Company, 5797
Maska USA, 5777
National Running Center, 5831
Ocean Hockey Supply Company, 5778
Kayaks
Great River Outfitters, 5633
Lacrosse
BSN Sports Lacrosse, 5795
Great Atlantic Lacrosse Company, 5796
Lacrosse International, 5798
Martial Arts
Artistic Video, 5800
Century Martial Art Supply, 5802
International Taekwondo Association, 5804
Jukado International, 5805

A

A&A Manufacturing, 443
A&A Manufacturing Parts, 443
A&D Bookstore & Supply, 2045
A&D Bookstore & Supply Educational, 2045
A&H Abrasives, 6012
A. Daigger & Company, 2134
A.L. Ellis, Inc., 4932
A.L.P. Lighting Components, Inc., 4595
A.M. Leonard, 4593
A.M. Leonard Gardeners Edge, 3017
A.M. Leonard Master Guide, 4593
A.M. Leonard, Inc., 3017
A.R.T. Studio Clay Company, Inc., 3814
A.S.L. & Associates, 4691
AA Clouet, 3855
AAVIM, 956, 2171
ABA Sales, 56, 1118
ABC Distributing, 3514
ABC Feelings, 2046, 2322
ABC Supply Co., Inc., 4594
ABP/Pharmex, 5502
ABaby, 656, 6142
ACA Corporate Awards, 5373
ACA For Churches Only, 5374
ACA School Essentials, 5375
ACE Educational Supplies, 2047
ACM Technologies Inc, 5352
ACP Composites, 636
ACS Publications, 1027
ACS Solutions Inc., 1973
AD Trophy, 3412
AD Trophy Manufacturing Corporation, 3412
ADCOLE, 444
AERCO, 5503
AG Russell, 5209
AG Russell Knives, Inc., 5209
AGV Sport, 277
AGV Sports Group, Inc., 277
AIAA Winter/Spring Publication Catalog, 957
AICPA, 876
AICPA Self-Study & On-Site Training Catalog, 876
AIChE, 2125
AIIM, 877
AIM Kilns, 3813
AIMS Education Foundation, 2120
AIRE, Inc., 749
AKA Gourmet, 2980
AL Ellis, 4932
ALP Lighting, 4595
ALPHA Sound & Lighting Co., 5461
AMC Sales, 5135
AMC Sales, Inc., 5135
AMES Taping Tools, 6029
AMSOIL, 405, 790
AP Sound, Inc., 2208, 5037, 5285
API Outdoors, 2460
APR Prop and Background, 5472
APSCO Catalog, 2288
ARE Press, 1097
ART Studio Clay Company, 3814
ARTA River Trips, 6229
ASCP Catalog, 1098
ASHA, 4225
ASI Home, 4797
ASL Associates, 4691
ASN Publishing, 1119
ATD-AMERICAN, 5324
ATD-American, 5325
ATD-American Catalog, 5324
ATD-American School Catalog, 5325
ATI Performance Products, 278
ATI Performance Products, Inc., 278
ATS Sports, 5868
AU-RUS Wax Patterns, 3856
AVAC Corporation, 4874
AVI-SPL, 257
AVW Equipment Company, 406
AVW Equipment Company, Inc., 406
AW Direct, 279
Aazida, Inc., 4420
Abatron, Inc., 2104
Abbeon Cal Plastic Working Tools, 2121

Abbeon Cal, Inc., 2121
Abbey Press, 3636
Abbey Press Trade Marketing, 3636
AbeBooks.com, 903
Abel, 2356
Ablenet, 1991
Ablenet Inc, 1991
Absolutely Natural, 4416
Acacia, 671, 3569
Academic Superstore, 2048, 2172
Accelerated Development, 958
Access to Recreation, 1992, 6227
Access to Recreation, Inc., 1992, 6227
Accessory Center, 280
Accon Marine, 748
Accordion-O-Rama, 5283
Accountant Stationers & Printers, 5903
Accu Trak Tool, 6013
Accu Trak Tool Corporation, 6013
Accu-Tech, 2207
Accu-Tech Cable, 2207
Accu-Time Systems, 1944
AccuCut Craft, 3712, 6014
AccuCut Systems, 3712, 6014
Accurate Metal Weather Strip Company, 4596
Accurate Metal Weatherstrip Co., 4596
Ace Tank, 6015
Ace Tank & Equipment Company, 6015
Achievement Products For Children, 4282
Achievement Products for Special Needs, 4282
Acme Manufacturing, 6016
Acme Tools, 6017
Acorn, 1859
Acorn Deck House, 4692
Acorn Deck House Company, 4692
Acoustic Sounds, 2289
Acoustic Sounds, Inc., 2289
Action Lighting, 4582
Action Lighting Holiday Catalog, 4582
Action Party Rentals, 1886
Action Sports Systems, 5774
Action Sports Systems Inc, 5774
Actionjetz LLC, 4528
Activa Sports, 1451, 1554
Active Forever, 4283
Active Parenting Publishers, 1082
Active Ride Shop, 5840, 5845, 5846
Active Ride Skate Shop, 5840
Active Ride Snow Shop, 5845
Active Ride Women's Shop, 5846
ActiveForever, 4292, 4313, 4326, 4328
Adage Publications/ABC Feelings, 2046, 2322
Adam Wood Products, 4683, 4714
Adams County Nursery, 3078
Adams Wood Products, 4683, 4714
Adaptive Seeds, 2267
Adcole Corporation, 444
Added Touch, 3413
The Added Touch, 3413
Addison, 4597
Addison Products Company, 4597
Adjustable Clamp, 6018
Adler's, 5159
Adolph Kiefer & Associates, 1452
Adolph Kiefer & Associates Inc, 791, 1452
Adolph Kiefer and Associates, Inc., 791
Adoption Book, 1083
Adorama, 1972
Advance Adapters Buyer's Guide, 388
Advance Adapters, Inc., 388
Advanced Graphics, 281
Advanced Graphics Inc., 281
Advanced Machinery, 6019
Advantage Bag Company, 2040
Advantage Bags, 2040
Advantage Medical, 2016, 2030, 2041
Adventure Cycling Association, 5721, 5722
Adventure Edge, 1249, 1555
Adventure Life, 1194
Adventure Motorcycle Gear, 1556
Adventure Publications, 920
Advertising Specialties & Business Gifts, 3515
Aerco International, 5503
Aerial Lift, 6020

Aero Design & Mfg. Co., Inc., 5242
AeroGarden, 3018, 3326
AeroGrow International Inc., 3018, 3326
Aerogroup International, LLC, 5555
Aerosoles, 5555
Aerospace Composite Products, 636
Aerospace Products International, 637
Aerostich Rider Wearhouse, 5242
Affinity Tool Works, LLC, 4128
Afro World Hair Company, 4468
Afro World Hair and Fashion Company, 4468
Aftosa, 3815
Age Comfort, 1993
Aged Woods, 4715
Aged Woods, Inc., 4715
Aging Resources, 1099, 2323
Agri Supply Co., 109
Agri Supply Company, 109
Agricultural Sciences, 110, 2049
Ahee, 5160
Aim Kiln Manufacturing Co., 3816
Aim Kiln Manufacturing Company, 3813
Aim Kilns, 3816
Aims International Books, 1195
Air Craft Spruce & Specialty Company, 648
Air Drive, Inc., 445
Air Tools, Hand Tools, Sheet Metal Tools, 6021
Air-Drive, 445
Air-Tite Holders, 1781
Air-Tite Holders Inc, 1781
Aircraft Spruce & Specialty Company, 605
Aircraft Spruce West, 605
Aircraft Tool Supply Company, 606, 6022
Aire Catalog, 749
Airline International, 3616
Airline International Luggage, 3476
Airline International Luggage & Gifts, 3616
Airplane Shop, 3637
The Airplane Shop, 3637
Airtex, 4007
Airtex Consumer Products, 4007
Aitken's Salmon Creek Garden, 3079
Akers Ski, 5847
Akers Ski, Inc., 5847
Al's Farm Toys, 6143
Al's Farm Toys & The Toy Box, 6143
Al's Goldfish Lure Company, 2357
Alan Furman & Co., Inc., 5161
Alan Furman & Company, 5161
Alan Sloane & Company, 1303
Alan Sloane & Company, Inc., 1303
Alaska Herb Tea Company, 2621
Alaska Wild Berry Products, 1728, 3638
Alaska Wild Berry Products, Inc., 1728, 3638
Albany Woodworks, 4716
Albany Woodworks, Inc., 4716
Alberene Royal Mail, 3414
Albion Engineering, 6023
Albion Industries, 6024
Albion Industries Full Line Catalog, 6024
Albritton Fruit Company, 2765
AlcoPro, 4343
Alcone Company, 5462
Alcone LIC, 5462
Alden Lee Company, 5284
Alden Lee Company, Inc., 5284
Alden Rowing Shells, 5827
Alden Rowing Shells, LLC, 5827
Alethea's Chocolates, 2544
Alexandra's Homespun Textiles, 4149
Alfa Aesar, 2268
Alfax Furniture, 5326
Alfred Angelo, 1408
Algy, 1625
Algy Team Collection, 1625
AliMed, 4320
AliMed Operating Room Products, 4226
AliMed, Inc, 4226, 4344
AliMed, Inc., 4235, 4348
Alimed, 4344
All About Dance, 607, 5443
All About Dog Grooming, 32
All About Dolls, 6174
All Pro Sound, 2208, 5037, 5285

Davidson's Organics, 2630
Davies, 1105
Davies Publishing, 1105
Davis, 300, 816, 2071, 2273
Davis Instruments, 816, 2273
Davis Instruments Corp., 300, 5552
Davis Publications, 2071
Day One Camouflage, 1218
Day Runner, 5361
Day Runner Direct, 5361
Day Timer, 5362
Day-Ray Products, 5047
Daylily Discounters, 3250
Daystone International Corporation, 5714
Dayton Wheel Products, 301
Dayton Wire Wheels, 301
Dazian Fabrics, 4163
Dazor Manufacturing Corporation, 5048
De Soto Sport Company, 1570
DeSantis Collection, 1526
DeSantis Gunhide, 2429
DeSantis Holster, 2429
Dean & DeLuca, 2511
Dean & DeLuca, Inc., 2511
Debbie Burk Optical, 5421
Decent Exposures, 1493
Decor Time Products, 3840
Decor by Dobry, 4729
Decorative Hardware Studio, 5011
Decorative Home, 4813
Decorative Painting by P.J.!, 4051
Decorators Supply Corporation, 4730
Dee Engineering, 420
Dee's Delight Inc, 1805, 4512
Dee's Delights, 1805, 4512
Deer & Deer Hunting Catalog, 2474
Deer & Hunting Books Catalog, 1148
The Deer Shack, 2475
Deer-Resistant Landscape Nursery, 3140, 3360
Deering, 5294
Deering Banjo Company, 5294
Deershack, 2475
Defender Industries, Inc., 795
Defender Marine Buyer's Guide, 795
Definitely Decorative, 3727
Deja Vu Collector's Gallery, 1149
Del Arbour Designs, 5842
Delia's, 1265, 1693, 5100
Delia's Contents, 5012
Delias, 5012
Delicious Orchards, 2770
Delphi Glass Corporation, 4032
Delphi's Annual Supply Catalog, 4032
Delta Consolidated Industries, 302, 307
Delta Creative, 1872
Delta Creative, Inc., 1872
Delta Education LLC, 2135
Delta Force, 2430
Delta Group, 2430
Delta Lights, 484
Delta Picture Frame Company, 160
Delta Pre-K - 6 Science and Math, 2135
Delta Press, 1150
Delta Press LTD., 1150
Delta Tech Industries, 484
Delta Truck Storage Solutions, 302
Deltec Homes, 4693
Deluxe Business Corporation, 1906
Deluxe For Business, 5944
Deluxe Small Business Services, 2219
Demco, 5333
Demco Furniture Catalog, 4974
Demco imagine whats possible, 5330
Deneen Pottery, 3997
Dennis Carpenter, 485
Dennis Carpenter Ford Restoration, 485
Dennis K Burk, 486
Dennis K. Burk Inc., 486
Dennis Kirk, 392, 1315, 1571, 5253, 5254
Dennis Kirk Inc, 5269
Dennis Kirk Metric Motorcycle Catalog, 5253
Dennis Kirk Off Road Catalog, 392, 5254
Dennis Kirk Snowmobile Catalog, 1315
Dennis Kirk Watercraft Catalog, 1571

Dennis Kirk, Inc., 716
Denny Manufacturing Company, 5464
The Denny Manufacturing Company, Inc., 5464
Deseret Book Company, 1053
Deseret Books, 1054, 1053
Desert Rat Off Road Centers, 393
Desert Rat Off-Road, 393
Design Group, 6170
Design Group Pattern, 6170
Design Originals, 1151
Design Toscano, 4975
Design Within Reach, 4976
Designer Culinary Stensils, 4045
Designer Stencils, 4045
Designs by Joan Green, 3948
Designs by Margarita, 5843
Desperate Enterprises, 1773
Desperate.com, 1773
Desserts by David Glass, 2671
Detailed Play Systems, 6171
Detroit Body Products, 487
Detta's Spindle, 4077
Detwiler Tractor Parts, 6045
Development Studies, 972
Dharma Communications, 1071, 2336
Dharma Trading Co., 4169
Dharma Trading Company, 186
DharmaCrafts, 1047
DiCamillo, 2534
DiCamillo Bakery, 2534
Dialogic Corporation, 1962
Diamond Essence, 5174
Diamond Machining Technology, 6046
Diamond Nexus, 1316
Diamond Pacific Tool, 3863
Diamond Pacific Tool Corporation, 3863
Diamond Tour Golf, 5746
Dick Blick Art Materials, 187
Dick Pond Athletics, 5830
Dick Pond Athletics, Inc, 5830
Dickies, 1666
Dickson Company, 5517
Didax, 2072
Didax Educational Resources, 2072
Diecast Direct, 1740, 6172
Diefenbacher Tools, 6047
Different Roads to Learning, 2073
Digging Dog Nursery, 3113
Digi International Inc., 1943
Dinkel's Bakery, 2672
Dinn Brothers, 5623
Dinn Brothers Trophies, 5623
Direct Gardening, 3114
Direct Promotions, 3530
Directory of Life Extension Nutrients and Dru gs, 4294
Disability Bookshop Catalog, 886
Disc Makers, 2192, 2299
Discount Dance Supply, 1317
Discount Inboard Marine, 796
Discount School Supply, 188, 2074, 3728
Discount Snow Plow Parts, 6048
Discover Magnetics, 4295
Discovery Channel, 2177, 3531, 3649
The Discovery Channel, 2097
Discovery Corner, 6173
Discovery Store, 2177, 3531, 3649
Displays2Go, 5383
Dissection Materials Catalog, 2136
Diva Beauty Products, 4441
Divers Direct, 5836
Divine Delights, 2673
Dixie Art Airbrush, 189
Dixon Industries, 3031
Dixondale Farms, 3066
Dock Builders Supply, 797
Dock Doctors, 798
Doctors Foster & Smith, 6
Dogs Unlimited, 96
Dogs Unlimited LLC, 96
Doheny's, 3032
Doheny's Water Warehouse, 3032, 3060, 4648
Doll Lover Catalog, 6174
Dollmasters, 1806
Domestic Trucks Performance Products, 303

Don Aslett's Cleaning Center, 4810
Donahue's Greenhouse, 3115
Donna Salyers Fabulous-Furs, 1481
Donnelly/Colt Progressive Resources, 1318
Doolco, 887
Dorothy Biddle Service, 3340
Dos De Tejas Patterns, 3949
Dos de Tejas / The Pattern Co., 3949
Double A Vineyards, 2996, 3116
Douglas Battery, 488
Douglas Battery Manufacturing Company, 488
Dove Brushes, 190
Dover Publications, 229, 932, 935, 977, 993, 995, 1073, 3724, 5320
Dover Saddlery, 117
Down Under Saddle Supply, 5784
Doyle's Thornless Blackberry, 2746
Dr Cookie, 2674
Dr Leonard's, 4296
Dr Leonard's Healthcare Corporation, 4296, 4297
Dr. Cookie Gourmet Cookies, 2674
Dr. Leonard's Healthcare, 4297
Dr. Slick, 2373
Dr. Slick Co., 2373
Dragon Door, 2234, 4240
Dramm Corporation of Manitowoc, 3341
Dramm Professional Watering Tools, 3341
Draper's & Damon's, 1694
Draper's Super Bee Apiaries, 4494
Drawing Board, 5384, 5922
Drawing Board Printing, 5384
Dream Products, 3432
DreamHaven Books, 834
Dremel, 6049
Drenon Jewelry, 5175
Drenon Jewelry Holiday, 5175
Drip Irrigation, 3033
DripWorks, 3067
Driwood Moulding Company, 4731
Droll Yankees, 61
Drug Package, 4298
Drumbeat Indian Arts, 3864
Drumbeat Indian Arts, Inc., 3864
Dry Goods for a Wet World, 5837
Drysdales, 1669
DuPont Pioneer, 1910, 1961
Ducks, Ducks & More Ducks Catalog, 1873
Dufour Pastry Kitchens, 2675
Dufour Pastry Kitchens, Inc., 2675
Duke Medical Supply, 4354
Dulcimer Shoppe, 5295
Duluth Trading Catalog for Men, 1319, 5569
Duluth Trading Catalog for Women, 1320, 5570
Duluth Trading Company, 1695, 5624, 1319, 1320, 1726, 5569, 5570, 6255
Dunbrooke Apparel Corp, 5881
Dunbrooke Sportswear Company, 5881
Duncan Enterprises, 3824
Duncraft, 62
Duncraft-Wild Bird Superstore, 62
Dundee Groves, 2564
Dunkin's Diamonds, 4586
Duralite, 3825
Duralite Inc., 3825
Durey Libby Edible Nuts, 2947
Durey Libby Edible Nuts Inc., 2947
Durham Boat Company, 5828
Dust Collection, 4098
Dutch Gardens, 3117
Dutchguard, 4299
Dutchman 1955-1957 Chevy Car Catalog, 360
Dutchman Motorsports, 361, 360
Dutchman Motorsports, Inc., 361
DwellStudio, 4814, 4910, 5101
Dwyer, 5518
Dwyer Instruments International, 5518
Dyna King, 2374
Dyna-King, Inc., 2374
DynaPro International, 4300
Dynamic Systems, Inc., 2013

E

E.A. Carey's Smokeshop, 5994
E.M.F Company, 2431
E.O.N.S. Inc, 3119
E.V. Roberts, 653
EAA Corporation, 2432
EC Kraus, 4532
EC Kraus Home Wine Making, 2997
EC Kraus Wine & Beermaking Supplies, 4532
EFDYN, 489
EGT Exhaust Gas Technologies, 490
ELK Group International, 4995
ELMS Jigsaw Puzzles, 6175
ELMS Puzzles, 6175
ELS Audio Publishing, LLC, 2301
EMF Company, Inc., 2431
ETA/Cuisenaire, 988, 1009, 1010
ETS Home Tanning Beds, 4233
ETS Tan, 4233
EV Roberts & Associates, 653
EZ-Dock, 2375
EZ-Dock, Inc., 2375
EZAutomation, 1950, 2220
EZAutomation.net, 1950, 2220
Eagle America, 4099
Eagle Creek, 6235
Eagle Creek Travel Gear, 6235
Eagle Equipment, 491
Eagle Equipment-Automotive Equipment, 491
Eagle Optics, 5433
Eagle Wings Catalog, 304
Earl P L Apfelbaum, 1874
Early Advantage, 2075
Early Bronco Catalog, 394
Early Childhood Collections, 973
Early Learning Essentials, 937
Early's Farm & Garden Centre, 3034, 3251
Early's Seed Catalog, 3034, 3251
Earth & Vine Provisions, 2512
Earthbox, 3342
Earthly Pursuits, 3118
Earthly Pursuits, Inc. , 3118
Earthstone Wood-Fire Ovens, 4877
East Coast Chevy, 362
East Coast Gourmet, 2719
East West DyeCom, 3916
Eastbay, 1572, 5571
Eastern Emblem, 3532
Eastern Emblem Mfg Corp, 3532
Eastern Mountain Sports, 5812
Easton Press, 835
Easton Press Leather Bound Books, 835
The Eastwood Company, 492
Eastwood Unique Automotive Tools & Supplies, 492
Easy Closets.Com, 4815
Easy Comforts, 4259, 4301, 4384
Easy Fire Kilns, 3998
Easy Leaf Products, 3865
Easy Stand Catalog, 2032
EasyClosets, 4815
Easyriders Roadware Catalog, 5255
EatRaw, 2839
Eaton, 2221, 480
Eaton Corporation, 493, 2221
Eaton Corporation World Headquarters, 493
Ebags, 1198, 3617
Ebbets Field Flannels, 1266, 1631
Ebersole Lapidary Supply, 1820
Eccentricks, 3729
Eckler's 1953-2001 Corvette Parts and Accesso ries, 363
Eckler's Classic Chevy, 494
Eckler's Corvette, 363
Eckler's Corvette Parts, 495
Eckler's El Camino, 496
Eckler's Industries Inc, 495
Ecology Action of the Mid-Peninsula, 3092
Ecommerce Innovations, 5183
Econ-Abrasives, 4100
Economy Handicrafts 99 Cents Catalog, 3730
Economy Handicrafts Annual Catalog, 3731
Economy Handicrafts, Inc., 3730, 3731
Ecoseeds Catalog, 3252
Ecotour Expeditions, 6236

Ecstasy Crafts, 191
Edelbrock Corporation, 497
Edelweiss, 6237
Edelweiss Bike Travel, 6237
Eden Organic Nursery Services, 3119
Eden Press, 915, 1116
Eden Ranch, 4385
Eder, Inc., 2463
Edgar Cayce's A.R.E., 1097
EdgeWater Power Boats, 757
Edgepark Continence Catalog, 4302, 4355
Edgepark Diabetes Catalog, 4303, 4356
Edgepark Full-line Catalog, 4304, 4357
Edgepark Medical Supplies, 4302, 4303, 4304, 4305, 4355, 4356, 4357, 4358
Edgepark Ostomy Catalog, 4305, 4358
Edible Arrangements, 2565, 2771, 2800
Edible Landscaping, 3120
Edinburgh Imports, 1807, 4164
Editions Limited, 228, 240
Edmund Industrial Optics, 5479
Edmund Optics, 5479
Edmund Roses, 3121
Edmunds' Roses, 3121
Edson Accessories Catalog, 730
Edson Marine Accessory Store, 730
Education Connection, 2080
Educational Activities, 2193
Educational Insights, 2076, 6176
Edupress Catalog, 974, 2077
Edward R Hamilton Bookseller, 836, 2300
Efdyn Incorporated, 489
Effective Learning Systems, 2301
EggCartons.Com, 63, 118
Egge Machine Company, 364
Egge Machine and Speed Shop, 364
Ehrman Tapestry, 3950
EiPrinting, 5913
Eichten's Hidden Acres Cheese Farm, 2604
Eichten's Market & Grill, 2604
Eilenberger Bakery, 2676, 2801, 2948
Ekone Oyster Company, 2720
El Camino Store, 365, 496
Elan Buttons, 3732
ElderSong Fall 2015 Catalog, 868
ElderSong Publications, 1199
ElderSong Publications, Inc., 868
Elderly Instruments, 5296
Eldred Wheeler, 4977
The Electric Quilt Company, 4022, 4929
Electric Time Company, 3841
Electric Time Company, Inc., 3841
The Electricity Forum, 2236
Electro Enterprises, 2222
Electro Medical Equipment, 1999
Electronix Express, 2223
The Elegant Office, 5369
Elemental Scientific, 5519
Elemental Scientific, LLC, 5519
Elementary STEM Catalog, 975, 2137
Eli's Cheesecake, 2677
The Eli's Cheesecake Company, 2677
Eliminator Lighting, 5465
Elite Sportswear LP, 688, 1429, 1430, 1576, 1577, 1578, 1579, 1580, 1632, 1698
Elizabeth Eakins, 5102
Elizabeth Eakins Inc., 5102
Elizabeth Van Buren Aromatherapy, 4260
Elizabeth Van Buren Essential Oil Therap, 4260
Elkes, 5103
Ellis Office Supply, 5385
Elmer Hinckley, 2376
Elmer Hinkley Fishing Tackle, 2376
Eloxite Corporation, 1815
Elrick-Manley Fine Art, 224
Elvee Rosen Berge Inc, 3870
Elvee Rosenberg, 3866
Elvee/Rosenberg Inc., 3866
Embroidery Research Press, 837
Emedco Buyer's Guide, 3533
Emedco, Inc., 3533
Emerald Collection, 3583
Emergency Medical Products, 4359
Emergency Medical Products, Inc , 4359

Emmett Miller MD, 1113, 2317
Emperor Clock, LLC, 3842, 4686
Empire Books, 838
Empire Motor Sports, 498
Empire Vehicle Accessories, 498
Empress Chocolates Company, 2566
EnableMart, 2000
Endless Pools, 4234
Ener-G-Foods, 2840
Ener-G-Foods, Inc., 2840
Enertia Building Systems, Inc., 4662
Engagement, 5176
English Basketry Willows, 3788
The English Company, Inc., 3698
The English Company, Inc. 2012 - 13 Catalog K night, 3698
English as a Second Language, 2194, 2329
Engraving Arts, 3733
Engraving Arts Custom Branding Irons, 3733
Engraving Connection, 3534
Enslow Publishers, 992
Enstrom Candies, 2567
Entertainment Earth, 6177
Entertainment Earth Inc, 6177
Entertainment You Can Believe In, 2330
EntirelyPets, 7, 36
Environmental Concern, Inc., 3232
Environmental Geothermal Houses, 4662
Environmental Media Corporation, 976
Environments, 2078
Ephemera Magnets Button & Stickers, 3433
Ephemera, Inc., 3433
Ephraim Pottery, 3999
Epicomm, 2308
Epoch Designs, 4046
Epson Accessories, 5386
Epson America, Inc., 5386
Equestrian Enterprise Inc, 5786
Equine Breeding Supply, 119
Equissage, 120
Erbaviva, 4261
Ercole, 4732
Ercole, Inc., 4732
Ergonomics/Occupational Health & Safety, 4235
Erie Dearie Lure Company, 2377
Erie Dearie Lure Inc, 2377
Erie Landmark, 5013
Erie Landmark Company, 5013
Erik Organic, 2274
Erik Organic Dining Table Catalog, 2274
Ernst Conservation Seeds, 3253
Ernst Flow Industries , 6050
Ertl Toy Catalog, 6178
Escape Adventures, 6238
Escort Lighting, 3343
Especially Yours, 1267, 4471, 5572
Espresso Gourmet, 2631
Espresso Supply, 2632
Espresso Zone, 2633
Esprit, 683, 731
Esprit International, LLP, 683, 731
Essential Oil Company, 4262
The Essential Oil Company, 4262
Essential Skills Software, 2178
Essentials by Anthony Richards, 1268
Ethnobotanical Catalog of Seeds, 3254
Eugene Ernst Products Company, 6050
Eureka Stamps, 3734
Euro Bike & Walking, 6239
European American Armory Corp., 2432
Eurosport, The Fabled Soccer Traders, 5867
Evangel Wedding Service, 5974
Eve Alexander, 1509
Evenheat Kiln, 3826
Evenheat Kiln, Inc., 3820
Evenheat Kilns & Ovens, 3826
Events by Paper Direct, 3434
Everett-Morrison Motorcars, 499
Everlast Worldwide, 5625
Everlast Worldwide Inc, 5625
Everything Carts, 5747
Everything Furniture, 5334
Everything Office Furniture, 5334
Everything Track & Field - 2015, 5626
Everything for the Lilypool, 3344

Exair Corporation, 4816
Examplarery, 3951
The Examplarery, 3951
Excalibur Collection, 4733
Excel Sports Products, 5882
Excel Technologies, 5520
Excel Technologies Inc, 5520
Exclusive Sports Jewelry, 5137
Exclusively Weddings, 5975
Exotic Houseplants, 3122
Exotic Nutrition Pet Company, 154
Exotic Silks, 4165
Exotic Silks, Inc., 4165
Explorations, 1055
Exposures, 161, 4734
Express Medical Supply, Inc, 4360
Expressions, 3650
Extech Instruments, 5521
Extrema, 6051
Extrema Machinery Co., 6051
Eye Communication Systems Inc, 2247

F

F. W. Schumacher Co., Inc., 3255
F.A.S.T. Corporation, 4735
FAST Corporation, 4735
FNT 2015 Product Catalog, 6052
FOTODYNE Incorporated, 2138
FSA Plus Woman, 702
FW Schumacher Company, 3255
Fabrics Catalog, 4013, 4166
Fabulous-Furs, 1481
Factory Direct Table Pad Company, 5104
Faganarms, 1741
Faganarms Inc., 1741
Fahrney's Pens, 5387
Fair Oak Workshops, 3735
Fairbury Steaks, 2721
Fairchild Books, 888
Fairchild Books & Visuals, 888
Fairfield, 4014
Fairfield Processing, 4014
Fairgate Rule, 2224
Fairytale Brownies Bakery, 2678, 2802
Falcon Fine Wire and Wire Products, 2225
Fall 2015 Eerdmans Books for Young Readers Ca talog, 938
Fall 2015 Eerdmans Trade Catalog, 889
Fall Angler, 2378
Fall Bright, 4533
Fall Bright Winemakers Shop, 4533
Fall Hunting II, 2476, 5690
Fall Planting, 3345
Family Album, 1152
Family Crest Jewelry Catalog, 5177
Family Heir-Loom Weavers, 4024
Family Labels, 1875
Family Medallion, 5976
Famous Smoke Shop, 5995
Fan Fair, 3346
Fan Man, 3584
Fancifuls, 4167
Fancifuls Inc., 4167
Fancy Flours, 5220
Fannie May, 2568, 2575
Farm Basket, 2803
The Farm Basket, 2803
FarmTek, 3035
Farmer Boy AG, 4785
Farmer Seed & Nursery, 3123
Farmer Seed & Nursery Company, 3123
Farriers' Greeting Cards, 8
Farriers' Greeting Cards-Hoofprints, 8
Fashion Fabrics Club, 4168
Fashionable Canes, 2001
Fashionable Canes & Walking Sticks, 2001
Fat Brain Toys, 662, 2079, 3651
Fat Brain Toys, LLC, 662, 2079, 3651
Father Flanagan's Boy's Home, 963
Faucet Outlet, 4786
Feather Craft Fly Fishing, 1153, 2379
Fedco Co-op Garden Supplies, 3256, 3257
Fedco Seeds, 3256

Fedco Trees, 3257
Feel Good Store, 1269
FeelGood Store, 1269
Fein Power Tools, 4101
Fein Power Tools Inc., 4101
Felber Ornamental Plastering, 4736
Felber Ornamental Plastering Corporation, 4736
Feldheim Publishers, 1088
Feller LLC, 4878
Feller US Corporation, 4878
Femail Creations, 732
Fence PBT, 5740
Ferdco Corporation, 3585
Feridies, 2949
Ferno Physical Therapy & Sports Equipment, 4306
Ferno-Washington, Inc, 4306
Ferrara Cafe, 2705
Ferrara Foods & Confections, 2705
Fertrell, 3068
Fertrell Company, 3068
Fest for Beatles Fans, 1742
Festal Creations, 1743
Festal Creations Catalog, 1743
Festool Catalog, 6053
FetchDog, 97
Fiber Arts Supplies Catalog, 4169
The Fiber Loft, 4210
Fiber Network Tools & Telecom Supplies,, 6052
Fiberglass Trends, 500
Fiberglass Trends Mitcom, 500
Fiddyment Farms, 2950
Field Outfitting, 2477
Field and Forest Products, 3258
Field's Fabrics, 4170
Fieldline, 5813
Fieldstone Gardens, 3124
Fiesta Yarns, 4171
Figi's Gifts in Good Taste, 2679, 2804, 2680, 2805
Figi's Sugar Free & More, 2680, 2805
Filaree Farms Seed Garlic Catalog, 3259
Filaree Garlic Farm, 3259
Filing Supplies from A-Z, 5388
Filling Station, 366
Films Media Group, 912, 1096, 2200, 2293
Filson, 1573, 1566
Final Flight Outfitters, 64, 2380, 5691
Finals, 1574
The Finals, 1574
Finck Cigar, 5996
Findings & Metals, 3867, 3917
Fine Architectural Metalsmiths, 4618
Fine Art & Art Instruction, 229, 977
Fine Art Presses Etching & Lithography, 230
Fine Foods & Accompaniments, 2903
Fine Impressions, 5939
Fine Lines, 501
Fine Lines, Inc., 501
Fine Wood Source Book, 4978
Fingerhut, 258
Fingerhut Spring Big Book, 258
Fingerlakes Woolen Mill, 4172
Finish Line, 502
Finish Line, Inc., 502
Finnottes, 2951
Fiorella's Jack Stack Barbecue, 2860, 2904
Fire End & Croker Corporation , 3736
Fire Mountain Gems & Beads Jewelry Maker's Ca talog, 3868
Fire Mountain Gems and Beads, 3868
Fire Protection Products, 3736
Fire Protection Publications (FPP), 894, 986
Fireside Fiberarts, 4078
Fireside Looms for Fiber Artists, 4078
Firewheel Classics, 503
Firewheel Classics, Inc., 503
Fireworks Popcorn, 2527
First Choice, 5914
First Frost, 1696, 3435, 4817
First Position Dancewear, 5627
First Position Dancewear Inc., 5627
First Street Catalog, 3436
First Street for Boomers and Beyond, 3436
First Wishes, 6179
FirstSTREET, 2226, 3586
FirstSTREET for Boomers & Beyond, 2226, 3586

Fischer & Jirouch Company, 3347
Fischer & Wieser Specialty Foods, 2745
Fish Place Catalog, 155
Fisher Science Education, 5522
Fisher-Price, 663, 6180
Fishing Components Catalog, 2381
Fishing Hot Spots, Inc., 1154, 2382
Fit Maternity & Beyond, 1510
Fitness Factory, 4236
Fitness Factory Outlet, 4236
Fitness Systems, 4386
Fitness Systems Manufacturing Corporatio, 4386
Fiutterby Garden Landscaping LLC, 3349
5 T'S Embroidery Supply, 1117
5.11 Inc., 1407
5.11 Tactical, 1407
Flag Fables Inc., 4959
Flag-Works, 4957
Flag-Works over America, LLC, 4957
FlagFables, 4961
FlagHouse Physical Education and Recreation, 5628
Flaghouse, 5659
Flaghouse Inc, 5628
Flaming River, 504
Flanders, 4619
Flanders/CSC Corporation, 4619
Flatt Stationers, 1951
Flemington Aluminum & Brass, 3535
Flemington Aluminum and Brass Inc , 3535
Flexbar Machine Corporation, 6054
Flexcut Carving Tools, 4102
Flexcut Tool Company., 4102
Flickinger's Nursery, 3125
Flinn Scientific Inc, 2164
Flirt, 1494, 1697
Florence & George, 1854
Florentine Craftsmen, 3348
Floria Designs, 83
Floriana, 1321
Florida Clay Art Company, 3827
Florida Gold Fruit Co., 2772
Flower & Herb Exchange, 3260
Fluke Corporation, 2227
Flutterbye Garden, 3349
Fly Rod and Reel Distributors LLC, 2391
Fly Shop, 2383
Flyfisher's Paradise, 1155
Flying Noodle, 2984
Focus Camera, 2228, 5486
Focus Camera Inc, 2228, 5486
Focusers, 5422
Focusers, Inc., 5422
Folbot Corporation, 758
Foley-Belsaw Co., 6102
Foliage Gardens, 3126
Folktale & Story Catalog, 6181
Folkwear, 3952
Food Catalog, 2773, 2905
Foodcrafter's Supply Catalog, 5221
Foot Traffic, 1322
FootSmart, 684, 733
FootSmart.com, 684, 733
Football America, 5629
Foothills Adult Education, 2080
Footprints, 5573
Footwear by Footskins, 5574
Footwise, 5575
For Counsel: Catalog for Lawyers, 1744
For Counsel: Products And Gifts for Lawy, 1744
For Small Hands Family Resource Catalog, 4079, 4103
Force Control, 505
Force Control Industries, 505
Ford Parts Specialists, 506
Fordham Equipment Company, 5335
Forecast International, 869
Foredom Electric Company Power Tool Catalog, 6055
Forespar, 799
Forest Farm At Pacifica, 3127
Forestfarm Catalog, 3127
Forever & Always, 5977
Forever & Always Inc, 5977
Formula Boats, 745
Forster Products, 2478
Fort Brands, 685, 686

Holabird Sports, 5874
Holbein, 260
Holden's Latex Corp., 3805
Holiday Cards for Businesses, 3660, 5917
Holiday Classics, 5941
Holiday Collection, 1432, 5943
Holiday Driver Inc., 5838
Holiday Expeditions, 1204
Holiday Expressions, 5944
Holiday Foods Catalogue Division, 2811
Holiday Gift Basket, 2999
Holiday Mini Catalog, 3739
Holland Bulb Farms, 3269
Holly Yashi, 5143
Holts Cigar Company, 5999
Holts Tobacconist, 5999
Holum & Sons Company, 194
Holum & Sons Company Inc, 194
Home & Garden, 5016
Home Brewery, 3000
The Home Brewery, 4540
Home Controls, 1982
Home Decorators Collection, 4825, 4889, 5106
Home Delivery Incontinent Supplies, 4312
Home Gardener's Vegetable, Flower & Supplies, 3270
Home Improvements, 4624
Home Lumber, 4105
Home Place Products, 3364
Home Place Products.com, 3364
Home Science Tools, 1816
Home Sew, 3960
Home Sew, Inc., 3960
Home Trends, 4890
Home at Five, 4826
HomePortfolio Insider, 4687
HomePortfolio, Inc., 4687
HomeRoom, 3538
HomeRoom Direct, 3538
HomeTops, 4105
Homecraft Veneer & Woodworker's Supplies, 4741
Homeopathic Reference Catalog, 4317
Homes by Vanderbilt, 4697
Homeschool Catalog, 1898
Homespun Music Instruction, 984, 2331, 5392
Homespun Tapes, 984, 2331, 5392
Homestead Communications Corp, 4699
The Hon Company, 5354
Honey Baked Ham, 2683, 2913
Honey Baked Ham Company, 2684, 2914
HoneyBaked Ham Company, 2684, 2914
Honeyville, 2748
Honeywax / Candle-Flex Molds, 3807
Honors Military Catalog, 1328, 1845
Hood Finishing Products, 4106
Hook & Hackle Company, 2387
Hoop House Greenhouse Kits, 4698
Hoops King, 5636
Hoosier Trapper Supply, 2480, 4062
Hoosier Trapper Supply, Inc., 2480, 4062
Hoover's Hatchery, 11, 69, 124
Hoovers Manufacturing Company, 1328, 1845
Hopkin's Medical Products, 4363
Horchow Catalog, 2812, 3452
Horchow Mail Order, 3452
Horizon Dart Supply, 4485
Horizon Darts, 4485
Horn USA, 6076
Horn, Inc., 6076
Hornady, 2348, 2435
Hornady Manufacturing, 2348, 2435
Horse Catalog, 125, 5785
Horse Health USA, 126
Horse Lover's Gift Guide, 5786
Horse Supply Catalog, 127, 5787
Horse.com, 12
Horses Prefer, 128
Hortense B. Hewitt Co., 5979
Horticultural Products & Services, 3271
Horton Brasses, 5017
Horton Brasses, Inc., 5017
Hoss Tools, 6077
Hostess Brands, 4895
Hot Deals, 1359
Hot Off The Press, Inc., 206

Hot Off the Ice, 5637
Hot Tools, 4107
Hotronic, Inc., 2180
House, 5638
The House, 5638, 5851
House Boardshop, 5851
House Parts, 3592
House of Webster, 2515, 3453
House of Caron, 1810
House of Conception Abbey, 5945
House of Fragrances, 4266
House of Onyx, 3878
House of Oxford Wholesale Cigars, 6000
House of Spices, 2706
House of Troy, 5053
House of Webster, 2515, 3453
House of Wesley, 3148
Houston Glass Craft Supply, 4036
Houston Stained Glass Supply, 4036
Hove Parfumeur, 4267
Howard Decorative Packaging, 195, 3740
Howard Hill Archery, 5692
Howard Miller Clock Company, 4742
Howell Book House, 13
Hubbard Peanut Company, 2956
Huckleberry Haven, 2749
Huckleberry Haven, Inc., 2749
Hudson Valley Seed Library, 3272, 3365
Hugger Mugger, 1329, 1464
Hugger-Mugger Yoga Products, 1329, 1464
Huggins and Scott Auctions, 1776
Hulme Sporting Goods & MFG Company, 5639
Human Kinetics, 892, 985, 1166
Human Kinetics Academic & Professional Resour ces, 892
Human Kinetics Physical Education and Dance, 985
Human Kinetics Sports and Fitness, 1166
Human Relations Media, 2197
HumanWare, 2005
Hundelrut Studio, 942
Hunt Country Foods, 2685
Hunt Country Foods Inc., 2685
Hunter Associates Laboratory, Inc,, 5525
Hunter Dan, 2349
Hunter Douglas, 4943
Hunter Douglas Window Fashions, 4943
HunterLab, 5525
The Huntington, 842
Huntington Library Press, 842
Hurley Patentee Lighting, 5054
Hurley Patentee Manor Lighting, 5054
Hut Products, 6078, 6066
Hyatt Fruit, 2777
Hyde, 4827
Hyde Drift Boats, 761
Hyde Tools, 4827
Hydrangeas Plus, 3149
Hydro-E-Lectric, 524
Hydro-Farm West, 3366
Hydro-Fit, Inc, 1463, 5635
Hydro-e-lectric, 524
Hyland's Inc, 4317
H„fele, 6079
H„fele America Co., 6079

I

I Do Collection, 5182
I.O. Metro, 4828, 4982
IBASE Techonology (USA), Inc., 1921
IBM, 893
IBM, Training Solutions, 893
IFSTA, 894, 986
IGO, 1904
IHC Hobby Texas, 4516
IHS Jane's 360 Inc., 896
IKEA, 4829
IPD, 598
ITW Automotive Products, 412
ITW Consumer, 412
IVP Academic Catalog, 987
IWA, 3001
Ibex Outdoor Clothing, 1272
Ibex Outdoor Clothing, LLC, 1272

Iccoin, 1790
Idaho Wood Lighting, 5055
Idea Book & Catalog, 3741
Ideal Industries, 2236
Ikegami Electronics, Inc., 5488
Illuminations, 3808
Impact Gift Collection, 3539
Imperial Sprinkler Supply, 3045
Imprints Publication, 6214
Impromptu Gourmet, 2813
Improvements, 4983, 5125, 4624
In The Company Of Dogs, 97
In The Company of Dogs, 14
In the Company of Dogs, 14
In the Swim, 6243
Inca, 2237
Inca TV Lifts, 2237
Inclinator, 2035
Inclinator Company of America, 2035
Indco, 3046
Indco Catalog, 3046
Independent Living Aids, 4318, 4319, 5424
Independent Living Aids Comprehensive Catalog, 5424
Independent Living Aids Low Vision Catalog, 4319
Indian Wells Date Gardens & Chocolatier, 2576
Indiana Berry, 3150, 3454
Indiana Berry & Plant Company, 3150, 3454
Indiana Botanic Gardens, 4436
Indiana Botanic Gardens, Inc, 4381, 4436
Indiana Botanic Gardens, Inc., 4429
Indigo Wild, 2277, 4437, 4891
Indus, 1899
Indus International, 1899
Industrial Abrasives, 4108
Industrial Arts Supply Company, 261
Industrial Lab & Plastics, 5526
The Industry Source, 4425
Infogroup, 4053
Information Packaging, 5393
Infosource, 1900, 1955
Infosource Inc., 1900, 1955
Inline Tube, 413
Inlinetube, 413
InnerBalance, 4242
Insect Lore, 1167, 2147
Inspire, 3742, 4015
Inspired Silver, 5183
Institute for Vibrant Living, 4394
Intarsia, 4109
Intarsia Times, 4109
Integrated Medical, 4243
Intelligent Outfitters, 6185
InterVarsity Press, 987
Interactive Therapeutics, 4320
Intercal Trading Group, 1811
Intercollegiate Designs, 3540
Interface Flooring Systems, Inc., 5107
InterfaceFlor, 5107
Interlink Publishing, 1211
Intermountain Cactus, 3151
International Auto Parts, 414, 431
International Autosport, 306
International Bible Society, 1065
International Bronze Manufacturers, 3541
International Bronze Manufacturers & Des, 3541
International Center Of Photography, 1168
International Center of Photography, 1168
International Coins and Currency, 1790
International Hobby Corporation, 4516
International Homes of Cedar, 4710
International Marine Boating Books, 1169
International Marine-Ragged Mt. Press, 1169
International Military Antiques, 1830, 1846
International Plastics, Inc., 5407
International Spy Museum, 3628
International Taekwondo Association, 5804
International Tea Importers, 2639
International Watch Company, 3528
International Wealth Success, 895
International Wine Accessories, 4535, 3001
International Wood Products, 6080
Internatural, 4321, 4395
Internatural Health & Wellness, 4321, 4395
Into The Wind Inc., 4504

Consumer Catalog & Company Index

K2 Sports, 5852
KBC Tools, 6086
KD Bridal Collection, 4589
KEH Camera Brokers, 5489
KGS Electronics, 2239
KHS Bicycles, 5729
KKFlyfisher, 2389
KP Creek Gifts, 3459
KRS Edstrom, 4311
KSA Jojoba, 4438
KV Supply, 85
KV Vet Supply, 40
KYTEC Athletic Speed Equipment, 5642, 5822
Kaehler Luggage, 6246
Kaehler Luggage Inc, 6246
Kansas City Steak Company, 2916
Kansas Wind Power, 2773, 2905, 5034
Kanson Electronics, 2240
Kanter Auto Products, 530
Kapla USA, 6186
Kapla USA LP, 6186
Kaplan, 6187
Kaplan Early Learning Company, 6187
Kappa Map Group, LLC, 1834, 6228
Karl Performance, 433
Karmaloop, 3299
Kasper Organics, 1549
Kassoy, 3883
Kast-A-Way Swimwear, 1589
Kava Kauai, 4396
Kay Jewelers, 5190
Keen Ovens, 5224
Keepsake Needle Arts, 3962
Keepsake NeedleArts, 4486
Keepsake Quilting, 4016
Keh Camera, 5489
Keith Keppel, 3156
Keith Keppel Irises, 3156
Keithley Instruments, 2241
Kelli's Gift Shop Suppliers, 3661
Kelly Brothers Nurseries, 3157
Kelly Herd, 5191
Kelly Nurseries, 3157
Kelly's Kids, 1388
Kellyco Metal Detector Superstore, 4487
Kelvin, 2148
Kemp's Hockey Supply Company, 5797
Ken's Fish Farm, 156
Ken's Hatchery and Fish Farm, Inc., 156
Ken-A-Vision Manufacturing Company, 2149
Ken-a-vision, 2149
Kenmore Stamp Company, 1878
Kennedy Hardware, 5018
Kennedy Hardware LLC, 4629
Kennedy Hardware, LLC, 5018
Kennel-Aire, 103
Kenneth Lynch & Sons, 3368
Kent-Moore Automotive, 531
Kentwood Manufacturing, 4892, 4912
Kenyon's Grist Mill, 2536
Kepco, Inc., 2242
Kester's Wild Game Food Nurseries, 3280
Kester's Wild Game Food Nurseries Inc, 3280
Kett Tool, 6087
Kett Tool Company, 6087
Kettle Care Inc, 4440
Kettle Care Organics, 4452
Kettle Care-Pure Herbal Body Care, 4440
Kevin's Fine Outdoor Gear & Apparel, 1590
Kewaunee, 2150
Kewaunee Scientific Corporation, 2150
Key West Aloe, 4268
Kicker, 1983
Kid Stuff Marketing, 6188
KidSafety of America, 989, 1092, 2087
Kimber, 2481
Kimbo, 2305
Kimbo Educational, 2305
KinderMark, 2088
King Arthur Flour & The Bakers, 2517, 5225
King Louie America, 1591
King Louie Sports, 1591
King Motorsports, 532
King Motorsports Unlimited, Inc., 532

King Ranch Saddle Shop, 1671
King School, 655
King's Chandelier, 5057
King's Mums, 3158
KingSize, 1365, 1529
Kings Chandelier, 3594
Kings Way Archery, 5693
Kingsley North Jewelry Supply, 3884
Kingsley North Lapidary Supply, 3885
Kingsley North, Inc., 3884, 3885
Kinsman Company, 3353
Kipp, 619, 1389, 3662
Kipp Toys, 619, 1389, 3662
Kirkpatrick Leather, 2438
Kirkpatrick Leather Company, 2438
Kitchen Garden Seeds, 3281
Kitchen Krafts, Inc., 5221
Kitts Industrial Tools, 6088
Kitty Hawk Kites, 4505
Kiwi Indian Motorcycle, 5261
Klass,, 3963, 4017
Klehm's Song Sparrow, 3159
Klehm's Song Sparrow Perennial Farm, 3159
Klingspor's Woodworking Shop, 4112
Klise Manufacturing Company, 3923
KlockIt, 3843
Klutz, 943
Knife Merchant, 5226
Knights Edge, 1847
Knit Knack Shop, 4182
Knit Knack Shop, Inc., 4182
Knit Picks, 3964
Knit it Now, 4155
Knitted Heirloom Lace, 3958
Knitting & Crochet Catalog, 4183
Knitting Basket, 3965
Knollwood Books, 1172
Knot Head Wood Crafts, 6089
Knott's Berry Farm, 2750
Knott's Berry Farm Food, 2750
Knowledge Unlimited, 990
Kodak, 5493
Kodak Professional Photographic Catalog, 5493
Koehler Bright Star, 5058
Koeze Company, 2958
Koeze Direct, 3543
Kogle Cards, 3544
Koinonia Farm, 2959
Koinonia Partners, 2959
Kol Ami, Inc., 1076, 2316
Kolick's Jewelers, 4590
Kolo, 198, 4488
Kolo Retail LLC, 198, 4488
Kolobags, 1902
Komet of America, 6090
Koo Koo Bear Kids, 666
Koo Koo Bear Kids, Inc, 666
KooKoo Bear Kids, 1390
Korman Autoworks, 434
Kosher Connection, 2707
Kotula's, 4831, 6189
Kozlowski Farms, 2751, 2864
Kraftbilt, 5918
Kraftsman Commercial Playgrounds & Water, 3595
Kraftsman Playground and Park Equipment, 3595
Kraftware, 5227
Krause Publications, 2474
Krause Publications Inc, 1148
Kreg, 6091
Kreg Tool Company, 6091
Kreiss Collection, 5084
Kreiss Furniture Collections Folio, 5084
Kron Chocolatier, 3663
Krout & Company, 5192
Kudos by Paper Direct, 5394
Kultur Films, 2333, 5450
Kultur Performing Arts DVD's, 2333, 5450
Kustom King Archery, 5694
Kustom King Traditional Archery, 5694
Kwik Sew, 3966

L

L & J G Stickley, 4996
L&L Kiln Manufacturing, 3830
L&L Kiln Mfg Inc, 3830
L&L Kiln Mfg., Inc., 3998
L.H. Selman, Ltd., 1735
L.L.Bean Back to School, 1391
L.L.Bean Christmas, 1275, 4556
L.L.Bean Fishing, 2390
L.L.Bean Hunting, 2482
L.L.Bean Inc., 1275, 1276, 1335, 1391, 1592, 2390, 2482, 4556
L.L.Bean Outsider, 1276, 1335, 1592
LA Stencilworks, 4048
LAT Apparel, 1277
LC Engineering, 403
LEDGlow, 5262
LEGO Shop at Home, 6190
LH Selman Ltd, 4746
LLT Products, 5395
LMC Right Start, 670, 704
LMC Truck, 533, 318
LS & S, 2006
LS&S, 2006
LTD Commodities, 3514
La Pelleterie, 1482
La Sportiva, 5814
La Tienda, 2960
A La Zing, 2503
La-Tee-Da, 4269
LaMotte Company, 2151, 2285
LaMotte Environmental Science Products, 2151
LabMart Catalog, 5528
The Labmart, 5528
Laboratory Equipment for the Life Sciences Catalog, 5529
Laboratory Glassware and Supplies Catalog, 5530
Laboratory Sampling Products Catalog, 130
Lacis, 1173, 3967
Lacrosse International, 5798
Ladies Collection 2, 1703
Lady & the Stamp, 1879
Lady Grace, 1499
Lafayette 148 New York, 1704
Lafayette Interior Fashions Inc., 4747
Lafayette Venetian Blind, 4747
Lafeber Company, 15, 71
Lafeber Pet Bird Food Catalog, 15, 71
Lake Champlain Chocolates, 4572
Lake City Craft Company, 3745
Lake Shore Industries Inc, 1051
Lakeshore, 2089
Lakeshore Learning Materials, 2089
Lakeside Collection, 3460
The Lakeside Collection, 3460
Lambert Vet Supply, 41
Lambspun, 4184
Lambspun of Colorado, 4184
Lammes Candies, 2580
Lamp Glass, 5059
Lamps Plus, 5060
Lancaster Archery, 5695
Lancaster Archery Supply, 1593
Lancaster Archery Supply 2015 - 16 Archer's Wishbo, 1593
Lance Camper Manufacturing, 397
Land & Sea Inc, 734
Land of Nod, 667, 4984
The Land of Nod, 5370
Landmark Creations, 4748
Lands' End, 1278
Lands' End Home, 4832, 4893, 4913
Lands' End Kids, 1336, 1392
Lands' End Men, 1337, 1366, 1530
Lands' End Plus, 1338, 1367, 1705
Lands' End School Outfitters, 1393, 1636
Lands' End, Inc., 1278, 1336, 1337, 1338, 1366, 1367, 1392, 1393, 1530, 1636, 1705, 4832, 4893, 4913
Lang, 3461
The Lang Company, 3461
Langlitz Leathers, 3924, 5263
Lansky Sharpeners, 5228
Larry Fox and Company Ltd, 3529
Laser Labels Technology, 5395
Latest Products Corporation, 4364
Latin Percussion, 5301

M

VIEW Video, 2343
VISTA, 597
VPC, 1969
VS Athletics Cross Country, 5600
Valiant IMC, 273, 1970
Valiant National AV Supply, 273, 1970
Valley Naturals, 4408
Valley Traditional Archery, 5707
Valley Traditional Archery Supply, Inc., 5707
Valley Vet Supply, 30, 51, 151, 52, 152
Valley Vet Supply Catalog, 52, 152
Van Bourgondien Brothers, 3223
Van Dyck's Flower Farm, 3315
Van Dyke's, 4072
Van Dyke's Restorers, 5031
Van Dyke's Supply Co., 4072
Van Dykes Restorers, 5031
Van Engelen, 3316
Van Engelen, Inc., 3316
Van Ness Water Gardens, 3408
Van's Aircraft Accessories, 650
Van's Aircraft, Inc., 650
Van's Gifts, 2829
Van's Gifts, Inc., 2829
VanWell Nursery, 3225
Vance & Hines, 5737
Vance & Hines Dirtbike Catalog, 5278
Vance & Hines Harley Davidson Catalog, 5279
Vance & Hines Metric Cruiser Catalog, 5280
Vance & Hines Sportbike Catalog, 5281
Vance and Hines, 5278, 5279, 5280, 5281
Vanguard Furniture Company, 4999
Vans Pines Nursery, 3224
Vantage Apparel, 1661
Vantage Deluxe World Travel, 6258
Vantage PRO Wireless Weather Station Catalog, 5552
Vanwell Nursery, 3225
Varsity Spirit Corporation, 5884
Vasa, 5677
Vasa Trainers, 5677
Veldheer Tulip Gardens, 3317
Veldheers, 3317
Veneering Catalog, 4132
Venue Sports Athletics, 5600
Venus, 1475
Veon Creations, 3703, 3854
Veranda Marine, 746
Veridian Healthcare, 4378
Verilux Healthy Lighting Products, 5075
Vermont Bean Seed Company, 3318
Vermont Castings, 4670
Vermont Christmas Company, 3505
The Vermont Country Store, 1352, 1297, 5091
Vermont Country Store, 1297, 5091
Vermont Hardwoods, 169
Vermont Industries, 5076
Vermont Life Green Mountain Gifts, 3704
Vermont Life Magazine, 3704
Vermont Log Buildings, 4708
Vermont Maple Outlet, 2762
The Vermont Maple Sugar Company, 2738
Vermont Nut Free Chocolates, 4575
Vermont Teddy Bear Company, 6220
Vermont Ware, 3403
Vermont Wildflower Farm, 3234
Vesey's Seeds, 3319
Veseys, 3319
Vesterheim, 4133, 4767
Vesterheim Norwegian American Museum, 4133, 4767
Vet-Vax, Inc., 53
Veteran Leather Co., Inc., 3929
Veteran Leather Corporation, 3929
Veterinary Apparel Company, 1662
Vets Plus, Inc., 128
Vetus America, 810
Vi Bella Jewelry, 5157
Victor Machinery Exchange, 3930
Victor Machinery Exchange Inc, 3930
Victorian Bride, 5986
Victorian Furniture, 5000
Victorian Furniture Company, 5000
Victorian Heart Company, Inc., 1307, 4008, 4023, 5090
Victorian Papers, 5965
Victorian Trading Company, 5965

Victoriana East, 4646
Video Artists International, 2320
The Video Collection, 2319
Video Learning Library, 2204
Video/Entertainment, 2205
Viking Folk Art Publications, 4768
Viking Folk Art Publications, Inc., 4768
Viking Woodcrafts Inc, 4134
Viking Woodcrafts, Inc., 4134
Village Coin Shop, 1794
Village Discount Drapery, 4940
Village Interiors Carpet One, 5116
Village Interiors Carpet One Floor & Hom, 5116
Village Spinning & Weaving, 4202
The Village Spinning & Weaving Shop, 4183
VinMaps, 1835
Vineyard Vines, 1298
Vinotemp, 3007
Vinotemp International, 3007
Vintage, 384
Vintage Cellars, 3008
Vintage Hardware, 5032
Vintage Hardware & Lighting, 5032
Vintage Model Catalog, 598
Vintage Tire Hotline, 385
Vintage Wood Works, 4681
Vintage Woodworks, 4681
VintageView, 3009
VintageView Wine Storage Systems, 3009
Vinten, 1989, 5483
Violet House of Pots, 3405
Violet Pots, 3405
The Violet Showcase, 3226
Violet Showcase, 3226, 3139
Virginia Classic Mustang, 386
Virginia Diner, 2975
Virginia Diner, Inc., 2975
Virginia Panel Corporation, 1969
Virginia Traditions, 2940
Viridian Bay, 4864, 4930, 5001
Vis-Ed, 2118
Vision Video, 1056
Visions Espresso Service, 2655
Visions Espresso Service, Inc., 2655
Visual Education, 2118
Vitacost, 4463
Vitamin Direct, 4409
Vitamin Direct Inc, 4409
Vitamin Research Products, 4410
VivaTerra, 4865
Vivre, 1545, 3611, 5601
Vixen Hill Gazebos, 3406
Vixen Hill Manufacturing Co., 3406
Viziflex Seels Computer Protection Products, 1923
Viziflex Seels, Inc., 1923
Vogue Patterns, 3983
Volleyball America Catalog, 5896
Voltexx, 1926
Voltexx, LLC, 1926
Voyager Spirit, 1545, 3611, 5601

W

W Atlee Burpee & Company, 2789, 3244, 3320
W Atlee Burpee and Company, 2789, 3320
W.D. Lockwood, 4213
W.D. Lockwood & Company, Inc., 4213
W.F. Norman Corp., 4769
W.L. Fuller Co., Inc., 4135
W.S. Badger Company, 4464
WA Charnstrom Mail Center Solutions, 5372, 5419
WAG Aero Group, 651
WASCO, 4073
WAWAK Sewing, 3934, 4201
WEBS - America's Yarn Store, 214, 3984, 4214, 4150
WEBS-America's Yarn Store, 214, 3984, 4214
WF Norman Corporation, 4769
WL Fuller, 4135
WM Berg, 6131, 6036
WSU Creamery, 2619
WTS Media, 256
WTSmedia Catalog, 2266

WW Grainger, 3059
Wafer Warehouse, 3060
Wag-Aero, 651
Wake Up Frankie, 4931
Wakefield Peanut Co., LLC, 2976
Wakefield Peanut Company, 2976
Walden Farms, Inc., 2528
Walden Foods, 2528
Walker Display, Inc., 4794
Wallis Stained Glass, Doors, Cabinets, Art, G lass, 4647
Walpole Woodworkers, 3407
Walpole Woodworkers Fence Master Catalog, 3407
Walter Drake, 3506, 4339, 4866
Walter T Kelley Bee Co., 4496
Walter T Kelley Company, 4496
Wandering Star Astrology Jewelry, 3705, 5207
Wandering Star Designs, 3705, 5207
War Eagle Boats, 785
War Eagle Mill, 2891
War Eagle Mill Product & Gift, 2891
Ward Cedar Log Homes, 4709
Ward Log Homes, 4709
Ward's Science, 5441
Warm Biscuit Bedding, 5002
Warm Biscuit Bedding Catalog, 5002
The Warm Company, 4215, 5092
Warm Company, 4215, 5092
Warm Things, 5093
Warms Things, 5093
Warner Electric, 599
Warner Stained Glass, 4040
Warner-Crivellaro, 4040
Warplanes, 4528
Warren Cutlery, 4491
Warren Tool Catalog, 4491
Warrior Lures, 2414
Wasserman Uniforms, 1663
Water Master Rafts, 786
Water Quality Testing Products, 2285
Water Tanks.com, 3020
Water Visions, 3408
Water Warehouse, 4648
WaterRower, 4252
WaterRower US, 4252
Watercolors Inc, 4793
Watercraft by Dennis Kirk Catalog, 716
Waterfowl Hunting, 2457, 2502
Waterwise, 4340, 4649
Waterwise Inc, 4340, 4649
Watts Heatway Catalog, 3061
Watts Radiant, Inc., 3061
Wavelength Catalog, 2206
Wavelength Inc, 2206
Wax Patterns, 3908
Way Out Wax Catalog, 3507
Way Out Wax Inc, 3507
Wayfair, 4867, 4885, 4905
Wayne Green Book, 5446
Wayside Gardens, 3227
Wayside Gardens Catalog, 3227
WearGuard Catalog, 717, 1664
WearGuard Corp, 717, 1664
Weather Shield, 4650
Weather Shield Windows and Doors, 4650
WeatherPort Shelter Systems, 3062
Weatherby, 2458
Weathervane Seafoo, 2733
Weathervane Seafoods, 2733
Weaver Leather, 3931
Weaver Leather, LLC, 3623, 3931
Weaver West, 3623
Weaver's Catalog, 2942
Web-Sters, 3985, 4086
The Websters, 3985, 4086
Webway Album Catalog, 5966
Wedding Wire, 5974
Weddingstar Catalog, 3706
Weddingstar Inc., 3706
Weekender, 3508
Welcome to the Best of Lillian Vernon, 3509
Weleda, 4341
Weleda North America, 4341
Well-Sweep Herb Farm Catalog, 3228
Well-Sweep Herb Farm Inc, 3228

Consumer Catalog & Company Index

A

A&H Abrasives, 8462
A&M Industries, 8042
A-J Manufacturing Company, 7342
A-J Manufacturing Company, Inc., 7342
A. Daigger & Company, 7546
A. Fleisig Paper Box Corporation, 7954
A.L. Ellis, Inc., 7498
A.L.P. Lighting Components, Inc., 7724
A/C Fabricating Corporation, 7767
AAA Acme Rubber Company, 8255
AAF-Environmental Commercial Product Group, 7270
ABB, 7343
ABB Drives, 7343
ABCO Industries, 7391
ABP/Pharmex, 7536
ABRISA, 7911
ACA Corporate Awards, 7141, 7876
ACA For Churches Only, 7142, 7877
ACA School Essentials, 7143, 7878
ACM Technologies Inc, 7831
ACS Publications, 6907
ACS Solutions Inc., 6385, 8448
ADCOA, 6554
ADCOLE, 6514
AEC, 7392, 7406
AEC, Inc., 7392
AERCO, 7397
AFTL, Inc., 7302
AGCO, 6260
AGET Dust/Mist Collectors, 7301
AICPA, 6890, 6900
AICPA Self Study/Video Catalog, 6900
AICPA Self-Study & On-Site Training Catalog, 6890
AIChE, 6908
AIIM, 6599
AIN Plastics of Michigan, 8102
AJ Abrams Company, 7271
AJ Abrams company inc., 7271
AK Ltd, 8256
AL Ellis, 7498
ALDATA, 7740
ALLMEDIA INC, 7741
ALLMEDIA International, 7741
ALP Lighting, 7724
AME International, 6643
AMPCO Safety Tools, 7344
AMSOIL, 6439
APS Packaging Systems, 8043
APW Wyott Corporation, 8234
ASICO, 7927
ATD-AMERICAN, 7879
ATD-American Catalog, 7879
ATL, 6906
ATSCO Alamo Transformer Supply Company, 8463
AVI-SPL, 6393
AVW Equipment Company, 6448
AVW Equipment Company, Inc., 6448
Aaladin Cleaning Systems, 8358
Aaladin Industries, 8358
Abatron Building & Restoration, 6644
Abatron Inc, 6720
Abatron, Inc., 6644, 6741
Abbeon Cal Plastic Working Tools, 8103, 8464
Abbeon Cal, Inc., 8103, 8464
Abnote North America, 8128
Above & Beyond, 6851
Above & Beyond Balloons, 6851
Abrisa Industrial Glass, 7911
Academic Superstore, 6950, 6969
Acco Chain & Lifting Products, 7010
Accountant Stationers & Printers, 7841
Accu Seal Corporation, 7993
Accu Trak Tool, 8465
Accu Trak Tool Corporation, 8465
Accu-Seal Corporation, 7993
Accu-Tech, 7013
Accu-Tech Cable, 7013
Accu-Time Systems, 6970
Accu-line, 8044
Accuform, 8306
Accurate Industries, 8466
Accurate Industries Commercial Products, 8466

Accurate Metal Weather Strip Company, 6790
Accurate Metal Weatherstrip Co., 6790
Accurate Plastics, 8045
Accurate Plastics, Inc., 8045
Accutherm, 7393
Accutherm, Inc., 7393
Ace Bag & Burlap Co, 8046
Ace Industrial Products, 7257
Ace Pump Corporation, 7272
Ace Tank, 7273
Ace Tank & Equipment Company, 7273
Aceco Industrial Packaging Company, 8046
Achim Importing Company, 7499
Acme, 6455, 7274
Acme Engineering & Manufacturing Corporation, 7274
Acme Manufacturing, 8467
Acme Miami, 6455
Acorn Manufacturing Company, 6763
Acorn Manufacturing Company, Inc., 6763
Acra Electric Corporation, 7394
Acrocrete, 6645
Adams County Nursery, 7638
Adams Manufacturing Company, 7395
Adapt Plastics, 8104
Adapt Plastics Inc, 8104
Adaptive, 8257
Adaptive Micro Systems, 8257
Adcoa Absorbents & Desicants, 6554
Adcole Corporation, 6514
Addison, 7275, 7396
Addison Products Company, 7275, 7396
Adjustable Clamp, 8468
Adrick Cooling Corporation, 7322
Adrick Marine Group, 7322
Advance Energy Technologies, Inc., 7323
Advance Energy Technology, 7323
Advanced Graphics, 6412
Advanced Graphics Inc., 6412
Advanced Paper Systems, 8043
Advanced Solutions Group, 6901
Advanced Thermal Systems, 7345
Advantage Bag Company, 7012
Advantage Bags, 7012
Advertising Specialties & Business Gifts, 7144
Aerco International, 7397
Aerial Lift, 8469
Aero Tec Laboratories, 6906
Aerofin, 7398
Aerofin Corporation, 7398
Aeroflash Signal, 8429
Aesthetic Procedure & Treatment Guide, 7202
Aesthetic Video source, 6408
Aetna, 6302
Aetna Bearing Company, 6302
Aftermarket Specialties, 7276
Aftermarket Specialties, Inc., 7276
Agco, 6260
Aged Woods, 6750
Aged Woods, Inc., 6750
Aget Manufacturing, 7301
Aggreko, 7399
Aggreko North America, 7399
Agricultural Sciences, 7709
Air Balance, 6791
Air Balance, Inc., 6791
Air Comfort, 7400
Air Conditioning Products Company, 7346
Air Craft Spruce & Specialty Company, 6585
Air Drive, Inc., 6515
Air Dry Co. of America, LLC., 7305
Air Filter Testing Laboratories, 7302
Air Filtronix, 7258
Air Fixtures, 7994
Air Fixtures, Inc., 7994
Air Handling Systems, 7259
Air Monitor Corporation, 7347
Air Quality Engineering, 7303
Air Rite Service Supply, 7304
Air Rover Company, 7324
Air Rover, Inc., 7324
Air Tools, Hand Tools, Sheet Metal Tools, 8470
Air-Drive, 6515
Air-Dry Corporation of America, 7305
Air-Jet, 7260

Air-Jet, Inc., 7260
Air-Lec Industries, 6764
AirCorrect Inc., 7418
Aircondex, 7277
Aircraft Tool Supply Company, 6555
Airguard Industries, 7306
Airmaster Fan Company, 7261
Airmo Hydraulics, 8471
Airmo, Inc., 8471
Airsan Corporation, 7307
Aitken Products, 7262
Aitken's Salmon Creek Garden, 7639
Ajax Tocco Magnethermic Corporation, 7471
Akro-Mills, 7938
Alameda Commons, 8047
Alameda Packaging, 8047
Alamo Transformer Supply Company (ATSCO), 8463
Alarm Controls Corporation, 8430
Alarm Monitoring Services, 8431
Alarm Monitoring Services, Inc., 8431
Alarmax Distributors Inc., 8432
Albany International, 6792
Albion Engineering, 8472
Albion Industries, 8473
Albion Industries Full Line Catalog, 8473
AlcoPro, 7203, 7710
Alconox, 8359
Alemite LLC, 6516
Alert Stamping & Manufacturing Company, 7725
Alfa-Laval Thermal, 7401
Alfax Furniture, 7111
Algy, 8657
Algy Team Collection, 8657
Ahern Martin Industrial Furnace Company, 7402
AliMed, 7234
AliMed Operating Room Products, 7204
AliMed, Inc, 7204
AliMed, Inc., 7206, 7224
Aline Systems Corporation, 7995
All About Dog Grooming, 6261
All Packaging Machinery & Supplies, 7996
All Packaging Machinery Corporation, 7996
All-Fill, 7997
All-Fill, Inc., 7997
All-Pac, Inc, 8063
Allen Brothers, 8218
Allen Filters, 7308
Allen Global Companies, 7308
Allen, Sterling & Lothrop, 7600
Allen, Sterling, & Lothrop, 7600
Allied Engineering & Production Corporat, 8474
Allied Engineering & Production Corporation, 8474
Allied Glove & Safety Products Corporati, 8258
Allied Glove & Safety Products Corporation, 8258
Allied Healthcare Products, 7205
Allied Plastic Supply, 8105
Allied Plastic Supply, Inc., 8105
Allied-Signal & Aerospace Company, 6556
Allometrics, 7537
Alloy Fabricators of New England, 7403
Allstate Can Corporation, 7939
Almore International, 6985
Almore International, Inc., 6985
Alpha American Co, 6714
Alphabroder Buyer's Guide, 8658
Alstrom Corporation, 7404
Altec NUECO, 8469
Altech Controls Corporation, 7348
Altek Manufacturing Company, 7998
Althor Products, 7940
Altimate Medical Inc, 7001
Alto Manufacturing Company, 7768
Alto Manufacturing Company, Inc., 7768
Aluminum Case Company, 7941
Alyan Pump Company, 7294
Am Cast, Inc., 7379
Amaryllis & Caladium Bulb Company, 7640
Amaryllis Bulb Company, 7640
Amazon Exotic Hardwoods, 7641
Amcest, 8433
Ameri Stamp/Sign-A-Rama, 6356
AmeriStamp - Sign-A-Rama, 6356
American Academy-Medical Administrators, 6891
American Acrylics, 8106

American Aerospace Controls, 6557
American Aluminum Company, 7942
American Arbitration Association, 6594
American Arborist Supplies, 7573
American Autoclave Company, 6558
American Autowire, 6413, 6456
American Autowire, Inc., 6413, 6456
American Business Systems, 6971
American Casting & Manufacturing Corporation, 8475
American Casting & Manufacturing, Corpor, 8475
American Chemical Society Publication Guide, 6907
American Color, 8158
American Color Printing, 8158
American Coolair Corporation, 7263
American Dental Association, 6986
American Diamond Instruments, 6987
American Durafilm, 8107
American Durafilm Company, 8107
American Gas & Chemical Company, 7087
American Health & Safety, 8259
American Healthcare Supply, 7229
American Hotel Register Company, 7122, 8203
The American Institute of Architects, 6357
American Institute of Architects Press, 6357
American Institute of Chemical Engineers, 6908
American List Counsel, 7742
American Machine & Hydraulics, 8476
American Management Association, 6382
American Metal Door Company, 6833
American Metal Products, 7309
American Panel Corporation, 7325
American Precision Glass Corporation, 6765
American Safety Razor Company, 8477
American Saw & Manufacturing, 8478
American Scientific Lighting Corporation, 7726
American Stationery, 7842
American Stationery Company, 7842
American Tank Company, 7570, 7574
American Technical Publishers, 6595
American Technologies Network, 7711
American Thermoplastic Company, 7843
American Tubing, 7349
American Van Equipment, 6517
American Van Equipment, Inc., 6517
American Weather Enterprises, 7575
Ames Performance Engineering, 6457
Ametek, 7372
Amglo Kemlite Laboratories, 7727
Amsterdam Printing, 6888, 7167, 7200
Amtrol, 7405
Analytical Measurements, 7538
Anchor Box Company, 7943
Andersen Corporation, 6834
Anderson Fabrics, 7500
Anderson Instrument Company, 7350
Anderson-Snow Corporation, 7351
The Andersons Cob Products, 6330
The Andersons Inc., 7500
Androck Hardware Corporation, 6766
Andy's Auto Sport, 6414, 6518
Andy's Autosport, 6414, 6518
Anel Corpration, 7769
Animal Health International, 6277
Annual Reviews, 6596
Ansell Healthcare, 8659
Ansell Protective Products, 8659
Anthony Forest Products, 6730
Anti-Seize Technology, 6715
Apco/Valve & Primer Corporation, 7352
Apollo Valves, 7088
Apollo Valves Commercial Catalog, 7088
Appalachian Stove, 6700
Applewood Seed Company, 7601
Application Engineering, 7406
Aprilaire, 7320
Aqua Quest Publications, 6597
Aqua Quest Publications, Incorporated, 6597
Aqua-Therm, 6701
Aqua-Therm, LLC, 6701
Aquatic Eco-Systems, 7278
Arbico Organics, 7576
Arbill, 7908, 8260, 8360
Arbill Safety Products, 7908, 8260, 8360
Archie McPhee & Company, 7145

Ardmore Textured Metals, 7770
Arista Surgical Supply Company, 7206
Arlington Machine and Tool Co., 8075
Armstrong Medical Industries, 7207
Armstrong Medical Industries, Inc., 7207
Art Brown's International Pen, 6598
Art Institute of Chicago, 7864
Art Supply Warehouse, 6358
Art Supply Wholesale Club, 6358
Artistic Labels, 7844
Arts & Crafts, 6359
Asprey, 7146
Asprey New York, 7146
Associated Bag, 8048
Associated Bag Company, 8048
Associated Environmental Systems, 7540
Associated Equipment Corporation, 7257
Association for Information & Image Managemen t, 6599
Association of Rotational Molders, 7944
Astrographics, 6948
Astrup Company, 6767, 6835
At-A-Glance, 7845
Athletics & Schools Sports Medicine Catalog, 7208
Atkins Technical, 7353
Atkins Technical Services, 7353
Atkinson Dynamics, 8447
Atlanta Cable Sales, 6385, 8448
Atlanta Models & Exhibits, 7816
Atlas Fibre Company, 8108
Atlas Greenhouse Systems, 6303, 6819, 7577
Atlas Manufacturing, Inc., 6303, 6819, 7577
Atlas Metal Industries, 7771
Atomizing Systems, 6296, 7407
Atomizing Systems Inc., 6296, 7407
Audio Accessories, 6386
Audio Accessories, Inc., 6386
AudioGo, 6600
Auto Custom Carpets, 6415
Auto Custom Carpets, Inc, 6415
Auto Labe, 7999
Auto Label, 7999
Auto Meter, 6538
Autoflo, 7361
Autom, 7112
Autom Inspirational Gifts, 7112
Automated Conveyor Systems, 8000
Automatic Devices Company, 7501
Automotive Airfilters, 6519
Aviator's Store, 6559
The Aviator's Store, 6559
Avid Reader, 6638
Award Company of America, 7141, 7142, 7143, 7876, 7877, 7878
Awards.com, 7147
Aztec Grill Corporation, 8192
Aztec Machinery Company, 7408

B

B & F System, Inc., 8711
B&B ARMR, 8399
B&B Electronics Manufacturing Company, 6934, 7354
B&H Photo Video, 6360, 6387, 7935
B&H Photo Video Pro-Audio, 6360, 6387, 7935
B&J Food Service Equipment, Inc., 8193
B&J Peerless Restaurant Supply, 8193
B&R Industrial Automation Corp., 6935, 6951, 6972
B&R Industrial Automation Corporation, 6935, 6951, 6972
B&R Moll, 8159
BAG Corporation, 8001
BASF Construction Chemicals, LLC, 6645
BAT Inc., 6543
BBC Audiobooks America, 6600
BEC Controls Corporation, 7539
BG Micro, 6952
BGK Finishing Systems, 7436
BGMicro.com, 6952
BIRD-X, 7571
BMA Environmental Chambers, 7540
BNZ Materials, 6793
BP Barco Products, 8261, 8361
BP Lubricants USA, 6443
BSN Sports, 7209, 7210, 8660, 8661, 8662, 8663, 8664, 8665

BSN Sports Athletic Performance, 7209
BSN Sports Direct, 7210
BSN Sports Equipment, 8660
BSN Sports Lacrosse, 8661
BSN Sports League, 8662
BSN Sports Middle School-Junior High, 8663
BSN Sports Team-Work, 8664
BSN Sports TeamWear, 8665
BTI-Coopermatics Inc., 7314
BVS Inc, 8362, 8479
BVS Samplers, 8362, 8479
BYK Gardner Catalog, 6909
BYK USA, Inc., 6909
Backdrop Outlet, 6936, 7048
Backwoods Solar Electric Systems, 6702
Backyard Buddy, 6520
Badge-A-Minit, 6852
Badger Fire Protection, 7089
Bagmaster Manufacturing, 7712
Bagmaster Quality Bags, Cases & Holsters, 7712
Bailey Refrigeration Company, 7326
Bailey's, 8480
Bailey's Master Catalog, 8480
Baker & Taylor, 6631
Baker Creek Heirloom seed Co., 7606
Baker Hughes Incorporated, 8481
Baker Hughes Mining Tools, 8481
Balcrank Corporation, 8169
Baldwin, 8160
Bale Bonnet Slip Ons Round Bale Covers, 6339
Ballymore, 8482
Baltimore Aircoil Company, 7327
Bamert Seed, 7602
Bamert Seed Company, 7602
Bar's Leaks, 6521
Bar's Products, Inc., 6521
Barco Products, 6646, 7113, 8363
Barco Products Company, 6646, 7113, 8363
Bare Root Fruit Trees, 7603
Barksdale Control Products, 7014
Barksdale Inc., 7014
Barnes Engineering Company, 8483
Barnett Rotor Craft, 6560
Bartlett Arborist Supply & Manufacturing Comp any, 7578
Bartlett Manufacturing Company, 7578
Base-Line, 8161
Baseball Express, 6388, 6937
Baseball, Softball, Football Superstore, 6388, 6937
Basement De-Watering Systems, Inc., 8325
Basic Adhesives, 6810
Bass Equipment Company, 6304
Bates Leathers, 8666
Bates Metal Products, 7049
Battelle, 6601
Battelle Press, 6601
Baudville, 6361, 6416, 7050
Baumfolder Corporation, 8185
Bcc Research, 6602, 6902
Bean Farm, 6262
The Bean Farm, 6262
Bearse Manufacturing Company, 8049
Bearse USA, 8049
Beauti-Vue Products Corporation, 7502
Beck-Lee, 7211
Becker's School Supplies, 7114, 8050, 8152
Beer, Beer & More Beer, 8219
Bel-Art Products, 7541
Bell Springs Publishing, 6603
Benchmark Displays, 7051
Benchmark Industrial Supply, 8667
Bennett Industries, 6836
Bergeman USA, 7310
Berkebile Oil Company, 6440
Berridge Manufacturing Company, 6647
Berry Metal Company, 7279
Best Access Systems, 8400, 8434
Best Impressions, 6853
Best of Blue Print, 6604
Bete Fog Nozzle, 8364
Better Lists, Inc., 7743
Betty Mills Catalog, 7880, 8365
The Betty Mills Company, 7880, 8365
Beyond.Com, 6973
Bib Pak, 8051

Mars Air Systems, 8376
Marsh Shipping Supply Company, 8070
Marshall Domestics, 8250
Martguild, 7787
Martin Yale Industries Inc, 7828
Marugg Company, 7719
Maryland Aquatic Nurseries, 7679
Marzetta Signs, 8306
Masco Corporation, 7309
Mason Box Catalog, 7967
Mason Box Company, 7967
Mason Company, 6279
Massa Products Corporation, 8411
Master Builder, 6737
Master Catalogue, 6670
Master Disposers, 8237
Mastercut Tool Corporation, 6992
Masune First Aid & Safety, 8307
Material Flow & Conveyor Systems, 7968
Mathews Wire Giftware Catalog, 7179
Matticks Industries, 7449
Mauser, 7969
Mauser USA, LLC., 7969
Mavidon Catalog, 6671
Maxcess, 8140
Maxcess International, Inc, 7448
Maxell Corporation of America, 6381
Maysteel, 6963
Maysteel LLC, 6963
McFeely's Square Drive Screws, 8542
McGlaughlin Company, 8238
The McGlaughlin Oil Company, 8238
McGraw-Hill Education, 6943
McIlhenny Company, 8228
McNaughton & Gunn, 8170
McNeil Inc., 7371
McNeil Insulation Company, 7371
MeadWestvaco Corporation, 8157
Measurement Specialists, 8543
Measurement Specialists, Inc., 8543
Mech-Chem Associates, 6918
Mech-Chem Associates, Inc., 6918
Medallic Art Company, Ltd, 7180
Medeco, 8412
Medeco Security Locks, 8412
Medical Arts Press, 6295
Medical Arts Press® Corporation, 7219, 7869, 7887, 7890
Medical-Diagnostic Specialty Gases, 7237, 7560
Meller Optics, 7924
Memco Supply, 7450
Merchandising Solutions, 6628
Merchant Circle, 6831
Merco, 8207
Merco/Savory, 8207
Merrill Manufacturing Corporation, 7788
Merrimade, 7863
Metal Edge International, 7970
Metal Edge International, Inc., 7970
Metal Sales Manufacturing Corporation, 6738, 7802
Metem Corporation, 6575
Metro Shelving & Warehouse Products, 7068
Meyer Drapery Services, 7520
Meyer Drapery Services,Inc., 7520
Meyer Industries, Inc., 8019
Meyer Machine Company, 8019
Meyer Seed, 7618
Meyer Seed Company of Baltimore, Inc, 7618
Meylan Corporation, 8544
Mica-Tron Products Corp., 7789
Mica-Tron Products Corporation, 7789
Micro-Brush Hand Scrub, 8377
Micro-Mark, 6778
Micro-Mark, The Small Tool Specialists, 6778
MicroGroup, 6739
MicroGroup Small Diameter Tubing Specialists, 6739
Micron Industries Corporation, 8545
Mid America Motorworks, 6487
Mid America Motorworks Air-Cooled VW, 6487
Mid Atlantic Packaging, 8071
Midland, 6434
Midland Radio Corporation, 6434
Midwest Metal Products Company, 7790
Midwest Plastics, 8117
Midwest Supplies, 7720

Mil-Spec Packaging Supply, 8072
Mil-Spec Packaging of Georgia, 8073
Milcare Company, 6280
MilesTek, 7031
MilesTek Catalog, 7031
Militex Industries Corporation, 7485
Mill Supply Inc, 6310
Miller Edge, 8308
The Miller Group, 7071, 7839
MillerEdge, 8308
Milliken & Company, 8251
Milton W Bosley Company, 6353, 6808
Mini-Edition Iris Lover's, 7680
Minwax, 6812
Minwax Wood Finishing Products, 6812
Mirage Dental Systems, 6993
Mitchellace, 7521
Mo' Money Associates, 6872
Mocal Oil Control Systems, 6543
ModSpace, 6733
Modern Chemical, 8378
Modular Devices, 8455
Moen Industries, 8020
Molded Fiber Glass Tray Company, 8379
Moli-International, 8208
Monarch, 7898
Monarch Accounting Supplies, 7898
Monitor Products, 7297
Monitor Products, Inc., 7297
MonlanGroup Division, 7317
Moore Fabrication, 8118
Moore Medical Corporation, 7238
Moore Medical LLC, 7238
MoreFlavor, 8219
Morgan Manufacturing & Engineering Compa, 7522
Morgan Manufacturing & Engineering Company, 7522
Morion Company, 6371
Morton Machine Works, 7451
Moss, 7069
Moss Inc, 7069
Mossburg's Sign Products, 7070, 7899
Motomco, 6298
Motorbooks, 6435
Motorsport Auto, 6488
Mount Pulaski Products, 6330
Mountain Rose Herbs, 8229
Mountain States Equipment Company, 7452
Mr G's Fasteners, 6779
Mr. G's Enterprises, 6779
Mrs Fields Gourmet Gifts, 7181
Mrs. Fields, 7181
Multiplex Versatile Display Systems, 7071, 7839
Multistack, 7335
Munroe, 8546
Murray McMurray Hatchery, 6281
Museum Shop Catalog, 7864
Musser Forests, 7681
Musser Forests Inc, 6331
Musser Forests, Inc., 7681
Musserforests, 6331
Musson, 6672
Musson Rubber Company, 6672
My Magic Kitchen, Inc., 8227
Myers Sheetmetal, 7791
Mystic Valley Traders, 7495
MysticValleyTraders, 7495

N

NAED, 6904
NAED Education Foundation, 6904
NALCO, 7318
NALPAK, 7971
NANMAC, 8547
NANMAC Corporation, 8547
NC Textile Connect, 7526
NEB Catalog, 7561
NELCO, 8548
NELCO Wiring Accessory Specialists, 8548
NEPTUNE, 7545
NGK Berylco, 8309
NGK Metals Corporation, 8309
NTE ELECTRONICS, 7032

NTE Electronics, 7032
NUCON International,Inc, 7319
NWL, 8549
NWL Transformers, 8549
Nalco Company, 7318
Nalpak Sales, 7971
Nanik, 7523
Nasco Arts & Crafts Store, 6328, 6359, 7709
Nasco International, 8135
Nashville Wraps, 7182
Nashville Wraps Catalog, 7182
Natchez Shooters Supply, 7721, 8413
Nation/Ruskin, 6451
Nation/Ruskin, Inc., 6451
National AV Supply, 6400
National Association of Printers & Lithograph ers, 6629, 6897
National Bridle Shop, 6282
National Bullet Proof, 8414
National Bullet Proof, Inc., 8414
National Business Furniture, 7131
National Coating Corporation, 8155
National Communications, 8456
National Controls Corporation, 7372
National Draeger Detector Tube Products, 8310
National Drying Machinery Company, 8209
National Hospitality Supply, 7132, 7562
National Hospitality Supply, Inc., 7132, 7562
National Manufacturing Co, 6780
National Metal Fabricators, 7818
National Parts Depot, 6489
National Pen, 7183
National Pen Company, 7183
National Seminars Training, 6905
National Starch & Chemical Corporation, 8074
National Technical Information Service, 6640
National Wildlife Federation, 7169, 7858, 7859
Nationwide Boiler Catalog, 7453
Nationwide Boiler, Inc., 7453
Natural & Organic Fertilizers, 7619, 7682
Natural INSECTO Products, 6299
Natural INSECTO Products, Inc., 6299
Natural Spaces Domes, 6673
Naugatuck Glass Company, 6576
Neider Company, 8550
Neil Enterprises, 6372, 6873, 6373, 6874, 8146
Neil Holiday Catalog, 6373, 6874, 8146
Nemco Food Equipment, 8210
Nemco Food Equipment Inc., 8210
Network Access & Connectivity Product Line, 6942
Neuberg & Neuberg Importers Group, Inc. , 6349
Neuhaus Corporation, 8551
New England BioLabs, Inc., 7561
New England Business Service, Inc. (NEBS, 6860, 7850, 7886
New England Etching Company, 7900
New England Solar Electric, 6709
New England Solar Electric, Inc., 6709
New Jersey Machine, 8075
NewHaven Software, 6979
Newell Rubbermaid, 7524
Newell Window Furnishings, 7524
Newport, 7486
Newport Layton Home Fashions, 7486
Newport Thin Film Laboratory, 7925
Newport Thin Film Laboratory, Inc., 7925
Next Level, 8692
Niagara Fiberboard, 6674
Niagara Fiberboard, Inc., 6674
Nichols Garden Nursery, 7620, 7683
Nikro Industries, 8380
Nikro Industries, Inc., 8380
Nimlok Company, 7072
Nmc-Wollard,Inc., 6577
Noco Company, 6544
The Noco Company, 6544
Nor-Lake, 8211
Nordic Air, 7454
Nordson Corporation, 8035
Nordson EFD, 8502
Norment Security Group, 8441
Norpin Deep Drawn Enclosures, 8552
Norpin Manufacturing Co. Inc, 7792, 8552
Norpin Manufacturing Company, 7792
Nortel Machinery, 8553
Nortel Manufacturing Limited, 8553

Solo Horton Brushes, 6376
Solo Horton Brushes, Inc., 6376
Somat Company, 8237
Somay Paint Factory Catalog, 6689
Somay Products, Inc., 6689
Sonoco, 7983
Sonoco Products Company, 7983
Source, 6404
Source Northwest Inc., 7531
Source Window Coverings, 7531
South-Port Systems, 7463
Southport Engineered Systems, LLC., 7463
Southwire Company ,LLC, 7464
Southwire Machinery Divison, 7464
Sovernet Communications, 6755
Space Age Plastic Fabricators, 8131
Space Age Plastic Fabricators, Inc., 8131
Sparyway, Inc., 8178
Speciality Store Services, 7083, 7106
Speciality Woodworks Co., 6847
Specialty Store Services, 7083, 7106
Specialty Woodworks Company, 6847
Speco Audio Products, 6405
Speco Technologies, 6405
Spectronics Corporation, 7338
Spectronics Corporation Catalog, 7338
Spectrum Corporation, 7084
Speed Tools, 8606
Spex Certiprep, 7567
Spokane Hardware Supply, 8607
Spokane Hardware Supply, Inc., 8607
Sportime Catalog, 7107, 8094
Spraying Systems Company, 6341
Sprayway, 8178
Spring Hill Nurseries, 7696
Spring Hill Nursery, 7696
Springbrook Gardens, 7697
Springbrook Gardens, Inc., 7697
Springer, 6604
Springfield Rod & Custom, 6500, 6549
Springs Global, 7490
Srem Chemicals, Inc., 6925
Srewart R. Browne Manufacuring Company,, 8338
St Lawrence Nurseries, 7684
St. John Companies, 7251
St. Lawrence Nurseries, 7698
Sta-Warm Electric Co., 7465
Sta-Warm Electric Company, 7465
Stafford Manufacturing Corp., 7806, 8608
Stafford Manufacturing Corporation, 7806, 8608
Stagestep, 6761
Stagestep, Inc., 6761
Stamp Inc, 8510
Standard Industrial Products Company, 8609
Standard Rate and Data Services, Inc., 7763
Standard Rubber Products, 8610
Standard Rubber Products Co., 8610
Standard Safety Equipment Company, 8337
Standard Tar Products Catalog, 6690
Stanley Fastening Systems,L.P., 7820, 7881
Stanley Security Solutions Inc., 8400, 8434
Stanley Supplies and Services, 6342
Stanley Supply &Services, Inc., 6342
Stant, 6550
Stant Corporation, 6550
Starduster Catalog, 6585
Stark Bro's, 7699
Stark Bro's Nurseries & Orchards Co., 7699
Starlight Skylights, 6848
State Line Tack, 6289
State Line Talk, 6289
The Stationery Studio, 7868
Stefan Sydor Optics, 7932
Steiner Tractor Parts, 6501
Stencil Ease, 6377
Stencil Ease International, 6377
Stephen Bader Co., Inc., 8611
Stephen Bader and Company, 8611
Stephens Instruments, 7252
Sterling Production Control Units, 7040
Stevenson & Vestalury, 7491, 7532
Stevenson Vestal, 7491, 7532
Stewart R Browne Manufacturing Company, 8338
Stiles Enterprises, Inc., 8036

Stiles Rubber Company, 8036
Stimpson Company, 8612
Stock Drive Products, 6502
Stock Drive Products / Sterling Instuume, 6502
Stock Parts List, 7807
Stock Seed Farms, 6343, 7700
Stockton Products, 6742
Stolle Corporation, 7808
Stolle Machinery Company, LLC, 7808
StoreSMART, 6946, 6983
Storesmart, 6946, 6983
Stranco Inc., 8421
Stranco Products, 8421
Streamlight, 7739
Streamlight, Inc, 7739
Strem Chemicals, 6925
Stromberg's Chicks, 6290
Stromberg's Chicks & Game Birds, 6290
Strongbox, 7041
Stuc-O-Flex International, Inc., 6691
Stuc-O-Flex, International, 6691
Stulz Air Technology Systems, Inc., 7339
Stulz-ATS, 7339
Submatic Irrigation Systems, 7585
Subminiature Instruments Corp., 8613
Subminiature Instruments Corporation, 8613
Successories, 7905
Sullair, 7299
Sullivan Dental Products, 6998
Sullivan Dental Products, Inc., 6998
Sun Precautions, 8339, 8700
Sun Precautions, Inc., 8339, 8700
Sun Process Converting, 8179
Sun Process Converting, Inc., 8179
Sun-Mar Corp., 6926, 8388
Sun-Mar Corporation, 6926, 8388
SunMate & Pudgee Orthopedic Cushions, 7007
Sunelco, 6711
Sunelco, Inc., 6711
Sunhill Insider, 8614
Sunhill Machinery, 8614
Sunlawn, Inc, 7599
Sunlawn, Inc., 7599
Sunshine Farm & Gardens Perennial Plants, 7701
Sunshine Farm and Gardens, 7701
Sunshine Rooms, 6824
Sunshine Rooms, Inc., 6824
Super Box by Plant Service Corporation, 7984
Super Duper Publications, 8701
Super Radiator Coils, 7378
Super Shop, 8615
Superfos Packaging, 7985
Superfuture Corporation, 8615
Superior Pneumatic, 8616
Superior Pneumatic Air Tools, 8616
Superior Signal Company, 7108
Superior Signal Company LLC, 7108
Superior Valve Company, 7379
Support Plus, 7253
Support Products, 8189
Support Products, Inc., 8189
Support Services Alliance, 6898
Surface Finishes Company, 7933
SurgiTEI, 7918
Surgical Products Guide, 7254
Surgical Solutions Group, 7254
Surry Gardens, 7702
Surry Gardens' Bedding Plant Catalog, 7702
Survivair, 7109
Sussman Aquamatic Steam Products Corporation, 7466
Sussman Electric Boilers, 7466
Swanson Tool Co., Inc., 8606
Sweet Impressions, 7194
Sweet Impressions Catalog, 7194
Swest Inc., 7777
Swiss Precision Instrument, Inc., 8617
Swiss Precision Instruments, 8617
Sydor Optics, 7932
Symphony EYC, 7740
Syntechnics, 8340, 8389, 8422

T

T Marzetti Company, 8230
T&J Incorporated, 8618
T. J. Incorporated, 8618
T. Marzetti Company, 8230
T/C Press, 8132
T/J Fabricators, 8180
T/J Fabricators, Inc., 8180
TANDEMLOC, Inc., 8621
TDI Drapery Importing Corp., 7533
TDI Drapery Importing Corporation, 7533
THERM-O-TYPE Corp., 8181
TIF International, 8341
TIGG Corporate Headquarters, 8346
TMC-Ametek, 8624
TOCOS America, Inc., 8630
TOMAR Electronics, Inc., 8348
TP Tools & Equipment, 8619, 8620
TP Tools and Equipment, 8620
TRIMCO, 7871
TRS RenTelco, 7042
TRS-Ren Telco, 7042
TRUSSFRAME-3, 6743
TURFER, 8705
TableCraft, 8253
Tablecraft Products Company, 8253
Tadiran Batteries, 8342
Tadiran Electronic Industries, 8342
Tampa Sheet Metal Company, 7809
Tampa Sheet Metal Company, 7809
TandemLoc, 8621
Tandy Leather Factory, Inc., 8690
Tapes And Seminars, 6905
Tapeswitch Corporation, 8622
Taylor Wings, Inc., 6458
Teachers College Press, 8132
Team 365, 8702
Tec Art Industries Inc., 7085
Tec Systems, 8150
TecArt Industries, 7085
Techical Manufacturing Corporation, 7934, 8623
Technical Furniture Systems, 8423
Technical Manufacturing Corporation, 7934, 8623
Technobrands, 8624
Telular Corporation, 8424
Tempco Electric Heater Corporation, 7387, 7476
Tempo Decorative Fabrics, 7534
Tenco Assemblies, 8095
Tenco Assemblies, Inc, 8095
Tenenz, 7872
Tenenz, Inc., 7872
Tennant, 8390
Tennant Company, 8390
Tepromark International, 8343
Tepromark International, Inc., 8343
Terra Universal, 6927
Terra Universal, Inc., 6927
TerraQuip Construction Products, Inc., 8626
Terracon Corporation, 8625
Terramite Corporation, 8626
Territorial Seed Company, 7634
Tesa Tape, 6692
Tesa Tape, Inc., 6692
Testrite Visual, 6378
Testrite Visual Products, 6378
Texas Instruments, 7380
Texas Instruments, Inc., 7380
Therm-O-Disc, 7381
Therm-O-Type Corporation, 8181
Thermadyne, 8344
Thermal Engineering Co., 7467
Thermal Engineering Company, 7467
Thermal Gas Systems, 8345
Thermal Gas systems, Inc., 8345
Thermal Transfer Corporation, 7468
Thermo ALKO, 7043, 7568
Thermo Kinetics, 7469
Thermo-Kinetics, 7469
Thermofisher,Inc, 7566
Thermographed Business Cards, 7873
Things Remembered, 7195
Things You Never Knew Existed, 7196
Thmpson & Morgan Seeds, 7635

Alabama

ACA Corporate Awards, 5373
ACA For Churches Only, 5374
ACA School Essentials, 5375
ALPHA Sound & Lighting Co., 5461
American Thermoplastic Company, 5376
Auto Custom Carpets, 286
Bates Turkey Farm, 2896
Bear & Son Cutlery, 1215
Bell Company, 1730
CGS Aviation, 640
Conde Systems, 1893
Crane Hill, 833
Denny Manufacturing Company, 5464
Foster Taxidermy Supply, 4060
GameTime, 3536
Greenhouses & Horticultural Supply, 3041
Jeffers Livestock, 129
Joe C Williams, 2957
Logan Kits, 4186
MediRest, Inc, 4366
Medical Supplies Depot, 4367
Opening Night, 1440
Para USA, 2448, 2490
Priester's Pecans, 2590, 2696
Regitar USA, 569
Siegel Display, 3561
Summit Stands Catalog, 2497
TNT Fireworks, 4502
Tandems, Ltd, 5736
Teacher Direct, 1940
US Chess Federation, 1190
Victorian Furniture, 5000
Wilderness Press Catalog, 1836

Alaska

A Taste of Juneau, 2715
Alaska Herb Tea Company, 2621
Alaska Wild Berry Products, 1728, 3638
Big Ray's, 1217, 1355
Musk Ox Producers Cooperative, 1341
White Pass Railroad, 3511

Arizona

2015 Sper Scientific Catalog, 5501
Active Forever, 4283
Adventure Motorcycle Gear, 1556
America's Foremost Sporting Books, 1120
Anthony's Cigar Emporium, 5987
AppetizersUSA, 2895
Arbico Organics, 3064
Autom Inspirational Gifts, 1032
Azida, 4420
Baer Claw Brake Systems, 289
Bob's Classic Chevy Catalog, 459
Buckaroo Bobbins, 1415, 1668
Canyon Records, 2294
Caregiver Education Catalog, 4292
Christian Brands Gifts, 3426
Coach Lift Catalog, 2018
Cotton Clouds, 4160
Desert Rat Off-Road, 393
Drumbeat Indian Arts, 3864
FNT 2015 Product Catalog, 6052
Fairytale Brownies Bakery, 2678, 2802
Goober Pet Direct, 9, 37
Grumpy's Truck Parts, 518
Halstead Bead, 3877
HealthWatchers System, 2862
Healthcare Innovations, 4313
Hobe Laboratories, 4435
Hohm Press, 1064
Institute for Vibrant Living, 4394
J&G Sales, 2436
Just for Redheads Beauty Products, 4439
Lazzeroni, 2350
Living Grace Catalog, 3666
Low Vision/Hearing Loss Catalog, 4326
MMS Medical Supply, 5531

Military Book, 847
Military Video, 2335
Mobility Electronics, 1904
Movement Disorder, 4328
NA Information and Trade Center, 3669
Native Seeds, 3285
Paul Gaudette Books, 903
Phoenix Graphix, 559
Professional River Outfitters, 772
Reactive Metals Studio, 3898
Rigging Innovations, 5825
Scottsdale Bead Supply & Imports, 3902
Shepard Iris Garden, 3306
Sphinx Date Ranch & Southwest Market, 2788, 2970
Stanton Video Services, 2260
Star Ridge, 48
Sunland Home, 4858
TA Performance, 588
Toyota Power, 403
TriVita, 4406
Ultimate Systems, Limited, 5895
Universal Fog Systems, 5030
Victorian Bride, 5986
Warplanes, 4528
White Cap Industries, 6221
Woodworkers Source - Scottsdale/Corporate, 4146

Arkansas

2015 Veranda Marine Boats Catalog, 746
2015 Xpress Boats Catalog, 747
AG Russell, 5209
American Tubing, 246
Baptist Spanish Publishing House, 1035
Burge's Hickory Smoked Turkeys & Hams, 2898
Cat Claws, 81, 93
Creations and Collections, 1737, 4059
Creative Irish Gifts, 2799, 3647
Delta Force, 2430
Delta Press, 1150
Dulcimer Shoppe, 5295
Femail Creations, 732
Heifer International, 2276
Herbal Healer Academy, 4316
House of Webster, 2515, 3453
I.O. Metro, 4828, 4982
Legend Boats, 762
Mack's Prairie Wing, 2392
Nite-Lite Company, 1598, 2488
NiteLite, 1469
Pine Ridge Gardens, 3190
Promolife, 4248, 4844
Ranger's Bass Series Catalogs, 774
Redbook Volume 5, 5112
Rojek Woodworking Machinery, 4689
SeaArk Catalog, 780
ShopIrish, 1443, 1758
Stratos Boats, 783
TOMAR Electronics, 2263
Tipton & Hurst, 3501
Universal Art Images, 272
War Eagle Boats, 785
War Eagle Mill Product & Gift, 2891

California

1965-1973 Mustang Parts, 344
1979-1993 Mustang Parts, 346
4 Wheel Parts, 276
5.11 Tactical, 1407
ABP/Pharmex, 5502
AIMS Education Foundation, 2120
AKA Gourmet, 2980
ASN Publishing, 1119
Abbeon Cal Plastic Working Tools, 2121
Abel, 2356
Access to Recreation, 1992, 6227
Accessory Center, 280
Accountant Stationers & Printers, 5903
Activa Sports, 1451, 1554
Active Ride Skate Shop, 5840
Active Ride Snow Shop, 5845

Active Ride Women's Shop, 5846
Advance Adapters Buyer's Guide, 388
Advantage Bags, 2040
Advertising Specialties & Business Gifts, 3515
Aerospace Composite Products, 636
Aftosa, 3815
Air Tools, Hand Tools, Sheet Metal Tools, 6021
Aircraft Spruce & Specialty Company, 605
Alden Lee Company, 5284
All Weather Inc, 5504
Allett, 1477
Allman Products, 2017, 2031
Aloha Tropicals, 3080
Alpen Outdoor, 5430
Alphabet Alley, 6144
Amador Flower Farm, 3081
America's Finest Pet Doors, 1
American Acrylic Awards & Gifts, 3415
American Fencers Supply, 5739
American Flag and Gift Catalog, 1767, 3639
American Furniture Design, 4088, 5007
American Pet Pro, 33
American Rotary Tools Company, 6026
American Technologies Network, 2419, 2462
American Weather Enterprises, 2126
AnB Stationery, 5932
Andy's Autosport, 285, 449
Antique Art Carpets, 5095
Any Mountain, 5848
Apricot Farm, 2766
Arcal, 2290
Are You Game.Com, 6149
ArtFox Lighting, 5463
Arta River Trips, 6229
Arthur Beren Shoes, 5557
Arts & Crafts Textiles, 4934
Astro Communication Services, 961
At Risk Resources, 2054, 2187
Athleta, 1454, 1559, 1682
Audio Editions, 858
Aunt Lute Books, 1101
Auromere Ayurvedic Products, 4419
Auromere Books, 1030
Aussie Dogs, 5559
Autograph Collector, 1123
Automotive Airfilters, 453
Available Plastics, 4963
Aviation Book Company, 609
Aviator's Store, 610
Avocado of the Month Club, 2767
B Coole Designs, 1383
B&W Tile Company, 4718
B-52 Professional / E.T.I. Sound Systems, 5287
BJB Enterprises, 4607
BTO Sports, 5243
BUYnail.com, 4421
Baby News, 673
Babystyle, 659, 1508
Backdrop Outlet, 181, 5474
Backroads-Bicycling Vacations, 6231
Bailey's Master Catalog, 879, 6031
Balsam Hill, 4672
Barbie Top 10 Holiday Picks, 1803
Bare Root Fruit Trees, 4592
Barksdale Control Products, 2210
Barnett Rotor Craft, 638
Baroni, 5166
Barska, 5431
Bates Leathers, 1478
Bates Nut Farm, 2547, 2945
Beauty Naturally, 4427
Beer, Beer & More Beer, 4531
Bellerophon Books, 925
Besame Cosmetics Inc., 3419
Betty Mills Catalog, 5380
Big Red Catalog, 457
Biordi Art Imports, 1732, 3817
Birkenstock Express, 5563
Biscoff Gourmet Catalog, 2548, 2659, 2793
Blind Butler, 4720
Blue Ox Millworks, 4610
Bonnie Triola Yarns, 4155
Book Publishing Resources, 880
Bountiful Gardens, 3092

Williams-Sonoma, 5240
Williams-Sonoma Home, 5241
Wine Appreciation Guild Store, 4543
Wine Country Gift Baskets Catalog, 3012
Wine.com - Holiday Catalog, 3016
Wireless Emporium Catalog, 1990
WomenSuits Catalog, 1727
Wood Screen Doors, 4651
Woodland Hills Camera, 5442, 5490
Woodwind Catalog, 5313
X-Stamper, 3779
XUMP Science Toys, 2169
Y Catalog, 1476, 4253
Yamaha Music Corporation, 5314
Yoshimura Catalog, 5282
Z Gallerie, 4951
Z&ZX Parts & Accessories Catalog, 441
Zoo Med Product Catalog, 54
Zymo Research, 4379
danzia, 5460
eMarinePX Catalog, 1667

Colorado

ABA Sales, 56, 1118
AeroGarden, 3018, 3326
Alpine Casting Company, 3857
Alpines Seed Catalog, 3240
American Educational Products, 2050, 2123, 5506
Applewood Seed Company, 3241
Artistic Labels, 5905
Asia Transpacific Journeys, 6230
Baby-Go-To-Sleep Parenting Resources, 923, 2325
Beyond Sight, 1996
Big Agnes, 5810
Black Pines Sheep, 4075
Brunton, 1227
Burris Optics Catalog, 2465
B"Ker, 5213
Centerline Alfa Products, 429
Cheryl Oberle Designs, 3721
Colorado Yurt, 1232
Colorful Images, 5936
Crystal Farm, 5046
Current, 3431, 3648
Custom Address Labels, 5937
Dogs Unlimited, 96
Down Under Saddle Supply, 5784
Ebags, 1198, 3617
Enstrom Candies, 2567
Espresso Gourmet, 2631
Eureka Stamps, 3734
Events by Paper Direct, 3434
Explorations, 1055
Gaiam Living, 1460, 2275, 3440
Gates Product Corporation, 509
Gibson Athletic, 5767
Glass Craft, 4034
Gorsuch, 1582
Growing Supplies, 3139
Hach Company, 2141
Hangouts, 3361
High Plains Bison, 2912, 2985
InnerBalance, 4242
Integrated Medical, 4243
International Auto Parts, 414, 431
International Bible Society, 1065
IntoTheWind Catalog, 4504
J and J Dog Supplies, 102
J.L. Powell The Sporting Life, 691, 1361, 1527
Jim Morris Environmental T-Shirt Company, 1363
Jonas Supply Company, 4065
Just Cases, 6245
Kudos by Paper Direct, 5394
La Sportiva, 5814
Lambspun, 4184
Leanin' Tree, 3462
Lillian Vernon, 1279, 3464
Lillian Vernon Big Sale, 4834
Lillian Vernon Personalized Gifts, 3465
Lillian Vernon Sales & Bargains, 3466
Lilly's Kids, 1394
Love and Logic, 1093

Message!Products, 5948
Morning Light Emporium, 3890
Mountain Woodcarvers, 4118
My Sentiments Exactly, 3749
Nostalgic Warehouse Door Hardware, 4752
Obermeyer, 5854
Only Natural Pet Store, 86, 105
Ornamental Resources, 3893
Ostrich Baskets & Custom Gifts, 3549
Paladin Press, 1178
PoolDawg, 5661
RTS Unlimited, 1179
Rage Fitness Supply, 5771
Reese Tipis, 1246
Right Start, 670, 704
RockWare, 1965
Rocky Mountain Chocolate Factory, 2593
Rocky Mountain Connection, 1288, 1605
Rocky Mountain Rare Plants, 3299
Schacht Spindle Co., 4085
Seeds Trust, 2786, 2884, 3303
Shop at Home Catalog Directory, 3491
Smith & Hawken, 3395
Sounds True, 2318
Stamp of Excellence, 3767
Stockyards Ranch Supply, 145
Styles Checks, 5414
Tecra Tools, 6125
The Golden Bear, 5203
Times to Cherish, 3774
Trumble Greetings, 5964
Univair Aircraft Corporation, 633
Valley Traditional Archery, 5707
VintageView, 3009
Violet Showcase, 3226
WeatherPort Shelter Systems, 3062
Welcome to the Best of Lillian Vernon, 3509
White Cloud Lodging, 5861
WildWasser Sport USA, 788
Yeti Cycles, 5738
Youcan Toocan Catalog, 4342
Zia Natural Skincare, 4467
eBags Catalog, 1214, 3624

Connecticut

Accu-Time Systems, 1944
Aerial Lift, 6020
At Peace Media, 2291
Audio Forum, 859
Balticshop.com, 863
Barker Animation Art Galleries, 1729
Baronet Coffee, 2623
Best of Cards, 6152
Blackstone Industries, 6037
Borgeson Universal Company, 460
BrandTech Scientific, 5511
Bridgewater Chocolate, 2550, 2794
Brooks Brothers, 1385, 1519, 1685
CM Almy General, 1046
Ceramica Direct, 5216
Chadwicks of Boston, 1313, 1687
Challah Connection, 2510, 2555, 2795
City Chemical, 5512
Classic Mustang, 476
Coastal Tool & Supply, 6043
Colonial Redi Record Corporation, 5359
Colorblends Catalog, 3248
Connecticut Cane & Reed Company, 3787
Cooking Enthusiast, 5218
Cottage Shop, 1736, 3430
Createx Colors, 4162
Creative Learning Institute, 2069
Cricket Hill Garden, 3110
Danbury Mint, 1785
Defender Marine Buyer's Guide, 795
Del Arbour Designs, 5842
Design Within Reach, 4976
Desserts by David Glass, 2671
Donnelly/Colt Progressive Resources, 1318
Droll Yankees, 61
Duralite, 3825
Early Advantage, 2075

Easton Press Leather Bound Books, 835
Edible Arrangements, 2565, 2771, 2800
Edward R Hamilton Bookseller, 836, 2300
English as a Second Language, 2194, 2329
Excel Technologies, 5520
Exclusive Sports Jewelry, 5137
Fairfield Processing, 4014
Florentine Craftsmen, 3348
Flying Noodle, 2984
Foothills Adult Education, 2080
Foredom Electric Company Power Tool Catalog, 6055
Frames & Insignia Products Catalog, 162
GCI Outdoor, 1234
Garden Book, 3350
Goal Sporting Goods, 5632
Godiva Chocolatier, 2570
H H Perkins, 3790
Harriets, 3957, 4178
Historic Housefitters Company, 5052
Hobbytyme, 4515
HomeRoom Direct, 3538
Horton Brasses, 5017
ITW Automotive Products, 412
Isabella Bird Collection, 1699
JB Tackle Co., 2388
JC Penney Baby Book, 665
Janice Corporation, 4324
Jaypro Sports, 5641, 5769
John Scheeper's Beauty from Bulbs, 3276
Kenneth Lynch & Sons, 3368
Kitchen Garden Seeds, 3281
Kolo, 198, 4488
LEGO Shop at Home, 6190
Lazy Hill Farm Designs, 4833
Logee's Greenhouses, 3164
Lux Bond & Green, 5196
Lyman Products Corporation, 5645
Masecraft Supply, 6095
Matthews 1812 House, 2688
McDonnell Marine Service, 804, 817
Metrostyle, 1708
Moore Medical Corporation, 4368
Mossberg Catalog, 1850, 2444, 2486
Mostly Mustangs, 541
Munchkin Motors, 542
Mustangs Unlimited, 316
Nodine's Smokehouse, 2922
PC Systems Handbook, 1934
PCS Stamps & Coins, 1881
PIC Design, 550
PTI Pyramid Technologies, 3845
Pleasant Valley Glads & Dahlias, 3292
Plumbridge Confections & Gifts, 2589
Radio Spirits, 2312
Rainhandler, 4634
S&S Worldwide, 207, 267
Sally Distributors, 3763
Select Seeds, 3208
Select Seeds Antique Flowers, 3305
Seton Catalog, 5924
Shuttercraft, 4638
Simpson & Vail, 2650
Skydog Kites, 4506
Solo Horton Brushes, 210
Soundprints, 951
Starstruck, 3906
Stencil Ease International, 4055
Stew Leonard's, 3006
Sudberry House, 3982
Territory Ahead, 714
The Pet Health and Nutrition Center, 89
Tuttle Distinctive Sportswear, 1619
US Games Systems Inc, 6218
USI Inc., 5356
Van Engelen, 3316
Vineyard Vines, 1298
Whelen Engineering, 600
Whispering Pines, 4869
White Flower Farm Catalog, 3229
Whole World Music Catalog, 2321
Wildlife Control Supplies, 31, 3077
Willabee & Ward, 1795
Woodbury Pewterers, 3615

Delaware

Advanced Machinery, 6019
Chick's Harness & Supply, 5783
Designer Culinary Stencils, 4045
Gevalia Coffee, 2635
Intelligent Outfitters, 6185
LA Stencilworks, 4048
Mid Shore Boat Sales, 766
Prestwick House, 2105
Stallard Chassis and Components, 582

District of Columbia

Biblical Archaeology Society Collection, 1038
Brass Knob, 4675
CQ Press, 966
Essential Skills Software, 2178
Fan Fair, 3346
Gallaudet University Press, 939, 1090
Hanley-Wood, 6068
International Spy Museum, 3628
National Geographic Society, 2096
Smithsonian Business Ventures, 5154
Smithsonian Journeys, 6253

Florida

1967-1969 Camaro Parts & Accessories, 345
ACE Educational Supplies, 2047
Absolutely Natural, 4416
Accon Marine, 748
Addison Products Company, 4597
Advanced Graphics, 281
Albritton Fruit Company, 2765
Alfred Angelo, 1408
Algy Team Collection, 1625
All About Dog Grooming, 32
All Pro Sound, 2208, 5037, 5285
Amaryllis Bulb Company, 3082
Amazon Exotic Hardwoods, 2269
Aqua Supercenter, 4600
Atlantic Publishing Company, 878
Atlantic Publishing Group, 1084
Aubrey Organics, 4418
Awards.com, 3520
Axner Company, 3988
B Lazarus, 3570, 4717
Baitmasters of South Florida, 2359
Barnie's Coffee & Tea Company, 2622
Betty's Attic, 613, 828, 3643
Biomagnetics, 4290
Blue Sky Swimwear, 1455
Bluewater Books & Charts, 725, 814
Boston Proper, 677, 727
Boston Proper Travel Clothing, 678
Boston Whaler, 750, 2361
Brinsea Products, 60
Buggies Unlimited, 615, 5475, 5742
Business Boosters Catalog, 2212
CCR Medical, 4351
Cable Organizer Office and Home, 290, 464
Caladium World, 3100, 3245
Call One, 3526
Captain Harry's Fishing Supply, 2369
Catherines, Inc., 680
Certified Steak and Seafood, 2900
Cerwin-Vega!, 291
Champs Software, 1892
Chestnut Hill Nursery, 3105
Chico's, 1689
Citrus Country Groves, 2769
Classic Airboaters Catalog, 755
Classic Auto Air Manufacturing, 471
Clientele, 4232
Coconut Telegraph, 1423
Collector Car Restorations, 358
Concept Catalog, 257
Concession Equipment Depot, 3626
Corona Cigar Company, 5993
Country Iron Foundry, 4954
Crafty Needle, 3946

Crystek, 2218
DB Enterprises, 5862
DJ Inkers, 3726
Dacasso, 5360
Davidson of Dundee, 2564
DeSantis Collection, 1526
Delta Picture Frame Company, 160
Directory of Life Extension Nutrients and Dru, 4294
Divers Direct, 5836
Dock Builders Supply, 797
Dove Brushes, 190
Dunkin's Diamonds, 4586
EAA Corporation, 2432
Eckler's 1953-2001 Corvette Parts and Accesso, 363
Eckler's Classic Chevy, 494
Eckler's Corvette Parts, 495
Eckler's El Camino, 496
Eden Organic Nursery Services, 3119
EdgeWater Power Boats, 757
El Camino Store, 365
Empire Books, 838
Everything Carts, 5747
Everything for the Lilypool, 3344
Fashionable Canes & Walking Sticks, 2001
Florida Clay Art Company, 3827
Florida Gold Fruit Co., 2772
Four Corners, 4307
Four Corners Direct, 1495
Full Of Life, 4237, 4308, 4388
Full of Life, 4309
G Neil Direct Mail, 5390
G. Neil, 5915
Going Bananas, 3134
Gold Effects, 511
Golf Around the World, 5748
Golfpac Golf Tours, 5752
Good Fortunes, 2571
Gourmet Food Store, 2808
Graphics 3, 4547, 4555, 4587
Graves Company, 1821
Gray & Sons, 5180
Guidance, Life Skills and Work, work, work!, 1106
Gulf Coast Avionics Products, 618
GymRats, 5889
HJ Saunders/US Military Insignia, 1844
HOVER-LURE, 2386
HR Direct, 1953
Hale Groves, 2774
Hale Indian River Groves, 2775
Hammond Electronics, 2233
Harvey's Groves, 2955
Hawk Racing, 5727
Hecht Rubber Corporation, 193
High Quality Tools High Quality Import Catalo, 6073
High Quality Tools Master Catalog, 6074
Hoffman Mint, 1789
Holiday Gift Basket, 2999
Hyatt Fruit, 2777
Hydro-E-Lectric, 524
Infosource, 1900, 1955
Jesada Tools, 6084
Jodee Post-Mastectomy Fashions Catalog, 1497
Joe's Goes Direct, 2723
Jonathan Arthur Ciener, 2437
Just Fruits and Exotics, 3155
Kellyco Metal Detector Superstore, 4487
Key West Aloe, 4268
Laboratory Equipment for the Life Sciences Ca, 5529
Laboratory Glassware and Supplies Catalog, 5530
Levenger, 3463, 4985
Life Uniform, 694
Lighter Side, 3596, 3664
Lockwood Aviation Supply, 620
Loop Fly Fishing, 2391
Luis Martinez Gallery of Fine Cigars, 6003
Marisota, 695, 1500, 1707
McMillan Optical Company, 2153
Mercedes Performance Products, 310, 537
Mike's Cigars, 6004
Mission Supply House, 4518
Mixon Fruit Farms, 2780
Model Expo, 4520
NASCAR Superstore, 1597
National Parts Depot, 543

P&H Crystalite, 5064
PRO-TOOLS, 551
Palm Beach Jewelry, 5198
Palm Beach Jewelry Signature Collection, 4277
PalmBeach Jewelry, 1343
Panama Marine, 735
Paper Crafts Magazine, 3753
Pelican Bay Ltd, 2538, 2875
Pepper Gal, 3290
Perfectly Sweet, 2588
Performance, 555
Performance Diver, 5838
Pet Doors USA, 20
PetMeds, 47
Pioneer Linens, 3552, 4900, 4919
Plus Skate Shop, 5844
Poinsettia Groves, 2783
Polart Distribution, 4842
Polart by Mail, 3485
Polart: Poland by Mail, 1754, 3680
Polka Dots, 6206
Possum Trot Tropical Fruit Nursery, 3194
Prima Bead, 3388, 3897, 3926
Pronto Business Cards, 5923
Quest Outfitters, 4193
Race Quip Safety Systems, 5664
Racer Walsh Company, 565
Rare Fruiting Plants & Trees, 3198, 3295
Regency Cap & Gown, 1646
Renco Electronics, 2254
Room It Up, 3559
Safari Ltd, 1819
Safariland Forensics Source Catalog, 5545
Safariland Master Catalog, 2452
Safariland Shooting Gear Catalog, 2453
Sarah's Sewing Supplies, 4196
Sarasota Avionics, 628
Script and Scribble, 5957
Seaway China, 1814
Self Publishing Catalog, 910
Shoes for Crews, 5595
Silver Queen, 3603
Soma, 1504
Star Styled Dancewear, 5454
Stork Avenue Catalog, 5960
Successories, 5415
Sun Harvest Citrus, 3495
Sunshine Discount Crafts, 3772
Sunshine Jewelry, 5155
Sunup/Sundown, 1473
Terrapin Ridge Farms, 2889
The Big Book, 5353, 5368, 5416
The Elegant Office, 5369
The Learning Connection, 953, 1021
The Lighter Side Catalog, 2524, 3400, 3699
Things You Never Knew Existed, 2525, 3401, 3700
Thompson Cigar Company, 6009
Tiger Direct, 1988
Timepieces International, 5206
Tomato Growers Supply, 3312
Tortuga Rum Cake Company, 2699
Travel Video Store Catalog, 6256
Trias Flowers, Weddings & Events, 3608
Trophyland USA, 3565
Tupperware, 5237
Tupperware Fundraiser Brochure, 5238
Tupperware Mid-Month Brochure, 5239
US Buildings, 4707
USA Scientific, 5551
Uniform Advantage Medical Uniforms, 1659
Uniform Wizard, 1660
Venus, 1475
Violet House of Pots, 3405
Wasserman Uniforms, 1663
Whip N Spur, 5794
Wicks Unlimited, 3810
Windjammer Barefoot Cruises, 1213
Wood Carvers Supply Catalog, 4139
Woodcarvers Supply Catalog, 6137
Worthington Architectural Details Catalog, 4772
Wrestler's Express, 5681
Wrestling Superstore Catalog, 1192
Wrisco Industries, 4654
Zarlene Imports, 3910

Georgia

AAVIM, 956, 2171
Accu-Tech Cable, 2207
Active Parenting Publishers, 1082
Alzheimer's Store Catalog, 1994, 4285
American 3B Scientific, 2122
American Light Source, 5038
Americana Catalog, 1768
Ames Taping Tool System, 6029
Apollo: Your Packaging Expert, 5008
Atlanta Cable Sales, 1973
Atlanta Cutlery, 1837
Atlas Greenhouse Systems, 2055, 4605
Augusta Office Solutions, 5379
Augusta Sportswear, 1561
B&R Industrial Automation Corporation, 1887
BIKE Football, 5605
Beverly Bremer Silver Shop, 3572
Bud K Worldwide, 5801
Byrd Cookie Company, 2661
Cali and York, 1686
Callaway Gardens Country Store, 2740
Carolina Skiff, 752, 2370
ChutingStar, 5821
Claxton Bakery, Inc., 2664
Collector's Armoury, 1841
Cooper Jones, 1525
Coronet Carpets, 5099
Electro Medical Equipment, 1999
Embroidery Research Press, 837
Eve Alexander, 1509
Folktale & Story Catalog, 6181
Fran's Gifts to Go, 2952
Global Pigeon Supplies, 65
Goodmark Retail Catalog, 513
Green Frog Railroad Catalog, 4513
Grill Lovers Catalog, 5223
HE Harris & Company, 1876
Heidelberg News, 5492
Highland Hardware, 6075
Hobby Builder's Supply, 1855
Home Decorators Collection, 4825, 4889, 5106
Honey Baked Ham, 2683, 2913
HoneyBaked Ham Company, 2684, 2914
Horse Lover's Gift Guide, 5786
Hoss Tools, 6077
House Parts, 3592
InterfaceFlor, 5107
Ison's Nursery & Vineyards, 3152
Johnson Nursery Fruit Trees & Small Fruit, 3153
Justin Charles, 3620
KEH Camera Brokers, 5489
Kapla USA, 6186
Ken's Fish Farm, 156
Kevin's Fine Outdoor Gear & Apparel, 1590
Koinonia Partners, 2959
Koo Koo Bear Kids, 666
KooKoo Bear Kids, 1390
LAT Apparel, 1277
Lazy K Nursery, 3161
Linksoul, 1532
Magnolia Hall, 4986
Mascot Pecan Shelling Company, 2961
Men's Catalog, 5584
Merritt Pecan Company, 2962
Mike's A Ford-able Parts, 538
Mo Hotta Mo Betta, 2868
Mori Luggage & Gifts, 3621
Muggins Math Series, 2094
Museum Replicas Limited, 3629
NetKnacks, 5875
Obsolete Chevrolet Parts Company, 547
Osborne Wood Products, 4688
Ozone Billiards, 5656
PMI, 5816
Pirelli Armstrong Tire Corporation, 561
Poultry & Gamebreeders Catalog, 137
Prevail Sport, 1471
Ranger Joe's, 1223
Ranger Joes, 5901
Rare Coin & Currency, 1792
Red Baron Antiques, 233
River Street Sweets, 2592, 2966

Rocker Shop, 6115
SafeShowroom.com, 5129
Savannah's Candy Kitchen, 2594
Showtime Dance Shoes, 5452
Spices Etc, 2888
Sportaid, 2012
Stafford's, 711
Stafford's Catalog, 1611
Sunnyland Farms, 2827, 2973
Swordsswords.com, 1248
Ten.o, 5772, 5808
Textile Enterprises, 4208
U.S. School Supply, 2117
Westport Big & Tall Catalog, 1546
Whitman Publishing Catalog, 1885
Wilkerson Mill Gardens Catalog, 3235
Williams & Kent, 1547
XYLO Molding Catalog, 170
YearOne Catalog, 387

Hawaii

Bess Press, 1196
Crazy Shirts, 1358
Hawaii Coffee Company, 2638
Hawaii's Flowers Catalog, 3142
Islands Tropicals, 3455
Kava Kauai, 4396
Sylvia Woods Harp Center, 5312

Idaho

A Child's Dream, 3932
ABC Feelings, 2046, 2322
AU-RUS Wax Patterns, 3856
Aire Catalog, 749
Alpine Archery, 5683
Anglers Catalog, 2358
Backwoods Solar Electric Systems, 4660
Beans Without the Bang, 2834
Big Sky Leatherworks, 5780
Bluster Bay Woodworks, 4076
Bosom Buddy Breast Forms, 4349
Cascade Outfitters, 753, 5620
Clean Report, 4810
Cranberry Junction Designs, 3725
Dutchman 1955-1957 Chevy Car Catalog, 360
Dutchman Motorsports, 361
Evangel Wedding Service, 5974
First Choice, 5914
Flutterbye Garden, 3349
GA Labs, 4432
H Potter, 67
Hortense B. Hewitt Co., 5979
Hyde Drift Boats, 761
Idaho Wood Lighting, 5055
Jensen Jewelers Current Bridal Catalog, 5185
Jensen Jewelers Elk Ivory Catalog, 5186
Mountain Archery, 5697
NRS, 5651
National Wildlife Federation, 3600, 6197
Northwest Pack Goats & Supplies, 18
Northwest River Supplies, 767
Rexcraft, 5984
Selkirk Aviation, 629
Snug Fleece Woolens, 4927
The Golden Egg of Idaho, 1858
Woodland Smoky Bear Catalog, 3568

Illinois

1 Stop Square, 173
ABC Distributing, 3514
ALP Lighting, 4595
ASCP Catalog, 1098
AVW Equipment Company, 406
Achievement Products for Special Needs, 4282
Adjustable Clamp, 6018
Adolph Kiefer & Associates, 1452
Adolph Kiefer and Associates, Inc., 791

Advantage Medical, 2016, 2030, 2041
Air-Drive, 445
Allen Brothers, 2716, 2893
Allergy Asthma Technology, 4284
American Health Information Management Catalo, 1100
American Rugby Outfitters, 1558
American Science & Surplus, 5507, 6146
American Tailgater, 389
Anti-Seize Technology, 450
Areoflash Signal, 608
Armstrong Medical Industries, 4227
Art Institute of Chicago, 3625
Ash-Dome, 5509
Ashro Lifestyle, 1681
Atkinson Dynamics, 6030
Auto Body Toolmart, 451
B&B Electronics Manufacturing Company, 813
BIRD-X, 57, 3065
Badge-A-Minit, 3715
Bahai Publishing Trust, 924, 1034
Barco Products Company, 3331
Basket Works, 2792, 3417
Berry Scuba Company, 5835
Billet Specialties, 458
Bretford, 1976
Brewer Sewing Supplies, 3938
Buck Brothers, 6039
Burgess Seed and Plant Company, 3097
CARL Manufacturing, 6040
CB2, 4807, 4968, 5078
CDW, 1927
CatfishConnection, 794, 1230
Ceramic Bug Supplies, 3819
Chefwear, 1629
Chicago Corvette Supply, 470
Child Management, 1086
Children's Book of the Month, 930
Clinton Electronics, 2215
Clubs of America, 2797
Cole-Parmer, 5513
Cole-Parmer Instruments Product Catalog, 5514
Collections Etc, 3577
Collections Etc., 3338, 3427
Collector's Paperweights, 1735
Commodity Traders International, 3028
Cookie Garden, 2559
Corvette/Volkswagen, 430
Court Products, 5621
Cozzini, 2902
Crate & Barrel, 4812
Creations by Elaine, 5973
Crown Galleries, 729
Custom Accessories, 297
Daigger & Company Lab Supply, 2134
Daigger Scientific, 5516
Decorators Supply Corporation, 4730
Design Toscano, 4975
Diamond Tour Golf, 5746
Dick Blick Art Materials, 187
Dick Pond Athletics, 5830
Dickson Company, 5517
Dinkel's Bakery, 2672
Direct Gardening, 3114
Discount School Supply, 188, 2074, 3728
Eli's Cheesecake, 2677
EnableMart, 2000
Fair Oak Workshops, 3735
Fannie May, 2568
Ferdco Corporation, 3585
Fitness Factory Outlet, 4236
Forster Products, 2478
Four Season's Nursery, 3128, 3261
Fox Valley Systems, 4775
Freedom Outdoor Furniture, 4818
Frontier Soups, 2513
Fruitful Yield, 4387
Fun-Tronics, 1746
G.H. Meiser & Company, 507
GC Electronics, 2229
General Association of Regular Baptist Church, 1057
Ghirelli Rosaries, 1058, 3873
GiftsForYouNow.com, 1748, 5940, 5997
Goodheart-Willcox Publisher, 1091
HRP World, 519

Handi-Ramp, 2034
Handy Hands, 4177
Harry London's Candies, 2575
Heartland Steaks, 2910
Heathrow Scientific, 2145
Heidts Suspension Systems, 521
High Performance Catalog, 522
Hodgson Mill, 2514, 2847
Holum & Sons Company, 194
Honors Military Catalog, 1328, 1845
Hot Off the Ice, 5637
House of Wesley, 3148
Howard Decorative Packaging, 195, 3740
Human Kinetics Academic & Professional Resour, 892
Human Kinetics Physical Education and Dance, 985
Human Kinetics Sports and Fitness, 1166
IVP Academic Catalog, 987
In the Swim, 6243
Iroquois Products Catalog, 415
Irv's Luggage, 3618
JC Whitney Motorcycle, 5258
Jasco Uniform Catalog, 692
Jayson Home, 4944, 5083, 5108
John Deere Construction Equipment, 3367
Johnson Bros Metal Forming Catalog, 197
Justrite Manufacturing Company, 5126
K-9 Science Catalog, 988
Kaehler Luggage, 6246
Knights Edge, 1847
Komet of America, 6090
LH Selman Ltd, 4746
Lafeber Pet Bird Food Catalog, 15, 71
Lakeside Collection, 3460
Land of Nod, 667, 4984
Learning Resources, 2090
Leather Coats Etc, 1483
Lee's Gardens, 3162
Lesman Instrument, 2279
Life Fitness Products, 4245
Light Up Your Holidays, 4577
Limoges Jewelry, 5145
Lindsay's Technical Books, 897
Lobster Gram, 2726
Lots and Lots of DVD Gifts for Kids, 945, 2306
Lou Malnati's Tastes Of Chicago, 2708
Lyon & Healy Harps, Inc., 5318
MacNeil Automotive Products, 309
Mallory Lane, 4896, 4916, 5085
Massage Warehouse & Spa Essentials, 1369, 3467
Methode Electronics, 2244
Mid America Motorworks, 311
Mid America Motorworks Air-Cooled VW, 435
Midwest TurkeyCall Supply, 2485
Modern Track Machinery, 6098
Museum Shop Catalog, 3630
Music Direct, 265, 315, 2307
National Manufacturing Co, 4627
Neil Enterprises, 202, 5496
Neil Holiday Catalog, 203, 4560, 5497
Nevco Scoreboard, 5652
New Life Systems, 4247, 4446
Niehaus Cycle, 5267
Nixalite of America, 72
Oak Hill Gardens, 3181
Office Specialists, Inc, 5402
OfficeDesigns.com, 5350
Oly-Ola Sales, 3377
Palos Sports, 5892
Para-Gear Equipment, 5823
Peerless Imported Rugs, 5110
Pickens Minerals, 3894
Pierce Biotechnology, 5540
Piper's Corvette Specialties, 560
Pit Pal Products, 320, 419, 562
Polana, 2710
Polyline, 2341
Pre K-12 Math & Science Catalog, 1009
Pre K-8 Literacy Solutions Catalog, 1010
Pro-Med Products, 4330
ProMed Products Xpress, 4371
Pure 'n Natural Systems, 4883
Quad City Ultralight Aircraft, 644
Quill.com, 5409
RCV Performance Products, 399

Rabbit Tool USA, 6111
Rainbow Resource Center, 1800, 1828, 1831
Rand McNally, 906
Rebechini Studios, 3558
Rediscover Music, 2314
Research Press Publishers, 1112
Richard Owen Nursery, 3201
Riley's Seasoning and Spices, 2880
Samantha's Style Shoppe, 1348, 1373, 1717
Sammons Preston, 4334
San Sun Hat and Cap Group, 5714
Schaul's Signature Gourmet Foods, 2822, 2933, 2967
School Health Sports Medicine, 4373
Scientific Chemical & Biological Catalog, 2164
ScripHessco, 3688
ScripHessco 2015 Catalog, 2011
Sellstrom Manufacturing Company, 5427
Sewbaby, 4199
Shop Wright, 5958
Simple Truths, 1114
Sipco Products, 2165
Source for Everything Jewish, 1759
Specialty Store Services, 5412
Spectrum Technologies, 5440
Steinland Gifts & Collectibles, 1760
Stencils & Stripes, 584
Stratford Hall, 5925
Tape Resources, 271
The Land of Nod, 5370
The Popcorn Factory, 3500
Tower Hobbies, 4527
USA Weld, 424
Unison Fall 2015, 3609
Veridian Healthcare, 4378
Video/Entertainment, 2205
Voltexx, 1926
WW Grainger, 3059
Wake Up Frankie, 4931
Warner Electric, 599
Wavelength Catalog, 2206
Wick's Aircraft Supply Catalog, 634
Wild Bird Supplies, 79
Wilkens-Anderson Company Catalog, 5554
Windy City Novelties Catalog, 3709
Wittek Golf Supply, 5766
Working Library, 917
World's Finest Chocolate, 2601
Worldwide Cigar Club Catalog, 6010
eDietShop, 2857

Indiana

2015 Formula Catalog, 745
3Rivers Archery, 2459, 5682
A Taste of Indiana, 3635
Abbey Press, 3636
Amazon Drygoods, 1548
Ameri Stamp/Sign-A-Rama, 1868
American Playground, 6145
American Stationery, 3416, 5931
American Wedding, 5969
Atwood Mobile Products, 723
Bargain Catalog Outlet, 675, 724
Bart's Watersports, 5612
Basket Basics, 3782
Bits & Pieces, 6153
Bits and Pieces, 1770
Botanic Choice, 4381
Botanic Gardens, 4429
Breck's Bulbs, 3094
Brickyard Ceramics & Crafts, 3818
Catalog of Antique Replica Ordinance, 1839
Central Metal Products: Dog Kennels, 94
Childlife, 6159
Country Kitchen SweetArt, 2560
Da-Lite Screen Company, 1979
Davidson Greenhouse & Nursery, 3112
Day One Camouflage, 1218
Doyle's Thornless Blackberry, 2746
Dwyer, 5518
ETS Home Tanning Beds, 4233
Factory Direct Table Pad Company, 5104
Family Labels, 1875

Farriers' Greeting Cards, 8
Festool Catalog, 6053
Fullbeauty, 687, 1496
Gardens Alive!, 3069
Garfield, 3654
Gator Grip, 2385
George F Cram Company, 1201
Glas-Col, 5523
Good Scents, 3356
Greenwoods Collection, 5941
Gurney's Seeds & Nursery, 3266
Henry Field's Seed & Nursery, 3267
HomePortfolio Insider, 4687
Hoosier Trapper Supply, 2480, 4062
Howell Book House, 13
Hunter Dan, 2349
Indco Catalog, 3046
Indiana Berry & Plant Company, 3150, 3454
Indiana Botanic Gardens, 4436
James Townsend & Son, 1433
Kennedy Hardware, 5018
Kipp, 619, 1389, 3662
Knit Knack Shop, 4182
Kustom King Archery, 5694
Lady & the Stamp, 1879
Lafayette Venetian Blind, 4747
Liberty Fund Books, 843
Map, Globe and Atlas Catalog, 2092
Max Merritt Auto-Parts Master Catalog, 372
Merrell, 696, 1594
Merrimade, 5947
Michigan Bulb Company, 3168, 3373
Mid-America Sports Advantage, 5647
Midwest Gym Supply, 5770
National Automotive Lines, Inc., 317
National Office Furniture, 5346
Notre Dame: BGI Sport Shop, 5654
Now & Forever, 3670
OneStopPlus.com, 1710
Paragon Gift Catalog, 1344
Paragon-Gifts, 6204
Photo Materials Company, 5351
Phyllis Kennedy, 4629
Racer Wholesale, 566
Ray Baker Classics, 6112
Red Saltbox, 2492
Romans, 705
Rytex Catalog, 5955
Sailrite Home Catalog, 777, 3978, 4195
Sailrite Marine Catalog, 743, 778, 808
Sechlers Fine Pickles, 2854
Slavica Catalog, 1209
Special Ideas, 237
Spilsbury, 952
Stumps, 3695
Stumps Spirit & Homecoming, 1447
Sur la Table, 5235
The American Wedding, 5985
The Office Shop, 5417
The Working Person's Store, 1678
Thompson & Morgan Seedsmen, 3311
Touch of Class, 4861
Twinrocker Handmade Paper, 3777
Urban Farmer Seeds, 3314, 3404
Willowes Basketry & Yarn, 3801, 4217
Woman Within Catalog, 1382
Wood-Mizer Products Catalog, 6136
Woodplay, 4143
World's Largest Party Superstore Catalog, 3512
Worms Way Catalog, 2286

Iowa

Amana Meat Shop & Smokehouse, 2894
American Athletic, 5708
Amsco School Publications, 960
Archival Products, 174, 721, 2505
Bridal / Anniversary Catalog 2012, 5169
Bridal / Anniversary Catalog 2013, 5170
Brownells, 2423, 5687
CR's Bear & Doll Supply, 1804
CT Farm & Country, 3026
Championship Productions Baseball Catalog, 1131

L.L.Bean Outsider, 1276, 1335, 1592
Lie-Nielsen Toolworks, 4114
Lovell Designs Earthsong Collection, 5195
Macomber Looms, 4083
Maine Balsam Fir Products, 4272
Maine Coast Sea Vegetables, 2852
Maine Potato Catalog, 2778
Nowetah's American Indian Store & Museum, 3631
Oompa Toys, 6201
Pinetree Garden Seeds, 3291
RB Swan & Son, 2757
Shaw & Tenney, 738
Shearwater Boats, 781
Stenhouse Publishers, 1210
Stonewall Kitchen, 2826, 4763
Sturbridge Yankee Workshop, 3606
Surry Gardens' Bedding Plant Catalog, 3220
Swans Island Company, 5089
US Bells, 4765
Up The Country Creations, 2890
Ward Log Homes, 4709
Weathervane Seafoods, 2733
Wood Prairie Farm, 2763, 2832, 3325
WoodenBoat Store, 789

Maryland

AGV Sport, 277
ASHA, 4225
ATI Performance Products, 278
Alan Furman & Company, 5161
All Pro Team Sports, 1557, 5603, 5878
Anatomical Chart Company, 4346
Association for Information & Image Managemen, 877
Atlantic Fitness Products, 4228
Bartley Collection, 4673, 4684
Bean Bag Deli & Catering Co., 2624
Bedwetting Store, 4289
Before & After, 3418, 3642
Beretta Product Guide, 2420
Beretta Rifle Product Guide, 2421
Beretta Seasonal Catalog, 1256
Blaine Window Hardware, 5010
Bob's BMW, 5245
Books for Cooks, 1127
Books on Tape, 865
Bostitch, 4611
Brookes Publishing, 964, 2188
Chesapeake Bay Crab Cakes & More, 2718
Chesapeake Light Craft, 740, 754
Clearfield Company, 831
Coast to Coast Coins and Currency, 1783
Country Casual, 4972
Country House, 3580
Daedalus Books & Music, 1197
Decor by Dobry, 4729
Delta Truck Storage Solutions, 302
Dollmasters, 1806
Earthly Pursuits, 3118
Ehrman Tapestry, 3950
ElderSong Fall 2015 Catalog, 868
ElderSong Publications, 1199
Florence & George, 1854
Garden Artisans, 3037
Genealogical Publishing Company, 1159
GovConnection, 1952
Gr8 Dogs, 10, 38, 99
Great Windows, 4941
Healthy Back, 4314
Heritage Books, 841
Hidden Camera Surveillance Catalog, 5124
Hobby House Press, 1165
Holabird Sports, 5874
Hopkin's Medical Products, 4363
Huggins and Scott Auctions, 1776
Impromptu Gourmet, 2813
JOBOX Premium Storage Solutions, 307
Janco Greenhouses, 3047
Jos. A. Bank Clothiers, 1332, 1528
Joseph Sheppard, 218
LaMotte Environmental Science Products, 2151
League Outfitters 2015 Football Equipment & U, 5644
Lilypons Water Gardens, 3163, 3369

Mackenzie Limited, 2815
Marketplace: Handwork of India, 1436
McCutcheon's Apple Products, 2754
Messianic Jewish Resources International Cata, 846
Meyer Seed, 3284
Milton W Bosley Company, 4750
National Archives-Pub. & Distribution, 2095
Neet Archery, 5698
Network Access & Connectivity Product Line, 1905
Phillips Harborplace, 2729
Raymond Geddes & Company, 3685
Redding Medical, 4372
Richlee Shoe, 5589
Robert A Madle Sci-Fi/Fantasy Books, 1181
Scarecrow Press, 909
Serrv Handcrafts, 3765
SimplySoles, 1719
Smyth Jewelers, 1824
Stoeger Airguns, 2455
SuspenderStore, 1351
Sweetbrier Waterfalls & Ponds, 3397
Tiffin Athletic Mats, 5773
US Naval Institute Holiday, 855
Ulla Popken, 1724
VETUS, 810
Water Quality Testing Products, 2285
Wholesale Nursery Catalog of Native Wetland P, 3232
Wicklein's Water Gardens, 3233
Yale Sportswear Catalog, 1624
Yellow Awning Fold Out Brochure, 2702

Massachusetts

AL Ellis, 4932
Accu Trak Tool, 6013
Acorn Deck House, 4692
Adcole Corporation, 444
Air-Tite Holders, 1781
Alden Rowing Shells, 5827
Alfa Aesar, 2268
AliMed Operating Room Products, 4226
Alimed, 4344
Allergy Buyers Club, 4875
AltE Catalog, 4657
America's Yarn Store, 4150
American Business Systems, 1945
American Marine Model Gallery, 4507
American Press, 959
American Saw & Manufacturing, 6028
Animal, Organ & Cell Physiology, 2127
Antique Auto Parts & Accessories, 349
Appalachian Mountain Club Books & Maps, 1121
Appleseed's, 1354
Applewood Books, 824
Architectural Components, 4601
Arista Surgical Supply Company, 4348
Armstrong Flag, 4956
Atlantic Spice, 2858
Avant Gardens, 3085, 3330
AzureGreen, 1033
Back In The Saddle, 611, 5779, 5988
Back in the Saddle, 674
Bigelow Nurseries, 3087
Bill Cole Enterprises, 4481
Boston Coffee Cake, 4584
Brahmin, 614, 728, 1684
Brigger Furniture, 4965
Bruce Medical Supply, 4350
CABI North America, 965
CBD Academic, 1040
CBD Bible, 1041
CBD Clearance, 1042
CBD Gift, 1043
CBD Home School, 2056, 2190
CBD Kid's, 2326, 6155
CBD Pastor, 1044
CBD Supply, 1045, 5382
Cambridge Soft Products Catalog, 2173
Cape Cod Cupola Company, 4677
Cape Cod Treasure Chest, 4969
Catalog Favorites, 3423
Catalog of Meditation Supplies, 1047
Channing Bete Company, 970

Chapman, 3575
Charles Ro Supply Company, 4511
Chem Scientific, 2131
Cheng & Tsui Company, 2174
Clark's Corvair Parts, 355
Clematis Specialty Nursery, 3106
Clifford's, 4546
Cohasset Colonials, 4971, 5044, 5080
Copperbeech Millwork, 4727
Country Bed Shop, 4908
Country Curtains, 4939
Crafts Manufacturing Company, 4044
Crossroads, 5136
Curriculum Associates, 2070
Cutting Tools C, 6044
Dancing Deer Baking Company, 2669
Davis Publications, 2071
Deluxe Small Business Services, 2219
Dennis K Burk, 486
Diamond Machining Technology, 6046
Didax Educational Resources, 2072
Dinn Brothers Trophies, 5623
Dover Saddlery, 117
East Coast Gourmet, 2719
Edson Accessories Catalog, 730
EggCartons.Com, 63, 118
Eldred Wheeler, 4977
Electric Time Company, 3841
Emerald Collection, 3583
Ergonomics/Occupational Health & Safety, 4235
Especially Yours, 1267, 4471, 5572
Expressions, 3650
FW Schumacher Company, 3255
FetchDog, 97
Franklin Sports, 5630, 5886
GardenTalk Catalog, 3352
Go Ahead Vacations, 6241
Good Time Stove, 4880
Grace Tea Company, 2636
Graphique de France, 5916
Guterman International, 5873
Habitat Post & Beam, 4695
Hammerworks, 5050
Hampden Engineering, 2142
Hampton Roads Publishing Company, 1062
Handcrafted Applique Flags, 4959
Hapco, 3446
Harbor Sweets, 2574
Hartman's Herb Farm, 3141
Harvest Direct, 2845
Health Management Resources, 4390
Hoop House Greenhouse Kits, 4698
Hot Tools, 4107
Hyde Tools, 4827
In the Company of Dogs, 14
Interactive Therapeutics, 4320
JR Burrows, 4179
Jensen Tools Master Sourcebook, 6083
Jewel of the Isle, 3880
Johnson String Instrument, 5300
Lady Grace, 1499
Lamp Glass, 5059
Legal Sea Foods, 2725
LobsterAnywhere.com, 2727
Lumenpulse, 5061
Magellan's, 1206
Military & Law Enforcement Product Catalog, 1849, 2352, 2443
Monarch Accounting Supplies, 5398
Morion Company, 3889
Motherwear, 1512
Mustang Replacement Seats for Metric Cruisers, 5265
Mustang Replacement Seats for Victory, 5266
My Grandma's of New England, 2691
NYR Organic, 4445
National Coating Corporation, 5495
National Geographic Learning PreK-12 Catalog, 947, 1002
Nature's Jewelry, 3891
New England Bamboo Company, 3174
New England Office Supply, 3471
New England Solar Electric, 4666
New Miller Harness, 5789
NorthStyle, 1753, 5150
Nourse Farms, 3179
Old-Fashioned Milk Paint Company, 4777

Ann's Wedding Stationary, 5971
Aqua-Therm, 4659
Art-In-A-Pinch, 178
Astragal Press, 826
Augsburg Fortress, 1029
BW Inc, 288
Ballistic Products, 2345
Bemidji Woolen Mills, 1308
BestBuy, 1975
Birchwood Casey, 2422
BlueStone Garden, 3022
Bluestem Brands, 4805
Bucilla Stocking Kits, 3939, 4156
Cannon Downriggers, 2368
Capstone Classroom, 927, 967
Capstone Library, 866, 928, 968
Capstone Young Readers, 929, 969
Casual Wear Catalog, 1263, 5247
Celtic Croft, 1417, 5173
Charmaster Products, 4953
Charnstrom, 5358
Continental Clay Company, 3822
Coolibar, 1458
Cordial Greetings, 5911
Courage Kenny Cards Corporate Holiday Card Ca, 5912
Cumberland's Northwest Trappers Supply, 2473
Deneen Pottery, 3997
Dennis Kirk Metric Motorcycle Catalog, 5253
Dennis Kirk Off Road Catalog, 392, 5254
Dennis Kirk Snowmobile Catalog, 1315
Dennis Kirk Watercraft Catalog, 1571
Detta's Spindle, 4077
Donahue's Greenhouse, 3115
DreamHaven Books, 834
Easy Stand Catalog, 2032
Effective Learning Systems, 2301
Eichten's Hidden Acres Cheese Farm, 2604
Elmer Hinckley, 2376
Erik Organic Dining Table Catalog, 2274
Farmer Seed & Nursery Company, 3123
Filing Supplies from A-Z, 5388
Fine Impressions, 5939
Footwear by Footskins, 5574
Free Spirit Publishing, 978, 1089
From the Neck Up, 1156
GS Direct, 5337
GS Direct Graphic Supplies, 192
Golden Ratio Woodworks, 4238
Goodson Tools & Supplies for Engine Builders, 514
Gopher Sports Equipment, 1461
GovMint.com, 1787
Grady-White Boats, 760
Greenworld Project, 3265
H. Christiansen Co, 5634
HED Cycling Products, 5725
HG Forms/Tenenz, 1877
HMI Marketing, 4362
Harris Communications, 2002
Haverhill's, 5434, 5487
Header Parts, 520
Heartland America, 3449, 5342
Heatmor, 4665
Historic Rail Product Catalog, 4484, 6184
Holiday Expressions, 5944
Holiday Foods Catalogue Division, 2811
Honeywax / Candle-Flex Molds, 3807
House, 5638
House Boardshop, 5851
Industrial Arts Supply Company, 261
J-Mark, 526
J.R. Watkins, 2848, 2863, 4323
JM Cremps, 1236
JW Hulmeco, 5640
Jennings Decoy Company, 4111
Jist Publishing, 1109
Jordan Seeds Inc., 3278
Junonia, 1588, 1702
Just For Kix, 1434
Just Two Bikes, 5728
Just for Kix, 1467
KYTEC Athletic Speed Equipment, 5642, 5822
Kelly Brothers Nurseries, 3157
KinderMark, 2088
Kogle Cards, 3544

Kotula's, 4831, 6189
Leaflet Missal Annual Catalog, 944
Learning ZoneXpress, 4397
Llewellyn Worldwide, 1067
Magus Books, 1069
Marvin Windows & Doors, 3597
Meadowbrook Press, 1094
Medical Arts Press Medical Reference Catalog, 1956
Meisel Hardware Specialties, 4116, 4700
Midwest Homebrewing and Winemaking, 4536
Midwest Supplies, 3375
Midwest Volleyball Warehouse, 3668
Midwest Volleyball Warehouse Volleyball Catal, 1595
Military Issue, 4517
Ministry Resources, 1070
Minn Kota, 805, 818, 2398
Minnesota Historical Society, 848
Minnesota Lapidary Supply, 3888
Modern Office Furniture, 5344
MotorStyles, 4521
Motorbooks, 899
Motorbooks Catalog, 314
Musicmaker's Kits, 5307
Native Gardener's Companion, 3173
Natural Spaces Domes, 4701
New England Business Service, 1906
Nordic Shop, 3472, 5149
Norm Thompson, 699, 1533, 1709
Northern Brewer, 4538
Northern Hydraulics, 546
Northern Sun, 3473
Northern Tool & Equipment Master Catalog, 6100
OPTP Tools for Fitness Catalog, 1110, 2338
Oakwood Game Farm, 2925
Offroad Catalog, 1282, 1599, 5268
Oklee Quilting, 4019
Old Pueblo Traders, 1283
Paper Showcase, 5919
PaperDirect, 3479, 5404
PaperDirect Events, 5920, 5983
Par Aide, 5761
Parts & Accessories for Harley-Davidson, 5269
Peytral Publications, 1006
Pipestone Indian Shrine Association, 3852
Prairie Moon Nursery Catalog and Cultural Gui, 3195
Print Craft, Inc., 3555
QA1, 5274, 5900
Redleaf Press 2015 Fall, 949
Rockabilia, 1757
Rockler Woodworking & Hardware, 4125
Room & Board, 4852, 4924, 4992
Rubber Parts for Classic Cars, 377
Sahalie, 627, 1289, 1347
Schroeder Log Home Supply, 4758
Seven Corners Ace Hardware, 6118
Shady Oaks Nursery, 3209
Signs Plus Banners, 5411
Skyvision, 2257
Solid Gold Northland Health Products for Pets, 88
SoulFlower, 1401, 1721
Spring Creek Canoe Accessories, 744
St. Patrick's Guild Book Catalog, 1079
Stampin' Place, 3768
Stauer, 1350, 1793
Street Catalog, 1291, 5277
Stromberg's Chicks, 146
Sunrise Bakery & Gourmet Foods, 2540, 2697
Sunrise River Press, 1115
Tenenz, 1967, 5927
The Sportsman's Guide, 2412, 2500
Thumb Things, 3564
Tog Shop, 1379
Touche Rubber Stamps, 3775
Triarco Arts & Crafts, 3776
Turncraft Clocks, 3847
Uber, 1489
United Vet Equine, 50
Viking Folk Art Publications, 4768
Viking Woodcrafts Inc, 4134
WA Charnstrom Mail Center Solutions, 5372, 5419
Watercraft by Dennis Kirk Catalog, 716
Webway Album Catalog, 5966
Weekender, 3508
Wenonah Canoe Catalog, 787

Wild Wings Collection, 4041
Wilderness Dreams, 1623
Willow Tree Lane, 5967
Wimmer-Ferguson, 6223
WinCraft, 3708
Winter Silks Catalog, 1507
Wintergreen Northern Wear Catalog, 1301
Wood & Parts for Classic Pickups, 604
Wood Workers Store Catalog, 4653
Yellow Jacket Solar, 4671
Yukon/Eagle Furnace, 4656
Z-World, 1943

Mississippi

Brussel's Bonsai Nursery, 3096
Classroom Supplymart Catalog, 2064
Historical Replications, 4696
Kelly's Kids, 1388
MFJ Enterprises, Inc., 264
Malaco, 5319
Malaco Records, 2334
Power Shack, 4401
Sherard Plantation, 2969
The Wright Stuff Daily Living Aids, 2014
Thunderbird and Lincoln Catalogs, 383

Missouri

2015 - 2016 Christian Education Catalog, 1026
2015 Music Catalog, 2287
2015 Professional & Academic Catalog, 955
Afro World Hair Company, 4468
American Audio Prose Library, 856
American Carnival Mart Key Items, 4043
American Daylily & Perennials, 3083
Anji Mountain, 5094
Aunt Vera's Attic, 3641
Bass Equipment Company, 2
Beacon Hill Press, 1036
BeautyTrends, 4469
Bella Taylor, 1307, 4008
Bissinger French Confectioners, 2549
Black Widow Bows, 5685
Books For Global Mindfulness, 962
Burgers' Smokehouse, 2899
Canine Training Systems, 91
Chocolate Catalogue, 2556, 2663
Christian Tools of Affirmation, 1050
Christmas, 1264, 4554, 6162
Classic Equine Equipment, 115
Classic Parts of America, 477
Common Core State Standards, 971
Comstock, Ferre & Company, 3108
Conklin Guitars, 5292
Constructive Playthings, 2065, 6163
Constructive Playthings Playground Catalog, 2066, 6164
Cruisin USA/Bowlingshirt, 1426
Dancewear Solutions, 1427
Dazor Manufacturing Corporation, 5048
Diefenbacher Tools, 6047
Discover Magnetics, 4295
Drenon Jewelry Holiday, 5175
Drug Package, 4298
Duke Medical Supply, 4354
Dunbrooke Sportswear Company, 5881
Dutchguard, 4299
EC Kraus Home Wine Making, 2997
EC Kraus Wine & Beermaking Supplies, 4532
EZ-Dock, 2375
Early Childhood Collections, 973
Everlast Worldwide, 5625
Express Medical Supply, Inc, 4360
Fall Angler, 2378
Fall Hunting II, 2476, 5690
Family Medallion, 5976
Fashion Fabrics Club, 4168
Feather Craft Fly Fishing, 1153, 2379
Fiorella's Jack Stack Barbecue, 2860, 2904
Foot Traffic, 1322
G3 Boats, 741, 759
Galati International, 1843

Kenmore Stamp Company, 1878
MacConnection, 2183
Marine Performance Accessories, 734
Merchandising Solutions, 5397
Nashua Nutrition, 4399
Newfound Woodworks, 4119
Nordic Fiber Arts, 4188
PC & MacConnection, 1933
PC Connection Express, 1909
Patternworks, 3755
Performance Years, 556
Peter Limmer & Sons, 5818
Pompanette, 736
Professional Resources for Teachers K-8, 1011
Scottish Lion Import, 707
Shelter-Kit, 4704
Soapstone, 3604
Stone River Outfitters, 1446
Supreme Audio, 5455
The Wooden Soldier Fall/Winter 2015 Catalog, 1403
The Wooden Soldier Spring/Easter 2015 Catalog, 1404
Vermont Log Buildings, 4708
Village Coin Shop, 1794
W.S. Badger Company, 4464
White Mountain Puzzles, 6222
Whitehorse Gear, 1299
Williams & Hussey Machine Co., 4137
Wooden Soldier, 1405
Woodstock Soapstone Company, 4955
YMAA Products Catalog, 1193

New Jersey

2015 Security & Builder's Hardware Catalog, 4713
2015 Spring/Summer HBC Catalog, 4783
Accordion-O-Rama, 5283
Aerosoles, 5555
Airplane Shop, 3637
Albion Engineering, 6023
American Autowire, 348
American Safety Razor Company, 6027
American Standard, 4887
American Van Equipment, 284
Analytical Measurements, 5508
Art Display Essentials, 159
Art Stone the Competitor, 5445
Atlas Model Railroad Company, 4508
Atomizing Systems, 4606
Becker's School Supplies, 182
Bed Bath & Beyond, 5210, 5244
Bedlam Architectural Metal, 6034
Bel-Art Products, 2130
Belleville Wire Cloth, 252
Benjamin Moore & Co., 4719
Bill Hirsch Automotive, 351
Bowling Delights, 1733
Broadway Basketeers, 4544
Brusso Hardware, 4612
Buttons Galore & More, 3719
CS Osborne Tools, 3912
Cable Design Guide, 3027
Campmor, 1229, 5617
Canare Catalog 13, 2214
Candy & Craft Molds Catalog, 2552
Capalbo's Gift Baskets, 2995
Carol Wright Gifts, 1262, 3422
Carpet Hardware Systems, 4723
Cases By Source, 5476
Castlegate Farm, 4159
Caswell-Massey, 4257
Ceramic Supply of New York & New Jersey, 3991
Charles GG Schmidt & Company, 6041
Cheeks Cape May, 1688
Cherrybrook Chris Christensen Catalog, 5, 35
Cloudveil, 1231, 1422
Coffee Bean Direct, 2628
Comfort House, 3428, 4293
Creative Hobbies, 3823
Creative Playthings, 6167
D&E Pharmaceuticals, 4413
Dale and Thomas Popcorn, 2563, 2838
Dance Horizons, 1147
Dante Zeller Tuxedo & Menswear, 4585

David's Cookies, 2670
Dazian Fabrics, 4163
Delicious Orchards, 2770
Detailed Play Systems, 6171
Diamond Essence, 5174
Dr Leonard's, 4296
Dr. Leonard's Healthcare, 4297
Durey Libby Edible Nuts, 2947
Eastern Emblem, 3532
Easy Closets.Com, 4815
Easy Fire Kilns, 3998
Economy Handicrafts 99 Cents Catalog, 3730
Economy Handicrafts Annual Catalog, 3731
Edmund Industrial Optics, 5479
Electronix Express, 2223
Eugene Ernst Products Company, 6050
Fest for Beatles Fans, 1742
Fingerhut Spring Big Book, 258
FlagHouse Physical Education and Recreation, 5628
Flemington Aluminum & Brass, 3535
Fran's Wicker & Rattan Furniture, 3587
Fright Catalog.com, 1428
General Military History, 840
Gift Box, 3441
Global Datacom, 1929
Grand Tool Supply Corporation, 6061
Happy Chef, 1634
Hard-to-Find Needlework Books, 1160
Heavenly Treasures, 5181
Henry Repeating Arms, 2433, 2479
Herbach & Rademan Company, 2146
Hitran Corporation, 523
Hood Finishing Products, 4106
Hunter Douglas Window Fashions, 4943
Ikegami Electronics, Inc., 5488
International Military Antiques, 1830, 1846
James and Fralinger's Catalog, 2577
Kanter Auto Products, 530
Kimbo Educational, 2305
Kraftware, 5227
Kultur Performing Arts DVD's, 2333, 5450
L&L Kiln Manufacturing, 3830
LEDGlow, 5262
LabMart Catalog, 5528
Latin Percussion, 5301
Laylas Dance Costumes, 5451
Lee Sims Chocolates, 4573
Linda's Lollies Company, 2581
Lion Brand Yarn, 4028, 4185
Lipsense Catalog, 4441
Long Elegant Legs, 1706
MECA ELECTRONICS, 2243
Maddak, 2020, 2027, 2036
Margola Corporation, 3886
Med-Plus, 2043
Mega Hobby, 3747
Micro Mark, 3748
Micro-Mark, The Small Tool Specialists, 1856
Mon Cheri Bridals, 1437
NTE Electronics, 2246
National Association of Printers & Lithograph, 2308
Norcostco, 5469
Norsons Industries, 5347
Ocean Hockey Supply Company, 5778
Office Penny, 5401
Old Durham Road, 3474, 4276
Outwater Plastics Industries, 266
Panaram International Trading Company, 4840
Pengad, 5405
Physical Education & Recreation, 5659
Plast-O-Matic Valves, 4788
Potdevin Machine Company, 166
Prime Time Toys, 6207
Product Pak, 1962
Quark Glass, 5541
Rainbow Industries, 3557
Raritan, 807
Reinco, 3054
Relay Specialties, 5026
Renton's, 5954
Repco, 570
Retail Winemaking, 4539
Reviva Labs, 4454
Rocket Age Enterprises, 5543

Rose Brand, 3977, 4194
Rosie Hippo, 6208
SQP, 3687
Salescaster Displays Corporation, 1918
Saniflo, 4789
Scholar's Bookshelf, 854, 2342
Show Your Pride Catalog, 325
Siebert & Rice, 3394
Silhouettes Catalog, 709
SkyMall, 28
Some's Uniforms, 1653
Speedgear, 327
Spex Certiprep, 5547
Standard Hobby Supply, 3771
Stencil Planet, 4056
TackleDirect, 809, 821
Testrite Visual Products, 212
Thomas Scientific, 2168
Tidewater Workshop, 3402
Tumi, Inc., 1353, 3622
US Bronze Powders, 4781
Ultimate Office, 5371
Utrecht Art & Drafting Supply, 213
Valiant IMC, 273, 1970
Vantage Apparel, 1661
Victoriana East, 4646
Viziflex Seels Computer Protection Products, 1923
Walden Foods, 2528
Well-Sweep Herb Farm Catalog, 3228
Wheaton Science Products Catalog, 5553
Wicker Furniture Catalog, 5004
Wicker Warehouse, 5005
Willys & Jeep Parts Catalog, 601
zZsounds Music Catalog, 5315

New Mexico

Amazing Gates, 4598
Aurora Press, 1031
Burst Electronics, 2211
Chamisa Ridge, 5782
Chile Shop, 2981, 3993
Cibolo Junction, 2703
Creative Consumers Products, 295
Fiesta Yarns, 4171
High-Lonesome Books, 1163, 1203
Jewelry Maker's Catalog, 3881
Los Chileros De Nuevo Mexico, 2987
NIC Law Enforcement Supply, 2445, 2487
New Mexico Pinon Coffee 2014 Catalog, 2644
Office Center, 5348
Plants of the Southwest, 3192
Sandifer Sculpture, 3391
Senor Murphy Candymaker, 2596
Southwest Indian Foundation, 5202
Stahmanns, 2971
Stahmanns Pecans, 2598, 2972
Stone Forest, 3396
Turtle Press, 1189

New York

1-877-Spirits.com, 2993, 3411
1909-1927 Model T & TT - 2014-2015 Issue, 334
1928-1931 Model A & AA - 2014-15 Issue, 335
1932-1948 Early V8 - 2014-2015 Issue, 336
1948-1979 Pickup Truck - 2014-2015 Issue, 337
1949-1959 Full-Size Ford & Mercury - Includes, 338
1955-1979 Thunderbird - 2014-2015 Issue, 339
1960-1970 Falcon & Comet - 2014-2015 Issue, 340
1960-1972 Full-Size Ford & Mercury - 2013-201, 341
1962-1971 Fairlane & Torino - 2014-2015 Issue, 342
1964-1973 Mustang - 2014-2015 Issue, 343
5 T'S Embroidery Supply, 1117
A Liss & Company, 4873
ABaby, 656, 6142
AD Trophy, 3412
AICPA Self-Study & On-Site Training Catalog, 876
APSCO Catalog, 2288
Accurate Metal Weather Strip Company, 4596
Adoption Book, 1083
Adorama, 1972

Aerco International, 5503
Alan Sloane & Company, 1303
Alcone Company, 5462
Alethea's Chocolates, 2544
Amana Tool, 4087, 6025
American Coin and Stamp Brokerage, 1782
American Cycle Express, 5717
American Diamond, 5162
American Institute of Chemical Engineers, 2125
American Pearl, 5163
Ames & Rollinson, 4480
Amplestuff, 1252
Archery, 2463
Army Navy Store Catalog, 5899
Art Brown's International Pen, 5377
Art Tech Casting Company, 3714
Artistic Video, 5800
Arts and Crafts, 1122
Artscroll, 1028
Asprey, 3518
Atlanta Thread & Supply, 3934
Aufhauser Brothers Corporation, 251
Avery Health Books, 1102
Azerty, 180
B&H Photo Video Pro-Audio, 5473, 5491
BMI Supply, 4608
Baccarat, 3571
Bachrach, 1515
Bailey Ceramic Supply & Pottery Equipment, 3989
Belgian Shoes, 5562
Berger Brothers Camera Video Digital, 5432, 5484
Best Made Company, 1226, 1257, 1310
Beth's Farm Kitchen, 2736
Betterbee, 4492
Big Apple Florist, 3086
Bill Levkoff, 5972
Blossom Flower Shop, 3089
Blue Book, 5168
Brass Center, 4721
Bread Alone, 2533
Brisky Pet Products, 4
BrylaneHome, 4806, 4876, 4967
Buffalo Batt & Felt Company, 4009
Bulbtronics, 5042
Bureau for At-Risk Youth, 1085, 2189
Butterick, 3941
CQ VHF Ham Radio Magazine, 1129, 2327
CSI\SPECO, 255
CUTCO, 5214
CWI Medical, 4231, 4291
Cablexpress Technologies, 1891
Cafe La Semeuse, 2626
Camaro Connection, 467
Cambridge Camera Exchange, 5485
Cambridge Educational Catalog, 2293
Car-Freshner Catalog, 409
Cartier, 5172
Castrol USA Catalog, 468
Catherine Knits, 3942
Celtic Treasures, 1734
Cementex Latex Corporation, 3805
Century Photo Products, 5477
Charles Lubin Company, 4724
Charles P Rogers, 4906
Charles Tyrwhitt, 1524, 5565
Charles W Jacobsen, 4678, 5098
Charleston Gardens, 3576
Check-Line, 6042
Chelsea Market Baskets, 4545
Chem Tainer Industries, 4784
Children's Books, 931
Children's Books & Activities, 932
Childswork/Childsplay, 1087, 6160
Chinese Porcelain Company, 3821
Chock Catalog.com, 1492
Chocolate Inn, 2557
Chocolate by Design, 2558
Church's English Shoes, 5566
Cigars for Aficionados, 5991
City Stationers Corporation, 5935
Clary's Wig, 4470
Cohasco, 1827
Coloring Books, 935
Comfortex Blindcrafter Center, 4811

Community Playthings, 1998
Compleat Sculptor, 3996
Costume Armour, 1425
Country Music Treasures, 5293
Crafts, Needlework and Hobbies, 3724
Crown Awards and Trophies, 5622
Custom Gifts & More, 83
Custom-Printed Promotional Items, 3529
Dallek, Inc., 5332
Dante Cozzi Sports, 5841
Dart Mart, 6169
Day Runner Direct, 5361
DeSantis Holster, 2429
Debbie Burk Optical, 5421
Decorative Hardware Studio, 5011
Decorative Home, 4813
Delia's, 1265, 1693, 5100
DiCamillo Bakery, 2534
Different Roads to Learning, 2073
Disc Makers, 2192, 2299
Double A Vineyards, 2996, 3116
Dufour Pastry Kitchens, 2675
DwellStudio, 4814, 4910, 5101
EatRaw, 2839
Eccentricks, 3729
Educational Activities, 2193
Elizabeth Eakins, 5102
Elvee Rosenberg, 3866
Emedco Buyer's Guide, 3533
Empress Chocolates Company, 2566
Engagement, 5176
English Basketry Willows, 3788
Ercole, 4732
Esprit, 683, 731
Everything Office Furniture, 5334
Excalibur Collection, 4733
Fairchild Books & Visuals, 888
Fairgate Rule, 2224
Fall Bright, 4533
Family Crest Jewelry Catalog, 5177
Fancifuls, 4167
Feldheim Publishers, 1088
Ferrara Foods & Confections, 2705
Finals, 1574
Fine Architectural Metalsmiths, 4618
Fine Art & Art Instruction, 229, 977
Fingerlakes Woolen Mill, 4172
Fire Protection Products, 3736
First Position Dancewear, 5627
Fisher-Price, 663, 6180
Flexbar Machine Corporation, 6054
Focus Camera, 2228, 5486
Ford Parts Specialists, 506
Fordham Equipment Company, 5335
Forever & Always, 5977
Fountain Pen Hospital, 5389
Four Seasons Sunrooms, 4694
Freeport Marine Supply Company, 800
Frette, 4263, 5081
Fuji Photo Film USA, 5480
GEI International, 1928
Galaxy Army Navy, 1219
Gampel Supply, 3870
Garden Catalog, 3038
Garden Tools by Lee Valley, 3039
Gardening Books, 1158
Gaylord Archival, 5338
Gentle Wind, 2302
Gerald Fried Display & Packaging, 1747
Giant Industrial Corporation, 510
Giordano's Petite Shoes, 5576
Girls Got Game Volleyball, 5887
Glamour Costumes, 5449
Global Industrial, 5339
Global Industrial Catalog, 5340, 6059
Gold Medal Hair Products, 4433
Golden Age Comics, 1799
Gourmet Fantasy, 2807
Graphite Metalizing Corporation, 516
Great Gardens, 3357
Great Skate Hockey Supply Company, 5775
Green Book of Natural Beauty, 4434
Grey Flannel Auctions, 1861
Grey House Publishing, 890

Griffin Manufacturing Company, 259
Grifhold, 6062
Gudrun Sjoden, 1270, 1325, 4823
Guildcraft Arts and Crafts, 3875, 3919, 4035
Guilford Psychology Catalog, 1107
HA Guden Company, 4739
HW Wilson Company, 891
Hammacher Schlemmer, 4824
Hank's Clothing, 1584
Hansen Caviar Company, 2722
Happy Kids Personalized Catalog, 3447
Hardware Catalog, 5014
Harney & Sons Fine Teas, 2637
Harper Audio/Caedmon, 871
Have Inc, 2235
Hear More, 2004
Herbal Actives, 4393
Hermes, 3921
Home Gardener's Vegetable, Flower & Supplies, 3270
Home Trends, 4890
Homespun Music Instruction, 984, 2331, 5392
House of Oxford Wholesale Cigars, 6000
House of Spices, 2706
Hudson Valley Seed Library, 3272, 3365
Human Relations Media, 2197
Hurley Patentee Manor Lighting, 5054
IBM, Training Solutions, 893
Ideal Industries, 2236
Independent Living Aids, 4318
Independent Living Aids Comprehensive Catalog, 5424
Independent Living Aids Low Vision Catalog, 4319
Information Packaging, 5393
Intercollegiate Designs, 3540
International Bronze Manufacturers, 3541
International Center of Photography, 1168
International Wealth Success, 895
Island Cases, 2304
J Sussman, 4744
J.Crew Style Guide, 1274, 1330, 1360
JJ Hat Center, 1331
Jacques Moret Bodywear, 1465
Jax Chemical Company, 4037
Jessica London, 1362, 1701
Jewelry Care, 5187
Joblot Automotive, 529
John Robshaw Textiles, 4181
Josh Bach Neckties, 1333
Judith Bowman Books, 1171
Just the Thing, 5189
Kassoy, 3883
Kelvin, 2148
Kemp's Hockey Supply Company, 5797
Kepco, Inc., 2242
Kimber, 2481
KingSize, 1365, 1529
Kodak Professional Photographic Catalog, 5493
Kosher Connection, 2707
Kron Chocolatier, 3663
Kwik Sew, 3966
LS&S, 2006
Lafayette 148 New York, 1704
Lansky Sharpeners, 5228
Latest Products Corporation, 4364
Lee Valley Tools, 4113
Leisure Living, 4625
Liberty Seed Company, 3282
Library Books K-12, 992
Light Impressions, 199, 5494
Light Livestock Equipment, 16, 131
Literature & Humanities, 993
LittleMissMatched, 1395, 4915
Long Island Corvette Supply, 370
Lowel-Lighting Equipment, 262
Luxury Made Easy, 263
Lynch & Kelly, 1068
Lyndon Lyon Greenhouses, 3166
MSC Industrial Supply Company, 6094
MacKenzie-Childs, 3831
Madison Industries, 4895
MadisonAveMall, 1864
Manhattan Fruitier, 2779
Master Mount, 5481
Mathematics & Science, 995
Matt McGhee, 4836

Maukilo European Toys, 6193
Maurice Badler Fine Jewelry, 5197
Maxi Aids, 2007
McCall's, 3969
McCall's Patterns, 3970
McNulty's Tea and Coffee Company, 2642
Meadows Medical Supply, 5435
Medco Sports Medicine, 4365
Met Kids Catalog, 6195
Michael C Fina, 3598
Modern Digital Canvas, 232
Mohawk Lifts, 2037
Monastery Store, 1071, 2336
Morrell & Company, 3003
Mother-Ease Cloth Diapers, 669
Mt Nebo Gallery, 219
Music Books & Scores, 5320
Mystic Stamp, 1880
Nat Sherman, 6006
National Collector's Mint, 1791
New Book Catalog, 1073
New Skete, 2921
New York Central Art Supply, 204
Newport News, 698
Nicholson Steam Trap, 4787
Nortel Machinery, 6099
Northern Climate Fruit & Nut Trees Catalog, 3178
Novel Box, 5151
Old World Mouldings, 4753
Olden Lighting, 5436
One World Projects, 3477
Oneida Air Systems, 5230
Option PC, 1932
Origami USA, 3752
P.E. Guerin, 4898
PC America, 1908
PM Research, 1778
Pacific Sports Warehouse, 5876
Packaged Lighting Systems, 5065
Palmer Electric Transporters, 3052
Paper Access, 1960, 5982
Parenting & Family Life, 1096
Paul Stuart, 1536
Pedifix Footcare Products, 4449
Peekskill Nurseries, 3187
Perfumax, 1986, 4278, 5950
Pet King, Inc., 87
Physical Education & Health, 2200
Pico Electronics, 6106
Plaster Gallery, 4756
Plaza Sweets, 2695
Positive Impressions Idea Showcase, 3554
Power Up!, 1936
Pratesi, 5086
Precious Metal Jewelry Findings, 3895
Prestons - Ships & Sea, 737, 3681
Pretty Personal, 3602, 3682
Prime Packaging Corp, 5408
ProTech Systems, 4630
Pure Collection, 1715
Puritan's Pride, 4331, 4402, 4453
Purple Mountain Press, 852
Putnam Rolling Ladder Company, 4632
QCI Direct, 3053
QTC Metric Gears, 6110
Qualiton Imports, 2311
Quality Saw & Knife Company, 5021
RMS Technology, 1917
Raceline Direct, 322
Rao's Specialty Foods, 2990
Red Ribbon Resources, 2106, 2201
Rego Irish Records and Tapes, 2315
Reliable Racing Winter Sports, 5857
Renaissance Carpet & Tapestries, 5113
Ressler Importers, 4851
Rifton Equipment, 2039
Rizzoli Lifestyles & Interior Design, 1208
Roaman's, 1372, 1716
Rosenzweig Lumber Corporation, 4636
Ross Metals Corporation, 5199
Royal Athena Galleries, 221
Rugs USA, 5115
Rush Industries, 4456
S&H Uniforms, 1649

S&P of New York Budo, 5807
SISU Home Entertainment/Sifriyat Ami, 1076, 2316
Sadigh Gallery Ancient Art, 1822, 3901
Saks Fifth Avenue, 706
Salem Press, 908
Sargent Welch, 1015
Sausage Maker, 2932
Scandinavian Ski Shops, 5858
Schaller & Weber, 2712
Scholastic Reading Club, 950
Schweitzer Linen, 5087
Schweitzer Nightwear, 1374, 1503
Scully & Scully, 4993
Sculpture in Contemporary Garden, 3393
Sea Eagle Inflatable Boats, 779
See More Vision, 5425
SeeMoreVision.com, 5426
Semrock, 5439
Sepp Leaf Products, 4779
Sequoyah Soaps, 2282
Sherry Lehmann Wine & Spirits, 3005
Simmons-Boardman Publishing Corporation, 911
Simon's Kitchen & Bath, 4903
Slosson Educational Publications, 1016
Social Studies Catalog, 912
Solo Slide Fasteners, 4201
SoundBytes, 4336
Speco Audio Products, 1987
Spiegel, 710, 3905
Spring at MoMA, 238
St. Lawrence Nurseries, 3213
Stamp & Collectibles, 1884
Stickley, 4996
Stock Drive Products, 585
Stokes Seeds, 3309
Storesmart, 5413
Stu-Art Supplies, 167
Sun-Mar Corporation, 2283, 4904
SunDog Solar, 4668
SunFeather Natural Soap Company, 4459
Super Silk, 4206
Surma Book & Music, 3696
Sycamore Creek, 3398
TNVitamins, 4405
TRIMCO, 5926
Team Cheer, 1448
Telescope Casual Consumer Furniture, 4998
Telstar Products, 1922
Terminal Tackle Co., 2411
Tesseract, 5550
The Craft Shop, 5673
The English Company, Inc. 2012 - 13 Catalog K, 3698
The Met Store, 914, 5156, 5962
Things Deco, 241, 1187
This Is Tiffany, 5204
Tic-Tac-Toes, 5456
Tiffany Watches, 5205
Tinsel Trading Company, 4211
Todaro Brothers, 2714
Tourneau Watch, 3503
Toy Connection, 6213
Toy Soldier Catalog, 6214
Transcat, 2265
Trienawear, 5458
Turf, Tree & Ornamental Catalog, 3076
UNICEF Catalog, 3504, 5929
Uncommon Goods, 1295
Underwater Equipment Guide, 5839
Unicef Corporate Card Collection, 5930
Union Pen Company Full Line Catalog, 3566
Urban Archeology, 4766
VAI Direct, 2320
VIEW Video, 2343
Veteran Leather Corporation, 3929
Victor Machinery Exchange, 3930
Vinten, 1989, 5483
Vivre, 1545, 3611, 5601
Vogue Patterns, 3983
W.D. Lockwood, 4213
Ward's Science, 5441
Warm Biscuit Bedding Catalog, 5002
Warren Tool Catalog, 4491
Watercolors Inc, 4793
Weleda, 4341

West Penn Hardwoods, 4136
Wickers America Catalog, 1506
Wild Thymes Farm, 2529, 2892
William Greenberg Desserts, 2701
Wine Enthusiast Catalog, 3013
Wine Express Catalog, 3014
Wine Merchant Catalog, 3015
Wittus, 4886
Woman Within, 1381, 1725
Womanswork, 3410
Wood Window Workshop, 4652
Woodard Weave, 5117
Works on Paper: 20th Anniversary Catalog, 224
Worldwide Sport Supply Volleyball, 5897
Worldwide Sport Supply Volleyball Coach, 5898
Worldwide Sport Supply Wrestling, 5679
Worldwide Sport Supply Wrestling Coach, 5680
Xander Blue, 4872
YesterYear's Vintage Doors, 4773
Yesteryear Toys & Books Catalog, 1780, 6225
York Ladder, 4655
Yves Rocher, 4466
Zabar's Catalog, 2833
Zahler, 4412
Zahn Dental, 1924

North Carolina

Action Sports Systems, 5774
Ames Walker Support Hosiery, 1304, 4286
Appalachian Stove, 4658
Art Supply Warehouse, 177
Atlantic Tan, 4288
Aunt Ruby's Peanuts, 2944
Belk New Directions, 1255, 1384, 4800
Belk Wedding Catalog, 4583, 4801
Bridal Collection, 5171
Brooks Equipment, 5119
Brushy Mountain Bee Farm, 3803, 4493
Cakes by Jane, 2551
Camellia Forest Nursery, 3102
Canyon Creek Nursery, 3104
Carolina Cookie Company, 2662
Carson-Dellosa Publishing, 2059
Cheap Joe's Art Stuff, 3720, 3992
Choir Robes Online Choral Attire Catalog, 1418
Choir Robes Online Church Dresses Catalog, 1419
Choir Robes Online Church Wear Catalog, 1420
Choir Robes Online Qwick-Ship Catalog, 1421
Columns Catalog, 4726
Compassion Books, 1104
Crow's Nest Trading Company, 1691, 4973
Crown Heritage, 4616
Custom Hardware by Kayne & Son, 4617
Deltec Homes, 4693
Dennis Carpenter Ford Restoration, 485
Dixon Industries, 3031
Douglas Battery Manufacturing Company, 488
Eagle Equipment-Automotive Equipment, 491
Elkes, 5103
Environmental Geothermal Houses, 4662
Exclusively Weddings, 5975
Feller US Corporation, 4878
Fence PBT, 5740
Fine Wood Source Book, 4978
Flanders, 4619
Folkwear, 3952
Forecast International, 869
Freud, 6058
Gardens of the Blue Ridge, 3131
Gold's Artworks, 3738
Golden Cockerel, 3655
Gould and Goodrich, 2082
Grapestompers, 4534
Great Atlantic Lacrosse Company, 5796
Hallelujah Diet, 2844
Head Quarters Taxidermy Supply, 4061
Homes by Vanderbuilt, 4697
House of Fragrances, 4266
H,fele, 6079
International Wood Products, 6080
Irwin Tools, 6081
JR Cigars, 6001

Consumer Geographic Index

RSH Catalog, 4579
Rachel Davis Fine Arts, 220
Ralph Maltby's GolfWorks, 5763
Ramm Fence, 139
RapidStart, 4122
Regent Sports Corporation, 5667
Ridge Tool Company, 6114
Ridgeway Hatchery, 141
Rod's Western Palace, 1675
Rodale's, 4455
Rods Western Palace, 1346
Rossi Pasta, 2711
Royalwood Basket Weaving & Caning Supply, 3796
Rupp Seeds, 3301
SGD Golf, 5764
Schneider Saddlery, 142
Shade Tree Powersports Metric Bikes, 5276
ShadeTree Canopies, 4637
Share the Spirit!, 1718, 3488, 4854
Signals, 5088
Silkflowers.Com, 4856
Slusher's Jewelry Holiday, 5201
Smucker's Catalog, 2759
Snyder's Antique Parts, 379
Soupbase.com, 2886
Sporty's Pilot Shop, 647
Sporty's Preferred Living Catalog, 3055
Sporty's Tool Shop Catalog, 3605
Spring Hill Nursery, 3210
Springbrook Gardens, 3211
Springfield Rod & Custom, 580
Standardbred Catalog, 144
Sterling Production Control Units, 2261
StewMac, 5310
Stoddard Imported Car Parts, 439
Summit Racing Equipment, 586
Support Plus, 4376
TP Tools & Equipment, 423
TP Tools and Equipment, 6124
TenPoint Crossbows, 2456, 2498, 5704
The Cruise Uniform Book, 1655
The Electric Quilt Company, 4022, 4929
The Security Uniform Book, 1656
The Sourcebook, 1657
The Uniform Book, 1658
Things Remembered, 3563
Thoroughbred Catalog, 149
Time for Me, 1722
Toledo Physical Education Supply, 5675
TouchStone Catalog, 3502
Touchstone, 4862
Touchstone Woodworks, 4643
Trophy Nut, 2526, 2974
True Choice, 592
Twin Sister's Productions LLC, 2116
Universal Radio, 822
Van Bourgondien Brothers, 3223
Van Dyck's Flower Farm, 3315
Visual Education, 2118
Weaver Leather, 3931
Weaver West, 3623
Western Fashions & Gifts, 5793
What on Earth, 1380, 3612
William Tricker Catalog, 3236
Windsor Collection, 5158, 5208
Wine Cellar Innovations Catalog, 3011
Wireless, 3710
Wood Classics, 4140
Woodcraft Plans Catalog, 4690, 4712
Woodcreek Drieds Inc, 3778
Wooster Products, 5036
World Quest Learning Catalog, 1025
Yukon Fitness Equipment, 4255

Oklahoma

Artisan Design, 4603
Bella Coastal D,cor, 4936, 4952, 5009
Bella Coastal Décor, 4802
Black Forest Decor, 4029, 4937, 5077
Brown Aviation Tool Supply, 639
Bustani Plant Farm, 3099, 3333
Camo Trading, 1567

Carlisle Food Service Products, 2509
Century Martial Art Supply, 5802
Cheyenne Pick Up Parts, 469
Classic Chevrolet Parts, 472
Coco Bidets Catalog, 4888
Drysdales, 1669
EFDYN, 489
Electro Enterprises, 2222
Fraser-Johnston Heating/Air Conditioning, 4620
Geological Highway Maps, 1200
Greenleaf Nursery Company, 3135
IFSTA, 894, 986
Jantz Supply, 6082
Kicker, 1983
King's Mums, 3158
Knot Head Wood Crafts, 6089
Kraftbilt, 5918
Lone Star Western D,cor, 4835
Lone Star Western Décor Fall 2015 Catalog, 231
Moore Norman Technology Center, 4327
Obsolete & Classic Auto Parts, 374, 418, 851
Par-Buster, 5762
Pharmaceutical Systems, Inc, 4370
Ralph's Packing, 2930
Red Devil, 6113
Sgt Grit's Marine Specialties, 1290, 1652
Skulls Unlimited International, 2166
Sportsmith, 4249
Supernaw's Oklahoma Indian Supply, 3853
Xtreme Rhythmic, 5459

Oregon

2015 Nosler Upfront, 2344
Adaptive Seeds, 2267
Antina's Doll Supply, 1802
Art Impressions, 3713
Art Video Productions, 2324
Aurora Silk, 4151
Authentic Models Holland, 4509
Azure Standard, 2507, 4380
Azure Standard Product Catalog, 80
Baby Works, 658
Barracuda USA, 1562
Beadcats, 3861
Beeswax Candle Works, 3802
Benchmade Catalog, 1216, 1838, 5614
Blackstone Audio Books, 864
Bovees Nursery, 3093
Burley Design Cooperative, 5719
CRKT Mid Year Catalog, 2362, 2466, 5615
CRKT Product Catalog, 2363, 2467, 5616
Cardphile, 5908
Celebrate the Wonder, 1048, 3424
Chief Aircraft, 617
Chief Supply, 5121
Clay In Motion, 3995
Cliff's Classic Chevrolet, 357
Corbin Manufacturing & Supply, 2346
Crimson Trace, 2428, 2472
Ephemera Magnets Button & Stickers, 3433
Essential Oil Company, 4262
Filling Station, 366
Fire Mountain Gems & Beads Jewelry Maker's Ca, 3868
Footwise, 5575
For Counsel: Catalog for Lawyers, 1744
Forestfarm Catalog, 3127
Fox Hollow Farm & Fiber, 4173
Fry Designs of Plastic Canvas Patterns, 3953
Georgies Ceramic & Clay Company, 3829
Glimakra Looms & Weaving Equipment, 4080
GloryBee Natural Foods and Crafts, 2842, 3737
Good Fortune, 3656
Goodwin Creek Gardens, 3264
Graphic Arts Center Publishing Company, 1202
Green Pepper, 1583
Greenhouse Catalog, 3358
Greenhouses Catalog, 3042
HYDRO-FIT Gear, 1463, 5635
Hanna Andersson, 1387
Harry & David, 2810
Heirloom Roses, 3143
Hired Bugs, 3070

Hydrangeas Plus, 3149
Italian Car Parts, 367
Josephsons Smokehouse & Specialty Seafood, 2724
Joy Creek Nursery, 3154
Keith Keppel, 3156
Langlitz Leathers, 3924, 5263
Learning Services, 2181
Leupold & Stevens, 2440, 2483
Littman Jewelers, 5194
Loc-Line, 3049
Loose Screws Bicycle Small Parts, 5731
McClain's Printmaking Supplies, 201
Mini-Edition Iris Lover's, 3169
Motosport Off Road, 398
Motosport, Inc., 5264
Mountain High Equipment & Supply Company, 623
Mountain Rose Herbs, 2643, 4444
Mystic Trader, 1072
Nichols Garden Nursery, 3287
Nike Footwear, 5586
Nomadics Tipi Makers, 4702
North Sports, 806
One Green World, 3186
Ornaments to Remember, 4838
Pacific Botanicals, 2874
Pacific Coast Avionics, 625
Pacific Spirit, 1074
Paper Parachute, 3754
Paper Wishes, 206
Paradigm Foodworks, 2587
Pendleton Woolen Mills, 1537
ProMotion Wetsuits, 1472
Pure Country Pet Boutique, 25
Quantum Medicine, 4403
Race Place, 5856
Raven Maps & Images, 1832
Red's Rhodies, 3200
Rejuvenation Lamp & Fixture Company, 5069
Research Mannikins, 4069
Rose Catalog/Rose Reference Guide, 3205
Schreiners Gardens, 3207
Security Chain Company, 324
Sporthill, 1608, 5834
Stackhouse Athletic, 1610, 5548
Stackhouse Athletic Equipment, 5715, 5866
Stash Tea, 2651
Stefani Photography, 239
Stock Yards, 2936
Sturdi-Built Greenhouse, 3057
Sugar Pine Woodcarving Supplies, 4129
Swan Island Dahlias, 3221
Territorial Seed Company, 3310
The Fruit Company, 2698, 2828
The Parks Company, 1762
Timber Press, 1188
Tognar Ski & Snowboard Tools, 5860
Unabridged Audiobooks, 874
V-Infinity Power Quick Guide Catalog, 1942
Van's Aircraft Accessories, 650
Video Learning Library, 2204
Vintage Model Catalog, 598
Wandering Star Astrology Jewelry, 3705, 5207
Web-Sters, 3985, 4086
White's Metal Detectors, 274, 3063, 5134
Whitman Farms Catalog, 3230
Wild Garden Seed, 3321
Wolferman's, 2542
Yakima-Destination Hardware, 333

Pennsylvania

75th Historical Document Catalog, 1826
ATD-American Catalog, 5324
ATD-American School Catalog, 5325
ATS Sports, 5868
Action Party Rentals, 1886
Adams County Nursery, 3078
Aged Woods, 4715
Alloy Apparel & Accessories, 1251
American Arborist Supplies, 3019
American Map, 6228
American Muscle, 283, 447
Ametek Equipment Gauges, 247

Displays2Go, 5383
Ecotour Expeditions, 6236
Everything Track & Field - 2015, 5626
Gowdey Reed Company, 4081
Great River Outfitters, 5633
Hodges Badge Company, 3659
JH Breakell & Company, 5184
Jamestown Distributors, 802
Kenyon's Grist Mill, 2536
MF Athletic Company, 1174
Meadow View Imports, 6194
Ostheimer Toys, 6202
Perform Better, 5824
Perform Better - Fitness Edition 2015, 5658
Practica, 4329
RBC Industries, 4633
READE, 3833
Ross-Simons, 5200
US Military Insignia, 1853
WL Fuller, 4135
WaterRower, 4252
Wild Horsefeathers Catalog, 1764, 3707

South Carolina

A Taste of the South, 2943
Atlas Copco Industrial Compressors, 249
Ben Silver, 1309, 1516
Boatlife, 726
Charleston Battery Bench, 3336
Chef Revival, 682
Discount Inboard Marine, 796
Doll Lover Catalog, 6174
Driwood Moulding Company, 4731
Environmental Media Corporation, 976
Environments, 2078
Folbot Corporation, 758
Four Oaks Farm, 2906
Golden Kernel Pecan Company, 2953
Jackson & Perkins, 3275
Jeffers Handbell Supply, 3619
Jones School Supply, 3542
Maurice's Piggie Park Barbeque, 2866
Medals of America, 1848
Midlothian, 3374
Nick's Cigar World, 6007
Otis S Twilley Seed Company, 3288
Park Seed Company, 3289
Perception Kayaks, 770
Piggie Park Enterprises, 2878
Plastic Bag and Packaging, 5407
Sarkis Studio, 222
Sealevel Systems, 1919
Shakespeare Electronic Products Group, 2256
SmileMakers, 3693
Solid Gold Products, 108
Spartina 449, 1349
Super Duper Publications, 2112
US Patriot Tactical, 1225
Urban Outfitters, 1296, 4863
Wayside Gardens Catalog, 3227
Write Touch, 5968
Wyco Sales, 6141
Young Plantations, 2978
Young Plantations Catalog, 2979

South Dakota

Big Country Fireworks, 4497
Cheval International, 114
Dakota Alert, 5122
Dakotah Toys, 6168
Fishing Components Catalog, 2381
Jerry Greer's Indian Engineering, 5260
Precision Reloading, 2353, 2491
RBE Electronics, 2253

Tennessee

Adams Wood Products, 4683, 4714

AlcoPro, 4343
Atlas Pen Catalog, 3519
Avionics International Supply, 637
Bible Study Planning Guide, 2292
Big Frog Mountain Corporation, 4661
Cardsone, 1771
Catalog of Professional Audio/Video Services, 256
Coker Tire, 479
Col. Littleton, 1480
Comfort Products, 293
Country Music Greats, 2296
Country Ruffles, 4940
DAIDO Corporation, 3029
Final Flight Outfitters, 64, 2380, 5691
FootSmart, 684, 733
Freedom Tree Farms, 3129
General Shale Brick, 4622
Gospel Advocate Bookstores, 1060
Graceland Gifts, 3657
Growbiz-Abco, 3138
Harrison's Bird Foods, 68
Hartmann by Design, 3537
Healthy Eating, 2846
Horn USA, 6076
Hulme Sporting Goods & MFG Company, 5639
Intarsia Times, 4109
Jim Barna Log & Timber Homes, 4699
Johnston & Murphy Catalog, 5577
Kanson Electronics, 2240
Lokar Performance Products, 535
Long Hungry Creek Nursery, 3370
Loveless Cafe, 2917
Lucky Heart Cosmetics, 4442
Marugg Company, 3372
Memphis Net & Twine Company, 2396
Memphis Net & Twine Company-Sports, 5890
Natchez Shooters Supply, 2446
Nate's Nantuckets, 3793
National Bridle Shop, 135
Nylon Net Company, 2404
Oakes Daylilies, 3182
Official US Chess Federation Catalog, 6199
Ortho-Flex Saddles, 5790
PS Engineering, 624
Praise Banners, 4960
Reemay, 5025
ShindigZ, 3692
Simonton's Cheese & Gourmet House, 2992
Smoky Mountain Knife Works, 1183, 2258, 2496
Source, 270
Spy Gear Products, 5132
St. Jude Gift Shop, 3494
Steele Plant Company, 3216
Sunco Tanning, 4460
Sunlight Gardens, 3218
Tractor Supply Blue Book, 49, 150
Trask, 1488
Triton Boats, 784
TruMedical Solutions, 4251
US Cavalry, 1224
Varsity Spirit Corporation, 5884
Vintage Tire Hotline, 385
WTSmedia Catalog, 2266
Willa's Shortbread, 2700
Wonder Laboratories, 4465
Woodline USA, 4142

Texas

2JP Ranch, 4148
A&D Bookstore & Supply Educational, 2045
APR Prop and Background, 5472
Academic Superstore, 2048, 2172
Airline International Luggage & Gifts, 3616
Alfax Furniture, 5326
Aluminum Tank & Truck Accessories, 446
American Blind & Wallpaper Factory, 4933
Amy Lee Bridal, 1410
Annie's Attic Needlecraft, 3933
Apparel World, 1514
Assessments Catalog, 2053
Athletic Connection, 1560, 5604, 5879
BEAR-COM Motorola Affordable Communication Sy, 2209

BG Micro, 1888
BSN Sports Athletic Performance, 5606
BSN Sports Baseball-Fastpitch, 5709
BSN Sports Direct, 5607
BSN Sports Equipment, 5608
BSN Sports Gear Pro-Tec, 5609
BSN Sports Lacrosse, 5795
BSN Sports League, 5610
BSN Sports Middle School-Junior High, 5611
BSN Sports TeamWear, 5880
Balcony Publishing, 862
Bamert Seed Company, 3242
Barlow's Fishing Tackle, 2360
Barnmaster, 111
Baseball Express, 1626
Baseball, Softball, Football Superstore, 5711
Basket Case Needlework Therapy, 3936
Basketball Express, 5613
Bayou Publishing, 1103
Bear Creek Smokehouse, 2508
Berridge Manufacturing Company, 4674
Big Little Fudge, 3523
Block Division, 1259
Bob Lee Bows, 5686
Bob Wells Nursery, 3091
Bowie Industries, 3023
Bra Smyth, 1491
Brookhollow Collection, 3645, 5907
Brown's Omaha Plant Farms, 3095
Brumbaugh's Furniture & Rug Catalog, 4966
Captain Bijou, 2328
CardsDirect.com, 5909
Carol Bond Health Foods, 4383
Casa Zia Saddlery, 5781
Cattle Kate Catalog, 681
Center Court, 5870
Cheaper Than Dirt, 1840
Chelsea Decorative Metal Company, 4725
Clacritter Designs, 1871
Clotilde, LLC, 3944
Collin Street Bakery, 2665
Comic Heaven Auction Catalog, 1797
Complete Environmental Products, 2272
Cookies by Design's Cookie Gift Book, 2667
Cooper Industries, 480
Crazy Crow Trading Post, 3849
Creme Lure Company, 2372
Crockett Farms, 2982
Cryer Creek Kitchens, 2561
Dallas Midwest, 5331
Dallas Mustang Parts, 299
Das Peach Haus, 2745
David Austin Handbook of Roses, 3111
Dixondale Farms, 3066
Doolco, 887
Dos De Tejas Patterns, 3949
Drip Irrigation, 3033
Early Bronco Catalog, 394
Econ-Abrasives, 4100
Eilenberger Bakery, 2676, 2801, 2948
Entertainment You Can Believe In, 2330
Everett-Morrison Motorcars, 499
Exotic Houseplants, 3122
Falcon Fine Wire and Wire Products, 2225
Fan Man, 3584
Finck Cigar, 5996
Findings & Metals, 3867, 3917
Firewheel Classics, 503
Flatt Stationers, 1951
Football America, 5629
Fossil, 2025
Friedrich Air Conditioning, 4621
Furniture for Teaching & Technology, 5336
Future Horizons, 2081
Gear Pro-Tec, 1581, 5631
Gems & Minerals Catalog, 3872
Glass Goose Catalog, 641
Golfsmith, 5872
Golfsmith Store, 5754
Gompa, 1059
Goodies from Goodman, 2806
Graham Embroidery, 3955
Gregor's Studios, 4738
HHH Enterprises, 3876

Wisconsin Cheese Mart, 2830
Wisconsin Cheeseman, 2620, 2831
Wisconsin Log & Cedar Homes, 4711
Wisconsin Wagon Company, 6224
Women's Catalog, 1726
Wood Violet Books, 1191
Wool Gathering, 4218
Xtreme Fireworks, 4503
Ziabicki Import Company Catalog, 171

Wyoming

2015 Auction Catalog, 216
A&H Abrasives, 6012
Adventure Edge, 1249, 1555
Border Collies in Action, 90
Eloxite Corporation, 1815
Gourmet Honey Candies from Queen Bee Gardens, 2572
Hot Deals, 1359
Jackson Hole Buffalo Meat, 2915
Marquis Awards & Specialties, 3545
Online Dancewear, 1439

Rendezvous River Sports, 775
Sierra Home and Gift, 1541, 4855
Sierra Shoes, 5596
Sierra Trading Post, 1606, 5670
Sierra Traditions For Men, 1542
Sierra Woman Catalog, 1376
Sleeping Indian Designs, 1444
Stone Age Industries, 1825
Westbank Anglers Catalog, 2415
Whitechapel Limited, 5003
Woodworker's Supply, 4145
Woodworkers Supply, 4147

Alabama

ACA Corporate Awards, 7141, 7876
ACA For Churches Only, 7142, 7877
ACA School Essentials, 7143, 7878
American Thermoplastic Company, 7843
Auto Custom Carpets, 6415
Expo Displays & Exhibits Catalog, 7058
Jeffers Livestock, 6275
Marathon Equipment Company Catalog, 8017
Norment Security Group, 8441
Ovalstrapping, 8021
Regitar USA, 8587
Siegel Display, 7081
Trenway Textiles, 8704
Wayne Industries, 6889

Arizona

AAA Acme Rubber Company, 8255
Arbico Organics, 7576
Autom Inspirational Gifts, 7112
Empire Communications Corporation, 6612
Farnam Companies, 6297
Farnam Horse & Livestock Equipment, 6315
Great Potential Press, 6615
Lawyers & Judges Publishing Company, 6625
MMS Medical Supply, 7559
Mandall Armor Design & Manufacturing, 8305
Phoenix Heat Treating, 6921
Pollard Dental Products, 6995
Rigging Innovations, 6583
Smart Practice, 6997
Tomar Electronics, 8348
White Cap Industries, 6747, 8652

Arkansas

American Tubing, 7349
Anthony Forest Products, 6730
Automated Conveyor Systems, 8000
Carlton-Bates Company, 7017, 7413, 7728
Cat Claws, 6265
Duro-Felt Products Catalog, 6775
House of Webster, 7172
Modern Chemical, 8378
Tyson Foods, 8232

California

5.11 Tactical, 8656
ABP/Pharmex, 7536
APS Packaging Systems, 8043
Abbeon Cal Plastic Working Tools, 8103, 8464
Above & Beyond Balloons, 6851
Abrisa Industrial Glass, 7911
Accountant Stationers & Printers, 7841
Accu-Seal Corporation, 7993
Adcoa Absorbents & Desicants, 6554
Advantage Bags, 7012
Advertising Specialties & Business Gifts, 7144
Air Monitor Corporation, 7347
Air Tools, Hand Tools, Sheet Metal Tools, 8470
Air-Dry Corporation of America, 7305
Alameda Commons, 8047
Aline Systems Corporation, 7995
Allied Engineering & Production Corporation, 8474
Allied-Signal & Aerospace Company, 6556
American Diamond Instruments, 6987
American Machine & Hydraulics, 8476
American Technologies Network, 7711
American Weather Enterprises, 7575
Andy's Autosport, 6414, 6518
Annual Reviews, 6596
Automotive Airfilters, 6519
Aviator's Store, 6559
Backdrop Outlet, 6936, 7048
Bailey's Master Catalog, 8480
Bare Root Fruit Trees, 7603
Barksdale Control Products, 7014

Barnett Rotor Craft, 6560
Bates Leathers, 8666
Beer, Beer & More Beer, 8219
Bell Springs Publishing, 6603
Benchmark Displays, 7051
Betty Mills Catalog, 7880, 8365
Big Red Catalog, 6458
Blue White Industries, 6910
Buick Parts Catalog, 6463
CCi Scale, 8002
CFW/Precision Metal Components, 7773
CH Products, 6961
CMC Rescue Equipment, 8263
CPR Industries, 7283
Cablescan, 7015
California Car Cover, 6418, 6441
California Power Systems, 6561
California Vibratory Feeders, 8003
Cambria Bicycle Outfitter, 6419
Carlisle Company, 7153
Catalina Plastics & Coating, 6362
Center for Management Effectiveness, 6894
Cirecast, 6771
Coast Distribution RV Catalog, 6471
Coffin World Water Systems, 8367
Collimated Holes, 7913
Colvin-Friedman Company, 8109
Continental Lab Products, 7545
Count Numbering Machine, 8162
Courtaulds Aerospace, 6562
Covoc Corporation, 7506
Creation Engine, 6978
Danchuk Manufacturing, 6474
Dharma Trading Company, 6366
Davis Instruments Corp., 6424
Direct Promotions, 6861, 7158
Dominar, 7915
Duniway Stockroom Corporation, 8501
EV Roberts & Associates, 6719
Easy Leaf Products, 6349
Eaton Lighted Pushbutton Switches, 6563
Edelbrock Corporation, 6476
Egge Machine Company, 6477
Electrosonic, 7023
Elliott Manufacturing Company, 8006
Entrepreneur Magazine, 6613
Exponents, 7059
Fall Planting, 7610
Fibre Container Company, 7953
Fiddyment Farms, 7657
Force, 7917
G&B Orchid Laboratory, 7660
G&N Gear, 8518
Garrett Callahan, 6914
Gibson & Barnes Flight Suits, 6566, 7715, 8681
Giggletime Toy Company, 7164
Greenwood Daylily Gardens, 7666
HB Distributors, 8452
Hardy Diesels, 6319, 6705, 8526
Harmony Farm Supply & Nursery, 6320
Harvesting & Country Living, 7614
Hayden, 7432
Haynes Publications, 6428
Headsets.com, 7920
Heat & Control, 8012
Hirsch Electronics Corporation, 8439
Impact Gift Collection, 7173
Imperial Sprinkler Supply, 7589
Industrial Pipe & Steel, 7367
International Sensor Technology, 8294
Interscan Corporation, 8295
JC Gury Company, 8410
Kal Plastics, 7965
Kaslen Textiles, 7516
KidSafety of America, 7235
Kikkoman International, 8223
Krames Health & Safety Education, 6623
Laval Lakos Corporation, 7316
LifeStock Stock Photography Management, 8187
LittleMachineShop.com Catalog, 8538
M&T Plastics Industrial Products Catalog, 8116
M&W Systems, 7446
Machinery & Equipment Company, 8068
Macro Plastics, 7966

MagicKitchen.Com, 8227
Mailboxes Catalog, 6991, 7066, 7130
Mars Air Door, 8376
Master Builder, 6737
Moen Industries, 8020
Motorsport Auto, 6488
Nalpak Sales, 7971
National Pen, 7183
Nationwide Boiler Catalog, 7453
Natural & Organic Fertilizers, 7619, 7682
Natural INSECTO Products, 6299
Newport Thin Film Laboratory, 7925
OLEA Exhibits/Displays, 7074
Organic Gardening Essentials, 7621
Organic Seeds, 7622, 7688
Orion Telescopes & Binoculars, 7937
PJ Catalog, 8563
Pacer Performance, 6453
Pacific Sportswear & Emblem Company, 6875, 7185
Pacific States Felt & Manufacturing Company, 8120
Package Devices, 8023
Paper White, 7487, 7528
Paradise Water Gardens & Landscape, 7593
Parker Boiler Company, 7455
Parlay International, 6632, 7240
Peabody Engineering, 8024
Pest & Weed Control, 7624
Pipe End Finishing Equipment & Tooling, 8573
Plas-Ties, 8025
Plastruct, 7034, 7076
Poly Fiber Aircraft Coatings, 6580
Poly-Fiber Aircraft Coatings Catalog, 6581
Polywell Computers, 6956, 6965
PoolSupplyWorld, 7595
Precision Dynamics Corporation, 7243
Premise Wiring, 6944
Preserva-Products, 6725, 6813
Pro Sound & Stage Lighting, 6401
Professional Products Company, 6996
Proprocess Corporation, 8212
Protech Systems, 8317
Prothane Motion Control, 6546
Protolab, 8580
Quality Tools & Drip Irrigation Supplies, 7628, 7692
Quartermaster, 8695
Quick Draw & Machining, 8175
Rad Care Products, 7246
Red Line, 6403
Redwood City Seed Company, 7630
Rightlook.com, 6447
Rollem Corporation of America, 8177
Roses of Yesterday & Today, 7694
Rug Market, 7496
SECO-LARM USA, 8442
SKB Corporation, 7976
Seeds of Change, 7632
Servall Packaging Industries, 8090
Sierra Monitor Corporation, 8335
Simple Green, 8387
Simplex, 8034
Simplex Strip Doors, 6846
Small Business Development Catalog, 6635
Solar Flare, 6710
St. John Companies, 7251
Starduster Catalog, 6585
Strongbox, 7041
Sweet Impressions Catalog, 7194
Swiss Precision Instruments, 8617
Tempo Decorative Fabrics, 7534
Terra Universal, 6927
The Original Privacy Catalog, 6636
Thunderbird Price and Accessory Catalog, 6437, 6503
Time Motion Tools, 8458, 8627
Tiodize Catalog, 6693
Torque Tech, 6505
Towers Club Book Store, 6638
Trans Lectric Corporation, 6586
Trees of Antiquity, 7703
Tubular Specialties Manufacturing, 6696
Twinhead Corporation, 6959, 6967
Two Brothers Racing, 6508
US Industrial Tool, 7045, 8636
US Radiator Corporation, 7474
United Testing Systems, 8639

Uvexs, 6930
VDO Automotive Instruments, 6509
VECO Chip Thermistors, 7046
Vacuum Parts Supply, 6831
Ver Sales Catalog, 8644
Vertrod Corporation, 8037
Waterwise, 7139, 7321
West Elm, 8217
West-Link Corporation, 8039
Wholesale Buyers Guide, 7835
Wilden Pump & Engineering Company, 8395
Williams Lowbuck Tools, 7815
Wine Country Gift Baskets Catalog, 7256
Zwick Energy Research, 7341

Colorado

Applewood Seed Company, 7601
Artistic Labels, 7844
BNZ Materials, 6793
Barnes Engineering Company, 8483
Continental Sports Supply, 8675
DSC Fabrics, 7508
Elsro, 6753
Flexoveyor Industries, 8008
Hach Company, 7551
Just Cases, 7964
Kudos by Paper Direct, 7895
Leanin' Tree, 7862
Lextron, 6277
Manne-King Catalog, 7067
Moli-International, 8208
Mountain States Equipment Company, 7452
Pueblo Diversified Industries, 8129
RockWare, 6982
Sashco Sealants Catalog, 6726
Sunlawn, Inc, 7599
Surgical Products Guide, 7254
Vacmasters of Denver, 8641
WeatherPort Shelter Systems, 6826
Wesco Fabrics, 7493

Connecticut

AJ Abrams Company, 7271
Accu-Time Systems, 6970
Aerial Lift, 8469
Air Handling Systems, 7259
Althor Products, 7940
BYK Gardner Catalog, 6909
Base-Line, 8161
Beck-Lee, 7211
Better Lists, Inc., 7743
Blackstone Industries, 8485
Borgeson Universal Company, 6461
Branson Ultrasonics Corporation, 8052
Bridgewater Chocolate, 7148
Brookfield Industries, 6768
CM Almy General, 6892, 6939, 7216
Carey Manufacturing, 6770, 6940
Champion America, 8268
Champion America Safety Essentials, 8269
Clinical Health Products, 7218
Coastal Tool & Supply, 8495
Colonial Bronze Company, 6773
Colonial Redi Record Corporation, 7836, 7848
Copley's, 8676
DAWG, Inc., 8369
Del-Tron Precision, 8497
Design Within Reach, 7119
Differential Pressure Instruments, 8500
Durham Manufacturing Company, 8112
EBM Industries, 7264
Ecometics, 8057
Emery Winslow Scale Company Catalog, 8507
Excel Technologies, 7548
Farmington Displays, 7060
Fischer Technology, 8515
Goodway Technologies Catalog, 6915
Gordon Engineering Corporation, 8284
Habco, 6569
High Precision, 8288

Horberg Gage & Grinding Industries, 6570
ITW Automotive Products, 6446
Jaypro Sports, 8685
Linemaster Switch Corporation, 8303
Logee's Greenhouses, 7677
Macton Corporation, 6668
Marion Manufacturing Company, 7786
Market Data Retrieval, 7757
Moore Medical Corporation, 7238
Naugatuck Glass Company, 6576
North American Plastic Manufacturing Company, 7073
PC Systems Handbook, 6964
PDC International Corporation, 8022
Paul Leibinger Numbering Machine, 8171
Permatex Industrial Catalog, 6680
RollEase, 7530
Select Seeds Antique Flowers, 7633
Seton Catalog, 6375
Seton Essentials, 8334
Solid State Heating, 7462
Solo Horton Brushes, 6376
Stencil Ease International, 6377
Thomas Industries, 7300
Turbotec Products Catalog, 7473
Van Engelen, 7637
Visonic, 8426
Whelen Engineering, 8354
White Flower Farm Catalog, 7705

Delaware

El Dupont De Nemours & Company, 6312
Felder USA, 8513
Franklin Fibre-Lamitex Company, 8113
Maintenance Troubleshooting, 6627
Mid Atlantic Packaging, 8071
Wilmington Fibre Specialty Company, 8136

District of Columbia

American Chemical Society Publication Guide, 6907
American Institute of Architects Press, 6357
Brass Knob, 6648
Fan Fair, 7588
List America, 7756

Florida

AME International, 6643
Acme, 6455
Acrocrete, 6645
Addison Products Company, 7275, 7396
Adrick Cooling Corporation, 7322
Advanced Graphics, 6412
Algy Team Collection, 8657
All About Dog Grooming, 6261
Amaryllis Bulb Company, 7640
Amazon Exotic Hardwoods, 7641
American Coolair Corporation, 7263
American Panel Corporation, 7325
Aquatic Eco-Systems, 7278
Atkins Technical, 7353
Atlas Metal Industries, 7771
Auto Label, 7999
Awards.com, 7147
Brinsea Products, 6264, 6305
Cable Organizer Office and Home, 6417
Call One, 6855, 7151
Camp Lot a Noise Tropicals, 7650
Cerwin-Vega!, 6420
Chestnut Hill Nursery, 7651
Classic Auto Air Manufacturing, 6468
Comfort Telecommunications, 7821, 7883
Concept Catalog, 6393
Deltran-Battery Tender, 6524
Directory Marketplace, 6611
Easy Picker Golf Products, 8504
Encoder Line Card, 7024
Everything for the Lilypool, 7587
FHP Bosch Group Catalog, 7288

Fi-Foil Company, 6797
G Neil Direct Mail, 6913
G. Neil, 7837
Going Bananas, 7664
Graphics 3, 6865
Guardian Fire Equipment, 7094
Gulf Coast Avionics Products, 6568
Hafner World Wide, 7717
Hecht Rubber Corporation, 6429
Just Fruits and Exotics, 7672
Levenger, 7177, 7733, 7827
Lockwood Aviation Supply, 6574
Ludeca, 7445
Magga Products, 7785
Maintenance USA, 6669, 7735
Marden Industries, 6329
Marine World Warehouse, 6278
Marzetta Signs, 8306
Mastercut Tool Corporation, 6992
Mavidon Catalog, 6671
Mo' Money Associates, 6872
Mocal Oil Control Systems, 6543
National Parts Depot, 6489
P&H Crystalite, 7736
Polart by Mail, 6681
Precision Response Corporation, 7760
Pronto Business Cards, 8174
Quality Business Cards, 8188
Quality Engineering Products Corporation, 7375
Renco Electronics, 7038
Safariland Forensics Source Catalog, 8715
Safariland Master Catalog, 8356
Safariland Shooting Gear Catalog, 8357
Scott Sign Systems Catalog, 6884
Sentrol Products, 8444
Shoes for Crews, 8699
Sigalarm, 8336
Somay Paint Factory Catalog, 6689
Stimpson Company, 8612
Successories, 7905
T&J Incorporated, 8618
Tampa Sheet Metal Company, 7809
The Big Book, 6958, 7135, 7832
Therm-O-Type Corporation, 8181
Things You Never Knew Existed, 7196
Tiger Direct, 6406
Tri-Motion Industrial, 8631
Trophyland USA, 7199
US Crane, 8635
Uniform Advantage Medical Uniforms, 8709
Uniweld Products, 7384
Wasserman Uniforms, 8712
Wealth Unlimited, 6641
Wrisco Industries, 6699, 6748, 6800

Georgia

ABCO Industries, 7391
ALDATA, 7740
Accu-Tech Cable, 7013
Aftermarket Specialties, 7276
Agco, 6260
Atlanta Cable Sales, 6385, 8448
Atlanta Models & Exhibits, 7816
Atlas Greenhouse Systems, 6303, 6819, 7577
B&R Industrial Automation Corporation, 6935, 6951, 6972
Bergeman USA, 7310
CoLinear Systems, 6975
Custom Bottle, 7952
DeLong Equipment Company, 7776
Galileo Vacuum Systems, 7333
Georgia-Pacific, 8154
Global Pigeon Supplies, 6317
Goodmark Retail Catalog, 6479
Heidelberg News, 8144
Honey Baked Ham, 7171
Imagers, 8167
Joe M Almand, 7962
Lazy K Nursery, 7676
Magnolia Plastics Catalog, 6721
Mil-Spec Packaging of Georgia, 8073
Pirelli Armstrong Tire Corporation, 6335, 6492
Poultry & Gamebreeders Catalog, 6285

Ronson Technical Products, 7801, 8594
Southwire Machinery Divison, 7464
Stewart R Browne Manufacturing Company, 8338
Thermal Gas Systems, 8345
William Bonnell Company, 8183

Hawaii

Hawaii Wholesale Company, 7168

Idaho

A Child's Dream, 6355
Backwoods Solar Electric Systems, 6702
Initial-Attack Firefighting, 7098
Quality Thermistor, 7035
Snug Fleece Woolens, 7489, 7497

Illinois

ALP Lighting, 7724
AVW Equipment Company, 6448
Accurate Industries Commercial Products, 8466
Adapt Plastics, 8104
Adjustable Clamp, 8468
Aeroflash Signal, 8429
Aetna Bearing Company, 6302
Air Comfort, 7400
Air-Drive, 6515
Allen Brothers, 8218
Allied Glove & Safety Products Corporation, 8258
Alto Manufacturing Company, 7768
Aluminum Case Company, 7941
American Academy-Medical Administrators, 6891
American Acrylics, 8106
American Color Printing, 8158
American Dental Association, 6986
American Technical Publishers, 6595
Amglo Kemlite Laboratories, 7727
Anderson-Snow Corporation, 7351
Androck Hardware Corporation, 6766
Anti-Seize Technology, 6715
Armstrong Medical Industries, 7207
Association of Rotational Molders, 7944
Atkinson Dynamics, 8447
Atlas Fibre Company, 8108
B&B Electronics Manufacturing Company, 6934, 7354
BIRD-X, 7571
BP Barco Products, 8261, 8361
Badge-A-Minit, 6852
Baldwin, 8160
Barco Products Company, 6646, 7113, 8363
Bearse Manufacturing Company, 8049
Best Impressions, 6853
Braeside Displays, 7052
Bretford, 6389
Burgess Seed and Plant Company, 7605, 7647
CARL Manufacturing, 8489
CCH Tax & Business Law Subscription, 6607
CDW Solutions, 6938, 6953, 6974
CME Gifts, 7150
Castell Safety, 8266
Central Sheet Metal Products, 7775
Champaign Plastics Company, 8673
Chefwear, 8243, 8674
Chicago Corvette Supply, 6467
Circle K Industries, 6308
Clark & Barlow Hardware Company, 6772
Cole-Parmer, 7542, 8272
Cole-Parmer Instruments Product Catalog, 7543
Cole-Parmer-Temperature Measurement & Control, 7018, 7357
Coleman Cable, 6392
Commodity Traders International, 7581
Cotton Goods Manufacturing Company, 8274
Cozzini, 8197
Cozzini Knives, 8198
Cresswood Recycling Systems, 8368
Custom Accessories, 6423
D&R Classic Automotive Camaro Catalog, 6444
Daigger & Company Lab Supply, 7546

Dick Blick Art Materials, 6367
Dickson Company, 7021
Direct Gardening, 7653
Dukane Corporation, 6395
Early Childhood Manufacturers' Direct, 7120, 7586
Everpure, 7315
Federal Signal Corporation, 8403
Figaro USA, 8282
Flex-O-Glass, 8060
Flight Form Cases, 8061
Fox Valley Systems, 8141
G.H. Meiser & Company, 6533
Good-Lite Company, 7228
Grieve Corporation, 7429
Guzzler Manufacturing, 6828
H Wilson Company, 7824
Handi-Ramp, 7002
Healthcare Supplies, 7229
Hesco, 8373
High Performance Catalog, 6538
Honeywell Analytics, 8289
House of Cans, 7958
House of Wesley, 7670
Howard Decorative Packaging, 7959
Human Kinetics Academic & Professional Resour, 7233
Identatronics, 8406
Indeck Power Equipment Company, 7437
Inspired, 7122, 8203
Iroquois Products Catalog, 8066
Jackson Marking Products Catalog, 8531
Jessup Manufacturing Company, 6665
JeweLite, 6870
Johnson Bros Metal Forming Catalog, 7783
Justrite Manufacturing Company, 7100, 8296
KH Huppert Company, 7439
Kamflex Corporation, 8374
Komet of America, 8536
LTD Commodities, 7176
Label Master, 8299
Landauer, 8300
Lester L Brossard Company, 8301
Loeb Equipment & Appraisal Company, 8016
MacNeil Automotive Products, 6433
Magenta Closure Division, 8069
Man Roland, 8145
Marsh Shipping Supply Company, 8070
Meyer Drapery Services, 7520
Micron Industries Corporation, 8545
Mid America Motorworks Air-Cooled VW, 6487
Moss, 7069
Multiplex Versatile Display Systems, 7071, 7839
Museum Shop Catalog, 7864
Nalco Company, 7318
National Bullet Proof, 8414
National Manufacturing Co, 6780
National Metal Fabricators, 7818
Neil Enterprises, 6372, 6873
Neil Holiday Catalog, 6373, 6874, 8146
Newell Window Furnishings, 7524
Nikro Industries, 8380
Nimlok Company, 7072
Olin Brass, 7794
Oly-Ola Sales, 7592
Ophthalmic Surgical Instruments, 7927
Paket Contract Packaging, 8080
Panduit Electrical Group, 8312
Paslode Corporation, 6740
Peacock Engineering Company, 8082
Personal Protection/Safety Products, 8314
Petra Manufacturing Company, 8122
Pierce Biotechnology, 7566
Piper Plastics, 8125
Platt Cases, 7829
Products Filling & Packaging Company Catalog, 8087
Promaco, 8316, 8384, 8417
Quill.com, 7830, 7904
Raani Corporation, 8088
Rabbit Tool USA, 8583
Rand McNally, 6633
Rawhide Brand, 6286
Rebechini Studios, 7192
Reid Tool Supply, 7800
Rock-Tred Corporation, 6760
Rowald Refrigeration Systems Catalog, 7336

Ryerson Wholesale Industrial Catalog, 8089
S&D Continuous Hinges, 8598
SRDS Media Solutions, 7763
Saf-T-Gard, 8324
Safe-Aire Radon Mitigation Products, 8325
Sammons Preston, 7006, 7248
Sauk Valley Equipment, 6923
School Health Corporation, 7249
Scientific Technologies, 8329
See All, 8331
Sellstrom Manufacturing Company, 8332
Service Packaging, 7979
Siltron Emergency Systems, 8446
Solberg Manufacturers Catalog, 8605
Specialty Store Services, 7083, 7106
Speed Tools, 8606
Spraying Systems Company, 6341
Sprayway, 8178
Standard Rubber Products, 8610
Sun Process Converting, 8179
Support Products, 8189
Surface Finishes Company, 7933
T/J Fabricators, 8180
Tablecraft Products Company, 8253
Telular Corporation, 8424
TitleWaves Publishing, 6637
Tocos America, 8630
Triad Controls, 8632
Tridan Tool & Machine, 7382
USABlue Book, 8637
United Ad Label, 6999
United Facilities, 8392
United Logistics, 7765
Varn, 8182
Vee Pak, 8100
Vijuk Equipment, 8191
Vinylweld, 8101
Viprofix, 7047
Visionary Solutions, 7387, 7476
WH Salisbury & Company, 8353
Warner Electric, 6512
Wick's Aircraft Supply Catalog, 6591
Wicks Aircraft Supply, 6592
William W Meyer & Sons, 6832
World Dryer Corporation, 8398

Indiana

A/C Fabricating Corporation, 7767
Air Fixtures, 7994
Air-Jet, 7260
Airguard Industries, 7306
Ameri Stamp/Sign-A-Rama, 6356
American Stationery, 7842
Best Access Systems, 8400, 8434
Breck's Bulbs, 7604
Central Metal Products: Dog Kennels, 6266
Colorimetric Catalog, 6716
Crown Packaging International/Polycon Industr, 7951
Da-Lite Screen Company, 7020
Davidson Greenhouse & Nursery, 7652
Farriers' Greeting Cards, 7852
Girtz Industries, 7779
Glas-Col, 7550
Gosport Manufacturing Company, 6659
Greenwoods Collection, 7856
Hawthorne Horse Care Products, 6272
Indco Pharma, 6735
Indiana Mills & Manufacturing, 6431
Madden Manufacturing, 7296
Martguild, 7787
Mathews Wire Giftware Catalog, 7179
Merrimade, 7863
Morgan Manufacturing & Engineering Company, 7522
Osborn Manufacturing Corporation, 8561
Personalized Acknowledgement Cards, 7868
Photo Materials Company, 7828
Racer Wholesale, 6547
SafetyWear, 8327
Signcrafters, 6886
Sillair Corporation, 7299
Stant, 6550
Stranco Products, 8421

Thompson & Morgan Seedsmen, 7635
Tyler Machinery Company, 8633
Weatherall Catalog, 6729
Wood-Mizer Products Catalog, 8654

Iowa

CT Farm & Country, 6306
Comco DataNet, 7746
Competitive Edge, 6857
FarmTek, 6270, 6314
G&R Publishing Company, 6863
Harper Brush Industrial Catalog, 8372
Hoover's Hatchery, 6274, 6323
JMF Company, 7368
Kent Feeds, 6327
Kitchen Krafts Catalog, 8206
Lattner Boilers Manufacturing, 7441
Lisle Corporation, 6542
Midwest Metal Products Company, 7790
Murray McMurray Hatchery, 6281
Novations Training Solutions Catalog, 6384
Seed Savers Exchange, 7631
Triple F Products, 6344
Woodhaven, 6411

Kansas

Career Track, 6383
Dedicated Distribution, 7222
Fantech, 7265
Fred Pryor Seminars, 6903
Garsite Division of America, 6565
Great Plains All Product Catalog, 6318
Kansas Wind Power, 6708
King Louie Sports, 8687
LMC Truck, 6483
Leslie Company, 7896
M-E-C Company, 7447
Mirage Dental Systems, 6993
SafeMart, 8419, 8443
Sunshine Rooms, 6824
Tapes And Seminars, 6905
US Safety, 8351
Valley Vet Supply Catalog, 6292
Vet-Vax, Inc., 6294
Waffle-Crete International, 6746

Kentucky

Air Filter Testing Laboratories, 7302
Campbellsville Industries, Inc, 6801
Gall's, 8200, 8283
Hard Hat Unique American Products, 8683
Hasco Tag Company, 6321
House of Winston, 8202
Kelley Technical Coatings, 8297
Krazy Duck Productions Catalog, 6624
Louisville Ladder, 6667
Metal Sales Manufacturing Corporation, 6738
Palmer Products Corporation, 6678
Parks Repair Parts, 8566
Rev-a-Shelf Specification Guide, 6784
Roof & Wall Systems, 7802
Skilcraft Sheetmetal, 7805
Stephens Instruments, 7252
Syntechnics, 8340, 8389, 8422
Wallis Stained Glass, Doors, Cabinets, Art, G, 6850

Louisiana

Alarm Monitoring Services, 8431
Allometrics, 7537
American Tank Company, 7570, 7574
Dixie Art Airbrush, 6368
Kim Kool, 7440
Laitram Corporation, 6818
Louisiana Nursery, 7678
McIlhenny Company, 8228

Poly Processing Company, 7975
Scientific Systems Corporation, 7337

Maine

Allen, Sterling, & Lothrop, 7600
Dingley Press, 8164
Fedco Seeds, 7611
Fedco Trees, 7612
Fieldstone Gardens, 7658
Johnny's Selected Seeds, 7615
Memco Supply, 7450
Pinetree Garden Seeds, 7625
Puritan Medical Products, 7245
Surry Gardens' Bedding Plant Catalog, 7702

Maryland

Association for Information & Image Managemen, 6599
Baltimore Aircoil Company, 7327
Bob's BMW, 6460
Bostitch, 7820, 7881
Cambridge Metal Belts, 8492
Chesapeake Ceramic Supply, 6363
Clean Fuel, 7313
Delta Truck Storage Solutions, 6426
Filamatic, 8007
GovConnection, 6941, 6954
Hopkin's Medical Products, 7232
JOBOX Premium Storage Solutions, 6432
Jamison Door Company, 6842
Knox Video, 6396
LaMotte Soil Testing Products, 6666
MMI Catalog, 7558
Maryland Aquatic Nurseries, 7679
Metro Shelving & Warehouse Products, 7068
Meyer Seed, 7618
Milton W Bosley Company, 6353, 6808
Network Access & Connectivity Product Line, 6942
Neuhaus Corporation, 8551
Protection People, 7102, 8318
Redding Medical, 7247
Starlight Skylights, 6848
Stulz-ATS, 7339
Water Quality Testing Products, 6931, 8394, 8649
Whitaker Brothers, 7834

Massachusetts

AL Ellis, 7498
Accu Trak Tool, 8465
Accu-line, 8044
Acorn Manufacturing Company, 6763
Adcole Corporation, 6514
AliMed Operating Room Products, 7204
Alloy Fabricators of New England, 7403
American Business Systems, 6971
American Durafilm Company, 8107
American Saw & Manufacturing, 8478
Arista Surgical Supply Company, 7206
BMA Environmental Chambers, 7540
Bcc Research, 6602, 6902
Bete Fog Nozzle, 8364
Bigelow Nurseries, 7642
Brooktrout Technology, 8449
Bruce Medical Supply, 7212
Cape Cod Cupola Company, 6802
Career Works, 6608
Computalabel, 6977
Contemporary Structures, 6820
Custom Paper Group, 8153
Cutting Tools C, 8496
Data Translation Product Handbook, 6949
Deluxe Small Business Services, 6860, 7850, 7886
Dennis K Burk, 6525
Diamond Machining Technology, 8499
Dinn Brothers Trophies, 7157
Dover Saddlery, 6269, 8276
ELCOM Systems, 7750
EggCartons.Com, 6313

Ergonomics/Occupational Health & Safety, 7224
FW Schumacher Company, 7609
Fireslate-2, 6754
Fulfillment America, 7752
Graphique de France, 7855
Gregstrom Corporation, 8142
GuardAir Corporation, 8404
HNU Systems, 7095
Hoop House Greenhouse Kits, 6822
Hotwatt.com, 7366
Hyde Tools, 8528
Incom, 7922
Industrial Packaging Supply, 8065
Interactive Therapeutics, 7234
International Light, 7553
K&R Equipment, 8013
Lamp Glass, 7732
Landrigan Corporation, 7101
Lock Inspection Systems, 8015
Lumenpulse, 7734
MIT Press, 6626
Mason Box Catalog, 7967
Massa Products Corporation, 8411
Mech-Chem Associates, 6918
Mica-Tron Products Corporation, 7789
MicroGroup Small Diameter Tubing Specialists, 6739
Monarch Accounting Supplies, 7898
Morion Company, 6371
Mystic Valley Traders, 7495
NANMAC Corporation, 8547
NEB Catalog, 7561
NELCO Wiring Accessory Specialists, 8548
National Coating Corporation, 8155
New England Etching Company, 7900
New England Solar Electric, 6709
Norpin Deep Drawn Enclosures, 8552
Norpin Manufacturing Company, 7792
Nourse Farms, 7685
Nye, 8555
Ophthalmic Instrument Company, 7909
POBCO Plastics & Hardwood, 6545, 8119
PetEdge, 6284
Plasticad Line, 8128
Precision Optics Corporation, 7930
Reliable Fabrics, 7488
Renbrandt-Flexible Couplings, 7037, 8588
Repromat Catalog, 7831
Stafford Manufacturing Corporation, 7806, 8608
Stanley Supplies and Services, 6342
Strem Chemicals, 6925
Technical Manufacturing Corporation, 7934, 8623
Technobrands, 8624
Terracon Corporation, 8625
Thermo ALKO, 7043, 7568
UMG Technologies, Inc., 8634
Williamsburg Blacksmiths, 6789
Windjammer Promotions, 7201
Window Imagination, 7535

Michigan

AGET Dust/Mist Collectors, 7301
AIN Plastics of Michigan, 8102
Acme Manufacturing, 8467
Air Conditioning Products Company, 7346
Aircraft Tool Supply Company, 6555
Airmaster Fan Company, 7261
Albion Industries Full Line Catalog, 8473
Ahern Martin Industrial Furnace Company, 7402
American Metal Products, 7309
Bar's Leaks, 6521
Bartlett Arborist Supply & Manufacturing Comp, 7578
Baudville, 6361, 6416, 7050
BrittenMedia, 6854, 7053
Brown-Campbell Steel Corporation, 6751
Burr Oak Tool & Gauge Company, 7412
Burton Press Company, 8487
Challenge Machinery, 8138
Cone Instruments, 7220
Corvette Central, 7008, 7019
DQB Industries, 6450
De-Sta-Co, 7360
Detroit Body Products, 6526

Display Pack, 8055
Douthitt Corporation, 8139
Dry Coolers, 7420
EJ, 6654
Elemental Scientific, 7547
Eliason Corporation, 7330
Engraving Connection, 7162
Environtronics, 6911
Federal APD, 8402
Feeny, 8511
Gast Manufacturing Corporation, 7292
General Scientific Corporation, 7918
Grant Industries, 8522
Gresham Driving Aids, 7009
Hilltop Nurseries, 7669
Humphrey Pneumatic Valves, 7782
Inductoheat, 7438
Installations, 8292
Inter-Lakes Bases, 8529
Jonesville Paper Tube Company, 7963
KBC Tools, 8533
Kentwood Manufacturing, 7128
Kitts Industrial Tools, 8535
Knape & Vogt, 7129
McNaughton & Gunn, 8170
Merco/Savory, 8207
MonlanGroup Division, 7317
Oikos Tree Crops, 7687
Onodi Tool & Engineering Company, 7795
Oxford Biomedical Research, 7563
Parco Scientific Company, 7564, 7928
Patco Air Tool, 8567
Permaloc Aluminum Edging, 7594
Plasteel Coporation, 8084
Prab Conveyor, 8027
Primore, 7374
Quantum Composites Catalog, 6685
RWC, 7799
Rare Earth Hardwoods, 6759
Reliable Products, 7376
Risdon Rigs, 6287
Rosedale Products, 8595
SLP Performance Parts, 6496
Schoolmasters Safety, 8328
Sherman & Associates, 6497
Shorty's Tooling & Equipment, 6498, 8033
Skidmore, 7459
Solaronics, 7461
Steiner Tractor Parts, 6501
TecArt Industries, 7085
Tocco, 7471
Tri-Mer Corporation, 8350
USA Manufacturing Corporation, 7383
Ultimate Hydroforming, 6589
Unist, 7475
Unistrut Illinois, 8352
United Resin Products, 8099
Van F Belknap, 8642
Weltronic/Technitron, 8650
Wholesale Tool Catalog, 8653
Z-Rite, 8184

Minnesota

3M Accessories for Abrasive Products, 8461
A Great Idea to Hang Onto, 6348
AAF-Environmental Commercial Product Group, 7270
Air Quality Engineering, 7303
Airmo Hydraulics, 8471
American Metal Door Company, 6833
Andersen Corporation, 6834
Apco/Valve & Primer Corporation, 7352
Aqua-Therm, 6701
Blanks USA, 8186
Charnstrom Company, 7115
Chief Manufacturing, 6650
Complimentary Health Reference Catalog, 7219
Continental Clay Company, 6365
Daro Industries, 6774
Daydots, 8235
Deluxe Enterprise, 7156, 7885
Dental Reference Catalog, 7887
Easy Stand Catalog, 7001

Eye Care Reference Catalog, 7890
Farmer Seed & Nursery Company, 7656
GE Interlogix, 8438
GS Direct Graphic Supplies, 6369
Glass, Plastic, Metal Packaging, 8063
Glenn Metalcraft, 7363
Great Plains Wholesale, 7293
H&H Exports, 8524
Header Parts, 6445, 6537
Heatmor, 6707
Home Business Startup Handbook, 6620
Hornell Speedglas Catalog, 7921
Hubbard Milling Company, 6324
Hypro Pressure, 6325
ITW BGK Finishing Systems, 7436
Industrial Arts Supply Company, 8114
J-Mark, 6540
Jennfan Commercial Products Group, 7268
Jones Metal Products, 7784
Kogle Cards, 7860
MacKenzie Nursery Supply, 7591
Midwest Supplies, 7720
Milcare Company, 6280
Motorbooks, 6435
Natural Spaces Domes, 6673
Northern Hydraulics, 6490
PaperDirect, 7901
PaperDirect Events, 7866
Podiatry Reference Catalog, 7869
Print Craft, Inc., 6877, 7188
Process Measurement Company, 8577
SJF Material Handling, 8031, 8599
SafeWay Hydraulics, 8601
Scott Equipment Company, 6924
Shady Oaks Nursery, 7695
Signs Plus Banners Catalog, 6887
Skyline Displays, 7082
Stromberg's Chicks, 6290
Super Radiator Coils, 7378
TIF International, 8341
Technical Furniture Systems, 8423
Tenenz, 7872
Tennant, 8390
Tepromark International, 8343
Thumb Things, 7197
Veterinary & Pet Care Reference Catalog, 6295
Viking Acoustical Corporation, 7137
WA Charnstrom Company, 7138
WA Charnstrom Mail Center Solutions, 8038
Watlow Electric Manufacturing Company, 7388
World Confederation of Productivity, 6899
Yellow Jacket Solar, 6713
Yukon/Eagle Furnace, 6714

Mississippi

Anel Corpration, 7769
Forestry Suppliers 61 Catalog, 8517
Heatcraft, 7364
MFJ Enterprises, Inc., 6399

Missouri

A-J Manufacturing Company, 7342
Accutherm, 7393
Ace Industrial Products, 7257
Alemite LLC, 6516
Allen Filters, 7308
Allied Healthcare Products, 7205
B&J Peerless Restaurant Supply, 8193
Bagmaster Quality Bags, Cases & Holsters, 7712
Bass Equipment Company, 6304
Chocolate Catalogue, 7154
Christian Tools of Affirmation, 6895, 8244
Classic Parts of America, 6469
Comstock, Ferre & Company, 7606
Convenience Products, 6717
Copeland Corporation, 7286
Dazor Manufacturing Corporation, 7729
Diansupply, 8163
Dunbrooke Sportswear Company, 8678
Fasco Industries, 7266

Gilbert H Wild & Son, 7663
Hantover, 8221
Ken-A-Vision Manufacturing Company, 7555
Magna Visual, 7838
Midland Radio Corporation, 6434
NAED Education Foundation, 6904
Ohmic Instruments Company, 7373
Parker McCrory Manufacturing Company, 6333
Posty Cards, 7870
Raven Environmental Products, 6922, 8385, 8585
SM Arnold, 6452
Scrubs & Beyond, 8698
Sealers Catalog, 6727
Semi-Bulk Systems, 7978
Silgan Plastics, 8092
Stark Bro's, 7699
Tomco, 6504
UPCO Wholesale Pet Supplies, 6291
Upbeat, 7833
VisiPak, 7988
WSI Distributors, 6788
Wilen Brushworx, 8396

Montana

Blake Nursery Catalog, 7643
Lawyer Nursery, 7675
Specialty Woodworks Company, 6847
Sunelco, 6711
Vacuum Lifters for Materials Handling, 6830

Nebraska

Cabela's Corporate Outfitter, 8670
Dutton-Lainson Company Catalog, 6311
Folder Express Catalog, 7891
Heartland Veterinary Supply & Pharmacy, 6273
InfoUSA, 6867, 7753
Labels Catalog, 8014
Midwest Plastics, 8117
Omaha Fixture International, 6676, 6844
Omaha Vaccine Company/Pet Supplies Delivered, 6283, 6332
Oriental Trading Business Edition, 7184
Snyder Industries, 8604
Stock Seed Farms, 6343, 7700
Vet Med Direct Catalog, 6293
Walter Karl Companies, 7766

Nevada

Corporate Service Center, 6858
Festo Tooltecnic, 8514
Haws Corporation, 6661
Heat Treating & America's Finest, 7433
Hogue Grip, 7718
Keystone View Company, 7923
Medallic Art Company, Ltd, 7180
Promo Direct Catalog, 6878
Promo Unlimited, 6879
Reliapon Police Products, 7722
Rice Hydro Equipment Manufacturing, 8590
Stockton Products, 6742
Weather-Bos Catalog, 6815

New Hampshire

Albany International, 6792
Ames Performance Engineering, 6457
Audio Accessories, 6386
Bond Optics, 7912
Copper House, 6804
Extech Instruments, 7549
Harris Graphics, 8143
Hello Direct, 6989
Herrington, 8527
Merchandising Solutions, 6628
Northeast Hinge Distributors Catalog, 6781
Production Process, 8029
Vibrac Corporation Catalog, 8645

Lourdes Industries, 8454
Lowel-Lighting Equipment, 6397
Luckner Steel Shelving, 7897
Masune First Aid & Safety, 8307
Newport, 7486
Niagara Fiberboard, 6674
Nortel Machinery, 8553
Northeast Dental Supplies, 6994
Northern Climate Fruit & Nut Trees Catalog, 7684
Northern Safety Company, 7133, 8311
Norton-Performance Plastics Catalog, 6675
Noteworthy Company, 8076
Oneida Air Systems, 8560
Overnight Labels, 8077
PM Research, 8564
Paper Access, 7865
Pawling Corporation, 8121
Penton Lists, 7759
Perretta Graphic, 8172
Pico Electronics, 8572
Positive Impressions Idea Showcase, 7187
ProTech Systems, 6682
Products in, on and Around Concrete, 6683, 8578
Professional Insurance Agents, 7903
Putnam Rolling Ladder Company, 6684
Putnam's, 8694
RKL Building Specialties Company, 6783
RPM Displays, 7077
Reed Business Lists, 7761
Regency Service Cart, 8252
Rigidized Metals Corporation, 6785
Roberts-Gordon, 8592
Russell Industries, 8597
S&H Uniforms, 8696
Safety Premiums, 8326
Salem Press, 6634
Sargent Welch, 8697
Sausage Maker, 8213
Scott Machine Development Corporation, 6686
Simon's Kitchen & Bath, 6786
Skydyne, 7982
Space Age Plastic Fabricators, 8131
Speco Audio Products, 6405
Spectronics Corporation Catalog, 7338
St. Lawrence Nurseries, 7698
Stefan Sydor Optics, 7932
Stephen Bader and Company, 8611
Stock Drive Products, 6502
Storesmart, 6946, 6983
Sun-Mar Corporation, 6926, 8388
Super Shop, 8615
Support Services Alliance, 6898
Sussman Aquamatic Steam Products Corporation, 7466
TDI Drapery Importing Corporation, 7533
TRIMCO, 7871
Tadiran Electronic Industries, 8342
Tapeswitch Corporation, 8622
Titan Tool Supply Company, 6928, 8629
Tobart Mannequins, 7086
Tourneau Watch, 7198
Transcat, 7044
Turf, Tree & Ornamental Catalog, 7572
UNICEF Catalog, 7874
US Monitor, 7764
USATCO, 6588, 7811
Unicef Corporate Card Collection, 7875
Union Pen Company Full Line Catalog, 6888, 7200
Van Son Holland Ink Corporation of America, 8190
Victor Machinery Exchange, 7812, 8646
Vinten, 6409
Watercolors Inc, 6698
West Point Pepperell, 7494
Wittus, 6712
World Guide to Gun Parts, 7723
York Industries Catalog, 6749
Yula Corporation, 7483
Zeller International, 6933

North Carolina

Apollo Valves Commercial Catalog, 7088
Appalachian Stove, 6700
Art Supply Warehouse, 6358

CEO Cards, 7847
Carolina Brush Company, 8366
Center for Creative Leadership, 6893
City Compressor Remanufacturers, 7284
Dennis Carpenter Ford Restoration, 6475
Dixon Industries, 7583
Douglas Battery Manufacturing Company, 6527
Eagle Equipment-Automotive Equipment, 6529
Environmental Geothermal Houses, 6704
Exclusively Weddings, 6805, 7851
Fairchild Products, 8509
Gardens of the Blue Ridge, 7661
Gas Fired Products, 7427
Hockmeyer Equipment Corporation, 6916
Hospitality Mints, 8222
Interlogix Security & Life Safety Group, 7099, 8293, 8407
Irwin Industrial Tools, 8530
Kent-Moore Automotive, 6541
Kewaunee Scientific Corporation, 7556
Korman Autoworks, 6482
Levelor Home Fashion, 7518
Levolor Kirsch Window Fashions, 7519
Lubrication Equipment & Accessories, 8169
Militex Industries Corporation, 7485
National Drying Machinery Company, 8209
Norton Diamond Pressing Tools, 8554
Nurses' Choice, 8693
P Collins Fabrics, 7526
Paper Clips, 6631
Penco Products Catalog, 6679
Rochling Engineered Plastics, 8130
Sales Promotion Tool Book, 6883, 7078
Scott Instruments, 8330
Shamrock Paper, 6885
Shurtape, 8091
Sirchie Product Catalog, 7931
Stevenson & Vestalury, 7491, 7532
SunMate & Pudgee Orthopedic Cushions, 7007
TandemLoc, 8621
Tesa Tape, 6692
Touch America, 6551, 6694
Turner Greenhouses, 6825
Ultimate HVAC and Door Products, 8638

Ohio

Adams Manufacturing Company, 7395
Air Rite Service Supply, 7304
Aitken Products, 7262
Akro-Mills, 7938
Alert Stamping & Manufacturing Company, 7725
Anderson Fabrics, 7500
Astrup Company, 6767, 6835
Backyard Buddy, 6520
Bates Metal Products, 7049
Battelle Press, 6601
Baumfolder Corporation, 8185
Benchmark Industrial Supply, 8667
Big Dee's Tack & Vet Supplies, 6263
Bluestone Perennials, 7644
Bottles, Containers, & Bags, 8194
Brown Fired Heater Division, 7411
Buckhorn, 7946
CED Process Minerals-Engineering & Sales, 7214
Campbell Tool Company, 8493
Caravan Protective Cases, 7947
Central Ohio Bag & Burlap, 7948
Cincinnati Sub-Zero Products, 7356
Cleveland Steel Specialty, 6651
Clopay Building Products, 6837
Commercial Mats and Matting, 8195
Consolidated Plastics Company, 8054
Cookie Bouquets, 7155
Country Manufacturing, 6309
Dayton Wheel Products, 6425
Discount Snow Plow Parts, 6310
Dove Enterprises, 6380
Downing Displays, 7057
Eaton, 7022
Eaton Corporation World Headquarters, 6531, 8505
Electric-Eel Manufacturing Company, 8236
FOMO Products, 6796
Ferno Physical Therapy & Sports Equipment, 7225

Flexi USA, Inc., 6271
Fluke Biomedical, 7226
Force Control Industries, 6532
Fox Lite, 6840
GVS Industries, 6564
Gallo Displays, 7061
Garrett Wade, 8520
Glo-Quartz Electric Heater Company, 7428
Gold Medal, 8201, 8220, 8246
Hadronics, 8166
Hamilton Manufacturing Corporation, 8525
Hanco International, 8287
Hardwood Flooring & Paneling, 6756
Head-To-Toe Catalog, 8684
Home Improvements, 6662
Home Office Direct, 7825
Keithley Instruments, 7028
Kett Tool, 8534
Kindt Collins Company, 7817
Lancaster Colony Commercial Products, 8249
Lintern Corporation, 7444
MCM Business to Business, 6398, 6955
MTM Molded Products, 7369
Marathon Special Products, 7370
Mason Company, 6279
McGlaughlin Company, 8238
Mitchellace, 7521
Mount Pulaski Products, 6330
Musson Rubber Company, 6672
Nemco Food Equipment, 8210
Noco Company, 6544
Nordic Air, 7454
Northern States Metals Corporation, 7793
Nucon International, 7319
OPW Aboveground Storage Tank Equipment, 8556
OPW Service Station Equipment, 8557
Office Scapes Direct, 7525, 7686
Ohio Earth Food, 6300
Ohio Nut & Bolt Company, 8558
Osborne/McGraw-Hill, 6943
Packaging Machinery Services, 8079
Pease Industries, 6845
Pecco Premiums, 6876
Pioneer Athletics, 6758
Pioneer National Latex, 7186
Plas-Tanks Industries, 8126
Pneumatic Scale, 8026
Porter Punch Catalog, 8575
Positive Safety Manufacturing Company, 8315
ProVantage, 6957, 6981
Puritas Metal Products Company, 7797
Ramm Fence, 6336
Revere, 7597
Ridge Tool Company, 8240
Rubber Queen, 6337
SGD Golf, 6882
SSP Product Catalog, 8600
Sentronic International, 8445
Servo Products Company, 7803
ShowTopper Exhibits, 7080
Sifco Forge Group, 7804
Skuttle Manufacturing Company, 7460
Slautterback Products, 8035
Slip-Ons Round Bale Covers, 6339
Spring Hill Nursery, 7696
Springbrook Gardens, 7697
Springfield Rod & Custom, 6500, 6549
Sta-Warm Electric Company, 7465
Sterling Production Control Units, 7040
Stock Parts List, 7807
Stolle Corporation, 7808
Superior Pneumatic Air Tools, 8616
Support Plus, 7253
T Marzetti Company, 8230
TP Tools & Equipment, 8619
TP Tools and Equipment, 8620
Therm-O-Disc, 7381
Thermal Engineering Company, 7467
Things Remembered, 7195
Timken Company, 8628
Total Ultimate Foods, 8231
Tronair, 6587
True Choice, 6506
United States Plastic Corporation, 8133

Universal Plastics, 8134
Van Dyck's Flower Farm, 7636
Vortec Corporation, 7477
WL Jenkins Company, 8427
WeatherKing Air Conditioning, 7481
Weaver Leather, 6347
Western States Machine Company, 6932
Witt Company, 8241
YSI Temperature, 7390
Youngstown Barrel & Drum Company, 7992

Oklahoma

Acme Engineering & Manufacturing Corporation, 7274
Acra Electric Corporation, 7394
CMP Corporation, 7282
Carlisle Food Service Products, 8242
Chilcutt Direct Marketing, 6268, 7745
ClimateMaster, 7415
Cookshack, 8196
EFDYN, 6528
Fife Corporation, 8140
Fraser-Johnston Heating/Air Conditioning, 7289, 7423
GC Broah Company, 7426
Greenleaf Nursery Company, 7665
Holland, RW, 7435
IFSTA, 7097, 8290
Kraftbilt, 7861
Magnat-Fairview, 7448
Red Devil, 8586

Oregon

AK Ltd, 8256
Almore International, 6985
Bovees Nursery, 7645
Chief Supply, 7090, 7217, 7713
Cliff's Classic Chevrolet, 6470
Coolers/Freezers & Refrigeration Systems, 7358
Forestfarm Catalog, 7659
Greenhouse Catalog, 6821, 7716
Hardin Optical Company, 7919
Keith Keppel, 7673
Material Flow & Conveyor Systems, 7968
Mini-Edition Iris Lover's, 7680
Mountain Rose Herbs, 8229
Nichols Garden Nursery, 7620, 7683
O'Brien Manufacturing, 7819
PSI Research, 6630
Pacific Coast Avionics, 6579
Pro Supply Catalog, 7244
Rol-Away Truck Manufacturing, 8030
Security Chain Company, 6436
Silver Springs Nursery, 6338
Siskiyou Fine Pewter & Gifts, 7193
Territorial Seed Company, 7634
Thermographed Business Cards, 7873
V-Infinity Power Quick Guide Catalog, 6968
Van's Aircraft Accessories, 6590
Vintage Model Catalog, 6510
Westview Products, 6827
Whitman Farms Catalog, 7706
Yakima-Destination Hardware, 6438

Pennsylvania

ATD-American Catalog, 7879
Acco Chain & Lifting Products, 7010
Adams County Nursery, 7638
Aged Woods, 6750
Air Balance, 6791
Alarmax Distributors Inc., 8432
All-Fill, 7997
Alphabroder Buyer's Guide, 8658
American Arborist Supplies, 7573
American Precision Glass Corporation, 6765
Arbill Safety Products, 7908, 8260, 8360
Astrographics, 6948
Automatic Devices Company, 7501
Aztec Machinery Company, 7408

B&R Moll, 8159
BVS Samplers, 8362, 8479
Ballymore, 8482
Berkebile Oil Company, 6440
Berry Metal Company, 7279
Beyond.Com, 6973
Bodek & Rhodes, 8668
Bon Tool, 6731
Bradish Tractor Parts, 6462
Brody Professional Development, 6605
Bustin Safety Grating & Platforms, 6649
C & P 55-57 Chevy Passenger Cars, 6464
C & P 55-59 Chevrolet Trucks, 6465
CID Associates, 6732
Cabinet Hardware from Cliffside Industries, 6769
Cairns & Brother Fire Helmets, 8671
Calgon Carbon Corporation, 7312
Cannon Technology, 7355
CertainTeed Corporation, 6752
Church Identification Products, 7054, 7882
Closeout City Office Furniture, 7116
Cook's Garden, 7608
Coopermatics, 7314
Corporate Outfitting Guide, 8677
Corvette World, 6472
Curtron Products, 6839
Day Timer, 7849
Doucette Industries, 7287
Drawing Board, 7888
Eagle America, 8503
Eastwood Unique Automotive Tools & Supplies, 6530
Ellwood Safety Appliance Company Catalog, 8278
Eriez Magnetics, 8279
Evaporated Coatings, 7916
Exclusive Apparel, 8680
Expanded Seal Tools, 7421
Fein Power Tools, 8512
FloAire, 7267
Follett Corporation, 7332
Foster Manufacturing Company, 8165
Fres-Co System USA, 8009
GE Modular Space, 6733
Gary's Perennials, 7662
Gem Refrigerator Company, 7334
Grace Industries, 8285
Gupta Permold Corporation, 6660
H-B Instrument Company, 8405
Hannmann Machinery/Alyan Pump Company, 7294
Havis Inc, 7731
Heritage Fence Company, 6807
Hoffman Hatchery, 6322
Holiday Gift Guide, 7170
ITW Philadelphia Resins Catalog, 6811
Industrial Abrasives, 6664
Instech Laboratories, 7295
Iris Limited, 8408
Iron Shop, 6816
JanWay Company, 7175
Jay Group, 6869
Karol Media, 7754
Knoll Essentials, 7826
Life Support International, 8302
Lindberg: A Unit of General Signal, 7443
Luttys Chevys - Warehouse Catalog, 6486
M&C Specialties Company, 8540
Mac-It Corporation, 8541
Master Catalogue, 6670
Master Disposers, 8237
Medical-Diagnostic Specialty Gases, 7237, 7560
Metal Edge International, 7970
Mil-Spec Packaging Supply, 8072
Miller Edge, 8308
Molded Fiber Glass Tray Company, 8379
Monitor Products, 7297
Morton Machine Works, 7451
Munroe, 8546
Musser Forests, 7681
Musserforests, 6331
Myers Sheetmetal, 7791
Nanik, 7523
Nation/Ruskin, 6451
National Controls Corporation, 7372
National Draeger Detector Tube Products, 8310
Next Level, 8692

PAC/TEC Electronic Enclosures, 8078
Pacer Pumps, 7298
Parking Products, 8565
Pecora Catalog, 6723
Peerless Hardware Manufacturing Company, 6782
Pendergast Safety, 8313
Pennfield Feeds, 8569
Pennsylvania Scale Company, 8570
Pennwood Products Company, 6757
Permabond International Catalog, 6724
Philips Lighting Company, 6454
Phoenix Contact USA, 7033
Pike's Peak Nurseries, 7689
Printing Industries of America, 8173
Promotional Ideabook, 6880, 7189
Pulva Corporation, 8581
Quill Full Line, 7190
RACO International, 8582
Ralmark Company, 6582
Rapidocolor Corporation, 8176
Raybuck Autobody Parts, 6493
Rock-N-Rescue, 8321
Ron Francis Wiring, 6495
Sharpsville Container Corporation, 7981
Shenango Steel Buildings, 6688
Slingmax, 8602
Stagestep, 6761
State Line Tack, 6289
Streamlight, 7739
Superior Valve Company, 7379
Team 365, 8702
Tenco Assemblies, 8095
Thermadyne, 8344
Thermal Transfer Corporation, 7468
Tigg Corporation, 8346
Tobias Associates, 8151
Toner Cable Equipment, 8459
Tools & Equipment Catalog, 6744
Tray-Pak Corporation, 7986
Tri-Boro Construction Supplies, 6695, 6745
Tuscarora Plastics, 7810
UN Publications, 6639
UltraClub Corporate Outfitting, 8707
UltraClub Performance Wear, 8708
Uniflow Manufacturing Corporation, 8215
Vixen Hill Manufacturing, 6849
Wayne Products, 7389
What's New, 8714
Wilson Safe Company, 8428
Yazoo Mills Catalog, 7991
Ziamatic Corporation, 7110

Rhode Island

Amtrol, 7405
BBC Audiobooks America, 6600
Complete Real Estate Software Catalog, 6976
EFD, 8502
Ferro Weathervanes, 6806
Glenncraft Corporation, 6864, 7165
Marshall Domestics, 8250
Meller Optics, 7924
READE, 6402
Survivair, 7109
Turfer Sportswear, 8705
WL Fuller, 7813, 8648

South Carolina

Advanced Solutions Group, 6901
Coastal Technologies, 7285
Container Salvage Company, 7950
EKO, 7511
International Knife & Saw, 8168
Jameson, 8453
Mar Mac Manufacturing Company, 8691
Milliken & Company, 8251
Mossburg's Sign Products, 7070, 7899
Oakwood Products, 6919
Plastic Bag and Packaging, 8085, 8127
Sealevel Systems, 6945
Shakespeare Electronic Products Group, 7039

Sonoco Products Company, 7983
Springs Global, 7490
Super Duper Publications, 8701

South Dakota

A&M Industries, 8042
Aaladin Industries, 8358
Dakota Alert, 8435
Dakotah Toys, 6473
Enercept, 6655
Feterl Manufacturing Company, 6316
RBE Electronics, 7036

Tennessee

Ace Pump Corporation, 7272
AlcoPro, 7203, 7710
Big Frog Mountain Corporation, 6703
Can-Do National Tape, 8053
Catalog of Professional Audio/Video Services, 6391
Clarage, 8270
Comfort Products, 6421
Country Ruffles, 7505
Eastman Chemical Products, 8056
Fostoria Industries, 7422
General Shale Brick, 6351
Growbiz-Abco, 7667
Heatec, 7434
International Paper Company, 7960
Johnsey's Sporting Goods, 8686
KaTom Catalog, 8204, 8247
KaTom Restaurant Supply, 8205
Kano Laboratories, 6917
Kanson Electronics, 7027
Lokar Performance Products, 6484
Marugg Company, 7719
NGK Metals Corporation, 8309
Nashville Wraps Catalog, 7182
Natchez Shooters Supply, 7721, 8413
National Bridle Shop, 6282
PS Engineering, 6578
Pierce Socbox, 8147
Powermatic, 8576
Prentice Machine Work, 7796
Reemay, 6799
Robertshaw Industrial Instrumentation, 8593
Setco, 7980
Source, 6404
US Cavalry, 8706
United Technologies Catalog, 7136
Vintage Tire Hotline, 6511
Water Systems, 7479
White Manufacturing Company, 6301
Wholesale Tape & Supply, 6410

Texas

ALLMEDIA International, 7741
AMPCO Safety Tools, 7344
APW Wyott Corporation, 8234
ATSCO Alamo Transformer Supply Company, 8463
Academic Superstore, 6950, 6969
Aggreko, 7399
Air Rover Company, 7324
Aircondex, 7277
Alfax Furniture, 7111
Allied Plastic Supply, 8105
Altech Controls Corporation, 7348
Anchor Box Company, 7943
Aztec Grill Corporation, 8192
B&B ARMR, 8399
BAG Corporation, 8001
BG Micro, 6952
BSN Sports Athletic Performance, 7209
BSN Sports Direct, 7210
BSN Sports Equipment, 8660
BSN Sports Lacrosse, 8661
BSN Sports League, 8662
BSN Sports Middle School-Junior High, 8663

BSN Sports Team-Work, 8664
BSN Sports TeamWear, 8665
Baker Hughes Mining Tools, 8481
Bamert Seed Company, 7602
Baseball, Softball, Football Superstore, 6388, 6937
Berridge Manufacturing Company, 6647
Bowie Industries, 7579
Bowie Industries, Inc., 7280
Bradleys' Hermetics, 7328
Brookhollow Collection, 7846
Brown's Omaha Plant Farms, 7646
Butcher Boy Door Company, 7329
Carlton Industries, 8265
Chelsea Decorative Metal Company, 6803
Citgo Petroleum Corporation, 6522
Compressors Unlimited, 7416
Cooper Industries, 6523
Culinary & Hospitality Industry Publications, 6609
D & B Hoovers, 6610
Dallas Midwest, 7822
Detcon, 8437
Detex Corporation, 7092
Drip Irrigation, 7585
Eagle Metal Products, 8401
Entech Sales & Service, 7331
Exotic Houseplants, 7655
FabEnCo, 8280
Falcon Fine Wire and Wire Products, 7025
Findings & Metals, 7777
Flexmaster USA, 6798
Flow Design, 7362
Friedrich Air Conditioning, 7290, 7424
General Packaging Equipment Company, 8010
Glass Goose Catalog, 6567
Gresco Products, 6988
Guard Rail Systems, 8286
Harris InfoSource, 6618
Hart Publications, 6619
Hoover Materials Handling Group, 7957
Houston Wire Works, 7063
Huckster Packaging & Supply Catalog, 8064
IKG Industries, 6663
International Crystal Company, 7064
Kemlon Products & Development Corporation, 8298
Kennel-Aire, 6276
Kraftsman Playground and Park Equipment, 7004
Leather Factory, 8690
Lennox International, 7442
LinguiSystems Catalog, 7005
Matticks Industries, 7449
Meyer Machine Company, 8019
Micro-Brush Hand Scrub, 8377
MilesTek Catalog, 7031
Moore Fabrication, 8118
Mr G's Fasteners, 6779
Payne Fabrics, 7529
Perimeter Exhibits, 7075
Perry Company, 6334, 6491
Phoenix Plastics, 8124
Photon Technologies, 7929
R Stahl Automation Catalog, 8319
R Stahl Explosion Proof/Protected Electrical, 8320
SA-SO Catalog, 8322, 8386
Security Cameras Direct, 8420
Server Management Products, 6966
Smith Brothers, 6288, 6340
Spectrum Corporation, 7084
Standard Industrial Products Company, 8609
TRS RenTelco, 7042
Texas Instruments, 7380
The Clean Team, 8391
Tisdale Company, 7470
Troy-Bilt, 6345
VICI Valco Instruments, 7340
VOSSTechnologies SingleSample, 8640
Vintage Wood Works, 6809
Virginia KMP Corporation, 7386
Vista: Something for Everyone, 8711
Whirlwind, 8651
Womack's Nursery Catalog, 7707
Yazaki Energy Systems, 7482
Yucca Do Nursery Catalog, 7708
Zig Ziglar Corporation, 6642

Utah

Intermountain Cactus, 7671
Mrs Fields Gourmet Gifts, 7181
Subminiature Instruments Corporation, 8613
The Parthenon Company, 7255
Tuff Country E-Z Ride Suspension, 6507
Video Source, 6408
Western Promotion Sportswear, 8713

Vermont

Calyx Flowers, 7649
DR Power Equipment, 7582, 7714
Foam Laminates of Vermont, 6755
HearthStone Catalog: Wood & Pellet Products, 6706
Hemming's Motor News, 6430
High Country Gardens, 7668
King Arthur Flour & The Bakers, 8224, 8248
Perennial Pleasures Nursery, 7623
PortaBrace, 8574
T/C Press, 8132
Vermont Frames, 6697

Virginia

Aerofin Corporation, 7398
Alfa-Laval Thermal, 7401
At-A-Glance, 7845
Badger Fire Protection, 7089
Bristol Compressors, 7281
C&C Tool Supply Company, 8488
CAI's Bookstore, 6606
CED Process Minerals-Manufacturing, 7215
Cardinal Jackets, 6856, 7152, 8672
Coastal Safety & Health Services, 8271
Crutchfield, 6394
Dan River, 7509
Davis & Warshow, 7359
Edible Landscaping, 7654
Executive Systems, 8451
First Street Catalog, 7163
Folder Factory-Presentation Products, 7853
Fraser Publishing Company, 6614
Fremont Die Consumer Products, 6427
Holiday Cards for Businesses, 7169, 7858
Holiday Collection, 7859
HunterLab, 7552
Institute of Certified Professional Managers, 6896
Jane's Catalog, 6572
Measurement Specialists, 8543
Medeco Security Locks, 8412
Response Unlimited, 7762
Shades of Light, 7738
Simplimatic Engineering Company, 8093
Sinclair's, 6499
Standard Safety Equipment Company, 8337
Superfos Packaging, 7985
Titmus Optical, 7910, 8347
Tomorrow's World Catalog, 7492
US Department of Commerce, 6640
Universal Air Precipitator Corporation, 8393
Westvaco, 8157
Zenith Aviation, 6593

Washington

Ace Tank, 7273
Aitken's Salmon Creek Garden, 7639
American Autoclave Company, 6558
Archie McPhee & Company, 7145
Bean Farm, 6262
Buffalo Industries, 6449
Bunnies by the Bay and Friends, 7149
Burnt Ridge Nursery, 7648
CC Filson Company, 8669
CCI Solutions, 6390
Complete Line of Architectural & Engineering, 6364
Connell's Dahlias, 7607
Conterra, 7544
Creative Openings, 6838
Drytac, 8111
Ebbets Field Flannels, 8679

Fluke Corporation, 7026
Fungi Perfecti, 7613
Garaventa Lift, 7011
Griot's Garage, 8523
Hydro-Tempo, 7096
Lamb-Weston, 8225
Lortone, 8539
Mallory Company, 8304
Marketry, 7758
Marq Packaging Systems, 8018
Neider Company, 8550
NewHaven Software, 6979
PCS Catalog, 6722
Plants of the Wild, 7691
Pressure Washer and Water Treatment Catalog, 8383
Raintree Nursery, 7693
Sensitech, 7377
Six Chuter International LLC, 6584
Source Window Coverings, 7531
Spokane Hardware Supply, 8607
Stuc-O-Flex, International, 6691
Sun Precautions, 8339, 8700
Sunhill Insider, 8614
True Brands, 8254
Visions Espresso Service, 8216
WESPUR, 8647
Weyerhaeuser, 6762
Wilmar Corporation, 6552

West Virginia

Blue Ridge Machinery and Tools, 8486
CWS Parts Company, 8490
Commercial Optical Manufacturing, 7914
Cyclope Industries, 8275
Sunshine Farm & Gardens Perennial Plants, 7701
Terramite Corporation, 8626
Vimasco Catalog, 6728
Woodcraft Supply Catalog, 8655

Wisconsin

ABB Drives, 7343
AEC, 7392
AMSOIL, 6439
Abatron Building & Restoration, 6644
Adaptive Micro Systems, 8257
Agricultural Sciences, 7709
Air-Lec Industries, 6764
Airsan Corporation, 7307
American Health & Safety, 8259

Application Engineering, 7406
Arts & Crafts, 6359
Associated Bag, 8048
BEC Controls Corporation, 7539
Beauti-Vue Products Corporation, 7502
Bib Pak, 8051
Bilt-Rite Conveyors, 8484
Bock Water Heaters, 7409
Brandtjen & Kluge, 8137
CF Struck Corporation, 7580
Carlin Horticultural Supplies, 6307
Chiller Rentals & Manufacturing, 7414
Conflex Packaging, 8005
Conney Safety, 8273
Cornell Corporation, 6795
DEMCO Library Supplies & Equipment, 7117, 7884
Decorator Industries, 7510
Decton Iron Works, 8370
Demco Furniture Catalog, 7118
Desert Aire Corporation, 7419
Detwiler Tractor Parts, 8498
Dramm Professional Watering Tools, 7584
Ega Products, 8506
Electronic Tele-Communications, 8450
Emergency Medical Products, 7889
Enercon Industries Corporation, 8058
Enzymatic Natural Medicines, 7223
Exposures, 6350
Fast Service For Food Service, 8245
Gempler's Catalog, 6658
Grove Gear Industrial Gear Drives, 6536
Hansen Refrigeration Machinery Company, 7430
Indus International, 6962
Industrial Epoxies & Other Compounds Catalog, 6720
Inpak-Systems, 6326
JG Braun Company, 6817
Johnson Brass & Machine Foundry, 8532
Julien Shade Shop, 7484
Jung Seeds & Plants, 7616
KI Business Solutions, 7123
KI Government Solutions, 7124
KI Healthcare, 7125
KI Higher Education Solutions, 7126
KI K-12 Solutions, 7127
Kester's Wild Game Food Nurseries, 7617
King Motorsports, 6481
Klehm's Song Sparrow Perennial Farm, 7674
LC Thomsen, 8375
Lab Safety Supply Company, 7557
Laboratory Sampling Products Catalog, 6328
Lands' End Business Outfitters, 8688
Lands' End School Outfitters, 8689
Leading Edge Air Foils, 6573
Maysteel, 6963

McFeely's Square Drive Screws, 8542
Merrill Manufacturing Corporation, 7788
Motomco, 6298
Multistack, 7335
National Business Furniture, 7131
National Hospitality Supply, 7132, 7562
Nor-Lake, 8211
Northwestern Motor Company, 6577
Oil-Rite Lubricating Equipment, 8559
Outdoor Power Equipment, 8562
PC/Nametag, 6980
Packrite, 7972
Panef Corporation, 8081
Panoramic, 7973
Performance Zone, 6741
Petersen Products Co., 8571
Petersen Products Company, 8382
Polar Ware Health Care, 7242
Prairie Nursery, 7627
Pro Video, 8457
Professional Equipment, 7456, 8416, 8579
Pyro-Chem, 7103
Quest Technologies, 7798
RH Shumway, 7629
Research Products Corporation, 7320
Rudd Lighting Catalog, 7737
Sax Arts & Crafts, 6374
School Kids Healthcare, 7250
Seco Mini Catalog, 8214
Sentry Equipment Corporation, 7458
Snap-On Tools, 8603
South-Port Systems, 7463
Sportime Catalog, 7107, 8094
Standard Tar Products Catalog, 6690
Sullivan Dental Products, 6998
Tec Systems, 8150
Uline Shipping Supply Corporate Office Catalo, 7906
Uline Shipping Supply Specialists, 7907, 7987, 8096
Velvit Products Catalog, 6814
Vermont Bean Seed Company, 7704
WB Bottle Supply Company, 7989
Whirl-Pak, 8135
Wisconsin Converting of Green Bay, 7990
Wisconsin Milk Marketing Board, 8233
Ziabicki Import Company Catalog, 6354

Wyoming

A&H Abrasives, 8462
Marquis Awards & Specialties, 6871, 7178
Woodworkers Supply, 6379, 6553, 8041

General Reference
America's College Museums
American Environmental Leaders: From Colonial Times to the Present
Encyclopedia of African-American Writing
Encyclopedia of Constitutional Amendments
Encyclopedia of Human Rights and the United States
Encyclopedia of Invasions & Conquests
Encyclopedia of Prisoners of War & Internment
Encyclopedia of Religion & Law in America
Encyclopedia of Rural America
Encyclopedia of the Continental Congress
Encyclopedia of the United States Cabinet, 1789-2010
Encyclopedia of War Journalism
Encyclopedia of Warrior Peoples & Fighting Groups
The Environmental Debate: A Documentary History
The Evolution Wars: A Guide to the Debates
From Suffrage to the Senate: America's Political Women
Gun Debate: An Encyclopedia of Gun Rights & Gun Control in the U.S.
Opinions throughout History: National Security vs. Civil and Privacy Rights
Opinions throughout History: Immigration
Opinions throughout History: Drug Abuse & Drug Epidemics
Political Corruption in America
Privacy Rights in the Digital Era
The Religious Right: A Reference Handbook
Speakers of the House of Representatives, 1789-2009
This is Who We Were: 1880-1900
This is Who We Were: A Companion to the 1940 Census
This is Who We Were: In the 1900s
This is Who We Were: In the 1910s
This is Who We Were: In the 1920s
This is Who We Were: In the 1940s
This is Who We Were: In the 1950s
This is Who We Were: In the 1960s
This is Who We Were: In the 1970s
This is Who We Were: In the 1980s
This is Who We Were: In the 1990s
This is Who We Were: In the 2000s
U.S. Land & Natural Resource Policy
The Value of a Dollar 1600-1865: Colonial Era to the Civil War
The Value of a Dollar: 1860-2014
Working Americans 1770-1869 Vol. IX: Revolutionary War to the Civil War
Working Americans 1880-1999 Vol. I: The Working Class
Working Americans 1880-1999 Vol. II: The Middle Class
Working Americans 1880-1999 Vol. III: The Upper Class
Working Americans 1880-1999 Vol. IV: Their Children
Working Americans 1880-2015 Vol. V: Americans At War
Working Americans 1880-2005 Vol. VI: Women at Work
Working Americans 1880-2006 Vol. VII: Social Movements
Working Americans 1880-2007 Vol. VIII: Immigrants
Working Americans 1880-2009 Vol. X: Sports & Recreation
Working Americans 1880-2010 Vol. XI: Inventors & Entrepreneurs
Working Americans 1880-2011 Vol. XII: Our History through Music
Working Americans 1880-2012 Vol. XIII: Education & Educators
Working Americans 1880-2016 Vol. XIV: Industry Through the Ages
Working Americans 1880-2017 Vol. XV: Politics & Politicians
World Cultural Leaders of the 20th & 21st Centuries

Education Information
Charter School Movement
Comparative Guide to American Elementary & Secondary Schools
Complete Learning Disabilities Directory
Educators Resource Handbook
Special Education: Policy and Curriculum Development

Health Information
Comparative Guide to American Hospitals
Complete Directory for Pediatric Disorders
Complete Directory for People with Chronic Illness
Complete Directory for People with Disabilities
Complete Mental Health Directory
Diabetes in America: Analysis of an Epidemic
Guide to Health Care Group Purchasing Organizations
Guide to U.S. HMO's & PPO's
Medical Device Market Place
Older Americans Information Directory

Business Information
Complete Television, Radio & Cable Industry Directory
Directory of Business Information Resources
Directory of Mail Order Catalogs
Directory of Venture Capital & Private Equity Firms
Environmental Resource Handbook
Financial Literacy Starter Kit
Food & Beverage Market Place
Grey House Homeland Security Directory
Grey House Performing Arts Directory
Grey House Safety & Security Directory
Hudson's Washington News Media Contacts Directory
New York State Directory
Sports Market Place Directory

Statistics & Demographics
American Tally
America's Top-Rated Cities
America's Top-Rated Smaller Cities
Ancestry & Ethnicity in America
The Asian Databook
Comparative Guide to American Suburbs
The Hispanic Databook
Profiles of America
"Profiles of" Series - State Handbooks
Weather America

Financial Ratings Series
Financial Literacy Basics
TheStreet Ratings' Guide to Bond & Money Market Mutual Funds
TheStreet Ratings' Guide to Common Stocks
TheStreet Ratings' Guide to Exchange-Traded Funds
TheStreet Ratings' Guide to Stock Mutual Funds
TheStreet Ratings' Ultimate Guided Tour of Stock Investing
Weiss Ratings' Consumer Guides
Weiss Ratings' Financial Literary Basic Guides
Weiss Ratings' Guide to Banks
Weiss Ratings' Guide to Credit Unions
Weiss Ratings' Guide to Health Insurers
Weiss Ratings' Guide to Life & Annuity Insurers
Weiss Ratings' Guide to Property & Casualty Insurers

Bowker's Books In Print® Titles
American Book Publishing Record® Annual
American Book Publishing Record® Monthly
Books In Print®
Books In Print® Supplement
Books Out Loud™
Bowker's Complete Video Directory™
Children's Books In Print®
El-Hi Textbooks & Serials In Print®
Forthcoming Books®
Law Books & Serials In Print™
Medical & Health Care Books In Print™
Publishers, Distributors & Wholesalers of the US™
Subject Guide to Books In Print®
Subject Guide to Children's Books In Print®

Canadian General Reference
Associations Canada
Canadian Almanac & Directory
Canadian Environmental Resource Guide
Canadian Parliamentary Guide
Canadian Venture Capital & Private Equity Firms
Canadian Who's Who
Financial Post Directory of Directors
Financial Services Canada
Governments Canada
Health Guide Canada
The History of Canada
Libraries Canada
Major Canadian Cities

2018 Title List

Visit www.SalemPress.com for Product Information, Table of Contents, and Sample Pages

Science, Careers & Mathematics

Ancient Creatures
Applied Science
Applied Science: Engineering & Mathematics
Applied Science: Science & Medicine
Applied Science: Technology
Biomes and Ecosystems
Careers in the Arts: Fine, Performing & Visual
Careers in Building Construction
Careers in Business
Careers in Chemistry
Careers in Communications & Media
Careers in Environment & Conservation
Careers in Financial Services
Careers in Green Energy
Careers in Healthcare
Careers in Hospitality & Tourism
Careers in Human Services
Careers in Law, Criminal Justice & Emergency Services
Careers in Manufacturing
Careers in Outdoor Jobs
Careers in Overseas Jobs
Careers in Physics
Careers in Sales, Insurance & Real Estate
Careers in Science & Engineering
Careers in Sports & Fitness
Careers in Social Media
Careers in Sports Medicine & Training
Careers in Technology Services & Repair
Computer Technology Innovators
Contemporary Biographies in Business
Contemporary Biographies in Chemistry
Contemporary Biographies in Communications & Media
Contemporary Biographies in Environment & Conservation
Contemporary Biographies in Healthcare
Contemporary Biographies in Hospitality & Tourism
Contemporary Biographies in Law & Criminal Justice
Contemporary Biographies in Physics
Earth Science
Earth Science: Earth Materials & Resources
Earth Science: Earth's Surface and History
Earth Science: Physics & Chemistry of the Earth
Earth Science: Weather, Water & Atmosphere
Encyclopedia of Energy
Encyclopedia of Environmental Issues
Encyclopedia of Environmental Issues: Atmosphere and Air Pollution
Encyclopedia of Environmental Issues: Ecology and Ecosystems
Encyclopedia of Environmental Issues: Energy and Energy Use
Encyclopedia of Environmental Issues: Policy and Activism
Encyclopedia of Environmental Issues: Preservation/Wilderness Issues
Encyclopedia of Environmental Issues: Water and Water Pollution
Encyclopedia of Global Resources
Encyclopedia of Global Warming
Encyclopedia of Mathematics & Society
Encyclopedia of Mathematics & Society: Engineering, Tech, Medicine
Encyclopedia of Mathematics & Society: Great Mathematicians
Encyclopedia of Mathematics & Society: Math & Social Sciences
Encyclopedia of Mathematics & Society: Math Development/Concepts
Encyclopedia of Mathematics & Society: Math in Culture & Society
Encyclopedia of Mathematics & Society: Space, Science, Environment
Encyclopedia of the Ancient World
Forensic Science
Geography Basics
Internet Innovators
Inventions and Inventors
Magill's Encyclopedia of Science: Animal Life
Magill's Encyclopedia of Science: Plant life
Notable Natural Disasters
Principles of Artificial Intelligence & Robotics
Principles of Astronomy
Principles of Biology
Principles of Biotechnology
Principles of Chemistry
Principles of Climatology
Principles of Physical Science
Principles of Physics
Principles of Programming & Coding
Principles of Research Methods
Principles of Sustainability
Science and Scientists
Solar System
Solar System: Great Astronomers

Solar System: Study of the Universe
Solar System: The Inner Planets
Solar System: The Moon and Other Small Bodies
Solar System: The Outer Planets
Solar System: The Sun and Other Stars
World Geography

Literature

American Ethnic Writers
Classics of Science Fiction & Fantasy Literature
Critical Approaches: Feminist
Critical Approaches: Multicultural
Critical Approaches: Moral
Critical Approaches: Psychological
Critical Insights: Authors
Critical Insights: Film
Critical Insights: Literary Collection Bundles
Critical Insights: Themes
Critical Insights: Works
Critical Survey of American Literature
Critical Survey of Drama
Critical Survey of Graphic Novels: Heroes & Super Heroes
Critical Survey of Graphic Novels: History, Theme & Technique
Critical Survey of Graphic Novels: Independents/Underground Classics
Critical Survey of Graphic Novels: Manga
Critical Survey of Long Fiction
Critical Survey of Mystery & Detective Fiction
Critical Survey of Mythology and Folklore: Heroes and Heroines
Critical Survey of Mythology and Folklore: Love, Sexuality & Desire
Critical Survey of Mythology and Folklore: World Mythology
Critical Survey of Novels into Film
Critical Survey of Poetry
Critical Survey of Poetry: American Poets
Critical Survey of Poetry: British, Irish & Commonwealth Poets
Critical Survey of Poetry: Cumulative Index
Critical Survey of Poetry: European Poets
Critical Survey of Poetry: Topical Essays
Critical Survey of Poetry: World Poets
Critical Survey of Science Fiction & Fantasy
Critical Survey of Shakespeare's Plays
Critical Survey of Shakespeare's Sonnets
Critical Survey of Short Fiction
Critical Survey of Short Fiction: American Writers
Critical Survey of Short Fiction: British, Irish, Commonwealth Writers
Critical Survey of Short Fiction: Cumulative Index
Critical Survey of Short Fiction: European Writers
Critical Survey of Short Fiction: Topical Essays
Critical Survey of Short Fiction: World Writers
Critical Survey of World Literature
Critical Survey of Young Adult Literature
Cyclopedia of Literary Characters
Cyclopedia of Literary Places
Holocaust Literature
Introduction to Literary Context: American Poetry of the 20th Century
Introduction to Literary Context: American Post-Modernist Novels
Introduction to Literary Context: American Short Fiction
Introduction to Literary Context: English Literature
Introduction to Literary Context: Plays
Introduction to Literary Context: World Literature
Magill's Literary Annual 2018
Masterplots
Masterplots II: African American Literature
Masterplots II: American Fiction Series
Masterplots II: British & Commonwealth Fiction Series
Masterplots II: Christian Literature
Masterplots II: Drama Series
Masterplots II: Juvenile & Young Adult Literature, Supplement
Masterplots II: Nonfiction Series
Masterplots II: Poetry Series
Masterplots II: Short Story Series
Masterplots II: Women's Literature Series
Notable African American Writers
Notable American Novelists
Notable Playwrights
Notable Poets
Recommended Reading: 600 Classics Reviewed
Short Story Writers

Grey House Publishing | Salem Press | H.W. Wilson | 4919 Route, 22 PO Box 56, Amenia NY 12501-0056

History and Social Science

The 2000s in America
50 States
African American History
Agriculture in History
American First Ladies
American Heroes
American Indian Culture
American Indian History
American Indian Tribes
American Presidents
American Villains
America's Historic Sites
Ancient Greece
The Bill of Rights
The Civil Rights Movement
The Cold War
Countries, Peoples & Cultures
Countries, Peoples & Cultures: Central & South America
Countries, Peoples & Cultures: Central, South & Southeast Asia
Countries, Peoples & Cultures: East & South Africa
Countries, Peoples & Cultures: East Asia & the Pacific
Countries, Peoples & Cultures: Eastern Europe
Countries, Peoples & Cultures: Middle East & North Africa
Countries, Peoples & Cultures: North America & the Caribbean
Countries, Peoples & Cultures: West & Central Africa
Countries, Peoples & Cultures: Western Europe
Defining Documents: American Revolution
Defining Documents: American West
Defining Documents: Ancient World
Defining Documents: Asia
Defining Documents: Civil Rights
Defining Documents: Civil War
Defining Documents: Court Cases
Defining Documents: Dissent & Protest
Defining Documents: Emergence of Modern America
Defining Documents: Exploration & Colonial America
Defining Documents: Immigration & Immigrant Communities
Defining Documents: LGBTQ
Defining Documents: Manifest Destiny
Defining Documents: Middle Ages
Defining Documents: Middle East
Defining Documents: Nationalism & Populism
Defining Documents: Native Americans
Defining Documents: Political Campaigns, Candidates & Discourse
Defining Documents: Postwar 1940s
Defining Documents: Reconstruction
Defining Documents: Renaissance & Early Modern Era
Defining Documents: Secrets, Leaks & Scandals
Defining Documents: 1920s
Defining Documents: 1930s
Defining Documents: 1950s
Defining Documents: 1960s
Defining Documents: 1970s
Defining Documents: The 17th Century
Defining Documents: The 18th Century
Defining Documents: The 19th Century
Defining Documents: The 20th Century: 1900-1950
Defining Documents: Vietnam War
Defining Documents: Women
Defining Documents: World War I
Defining Documents: World War II
Education Today
The Eighties in America
Encyclopedia of American Immigration
Encyclopedia of Flight
Encyclopedia of the Ancient World
Fashion Innovators
The Fifties in America
The Forties in America
Great Athletes
Great Athletes: Baseball
Great Athletes: Basketball
Great Athletes: Boxing & Soccer
Great Athletes: Cumulative Index
Great Athletes: Football
Great Athletes: Golf & Tennis
Great Athletes: Olympics

Great Athletes: Racing & Individual Sports
Great Contemporary Athletes
Great Events from History: 17th Century
Great Events from History: 18th Century
Great Events from History: 19th Century
Great Events from History: 20th Century (1901-1940)
Great Events from History: 20th Century (1941-1970)
Great Events from History: 20th Century (1971-2000)
Great Events from History: 21st Century (2000-2016)
Great Events from History: African American History
Great Events from History: Cumulative Indexes
Great Events from History: LGBTG
Great Events from History: Middle Ages
Great Events from History: Secrets, Leaks & Scandals
Great Events from History: Renaissance & Early Modern Era
Great Lives from History: 17th Century
Great Lives from History: 18th Century
Great Lives from History: 19th Century
Great Lives from History: 20th Century
Great Lives from History: 21st Century (2000-2017)
Great Lives from History: American Women
Great Lives from History: Ancient World
Great Lives from History: Asian & Pacific Islander Americans
Great Lives from History: Cumulative Indexes
Great Lives from History: Incredibly Wealthy
Great Lives from History: Inventors & Inventions
Great Lives from History: Jewish Americans
Great Lives from History: Latinos
Great Lives from History: Notorious Lives
Great Lives from History: Renaissance & Early Modern Era
Great Lives from History: Scientists & Science
Historical Encyclopedia of American Business
Issues in U.S. Immigration
Magill's Guide to Military History
Milestone Documents in African American History
Milestone Documents in American History
Milestone Documents in World History
Milestone Documents of American Leaders
Milestone Documents of World Religions
Music Innovators
Musicians & Composers 20th Century
The Nineties in America
The Seventies in America
The Sixties in America
Sociology Today
Survey of American Industry and Careers
The Thirties in America
The Twenties in America
United States at War
U.S. Court Cases
U.S. Government Leaders
U.S. Laws, Acts, and Treaties
U.S. Legal System
U.S. Supreme Court
Weapons and Warfare
World Conflicts: Asia and the Middle East

Health

Addictions & Substance Abuse
Adolescent Health & Wellness
Cancer
Complementary & Alternative Medicine
Community & Family Health
Genetics & Inherited Conditions
Health Issues
Infectious Diseases & Conditions
Magill's Medical Guide
Nutrition
Nursing
Psychology & Behavioral Health
Psychology Basics

2018 Title List
Visit www.HWWilsonInPrint.com for Product Information, Table of Contents and Sample Pages

Current Biography
Current Biography Cumulative Index 1946-2013
Current Biography Monthly Magazine
Current Biography Yearbook: 2003
Current Biography Yearbook: 2004
Current Biography Yearbook: 2005
Current Biography Yearbook: 2006
Current Biography Yearbook: 2007
Current Biography Yearbook: 2008
Current Biography Yearbook: 2009
Current Biography Yearbook: 2010
Current Biography Yearbook: 2011
Current Biography Yearbook: 2012
Current Biography Yearbook: 2013
Current Biography Yearbook: 2014
Current Biography Yearbook: 2015
Current Biography Yearbook: 2016
Current Biography Yearbook: 2017

Core Collections
Children's Core Collection
Fiction Core Collection
Graphic Novels Core Collection
Middle & Junior High School Core
Public Library Core Collection: Nonfiction
Senior High Core Collection
Young Adult Fiction Core Collection

The Reference Shelf
Aging in America
Alternative Facts: Post Truth & the Information War
The American Dream
American Military Presence Overseas
The Arab Spring
Artificial Intelligence
The Brain
The Business of Food
Campaign Trends & Election Law
Conspiracy Theories
The Digital Age
Dinosaurs
Embracing New Paradigms in Education
Faith & Science
Families: Traditional and New Structures
The Future of U.S. Economic Relations: Mexico, Cuba, and Venezuela
Global Climate Change
Graphic Novels and Comic Books
Guns in America
Immigration
Immigration in the U.S.
Internet Abuses & Privacy Rights
Internet Safety
LGBTQ in the 21st Century
Marijuana Reform
The News and its Future
The Paranormal
Politics of the Ocean
Prescription Drug Abuse
Racial Tension in a "Postracial" Age
Reality Television
Representative American Speeches: 2008-2009
Representative American Speeches: 2009-2010
Representative American Speeches: 2010-2011
Representative American Speeches: 2011-2012
Representative American Speeches: 2012-2013
Representative American Speeches: 2013-2014
Representative American Speeches: 2014-2015
Representative American Speeches: 2015-2016
Representative American Speeches: 2016-2017
Representative American Speeches: 2017-2018
Rethinking Work
Revisiting Gender
Robotics
Russia
Social Networking
Social Services for the Poor
South China Seas Conflict
Space Exploration & Development
Sports in America

The Supreme Court
The Transformation of American Cities
U.S. Infrastructure
U.S. National Debate Topic: Educational Reform
U.S. National Debate Topic: Surveillance
U.S. National Debate Topic: The Ocean
U.S. National Debate Topic: Transportation Infrastructure
Whistleblowers

Readers' Guide
Abridged Readers' Guide to Periodical Literature
Readers' Guide to Periodical Literature

Indexes
Index to Legal Periodicals & Books
Short Story Index
Book Review Digest

Sears List
Sears List of Subject Headings
Sears: Lista de Encabezamientos de Materia

Facts About Series
Facts About American Immigration
Facts About China
Facts About the 20th Century
Facts About the Presidents
Facts About the World's Languages

Nobel Prize Winners
Nobel Prize Winners: 1901-1986
Nobel Prize Winners: 1987-1991
Nobel Prize Winners: 1992-1996
Nobel Prize Winners: 1997-2001

World Authors
World Authors: 1995-2000
World Authors: 2000-2005

Famous First Facts
Famous First Facts
Famous First Facts About American Politics
Famous First Facts About Sports
Famous First Facts About the Environment
Famous First Facts: International Edition

American Book of Days
The American Book of Days
The International Book of Days

Monographs
American Reformers
The Barnhart Dictionary of Etymology
Celebrate the World
Guide to the Ancient World
Indexing from A to Z
Nobel Prize Winners
The Poetry Break
Radical Change: Books for Youth in a Digital Age
Speeches of American Presidents

Wilson Chronology
Wilson Chronology of Asia and the Pacific
Wilson Chronology of Human Rights
Wilson Chronology of Ideas
Wilson Chronology of the Arts
Wilson Chronology of the World's Religions
Wilson Chronology of Women's Achievements

Grey House Publishing | Salem Press | H.W. Wilson | 4919 Route, 22 PO Box 56, Amenia NY 12501-0056